Sporting News
BOOKS

BASEBALL REGISTER

2003 EDITION

Editors/Baseball Register
TONY NISTLER
DAVID WALTON

ON THE COVER: Top: Barry Bonds photo by Dilip Vishwanat/The Sporting News; bottom left to right: Albert Pujols photo by Dilip Vishwanat/The Sporting News, Curt Schilling photo by Dilip Vishwanat/The Sporting News, Manny Ramirez photo by Mark Bolton for The Sporting News, Miguel Tejada photo by Dilip Vishwanat/The Sporting News; spine: Barry Bonds photo by John Cordes for The Sporting News.

Major league statistics compiled by STATS, Inc., a News Corporation company, 8130 Lehigh Avenue, Morton Grove, IL 60053. STATS is a trademark of Sports Team Analysis and Tracking Systems, Inc.

Minor league statistics provided by SportsTicker.

ISBN: 0-89204-699-6

10 9 8 7 6 5 4 3 2 1

CONTENTS

EXPLANATION OF FOOTNOTES AND ABBREVIATIONS

Note for statistical comparisons: Player strikes forced the cancellation of games in the 1972 season (10 days missed), the 1981 season (50 days missed), the 1994 season (52 days missed) and the 1995 season (18 games missed).

Positions are listed in descending order of games played; because of limited space, pinch-hitter and pinch-runner are listed in the regular-season section only if a player did not play a defensive position.

- * Led league. For fielding statistics, the player led the league at the position shown.
- • Tied for league lead. For fielding statistics, the player tied for the league lead at the position shown.
- † Led league, but number indicated is total figure for two or more positions. Actual league-leading figure for a position is mentioned in "Statistical Notes" section.
- ‡ Tied for league lead, but number indicated is total figure for two or more positions. Actual league-tying figure for a position is mentioned in "Statistical Notes" section.
- § Led or tied for league lead, but total figure is divided between two different teams. Actual league-leading or league-tying figure is mentioned in "Statistical Notes" section.
- ■ Indicates a player's movement from one major league organization to another major league organization or to an independent minor league organization.
- ... Statistic unavailable, inapplicable, unofficial or mathematically impossible to calculate.
- — Manager statistic inapplicable.

LEAGUES: A.A., Am. Assoc.—American Association. **A.L.**—American. **App., Appal.**—Appalachian. **Ar., Ariz.**—Arizona. **Atl.**—Atlantic. **Cal., Calif.**—California. **Car., Caro.**—Carolina. **CRL**—Cocoa Rookie. **DSL**—Dominican Summer. **East.**—Eastern. **Evan.**—Evangeline. **Fla. St., Florida St., FSL**—Florida State. **GCL**—Gulf Coast. **GSL**—Gulf States. **In.-Am.**—Inter-American. **Int'l., I.L.**—International. **J.P., Jap. Pac., Jp. Pac.**—Japan Pacific. **Jp. Cen., Jp. Cn.**—Japan Central. **Jp. East**—Japan East. **Jp. West**—Japan West. **Mex.**—Mexican. **Mex. Cen.**—Mexican Center. **Mid., Midw.**—Midwest. **Miss.-O.V.**—Mississippi-Ohio Valley. **N.C. St.**—North Carolina State. **N.L.**—National. **North.**—Northern. **N'West, NW**—Northwest. **NYP, NY-P, NY-Penn**—New York-Pennsylvania. **Pac. Coast, PCL**—Pacific Coast. **Pio.**—Pioneer. **S. Atl., SAL**—South Atlantic. **Soph.**—Sophomore. **Sou., South.**—Southern. **Taiw.**—Taiwan. **Tex.**—Texas. **West.**—Western. **W. Car., W. Caro.**—Western Carolinas.

TEAMS: Aguas.—Aguascalientes. **Alb./Colon., Alb./Colonie**—Albany/Colonie. **Ariz.**—Arizona. **Ariz. D-backs**—Arizona League Diamondbacks. **Belling.**—Bellingham. **Birm.**—Birmingham. **Brevard Co.**—Brevard County. **Cant./Akr.**—Canton/Akron. **Ced. Rap.**—Cedar Rapids. **Cent. Ore.**—Central Oregon. **Central Vall.**—Central Valley. **Char., Charl.**—Charleston. **Chatt.**—Chattanooga. **Chiba Lot.**—Chiba Lotte. **Ciu. Juarez**—Ciudad Juarez. **Colo. Spr., Colo. Springs**—Colorado Springs. **Dall./Fort W.**—Dallas/Fort Worth. **Day. Beach.**—Daytona Beach. **Dm., Dom.**—Dominican. **Dom. B. Jays**—Dominican Blue Jays. **Dom. Orioles/WS**—Dominican Orioles/White Sox. **Elizabeth.**—Elizabethton. **Estadio Quis.**—Estadio Quisqueya. **Eve.**—Everett. **Fort Lauder., Fort Laud.**—Fort Lauderdale. **Fukuoka**—Fukuoka Daiei. **GC**—Gulf Coast. **GC Astros-Or.**—Gulf Coast Astros-Orange. **GC Royals-Bl.**—Gulf Coast Royals-Blue. **GC Whi. Sox**—Gulf Coast White Sox. **Grays Har.**—Grays Harbor. **Greens.**—Greensboro. **Greenw.**—Greenwood. **Guana.**—Guanajuato. **H.P.-Thomas.**—High Point-Thomasville. **Hunting.**—Huntington. **Jacksonv.**—Jacksonville. **Johns. City**—Johnson City. **Kane Co.**—Kane County. **Lake Charl.**—Lake Charles. **Matt.**—Mattoon. **M.C., Mex. City**—Mexico City. **Med. Hat**—Medicine Hat. **Monc.**—Monclova. **Niag. F., Niag. Falls**—Niagara Falls. **Okla. City**—Oklahoma City. **Pan. City**—Panama City. **Phoe.**—Phoenix. **Pomp. Beach**—Pompano Beach. **Pres. Lions**—President Lions. **Prin. Will., Prin. William**—Prince William. **Ral./Dur.**—Raleigh/Durham. **Rancho Cuca.**—Rancho Cucamonga. **Rocky Mount.**—Rocky Mountain. **Salt.**—Saltillo. **Salt.-Monc.**—Saltillo-Monclova. **San. Dom., San. Domingo**—Santo Domingo. **San Bern.**—San Bernardino. **San Fran.**—San Francisco. **Schen.**—Schenectady. **Scran./W.B.**—Scranton/Wilkes-Barre. **S.C.**—South Carolina. **S.F. de Mac.**—San Francisco de Macoris. **San Luis Pot.**—San Luis Potosi. **Sonoma Co.**—Sonoma County. **S. Oregon**—Southern Oregon. **Spartan.**—Spartanburg. **St. Cath., St. Cathar.**—St. Catharines. **St. Peters., St. Pete.**—St. Petersburg. **States.**—Statesville. **Stock.**—Stockton. **T.-C.**—Tri-Cities. **Vanc.**—Vancouver. **Ven.**—Venezuelan. **Vent. Co.**—Ventura County. **W. Mich.**—West Michigan. **Win.-Salem, Winst.-Salem**—Winston-Salem. **Wis. Rap., Wis. Rapids**—Wisconsin Rapids. **W.P. Beach**—West Palm Beach. **W.Va.**—West Virgina. **Yuc.**—Yucatan.

STATISTICS: A—assists. **AB**—at-bats. **Avg.**—average. **BB**—bases on balls. **CG**—complete games. **CS**—caught stealing. **E**—errors. **ER**—earned runs. **ERA**—earned-run average. **G**—games. **GS**—games started. **H**—hits. **HR**—home runs. **IBB**—intentional bases on balls. **IP**—innings pitched. **L**—losses. **OBP**—on-base percentage. **Pct.**—winning percentage. **PO**—putouts. **Pos.**—position. **R**—runs. **RBI**—runs batted in. **SB**—stolen bases. **ShO**—shutouts. **SLG**—slugging percentage. **SO**—strikeouts. **Sv.**—saves. **Sv.Opp.**—save opportunities. **W**—wins. **2B**—doubles. **3B**—triples.

PLAYERS

A

ABBOTT, PAUL — P — MARINERS

PERSONAL: Born September 15, 1967, in Van Nuys, Calif. ... 6-3/204. ... Throws right, bats right. ... Full name: Paul David Abbott.

HIGH SCHOOL: Sunny Hills (Fullerton, Calif.).

TRANSACTIONS/CAREER NOTES: Selected by Minnesota Twins organization in third round of free-agent draft (June 3, 1985). ... On Minnesota disabled list (March 28-June 5 and August 14-September 1, 1992). ... Released by Twins (March 2, 1993). ... Signed by Cleveland Indians organization (March 27, 1993). ... On Canton/Akron disabled list (April 8-May 6, 1993). ... Granted free agency (October 15, 1993). ... Signed by Kansas City Royals organization (November 21, 1993). ... On disabled list (March 18-May 25 and June 16-30, 1994). ... Released by Royals (June 30, 1994). ... Signed by Chicago Cubs organization (March 17, 1995). ... Granted free agency (October 16, 1995). ... Signed by San Diego Padres organization (November 29, 1995). ... Granted free agency (October 15, 1996). ... Signed by Seattle Mariners organization (January 10, 1997). ... On Tacoma disabled list (May 23-July 14, 1997). ... On Orlando disabled list (April 2-August 21, 1998); included rehabilitation assignment to Arizona League Mariners (August 19-21). ... Released by Mariners (December 14, 1998). ... Re-signed by Mariners (January 21, 1999). ... On New Haven disabled list (April 9-June 12, 1999). ... On Seattle disabled list (April 1-28, 2001); included rehabilitation assignment to Tacoma (April 23-28). ... On Seattle disabled list (May 6, 2002-remainder of season); included rehabilitation assignment to San Bernardino (June 3-9) and Tacoma (June 10-17).

STATISTICAL NOTES: Pitched 3-0 no-hit victory against Palm Springs (June 26, 1988, seven innings).

CAREER HITTING (MLB): 3-for-9 (.333), 1 R, 1 2B, 0 3B, 0 HR, 0 RBI.

Year League	W	L	Pct.	ERA	G	GS	CG	ShO	Sv.-Opp.	IP	H	R	ER	HR	BB-IBB	SO
1985— Elizabethton (Appl.)	1	5	.167	6.94	10	10	1	0	0-...	35.0	33	32	27	3	32-0	34
1986— Kenosha (Midw.)	6	10	.375	4.50	25	15	1	0	0-...	98.0	102	62	49	13	73-3	73
1987— Kenosha (Midw.)	13	6	.684	3.65	26	25	1	0	0-...	145.1	102	76	59	11	103-0	138
1988— Visalia (Calif.)	11	9	.550	4.18	28	•28	4	2	0-...	172.1	141	95	80	9	*143-5	*205
1989— Orlando (Sou.)	9	3	.750	4.37	17	17	1	0	0-...	90.2	71	48	44	6	48-0	102
1990— Portland (PCL)	5	14	.263	4.56	23	23	4	1	0-...	128.1	110	75	65	9	82-0	129
— Minnesota (A.L.)	0	5	.000	5.97	7	7	0	0	0-0	34.2	37	24	23	0	28-0	25
1991— Portland (PCL)	2	3	.400	3.89	8	8	1	1	0-...	44.0	36	19	19	2	28-0	40
— Minnesota (A.L.)	3	1	.750	4.75	15	3	0	0	0-0	47.1	38	27	25	5	36-1	43
1992— Portland (PCL)	4	1	.800	2.33	7	7	0	0	0-...	46.1	30	13	12	2	31-0	46
— Minnesota (A.L.)	0	0	...	3.27	6	0	0	0	0-0	11.0	12	4	4	1	5-0	13
1993— Canton/Akron (East.)■	4	5	.444	4.06	13	12	1	0	0-...	75.1	72	34	34	4	28-2	86
— Cleveland (A.L.)	0	1	.000	6.38	5	5	0	0	0-0	18.1	19	15	13	5	11-1	7
— Charlotte (I.L.)	0	1	.000	6.63	4	4	0	0	0-...	19.0	25	16	14	4	7-0	12
1994— Omaha (A.A.)■	4	1	.800	4.87	15	10	0	0	0-...	57.1	57	32	31	8	45-0	48
1995— Iowa (A.A.)■	7	7	.500	3.67	46	11	0	0	0-...	115.1	104	50	47	12	64-4	*127
1996— Las Vegas (PCL)■	4	2	.667	4.18	28	0	0	0	7-...	28.0	27	14	13	4	12-4	37
1997— Tacoma (PCL)■	8	4	.667	4.13	17	14	3	0	0-...	93.2	80	48	43	11	29-1	117
— Arizona Mariners (Ariz.)	0	0	...	0.93	3	3	0	0	0-...	9.2	0	2	1	0	7-0	13
1998— Arizona Mariners (Ariz.)	0	0	...	0.00	1	0	0	0	0-...	3.0	1	0	0	0	0-0	6
— Tacoma (PCL)	1	0	1.000	1.20	3	3	0	0	0-...	15.0	9	2	2	2	5-0	20
— Seattle (A.L.)	3	1	.750	4.01	4	4	0	0	0-0	24.2	24	11	11	2	10-0	22
1999— Tacoma (PCL)	1	1	.500	6.43	2	2	0	0	0-...	14.0	21	11	10	1	4-0	10
— Seattle (A.L.)	6	2	.750	3.10	25	7	0	0	0-2	72.2	50	31	25	9	32-3	68
2000— Seattle (A.L.)	9	7	.563	4.22	35	27	0	0	0-0	179.0	164	89	84	23	80-4	100
2001— Tacoma (PCL)	0	0	...	0.00	1	1	0	0	0-...	4.0	1	0	0	0	4-0	4
— Seattle (A.L.)	17	4	.810	4.25	28	27	1	0	0-0	163.0	145	79	77	21	87-5	118
2002— Seattle (A.L.)	1	3	.250	11.96	7	5	0	0	0-0	26.1	40	36	35	5	20-0	22
— San Bernardino (Calif.)	0	0	...	0.00	1	1	0	0	0-...	5.0	3	0	0	0	2-0	5
— Tacoma (PCL)	0	1	.000	6.23	2	2	0	0	0-...	8.2	13	10	6	3	3-0	8
Major League totals (9 years)	39	24	.619	4.63	132	85	1	0	0-2	577.0	529	316	297	71	309-14	418

DIVISION SERIES RECORD

Year League	W	L	Pct.	ERA	G	GS	CG	ShO	Sv.-Opp.	IP	H	R	ER	HR	BB-IBB	SO
2000— Seattle (A.L.)	1	0	1.000	1.59	1	1	0	0	0-0	5.2	5	2	1	0	3-0	1
2001— Seattle (A.L.)	0	0	...	24.00	1	0	0	0	0-0	3.0	9	8	8	3	5-0	3
Division series totals (2 years)	1	0	1.000	9.35	2	1	0	0	0-0	8.2	14	10	9	3	8-0	4

CHAMPIONSHIP SERIES RECORD

Year League	W	L	Pct.	ERA	G	GS	CG	ShO	Sv.-Opp.	IP	H	R	ER	HR	BB-IBB	SO
2000— Seattle (A.L.)	0	1	.000	5.40	1	1	0	0	0-0	5.0	3	3	3	1	3-0	3
2001— Seattle (A.L.)	0	0	...	0.00	1	1	0	0	0-0	5.0	0	0	0	0	8-0	2
Champ. series totals (2 years)	0	1	.000	2.70	2	2	0	0	0-0	10.0	3	3	3	1	11-0	5

ABERNATHY, BRENT — 2B — DEVIL RAYS

PERSONAL: Born September 23, 1977, in Atlanta, Ga. ... 6-1/191. ... Bats right, throws right. ... Full name: Michael Brent Abernathy.

HIGH SCHOOL: Lovett School (Atlanta, Ga.).

TRANSACTIONS/CAREER NOTES: Selected by Toronto Blue Jays organization in second round of free-agent draft (June 4, 1996); pick received as part of compensation from Florida Marlins for signing of Type B free agent OF Devon White. ... On Syracuse disabled list (June 21-28, 2000). ... Traded by Blue Jays with player to be named later to Tampa Bay Devil Rays for P Steve Trachsel and P Mark Guthrie (July 31, 2000). ... On Durham disabled list (April 15-May 2, 2001).

STATISTICAL NOTES: Led Southern League second basemen with 292 putouts, 361 assists and 669 total chances in 1999.

MISCELLANEOUS: Member of 2000 U.S. Olympic baseball team.

2002 GAMES PLAYED BY POSITION (MLB): 2B—116; DH—1.

Year	Team (League)	Pos.	G	AB	R	H	2B	3B	HR	RBI	BB	SO	SB-CS	Avg.	OBP	SLG	E	Avg.
			BATTING														FIELDING	
1997—	Hagerstown (S.Atl.)....	2B	99	379	69	117	27	2	1	26	30	32	22-13	.309	.367	.398	12	.973
1998—	Dunedin (FSL)...........	2B	124	485	85	169	36	1	3	65	44	38	35-13	.348	.399	.445	16	.973
1999—	Knoxville (Sou.)..........	2B	136	*577	*108	*168	42	1	13	62	55	47	34-15	.291	.355	.435	16	.976
2000—	Syracuse (I.L.)............	2B	92	358	47	106	21	2	4	35	36	32	14-13	.296	.359	.399	11	.973
	—Durham (I.L.)■.........	2B	27	91	14	24	6	0	1	15	11	11	9-2	.264	.351	.363	3	.973
2001—	Durham (I.L.).............	2B	61	252	45	76	20	0	4	23	16	23	11-4	.302	.346	.429	9	.969
	—Tampa Bay (A.L.)........	2B	79	304	43	82	17	1	5	33	27	35	8-3	.270	.328	.382	7	.981
2002—	Tampa Bay (A.L.)........	2B-DH	117	463	46	112	18	4	2	40	25	46	10-4	.242	.288	.311	12	.979
Major League totals (2 years)			196	767	89	194	35	5	7	73	52	81	18-7	.253	.304	.339	19	.980

ABREU, BOBBY — OF — PHILLIES

PERSONAL: Born March 11, 1974, in Aragua, Venezuela. ... 6-0/195. ... Bats left, throws right. ... Full name: Bob Kelly Abreu. ... Name pronounced uh-BRAY-yew.

TRANSACTIONS/CAREER NOTES: Signed as non-drafted free agent by Houston Astros organization (August 21, 1990). ... On Houston disabled list (May 25-July 1, 1997); included rehabilitation assignments to Jackson (June 23-26) and New Orleans (June 27-July 1). ... Selected by Tampa Bay Devil Rays in first round (sixth pick overall) of expansion draft (November 18, 1997). ... Traded by Devil Rays to Philadelphia Phillies for SS Kevin Stocker (November 18, 1997).

STATISTICAL NOTES: Led Gulf Coast League outfielders with 11 assists in 1991. ... Led Pacific Coast League outfielders with 18 assists in 1995. ... Led Pacific Coast League in caught stealing with 18 in 1996. ... Had 17-game hitting streak (September 5-24, 2002). ... Career major league grand slams: 2.

2002 GAMES PLAYED BY POSITION (MLB): OF—154.

Year	Team (League)	Pos.	G	AB	R	H	2B	3B	HR	RBI	BB	SO	SB-CS	Avg.	OBP	SLG	E	Avg.
			BATTING														FIELDING	
1991—	GC Astros (GCL)........	OF-SS	56	183	21	55	7	3	0	20	17	27	10-6	.301	.358	.372	5	.943
1992—	Asheville (S.Atl.).........	OF	135	480	81	140	21	4	8	48	63	79	15-11	.292	.375	.402	11	.943
1993—	Osceola (FSL).............	OF	129	474	62	134	21	17	5	55	51	90	10-14	.283	.352	.430	8	.961
1994—	Jackson (Texas).........	OF	118	400	61	121	25	9	16	73	42	81	12-10	.303	.368	*.530	4	.967
1995—	Tucson (PCL).............	OF-2B	114	415	72	126	24	*17	10	75	67	120	16-14	.304	.395	.516	7	.970
1996—	Tucson (PCL).............	OF-DH	132	484	86	138	14	*16	13	68	83	111	24-18	.285	.391	.461	7	.969
	—Houston (N.L.)...........	OF	15	22	1	5	1	0	0	1	2	3	0-0	.227	.292	.273	0	1.000
1997—	Houston (N.L.)...........	OF	59	188	22	47	10	2	3	26	21	48	7-2	.250	.329	.372	2	.978
	—Jackson (Texas).........	OF	3	12	2	2	1	0	0	0	1	5	0-0	.167	.231	.250	0	1.000
	—New Orleans (A.A.).....	OF	47	194	25	52	9	4	2	22	21	49	7-4	.268	.335	.387	1	.990
1998—	Philadelphia (N.L.)■..	OF	151	497	68	155	29	6	17	74	84	133	19-10	.312	.409	.497	8	.973
1999—	Philadelphia (N.L.)......	OF-DH	152	546	118	183	35	•11	20	93	109	113	27-9	.335	.446	.549	3	.989
2000—	Philadelphia (N.L.)......	OF	154	576	103	182	42	10	25	79	100	116	28-8	.316	.416	.554	4	.989
2001—	Philadelphia (N.L.)......	OF	•162	588	118	170	48	4	31	110	106	137	36-14	.289	.393	.543	8	.976
2002—	Philadelphia (N.L.)......	OF	157	572	102	176	*50	6	20	85	104	117	31-12	.308	.413	.521	5	.983
Major League totals (7 years)			850	2989	532	918	215	39	116	468	526	667	148-55	.307	.409	.522	30	.982

DIVISION SERIES RECORD

Year	Team (League)	Pos.	G	AB	R	H	2B	3B	HR	RBI	BB	SO	SB-CS	Avg.	OBP	SLG	E	Avg.
			BATTING														FIELDING	
1997—	Houston (N.L.)...........	PH	3	3	0	1	0	0	0	0	0	2	1-0	.333	.333	.333	...	...

ACEVEDO, JOSE — P — REDS

PERSONAL: Born December 18, 1977, in Santo Domingo, Dominican Republic. ... 6-0/185. ... Throws right, bats right. ... Full name: Jose Omar Acevedo. ... Cousin of Juan Marichal, pitcher with San Francisco Giants (1960-73), Boston Red Sox (1974) and Los Angeles Dodgers (1975).

TRANSACTIONS/CAREER NOTES: Signed as non-drafted free agent by Cincinnati Reds organization (December 7, 1996).

CAREER HITTING (MLB): 5-for-41 (.122), 2 R, 2 2B, 0 3B, 0 HR, 3 RBI.

Year	League	W	L	Pct.	ERA	G	GS	CG	ShO	Sv.-Opp.	IP	H	R	ER	HR	BB-IBB	SO
1997—	Charleston, W.Va. (S.Atl.).	3	3	.500	3.92	15	8	0	0	0-...	57.1	61	29	25	8	9-0	34
1998—	Charleston, W.Va. (S.Atl.).	9	9	.500	3.91	25	25	2	0	0-...	158.2	169	74	69	9	40-0	132
1999—	Clinton (Midw.)...............	8	6	.571	3.77	24	24	1	1	0-...	133.2	119	65	56	14	43-0	136
2000—	Dayton (Midw.)...............	11	5	.688	3.89	25	23	0	0	0-...	141.0	135	74	61	16	53-0	123
2001—	Chattanooga (Sou.)..........	4	4	.500	3.69	16	11	0	0	0-...	78.0	68	34	32	6	25-1	82
	—Cincinnati (N.L.)............	5	7	.417	5.44	18	18	0	0	0-0	96.0	101	61	58	17	34-2	68
2002—	Cincinnati (N.L.).............	4	2	.667	7.23	6	5	0	0	0-0	23.2	28	21	19	8	12-0	14
	—Louisville (I.L.)................	12	7	.632	3.20	23	23	0	0	0-...	154.2	146	61	55	16	34-0	128
Major League totals (2 years).....		9	9	.500	5.79	24	23	0	0	0-0	119.2	129	82	77	25	46-2	82

ACEVEDO, JUAN — P

PERSONAL: Born May 5, 1970, in Juarez, Mexico. ... 6-2/228. ... Throws right, bats right. ... Full name: Juan Carlos Lara Acevedo. ... Name pronounced ah-sah-VAY-doh.

HIGH SCHOOL: Dundee-Crown (Carpentersville, Ill.).

JUNIOR COLLEGE: Parkland College (Ill.).

TRANSACTIONS/CAREER NOTES: Selected by Colorado Rockies organization in 14th round of free-agent draft (June 1, 1992). ... Traded by Rockies with P Arnold Gooch to New York Mets for P Bret Saberhagen and a player to be named later (July 31, 1995); Rockies acquired P David Swanson to complete deal (August 4, 1995). ... On New York disabled list (March 26-May 9, 1996); included rehabilitation assignment to Norfolk (April 10-May 9). ... Traded by Mets to St. Louis Cardinals for P Rigo Beltran (March 29, 1998). ... On St. Louis disabled list (July 18-August 16, 1998); included rehabilitation assignment to Memphis (August 6-16). ... Traded by Cardinals with two players to be named later to Milwaukee Brewers for 2B Fernando Vina (December 20, 1999); Brewers acquired P Matt Parker and C Eliezer Alfonzo to complete deal

(June 13, 2000). ... On Milwaukee disabled list (April 7-30, 2000); included rehabilitation assignment to Indianapolis (April 25-29). ... Traded by Brewers with P Kane Davis and IF Jose Flores to Rockies for P Mark Leiter, P Mike DeJean and 2B/SS Elvis Pena (April 4, 2001). ... On Colorado disabled list (April 7-22 and April 29-May 24, 2001); included rehabilitation assignments to Colorado Springs (April 17-22 and May 17-24). ... Traded by Rockies to Florida Marlins for IF Josue Espada (August 6, 2001). ... Granted free agency (November 26, 2001). ... Signed by Detroit Tigers organization (December 20, 2001). ... Granted free agency (October 28, 2002).

HONORS: Named Eastern League Pitcher of the Year (1994).

STATISTICAL NOTES: Tied for Eastern League lead with five balks in 1994. ... Tied for International League lead with four balks in 1997.

CAREER HITTING (MLB): 6-for-65 (.092), 4 R, 2 2B, 0 3B, 0 HR, 0 RBI.

Year League	W	L	Pct.	ERA	G	GS	CG	ShO	Sv.-Opp.	IP	H	R	ER	HR	BB-IBB	SO
1992—Bend (N'West)	0	0	...	13.50	1	0	0	0	0-...	2.0	4	3	3	0	1-0	3
—Visalia (Calif.)	3	4	.429	5.43	12	12	1	0	0-...	64.2	75	46	39	2	33-0	37
1993—Central Valley (Calif.)	9	8	.529	4.40	27	20	1	0	0-...	118.2	119	68	58	8	58-0	107
1994—New Haven (East.)	*17	6	.739	*2.37	26	26	5	2	0-...	174.2	142	56	46	16	38-0	161
1995—Colorado (N.L.)	4	6	.400	6.44	17	11	0	0	0-0	65.2	82	53	47	15	20-2	40
—Colorado Springs (PCL)	1	1	.500	6.14	3	3	0	0	0-...	14.2	18	11	10	0	7-0	7
—Norfolk (I.L.)■	0	0	...	0.00	2	2	0	0	0-...	3.0	0	0	0	0	1-0	2
1996—Norfolk (I.L.)	4	8	.333	5.96	19	19	2	1	0-...	102.2	116	70	68	15	53-0	83
1997—Norfolk (I.L.)	6	6	.500	3.86	18	18	1	0	0-...	116.2	111	55	50	7	34-1	99
—New York (N.L.)	3	1	.750	3.59	25	2	0	0	0-4	47.2	52	24	19	6	22-2	33
1998—St. Louis (N.L.)■	8	3	.727	2.56	50	9	0	0	15-16	98.1	83	30	28	7	29-2	56
—Memphis (PCL)	0	0	...	0.00	2	2	0	0	0-...	8.2	5	0	0	0	1-0	6
1999—St. Louis (N.L.)	6	8	.429	5.89	50	12	0	0	4-6	102.1	115	71	67	17	48-3	52
2000—Milwaukee (N.L.)■	3	7	.300	3.81	62	0	0	0	0-2	82.2	77	38	35	11	31-9	51
—Indianapolis (I.L.)	0	0	...	0.00	2	2	0	0	0-...	4.0	3	0	0	0	0-0	4
2001—Colorado (N.L.)■	0	2	.000	5.63	39	0	0	0	0-5	32.0	37	24	20	4	19-6	26
—Colorado Springs (PCL)	0	0	...	1.29	6	0	0	0	1-...	7.0	3	2	1	0	4-0	7
—Florida (N.L.)■	2	3	.400	2.54	20	0	0	0	0-0	28.1	31	11	8	2	16-3	21
2002—Detroit (A.L.)■	1	5	.167	2.65	65	0	0	0	28-35	74.2	68	33	22	4	23-3	43
A.L. totals (1 year)	1	5	.167	2.65	65	0	0	0	28-35	74.2	68	33	22	4	23-3	43
N.L. totals (6 years)	26	30	.464	4.41	263	34	0	0	19-33	457.0	477	251	224	62	185-27	279
Major League totals (7 years)	27	35	.435	4.16	328	34	0	0	47-68	531.2	545	284	246	66	208-30	322

ADAMS, TERRY P

PERSONAL: Born March 6, 1973, in Mobile, Ala. ... 6-3/215. ... Throws right, bats right. ... Full name: Terry Wayne Adams.

HIGH SCHOOL: Mary G. Montgomery (Semmes, Ala.).

TRANSACTIONS/CAREER NOTES: Selected by Chicago Cubs organization in fourth round of free-agent draft (June 3, 1991). ... On disabled list (June 21-September 21, 1993). ... On Chicago disabled list (March 26-May 8 and June 19-July 4, 1999); included rehabilitation assignments to West Tenn (April 30-May 4) and Iowa (May 6-8). ... Traded by Cubs with P Chad Ricketts and a player to be named later to Los Angeles Dodgers for P Ismael Valdes and 2B Eric Young (December 12, 1999); Dodgers acquired P Brian Stephenson to complete deal (December 16, 1999). ... Granted free agency (November 5, 2001). ... Signed by Philadelphia Phillies (January 17, 2002). ... Granted free agency (October 29, 2002).

CAREER HITTING (MLB): 4-for-77 (.052), 2 R, 1 2B, 0 3B, 0 HR, 2 RBI.

Year League	W	L	Pct.	ERA	G	GS	CG	ShO	Sv.-Opp.	IP	H	R	ER	HR	BB-IBB	SO
1991—Huntington (Appl.)	0	*9	.000	5.77	14	13	0	0	0-...	57.2	67	*56	37	1	62-0	52
1992—Peoria (Midw.)	7	12	.368	4.41	25	25	3	1	0-...	157.0	144	95	77	7	86-0	96
1993—Daytona (FSL)	3	5	.375	4.97	13	13	0	0	0-...	70.2	78	47	39	2	43-0	35
1994—Daytona (FSL)	9	10	.474	4.38	39	7	0	0	7-...	84.1	87	47	41	5	46-3	64
1995—Orlando (Sou.)	2	3	.400	1.43	37	0	0	0	19-...	37.2	23	9	6	2	16-1	26
—Iowa (A.A.)	0	0	...	0.00	7	0	0	0	5-...	6.1	3	0	0	0	2-0	10
—Chicago (N.L.)	1	1	.500	6.50	18	0	0	0	1-1	18.0	22	15	13	0	10-1	15
1996—Chicago (N.L.)	3	6	.333	2.94	69	0	0	0	4-8	101.0	84	36	33	6	49-6	78
1997—Chicago (N.L.)	2	9	.182	4.62	74	0	0	0	18-22	74.0	91	43	38	3	40-6	64
1998—Chicago (N.L.)	7	7	.500	4.33	63	0	0	0	1-7	72.2	72	39	35	7	41-3	73
—Iowa (PCL)	0	0	...	0.00	3	0	0	0	0-...	4.0	1	1	0	0	3-0	5
1999—West Tenn (Sou.)	0	0	...	16.88	2	1	0	0	0-...	2.2	5	6	5	0	2-0	2
—Chicago (N.L.)	6	3	.667	4.02	52	0	0	0	13-18	65.0	60	33	29	9	28-2	57
2000—Los Angeles (N.L.)■	6	9	.400	3.52	66	0	0	0	2-7	84.1	80	42	33	6	39-0	56
2001—Los Angeles (N.L.)	12	8	.600	4.33	43	22	0	0	0-1	166.1	172	84	80	9	54-1	141
2002—Philadelphia (N.L.)■	7	9	.438	4.35	46	19	0	0	0-1	136.2	132	76	66	9	58-5	96
Major League totals (8 years)	44	52	.458	4.10	431	41	0	0	39-65	718.0	713	368	327	49	319-24	580

AFFELDT, JEREMY P ROYALS

PERSONAL: Born June 6, 1979, in Phoenix, Ariz. ... 6-4/215. ... Throws left, bats left. ... Full name: Jeremy David Affeldt.

HIGH SCHOOL: Northwest Christian (Spokane, Wash.).

TRANSACTIONS/CAREER NOTES: Selected by Kansas City Royals organization in third round of free-agent draft (June 3, 1997). ... On Kansas City disabled list (June 9-August 1, 2002); included rehabilitation assignment to Wichita (July 24-August 1).

CAREER HITTING (MLB): 0-for-0 (.000), 0 R, 0 2B, 0 3B, 0 HR, 0 RBI.

Year League	W	L	Pct.	ERA	G	GS	CG	ShO	Sv.-Opp.	IP	H	R	ER	HR	BB-IBB	SO
1997—Gulf Coast Royals (GCL)	2	0	1.000	4.50	10	9	0	0	0-...	40.0	34	24	20	3	21-0	36
1998—Lansing (Midw.)	0	3	.000	9.53	6	3	0	0	0-...	17.0	27	21	18	1	12-0	8
—Gulf Coast Royals (GCL)	4	3	.571	2.89	12	9	0	0	0-...	56.0	50	24	18	1	24-0	67
1999—Charleston, W.Va. (S.Atl.)	7	7	.500	3.83	27	24	2	1	0-...	143.1	140	78	61	4	80-0	111
2000—Wilmington (Caro.)	5	15	.250	4.09	27	26	0	0	0-...	147.1	158	87	67	7	59-0	92
2001—Wichita (Texas)	10	6	.625	3.90	25	25	0	0	0-...	145.1	153	74	63	9	46-0	128
2002—Kansas City (A.L.)	3	4	.429	4.64	34	7	0	0	0-1	77.2	85	41	40	8	37-4	67
—Wichita (Texas)	0	0	...	1.50	3	3	0	0	0-...	6.0	1	1	1	0	3-0	3
Major League totals (1 year)	3	4	.429	4.64	34	7	0	0	0-1	77.2	85	41	40	8	37-4	67

AGBAYANI, BENNY — OF — RED SOX

PERSONAL: Born December 28, 1971, in Honolulu, Hawaii. ... 6-0/225. ... Bats right, throws right. ... Full name: Benny Peter Agbayani Jr.
HIGH SCHOOL: St. Louis (Honolulu, Hawaii).
COLLEGE: Oregon Tech, then Hawaii Pacific.
TRANSACTIONS/CAREER NOTES: Selected by California Angels organization in 25th round of free-agent draft (June 1, 1992); did not sign. ... Selected by New York Mets organization in 30th round of free-agent draft (June 3, 1993). ... On Norfolk disabled list (May 10-June 6, 1998). ... On New York disabled list (April 9-24 and September 18, 2001-remainder of season); included rehabilitation assignment to Norfolk (April 20-24). ... Traded by Mets to Colorado Rockies as part of three-way deal in which Mets traded P Glendon Rusch to Milwaukee Brewers, Rockies traded 1B/OF Ross Gload and P Craig House to Mets, Brewers traded P Jeff D'Amico, OF Jeromy Burnitz, IF Lou Collier, OF/1B Mark Sweeney and cash to Mets, Mets traded 1B/3B Todd Zeile, IF/OF Lenny Harris and cash to Rockies and Rockies traded OF Alex Ochoa to Brewers (January 21, 2002). ... On Colorado disabled list (May 13-June 5, 2002); included rehabilitation assignment to Colorado Springs (May 28-June 5). ... Claimed on waivers by Boston Red Sox (August 26, 2002).
STATISTICAL NOTES: Tied for International League lead in caught stealing with 14 in 1997. ... Career major league grand slams: 2.
2002 GAMES PLAYED BY POSITION (MLB): OF—50; DH—1.

		BATTING														FIELDING	
Year Team (League)	Pos.	G	AB	R	H	2B	3B	HR	RBI	BB	SO	SB-CS	Avg.	OBP	SLG	E	Avg.
1993— Pittsfield (NY-Penn)	OF	51	167	26	42	6	3	2	22	20	43	7-2	.251	.332	.359	2	.969
1994— St. Lucie (FSL)	OF	119	411	72	115	13	5	5	63	58	67	8-6	.280	.378	.372	1	.993
1995— Binghamton (East.)	OF	88	295	38	81	11	2	1	26	39	51	12-3	.275	.368	.336	3	.972
— St. Lucie (FSL)	OF	44	155	24	48	9	3	2	29	26	27	8-3	.310	.416	.445	2	.950
1996— Binghamton (East.)	OF	21	53	7	9	1	0	2	8	11	13	1-0	.170	.318	.302	1	.952
— Norfolk (I.L.)	OF-1B	99	331	43	92	13	9	7	56	30	57	14-5	.278	.339	.435	2	.989
1997— Norfolk (I.L.)	OF	127	468	90	145	24	2	11	51	67	106	29-14	.310	.401	.440	5	.978
1998— Norfolk (I.L.)	OF-1B	90	322	43	91	20	5	11	53	50	58	16-6	.283	.381	.478	4	.975
— New York (N.L.)	OF	11	15	1	2	0	0	0	0	1	5	0-2	.133	.188	.133	0	1.000
1999— Norfolk (I.L.)	OF-1B-DH	28	101	21	36	8	1	8	32	16	19	5-3	.356	.446	.693	2	.983
— New York (N.L.)	OF-DH	101	276	42	79	18	3	14	42	32	60	6-4	.286	.363	.525	2	.984
2000— New York (N.L.)	OF-DH	119	350	59	101	19	1	15	60	54	68	5-5	.289	.391	.477	4	.975
2001— New York (N.L.)	OF	91	296	28	82	14	2	6	27	36	73	4-5	.277	.364	.399	6	.954
— Norfolk (I.L.)	OF	4	16	3	5	1	0	1	3	1	0	0-0	.313	.353	.563	0	1.000
2002— Colorado (N.L.)■	OF-DH	48	117	10	24	5	0	4	19	10	35	1-0	.205	.266	.350	0	1.000
— Colo. Springs (PCL)	OF	43	147	28	40	8	1	11	32	28	32	1-0	.272	.391	.565	0	1.000
— Pawtucket (I.L.)■	OF	5	17	1	3	1	0	0	2	3	6	0-0	.176	.300	.235	0	1.000
— Boston (A.L.)	OF	13	37	5	11	1	0	0	8	6	5	0-0	.297	.395	.324	1	.962
American League totals (1 year)		13	37	5	11	1	0	0	8	6	5	0-0	.297	.395	.324	1	.962
National League totals (5 years)		370	1054	140	288	56	6	39	148	133	241	16-16	.273	.360	.449	12	.975
Major League totals (5 years)		383	1091	145	299	57	6	39	156	139	246	16-16	.274	.362	.445	13	.974

DIVISION SERIES RECORD

		BATTING														FIELDING	
Year Team (League)	Pos.	G	AB	R	H	2B	3B	HR	RBI	BB	SO	SB-CS	Avg.	OBP	SLG	E	Avg.
1999— New York (N.L.)	OF-PH	4	10	1	3	1	0	0	1	0	3	0-0	.300	.300	.400	0	1.000
2000— New York (N.L.)	OF	4	15	1	5	1	0	1	1	3	3	0-0	.333	.444	.600	0	1.000
Division series totals (2 years)		8	25	2	8	2	0	1	2	3	6	0-0	.320	.393	.520	0	1.000

CHAMPIONSHIP SERIES RECORD

		BATTING														FIELDING	
Year Team (League)	Pos.	G	AB	R	H	2B	3B	HR	RBI	BB	SO	SB-CS	Avg.	OBP	SLG	E	Avg.
1999— New York (N.L.)	OF-PH	4	7	2	1	0	0	0	0	4	2	1-1	.143	.455	.143	0	1.000
2000— New York (N.L.)	OF	5	17	0	6	2	0	0	3	4	0	0-0	.353	.476	.471	1	.917
Championship series totals (2 years)		9	24	2	7	2	0	0	3	8	2	1-1	.292	.469	.375	1	.938

WORLD SERIES RECORD

		BATTING														FIELDING	
Year Team (League)	Pos.	G	AB	R	H	2B	3B	HR	RBI	BB	SO	SB-CS	Avg.	OBP	SLG	E	Avg.
2000— New York (N.L.)	OF	5	18	2	5	2	0	0	2	3	6	0-0	.278	.381	.389	0	1.000

AINSWORTH, KURT — P — GIANTS

PERSONAL: Born September 9, 1978, in Baton Rouge, La. ... 6-3/192. ... Throws right, bats right. ... Full name: Kurt Harold Ainsworth.
HIGH SCHOOL: Catholic (Baton Rouge, La.).
COLLEGE: Louisiana State.
TRANSACTIONS/CAREER NOTES: Selected by San Francisco Giants organization in first round (24th pick overall) of free-agent draft (June 2, 1999). ... On Fresno disabled list (June 16-July 15, 2002).
MISCELLANEOUS: Member of 2000 Olympic baseball team.
CAREER HITTING (MLB): 1-for-6 (.167), 1 R, 1 2B, 0 3B, 0 HR, 0 RBI.

Year League	W	L	Pct.	ERA	G	GS	CG	ShO	Sv.-Opp.	IP	H	R	ER	HR	BB-IBB	SO
1999— Salem-Kaizer (N'West)	3	3	.500	1.61	10	10	1	0	0-...	44.2	34	18	8	1	18-0	64
2000— Shreveport (Texas)	10	9	.526	3.30	28	28	0	0	0-...	158.0	138	67	58	12	63-3	130
2001— Fresno (PCL)	10	9	.526	5.07	27	26	0	0	0-...	149.0	139	91	84	22	54-1	157
— San Francisco (N.L.)	0	0	...	13.50	2	0	0	0	0-0	2.0	3	3	3	1	2-0	3
2002— Fresno (PCL)	8	6	.571	3.41	20	19	1	0	0-...	116.0	101	49	44	7	43-0	119
— San Francisco (N.L.)	1	2	.333	2.10	6	4	0	0	0-0	25.2	22	7	6	1	12-0	15
Major League totals (2 years)	1	2	.333	2.93	8	4	0	0	0-0	27.2	25	10	9	2	14-0	18

ALCANTARA, ISRAEL 1B/OF

PERSONAL: Born May 6, 1973, in Bani, Dominican Republic. ... 6-2/210. ... Bats right, throws right. ... Full name: Israel Cristostomo Alcantara.
TRANSACTIONS/CAREER NOTES: Signed as non-drafted free agent by Montreal Expos organization (July 2, 1990). ... On Harrisburg disabled list (June 24-August 16, 1996). ... Granted free agency (October 15, 1997). ... Signed by Tampa Bay Devil Rays organization (December 16, 1997). ... On Durham disabled list (April 9-May 9, 1998). ... Granted free agency (October 15, 1998). ... Signed by Boston Red Sox organization (December 14, 1998). ... Granted free agency (October 15, 1999). ... Re-signed by Red Sox organization (January 4, 2000). ... On Pawtucket disabled list (May 15-22, 2001). ... On Boston disabled list (August 14-September 1, 2000); included rehabilitation assignment to Pawtucket (August 19-September 1). ... Granted free agency (December 21, 2000). ... Re-signed by Red Sox organization (January 11, 2001). ... Granted free agency (December 21, 2001). ... Signed by Milwaukee Brewers organization (February 8, 2002). ... Released by Brewers (September 30, 2002).
STATISTICAL NOTES: Led Gulf Coast League with four intentional bases on balls received in 1992. ... Led Midwest League third basemen with 98 putouts and 371 total chances in 1993. ... Led International League with 270 total bases and .599 slugging percentage in 2001.
2002 GAMES PLAYED BY POSITION (MLB): OF—7; 1B—2.

			BATTING														FIELDING	
Year	Team (League)	Pos.	G	AB	R	H	2B	3B	HR	RBI	BB	SO	SB-CS	Avg.	OBP	SLG	E	Avg.
1991—	Dom. Expos (DSL)		68	239	42	68	9	2	•13	51	32	41	8-...	.285	...	.502	...	...
1992—	GC Expos (GCL)	3B-2B-SS	59	224	29	62	14	2	3	37	17	35	6-5	.277	.328	.397	14	.932
1993—	Burlington (Midw.)	3B	126	470	65	115	26	3	18	73	20	125	6-7	.245	.283	.428	*57	.846
1994—	W. Palm Beach (FSL)	3B	125	471	65	134	26	4	15	69	26	130	9-3	.285	.324	.452	*32	.902
1995—	Harrisburg (East.)	3B-DH	71	237	25	50	12	2	10	29	21	81	1-1	.211	.280	.405	20	.892
—	W. Palm Beach (FSL)	3B-DH-OF	39	134	16	37	7	2	3	22	9	35	3-0	.276	.329	.425	9	.911
1996—	Harrisburg (East.)	3B-DH	62	218	26	46	5	0	8	19	14	62	1-1	.211	.261	.344	16	.912
—	GC Expos (GCL)	3B-DH	7	30	4	9	2	0	2	10	3	6	0-1	.300	.364	.567	3	.880
—	W. Palm Beach (FSL)	3B-DH	15	61	11	19	2	0	4	14	3	13	0-0	.311	.348	.541	4	.897
1997—	Harrisburg (East.)	3B-1B-DH-OF	89	301	48	85	9	2	27	68	29	84	4-5	.282	.348	.595	19	.946
1998—	St. Pete. (FSL)■	3B-OF-DH	38	141	21	47	5	0	10	26	21	29	1-0	.333	.427	.582	8	.908
—	Reading (East.)	DH-1B-3B-OF	53	203	36	63	12	2	15	44	17	37	0-1	.310	.368	.611	7	.962
—	Orlando (Sou.)	DH-1B-OF-3B	15	55	8	13	4	0	3	18	7	15	0-1	.236	.308	.473	1	.963
1999—	Trenton (East.)■	OF-DH-1B	77	293	48	86	26	0	20	60	27	78	4-2	.294	.361	.587	2	.990
—	Pawtucket (I.L.)	OF-DH-1B	24	81	13	22	3	0	9	23	9	29	0-0	.272	.366	.642	0	1.000
2000—	Pawtucket (I.L.)	OF-1B	78	299	60	92	17	1	29	76	25	84	2-1	.308	.364	.662	8	.941
—	Boston (A.L.)	DH-OF-1B	21	45	9	13	1	0	4	7	3	7	0-0	.289	.333	.578	1	.944
2001—	Pawtucket (I.L.)	OF-1B	119	451	80	134	26	1	*36	90	57	107	9-2	.297	.380	.599	5	.975
—	Boston (A.L.)	OF-1B-DH	14	38	3	10	1	0	0	3	3	13	1-0	.263	.317	.289	2	.933
2002—	Indianapolis (I.L.)■	OF-1B-3B	110	410	61	110	21	2	*27	65	51	88	9-3	.268	.350	.527	5	.983
—	Milwaukee (N.L.)	OF-1B	16	32	3	8	1	0	2	5	0	6	0-1	.250	.250	.469	1	.952
American League totals (2 years)			35	83	12	23	2	0	4	10	6	20	1-0	.277	.326	.446	3	.938
National League totals (1 year)			16	32	3	8	1	0	2	5	0	6	0-1	.250	.250	.469	1	.952
Major League totals (3 years)			51	115	15	31	3	0	6	15	6	26	1-1	.270	.306	.452	4	.942

ALDRIDGE, CORY OF BRAVES

PERSONAL: Born June 13, 1979, in San Angelo, Texas. ... 6-0/210. ... Bats left, throws right. ... Full name: Cory Coty Jerome Aldridge.
HIGH SCHOOL: Cooper (Abilene, Texas).
TRANSACTIONS/CAREER NOTES: Selected by Atlanta Braves organization in fourth round of free-agent draft (June 3, 1997). ... On disabled list (June 13-July 10, 2000). ... On Atlanta disabled list (March 30, 2002-entire season); included rehabilitation assignment to Gulf Coast Braves (August 5-24).

			BATTING														FIELDING	
Year	Team (League)	Pos.	G	AB	R	H	2B	3B	HR	RBI	BB	SO	SB-CS	Avg.	OBP	SLG	E	Avg.
1997—	GC Braves (GCL)	OF	46	169	26	47	8	1	3	37	14	37	1-0	.278	.337	.391	1	.955
1998—	Danville (Appl.)	OF	60	214	37	63	16	1	3	33	29	48	16-2	.294	.382	.421	3	.955
1999—	Macon (S.Atl.)	OF	124	443	48	111	19	4	12	65	33	123	9-5	.251	.308	.393	7	.963
2000—	Myrtle Beach (Caro.)	OF	109	401	51	100	18	5	15	64	33	118	10-5	.249	.302	.431	4	.977
2001—	Greenville (Sou.)	OF	131	452	57	111	19	2	19	56	48	139	12-6	.246	.323	.423	8	.964
—	Atlanta (N.L.)	OF	8	5	1	0	0	0	0	0	0	4	0-0	.000	.000	.000	0	1.000
2002—	GC Braves (GCL)		17	59	10	17	5	3	3	13	11	17	0-0	.288	.394	.627	0	...
Major League totals (1 year)			8	5	1	0	0	0	0	0	0	4	0-0	.000	.000	.000	0	1.000

ALFONSECA, ANTONIO P CUBS

PERSONAL: Born April 16, 1972, in La Romana, Dominican Republic. ... 6-5/250. ... Throws right, bats right.
TRANSACTIONS/CAREER NOTES: Signed as non-drafted free agent by Montreal Expos organization (July 3, 1989). ... Selected by Florida Marlins organization from Expos organization in Rule 5 minor league draft (December 13, 1993). ... On disabled list (May 15-June 15, 1995). ... On disabled list (July 12-September 3, 1996). ... On disabled list (May 14-31, 1998). ... Traded by Marlins with P Matt Clement to Chicago Cubs for P Julian Tavarez, P Jose Cueto, P Dontrelle Willis and C Ryan Jorgensen (March 27, 2002).
HONORS: Named N.L. Fireman of the Year by The Sporting News (2000).
CAREER HITTING (MLB): 2-for-12 (.167), 0 R, 0 2B, 0 3B, 0 HR, 2 RBI.

Year	League	W	L	Pct.	ERA	G	GS	CG	ShO	Sv.-Opp.	IP	H	R	ER	HR	BB-IBB	SO
1990—	Dominican Expos (DSL)	3	5	.375	3.60	13	13	1	0	0-...	60.0	60	29	24	...	32-...	19
1991—	Gulf Coast Expos (GCL)	3	3	.500	3.88	11	10	0	0	0-...	51.0	46	33	22	2	25-0	38
1992—	Gulf Coast Expos (GCL)	3	4	.429	3.68	12	10	1	1	0-...	66.0	55	31	27	0	35-0	62
1993—	Jamestown (NY-Penn)	2	2	.500	6.15	15	4	0	0	1-...	33.2	31	26	23	3	22-1	29
1994—	Kane County (Midw.)■	6	5	.545	4.07	32	9	0	0	0-...	86.1	78	41	39	5	21-1	74
1995—	Portland (East.)	9	3	.750	3.64	19	17	1	0	0-...	96.1	81	43	39	6	42-1	75
1996—	Charlotte (I.L.)	4	4	.500	5.53	14	13	0	0	1-...	71.2	86	47	44	6	22-0	51
1997—	Charlotte (I.L.)	7	2	.778	4.32	46	0	0	0	7-...	58.1	58	34	28	8	20-3	45
—	Florida (N.L.)	1	3	.250	4.91	17	0	0	0	0-2	25.2	36	16	14	3	10-3	19

Year	League	W	L	Pct.	ERA	G	GS	CG	ShO	Sv.-Opp.	IP	H	R	ER	HR	BB-IBB	SO
1998—	Florida (N.L.)	4	6	.400	4.08	58	0	0	0	8-14	70.2	75	36	32	10	33-9	46
1999—	Florida (N.L.)	4	5	.444	3.24	73	0	0	0	21-25	77.2	79	28	28	4	29-6	46
2000—	Florida (N.L.)	5	6	.455	4.24	68	0	0	0	*45-49	70.0	82	35	33	7	24-3	47
2001—	Florida (N.L.)	4	4	.500	3.06	58	0	0	0	28-34	61.2	68	24	21	6	15-3	40
2002—	Chicago (N.L.)■	2	5	.286	4.00	66	0	0	0	19-28	74.1	73	34	33	5	36-3	61
Major League totals (6 years)		20	29	.408	3.81	340	0	0	0	121-152	380.0	413	173	161	35	147-27	259

DIVISION SERIES RECORD

Year	League	W	L	Pct.	ERA	G	GS	CG	ShO	Sv.-Opp.	IP	H	R	ER	HR	BB-IBB	SO
1997—	Florida (N.L.)									Did not play.							

CHAMPIONSHIP SERIES RECORD

Year	League	W	L	Pct.	ERA	G	GS	CG	ShO	Sv.-Opp.	IP	H	R	ER	HR	BB-IBB	SO
1997—	Florida (N.L.)									Did not play.							

WORLD SERIES RECORD

NOTES: Member of World Series championship team (1997).

Year	League	W	L	Pct.	ERA	G	GS	CG	ShO	Sv.-Opp.	IP	H	R	ER	HR	BB-IBB	SO
1997—	Florida (N.L.)	0	0	...	0.00	3	0	0	0	0-0	6.1	6	0	0	0	1-0	5

ALFONZO, EDGARDO 3B

PERSONAL: Born November 8, 1973, in St. Teresa, Venezuela. ... 5-11/187. ... Bats right, throws right. ... Full name: Edgardo Antonio Alfonzo. ... Brother of Roberto Alfonzo, second baseman with New York Mets organization (1993-94).

HIGH SCHOOL: Cecilio Acosto (Venezuela).

TRANSACTIONS/CAREER NOTES: Signed as non-drafted free agent by New York Mets organization (February 19, 1991). ... On disabled list (August 11, 1995-remainder of season; and May 4-19, 1998). ... On New York disabled list (June 14-July 3, 2001); included rehabilitation assignment to Norfolk (June 30-July 3). ... On disabled list (August 4-24, 2002). ... Granted free agency (October 28, 2002).

RECORDS: Shares major league single-game records for most runs scored—6 (August 30, 1999); and most double plays by third basemen—4 (May 14, 1997).

HONORS: Named second baseman on The Sporting News N.L. All-Star team (1999). ... Named second baseman on The Sporting News N.L. Silver Slugger team (1999).

STATISTICAL NOTES: Led New York-Pennsylvania League shortstops with 126 putouts, 237 assists, 389 total chances and 39 double plays in 1992. ... Had 20-game hitting streak (June 10-July 10, 1997). ... Hit three home runs in one game (August 30, 1999). ... Collected six hits in one game (August 30, 1999). ... Had 15-game hitting streak (August 28-September 23, 2001). ... Career major league grand slams: 1.

2002 GAMES PLAYED BY POSITION (MLB): 3B—134.

			BATTING														FIELDING	
Year	Team (League)	Pos.	G	AB	R	H	2B	3B	HR	RBI	BB	SO	SB-CS	Avg.	OBP	SLG	E	Avg.
1991—	GC Mets (GCL)	2B-SS-3B	54	175	29	58	8	4	0	27	34	12	6-4	.331	.431	.423	9	.958
1992—	St. Lucie (FSL)	2B	4	5	0	0	0	0	0	0	0	0	0-0	.000	.000	.000	0	1.000
—	Pittsfield (NY-Penn)	SS	74	*298	44	*106	13	5	1	44	18	31	7-5	*.356	.388	.443	*26	.933
1993—	St. Lucie (FSL)	SS	128	494	75	145	18	3	11	86	57	51	26-16	.294	.366	.409	29	.954
1994—	Binghamton (East.)	SS-2B-1B	127	498	89	146	34	2	15	75	64	55	14-11	.293	.369	.460	27	.958
1995—	New York (N.L.)	3B-2B-SS	101	335	26	93	13	5	4	41	12	37	1-1	.278	.301	.382	7	.973
1996—	New York (N.L.)	2B-3B-SS	123	368	36	96	15	2	4	40	25	56	2-0	.261	.304	.345	11	.973
1997—	New York (N.L.)	3B-SS-2B	151	518	84	163	27	2	10	72	63	56	11-6	.315	.391	.432	12	.970
1998—	New York (N.L.)	3B-SS	144	557	94	155	28	2	17	78	65	77	8-3	.278	.355	.427	9	.976
1999—	New York (N.L.)	2B	158	628	123	191	41	1	27	108	85	85	9-2	.304	.385	.502	5	*.993
2000—	New York (N.L.)	2B-DH	150	544	109	176	40	2	25	94	95	70	3-2	.324	.425	.542	10	.985
2001—	New York (N.L.)	2B	124	457	64	111	22	0	17	49	51	62	5-0	.243	.322	.403	7	.987
—	Norfolk (I.L.)	2B	2	8	0	0	0	0	0	0	0	0	0-0	.000	.000	.000	0	1.000
2002—	New York (N.L.)	3B	135	490	78	151	26	0	16	56	62	55	6-0	.308	.391	.459	12	.969
Major League totals (8 years)			1086	3897	614	1136	212	14	120	538	458	498	45-14	.292	.367	.445	73	.980

DIVISION SERIES RECORD

RECORDS: Shares N.L. single-series record for most runs scored—6 (1999). ... Shares single-game records for most home runs—2; most grand slams—1; and most runs batted in—5 (October 5, 1999). ... Shares single-inning record for most runs batted in—4 (October 5, 1999, ninth inning).

			BATTING														FIELDING	
Year	Team (League)	Pos.	G	AB	R	H	2B	3B	HR	RBI	BB	SO	SB-CS	Avg.	OBP	SLG	E	Avg.
1999—	New York (N.L.)	2B	4	16	6	4	1	0	3	6	3	2	0-0	.250	.368	.875	0	1.000
2000—	New York (N.L.)	2B	4	18	1	5	2	0	1	5	1	2	0-1	.278	.316	.556	0	1.000
Division series totals (2 years)			8	34	7	9	3	0	4	11	4	4	0-1	.265	.342	.706	0	1.000

CHAMPIONSHIP SERIES RECORD

			BATTING														FIELDING	
Year	Team (League)	Pos.	G	AB	R	H	2B	3B	HR	RBI	BB	SO	SB-CS	Avg.	OBP	SLG	E	Avg.
1999—	New York (N.L.)	2B	6	27	2	6	4	0	0	1	1	9	0-0	.222	.250	.370	1	.971
2000—	New York (N.L.)	2B	5	18	5	8	1	1	0	4	4	1	0-0	.444	.565	.611	0	1.000
Championship series totals (2 years)			11	45	7	14	5	1	0	5	5	10	0-0	.311	.392	.467	1	.979

WORLD SERIES RECORD

			BATTING														FIELDING	
Year	Team (League)	Pos.	G	AB	R	H	2B	3B	HR	RBI	BB	SO	SB-CS	Avg.	OBP	SLG	E	Avg.
2000—	New York (N.L.)	2B	5	21	1	3	0	0	0	1	1	5	0-0	.143	.217	.143	0	1.000

ALL-STAR GAME RECORD

	AB	R	H	2B	3B	HR	RBI	BB	SO	SB-CS	Avg.	OBP	SLG	E	Avg.
All-Star Game totals (1 year)	2	0	0	0	0	0	0	0	1	0-0	.000	.000	.000	0	1.000

ALICEA, LUIS 2B

PERSONAL: Born July 29, 1965, in Santurce, Puerto Rico. ... 5-9/175. ... Bats both, throws right. ... Full name: Luis Rene Alicea. ... Brother of Ed Alicea, minor league infielder with Atlanta Braves (1988-93), Colorado Rockies (1993) and New York Mets (1995). ... Name pronounced AH-la-SAY-uh.

HIGH SCHOOL: Liceo Castro (Rio Piedras, Puerto Rico).

COLLEGE: Florida State.

TRANSACTIONS/CAREER NOTES: Selected by St. Louis Cardinals organization in first round (23rd pick overall) of free-agent draft (June 2, 1986). ... On St. Petersburg disabled list (April 6-June 4, 1990). ... On Louisville disabled list (April 25-May 25, 1991). ... On St. Louis disabled list (June 1-July 6, 1992); included rehabilitation assignment to Louisville (July 2-6). ... Traded by Cardinals to Boston Red Sox for P Nate Minchey and OF Jeff McNeely (December 7, 1994). ... Claimed on waivers by Cardinals (March 19, 1996). ... Granted free agency (October 31, 1996). ... Signed by Anaheim Angels organization (January 20, 1997). ... Granted free agency (October 30, 1997). ... Signed by Texas Rangers (December 9, 1997). ... Granted free agency (October 28, 1999). ... Re-signed by Rangers (December 7, 1999). ... Granted free agency (October 31, 2000). ... Signed by Kansas City Royals (January 26, 2001). ... Granted free agency (November 5, 2001). ... Re-signed by Royals (December 7, 2001). ... Granted free agency (October 28, 2002).

HONORS: Named second baseman on The Sporting News college All-America team (1986).

STATISTICAL NOTES: Switch-hit home runs in one game (July 28, 1995). ... Led A.L. second basemen with 699 total chances and 103 double plays in 1995. ... Career major league grand slams: 1.

2002 GAMES PLAYED BY POSITION (MLB): 2B—32; 3B—32; DH—17; 1B—2; SS—1; OF—1.

		BATTING														FIELDING	
Year Team (League)	**Pos.**	**G**	**AB**	**R**	**H**	**2B**	**3B**	**HR**	**RBI**	**BB**	**SO**	**SB-CS**	**Avg.**	**OBP**	**SLG**	**E**	**Avg.**
1986—Erie (NY-Penn)	2B	47	163	40	46	6	1	3	18	37	20	27-4	.282	.418	.387	12	.955
—Arkansas (Texas)	2B-SS	25	68	8	16	3	0	0	3	5	11	0-3	.235	.280	.279	4	.962
1987—Arkansas (Texas)	2B	101	337	57	91	14	3	4	47	49	28	13-8	.270	.361	.365	11	*.975
—Louisville (A.A.)	2B	29	105	18	32	10	2	2	20	9	9	4-2	.305	.362	.495	4	.974
1988—Louisville (A.A.)	2B-SS-OF	49	191	21	53	11	6	1	21	11	21	8-4	.277	.316	.414	0	1.000
—St. Louis (N.L.)	2B	93	297	20	63	10	4	1	24	25	32	1-1	.212	.276	.283	14	.970
1989—Louisville (A.A.)	2B	124	412	53	102	20	3	8	48	59	55	13-5	.248	.344	.369	16	.972
1990—St. Petersburg (FSL)	2B	29	95	14	22	1	4	0	12	20	14	9-3	.232	.388	.326	0	1.000
—Arkansas (Texas)	2B	14	49	11	14	3	1	0	4	7	8	2-2	.286	.386	.388	4	.935
—Louisville (A.A.)	3B	25	92	10	32	6	3	0	10	5	12	0-4	.348	.388	.478	6	.898
1991—Louisville (A.A.)	2B	31	112	26	44	6	3	4	16	14	8	5-3	.393	.462	.607	5	.970
—St. Louis (N.L.)	2B-3B-SS	56	68	5	13	3	0	0	0	8	19	0-1	.191	.276	.235	0	1.000
1992—Louisville (A.A.)	2B-SS	20	71	11	20	8	0	0	6	16	6	0-0	.282	.409	.394	4	.960
—St. Louis (N.L.)	2B-SS	85	265	26	65	9	11	2	32	27	40	2-5	.245	.320	.385	7	.981
1993—St. Louis (N.L.)	2B-OF-3B	115	362	50	101	19	3	3	46	47	54	11-1	.279	.362	.373	11	.978
1994—St. Louis (N.L.)	2B-OF	88	205	32	57	12	5	5	29	30	38	4-5	.278	.373	.459	4	.986
1995—Boston (A.L.)■	2B	132	419	64	113	20	3	6	44	63	61	13-10	.270	.367	.375	16	.977
1996—St. Louis (N.L.)■	2B	129	380	54	98	26	3	5	42	52	78	11-3	.258	.350	.382	*24	.957
1997—Anaheim (A.L.)■	2B-3B-DH	128	388	59	98	16	7	5	37	69	65	22-8	.253	.375	.369	12	.977
1998—Texas (A.L.)■	2-3-DH-O	101	259	51	71	15	3	6	33	37	40	4-3	.274	.372	.425	9	.964
1999—Texas (A.L.)	2B-3B-DH-OF	68	164	33	33	10	0	3	17	28	32	2-1	.201	.316	.317	5	.971
2000—Texas (A.L.)	2-3-DH-S	139	540	85	159	25	8	6	63	59	75	1-3	.294	.365	.404	18	.970
2001—Kansas City (A.L.)■	2B-DH-3B	113	387	44	106	16	4	4	32	23	56	8-6	.274	.320	.367	14	.960
2002—Kansas City (A.L.)	IF-DH-OF	94	237	28	54	8	2	1	23	32	34	2-3	.228	.322	.291	8	.962
American League totals (7 years)		775	2394	364	634	110	27	31	249	311	363	52-34	.265	.354	.372	82	.971
National League totals (6 years)		566	1577	187	397	79	26	16	173	189	261	29-16	.252	.334	.365	60	.973
Major League totals (13 years)		1341	3971	551	1031	189	53	47	422	500	624	81-50	.260	.346	.369	142	.972

DIVISION SERIES RECORD

		BATTING														FIELDING	
Year Team (League)	**Pos.**	**G**	**AB**	**R**	**H**	**2B**	**3B**	**HR**	**RBI**	**BB**	**SO**	**SB-CS**	**Avg.**	**OBP**	**SLG**	**E**	**Avg.**
1995—Boston (A.L.)	2B	3	10	1	6	1	0	1	1	2	2	1-0	.600	.667	1.000	1	.944
1996—St. Louis (N.L.)	2B	3	11	1	2	2	0	0	0	1	4	0-2	.182	.250	.364	1	.875
1998—Texas (A.L.)	PH-DH	1	1	0	0	0	0	0	0	0	0	0-0	.000	.000	.000	...	...
1999—Texas (A.L.)								Did not play.									
Division series totals (3 years)		7	22	2	8	3	0	1	1	3	6	1-2	.364	.440	.636	2	.923

CHAMPIONSHIP SERIES RECORD

		BATTING														FIELDING	
Year Team (League)	**Pos.**	**G**	**AB**	**R**	**H**	**2B**	**3B**	**HR**	**RBI**	**BB**	**SO**	**SB-CS**	**Avg.**	**OBP**	**SLG**	**E**	**Avg.**
1996—St. Louis (N.L.)	2B-PH	5	8	0	0	0	0	0	0	2	1	0-0	.000	.200	.000	1	.923

ALLEN, CHAD OF

PERSONAL: Born February 6, 1975, in Dallas. ... 6-1/195. ... Bats right, throws right. ... Full name: John Chad Allen.

HIGH SCHOOL: Duncanville (Texas).

COLLEGE: Texas A&M.

TRANSACTIONS/CAREER NOTES: Selected by Cincinnati Reds organization in 38th round of free-agent draft (June 3, 1993); did not sign. ... Selected by Minnesota Twins organization in fourth round of free-agent draft (June 4, 1996). ... On Salt Lake disabled list (April 11-22, 2000). ... On Minnesota disabled list (June 4-19 and August 15, 2001-remainder of season). ... Granted free agency (October 24, 2001). ... Signed by Baltimore Orioles organization (March 27, 2002). ... Released by Orioles (April 16, 2002). ... Signed by Cleveland Indians organization (May 13, 2002). ... Released by Indians (September 30, 2002).

MISCELLANEOUS: Member of 1996 U.S. Olympic baseball team.

2002 GAMES PLAYED BY POSITION (MLB): OF—4.

		BATTING														FIELDING	
Year Team (League)	**Pos.**	**G**	**AB**	**R**	**H**	**2B**	**3B**	**HR**	**RBI**	**BB**	**SO**	**SB-CS**	**Avg.**	**OBP**	**SLG**	**E**	**Avg.**
1996—Fort Wayne (Midw.)	OF	7	21	2	9	0	0	0	2	3	2	1-1	.429	.480	.429	0	1.000
1997—Fort Myers (FSL)	OF	105	401	66	124	18	4	3	45	40	51	27-15	.309	.373	.397	5	.977
—New Britain (East.)	OF	30	115	20	29	9	1	4	18	9	21	2-0	.252	.304	.452	1	.973

Year Team (League)	Pos.	BATTING G	AB	R	H	2B	3B	HR	RBI	BB	SO	SB-CS	Avg.	OBP	SLG	FIELDING E	Avg.
1998—New Britain (East.)	OF	137	504	70	132	31	7	8	82	51	78	21-9	.262	.334	.399	4	.980
1999—Minnesota (A.L.)	OF-DH	137	481	69	133	21	3	10	46	37	89	14-7	.277	.330	.395	7	.975
2000—Salt Lake (PCL)	OF	96	389	71	121	21	5	9	67	31	72	10-2	.311	.363	.460	1	.993
—Minnesota (A.L.)	OF	15	50	2	15	3	0	0	7	3	14	0-2	.300	.345	.360	0	1.000
2001—Minnesota (A.L.)	OF-DH	57	175	20	46	13	2	4	20	19	37	1-2	.263	.333	.429	2	.968
—Edmonton (PCL)	OF	6	22	4	8	2	0	1	1	4	1	2-0	.364	.481	.591	0	1.000
2002—Rochester (I.L.)■	OF	8	32	1	7	2	1	0	1	0	6	0-0	.219	.219	.344	0	1.000
—Buffalo (I.L.)■	OF	70	279	45	84	20	1	10	62	15	34	0-1	.301	.340	.487	0	1.000
—Cleveland (A.L.)	OF	5	10	0	1	1	0	0	0	0	2	0-0	.100	.100	.200	0	1.000
Major League totals (4 years)		214	716	91	195	38	5	14	73	59	142	15-11	.272	.329	.398	9	.976

ALLEN, LUKE — OF — DODGERS

PERSONAL: Born August 4, 1978, in Covington, Ga. ... 6-2/208. ... Bats left, throws right. ... Full name: Lucas G. Allen.
HIGH SCHOOL: Newton County (Covington, Ga.).
TRANSACTIONS/CAREER NOTES: Signed as non-drafted free agent by Los Angeles Dodgers organization (August 4, 1996).
STATISTICAL NOTES: Tied for Southern League lead in assists by outfielder with 15 in 2001. ... Led Pacific Coast League outfielders with 23 assists and seven double plays in 2002.
2002 GAMES PLAYED BY POSITION (MLB): OF—3.

Year Team (League)	Pos.	BATTING G	AB	R	H	2B	3B	HR	RBI	BB	SO	SB-CS	Avg.	OBP	SLG	FIELDING E	Avg.
1997—Great Falls (Pio.)	3B-OF	67	258	50	89	12	6	7	40	19	53	12-11	.345	.390	.519	22	.868
1998—San Bern. (Calif.)	OF	105	399	51	119	25	6	4	46	30	93	18-11	.298	.349	.421	6	.971
—San Antonio (Texas)	OF	23	78	9	26	3	1	3	10	6	16	1-2	.333	.381	.513	4	.918
1999—San Antonio (Texas)	3B	137	533	90	150	16	12	14	82	44	102	14-8	.281	.336	.435	53	.851
2000—San Antonio (Texas)	1B-3B	90	339	55	90	15	5	7	60	40	71	14-5	.265	.340	.401	27	.895
2001—Jacksonville (Sou.)	OF	125	486	74	141	32	6	16	73	42	111	13-3	.290	.345	.479	7	.972
—Las Vegas (PCL)	OF	2	9	1	2	1	0	0	0	0	0	0-0	.222	.222	.333	1	.667
2002—Las Vegas (PCL)	OF	137	501	85	165	28	3	12	78	56	77	4-6	.329	.395	.469	*9	.969
—Los Angeles (N.L.)	OF	6	7	2	1	1	0	0	0	2	3	0-0	.143	.333	.286	0	1.000
Major League totals (1 year)		6	7	2	1	1	0	0	0	2	3	0-0	.143	.333	.286	0	1.000

ALMANZA, ARMANDO — P — MARLINS

PERSONAL: Born October 26, 1972, in El Paso, Texas. ... 6-3/240. ... Throws left, bats left.
HIGH SCHOOL: Bel Air (El Paso, Texas).
JUNIOR COLLEGE: New Mexico Junior College.
TRANSACTIONS/CAREER NOTES: Selected by St. Louis Cardinals organization in 21st round of free-agent draft (June 3, 1993). ... On disabled list (April 8, 1994-entire season). ... On Memphis disabled list (July 10-21, 1998). ... Traded by Cardinals with P Braden Looper and SS Pablo Ozuna to Florida Marlins for SS Edgar Renteria (December 14, 1998). ... On Calgary disabled list (May 10-June 2, 1999). ... On Florida disabled list (March 30-May 21, 2002); included rehabilitation assignment to Jupiter (May 2-21).
STATISTICAL NOTES: Tied for Arizona League lead with 14 wild pitches in 1993.
CAREER HITTING (MLB): 0-for-4 (.000), 0 R, 0 2B, 0 3B, 0 HR, 0 RBI.

Year League	W	L	Pct.	ERA	G	GS	CG	ShO	Sv.-Opp.	IP	H	R	ER	HR	BB-IBB	SO
1993—Arizona Cardinals (Ariz.)	4	1	.800	3.21	20	4	0	0	0-...	42.0	38	19	15	2	14-0	56
—Johnson City (Appl.)	1	1	.500	4.15	3	3	0	0	0-...	4.1	6	2	2	1	3-0	4
1994—Madison (Midw.)	Did not play.															
1995—Savannah (S.Atl.)	3	9	.250	3.92	20	20	0	0	0-...	108.0	108	62	47	13	40-1	72
1996—Peoria (Midw.)	8	6	.571	2.76	52	1	0	0	0-...	62.0	50	27	19	2	32-5	67
1997—Prince William (Caro.)	2	3	.400	1.67	•58	0	0	0	*36-...	64.2	38	18	12	3	32-1	83
1998—Arkansas (Texas)	4	1	.800	3.31	28	0	0	0	8-...	32.2	27	13	12	2	18-0	46
—Memphis (PCL)	3	1	.750	3.03	31	0	0	0	1-...	35.2	35	18	12	1	19-1	45
1999—Calgary (PCL)■	2	2	.500	10.90	15	0	0	0	0-...	17.1	29	27	21	3	18-0	20
—Portland (East.)	0	1	.000	3.97	10	0	0	0	3-...	11.1	5	5	5	1	4-0	20
—Florida (N.L.)	0	1	.000	1.72	14	0	0	0	0-0	15.2	8	4	3	1	9-1	20
2000—Florida (N.L.)	4	2	.667	4.86	67	0	0	0	0-4	46.1	38	27	25	3	43-6	46
2001—Florida (N.L.)	2	2	.500	4.83	52	0	0	0	0-2	41.0	34	24	22	8	26-1	45
2002—Jupiter (FSL)	0	0	...	0.00	6	5	0	0	0-...	6.2	1	0	0	0	3-0	6
—Florida (N.L.)	3	2	.600	4.34	51	0	0	0	2-4	45.2	36	22	22	8	23-1	57
Major League totals (4 years)	9	7	.563	4.36	184	0	0	0	2-10	148.2	116	77	72	20	101-9	168

ALMANZAR, CARLOS — P — REDS

PERSONAL: Born November 6, 1973, in Santiago, Dominican Republic. ... 6-2/200. ... Throws right, bats right. ... Full name: Carlos Manuel Almanzar.
TRANSACTIONS/CAREER NOTES: Signed as non-drafted free agent by Toronto Blue Jays organization (December 10, 1990). ... On Knoxville disabled list (May 27-June 3, 1997). ... Traded by Blue Jays with P Woody Williams and OF Peter Tucci to San Diego Padres for P Joey Hamilton (December 13, 1998). ... On San Diego disabled list (April 24-May 27, 1999); included rehabilitation assignment to Las Vegas (May 22-27). ... Traded by Padres to New York Yankees for P David Lee (March 25, 2001). ... Granted free agency (October 15, 2001). ... Signed by Colorado Rockies organization (January 20, 2002). ... Claimed on waivers by Cincinnati Reds (March 30, 2002). ... On Cincinnati disabled list (June 11, 2002-remainder of season); included rehabilitation assignment to Louisville (August 16-September 13).
CAREER HITTING (MLB): 0-for-4 (.000), 0 R, 0 2B, 0 3B, 0 HR, 0 RBI.

Year League	W	L	Pct.	ERA	G	GS	CG	ShO	Sv.-Opp.	IP	H	R	ER	HR	BB-IBB	SO
1991—Dom. Blue Jays (DSL)......	3	1	.750	2.83	6	6	1	0	0-...	35.0	36	17	11	...	11-...	20
1992—Dom. Blue Jays (DSL)......	10	0	1.000	2.01	13	11	2	1	1-...	67.0	45	26	15	...	31-...	60
1993—Dom. Blue Jays (DSL)......	5	2	.714	3.38	16	9	0	0	2-...	69.1	60	35	26	...	32-...	59
1994—Medicine Hat (Pio.)	7	4	.636	2.87	14	14	0	0	0-...	84.2	82	38	27	2	19-0	77
1995—Knoxville (Sou.)................	3	12	.200	3.99	35	19	0	0	2-...	126.1	144	77	56	10	32-1	93
1996—Knoxville (Sou.)................	7	8	.467	4.85	54	0	0	0	9-...	94.2	106	58	51	13	33-6	105
1997—Knoxville (Sou.)................	1	1	.500	4.91	21	0	0	0	8-...	25.2	30	14	14	2	5-1	25
—Syracuse (I.L.)..................	5	1	.833	1.41	32	0	0	0	3-...	51.0	30	9	8	2	8-0	47
—Toronto (A.L.)....................	0	1	.000	2.70	4	0	0	0	0-0	3.1	1	1	1	1	1-0	4
1998—Toronto (A.L.)....................	2	2	.500	5.34	25	0	0	0	0-3	28.2	34	18	17	4	8-2	20
—Syracuse (I.L.)..................	3	6	.333	2.31	30	0	0	0	10-...	50.2	44	21	13	7	13-2	53
1999—San Diego (N.L.)■	0	0	...	7.47	28	0	0	0	0-0	37.1	48	32	31	6	15-2	30
—Las Vegas (PCL)	1	3	.250	9.53	11	3	0	0	0-...	22.2	32	25	24	11	8-1	18
2000—San Diego (N.L.)	4	5	.444	4.39	62	0	0	0	0-3	69.2	73	35	34	12	25-2	56
—Las Vegas (PCL)	0	0	...	4.50	4	0	0	0	0-...	6.0	9	4	3	1	0-0	7
2001—New York (A.L.)■............	0	1	.000	3.38	10	0	0	0	0-2	10.2	14	4	4	2	2-1	6
—Columbus (I.L.)..................	2	1	.667	2.43	35	0	0	0	18-...	33.1	36	10	9	2	6-2	26
2002—Louisville (I.L.)■.............	1	0	1.000	2.74	21	0	0	0	11-...	23.0	21	7	7	0	5-0	19
—Cincinnati (N.L.)..............	0	1	.000	2.31	8	1	0	0	0-0	11.2	6	4	3	0	5-1	7
A.L. totals (3 years)	2	4	.333	4.64	39	0	0	0	0-5	42.2	49	23	22	7	11-3	30
N.L. totals (3 years)	4	6	.400	5.16	98	1	0	0	0-3	118.2	127	71	68	18	45-5	93
Major League totals (6 years).....	6	10	.375	5.02	137	1	0	0	0-8	161.1	176	94	90	25	56-8	123

ALMONTE, EDWIN — P — WHITE SOX

PERSONAL: Born December 17, 1976, in Santiago, Dominican Republic. ... 6-3/200. ... Throws right, bats right.
HIGH SCHOOL: Seward Park (New York, N.Y.).
COLLEGE: St. Francis (N.Y.).
TRANSACTIONS/CAREER NOTES: Selected by Chicago White Sox organization in 26th round of free-agent draft (June 2, 1998).

Year League	W	L	Pct.	ERA	G	GS	CG	ShO	Sv.-Opp.	IP	H	R	ER	HR	BB-IBB	SO
1998—Arizona White Sox (Ariz.) .	0	0	...	0.93	5	0	0	0	0-...	9.2	6	5	1	0	1-0	6
—Bristol (Appl.)..................	3	0	1.000	3.38	8	3	0	0	0-...	26.2	29	14	10	3	4-0	26
1999—Burlington (Midw.)...........	9	12	.429	3.03	37	5	2	0	5-...	115.2	107	48	39	5	28-4	85
2000—Winston-Salem (Caro.).....	3	1	.750	3.16	33	7	0	0	2-...	77.0	66	32	27	2	20-0	73
—Birmingham (Sou.)...........	1	3	.250	4.54	7	6	0	0	0-...	39.2	45	22	20	5	9-0	21
2001—Birmingham (Sou.)...........	1	4	.200	1.49	54	0	0	0	*36-...	66.1	58	16	11	4	16-4	62
2002—Charlotte (I.L.).................	2	3	.400	2.24	50	0	0	0	*26-...	60.1	52	16	15	6	12-2	56

ALMONTE, ERICK — SS — YANKEES

PERSONAL: Born February 1, 1978, in Santo Domingo, Dominican Republic. ... 6-2/180. ... Bats right, throws right. ... Full name: Erick R. Almonte.
TRANSACTIONS/CAREER NOTES: Signed as non-drafted free agent by New York Yankees organization (February 12, 1996). ... On Norwich disabled list (June 14-26, 2001). ... On Columbus disabled list (July 23-August 4, 2001; and April 7-19, 2002).
STATISTICAL NOTES: Led Gulf Coast League third basemen with 53 putouts and 163 total chances in 1998. ... Led South Atlantic League in grounding into double plays with 17 in 1999.

		BATTING														FIELDING	
Year Team (League)	Pos.	G	AB	R	H	2B	3B	HR	RBI	BB	SO	SB-CS	Avg.	OBP	SLG	E	Avg.
1996—Dom. Yankees (DSL)..	3B	58	216	37	61	7	0	8	36	15	30	3-...	.282	...	.426	36	.848
1997—GC Yankees (GCL)......	3B	52	180	32	51	4	4	3	31	21	27	8-2	.283	.355	.400	18	.890
1998—Greensboro (S.Atl.)....	SS	120	450	53	94	13	0	6	33	29	121	6-2	.209	.260	.278	47	.911
1999—Tampa (FSL)...............	SS	61	230	36	59	8	2	5	25	18	49	3-1	.257	.313	.374	20	.938
—GC Yankees (GCL)......	SS	9	30	5	9	2	0	2	9	3	10	1-0	.300	.343	.567	2	.931
2000—Norwich (East.)	3B	131	454	56	123	18	4	15	77	35	129	12-2	.271	.326	.427	*33	.943
2001—Columbus (I.L.)..........	SS	97	345	55	99	19	3	12	55	44	90	4-5	.287	.369	.464	*27	.936
—Norwich (East.)	SS	3	12	2	3	0	0	0	0	1	6	1-0	.250	.308	.250	1	.900
—New York (A.L.)..........	SS-DH	8	4	0	2	1	0	0	0	0	1	2-0	.500	.500	.750	1	.875
2002—Columbus (I.L.)..........	3B-SS	66	221	25	52	10	1	9	28	15	60	2-1	.235	.282	.412	18	.937
—Norwich (East.)	SS-3B	53	187	28	45	7	0	8	33	30	59	10-2	.241	.342	.406	8	.963
Major League totals (1 year)		8	4	0	2	1	0	0	0	0	1	2-0	.500	.500	.750	1	.875

ALOMAR, ROBERTO — 2B — METS

PERSONAL: Born February 5, 1968, in Ponce, Puerto Rico. ... 6-0/185. ... Bats both, throws right. ... Full name: Roberto Velazquez Alomar. ... Son of Sandy Alomar Sr., major league infielder with six teams (1964-78) and coach, Chicago Cubs; and brother of Sandy Alomar Jr., catcher, Colorado Rockies.
TRANSACTIONS/CAREER NOTES: Signed as non-drafted free agent by San Diego Padres organization (February 16, 1985). ... Traded by Padres with OF Joe Carter to Toronto Blue Jays for 1B Fred McGriff and SS Tony Fernandez (December 5, 1990). ... On suspended list (May 23-24, 1995). ... Granted free agency (October 30, 1995). ... Signed by Baltimore Orioles (December 21, 1995). ... On suspended list (April 1-7, 1997). ... On disabled list (July 30-August 26, 1997; and July 19-August 4, 1998). ... Granted free agency (October 26, 1998). ... Signed by Cleveland Indians (December 1, 1998). ... Traded by Indians with P Mike Bacsik and OF Danny Peoples to New York Mets for OF Matt Lawton, OF Alex Escobar, P Jerrod Riggan and two players to be named later (December 11, 2001); Indians acquired P Billy Traber and 1B Earl Snyder to complete deal (December 13, 2001).
RECORDS: Holds A.L. career records for highest fielding percentage by second basemen—.987; and most consecutive errorless games by second baseman—104 (June 21, 1994 through July 3, 1995). ... Holds A.L. single-season records for fewest double plays by second baseman (150 or more games)—66 (1992); and most runs by switch-hitter—138 (1999). ... Shares A.L. single-season records for most games with switch-hit home runs—2 (1996); and fewest errors by second baseman (150 or more games)—5 (1992 and 2001).

HONORS: Won A.L. Gold Glove at second base (1991-96 and 1998-2001). ... Named second baseman on The Sporting News A.L. All-Star team (1992, 1996, 1998, 1999 and 2000). ... Named second baseman on The Sporting News A.L. Silver Slugger team (1992, 1996, 1999 and 2000).
STATISTICAL NOTES: Led South Atlantic League second basemen with 35 errors in 1985. ... Led Texas League shortstops with 167 putouts and 34 errors in 1987. ... Led N.L. with 17 sacrifice hits in 1989. ... Led N.L. second basemen with 17 errors in 1990. ... Switch-hit home runs in one game five times (May 10, 1991; May 3, 1995; July 25 and August 14, 1996; and July 16, 2001). ... Led A.L. second basemen with 272 assists in 1995, 449 in 1998 and 437 in 2000. ... Had 22-game hitting streak (May 12-June 8, 1996). ... Hit three home runs in one game (April 26, 1997). ... Led A.L. with 13 sacrifice flies in 1999. ... Had 17-game hitting streak (May 5-25, 2000). ... Had 18-game hitting streak (September 17-October 1, 2000). ... Had 15-game hitting streak (May 28-June 13, 2001). ... Career major league grand slams: 6.
MISCELLANEOUS: Holds Toronto Blue Jays all-time record for highest career batting average (.307).
2002 GAMES PLAYED BY POSITION (MLB): 2B—147.

		BATTING														FIELDING	
Year Team (League)	**Pos.**	**G**	**AB**	**R**	**H**	**2B**	**3B**	**HR**	**RBI**	**BB**	**SO**	**SB-CS**	**Avg.**	**OBP**	**SLG**	**E**	**Avg.**
1985—Charl., S.C. (S.Atl.).....	2B-SS	*137	*546	89	160	14	3	0	54	61	73	36-19	.293	.362	.330	†36	.947
1986—Reno (Calif.)...............	2B	90	356	53	123	16	4	4	49	32	38	14-8	*.346	.397	.447	18	.963
1987—Wichita (Texas)..........	SS-2B	130	536	88	171	41	4	12	68	49	74	43-15	.319	.374	.478	†36	.932
1988—Las Vegas (PCL)........	2B	9	37	5	10	1	0	2	14	1	4	3-0	.270	.282	.459	1	.981
—San Diego (N.L.)........	2B	143	545	84	145	24	6	9	41	47	83	24-6	.266	.328	.382	16	.980
1989—San Diego (N.L.)........	2B	158	623	82	184	27	1	7	56	53	76	42-17	.295	.347	.376	*28	.967
1990—San Diego (N.L.)........	2B-SS	147	586	80	168	27	5	6	60	48	72	24-7	.287	.340	.381	†19	.974
1991—Toronto (A.L.)■..........	2B	161	637	88	188	41	11	9	69	57	86	53-11	.295	.354	.436	15	.981
1992—Toronto (A.L.).............	2B-DH	152	571	105	177	27	8	8	76	87	52	49-9	.310	.405	.427	5	.993
1993—Toronto (A.L.).............	2B	153	589	109	192	35	6	17	93	80	67	55-15	.326	.408	.492	14	.980
1994—Toronto (A.L.).............	2B	107	392	78	120	25	4	8	38	51	41	19-8	.306	.386	.452	4	.991
1995—Toronto (A.L.).............	2B	130	517	71	155	24	7	13	66	47	45	30-3	.300	.354	.449	4	*.993
1996—Baltimore (A.L.)■.......	2B-DH	153	588	132	193	43	4	22	94	90	65	17-6	.328	.411	.527	11	.985
1997—Baltimore (A.L.)..........	2B-DH	112	412	64	137	23	2	14	60	40	43	9-3	.333	.390	.500	6	.988
1998—Baltimore (A.L.)..........	2B-DH	147	588	86	166	36	1	14	56	59	70	18-5	.282	.347	.418	11	.985
1999—Cleveland (A.L.)■.......	2B-DH	159	563	*138	182	40	3	24	120	99	96	37-6	.323	.422	.533	6	*.992
2000—Cleveland (A.L.)..........	2B	155	610	111	189	40	2	19	89	64	82	39-4	.310	.378	.475	15	.980
2001—Cleveland (A.L.)..........	2B	157	575	113	193	34	12	20	100	80	71	30-6	.336	.415	.541	5	.993
2002—New York (N.L.)■......	2B	149	590	73	157	24	4	11	53	57	83	16-4	.266	.331	.376	11	.983
American League totals (11 years)		1586	6042	1095	1892	368	60	168	861	754	718	356-76	.313	.389	.477	96	.987
National League totals (4 years)		597	2344	319	654	102	16	33	210	205	314	106-34	.279	.337	.378	74	.975
Major League totals (15 years)		2183	8386	1414	2546	470	76	201	1071	959	1032	462-110	.304	.375	.450	170	.984

DIVISION SERIES RECORD

RECORDS: Shares single-series record for most doubles—4 (1999).

		BATTING														FIELDING	
Year Team (League)	**Pos.**	**G**	**AB**	**R**	**H**	**2B**	**3B**	**HR**	**RBI**	**BB**	**SO**	**SB-CS**	**Avg.**	**OBP**	**SLG**	**E**	**Avg.**
1996—Baltimore (A.L.)..........	2B	4	17	2	5	0	0	1	4	2	3	0-0	.294	.350	.471	0	1.000
1997—Baltimore (A.L.)..........	2B-PH	4	10	1	3	2	0	0	2	1	1	0-0	.300	.364	.500	0	1.000
1999—Cleveland (A.L.)..........	2B	5	19	4	7	4	0	0	3	2	3	2-0	.368	.409	.579	1	.964
2001—Cleveland (A.L.)..........	2B	5	21	3	4	3	0	0	3	2	5	0-0	.190	.261	.333	0	1.000
Division series totals (4 years)		18	67	10	19	9	0	1	12	7	12	2-0	.284	.342	.463	1	.986

CHAMPIONSHIP SERIES RECORD

RECORDS: Shares career record for most times grounded into double play—5.
NOTES: Named Most Valuable Player (1992).

		BATTING														FIELDING	
Year Team (League)	**Pos.**	**G**	**AB**	**R**	**H**	**2B**	**3B**	**HR**	**RBI**	**BB**	**SO**	**SB-CS**	**Avg.**	**OBP**	**SLG**	**E**	**Avg.**
1991—Toronto (A.L.).............	2B	5	19	3	9	0	0	0	4	2	3	2-0	.474	.524	.474	0	1.000
1992—Toronto (A.L.).............	2B	6	26	4	11	1	0	2	4	2	1	5-0	.423	.464	.692	0	1.000
1993—Toronto (A.L.).............	2B	6	24	3	7	1	0	0	4	4	3	4-0	.292	.393	.333	0	1.000
1996—Baltimore (A.L.)..........	2B	5	23	2	5	2	0	0	1	0	4	0-0	.217	.208	.304	2	.953
1997—Baltimore (A.L.)..........	2B	6	22	2	4	0	0	1	2	7	3	0-0	.182	.379	.318	2	.931
Championship series totals (5 years)		28	114	14	36	4	0	3	15	15	14	11-0	.316	.392	.430	4	.975

WORLD SERIES RECORD

RECORDS: Shares record for most at-bats in one inning—2 (October 20, 1993, eighth inning).
NOTES: Member of World Series championship team (1992 and 1993).

		BATTING														FIELDING	
Year Team (League)	**Pos.**	**G**	**AB**	**R**	**H**	**2B**	**3B**	**HR**	**RBI**	**BB**	**SO**	**SB-CS**	**Avg.**	**OBP**	**SLG**	**E**	**Avg.**
1992—Toronto (A.L.).............	2B	6	24	3	5	1	0	0	0	3	3	3-0	.208	.296	.250	0	1.000
1993—Toronto (A.L.).............	2B	6	25	5	12	2	1	0	6	2	3	4-2	.480	.519	.640	2	.938
World Series totals (2 years)		12	49	8	17	3	1	0	6	5	6	7-2	.347	.407	.449	2	.959

ALL-STAR GAME RECORD

RECORDS: Shares single-game record for most stolen bases—2 (July 14, 1992).
NOTES: Named Most Valuable Player (1998).

	AB	**R**	**H**	**2B**	**3B**	**HR**	**RBI**	**BB**	**SO**	**SB-CS**	**Avg.**	**OBP**	**SLG**	**E**	**Avg.**
All-Star Game totals (12 years)	30	5	7	0	0	2	3	2	1	5-0	.233	.281	.433	1	.971

ALOMAR, SANDY C ROCKIES

PERSONAL: Born June 18, 1966, in Salinas, Puerto Rico. ... 6-5/235. ... Bats right, throws right. ... Full name: Santos Velazquez Alomar Jr. ... Son of Sandy Alomar Sr., major league infielder with six teams (1964-78) and coach, Chicago Cubs; and brother of Roberto Alomar, second baseman, New York Mets.
HIGH SCHOOL: Luis Munoz Rivera (Salinas, Puerto Rico).
TRANSACTIONS/CAREER NOTES: Signed as non-drafted free agent by San Diego Padres organization (October 21, 1983). ... Traded by Padres with OF Chris James and 3B Carlos Baerga to Cleveland Indians for OF Joe Carter (December 6, 1989). ... On Cleveland disabled list (May 15-

June 17 and July 29, 1991-remainder of season); included rehabilitation assignments to Colorado Springs (June 8-17 and August 9-12). ... On disabled list (May 2-18, 1992). ... On suspended list (July 29-August 2, 1992). ... On Cleveland disabled list (May 1-August 7, 1993); included rehabilitation assignment to Charlotte, S.C. (July 22-August 7). ... On disabled list (April 24-May 11, 1994). ... On Cleveland disabled list (April 19-June 29, 1995); included rehabilitation assignment to Canton/Akron (June 22-29). ... On Cleveland disabled list (May 11-September 6, 1999); included rehabilitation assignments to Akron (July 5-19 and September 3-6) and Buffalo (August 10-27). ... On disabled list (April 19-May 8, 2000). ... Granted free agency (October 27, 2000). ... Signed by Chicago White Sox (December 18, 2000). ... On disabled list (August 8-September 18, 2001). ... On Chicago disabled list (June 13-July 1, 2002); included rehabilitation assignment to Charlotte (June 28-July 1). ... Traded by White Sox to Colorado Rockies for P Enemencio Pacheco (July 29, 2002).

RECORDS: Shares major league single-game record for most doubles—4 (June 6, 1997).

HONORS: Named Minor League co-Player of the Year by The Sporting News (1988). ... Named Pacific Coast League Player of the Year (1988 and 1989). ... Named Minor League Player of the Year by The Sporting News (1989). ... Named A.L. Rookie Player of the Year by The Sporting News (1990). ... Won A.L. Gold Glove at catcher (1990). ... Named A.L. Rookie of the Year by Baseball Writers' Association of America (1990).

STATISTICAL NOTES: Led Northwest League catchers with 421 putouts and .985 fielding percentage in 1984. ... Led Texas League catchers with 606 putouts in 1987. ... Led Pacific Coast League catchers with 14 errors in 1988. ... Led Pacific Coast League catchers with 573 putouts in 1988 and 702 in 1989. ... Led Pacific Coast League catchers with 633 total chances in 1988 and 761 in 1989. ... Had 30-game hitting streak (May 25-July 6, 1997). ... Career major league grand slams: 2.

MISCELLANEOUS: Batted as switch hitter (1984-86).

2002 GAMES PLAYED BY POSITION (MLB): C—88.

			BATTING														FIELDING	
Year	**Team (League)**	**Pos.**	**G**	**AB**	**R**	**H**	**2B**	**3B**	**HR**	**RBI**	**BB**	**SO**	**SB-CS**	**Avg.**	**OBP**	**SLG**	**E**	**Avg.**
1984—	Spokane (N'West)	C-1B	59	219	13	47	5	0	0	21	13	20	3-0	.215	.260	.237	8	†.985
1985—	Charl., S.C. (S.Atl.)	C-OF	100	352	38	73	7	0	3	43	31	30	3-1	.207	.276	.253	18	.979
1986—	Beaumont (Texas)	C	100	346	36	83	15	1	4	27	15	35	2-6	.240	.271	.324	*18	.969
1987—	Wichita (Texas)	C	103	375	50	115	19	1	8	65	21	37	1-5	.307	.346	.427	*15	.978
1988—	Las Vegas (PCL)	C-OF	93	337	59	100	9	5	16	71	28	35	1-1	.297	.354	.496	†14	.978
—	San Diego (N.L.)	PH	1	1	0	0	0	0	0	0	0	1	0-0	.000	.000	.000	...	...
1989—	Las Vegas (PCL)	C-OF	131	*523	88	160	33	8	13	101	42	58	3-1	.306	.358	.474	12	.984
—	San Diego (N.L.)	C	7	19	1	4	1	0	1	6	3	3	0-0	.211	.318	.421	0	1.000
1990—	Cleveland (A.L.)■	C	132	445	60	129	26	2	9	66	25	46	4-1	.290	.326	.418	*14	.981
1991—	Cleveland (A.L.)	C-DH	51	184	10	40	9	0	0	7	8	24	0-4	.217	.264	.266	4	.987
—	Colo. Springs (PCL)	C	12	35	5	14	2	0	1	10	5	0	0-0	.400	.463	.543	1	.833
1992—	Cleveland (A.L.)	C-DH	89	299	22	75	16	0	2	26	13	32	3-3	.251	.293	.324	2	.996
1993—	Cleveland (A.L.)	C	64	215	24	58	7	1	6	32	11	28	3-1	.270	.318	.395	6	.984
—	Charlotte (I.L.)	C	12	44	8	16	5	0	1	8	5	8	0-0	.364	.440	.545	0	1.000
1994—	Cleveland (A.L.)	C	80	292	44	84	15	1	14	43	25	31	8-4	.288	.347	.490	2	.996
1995—	Canton/Akron (East.)	C-DH	6	15	3	6	1	0	0	1	1	1	0-0	.400	.438	.467	1	.958
—	Cleveland (A.L.)	C	66	203	32	61	6	0	10	35	7	26	3-1	.300	.332	.478	2	.995
1996—	Cleveland (A.L.)	C-1B	127	418	53	110	23	0	11	50	19	42	1-0	.263	.299	.397	9	.988
1997—	Cleveland (A.L.)	C-DH	125	451	63	146	37	0	21	83	19	48	0-2	.324	.354	.545	*12	.985
1998—	Cleveland (A.L.)	C-DH	117	409	45	96	26	2	6	44	18	45	0-3	.235	.270	.352	6	.992
1999—	Cleveland (A.L.)	C-DH	37	137	19	42	13	0	6	25	4	23	0-1	.307	.322	.533	7	.974
—	Akron (East.)	DH-C	10	29	8	9	0	0	1	6	3	2	1-0	.310	.353	.414	1	.929
—	Buffalo (I.L.)	C-DH	10	33	9	9	2	1	2	10	6	3	0-0	.273	.400	.576	3	.921
2000—	Cleveland (A.L.)	C-DH	97	356	44	103	16	2	7	42	16	41	2-2	.289	.324	.404	8	.989
2001—	Chicago (A.L.)■	C	70	220	17	54	8	1	4	21	12	17	1-2	.245	.288	.345	4	.990
2002—	Chicago (A.L.)	C	51	167	21	48	10	1	7	25	5	14	0-0	.287	.309	.485	2	.994
—	Charlotte (I.L.)	C	3	8	0	1	0	0	0	0	0	0	0-0	.125	.125	.125	0	1.000
—	Colorado (N.L.)■	C	38	116	8	31	4	0	0	12	4	19	0-0	.267	.292	.302	0	1.000
American League totals (13 years)			1106	3796	454	1046	212	10	103	499	182	417	25-24	.276	.313	.418	78	.989
National League totals (3 years)			46	136	9	35	5	0	1	18	7	23	0-0	.257	.294	.316	0	1.000
Major League totals (15 years)			1152	3932	463	1081	217	10	104	517	189	440	25-24	.275	.312	.415	78	.989

DIVISION SERIES RECORD

			BATTING														FIELDING	
Year	**Team (League)**	**Pos.**	**G**	**AB**	**R**	**H**	**2B**	**3B**	**HR**	**RBI**	**BB**	**SO**	**SB-CS**	**Avg.**	**OBP**	**SLG**	**E**	**Avg.**
1995—	Cleveland (A.L.)	C	3	11	1	2	1	0	0	1	0	1	0-0	.182	.182	.273	0	1.000
1996—	Cleveland (A.L.)	C	4	16	0	2	0	0	0	3	0	2	0-1	.125	.125	.125	1	.978
1997—	Cleveland (A.L.)	C	5	19	4	6	1	0	2	5	0	2	0-0	.316	.316	.684	1	.967
1998—	Cleveland (A.L.)	C	4	13	2	3	3	0	0	2	1	4	0-0	.231	.286	.462	1	.967
1999—	Cleveland (A.L.)	C	5	14	1	2	0	0	0	1	2	6	0-0	.143	.235	.143	1	.971
Division series totals (5 years)			21	73	8	15	5	0	2	12	3	15	0-1	.205	.234	.356	4	.975

CHAMPIONSHIP SERIES RECORD

			BATTING														FIELDING	
Year	**Team (League)**	**Pos.**	**G**	**AB**	**R**	**H**	**2B**	**3B**	**HR**	**RBI**	**BB**	**SO**	**SB-CS**	**Avg.**	**OBP**	**SLG**	**E**	**Avg.**
1995—	Cleveland (A.L.)	C	5	15	0	4	1	1	0	1	1	1	0-0	.267	.313	.467	1	.971
1997—	Cleveland (A.L.)	C	6	24	3	3	0	0	1	4	1	3	0-0	.125	.160	.250	0	1.000
1998—	Cleveland (A.L.)	C	5	16	1	1	0	0	0	0	0	2	0-0	.063	.118	.063	2	.938
Championship series totals (3 years)			16	55	4	8	1	1	1	5	2	6	0-0	.145	.190	.255	3	.974

WORLD SERIES RECORD

			BATTING														FIELDING	
Year	**Team (League)**	**Pos.**	**G**	**AB**	**R**	**H**	**2B**	**3B**	**HR**	**RBI**	**BB**	**SO**	**SB-CS**	**Avg.**	**OBP**	**SLG**	**E**	**Avg.**
1995—	Cleveland (A.L.)	C	5	15	0	3	2	0	0	1	0	2	0-0	.200	.200	.333	0	1.000
1997—	Cleveland (A.L.)	C	7	30	5	11	1	0	2	10	2	3	0-0	.367	.406	.600	0	1.000
World Series totals (2 years)			12	45	5	14	3	0	2	11	2	5	0-0	.311	.340	.511	0	1.000

ALL-STAR GAME RECORD

NOTES: Named Most Valuable Player (1997).

	AB	**R**	**H**	**2B**	**3B**	**HR**	**RBI**	**BB**	**SO**	**SB-CS**	**Avg.**	**OBP**	**SLG**	**E**	**Avg.**
All-Star Game totals (6 years)	12	2	5	0	0	1	3	0	0	0-0	.417	.417	.667	0	1.000

ALOU, MOISES — OF — CUBS

PERSONAL: Born July 3, 1966, in Atlanta. ... 6-3/220. ... Bats right, throws right. ... Full name: Moises Rojas Alou. ... Son of Felipe Alou, manager, San Francisco Giants and outfielder with six major league teams (1958-1974); nephew of Jesus Alou, outfielder with four major league teams (1963-75 and 1978-79); nephew of Matty Alou, outfielder with six major league teams (1960-74); and cousin of Mel Rojas, pitcher with five major league teams (1990-99). ... Name pronounced moy-SEZZ ah-LOO.

HIGH SCHOOL: C.E.E. (Santo Domingo, Dominican Republic).

JUNIOR COLLEGE: Canada College (Calif.).

TRANSACTIONS/CAREER NOTES: Selected by Pittsburgh Pirates organization in first round (second pick overall) of free-agent draft (January 14, 1986). ... Traded by Pirates to Montreal Expos (August 16, 1990), completing deal in which Expos traded P Zane Smith to Pirates for P Scott Ruskin, SS Willie Greene and a player to be named later (August 8, 1990). ... On Montreal disabled list (March 19, 1991-entire season; July 7-27, 1992; September 18, 1993-remainder of season; August 18-September 5 and September 11, 1995-remainder of season). ... On disabled list (July 8-23, 1996). ... On suspended list (August 23-27, 1996). ... Granted free agency (December 7, 1996). ... Signed by Florida Marlins (December 12, 1996). ... Traded by Marlins to Houston Astros for P Oscar Henriquez, P Manuel Barrios and a player to be named later (November 11, 1997); Marlins acquired P Mark Johnson to complete deal (December 16, 1997). ... On disabled list (April 3, 1999-entire season; April 27-May 14, 2000; and March 29-April 16, 2001). ... Granted free agency (November 5, 2001). ... Signed by Chicago Cubs (December 19, 2001). ... On Chicago disabled list (March 31-April 15, 2002); included rehabilitation assignment to Daytona (April 10-15).

HONORS: Named outfielder on The Sporting News N.L. All-Star team (1994 and 1998). ... Named outfielder on The Sporting News N.L. Silver Slugger team (1994 and 1998).

STATISTICAL NOTES: Led American Association outfielders with seven double plays in 1990. ... Led N.L. in grounding into double plays with 21 in 2000. ... Had 23-game hitting streak (June 22-July 18, 2001). ... Career major league grand slams: 2.

2002 GAMES PLAYED BY POSITION (MLB): OF—124; DH—2.

		BATTING														FIELDING	
Year Team (League)	**Pos.**	**G**	**AB**	**R**	**H**	**2B**	**3B**	**HR**	**RBI**	**BB**	**SO**	**SB-CS**	**Avg.**	**OBP**	**SLG**	**E**	**Avg.**
1986—Watertown (NY-Penn)	OF	69	254	30	60	9	*8	6	35	22	72	14-8	.236	.300	.406	7	.952
1987—Macon (S.Atl.)	OF	4	8	1	1	0	0	0	0	2	4	0-0	.125	.300	.125	0	1.000
—Watertown (NY-Penn)	OF	39	117	20	25	6	2	4	8	16	36	6-3	.214	.324	.402	2	.957
1988—Augusta (S.Atl.)	OF	105	358	58	112	23	5	7	62	51	84	24-12	.313	.399	.464	9	.962
1989—Salem (Caro.)	OF	86	321	50	97	29	2	14	53	35	69	12-5	.302	.374	.536	10	.947
—Harrisburg (East.)	OF	54	205	36	60	5	2	3	19	17	38	8-4	.293	.344	.380	2	.978
1990—Harrisburg (East.)	OF	36	132	19	39	12	2	3	22	16	21	7-4	.295	.373	.485	1	.990
—Buffalo (A.A.)	OF	75	271	38	74	4	6	5	31	30	43	9-4	.273	.345	.387	8	.957
—Pittsburgh (N.L.)	OF	2	5	0	1	0	0	0	0	0	0	0-0	.200	.200	.200	0	1.000
—Indianapolis (A.A.)■	OF	15	55	6	12	1	0	0	6	3	7	4-3	.218	.254	.236	0	1.000
—Montreal (N.L.)	OF	14	15	4	3	0	1	0	0	0	3	0-0	.200	.200	.333	0	1.000
1991—Montreal (N.L.)		Did not play.															
1992—Montreal (N.L.)	OF	115	341	53	96	28	2	9	56	25	46	16-2	.282	.328	.455	4	.978
1993—Montreal (N.L.)	OF	136	482	70	138	29	6	18	85	38	53	17-6	.286	.340	.483	4	.985
1994—Montreal (N.L.)	OF	107	422	81	143	31	5	22	78	42	63	7-6	.339	.397	.592	3	.986
1995—Montreal (N.L.)	OF	93	344	48	94	22	0	14	58	29	56	4-3	.273	.342	.459	3	.981
1996—Montreal (N.L.)	OF	143	540	87	152	28	2	21	96	49	83	9-4	.281	.339	.457	3	.989
1997—Florida (N.L.)■	OF	150	538	88	157	29	5	23	115	70	85	9-5	.292	.373	.493	3	.988
1998—Houston (N.L.)■	OF-DH	159	584	104	182	34	5	38	124	84	87	11-3	.312	.399	.582	5	.980
1999—Houston (N.L.)		Did not play.															
2000—Houston (N.L.)	OF-DH	126	454	82	161	28	2	30	114	52	45	3-3	.355	.416	.623	6	.970
2001—Houston (N.L.)	OF-DH	136	513	79	170	31	1	27	108	57	57	5-1	.331	.396	.554	2	.991
2002—Daytona (FSL)■	OF	2	8	0	5	1	0	0	2	1	1	0-0	.625	.667	.750	0	1.000
—Chicago (N.L.)	OF-DH	132	484	50	133	23	1	15	61	47	61	8-0	.275	.337	.419	2	.991
Major League totals (11 years)		1313	4722	746	1430	283	30	217	895	493	639	89-33	.303	.368	.513	35	.984

DIVISION SERIES RECORD

		BATTING														FIELDING	
Year Team (League)	**Pos.**	**G**	**AB**	**R**	**H**	**2B**	**3B**	**HR**	**RBI**	**BB**	**SO**	**SB-CS**	**Avg.**	**OBP**	**SLG**	**E**	**Avg.**
1997—Florida (N.L.)	OF	3	14	1	3	1	0	0	1	0	3	0-0	.214	.214	.286	0	1.000
1998—Houston (N.L.)	OF	4	16	0	3	0	0	0	0	0	2	0-0	.188	.188	.188	0	1.000
2001—Houston (N.L.)	OF	3	12	0	2	1	0	0	1	0	1	0-0	.167	.167	.250	0	1.000
Division series totals (3 years)		10	42	1	8	2	0	0	2	0	6	0-0	.190	.190	.238	0	1.000

CHAMPIONSHIP SERIES RECORD

		BATTING														FIELDING	
Year Team (League)	**Pos.**	**G**	**AB**	**R**	**H**	**2B**	**3B**	**HR**	**RBI**	**BB**	**SO**	**SB-CS**	**Avg.**	**OBP**	**SLG**	**E**	**Avg.**
1997—Florida (N.L.)	OF-PH	5	15	0	1	1	0	0	5	1	3	0-0	.067	.125	.133	0	1.000

WORLD SERIES RECORD

NOTES: Member of World Series championship team (1997).

		BATTING														FIELDING	
Year Team (League)	**Pos.**	**G**	**AB**	**R**	**H**	**2B**	**3B**	**HR**	**RBI**	**BB**	**SO**	**SB-CS**	**Avg.**	**OBP**	**SLG**	**E**	**Avg.**
1997—Florida (N.L.)	OF	7	28	6	9	2	0	3	9	3	6	1-0	.321	.387	.714	0	1.000

ALL-STAR GAME RECORD

	AB	**R**	**H**	**2B**	**3B**	**HR**	**RBI**	**BB**	**SO**	**SB-CS**	**Avg.**	**OBP**	**SLG**	**E**	**Avg.**
All-Star Game totals (4 years)	7	1	3	1	0	0	1	0	3	0-0	.429	.429	.571	0	1.000

ALVAREZ, JUAN — P — RANGERS

PERSONAL: Born August 9, 1973, in Coral Gables, Fla. ... 6-0/184. ... Throws left, bats left. ... Full name: Juan M. Alvarez.

HIGH SCHOOL: Coral Gables (Fla.).

COLLEGE: St. Thomas.

TRANSACTIONS/CAREER NOTES: Signed as non-drafted free agent by California Angels organization (July 25, 1995). ... Angels franchise renamed Anaheim Angels for 1997 season. ... Granted free agency (October 15, 2001). ... Signed by Texas Rangers organization (December 6, 2001).

CAREER HITTING (MLB): 0-for-0 (.000), 0 R, 0 2B, 0 3B, 0 HR, 0 RBI.

Year League	W	L	Pct.	ERA	G	GS	CG	ShO	Sv.-Opp.	IP	H	R	ER	HR	BB-IBB	SO
1995—Boise (N'West)	0	0	...	0.77	9	0	0	0	0-...	11.2	12	1	1	0	2-0	11
1996—Cedar Rapids (Midw.)	1	2	.333	3.40	40	0	0	0	3-...	53.0	50	25	20	0	30-1	53
1997—Lake Elsinore (Calif.)	4	2	.667	1.40	27	0	0	0	3-...	51.1	33	9	8	2	13-2	46
—Midland (Texas)	4	1	.800	8.27	24	0	0	0	0-...	37.0	63	42	34	5	22-1	27
1998—Midland (Texas)	3	4	.429	4.30	40	0	0	0	12-...	46.0	40	26	22	5	21-3	41
—Vancouver (PCL)	1	1	.500	5.02	18	0	0	0	0-...	14.1	14	9	8	2	8-0	12
1999—Erie (East.)	1	2	.333	2.05	23	0	0	0	4-...	30.2	20	14	7	4	6-0	22
—Edmonton (PCL)	0	3	.000	3.49	27	0	0	0	0-...	28.1	30	13	11	2	8-0	25
—Anaheim (A.L.)	0	1	.000	3.00	8	0	0	0	0-0	3.0	1	1	1	0	4-0	4
2000—Edmonton (PCL)	3	1	.750	2.82	44	0	0	0	0-...	38.1	30	12	12	3	19-1	27
—Anaheim (A.L.)	0	0	...	13.50	11	0	0	0	0-0	6.0	14	9	9	3	7-1	2
2001—Salt Lake (PCL)	2	2	.500	4.95	48	1	0	0	0-...	67.1	68	42	37	13	27-0	44
2002—Tulsa (Texas)■	0	0	...	0.00	2	0	0	0	0-...	1.2	1	0	0	0	0-0	0
—Oklahoma (PCL)	0	0	...	3.63	15	0	0	0	1-...	17.1	19	7	7	1	9-1	13
—Texas (A.L.)	0	4	.000	4.76	52	0	0	0	0-3	39.2	35	22	21	7	21-0	30
Major League totals (3 years)	0	5	.000	5.73	71	0	0	0	0-3	48.2	50	32	31	10	32-1	36

ALVAREZ, TONY — OF/IF — PIRATES

PERSONAL: Born May 10, 1979, in Caracas, Venezuela. ... 6-1/200. ... Bats right, throws right. ... Full name: Antonio Enrique Alvarez.

TRANSACTIONS/CAREER NOTES: Signed as non-drafted free agent by Pittsburgh Pirates organization (September 27, 1995).

HONORS: Named Most Valuable Player in New York-Pennsylvania League Pinckney Division (1999).

STATISTICAL NOTES: Tied for Gulf Coast League lead in sacrifice flies with five in 1998. ... Led New York-Pennsylvania League in being hit by pitch with 16 in 1999. ... Led South Atlantic League with 21 caught stealing in 2000.

2002 GAMES PLAYED BY POSITION (MLB): OF—8.

		BATTING														FIELDING	
Year Team (League)	Pos.	G	AB	R	H	2B	3B	HR	RBI	BB	SO	SB-CS	Avg.	OBP	SLG	E	Avg.
1996—Dom. Pirates (DSL)	3B	39	109	12	15	2	0	1	9	8	12	6-...	.138	...	.183	15	.892
1997—Guacara 1 (VSL)		38	91	15	20	3	0	0	6	9	10	3-...	.220	...	.253	...	...
1998—GC Pirates (GCL)	3-1-2-S-0	50	190	27	47	13	1	4	29	13	24	19-1	.247	.299	.389	14	.941
1999—Williamsport (NY-P)	3-2-0-1-C-S	58	196	44	63	14	1	7	45	21	36	38-9	.321	.418	.510	21	.871
2000—Hickory (S.Atl.)	OF-1B	118	442	75	126	25	4	15	77	39	93	52-21	.285	.357	.462	14	.951
2001—Lynchburg (Caro.)	OF	25	93	10	32	4	0	2	11	7	11	7-3	.344	.390	.452	3	.893
—Altoona (East.)	OF-2B	67	254	34	81	16	1	6	25	9	30	17-11	.319	.359	.461	4	.968
2002—Altoona (East.)	OF	125	507	79	161	37	1	15	59	27	71	29-•18	.318	.361	.483	6	.978
—Pittsburgh (N.L.)	OF	14	26	6	8	2	0	1	2	3	5	1-0	.308	.379	.500	0	1.000
Major League totals (1 year)		14	26	6	8	2	0	1	2	3	5	1-0	.308	.379	.500	0	1.000

ALVAREZ, VICTOR — P — DODGERS

PERSONAL: Born November 8, 1976, in Culiacan, Mexico. ... 5-10/150. ... Throws left, bats left.

TRANSACTIONS/CAREER NOTES: Signed as non-drafted free agent by Los Angeles Dodgers organization (May 16, 1997). ... Loaned by Dodgers organization to Mexico City Reds, Mexican League (March 18-October 28, 1998; and April 2-June 12, 2000).

CAREER HITTING (MLB): 0-for-2 (.000), 0 R, 0 2B, 0 3B, 0 HR, 0 RBI.

Year League	W	L	Pct.	ERA	G	GS	CG	ShO	Sv.-Opp.	IP	H	R	ER	HR	BB-IBB	SO
1997—Dom. Dodgers (DSL)	2	0	1.000	0.90	3	0	0	0	1-...	10.0	4	1	1	...	5-...	18
—Great Falls (Pio.)	4	1	.800	3.35	12	8	0	0	0-...	48.1	49	30	18	0	17-0	50
1998—Mex. City Reds (Mex.)■	3	4	.429	3.62	22	12	0	0	2-...	79.2	93	39	32	3	49-2	36
1999—Vero Beach (FSL)■	4	4	.500	1.97	12	12	1	0	0-...	73.0	56	21	16	4	16-0	57
—San Antonio (Texas)	4	3	.571	3.67	9	9	0	0	0-...	56.1	58	27	23	5	10-0	43
2000—Mex. City Reds (Mex.)■	0	2	.000	6.33	7	6	0	0	0-...	21.1	30	15	15	3	14-0	14
—San Antonio (Texas)■	0	3	.000	3.91	11	8	0	0	0-...	48.1	44	27	21	3	30-1	43
—Vero Beach (FSL)	1	1	.500	5.16	4	4	0	0	0-...	22.2	17	14	13	6	11-0	20
2001—Jacksonville (Sou.)	2	0	1.000	1.20	8	8	0	0	0-...	45.0	27	6	6	1	7-0	40
—Las Vegas (PCL)	7	4	.636	4.27	20	20	0	0	0-...	118.0	115	63	56	12	41-0	94
2002—Las Vegas (PCL)	10	7	.588	4.70	34	15	0	0	3-...	122.2	132	69	64	11	39-1	106
—Los Angeles (N.L.)	0	1	.000	4.35	4	1	0	0	0-0	10.1	9	5	5	1	2-0	7
Major League totals (1 year)	0	1	.000	4.35	4	1	0	0	0-0	10.1	9	5	5	1	2-0	7

ALVAREZ, WILSON — P

PERSONAL: Born March 24, 1970, in Maracaibo, Venezuela. ... 6-1/245. ... Throws left, bats left. ... Full name: Wilson Eduardo Alvarez.

TRANSACTIONS/CAREER NOTES: Signed as non-drafted free agent by Texas Rangers organization (September 23, 1986). ... Traded by Rangers with IF Scott Fletcher and OF Sammy Sosa to Chicago White Sox for OF Harold Baines and IF Fred Manrique (July 29, 1989). ... Traded by White Sox with P Danny Darwin and P Roberto Hernandez to San Francisco Giants for SS Michael Caruso, OF Brian Manning, P Lorenzo Barcelo, P Keith Foulke, P Bobby Howry and P Ken Vining (July 31, 1997). ... Granted free agency (November 1, 1997). ... Signed by Tampa Bay Devil Rays (December 3, 1997). ... On Tampa Bay disabled list (May 21-July 6, 1998); included rehabilitation assignments to Gulf Coast Devil Rays (June 26-29), St. Petersburg (June 30-July 4) and Durham (July 5-6). ... On disabled list (April 12-29 and July 24-August 8, 1999). ... On Tampa Bay disabled list (March 25, 2000-entire season); included rehabilitation assignment to St. Petersburg (April 15). ... On Tampa Bay disabled list (March 23, 2001-entire season); included to rehabilitation assignments to Orlando (June 9-18 and July 29-August 13) and Durham (June 19-July 3 and August 14-27). ... On Tampa Bay disabled list (April 15-May 31 and July 15-August 5, 2002); included rehabilitation assignment to Orlando (May 19-31). ... Released by Devil Rays (September 30, 2002).

RECORDS: Shares major league single-inning record for most strikeouts—4 (July 21, 1997, seventh inning).

STATISTICAL NOTES: Pitched 7-0 no-hit victory for Chicago against Baltimore (August 11, 1991).
CAREER HITTING (MLB): 3-for-33 (.091), 1 R, 0 2B, 0 3B, 0 HR, 1 RBI.

Year League	W	L	Pct.	ERA	G	GS	CG	ShO	Sv.-Opp.	IP	H	R	ER	HR	BB-IBB	SO
1987—Gastonia (S.Atl.)	1	5	.167	6.47	8	6	0	0	0-...	32.0	39	24	23	5	23-0	19
—Gulf Coast Rangers (GCL)	2	5	.286	5.24	10	10	0	0	0-...	44.2	41	29	26	•6	21-0	46
1988—Gastonia (S.Atl.)	4	11	.267	2.98	23	23	1	0	0-...	127.0	113	63	42	5	49-1	134
—Oklahoma City (A.A.)	1	1	.500	3.78	5	3	0	0	0-...	16.2	17	8	7	2	6-0	9
1989—Charlotte (FSL)	7	4	.636	2.11	13	13	3	2	0-...	81.0	68	29	19	2	21-0	51
—Tulsa (Texas)	2	2	.500	2.06	7	7	1	1	0-...	48.0	40	14	11	1	16-3	29
—Texas (A.L.)	0	1	.000	...	1	1	0	0	0-0	.0	3	3	3	2	2-0	0
—Birmingham (Sou.)■	2	1	.667	3.03	6	6	0	0	0-...	35.2	32	12	12	2	16-0	18
1990—Vancouver (PCL)	7	7	.500	6.00	17	15	1	0	0-...	75.0	91	54	50	7	51-0	35
—Birmingham (Sou.)	5	1	.833	4.27	7	7	1	0	0-...	46.1	44	24	22	5	25-0	36
1991—Birmingham (Sou.)	10	6	.625	1.83	23	23	3	2	0-...	152.1	109	46	31	6	74-0	165
—Chicago (A.L.)	3	2	.600	3.51	10	9	2	1	0-0	56.1	47	26	22	9	29-0	32
1992—Chicago (A.L.)	5	3	.625	5.20	34	9	0	0	1-1	100.1	103	64	58	12	65-2	66
1993—Chicago (A.L.)	15	8	.652	2.95	31	31	1	1	0-0	207.2	168	78	68	14	*122-8	155
—Nashville (A.A.)	0	1	.000	2.84	1	1	0	0	0-...	6.1	7	7	2	0	2-0	8
1994—Chicago (A.L.)	12	8	.600	3.45	24	24	2	1	0-0	161.2	147	72	62	16	62-1	108
1995—Chicago (A.L.)	8	11	.421	4.32	29	29	3	0	0-0	175.0	171	96	84	21	93-4	118
1996—Chicago (A.L.)	15	10	.600	4.22	35	35	0	0	0-0	217.1	216	106	102	21	97-3	181
1997—Chicago (A.L.)	9	8	.529	3.03	22	22	2	1	0-0	145.2	126	61	49	9	55-1	110
—San Francisco (N.L.)■	4	3	.571	4.48	11	11	0	0	0-0	66.1	54	36	33	9	36-3	69
1998—Tampa Bay (A.L.)■	6	14	.300	4.73	25	25	0	0	0-0	142.2	130	78	75	18	68-0	107
—GC Devil Rays (GCL)	0	0	...	0.00	1	1	0	0	0-...	3.0	2	0	0	0	1-0	4
—St. Petersburg (FSL)	0	1	.000	27.00	1	1	0	0	0-...	1.2	5	5	5	1	2-0	2
—Durham (I.L.)	0	0	...	3.86	1	1	0	0	0-...	4.2	4	2	2	0	2-0	6
1999—Tampa Bay (A.L.)	9	9	.500	4.22	28	28	1	0	0-0	160.0	159	92	75	22	79-1	128
2000—St. Petersburg (FSL)	0	0	...	0.00	1	1	0	0	0-...	4.0	0	0	0	0	0-0	2
2001—Orlando (Sou.)	1	3	.250	4.43	5	5	0	0	0-...	20.1	24	10	10	2	6-0	18
—Durham (I.L.)	1	1	.500	3.00	4	4	0	0	0-...	18.0	20	8	6	2	6-0	16
2002—Tampa Bay (A.L.)	2	3	.400	5.28	23	10	0	0	1-1	75.0	80	47	44	13	36-3	56
—Orlando (Sou.)	1	0	1.000	1.13	2	2	0	0	0-...	8.0	6	1	1	0	2-0	7
A.L. totals (11 years)	84	77	.522	4.01	262	223	11	4	2-2	1441.2	1350	723	642	157	708-23	1061
N.L. totals (1 year)	4	3	.571	4.48	11	11	0	0	0-0	66.1	54	36	33	9	36-3	69
Major League totals (11 years)	88	80	.524	4.03	273	234	11	4	2-2	1508.0	1404	759	675	166	744-26	1130

DIVISION SERIES RECORD

Year League	W	L	Pct.	ERA	G	GS	CG	ShO	Sv.-Opp.	IP	H	R	ER	HR	BB-IBB	SO
1997—San Francisco (N.L.)	0	1	.000	6.00	1	1	0	0	0-0	6.0	6	4	4	1	4-0	4

CHAMPIONSHIP SERIES RECORD

Year League	W	L	Pct.	ERA	G	GS	CG	ShO	Sv.-Opp.	IP	H	R	ER	HR	BB-IBB	SO
1993—Chicago (A.L.)	1	0	1.000	1.00	1	1	1	0	0-0	9.0	7	1	1	0	2-0	6

ALL-STAR GAME RECORD

	W	L	Pct.	ERA	GS	CG	ShO	Sv.-Opp.	IP	H	R	ER	HR	BB-IBB	SO
All-Star Game totals (1 year)	0	0	...	0.00	0	0	0	0-0	1.0	0	0	0	0	0-0	0

AMEZAGA, ALFREDO — SS/2B — ANGELS

PERSONAL: Born January 16, 1978, in Obregon, Mexico. ... 5-10/165. ... Bats both, throws right.
HIGH SCHOOL: Miami Senior (Miami).
JUNIOR COLLEGE: St. Petersburg (Fla.).
TRANSACTIONS/CAREER NOTES: Selected by Anaheim Angels organization in 13th round of free-agent draft (June 2, 1999). ... On Arkansas disabled list (April 21-May 4, 2001).
STATISTICAL NOTES: Tied for Texas League lead with 15 caught stealing in 2001. ... Led Pacific Coast League shortstops with 24 errors and 90 double plays in 2002.
2002 GAMES PLAYED BY POSITION (MLB): SS—5; DH—1.

		BATTING														FIELDING	
Year Team (League)	Pos.	G	AB	R	H	2B	3B	HR	RBI	BB	SO	SB-CS	Avg.	OBP	SLG	E	Avg.
1999—Butte (Pio.)	2B-SS	8	34	11	10	2	0	0	5	5	5	6-2	.294	.400	.353	0	1.000
—Boise (N'West)	2B-SS	48	205	52	66	6	4	2	29	23	29	14-3	.322	.402	.420	12	.953
2000—Lake Elsinore (Calif.)	2B-SS	108	420	90	117	13	4	4	44	63	70	73-21	.279	.374	.357	22	.961
2001—Arkansas (Texas)	SS	70	285	50	89	10	5	4	21	22	55	24-15	.312	.370	.425	13	.964
—Salt Lake (PCL)	SS	49	200	28	50	5	4	1	16	14	45	9-6	.250	.307	.330	11	.954
2002—Salt Lake (PCL)	SS-2B	128	518	77	130	25	7	6	51	45	100	23-14	.251	.317	.361	†24	.962
—Anaheim (A.L.)	SS-DH	12	13	3	7	2	0	0	2	0	1	1-0	.538	.538	.692	0	1.000
Major League totals (1 year)		12	13	3	7	2	0	0	2	0	1	1-0	.538	.538	.692	0	1.000

ANDERSON, BRADY — OF

PERSONAL: Born January 18, 1964, in Silver Spring, Md. ... 6-1/202. ... Bats left, throws left. ... Full name: Brady Kevin Anderson.
HIGH SCHOOL: Carlsbad (Calif.).
COLLEGE: UC Irvine.
TRANSACTIONS/CAREER NOTES: Selected by Boston Red Sox organization in 10th round of free-agent draft (June 3, 1985). ... Traded by Red Sox with P Curt Schilling to Baltimore Orioles for P Mike Boddicker (July 29, 1988). ... On Baltimore disabled list (June 8-July 20, 1990); included rehabilitation assignments to Hagerstown (July 5-12) and Frederick (July 13-17). ... On Baltimore disabled list (May 28-June 14, 1991 and June 23-July 8, 1993). ... Granted free agency (October 27, 1997). ... Re-signed by Orioles (December 7, 1997). ... On disabled list (April 20-May 8, 1998). ... Released by Orioles (November 16, 2001). ... Signed by Cleveland Indians (December 6, 2001). ... Released by Indians (May 21, 2002).

RECORDS: Holds major league single-season record for most home runs leading off game—12 (1996). ... Shares major league single-inning record for most times hit by pitch—2 (May 23, 1999, first inning).

STATISTICAL NOTES: Led A.L. outfielders with six double plays in 1992. ... Led A.L. in being hit by pitch with 22 in 1996, 19 in 1997 and 24 in 1999. ... Career major league grand slams: 3.

MISCELLANEOUS: Holds Baltimore Orioles all-time record for stolen bases (307).

2002 GAMES PLAYED BY POSITION (MLB): OF—29; DH—1.

			BATTING													FIELDING	
Year	**Team (League)**	**Pos.**	**G**	**AB**	**R**	**H**	**2B**	**3B**	**HR**	**RBI**	**BB**	**SO**	**SB-CS**	**Avg.**	**OBP**	**SLG**	**E**	**Avg.**
1985—	Elmira (NY-Penn)	OF	71	215	36	55	7	•6	5	21	*67	32	13-9	.256	.437	.414	3	.976
1986—	Winter Haven (FSL)	OF	126	417	86	133	19	11	12	87	*107	47	44-19	.319	.459	.504	1	*.997
1987—	New Britain (East.)	OF	52	170	30	50	4	3	6	35	45	24	7-3	.294	.445	.459	2	.985
—	Pawtucket (I.L.)	OF	23	79	18	30	4	0	2	8	16	8	2-1	.380	.484	.506	0	1.000
1988—	Boston (A.L.)	OF	41	148	14	34	5	3	0	12	15	35	4-2	.230	.315	.304	1	.989
—	Pawtucket (I.L.)	OF	49	167	27	48	6	1	4	19	26	33	8-3	.287	.393	.407	2	.983
—	Baltimore (A.L.)■	OF	53	177	17	35	8	1	1	9	8	40	6-4	.198	.232	.271	3	.981
1989—	Baltimore (A.L.)	OF-DH	94	266	44	55	12	2	4	16	43	45	16-4	.207	.324	.312	3	.985
—	Rochester (I.L.)	OF	21	70	14	14	1	2	1	8	12	13	2-2	.200	.333	.314	0	1.000
1990—	Baltimore (A.L.)	OF-DH	89	234	24	54	5	2	3	24	31	46	15-2	.231	.327	.308	2	.987
—	Hagerstown (East.)	OF	9	34	8	13	0	2	1	5	5	5	2-1	.382	.450	.588	0	1.000
—	Frederick (Caro.)	OF	2	7	2	3	1	0	0	3	1	1	0-0	.429	.500	.571	0	1.000
1991—	Baltimore (A.L.)	OF-DH	113	256	40	59	12	3	2	27	38	44	12-5	.230	.338	.324	3	.981
—	Rochester (I.L.)	OF	7	26	5	10	3	0	0	2	7	4	4-1	.385	.515	.500	0	1.000
1992—	Baltimore (A.L.)	OF	159	623	100	169	28	10	21	80	98	98	53-16	.271	.373	.449	8	.980
1993—	Baltimore (A.L.)	OF-DH	142	560	87	147	36	8	13	66	82	99	24-12	.263	.363	.425	2	.993
1994—	Baltimore (A.L.)	OF	111	453	78	119	25	5	12	48	57	75	31-1	.263	.356	.419	1	.996
1995—	Baltimore (A.L.)	OF	143	554	108	145	33	10	16	64	87	111	26-7	.262	.371	.444	3	.989
1996—	Baltimore (A.L.)	OF-DH	149	579	117	172	37	5	50	110	76	106	21-8	.297	.396	.637	3	.992
1997—	Baltimore (A.L.)	OF-DH	151	590	97	170	39	7	18	73	84	105	18-12	.288	.393	.469	3	.989
1998—	Baltimore (A.L.)	OF-DH	133	479	84	113	28	3	18	51	75	78	21-7	.236	.356	.420	4	.985
1999—	Baltimore (A.L.)	OF-DH	150	564	109	159	28	5	24	81	96	105	36-7	.282	.404	.477	1	.997
2000—	Baltimore (A.L.)	OF-DH	141	506	89	130	26	0	19	50	92	103	16-9	.257	.375	.421	1	.997
2001—	Baltimore (A.L.)	OF-DH	131	430	50	87	12	3	8	45	60	77	12-4	.202	.311	.300	3	.988
2002—	Cleveland (A.L.)■	OF-DH	34	80	4	13	4	0	1	5	18	23	4-0	.163	.327	.250	1	.981
Major League totals (15 years)			1834	6499	1062	1661	338	67	210	761	960	1190	315-100	.256	.362	.425	42	.989

DIVISION SERIES RECORD

NOTES: Hit home run in first at-bat (October 1, 1996).

			BATTING													FIELDING	
Year	**Team (League)**	**Pos.**	**G**	**AB**	**R**	**H**	**2B**	**3B**	**HR**	**RBI**	**BB**	**SO**	**SB-CS**	**Avg.**	**OBP**	**SLG**	**E**	**Avg.**
1996—	Baltimore (A.L.)	OF	4	17	3	5	0	0	2	4	2	3	0-1	.294	.381	.647	0	1.000
1997—	Baltimore (A.L.)	OF	4	17	3	6	1	0	1	4	1	4	1-0	.353	.389	.588	0	1.000
Division series totals (2 years)			8	34	6	11	1	0	3	8	3	7	1-1	.324	.385	.618	0	1.000

CHAMPIONSHIP SERIES RECORD

			BATTING													FIELDING	
Year	**Team (League)**	**Pos.**	**G**	**AB**	**R**	**H**	**2B**	**3B**	**HR**	**RBI**	**BB**	**SO**	**SB-CS**	**Avg.**	**OBP**	**SLG**	**E**	**Avg.**
1996—	Baltimore (A.L.)	OF	5	21	5	4	1	0	1	1	3	5	0-0	.190	.292	.381	0	1.000
1997—	Baltimore (A.L.)	OF	6	25	5	9	2	0	2	3	4	4	2-0	.360	.448	.680	1	.929
Championship series totals (2 years)			11	46	10	13	3	0	3	4	7	9	2-0	.283	.377	.543	1	.955

ALL-STAR GAME RECORD

	AB	**R**	**H**	**2B**	**3B**	**HR**	**RBI**	**BB**	**SO**	**SB-CS**	**Avg.**	**OBP**	**SLG**	**E**	**Avg.**
All-Star Game totals (3 years)	9	0	2	1	0	0	0	0	0	0-0	.222	.222	.333	0	1.000

ANDERSON, BRIAN — P

PERSONAL: Born April 26, 1972, in Geneva, Ohio. ... 6-1/183. ... Throws left, bats right. ... Full name: Brian James Anderson.

HIGH SCHOOL: Geneva (Ohio).

COLLEGE: Wright State.

TRANSACTIONS/CAREER NOTES: Selected by California Angels organization in first round (third pick overall) of free-agent draft (June 3, 1993). ... On California disabled list (May 7-June 7, 1994); included rehabilitation assignment to Lake Elsinore (May 27-June 7). ... On California disabled list (May 6-June 20, 1995); included rehabilitation assignment to Lake Elsinore (June 4-20). ... Traded by Angels to Cleveland Indians for P Jason Grimsley and P Pep Harris (February 15, 1996). ... On Cleveland disabled list (July 5-August 12, 1997); included rehabilitation assignment to Buffalo (August 3-13). ... Selected by Arizona Diamondbacks in first round (second pick overall) of expansion draft (November 18, 1997). ... On Arizona disabled list (April 12-May 2 and June 3-July 1, 2001); included rehabilitation assignments to Tuscon (April 27-May 2 and June 26-27). ... Granted free agency (October 28, 2002).

RECORDS: Shares major league single-inning record for most home runs allowed—4 (September 5, 1995, second inning). ... Shares N.L. single-inning record for most consecutive home runs allowed—3 (July 22, 2001).

HONORS: Named A.L. Rookie Pitcher of the Year by The Sporting News (1994).

STATISTICAL NOTES: Tied for A.L. lead with five balks in 1994 and three in 1995. ... Tied for American Association lead with three balks in 1996. ... Led N.L. with six balks in 1998 and five in 2002.

MISCELLANEOUS: Scored one run in three appearances as pinch runner (1998). ... Scored a run in only appearance as pinch runner (1999). ... Walked and grounded into fielder's choice in two appearances as pinch hitter and scored one run in two appearances as pinch runner (2000). ... Appeared in one game as pinch hitter (2001). ... Appeared in three games as pinch runner (2001).

CAREER HITTING (MLB): 35-for-253 (.138), 15 R, 5 2B, 3 3B, 1 HR, 10 RBI.

Year	**League**	**W**	**L**	**Pct.**	**ERA**	**G**	**GS**	**CG**	**ShO**	**Sv.-Opp.**	**IP**	**H**	**R**	**ER**	**HR**	**BB-IBB**	**SO**
1993—	Midland (Texas)	0	1	.000	3.38	2	2	0	0	0-...	10.2	16	5	4	2	0-0	9
—	Vancouver (PCL)	0	1	.000	12.38	2	2	0	0	0-...	8.0	13	12	11	3	6-0	2
—	California (A.L.)	0	0	...	3.97	4	1	0	0	0-0	11.1	11	5	5	1	2-0	4
1994—	California (A.L.)	7	5	.583	5.22	18	18	0	0	0-0	101.2	120	63	59	13	27-0	47
—	Lake Elsinore (Calif.)	0	1	.000	3.00	2	2	0	0	0-...	12.0	6	4	4	1	0-0	9

Year	League	W	L	Pct.	ERA	G	GS	CG	ShO	Sv.-Opp.	IP	H	R	ER	HR	BB-IBB	SO
1995—	California (A.L.)	6	8	.429	5.87	18	17	1	0	0-0	99.2	110	66	65	24	30-2	45
—	Lake Elsinore (Calif.)	1	1	.500	1.93	3	3	0	0	0-...	14.0	10	3	3	0	1-0	13
1996—	Buffalo (A.A.)■	11	5	.688	3.59	19	19	2	0	0-...	128.0	125	57	51	14	28-0	85
—	Cleveland (A.L.)	3	1	.750	4.91	10	9	0	0	0-0	51.1	58	29	28	9	14-1	21
1997—	Buffalo (A.A.)	7	1	.875	3.05	15	15	1	1	0-...	85.2	78	33	29	13	15-0	60
—	Cleveland (A.L.)	4	2	.667	4.69	8	8	0	0	0-0	48.0	55	28	25	7	11-0	22
1998—	Arizona (N.L.)■	12	13	.480	4.33	32	32	2	1	0-0	208.0	221	109	100	•39	24-2	95
1999—	Arizona (N.L.)	8	2	.800	4.57	31	19	2	1	1-2	130.0	144	69	66	18	28-3	75
—	Tucson (PCL)	0	1	.000	5.40	2	2	0	0	0-...	6.2	9	5	4	1	1-0	8
2000—	Arizona (N.L.)	11	7	.611	4.05	33	32	2	0	0-0	213.1	226	101	96	38	39-7	104
2001—	Arizona (N.L.)	4	9	.308	5.20	29	22	1	0	0-1	133.1	156	93	77	25	30-2	55
—	Tucson (PCL)	1	0	1.000	1.50	2	2	0	0	0-...	12.0	7	2	2	0	2-0	8
2002—	Arizona (N.L.)	6	11	.353	4.79	35	24	0	0	0-0	156.0	174	86	83	23	32-3	81
A.L. totals (5 years)		20	16	.556	5.25	58	53	1	0	0-0	312.0	354	191	182	54	84-3	139
N.L. totals (5 years)		41	42	.494	4.52	160	129	7	2	1-3	840.2	921	458	422	143	153-17	410
Major League totals (10 years)		61	58	.513	4.72	218	182	8	2	1-3	1152.2	1275	649	604	197	237-20	549

DIVISION SERIES RECORD

Year	League	W	L	Pct.	ERA	G	GS	CG	ShO	Sv.-Opp.	IP	H	R	ER	HR	BB-IBB	SO
1999—	Arizona (N.L.)	0	0	...	2.57	1	1	0	0	0-0	7.0	7	2	2	1	0-0	4
2001—	Arizona (N.L.)	0	0	...	2.25	2	0	0	0	0-0	4.0	3	1	1	1	0-0	3
Division series totals (2 years)		0	0	...	2.45	3	1	0	0	0-0	11.0	10	3	3	2	0-0	7

CHAMPIONSHIP SERIES RECORD

Year	League	W	L	Pct.	ERA	G	GS	CG	ShO	Sv.-Opp.	IP	H	R	ER	HR	BB-IBB	SO
1997—	Cleveland (A.L.)	1	0	1.000	1.42	3	0	0	0	0-0	6.1	1	1	1	0	3-1	7
2001—	Arizona (N.L.)	1	0	1.000	2.70	1	0	0	0	0-0	3.1	4	1	1	0	1-0	0
Champ. series totals (2 years)		2	0	1.000	1.86	4	0	0	0	0-0	9.2	5	2	2	0	4-1	7

WORLD SERIES RECORD

NOTES: Member of World Series championship team (2001).

Year	League	W	L	Pct.	ERA	G	GS	CG	ShO	Sv.-Opp.	IP	H	R	ER	HR	BB-IBB	SO
1997—	Cleveland (A.L.)	0	0	...	2.45	3	0	0	0	1-1	3.2	2	1	1	0	0-0	2
2001—	Arizona (N.L.)	0	1	.000	3.38	1	1	0	0	0-0	5.1	5	2	2	1	3-0	1
World Series totals (2 years)		0	1	.000	3.00	4	1	0	0	1-1	9.0	7	3	3	1	3-0	3

ANDERSON, GARRET — OF — ANGELS

PERSONAL: Born June 30, 1972, in Los Angeles. ... 6-3/228. ... Bats left, throws left. ... Full name: Garret Joseph Anderson.

HIGH SCHOOL: John F. Kennedy (Granada Hills, Calif.).

TRANSACTIONS/CAREER NOTES: Selected by California Angels organization in fourth round of free-agent draft (June 4, 1990). ... Angels franchise renamed Anaheim Angels for 1997 season.

HONORS: Named A.L. Rookie Player of the Year by The Sporting News (1995). ... Named outfielder on The Sporting News A.L. All-Star team (2002). ... Named outfielder on A.L. Silver Slugger team (2002).

STATISTICAL NOTES: Collected six hits in one game (September 27, 1996). ... Had 28-game hitting streak (June 28-July 31, 1998). ... Led A.L. outfielders with 406 putouts in 1999. ... Had 16-game hitting streak (July 6-25, 1999). ... Had 17-game hitting streak (August 30-September 17, 1999). ... Had 15-game hitting streak (July 14-29, 2002). ... Career major league grand slams: 5.

MISCELLANEOUS: Holds Anaheim Angels franchise all-time record for doubles (300).

2002 GAMES PLAYED BY POSITION (MLB): OF—147; DH—10.

			BATTING														FIELDING	
Year	Team (League)	Pos.	G	AB	R	H	2B	3B	HR	RBI	BB	SO	SB-CS	Avg.	OBP	SLG	E	Avg.
1990—	Arizona Angels (Ariz.)	OF	32	127	5	27	2	0	0	14	2	24	3-0	.213	.231	.228	2	.965
—	Boise (N'West)	OF	25	83	11	21	3	1	1	8	4	18	0-1	.253	.284	.349	2	.950
1991—	Quad City (Midw.)	OF	105	392	40	102	22	2	2	42	20	89	5-6	.260	.295	.342	10	.943
1992—	Palm Springs (Calif.)	OF	81	322	46	104	15	2	1	62	21	61	1-1	.323	.366	.391	6	.959
—	Midland (Texas)	OF	39	146	16	40	5	0	2	19	9	30	2-1	.274	.316	.349	1	.986
1993—	Vancouver (PCL)	OF-1B	124	467	57	137	34	4	4	71	31	95	3-4	.293	.334	.409	2	.991
1994—	Vancouver (PCL)	OF-DH-1B	123	505	75	162	42	6	12	102	28	93	3-3	.321	.356	.499	2	.990
—	California (A.L.)	OF	5	13	0	5	0	0	0	1	0	2	0-0	.385	.385	.385	0	1.000
1995—	California (A.L.)	OF-DH	106	374	50	120	19	1	16	69	19	65	6-2	.321	.352	.505	5	.978
—	Vancouver (PCL)	OF-DH	14	61	9	19	7	0	0	12	5	14	0-0	.311	.364	.426	1	.957
1996—	California (A.L.)	OF-DH	150	607	79	173	33	2	12	72	27	84	7-9	.285	.314	.405	7	.979
1997—	Anaheim (A.L.)	OF-DH	154	624	76	189	36	3	8	92	30	70	10-4	.303	.334	.409	3	.992
1998—	Anaheim (A.L.)	OF	156	622	62	183	41	7	15	79	29	80	8-3	.294	.325	.455	6	.983
1999—	Anaheim (A.L.)	OF-DH	157	620	88	188	36	2	21	80	34	81	3-4	.303	.336	.469	3	.993
2000—	Anaheim (A.L.)	OF-DH-1B	159	647	92	185	40	3	35	117	24	87	7-6	.286	.307	.519	4	.990
2001—	Anaheim (A.L.)	OF-DH	161	672	83	194	39	2	28	123	27	100	13-6	.289	.314	.478	2	.994
2002—	Anaheim (A.L.)	OF-DH	158	638	93	195	•56	3	29	123	30	80	6-4	.306	.332	.539	2	.994
Major League totals (9 years)			1206	4817	623	1432	300	23	164	756	220	649	60-38	.297	.326	.471	32	.988

DIVISION SERIES RECORD

			BATTING														FIELDING	
Year	Team (League)	Pos.	G	AB	R	H	2B	3B	HR	RBI	BB	SO	SB-CS	Avg.	OBP	SLG	E	Avg.
2002—	Anaheim (A.L.)	OF	4	18	5	7	2	0	1	4	1	3	0-0	.389	.421	.667	0	1.000

CHAMPIONSHIP SERIES RECORD

			BATTING														FIELDING	
Year	Team (League)	Pos.	G	AB	R	H	2B	3B	HR	RBI	BB	SO	SB-CS	Avg.	OBP	SLG	E	Avg.
2002—	Anaheim (A.L.)	OF	5	20	3	5	1	0	1	3	1	0	0-1	.250	.286	.450	0	1.000

WORLD SERIES RECORD

NOTES: Member of World Series championship team (2002).

			BATTING														FIELDING	
Year	Team (League)	Pos.	G	AB	R	H	2B	3B	HR	RBI	BB	SO	SB-CS	Avg.	OBP	SLG	E	Avg.
2002—	Anaheim (A.L.)	OF	7	32	3	9	1	0	0	6	0	3	0-0	.281	.281	.313	1	.947

ALL-STAR GAME RECORD

	AB	R	H	2B	3B	HR	RBI	BB	SO	SB-CS	Avg.	OBP	SLG	E	Avg.
All-Star Game totals (1 year)	4	0	0	0	0	0	1	0	0	0-0	.000	.000	.000	0	...

ANDERSON, JIMMY — P — PIRATES

PERSONAL: Born January 22, 1976, in Portsmouth, Va. ... 6-1/218. ... Throws left, bats left. ... Full name: James Drew Anderson Jr.
HIGH SCHOOL: Western Branch (Chesapeake, Va.).
TRANSACTIONS/CAREER NOTES: Selected by Pittsburgh Pirates organization in ninth round of free-agent draft (June 2, 1994). ... On disabled list (July 5-12, 1998).
STATISTICAL NOTES: Tied for Pacific Coast League lead with four balks in 1997.
CAREER HITTING (MLB): 22-for-160 (.138), 10 R, 3 2B, 0 3B, 0 HR, 6 RBI.

Year	League	W	L	Pct.	ERA	G	GS	CG	ShO	Sv.-Opp.	IP	H	R	ER	HR	BB-IBB	SO
1994—	Gulf Coast Pirates (GCL)	5	1	.833	1.60	10	10	0	0	0-...	56.1	35	21	10	1	27-0	66
1995—	Augusta (S.Atl.)	4	2	.667	1.53	14	14	0	0	0-...	76.2	51	15	13	1	31-0	75
—	Lynchburg (Caro.)	1	5	.167	4.13	10	9	0	0	0-...	52.1	56	29	24	1	21-1	32
1996—	Lynchburg (Caro.)	5	3	.625	1.93	11	11	1	1	0-...	65.1	51	25	14	2	21-0	56
—	Carolina (Sou.)	8	5	.615	3.34	17	16	0	0	0-...	97.0	92	40	36	3	44-3	79
1997—	Carolina (Sou.)	2	1	.667	1.46	4	4	0	0	0-...	24.2	16	6	4	1	9-0	23
—	Calgary (PCL)	7	6	.538	5.68	21	21	0	0	0-...	103.0	124	78	65	9	64-3	71
1998—	Nashville (PCL)	9	10	.474	5.02	35	17	0	0	0-...	123.2	144	87	69	8	72-6	63
1999—	Nashville (PCL)	11	2	*.846	3.84	21	21	1	0	0-...	133.2	153	67	57	5	41-0	93
—	Pittsburgh (N.L.)	2	1	.667	3.99	13	4	0	0	0-0	29.1	25	15	13	2	16-2	13
2000—	Pittsburgh (N.L.)	5	11	.313	5.25	27	26	1	0	0-0	144.0	169	94	84	13	58-2	73
—	Nashville (PCL)	0	0	...	4.15	2	2	0	0	0-...	13.0	18	6	6	0	4-0	7
—	Altoona (East.)	1	0	1.000	0.00	1	1	1	0	0-...	9.0	7	1	0	0	1-0	6
2001—	Pittsburgh (N.L.)	9	17	.346	5.10	34	34	1	0	0-0	206.1	232	123	117	15	83-14	89
2002—	Pittsburgh (N.L.)	8	13	.381	5.44	28	25	1	0	0-0	140.2	167	91	85	20	63-5	47
Major League totals (4 years)		24	42	.364	5.17	102	89	3	0	0-0	520.1	593	323	299	50	220-23	222

ANDERSON, MARLON — 2B — PHILLIES

PERSONAL: Born January 6, 1974, in Montgomery, Ala. ... 5-11/200. ... Bats left, throws right. ... Full name: Marlon Ordell Anderson.
HIGH SCHOOL: Prattville (Ala.).
COLLEGE: South Alabama.
TRANSACTIONS/CAREER NOTES: Selected by Philadelphia Phillies organization in second round of free-agent draft (June 1, 1995); choice received from St. Louis Cardinals as part of compensation for Cardinals signing Type A free-agent P Danny Jackson.
STATISTICAL NOTES: Led New York-Pennsylvania League second basemen with 153 putouts, 231 assists, 398 total chances and 67 double plays in 1995. ... Led Eastern League second basemen with 323 putouts, 396 assists and 748 total chances in 1997. ... Hit home run in first major league at-bat (September 8, 1998). ... Led International League second basemen with 681 total chances in 1998. ... Led International League in intentional bases on balls received with 12 in 2000.
2002 GAMES PLAYED BY POSITION (MLB): 2B—143.

			BATTING														FIELDING	
Year	Team (League)	Pos.	G	AB	R	H	2B	3B	HR	RBI	BB	SO	SB-CS	Avg.	OBP	SLG	E	Avg.
1995—	Batavia (NY-Penn)	2B	74	*312	52	92	13	4	3	40	15	20	22-8	.295	.331	.391	14	*.965
1996—	Clearwater (FSL)	2B	60	257	37	70	10	3	2	22	14	18	26-1	.272	.315	.358	16	.958
—	Reading (East.)	2B	75	314	38	86	14	3	3	28	26	44	17-9	.274	.330	.366	18	.957
1997—	Reading (East.)	2B	137	*553	88	147	18	6	10	62	42	77	27-15	.266	.328	.374	*29	.961
1998—	Scranton/W.B. (I.L.)	2B	136	575	104	*176	32	*14	16	86	28	77	24-12	.306	.343	.494	*28	.959
—	Philadelphia (N.L.)	2B	17	43	4	14	3	0	1	4	1	6	2-0	.326	.333	.465	1	.978
1999—	Philadelphia (N.L.)	2B	129	452	48	114	26	4	5	54	24	61	13-2	.252	.292	.361	11	.979
2000—	Scranton/W.B. (I.L.)	2B	103	397	57	121	18	8	8	53	39	43	24-10	.305	.370	.451	•14	.969
—	Philadelphia (N.L.)	2B	41	162	10	37	8	1	1	15	12	22	2-2	.228	.282	.309	2	.989
2001—	Philadelphia (N.L.)	2B	147	522	69	153	30	2	11	61	35	74	8-5	.293	.337	.421	12	.982
2002—	Philadelphia (N.L.)	2B	145	539	64	139	30	6	8	48	42	71	5-1	.258	.315	.380	*20	.970
Major League totals (5 years)			479	1718	195	457	97	13	26	182	114	234	30-10	.266	.313	.383	46	.978

ANDERSON, MATT — P — TIGERS

PERSONAL: Born August 17, 1976, in Louisville, Ky. ... 6-4/190. ... Throws right, bats right. ... Full name: Matthew Jason Anderson.
HIGH SCHOOL: St. Xavier (Louisville, Ky.).
COLLEGE: Rice.
TRANSACTIONS/CAREER NOTES: Selected by Detroit Tigers organization in first round (first pick overall) of free-agent draft (June 3, 1997). ... On disabled list (April 27-May 18 and May 19-September 20, 2002).
CAREER HITTING (MLB): 0-for-0 (.000), 0 R, 0 2B, 0 3B, 0 HR, 0 RBI.

Year	League	W	L	Pct.	ERA	G	GS	CG	ShO	Sv.-Opp.	IP	H	R	ER	HR	BB-IBB	SO
1998—	Lakeland (FSL)	1	0	1.000	0.69	17	0	0	0	3-...	26.0	18	4	2	0	8-0	34
—	Jacksonville (Sou.)	1	0	1.000	0.60	13	0	0	0	10-...	15.0	7	1	1	1	5-0	11
—	Detroit (A.L.)	5	1	.833	3.27	42	0	0	0	0-4	44.0	38	16	16	3	31-4	44
1999—	Detroit (A.L.)	2	1	.667	5.68	37	0	0	0	0-2	38.0	33	27	24	8	35-1	32
—	Toledo (I.L.)	0	4	.000	6.39	24	4	0	0	5-...	38.0	32	27	27	9	31-0	35
2000—	Detroit (A.L.)	3	2	.600	4.72	69	0	0	0	1-1	74.1	61	44	39	8	45-4	71
2001—	Detroit (A.L.)	3	1	.750	4.82	62	0	0	0	22-24	56.0	56	33	30	2	18-4	52
2002—	Detroit (A.L.)	2	1	.667	9.00	12	0	0	0	0-2	11.0	17	13	11	1	8-1	8
Major League totals (5 years)		15	6	.714	4.84	222	0	0	0	23-33	223.1	205	133	120	22	137-14	207

ANDREWS, SHANE — 3B

PERSONAL: Born August 28, 1971, in Dallas. ... 6-1/220. ... Bats right, throws right. ... Full name: Darrell Shane Andrews.
HIGH SCHOOL: Carlsbad (N.M.) Senior.
TRANSACTIONS/CAREER NOTES: Selected by Montreal Expos organization in first round (11th pick overall) of free-agent draft (June 4, 1990). ... On disabled list (August 3-11, 1993). ... On Montreal disabled list (May 1, 1997-remainder of season); included rehabilitation assignments to Ottawa (May 14-18) and West Palm Beach (July 26-August 10). ... On Montreal disabled list (May 11-June 1, 1999); included rehabilitation assignment to Ottawa (May 30-June 1). ... Released by Expos (September 7, 1999). ... Signed by Chicago Cubs (September 10, 1999). ... On Chicago disabled list (May 15-August 25, 2000); included rehabilitation assignment to Iowa (August 7-25). ... Granted free agency (October 31, 2000). ... Signed by St. Louis Cardinals organization (January 5, 2001). ... On disabled list (June 21-28, 2001). ... Released by Cardinals (June 28, 2001). ... Signed by Boston Red Sox organization (February 1, 2002). ... Granted free agency (October 31, 2002).
STATISTICAL NOTES: Led South Atlantic League third basemen with 98 putouts in 1992. ... Led International League third basemen with 320 assists and 436 total chances in 1994. ... Career major league grand slams: 3.
2002 GAMES PLAYED BY POSITION (MLB): 3B—4; 1B—2; OF—1; DH—1.

			BATTING													FIELDING	
Year Team (League)	Pos.	G	AB	R	H	2B	3B	HR	RBI	BB	SO	SB-CS	Avg.	OBP	SLG	E	Avg.
1990— GC Expos (GCL)	3B	56	190	31	46	7	1	3	24	29	46	11-4	.242	.350	.337	17	.896
1991— Sumter (S.Atl.)	3B	105	356	46	74	16	7	11	49	65	132	5-4	.208	.335	.385	29	.905
1992— Albany (S.Atl.)	3B-1B	136	453	76	104	18	1	*25	87	*107	*174	8-3	.230	.382	.439	26	.928
1993— Harrisburg (East.)	3B-SS	124	442	77	115	29	2	18	70	64	118	10-6	.260	.352	.457	23	.927
1994— Ottawa (I.L.)	3B-DH	137	460	79	117	25	2	16	85	80	126	6-5	.254	.367	.422	*32	.927
1995— Montreal (N.L.)	3B-1B	84	220	27	47	10	1	8	31	17	68	1-1	.214	.271	.377	7	.976
1996— Montreal (N.L.)	3B	127	375	43	85	15	2	19	64	35	119	3-1	.227	.295	.429	15	.955
1997— Montreal (N.L.)	3B	18	64	10	13	3	0	4	9	3	20	0-0	.203	.232	.438	6	.895
— Ottawa (I.L.)	3B	3	12	3	3	0	0	1	1	1	0	0-0	.250	.308	.500	0	1.000
— W. Palm Beach (FSL)	DH-3B	5	17	2	3	2	0	1	5	2	7	0-1	.176	.250	.471	1	.917
1998— Montreal (N.L.)	3B	150	492	48	117	30	1	25	69	58	137	1-6	.238	.314	.455	20	.954
1999— Montreal (N.L.)	3B-1B-DH	98	281	28	51	8	0	11	37	43	88	1-0	.181	.287	.327	14	.954
— Ottawa (I.L.)	3B	2	8	1	2	0	0	1	4	0	2	0-0	.250	.250	.625	0	1.000
— Chicago (N.L.)■	3B-1B	19	67	13	17	4	0	5	14	7	21	0-1	.254	.329	.537	2	.955
2000— Chicago (N.L.)	3B-1B	66	192	25	44	5	0	14	39	27	59	1-1	.229	.329	.474	12	.930
— Iowa (PCL)	3B	15	38	5	7	3	0	2	7	7	10	0-0	.184	.304	.421	0	1.000
2001— Memphis (PCL)■	1B-3B	62	193	30	42	9	1	9	31	33	63	2-0	.218	.339	.415	7	.982
2002— Pawtucket (I.L.)■	3B-1B-OF-2B	116	390	61	100	19	1	22	63	52	123	1-1	.256	.346	.479	10	.971
— Boston (A.L.)	3B-1B-OF-DH	7	13	2	1	1	0	0	0	1	3	0-0	.077	.200	.154	0	1.000
American League totals (1 year)		7	13	2	1	1	0	0	0	1	3	0-0	.077	.200	.154	0	1.000
National League totals (6 years)		562	1691	194	374	75	4	86	263	190	512	7-10	.221	.299	.423	76	.954
Major League totals (7 years)		569	1704	196	375	76	4	86	263	191	515	7-10	.220	.298	.421	76	.954

ANKIEL, RICK — P — CARDINALS

PERSONAL: Born July 19, 1979, in Fort Pierce, Fla. ... 6-1/210. ... Throws left, bats left. ... Full name: Richard Alexander Ankiel.
HIGH SCHOOL: Port St. Lucie (Fla.).
TRANSACTIONS/CAREER NOTES: Selected by St. Louis Cardinals organization in second round of free-agent draft (June 3, 1997). ... On St. Louis disabled list (March 29-June 5, 2002). ... On Peoria disabled list (July 15, 2002-remainder of season).
HONORS: Named Carolina League Pitcher of the Year (1998). ... Named Minor League Player of the Year by The Sporting News (1999). ... Named N.L. Rookie Pitcher of the Year by The Sporting News (2000). ... Named Appalachian League Pitcher of the Year (2001).
MISCELLANEOUS: Appeared in one game as pinch runner (2000). ... Struck out three times in three appearances as pinch hitter (2000).
CAREER HITTING (MLB): 18-for-86 (.209), 9 R, 1 2B, 1 3B, 2 HR, 9 RBI.

Year League	W	L	Pct.	ERA	G	GS	CG	ShO	Sv.-Opp.	IP	H	R	ER	HR	BB-IBB	SO
1998— Peoria (Midw.)	3	0	1.000	2.06	7	7	0	0	0-...	35.0	15	8	8	0	12-0	41
— Prince William (Caro.)	9	6	.600	2.79	21	21	1	0	0-...	126.0	91	46	39	8	38-0	181
1999— Arkansas (Texas)	6	0	1.000	0.91	8	8	1	•1	0-...	49.1	25	6	5	2	16-0	75
— Memphis (PCL)	7	3	.700	3.16	16	16	0	0	0-...	88.1	73	37	31	7	46-1	119
— St. Louis (N.L.)	0	1	.000	3.27	9	5	0	0	1-1	33.0	26	12	12	2	14-0	39
2000— St. Louis (N.L.)	11	7	.611	3.50	31	30	0	0	0-0	175.0	137	80	68	21	90-2	194
2001— St. Louis (N.L.)	1	2	.333	7.13	6	6	0	0	0-0	24.0	25	21	19	7	25-0	27
— Memphis (PCL)	0	2	.000	20.77	3	3	0	0	0-...	4.1	3	10	10	0	17-0	4
— Johnson City (Appl.)	5	3	.625	*1.33	14	•14	1	0	0-...	*87.2	42	20	13	1	18-0	*158
2002— St. Louis (N.L.)									Did not play.							
— Peoria (Midw.)									Did not play.							
Major League totals (3 years)	12	10	.545	3.84	46	41	0	0	1-0	232.0	188	113	99	30	129-2	260

DIVISION SERIES RECORD

Year League	W	L	Pct.	ERA	G	GS	CG	ShO	Sv.-Opp.	IP	H	R	ER	HR	BB-IBB	SO
2000— St. Louis (N.L.)	0	0	...	13.50	1	1	0	0	0-0	2.2	4	4	4	0	6-0	3

CHAMPIONSHIP SERIES RECORD

RECORDS: Shares career record for most wild pitches—4. ... Shares single-inning record for most wild pitches—2 (October 12, 2000, first inning and October 16, 2000, seventh inning).

Year League	W	L	Pct.	ERA	G	GS	CG	ShO	Sv.-Opp.	IP	H	R	ER	HR	BB-IBB	SO
2000— St. Louis (N.L.)	0	0	...	20.25	2	1	0	0	0-0	1.1	1	3	3	0	5-0	2

RECORD AS POSITION PLAYER

			BATTING													FIELDING	
Year Team (League)	Pos.	G	AB	R	H	2B	3B	HR	RBI	BB	SO	SB-CS	Avg.	OBP	SLG	E	Avg.
2001— Johnson City (Appl.)	DH	41	105	21	30	7	0	10	35	11	26	0-0	.286	.364	.638	...	...

APPIER, KEVIN P ANGELS

PERSONAL: Born December 6, 1967, in Lancaster, Calif. ... 6-2/200. ... Throws right, bats right. ... Full name: Robert Kevin Appier. ... Name pronounced APE-ee-er.

HIGH SCHOOL: Antelope Valley (Lancaster, Calif.).

JUNIOR COLLEGE: Antelope Valley College (Calif.).

COLLEGE: Fresno State.

TRANSACTIONS/CAREER NOTES: Selected by Kansas City Royals organization in first round (ninth pick overall) of free-agent draft (June 2, 1987). ... On disabled list (July 26-August 12, 1995). ... On Kansas City disabled list (March 20-September 1, 1998); included rehabilitation assignments to Gulf Coast Royals (July 16-21), Lansing (July 22-26), Wichita (July 27-30) and Omaha (July 31-August 27). ... Traded by Royals to Oakland Athletics for P Blake Stein, P Jeff D'Amico, and P Brad Rigby (July 31, 1999). ... On disabled list (April 25-May 13, 2000). ... Granted free agency (October 31, 2000). ... Signed by New York Mets (December 11, 2000). ... Traded by Mets to Anaheim Angels for 1B Mo Vaughn (December 27, 2001).

RECORDS: Shares major league record for most strikeouts in one inning—4 (September 3, 1996, fourth inning).

HONORS: Named A.L. Rookie Pitcher of the Year by The Sporting News (1990).

STATISTICAL NOTES: Pitched 4-0 one-hit, complete-game victory for Kansas City against Detroit (July 7, 1990). ... Pitched 1-0 one-hit, complete-game loss against Texas (July 27, 1993). ... Tied for A.L. lead with 14 wild pitches in 1997.

MISCELLANEOUS: Holds Kansas City Royals all-time record for strikeouts (1,451).

CAREER HITTING (MLB): 8-for-78 (.103), 4 R, 0 2B, 0 3B, 0 HR, 4 RBI.

Year League	W	L	Pct.	ERA	G	GS	CG	ShO	Sv.-Opp.	IP	H	R	ER	HR	BB-IBB	SO
1987— Eugene (N'West)	5	2	.714	3.04	15	•15	0	0	0-...	77.0	81	43	26	2	29-0	72
1988— Baseball City (FSL)	10	9	.526	2.75	24	24	1	0	0-...	147.1	134	58	45	1	39-5	112
— Memphis (Sou.)	2	0	1.000	1.83	3	3	0	0	0-...	19.2	11	5	4	0	7-0	18
1989— Omaha (A.A.)	8	8	.500	3.95	22	22	3	2	0-...	139.0	141	70	61	6	42-1	109
— Kansas City (A.L.)	1	4	.200	9.14	6	5	0	0	0-0	21.2	34	22	22	3	12-1	10
1990— Omaha (A.A.)	2	0	1.000	1.50	3	3	0	0	0-...	18.0	15	3	3	0	3-0	17
— Kansas City (A.L.)	12	8	.600	2.76	32	24	3	3	0-0	185.2	179	67	57	13	54-2	127
1991— Kansas City (A.L.)	13	10	.565	3.42	34	31	6	3	0-0	207.2	205	97	79	13	61-3	158
1992— Kansas City (A.L.)	15	8	.652	2.46	30	30	3	0	0-0	208.1	167	59	57	10	68-5	150
1993— Kansas City (A.L.)	18	8	.692	*2.56	34	34	5	1	0-0	238.2	183	74	68	8	81-3	186
1994— Kansas City (A.L.)	7	6	.538	3.83	23	23	1	0	0-0	155.0	137	68	66	11	63-7	145
1995— Kansas City (A.L.)	15	10	.600	3.89	31	31	4	1	0-0	201.1	163	90	87	14	80-1	185
1996— Kansas City (A.L.)	14	11	.560	3.62	32	32	5	1	0-0	211.1	192	87	85	17	75-2	207
1997— Kansas City (A.L.)	9	13	.409	3.40	34	34	4	1	0-0	235.2	215	96	89	24	74-2	196
1998— Gulf Coast Royals (GCL)	0	1	.000	2.70	1	1	0	0	0-...	3.1	3	3	1	0	1-0	2
— Lansing (Midw.)	0	0	...	2.25	1	1	0	0	0-...	4.0	4	1	1	0	0-0	5
— Wichita (Texas)	0	1	.000	6.00	1	1	0	0	0-...	6.0	8	4	4	1	2-0	1
— Omaha (PCL)	3	2	.600	7.03	6	6	0	0	0-...	32.0	41	25	25	7	12-1	22
— Kansas City (A.L.)	1	2	.333	7.80	3	3	0	0	0-0	15.0	21	13	13	3	5-1	9
1999— Kansas City (A.L.)	9	9	.500	4.87	22	22	1	0	0-0	140.1	153	81	76	18	51-3	78
— Oakland (A.L.)■	7	5	.583	5.77	12	12	0	0	0-0	68.2	77	50	44	9	33-1	53
2000— Oakland (A.L.)	15	11	.577	4.52	31	31	1	1	0-0	195.1	200	109	98	23	*102-10	129
2001— New York (N.L.)■	11	10	.524	3.57	33	33	1	1	0-0	206.2	181	89	82	22	64-4	172
2002— Anaheim (A.L.)■	14	12	.538	3.92	32	32	0	0	0-0	188.1	191	89	82	23	64-2	132
A.L. totals (13 years)	150	117	.562	3.65	356	344	33	11	0-0	2273.0	2117	1002	923	189	823-43	1765
N.L. totals (1 year)	11	10	.524	3.57	33	33	1	1	0-0	206.2	181	89	82	22	64-4	172
Major League totals (14 years)	161	127	.559	3.65	389	377	34	12	0-0	2479.2	2298	1091	1005	211	887-47	1937

DIVISION SERIES RECORD

Year League	W	L	Pct.	ERA	G	GS	CG	ShO	Sv.-Opp.	IP	H	R	ER	HR	BB-IBB	SO
2000— Oakland (A.L.)	0	1	.000	3.48	2	1	0	0	0-0	10.1	10	4	4	1	6-1	13
2002— Anaheim (A.L.)	0	0	...	5.40	1	1	0	0	0-0	5.0	5	3	3	1	3-0	3
Division series totals (2 years)	0	1	.000	4.11	3	2	0	0	0-0	15.1	15	7	7	2	9-1	16

CHAMPIONSHIP SERIES RECORD

Year League	W	L	Pct.	ERA	G	GS	CG	ShO	Sv.-Opp.	IP	H	R	ER	HR	BB-IBB	SO
2002— Anaheim (A.L.)	0	1	.000	3.48	2	2	0	0	0-0	10.1	10	4	4	0	4-0	3

WORLD SERIES RECORD

NOTES: Member of World Series championship team (2002).

Year League	W	L	Pct.	ERA	G	GS	CG	ShO	Sv.-Opp.	IP	H	R	ER	HR	BB-IBB	SO
2002— Anaheim (A.L.)	0	0	...	11.37	2	2	0	0	0-0	6.1	9	8	8	4	5-1	4

ALL-STAR GAME RECORD

	W	L	Pct.	ERA	GS	CG	ShO	Sv.-Opp.	IP	H	R	ER	HR	BB-IBB	SO
All-Star Game totals (1 year)	0	0	...	0.00	0	0	0	0-0	2.0	0	0	0	0	0-0	1

ARIAS, ALEX SS

PERSONAL: Born November 20, 1967, in New York. ... 6-3/202. ... Bats right, throws right. ... Full name: Alejandro Arias. ... Name pronounced air-REE-ahs.

HIGH SCHOOL: George Washington (New York).

TRANSACTIONS/CAREER NOTES: Selected by Chicago Cubs organization in third round of free-agent draft (June 2, 1987). ... Traded by Cubs with 3B Gary Scott to Florida Marlins for P Greg Hibbard (November 17, 1992). ... On disabled list (June 14-July 2, 1997). ... Released by Marlins (December 12, 1997). ... Signed by Philadelphia Phillies (December 26, 1997). ... Granted free agency (October 30, 2000). ... Signed by San Diego Padres (December 13, 2000). ... On disabled list (August 20-September 4, 2001). ... Traded by Padres for with C Ben Davis and P Wascar Serrano to Seattle Mariners for P Brett Tomko, C Tom Lampkin and SS Ramon Vazquez (December 11, 2001). ... Released by Mariners (April 4, 2002). ... Signed by Baltimore Orioles organization (April 27, 2002). ... Released by Orioles (May 28, 2002). ... Signed by New York Yankees organization (June 6, 2002). ... Granted free agency (October 28, 2002).

STATISTICAL NOTES: Led Midwest League shortstops with 210 putouts, 408 assists, 655 total chances and 83 double plays in 1989. ... Led Southern League shortstops with 203 putouts, 351 assists, 583 total chances and 81 double plays in 1991.

2002 GAMES PLAYED BY POSITION (MLB): 3B—4; SS—1.

Year	Team (League)	Pos.	G	AB	R	H	2B	3B	HR	RBI	BB	SO	SB-CS	Avg.	OBP	SLG	E	Avg.
			BATTING														FIELDING	
1987—	Wytheville (Appl.)	SS-3B	61	233	41	69	7	0	0	24	27	29	16-6	.296	.370	.326	16	.932
1988—	Charl., W.Va. (S.Atl.)	SS-3B-2B	127	472	57	122	12	1	0	33	54	44	41-12	.258	.336	.288	32	.948
1989—	Peoria (Midw.)	SS	*136	506	74	140	10	*11	2	64	49	67	31-6	.277	.348	.352	37	.944
1990—	Charlotte (Sou.)	SS	119	419	55	103	16	3	4	38	42	53	12-5	.246	.315	.327	*42	.915
1991—	Charlotte (Sou.)	SS	134	488	69	134	26	0	4	47	47	42	23-9	.275	.340	.352	29	*.950
1992—	Iowa (A.A.)	SS-2B	106	409	52	114	23	3	5	40	44	27	14-3	.279	.357	.386	14	.971
—	Chicago (N.L.)	SS	32	99	14	29	6	0	0	7	11	13	0-0	.293	.375	.354	4	.967
1993—	Florida (N.L.)■	2B-3B-SS	96	249	27	67	5	1	2	20	27	18	1-1	.269	.344	.321	6	.975
1994—	Florida (N.L.)	SS-3B	59	113	4	27	5	0	0	15	9	19	0-1	.239	.298	.283	2	.978
1995—	Florida (N.L.)	SS-3B-2B	94	216	22	58	9	2	3	26	22	20	1-0	.269	.337	.370	9	.953
1996—	Florida (N.L.)	3-S-1-2	100	224	27	62	11	2	3	26	17	28	2-0	.277	.335	.384	7	.962
1997—	Florida (N.L.)	3B-SS	74	93	13	23	2	0	1	11	12	12	0-1	.247	.352	.301	2	.970
1998—	Philadelphia (N.L.)■	SS-3B-2B	56	133	17	39	8	0	1	16	13	18	2-0	.293	.358	.376	2	.985
1999—	Philadelphia (N.L.)	SS-3B-2B	118	347	43	105	20	1	4	48	36	31	2-2	.303	.373	.401	4	.988
2000—	Philadelphia (N.L.)	SS-3B-2B	70	155	17	29	9	0	2	15	16	28	1-0	.187	.271	.284	5	.966
2001—	San Diego (N.L.)■	3B-1B-2B-SS	70	137	19	31	9	0	2	12	17	22	1-0	.226	.312	.336	5	.975
2002—	Rochester (I.L.)■	2B-3B-SS-1B	16	52	2	7	2	0	0	3	5	11	0-0	.135	.211	.173	2	.947
—	Columbus (I.L.)■	SS-3B-2B	61	211	32	56	16	0	1	22	16	15	3-2	.265	.322	.355	2	.992
—	New York (A.L.)	3B-SS	6	7	0	0	0	0	0	0	1	2	0-0	.000	.125	.000	1	.857
American League totals (1 year)			6	7	0	0	0	0	0	0	1	2	0-0	.000	.125	.000	1	.857
National League totals (10 years)			769	1766	203	470	84	6	18	196	180	209	10-5	.266	.339	.351	46	.973
Major League totals (11 years)			775	1773	203	470	84	6	18	196	181	211	10-5	.265	.338	.350	47	.973

DIVISION SERIES RECORD

Year	Team (League)	Pos.	G	AB	R	H	2B	3B	HR	RBI	BB	SO	SB-CS	Avg.	OBP	SLG	E	Avg.
			BATTING														FIELDING	
1997—	Florida (N.L.)	PH	1	1	0	1	0	0	0	1	0	0	0-0	1.000	1.000	1.000	...	...

CHAMPIONSHIP SERIES RECORD

Year	Team (League)	Pos.	G	AB	R	H	2B	3B	HR	RBI	BB	SO	SB-CS	Avg.	OBP	SLG	E	Avg.
			BATTING														FIELDING	
1997—	Florida (N.L.)	3B-PH	3	1	0	1	0	0	0	0	0	0	0-0	1.000	1.000	1.000	0	...

WORLD SERIES RECORD

NOTES: Member of World Series championship team (1997).

Year	Team (League)	Pos.	G	AB	R	H	2B	3B	HR	RBI	BB	SO	SB-CS	Avg.	OBP	SLG	E	Avg.
			BATTING														FIELDING	
1997—	Florida (N.L.)	3B-PR	2	1	1	0	0	0	0	0	0	0	0-0	.000	.000	.000	0	...

ARMAS, TONY — P — EXPOS

PERSONAL: Born April 29, 1978, in Puerto Piritu, Venezuela. ... 6-4/215. ... Throws right, bats right. ... Full name: Antonio Jose Armas Jr. ... Son of Tony Armas, outfielder with four major league teams (1976-89).

TRANSACTIONS/CAREER NOTES: Signed as non-drafted free agent by New York Yankees organization (August 16, 1994). ... Traded by Yankees with a player to be named later to Boston Red Sox for C Mike Stanley and SS Randy Brown (August 13, 1997); Red Sox acquired P Jim Mecir to complete deal (September 29, 1997). ... Traded by Red Sox to Montreal Expos (December 18, 1997), completing deal in which Red Sox traded P Carl Pavano and a player to be named later to Expos for P Pedro Martinez (November 18, 1997). ... On Montreal disabled list (April 1-28 and July 19-September 6, 2000); included rehabilitation assignments to Jupiter (April 22-28) and Ottawa (August 27-September 4). ... On disabled list (July 27-August 19, 2002).

STATISTICAL NOTES: Led N.L. with 12 intentional bases on balls issued in 2002. ... Tied for N.L. lead with 14 wild pitches in 2002.

CAREER HITTING (MLB): 14-for-131 (.107), 4 R, 1 2B, 1 3B, 0 HR, 7 RBI.

Year	League	W	L	Pct.	ERA	G	GS	CG	ShO	Sv.-Opp.	IP	H	R	ER	HR	BB-IBB	SO
1995—	Gulf Coast Yankees (GCL)	0	1	.000	0.64	5	4	0	0	0-...	14.0	12	9	1	1	6-0	13
1996—	Oneonta (NY-Penn)	1	1	.500	5.74	3	3	0	0	0-...	15.2	14	12	10	1	11-0	14
—	Gulf Coast Yankees (GCL)	4	1	.800	3.15	8	7	0	0	1-...	45.2	41	18	16	1	13-0	45
1997—	Greensboro (S.Atl.)	5	2	.714	1.05	9	9	2	1	0-...	51.2	36	13	6	3	13-0	64
—	Tampa (FSL)	3	1	.750	3.33	9	9	0	0	0-...	46.0	43	23	17	1	16-3	26
—	Sarasota (FSL)■	2	1	.667	6.62	3	3	0	0	0-...	17.2	18	13	13	2	12-0	9
1998—	Jupiter (FSL)■	12	8	.600	2.88	27	27	1	1	0-...	153.1	140	63	49	11	59-0	136
1999—	Harrisburg (East.)	9	7	.563	2.89	24	24	2	1	0-...	149.2	123	62	48	10	55-0	106
—	Montreal (N.L.)	0	1	.000	1.50	1	1	0	0	0-0	6.0	8	4	1	0	2-1	2
2000—	Jupiter (FSL)	0	0	...	0.00	1	1	0	0	0-...	4.2	4	0	0	0	0-0	8
—	Ottawa (I.L.)	1	2	.333	3.79	4	4	0	0	0-...	19.0	22	11	8	3	4-0	12
—	Montreal (N.L.)	7	9	.438	4.36	17	17	0	0	0-0	95.0	74	49	46	10	50-2	59
2001—	Montreal (N.L.)	9	14	.391	4.03	34	34	0	0	0-0	196.2	180	101	88	18	91-6	176
2002—	Montreal (N.L.)	12	12	.500	4.44	29	29	0	0	0-0	164.1	149	87	81	22	78-12	131
Major League totals (4 years)		28	36	.438	4.21	81	81	0	0	0-0	462.0	411	241	216	50	221-21	368

ARROJO, ROLANDO — P — RED SOX

PERSONAL: Born July 18, 1968, in Havana, Cuba. ... 6-4/236. ... Throws right, bats right. ... Full name: Luis Rolando Arrojo.

TRANSACTIONS/CAREER NOTES: Signed as non-drafted free agent by Tampa Bay Devil Rays organization (April 21, 1997). ... On disabled list (September 21, 1998-remainder of season). ... On Tampa Bay disabled list (May 25-July 15, 1999); included rehabilitation assignment to St. Petersburg (July 2-15). ... Traded by Devil Rays with IF Aaron Ledesma to Colorado Rockies for 3B Vinny Castilla (December 13, 1999). ... On Colorado disabled list (April 21-May 6, 2000). ... Traded by Rockies with P Rick Croushore, 2B Mike Lansing and cash to Boston Red Sox for P Brian Rose, P John Wasdin, P Jeff Taglienti and 2B Jeff Frye (July 27, 2000). ... On Boston disabled list (August 13-September 2, 2001); included rehabilitation assignment to Sarasota (August 27-September 2). ... On Boston disabled list (June 17-July 15 and August 7-September 13, 2002); included rehabilitation assignments to Gulf Coast Red Sox (July 11-15) and Sarasota (September 1-9).

HONORS: Named A.L. Rookie Pitcher of the Year by The Sporting News (1998).

STATISTICAL NOTES: Led A.L. with 19 hit batsmen in 1998.

MISCELLANEOUS: Member of Cuban national baseball team (1986-96). ... Shares Tampa Bay Devil Rays all-time record for most shutouts (2).

CAREER HITTING (MLB): 3-for-37 (.081), 2 R, 1 2B, 0 3B, 0 HR, 3 RBI.

Year League	W	L	Pct.	ERA	G	GS	CG	ShO	Sv.-Opp.	IP	H	R	ER	HR	BB-IBB	SO
1997— St. Petersburg (FSL)	5	6	.455	3.43	16	16	4	1	0-...	89.1	73	40	34	6	13-0	73
1998— Tampa Bay (A.L.)	14	12	.538	3.56	32	32	2	2	0-0	202.0	195	84	80	21	65-2	152
1999— Tampa Bay (A.L.)	7	12	.368	5.18	24	24	2	0	0-0	140.2	162	84	81	23	60-2	107
— St. Petersburg (FSL)	0	1	.000	4.50	2	2	0	0	0-...	10.0	11	6	5	0	1-0	10
2000— Colorado (N.L.)■	5	9	.357	6.04	19	19	0	0	0-0	101.1	120	77	68	14	46-6	80
— Boston (A.L.)■	5	2	.714	5.05	13	13	0	0	0-0	71.1	67	41	40	10	22-0	44
2001— Boston (A.L.)	5	4	.556	3.48	41	9	0	0	5-7	103.1	88	44	40	8	35-4	78
— Sarasota (FSL)	0	1	.000	6.00	2	2	0	0	0-...	3.0	4	2	2	2	1-0	5
2002— Boston (A.L.)	4	3	.571	4.98	29	8	0	0	1-4	81.1	83	47	45	7	27-1	51
— Gulf Coast Red Sox (GCL)	0	0	...	0.00	1	1	0	0	0-...	3.0	3	0	0	0	0-0	1
— Sarasota (FSL)	0	0	...	0.00	1	0	0	0	0-...	2.0	2	0	0	0	0-0	2
A.L. totals (5 years)	35	33	.515	4.30	139	86	4	2	6-11	598.2	595	300	286	69	209-9	432
N.L. totals (1 year)	5	9	.357	6.04	19	19	0	0	0-0	101.1	120	77	68	14	46-6	80
Major League totals (5 years)	40	42	.488	4.55	158	105	4	2	6-11	700.0	715	377	354	83	255-15	512

ALL-STAR GAME RECORD

	W	L	Pct.	ERA	GS	CG	ShO	Sv.-Opp.	IP	H	R	ER	HR	BB-IBB	SO
All-Star Game totals (1 year)	0	0	...	0.00	0	0	0	0-0	1.0	2	0	0	0	0-0	1

ARROYO, BRONSON — P — PIRATES

PERSONAL: Born February 24, 1977, in Key West, Fla. ... 6-5/194. ... Throws right, bats right. ... Full name: Bronson Anthony Arroyo.

HIGH SCHOOL: Hernando (Fla.).

TRANSACTIONS/CAREER NOTES: Selected by Pittsburgh Pirates organization in third round of free-agent draft (June 1, 1995). ... On suspended list (May 29-June 1, 1996). ... On disabled list (May 18-June 7 and June 18-July 4, 1998).

MISCELLANEOUS: Appeared in one game as pinch runner and grounded out in only appearance as pinch hitter (2000).

CAREER HITTING (MLB): 4-for-48 (.083), 2 R, 2 2B, 0 3B, 0 HR, 1 RBI.

Year League	W	L	Pct.	ERA	G	GS	CG	ShO	Sv.-Opp.	IP	H	R	ER	HR	BB-IBB	SO
1995— Gulf Coast Pirates (GCL)	5	4	.556	4.26	13	9	0	0	1-...	61.1	72	39	29	4	9-0	48
1996— Augusta (S.Atl.)	8	6	.571	3.52	26	26	0	0	0-...	135.2	123	64	53	11	36-0	107
1997— Lynchburg (Caro.)	•12	4	.750	3.31	24	24	3	1	0-...	160.1	154	69	59	17	33-0	121
1998— Carolina (Sou.)	9	8	.529	5.46	23	22	1	0	0-...	127.0	158	91	77	18	51-0	90
1999— Altoona (East.)	•15	4	.789	3.65	25	25	2	1	0-...	153.0	167	73	62	15	58-1	100
— Nashville (PCL)	0	2	.000	10.38	3	3	0	0	0-...	13.0	22	15	15	1	10-0	11
2000— Nashville (PCL)	8	2	.800	3.65	13	13	1	0	0-...	88.2	82	43	36	7	25-3	52
— Pittsburgh (N.L.)	2	6	.250	6.40	20	12	0	0	0-0	71.2	88	61	51	10	36-6	50
— Lynchburg (Caro.)	0	0	...	3.86	1	1	0	0	0-...	7.0	8	3	3	0	2-0	3
2001— Pittsburgh (N.L.)	5	7	.417	5.09	24	13	1	0	0-0	88.1	99	54	50	12	34-6	39
— Nashville (PCL)	6	2	.750	3.93	9	9	2	1	0-...	66.1	63	32	29	6	15-1	49
2002— Nashville (PCL)	8	6	.571	2.96	22	21	•3	•2	0-...	143.0	126	57	47	10	28-1	116
— Pittsburgh (N.L.)	2	1	.667	4.00	9	4	0	0	0-0	27.0	30	14	12	1	15-3	22
Major League totals (3 years)	9	14	.391	5.44	53	29	1	0	0-0	187.0	217	129	113	23	85-15	111

ASENCIO, MIGUEL — P — ROYALS

PERSONAL: Born September 29, 1980, in Villa Mella, Dominican Republic. ... 6-2/160. ... Throws right, bats right. ... Full name: Miguel Depaula Asencio.

HIGH SCHOOL: Liceo Tiro Al Blanco (La Victoria, Dominican Republic).

TRANSACTIONS/CAREER NOTES: Signed as non-drafted free agent by Philadelphia Phillies organization (March 2, 1998). ... Selected by Kansas City Royals from Phillies organization in Rule 5 major league draft (December 13, 2001).

CAREER HITTING (MLB): 0-for-2 (.000), 0 R, 0 2B, 0 3B, 0 HR, 0 RBI.

Year League	W	L	Pct.	ERA	G	GS	CG	ShO	Sv.-Opp.	IP	H	R	ER	HR	BB-IBB	SO
1998— Dominican Phillies (DSL)	0	2	.000	6.55	11	4	0	0	0-...	22.0	39	29	16	...	12-...	7
1999— Gulf Coast Phillies (GCL)	1	4	.200	5.97	9	5	0	0	0-...	28.2	35	24	19	1	16-0	14
2000— Clearwater (FSL)	2	1	.667	2.73	5	5	0	0	0-...	33.0	22	10	10	2	17-0	24
— Batavia (NY-Penn)	2	2	.500	4.99	7	7	1	0	0-...	39.2	32	23	22	3	17-0	28
2001— Clearwater (FSL)	12	5	.706	2.84	28	21	2	1	0-...	155.1	124	62	49	7	70-1	123
2002— Kansas City (A.L.)■	4	7	.364	5.11	31	21	0	0	0-0	123.1	136	73	70	17	64-2	58
Major League totals (1 year)	4	7	.364	5.11	31	21	0	0	0-0	123.1	136	73	70	17	64-2	58

ASHBY, ANDY — P — DODGERS

PERSONAL: Born July 11, 1967, in Kansas City, Mo. ... 6-1/202. ... Throws right, bats right. ... Full name: Andrew Jason Ashby.

HIGH SCHOOL: Park Hill (Kansas City, Mo.).

JUNIOR COLLEGE: Crowder College (Mo.).

TRANSACTIONS/CAREER NOTES: Signed as non-drafted free agent by Philadelphia Phillies organization (May 4, 1986). ... On Spartanburg disabled list (April 7-July 10, 1988). ... On Spartanburg disabled list (April 6-26, 1989). ... On Philadelphia disabled list (April 27-August 11, 1992); included rehabilitation assignments to Scranton/Wilkes-Barre (July 8-August 2 and August 6-10). ... Selected by Colorado Rockies in first round (25th pick overall) of expansion draft (November 17, 1992). ... Traded by Rockies to San Diego Padres (July 27, 1993), completing deal in which Padres traded P Bruce Hurst and P Greg W. Harris to Rockies for C Brad Ausmus, P Doug Bochtler and a player to be named later (July 26, 1993). ... On disabled list (June 6-22, June 29-July 15 and July 27-September 1, 1996; May 20-June 15, 1997; and June 7-24, 1999). ... Traded by Padres to Phillies for P Carlton Loewer, P Steve Montgomery and P Adam Eaton (November 10, 1999). ... On Philadelphia disabled list (June 12-27, 2000). ... Traded by Phillies to Atlanta Braves for P Bruce Chen and P Jimmy Osting (July 12, 2000). ... Granted free agency (November 1, 2000). ... Signed by Los Angeles Dodgers (December 6, 2000). ... On disabled list (April 16, 2001-remainder of season).

RECORDS: Shares major league record by striking out side on nine pitches (June 15, 1991, fourth inning).

MISCELLANEOUS: Had sacrifice hit in only appearance as pinch-hitter (1996). ... Appeared in one game as pinch runner (1997). ... Appeared in one game as pinch runner with Atlanta (2000). ... Appeared in one game as pinch runner (2001).

CAREER HITTING (MLB): 70-for-507 (.138), 26 R, 13 2B, 0 3B, 1 HR, 26 RBI.

Year League	W	L	Pct.	ERA	G	GS	CG	ShO	Sv.-Opp.	IP	H	R	ER	HR	BB-IBB	SO
1986—Bend (N'West)	1	2	.333	4.95	16	6	0	0	2-...	60.0	56	40	33	3	34-1	45
1987—Spartanburg (S.Atl.)	4	6	.400	5.60	13	13	1	0	0-...	64.1	73	45	40	8	38-2	52
—Utica (NY-Penn)	3	7	.300	4.05	13	13	0	0	0-...	60.0	56	38	27	3	36-3	51
1988—Spartanburg (S.Atl.)	1	1	.500	2.70	3	3	0	0	0-...	16.2	13	7	5	0	7-0	16
—Batavia (NY-Penn)	3	1	.750	1.61	6	6	2	1	0-...	44.2	25	11	8	3	16-0	32
1989—Spartanburg (S.Atl.)	5	9	.357	2.87	17	17	3	1	0-...	106.2	95	48	34	8	49-0	100
—Clearwater (FSL)	1	4	.200	1.24	6	6	2	1	0-...	43.2	28	9	6	0	21-0	44
1990—Reading (East.)	10	7	.588	3.42	23	23	4	1	0-...	139.2	134	65	53	3	48-0	94
1991—Scranton/W.B. (I.L.)	11	11	.500	3.46	26	26	•6	•3	0-...	161.1	144	78	62	12	60-2	113
—Philadelphia (N.L.)	1	5	.167	6.00	8	8	0	0	0-0	42.0	41	28	28	5	19-0	26
1992—Philadelphia (N.L.)	1	3	.250	7.54	10	8	0	0	0-0	37.0	42	31	31	6	21-0	24
—Scranton/W.B. (I.L.)	0	3	.000	3.00	7	7	1	0	0-...	33.0	23	13	11	4	14-0	18
1993—Colorado (N.L.)■	0	4	.000	8.50	20	9	0	0	1-1	54.0	89	54	51	5	32-4	33
—Colorado Springs (PCL)	4	2	.667	4.10	7	6	1	0	0-...	41.2	45	25	19	2	12-0	35
—San Diego (N.L.)■	3	6	.333	5.48	12	12	0	0	0-0	69.0	79	46	42	14	24-1	44
1994—San Diego (N.L.)	6	11	.353	3.40	24	24	4	0	0-0	164.1	145	75	62	16	43-12	121
1995—San Diego (N.L.)	12	10	.545	2.94	31	•31	2	2	0-0	192.2	180	79	63	17	62-3	150
1996—San Diego (N.L.)	9	5	.643	3.23	24	24	1	0	0-0	150.2	147	60	54	17	34-1	85
1997—San Diego (N.L.)	9	11	.450	4.13	30	30	2	0	0-0	200.2	207	108	92	17	49-2	144
1998—San Diego (N.L.)	17	9	.654	3.34	33	33	5	1	0-0	226.2	223	90	84	23	58-8	151
1999—San Diego (N.L.)	14	10	.583	3.80	31	31	4	*3	0-0	206.0	204	95	87	26	54-4	132
2000—Philadelphia (N.L.)■	4	7	.364	5.68	16	16	1	0	0-0	101.1	113	75	64	17	38-5	51
—Atlanta (N.L.)■	8	6	.571	4.13	15	15	2	1	0-0	98.0	103	49	45	12	23-4	55
2001—Los Angeles (N.L.)■	2	0	1.000	3.86	2	2	0	0	0-0	11.2	14	5	5	2	1-0	7
2002—Los Angeles (N.L.)	9	13	.409	3.91	30	30	0	0	0-0	181.2	179	85	79	20	65-3	107
Major League totals (12 years)	95	100	.487	4.08	286	273	21	7	1-1	1735.2	1766	880	787	197	523-47	1130

DIVISION SERIES RECORD

Year League	W	L	Pct.	ERA	G	GS	CG	ShO	Sv.-Opp.	IP	H	R	ER	HR	BB-IBB	SO
1996—San Diego (N.L.)	0	0	...	6.75	1	1	0	0	0-0	5.1	7	4	4	1	1-0	5
1998—San Diego (N.L.)	0	0	...	6.75	1	1	0	0	0-0	4.0	6	3	3	0	1-0	4
2000—Atlanta (N.L.)	0	0	...	2.45	2	0	0	0	0-0	3.2	1	1	1	0	3-2	5
Division series totals (3 years)	0	0	...	5.54	4	2	0	0	0-0	13.0	14	8	8	1	5-2	14

CHAMPIONSHIP SERIES RECORD

Year League	W	L	Pct.	ERA	G	GS	CG	ShO	Sv.-Opp.	IP	H	R	ER	HR	BB-IBB	SO
1998—San Diego (N.L.)	0	0	...	2.08	2	2	0	0	0-0	13.0	14	3	3	1	2-0	5

WORLD SERIES RECORD

Year League	W	L	Pct.	ERA	G	GS	CG	ShO	Sv.-Opp.	IP	H	R	ER	HR	BB-IBB	SO
1998—San Diego (N.L.)	0	1	.000	13.50	1	1	0	0	0-0	2.2	10	7	4	1	1-0	1

ALL-STAR GAME RECORD

	W	L	Pct.	ERA	GS	CG	ShO	Sv.-Opp.	IP	H	R	ER	HR	BB-IBB	SO
All-Star Game totals (2 years)	0	0	...	6.75	0	0	0	0-0	1.1	1	1	1	2	1-0	0

ASTACIO, PEDRO — P — METS

PERSONAL: Born November 28, 1969, in Hato Mayor, Dominican Republic. ... 6-2/210. ... Throws right, bats right. ... Full name: Pedro Julio Astacio. ... Name pronounced ah-STA-see-oh.

HIGH SCHOOL: Pilar Rondon (Dominican Republic).

TRANSACTIONS/CAREER NOTES: Signed as non-drafted free agent by Los Angeles Dodgers organization (November 21, 1987). ... On Albuquerque disabled list (April 26-May 21, 1992). ... Traded by Dodgers to Colorado Rockies for 2B Eric Young (August 19, 1997). ... Traded by Rockies to Houston Astros for P Scott Elarton and a player to be named later (July 31, 2001). ... On Houston disabled list (August 29, 2001-remainder of season). ... Granted free agency (November 8, 2001). ... Signed by New York Mets (January 16, 2002).

STATISTICAL NOTES: Led N.L. with nine balks in 1993. ... Led N.L. with 17 hit batsmen in 1998 and tied for lead with 16 in 2002.

MISCELLANEOUS: Holds Colorado Rockies all-time record for most wins (53), most innings pitched ($827^1/_3$) and most strikeouts (749). ... Struck out in both appearances as pinch hitter and appeared in one game as pinch runner (1999).

CAREER HITTING (MLB): 83-for-624 (.133), 27 R, 8 2B, 1 3B, 0 HR, 27 RBI.

Year League	W	L	Pct.	ERA	G	GS	CG	ShO	Sv.-Opp.	IP	H	R	ER	HR	BB-IBB	SO
1988—Dom. Dodgers (DSL)	4	2	.667	2.08	8	7	1	...	0-...	47.2	43	21	11	...	18-...	20
1989—Gulf Coast Dodgers (GCL)	7	3	.700	3.17	12	12	1	•1	0-...	76.2	77	30	27	3	12-0	52
1990—Vero Beach (FSL)	1	5	.167	6.32	8	8	0	0	0-...	47.0	54	39	33	3	23-0	41
—Yakima (N'West)	2	0	1.000	1.74	3	3	0	0	0-...	20.2	9	8	4	0	4-0	22
—Bakersfield (Calif.)	5	2	.714	2.77	10	7	1	0	0-...	52.0	46	22	16	3	15-1	34
1991—Vero Beach (FSL)	5	3	.625	1.67	9	9	3	1	0-...	59.1	44	19	11	0	8-0	45
—San Antonio (Texas)	4	11	.267	4.78	19	19	2	1	0-...	113.0	142	67	60	9	39-3	62
1992—Albuquerque (PCL)	6	6	.500	5.47	24	15	1	0	0-...	98.2	115	68	60	8	44-1	66
—Los Angeles (N.L.)	5	5	.500	1.98	11	11	4	4	0-0	82.0	80	23	18	1	20-4	43
1993—Los Angeles (N.L.)	14	9	.609	3.57	31	31	3	2	0-0	186.1	165	80	74	14	68-5	122
1994—Los Angeles (N.L.)	6	8	.429	4.29	23	23	3	1	0-0	149.0	142	77	71	18	47-4	108
1995—Los Angeles (N.L.)	7	8	.467	4.24	48	11	1	1	0-1	104.0	103	53	49	12	29-5	80
1996—Los Angeles (N.L.)	9	8	.529	3.44	35	32	0	0	0-0	211.2	207	86	81	18	67-9	130
1997—Los Angeles (N.L.)	7	9	.438	4.10	26	24	2	1	0-0	153.2	151	75	70	15	47-0	115
—Colorado (N.L.)■	5	1	.833	4.25	7	7	0	0	0-0	48.2	49	23	23	9	14-0	51
1998—Colorado (N.L.)	13	14	.481	6.23	35	34	0	0	0-0	209.1	245	*160	*145	•39	74-0	170
1999—Colorado (N.L.)	17	11	.607	5.04	34	34	7	0	0-0	232.0	258	140	130	*38	75-6	210
2000—Colorado (N.L.)	12	9	.571	5.27	32	32	3	0	0-0	196.1	217	119	115	32	77-5	193
2001—Colorado (N.L.)	6	13	.316	5.49	22	22	4	1	0-0	141.0	151	91	86	21	50-3	125
—Houston (N.L.)■	2	1	.667	3.14	4	4	0	0	0-0	28.2	30	10	10	1	4-0	19
2002—New York (N.L.)■	12	11	.522	4.79	31	31	3	1	0-0	191.2	192	106	102	*32	63-5	152
Major League totals (11 years)	115	107	.518	4.53	339	296	30	11	0-1	1934.1	1990	1043	974	250	635-46	1518

DIVISION SERIES RECORD

Year League	W	L	Pct.	ERA	G	GS	CG	ShO	Sv.-Opp.	IP	H	R	ER	HR	BB-IBB	SO
1995—Los Angeles (N.L.)	0	0	...	0.00	3	0	0	0	0-0	3.1	1	0	0	0	0-0	5
1996—Los Angeles (N.L.)	0	0	...	0.00	1	0	0	0	0-0	1.2	0	0	0	0	0-0	1
Division series totals (2 years)	0	0	...	0.00	4	0	0	0	0-0	5.0	1	0	0	0	0-0	6

AURILIA, RICH — SS — GIANTS

PERSONAL: Born September 2, 1971, in Brooklyn, N.Y. ... 6-1/185. ... Bats right, throws right. ... Full name: Richard Santo Aurilia. ... Name pronounced uh-REEL-yuh.

HIGH SCHOOL: Xaverian (Brooklyn, N.Y.).

COLLEGE: St. John's.

TRANSACTIONS/CAREER NOTES: Selected by Texas Rangers organization in 24th round of free-agent draft (June 1, 1992). ... On disabled list (April 9-16, 1993). ... Traded by Rangers with IF/OF Desi Wilson to San Francisco Giants for P John Burkett (December 24, 1994). ... On San Francisco disabled list (September 24, 1996-remainder of season). ... On disabled list (July 4-20, 1998; and May 20-June 4, 2002).

HONORS: Named shortstop on N.L. Silver Slugger team (2001). ... Named shortstop on The Sporting News N.L. All-Star team (2001).

STATISTICAL NOTES: Led Texas League shortstops with 237 putouts and 635 total chances and tied for lead with 82 double plays in 1994. ... Career major league grand slams: 1.

2002 GAMES PLAYED BY POSITION (MLB): SS—131.

		BATTING														FIELDING	
Year Team (League)	Pos.	G	AB	R	H	2B	3B	HR	RBI	BB	SO	SB-CS	Avg.	OBP	SLG	E	Avg.
1992—Butte (Pio.)	SS	59	202	37	68	11	3	3	30	42	18	13-9	.337	.447	.465	14	*.943
1993—Charlotte (FSL)	SS	122	440	80	136	16	5	5	56	75	57	15-18	.309	.408	.402	24	.964
1994—Tulsa (Texas)	SS	129	458	67	107	18	6	12	57	53	74	10-13	.234	.315	.378	24	*.962
1995—Shreveport (Texas)■	SS	64	226	29	74	17	1	4	42	27	26	10-3	.327	.398	.465	14	.962
—Phoenix (PCL)	SS	71	258	42	72	12	0	5	34	35	29	2-2	.279	.361	.384	9	.975
—San Francisco (N.L.)	SS	9	19	4	9	3	0	2	4	1	2	1-0	.474	.476	.947	0	1.000
1996—Phoenix (PCL)	SS-2B	7	30	9	13	7	0	0	4	2	3	1-1	.433	.469	.667	1	.972
—San Francisco (N.L.)	SS-2B	105	318	27	76	7	1	3	26	25	52	4-1	.239	.295	.296	10	.975
1997—San Francisco (N.L.)	SS	46	102	16	28	8	0	5	19	8	15	1-1	.275	.321	.500	3	.979
—Phoenix (PCL)	SS	8	34	9	10	2	0	1	5	5	4	2-1	.294	.385	.441	0	1.000
1998—San Francisco (N.L.)	SS	122	413	54	110	27	2	9	49	31	62	3-3	.266	.319	.407	10	.979
1999—San Francisco (N.L.)	SS	152	558	68	157	23	1	22	80	43	71	2-3	.281	.336	.444	*28	.957
2000—San Francisco (N.L.)	SS	141	509	67	138	24	2	20	79	54	90	1-2	.271	.339	.444	21	.967
2001—San Francisco (N.L.)	SS	156	636	114	*206	37	5	37	97	47	83	1-3	.324	.369	.572	17	.975
2002—San Francisco (N.L.)	SS	133	538	76	138	35	2	15	61	37	90	1-2	.257	.305	.413	11	*.980
Major League totals (8 years)		864	3093	426	862	164	13	113	415	246	465	14-15	.279	.332	.450	100	.972

DIVISION SERIES RECORD

		BATTING														FIELDING	
Year Team (League)	Pos.	G	AB	R	H	2B	3B	HR	RBI	BB	SO	SB-CS	Avg.	OBP	SLG	E	Avg.
2000—San Francisco (N.L.)	SS	4	15	0	2	1	0	0	0	0	3	0-0	.133	.133	.200	1	.955
2002—San Francisco (N.L.)	SS	5	21	4	5	1	0	2	7	1	5	0-0	.238	.273	.571	0	1.000
Division series totals (2 years)		9	36	4	7	2	0	2	7	1	8	0-0	.194	.216	.417	1	.978

CHAMPIONSHIP SERIES RECORD

		BATTING														FIELDING	
Year Team (League)	Pos.	G	AB	R	H	2B	3B	HR	RBI	BB	SO	SB-CS	Avg.	OBP	SLG	E	Avg.
2002—San Francisco (N.L.)	SS	5	15	4	5	1	0	2	5	2	2	0-0	.333	.421	.800	1	.955

WORLD SERIES RECORD

RECORDS: Shares single-game record for most at-bats—6 (October 24, 2002).

		BATTING														FIELDING	
Year Team (League)	Pos.	G	AB	R	H	2B	3B	HR	RBI	BB	SO	SB-CS	Avg.	OBP	SLG	E	Avg.
2002—San Francisco (N.L.)	SS	7	32	5	8	2	0	2	5	1	9	0-0	.250	.273	.500	0	1.000

ALL-STAR GAME RECORD

	AB	R	H	2B	3B	HR	RBI	BB	SO	SB-CS	Avg.	OBP	SLG	E	Avg.
All-Star Game totals (1 year)	2	0	0	0	0	0	0	0	0	0-0	.000	.000	.000	0	1.000

AUSMUS, BRAD — C — ASTROS

PERSONAL: Born April 14, 1969, in New Haven, Conn. ... 5-11/200. ... Bats right, throws right. ... Full name: Bradley David Ausmus.

HIGH SCHOOL: Cheshire (Conn.).

COLLEGE: Dartmouth.

TRANSACTIONS/CAREER NOTES: Selected by New York Yankees organization in 48th round of free-agent draft (June 2, 1987). ... Selected by Colorado Rockies in third round (54th pick overall) of expansion draft (November 17, 1992). ... Traded by Rockies with P Doug Bochtler and a player to be named later to San Diego Padres for P Bruce Hurst and P Greg W. Harris (July 26, 1993); Padres acquired P Andy Ashby to complete deal (July 27, 1993). ... Traded by Padres with SS Andujar Cedeno and P Russ Spear to Detroit Tigers for C John Flaherty and SS Chris Gomez (June 18, 1996). ... On Detroit suspended list (September 4-5, 1996). ... Traded by Tigers with P Jose Lima, P C.J. Nitkowski, P Trever Miller and IF Daryle Ward to Houston Astros for OF Brian L. Hunter, IF Orlando Miller, P Doug Brocail, P Todd Jones and cash (December 10, 1996). ... Traded by Astros with P C.J. Nitkowski to Tigers for C Paul Bako, P Dean Crow, P Mark Persails, P Brian Powell, and 3B Carlos Villalobos (January 14, 1999). ... Traded by Tigers with P Doug Brocail and P Nelson Cruz to Astros for C Mitch Meluskey, P Chris Holt and OF Roger Cedeno (December 11, 2000).

RECORDS: Holds A.L. single-season record for fewest passed balls (150 or more games)—3 (2000). ... Shares N.L. single-season record for most grounding into double plays—30 (2002).

HONORS: Won N.L. Gold Glove at catcher (2001-02).

STATISTICAL NOTES: Led Gulf Coast League catchers with 378 putouts, 47 assists and 434 total chances in 1988. ... Led International League catchers with 666 putouts and 738 total chances in 1992. ... Led N.L. catchers with 683 putouts and 749 total chances in 1994. ... Led N.L. catchers with 14 double plays in 1995. ... Tied for N.L. lead in assists by catcher with 63 in 1995. ... Led A.L. catchers with 898 putouts, 68 assists and 974 total chances in 2000. ... Led N.L. with 30 grounded into double plays in 2002. ... Career major league grand slams: 1.
2002 GAMES PLAYED BY POSITION (MLB): C—129.

		BATTING														FIELDING	
Year Team (League)	Pos.	G	AB	R	H	2B	3B	HR	RBI	BB	SO	SB-CS	Avg.	OBP	SLG	E	Avg.
1988—GC Yankees (GCL)	C	43	133	22	34	2	0	0	15	11	25	5-2	.256	.320	.271	9	.979
—Oneonta (NY-Penn)	C	2	4	0	1	0	0	0	0	0	2	0-0	.250	.250	.250	0	...
1989—Oneonta (NY-Penn)	C-3B	52	165	29	43	6	0	1	18	22	28	6-4	.261	.348	.315	7	.984
1990—Prince William (Caro.)	C	107	364	46	86	12	2	0	27	32	73	2-8	.236	.303	.280	5	*.993
1991—Prince William (Caro.)	C	63	230	28	70	14	3	2	30	24	37	17-6	.304	.366	.417	5	.990
—Albany/Colonie (East.)	C	67	229	36	61	9	2	1	29	27	36	14-3	.266	.345	.336	4	.992
1992—Albany/Colonie (East.)	C	5	18	0	3	0	1	0	1	2	3	2-1	.167	.250	.278	1	.970
—Columbus (I.L.)	C-OF	111	364	48	88	14	3	2	35	40	56	19-5	.242	.317	.313	9	.988
1993—Colo. Springs (PCL)■	C-DH-OF	76	241	31	65	10	4	2	33	27	41	10-6	.270	.342	.369	6	.987
—San Diego (N.L.)■	C	49	160	18	41	8	1	5	12	6	28	2-0	.256	.283	.413	8	.975
1994—San Diego (N.L.)	C-1B	101	327	45	82	12	1	7	24	30	63	5-1	.251	.314	.358	7	.991
1995—San Diego (N.L.)	C-1B	103	328	44	96	16	4	5	34	31	56	16-5	.293	.353	.412	6	.992
1996—San Diego (N.L.)	C	50	149	16	27	4	0	1	13	13	27	1-4	.181	.261	.228	6	.982
—Detroit (A.L.)■	C	75	226	30	56	12	0	4	22	26	45	3-4	.248	.328	.354	4	.992
1997—Houston (N.L.)■	C	130	425	45	113	25	1	4	44	38	78	14-6	.266	.326	.358	7	.992
1998—Houston (N.L.)	C	128	412	62	111	10	4	6	45	53	60	10-3	.269	.356	.357	7	.992
1999—Detroit (A.L.)■	C	127	458	62	126	25	6	9	54	51	71	12-9	.275	.365	.415	2	*.998
2000—Detroit (A.L.)	C-1B-2B-3B	150	523	75	139	25	3	7	51	69	79	11-5	.266	.357	.365	8	.992
2001—Houston (N.L.)■	C	128	422	45	98	23	4	5	34	30	64	4-1	.232	.284	.341	3	.997
2002—Houston (N.L.)	C	130	447	57	115	19	3	6	50	38	71	2-3	.257	.322	.353	3	.997
American League totals (3 years)		352	1207	167	321	62	9	20	127	146	195	26-18	.266	.354	.382	14	.994
National League totals (8 years)		819	2670	332	683	117	18	39	256	239	447	54-23	.256	.319	.357	47	.992
Major League totals (10 years)		1171	3877	499	1004	179	27	59	383	385	642	80-41	.259	.331	.365	61	.993

DIVISION SERIES RECORD

		BATTING														FIELDING	
Year Team (League)	Pos.	G	AB	R	H	2B	3B	HR	RBI	BB	SO	SB-CS	Avg.	OBP	SLG	E	Avg.
1997—Houston (N.L.)	C	2	5	1	2	1	0	0	2	0	1	0-0	.400	.400	.600	0	1.000
1998—Houston (N.L.)	C	4	9	0	2	0	0	0	0	0	4	0-0	.222	.222	.222	0	1.000
2001—Houston (N.L.)	C-PH	3	8	1	2	0	0	1	2	0	0	0-0	.250	.250	.625	0	1.000
Division series totals (3 years)		9	22	2	6	1	0	1	4	0	5	0-0	.273	.273	.455	0	1.000

ALL-STAR GAME RECORD

	AB	R	H	2B	3B	HR	RBI	BB	SO	SB-CS	Avg.	OBP	SLG	E	Avg.
All-Star Game totals (1 year)	1	0	0	0	0	0	0	0	0	0-0	.000	.000	.000	0	1.000

AUSTIN, JEFF — P — ROYALS

PERSONAL: Born October 19, 1976, in San Bernardino, Calif. ... 6-0/185. ... Throws right, bats right. ... Full name: Jeffrey Wellington Austin.
HIGH SCHOOL: Kingwood (Texas).
COLLEGE: Stanford.
TRANSACTIONS/CAREER NOTES: Selected by Montreal Expos organization in 10th round of free-agent draft (June 1, 1995); did not sign. ... Selected by Kansas City Royals organization in first round (fourth pick overall) of free-agent draft (June 2, 1998).
CAREER HITTING (MLB): 0-for-0 (.000), 0 R, 0 2B, 0 3B, 0 HR, 0 RBI.

Year League	W	L	Pct.	ERA	G	GS	CG	ShO	Sv.-Opp.	IP	H	R	ER	HR	BB-IBB	SO
1999—Wilmington (Caro.)	7	2	.778	3.77	18	18	0	0	0-...	112.1	108	52	47	10	39-0	97
—Wichita (Texas)	3	1	.750	4.46	6	6	0	0	0-...	34.1	40	19	17	1	11-1	21
2000—Wichita (Texas)	2	2	.500	2.93	6	6	1	0	0-...	43.0	33	16	14	3	4-0	31
—Omaha (PCL)	7	9	.438	4.48	23	19	1	1	0-...	126.2	150	85	63	16	35-1	57
2001—Omaha (PCL)	3	7	.300	6.88	28	8	0	0	2-...	70.2	89	56	54	14	27-1	55
—Kansas City (A.L.)	0	0	...	5.54	21	0	0	0	0-0	26.0	27	17	16	4	14-2	27
2002—Kansas City (A.L.)	0	0	...	4.91	10	0	0	0	0-0	11.0	14	6	6	0	6-1	6
—Omaha (PCL)	4	0	1.000	3.27	39	0	0	0	2-...	52.1	54	24	19	2	15-2	44
Major League totals (2 years)	0	0	...	5.35	31	0	0	0	0-0	37.0	41	23	22	4	20-3	33

AVEN, BRUCE — OF — BLUE JAYS

PERSONAL: Born March 4, 1972, in Orange, Texas. ... 5-9/180. ... Bats right, throws right. ... Full name: David Bruce Aven.
HIGH SCHOOL: West Orange-Stark (Orange, Texas).
COLLEGE: Lamar.
TRANSACTIONS/CAREER NOTES: Selected by Cleveland Indians organization in 30th round of free-agent draft (June 2, 1994). ... On Buffalo disabled list (April 9-17, April 23-May 23 and May 27, 1998-remainder of season). ... Claimed on waivers by Florida Marlins (October 20, 1998). ... Traded by Marlins to Pittsburgh Pirates for OF Brant Brown (December 13, 1999). ... On Pittsburgh disabled list (June 30-July 18, 2000); included rehabilitation assignment to Nashville (July 14-18). ... Traded by Pirates to Los Angeles Dodgers for a player to be named later (August 6, 2000). ... Granted free agency (October 17, 2001). ... Signed by Indians organization (February 1, 2002). ... On Buffalo disabled list (June 10-25, 2002). ... Traded by Indians to Philadelphia Phillies for P Jeff D'Amico (June 25, 2002). ... Released by Phillies (September 30, 2002). ... Signed by Toronto Blue Jays organization (November 8, 2002).
STATISTICAL NOTES: Led Eastern League outfielders with 289 total chances in 1996. ... Tied for American Association lead in being hit by pitch with 11 in 1997. ... Career major league grand slams: 2.
2002 GAMES PLAYED BY POSITION (MLB): OF—7.

Year Team (League)	Pos.	G	AB	R	H	2B	3B	HR	RBI	BB	SO	SB-CS	Avg.	OBP	SLG	E	Avg.
		BATTING														FIELDING	
1994—Watertown (NY-Penn)	OF	61	220	49	73	14	5	5	33	20	45	12-3	.332	.409	.509	1	.989
1995—Kinston (Caro.)..........	OF	130	479	70	125	23	5	23	69	41	109	15-9	.261	.335	.474	3	.983
1996—Canton/Akron (East.)..	OF	131	481	91	143	31	4	23	79	43	101	22-6	.297	.373	.522	6	.979
—Buffalo (A.A.)............	OF	3	9	5	6	0	0	1	2	1	1	0-1	.667	.727	1.000	0	1.000
1997—Buffalo (A.A.)............	OF-DH	121	432	69	124	27	3	17	77	50	99	10-3	.287	.371	.481	2	.991
—Cleveland (A.L.)..........	OF	13	19	4	4	1	0	0	2	1	5	0-1	.211	.250	.263	0	1.000
1998—Buffalo (I.L.).............	DH	5	15	4	3	1	0	1	1	6	5	3-0	.200	.429	.467	0	...
1999—Florida (N.L.)■..........	OF-DH	137	381	57	110	19	2	12	70	44	82	3-0	.289	.370	.444	3	.984
2000—Pittsburgh (N.L.)■.....	OF	72	148	18	37	11	0	5	25	5	31	2-3	.250	.275	.426	1	.980
—Nashville (PCL)	OF	3	10	1	3	1	0	0	3	1	3	0-0	.300	.364	.400	0	1.000
—Albuquerque (PCL)■..	OF	9	32	7	9	1	0	0	3	6	6	0-0	.281	.395	.313	0	1.000
—Los Angeles (N.L.)	OF	9	20	2	5	0	0	2	4	3	8	0-0	.250	.348	.550	0	1.000
2001—Las Vegas (PCL)	OF	86	292	43	76	17	0	8	32	24	59	5-1	.260	.325	.401	2	.983
—Los Angeles (N.L.)	OF	21	24	3	8	2	0	1	2	0	5	0-0	.333	.385	.542	0	1.000
2002—Buffalo (I.L.)■...........	OF	35	119	17	34	5	0	5	16	14	21	1-0	.286	.375	.454	0	1.000
—Cleveland (A.L.)..........	OF	7	17	1	2	0	0	0	0	4	4	1-0	.118	.286	.118	0	1.000
—Scranton/W.B. (I.L.)■	OF	59	205	26	50	11	0	8	42	36	35	3-1	.244	.375	.415	0	1.000
American League totals (2 years)		20	36	5	6	1	0	0	2	5	9	1-1	.167	.268	.194	0	1.000
National League totals (3 years)		239	573	80	160	32	2	20	101	52	126	5-3	.279	.347	.447	4	.984
Major League totals (5 years)		259	609	85	166	33	2	20	103	57	135	6-4	.273	.343	.432	4	.986

AYBAR, MANNY — P — GIANTS

PERSONAL: Born May 4, 1972, in Bani, Dominican Republic. ... 6-1/177. ... Throws right, bats right. ... Full name: Manuel Antonio Aybar. ... Name pronounced I-bar.

TRANSACTIONS/CAREER NOTES: Signed as non-drafted free agent by St. Louis Cardinals organization (October 21, 1991). ... Traded by Cardinals with P Jose Jimenez, P Rick Croushore and IF Brent Butler to Colorado Rockies for P Darryl Kile, P Dave Veres and P Luther Hackman (November 16, 1999). ... Traded by Rockies to Cincinnati Reds for P Gabe White (April 7, 2000). ... On Cincinnati disabled list (July 2-24, 2000); included rehabilitation assignment to Louisville (July 8-23). ... Traded by Reds to Florida Marlins for P Jorge Cordova (July 26, 2000). ... Traded by Marlins to Chicago Cubs for P Oswaldo Mairena (March 30, 2001). ... Traded by Cubs with a player to be named later to Tampa Bay Devil Rays for 1B Fred McGriff (July 27, 2001); Devil Rays acquired SS Jason Smith to complete deal (August 5, 2001). ... Granted free agency (October 12, 2001). ... Signed by San Francisco Giants (February 2, 2002). ... On San Francisco disabled list (August 15-September 1, 2002); included rehabilitation assignment to Fresno (August 27-September 1).

MISCELLANEOUS: Appeared in two games as pinch runner (1999).

CAREER HITTING (MLB): 13-for-70 (.186), 6 R, 0 2B, 0 3B, 1 HR, 5 RBI.

Year League	W	L	Pct.	ERA	G	GS	CG	ShO	Sv.-Opp.	IP	H	R	ER	HR	BB-IBB	SO
1992—Dom. Cardinals (DSL)......	1	0	1.000	0.00	1	0	0	0	0-...	3.0	1	0	0	...	3-...	1
1993—Dom. Cardinals (DSL)......	4	4	.500	3.15	13	11	1	0	0-...	71.1	54	33	25	...	33-...	66
1994—Arizona Cardinals (Ariz.)...	6	1	.857	2.12	13	13	1	0	0-...	72.1	69	25	17	0	9-0	79
1995—Savannah (S.Atl.)............	3	8	.273	3.04	18	18	2	1	0-...	112.2	82	46	38	8	36-0	99
—St. Petersburg (FSL)........	2	5	.286	3.35	9	9	0	0	0-...	48.1	42	27	18	4	16-0	43
1996—Arkansas (Texas).............	8	6	.571	3.05	20	20	0	0	0-...	121.0	120	53	41	10	34-0	83
—Louisville (A.A.)...............	2	2	.500	3.23	5	5	0	0	0-...	30.2	26	12	11	1	7-0	25
1997—Louisville (A.A.)...............	5	8	.385	3.48	22	22	3	•2	0-...	137.0	131	60	53	10	45-2	114
—St. Louis (N.L.)................	2	4	.333	4.24	12	12	0	0	0-0	68.0	66	33	32	8	29-0	41
1998—St. Louis (N.L.)................	6	6	.500	5.98	20	14	0	0	0-0	81.1	90	58	54	6	42-1	57
—Memphis (PCL)...............	10	0	*1.000	2.60	13	13	0	0	0-...	83.0	62	24	24	7	17-0	63
1999—St. Louis (N.L.)................	4	5	.444	5.47	65	1	0	0	3-5	97.0	104	67	59	13	36-3	74
2000—Colorado (N.L.)■............	0	1	.000	16.20	1	0	0	0	0-0	1.2	5	3	3	1	0-0	0
—Cincinnati (N.L.)■..........	1	1	.500	4.83	32	0	0	0	0-0	50.1	51	31	27	7	22-2	31
—Louisville (I.L.)................	0	2	.000	13.50	3	2	0	0	0-...	6.2	10	10	10	0	10-0	1
—Florida (N.L.)■................	1	0	1.000	2.63	21	0	0	0	0-1	27.1	18	8	8	3	13-1	14
2001—Chicago (N.L.)■..............	2	1	.667	6.35	17	1	0	0	0-0	22.2	28	19	16	5	17-0	16
—Iowa (PCL).....................	1	2	.333	5.02	8	7	1	1	0-...	43.0	42	26	24	8	16-1	32
—Durham (I.L.)■	1	3	.250	5.68	11	3	0	0	0-...	31.2	40	25	20	5	9-0	29
2002—Fresno (PCL)■................	1	4	.200	3.75	45	0	0	0	24-...	50.1	46	24	21	6	18-1	53
—San Francisco (N.L.)	1	0	1.000	2.51	15	0	0	0	0-0	14.1	16	6	4	1	3-2	11
Major League totals (6 years).....	17	18	.486	5.04	183	28	0	0	3-6	362.2	378	225	203	44	162-9	244

DIVISION SERIES RECORD

Year League	W	L	Pct.	ERA	G	GS	CG	ShO	Sv.-Opp.	IP	H	R	ER	HR	BB-IBB	SO
2002—San Francisco (N.L.)	0	0	...	6.75	2	0	0	0	0-0	2.2	2	2	2	1	1-0	3

RECORD AS POSITION PLAYER

Year Team (League)	Pos.	G	AB	R	H	2B	3B	HR	RBI	BB	SO	SB-CS	Avg.	OBP	SLG	E	Avg.
		BATTING														FIELDING	
1992—Dom. Cardinals (DSL)	IF	55	153	18	31	5	0	1	11	10	27	2-...	.203	...	.255	19	.906

BACKE, BRANDON — P — DEVIL RAYS

PERSONAL: Born April 5, 1978, in Galveston, Texas. ... 6-0/182. ... Throws right, bats right. ... Full name: Brandon Allen Backe.

HIGH SCHOOL: Ball (Galveston, Texas).

JUNIOR COLLEGE: Galveston (Texas).

TRANSACTIONS/CAREER NOTES: Selected by Tampa Bay Devil Rays organization in 18th round of free-agent draft (June 2, 1998). ... On Bakersfield disabled list (April 5-19, 2001).

CAREER HITTING (MLB): 0-for-0 (.000), 0 R, 0 2B, 0 3B, 0 HR, 0 RBI.

Year	League	W	L	Pct.	ERA	G	GS	CG	ShO	Sv.-Opp.	IP	H	R	ER	HR	BB-IBB	SO
1998—	Princeton (Appl.)	0	0	...	0.00	1	0	0	0	0-...	2.0	0	0	0	0	2-0	3
2001—	Char., S.C. (S.Atl.)	2	1	.667	2.92	16	0	0	0	7-...	24.2	17	8	8	2	7-1	20
—	Bakersfield (Calif.)	1	0	1.000	1.09	17	0	0	0	3-...	24.2	13	7	3	1	8-0	33
—	Orlando (Sou.)	1	0	1.000	5.73	14	0	0	0	0-...	22.0	20	14	14	1	11-0	20
2002—	Orlando (Sou.)	4	6	.400	4.68	20	14	•3	1	2-...	92.1	91	58	48	9	37-1	45
—	Tampa Bay (A.L.)	0	0	...	6.92	9	0	0	0	0-0	13.0	15	10	10	3	7-0	6
Major League totals (1 year)		0	0	...	6.92	9	0	0	0	0-0	13.0	15	10	10	3	7-0	6

RECORD AS POSITION PLAYER

			BATTING														FIELDING	
Year	Team (League)	Pos.	G	AB	R	H	2B	3B	HR	RBI	BB	SO	SB-CS	Avg.	OBP	SLG	E	Avg.
1998—	Princeton (Appl.)	OF-3B-2B-P	27	92	14	23	5	1	0	7	12	31	1-1	.250	.340	.326	3	.933
—	Hudson Valley (NY-P)	OF-SS-2B	11	26	3	6	2	0	0	1	2	7	0-0	.231	.310	.308	2	.889
1999—	Charl., S.C. (S.Atl.)	0-2-1-S-3	84	272	43	63	11	2	9	40	35	81	3-5	.232	.329	.386	9	.957
—	St. Petersburg (FSL)	OF-SS-2B-1B	41	132	21	26	6	1	1	11	21	34	0-3	.197	.316	.280	3	.971
2000—	St. Petersburg (FSL)	OF-SS-3B-2B	112	376	38	93	25	6	1	34	31	99	3-6	.247	.318	.354	2	.994
—	Orlando (Sou.)	OF-SS	4	8	1	2	0	0	0	0	2	1	0-2	.250	.400	.250	0	1.000

BACSIK, MIKE — P — METS

PERSONAL: Born November 11, 1977, in Dallas. ... 6-3/190. ... Throws left, bats left. ... Full name: Michael J. Bacsik.
HIGH SCHOOL: Duncanville (Texas).
TRANSACTIONS/CAREER NOTES: Selected by Cleveland Indians organization in 18th round of free-agent draft (June 4, 1996). ... Traded by Indians with 2B Roberto Alomar and OF Danny Peoples to New York Mets for OF Matt Lawton, OF Alex Escobar, P Jerrod Riggan and two players to be named later (December 11, 2001); Indians acquired P Billy Traber and 1B Earl Snyder to complete deal (December 13, 2001).
CAREER HITTING (MLB): 2-for-18 (.111), 0 R, 1 2B, 0 3B, 0 HR, 2 RBI.

Year	League	W	L	Pct.	ERA	G	GS	CG	ShO	Sv.-Opp.	IP	H	R	ER	HR	BB-IBB	SO
1996—	Burlington (Appl.)	4	2	.667	2.20	13	13	1	0	0-...	69.2	49	23	17	3	14-0	61
1997—	Columbus (S.Atl.)	4	14	.222	5.44	28	28	0	0	0-...	139.0	163	94	84	16	47-1	100
1998—	Kinston (Caro.)	10	9	.526	2.88	27	27	1	0	0-...	165.2	147	64	53	*17	37-3	128
1999—	Akron (East.)	11	11	.500	4.64	26	26	1	0	0-...	149.1	164	84	77	24	47-0	84
2000—	Kinston (Caro.)	3	6	.333	4.57	11	11	0	0	0-...	65.0	72	36	33	4	8-0	56
—	Akron (East.)	7	1	.875	2.78	11	11	1	1	0-...	71.1	61	23	22	3	15-0	44
—	Buffalo (I.L.)	0	3	.000	5.59	5	5	0	0	0-...	29.0	31	20	18	7	7-0	9
2001—	Buffalo (I.L.)	12	5	.706	3.26	21	20	2	0	0-...	121.1	115	47	44	13	25-0	81
—	Akron (East.)	1	1	.500	1.98	4	4	1	1	0-...	27.1	21	7	6	2	3-0	19
—	Cleveland (A.L.)	0	0	...	9.00	3	0	0	0	0-0	9.0	13	10	9	0	3-1	4
2002—	Norfolk (I.L.)■	5	5	.500	3.74	25	14	1	1	0-...	108.1	134	48	45	13	25-0	75
—	New York (N.L.)	3	2	.600	4.37	11	9	1	0	0-0	55.2	63	29	27	8	19-3	30
A.L. totals (1 year)		0	0	...	9.00	3	0	0	0	0-0	9.0	13	10	9	0	3-1	4
N.L. totals (1 year)		3	2	.600	4.37	11	9	1	0	0-0	55.2	63	29	27	8	19-3	30
Major League totals (2 years)		3	2	.600	5.01	14	9	1	0	0-0	64.2	76	39	36	8	22-4	34

BAERGA, CARLOS — 2B/3B — RED SOX

PERSONAL: Born November 4, 1968, in San Juan, Puerto Rico. ... 5-11/215. ... Bats both, throws right. ... Full name: Carlos Obed Ortiz Baerga. ... Name pronounced by-AIR-guh.
HIGH SCHOOL: Barbara Ann Rooshart (Rio Piedras, Puerto Rico).
TRANSACTIONS/CAREER NOTES: Signed as non-drafted free agent by San Diego Padres organization (November 4, 1985). ... Traded by Padres with C Sandy Alomar and OF Chris James to Cleveland Indians for OF Joe Carter (December 6, 1989). ... Traded by Indians with IF Alvaro Espinoza to New York Mets for IF Jose Vizcaino and IF Jeff Kent (July 29, 1996). ... Granted free agency (October 26, 1998). ... Signed by St. Louis Cardinals (January 27, 1999). ... Released by Cardinals (March 17, 1999). ... Signed by Cincinnati Reds organization (March 23, 1999). ... Released by Reds (June 4, 1999). ... Signed by San Diego Padres organization (June 6, 1999). ... Traded by Padres to Indians for cash (August 16, 1999). ... Granted free agency (October 29, 1999). ... Signed by Tampa Bay Devil Rays organization (February 24, 2000). ... Contract voided (March 21, 2000). ... Signed by Seattle Mariners organization (January 19, 2001). ... Released by Mariners (March 30, 2001). ... Signed by Samsung, Korean League (April 2001). ... Signed by Long Island, Atlantic League (April 19, 2001). ... Signed by Boston Red Sox organization (December 18, 2001). ... On disabled list (July 2-26, 2002).
RECORDS: Shares major league record for switch-hitting home runs in one inning (April 8, 1993, seventh inning). ... Shares major league single-inning record for most home runs—2 (April 8, 1993, seventh inning).
HONORS: Named second baseman on The Sporting News A.L. All-Star team (1993 and 1995). ... Named second baseman on The Sporting News A.L. Silver Slugger team (1993-94).
STATISTICAL NOTES: Tied for South Atlantic League lead with 29 errors by second basemen in 1987. ... Led Texas League shortstops with 61 double plays in 1988. ... Led Pacific Coast League third basemen with 92 putouts and 380 total chances in 1989. ... Led A.L. second basemen with 400 putouts, 475 assists and 138 double plays in 1992. ... Led A.L. second basemen with 347 putouts and 445 assists in 1993. ... Led A.L. second basemen with 894 total chances in 1992 and 809 in 1993. ... Collected six hits in one game (April 11, 1992). ... Switch-hit home runs in one game (April 8, 1993). ... Hit three home runs in one game (June 17, 1993). ... Led A.L. second basemen with 444 assists in 1995. ... Career major league grand slams: 1.
2002 GAMES PLAYED BY POSITION (MLB): DH—32; 2B—17; 3B—1.

			BATTING														FIELDING	
Year	Team (League)	Pos.	G	AB	R	H	2B	3B	HR	RBI	BB	SO	SB-CS	Avg.	OBP	SLG	E	Avg.
1986—	Charl., S.C. (S.Atl.)	2B-SS	111	378	57	102	14	4	7	41	26	60	6-1	.270	.321	.384	27	.943
1987—	Charl., S.C. (S.Atl.)	2B-SS	134	515	83	157	23	•9	7	50	38	107	26-21	.305	.365	.425	‡36	.943
1988—	Wichita (Texas)	SS-2B	122	444	67	121	28	1	12	65	31	83	4-4	.273	.331	.421	33	.943
1989—	Las Vegas (PCL)	3B	132	520	63	143	28	2	10	74	30	98	6-6	.275	.319	.394	*32	.916
1990—	Cleveland (A.L.)■	3B-SS-2B	108	312	46	81	17	2	7	47	16	57	0-2	.260	.300	.394	17	.935
—	Colo. Springs (PCL)	3B	12	50	11	19	2	1	1	11	5	4	1-0	.380	.436	.520	4	.925
1991—	Cleveland (A.L.)	3B-2B-SS	158	593	80	171	28	2	11	69	48	74	3-2	.288	.346	.398	27	.959
1992—	Cleveland (A.L.)	2B-DH	161	657	92	205	32	1	20	105	35	76	10-2	.312	.354	.455	19	.979

Year Team (League)	Pos.	G	AB	R	H	2B	3B	HR	RBI	BB	SO	SB-CS	Avg.	OBP	SLG	E	Avg.
							BATTING									FIELDING	
1993—Cleveland (A.L.)	2B-DH	154	624	105	200	28	6	21	114	34	68	15-4	.321	.355	.486	17	.979
1994—Cleveland (A.L.)	2B-DH	103	442	81	139	32	2	19	80	10	45	8-2	.314	.333	.525	*15	.973
1995—Cleveland (A.L.)	2B-DH	135	557	87	175	28	2	15	90	35	31	11-2	.314	.355	.452	19	.973
1996—Cleveland (A.L.)	2B	100	424	54	113	25	0	10	55	16	25	1-1	.267	.302	.396	15	.971
—New York (N.L.)■	1B-3B-2B	26	83	5	16	3	0	2	11	5	2	0-0	.193	.253	.301	4	.966
1997—New York (N.L.)	2B	133	467	53	131	25	1	9	52	20	54	2-6	.281	.311	.396	14	.978
1998—New York (N.L.)	2B	147	511	46	136	27	1	7	53	24	55	0-1	.266	.303	.364	9	.986
1999—Indianapolis (I.L.)■	3B-2B-1B-DH	52	221	32	64	10	0	3	27	10	18	2-1	.290	.321	.376	6	.975
—Las Vegas (PCL)■	3B-2B	21	91	15	26	7	0	2	9	9	5	0-0	.286	.356	.429	5	.919
—San Diego (N.L.)	2B-3B-1B-DH	33	80	6	20	1	0	2	5	6	14	1-0	.250	.318	.338	2	.962
—Cleveland (A.L.)■	3B-2B-DH	22	57	4	13	0	0	1	5	4	10	1-1	.228	.274	.281	1	.976
2000—								Did not play.									
2001—Samsung (Korean)■		...	120	18	33	...	...	4	17	10	12	...-...	.275	...	.375	...	...
—Long Island (Atl.)■		53	203	38	64	9	3	9	44	18	24	3-...	.315	...	.522	...	...
2002—Boston (A.L.)■	DH-2B-3B	73	182	17	52	11	0	2	19	7	20	6-0	.286	.316	.379	1	.983
American League totals (9 years)		1014	3848	566	1149	201	15	106	584	205	406	55-16	.299	.338	.441	131	.971
National League totals (4 years)		339	1141	110	303	56	2	20	121	55	125	3-7	.266	.304	.371	29	.980
Major League totals (11 years)		1353	4989	676	1452	257	17	126	705	260	531	58-23	.291	.330	.425	160	.973

DIVISION SERIES RECORD

Year Team (League)	Pos.	G	AB	R	H	2B	3B	HR	RBI	BB	SO	SB-CS	Avg.	OBP	SLG	E	Avg.
							BATTING									FIELDING	
1995—Cleveland (A.L.)	2B	3	14	2	4	1	0	0	1	0	1	0-0	.286	.333	.357	1	.929

CHAMPIONSHIP SERIES RECORD

Year Team (League)	Pos.	G	AB	R	H	2B	3B	HR	RBI	BB	SO	SB-CS	Avg.	OBP	SLG	E	Avg.
							BATTING									FIELDING	
1995—Cleveland (A.L.)	2B	6	25	3	10	0	0	1	4	2	3	0-0	.400	.444	.520	0	1.000

WORLD SERIES RECORD

Year Team (League)	Pos.	G	AB	R	H	2B	3B	HR	RBI	BB	SO	SB-CS	Avg.	OBP	SLG	E	Avg.
							BATTING									FIELDING	
1995—Cleveland (A.L.)	2B	6	26	1	5	2	0	0	4	1	1	0-0	.192	.222	.269	1	.975

ALL-STAR GAME RECORD

	AB	R	H	2B	3B	HR	RBI	BB	SO	SB-CS	Avg.	OBP	SLG	E	Avg.
All-Star Game totals (3 years)	6	3	4	2	0	0	1	0	1	0-1	.667	.667	1.000	0	1.000

BAEZ, BENITO — P

PERSONAL: Born May 6, 1977, in Bonao, Dominican Republic. ... 6-0/160. ... Throws left, bats left.

TRANSACTIONS/CAREER NOTES: Signed as non-drafted free agent by Oakland Athletics organization (November 8, 1993). ... On disabled list (April 11-May 1, 2000). ... Granted free agency (October 15, 2000). ... Signed by Florida Marlins organization (January 4, 2001). ... On Calgary disabled list (June 30-July 8, 2001). ... On Florida disabled list (March 22-July 20 and July 21, 2002-remainder of season); included rehabilitation assignment to Gulf Coast Marlins (July 11-20). ... Released by Marlins (October 3, 2002).

CAREER HITTING (MLB): 0-for-1 (.000), 0 R, 0 2B, 0 3B, 0 HR, 0 RBI.

Year League	W	L	Pct.	ERA	G	GS	CG	ShO	Sv.-Opp.	IP	H	R	ER	HR	BB-IBB	SO
1994—Dom. Athletics (DSL)	8	5	.615	2.93	16	3	0	0	1-...	58.1	44	34	19	...	30-...	44
1995—Arizona Athletics (Ariz.)	5	1	.833	3.34	14	11	1	0	0-...	70.0	64	35	26	2	28-0	83
1996—West Michigan (Midw.)	8	4	.667	3.47	32	20	0	0	4-...	129.2	123	60	50	6	52-1	92
1997—Visalia (Calif.)	5	5	.500	3.54	16	15	1	0	0-...	96.2	83	40	38	8	28-0	87
—Huntsville (Sou.)	2	4	.333	9.14	15	7	0	0	0-...	42.1	64	47	43	8	22-1	27
1998—Huntsville (Sou.)	3	8	.273	5.80	34	17	0	0	0-...	122.2	161	92	79	12	64-0	83
1999—Midland (Texas)	5	1	.833	5.47	37	0	0	0	3-...	54.1	68	35	33	5	15-2	51
—Vancouver (PCL)	0	2	.000	3.50	11	0	0	0	1-...	18.0	18	7	7	2	7-0	19
2000—Midland (Texas)	5	4	.556	4.89	37	0	0	0	0-...	53.1	61	35	29	4	27-3	50
2001—Calgary (PCL)■	7	1	.875	3.03	49	0	0	0	1-...	59.1	53	22	20	5	7-1	56
—Florida (N.L.)	0	0	...	13.50	8	0	0	0	0-0	9.1	22	14	14	3	6-0	14
2002—Gulf Coast Marlins (GCL)	0	0	...	3.86	5	3	0	0	0-...	4.2	3	2	2	0	2-0	5
Major League totals (1 year)	0	0	...	13.50	8	0	0	0	0-0	9.1	22	14	14	3	6-0	14

BAEZ, DANYS — P — INDIANS

PERSONAL: Born September 10, 1977, in Pinar del Rio, Cuba. ... 6-3/225. ... Throws right, bats right.

TRANSACTIONS/CAREER NOTES: Signed as non-drafted free agent by Cleveland Indians organization (November 5, 1999). ... On Buffalo disabled list (June 19-July 4, 2000; and June 4-29, 2001).

CAREER HITTING (MLB): 0-for-2 (.000), 0 R, 0 2B, 0 3B, 0 HR, 0 RBI.

Year League	W	L	Pct.	ERA	G	GS	CG	ShO	Sv.-Opp.	IP	H	R	ER	HR	BB-IBB	SO
2000—Kinston (Caro.)	2	2	.500	4.71	9	9	0	0	0-...	49.2	45	29	26	5	20-0	56
—Akron (East.)	4	9	.308	3.68	18	18	0	0	0-...	102.2	98	46	42	6	32-0	77
2001—Buffalo (I.L.)	2	0	1.000	3.20	16	0	0	0	3-...	25.1	18	9	9	2	9-0	30
—Akron (East.)	0	0	...	0.00	1	0	0	0	0-...	2.0	1	0	0	0	0-0	2
—Cleveland (A.L.)	5	3	.625	2.50	43	0	0	0	0-1	50.1	34	22	14	5	20-4	52
2002—Cleveland (A.L.)	10	11	.476	4.41	39	26	1	0	6-8	165.1	160	84	81	14	82-5	130
Major League totals (2 years)	15	14	.517	3.96	82	26	1	0	6-9	215.2	194	106	95	19	102-9	182

DIVISION SERIES RECORD

Year League	W	L	Pct.	ERA	G	GS	CG	ShO	Sv.-Opp.	IP	H	R	ER	HR	BB-IBB	SO
2001—Cleveland (A.L.)	0	0	...	2.45	3	0	0	0	0-0	3.2	4	1	1	0	0-0	6

BAGWELL, JEFF — 1B — ASTROS

PERSONAL: Born May 27, 1968, in Boston. ... 6-0/215. ... Bats right, throws right. ... Full name: Jeffrey Robert Bagwell.
HIGH SCHOOL: Xavier (Middletown, Conn.).
COLLEGE: Hartford.
TRANSACTIONS/CAREER NOTES: Selected by Boston Red Sox organization in fourth round of free-agent draft (June 5, 1989). ... Traded by Red Sox to Houston Astros for P Larry Andersen (August 31, 1990). ... On Houston disabled list (July 31-September 1, 1995); included rehabilitation assignment to Jackson (August 28-September 1). ... On disabled list (May 13-28, 1998).
RECORDS: Shares major league single-game records for most doubles—4 (June 14, 1996); and most bases on balls—6 (August 20, 1999, 16 innings). ... Shares major league single-inning record for most home runs—2 (June 24, 1994, sixth inning).
HONORS: Named Eastern League Most Valuable Player (1990). ... Named N.L. Rookie Player of the Year by The Sporting News (1991). ... Named N.L. Rookie of the Year by Baseball Writers' Association of America (1991). ... Named Major League Player of the Year by The Sporting News (1994). ... Named first baseman on The Sporting News N.L. All-Star team (1994, 1996, 1997 and 1999). ... Won N.L. Gold Glove at first base (1994). ... Named first baseman on The Sporting News N.L. Silver Slugger team (1994, 1997 and 1999). ... Named N.L. Most Valuable Player by Baseball Writers' Association of America (1994).
STATISTICAL NOTES: Led Eastern League with 220 total bases and 12 intentional bases on balls received in 1990. ... Led N.L. in being hit by pitch with 13 in 1991. ... Led N.L. with 13 sacrifice flies in 1992. ... Hit three home runs in one game (June 24, 1994; and April 21 and June 9, 1999). ... Led N.L. first basemen with 120 assists in 1994. ... Tied for N.L. lead in errors by first basemen with nine and double plays by first basemen with 94 in 1994. ... Led N.L. first basemen with 129 assists in 1995, 136 in 1996 and 137 in 1997. ... Had 18-game hitting streak (August 2-20, 2000). ... Hit for the cycle (July 18, 2001). ... Had 15-game hitting streak (August 10-24, 2002). ... Career major league grand slams: 5.
MISCELLANEOUS: Holds Houston Astros all-time records for most home runs (380), most runs batted in (1,321) and highest career batting average (.302).
2002 GAMES PLAYED BY POSITION (MLB): 1B—153; DH—4.

			BATTING														FIELDING	
Year	Team (League)	Pos.	G	AB	R	H	2B	3B	HR	RBI	BB	SO	SB-CS	Avg.	OBP	SLG	E	Avg.
1989—	GC Red Sox (GCL)	3B-2B	5	19	3	6	1	0	0	3	3	0	0-0	.316	.409	.368	2	.875
—	Winter Haven (FSL)	3B-2B-1B	64	210	27	65	13	2	2	19	22	25	1-1	.310	.381	.419	12	.931
1990—	New Britain (East.)	3B	136	481	63	*160	•34	7	4	61	73	57	5-7	.333	.423	.457	34	.914
1991—	Houston (N.L.)■	1B	156	554	79	163	26	4	15	82	75	116	7-4	.294	.387	.437	12	.991
1992—	Houston (N.L.)	1B	•162	586	87	160	34	6	18	96	84	97	10-6	.273	.368	.444	7	.995
1993—	Houston (N.L.)	1B	142	535	76	171	37	4	20	88	62	73	13-4	.320	.388	.516	9	.993
1994—	Houston (N.L.)	1B-OF	110	400	*104	147	32	2	39	*116	65	65	15-4	.368	.451	*.750	‡9	.991
1995—	Houston (N.L.)	1B	114	448	88	130	29	0	21	87	79	102	12-5	.290	.399	.496	7	.994
—	Jackson (Texas)	1B-DH	4	12	0	2	0	0	0	0	3	2	0-0	.167	.375	.167	0	1.000
1996—	Houston (N.L.)	1B	*162	568	111	179	*48	2	31	120	135	114	21-7	.315	.451	.570	*16	.989
1997—	Houston (N.L.)	1B-DH	•162	566	109	162	40	2	43	135	127	122	31-10	.286	.425	.592	11	.993
1998—	Houston (N.L.)	1B	147	540	124	164	33	1	34	111	109	90	19-7	.304	.424	.557	7	.995
1999—	Houston (N.L.)	1B-DH	•162	562	*143	171	35	0	42	126	*149	127	30-11	.304	.454	.591	8	.994
2000—	Houston (N.L.)	1B-DH	159	590	*152	183	37	1	47	132	107	116	9-6	.310	.424	.615	9	.994
2001—	Houston (N.L.)	1B	161	600	126	173	43	4	39	130	106	135	11-3	.288	.397	.568	12	.992
2002—	Houston (N.L.)	1B-DH	158	571	94	166	33	2	31	98	101	130	7-3	.291	.401	.518	7	.995
Major League totals (12 years)			1795	6520	1293	1969	427	28	380	1321	1199	1287	185-70	.302	.414	.551	114	.993

DIVISION SERIES RECORD

			BATTING														FIELDING	
Year	Team (League)	Pos.	G	AB	R	H	2B	3B	HR	RBI	BB	SO	SB-CS	Avg.	OBP	SLG	E	Avg.
1997—	Houston (N.L.)	1B	3	12	0	1	0	0	0	0	1	5	0-0	.083	.154	.083	2	.920
1998—	Houston (N.L.)	1B	4	14	0	2	0	0	0	4	1	6	0-0	.143	.250	.143	0	1.000
1999—	Houston (N.L.)	1B	4	13	3	2	0	0	0	0	5	4	0-0	.154	.421	.154	0	1.000
2001—	Houston (N.L.)	1B	3	7	0	3	0	0	0	0	5	1	0-1	.429	.667	.429	0	1.000
Division series totals (4 years)			14	46	3	8	0	0	0	4	12	16	0-1	.174	.367	.174	2	.984

ALL-STAR GAME RECORD

	AB	R	H	2B	3B	HR	RBI	BB	SO	SB-CS	Avg.	OBP	SLG	E	Avg.
All-Star Game totals (4 years)	12	1	3	0	0	0	0	0	4	0-0	.250	.250	.250	0	1.000

BAILEY, CORY — P

PERSONAL: Born January 24, 1971, in Herrin, Ill. ... 6-1/210. ... Throws right, bats right. ... Full name: Phillip Cory Bailey.
HIGH SCHOOL: Marion (Ill.).
COLLEGE: Southeastern Illinois.
TRANSACTIONS/CAREER NOTES: Selected by Boston Red Sox organization in 15th round of free-agent draft (June 3, 1991). ... Traded by Red Sox with 3B Scott Cooper and a player to be named later to St. Louis Cardinals for P Rheal Cormier and OF Mark Whiten (April 8, 1995). ... Traded by Cardinals to Texas Rangers for P David Chavarria and a player to be named later (December 16, 1996). ... Traded by Rangers to San Francisco Giants for P Chad Hartvigson (July 29, 1997). ... On disabled list (August 14-September 1, 1999). ... Granted free agency (October 4, 1999). ... Signed by Pittsburgh Pirates organization (January 18, 2000). ... Granted free agency (October 18, 2000). ... Signed by Kansas City Royals organization (January 7, 2001). ... Released by Royals (March 25, 2001). ... Re-signed by Royals organization (April 2, 2001). ... Released by Royals (October 7, 2002).
CAREER HITTING (MLB): 1-for-2 (.500), 2 R, 0 2B, 0 3B, 0 HR, 0 RBI.

Year	League	W	L	Pct.	ERA	G	GS	CG	ShO	Sv.-Opp.	IP	H	R	ER	HR	BB-IBB	SO
1991—	Gulf Coast Red Sox (GCL)	0	0	...	0.00	1	0	0	0	1-...	2.0	2	1	0	0	1-0	1
—	Elmira (NY-Penn)	2	4	.333	1.85	28	0	0	0	*15-...	39.0	19	10	8	2	12-0	54
1992—	Lynchburg (Caro.)	5	7	.417	2.44	49	0	0	0	*23-...	66.1	43	20	18	3	30-2	87
1993—	Pawtucket (I.L.)	4	5	.444	2.88	52	0	0	0	20-...	65.2	48	21	21	1	31-3	59
—	Boston (A.L.)	0	1	.000	3.45	11	0	0	0	0-0	15.2	12	7	6	0	12-3	11
1994—	Pawtucket (I.L.)	4	3	.571	3.23	53	0	0	0	19-...	61.1	44	25	22	4	38-2	52
—	Boston (A.L.)	0	1	.000	12.46	5	0	0	0	0-1	4.1	10	6	6	2	3-1	4
1995—	Louisville (A.A.)■	5	3	.625	4.55	55	0	0	0	*25-...	59.1	51	30	30	6	30-4	49
—	St. Louis (N.L.)	0	0	...	7.36	3	0	0	0	0-0	3.2	2	3	3	0	2-1	5

Year League	W	L	Pct.	ERA	G	GS	CG	ShO	Sv.-Opp.	IP	H	R	ER	HR	BB-IBB	SO
1996—St. Louis (N.L.)................	5	2	.714	3.00	51	0	0	0	0-1	57.0	57	21	19	1	30-3	38
—Louisville (A.A.)...............	2	4	.333	5.82	22	0	0	0	1-...	34.0	29	22	22	1	20-5	27
1997—Oklahoma City (A.A.)■.....	3	4	.429	3.40	42	0	0	0	15-...	50.1	49	20	19	1	23-7	38
—Phoenix (PCL)■...............	4	0	1.000	1.56	13	0	0	0	3-...	17.1	16	4	3	0	6-1	14
—San Francisco (N.L.)........	0	1	.000	8.38	7	0	0	0	0-0	9.2	15	9	9	1	4-0	5
1998—Fresno (PCL)....................	7	2	.778	2.47	57	0	0	0	10-...	94.2	79	31	26	4	18-4	76
—San Francisco (N.L.)........	0	0	...	2.70	5	0	0	0	0-0	3.1	2	1	1	1	1-0	2
1999—Fresno (PCL)....................	2	1	.667	3.30	43	0	0	0	18-...	46.1	47	24	17	7	17-0	52
2000—Nashville (PCL)■............	2	4	.333	3.47	55	0	0	0	12-...	72.2	76	32	28	2	35-10	62
2001—Omaha (PCL)■................	1	0	1.000	0.00	5	0	0	0	1-...	10.0	2	0	0	0	5-0	7
—Kansas City (A.L.)............	1	1	.500	3.48	53	0	0	0	0-1	67.1	57	28	26	3	33-2	61
2002—Kansas City (A.L.)............	3	4	.429	4.11	37	0	0	0	1-7	46.0	53	24	21	5	31-7	24
—Omaha (PCL)...................	1	0	1.000	1.83	18	0	0	0	9-...	19.2	13	4	4	0	10-0	17
A.L. totals (4 years)....................	4	7	.364	3.98	106	0	0	0	1-9	133.1	132	65	59	10	79-13	100
N.L. totals (4 years)....................	5	3	.625	3.91	66	0	0	0	0-1	73.2	76	34	32	3	37-4	50
Major League totals (8 years).....	9	10	.474	3.96	172	0	0	0	1-10	207.0	208	99	91	13	116-17	150

BAKO, PAUL — C — BREWERS

PERSONAL: Born June 20, 1972, in Lafayette, La. ... 6-2/205. ... Bats left, throws right. ... Full name: Gabor Paul Bako.

HIGH SCHOOL: Lafayette (La.).

COLLEGE: Southwestern Louisiana.

TRANSACTIONS/CAREER NOTES: Selected by Cincinnati Reds organization in fifth round of free-agent draft (June 3, 1993). ... Traded by Reds with P Donne Wall to Detroit Tigers for OF Melvin Nieves (November 11, 1997). ... Traded by Tigers with P Dean Crow, P Mark Persails, P Brian Powell and 3B Carlos Villalobos to Houston Astros for C Brad Ausmus and P C.J. Nitkowski (January 14, 1999). ... Traded by Astros to Florida Marlins for a player to be named to later (April 11, 2000); Astros acquired cash to complete deal (October 10, 2000). ... Claimed on waivers by Atlanta Braves (July 21, 2000). ... Traded by Braves with P Jose Cabrera to Milwaukee Brewers for C Henry Blanco (March 20, 2002). ... On disabled list (June 9-24, 2002).

STATISTICAL NOTES: Tied for Carolina League lead with 15 passed balls in 1995. ... Led Southern League catchers with 694 putouts, 84 assists and 791 total chances in 1996. ... Tied for American Association lead in double plays with 10 by catcher and nine passed balls in 1997.

2002 GAMES PLAYED BY POSITION (MLB): C—76.

		BATTING														FIELDING	
Year Team (League)	Pos.	G	AB	R	H	2B	3B	HR	RBI	BB	SO	SB-CS	Avg.	OBP	SLG	E	Avg.
1993—Billings (Pio.).............	C-1B	57	194	34	61	11	0	4	30	22	37	5-1	.314	.382	.433	6	.984
1994—Win.-Salem (Caro.)....	C	90	289	29	59	9	1	3	26	35	81	2-2	.204	.299	.273	15	.977
1995—Win.-Salem (Caro.)....	C	82	249	29	71	11	2	7	27	42	66	3-1	.285	.389	.430	6	.989
1996—Chattanooga (Sou.)....	C	110	360	53	106	27	0	8	48	48	93	1-0	.294	.381	.436	13	.984
1997—Indianapolis (A.A.)......	C	104	321	34	78	14	1	8	43	34	81	0-5	.243	.316	.368	6	.991
1998—Toledo (I.L.)■............	C	13	48	5	14	3	1	1	6	1	13	0-0	.292	.300	.458	1	.988
—Detroit (A.L.).............	C	96	305	23	83	12	1	3	30	23	82	1-1	.272	.319	.348	6	.989
1999—New Orleans (PCL)■..	C	12	47	2	9	3	1	1	4	1	11	0-0	.191	.208	.362	1	.984
—Houston (N.L.)..........	C	73	215	16	55	14	1	2	17	26	57	1-1	.256	.332	.358	6	.988
2000—Houston (N.L.)..........	C	1	2	0	0	0	0	0	0	0	1	0-0	.000	.000	.000	0	1.000
—Florida (N.L.)■..........	C	56	161	10	39	6	1	0	14	22	48	0-0	.242	.335	.292	3	.991
—Atlanta (N.L.)■..........	C-1B	24	58	8	11	4	0	2	6	5	15	0-0	.190	.254	.362	1	.992
2001—Atlanta (N.L.)............	C	61	137	19	29	10	1	2	15	20	34	1-0	.212	.312	.343	3	.991
2002—Milwaukee (N.L.)■.....	C	87	234	24	55	8	1	4	20	20	46	0-2	.235	.295	.329	4	.991
American League totals (1 year)		96	305	23	83	12	1	3	30	23	82	1-1	.272	.319	.348	6	.989
National League totals (4 years)		302	807	77	189	42	4	10	72	93	201	2-3	.234	.313	.333	17	.990
Major League totals (5 years)		398	1112	100	272	54	5	13	102	116	283	3-4	.245	.314	.337	23	.990

DIVISION SERIES RECORD

		BATTING														FIELDING	
Year Team (League)	Pos.	G	AB	R	H	2B	3B	HR	RBI	BB	SO	SB-CS	Avg.	OBP	SLG	E	Avg.
2000—Atlanta (N.L.).............	C	2	1	0	0	0	0	0	0	0	1	0-0	.000	.000	.000	1	.800
2001—Atlanta (N.L.).............	C	3	7	1	2	1	0	1	3	1	0	0-0	.286	.375	.857	0	1.000
Division series totals (2 years)		5	8	1	2	1	0	1	3	1	1	0-0	.250	.333	.750	1	.955

CHAMPIONSHIP SERIES RECORD

		BATTING														FIELDING	
Year Team (League)	Pos.	G	AB	R	H	2B	3B	HR	RBI	BB	SO	SB-CS	Avg.	OBP	SLG	E	Avg.
2001—Atlanta (N.L.).............	C	3	3	0	0	0	0	0	0	0	0	0-0	.000	.000	.000	0	1.000

BALDELLI, ROCCO — OF — DEVIL RAYS

PERSONAL: Born September 25, 1981, in Woonsocket, R.I. ... 6-4/187. ... Bats right, throws right. ... Full name: Rocco Daniel Baldelli.

HIGH SCHOOL: Bishop Hendrickson (Warwick, R.I.).

TRANSACTIONS/CAREER NOTES: Selected by Tampa Bay Devil Rays organization in first round (sixth pick overall) of free-agent draft (June 5, 2000).

HONORS: Named California League Most Valuable Player (2002).

		BATTING														FIELDING	
Year Team (League)	Pos.	G	AB	R	H	2B	3B	HR	RBI	BB	SO	SB-CS	Avg.	OBP	SLG	E	Avg.
2000—Princeton (Appl.)........	OF	60	232	33	50	9	2	3	25	12	56	11-3	.216	.269	.310	4	.966
2001—Charl., S.C. (S.Atl.).....	OF	113	406	58	101	23	6	8	55	23	89	25-9	.249	.303	.394	9	.964
2002—Bakersfield (Calif.)......	OF	77	312	63	104	19	1	14	51	18	63	21-6	.333	.382	.535	3	.975
—Orlando (Sou.)...........	OF	17	70	10	26	3	1	2	13	5	11	3-2	.371	.413	.529	1	.967
—Durham (I.L.)............	OF	23	96	13	28	6	1	3	7	0	23	2-5	.292	.292	.469	0	1.000

BALDWIN, JAMES — P

PERSONAL: Born July 15, 1971, in Southern Pines, N.C. ... 6-3/235. ... Throws right, bats right. ... Full name: James Baldwin Jr.
HIGH SCHOOL: Pinecrest (Southern Pines, N.C.).
TRANSACTIONS/CAREER NOTES: Selected by Chicago White Sox organization in fourth round of free-agent draft (June 4, 1990). ... On disabled list (August 3-19, 1994). ... On Chicago disabled list (March 23-April 21, 2001); included rehabilitation assignment to Charlotte (April 11-17). ... Traded by White Sox to Los Angeles Dodgers for P Onan Masaoka, P Gary Majewski and OF Jeff Barry (July 26, 2001). ... Granted free agency (November 5, 2001). ... Signed by Seattle Mariners (February 1, 2002). ... Granted free agency (October 29, 2002).
RECORDS: Shares A.L. single-game record for most hit batsmen (nine innings)—4 (August 17, 2000).
HONORS: Named A.L. Rookie Pitcher of the Year by The Sporting News (1996).
STATISTICAL NOTES: Tied for American Association lead with three balks in 1995.. ... Tied for A.L. lead with 14 wild pitches and three balks in 1997.
CAREER HITTING (MLB): 4-for-41 (.098), 1 R, 1 2B, 1 3B, 0 HR, 2 RBI.

Year League	W	L	Pct.	ERA	G	GS	CG	ShO	Sv.-Opp.	IP	H	R	ER	HR	BB-IBB	SO
1990— GC White Sox (GCL)	1	6	.143	4.10	9	7	0	0	0-...	37.1	32	29	17	1	18-0	32
1991— GC White Sox (GCL)	3	1	.750	2.12	6	6	0	0	0-...	34.0	16	8	8	0	16-0	48
— Utica (NY-Penn)	1	4	.200	5.30	7	7	1	0	0-...	37.1	40	26	22	0	27-0	23
1992— South Bend (Midw.)	9	5	.643	2.42	21	21	1	1	0-...	137.2	118	53	37	6	45-0	137
— Sarasota (FSL)	1	2	.333	2.87	6	6	1	0	0-...	37.2	31	13	12	2	7-0	39
1993— Birmingham (Sou.)	8	5	.615	*2.25	17	17	•4	0	0-...	120.0	94	48	30	6	43-0	107
— Nashville (A.A.)	5	4	.556	2.61	10	10	1	0	0-...	69.0	43	21	20	5	36-0	61
1994— Nashville (A.A.)	12	6	.667	3.72	26	26	2	0	0-...	162.0	144	75	67	14	83-1	*156
1995— Chicago (A.L.)	0	1	.000	12.89	6	4	0	0	0-0	14.2	32	22	21	6	9-1	10
— Nashville (A.A.)	5	9	.357	5.85	18	18	0	0	0-...	95.1	120	76	62	*27	44-1	89
1996— Nashville (A.A.)	1	1	.500	0.64	2	2	1	0	0-...	14.0	5	1	1	0	4-0	15
— Chicago (A.L.)	11	6	.647	4.42	28	28	0	0	0-0	169.0	168	88	83	24	57-3	127
1997— Chicago (A.L.)	12	•15	.444	5.26	32	32	1	0	0-0	200.0	205	128	117	19	83-3	140
1998— Chicago (A.L.)	13	6	.684	5.32	37	24	1	0	0-1	159.0	176	103	94	18	60-2	108
1999— Chicago (A.L.)	12	13	.480	5.10	35	33	1	0	0-0	199.1	219	119	113	34	81-1	123
2000— Chicago (A.L.)	14	7	.667	4.65	29	28	2	1	0-0	178.0	185	96	92	34	59-3	116
2001— Charlotte (I.L.)	1	0	1.000	5.25	2	2	0	0	0-...	12.0	12	7	7	2	2-0	11
— Chicago (A.L.)	7	5	.583	4.61	17	16	2	1	0-0	95.2	109	56	49	15	38-0	42
— Los Angeles (N.L.)■	3	6	.333	4.20	12	12	0	0	0-0	79.1	82	39	37	10	25-1	53
2002— Seattle (A.L.)	7	10	.412	5.28	30	23	0	0	0-0	150.0	179	95	88	26	49-2	88
A.L. totals (8 years)	76	63	.547	5.07	214	188	7	2	0-1	1165.2	1273	707	657	176	436-15	754
N.L. totals (1 year)	3	6	.333	4.20	12	12	0	0	0-0	79.1	82	39	37	10	25-1	53
Major League totals (8 years)	79	69	.534	5.02	226	200	7	2	0-1	1245.0	1355	746	694	186	461-16	807

DIVISION SERIES RECORD

Year League	W	L	Pct.	ERA	G	GS	CG	ShO	Sv.-Opp.	IP	H	R	ER	HR	BB-IBB	SO
2000— Chicago (A.L.)	0	0	...	1.50	1	1	0	0	0-0	6.0	3	1	1	0	3-0	2

ALL-STAR GAME RECORD

	W	L	Pct.	ERA	GS	CG	ShO	Sv.-Opp.	IP	H	R	ER	HR	BB-IBB	SO
All-Star Game totals (1 year)	1	0	1.000	9.00	0	0	0	0-0	1.0	2	1	1	1	0-0	0

BALFOUR, GRANT — P — TWINS

PERSONAL: Born December 30, 1977, in Sydney, Australia. ... 6-2/170. ... Throws right, bats right. ... Full name: Grant Robert Balfour.
HIGH SCHOOL: William Clarke College (Kellyville, New South Wales, Australia).
TRANSACTIONS/CAREER NOTES: Signed as non-drafted free agent by Minnesota Twins organization (January 19, 1997). ... On New Britain disabled list (April 6-26, 2001).
CAREER HITTING (MLB): 0-for-0 (.000), 0 R, 0 2B, 0 3B, 0 HR, 0 RBI.

Year League	W	L	Pct.	ERA	G	GS	CG	ShO	Sv.-Opp.	IP	H	R	ER	HR	BB-IBB	SO
1997— Gulf Coast Twins (GCL)	2	4	.333	3.76	13	12	0	0	0-...	67.0	*73	31	28	1	20-0	43
1998— Elizabethton (Appl.)	*7	2	.778	3.36	13	13	0	0	0-...	77.2	70	36	29	7	27-0	75
1999— Quad City (Midw.)	8	5	.615	3.53	19	14	0	0	1-...	91.2	66	39	36	7	37-0	95
2000— Fort Myers (FSL)	8	5	.615	4.25	35	10	0	0	6-...	89.0	91	46	42	8	34-2	90
2001— New Britain (East.)	2	1	.667	1.08	35	0	0	0	13-...	50.0	26	6	6	1	22-2	72
— Minnesota (A.L.)	0	0	...	13.50	2	0	0	0	0-0	2.2	3	4	4	2	3-0	2
— Edmonton (PCL)	2	2	.500	5.51	11	0	0	0	0-...	16.1	18	11	10	2	10-1	17
2002— Edmonton (PCL)	2	4	.333	4.16	58	0	0	0	8-...	71.1	60	34	33	3	30-1	88
Major League totals (1 year)	0	0	...	13.50	2	0	0	0	0-0	2.2	3	4	4	2	3-0	2

BANKS, BRIAN — OF/1B — MARLINS

PERSONAL: Born September 28, 1970, in Mesa, Ariz. ... 6-3/210. ... Bats both, throws right. ... Full name: Brian Glen Banks.
HIGH SCHOOL: Mountain View (Mesa, Ariz.).
COLLEGE: Brigham Young.
TRANSACTIONS/CAREER NOTES: Selected by Milwaukee Brewers organization in second round of free-agent draft (June 3, 1993); pick received as part of compensation for Seattle Mariners signing Type A free-agent P Chris Bosio. ... Released by Brewers (March 28, 2000). ... Signed by Fukuoka Daiei Hawks of Japan Pacific League (2000). ... Signed by Chicago Cubs organization (December 13, 2000). ... Released by Cubs (May 2, 2001). ... Signed by Florida Marlins organization (May 6, 2001). ... On Calgary disabled list (July 22-August 4, 2001). ... Granted free agency (October 15, 2001). ... Re-signed by Marlins organization (November 14, 2001).
STATISTICAL NOTES: Career major league grand slams: 1.
2002 GAMES PLAYED BY POSITION (MLB): OF—8; 3B—1; 1B—1.

Year	Team (League)	Pos.	G	AB	R	H	2B	3B	HR	RBI	BB	SO	SB-CS	Avg.	OBP	SLG	E	Avg.
			BATTING														FIELDING	
1993—	Helena (Pio.)	OF	12	48	8	19	1	1	2	8	11	8	1-2	.396	.500	.583	1	.962
—	Beloit (Midw.)	OF	38	147	21	36	5	1	4	19	7	34	1-2	.245	.284	.374	1	.980
1994—	Beloit (Midw.)	OF-1B-3B	65	237	41	71	13	1	9	47	29	40	11-1	.300	.375	.477	2	.985
—	Stockton (Calif.)	OF	67	246	29	58	9	1	4	28	38	46	3-8	.236	.340	.329	4	.966
1995—	El Paso (Texas)	OF-1B-3B	128	441	81	136	*39	10	12	78	*81	113	9-9	.308	.413	.524	10	.962
1996—	New Orleans (A.A.)	O-3-DH-C	137	487	71	132	29	7	16	64	66	105	17-8	.271	.356	.458	8	.972
—	Milwaukee (A.L.)	OF-1B	4	7	2	4	2	0	1	2	1	2	0-0	.571	.625	1.286	0	1.000
1997—	Tucson (PCL)	OF-C-DH	98	378	53	112	26	3	10	63	35	83	7-3	.296	.353	.460	3	.986
—	Milwaukee (A.L.)	OF-1B-DH-3B	28	68	9	14	1	0	1	8	6	17	0-1	.206	.267	.265	2	.949
1998—	Louisville (I.L.)	O-DH-C-1-3	85	299	58	87	18	1	21	66	52	72	14-3	.291	.397	.569	6	.979
—	Milwaukee (N.L.)	C-1B-3B-OF	24	24	3	7	2	0	1	5	4	7	0-0	.292	.393	.500	1	.929
1999—	Milwaukee (N.L.)	1B-C-OF	105	219	34	53	7	1	5	22	25	59	6-1	.242	.317	.352	5	.988
—	Louisville (I.L.)	1B-OF-C	6	24	3	5	2	1	1	6	2	5	0-0	.208	.259	.500	1	.968
2000—	Fukuoka (Jp. West.)■		48	157	23	42	6	0	7	29	26	28	3-...	.268	...	.439	...	...
—	Fukuoka (Jap. Pac.)		32	74	6	11	2	0	0	4	8	23	0-...	.149	...	.176	...	...
2001—	Iowa (PCL)■	OF-1B	17	39	2	7	2	0	1	4	4	11	0-0	.179	.256	.308	0	1.000
—	Calgary (PCL)■	1B-OF-C	101	357	70	104	27	4	23	63	32	97	5-4	.291	.352	.583	8	.989
2002—	Calgary (PCL)	1B-OF-C-3B	130	439	90	136	38	3	19	89	73	77	10-5	.310	.410	.540	9	.988
—	Florida (N.L.)	OF-3B-1B	20	28	3	9	1	0	1	4	1	6	0-0	.321	.345	.464	1	.923
American League totals (2 years)			32	75	11	18	3	0	2	10	7	19	0-1	.240	.301	.360	2	.964
National League totals (3 years)			149	271	40	69	10	1	7	31	30	72	6-1	.255	.327	.376	7	.984
Major League totals (5 years)			181	346	51	87	13	1	9	41	37	91	6-2	.251	.321	.373	9	.982

BANKS, WILLIE — P

PERSONAL: Born February 27, 1969, in Jersey City, N.J. ... 6-1/200. ... Throws right, bats right. ... Full name: Willie Anthony Banks.
HIGH SCHOOL: St. Anthony (Jersey City, N.J.).
TRANSACTIONS/CAREER NOTES: Selected by Minnesota Twins organization in first round (third pick overall) of free-agent draft (June 2, 1987). ... Traded by Twins to Chicago Cubs for P Dave Stevens and C Matt Walbeck (November 24, 1993). ... Traded by Cubs to Los Angeles Dodgers for P Dax Winslett (June 19, 1995). ... Claimed on waivers by Florida Marlins (August 10, 1995). ... Claimed on waivers by Philadelphia Phillies (October 4, 1995). ... Released by Phillies (March 8, 1996). ... Signed by New York Yankees organization (January 3, 1997). ... Traded by Yankees to Arizona Diamondbacks for P Scott Brow and P Joe Lisio (June 3, 1998). ... Granted free agency (December 21, 1998). ... Signed by Orix Blue Wave of Japan Pacific League (1999). ... Signed by New York Mets organization (July 12, 2000). ... Granted free agency (October 18, 2000). ... Signed by Toronto Blue Jays organization (April 2, 2001). ... Released by Blue Jays (August 15, 2001). ... Signed by Boston Red Sox organization (August 23, 2001). ... Granted free agency (November 6, 2002).
STATISTICAL NOTES: Led Appalachian League with 28 wild pitches and tied for lead with three balks in 1987. ... Pitched 1-0 no-hit victory for Visalia against Palm Springs (May 24, 1989). ... Led California League with 22 wild pitches in 1989. ... Tied for Pacific Coast League lead with 14 wild pitches in 1991. ... Tied for A.L. lead with five balks in 1993.
MISCELLANEOUS: Appeared in two games as pinch runner and struck out in only appearance as pinch hitter with Florida (1995).
CAREER HITTING (MLB): 12-for-68 (.176), 5 R, 2 2B, 0 3B, 0 HR, 1 RBI.

Year	League	W	L	Pct.	ERA	G	GS	CG	ShO	Sv.-Opp.	IP	H	R	ER	HR	BB-IBB	SO
1987—	Elizabethton (Appl.)	1	8	.111	6.99	13	13	0	0	0-...	65.2	73	*71	*51	3	*62-0	71
1988—	Kenosha (Midw.)	10	10	.500	3.72	24	24	0	0	0-...	125.2	109	73	52	3	*107-2	113
1989—	Visalia (Calif.)	12	9	.571	2.59	27	27	7	•4	0-...	174.0	122	70	50	5	85-0	*173
—	Orlando (Sou.)	1	0	1.000	5.14	1	1	0	0	0-...	7.0	10	4	4	0	0-0	9
1990—	Orlando (Sou.)	7	9	.438	3.93	28	28	1	0	0-...	162.2	161	93	71	15	98-0	114
1991—	Portland (PCL)	9	8	.529	4.55	25	24	1	1	0-...	146.1	156	81	74	6	76-1	63
—	Minnesota (A.L.)	1	1	.500	5.71	5	3	0	0	0-0	17.1	21	15	11	1	12-0	16
1992—	Portland (PCL)	6	1	.857	1.92	11	11	2	1	0-...	75.0	62	20	16	2	34-0	41
—	Minnesota (A.L.)	4	4	.500	5.70	16	12	0	0	0-0	71.0	80	46	45	6	37-0	37
1993—	Minnesota (A.L.)	11	12	.478	4.04	31	30	0	0	0-0	171.1	186	91	77	17	78-2	138
1994—	Chicago (N.L.)■	8	12	.400	5.40	23	23	1	1	0-0	138.1	139	88	83	16	56-3	91
1995—	Chicago (N.L.)	0	1	.000	15.43	10	0	0	0	0-1	11.2	27	23	20	5	12-4	9
—	Los Angeles (N.L.)■	0	2	.000	4.03	6	6	0	0	0-0	29.0	36	21	13	2	16-2	23
—	Florida (N.L.)■	2	3	.400	4.32	9	9	0	0	0-0	50.0	43	27	24	7	30-1	30
1996—								Out of organized baseball.									
1997—	Columbus (I.L.)■	14	5	.737	4.27	33	24	1	0	3-...	154.0	164	87	73	18	45-0	130
—	New York (A.L.)	3	0	1.000	1.93	5	1	0	0	0-1	14.0	9	3	3	0	6-0	8
1998—	New York (A.L.)	1	1	.500	10.05	9	0	0	0	0-0	14.1	20	16	16	4	12-2	8
—	Arizona (N.L.)■	1	2	.333	3.09	33	0	0	0	1-2	43.2	34	21	15	2	25-2	32
1999—	Orix (Jp. West.)■	4	1	.800	3.23	10	6	0	0	0-...	39.0	36	15	14	...	23-...	35
—	Orix (Jap. Pac.)	3	3	.500	3.90	13	2	0	0	1-...	30.0	27	16	13	...	21-...	26
2000—	Surpass (Jp. West.)■	0	5	.000	6.36	13	10	0	0	0-...	58.0	69	44	41	...	55-...	37
—	Norfolk (I.L.)■	2	4	.333	5.08	9	9	0	0	0-...	51.1	56	32	29	5	25-2	20
2001—	Syracuse (I.L.)■	8	5	.615	3.25	24	23	0	0	0-...	146.2	151	63	53	12	53-0	121
—	Pawtucket (I.L.)■	2	0	1.000	1.42	2	2	0	0	0-...	12.2	8	3	2	0	3-0	12
—	Boston (A.L.)	0	0	...	0.84	5	0	0	0	0-0	10.2	5	4	1	0	4-0	10
2002—	Boston (A.L.)	2	1	.667	3.23	29	0	0	0	1-1	39.0	32	15	14	5	14-0	26
—	Pawtucket (I.L.)	1	2	.333	4.50	6	4	0	0	1-...	26.0	20	14	13	2	9-0	15
A.L. totals (7 years)		22	19	.537	4.45	100	46	0	0	1-2	337.2	353	190	167	33	163-4	243
N.L. totals (3 years)		11	20	.355	5.12	81	38	1	1	1-3	272.2	279	180	155	32	139-12	185
Major League totals (9 years)		33	39	.458	4.75	181	84	1	1	2-5	610.1	632	370	322	65	302-16	428

BARAJAS, ROD — C — DIAMONDBACKS

PERSONAL: Born September 5, 1975, in Ontario, Calif. ... 6-2/229. ... Bats right, throws right. ... Full name: Rodrigo Richard Barajas.
HIGH SCHOOL: Sante Fe Springs (Calif.).
JUNIOR COLLEGE: Cerritos.
TRANSACTIONS/CAREER NOTES: Signed as non-drafted free agent by Arizona Diamondbacks organization (January 23, 1996). ... Loaned by Diamondbacks to Visalia, Oakland Athletics organization (April 5-June 16, 1996).

STATISTICAL NOTES: Led Pioneer League catchers with .985 fielding percentage in 1996. ... Led Texas League catchers with 787 putouts, 95 assists, 14 errors and 896 total chances in 1999. ... Tied Pacific Coast League lead with 11 sacrifice flies in 2000. ... Led Pacific Coast League catchers with 69 assists and tied for lead with 11 errors in 2000.
2002 GAMES PLAYED BY POSITION (MLB): C—69; 1B—1.

			BATTING														FIELDING	
Year	**Team (League)**	**Pos.**	**G**	**AB**	**R**	**H**	**2B**	**3B**	**HR**	**RBI**	**BB**	**SO**	**SB-CS**	**Avg.**	**OBP**	**SLG**	**E**	**Avg.**
1996—	Visalia (Calif.)■	C	27	74	6	12	3	0	0	8	7	21	0-0	.162	.244	.203	0	1.000
—	Lethbridge (Pio.)■	C-1B	51	175	47	59	9	3	10	50	12	24	2-1	.337	.378	.594	5	†.986
1997—	High Desert (Calif.)	C-1B	57	199	24	53	11	0	7	30	8	41	0-2	.266	.297	.427	3	.993
1998—	High Desert (Calif.)	C	113	442	67	134	26	0	23	81	25	81	1-1	.303	.345	.518	14	.983
1999—	El Paso (Texas)	C-DH-1B	127	510	77	162	41	2	14	95	24	73	2-0	.318	.354	.488	†14	.985
—	Arizona (N.L.)	C	5	16	3	4	1	0	1	3	1	1	0-0	.250	.294	.500	0	1.000
2000—	Tucson (PCL)	C-1B-3B	110	416	43	94	25	0	13	75	14	65	4-3	.226	.253	.380	‡14	.980
—	Arizona (N.L.)	C	5	13	1	3	0	0	1	3	0	4	0-0	.231	.231	.462	0	1.000
2001—	Arizona (N.L.)	C	51	106	9	17	3	0	3	9	4	26	0-0	.160	.191	.274	1	.995
—	Tucson (PCL)	C-1B-3B	45	162	23	52	13	0	9	32	9	23	3-1	.321	.366	.568	3	.990
2002—	Arizona (N.L.)	C-1B	70	154	12	36	10	0	3	23	10	25	1-0	.234	.288	.357	1	.997
—	Tucson (PCL)	C-1B	5	16	2	7	1	0	1	1	1	2	0-0	.438	.471	.688	0	1.000
Major League totals (4 years)			131	289	25	60	14	0	8	38	15	56	1-0	.208	.252	.339	2	.996

DIVISION SERIES RECORD

			BATTING														FIELDING	
Year	**Team (League)**	**Pos.**	**G**	**AB**	**R**	**H**	**2B**	**3B**	**HR**	**RBI**	**BB**	**SO**	**SB-CS**	**Avg.**	**OBP**	**SLG**	**E**	**Avg.**
2001—	Arizona (N.L.)	C	1	0	0	0	0	0	0	0	0	0	0-0	...	...	...	0	...
2002—	Arizona (N.L.)	C	2	4	1	1	0	0	1	1	0	1	0-0	.250	.250	1.000	0	1.000
Division series totals (2 years)			3	4	1	1	0	0	1	1	0	1	0-0	.250	.250	1.000	0	1.000

CHAMPIONSHIP SERIES RECORD

			BATTING														FIELDING	
Year	**Team (League)**	**Pos.**	**G**	**AB**	**R**	**H**	**2B**	**3B**	**HR**	**RBI**	**BB**	**SO**	**SB-CS**	**Avg.**	**OBP**	**SLG**	**E**	**Avg.**
2001—	Arizona (N.L.)								Did not play.									

WORLD SERIES RECORD

NOTES: Member of World Series championship team (2001).

			BATTING														FIELDING	
Year	**Team (League)**	**Pos.**	**G**	**AB**	**R**	**H**	**2B**	**3B**	**HR**	**RBI**	**BB**	**SO**	**SB-CS**	**Avg.**	**OBP**	**SLG**	**E**	**Avg.**
2001—	Arizona (N.L.)	C	2	5	1	2	0	0	1	1	0	0	0-0	.400	.400	1.000	0	1.000

BARCELO, LORENZO P

PERSONAL: Born August 10, 1977, in San Pedro de Macoris, Dominican Republic. ... 6-4/230. ... Throws right, bats right. ... Full name: Lorenzo A. Barcelo. ... Brother of Orger Barcelo, player in Atlanta Braves organization (1990).
HIGH SCHOOL: Sanatonio (San Pedro de Macoris, Dominican Republic).
TRANSACTIONS/CAREER NOTES: Signed as non-drafted free agent by San Francisco Giants organization (May 23, 1994). ... Traded by Giants with SS Mike Caruso, OF Brian Manning, P Keith Foulke, P Bob Howry and P Ken Vining by Giants to Chicago White Sox for P Wilson Alvarez, P Danny Darwin and P Roberto Hernandez (July 31, 1997). ... On Birmingham disabled list (April 2, 1998-entire season); included rehabilitation assignment to Arizona League White Sox (June 29-July 9). ... On Birmingham disabled list (April 8-August 13, 1999); included rehabilitation assignment to Burlington (August 11-13). ... On Chicago disabled list (June 4, 2001-remainder of season). ... On Charlotte disabled list (May 4, 2002-remainder of season). ... Granted free agency (October 15, 2002).
STATISTICAL NOTES: Led Midwest League with 19 home runs allowed in 1996.
CAREER HITTING (MLB): 0-for-0 (.000), 0 R, 0 2B, 0 3B, 0 HR, 0 RBI.

Year	**League**	**W**	**L**	**Pct.**	**ERA**	**G**	**GS**	**CG**	**ShO**	**Sv.-Opp.**	**IP**	**H**	**R**	**ER**	**HR**	**BB-IBB**	**SO**
1994—	Dominican Giants (DSL)	0	0	...	4.32	22	0	0	0	0-...	41.2	45	37	20	...	28-...	25
1995—	Bellingham (N'West)	3	2	.600	3.45	12	11	0	0	0-...	47.0	43	23	18	3	19-0	34
1996—	Burlington (Midw.)	12	10	.545	3.54	26	26	1	0	0-...	152.2	138	70	60	19	46-0	139
1997—	San Jose (Calif.)	5	4	.556	3.94	16	16	1	1	0-...	89.0	91	45	39	13	30-2	89
—	Shreveport (Texas)	2	0	1.000	4.02	5	5	0	0	0-...	31.1	30	19	14	4	8-0	20
—	Birmingham (Sou.)■	2	1	.667	4.86	6	6	0	0	0-...	33.1	36	20	18	2	9-0	29
1998—	Arizona White Sox (Ariz.)	0	1	.000	1.50	3	3	0	0	0-...	6.0	6	1	1	0	0-0	9
1999—	Arizona White Sox (Ariz.)	2	1	.667	1.69	9	9	0	0	0-...	42.2	36	14	8	0	6-0	57
—	Burlington (Midw.)	1	0	1.000	3.60	1	1	0	0	0-...	5.0	3	2	2	1	0-0	6
—	Birmingham (Sou.)	0	1	.000	3.60	4	4	0	0	0-...	20.0	14	8	8	0	6-0	14
2000—	Charlotte (I.L.)	5	6	.455	4.26	17	17	0	0	0-...	99.1	114	53	47	20	17-1	62
—	Chicago (A.L.)	4	2	.667	3.69	22	1	0	0	0-1	39.0	34	17	16	5	9-1	26
2001—	Charlotte (I.L.)	1	0	1.000	5.40	2	0	0	0	0-...	5.0	6	3	3	2	1-1	5
—	Chicago (A.L.)	1	0	1.000	4.71	17	0	0	0	0-0	21.0	24	13	11	1	8-2	15
2002—	Chicago (A.L.)	0	1	.000	9.00	4	0	0	0	0-0	6.0	9	6	6	1	1-0	1
—	Charlotte (I.L.)	0	0	...	6.75	2	1	0	0	0-...	5.1	5	4	4	1	1-0	1
Major League totals (3 years)		5	3	.625	4.50	43	1	0	0	0-1	66.0	67	36	33	7	18-3	42

DIVISION SERIES RECORD

Year	**League**	**W**	**L**	**Pct.**	**ERA**	**G**	**GS**	**CG**	**ShO**	**Sv.-Opp.**	**IP**	**H**	**R**	**ER**	**HR**	**BB-IBB**	**SO**
2000—	Chicago (A.L.)	0	0	...	0.00	1	0	0	0	0-0	1.2	0	0	0	0	1-0	0

BARD, JOSH C INDIANS

PERSONAL: Born March 30, 1978, in Ithaca, N.Y. ... 6-3/215. ... Bats both, throws right. ... Full name: Joshua David Bard.
HIGH SCHOOL: Cherry Creek (Englewood, Colo.).
COLLEGE: Texas Tech.
TRANSACTIONS/CAREER NOTES: Selected by Minnesota Twins organization in 35th round of free-agent draft (June 4, 1996); did not sign. ... Selected by Colorado Rockies organization in third round of free-agent draft (June 2, 1999). ... Traded by Rockies with OF Jody Gerut to Cleveland Indians for OF Jacob Cruz (June 2, 2001).

STATISTICAL NOTES: Led International League catchers with 60 assists in 2002.
2002 GAMES PLAYED BY POSITION (MLB): C—24.

		BATTING														FIELDING	
Year Team (League)	**Pos.**	**G**	**AB**	**R**	**H**	**2B**	**3B**	**HR**	**RBI**	**BB**	**SO**	**SB-CS**	**Avg.**	**OBP**	**SLG**	**E**	**Avg.**
2000—Salem (Caro.)	C	93	309	40	88	17	0	2	25	32	33	3-1	.285	.352	.359	10	.987
—Colo. Springs (PCL)	C	4	17	0	4	0	0	0	1	0	2	0-0	.235	.235	.235	1	.923
2001—Carolina (Sou.)	C	35	124	14	32	13	0	1	24	19	23	0-1	.258	.359	.387	2	.993
—Akron (East.)■	C	51	194	26	54	11	0	4	25	16	27	0-0	.278	.338	.397	4	.986
—Mahoning Val. (NY-P)	C	13	44	7	12	4	0	2	8	6	2	0-1	.273	.373	.500	3	.769
—Buffalo (I.L.)	DH	1	4	0	0	0	0	0	0	0	1	0-0	.000	.000	.000	...	...
2002—Buffalo (I.L.)	C	94	344	36	102	26	2	6	53	20	45	0-0	.297	.332	.436	*11	.984
—Cleveland (A.L.)	C	24	90	9	20	5	0	3	12	4	13	0-0	.222	.255	.378	2	.988
Major League totals (1 year)		24	90	9	20	5	0	3	12	4	13	0-0	.222	.255	.378	2	.988

BARKER, KEVIN 1B

PERSONAL: Born July 26, 1975, in Bristol, Va. ... 6-3/205. ... Bats left, throws left. ... Full name: Kevin Stewart Barker.
HIGH SCHOOL: Virginia (Bristol, Va.).
COLLEGE: Virginia Tech.
TRANSACTIONS/CAREER NOTES: Selected by Milwaukee Brewers organization in third round of free-agent draft (June 4, 1996). ... Traded by Brewers to San Diego Padres for C Dusty Wathan (March 20, 2002). ... Released by Padres (September 30, 2002).
STATISTICAL NOTES: Led Pioneer League first basemen with 44 assists in 1996. ... Led International League first basemen with 73 assists in 1998.
2002 GAMES PLAYED BY POSITION (MLB): 1B—6.

		BATTING														FIELDING	
Year Team (League)	**Pos.**	**G**	**AB**	**R**	**H**	**2B**	**3B**	**HR**	**RBI**	**BB**	**SO**	**SB-CS**	**Avg.**	**OBP**	**SLG**	**E**	**Avg.**
1996—Ogden (Pio.)	1B	71	281	61	89	19	4	9	56	46	54	0-2	.317	.412	.509	11	.982
1997—Stockton (Calif.)	1B	70	267	47	81	20	5	13	45	25	60	4-3	.303	.362	.562	6	.988
—El Paso (Texas)	1B	65	238	37	66	15	6	10	63	28	40	3-3	.277	.352	.517	9	.982
1998—El Paso (Texas)	1B	20	85	14	26	6	0	5	14	3	21	2-1	.306	.337	.553	1	.995
—Louisville (I.L.)	1B-OF	124	463	59	128	26	4	23	96	36	97	2-5	.276	.330	.499	9	.991
1999—Louisville (I.L.)	1B-OF	121	442	89	123	27	5	23	87	59	94	2-2	.278	.363	.518	10	.991
—Milwaukee (N.L.)	1B	38	117	13	33	3	0	3	23	9	19	1-0	.282	.331	.385	1	.996
2000—Milwaukee (N.L.)	1B	40	100	14	22	5	0	2	9	20	21	1-0	.220	.352	.330	2	.993
—Indianapolis (I.L.)	1B	85	286	41	56	10	1	11	44	52	76	0-1	.196	.316	.353	3	.995
2001—Indianapolis (I.L.)	OF-1B	51	159	12	30	5	0	4	20	20	40	0-0	.189	.282	.296	0	1.000
—Huntsville (Sou.)	1B-OF	66	232	42	75	16	1	8	38	35	51	0-2	.323	.410	.504	4	.992
2002—Portland (PCL)■	1B-OF	113	390	54	98	14	1	14	48	46	70	1-1	.251	.333	.400	4	.996
—San Diego (N.L.)	1B	7	19	0	3	0	0	0	0	1	6	1-0	.158	.200	.158	0	1.000
Major League totals (3 years)		85	236	27	58	8	0	5	32	30	46	3-0	.246	.331	.343	3	.995

BARRETT, MICHAEL C EXPOS

PERSONAL: Born October 22, 1976, in Atlanta. ... 6-2/200. ... Bats right, throws right. ... Full name: Michael Patrick Barrett.
HIGH SCHOOL: Pace Academy (Atlanta).
TRANSACTIONS/CAREER NOTES: Selected by Montreal Expos organization in first round (28th pick overall) of free-agent draft (June 1, 1995). ... On Montreal disabled list (June 24-July 11, 1999); included rehabilitation assignment to Ottawa (July 9-10).
2002 GAMES PLAYED BY POSITION (MLB): C—110; 1B—6.

		BATTING														FIELDING	
Year Team (League)	**Pos.**	**G**	**AB**	**R**	**H**	**2B**	**3B**	**HR**	**RBI**	**BB**	**SO**	**SB-CS**	**Avg.**	**OBP**	**SLG**	**E**	**Avg.**
1995—GC Expos (GCL)	SS-3B	50	183	22	57	13	4	0	19	15	19	7-6	.311	.362	.426	25	.893
—Vermont (NY-Penn)	SS	3	10	0	1	0	0	0	1	1	1	0-0	.100	.167	.100	0	1.000
1996—Delmarva (S.Atl.)	C-DH-3B	129	474	57	113	29	4	4	62	18	42	5-11	.238	.277	.342	15	.978
1997—W. Palm Beach (FSL)	C-DH	119	423	52	120	30	0	8	61	36	49	7-4	.284	.340	.411	13	.982
1998—Harrisburg (East.)	C-3B-DH	120	453	78	145	32	2	19	87	27	43	7-6	.320	.358	.525	12	.981
—Montreal (N.L.)	C-3B	8	23	3	7	2	0	1	2	3	6	0-0	.304	.407	.522	3	.912
1999—Montreal (N.L.)	3B-C-SS	126	433	53	127	32	3	8	52	32	39	0-2	.293	.345	.436	14	.973
—Ottawa (I.L.)	3B	2	7	1	3	0	0	0	2	1	0	0-1	.429	.500	.429	1	.800
2000—Ottawa (I.L.)	3B-C	31	120	21	43	7	0	2	19	13	10	1-0	.358	.430	.467	5	.945
—Montreal (N.L.)	3B-C	89	271	28	58	15	1	1	22	23	35	0-1	.214	.277	.288	15	.949
2001—Montreal (N.L.)	C	132	472	42	118	33	2	6	38	25	54	2-1	.250	.289	.367	7	.993
2002—Montreal (N.L.)	C-1B	117	376	41	99	20	1	12	49	40	65	6-3	.263	.332	.418	9	.989
Major League totals (5 years)		472	1575	167	409	102	7	28	163	123	199	8-7	.260	.315	.387	48	.982

BARTOSH, CLIFF P PADRES

PERSONAL: Born September 5, 1979, in West, Texas. ... 6-2/175. ... Throws left, bats left. ... Full name: Clifford Paul Bartosh.
HIGH SCHOOL: Duncanville (Texas).
TRANSACTIONS/CAREER NOTES: Selected by San Diego Padres organization in 29th round of free-agent draft (June 27, 1998).

Year League	**W**	**L**	**Pct.**	**ERA**	**G**	**GS**	**CG**	**ShO**	**Sv.-Opp.**	**IP**	**H**	**R**	**ER**	**HR**	**BB-IBB**	**SO**
1998—Arizona Padres (Ariz.)	3	2	.600	3.48	13	5	0	0	0-...	44.0	43	23	17	2	16-0	43
1999—Fort Wayne (Midw.)	5	12	.294	4.44	35	20	1	1	0-...	129.2	136	76	64	14	49-0	100
2000—Fort Wayne (Midw.)	8	4	.667	3.04	50	4	0	0	1-...	77.0	50	40	26	6	44-3	94
2001—Lake Elsinore (Calif.)	6	2	.750	1.58	38	0	0	0	10-...	45.2	42	17	8	2	12-5	66
—Mobile (Sou.)	1	2	.333	3.97	20	0	0	0	2-...	22.2	20	12	10	5	13-1	20
2002—Mobile (Sou.)	2	4	.333	3.18	62	0	0	0	25-...	70.2	54	28	25	4	32-5	70

BATISTA, MIGUEL P DIAMONDBACKS

PERSONAL: Born February 19, 1971, in Santo Domingo, Dominican Republic. ... 6-2/195. ... Throws right, bats right. ... Full name: Miguel Jerez Decartes Batista.

HIGH SCHOOL: Nuevo Horizondes (San Pedro de Macoris, Dominican Republic).

TRANSACTIONS/CAREER NOTES: Signed as non-drafted free agent by Montreal Expos organization (February 29, 1988). ... Selected by Pittsburgh Pirates from Expos organization in Rule 5 major league draft (December 9, 1991). ... Returned to Expos organization (April 23, 1992). ... On disabled list (April 14-30 and May 7, 1994-remainder of season). ... Released by Expos (November 18, 1994). ... Signed by Florida Marlins organization (December 9, 1994). ... Claimed on waivers by Chicago Cubs (December 17, 1996). ... Traded by Cubs to Expos for OF Henry Rodriguez (December 12, 1997). ... On Montreal disabled list (July 16-August 10, 1999); included rehabilitation assignment to Ottawa (July 30-August 8). ... Traded by Expos to Kansas City Royals for P Brad Rigby (April 25, 2000). ... Granted free agency (October 2, 2000). ... Signed by Arizona Diamondbacks organization (November 3, 2000).

CAREER HITTING (MLB): 17-for-162 (.105), 13 R, 3 2B, 0 3B, 2 HR, 5 RBI.

Year League	W	L	Pct.	ERA	G	GS	CG	ShO	Sv.-Opp.	IP	H	R	ER	HR	BB-IBB	SO
1988—	Dominican Summer League statistics unavailable.															
1989—Dominican Expos (DSL)	1	7	.125	4.24	13	11	0	0	0-...	68.0	56	46	32	...	50-...	60
1990—Gulf Coast Expos (GCL)	4	3	.571	2.06	9	6	0	0	0-...	39.1	33	16	9	0	17-0	21
—Rockford (Midw.)	0	1	.000	8.76	3	2	0	0	0-...	12.1	16	13	12	2	5-0	7
1991—Rockford (Midw.)	11	5	.688	4.04	23	23	2	1	0-...	133.2	126	74	60	1	57-0	90
1992—Pittsburgh (N.L.)■	0	0	...	9.00	1	0	0	0	0-0	2.0	4	2	2	1	3-0	1
—West Palm Beach (FSL)■	7	7	.500	3.79	24	24	1	0	0-...	135.1	130	69	57	3	54-1	92
1993—Harrisburg (East.)	13	5	.722	4.34	26	26	0	0	0-...	141.0	139	79	68	11	86-0	91
1994—Harrisburg (East.)	0	1	.000	2.38	3	3	0	0	0-...	11.1	8	3	3	0	9-0	5
1995—Charlotte (I.L.)■	6	12	.333	4.80	34	18	0	0	0-...	116.1	118	79	62	11	60-2	58
1996—Charlotte (I.L.)	4	3	.571	5.38	47	2	0	0	4-...	77.0	93	57	46	4	39-0	56
—Florida (N.L.)	0	0	...	5.56	9	0	0	0	0-0	11.1	9	8	7	0	7-2	6
1997—Iowa (A.A.)■	9	4	.692	4.20	31	14	2	•2	0-...	122.0	117	60	57	19	38-1	95
—Chicago (N.L.)	0	5	.000	5.70	11	6	0	0	0-0	36.1	36	24	23	4	24-2	27
1998—Montreal (N.L.)■	3	5	.375	3.80	56	13	0	0	0-0	135.0	141	66	57	12	65-7	92
1999—Montreal (N.L.)	8	7	.533	4.88	39	17	2	1	1-1	134.2	146	88	73	10	58-2	95
—Ottawa (I.L.)	0	1	.000	2.25	3	3	0	0	0-...	8.0	3	2	2	1	4-0	7
2000—Montreal (N.L.)	0	1	.000	14.04	4	0	0	0	0-2	8.1	19	14	13	2	3-0	7
—Kansas City (A.L.)■	2	6	.250	7.74	14	9	0	0	0-0	57.0	66	54	49	17	34-2	30
—Omaha (PCL)	2	2	.500	6.04	18	1	0	0	3-...	28.1	35	20	19	6	7-0	27
2001—Arizona (N.L.)■	11	8	.579	3.36	48	18	0	0	0-0	139.1	113	57	52	13	60-2	90
2002—Arizona (N.L.)	8	9	.471	4.29	36	29	1	0	0-0	184.2	172	99	88	12	70-3	112
A.L. totals (1 year)	2	6	.250	7.74	14	9	0	0	0-0	57.0	66	54	49	17	34-2	30
N.L. totals (8 years)	30	35	.462	4.35	204	83	3	1	1-3	651.2	640	358	315	54	290-18	430
Major League totals (8 years)	32	41	.438	4.62	218	92	3	1	1-3	708.2	706	412	364	71	324-20	460

DIVISION SERIES RECORD

Year League	W	L	Pct.	ERA	G	GS	CG	ShO	Sv.-Opp.	IP	H	R	ER	HR	BB-IBB	SO
2001—Arizona (N.L.)	1	0	1.000	2.70	2	1	0	0	0-0	6.2	3	2	2	1	1-0	4
2002—Arizona (N.L.)	0	1	.000	9.82	1	1	0	0	0-0	3.2	5	4	4	0	3-0	1
Division series totals (2 years)	1	1	.500	5.23	3	2	0	0	0-0	10.1	8	6	6	1	4-0	5

CHAMPIONSHIP SERIES RECORD

Year League	W	L	Pct.	ERA	G	GS	CG	ShO	Sv.-Opp.	IP	H	R	ER	HR	BB-IBB	SO
2001—Arizona (N.L.)	0	1	.000	5.14	2	1	0	0	0-0	7.0	5	4	4	2	2-0	3

WORLD SERIES RECORD

NOTES: Member of World Series championship team (2001).

Year League	W	L	Pct.	ERA	G	GS	CG	ShO	Sv.-Opp.	IP	H	R	ER	HR	BB-IBB	SO
2001—Arizona (N.L.)	0	0	...	0.00	2	1	0	0	0-0	8.0	5	0	0	0	5-0	6

BATISTA, TONY 3B ORIOLES

PERSONAL: Born December 9, 1973, in Puerto Plata, Dominican Republic. ... 6-0/205. ... Bats right, throws right. ... Full name: Leocadio Francisco Batista.

TRANSACTIONS/CAREER NOTES: Signed as non-drafted free agent by Oakland Athletics organization (February 8, 1991). ... On Tacoma disabled list (July 29, 1993-remainder of season). ... On Oakland disabled list (August 27-September 12, 1997); included rehabilitation assignment to Edmonton (September 11-12). ... Selected by Arizona Diamondbacks in first round (27th pick overall) of expansion draft (November 18, 1997). ... Traded by Diamondbacks with P John Frascatore to Toronto Blue Jays for P Dan Plesac (June 12, 1999). ... Claimed on waivers by Baltimore Orioles (June 25, 2001).

STATISTICAL NOTES: Led California League shortstops with .950 fielding percentage in 1994. ... Had 17-game hitting streak (July 30-August 16, 1999). ... Led A.L. third basemen with 35 double plays in 2000 and 35 in 2002. ... Career major league grand slams: 5.

2002 GAMES PLAYED BY POSITION (MLB): 3B—154; DH—7.

		BATTING														FIELDING	
Year Team (League)	Pos.	G	AB	R	H	2B	3B	HR	RBI	BB	SO	SB-CS	Avg.	OBP	SLG	E	Avg.
1991—Dom. Athletics (DSL)		46	166	16	31	5	1	2	15	23	16	4-...	.187	...	.265	...	...
1992—Ariz. Athletics (Ariz.)	2B-SS-OF	45	167	32	41	6	2	0	22	15	29	1-0	.246	.315	.305	8	.960
1993—Ariz. Athletics (Ariz.)	3B-2B-SS	24	104	21	34	6	2	2	17	6	14	6-2	.327	.357	.481	3	.967
—Tacoma (PCL)	OF	4	12	1	2	1	0	0	1	1	4	0-0	.167	.286	.250	0	1.000
1994—Modesto (Calif.)	SS-2B	119	466	91	131	26	3	17	68	54	108	7-7	.281	.359	.459	30	†.949
1995—Huntsville (Sou.)	SS-2B	120	419	55	107	23	1	16	61	29	98	7-8	.255	.305	.430	29	.949
1996—Edmonton (PCL)	SS	57	205	33	66	17	4	8	40	15	30	2-1	.322	.372	.561	8	.973
—Oakland (A.L.)	2-3-DH-S	74	238	38	71	10	2	6	25	19	49	7-3	.298	.350	.433	5	.983
1997—Oakland (A.L.)	S-3-DH-2	68	188	22	38	10	1	4	18	14	31	2-2	.202	.265	.330	8	.971
—Edmonton (PCL)	SS-DH	33	124	25	39	10	1	3	21	17	18	2-2	.315	.396	.484	6	.952
1998—Arizona (N.L.)■	2B-SS-3B	106	293	46	80	16	1	18	41	18	52	1-1	.273	.318	.519	6	.982
1999—Arizona (N.L.)	SS	44	144	16	37	5	0	5	21	16	17	2-0	.257	.335	.396	4	.979
—Toronto (A.L.)■	SS	98	375	61	107	25	1	26	79	22	79	2-0	.285	.328	.565	12	.975

Year Team (League)	Pos.	G	AB	R	H	2B	3B	HR	RBI	BB	SO	SB-CS	Avg.	OBP	SLG	E	Avg.
		BATTING														FIELDING	
2000—Toronto (A.L.)	3B	154	620	96	163	32	2	41	114	35	121	5-4	.263	.307	.519	17	.963
2001—Toronto (A.L.)	3B	72	271	29	56	11	1	13	45	13	66	0-1	.207	.251	.399	10	.953
—Baltimore (A.L.)■	DH-3B-SS	84	308	41	82	16	5	12	42	19	47	5-1	.266	.305	.468	6	.965
2002—Baltimore (A.L.)	3B-DH	161	615	90	150	36	1	31	87	50	107	5-4	.244	.309	.457	16	.962
American League totals (6 years)		711	2615	377	667	140	13	133	410	172	500	26-15	.255	.305	.471	74	.968
National League totals (2 years)		150	437	62	117	21	1	23	62	34	69	3-1	.268	.324	.478	10	.981
Major League totals (7 years)		861	3052	439	784	161	14	156	472	206	569	29-16	.257	.308	.472	84	.970

ALL-STAR GAME RECORD

	AB	R	H	2B	3B	HR	RBI	BB	SO	SB-CS	Avg.	OBP	SLG	E	Avg.
All-Star Game totals (2 years)	4	1	1	0	0	0	1	0	2	0-0	.250	.250	.250	0	1.000

BAUER, RICK — P — ORIOLES

PERSONAL: Born January 10, 1977, in Garden Grove, Calif. ... 6-6/212. ... Throws right, bats right. ... Full name: Richard Edward Bauer.
HIGH SCHOOL: Centennial (Meridian, Idaho).
JUNIOR COLLEGE: Treasure Valley (Ore.).
TRANSACTIONS/CAREER NOTES: Selected by Baltimore Orioles organization in fifth round of free-agent draft (June 3, 1997).
CAREER HITTING (MLB): 0-for-0 (.000), 0 R, 0 2B, 0 3B, 0 HR, 0 RBI.

Year League	W	L	Pct.	ERA	G	GS	CG	ShO	Sv.-Opp.	IP	H	R	ER	HR	BB-IBB	SO
1997—Bluefield (Appl.)	8	3	.727	2.86	13	13	0	0	0-...	72.1	58	31	23	1	20-0	67
—Delmarva (S.Atl.)	0	0	...	0.00	1	0	0	0	1-...	2.0	0	0	0	0	1-0	2
1998—Delmarva (S.Atl.)	5	8	.385	4.73	22	22	1	1	0-...	118.0	127	69	62	11	44-0	81
1999—Frederick (Caro.)	10	9	.526	4.56	26	26	•4	0	0-...	152.0	159	85	77	17	54-2	123
2000—Bowie (East.)	6	8	.429	5.30	26	23	1	0	1-...	129.0	154	89	76	16	39-1	87
—Frederick (Caro.)	0	1	.000	5.21	3	3	0	0	0-...	19.0	20	13	11	1	6-0	15
2001—Bowie (East.)	2	6	.250	3.54	9	9	2	0	0-...	61.0	52	27	24	8	10-0	34
—Rochester (I.L.)	10	4	.714	3.89	19	18	1	1	0-...	113.1	119	63	49	10	28-0	89
—Baltimore (A.L.)	0	5	.000	4.64	6	6	0	0	0-0	33.0	35	22	17	7	9-0	16
2002—Baltimore (A.L.)	6	7	.462	3.98	56	1	0	0	1-5	83.2	84	41	37	12	36-4	45
—Rochester (I.L.)	0	1	.000	6.75	1	1	0	0	0-...	4.0	4	4	3	2	2-0	1
Major League totals (2 years)	6	12	.333	4.17	62	7	0	0	1-5	116.2	119	63	54	19	45-4	61

BAUTISTA, DANNY — OF — DIAMONDBACKS

PERSONAL: Born May 24, 1972, in Santo Domingo, Dominican Republic. ... 5-11/204. ... Bats right, throws right. ... Full name: Daniel Bautista. ... Stepson of Jesus de la Rosa, outfielder with Houston Astros (1974). ... Name pronounced bough-TEES-tuh.
TRANSACTIONS/CAREER NOTES: Signed as non-drafted free agent by Detroit Tigers organization (June 24, 1989). ... On disabled list (May 24-July 10, 1991). ... On Toledo disabled list (June 8-July 31, 1994). ... Traded by Tigers to Atlanta Braves for OF Anton French (May 31, 1996). ... On Atlanta disabled list (June 28, 1996-remainder of season). ... On Atlanta disabled list (March 23-April 23, 1997); included rehabilitation assignment to Richmond (April 18-23). ... On Atlanta disabled list (April 17-May 7 and August 25-September 17, 1998); included rehabilitation assignment to Greenville (May 5-7). ... Released by Braves (April 2, 1999). ... Signed by Florida Marlins organization (April 8, 1999). ... On Calgary disabled list (June 1-8, 1999). ... Traded by Marlins to Arizona Diamondbacks for IF Andy Fox (June 10, 2000). ... Granted free agency (November 8, 2001). ... Re-signed by Diamondbacks (December 19, 2001). ... On disabled list (May 23, 2002-remainder of season).
RECORDS: Shares major league single-game record for most strikeouts (nine-inning game)—5 (May 28, 1995).
STATISTICAL NOTES: Had 15-game hitting streak (August 13-September 1, 2000).
2002 GAMES PLAYED BY POSITION (MLB): OF—39.

Year Team (League)	Pos.	G	AB	R	H	2B	3B	HR	RBI	BB	SO	SB-CS	Avg.	OBP	SLG	E	Avg.
		BATTING														FIELDING	
1989—					Dominican Summer League statistics unavailable.												
1990—Bristol (Appl.)	OF	27	95	9	26	3	0	2	12	8	21	2-3	.274	.330	.368	0	1.000
1991—Fayetteville (S.Atl.)	OF	69	234	21	45	6	4	1	30	21	65	7-7	.192	.259	.265	4	.973
1992—Fayetteville (S.Atl.)	OF	121	453	59	122	22	0	5	52	29	76	18-20	.269	.319	.351	6	.974
1993—London (East.)	OF-DH	117	424	55	121	21	1	6	48	32	69	28-12	.285	.334	.382	3	.989
—Detroit (A.L.)	OF-DH	17	61	6	19	3	0	1	9	1	10	3-1	.311	.317	.410	0	1.000
1994—Detroit (A.L.)	OF-DH	31	99	12	23	4	1	4	15	3	18	1-2	.232	.255	.414	0	1.000
—Toledo (I.L.)	OF	27	98	7	25	7	0	2	14	6	23	2-3	.255	.292	.388	1	.982
1995—Detroit (A.L.)	OF	89	271	28	55	9	0	7	27	12	68	4-1	.203	.237	.314	2	.988
—Toledo (I.L.)	OF	18	58	6	14	3	0	0	4	1	10	1-2	.241	.290	.293	2	.943
1996—Detroit (A.L.)	OF-DH	25	64	12	16	2	0	2	8	9	15	1-2	.250	.342	.375	1	.974
—Atlanta (N.L.)■	OF	17	20	1	3	0	0	0	1	2	5	0-0	.150	.261	.150	0	1.000
1997—Richmond (I.L.)	OF-DH	46	170	28	48	10	3	2	28	19	30	1-0	.282	.356	.412	0	1.000
—Atlanta (N.L.)	OF	64	103	14	25	3	2	3	9	5	24	2-0	.243	.282	.398	1	.984
1998—Atlanta (N.L.)	OF-DH	82	144	17	36	11	0	3	17	7	21	1-0	.250	.281	.389	2	.959
—Greenville (Sou.)	OF	2	6	1	2	0	0	1	2	1	1	0-0	.333	.429	.833	0	1.000
1999—Calgary (PCL)■	OF-DH	38	135	25	43	8	1	8	28	11	18	3-3	.319	.374	.570	3	.969
—Florida (N.L.)	OF	70	205	32	59	10	1	5	24	4	30	3-0	.288	.303	.420	3	.979
2000—Florida (N.L.)	OF	44	89	9	17	4	0	4	12	5	20	1-0	.191	.234	.371	1	.980
—Arizona (N.L.)■	OF	87	262	45	83	16	7	7	47	20	30	5-2	.317	.366	.511	2	.987
2001—Arizona (N.L.)	OF	100	222	26	67	11	2	5	26	14	31	3-2	.302	.346	.437	0	1.000
2002—Arizona (N.L.)	OF	40	154	22	50	5	2	6	23	11	21	4-2	.325	.367	.500	1	.985
American League totals (4 years)		162	495	58	113	18	1	14	59	25	111	9-6	.228	.265	.354	3	.990
National League totals (7 years)		504	1199	166	340	60	14	33	159	68	182	19-6	.284	.323	.440	10	.984
Major League totals (10 years)		666	1694	224	453	78	15	47	218	93	293	28-12	.267	.306	.414	13	.986

DIVISION SERIES RECORD

Year Team (League)	Pos.	G	AB	R	H	2B	3B	HR	RBI	BB	SO	SB-CS	Avg.	OBP	SLG	E	Avg.
		BATTING														FIELDING	
1997—Atlanta (N.L.)	OF	3	3	0	1	0	0	0	2	0	1	0-0	.333	.333	.333	0	...
1998—Atlanta (N.L.)	OF	2	2	0	1	1	0	0	0	0	0	0-0	.500	.500	1.000	0	1.000
2001—Arizona (N.L.)	PH-OF-PR	3	6	1	0	0	0	0	1	0	1	0-0	.000	.000	.000	0	1.000
Division series totals (3 years)		8	11	1	2	1	0	0	3	0	2	0-0	.182	.182	.273	0	1.000

CHAMPIONSHIP SERIES RECORD

Year Team (League)	Pos.	G	AB	R	H	2B	3B	HR	RBI	BB	SO	SB-CS	Avg.	OBP	SLG	E	Avg.
		BATTING														FIELDING	
1997—Atlanta (N.L.)	OF	2	4	0	1	0	0	0	0	0	0	0-0	.250	.250	.250	0	1.000
1998—Atlanta (N.L.)	PR-OF	5	5	0	0	0	0	0	0	0	1	0-0	.000	.000	.000	1	.667
2001—Arizona (N.L.)	OF	2	4	1	1	0	0	0	1	1	1	0-0	.250	.400	.250	0	1.000
Championship series totals (3 years)		9	13	1	2	0	0	0	1	1	2	0-0	.154	.214	.154	1	.889

WORLD SERIES RECORD

NOTES: Member of World Series championship team (2001).

Year Team (League)	Pos.	G	AB	R	H	2B	3B	HR	RBI	BB	SO	SB-CS	Avg.	OBP	SLG	E	Avg.
		BATTING														FIELDING	
2001—Arizona (N.L.)	OF-PH-DH	5	12	1	7	2	0	0	7	1	1	0-0	.583	.615	.750	0	1.000

BECHLER, STEVE — P — ORIOLES

PERSONAL: Born November 18, 1979, in Medford, Ore. ... 6-2/239. ... Throws right, bats right. ... Full name: Steven Scott Bechler.
HIGH SCHOOL: South Medford (Medford, Ore.).
TRANSACTIONS/CAREER NOTES: Selected by Baltimore Orioles organization in third round of free-agent draft (June 2, 1998).
CAREER HITTING (MLB): 0-for-0 (.000), 0 R, 0 2B, 0 3B, 0 HR, 0 RBI.

Year League	W	L	Pct.	ERA	G	GS	CG	ShO	Sv.-Opp.	IP	H	R	ER	HR	BB-IBB	SO
1998—Gulf Coast Orioles (GCL)	2	4	.333	2.72	9	9	0	0	0-...	49.2	51	22	15	4	8-0	39
1999—Delmarva (S.Atl.)	8	12	.400	3.54	26	26	1	1	0-...	152.1	137	69	60	12	58-0	139
2000—Frederick (Caro.)	8	12	.400	4.83	27	27	2	0	0-...	162.0	*179	*98	*87	*19	57-1	137
2001—Frederick (Caro.)	5	2	.714	2.27	13	13	1	1	0-...	83.1	73	24	21	3	22-0	71
—Rochester (I.L.)	1	1	.500	15.95	2	2	0	0	0-...	7.1	14	14	13	4	5-0	6
—Bowie (East.)	3	5	.375	3.08	12	12	2	0	0-...	79.0	63	31	27	14	15-0	58
2002—Bowie (East.)	2	1	.667	3.42	4	4	0	0	0-...	23.2	28	11	9	2	6-0	13
—Rochester (I.L.)	6	11	.353	4.09	24	24	2	1	0-...	149.2	154	78	68	15	52-2	77
—Baltimore (A.L.)	0	0	...	13.50	3	0	0	0	0-0	4.2	6	7	7	3	4-0	3
Major League totals (1 year)	0	0	...	13.50	3	0	0	0	0-0	4.2	6	7	7	3	4-0	3

BECKETT, JOSH — P — MARLINS

PERSONAL: Born May 15, 1980, in Spring, Texas. ... 6-5/216. ... Throws right, bats right. ... Full name: Joshua Patrick Beckett.
HIGH SCHOOL: Spring (Texas).
TRANSACTIONS/CAREER NOTES: Selected by Florida Marlins organization in first round (second pick overall) of free-agent draft (June 2, 1999). ... On Brevard County disabled list (April 17-May 30 and August 16-September 11, 2000). ... On Florida disabled list (April 29-May 14, June 5-July 16 and August 23-September 11, 2002); included rehabilitation assignments to Gulf Coast Marlins (July 6-11) and Jupiter (July 12-16).
RECORDS: Shares N.L. single-inning record for most consecutive home runs allowed—3 (April 28, 2002, sixth inning).
CAREER HITTING (MLB): 3-for-38 (.079), 1 R, 2 2B, 0 3B, 0 HR, 0 RBI.

Year League	W	L	Pct.	ERA	G	GS	CG	ShO	Sv.-Opp.	IP	H	R	ER	HR	BB-IBB	SO
2000—Kane County (Midw.)	2	3	.400	2.12	13	12	0	0	0-...	59.1	45	18	14	4	15-0	61
2001—Brevard County (FSL)	6	0	1.000	1.23	13	12	0	0	0-...	65.2	32	13	9	0	15-0	101
—Portland (East.)	8	1	.889	1.82	13	13	0	0	0-...	74.1	50	16	15	8	19-0	102
—Florida (N.L.)	2	2	.500	1.50	4	4	0	0	0-0	24.0	14	9	4	3	11-0	24
2002—Florida (N.L.)	6	7	.462	4.10	23	21	0	0	0-0	107.2	93	56	49	13	44-2	113
—Gulf Coast Marlins (GCL)	0	0	...	4.50	1	1	0	0	0-...	4.0	5	2	2	0	1-0	7
—Jupiter (FSL)	1	0	1.000	0.00	1	1	0	0	0-...	6.0	4	0	0	0	1-0	12
Major League totals (2 years)	8	9	.471	3.62	27	25	0	0	0-0	131.2	107	65	53	16	55-2	137

BEDARD, ERIK — P — ORIOLES

PERSONAL: Born March 6, 1979, in Naum, Ont. ... 6-1/186. ... Throws left, bats left. ... Full name: Erik Joseph Bedard.
JUNIOR COLLEGE: Norwalk Tech (Conn.).
TRANSACTIONS/CAREER NOTES: Selected by Baltimore Orioles organization in sixth round of free-agent draft (June 2, 1999). ... On Frederick disabled list (July 3-23, 2001). ... On Bowie disabled list (July 1, 2002-remainder of season).
CAREER HITTING (MLB): 0-for-0 (.000), 0 R, 0 2B, 0 3B, 0 HR, 0 RBI.

Year League	W	L	Pct.	ERA	G	GS	CG	ShO	Sv.-Opp.	IP	H	R	ER	HR	BB-IBB	SO
1999—Gulf Coast Orioles (GCL)	2	1	.667	1.86	8	6	0	0	0-...	29.0	20	7	6	1	13-0	41
2000—Delmarva (S.Atl.)	9	4	.692	3.57	29	22	1	1	2-...	111.0	98	48	44	2	35-0	131
2001—Frederick (Caro.)	9	2	.818	2.15	17	17	0	0	0-...	96.1	68	27	23	4	26-0	130
—Gulf Coast Orioles (GCL)	0	1	.000	3.00	2	2	0	0	0-...	6.0	4	2	2	0	3-0	7
2002—Bowie (East.)	6	3	.667	1.97	13	12	0	0	0-...	68.2	43	18	15	0	30-0	66
—Baltimore (A.L.)	0	0	...	13.50	2	0	0	0	0-0	.2	2	1	1	0	0-0	1
Major League totals (1 year)	0	0	...	13.50	2	0	0	0	0-0	.2	2	1	1	0	0-0	1

BEIMEL, JOE — P — PIRATES

PERSONAL: Born April 19, 1977, in St. Mary's, Pa. ... 6-3/215. ... Throws left, bats left. ... Full name: Joseph Ronald Beimel.
HIGH SCHOOL: St. Mary's Area (St. Mary's, Pa.).
JUNIOR COLLEGE: Allegany (Md.).
COLLEGE: Duquesne.
TRANSACTIONS/CAREER NOTES: Selected by Pittsburgh Pirates organization in 18th round of free-agent draft (June 3, 1998).
CAREER HITTING (MLB): 10-for-36 (.278), 3 R, 1 2B, 0 3B, 0 HR, 1 RBI.

Year	League	W	L	Pct.	ERA	G	GS	CG	ShO	Sv.-Opp.	IP	H	R	ER	HR	BB-IBB	SO
1998—	Erie (NY-Penn)	1	4	.200	6.32	17	6	0	0	0-...	47.0	56	39	33	6	22-0	37
1999—	Hickory (S.Atl.)	5	11	.313	4.43	29	22	0	0	0-...	130.0	146	81	64	12	43-0	102
2000—	Lynchburg (Caro.)	10	6	.625	3.36	18	18	2	1	0-...	120.2	111	49	45	6	44-1	82
—	Altoona (East.)	1	6	.143	4.16	10	10	1	0	0-...	62.2	72	38	29	8	21-0	28
2001—	Pittsburgh (N.L.)	7	11	.389	5.23	42	15	0	0	0-0	115.1	131	72	67	12	49-4	58
2002—	Pittsburgh (N.L.)	2	5	.286	4.64	53	8	0	0	0-1	85.1	88	49	44	9	45-12	53
Major League totals (2 years)		9	16	.360	4.98	95	23	0	0	0-1	200.2	219	121	111	21	94-16	111

BEIRNE, KEVIN — P — DODGERS

PERSONAL: Born January 1, 1974, in Houston. ... 6-4/210. ... Throws right, bats left. ... Full name: Kevin P. Beirne. ... Son of Jim Beirne, wide receiver/tight end with Houston Oilers (1968-73, 1975 and 1976) and San Diego Chargers (1974).
HIGH SCHOOL: McCollough (The Woodlands, Texas).
COLLEGE: Texas A&M.
TRANSACTIONS/CAREER NOTES: Selected by Cincinnati Reds organization in 43rd round of free-agent draft (June 2, 1992); did not sign. ... Selected by Chicago White Sox organization in 11th round of free-agent draft (June 1, 1995). ... On Charlotte disabled list (May 6-14 and August 6, 1999-remainder of season). ... Traded by White Sox with P Mike Sirotka, OF Brian Simmons, P Mike Williams to Toronto Blue Jays for P David Wells and P Matt DeWitt (January 14, 2001). ... On Syracuse disabled list (April 26-July 27, 2001). ... Granted free agency (October 19, 2001). ... Signed by Los Angeles Dodgers organization (December 3, 2001).
CAREER HITTING (MLB): 2-for-5 (.400), 1 R, 0 2B, 0 3B, 0 HR, 0 RBI.

Year	League	W	L	Pct.	ERA	G	GS	CG	ShO	Sv.-Opp.	IP	H	R	ER	HR	BB-IBB	SO
1995—	GC White Sox (GCL)	0	0	...	2.45	2	0	0	0	2-...	3.2	2	2	1	0	1-0	3
—	Bristol (Appl.)	1	0	1.000	0.00	9	0	0	0	2-...	9.0	4	0	0	0	4-0	12
—	Hickory (S.Atl.)	0	0	...	4.50	3	0	0	0	1-...	4.0	7	2	2	0	0-0	4
1996—	South Bend (Midw.)	4	11	.267	4.15	26	25	1	0	0-...	145.1	153	85	67	5	60-0	110
1997—	Winston-Salem (Caro.)	4	4	.500	3.05	13	13	1	0	0-...	82.2	66	38	28	7	28-1	75
—	Birmingham (Sou.)	6	4	.600	4.92	13	12	0	0	0-...	75.0	76	51	41	4	41-0	49
1998—	Birmingham (Sou.)	13	9	.591	3.44	26	26	2	1	0-...	167.1	142	77	64	12	87-2	153
—	Calgary (PCL)	0	0	...	4.50	2	2	0	0	0-...	8.0	12	5	4	1	4-0	6
1999—	Charlotte (I.L.)	5	5	.500	5.42	20	20	0	0	0-...	113.0	134	75	68	14	36-0	63
2000—	Charlotte (I.L.)	1	2	.333	3.51	7	7	0	0	0-...	33.1	39	13	13	3	7-0	28
—	Chicago (A.L.)	1	3	.250	6.70	29	1	0	0	0-1	49.2	50	41	37	9	20-1	41
2001—	Toronto (A.L.)■	0	0	...	12.86	5	0	0	0	0-0	7.0	13	10	10	1	6-1	5
—	Syracuse (I.L.)	1	1	.500	1.57	18	0	0	0	0-...	28.2	24	6	5	2	3-1	17
—	Auburn (NY-Penn)	0	0	...	5.40	2	2	0	0	0-...	3.1	6	2	2	0	1-0	2
2002—	Las Vegas (PCL)■	10	3	.769	4.15	22	22	0	0	0-...	125.2	129	64	58	12	41-0	88
—	Los Angeles (N.L.)	2	0	1.000	3.41	12	3	0	0	0-1	29.0	26	11	11	4	17-2	17
—	Vero Beach (FSL)	0	0	...	0.00	1	0	0	0	0-...	2.0	1	0	0	0	0-0	2
A.L. totals (2 years)		1	3	.250	7.46	34	1	0	0	0-1	56.2	63	51	47	10	26-2	46
N.L. totals (1 year)		2	0	1.000	3.41	12	3	0	0	0-1	29.0	26	11	11	4	17-2	17
Major League totals (3 years)		3	3	.500	6.09	46	4	0	0	0-2	85.2	89	62	58	14	43-4	63

BELL, DAVID — 3B

PERSONAL: Born September 14, 1972, in Cincinnati. ... 5-10/195. ... Bats right, throws right. ... Full name: David Michael Bell. ... Son of Buddy Bell, major league third baseman with four teams (1972-89) and manager with Detroit Tigers (1996-98) and Colorado Rockies (2000-April 26, 2002); brother of Mike Bell, third baseman with Cincinnati Reds (2000); and grandson of Gus Bell, major league outfielder with four teams (1950-64).
HIGH SCHOOL: Moeller (Cincinnati).
TRANSACTIONS/CAREER NOTES: Selected by Cleveland Indians organization in seventh round of free-agent draft (June 4, 1990). ... Traded by Indians with C Pepe McNeal and P Rick Heiserman to St. Louis Cardinals for P Ken Hill (July 27, 1995). ... On St. Louis disabled list (April 29-June 30, 1997); included rehabilitation assignments to Arkansas (June 10-19) and Louisville (June 20-26). ... Claimed on waivers by Indians (April 14, 1998). ... Traded by Indians to Seattle Mariners for 2B Joey Cora (August 31, 1998). ... Granted free agency (November 7, 2001). ... Re-signed by Mariners (December 19, 2001). ... Traded by Mariners to San Francisco Giants for SS Desi Relaford and cash (January 25, 2002). ... Granted free agency (October 31, 2002).
STATISTICAL NOTES: Led South Atlantic League in grounding into double plays with 22 in 1991. ... Led South Atlantic League third basemen with 268 assists and 389 total chances in 1991. ... Led Eastern League third basemen with 32 double plays in 1993. ... Led International League third basemen with .950 fielding percentage in 1994. ... Led A.L. second baseman with 313 putouts and 118 double plays in 1999.
2002 GAMES PLAYED BY POSITION (MLB): 3B—139; 2B—12; SS—3; 1B—2.

			BATTING														FIELDING	
Year	Team (League)	Pos.	G	AB	R	H	2B	3B	HR	RBI	BB	SO	SB-CS	Avg.	OBP	SLG	E	Avg.
1990—	GC Indians (GCL)	3B	30	111	18	29	5	1	0	13	10	8	1-1	.261	.341	.324	7	.919
—	Burlington (Appl.)	3B	12	42	4	7	1	1	0	2	2	5	2-1	.167	.217	.238	3	.921
1991—	Columbus (S.Atl.)	3B	136	491	47	113	24	1	5	63	37	50	3-2	.230	.287	.314	31	.920
1992—	Kinston (Caro.)	3B	123	464	52	117	17	2	6	47	54	66	3-2	.252	.327	.336	20	.946
1993—	Canton/Akron (East.)	3B-2B-SS	129	483	69	141	20	2	9	60	43	54	2-4	.292	.350	.398	21	.950
1994—	Charlotte (I.L.)	3B-SS-2B	134	481	66	141	17	4	18	88	41	54	2-5	.293	.355	.457	20	†.956

Year Team (League)	Pos.	G	AB	R	H	2B	3B	HR	RBI	BB	SO	SB-CS	Avg.	OBP	SLG	E	Avg.
		BATTING														FIELDING	
1995— Buffalo (A.A.)	3B-SS-2B	70	254	34	69	11	1	8	34	22	37	0-3	.272	.336	.417	11	.952
— Cleveland (A.L.)	3B	2	2	0	0	0	0	0	0	0	0	0-0	.000	.000	.000	0	1.000
— Louisville (A.A.)■	2B	18	76	9	21	3	1	1	9	2	10	4-0	.276	.321	.382	1	.989
— St. Louis (N.L.)	2B-3B	39	144	13	36	7	2	2	19	4	25	1-2	.250	.278	.368	7	.964
1996— St. Louis (N.L.)	3B-2B-SS	62	145	12	31	6	0	1	9	10	22	1-1	.214	.268	.276	5	.969
— Louisville (A.A.)	2B-3B-SS	42	136	9	24	5	1	0	7	7	15	1-2	.176	.217	.228	5	.973
1997— St. Louis (N.L.)	3B-2B-SS	66	142	9	30	7	2	1	12	10	28	1-0	.211	.261	.310	8	.949
— Arkansas (Texas)	3B-2B	9	32	3	7	2	0	1	3	2	2	1-0	.219	.265	.375	1	.947
— Louisville (A.A.)	2B-3B-DH-SS	6	22	3	5	0	0	1	4	0	6	0-0	.227	.250	.364	1	.941
1998— St. Louis (N.L.)	3B-2B	4	9	0	2	1	0	0	0	0	3	0-0	.222	.222	.333	0	1.000
— Cleveland (A.L.)■	2-3-1-S	107	340	37	89	21	2	10	41	22	54	0-4	.262	.306	.424	9	.983
— Seattle (A.L.)■	2B-1B-3B-OF	21	80	11	26	8	0	0	8	5	8	0-0	.325	.365	.425	1	.991
1999— Seattle (A.L.)	2B-1B-SS	157	597	92	160	31	2	21	78	58	90	7-4	.268	.331	.432	17	.978
2000— Seattle (A.L.)	3-2-1-DH-S	133	454	57	112	24	2	11	47	42	66	2-3	.247	.316	.381	15	.963
2001— Seattle (A.L.)	3B-1B	135	470	62	122	28	0	15	64	28	59	2-1	.260	.303	.415	14	.962
2002— San Fran. (N.L.)■	3-2-S-1	154	552	82	144	29	2	20	73	54	80	1-2	.261	.333	.429	12	.971
American League totals (5 years)		555	1943	259	509	112	6	57	238	155	277	11-12	.262	.318	.414	56	.974
National League totals (5 years)		325	992	116	243	50	6	24	113	78	158	4-5	.245	.305	.380	32	.966
Major League totals (8 years)		880	2935	375	752	162	12	81	351	233	435	15-17	.256	.313	.402	88	.972

DIVISION SERIES RECORD

Year Team (League)	Pos.	G	AB	R	H	2B	3B	HR	RBI	BB	SO	SB-CS	Avg.	OBP	SLG	E	Avg.
		BATTING														FIELDING	
2000— Seattle (A.L.)	3B	3	11	0	4	1	0	0	1	2	2	0-0	.364	.462	.455	0	1.000
2001— Seattle (A.L.)	3B	5	16	2	5	1	0	1	2	1	6	0-0	.313	.333	.563	0	1.000
2002— San Francisco (N.L.)	3B	5	16	3	3	0	0	0	1	3	4	0-0	.188	.316	.188	1	.944
Division series totals (3 years)		13	43	5	12	2	0	1	4	6	12	0-0	.279	.360	.395	1	.969

CHAMPIONSHIP SERIES RECORD

Year Team (League)	Pos.	G	AB	R	H	2B	3B	HR	RBI	BB	SO	SB-CS	Avg.	OBP	SLG	E	Avg.
		BATTING														FIELDING	
2000— Seattle (A.L.)	3B	5	18	0	4	0	0	0	0	0	0	0-0	.222	.222	.222	0	1.000
2001— Seattle (A.L.)	3B	5	16	1	3	0	0	0	4	0	3	0-0	.188	.188	.188	1	.923
2002— San Francisco (N.L.)	3B	5	17	4	7	1	0	1	1	2	3	0-0	.412	.474	.647	0	1.000
Championship series totals (3 years)		15	51	5	14	1	0	1	5	2	6	0-0	.275	.302	.353	1	.974

WORLD SERIES RECORD

Year Team (League)	Pos.	G	AB	R	H	2B	3B	HR	RBI	BB	SO	SB-CS	Avg.	OBP	SLG	E	Avg.
		BATTING														FIELDING	
2002— San Francisco (N.L.)	3B	7	23	4	7	0	0	1	4	5	4	0-1	.304	.448	.435	2	.889

BELL, JAY 2B

PERSONAL: Born December 11, 1965, in Eglin AFB, Fla. ... 6-0/184. ... Bats right, throws right. ... Full name: Jay Stuart Bell.

HIGH SCHOOL: Tate (Gonzalez, Fla.).

TRANSACTIONS/CAREER NOTES: Selected by Minnesota Twins organization in first round (eighth pick overall) of free-agent draft (June 4, 1984). ... Traded by Twins with P Curt Wardle, OF Jim Weaver and a player to be named later to Cleveland Indians for P Bert Blyleven (August 1, 1985); Indians acquired P Rich Yett to complete deal (September 17, 1985). ... Traded by Indians to Pittsburgh Pirates for SS Felix Fermin (March 25, 1989). ... Traded by Pirates with 1B/3B Jeff King to Kansas City Royals for 3B Joe Randa, P Jeff Granger, P Jeff Martin and P Jeff Wallace (December 13, 1996). ... Granted free agency (November 4, 1997). ... Signed by Arizona Diamondbacks (November 17, 1997). ... On Arizona disabled list (March 28-July 19, 2002); included rehabilitation assignments to Tucson (April 29-May 6) and Lancaster (July 9-19). ... Granted free agency (October 29, 2002).

HONORS: Named shortstop on The Sporting News N.L. All-Star team (1993). ... Won N.L. Gold Glove at shortstop (1993). ... Named shortstop on The Sporting News N.L. Silver Slugger team (1993).

STATISTICAL NOTES: Led Appalachian League shortstops with 109 putouts, 218 assists, 352 total chances and 43 double plays in 1984. ... Led California League shortstops with 84 double plays in 1985. ... Hit home run in first major league at-bat on first pitch (September 29, 1986). ... Led Eastern League shortstops with 371 assists and 613 total chances in 1986. ... Led American Association shortstops with 198 putouts, 322 assists, 30 errors and 550 total chances in 1987. ... Led N.L. shortstops with 260 putouts in 1990, 268 in 1992 and 256 in 1993. ... Led N.L. with 39 sacrifice hits in 1990 and 30 in 1991. ... Led N.L. shortstops with 491 assists in 1991, 526 in 1992, 527 in 1993, 380 in 1994 and 478 in 1996. ... Had 22-game hitting streak (August 24-September 17, 1992). ... Led N.L. shortstops with 741 total chances in 1990, 754 in 1991, 816 in 1992, 794 in 1993 and 547 in 1994.. ... Led N.L. shortstops with 94 double plays in 1992. ... Led N.L. second basemen with 22 errors in 1999. ... Career major league grand slams: 6.

2002 GAMES PLAYED BY POSITION (MLB): 3B—6; 1B—5; 2B—2; SS—2.

Year Team (League)	Pos.	G	AB	R	H	2B	3B	HR	RBI	BB	SO	SB-CS	Avg.	OBP	SLG	E	Avg.
		BATTING														FIELDING	
1984— Elizabethton (Appl.)	SS	66	245	43	54	12	1	6	30	42	50	4-2	.220	.334	.351	25	.929
1985— Visalia (Calif.)	SS	106	376	56	106	16	6	9	59	41	73	10-6	.282	.353	.428	53	.905
— Waterbury (East.)■	SS	29	114	13	34	11	2	1	14	9	16	3-3	.298	.350	.456	6	.952
1986— Waterbury (East.)	SS	138	494	86	137	28	4	7	74	87	65	10-9	.277	.378	.393	*45	.927
— Cleveland (A.L.)	2B-DH	5	14	3	5	2	0	1	4	2	3	0-0	.357	.438	.714	2	.778
1987— Buffalo (A.A.)	SS-2B	110	362	71	94	15	4	17	60	70	84	6-5	.260	.380	.464	†30	.946
— Cleveland (A.L.)	SS	38	125	14	27	9	1	2	13	8	31	2-0	.216	.269	.352	9	.947
1988— Cleveland (A.L.)	SS-DH	73	211	23	46	5	1	2	21	21	53	4-2	.218	.289	.280	10	.965
— Colo. Springs (PCL)	SS	49	181	35	50	12	2	7	24	26	27	3-1	.276	.368	.481	18	.935
1989— Pittsburgh (N.L.)■	SS	78	271	33	70	13	3	2	27	19	47	5-3	.258	.307	.351	10	.968
— Buffalo (A.A.)	SS-3B	86	298	49	85	15	3	10	54	38	55	12-5	.285	.370	.456	16	.954
1990— Pittsburgh (N.L.)	SS	159	583	93	148	28	7	7	52	65	109	10-6	.254	.329	.362	22	.970
1991— Pittsburgh (N.L.)	SS	157	608	96	164	32	8	16	67	52	99	10-6	.270	.330	.428	*24	.968
1992— Pittsburgh (N.L.)	SS	159	632	87	167	36	6	9	55	55	103	7-5	.264	.326	.383	22	.973

Year Team (League)	Pos.	G	AB	R	H	2B	3B	HR	RBI	BB	SO	SB-CS	Avg.	OBP	SLG	E	Avg.
		BATTING														FIELDING	
1993—Pittsburgh (N.L.)	SS	154	604	102	187	32	9	9	51	77	122	16-10	.310	.392	.437	11	*.986
1994—Pittsburgh (N.L.)	SS	110	424	68	117	35	4	9	45	49	82	2-0	.276	.353	.441	15	.973
1995—Pittsburgh (N.L.)	SS-3B	138	530	79	139	28	4	13	55	55	110	2-5	.262	.336	.404	14	.978
1996—Pittsburgh (N.L.)	SS	151	527	65	132	29	3	13	71	54	108	6-4	.250	.323	.391	10	*.986
1997—Kansas City (A.L.)■	SS-3B	153	573	89	167	28	3	21	92	71	101	10-6	.291	.368	.461	10	.985
1998—Arizona (N.L.)■	SS-2B	155	549	79	138	29	5	20	67	81	129	3-5	.251	.353	.432	19	.972
1999—Arizona (N.L.)	2B-DH-SS	151	589	132	170	32	6	38	112	82	132	7-4	.289	.374	.557	†22	.968
2000—Arizona (N.L.)	2B-DH	149	565	87	151	30	6	18	68	70	88	7-3	.267	.348	.437	8	.988
2001—Arizona (N.L.)	2B-3B-DH	129	428	59	106	24	1	13	46	65	79	0-1	.248	.349	.400	7	.983
2002—Tucson (PCL)	3B	7	22	4	5	3	0	0	2	4	1	0-0	.227	.346	.364	2	.833
—Lancaster (Calif.)	SS	7	20	4	4	1	0	1	7	4	6	0-0	.200	.333	.400	0	1.000
—Arizona (N.L.)	3B-1B-2B-SS	32	49	3	8	1	0	2	11	5	9	0-0	.163	.250	.306	0	1.000
American League totals (4 years)		269	923	129	245	44	5	26	130	102	188	16-8	.265	.339	.408	31	.973
National League totals (13 years)		1722	6359	983	1697	349	62	169	727	729	1217	75-52	.267	.345	.421	184	.976
Major League totals (17 years)		1991	7282	1112	1942	393	67	195	857	831	1405	91-60	.267	.344	.419	215	.976

DIVISION SERIES RECORD

Year Team (League)	Pos.	G	AB	R	H	2B	3B	HR	RBI	BB	SO	SB-CS	Avg.	OBP	SLG	E	Avg.
		BATTING														FIELDING	
1999—Arizona (N.L.)	2B	4	14	3	4	1	0	0	3	1	0	0-1	.286	.353	.357	1	.950
2001—Arizona (N.L.)	2B-PH	2	4	0	1	0	0	0	0	0	1	0-0	.250	.250	.250	0	1.000
Division series totals (2 years)		6	18	3	5	1	0	0	3	1	1	0-1	.278	.333	.333	1	.960

CHAMPIONSHIP SERIES RECORD

RECORDS: Shares N.L. single-series record for most singles—9 (1991).

Year Team (League)	Pos.	G	AB	R	H	2B	3B	HR	RBI	BB	SO	SB-CS	Avg.	OBP	SLG	E	Avg.
		BATTING														FIELDING	
1990—Pittsburgh (N.L.)	SS	6	20	3	5	1	0	1	1	4	3	0-0	.250	.400	.450	1	.963
1991—Pittsburgh (N.L.)	SS	7	29	2	12	2	0	1	1	0	10	0-1	.414	.414	.586	1	.970
1992—Pittsburgh (N.L.)	SS	7	29	3	5	2	0	1	4	3	4	0-0	.172	.273	.345	1	.933
2001—Arizona (N.L.)	2B	1	4	0	0	0	0	0	0	0	0	0-0	.000	.000	.000	0	1.000
Championship series totals (4 years)		21	82	8	22	5	0	3	6	7	17	0-1	.268	.341	.439	3	.962

WORLD SERIES RECORD

NOTES: Member of World Series championship team (2001).

Year Team (League)	Pos.	G	AB	R	H	2B	3B	HR	RBI	BB	SO	SB-CS	Avg.	OBP	SLG	E	Avg.
		BATTING														FIELDING	
2001—Arizona (N.L.)	PH-2B	3	7	3	1	0	0	0	1	0	2	0-0	.143	.143	.143	0	1.000

ALL-STAR GAME RECORD

	AB	R	H	2B	3B	HR	RBI	BB	SO	SB-CS	Avg.	OBP	SLG	E	Avg.
All-Star Game totals (2 years)	2	0	0	0	0	0	0	1	1	0-0	.000	.333	.000	0	1.000

BELL, ROB — P — RANGERS

PERSONAL: Born January 17, 1977, in Newburgh, N.Y. ... 6-5/225. ... Throws right, bats right. ... Full name: Robert Allen Bell.
HIGH SCHOOL: Marlboro (N.Y.) Central.
TRANSACTIONS/CAREER NOTES: Selected by Atlanta Braves organization in third round of free-agent draft (June 1, 1995). ... Traded by Braves with OF Michael Tucker and P Denny Neagle to Cincinnati Reds for 2B Bret Boone and P Mike Remlinger (November 10, 1998). ... On Chattanooga disabled list (April 20-July 20, 1999). ... Traded by Reds to Texas Rangers for OF Ruben Mateo and 3B Edwin Encarnacion (June 15, 2001).
CAREER HITTING (MLB): 4-for-53 (.075), 1 R, 1 2B, 0 3B, 0 HR, 0 RBI.

Year League	W	L	Pct.	ERA	G	GS	CG	ShO	Sv.-Opp.	IP	H	R	ER	HR	BB-IBB	SO
1995—Gulf Coast Braves (GCL)	1	6	.143	6.88	10	8	0	0	0-...	34.0	38	29	26	2	14-0	33
1996—Eugene (N'West)	5	6	.455	5.11	16	*16	0	0	0-...	81.0	89	49	46	5	29-1	74
1997—Macon (S.Atl.)	•14	7	.667	3.68	27	27	1	0	0-...	146.2	144	72	60	15	41-1	140
1998—Danville (Caro.)	7	9	.438	3.28	28	•28	2	0	0-...	*178.1	169	79	65	8	46-0	*197
1999—Chattanooga (Sou.)■	3	6	.333	3.13	12	12	2	1	0-...	72.0	75	30	25	7	17-0	68
—Gulf Coast Reds (GCL)	0	0	...	1.13	2	2	0	0	0-...	8.0	3	1	1	0	0-0	11
2000—Cincinnati (N.L.)	7	8	.467	5.00	26	26	1	0	0-0	140.1	130	84	78	32	73-6	112
—Louisville (I.L.)	4	0	1.000	3.73	6	6	0	0	0-...	41.0	35	18	17	6	13-0	47
2001—Cincinnati (N.L.)	0	5	.000	5.48	9	9	0	0	0-0	44.1	46	28	27	9	17-1	33
—Louisville (I.L.)	2	2	.500	3.33	5	4	0	0	0-...	27.0	32	10	10	4	4-0	26
—Texas (A.L.)■	5	5	.500	7.18	18	18	0	0	0-0	105.1	130	87	84	23	47-0	64
2002—Oklahoma (PCL)	5	0	1.000	4.06	12	11	2	•2	0-...	75.1	70	36	34	10	25-0	55
—Texas (A.L.)	4	3	.571	6.22	17	15	0	0	0-0	94.0	113	69	65	16	35-0	70
—Tulsa (Texas)	1	0	1.000	0.00	1	1	0	0	0-...	8.0	4	0	0	0	0-0	5
A.L. totals (2 years)	9	8	.529	6.73	35	33	0	0	0-0	199.1	243	156	149	39	82-0	134
N.L. totals (2 years)	7	13	.350	5.12	35	35	1	0	0-0	184.2	176	112	105	41	90-7	145
Major League totals (3 years)	16	21	.432	5.95	70	68	1	0	0-0	384.0	419	268	254	80	172-7	279

BELLHORN, MARK — 2B — CUBS

PERSONAL: Born August 23, 1974, in Boston. ... 6-1/205. ... Bats both, throws right. ... Full name: Mark Christian Bellhorn.
HIGH SCHOOL: Oviedo (Fla.).
COLLEGE: Auburn.
TRANSACTIONS/CAREER NOTES: Selected by Oakland Athletics organization in second round of free agent draft (June 1, 1995). ... On Vancouver disabled list (April 8-July 29, 1999). ... On Sacramento disabled list (May 12-24, 2000). ... Traded by A's to Chicago Cubs for IF Adam Morrissey (November 2, 2001).

RECORDS: Shares major league single-game record for most home runs in one inning—2 (August 29, 2002, fourth inning).
STATISTICAL NOTES: Tied for Arizona League lead with two intentional bases on balls received in 1999. ... Switch-hit home runs in one game twice (June 30 and August 29, 2002). ... Career major league grand slams: 1.
2002 GAMES PLAYED BY POSITION (MLB): 2B—77; 3B—36; 1B—22; SS—12; OF—1.

		BATTING														FIELDING	
Year Team (League)	Pos.	G	AB	R	H	2B	3B	HR	RBI	BB	SO	SB-CS	Avg.	OBP	SLG	E	Avg.
1995—Modesto (Calif.)	SS	56	229	35	59	12	0	6	31	27	52	5-2	.258	.346	.389	21	.927
1996—Huntsville (Sou.)	IF	131	468	84	117	24	5	10	71	73	124	19-2	.250	.353	.387	32	.945
1997—Edmonton (PCL)	2B-SS-3B-DH	70	241	54	79	18	3	11	46	64	59	6-6	.328	.472	.564	13	.957
—Oakland (A.L.)	3B-2B-DH-SS	68	224	33	51	9	1	6	19	32	70	7-1	.228	.324	.357	9	.956
1998—Edmonton (PCL)	3-2-DH-S-1	87	309	57	77	20	4	10	44	62	90	6-2	.249	.384	.437	11	.965
—Oakland (A.L.)	3B-DH-SS-2B	11	12	1	1	1	0	0	1	3	4	2-0	.083	.313	.167	0	1.000
1999—Ariz. Athletics (Ariz.)	2B-DH	12	43	11	10	3	0	0	5	11	9	0-0	.233	.389	.302	0	1.000
—Midland (Texas)	2B	17	57	12	17	3	0	2	8	11	13	1-0	.298	.412	.456	2	.973
2000—Sacramento (PCL)	3B-2B-SS-1B	117	436	*111	116	17	11	24	73	*94	121	20-5	.266	.399	.521	15	.956
—Oakland (A.L.)	2B-3B-SS	9	13	2	2	0	0	0	0	2	6	0-0	.154	.267	.154	0	1.000
2001—Sacramento (PCL)	OF-2B-SS-3B	43	156	30	42	6	0	12	36	22	60	3-0	.269	.370	.538	2	.985
—Oakland (A.L.)	2-3-S-DH-O	38	74	11	10	1	2	1	4	7	37	0-0	.135	.210	.243	5	.932
2002—Chicago (N.L.)■	2-3-1-S-O	146	445	86	115	24	4	27	56	76	144	7-5	.258	.374	.512	11	.977
American League totals (4 years)		126	323	47	64	11	3	7	24	44	117	9-1	.198	.296	.316	14	.952
National League totals (1 year)		146	445	86	115	24	4	27	56	76	144	7-5	.258	.374	.512	11	.977
Major League totals (5 years)		272	768	133	179	35	7	34	80	120	261	16-6	.233	.342	.430	25	.968

BELLIARD, RON 2B BREWERS

PERSONAL: Born April 7, 1975, in Bronx, N.Y. ... 5-8/197. ... Bats right, throws right. ... Full name: Ronald Belliard. ... Name pronounced BELL-ee-ard.
HIGH SCHOOL: Central (Miami).
TRANSACTIONS/CAREER NOTES: Selected by Milwaukee Brewers organization in eighth round of free-agent draft (June 2, 1994). ... On disabled list (August 8-September 30, 2001).
STATISTICAL NOTES: Led Midwest League second basemen with 25 errors in 1995. ... Led Pacific Coast League second basemen with 229 putouts, 358 assists, 24 errors and 611 total chances and tied for league lead with 92 double plays in 1997. ... Led International League second basemen with 401 assists and 98 double plays in 1998. ... Led N.L. second basemen with 336 putouts, 793 total chances and 130 double plays in 2000.
2002 GAMES PLAYED BY POSITION (MLB): 2B—49; 3B—42.

		BATTING														FIELDING	
Year Team (League)	Pos.	G	AB	R	H	2B	3B	HR	RBI	BB	SO	SB-CS	Avg.	OBP	SLG	E	Avg.
1994—Ariz. Brewers (Ariz.)	2B-3B-SS	39	143	32	42	7	3	0	27	14	25	7-0	.294	.366	.385	12	.935
1995—Beloit (Midw.)	2B-3B	130	461	76	137	28	5	13	76	36	67	16-12	.297	.356	.464	†26	.956
1996—El Paso (Texas)	2B-DH	109	416	73	116	20	8	3	57	60	51	26-10	.279	.373	.387	16	.972
1997—Tucson (PCL)	2B-SS	118	443	80	125	35	4	4	55	61	69	10-7	.282	.379	.406	†26	.959
1998—Louisville (I.L.)	2B-SS	133	507	*114	163	36	7	14	73	69	77	33-12	.321	.408	.503	14	.979
—Milwaukee (N.L.)	2B	8	5	1	1	0	0	0	0	0	0	0-0	.200	.200	.200	0	...
1999—Louisville (I.L.)	2B	29	108	14	26	4	0	1	8	14	13	12-2	.241	.331	.306	3	.975
—Milwaukee (N.L.)	2B-3B-SS	124	457	60	135	29	4	8	58	64	59	4-5	.295	.379	.429	13	.978
2000—Milwaukee (N.L.)	2B	152	571	83	150	30	9	8	54	82	84	7-5	.263	.354	.389	*19	.976
2001—Milwaukee (N.L.)	2B	101	364	69	96	30	3	11	36	35	65	5-2	.264	.335	.453	5	.990
2002—Milwaukee (N.L.)	2B-3B	104	289	30	61	13	0	3	26	18	46	2-3	.211	.257	.287	10	.963
Major League totals (5 years)		489	1686	243	443	102	16	30	174	199	254	18-15	.263	.341	.396	47	.978

BELLINGER, CLAY OF/IF

PERSONAL: Born November 18, 1968, in Oneonta, N.Y. ... 6-3/215. ... Bats right, throws right. ... Full name: Clayton Daniel Bellinger.
HIGH SCHOOL: Oneonta (N.Y.).
COLLEGE: Rollins.
TRANSACTIONS/CAREER NOTES: Selected by San Francisco Giants organization in second round of free-agent draft (June 5, 1989). ... Granted free agency (October 16, 1995). ... Signed by Baltimore Orioles organization (November 22, 1995). ... Granted free agency (October 15, 1996). ... Signed by New York Yankees organization (November 4, 1996). ... Released by Yankees (January 17, 2002). ... Signed by Anaheim Angels organization (January 31, 2002). ... Granted free agency (October 15, 2002).
2002 GAMES PLAYED BY POSITION (MLB): 1B—2.

		BATTING														FIELDING	
Year Team (League)	Pos.	G	AB	R	H	2B	3B	HR	RBI	BB	SO	SB-CS	Avg.	OBP	SLG	E	Avg.
1989—Everett (N'West)	SS	51	185	29	37	8	1	4	16	19	47	3-2	.200	.278	.319	24	.874
1990—Clinton (Midw.)	SS-3B	109	383	52	83	17	4	10	48	27	102	13-6	.217	.279	.360	29	.928
1991—San Jose (Calif.)	SS	105	368	65	95	29	2	8	62	53	88	13-4	.258	.363	.413	32	.934
1992—Shreveport (Texas)	SS	126	433	45	90	18	3	13	50	36	82	7-8	.208	.271	.353	*41	.928
1993—Phoenix (PCL)	3B-SS-1B	122	407	50	104	20	3	6	49	38	81	7-7	.256	.322	.364	28	.934
1994—Phoenix (PCL)	O-S-1-3-2-C	106	337	48	90	15	1	7	50	18	56	6-1	.267	.315	.380	8	.980
1995—Phoenix (PCL)	S-3-0-2-1-C	97	277	34	76	16	1	2	32	27	52	3-2	.274	.340	.361	8	.970
1996—Rochester (I.L.)■	SS-1B-2B	125	459	68	138	34	4	15	78	33	90	8-4	.301	.348	.490	22	.968
1997—Columbus (I.L.)■	3-O-S-1-2	111	416	55	114	31	3	12	59	34	74	10-4	.274	.338	.450	15	.956
1998—Columbus (I.L.)	1-S-3-2-O-C	115	397	35	89	20	2	9	40	35	79	6-3	.224	.293	.353	14	.974
1999—New York (A.L.)	3-1-DH-O-2-S	32	45	12	9	2	0	1	2	1	10	1-0	.200	.217	.311	0	1.000
—Columbus (I.L.)	3-S-O-2-1	40	141	19	33	10	1	2	14	13	32	6-0	.234	.300	.362	2	.987
2000—New York (A.L.)	O-2-3-1-S	98	184	33	38	8	2	6	21	17	48	5-0	.207	.288	.370	5	.977
—Columbus (I.L.)	1B-OF-SS-C	8	28	3	9	2	0	0	2	2	5	1-0	.321	.367	.393	1	.976
2001—New York (A.L.)	O-3-1-S-DH	51	81	12	13	1	1	5	12	4	23	1-2	.160	.207	.383	3	.963
—Columbus (I.L.)	O-S-3-1-2	26	98	13	21	10	0	1	9	5	22	3-0	.214	.260	.347	3	.961
2002—Salt Lake (PCL)■	OF-3B-1B-C	89	324	45	83	17	5	13	41	13	87	4-2	.256	.289	.460	6	.981
—Anaheim (A.L.)	1B	2	1	0	0	0	0	0	0	0	1	0-0	.000	.000	.000	0	1.000
Major League totals (4 years)		183	311	57	60	11	3	12	35	22	82	7-2	.193	.257	.363	8	.977

DIVISION SERIES RECORD

							BATTING									FIELDING	
Year Team (League)	Pos.	G	AB	R	H	2B	3B	HR	RBI	BB	SO	SB-CS	Avg.	OBP	SLG	E	Avg.
1999— New York (A.L.)	PR-DH	1	0	0	0	0	0	0	0	0	0	0-0	...	...	...	...	...
2000— New York (A.L.)	OF	2	1	0	1	1	0	0	1	0	0	0-0	1.000	1.000	2.000	0	...
2001— New York (A.L.)	PR	1	0	0	0	0	0	0	0	0	0	0-0	...	...	...	...	...
Division series totals (3 years)		4	1	0	1	1	0	0	1	0	0	0-0	1.000	1.000	2.000	0	...

CHAMPIONSHIP SERIES RECORD

							BATTING									FIELDING	
Year Team (League)	Pos.	G	AB	R	H	2B	3B	HR	RBI	BB	SO	SB-CS	Avg.	OBP	SLG	E	Avg.
1999— New York (A.L.)	PH-SS-PR-DH	3	1	0	0	0	0	0	0	0	1	0-0	.000	.000	.000	0	1.000
2000— New York (A.L.)	OF-PR	5	0	0	0	0	0	0	0	0	0	0-0	...	...	...	0	1.000
2001— New York (A.L.)	OF	1	1	0	0	0	0	0	0	0	0	0-0	.000	.000	.000	0	1.000
Championship series totals (3 years)		9	2	0	0	0	0	0	0	0	1	0-0	.000	.000	.000	0	1.000

WORLD SERIES RECORD

NOTES: Member of World Series championship team (1999 and 2000).

							BATTING									FIELDING	
Year Team (League)	Pos.	G	AB	R	H	2B	3B	HR	RBI	BB	SO	SB-CS	Avg.	OBP	SLG	E	Avg.
1999— New York (A.L.)								Did not play.									
2000— New York (A.L.)	PR-OF	4	0	0	0	0	0	0	0	0	0	0-0	...	...	...	0	1.000
2001— New York (A.L.)	PR-OF-PH	2	2	0	0	0	0	0	0	0	2	0-0	.000	.000	.000	0	1.000
World Series totals (2 years)		6	2	0	0	0	0	0	0	0	2	0-0	.000	.000	.000	0	1.000

RECORD AS PITCHER

Year League	W	L	Pct.	ERA	G	GS	CG	ShO	Sv.	IP	H	R	ER	BB	SO
1994— Phoenix (PCL)	0	0	...	9.00	2	0	0	0	0	2.0	6	2	2	0	0
1998— Columbus (I.L.)	0	0	...	0.00	1	0	0	0	0	.1	1	0	0	1	0

BELTRAN, CARLOS OF ROYALS

PERSONAL: Born April 24, 1977, in Manati, Puerto Rico. ... 6-1/190. ... Bats both, throws right. ... Full name: Carlos Ivan Beltran.
HIGH SCHOOL: Fernando Callejas (Manati, Puerto Rico).
TRANSACTIONS/CAREER NOTES: Selected by Kansas City Royals organization in second round of free-agent draft (June 1, 1995). ... On Kansas City disabled list (July 4-September 4, 2000); included rehabilitation assignments to Gulf Coast Royals (August 21-24), Wilmington (August 25-30) and Omaha (August 31-September 4).
RECORDS: Holds A.L. single-season record for most extra-base hits by switch-hitter—80 (2002).
HONORS: Named A.L. Rookie Player of the Year by The Sporting News (1999). ... Named A.L. Rookie of the Year by Baseball Writers' Association of America (1999).
STATISTICAL NOTES: Led A.L. outfielders with 423 total chances in 1999. ... Switch-hit home runs in one game twice (June 29, 2000; September 6, 2002). ... Career major league grand slams: 4.
2002 GAMES PLAYED BY POSITION (MLB): OF—149; DH—12.

							BATTING									FIELDING	
Year Team (League)	Pos.	G	AB	R	H	2B	3B	HR	RBI	BB	SO	SB-CS	Avg.	OBP	SLG	E	Avg.
1995— GC Royals (GCL)	OF	52	180	29	50	9	0	0	23	13	30	5-3	.278	.332	.328	2	.977
1996— Lansing (Midw.)	OF	11	42	3	6	2	0	0	0	1	11	1-0	.143	.163	.190	2	.938
— Spokane (N'West)	OF	59	215	29	58	8	3	7	29	31	65	10-2	.270	.359	.433	7	.938
1997— Wilmington (Caro.)	OF	120	419	57	96	15	4	11	46	46	96	17-7	.229	.311	.363	8	.968
1998— Wilmington (Caro.)	OF	52	192	32	53	14	0	5	32	25	39	11-7	.276	.364	.427	2	.983
— Wichita (Texas)	OF	47	182	50	64	13	3	14	44	23	30	7-1	.352	.427	.687	4	.960
— Kansas City (A.L.)	OF	14	58	12	16	5	3	0	7	3	12	3-0	.276	.317	.466	1	.978
1999— Kansas City (A.L.)	OF-DH	156	663	112	194	27	7	22	108	46	123	27-8	.293	.337	.454	*12	.972
2000— Kansas City (A.L.)	OF-DH	98	372	49	92	15	4	7	44	35	69	13-0	.247	.309	.366	6	.975
— GC Royals (GCL)	DH	1	4	3	2	1	0	1	1	1	0	0-0	.500	.600	1.500	...	...
— Wilmington (Caro.)	OF	3	13	2	4	0	1	2	6	0	5	0-0	.308	.308	.923	0	1.000
— Omaha (PCL)	OF	5	18	4	6	1	0	2	2	3	3	1-0	.333	.455	.722	0	1.000
2001— Kansas City (A.L.)	OF-DH	155	617	106	189	32	12	24	101	52	120	31-1	.306	.362	.514	5	.988
2002— Kansas City (A.L.)	OF-DH	•162	637	114	174	44	7	29	105	71	135	35-7	.273	.346	.501	7	.983
Major League totals (5 years)		585	2347	393	665	123	33	82	365	207	459	109-16	.283	.341	.469	31	.980

BELTRAN, FRANCIS P CUBS

PERSONAL: Born November 29, 1979, in Santo Domingo, Dominican Republic. ... 6-5/220. ... Throws right, bats right. ... Full name: Francis Lebron Beltran.
TRANSACTIONS/CAREER NOTES: Signed as non-drafted free agent by Chicago Cubs organization (November 15, 1996). ... On disabled list (June 9-July 24, 2001). ... On West Tenn disabled list (April 4-May 11, 2002).
CAREER HITTING (MLB): 0-for-1 (.000), 0 R, 0 2B, 0 3B, 0 HR, 0 RBI.

Year League	W	L	Pct.	ERA	G	GS	CG	ShO	Sv.-Opp.	IP	H	R	ER	HR	BB-IBB	SO
1997— Arizona Cubs (Ariz.)	0	1	.000	3.42	16	0	0	0	1-...	23.2	27	18	9	1	8-0	17
1998— Arizona Cubs (Ariz.)	1	1	.500	5.55	12	5	0	0	0-...	35.2	49	23	22	1	14-1	26
1999— Arizona Cubs (Ariz.)	0	1	.000	0.00	7	7	0	0	2-...	10.2	5	3	0	0	1-0	8
— Eugene (N'West)	0	2	.000	8.36	16	0	0	0	0-...	28.0	41	32	26	2	14-0	28
2000— Lansing (Midw.)	1	1	.500	9.68	16	0	0	0	0-...	17.2	24	22	19	0	19-0	16
— Eugene (N'West)	2	2	.500	2.68	25	0	0	0	8-...	43.2	28	16	13	1	20-2	52
2001— Daytona (FSL)	6	9	.400	5.00	21	18	0	0	0-...	95.1	93	62	53	10	40-1	72
2002— West Tenn (Sou.)	2	2	.500	2.59	39	0	0	0	23-...	41.2	28	14	12	2	19-2	43
— Chicago (N.L.)	0	0	...	7.50	11	0	0	0	0-0	12.0	14	11	10	2	16-1	11
Major League totals (1 year)	0	0	...	7.50	11	0	0	0	0-0	12.0	14	11	10	2	16-1	11

BELTRE, ADRIAN — 3B — DODGERS

PERSONAL: Born April 7, 1979, in Santo Domingo, Dominican Republic. ... 5-11/170. ... Bats right, throws right. ... Full name: Adrian Perez Beltre. ... Name pronounced bell-TREE.

HIGH SCHOOL: Liceo Maximo Gomez (Santo Domingo, Dominican Republic).

TRANSACTIONS/CAREER NOTES: Signed as non-drafted free agent by Los Angeles Dodgers (July 7, 1994). ... On San Bernardino disabled list (June 25-July 2, 1996). ... On Albuquerque disabled list (April 23-May 1 and May 12-19, 1998). ... On disabled list (May 28-June 17, 2000). ... On Los Angeles disabled list (March 23-May 12, 2001); included rehabilitation assignments to Vero Beach (May 6-9) and Las Vegas (May 10-12).

HONORS: Named Florida State League Most Valuable Player (1997).

STATISTICAL NOTES: Led Florida State League with 12 intentional bases on balls received in 1997. ... Led Florida State League third basemen with 26 double plays in 1997. ... Led N.L. third basemen with 116 putouts and 412 total chances in 2000. ... Had 17-game hitting streak (August 25-September 18, 2001). ... Career major league grand slams: 2.

2002 GAMES PLAYED BY POSITION (MLB): 3B—157.

		BATTING														FIELDING	
Year Team (League)	Pos.	G	AB	R	H	2B	3B	HR	RBI	BB	SO	SB-CS	Avg.	OBP	SLG	E	Avg.
1995—Dom. Dodgers (DSL)	3B	62	218	56	67	15	3	8	40	54	26	2-1	.307	.452	.514	19	.920
1996—Savannah (S.Atl.)	3B-2B	68	244	48	75	14	3	16	59	35	46	4-3	.307	.406	.586	19	.912
—San Bern. (Calif.)	3B-DH	63	238	40	62	13	1	10	40	19	44	3-4	.261	.322	.450	7	.953
1997—Vero Beach (FSL)	3B-OF	123	435	95	138	24	2	*26	*104	67	66	25-9	.317	.407	*.561	37	.895
1998—San Antonio (Texas)	3B-DH	64	246	49	79	21	2	13	56	39	37	20-4	.321	.411	.581	17	.910
—Los Angeles (N.L.)	3B-SS	77	195	18	42	9	0	7	22	14	37	3-1	.215	.278	.369	13	.926
1999—Los Angeles (N.L.)	3B	152	538	84	148	27	5	15	67	61	105	18-7	.275	.352	.428	•29	.932
2000—Los Angeles (N.L.)	3B-SS	138	510	71	148	30	2	20	85	56	80	12-5	.290	.360	.475	23	.944
2001—Vero Beach (FSL)	3B	3	9	0	4	1	0	0	1	2	1	0-0	.444	.583	.556	0	1.000
—Las Vegas (PCL)	3B	2	5	2	3	1	0	1	2	2	0	0-0	.600	.714	1.400	1	.833
—Los Angeles (N.L.)	3B-SS	126	475	59	126	22	4	13	60	28	82	13-4	.265	.310	.411	16	.953
2002—Los Angeles (N.L.)	3B	159	587	70	151	26	5	21	75	37	96	7-5	.257	.303	.426	20	.954
Major League totals (5 years)		652	2305	302	615	114	16	76	309	196	400	53-22	.267	.327	.429	101	.943

BENARD, MARVIN — OF — GIANTS

PERSONAL: Born January 20, 1970, in Bluefields, Nicaragua. ... 5-9/191. ... Bats left, throws left. ... Full name: Marvin Larry Benard. ... Name pronounced buh-NARD.

HIGH SCHOOL: Bell (Bell Gardens, Calif.).

JUNIOR COLLEGE: Los Angeles Harbor College.

COLLEGE: Lewis-Clark State (Idaho).

TRANSACTIONS/CAREER NOTES: Selected by Philadelphia Phillies organization in 20th round of free-agent draft (June 4, 1990); did not sign. ... Selected by San Francisco Giants organization in 50th round of free-agent draft (June 1, 1992). ... On disabled list (April 17-28, 1993). ... On disabled list (July 2-September 1, 2002).

STATISTICAL NOTES: Tied for Texas League lead in grounding into double plays with 15 in 1994. ... Led Texas League outfielders with five double plays in 1994. ... Career major league grand slams: 1.

2002 GAMES PLAYED BY POSITION (MLB): OF—38.

		BATTING														FIELDING	
Year Team (League)	Pos.	G	AB	R	H	2B	3B	HR	RBI	BB	SO	SB-CS	Avg.	OBP	SLG	E	Avg.
1992—Everett (N'West)	OF	64	161	31	38	10	2	1	17	24	39	17-3	.236	.356	.342	3	.970
1993—Clinton (Midw.)	OF	112	349	84	105	14	2	5	50	56	66	42-10	.301	.403	.395	5	.974
1994—Shreveport (Texas)	OF	125	454	66	143	32	3	4	48	31	58	24-13	.315	.361	.425	*12	.958
1995—Phoenix (PCL)	OF-DH	111	378	70	115	14	6	6	32	50	66	10-13	.304	.390	.421	8	.959
—San Francisco (N.L.)	OF	13	34	5	13	2	0	1	4	1	7	1-0	.382	.400	.529	0	1.000
1996—Phoenix (PCL)	OF	4	19	2	7	0	0	0	4	2	2	1-0	.368	.429	.368	0	1.000
—San Francisco (N.L.)	OF	135	488	89	121	17	4	5	27	59	84	25-11	.248	.333	.330	5	.984
1997—San Francisco (N.L.)	OF-DH	84	114	13	26	4	0	1	13	13	29	3-1	.228	.315	.289	1	.967
—Phoenix (PCL)	OF	17	60	14	20	5	0	0	5	11	9	4-3	.333	.444	.417	1	.966
1998—San Francisco (N.L.)	OF-DH	121	286	41	92	21	1	3	36	34	39	11-4	.322	.396	.434	2	.982
1999—San Francisco (N.L.)	OF	149	562	100	163	36	5	16	64	55	97	27-14	.290	.359	.457	4	.988
2000—San Francisco (N.L.)	OF	149	560	102	147	27	6	12	55	63	97	22-7	.263	.342	.396	1	.997
2001—San Francisco (N.L.)	OF	129	392	70	104	19	2	15	44	29	66	10-5	.265	.320	.439	8	.965
2002—San Francisco (N.L.)	OF	65	123	16	34	9	2	1	13	7	26	5-1	.276	.321	.407	0	1.000
Major League totals (8 years)		845	2559	436	700	135	20	54	256	261	445	104-43	.274	.345	.405	21	.985

DIVISION SERIES RECORD

		BATTING														FIELDING	
Year Team (League)	Pos.	G	AB	R	H	2B	3B	HR	RBI	BB	SO	SB-CS	Avg.	OBP	SLG	E	Avg.
1997—San Francisco (N.L.)	PH	2	2	0	0	0	0	0	0	0	1	0-0	.000	.000	.000	...	...
2000—San Francisco (N.L.)	OF-PH	4	14	0	1	0	0	0	1	1	7	0-0	.071	.133	.071	0	1.000
Division series totals (2 years)		6	16	0	1	0	0	0	1	1	8	0-0	.063	.118	.063	0	1.000

BENES, ALAN — P — CUBS

PERSONAL: Born January 21, 1972, in Evansville, Ind. ... 6-5/235. ... Throws right, bats right. ... Full name: Alan Paul Benes. ... Brother of Andy Benes, pitcher with five major league teams (1989-2002); and brother of Adam Benes, pitcher with Cardinals organization (1995-2000). ... Name pronounced BEN-es.

HIGH SCHOOL: Lake Forest (Ill.).

COLLEGE: Creighton.

TRANSACTIONS/CAREER NOTES: Selected by San Diego Padres organization in 49th round of free-agent draft (June 4, 1990); did not sign. ... Selected by St. Louis Cardinals organization in first round (16th pick overall) of free-agent draft (June 3, 1993). ...

On Louisville disabled list (May 3-August 9, 1995). ... On disabled list (July 31, 1997-remainder of season; and March 22, 1998-entire season). ... On St. Louis disabled list (March 26-September 5, 1999); included rehabilitation assignments to Arkansas (August 5-10 and August 26-30), Potomac (August 11-15 and August 31-September 3) and Memphis (August 16-25 and September 4-5). ... Granted free agency (December 21, 2001). ... Signed by Chicago Cubs organization (January 16, 2002). ... On Iowa disabled list (May 7-14, 2002).

HONORS: Named N.L. Rookie Pitcher of the Year by The Sporting News (1996).

CAREER HITTING (MLB): 22-for-138 (.159), 6 R, 6 2B, 0 3B, 0 HR, 8 RBI.

Year League	W	L	Pct.	ERA	G	GS	CG	ShO	Sv.-Opp.	IP	H	R	ER	HR	BB-IBB	SO
1993—Glens Falls (NY-Penn)	0	4	.000	3.65	7	7	0	0	0-...	37.0	39	20	15	2	14-0	29
1994—Savannah (S.Atl.)	2	0	1.000	1.48	4	4	0	0	0-...	24.1	21	5	4	1	7-0	24
—St. Petersburg (FSL)	7	1	.875	1.61	11	11	0	0	0-...	78.1	55	18	14	0	15-0	69
—Arkansas (Texas)	7	2	.778	2.98	13	13	1	0	0-...	87.2	58	38	29	8	26-0	75
—Louisville (A.A.)	1	0	1.000	2.93	2	2	1	0	0-...	15.1	10	5	5	1	4-0	16
1995—Louisville (A.A.)	4	2	.667	2.41	11	11	2	1	0-...	56.0	37	16	15	5	14-1	54
—St. Louis (N.L.)	1	2	.333	8.44	3	3	0	0	0-0	16.0	24	15	15	2	4-0	20
1996—St. Louis (N.L.)	13	10	.565	4.90	34	32	3	1	0-0	191.0	192	120	104	27	87-3	131
1997—St. Louis (N.L.)	9	9	.500	2.89	23	23	2	0	0-0	161.2	128	60	52	13	68-3	160
1998—St. Louis (N.L.)									Did not play.							
1999—Arkansas (Texas)	0	0	...	6.23	2	2	0	0	0-...	4.1	6	3	3	0	1-0	0
—Potomac (Caro.)	0	0	...	1.80	2	2	0	0	0-...	5.0	1	1	1	0	4-0	2
—Memphis (PCL)	0	1	.000	3.18	3	3	0	0	0-...	5.2	8	3	2	0	2-0	3
—St. Louis (N.L.)	0	0	...	0.00	2	0	0	0	0-0	2.0	2	0	0	0	0-0	2
2000—Memphis (PCL)	1	2	.333	5.95	9	8	0	0	0-...	39.1	45	31	26	7	21-0	26
—St. Louis (N.L.)	2	2	.500	5.67	30	0	0	0	0-1	46.0	54	33	29	7	23-2	26
2001—Memphis (PCL)	7	6	.538	3.55	25	25	1	0	0-...	142.0	164	71	56	13	51-1	96
—St. Louis (N.L.)	2	0	1.000	7.36	9	1	0	0	0-0	14.2	14	12	12	5	12-0	10
2002—Iowa (PCL)■	10	9	.526	5.65	28	19	0	0	0-...	113.0	130	79	71	17	53-0	85
—Chicago (N.L.)	2	2	.500	4.35	7	7	0	0	0-0	39.1	42	22	19	3	12-1	32
Major League totals (7 years)	29	25	.537	4.42	108	66	5	1	0-1	470.2	456	262	231	57	206-9	381

CHAMPIONSHIP SERIES RECORD

Year League	W	L	Pct.	ERA	G	GS	CG	ShO	Sv.-Opp.	IP	H	R	ER	HR	BB-IBB	SO
1996—St. Louis (N.L.)	0	1	.000	2.84	2	1	0	0	0-0	6.1	3	2	2	0	2-1	5

BENES, ANDY P

PERSONAL: Born August 20, 1967, in Evansville, Ind. ... 6-6/245. ... Throws right, bats right. ... Full name: Andrew Charles Benes. ... Brother of Alan Benes, pitcher, Chicago Cubs; and brother of Adam Benes, pitcher with Cardinals organization (1995-2000). ... Name pronounced BEN-ess.

HIGH SCHOOL: Central (Evansville, Ind.).

COLLEGE: Evansville.

TRANSACTIONS/CAREER NOTES: Selected by San Diego Padres organization in first round (first pick overall) of free-agent draft (June 1, 1988). ... On suspended list (September 28, 1993-remainder of season). ... Traded by Padres with a player to be named later to Seattle Mariners for P Ron Villone and OF Marc Newfield (July 31, 1995); Mariners acquired P Greg Keagle to complete deal (September 16, 1995). ... Granted free agency (October 31, 1995). ... Signed by St. Louis Cardinals (December 23, 1995). ... On St. Louis disabled list (March 23-April 28, 1997); included rehabilitation assignments to Prince William (April 11), Louisville (April 16) and Arkansas (April 22). ... Granted free agency (October 29, 1997). ... Signed by Arizona Diamondbacks (February 3, 1998). ... Granted free agency (October 29, 1999). ... Signed by Cardinals (January 7, 2000). ... On disabled list (August 15-September 3, 2000). ... On St. Louis disabled list (April 16-July 16, 2002); included rehabilitation assignments to Memphis (June 15-July 8 and July 10-16) and Potomac (July 9). ... Granted free agency (October 31, 2002).

RECORDS: Holds major league single-season record for fewest hits allowed for leader in most hits allowed—230 (1992). ... Shares major league record for most home runs allowed in one inning—4 (July 23, 2000, second inning).

HONORS: Named N.L. Rookie Pitcher of the Year by The Sporting News (1989). ... Named Texas League Pitcher of the Year (1989).

STATISTICAL NOTES: Tied for N.L. lead with five balks in 1990. ... Pitched 7-0 one-hit, complete-game victory against New York (July 3, 1994).

MISCELLANEOUS: Holds San Diego Padres all-time record for most strikeouts (1,036). ... Member of 1988 U.S. Olympic baseball team (1988). ... Made an out in only appearance as pinch hitter (1998).

CAREER HITTING (MLB): 106-for-741 (.143), 48 R, 21 2B, 0 3B, 8 HR, 50 RBI.

Year League	W	L	Pct.	ERA	G	GS	CG	ShO	Sv.-Opp.	IP	H	R	ER	HR	BB-IBB	SO
1989—Wichita (Texas)	8	4	.667	2.16	16	16	5	*3	0-...	108.1	79	32	26	6	39-1	115
—Las Vegas (PCL)	2	1	.667	8.10	5	5	0	0	0-...	26.2	41	29	24	8	12-0	29
—San Diego (N.L.)	6	3	.667	3.51	10	10	0	0	0-0	66.2	51	28	26	7	31-0	66
1990—San Diego (N.L.)	10	11	.476	3.60	32	31	2	0	0-0	192.1	177	87	77	18	69-5	140
1991—San Diego (N.L.)	15	11	.577	3.03	33	33	4	1	0-0	223.0	194	76	75	23	59-7	167
1992—San Diego (N.L.)	13	14	.481	3.35	34	34	2	2	0-0	231.1	*230	90	86	14	61-6	169
1993—San Diego (N.L.)	15	15	.500	3.78	34	34	4	2	0-0	230.2	200	111	97	23	86-7	179
1994—San Diego (N.L.)	6	*14	.300	3.86	25	25	2	2	0-0	172.1	155	82	74	20	51-2	*189
1995—San Diego (N.L.)	4	7	.364	4.17	19	19	1	1	0-0	118.2	121	65	55	10	45-3	126
—Seattle (A.L.)■	7	2	.778	5.86	12	12	0	0	0-0	63.0	72	42	41	8	33-2	45
1996—St. Louis (N.L.)■	18	10	.643	3.83	36	34	3	1	1-1	230.1	215	107	98	28	77-7	160
1997—Prince William (Caro.)	0	0	...	0.00	1	1	0	0	0-...	5.0	3	1	0	0	1-0	9
—Louisville (A.A.)	0	0	...	1.80	1	1	0	0	0-...	5.0	3	1	1	1	1-0	5
—Arkansas (Texas)	1	0	1.000	1.29	1	1	0	0	0-...	7.0	2	1	1	0	2-0	6
—St. Louis (N.L.)	10	7	.588	3.10	26	26	0	0	0-0	177.0	149	64	61	9	61-4	175
1998—Arizona (N.L.)■	14	13	.519	3.97	34	34	1	0	0-0	231.1	221	111	102	25	74-3	164
1999—Arizona (N.L.)	13	12	.520	4.81	33	32	0	0	0-0	198.1	216	117	106	34	82-3	141
2000—St. Louis (N.L.)■	12	9	.571	4.88	30	27	1	0	0-0	166.0	174	95	90	30	68-0	137
2001—St. Louis (N.L.)	7	7	.500	7.38	27	19	0	0	0-1	107.1	122	92	88	30	61-0	78
2002—St. Louis (N.L.)	5	4	.556	2.78	18	17	1	0	0-0	97.0	80	39	30	10	51-3	64
—Memphis (PCL)	1	1	.500	3.12	4	4	0	0	0-...	17.1	17	7	6	2	4-0	8
—Potomac (Caro.)	0	0	...	9.00	1	1	0	0	0-...	7.0	8	7	7	2	6-0	3
A.L. totals (1 year)	7	2	.778	5.86	12	12	0	0	0-0	63.0	72	42	41	8	33-2	45
N.L. totals (14 years)	148	137	.519	3.92	391	375	21	9	1-2	2442.1	2305	1164	1065	281	876-50	1955
Major League totals (14 years)	155	139	.527	3.97	403	387	21	9	1-2	2505.1	2377	1206	1106	289	909-52	2000

DIVISION SERIES RECORD

Year League	W	L	Pct.	ERA	G	GS	CG	ShO	Sv.-Opp.	IP	H	R	ER	HR	BB-IBB	SO
1995—Seattle (A.L.)	0	0	...	5.40	2	2	0	0	0-0	11.2	10	7	7	3	9-1	8
1996—St. Louis (N.L.)	0	0	...	5.14	1	1	0	0	0-0	7.0	6	4	4	1	1-0	9
2000—St. Louis (N.L.)									Did not play.							
2001—St. Louis (N.L.)									Did not play.							
2002—St. Louis (N.L.)	0	0	...	5.79	1	1	0	0	0-0	4.2	2	3	3	2	4-0	5
Division series totals (3 years)	0	0	...	5.40	4	4	0	0	0-0	23.1	18	14	14	6	14-1	22

CHAMPIONSHIP SERIES RECORD

RECORDS: Shares N.L. single-series record for most hits allowed—19 (1996).

Year League	W	L	Pct.	ERA	G	GS	CG	ShO	Sv.-Opp.	IP	H	R	ER	HR	BB-IBB	SO
1995—Seattle (A.L.)	0	1	.000	23.14	1	1	0	0	0-0	2.1	6	6	6	2	2-0	3
1996—St. Louis (N.L.)	0	0	...	5.28	3	2	0	0	0-0	15.1	19	9	9	3	3-0	9
2000—St. Louis (N.L.)	1	0	1.000	2.25	1	1	0	0	0-0	8.0	6	2	2	0	3-0	5
2002—St. Louis (N.L.)	0	0	...	3.38	1	1	0	0	0-0	5.1	2	2	2	0	4-0	5
Champ. series totals (4 years)	1	1	.500	5.52	6	5	0	0	0-0	31.0	33	19	19	5	12-0	22

ALL-STAR GAME RECORD

	W	L	Pct.	ERA	GS	CG	ShO	Sv.-Opp.	IP	H	R	ER	HR	BB-IBB	SO
All-Star Game totals (1 year)	0	0	...	4.50	0	0	0	0-0	2.0	2	1	1	1	0-0	2

BENITEZ, ARMANDO — P — METS

PERSONAL: Born November 3, 1972, in Ramon Santana, Dominican Republic. ... 6-4/229. ... Throws right, bats right. ... Full name: Armando German Benitez.

TRANSACTIONS/CAREER NOTES: Signed as non-drafted free agent by Baltimore Orioles organization (April 1, 1990). ... On Baltimore disabled list (April 20-August 26, 1996); included rehabilitation assignments to Bowie (May 17-19) and Gulf Coast Orioles (August 13-26). ... On suspended list (May 20-28, 1998). ... Traded by Orioles to New York Mets for C Charles Johnson (December 1, 1998).

HONORS: Named N.L. co-Reliever of the Year by The Sporting News (2001).

CAREER HITTING (MLB): 0-for-6 (.000), 0 R, 0 2B, 0 3B, 0 HR, 2 RBI.

Year League	W	L	Pct.	ERA	G	GS	CG	ShO	Sv.-Opp.	IP	H	R	ER	HR	BB-IBB	SO
1990—Dom. Orioles/WS (DSL)	3	1	.750	2.72	19	0	0	0	8-...	43.0	39	23	13	...	20-...	34
1991—Gulf Coast Orioles (GCL)	3	2	.600	2.72	14	3	0	0	0-...	36.1	35	16	11	2	11-0	33
1992—Bluefield (Appl.)	1	2	.333	4.31	25	0	0	0	5-...	31.1	35	31	15	1	23-0	37
1993—Albany (S.Atl.)	5	1	.833	1.52	40	0	0	0	14-...	53.1	31	10	9	2	19-0	83
—Frederick (Caro.)	3	0	1.000	0.66	12	0	0	0	4-...	13.2	7	1	1	0	4-0	29
1994—Bowie (East.)	8	4	.667	3.14	53	0	0	0	16-...	71.2	41	29	25	6	39-0	106
—Baltimore (A.L.)	0	0	...	0.90	3	0	0	0	0-0	10.0	8	1	1	0	4-0	14
1995—Baltimore (A.L.)	1	5	.167	5.66	44	0	0	0	2-5	47.2	37	33	30	8	37-2	56
—Rochester (I.L.)	2	2	.500	1.25	17	0	0	0	8-...	21.2	10	4	3	2	7-0	37
1996—Baltimore (A.L.)	1	0	1.000	3.77	18	0	0	0	4-5	14.1	7	6	6	2	6-0	20
—Bowie (East.)	0	0	...	4.50	4	4	0	0	0-...	6.0	7	3	3	0	0-0	8
—Gulf Coast Orioles (GCL)	1	0	1.000	0.00	1	0	0	0	0-...	2.0	1	0	0	0	0-0	5
—Rochester (I.L.)	0	0	...	2.25	2	0	0	0	0-...	4.0	3	1	1	1	1-0	5
1997—Baltimore (A.L.)	4	5	.444	2.45	71	0	0	0	9-10	73.1	49	22	20	7	43-5	106
1998—Baltimore (A.L.)	5	6	.455	3.82	71	0	0	0	22-26	68.1	48	29	29	10	39-2	87
1999—New York (N.L.)■	4	3	.571	1.85	77	0	0	0	22-28	78.0	40	17	16	4	41-4	128
2000—New York (N.L.)	4	4	.500	2.61	76	0	0	0	41-46	76.0	39	24	22	10	38-2	106
2001—New York (N.L.)	6	4	.600	3.77	73	0	0	0	43-46	76.1	59	32	32	12	40-6	93
2002—New York (N.L.)	1	0	1.000	2.27	62	0	0	0	33-37	67.1	46	20	17	8	25-0	79
A.L. totals (5 years)	11	16	.407	3.62	207	0	0	0	37-46	213.2	149	91	86	27	129-9	283
N.L. totals (4 years)	15	11	.577	2.63	288	0	0	0	139-157	297.2	184	93	87	34	144-12	406
Major League totals (9 years)	26	27	.491	3.04	495	0	0	0	176-203	511.1	333	184	173	61	273-21	689

DIVISION SERIES RECORD

Year League	W	L	Pct.	ERA	G	GS	CG	ShO	Sv.-Opp.	IP	H	R	ER	HR	BB-IBB	SO
1996—Baltimore (A.L.)	2	0	1.000	2.25	3	0	0	0	0-1	4.0	1	1	1	1	2-0	6
1997—Baltimore (A.L.)	0	0	...	3.00	3	0	0	0	0-0	3.0	3	1	1	1	2-0	4
1999—New York (N.L.)	0	0	...	0.00	2	0	0	0	0-1	2.1	2	0	0	0	1-1	2
2000—New York (N.L.)	1	0	1.000	6.00	2	0	0	0	0-1	3.0	4	2	2	1	1-1	3
Division series totals (4 years)	3	0	1.000	2.92	10	0	0	0	0-3	12.1	10	4	4	3	6-2	15

CHAMPIONSHIP SERIES RECORD

Year League	W	L	Pct.	ERA	G	GS	CG	ShO	Sv.-Opp.	IP	H	R	ER	HR	BB-IBB	SO
1996—Baltimore (A.L.)	0	0	...	7.71	3	0	0	0	1-2	2.1	3	2	2	2	3-1	2
1997—Baltimore (A.L.)	0	2	.000	12.00	4	0	0	0	0-1	3.0	3	4	4	2	4-0	6
1999—New York (N.L.)	0	0	...	1.35	5	0	0	0	1-1	6.2	3	1	1	0	2-0	9
2000—New York (N.L.)	0	0	...	0.00	3	0	0	0	1-1	3.0	3	2	0	0	2-0	2
Champ. series totals (4 years)	0	2	.000	4.20	15	0	0	0	3-5	15.0	12	9	7	4	11-1	19

WORLD SERIES RECORD

Year League	W	L	Pct.	ERA	G	GS	CG	ShO	Sv.-Opp.	IP	H	R	ER	HR	BB-IBB	SO
2000—New York (N.L.)	0	0	...	3.00	3	0	0	0	1-2	3.0	3	1	1	0	2-0	2

BENJAMIN, MIKE — IF

PERSONAL: Born November 22, 1965, in Euclid, Ohio. ... 6-0/172. ... Bats right, throws right. ... Full name: Michael Paul Benjamin.

HIGH SCHOOL: Bellflower (Calif.).

JUNIOR COLLEGE: Cerritos College (Calif.).

COLLEGE: Arizona State.

TRANSACTIONS/CAREER NOTES: Selected by Minnesota Twins organization in seventh round of free-agent draft (January 9, 1985); did not sign. ... Selected by San Francisco Giants organization in third round of free-agent draft (June 2, 1987). ... On San Francisco disabled list

(March 31-June 5, 1992); included rehabilitation assignment to Phoenix (April 20-May 10). ... On San Francisco disabled list (July 8-August 6, 1993); included rehabilitation assignment to San Jose (August 4-6). ... Traded by Giants to Philadelphia Phillies for P Jeff Juden and OF/1B Tommy Eason (October 6, 1995). ... On Philadelphia disabled list (March 23-April 26 and July 20, 1996-remainder of season); included rehabilitation assignments to Clearwater (April 8-17) and Scranton/Wilkes-Barre (April 21-26). ... Granted free agency (October 8, 1996). ... Signed by Boston Red Sox organization (January 31, 1997). ... Granted free agency (October 27, 1997). ... Re-signed by Red Sox (November 21, 1997). ... Granted free agency (October 26, 1998). ... Signed by Pittsburgh Pirates (November 17, 1998). ... On disabled list (July 24-August 11, 1999; and March 31, 2001-entire season). ... Granted free agency (October 29, 2002).

RECORDS: Holds modern major league record for most hits in three consecutive games—14 (June 11 [4], 13 [4] and 14 [6], 1995).

STATISTICAL NOTES: Led Pacific Coast League shortstops with 216 putouts, 386 assists and 626 total chances in 1990. ... Collected six hits in one game (June 14, 1995).

2002 GAMES PLAYED BY POSITION (MLB): 3B—62; SS—15; 2B—11; DH—1; OF—1; 1B—1.

			BATTING														FIELDING	
Year	**Team (League)**	**Pos.**	**G**	**AB**	**R**	**H**	**2B**	**3B**	**HR**	**RBI**	**BB**	**SO**	**SB-CS**	**Avg.**	**OBP**	**SLG**	**E**	**Avg.**
1987—	Fresno (Calif.)	SS	64	212	25	51	6	4	6	24	24	71	6-2	.241	.324	.392	21	.930
1988—	Shreveport (Texas)	SS	89	309	48	73	19	5	6	37	22	63	14-6	.236	.285	.388	11	.972
—	Phoenix (PCL)	SS	37	106	13	18	4	1	0	6	13	32	2-1	.170	.270	.226	4	.966
1989—	Phoenix (PCL)	SS-2B	113	363	44	94	17	6	3	36	18	82	10-4	.259	.303	.364	15	.970
—	San Francisco (N.L.)	SS	14	6	6	1	0	0	0	0	0	1	0-0	.167	.167	.167	0	1.000
1990—	Phoenix (PCL)	SS	118	419	61	105	21	7	5	39	25	89	13-7	.251	.297	.370	24	.962
—	San Francisco (N.L.)	SS	22	56	7	12	3	1	2	3	3	10	1-0	.214	.254	.411	1	.988
1991—	San Francisco (N.L.)	SS-3B	54	106	12	13	3	0	2	8	7	26	3-0	.123	.188	.208	3	.984
—	Phoenix (PCL)	SS	64	226	34	46	13	2	6	31	20	67	3-2	.204	.270	.358	9	.976
1992—	Phoenix (PCL)	SS-2B	31	108	15	33	10	2	0	17	3	18	4-2	.306	.342	.435	2	.986
—	San Francisco (N.L.)	SS-3B	40	75	4	13	2	1	1	3	4	15	1-0	.173	.215	.267	1	.991
1993—	San Francisco (N.L.)	SS-2B-3B	63	146	22	29	7	0	4	16	9	23	0-0	.199	.264	.329	5	.976
—	San Jose (Calif.)	SS-2B	2	8	1	0	0	0	0	0	1	0	0-0	.000	.200	.000	0	1.000
1994—	San Francisco (N.L.)	SS-2B-3B	38	62	9	16	5	1	1	9	5	16	5-0	.258	.343	.419	3	.972
1995—	San Francisco (N.L.)	3B-SS-2B	68	186	19	41	6	0	3	12	8	51	11-1	.220	.256	.301	4	.977
1996—	Clearwater (FSL)■	SS	8	23	3	4	1	0	0	0	3	4	1-0	.174	.269	.217	2	.935
—	Scranton/W.B. (I.L.)	SS	4	13	2	5	2	0	0	4	3	0	0-0	.385	.471	.538	0	1.000
—	Philadelphia (N.L.)	SS-2B	35	103	13	23	5	1	4	13	12	21	3-1	.223	.316	.408	6	.954
1997—	Pawtucket (I.L.)■	SS-DH-3B-2B	33	105	12	26	4	1	4	12	8	20	4-1	.248	.313	.419	5	.964
—	Boston (A.L.)	3-S-2-1-DH-P	49	116	12	27	9	1	0	7	4	27	2-3	.233	.262	.328	6	.956
1998—	Boston (A.L.)	2-S-3-1-DH	124	349	46	95	23	0	4	39	15	73	3-0	.272	.312	.372	3	.994
1999—	Pittsburgh (N.L.)■	SS-2B-3B	110	368	42	91	26	7	1	37	20	90	10-1	.247	.288	.364	8	.984
2000—	Pittsburgh (N.L.)	3B-SS-2B-1B	93	233	28	63	18	2	2	19	12	45	5-4	.270	.313	.391	4	.987
2001—	Pittsburgh (N.L.)								Did not play.									
2002—	Pittsburgh (N.L.)	IF-DH-OF-1B	108	120	7	18	2	1	0	3	7	31	0-4	.150	.202	.183	2	.987
American League totals (2 years)			173	465	58	122	32	1	4	46	19	100	5-3	.262	.300	.361	9	.986
National League totals (11 years)			645	1461	169	320	77	14	20	123	87	329	39-11	.219	.270	.332	37	.981
Major League totals (13 years)			818	1926	227	442	109	15	24	169	106	429	44-14	.229	.277	.339	46	.983

DIVISION SERIES RECORD

			BATTING														FIELDING	
Year	**Team (League)**	**Pos.**	**G**	**AB**	**R**	**H**	**2B**	**3B**	**HR**	**RBI**	**BB**	**SO**	**SB-CS**	**Avg.**	**OBP**	**SLG**	**E**	**Avg.**
1998—	Boston (A.L.)	2B-1B	4	11	1	1	0	0	0	0	1	3	0-0	.091	.167	.091	0	1.000

RECORD AS PITCHER

Year	League	W	L	Pct.	ERA	G	GS	CG	ShO	Sv.-Opp.	IP	H	R	ER	HR	BB-IBB	SO
1997—	Boston (A.L.)	0	0	...	0.00	1	0	0	0	0-0	1.0	0	0	0	0	0-0	0

BENNETT, GARY — C — ROCKIES

PERSONAL: Born April 17, 1972, in Waukegan, Ill. ... 6-0/208. ... Bats right, throws right. ... Full name: Gary David Bennett Jr.

HIGH SCHOOL: Waukegan East (Ill.).

TRANSACTIONS/CAREER NOTES: Selected by Philadelphia Phillies organization in 11th round of free-agent draft (June 4, 1990). ... On Clearwater disabled list (September 5-15, 1993). ... Granted free agency (October 8, 1996). ... Signed by Boston Red Sox organization (February 10, 1997). ... Granted free agency (October 15, 1997). ... Signed by Phillies organization (December 27, 1997). ... On Scranton/Wilkes-Barre disabled list (June 23-July 4, 2000). ... Traded by Phillies to New York Mets for C Todd Pratt (July 23, 2001). ... Traded by Mets to Colorado Rockies for a player to be named later (August 24, 2001); Mets acquired OF Ender Chavez to complete deal (December 27, 2001).

STATISTICAL NOTES: Led Eastern League with 22 passed balls in 1994. ... Led Eastern League catchers with 13 double plays in 1995.

2002 GAMES PLAYED BY POSITION (MLB): C—90.

			BATTING														FIELDING	
Year	**Team (League)**	**Pos.**	**G**	**AB**	**R**	**H**	**2B**	**3B**	**HR**	**RBI**	**BB**	**SO**	**SB-CS**	**Avg.**	**OBP**	**SLG**	**E**	**Avg.**
1990—	Martinsville (Appl.)	C	16	52	3	14	2	1	0	10	4	15	0-1	.269	.316	.346	3	.965
1991—	Martinsville (Appl.)	C	41	136	15	32	7	0	1	16	17	26	0-1	.235	.340	.309	2	.994
1992—	Batavia (NY-Penn)	C	47	146	22	30	2	0	0	12	15	27	2-1	.205	.288	.219	2	*.994
1993—	Spartanburg (S.Atl.)	C	42	126	18	32	4	1	0	15	12	22	0-2	.254	.321	.302	2	.992
—	Clearwater (FSL)	C	17	55	5	18	0	0	1	6	3	10	0-1	.327	.373	.382	0	1.000
1994—	Clearwater (FSL)	C	19	55	6	13	3	0	0	10	8	6	0-0	.236	.328	.291	1	.991
—	Reading (East.)	C	63	208	13	48	9	0	3	22	14	26	0-1	.231	.276	.317	2	.995
1995—	Reading (East.)	C-DH	86	271	27	64	11	0	4	40	22	36	0-0	.236	.299	.321	4	.994
—	Scranton/W.B. (I.L.)	C	7	20	1	3	0	0	0	1	2	2	0-0	.150	.227	.150	0	1.000
—	Philadelphia (N.L.)	PH	1	1	0	0	0	0	0	0	0	1	0-0	.000	.000	.000	...	...
1996—	Scranton/W.B. (I.L.)	C	91	286	37	71	15	1	8	37	24	43	1-0	.248	.310	.392	7	.988
—	Philadelphia (N.L.)	C	6	16	0	4	0	0	0	1	2	6	0-0	.250	.333	.250	0	1.000
1997—	Pawtucket (I.L.)■	C-1B	71	224	16	48	7	1	4	22	18	39	1-1	.214	.278	.308	8	.986
1998—	Scranton/W.B. (I.L.)■	C-DH-1B	86	282	33	72	18	0	10	40	25	41	0-0	.255	.316	.426	1	.998
—	Philadelphia (N.L.)	C	9	31	4	9	0	0	0	3	5	5	0-0	.290	.378	.290	0	1.000
1999—	Philadelphia (N.L.)	C	36	88	7	24	4	0	1	21	4	11	0-0	.273	.298	.352	4	.971

Year	Team (League)	Pos.	G	AB	R	H	2B	3B	HR	RBI	BB	SO	SB-CS	Avg.	OBP	SLG	E	Avg.
			BATTING														FIELDING	
2000—	Scranton/W.B. (I.L.) ...	C	92	317	47	97	24	0	12	52	40	44	1-0	.306	.393	.495	2	*.996
	—Philadelphia (N.L.)......	C	31	74	8	18	5	0	2	5	13	15	0-0	.243	.371	.392	1	.995
2001—	Philadelphia (N.L.)......	C	26	75	8	16	3	1	1	6	9	19	0-0	.213	.294	.320	2	.987
	—New York (N.L.)■	PH	1	1	0	1	0	0	0	0	0	0	0-0	1.000	1.000	1.000	...	...
	—Norfolk (I.L.)	C-3B	20	67	7	20	5	0	2	14	4	12	0-0	.299	.342	.463	0	1.000
	—Colorado (N.L.)■	C	19	55	7	15	3	0	1	4	3	5	0-0	.273	.317	.382	0	1.000
2002—	Colorado (N.L.)	C	90	291	26	77	10	2	4	26	15	45	1-3	.265	.314	.354	4	.992
Major League totals (7 years)			219	632	60	164	25	3	9	66	51	107	1-3	.259	.321	.351	11	.991

BENOIT, JOAQUIN — P — RANGERS

PERSONAL: Born July 26, 1977, in Santiago, Dominican Republic. ... 6-3/205. ... Throws right, bats right. ... Full name: Joaquin Antonio Benoit.

TRANSACTIONS/CAREER NOTES: Signed as non-drafted free agent by Texas Rangers organization (May 20, 1996). ... On disabled list (May 2-June 21, 2000).

CAREER HITTING (MLB): 0-for-0 (.000), 0 R, 0 2B, 0 3B, 0 HR, 0 RBI.

Year	League	W	L	Pct.	ERA	G	GS	CG	ShO	Sv.-Opp.	IP	H	R	ER	HR	BB-IBB	SO
1996—	Dom. Rangers (DSL)........	6	5	.545	2.28	14	13	2	1	0-...	75.0	63	26	19	...	23-...	63
1997—	Gulf Coast Rangers (GCL)	3	3	.500	2.05	10	10	1	0	0-...	44.0	40	14	10	0	11-0	38
1998—	Savannah (S.Atl.)	4	3	.571	3.83	15	1	0	0	0-...	80.0	79	41	34	8	18-0	68
1999—	Charlotte (FSL)................	7	4	.636	5.31	22	22	0	0	0-...	105.0	117	67	62	5	50-0	83
2000—	Tulsa (Texas)....................	4	4	.500	3.83	16	16	0	0	0-...	82.1	73	40	35	6	30-0	72
2001—	Tulsa (Texas)....................	1	0	1.000	3.32	4	4	0	0	0-...	21.2	23	8	8	1	6-0	23
	—Oklahoma (PCL)..............	9	5	.643	4.19	24	24	1	1	0-...	131.0	113	63	61	14	73-0	142
	—Texas (A.L.).....................	0	0	...	10.80	1	1	0	0	0-0	5.0	8	6	6	3	3-0	4
2002—	Oklahoma (PCL)..............	8	4	.667	3.56	16	16	0	0	0-...	98.2	74	42	39	8	37-0	103
	—Texas (A.L.).....................	4	5	.444	5.31	17	13	0	0	1-1	84.2	91	51	50	6	58-2	59
	—Charlotte (FSL)................	0	0	...	0.00	1	1	0	0	0-...	5.0	1	0	0	0	3-0	8
Major League totals (2 years).....		4	5	.444	5.62	18	14	0	0	1-1	89.2	99	57	56	9	61-2	63

BENSON, KRIS — P — PIRATES

PERSONAL: Born November 7, 1974, in Superior, Wis. ... 6-4/200. ... Throws right, bats right. ... Full name: Kristin James Benson.

HIGH SCHOOL: Spayberry (Marietta, Ga.).

COLLEGE: Clemson.

TRANSACTIONS/CAREER NOTES: Selected by Pittsburgh Pirates organization in first round (first pick overall) of free-agent draft (June 2, 1996). ... On disabled list (March 31, 2001-entire season). ... On Pittsburgh disabled list (March 22-May 13, 2002); included rehabilitation assignments to Nashville (April 4-19 and April 27-May 7) and Altoona (May 8-13).

MISCELLANEOUS: Member of 1996 U.S. Olympic baseball team.

CAREER HITTING (MLB): 23-for-170 (.135), 13 R, 6 2B, 0 3B, 0 HR, 9 RBI.

Year	League	W	L	Pct.	ERA	G	GS	CG	ShO	Sv.-Opp.	IP	H	R	ER	HR	BB-IBB	SO
1997—	Lynchburg (Caro.)...........	5	2	.714	2.58	10	10	0	0	0-...	59.1	49	20	17	1	13-0	72
	—Carolina (Sou.)................	3	5	.375	4.98	14	14	0	0	0-...	68.2	81	49	38	11	32-1	66
1998—	Nashville (PCL)................	8	10	.444	5.37	28	28	1	1	0-...	156.0	162	102	93	26	50-5	129
1999—	Pittsburgh (N.L.).............	11	14	.440	4.07	31	31	2	0	0-0	196.2	184	105	89	16	83-5	139
2000—	Pittsburgh (N.L.).............	10	12	.455	3.85	32	32	2	1	0-0	217.2	206	104	93	24	86-5	184
2001—	Pittsburgh (N.L.).............	Did not play.															
2002—	Nashville (PCL)................	0	2	.000	1.53	4	4	0	0	0-...	17.2	8	4	3	1	8-0	25
	—Altoona (East.)................	1	0	1.000	1.29	1	1	0	0	0-...	7.0	5	1	1	1	0-0	7
	—Pittsburgh (N.L.).............	9	6	.600	4.70	25	25	0	0	0-0	130.1	152	76	68	18	50-8	79
Major League totals (3 years).....		30	32	.484	4.13	88	88	4	1	0-0	544.2	542	285	250	58	219-18	402

BERE, JASON — P

PERSONAL: Born May 26, 1971, in Cambridge, Mass. ... 6-3/225. ... Throws right, bats right. ... Full name: Jason Phillip Bere. ... Name pronounced burr-AY.

HIGH SCHOOL: Wilmington (Mass.).

JUNIOR COLLEGE: Middlesex Community College (Mass.).

TRANSACTIONS/CAREER NOTES: Selected by Chicago White Sox organization in 36th round of free-agent draft (June 4, 1990). ... On Chicago disabled list (August 5-20, 1995); included rehabilitation assignment to South Bend (August 13-18). ... On Chicago disabled list (April 22-September 3 and September 14, 1996-remainder of season); included rehabilitation assignments to Nashville (May 14-19 and August 27-28), Gulf Coast White Sox (August 5-10), Hickory (August 10-16) and Birmingham (August 16-27). ... On Chicago disabled list (March 31-August 19, 1997); included rehabilitation assignments to Gulf Coast White Sox (July 2-7), Hickory (July 12), Birmingham (July 17-22) and Nashville (July 29-August 14). ... Released by White Sox (July 16, 1998). ... Signed by Cincinnati Reds organization (July 21, 1998). ... On Cincinnati disabled list (June 16-August 4, 1999); included rehabilitation assignment to Indianapolis (July 11-August 4). ... Released by Reds (August 4, 1999). ... Signed by Milwaukee Brewers organization (August 12, 1999). ... Granted free agency (November 1, 1999). ... Re-signed by Brewers (November 19, 1999). ... Traded by Brewers with P Bob Wickman and P Steve Woodard to Cleveland Indians for 1B/OF Richie Sexson, P Paul Rigdon, P Kane Davis and a player to be named later (July 28, 2000); Brewers acquired 2B Marcos Scutaro to complete deal (August 30, 2000). ... Granted free agency (October 31, 2000). ... Signed by Chicago Cubs (December 18, 2000). ... On Chicago disabled list (June 27-August 31 and September 6, 2002-remainder of season); included rehabilitation assignment to Iowa (August 25-26). ... Granted free agency (October 28, 2002).

CAREER HITTING (MLB): 30-for-161 (.186), 9 R, 6 2B, 1 3B, 0 HR, 5 RBI.

Year	League	W	L	Pct.	ERA	G	GS	CG	ShO	Sv.-Opp.	IP	H	R	ER	HR	BB-IBB	SO
1990	—GC White Sox (GCL)	0	4	.000	2.37	16	2	0	0	1-...	38.0	26	19	10	1	19-0	41
1991	—South Bend (Midw.)	9	12	.429	2.87	27	27	2	1	0-...	163.0	116	66	52	8	*100-0	158
1992	—Sarasota (FSL)	7	2	.778	2.41	18	18	1	1	0-...	116.0	84	35	31	3	34-3	106
	—Birmingham (Sou.)	4	4	.500	3.00	8	8	4	2	0-...	54.0	44	22	18	1	20-1	45
	—Vancouver (PCL)	0	0	...	0.00	1	0	0	0	0-...	1.0	2	0	0	0	0-0	2
1993	—Nashville (A.A.)	5	1	.833	2.37	8	8	0	0	0-...	49.1	36	19	13	1	25-1	52
	—Chicago (A.L.)	12	5	.706	3.47	24	24	1	0	0-0	142.2	109	60	55	12	81-0	129
1994	—Chicago (A.L.)	12	2	*.857	3.81	24	24	0	0	0-0	141.2	119	65	60	17	80-0	127
1995	—Chicago (A.L.)	8	•15	.348	7.19	27	27	1	0	0-0	137.2	151	120	110	21	106-6	110
	—Nashville (A.A.)	1	0	1.000	3.38	1	1	0	0	0-...	5.1	6	2	2	0	2-0	7
1996	—Chicago (A.L.)	0	1	.000	10.26	5	5	0	0	0-0	16.2	26	19	19	3	18-1	19
	—Nashville (A.A.)	0	0	...	1.42	3	3	0	0	0-...	12.2	9	2	2	1	4-0	15
	—GC White Sox (GCL)	0	1	.000	6.00	1	1	0	0	0-...	3.0	3	2	2	0	1-0	3
	—Hickory (S.Atl.)	1	0	1.000	0.00	1	1	0	0	0-...	5.0	3	0	0	0	0-0	5
	—Birmingham (Sou.)	0	0	...	4.15	1	1	0	0	0-...	4.1	4	2	2	2	4-0	5
1997	—GC White Sox (GCL)	0	0	...	0.00	2	2	0	0	0-...	5.0	2	0	0	0	0-0	5
	—Hickory (S.Atl.)	0	0	...	6.00	1	1	0	0	0-...	3.0	4	2	2	0	0-0	2
	—Birmingham (Sou.)	0	1	.000	7.71	2	2	0	0	0-...	7.0	8	7	6	2	2-0	7
	—Nashville (A.A.)	1	1	.500	5.59	4	4	0	0	0-...	19.1	23	13	12	2	7-0	13
	—Chicago (A.L.)	4	2	.667	4.71	6	6	0	0	0-0	28.2	20	15	15	4	17-0	21
1998	—Chicago (A.L.)	3	7	.300	6.45	18	15	0	0	0-0	83.2	98	71	60	14	58-0	53
	—Cincinnati (N.L.)■	3	2	.600	4.12	9	7	0	0	0-0	43.2	39	20	20	3	20-0	31
1999	—Cincinnati (N.L.)	3	0	1.000	6.85	12	10	0	0	0-0	43.1	56	37	33	6	40-3	28
	—Indianapolis (I.L.)	0	2	.000	10.19	5	4	0	0	0-...	17.2	25	20	20	3	19-0	8
	—Louisville (I.L.)■	2	1	.667	2.08	5	5	0	0	0-...	26.0	21	8	6	0	8-0	27
	—Milwaukee (N.L.)	2	0	1.000	4.63	5	4	0	0	0-0	23.1	23	15	12	3	10-0	19
2000	—Milwaukee (N.L.)	6	7	.462	4.93	20	20	0	0	0-0	115.0	115	66	63	19	63-7	98
	—Cleveland (A.L.)■	6	3	.667	6.63	11	11	0	0	0-0	54.1	65	41	40	6	26-0	44
2001	—Chicago (N.L.)■	11	11	.500	4.31	32	32	2	0	0-0	188.0	171	99	90	24	77-7	175
2002	—Chicago (N.L.)	1	10	.091	5.67	16	16	0	0	0-0	85.2	98	63	54	13	28-1	65
	—Iowa (PCL)	1	0	1.000	1.80	1	1	0	0	0-...	5.0	2	1	1	0	3-0	3
A.L. totals (7 years)		45	35	.563	5.34	115	112	2	0	0-0	605.1	588	391	359	77	386-7	503
N.L. totals (5 years)		26	30	.464	4.91	94	89	2	0	0-0	499.0	502	300	272	68	238-18	416
Major League totals (10 years)		71	65	.522	5.14	209	201	4	0	0-0	1104.1	1090	691	631	145	624-25	919

CHAMPIONSHIP SERIES RECORD

Year	League	W	L	Pct.	ERA	G	GS	CG	ShO	Sv.-Opp.	IP	H	R	ER	HR	BB-IBB	SO
1993	—Chicago (A.L.)	0	0	...	11.57	1	1	0	0	0-0	2.1	5	3	3	0	2-0	3

ALL-STAR GAME RECORD

	W	L	Pct.	ERA	GS	CG	ShO	Sv.-Opp.	IP	H	R	ER	HR	BB-IBB	SO
All-Star Game totals (1 year)	0	1	.000	...	0	0	0	0-0	.0	2	1	1	0	0-0	0

BERG, DAVID — IF — BLUE JAYS

PERSONAL: Born September 3, 1970, in Roseville, Calif. ... 5-11/196. ... Bats right, throws right. ... Full name: David Scott Berg.
HIGH SCHOOL: Roseville (Calif.).
JUNIOR COLLEGE: Sacramento City College.
COLLEGE: Miami (Fla.).
TRANSACTIONS/CAREER NOTES: Selected by California Angels organization in 32nd round of free-agent draft (June 4, 1990); did not sign. ... Selected by Florida Marlins organization in 38th round of free-agent draft (June 3, 1993). ... On Florida disabled list (April 2-25, 2000); included rehabilitation assignment to Brevard County (April 22-25). ... Granted free agency (December 21, 2001). ... Signed by Toronto Blue Jays organization (January 12, 2002).
STATISTICAL NOTES: Led New York-Penn League third basemen with 158 assists in 1993. ... Led Midwest League third basemen with .948 fielding percentage in 1994.
2002 GAMES PLAYED BY POSITION (MLB): 2B—52; 3B—20; OF—13; SS—13; 1B—10; DH—8.

			BATTING														FIELDING	
Year	Team (League)	Pos.	G	AB	R	H	2B	3B	HR	RBI	BB	SO	SB-CS	Avg.	OBP	SLG	E	Avg.
1993	—Elmira (NY-Penn)	3B-2B-OF	75	281	37	74	13	1	4	28	34	37	7-4	.263	.356	.359	20	.925
1994	—Kane County (Midw.)	3B-2B	121	437	80	117	27	8	9	53	54	80	8-6	.268	.354	.428	17	†.948
1995	—Brevard County (FSL)	SS-3B-2B	114	382	71	114	18	1	3	39	68	61	9-4	.298	.407	.374	26	.951
1996	—Portland (East.)	SS-3B	109	414	64	125	28	5	9	73	42	60	17-7	.302	.368	.459	26	.951
1997	—Charlotte (I.L.)	SS-2B-3B	117	424	76	125	26	6	9	47	55	71	16-7	.295	.377	.448	22	.954
1998	—Florida (N.L.)	2B-3B-SS	81	182	18	57	11	0	2	21	26	46	3-0	.313	.393	.407	7	.969
1999	—Florida (N.L.)	S-2-3-O	109	304	42	87	18	1	3	25	27	59	2-2	.286	.348	.382	8	.974
2000	—Brevard County (FSL)	2B-3B-SS	3	11	2	3	0	0	0	2	1	3	0-1	.273	.385	.273	0	1.000
	—Florida (N.L.)	SS-3B-2B	82	210	23	53	14	1	1	21	25	46	3-0	.252	.340	.343	8	.964
2001	—Florida (N.L.)	2B-SS-3B	82	215	26	52	12	1	4	16	14	39	0-1	.242	.292	.363	8	.961
2002	—Toronto (A.L.)■	IF-OF-DH	109	374	42	101	26	2	4	39	26	57	0-2	.270	.322	.382	10	.974
American League totals (1 year)			109	374	42	101	26	2	4	39	26	57	0-2	.270	.322	.382	10	.974
National League totals (4 years)			354	911	109	249	55	3	10	83	92	190	8-3	.273	.343	.373	31	.968
Major League totals (5 years)			463	1285	151	350	81	5	14	122	118	247	8-5	.272	.337	.376	41	.969

BERGER, BRANDON — OF — ROYALS

PERSONAL: Born February 21, 1975, in Covington, Ky. ... 5-11/205. ... Bats right, throws right. ... Full name: Brandon Charles Berger.
HIGH SCHOOL: Beechwood (Fort Mitchell, Ky.).
COLLEGE: Eastern Kentucky.
TRANSACTIONS/CAREER NOTES: Selected by Kansas City Royals organization in 14th round of free-agent draft (June 4, 1996).
2002 GAMES PLAYED BY POSITION (MLB): OF—36; DH—10; 1B—1.

Year	Team (League)	Pos.	G	AB	R	H	2B	3B	HR	RBI	BB	SO	SB-CS	Avg.	OBP	SLG	E	Avg.
			BATTING														FIELDING	
1996—	Spokane (N'West)	OF	71	283	46	87	12	1	13	58	31	64	17-5	.307	.376	.495	4	.967
1997—	Lansing (Midw.)	OF	107	393	64	115	22	6	12	73	42	79	13-1	.293	.368	.471	3	.979
1998—	Wilmington (Caro.).....	OF-P	110	338	53	75	18	3	8	50	53	94	13-3	.222	.332	.364	2	.986
1999—	Wilmington (Caro.).....	OF	119	450	73	132	27	4	16	73	45	93	29-7	.293	.363	.478	5	.964
2000—	Wichita (Texas)	OF	27	86	9	14	2	0	3	8	7	27	6-1	.163	.240	.291	0	1.000
—	Wilmington (Caro.).....	OF	102	379	63	108	18	4	15	71	40	71	12-4	.285	.376	.472	3	.983
2001—	Wichita (Texas)	OF	120	454	98	140	28	3	*40	118	43	91	14-6	.308	.383	*.648	4	.971
—	Kansas City (A.L.)	OF-DH	6	16	4	5	1	1	2	2	2	2	0-0	.313	.389	.875	0	1.000
2002—	Omaha (PCL)..............	OF-1B	68	261	34	76	16	1	13	47	25	43	11-2	.291	.363	.510	3	.975
—	Kansas City (A.L.)	OF-DH-1B	51	134	16	27	5	1	6	17	8	32	1-0	.201	.255	.388	0	1.000
Major League totals (2 years)			57	150	20	32	6	2	8	19	10	34	1-0	.213	.270	.440	0	1.000

RECORD AS PITCHER

Year	League	W	L	Pct.	ERA	G	GS	CG	ShO	Sv.	IP	H	R	ER	BB	SO
1998—	Wilmington (Caro.)............	0	0	...	13.50	1	0	0	0	0	2	3	3	3	4	0

BERGERON, PETER — OF — EXPOS

PERSONAL: Born November 9, 1977, in Greenfield, Mass. ... 6-0/190. ... Bats left, throws right. ... Full name: Peter Francis Bergeron.
HIGH SCHOOL: Greenfield (Mass.).
TRANSACTIONS/CAREER NOTES: Selected by Los Angeles Dodgers organization in fourth round of free-agent draft (June 4, 1996). ... Traded by Dodgers with 2B Wilton Guerrero, P Ted Lilly and 1B Jonathan Tucker to Montreal Expos for P Carlos Perez, SS Mark Grudzielanek and OF Hiram Bocachica (July 31, 1998).
STATISTICAL NOTES: Led Texas League outfielders with five double plays in 1998. ... Led N.L. outfielders with 16 assists in 2000. ... Had 19-game hitting streak (July 1-23, 2001).
2002 GAMES PLAYED BY POSITION (MLB): OF—31.

Year	Team (League)	Pos.	G	AB	R	H	2B	3B	HR	RBI	BB	SO	SB-CS	Avg.	OBP	SLG	E	Avg.
			BATTING														FIELDING	
1996—	Yakima (N'West)	OF	61	232	36	59	5	3	5	21	28	59	13-9	.254	.335	.366	1	*.990
1997—	Savannah (S.Atl.)	OF	131	492	89	138	18	5	5	36	67	110	32-21	.280	.367	.368	4	.984
—	San Bern. (Calif.)........	OF	2	8	1	2	0	0	0	1	0	2	2-0	.250	.250	.250	0	1.000
1998—	San Antonio (Texas)...	OF	109	416	81	132	17	8	8	54	61	69	33-9	.317	.406	.454	2	*.992
—	Harrisburg (East.)■ ...	OF	34	134	22	33	8	4	0	9	17	26	8-3	.246	.331	.366	0	1.000
1999—	Harrisburg (East.).......	OF-DH	42	162	29	53	14	2	4	18	24	29	9-7	.327	.407	.512	1	.986
—	Ottawa (I.L.)	OF-DH	58	194	36	61	12	3	3	20	23	40	14-8	.314	.386	.454	2	.973
—	Montreal (N.L.)...........	OF	16	45	12	11	2	0	0	1	9	5	0-0	.244	.370	.289	1	.967
2000—	Montreal (N.L.)...........	OF	148	518	80	127	25	7	5	31	58	100	11-13	.245	.320	.349	5	.985
2001—	Montreal (N.L.)...........	OF	102	375	53	79	11	4	3	16	28	87	10-7	.211	.275	.285	1	.996
—	Ottawa (I.L.)	OF	52	206	29	49	5	3	0	8	20	42	15-7	.238	.307	.291	2	.983
2002—	Montreal (N.L.)...........	OF	31	123	24	23	3	2	0	7	22	44	10-3	.187	.310	.244	2	.974
—	Ottawa (I.L.)	OF	104	340	51	99	9	4	1	29	39	65	7-7	.291	.364	.350	3	.984
Major League totals (4 years)			297	1061	169	240	41	13	8	55	117	236	31-23	.226	.305	.312	9	.986

BERKMAN, LANCE — OF — ASTROS

PERSONAL: Born February 10, 1976, in Waco, Texas. ... 6-1/220. ... Bats both, throws left. ... Full name: William Lance Berkman.
HIGH SCHOOL: Canyon (New Braunfels, Texas).
COLLEGE: Rice.
TRANSACTIONS/CAREER NOTES: Selected by Houston Astros organization in first round (16th pick overall) of free-agent draft (June 3, 1997). ... On New Orleans disabled list (April 13-May 14, 1999).
RECORDS: Holds major league single-season record for most doubles by switch-hitter—55 (2001); and most extra-base hits by switch-hitter—94 (2001).
HONORS: Named first baseman on The Sporting News college All-America first team (1997).
STATISTICAL NOTES: Led Texas League with 10 intentional bases on balls in 1998. ... Had 21-game hitting streak (June 17-July 8, 2001). ... Hit three home runs in one game (April 16, 2002). ... Career major league grand slams: 2.
2002 GAMES PLAYED BY POSITION (MLB): OF—156.

Year	Team (League)	Pos.	G	AB	R	H	2B	3B	HR	RBI	BB	SO	SB-CS	Avg.	OBP	SLG	E	Avg.
			BATTING														FIELDING	
1997—	Kissimmee (FSL)........	OF-DH	53	184	31	54	10	0	12	35	37	38	2-1	.293	.417	.543	0	1.000
1998—	Jackson (Texas)	OF-DH	122	425	82	130	34	0	24	89	85	82	6-4	.306	.424	.555	4	.980
—	New Orleans (PCL).....	OF	17	59	14	16	4	0	6	13	12	16	0-0	.271	.411	.644	0	1.000
1999—	New Orleans (PCL).....	OF-1B-DH	64	226	42	73	20	0	8	49	39	47	7-1	.323	.419	.518	4	.972
—	Houston (N.L.)	OF-1B	34	93	10	22	2	0	4	15	12	21	5-1	.237	.321	.387	2	.956
2000—	New Orleans (PCL).....	OF-1B	31	112	18	37	4	2	6	27	31	20	4-4	.330	.479	.563	2	.982
—	Houston (N.L.)	OF-1B	114	353	76	105	28	1	21	67	56	73	6-2	.297	.388	.561	6	.968
2001—	Houston (N.L.)	OF	156	577	110	191	*55	5	34	126	92	121	7-9	.331	.430	.620	6	.981
2002—	Houston (N.L.)	OF	158	578	106	169	35	2	42	*128	107	118	8-4	.292	.405	.578	7	.977
Major League totals (4 years)			462	1601	302	487	120	8	101	336	267	333	26-16	.304	.406	.578	21	.976

DIVISION SERIES RECORD

Year	Team (League)	Pos.	G	AB	R	H	2B	3B	HR	RBI	BB	SO	SB-CS	Avg.	OBP	SLG	E	Avg.
			BATTING														FIELDING	
2001—	Houston (N.L.)	OF	3	12	0	2	0	0	0	0	0	4	0-0	.167	.167	.167	0	1.000

ALL-STAR GAME RECORD

	AB	R	H	2B	3B	HR	RBI	BB	SO	SB-CS	Avg.	OBP	SLG	E	Avg.
All-Star Game totals (2 years)	5	0	2	0	0	0	2	0	0	1-0	.400	.400	.400	0	1.000

BERNERO, ADAM — P — TIGERS

PERSONAL: Born November 28, 1976, in San Jose, Calif. ... 6-4/205. ... Throws right, bats right. ... Full name: Adam G. Bernero.
HIGH SCHOOL: John F. Kennedy (Sacramento, Calif.).
COLLEGE: Armstrong Atlantic State (Ga.).
TRANSACTIONS/CAREER NOTES: Signed as non-drafted free agent by Detroit Tigers organization (May 21, 1999). ... On Jacksonville disabled list (April 10-28, 2000). ... On Toledo disabled list (June 18-July 4, 2001).
STATISTICAL NOTES: Tied for International League lead with five balks in 2001.
CAREER HITTING (MLB): 0-for-4 (.000), 0 R, 0 2B, 0 3B, 0 HR, 0 RBI.

Year League	W	L	Pct.	ERA	G	GS	CG	ShO	Sv.-Opp.	IP	H	R	ER	HR	BB-IBB	SO
1999—West Michigan (Midw.)	8	4	.667	2.54	15	15	2	1	0-...	95.2	75	36	27	8	23-0	80
2000—Jacksonville (Sou.)	2	5	.286	2.79	10	10	0	0	0-...	61.1	54	26	19	6	24-0	46
—Toledo (I.L.)	3	1	.750	2.47	7	7	1	1	0-...	47.1	34	16	13	5	10-0	37
—Detroit (A.L.)	0	1	.000	4.19	12	4	0	0	0-0	34.1	33	18	16	3	13-1	20
2001—Toledo (I.L.)	6	11	.353	5.13	26	25	1	0	0-...	140.1	172	90	80	13	54-0	99
—Detroit (A.L.)	0	0	...	7.30	5	0	0	0	0-0	12.1	13	13	10	4	4-0	8
2002—Toledo (I.L.)	2	2	.500	1.58	9	9	2	1	0-...	57.0	46	13	10	2	13-0	49
—Detroit (A.L.)	4	7	.364	6.20	28	11	0	0	0-0	101.2	128	74	70	17	31-1	69
Major League totals (3 years)	4	8	.333	5.82	45	15	0	0	0-0	148.1	174	105	96	24	48-2	97

BERROA, ANGEL — SS — ROYALS

PERSONAL: Born January 27, 1978, in Santo Domingo, Dominican Republic. ... 6-0/175. ... Bats right, throws right. ... Full name: Angel Maria Berroa.
TRANSACTIONS/CAREER NOTES: Signed as non-drafted free agent by Oakland Athletics organization (August 14, 1997). ... Traded by Athletics with C A.J. Hinch and cash to Kansas City Royals as part of three-way deal in which Royals received P Roberto Hernandez from Tampa Devil Rays, A's received P Cory Lidle from Devil Rays and OF Johnny Damon, IF Mark Ellis and player to be named from Royals and Devil Rays received OF Ben Grieve and a player to be named or cash from A's (January 8, 2001). ... On Omaha disabled list (April 15-June 9, 2002).
STATISTICAL NOTES: Led California League shortstops with 593 total chances and tied for league lead in putouts with 195 in 2000.
2002 GAMES PLAYED BY POSITION (MLB): SS—20.

		BATTING													FIELDING	
Year Team (League)	Pos.	G	AB	R	H	2B	3B	HR	RBI	BB	SO	SB-CS	Avg.	OBP	SLG	E	Avg.
1998—Dom. Athletics (DSL)		58	196	51	48	7	4	8	37	25	37	4-...	.245	...	.444	...	...
1999—Ariz. Athletics (Ariz.)	SS-2B-3B-OF	46	169	42	49	11	4	2	24	16	26	11-4	.290	.371	.438	18	.925
—Midland (Texas)	SS	4	17	3	1	1	0	0	0	0	2	0-0	.059	.059	.118	2	.889
2000—Visalia (Calif.)	SS	129	429	61	119	25	6	10	63	30	70	11-9	.277	.337	.434	*54	.909
2001—Wilmington (Caro.)■	SS	51	199	43	63	18	4	6	25	9	41	10-6	.317	.382	.538	17	.933
—Wichita (Texas)	SS	80	304	63	90	20	4	8	42	17	55	15-6	.296	.373	.467	13	.965
—Kansas City (A.L.)	SS	15	53	8	16	2	0	0	4	3	10	2-0	.302	.339	.340	3	.953
2002—Omaha (PCL)	SS	77	297	37	64	11	4	8	35	15	84	6-4	.215	.277	.360	16	.956
—Kansas City (A.L.)	SS	20	75	8	17	7	1	0	5	7	10	3-0	.227	.301	.347	4	.964
Major League totals (2 years)		35	128	16	33	9	1	0	9	10	20	5-0	.258	.317	.344	7	.960

BETEMIT, WILSON — SS — BRAVES

PERSONAL: Born November 2, 1981, in Santo Domingo, Dominican Republic. ... 6-2/155. ... Bats both, throws right.
TRANSACTIONS/CAREER NOTES: Signed as non-drafted free agent by Atlanta Braves organization (July 28, 1996). ... On Richmond disabled list (April 4-11, June 10-July 4 and July 14-15, 2002).
STATISTICAL NOTES: Led Appalachian League shortstops with 92 putouts and 326 total chances in 1999.

		BATTING													FIELDING	
Year Team (League)	Pos.	G	AB	R	H	2B	3B	HR	RBI	BB	SO	SB-CS	Avg.	OBP	SLG	E	Avg.
1997—GC Braves (GCL)	SS	32	113	12	24	6	1	0	15	9	32	0-0	.212	.270	.283	*20	.856
1998—GC Braves (GCL)	SS	51	173	23	38	8	4	5	16	20	49	6-5	.220	.301	.399	20	.908
1999—Danville (Appl.)	SS	67	259	39	83	18	2	5	53	27	63	6-3	.320	.383	.463	33	.899
2000—Jamestown (NY-P)	SS	69	269	54	89	15	2	5	37	30	37	3-4	.331	.393	.457	•29	.910
2001—Myrtle Beach (Caro.)	SS	84	318	38	88	20	1	7	43	23	71	8-5	.277	.324	.412	23	.944
—Greenville (Sou.)	SS	47	183	22	65	14	0	5	19	12	36	6-2	.355	.394	.514	9	.954
—Atlanta (N.L.)	SS	8	3	1	0	0	0	0	0	2	3	1-0	.000	.400	.000	0	...
2002—GC Braves (GCL)	SS	7	19	2	5	4	0	0	2	5	2	1-0	.263	.417	.474	2	.867
—Richmond (I.L.)	SS	93	343	43	84	17	1	8	34	34	82	8-5	.245	.312	.370	21	.946
Major League totals (1 year)		8	3	1	0	0	0	0	0	2	3	1-0	.000	.400	.000	0	...

BEVERLIN, JASON — P

PERSONAL: Born November 27, 1973, in Ashtabula, Ohio. ... 6-5/220. ... Throws right, bats left. ... Full name: Jason Robert Beverlin.
COLLEGE: Western Carolina.
TRANSACTIONS/CAREER NOTES: Selected by Oakland Athletics organization in fourth round of free-agent draft (June 2, 1994). ... Traded by A's with OF Danny Tartabull to New York Yankees for OF Ruben Sierra (July 28, 1995). ... Granted free agency (October 15, 2000). ... Signed by Anaheim Angels organization (November 17, 2000). ... Granted free agency (October 15, 2001). ... Signed by Cleveland Indians organization (November 7, 2001). ... Claimed on waivers by Detroit Tigers (August 16, 2002). ... Granted free agency (October 15, 2002).
CAREER HITTING (MLB): 0-for-0 (.000), 0 R, 0 2B, 0 3B, 0 HR, 0 RBI.

Year League	W	L	Pct.	ERA	G	GS	CG	ShO	Sv.-Opp.	IP	H	R	ER	HR	BB-IBB	SO
1994—West Michigan (Midw.)	3	2	.600	1.76	17	1	0	0	1-...	41.0	32	12	8	0	14-0	48
1995—West Michigan (Midw.)	3	9	.250	4.04	22	14	0	0	0-...	89.0	76	51	40	4	40-0	84
—Greensboro (S.Atl.)■	2	4	.333	2.65	7	7	1	1	0-...	51.0	49	15	15	1	6-0	31
1996—Tampa (FSL)	2	0	1.000	3.50	25	1	0	0	1-...	46.1	43	22	18	5	17-2	38
—Norwich (East.)	0	3	.000	8.44	8	4	0	0	0-...	16.0	25	21	15	2	6-1	17
1997—Norwich (East.)	1	0	1.000	7.78	25	0	0	0	0-...	41.2	50	38	36	10	24-0	42
—Tampa (FSL)	1	3	.250	4.79	7	6	0	0	0-...	41.1	37	26	22	4	13-1	24
1998—Tampa (FSL)	1	3	.250	5.63	7	5	0	0	0-...	32.0	37	23	20	2	16-2	15
—Norwich (East.)	3	5	.375	3.67	25	9	0	0	1-...	81.0	68	34	33	5	38-0	86
1999—Norwich (East.)	15	9	.625	3.69	28	27	1	0	0-...	173.1	153	91	71	16	81-0	147
2000—Columbus (I.L.)	0	3	.000	18.90	3	3	0	0	0-...	6.2	13	14	14	1	14-0	6
—Norwich (East.)	8	9	.471	2.82	24	24	1	0	0-...	143.2	110	61	45	7	87-2	100
2001—Salt Lake (PCL)■	6	2	.750	4.23	19	12	1	0	0-...	83.0	82	41	39	9	29-0	74
—Arkansas (Texas)	4	2	.667	2.75	6	6	0	0	0-...	39.1	36	15	12	4	11-0	30
2002—Buffalo (I.L.)■	10	8	.556	3.87	23	20	1	1	0-...	118.2	107	55	51	11	39-1	106
—Cleveland (A.L.)	0	0	...	7.36	4	0	0	0	0-0	7.1	9	7	6	1	4-0	9
—Toledo (I.L.)■	3	0	1.000	1.93	4	3	0	0	0-...	18.2	17	5	4	0	6-0	13
—Detroit (A.L.)	0	3	.000	9.49	3	3	0	0	0-0	12.1	18	15	13	2	5-0	7
Major League totals (1 year)	0	3	.000	8.69	7	3	0	0	0-0	19.2	27	22	19	3	9-0	16

BIDDLE, ROCKY — P — WHITE SOX

PERSONAL: Born May 21, 1976, in Las Vegas, Nev. ... 6-3/230. ... Throws right, bats right. ... Full name: Lee F. Biddle.
HIGH SCHOOL: Temple City (Calif.).
COLLEGE: Long Beach State.
TRANSACTIONS/CAREER NOTES: Selected by Chicago White Sox organization in supplemental round ("sandwich" pick between first and second round, 51st pick overall) of free-agent draft (June 3, 1997); pick received as compensation for failure to sign 1996 first-round pick P Bobby Seay. ... On disabled list (April 9, 1999-entire season). ... On disabled list (September 21, 2001-remainder of season). ... On Chicago disabled list (March 22-May 3, 2002); included rehabilitation assignment to Charlotte (April 25-May 3).
CAREER HITTING (MLB): 0-for-1 (.000), 0 R, 0 2B, 0 3B, 0 HR, 0 RBI.

Year League	W	L	Pct.	ERA	G	GS	CG	ShO	Sv.-Opp.	IP	H	R	ER	HR	BB-IBB	SO
1997—Hickory (S.Atl.)	0	1	.000	4.64	13	0	0	0	1-...	21.1	22	18	11	2	10-0	25
1998—Winston-Salem (Caro.)	4	5	.444	4.57	16	16	0	0	0-...	82.2	92	55	42	7	45-0	72
—Arizona White Sox (Ariz.)	1	0	1.000	3.94	5	2	0	0	0-...	16.0	15	9	7	2	8-0	18
1999—Winston-Salem (Caro.)									Did not play.							
2000—Birmingham (Sou.)	11	6	.647	3.08	23	23	2	2	0-...	146.1	138	63	50	10	54-0	118
—Chicago (A.L.)	1	2	.333	8.34	4	4	0	0	0-0	22.2	31	25	21	5	8-0	7
2001—Chicago (A.L.)	7	8	.467	5.39	30	21	0	0	0-3	128.2	137	87	77	16	52-3	85
2002—Charlotte (I.L.)	0	0	...	1.29	2	2	0	0	0-...	7.0	4	1	1	0	1-0	9
—Chicago (A.L.)	3	4	.429	4.06	44	7	0	0	1-3	77.2	72	42	35	13	39-4	64
Major League totals (3 years)	11	14	.440	5.23	78	32	0	0	1-6	229.0	240	154	133	34	99-7	156

BIERBRODT, NICK — P — DEVIL RAYS

PERSONAL: Born May 16, 1978, in Tarzana, Calif. ... 6-5/185. ... Throws left, bats left. ... Full name: Nicholas Raymond Bierbrodt.
HIGH SCHOOL: Millikan (Long Beach, Calif.).
TRANSACTIONS/CAREER NOTES: Selected by Arizona Diamondbacks organization in first round (30th pick overall) of free-agent draft (June 4, 1996). ... On Tucson disabled list (May 4-July 8 and July 23-28, 2000). ... On Arizona disabled list (March 23-April 19, 2001); included rehabilitation assignment to El Paso (May 1-19). ... Traded by Diamondbacks with OF Jason Conti to Tampa Bay Devil Rays for P Albie Lopez and C Mike Difelice (July 25, 2001). ... On disabled list (June 7, 2002-remainder of season).
MISCELLANEOUS: Appeared in one game as pinch runner (2001).
CAREER HITTING (MLB): 4-for-6 (.667), 3 R, 1 2B, 0 3B, 0 HR, 0 RBI.

Year League	W	L	Pct.	ERA	G	GS	CG	ShO	Sv.-Opp.	IP	H	R	ER	HR	BB-IBB	SO
1996—Ariz. D-backs (Ariz.)	1	1	.500	1.66	8	8	0	0	0-...	38.0	25	9	7	1	13-0	46
—Lethbridge (Pio.)	2	0	1.000	0.50	3	3	0	0	0-...	18.0	12	4	1	0	5-0	23
1997—South Bend (Midw.)	2	4	.333	4.04	15	15	0	0	0-...	75.2	77	43	34	4	37-0	64
1998—High Desert (Calif.)	8	7	.533	3.40	24	23	1	0	0-...	129.2	122	66	49	7	64-0	88
1999—El Paso (Texas)	5	6	.455	4.62	14	14	2	•1	0-...	76.0	78	45	39	3	37-0	55
—Tucson (PCL)	1	4	.200	7.27	11	11	0	0	0-...	43.1	57	42	35	9	30-0	43
2000—Tucson (PCL)	2	1	.667	4.82	4	3	0	0	0-...	18.2	13	10	10	3	14-0	11
—Ariz. D-backs (Ariz.)	0	0	...	4.50	4	3	0	0	0-...	8.0	4	4	4	0	5-0	10
—El Paso (Texas)	1	3	.250	7.13	7	7	0	0	0-...	35.1	37	30	28	1	24-0	36
2001—El Paso (Texas)	2	1	.667	1.37	4	4	0	0	0-...	19.2	13	3	3	1	6-0	18
—Tucson (PCL)	4	1	.800	2.18	7	6	0	0	0-...	45.1	48	15	11	0	9-1	56
—Arizona (N.L.)	2	2	.500	8.22	5	5	0	0	0-0	23.0	29	21	21	6	12-0	17
—Tampa Bay (A.L.)■	3	4	.429	4.55	11	11	0	0	0-0	61.1	71	38	31	11	27-1	56
2002—Charleston, S.C. (S.Atl.)									Did not play.							
A.L. totals (1 year)	3	4	.429	4.55	11	11	0	0	0-0	61.1	71	38	31	11	27-1	56
N.L. totals (1 year)	2	2	.500	8.22	5	5	0	0	0-0	23.0	29	21	21	6	12-0	17
Major League totals (1 year)	5	6	.455	5.55	16	16	0	0	0-0	84.1	100	59	52	17	39-1	73

BIGBIE, LARRY — OF — ORIOLES

PERSONAL: Born November 4, 1977, in Hobart, Ind. ... 6-4/190. ... Bats left, throws left. ... Full name: Larry R. Bigbie.
HIGH SCHOOL: Hobart (Ind.).
COLLEGE: Ball State.

TRANSACTIONS/CAREER NOTES: Selected by Baltimore Orioles organization in first round (21st pick overall) of free-agent draft (June 2, 1999); pick received from Texas Rangers as part of compensation for Type A free agent 1B Rafael Palmeiro. ... On Frederick disabled list (April 22-29, 2000). ... On Bowie disabled list (July 28, 2000-remainder of season). ... On Rochester disabled list (July 5-25, 2002).
STATISTICAL NOTES: Tied for International League lead with seven intentional bases on balls in 2002.
2002 GAMES PLAYED BY POSITION (MLB): OF—12.

			BATTING														FIELDING	
Year	Team (League)	Pos.	G	AB	R	H	2B	3B	HR	RBI	BB	SO	SB-CS	Avg.	OBP	SLG	E	Avg.
1999	Bluefield (Appl.)	OF	8	30	3	8	0	0	0	4	3	8	1-3	.267	.343	.267	0	1.000
—	Delmarva (S.Atl.)	OF	43	165	18	46	7	3	2	27	29	42	3-1	.279	.381	.394	3	.950
2000	Frederick (Caro.)	OF	55	201	33	59	11	0	2	28	23	34	7-3	.294	.360	.378	3	.975
—	Bowie (East.)	OF	31	112	11	27	6	0	0	5	11	28	3-0	.241	.309	.295	0	1.000
2001	Bowie (East.)	OF	71	262	41	77	13	3	8	33	40	54	10-7	.294	.386	.458	4	.972
—	Baltimore (A.L.)	OF	47	131	15	30	6	0	2	11	17	42	4-1	.229	.318	.321	0	1.000
—	Rochester (I.L.)	OF	10	42	5	13	4	0	1	2	3	8	1-1	.310	.356	.476	0	1.000
2002	Rochester (I.L.)	OF	98	348	42	105	23	2	2	35	35	79	7-3	.302	.363	.397	2	.990
—	Baltimore (A.L.)	OF	16	34	1	6	1	0	0	3	1	11	1-0	.176	.194	.206	0	1.000
Major League totals (2 years)			63	165	16	36	7	0	2	14	18	53	5-1	.218	.293	.297	0	1.000

BIGGIO, CRAIG 2B ASTROS

PERSONAL: Born December 14, 1965, in Smithtown, N.Y. ... 5-11/185. ... Bats right, throws right. ... Full name: Craig Alan Biggio. ... Name pronounced BEE-jee-oh.
HIGH SCHOOL: Kings Park (N.Y.).
COLLEGE: Seton Hall.
TRANSACTIONS/CAREER NOTES: Selected by Houston Astros organization in first round (22nd pick overall) of free-agent draft (June 2, 1987). ... Granted free agency (October 31, 1995). ... Re-signed by Astros (December 14, 1995). ... On disabled list (August 2, 2000-remainder of season).
RECORDS: Shares N.L. record for most years leading league in games by second baseman—8.
HONORS: Named catcher on The Sporting News college All-America team (1987). ... Named catcher on The Sporting News N.L. Silver Slugger team (1989). ... Named second baseman on The Sporting News N.L. All-Star team (1994-95, 1997-98 and 2001). ... Won N.L. Gold Glove at second base (1994-97). ... Named second baseman on The Sporting News N.L. Silver Slugger team (1994-95 and 1997-98).
STATISTICAL NOTES: Led N.L. catchers with 889 putouts, 963 total chances and 13 passed balls in 1991. ... Led N.L. second basemen with 344 putouts in 1992, 361 in 1996 and 341 in 1997. ... Led N.L. second basemen with 447 assists in 1993, 338 in 1994, 419 in 1995, 440 in 1996 and 504 in 1997. ... Led N.L. in being hit by pitch with 22 in 1995, 27 in 1996, 34 in 1997 and 28 in 2001. ... Led N.L. second basemen in total chances with 728 in 1995, 811 in 1996 and 863 in 1997. ... Led N.L. second basemen with 359 putouts, 430 assists, 801 total chances and 117 double plays in 1999. ... Had 16-game hitting streak (April 5-26, 2000). ... Had 18-game hitting streak (May 29-June 18, 2001). ... Hit for the cycle (April 8, 2002). ... Career major league grand slams: 2.
MISCELLANEOUS: Holds Houston Astros all-time records for most hits (2,295), most runs (1,401) and most doubles (473).
2002 GAMES PLAYED BY POSITION (MLB): 2B—142; OF—1.

			BATTING														FIELDING	
Year	Team (League)	Pos.	G	AB	R	H	2B	3B	HR	RBI	BB	SO	SB-CS	Avg.	OBP	SLG	E	Avg.
1987	Asheville (S.Atl.)	C-OF	64	216	59	81	17	2	9	49	39	33	31-10	.375	.471	.597	2	.995
1988	Tucson (PCL)	C-OF	77	281	60	90	21	4	3	41	40	39	19-4	.320	.408	.456	6	.983
—	Houston (N.L.)	C	50	123	14	26	6	1	3	5	7	29	6-1	.211	.254	.350	3	.991
1989	Houston (N.L.)	C-OF	134	443	64	114	21	2	13	60	49	64	21-3	.257	.336	.402	9	.989
1990	Houston (N.L.)	C-OF	150	555	53	153	24	2	4	42	53	79	25-11	.276	.342	.348	13	.982
1991	Houston (N.L.)	C-2B-OF	149	546	79	161	23	4	4	46	53	71	19-6	.295	.358	.374	11	.989
1992	Houston (N.L.)	2B	•162	613	96	170	32	3	6	39	94	95	38-15	.277	.378	.369	12	.984
1993	Houston (N.L.)	2B	155	610	98	175	41	5	21	64	77	93	15-17	.287	.373	.474	14	.982
1994	Houston (N.L.)	2B	114	437	88	139	*44	5	6	56	62	58	*39-4	.318	.411	.483	7	.988
1995	Houston (N.L.)	2B	141	553	*123	167	30	2	22	77	80	85	33-8	.302	.406	.483	10	.986
1996	Houston (N.L.)	2B	•162	605	113	174	24	4	15	75	75	72	25-7	.288	.386	.415	10	.988
1997	Houston (N.L.)	2B-DH	•162	619	*146	191	37	8	22	81	84	107	47-10	.309	.415	.501	18	.979
1998	Houston (N.L.)	2B-DH	160	646	123	210	*51	2	20	88	64	113	50-8	.325	.403	.503	15	.980
1999	Houston (N.L.)	2B-OF-DH	160	639	123	188	*56	0	16	73	88	107	28-14	.294	.386	.457	12	.985
2000	Houston (N.L.)	2B	101	377	67	101	13	5	8	35	61	73	12-2	.268	.388	.393	6	.987
2001	Houston (N.L.)	2B-DH	155	617	118	180	35	3	20	70	66	100	7-4	.292	.382	.455	11	.984
2002	Houston (N.L.)	2B-OF	145	577	96	146	36	3	15	58	50	111	16-2	.253	.330	.404	8	.988
Major League totals (15 years)			2100	7960	1401	2295	473	49	195	869	963	1257	381-112	.288	.377	.434	159	.985

DIVISION SERIES RECORD

			BATTING														FIELDING	
Year	Team (League)	Pos.	G	AB	R	H	2B	3B	HR	RBI	BB	SO	SB-CS	Avg.	OBP	SLG	E	Avg.
1997	Houston (N.L.)	2B	3	12	0	1	0	0	0	0	1	0	0-0	.083	.154	.083	1	.923
1998	Houston (N.L.)	2B	4	11	3	2	1	0	0	1	4	4	0-0	.182	.471	.273	1	.950
1999	Houston (N.L.)	2B	4	19	1	2	0	0	0	0	1	5	0-0	.105	.150	.105	0	1.000
2001	Houston (N.L.)	2B	3	12	0	2	0	0	0	0	0	1	0-0	.167	.167	.167	0	1.000
Division series totals (4 years)			14	54	4	7	1	0	0	1	6	10	0-0	.130	.242	.148	2	.971

ALL-STAR GAME RECORD

	AB	R	H	2B	3B	HR	RBI	BB	SO	SB-CS	Avg.	OBP	SLG	E	Avg.
All-Star Game totals (7 years)	15	2	1	0	0	1	2	0	5	0-0	.067	.176	.267	1	.957

BLAKE, CASEY 3B

PERSONAL: Born August 23, 1973, in Des Moines, Iowa. ... 6-2/205. ... Bats right, throws right. ... Full name: William Casey Blake.
HIGH SCHOOL: Indianola (Iowa).
COLLEGE: Wichita State.

TRANSACTIONS/CAREER NOTES: Selected by Philadelphia Phillies organization in 11th round of free-agent draft (June 1, 1992); did not sign. ... Selected by New York Yankees organization in 45th round of free-agent draft (June 1, 1995); did not sign. ... Selected by Toronto Blue Jays organization in seventh round of free-agent draft (June 4, 1996). ... Claimed on waivers by Minnesota Twins (May 23, 2000). ... On Salt Lake disabled list (June 28-July 7, 2000). ... Claimed on waivers by Baltimore Orioles (September 21, 2001). ... Claimed on waivers by Twins (October 12, 2001). ... Released by Twins (October 14, 2002).

STATISTICAL NOTES: Led Florida State League third basemen with 98 putouts and 39 errors in 1997. ... Led International League third basemen with .967 fielding percentage in 1999. ... Tied for International League lead with 94 putouts by third basemen in 1999.

2002 GAMES PLAYED BY POSITION (MLB): 3B—5; 1B—3; DH—1.

			BATTING														FIELDING	
Year	**Team (League)**	**Pos.**	**G**	**AB**	**R**	**H**	**2B**	**3B**	**HR**	**RBI**	**BB**	**SO**	**SB-CS**	**Avg.**	**OBP**	**SLG**	**E**	**Avg.**
1996—	Hagerstown (S.Atl.)	3B-1B-OF	48	172	29	43	13	1	2	18	11	40	5-3	.250	.318	.372	12	.906
1997—	Dunedin (FSL)	3B-SS	129	449	56	107	21	0	7	39	48	91	19-9	.238	.319	.332	†39	.895
1998—	Dunedin (FSL)	3B	88	340	62	119	28	3	11	65	30	81	9-6	*.350	.409	.547	16	.939
—	Knoxville (Sou.)	3B	45	172	41	64	15	4	7	38	22	25	10-0	.372	.442	.628	11	.913
1999—	Syracuse (I.L.)	3B-DH-SS	110	387	69	95	16	2	22	75	61	82	9-5	.245	.357	.468	10	†.963
—	Toronto (A.L.)	3B	14	39	6	10	2	0	1	1	2	7	0-0	.256	.293	.385	0	1.000
—	St. Catharines (NY-P)	3B	1	3	0	2	0	0	0	0	1	0	0-0	.667	.750	.667	0	1.000
2000—	Syracuse (I.L.)	3B-SS	30	106	10	23	6	1	2	7	8	23	0-3	.217	.291	.349	2	.971
—	Salt Lake (PCL)■	3B-SS-1B	80	293	59	93	22	2	12	52	39	59	7-2	.317	.406	.529	14	.934
—	Minnesota (A.L.)	3B-DH-1B	7	16	1	3	2	0	0	1	3	7	0-0	.188	.333	.313	0	1.000
2001—	Edmonton (PCL)	3-1-2-S-O	94	375	64	116	24	6	10	49	34	66	14-3	.309	.376	.485	11	.961
—	Minnesota (A.L.)	3B-DH-1B	13	22	1	7	1	0	0	2	3	8	1-0	.318	.400	.364	1	.955
—	Baltimore (A.L.)■	1B-DH	6	15	2	2	0	0	1	2	1	4	2-0	.133	.188	.333	1	.967
2002—	Edmonton (PCL)■	3B-2B-1B-OF	126	482	87	149	25	3	19	58	54	78	24-9	.309	.383	.492	12	.969
—	Minnesota (A.L.)	3B-1B-DH	9	20	2	4	1	0	0	1	2	7	0-0	.200	.273	.250	2	.920
Major League totals (4 years)			49	112	12	26	6	0	2	7	11	33	3-0	.232	.304	.339	4	.968

BLALOCK, HANK — 3B — RANGERS

PERSONAL: Born November 21, 1980, in San Diego. ... 6-1/192. ... Bats left, throws right. ... Full name: Hank Joe Blalock.

HIGH SCHOOL: Rancho Bernardo (San Diego).

TRANSACTIONS/CAREER NOTES: Selected by Texas Rangers organization in third round of free-agent draft (June 2, 1999). ... On Oklahoma disabled list (June 10-17, 2002).

2002 GAMES PLAYED BY POSITION (MLB): 3B—46.

			BATTING														FIELDING	
Year	**Team (League)**	**Pos.**	**G**	**AB**	**R**	**H**	**2B**	**3B**	**HR**	**RBI**	**BB**	**SO**	**SB-CS**	**Avg.**	**OBP**	**SLG**	**E**	**Avg.**
1999—	GC Rangers (GCL)	3B	51	191	34	69	17	6	3	38	25	23	3-2	.361	.428	.560	12	.914
—	Savannah (S.Atl.)	3B	7	25	3	6	1	0	1	2	1	3	0-0	.240	.286	.400	5	.762
2000—	Savannah (S.Atl.)	3B	139	512	66	153	32	2	10	77	62	53	31-8	.299	.373	.428	20	.942
2001—	Charlotte (FSL)	3B	63	237	46	90	19	1	7	47	26	31	7-4	.380	.437	.557	7	.963
—	Tulsa (Texas)	3B	68	272	50	89	18	4	11	61	39	38	3-3	.327	.413	.544	8	.953
2002—	Texas (A.L.)	3B	49	147	16	31	8	0	3	17	20	43	0-0	.211	.306	.327	6	.943
—	Oklahoma (PCL)	3B-2B	95	387	63	119	32	1	8	62	34	61	2-1	.307	.363	.457	16	.938
Major League totals (1 year)			49	147	16	31	8	0	3	17	20	43	0-0	.211	.306	.327	6	.943

BLANCO, HENRY — C — BRAVES

PERSONAL: Born August 29, 1971, in Caracas, Venezuela. ... 5-11/220. ... Bats right, throws right. ... Full name: Henry Ramon Blanco.

HIGH SCHOOL: Antonio Jose de Sucre (Venezuela).

TRANSACTIONS/CAREER NOTES: Signed as non-drafted free agent by Los Angeles Dodgers organization (November 12, 1989). ... On disabled list (June 16-25, 1993). ... On Los Angeles disabled list (March 22-July 29, 1998); included rehabilitation assignment to San Bernardino (May 19-27). ... Granted free agency (October 15, 1998). ... Signed by Colorado Rockies organization (December 18, 1998). ... Traded by Rockies with P Jamey Wright to Milwaukee Brewers as part of three-way deal in which Rockies received 3B Jeff Cirillo, P Scott Karl and cash from Brewers, Oakland Athletics received P Justin Miller and cash from Rockies and Brewers received P Jimmy Haynes from A's (December 13, 1999). ... On Milwaukee disabled list (April 14-May 2, 2000); included rehabilitation assignment to Indianapolis (April 30-May 2). ... Traded by Brewers to Atlanta Braves for C Paul Bako and P Jose Cabrera (March 20, 2002). ... On disabled list (August 12-27, 2002).

STATISTICAL NOTES: Led Gulf Coast League third basemen with 48 putouts in 1990. ... Led Pioneer League third basemen with .947 fielding percentage and 10 double plays in 1991. ... Led California League third basemen with 95 putouts, 236 assists, 345 total chances and 34 double plays in 1992. ... Led Texas League third basemen with .944 fielding percentage, 92 putouts and 270 total chances in 1993. ... Led Texas League catchers with 13 errors and 17 passed balls in 1996. ... Led Pacific Coast League catchers with 64 assists and 11 double plays in 1997. ... Career major league grand slams: 1.

2002 GAMES PLAYED BY POSITION (MLB): C—79.

			BATTING														FIELDING	
Year	**Team (League)**	**Pos.**	**G**	**AB**	**R**	**H**	**2B**	**3B**	**HR**	**RBI**	**BB**	**SO**	**SB-CS**	**Avg.**	**OBP**	**SLG**	**E**	**Avg.**
1990—	GC Dodgers (GCL)	3B	60	178	23	39	8	0	1	19	26	41	7-2	.219	.316	.281	11	.941
1991—	Vero Beach (FSL)	3B-SS	5	7	0	1	0	0	0	0	2	0	0-0	.143	.333	.143	0	1.000
—	Great Falls (Pio.)	3B-1B	62	216	35	55	7	1	5	28	27	39	3-6	.255	.336	.366	8	†.960
1992—	Bakersfield (Calif.)	3B	124	401	42	94	21	2	5	52	51	91	10-6	.234	.328	.334	14	*.959
1993—	San Antonio (Texas)	3B-1B-SS	117	374	33	73	19	1	10	42	29	80	3-3	.195	.260	.332	16	†.952
1994—	San Antonio (Texas)	3B-1B-P	*132	405	36	93	23	2	6	38	53	67	6-6	.230	.320	.341	21	.924
1995—	San Antonio (Texas)	3B-C	88	302	37	77	18	4	12	48	29	52	1-1	.255	.328	.460	11	.964
—	Albuquerque (PCL)	3B-1B-OF	29	97	11	22	4	1	2	13	10	23	0-0	.227	.294	.351	2	.988
1996—	San Antonio (Texas)	C-3B	92	307	39	82	14	1	5	40	28	38	2-3	.267	.324	.368	†13	.979
—	Albuquerque (PCL)	C	2	6	1	1	0	0	0	0	0	3	0-0	.167	.167	.167	0	1.000
1997—	Albuquerque (PCL)	C-1B-DH-OF	91	294	38	92	20	1	6	47	37	63	7-4	.313	.388	.449	3	.996
—	Los Angeles (N.L.)	1B-3B	3	5	1	2	0	0	1	1	0	1	0-0	.400	.400	1.000	0	1.000
1998—	San Bern. (Calif.)	C-DH	7	19	5	6	1	0	2	3	4	6	1-0	.316	.435	.684	0	1.000
—	Albuquerque (PCL)	C-DH	48	134	19	36	11	0	4	23	22	27	2-0	.269	.367	.440	4	.985

Year	Team (League)	Pos.	G	AB	R	H	2B	3B	HR	RBI	BB	SO	SB-CS	Avg.	OBP	SLG	E	Avg.
			BATTING														FIELDING	
1999—	Colo. Springs (PCL)■	C	15	57	8	19	4	0	3	12	1	12	0-1	.333	.339	.561	1	.990
—	Colorado (N.L.)	C-OF	88	263	30	61	12	3	6	28	34	38	1-1	.232	.320	.369	5	.992
2000—	Milwaukee (N.L.)■	C	93	284	29	67	24	0	7	31	36	60	0-3	.236	.318	.394	5	.991
—	Indianapolis (I.L.)	DH	1	3	1	1	1	0	0	0	1	0	0-0	.333	.500	.667	...	...
2001—	Milwaukee (N.L.)	C	104	314	33	66	18	3	6	31	34	72	3-1	.210	.290	.344	6	.992
2002—	Atlanta (N.L.)■	C	81	221	17	45	9	1	6	22	20	51	0-2	.204	.267	.335	3	.993
Major League totals (5 years)			369	1087	110	241	63	7	26	113	124	222	4-7	.222	.300	.364	19	.992

DIVISION SERIES RECORD

Year	Team (League)	Pos.	G	AB	R	H	2B	3B	HR	RBI	BB	SO	SB-CS	Avg.	OBP	SLG	E	Avg.
			BATTING														FIELDING	
2002—	Atlanta (N.L.)	C	2	6	0	1	0	0	0	0	0	2	0-0	.167	.167	.167	0	1.000

RECORD AS PITCHER

Year	League	W	L	Pct.	ERA	G	GS	CG	ShO	Sv.-Opp.	IP	H	R	ER	HR	BB-IBB	SO
1994—	San Antonio (Texas)	0	0	...	9.00	1	0	0	0	0-...	1.0	3	1	1	0	0-0	1

BLOOMQUIST, WILLIE — OF/2B — MARINERS

PERSONAL: Born November 27, 1977, in Bremerton, Wash. ... 5-11/180. ... Bats right, throws right. ... Full name: William Paul Bloomquist.
HIGH SCHOOL: South Kitsap (Port Orchard, Wash.).
COLLEGE: Arizona State.
TRANSACTIONS/CAREER NOTES: Selected by Seattle Mariners organization in eighth round of free-agent draft (June 4, 1996); did not sign. ... Selected by Mariners organization in third round of free-agent draft (June 2, 1999). ... On Lancaster disabled list (August 6, 2000-remainder of season). ... On Tacoma disabled list (April 22-May 3 and June 6-18, 2002).
2002 GAMES PLAYED BY POSITION (MLB): OF—7; 2B—4; DH—2.

Year	Team (League)	Pos.	G	AB	R	H	2B	3B	HR	RBI	BB	SO	SB-CS	Avg.	OBP	SLG	E	Avg.
			BATTING														FIELDING	
1999—	Everett (N'West)	2B-OF	42	178	35	51	10	3	2	27	22	25	17-5	.287	.366	.410	7	.954
2000—	Lancaster (Calif.)	2B-SS	64	256	63	97	19	6	2	51	37	27	22-12	.379	.456	.523	12	.961
—	Tacoma (PCL)	2B	51	191	17	43	5	1	1	23	7	28	5-0	.225	.249	.277	3	.987
2001—	San Antonio (Texas)	SS-2B	123	491	59	125	23	2	0	28	28	55	34-9	.255	.294	.310	24	.959
2002—	Tacoma (PCL)	OF-2B-3B-SS	104	337	47	91	14	3	6	47	29	44	20-10	.270	.331	.383	12	.961
—	Seattle (A.L.)	OF-2B-DH	12	33	11	15	4	0	0	7	5	2	3-1	.455	.526	.576	0	1.000
Major League totals (1 year)			12	33	11	15	4	0	0	7	5	2	3-1	.455	.526	.576	0	1.000

BLUM, GEOFF — 3B/OF — ASTROS

PERSONAL: Born April 26, 1973, in Redwood City, Calif. ... 6-3/200. ... Bats both, throws right. ... Full name: Geoffery Edward Blum.
HIGH SCHOOL: Chino (Calif.).
COLLEGE: California.
TRANSACTIONS/CAREER NOTES: Selected by Montreal Expos organization in seventh round of free-agent draft (June 2, 1994). ... On Ottawa disabled list (May 21-June 15, 1999). ... Traded by Expos to Houston Astros for 3B Chris Truby (March 12, 2002).
STATISTICAL NOTES: Switch-hit home runs in one game (July 5, 2001).
2002 GAMES PLAYED BY POSITION (MLB): 3B—104; OF—10; SS—2; 1B—1; 2B—1.

Year	Team (League)	Pos.	G	AB	R	H	2B	3B	HR	RBI	BB	SO	SB-CS	Avg.	OBP	SLG	E	Avg.
			BATTING														FIELDING	
1994—	Vermont (NY-Penn)	SS	63	241	48	83	15	1	3	38	33	21	5-5	.344	.428	.452	15	.948
1995—	W. Palm Beach (FSL)	2B-SS-3B	125	457	54	120	20	2	1	62	34	61	6-5	.263	.313	.322	18	.963
1996—	Harrisburg (East.)	2-S-1-0	120	396	47	95	22	2	1	41	59	51	6-7	.240	.341	.313	9	.984
1997—	Ottawa (I.L.)	2B-SS-3B	118	407	59	101	21	2	3	35	52	73	14-6	.248	.333	.332	17	.969
1998—	Ottawa (I.L.)	2B	8	23	1	4	0	0	0	1	3	6	0-0	.174	.269	.174	0	1.000
—	GC Expos (GCL)	2B	5	18	0	3	1	1	0	1	1	4	0-0	.167	.211	.333	0	1.000
—	Jupiter (FSL)	2B-3B-SS	17	58	13	16	6	0	0	5	13	14	1-0	.276	.411	.379	2	.976
—	Harrisburg (East.)	SS-3B-2B-1B	39	139	25	43	12	3	6	21	17	24	2-1	.309	.400	.568	2	.986
1999—	Ottawa (I.L.)	S-1-2-3-DH	77	268	43	71	14	1	10	37	37	39	6-1	.265	.350	.437	12	.965
—	Montreal (N.L.)	SS-2B	45	133	21	32	7	2	8	18	17	25	1-0	.241	.327	.504	10	.929
2000—	Montreal (N.L.)	3B-SS-2B-1B	124	343	40	97	20	2	11	45	26	60	1-4	.283	.335	.449	9	.974
2001—	Montreal (N.L.)	3-0-2-1-S	148	453	57	107	25	0	9	50	43	94	9-5	.236	.313	.351	8	.980
2002—	Houston (N.L.)■	3-0-S-1-2	130	368	45	104	20	4	10	52	49	70	2-0	.283	.367	.440	8	.972
Major League totals (4 years)			447	1297	163	340	72	8	38	165	135	249	13-9	.262	.336	.418	35	.970

BOCACHICA, HIRAM — OF/2B — TIGERS

PERSONAL: Born March 4, 1976, in Ponce, Puerto Rico. ... 5-11/165. ... Bats right, throws right. ... Full name: Hiram Colon Bocachica.
HIGH SCHOOL: Rexville (Bayamon, Puerto Rico).
TRANSACTIONS/CAREER NOTES: Selected by Montreal Expos organization in first round (21st pick overall) of free-agent draft (June 2, 1994). ... On West Palm Beach disabled list (May 16-July 12, 1996). ... On Harrisburg suspended list (June 15-18, 1997). ... On Harrisburg disabled list (June 18-25, 1997). ... Traded by Expos with P Carlos Perez and SS Mark Grudzielanek to Los Angeles Dodgers for 2B Wilton Guerrero, P Ted Lilly, OF Peter Bergeron and 1B Jonathan Tucker (July 31, 1998). ... On San Antonio suspended list (August 16-19, 1999). ... On Albuquerque disabled list (May 23-June 2, 2000). ... On disabled list (July 9-26, 2001). ... Traded by Dodgers to Detroit Tigers for P Tom Farmer and a player to be named later (July 25, 2002); Dodgers acquired P Jason Frasor to complete deal (September 18, 2002).
STATISTICAL NOTES: Led South Atlantic League shortstops with 58 errors in 1995. ... Led Texas League in being hit by pitch with 13 in 1999. ... Tied for Texas League lead with 77 double plays by second basemen in 1999. ... Led Pacific Coast League second basemen with 99 double plays in 2000. ... Tied for Pacific Coast League lead with nine sacrifice hits in 2000.
2002 GAMES PLAYED BY POSITION (MLB): OF—54; DH—2; 2B—2.

Year	Team (League)	Pos.	G	AB	R	H	2B	3B	HR	RBI	BB	SO	SB-CS	Avg.	OBP	SLG	E	Avg.
			BATTING														FIELDING	
1994—	GC Expos (GCL)	SS	43	168	31	47	9	0	5	16	15	42	11-4	.280	.346	.423	23	.896
1995—	Albany (S.Atl.)	SS-2B	96	380	65	108	20	10	2	30	52	78	47-17	.284	.381	.405	†58	.881
1996—	W. Palm Beach (FSL)	DH-SS	71	267	50	90	17	5	2	26	34	47	21-3	.337	.419	.461	24	.833
	— GC Expos (GCL)	DH	9	32	11	8	3	0	0	2	5	3	2-1	.250	.368	.344	...	...
1997—	Harrisburg (East.)	SS-2B-DH	119	443	82	123	19	3	11	35	41	98	29-12	.278	.354	.409	32	.909
1998—	Harrisburg (East.)	OF-DH	80	296	39	78	18	4	4	27	21	61	20-8	.264	.334	.392	10	.946
	— Ottawa (I.L.)	OF	12	41	5	8	3	1	0	5	6	14	2-0	.195	.313	.317	0	1.000
	— Albuquerque (PCL)■	OF	26	101	16	24	7	1	4	16	13	24	5-3	.238	.358	.446	2	.976
1999—	San Antonio (Texas)	2B-DH	123	477	84	139	22	10	11	60	60	71	30-15	.291	.382	.449	31	.946
2000—	Albuquerque (PCL)	2B	124	482	99	155	38	4	23	84	40	100	10-14	.322	.390	.560	23	.963
	— Los Angeles (N.L.)	2B	8	10	2	3	0	0	0	0	0	2	0-0	.300	.300	.300	0	1.000
2001—	Los Angeles (N.L.)	2B-OF-3B	75	133	15	31	11	1	2	9	9	33	4-1	.233	.287	.376	7	.919
2002—	Los Angeles (N.L.)	OF-DH	49	65	12	14	3	0	4	9	5	19	1-1	.215	.271	.446	1	.960
	— Detroit (A.L.)■	OF-2B-DH	34	103	14	23	4	0	4	8	5	22	2-2	.223	.259	.379	2	.969
American League totals (1 year)			34	103	14	23	4	0	4	8	5	22	2-2	.223	.259	.379	2	.969
National League totals (3 years)			132	208	29	48	14	1	6	18	14	54	5-2	.231	.283	.394	8	.935
Major League totals (3 years)			166	311	43	71	18	1	10	26	19	76	7-4	.228	.275	.389	10	.947

BOEHRINGER, BRIAN P

PERSONAL: Born January 8, 1970, in St. Louis. ... 6-2/190. ... Throws right, bats both. ... Full name: Brian Edward Boehringer. ... Name pronounced BO-ring-er.

HIGH SCHOOL: Northwest (House Springs, Mo.).

JUNIOR COLLEGE: St. Louis Community College at Meramec.

COLLEGE: UNLV.

TRANSACTIONS/CAREER NOTES: Selected by Houston Astros organization in 10th round of free-agent draft (June 4, 1990); did not sign. ... Selected by Chicago White Sox organization in fourth round of free-agent draft (June 3, 1991). ... On Utica disabled list (June 29-August 25, 1991). ... On disabled list (June 24-August 25, 1992). ... Traded by White Sox to New York Yankees for P Paul Assenmacher (March 21, 1994). ... On New York disabled list (May 27-August 19, 1997); included rehabilitation assignments to Gulf Coast Yankees (August 10-12) and Tampa (August 13-19). ... Selected by Tampa Bay Devil Rays in second round (30th pick overall) of expansion draft (November 18, 1997). ... Traded by Devil Rays with SS Andy Sheets to San Diego Padres for C John Flaherty (November 18, 1997). ... On disabled list (August 14, 1999-remainder of season). ... On San Diego disabled list (April 21-May 24 and July 4, 2000-remainder of season); included rehabilitation assignment to Rancho Cucamonga (May 17-24). ... Granted free agency (October 25, 2000). ... Signed by Yankees organization (December 14, 2000). ... Traded by Yankees to San Francisco Giants for C Bobby Estalella and P Joe Smith (July 5, 2001). ... Granted free agency (December 21, 2001). ... Signed by Pittsburgh Pirates organization (January 25, 2002). ... Granted free agency (October 28, 2002).

STATISTICAL NOTES: Tied for Eastern League lead with five balks in 1994. ... Led International League with 11 hit batsmen in 1996.

CAREER HITTING (MLB): 2-for-30 (.067), 0 R, 1 2B, 0 3B, 0 HR, 2 RBI.

Year	League	W	L	Pct.	ERA	G	GS	CG	ShO	Sv.-Opp.	IP	H	R	ER	HR	BB-IBB	SO
1991—	GC White Sox (GCL)	1	1	.500	6.57	5	1	0	0	0-...	12.1	14	9	9	1	5-0	10
	— Utica (NY-Penn)	1	1	.500	2.37	4	4	0	0	0-...	19.0	14	8	5	0	8-0	19
1992—	South Bend (Midw.)	6	7	.462	4.38	15	15	2	0	0-...	86.1	87	52	42	5	40-0	59
1993—	Sarasota (FSL)	10	4	.714	2.80	18	17	3	0	0-...	119.0	103	47	37	2	51-2	92
	— Birmingham (Sou.)	2	1	.667	3.54	7	7	1	0	0-...	40.2	41	20	16	3	14-0	29
1994—	Albany/Colonie (East.)■	10	11	.476	3.62	27	27	5	1	0-...	171.2	165	85	69	10	57-1	145
1995—	New York (A.L.)	0	3	.000	13.75	7	3	0	0	0-1	17.2	24	27	27	5	22-1	10
	— Columbus (I.L.)	8	6	.571	2.77	17	17	3	0	0-...	104.0	101	39	32	6	31-1	58
1996—	Columbus (I.L.)	11	7	.611	4.00	25	25	3	1	0-...	153.0	155	79	68	13	56-1	132
	— New York (A.L.)	2	4	.333	5.44	15	3	0	0	0-1	46.1	46	28	28	6	21-2	37
1997—	New York (A.L.)	3	2	.600	2.63	34	0	0	0	0-3	48.0	39	16	14	4	32-6	53
	— Gulf Coast Yankees (GCL)	0	0	...	0.00	1	1	0	0	0-...	2.0	1	0	0	0	0-0	2
	— Tampa (FSL)	0	1	.000	5.00	3	3	0	0	0-...	9.0	9	5	5	1	5-0	8
1998—	San Diego (N.L.)■	5	2	.714	4.36	56	1	0	0	0-1	76.1	75	38	37	10	45-4	67
1999—	San Diego (N.L.)	6	5	.545	3.24	33	11	0	0	0-2	94.1	97	38	34	10	35-4	64
2000—	San Diego (N.L.)	0	3	.000	5.74	7	3	0	0	0-1	15.2	18	15	10	4	10-0	9
	— Rancho Cuca. (Calif.)	0	2	.000	5.40	4	2	0	0	0-...	5.0	8	3	3	0	1-0	5
2001—	New York (A.L.)■	0	1	.000	3.12	22	0	0	0	1-1	34.2	35	15	12	3	12-0	33
	— San Francisco (N.L.)■	0	3	.000	4.19	29	0	0	0	1-1	34.1	32	20	16	4	17-5	27
2002—	Pittsburgh (N.L.)■	4	4	.500	3.39	70	0	0	0	1-6	79.2	65	30	30	5	33-6	65
A.L. totals (4 years)		5	10	.333	4.97	78	6	0	0	1-6	146.2	144	86	81	18	87-9	133
N.L. totals (5 years)		15	17	.469	3.81	195	15	0	0	2-11	300.1	287	141	127	33	140-19	232
Major League totals (8 years)		20	27	.426	4.19	273	21	0	0	3-17	447.0	431	227	208	51	227-28	365

DIVISION SERIES RECORD

Year	League	W	L	Pct.	ERA	G	GS	CG	ShO	Sv.-Opp.	IP	H	R	ER	HR	BB-IBB	SO
1996—	New York (A.L.)	1	0	1.000	6.75	2	0	0	0	0-0	1.1	3	2	1	1	2-0	0
1997—	New York (A.L.)	0	0	...	0.00	1	0	0	0	0-0	1.2	1	0	0	0	1-0	2
1998—	San Diego (N.L.)									Did not play.							
Division series totals (2 years)		1	0	1.000	3.00	3	0	0	0	0-0	3.0	4	2	1	1	3-0	2

CHAMPIONSHIP SERIES RECORD

Year	League	W	L	Pct.	ERA	G	GS	CG	ShO	Sv.-Opp.	IP	H	R	ER	HR	BB-IBB	SO
1998—	San Diego (N.L.)	0	0	...	0.00	3	0	0	0	0-0	3.0	3	0	0	0	1-0	1

WORLD SERIES RECORD

NOTES: Member of World Series championship team (1996).

Year	League	W	L	Pct.	ERA	G	GS	CG	ShO	Sv.-Opp.	IP	H	R	ER	HR	BB-IBB	SO
1996—	New York (A.L.)	0	0	...	5.40	2	0	0	0	0-0	5.0	5	5	3	2	0-0	5
1998—	San Diego (N.L.)	0	0	...	9.00	2	0	0	0	0-0	2.0	4	2	2	1	2-0	3
World Series totals (2 years)		0	0	...	6.43	4	0	0	0	0-0	7.0	9	7	5	3	2-0	8

BONDS, BARRY — OF — GIANTS

PERSONAL: Born July 24, 1964, in Riverside, Calif. ... 6-2/228. ... Bats left, throws left. ... Full name: Barry Lamar Bonds. ... Son of Bobby Bonds, outfielder with eight major league teams (1968-81); and coach with Cleveland Indians (1984-87) and San Francisco Giants (1993-96).

HIGH SCHOOL: Serra (San Mateo, Calif.).

COLLEGE: Arizona State.

TRANSACTIONS/CAREER NOTES: Selected by San Francisco Giants organization in second round of free-agent draft (June 7, 1982); did not sign. ... Selected by Pittsburgh Pirates organization in first round (sixth pick overall) of free-agent draft (June 3, 1985). ... On disabled list (June 15-July 4, 1992). ... Granted free agency (October 26, 1992). ... Signed by Giants (December 8, 1992). ... On suspended list (August 14-16, 1998). ... On disabled list (April 18-June 9, 1999). ... Granted free agency (November 5, 2001). ... Re-signed by Giants (January 17, 2002).

RECORDS: Holds major league career record for most intentional bases on balls—423. ... Holds N.L. career record for highest slugging percentage—.595; most home runs by lefthanded batter—613; most consecutive years leading league in bases on balls—4 (1994-97); most years leading in bases on balls—8 (1992, 1994-97 and 2000-02); and most consecutive years with 30 or more home runs—11 (1992-2002). ... Shares major league record for most seasons and consecutive seasons leading league in intentional bases on balls received—7 (1992-98). ... Shares major league single-season record for fewest assists by outfielder who led league in assists—14 (1990). ... Shares major league record for fewest double plays by outfielder (150 or more games)—0 (1997 and 1998); most consecutive home runs—4 (May 19 [2] and 20 [2], 2001); most home runs in two consecutive games—5 (May 19 [3] and 20 [2], 2001); most home runs in three consecutive games—6 (May 18, 19 [3], 20 [2], 2001 and May 19 [3], 20 [2], 21, 2001); most home runs in five consecutive games—8 (May 17, 18, 19 [3], 20 [2], 21, 2001 and May 18, 19 [3], 20 [2], 21, 22, 2001); and most consecutive games with two or more home runs, start of season—2 (April 2 [2] and 3 [2], 2002). ... Shares N.L. single-season records for most consecutive times reached base safely—15 (August 31 [1], September 1 [5], 2 [4], 4 [5], 1998 [5 singles, 2 doubles, 2 home runs, 6 bases on balls]; fewest assists by outfielder (150 or more games)—2 (1993 and 1998); and most extra base hits—102 (2001). ... Holds N.L. single-season record for most home runs in six consecutive games—9 (May 17, 18, 19 [3], 20 [2], 21, 22, 2001). ... Holds major league single-season records for most home runs—73 (2001); most home runs by outfielder—71 (2001); highest slugging percentage—.863 (2001); highest on-base percentage—.582 (2002); fewest singles in season (150 or more games)—49 (2001); most bases on balls—198 (2002); most intentional bases on balls—68 (2002); and extra bases on long hits—255 (2001). ... Holds major league single-month record for most home runs—17 (May 2001). ... Shares N.L. career records for most years with 100 or more runs batted in—11 (1990-93, 1995-98 and 2000-02); and most years with 100 or more bases on balls—10 (1991-93, 1995-98 and 2000-02). ... Holds N.L. record for most consecutive games with one or more bases on balls—18 (September 9-28, 2002, 34 bases on balls).

HONORS: Named outfielder on The Sporting News college All-America team (1985). ... Named Major League Player of the Year by The Sporting News (1990 and 2001). ... Named N.L. Player of the Year by The Sporting News (1990 and 1991). ... Named outfielder on The Sporting News N.L. All-Star team (1990-94, 1996-97 and 2000-02). ... Won N.L. Gold Glove as outfielder (1990-94 and 1996-98). ... Named outfielder on The Sporting News N.L. Silver Slugger team (1990-94, 1996, 1997 and 2000). ... Named N.L. Most Valuable Player by Baseball Writers' Association of America (1990, 1992-93 and 2001-02). ... Named outfielder on N.L. Silver Slugger team (2001 and 2002).

STATISTICAL NOTES: Tied for N.L. lead with 14 assists by outfielder in 1990. ... Led N.L. with 32 intentional bases on balls received in 1992, 43 in 1993, 18 in 1994, 22 in 1995, 30 in 1996, 34 in 1997, 29 in 1998 and 68 in 2002. ... Led N.L. with 365 total bases in 1993. ... Hit three home runs in one game (August 2, 1994; May 19 and September 9, 2001; and August 27, 2002). ... Tied N.L. outfielders for lead in double plays with four in 2000. ... Had 15-game hitting streak (May 11-27, 2001). ... Career major league grand slams: 11.

2002 GAMES PLAYED BY POSITION (MLB): OF—135; DH—5.

		BATTING														FIELDING	
Year Team (League)	Pos.	G	AB	R	H	2B	3B	HR	RBI	BB	SO	SB-CS	Avg.	OBP	SLG	E	Avg.
1985—Prince William (Caro.)	OF	71	254	49	76	16	4	13	37	37	52	15-3	.299	.383	.547	5	.976
1986—Hawaii (PCL)	OF	44	148	30	46	7	2	7	37	33	31	16-5	.311	.435	.527	2	.983
—Pittsburgh (N.L.)	OF	113	413	72	92	26	3	16	48	65	102	36-7	.223	.330	.416	5	.983
1987—Pittsburgh (N.L.)	OF	150	551	99	144	34	9	25	59	54	88	32-10	.261	.329	.492	5	.986
1988—Pittsburgh (N.L.)	OF	144	538	97	152	30	5	24	58	72	82	17-11	.283	.368	.491	6	.980
1989—Pittsburgh (N.L.)	OF	159	580	96	144	34	6	19	58	93	93	32-10	.248	.351	.426	6	.984
1990—Pittsburgh (N.L.)	OF	151	519	104	156	32	3	33	114	93	83	52-13	.301	.406	*.565	6	.983
1991—Pittsburgh (N.L.)	OF	153	510	95	149	28	5	25	116	107	73	43-13	.292	*.410	.514	3	.991
1992—Pittsburgh (N.L.)	OF	140	473	*109	147	36	5	34	103	*127	69	39-8	.311	*.456	*.624	3	.991
1993—San Fran. (N.L.)■	OF	159	539	129	181	38	4	*46	*123	126	79	29-12	.336	*.458	*.677	5	.984
1994—San Francisco (N.L.)	OF	112	391	89	122	18	1	37	81	*74	43	29-9	.312	.426	.647	3	.986
1995—San Francisco (N.L.)	OF	•144	506	109	149	30	7	33	104	*120	83	31-10	.294	*.431	.577	6	.980
1996—San Francisco (N.L.)	OF	158	517	122	159	27	3	42	129	*151	76	40-7	.308	.461	.615	6	.980
1997—San Francisco (N.L.)	OF	159	532	123	155	26	5	40	101	*145	87	37-8	.291	.446	.585	5	.984
1998—San Francisco (N.L.)	OF	156	552	120	167	44	7	37	122	130	92	28-12	.303	.438	.609	5	.984
1999—San Francisco (N.L.)	OF-DH	102	355	91	93	20	2	34	83	73	62	15-2	.262	.389	.617	3	.984
2000—San Francisco (N.L.)	OF	143	480	129	147	28	4	49	106	*117	77	11-3	.306	.440	.688	3	.989
2001—San Francisco (N.L.)	OF-DH	153	476	129	156	32	2	*73	137	*177	93	13-3	.328	*.515	*.863	6	.977
2002—San Francisco (N.L.)	OF-DH	143	403	117	149	31	2	46	110	*198	47	9-2	*.370	*.582	*.799	8	.968
Major League totals (17 years)		2439	8335	1830	2462	514	73	613	1652	1922	1329	493-140	.295	.428	.595	84	.983

DIVISION SERIES RECORD

		BATTING														FIELDING	
Year Team (League)	Pos.	G	AB	R	H	2B	3B	HR	RBI	BB	SO	SB-CS	Avg.	OBP	SLG	E	Avg.
1997—San Francisco (N.L.)	OF	3	12	0	3	2	0	0	2	0	3	1-0	.250	.231	.417	0	1.000
2000—San Francisco (N.L.)	OF	4	17	2	3	1	1	0	1	3	4	1-0	.176	.300	.353	0	1.000
2002—San Francisco (N.L.)	OF	5	17	5	5	0	0	3	4	4	1	0-1	.294	.409	.824	1	.909
Division series totals (3 years)		12	46	7	11	3	1	3	7	7	8	2-1	.239	.327	.543	1	.963

CHAMPIONSHIP SERIES RECORD

RECORDS: Shares career record for most bases on balls—24. ... Shares single-series record for most bases on balls—10 (2002). ... Shares single-inning record for most hits—2 (October 13, 1992, second inning).

		BATTING														FIELDING	
Year Team (League)	Pos.	G	AB	R	H	2B	3B	HR	RBI	BB	SO	SB-CS	Avg.	OBP	SLG	E	Avg.
1990—Pittsburgh (N.L.)	OF	6	18	4	3	0	0	0	1	6	5	2-0	.167	.375	.167	0	1.000
1991—Pittsburgh (N.L.)	OF	7	27	1	4	1	0	0	0	2	4	3-0	.148	.207	.185	1	.938
1992—Pittsburgh (N.L.)	OF	7	23	5	6	1	0	1	2	6	4	1-0	.261	.433	.435	0	1.000
2002—San Francisco (N.L.)	OF	5	11	5	3	0	1	1	6	10	2	0-0	.273	.591	.727	0	1.000
Championship series totals (4 years)		25	79	15	16	2	1	2	9	24	15	6-0	.203	.390	.329	1	.982

WORLD SERIES RECORD

RECORDS: Holds single-series record for most bases on balls—13 (2002).
NOTES: Hit home run in first at-bat (October 19, 2002).

		BATTING														FIELDING	
Year Team (League)	Pos.	G	AB	R	H	2B	3B	HR	RBI	BB	SO	SB-CS	Avg.	OBP	SLG	E	Avg.
2002— San Francisco (N.L.) ..	OF	7	17	8	8	2	0	4	6	13	3	0-0	.471	.700	1.294	1	.909

ALL-STAR GAME RECORD

RECORDS: Holds single-game record for most doubles—2 (July 13, 1993).

	AB	R	H	2B	3B	HR	RBI	BB	SO	SB-CS	Avg.	OBP	SLG	E	Avg.
All-Star Game totals (10 years)	24	5	6	3	0	2	7	3	5	1-1	.250	.321	.625	0	1.000

BONG, JUNG P BRAVES

PERSONAL: Born July 15, 1980, in Seoul, South Korea. ... 6-3/175. ... Throws left, bats left. ... Full name: Jung Kuen Bong.
TRANSACTIONS/CAREER NOTES: Signed as non-drafted free agent by Atlanta Braves organization (November 6, 1997).
CAREER HITTING (MLB): 0-for-2 (.000), 0 R, 0 2B, 0 3B, 0 HR, 0 RBI.

Year League	W	L	Pct.	ERA	G	GS	CG	ShO	Sv.-Opp.	IP	H	R	ER	HR	BB-IBB	SO
1998— Gulf Coast Braves (GCL) ..	1	1	.500	1.49	11	10	0	0	0-...	48.1	31	9	8	2	14-0	56
1999— Macon (S.Atl.)	6	5	.545	3.98	26	20	0	0	1-...	108.2	111	61	48	8	50-0	100
2000— Macon (S.Atl.)	7	7	.500	4.23	20	19	0	0	0-...	112.2	119	65	53	4	45-0	90
— Myrtle Beach (Caro.)	3	1	.750	2.18	7	6	0	0	0-...	41.1	33	14	10	1	7-0	37
2001— Myrtle Beach (Caro.)	13	9	.591	3.00	28	•28	0	0	0-...	168.0	151	67	56	7	47-0	145
2002— Greenville (Sou.)	7	8	.467	3.25	27	17	0	0	2-...	122.0	136	59	44	6	45-1	107
— Atlanta (N.L.)	0	1	.000	7.50	1	1	0	0	0-0	6.0	8	5	5	0	2-0	4
Major League totals (1 year)	0	1	.000	7.50	1	1	0	0	0-0	6.0	8	5	5	0	2-0	4

BONSER, BOOF P GIANTS

PERSONAL: Born October 14, 1981, in St. Petersburg, Fla. ... 6-4/230. ... Throws right, bats right. ... Full name: John P. Bonser.
HIGH SCHOOL: Gibbs (St. Petersburg, Fla.).
TRANSACTIONS/CAREER NOTES: Selected by San Francisco Giants in first round (21st pick overall) of free-agent draft (June 5, 2000).
HONORS: Named South Atlantic League Most Valuable Pitcher (2001).

Year League	W	L	Pct.	ERA	G	GS	CG	ShO	Sv.-Opp.	IP	H	R	ER	HR	BB-IBB	SO
2000— Salem-Kaizer (N'West)	1	4	.200	6.00	10	9	0	0	0-...	33.0	21	23	22	2	29-0	41
2001— Hagerstown (S.Atl.)	*16	4	.800	2.49	27	27	0	0	0-...	134.0	91	40	37	7	61-2	178
2002— Shreveport (Texas)	1	2	.333	5.55	5	5	0	0	0-...	24.1	30	15	15	3	14-0	23
— San Jose (Calif.)	8	6	.571	2.88	23	23	0	0	0-...	128.1	89	44	41	9	70-0	139

BOONE, AARON 3B REDS

PERSONAL: Born March 9, 1973, in La Mesa, Calif. ... 6-2/200. ... Bats right, throws right. ... Full name: Aaron John Boone. ... Son of Bob Boone, manager, Cincinnati Reds and catcher with three major league teams (1972-90); brother of Bret Boone, second baseman, Seattle Mariners; grandson of Ray Boone, major league infielder with six teams (1948-60); and nephew of Rodney Boone, minor league catcher/outfielder (1972-75).
HIGH SCHOOL: Villa Park (Calif.).
COLLEGE: Southern California.
TRANSACTIONS/CAREER NOTES: Selected by California Angels organization in 43rd round of free-agent draft (June 3, 1991); did not sign. ... Selected by Cincinnati Reds organization in third round of free-agent draft (June 2, 1994). ... On disabled list (July 10, 2000-remainder of season). ... On Cincinnati disabled list (May 15-June 15, August 15-September 1 and September 24, 2001-remainder of season); included rehabilitation assignment to Louisville (June 14-15).
RECORDS: Shares major league single-game record for most home runs in one inning—2 (August 9, 2002, first inning).
STATISTICAL NOTES: Led Pioneer League third basemen with 46 putouts, 156 assists, 220 total chances and 13 double plays in 1994. ... Led Carolina League third basemen with 272 assists in 1995. ... Led Southern League third basemen with 101 putouts, 347 total chances and 28 double plays in 1996. ... Led American Association third basemen with 76 putouts, 241 assists, 336 total chances and 27 double plays in 1997. ... Hit three home runs in one game (August 9, 2002). ... Led N.L. third basemen with 42 double plays in 2002. ... Career major league grand slams: 1.
2002 GAMES PLAYED BY POSITION (MLB): 3B—154; SS—16.

		BATTING														FIELDING	
Year Team (League)	Pos.	G	AB	R	H	2B	3B	HR	RBI	BB	SO	SB-CS	Avg.	OBP	SLG	E	Avg.
1994— Billings (Pio.)	3B-1B	67	256	48	70	15	5	7	55	36	35	6-3	.273	.362	.453	18	.924
1995— Chattanooga (Sou.)	3B	23	66	6	15	3	0	0	3	5	12	2-0	.227	.274	.273	6	.875
— Win.-Salem (Caro.)	3B	108	395	61	103	19	1	14	50	43	77	11-7	.261	.345	.420	21	*.940
1996— Chattanooga (Sou.)	3B-SS-DH	136	*548	86	158	*44	7	17	95	38	77	21-10	.288	.338	.487	22	.945
1997— Indianapolis (A.A.)	3B-SS-2B	131	476	79	138	30	4	22	75	40	81	12-4	.290	.344	.508	24	.941
— Cincinnati (N.L.)	3B-2B	16	49	5	12	1	0	0	5	2	5	1-0	.245	.275	.265	3	.917
1998— Cincinnati (N.L.)	3B-2B-SS	58	181	24	51	13	2	2	28	15	36	6-1	.282	.350	.409	8	.944
— Indianapolis (I.L.)	3B-2B-SS	87	332	56	80	18	1	7	38	31	71	17-5	.241	.316	.364	19	.943
1999— Cincinnati (N.L.)	3B-SS	139	472	56	132	26	5	14	72	30	79	17-6	.280	.330	.445	15	.958
— Indianapolis (I.L.)	3B-2B-SS	11	41	6	14	2	1	0	7	3	4	2-2	.341	.388	.439	3	.930
2000— Cincinnati (N.L.)	3B-SS	84	291	44	83	18	0	12	43	24	52	6-1	.285	.356	.471	8	.965
2001— Cincinnati (N.L.)	3B	103	381	54	112	26	2	14	62	29	71	6-3	.294	.351	.483	19	.936
— Louisville (I.L.)	3B	1	4	0	1	0	0	0	0	0	0	0-0	.250	.250	.250	0	1.000
2002— Cincinnati (N.L.)	3B-SS	•162	606	83	146	38	2	26	87	56	111	32-8	.241	.314	.439	22	.956
Major League totals (6 years)		562	1980	266	536	122	11	68	297	156	354	68-19	.271	.333	.446	75	.952

BOONE, BRET 2B MARINERS

PERSONAL: Born April 6, 1969, in El Cajon, Calif. ... 5-10/190. ... Bats right, throws right. ... Full name: Bret Robert Boone. ... Son of Bob Boone, manager, Cincinnati Reds and catcher with three major league teams (1972-90); brother of Aaron Boone, third baseman, Cincinnati Reds; grandson of Ray Boone, major league infielder with six teams (1948-60); and nephew of Rodney Boone, minor league catcher/outfielder (1972-75).

HIGH SCHOOL: El Dorado (Yorba Linda, Calif.).

COLLEGE: Southern California.

TRANSACTIONS/CAREER NOTES: Selected by Minnesota Twins organization in 28th round of free-agent draft (June 2, 1987); did not sign. ... Selected by Seattle Mariners organization in fifth round of free-agent draft (June 4, 1990). ... Traded by Mariners with P Erik Hanson to Cincinnati Reds for P Bobby Ayala and C Dan Wilson (November 2, 1993). ... On disabled list (April 1-16, 1996). ... Traded by Reds with P Mike Remlinger to Atlanta Braves for P Denny Neagle, OF Michael Tucker and P Rob Bell (November 10, 1998). ... Traded by Braves with OF/1B Ryan Klesko and P Jason Shiell to San Diego Padres for 2B Quilvio Veras, 1B Wally Joyner and OF Reggie Sanders (December 22, 1999). ... On disabled list (August 27, 2000-remainder of season). ... Granted free agency (October 31, 2000). ... Signed by Mariners (December 22, 2000). ... Granted free agency (November 5, 2001). ... Re-signed by Mariners (January 17, 2002).

RECORDS: Holds major league single-season record for highest fielding percentage by second baseman (100 or more games)—.997 (1997). ... Shares major league single-game record for most home runs in one inning—2 (May 2, 2002, first inning).

HONORS: Won N.L. Gold Glove at second base (1998). ... Named second baseman on A.L. Silver Slugger team (2001). ... Named second baseman on The Sporting News A.L. All-Star team (2001). ... Won A.L. Gold Glove at second base (2002).

STATISTICAL NOTES: Tied for Southern League lead in grounding into double plays with 21 in 1991. ... Led Southern League second basemen with 288 putouts in 1991. ... Led Pacific Coast League second basemen with 90 double plays in 1992. ... Led N.L. second basemen with 311 putouts and 106 double plays in 1995. ... Hit three home runs in one game (September 20, 1998; and June 23, 2000). ... Career major league grand slams: 3.

2002 GAMES PLAYED BY POSITION (MLB): 2B—153; DH—1.

		BATTING														FIELDING	
Year Team (League)	**Pos.**	**G**	**AB**	**R**	**H**	**2B**	**3B**	**HR**	**RBI**	**BB**	**SO**	**SB-CS**	**Avg.**	**OBP**	**SLG**	**E**	**Avg.**
1990—Peninsula (Caro.)	2B	74	255	42	68	13	2	8	38	47	57	5-2	.267	.383	.427	19	.951
1991—Jacksonville (Sou.)	2B-3B	•139	475	64	121	18	1	19	75	72	123	9-9	.255	.357	.417	21	.970
1992—Calgary (PCL)	2B-SS	118	439	73	138	26	5	13	73	60	88	17-12	.314	.398	.485	10	.984
—Seattle (A.L.)	2B-3B	33	129	15	25	4	0	4	15	4	34	1-1	.194	.224	.318	6	.966
1993—Calgary (PCL)	2B	71	274	48	91	18	3	8	56	28	58	3-8	.332	.388	.507	8	.976
—Seattle (A.L.)	2B-DH	76	271	31	68	12	2	12	38	17	52	2-3	.251	.301	.443	3	.991
1994—Cincinnati (N.L.)■	2B-3B	108	381	59	122	25	2	12	68	24	74	3-4	.320	.368	.491	12	.975
1995—Cincinnati (N.L.)	2B	138	513	63	137	34	2	15	68	41	84	5-1	.267	.326	.429	4	*.994
1996—Cincinnati (N.L.)	2B	142	520	56	121	21	3	12	69	31	100	3-2	.233	.275	.354	6	*.991
1997—Cincinnati (N.L.)	2B	139	443	40	99	25	1	7	46	45	101	5-5	.223	.298	.332	2	*.997
—Indianapolis (A.A.)	2B	3	7	1	2	1	0	0	1	2	2	1-0	.286	.444	.429	0	1.000
1998—Cincinnati (N.L.)	2B	157	583	76	155	38	1	24	95	48	104	6-4	.266	.324	.458	9	.988
1999—Atlanta (N.L.)■	2B	152	608	102	153	38	1	20	63	47	112	14-9	.252	.310	.416	13	.982
2000—San Diego (N.L.)■	2B	127	463	61	116	18	2	19	74	50	97	8-4	.251	.326	.421	15	.977
2001—Seattle (A.L.)■	2B-DH	158	623	118	206	37	3	37	*141	40	110	5-5	.331	.372	.578	10	.986
2002—Seattle (A.L.)	2B-DH	155	608	88	169	34	3	24	107	53	102	12-5	.278	.339	.462	7	*.989
American League totals (4 years)		422	1631	252	468	87	8	77	301	114	298	20-14	.287	.337	.492	26	.986
National League totals (7 years)		963	3511	457	903	199	12	109	483	286	672	44-29	.257	.316	.414	61	.987
Major League totals (11 years)		1385	5142	709	1371	286	20	186	784	400	970	64-43	.267	.323	.439	87	.986

DIVISION SERIES RECORD

RECORDS: Shares N.L. single-game record for most at-bats—6 (October 8, 1999).

		BATTING														FIELDING	
Year Team (League)	**Pos.**	**G**	**AB**	**R**	**H**	**2B**	**3B**	**HR**	**RBI**	**BB**	**SO**	**SB-CS**	**Avg.**	**OBP**	**SLG**	**E**	**Avg.**
1995—Cincinnati (N.L.)	2B	3	10	4	3	1	0	1	1	1	3	1-0	.300	.364	.700	0	1.000
1999—Atlanta (N.L.)	2B	4	19	3	9	1	0	0	1	0	4	1-0	.474	.474	.526	0	1.000
2001—Seattle (A.L.)	2B	5	21	1	2	0	0	0	0	1	11	1-0	.095	.136	.095	1	.960
Division series totals (3 years)		12	50	8	14	2	0	1	2	2	18	3-0	.280	.308	.380	1	.984

CHAMPIONSHIP SERIES RECORD

RECORDS: Shares A.L. single-game record for most runs batted in—5 (October 20, 2001).

		BATTING														FIELDING	
Year Team (League)	**Pos.**	**G**	**AB**	**R**	**H**	**2B**	**3B**	**HR**	**RBI**	**BB**	**SO**	**SB-CS**	**Avg.**	**OBP**	**SLG**	**E**	**Avg.**
1995—Cincinnati (N.L.)	2B	4	14	1	3	0	0	0	0	1	2	0-0	.214	.267	.214	0	1.000
1999—Atlanta (N.L.)	2B	6	22	2	4	1	0	0	1	1	7	2-1	.182	.250	.227	0	1.000
2001—Seattle (A.L.)	2B	5	19	2	6	0	0	2	6	2	2	0-0	.316	.381	.632	0	1.000
Championship series totals (3 years)		15	55	5	13	1	0	2	7	4	11	2-1	.236	.300	.364	0	1.000

WORLD SERIES RECORD

		BATTING														FIELDING	
Year Team (League)	**Pos.**	**G**	**AB**	**R**	**H**	**2B**	**3B**	**HR**	**RBI**	**BB**	**SO**	**SB-CS**	**Avg.**	**OBP**	**SLG**	**E**	**Avg.**
1999—Atlanta (N.L.)	2B-PH	4	13	1	7	4	0	0	3	1	3	0-1	.538	.571	.846	0	1.000

ALL-STAR GAME RECORD

	AB	**R**	**H**	**2B**	**3B**	**HR**	**RBI**	**BB**	**SO**	**SB-CS**	**Avg.**	**OBP**	**SLG**	**E**	**Avg.**
All-Star Game totals (1 year)	2	0	0	0	0	0	0	0	0	0-0	.000	.000	.000	0	1.000

BORBON, PEDRO P

PERSONAL: Born November 15, 1967, in Mao, Dominican Republic. ... 6-1/230. ... Throws left, bats left. ... Full name: Pedro Felix Borbon Jr. ... Son of Pedro Borbon, pitcher with four major league teams (1969-80). ... Name pronounced bor-BONE.

HIGH SCHOOL: DeWitt Clinton (Sioux, N.J.).

JUNIOR COLLEGE: Ranger (Texas) Junior College.

TRANSACTIONS/CAREER NOTES: Selected by Milwaukee Brewers organization in 35th round of free-agent draft (June 3, 1985); did not sign. ... Selected by Los Angeles Dodgers organization in secondary phase of free-agent draft (January 14, 1986); did not sign. ... Signed as non-drafted free agent by Chicago White Sox organization (June 4, 1988). ... Released by White Sox (April 1, 1989). ... Signed by Atlanta Braves organization (August 25, 1989). ... On Atlanta disabled list (April 8-26 and August 23, 1996-remainder of season); included rehabilitation assignment to Greenville (April 23-26). ... On disabled list (March 30, 1997-entire season). ... On Atlanta disabled list (March 29, 1998-entire season); included rehabilitation assignments to Macon (June 4-7), Greenville (June 9-July 5 and July 9-14) and Richmond (July 16-August 31 and September 1-8). ... Granted free agency (October 1, 1998). ... Signed by Dodgers organization (December 30, 1998). ... Traded by Dodgers with OF Raul Mondesi to Toronto Blue Jays for OF Shawn Green and 2B Jorge Nunez (November 8, 1999). ... Traded by Blue Jays to Houston Astros for a player to be named later (May 15, 2002). ... Granted free agency (October 28, 2002).

STATISTICAL NOTES: Led Gulf Coast League with 14 balks in 1988.

CAREER HITTING (MLB): 1-for-7 (.143), 0 R, 0 2B, 0 3B, 0 HR, 0 RBI.

Year League	W	L	Pct.	ERA	G	GS	CG	ShO	Sv.-Opp.	IP	H	R	ER	HR	BB-IBB	SO
1988— GC White Sox (GCL)	5	3	.625	2.41	16	11	1	1	1-...	74.2	52	28	20	1	17-0	67
1989—									Did not play.							
1990— Burlington (Midw.)■	11	3	.786	1.47	14	14	6	2	0-...	97.2	73	25	16	3	23-0	76
— Durham (Caro.)	4	5	.444	5.43	11	11	0	0	0-...	61.1	73	40	37	8	16-0	37
1991— Durham (Caro.)	4	3	.571	2.27	37	6	1	0	5-...	91.0	85	40	23	2	35-2	79
— Greenville (Sou.)	0	1	.000	2.79	4	4	0	0	0-...	29.0	23	12	9	1	10-0	22
1992— Greenville (Sou.)	8	2	.800	3.06	39	10	0	0	3-...	94.0	73	36	32	6	42-1	79
— Atlanta (N.L.)	0	1	.000	6.75	2	0	0	0	0-0	1.1	2	1	1	0	1-1	1
1993— Richmond (I.L.)	5	5	.500	4.23	52	0	0	0	1-...	76.2	71	40	36	7	42-9	95
— Atlanta (N.L.)	0	0	...	21.60	3	0	0	0	0-0	1.2	3	4	4	0	3-0	2
1994— Richmond (I.L.)	3	4	.429	2.79	59	0	0	0	4-...	80.2	66	29	25	3	41-5	82
1995— Atlanta (N.L.)	2	2	.500	3.09	41	0	0	0	2-4	32.0	29	12	11	2	17-4	33
1996— Atlanta (N.L.)	3	0	1.000	2.75	43	0	0	0	1-1	36.0	26	12	11	1	7-0	31
— Greenville (Sou.)	0	0	...	0.00	1	0	0	0	0-...	1.0	0	0	0	0	0-0	0
1997— Atlanta (N.L.)									Did not play.							
1998— Macon (S.Atl.)	0	0	...	9.00	3	0	0	0	0-...	3.0	4	3	3	1	1-0	3
— Greenville (Sou.)	0	2	.000	4.74	16	0	0	0	0-...	19.0	21	14	10	2	14-0	10
— Richmond (I.L.)	0	1	.000	5.70	20	0	0	0	0-...	23.2	29	17	15	1	8-0	15
1999— Los Angeles (N.L.)■	4	3	.571	4.09	70	0	0	0	1-2	50.2	39	23	23	5	29-1	33
2000— Toronto (A.L.)■	1	1	.500	6.48	59	0	0	0	1-1	41.2	45	37	30	5	38-5	29
2001— Toronto (A.L.)	2	4	.333	3.71	71	0	0	0	0-5	53.1	48	24	22	8	12-3	45
2002— Toronto (A.L.)	1	2	.333	4.97	16	0	0	0	0-2	12.2	12	8	7	3	6-3	11
— Houston (N.L.)■	3	2	.600	5.50	56	0	0	0	1-3	37.2	41	24	23	7	19-5	39
A.L. totals (3 years)	4	7	.364	4.93	146	0	0	0	1-8	107.2	105	69	59	16	56-11	85
N.L. totals (6 years)	12	8	.600	4.12	215	0	0	0	5-10	159.1	140	76	73	15	76-11	139
Major League totals (8 years)	16	15	.516	4.45	361	0	0	0	6-18	267.0	245	145	132	31	132-22	224

DIVISION SERIES RECORD

Year League	W	L	Pct.	ERA	G	GS	CG	ShO	Sv.-Opp.	IP	H	R	ER	HR	BB-IBB	SO
1995— Atlanta (N.L.)	0	0	...	0.00	1	0	0	0	0-0	1.0	1	0	0	0	0-0	3

CHAMPIONSHIP SERIES RECORD

Year League	W	L	Pct.	ERA	G	GS	CG	ShO	Sv.-Opp.	IP	H	R	ER	HR	BB-IBB	SO
1995— Atlanta (N.L.)									Did not play.							

WORLD SERIES RECORD

NOTES: Member of World Series championship team (1995).

Year League	W	L	Pct.	ERA	G	GS	CG	ShO	Sv.-Opp.	IP	H	R	ER	HR	BB-IBB	SO
1995— Atlanta (N.L.)	0	0	...	0.00	1	0	0	0	1-1	1.0	0	0	0	0	0-0	2

BORCHARD, JOE — OF — WHITE SOX

PERSONAL: Born November 25, 1978, in Panorama City, Calif. ... 6-5/220. ... Bats both, throws right. ... Full name: Joseph Edward Borchard.

HIGH SCHOOL: Camarillo (Calif.).

COLLEGE: Stanford.

TRANSACTIONS/CAREER NOTES: Selected by Baltimore Orioles organization in 20th round of free-agent draft (June 3, 1997); did not sign. ... Selected by Chicago White Sox organization in first round (12th pick overall) of free-agent draft (June 5, 2000). ... On Charlotte disabled list (April 4-22, 2002).

2002 GAMES PLAYED BY POSITION (MLB): OF—15.

		BATTING														FIELDING	
Year Team (League)	Pos.	G	AB	R	H	2B	3B	HR	RBI	BB	SO	SB-CS	Avg.	OBP	SLG	E	Avg.
2000— Ariz. White Sox (Ariz.)	OF	7	29	3	12	4	0	0	8	4	4	0-0	.414	.485	.552	0	1.000
— Win.-Salem (Caro.)	OF	14	52	7	15	3	0	2	7	6	9	0-0	.288	.377	.462	0	1.000
— Birmingham (Sou.)	OF	6	22	3	5	0	1	0	3	3	8	0-0	.227	.308	.318	1	.875
2001— Birmingham (Sou.)	OF	133	515	95	152	27	1	27	98	67	158	5-4	.295	.384	.509	12	.964
2002— Win.-Salem (Caro.)	OF	2	3	1	0	0	0	0	0	6	0	0-0	.000	.667	.000	0	1.000
— Charlotte (I.L.)	OF	117	438	62	119	35	2	20	59	49	139	2-4	.272	.349	.498	3	.990
— Chicago (A.L.)	OF	16	36	5	8	0	0	2	5	1	14	0-0	.222	.243	.389	0	1.000
Major League totals (1 year)		16	36	5	8	0	0	2	5	1	14	0-0	.222	.243	.389	0	1.000

BORDERS, PAT — C

PERSONAL: Born May 14, 1963, in Columbus, Ohio. ... 6-2/200. ... Bats right, throws right. ... Full name: Patrick Lance Borders. ... Brother of Todd Borders, minor league catcher (1988).

HIGH SCHOOL: Lake Wales (Fla.).

TRANSACTIONS/CAREER NOTES: Selected by Toronto Blue Jays organization in sixth round of free-agent draft (June 7, 1982). ... On Toronto disabled list (July 5-August 19, 1988); included rehabilitation assignment to Syracuse (July 30-August 19). ... Granted free agency (October 21, 1994). ... Signed by Kansas City Royals (April 10, 1995). ... Traded by Royals to Houston Astros for a player to be named later (August 12, 1995); Royals acquired P Rick Huisman to complete deal (August 17, 1995). ... On Houston suspended list (September 8-14, 1995). ...

Granted free agency (November 6, 1995). ... Signed by St. Louis Cardinals organization (January 10, 1996). ... Traded by Cardinals to California Angels for P Ben VanRyn (June 15, 1996). ... Traded by Angels to Chicago White Sox for P Robert Ellis (July 27, 1996). ... Granted free agency (November 8, 1996). ... Signed by Cleveland Indians organization (December 13, 1996). ... Granted free agency (November 7, 1997). ... Re-signed by Indians organization (December 17, 1997). ... Granted free agency (November 3, 1998). ... Re-signed by Indians organization (February 26, 1999). ... Released by Indians (August 30, 1999). ... Signed by Blue Jays (August 31, 1999). ... Granted free agency (November 11, 1999). ... Signed by Tampa Bay Devil Rays (January 27, 2000). ... Contract sold by Devil Rays to Seattle Mariners organization (August 27, 2001). ... Granted free agency (November 7, 2001). ... Signed by Texas Rangers organization (February 2, 2002). ... Released by Rangers (April 2, 2002). ... Signed by Mariners organization (April 8, 2002). ... Granted free agency (November 4, 2002).

STATISTICAL NOTES: Tied for Southern League lead with 16 passed balls in 1987. ... Led A.L. catchers with 880 total chances in 1992 and 962 in 1993. ... Led A.L. catchers with 88 assists in 1992, 80 in 1993 and 60 in 1994. ... Led A.L. with nine passed balls in 1994. ... Tied for Pacific Coast League lead with nine double plays in 2002. ... Career major league grand slams: 1.

MISCELLANEOUS: Member of 2000 U.S. Olympic baseball team.

2002 GAMES PLAYED BY POSITION (MLB): DH—2; C—2.

		BATTING														FIELDING	
Year Team (League)	**Pos.**	**G**	**AB**	**R**	**H**	**2B**	**3B**	**HR**	**RBI**	**BB**	**SO**	**SB-CS**	**Avg.**	**OBP**	**SLG**	**E**	**Avg.**
1982—Medicine Hat (Pio.)	3B	61	217	30	66	12	2	5	33	24	52	1-2	.304	.377	.447	*25	.826
1983—Florence (S.Atl.)	3B	131	457	62	125	31	4	5	54	46	116	4-1	.274	.341	.392	*41	.881
1984—Florence (S.Atl.)	1B-3B-OF	131	467	69	129	32	5	12	85	56	109	3-4	.276	.353	.443	25	.967
1985—Kinston (Caro.)	1B	127	460	43	120	16	1	10	60	45	116	6-5	.261	.327	.365	*20	.978
1986—Florence (S.Atl.)	C-OF	16	40	8	15	7	0	3	9	2	9	0-0	.375	.405	.775	0	1.000
—Knoxville (Sou.)	C-1B	12	34	3	12	1	0	2	5	1	6	0-3	.353	.371	.559	3	.943
—Kinston (Caro.)	C-1B-OF	49	174	24	57	10	0	6	26	10	42	0-0	.328	.366	.489	7	.971
1987—Dunedin (FSL)	1B	3	11	0	4	0	0	0	1	0	3	0-0	.364	.364	.364	0	1.000
—Knoxville (Sou.)	C-3B	94	349	44	102	14	1	11	51	20	56	2-5	.292	.332	.433	12	.976
1988—Toronto (A.L.)	C-DH-2B-3B	56	154	15	42	6	3	5	21	3	24	0-0	.273	.285	.448	7	.970
—Syracuse (I.L.)	C	35	120	11	29	8	0	3	14	16	22	0-0	.242	.326	.383	2	.991
1989—Toronto (A.L.)	C-DH	94	241	22	62	11	1	3	29	11	45	2-1	.257	.290	.349	6	.980
1990—Toronto (A.L.)	C-DH	125	346	36	99	24	2	15	49	18	57	0-1	.286	.319	.497	4	.993
1991—Toronto (A.L.)	C	105	291	22	71	17	0	5	36	11	45	0-0	.244	.271	.354	4	.993
1992—Toronto (A.L.)	C	138	480	47	116	26	2	13	53	33	75	1-1	.242	.290	.385	8	.991
1993—Toronto (A.L.)	C	138	488	38	124	30	0	9	55	20	66	2-2	.254	.285	.371	*13	.986
1994—Toronto (A.L.)	C	85	295	24	73	13	1	3	26	15	50	1-1	.247	.284	.329	8	.988
1995—Kansas City (A.L.)■	C-DH	52	143	14	33	8	1	4	13	7	22	0-0	.231	.267	.385	0	1.000
—Houston (N.L.)■	C	11	35	1	4	0	0	0	0	2	7	0-0	.114	.162	.114	1	.987
1996—St. Louis (N.L.)■	C-1B	26	69	3	22	3	0	0	4	1	14	0-1	.319	.329	.362	3	.977
—California (A.L.)■	C	19	57	6	13	3	0	2	8	3	11	0-1	.228	.267	.386	2	.984
—Chicago (A.L.)■	C-DH	31	94	6	26	1	0	3	6	5	18	0-0	.277	.313	.383	3	.982
1997—Cleveland (A.L.)■	C	55	159	17	47	7	1	4	15	9	27	0-2	.296	.341	.428	0	1.000
1998—Cleveland (A.L.)	C-3B	54	160	12	38	6	0	0	6	10	40	0-2	.238	.289	.275	8	.974
1999—Buffalo (I.L.)	C-DH	55	198	17	47	7	0	5	23	12	31	0-1	.237	.290	.348	5	.986
—Cleveland (A.L.)	C-3B	6	20	2	6	0	1	0	3	0	3	0-1	.300	.300	.400	2	.943
—Toronto (A.L.)■	DH-C	6	14	1	3	0	0	1	3	1	2	0-0	.214	.267	.429	0	1.000
2000—Durham (I.L.)■	C-1B	96	348	44	95	16	0	12	55	20	66	7-2	.273	.311	.422	3	.995
2001—Durham (I.L.)	C-1B	87	313	26	74	15	1	2	28	16	61	3-2	.236	.278	.310	4	.989
—Tacoma (PCL)■	C	3	11	2	3	0	0	1	2	1	1	0-0	.273	.385	.545	0	1.000
—Seattle (A.L.)	C	5	6	1	3	0	0	0	0	0	1	0-0	.500	.500	.500	1	.923
2002—Tacoma (PCL)	C-3B-1B	92	317	42	84	16	1	12	27	11	47	3-2	.265	.289	.435	5	.992
—Seattle (A.L.)	DH-C	4	4	0	2	1	0	0	1	0	1	0-0	.500	.500	.750	0	1.000
American League totals (14 years)		973	2952	263	758	153	12	67	324	146	487	6-12	.257	.292	.385	66	.988
National League totals (2 years)		37	104	4	26	3	0	0	4	3	21	0-1	.250	.271	.279	4	.980
Major League totals (14 years)		1010	3056	267	784	156	12	67	328	149	508	6-13	.257	.292	.381	70	.987

CHAMPIONSHIP SERIES RECORD

		BATTING														FIELDING	
Year Team (League)	**Pos.**	**G**	**AB**	**R**	**H**	**2B**	**3B**	**HR**	**RBI**	**BB**	**SO**	**SB-CS**	**Avg.**	**OBP**	**SLG**	**E**	**Avg.**
1989—Toronto (A.L.)	PH-C	1	1	0	1	0	0	0	1	0	0	0-0	1.000	1.000	1.000	0	1.000
1991—Toronto (A.L.)	C	5	19	0	5	1	0	0	2	0	0	0-0	.263	.263	.316	2	.955
1992—Toronto (A.L.)	C	6	22	3	7	0	0	1	3	1	1	0-0	.318	.320	.455	1	.976
1993—Toronto (A.L.)	C	6	24	1	6	1	0	0	3	0	6	1-0	.250	.250	.292	0	1.000
Championship series totals (4 years)		18	66	4	19	2	0	1	9	1	7	1-0	.288	.290	.364	3	.977

WORLD SERIES RECORD

NOTES: Named Most Valuable Player (1992). ... Member of World Series championship team (1992 and 1993).

		BATTING														FIELDING	
Year Team (League)	**Pos.**	**G**	**AB**	**R**	**H**	**2B**	**3B**	**HR**	**RBI**	**BB**	**SO**	**SB-CS**	**Avg.**	**OBP**	**SLG**	**E**	**Avg.**
1992—Toronto (A.L.)	C	6	20	2	9	3	0	1	3	2	1	0-0	.450	.500	.750	1	.981
1993—Toronto (A.L.)	C	6	23	2	7	0	0	0	1	2	1	0-0	.304	.360	.304	1	.981
World Series totals (2 years)		12	43	4	16	3	0	1	4	4	2	0-0	.372	.426	.512	2	.981

BORDICK, MIKE SS

PERSONAL: Born July 21, 1965, in Marquette, Mich. ... 5-11/175. ... Bats right, throws right. ... Full name: Michael Todd Bordick.

HIGH SCHOOL: Hampden (Maine) Academy.

COLLEGE: Maine.

TRANSACTIONS/CAREER NOTES: Signed as non-drafted free agent by Oakland Athletics organization (July 10, 1986). ... On Tacoma disabled list (April 14-May 13, 1991). ... On Oakland disabled list (May 8-27, 1995); included rehabilitation assignment to Modesto (May 23-26). ... Granted free agency (December 7, 1996). ... Signed by Baltimore Orioles (December 13, 1996). ... Traded by Orioles to New York Mets for OF Melvin Mora, 3B Mike Kinkade, P Lesli Brea and P Pat Gorman (July 28, 2000). ... Granted free agency (October 27, 2000). ... Signed by Orioles (December 20, 2000). ... On Baltimore disabled list (June 14, 2001-remainder of season); included rehabilitation assignments to Bowie (August 2-3) and Delmarva (August 4-10). ... On disabled list (July 16-August 17, 2002). ... Granted free agency (October 31, 2002).

RECORDS: Holds major league career records for most consecutive errorless games by shortstop—110 (April 11-September 29, 2002); and most chances accepted without an error—543 (April 10-September 29, 2002). ... Holds major league single-season records for highest fielding percentage by shortstop (150 or more games)—.998 (2002); most consecutive errorless games by shortstop—110 (April 11-September 29, 2002); and most chances accepted without an error—543 (April 10-September 29, 2002).

STATISTICAL NOTES: Led Pacific Coast League shortstops with .972 fielding percentage and 82 double plays in 1990. ... Led A.L. shortstops with 280 putouts and tied for lead with 108 double plays in 1993. ... Led A.L. shortstops with 245 putouts in 1995. ... Led A.L. shortstopts with 476 assists in 1996 and 446 in 1998. ... Led A.L. with 15 sacrifice hits in 1998. ... Led A.L. shortstops with 511 assists, 797 total chances and 132 double plays in 1999. ... Career major league grand slams: 1.

2002 GAMES PLAYED BY POSITION (MLB): SS—117.

			BATTING														FIELDING	
Year	Team (League)	Pos.	G	AB	R	H	2B	3B	HR	RBI	BB	SO	SB-CS	Avg.	OBP	SLG	E	Avg.
1986—	Medford (N'West)	SS	46	187	30	48	3	1	0	19	40	21	6-0	.257	.389	.283	18	.921
1987—	Modesto (Calif.)	SS	133	497	73	133	17	0	3	75	87	92	8-8	.268	.377	.320	17	*.968
1988—	Huntsville (Sou.)	2B-SS-3B	132	481	48	130	13	2	0	28	87	50	7-9	.270	.384	.306	24	.965
1989—	Tacoma (PCL)	2B-SS-3B	136	487	55	117	17	1	1	43	58	51	4-9	.240	.329	.285	33	.954
1990—	Oakland (A.L.)	3B-SS-2B	25	14	0	1	0	0	0	0	1	4	0-0	.071	.133	.071	0	1.000
—	Tacoma (PCL)	SS-2B	111	348	49	79	16	1	2	30	46	40	3-0	.227	.321	.296	16	†.973
1991—	Tacoma (PCL)	SS	26	81	15	22	4	1	2	14	17	10	0-1	.272	.404	.420	3	.974
—	Oakland (A.L.)	SS-2B-3B	90	235	21	56	5	1	0	21	14	37	3-4	.238	.289	.268	11	.970
1992—	Oakland (A.L.)	2B-SS	154	504	62	151	19	4	3	48	40	59	12-6	.300	.358	.371	16	.979
1993—	Oakland (A.L.)	SS-2B	159	546	60	136	21	2	3	48	60	58	10-10	.249	.332	.311	13	.982
1994—	Oakland (A.L.)	SS-2B	114	391	38	99	18	4	2	37	38	44	7-2	.253	.320	.335	14	.973
1995—	Oakland (A.L.)	SS-DH	126	428	46	113	13	0	8	44	35	48	11-3	.264	.325	.350	10	.983
—	Modesto (Calif.)	SS	1	2	0	0	0	0	0	0	0	0	0-1	.000	.333	.000	0	1.000
1996—	Oakland (A.L.)	SS	155	525	46	126	18	4	5	54	52	59	5-6	.240	.307	.318	16	.979
1997—	Baltimore (A.L.)■	SS	153	509	55	120	19	1	7	46	33	66	0-2	.236	.283	.318	13	.980
1998—	Baltimore (A.L.)	SS	151	465	59	121	29	1	13	51	39	65	6-7	.260	.328	.411	7	.990
1999—	Baltimore (A.L.)	SS	160	631	93	175	35	7	10	77	54	102	14-4	.277	.334	.403	9	*.989
2000—	Baltimore (A.L.)	SS	100	391	70	116	22	1	16	59	34	71	6-5	.297	.350	.481	9	.979
—	New York (N.L.)■	SS	56	192	18	50	8	0	4	21	15	28	3-1	.260	.321	.365	7	.968
2001—	Baltimore (A.L.)■	SS	58	229	32	57	13	0	7	30	17	36	9-3	.249	.314	.397	6	.977
—	Bowie (East.)	DH	1	4	0	1	0	0	0	0	0	1	0-0	.250	.250	.250	...	...
—	Delmarva (S.Atl.)	SS	3	8	0	0	0	0	0	1	2	1	0-0	.000	.200	.000	0	...
2002—	Baltimore (A.L.)	SS	117	367	37	85	19	3	8	36	35	63	7-4	.232	.302	.365	1	*.998
American League totals (13 years)			1562	5235	619	1356	231	28	82	551	452	712	90-56	.259	.322	.361	125	.983
National League totals (1 year)			56	192	18	50	8	0	4	21	15	28	3-1	.260	.321	.365	7	.968
Major League totals (13 years)			1618	5427	637	1406	239	28	86	572	467	740	93-57	.259	.322	.361	132	.982

DIVISION SERIES RECORD

			BATTING														FIELDING	
Year	Team (League)	Pos.	G	AB	R	H	2B	3B	HR	RBI	BB	SO	SB-CS	Avg.	OBP	SLG	E	Avg.
1997—	Baltimore (A.L.)	SS	4	10	4	4	1	0	0	4	4	2	0-1	.400	.571	.500	0	1.000
2000—	New York (N.L.)	SS	4	12	3	2	0	0	0	0	3	4	0-0	.167	.412	.167	0	1.000
Division series totals (2 years)			8	22	7	6	1	0	0	4	7	6	0-1	.273	.484	.318	0	1.000

CHAMPIONSHIP SERIES RECORD

			BATTING														FIELDING	
Year	Team (League)	Pos.	G	AB	R	H	2B	3B	HR	RBI	BB	SO	SB-CS	Avg.	OBP	SLG	E	Avg.
1990—	Oakland (A.L.)		Did not play.															
1992—	Oakland (A.L.)	SS-2B	6	19	1	1	0	0	0	0	1	2	1-0	.053	.100	.053	0	1.000
1997—	Baltimore (A.L.)	SS	6	19	0	3	1	0	0	2	0	6	0-0	.158	.158	.211	0	1.000
2000—	New York (N.L.)	SS	5	13	2	1	0	0	0	0	3	1	0-0	.077	.294	.077	0	1.000
Championship series totals (3 years)			17	51	3	5	1	0	0	2	4	9	1-0	.098	.179	.118	0	1.000

WORLD SERIES RECORD

			BATTING														FIELDING	
Year	Team (League)	Pos.	G	AB	R	H	2B	3B	HR	RBI	BB	SO	SB-CS	Avg.	OBP	SLG	E	Avg.
1990—	Oakland (A.L.)	SS-PR	3	0	0	0	0	0	0	0	0	0	0-0	...	...	...	0	1.000
2000—	New York (N.L.)	SS	4	8	0	1	0	0	0	0	0	3	0-0	.125	.125	.125	1	.917
World Series totals (2 years)			7	8	0	1	0	0	0	0	0	3	0-0	.125	.125	.125	1	.929

ALL-STAR GAME RECORD

	AB	R	H	2B	3B	HR	RBI	BB	SO	SB-CS	Avg.	OBP	SLG	E	Avg.
All-Star Game totals (1 year)	1	0	0	0	0	0	0	0	0	0-0	.000	.000	.000	0	...

BORLAND, TOBY — P — MARLINS

PERSONAL: Born May 29, 1969, in Ruston, La. ... 6-6/210. ... Throws right, bats right. ... Full name: Toby Shawn Borland.

HIGH SCHOOL: Quitman (La.).

TRANSACTIONS/CAREER NOTES: Selected by Philadelphia Phillies organization in 27th round of free-agent draft (June 2, 1987). ... On Philadelphia disabled list (June 14-July 8, 1995); included rehabilitation assignment to Scranton/Wilkes-Barre (June 22-July 8). ... Traded by Phillies with P Ricardo Jordan to New York Mets for 1B Rico Brogna (November 27, 1996). ... Traded by Mets to Boston Red Sox for P Rick Trlicek (May 12, 1997). ... Granted free agency (October 15, 1997). ... Signed by Cincinnati Reds organization (November 27, 1997). ... Released by Reds (March 5, 1998). ... Signed by Phillies organization (March 6, 1998). ... Released by Phillies (July 6, 1998). ... Signed by Florida Marlins organization (July 14, 1998). ... Granted free agency (October 15, 1998). ... Signed by Anaheim Angels organization (November 23, 1998). ... On Edmonton disabled list (June 1, 1999-remainder of season). ... Granted free agency (October 15, 1999). ... Re-signed by Angels organization (January 25, 2000). ... On Edmonton disabled list (April 7-July 25, 2000). ... Granted free agency (October 18, 2000). ... Re-signed by Angels organization (November 27, 2000). ... On Salt Lake disabled list (August 29, 2001-remainder of season). ... Granted free agency (October 8, 2001). ... Signed by Marlins organization (November 20, 2001).

STATISTICAL NOTES: Tied for Eastern League lead with three balks in 1991. ... Pitched one inning, combining with starter Craig Holman (two innings), Gregory Brown (two innings) and Ricky Bottalico (two innings) in seven-inning 2-0 no-hit victory for Reading against New Britain (September 4, 1993, first game).

CAREER HITTING (MLB): 1-for-12 (.083), 1 R, 0 2B, 0 3B, 0 HR, 2 RBI.

Year League	W	L	Pct.	ERA	G	GS	CG	ShO	Sv.-Opp.	IP	H	R	ER	HR	BB-IBB	SO
1988—Martinsville (Appl.)	2	3	.400	4.04	34	0	0	0	*12-...	49.0	42	26	22	1	29-1	43
1989—Spartanburg (S.Atl.)	4	5	.444	2.97	47	0	0	0	9-...	66.2	62	29	22	3	35-1	48
1990—Clearwater (FSL)	1	2	.333	2.26	44	0	0	0	5-...	59.2	44	21	15	1	35-4	44
—Reading (East.)	4	1	.800	1.44	14	0	0	0	0-...	25.0	16	6	4	1	11-1	26
1991—Reading (East.)	8	3	.727	2.70	*59	0	0	0	•24-...	76.2	68	31	23	2	56-5	72
1992—Scranton/W.B. (I.L.)	0	1	.000	7.24	27	0	0	0	1-...	27.1	25	23	22	2	26-3	25
—Reading (East.)	2	4	.333	3.43	32	0	0	0	5-...	42.0	39	23	16	2	32-3	45
1993—Reading (East.)	2	2	.500	2.52	44	0	0	0	13-...	53.2	38	17	15	2	20-1	74
—Scranton/W.B. (I.L.)	2	4	.333	5.76	26	0	0	0	1-...	29.2	31	20	19	4	20-3	26
1994—Scranton/W.B. (I.L.)	4	1	.800	1.68	27	1	0	0	4-...	53.2	36	12	10	2	21-7	61
—Philadelphia (N.L.)	1	0	1.000	2.36	24	0	0	0	1-1	34.1	31	10	9	1	14-3	26
1995—Philadelphia (N.L.)	1	3	.250	3.77	50	0	0	0	6-9	74.0	81	37	31	3	37-7	59
—Scranton/W.B. (I.L.)	0	0	...	0.00	8	0	0	0	1-...	11.1	5	0	0	0	6-1	15
1996—Philadelphia (N.L.)	7	3	.700	4.07	69	0	0	0	0-2	90.2	83	51	41	9	43-3	76
1997—New York (N.L.)■	0	1	.000	6.07	13	0	0	0	1-2	13.1	11	9	9	1	14-0	7
—Boston (A.L.)■	0	0	...	13.50	3	0	0	0	0-0	3.1	6	5	5	1	7-0	1
—Pawtucket (I.L.)	2	0	1.000	3.99	28	2	0	0	2-...	47.1	50	22	21	5	25-3	46
1998—Reading (East.)■	1	3	.250	9.64	8	0	0	0	3-...	9.1	18	12	10	4	5-0	13
—Scranton/W.B. (I.L.)	0	2	.000	5.68	13	0	0	0	5-...	12.2	14	8	8	1	3-0	15
—Philadelphia (N.L.)	0	0	...	5.00	6	0	0	0	0-0	9.0	8	5	5	1	5-0	9
—Charlotte (I.L.)■	3	0	1.000	2.70	19	0	0	0	1-...	36.2	33	12	11	3	21-1	26
1999—Edmonton (PCL)■	2	1	.667	7.00	21	0	0	0	0-...	27.0	31	24	21	5	23-2	34
2000—Erie (East.)	1	3	.250	4.50	9	1	0	0	1-...	12.0	12	8	6	0	7-0	12
2001—Salt Lake (PCL)	7	3	.700	2.30	45	1	0	0	3-...	74.1	53	25	19	2	29-0	92
—Anaheim (A.L.)	0	1	.000	10.80	2	0	0	0	0-1	3.1	8	5	4	1	1-0	0
2002—Calgary (PCL)■	5	2	.714	2.96	56	0	0	0	14-...	70.0	55	24	23	2	30-3	75
—Florida (N.L.)	1	0	1.000	5.27	15	0	0	0	0-0	13.2	14	8	8	3	5-0	11
A.L. totals (2 years)	0	1	.000	12.15	5	0	0	0	0-1	6.2	14	10	9	2	8-0	1
N.L. totals (6 years)	10	7	.588	3.94	177	0	0	0	8-14	235.0	228	120	103	18	118-13	188
Major League totals (7 years)	10	8	.556	4.17	182	0	0	0	8-15	241.2	242	130	112	20	126-13	189

BOROWSKI, JOE — P — CUBS

PERSONAL: Born May 4, 1971, in Bayonne, N.J. ... 6-2/240. ... Throws right, bats right. ... Full name: Joseph Thomas Borowski.

HIGH SCHOOL: Marist (Bayonne, N.J.).

COLLEGE: Rutgers.

TRANSACTIONS/CAREER NOTES: Selected by Chicago White Sox organization in 32nd round of free-agent draft (June 5, 1989). ... Traded by White Sox to Baltimore Orioles for IF Pete Rose Jr. (March 21, 1991). ... Traded by Orioles with P Rachaad Stewart to Atlanta Braves for P Kent Mercker (December 17, 1995). ... Claimed on waivers by New York Yankees (September 15, 1997). ... On New York disabled list (August 24-September 8, 1998). ... Claimed on waivers by Milwaukee Brewers (December 4, 1998). ... Granted free agency (October 15, 1999). ... Signed by Cincinnati Reds organization (November 9, 1999). ... Released by Reds (April 14, 2000). ... Signed by Newark, Atlantic League (2000). ... Signed by Monterrey, Mexican League (2000). ... Signed by Chicago Cubs organization (December 11, 2000). ... Granted free agency (October 10, 2001). ... Re-signed by Cubs organization (November 20, 2001).

CAREER HITTING (MLB): 2-for-9 (.222), 1 R, 0 2B, 0 3B, 0 HR, 0 RBI.

Year League	W	L	Pct.	ERA	G	GS	CG	ShO	Sv.-Opp.	IP	H	R	ER	HR	BB-IBB	SO
1990—GC White Sox (GCL)	2	•8	.200	5.58	12	11	0	0	0-...	61.1	74	*47	*38	3	25-0	67
1991—Kane County (Midw.)■	7	2	.778	2.56	49	0	0	0	13-...	81.0	60	26	23	2	43-2	76
1992—Frederick (Caro.)	5	6	.455	3.70	48	0	0	0	10-...	80.1	71	40	33	3	50-3	85
1993—Frederick (Caro.)	1	1	.500	3.61	42	2	0	0	11-...	62.1	61	30	25	5	37-0	70
—Bowie (East.)	3	0	1.000	0.00	9	0	0	0	0-...	17.2	11	0	0	0	11-3	17
1994—Bowie (East.)	3	4	.429	1.91	49	0	0	0	14-...	66.0	52	14	14	3	28-3	73
1995—Rochester (I.L.)	1	3	.250	4.04	28	0	0	0	6-...	35.2	32	16	16	3	18-2	32
—Bowie (East.)	2	2	.500	3.92	16	0	0	0	7-...	20.2	16	9	9	2	7-1	32
—Baltimore (A.L.)	0	0	...	1.23	6	0	0	0	0-0	7.1	5	1	1	0	4-0	3
1996—Richmond (I.L.)■	1	5	.167	3.71	34	0	0	0	7-...	53.1	42	25	22	4	30-1	40
—Atlanta (N.L.)	2	4	.333	4.85	22	0	0	0	0-0	26.0	33	15	14	4	13-4	15
1997—Atlanta (N.L.)	2	2	.500	3.75	20	0	0	0	0-0	24.0	27	11	10	2	16-4	6
—Richmond (I.L.)	1	2	.333	3.58	21	0	0	0	2-...	37.2	32	16	15	3	19-2	34
—New York (A.L.)■	0	1	.000	9.00	1	0	0	0	0-0	2.0	2	2	2	0	4-1	2
1998—Columbus (I.L.)	3	3	.500	2.93	45	0	0	0	4-...	73.2	66	25	24	6	39-1	67
—New York (A.L.)	1	0	1.000	6.52	8	0	0	0	0-0	9.2	11	7	7	0	4-0	7
1999—Louisville (I.L.)■	6	2	.750	5.46	58	0	0	0	4-...	89.0	94	59	54	7	44-3	70
2000—Newark (Atl.)■	6	3	.667	5.50	28	0	0	0	0-...	37.2	44	23	23	...	17-...	39
—Monterrey (Mex.)■	4	2	.667	3.19	12	5	0	0	1-...	42.1	31	15	15	5	18-1	44
2001—Iowa (PCL)■	8	7	.533	2.62	39	12	1	1	1-...	110.0	87	35	32	10	26-3	131
—Chicago (N.L.)	0	1	.000	32.40	1	1	0	0	0-0	1.2	6	6	6	1	3-0	1
2002—Chicago (N.L.)	4	4	.500	2.73	73	0	0	0	2-6	95.2	84	31	29	10	29-6	97
A.L. totals (3 years)	1	1	.500	4.74	15	0	0	0	0-0	19.0	18	10	10	0	12-1	12
N.L. totals (4 years)	8	11	.421	3.60	116	1	0	0	2-6	147.1	150	63	59	17	61-14	119
Major League totals (6 years)	9	12	.429	3.73	131	1	0	0	2-6	166.1	168	73	69	17	73-15	131

BOTTALICO, RICKY — P

PERSONAL: Born August 26, 1969, in New Britain, Conn. ... 6-1/215. ... Throws right, bats left. ... Full name: Richard Paul Bottalico. ... Name pronounced ba-TAL-eh-koh.

HIGH SCHOOL: South Catholic (Hartford, Conn.).

COLLEGE: Florida Southern, then Central Connecticut State.

TRANSACTIONS/CAREER NOTES: Signed as non-drafted free agent by Philadelphia Phillies organization (July 21, 1991). ... On Philadelphia disabled list (April 24-July 1, 1998); included rehabilitation assignment to Scranton/Wilkes-Barre (June 6-July 1). ... On suspended list (August 25-28, 1998). ... Traded by Phillies with P Garrett Stephenson to St. Louis Cardinals for OF Ron Gant, P Jeff Brantley and P Cliff Politte (November 19, 1998). ... Granted free agency (December 21, 1999). ... Signed by Kansas City Royals (January 27, 2000). ... Granted free agency (November 4, 2000). ... Signed by Phillies (December 15, 2000). ... On Philadelphia disabled list (June 29-July 20, 2001); included rehabilitation assignment to Reading (July 13-20). ... Granted free agency (November 5, 2001). ... Re-signed by Phillies (January 8, 2002). ... On disabled list (June 23, 2002-remainder of season). ... Granted free agency (October 30, 2002).

STATISTICAL NOTES: Pitched two innings, combining with starter Craig Holman (two innings), Gregory Brown (two innings) and Toby Borland (one inning) in seven-inning, 2-0 no-hit victory for Reading against New Britain (September 4, 1993, first game).

CAREER HITTING (MLB): 2-for-15 (.133), 1 R, 2 2B, 0 3B, 0 HR, 1 RBI.

Year League	W	L	Pct.	ERA	G	GS	CG	ShO	Sv.-Opp.	IP	H	R	ER	HR	BB-IBB	SO
1991—Martinsville (Appl.)	3	2	.600	4.09	7	6	2	•1	0-...	33.0	32	20	15	2	13-0	38
—Spartanburg (S.Atl.)	2	0	1.000	0.00	2	2	0	0	0-...	15.0	4	0	0	0	2-0	11
1992—Spartanburg (S.Atl.)	5	10	.333	2.41	42	11	1	0	13-...	119.2	94	41	32	6	56-0	118
1993—Clearwater (FSL)	1	0	1.000	2.75	13	0	0	0	4-...	19.2	19	6	6	0	5-0	19
—Reading (East.)	3	3	.500	2.25	49	0	0	0	20-...	72.0	63	22	18	4	26-3	65
1994—Scranton/W.B. (I.L.)	3	1	.750	8.87	19	0	0	0	3-...	22.1	32	27	22	4	22-2	22
—Reading (East.)	2	2	.500	2.53	38	0	0	0	22-...	42.2	29	13	12	6	10-0	51
—Philadelphia (N.L.)	0	0	...	0.00	3	0	0	0	0-0	3.0	3	0	0	0	1-0	3
1995—Philadelphia (N.L.)	5	3	.625	2.46	62	0	0	0	1-5	87.2	50	25	24	7	42-3	87
1996—Philadelphia (N.L.)	4	5	.444	3.19	61	0	0	0	34-38	67.2	47	24	24	6	23-2	74
1997—Philadelphia (N.L.)	2	5	.286	3.65	69	0	0	0	34-41	74.0	68	31	30	7	42-4	89
1998—Philadelphia (N.L.)	1	5	.167	6.44	39	0	0	0	6-7	43.1	54	31	31	7	25-5	27
—Scranton/W.B. (I.L.)	0	1	.000	2.92	10	5	0	0	1-...	12.1	8	4	4	1	9-0	4
1999—St. Louis (N.L.)■	3	7	.300	4.91	68	0	0	0	20-28	73.1	83	45	40	8	49-1	66
2000—Kansas City (A.L.)■	9	6	.600	4.83	62	0	0	0	16-23	72.2	65	40	39	12	41-3	56
2001—Philadelphia (N.L.)■	3	4	.429	3.90	66	0	0	0	3-7	67.0	58	31	29	11	25-2	57
—Reading (East.)	0	1	.000	1.80	3	3	0	0	0-...	5.0	3	2	1	1	1-0	5
2002—Philadelphia (N.L.)	0	3	.000	4.61	30	0	0	0	0-1	27.1	33	16	14	3	13-2	24
A.L. totals (1 year)	9	6	.600	4.83	62	0	0	0	16-23	72.2	65	40	39	12	41-3	56
N.L. totals (8 years)	18	32	.360	3.90	398	0	0	0	98-127	443.1	396	203	192	49	220-19	427
Major League totals (9 years)	27	38	.415	4.03	460	0	0	0	114-150	516.0	461	243	231	61	261-22	483

ALL-STAR GAME RECORD

	W	L	Pct.	ERA	GS	CG	ShO	Sv.-Opp.	IP	H	R	ER	HR	BB-IBB	SO
All-Star Game totals (1 year)	0	0	...	0.00	0	0	0	0-0	1.0	0	0	0	0	0-0	1

BOWIE, MICAH — P — ATHLETICS

PERSONAL: Born November 10, 1974, in Webster, Texas. ... 6-4/210. ... Throws left, bats left. ... Full name: Micah Andrew Bowie. ... Name pronounced bu-ee.

HIGH SCHOOL: Kingwood (Texas).

TRANSACTIONS/CAREER NOTES: Signed as non-drafted free agent by Atlanta Braves organization (July 15, 1993). ... On Durham disabled list (July 4, 1996-remainder of season). ... On Richmond disabled list (May 18-June 10, 1999). ... Traded by Braves with P Ruben Quevado and a player to be named later to Chicago Cubs for P Terry Mulholland and SS Jose Hernandez (July 31, 1999); Cubs acquired P Joey Nation to complete deal (August 24, 1999). ... Released by Cubs (November 27, 2000). ... Signed by Oakland Athletics organization (December 20, 2000).

CAREER HITTING (MLB): 3-for-14 (.214), 0 R, 0 2B, 0 3B, 0 HR, 3 RBI.

Year League	W	L	Pct.	ERA	G	GS	CG	ShO	Sv.-Opp.	IP	H	R	ER	HR	BB-IBB	SO
1994—Gulf Coast Braves (GCL)	0	3	.000	3.03	6	5	0	0	0-...	29.2	27	14	10	1	5-0	35
—Danville (Appl.)	3	1	.750	3.58	7	5	0	0	0-...	32.2	28	16	13	4	13-1	38
1995—Macon (S.Atl.)	4	1	.800	2.28	5	5	0	0	0-...	27.2	9	8	7	1	11-0	36
—Durham (Caro.)	4	11	.267	3.59	23	23	1	0	0-...	130.1	119	65	52	8	61-3	91
1996—Durham (Caro.)	3	6	.333	3.66	13	13	0	0	0-...	66.1	55	29	27	4	33-0	65
1997—Durham (Caro.)	2	2	.500	3.66	9	6	0	0	0-...	39.1	29	16	16	2	27-0	44
—Greenville (Sou.)	3	2	.600	3.50	8	7	0	0	0-...	43.2	34	19	17	3	26-1	41
1998—Greenville (Sou.)	11	6	.647	3.48	30	•29	1	0	0-...	163.0	132	73	63	12	64-0	160
1999—Richmond (I.L.)	4	4	.500	2.96	13	13	0	0	0-...	73.0	65	24	24	4	14-0	82
—Atlanta (N.L.)	0	1	.000	13.50	3	0	0	0	0-0	4.0	8	6	6	1	4-0	2
—Chicago (N.L.)■	2	6	.250	9.96	11	11	0	0	0-0	47.0	73	54	52	8	30-2	39
2000—Iowa (PCL)	1	7	.125	7.94	9	9	0	0	0-...	45.1	59	44	40	9	31-3	35
—West Tenn (Sou.)	7	6	.538	3.45	18	18	1	1	0-...	117.1	91	47	45	6	48-1	106
2001—Sacramento (PCL)■	6	8	.429	5.04	38	10	1	1	3-...	116.0	123	68	65	13	44-1	102
2002—Sacramento (PCL)	3	2	.600	3.13	46	0	0	0	4-...	54.2	40	21	19	2	24-2	64
—Oakland (A.L.)	2	0	1.000	1.50	13	0	0	0	0-0	12.0	12	2	2	1	8-1	8
A.L. totals (1 year)	2	0	1.000	1.50	13	0	0	0	0-0	12.0	12	2	2	1	8-1	8
N.L. totals (1 year)	2	7	.222	10.24	14	11	0	0	0-0	51.0	81	60	58	9	34-2	41
Major League totals (2 years)	4	7	.364	8.57	27	11	0	0	0-0	63.0	93	62	60	10	42-3	49

DIVISION SERIES RECORD

Year League	W	L	Pct.	ERA	G	GS	CG	ShO	Sv.-Opp.	IP	H	R	ER	HR	BB-IBB	SO
2002—Oakland (A.L.)	0	0	...	0.00	1	0	0	0	0-0	1.1	0	0	0	0	0-0	3

BOWLES, BRIAN — P — BLUE JAYS

PERSONAL: Born August 18, 1976, in Harbor City, Calif. ... 6-5/220. ... Throws right, bats right. ... Full name: Brian Christopher Bowles.

HIGH SCHOOL: Peninsula (Manhattan Beach, Calif.).

COLLEGE: UC-Santa Barbara.

TRANSACTIONS/CAREER NOTES: Selected by Toronto Blue Jays organization in 50th round of free-agent draft (June 2, 1994).

CAREER HITTING (MLB): 0-for-0 (.000), 0 R, 0 2B, 0 3B, 0 HR, 0 RBI.

Year League	W	L	Pct.	ERA	G	GS	CG	ShO	Sv.-Opp.	IP	H	R	ER	HR	BB-IBB	SO
1995—GC Blue Jays (GCL)	0	1	.000	2.40	8	0	0	0	0-...	15.0	18	12	4	2	3-0	11
1996—Medicine Hat (Pio.)	2	2	.500	6.35	24	0	0	0	1-...	39.2	53	35	28	5	21-1	29
1997—Hagerstown (S.Atl.)	1	0	1.000	6.97	4	0	0	0	0-...	10.1	14	10	8	2	5-0	9
—Dunedin (FSL)	0	2	.000	7.53	7	1	0	0	0-...	14.1	20	14	12	2	7-1	9
—St. Catharines (NY-Penn)	5	8	.385	5.03	16	16	0	0	0-...	78.2	76	53	44	6	35-0	64
1998—Dunedin (FSL)	1	2	.333	3.33	9	2	1	0	0-...	27.0	32	13	10	2	16-0	17
—Hagerstown (S.Atl.)	2	4	.333	4.52	31	4	0	0	0-...	67.2	80	41	34	4	18-1	48
1999—Hagerstown (S.Atl.)	6	2	.750	3.97	48	1	0	0	3-...	79.1	73	41	35	4	39-3	80
2000—Tennessee (Sou.)	4	4	.500	2.98	49	0	0	0	0-...	81.2	64	31	27	1	36-1	72
2001—Syracuse (I.L.)	3	5	.375	2.91	*66	0	0	0	6-...	77.1	56	30	25	3	44-4	81
—Toronto (A.L.)	0	0	...	0.00	2	0	0	0	0-0	3.2	4	0	0	0	1-0	4
2002—Syracuse (I.L.)	4	7	.364	3.36	59	0	0	0	14-...	59.0	46	24	22	4	32-5	53
—Toronto (A.L.)	2	1	.667	4.05	17	0	0	0	0-1	20.0	13	11	9	0	14-1	19
Major League totals (2 years)	2	1	.667	3.42	19	0	0	0	0-1	23.2	17	11	9	0	15-1	23

BOYD, JASON — P

PERSONAL: Born February 23, 1973, in St. Clair, Ill. ... 6-3/173. ... Throws right, bats right. ... Full name: Jason Pernell Boyd.
HIGH SCHOOL: Edwardsville (Ill.).
JUNIOR COLLEGE: John A. Logan College (Ill.).
TRANSACTIONS/CAREER NOTES: Selected by Philadelphia Phillies organization in eighth round of free-agent draft (June 2, 1994). ... Selected by Arizona Diamondbacks in first round (23rd pick overall) of expansion draft (November 18, 1997). ... On disabled list (May 22, 1998-remainder of season). ... Traded by Diamondbacks to Pittsburgh Pirates (August 25, 1999), completing deal in which Pirates traded 2B Tony Womack to Diamondbacks for OF Paul Weichard and a player to named later (February 26, 1999). ... Claimed on waivers by Milwaukee Brewers (March 29, 2000). ... Claimed on waivers by Philadelphia Phillies (March 31, 2000). ... On Philadelphia disabled list (March 25-May 4 and June 15-August 15, 2000); included rehabilitation assignments to Clearwater (April 7-15 and July 28-31) and Scranton (April 16-19, April 26-May 2 and August 1-15). ... Granted free agency (October 15, 2001). ... Signed by San Diego Padres organization (December 6, 2001). ... Released by Padres (August 4, 2002). ... Signed by Boston Red Sox organization (August 16, 2002). ... Granted free agency (October 15, 2002).
CAREER HITTING (MLB): 0-for-1 (.000), 0 R, 0 2B, 0 3B, 0 HR, 0 RBI.

Year League	W	L	Pct.	ERA	G	GS	CG	ShO	Sv.-Opp.	IP	H	R	ER	HR	BB-IBB	SO
1994—Martinsville (Appl.)	3	7	.300	4.17	14	13	1	0	0-...	69.0	65	46	32	6	32-0	45
1995—Piedmont (S.Atl.)	6	8	.429	3.58	26	24	1	0	0-...	151.0	151	77	60	8	44-0	129
1996—Clearwater (FSL)	11	8	.579	3.90	26	26	2	0	0-...	161.2	160	75	70	12	49-1	120
1997—Reading (East.)	10	6	.625	4.82	48	7	0	0	0-...	115.2	113	65	62	16	64-7	98
1998—Tucson (PCL)■	2	2	.500	6.23	15	0	0	0	0-...	21.2	28	22	15	4	14-1	13
1999—Tucson (PCL)	6	5	.545	4.52	44	0	0	0	5-...	75.2	76	42	38	6	27-2	60
—Nashville (PCL)■	0	0	...	0.00	5	0	0	0	0-...	4.2	2	0	0	0	0-0	2
—Pittsburgh (N.L.)	0	0	...	3.38	4	0	0	0	0-0	5.1	5	2	2	0	2-0	4
2000—Clearwater (FSL)■	1	0	1.000	2.38	6	3	0	0	0-...	11.1	11	4	3	0	4-0	12
—Scranton/W.B. (I.L.)	1	0	1.000	1.72	11	2	0	0	0-...	15.2	8	3	3	0	14-0	10
—Philadelphia (N.L.)	0	1	.000	6.55	30	0	0	0	0-1	34.1	39	28	25	2	24-4	32
2001—Scranton/W.B. (I.L.)	2	7	.222	1.97	52	0	0	0	12-...	59.1	44	17	13	4	22-1	66
2002—Portland (PCL)■	0	1	.000	1.04	19	0	0	0	4-...	26.0	19	4	3	2	7-0	22
—San Diego (N.L.)	1	0	1.000	7.94	23	0	0	0	0-3	28.1	33	29	25	6	15-1	18
—Pawtucket (I.L.)■	1	0	1.000	3.94	9	0	0	0	1-...	16.0	13	7	7	3	9-0	15
Major League totals (3 years)	1	1	.500	6.88	57	0	0	0	0-4	68.0	77	59	52	8	41-5	54

BRADFORD, CHAD — P — ATHLETICS

PERSONAL: Born September 14, 1974, in Jackson, Miss. ... 6-5/203. ... Throws right, bats right. ... Full name: Chadwick Lee Bradford.
HIGH SCHOOL: Byram (Jackson, Miss.).
JUNIOR COLLEGE: Hinds Community College (Miss.).
COLLEGE: Southern Mississippi.
TRANSACTIONS/CAREER NOTES: Selected by Chicago White Sox organization in 13th round of free-agent draft (June 4, 1996). ... On Charlotte disabled list (June 28-July 5, 2000). ... Traded by White Sox to Oakland Athletics for a player to be named later (December 7, 2000); White Sox acquired C Miguel Olivo to complete deal (December 13, 2000).
CAREER HITTING (MLB): 0-for-0 (.000), 0 R, 0 2B, 0 3B, 0 HR, 0 RBI.

Year League	W	L	Pct.	ERA	G	GS	CG	ShO	Sv.-Opp.	IP	H	R	ER	HR	BB-IBB	SO
1996—Hickory (S.Atl.)	0	2	.000	0.90	28	0	0	0	18-...	30.0	21	7	3	1	7-1	27
1997—Winston-Salem (Caro.)	3	7	.300	3.95	46	0	0	0	15-...	54.2	51	30	24	2	25-5	43
1998—Birmingham (Sou.)	1	1	.500	2.60	10	0	0	0	1-...	17.1	13	6	5	2	8-0	14
—Calgary (PCL)	4	1	.800	1.94	29	0	0	0	0-...	51.0	50	12	11	3	11-2	27
—Chicago (A.L.)	2	1	.667	3.23	29	0	0	0	1-3	30.2	27	16	11	0	7-0	11
1999—Charlotte (I.L.)	9	3	.750	1.94	47	0	0	0	5-...	74.1	63	19	16	2	15-0	56
—Chicago (A.L.)	0	0	...	19.64	3	0	0	0	0-0	3.2	9	8	8	1	5-0	0
2000—Charlotte (I.L.)	2	4	.333	1.51	55	0	0	0	10-...	53.2	38	18	9	2	12-1	42
—Chicago (A.L.)	1	0	1.000	1.98	12	0	0	0	0-0	13.2	13	4	3	0	1-1	9
2001—Sacramento (PCL)■	0	0	...	0.38	12	0	0	0	2-...	23.2	15	2	1	0	2-0	24
—Oakland (A.L.)	2	1	.667	2.70	35	0	0	0	1-4	36.2	41	12	11	6	6-0	34
2002—Oakland (A.L.)	4	2	.667	3.11	75	0	0	0	2-5	75.1	73	29	26	2	14-5	56
Major League totals (5 years)	9	4	.692	3.32	154	0	0	0	4-12	160.0	163	69	59	9	33-6	110

DIVISION SERIES RECORD

Year League	W	L	Pct.	ERA	G	GS	CG	ShO	Sv.-Opp.	IP	H	R	ER	HR	BB-IBB	SO
2000—Chicago (A.L.)	0	0	...	0.00	1	0	0	0	0-1	.2	2	0	0	0	0-0	0
2001—Oakland (A.L.)	0	0	...	0.00	1	0	0	0	0-0	1.0	0	0	0	0	0-0	1
2002—Oakland (A.L.)	0	0	...	0.00	2	0	0	0	0-0	3.0	1	0	0	0	0-0	1
Division series totals (3 years)	0	0	...	0.00	4	0	0	0	0-1	4.2	3	0	0	0	0-0	2

BRADLEY, MILTON OF INDIANS

PERSONAL: Born April 15, 1978, in Harbor City, Fla. ... 6-0/190. ... Bats both, throws right. ... Full name: Milton Obelle Bradley.
HIGH SCHOOL: Polytechnic (Long Beach, Calif.).
TRANSACTIONS/CAREER NOTES: Selected by Montreal Expos organization in second round of free-agent draft (June 4, 1996). ... On disabled list (June 14-25, 1999). ... Traded by Expos to Cleveland Indians for P Zach Day (July 31, 2001). ... On Cleveland disabled list (May 2-June 4 and August 14-30, 2002); included rehabilitation assignments to Buffalo (May 28-June 4) and Akron (August 27-30).
STATISTICAL NOTES: Career major league grand slams: 2.
2002 GAMES PLAYED BY POSITION (MLB): OF—94; DH—1.

		BATTING														FIELDING	
Year Team (League)	Pos.	G	AB	R	H	2B	3B	HR	RBI	BB	SO	SB-CS	Avg.	OBP	SLG	E	Avg.
1996—GC Expos (GCL)	OF	32	112	18	27	7	1	1	12	13	15	7-4	.241	.320	.348	3	.949
1997—Vermont (NY-Penn)	OF	50	200	29	60	7	5	3	30	17	34	7-7	.300	.352	.430	4	.967
—GC Expos (GCL)	OF	9	25	6	5	2	0	1	2	4	4	2-2	.200	.333	.400	1	.938
1998—Cape Fear (S.Atl.)	OF	75	281	54	85	21	4	6	50	23	57	13-8	.302	.360	.470	3	.968
—Jupiter (FSL)	OF	67	261	55	75	14	1	5	34	30	42	17-9	.287	.369	.406	1	.993
1999—Harrisburg (East.)	OF-DH	87	346	62	114	22	5	12	50	33	61	14-10	.329	.391	.526	5	.971
2000—Ottawa (I.L.)	OF	88	342	58	104	20	1	6	29	45	56	10-15	.304	.385	.421	3	.987
—Montreal (N.L.)	OF	42	154	20	34	8	1	2	15	14	32	2-1	.221	.288	.325	2	.979
2001—Montreal (N.L.)	OF	67	220	19	49	16	3	1	19	19	62	7-4	.223	.288	.336	2	.988
—Ottawa (I.L.)	OF	35	136	21	37	7	2	2	13	23	30	14-1	.272	.383	.397	3	.966
—Buffalo (I.L.)■	OF	30	114	18	29	3	0	5	15	19	31	9-2	.254	.361	.412	0	1.000
—Cleveland (A.L.)	OF-DH	10	18	3	4	1	0	0	0	2	3	1-1	.222	.300	.278	1	.929
2002—Cleveland (A.L.)	OF-DH	98	325	48	81	18	3	9	38	32	58	6-3	.249	.317	.406	4	.982
—Buffalo (I.L.)	OF	6	23	3	6	0	0	0	3	3	5	2-1	.261	.321	.261	0	1.000
—Akron (East.)	OF	3	11	1	3	1	0	0	1	1	1	0-1	.273	.333	.364	0	1.000
American League totals (2 years)		108	343	51	85	19	3	9	38	34	61	7-4	.248	.316	.399	5	.979
National League totals (2 years)		109	374	39	83	24	4	3	34	33	94	9-5	.222	.288	.332	4	.984
Major League totals (3 years)		217	717	90	168	43	7	12	72	67	155	16-9	.234	.301	.364	9	.982

BRAGG, DARREN OF

PERSONAL: Born September 7, 1969, in Waterbury, Conn. ... 5-9/180. ... Bats left, throws right. ... Full name: Darren William Bragg.
HIGH SCHOOL: Taft (Watertown, Conn.).
COLLEGE: Georgia Tech.
TRANSACTIONS/CAREER NOTES: Selected by Seattle Mariners organization in 22nd round of free-agent draft (June 30, 1991). ... Traded by Mariners to Boston Red Sox for P Jamie Moyer (July 30, 1996). ... Granted free agency (December 21, 1998). ... Signed by St. Louis Cardinals (January 12, 1999). ... On disabled list (August 3, 1999-remainder of season). ... Released by Cardinals (December 16, 1999). ... Signed by Colorado Rockies (February 1, 2000). ... Released by Rockies (July 24, 2000). ... Signed by New York Mets organization (January 9, 2001). ... Claimed on waivers by New York Yankees (June 12, 2001). ... Granted free agency (October 9, 2001). ... Signed by Mets organization (January 15, 2002). ... Released by Mets (April 2, 2002). ... Signed by Atlanta Braves organization (April 2, 2002). ... Granted free agency (October 30, 2002).
STATISTICAL NOTES: Led Carolina League in caught stealing with 19 in 1992. ... Led Pacific Coast League outfielders with 344 total chances and five double plays in 1994. ... Career major league grand slams: 2.
2002 GAMES PLAYED BY POSITION (MLB): OF—63; DH—3.

		BATTING														FIELDING	
Year Team (League)	Pos.	G	AB	R	H	2B	3B	HR	RBI	BB	SO	SB-CS	Avg.	OBP	SLG	E	Avg.
1991—Peninsula (Caro.)	OF-2B	69	237	42	53	14	0	3	29	66	72	21-9	.224	.395	.321	4	.978
1992—Peninsula (Caro.)	OF	135	428	*83	117	29	5	9	58	*105	76	44-19	.273	.418	.428	4	.986
1993—Jacksonville (Sou.)	OF-P	131	451	74	119	26	3	11	46	81	82	19-11	.264	.382	.408	10	.970
1994—Calgary (PCL)	OF	126	500	112	175	33	6	17	85	68	72	28-12	.350	.430	.542	7	.980
—Seattle (A.L.)	DH-OF	8	19	4	3	1	0	0	2	2	5	0-0	.158	.238	.211	0	1.000
1995—Seattle (A.L.)	OF-DH	52	145	20	34	5	1	3	12	18	37	9-0	.234	.331	.345	1	.989
—Tacoma (PCL)	OF-DH	53	212	24	65	13	3	4	31	23	39	10-3	.307	.373	.453	4	.968
1996—Seattle (A.L.)	OF	69	195	36	53	12	1	7	25	33	35	8-5	.272	.376	.451	1	.992
—Tacoma (PCL)	OF	20	71	17	20	8	0	3	8	14	14	1-0	.282	.414	.521	0	1.000
—Boston (A.L.)■	OF	58	222	38	56	14	1	3	22	36	39	6-4	.252	.357	.365	2	.986
1997—Boston (A.L.)	OF-3B	153	513	65	132	35	2	9	57	61	102	10-6	.257	.337	.386	5	.987
1998—Boston (A.L.)	OF-DH	129	409	51	114	29	3	8	57	42	99	5-3	.279	.351	.423	1	*.996
1999—St. Louis (N.L.)■	OF	93	273	38	71	12	1	6	26	44	67	3-0	.260	.369	.377	3	.982
2000—Colorado (N.L.)■	OF	71	149	16	33	7	1	3	21	17	41	4-1	.221	.296	.342	0	1.000
2001—Norfolk (I.L.)■	OF	32	99	22	33	4	0	4	7	23	22	5-2	.333	.468	.495	0	1.000
—New York (N.L.)	OF	18	57	4	15	6	0	0	5	4	23	3-2	.263	.323	.368	0	1.000
—New York (A.L.)■	OF	5	4	1	1	1	0	0	0	0	1	0-0	.250	.250	.500	0	1.000
—Columbus (I.L.)	OF	53	199	30	58	11	2	7	21	27	51	3-2	.291	.379	.472	0	1.000
2002—Richmond (I.L.)■	OF	22	75	15	22	5	0	1	8	20	15	4-2	.293	.442	.400	0	1.000
—Atlanta (N.L.)	OF-DH	109	212	34	57	15	2	3	15	24	52	5-2	.269	.347	.401	3	.971
American League totals (6 years)		474	1507	215	393	97	8	30	175	192	318	38-18	.261	.347	.395	10	.990
National League totals (4 years)		291	691	92	176	40	4	12	67	89	183	15-5	.255	.343	.376	6	.983
Major League totals (9 years)		765	2198	307	569	137	12	42	242	281	501	53-23	.259	.346	.389	16	.988

DIVISION SERIES RECORD

		BATTING														FIELDING	
Year Team (League)	Pos.	G	AB	R	H	2B	3B	HR	RBI	BB	SO	SB-CS	Avg.	OBP	SLG	E	Avg.
1998—Boston (A.L.)	OF	3	12	0	1	0	0	0	0	0	5	0-0	.083	.083	.083	0	1.000
2002—Atlanta (N.L.)	OF	4	3	0	0	0	0	0	0	0	0	0-0	.000	.000	.000	0	...
Division series totals (2 years)		7	15	0	1	0	0	0	0	0	5	0-0	.067	.067	.067	0	1.000

RECORD AS PITCHER

Year League	W	L	Pct.	ERA	G	GS	CG	ShO	Sv.-Opp.	IP	H	R	ER	HR	BB-IBB	SO
1993—Jacksonville (Sou.)	0	0	...	9.00	1	0	0	0	0-...	1.0	3	1	1	0	0-0	0

BRANYAN, RUSSELL — 3B — REDS

PERSONAL: Born December 19, 1975, in Warner Robins, Ga. ... 6-3/195. ... Bats left, throws right. ... Full name: Russell Oles Branyan.
HIGH SCHOOL: Stratford Academy (Warner Robins, Ga.).
TRANSACTIONS/CAREER NOTES: Selected by Cleveland Indians organization in seventh round of free-agent draft (June 2, 1994). ... On Akron disabled list (April 23-May 11 and May 16-August 15, 1998). ... Traded by Indians to Cincinnati Reds for OF Ben Broussard (June 7, 2002).
HONORS: Named Appalachian League Most Valuable Player (1996).
STATISTICAL NOTES: Led South Atlantic League third basemen with 24 double plays in 1996. ... Hit three home runs in one game (August 4, 2002). ... Career major league grand slams: 2.
2002 GAMES PLAYED BY POSITION (MLB): OF—67; 3B—24; 1B—18; DH—5.

			BATTING														FIELDING	
Year	Team (League)	Pos.	G	AB	R	H	2B	3B	HR	RBI	BB	SO	SB-CS	Avg.	OBP	SLG	E	Avg.
1994—	Burlington (Appl.)	3B	55	171	21	36	10	0	5	13	25	64	4-2	.211	.323	.357	21	.851
1995—	Columbus (S.Atl.)	3B	76	277	46	71	8	6	19	55	27	120	1-1	.256	.326	.534	26	.856
1996—	Columbus (S.Atl.)	3B-DH	130	482	102	129	20	4	*40	*106	62	166	7-4	.268	.355	*.575	44	.885
1997—	Kinston (Caro.)	3B-DH	83	297	59	86	26	2	27	75	52	94	3-1	.290	.398	.663	21	.897
	—Akron (East.)	3B-DH	41	137	26	32	4	0	12	30	28	56	0-0	.234	.369	.526	11	.921
1998—	Akron (East.)	3B-DH	43	163	35	48	11	3	16	46	35	58	1-1	.294	.417	.693	7	.932
	—Cleveland (A.L.)	3B	1	4	0	0	0	0	0	0	0	2	0-0	.000	.000	.000	0	1.000
1999—	Buffalo (I.L.)	3B-DH	109	395	51	82	11	1	30	67	52	*187	8-3	.208	.305	.468	23	.921
	—Cleveland (A.L.)	3B-DH	11	38	4	8	2	0	1	6	3	19	0-0	.211	.286	.342	1	.960
2000—	Buffalo (I.L.)	3B-OF	64	229	46	56	9	2	21	60	28	93	1-1	.245	.330	.576	9	.942
	—Cleveland (A.L.)	OF-DH-3B	67	193	32	46	7	2	16	38	22	76	0-0	.238	.327	.544	3	.954
2001—	Cleveland (A.L.)	3B-OF-DH	113	315	48	73	16	2	20	54	38	132	1-1	.232	.316	.486	14	.931
2002—	Cleveland (A.L.)	OF-3B-DH	50	161	16	33	4	0	8	17	17	65	1-2	.205	.278	.379	2	.976
	—Cincinnati (N.L.)■	OF-1B-3B-DH	84	217	34	53	9	1	16	39	34	86	3-1	.244	.349	.516	6	.977
American League totals (5 years)			242	711	100	160	29	4	45	115	80	294	2-3	.225	.307	.467	20	.947
National League totals (1 year)			84	217	34	53	9	1	16	39	34	86	3-1	.244	.349	.516	6	.977
Major League totals (5 years)			326	928	134	213	38	5	61	154	114	380	5-4	.230	.317	.478	26	.959

DIVISION SERIES RECORD

			BATTING														FIELDING	
Year	Team (League)	Pos.	G	AB	R	H	2B	3B	HR	RBI	BB	SO	SB-CS	Avg.	OBP	SLG	E	Avg.
2001—	Cleveland (A.L.)	OF-PH	2	3	1	1	0	0	0	0	0	1	0-0	.333	.333	.333	0	...

BRAZELTON, DEWON — P — DEVIL RAYS

PERSONAL: Born June 16, 1980, in Tullahoma, Tenn. ... 6-4/214. ... Throws right, bats right.
COLLEGE: Middle Tennessee State.
TRANSACTIONS/CAREER NOTES: Selected by Tampa Bay Devil Rays organization in first round (third pick overall) of free-agent draft (June 1, 2001).
CAREER HITTING (MLB): 0-for-0 (.000), 0 R, 0 2B, 0 3B, 0 HR, 0 RBI.

Year	League	W	L	Pct.	ERA	G	GS	CG	ShO	Sv.-Opp.	IP	H	R	ER	HR	BB-IBB	SO
2002—	Orlando (Sou.)	5	9	.357	3.33	26	26	1	0	0-...	146.0	129	69	54	7	67-1	109
	—Durham (I.L.)	1	0	1.000	0.00	1	1	0	0	0-...	5.0	5	0	0	0	1-0	6
	—Tampa Bay (A.L.)	0	1	.000	4.85	2	2	0	0	0-0	13.0	12	7	7	3	6-0	5
Major League totals (1 year)		0	1	.000	4.85	2	2	0	0	0-0	13.0	12	7	7	3	6-0	5

BRITO, JUAN — C — ROYALS

PERSONAL: Born November 7, 1979, in Santiago Rodriguez, Dominican Republic. ... 5-11/205. ... Bats right, throws right. ... Full name: Juan Ramon Brito.
HIGH SCHOOL: Liceo JuanPablo Duarte (Dominican Republic).
TRANSACTIONS/CAREER NOTES: Signed as non-drafted free agent by Kansas City Royals organization (November 13, 1996).
2002 GAMES PLAYED BY POSITION (MLB): C—9.

			BATTING														FIELDING	
Year	Team (League)	Pos.	G	AB	R	H	2B	3B	HR	RBI	BB	SO	SB-CS	Avg.	OBP	SLG	E	Avg.
1997—	GC Royals (GCL)	C	25	70	14	22	4	0	3	15	5	5	0-0	.314	.368	.500	3	.980
1998—	Lansing (Midw.)	C	63	212	16	52	7	0	0	22	17	41	2-2	.245	.305	.278	6	.989
1999—	Wilmington (Caro.)	C	14	46	3	13	1	0	0	1	1	11	0-0	.283	.298	.304	2	.984
	—Charl., W.Va. (S.Atl.)	C-1B	61	208	14	50	6	0	0	19	11	37	1-2	.240	.282	.269	5	.991
	—Omaha (PCL)	C	2	7	1	2	2	0	0	0	0	2	0-0	.286	.286	.571	0	1.000
	—Wichita (Texas)	C	4	11	0	1	0	0	0	0	2	3	0-0	.091	.231	.091	0	1.000
2000—	Wichita (Texas)	C	34	105	9	27	2	0	0	10	11	15	2-1	.257	.328	.276	2	.990
	—Wilmington (Caro.)	C	22	54	4	12	4	0	0	9	8	7	1-0	.222	.317	.296	4	.972
	—Omaha (PCL)	C	17	49	8	14	1	0	1	2	3	10	1-1	.286	.327	.367	0	1.000
2001—	Wichita (Texas)	C-OF	70	236	22	63	10	0	4	28	17	29	3-3	.267	.315	.360	2	.996
2002—	Omaha (PCL)	C	3	9	1	2	1	0	0	1	1	1	0-0	.222	.300	.333	0	1.000
	—Wichita (Texas)	C	89	302	40	77	11	0	7	38	21	46	1-1	.255	.303	.361	5	.992
	—Kansas City (A.L.)	C	9	23	1	7	2	0	0	1	0	3	0-0	.304	.304	.391	1	.978
Major League totals (1 year)			9	23	1	7	2	0	0	1	0	3	0-0	.304	.304	.391	1	.978

BROCAIL, DOUG — P

PERSONAL: Born May 16, 1967, in Clearfield, Pa. ... 6-5/235. ... Throws right, bats left. ... Full name: Douglas Keith Brocail.
HIGH SCHOOL: Lamar (Colo.).

JUNIOR COLLEGE: Lamar (Colo.) Community College.

TRANSACTIONS/CAREER NOTES: Selected by San Diego Padres organization in first round (12th pick overall) of free-agent draft (January 14, 1986). ... On Las Vegas disabled list (May 5-12, 1993). ... On San Diego disabled list (April 2-June 28, 1994); included rehabilitation assignments to Wichita (May 26-June 3) and Las Vegas (June 3-23). ... Traded by Padres with OF Phil Plantier, OF Derek Bell, P Pedro Martinez, IF Craig Shipley and SS Ricky Gutierrez to Houston Astros for 3B Ken Caminiti, OF Steve Finley, SS Andujar Cedeno, 1B Robert Petagine, P Brian Williams and a player to be named later (December 28, 1994); Padres acquired P Sean Fesh to complete deal (May 1, 1995). ... On Houston disabled list (May 11-August 15, 1996); included rehabilitation assignments to Jackson (May 27-June 4) and Tucson (July 29-August 15). ... Traded by Astros with OF Brian L. Hunter, IF Orlando Miller, P Todd Jones and cash to Detroit Tigers for C Brad Ausmus, P Jose Lima, P C.J. Nitkowski, P Trever Miller and IF Daryle Ward (December 10, 1996). ... On suspended list (June 10-13, 1998). ... On disabled list (August 9-24, 1998). ... On suspended list (April 28-May 1, 2000). ... On disabled list (August 14-September 1 and September 29, 2000-remainder of season). ... Traded by Tigers with C Brad Ausmus and P Nelson Cruz to Astros for C Mitch Meluskey, P Chris Holt and OF Roger Cedeno (December 11, 2000). ... On Houston disabled list (March 31, 2001-entire season); included rehabilitation assignments to New Orleans (April 3-5) and Round Rock (April 9-16). ... Granted free agency (November 8, 2001). ... Re-signed by Astros organization (December 7, 2001). ... On disabled list (March 22, 2002-entire season). ... Granted free agency (November 11, 2002).

MISCELLANEOUS: Appeared in six games as pinch runner with San Diego (1993). ... Appeared in two games as pinch runner with San Diego (1994). ... Appeared in one game as pinch runner with Houston (1995). ... Appeared in two games as pinch runner with Houston (1996).

CAREER HITTING (MLB): 11-for-67 (.164), 9 R, 0 2B, 1 3B, 0 HR, 1 RBI.

Year League	W	L	Pct.	ERA	G	GS	CG	ShO	Sv.-Opp.	IP	H	R	ER	HR	BB-IBB	SO
1986—Spokane (N'West)	5	4	.556	3.81	16	•15	0	0	0-...	85.0	85	52	36	4	53-1	77
1987—Charleston, S.C. (S.Atl.)	2	6	.250	4.09	19	18	0	0	0-...	92.1	94	51	42	6	28-0	68
1988—Charleston, S.C. (S.Atl.)	8	6	.571	2.69	22	13	5	0	2-...	107.0	107	40	32	3	25-0	107
1989—Wichita (Texas)	5	9	.357	5.21	23	22	1	1	0-...	134.2	158	88	78	11	50-4	95
1990—Wichita (Texas)	2	2	.500	4.33	12	9	0	0	0-...	52.0	53	30	25	7	24-0	27
1991—Wichita (Texas)	10	7	.588	3.87	34	16	3	•3	6-...	146.1	147	77	63	15	43-3	108
1992—Las Vegas (PCL)	10	10	.500	3.97	29	25	4	0	0-...	172.1	187	82	76	7	63-5	103
—San Diego (N.L.)	0	0	...	6.43	3	3	0	0	0-0	14.0	17	10	10	2	5-0	15
1993—Las Vegas (PCL)	4	2	.667	3.68	10	8	0	0	1-...	51.1	51	26	21	4	14-0	32
—San Diego (N.L.)	4	13	.235	4.56	24	24	0	0	0-0	128.1	143	75	65	16	42-4	70
1994—Wichita (Texas)	0	0	...	0.00	2	0	0	0	0-...	4.0	3	1	0	0	1-0	2
—Las Vegas (PCL)	0	0	...	7.11	7	3	0	0	0-...	12.2	21	12	10	1	2-0	8
—San Diego (N.L.)	0	0	...	5.82	12	0	0	0	0-1	17.0	21	13	11	1	5-3	11
1995—Houston (N.L.)■	6	4	.600	4.19	36	7	0	0	1-1	77.1	87	40	36	10	22-2	39
—Tucson (PCL)	1	0	1.000	3.86	3	3	0	0	0-...	16.1	18	9	7	1	4-0	16
1996—Houston (N.L.)	1	5	.167	4.58	23	4	0	0	0-0	53.0	58	31	27	7	23-1	34
—Jackson (Texas)	0	0	...	0.00	2	2	0	0	0-...	4.0	1	0	0	0	1-0	5
—Tucson (PCL)	0	1	.000	7.36	5	1	0	0	0-...	7.1	12	6	6	1	1-0	4
1997—Detroit (A.L.)■	3	4	.429	3.23	61	4	0	0	2-9	78.0	74	31	28	10	36-4	60
1998—Detroit (A.L.)	5	2	.714	2.73	60	0	0	0	0-1	62.2	47	23	19	2	18-3	55
1999—Detroit (A.L.)	4	4	.500	2.52	70	0	0	0	2-4	82.0	60	23	23	7	25-1	78
2000—Detroit (A.L.)	5	4	.556	4.09	49	0	0	0	0-5	50.2	57	25	23	5	14-2	41
2001—New Orleans (PCL)■	0	0	...	0.00	2	0	0	0	0-...	2.1	2	0	0	0	1-0	2
—Round Rock (Texas)	0	0	...	0.00	1	1	0	0	0-...	1.0	0	0	0	0	0-0	1
2002—Houston (N.L.)									Did not play.							
A.L. totals (4 years)	17	14	.548	3.06	240	4	0	0	4-19	273.1	238	102	93	24	93-10	234
N.L. totals (5 years)	11	22	.333	4.63	98	38	0	0	1-2	289.2	326	169	149	36	97-10	169
Major League totals (9 years)	28	36	.438	3.87	338	42	0	0	5-21	563.0	564	271	242	60	190-20	403

BROCK, CHRIS — P

PERSONAL: Born February 5, 1971, in Orlando. ... 6-0/185. ... Throws right, bats right. ... Full name: Terrence Christopher Brock.

HIGH SCHOOL: Lyman (Longwood, Fla.).

COLLEGE: Florida State.

TRANSACTIONS/CAREER NOTES: Selected by Atlanta Braves organization in 12th round of free-agent draft (June 1, 1992). ... On disabled list (July 26, 1995-remainder of season). ... Granted free agency (October 15, 1997). ... Signed by San Francisco Giants organization (December 20, 1997). ... On disabled list (July 24, 1999-remainder of season). ... Traded by Giants to Philadelphia Phillies for C Bobby Estalella (December 12, 1999). ... Traded by Phillies to Baltimore Orioles for P John Wasdin (December 13, 2001). ... On Baltimore disabled list (April 16-June 3, 2002); included rehabilitation assignment to Bowie (May 30-June 3). ... Released by Orioles (October 1, 2002).

CAREER HITTING (MLB): 12-for-63 (.190), 5 R, 1 2B, 0 3B, 1 HR, 7 RBI.

Year League	W	L	Pct.	ERA	G	GS	CG	ShO	Sv.-Opp.	IP	H	R	ER	HR	BB-IBB	SO
1992—Idaho Falls (Pio.)	6	4	.600	2.31	15	15	1	0	0-...	78.0	61	27	20	3	48-0	72
1993—Macon (S.Atl.)	7	5	.583	2.70	14	14	1	0	0-...	80.0	61	37	24	3	33-0	92
—Durham (Caro.)	5	2	.714	2.51	12	12	1	0	0-...	79.0	63	28	22	7	35-0	67
1994—Greenville (Sou.)	7	6	.538	3.74	25	23	2	2	0-...	137.1	128	68	57	9	47-0	94
1995—Richmond (I.L.)	2	8	.200	5.40	22	9	0	0	0-...	60.0	68	37	36	2	27-2	43
1996—Richmond (I.L.)	10	11	.476	4.67	26	25	3	0	0-...	150.1	137	95	78	20	61-0	112
1997—Richmond (I.L.)	10	6	.625	3.34	20	19	0	0	0-...	118.2	97	50	44	9	51-0	83
—Atlanta (N.L.)	0	0	...	5.58	7	6	0	0	0-0	30.2	34	23	19	2	19-2	16
1998—Fresno (PCL)■	11	3	.786	3.29	17	17	2	0	0-...	115.0	111	47	42	11	33-2	112
—San Francisco (N.L.)	0	0	...	3.90	13	0	0	0	0-0	27.2	31	13	12	3	7-1	19
1999—San Francisco (N.L.)	6	8	.429	5.48	19	19	0	0	0-0	106.2	124	69	65	18	41-2	76
2000—Philadelphia (N.L.)■	7	8	.467	4.34	63	5	0	0	1-3	93.1	85	48	45	21	41-0	69
2001—Philadelphia (N.L.)	3	0	1.000	4.13	24	0	0	0	0-1	32.2	35	16	15	6	15-2	26
—Scranton/W.B. (I.L.)	6	2	.750	3.55	13	13	2	0	0-...	78.2	75	31	31	9	16-0	56
2002—Baltimore (A.L.)■	2	1	.667	4.70	22	0	0	0	0-0	44.0	52	24	23	6	14-1	21
—Bowie (East.)	0	0	...	3.60	1	1	0	0	0-...	5.0	6	2	2	2	0-0	2
A.L. totals (1 year)	2	1	.667	4.70	22	0	0	0	0-0	44.0	52	24	23	6	14-1	21
N.L. totals (5 years)	16	16	.500	4.82	126	30	0	0	1-4	291.0	309	169	156	50	123-7	206
Major League totals (6 years)	18	17	.514	4.81	148	30	0	0	1-4	335.0	361	193	179	56	137-8	227

BROHAWN, TROY — P

PERSONAL: Born January 14, 1973, in Cambridge, Md. ... 6-1/190. ... Throws left, bats left. ... Full name: Michael Troy Brohawn.
HIGH SCHOOL: Cambridge South Dorchester (Cambridge, Md.).
COLLEGE: Nebraska.
TRANSACTIONS/CAREER NOTES: Selected by San Francisco Giants organization in fourth round of free-agent draft (June 2, 1994). ... Traded by Giants to Arizona Diamondbacks (December 21, 1998), completing deal in which Diamondbacks traded P Felix Rodriguez to Giants for future considerations (December 8, 1998). ... On Tucson disabled list (April 24-August 30, 1999). ... On Arizona disabled list (August 31, 1999-remainder of season). ... On Tucson disabled list (April 6-July 31, 2000). ... Released by Diamondbacks (March 27, 2002). ... Signed by Giants organization (March 28, 2002). ... Granted free agency (October 15, 2002).
CAREER HITTING (MLB): 0-for-1 (.000), 0 R, 0 2B, 0 3B, 0 HR, 0 RBI.

Year	League	W	L	Pct.	ERA	G	GS	CG	ShO	Sv.-Opp.	IP	H	R	ER	HR	BB-IBB	SO
1994—	San Jose (Calif.)	0	2	.000	7.02	4	4	0	0	0-...	16.2	27	15	13	2	5-0	13
1995—	San Jose (Calif.)	7	3	.700	1.65	11	10	0	0	0-...	65.1	45	14	12	4	20-0	57
1996—	Shreveport (Texas)	9	10	.474	4.60	28	28	0	0	0-...	156.2	163	99	80	30	49-0	82
1997—	Shreveport (Texas)	13	5	.722	*2.56	26	26	1	•1	0-...	169.0	148	57	48	10	64-0	98
1998—	Fresno (PCL)	10	8	.556	5.25	30	19	0	0	0-...	121.2	144	75	71	18	36-1	87
1999—	Tucson (PCL)■	1	0	1.000	3.29	3	2	0	0	0-...	13.2	22	8	5	1	3-0	12
2000—	Ariz. D-backs (Ariz.)	0	0	...	0.00	3	3	0	0	0-...	4.0	5	1	0	0	1-0	6
	—Tucson (PCL)	0	0	...	3.78	11	1	0	0	0-...	16.2	18	7	7	5	5-0	16
2001—	Tucson (PCL)	0	0	...	0.00	2	0	0	0	0-...	3.1	1	0	0	0	1-0	4
	—Arizona (N.L.)	2	3	.400	4.93	59	0	0	0	1-3	49.1	55	27	27	5	23-2	30
2002—	Fresno (PCL)■	3	3	.500	3.65	56	0	0	0	1-...	69.0	71	31	28	7	21-2	55
	—San Francisco (N.L.)	0	1	.000	6.35	11	0	0	0	0-0	5.2	5	4	4	1	1-0	3
Major League totals (2 years)		2	4	.333	5.07	70	0	0	0	1-3	55.0	60	31	31	6	24-2	33

DIVISION SERIES RECORD

Year	League	W	L	Pct.	ERA	G	GS	CG	ShO	Sv.-Opp.	IP	H	R	ER	HR	BB-IBB	SO
2001—	Arizona (N.L.)									Did not play.							

CHAMPIONSHIP SERIES RECORD

Year	League	W	L	Pct.	ERA	G	GS	CG	ShO	Sv.-Opp.	IP	H	R	ER	HR	BB-IBB	SO
2001—	Arizona (N.L.)									Did not play.							

WORLD SERIES RECORD

NOTES: Member of World Series championship team (2001).

Year	League	W	L	Pct.	ERA	G	GS	CG	ShO	Sv.-Opp.	IP	H	R	ER	HR	BB-IBB	SO
2001—	Arizona (N.L.)	0	0	...	0.00	1	0	0	0	0-0	1.0	1	0	0	0	0-0	1

BROUSSARD, BEN — OF — INDIANS

PERSONAL: Born September 24, 1976, in Beaumont, Texas. ... 6-2/220. ... Bats left, throws left. ... Full name: Benjamin Isaac Broussard.
COLLEGE: McNeese State.
TRANSACTIONS/CAREER NOTES: Selected by Cincinnati Reds organization in second round of free-agent draft (June 2, 1999). ... On disabled list (May 10-June 26, 2000). ... On Chattanooga disabled list (May 22-29, 2001). ... Traded by Reds to Cleveland Indians for 3B Russell Branyan (June 7, 2002).
2002 GAMES PLAYED BY POSITION (MLB): OF—32; 1B—4; DH—3.

			BATTING														FIELDING	
Year	Team (League)	Pos.	G	AB	R	H	2B	3B	HR	RBI	BB	SO	SB-CS	Avg.	OBP	SLG	E	Avg.
1999—	Billings (Pio.)	OF-1B	38	145	39	59	11	2	14	48	34	30	1-0	.407	.527	.800	5	.963
	—Clinton (Midw.)	1B-OF	5	20	8	11	4	1	2	6	3	4	0-0	.550	.609	1.150	2	.926
	—Chattanooga (Sou.)	OF-1B	35	127	26	27	5	0	8	21	11	41	1-0	.213	.291	.441	2	.987
2000—	Chattanooga (Sou.)	OF-1B	87	286	64	73	8	4	14	51	72	78	15-2	.255	.413	.458	10	.958
2001—	Mudville (Calif.)	1B	30	102	14	25	5	0	5	21	16	31	0-0	.245	.360	.441	2	.992
	—Chattanooga (Sou.)	1B-OF	100	353	81	113	27	0	23	69	61	69	10-3	.320	.428	*.592	8	.990
2002—	Louisville (I.L.)	1B	57	187	31	51	14	1	11	30	31	50	4-1	.273	.396	.535	2	.995
	—Buffalo (I.L.)■	OF-1B	42	153	30	37	8	0	5	21	24	30	0-0	.242	.354	.392	3	.975
	—Cleveland (A.L.)	OF-1B-DH	39	112	10	27	4	0	4	9	7	25	0-0	.241	.292	.384	2	.974
Major League totals (1 year)			39	112	10	27	4	0	4	9	7	25	0-0	.241	.292	.384	2	.974

BROWER, JIM — P — EXPOS

PERSONAL: Born December 29, 1972, in Edina, Minn. ... 6-3/215. ... Throws right, bats right. ... Full name: James Robert Brower.
HIGH SCHOOL: Minnetonka (Minn.).
COLLEGE: Minnesota.
TRANSACTIONS/CAREER NOTES: Selected by Texas Rangers organization in sixth round of free-agent draft (June 2, 1994). ... Released by Rangers (April 15, 1998). ... Signed by Cleveland Indians organization (April 18, 1998). ... Granted free agency (October 16, 1998). ... Re-signed by Indians organization (January 4, 1999). ... Traded by Indians with P Robert Pugmire to Cincinnati Reds for C Eddie Taubensee (November 16, 2000). ... Traded by Reds to Montreal Expos for P Bruce Chen (June 14, 2002).
MISCELLANEOUS: Appeared in two games as pinch runner (2001).
CAREER HITTING (MLB): 8-for-38 (.211), 6 R, 1 2B, 0 3B, 0 HR, 3 RBI.

Year	League	W	L	Pct.	ERA	G	GS	CG	ShO	Sv.-Opp.	IP	H	R	ER	HR	BB-IBB	SO
1994—	Hudson Valley (NY-Penn).	2	1	.667	3.20	4	4	1	0	0-...	19.2	14	10	7	0	6-0	15
	—Charleston, S.C. (S.Atl.)	7	3	.700	1.72	12	12	3	2	0-...	78.2	52	18	15	2	26-1	84
1995—	Charlotte (FSL)	7	10	.412	3.89	27	27	2	1	0-...	173.2	170	93	75	16	62-1	110
1996—	Charlotte (FSL)	9	8	.529	3.79	23	21	2	0	0-...	145.0	148	67	61	11	40-0	86
	—Tulsa (Texas)	3	2	.600	3.78	5	5	1	1	0-...	33.1	35	16	14	4	10-0	16

Year League	W	L	Pct.	ERA	G	GS	CG	ShO	Sv.-Opp.	IP	H	R	ER	HR	BB-IBB	SO
1997— Tulsa (Texas)	5	12	.294	5.21	23	23	1	0	0-...	140.0	156	99	81	13	42-1	103
— Oklahoma City (A.A.)	2	1	.667	7.23	4	3	0	0	0-...	18.2	30	17	15	3	8-0	7
1998— Akron (East.)■	13	5	.722	3.01	23	23	2	2	0-...	155.2	142	60	52	9	38-0	91
1999— Buffalo (I.L.)	11	11	.500	4.72	27	27	0	0	0-...	160.0	164	101	84	23	59-6	76
— Cleveland (A.L.)	3	1	.750	4.56	9	2	0	0	0-0	25.2	27	13	13	8	10-1	18
2000— Buffalo (I.L.)	9	4	.692	3.11	16	15	1	0	0-...	101.1	99	41	35	7	24-1	68
— Cleveland (A.L.)	2	3	.400	6.24	17	11	0	0	0-0	62.0	80	45	43	11	31-1	32
2001— Louisville (I.L.)■	1	0	1.000	4.09	2	2	0	0	0-...	11.0	12	5	5	1	2-0	11
— Cincinnati (N.L.)	7	10	.412	3.97	46	10	0	0	1-2	129.1	119	65	57	17	60-5	94
2002— Cincinnati (N.L.)	2	0	1.000	3.89	22	0	0	0	0-0	39.1	38	18	17	2	10-1	24
— Montreal (N.L.)■	1	2	.333	4.83	30	0	0	0	0-1	41.0	39	22	22	5	22-1	33
A.L. totals (2 years)	5	4	.556	5.75	26	13	0	0	0-0	87.2	107	58	56	19	41-2	50
N.L. totals (2 years)	10	12	.455	4.12	98	10	0	0	1-3	209.2	196	105	96	24	92-7	151
Major League totals (4 years)	15	16	.484	4.60	124	23	0	0	1-3	297.1	303	163	152	43	133-9	201

BROWN, ADRIAN OF DEVIL RAYS

PERSONAL: Born February 7, 1974, in McComb, Miss. ... 6-0/200. ... Bats both, throws right. ... Full name: Adrian Demond Brown.
HIGH SCHOOL: McComb (Miss.).
TRANSACTIONS/CAREER NOTES: Selected by Pittsburgh Pirates organization in 48th round of free-agent draft (June 1, 1992). ... Loaned by Pirates organization to Lethbridge of Pioneer League (June 11-September 19, 1993). ... On Pittsburgh disabled list (June 13-July 4 and July 6-August 7, 2000); included rehabilitation assignments to Altoona (July 2-4) and Nashville (July 30-August 7). ... On Pittsburgh disabled list (April 17, 2001-remainder of season); included rehabilitation assignments to Altoona (May 7-15), Lynchburg (August 28-September 2) and Williamsport (September 3-13). ... Released by Pirates (October 10, 2002). ... Signed by Tampa Bay Devil Rays organization (November 6, 2002).
2002 GAMES PLAYED BY POSITION (MLB): OF—71.

		BATTING														FIELDING	
Year Team (League)	Pos.	G	AB	R	H	2B	3B	HR	RBI	BB	SO	SB-CS	Avg.	OBP	SLG	E	Avg.
1992— GC Pirates (GCL)	OF-1B	39	121	11	31	2	2	0	12	0	12	8-4	.256	.268	.306	1	.985
1993— Lethbridge (Pio.)	OF	69	282	47	75	12	*9	3	27	17	34	22-7	.266	.319	.404	1	*.992
1994— Augusta (S.Atl.)	OF	79	308	41	80	17	1	1	18	14	38	19-12	.260	.292	.331	2	.984
1995— Augusta (S.Atl.)	OF	76	287	64	86	15	4	4	31	33	23	25-14	.300	.372	.422	7	.950
— Lynchburg (Caro.)	OF	54	215	30	52	5	2	1	14	12	20	11-6	.242	.284	.298	2	.983
1996— Lynchburg (Caro.)	OF	52	215	39	69	9	3	4	25	14	24	18-9	.321	.368	.447	2	.981
— Carolina (Sou.)	OF	84	341	48	101	11	3	3	25	25	40	27-11	.296	.345	.372	2	.990
1997— Carolina (Sou.)	OF	37	145	29	44	4	4	2	15	18	12	9-5	.303	.388	.428	3	.956
— Pittsburgh (N.L.)	OF	48	147	17	28	6	0	1	10	13	18	8-4	.190	.273	.252	1	.987
— Calgary (PCL)	OF	62	248	53	79	10	1	1	19	27	38	20-4	.319	.383	.379	1	.993
1998— Nashville (PCL)	OF	85	311	58	90	12	5	3	27	28	38	25-7	.289	.346	.389	5	.977
— Pittsburgh (N.L.)	OF	41	152	20	43	4	1	0	5	9	18	4-0	.283	.323	.322	2	.977
1999— Pittsburgh (N.L.)	OF	116	226	34	61	5	2	4	17	33	39	5-3	.270	.364	.363	4	.966
— Nashville (PCL)	OF	17	56	10	18	3	1	0	4	11	8	6-1	.321	.433	.411	1	.969
2000— Pittsburgh (N.L.)	OF	104	308	64	97	18	3	4	28	29	34	13-1	.315	.373	.432	4	.976
— Altoona (East.)	OF	2	5	1	0	0	0	0	0	3	1	0-0	.000	.375	.000	0	1.000
— Nashville (PCL)	OF	8	26	3	6	1	0	0	2	2	4	3-0	.231	.310	.269	0	1.000
2001— Pittsburgh (N.L.)	OF	8	31	3	6	0	0	1	2	3	3	2-1	.194	.265	.290	0	1.000
— Altoona (East.)	DH	7	30	7	10	1	1	0	1	1	7	1-2	.333	.344	.433	...	...
— Lynchburg (Caro.)	DH	4	18	2	6	0	0	0	1	1	3	2-0	.333	.400	.333	...	...
— Williamsport (NY-P)	DH	4	18	4	6	0	1	0	4	1	2	2-0	.333	.368	.444	...	...
2002— Pittsburgh (N.L.)	OF	91	208	20	45	10	2	1	21	19	34	10-6	.216	.284	.298	3	.974
— Nashville (PCL)	OF	51	184	36	62	7	1	3	16	23	18	22-6	.337	.409	.435	2	.975
Major League totals (6 years)		408	1072	158	280	43	8	11	83	106	146	42-15	.261	.330	.347	14	.976

BROWN, DEE OF ROYALS

PERSONAL: Born March 27, 1978, in Bronx, N.Y. ... 6-0/225. ... Bats left, throws right. ... Full name: Dermal Bram Brown.
HIGH SCHOOL: Marlboro (N.Y.) Central.
TRANSACTIONS/CAREER NOTES: Selected by Kansas City Royals organization in first round (14th pick overall) of free-agent draft (June 2, 1996). ... On Kansas City disabled list (June 17-July 27, 2001); included rehabilitation assignment to Omaha (July 12-27).
HONORS: Named Northwest League Most Valuable Player in 1997.
STATISTICAL NOTES: Led Northwest League with 168 total bases in 1997. ... Tied for Carolina League lead with five intentional bases on balls received in 1998 and six in 1999.
2002 GAMES PLAYED BY POSITION (MLB): OF—8; DH—5.

		BATTING														FIELDING	
Year Team (League)	Pos.	G	AB	R	H	2B	3B	HR	RBI	BB	SO	SB-CS	Avg.	OBP	SLG	E	Avg.
1996— GC Royals (GCL)	DH	7	20	1	1	1	0	0	1	0	6	0-2	.050	.095	.100	...	...
1997— Spokane (N'West)	OF	73	298	67	97	20	6	13	*73	38	65	17-4	.326	.404	*.564	7	.921
1998— Wilmington (Caro.)	OF	128	442	64	114	30	2	10	58	53	115	26-10	.258	.347	.403	13	.908
— Kansas City (A.L.)	DH-OF	5	3	2	0	0	0	0	0	0	1	0-0	.000	.000	.000	0	1.000
1999— Wilmington (Caro.)	OF-DH	61	221	49	68	10	2	13	46	44	56	20-7	.308	.431	.548	2	.979
— Wichita (Texas)	OF	65	235	58	83	14	3	12	56	35	41	10-8	.353	.440	.591	5	.958
— Kansas City (A.L.)	OF-DH	12	25	1	2	0	0	0	0	2	7	0-0	.080	.148	.080	1	.929
2000— Omaha (PCL)	OF	125	479	76	129	25	6	23	70	37	112	20-3	.269	.324	.491	7	.966
— Kansas City (A.L.)	OF	15	25	4	4	1	0	0	4	3	9	0-0	.160	.250	.200	0	1.000
2001— Kansas City (A.L.)	OF-DH	106	380	39	93	19	0	7	40	22	81	5-3	.245	.286	.350	2	.988
— Omaha (PCL)	OF	10	37	5	11	0	0	2	6	3	5	0-0	.297	.357	.459	1	.950
2002— Omaha (PCL)	OF	121	458	66	126	23	1	17	75	44	111	10-4	.275	.344	.441	5	.968
— Kansas City (A.L.)	OF-DH	16	51	5	12	3	1	1	7	4	20	0-0	.235	.291	.392	1	.923
Major League totals (5 years)		154	484	51	111	23	1	8	51	31	118	5-3	.229	.276	.331	4	.980

BROWN, KEVIN — P — DODGERS

PERSONAL: Born March 14, 1965, in McIntyre, Ga. ... 6-4/200. ... Throws right, bats right. ... Full name: James Kevin Brown.

HIGH SCHOOL: Wilkinson County (Irwinton, Ga.).

COLLEGE: Georgia Tech.

TRANSACTIONS/CAREER NOTES: Selected by Texas Rangers organization in first round (fourth pick overall) of free-agent draft (June 2, 1986). ... On disabled list (August 14-29, 1990 and March 27-April 11, 1993). ... Granted free agency (October 15, 1994). ... Signed by Baltimore Orioles (April 9, 1995). ... On disabled list (June 23-July 17, 1995). ... Granted free agency (November 3, 1995). ... Signed by Florida Marlins (December 22, 1995). ... On disabled list (May 13-28, 1996). ... Traded by Marlins to San Diego Padres for P Rafael Medina, P Steve Hoff and 1B Derrek Lee (December 15, 1997). ... Granted free agency (October 26, 1998). ... Signed by Los Angeles Dodgers (December 12, 1998). ... On disabled list (April 9-25, 2000; March 24-April 10, May 30-June 24 and July 16-August 28, 2001). ... On Los Angeles disabled list (April 14-30 and May 27-August 15, 2002); included rehabilitation assignment to Las Vegas (August 3-15).

HONORS: Named righthanded pitcher on The Sporting News college All-America team (1986). ... Named N.L. Pitcher of the Year by The Sporting News (1998). ... Named righthanded pitcher on The Sporting News N.L. All-Star team (1998).

STATISTICAL NOTES: Tied for A.L. lead with 13 hit batsmen in 1991. ... Tied for N.L. lead with 16 hit batsmen in 1996. ... Pitched 9-0 no-hit victory against San Francisco (June 10, 1997). ... Pitched 5-1 one-hit, complete-game victory against Los Angeles (July 16, 1997). ... Led N.L. with 14 hit batsmen in 1997. ... Pitched 4-0 one-hit, complete-game victory against Milwaukee (August 16, 1998).

MISCELLANEOUS: Holds Florida Marlins all-time record for lowest earned-run average (2.30). ... Made an out in only appearance as pinch hitter (1990). ... Appeared in one game as pinch runner (1993). ... Appeared in two games as pinch runner (1996).

CAREER HITTING (MLB): 53-for-430 (.123), 16 R, 6 2B, 0 3B, 2 HR, 27 RBI.

Year	League	W	L	Pct.	ERA	G	GS	CG	ShO	Sv.-Opp.	IP	H	R	ER	HR	BB-IBB	SO
1986	—Gulf Coast Rangers (GCL)	0	0	...	6.00	3	0	0	0	0-...	6.0	7	4	4	0	2-0	1
	—Tulsa (Texas)	0	0	...	4.50	3	2	0	0	0-...	10.0	9	7	5	0	5-0	10
	—Texas (A.L.)	1	0	1.000	3.60	1	1	0	0	0-0	5.0	6	2	2	0	0-0	4
1987	—Tulsa (Texas)	1	4	.200	7.29	8	8	0	0	0-...	42.0	53	36	34	3	18-1	26
	—Oklahoma City (A.A.)	0	5	.000	10.73	5	5	0	0	0-...	24.1	32	32	29	2	17-0	9
	—Charlotte (FSL)	0	2	.000	2.72	6	6	1	0	0-...	36.1	33	14	11	1	17-0	21
1988	—Tulsa (Texas)	12	10	.545	3.51	26	26	5	0	0-...	174.1	174	94	68	5	61-1	118
	—Texas (A.L.)	1	1	.500	4.24	4	4	1	0	0-0	23.1	33	15	11	2	8-0	12
1989	—Texas (A.L.)	12	9	.571	3.35	28	28	7	0	0-0	191.0	167	81	71	10	70-2	104
1990	—Texas (A.L.)	12	10	.545	3.60	26	26	6	2	0-0	180.0	175	84	72	13	60-3	88
1991	—Texas (A.L.)	9	12	.429	4.40	33	33	0	0	0-0	210.2	233	116	103	17	90-5	96
1992	—Texas (A.L.)	•21	11	.656	3.32	35	35	11	1	0-0	*265.2	*262	117	98	11	76-2	173
1993	—Texas (A.L.)	15	12	.556	3.59	34	34	12	3	0-0	233.0	228	105	93	14	74-5	142
1994	—Texas (A.L.)	7	9	.438	4.82	26	•25	3	0	0-0	170.0	*218	109	91	18	50-3	123
1995	—Baltimore (A.L.)■	10	9	.526	3.60	26	26	3	1	0-0	172.1	155	73	69	10	48-1	117
1996	—Florida (N.L.)■	17	11	.607	*1.89	32	32	5	*3	0-0	233.0	187	60	49	8	33-2	159
1997	—Florida (N.L.)	16	8	.667	2.69	33	33	6	2	0-0	237.1	214	77	71	10	66-7	205
1998	—San Diego (N.L.)■	18	7	.720	2.38	36	•35	7	3	0-0	257.0	225	77	68	8	49-4	257
1999	—Los Angeles (N.L.)■	18	9	.667	3.00	35	•35	5	1	0-0	252.1	210	99	84	19	59-1	221
2000	—Los Angeles (N.L.)	13	6	.684	*2.58	33	33	5	1	0-0	230.0	181	76	66	21	47-1	216
2001	—Los Angeles (N.L.)	10	4	.714	2.65	20	19	1	0	0-0	115.2	94	41	34	8	38-2	104
2002	—Los Angeles (N.L.)	3	4	.429	4.81	17	10	0	0	0-0	63.2	68	36	34	9	23-1	58
	—Las Vegas (PCL)	1	0	1.000	1.86	2	2	0	0	0-...	9.2	6	2	2	0	3-0	7
A.L. totals (9 years)		88	73	.547	3.78	213	212	43	7	0-0	1451.0	1477	702	610	95	476-21	859
N.L. totals (7 years)		95	49	.660	2.63	206	197	29	10	0-0	1389.0	1179	466	406	83	315-18	1220
Major League totals (16 years)		183	122	.600	3.22	419	409	72	17	0-0	2840.0	2656	1168	1016	178	791-39	2079

DIVISION SERIES RECORD

RECORDS: Holds N.L. career record for most hit batsmen—3. ... Holds N.L. single-game record for most strikeouts—16 (September 29, 1998).

Year	League	W	L	Pct.	ERA	G	GS	CG	ShO	Sv.-Opp.	IP	H	R	ER	HR	BB-IBB	SO
1997	—Florida (N.L.)	0	0	...	1.29	1	1	0	0	0-0	7.0	4	1	1	1	0-0	5
1998	—San Diego (N.L.)	1	0	1.000	0.61	2	2	0	0	0-0	14.2	5	1	1	0	7-0	21
Division series totals (2 years)		1	0	1.000	0.83	3	3	0	0	0-0	21.2	9	2	2	1	7-0	26

CHAMPIONSHIP SERIES RECORD

RECORDS: Shares single-game record for most hits allowed—11 (October 14, 1997).

Year	League	W	L	Pct.	ERA	G	GS	CG	ShO	Sv.-Opp.	IP	H	R	ER	HR	BB-IBB	SO
1997	—Florida (N.L.)	2	0	1.000	4.20	2	2	1	0	0-0	15.0	16	7	7	2	5-0	11
1998	—San Diego (N.L.)	1	1	.500	2.61	2	1	1	1	0-1	10.1	5	3	3	1	4-0	12
Champ. series totals (2 years)		3	1	.750	3.55	4	3	2	1	0-1	25.1	21	10	10	3	9-0	23

WORLD SERIES RECORD

NOTES: Member of World Series championship team (1997).

Year	League	W	L	Pct.	ERA	G	GS	CG	ShO	Sv.-Opp.	IP	H	R	ER	HR	BB-IBB	SO
1997	—Florida (N.L.)	0	2	.000	8.18	2	2	0	0	0-0	11.0	15	10	10	1	5-0	6
1998	—San Diego (N.L.)	0	1	.000	4.40	2	2	0	0	0-0	14.1	14	7	7	0	6-2	13
World Series totals (2 years)		0	3	.000	6.04	4	4	0	0	0-0	25.1	29	17	17	1	11-2	19

ALL-STAR GAME RECORD

	W	L	Pct.	ERA	GS	CG	ShO	Sv.-Opp.	IP	H	R	ER	HR	BB-IBB	SO
All-Star Game totals (5 years)	1	0	1.000	1.93	1	0	0	0-0	4.2	2	1	1	0	3-0	2

BROWN, KEVIN — C

PERSONAL: Born April 21, 1973, in Valparaiso, Ind. ... 6-2/231. ... Bats right, throws right. ... Full name: Kevin Lee Brown.

HIGH SCHOOL: Pike Central (Petersburg, Ind.).

COLLEGE: Southern Indiana.

TRANSACTIONS/CAREER NOTES: Selected by Texas Rangers organization in second round of free-agent draft (June 2, 1994). ... Traded by Rangers to Toronto Blue Jays for P Tim Crabtree (March 14, 1998). ... On Toronto disabled list (June 13-30, 1998); included rehabilitation assignment to Syracuse (June 28-30). ... On Syracuse disabled list (April 25-May 5, 2000). ... Traded by Blue Jays to Milwaukee Brewers for OF Alvin Morrow (July 25, 2000). ... Granted free agency (October 10, 2001). ... Signed by Tampa Bay Devil Rays organization (January 24, 2002). ... Released by Devil Rays (April 16, 2002). ... Signed by Boston Red Sox organization (April 19, 2002). ... Granted free agency (October 14, 2002).

STATISTICAL NOTES: Led American Association catchers with .991 fielding percentage and tied for the league lead with 10 double plays in 1997.

			BATTING														FIELDING	
Year	**Team (League)**	**Pos.**	**G**	**AB**	**R**	**H**	**2B**	**3B**	**HR**	**RBI**	**BB**	**SO**	**SB-CS**	**Avg.**	**OBP**	**SLG**	**E**	**Avg.**
1994	Hudson Valley (NY-P).	C	68	233	33	57	*19	1	6	32	23	•86	0-1	.245	.316	.412	7	.980
1995	Charlotte (FSL)..........	C-1B	107	355	48	94	25	1	11	57	50	96	2-3	.265	.366	.434	9	.985
	—Oklahoma City (A.A.)..	C	3	10	1	4	1	0	0	0	2	4	0-0	.400	.500	.500	2	.750
1996	Tulsa (Texas).............	C-DH-1B	128	460	77	121	27	1	26	86	73	*150	0-3	.263	.373	.496	13	.981
	—Texas (A.L.)................	C-DH	3	4	1	0	0	0	0	1	2	2	0-0	.000	.375	.000	0	1.000
1997	Oklahoma City (A.A.)..	C-1B-DH	116	403	56	97	18	2	19	50	38	111	2-2	.241	.313	.437	5	†.993
	—Texas (A.L.)................	C	4	5	1	2	0	0	1	1	0	0	0-0	.400	.400	1.000	1	.900
1998	Toronto (A.L.)■.........	C	52	110	17	29	7	1	2	15	9	31	0-0	.264	.320	.400	2	.993
	—Syracuse (I.L.)..........	C	2	8	2	5	2	0	0	0	0	2	0-0	.625	.625	.875	0	1.000
1999	Syracuse (I.L.)..........	C-DH	88	295	39	76	18	2	13	51	21	79	0-1	.258	.309	.464	*13	.979
	—Toronto (A.L.)............	C	2	9	1	4	2	0	0	1	0	3	0-0	.444	.444	.667	0	1.000
2000	Syracuse (I.L.)..........	C	51	179	26	60	15	1	7	29	8	46	0-0	.335	.362	.547	3	.990
	—Indianapolis (I.L.)■....	C	23	82	5	20	5	0	1	6	6	24	0-0	.244	.303	.341	0	1.000
	—Milwaukee (N.L.).......	C	5	17	3	4	3	0	0	1	1	5	0-0	.235	.278	.412	1	.957
2001	Indianapolis (I.L.)......	C	82	290	19	67	16	1	9	34	18	110	0-1	.231	.284	.386	4	.992
	—Milwaukee (N.L.).......	C	17	43	7	9	0	1	4	12	2	18	0-0	.209	.261	.535	0	1.000
2002	Durham (I.L.)■.........	C-1B	6	20	4	3	0	0	2	4	2	6	0-0	.150	.227	.450	0	1.000
	—Pawtucket (I.L.)■......	C	70	226	29	55	13	1	6	21	18	60	0-0	.243	.299	.389	4	.991
	—Boston (A.L.)............	PH	2	1	0	0	0	0	0	0	0	0	0-0	.000	.000	.000	...	...
American League totals (5 years)			63	129	20	35	9	1	3	18	11	36	0-0	.271	.331	.426	3	.990
National League totals (2 years)			22	60	10	13	3	1	4	13	3	23	0-0	.217	.266	.500	1	.990
Major League totals (7 years)			85	189	30	48	12	2	7	31	14	59	0-0	.254	.311	.450	4	.990

BROWN, ROOSEVELT OF CUBS

PERSONAL: Born August 3, 1975, in Vicksburg, Miss. ... 5-10/205. ... Bats left, throws right. ... Full name: Roosevelt Lawayne Brown. ... Cousin of Ellis Burks, designated hitter/outfielder, Cleveland Indians; cousin of Michael Carter, outfielder, Cubs organization.

HIGH SCHOOL: Vicksburg (Miss.).

TRANSACTIONS/CAREER NOTES: Selected by Atlanta Braves organization in 20th round of free-agent draft (June 3, 1993). ... Traded by Braves to Florida Marlins for 3B Terry Pendleton (August 13, 1996). ... Selected by Chicago Cubs organization from Marlins organization in Rule 5 minor league draft (December 15, 1997).

STATISTICAL NOTES: Career major league grand slams: 1.

2002 GAMES PLAYED BY POSITION (MLB): OF—64; DH—1.

			BATTING														FIELDING	
Year	**Team (League)**	**Pos.**	**G**	**AB**	**R**	**H**	**2B**	**3B**	**HR**	**RBI**	**BB**	**SO**	**SB-CS**	**Avg.**	**OBP**	**SLG**	**E**	**Avg.**
1993	GC Braves (GCL)........	OF	26	80	4	9	1	2	0	5	2	9	2-0	.113	.145	.175	4	.846
1994	Idaho Falls (Pio.)........	OF	48	160	28	53	8	1	3	22	17	15	8-6	.331	.397	.450	1	.985
1995	Eugene (N'West)........	OF	57	165	28	51	12	4	7	32	13	30	6-3	.309	.366	.558	8	.857
1996	Macon (S.Atl.)...........	OF	113	413	61	115	27	0	19	64	33	60	21-11	.278	.334	.482	•12	.930
	—Kane Co. (Midw.)■....	OF	11	40	1	6	2	0	0	3	1	10	0-1	.150	.190	.200	1	.933
1997	Kane County (Midw.)..	OF	61	211	29	50	7	1	4	30	22	52	5-4	.237	.312	.336	6	.930
	—Brevard County (FSL).	OF	33	114	8	28	7	1	1	12	7	31	0-3	.246	.287	.351	1	.980
1998	Daytona (FSL)■.........	OF	68	244	49	84	15	5	9	43	23	46	3-2	.344	.402	.557	2	.982
	—West Tenn (Sou.).......	OF	42	160	20	42	11	0	6	24	13	30	3-1	.263	.324	.444	3	.956
	—Iowa (PCL)................	DH	1	3	0	1	1	0	0	2	0	0	0-0	.333	.333	.667	...	...
1999	West Tenn (Sou.).......	OF	34	125	12	37	12	0	3	12	14	29	6-1	.296	.376	.464	1	.983
	—Chicago (N.L.)...........	OF	33	64	6	14	6	1	1	10	2	14	1-0	.219	.239	.391	1	.955
	—Iowa (PCL)................	OF-DH	74	268	50	96	25	2	22	79	19	54	3-3	.358	.401	.713	5	.959
2000	Chicago (N.L.)...........	OF	45	91	11	32	8	0	3	14	4	22	0-1	.352	.378	.538	0	1.000
	—Iowa (PCL)................	OF	100	363	67	112	32	0	12	55	37	60	10-3	.309	.381	.496	10	.943
2001	Chicago (N.L.)...........	OF-DH	39	83	13	22	6	1	4	22	7	12	0-0	.265	.326	.506	1	.952
	—Iowa (PCL)................	OF	88	364	68	126	34	1	22	77	14	67	3-5	.346	.381	.626	4	.971
2002	Chicago (N.L.)...........	OF-DH	111	204	14	43	12	0	3	23	23	50	2-2	.211	.299	.314	2	.975
Major League totals (4 years)			228	442	44	111	32	2	11	69	36	98	3-3	.251	.311	.407	4	.975

BUCHANAN, BRIAN OF PADRES

PERSONAL: Born July 21, 1973, in Miami. ... 6-4/230. ... Bats right, throws right. ... Full name: Brian James Buchanan.

HIGH SCHOOL: Fairfax (Va.).

COLLEGE: Virginia.

TRANSACTIONS/CAREER NOTES: Selected by New York Yankees organization in first round (24th pick overall) of free-agent draft (June 2, 1994). ... On disabled list (April 29, 1995-remainder of season). ... Traded by Yankees with P Eric Milton, P Danny Mota, SS Cristian Guzman and cash to Minnesota Twins for 2B Chuck Knoblauch (February 6, 1998). ... On disabled list (July 18-27 and July 29-August 9, 1999). ... On disabled list (June 29-July 14, 2001). ... On Minnesota disabled list (April 7-19, 2002); included rehabilitation assignment to Edmonton (April 18-19). ... Traded by Twins to San Diego Padres for SS Jason Bartlett (July 12, 2002).

STATISTICAL NOTES: Tied for Pacific Coast League lead with three double plays by outfielder in 1998. ... Tied Pacific Coast League lead with 11 sacrifice flies in 2000.

2002 GAMES PLAYED BY POSITION (MLB): OF—38; DH—17; 1B—15.

Year	Team (League)	Pos.	G	AB	R	H	2B	3B	HR	RBI	BB	SO	SB-CS	Avg.	OBP	SLG	E	Avg.
			BATTING														FIELDING	
1994—	Oneonta (NY-Penn)	OF	50	177	28	40	9	2	4	26	24	53	5-3	.226	.335	.367	0	1.000
1995—	Greensboro (S.Atl.)	OF	23	96	19	29	3	0	3	12	9	17	7-1	.302	.368	.427	1	.970
1996—	Tampa (FSL)	OF	131	526	65	137	22	4	10	58	37	108	23-8	.260	.321	.375	6	.969
1997—	Norwich (East.)	OF	116	470	75	145	25	2	10	69	32	85	11-9	.309	.362	.434	8	.962
	— Columbus (I.L.)	OF	18	61	8	17	1	0	4	7	4	11	2-1	.279	.348	.492	1	.947
1998—	Salt Lake (PCL)■	OF	133	500	74	139	29	3	17	82	36	90	14-2	.278	.337	.450	8	.969
1999—	Salt Lake (PCL)	OF-DH	107	391	67	116	24	1	10	60	28	85	11-2	.297	.355	.440	4	.980
2000—	Salt Lake (PCL)	OF-1B	95	364	82	108	20	1	27	103	41	75	5-1	.297	.363	.580	4	.980
	— Minnesota (A.L.)	OF-DH	30	82	10	19	3	0	1	8	8	22	0-2	.232	.301	.305	0	1.000
2001—	Minnesota (A.L.)	OF-DH	69	197	28	54	12	0	10	32	19	58	1-1	.274	.342	.487	2	.973
2002—	Minnesota (A.L.)	OF-DH	44	135	19	34	5	1	5	15	6	33	2-1	.252	.294	.415	0	1.000
	— Edmonton (PCL)	OF	1	3	0	0	0	0	0	0	0	0	0-0	.000	.000	.000	0	1.000
	— San Diego (N.L.)■	1B-OF	48	92	12	27	5	0	6	13	9	26	0-1	.293	.363	.543	1	.990
American League totals (3 years)			143	414	57	107	20	1	16	55	33	113	3-4	.258	.319	.428	2	.987
National League totals (1 year)			48	92	12	27	5	0	6	13	9	26	0-1	.293	.363	.543	1	.990
Major League totals (3 years)			191	506	69	134	25	1	22	68	42	139	3-5	.265	.327	.449	3	.988

BUCK, JOHN — C — ASTROS

PERSONAL: Born July 7, 1980, in Kemmerer, Wyo. ... 6-3/210. ... Bats right, throws right. ... Full name: Johnathan R. Buck.

HIGH SCHOOL: Taylorsville (Utah).

TRANSACTIONS/CAREER NOTES: Selected by Houston Astros organization in seventh round of free-agent draft (June 2, 1998). ... On Round Rock disabled list (April 6-16, 2002).

STATISTICAL NOTES: Led New York-Pennsylvania League catchers with 549 putouts, 52 assists and 617 total chances and tied for lead in double plays in 1999. ... Led Midwest League catchers with 748 putouts, 844 total chances and 11 double plays in 2000. ... Led South Atlantic League catchers with 1,006 putouts, 118 assists and 1,130 total chances in 2001. ... Led Texas League catchers with 727 putouts and 799 total chances in 2002.

Year	Team (League)	Pos.	G	AB	R	H	2B	3B	HR	RBI	BB	SO	SB-CS	Avg.	OBP	SLG	E	Avg.
			BATTING														FIELDING	
1998—	GC Astros (GCL)	C	36	126	24	36	9	0	3	15	13	22	2-2	.286	.362	.429	4	.983
1999—	Auburn (NY-Penn)	C	63	233	36	57	17	0	3	29	25	48	7-1	.245	.328	.356	*16	.974
	— Michigan (Midw.)	C	4	10	1	1	1	0	0	0	2	3	0-0	.100	.250	.200	0	1.000
2000—	Michigan (Midw.)	C	109	390	57	110	33	0	10	71	55	81	2-4	.282	.374	.444	•15	.982
2001—	Lexington (S.Atl.)	C	122	443	72	122	24	1	22	73	37	84	4-9	.275	.345	.483	6	*.995
2002—	Round Rock (Texas)	C	120	448	48	118	29	3	12	89	31	93	2-3	.263	.314	.422	8	.990

BUDDIE, MIKE — P

PERSONAL: Born December 12, 1970, in Berea, Ohio. ... 6-3/212. ... Throws right, bats right. ... Full name: Michael Joseph Buddie.

HIGH SCHOOL: St. Ignatius (Cleveland).

COLLEGE: Wake Forest.

TRANSACTIONS/CAREER NOTES: Selected by New York Yankees organization in fourth round of free-agent draft (June 1, 1992). ... Released by Yankees (June 9, 2000). ... Signed by Milwaukee Brewers organization (June 12, 2000). ... On Milwaukee disabled list (July 8-27, 2001). ... Released by Brewers (June 4, 2002). ... Signed by Montreal Expos organization (June 14, 2002). ... Granted free agency (October 15, 2002).

CAREER HITTING (MLB): 1-for-6 (.167), 1 R, 0 2B, 0 3B, 0 HR, 0 RBI.

Year	League	W	L	Pct.	ERA	G	GS	CG	ShO	Sv.-Opp.	IP	H	R	ER	HR	BB-IBB	SO
1992—	Oneonta (NY-Penn)	1	4	.200	3.88	13	13	1	0	0-...	67.1	69	36	29	3	34-0	87
1993—	Greensboro (S.Atl.)	13	10	.565	4.87	27	26	0	0	0-...	155.1	138	104	84	19	89-0	143
1994—	Tampa (FSL)	12	5	.706	4.01	25	24	2	0	0-...	150.1	143	75	67	7	66-2	113
1995—	Norwich (East.)	10	*12	.455	4.81	29	27	2	0	1-...	149.2	155	*102	80	4	81-2	106
1996—	Norwich (East.)	7	12	.368	4.45	29	26	4	0	0-...	159.2	176	101	79	10	71-5	103
1997—	Norwich (East.)	0	0	...	0.00	1	0	0	0	0-...	1.0	0	0	0	0	0-0	3
	— Columbus (I.L.)	6	6	.500	2.64	53	0	0	0	13-...	75.0	85	24	22	4	25-0	67
1998—	New York (A.L.)	4	1	.800	5.62	24	2	0	0	0-0	41.2	46	29	26	5	13-1	20
	— Columbus (I.L.)	5	0	1.000	2.74	26	0	0	0	4-...	42.2	35	15	13	0	15-0	30
1999—	Columbus (I.L.)	9	2	.818	2.86	49	2	0	0	0-...	78.2	80	30	25	2	22-2	68
	— New York (A.L.)	0	0	...	4.50	2	0	0	0	0-0	2.0	3	1	1	1	0-0	1
2000—	Columbus (I.L.)	1	3	.250	7.50	6	6	0	0	0-...	30.0	34	30	25	8	20-1	16
	— Indianapolis (I.L.)■	7	2	.778	2.62	30	0	0	0	2-...	58.1	40	20	17	4	29-1	39
	— Milwaukee (N.L.)	0	0	...	4.50	5	0	0	0	0-0	6.0	8	3	3	0	1-1	5
2001—	Indianapolis (I.L.)	4	1	.800	2.31	27	0	0	0	3-...	46.2	36	13	12	4	25-4	31
	— Milwaukee (N.L.)	0	1	.000	3.89	31	0	0	0	2-2	41.2	34	20	18	2	17-2	22
2002—	Milwaukee (N.L.)	1	2	.333	4.54	25	0	0	0	0-2	39.2	46	23	20	5	21-7	28
	— Ottawa (I.L.)■	4	4	.500	4.07	29	0	0	0	2-...	42.0	34	21	19	2	23-3	18
A.L. totals (2 years)		4	1	.800	5.56	26	2	0	0	0-0	43.2	49	30	27	6	13-1	21
N.L. totals (3 years)		1	3	.250	4.23	61	0	0	0	2-4	87.1	88	46	41	7	39-10	55
Major League totals (5 years)		5	4	.556	4.67	87	2	0	0	2-4	131.0	137	76	68	13	52-11	76

BUEHRLE, MARK — P — WHITE SOX

PERSONAL: Born March 23, 1979, in St. Charles, Mo. ... 6-2/200. ... Throws left, bats left. ... Full name: Mark A. Buehrle.

HIGH SCHOOL: Francis Howell North (St. Charles, Mo.).

JUNIOR COLLEGE: Jefferson College (Mo.).

TRANSACTIONS/CAREER NOTES: Selected by Chicago White Sox organization in 38th round of free-agent draft (June 2, 1998).

HONORS: Named Southern League Most Outstanding Pitcher (2000).

STATISTICAL NOTES: Pitched 4-0 one-hit, complete-game victory against Tampa Bay (August 3, 2001).

CAREER HITTING (MLB): 1-for-9 (.111), 1 R, 0 2B, 0 3B, 0 HR, 0 RBI.

Year League	W	L	Pct.	ERA	G	GS	CG	ShO	Sv.-Opp.	IP	H	R	ER	HR	BB-IBB	SO
1999— Burlington (Midw.)	7	4	.636	4.10	20	14	1	1	3-...	98.2	105	49	45	8	16-1	91
2000— Birmingham (Sou.)	8	4	.667	2.28	16	16	1	1	0-...	118.2	95	37	30	8	17-0	68
— Chicago (A.L.)	4	1	.800	4.21	28	3	0	0	0-2	51.1	55	27	24	5	19-1	37
2001— Chicago (A.L.)	16	8	.667	3.29	32	32	4	2	0-0	221.1	188	89	81	24	48-2	126
2002— Chicago (A.L.)	19	12	.613	3.58	34	34	5	2	0-0	239.0	236	102	95	25	61-7	134
Major League totals (3 years)	39	21	.650	3.52	94	69	9	4	0-2	511.2	479	218	200	54	128-10	297

DIVISION SERIES RECORD

Year League	W	L	Pct.	ERA	G	GS	CG	ShO	Sv.-Opp.	IP	H	R	ER	HR	BB-IBB	SO
2000— Chicago (A.L.)	0	0	...	0.00	1	0	0	0	0-0	.1	2	0	0	0	0-0	1

ALL-STAR GAME RECORD

	W	L	Pct.	ERA	GS	CG	ShO	Sv.-Opp.	IP	H	R	ER	HR	BB-IBB	SO
All-Star Game totals (1 year)	0	0	...	4.50	0	0	0	0-0	2.0	2	1	1	0	0-0	2

BUKVICH, RYAN — P — ROYALS

PERSONAL: Born May 13, 1978, in Naperville, Ill. ... 6-2/250. ... Throws right, bats right. ... Full name: Ryan Adrien Bukvich.
HIGH SCHOOL: Northwest Rankin (Brandon, Miss.).
COLLEGE: Mississippi.
TRANSACTIONS/CAREER NOTES: Selected by Kansas City Royals organization in 11th round of free-agent draft (June 5, 2000).
CAREER HITTING (MLB): 0-for-0 (.000), 0 R, 0 2B, 0 3B, 0 HR, 0 RBI.

Year League	W	L	Pct.	ERA	G	GS	CG	ShO	Sv.-Opp.	IP	H	R	ER	HR	BB-IBB	SO
2000— Spokane (N'West)	2	0	1.000	0.64	10	0	0	0	2-...	14.0	5	1	1	0	9-0	15
— Charleston, W.Va. (S.Atl.)	0	0	...	1.88	11	0	0	0	4-...	14.1	6	3	3	0	7-0	17
— Wilmington (Caro.)	0	1	.000	18.00	2	0	0	0	0-...	2.0	3	4	4	0	5-2	3
2001— Wilmington (Caro.)	0	1	.000	1.72	37	0	0	0	13-...	57.2	41	16	11	1	31-0	80
— Wichita (Texas)	0	0	...	3.75	7	0	0	0	0-...	12.0	9	6	5	2	2-0	14
2002— Wichita (Texas)	1	1	.500	1.31	23	0	0	0	8-...	34.1	17	8	5	0	15-1	47
— Omaha (PCL)	1	0	1.000	0.00	12	0	0	0	8-...	13.2	4	0	0	0	7-0	17
— Kansas City (A.L.)	1	0	1.000	6.12	26	0	0	0	0-1	25.0	26	19	17	2	19-3	20
Major League totals (1 year)	1	0	1.000	6.12	26	0	0	0	0-1	25.0	26	19	17	2	19-3	20

BURBA, DAVE — P

PERSONAL: Born July 7, 1966, in Dayton, Ohio. ... 6-4/240. ... Throws right, bats right. ... Full name: David Allen Burba. ... Nephew of Ray Hathaway, pitcher with Brooklyn Dodgers (1945).
HIGH SCHOOL: Kenton Ridge (Springfield, Ohio).
COLLEGE: Ohio State.
TRANSACTIONS/CAREER NOTES: Selected by Seattle Mariners organization in second round of free-agent draft (June 2, 1987). ... Traded by Mariners with P Bill Swift and P Mike Jackson to San Francisco Giants for OF Kevin Mitchell and P Mike Remlinger (December 11, 1991). ... Traded by Giants with OF Darren Lewis and P Mark Portugal to Cincinnati Reds for OF Deion Sanders, P John Roper, P Ricky Pickett, P Scott Service and IF Dave McCarty (July 21, 1995). ... On disabled list (August 7-27, 1997). ... Traded by Reds to Cleveland Indians for 1B Sean Casey (March 30, 1998). ... Granted free agency (November 6, 2001). ... Signed by Texas Rangers (December 19, 2001). ... Released by Rangers (July 29, 2002). ... Signed by Indians organization (August 7, 2002). ... Granted free agency (November 4, 2002).
RECORDS: Shares major league record for most home runs allowed in one inning—4 (June 29, 2001, fourth inning).
CAREER HITTING (MLB): 26-for-180 (.144), 10 R, 1 2B, 0 3B, 3 HR, 12 RBI.

Year League	W	L	Pct.	ERA	G	GS	CG	ShO	Sv.-Opp.	IP	H	R	ER	HR	BB-IBB	SO
1987— Bellingham (N'West)	3	1	.750	1.93	5	5	0	0	0-...	23.1	20	10	5	0	3-0	24
— Salinas (Calif.)	1	6	.143	4.61	9	9	0	0	0-...	54.2	53	31	28	3	29-0	46
1988— San Bernardino (Calif.)	5	7	.417	2.68	20	20	0	0	0-...	114.0	106	41	34	4	54-1	102
1989— Williamsport (East.)	11	7	.611	3.16	25	25	5	1	0-...	156.2	138	69	55	7	55-0	89
1990— Calgary (PCL)	10	6	.625	4.67	31	18	1	0	2-...	113.2	124	64	59	11	45-0	47
— Seattle (A.L.)	0	0	...	4.50	6	0	0	0	0-0	8.0	8	6	4	0	2-0	4
1991— Seattle (A.L.)	2	2	.500	3.68	22	2	0	0	1-1	36.2	34	16	15	6	14-3	16
— Calgary (PCL)	6	4	.600	3.53	23	9	0	0	4-...	71.1	82	35	28	4	27-0	42
1992— San Francisco (N.L.)■	2	7	.222	4.97	23	11	0	0	0-0	70.2	80	43	39	4	31-2	47
— Phoenix (PCL)	5	5	.500	4.72	13	13	0	0	0-...	74.1	86	40	39	5	24-2	44
1993— San Francisco (N.L.)	10	3	.769	4.25	54	5	0	0	0-0	95.1	95	49	45	14	37-5	88
1994— San Francisco (N.L.)	3	6	.333	4.38	57	0	0	0	0-3	74.0	59	39	36	5	45-3	84
1995— San Francisco (N.L.)	4	2	.667	4.98	37	0	0	0	0-1	43.1	38	26	24	5	25-2	46
— Cincinnati (N.L.)■	6	2	.750	3.27	15	9	1	1	0-0	63.1	52	24	23	4	26-1	50
1996— Cincinnati (N.L.)	11	13	.458	3.83	34	33	0	0	0-0	195.0	179	96	83	18	97-9	148
1997— Cincinnati (N.L.)	11	10	.524	4.72	30	27	2	0	0-0	160.0	157	88	84	22	73-10	131
1998— Cleveland (A.L.)■	15	10	.600	4.11	32	31	0	0	0-0	203.2	210	100	93	30	69-4	132
1999— Cleveland (A.L.)	15	9	.625	4.25	34	34	1	0	0-0	220.0	211	113	104	30	96-3	174
2000— Cleveland (A.L.)	16	6	.727	4.47	32	32	0	0	0-0	191.1	199	99	95	19	91-2	180
2001— Cleveland (A.L.)	10	10	.500	6.21	32	27	1	0	0-0	150.2	188	112	104	16	54-2	118
2002— Texas (A.L.)■	4	5	.444	5.42	23	18	1	0	0-1	111.1	125	71	67	13	40-3	70
— Akron (East.)■	0	0	...	0.00	1	1	0	0	0-...	4.2	2	0	0	0	1-0	1
— Cleveland (A.L.)	1	0	1.000	4.50	12	3	0	0	0-1	34.0	30	20	17	3	17-0	25
A.L. totals (7 years)	63	42	.600	4.70	193	147	3	0	1-3	955.2	1005	537	499	117	383-17	719
N.L. totals (6 years)	47	43	.522	4.28	250	85	3	1	0-4	701.2	660	365	334	72	334-32	594
Major League totals (13 years)	110	85	.564	4.52	443	232	6	1	1-7	1657.1	1665	902	833	189	717-49	1313

DIVISION SERIES RECORD

Year League	W	L	Pct.	ERA	G	GS	CG	ShO	Sv.-Opp.	IP	H	R	ER	HR	BB-IBB	SO
1995— Cincinnati (N.L.)	1	0	1.000	0.00	1	0	0	0	0-0	1.0	2	0	0	0	1-0	0
1998— Cleveland (A.L.)	1	0	1.000	5.06	1	0	0	0	0-0	5.1	4	3	3	0	2-0	4
1999— Cleveland (A.L.)	0	0	...	0.00	1	1	0	0	0-0	4.0	1	0	0	0	1-0	0
2001— Cleveland (A.L.)	0	0	...	0.00	1	0	0	0	0-0	1.0	0	0	0	0	0-0	1
Division series totals (4 years)	2	0	1.000	2.38	4	1	0	0	0-0	11.1	7	3	3	0	4-0	5

CHAMPIONSHIP SERIES RECORD

Year League	W	L	Pct.	ERA	G	GS	CG	ShO	Sv.-Opp.	IP	H	R	ER	HR	BB-IBB	SO
1995—Cincinnati (N.L.)	0	0	...	0.00	2	0	0	0	0-0	3.2	3	0	0	0	4-1	0
1998—Cleveland (A.L.)	1	0	1.000	3.00	3	0	0	0	0-0	6.0	3	4	2	0	5-0	8
Champ. series totals (2 years)	1	0	1.000	1.86	5	0	0	0	0-0	9.2	6	4	2	0	9-1	8

BURKETT, JOHN — P — RED SOX

PERSONAL: Born November 28, 1964, in New Brighton, Pa. ... 6-3/215. ... Throws right, bats right. ... Full name: John David Burkett. ... Name pronounced bur-KETT.

HIGH SCHOOL: Beaver (Pa.).

TRANSACTIONS/CAREER NOTES: Selected by San Francisco Giants organization in sixth round of free-agent draft (June 6, 1983). ... Traded by Giants to Texas Rangers for IF Rich Aurilia and OF Desi Wilson (December 22, 1994). ... Granted free agency (April 7, 1995). ... Signed by Florida Marlins (April 9, 1995). ... Traded by Marlins to Texas Rangers for P Ryan Dempster and a player to be named later (August 8, 1996); Marlins acquired P Rick Helling to complete deal (September 3, 1996). ... On Texas disabled list (August 6-31, 1997); included rehabilitation assignment to Oklahoma City (August 26). ... On Texas disabled list (April 21-May 9, 1999); included rehabilitation assignment to Tulsa (May 1-9). ... Granted free agency (November 1, 1999). ... Signed by Tampa Bay Devil Rays organization (January 17, 2000). ... Released by Devil Rays (March 29, 2000). ... Signed by Atlanta Braves (April 2, 2000). ... Granted free agency (October 31, 2000). ... Re-signed by Braves (December 20, 2000). ... Granted free agency (November 6, 2001). ... Signed by Boston Red Sox (December 20, 2001). ... On Boston disabled list (March 21-April 19, 2002); included rehabilitation assignment to Pawtucket (April 14-19).

STATISTICAL NOTES: Led N.L. 10 hit batsmen in 1991.

MISCELLANEOUS: Had sacrifice hit in only appearance as pinch hitter (1995).

CAREER HITTING (MLB): 50-for-539 (.093), 22 R, 6 2B, 0 3B, 0 HR, 18 RBI.

Year League	W	L	Pct.	ERA	G	GS	CG	ShO	Sv.-Opp.	IP	H	R	ER	HR	BB-IBB	SO
1983—Great Falls (Pio.)	2	6	.250	6.26	13	9	0	0	0-...	50.1	73	44	35	1	30-2	38
1984—Clinton (Midw.)	7	6	.538	4.33	20	20	2	0	0-...	126.2	128	81	61	5	38-1	83
1985—Fresno (Calif.)	7	4	.636	2.87	20	20	1	1	0-...	109.2	98	43	35	3	46-0	72
1986—Shreveport (Texas)	10	6	.625	2.66	22	21	4	2	0-...	128.2	99	46	38	7	42-0	73
—Fresno (Calif.)	0	3	.000	5.47	4	4	0	0	0-...	24.2	34	19	15	2	8-0	14
1987—Shreveport (Texas)	•14	8	.636	3.34	27	27	6	1	0-...	*177.2	181	75	66	11	53-2	126
—San Francisco (N.L.)	0	0	...	4.50	3	0	0	0	0-0	6.0	7	4	3	2	3-0	5
1988—Phoenix (PCL)	5	11	.313	5.21	21	21	0	0	0-...	114.0	141	79	66	7	49-3	74
—Shreveport (Texas)	5	1	.833	2.13	7	7	2	1	0-...	50.2	33	15	12	3	18-1	34
1989—Phoenix (PCL)	10	11	.476	5.05	28	•28	2	1	0-...	167.2	197	111	94	19	59-3	105
1990—Phoenix (PCL)	2	1	.667	2.74	3	3	2	1	0-...	23.0	18	8	7	2	3-0	9
—San Francisco (N.L.)	14	7	.667	3.79	33	32	2	0	1-1	204.0	201	92	86	18	61-7	118
1991—San Francisco (N.L.)	12	11	.522	4.18	36	34	3	1	0-0	206.2	223	103	96	19	60-2	131
1992—San Francisco (N.L.)	13	9	.591	3.84	32	32	3	1	0-0	189.2	194	96	81	13	45-6	107
1993—San Francisco (N.L.)	•22	7	.759	3.65	34	34	2	1	0-0	231.2	224	100	94	18	40-4	145
1994—San Francisco (N.L.)	6	8	.429	3.62	25	25	0	0	0-0	159.1	176	72	64	14	36-7	85
1995—Florida (N.L.)■	14	14	.500	4.30	30	30	4	0	0-0	188.1	208	95	90	22	57-5	126
1996—Florida (N.L.)	6	10	.375	4.32	24	24	1	0	0-0	154.0	154	84	74	15	42-2	108
—Texas (A.L.)■	5	2	.714	4.06	10	10	1	1	0-0	68.2	75	33	31	4	16-2	47
1997—Texas (A.L.)	9	12	.429	4.56	30	30	2	0	0-0	189.1	240	106	96	20	30-1	139
—Oklahoma City (A.A.)	1	0	1.000	3.60	1	1	0	0	0-...	5.0	6	2	2	1	2-0	3
1998—Texas (A.L.)	9	13	.409	5.68	32	32	0	0	0-0	195.0	230	131	*123	19	46-1	131
1999—Texas (A.L.)	9	8	.529	5.62	30	25	0	0	0-0	147.1	184	95	92	18	46-1	96
—Tulsa (Texas)	0	1	.000	2.70	2	2	0	0	0-...	6.2	7	5	2	0	3-0	3
2000—Atlanta (N.L.)■	10	6	.625	4.89	31	22	0	0	0-1	134.1	162	79	73	13	51-2	110
2001—Atlanta (N.L.)	12	12	.500	3.04	34	34	1	1	0-0	219.1	187	83	74	17	70-13	187
2002—Pawtucket (I.L.)■	0	1	.000	11.57	1	1	0	0	0-...	2.1	4	3	3	0	1-0	2
—Boston (A.L.)	13	8	.619	4.53	29	29	1	1	0-0	173.0	199	93	87	25	50-5	124
A.L. totals (5 years)	45	43	.511	4.99	131	126	4	2	0-0	773.1	928	458	429	86	188-10	537
N.L. totals (10 years)	109	84	.565	3.91	282	267	16	4	1-2	1693.1	1736	808	735	151	465-48	1122
Major League totals (14 years)	154	127	.548	4.25	413	393	20	6	1-2	2466.2	2664	1266	1164	237	653-58	1659

DIVISION SERIES RECORD

Year League	W	L	Pct.	ERA	G	GS	CG	ShO	Sv.-Opp.	IP	H	R	ER	HR	BB-IBB	SO
1996—Texas (A.L.)	1	0	1.000	2.00	1	1	1	0	0-0	9.0	10	2	2	0	1-0	7
1998—Texas (A.L.)									Did not play.							
1999—Texas (A.L.)									Did not play.							
2000—Atlanta (N.L.)	0	0	...	6.75	1	0	0	0	0-0	1.1	1	1	1	0	0-0	0
2001—Atlanta (N.L.)	1	0	1.000	2.84	1	1	0	0	0-0	6.1	6	2	2	1	2-0	4
Division series totals (3 years)	2	0	1.000	2.70	3	2	1	0	0-0	16.2	17	5	5	1	3-0	11

CHAMPIONSHIP SERIES RECORD

Year League	W	L	Pct.	ERA	G	GS	CG	ShO	Sv.-Opp.	IP	H	R	ER	HR	BB-IBB	SO
2001—Atlanta (N.L.)	0	1	.000	8.31	1	1	0	0	0-0	4.1	7	5	4	0	2-1	2

ALL-STAR GAME RECORD

	W	L	Pct.	ERA	GS	CG	ShO	Sv.-Opp.	IP	H	R	ER	HR	BB-IBB	SO
All-Star Game totals (2 years)	0	1	.000	16.20	0	0	0	0-0	1.2	4	3	3	0	0-0	2

BURKS, ELLIS — DH/OF — INDIANS

PERSONAL: Born September 11, 1964, in Vicksburg, Miss. ... 6-2/205. ... Bats right, throws right. ... Full name: Ellis Rena Burks. ... Cousin of Roosevelt Brown, outfielder, Chicago Cubs.

HIGH SCHOOL: Everman (Texas).

JUNIOR COLLEGE: Ranger (Texas) Junior College.

TRANSACTIONS/CAREER NOTES: Selected by Boston Red Sox organization in first round (20th pick overall) of free-agent draft (January 11, 1983). ... On disabled list (March 26-April 12, 1988). ... On Boston disabled list (June 15-August 1, 1989); included rehabilitation assignment to Pawtucket (July 26-August 1). ... On disabled list (June 25, 1992-remainder of season). ... Granted free agency (December 19, 1992). ...

Signed by Chicago White Sox (January 4, 1993). ... Granted free agency (October 27, 1993). ... Signed by Colorado Rockies (November 30, 1993). ... On Colorado disabled list (May 18-July 31, 1994); included rehabilitation assignment to Colorado Springs (July 18-20). ... On Colorado disabled list (April 17-May 5, 1995); included rehabilitation assignment to Colorado Springs (April 25-May 5). ... On disabled list (June 28-July 29, 1997). ... Traded by Rockies to San Francisco Giants for OF Darryl Hamilton, P James Stoops and a player to be named later (July 31, 1998); Rockies acquired P Jason Brester to complete deal (August 17, 1998). ... Granted free agency (November 2, 1998). ... Re-signed by Giants (November 13, 1998). ... On disabled list (June 9-26, 1999; and May 9-24, 2000). ... Granted free agency (October 30, 2000). ... Signed by Cleveland Indians (November 19, 2000). ... On disabled list (July 16-August 1, 2001).

RECORDS: Shares major league single-inning record for most home runs—2 (August 27, 1990, fourth inning).

HONORS: Named outfielder on The Sporting News A.L. All-Star team (1990). ... Named outfielder on The Sporting News A.L. Silver Slugger team (1990). ... Won A.L. Gold Glove as outfielder (1990). ... Named outfielder on The Sporting News N.L. All-Star team (1996). ... Named outfielder on The Sporting News N.L. Silver Slugger team (1996).

STATISTICAL NOTES: Tied for Florida State League lead in double plays by outfielder with six in 1984. ... Led N.L. with 392 total bases in 1996. ... Hit three home runs in one game (June 19, 2001). ... Career major league grand slams: 10.

2002 GAMES PLAYED BY POSITION (MLB): DH—127; OF—6.

								BATTING								FIELDING	
Year Team (League)	**Pos.**	**G**	**AB**	**R**	**H**	**2B**	**3B**	**HR**	**RBI**	**BB**	**SO**	**SB-CS**	**Avg.**	**OBP**	**SLG**	**E**	**Avg.**
1983—Elmira (NY-Penn)	OF	53	174	30	42	9	0	2	23	17	43	9-0	.241	.309	.328	2	.979
1984—Winter Haven (FSL)	OF	112	375	52	96	15	4	6	43	42	68	29-8	.256	.337	.365	5	.977
1985—New Britain (East.)	OF	133	476	66	121	25	7	10	61	42	85	17-14	.254	.316	.399	8	.975
1986—New Britain (East.)	OF	124	462	70	126	20	3	14	55	44	75	31-9	.273	.337	.420	5	.985
1987—Pawtucket (I.L.)	OF	11	40	11	9	3	1	3	6	7	7	1-0	.225	.340	.575	0	1.000
—Boston (A.L.)	OF-DH	133	558	94	152	30	2	20	59	41	98	27-6	.272	.324	.441	4	.988
1988—Boston (A.L.)	OF-DH	144	540	93	159	37	5	18	92	62	89	25-9	.294	.367	.481	9	.977
1989—Boston (A.L.)	OF-DH	97	399	73	121	19	6	12	61	36	52	21-5	.303	.365	.471	6	.977
—Pawtucket (I.L.)	OF	5	21	4	3	1	0	0	0	2	3	0-0	.143	.217	.190	0	1.000
1990—Boston (A.L.)	OF-DH	152	588	89	174	33	8	21	89	48	82	9-11	.296	.349	.486	2	.994
1991—Boston (A.L.)	OF-DH	130	474	56	119	33	3	14	56	39	81	6-11	.251	.314	.422	2	.993
1992—Boston (A.L.)	OF-DH	66	235	35	60	8	3	8	30	25	48	5-2	.255	.327	.417	2	.984
1993—Chicago (A.L.)■	OF	146	499	75	137	24	4	17	74	60	97	6-9	.275	.352	.441	6	.982
1994—Colorado (N.L.)■	OF	42	149	33	48	8	3	13	24	16	39	3-1	.322	.388	.678	3	.964
—Colo. Springs (PCL)	OF	2	8	4	4	1	0	1	2	2	1	0-0	.500	.600	1.000	0	1.000
1995—Colo. Springs (PCL)	OF-DH	8	29	9	9	2	1	2	6	4	8	0-0	.310	.394	.655	0	1.000
—Colorado (N.L.)	OF	103	278	41	74	10	6	14	49	39	72	7-3	.266	.359	.496	5	.970
1996—Colorado (N.L.)	OF	156	613	*142	211	45	8	40	128	61	114	32-6	.344	.408	*.639	5	.983
1997—Colorado (N.L.)	OF	119	424	91	123	19	2	32	82	47	75	7-2	.290	.363	.571	4	.982
1998—Colorado (N.L.)	OF	100	357	54	102	22	5	16	54	39	80	3-7	.286	.355	.510	5	.975
—San Fran. (N.L.)■	OF	42	147	22	45	6	1	5	22	19	31	8-1	.306	.387	.463	1	.989
1999—San Francisco (N.L.)	OF-DH	120	390	73	110	19	0	31	96	69	86	7-5	.282	.394	.569	2	.991
2000—San Francisco (N.L.)	OF-DH	122	393	74	135	21	5	24	96	56	49	5-1	.344	.419	.606	4	.982
2001—Cleveland (A.L.)■	DH-OF	124	439	83	123	29	1	28	74	62	85	5-1	.280	.369	.542	0	1.000
2002—Cleveland (A.L.)	DH-OF	138	518	92	156	28	0	32	91	44	108	2-3	.301	.362	.541	0	1.000
American League totals (9 years)		1130	4250	690	1201	241	32	170	626	417	740	106-57	.283	.349	.474	31	.985
National League totals (7 years)		804	2751	530	848	150	30	175	551	346	546	72-26	.308	.387	.575	29	.980
Major League totals (16 years)		1934	7001	1220	2049	391	62	345	1177	763	1286	178-83	.293	.364	.514	60	.983

DIVISION SERIES RECORD

								BATTING								FIELDING	
Year Team (League)	**Pos.**	**G**	**AB**	**R**	**H**	**2B**	**3B**	**HR**	**RBI**	**BB**	**SO**	**SB-CS**	**Avg.**	**OBP**	**SLG**	**E**	**Avg.**
1995—Colorado (N.L.)	OF	2	6	1	2	1	0	0	2	0	1	0-0	.333	.286	.500	1	.800
2000—San Francisco (N.L.)	OF	4	13	2	3	1	0	1	4	4	2	0-0	.231	.412	.538	0	1.000
2001—Cleveland (A.L.)	DH	5	19	4	6	1	0	1	1	1	3	0-0	.316	.350	.526	...	...
Division series totals (3 years)		11	38	7	11	3	0	2	7	5	6	0-0	.289	.364	.526	1	.941

CHAMPIONSHIP SERIES RECORD

								BATTING								FIELDING	
Year Team (League)	**Pos.**	**G**	**AB**	**R**	**H**	**2B**	**3B**	**HR**	**RBI**	**BB**	**SO**	**SB-CS**	**Avg.**	**OBP**	**SLG**	**E**	**Avg.**
1988—Boston (A.L.)	OF	4	17	2	4	1	0	0	1	0	3	0-0	.235	.235	.294	0	1.000
1990—Boston (A.L.)	OF	4	15	1	4	2	0	0	0	1	1	1-0	.267	.313	.400	0	1.000
1993—Chicago (A.L.)	OF	6	23	4	7	1	0	1	3	3	5	0-1	.304	.407	.478	0	1.000
Championship series totals (3 years)		14	55	7	15	4	0	1	4	4	9	1-1	.273	.333	.400	0	1.000

ALL-STAR GAME RECORD

NOTES: Named to A.L. All-Star team for 1990 game; replaced by Brook Jacoby due to injury.

	AB	**R**	**H**	**2B**	**3B**	**HR**	**RBI**	**BB**	**SO**	**SB-CS**	**Avg.**	**OBP**	**SLG**	**E**	**Avg.**
All-Star Game totals (1 year)	2	0	1	0	1	0	0	0	1	0-0	.500	.500	1.500	0	1.000

BURNETT, A.J. — P — MARLINS

PERSONAL: Born January 3, 1977, in North Little Rock, Ark. ... 6-4/229. ... Throws right, bats right. ... Full name: Allen James Burnett.

HIGH SCHOOL: Central Arkansas Christian (North Little Rock, Ark.).

TRANSACTIONS/CAREER NOTES: Selected by New York Mets organization in eighth round of free-agent draft (June 1, 1995). ... Traded by Mets with P Jesus Sanchez and OF Robert Stratton to Florida Marlins for P Al Leiter and 2B Ralph Milliard (February 6, 1998). ... On Florida disabled list (March 17-July 20, 2000); included rehabilitation assignments to Brevard County (July 4-14) and Calgary (July 15-20). ... On Florida disabled list (March 23-May 7, 2001); included rehabilitation assignment to Brevard County (April 24-May 1). ... On disabled list (August 19-September 14, 2002).

STATISTICAL NOTES: Tied for Appalachian League lead in wild pitches with 16 in 1996. ... Pitched 3-0 no-hit victory against San Diego (May 12, 2001). ... Tied for N.L. lead with 14 wild pitches in 2002.

MISCELLANEOUS: Holds Florida Marlins all-time record for most shutouts (6).

CAREER HITTING (MLB): 19-for-149 (.128), 5 R, 4 2B, 1 3B, 2 HR, 6 RBI.

Year	League	W	L	Pct.	ERA	G	GS	CG	ShO	Sv.-Opp.	IP	H	R	ER	HR	BB-IBB	SO
1995	—Gulf Coast Mets (GCL).....	2	3	.400	4.28	9	8	1	0	0-...	33.2	27	16	16	2	23-0	26
1996	—Kingsport (Appl.).............	4	0	1.000	3.88	12	12	0	0	0-...	58.0	31	26	25	0	*54-0	68
1997	—Gulf Coast Mets (GCL).....	0	1	.000	3.18	3	2	0	0	0-...	11.1	8	8	4	0	8-0	15
	—Pittsfield (NY-Penn)..........	3	1	.750	4.70	20	9	0	0	0-...	44.0	28	26	23	3	35-0	48
1998	—Kane County (Midw.)■.....	10	4	.714	1.97	20	20	0	0	0-...	119.0	74	27	26	3	45-0	186
1999	—Portland (East.)...............	6	12	.333	5.52	26	23	0	0	0-...	120.2	132	91	74	15	71-0	121
	—Florida (N.L.).....................	4	2	.667	3.48	7	7	0	0	0-0	41.1	37	23	16	3	25-2	33
2000	—Brevard County (FSL).......	0	0	...	3.68	2	2	0	0	0-...	7.1	4	3	3	0	6-0	6
	—Calgary (PCL).....................	0	0	...	0.00	1	1	0	0	0-...	5.0	0	0	0	0	3-0	6
	—Florida (N.L.).....................	3	7	.300	4.79	13	13	0	0	0-0	82.2	80	46	44	8	44-3	57
2001	—Brevard County (FSL).......	0	0	...	1.93	2	2	0	0	0-...	9.1	4	2	2	0	4-0	10
	—Florida (N.L.).....................	11	12	.478	4.05	27	27	2	1	0-0	173.1	145	82	78	20	83-3	128
2002	—Florida (N.L.).....................	12	9	.571	3.30	31	29	7	*5	0-1	204.1	153	84	75	12	90-5	203
Major League totals (4 years).....		30	30	.500	3.82	78	76	9	6	0-1	501.2	415	235	213	43	242-13	421

B

BURNITZ, JEROMY OF METS

PERSONAL: Born April 15, 1969, in Westminster, Calif. ... 6-0/213. ... Bats left, throws right. ... Full name: Jeromy Neal Burnitz.
HIGH SCHOOL: Conroe (Texas).
COLLEGE: Oklahoma State.
TRANSACTIONS/CAREER NOTES: Selected by Milwaukee Brewers organization in 24th round of free-agent draft (June 2, 1987); did not sign. ... Selected by New York Mets organization in first round (17th pick overall) of free-agent draft (June 4, 1990). ... On disabled list (August 23-September 18, 1992). ... On Norfolk suspended list (August 11-13, 1994). ... Traded by Mets with P Joe Roa to Cleveland Indians for P Paul Byrd, P Jerry DiPoto, P Dave Mlicki and a player to be named later (November 18, 1994); Mets acquired 2B Jesus Azuaje to complete deal (December 6, 1994). ... Traded by Indians to Milwaukee Brewers for 3B/1B Kevin Seitzer (August 31, 1996). ... On disabled list (July 18-August 20, 1999). ... Traded by Brewers to Mets as part of three-way deal in which Mets traded P Glendon Rusch to Brewers, Colorado Rockies traded 1B/OF Ross Gload and P Craig House to Mets, Brewers traded P Jeff D'Amico, IF Lou Collier, OF/1B Mark Sweeney and cash to Mets, Mets traded 1B/3B Todd Zeile, OF Benny Agbayani, IF/OF Lenny Harris and cash to Rockies and Rockies traded OF Alex Ochoa to Brewers (January 21, 2002).
RECORDS: Shares A.L. record for most home runs by pinch-hitter in consecutive at-bats—2 (August 2 and 3, 1997).
STATISTICAL NOTES: Tied for New York-Pennsylvania League lead with six intentional bases on balls received in 1990. ... Led American Association with eight intentional bases on balls received in 1995. ... Hit three home runs in one game (May 10, 2001 and September 25, 2001). ... Career major league grand slams: 6.
2002 GAMES PLAYED BY POSITION (MLB): OF—140; DH—1.

			BATTING														FIELDING	
Year	Team (League)	Pos.	G	AB	R	H	2B	3B	HR	RBI	BB	SO	SB-CS	Avg.	OBP	SLG	E	Avg.
1990	—Pittsfield (NY-Penn)....	OF	51	173	37	52	6	5	6	22	45	39	12-5	.301	*.444	.497	0	1.000
	—St. Lucie (FSL)...........	OF	11	32	6	5	1	0	0	3	7	12	1-0	.156	.372	.188	0	1.000
1991	—Williamsport (East.)...	OF	135	457	80	103	16	•10	*31	•85	*104	127	31-13	.225	.368	.508	•11	.958
1992	—Tidewater (I.L.)...........	OF	121	445	56	108	21	3	8	40	33	84	30-7	.243	.298	.357	8	.967
1993	—Norfolk (I.L.)..............	OF	65	255	33	58	15	3	8	44	25	53	10-7	.227	.298	.404	1	.993
	—New York (N.L.)..........	OF	86	263	49	64	10	6	13	38	38	66	3-6	.243	.339	.475	4	.977
1994	—New York (N.L.)..........	OF	45	143	26	34	4	0	3	15	23	45	1-1	.238	.347	.329	2	.970
	—Norfolk (I.L.)..............	OF-DH	85	314	58	75	15	5	14	49	49	82	18-6	.239	.340	.452	4	.979
1995	—Buffalo (A.A.)■..........	OF	128	443	72	126	26	7	19	*85	50	83	13-5	.284	.359	*.503	5	.981
	—Cleveland (A.L.)..........	OF-DH	9	7	4	4	1	0	0	0	0	0	0-0	.571	.571	.714	0	1.000
1996	—Cleveland (A.L.)..........	OF-DH	71	128	30	36	10	0	7	26	25	31	2-1	.281	.406	.523	0	1.000
	—Milwaukee (A.L.)■.....	OF	23	72	8	17	4	0	2	14	8	16	2-0	.236	.321	.375	1	.975
1997	—Milwaukee (A.L.)........	OF	153	494	85	139	37	8	27	85	75	111	20-13	.281	.382	.553	7	.975
1998	—Milwaukee (N.L.)........	OF	161	609	92	160	28	1	38	125	70	158	7-4	.263	.339	.499	9	.972
1999	—Milwaukee (N.L.)........	OF-DH	130	467	87	126	33	2	33	103	91	124	7-3	.270	.402	.561	5	.982
2000	—Milwaukee (N.L.)........	OF-DH	161	564	91	131	29	2	31	98	99	121	6-4	.232	.356	.456	7	.979
2001	—Milwaukee (N.L.)........	OF	154	562	104	141	32	4	34	100	80	150	0-4	.251	.347	.504	6	.981
2002	—New York (N.L.)■......	OF-DH	154	479	65	103	15	0	19	54	58	135	10-7	.215	.311	.365	9	.966
American League totals (3 years)			256	701	127	196	52	8	36	125	108	158	24-14	.280	.382	.531	8	.978
National League totals (7 years)			891	3087	514	759	151	15	171	533	459	799	34-29	.246	.350	.471	42	.976
Major League totals (10 years)			1147	3788	641	955	203	23	207	658	567	957	58-43	.252	.356	.482	50	.977

ALL-STAR GAME RECORD

	AB	R	H	2B	3B	HR	RBI	BB	SO	SB-CS	Avg.	OBP	SLG	E	Avg.
All-Star Game totals (1 year)	2	1	1	1	0	0	0	0	0	0-0	.500	.500	1.000	0	...

BURRELL, PAT OF PHILLIES

PERSONAL: Born October 10, 1976, in Eureka Springs, Ark. ... 6-4/222. ... Bats right, throws right. ... Full name: Patrick B. Burrell. ... Name pronounced BURL.
HIGH SCHOOL: Bellarmine Prep (San Jose, Calif.).
COLLEGE: Miami (Fla.).
TRANSACTIONS/CAREER NOTES: Selected by Boston Red Sox organization in 43rd round of free-agent draft (June 1, 1995); did not sign. ... Selected by Philadelphia Phillies organization in first round (first pick overall) of free-agent draft (June 2, 1998).
STATISTICAL NOTES: Career major league grand slams: 4.
2002 GAMES PLAYED BY POSITION (MLB): OF—157.

			BATTING														FIELDING	
Year	Team (League)	Pos.	G	AB	R	H	2B	3B	HR	RBI	BB	SO	SB-CS	Avg.	OBP	SLG	E	Avg.
1998	—Clearwater (FSL)........	1B	37	132	29	40	7	1	7	30	27	22	2-0	.303	.416	.530	1	.995
1999	—Reading (East.)...........	1B-OF-DH	117	417	84	139	28	6	28	90	79	103	3-1	.333	.438	.631	12	.985
	—Scranton/W.B. (I.L.)...	1B-OF	10	33	4	5	0	0	1	4	4	8	0-1	.152	.263	.242	0	1.000
2000	—Scranton/W.B. (I.L.)...	OF-1B	40	143	31	42	15	1	4	25	32	36	1-1	.294	.420	.497	2	.987
	—Philadelphia (N.L.)......	1B-OF-DH	111	408	57	106	27	1	18	79	63	139	0-0	.260	.359	.463	8	.986
2001	—Philadelphia (N.L.)......	OF-DH	155	539	70	139	29	2	27	89	70	162	2-1	.258	.346	.469	7	.972
2002	—Philadelphia (N.L.)......	OF	157	586	96	165	39	2	37	116	89	153	1-0	.282	.376	.544	6	.979
Major League totals (3 years)			423	1533	223	410	95	5	82	284	222	454	3-1	.267	.361	.496	21	.981

BURROUGHS, SEAN — 3B/2B — PADRES

PERSONAL: Born September 12, 1980, in Atlanta. ... 6-2/200. ... Bats left, throws right. ... Full name: Sean Patrick Burroughs.
HIGH SCHOOL: Wilson (Long Beach, Calif.).
TRANSACTIONS/CAREER NOTES: Selected by San Diego Padres organization in first round (ninth pick overall) of free-agent draft (June 2, 1998). ... On San Diego disabled list (May 29-July 15, 2002); included rehabilitation assignment to Portland (June 28-July 15). ... On Portland disabled list (August 4-11, 2002).
STATISTICAL NOTES: Led Midwest League with seven intentional bases on balls received in 1999.
2002 GAMES PLAYED BY POSITION (MLB): 3B—48; 2B—13.

		BATTING														FIELDING	
Year Team (League)	**Pos.**	**G**	**AB**	**R**	**H**	**2B**	**3B**	**HR**	**RBI**	**BB**	**SO**	**SB-CS**	**Avg.**	**OBP**	**SLG**	**E**	**Avg.**
1999—Fort Wayne (Midw.)....	3B	122	426	65	153	30	3	5	80	74	59	17-15	.359	.464	.479	37	.898
—Rancho Cuca. (Calif.) .	3B	6	23	3	10	3	0	1	5	3	3	0-1	.435	.519	.696	0	1.000
2000—Mobile (Sou.)	3B	108	392	46	114	29	4	2	42	58	45	6-8	.291	.383	.401	16	.947
2001—Portland (PCL)	3B	104	394	60	127	28	1	9	55	37	54	9-2	.322	.386	.467	10	.964
2002—San Diego (N.L.)	3B-2B	63	192	18	52	5	1	1	11	12	30	2-0	.271	.317	.323	8	.949
—Portland (PCL)	2B-3B	50	179	29	54	16	2	2	23	21	16	1-0	.302	.380	.447	6	.969
Major League totals (1 year)		63	192	18	52	5	1	1	11	12	30	2-0	.271	.317	.323	8	.949

BUSH, HOMER — 2B

PERSONAL: Born November 12, 1972, in East St. Louis, Ill. ... 5-10/185. ... Bats right, throws right. ... Full name: Homer Giles Bush.
HIGH SCHOOL: East St. Louis (Ill.).
COLLEGE: Southern Illinois-Edwardsville.
TRANSACTIONS/CAREER NOTES: Selected by San Diego Padres organization in seventh round of free-agent draft (June 3, 1991). ... On Rancho Cucamonga disabled list (April 27-May 4 and May 9-26, 1994). ... On disabled list (May 20, 1996-remainder of season). ... Traded by Padres with rights to P Hideki Irabu, OF Gordon Amerson and player to be named later to New York Yankees for OF Ruben Rivera, P Rafael Medina and cash (April 22, 1997); Yankees acquired OF Vernon Maxwell to complete deal (June 9, 1997). ... Traded by Yankees with P David Wells and P Graeme Lloyd to Toronto Blue Jays for P Roger Clemens (February 18, 1999). ... On Toronto disabled list (April 11-May 14, 1999); included rehabilitation assignment to Dunedin (May 9-14). ... On disabled list (May 22-June 6 and July 31, 2000-remainder of season). ... On Toronto disabled list (April 5-May 18 and June 26-August 1, 2001); included rehabilitation assignments to Dunedin (May 7-18) and Syracuse (July 28-August 1). ... Released by Blue Jays (May 10, 2002). ... Signed by Florida Marlins (May 21, 2002). ... Released by Marlins (September 1, 2002).
2002 GAMES PLAYED BY POSITION (MLB): 2B—34; SS—4; DH—1.

		BATTING														FIELDING	
Year Team (League)	**Pos.**	**G**	**AB**	**R**	**H**	**2B**	**3B**	**HR**	**RBI**	**BB**	**SO**	**SB-CS**	**Avg.**	**OBP**	**SLG**	**E**	**Avg.**
1991—Arizona Padres (Ariz.)	3B	32	127	16	41	3	2	0	16	4	33	11-7	.323	.348	.378	10	.895
1992—Charl., S.C. (S.Atl.).....	2B	108	367	37	86	10	5	0	18	13	85	14-11	.234	.265	.289	*34	.935
1993—Waterloo (Midw.)	2B	130	472	63	*152	19	3	5	51	19	87	39-14	.322	.349	.407	38	.930
1994—Rancho Cuca. (Calif.) .	2B	39	161	37	54	10	3	0	16	9	29	9-2	.335	.383	.435	7	.961
—Wichita (Texas)	2B	59	245	35	73	11	4	3	14	10	39	20-7	.298	.333	.412	8	.967
1995—Memphis (Sou.)	2B-DH	108	432	53	121	12	5	5	37	15	83	34-12	.280	.307	.366	16	.969
1996—Las Vegas (PCL)	2B-DH	32	116	24	42	11	1	2	3	3	33	3-5	.362	.388	.526	5	.969
1997—Las Vegas (PCL)	2B-DH	38	155	25	43	10	1	3	14	7	40	5-1	.277	.310	.413	4	.978
—Columbus (I.L.)■.......	2B	74	275	36	68	10	3	2	26	25	56	12-7	.247	.308	.327	9	.978
—New York (A.L.)..........	2B-DH	10	11	2	4	0	0	0	3	0	0	0-0	.364	.364	.364	2	.913
1998—New York (A.L.)..........	2-DH-3-S	45	71	17	27	3	0	1	5	5	19	6-3	.380	.421	.465	2	.974
1999—Toronto (A.L.)■..........	2B-SS	128	485	69	155	26	4	5	55	21	82	32-8	.320	.353	.421	16	.976
—Dunedin (FSL)............	2B-DH	4	14	3	5	2	0	0	0	1	1	1-0	.357	.438	.500	0	1.000
2000—Toronto (A.L.)............	2B	76	297	38	64	8	0	1	18	18	60	9-4	.215	.271	.253	6	.986
2001—Toronto (A.L.)............	2B	78	271	32	83	11	1	3	27	8	50	13-4	.306	.336	.387	4	.990
—Dunedin (FSL)............	2B	4	17	4	6	0	0	0	2	2	3	1-0	.353	.421	.353	0	1.000
—Syracuse (I.L.)............	2B	9	32	11	8	2	0	0	3	3	6	0-0	.250	.342	.313	0	1.000
2002—Toronto (A.L.)............	2B-DH	23	78	9	18	2	0	1	2	2	12	2-0	.231	.268	.295	1	.990
—Florida (N.L.)■...........	2B-SS	40	54	7	12	0	0	0	5	3	13	2-1	.222	.263	.222	1	.962
American League totals (6 years)		360	1213	167	351	50	5	11	110	54	223	62-19	.289	.328	.366	31	.982
National League totals (1 year)		40	54	7	12	0	0	0	5	3	13	2-1	.222	.263	.222	1	.962
Major League totals (6 years)		400	1267	174	363	50	5	11	115	57	236	64-20	.287	.325	.360	32	.981

DIVISION SERIES RECORD

		BATTING														FIELDING	
Year Team (League)	**Pos.**	**G**	**AB**	**R**	**H**	**2B**	**3B**	**HR**	**RBI**	**BB**	**SO**	**SB-CS**	**Avg.**	**OBP**	**SLG**	**E**	**Avg.**
1998—New York (A.L.)..........	PR-DH	1	0	0	0	0	0	0	0	0	0	1-0	...	...	...	...	...

CHAMPIONSHIP SERIES RECORD

		BATTING														FIELDING	
Year Team (League)	**Pos.**	**G**	**AB**	**R**	**H**	**2B**	**3B**	**HR**	**RBI**	**BB**	**SO**	**SB-CS**	**Avg.**	**OBP**	**SLG**	**E**	**Avg.**
1998—New York (A.L.)..........	PR-DH	2	0	1	0	0	0	0	0	0	0	1-0	...	...	...	...	...

WORLD SERIES RECORD

NOTES: Member of World Series championship team (1998).

		BATTING														FIELDING	
Year Team (League)	**Pos.**	**G**	**AB**	**R**	**H**	**2B**	**3B**	**HR**	**RBI**	**BB**	**SO**	**SB-CS**	**Avg.**	**OBP**	**SLG**	**E**	**Avg.**
1998—New York (A.L.)..........	PR-DH	2	0	0	0	0	0	0	0	0	0	0-0	...	...	...	...	...

BUTLER, BRENT — 2B/SS — ROCKIES

PERSONAL: Born February 11, 1978, in Laurinburg, N.C. ... 6-0/180. ... Bats right, throws right. ... Full name: Justin Brent Butler.
HIGH SCHOOL: Scotland County (Laurinburg, N.C.).
TRANSACTIONS/CAREER NOTES: Selected by St. Louis Cardinals organization in third round of free-agent draft (June 2, 1996). ... On disabled list (June 21-June 28, 1998). ... Traded by Cardinals with P Jose Jimenez, P Manny Aybar and P Rick Croushore to Colorado Rockies for P Darryl Kile, P Dave Veres and P Luther Hackman (November 16, 1999). ... On Colorado Springs disabled list (August 29-September 12, 2000). ... On Colorado Springs disabled list (April 17-28, 2002).
STATISTICAL NOTES: Led Midwest League shortstops with 220 putouts in 1997.
2002 GAMES PLAYED BY POSITION (MLB): 2B—72; 3B—33; SS—13.

			BATTING														FIELDING	
Year	Team (League)	Pos.	G	AB	R	H	2B	3B	HR	RBI	BB	SO	SB-CS	Avg.	OBP	SLG	E	Avg.
1996—	Johnson City (Appl.)	SS	62	248	45	*85	21	1	8	50	25	29	8-1	.343	.404	.532	12	*.945
1997—	Peoria (Midw.)	SS	129	480	81	147	37	2	15	71	63	69	6-4	.306	.388	.485	35	.942
1998—	Prince William (Caro.)	S-3-DH-2	126	475	63	136	27	2	11	76	39	74	3-4	.286	.347	.421	29	.945
1999—	Arkansas (Texas)	SS-3B-2B	•139	528	68	142	21	1	13	54	26	47	0-4	.269	.308	.386	17	.968
2000—	Colo. Springs (PCL)■	2B-SS	122	438	73	128	35	1	8	54	44	46	1-3	.292	.356	.432	16	.971
2001—	Colo. Springs (PCL)	2B-SS-3B	65	272	51	91	20	3	7	38	15	26	4-2	.335	.375	.507	5	.982
—	Colorado (N.L.)	2B-SS-3B	53	119	17	29	7	1	1	14	7	7	1-1	.244	.287	.345	5	.960
2002—	Colorado (N.L.)	2B-3B-SS	113	344	55	89	18	4	9	42	10	40	2-6	.259	.287	.413	9	.975
—	Colo. Springs (PCL)	SS-2B	24	105	20	35	9	1	2	17	6	12	0-0	.333	.375	.495	4	.965
Major League totals (2 years)			166	463	72	118	25	5	10	56	17	47	3-7	.255	.287	.395	14	.972

BYNUM, MIKE — P — PADRES

PERSONAL: Born March 20, 1978, in Tampa, Fla. ... 6-4/200. ... Throws left, bats left. ... Full name: Michael Alan Bynum.
COLLEGE: North Carolina.
TRANSACTIONS/CAREER NOTES: Selected by San Diego Padres organization in first round (19th pick overall) of free-agent draft (June 2, 1999). ... On Mobile disabled list (April 4-May 31 and June 4-17, 2002).
CAREER HITTING (MLB): 0-for-8 (.000), 0 R, 0 2B, 0 3B, 0 HR, 0 RBI.

Year	League	W	L	Pct.	ERA	G	GS	CG	ShO	Sv.-Opp.	IP	H	R	ER	HR	BB-IBB	SO
1999—	Idaho Falls (Pio.)	1	0	1.000	0.00	5	3	0	0	0-...	17.0	7	0	0	0	4-0	21
—	Rancho Cuca. (Calif.)	3	1	.750	3.29	7	7	0	0	0-...	38.1	35	17	14	1	8-0	44
2000—	Rancho Cuca. (Calif.)	9	6	.600	3.00	21	21	0	0	0-...	126.0	101	55	42	4	51-0	129
—	Mobile (Sou.)	3	1	.750	2.91	6	6	0	0	0-...	34.0	31	12	11	2	16-0	27
2001—	Mobile (Sou.)	2	7	.222	5.02	16	15	0	0	0-...	84.1	90	53	47	14	35-0	69
2002—	Mobile (Sou.)	4	0	1.000	0.82	6	5	0	0	0-...	33.0	17	5	3	0	7-0	29
—	Portland (PCL)	3	2	.600	3.51	7	7	0	0	0-...	41.0	36	19	16	6	7-0	35
—	San Diego (N.L.)	1	0	1.000	5.27	14	3	0	0	0-0	27.1	33	16	16	3	15-2	17
Major League totals (1 year)		1	0	1.000	5.27	14	3	0	0	0-0	27.1	33	16	16	3	15-2	17

BYRD, MARLON — OF — PHILLIES

PERSONAL: Born August 30, 1977, in Boynton Beach, Fla. ... 6-0/225. ... Bats right, throws right. ... Full name: Marlon Jerrard Byrd.
HIGH SCHOOL: Sprayberry (Marietta, Ga.).
JUNIOR COLLEGE: Georgia Perimeter.
TRANSACTIONS/CAREER NOTES: Selected by Philadelphia Phillies organization in 10th round of free-agent draft (June 2, 1999).
HONORS: Named Eastern League Most Valuable Player (2001).
STATISTICAL NOTES: Led South Atlantic League with 265 total bases in 2000. ... Led International League with 256 total bases in 2002.
2002 GAMES PLAYED BY POSITION (MLB): OF—10.

			BATTING														FIELDING	
Year	Team (League)	Pos.	G	AB	R	H	2B	3B	HR	RBI	BB	SO	SB-CS	Avg.	OBP	SLG	E	Avg.
1999—	Batavia (NY-Penn)	OF	65	243	40	72	7	6	13	50	28	70	8-2	.296	.376	.535	7	.926
2000—	Piedmont (S.Atl.)	OF	133	515	104	159	29	*13	17	93	51	110	41-5	.309	.379	.515	4	.980
2001—	Reading (East.)	OF	137	510	108	161	22	8	28	89	52	93	32-5	.316	.386	.555	2	*.994
2002—	Scranton/W.B. (I.L.)	OF	136	538	*103	160	37	7	15	63	46	98	15-1	.297	.362	.476	8	.975
—	Philadelphia (N.L.)	OF	10	35	2	8	2	0	1	1	1	8	0-2	.229	.250	.371	0	1.000
Major League totals (1 year)			10	35	2	8	2	0	1	1	1	8	0-2	.229	.250	.371	0	1.000

BYRD, PAUL — P

PERSONAL: Born December 3, 1970, in Louisville, Ky. ... 6-1/185. ... Throws right, bats right. ... Full name: Paul Gregory Byrd.
HIGH SCHOOL: St. Xavier (Louisville, Ky.).
COLLEGE: Louisiana State.
TRANSACTIONS/CAREER NOTES: Selected by Cincinnati Reds organization in 13th round of free-agent draft (June 1, 1988); did not sign. ... Selected by Cleveland Indians organization in fourth round of free-agent draft (June 3, 1991). ... On disabled list (August 12, 1992-remainder of season). ... On disabled list (May 23-July 24, 1993). ... Traded by Indians organization with P Dave Mlicki, P Jerry DiPoto and a player to be named later to New York Mets organization for OF Jeromy Burnitz and P Joe Roa (November 18, 1994); Mets acquired 2B Jesus Azuaje to complete deal (December 6, 1994). ... On Norfolk disabled list (June 1-19, 1995). ... On New York disabled list (March 22-June 9, 1996); included rehabilitation assignment to Norfolk (May 27-June 9). ... Traded by Mets with a player to be named later to Atlanta Braves for P Greg McMichael (November 25, 1996); Braves acquired P Andy Zwirchitz to complete deal (May 25, 1997). ... On Richmond disabled list (June 3-July 2, 1998). ... Claimed on waivers by Philadelphia Phillies (August 14, 1998). ... On Philadelphia disabled list (July 27, 2000-remainder of season). ... Granted free agency (October 12, 2000). ... Re-signed by Phillies organization (January 29, 2001). ... Traded by Phillies to Kansas City Royals for P Jose Santiago (June 5, 2001). ... On Kansas City disabled list (September 22, 2001-remainder of season). ... Granted free agency (December 21, 2001). ... Re-signed by Royals (January 10, 2002). ... Granted free agency (October 28, 2002).
RECORDS: Shares major league single-season record for fewest complete games for leader—7 (2002).

STATISTICAL NOTES: Led Carolina League with seven balks in 1991. ... Led N.L. with 17 hit batsmen in 1999.
MISCELLANEOUS: Appeared in one game as pinch runner (2001).
CAREER HITTING (MLB): 16-for-111 (.144), 9 R, 0 2B, 0 3B, 0 HR, 6 RBI.

Year League	W	L	Pct.	ERA	G	GS	CG	ShO	Sv.-Opp.	IP	H	R	ER	HR	BB-IBB	SO
1991—Kinston (Caro.)	4	3	.571	3.16	14	11	0	0	0-...	62.2	40	27	22	7	36-0	62
1992—Canton/Akron (East.)	14	6	.700	3.01	24	24	4	0	0-...	152.1	122	68	51	4	75-2	118
1993—Charlotte (I.L.)	7	4	.636	3.89	14	14	1	1	0-...	81.0	80	43	35	9	30-0	54
—Canton/Akron (East.)	0	0	...	3.60	2	1	0	0	0-...	10.0	7	4	4	1	3-0	8
1994—Canton/Akron (East.)	5	9	.357	3.81	21	20	4	1	0-...	139.1	135	70	59	10	52-3	106
—Charlotte (I.L.)	2	2	.500	3.93	9	4	0	0	1-...	36.2	33	19	16	5	11-1	15
1995—Norfolk (I.L.)■	3	5	.375	2.79	22	10	1	0	6-...	87.0	71	29	27	6	21-0	61
—New York (N.L.)	2	0	1.000	2.05	17	0	0	0	0-0	22.0	18	6	5	1	7-1	26
1996—Norfolk (I.L.)	2	0	1.000	3.52	5	0	0	0	1-...	7.2	4	3	3	0	4-1	8
—New York (N.L.)	1	2	.333	4.24	38	0	0	0	0-2	46.2	48	22	22	7	21-4	31
1997—Atlanta (N.L.)■	4	4	.500	5.26	31	4	0	0	0-0	53.0	47	34	31	6	28-4	37
—Richmond (I.L.)	2	1	.667	3.18	3	3	0	0	0-...	17.0	14	6	6	2	1-0	14
1998—Richmond (I.L.)	5	5	.500	3.69	17	17	2	0	0-...	102.1	92	44	42	9	36-2	84
—Atlanta (N.L.)	0	0	...	13.50	1	0	0	0	0-0	2.0	4	3	3	0	1-0	1
—Philadelphia (N.L.)■	5	2	.714	2.29	8	8	2	1	0-0	55.0	41	16	14	6	17-1	38
1999—Philadelphia (N.L.)	15	11	.577	4.60	32	32	1	0	0-0	199.2	205	119	102	34	70-2	106
2000—Philadelphia (N.L.)	2	9	.182	6.51	17	15	0	0	0-0	83.0	89	67	60	17	35-2	53
—Scranton/W.B. (I.L.)	2	0	1.000	1.73	3	3	2	0	0-...	26.0	20	6	5	2	6-0	10
2001—Clearwater (FSL)	0	3	.000	3.42	4	4	0	0	0-...	23.2	24	10	9	1	5-0	17
—Scranton/W.B. (I.L.)	1	3	.250	3.65	5	5	0	0	0-...	37.0	34	18	15	4	7-0	35
—Philadelphia (N.L.)	0	1	.000	8.10	3	1	0	0	0-0	10.0	10	9	9	1	4-0	3
—Kansas City (A.L.)■	6	6	.500	4.05	16	15	1	0	0-0	93.1	110	45	42	11	22-1	49
2002—Kansas City (A.L.)	17	11	.607	3.90	33	33	*7	2	0-0	228.1	224	111	99	36	38-1	129
A.L. totals (2 years)	23	17	.575	3.95	49	48	8	2	0-0	321.2	334	156	141	47	60-2	178
N.L. totals (7 years)	29	29	.500	4.70	147	60	3	1	0-2	471.1	462	276	246	72	183-14	295
Major League totals (8 years)	52	46	.531	4.39	196	108	11	3	0-2	793.0	796	432	387	119	243-16	473

ALL-STAR GAME RECORD

	W	L	Pct.	ERA	GS	CG	ShO	Sv.-Opp.	IP	H	R	ER	HR	BB-IBB	SO
All-Star Game totals (1 years)	1999—Selected, did not play.														

BYRNES, ERIC — OF — ATHLETICS

PERSONAL: Born February 16, 1976, in Redwood City, Calif. ... 6-2/210. ... Bats right, throws right. ... Full name: Eric James Byrnes.
HIGH SCHOOL: St. Francis (Mountain View, Calif.).
COLLEGE: UCLA.
TRANSACTIONS/CAREER NOTES: Selected by Oakland Athletics organization in eighth round of free-agent draft (June 2, 1998).
STATISTICAL NOTES: Led Pacific Coast League outfielders with five double plays in 2001.
2002 GAMES PLAYED BY POSITION (MLB): OF—79; DH—7.

					BATTING											FIELDING	
Year Team (League)	Pos.	G	AB	R	H	2B	3B	HR	RBI	BB	SO	SB-CS	Avg.	OBP	SLG	E	Avg.
1998—S. Oregon (N'West)	OF	42	169	36	53	10	2	7	31	16	16	6-1	.314	.378	.521	1	.986
—Visalia (Calif.)	OF	29	108	26	46	9	2	4	21	18	15	11-1	.426	.504	.657	3	.952
1999—Modesto (Calif.)	OF	96	365	86	123	28	1	6	66	58	37	28-8	.337	.433	.468	6	.960
—Midland (Texas)	OF	43	164	25	39	14	0	1	22	17	32	6-3	.238	.316	.341	5	.923
2000—Midland (Texas)	OF	67	259	49	78	25	2	5	37	43	38	21-11	.301	.395	.471	2	.983
—Sacramento (PCL)	OF	67	243	55	81	23	1	9	47	31	30	12-5	.333	.410	.547	2	.980
—Oakland (A.L.)	OF-DH	10	10	5	3	0	0	0	0	0	1	2-1	.300	.364	.300	0	1.000
2001—Sacramento (PCL)	OF	100	415	81	120	23	2	20	51	33	66	25-3	.289	.343	.499	5	.973
—Oakland (A.L.)	OF-DH	19	38	9	9	1	0	3	5	4	6	1-0	.237	.326	.500	1	.933
2002—Sacramento (PCL)	OF	31	119	16	31	7	0	4	16	7	15	5-1	.261	.302	.420	2	.971
—Oakland (A.L.)	OF-DH	90	94	24	23	4	2	3	11	4	17	3-0	.245	.291	.426	1	.982
Major League totals (3 years)		119	142	38	35	5	2	6	16	8	24	6-1	.246	.306	.437	2	.973

DIVISION SERIES RECORD

					BATTING											FIELDING	
Year Team (League)	Pos.	G	AB	R	H	2B	3B	HR	RBI	BB	SO	SB-CS	Avg.	OBP	SLG	E	Avg.
2001—Oakland (A.L.)	PH	2	2	0	0	0	0	0	0	0	1	0-0	.000	.000	.000	...	...
2002—Oakland (A.L.)	OF	2	1	0	0	0	0	0	0	0	1	0-0	.000	.000	.000	0	1.000
Division series totals (2 years)		4	3	0	0	0	0	0	0	0	2	0-0	.000	.000	.000	0	1.000

CABRERA, JOLBERT — IF/OF — DODGERS

PERSONAL: Born December 8, 1972, in Cartagena, Colombia. ... 6-1/190. ... Bats right, throws right. ... Full name: Jolbert Alexis Cabrera. ... Brother of Orlando Cabrera, shortstop, Montreal Expos.
HIGH SCHOOL: Confenalco (Cartagena, Colombia).
TRANSACTIONS/CAREER NOTES: Signed as non-drafted free agent by Montreal Expos organization (July 3, 1990). ... Loaned by Expos organization to San Bernardino, California League (July 27-September 1, 1994). ... Granted free agency (October 17, 1997). ... Signed by Cleveland Indians organization (January 19, 1998). ... On Cleveland disabled list (March 28-May 2, 2002); included rehabilitation assignment to Buffalo (April 25-May 2). ... Traded by Indians to Los Angeles Dodgers for P Lance Caraccioli (July 22, 2002).
STATISTICAL NOTES: Tied for Midwest League lead with 173 putouts by shortstop in 1993. ... Tied for International League lead in caught stealing with 15 in 1998.
2002 GAMES PLAYED BY POSITION (MLB): OF—38; 2B—4; 3B—3; DH—1.

Year	Team (League)	Pos.	G	AB	R	H	2B	3B	HR	RBI	BB	SO	SB-CS	Avg.	OBP	SLG	E	Avg.
			BATTING														FIELDING	
1990—	Dom. Expos (DSL)	SS	29	115	31	36	3	2	0	12	14	10	14-...	.313	...	.374	...	...
1991—	Sumter (S.Atl.)	SS	101	324	33	66	4	0	1	20	19	62	10-11	.204	.255	.225	28	.934
1992—	Albany (S.Atl.)	SS	118	377	44	86	9	2	0	23	34	77	22-11	.228	.294	.263	35	.927
1993—	Burlington (Midw.)	SS	128	507	62	129	24	2	0	38	39	93	31-11	.254	.314	.310	*36	.929
1994—	W. Palm Beach (FSL)	SS	83	266	32	54	4	0	0	13	14	48	7-10	.203	.264	.218	26	.933
—	San Bern. (Calif.)■	SS	30	109	14	27	5	1	0	11	14	24	2-2	.248	.328	.312	7	.950
—	Harrisburg (East.)■	SS	3	2	0	0	0	0	0	0	0	1	0-0	.000	.000	.000	0	1.000
1995—	W. Palm Beach (FSL)	SS-2B-3B	103	357	62	102	23	2	1	25	38	61	19-12	.286	.364	.370	29	.938
—	Harrisburg (East.)	SS	9	35	4	10	2	0	0	1	1	3	3-1	.286	.306	.343	2	.935
1996—	Harrisburg (East.)	SS-OF-3B	107	354	40	85	18	2	3	29	23	63	10-5	.240	.285	.328	25	.951
1997—	Harrisburg (East.)	2B-SS-OF	48	171	28	43	9	0	2	11	28	28	5-4	.251	.360	.339	9	.951
—	Ottawa (I.L.)	3B-2B-SS-OF	68	191	28	54	10	4	0	12	11	31	15-5	.283	.320	.377	7	.962
1998—	Cleveland (A.L.)■	SS	1	2	0	0	0	0	0	0	0	1	0-0	.000	.000	.000	0	1.000
—	Buffalo (I.L.)	SS-OF-2B	129	494	94	157	24	1	10	45	68	71	25-15	.318	.412	.431	27	.956
1999—	Cleveland (A.L.)	OF-2B-DH	30	37	6	7	1	0	0	0	1	8	3-0	.189	.231	.216	1	.968
—	Buffalo (I.L.)	OF-SS-2B-3B	71	279	44	74	13	4	0	27	26	43	20-4	.265	.327	.341	6	.975
2000—	Buffalo (I.L.)	OF-SS-2B	20	74	18	25	6	1	3	11	5	8	2-1	.338	.383	.568	0	1.000
—	Cleveland (A.L.)	O-2-S-D	100	175	27	44	3	1	2	15	8	15	6-4	.251	.290	.314	1	.993
2001—	Cleveland (A.L.)	O-2-3-S-DH	141	287	50	75	16	3	1	38	16	41	10-4	.261	.312	.348	6	.973
2002—	Buffalo (I.L.)	O-S-1-3-2	23	91	16	26	5	0	0	7	9	10	4-2	.286	.353	.341	0	1.000
—	Cleveland (A.L.)	OF-2B-DH	38	72	5	8	1	0	0	7	5	13	1-1	.111	.177	.125	0	1.000
—	Las Vegas (PCL)■	OF-3B-SS-2B	27	102	22	35	8	1	2	11	14	18	2-3	.343	.417	.500	2	.969
—	Los Angeles (N.L.)	OF-3B-2B	10	12	3	4	1	0	0	1	2	2	0-0	.333	.429	.417	0	1.000
American League totals (5 years)			310	573	88	134	21	4	3	60	30	78	20-9	.234	.282	.300	8	.983
National League totals (1 year)			10	12	3	4	1	0	0	1	2	2	0-0	.333	.429	.417	0	1.000
Major League totals (5 years)			320	585	91	138	22	4	3	61	32	80	20-9	.236	.285	.303	8	.983

DIVISION SERIES RECORD

Year	Team (League)	Pos.	G	AB	R	H	2B	3B	HR	RBI	BB	SO	SB-CS	Avg.	OBP	SLG	E	Avg.
			BATTING														FIELDING	
2001—	Cleveland (A.L.)	OF-PH	2	1	1	1	0	0	0	1	0	0	0-0	1.000	1.000	1.000	0	...

CABRERA, JOSE — P — BREWERS

PERSONAL: Born March 24, 1969, in Santiago, Dominican Republic. ... 6-0/180. ... Throws right, bats right. ... Full name: Jose Alberto Cabrera.

TRANSACTIONS/CAREER NOTES: Signed as non-drafted free agent by Cleveland Indians organization (October 12, 1990). ... On disabled list (May 11-28, 1993). ... On disabled list (April 25-May 24, 1995). ... Loaned by Indians organization to Bakersfield, California League (April 4-May 9, 1996). ... On Buffalo disabled list (April 4-13 and 17-25, 1997). ... Traded by Indians to Houston Astros for P Alvin Morman (May 10, 1997). ... On Houston disabled list (April 5, 1998-remainder of season); included rehabilitation assignment to New Orleans (July 4-20). ... Claimed on waivers by Atlanta Braves (April 12, 2001). ... Traded by Braves with C Paul Bako to Milwaukee Brewers for C Henry Blanco (March 20, 2002).

RECORDS: Shares N.L. single-inning record for most consecutive home runs allowed—3 (May 23, 2002, ninth inning).

CAREER HITTING (MLB): 2-for-23 (.087), 1 R, 0 2B, 0 3B, 0 HR, 0 RBI.

Year	League	W	L	Pct.	ERA	G	GS	CG	ShO	Sv.-Opp.	IP	H	R	ER	HR	BB-IBB	SO
1991—	Dominican Indians (DSL)	6	4	.600	3.07	16	12	1	0	0-...	73.1	64	32	25	...	17-...	40
1992—	Burlington (Appl.)	•8	3	.727	1.75	13	13	1	0	0-...	92.1	74	27	18	6	18-0	79
1993—	Columbus (S.Atl.)	11	6	.647	2.67	26	26	1	0	0-...	155.1	122	54	46	8	53-2	105
1994—	Kinston (Caro.)	4	13	.235	4.44	24	24	0	0	0-...	133.2	134	84	66	15	43-0	110
1995—	Canton/Akron (East.)	1	1	.500	1.02	4	3	0	0	0-...	17.2	7	2	2	7	8-1	19
1996—	Bakersfield (Calif.)■	2	2	.500	3.95	7	7	0	0	0-...	41.0	40	25	18	7	21-0	52
—	Kinston (Caro.)■	1	1	.500	1.00	4	3	0	0	0-...	18.0	7	2	2	0	8-0	19
—	Canton/Akron (East.)	4	3	.571	5.63	15	7	0	0	0-...	62.1	78	45	39	10	17-2	40
1997—	Buffalo (A.A.)	3	0	1.000	1.20	5	0	0	0	0-...	15.0	8	2	2	2	7-1	11
—	New Orleans (A.A.)■	2	2	.500	2.54	31	0	0	0	0-...	46.0	31	13	13	2	13-3	48
—	Houston (N.L.)	0	0	...	1.17	12	0	0	0	0-1	15.1	6	2	2	1	6-0	18
1998—	Houston (N.L.)	0	0	...	8.31	3	0	0	0	0-0	4.1	7	4	4	0	1-1	1
—	New Orleans (PCL)	0	0	...	5.40	5	0	0	0	1-...	5.0	2	3	3	2	1-0	6
1999—	New Orleans (PCL)	3	1	.750	2.82	31	0	0	0	7-...	51.0	34	18	16	3	12-3	41
—	Houston (N.L.)	4	0	1.000	2.15	26	0	0	0	0-1	29.1	21	7	7	3	9-2	28
2000—	Houston (N.L.)	2	3	.400	5.92	52	0	0	0	2-3	59.1	74	40	39	10	17-2	41
—	New Orleans (PCL)	0	1	.000	2.93	12	0	0	0	4-...	15.1	15	6	5	0	5-2	12
2001—	Atlanta (N.L.)■	7	4	.636	2.88	55	0	0	0	2-8	59.1	52	24	19	5	25-4	43
2002—	Milwaukee (N.L.)■	6	10	.375	6.79	50	11	0	0	0-1	103.1	131	84	78	23	36-9	61
Major League totals (6 years)		19	17	.528	4.95	198	11	0	0	4-14	271.0	291	161	149	42	94-18	192

DIVISION SERIES RECORD

Year	League	W	L	Pct.	ERA	G	GS	CG	ShO	Sv.-Opp.	IP	H	R	ER	HR	BB-IBB	SO
1999—	Houston (N.L.)	0	0	...	0.00	1	0	0	0	0-0	2.0	2	0	0	0	0-0	6

CABRERA, ORLANDO — SS — EXPOS

PERSONAL: Born November 2, 1974, in Cartagena, Columbia. ... 5-10/185. ... Bats right, throws right. ... Full name: Orlando Luis Cabrera. ... Brother of Jolbert Cabrera, infielder/outfielder, Cleveland Indians.

TRANSACTIONS/CAREER NOTES: Signed as non-drafted free agent by Montreal Expos organization (June 1, 1993). ... On disabled list (August 9, 1999-remainder of season). ... On Montreal disabled list (July 15-August 15, 2000); included rehabilitation assignment to Ottawa (August 12-15).

HONORS: Won N.L. Gold Glove at shortstop (2001).

2002 GAMES PLAYED BY POSITION (MLB): SS—153.

Year	Team (League)	Pos.	G	AB	R	H	2B	3B	HR	RBI	BB	SO	SB-CS	Avg.	OBP	SLG	E	Avg.
			BATTING														FIELDING	
1993—	Dom. Expos (DSL)	IF	38	122	24	42	6	1	1	17	18	11	14-...	.344	...	.434	3	.982
1994—	GC Expos (GCL)	2B-SS-OF	22	73	13	23	4	1	0	11	5	8	6-0	.315	.359	.397	4	.941
1995—	Vermont (NY-Penn)	2B-SS	65	248	37	70	12	5	3	33	16	28	15-8	.282	.323	.407	17	.950
—	W. Palm Beach (FSL)	SS	3	5	0	1	0	0	0	0	0	1	0-0	.200	.200	.200	1	.833
1996—	Delmarva (S.Atl.)	SS-2B	134	512	86	129	28	4	14	65	54	63	51-18	.252	.327	.404	27	.953
1997—	W. Palm Beach (FSL)	SS-DH-2B	69	279	56	77	19	2	5	26	27	33	32-12	.276	.340	.412	20	.927
—	Harrisburg (East.)	SS-2B	35	133	34	41	13	2	5	20	15	18	7-2	.308	.378	.549	5	.966
—	Ottawa (I.L.)	SS-2B	31	122	17	32	5	2	2	14	7	16	8-1	.262	.306	.385	3	.979
—	Montreal (N.L.)	SS-2B	16	18	4	4	0	0	0	2	1	3	1-2	.222	.263	.222	1	.963
1998—	Ottawa (I.L.)	SS-2B	66	272	31	63	9	4	0	26	28	27	19-9	.232	.298	.294	12	.963
—	Montreal (N.L.)	SS-2B	79	261	44	73	16	5	3	22	18	27	6-2	.280	.325	.414	7	.978
1999—	Montreal (N.L.)	SS	104	382	48	97	23	5	8	39	18	38	2-2	.254	.293	.403	10	.979
2000—	Montreal (N.L.)	SS-2B	125	422	47	100	25	1	13	55	25	28	4-4	.237	.279	.393	10	.981
—	Ottawa (I.L.)	SS	2	6	1	4	0	0	0	0	1	0	1-0	.667	.750	.667	0	1.000
2001—	Montreal (N.L.)	SS	•162	626	64	173	41	6	14	96	43	54	19-7	.276	.324	.428	11	.986
2002—	Montreal (N.L.)	SS	153	563	64	148	43	1	7	56	48	53	25-7	.263	.321	.380	*29	.962
Major League totals (6 years)			639	2272	271	595	148	18	45	270	153	203	57-24	.262	.309	.402	68	.976

CAIRO, MIGUEL — 2B — CARDINALS

PERSONAL: Born May 4, 1974, in Anaco, Venezuela. ... 6-1/200. ... Bats right, throws right. ... Full name: Miguel Jesus Cairo. ... Name pronounced KI-ro.

HIGH SCHOOL: Escuela Anaco (Anaco, Venezuela).

TRANSACTIONS/CAREER NOTES: Signed as non-drafted free agent by Los Angeles Dodgers organization (September 20, 1990). ... Traded by Dodgers with 3B Willis Otanez to Seattle Mariners for 3B Mike Blowers (November 29, 1995). ... Traded by Mariners with P Bill Risley to Toronto Blue Jays for P Edwin Hurtado and P Paul Menhart (December 18, 1995). ... Traded by Blue Jays to Chicago Cubs for P Jason Stevenson (November 20, 1996). ... Selected by Tampa Bay Devil Rays in first round (eighth pick overall) of expansion draft (November 18, 1997). ... On Tampa Bay disabled list (April 24-May 17 and July 26-August 11, 1999); included rehabilitation assignments to Orlando (May 14-17) and St. Petersburg (August 7-11). ... Released by Devil Rays (November 27, 2000). ... Signed by Oakland Athletics organization (January 7, 2001). ... Traded by A's to Chicago Cubs for 3B/1B Eric Hinske (March 28, 2001). ... Claimed on waivers by St. Louis Cardinals (August 10, 2001).

STATISTICAL NOTES: Led California League in caught stealing with 23 in 1994. ... Led International League second basemen with 64 double plays in 1996. ... Tied for American Association lead in caught stealing with 15 in 1997.

MISCELLANEOUS: Holds Tampa Bay Devil Rays all-time record for most stolen bases (69).

2002 GAMES PLAYED BY POSITION (MLB): OF—24; 2B—18; 3B—7; SS—6; 1B—4; DH—3.

Year	Team (League)	Pos.	G	AB	R	H	2B	3B	HR	RBI	BB	SO	SB-CS	Avg.	OBP	SLG	E	Avg.
			BATTING														FIELDING	
1991—	Dom. Dodgers (DSL)	IF	57	203	16	45	5	1	0	17	0	17	8-...	.222	...	.256	...	...
1992—	GC Dodgers (GCL)	SS-3B	21	76	10	23	5	2	0	9	2	6	1-0	.303	.333	.421	4	.953
—	Vero Beach (FSL)	2B-3B	36	125	7	28	0	0	0	7	11	12	5-3	.224	.285	.224	10	.935
1993—	Vero Beach (FSL)	2B-SS-3B	90	346	50	109	10	1	1	23	28	22	23-16	.315	.378	.358	18	.959
1994—	Bakersfield (Calif.)	2B-SS	133	533	76	155	23	4	2	48	34	37	44-23	.291	.338	.360	28	.958
1995—	San Antonio (Texas)	2B-SS-DH	107	435	53	121	20	1	1	41	26	31	33-16	.278	.323	.336	23	.958
1996—	Syracuse (I.L.)■	2B-3B-SS	120	465	71	129	14	4	3	48	26	44	27-9	.277	.323	.344	23	.955
—	Toronto (A.L.)	2B	9	27	5	6	2	0	0	1	2	9	0-0	.222	.300	.296	0	1.000
1997—	Iowa (A.A.)■	2B-SS	135	*569	82	159	35	4	5	46	24	54	*40-15	.279	.314	.381	20	.969
—	Chicago (N.L.)	2B-SS	16	29	7	7	1	0	0	1	2	3	0-0	.241	.313	.276	0	1.000
1998—	Tampa Bay (A.L.)■	2B-DH	150	515	49	138	26	5	5	46	24	44	19-8	.268	.307	.367	16	.978
1999—	Tampa Bay (A.L.)	2B-DH	120	465	61	137	15	5	3	36	24	46	22-7	.295	.335	.368	9	.986
—	Orlando (Sou.)	2B	3	13	1	5	2	0	0	1	0	1	0-1	.385	.385	.538	0	1.000
—	St. Petersburg (FSL)	2B	3	13	2	5	0	0	0	0	1	2	1-1	.385	.429	.385	1	.958
2000—	Tampa Bay (A.L.)	2B-DH	119	375	49	98	18	2	1	34	29	34	28-7	.261	.314	.328	9	.983
2001—	Iowa (PCL)■	2B-SS-3B	34	123	22	37	7	1	3	14	8	11	3-4	.301	.348	.447	3	.978
—	Chicago (N.L.)	3B-2B-SS	66	123	20	35	3	1	2	9	16	21	2-1	.285	.364	.374	7	.917
—	St. Louis (N.L.)■	O-2-3-1-S	27	33	5	11	5	0	1	7	2	2	0-0	.333	.371	.576	1	.929
2002—	St. Louis (N.L.)	OF-IF-DH	108	184	28	46	9	2	2	23	13	36	1-1	.250	.307	.353	4	.963
American League totals (4 years)			398	1382	164	379	61	12	9	117	79	133	69-22	.274	.318	.355	34	.982
National League totals (3 years)			217	369	60	99	18	3	5	40	33	62	3-2	.268	.333	.374	12	.950
Major League totals (7 years)			615	1751	224	478	79	15	14	157	112	195	72-24	.273	.321	.359	46	.979

DIVISION SERIES RECORD

Year	Team (League)	Pos.	G	AB	R	H	2B	3B	HR	RBI	BB	SO	SB-CS	Avg.	OBP	SLG	E	Avg.
			BATTING														FIELDING	
2001—	St. Louis (N.L.)	PH-OF	3	5	0	1	0	0	0	0	0	1	1-0	.200	.200	.200	0	1.000
2002—	St. Louis (N.L.)	3B	2	4	2	4	1	0	0	3	0	0	0-1	1.000	1.000	1.250	0	1.000
Division series totals (2 years)			5	9	2	5	1	0	0	3	0	1	1-1	.556	.600	.667	0	1.000

CHAMPIONSHIP SERIES RECORD

Year	Team (League)	Pos.	G	AB	R	H	2B	3B	HR	RBI	BB	SO	SB-CS	Avg.	OBP	SLG	E	Avg.
			BATTING														FIELDING	
2002—	St. Louis (N.L.)	3B	3	13	2	5	0	0	1	2	0	2	0-0	.385	.385	.615	0	1.000

CALLAWAY, MICKEY — P — ANGELS

PERSONAL: Born May 13, 1975, in Memphis, Tenn. ... 6-2/200. ... Throws right, bats right. ... Full name: Michael Christopher Callaway.

HIGH SCHOOL: Germantown (Tenn.).

COLLEGE: Mississippi.

TRANSACTIONS/CAREER NOTES: Selected by Tampa Bay Devil Rays organization in seventh round of free-agent draft (June 4, 1996). ... Loaned by Devil Rays to Orlando, Seattle Mariners organization (April 2-July 21, 1998). ... On Tampa Bay disabled list (June 19-July 6, 1999). ... On disabled list (May 22-June 5, 2000). ... Traded by Devil Rays to Anaheim Angels for SS/2B Wilmy Caceres (December 17, 2001). ... On Salt Lake disabled list (May 25-June 11 and June 15-July 28, 2002).
STATISTICAL NOTES: Tied for Florida State League lead with seven balks in 1997.
MISCELLANEOUS: Appeared in one game as pinch runner (1999).
CAREER HITTING (MLB): 2-for-3 (.667), 0 R, 0 2B, 0 3B, 0 HR, 1 RBI.

Year League	W	L	Pct.	ERA	G	GS	CG	ShO	Sv.-Opp.	IP	H	R	ER	HR	BB-IBB	SO
1996—Butte (Pio.)	6	2	.750	3.71	16	11	0	0	0-...	63.0	70	37	26	5	25-0	57
1997—St. Petersburg (FSL)	11	7	.611	3.22	28	•28	3	0	0-...	170.2	162	74	61	9	39-0	109
1998—Orlando (Sou.)■	5	6	.455	4.42	18	17	0	0	0-...	89.2	103	56	44	8	44-0	57
—Durham (I.L.)■	5	3	.625	4.53	9	8	0	0	0-...	47.2	49	27	24	6	17-0	19
1999—Orlando (Sou.)	1	1	.500	4.50	2	2	0	0	0-...	10.0	15	6	5	1	2-0	7
—Durham (I.L.)	7	1	.875	4.20	15	15	0	0	0-...	81.1	86	45	38	5	28-0	56
—Tampa Bay (A.L.)	1	2	.333	7.45	5	4	0	0	0-0	19.1	30	20	16	2	14-1	11
2000—Durham (I.L.)	11	6	.647	5.29	26	20	0	0	0-...	117.1	151	88	69	11	50-2	64
2001—Durham (I.L.)	11	7	.611	3.07	29	21	2	1	0-...	129.0	131	50	44	9	24-0	81
—Tampa Bay (A.L.)	0	0	...	7.20	2	0	0	0	0-0	5.0	3	4	4	2	2-0	2
2002—Salt Lake (PCL)■	9	2	.818	1.68	17	14	1	0	0-...	91.1	79	26	17	7	22-0	75
—Anaheim (A.L.)	2	1	.667	4.19	6	6	0	0	0-0	34.1	31	20	16	4	11-0	23
Major League totals (3 years)	3	3	.500	5.52	13	10	0	0	0-0	58.2	64	44	36	8	27-1	36

CALLOWAY, RON OF EXPOS

PERSONAL: Born September 4, 1976, in San Jose, Calif. ... 6-0/190. ... Bats left, throws left. ... Full name: Ronald Isiah Calloway.
HIGH SCHOOL: James Lick (San Jose, Calif.).
JUNIOR COLLEGE: Canada (Calif.).
TRANSACTIONS/CAREER NOTES: Selected by Arizona Diamondbacks organization in eighth round of free-agent draft (June 3, 1997). ... Traded by Diamondbacks to Montreal Expos (July 5, 1999), completing deal in which Expos traded C John Pachot to Diamondbacks for future considerations (May 21, 1999).
STATISTICAL NOTES: Led International League outfielders with five double plays in 2002.

		BATTING													FIELDING	
Year Team (League)	Pos.	G	AB	R	H	2B	3B	HR	RBI	BB	SO	SB-CS	Avg.	OBP	SLG	E	Avg.
1997—Lethbridge (Pio.)	OF	43	148	23	37	5	0	0	9	14	29	5-8	.250	.323	.284	3	.954
—South Bend (Midw.)	OF	9	25	3	7	1	0	0	1	2	8	1-0	.280	.333	.320	2	.846
1998—South Bend (Midw.)	OF	69	251	29	66	12	2	3	33	25	50	6-5	.263	.331	.363	6	.944
—High Desert (Calif.)	OF	44	156	30	44	8	2	3	27	12	38	2-4	.282	.337	.417	4	.946
1999—High Desert (Calif.)	OF	60	196	41	62	14	1	3	23	30	34	22-7	.316	.412	.444	3	.962
—El Paso (Texas)	OF	11	32	4	7	0	0	0	1	7	7	1-2	.219	.359	.219	0	1.000
—Jupiter (FSL)■	OF	54	211	30	57	8	4	3	25	15	45	5-6	.270	.325	.389	0	1.000
2000—Jupiter (FSL)	OF	135	530	78	147	24	6	6	65	55	89	34-14	.277	.346	.379	2	.994
2001—Harrisburg (East.)	OF	74	279	48	92	22	4	9	47	24	46	25-7	.330	.385	.534	4	.969
—Ottawa (I.L.)	OF	61	239	27	63	12	0	10	35	16	64	11-1	.264	.323	.439	5	.959
2002—Ottawa (I.L.)	OF	128	447	72	118	21	5	14	60	44	89	16-12	.264	.335	.427	3	.988

CAMERON, MIKE OF MARINERS

PERSONAL: Born January 8, 1973, in La Grange, Ga. ... 6-2/195. ... Bats right, throws right. ... Full name: Michael Terrance Cameron.
HIGH SCHOOL: La Grange (Ga.).
TRANSACTIONS/CAREER NOTES: Selected by Chicago White Sox organization in 18th round of free-agent draft (June 3, 1991). ... Traded by White Sox to Cincinnati Reds for 1B/3B Paul Konerko (November 11, 1998). ... Traded by Reds with P Brett Tomko, IF Antonio Perez and P Jake Meyer to Seattle Mariners for OF Ken Griffey Jr. (February 10, 2000).
RECORDS: Shares major league single-game records for most home runs in one game—4 (May 2, 2002); most consecutive home runs hit in one game—4 (May 2, 2002); and for most home runs in one inning—2 (May 2, 2002, first inning). ... Shares major league single-season record for fewest double plays by outfielder (150 or more games)—0 (2002).
HONORS: Won A.L. Gold Glove as outfielder (2001).
STATISTICAL NOTES: Tied for Carolina League lead in double plays by outfielder with four in 1994. ... Tied for Southern League lead with 15 caught stealing in 1996. ... Led Southern League outfielders with 249 putouts and 264 total chances in 1996. ... Hit four home runs in one game (May 2, 2002). ... Career major league grand slams: 3.
2002 GAMES PLAYED BY POSITION (MLB): OF—155; DH—1.

		BATTING													FIELDING	
Year Team (League)	Pos.	G	AB	R	H	2B	3B	HR	RBI	BB	SO	SB-CS	Avg.	OBP	SLG	E	Avg.
1991—GC White Sox (GCL)	OF	44	136	20	30	3	0	0	11	17	29	13-2	.221	.325	.243	3	.951
1992—Utica (NY-Penn)	OF	26	87	15	24	1	4	2	12	11	26	3-7	.276	.354	.448	0	1.000
—South Bend (Midw.)	OF	35	114	19	26	8	1	1	9	10	37	2-3	.228	.310	.342	3	.957
1993—South Bend (Midw.)	OF	122	411	52	98	14	5	0	30	27	101	19-10	.238	.292	.297	4	.985
1994—Prince William (Caro.)	OF	131	468	86	116	15	*17	6	48	60	101	22-10	.248	.343	.391	6	.979
1995—Birmingham (Sou.)	OF	107	350	64	87	20	5	11	60	54	104	21-12	.249	.355	.429	4	.985
—Chicago (A.L.)	OF	28	38	4	7	2	0	1	2	3	15	0-0	.184	.244	.316	0	1.000
1996—Birmingham (Sou.)	OF-DH	123	473	*120	142	34	12	28	77	71	117	*39-15	.300	.402	*.600	7	.973
—Chicago (A.L.)	OF-DH	11	11	1	1	0	0	0	0	1	3	0-1	.091	.167	.091	0	1.000
1997—Nashville (A.A.)	OF-DH	30	120	21	33	7	3	6	17	18	31	4-2	.275	.378	.533	1	.985
—Chicago (A.L.)	OF-DH	116	379	63	98	18	3	14	55	55	105	23-2	.259	.356	.433	5	.985
1998—Chicago (A.L.)	OF	141	396	53	83	16	5	8	43	37	101	27-11	.210	.285	.336	4	.988
1999—Cincinnati (N.L.)■	OF	146	542	93	139	34	9	21	66	80	145	38-12	.256	.357	.469	8	.979
2000—Seattle (A.L.)■	OF	155	543	96	145	28	4	19	78	78	133	24-7	.267	.365	.438	6	.985
2001—Seattle (A.L.)	OF-DH	150	540	99	144	30	5	25	110	69	155	34-5	.267	.353	.480	6	.986
2002—Seattle (A.L.)	OF-DH	158	545	84	130	26	5	25	80	79	*176	31-8	.239	.340	.442	5	.988
American League totals (7 years)		759	2452	400	608	120	22	92	368	322	688	139-34	.248	.340	.427	26	.987
National League totals (1 year)		146	542	93	139	34	9	21	66	80	145	38-12	.256	.357	.469	8	.979
Major League totals (8 years)		905	2994	493	747	154	31	113	434	402	833	177-46	.249	.343	.435	34	.986

DIVISION SERIES RECORD

Year Team (League)	Pos.	G	AB	R	H	2B	3B	HR	RBI	BB	SO	SB-CS	Avg.	OBP	SLG	E	Avg.
		BATTING														FIELDING	
2000—Seattle (A.L.)	OF	3	12	2	3	0	0	0	2	0	0	1-0	.250	.308	.250	0	1.000
2001—Seattle (A.L.)	OF	5	18	2	4	3	0	1	3	2	7	0-1	.222	.333	.556	0	1.000
Division series totals (2 years)		8	30	4	7	3	0	1	5	2	7	1-1	.233	.324	.433	0	1.000

CHAMPIONSHIP SERIES RECORD

Year Team (League)	Pos.	G	AB	R	H	2B	3B	HR	RBI	BB	SO	SB-CS	Avg.	OBP	SLG	E	Avg.
		BATTING														FIELDING	
2000—Seattle (A.L.)	OF	6	18	3	2	0	0	0	1	2	7	1-0	.111	.200	.111	0	1.000
2001—Seattle (A.L.)	OF	5	17	3	3	2	0	0	0	4	4	0-0	.176	.364	.294	0	1.000
Championship series totals (2 years)		11	35	6	5	2	0	0	1	6	11	1-0	.143	.286	.200	0	1.000

ALL-STAR GAME RECORD

	AB	R	H	2B	3B	HR	RBI	BB	SO	SB-CS	Avg.	OBP	SLG	E	Avg.
All-Star Game totals (1 year)	3	0	1	1	0	0	0	0	1	0-0	.333	.333	.667	0	1.000

CANIZARO, JAY — 2B — DEVIL RAYS

PERSONAL: Born July 4, 1973, in Orange, Texas. ... 5-9/178. ... Bats right, throws right. ... Full name: Jason Kyle Canizaro.
HIGH SCHOOL: West Orange-Stark (Orange, Texas).
JUNIOR COLLEGE: Blinn College (Texas).
COLLEGE: Oklahoma State.
TRANSACTIONS/CAREER NOTES: Selected by San Francisco Giants organization in fourth round of free-agent draft (June 3, 1993). ... On Fresno disabled list (July 10-August 15, 1999). ... Released by Giants (April 3, 2000). ... Signed by Minnesota Twins organization (April 4, 2000). ... On disabled list (March 24, 2001-entire season). ... Released by Twins (September 30, 2002). ... Signed by Tampa Bay Devil Rays organization (November 6, 2002).
STATISTICAL NOTES: Led Arizona League second basemen with 33 double plays in 1993. ... Led Texas League second basemen with 19 errors in 1995. ... Career major league grand slams: 2.
2002 GAMES PLAYED BY POSITION (MLB): 2B—30; 3B—8.

Year Team (League)	Pos.	G	AB	R	H	2B	3B	HR	RBI	BB	SO	SB-CS	Avg.	OBP	SLG	E	Avg.
		BATTING														FIELDING	
1993—Arizona Giants (Ariz.)	2B-SS	49	180	34	47	10	•6	3	*41	22	40	12-3	.261	.337	.433	10	.954
1994—San Jose (Calif.)	2-S-3-O	126	464	77	117	16	2	15	69	46	98	12-6	.252	.324	.392	30	.954
1995—Shreveport (Texas)	2B-SS	126	440	83	129	25	7	12	60	58	98	16-9	.293	.379	.464	†23	.962
1996—Phoenix (PCL)	2-S-3-DH	102	363	50	95	21	2	7	64	46	77	14-4	.262	.347	.388	14	.973
—San Francisco (N.L.)	2B-SS	43	120	11	24	4	1	2	8	9	38	0-2	.200	.260	.300	6	.963
1997—Phoenix (PCL)	2B-3B	23	81	12	16	7	0	2	12	9	24	2-2	.198	.278	.358	2	.975
—Shreveport (Texas)	2-S-3-DH	50	176	36	45	9	0	11	38	26	44	2-2	.256	.354	.494	6	.971
1998—Shreveport (Texas)	2B	83	281	47	63	7	1	12	32	53	46	5-2	.224	.352	.384	10	.976
—Fresno (PCL)	2-DH-O-S	45	106	23	24	6	2	6	14	17	23	0-1	.226	.336	.491	2	.983
1999—Fresno (PCL)	2B-SS-3B	105	364	76	102	20	2	26	78	49	79	16-5	.280	.364	.560	15	.968
—San Francisco (N.L.)	2B	12	18	5	8	2	0	1	9	1	2	1-0	.444	.474	.722	0	1.000
2000—Salt Lake (PCL)■	2B-SS-3B	27	101	21	36	9	2	6	32	17	17	4-1	.356	.439	.663	7	.949
—Minnesota (A.L.)	2B-DH	102	346	43	93	21	1	7	40	24	57	4-2	.269	.318	.396	6	.982
2001—Minnesota (A.L.)								Did not play.									
2002—Minnesota (A.L.)	2B-3B	38	112	14	24	8	1	0	11	10	22	0-1	.214	.280	.304	3	.976
—Edmonton (PCL)	2B-3B	66	247	43	71	11	2	14	37	30	46	6-3	.287	...	.518	7	.972
American League totals (2 years)		140	458	57	117	29	2	7	51	34	79	4-3	.255	.308	.373	9	.980
National League totals (2 years)		55	138	16	32	6	1	3	17	10	40	1-2	.232	.287	.355	6	.964
Major League totals (4 years)		195	596	73	149	35	3	10	68	44	119	5-5	.250	.303	.369	15	.976

CARDONA, JAVIER — C

PERSONAL: Born September 15, 1975, in Santurce, Puerto Rico. ... 6-1/210. ... Bats right, throws right. ... Full name: Javier Peterson Cardona.
HIGH SCHOOL: Jose Alegria (Barrio Maguayo, Puerto Rico).
JUNIOR COLLEGE: Lake Land Community College (Ill.).
TRANSACTIONS/CAREER NOTES: Selected by Detroit Tigers organization in 19th round of free-agent draft (June 3, 1993); did not sign. ... Selected by Tigers organization in 23rd round of free-agent draft (June 4, 1994). ... Traded by Tigers with OF Rich Gomez to San Diego Padres for IF Damian Jackson and C Matt Walbeck (March 24, 2002). ... On Portland disabled list (July 1, 2002-remainder of season). ... Granted free agency (October 15, 2002).
2002 GAMES PLAYED BY POSITION (MLB): C—14.

Year Team (League)	Pos.	G	AB	R	H	2B	3B	HR	RBI	BB	SO	SB-CS	Avg.	OBP	SLG	E	Avg.
		BATTING														FIELDING	
1994—Jamestown (NY-P)	C	19	46	6	12	2	0	0	5	7	9	0-0	.261	.358	.304	4	.964
1995—Fayetteville (S.Atl.)	C	51	165	18	34	8	0	3	19	13	30	1-0	.206	.268	.309	4	.990
1996—Fayetteville (S.Atl.)	C	97	348	42	98	21	0	4	28	28	53	1-5	.282	.336	.376	15	.981
1997—Lakeland (FSL)	C	85	284	28	82	15	0	7	38	25	51	1-3	.289	.346	.415	12	.979
1998—Jacksonville (Sou.)	C	46	163	31	54	16	1	4	40	15	29	0-0	.331	.387	.515	6	.976
—Toledo (I.L.)	C	47	162	12	31	4	0	5	16	9	32	0-0	.191	.238	.309	5	.983
1999—Jacksonville (Sou.)	C	108	418	84	129	31	0	*26	92	46	69	4-2	.309	.384	*.569	11	.983
2000—Toledo (I.L.)	C	56	218	29	60	10	0	11	43	15	33	0-1	.275	.325	.472	5	.986
—Detroit (A.L.)	C	26	40	1	7	1	0	1	2	0	9	0-0	.175	.190	.275	2	.973
2001—Detroit (A.L.)	C-DH	46	96	10	25	8	0	1	10	2	12	0-1	.260	.280	.375	3	.980
—Toledo (I.L.)	C	26	98	7	23	2	0	1	10	8	18	1-0	.235	.292	.286	2	.989
2002—Portland (PCL)■	C	20	63	7	18	1	2	1	6	2	12	0-0	.286	.313	.413	0	1.000
—San Diego (N.L.)	C	15	39	2	4	1	0	0	2	2	10	0-0	.103	.143	.128	2	.976
American League totals (2 years)		72	136	11	32	9	0	2	12	2	21	0-1	.235	.254	.346	5	.978
National League totals (1 year)		15	39	2	4	1	0	0	2	2	10	0-0	.103	.143	.128	2	.976
Major League totals (3 years)		87	175	13	36	10	0	2	14	4	31	0-1	.206	.228	.297	7	.977

CARPENTER, CHRIS — P

PERSONAL: Born April 27, 1975, in Exeter, N.H. ... 6-6/215. ... Throws right, bats right. ... Full name: Christopher John Carpenter.
HIGH SCHOOL: Trinity (Manchester, N.H.).
TRANSACTIONS/CAREER NOTES: Selected by Toronto Blue Jays organization in first round (15th pick overall) of free-agent draft (June 3, 1993). ... On Toronto disabled list (June 3-28, 1999); included rehabilitation assignment to St. Catharines (June 23-28). ... On Toronto disabled list (April 2-20, April 22-June 21 and August 14, 2002-remainder of season); included rehabilitation assignments to Tennessee (May 23-June 12) and Syracuse (June 13-18). ... Released by Blue Jays (October 9, 2002).
CAREER HITTING (MLB): 2-for-11 (.182), 1 R, 0 2B, 0 3B, 0 HR, 0 RBI.

Year League	W	L	Pct.	ERA	G	GS	CG	ShO	Sv.-Opp.	IP	H	R	ER	HR	BB-IBB	SO
1994—Medicine Hat (Pio.)	6	3	.667	2.76	15	15	0	0	0-...	84.2	76	40	26	3	39-0	80
1995—Dunedin (FSL)	3	5	.375	2.17	15	15	0	0	0-...	99.1	83	29	24	3	50-0	56
—Knoxville (Sou.)	3	7	.300	5.18	12	12	0	0	0-...	64.1	71	47	37	3	31-1	53
1996—Knoxville (Sou.)	7	9	.438	3.94	28	28	1	0	0-...	171.1	161	94	75	13	91-4	150
1997—Syracuse (I.L.)	4	9	.308	4.50	19	19	3	2	0-...	120.0	113	64	60	16	53-0	97
—Toronto (A.L.)	3	7	.300	5.09	14	13	1	1	0-0	81.1	108	55	46	7	37-0	55
1998—Toronto (A.L.)	12	7	.632	4.37	33	24	1	1	0-0	175.0	177	97	85	18	61-1	136
1999—Toronto (A.L.)	9	8	.529	4.38	24	24	4	1	0-0	150.0	177	81	73	16	48-1	106
—St. Catharines (NY-Penn)	0	0	...	4.50	1	1	0	0	0-...	4.0	5	2	2	0	1-0	6
2000—Toronto (A.L.)	10	12	.455	6.26	34	27	2	0	0-0	175.1	204	*130	*122	30	83-1	113
2001—Toronto (A.L.)	11	11	.500	4.09	34	34	3	2	0-0	215.2	229	112	98	29	75-5	157
2002—Toronto (A.L.)	4	5	.444	5.28	13	13	1	0	0-0	73.1	89	45	43	11	27-0	45
—Tennessee (Sou.)	0	1	.000	8.20	5	5	0	0	0-...	18.2	26	18	17	5	8-0	9
—Syracuse (I.L.)	0	1	.000	4.50	1	1	0	0	0-...	6.0	8	3	3	1	2-0	6
Major League totals (6 years)	49	50	.495	4.83	152	135	12	5	0-0	870.2	984	520	467	111	331-8	612

CARRARA, GIOVANNI — P — DODGERS

PERSONAL: Born March 4, 1968, in Edo Anzuategni, Venezuela. ... 6-2/235. ... Throws right, bats right. ... Full name: Giovanni Jimenez Carrara.
TRANSACTIONS/CAREER NOTES: Signed as non-drafted free agent by Toronto Blue Jays organization (January 23, 1990). ... Claimed on waivers by Cincinnati Reds (July 3, 1996). ... Granted free agency (October 15, 1996). ... Signed by Baltimore Orioles organization (November 12, 1996). ... Released by Orioles (May 14, 1997). ... Signed by Reds organization (May 17, 1997). ... Granted free agency (September 11, 1997). ... Played for Seibu Lions of Japan Pacific League (1998). ... Signed by Reds organization (December 23, 1998). ... Granted free agency (October 15, 1999). ... Signed by Colorado Rockies organization (December 1, 1999). ... On Colorado Springs disabled list (May 29-June 21, 2000). ... On Colorado disabled list (August 3-September 4, 2000); included rehabilitation assignment to Colorado Springs (August 29-September 4). ... Granted free agency (October 4, 2000). ... Signed by Los Angeles Dodgers organization (January 4, 2001). ... On disabled list (August 11-September 1, 2002).
CAREER HITTING (MLB): 3-for-28 (.107), 2 R, 0 2B, 0 3B, 0 HR, 0 RBI.

Year League	W	L	Pct.	ERA	G	GS	CG	ShO	Sv.-Opp.	IP	H	R	ER	HR	BB-IBB	SO
1990—Dom. Blue Jays (DSL)	2	2	.500	2.62	15	14	4	0	0-...	86.0	88	31	25	...	28-...	55
1991—St. Catharines (NY-Penn)	5	2	.714	1.71	15	13	2	•2	0-...	89.2	66	26	17	5	21-0	83
1992—Dunedin (FSL)	0	1	.000	4.63	5	4	0	0	0-...	23.1	22	13	12	1	11-0	16
—Myrtle Beach (S.Atl.)	11	7	.611	3.14	22	16	1	1	0-...	100.1	86	40	35	12	36-0	100
1993—Dunedin (FSL)	6	11	.353	3.45	27	24	1	0	0-...	140.2	136	69	54	14	59-0	108
1994—Knoxville (Sou.)	13	7	.650	3.89	26	26	1	0	0-...	164.1	158	85	71	16	59-0	96
1995—Syracuse (I.L.)	7	7	.500	3.96	21	21	0	0	0-...	131.2	116	72	58	11	56-2	81
—Toronto (A.L.)	2	4	.333	7.21	12	7	1	0	0-0	48.2	64	46	39	10	25-1	27
1996—Toronto (A.L.)	0	1	.000	11.40	11	0	0	0	0-1	15.0	23	19	19	5	12-2	10
—Syracuse (I.L.)	4	4	.500	3.58	9	6	1	0	0-...	37.2	37	16	15	2	12-1	28
—Indianapolis (A.A.)■	4	0	1.000	0.76	9	6	1	1	1-...	47.2	25	6	4	2	9-0	45
—Cincinnati (N.L.)	1	0	1.000	5.87	8	5	0	0	0-0	23.0	31	17	15	6	13-1	13
1997—Rochester (I.L.)■	4	2	.667	4.44	8	8	1	0	0-...	46.2	45	23	23	4	16-0	48
—Indianapolis (A.A.)■	12	5	.706	3.51	19	18	2	0	0-...	120.2	111	50	47	12	51-3	105
—Cincinnati (N.L.)	0	1	.000	7.84	2	2	0	0	0-0	10.1	14	9	9	4	6-1	5
1998—Seibu (Jp. East.)■	2	0	1.000	4.50	4	0	0	0	0-...	8.0	8	4	4	...	1-...	8
—Seibu (Jap. Pac.)	1	2	.333	4.91	33	5	0	0	1-...	73.1	68	44	40	...	40-...	50
1999—Indianapolis (I.L.)■	12	7	.632	•3.47	39	21	2	1	0-...	158.0	144	68	61	20	58-3	114
2000—Colorado Springs (PCL)■	7	2	.778	3.26	18	15	0	0	0-...	96.2	89	39	35	8	30-1	89
—Colorado (N.L.)	0	1	.000	12.82	8	0	0	0	0-1	13.1	21	19	19	5	11-2	15
2001—Las Vegas (PCL)■	1	2	.333	3.10	6	6	0	0	0-...	29.0	27	10	10	5	9-0	35
—Los Angeles (N.L.)	6	1	.857	3.16	47	3	0	0	0-3	85.1	73	30	30	12	24-3	70
2002—Los Angeles (N.L.)	6	3	.667	3.28	63	1	0	0	1-6	90.2	83	34	33	14	32-4	56
A.L. totals (2 years)	2	5	.286	8.20	23	7	1	0	0-1	63.2	87	65	58	15	37-3	37
N.L. totals (5 years)	13	6	.684	4.28	128	11	0	0	1-10	222.2	222	109	106	41	86-11	159
Major League totals (6 years)	15	11	.577	5.15	151	18	1	0	1-11	286.1	309	174	164	56	123-14	196

CARROLL, JAMEY — 2B — EXPOS

PERSONAL: Born February 18, 1974, in Evansville, Ind. ... 5-10/175. ... Bats right, throws right. ... Full name: Jamey Blake Carroll.
HIGH SCHOOL: Castle (Newburgh, Ind.).
COLLEGE: Evansville.
TRANSACTIONS/CAREER NOTES: Selected by Montreal Expos organization in 14th round of free-agent draft (June 4, 1996).
STATISTICAL NOTES: Led International League third basemen with 26 double plays in 2002.
2002 GAMES PLAYED BY POSITION (MLB): 3B—13; SS—3; 2B—1.

		BATTING														FIELDING	
Year Team (League)	Pos.	G	AB	R	H	2B	3B	HR	RBI	BB	SO	SB-CS	Avg.	OBP	SLG	E	Avg.
1996— Vermont (NY-Penn)	SS-2B-3B	54	203	40	56	6	1	0	17	29	25	16-11	.276	.363	.315	9	.960
1997— W. Palm Beach (FSL)	SS-2B	121	407	56	99	19	1	0	38	43	48	17-11	.243	.319	.295	22	.951
1998— Jupiter (FSL)	2B-SS	55	222	40	58	5	0	0	14	24	26	11-4	.261	.345	.284	6	.977
— Harrisburg (East.)	2B-SS	75	261	43	66	11	3	0	20	41	29	11-5	.253	.365	.318	17	.953
1999— Harrisburg (East.)	2B-SS	141	561	78	164	34	5	5	63	48	58	21-10	.292	.351	.398	14	.979
2000— Ottawa (I.L.)	2B-3B-SS	91	349	53	97	17	2	2	23	33	32	6-3	.278	.342	.355	13	.967
— Harrisburg (East.)	3B-SS-2B	45	169	23	49	5	3	0	18	12	13	8-2	.290	.335	.355	6	.960
2001— Ottawa (I.L.)	2B-SS-3B	83	267	26	64	8	2	0	16	18	41	5-5	.240	.292	.285	9	.972
2002— Harrisburg (East.)	2B-3B	3	9	1	4	0	0	0	1	3	0	0-0	.444	.583	.444	0	1.000
— Ottawa (I.L.)	3B-2B-SS	117	421	57	118	19	2	8	49	37	39	6-10	.280	.342	.392	7	.983
— Montreal (N.L.)	3B-SS-2B	16	71	16	22	5	3	1	6	4	12	1-0	.310	.347	.507	4	.925
Major League totals (1 year)		16	71	16	22	5	3	1	6	4	12	1-0	.310	.347	.507	4	.925

CARTER, LANCE — P — DEVIL RAYS

PERSONAL: Born December 18, 1974, in Bradenton, Fla. ... 6-1/190. ... Throws right, bats right. ... Full name: Lance David Carter.
HIGH SCHOOL: Manatee (Bradenton, Fla.).
JUNIOR COLLEGE: Manatee Community College (Fla.).
TRANSACTIONS/CAREER NOTES: Selected by Kansas City Royals organization in 21st round of free-agent draft (June 21, 1994). ... On disabled list (June 12-September 15, 1997). ... On Omaha disabled list (August 7-September 12, 2000). ... Granted free agency (October 10, 2000). ... Signed by Tampa Bay Devil Rays organization (January 22, 2002). ... On Durham disabled list (May 14-23, 2002).
CAREER HITTING (MLB): 0-for-0 (.000), 0 R, 0 2B, 0 3B, 0 HR, 0 RBI.

Year League	W	L	Pct.	ERA	G	GS	CG	ShO	Sv.-Opp.	IP	H	R	ER	HR	BB-IBB	SO
1994— Eugene (N'West)	1	0	1.000	5.47	8	7	0	0	0-...	26.1	26	17	16	2	15-0	23
— Gulf Coast Royals (GCL)	3	0	1.000	0.29	5	5	0	0	0-...	31.0	19	1	1	1	3-0	36
1995— Springfield (Midw.)	9	5	.643	3.99	27	24	1	1	0-...	137.2	151	77	61	14	22-0	118
1996— Wilmington (Caro.)	3	6	.333	6.34	16	12	0	0	0-...	65.1	81	50	46	8	17-2	49
1997— Kingsport (Appl.)									Did not play.							
1998— Lansing (Midw.)	3	1	.750	0.67	15	2	0	0	2-...	40.1	34	6	3	0	9-1	37
— Wilmington (Caro.)	1	4	.200	3.29	28	1	0	0	5-...	52.0	50	21	19	5	14-1	61
1999— Wichita (Texas)	5	2	.714	0.78	44	0	0	0	13-...	69.2	49	10	6	1	27-5	77
— Kansas City (A.L.)	0	1	.000	5.06	6	0	0	0	0-0	5.1	3	3	3	2	3-0	3
2000— Omaha (PCL)	2	8	.200	4.95	34	6	0	0	5-...	76.1	88	46	42	13	18-1	51
2001—									Did not play.							
2002— Durham (I.L.)■	12	2	.857	2.80	33	18	2	1	1-...	132.0	111	43	41	15	12-0	90
— Tampa Bay (A.L.)	2	0	1.000	1.33	8	0	0	0	2-2	20.1	15	3	3	2	5-1	14
Major League totals (2 years)	2	1	.667	2.10	14	0	0	0	2-2	25.2	18	6	6	4	8-1	17

CARUSO, MIKE — SS

PERSONAL: Born May 27, 1977, in Queens, N.Y. ... 6-1/172. ... Bats left, throws right. ... Full name: Michael John Caruso.
HIGH SCHOOL: Stoneman Douglas (Parkland, Fla.).
TRANSACTIONS/CAREER NOTES: Selected by San Francisco Giants organization in second round of free-agent draft (June 2, 1996). ... Traded by Giants with P Keith Foulke, P Lorenzo Barcelo, P Bobby Howry, P Ken Vining and OF Brian Manning to Chicago White Sox for P Danny Darwin, P Wilson Alvarez and P Roberto Hernandez (July 31, 1997). ... On Charlotte disabled list (August 1-9, 2000). ... On Chicago disabled list (August 10, 2000-remainder of season). ... Claimed on waivers by Seattle Mariners (December 14, 2000). ... Granted free agency (December 21, 2000). ... Signed by Tampa Bay Devil Rays organization (February 13, 2001). ... On disabled list (May 2-16, 2001). ... Granted free agency (October 15, 2001). ... Signed by Cincinnati Reds organization (December 21, 2001). ... On Louisville disabled list (April 4-26, 2002). ... Claimed on waivers by Kansas City Royals (April 28, 2002). ... Granted free agency (October 15, 2002).
STATISTICAL NOTES: Led Northwest League in caught stealing with 10 in 1996. ... Led Northwest League shortstops with 106 putouts, 230 assists, 374 total chances and 43 double plays and tied for lead with 38 errors in 1996. ... Tied for A.L. lead in caught stealing with 14 in 1999.
2002 GAMES PLAYED BY POSITION (MLB): SS—5; 2B—4; 3B—2.

		BATTING														FIELDING	
Year Team (League)	Pos.	G	AB	R	H	2B	3B	HR	RBI	BB	SO	SB-CS	Avg.	OBP	SLG	E	Avg.
1996— Bellingham (N'West)	SS-3B	73	312	48	91	13	1	2	24	16	23	•24-10	.292	.324	.359	‡40	.894
1997— San Jose (Calif.)	SS-DH	108	441	76	147	24	11	2	50	38	19	11-16	.333	.391	.451	33	.934
— Win.-Salem (Caro.)■	SS-DH	28	119	12	27	3	2	0	14	4	8	3-0	.227	.264	.286	7	.941
1998— Chicago (A.L.)	SS	133	523	81	160	17	6	5	55	14	38	22-6	.306	.331	.390	*35	.944
1999— Chicago (A.L.)	SS-DH	136	529	60	132	11	4	2	35	20	36	12-14	.250	.280	.297	24	.957
2000— Charlotte (I.L.)	SS-2B	88	309	38	76	11	5	0	26	22	23	5-7	.246	.301	.314	16	.960
2001— Durham (I.L.)■	2B-SS	110	387	62	113	10	9	0	35	22	22	11-9	.292	.340	.364	17	.966
2002— Chattanooga (Sou.)■	2B-OF	3	14	4	5	0	0	1	4	1	0	1-0	.357	.400	.571	2	.882
— Omaha (PCL)■	SS-2B-3B	60	219	28	67	3	2	3	23	12	14	10-3	.306	.350	.379	12	.947
— Kansas City (A.L.)	SS-2B-3B	12	20	3	2	0	0	0	0	1	2	0-0	.100	.143	.100	1	.967
Major League totals (3 years)		281	1072	144	294	28	10	7	90	35	76	34-20	.274	.302	.339	60	.951

CASANOVA, RAUL — C

PERSONAL: Born August 23, 1972, in Humacao, Puerto Rico. ... 6-0/216. ... Bats both, throws right.
HIGH SCHOOL: Ponce (Puerto Rico).
TRANSACTIONS/CAREER NOTES: Selected by New York Mets organization in eighth round of free-agent draft (June 4, 1990). ... Traded by Mets to San Diego Padres (December 7, 1992), completing deal in which Padres traded SS Tony Fernandez to Mets for P Wally Whitehurst, OF D.J. Dozier and a player to be named later (October 26, 1992). ... Traded by Padres with P Richie Lewis and OF Melvin Nieves to Detroit Tigers for P Sean Bergman, P Cade Gaspar and OF Todd Steverson (March 22, 1996). ... On Toledo disabled list (May 3-14, 1996). ... On Detroit disabled list (June 19-August 13, 1996); included rehabilitation assignments to Jacksonville (July 31-August 9) and Toledo (August 9-13). ... On Detroit disabled list (April 25-May 28 and July 21, 1998-remainder of season); included rehabilitation assignments to Toledo (May

8-27 and July 30-August 3). ... On Detroit disabled list (March 31-July 12, 1999); included rehabilitation assignments to the Gulf Coast Tigers (June 24-28), Lakeland (June 29-July 4) and Toledo (July 5-July 12). ... Granted free agency (October 15, 1999). ... Signed by Colorado Rockies organization (December 15, 1999). ... Released by Rockies (March 24, 2000). ... Signed by Milwaukee Brewers organization (March 25, 2000). ... On disabled list (August 11, 2001-remainder of season). ... On Milwaukee disabled list (May 17-August 23, 2002); included rehabilitation assignment to Indianapolis (July 29-August 17). ... Released by Brewers (September 3, 2002). ... Signed by Baltimore Orioles (September 11, 2002). ... Released by Orioles (October 1, 2002).

STATISTICAL NOTES: Switch-hit home runs in one game (June 6, 1996). ... Career major league grand slams: 3.

2002 GAMES PLAYED BY POSITION (MLB): C—30.

			BATTING														FIELDING	
Year	**Team (League)**	**Pos.**	**G**	**AB**	**R**	**H**	**2B**	**3B**	**HR**	**RBI**	**BB**	**SO**	**SB-CS**	**Avg.**	**OBP**	**SLG**	**E**	**Avg.**
1990—	GC Mets (GCL)	C	23	65	4	5	0	0	0	1	4	16	0-1	.077	.130	.077	8	.953
1991—	GC Mets (GCL)	C	32	111	19	27	4	2	0	9	12	22	3-0	.243	.325	.315	5	.979
	—Kingsport (Appl.)	C	5	18	0	1	0	0	0	0	1	10	0-0	.056	.105	.056	1	.975
1992—	Columbia (S.Atl.)	C	5	18	2	3	0	0	0	1	1	4	0-0	.167	.211	.167	0	1.000
	—Kingsport (Appl.)	C	42	137	25	37	9	1	4	27	26	25	3-1	.270	.401	.438	6	.982
1993—	Waterloo (Midw.)■	C-3B	76	227	32	58	12	0	6	30	21	46	0-1	.256	.321	.388	10	.976
1994—	Rancho Cuca. (Calif.)	C	123	471	83	*160	27	2	23	120	43	97	1-4	*.340	.403	.552	14	.979
1995—	Memphis (Sou.)	C-DH	89	306	42	83	18	0	12	44	25	51	4-1	.271	.330	.448	*12	.980
1996—	Toledo (I.L.)■	C-DH	49	161	23	44	11	0	8	28	20	24	0-1	.273	.353	.491	2	.992
	—Detroit (A.L.)	C-DH	25	85	6	16	1	0	4	9	6	18	0-0	.188	.242	.341	3	.978
	—Jacksonville (Sou.)	DH-C	8	30	5	10	2	0	4	9	2	7	0-0	.333	.375	.800	0	1.000
1997—	Toledo (I.L.)	C	12	41	1	8	0	0	1	3	3	8	0-0	.195	.244	.268	2	.977
	—Detroit (A.L.)	C-DH	101	304	27	74	10	1	5	24	26	48	1-1	.243	.308	.332	9	.985
1998—	Detroit (A.L.)	C	16	42	4	6	2	0	1	3	5	10	0-0	.143	.250	.262	3	.967
	—Toledo (I.L.)	C-DH	50	171	17	44	8	0	7	26	22	28	0-1	.257	.350	.427	9	.973
1999—	GC Tigers (GCL)	C	2	5	1	4	0	0	1	1	0	0	0-1	.800	.800	1.400	0	1.000
	—Lakeland (FSL)	C-DH	4	12	3	6	2	0	1	6	0	1	0-0	.500	.538	.917	0	1.000
	—Toledo (I.L.)	C-DH	44	160	21	33	9	0	6	23	7	28	0-0	.206	.243	.375	3	.985
2000—	Indianapolis (I.L.)■	C	20	73	10	21	2	0	5	12	7	10	0-1	.288	.354	.521	2	.985
	—Milwaukee (N.L.)	C-DH	86	231	20	57	13	3	6	36	26	48	1-2	.247	.331	.407	4	.990
2001—	Milwaukee (N.L.)	C-DH	71	192	21	50	10	0	11	33	12	29	0-0	.260	.303	.484	3	.991
2002—	Milwaukee (N.L.)	C	31	87	3	16	1	0	1	8	10	18	0-0	.184	.273	.230	1	.994
	—Indianapolis (I.L.)	C	14	43	2	12	4	0	0	8	3	8	0-0	.279	.313	.372	0	1.000
	—Baltimore (A.L.)■	C	2	1	0	0	0	0	0	0	0	1	0-0	.000	.000	.000	0	1.000
American League totals (4 years)			144	432	37	96	13	1	10	36	37	77	1-1	.222	.289	.326	15	.982
National League totals (3 years)			188	510	44	123	24	3	18	77	48	95	1-2	.241	.311	.406	8	.991
Major League totals (6 years)			332	942	81	219	37	4	28	113	85	172	2-3	.232	.301	.369	23	.987

CASEY, SEAN — 1B — REDS

PERSONAL: Born July 2, 1974, in Willingsboro, N.J. ... 6-4/225. ... Bats left, throws right. ... Full name: Sean Thomas Casey.

HIGH SCHOOL: Upper St. Clair (Pittsburgh).

COLLEGE: Richmond.

TRANSACTIONS/CAREER NOTES: Selected by Cleveland Indians organization in second round of free-agent draft (June 1, 1995). ... On disabled list (July 23-September 23, 1996). ... On Akron disabled list (April 4-June 8, 1997). ... Traded by Indians to Cincinnati Reds for P Dave Burba (March 30, 1998). ... On Cincinnati disabled list (April 2-May 5, 1998); included rehabilitation assignment to Indianapolis (April 30-May 5). ... On disabled list (April 2-19, 2000). ... On Cincinnati disabled list (July 23-August 9 and September 10, 2002-remainder of season); included rehabilitation assignment to Louisville (August 7-9).

RECORDS: Shares major league single-game record for most times reached base (nine-inning game)—7 (May 19, 1999).

STATISTICAL NOTES: Had 21-game hitting streak (July 4-30, 2000).

2002 GAMES PLAYED BY POSITION (MLB): 1B—108; DH—1.

			BATTING														FIELDING	
Year	**Team (League)**	**Pos.**	**G**	**AB**	**R**	**H**	**2B**	**3B**	**HR**	**RBI**	**BB**	**SO**	**SB-CS**	**Avg.**	**OBP**	**SLG**	**E**	**Avg.**
1995—	Watertown (NY-Penn)	1B	55	207	26	68	18	0	2	37	18	21	3-0	.329	.380	.444	8	.985
1996—	Kinston (Caro.)	1B-DH	92	344	62	114	31	3	12	57	36	47	1-1	*.331	.402	*.544	6	.991
1997—	Akron (East.)	1B-DH	62	241	38	93	19	1	10	66	23	34	0-1	.386	.448	.598	5	.988
	—Buffalo (A.A.)	DH-1B	20	72	12	26	7	0	5	18	9	11	0-0	.361	.439	.667	0	1.000
	—Cleveland (A.L.)	DH-1B	6	10	1	2	0	0	0	1	1	2	0-0	.200	.333	.200	0	1.000
1998—	Cincinnati (N.L.)■	1B	96	302	44	82	21	1	7	52	43	45	1-1	.272	.365	.417	4	.994
	—Indianapolis (I.L.)	1B-DH	27	95	14	31	8	1	1	13	14	10	0-0	.326	.418	.463	2	.991
1999—	Cincinnati (N.L.)	1B-DH	151	594	103	197	42	3	25	99	61	88	0-2	.332	.399	.539	6	.995
2000—	Cincinnati (N.L.)	1B	133	480	69	151	33	2	20	85	52	80	1-0	.315	.385	.517	6	.995
2001—	Cincinnati (N.L.)	1B-DH	145	533	69	165	40	0	13	89	43	63	3-1	.310	.369	.458	7	.994
2002—	Cincinnati (N.L.)	1B-DH	120	425	56	111	25	0	6	42	43	47	2-1	.261	.334	.362	7	.993
	—Louisville (I.L.)	DH	2	8	2	4	0	0	1	3	1	0	0-0	.500	.556	.875	...	...
American League totals (1 year)			6	10	1	2	0	0	0	1	1	2	0-0	.200	.333	.200	0	1.000
National League totals (5 years)			645	2334	341	706	161	6	71	367	242	323	7-5	.302	.373	.468	30	.994
Major League totals (6 years)			651	2344	342	708	161	6	71	368	243	325	7-5	.302	.373	.467	30	.994

ALL-STAR GAME RECORD

	AB	**R**	**H**	**2B**	**3B**	**HR**	**RBI**	**BB**	**SO**	**SB-CS**	**Avg.**	**OBP**	**SLG**	**E**	**Avg.**
All-Star Game totals (2 years)	2	0	0	0	0	0	0	0	1	0-0	.000	.000	.000	0	1.000

CASH, KEVIN — C — BLUE JAYS

PERSONAL: Born December 6, 1977, in Tampa, Fla. ... 6-0/185. ... Bats right, throws right. ... Full name: Kevin Forrest Cash.

COLLEGE: Florida State.

TRANSACTIONS/CAREER NOTES: Signed as non-drafted free agent by Toronto Blue Jays organization (August 7, 1999).

STATISTICAL NOTES: Tied for International League lead with six double plays by catcher in 2002.

2002 GAMES PLAYED BY POSITION (MLB): C—7.

Year	Team (League)	Pos.	G	AB	R	H	2B	3B	HR	RBI	BB	SO	SB-CS	Avg.	OBP	SLG	E	Avg.
			BATTING														FIELDING	
2000—	Hagerstown (S.Atl.)....	C	59	196	28	48	10	1	10	27	22	54	5-3	.245	.323	.459	10	.974
2001—	Dunedin (FSL)...........	C	105	371	55	105	27	0	12	66	43	80	4-3	.283	.369	.453	12	.979
2002—	Syracuse (I.L.)...........	C	67	236	27	52	18	0	10	26	25	72	0-1	.220	.299	.424	4	.989
—	Toronto (A.L.)............	C	7	14	1	2	0	0	0	0	1	4	0-0	.143	.200	.143	1	.968
Major League totals (1 year)			7	14	1	2	0	0	0	0	1	4	0-0	.143	.200	.143	1	.968

CASSIDY, SCOTT — P — BLUE JAYS

PERSONAL: Born October 3, 1975, in Syracuse, N.Y. ... 6-2/175. ... Throws right, bats right. ... Full name: Scott Robert Cassidy.
COLLEGE: LeMoyne (N.Y.).
TRANSACTIONS/CAREER NOTES: Signed as non-drafted free agent by Toronto Blue Jays organization (May 21, 1998).
STATISTICAL NOTES: Led South Atlantic League with 21 hit batsmen in 1999.
CAREER HITTING (MLB): 0-for-0 (.000), 0 R, 0 2B, 0 3B, 0 HR, 0 RBI.

Year	League	W	L	Pct.	ERA	G	GS	CG	ShO	Sv.-Opp.	IP	H	R	ER	HR	BB-IBB	SO
1998—	Medicine Hat (Pio.)..........	8	1	.889	2.43	15	14	0	0	0-...	81.1	71	31	22	4	14-0	82
1999—	Hagerstown (S.Atl.)..........	13	7	.650	3.27	27	27	1	0	0-...	170.2	151	78	62	13	30-0	178
2000—	Dunedin (FSL)..................	9	3	.750	1.33	14	13	1	0	0-...	88.0	53	15	13	4	34-2	89
—	Tennessee (Sou.)............	2	2	.500	5.91	8	7	0	0	0-...	42.2	48	30	28	7	15-0	39
2001—	Tennessee (Sou.)............	6	6	.500	3.44	16	15	•4	*3	0-...	96.2	78	45	37	10	27-0	81
—	Syracuse (I.L.)..................	3	3	.500	2.71	11	11	0	0	0-...	63.0	60	24	19	6	26-0	48
2002—	Syracuse (I.L.)..................	1	0	1.000	4.00	3	2	0	0	0-...	9.0	8	4	4	2	0-0	4
—	Toronto (A.L.)..................	1	4	.200	5.73	58	0	0	0	0-7	66.0	52	42	42	12	32-3	48
Major League totals (1 year).......		1	4	.200	5.73	58	0	0	0	0-7	66.0	52	42	42	12	32-3	48

CASTILLA, VINNY — 3B — BRAVES

PERSONAL: Born July 4, 1967, in Oaxaca, Mexico. ... 6-1/205. ... Bats right, throws right. ... Full name: Vinicio Soria Castilla. ... Name pronounced kass-TEE-uh.
HIGH SCHOOL: Instituto Carlos Gracida (Oaxaca, Mexico).
COLLEGE: Benito Suarez.
TRANSACTIONS/CAREER NOTES: Signed as non-drafted free agent by Saltillo, Mexican League (1987). ... Contract sold by Saltillo to Atlanta Braves organization (March 19, 1990). ... Selected by Colorado Rockies in second round (40th pick overall) of expansion draft (November 17, 1992). ... On disabled list (May 20-June 4, 1993). ... Traded by Rockies to Tampa Bay Devil Rays for P Rolando Arrojo and IF Aaron Ledesma (December 13, 1999). ... On Tampa Bay disabled list (March 25-April 11, June 14-July 3 and July 30-September 4, 2000); included rehabilitation assignment to Durham (July 1-3). ... Released by Devil Rays (May 10, 2001). ... Signed by Houston Astros (May 15, 2001). ... Granted free agency (November 6, 2001). ... Signed by Braves (December 11, 2001).
RECORDS: Holds major league single-month record for most home runs—2 (March 2001).
HONORS: Named third baseman on The Sporting News N.L. All-Star team (1995 and 1997-98). ... Named third baseman on The Sporting News N.L. Silver Slugger team (1995 and 1997-98).
STATISTICAL NOTES: Led International League shortstops with 550 total chances and 72 double plays in 1992. ... Led N.L. third basemen with 389 assists, 506 total chances and 43 double plays in 1996. ... Had 22-game hitting streak (August 9-September 1, 1997). ... Led N.L. third basemen with 323 assists and 41 double plays in 1997. ... Hit three home runs in one game (June 5, 1999; and July 28, 2001). ... Career major league grand slams: 4.
2002 GAMES PLAYED BY POSITION (MLB): 3B—139.

Year	Team (League)	Pos.	G	AB	R	H	2B	3B	HR	RBI	BB	SO	SB-CS	Avg.	OBP	SLG	E	Avg.
			BATTING														FIELDING	
1987—	Saltillo (Mex.)............	3B	13	27	0	5	2	0	0	1	0	5	0-0	.185	.222	.259	1	.976
1988—	Salt.-Monc. (Mex.)■..	SS	50	124	22	30	2	2	5	18	8	29	1-4	.242	.286	.411	13	.924
1989—	Saltillo (Mex.)■..........	SS-3B	128	462	70	142	25	13	10	58	33	70	11-12	.307	.356	.483	34	.950
1990—	Sumter (S.Atl.)■........	SS	93	339	47	91	15	2	9	53	28	54	2-5	.268	.334	.404	23	.952
—	Greenville (Sou.)........	SS	46	170	20	40	5	1	4	16	13	23	4-4	.235	.296	.347	7	.971
1991—	Greenville (Sou.)........	SS	66	259	34	70	17	3	7	44	9	35	0-1	.270	.296	.440	11	.965
—	Richmond (I.L.)..........	SS	67	240	25	54	7	4	7	36	14	32	1-1	.225	.271	.375	12	.962
—	Atlanta (N.L.)..............	SS	12	5	1	1	0	0	0	0	0	2	0-0	.200	.200	.200	0	1.000
1992—	Richmond (I.L.)..........	SS	127	449	49	113	29	1	7	44	21	68	1-2	.252	.288	.367	*31	.944
—	Atlanta (N.L.)..............	SS-3B	9	16	1	4	1	0	0	1	1	4	0-0	.250	.333	.313	1	.933
1993—	Colorado (N.L.)■.......	SS	105	337	36	86	9	7	9	30	13	45	2-5	.255	.283	.404	11	.975
1994—	Colorado (N.L.)..........	SS-2B-3B-1B	52	130	16	43	11	1	3	18	7	23	2-1	.331	.357	.500	2	.986
—	Colo. Springs (PCL)...	3B-2B-SS	22	78	13	19	6	1	1	11	7	11	0-0	.244	.303	.385	3	.964
1995—	Colorado (N.L.)..........	3B-SS	139	527	82	163	34	2	32	90	30	87	2-8	.309	.347	.564	15	.959
1996—	Colorado (N.L.)..........	3B	160	629	97	191	34	0	40	113	35	88	7-2	.304	.343	.548	20	.960
1997—	Colorado (N.L.)..........	3B	159	612	94	186	25	2	40	113	44	108	2-4	.304	.356	.547	21	.954
1998—	Colorado (N.L.)..........	3B-SS	•162	645	108	206	28	4	46	144	40	89	5-9	.319	.362	.589	13	.970
1999—	Colorado (N.L.)..........	3B	158	615	83	169	24	1	33	102	53	75	2-3	.275	.331	.478	19	.954
2000—	Tampa Bay (A.L.)■.....	3B	85	331	22	73	9	1	6	42	14	41	1-2	.221	.254	.308	8	.967
—	Durham (I.L.).............	3B	2	8	1	3	1	0	1	3	0	1	0-0	.375	.375	.875	0	1.000
2001—	Tampa Bay (A.L.)........	3B	24	93	7	20	6	0	2	9	3	22	0-0	.215	.247	.344	5	.934
—	Houston (N.L.)■........	3B-SS	122	445	62	120	28	1	23	82	32	86	1-4	.270	.320	.492	12	.963
2002—	Atlanta (N.L.)■...........	3B	143	543	56	126	23	2	12	61	22	69	4-1	.232	.268	.348	6	*.982
American League totals (2 years)			109	424	29	93	15	1	8	51	17	63	1-2	.219	.253	.316	13	.959
National League totals (11 years)			1221	4504	636	1295	217	20	238	754	277	676	27-37	.288	.331	.503	120	.965
Major League totals (12 years)			1330	4928	665	1388	232	21	246	805	294	739	28-39	.282	.324	.487	133	.965

DIVISION SERIES RECORD

Year	Team (League)	Pos.	G	AB	R	H	2B	3B	HR	RBI	BB	SO	SB-CS	Avg.	OBP	SLG	E	Avg.
								BATTING									FIELDING	
1995—	Colorado (N.L.)	3B	4	15	3	7	1	0	3	6	0	1	0-0	.467	.500	1.133	1	.941
2001—	Houston (N.L.)	3B	3	11	1	3	0	0	1	1	0	3	0-0	.273	.273	.545	0	1.000
2002—	Atlanta (N.L.)	3B	5	18	5	7	0	0	1	4	2	2	0-0	.389	.450	.556	0	1.000
Division series totals (3 years)			12	44	9	17	1	0	5	11	2	6	0-0	.386	.426	.750	1	.977

ALL-STAR GAME RECORD

	AB	R	H	2B	3B	HR	RBI	BB	SO	SB-CS	Avg.	OBP	SLG	E	Avg.
All-Star Game totals (2 years)	4	0	0	0	0	0	0	0	1	0-0	.000	.000	.000	0	1.000

CASTILLO, ALBERTO C

PERSONAL: Born February 10, 1970, in San Juan de la Maguana, Dominican Republic. ... 6-0/200. ... Bats right, throws right. ... Full name: Alberto Terrero Castillo.

HIGH SCHOOL: Mercedes Maria Mateo (Dominican Republic).

TRANSACTIONS/CAREER NOTES: Signed as non-drafted free agent by New York Mets organization (April 15, 1987). ... On disabled list (July 3, 1992-remainder of season; and June 1-July 13, 1994). ... On suspended list (August 27-29, 1994). ... Granted free agency (October 15, 1998). ... Signed by Philadelphia Phillies organization (November 5, 1998). ... Selected by St. Louis Cardinals from Phillies organization in Rule 5 major league draft (December 14, 1998). ... Traded by Cardinals with P Lance Painter and P Matt DeWitt to Toronto Blue Jays for P Pat Hentgen and P Paul Spoljaric (November 11, 1999). ... Released by Blue Jays (December 12, 2001). ... Signed by New York Yankees organization (December 21, 2001). ... Released by Yankees (October 10, 2002).

STATISTICAL NOTES: Led South Atlantic League catchers with 734 putouts in 1991. ... Led Florida State League catchers with 604 putouts in 1993. ... Led International League catchers with 747 putouts, 72 assists, 827 total chances and nine double plays in 1996.

2002 GAMES PLAYED BY POSITION (MLB): C—14.

Year	Team (League)	Pos.	G	AB	R	H	2B	3B	HR	RBI	BB	SO	SB-CS	Avg.	OBP	SLG	E	Avg.
								BATTING									FIELDING	
1987—	Kingsport (Appl.)	C	7	9	1	1	0	0	0	0	5	3	1-0	.111	.429	.111	0	1.000
1988—	GC Mets (GCL)	C	22	68	7	18	4	0	0	10	4	4	2-0	.265	.312	.324	1	.993
—	Kingsport (Appl.)	C	24	75	7	22	3	0	1	14	15	14	0-1	.293	.407	.373	5	.973
1989—	Kingsport (Appl.)	C-1B	27	74	15	19	4	0	3	12	11	14	2-1	.257	.360	.432	1	.994
—	Pittsfield (NY-Penn)	C	34	123	13	29	8	0	1	13	7	26	2-0	.236	.278	.325	2	.991
1990—	Columbia (S.Atl.)	C	30	103	8	24	4	3	1	14	10	21	1-1	.233	.296	.359	5	.977
—	Pittsfield (NY-Penn)	C-OF-1B	58	187	19	41	8	1	4	24	26	35	3-3	.219	.327	.337	9	.980
—	St. Lucie (FSL)	C	3	11	4	4	0	0	1	3	1	1	0-0	.364	.417	.636	0	1.000
1991—	Columbia (S.Atl.)	C	90	267	35	74	20	3	3	47	43	44	6-6	.277	.382	.408	15	.982
1992—	St. Lucie (FSL)	C	60	162	11	33	6	0	3	17	16	37	0-0	.204	.280	.296	12	.967
1993—	St. Lucie (FSL)	C	105	333	37	86	21	0	5	42	28	46	0-2	.258	.315	.366	12	.983
1994—	Binghamton (East.)	C-1B	90	315	33	78	14	0	7	42	41	46	1-3	.248	.333	.359	6	.991
1995—	Norfolk (I.L.)	C-DH	69	217	23	58	13	1	4	31	26	32	2-3	.267	.346	.392	7	.987
—	New York (N.L.)	C	13	29	2	3	0	0	0	0	3	9	1-0	.103	.212	.103	2	.974
1996—	New York (N.L.)	C	6	11	1	4	0	0	0	0	0	4	0-0	.364	.364	.364	0	1.000
—	Norfolk (I.L.)	C	113	341	34	71	12	1	11	39	39	67	2-2	.208	.295	.346	8	.990
1997—	New York (N.L.)	C	35	59	3	12	1	0	0	7	9	16	0-1	.203	.304	.220	2	.987
—	Norfolk (I.L.)	C-OF	34	83	4	18	1	0	1	8	17	16	1-0	.217	.347	.265	7	.968
1998—	New York (N.L.)	C-DH	38	83	13	17	4	0	2	7	9	17	0-2	.205	.290	.325	2	.990
—	Norfolk (I.L.)	C-OF	21	49	4	9	2	0	1	6	11	12	0-0	.184	.333	.286	1	.991
1999—	St. Louis (N.L.)■	C	93	255	21	67	8	0	4	31	24	48	0-0	.263	.326	.341	5	.991
2000—	Toronto (A.L.)■	C	66	185	14	39	7	0	1	16	21	36	0-0	.211	.287	.265	3	.993
2001—	Toronto (A.L.)	C	66	131	9	26	4	0	1	4	7	30	1-1	.198	.255	.252	4	.989
2002—	New York (A.L.)■	C	15	37	3	5	1	1	0	4	1	12	0-0	.135	.158	.216	1	.990
—	Columbus (I.L.)	C	30	91	7	25	7	0	0	8	9	8	1-0	.275	.350	.352	4	.984
American League totals (3 years)			147	353	26	70	12	1	2	24	29	78	1-1	.198	.263	.255	8	.991
National League totals (5 years)			185	437	40	103	13	0	6	45	45	94	1-3	.236	.310	.307	11	.989
Major League totals (8 years)			332	790	66	173	25	1	8	69	74	172	2-4	.219	.289	.284	19	.990

CASTILLO, FRANK P

PERSONAL: Born April 1, 1969, in El Paso, Texas. ... 6-1/198. ... Throws right, bats right. ... Full name: Frank Anthony Castillo.

HIGH SCHOOL: Eastwood (El Paso, Texas).

TRANSACTIONS/CAREER NOTES: Selected by Chicago Cubs organization in sixth round of free-agent draft (June 2, 1987). ... On disabled list (April 1-July 23, 1988). ... On Iowa disabled list (April 12-June 6, 1991). ... On Chicago disabled list (August 11-27, 1991). ... On suspended list (September 20-24, 1993). ... On Chicago disabled list (March 20-May 12, 1994); included rehabilitation assignments to Daytona (April 24), Orlando (April 25-May 2) and Iowa (May 2-10). ... On Iowa disabled list (June 21-July 1, 1994). ... Traded by Cubs to Colorado Rockies for P Matt Pool (July 15, 1997). ... Granted free agency (October 30, 1997). ... Signed by Detroit Tigers (December 11, 1997). ... On Detroit disabled list (March 24-April 28, 1998); included rehabilitation assignment to Lakeland (April 18-28). ... Granted free agency (October 27, 1998). ... Signed by Arizona Diamondbacks organization (January 12, 1999). ... Released by Diamondbacks (March 27, 1999). ... Signed by Pittsburgh Pirates organization (April 20, 1999). ... Granted free agency (October 15, 1999). ... Signed by Toronto Blue Jays organization (December 21, 1999). ... On disabled list (August 14-September 16, 2000). ... Granted free agency (October 31, 2000). ... Signed by Boston Red Sox (December 7, 2000). ... On Boston disabled list (June 29-August 8, 2001); included rehabilitation assignment to Pawtucket (July 28-August 7). ... On suspended list (May 17-22 and July 1-5, 2002). ... Granted free agency (October 31, 2002).

HONORS: Named Appalachian League Player of the Year (1987).

STATISTICAL NOTES: Pitched 4-0 no-hit victory against Huntsville (July 13, 1990, first game). ... Pitched 7-0 one-hit, complete-game victory against St. Louis (September 25, 1995).

CAREER HITTING (MLB): 37-for-337 (.110), 7 R, 0 2B, 0 3B, 0 HR, 13 RBI.

Year League	W	L	Pct.	ERA	G	GS	CG	ShO	Sv.-Opp.	IP	H	R	ER	HR	BB-IBB	SO
1987—Wytheville (Appl.)	*10	1	*.909	2.29	12	12	•5	0	0-...	90.1	86	31	23	4	21-0	83
—Geneva (NY-Penn)	1	0	1.000	0.00	1	1	0	0	0-...	6.0	3	1	0	0	1-0	6
1988—Peoria (Midw.)	6	1	.857	0.71	9	8	2	2	0-...	51.0	25	5	4	1	10-0	58
1989—Winston-Salem (Caro.)	9	6	.600	2.51	18	18	8	1	0-...	129.1	118	42	36	5	24-1	114
—Charlotte (Sou.)	3	4	.429	3.84	10	10	4	0	0-...	68.0	73	35	29	7	12-3	43
1990—Charlotte (Sou.)	6	6	.500	3.88	18	18	4	1	0-...	111.1	113	54	48	8	27-4	112
1991—Iowa (A.A.)	3	1	.750	2.52	4	4	1	1	0-...	25.0	20	7	7	0	7-0	20
—Chicago (N.L.)	6	7	.462	4.35	18	18	4	0	0-0	111.2	107	56	54	5	33-2	73
1992—Chicago (N.L.)	10	11	.476	3.46	33	33	0	0	0-0	205.1	179	91	79	19	63-6	135
1993—Chicago (N.L.)	5	8	.385	4.84	29	25	2	0	0-0	141.1	162	83	76	20	39-4	84
1994—Daytona (FSL)	0	1	.000	4.50	1	1	0	0	0-...	4.0	7	3	2	0	0-0	1
—Orlando (Sou.)	1	0	1.000	1.29	1	1	0	0	0-...	7.0	4	2	1	0	1-0	2
—Iowa (A.A.)	4	2	.667	3.27	11	11	0	0	0-...	66.0	57	30	24	9	10-0	64
—Chicago (N.L.)	2	1	.667	4.30	4	4	1	0	0-0	23.0	25	13	11	3	5-0	19
1995—Chicago (N.L.)	11	10	.524	3.21	29	29	2	2	0-0	188.0	179	75	67	22	52-4	135
1996—Chicago (N.L.)	7	•16	.304	5.28	33	33	1	1	0-0	182.1	209	112	107	28	46-4	139
1997—Chicago (N.L.)	6	9	.400	5.42	20	19	0	0	0-0	98.0	113	64	59	9	44-1	67
—Colorado (N.L.)■	6	3	.667	5.42	14	14	0	0	0-0	86.1	107	57	52	16	25-3	59
1998—Lakeland (FSL)■	1	0	1.000	0.00	1	1	0	0	0-...	5.0	2	0	0	0	0-0	4
—Detroit (A.L.)	3	9	.250	6.83	27	19	0	0	1-1	116.0	150	91	88	17	44-0	81
1999—Nashville (PCL)■	7	5	.583	4.68	19	19	0	0	0-...	119.1	139	72	62	15	32-4	90
2000—Toronto (A.L.)■	10	5	.667	3.59	25	24	0	0	0-0	138.0	112	58	55	18	56-0	104
2001—Boston (A.L.)■	10	9	.526	4.21	26	26	0	0	0-0	136.2	138	72	64	14	35-2	89
—Pawtucket (I.L.)	0	0	...	0.00	2	2	0	0	0-...	7.2	7	1	0	0	0-0	3
2002—Boston (A.L.)	6	15	.286	5.07	36	23	0	0	1-2	163.1	174	101	92	19	58-6	112
A.L. totals (4 years)	29	38	.433	4.86	114	92	0	0	2-3	554.0	574	322	299	68	193-8	386
N.L. totals (7 years)	53	65	.449	4.39	180	175	10	3	0-0	1036.0	1081	551	505	122	307-24	711
Major League totals (11 years)	82	103	.443	4.55	294	267	10	3	2-3	1590.0	1655	873	804	190	500-32	1097

CASTILLO, LUIS 2B MARLINS

PERSONAL: Born September 12, 1975, in San Pedro de Macoris, Dominican Republic. ... 5-11/190. ... Bats both, throws right. ... Full name: Luis Antonio Donato Castillo.

HIGH SCHOOL: Colegio San Benito Abad (San Pedro de Macoris, Dominican Republic).

TRANSACTIONS/CAREER NOTES: Signed as non-drafted free agent by Florida Marlins organization (August 19, 1992). ... On disabled list (July 20-September 11, 1995). ... On Florida disabled list (May 7-22, 1997). ... On Florida disabled list (April 16-May 5, 2000); included rehabilitation assignment to Calgary (April 28-May 5).

RECORDS: Holds N.L. single-season record for fewest errors for leader by second baseman—13 (2001).

STATISTICAL NOTES: Tied for Gulf Coast League lead in caught stealing with 12 in 1994. ... Led Gulf Coast League second basemen with 142 putouts, 318 total chances, 40 double plays and .972 fielding percentage in 1994. ... Led Eastern League in caught stealing with 28 in 1996. ... Led Eastern League second basemen with 326 assists, 557 total chances and 87 double plays in 1996. ... Tied for International League lead in caught stealing with 15 in 1998. ... Had 22-game hitting streak (August 9-September 3, 1999). ... Had 19-game hitting streak (July 3-28, 2000). ... Led N.L. in caught stealing with 22 in 2000. ... Had 35-game hitting streak (May 8-June 21, 2002).

MISCELLANEOUS: Holds Florida Marlins all-time records for most hits (790), most runs (413), most triples (25) and most stolen bases (229).

2002 GAMES PLAYED BY POSITION (MLB): 2B—144.

		BATTING														FIELDING	
Year Team (League)	Pos.	G	AB	R	H	2B	3B	HR	RBI	BB	SO	SB-CS	Avg.	OBP	SLG	E	Avg.
1993—Dom. Marlins (DSL)	IF	69	266	48	75	7	1	4	31	36	22	21-...	.282	...	.361	20	.943
1994—GC Marlins (GCL)	2B-SS	57	216	49	57	8	0	0	16	37	36	31-12	.264	.371	.301	9	†.972
1995—Kane County (Midw.)	2B	89	340	71	111	4	4	0	23	55	50	41-18	.326	.419	.362	17	.962
1996—Portland (East.)	2B	109	420	83	133	15	7	1	35	66	68	*51-28	.317	.411	.393	14	*.975
—Florida (N.L.)	2B	41	164	26	43	2	1	1	8	14	46	17-4	.262	.320	.305	3	.986
1997—Florida (N.L.)	2B	75	263	27	63	8	0	0	8	27	53	16-10	.240	.310	.270	9	.971
—Charlotte (I.L.)	2B	37	130	25	46	5	0	0	5	16	22	8-6	.354	.425	.392	5	.970
1998—Charlotte (I.L.)	2B	100	381	74	109	11	2	0	15	75	68	41-15	.286	.403	.325	16	.970
—Florida (N.L.)	2B	44	153	21	31	3	2	1	10	22	33	3-0	.203	.307	.268	7	.970
1999—Florida (N.L.)	2B	128	487	76	147	23	4	0	28	67	85	50-17	.302	.384	.366	15	.976
2000—Florida (N.L.)	2B	136	539	101	180	17	3	2	17	78	86	*62-22	.334	.418	.388	11	.983
—Calgary (PCL)	2B	4	13	4	4	1	1	0	0	4	2	1-0	.308	.471	.538	1	.944
2001—Florida (N.L.)	2B	134	537	76	141	16	10	2	45	67	90	33-16	.263	.344	.341	*13	.980
2002—Florida (N.L.)	2B	146	606	86	185	18	5	2	39	55	76	*48-15	.305	.364	.361	13	.981
Major League totals (7 years)		704	2749	413	790	87	25	8	155	330	469	229-84	.287	.364	.346	71	.979

ALL-STAR GAME RECORD

	AB	R	H	2B	3B	HR	RBI	BB	SO	SB-CS	Avg.	OBP	SLG	E	Avg.
All-Star Game totals (1 year)	2	0	0	0	0	0	0	0	0	0-0	.000	.000	.000	0	1.000

CASTRO, JUAN SS/2B REDS

PERSONAL: Born June 20, 1972, in Los Mochis, Mexico. ... 5-11/195. ... Bats right, throws right. ... Full name: Juan Gabriel Castro.

HIGH SCHOOL: CBTIS 43 (Los Mochis, Mexico).

TRANSACTIONS/CAREER NOTES: Signed as non-drafted free agent by Los Angeles Dodgers organization (June 13, 1991). ... On Los Angeles disabled list (June 5-August 1, 1997). ... Traded by Dodgers to Cincinnati Reds for a player to be named later and cash (April 1, 2000); Dodgers acquired P Kenny Lutz to complete deal (June 8, 2000). ... On Cincinnati disabled list (March 27-June 1, 2002); included rehabilitation assignments to Louisville (April 10-11 and May 27-June 1).

STATISTICAL NOTES: Tied for Texas League lead in double plays by shortstop with 82 in 1994.

2002 GAMES PLAYED BY POSITION (MLB): SS—25; 2B—17; 3B—1; 1B—1.

Year	Team (League)	Pos.	G	AB	R	H	2B	3B	HR	RBI	BB	SO	SB-CS	Avg.	OBP	SLG	E	Avg.
			BATTING														FIELDING	
1991—	Great Falls (Pio.)	SS-2B	60	217	36	60	4	2	1	27	33	31	7-6	.276	.369	.327	21	.921
1992—	Bakersfield (Calif.)	SS	113	446	56	116	15	4	4	42	37	64	14-11	.260	.314	.339	38	.928
1993—	San Antonio (Texas)	SS-2B	118	424	55	117	23	8	7	41	30	40	12-11	.276	.325	.417	28	.945
1994—	San Antonio (Texas)	SS	123	445	55	128	25	4	4	44	31	66	4-7	.288	.334	.389	29	.951
1995—	Albuquerque (PCL)	SS-2B	104	341	51	91	18	4	3	43	20	42	4-4	.267	.307	.370	14	.973
—	Los Angeles (N.L.)	3B-SS	11	4	0	1	0	0	0	0	1	1	0-0	.250	.400	.250	0	1.000
1996—	Albuquerque (PCL)	3B-SS-2B	17	56	12	21	4	2	1	8	6	7	1-1	.375	.444	.571	2	.962
—	Los Angeles (N.L.)	S-3-2-O	70	132	16	26	5	3	0	5	10	27	1-0	.197	.254	.280	3	.979
1997—	Los Angeles (N.L.)	SS-2B-3B	40	75	3	11	3	1	0	4	7	20	0-0	.147	.220	.213	1	.990
—	Albuquerque (PCL)	SS-2B	27	101	11	31	5	2	2	11	4	20	1-0	.307	.327	.455	9	.928
1998—	Los Angeles (N.L.)	SS-2B-3B	89	220	25	43	7	0	2	14	15	37	0-0	.195	.245	.255	10	.965
1999—	Albuquerque (PCL)	S-3-2-DH	116	423	52	116	25	4	7	51	34	70	2-3	.274	.325	.402	19	.956
—	Los Angeles (N.L.)	2B-SS	2	1	0	0	0	0	0	0	0	1	0-0	.000	.000	.000	0	1.000
2000—	Louisville (I.L.)■	SS-2B-3B	19	60	9	19	5	1	2	10	12	12	0-1	.317	.425	.533	4	.956
—	Cincinnati (N.L.)	SS-2B-3B	82	224	20	54	12	2	4	23	14	33	0-2	.241	.283	.366	2	.993
2001—	Cincinnati (N.L.)	SS-2B-3B-1B	96	242	27	54	10	0	3	13	13	50	0-0	.223	.261	.302	8	.970
2002—	Louisville (I.L.)	SS-2B	5	17	2	3	0	0	0	2	1	3	0-0	.176	.222	.176	1	.962
—	Cincinnati (N.L.)	SS-2B-3B-1B	54	82	5	18	3	0	2	11	7	18	0-0	.220	.278	.329	3	.971
Major League totals (8 years)			444	980	96	207	40	6	11	70	67	187	1-2	.211	.260	.298	27	.977

DIVISION SERIES RECORD

Year	Team (League)	Pos.	G	AB	R	H	2B	3B	HR	RBI	BB	SO	SB-CS	Avg.	OBP	SLG	E	Avg.
			BATTING														FIELDING	
1996—	Los Angeles (N.L.)	2B	2	5	0	1	1	0	0	1	1	1	0-0	.200	.333	.400	0	1.000

CASTRO, RAMON — C — MARLINS

PERSONAL: Born March 1, 1976, in Vega Baja, Puerto Rico. ... 6-3/235. ... Bats right, throws right. ... Full name: Ramon Abraham Castro.
HIGH SCHOOL: Lino P. Rivera (Vega Baja, Puerto Rico).
TRANSACTIONS/CAREER NOTES: Selected by Houston Astros organization in first round (17th pick overall) of free-agent draft (June 2, 1994). ... On Jackson disabled list (April 27-May 15, 1998). ... Traded by Astros to Florida Marlins for P Jay Powell and C Scott Makarewicz (July 6, 1998). ... On Calgary disabled list (April 20-May 5, 2000). ... On disabled list (May 17-June 8, 2002).
2002 GAMES PLAYED BY POSITION (MLB): C—37; DH—1.

Year	Team (League)	Pos.	G	AB	R	H	2B	3B	HR	RBI	BB	SO	SB-CS	Avg.	OBP	SLG	E	Avg.
			BATTING														FIELDING	
1994—	GC Astros (GCL)	C	37	123	17	34	7	0	3	14	17	14	5-5	.276	.373	.407	4	.983
1995—	Kissimmee (FSL)	C	36	120	6	25	5	0	0	8	6	21	0-0	.208	.250	.250	7	.967
—	Auburn (NY-Penn)	C	63	224	40	67	17	0	9	49	24	27	0-1	.299	.358	.496	2	.994
1996—	Quad City (Midw.)	C	96	314	38	78	15	0	7	43	31	61	2-0	.248	.317	.363	10	.987
1997—	Kissimmee (FSL)	C	115	410	53	115	22	1	8	65	53	73	1-0	.280	.357	.398	6	*.992
1998—	Jackson (Texas)	C	48	168	27	43	6	0	8	25	13	31	0-1	.256	.324	.435	10	.974
—	Portland (East.)■	C	31	88	9	22	3	0	3	11	8	21	0-0	.250	.306	.386	5	.946
1999—	Calgary (PCL)	C-DH	97	349	43	90	22	0	15	61	24	64	0-0	.258	.307	.450	7	.989
—	Florida (N.L.)	C	24	67	4	12	4	0	2	4	10	14	0-0	.179	.282	.328	1	.992
2000—	Calgary (PCL)	C	67	218	44	73	22	0	14	45	16	38	0-0	.335	.380	.628	4	.990
—	Florida (N.L.)	C	50	138	10	33	4	0	2	14	16	36	0-0	.239	.318	.312	6	.980
2001—	Florida (N.L.)	C	7	11	0	2	0	0	0	1	1	1	0-0	.182	.250	.182	0	1.000
—	Calgary (PCL)	C	108	390	81	131	33	0	27	90	38	74	1-1	.336	.393	.628	7	.989
2002—	Florida (N.L.)	C-DH	54	101	11	24	4	0	6	18	14	24	0-0	.238	.322	.455	0	1.000
Major League totals (4 years)			135	317	25	71	12	0	10	37	41	75	0-0	.224	.310	.356	7	.988

CATALANOTTO, FRANK — OF/IF — RANGERS

PERSONAL: Born April 27, 1974, in Smithtown, N.Y. ... 5-11/195. ... Bats left, throws right. ... Full name: Frank John Catalanotto.
HIGH SCHOOL: Smithtown (N.Y.) East.
COLLEGE: C.W. Post (Brookville, N.Y.).
TRANSACTIONS/CAREER NOTES: Selected by Detroit Tigers organization in 10th round of free-agent draft (June 1, 1992). ... Selected by Oakland Athletics from Tigers organization in Rule 5 major league draft (December 9, 1996). ... Returned to Tigers organization (March 21, 1997). ... On Toledo disabled list (June 18-25, 1998). ... Traded by Tigers with P Justin Thompson, P Francisco Cordero, OF Gabe Kapler, C Bill Haselman and P Alan Webb to Texas Rangers for OF Juan Gonzalez, P Danny Patterson and C Gregg Zaun (November 2, 1999). ... On Texas disabled list (April 22-May 15, 2000); included rehabilitation assignment to Oklahoma (May 12-15). ... On Texas disabled list (May 11-June 28 and August 17, 2002-remainder of season); included rehabilitation assignment to Tulsa (June 24-28).
STATISTICAL NOTES: Led Southern League second basemen with 411 assists, 681 total chances and 98 double plays in 1995. ... Led Southern League second basemen with 421 assists, 689 total chances and 99 double plays in 1996. ... Led International League second basemen with .984 fielding percentage in 1997. ... Career major league grand slams: 1.
2002 GAMES PLAYED BY POSITION (MLB): OF—26; 2B—23; 1B—15; DH—8.

Year	Team (League)	Pos.	G	AB	R	H	2B	3B	HR	RBI	BB	SO	SB-CS	Avg.	OBP	SLG	E	Avg.
			BATTING														FIELDING	
1992—	Bristol (Appl.)	2B	21	50	6	10	2	0	0	4	8	8	0-1	.200	.310	.240	2	.875
1993—	Bristol (Appl.)	2B	55	199	37	61	9	5	3	22	15	19	3-6	.307	.364	.447	10	.957
1994—	Fayetteville (S.Atl.)	2B	119	458	72	149	24	8	3	56	37	54	4-5	.325	.379	.432	15	.973
1995—	Jacksonville (Sou.)	2B	134	491	66	111	19	5	8	48	49	56	13-8	.226	.306	.334	18	*.974
1996—	Jacksonville (Sou.)	2B	132	497	105	148	34	6	17	67	74	69	15-14	.298	.398	.493	•22	.968
1997—	Toledo (I.L.)	2-3-O-DH	134	500	75	150	32	3	16	68	47	80	12-11	.300	.368	.472	18	†.966
—	Detroit (A.L.)	2B-DH	13	26	2	8	2	0	0	3	3	7	0-0	.308	.379	.385	0	1.000
1998—	Detroit (A.L.)	2-DH-1-3	89	213	23	60	13	2	6	25	12	39	3-2	.282	.325	.446	3	.986
—	Toledo (I.L.)	1B-2B-DH	28	105	20	35	6	3	4	28	14	21	0-0	.333	.438	.562	2	.989

Year	Team (League)	Pos.	G	AB	R	H	2B	3B	HR	RBI	BB	SO	SB-CS	Avg.	OBP	SLG	E	Avg.
								BATTING									FIELDING	
1999—	Detroit (A.L.)	1-2-3-DH	100	286	41	79	19	0	11	35	15	49	3-4	.276	.327	.458	5	.986
2000—	Texas (A.L.)■	2-DH-1-O	103	282	55	82	13	2	10	42	33	36	6-2	.291	.375	.457	9	.969
—	Oklahoma (PCL)	OF-2B	3	11	2	3	0	0	0	1	0	4	0-0	.273	.333	.273	0	1.000
2001—	Texas (A.L.)	0-2-3-1-DH	133	463	77	153	31	5	11	54	39	55	15-5	.330	.391	.490	4	.985
2002—	Texas (A.L.)	OF-2B-1B-DH	68	212	42	57	16	6	3	23	25	27	9-5	.269	.364	.443	2	.990
—	Tulsa (Texas)	1B-2B-OF	4	16	1	2	0	1	0	3	1	1	0-0	.125	.222	.250	0	1.000
Major League totals (6 years)			506	1482	240	439	94	15	41	182	127	213	36-18	.296	.362	.463	23	.983

CEDENO, JOVANNY — P — RANGERS

PERSONAL: Born October 25, 1979, in La Romana, Domincan Republic. ... 6-0/170. ... Throws right, bats right. ... Full name: Jovanny R. Cedeno.
TRANSACTIONS/CAREER NOTES: Signed as non-drafted free agent by Texas Rangers organization (February 2, 1997). ... On disabled list (September 1, 2000-remainder of season). ... On disabled list (April 22, 2001-remainder of season). ... On Texas disabled list (March 29, 2002-entire season); included rehabilitation assignment to Gulf Coast Rangers (August 20-25).

Year	League	W	L	Pct.	ERA	G	GS	CG	ShO	Sv.-Opp.	IP	H	R	ER	HR	BB-IBB	SO
1997—	Dom. Rangers (DSL)	10	2	.833	2.56	14	14	1	0	0-...	84.1	70	29	24	...	23-...	73
1998—	Dom. Rangers (DSL)	1	0	1.000	1.42	5	2	0	0	1-...	19.0	14	5	3	...	5-...	22
1999—	GC Rangers (GCL)	3	0	1.000	0.33	6	6	1	•1	0-...	27.1	13	3	1	0	4-0	32
—	Charlotte (FSL)	1	0	1.000	5.40	1	1	0	0	0-...	5.0	7	3	3	1	1-0	5
2000—	Savannah (S.Atl.)	11	4	.733	2.42	24	22	0	0	0-...	130.1	95	40	35	1	53-0	153
2001—	Texas (A.L.)									Did not play.							
—	Charlotte (FSL)	0	0	...	1.86	3	3	0	0	0-...	9.2	3	2	2	0	5-0	12
2002—	Gulf Coast Rangers (GCL)	0	0	...	0.00	3	1	0	0	0-...	5.0	3	0	0	0	1-0	4

CEDENO, ROGER — OF — METS

PERSONAL: Born August 16, 1974, in Valencia, Venezuela. ... 6-1/205. ... Bats both, throws right. ... Full name: Roger Leandro Cedeno.
TRANSACTIONS/CAREER NOTES: Signed as non-drafted free agent by Los Angeles Dodgers organization (March 28, 1991). ... On disabled list (June 27-July 14, 1994). ... On Los Angeles disabled list (March 25-April 17 and August 25, 1997-remainder of season); included rehabilitation assignment to Albuquerque (April 17-21). ... On Los Angeles disabled list (March 22-April 24, 1998); included rehabilitation assignment to Vero Beach (April 16-24). ... Traded by Dodgers with C Charles Johnson to New York Mets for C Todd Hundley and P Arnold Gooch (December 1, 1998). ... Traded by Mets with P Octavio Dotel and P Kyle Kessel to Houston Astros for P Mike Hampton and OF Derek Bell (December 23, 1999). ... On Houston disabled list (May 26-August 18, 2000); included rehabilitation assignment to New Orleans (August 10-18). ... Traded by Astros with C Mitch Meluskey and P Chris Holt to Detroit Tigers for C Brad Ausmus, P Doug Brocail and P Nelson Cruz (December 11, 2000). ... Granted free agency (November 5, 2001). ... Signed by Mets (December 17, 2001).
STATISTICAL NOTES: Tied for Pioneer League lead with three intentional bases on balls received in 1992. ... Led Texas League in caught stealing with 20 in 1993. ... Led Pacific Coast League in caught stealing with 18 in 1995. ... Led A.L. in caught stealing with 15 in 2001.
2002 GAMES PLAYED BY POSITION (MLB): OF—132.

Year	Team (League)	Pos.	G	AB	R	H	2B	3B	HR	RBI	BB	SO	SB-CS	Avg.	OBP	SLG	E	Avg.
								BATTING									FIELDING	
1991—	Dom. Dodgers (DSL)	OF	58	209	25	50	1	1	0	7	0	0	26-13	.239	...	.254	...	...
1992—	Great Falls (Pio.)	OF	69	256	60	81	6	5	2	27	51	53	*40-9	.316	.431	.402	8	.937
1993—	San Antonio (Texas)	OF	122	465	70	134	12	8	4	30	45	90	28-20	.288	.352	.374	9	.961
—	Albuquerque (PCL)	OF	6	18	1	4	1	1	0	4	3	3	0-1	.222	.333	.389	1	.923
1994—	Albuquerque (PCL)	OF	104	383	84	123	18	5	4	49	51	57	30-13	.321	.395	.426	8	.962
1995—	Albuquerque (PCL)	OF-DH	99	367	67	112	19	9	2	44	53	56	23-18	.305	.393	.422	3	.985
—	Los Angeles (N.L.)	OF	40	42	4	10	2	0	0	3	3	10	1-0	.238	.283	.286	1	.977
1996—	Los Angeles (N.L.)	OF	86	211	26	52	11	1	2	18	24	47	5-1	.246	.326	.336	2	.983
—	Albuquerque (PCL)	OF	33	125	16	28	2	3	1	10	15	22	6-5	.224	.307	.312	0	1.000
1997—	Albuquerque (PCL)	OF	29	113	21	40	4	4	2	9	22	16	5-5	.354	.463	.513	2	.964
—	Los Angeles (N.L.)	OF	80	194	31	53	10	2	3	17	25	44	9-1	.273	.362	.392	2	.987
1998—	Vero Beach (FSL)	OF	6	21	5	9	0	1	1	6	5	5	1-0	.429	.538	.667	1	.933
—	Los Angeles (N.L.)	OF	105	240	33	58	11	1	2	17	27	57	8-2	.242	.317	.321	2	.978
1999—	New York (N.L.)■	OF-2B	155	453	90	142	23	4	4	36	60	100	66-17	.313	.396	.408	3	.989
2000—	Houston (N.L.)■	OF	74	259	54	73	2	5	6	26	43	47	25-11	.282	.383	.398	3	.978
—	New Orleans (PCL)	OF	6	20	2	7	0	1	0	3	2	5	1-1	.350	.391	.450	0	1.000
2001—	Detroit (A.L.)■	OF-DH	131	523	79	153	14	11	6	48	36	83	55-15	.293	.337	.396	12	.953
2002—	New York (N.L.)■	OF	149	511	65	133	19	2	7	41	42	92	25-4	.260	.318	.346	8	.966
American League totals (1 year)			131	523	79	153	14	11	6	48	36	83	55-15	.293	.337	.396	12	.953
National League totals (7 years)			689	1910	303	521	78	15	24	158	224	397	139-36	.273	.350	.367	21	.980
Major League totals (8 years)			820	2433	382	674	92	26	30	206	260	480	194-51	.277	.348	.373	33	.975

DIVISION SERIES RECORD

Year	Team (League)	Pos.	G	AB	R	H	2B	3B	HR	RBI	BB	SO	SB-CS	Avg.	OBP	SLG	E	Avg.
								BATTING									FIELDING	
1999—	New York (N.L.)	OF-PH	4	7	1	2	0	0	0	2	1	1	1-0	.286	.333	.286	0	1.000

CHAMPIONSHIP SERIES RECORD

Year	Team (League)	Pos.	G	AB	R	H	2B	3B	HR	RBI	BB	SO	SB-CS	Avg.	OBP	SLG	E	Avg.
								BATTING									FIELDING	
1999—	New York (N.L.)	OF-PR	5	12	2	6	1	0	0	1	0	1	2-1	.500	.500	.583	0	1.000

CEPICKY, MATT — OF — EXPOS

PERSONAL: Born November 10, 1977, in St. Louis, Mo. ... 6-2/215. ... Bats left, throws right. ... Full name: Matthew William Cepicky. ... Cousin of Scott Cepicky, first baseman in Chicago White Sox organization (1989-94).
HIGH SCHOOL: Vianney (Kirkwood, Mo.).
COLLEGE: Southwest Missouri State.

TRANSACTIONS/CAREER NOTES: Selected by Montreal Expos organization in fourth round of free-agent draft (June 2, 1999).
STATISTICAL NOTES: Tied for New York-Pennsylvania League lead with 160 total bases in 1999. ... Career major league grand slams: 1.
2002 GAMES PLAYED BY POSITION (MLB): OF—17.

			BATTING														FIELDING	
Year	**Team (League)**	**Pos.**	**G**	**AB**	**R**	**H**	**2B**	**3B**	**HR**	**RBI**	**BB**	**SO**	**SB-CS**	**Avg.**	**OBP**	**SLG**	**E**	**Avg.**
1999—	Vermont (NY-Penn)	OF	74	323	50	99	15	5	12	53	20	49	10-9	.307	.349	.495	1	.986
2000—	Jupiter (FSL)	OF	131	*536	61	160	32	7	5	88	24	64	32-13	.299	.328	.412	4	.983
2001—	Harrisburg (East.)	OF	122	459	59	121	23	8	15	77	21	97	5-12	.264	.296	.447	3	.986
2002—	Harrisburg (East.)	OF	109	419	54	116	25	2	16	76	33	94	7-1	.277	.327	.461	2	.988
	—Montreal (N.L.)	OF	32	74	7	16	3	0	3	15	4	21	0-0	.216	.256	.378	0	1.000
Major League totals (1 year)			32	74	7	16	3	0	3	15	4	21	0-0	.216	.256	.378	0	1.000

CERDA, JAIME — P — METS

PERSONAL: Born October 26, 1978, in Fresno, Calif. ... 6-0/175. ... Throws left, bats left. ... Full name: Jaime M. Cerda.
JUNIOR COLLEGE: Fresno City.
TRANSACTIONS/CAREER NOTES: Selected by New York Mets organization in 23rd round of free-agent draft (June 2, 1998). ... On disabled list (June 18, 1999-entire season).
CAREER HITTING (MLB): 0-for-1 (.000), 0 R, 0 2B, 0 3B, 0 HR, 0 RBI.

Year	**League**	**W**	**L**	**Pct.**	**ERA**	**G**	**GS**	**CG**	**ShO**	**Sv.-Opp.**	**IP**	**H**	**R**	**ER**	**HR**	**BB-IBB**	**SO**
1999—										Did not play.							
2000—	Pittsfield (NY-Penn)	4	1	.800	0.57	20	1	0	0	5-...	47.0	33	6	3	0	6-1	51
2001—	St. Lucie (FSL)	2	1	.667	0.97	28	0	0	0	6-...	55.2	40	8	6	3	12-0	53
	—Binghamton (East.)	1	0	1.000	3.10	12	0	0	0	3-...	20.1	17	7	7	1	6-0	22
	—Norfolk (I.L.)	0	0	...	3.86	3	0	0	0	0-...	4.2	2	2	2	0	2-0	4
2002—	Binghamton (East.)	5	1	.833	2.27	14	0	0	0	0-...	31.2	21	8	8	0	10-0	33
	—Norfolk (I.L.)	0	0	...	0.43	12	0	0	0	1-...	21.0	10	2	1	0	7-1	17
	—New York (N.L.)	0	0	...	2.45	32	0	0	0	0-0	25.2	22	7	7	0	14-0	21
Major League totals (1 year)		0	0	...	2.45	32	0	0	0	0-0	25.2	22	7	7	0	14-0	21

CHACON, SHAWN — P — ROCKIES

PERSONAL: Born December 23, 1977, in Anchorage, Alaska. ... 6-3/212. ... Throws right, bats right. ... Full name: Shawn A. Chacon.
HIGH SCHOOL: Greeley (Colo.) Central.
TRANSACTIONS/CAREER NOTES: Selected by Colorado Rockies organization in third round of free-agent draft (June 4, 1996). ... On Colorado disabled list (May 10-June 6, 2002); included rehabilitation assignment to Colorado Springs (May 29-June 6).
CAREER HITTING (MLB): 11-for-82 (.134), 5 R, 1 2B, 0 3B, 0 HR, 3 RBI.

Year	**League**	**W**	**L**	**Pct.**	**ERA**	**G**	**GS**	**CG**	**ShO**	**Sv.-Opp.**	**IP**	**H**	**R**	**ER**	**HR**	**BB-IBB**	**SO**
1996—	Arizona Rockies (Ariz.)	1	2	.333	*1.60	11	11	1	0	0-...	56.1	46	17	10	1	15-0	64
	—Portland (N'West)	0	2	.000	6.86	4	4	0	0	0-...	19.2	24	18	15	2	9-0	17
1997—	Asheville (S.Atl.)	11	7	.611	3.89	28	27	1	0	0-...	162.0	155	80	70	13	63-1	149
1998—	Salem (Caro.)	0	4	.000	5.30	12	12	0	0	0-...	56.0	53	35	33	5	31-0	54
1999—	Salem (Caro.)	5	5	.500	4.13	12	12	0	0	0-...	72.0	69	44	33	3	34-0	66
2000—	Carolina (Sou.)	10	10	.500	3.16	27	•27	4	*3	0-...	173.2	151	71	61	10	*85-1	*172
2001—	Colorado Springs (PCL)	2	0	1.000	2.25	4	4	0	0	0-...	24.0	18	6	6	3	7-0	28
	—Colorado (N.L.)	6	10	.375	5.06	27	27	0	0	0-0	160.0	157	96	90	26	87-10	134
2002—	Colorado (N.L.)	5	11	.313	5.73	21	21	0	0	0-0	119.1	122	84	76	25	60-3	67
	—Colorado Springs (PCL)	2	0	1.000	4.79	4	4	0	0	0-...	20.2	23	12	11	3	10-0	15
Major League totals (2 years)		11	21	.344	5.35	48	48	0	0	0-0	279.1	279	180	166	51	147-13	201

CHARLTON, NORM — P

PERSONAL: Born January 6, 1963, in Fort Polk, La. ... 6-3/205. ... Throws left, bats both. ... Full name: Norman Wood Charlton III.
HIGH SCHOOL: James Madison (San Antonio).
COLLEGE: Rice.
TRANSACTIONS/CAREER NOTES: Selected by Montreal Expos organization in supplemental round ("sandwich pick" between first and second round, 28th pick overall) of free-agent draft (June 4, 1984); pick received as compensation for San Francisco Giants signing Type B free-agent 2B Manny Trillo. ... Traded by Expos with a player to be named later to Cincinnati Reds for IF Wayne Krenchicki (March 31, 1986); Reds acquired 2B Tim Barker to complete deal (April 2, 1986). ... On Cincinnati disabled list (April 6-June 26, 1987); included rehabilitation assignment to Nashville (June 9-26). ... On disabled list (May 26-June 11 and June 17-July 19, 1991). ... On suspended list (September 29 and October 4-6, 1991). ... Traded by Reds to Seattle Mariners for OF Kevin Mitchell (November 17, 1992). ... On suspended list (July 9-16, 1993). ... On disabled list (July 21-August 5 and August 8, 1993-remainder of season). ... Granted free agency (November 18, 1993). ... Signed by Philadelphia Phillies organization (February 3, 1994). ... On disabled list (March 31, 1994-entire season). ... Granted free agency (October 28, 1994). ... Re-signed by Phillies organization (December 22, 1994). ... Released by Phillies (July 10, 1995). ... Signed by Mariners (July 14, 1995). ... Granted free agency (November 7, 1997). ... Signed by Baltimore Orioles organization (December 15, 1997). ... Released by Orioles (July 28, 1998). ... Signed by Atlanta Braves organization (August 5, 1998). ... Granted free agency (October 27, 1998). ... Signed by Tampa Bay Devil Rays organization (January 20, 1999). ... On Durham disabled list (April 8-17, 1999). ... Granted free agency (November 2, 1999). ... Re-signed by Devil Rays organization (January 7, 2000). ... Released by Devil Rays (March 31, 2000). ... Signed by Reds organization (April 9, 2000). ... Released by Reds (April 28, 2000). ... Signed by Mariners organization (December 19, 2000). ... On Seattle disabled list (May 31-June 15 and June 23-July 26, 2001); included rehabilitation assignment to Tacoma (July 22-26). ... Granted free agency (November 5, 2001). ... Re-signed by Mariners (December 18, 2001). ... Released by Mariners (February 7, 2002). ... Re-signed by Mariners (May 15, 2002). ... On disabled list (May 15, 2002-entire season). ... Granted free agency (October 29, 2002).
STATISTICAL NOTES: Led American Association with 13 wild pitches in 1988.
MISCELLANEOUS: Appeared in one game as pinch runner (1990). ... Appeared in two games as pinch runner (1991).
CAREER HITTING (MLB): 8-for-87 (.092), 6 R, 2 2B, 0 3B, 0 HR, 1 RBI.

Year League	W	L	Pct.	ERA	G	GS	CG	ShO	Sv.-Opp.	IP	H	R	ER	HR	BB-IBB	SO
1984—West Palm Beach (FSL)	1	4	.200	4.58	8	8	0	0	0-...	39.1	51	27	20	2	22-0	27
1985—West Palm Beach (FSL)	7	10	.412	4.57	24	23	5	2	0-...	128.0	135	79	65	7	79-1	71
1986—Vermont (East.)■	10	6	.625	2.83	22	22	6	1	0-...	136.2	109	55	43	4	74-2	96
1987—Nashville (A.A.)	2	8	.200	4.30	18	17	3	1	0-...	98.1	97	57	47	8	44-1	74
1988—Nashville (A.A.)	11	10	.524	3.02	27	27	8	1	0-...	182.0	149	69	61	7	56-1	*161
—Cincinnati (N.L.)	4	5	.444	3.96	10	10	0	0	0-0	61.1	60	27	27	6	20-2	39
1989—Cincinnati (N.L.)	8	3	.727	2.93	69	0	0	0	0-1	95.1	67	38	31	5	40-7	98
1990—Cincinnati (N.L.)	12	9	.571	2.74	56	16	1	1	2-3	154.1	131	53	47	10	70-4	117
1991—Cincinnati (N.L.)	3	5	.375	2.91	39	11	0	0	1-4	108.1	92	37	35	6	34-4	77
1992—Cincinnati (N.L.)	4	2	.667	2.99	64	0	0	0	26-34	81.1	79	39	27	7	26-4	90
1993—Seattle (A.L.)■	1	3	.250	2.34	34	0	0	0	18-21	34.2	22	12	9	4	17-0	48
1994—Philadelphia (N.L.)■									Did not play.							
1995—Philadelphia (N.L.)	2	5	.286	7.36	25	0	0	0	0-1	22.0	23	19	18	2	15-3	12
—Seattle (A.L.)■	2	1	.667	1.51	30	0	0	0	14-15	47.2	23	12	8	2	16-0	58
1996—Seattle (A.L.)	4	7	.364	4.04	70	0	0	0	20-27	75.2	68	37	34	7	38-1	73
1997—Seattle (A.L.)	3	8	.273	7.27	71	0	0	0	14-25	69.1	89	59	56	7	47-2	55
1998—Baltimore (A.L.)■	2	1	.667	6.94	36	0	0	0	0-1	35.0	46	27	27	5	25-0	41
—Richmond (I.L.)■	0	0	...	0.00	2	0	0	0	0-...	2.0	2	0	0	0	0-0	1
—Atlanta (N.L.)	0	0	...	1.38	13	0	0	0	1-1	13.0	7	2	2	0	8-0	6
1999—Durham (I.L.)■	3	2	.600	3.69	18	0	0	0	1-...	31.2	27	13	13	7	10-1	29
—Tampa Bay (A.L.)	2	3	.400	4.44	42	0	0	0	0-1	50.2	49	29	25	4	36-0	45
2000—Louisville (I.L.)■	0	0	...	0.00	4	0	0	0	1-...	2.2	0	0	0	0	2-0	5
—Cincinnati (N.L.)	0	0	...	27.00	2	0	0	0	0-0	3.0	6	9	9	1	6-0	1
2001—Seattle (A.L.)■	4	2	.667	3.02	44	0	0	0	1-2	47.2	36	19	16	4	11-0	48
—Tacoma (PCL)	0	1	.000	3.00	4	2	0	0	0-...	6.0	4	2	2	0	2-0	9
2002—Seattle (A.L.)									Did not play.							
A.L. totals (7 years)	18	25	.419	4.37	327	0	0	0	67-92	360.2	333	195	175	33	190-3	368
N.L. totals (8 years)	33	29	.532	3.27	278	37	1	1	30-44	538.2	465	224	196	37	219-24	440
Major League totals (13 years)	51	54	.486	3.71	605	37	1	1	97-136	899.1	798	419	371	70	409-27	808

DIVISION SERIES RECORD

Year League	W	L	Pct.	ERA	G	GS	CG	ShO	Sv.-Opp.	IP	H	R	ER	HR	BB-IBB	SO
1995—Seattle (A.L.)	1	0	1.000	2.45	4	0	0	0	1-3	7.1	4	2	2	1	3-0	9
1997—Seattle (A.L.)	0	0	...	0.00	2	0	0	0	0-0	2.1	2	0	0	0	0-0	1
2001—Seattle (A.L.)	0	0	...	0.00	1	0	0	0	0-0	1.2	0	0	0	0	0-0	2
Division series totals (3 years)	1	0	1.000	1.59	7	0	0	0	1-3	11.1	6	2	2	1	3-0	12

CHAMPIONSHIP SERIES RECORD

Year League	W	L	Pct.	ERA	G	GS	CG	ShO	Sv.-Opp.	IP	H	R	ER	HR	BB-IBB	SO
1990—Cincinnati (N.L.)	1	1	.500	1.80	4	0	0	0	0-0	5.0	4	2	1	0	3-0	3
1995—Seattle (A.L.)	1	0	1.000	0.00	3	0	0	0	1-1	6.0	1	0	0	0	1-0	5
2001—Seattle (A.L.)	0	0	...	0.00	2	0	0	0	0-0	1.2	1	0	0	0	2-1	2
Champ. series totals (3 years)	2	1	.667	0.71	9	0	0	0	1-1	12.2	6	2	1	0	6-1	10

WORLD SERIES RECORD

NOTES: Member of World Series championship team (1990).

Year League	W	L	Pct.	ERA	G	GS	CG	ShO	Sv.-Opp.	IP	H	R	ER	HR	BB-IBB	SO
1990—Cincinnati (N.L.)	0	0	...	0.00	1	0	0	0	0-0	1.0	1	0	0	0	0-0	0

ALL-STAR GAME RECORD

	W	L	Pct.	ERA	GS	CG	ShO	Sv.-Opp.	IP	H	R	ER	HR	BB-IBB	SO
All-Star Game totals (1 year)	0	0	...	0.00	0	0	0	0-0	1.0	0	0	0	0	0-0	1

CHAVEZ, ENDY — OF — EXPOS

PERSONAL: Born February 7, 1978, in Valencia, Venezuela. ... 6-0/165. ... Bats left, throws left. ... Full name: Endy DeJesus Chavez.

HIGH SCHOOL: Liceo Bataila Carabobo (Venezuela).

TRANSACTIONS/CAREER NOTES: Signed as non-drafted free agent by New York Mets organization (April 29, 1996). ... Selected by Kansas City Royals from Mets organization in Rule 5 major league draft (December 11, 2000). ... Returned to Mets organization (March 30, 2001). ... Traded by Mets to Royals for OF Michael Curry (March 30, 2001). ... Claimed on waivers by Detroit Tigers (December 20, 2001). ... Claimed on waivers by Mets (February 1, 2002). ... Claimed on waivers by Montreal Expos (February 22, 2002).

STATISTICAL NOTES: Had 16-game hitting streak (September 10-27, 2002).

2002 GAMES PLAYED BY POSITION (MLB): OF—35.

		BATTING														FIELDING	
Year Team (League)	Pos.	G	AB	R	H	2B	3B	HR	RBI	BB	SO	SB-CS	Avg.	OBP	SLG	E	Avg.
1996—Dom. Mets (DSL)	OF	48	164	42	58	11	1	7	29	22	16	3-...	.354	...	.561	3	.963
1997—GC Mets (GCL)	OF	33	119	26	33	6	3	0	15	20	10	1-2	.277	.379	.378	2	.967
—Kingsport (Appl.)	OF	19	73	16	22	4	0	0	4	13	10	5-2	.301	.407	.356	2	.957
1998—Kingsport (Appl.)	OF	33	114	26	33	8	4	0	16	17	17	10-5	.289	.373	.430	2	.941
1999—Capital City (S.Atl.)	OF	73	253	40	64	8	1	0	15	34	36	20-12	.253	.340	.292	5	.967
—St. Lucie (FSL)	OF	45	183	33	57	8	3	2	18	22	22	9-3	.311	.383	.421	2	.980
2000—St. Lucie (FSL)	OF	111	433	84	129	20	2	1	43	47	48	38-16	.298	.364	.360	5	.980
2001—Wichita (Texas)■	OF	43	168	27	50	6	1	1	13	16	13	11-6	.298	.353	.363	1	.990
—Kansas City (A.L.)	OF	29	77	4	16	2	0	0	5	3	8	0-2	.208	.238	.234	0	1.000
—Omaha (PCL)	OF	23	104	18	35	6	0	0	4	0	13	4-3	.337	.333	.394	0	1.000
2002—Ottawa (I.L.)■	OF	103	405	67	139	28	5	4	41	33	37	21-13	*.343	.392	.467	4	.985
—Montreal (N.L.)	OF	36	125	20	37	8	5	1	9	5	16	3-5	.296	.321	.464	1	.989
American League totals (1 year)		29	77	4	16	2	0	0	5	3	8	0-2	.208	.238	.234	0	1.000
National League totals (1 year)		36	125	20	37	8	5	1	9	5	16	3-5	.296	.321	.464	1	.989
Major League totals (2 years)		65	202	24	53	10	5	1	14	8	24	3-7	.262	.289	.376	1	.992

CHAVEZ, ERIC — 3B — ATHLETICS

PERSONAL: Born December 7, 1977, in Los Angeles. ... 6-1/206. ... Bats left, throws right. ... Full name: Eric Cesar Chavez.
HIGH SCHOOL: Mount Carmel (San Diego).
TRANSACTIONS/CAREER NOTES: Selected by Oakland Athletics organization in first round (10th pick overall) of free-agent draft (June 2, 1996). ... On Oakland disabled list (August 21-September 19, 1999); included rehabilitation assignment to Vancouver (September 14-19).
HONORS: Won A.L. Gold Glove at third base (2001-02). ... Named third baseman on The Sporting News A.L. All-Star team (2002). ... Named third baseman on A.L. Silver Slugger team (2002).
STATISTICAL NOTES: Had 15-game hitting streak (May 27-June 18, 2000). ... Hit for the cycle (June 21, 2000). ... Led A.L. third basemen with 120 putouts, 301 assists and 438 total chances in 2002. ... Career major league grand slams: 4.
2002 GAMES PLAYED BY POSITION (MLB): 3B—143; DH—9; OF—1.

		BATTING														FIELDING	
Year Team (League)	Pos.	G	AB	R	H	2B	3B	HR	RBI	BB	SO	SB-CS	Avg.	OBP	SLG	E	Avg.
1997—Visalia (Calif.)	3B-DH	134	520	67	141	30	3	18	100	37	91	13-7	.271	.321	.444	*32	.917
1998—Huntsville (Sou.)	3B-DH	88	335	66	110	27	1	22	86	42	61	12-4	.328	.402	.612	14	.935
—Edmonton (PCL)	3B-DH	47	194	38	63	18	0	11	40	12	32	2-3	.325	.364	.588	7	.935
—Oakland (A.L.)	3B	16	45	6	14	4	1	0	6	3	5	1-1	.311	.354	.444	0	1.000
1999—Oakland (A.L.)	3B-DH-SS	115	356	47	88	21	2	13	50	46	56	1-1	.247	.333	.427	9	.961
2000—Oakland (A.L.)	3B-SS-DH	153	501	89	139	23	4	26	86	62	94	2-2	.277	.355	.495	18	.951
2001—Oakland (A.L.)	3-1-S-DH	151	552	91	159	43	0	32	114	41	99	8-2	.288	.338	.540	12	.972
2002—Oakland (A.L.)	3B-DH-OF	153	585	87	161	31	3	34	109	65	119	8-3	.275	.348	.513	17	.961
Major League totals (5 years)		588	2039	320	561	122	10	105	365	217	373	20-9	.275	.344	.499	56	.963

DIVISION SERIES RECORD

		BATTING														FIELDING	
Year Team (League)	Pos.	G	AB	R	H	2B	3B	HR	RBI	BB	SO	SB-CS	Avg.	OBP	SLG	E	Avg.
2000—Oakland (A.L.)	3B	5	21	4	7	3	0	0	4	0	5	0-0	.333	.333	.476	0	1.000
2001—Oakland (A.L.)	3B	5	21	0	3	1	0	0	0	0	5	0-0	.143	.143	.190	1	.938
2002—Oakland (A.L.)	3B	5	21	3	8	0	0	1	5	2	1	0-0	.381	.435	.524	0	1.000
Division series totals (3 years)		15	63	7	18	4	0	1	9	2	11	0-0	.286	.308	.397	1	.977

CHAVEZ, RAUL — C — ASTROS

PERSONAL: Born March 18, 1973, in Valencia, Venezuela. ... 5-11/210. ... Bats right, throws right. ... Full name: Raul Alexander Chavez.
TRANSACTIONS/CAREER NOTES: Signed as non-drafted free agent by Houston Astros organization (January 10, 1990). ... Traded by Astros with P Dave Veres to Montreal Expos for 3B Sean Berry (December 20, 1995). ... Traded by Expos to Seattle Mariners for OF Robert Perez (May 8, 1998). ... Granted free agency (October 15, 1999). ... Signed by Astros organization (January 5, 2000). ... On disabled list (August 10-19, 2001).
STATISTICAL NOTES: Led Texas League catchers with 563 putouts in 1994. ... Led International League catchers with 77 assists in 1997. ... Tied for International League lead in double plays by catcher with nine in 1997. ... Led Pacific Coast League catchers with 12 double plays in 1998. ... Led Pacific Coast League catchers with 74 assists in 1999. ... Tied for Pacific Coast League lead in assists by catcher with 62 and double plays with 10 in 2001. ... Led Pacific Coast League catchers with 734 putouts, 77 assists and 818 total chances and tied for league lead with nine double plays in 2002.
2002 GAMES PLAYED BY POSITION (MLB): C—2.

		BATTING														FIELDING	
Year Team (League)	Pos.	G	AB	R	H	2B	3B	HR	RBI	BB	SO	SB-CS	Avg.	OBP	SLG	E	Avg.
1990—GC Astros (GCL)	SS-2B-3B	48	155	23	50	8	1	0	23	7	12	5-3	.323	.358	.387	9	.954
1991—Burlington (Midw.)	SS-3B	114	420	54	108	17	0	3	41	25	65	1-4	.257	.312	.319	41	.914
1992—Asheville (S.Atl.)	C	95	348	37	99	22	1	2	40	16	39	1-0	.284	.320	.371	13	.976
1993—Osceola (FSL)	C	58	197	13	45	5	1	0	16	8	19	1-1	.228	.261	.264	5	.986
1994—Jackson (Texas)	C	89	251	17	55	7	0	1	22	17	41	1-0	.219	.273	.259	9	.986
1995—Jackson (Texas)	C	58	188	16	54	8	0	4	25	8	17	0-4	.287	.323	.394	5	.987
—Tucson (PCL)	C	32	103	14	27	5	0	0	10	8	13	0-1	.262	.325	.311	5	.980
1996—Ottawa (I.L.)■	C	60	198	15	49	10	0	2	24	11	31	0-2	.247	.290	.328	4	.990
—Montreal (N.L.)	C	4	5	1	1	0	0	0	0	1	1	1-0	.200	.333	.200	0	1.000
1997—Ottawa (I.L.)	C-DH	92	310	31	76	17	0	4	46	18	42	1-3	.245	.293	.339	*15	.978
—Montreal (N.L.)	C	13	26	0	7	0	0	0	2	0	5	1-0	.269	.259	.269	0	1.000
1998—Ottawa (I.L.)	C	11	31	2	7	0	0	0	1	5	5	0-0	.226	.333	.226	0	1.000
—Tacoma (PCL)■	C-DH	76	233	27	52	6	0	4	34	22	41	1-2	.223	.294	.300	6	.990
—Seattle (A.L.)	C	1	1	0	0	0	0	0	0	0	0	0-0	.000	.000	.000	0	1.000
1999—Tacoma (PCL)	C-D-1-2-3-S	102	354	39	95	20	1	3	40	28	63	1-3	.268	.331	.356	10	.987
2000—New Orleans (PCL)■	C	99	303	31	74	13	0	2	36	34	44	3-0	.244	.325	.307	8	.987
—Houston (N.L.)	C	14	43	3	11	2	0	1	5	3	6	0-0	.256	.298	.372	1	.986
2001—New Orleans (PCL)	C-1B-3B	85	278	38	84	17	0	8	40	19	34	1-1	.302	.361	.450	5	.992
2002—New Orleans (PCL)	C	111	373	24	85	10	0	3	36	21	50	3-4	.228	.278	.279	7	.991
—Houston (N.L.)	C	2	4	1	1	1	0	0	0	1	0	0-0	.250	.500	.500	0	1.000
American League totals (1 year)		1	1	0	0	0	0	0	0	0	0	0-0	.000	.000	.000	0	1.000
National League totals (4 years)		33	78	5	20	3	0	1	7	5	12	2-0	.256	.302	.333	1	.993
Major League totals (5 years)		34	79	5	20	3	0	1	7	5	12	2-0	.253	.299	.329	1	.994

CHEN, BRUCE — P — REDS

PERSONAL: Born June 19, 1977, in Panama City, Panama. ... 6-2/210. ... Throws left, bats left. ... Full name: Bruce Kastulo Chen.
HIGH SCHOOL: Instituto Panamericano (Panama).
TRANSACTIONS/CAREER NOTES: Signed as non-drafted free agent by Atlanta Braves organization (July 1, 1993). ... Traded by Braves with P Jimmy Osting to Philadelphia Phillies for P Andy Ashby (July 12, 2000). ... Traded by Phillies with P Adam Walker to New York Mets for P Turk Wendell and P Dennis Cook (July 27, 2001). ... Traded by Mets with P Dicky Gonzalez and SS/2B Luis Figueroa to Montreal Expos for P Scott Strickland, OF Matt Watson and P Philip Seibel (April 5, 2002). ... Traded by Expos to Cincinnati Reds for P Jim Brower (June 14, 2002).
RECORDS: Shares N.L. single-inning record for most consecutive home runs allowed—3 (May 3, 2002, first inning).
HONORS: Named Southern League Most Outstanding Pitcher (1998).
CAREER HITTING (MLB): 13-for-110 (.118), 4 R, 1 2B, 0 3B, 0 HR, 3 RBI.

Year League	W	L	Pct.	ERA	G	GS	CG	ShO	Sv.-Opp.	IP	H	R	ER	HR	BB-IBB	SO
1994—Gulf Coast Braves (GCL)	1	4	.200	3.80	9	7	0	0	1-...	42.2	42	21	18	2	3-0	26
1995—Danville (Appl.)	4	4	.500	3.97	14	13	1	0	0-...	70.1	78	42	31	3	19-1	56
1996—Eugene (N'West)	4	1	.800	2.27	11	8	0	0	0-...	35.2	23	13	9	1	14-0	55
1997—Macon (S.Atl.)	12	7	.632	3.51	28	28	1	1	0-...	146.1	120	67	57	*19	44-0	*182
1998—Greenville (Sou.)	13	7	.650	3.29	24	23	1	0	0-...	139.1	106	57	51	12	48-0	164
—Richmond (I.L.)	2	1	.667	1.88	4	4	0	0	0-...	24.0	17	5	5	1	19-0	29
—Atlanta (N.L.)	2	0	1.000	3.98	4	4	0	0	0-0	20.1	23	9	9	3	9-1	17
1999—Richmond (I.L.)	6	3	.667	3.81	14	14	0	0	0-...	78.0	73	36	33	10	26-0	90
—Atlanta (N.L.)	2	2	.500	5.47	16	7	0	0	0-0	51.0	38	32	31	11	27-3	45
2000—Atlanta (N.L.)	4	0	1.000	2.50	22	0	0	0	0-0	39.2	35	15	11	4	19-2	32
—Richmond (I.L.)	1	0	1.000	0.00	1	1	0	0	0-...	6.0	5	0	0	0	1-0	6
—Philadelphia (N.L.)■	3	4	.429	3.63	15	15	0	0	0-0	94.1	81	39	38	14	27-2	80
2001—Philadelphia (N.L.)	4	5	.444	5.00	16	16	0	0	0-0	86.1	90	53	48	19	31-4	79
—Reading (East.)	1	0	1.000	0.00	1	1	0	0	0-...	6.0	3	0	0	0	0-0	7
—Scranton/W.B. (I.L.)	1	0	1.000	3.86	3	3	0	0	0-...	18.2	14	8	8	2	5-0	14
—New York (N.L.)■	3	2	.600	4.68	11	11	0	0	0-0	59.2	56	37	31	10	28-0	47
2002—New York (N.L.)	0	0	...	0.00	1	0	0	0	0-0	.2	1	0	0	0	0-0	0
—Montreal (N.L.)■	2	3	.400	6.99	15	5	0	0	0-0	37.1	47	29	29	9	23-3	43
—Cincinnati (N.L.)■	0	2	.000	4.31	39	1	0	0	0-0	39.2	37	24	19	7	20-2	37
Major League totals (5 years)	20	18	.526	4.53	139	59	0	0	0-0	429.0	408	238	216	77	184-17	380

DIVISION SERIES RECORD

Year League	W	L	Pct.	ERA	G	GS	CG	ShO	Sv.-Opp.	IP	H	R	ER	HR	BB-IBB	SO
1999—Atlanta (N.L.)									Did not play.							

CHAMPIONSHIP SERIES RECORD

Year League	W	L	Pct.	ERA	G	GS	CG	ShO	Sv.-Opp.	IP	H	R	ER	HR	BB-IBB	SO
1999—Atlanta (N.L.)									Did not play.							

WORLD SERIES RECORD

Year League	W	L	Pct.	ERA	G	GS	CG	ShO	Sv.-Opp.	IP	H	R	ER	HR	BB-IBB	SO
1999—Atlanta (N.L.)									Did not play.							

CHEN, CHIN-FENG — OF — DODGERS

PERSONAL: Born October 28, 1977, in Tainan City, Taiwan. ... 6-1/189. ... Bats right, throws right.
TRANSACTIONS/CAREER NOTES: Signed as non-drafted free agent by Los Angeles Dodgers organization (January 5, 1999).
HONORS: Named California League Most Valuable Player (1999).
2002 GAMES PLAYED BY POSITION (MLB): OF—1.

		BATTING														FIELDING	
Year Team (League)	Pos.	G	AB	R	H	2B	3B	HR	RBI	BB	SO	SB-CS	Avg.	OBP	SLG	E	Avg.
1999—San Bern. (Calif.)	OF	131	510	98	161	22	10	31	•123	75	129	31-7	.316	.404	.580	6	.971
2000—San Antonio (Texas)	OF	133	516	66	143	27	3	6	67	61	131	23-15	.277	.355	.376	3	.988
2001—Vero Beach (FSL)	OF	62	235	38	63	15	3	5	41	28	56	2-0	.268	.359	.421	0	1.000
—Jacksonville (Sou.)	OF	66	224	47	70	16	2	17	50	41	65	5-4	.313	.422	.629	3	.966
2002—Las Vegas (PCL)	1B-OF	137	511	90	145	26	4	26	84	58	*160	1-0	.284	.352	.503	11	.988
—Los Angeles (N.L.)	OF	3	5	1	0	0	0	0	0	1	3	0-0	.000	.167	.000	0	1.000
Major League totals (1 year)		3	5	1	0	0	0	0	0	1	3	0-0	.000	.167	.000	0	1.000

CHIASSON, SCOTT — P — CUBS

PERSONAL: Born August 14, 1977, in Norwich, Conn. ... 6-3/200. ... Throws right, bats right. ... Full name: Scott Christopher Chiasson.
HIGH SCHOOL: Norwich Free Academy (Conn.).
COLLEGE: Eastern Connecticut College.
TRANSACTIONS/CAREER NOTES: Selected by Kansas City Royals organization in fifth round of free-agent draft (June 2, 1998). ... Traded by Royals to Oakland Atheltics (June 10, 1999), completing deal in which A's sent P Jay Witasick to Royals for a player to be named later and cash (March 30, 1999). ... Selected by Chicago Cubs from A's organization in Rule 5 major league draft (December 11, 2000). ... On Iowa disabled list (June 4-13, 2002). ... On West Tenn disabled list (July 6, 2002-remainder of season).
CAREER HITTING (MLB): 0-for-0 (.000), 0 R, 0 2B, 0 3B, 0 HR, 0 RBI.

Year League	W	L	Pct.	ERA	G	GS	CG	ShO	Sv.-Opp.	IP	H	R	ER	HR	BB-IBB	SO
1998—Gulf Coast Royals (GCL)	2	0	1.000	4.88	13	0	0	0	1-...	24.0	24	17	13	2	11-0	26
1999—S. Oregon (N'West)■	2	2	.500	5.22	15	13	0	0	0-...	69.0	80	52	40	6	39-0	51
2000—Visalia (Calif.)	11	4	.733	3.06	31	23	0	0	2-...	156.0	146	66	53	17	57-2	150
2001—West Tenn (Sou.)■	3	4	.429	1.76	52	0	0	0	24-...	61.1	43	15	12	2	20-4	62
—Iowa (PCL)	0	0	...	2.25	11	0	0	0	10-...	12.0	11	3	3	1	0-0	14
—Chicago (N.L.)	1	1	.500	2.70	6	0	0	0	0-0	6.2	5	2	2	2	2-0	6
2002—Iowa (PCL)	1	4	.200	7.94	27	0	0	0	7-...	28.1	34	26	25	9	13-1	26
—Chicago (N.L.)	0	0	...	23.14	4	0	0	0	0-0	4.2	11	12	12	2	6-1	3
—West Tenn (Sou.)	0	0	...	3.00	3	0	0	0	0-...	3.0	5	2	1	0	1-0	5
Major League totals (2 years)	1	1	.500	11.12	10	0	0	0	0-0	11.1	16	14	14	4	8-1	9

CHIAVIACCI, RON — P — EXPOS

PERSONAL: Born September 5, 1977, in Scranton, Pa. ... 6-2/220. ... Throws right, bats right. ... Full name: Ronald Joseph Chiaviacci.
HIGH SCHOOL: Scranton (Pa.).
COLLEGE: Kutztown.
TRANSACTIONS/CAREER NOTES: Selected by Montreal Expos organization in 44th round of free-agent draft (June 2, 1998). ... On disabled list (June 27-July 14, 2001). ... On Harrisburg disabled list (May 22-29, 2002).

Year	League	W	L	Pct.	ERA	G	GS	CG	ShO	Sv.-Opp.	IP	H	R	ER	HR	BB-IBB	SO
1998—	Gulf Coast Expos (GCL) ...	6	3	.667	2.13	13	6	0	0	0-...	55.0	43	17	13	1	13-0	42
—	Jupiter (FSL)	0	1	.000	2.35	4	0	0	0	1-...	7.2	5	2	2	0	2-0	5
1999—	Cape Fear (S.Atl.)	5	3	.625	3.59	20	8	0	0	1-...	62.2	60	39	25	5	34-0	67
—	Jupiter (FSL)	4	4	.500	2.33	8	8	0	0	0-...	46.1	36	15	12	5	17-0	32
2000—	Jupiter (FSL)	11	11	.500	3.65	28	26	1	0	0-...	158.0	145	80	64	12	59-0	131
2001—	Harrisburg (East.)............	3	11	.214	3.97	25	25	2	1	0-...	147.1	137	77	65	12	76-2	161
2002—	Harrisburg (East.)............	6	9	.400	4.27	35	10	0	0	0-...	111.2	105	70	53	6	65-1	98

CHILDERS, MATT — P — BREWERS

PERSONAL: Born December 3, 1978, in Douglas, Ga. ... 6-5/195. ... Throws right, bats right. ... Full name: Matthew William Childers.
HIGH SCHOOL: Westside (Augusta, Ga.).
TRANSACTIONS/CAREER NOTES: Selected by Milwaukee Brewers organization in ninth round of free-agent draft (June 3, 1997).
CAREER HITTING (MLB): 0-for-1 (.000), 0 R, 0 2B, 0 3B, 0 HR, 0 RBI.

Year	League	W	L	Pct.	ERA	G	GS	CG	ShO	Sv.-Opp.	IP	H	R	ER	HR	BB-IBB	SO
1997—	Helena (Pio.)	1	4	.200	6.20	14	10	0	0	1-...	61.0	81	49	42	5	24-0	19
1998—	Helena (Pio.)	1	0	1.000	0.64	2	2	1	1	0-...	14.0	9	1	1	0	4-1	4
—	Beloit (Midw.)..................	3	7	.300	5.10	14	14	3	0	0-...	67.0	89	55	38	5	20-0	49
1999—	Beloit (Midw.)..................	3	10	.231	5.94	20	19	0	0	0-...	100.0	129	72	66	9	30-1	32
2000—	Beloit (Midw.)..................	8	2	.800	2.71	12	12	1	1	0-...	73.0	64	33	22	4	17-0	47
—	Mudville (Calif.)...............	3	9	.250	4.75	15	15	0	0	0-...	85.1	103	59	45	10	32-0	43
2001—	High Desert (Calif.)..........	6	11	.353	6.44	20	20	0	0	0-...	117.1	155	95	84	19	29-0	76
—	Huntsville (Sou.)	2	2	.500	3.43	7	7	0	0	0-...	39.1	41	19	15	3	12-0	21
2002—	Huntsville (Sou.)	2	5	.286	4.50	35	10	0	0	12-...	82.0	103	47	41	6	27-0	57
—	Milwaukee (N.L.).............	0	0	...	12.00	8	0	0	0	0-0	9.0	13	12	12	2	8-1	6
—	Indianapolis (I.L.)............	0	0	...	0.00	3	0	0	0	0-...	5.0	1	0	0	0	2-0	4
Major League totals (1 year).......		0	0	...	12.00	8	0	0	0	0-0	9.0	13	12	12	2	8-1	6

CHOATE, RANDY — P — YANKEES

PERSONAL: Born September 5, 1975, in San Antonio. ... 6-1/180. ... Throws left, bats left. ... Full name: Randol Doyol Choate.
HIGH SCHOOL: Winston Churchill (San Antonio).
COLLEGE: Florida State.
TRANSACTIONS/CAREER NOTES: Selected by New York Yankees organization in fifth round of free-agent draft (June 3, 1997).
CAREER HITTING (MLB): 0-for-4 (.000), 0 R, 0 2B, 0 3B, 0 HR, 0 RBI.

Year	League	W	L	Pct.	ERA	G	GS	CG	ShO	Sv.-Opp.	IP	H	R	ER	HR	BB-IBB	SO
1997—	Oneonta (NY-Penn)	5	1	.833	1.73	10	10	0	0	0-...	62.1	49	12	12	1	12-1	61
1998—	Tampa (FSL)......................	1	8	.111	5.27	13	13	0	0	0-...	70.0	83	57	41	6	22-2	55
—	Greensboro (S.Atl.)	1	5	.167	3.00	8	8	1	0	0-...	39.0	46	21	13	1	7-0	32
1999—	Tampa (FSL)......................	2	2	.500	4.50	47	0	0	0	1-...	50.0	51	25	25	4	24-5	62
2000—	Columbus (I.L.).................	2	0	1.000	2.04	33	0	0	0	1-...	35.1	34	8	8	2	14-3	37
—	New York (A.L.)................	0	1	.000	4.76	22	0	0	0	0-0	17.0	14	10	9	3	8-0	12
2001—	New York (A.L.)................	3	1	.750	3.35	37	0	0	0	0-0	48.1	34	21	18	0	27-2	35
—	Columbus (I.L.).................	1	1	.500	2.08	4	0	0	0	0-...	4.1	7	1	1	0	3-0	4
2002—	Columbus (I.L.).................	3	2	.600	1.72	31	0	0	0	1-...	36.2	25	8	7	0	15-1	32
—	New York (A.L.)................	0	0	...	6.04	18	0	0	0	0-0	22.1	18	18	15	1	15-0	17
Major League totals (3 years).....		3	2	.600	4.31	77	0	0	0	0-0	87.2	66	49	42	4	50-2	64

DIVISION SERIES RECORD

Year	League	W	L	Pct.	ERA	G	GS	CG	ShO	Sv.-Opp.	IP	H	R	ER	HR	BB-IBB	SO
2000—	New York (A.L.)................	0	0	...	6.75	1	0	0	0	0-0	1.1	0	1	1	0	1-0	1
2001—	New York (A.L.)................									Did not play.							

CHAMPIONSHIP SERIES RECORD

Year	League	W	L	Pct.	ERA	G	GS	CG	ShO	Sv.-Opp.	IP	H	R	ER	HR	BB-IBB	SO
2000—	New York (A.L.)................	0	0	...	0.00	1	0	0	0	0-0	.1	0	0	0	0	0-0	1
2001—	New York (A.L.)................									Did not play.							

WORLD SERIES RECORD

NOTES: Member of World Series championship team (2000).

Year	League	W	L	Pct.	ERA	G	GS	CG	ShO	Sv.-Opp.	IP	H	R	ER	HR	BB-IBB	SO
2000—	New York (A.L.)................									Did not play.							
2001—	New York (A.L.)................	0	0	...	2.45	2	0	0	0	0-0	3.2	7	4	1	0	1-1	2

CHOI, HEE SEOP — 1B — CUBS

PERSONAL: Born March 16, 1979, in Chun-Nam, Korea. ... 6-5/235. ... Bats left, throws left.
HIGH SCHOOL: Kwang-Ju Jae (Kwang-Ju, Korea).
COLLEGE: Korea University.
TRANSACTIONS/CAREER NOTES: Signed as non-drafted free agent by Chicago Cubs organization (March 8, 1999). ... On disabled list (May 24-June 17 and June 25-August 3, 2001).
STATISTICAL NOTES: Led Pacific Coast League first basmen with 1,074 putouts and 1,161 total chances in 2002.
2002 GAMES PLAYED BY POSITION (MLB): 1B—22.

			BATTING														FIELDING	
Year	Team (League)	Pos.	G	AB	R	H	2B	3B	HR	RBI	BB	SO	SB-CS	Avg.	OBP	SLG	E	Avg.
1999—	Lansing (Midw.).........	1B	79	290	71	93	18	6	18	70	50	68	2-1	.321	.422	.610	18	.976
2000—	Daytona (FSL)............	1B	96	345	60	102	25	6	15	70	37	78	4-1	.296	.369	.533	4	.995
—	West Tenn (Sou.)	1B	36	122	25	37	9	0	10	25	25	38	3-1	.303	.419	.623	1	.997
2001—	Iowa (PCL).................	1B	77	266	38	61	11	0	13	45	34	67	5-1	.229	.313	.417	3	.995
2002—	Iowa (PCL).................	1B	135	478	94	137	24	3	26	97	*95	119	3-2	.287	.406	.513	12	.990
—	Chicago (N.L.)...........	1B	24	50	6	9	1	0	2	4	7	15	0-0	.180	.281	.320	2	.983
Major League totals (1 year)			24	50	6	9	1	0	2	4	7	15	0-0	.180	.281	.320	2	.983

CHRISTENSEN, McKAY — OF

PERSONAL: Born August 14, 1975, in Upland, Calif. ... 5-11/180. ... Bats left, throws left. ... Full name: McKay A. Christensen.
HIGH SCHOOL: Clovis West (Fresno, Calif.).
TRANSACTIONS/CAREER NOTES: Selected by California Angels organization in first round (sixth pick overall) of free-agent draft (June 2, 1994). ... Traded by Angels with P Andrew Lorraine, P Bill Simas and P John Snyder to Chicago White Sox for P Jim Abbott and P Tim Fortugno (July 27, 1995). ... On disabled list (April 10-28 and June 2-17, 1998). ... On Birmingham disabled list (July 13-August 1, 1999). ... On Charlotte disabled list (August 2-26, 2000). ... Traded by White Sox to Los Angeles Dodgers for P Wade Parrish (July 13, 2001). ... Claimed on waivers by New York Mets (April 3, 2002). ... On Norfolk disabled list (June 22-July 5, 2002). ... Granted free agency (October 15, 2002).
STATISTICAL NOTES: Led South Atlantic League outfielders with 280 putouts in 1997. ... Tied for Carolina League lead with three double plays by outfielder in 1998.
2002 GAMES PLAYED BY POSITION (MLB): OF—3.

			BATTING														FIELDING	
Year	Team (League)	Pos.	G	AB	R	H	2B	3B	HR	RBI	BB	SO	SB-CS	Avg.	OBP	SLG	E	Avg.
1996—	GC White Sox (GCL)	OF	35	133	17	35	7	5	1	16	10	23	10-3	.263	.327	.414	1	.982
—	Hickory (S.Atl.)	OF	6	11	0	0	0	0	0	0	1	4	0-0	.000	.083	.000	0	1.000
1997—	Hickory (S.Atl.)	OF	127	503	95	141	12	*12	5	47	52	81	28-20	.280	.357	.382	9	.969
1998—	Win.-Salem (Caro.)	OF	95	361	69	103	17	6	4	32	53	54	20-10	.285	.391	.399	4	.981
1999—	Chicago (A.L.)	OF	28	53	10	12	1	0	1	6	4	7	2-1	.226	.271	.302	3	.943
—	Birmingham (Sou.)	OF	75	293	53	85	8	6	3	28	31	46	18-6	.290	.372	.389	2	.990
—	Charlotte (I.L.)	OF	1	4	0	1	0	0	0	0	0	0	1-0	.250	.250	.250	0	1.000
2000—	Chicago (A.L.)	OF	32	19	4	2	0	0	0	1	2	6	1-1	.105	.227	.105	0	1.000
—	Charlotte (I.L.)	OF	90	337	49	89	13	2	6	29	32	51	28-6	.264	.325	.368	7	.964
2001—	Charlotte (I.L.)	OF	69	273	53	75	15	6	7	25	30	52	17-3	.275	.347	.451	3	.981
—	Chicago (A.L.)	OF	7	4	0	1	0	0	0	0	0	2	0-0	.250	.400	.250	0	1.000
—	Las Vegas (PCL)■	OF	16	57	8	14	2	1	1	3	5	11	3-1	.246	.317	.368	2	.943
—	Los Angeles (N.L.)	OF	28	49	7	16	2	0	1	7	3	10	3-2	.327	.400	.429	2	.917
2002—	New York (N.L.)■	OF	4	3	1	1	0	0	0	0	1	1	0-0	.333	.500	.333	0	1.000
—	Norfolk (I.L.)	OF	97	377	52	107	23	6	5	30	26	72	20-13	.284	.341	.416	1	.995
American League totals (3 years)			67	76	14	15	1	0	1	7	6	15	3-2	.197	.267	.250	3	.961
National League totals (2 years)			32	52	8	17	2	0	1	7	4	11	3-2	.327	.407	.423	2	.926
Major League totals (4 years)			99	128	22	32	3	0	2	14	10	26	6-4	.250	.324	.320	5	.951

DIVISION SERIES RECORD

			BATTING														FIELDING	
Year	Team (League)	Pos.	G	AB	R	H	2B	3B	HR	RBI	BB	SO	SB-CS	Avg.	OBP	SLG	E	Avg.
2000—	Chicago (A.L.)	OF	1	0	0	0	0	0	0	0	0	0	0-0	...	...	...	0	...

CHRISTENSON, RYAN — OF

PERSONAL: Born March 28, 1974, in Redlands, Calif. ... 6-0/191. ... Bats right, throws right. ... Full name: Ryan Alan Christenson.
HIGH SCHOOL: Apple Valley (Calif.).
COLLEGE: Pepperdine.
TRANSACTIONS/CAREER NOTES: Selected by Oakland Athletics organization in 10th round of free-agent draft (June 1, 1995). ... On Sacramento disabled list (May 20-June 9, 2001). ... Traded by A's to Arizona Diamondbacks for OF Rob Ryan (June 19, 2001). ... Selected by Milwaukee Brewers from Diamondbacks organization in Rule 5 major league draft (December 13, 2001). ... On Indianapolis disabled list (June 24-August 14, 2002). ... Released by Brewers (October 15, 2002).
2002 GAMES PLAYED BY POSITION (MLB): OF—21.

			BATTING														FIELDING	
Year	Team (League)	Pos.	G	AB	R	H	2B	3B	HR	RBI	BB	SO	SB-CS	Avg.	OBP	SLG	E	Avg.
1995—	S. Oregon (N'West)	OF	49	158	14	30	4	1	1	16	22	33	5-5	.190	.286	.247	2	.978
1996—	S. Oregon (N'West)	OF	36	136	31	39	11	0	5	21	19	21	8-6	.287	.376	.478	4	.954
—	West Mich. (Midw.)	OF-3B	33	122	21	38	2	2	2	18	13	22	2-4	.311	.387	.410	3	.956
1997—	Visalia (Calif.)	OF	83	308	69	90	18	8	13	54	70	72	20-11	.292	.425	.529	3	.982
—	Huntsville (Sou.)	OF	29	120	39	44	9	3	2	18	24	23	5-4	.367	.469	.542	1	.988
—	Edmonton (PCL)	OF	16	49	12	14	2	2	2	5	11	11	2-0	.286	.435	.531	0	1.000
1998—	Edmonton (PCL)	OF	22	88	17	23	6	1	1	7	15	24	4-1	.261	.365	.386	0	1.000
—	Oakland (A.L.)	OF	117	370	56	95	22	2	5	40	36	106	5-6	.257	.321	.368	5	.983
1999—	Oakland (A.L.)	OF-DH	106	268	41	56	12	1	4	24	38	58	7-5	.209	.305	.306	7	.969
—	Vancouver (PCL)	OF	33	128	30	44	8	1	1	16	22	21	7-2	.344	.440	.445	2	.978
2000—	Oakland (A.L.)	OF	121	129	31	32	2	2	4	18	19	33	1-2	.248	.349	.388	5	.951
2001—	Oakland (A.L.)	OF-DH	7	4	1	0	0	0	0	0	0	1	0-0	.000	.000	.000	0	1.000
—	Sacramento (PCL)	OF	19	70	7	12	4	0	1	3	4	13	2-0	.171	.216	.271	0	1.000
—	Arizona (N.L.)■	OF	19	4	3	1	1	0	0	1	1	1	1-0	.250	.400	.500	0	1.000
—	Tucson (PCL)	OF	57	215	32	62	17	0	6	27	23	43	5-2	.288	.353	.451	7	.950
2002—	Indianapolis (I.L.)■	OF	67	260	38	66	17	2	5	30	18	28	11-5	.254	.306	.392	0	1.000
—	Ariz. Brewers (Ariz.)	OF	4	10	1	4	2	0	0	2	0	2	0-0	.400	.364	.000	0	1.000
—	Milwaukee (N.L.)	OF	22	58	5	9	4	0	1	3	5	13	0-0	.155	.222	.276	0	1.000
American League totals (4 years)			351	771	129	183	36	5	13	82	93	198	13-13	.237	.319	.348	17	.973
National League totals (2 years)			41	62	8	10	5	0	1	4	6	14	1-0	.161	.235	.290	0	1.000
Major League totals (5 years)			392	833	137	193	41	5	14	86	99	212	14-13	.232	.313	.343	17	.974

DIVISION SERIES RECORD

			BATTING														FIELDING	
Year	Team (League)	Pos.	G	AB	R	H	2B	3B	HR	RBI	BB	SO	SB-CS	Avg.	OBP	SLG	E	Avg.
2000—	Oakland (A.L.)	OF-PR	2	2	0	1	0	0	0	1	0	1	0-0	.500	.500	.500	0	1.000

CHRISTIANSEN, JASON — P — GIANTS

PERSONAL: Born September 21, 1969, in Omaha, Neb. ... 6-5/241. ... Throws left, bats right. ... Full name: Jason Samuel Christiansen.
HIGH SCHOOL: Elkhorn (Neb.).
JUNIOR COLLEGE: Iowa Western College.
COLLEGE: Cameron (Okla.).
TRANSACTIONS/CAREER NOTES: Signed as non-drafted free agent by Pittsburgh Pirates organization (July 5, 1991). ... On Calgary disabled list (August 12-September 5, 1996). ... On Pittsburgh disabled list (March 31-June 19, 1997). ... On Pittsburgh disabled list (May 7-28, July 29-August 21 and August 24-September 23, 1999); included rehabilitation assignments to Altoona (May 22-28) and Nashville (August 16-21). ... Traded by Pirates to St. Louis Cardinals for SS Jack Wilson (July 30, 2000). ... On St. Louis disabled list (March 23-May 7, 2001); included rehabilitation assignment to Memphis (April 17-May 7). ... Traded by Cardinals to San Francisco Giants for P Kevin Joseph and a player to be named later or cash (July 31, 2001). ... Granted free agency (November 6, 2001). ... Re-signed by Giants (December 5, 2001). ... On disabled list (April 16, 2002-remainder of season).
CAREER HITTING (MLB): 1-for-10 (.100), 0 R, 0 2B, 0 3B, 0 HR, 1 RBI.

Year League	W	L	Pct.	ERA	G	GS	CG	ShO	Sv.-Opp.	IP	H	R	ER	HR	BB-IBB	SO
1991—Gulf Coast Pirates (GCL)..	1	0	1.000	0.00	6	0	0	0	1-...	8.0	4	0	0	0	1-0	8
—Welland (NY-Penn)..........	0	1	.000	2.53	8	1	0	0	0-...	21.1	15	9	6	1	12-1	17
1992—Augusta (S.Atl.)...............	1	0	1.000	1.80	10	0	0	0	2-...	20.0	12	4	4	0	8-0	21
—Salem (Caro.)..................	3	1	.750	3.24	38	0	0	0	2-...	50.0	47	20	18	7	22-2	59
1993—Salem (Caro.)..................	1	1	.500	3.15	57	0	0	0	4-...	71.1	48	30	25	5	24-2	70
—Carolina (Sou.)................	0	0	...	0.00	2	0	0	0	0-...	2.2	3	0	0	0	1-0	2
1994—Carolina (Sou.)................	2	1	.667	2.09	28	0	0	0	2-...	38.2	30	10	9	2	14-1	43
—Buffalo (A.A.)...................	3	1	.750	2.41	33	0	0	0	0-...	33.2	19	9	9	3	16-0	39
1995—Pittsburgh (N.L.).............	1	3	.250	4.15	63	0	0	0	0-4	56.1	49	28	26	5	34-9	53
1996—Pittsburgh (N.L.).............	3	3	.500	6.70	33	0	0	0	0-2	44.1	56	34	33	7	19-2	38
—Calgary (PCL)..................	1	0	1.000	3.27	2	2	0	0	0-...	11.0	9	4	4	1	1-0	10
1997—Carolina (Sou.)................	0	1	.000	4.20	8	1	0	0	1-...	15.0	17	7	7	1	5-0	25
—Pittsburgh (N.L.).............	3	0	1.000	2.94	39	0	0	0	0-2	33.2	37	11	11	2	17-3	37
1998—Pittsburgh (N.L.).............	3	3	.500	2.51	60	0	0	0	6-10	64.2	51	22	18	2	27-7	71
1999—Pittsburgh (N.L.).............	2	3	.400	4.06	39	0	0	0	3-5	37.2	26	17	17	2	22-4	35
—Altoona (East.)................	0	0	...	0.00	2	1	0	0	0-...	3.0	1	0	0	0	1-0	2
—Nashville (PCL)................	0	0	...	0.00	2	0	0	0	0-...	2.0	0	0	0	0	0-0	1
2000—Pittsburgh (N.L.).............	2	8	.200	4.97	44	0	0	0	1-3	38.0	28	22	21	2	25-4	41
—St. Louis (N.L.)■............	1	0	1.000	5.40	21	0	0	0	0-1	10.0	13	7	6	1	2-1	12
2001—Memphis (PCL)................	0	0	...	2.25	7	1	0	0	0-...	8.0	9	2	2	0	0-0	9
—St. Louis (N.L.)................	1	1	.500	4.66	30	0	0	0	3-3	19.1	15	10	10	4	10-1	19
—San Francisco (N.L.)■.....	1	0	1.000	1.59	25	0	0	0	0-1	17.0	14	3	3	1	5-0	12
2002—San Francisco (N.L.)........	0	1	.000	5.40	6	0	0	0	0-0	5.0	6	3	3	1	2-0	1
Major League totals (8 years).....	17	22	.436	4.09	360	0	0	0	13-31	326.0	295	157	148	27	163-31	319

DIVISION SERIES RECORD

Year League	W	L	Pct.	ERA	G	GS	CG	ShO	Sv.-Opp.	IP	H	R	ER	HR	BB-IBB	SO
2000—St. Louis (N.L.)................	0	0	...	0.00	1	0	0	0	0-0	.1	0	0	0	0	0-0	0

CHAMPIONSHIP SERIES RECORD

Year League	W	L	Pct.	ERA	G	GS	CG	ShO	Sv.-Opp.	IP	H	R	ER	HR	BB-IBB	SO
2000—St. Louis (N.L.)................	0	0	...	0.00	2	0	0	0	0-0	2.0	0	0	0	0	0-0	1

CHULK, VINNY — P — BLUE JAYS

PERSONAL: Born December 19, 1978, in Miami. ... 6-2/185. ... Throws right, bats right. ... Full name: Charles Vincent Chulk.
COLLEGE: St. Thomas (Fla.).
TRANSACTIONS/CAREER NOTES: Selected by Toronto Blue Jays organization in 12th round of free-agent draft (June 5, 2000).
HONORS: Named Southern League Most Outstanding Pitcher (2002).

Year League	W	L	Pct.	ERA	G	GS	CG	ShO	Sv.-Opp.	IP	H	R	ER	HR	BB-IBB	SO
2000—Medicine Hat (Pio.)..........	2	4	.333	3.80	14	13	0	0	0-...	68.2	75	36	29	5	20-0	51
2001—Dunedin (FSL)..................	1	2	.333	3.12	16	1	0	0	1-...	34.2	38	16	12	2	13-1	50
—Syracuse (I.L.).................	1	0	.500	1.50	5	0	0	0	0-...	6.0	5	1	1	0	4-0	4
—Tennessee (Sou.).............	2	5	.286	3.14	24	1	0	0	2-...	43.0	34	15	15	5	8-1	43
2002—Tennessee (Sou.).............	•13	5	.722	*2.96	25	24	0	0	1-...	152.0	133	55	50	12	53-0	108
—Syracuse (I.L.).................	0	1	.000	5.79	2	1	0	0	0-...	4.2	6	6	3	0	6-0	2

CINTRON, ALEX — SS — DIAMONDBACKS

PERSONAL: Born December 17, 1978, in Humacao, Puerto Rico. ... 6-2/185. ... Bats both, throws right. ... Full name: Alexander Cintron.
HIGH SCHOOL: Mech-Tech (Caguas, Puerto Rico).
TRANSACTIONS/CAREER NOTES: Selected by Arizona Diamondbacks organization in 36th round of free-agent draft (June 3, 1997). ... On Tucson disabled list (April 30-May 8, 2001).
STATISTICAL NOTES: Led Pacific Coast League with 20 sacrifice hits in 2001. ... Led Pacific Coast League shortstops with 30 errors in 2001.
2002 GAMES PLAYED BY POSITION (MLB): 2B—18; 3B—9; SS—8.

		BATTING														FIELDING	
Year Team (League)	Pos.	G	AB	R	H	2B	3B	HR	RBI	BB	SO	SB-CS	Avg.	OBP	SLG	E	Avg.
1997—Ariz. D-backs (Ariz.)...	SS	43	152	23	30	6	1	0	20	21	32	1-4	.197	.301	.250	15	.931
—Lethbridge (Pio.)........	SS	1	3	0	1	0	0	0	0	0	1	0-0	.333	.333	.333	1	.857
1998—Lethbridge (Pio.)........	SS	67	258	41	68	11	4	3	34	20	32	8-4	.264	.319	.372	27	.921
1999—High Desert (Calif.).....	SS	128	499	78	153	25	4	3	64	19	65	15-8	.307	.333	.391	28	.950
2000—El Paso (Texas)...........	SS	125	522	83	157	30	6	4	59	29	56	9-9	.301	.336	.404	32	.950
2001—Tucson (PCL)............	SS-2B	107	425	53	124	24	3	3	35	15	48	9-6	.292	.315	.384	†32	.936
—Arizona (N.L.)............	SS	8	7	0	2	0	1	0	0	0	0	0-0	.286	.286	.571	0	1.000
2002—Tucson (PCL)............	SS-2B	85	351	53	113	22	3	4	26	11	33	9-5	.322	.345	.436	14	.960
—Arizona (N.L.)............	2B-3B-SS	38	75	11	16	6	0	0	4	12	13	0-0	.213	.322	.293	1	.989
Major League totals (2 years)		46	82	11	18	6	1	0	4	12	13	0-0	.220	.319	.317	1	.990

DIVISION SERIES RECORD

		BATTING														FIELDING	
Year Team (League)	Pos.	G	AB	R	H	2B	3B	HR	RBI	BB	SO	SB-CS	Avg.	OBP	SLG	E	Avg.
2002—Arizona (N.L.)............	3B	2	0	0	0	0	0	0	0	0	0	0-0	...	...	...	0	...

CIRILLO, JEFF — 3B — MARINERS

PERSONAL: Born September 23, 1969, in Pasadena, Calif. ... 6-1/190. ... Bats right, throws right. ... Full name: Jeffrey Howard Cirillo.
HIGH SCHOOL: Providence (Burbank, Calif.).
COLLEGE: Southern California.
TRANSACTIONS/CAREER NOTES: Selected by Chicago Cubs organization in 37th round of free-agent draft (June 2, 1987); did not sign. ... Selected by Milwaukee Brewers organization in 11th round of free-agent draft (June 3, 1991). ... On New Orleans disabled list (July 22-August 6, 1993). ... Traded by Brewers with P Scott Karl and cash to Colorado Rockies as part of three-way deal in which Brewers received P Jamey Wright and C Henry Blanco from Rockies, Oakland Athletics received P Justin Miller and cash from Rockies and Brewers received P Jimmy Haynes from A's (December 13, 1999). ... On Colorado disabled list (April 27-May 13, 2001); included rehabilitation assignment to Colorado Springs (May 12-13). ... Traded by Rockies to Seattle Mariners for P Jose Paniagua, P Dennis Stark and P Brian Fuentes (December 15, 2001).
RECORDS: Shares major league career record for most consecutive errorless games—99 (June 20, 2001-April 19, 2002). ... Holds N.L. single-season record for most consecutive errorless games by third baseman—85 (June 20 through October 7, 2001); and most consecutive chances accepted without an error by third baseman—85 (June 20 through October 7, 2001). ... Shares N.L. single-season record for most double plays by third baseman—45 (1998).
STATISTICAL NOTES: Led Pioneer League in grounding into double plays with 11 in 1991. ... Led Pioneer League third basemen with 60 putouts, 104 assists and 179 total chances in 1991. ... Tied for Midwest League lead with six intentional bases on balls received in 1992. ... Led A.L. third basemen with 18 errors in 1996. ... Led A.L. third basemen with 320 assists, 463 total chances and 29 double plays and tied for lead with 126 putouts in 1997. ... Led N.L. in grounding into double plays with 26 in 1998. ... Led N.L. third basemen with 340 assists and 45 double plays in 1998. ... Led N.L. third basemen with 124 putouts in 1999. ... Led N.L. third basemen in double plays with 35 in 1999 and 41 in 2000. ... Led N.L. third basemen with 304 assists in 2000. ... Had 15-game hitting streak (April 21-May 9, 2000). ... Hit three home runs in one game (June 28, 2000). ... Career major league grand slams: 1.
MISCELLANEOUS: Holds Milwaukee Brewers all-time record for highest career batting average (.307).
2002 GAMES PLAYED BY POSITION (MLB): 3B—141; 1B—11.

			BATTING														FIELDING	
Year	Team (League)	Pos.	G	AB	R	H	2B	3B	HR	RBI	BB	SO	SB-CS	Avg.	OBP	SLG	E	Avg.
1991	—Helena (Pio.)	3B-OF	•70	286	60	100	16	2	10	51	31	28	3-1	.350	.418	.524	15	.921
1992	—Stockton (Calif.)	3B	7	27	2	6	1	0	0	5	2	0	0-0	.222	.323	.259	0	1.000
	—Beloit (Midw.)	3B-2B	126	444	65	135	27	3	9	71	84	85	21-12	.304	.417	.439	26	.942
1993	—El Paso (Texas)	2B-3B	67	249	53	85	16	2	9	41	26	37	2-3	.341	.410	.530	9	.962
	—New Orleans (A.A.)	3-2-S-DH	58	215	31	63	13	2	3	32	29	33	2-1	.293	.385	.414	5	.974
1994	—New Orleans (A.A.)	3-2-DH-S	61	236	45	73	18	2	10	46	28	39	4-0	.309	.386	.530	8	.963
	—Milwaukee (A.L.)	3B-2B	39	126	17	30	9	0	3	12	11	16	0-1	.238	.309	.381	3	.965
1995	—Milwaukee (A.L.)	3-2-1-S	125	328	57	91	19	4	9	39	47	42	7-2	.277	.371	.442	15	.958
1996	—Milwaukee (A.L.)	3-DH-1-2	158	566	101	184	46	5	15	83	58	69	4-9	.325	.391	.504	†18	.952
1997	—Milwaukee (A.L.)	3B-DH	154	580	74	167	46	2	10	82	60	74	4-3	.288	.367	.426	17	.963
1998	—Milwaukee (N.L.)	3B-1B	156	604	97	194	31	1	14	68	79	88	10-4	.321	.402	.445	11	.979
1999	—Milwaukee (N.L.)	3B	157	607	98	198	35	1	15	88	75	83	7-4	.326	.401	.461	15	.967
2000	—Colorado (N.L.)■	3B	157	598	111	195	53	2	11	115	67	72	3-4	.326	.392	.477	15	.964
2001	—Colorado (N.L.)	3B	138	528	72	165	26	4	17	83	43	63	12-2	.313	.364	.473	7	.982
	—Colo. Springs (PCL)	3B	1	4	2	3	1	0	0	3	1	0	0-0	.750	.800	1.000	0	1.000
2002	—Seattle (A.L.)■	3B-1B	146	485	51	121	20	0	6	54	31	67	8-4	.249	.301	.328	9	*.976
American League totals (5 years)			622	2085	300	593	140	11	43	270	207	268	23-19	.284	.356	.424	62	.963
National League totals (4 years)			608	2337	378	752	145	8	57	354	264	306	32-14	.322	.391	.464	48	.973
Major League totals (9 years)			1230	4422	678	1345	285	19	100	624	471	574	55-33	.304	.374	.445	110	.968

ALL-STAR GAME RECORD

	AB	R	H	2B	3B	HR	RBI	BB	SO	SB-CS	Avg.	OBP	SLG	E	Avg.
All-Star Game totals (2 years)	2	0	0	0	0	0	0	0	1	0-0	.000	.000	.000	0	1.000

CLARK, BRADY — OF — METS

PERSONAL: Born April 18, 1973, in Portland, Ore. ... 6-2/195. ... Bats right, throws right. ... Full name: Brady William Clark.
HIGH SCHOOL: Sunset (Beaverton, Ore.).
COLLEGE: University of San Diego.
TRANSACTIONS/CAREER NOTES: Signed as non-drafted free agent by Cincinnati Reds organization (January 13, 1996). ... Released by Reds (April 10, 1996). ... Re-signed by Reds organization (February 15, 1997). ... On Louisville disabled list (June 20-July 11 and August 22-29, 2002). ... Traded by Reds to New York Mets (September 9, 2002), completing deal in which Reds traded P Pedro Feliciano, OF Elvin Andujar and two players to be named later to Mets for P Shawn Estes (August 15, 2002); Mets acquired OF Raul Gonzalez as partial completion (August 20, 2002).
HONORS: Named Southern League Most Valuable Player (1999).
STATISTICAL NOTES: Led Midwest League outfielders with 265 putouts and 278 total chances in 1997. ... Led Southern League with 261 total bases in 1999. ... Tied for International League lead with nine sacrifice flies in 2000. ... Led International League outfielders with 298 putouts and tied for lead with 314 total chances and four double plays in 2000.
2002 GAMES PLAYED BY POSITION (MLB): OF—28.

			BATTING														FIELDING	
Year	Team (League)	Pos.	G	AB	R	H	2B	3B	HR	RBI	BB	SO	SB-CS	Avg.	OBP	SLG	E	Avg.
1997	—Burlington (Midw.)	OF	126	459	108	149	29	7	11	63	76	71	31-18	.325	.423	.490	4	.986
1998	—Chattanooga (Sou.)	OF	64	222	41	60	13	1	2	16	31	34	12-4	.270	.370	.365	1	.993
1999	—Chattanooga (Sou.)	OF-3B	*138	506	103	165	37	4	17	75	89	58	25-17	.326	.425	.516	5	.981
2000	—Louisville (I.L.)	OF	132	487	90	148	*41	6	16	79	72	51	12-8	.304	.397	.511	6	.981
	—Cincinnati (N.L.)	OF	11	11	1	3	1	0	0	2	0	2	0-0	.273	.273	.364	0	1.000
2001	—Louisville (I.L.)	OF	49	167	24	44	5	1	2	18	18	17	6-2	.263	.354	.341	2	.981
	—Cincinnati (N.L.)	OF-DH	89	129	22	34	3	0	6	18	22	16	4-1	.264	.373	.426	1	.981
2002	—Cincinnati (N.L.)	OF	51	66	6	10	3	0	0	9	6	9	1-2	.152	.233	.197	1	.938
	—Louisville (I.L.)	OF-3B	25	109	17	33	7	0	1	17	3	9	0-2	.303	.328	.394	3	.955
	—New York (N.L.)■	OF	10	12	3	5	1	0	0	1	1	2	0-0	.417	.462	.500	0	1.000
Major League totals (3 years)			161	218	32	52	8	0	6	30	29	29	5-3	.239	.332	.358	2	.975

CLARK, HOWIE — OF — BLUE JAYS

PERSONAL: Born February 13, 1974, in San Diego. ... 5-10/191. ... Bats left, throws right. ... Full name: Howard Roddy Clark.
HIGH SCHOOL: Huntington Beach (Calif.).
TRANSACTIONS/CAREER NOTES: Selected by Baltimore Orioles organization in 27th round of free-agent draft (June 1, 1992). ... Granted free agency (October 15, 1999). ... Re-signed by Orioles organization (December 4, 1999). ... Granted free agency (October 15, 2000). ... Signed by Yucatan, Mexican League (April 2001). ... Signed by Chico, Western League (August 2001). ... Signed by Orioles organization (October 8, 2001). ... Granted free agency (October 15, 2002). ... Signed by Toronto Blue Jays organization (November 5, 2002).
2002 GAMES PLAYED BY POSITION (MLB): DH—8; OF—4; 1B—1.

		BATTING														FIELDING	
Year Team (League)	Pos.	G	AB	R	H	2B	3B	HR	RBI	BB	SO	SB-CS	Avg.	OBP	SLG	E	Avg.
1992—GC Orioles (GCL)	2B-3B-1B	43	138	12	33	7	1	0	6	12	21	1-2	.239	.309	.304	7	.948
1993—Albany (S.Atl.)	2B	7	17	2	4	0	0	0	1	0	3	1-0	.235	.235	.235	2	.833
—Bluefield (Appl.)	2B-OF-1B	58	180	29	53	10	1	3	30	26	34	2-2	.294	.388	.411	10	.900
1994—Albany (S.Atl.)	1B-2B	108	353	56	95	22	7	2	47	51	58	5-4	.269	.371	.388	14	.978
—Frederick (Caro.)	2B	2	7	1	1	1	0	0	0	0	2	0-0	.143	.143	.286	0	1.000
1995—High Desert (Calif.)	3-2-O-C-1-S	100	329	50	85	20	2	5	40	32	51	12-6	.258	.329	.377	21	.920
1996—Bowie (East.)	2-O-C-1-3-S	127	449	55	122	29	3	4	52	59	54	2-8	.272	.354	.376	14	.975
1997—Bowie (East.)	3B-2B-1B	105	314	39	90	16	0	9	37	32	38	2-2	.287	.351	.424	20	.909
1998—Bowie (East.)	O-2-1-3	88	276	37	79	16	0	9	45	29	42	1-1	.286	.359	.442	6	.954
—Rochester (I.L.)	1B-2B-3B	30	95	13	22	4	1	3	8	9	11	1-2	.232	.298	.389	2	.983
1999—Rochester (I.L.)	O-2-3-1	79	279	33	82	19	4	6	28	34	24	1-2	.294	.370	.455	2	.988
—Bowie (East.)	2B-1B-OF-C	39	126	17	37	6	0	2	12	10	12	2-0	.294	.360	.389	0	1.000
2000—Bowie (East.)	OF-1B	13	53	11	18	6	0	1	9	3	6	0-0	.340	.379	.509	0	1.000
—Rochester (I.L.)	2-O-3-1	54	189	25	54	10	0	3	21	26	14	3-1	.286	.373	.386	5	.966
2001—Yucatan (Mex.)■	OF-2B-1B	121	493	68	164	42	7	5	64	43	47	5-4	.333	.385	.477	2	.993
—Chico (West.)■		4	15	3	8	0	1	0	0	1	1	0-...	.533	...	.667	...	...
2002—Rochester (I.L.)■	OF-1B-2B-3B	108	418	57	129	21	4	7	43	41	28	3-4	.309	.369	.428	8	.976
—Baltimore (A.L.)	DH-OF-1B	14	53	3	16	5	0	0	4	3	6	0-0	.302	.362	.396	0	1.000
Major League totals (1 year)		14	53	3	16	5	0	0	4	3	6	0-0	.302	.362	.396	0	1.000

CLARK, TONY — 1B/DH

PERSONAL: Born June 15, 1972, in Newton, Kan. ... 6-7/245. ... Bats both, throws right. ... Full name: Anthony Christopher Clark.
HIGH SCHOOL: Valhalla (El Cajon, Calif.), then Christian (El Cajon, Calif.).
COLLEGE: Arizona (did not play baseball), then San Diego State.
TRANSACTIONS/CAREER NOTES: Selected by Detroit Tigers organization in first round (second pick overall) of free-agent draft (June 4, 1990). ... On Niagara Falls temporarily inactive list (June 17, 1991-remainder of season; and August 17, 1992-remainder of season). ... On disabled list (August 24, 1993-remainder of season). ... On Detroit disabled list (May 26-June 10, 1999); included rehabilitation assignment to Toledo (June 8-10). ... On Detroit disabled list (May 13-June 12, July 15-September 1 and September 19, 2000-remainder of season); included rehabilitation assignments to Toledo (June 9-12 and August 28-September 1). ... Claimed on waivers by Boston Red Sox (November 20, 2001). ... Granted free agency (October 30, 2002).
RECORDS: Holds A.L. single-season record for most games with switch-hit home runs—3 (1998).
STATISTICAL NOTES: Switch-hit home runs in one game six times (April 5, 1997; June 17, July 26 and August 1, 1998; and July 18 and July 25, 1999). ... Led A.L. first basemen with 1,423 putouts and 1,533 total chances in 1997. ... Had 19-game hitting streak (July 10-August 1, 1999). ... Career major league grand slams: 2.
2002 GAMES PLAYED BY POSITION (MLB): 1B—85; DH—2.

		BATTING														FIELDING	
Year Team (League)	Pos.	G	AB	R	H	2B	3B	HR	RBI	BB	SO	SB-CS	Avg.	OBP	SLG	E	Avg.
1990—Bristol (Appl.)	OF	25	73	2	12	2	0	1	8	6	28	0-0	.164	.238	.233	0	1.000
1991—Niagara Falls (NY-P)								Did not play.									
1992—Niagara Falls (NY-P)	OF	27	85	12	26	9	0	5	17	9	34	1-0	.306	.372	.588	0	1.000
1993—Lakeland (FSL)	OF	36	117	14	31	4	1	1	22	18	32	0-1	.265	.358	.342	2	.944
1994—Trenton (East.)	DH-1B	107	394	50	110	25	0	21	86	40	113	0-4	.279	.346	.503	•13	.977
—Toledo (I.L.)	1B-DH	25	92	10	24	4	0	2	13	12	25	2-0	.261	.340	.370	0	1.000
1995—Toledo (I.L.)	1B-DH	110	405	50	98	17	2	14	63	52	*129	0-2	.242	.330	.398	*13	.981
—Detroit (A.L.)	1B	27	101	10	24	5	1	3	11	8	30	0-0	.238	.294	.396	4	.985
1996—Toledo (I.L.)	1B-DH	55	194	42	58	7	1	14	36	31	58	1-1	.299	.396	.562	3	.993
—Detroit (A.L.)	1B-DH	100	376	56	94	14	0	27	72	29	127	0-1	.250	.299	.503	6	.993
1997—Detroit (A.L.)	1B-DH	159	580	105	160	28	3	32	117	93	144	1-3	.276	.376	.500	10	.993
1998—Detroit (A.L.)	1B-DH	157	602	84	175	37	0	34	103	63	128	3-3	.291	.358	.522	13	.991
1999—Detroit (A.L.)	1B-DH	143	536	74	150	29	0	31	99	64	133	2-1	.280	.361	.507	10	.992
—Toledo (I.L.)	1B	1	3	0	0	0	0	0	0	1	1	0-0	.000	.250	.000	0	1.000
2000—Detroit (A.L.)	1B-DH	60	208	32	57	14	0	13	37	24	51	0-0	.274	.349	.529	4	.993
—Toledo (I.L.)	1B	6	22	1	2	1	0	1	2	1	1	0-0	.091	.130	.273	0	1.000
2001—Detroit (A.L.)	1B-DH	126	428	67	123	29	3	16	75	62	108	0-1	.287	.374	.481	3	.996
2002—Boston (A.L.)■	1B-DH	90	275	25	57	12	1	3	29	21	57	0-0	.207	.265	.291	6	.992
Major League totals (8 years)		862	3106	453	840	168	8	159	543	364	778	6-9	.270	.347	.483	56	.992

ALL-STAR GAME RECORD

	AB	R	H	2B	3B	HR	RBI	BB	SO	SB-CS	Avg.	OBP	SLG	E	Avg.
All-Star Game totals (1 year)	1	0	0	0	0	0	0	0	1	0-0	.000	.000	.000	0	...

CLAUSSEN, BRANDON — P — YANKEES

PERSONAL: Born May 1, 1979, in Rapid City, S.D. ... 6-2/175. ... Throws left, bats left. ... Full name: Brandon A. Claussen.
HIGH SCHOOL: Goddard (Roswell, N.M.).
JUNIOR COLLEGE: Howard (Texas).

TRANSACTIONS/CAREER NOTES: Selected by New York Yankees oranization in 34th round of free-agent draft (June 2, 1998). ... On Columbus disabled list (June 18, 2002-remainder of season).

Year	League	W	L	Pct.	ERA	G	GS	CG	ShO	Sv.-Opp.	IP	H	R	ER	HR	BB-IBB	SO
1999—	Gulf Coast Yankees (GCL)	0	1	.000	3.18	2	2	0	0	0-...	11.1	7	4	4	2	2-0	16
—	Staten Island (NY-Penn)...	6	4	.600	3.38	12	12	1	0	0-...	72.0	70	30	27	4	12-2	89
—	Greensboro (S.Atl.)	0	1	.000	10.50	1	1	1	0	0-...	6.0	8	7	7	1	2-0	5
2000—	Greensboro (S.Atl.)	8	5	.615	4.05	17	17	1	0	0-...	97.2	91	49	44	9	44-0	98
—	Tampa (FSL)......................	2	5	.286	3.10	9	9	1	1	0-...	52.1	49	24	18	1	17-0	44
2001—	Tampa (FSL)......................	5	2	.714	2.73	8	8	0	0	0-...	56.0	47	21	17	2	13-0	69
—	Norwich (East.)	9	2	.818	2.13	21	21	1	1	0-...	131.0	101	42	31	6	55-0	151
2002—	Columbus (I.L.)	2	8	.200	3.28	15	15	0	0	0-...	93.1	85	47	34	4	46-3	73

CLAYTON, ROYCE — SS

PERSONAL: Born January 2, 1970, in Burbank, Calif. ... 6-0/185. ... Bats right, throws right. ... Full name: Royce Spencer Clayton.

HIGH SCHOOL: St. Bernard (Playa del Ray, Calif.).

TRANSACTIONS/CAREER NOTES: Selected by San Francisco Giants organization in first round (15th pick overall) of free-agent draft (June 1, 1988); pick received as compensation for Cincinnati Reds signing Type B free-agent OF Eddie Milner. ... Traded by Giants with a player to be named later to St. Louis Cardinals for P Allen Watson, P Rich DeLucia and P Doug Creek (December 14, 1995); Cardinals acquired 2B Chris Wimmer to complete deal (January 16, 1996). ... On St. Louis disabled list (June 24-July 9, 1998). ... Traded by Cardinals with P Todd Stottlemyre to Texas Rangers for P Darren Oliver, 3B Fernando Tatis and a player to be named later (July 31, 1998); Cardinals acquired OF Mark Little to complete deal (August 9, 1998). ... Granted free agency (October 23, 1998). ... Re-signed by Rangers (December 2, 1998). ... On Texas disabled list (May 1-21, 1999); included rehabilitation assignment to Oklahoma (May 18-21). ... Traded by Rangers to Chicago White Sox for P Aaron Myette and P Brian Schmack (December 14, 2000). ... Released by White Sox (September 8, 2002).

STATISTICAL NOTES: Led California League shortstops with 202 putouts in 1990. ... Led Texas League shortstops with 80 double plays in 1991. ... Led N.L. shortstops with 103 double plays in 1993. ... Led N.L. shortstops with 223 putouts and 654 total chances and tied for league lead with 411 assists in 1995. ... Led N.L. shortstops with 452 assists in 1997. ... Led A.L. shortstops with 265 putouts in 2000. ... Career major league grand slams: 1.

2002 GAMES PLAYED BY POSITION (MLB): SS—109.

			BATTING														FIELDING	
Year	Team (League)	Pos.	G	AB	R	H	2B	3B	HR	RBI	BB	SO	SB-CS	Avg.	OBP	SLG	E	Avg.
1988—	Everett (N'West).........	SS	60	212	35	55	4	0	3	29	27	54	10-4	.259	.348	.321	35	.873
1989—	Clinton (Midw.)	SS	104	385	39	91	13	3	0	24	39	101	28-16	.236	.309	.286	31	.943
—	San Jose (Calif.).........	SS	28	92	5	11	2	0	0	4	13	27	10-1	.120	.236	.141	8	.939
1990—	San Jose (Calif.).........	SS	123	460	80	123	15	10	7	71	68	98	33-15	.267	.364	.389	37	.938
1991—	Shreveport (Texas).....	SS	126	485	84	136	22	8	5	68	61	104	36-10	.280	.361	.390	29	.950
—	San Francisco (N.L.) ..	SS	9	26	0	3	1	0	0	2	1	6	0-0	.115	.148	.154	3	.880
1992—	San Francisco (N.L.) ..	SS-3B	98	321	31	72	7	4	4	24	26	63	8-4	.224	.281	.308	11	.973
—	Phoenix (PCL)...........	SS	48	192	30	46	6	2	3	18	17	25	15-6	.240	.300	.339	7	.971
1993—	San Francisco (N.L.) ..	SS	153	549	54	155	21	5	6	70	38	91	11-10	.282	.331	.372	27	.963
1994—	San Francisco (N.L.) ..	SS	108	385	38	91	14	6	3	30	30	74	23-3	.236	.295	.327	14	.973
1995—	San Francisco (N.L.) ..	SS	138	509	56	124	29	3	5	58	38	109	24-9	.244	.298	.342	20	.969
1996—	St. Louis (N.L.)■	SS	129	491	64	136	20	4	6	35	33	89	33-15	.277	.321	.371	15	.972
1997—	St. Louis (N.L.)..........	SS	154	576	75	153	39	5	9	61	33	109	30-10	.266	.306	.398	19	.973
1998—	St. Louis (N.L.)..........	SS	90	355	59	83	19	1	4	29	40	51	19-6	.234	.313	.327	13	.970
—	Texas (A.L.)■............	SS	52	186	30	53	12	1	5	24	13	32	5-5	.285	.330	.441	7	.972
1999—	Texas (A.L.)	SS	133	465	69	134	21	5	14	52	39	100	8-6	.288	.346	.445	*25	.961
—	Oklahoma (PCL).........	SS	2	7	1	1	0	0	0	1	3	3	0-0	.143	.400	.143	0	1.000
2000—	Texas (A.L.)	SS	148	513	70	124	21	5	14	54	42	92	11-7	.242	.301	.384	16	.977
2001—	Chicago (A.L.)■.........	SS	135	433	62	114	21	4	9	60	33	72	10-7	.263	.315	.393	7	.988
2002—	Chicago (A.L.)	SS	112	342	51	86	14	2	7	35	20	67	5-1	.251	.295	.365	5	.989
American League totals (5 years)			580	1939	282	511	89	17	49	225	147	363	39-26	.264	.317	.403	60	.977
National League totals (8 years)			879	3212	377	817	150	28	37	309	239	592	148-57	.254	.307	.353	122	.970
Major League totals (12 years)			1459	5151	659	1328	239	45	86	534	386	955	187-83	.258	.311	.372	182	.972

DIVISION SERIES RECORD

			BATTING														FIELDING	
Year	Team (League)	Pos.	G	AB	R	H	2B	3B	HR	RBI	BB	SO	SB-CS	Avg.	OBP	SLG	E	Avg.
1996—	St. Louis (N.L.)..........	SS	2	6	1	2	0	0	0	0	3	1	0-1	.333	.556	.333	0	1.000
1998—	Texas (A.L.)	SS	3	9	0	2	0	0	0	0	0	4	0-0	.222	.222	.222	1	.929
1999—	Texas (A.L.)	SS	3	10	0	0	0	0	0	0	0	1	0-0	.000	.000	.000	0	1.000
Division series totals (3 years)			8	25	1	4	0	0	0	0	3	6	0-1	.160	.250	.160	1	.973

CHAMPIONSHIP SERIES RECORD

			BATTING														FIELDING	
Year	Team (League)	Pos.	G	AB	R	H	2B	3B	HR	RBI	BB	SO	SB-CS	Avg.	OBP	SLG	E	Avg.
1996—	St. Louis (N.L.)..........	SS	5	20	4	7	0	0	0	1	1	4	1-1	.350	.381	.350	2	.913

ALL-STAR GAME RECORD

	AB	R	H	2B	3B	HR	RBI	BB	SO	SB-CS	Avg.	OBP	SLG	E	Avg.
All-Star Game totals (1 year)	1	0	0	0	0	0	0	0	1	0-0	.000	.000	.000	0	1.000

CLEMENS, ROGER — P

PERSONAL: Born August 4, 1962, in Dayton, Ohio. ... 6-4/235. ... Throws right, bats right. ... Full name: William Roger Clemens.

HIGH SCHOOL: Spring Woods (Houston).

JUNIOR COLLEGE: San Jacinto (North) College (Texas).

COLLEGE: Texas.

TRANSACTIONS/CAREER NOTES: Selected by New York Mets organization in 12th round of free-agent draft (June 8, 1981); did not sign. ... Selected by Boston Red Sox organization in first round (19th pick overall) of free-agent draft (June 6, 1983). ... On disabled list (July 8-August 3 and August 21, 1985-remainder of season). ... On suspended list (April 26-May 3, 1991). ... On Boston disabled list (June 19-July 16, 1993); included rehabilitation assignment to Pawtucket (July 11-16). ... On Boston disabled list (April 16-June 2, 1995); included rehabilitation assignments to Sarasota (May 25-28) and Pawtucket (May 28-June 2). ... Granted free agency (November 5, 1996). ... Signed by Toronto Blue Jays (December 13, 1996). ... Traded by Blue Jays to New York Yankees for P David Wells, P Graeme Lloyd and 2B Homer Bush (February 18, 1999). ... On disabled list (April 28-May 21, 1999; and June 15-July 2, 2000). ... On New York disabled list (July 13-August 7, 2002); included rehabilitation assignments to Tampa (July 27-31) and Norwich (August 1-7). ... Granted free agency (November 7, 2002).

RECORDS: Holds A.L. record for most consecutive seasons with 100 or more strikeouts—17 (1986-2002). ... Shares major league single-game record for most strikeouts (nine-inning game)—20 (April 29, 1986; and September 18, 1996). ... Shares major league record for most putouts by pitcher in one inning—3 (June 27, 1992, sixth inning). ... Holds A.L. record for most consecutive games won—20 (June 3, 1998-June 1, 1999). ... Shares A.L. records for most consecutive seasons with 200 or more strikeouts—7 (1986-92); most seasons with 200 or more strikeouts—11; and most years with 100 or more strikeouts—18 (1984 and 1986-2002). ... Shares A.L. single-game record for most consecutive strikeouts—8 (April 29, 1986). ... Holds A.L. career record for most strikeouts—3,909; most consecutive starting assignments—561 (July 26, 1984-present); and most consecutive years with 100 or more strikeouts—17 (1986-2002). ... Shares A.L. single-season record for most consecutive games won—16 (May 26-September 19, 2001).

HONORS: Named Major League Player of the Year by The Sporting News (1986). ... Named A.L. Pitcher of the Year by The Sporting News (1986, 1991, 1997, 1998 and 2001). ... Named righthanded pitcher on The Sporting News A.L. All-Star team (1986-87, 1991, 1997 and 2001). ... Named A.L. Most Valuable Player by Baseball Writers' Association of America (1986). ... Named A.L. Cy Young Award winner by Baseball Writers' Association of America (1986, 1987, 1991, 1997, 1998 and 2001).

STATISTICAL NOTES: Struck out 15 batters in one game (August 21, 1984; July 9, 1988; August 15 and September 21, 1998). ... Struck out 20 batters in one game (April 29, 1986; and September 18, 1996). ... Struck out 16 batters in one game (May 9 and July 15, 1988; and July 12, 1997). ... Pitched 6-0 one-hit, complete-game victory against Cleveland (September 10, 1988). ... Led A.L. with 14 hit batsmen in 1995. ... Struck out 18 batters in one game (August 25, 1998). ... Tied for A.L. lead with 14 wild pitches in 2001.

MISCELLANEOUS: Holds Boston Red Sox all-time records for most innings pitched (2,776) and most strikeouts (2,590). ... Shares Boston Red Sox all-time records for most wins (192) and most shuouts (38). ... Singled in only appearance as pinch hitter (1996).

CAREER HITTING (MLB): 4-for-19 (.211), 2 R, 2 2B, 0 3B, 0 HR, 1 RBI.

Year League	W	L	Pct.	ERA	G	GS	CG	ShO	Sv.-Opp.	IP	H	R	ER	HR	BB-IBB	SO
1983—Winter Haven (FSL)	3	1	.750	1.24	4	4	3	1	0-...	29.0	22	4	4	0	0-0	36
—New Britain (East.)	4	1	.800	1.38	7	7	1	1	0-...	52.0	31	8	8	1	12-0	59
1984—Pawtucket (I.L.)	2	3	.400	1.93	7	6	3	1	0-...	46.2	39	12	10	3	14-0	50
—Boston (A.L.)	9	4	.692	4.32	21	20	5	1	0-0	133.1	146	67	64	13	29-3	126
1985—Boston (A.L.)	7	5	.583	3.29	15	15	3	1	0-0	98.1	83	38	36	5	37-0	74
1986—Boston (A.L.)	*24	4	*.857	*2.48	33	33	10	1	0-0	254.0	179	77	70	21	67-0	238
1987—Boston (A.L.)	•20	9	.690	2.97	36	36	*18	*7	0-0	281.2	248	100	93	19	83-4	256
1988—Boston (A.L.)	18	12	.600	2.93	35	35	•14	*8	0-0	264.0	217	93	86	17	62-4	*291
1989—Boston (A.L.)	17	11	.607	3.13	35	35	8	3	0-0	253.1	215	101	88	20	93-5	230
1990—Boston (A.L.)	21	6	.778	*1.93	31	31	7	•4	0-0	228.1	193	59	49	7	54-3	209
1991—Boston (A.L.)	18	10	.643	*2.62	35	•35	13	*4	0-0	*271.1	219	93	79	15	65-12	*241
1992—Boston (A.L.)	18	11	.621	*2.41	32	32	11	*5	0-0	246.2	203	80	66	11	62-5	208
1993—Boston (A.L.)	11	14	.440	4.46	29	29	2	1	0-0	191.2	175	99	95	17	67-4	160
—Pawtucket (I.L.)	0	0	...	0.00	1	1	0	0	0-...	3.2	1	0	0	0	4-0	8
1994—Boston (A.L.)	9	7	.563	2.85	24	24	3	1	0-0	170.2	124	62	54	15	71-1	168
1995—Sarasota (FSL)	0	0	...	0.00	1	1	0	0	0-...	4.0	0	0	0	0	2-0	7
—Pawtucket (I.L.)	0	0	...	0.00	1	1	0	0	0-...	5.0	1	0	0	0	3-0	5
—Boston (A.L.)	10	5	.667	4.18	23	23	0	0	0-0	140.0	141	70	65	15	60-0	132
1996—Boston (A.L.)	10	13	.435	3.63	34	34	6	2	0-0	242.2	216	106	98	19	106-2	*257
1997—Toronto (A.L.)■	*21	7	.750	*2.05	34	34	•9	•3	0-0	•264.0	204	65	60	9	68-1	*292
1998—Toronto (A.L.)	•20	6	.769	*2.65	33	33	5	3	0-0	234.2	169	78	69	11	88-0	*271
1999—New York (A.L.)■	14	10	.583	4.60	30	30	1	1	0-0	187.2	185	101	96	20	90-0	163
2000—New York (A.L.)	13	8	.619	3.70	32	32	1	0	0-0	204.1	184	96	84	26	84-0	188
2001—New York (A.L.)	20	3	*.870	3.51	33	33	0	0	0-0	220.1	205	94	86	19	72-1	213
2002—New York (A.L.)	13	6	.684	4.35	29	29	0	0	0-0	180.0	172	94	87	18	63-6	192
—Tampa (FSL)	1	0	1.000	5.40	1	1	0	0	0-...	5.0	5	3	3	1	2-0	6
—Norwich (East.)	0	1	.000	1.29	1	1	0	0	0-...	7.0	5	1	1	0	0-0	7
Major League totals (19 years)	293	151	.660	3.15	574	573	116	45	0-0	4067.0	3478	1573	1425	297	1321-51	3909

DIVISION SERIES RECORD

RECORDS: Shares A.L. career records for most losses—3; and bases on balls allowed—18.

Year League	W	L	Pct.	ERA	G	GS	CG	ShO	Sv.-Opp.	IP	H	R	ER	HR	BB-IBB	SO
1995—Boston (A.L.)	0	0	...	3.86	1	1	0	0	0-0	7.0	5	3	3	0	1-0	5
1999—New York (A.L.)	1	0	1.000	0.00	1	1	0	0	0-0	7.0	3	0	0	0	2-0	2
2000—New York (A.L.)	0	2	.000	8.18	2	2	0	0	0-0	11.0	13	10	10	1	8-1	10
2001—New York (A.L.)	0	1	.000	5.40	2	2	0	0	0-0	8.1	9	5	5	1	4-0	6
2002—New York (A.L.)	0	0	...	6.35	1	1	0	0	0-0	5.2	8	4	4	1	3-0	5
Division series totals (5 years)	1	3	.250	5.08	7	7	0	0	0-0	39.0	38	22	22	3	18-1	28

CHAMPIONSHIP SERIES RECORD

RECORDS: Holds A.L. career record for most strikeouts—53. ... Holds single-series record for most hits allowed—22 (1986). ... Shares single-series record for most earned runs allowed—11 (1986). ... Shares single-game records for most earned runs allowed—7 (October 7, 1986); and most consecutive strikeouts—4 (October 6, 1988). ... Holds A.L. single-series record for most innings pitched—22 2/3 (1986). ... Shares A.L. single-game record for most runs allowed—8 (October 7, 1986). ... Holds single-game record for fewest hits allowed—1 (October 14, 2000).

Year League	W	L	Pct.	ERA	G	GS	CG	ShO	Sv.-Opp.	IP	H	R	ER	HR	BB-IBB	SO
1986—Boston (A.L.)	1	1	.500	4.37	3	3	0	0	0-0	22.2	22	12	11	1	7-0	17
1988—Boston (A.L.)	0	0	...	3.86	1	1	0	0	0-0	7.0	6	3	3	1	0-0	8
1990—Boston (A.L.)	0	1	.000	3.52	2	2	0	0	0-0	7.2	7	3	3	0	5-0	4
1999—New York (A.L.)	0	1	.000	22.50	1	1	0	0	0-0	2.0	6	5	5	1	2-0	2
2000—New York (A.L.)	1	0	1.000	0.00	1	1	1	1	0-0	9.0	1	0	0	0	2-0	15
2001—New York (A.L.)	0	0	...	0.00	1	1	0	0	0-0	5.0	1	0	0	0	4-0	7
Champ. series totals (6 years)	2	3	.400	3.71	9	9	1	1	0-0	53.1	43	23	22	3	20-0	53

WORLD SERIES RECORD

NOTES: Member of World Series championship team (1999 and 2000).

Year League	W	L	Pct.	ERA	G	GS	CG	ShO	Sv.-Opp.	IP	H	R	ER	HR	BB-IBB	SO
1986—Boston (A.L.)	0	0	...	3.18	2	2	0	0	0-0	11.1	9	5	4	0	6-0	11
1999—New York (A.L.)	1	0	1.000	1.17	1	1	0	0	0-0	7.2	4	1	1	0	2-0	4
2000—New York (A.L.)	1	0	1.000	0.00	1	1	0	0	0-0	8.0	2	0	0	0	0-0	9
2001—New York (A.L.)	1	0	1.000	1.35	2	2	0	0	0-0	13.1	10	2	2	0	4-0	19
World Series totals (4 years)	3	0	1.000	1.56	6	6	0	0	0-0	40.1	25	8	7	0	12-0	43

ALL-STAR GAME RECORD

NOTES: Named Most Valuable Player (1986).

	W	L	Pct.	ERA	GS	CG	ShO	Sv.-Opp.	IP	H	R	ER	HR	BB-IBB	SO
All-Star Game totals (7 years)	1	0	1.000	2.70	2	0	0	0-0	10.0	6	3	3	1	1-0	5

CLEMENT, MATT P CUBS

PERSONAL: Born August 12, 1974, in McCandless Township, Pa. ... 6-3/213. ... Throws right, bats right. ... Full name: Matthew Paul Clement.
HIGH SCHOOL: Butler (Pa.).
TRANSACTIONS/CAREER NOTES: Selected by San Diego Padres organization in third round of free-agent draft (June 3, 1993). ... Traded by Padres with OF Eric Owens and P Omar Ortiz to Florida Marlins for OF Mark Kotsay and OF Cesar Crespo (March 28, 2001). ... Traded by Marlins with P Antonio Alfonseca to Chicago Cubs for P Julian Tavarez, P Jose Cueto, P Dontrelle Willis and C Ryan Jorgensen (March 27, 2002).
RECORDS: Shares major league single-season record for most grand slams allowed—4 (2000).
STATISTICAL NOTES: Led Pioneer League with 19 wild pitches in 1995. ... Led Pacific Coast League with 30 hit batsmen in 1998. ... Led N.L. with 23 wild pitches in 2000 and 15 in 2001.
MISCELLANEOUS: Appeared one game as pinch hitter (2001).
CAREER HITTING (MLB): 15-for-225 (.067), 16 R, 2 2B, 1 3B, 0 HR, 7 RBI.

Year League	W	L	Pct.	ERA	G	GS	CG	ShO	Sv.-Opp.	IP	H	R	ER	HR	BB-IBB	SO
1994—Spokane (N'West)	1	1	.500	6.14	2	2	0	0	0-...	7.1	8	7	5	0	11-0	4
—Arizona Padres (Ariz.)	•8	5	.615	4.43	13	13	0	0	0-...	67.0	65	38	33	0	17-0	76
1995—Rancho Cuca. (Calif.)	3	4	.429	4.24	12	12	0	0	0-...	57.1	61	37	27	1	49-0	33
—Idaho Falls (Pio.)	6	3	.667	4.33	14	14	0	0	0-...	81.0	61	53	39	3	42-0	65
1996—Clinton (Midw.)	8	3	.727	2.80	16	16	1	•1	0-...	96.1	66	31	30	3	52-0	109
—Rancho Cuca. (Calif.)	4	5	.444	5.59	11	11	0	0	0-...	56.1	61	40	35	8	26-0	75
1997—Rancho Cuca. (Calif.)	6	3	.667	1.60	14	14	2	1	0-...	101.0	74	30	18	3	31-1	109
—Mobile (Sou.)	6	5	.545	2.56	13	13	1	1	0-...	88.0	83	37	25	4	32-0	92
1998—Las Vegas (PCL)	10	9	.526	3.98	27	27	1	0	0-...	171.2	157	94	76	12	85-2	*160
—San Diego (N.L.)	2	0	1.000	4.61	4	2	0	0	0-0	13.2	15	8	7	0	7-1	13
1999—San Diego (N.L.)	10	12	.455	4.48	31	31	0	0	0-0	180.2	190	106	90	18	86-2	135
2000—San Diego (N.L.)	13	17	.433	5.14	34	34	0	0	0-0	205.0	194	131	117	22	*125-4	170
2001—Florida (N.L.)■	9	10	.474	5.05	31	31	0	0	0-0	169.1	172	102	95	15	85-2	134
2002—Chicago (N.L.)■	12	11	.522	3.60	32	32	3	2	0-0	205.0	162	84	82	18	85-7	215
Major League totals (5 years)	46	50	.479	4.55	132	130	3	2	0-0	773.2	733	431	391	73	388-16	667

COCO, PASQUAL P BLUE JAYS

PERSONAL: Born September 24, 1977, in Santo Domingo, Dominican Republic. ... 6-1/180. ... Throws right, bats right. ... Full name: Pasqual Reynoso Coco.
TRANSACTIONS/CAREER NOTES: Signed as non-drafted free agent by Toronto Blue Jays organization (August 10, 1994).
STATISTICAL NOTES: Pitched 3-1 no-hit loss for St. Catharines against Jamestown (August 16, 1998). ... Led Southern League with 17 hit batsmen in 2000. ... Tied for Southern League lead with three balks in 2000. ... Led International League with 10 sacrifice flies allowed in 2002.
CAREER HITTING (MLB): 0-for-0 (.000), 0 R, 0 2B, 0 3B, 0 HR, 0 RBI.

Year League	W	L	Pct.	ERA	G	GS	CG	ShO	Sv.-Opp.	IP	H	R	ER	HR	BB-IBB	SO
1995—Dom. Blue Jays (DSL)	7	1	.875	2.78	11	11	0	0	0-...	58.1	51	30	18	...	36-...	38
1996—Dom. Blue Jays (DSL)	7	2	.778	2.99	17	16	2	2	0-...	96.1	77	46	32	...	53-...	92
1997—St. Catharines (NY-Penn)	1	4	.200	4.89	10	8	0	0	0-...	46.0	48	32	25	5	16-1	44
1998—St. Catharines (NY-Penn)	3	7	.300	3.20	15	15	1	0	0-...	81.2	62	52	29	4	32-0	84
1999—Hagerstown (S.Atl.)	11	1	*.917	2.21	14	14	0	0	0-...	97.2	67	29	24	4	25-1	83
—Dunedin (FSL)	4	6	.400	5.28	13	13	2	0	0-...	75.0	79	52	44	7	33-0	44
2000—Tennessee (Sou.)	12	7	.632	3.76	27	26	2	0	0-...	167.2	154	83	70	16	68-0	142
—Toronto (A.L.)	0	0	...	9.00	1	1	0	0	0-0	4.0	5	4	4	1	5-0	2
2001—Tennessee (Sou.)	0	1	.000	3.94	3	3	0	0	0-...	16.0	13	7	7	3	5-0	13
—Toronto (A.L.)	1	0	1.000	4.40	7	1	0	0	0-0	14.1	12	8	7	0	6-0	9
—Syracuse (I.L.)	8	6	.571	4.66	22	22	0	0	0-...	121.2	128	67	63	11	50-0	82
2002—Syracuse (I.L.)	4	9	.308	4.98	30	23	1	0	0-...	141.0	145	91	78	17	57-0	98
—Toronto (A.L.)	0	1	.000	18.00	2	0	0	0	0-0	1.0	4	2	2	0	3-1	0
Major League totals (3 years)	1	1	.500	6.05	10	2	0	0	0-0	19.1	21	14	13	1	14-1	11

COGGIN, DAVE P PHILLIES

PERSONAL: Born October 30, 1976, in Covina, Calif. ... 6-4/205. ... Throws right, bats right. ... Full name: David Raymond Coggin.
HIGH SCHOOL: Upland (Calif.).
TRANSACTIONS/CAREER NOTES: Selected by Philadelphia Phillies organization in supplemental round ("sandwich pick" between first and second round, 30th pick overall) of free-agent draft (June 1, 1995). ... On disabled list (April 20-May 25, 1998; May 14-June 4 and June 26, 1999-remainder of season). ... On Scranton/Wilkes-Barre disabled list (June 5-15, 2001).
STATISTICAL NOTES: Led Florida State League with 24 wild pitches in 1997.
CAREER HITTING (MLB): 2-for-48 (.042), 1 R, 1 2B, 0 3B, 0 HR, 1 RBI.

Year	League	W	L	Pct.	ERA	G	GS	CG	ShO	Sv.-Opp.	IP	H	R	ER	HR	BB-IBB	SO
1995—	Martinsville (Appl.)	5	3	.625	3.00	11	11	0	0	0-...	48.0	45	25	16	1	31-0	37
1996—	Piedmont (S.Atl.)	9	12	.429	4.31	28	28	3	3	0-...	169.1	156	87	81	12	46-1	129
1997—	Clearwater (FSL)	11	8	.579	4.70	27	27	3	•2	0-...	155.0	160	96	81	12	86-0	110
1998—	Reading (East.)	4	8	.333	4.14	20	20	0	0	0-...	108.2	106	58	50	8	62-1	65
1999—	Reading (East.)	2	5	.286	7.50	9	9	0	0	0-...	42.0	55	37	35	8	20-0	21
2000—	Clearwater (FSL)	2	2	.500	2.67	6	5	0	0	0-...	33.2	25	11	10	1	13-0	26
—	Reading (East.)	2	3	.400	4.93	7	7	0	0	0-...	42.0	49	24	23	5	13-0	30
—	Philadelphia (N.L.)	2	0	1.000	5.33	5	5	0	0	0-0	27.0	35	20	16	2	12-0	17
—	Scranton/W.B. (I.L.)	3	2	.600	4.34	9	9	0	0	0-...	45.2	35	27	22	2	33-0	27
2001—	Scranton/W.B. (I.L.)	5	5	.500	3.05	15	15	0	0	0-...	97.1	93	36	33	6	31-0	53
—	Philadelphia (N.L.)	6	7	.462	4.17	17	17	0	0	0-0	95.0	99	46	44	7	39-6	62
2002—	Philadelphia (N.L.)	2	5	.286	4.68	38	7	0	0	0-0	77.0	65	42	40	4	51-3	64
Major League totals (3 years)		10	12	.455	4.52	60	29	0	0	0-0	199.0	199	108	100	13	102-9	143

COLANGELO, MIKE OF

PERSONAL: Born October 22, 1976, in Teaneck, N.J. ... 6-1/185. ... Bats right, throws right. ... Full name: Michael Gus Colangelo.
HIGH SCHOOL: C.D. Hylton (Woodbridge, Va.).
COLLEGE: George Mason.
TRANSACTIONS/CAREER NOTES: Selected by Anaheim Angels organization in 21st round of free-agent draft (June 3, 1997). ... On Anaheim disabled list (June 14, 1999-remainder of season). ... On disabled list (March 20, 2000-entire season). ... Claimed on waivers by Arizona Diamondbacks (October 5, 2000). ... Claimed on waivers by San Diego Padres (October 17, 2000). ... Granted free agency (October 18, 2001). ... Signed by Oakland Athletics (November 15, 2001). ... On Sacramento disabled list (June 5-29, 2002). ... Released by A's (October 1, 2002).
2002 GAMES PLAYED BY POSITION (MLB): OF—19.

			BATTING													FIELDING	
Year	Team (League)	Pos.	G	AB	R	H	2B	3B	HR	RBI	BB	SO	SB-CS	Avg.	OBP	SLG	E	Avg.
1998—	Cedar Rapids (Midw.)	OF	22	83	13	23	8	0	4	8	12	16	5-1	.277	.378	.518	1	.933
—	Lake Elsinore (Calif.)	OF	36	145	33	55	11	3	5	21	13	24	2-6	.379	.448	.600	0	1.000
1999—	Erie (East.)	OF-DH	28	109	24	37	10	3	1	13	14	22	3-3	.339	.433	.514	2	.950
—	Edmonton (PCL)	OF	26	105	13	38	7	1	0	9	13	18	2-1	.362	.442	.448	2	.941
—	Anaheim (A.L.)	OF	1	2	0	1	0	0	0	0	1	0	0-0	.500	.667	.500	0	1.000
2000—	Anaheim (A.L.)								Did not play.									
2001—	Mobile (Sou.)■	OF	9	34	5	9	0	1	1	4	4	8	0-0	.265	.342	.412	1	.909
—	Portland (PCL)	OF	61	180	27	47	11	1	3	22	31	44	5-3	.261	.385	.383	1	.991
—	San Diego (N.L.)	OF	50	91	10	22	3	3	2	8	8	30	0-0	.242	.310	.407	1	.979
2002—	Oakland (A.L.)	OF	20	23	2	4	1	0	0	0	1	2	0-0	.174	.240	.217	0	1.000
—	Sacramento (PCL)	OF	70	217	22	46	9	0	0	22	33	36	3-3	.212	.331	.253	2	.986
American League totals (2 years)			21	25	2	5	1	0	0	0	2	2	0-0	.200	.286	.240	0	1.000
National League totals (1 year)			50	91	10	22	3	3	2	8	8	30	0-0	.242	.310	.407	1	.979
Major League totals (3 years)			71	116	12	27	4	3	2	8	10	32	0-0	.233	.305	.371	1	.985

COLBRUNN, GREG 1B

PERSONAL: Born July 26, 1969, in Fontana, Calif. ... 6-0/212. ... Bats right, throws right. ... Full name: Gregory Joseph Colbrunn.
HIGH SCHOOL: Fontana (Calif.).
TRANSACTIONS/CAREER NOTES: Selected by Montreal Expos organization in sixth round of free-agent draft (June 2, 1987). ... On disabled list (April 10, 1991-entire season). ... On Indianapolis disabled list (April 9-May 5, 1992). ... On Montreal disabled list (August 2-18, 1992); included rehabilitation assignment to Indianapolis (August 13-18). ... On Montreal disabled list (April 5-21, 1993); included rehabilitation assignment to West Palm Beach (April 9-20). ... On Montreal disabled list (July 12, 1993-remainder of season); included rehabilitation assignment to Ottawa (July 27-August 2). ... Claimed on waivers by Florida Marlins (October 7, 1993). ... On Florida disabled list (April 9-May 27, and July 15-30, 1994); included rehabilitation assignments to Brevard County (May 12-18 and July 28-30) and Edmonton (May 18-27). ... On disabled list (July 24-August 8, 1996). ... Granted free agency (December 20, 1996). ... Signed by Minnesota Twins organization (January 24, 1997). ... Traded by Twins to Atlanta Braves for a player to be named later (August 14, 1997); Twins acquired OF Marc Lewis to complete deal (October 1, 1997). ... Granted free agency (October 23, 1997). ... Signed by Colorado Rockies organization (December 23, 1997). ... Traded by Rockies to Braves for P David Cortes, P Mike Porzio and a player to be named later (July 30, 1998); Rockies acquired P Anthony Briggs to complete deal (September 9, 1998). ... Granted free agency (October 23, 1998). ... Signed by Arizona Diamondbacks (November 17, 1998). ... On Arizona disabled list (June 6-25 and June 27-August 17, 2001); included rehabilitation assignment to Tucson (August 10-17). ... On Arizona disabled list (March 22-April 10 and July 18-August 2, 2002); included rehabilitation assignment to Tucson (April 4-10). ... Granted free agency (October 28, 2002).
STATISTICAL NOTES: Had 21-game hitting streak (May 31-June 23, 1996). ... Hit for the cycle (September 18, 2002). ... Career major league grand slams: 2.
MISCELLANEOUS: Holds Arizona Diamondbacks record for highest career batting average (.317).
2002 GAMES PLAYED BY POSITION (MLB): 1B—40; 3B—5; DH—3.

			BATTING													FIELDING	
Year	Team (League)	Pos.	G	AB	R	H	2B	3B	HR	RBI	BB	SO	SB-CS	Avg.	OBP	SLG	E	Avg.
1988—	Rockford (Midw.)	C	115	417	55	111	18	2	7	46	22	60	5-3	.266	.318	.369	15	.978
1989—	W. Palm Beach (FSL)	C	59	228	20	54	8	0	0	25	6	29	3-1	.237	.261	.272	5	.988
—	Jacksonville (Sou.)	C	55	178	21	49	11	1	3	18	13	33	0-1	.275	.330	.399	4	.988
1990—	Jacksonville (Sou.)	C	125	458	57	138	29	1	13	76	38	78	1-2	.301	.358	.454	15	.981
1991—									Did not play.									
1992—	Indianapolis (A.A.)	1B	57	216	32	66	19	1	11	48	7	41	1-0	.306	.333	.556	4	.992
—	Montreal (N.L.)	1B	52	168	12	45	8	0	2	18	6	34	3-2	.268	.294	.351	3	.992
1993—	W. Palm Beach (FSL)	1B	8	31	6	12	2	1	1	5	4	1	0-0	.387	.457	.613	1	.988
—	Montreal (N.L.)	1B	70	153	15	39	9	0	4	23	6	33	4-2	.255	.282	.392	2	.995
—	Ottawa (I.L.)	1B	6	22	4	6	1	0	0	8	1	2	1-0	.273	.292	.318	0	1.000
1994—	Florida (N.L.)■	1B	47	155	17	47	10	0	6	31	9	27	1-1	.303	.345	.484	4	.988
—	Brevard County (FSL)	DH-1B	7	11	3	6	2	0	1	2	1	0	0-0	.545	.583	1.000	1	.944
—	Edmonton (PCL)	1B-DH	7	17	2	4	0	0	1	2	0	1	0-0	.235	.278	.412	1	.967

		BATTING														FIELDING	
Year Team (League)	Pos.	G	AB	R	H	2B	3B	HR	RBI	BB	SO	SB-CS	Avg.	OBP	SLG	E	Avg.
1995— Florida (N.L.)	1B	138	528	70	146	22	1	23	89	22	69	11-3	.277	.311	.453	5	.996
1996— Florida (N.L.)	1B	141	511	60	146	26	2	16	69	25	76	4-5	.286	.333	.438	6	.995
1997— Minnesota (A.L.)■	1B-DH	70	217	24	61	14	0	5	26	8	38	1-2	.281	.307	.415	6	.988
— Atlanta (N.L.)■	1B-DH	28	54	3	15	3	0	2	9	2	11	0-0	.278	.316	.444	1	.984
1998— Colorado (N.L.)■	1B-OF-DH-C	62	122	12	38	8	2	2	13	8	23	3-3	.311	.359	.459	2	.992
— Atlanta (N.L.)■	1B-OF	28	44	6	13	3	0	1	10	2	11	1-0	.295	.367	.432	0	1.000
1999— Arizona (N.L.)■	1B-DH-3B	67	135	20	44	5	3	5	24	12	23	1-1	.326	.392	.519	1	.996
2000— Arizona (N.L.)	1B-DH-3B	116	329	48	103	22	1	15	57	43	45	0-1	.313	.405	.523	8	.989
2001— Arizona (N.L.)	1B-3B	59	97	12	28	8	0	4	18	9	14	0-0	.289	.373	.495	3	.968
— Tucson (PCL)	1B	5	13	1	5	1	0	0	4	2	0	0-0	.385	.467	.462	0	1.000
2002— Tucson (PCL)	1B-3B	6	25	6	9	3	0	2	7	3	3	0-0	.360	.429	.720	1	.960
— Arizona (N.L.)	1B-3B-DH	72	171	30	57	16	2	10	27	13	19	0-0	.333	.378	.626	2	.993
American League totals (1 year)		70	217	24	61	14	0	5	26	8	38	1-2	.281	.307	.415	6	.988
National League totals (11 years)		880	2467	305	721	140	11	90	388	157	385	28-18	.292	.343	.467	37	.993
Major League totals (11 years)		950	2684	329	782	154	11	95	414	165	423	29-20	.291	.341	.463	43	.993

DIVISION SERIES RECORD

RECORDS: Shares N.L. career record for most pinch hits—3.

		BATTING														FIELDING	
Year Team (League)	Pos.	G	AB	R	H	2B	3B	HR	RBI	BB	SO	SB-CS	Avg.	OBP	SLG	E	Avg.
1997— Atlanta (N.L.)	PH	1	1	0	1	0	0	0	2	0	0	0-0	1.000	1.000	1.000	...	...
1998— Atlanta (N.L.)	PH	2	2	0	0	0	0	0	0	0	0	0-0	.000	.000	.000	...	...
1999— Arizona (N.L.)	1B	2	5	1	2	1	0	1	2	2	2	0-0	.400	.625	1.200	0	1.000
2001— Arizona (N.L.)	PH-1B	4	6	0	2	0	0	0	1	1	0	0-0	.333	.429	.333	0	1.000
2002— Arizona (N.L.)	1B	1	3	1	0	0	0	0	0	1	1	0-0	.000	.250	.000	0	1.000
Division series totals (5 years)		10	17	2	5	1	0	1	5	4	3	0-0	.294	.455	.529	0	1.000

CHAMPIONSHIP SERIES RECORD

		BATTING														FIELDING	
Year Team (League)	Pos.	G	AB	R	H	2B	3B	HR	RBI	BB	SO	SB-CS	Avg.	OBP	SLG	E	Avg.
1997— Atlanta (N.L.)	PH	3	3	0	2	0	0	0	0	0	0	0-0	.667	.667	.667	...	...
1998— Atlanta (N.L.)	PH	6	6	0	2	0	0	0	0	0	2	0-0	.333	.333	.333	...	...
2001— Arizona (N.L.)	PH	1	1	0	0	0	0	0	0	0	0	0-0	.000	.000	.000	...	...
Championship series totals (3 years)		10	10	0	4	0	0	0	0	0	2	0-0	.400	.400	.400	0	...

WORLD SERIES RECORD

RECORDS: Shares single-inning record for most runs—2 (November 3, 2001, third inning).
NOTES: Member of World Series championship team (2001).

		BATTING														FIELDING	
Year Team (League)	Pos.	G	AB	R	H	2B	3B	HR	RBI	BB	SO	SB-CS	Avg.	OBP	SLG	E	Avg.
2001— Arizona (N.L.)	1B	1	5	2	2	0	0	0	1	1	1	0-0	.400	.500	.400	0	1.000

COLLIER, LOU IF/OF

PERSONAL: Born August 21, 1973, in Chicago. ... 5-10/191. ... Bats right, throws right. ... Full name: Louis Keith Collier.
HIGH SCHOOL: Vocational (Chicago).
JUNIOR COLLEGE: Kishwaukee Junior College (Ill.), then Triton Community College (Ill.).
TRANSACTIONS/CAREER NOTES: Selected by Pittsburgh Pirates organization in 31st round of free-agent draft (June 1, 1992). ... On Pittsburgh disabled list (May 22-June 7, 1998); included rehabilitation assignment to Lynchburg (June 3-7). ... Claimed on waivers by Milwaukee Brewers (December 18, 1998). ... On Indianapolis disabled list (April 27-July 7, 2000). ... Traded by Brewers to New York Mets as part of three-way deal in which Mets traded P Glendon Rusch to Brewers, Colorado Rockies traded 1B/OF Ross Gload and P Craig House to Mets, Brewers traded P Jeff D'Amico, OF Jeromy Burnitz, OF/1B Mark Sweeney and cash to Mets, Mets traded 1B/3B Todd Zeile, OF Benny Agbayani, IF/OF Lenny Harris and cash to Rockies and Rockies traded OF Alex Ochoa to Brewers (January 21, 2002). ... Traded by Mets to Montreal Expos for P Jimmy Serrano and OF Jason Bay (March 26, 2002). ... Released by Expos (September 30, 2002).
2002 GAMES PLAYED BY POSITION (MLB): OF—7; 2B—2; 3B—1.

		BATTING														FIELDING	
Year Team (League)	Pos.	G	AB	R	H	2B	3B	HR	RBI	BB	SO	SB-CS	Avg.	OBP	SLG	E	Avg.
1993— Welland (NY-Penn)	SS	50	201	35	61	6	2	1	19	12	31	8-7	.303	.356	.368	27	.887
1994— Augusta (S.Atl.)	SS	85	318	48	89	17	4	7	40	25	53	32-10	.280	.345	.425	34	.915
— Salem (Caro.)	SS	43	158	25	42	4	1	6	16	15	29	5-8	.266	.348	.418	11	.946
1995— Lynchburg (Caro.)	SS	114	399	68	110	19	3	4	38	51	60	31-11	.276	.365	.368	35	.937
1996— Carolina (Sou.)	SS-DH	119	443	76	124	20	3	3	49	48	73	29-9	.280	.355	.359	30	.943
1997— Calgary (PCL)	SS-2B-DH	112	397	65	131	31	5	1	48	37	47	12-7	.330	.393	.441	34	.937
— Pittsburgh (N.L.)	SS	18	37	3	5	0	0	0	3	1	11	1-0	.135	.158	.135	0	1.000
1998— Pittsburgh (N.L.)	SS	110	334	30	82	13	6	2	34	31	70	2-2	.246	.316	.338	18	.960
— Lynchburg (Caro.)	SS	5	18	4	3	2	0	0	0	2	0	2-0	.167	.286	.278	4	.840
1999— Milwaukee (N.L.)■	SS-OF-3B-2B	74	135	18	35	9	0	2	21	14	32	3-2	.259	.325	.370	5	.951
— Louisville (I.L.)	3B-SS-OF	27	91	25	35	10	0	4	11	15	14	6-3	.385	.472	.626	3	.962
2000— Indianapolis (I.L.)	OF-2B-3B	17	56	7	14	4	1	0	12	11	9	2-2	.250	.371	.357	3	.933
— Huntsville (Sou.)	3B-OF-2B-SS	50	172	29	46	4	2	2	29	30	44	7-3	.267	.374	.349	8	.929
— Milwaukee (N.L.)	OF-3B	14	32	9	7	1	0	1	2	6	4	0-0	.219	.333	.344	0	1.000
2001— Indianapolis (I.L.)	OF-2B-3B	86	312	48	90	17	2	14	36	24	64	9-3	.288	.350	.490	6	.976
— Milwaukee (N.L.)	OF-3B-DH	50	127	19	32	8	1	2	14	17	30	5-1	.252	.340	.378	4	.948
2002— Montreal (N.L.)■	OF-2B-3B	13	11	3	1	1	0	0	0	1	3	0-0	.091	.231	.182	0	1.000
— Ottawa (I.L.)	O-3-2-S-1	89	307	48	97	26	6	6	52	37	69	5-2	.316	.394	.498	14	.932
Major League totals (6 years)		279	676	82	162	32	7	7	74	70	150	11-5	.240	.314	.339	27	.962

COLOME, JESUS — P — DEVIL RAYS

PERSONAL: Born December 23, 1977, in San Pedro de Macoris, Dominican Republic. ... 6-4/205. ... Throws right, bats right. ... Full name: Jesus Colome De La Cruz.

TRANSACTIONS/CAREER NOTES: Signed as non-drafted free agent by Oakland Athletics organization (September 29, 1996). ... Traded by A's with player to be named to Tampa Bay Devil Rays for P Jim Mecir and P Todd Belitz (July 28, 2000). ... On Durham disabled list (April 5-May 20, 2001).

CAREER HITTING (MLB): 0-for-0 (.000), 0 R, 0 2B, 0 3B, 0 HR, 0 RBI.

Year League	W	L	Pct.	ERA	G	GS	CG	ShO	Sv.-Opp.	IP	H	R	ER	HR	BB-IBB	SO
1997— Dom. Athletics (DSL)	9	3	.750	2.70	18	7	3	0	0-...	90.0	73	33	27	...	22-...	55
1998— Arizona Athletics (Ariz.)	2	5	.286	3.18	12	11	0	0	0-...	56.2	47	27	20	1	16-0	62
1999— Modesto (Calif.)	8	4	.667	3.36	31	22	0	0	1-...	128.2	125	63	48	6	60-2	127
2000— Midland (Texas)	9	4	.692	3.59	20	20	0	0	0-...	110.1	99	62	44	10	50-0	95
— Orlando (Sou.)■	1	2	.333	6.75	3	3	0	0	0-...	14.2	18	12	11	2	7-0	9
2001— Durham (I.L.)	0	3	.000	6.23	13	0	0	0	0-...	17.1	22	13	12	1	6-0	18
— Tampa Bay (A.L.)	2	3	.400	3.33	30	0	0	0	0-0	48.2	37	22	18	8	25-4	31
2002— Tampa Bay (A.L.)	2	7	.222	8.27	32	0	0	0	0-5	41.1	56	41	38	6	33-5	33
— Durham (I.L.)	2	2	.500	2.17	18	0	0	0	1-...	29.0	18	8	7	1	13-0	30
Major League totals (2 years)	4	10	.286	5.60	62	0	0	0	0-5	90.0	93	63	56	14	58-9	64

COLON, BARTOLO — P — EXPOS

PERSONAL: Born May 24, 1973, in Altamira, Dominican Republic. ... 6-0/235. ... Throws right, bats right.

TRANSACTIONS/CAREER NOTES: Signed as non-drafted free agent by Cleveland Indians organization (June 26, 1993). ... On Canton/Akron disabled list (May 30-July 24, 1996). ... On Cleveland disabled list (April 16-May 12, 2000); included rehabilitation assignment to Buffalo (May 7-12). ... On suspended list (July 28-August 2, 2001). ... Traded by Indians with future considerations to Montreal Expos for 1B Lee Stevens, SS Brandon Phillips, P Cliff Lee and OF Grady Sizemore (June 27, 2002); Expos acquired P Tim Drew to complete deal (June 28, 2002).

HONORS: Named Carolina League Pitcher of the Year (1995).

STATISTICAL NOTES: Pitched 4-0 no-hit victory against New Orleans (June 20, 1997). ... Pitched 2-0 one-hit, complete-game victory against New York Yankees (September 18, 2000).

CAREER HITTING (MLB): 9-for-67 (.134), 1 R, 0 2B, 0 3B, 0 HR, 4 RBI.

Year League	W	L	Pct.	ERA	G	GS	CG	ShO	Sv.-Opp.	IP	H	R	ER	HR	BB-IBB	SO
1993— Santiago (DSL)	6	1	.857	2.59	11	10	2	1	1-...	66.0	44	24	19	...	33-...	48
1994— Burlington (Appl.)	7	4	.636	3.14	12	12	0	0	0-...	66.0	46	32	23	3	44-0	84
1995— Kinston (Caro.)	13	3	*.813	1.96	21	21	0	0	0-...	128.2	91	31	28	8	39-0	*152
1996— Canton/Akron (East.)	2	2	.500	1.74	13	12	0	0	0-...	62.0	44	17	12	2	25-0	56
— Buffalo (A.A.)	0	0	...	6.00	8	0	0	0	0-...	15.0	16	10	10	2	8-0	19
1997— Cleveland (A.L.)	4	7	.364	5.65	19	17	1	0	0-0	94.0	107	66	59	12	45-1	66
— Buffalo (A.A.)	7	1	.875	2.22	10	10	1	1	0-...	56.2	45	15	14	4	23-0	54
1998— Cleveland (A.L.)	14	9	.609	3.71	31	31	6	2	0-0	204.0	205	91	84	15	79-5	158
1999— Cleveland (A.L.)	18	5	.783	3.95	32	32	1	1	0-0	205.0	185	97	90	24	76-5	161
2000— Cleveland (A.L.)	15	8	.652	3.88	30	30	2	1	0-0	188.0	163	86	81	21	98-4	212
— Buffalo (I.L.)	1	0	1.000	1.80	1	1	0	0	0-...	5.0	6	1	1	0	0-0	4
2001— Cleveland (A.L.)	14	12	.538	4.09	34	34	1	0	0-0	222.1	220	106	101	26	90-2	201
2002— Cleveland (A.L.)	10	4	.714	2.55	16	16	4	2	0-0	116.1	104	37	33	11	31-1	75
— Montreal (N.L.)■	10	4	.714	3.31	17	17	4	1	0-0	117.0	115	48	43	9	39-4	74
A.L. totals (6 years)	75	45	.625	3.92	162	160	15	6	0-0	1029.2	984	483	448	109	419-18	873
N.L. totals (1 year)	10	4	.714	3.31	17	17	4	1	0-0	117.0	115	48	43	9	39-4	74
Major League totals (6 years)	85	49	.634	3.85	179	177	19	7	0-0	1146.2	1099	531	491	118	458-22	947

DIVISION SERIES RECORD

Year League	W	L	Pct.	ERA	G	GS	CG	ShO	Sv.-Opp.	IP	H	R	ER	HR	BB-IBB	SO
1997— Cleveland (A.L.)									Did not play.							
1998— Cleveland (A.L.)	0	0	...	1.59	1	1	0	0	0-0	5.2	5	1	1	1	3-1	3
1999— Cleveland (A.L.)	0	1	.000	9.00	2	2	0	0	0-0	9.0	11	9	9	3	4-0	12
2001— Cleveland (A.L.)	1	1	.500	1.84	2	2	0	0	0-0	14.2	12	3	3	0	6-0	13
Division series totals (3 years)	1	2	.333	3.99	5	5	0	0	0-0	29.1	28	13	13	4	13-1	28

CHAMPIONSHIP SERIES RECORD

Year League	W	L	Pct.	ERA	G	GS	CG	ShO	Sv.-Opp.	IP	H	R	ER	HR	BB-IBB	SO
1997— Cleveland (A.L.)									Did not play.							
1998— Cleveland (A.L.)	1	0	1.000	1.00	1	1	1	0	0-0	9.0	4	1	1	0	4-0	3

WORLD SERIES RECORD

Year League	W	L	Pct.	ERA	G	GS	CG	ShO	Sv.-Opp.	IP	H	R	ER	HR	BB-IBB	SO
1997— Cleveland (A.L.)									Did not play.							

ALL-STAR GAME RECORD

	W	L	Pct.	ERA	GS	CG	ShO	Sv.-Opp.	IP	H	R	ER	HR	BB-IBB	SO
All-Star Game totals (1 year)	1	0	1.000	27.00	0	0	0	0-0	1.0	2	3	3	2	1-0	1

CONDREY, CLAY — P — PADRES

PERSONAL: Born November 19, 1975, in Beaumont, Texas. ... 6-3/195. ... Throws right, bats right. ... Full name: Clayton Lee Condrey.

HIGH SCHOOL: Navasota (Texas).

COLLEGE: McNeese State.

TRANSACTIONS/CAREER NOTES: Signed as non-drafted free agent by San Diego Padres organization (June 29, 1998).

CAREER HITTING (MLB): 0-for-6 (.000), 0 R, 0 2B, 0 3B, 0 HR, 0 RBI.

Year	League	W	L	Pct.	ERA	G	GS	CG	ShO	Sv.-Opp.	IP	H	R	ER	HR	BB-IBB	SO
1998—	Arizona Padres (Ariz.)	0	1	.000	3.38	5	0	0	0	0-...	5.1	6	4	2	0	5-1	4
—	Idaho Falls (Pio.)	2	1	.667	2.55	18	0	0	0	5-...	24.2	31	12	7	2	4-0	19
1999—	Fort Wayne (Midw.)	2	3	.400	3.78	42	0	0	0	20-...	47.2	40	24	20	5	19-4	47
—	Rancho Cuca. (Calif.)	0	0	...	3.68	6	0	0	0	0-...	7.1	4	3	3	1	3-0	9
2000—	Rancho Cuca. (Calif.)	1	1	.500	3.48	18	0	0	0	4-...	20.2	18	9	8	1	7-0	21
—	Mobile (Sou.)	2	2	.500	5.36	35	0	0	0	6-...	43.2	41	27	26	4	20-0	25
2001—	Mobile (Sou.)	2	2	.500	4.54	27	0	0	0	12-...	33.2	33	23	17	1	15-4	21
—	Portland (PCL)	1	3	.250	4.75	39	0	0	0	2-...	53.0	63	37	28	7	13-1	45
2002—	Portland (PCL)	10	4	.714	3.50	25	23	0	0	0-...	133.2	128	55	52	12	40-1	73
—	San Diego (N.L.)	1	2	.333	1.69	9	3	0	0	0-0	26.2	20	7	5	1	8-1	16
Major League totals (1 year)		1	2	.333	1.69	9	3	0	0	0-0	26.2	20	7	5	1	8-1	16

CONINE, JEFF — 1B/OF — ORIOLES

PERSONAL: Born June 27, 1966, in Tacoma, Wash. ... 6-1/220. ... Bats right, throws right. ... Full name: Jeffrey Guy Conine.
HIGH SCHOOL: Eisenhower (Rialto, Calif.).
COLLEGE: UCLA.
TRANSACTIONS/CAREER NOTES: Selected by Kansas City Royals organization in 58th round of free-agent draft (June 2, 1987). ... On disabled list (June 28, 1991-remainder of season). ... Selected by Florida Marlins in first round (22nd pick overall) of expansion draft (November 17, 1992). ... Traded by Marlins to Royals for P Blaine Mull (November 20, 1997). ... On Kansas City disabled list (March 25-May 5 and July 27-August 19, 1998); included rehabilitation assignment to Omaha (August 17-19). ... Traded by Royals to Baltimore Orioles for P Chris Fussell (April 2, 1999). ... Granted free agency (November 5, 1999). ... Re-signed by Orioles (December 15, 1999). ... On disabled list (June 15-August 7, 2002).
RECORDS: Shares major league rookie-season record for most games—162 (1993).
HONORS: Named Southern League Most Valuable Player (1990).
STATISTICAL NOTES: Led Southern League first basemen with 1,164 putouts, 95 assists, 22 errors, 1,281 total chances and 108 double plays in 1990. ... Led N.L. with 12 sacrifice flies in 1995. ... Career major league grand slams: 5.
MISCELLANEOUS: Holds Florida Marlins all-time record for most runs batted in (422).
2002 GAMES PLAYED BY POSITION (MLB): 1B—103; DH—7; OF—6.

			BATTING															FIELDING	
Year	Team (League)	Pos.	G	AB	R	H	2B	3B	HR	RBI	BB	SO	SB-CS	Avg.	OBP	SLG	E	Avg.
1988—	Baseball City (FSL)	1B-3B	118	415	63	113	23	9	10	59	46	77	26-12	.272	.342	.443	22	.970
1989—	Baseball City (FSL)	1B	113	425	68	116	12	7	14	60	40	91	32-13	.273	.338	.433	18	.980
1990—	Memphis (Sou.)	1B-3B	137	487	89	156	37	8	15	95	94	88	21-6	.320	.425	.522	†22	.983
—	Kansas City (A.L.)	1B	9	20	3	5	2	0	0	2	2	5	0-0	.250	.318	.350	1	.977
1991—	Omaha (A.A.)	1B-OF	51	171	23	44	9	1	3	15	26	39	0-6	.257	.359	.374	7	.984
1992—	Omaha (A.A.)	1B-OF	110	397	69	120	24	5	20	72	54	67	4-5	.302	.383	.539	6	.993
—	Kansas City (A.L.)	OF-1B	28	91	10	23	5	2	0	9	8	23	0-0	.253	.313	.352	0	1.000
1993—	Florida (N.L.)■	OF-1B	*162	595	75	174	24	3	12	79	52	135	2-2	.292	.351	.403	2	.995
1994—	Florida (N.L.)	OF-1B	115	451	60	144	27	6	18	82	40	92	1-2	.319	.373	.525	6	.986
1995—	Florida (N.L.)	OF-1B	133	483	72	146	26	2	25	105	66	94	2-0	.302	.379	.520	6	.981
1996—	Florida (N.L.)	OF-1B	157	597	84	175	32	2	26	95	62	121	1-4	.293	.360	.484	8	.985
1997—	Florida (N.L.)	1B-OF	151	405	46	98	13	1	17	61	57	89	2-0	.242	.337	.405	8	.992
1998—	Kansas City (A.L.)■	OF-1B-DH	93	309	30	79	26	0	8	43	26	68	3-0	.256	.312	.417	1	.996
—	Omaha (PCL)	DH-OF	2	9	0	0	0	0	0	0	0	3	0-0	.000	.000	.000	0	1.000
1999—	Baltimore (A.L.)■	1-DH-O-3	139	444	54	129	31	1	13	75	30	40	0-3	.291	.335	.453	7	.992
2000—	Baltimore (A.L.)	3-1-DH-O	119	409	53	116	20	2	13	46	36	53	4-3	.284	.341	.438	15	.969
2001—	Baltimore (A.L.)	1B-OF-3B-DH	139	524	75	163	23	2	14	97	64	75	12-8	.311	.386	.443	4	.995
2002—	Baltimore (A.L.)	1B-DH-OF	116	451	44	123	26	4	15	63	25	66	8-0	.273	.307	.448	10	.990
American League totals (7 years)			643	2248	269	638	133	11	63	335	191	330	27-14	.284	.339	.437	38	.989
National League totals (5 years)			718	2531	337	737	122	14	98	422	277	531	8-8	.291	.360	.467	30	.989
Major League totals (12 years)			1361	4779	606	1375	255	25	161	757	468	861	35-22	.288	.350	.453	68	.989

DIVISION SERIES RECORD

			BATTING														FIELDING	
Year	Team (League)	Pos.	G	AB	R	H	2B	3B	HR	RBI	BB	SO	SB-CS	Avg.	OBP	SLG	E	Avg.
1997—	Florida (N.L.)	1B	3	11	3	4	1	0	0	0	1	0	0-0	.364	.417	.455	1	.964

CHAMPIONSHIP SERIES RECORD

			BATTING														FIELDING	
Year	Team (League)	Pos.	G	AB	R	H	2B	3B	HR	RBI	BB	SO	SB-CS	Avg.	OBP	SLG	E	Avg.
1997—	Florida (N.L.)	1B	6	18	1	2	0	0	0	1	1	4	0-0	.111	.158	.111	0	1.000

WORLD SERIES RECORD

NOTES: Member of World Series championship team (1997).

			BATTING														FIELDING	
Year	Team (League)	Pos.	G	AB	R	H	2B	3B	HR	RBI	BB	SO	SB-CS	Avg.	OBP	SLG	E	Avg.
1997—	Florida (N.L.)	1B-PH	6	13	1	3	0	0	0	2	0	0	0-0	.231	.231	.231	0	1.000

ALL-STAR GAME RECORD

NOTES: Hit home run in first at-bat (July 11, 1995). ... Named Most Valuable Player (1995).

	AB	R	H	2B	3B	HR	RBI	BB	SO	SB-CS	Avg.	OBP	SLG	E	Avg.
All-Star Game totals (1 year)	1	1	1	0	0	1	1	0	0	0-0	1.000	1.000	4.000	0	...

CONTI, JASON — OF — DEVIL RAYS

PERSONAL: Born January 27, 1975, in Pittsburgh. ... 5-11/175. ... Bats left, throws right. ... Full name: Stanley Jason Conti.
HIGH SCHOOL: Seneca Valley (Harmony, Pa.).
COLLEGE: Pittsburgh.

TRANSACTIONS/CAREER NOTES: Selected by Arizona Diamondbacks organization in 32nd round of free-agent draft (June 4, 1996). ... Loaned by Diamondbacks to Tulsa, Texas Rangers organization (April 1-September 14, 1998). ... Traded by Diamondbacks with P Nick Bierbrodt to Tampa Bay Devil Rays for P Albie Lopez and C Mike Difelice (July 25, 2001).

STATISTICAL NOTES: Tied for Midwest League lead in double plays by outfielder with six in 1997. ... Led Texas League outfielders with 20 assists in 1998. ... Led Pacific Coast League outfielders with 303 total chances in 1999.

2002 GAMES PLAYED BY POSITION (MLB): OF—74.

			BATTING														FIELDING	
Year	Team (League)	Pos.	G	AB	R	H	2B	3B	HR	RBI	BB	SO	SB-CS	Avg.	OBP	SLG	E	Avg.
1996—	Lethbridge (Pio.)	OF	63	226	63	83	15	1	4	49	30	29	30-7	.367	.449	.496	4	.955
1997—	South Bend (Midw.)	OF	117	458	78	142	22	10	3	43	45	99	30-18	.310	.383	.421	5	.981
—	High Desert (Calif.)	OF	14	59	15	21	5	1	2	8	10	12	1-2	.356	.457	.576	5	.853
1998—	Tulsa (Texas)■	OF	130	530	*125	167	31	12	15	67	63	96	19-13	.315	.396	.504	5	.976
1999—	Tucson (PCL)■	OF	133	520	100	151	23	8	9	57	55	89	22-7	.290	.360	.417	8	.974
2000—	Tucson (PCL)	OF	93	383	75	117	20	5	11	57	23	57	11-3	.305	.349	.470	10	.950
—	Arizona (N.L.)	OF	47	91	11	21	4	3	1	15	7	30	3-0	.231	.293	.374	1	.983
2001—	Tucson (PCL)	OF	92	362	68	120	23	6	9	52	33	54	2-5	.331	.402	.503	2	.991
—	Arizona (N.L.)	OF	5	4	1	1	0	0	0	0	1	2	0-0	.250	.400	.250	0	...
—	Durham (I.L.)■	OF	38	157	24	48	12	0	5	18	9	31	3-1	.306	.347	.478	1	.987
2002—	Tampa Bay (A.L.)	OF	78	222	26	57	15	2	3	21	18	55	4-2	.257	.315	.383	6	.966
American League totals (1 year)			78	222	26	57	15	2	3	21	18	55	4-2	.257	.315	.383	6	.966
National League totals (2 years)			52	95	12	22	4	3	1	15	8	32	3-0	.232	.298	.368	1	.983
Major League totals (3 years)			130	317	38	79	19	5	4	36	26	87	7-2	.249	.310	.379	7	.970

COOK, AARON — P — ROCKIES

PERSONAL: Born February 8, 1979, in Fort Campbell, Ky. ... 6-3/175. ... Throws right, bats right. ... Full name: Aaron Lane Cook.

HIGH SCHOOL: Hamilton (Ohio).

TRANSACTIONS/CAREER NOTES: Selected by Colorado Rockies organization in second round of free-agent draft (June 3, 1997).

CAREER HITTING (MLB): 1-for-11 (.091), 0 R, 0 2B, 0 3B, 0 HR, 1 RBI.

Year	League	W	L	Pct.	ERA	G	GS	CG	ShO	Sv.-Opp.	IP	H	R	ER	HR	BB-IBB	SO
1997—	Arizona Rockies (Ariz.)	1	3	.250	3.13	9	8	0	0	0-...	46.0	48	27	16	1	17-0	35
1998—	Portland (N'West)	5	8	.385	4.88	15	15	•1	0	0-...	79.1	87	50	43	8	39-0	38
1999—	Asheville (S.Atl.)	4	12	.250	6.44	25	25	2	0	0-...	121.2	157	•99	87	17	42-0	73
2000—	Asheville (S.Atl.)	10	7	.588	2.96	21	21	4	•2	0-...	142.2	130	54	47	10	23-0	118
—	Salem (Caro.)	1	6	.143	5.44	7	7	1	0	0-...	43.0	52	33	26	4	12-0	37
2001—	Salem (Caro.)	11	11	.500	3.08	27	27	0	0	0-...	155.0	157	73	53	4	38-0	122
2002—	Carolina (Sou.)	7	2	.778	1.42	14	14	2	2	0-...	95.0	73	24	15	4	19-0	58
—	Colorado Springs (PCL)	4	4	.500	3.78	10	10	1	0	0-...	64.1	67	40	27	6	18-0	32
—	Colorado (N.L.)	2	1	.667	4.54	9	5	0	0	0-0	35.2	41	18	18	4	13-0	14
Major League totals (1 year)		2	1	.667	4.54	9	5	0	0	0-0	35.2	41	18	18	4	13-0	14

COOK, DENNIS — P

PERSONAL: Born October 4, 1962, in Lamarque, Texas. ... 6-3/190. ... Throws left, bats left. ... Full name: Dennis Bryan Cook.

HIGH SCHOOL: Dickinson (Texas).

JUNIOR COLLEGE: Angelina College (Texas).

COLLEGE: Texas.

TRANSACTIONS/CAREER NOTES: Selected by San Diego Padres organization in sixth round of free-agent draft (January 11, 1983); did not sign. ... Selected by San Francisco Giants organization in 18th round of free-agent draft (June 3, 1985). ... Traded by Giants with P Terry Mulholland and 3B Charlie Hayes to Philadelphia Phillies for P Steve Bedrosian and a player to be named later (June, 18, 1989); Giants acquired IF Rick Parker to complete deal (August 7, 1989). ... Traded by Phillies to Los Angeles Dodgers for C Darrin Fletcher (September 13, 1990). ... Traded by Dodgers with P Mike Christopher to Cleveland Indians for P Rudy Seanez (December 10, 1991). ... Granted free agency (October 15, 1993). ... Signed by Chicago White Sox organization (January 5, 1994). ... Claimed on waivers by Indians (October 17, 1994). ... Traded by Indians to Texas Rangers for SS Guillermo Mercedes (June 22, 1995). ... Granted free agency (October 29, 1996). ... Signed by Florida Marlins (December 10, 1996). ... On suspended list (July 4-5, 1997). ... Traded by Marlins to New York Mets for OF Fletcher Bates and P Scott Comer (December 18, 1997). ... Granted free agency (October 23, 1998). ... Re-signed by Mets (November 18, 1998). ... Traded by Mets with P Turk Wendell to Phillies for P Bruce Chen and P Adam Walker (July 27, 2001). ... On Philadelphia disabled list (July 30-August 14, 2001); included rehabilitation assignment to Scranton (August 13-14). ... Granted free agency (November 5, 2001). ... Signed by Anaheim Angels (December 20, 2001). ... On Anaheim disabled list (March 22-April 10 and July 5-September 1, 2002); included rehabilitation assignment to Rancho Cucamonga (August 27-September 1). ... Granted free agency (November 6, 2002).

HONORS: Named Texas League Pitcher of the Year (1987).

STATISTICAL NOTES: Led A.L. with five balks in 1992.

MISCELLANEOUS: Appeared in one game as pinch runner with Philadelphia (1989). ... Singled once and scored once in five games as pinch hitter and appeared in one game as pinch runner with Philadelphia (1990). ... Appeared in one game as pinch runner (1997). ... Singled twice, scored once and had an RBI in two games as pinch hitter (1997).

CAREER HITTING (MLB): 29-for-110 (.264), 15 R, 2 2B, 1 3B, 2 HR, 9 RBI.

Year	League	W	L	Pct.	ERA	G	GS	CG	ShO	Sv.-Opp.	IP	H	R	ER	HR	BB-IBB	SO
1985—	Clinton (Midw.)	5	4	.556	3.36	13	13	1	0	0-...	83.0	73	35	31	7	27-0	40
1986—	Fresno (Calif.)	12	7	.632	3.97	27	25	2	1	1-...	170.0	141	92	75	16	100-1	*173
1987—	Shreveport (Texas)	9	2	.818	2.13	16	16	1	1	0-...	105.2	94	32	25	1	20-1	98
—	Phoenix (PCL)	2	5	.286	5.23	12	11	1	0	0-...	62.0	72	45	36	8	26-2	24
1988—	Phoenix (PCL)	11	9	.550	3.88	26	25	5	1	0-...	141.1	138	73	61	14	51-1	110
—	San Francisco (N.L.)	2	1	.667	2.86	4	4	1	1	0-0	22.0	9	8	7	1	11-1	13
1989—	Phoenix (PCL)	7	4	.636	3.12	12	12	3	1	0-...	78.0	73	29	27	4	19-0	85
—	San Francisco (N.L.)	1	0	1.000	1.80	2	2	1	0	0-0	15.0	13	3	3	1	5-0	9
—	Philadelphia (N.L.)■	6	8	.429	3.99	21	16	1	1	0-0	106.0	97	56	47	17	33-6	58
1990—	Philadelphia (N.L.)	8	3	.727	3.56	42	13	2	1	1-2	141.2	132	61	56	13	54-9	58
—	Los Angeles (N.L.)■	1	1	.500	7.53	5	3	0	0	0-0	14.1	23	13	12	7	2-0	6

Year League	W	L	Pct.	ERA	G	GS	CG	ShO	Sv.-Opp.	IP	H	R	ER	HR	BB-IBB	SO
1991—Albuquerque (PCL)	7	3	.700	3.63	14	14	1	0	0-...	91.2	73	46	37	9	32-0	84
—Los Angeles (N.L.)	1	0	1.000	0.51	20	1	0	0	0-1	17.2	12	3	1	0	7-1	8
—San Antonio (Texas)	1	3	.250	2.49	7	7	1	0	0-...	50.2	43	20	14	2	10-1	45
1992—Cleveland (A.L.)■	5	7	.417	3.82	32	25	1	0	0-0	158.0	156	79	67	29	50-2	96
1993—Cleveland (A.L.)	5	5	.500	5.67	25	6	0	0	0-2	54.0	62	36	34	9	16-1	34
—Charlotte (I.L.)	3	2	.600	5.06	12	6	0	0	0-...	42.2	46	26	24	6	6-1	40
1994—Chicago (A.L.)■	3	1	.750	3.55	38	0	0	0	0-1	33.0	29	17	13	4	14-3	26
1995—Cleveland (A.L.)■	0	0	...	6.39	11	0	0	0	0-0	12.2	16	9	9	3	10-2	13
—Texas (A.L.)■	0	2	.000	4.00	35	1	0	0	2-2	45.0	47	23	20	6	16-1	40
1996—Texas (A.L.)	5	2	.714	4.09	60	0	0	0	0-2	70.1	53	34	32	2	35-7	64
1997—Florida (N.L.)■	1	2	.333	3.90	59	0	0	0	0-2	62.1	64	28	27	4	28-4	63
1998—New York (N.L.)■	8	4	.667	2.38	73	0	0	0	1-5	68.0	60	21	18	5	27-4	79
1999—New York (N.L.)	10	5	.667	3.86	71	0	0	0	3-6	63.0	50	27	27	11	27-1	68
2000—New York (N.L.)	6	3	.667	5.34	68	0	0	0	2-8	59.0	63	35	35	8	31-4	53
2001—New York (N.L.)	1	1	.500	4.25	43	0	0	0	0-2	36.0	28	18	17	6	10-1	34
—Philadelphia (N.L.)■	0	0	...	5.59	19	0	0	0	0-1	9.2	15	6	6	2	4-2	4
—Scranton/W.B. (I.L.)	0	0	...	9.00	1	1	0	0	0-...	1.0	1	1	1	0	2-0	1
2002—Anaheim (A.L.)■	1	1	.500	3.38	37	0	0	0	0-1	24.0	21	9	9	2	10-0	13
—Rancho Cuca. (Calif.)	0	1	.000	17.18	4	3	0	0	0-...	3.2	8	7	7	3	1-0	5
A.L. totals (6 years)	19	18	.514	4.17	238	32	1	0	2-8	397.0	384	207	184	55	151-16	286
N.L. totals (9 years)	45	28	.616	3.75	427	39	5	3	7-27	614.2	566	279	256	75	239-33	453
Major League totals (15 years)	64	46	.582	3.91	665	71	6	3	9-35	1011.2	950	486	440	130	390-49	739

C

DIVISION SERIES RECORD

Year League	W	L	Pct.	ERA	G	GS	CG	ShO	Sv.-Opp.	IP	H	R	ER	HR	BB-IBB	SO
1996—Texas (A.L.)	0	0	...	0.00	2	0	0	0	0-0	1.1	0	0	0	0	1-0	0
1997—Florida (N.L.)	1	0	1.000	0.00	2	0	0	0	0-0	3.0	0	0	0	0	1-0	3
1999—New York (N.L.)	0	0	...	0.00	1	0	0	0	0-0	1.2	1	0	0	0	1-0	1
2000—New York (N.L.)	0	0	...	0.00	2	0	0	0	0-0	1.1	0	0	0	0	2-0	1
Division series totals (4 years)	1	0	1.000	0.00	7	0	0	0	0-0	7.1	1	0	0	0	5-0	5

CHAMPIONSHIP SERIES RECORD

Year League	W	L	Pct.	ERA	G	GS	CG	ShO	Sv.-Opp.	IP	H	R	ER	HR	BB-IBB	SO
1997—Florida (N.L.)	0	0	...	0.00	2	0	0	0	0-0	2.1	0	0	0	0	0-0	2
1999—New York (N.L.)	0	0	...	0.00	3	0	0	0	0-0	1.1	1	0	0	0	2-1	1
2000—New York (N.L.)	0	0	...	0.00	1	0	0	0	0-0	1.0	1	0	0	0	0-0	2
Champ. series totals (3 years)	0	0	...	0.00	6	0	0	0	0-0	4.2	2	0	0	0	2-1	5

WORLD SERIES RECORD

NOTES: Member of World Series championship team (1997).

Year League	W	L	Pct.	ERA	G	GS	CG	ShO	Sv.-Opp.	IP	H	R	ER	HR	BB-IBB	SO
1997—Florida (N.L.)	1	0	1.000	0.00	3	0	0	0	0-0	3.2	1	0	0	0	1-0	5
2000—New York (N.L.)	0	0	...	0.00	3	0	0	0	0-0	.2	1	0	0	0	3-0	1
World Series totals (2 years)	1	0	1.000	0.00	6	0	0	0	0-0	4.1	2	0	0	0	4-0	6

COOLBAUGH, MIKE 3B PHILLIES

PERSONAL: Born June 5, 1972, in Binghamton, N.Y. ... 6-1/190. ... Bats right, throws right. ... Full name: Michael Robert Coolbaugh. ... Brother of Scott Coolbaugh, third baseman with Texas Rangers (1989-1990), San Diego Padres (1991) and St. Louis Cardinals (1994).

HIGH SCHOOL: Theodore Roosevelt (San Antonio).

TRANSACTIONS/CAREER NOTES: Selected by Toronto Blue Jays organization in 16th round of free-agent draft (June 4, 1990). ... On disabled list (June 23-August 21, 1993). ... Selected by Texas Rangers organization from Blue Jays organization in Rule 5 minor league draft (December 4, 1996). ... Granted free agency (October 18, 1996). ... Signed by Oakland Athletics organization (November 4, 1996). ... Granted free agency (October 17, 1997). ... Signed by Colorado Rockies organization prior to 1998 season. ... On Colorado Springs disabled list (April 18-May 5 and July 23-31, 1998). ... Granted free agency (October 16, 1998). ... Signed by New York Yankees (November 17, 1998). ... Granted free agency (October 15, 1999). ... Re-signed by Yankees organization (October 22, 1999). ... Granted free agency (October 18, 2000). ... Signed by Milwaukee Brewers organization (November 13, 2000). ... Granted free agency (October 15, 2001). ... Signed by St. Louis Cardinals organization (November 21, 2001). ... Released by Cardinals (September 30, 2002). ... Signed by Philadelphia Phillies organization (November 13, 2002).

STATISTICAL NOTES: Led Southern League with 303 total bases in 1997. ... Led Southern League third basemen with 94 putouts, 302 assists, 420 total chances, .943 fielding percentage and 35 double plays in 1997.

2002 GAMES PLAYED BY POSITION (MLB): 3B—4.

		BATTING														FIELDING	
Year Team (League)	Pos.	G	AB	R	H	2B	3B	HR	RBI	BB	SO	SB-CS	Avg.	OBP	SLG	E	Avg.
1990—Medicine Hat (Pio.)	SS-2B-3B	58	211	21	40	9	0	2	16	13	47	3-2	.190	.238	.261	33	.866
1991—St. Catharines (NY-P)	1B-2B-3B-OF	71	256	28	59	13	2	3	25	17	40	4-5	.230	.282	.332	12	.978
1992—St. Catharines (NY-P)	3B-OF	15	49	3	14	1	1	0	2	3	12	0-2	.286	.327	.347	4	.889
1993—Hagerstown (S.Atl.)	2B-3B-1B-OF	112	389	58	95	23	1	16	62	32	94	4-3	.244	.304	.432	17	.958
1994—Dunedin (FSL)	3-S-O-1-2	122	456	53	120	33	3	16	66	28	94	3-4	.263	.313	.454	22	.945
1995—Knoxville (Sou.)	3-1-2-O	•142	500	71	120	32	2	9	56	37	110	7-11	.240	.305	.366	25	.948
1996—Charlotte (FSL)■	S-1-3-O-P	124	449	76	129	33	4	15	75	42	80	8-10	.287	.357	.479	22	.961
—Tulsa (Texas)	2B-1B	7	23	6	8	3	0	2	9	2	3	1-0	.348	.444	.739	0	1.000
1997—Huntsville (Sou.)■	3B-SS-2B	*139	*559	100	172	37	2	•30	*132	52	105	8-3	.308	.369	.542	26	†.944
1998—Colo. Springs (PCL)■	3-1-2-O	108	386	62	107	35	2	16	75	32	93	0-3	.277	.331	.503	26	.935
1999—Columbus (I.L.)■	3-O-1-D	114	391	65	108	31	2	15	66	38	112	5-7	.276	.340	.481	21	.934
2000—Columbus (I.L.)	S-2-O-3-1	117	387	63	105	28	0	23	61	67	96	6-3	.271	.380	.522	17	.966
2001—Indianapolis (I.L.)■	3B-SS	94	347	49	93	24	3	10	50	39	92	3-2	.268	.347	.441	14	.960
—Milwaukee (N.L.)	3B-SS	39	70	10	14	6	0	2	7	5	16	0-0	.200	.273	.371	1	.976
2002—Memphis (PCL)■	3B-SS-1B-C	116	411	62	100	20	1	29	75	51	126	9-3	.243	.338	.509	12	.965
—St. Louis (N.L.)	3B	5	12	0	1	0	0	0	0	1	3	0-0	.083	.154	.083	0	1.000
Major League totals (2 years)		44	82	10	15	6	0	2	7	6	19	0-0	.183	.256	.329	1	.980

RECORD AS PITCHER

Year League	W	L	Pct.	ERA	G	GS	CG	ShO	Sv.-Opp.	IP	H	R	ER	HR	BB-IBB	SO
1996—Charlotte (FSL)	0	0	...	36.00	1	0	0	0	0-...	1.0	5	4	4	0	0-0	2

COOMER, RON 1B

PERSONAL: Born November 18, 1966, in Chicago. ... 6-0/215. ... Bats right, throws right. ... Full name: Ronald Bryan Coomer.
HIGH SCHOOL: Lockport (Ill.).
JUNIOR COLLEGE: Taft (Calif.) Junior College.
TRANSACTIONS/CAREER NOTES: Selected by Oakland Athletics organization in 14th round of free-agent draft (June 2, 1987). ... Released by A's (August 1, 1990). ... Signed by Chicago White Sox organization (March 18, 1991). ... On disabled list (June 5-19, 1992). ... On Birmingham disabled list (June 12-21, 1993). ... Traded by White Sox to Los Angeles Dodgers for P Isidro Martinez (December 27, 1993). ... Traded by Dodgers with P Greg Hansell, P Jose Parra and a player to be named later to Minnesota Twins for P Kevin Tapani and P Mark Guthrie (July 31, 1995); Twins acquired OF Chris Latham to complete deal (October 30, 1995). ... Granted free agency (December 21, 2000). ... Signed by Chicago Cubs (January 10, 2001). ... On Chicago disabled list (April 3-25, 2001); included rehabilitation assignment to Iowa (April 21-25). ... Granted free agency (November 7, 2001). ... Signed by New York Yankees organization (January 25, 2002). ... Granted free agency (October 29, 2002).
STATISTICAL NOTES: Led Southern League with eight sacrifice flies and tied for lead in grounding into double plays with 21 in 1991. ... Led Southern League third basemen with 94 putouts, 396 total chances, 24 double plays and tied for lead with 26 errors in 1991. ... Led Pacific Coast League with 293 total bases in 1994. ... Led Pacific Coast League third basemen with .952 fielding percentage, 399 total chances and 299 assists in 1994. ... Tied for A.L. lead in grounding into double plays with 22 in 1998. ... Career major league grand slams: 1.
2002 GAMES PLAYED BY POSITION (MLB): 3B—26; DH—15; 1B—11.

			BATTING														FIELDING	
Year	Team (League)	Pos.	G	AB	R	H	2B	3B	HR	RBI	BB	SO	SB-CS	Avg.	OBP	SLG	E	Avg.
1987—	Medford (N'West)	3B-1B	45	168	23	58	10	2	1	26	19	22	1-1	.345	.410	.446	11	.923
1988—	Modesto (Calif.)	3B-1B	131	495	67	138	23	2	17	85	60	88	2-6	.279	.357	.436	16	.920
1989—	Madison (Midw.)	3B-1B	61	216	28	69	15	0	4	28	30	34	0-1	.319	.401	.444	6	.956
1990—	Huntsville (Sou.)	2B-1B-3B	66	194	22	43	7	0	3	27	21	40	3-1	.222	.297	.304	11	.965
1991—	Birmingham (Sou.)■	3B-1B	137	505	*81	129	27	5	13	76	59	78	0-3	.255	.330	.406	‡26	.938
1992—	Vancouver (PCL)	3B	86	262	29	62	10	0	9	40	16	36	3-0	.237	.277	.378	13	.927
1993—	Birmingham (Sou.)	3B-1B	69	262	44	85	18	0	13	50	15	43	1-1	.324	.358	.542	11	.931
—	Nashville (A.A.)	3B	59	211	34	66	19	0	13	51	10	29	1-2	.313	.342	.588	16	.895
1994—	Albuquerque (PCL)■	3B-DH-2B	127	535	89	181	34	6	22	*123	26	62	4-3	.338	.367	.548	19	†.952
1995—	Albuquerque (PCL)	3B-1B-DH	85	323	54	104	23	2	16	76	18	28	5-2	.322	.357	.554	9	.979
—	Minnesota (A.L.)■	1-3-DH-O	37	101	15	26	3	1	5	19	9	11	0-1	.257	.324	.455	2	.988
1996—	Minnesota (A.L.)	1-O-3-DH	95	233	34	69	12	1	12	41	17	24	3-0	.296	.340	.511	4	.988
1997—	Minnesota (A.L.)	3-1-DH-O	140	523	63	156	30	2	13	85	22	91	4-3	.298	.324	.438	11	.969
1998—	Minnesota (A.L.)	3-1-DH-O	137	529	54	146	22	1	15	72	18	72	2-2	.276	.295	.406	6	.990
1999—	Minnesota (A.L.)	1-3-DH-O	127	467	53	123	25	1	16	65	30	69	2-1	.263	.307	.424	6	.991
2000—	Minnesota (A.L.)	1B-DH-3B	140	544	64	147	29	1	16	82	36	50	2-0	.270	.317	.415	5	.995
2001—	Chicago (N.L.)■	3B-1B-DH	111	349	25	91	19	1	8	53	29	70	0-0	.261	.316	.390	7	.977
—	Iowa (PCL)	1B-3B	4	12	0	4	0	0	0	0	1	3	0-0	.333	.385	.333	0	1.000
2002—	New York (A.L.)■	3B-DH-1B	55	148	14	39	7	0	3	17	6	23	0-0	.264	.290	.372	7	.941
American League totals (7 years)			731	2545	297	706	128	7	80	381	138	340	13-7	.277	.313	.428	41	.988
National League totals (1 year)			111	349	25	91	19	1	8	53	29	70	0-0	.261	.316	.390	7	.977
Major League totals (8 years)			842	2894	322	797	147	8	88	434	167	410	13-7	.275	.314	.423	48	.987

DIVISION SERIES RECORD

			BATTING														FIELDING	
Year	Team (League)	Pos.	G	AB	R	H	2B	3B	HR	RBI	BB	SO	SB-CS	Avg.	OBP	SLG	E	Avg.
2002—	New York (A.L.)	DH	1	2	0	1	0	0	0	0	0	0	0-0	.500	.500	.500	0	...

ALL-STAR GAME RECORD

	AB	R	H	2B	3B	HR	RBI	BB	SO	SB-CS	Avg.	OBP	SLG	E	Avg.
All-Star Game totals (1 year)	1	0	0	0	0	0	0	0	1	0-0	.000	.000	.000	0	1.000

COOPER, BRIAN P

PERSONAL: Born August 19, 1974, in North Hollywood, Calif. ... 6-1/185. ... Throws right, bats right. ... Full name: Brian John Cooper.
HIGH SCHOOL: Glendora (Calif.).
COLLEGE: Southern California.
TRANSACTIONS/CAREER NOTES: Selected by California Angels organization in fourth round of free-agent draft (June 1, 1995). ... Angels franchise renamed Anaheim Angels for 1997 season. ... On Salt Lake disabled list (June 24-July 2, 2001). ... Traded by Angels to Toronto Blue Jays for DH/1B Brad Fullmer (January 17, 2002). ... Released by Blue Jays (September 30, 2002).
CAREER HITTING (MLB): 0-for-4 (.000), 0 R, 0 2B, 0 3B, 0 HR, 0 RBI.

Year	League	W	L	Pct.	ERA	G	GS	CG	ShO	Sv.-Opp.	IP	H	R	ER	HR	BB-IBB	SO
1995—	Boise (N'West)	3	2	.600	3.92	13	11	0	0	1-...	62.0	60	31	27	5	22-1	66
1996—	Lake Elsinore (Calif.)	7	9	.438	4.21	26	23	1	1	0-...	162.1	177	100	76	17	39-0	155
1997—	Lake Elsinore (Calif.)	7	3	.700	3.54	17	17	1	0	0-...	117.0	111	56	46	7	27-0	104
1998—	Midland (Texas)	8	10	.444	7.13	32	24	5	0	1-...	161.2	*215	*138	*128	*35	59-1	*141
1999—	Erie (East.)	10	5	.667	3.30	22	22	*6	0	0-...	158.0	146	61	58	17	29-0	143
—	Edmonton (PCL)	2	1	.667	3.77	5	5	0	0	0-...	31.0	30	17	13	0	10-0	32
—	Anaheim (A.L.)	1	1	.500	4.88	5	5	0	0	0-0	27.2	23	15	15	3	18-0	15
2000—	Edmonton (PCL)	3	7	.300	7.23	11	11	1	1	0-...	61.0	87	51	49	12	18-0	37
—	Anaheim (A.L.)	4	8	.333	5.90	15	15	1	1	0-0	87.0	105	66	57	18	35-1	36
—	Lake Elsinore (Calif.)	0	0	...	0.00	1	1	0	0	0-...	7.0	4	1	0	0	2-0	3
2001—	Salt Lake (PCL)	12	8	.600	4.63	28	28	1	0	0-...	173.0	181	98	89	26	58-0	109
—	Anaheim (A.L.)	0	1	.000	2.63	7	1	0	0	0-0	13.2	10	5	4	2	4-0	7
2002—	Syracuse (I.L.)■	9	9	.500	5.09	27	25	1	0	0-...	155.2	176	98	88	19	46-1	71
—	Toronto (A.L.)	0	1	.000	14.04	2	2	0	0	0-0	8.1	14	13	13	5	4-0	3
Major League totals (4 years)		5	11	.313	5.86	29	23	1	1	0-0	136.2	152	99	89	28	61-1	61

CORA, ALEX — SS — DODGERS

PERSONAL: Born October 18, 1975, in Caguas, Puerto Rico. ... 6-0/180. ... Bats left, throws right. ... Full name: Jose Alexander Cora. ... Brother of Joey Cora, second baseman with four major league teams (1987-98).
HIGH SCHOOL: Bautista (Caguas, Puerto Rico).
COLLEGE: Miami (Fla.).
TRANSACTIONS/CAREER NOTES: Selected by Los Angeles Dodgers organization in third round of free-agent draft (June 4, 1996). ... On Los Angeles disabled list (March 25-June 27, 1999); included rehabilitation assignment to Albuquerque (June 8-27).
STATISTICAL NOTES: Led Texas League shortstops with 629 total chances and 88 double plays in 1997.
2002 GAMES PLAYED BY POSITION (MLB): SS—61; 2B—40.

			BATTING														FIELDING	
Year Team (League)	Pos.	G	AB	R	H	2B	3B	HR	RBI	BB	SO	SB-CS	Avg.	OBP	SLG	E	Avg.
1996—Vero Beach (FSL)	SS-OF	61	214	26	55	5	4	0	26	12	36	5-5	.257	.306	.318	16	.940
1997—San Antonio (Texas)	SS	127	448	52	105	20	4	3	48	25	60	12-9	.234	.279	.317	20	*.968
1998—Albuquerque (PCL)	SS-2B	81	299	42	79	17	5	5	45	15	38	10-7	.264	.303	.405	18	.957
—Los Angeles (N.L.)	SS-2B	29	33	1	4	0	1	0	0	2	8	0-0	.121	.194	.182	2	.965
1999—Albuquerque (PCL)	SS-DH-2B	80	302	51	93	11	7	4	37	12	37	9-5	.308	.348	.430	12	.968
—Los Angeles (N.L.)	SS-2B	11	30	2	5	1	0	0	3	0	4	0-0	.167	.194	.200	2	.943
2000—Albuquerque (PCL)	SS	30	110	18	41	8	3	0	20	7	10	5-3	.373	.417	.500	7	.959
—Los Angeles (N.L.)	SS-2B	109	353	39	84	18	6	4	32	26	53	4-1	.238	.302	.357	12	.973
2001—Los Angeles (N.L.)	SS-2B	134	405	38	88	18	3	4	29	31	58	0-2	.217	.285	.306	20	.962
2002—Los Angeles (N.L.)	SS-2B	115	258	37	75	14	4	5	28	26	38	7-2	.291	.371	.434	7	.977
Major League totals (5 years)		398	1079	117	256	51	14	13	92	85	161	11-5	.237	.306	.347	43	.969

CORDERO, FRANCISCO — P — RANGERS

PERSONAL: Born May 11, 1975, in Santo Domingo, Dominican Republic. ... 6-2/200. ... Throws right, bats right. ... Full name: Francisco Javier Cordero.
HIGH SCHOOL: Colegio Luz de Arroyo Hondo (Dominican Republic).
TRANSACTIONS/CAREER NOTES: Signed as non-drafted free agent by Detroit Tigers organization (June 18, 1994). ... On Jamestown disabled list (June 28, 1996-remainder of season). ... On Jacksonville disabled list (May 22-June 18 and June 26, 1998-remainder of season). ... Traded by Tigers with P Justin Thompson, OF Gabe Kapler, C Bill Haselman, 2B Frank Catalanotto and P Alan Webb to Texas Rangers for OF Juan Gonzalez, P Danny Patterson and C Gregg Zaun (November 2, 1999). ... On Texas disabled list (March 23-June 19 and June 26, 2001-remainder of season); included rehabilitation assignment to Oklahoma (May 21-June 19). ... On Texas disabled list (June 25-July 27, 2002); included rehabilitation assignment to Oklahoma (July 20-27).
HONORS: Named Southern League Most Outstanding Pitcher (1999).
CAREER HITTING (MLB): 0-for-1 (.000), 0 R, 0 2B, 0 3B, 0 HR, 0 RBI.

Year League	W	L	Pct.	ERA	G	GS	CG	ShO	Sv.-Opp.	IP	H	R	ER	HR	BB-IBB	SO
1994—Dominican Tigers (DSL)	4	3	.571	3.90	12	12	0	0	0-...	60.0	65	47	26	...	27-...	36
1995—Fayetteville (S.Atl.)	0	3	.000	6.30	4	4	0	0	0-...	20.0	26	16	14	1	12-0	19
—Jamestown (NY-Penn)	4	7	.364	5.22	15	14	0	0	0-...	88.0	96	62	51	3	37-0	54
1996—Fayetteville (S.Atl.)	0	0	...	2.57	2	1	0	0	0-...	7.0	2	2	2	0	6-0	7
—Jamestown (NY-Penn)	0	0	...	0.82	2	2	0	0	0-...	11.0	5	1	1	0	2-0	10
1997—West Michigan (Midw.)	6	1	.857	0.99	50	0	0	0	*35-...	54.1	36	13	6	2	15-2	67
1998—Jacksonville (Sou.)	1	1	.500	4.86	17	0	0	0	8-...	16.2	19	12	9	1	9-0	18
—Lakeland (FSL)	0	0	...	0.00	1	0	0	0	0-...	...	1	0	0	0	0-0	0
1999—Jacksonville (Sou.)	4	1	.800	1.38	47	0	0	0	*27-...	52.1	35	9	8	3	22-0	58
—Detroit (A.L.)	2	2	.500	3.32	20	0	0	0	0-0	19.0	19	7	7	2	18-2	19
2000—Texas (A.L.)■	1	2	.333	5.35	56	0	0	0	0-3	77.1	87	51	46	11	48-3	49
—Oklahoma (PCL)	0	0	...	4.15	3	0	0	0	1-...	4.1	7	3	2	0	3-0	5
2001—Oklahoma (PCL)	0	1	.000	0.59	12	0	0	0	6-...	15.1	8	2	1	0	3-0	20
—Texas (A.L.)	0	1	.000	3.86	3	0	0	0	0-0	2.1	3	1	1	0	2-1	1
2002—Texas (A.L.)	2	0	1.000	1.79	39	0	0	0	10-12	45.1	33	12	9	2	13-1	41
—Oklahoma (PCL)	0	2	.000	5.84	11	1	0	0	2-...	12.1	15	14	8	2	7-1	21
Major League totals (4 years)	5	5	.500	3.94	118	0	0	0	10-15	144.0	142	71	63	15	81-7	110

CORDERO, WIL — OF

PERSONAL: Born October 3, 1971, in Mayaguez, Puerto Rico. ... 6-2/200. ... Bats right, throws right. ... Full name: Wilfredo Nieva Cordero. ... Name pronounced cor-DARE-oh.
HIGH SCHOOL: Centro de Servicios Education de Mayaguez (Puerto Rico).
TRANSACTIONS/CAREER NOTES: Signed as non-drafted free agent by Montreal Expos organization (May 24, 1988). ... On Indianapolis disabled list (August 1, 1991-remainder of season; and May 12-June 11 and July 7-20, 1992). ... Traded by Expos with P Bryan Eversgerd to Boston Red Sox for P Rheal Cormier, 1B Ryan McGuire and P Shayne Bennett (January 10, 1996). ... On Boston disabled list (May 21-August 12, 1996); included rehabilitation assignments to Gulf Coast Red Sox (July 23-27) and Pawtucket (July 27-August 6). ... Released by Red Sox (September 28, 1997). ... Signed by Chicago White Sox (March 23, 1998). ... Granted free agency (November 3, 1998). ... Signed by Cleveland Indians (February 3, 1999). ... On Cleveland disabled list (June 9-September 8, 1999); included rehabilitation assignment to Akron (September 3-8). ... Granted free agency (October 29, 1999). ... Signed by Pittsburgh Pirates (December 14, 1999). ... Traded by Pirates to Indians for OF Alex Ramirez and IF Enrique Wilson (July 28, 2000). ... On suspended list (September 19-23, 2000). ... On disabled list (June 11-26, 2001). ... Released by Indians (April 29, 2002). ... Signed by Expos (May 12, 2002). ... On Montreal disabled list (August 1-16, 2002). ... Granted free agency (October 28, 2002).
HONORS: Named shortstop on The Sporting News N.L. Silver Slugger team (1994).
STATISTICAL NOTES: Had 15-game hitting streak (April 29-May 23, 2000). ... Career major league grand slams: 3.
2002 GAMES PLAYED BY POSITION (MLB): OF—32; 1B—11; DH—2.

			BATTING														FIELDING	
Year	**Team (League)**	**Pos.**	**G**	**AB**	**R**	**H**	**2B**	**3B**	**HR**	**RBI**	**BB**	**SO**	**SB-CS**	**Avg.**	**OBP**	**SLG**	**E**	**Avg.**
1988	—Jamestown (NY-P)	SS	52	190	18	49	3	0	2	22	15	44	3-3	.258	.322	.305	31	.886
1989	—W. Palm Beach (FSL)	SS	78	289	37	80	12	2	6	29	33	58	2-5	.277	.355	.394	29	.922
	—Jacksonville (Sou.)	SS	39	121	9	26	6	1	3	17	12	33	1-2	.215	.284	.355	7	.957
1990	—Jacksonville (Sou.)	SS	131	444	63	104	18	4	7	40	56	122	9-4	.234	.326	.340	41	.928
1991	—Indianapolis (A.A.)	SS	98	360	48	94	16	4	11	52	26	89	9-3	.261	.315	.419	27	.943
1992	—Indianapolis (A.A.)	SS	52	204	32	64	11	1	6	27	24	54	6-7	.314	.384	.466	12	.948
	—Montreal (N.L.)	SS-2B	45	126	17	38	4	1	2	8	9	31	0-0	.302	.353	.397	8	.947
1993	—Montreal (N.L.)	SS-3B	138	475	56	118	32	2	10	58	34	60	12-3	.248	.308	.387	36	.937
1994	—Montreal (N.L.)	SS	110	415	65	122	30	3	15	63	41	62	16-3	.294	.363	.489	22	.952
1995	—Montreal (N.L.)	SS-OF	131	514	64	147	35	2	10	49	36	88	9-5	.286	.341	.420	22	.953
1996	—Boston (A.L.)■	2B-DH-1B	59	198	29	57	14	0	3	37	11	31	2-1	.288	.330	.404	10	.950
	—GC Red Sox (GCL)	DH-2B	3	10	1	3	0	0	1	3	0	2	0-0	.300	.273	.600	0	1.000
	—Pawtucket (I.L.)	2B-DH	4	10	2	3	1	0	1	2	2	3	0-0	.300	.417	.700	0	1.000
1997	—Boston (A.L.)	OF-DH-2B	140	570	82	160	26	3	18	72	31	122	1-3	.281	.320	.432	2	.992
1998	—Birmingham (Sou.)■	1B-DH	11	35	6	10	2	0	2	11	7	3	0-0	.286	.405	.514	1	.989
	—Chicago (A.L.)	1B-OF	96	341	58	91	18	2	13	49	22	66	2-1	.267	.314	.446	7	.991
1999	—Cleveland (A.L.)■	OF-DH	54	194	35	58	15	0	8	32	15	37	2-0	.299	.364	.500	1	.981
	—Akron (East.)	OF-DH	3	11	2	4	2	0	0	0	0	3	0-0	.364	.417	.545	0	...
2000	—Pittsburgh (N.L.)■	OF-DH	89	348	46	98	24	3	16	51	25	58	1-2	.282	.336	.506	2	.983
	—Cleveland (A.L.)■	OF	38	148	18	39	11	2	0	17	7	18	0-0	.264	.310	.365	0	1.000
2001	—Cleveland (A.L.)	OF-1B-DH	89	268	30	67	11	1	4	21	22	50	0-0	.250	.313	.343	2	.992
2002	—Cleveland (A.L.)	OF-1B	6	18	1	4	0	0	0	1	0	3	0-0	.222	.222	.222	0	1.000
	—Montreal (N.L.)■	OF-1B-DH	66	143	21	39	9	0	6	29	17	26	2-0	.273	.349	.462	2	.983
American League totals (7 years)			482	1737	253	476	95	8	46	229	108	327	7-5	.274	.322	.417	22	.987
National League totals (6 years)			579	2021	269	562	134	11	59	258	162	325	40-13	.278	.338	.443	92	.951
Major League totals (11 years)			1061	3758	522	1038	229	19	105	487	270	652	47-18	.276	.331	.431	114	.968

DIVISION SERIES RECORD

			BATTING														FIELDING	
Year	**Team (League)**	**Pos.**	**G**	**AB**	**R**	**H**	**2B**	**3B**	**HR**	**RBI**	**BB**	**SO**	**SB-CS**	**Avg.**	**OBP**	**SLG**	**E**	**Avg.**
1999	—Cleveland (A.L.)	PH-DH-OF	3	9	3	5	0	0	1	2	1	2	0-0	.556	.600	.889	0	1.000
2001	—Cleveland (A.L.)	PH-OF	1	1	0	0	0	0	0	0	0	0	0-0	.000	.000	.000	0	1.000
Division series totals (2 years)			4	10	3	5	0	0	1	2	1	2	0-0	.500	.545	.800	0	1.000

ALL-STAR GAME RECORD

	AB	**R**	**H**	**2B**	**3B**	**HR**	**RBI**	**BB**	**SO**	**SB-CS**	**Avg.**	**OBP**	**SLG**	**E**	**Avg.**
All-Star Game totals (1 year)	2	0	0	0	0	0	0	0	0	0-0	.000	.000	.000	0	1.000

CORDOVA, MARTY — OF — ORIOLES

PERSONAL: Born July 10, 1969, in Las Vegas. ... 6-0/206. ... Bats right, throws right. ... Full name: Martin Keevin Cordova.

HIGH SCHOOL: Bishop Gorman (Las Vegas).

JUNIOR COLLEGE: Orange Coast College (Calif.).

COLLEGE: UNLV.

TRANSACTIONS/CAREER NOTES: Selected by San Diego Padres organization in eighth round of free-agent draft (June 2, 1987); did not sign. ... Selected by Minnesota Twins organization in 10th round of free-agent draft (June 5, 1989). ... On Visalia disabled list (April 12-May 20, 1991). ... On Salt Lake disabled list (April 17-May 11, 1994). ... On Minnesota disabled list (April 11-May 26, 1997); included rehabilitation assignment to Salt Lake (May 20-26). ... On disabled list (April 27-May 12, 1998). ... Granted free agency (October 7, 1999). ... Signed by Boston Red Sox organization (January 19, 2000). ... Released by Red Sox (March 26, 2000). ... Signed by Toronto Blue Jays organization (March 27, 2000). ... Granted free agency (October 4, 2000). ... Signed by Cleveland Indians organization (December 20, 2000). ... Granted free agency (November 5, 2001). ... Signed by Baltimore Orioles (December 6, 2001). ... On disabled list (March 31-April 12, 2002).

HONORS: Named California League Most Valuable Player (1992). ... Named A.L. Rookie of the Year by Baseball Writers' Association of America (1995).

STATISTICAL NOTES: Led California League with 302 total bases and tied for lead in grounding into double plays with 20 in 1992. ... Had 23-game hitting streak (June 5-29, 1996). ... Had 22-game hitting streak (April 22-May 18, 2001). ... Career major league grand slams: 1.

2002 GAMES PLAYED BY POSITION (MLB): OF—72; DH—56.

			BATTING														FIELDING	
Year	**Team (League)**	**Pos.**	**G**	**AB**	**R**	**H**	**2B**	**3B**	**HR**	**RBI**	**BB**	**SO**	**SB-CS**	**Avg.**	**OBP**	**SLG**	**E**	**Avg.**
1989	—Elizabethton (Appl.)	OF-3B	38	148	32	42	2	3	8	29	14	29	2-1	.284	.358	.500	4	.789
1990	—Kenosha (Midw.)	OF	81	269	35	58	7	5	7	25	28	73	6-3	.216	.300	.357	5	.948
1991	—Visalia (Calif.)	OF	71	189	31	40	6	1	7	19	17	46	2-3	.212	.284	.365	5	.923
1992	—Visalia (Calif.)	OF	134	513	103	175	31	6	*28	*131	76	99	13-5	.341	.431	*.589	3	.984
1993	—Nashville (Sou.)	OF	138	508	83	127	30	5	19	77	64	*153	10-5	.250	.347	.441	2	*.991
1994	—Salt Lake (PCL)	OF-DH	103	385	69	138	25	4	19	66	39	63	17-6	.358	.426	.592	8	.962
1995	—Minnesota (A.L.)	OF	137	512	81	142	27	4	24	84	52	111	20-7	.277	.352	.486	5	.986
1996	—Minnesota (A.L.)	OF	145	569	97	176	46	1	16	111	53	96	11-5	.309	.371	.478	3	.991
1997	—Minnesota (A.L.)	OF-DH	103	378	44	93	18	4	15	51	30	92	5-3	.246	.305	.434	2	.991
	—Salt Lake (PCL)	DH-OF	6	24	5	9	4	0	1	4	2	3	1-0	.375	.423	.667	1	.750
1998	—Minnesota (A.L.)	OF-DH	119	438	52	111	20	2	10	69	50	103	3-6	.253	.333	.377	6	.978
1999	—Minnesota (A.L.)	DH-OF	124	425	62	121	28	3	14	70	48	96	13-4	.285	.365	.464	3	.927
2000	—Toronto (A.L.)■	OF-DH	62	200	23	49	7	0	4	18	18	35	3-2	.245	.317	.340	1	.982
2001	—Cleveland (A.L.)■	OF-DH	122	409	61	123	20	2	20	69	23	81	0-3	.301	.348	.506	2	.990
2002	—Baltimore (A.L.)■	OF-DH	131	458	55	116	25	2	18	64	47	111	1-6	.253	.325	.434	4	.971
Major League totals (8 years)			943	3389	475	931	191	18	121	536	321	725	56-36	.275	.343	.449	26	.984

DIVISION SERIES RECORD

			BATTING														FIELDING	
Year	**Team (League)**	**Pos.**	**G**	**AB**	**R**	**H**	**2B**	**3B**	**HR**	**RBI**	**BB**	**SO**	**SB-CS**	**Avg.**	**OBP**	**SLG**	**E**	**Avg.**
2001	—Cleveland (A.L.)	OF	4	12	0	3	0	0	0	1	0	5	0-0	.250	.250	.250	0	1.000

COREY, BRYAN — P

PERSONAL: Born October 21, 1973, in Thousand Oaks, Calif. ... 6-0/170. ... Throws right, bats right. ... Full name: Bryan Scott Corey.
HIGH SCHOOL: Thousand Oaks (Calif.).
JUNIOR COLLEGE: Pierce Junior College (Calif.).
TRANSACTIONS/CAREER NOTES: Selected by Detroit Tigers organization in 12th round of free-agent draft (June 3, 1993). ... Selected by Arizona Diamondbacks in third round (63rd pick overall) of expansion draft (November 18, 1997). ... Claimed on waivers by Tigers (December 4, 1998). ... Granted free agency (October 15, 1999). ... Signed by Oakland Athletics organization (December 3, 1999). ... Granted free agency (October 18, 2000). ... Signed by San Diego Padres organization (November 20, 2000). ... Granted free agency (October 15, 2001). ... Signed by Los Angeles Dodgers organization (January 7, 2002). ... On Las Vegas disabled list (April 4-May 6, 2002). ... On Los Angeles disabled list (May 29-June 13, 2002). ... Released by Dodgers (October 8, 2002).
CAREER HITTING (MLB): 0-for-0 (.000), 0 R, 0 2B, 0 3B, 0 HR, 0 RBI.

Year	League	W	L	Pct.	ERA	G	GS	CG	ShO	Sv.-Opp.	IP	H	R	ER	HR	BB-IBB	SO
1995—	Jamestown (NY-Penn)	2	2	.500	3.86	29	0	0	0	10-...	28.0	21	14	12	2	12-1	41
1996—	Fayetteville (S.Atl.)	6	4	.600	1.21	60	0	0	0	34-...	82.0	50	19	11	2	17-3	101
1997—	Jacksonville (Sou.)	3	8	.273	4.76	52	0	0	0	9-...	68.0	74	42	36	8	21-3	37
1998—	Tucson (PCL)■	4	6	.400	5.44	39	10	0	0	2-...	87.2	116	61	53	14	24-0	50
—	Arizona (N.L.)	0	0	...	9.00	3	0	0	0	0-0	4.0	6	4	4	1	2-0	1
1999—	Toledo (I.L.)■	5	2	.714	2.86	48	0	0	0	2-...	69.1	63	27	22	6	34-4	36
2000—	Sacramento (PCL)■	8	3	.727	4.24	47	6	0	0	4-...	85.0	88	43	40	11	29-2	55
2001—	Portland (PCL)■	8	7	.533	4.67	47	12	0	0	6-...	106.0	124	55	55	12	31-3	66
2002—	Las Vegas (PCL)■	5	4	.556	4.36	37	0	0	0	1-...	53.2	79	31	26	5	18-1	33
—	Los Angeles (N.L.)	0	0	...	0.00	1	0	0	0	0-0	1.0	0	0	0	0	0-0	0
Major League totals (2 years)		0	0	...	7.20	4	0	0	0	0-0	5.0	6	4	4	1	2-0	1

RECORD AS POSITION PLAYER

			BATTING													FIELDING	
Year	Team (League)	Pos.	G	AB	R	H	2B	3B	HR	RBI	BB	SO	SB-CS	Avg.	OBP	SLG	E	Avg.
1993—	Bristol (Appl.)	SS-2B	39	95	14	10	3	0	0	3	26	35	2-3	.105	.309	.137	10	.930
1994—	Jamestown (NY-P)	2B-SS-3B	41	85	14	13	1	1	0	3	13	27	2-3	.153	.280	.188	10	.911

COREY, MARK — P

PERSONAL: Born November 16, 1974, in Coudersport, Pa. ... 6-3/210. ... Throws right, bats right. ... Full name: Mark Franklin Corey.
HIGH SCHOOL: Austin Area (Austin, Pa.).
COLLEGE: Edinboro.
TRANSACTIONS/CAREER NOTES: Selected by Cincinnati Reds organization in fourth round of free-agent draft (June 1, 1995). ... On disabled list (June 12, 1996-entire season). ... Traded by Reds to New York Mets for IF Ralph Millard (February 4, 1999). ... On New York disabled list (June 27-July 12, 2002); included rehabilitation assignment to Norfolk (July 5-12). ... Traded by Mets with OF Jay Payton and OF Robert Stratton to Colorado Rockies for P John Thomson and OF Mark Little (July 31, 2002). ... Granted free agency (October 15, 2002).
CAREER HITTING (MLB): 0-for-2 (.000), 0 R, 0 2B, 0 3B, 0 HR, 0 RBI.

Year	League	W	L	Pct.	ERA	G	GS	CG	ShO	Sv.-Opp.	IP	H	R	ER	HR	BB-IBB	SO
1995—	Princeton (Appl.)	1	1	.500	3.68	4	3	0	0	0-...	14.2	12	7	6	1	6-0	8
1996—										Did not play.							
1997—	Charleston, W.Va. (S.Atl.)	8	13	.381	4.57	26	26	1	0	0-...	136.0	169	87	69	7	42-3	97
1998—	Burlington (Midw.)	12	6	.667	2.44	20	20	•6	•2	0-...	140.0	125	55	38	9	36-0	109
—	Chattanooga (Sou.)	0	4	.000	8.20	6	6	0	0	0-...	26.1	32	25	24	6	16-1	6
—	Indianapolis (I.L.)	0	1	.000	4.50	1	1	1	0	0-...	6.0	4	3	3	1	3-0	2
1999—	Binghamton (East.)■	7	13	.350	5.40	29	27	0	0	0-...	155.0	175	108	93	18	64-0	111
2000—	Binghamton (East.)	0	0	...	1.05	14	2	0	0	0-...	25.2	15	5	3	0	11-0	19
—	Norfolk (I.L.)	3	7	.300	6.79	20	11	0	0	1-...	63.2	80	52	48	11	29-1	43
2001—	Binghamton (East.)	1	2	.333	1.80	25	0	0	0	17-...	35.0	23	10	7	1	12-0	50
—	Norfolk (I.L.)	8	2	.800	1.47	28	0	0	0	10-...	36.2	24	7	6	1	22-0	42
—	New York (N.L.)	0	0	...	16.20	2	0	0	0	0-0	1.2	5	3	3	0	3-1	3
2002—	Norfolk (I.L.)	3	1	.750	1.03	25	0	0	0	7-...	26.1	14	3	3	1	7-1	37
—	New York (N.L.)	0	3	.000	4.50	12	0	0	0	0-0	10.0	10	7	5	2	8-1	9
—	St. Lucie (FSL)	0	0	...	0.00	1	0	0	0	0-...	2.0	0	0	0	0	0-0	3
—	Colorado (N.L.)■	0	0	...	12.00	14	0	0	0	0-0	12.0	22	16	16	7	8-1	12
Major League totals (2 years)		0	3	.000	9.13	28	0	0	0	0-0	23.2	37	26	24	9	19-3	24

CORMIER, RHEAL — P — PHILLIES

PERSONAL: Born April 23, 1967, in Moncton, New Brunswick. ... 5-10/187. ... Throws left, bats left. ... Full name: Rheal Paul Cormier. ... Name pronounced ree-AL COR-mee-AY.
HIGH SCHOOL: Polyvalente Louis J. Robichaud.
JUNIOR COLLEGE: Community College of Rhode Island.
TRANSACTIONS/CAREER NOTES: Selected by St. Louis Cardinals organization in sixth round of free-agent draft (June 6, 1988). ... On Louisville disabled list (April 10-29, 1991). ... On disabled list (August 12-September 7, 1993). ... On St. Louis disabled list (April 28-May 13 and May 21-August 3, 1994); included rehabilitation assignments to Arkansas (July 7-18) and Louisville (July 18-30). ... Traded by Cardinals with OF Mark Whiten to Boston Red Sox for 3B Scott Cooper, P Cory Bailey and a player to be named later (April 8, 1995). ... Traded by Red Sox with 1B Ryan McGuire and P Shayne Bennett to Montreal Expos for SS Wil Cordero and P Bryan Eversgerd (Jauary 10, 1996). ... On disabled list (August 26-September 10, 1996). ... Granted free agency (October 30, 1997). ... Signed by Cleveland Indians organization (December 18, 1997). ... On Buffalo disabled list (April 9-June 2, 1998). ... On Akron disabled list (June 18, 1998-remainder of season). ... Granted free agency (October 15, 1998). ... Signed by Red Sox organization (January 5, 1999). ... On suspended list (May 7-10, 1999). ... Granted free agency (November 1, 2000). ... Signed by Philadelphia Phillies (November 29, 2000). ... On Philadelphia disabled list (August 10-29, 2001); included rehabilitation assignment to Reading (August 27-29).
MISCELLANEOUS: Member of 1988 Canadian Olympic baseball team.
CAREER HITTING (MLB): 35-for-188 (.186), 14 R, 4 2B, 1 3B, 0 HR, 12 RBI.

Year	League	W	L	Pct.	ERA	G	GS	CG	ShO	Sv.-Opp.	IP	H	R	ER	HR	BB-IBB	SO
1989	—St. Petersburg (FSL)	12	7	.632	2.23	26	26	4	1	0-...	169.2	141	63	42	9	33-2	122
1990	—Arkansas (Texas)	5	•12	.294	5.04	22	21	3	1	0-...	121.1	133	81	68	9	30-2	102
	—Louisville (A.A.)	1	1	.500	2.25	4	4	0	0	0-...	24.0	18	8	6	1	3-0	9
1991	—Louisville (A.A.)	7	9	.438	4.23	21	21	3	*3	0-...	127.2	140	64	60	5	31-1	74
	—St. Louis (N.L.)	4	5	.444	4.12	11	10	2	0	0-0	67.2	74	35	31	5	8-1	38
1992	—St. Louis (N.L.)	10	10	.500	3.68	31	30	3	0	0-0	186.0	194	83	76	15	33-2	117
	—Louisville (A.A.)	0	1	.000	6.75	1	1	0	0	0-...	4.0	8	4	3	0	0-0	1
1993	—St. Louis (N.L.)	7	6	.538	4.33	38	21	1	0	0-0	145.1	163	80	70	18	27-3	75
1994	—St. Louis (N.L.)	3	2	.600	5.45	7	7	0	0	0-0	39.2	40	24	24	6	7-0	26
	—Arkansas (Texas)	1	0	1.000	1.93	2	2	0	0	0-...	9.1	9	2	2	0	0-0	11
	—Louisville (A.A.)	1	2	.333	4.50	3	3	1	0	0-...	22.0	21	11	11	3	8-1	13
1995	—Boston (A.L.)■	7	5	.583	4.07	48	12	0	0	0-2	115.0	131	60	52	12	31-2	69
1996	—Montreal (N.L.)■	7	10	.412	4.17	33	27	1	1	0-0	159.2	165	80	74	16	41-3	100
1997	—Montreal (N.L.)	0	1	.000	33.75	1	1	0	0	0-0	1.1	4	5	5	1	1-0	0
1998	—Akron (East.)■	0	0	...	6.52	3	3	0	0	0-...	9.2	15	7	7	3	2-0	6
1999	—Boston (A.L.)■	2	0	1.000	3.69	60	0	0	0	0-3	63.1	61	34	26	4	18-2	39
2000	—Boston (A.L.)	3	3	.500	4.61	64	0	0	0	0-2	68.1	74	40	35	7	17-2	43
2001	—Philadelphia (N.L.)■	5	6	.455	4.21	60	0	0	0	1-6	51.1	49	26	24	5	17-4	37
	—Reading (East.)	0	0	...	0.00	1	1	0	0	0-...	2.0	0	0	0	0	1-0	2
2002	—Philadelphia (N.L.)	5	6	.455	5.25	54	0	0	0	0-3	60.0	61	38	35	6	32-6	49
A.L. totals (3 years)		12	8	.600	4.12	172	12	0	0	0-7	246.2	266	134	113	23	66-6	151
N.L. totals (8 years)		41	46	.471	4.29	235	96	7	1	1-9	711.0	750	371	339	72	166-19	442
Major League totals (11 years)		53	54	.495	4.25	407	108	7	1	1-16	957.2	1016	505	452	95	232-25	593

DIVISION SERIES RECORD

Year	League	W	L	Pct.	ERA	G	GS	CG	ShO	Sv.-Opp.	IP	H	R	ER	HR	BB-IBB	SO
1995	—Boston (A.L.)	0	0	...	13.50	2	0	0	0	0-0	.2	2	1	1	0	1-0	2
1999	—Boston (A.L.)	0	0	...	0.00	2	0	0	0	0-0	4.0	2	0	0	0	1-0	4
Division series totals (2 years)		0	0	...	1.93	4	0	0	0	0-0	4.2	4	1	1	0	2-0	6

CHAMPIONSHIP SERIES RECORD

Year	League	W	L	Pct.	ERA	G	GS	CG	ShO	Sv.-Opp.	IP	H	R	ER	HR	BB-IBB	SO
1999	—Boston (A.L.)	0	0	...	0.00	4	0	0	0	0-0	3.2	3	0	0	0	3-1	4

CORNEJO, NATE — P — TIGERS

PERSONAL: Born September 24, 1979, in Wellington, Kan. ... 6-5/240. ... Throws right, bats right. ... Full name: Nathan J. Cornejo.
HIGH SCHOOL: Wellington (Kan.).
TRANSACTIONS/CAREER NOTES: Selected by Detroit Tigers organization in supplemental round ("sandwich pick" between first and second round, 34th pick overall) of free-agent draft (June 2, 1998); pick received as part of compensation for Arizona Diamondbacks signing Type A free-agent P Willie Blair.
CAREER HITTING (MLB): 0-for-0 (.000), 0 R, 0 2B, 0 3B, 0 HR, 0 RBI.

Year	League	W	L	Pct.	ERA	G	GS	CG	ShO	Sv.-Opp.	IP	H	R	ER	HR	BB-IBB	SO
1998	—Gulf Coast Tigers (GCL)	1	0	1.000	1.26	5	0	0	0	1-...	14.1	12	2	2	0	2-0	9
1999	—West Michigan (Midw.)	9	11	.450	3.71	28	•28	4	1	0-...	174.2	173	87	72	4	67-0	125
2000	—Lakeland (FSL)	5	5	.500	3.04	12	12	1	0	0-...	77.0	67	37	26	5	31-0	60
	—Jacksonville (Sou.)	5	7	.417	4.61	16	16	0	0	0-...	91.2	91	52	47	6	43-1	60
2001	—Erie (East.)	12	3	.800	2.68	19	19	3	1	0-...	124.1	107	47	37	12	41-0	105
	—Toledo (I.L.)	4	0	1.000	2.12	4	4	0	0	0-...	29.2	24	8	7	1	7-0	22
	—Detroit (A.L.)	4	4	.500	7.38	10	10	0	0	0-0	42.2	63	38	35	10	28-4	22
2002	—Toledo (I.L.)	9	8	.529	4.42	21	20	1	0	0-...	132.1	163	72	65	11	31-1	86
	—Detroit (A.L.)	1	5	.167	5.04	9	9	1	0	0-0	50.0	63	33	28	6	18-0	23
Major League totals (2 years)		5	9	.357	6.12	19	19	1	0	0-0	92.2	126	71	63	16	46-4	45

COTA, HUMBERTO — C — PIRATES

PERSONAL: Born February 7, 1979, in San Luis Rio Colorado, Mexico. ... 6-0/205. ... Bats right, throws right. ... Full name: Humberto Figueroa Cota.
HIGH SCHOOL: Preparatoria Abierta.
TRANSACTIONS/CAREER NOTES: Signed as non-drafted free agent by Atlanta Braves organization (December 22, 1995). ... Loaned by Braves organization to Mexico City Tigres, Mexican League (June 23-September 23, 1996); did not play. ... Released by Braves (January 27, 1997). ... Signed by Tampa Bay Devil Rays organization (May 22, 1997). ... Traded by Devil Rays with C Joe Oliver to Pittsburgh Pirates for OF Jose Guillen and P Jeff Sparks (July 23, 1999). ... On Nashville disabled list (April 18-26, 2001).
STATISTICAL NOTES: Tied for Gulf Coast League lead in double plays by catcher with four in 1997. ... Led Appalachian League catchers with 382 putouts in 1998. ... Led Eastern League catchers with 15 passed balls in 2000.
2002 GAMES PLAYED BY POSITION (MLB): C—7.

			BATTING														FIELDING	
Year	Team (League)	Pos.	G	AB	R	H	2B	3B	HR	RBI	BB	SO	SB-CS	Avg.	OBP	SLG	E	Avg.
1996	— MC Tigres (Mex.)								Did not play.									
1997	—GC Devil Rays (GCL)■	C	44	133	14	32	6	1	2	20	17	27	3-1	.241	.333	.346	5	.985
	—Hudson Valley (NY-P)	C	3	9	0	2	0	0	0	2	0	1	0-0	.222	.222	.222	0	1.000
1998	—Princeton (Appl.)	C	67	245	48	76	13	4	15	61	32	59	4-4	.310	.399	.580	•12	.973
1999	—Charl., S.C. (S.Atl.)	C-1B	85	336	42	94	21	1	9	61	20	51	1-1	.280	.320	.429	7	.986
	—Hickory (S.Atl.)■	C	37	133	28	36	11	2	2	20	21	20	3-1	.271	.365	.429	2	.992
2000	—Altoona (East.)	C-1B	112	429	49	112	20	1	8	44	21	80	6-4	.261	.297	.368	*17	.973
2001	—Nashville (PCL)	C	111	377	61	112	22	2	14	72	25	74	7-2	.297	.351	.477	8	.986
	—Pittsburgh (N.L.)	C	7	9	0	2	0	0	0	1	0	5	0-0	.222	.222	.222	0	1.000
2002	—Nashville (PCL)	C-1B	118	404	51	108	27	1	9	54	31	106	5-8	.267	.321	.406	4	.994
	—Pittsburgh (N.L.)	C	7	17	2	5	1	0	0	0	1	4	0-0	.294	.333	.353	0	1.000
Major League totals (2 years)			14	26	2	7	1	0	0	1	1	9	0-0	.269	.296	.308	0	1.000

COUNSELL, CRAIG — 2B — DIAMONDBACKS

PERSONAL: Born August 21, 1970, in South Bend, Ind. ... 6-0/175. ... Bats left, throws right. ... Full name: Craig John Counsell. ... Son of John Counsell, outfielder in Minnesota Twins organization (1964-68).

HIGH SCHOOL: Whitefish Bay (Milwaukee).

COLLEGE: Notre Dame.

TRANSACTIONS/CAREER NOTES: Selected by Colorado Rockies organization in 11th round of free-agent draft (June 1, 1992). ... On disabled list (April 7-May 13, July 30-August 6 and August 7-27, 1994). ... On disabled list (May 1-July 15 and July 18-September 3, 1996). ... Traded by Rockies to Florida Marlins for P Mark Hutton (July 27, 1997). ... On disabled list (August 4, 1998-remainder of season). ... Traded by Marlins to Los Angeles Dodgers for a player to be named later (June 15, 1999); Marlins acquired P Ryan Moskau to complete deal (July 15, 1999). ... Released by Dodgers (March 15, 2000). ... Signed by Arizona Diamondbacks organization (March 20, 2000). ... On disabled list (August 9, 2002-remainder of season).

STATISTICAL NOTES: Led California League shortstops with 233 putouts and 621 total chances in 1993. ... Led Pacific Coast League shortstops with 598 total chances and 86 double plays in 1995. ... Career major league grand slams: 2.

2002 GAMES PLAYED BY POSITION (MLB): 3B—94; SS—22; 2B—13.

			BATTING														FIELDING	
Year	Team (League)	Pos.	G	AB	R	H	2B	3B	HR	RBI	BB	SO	SB-CS	Avg.	OBP	SLG	E	Avg.
1992—	Bend (N'West)	2B-SS	18	61	11	15	6	1	0	8	9	10	1-2	.246	.352	.377	2	.967
1993—	Central Valley (Calif.)	SS	131	471	79	132	26	3	5	59	95	68	14-8	.280	.401	.380	35	.944
1994—	New Haven (East.)	SS-2B	83	300	47	84	20	1	5	37	37	32	4-1	.280	.366	.403	27	.931
1995—	Colo. Springs (PCL)	SS	118	399	60	112	22	6	5	53	34	47	10-2	.281	.336	.404	30	.950
—	Colorado (N.L.)	SS	3	1	0	0	0	0	0	0	1	0	0-0	.000	.500	.000	0	1.000
1996—	Colo. Springs (PCL)	2B-3B-SS	25	75	17	18	3	0	2	10	24	7	4-3	.240	.424	.360	4	.961
1997—	Colo. Springs (PCL)	2B-SS	96	376	77	126	31	6	5	63	45	38	12-2	.335	.409	.489	9	.981
—	Colorado (N.L.)	PR	1	0	0	0	0	0	0	0	0	0	0-0	...	...	...	...	...
—	Florida (N.L.)■	2B	51	164	20	49	9	2	1	16	18	17	1-1	.299	.376	.396	3	.989
1998—	Florida (N.L.)	2B	107	335	43	84	19	5	4	40	51	47	3-0	.251	.355	.373	5	.991
1999—	Florida (N.L.)	2B	37	66	4	10	1	0	0	2	5	10	0-0	.152	.211	.167	1	.980
—	Los Angeles (N.L.)■	2B-SS	50	108	20	28	6	0	0	9	9	14	1-0	.259	.311	.315	1	.993
2000—	Tucson (PCL)■	2B-3B-SS	50	198	45	69	14	3	3	27	22	20	4-1	.348	.413	.495	4	.981
—	Arizona (N.L.)	2B-3B-SS	67	152	23	48	8	1	2	11	20	18	3-3	.316	.400	.421	6	.957
2001—	Arizona (N.L.)	S-2-3-1	141	458	76	126	22	3	4	38	61	76	6-8	.275	.359	.362	8	.985
2002—	Arizona (N.L.)	3B-SS-2B	112	436	63	123	22	1	2	51	45	52	7-5	.282	.348	.351	8	.979
Major League totals (7 years)			569	1720	249	468	87	12	13	167	210	234	21-17	.272	.353	.359	32	.984

DIVISION SERIES RECORD

			BATTING														FIELDING	
Year	Team (League)	Pos.	G	AB	R	H	2B	3B	HR	RBI	BB	SO	SB-CS	Avg.	OBP	SLG	E	Avg.
1997—	Florida (N.L.)	2B	3	5	0	2	1	0	0	1	1	0	0-0	.400	.500	.600	1	.875
2001—	Arizona (N.L.)	2B-PH	5	16	2	3	0	0	1	3	2	2	0-0	.188	.278	.375	0	1.000
Division series totals (2 years)			8	21	2	5	1	0	1	4	3	2	0-0	.238	.333	.429	1	.963

CHAMPIONSHIP SERIES RECORD

RECORDS: Shares N.L. single-game record for most at-bats—6 (October 20, 2001).

NOTES: Named Most Valuable Player (2001).

			BATTING														FIELDING	
Year	Team (League)	Pos.	G	AB	R	H	2B	3B	HR	RBI	BB	SO	SB-CS	Avg.	OBP	SLG	E	Avg.
1997—	Florida (N.L.)	2B-PH	5	14	0	6	0	0	0	2	3	3	0-0	.429	.529	.429	1	.941
2001—	Arizona (N.L.)	2B-SS	5	21	5	8	3	0	0	4	0	3	1-0	.381	.381	.524	0	1.000
Championship series totals (2 years)			10	35	5	14	3	0	0	6	3	6	1-0	.400	.447	.486	1	.972

WORLD SERIES RECORD

NOTES: Member of World Series championship team (1997 and 2001).

			BATTING														FIELDING	
Year	Team (League)	Pos.	G	AB	R	H	2B	3B	HR	RBI	BB	SO	SB-CS	Avg.	OBP	SLG	E	Avg.
1997—	Florida (N.L.)	2B	7	22	4	4	1	0	0	2	6	5	1-0	.182	.345	.227	1	.971
2001—	Arizona (N.L.)	2B	6	24	1	2	0	0	1	1	0	7	0-0	.083	.120	.208	0	1.000
World Series totals (2 years)			13	46	5	6	1	0	1	3	6	12	1-0	.130	.241	.217	1	.984

COX, STEVE — 1B — DEVIL RAYS

PERSONAL: Born October 31, 1974, in Delano, Calif. ... 6-4/225. ... Bats left, throws left. ... Full name: Charles Steven Cox.

HIGH SCHOOL: Monache (Porterville, Calif.).

TRANSACTIONS/CAREER NOTES: Selected by Oakland Athletics organization in fifth round of free-agent draft (June 1, 1992). ... On disabled list (July 23, 1993-remainder of season). ... Selected by Tampa Bay Devil Rays in second round (46th pick overall) of expansion draft (November 18, 1997). ... On disabled list (April 12-26, 1998). ... On Tampa Bay disabled list (August 6-23, 2001); included rehabilitation assignment to Orlando (August 19-23).

HONORS: Named International League Most Valuable Player (1999).

STATISTICAL NOTES: Led California League with 10 sacrifice flies in 1995. ... Tied for Pacific Coast League lead with nine sacrifice flies in 1997. ... Led International League first basemen with 1,079 total chances in 1998. ... Led International League with 314 total bases and 11 intentional bases on balls received in 1999. ... Led International League first basemen with 1,125 putouts, 1,203 total chances and 121 double plays in 1999. ... Career major league grand slams: 1.

2002 GAMES PLAYED BY POSITION (MLB): 1B—110; DH—35.

			BATTING														FIELDING	
Year	Team (League)	Pos.	G	AB	R	H	2B	3B	HR	RBI	BB	SO	SB-CS	Avg.	OBP	SLG	E	Avg.
1992—	Ariz. Athletics (Ariz.)	1B	52	184	30	43	4	1	1	35	27	51	2-1	.234	.338	.283	11	.975
1993—	S. Oregon (N'West)	1B	15	57	10	18	4	1	2	16	5	15	0-0	.316	.359	.526	2	.983
1994—	West Mich. (Midw.)	1B-OF	99	311	37	75	19	2	6	32	41	95	2-6	.241	.334	.373	10	.987
1995—	Modesto (Calif.)	1B	132	483	95	144	29	3	*30	*110	84	88	5-4	.298	.409	.557	17	.984

		BATTING														FIELDING	
Year Team (League)	Pos.	G	AB	R	H	2B	3B	HR	RBI	BB	SO	SB-CS	Avg.	OBP	SLG	E	Avg.
1996—Huntsville (Sou.)	1B-DH	104	381	59	107	21	1	12	61	51	65	2-2	.281	.372	.436	15	.985
1997—Edmonton (PCL)	1B-DH	131	467	84	128	34	1	15	93	*88	90	1-3	.274	.385	.448	*10	.991
1998—Durham (I.L.)■	1B-OF-DH	119	430	64	109	23	2	13	67	56	100	3-4	.253	.339	.407	7	.994
1999—Durham (I.L.)	1B-DH	134	534	*107	*182	*49	4	25	*127	67	74	3-3	*.341	.415	*.588	5	.996
—Tampa Bay (A.L.)	1B-OF	6	19	0	4	1	0	0	0	0	2	0-0	.211	.211	.263	0	1.000
2000—Tampa Bay (A.L.)	OF-1B-DH	116	318	44	90	19	1	11	35	46	47	1-2	.283	.379	.453	8	.972
2001—Tampa Bay (A.L.)	1B-OF-DH	108	342	37	88	22	0	12	51	24	75	2-2	.257	.323	.427	1	.998
—Orlando (Sou.)	1B	4	14	2	3	1	0	1	3	2	1	0-0	.214	.313	.500	1	.962
2002—Tampa Bay (A.L.)	1B-DH	148	560	65	142	30	1	16	72	60	116	5-0	.254	.330	.396	7	.993
Major League totals (4 years)		378	1239	146	324	72	2	39	158	130	240	8-4	.262	.340	.417	16	.992

CRAWFORD, CARL — OF — DEVIL RAYS

PERSONAL: Born August 5, 1981, in Houston, Texas. ... 6-2/219. ... Bats left, throws left. ... Full name: Carl Demonte Crawford.
HIGH SCHOOL: Jefferson Davis (Houston).
TRANSACTIONS/CAREER NOTES: Selected by Tampa Bay Devil Rays organization in second round of free-agent draft (June 2, 1999). ... On Durham disabled list (May 21-30, 2002).
2002 GAMES PLAYED BY POSITION (MLB): OF—63.

		BATTING														FIELDING	
Year Team (League)	Pos.	G	AB	R	H	2B	3B	HR	RBI	BB	SO	SB-CS	Avg.	OBP	SLG	E	Avg.
1999—Princeton (Appl.)	OF	60	260	62	83	14	4	0	25	13	47	17-2	.319	.350	.404	8	.934
2000—Charl., S.C. (S.Atl.)	OF	135	564	99	170	21	11	6	57	32	102	55-9	.301	.342	.410	8	.968
2001—Orlando (Sou.)	OF	132	537	64	147	24	3	4	51	36	90	36-20	.274	.323	.352	6	.981
2002—Durham (I.L.)	OF	85	353	59	105	17	9	7	52	20	69	26-8	.297	.335	.456	1	.994
—Tampa Bay (A.L.)	OF	63	259	23	67	11	6	2	30	9	41	9-5	.259	.290	.371	1	.994
Major League totals (1 year)		63	259	23	67	11	6	2	30	9	41	9-5	.259	.290	.371	1	.994

CREDE, JOE — 3B — WHITE SOX

PERSONAL: Born April 26, 1978, in Jefferson City, Mo. ... 6-2/195. ... Bats right, throws right. ... Full name: Joseph Crede.
HIGH SCHOOL: Fatima (Westphalia, Mo.).
TRANSACTIONS/CAREER NOTES: Selected by Chicago White Sox organization in fifth round of free-agent draft (June 2, 1996). ... On Birmingham disabled list (July 2, 1999-remainder of season).
HONORS: Named Carolina League Most Valuable Player (1998). ... Named Southern League Most Valuable Player (2000).
STATISTICAL NOTES: Led Gulf Coast League third basemen with 42 putouts, 108 assists and 175 total chances in 1996. ... Led Carolina League with 253 total bases and 11 sacrifice flies in 1998. ... Led Carolina League third basemen with 100 putouts, 290 assists and 420 total chances in 1998. ... Led Southern League with 261 total bases and in grounding into double play with 18 in 2000. ... Led Southern League third basemen with 328 total chances in 2000. ... Career major league grand slams: 1.
2002 GAMES PLAYED BY POSITION (MLB): 3B—53.

		BATTING														FIELDING	
Year Team (League)	Pos.	G	AB	R	H	2B	3B	HR	RBI	BB	SO	SB-CS	Avg.	OBP	SLG	E	Avg.
1996—GC White Sox (GCL)	3B	56	221	30	66	17	1	4	32	9	41	1-1	.299	.326	.439	*25	.857
1997—Hickory (S.Atl.)	3B	113	402	45	109	25	0	5	62	24	83	3-1	.271	.319	.371	33	.905
1998—Win.-Salem (Caro.)	3B	*137	492	•92	155	32	3	20	*88	53	98	9-7	*.315	.387	.514	*30	.929
1999—Birmingham (Sou.)	3B-DH	74	291	37	73	14	1	4	42	22	47	2-6	.251	.303	.347	20	.910
2000—Birmingham (Sou.)	3B	138	533	84	*163	35	0	21	94	56	111	3-4	.306	.384	.490	19	.942
—Chicago (A.L.)	3B-DH	7	14	2	5	1	0	0	3	0	3	0-0	.357	.333	.429	1	.933
2001—Charlotte (I.L.)	3B	124	463	67	128	34	1	17	65	46	88	2-1	.276	.349	.464	20	.946
—Chicago (A.L.)	3B	17	50	1	11	1	1	0	7	3	11	1-0	.220	.273	.280	0	1.000
2002—Charlotte (I.L.)	3B	95	359	57	112	21	0	24	65	26	48	0-1	.312	.359	.571	15	.944
—Chicago (A.L.)	3B	53	200	28	57	10	0	12	35	8	40	0-2	.285	.311	.515	8	.938
Major League totals (3 years)		77	264	31	73	12	1	12	45	11	54	1-2	.277	.305	.466	9	.950

CREEK, DOUG — P — BLUE JAYS

PERSONAL: Born March 1, 1969, in Winchester, Va. ... 6-0/227. ... Throws left, bats left. ... Full name: Paul Douglas Creek.
HIGH SCHOOL: Martinsburg (W.Va.).
COLLEGE: Georgia Tech.
TRANSACTIONS/CAREER NOTES: Selected by California Angels organization in fifth round of free-agent draft (June 4, 1990); did not sign. ... Selected by St. Louis Cardinals organization in seventh round of free-agent draft (June 3, 1991). ... On Arkansas disabled list (April 10-May 21, 1992; July 25-August 1, 1993; and June 25-July 10, 1994). ... Traded by Cardinals with P Allen Watson and P Rich DeLucia to San Francisco Giants for SS Royce Clayton and a player to be named later (December 14, 1995); Cardinals acquired 2B Chris Wimmer to complete deal (January 16, 1996). ... Contract purchased by Chicago White Sox from Giants organization (November 7, 1997). ... Contract sold by White Sox to Hanshin Tigers of Japan Central League (December 4, 1997). ... Signed by Chicago Cubs organization (January 29, 1999). ... Released by Cubs (September 13, 1999). ... Signed by Tampa Bay Devil Rays organization (February 1, 2000). ... On Durham disabled list (April 6-25, 2000). ... Traded by Devil Rays to Seattle Mariners for cash considerations (July 24, 2002). ... Released by Mariners (October 15, 2002). ... Signed by Toronto Blue Jays organization (October 29, 2002).
STATISTICAL NOTES: Tied for Pacific Coast League lead with 12 hit batsmen in 1999.
CAREER HITTING (MLB): 1-for-5 (.200), 1 R, 0 2B, 0 3B, 0 HR, 0 RBI.

Year League	W	L	Pct.	ERA	G	GS	CG	ShO	Sv.-Opp.	IP	H	R	ER	HR	BB-IBB	SO
1991—Hamilton (NY-Penn)	3	2	.600	5.12	7	6	0	0	0-...	38.2	39	22	22	2	18-0	45
—Savannah (S.Atl.)	2	1	.667	4.45	5	5	0	0	0-...	28.1	24	14	14	2	17-0	32
1992—Springfield (Midw.)	4	1	.800	2.58	6	6	0	0	0-...	38.1	32	11	11	4	13-1	43
—St. Petersburg (FSL)	5	4	.556	2.82	13	13	0	0	0-...	73.1	57	31	23	5	37-1	63

Year League	W	L	Pct.	ERA	G	GS	CG	ShO	Sv.-Opp.	IP	H	R	ER	HR	BB-IBB	SO
1993— Arkansas (Texas)	11	10	.524	4.02	25	25	1	1	0-...	147.2	142	75	66	15	48-1	128
— Louisville (A.A.)	0	0	...	3.21	2	2	0	0	0-...	14.0	10	5	5	0	9-0	9
1994— Louisville (A.A.)	1	4	.200	8.54	7	7	0	0	0-...	26.1	37	26	25	2	23-0	16
— Arkansas (Texas)	3	10	.231	4.40	17	17	1	0	0-...	92.0	96	54	45	8	36-0	65
1995— Louisville (A.A.)	3	2	.600	3.23	26	0	0	0	0-...	30.2	20	12	11	1	21-0	29
— Arkansas (Texas)	4	2	.667	2.88	26	0	0	0	1-...	34.1	24	12	11	4	16-2	50
— St. Louis (N.L.)	0	0	...	0.00	6	0	0	0	0-0	6.2	2	0	0	0	3-0	10
1996— San Francisco (N.L.)■	0	2	.000	6.52	63	0	0	0	0-1	48.1	45	41	35	11	32-2	38
1997— Phoenix (PCL)	8	6	.571	4.93	25	23	2	1	0-...	129.2	140	76	71	15	66-0	*137
— San Francisco (N.L.)	1	2	.333	6.75	3	3	0	0	0-0	13.1	12	12	10	1	14-0	14
1998— Hanshin (Jp. West.)■	9	1	.900	2.16	17	16	2	...	0-...	100.0	77	28	24	...	52-...	101
— Hanshin (Jap. Cen.)	0	4	.000	5.65	7	6	0	0	0-...	28.2	23	21	18	...	25-...	24
1999— Iowa (PCL)■	7	3	.700	3.79	25	20	0	0	1-...	130.2	116	66	55	20	62-0	140
— Chicago (N.L.)	0	0	...	10.50	3	0	0	0	0-0	6.0	6	7	7	1	8-1	6
2000— Durham (I.L.)■	0	0	...	1.96	10	1	0	0	0-...	18.1	10	5	4	1	14-0	22
— Tampa Bay (A.L.)	1	3	.250	4.60	45	0	0	0	1-3	60.2	49	33	31	10	39-3	73
2001— Tampa Bay (A.L.)	2	5	.286	4.31	66	0	0	0	0-3	62.2	51	34	30	7	49-5	66
2002— Tampa Bay (A.L.)	2	1	.667	6.27	29	0	0	0	0-2	37.1	39	27	26	8	21-1	37
— Seattle (A.L.)■	1	1	.500	4.91	23	0	0	0	0-0	18.1	18	10	10	2	14-1	19
A.L. totals (3 years)	6	10	.375	4.88	163	0	0	0	1-8	179.0	157	104	97	27	123-10	195
N.L. totals (4 years)	1	4	.200	6.30	75	3	0	0	0-1	74.1	65	60	52	13	57-3	68
Major League totals (7 years)	7	14	.333	5.29	238	3	0	0	1-9	253.1	222	164	149	40	180-13	263

CRESPO, CESAR — OF/IF — PADRES

PERSONAL: Born May 23, 1979, in Rio Piedras, Puerto Rico. ... 5-11/170. ... Bats both, throws right. ... Full name: Cesar Antonio Crespo. ... Brother of Felipe Crespo, infielder/outfielder with Toronto Blue Jays (1996-98), San Francisco Giants (2000 and 2001) and Philadelphia Phillies (2001).

HIGH SCHOOL: Notre Dame (Caguas, Puerto Rico).

TRANSACTIONS/CAREER NOTES: Selected by New York Mets organization in third round of free-agent draft (June 3, 1997). ... Traded by Mets to Florida Marlins (September 12, 1998), completing deal in which Marlins traded OF Robert Stratton to Mets for a player to be named later (March 20, 1998). ... On disabled list (May 19-31, 1999). ... Traded by Marlins with OF Mark Kotsay to San Diego Padres for OF Eric Owens, P Matt Clement and P Omar Ortiz (March 28, 2001). ... On Portland disabled list (May 11-21, 2001). ... On Portland disabled list (June 28-July 11, 2002).

STATISTICAL NOTES: Tied for Eastern League lead in assists by outfielder with nine in 2000.

2002 GAMES PLAYED BY POSITION (MLB): OF—7; 3B—4; 2B—4; SS—1.

		BATTING														FIELDING	
Year Team (League)	Pos.	G	AB	R	H	2B	3B	HR	RBI	BB	SO	SB-CS	Avg.	OBP	SLG	E	Avg.
1998— Capital City (S.Atl.)	2B-SS	116	428	61	108	18	4	6	48	44	114	47-14	.252	.326	.355	27	.948
1999— Brevard Co. (FSL)■	2B	115	427	63	122	17	2	6	40	62	86	22-8	.286	.376	.377	22	.958
2000— Portland (East.)	OF-2B-SS	134	482	96	124	21	6	9	60	77	118	41-15	.257	.359	.382	15	.958
2001— Portland (PCL)■	2B-OF-SS-3B	78	273	46	71	18	3	8	29	39	66	23-3	.260	.354	.436	4	.986
— San Diego (N.L.)	2B-OF-3B-SS	55	153	27	32	6	0	4	12	25	50	6-2	.209	.320	.327	4	.976
2002— Portland (PCL)	2B-OF-SS-3B	92	322	43	83	17	2	9	37	50	78	21-7	.258	.363	.407	12	.967
— San Diego (N.L.)	OF-3B-2B-SS	25	29	5	5	2	0	0	0	3	6	3-2	.172	.250	.241	1	.923
Major League totals (2 years)		80	182	32	37	8	0	4	12	28	56	9-4	.203	.310	.313	5	.972

CRESSEND, JACK — P — INDIANS

PERSONAL: Born May 13, 1975, in New Orleans. ... 6-1/185. ... Throws right, bats right. ... Full name: John Baptiste Cressend III.

HIGH SCHOOL: Mandeville (La.).

COLLEGE: Tulane.

TRANSACTIONS/CAREER NOTES: Signed as non-drafted free agent by Boston Red Sox organization (July 24, 1996). ... Claimed on waivers by Minnesota Twins (April 22, 1999). ... On Minnesota disabled list (June 8-September 30, 2002); included rehabilitation assignments to Gulf Coast Twins (August 9-21) and Fort Myers (August 22-September 1). ... Claimed on waivers by Cleveland Indians (October 17, 2002).

CAREER HITTING (MLB): 0-for-0 (.000), 0 R, 0 2B, 0 3B, 0 HR, 0 RBI.

Year League	W	L	Pct.	ERA	G	GS	CG	ShO	Sv.-Opp.	IP	H	R	ER	HR	BB-IBB	SO
1996— Lowell (NY-Penn)	3	2	.600	2.36	9	8	0	0	0-...	45.2	37	15	12	0	17-1	57
1997— Sarasota (FSL)	8	11	.421	3.80	28	25	2	1	0-...	165.2	163	98	70	15	56-1	149
1998— Trenton (East.)	10	11	.476	4.34	29	29	1	1	0-...	149.1	168	86	72	13	55-0	130
1999— Trenton (East.)	1	0	1.000	7.20	3	3	0	0	0-...	15.0	19	12	12	3	7-0	11
— New Britain (East.)■	7	10	.412	4.34	25	24	2	*2	0-...	145.0	152	79	70	10	50-0	125
2000— Salt Lake (PCL)	4	4	.500	3.44	54	1	0	0	8-...	86.1	87	40	33	3	39-4	87
— Minnesota (A.L.)	0	0	...	5.27	11	0	0	0	0-0	13.2	20	8	8	0	6-0	6
2001— Edmonton (PCL)	2	2	.500	3.50	12	0	0	0	1-...	18.0	19	12	7	2	7-2	9
— Minnesota (A.L.)	3	2	.600	3.67	44	0	0	0	0-2	56.1	50	24	23	6	16-0	40
2002— Minnesota (A.L.)	0	1	.000	5.91	23	0	0	0	0-0	32.0	40	25	21	6	19-4	22
— Gulf Coast Twins (GCL)	0	0	...	7.11	3	3	0	0	0-...	6.1	10	7	5	0	1-0	8
— Fort Myers (FSL)	1	0	1.000	3.60	3	1	0	0	0-...	5.0	4	2	2	0	2-0	5
Major League totals (3 years)	3	3	.500	4.59	78	0	0	0	0-2	102.0	110	57	52	12	41-4	68

CRISP, COCO — OF — INDIANS

PERSONAL: Born November 1, 1979, in Los Angeles. ... 6-0/185. ... Bats both, throws right. ... Full name: Covelli Loyce Crisp.

JUNIOR COLLEGE: Pierce Junior College (Calif.).

TRANSACTIONS/CAREER NOTES: Selected by St. Louis Cardinals organization in seventh round of free-agent draft (June 2, 1999). ... Traded by Cardinals to Cleveland Indians (August 6, 2002), completing deal in which Cardinals traded 1B Luis Garcia and a player to be named later for P Chuck Finley (July 19, 2002).

2002 GAMES PLAYED BY POSITION (MLB): OF—32.

		BATTING														FIELDING	
Year Team (League)	Pos.	G	AB	R	H	2B	3B	HR	RBI	BB	SO	SB-CS	Avg.	OBP	SLG	E	Avg.
1999—Johnson City (Appl.) ..	2B	65	229	55	59	5	4	3	22	44	41	27-5	.258	.379	.354	24	.912
2000—New Jersey (NY-P).....	OF-2B	36	134	18	32	5	0	0	14	11	22	25-3	.239	.301	.276	2	.972
—Peoria (Midw.)...........	OF	27	98	14	27	9	0	0	7	16	15	7-3	.276	.377	.367	0	1.000
2001—Potomac (Caro.).........	OF	139	530	80	162	23	3	11	47	52	64	39-21	.306	.368	.423	6	.975
2002—New Haven (East.)......	OF	89	355	61	107	16	1	9	47	36	56	26-10	.301	.365	.428	3	.985
—Akron (East.)■...........	OF	7	32	9	13	1	0	1	4	3	3	4-0	.406	.457	.531	0	1.000
—Cleveland (A.L.)..........	OF	32	127	16	33	9	2	1	9	11	19	4-1	.260	.314	.386	1	.988
—Buffalo (I.L.)..............	OF	4	21	3	5	1	0	0	2	0	2	1-0	.238	.238	.286	0	1.000
Major League totals (1 year)		32	127	16	33	9	2	1	9	11	19	4-1	.260	.314	.386	1	.988

CRUDALE, MIKE — P — CARDINALS

PERSONAL: Born January 3, 1977, in San Diego. ... 6-0/205. ... Throws right, bats right. ... Full name: Michael Christopher Crudale.
HIGH SCHOOL: Monte Vista (Danville, Calif.).
COLLEGE: Santa Clara.
TRANSACTIONS/CAREER NOTES: Selected by St. Louis Cardinals organization in 24th round of free-agent draft (June 2, 1999).
CAREER HITTING (MLB): 0-for-2 (.000), 0 R, 0 2B, 0 3B, 0 HR, 0 RBI.

Year League	W	L	Pct.	ERA	G	GS	CG	ShO	Sv.-Opp.	IP	H	R	ER	HR	BB-IBB	SO
1999—Johnson City (Appl.)	0	1	.000	3.27	24	0	0	0	1-...	33.0	29	15	12	1	14-0	36
2000—Peoria (Midw.).................	6	1	.857	2.31	38	0	0	0	5-...	50.2	40	17	13	2	16-3	45
—Potomac (Caro.)..............	2	4	.333	4.56	21	0	0	0	2-...	25.2	31	17	13	3	11-1	28
2001—New Haven (East.)...........	4	9	.308	3.25	62	0	0	0	9-...	80.1	76	42	29	7	22-4	85
2002—Memphis (PCL)..............	1	0	1.000	1.84	13	0	0	0	7-...	14.2	10	3	3	1	5-1	16
—St. Louis (N.L.)................	3	0	1.000	1.88	49	1	0	0	0-1	52.2	43	11	11	3	14-2	47
Major League totals (1 year).......	3	0	1.000	1.88	49	1	0	0	0-1	52.2	43	11	11	3	14-2	47

DIVISION SERIES RECORD

Year League	W	L	Pct.	ERA	G	GS	CG	ShO	Sv.-Opp.	IP	H	R	ER	HR	BB-IBB	SO
2002—St. Louis (N.L.)................	0	0	...	0.00	1	0	0	0	0-0	1.0	0	0	0	0	1-0	2

CHAMPIONSHIP SERIES RECORD

Year League	W	L	Pct.	ERA	G	GS	CG	ShO	Sv.-Opp.	IP	H	R	ER	HR	BB-IBB	SO
2002—St. Louis (N.L.)................	0	0	...	10.80	1	0	0	0	0-0	1.2	1	2	2	1	1-0	2

CRUZ, DEIVI — SS

PERSONAL: Born November 6, 1972, in Nizao de Bani, Dominican Republic. ... 6-0/184. ... Bats right, throws right. ... Full name: Deivi Garcia Cruz.
HIGH SCHOOL: Liceo Aliro Paulino Nizao (Dominican Republic).
TRANSACTIONS/CAREER NOTES: Signed as non-drafted free agent by San Francisco Giants organization (April 23, 1993). ... Selected by Los Angeles Dodgers from Giants organization in Rule 5 major league draft (December 9, 1996). ... Traded by Dodgers with OF Juan Hernaiz to Detroit Tigers for 2B Jeff Berblinger (December 9, 1996). ... On Detroit disabled list (March 20-April 27, 1998); included rehabilitation assignments to Lakeland (April 21-23) and Toledo (April 24-27). ... On Detroit disabled list (June 8-July 18, 2001); included rehabilitation assignment to Erie (July 14-18). ... Granted free agency (December 21, 2001). ... Signed by San Diego Padres (January 30, 2002). ... Granted free agency (October 29, 2002).
STATISTICAL NOTES: Led Northwest League third basemen with 47 putouts and .941 fielding percentage in 1995. ... Led Midwest League shortstops with 427 assists and .980 fielding percentage in 1996. ... Had 15-game hitting streak (May 17-June 2, 2002). ... Career major league grand slams: 2.
2002 GAMES PLAYED BY POSITION (MLB): SS—147; 1B—1.

		BATTING														FIELDING	
Year Team (League)	Pos.	G	AB	R	H	2B	3B	HR	RBI	BB	SO	SB-CS	Avg.	OBP	SLG	E	Avg.
1993—Arizona Giants (Ariz.).	3B-SS-1B	28	82	8	28	3	0	0	15	4	5	3-0	.341	.368	.378	2	.972
1994—Arizona Giants (Ariz.).	SS-3B	18	53	10	16	8	0	0	5	5	3	0-1	.302	.367	.453	1	.980
1995—Burlington (Midw.).....	2B-3B-SS	16	58	2	8	1	0	1	9	4	7	1-1	.138	.194	.207	2	.969
—Bellingham (N'West) ..	3B-2B	62	223	32	66	17	0	3	28	19	21	6-3	.296	.348	.413	10	†.947
1996—Burlington (Midw.).....	SS-3B	127	517	72	152	27	2	9	64	35	49	12-5	.294	.342	.406	13	†.979
1997—Detroit (A.L.)■..........	SS	147	436	35	105	26	0	2	40	14	55	3-6	.241	.263	.314	13	.979
1998—Lakeland (FSL)..........	SS	2	9	0	0	0	0	0	1	0	1	0-0	.000	.000	.000	0	1.000
—Toledo (I.L.)...............	SS	2	9	1	1	1	0	0	2	2	3	0-0	.111	.273	.222	0	1.000
—Detroit (A.L.).............	SS	135	454	52	118	22	3	5	45	13	55	3-4	.260	.284	.355	11	.983
1999—Detroit (A.L.).............	SS	155	518	64	147	35	0	13	58	12	57	1-4	.284	.302	.427	12	.983
2000—Detroit (A.L.).............	SS	156	583	68	176	46	5	10	82	13	43	1-4	.302	.318	.449	13	.982
2001—Detroit (A.L.).............	SS-3B	110	414	39	106	28	1	7	52	17	46	4-1	.256	.291	.379	17	.964
—Erie (East.)................	SS-3B	4	12	2	5	1	0	1	3	0	0	1-0	.417	.417	.750	1	.929
2002—San Diego (N.L.)■.....	SS-1B	151	514	49	135	28	2	7	47	22	58	2-3	.263	.294	.366	15	.973
American League totals (5 years)		703	2405	258	652	157	9	37	277	69	256	12-19	.271	.293	.390	66	.979
National League totals (1 year)		151	514	49	135	28	2	7	47	22	58	2-3	.263	.294	.366	15	.973
Major League totals (6 years)		854	2919	307	787	185	11	44	324	91	314	14-22	.270	.294	.386	81	.978

CRUZ, IVAN — 1B — CARDINALS

PERSONAL: Born May 3, 1968, in Fajardo, Puerto Rico. ... 6-2/219. ... Bats left, throws left. ... Full name: Luis Ivan Cruz.
HIGH SCHOOL: Colegio Santiago Apostal (Fajardo, Puerto Rico).
COLLEGE: Jacksonville.
TRANSACTIONS/CAREER NOTES: Selected by Detroit Tigers organization in 28th round of free-agent draft (June 5, 1989). ... Granted free agency (October 16, 1995). ... Signed by New York Yankees organization (November 27, 1995). ... Granted free agency (October 3, 1998). ... Signed by Pittsburgh Pirates organization (December 22, 1998). ... On Pittsburgh disabled list (July 4, 1999-remainder of season);

included rehabilitation assignments to Altoona (July 23-25) and Nashville (July 26-August 9). ... Loaned by Pirates to Mexico City Reds, Mexican League (June 17-September 6, 2000). ... Granted free agency (October 2, 2000). ... Signed by Hanshin Tigers, Japan Central League (2001). ... Signed by Montreal Expos organization (January 11, 2002). ... Released by Expos (March 20, 2002). ... Signed by St. Louis Cardinals organization (March 30, 2002).

STATISTICAL NOTES: Tied for Florida State League lead in double plays by first baseman with 75 in 1990. ... Led Southern League with .564 slugging percentage in 1995. ... Tied for Southern League lead in intentional bases on balls received with 15 in 1995. ... Led International League first basemen with 1,098 putouts, 94 assists and 1,127 total chances and 88 double plays in 1996. ... Tied for Pacific Coast League lead in sacrifice flies with nine in 1999. ... Led Pacific Coast League first basemen with 129 double plays in 2002.

2002 GAMES PLAYED BY POSITION (MLB): 1B—7.

		BATTING														FIELDING	
Year Team (League)	Pos.	G	AB	R	H	2B	3B	HR	RBI	BB	SO	SB-CS	Avg.	OBP	SLG	E	Avg.
1989—Niagara Falls (NY-P)...	1B	64	226	43	62	11	2	7	40	27	29	2-0	.274	.358	.434	5	.989
1990—Lakeland (FSL)...........	1B	118	414	61	118	23	2	11	73	49	71	8-1	.285	.364	.430	11	.989
1991—London (East.)...........	1B	121	443	46	110	21	0	9	47	36	73	3-3	.248	.309	.357	12	.987
—Toledo (I.L.)................	1B	8	29	2	4	0	0	1	4	2	12	0-0	.138	.219	.241	0	1.000
1992—London (East.)...........	1B	134	*524	71	143	25	1	14	*104	37	102	1-1	.273	.322	.405	8	.986
1993—Toledo (I.L.)................	1B	115	402	44	91	18	4	13	50	30	85	1-1	.226	.284	.388	2	.993
1994—Toledo (I.L.)................	1B-DH	97	303	36	75	11	2	15	43	28	83	1-0	.248	.313	.446	6	.987
1995—Toledo (I.L.)................	1B-DH	11	36	5	7	2	0	0	3	6	9	0-0	.194	.302	.250	3	.969
—Jacksonville (Sou.).....	1B-DH	108	397	65	112	17	1	*31	93	60	94	0-0	.282	.374	.564	7	.992
1996—Columbus (I.L.)■.......	1B-DH	130	446	84	115	26	0	28	96	48	99	2-4	.258	.335	.504	5	*.996
1997—Columbus (I.L.)..........	1B-DH	116	417	69	125	35	1	24	95	65	78	4-5	.300	.404	.561	8	.992
—New York (A.L.)..........	DH-1B-OF	11	20	0	5	1	0	0	3	2	4	0-0	.250	.318	.300	0	1.000
1998—Columbus (I.L.)..........	1B-DH-OF	56	204	34	54	10	0	13	36	29	44	0-0	.265	.360	.505	5	.991
—GC Yankees (GCL)......	1B-DH	5	10	2	6	3	0	1	5	3	3	0-0	.600	.692	1.200	0	1.000
1999—Nashville (PCL)■.......	1B-DH	75	273	57	89	20	1	25	81	21	56	0-2	.326	.365	.681	4	.993
—Pittsburgh (N.L.)........	1B-OF	5	10	3	4	0	0	1	2	0	2	0-0	.400	.400	.700	0	1.000
—Altoona (East.)...........	DH	3	13	1	2	1	0	0	3	1	8	0-0	.154	.214	.231	0	...
2000—Nashville (PCL)..........	1B	36	121	15	38	11	0	7	28	15	26	0-0	.314	.391	.579	2	.992
—Pittsburgh (N.L.)........	1B	8	11	0	1	0	0	0	0	0	8	0-0	.091	.091	.091	0	1.000
—Mex. City Reds (Mex.)■	OF-1B	51	199	52	80	16	1	20	49	20	29	0-0	.402	.449	.794	0	1.000
2001—Hanshin (Jap. Cen.)■		70	239	19	56	5	0	14	34	25	62	0-...	.234			...	...
2002—Memphis (PCL)■.......	1B	125	461	83	129	27	0	*35	100	49	96	0-0	.280	.349	.566	5	.995
—St. Louis (N.L.).........	1B	17	14	2	5	0	0	1	3	1	3	0-0	.357	.400	.571	0	1.000
American League totals (1 year)		11	20	0	5	1	0	0	3	2	4	0-0	.250	.318	.300	0	1.000
National League totals (3 years)		30	35	5	10	0	0	2	5	1	13	0-0	.286	.306	.457	0	1.000
Major League totals (4 years)		41	55	5	15	1	0	2	8	3	17	0-0	.273	.310	.400	0	1.000

CRUZ, JACOB OF

PERSONAL: Born January 28, 1973, in Oxnard, Calif. ... 6-0/210. ... Bats left, throws left.

HIGH SCHOOL: Channel Islands (Oxnard, Calif.).

COLLEGE: Arizona State.

TRANSACTIONS/CAREER NOTES: Selected by California Angels organization in 45th round of free-agent draft (June 3, 1991); did not sign. ... Selected by San Francisco Giants organization in supplemental round ("sandwich pick" between first and second round; 32nd pick overall) of free-agent draft (June 2, 1994); pick received as part of compensation for Texas Rangers signing Type A free agent 1B Will Clark. ... Traded by Giants with P Steve Reed to Cleveland Indians for P Jose Mesa, IF Shawon Dunston and P Alvin Morman (July 24, 1998). ... On Cleveland disabled list (March 30-April 29 and August 3, 1999-remainder of season); included rehabilitation assignment to Buffalo (April 18-29). ... On disabled list (April 30, 2000-remainder of season). ... Traded by Indians to Colorado Rockies for C Josh Bard and OF Jody Gerut (June 2, 2001). ... On Colorado disabled list (July 17-August 17, 2001); included rehabilitation assignment to Colorado Springs (July 30-August 13). ... Released by Rockies (November 30, 2001). ... Signed by Detroit Tigers organization (December 21, 2001). ... On Detroit disabled list (June 1-18 and June 23, 2002-remainder of season); included rehabilitation assignment to Toledo (June 7-18). ... Released by Tigers (October 3, 2002).

STATISTICAL NOTES: Led Pacific Coast League with 11 sacrifice flies in 1996. ... Tied Pacific Coast League lead with nine intentional bases on balls received in 1997. ... Led Pacific Coast League outfielders with 16 assists in 1997.

2002 GAMES PLAYED BY POSITION (MLB): DH—15; OF—12; 1B—4.

		BATTING														FIELDING	
Year Team (League)	Pos.	G	AB	R	H	2B	3B	HR	RBI	BB	SO	SB-CS	Avg.	OBP	SLG	E	Avg.
1994—San Jose (Calif.).........	OF	31	118	14	29	7	0	0	12	9	22	0-2	.246	.305	.305	2	.957
1995—Shreveport (Texas).....	OF	127	458	88	136	33	1	13	77	57	72	9-8	.297	.383	.459	1	*.996
1996—Phoenix (PCL)...........	OF-DH	121	435	60	124	26	4	7	75	62	77	5-9	.285	.378	.411	3	.989
—San Francisco (N.L.)..	OF	33	77	10	18	3	0	3	10	12	24	0-1	.234	.352	.390	1	.977
1997—Phoenix (PCL)...........	OF-DH	127	493	97	178	*45	3	12	95	64	64	18-3	*.361	*.434	.538	8	.970
—San Francisco (N.L.)..	OF	16	25	3	4	1	0	0	3	3	4	0-0	.160	.241	.200	1	.933
1998—Fresno (PCL).............	OF-DH	89	342	60	102	17	3	18	62	46	57	12-5	.298	.393	.523	6	.963
—San Francisco (N.L.)..	PH	3	3	0	0	0	0	0	0	0	2	0-0	.000	.000	.000	0	...
—Buffalo (I.L.)■...........	OF	43	169	32	56	8	2	13	36	13	26	2-3	.331	.380	.633	4	.949
—Cleveland (A.L.)..........	PH	1	1	0	0	0	0	0	0	0	1	0-0	.000	.000	.000	0	...
1999—Buffalo (I.L.)..............	OF-DH	54	202	29	55	7	2	7	31	21	39	4-2	.272	.348	.431	4	.953
—Cleveland (A.L.)..........	OF-DH	32	88	14	29	5	1	3	17	5	13	0-2	.330	.368	.511	0	1.000
2000—Cleveland (A.L.)..........	OF-DH	11	29	3	7	3	0	0	5	5	4	1-0	.241	.361	.345	0	1.000
2001—Cleveland (A.L.)..........	OF	28	68	12	15	4	0	3	11	5	23	0-2	.221	.303	.412	1	.976
—Colorado (N.L.)■.......	OF	44	76	7	16	1	0	1	7	10	27	0-2	.211	.303	.263	2	.931
—Colo. Springs (PCL)...	OF	20	86	18	28	5	2	6	25	1	23	1-0	.326	.337	.640	0	1.000
2002—Detroit (A.L.)■..........	DH-OF-1B	35	88	12	24	3	1	2	6	13	20	3-1	.273	.377	.398	1	.976
—Toledo (I.L.)...............	OF	11	43	6	7	1	1	0	5	8	14	1-0	.163	.302	.233	0	1.000
American League totals (5 years)		107	274	41	75	15	2	8	39	28	61	4-5	.274	.354	.431	2	.986
National League totals (4 years)		96	181	20	38	5	0	4	20	25	57	0-3	.210	.311	.304	4	.954
Major League totals (7 years)		203	455	61	113	20	2	12	59	53	118	4-8	.248	.337	.380	6	.974

CRUZ, JOSE — OF — BLUE JAYS

PERSONAL: Born April 19, 1974, in Arroyo, Puerto Rico. ... 6-0/210. ... Bats both, throws right. ... Full name: Jose Cruz Jr. ... Son of Jose Cruz Sr., outfielder with St. Louis Cardinals (1970-1974), Houston Astros (1975-1987) and New York Yankees (1988); and coach, Houston Astros; nephew of Hector Cruz, outfielder/third baseman with four major league teams (1973, 1975-82); and nephew of Tommy Cruz, outfielder with St. Louis Cardinals (1973), Chicago White Sox (1977) and Nippon Ham Fighters of Japan League (1980-85).

HIGH SCHOOL: Bellaire (Houston).

COLLEGE: Rice.

TRANSACTIONS/CAREER NOTES: Selected by Atlanta Braves organization in 15th round of free-agent draft (June 1, 1992); did not sign. ... Selected by Seattle Mariners organization in first round (third pick overall) of free-agent draft (June 1, 1995). ... Traded by Mariners to Toronto Blue Jays for P Mike Timlin and P Paul Spoljaric (July 31, 1997). ... On Toronto disabled list (June 24-July 9, 1999); included rehabilitation assignment to Syracuse (July 5-9). ... On disabled list (May 6-21, 2001; and August 10-September 15, 2002).

RECORDS: Shares A.L. single-month record for most home runs—4 (October 2001).

STATISTICAL NOTES: Switch-hit home runs in one game (August 24, 1997). ... Had 18-game hitting streak (August 5-24, 1998). ... Led A.L. outfielders with 405 putouts and 417 total chances in 2000. ... Had 19-game hitting streak (April 4-27, 2001). ... Career major league grand slams: 1.

2002 GAMES PLAYED BY POSITION (MLB): OF—119; DH—2.

			BATTING														FIELDING	
Year	Team (League)	Pos.	G	AB	R	H	2B	3B	HR	RBI	BB	SO	SB-CS	Avg.	OBP	SLG	E	Avg.
1995—	Everett (N'West)	OF	3	11	6	5	0	0	0	2	3	3	1-0	.455	.571	.455	0	1.000
—	Riverside (Calif.)	OF	35	144	34	37	7	1	7	29	24	50	3-1	.257	.359	.465	3	.961
1996—	Lancaster (Calif.)	OF-DH	53	203	38	66	17	1	6	43	39	33	7-1	.325	.423	.507	1	.986
—	Port City (Sou.)	OF-DH	47	181	39	51	10	2	3	31	27	38	5-0	.282	.373	.409	1	.990
—	Tacoma (PCL)	OF	22	76	15	18	1	2	6	15	18	12	1-1	.237	.383	.539	0	1.000
1997—	Tacoma (PCL)	OF-DH	50	190	33	51	16	2	6	30	34	44	3-0	.268	.382	.468	0	1.000
—	Seattle (A.L.)	OF	49	183	28	49	12	1	12	34	13	45	1-0	.268	.315	.541	3	.966
—	Toronto (A.L.)■	OF	55	212	31	49	7	0	14	34	28	72	6-2	.231	.316	.462	2	.981
1998—	Toronto (A.L.)	OF	105	352	55	89	14	3	11	42	57	99	11-4	.253	.354	.403	4	.984
—	Syracuse (I.L.)	OF	40	141	29	42	14	1	7	23	32	32	8-4	.298	.425	.560	1	.991
1999—	Toronto (A.L.)	OF	106	349	63	84	19	3	14	45	64	91	14-4	.241	.358	.433	3	.990
—	Syracuse (I.L.)	OF-DH	31	103	17	19	3	1	3	14	28	20	5-0	.184	.356	.320	0	1.000
2000—	Toronto (A.L.)	OF	•162	603	91	146	32	5	31	76	71	129	15-5	.242	.323	.466	3	.993
2001—	Toronto (A.L.)	OF-DH	146	577	92	158	38	4	34	88	45	138	32-5	.274	.326	.530	3	.990
2002—	Toronto (A.L.)	OF-DH	124	466	64	114	26	5	18	70	51	106	7-1	.245	.317	.438	2	.992
Major League totals (6 years)			747	2742	424	689	148	21	134	389	329	680	86-21	.251	.330	.467	20	.988

CRUZ, JUAN — P — CUBS

PERSONAL: Born October 15, 1978, in Bonao, Dominican Republic. ... 6-2/165. ... Throws right, bats right. ... Full name: Juan Carlos Cruz.

TRANSACTIONS/CAREER NOTES: Signed as non-drafted free agent by Chicago Cubs organization (July 4, 1997). ... On disabled list (August 10-25, 2002).

STATISTICAL NOTES: Led Southern League with 16 hit batsmen in 2001.

MISCELLANEOUS: Appeared in three games as pinch runner (2001).

CAREER HITTING (MLB): 4-for-30 (.133), 0 R, 0 2B, 0 3B, 0 HR, 1 RBI.

Year	League	W	L	Pct.	ERA	G	GS	CG	ShO	Sv.-Opp.	IP	H	R	ER	HR	BB-IBB	SO
1998—	Arizona Cubs (Ariz.)	2	4	.333	6.10	12	6	0	0	0-...	41.1	61	48	28	2	14-0	36
1999—	Eugene (N'West)	5	6	.455	5.94	15	15	0	0	0-...	80.1	97	59	53	11	33-0	65
2000—	Lansing (Midw.)	5	5	.500	3.28	17	17	2	1	0-...	96.0	75	50	35	6	60-0	106
—	Daytona (FSL)	3	0	1.000	3.25	8	7	1	0	0-...	44.1	30	22	16	5	18-0	54
2001—	West Tenn (Sou.)	9	6	.600	4.01	23	23	0	0	0-...	121.1	107	56	54	6	60-0	137
—	Chicago (N.L.)	3	1	.750	3.22	8	8	0	0	0-0	44.2	40	16	16	4	17-1	39
2002—	Chicago (N.L.)	3	11	.214	3.98	45	9	0	0	1-4	97.1	84	56	43	11	59-4	81
Major League totals (2 years)		6	12	.333	3.74	53	17	0	0	1-4	142.0	124	72	59	15	76-5	120

CRUZ, NELSON — P — ASTROS

PERSONAL: Born September 13, 1972, in Puerta Plata, Dominican Republic. ... 6-1/185. ... Throws right, bats right. ... Cousin of Jose Roman, pitcher with Cleveland Indians (1984-86).

HIGH SCHOOL: Liceo Jose Castellanos (Puerto Plata, Dominican Republic).

TRANSACTIONS/CAREER NOTES: Signed as non-drafted free agent by Montreal Expos organization (July 5, 1989). ... Released by Expos (March 27, 1992). ... Signed by Chicago White Sox organization (December 10, 1994). ... Granted free agency (October 15, 1998). ... Signed by Detroit Tigers (November 19, 1998). ... On Toledo disabled list (May 7-24, 2000). ... Traded by Tigers with C Brad Ausmus and P Doug Brocail to Houston Astros for C Mitch Meluskey, P Chris Holt and OF Roger Cedeno (December 11, 2000). ... On Houston disabled list (April 19-May 4, 2002); included rehabilitation assignment to New Orleans (April 22-May 3).

CAREER HITTING (MLB): 1-for-20 (.050), 0 R, 0 2B, 0 3B, 0 HR, 1 RBI.

Year	League	W	L	Pct.	ERA	G	GS	CG	ShO	Sv.-Opp.	IP	H	R	ER	HR	BB-IBB	SO
1990—	Dominican Expos (DSL)	9	2	.818	2.62	16	16	0	0	0-...	103.0	105	49	30	...	42-...	83
1991—	Gulf Coast Expos (GCL)	2	4	.333	2.40	12	8	1	1	0-...	48.2	40	18	13	1	19-0	34
1992—		Out of organized baseball.															
1993—		Out of organized baseball.															
1994—		Out of organized baseball.															
1995—	Bristol (Appl.)■	0	0	...	9.00	1	0	0	0	0-...	1.0	2	1	1	0	0-0	0
—	Hickory (S.Atl.)	2	7	.222	2.70	44	0	0	0	9-...	66.2	65	31	20	6	15-2	68
—	Prince William (Caro.)	2	1	.667	0.47	9	0	0	0	1-...	19.1	12	1	1	1	6-0	15
1996—	Birmingham (Sou.)	6	6	.500	3.20	37	18	2	1	1-...	149.0	150	65	53	10	41-2	142
1997—	Nashville (A.A.)	11	7	.611	5.11	21	20	1	0	0-...	123.1	139	75	70	20	31-0	93
—	Chicago (A.L.)	0	2	.000	6.49	19	0	0	0	0-0	26.1	29	19	19	6	9-1	23
1998—	Calgary (PCL)	10	6	.625	5.33	35	18	2	1	0-...	126.2	159	85	75	18	40-1	101

Year	League	W	L	Pct.	ERA	G	GS	CG	ShO	Sv.-Opp.	IP	H	R	ER	HR	BB-IBB	SO
1999—	Toledo (I.L.)■	7	1	.875	2.73	10	10	4	•2	0-...	62.2	47	20	19	5	21-0	41
—	Detroit (A.L.)	2	5	.286	5.67	29	6	0	0	0-0	66.2	74	44	42	11	23-1	46
2000—	Toledo (I.L.)	2	4	.333	4.82	11	10	0	0	0-...	52.1	54	37	28	9	17-0	39
—	Detroit (A.L.)	5	2	.714	3.07	27	0	0	0	0-1	41.0	39	14	14	4	13-3	34
2001—	Houston (N.L.)■	3	3	.500	4.15	66	0	0	0	2-4	82.1	72	41	38	11	24-4	75
2002—	Houston (N.L.)	2	6	.250	4.48	43	5	0	0	0-2	78.1	90	44	39	12	29-4	61
—	New Orleans (PCL)	0	1	.000	4.50	6	0	0	0	1-...	8.0	4	4	4	2	4-0	8
A.L. totals (3 years)		7	9	.438	5.04	75	6	0	0	0-1	134.0	142	77	75	21	45-5	103
N.L. totals (2 years)		5	9	.357	4.31	109	5	0	0	2-6	160.2	162	85	77	23	53-8	136
Major League totals (5 years)		12	18	.400	4.64	184	11	0	0	2-7	294.2	304	162	152	44	98-13	239

DIVISION SERIES RECORD

Year	League	W	L	Pct.	ERA	G	GS	CG	ShO	Sv.-Opp.	IP	H	R	ER	HR	BB-IBB	SO
2001—	Houston (N.L.)	0	0	...	0.00	2	0	0	0	0-0	2.2	1	0	0	0	1-1	1

CUDDYER, MIKE — OF/3B — TWINS

PERSONAL: Born March 27, 1979, in Norfolk, Va. ... 6-2/215. ... Bats right, throws right. ... Full name: Michael Brent Cuddyer.

HIGH SCHOOL: Great Bridge (Chesapeake, Va.).

TRANSACTIONS/CAREER NOTES: Selected by Minnesota Twins organization in first round (ninth pick overall) of free-agent draft (June 3, 1997). ... On Edmonton disabled list (April 27-May 10, 2002).

STATISTICAL NOTES: Led Midwest League shortstops with 61 errors and 654 total chances in 1998. ... Led Florida State League in grounding into double plays with 20 in 1999. ... Tied for Florida State League lead in double plays by third baseman with 25 in 1999. ... Career major league grand slams: 1.

2002 GAMES PLAYED BY POSITION (MLB): OF—25; 3B—10; 1B—6; DH—3.

			BATTING														FIELDING	
Year	Team (League)	Pos.	G	AB	R	H	2B	3B	HR	RBI	BB	SO	SB-CS	Avg.	OBP	SLG	E	Avg.
1998—	Fort Wayne (Midw.)	SS-2B	129	497	82	137	37	7	12	81	61	107	16-7	.276	.364	.451	†61	.907
1999—	Fort Myers (FSL)	3B	130	466	87	139	24	4	16	82	•76	91	14-4	.298	.403	.470	28	.921
2000—	New Britain (East.)	3B	138	490	72	129	30	8	6	61	55	93	5-4	.263	.351	.394	*34	.903
2001—	New Britain (East.)	3B-1B-OF	141	509	95	153	36	3	30	87	75	106	5-9	.301	.395	.560	28	.963
—	Minnesota (A.L.)	1B-3B-DH	8	18	1	4	2	0	0	1	2	6	1-0	.222	.300	.333	1	.975
2002—	Edmonton (PCL)	OF-1B-3B	86	330	70	102	16	9	20	53	36	79	12-7	.309	.379	.594	7	.970
—	Minnesota (A.L.)	OF-3B-1B-DH	41	112	12	29	7	0	4	13	8	30	2-0	.259	.311	.429	1	.990
Major League totals (2 years)			49	130	13	33	9	0	4	14	10	36	3-0	.254	.310	.415	2	.985

DIVISION SERIES RECORD

			BATTING														FIELDING	
Year	Team (League)	Pos.	G	AB	R	H	2B	3B	HR	RBI	BB	SO	SB-CS	Avg.	OBP	SLG	E	Avg.
2002—	Minnesota (A.L.)	OF	5	13	1	5	1	0	0	1	3	3	0-0	.385	.500	.462	0	1.000

CHAMPIONSHIP SERIES RECORD

			BATTING														FIELDING	
Year	Team (League)	Pos.	G	AB	R	H	2B	3B	HR	RBI	BB	SO	SB-CS	Avg.	OBP	SLG	E	Avg.
2002—	Minnesota (A.L.)	OF	3	5	0	1	0	0	0	0	1	1	0-0	.200	.333	.200	0	1.000

CUNNANE, WILL — P — CUBS

PERSONAL: Born April 24, 1974, in Suffern, N.Y. ... 6-1/205. ... Throws right, bats right. ... Full name: William Joseph Cunnane.

HIGH SCHOOL: Clarkstown North (New City, N.Y.).

TRANSACTIONS/CAREER NOTES: Signed as non-drafted free agent by Florida Marlins organization (August 18, 1992). ... On Portland disabled list (August 7-23, 1996). ... Selected by San Diego Padres from Marlins organization in Rule 5 major league draft (December 9, 1996). ... On San Diego disabled list (March 29-June 21, 1998); included rehabilitation assignment to Las Vegas (June 9-21). ... Traded by Padres to Milwaukee Brewers for OF Chad Green (December 20, 2000), completing deal in which Brewers traded SS Santiago Perez and a player to be named later or cash to San Deigo Padres for P Brandon Kolb (December 1, 2000). ... Granted free agency (October 8, 2001). ... Signed by Chicago Cubs organization (December 17, 2001).

MISCELLANEOUS: Appeared in one game as pinch runner (1997). ... Appeared in one game as pinch runner (2001).

CAREER HITTING (MLB): 7-for-35 (.200), 6 R, 1 2B, 1 3B, 0 HR, 4 RBI.

Year	League	W	L	Pct.	ERA	G	GS	CG	ShO	Sv.-Opp.	IP	H	R	ER	HR	BB-IBB	SO
1993—	Gulf Coast Marlins (GCL)	3	3	.500	2.70	16	9	0	0	2-...	66.2	75	32	20	1	8-0	64
1994—	Kane County (Midw.)	11	3	.786	*1.43	32	16	5	*4	1-...	138.2	110	27	22	2	23-4	106
1995—	Portland (East.)	9	2	.818	3.67	21	21	1	1	0-...	117.2	120	48	48	10	34-1	83
1996—	Portland (East.)	10	12	.455	3.74	25	25	4	0	0-...	151.2	156	73	63	15	30-6	101
1997—	San Diego (N.L.)■	6	3	.667	5.81	54	8	0	0	0-2	91.1	114	69	59	11	49-3	79
1998—	Las Vegas (PCL)	1	2	.333	5.25	33	0	0	0	4-...	36.0	45	26	21	1	19-4	30
—	San Diego (N.L.)	0	0	...	6.00	3	0	0	0	0-0	3.0	4	2	2	1	1-1	1
1999—	Las Vegas (PCL)	2	1	.667	0.98	28	0	0	0	11-...	36.2	30	5	4	0	16-2	54
—	San Diego (N.L.)	2	1	.667	5.23	24	0	0	0	0-0	31.0	34	19	18	8	12-3	22
2000—	San Diego (N.L.)	1	1	.500	4.23	27	3	0	0	0-0	38.1	35	21	18	2	21-0	34
—	Las Vegas (PCL)	7	4	.636	3.98	17	17	1	1	0-...	97.1	96	46	43	7	26-0	97
2001—	Milwaukee (N.L.)■	0	3	.000	5.40	31	1	0	0	0-0	51.2	66	34	31	6	22-6	37
—	Indianapolis (I.L.)	0	1	.000	3.86	7	3	0	0	1-...	23.1	25	10	10	2	6-1	25
2002—	Iowa (PCL)■	4	1	.800	2.20	43	0	0	0	2-...	73.2	67	23	18	3	23-3	69
—	Chicago (N.L.)	1	1	.500	5.47	16	0	0	0	0-1	26.1	27	16	16	5	13-1	30
Major League totals (6 years)		10	9	.526	5.36	155	12	0	0	0-3	241.2	280	161	144	33	118-14	203

CUST, JACK — OF — ROCKIES

PERSONAL: Born January 16, 1979, in Flemington, N.J. ... 6-1/205. ... Bats left, throws right. ... Full name: John Joseph Cust.
HIGH SCHOOL: Immaculata (Somerville, N.J.).
TRANSACTIONS/CAREER NOTES: Selected by Arizona Diamondbacks organization in first round (30th pick overall) of free-agent draft (June 3, 1997). ... Traded by Diamondbacks with C J.D. Closser to Colorado Rockies for P Mike Myers (January 7, 2002).
2002 GAMES PLAYED BY POSITION (MLB): OF—18.

			BATTING														FIELDING	
Year	Team (League)	Pos.	G	AB	R	H	2B	3B	HR	RBI	BB	SO	SB-CS	Avg.	OBP	SLG	E	Avg.
1997—	Ariz. D-backs (Ariz.)	OF	35	121	26	37	11	1	3	33	31	39	2-0	.306	.447	.488	5	.902
1998—	South Bend (Midw.)	OF	16	62	5	15	3	0	0	4	5	20	0-1	.242	.294	.290	4	.975
—	Lethbridge (Pio.)	OF	73	223	75	77	20	2	11	56	86	71	15-8	.345	.530	.601	0	1.000
1999—	High Desert (Calif.)	OF	125	455	107	152	42	3	32	112	96	145	1-4	.334	.450	.651	12	.922
2000—	El Paso (Texas)	OF	129	447	100	131	32	6	20	75	117	150	12-9	.293	.440	.526	11	.944
2001—	Tucson (PCL)	OF	135	442	81	123	24	2	27	79	102	160	6-3	.278	.415	.525	*11	.948
—	Arizona (N.L.)	OF	3	2	0	1	0	0	0	0	1	0	0-0	.500	.667	.500	0	...
2002—	Colo. Springs (PCL)■	OF	105	359	74	95	24	0	23	55	83	121	6-3	.265	.407	.524	6	.961
—	Colorado (N.L.)	OF	35	65	8	11	2	0	1	8	12	32	0-1	.169	.295	.246	1	.960
Major League totals (2 years)			38	67	8	12	2	0	1	8	13	32	0-1	.179	.309	.254	1	.960

CYR, ERIC — P — PADRES

PERSONAL: Born February 11, 1979, in Montreal. ... 6-4/200. ... Throws left, bats right.
HIGH SCHOOL: Polyvalente Edouard Montpetit (Montreal).
JUNIOR COLLEGE: Seminole (Okla.).
TRANSACTIONS/CAREER NOTES: Selected by San Diego Padres organization in 30th round of free-agent draft (June 2, 1998). ... On Fort Wayne disabled list (May 8-August 25, 2000). ... On San Diego disabled list (July 3-August 3, 2002).
CAREER HITTING (MLB): 0-for-1 (.000), 0 R, 0 2B, 0 3B, 0 HR, 0 RBI.

Year	League	W	L	Pct.	ERA	G	GS	CG	ShO	Sv.-Opp.	IP	H	R	ER	HR	BB-IBB	SO
1999—	Arizona Padres (Ariz.)	2	1	.667	3.26	11	5	0	0	0-...	38.2	34	19	14	2	15-0	39
—	Idaho Falls (Pio.)	1	0	1.000	1.80	1	1	0	0	0-...	5.0	5	1	1	0	1-0	3
2000—	Fort Wayne (Midw.)	2	2	.500	4.68	9	6	0	0	0-...	32.2	28	18	17	2	15-0	31
—	Arizona Padres (Ariz.)	0	0	...	3.00	2	1	0	0	0-...	3.0	4	1	1	0	2-0	4
2001—	Lake Elsinore (Calif.)	7	4	.636	1.61	21	16	0	0	0-...	100.2	68	28	18	1	24-0	131
2002—	Mobile (Sou.)	4	6	.400	3.24	14	14	0	0	0-...	72.1	62	37	26	6	34-0	65
—	San Diego (N.L.)	0	1	.000	10.50	5	0	0	0	0-0	6.0	6	7	7	0	6-1	4
—	Portland (PCL)	0	0	...	3.14	9	2	0	0	0-...	14.1	14	6	5	0	10-0	11
Major League totals (1 year)		0	1	.000	10.50	5	0	0	0	0-0	6.0	6	7	7	0	6-1	4

D'AMICO, JEFF — P

PERSONAL: Born December 27, 1975, in St. Petersburg, Fla. ... 6-7/250. ... Throws right, bats right. ... Full name: Jeffrey Charles D'Amico.
HIGH SCHOOL: Northeast (St. Petersburg, Fla.).
TRANSACTIONS/CAREER NOTES: Selected by Milwaukee Brewers organization in first round (23rd pick overall) of free-agent draft (June 3, 1993). ... On disabled list (June 24, 1994-entire season). ... On Milwaukee disabled list (July 28-September 2, 1997; and January 14, 1998-entire season). ... On Milwaukee disabled list (March 29-September 25, 1999); included rehabilitation assignments to Beloit (July 6-15), Huntsville (July 16-21) and Louisville (August 12-25). ... On Milwaukee disabled list (June 6-30, 2000). ... On Milwaukee disabled list (April 23-September 1, 2001); included rehabilitation assignments to Beloit (June 6-11 and August 29-31) and Huntsville (June 12). ... Traded by Brewers to New York Mets as part of three-way deal in which Mets traded P Glendon Rusch to Brewers, Colorado Rockies traded 1B/OF Ross Gload and P Craig House to Mets, Brewers traded OF Jeromy Burnitz, IF Lou Collier, OF/1B Mark Sweeney and cash to Mets, Mets traded 1B/3B Todd Zeile, OF Benny Agbayani, IF/OF Lenny Harris and cash to Rockies and Rockies traded OF Alex Ochoa to Brewers (January 21, 2002). ... Granted free agency (October 28, 2002).
CAREER HITTING (MLB): 9-for-100 (.090), 4 R, 1 2B, 1 3B, 1 HR, 2 RBI.

Year	League	W	L	Pct.	ERA	G	GS	CG	ShO	Sv.-Opp.	IP	H	R	ER	HR	BB-IBB	SO
1994—	Arizona Brewers (Ariz.)									Did not play.							
1995—	Beloit (Midw.)	13	3	*.813	2.39	21	20	3	1	0-...	132.0	102	40	35	7	31-2	119
1996—	El Paso (Texas)	5	4	.556	3.19	13	13	3	0	0-...	96.0	89	42	34	10	13-0	76
—	Milwaukee (A.L.)	6	6	.500	5.44	17	17	0	0	0-0	86.0	88	53	52	21	31-0	53
1997—	Milwaukee (A.L.)	9	7	.563	4.71	23	23	1	1	0-0	135.2	139	81	71	25	43-2	94
—	Beloit (Midw.)	0	0	...	0.00	1	1	0	0	0-...	3.0	0	0	0	0	1-0	7
1998—	Milwaukee (A.L.)									Did not play.							
1999—	Beloit (Midw.)	1	0	1.000	0.00	2	2	0	0	0-...	8.0	7	0	0	0	1-0	6
—	Huntsville (Sou.)	0	0	...	36.00	1	1	0	0	0-...	2.0	6	8	8	3	1-0	2
—	Louisville (I.L.)	0	0	...	13.50	1	1	0	0	0-...	3.1	6	5	5	0	2-0	1
—	Milwaukee (N.L.)	0	0	...	0.00	1	0	0	0	0-0	1.0	1	0	0	0	0-0	1
2000—	Indianapolis (I.L.)	1	1	.500	3.16	6	6	0	0	0-...	31.1	25	11	11	6	11-0	20
—	Milwaukee (N.L.)	12	7	.632	2.66	23	23	1	1	0-0	162.1	143	55	48	14	46-5	101
2001—	Milwaukee (N.L.)	2	4	.333	6.08	10	10	0	0	0-0	47.1	60	42	32	11	16-4	32
—	Beloit (Midw.)	0	0	...	5.40	2	2	0	0	0-...	8.1	11	6	5	1	1-0	6
—	Huntsville (Sou.)	1	0	1.000	2.57	1	1	0	0	0-...	7.0	3	2	2	2	2-0	5
2002—	New York (N.L.)■	6	10	.375	4.94	29	22	1	1	0-0	145.2	152	84	80	20	37-8	101
A.L. totals (2 years)		15	13	.536	4.99	40	40	1	1	0-0	221.2	227	134	123	46	74-2	147
N.L. totals (4 years)		20	21	.488	4.04	63	55	2	2	0-0	356.1	356	181	160	45	99-17	235
Major League totals (6 years)		35	34	.507	4.41	103	95	3	3	0-0	578.0	583	315	283	91	173-19	382

DAAL, OMAR — P

PERSONAL: Born March 1, 1972, in Maracaibo, Venezuela. ... 6-3/204. ... Throws left, bats left. ... Full name: Omar Jose Cordaro Daal.
HIGH SCHOOL: Valencia (Venezuela) Superior.
TRANSACTIONS/CAREER NOTES: Signed as non-drafted free agent by Los Angeles Dodgers organization (August 24, 1990). ... Traded by Dodgers to Montreal Expos for P Rick Clelland (December 14, 1995). ... Claimed on waivers by Toronto Blue Jays (July 25, 1997). ... Selected by Arizona Diamondbacks in second round (31st pick overall) of expansion draft (November 18, 1997). ... On Arizona disabled list (June 22-July 11, 1998); included rehabilitation assignment to Tucson (July 9-11). ... Traded by Diamondbacks with OF Travis Lee, P Vicente Padilla and P Nelson Figueroa to Philadelphia Phillies for P Curt Schilling (July 26, 2000). ... Traded by Phillies to Dodgers for P Eric Junge and P Jesus Cordero (November 9, 2001). ... Granted free agency (October 28, 2002).
STATISTICAL NOTES: Led N.L. with 19 losses in 2000. ... Tied for N.L. lead with three balks in 2001.
CAREER HITTING (MLB): 53-for-270 (.196), 23 R, 8 2B, 0 3B, 2 HR, 21 RBI.

Year League	W	L	Pct.	ERA	G	GS	CG	ShO	Sv.-Opp.	IP	H	R	ER	HR	BB-IBB	SO
1990— Dom. Dodgers (DSL)	3	6	.333	1.18	17	13	6	0	2-...	91.2	61	29	12	...	29-...	91
1991— Dom. Dodgers (DSL)	7	2	.778	1.16	13	13	0	0	0-...	93.0	30	17	12	...	32-...	81
1992— San Antonio (Texas)	2	6	.250	5.02	35	5	0	0	5-...	57.1	60	39	32	3	33-1	52
— Albuquerque (PCL)	0	2	.000	7.84	12	0	0	0	0-...	10.1	14	9	9	1	11-1	9
1993— Albuquerque (PCL)	1	1	.500	3.38	6	0	0	0	2-...	5.1	5	2	2	1	3-1	2
— Los Angeles (N.L.)	2	3	.400	5.09	47	0	0	0	0-1	35.1	36	20	20	5	21-3	19
1994— Albuquerque (PCL)	4	2	.667	5.19	11	5	0	0	1-...	34.2	38	20	20	6	16-0	28
— Los Angeles (N.L.)	0	0	...	3.29	24	0	0	0	0-0	13.2	12	5	5	1	5-0	9
1995— Albuquerque (PCL)	2	3	.400	4.05	17	9	0	0	1-...	53.1	56	28	24	3	26-2	46
— Los Angeles (N.L.)	4	0	1.000	7.20	28	0	0	0	0-1	20.0	29	16	16	1	15-4	11
1996— Montreal (N.L.)■	4	5	.444	4.02	64	6	0	0	0-4	87.1	74	40	39	10	37-3	82
1997— Montreal (N.L.)	1	2	.333	9.79	33	0	0	0	1-3	30.1	48	35	33	4	15-3	16
— Ottawa (I.L.)	0	1	.000	5.63	2	2	0	0	0-...	8.0	10	6	5	1	1-0	9
— Toronto (A.L.)■	1	1	.500	4.00	9	3	0	0	0-0	27.0	34	13	12	3	6-0	28
— Syracuse (I.L.)	3	0	1.000	0.53	5	5	1	1	0-...	34.0	18	2	2	0	10-0	29
1998— Arizona (N.L.)■	8	12	.400	2.88	33	23	3	1	0-0	162.2	146	60	52	12	51-3	132
— Tucson (PCL)	0	0	...	3.00	1	1	0	0	0-...	3.0	3	2	1	0	1-0	4
1999— Arizona (N.L.)	16	9	.640	3.65	32	32	2	1	0-0	214.2	188	92	87	21	79-3	148
2000— Arizona (N.L.)	2	10	.167	7.22	20	16	0	0	0-0	96.0	127	88	77	17	42-11	45
— Philadelphia (N.L.)■	2	§9	.182	4.69	12	12	0	0	0-0	71.0	81	40	37	9	30-0	51
2001— Philadelphia (N.L.)	13	7	.650	4.46	32	32	0	0	0-0	185.2	199	100	92	26	56-3	107
2002— Los Angeles (N.L.)■	11	9	.550	3.90	39	23	0	0	0-0	161.1	142	73	70	20	54-3	105
A.L. totals (1 year)	1	1	.500	4.00	9	3	0	0	0-0	27.0	34	13	12	3	6-0	28
N.L. totals (10 years)	63	66	.488	4.41	364	144	5	2	1-9	1078.0	1082	569	528	126	405-36	725
Major League totals (10 years)	64	67	.489	4.40	373	147	5	2	1-9	1105.0	1116	582	540	129	411-36	753

DIVISION SERIES RECORD

Year League	W	L	Pct.	ERA	G	GS	CG	ShO	Sv.-Opp.	IP	H	R	ER	HR	BB-IBB	SO
1999— Arizona (N.L.)	0	1	.000	6.75	1	1	0	0	0-0	4.0	6	3	3	0	3-0	4

DAMON, JOHNNY — OF — RED SOX

PERSONAL: Born November 5, 1973, in Fort Riley, Kan. ... 6-2/190. ... Bats left, throws left. ... Full name: Johnny David Damon.
HIGH SCHOOL: Dr. Phillips (Orlando).
TRANSACTIONS/CAREER NOTES: Selected by Kansas City Royals organization in supplemental round ("sandwich pick" between first and second round, 35th pick overall) of free-agent draft (June 1, 1992); pick received as part of compensation for San Diego Padres signing Type A free-agent IF Kurt Stillwell. ... On suspended list (September 5-7, 1997). ... Traded by Royals with IF Mark Ellis and a player to be named later to Oakland Athletics as part of three-way deal in which Royals received P Roberto Hernandez from Tampa Bay Devil Rays, A's received P Cory Lidle from Devil Rays, Royals received C A.J. Hinch, IF Angel Berroa and cash from A's and Devil Rays received OF Ben Grieve and a player to be named later or cash from A's (January 8, 2001). ... Granted free agency (November 5, 2001). ... Signed by Boston Red Sox (December 21, 2001).
RECORDS: Holds A.L. career record for most consecutive chances accepted without an error by outfielder—593 (May 4, 2001-August 31, 2002). ... Shares major league single-game record for most doubles—4 (July 18, 2000). ... Shares A.L. record for most hits in four consecutive games—15 (July 18-21, 2000).
HONORS: Named Texas League Player of the Year (1995).
STATISTICAL NOTES: Led Gulf Coast League with 109 total bases in 1992. ... Led Midwest League outfielders with five double plays in 1993. ... Led Texas League with 13 intentional bases on balls received in 1995. ... Had 16-game hitting streak (April 27-May 12, 1999). ... Had 16-game hitting streak (August 5-21, 2000). ... Had 18-game hitting streak (April 15-May 8, 2002). ... Career major league grand slams: 4.
2002 GAMES PLAYED BY POSITION (MLB): OF—151; DH—1.

					BATTING											FIELDING	
Year Team (League)	Pos.	G	AB	R	H	2B	3B	HR	RBI	BB	SO	SB-CS	Avg.	OBP	SLG	E	Avg.
1992— GC Royals (GCL)	OF	50	192	*58	67	12	*9	4	24	31	21	33-6	*.349	.449	.568	1	.988
— Baseball City (FSL)	OF	1	1	0	0	0	0	0	0	0	0	0-0	.000	.000	.000	0	...
1993— Rockford (Midw.)	OF	127	511	82	148	25	*13	5	50	52	83	59-18	.290	.360	.419	6	.977
1994— Wilmington (Caro.)	OF	119	472	96	149	25	13	6	75	62	55	44-9	.316	.399	.462	3	.989
1995— Wichita (Texas)	OF-DH	111	423	83	145	15	9	16	54	67	35	26-15	.343	*.434	*.534	5	.984
— Kansas City (A.L.)	OF	47	188	32	53	11	5	3	23	12	22	7-0	.282	.324	.441	1	.991
1996— Kansas City (A.L.)	OF-DH	145	517	61	140	22	5	6	50	31	64	25-5	.271	.313	.368	6	.983
1997— Kansas City (A.L.)	OF-DH	146	472	70	130	12	8	8	48	42	70	16-10	.275	.338	.386	4	.988
1998— Kansas City (A.L.)	OF	161	642	104	178	30	10	18	66	58	84	26-12	.277	.339	.439	4	.990
1999— Kansas City (A.L.)	OF-DH	145	583	101	179	39	9	14	77	67	50	36-6	.307	.379	.477	4	.987
2000— Kansas City (A.L.)	OF-DH	159	655	*136	214	42	10	16	88	65	60	*46-9	.327	.382	.495	5	.986
2001— Oakland (A.L.)■	OF	155	644	108	165	34	4	9	49	61	70	27-12	.256	.324	.363	3	.991
2002— Boston (A.L.)	OF-DH	154	623	118	178	34	*11	14	63	65	70	31-6	.286	.356	.443	1	.997
Major League totals (8 years)		1112	4324	730	1237	224	62	88	464	401	490	214-60	.286	.348	.428	28	.989

DIVISION SERIES RECORD

Year	Team (League)	Pos.	G	AB	R	H	2B	3B	HR	RBI	BB	SO	SB-CS	Avg.	OBP	SLG	E	Avg.
			BATTING														FIELDING	
2001—	Oakland (A.L.)	OF	5	22	3	9	2	1	0	0	1	1	2-0	.409	.435	.591	0	1.000

ALL-STAR GAME RECORD

	AB	R	H	2B	3B	HR	RBI	BB	SO	SB-CS	Avg.	OBP	SLG	E	Avg.
All-Star Game totals (1 year)	3	1	1	0	0	0	0	0	1	1-0	.333	.333	.333	0	1.000

DARENSBOURG, VIC — P

PERSONAL: Born November 13, 1970, in Los Angeles. ... 5-8/170. ... Throws left, bats left. ... Full name: Victor Anthony Darensbourg.
HIGH SCHOOL: Westchester (Los Angeles).
COLLEGE: Lewis and Clark State (Idaho).
TRANSACTIONS/CAREER NOTES: Signed as non-drafted free agent by Florida Marlins organization (June 11, 1992). ... On disabled list entire 1995 season. ... On Portland disabled list (April 4-15, 1996). ... On disabled list (April 25-June 21 and July 29-September 6, 1997). ... On disabled list (August 20-September 17, 2001). ... Granted free agency (October 15, 2002).
MISCELLANEOUS: Appeared in one game as pinch runner (2001).
CAREER HITTING (MLB): 2-for-17 (.118), 0 R, 0 2B, 0 3B, 0 HR, 0 RBI.

Year	League	W	L	Pct.	ERA	G	GS	CG	ShO	Sv.-Opp.	IP	H	R	ER	HR	BB-IBB	SO
1992—	Gulf Coast Marlins (GCL)	2	1	.667	0.64	8	4	0	0	2-...	42.0	28	5	3	1	11-2	37
1993—	Kane County (Midw.)	9	1	.900	2.14	46	0	0	0	16-...	71.1	58	17	17	3	28-3	89
—	High Desert (Calif.)	0	0	...	0.00	1	0	0	0	0-...	1.0	0	0	0	0	0-0	1
1994—	Portland (East.)	10	7	.588	3.81	35	21	1	1	4-...	149.0	146	76	63	18	60-3	103
1995—	Florida (N.L.)									Did not play.							
1996—	Brevard County (FSL)	0	0	...	0.00	2	0	0	0	0-...	3.0	1	0	0	0	1-0	5
—	Charlotte (I.L.)	1	5	.167	3.69	47	0	0	0	7-...	63.1	61	30	26	7	32-3	66
1997—	Charlotte (I.L.)	4	2	.667	4.38	27	0	0	0	2-...	24.2	22	12	12	4	15-3	21
1998—	Florida (N.L.)	0	7	.000	3.68	59	0	0	0	1-2	71.0	52	29	29	5	30-6	74
1999—	Florida (N.L.)	0	1	.000	8.83	56	0	0	0	0-1	34.2	50	36	34	3	21-1	16
—	Calgary (PCL)	0	0	...	4.63	9	0	0	0	1-...	11.2	13	6	6	0	0-0	12
2000—	Florida (N.L.)	5	3	.625	4.06	56	0	0	0	0-1	62.0	61	32	28	7	28-1	59
2001—	Florida (N.L.)	1	2	.333	4.25	58	0	0	0	1-3	48.2	52	24	23	4	10-6	33
2002—	Florida (N.L.)	1	2	.333	6.14	42	0	0	0	0-0	48.1	61	34	33	10	26-4	33
Major League totals (5 years)		7	15	.318	5.00	271	0	0	0	2-7	264.2	276	155	147	29	115-18	215

DAUBACH, BRIAN — 1B/DH — RED SOX

PERSONAL: Born February 11, 1972, in Belleville, Ill. ... 6-1/233. ... Bats left, throws right. ... Full name: Brian Michael Daubach.
HIGH SCHOOL: Belleville (Ill.) West.
TRANSACTIONS/CAREER NOTES: Selected by New York Mets organization in 17th round of free-agent draft (June 4, 1990). ... Granted free agency (October 15, 1996). ... Signed by Florida Marlins organization (November 7, 1996). ... Granted free agency (October 17, 1997). ... Re-signed by Marlins organization (January 6, 1998). ... Released by Marlins (November 19, 1998). ... Signed by Boston Red Sox organization (December 18, 1998). ... On Boston disabled list (August 15-September 2, 2001); included rehabilitation assignments to Pawtucket (August 29-30) and Lowell (August 31-September 1).
STATISTICAL NOTES: Tied for Appalachian League lead in intentional bases on balls received with five in 1991. ... Led Appalachian League first basemen with 562 putouts, 52 assists, 623 total chances and 41 double plays in 1991. ... Tied for New York-Penn League lead with 44 assists by first basemen in 1992. ... Led Florida State League first basemen with 115 assists in 1994. ... Tied for Florida State League lead in double plays by first basemen with 127 in 1994. ... Led Eastern League first basemen with 111 double plays and .992 fielding percentage and tied for lead with 98 assists in 1995. ... Led Eastern League first basemen with 115 assists in 1996. ... Led International League with 10 sacrifice flies in 1997. ... Led International League with 315 total bases and nine intentional bases on balls received and tied for lead in being hit by pitch with 15 in 1998. ... Career major league grand slams: 1.
2002 GAMES PLAYED BY POSITION (MLB): 1B—60; OF—48; DH—28.

Year	Team (League)	Pos.	G	AB	R	H	2B	3B	HR	RBI	BB	SO	SB-CS	Avg.	OBP	SLG	E	Avg.
			BATTING														FIELDING	
1990—	GC Mets (GCL)	1B	45	152	26	41	8	4	1	19	22	41	2-1	.270	.363	.395	7	.976
1991—	Kingsport (Appl.)	1B	65	218	30	53	9	1	7	42	33	64	1-3	.243	.355	.390	9	.986
1992—	Pittsfield (NY-Penn)	1B	72	260	26	63	15	2	2	40	30	61	4-0	.242	.323	.338	12	.982
1993—	Capital City (S.Atl.)	1B-OF	102	379	50	106	19	3	7	72	52	84	6-1	.280	.368	.401	5	.989
1994—	St. Lucie (FSL)	1B	129	450	52	123	30	2	6	74	58	120	14-9	.273	.360	.389	12	.991
1995—	Binghamton (East.)	1B-3B	135	469	61	115	25	2	10	72	51	104	6-2	.245	.324	.371	10	†.992
—	Norfolk (I.L.)	1B	2	7	0	0	0	0	0	0	1	0	0-0	.000	.125	.000	0	1.000
1996—	Binghamton (East.)	1B-3B	122	436	80	129	24	1	22	76	74	103	7-9	.296	.403	.507	11	.991
—	Norfolk (I.L.)	1B	17	54	7	11	2	0	0	6	6	14	1-1	.204	.279	.241	0	1.000
1997—	Charlotte (I.L.)■	1B	136	461	66	128	40	2	21	93	65	126	1-8	.278	.367	.510	8	.991
1998—	Charlotte (I.L.)	OF-1B	140	497	102	157	*45	4	*35	*124	80	114	9-3	.316	.421	*.634	3	.992
—	Florida (N.L.)	1B	10	15	0	3	1	0	0	3	1	5	0-0	.200	.294	.267	0	1.000
1999—	Boston (A.L.)■	1-DH-O-3	110	381	61	112	33	3	21	73	36	92	0-1	.294	.360	.562	8	.983
—	Pawtucket (I.L.)	DH-1B-OF	9	31	4	9	2	0	1	6	6	8	0-0	.290	.436	.452	1	.971
2000—	Boston (A.L.)	1-DH-O-3	142	495	55	123	32	2	21	76	44	130	1-1	.248	.315	.448	3	.996
2001—	Boston (A.L.)	1B-OF	122	407	54	107	28	3	22	71	53	108	1-0	.263	.350	.509	11	.988
—	Pawtucket (I.L.)	DH	1	4	0	1	0	0	0	0	0	2	0-0	.250	.250	.250	...	...
—	Lowell (NY-Penn)	1B	1	2	0	0	0	0	0	0	1	1	0-0	.000	.333	.000	0	1.000
2002—	Boston (A.L.)	1B-OF-DH	137	444	62	118	24	2	20	78	51	126	2-1	.266	.348	.464	5	.991
American League totals (4 years)			511	1727	232	460	117	10	84	298	184	456	4-3	.266	.342	.492	27	.990
National League totals (1 year)			10	15	0	3	1	0	0	3	1	5	0-0	.200	.294	.267	0	1.000
Major League totals (5 years)			521	1742	232	463	118	10	84	301	185	461	4-3	.266	.341	.490	27	.990

DIVISION SERIES RECORD

RECORDS: Holds single-game record for most at-bats with no hits—6 (October 10, 1999). ... Shares single-game record for most at-bats (nine-inning game)—6 (October 10, 1999).

			BATTING														FIELDING	
Year	**Team (League)**	**Pos.**	**G**	**AB**	**R**	**H**	**2B**	**3B**	**HR**	**RBI**	**BB**	**SO**	**SB-CS**	**Avg.**	**OBP**	**SLG**	**E**	**Avg.**
1999—	Boston (A.L.)	DH-PH-1B	4	16	3	4	2	0	1	3	0	7	0-0	.250	.250	.563	0	1.000

CHAMPIONSHIP SERIES RECORD

			BATTING														FIELDING	
Year	**Team (League)**	**Pos.**	**G**	**AB**	**R**	**H**	**2B**	**3B**	**HR**	**RBI**	**BB**	**SO**	**SB-CS**	**Avg.**	**OBP**	**SLG**	**E**	**Avg.**
1999—	Boston (A.L.)	DH-1B-PH	5	17	2	3	1	0	1	3	1	4	0-0	.176	.222	.412	0	...

DaVANON, JEFF — OF — ANGELS

PERSONAL: Born December 8, 1973, in San Diego. ... 6-0/185. ... Bats both, throws right. ... Full name: Jeffrey Graham DaVanon. ... Son of Jerry DaVanon, infielder with five major league teams (1969-77).
HIGH SCHOOL: Bellaire (Texas).
COLLEGE: San Diego State.
TRANSACTIONS/CAREER NOTES: Selected by Oakland Athletics organization in 26th round of free-agent draft (June 1, 1995). ... Traded by Athletics with P Elvin Nina and OF Nathan Haynes to Anaheim Angels for P Omar Olivares and 2B Randy Velarde (July 29, 1999). ... On disabled list (March 20, 2000-entire season). ... On Salt Lake disabled list (April 14-21, 2001). ... On Salt Lake disabled list (May 25-August 23 and August 29, 2002-remainder of season).
STATISTICAL NOTES: Led California League outfielders with 17 assists in 1997.
2002 GAMES PLAYED BY POSITION (MLB): OF—10; DH—4.

			BATTING														FIELDING	
Year	**Team (League)**	**Pos.**	**G**	**AB**	**R**	**H**	**2B**	**3B**	**HR**	**RBI**	**BB**	**SO**	**SB-CS**	**Avg.**	**OBP**	**SLG**	**E**	**Avg.**
1995—	S. Oregon (N'West)	OF	57	167	29	42	6	2	1	17	34	49	6-5	.251	.376	.329	8	.864
1996—	West Mich. (Midw.)	OF-1B-2B	89	289	43	70	13	4	2	33	49	66	5-7	.242	.353	.336	2	.976
1997—	Visalia (Calif.)	OF	119	408	70	104	17	3	6	38	81	101	23-14	.255	.377	.355	10	.948
1998—	Modesto (Calif.)	OF	84	301	66	101	17	4	5	60	59	69	33-10	.336	.439	.468	13	.902
1999—	Midland (Texas)	OF-DH	100	374	87	128	29	11	11	60	53	68	18-10	.342	.424	.567	7	.960
	—Edmonton (PCL)■	OF-DH	34	132	35	43	8	3	6	19	20	27	11-4	.326	.416	.568	0	1.000
	—Anaheim (A.L.)	OF-DH	7	20	4	4	0	1	1	4	2	7	0-1	.200	.273	.450	0	1.000
2000—	Anaheim (A.L.)								Did not play.									
2001—	Salt Lake (PCL)	OF	69	256	46	80	19	8	10	48	32	57	8-3	.313	.390	.566	1	.992
	—Anaheim (A.L.)	OF-DH	40	88	7	17	2	1	5	9	11	29	1-3	.193	.280	.409	1	.980
2002—	Anaheim (A.L.)	OF-DH	16	30	3	5	3	0	1	4	2	6	1-0	.167	.219	.367	0	1.000
	—Salt Lake (PCL)	OF	25	100	21	33	10	1	5	18	17	24	5-3	.330	.429	.600	2	.962
	—Arizona Angels (Ariz.)	OF	5	15	5	10	6	1	0	4	5	2	2-0	.667	.714	1.200	0	1.000
Major League totals (3 years)			63	138	14	26	5	2	7	17	15	42	2-4	.188	.266	.406	1	.985

DAVEY, TOM — P

PERSONAL: Born September 11, 1973, in Garden City, Mich. ... 6-7/230. ... Throws right, bats right. ... Full name: Thomas Joseph Davey.
HIGH SCHOOL: Plymouth Salem (Canton, Mich.).
JUNIOR COLLEGE: Henry Ford Community College (Mich.).
TRANSACTIONS/CAREER NOTES: Selected by Toronto Blue Jays organization in fifth round of free-agent draft (June 2, 1994). ... Selected by Baltimore Orioles from Blue Jays organization in Rule 5 major league draft (December 9, 1996). ... Returned to Blue Jays organization (March 20, 1997). ... Traded by Blue Jays with P Steve Sinclair to Seattle Mariners for 1B David Segui (July 28, 1999). ... Traded by Mariners with OF/3B John Mabry to San Diego Padres for OF Al Martin (July 31, 2000). ... On disabled list (July 28, 2001-remainder of season). ... On disabled list (March 27-May 15, 2002). ... Released by Padres (September 30, 2002).
CAREER HITTING (MLB): 0-for-0 (.000), 0 R, 0 2B, 0 3B, 0 HR, 0 RBI.

Year	**League**	**W**	**L**	**Pct.**	**ERA**	**G**	**GS**	**CG**	**ShO**	**Sv.-Opp.**	**IP**	**H**	**R**	**ER**	**HR**	**BB-IBB**	**SO**
1994—	Medicine Hat (Pio.)	2	•8	.200	5.12	14	14	0	0	0-...	65.0	76	59	37	3	*59-0	35
1995—	St. Catharines (NY-Penn)	4	3	.571	3.32	7	7	0	0	0-...	38.0	27	19	14	2	21-0	29
	—Hagerstown (S.Atl.)	4	1	.800	3.38	8	8	0	0	0-...	37.1	29	23	14	2	31-0	25
1996—	Hagerstown (S.Atl.)	10	9	.526	3.87	26	26	2	1	0-...	155.2	132	76	67	7	91-0	98
1997—	Dunedin (FSL)	1	3	.250	4.31	7	6	0	0	0-...	39.2	44	21	19	4	15-0	36
	—Knoxville (Sou.)	6	7	.462	5.83	20	16	0	0	0-...	92.2	108	65	60	5	50-0	72
1998—	Knoxville (Sou.)	5	3	.625	3.87	48	9	0	0	16-...	76.2	70	35	33	2	52-3	78
1999—	Toronto (A.L.)	1	1	.500	4.70	29	0	0	0	1-1	44.0	40	28	23	5	26-0	42
	—Syracuse (I.L.)	1	2	.333	3.48	6	6	0	0	0-...	33.2	30	15	13	1	19-0	20
	—Seattle (A.L.)■	1	0	1.000	4.71	16	0	0	0	0-0	21.0	22	13	11	0	14-1	17
2000—	Tacoma (PCL)	8	6	.571	4.61	28	12	0	0	2-...	93.2	104	59	48	10	37-0	77
	—Las Vegas (PCL)■	1	2	.333	4.02	13	0	0	0	0-...	15.2	27	13	7	0	7-0	17
	—San Diego (N.L.)	2	1	.667	0.71	11	0	0	0	0-1	12.2	12	1	1	0	2-0	6
2001—	San Diego (N.L.)	2	4	.333	4.50	39	0	0	0	0-4	38.0	41	22	19	3	17-3	37
2002—	San Diego (N.L.)	1	0	1.000	5.57	19	0	0	0	0-1	21.0	23	14	13	2	11-1	21
A.L. totals (1 year)		2	1	.667	4.71	45	0	0	0	1-1	65.0	62	41	34	5	40-1	59
N.L. totals (3 years)		5	5	.500	4.14	69	0	0	0	0-6	71.2	76	37	33	5	30-4	64
Major League totals (4 years)		7	6	.538	4.41	114	0	0	0	1-7	136.2	138	78	67	10	70-5	123

DAVIS, BEN — C — MARINERS

PERSONAL: Born March 10, 1977, in Chester, Pa. ... 6-4/214. ... Bats both, throws right. ... Full name: Mark Christopher Davis.
HIGH SCHOOL: Malvern (Pa.) Prep.
TRANSACTIONS/CAREER NOTES: Selected by San Diego Padres organization in first round (second pick overall) of free-agent draft (June 3, 1995). ... On San Diego disabled list (August 13-September 1, 2000). ... Traded by Padres for with P Wascar Serrano and SS Alex Arias to Seattle Mariners for P Brett Tomko, C Tom Lampkin and SS Ramon Vazquez (December 11, 2001).

STATISTICAL NOTES: Led Pioneer League catchers with 362 putouts and 412 total chances in 1995. ... Led California League catchers with 992 putouts and 1,109 total chances in 1997. ... Led Southern League catchers with 920 putouts and 1,002 total chances in 1998. ... Career major league grand slams: 3.
2002 GAMES PLAYED BY POSITION (MLB): C—77; 1B—2.

		BATTING														FIELDING	
Year Team (League)	Pos.	G	AB	R	H	2B	3B	HR	RBI	BB	SO	SB-CS	Avg.	OBP	SLG	E	Avg.
1995—Idaho Falls (Pio.)........	C	52	197	36	55	8	3	5	46	17	36	0-0	.279	.338	.426	6	.985
1996—Rancho Cuca. (Calif.) .	C-DH	98	353	35	71	10	1	6	41	31	89	1-1	.201	.264	.286	9	.987
1997—Rancho Cuca. (Calif.) .	C-DH-1B	122	474	67	132	30	1	17	76	28	107	3-1	.278	.320	.454	14	.987
1998—Mobile (Sou.).............	C-DH	116	433	65	124	29	2	14	75	42	60	4-2	.286	.352	.460	6	.994
—San Diego (N.L.)........	C	1	1	0	0	0	0	0	0	0	0	0-0	.000	.000	.000	0	1.000
1999—Las Vegas (PCL)........	C	58	201	27	62	18	1	7	44	24	41	4-1	.308	.384	.512	4	.992
—San Diego (N.L.)........	C	76	266	29	65	14	1	5	30	25	70	2-1	.244	.307	.361	7	.986
2000—Las Vegas (PCL)........	C	59	221	38	58	16	1	7	40	38	43	5-2	.262	.373	.439	7	.986
—San Diego (N.L.)........	C-DH	43	130	12	29	6	0	3	14	14	35	1-1	.223	.297	.338	1	.996
2001—San Diego (N.L.)........	C-1B	138	448	56	107	20	0	11	57	66	112	4-4	.239	.337	.357	9	.990
2002—Seattle (A.L.)■...........	C-1B	80	228	24	59	10	1	7	43	18	58	1-1	.259	.313	.404	1	.998
American League totals (1 year)		80	228	24	59	10	1	7	43	18	58	1-1	.259	.313	.404	1	.998
National League totals (4 years)		258	845	97	201	40	1	19	101	105	217	7-6	.238	.322	.355	17	.990
Major League totals (5 years)		338	1073	121	260	50	2	26	144	123	275	8-7	.242	.320	.365	18	.992

DAVIS, DOUG — P — RANGERS

PERSONAL: Born September 21, 1975, in Sacramento. ... 6-4/190. ... Throws left, bats right. ... Full name: Douglas P. Davis.
HIGH SCHOOL: Northgate (Walnut Creek, Calif.).
JUNIOR COLLEGE: City College of San Francisco.
TRANSACTIONS/CAREER NOTES: Selected by Texas Rangers organization in 10th round of free-agent draft (June 4, 1996). ... On Oklahoma disabled list (July 24, 2002-remainder of season).
CAREER HITTING (MLB): 0-for-3 (.000), 0 R, 0 2B, 0 3B, 0 HR, 0 RBI.

Year League	W	L	Pct.	ERA	G	GS	CG	ShO	Sv.-Opp.	IP	H	R	ER	HR	BB-IBB	SO
1996—Gulf Coast Rangers (GCL)	3	1	.750	1.90	8	7	0	0	0-...	42.2	28	13	9	0	26-1	49
1997—Gulf Coast Rangers (GCL)	3	1	.750	1.71	4	4	0	0	0-...	21.0	14	5	4	0	15-0	27
—Charlotte (FSL)................	5	3	.625	3.10	9	8	1	0	0-...	49.1	29	19	17	2	33-1	52
1998—Charlotte (FSL)................	11	7	.611	3.24	27	27	1	1	0-...	155.1	129	69	56	8	74-0	*173
1999—Tulsa (Texas)..................	4	4	.500	2.42	12	12	1	0	0-...	74.1	65	26	20	9	25-0	79
—Oklahoma (PCL)..............	7	0	1.000	3.00	13	11	0	0	0-...	78.0	77	27	26	4	31-0	74
—Texas (A.L.).....................	0	0	...	33.75	2	0	0	0	0-0	2.2	12	10	10	3	0-0	3
2000—Oklahoma (PCL)..............	8	3	.727	2.84	12	12	2	0	0-...	69.2	62	32	22	8	34-1	53
—Texas (A.L.).....................	7	6	.538	5.38	30	13	1	0	0-3	98.2	109	61	59	14	58-3	66
2001—Texas (A.L.).....................	11	10	.524	4.45	30	30	1	0	0-0	186.0	220	103	92	14	69-1	115
—Oklahoma (PCL)..............	2	0	1.000	2.87	2	2	0	0	0-...	15.2	10	5	5	1	4-0	14
2002—Texas (A.L.).....................	3	5	.375	4.98	10	10	1	1	0-0	59.2	67	36	33	7	22-0	28
—Oklahoma (PCL)..............	4	3	.571	4.99	9	9	0	0	0-...	61.1	70	38	34	7	11-0	48
Major League totals (4 years).....	21	21	.500	5.03	72	53	3	1	0-3	347.0	408	210	194	38	149-4	212

DAVIS, J.J. — OF — PIRATES

PERSONAL: Born October 25, 1978, in Glendora, Calif. ... 6-5/250. ... Bats right, throws right. ... Full name: Jerry C. Davis.
HIGH SCHOOL: Baldwin Park (Calif.).
TRANSACTIONS/CAREER NOTES: Selected by Pittsburgh Pirates organization in first round (eighth pick overall) of free-agent draft (June 3, 1997). ... On Altoona disabled list (June 22-August 23, 2001). ... On Altoona disabled list (April 9-May 13, 2002).
2002 GAMES PLAYED BY POSITION (MLB): OF—4.

		BATTING														FIELDING	
Year Team (League)	Pos.	G	AB	R	H	2B	3B	HR	RBI	BB	SO	SB-CS	Avg.	OBP	SLG	E	Avg.
1997—GC Pirates (GCL)........	OF	45	165	19	42	10	2	1	18	14	44	0-0	.255	.315	.358	0	1.000
—Erie (NY-Penn)...........	DH	4	13	1	1	0	0	0	0	0	4	0-0	.077	.077	.077	...	...
1998—Augusta (S.Atl.)..........	OF	30	106	11	21	6	0	4	11	3	24	1-1	.198	.220	.368	3	.923
—Erie (NY-Penn)...........	OF	52	196	25	53	12	2	8	39	20	54	4-1	.270	.341	.474	7	.932
1999—Hickory (S.Atl.)...........	OF	86	317	58	84	26	1	19	65	44	99	2-5	.265	.360	.533	4	.950
2000—Lynchburg (Caro.)......	OF	130	485	77	118	36	1	20	80	52	171	9-4	.243	.319	.445	18	.925
2001—Altoona (East.)...........	OF	67	228	21	57	13	3	4	26	21	79	2-5	.250	.317	.386	0	1.000
—GC Pirates (GCL)........	OF	4	17	3	8	1	0	2	6	1	2	0-0	.471	.500	.882	1	.667
2002—Altoona (East.)...........	OF	101	348	51	100	17	3	20	62	33	101	7-4	.287	.351	.526	6	.971
—Pittsburgh (N.L.)........	OF	9	10	1	1	0	0	0	0	0	4	0-0	.100	.182	.100	0	1.000
Major League totals (1 year)		9	10	1	1	0	0	0	0	0	4	0-0	.100	.182	.100	0	1.000

DAVIS, JASON — P — INDIANS

PERSONAL: Born May 8, 1980, in Chattanooga, Tenn. ... 6-6/195. ... Throws right, bats right. ... Full name: Jason T. Davis.
JUNIOR COLLEGE: Cleveland State Junior College.
TRANSACTIONS/CAREER NOTES: Selected by Cleveland Indians organization in 21st round of free-agent draft (June 5, 1999).
CAREER HITTING (MLB): 0-for-0 (.000), 0 R, 0 2B, 0 3B, 0 HR, 0 RBI.

Year League	W	L	Pct.	ERA	G	GS	CG	ShO	Sv.-Opp.	IP	H	R	ER	HR	BB-IBB	SO
2000—Burlington (Appl.)............	4	4	.500	4.40	10	10	0	0	0-...	45.0	48	27	22	5	16-0	35
2001—Columbus (S.Atl.)..............	14	6	.700	2.70	27	27	1	1	0-...	160.0	147	72	48	9	51-1	115
2002—Kinston (Caro.).................	3	6	.333	4.15	17	17	1	1	0-...	99.2	107	64	46	7	31-2	68
—Akron (East.).....................	6	2	.750	3.51	10	10	0	0	0-...	59.0	63	26	23	2	16-0	45
—Cleveland (A.L.)...............	1	0	1.000	1.84	3	2	0	0	0-0	14.2	12	3	3	1	4-0	11
Major League totals (1 year).......	1	0	1.000	1.84	3	2	0	0	0-0	14.2	12	3	3	1	4-0	11

DAVIS, KANE — P

PERSONAL: Born June 25, 1975, in Ripley, W.Va. ... 6-3/194. ... Throws right, bats right. ... Full name: Kane Thomas Davis.
HIGH SCHOOL: Spencer (W.Va.).
TRANSACTIONS/CAREER NOTES: Selected by Pittsburgh Pirates organization in 13th round of free-agent draft (June 3, 1993). ... On Pittsburgh disabled list (March 22-May 1, 1998). ... On Carolina disabled list (May 17-June 6, 1998). ... On Nashville disabled list (August 25-September 2, 1999). ... Granted free agency (October 15, 1999). ... Signed by Cleveland Indians organization (December 22, 1999). ... On Buffalo disabled list (April 7-24, 2000). ... Traded by Indians with P Paul Rigdon, 1B/OF Richie Sexson and a player to be named later to Milwaukee Brewers for P Bob Wickman, P Steve Woodard and P Jason Bere (July 28, 2000); Brewers acquired 2B Marcos Scutaro to complete deal (August 30, 2000). ... Traded by Brewers with P Juan Acevedo and IF Jose Flores to Colorado Rockies for P Mark Leiter, P Mike DeJean and 2B/SS Elvis Pena (April 4, 2001). ... On Colorado disabled list (July 8-August 6, 2001); included rehabilitation assignment to Colorado Springs (July 27-August 6). ... Traded by Rockies to New York Mets for P Corey Brittan (February 21, 2002). ... On New York disabled list (May 13, 2002-remainder of season); included rehabilitation assignment to Norfolk (May 23-24). ... Granted free agency (October 15, 2002).
CAREER HITTING (MLB): 0-for-6 (.000), 0 R, 0 2B, 0 3B, 0 HR, 0 RBI.

Year League	W	L	Pct.	ERA	G	GS	CG	ShO	Sv.-Opp.	IP	H	R	ER	HR	BB-IBB	SO
1993— Gulf Coast Pirates (GCL)	0	4	.000	7.07	11	4	0	0	0-...	28.0	34	30	22	0	19-1	24
1994— Welland (NY-Penn)	5	5	.500	2.65	15	•15	0	0	0-...	98.1	90	36	29	4	32-1	74
1995— Augusta (S.Atl.)	12	6	.667	3.75	26	25	1	0	0-...	139.1	136	73	58	4	43-0	78
1996— Lynchburg (Caro.)	11	9	.550	4.29	26	26	3	1	0-...	157.1	160	84	75	12	56-0	116
1997— Carolina (Sou.)	0	3	.000	3.77	6	6	0	0	0-...	28.2	22	17	12	2	16-1	23
1998— Augusta (S.Atl.)	0	0	...	6.00	2	2	0	0	0-...	9.0	8	6	6	0	3-0	6
— Carolina (Sou.)	1	11	.083	9.24	18	16	0	0	0-...	74.0	102	84	76	12	38-2	39
1999— Altoona (East.)	4	6	.400	3.78	16	16	0	0	0-...	95.1	97	51	40	5	41-1	53
— Nashville (PCL)	3	2	.600	6.75	12	9	0	0	0-...	49.1	65	38	37	8	17-1	31
2000— Akron (East.)■	0	1	.000	2.70	5	5	0	0	0-...	20.0	17	7	6	2	5-0	13
— Buffalo (I.L.)	2	0	1.000	4.20	6	4	0	0	0-...	30.0	30	16	14	2	12-0	19
— Cleveland (A.L.)	0	3	.000	14.73	5	2	0	0	0-0	11.0	20	21	18	3	8-0	2
— Milwaukee (N.L.)■	0	0	...	6.75	3	0	0	0	0-0	4.0	7	3	3	1	5-0	2
— Indianapolis (I.L.)	1	1	.500	3.54	4	4	0	0	0-...	20.1	19	8	8	2	7-0	12
2001— Colorado (N.L.)■	2	4	.333	4.35	57	0	0	0	0-5	68.1	66	36	33	11	32-4	47
— Colorado Springs (PCL)	0	0	...	3.60	4	0	0	0	0-...	5.0	5	2	2	0	3-1	7
2002— New York (N.L.)■	1	1	.500	7.07	16	0	0	0	0-0	14.0	15	11	11	2	11-2	24
— Norfolk (I.L.)	0	0	...	0.00	1	0	0	0	0-...	1.0	1	0	0	0	0-0	2
A.L. totals (1 year)	0	3	.000	14.73	5	2	0	0	0-0	11.0	20	21	18	3	8-0	2
N.L. totals (3 years)	3	5	.375	4.90	76	0	0	0	0-5	86.1	88	50	47	14	48-6	73
Major League totals (3 years)	3	8	.273	6.01	81	2	0	0	0-5	97.1	108	71	65	17	56-6	75

DAWKINS, GOOKIE — SS — REDS

PERSONAL: Born May 12, 1979, in Newberry, S.C. ... 6-1/180. ... Bats right, throws right. ... Full name: Travis Sentell Dawkins.
HIGH SCHOOL: Newberry (S.C.).
TRANSACTIONS/CAREER NOTES: Selected by Cincinnati Reds organization in second round of free-agent draft (June 3, 1997). ... On Louisville disabled list (August 1-8, 2000). ... On disabled list (April 5-12 and April 28-May 9, 2001).
STATISTICAL NOTES: Led Pioneer League shortstops with 118 putouts, 216 assists and 368 total chances in 1997.
MISCELLANEOUS: Member of 2000 U.S. Olympic baseball team.
2002 GAMES PLAYED BY POSITION (MLB): SS—21; 2B—3.

								BATTING								FIELDING	
Year Team (League)	Pos.	G	AB	R	H	2B	3B	HR	RBI	BB	SO	SB-CS	Avg.	OBP	SLG	E	Avg.
1997— Billings (Pio.)	SS	70	253	47	61	5	0	4	37	30	38	16-6	.241	.315	.308	34	.908
1998— Burlington (Midw.)	SS	102	367	52	97	7	6	1	30	37	60	37-10	.264	.332	.324	36	.925
1999— Rockford (Midw.)	SS	76	305	56	83	10	6	8	32	35	38	38-13	.272	.346	.423	17	.950
— Chattanooga (Sou.)	SS	32	129	24	47	7	0	2	13	14	17	15-5	.364	.427	.465	3	.979
— Cincinnati (N.L.)	SS	7	7	1	1	0	0	0	0	0	4	0-0	.143	.250	.143	0	1.000
2000— Chattanooga (Sou.)	SS-2B	95	368	54	85	20	6	6	31	40	71	22-10	.231	.310	.367	19	.962
— Cincinnati (N.L.)	SS	14	41	5	9	2	0	0	3	2	7	0-0	.220	.256	.268	2	.965
2001— Chattanooga (Sou.)	SS	104	394	59	89	16	3	8	40	32	88	14-4	.226	.285	.343	16	*.964
2002— Cincinnati (N.L.)	SS-2B	31	48	2	6	2	0	0	0	6	21	2-1	.125	.222	.167	4	.927
— Chattanooga (Sou.)	SS-2B	40	155	21	42	10	1	1	12	25	28	5-5	.271	.372	.368	6	.968
— Louisville (I.L.)	SS-2B	47	167	14	42	5	2	0	8	12	34	2-3	.251	.302	.305	4	.983
Major League totals (3 years)		52	96	8	16	4	0	0	3	8	32	2-1	.167	.238	.208	6	.949

DAWLEY, JOEY — P — BRAVES

PERSONAL: Born September 19, 1971, in Riverside, Calif. ... 6-4/205. ... Throws right, bats right. ... Full name: Joseph Thomas Dawley.
JUNIOR COLLEGE: Riverside (Calif.) Community College.
TRANSACTIONS/CAREER NOTES: Selected by Baltimore Orioles organization in 28th round of free-agent draft (June 1, 1992). ... Released by Orioles (July 9, 1995). ... Signed by Palm Springs, Western League (July 1995). ... Signed by Chico, Western League (May 1997). ... Signed by Atlanta Braves organization (September 19, 1998). ... Granted free agency (October 15, 1999). ... Re-signed by Braves organization (November 9, 1999). ... On disabled list (April 6, 2000-entire season). ... Granted free agency (October 15, 2000). ... Re-signed by Braves organization (November 1, 2000).
CAREER HITTING (MLB): 0-for-0 (.000), 0 R, 0 2B, 0 3B, 0 HR, 0 RBI.

Year League	W	L	Pct.	ERA	G	GS	CG	ShO	Sv.-Opp.	IP	H	R	ER	HR	BB-IBB	SO
1993— Bluefield (Appl.)	3	1	.750	3.52	20	0	0	0	3-...	30.2	34	20	12	1	14-3	30
1994— Bluefield (Appl.)	1	2	.333	5.70	11	2	0	0	2-...	23.2	20	18	15	2	18-0	18
— Albany (S.Atl.)	0	0	...	6.14	5	0	0	0	0-...	7.1	7	6	5	0	7-1	4
1995— Frederick (Caro.)	1	2	.333	6.34	24	0	0	0	1-...	32.2	41	28	23	4	22-1	29
— Palm Springs (West.)■	1	0	1.000	3.86	15	0	0	0	0-...	28.0	28	14	12	2	9-0	20

Year	League	W	L	Pct.	ERA	G	GS	CG	ShO	Sv.-Opp.	IP	H	R	ER	HR	BB-IBB	SO
1996—	Palm Springs (West.)	2	1	.667	1.59	27	0	0	0	4-...	34.0	26	14	6	3	18-1	29
1997—	Chico (West.)■	1	4	.200	4.39	41	0	0	0	14-...	41.0	42	24	20	2	18-2	51
1998—	Chico (West.)	2	4	.333	3.35	45	0	0	0	26-...	43.0	43	22	16	2	27-2	36
1999—	Greenville (Sou.)■	5	3	.625	4.03	26	11	0	0	0-...	91.2	76	54	41	5	37-3	89
	—Richmond (I.L.)	0	3	.000	5.18	7	7	1	0	0-...	40.0	43	26	23	5	12-0	31
2000—										Did not play.							
2001—	Myrtle Beach (Caro.)	1	0	1.000	1.80	5	0	0	0	0-...	10.0	4	2	2	0	0-0	16
	—Richmond (I.L.)	1	0	1.000	2.84	3	0	0	0	0-...	6.1	3	2	2	1	1-0	5
	—Greenville (Sou.)	7	5	.583	3.04	22	21	1	0	0-...	127.1	95	50	43	15	46-0	130
2002—	Richmond (I.L.)	9	7	.563	2.63	24	23	1	1	0-...	140.1	113	44	41	10	36-0	136
	—Atlanta (N.L.)	0	0	...	0.00	1	0	0	0	0-0	.1	0	0	0	0	0-0	1
Major League totals (1 year)		0	0	...	0.00	1	0	0	0	0-0	.1	0	0	0	0	0-0	1

DAY, ZACH — P — EXPOS

PERSONAL: Born June 15, 1978, in Cincinnati. ... 6-4/185. ... Throws right, bats right. ... Full name: Stephen Zachary Day.

HIGH SCHOOL: La Salle (Cincinnati).

TRANSACTIONS/CAREER NOTES: Selected by New York Yankees organization in fifth round of free-agent draft (June 4, 1996). ... Traded by Yankees to Cleveland Indians with P Jake Westbrook (July 24, 2000), completing deal in which Indians traded OF David Justice to Yankees for OF Ricky Ledee and two players to be named later (June 29, 2000). ... Traded by Indians to Montreal Expos for OF Milton Bradley (July 31, 2001).

CAREER HITTING (MLB): 1-for-6 (.167), 1 R, 0 2B, 0 3B, 0 HR, 0 RBI.

Year	League	W	L	Pct.	ERA	G	GS	CG	ShO	Sv.-Opp.	IP	H	R	ER	HR	BB-IBB	SO
1996—	Gulf Coast Yankees (GCL)	5	2	.714	5.61	7	5	0	0	0-...	33.2	41	26	21	3	3-0	23
1997—	Oneonta (NY-Penn)	7	2	.778	2.15	14	14	0	0	0-...	92.0	82	26	22	2	23-0	92
1998—	Tampa (FSL)	5	8	.385	5.49	18	17	0	0	0-...	100.0	142	89	61	5	32-4	69
	—Greensboro (S.Atl.)	1	2	.333	2.75	7	6	1	0	0-...	36.0	35	22	11	1	6-0	37
1999—	Gulf Coast Yankees (GCL)	1	1	.500	3.78	5	4	0	0	0-...	16.2	20	10	7	1	4-0	17
	—Greensboro (S.Atl.)	0	1	.000	2.25	2	2	0	0	0-...	8.0	14	11	2	0	1-0	4
2000—	Greensboro (S.Atl.)	9	3	.750	1.90	13	13	1	1	0-...	85.1	72	29	18	6	31-0	101
	—Tampa (FSL)	2	4	.333	4.19	7	7	0	0	0-...	34.1	33	22	16	2	15-1	36
	—Akron (East.)■	4	2	.667	3.52	8	8	0	0	0-...	46.0	38	20	18	1	21-0	43
2001—	Akron (East.)	9	10	.474	3.10	22	22	2	0	0-...	136.2	123	57	47	8	45-1	94
	—Buffalo (I.L.)	1	0	1.000	1.50	1	1	0	0	0-...	6.0	3	1	1	0	1-0	4
	—Ottawa (I.L.)■	2	2	.500	7.43	6	5	0	0	0-...	26.2	38	23	22	2	8-0	15
2002—	Ottawa (I.L.)	5	6	.455	3.50	17	16	1	0	0-...	90.0	77	38	35	5	32-0	68
	—Montreal (N.L.)	4	1	.800	3.62	19	2	0	0	1-2	37.1	28	18	15	3	15-2	25
Major League totals (1 year)		4	1	.800	3.62	19	2	0	0	1-2	37.1	28	18	15	3	15-2	25

DE LOS SANTOS, LUIS — P — DEVIL RAYS

PERSONAL: Born November 1, 1977, in Santo Domingo, Dominican Republic. ... 6-2/216. ... Throws right, bats right.

TRANSACTIONS/CAREER NOTES: Signed as non-drafted free agent by New York Yankees organization (February 11, 1995). ... On Norwich disabled list (April 23-May 22, 1998). ... On Columbus disabled list (May 6-July 5 and August 5-September 14, 1999). ... On New York disabled list (September 16, 1999-remainder of season). ... On New York disabled list (April 2, 2000-entire season); included rehabilitation assignment to Gulf Coast Yankees (June 24-July 13). ... On Norwich disabled list (April 5-July 2, 2001). ... Released by Yankees (July 2, 2001). ... Signed by Tampa Bay Devil Rays organization (November 7, 2001). ... On Orlando disabled list (April 4-28, 2002).

STATISTICAL NOTES: Pitched 4-0 no-hit victory against Batavia (July 28, 1996).

CAREER HITTING (MLB): 0-for-0 (.000), 0 R, 0 2B, 0 3B, 0 HR, 0 RBI.

Year	League	W	L	Pct.	ERA	G	GS	CG	ShO	Sv.-Opp.	IP	H	R	ER	HR	BB-IBB	SO
1995—	Dominican Yankees (DSL)	3	4	.429	3.92	12	11	0	0	0-...	64.0	64	41	28	...	27-...	40
	—Gulf Coast Yankees (GCL)	0	0	...	0.00	2	0	0	0	0-...	5.0	5	2	0	0	2-0	6
1996—	Greensboro (S.Atl.)	4	1	.800	4.83	7	6	0	0	0-...	31.2	39	17	17	4	11-0	21
	—Oneonta (NY-Penn)	4	4	.500	3.72	10	10	3	*2	0-...	58.0	44	28	24	3	21-0	62
1997—	Greensboro (S.Atl.)	5	6	.455	3.05	14	14	1	0	0-...	88.2	91	45	30	3	13-0	62
	—Tampa (FSL)	5	0	1.000	2.34	10	10	0	0	0-...	61.2	49	19	16	4	8-0	39
	—Norwich (East.)	1	1	.500	2.52	4	4	0	0	0-...	25.0	23	9	7	4	7-0	15
1998—	Norwich (East.)	2	6	.250	4.90	13	13	2	0	0-...	79.0	97	49	43	4	23-2	51
	—Tampa (FSL)	4	2	.667	4.18	10	10	1	0	0-...	66.2	69	40	31	2	11-0	33
1999—	Columbus (I.L.)	6	3	.667	4.77	12	12	0	0	0-...	66.0	81	42	35	11	24-0	45
	—Gulf Coast Yankees (GCL)	0	0	...	0.00	2	2	0	0	0-...	8.0	5	0	0	0	0-0	7
2000—	Gulf Coast Yankees (GCL)	2	0	1.000	3.00	4	3	0	0	0-...	15.0	15	5	5	0	6-0	19
2001—									Did not play—injured.								
2002—	Durham (I.L.)■	9	2	.818	*2.42	24	16	1	1	0-...	115.1	105	38	31	8	21-0	68
	—Tampa Bay (A.L.)	0	3	.000	11.57	3	3	0	0	0-0	14.0	24	19	18	5	4-0	7
Major League totals (1 year)		0	3	.000	11.57	3	3	0	0	0-0	14.0	24	19	18	5	4-0	7

DE LOS SANTOS, VALERIO — P — BREWERS

PERSONAL: Born October 6, 1972, in Las Matas, Dominican Republic. ... 6-2/206. ... Throws left, bats left. ... Full name: Valerio Lorenzo De Los Santos.

TRANSACTIONS/CAREER NOTES: Signed as non-drafted free agent by Milwaukee Brewers organization (January 26, 1993). ... On El Paso disabled list (April 27-May 4, 1998). ... On Milwaukee disabled list (April 29-September 23, 1999). ... On disabled list (April 4, 2001-remainder of season).

STATISTICAL NOTES: Tied for Arizona League lead with two intentional bases on balls issued in 1995.

CAREER HITTING (MLB): 0-for-8 (.000), 0 R, 0 2B, 0 3B, 0 HR, 0 RBI.

Year League	W	L	Pct.	ERA	G	GS	CG	ShO	Sv.-Opp.	IP	H	R	ER	HR	BB-IBB	SO
1993— Dominican Brewers (DSL)	1	7	.125	6.50	19	6	1	0	0-...	63.2	91	57	46	...	37-...	39
1994— Dominican Brewers (DSL)	7	6	.538	3.69	17	•16	1	1	0-...	90.1	90	52	37	...	35-...	50
1995— Arizona Brewers (Ariz.)	4	6	.400	2.20	14	12	0	0	0-...	82.0	*81	34	20	3	12-2	57
1996— Beloit (Midw.)	10	8	.556	3.55	33	23	•5	•1	4-...	164.2	164	83	65	11	59-4	137
1997— El Paso (Texas)	6	10	.375	5.75	26	16	1	0	2-...	114.1	146	83	73	6	38-2	61
1998— El Paso (Texas)	6	2	.750	3.91	42	4	0	0	10-...	66.2	81	34	29	2	25-1	62
— Milwaukee (N.L.)	0	0	...	2.91	13	0	0	0	0-0	21.2	11	7	7	4	2-0	18
— Louisville (I.L.)	0	0	...	3.60	5	0	0	0	0-...	5.0	4	2	2	0	0-0	0
1999— Milwaukee (N.L.)	0	1	.000	6.48	7	0	0	0	0-0	8.1	12	6	6	1	7-0	5
2000— Milwaukee (N.L.)	2	3	.400	5.13	66	2	0	0	0-1	73.2	72	43	42	15	33-7	70
2001— Milwaukee (N.L.)	0	0	...	9.00	1	0	0	0	0-0	1.0	1	1	1	0	1-0	1
2002— Indianapolis (I.L.)	1	0	1.000	0.00	2	0	0	0	0-...	2.0	1	0	0	0	1-0	5
— Milwaukee (N.L.)	2	3	.400	3.12	51	0	0	0	0-0	57.2	42	21	20	4	26-3	38
Major League totals (5 years)	4	7	.364	4.21	138	2	0	0	0-1	162.1	138	78	76	24	69-10	132

DeHAAN, KORY — OF — PADRES

PERSONAL: Born July 16, 1976, in Pella, Iowa. ... 6-2/187. ... Bats left, throws right. ... Full name: Korwin Jay DeHaan.
HIGH SCHOOL: Pella (Iowa) Christian.
COLLEGE: Morningside College (Iowa).
TRANSACTIONS/CAREER NOTES: Selected by Pittsburgh Pirates organization in seventh round of free-agent draft (June 3, 1997). ... Selected by San Diego Padres from Pirates organization in Rule 5 major league draft (December 13, 1999). ... On San Diego disabled list (April 1-24, 2000); included rehabilitation assignments to Rancho Cucamonga (April 11-15) and Las Vegas (April 16-24).
2002 GAMES PLAYED BY POSITION (MLB): OF—9.

		BATTING														FIELDING	
Year Team (League)	Pos.	G	AB	R	H	2B	3B	HR	RBI	BB	SO	SB-CS	Avg.	OBP	SLG	E	Avg.
1997— Erie (NY-Penn)	OF	58	205	43	49	8	6	1	18	38	43	14-9	.239	.357	.351	1	.991
1998— Augusta (S.Atl.)	OF	132	475	85	149	*39	8	8	75	69	114	33-13	.314	.404	.480	4	.984
1999— Lynchburg (Caro.)	OF	78	295	55	96	19	5	7	42	36	63	32-10	.325	.405	.495	4	.976
— Altoona (East.)	OF	47	190	26	51	13	2	3	24	11	46	14-6	.268	.311	.405	1	.989
2000— Rancho Cuca. (Calif.)■	OF	4	14	2	3	1	0	1	1	1	4	0-0	.214	.267	.500	0	1.000
— Las Vegas (PCL)	OF	10	41	7	12	4	0	0	3	2	11	3-0	.293	.333	.390	0	1.000
— San Diego (N.L.)	OF-DH	90	103	19	21	7	0	2	13	5	39	4-2	.204	.239	.330	0	1.000
2001— Portland (PCL)	OF	87	304	35	77	9	5	7	28	20	71	12-9	.253	.303	.385	2	.990
— Mobile (Sou.)	OF	42	159	29	47	8	2	4	23	22	27	12-4	.296	.382	.447	1	.988
2002— Portland (PCL)	OF	120	442	64	125	31	14	2	39	31	96	23-9	.283	.340	.430	3	.990
— San Diego (N.L.)	OF	12	11	1	1	0	0	0	0	0	6	0-0	.091	.091	.091	0	1.000
Major League totals (2 years)		102	114	20	22	7	0	2	13	5	45	4-2	.193	.225	.307	0	1.000

DeJEAN, MIKE — P — BREWERS

PERSONAL: Born September 28, 1970, in Baton Rouge, La. ... 6-4/219. ... Throws right, bats right. ... Full name: Michel Dwain DeJean.
HIGH SCHOOL: Walker (La.).
JUNIOR COLLEGE: Mississippi Delta Community College.
COLLEGE: Livingston (La.).
TRANSACTIONS/CAREER NOTES: Selected by New York Yankees organization in 24th round of free-agent draft (June 1, 1992). ... On disabled list (June 4-July 21 and July 26, 1993-remainder of season). ... Traded by Yankees with a player to be named later to Colorado Rockies for C Joe Girardi (November 20, 1995); Rockies acquired P Steve Shoemaker to complete deal (December 6, 1995). ... On Colorado disabled list (July 18-August 8, 1997); included rehabilitation assignment to New Haven (July 30-August 8). ... On disabled list (September 2, 1998-remainder of season). ... On Colorado disabled list (August 14-September 1, 1999); included rehabilitation assignment to Colorado Springs (August 30-September 1). ... On Colorado disabled list (March 29-April 28 and July 25-August 15, 2000); included rehabilitation assignment to Colorado Springs (April 6-28 and August 10-13). ... Traded by Rockies with P Mark Leiter and 2B/SS Elvis Pena to Milwaukee Brewers for P Juan Acevedo, P Kane Davis and IF Jose Flores (April 4, 2001).
CAREER HITTING (MLB): 1-for-16 (.063), 0 R, 1 2B, 0 3B, 0 HR, 0 RBI.

Year League	W	L	Pct.	ERA	G	GS	CG	ShO	Sv.-Opp.	IP	H	R	ER	HR	BB-IBB	SO
1992— Oneonta (NY-Penn)	0	0	...	0.44	20	0	0	0	16-...	20.2	12	3	1	1	3-0	20
1993— Greensboro (S.Atl.)	2	3	.400	5.00	20	0	0	0	9-...	18.0	22	12	10	1	8-2	16
1994— Tampa (FSL)	0	2	.000	2.38	34	0	0	0	16-...	34.0	39	15	9	1	13-0	22
— Albany (East.)	0	2	.000	4.38	16	0	0	0	4-...	24.2	22	14	12	1	15-3	13
1995— Norwich (East.)	5	5	.500	2.99	59	0	0	0	20-...	78.1	58	29	26	5	34-2	57
1996— Colorado Springs (PCL)■	0	2	.000	5.13	30	0	0	0	1-...	40.1	52	24	23	3	21-3	31
— New Haven (East.)	0	0	...	3.22	16	0	0	0	11-...	22.1	20	9	8	2	8-0	12
1997— Colorado Springs (PCL) ...	0	1	.000	5.40	10	0	0	0	4-...	10.0	17	6	6	0	7-1	9
— Colorado (N.L.)	5	0	1.000	3.99	55	0	0	0	2-4	67.2	74	34	30	4	24-2	38
— New Haven (East.)	0	1	.000	6.00	2	0	0	0	0-...	3.0	3	2	2	0	2-0	2
1998— Colorado (N.L.)	3	1	.750	3.03	59	1	0	0	2-3	74.1	78	29	25	4	24-1	27
1999— Colorado (N.L.)	2	4	.333	8.41	56	0	0	0	0-4	61.0	83	61	57	13	32-8	31
— Colorado Springs (PCL) ...	0	0	...	0.00	1	0	0	0	0-...	1.0	1	0	0	0	0-0	0
2000— Colorado Springs (PCL) ...	1	1	.500	2.51	12	0	0	0	5-...	14.1	15	4	4	0	4-0	12
— Colorado (N.L.)	4	4	.500	4.89	54	0	0	0	0-4	53.1	54	31	29	9	30-6	34
2001— Milwaukee (N.L.)■	4	2	.667	2.77	75	0	0	0	2-4	84.1	75	31	26	4	39-7	68
2002— Milwaukee (N.L.)	1	5	.167	3.12	68	0	0	0	27-30	75.0	66	28	26	7	39-8	65
Major League totals (6 years)	19	16	.543	4.18	367	1	0	0	33-49	415.2	430	214	193	41	188-32	263

DELGADO, CARLOS — 1B — BLUE JAYS

PERSONAL: Born June 25, 1972, in Aguadilla, Puerto Rico. ... 6-3/230. ... Bats left, throws right. ... Full name: Carlos Juan Delgado.
HIGH SCHOOL: Jose de Diego (Aguadilla, Puerto Rico).
TRANSACTIONS/CAREER NOTES: Signed as non-drafted free agent by Toronto Blue Jays organization (October 9, 1988). ... On Toronto disabled list (March 15-April 24, 1998); included rehabilitation assignments to Dunedin (April 17-19) and Syracuse (April 20-24). ... On disabled list (August 9-25, 2002).

HONORS: Named Florida State League Most Valuable Player (1992). ... Named Southern League Most Valuable Player (1993). ... Named first baseman on The Sporting News A.L. Silver Slugger team (1999 and 2000). ... Named Major League Player of the Year by The Sporting News (2000). ... Named first baseman on The Sporting News A.L. All-Star team (2000).

STATISTICAL NOTES: Led New York-Pennsylvania League catchers with 471 putouts, 62 assists, 540 total chances and six double plays in 1990. ... Led South Atlantic League catchers with 100 assists and 29 passed balls in 1991. ... Led Florida State League with 281 total bases and 11 intentional bases on balls received in 1992. ... Led Florida State League catchers with 684 putouts and 784 total chances in 1992. ... Led Southern League catchers with 683 putouts, 103 assists and 800 total chances in 1993. ... Led International League with seven intentional bases on balls received in 1995. ... Had 19-game hitting streak (May 21-June 9, 1998). ... Hit three home runs in one game (August 4, 1998; August 6, 1999; April 4, 2001; and April 20, 2001). ... Led A.L. first baseman with 1,306 putouts and 134 double plays in 1999. ... Had 22-game hitting streak (June 4-29, 2000). ... Led A.L. first baseman with 1,416 putouts, 1,511 total chances and 157 double plays in 2000. ... Led A.L. with 378 total bases in 2000. ... Tied for A.L. lead in being hit by pitch with 15 in 2000. ... Led A.L. first basemen with 1,231 putouts and 1,338 total chances in 2002. ... Career major league grand slams: 7.

MISCELLANEOUS: Holds Toronto Blue Jays all-time records for most home runs (262) and most runs batted in (814).

2002 GAMES PLAYED BY POSITION (MLB): 1B—140; DH—3.

		BATTING														FIELDING	
Year Team (League)	**Pos.**	**G**	**AB**	**R**	**H**	**2B**	**3B**	**HR**	**RBI**	**BB**	**SO**	**SB-CS**	**Avg.**	**OBP**	**SLG**	**E**	**Avg.**
1989—St. Catharines (NY-P)	C	31	89	9	16	5	0	0	11	23	39	0-0	.180	.345	.236	2	.974
1990—St. Catharines (NY-P)	C	67	228	30	64	13	0	6	39	35	65	2-7	.281	.382	.417	7	.987
1991—Myrtle Beach (S.Atl.)	C	132	441	72	126	18	2	18	70	75	97	9-10	.286	.396	.458	19	.976
—Syracuse (I.L.)	C	1	3	0	0	0	0	0	0	0	2	0-0	.000	.000	.000	0	1.000
1992—Dunedin (FSL)	C	133	485	83	*157	•30	2	*30	*100	59	91	2-5	.324	*.402	*.579	11	.986
1993—Knoxville (Sou.)	C	140	468	91	142	28	0	*25	*102	*102	98	10-3	.303	*.430	*.524	*14	.983
—Toronto (A.L.)	DH-C	2	1	0	0	0	0	0	0	1	0	0-0	.000	.500	.000	0	1.000
1994—Toronto (A.L.)	OF-C	43	130	17	28	2	0	9	24	25	46	1-1	.215	.352	.438	2	.967
—Syracuse (I.L.)	DH-C-1B	85	307	52	98	11	0	19	58	42	58	1-0	.319	.404	.541	7	.974
1995—Toronto (A.L.)	OF-DH-1B	37	91	7	15	3	0	3	11	6	26	0-0	.165	.212	.297	0	1.000
—Syracuse (I.L.)	1B-OF	91	333	59	106	23	4	22	74	45	78	0-4	.318	.403	*.610	4	.995
1996—Toronto (A.L.)	DH-1B	138	488	68	132	28	2	25	92	58	139	0-0	.270	.353	.490	4	.983
1997—Toronto (A.L.)	1B-DH	153	519	79	136	42	3	30	91	64	133	0-3	.262	.350	.528	12	.988
1998—Dunedin (FSL)	DH-1B	4	16	4	5	1	0	2	7	2	4	0-0	.313	.389	.750	0	1.000
—Syracuse (I.L.)	1B	2	7	4	4	2	0	1	6	2	0	0-0	.571	.667	1.286	0	1.000
—Toronto (A.L.)	1B-DH	142	530	94	155	43	1	38	115	73	139	3-0	.292	.385	.592	10	.992
1999—Toronto (A.L.)	1B-DH	152	573	113	156	39	0	44	134	86	141	1-1	.272	.377	.571	*14	.990
2000—Toronto (A.L.)	1B	•162	569	115	196	*57	1	41	137	123	104	0-1	.344	.470	.664	13	.991
2001—Toronto (A.L.)	1B	•162	574	102	160	31	1	39	102	111	136	3-0	.279	.408	.540	9	.994
2002—Toronto (A.L.)	1B-DH	143	505	103	140	34	2	33	108	102	126	1-0	.277	.406	.549	12	.991
Major League totals (10 years)		1134	3980	698	1118	279	10	262	814	649	990	9-6	.281	.390	.554	76	.991

ALL-STAR GAME RECORD

	AB	R	H	2B	3B	HR	RBI	BB	SO	SB-CS	Avg.	OBP	SLG	E	Avg.
All-Star Game totals (1 year)	1	0	1	1	0	0	0	0	0	0-0	1.000	1.000	2.000	0	1.000

DELGADO, WILSON — SS/2B — CARDINALS

PERSONAL: Born July 15, 1972, in San Cristobal, Dominican Republic. ... 5-11/165. ... Bats both, throws right. ... Full name: Wilson Duran Delgado.

TRANSACTIONS/CAREER NOTES: Signed as non-drafted free agent by Seattle Mariners organization (October 29, 1992). ... Traded by Mariners with P Shawn Estes to San Francisco Giants for P Salomon Torres (May 21, 1995). ... Traded by Giants to New York Yankees for SS Juan Melo (March 23, 2000). ... Traded by Yankees to Kansas City Royals for SS Nick Ortiz (August 11, 2000). ... Granted free agency (October 9, 2001). ... Signed by St. Louis Cardinals organization (December 23, 2001). ... On Memphis disabled list (June 12-July 29, 2002).

STATISTICAL NOTES: Led Pacific Coast League shortstops with 197 putouts, 547 total chances and 86 double plays in 1997.

2002 GAMES PLAYED BY POSITION (MLB): SS—8.

		BATTING														FIELDING	
Year Team (League)	**Pos.**	**G**	**AB**	**R**	**H**	**2B**	**3B**	**HR**	**RBI**	**BB**	**SO**	**SB-CS**	**Avg.**	**OBP**	**SLG**	**E**	**Avg.**
1993—Dom. Mariners (DSL)	IF	60	171	19	50	8	0	0	26	34	25	5-...	.292	...	.339	16	.938
1994—Ariz. Mariners (Ariz.)	SS-2B	39	149	30	56	5	4	0	10	15	24	13-5	*.376	.436	.463	10	.945
—Appleton (Midw.)	SS	9	31	2	6	0	0	0	0	0	8	0-0	.194	.194	.194	1	.967
1995—Port City (Sou.)	SS	13	41	3	8	4	0	0	1	6	8	0-0	.195	.298	.293	5	.917
—Wisconsin (Midw.)	SS	19	70	13	17	3	0	0	7	3	15	3-0	.243	.274	.286	6	.940
—Burlington (Midw.)■	SS	93	365	52	113	20	3	5	37	32	57	9-9	.310	.368	.422	19	.956
—San Jose (Calif.)	SS	1	2	1	0	0	0	0	0	0	0	0-0	.000	.000	.000	0	1.000
1996—San Jose (Calif.)	SS	121	462	59	124	19	6	2	54	48	89	8-2	.268	.337	.348	24	.957
—Phoenix (PCL)	SS	12	43	1	6	0	1	0	1	3	7	0-1	.140	.196	.186	2	.975
—San Francisco (N.L.)	SS	6	22	3	8	0	0	0	2	1	5	1-0	.364	.440	.364	1	.960
1997—San Francisco (N.L.)	2B-SS	8	7	1	1	1	0	0	0	0	2	0-0	.143	.143	.286	0	1.000
—Phoenix (PCL)	SS-2B	119	416	47	120	22	4	9	59	24	70	9-3	.288	.326	.425	18	.969
1998—Fresno (PCL)	SS	127	512	87	142	22	2	12	63	52	92	9-5	.277	.345	.398	23	.962
—San Francisco (N.L.)	SS	10	12	1	2	1	0	0	1	1	3	0-0	.167	.231	.250	0	1.000
1999—Fresno (PCL)	SS-DH-2B	57	213	28	64	10	3	1	33	18	35	4-2	.300	.355	.390	15	.944
—San Francisco (N.L.)	SS-2B	35	71	7	18	2	1	0	3	5	9	1-0	.254	.312	.310	5	.942
2000—New York (A.L.)■	2B-SS-3B	31	45	6	11	1	0	1	4	5	9	1-0	.244	.314	.333	3	.952
—Kansas City (A.L.)■	2B-SS-3B	33	83	15	22	1	0	0	7	6	17	1-1	.265	.311	.277	1	.993
2001—Omaha (PCL)	2B-3B-SS	76	255	24	63	11	2	4	30	16	43	8-3	.247	.293	.353	11	.963
—Kansas City (A.L.)	SS-3B-2B	14	25	1	3	0	0	0	1	3	10	0-0	.120	.214	.120	0	1.000
2002—Memphis (PCL)■	SS	98	365	31	95	19	2	7	35	23	54	2-5	.260	.309	.381	10	.977
—St. Louis (N.L.)	SS	12	20	2	4	2	0	2	5	0	6	0-0	.200	.200	.600	0	1.000
American League totals (2 years)		78	153	22	36	2	0	1	12	14	36	2-1	.235	.296	.268	4	.982
National League totals (5 years)		71	132	14	33	6	1	2	11	7	25	2-0	.250	.303	.356	6	.958
Major League totals (7 years)		149	285	36	69	8	1	3	23	21	61	4-1	.242	.299	.309	10	.973

DELLUCCI, DAVID — OF — DIAMONDBACKS

PERSONAL: Born October 31, 1973, in Baton Rouge, La. ... 5-11/198. ... Bats left, throws left. ... Full name: David Michael Dellucci. ... Name pronounced duh-LOO-chee.
HIGH SCHOOL: Catholic (Baton Rouge, La.).
COLLEGE: Mississippi.
TRANSACTIONS/CAREER NOTES: Selected by Baltimore Orioles organization in 10th round of free agent draft (June 1, 1995). ... Selected by Arizona Diamondbacks in second round (45th pick overall) of expansion draft (November 18, 1997). ... On disabled list (July 25, 1999-remainder of season). ... On Tucson disabled list (May 8-July 26, 2000). ... On Arizona disabled list (May 3-24, 2002); included rehabilitation assignment to Tucson (May 20-24).
STATISTICAL NOTES: Career major league grand slams: 1.
2002 GAMES PLAYED BY POSITION (MLB): OF—64; DH—3.

		BATTING														FIELDING	
Year Team (League)	Pos.	G	AB	R	H	2B	3B	HR	RBI	BB	SO	SB-CS	Avg.	OBP	SLG	E	Avg.
1995—Bluefield (Appl.)	OF	20	69	11	23	5	1	2	12	6	7	3-1	.333	.390	.522	2	.846
—Frederick (Caro.)	OF	28	96	16	27	3	0	1	10	12	10	1-2	.281	.378	.344	1	.966
1996—Frederick (Caro.)	OF	59	185	33	60	11	1	4	28	38	34	5-6	.324	.438	.459	3	.972
—Bowie (East.)	OF	66	251	27	73	14	1	2	33	28	56	2-7	.291	.363	.378	3	.979
1997—Bowie (East.)	OF-DH	107	385	71	126	29	3	20	55	58	69	11-4	.327	.421	.574	1	.994
—Baltimore (A.L.)	OF-DH	17	27	3	6	1	0	1	3	4	7	0-0	.222	.344	.370	0	1.000
1998—Tucson (PCL)■	OF	17	72	17	22	4	3	1	11	5	8	4-0	.306	.346	.486	0	1.000
—Arizona (N.L.)	OF	124	416	43	108	19	*12	5	51	33	103	3-5	.260	.318	.399	3	.987
1999—Arizona (N.L.)	OF-DH	63	109	27	43	7	1	1	15	11	24	2-0	.394	.463	.505	0	1.000
2000—Arizona (N.L.)	OF	34	50	2	15	3	0	0	2	4	9	0-2	.300	.352	.360	0	1.000
—Tucson (PCL)	OF	33	122	16	28	6	3	3	17	13	15	4-0	.230	.301	.402	2	.966
—Ariz. D-backs (Ariz.)	OF	2	6	0	2	1	0	0	2	0	1	0-0	.333	.333	.500	0	...
—South Bend (Midw.)	OF	2	5	3	1	1	0	0	1	2	0	0-1	.200	.375	.400	0	1.000
2001—Arizona (N.L.)	OF	115	217	28	60	10	2	10	40	22	52	2-1	.276	.349	.479	1	.989
2002—Arizona (N.L.)	OF-DH	97	229	34	56	11	2	7	29	28	55	2-4	.245	.326	.402	3	.967
—Tucson (PCL)	OF	4	15	2	2	1	0	0	1	2	4	0-0	.133	.235	.200	0	1.000
American League totals (1 year)		17	27	3	6	1	0	1	3	4	7	0-0	.222	.344	.370	0	1.000
National League totals (5 years)		433	1021	134	282	50	17	23	137	98	243	9-12	.276	.344	.426	7	.985
Major League totals (6 years)		450	1048	137	288	51	17	24	140	102	250	9-12	.275	.344	.425	7	.986

DIVISION SERIES RECORD

		BATTING														FIELDING	
Year Team (League)	Pos.	G	AB	R	H	2B	3B	HR	RBI	BB	SO	SB-CS	Avg.	OBP	SLG	E	Avg.
2001—Arizona (N.L.)	PH	2	0	0	0	0	0	0	0	0	0	0-0	...	...	...	...	...
2002—Arizona (N.L.)	OF	3	7	1	2	0	0	1	2	0	1	0-0	.286	.286	.714	0	1.000
Division series totals (2 years)		5	7	1	2	0	0	1	2	0	1	0-0	.286	.286	.714	0	1.000

CHAMPIONSHIP SERIES RECORD

		BATTING														FIELDING	
Year Team (League)	Pos.	G	AB	R	H	2B	3B	HR	RBI	BB	SO	SB-CS	Avg.	OBP	SLG	E	Avg.
2001—Arizona (N.L.)	PH	2	2	1	1	0	0	0	0	0	0	0-0	.500	.500	.500	...	...

WORLD SERIES RECORD

NOTES: Member of World Series championship team (2001).

		BATTING														FIELDING	
Year Team (League)	Pos.	G	AB	R	H	2B	3B	HR	RBI	BB	SO	SB-CS	Avg.	OBP	SLG	E	Avg.
2001—Arizona (N.L.)	PR-OF	2	2	0	1	0	0	0	0	0	0	0-0	.500	.500	.500	0	1.000

DEMPSTER, RYAN — P — REDS

PERSONAL: Born May 3, 1977, in Sechelt, B.C. ... 6-3/215. ... Throws right, bats right. ... Full name: Ryan Scott Dempster.
HIGH SCHOOL: Elphinstone (Gibsons, B.C.).
TRANSACTIONS/CAREER NOTES: Selected by Texas Rangers organization in third round of free-agent draft (June 1, 1995). ... Traded by Rangers with a player to be named later to Florida Marlins for P John Burkett (August 8, 1996); Marlins acquired P Rick Helling to complete deal (September 3, 1996). ... Traded by Marlins to Cincinnati Reds for OF Juan Encarnacion, OF/2B Wilton Guerrero and P Ryan Snare (July 11, 2002).
STATISTICAL NOTES: Pitched 3-0 one-hit, complete-game victory against New York Mets (May 7, 2000). ... Led N.L. with 125 earned runs in 2002.
MISCELLANEOUS: Holds Florida Marlins all-time records for most wins (42), most innings pitched (759 2/3) and most strikeouts (628). ... Appeared in one game as pinch runner (1999).
CAREER HITTING (MLB): 22-for-263 (.084), 11 R, 5 2B, 1 3B, 0 HR, 7 RBI.

Year League	W	L	Pct.	ERA	G	GS	CG	ShO	Sv.-Opp.	IP	H	R	ER	HR	BB-IBB	SO
1995—Gulf Coast Rangers (GCL)	3	1	.750	2.36	8	6	1	0	0-...	34.1	34	21	9	1	17-0	37
—Hudson Valley (NY-Penn)	1	0	1.000	3.18	1	1	0	0	0-...	5.2	7	2	2	0	1-0	6
1996—Charleston, S.C. (S.Atl.)	7	11	.389	3.30	23	23	2	0	0-...	144.1	120	71	53	13	58-1	141
—Kane County (Midw.)■	2	1	.667	2.73	4	4	1	1	0-...	26.1	18	10	8	0	18-0	16
1997—Brevard County (FSL)	10	9	.526	4.90	28	26	2	1	0-...	165.1	190	100	90	19	46-1	131
1998—Portland (East.)	4	3	.571	3.22	7	7	0	0	0-...	44.2	34	20	16	8	15-0	33
—Florida (N.L.)	1	5	.167	7.08	14	11	0	0	0-1	54.2	72	47	43	6	38-1	35
—Charlotte (I.L.)	3	1	.750	3.27	5	5	1	0	0-...	33.0	33	14	12	4	12-1	24
1999—Calgary (PCL)	1	1	.500	4.99	5	5	0	0	0-...	30.2	30	17	17	6	10-1	29
—Florida (N.L.)	7	8	.467	4.71	25	25	0	0	0-0	147.0	146	77	77	21	93-2	126
2000—Florida (N.L.)	14	10	.583	3.66	33	33	2	1	0-0	226.1	210	102	92	30	97-7	209
2001—Florida (N.L.)	15	12	.556	4.94	34	34	2	1	0-0	211.1	218	123	116	21	*112-5	171
2002—Florida (N.L.)	5	8	.385	4.79	18	18	3	0	0-0	120.1	126	66	64	12	55-1	87
—Cincinnati (N.L.)■	5	5	.500	6.19	15	15	1	0	0-0	88.2	102	61	§61	16	38-1	66
Major League totals (5 years)	47	48	.495	4.81	139	136	8	2	0-1	848.1	874	476	453	106	433-17	694

ALL-STAR GAME RECORD

	W	L	Pct.	ERA	GS	CG	ShO	Sv.-Opp.	IP	H	R	ER	HR	BB-IBB	SO
All-Star Game totals (0 years)	2000—Selected, did not play.														

DePAULA, SEAN — P

PERSONAL: Born November 7, 1973, in Newton, Mass. ... 6-4/220. ... Throws right, bats right. ... Full name: Sean Michael DePaula.
HIGH SCHOOL: Pinkerton Academy (Derry, N.H.), then Cushing Academy (Ashburnham, Mass.).
COLLEGE: Wake Forest.
TRANSACTIONS/CAREER NOTES: Selected by Boston Red Sox organization in eighth round of free-agent draft (June 3, 1993); did not sign. ... Selected by Cleveland Indians organization in ninth round of free-agent draft (June 4, 1996). ... On Cleveland disabled list (May 28-July 9 and September 8, 2000-remainder of season); included rehabilitation assignment to Akron (June 24-July 9). ... On Buffalo disabled list (August 2-September 6, 2000). ... On disabled list (April 23, 2001-remainder of season). ... Granted free agency (October 15, 2002).
CAREER HITTING (MLB): 0-for-0 (.000), 0 R, 0 2B, 0 3B, 0 HR, 0 RBI.

Year	League	W	L	Pct.	ERA	G	GS	CG	ShO	Sv.-Opp.	IP	H	R	ER	HR	BB-IBB	SO
1996—	Burlington (Appl.)	4	2	.667	3.82	23	0	0	0	1-...	35.1	31	16	15	3	13-0	42
—	Watertown (NY-Penn)	0	0	...	0.00	1	0	0	0	0-...	2.0	0	0	0	0	0-0	5
1997—	Columbus (S.Atl.)	4	5	.444	5.20	29	1	0	0	0-...	71.0	71	56	41	4	43-3	75
—	Watertown (NY-Penn)	1	1	.500	2.84	9	0	0	0	0-...	19.0	21	6	6	1	8-0	17
1998—	Kinston (Caro.)	3	2	.600	2.36	28	1	0	0	1-...	49.2	50	20	13	0	18-3	59
—	Akron (East.)	1	1	.500	4.76	8	1	0	0	0-...	17.0	16	10	9	0	15-0	17
1999—	Kinston (Caro.)	4	2	.667	2.28	23	0	0	0	7-...	51.1	36	17	13	6	17-0	75
—	Akron (East.)	1	0	1.000	3.54	14	0	0	0	1-...	28.0	20	11	11	2	17-0	31
—	Buffalo (I.L.)	0	0	...	0.00	5	0	0	0	2-...	5.0	0	0	0	0	3-0	7
—	Cleveland (A.L.)	0	0	...	4.63	11	0	0	0	0-0	11.2	8	6	6	0	3-0	18
2000—	Buffalo (I.L.)	1	0	1.000	5.54	9	0	0	0	1-...	13.0	16	10	8	1	7-0	11
—	Cleveland (A.L.)	0	0	...	5.94	13	0	0	0	0-2	16.2	20	11	11	3	14-2	16
—	Akron (East.)	0	0	...	1.80	4	0	0	0	0-...	5.0	1	1	1	0	2-0	4
2001—	Buffalo (I.L.)	1	0	1.000	1.04	6	0	0	0	1-...	8.2	2	1	1	0	4-0	6
2002—	Buffalo (I.L.)	2	3	.400	3.95	34	0	0	0	9-...	57.0	55	26	25	6	18-2	53
—	Cleveland (A.L.)	1	1	.500	12.79	5	0	0	0	0-2	6.1	11	9	9	3	3-0	8
Major League totals (3 years)		1	1	.500	6.75	29	0	0	0	0-4	34.2	39	26	26	6	20-2	42

DIVISION SERIES RECORD

Year	League	W	L	Pct.	ERA	G	GS	CG	ShO	Sv.-Opp.	IP	H	R	ER	HR	BB-IBB	SO
1999—	Cleveland (A.L.)	0	0	...	1.80	3	0	0	0	0-0	5.0	2	1	1	0	3-0	5

DeROSA, MARK — SS — BRAVES

PERSONAL: Born February 26, 1975, in Passaic, N.J. ... 6-1/205. ... Bats right, throws right. ... Full name: Mark Thomas DeRosa.
HIGH SCHOOL: Bergen Catholic (Oradell, N.J.).
COLLEGE: Pennsylvania.
TRANSACTIONS/CAREER NOTES: Selected by Atlanta Braves organization in seventh round of free-agent draft (June 4, 1996). ... On Atlanta disabled list (May 18-July 17, 2002); included rehabilitation assignment to Richmond (June 28-July 8) and Myrtle Beach (July 9-17).
STATISTICAL NOTES: Led Northwest League in grounding into double plays with 10 in 1996.
2002 GAMES PLAYED BY POSITION (MLB): 2B—32; SS—19; OF—7; 3B—4.

			BATTING														FIELDING	
Year	Team (League)	Pos.	G	AB	R	H	2B	3B	HR	RBI	BB	SO	SB-CS	Avg.	OBP	SLG	E	Avg.
1996—	Eugene (N'West)	SS	70	255	43	66	13	1	2	28	38	48	3-4	.259	.363	.341	24	.921
1997—	Durham (Caro.)	SS	92	346	51	93	11	3	8	37	25	73	6-8	.269	.332	.387	21	.948
1998—	Greenville (Sou.)	SS	125	461	67	123	26	2	8	49	60	57	7-13	.267	.356	.384	20	*.964
—	Atlanta (N.L.)	SS	5	3	2	1	0	0	0	0	0	1	0-0	.333	.333	.333	0	1.000
1999—	Richmond (I.L.)	SS-DH	105	364	41	99	16	2	1	40	21	49	7-6	.272	.317	.335	20	.951
—	Atlanta (N.L.)	SS	7	8	0	0	0	0	0	0	0	2	0-0	.000	.000	.000	0	1.000
2000—	Richmond (I.L.)	SS-2B-3B	101	370	62	108	22	3	3	35	38	36	13-4	.292	.359	.392	19	.958
—	Atlanta (N.L.)	SS	22	13	9	4	1	0	0	3	2	1	0-0	.308	.400	.385	0	1.000
2001—	Richmond (I.L.)	SS-3B-2B	49	186	31	55	18	0	2	17	17	22	7-3	.296	.351	.425	4	.978
—	Atlanta (N.L.)	S-2-DH-3-O	66	164	27	47	8	0	3	20	12	19	2-1	.287	.350	.390	7	.966
2002—	Atlanta (N.L.)	2B-SS-OF-3B	72	212	24	63	9	2	5	23	12	24	2-3	.297	.339	.429	6	.976
—	Richmond (I.L.)	2B-SS	16	55	9	14	3	0	0	6	5	2	2-0	.255	.339	.309	3	.952
—	Myrtle Beach (Caro.)	2B	2	7	0	0	0	0	0	0	1	1	0-0	.000	.125	.000	1	.889
Major League totals (5 years)			172	400	62	115	18	2	8	46	26	47	4-4	.288	.339	.403	13	.972

DIVISION SERIES RECORD

			BATTING														FIELDING	
Year	Team (League)	Pos.	G	AB	R	H	2B	3B	HR	RBI	BB	SO	SB-CS	Avg.	OBP	SLG	E	Avg.
2001—	Atlanta (N.L.)	SS	1	1	0	1	0	0	0	0	0	0	0-0	1.000	1.000	1.000	0	1.000
2002—	Atlanta (N.L.)	2B	4	7	2	3	1	1	0	3	1	1	0-0	.429	.500	.857	0	1.000
Division series totals (2 years)			5	8	2	4	1	1	0	3	1	1	0-0	.500	.556	.875	0	1.000

CHAMPIONSHIP SERIES RECORD

			BATTING														FIELDING	
Year	Team (League)	Pos.	G	AB	R	H	2B	3B	HR	RBI	BB	SO	SB-CS	Avg.	OBP	SLG	E	Avg.
2001—	Atlanta (N.L.)	PH-SS	4	4	0	0	0	0	0	0	0	0	0-0	.000	.000	.000	0	1.000

DeSHIELDS, DELINO — 2B/OF

PERSONAL: Born January 15, 1969, in Seaford, Del. ... 6-1/180. ... Bats left, throws right. ... Full name: Delino Lamont DeShields. ... Name pronounced duh-LINE-oh.
HIGH SCHOOL: Seaford (Del.).
COLLEGE: Villanova.
TRANSACTIONS/CAREER NOTES: Selected by Montreal Expos organization in first round (12th pick overall) of free-agent draft (June 2, 1987). ... On disabled list (June 16-July 12, 1990 and August 12-September 11, 1993). ... Traded by Expos to Los Angeles Dodgers for P Pedro J.

Martinez (November 19, 1993). ... On disabled list (May 26-June 20, 1994). ... Granted free agency (October 29, 1996). ... Signed by St. Louis Cardinals (November 20, 1996). ... On St. Louis disabled list (July 5-August 10, 1998); included rehabilitation assignment to Arkansas (August 5-10). ... Granted free agency (October 23, 1998). ... Signed by Baltimore Orioles (December 7, 1998). ... On Baltimore disabled list (March 25-April 11, June 21-July 23 and October 1, 1999-remainder of season); included rehabilitation assignments to Bowie (April 9-11 and July 20-22), Delmarva (July 15-16) and Frederick (July 17-19). ... Released by Orioles (July 2, 2001). ... Signed by Chicago Cubs (July 7, 2001). ... Granted free agency (November 5, 2001). ... Re-signed by Cubs (December 6, 2001). ... On disabled list (May 28-June 12, 2002). ... Released by Cubs (August 9, 2002).

RECORDS: Shares modern N.L. record for most hits in first major league game—4 (April 9, 1990). ... Shares major league single-game record for most strikeouts (nine-inning game)—5 (September 17, 1991, second game).

STATISTICAL NOTES: Led Gulf Coast League shortstops with 22 errors in 1987. ... Had 21-game hitting streak (June 28-July 21, 1993). ... Had 18-game hitting streak (May 30-June 20, 1998). ... Career major league grand slams: 1.

2002 GAMES PLAYED BY POSITION (MLB): 2B—41; OF—1.

								BATTING								FIELDING	
Year Team (League)	**Pos.**	**G**	**AB**	**R**	**H**	**2B**	**3B**	**HR**	**RBI**	**BB**	**SO**	**SB-CS**	**Avg.**	**OBP**	**SLG**	**E**	**Avg.**
1987—GC Expos (GCL)	SS-3B	31	111	17	24	5	2	1	4	21	30	16-5	.216	.351	.324	22	.862
—Jamestown (NY-P)	SS	34	96	16	21	1	2	1	5	24	28	14-4	.219	.377	.302	21	.796
1988—Rockford (Midw.)	SS	129	460	97	116	26	6	12	46	95	110	59-18	.252	.380	.413	42	.925
1989—Jacksonville (Sou.)	SS	93	307	55	83	10	6	3	35	76	80	37-12	.270	.413	.371	34	.910
—Indianapolis (A.A.)	SS	47	181	29	47	8	4	2	14	16	53	16-7	.260	.320	.381	13	.930
1990—Montreal (N.L.)	2B	129	499	69	144	28	6	4	45	66	96	42-22	.289	.375	.393	12	.981
1991—Montreal (N.L.)	2B	151	563	83	134	15	4	10	51	95	*151	56-23	.238	.347	.332	*27	.962
1992—Montreal (N.L.)	2B	135	530	82	155	19	8	7	56	54	108	46-15	.292	.359	.398	15	.976
1993—Montreal (N.L.)	2B	123	481	75	142	17	7	2	29	72	64	43-10	.295	.389	.372	11	.983
1994—Los Angeles (N.L.)■	2B-SS	89	320	51	80	11	3	2	33	54	53	27-7	.250	.357	.322	7	.984
1995—Los Angeles (N.L.)	2B	127	425	66	109	18	3	8	37	63	83	39-14	.256	.353	.369	•11	.980
1996—Los Angeles (N.L.)	2B	154	581	75	130	12	8	5	41	53	124	48-11	.224	.288	.298	17	.975
1997—St. Louis (N.L.)■	2B	150	572	92	169	26	*14	11	58	55	72	55-14	.295	.357	.448	19	.972
1998—St. Louis (N.L.)	2B-1B	117	420	74	122	21	8	7	44	56	61	26-10	.290	.371	.429	9	.983
—Arkansas (Texas)	2B-DH	4	13	1	2	0	0	0	0	2	6	0-1	.154	.267	.154	0	1.000
1999—Bowie (East.)■	2B-DH	4	15	2	4	1	0	0	0	3	2	0-0	.267	.421	.333	0	1.000
—Baltimore (A.L.)	2B	96	330	46	87	11	2	6	34	37	52	11-8	.264	.339	.364	10	.977
—Delmarva (S.Atl.)	2B	2	7	1	2	0	0	1	2	1	1	0-1	.286	.375	.714	0	1.000
—Frederick (Caro.)	2B	2	8	1	1	0	0	1	2	0	1	0-0	.125	.125	.500	0	1.000
2000—Baltimore (A.L.)	2B-OF-DH	151	561	84	166	43	5	10	86	69	82	37-10	.296	.369	.444	13	.975
2001—Baltimore (A.L.)	OF-DH	58	188	29	37	8	2	3	21	31	42	11-1	.197	.312	.309	3	.967
—Chicago (N.L.)■	OF-2B-3B-1B	68	163	26	45	9	3	2	16	28	35	12-1	.276	.380	.405	3	.969
2002—Chicago (N.L.)	2B-OF	67	146	20	28	6	1	3	10	21	38	10-1	.192	.292	.308	5	.971
American League totals (3 years)		305	1079	159	290	62	9	19	141	137	176	59-19	.269	.350	.396	26	.975
National League totals (11 years)		1310	4700	713	1258	182	65	61	420	617	885	404-128	.268	.353	.373	136	.976
Major League totals (13 years)		1615	5779	872	1548	244	74	80	561	754	1061	463-147	.268	.352	.377	162	.976

DIVISION SERIES RECORD

								BATTING								FIELDING	
Year Team (League)	**Pos.**	**G**	**AB**	**R**	**H**	**2B**	**3B**	**HR**	**RBI**	**BB**	**SO**	**SB-CS**	**Avg.**	**OBP**	**SLG**	**E**	**Avg.**
1995—Los Angeles (N.L.)	2B	3	12	1	3	0	0	0	0	1	3	0-0	.250	.308	.250	0	1.000
1996—Los Angeles (N.L.)	2B	2	4	0	0	0	0	0	0	0	1	0-0	.000	.000	.000	0	1.000
Division series totals (2 years)		5	16	1	3	0	0	0	0	1	4	0-0	.188	.235	.188	0	1.000

DESSENS, ELMER — P — REDS

PERSONAL: Born January 13, 1972, in Hermosillo, Mexico. ... 6-0/187. ... Throws right, bats right. ... Full name: Elmer Dessens Jusaino. ... Name pronounced DAH-cenz.

HIGH SCHOOL: Carrera Technica (Hermosillo, Mexico).

TRANSACTIONS/CAREER NOTES: Signed as non-drafted free agent by Pittburgh Pirates organization (January 27, 1993). ... Loaned by Pirates organization to Mexico City Red Devils, Mexican League for 1993 and 1994 seasons; returned to Pirates organization for 1995 season. ... Loaned by Pirates organization to Red Devils (May 7, 1996). ... Returned to Pirates organization (June 21, 1996). ... On Pittsburgh disabled list (July 31-September 10, 1996); included rehabilitation assignment to Carolina (August 16-September 10). ... Loaned by Pirates to Red Devils (March 27-September 5, 1997). ... On Pittsburgh disabled list (April 8-24, 1998); included rehabilitation assignment to Nashville (April 21-24). ... Released by Pirates (March 31, 1999). ... Played for Yomiuri Giants of Japan Central League (1999). ... Signed by Cincinnati Reds (December 15, 1999). ... On disabled list (August 2-27, 2002).

MISCELLANEOUS: Appeared in one game as pinch hitter (2001).

CAREER HITTING (MLB): 26-for-155 (.168), 11 R, 1 2B, 0 3B, 0 HR, 10 RBI.

Year League	**W**	**L**	**Pct.**	**ERA**	**G**	**GS**	**CG**	**ShO**	**Sv.-Opp.**	**IP**	**H**	**R**	**ER**	**HR**	**BB-IBB**	**SO**
1993—MC Red Devils (Mex.)	3	1	.750	2.35	14	0	0	0	2-...	30.2	31	8	8	2	5-1	16
1994—MC Red Devils (Mex.)	11	4	.733	2.04	37	15	4	1	3-...	127.2	121	37	29	5	32-1	51
1995—Carolina (Sou.)■	*15	8	.652	*2.49	27	27	1	0	0-...	152.0	170	62	42	10	21-3	68
1996—Calgary (PCL)	2	2	.500	3.15	6	6	0	0	0-...	34.1	40	14	12	5	15-1	15
—MC Red Devils (Mex.)■	7	0	1.000	1.26	7	7	1	0	0-...	50.0	44	12	7	1	10-0	17
—Pittsburgh (N.L.)■	0	2	.000	8.28	15	3	0	0	0-0	25.0	40	23	23	2	4-0	13
—Carolina (Sou.)	0	1	.000	5.40	5	1	0	0	0-...	11.2	15	8	7	1	4-0	7
1997—MC Red Devils (Mex.)■	•16	5	.762	3.56	26	25	3	1	0-...	159.1	156	73	63	1	51-1	61
—Pittsburgh (N.L.)■	0	0	...	0.00	3	0	0	0	0-0	3.1	2	0	0	0	0-0	2
1998—Pittsburgh (N.L.)	2	6	.250	5.67	43	5	0	0	0-1	74.2	90	50	47	10	25-2	43
—Nashville (PCL)	3	1	.750	3.30	6	5	0	0	0-...	30.0	32	12	11	2	6-1	13
1999—Yomiuri (Jp. East.)■	4	3	.571	2.08	15	14	2	...	0-...	95.0	67	26	22	...	24-...	58
—Yomiuri (Jap. Cen.)	0	1	.000	3.86	8	0	0	0	0-...	16.1	24	7	7	...	4-...	6
2000—Louisville (I.L.)■	2	0	1.000	3.18	4	4	0	0	0-...	22.2	24	10	8	1	7-0	14
—Cincinnati (N.L.)	11	5	.688	4.28	40	16	1	0	1-1	147.1	170	73	70	10	43-7	85
2001—Cincinnati (N.L.)	10	14	.417	4.48	34	34	1	1	0-0	205.0	221	103	102	32	56-1	128
2002—Cincinnati (N.L.)	7	8	.467	3.03	30	30	0	0	0-0	178.0	173	70	60	24	49-8	93
Major League totals (6 years)	30	35	.462	4.29	165	88	2	1	1-2	633.1	696	319	302	78	177-18	364

DeWITT, MATT — P

PERSONAL: Born September 4, 1977, in San Bernardino, Calif. ... 6-3/225. ... Throws right, bats right. ... Full name: Matthew Brian DeWitt.
HIGH SCHOOL: Valley (Las Vegas).
TRANSACTIONS/CAREER NOTES: Selected by St. Louis Cardinals organization in 10th round of free-agent draft (June 1, 1995). ... Traded by Cardinals with P Lance Painter and C Alberto Castillo to Toronto Blue Jays for P Pat Hentgen and P Paul Spoljaric (November 11, 1999). ... On Toronto disabled list (August 23, 2000-remainder of season). ... Traded by Blue Jays with P David Wells to Chicago White Sox for P Mike Sirotka, P Kevin Beirne, OF Brian Simmons and P Mike Williams (January 14, 2001). ... Traded by White Sox to Blue Jays for P Mike Williams (March 20, 2001). ... Granted free agency (October 19, 2001). ... Signed by San Diego Padres organization (December 23, 2001). ... On San Diego disabled list (May 3, 2002-remainder of season). ... Released by Padres (October 2, 2002).
CAREER HITTING (MLB): 0-for-0 (.000), 0 R, 0 2B, 0 3B, 0 HR, 0 RBI.

Year	League	W	L	Pct.	ERA	G	GS	CG	ShO	Sv.-Opp.	IP	H	R	ER	HR	BB-IBB	SO
1995—	Johnson City (Appl.)	2	6	.250	7.04	13	12	0	0	0-...	62.2	84	56	*49	10	32-0	45
1996—	Johnson City (Appl.)	5	5	.500	5.42	14	*14	0	0	0-...	*79.2	66	53	48	*17	26-0	58
1997—	Peoria (Midw.)	9	9	.500	4.09	27	•27	1	0	0-...	158.1	152	84	72	16	57-2	121
1998—	Prince William (Caro.)	6	9	.400	3.64	24	24	1	0	0-...	148.1	132	65	60	13	18-0	118
1999—	Arkansas (Texas)	9	8	.529	4.43	26	26	0	0	0-...	148.1	153	87	73	21	59-0	107
2000—	Syracuse (I.L.)■	4	5	.444	4.87	31	7	0	0	15-...	64.2	78	42	35	6	25-0	41
	—Toronto (A.L.)	1	0	1.000	8.56	8	0	0	0	0-0	13.2	20	13	13	4	9-0	6
2001—	Syracuse (I.L.)	3	2	.600	2.78	53	0	0	0	*27-...	58.1	45	20	18	4	17-1	44
	—Toronto (A.L.)	0	2	.000	3.79	16	0	0	0	0-0	19.0	22	8	8	2	10-5	13
2002—	Portland (PCL)■	1	0	1.000	1.00	2	2	0	0	0-...	9.0	5	1	1	1	2-0	7
	—San Diego (N.L.)	0	1	.000	1.23	5	0	0	0	0-0	7.1	6	2	1	1	3-0	5
A.L. totals (2 years)		1	2	.333	5.79	24	0	0	0	0-0	32.2	42	21	21	6	19-5	19
N.L. totals (1 year)		0	1	.000	1.23	5	0	0	0	0-0	7.1	6	2	1	1	3-0	5
Major League totals (3 years)		1	3	.250	4.95	29	0	0	0	0-0	40.0	48	23	22	7	22-5	24

DIAZ, EINAR — C — INDIANS

D

PERSONAL: Born December 28, 1972, in Chiniqui, Panama. ... 5-10/190. ... Bats right, throws right. ... Full name: Einar Antonio Diaz.
TRANSACTIONS/CAREER NOTES: Signed as non-drafted free agent by Cleveland Indians organization (October 5, 1990). ... On Cleveland disabled list (August 23-September 30, 2002); included rehabilitation assignment to Mahoning Valley (September 2-6).
STATISTICAL NOTES: Led Appalachian League third basemen with 125 assists and .959 fielding percentage in 1992. ... Led Appalachian League catchers with 54 assists and nine errors in 1993. ... Led South Atlantic League in grounding into double plays with 18 in 1994. ... Led South Atlantic League catchers with 845 putouts, 112 assists, 966 total chances and tied for lead with eight double plays in 1994. ... Led Carolina League catchers with 107 assists and .992 fielding percentage in 1995. ... Led Eastern League catchers with 15 errors in 1996. ... Led American Association catchers with 18 errors in 1997. ... Led International League catchers with 791 putouts, 70 assists and 873 total chances in 1998. ... Led A.L. catchers with 77 assists in 2002.
2002 GAMES PLAYED BY POSITION (MLB): C—100.

			BATTING														FIELDING	
Year	Team (League)	Pos.	G	AB	R	H	2B	3B	HR	RBI	BB	SO	SB-CS	Avg.	OBP	SLG	E	Avg.
1991—	Dom. Indians (DSL)		62	239	35	67	6	3	1	29	14	5	10-...	.280	...	.343	...	...
1992—	Burlington (Appl.)	3B-SS	52	178	19	37	3	0	1	14	20	9	2-3	.208	.296	.242	7	†.959
1993—	Burlington (Appl.)	C-3B	60	231	40	69	15	3	5	33	8	7	7-3	.299	.328	.455	†10	.974
	—Columbus (S.Atl.)	C	1	5	0	0	0	0	0	0	0	1	0-0	.000	.000	.000	0	1.000
1994—	Columbus (S.Atl.)	C-3B	120	491	67	137	23	2	16	71	17	34	4-4	.279	.330	.432	9	.991
1995—	Kinston (Caro.)	C-3B-DH	104	373	46	98	21	0	6	43	12	29	3-6	.263	.297	.367	7	†.991
1996—	Canton/Akron (East.)	C-3B	104	395	47	111	26	2	3	35	12	22	3-2	.281	.317	.380	†15	.983
	—Cleveland (A.L.)	C	4	1	0	0	0	0	0	0	0	0	0-0	.000	.000	.000	0	1.000
1997—	Buffalo (A.A.)	C-3B	109	336	40	86	18	2	3	31	18	34	2-6	.256	.302	.348	†19	.974
	—Cleveland (A.L.)	C	5	7	1	1	1	0	0	1	0	2	0-0	.143	.143	.286	1	.955
1998—	Buffalo (I.L.)	C	115	415	62	130	21	3	8	63	21	33	3-3	.313	.354	.436	*12	.986
	—Cleveland (A.L.)	C	17	48	8	11	1	0	2	9	3	2	0-0	.229	.286	.375	3	.973
1999—	Cleveland (A.L.)	C	119	392	43	110	21	1	3	32	23	41	11-4	.281	.328	.362	10	.988
2000—	Cleveland (A.L.)	C-3B	75	250	29	68	14	2	4	25	11	29	4-2	.272	.323	.392	4	.994
2001—	Cleveland (A.L.)	C-2B	134	437	54	121	34	1	4	56	17	44	1-2	.277	.328	.387	8	.992
2002—	Cleveland (A.L.)	C	102	320	34	66	19	0	2	16	17	27	0-1	.206	.258	.284	8	.989
Major League totals (7 years)			456	1455	169	377	90	4	15	139	71	145	16-9	.259	.309	.357	34	.990

DIVISION SERIES RECORD

			BATTING														FIELDING	
Year	Team (League)	Pos.	G	AB	R	H	2B	3B	HR	RBI	BB	SO	SB-CS	Avg.	OBP	SLG	E	Avg.
1998—	Cleveland (A.L.)								Did not play.									
1999—	Cleveland (A.L.)	C-PH	2	1	0	0	0	0	0	0	0	0	0-0	.000	.000	.000	0	1.000
2001—	Cleveland (A.L.)	C	5	16	3	5	0	0	0	2	2	1	0-0	.313	.389	.313	1	.982
Division series totals (2 years)			7	17	3	5	0	0	0	2	2	1	0-0	.294	.368	.294	1	.983

CHAMPIONSHIP SERIES RECORD

			BATTING														FIELDING	
Year	Team (League)	Pos.	G	AB	R	H	2B	3B	HR	RBI	BB	SO	SB-CS	Avg.	OBP	SLG	E	Avg.
1998—	Cleveland (A.L.)	C	4	4	0	0	0	0	0	0	0	1	0-0	.000	.000	.000	0	1.000

DIAZ, JUAN — 1B — RED SOX

PERSONAL: Born February 19, 1974, in San Jose de las Lajas, Cuba. ... 6-2/228. ... Bats right, throws right. ... Full name: Juan Carlos Diaz.
TRANSACTIONS/CAREER NOTES: Signed as non-drafted free agent by Los Angeles Dodgers organization (May 19, 1996). ... Contract voided by Major League Baseball (June 25, 1999). ... Signed by Boston Red Sox organization (March 4, 2000). ... On disabled list (April 5-June 3, 2001).
2002 GAMES PLAYED BY POSITION (MLB): DH—1; 1B—1.

Year	Team (League)	Pos.	G	AB	R	H	2B	3B	HR	RBI	BB	SO	SB-CS	Avg.	OBP	SLG	E	Avg.
			BATTING														FIELDING	
1996—	Dom. Dodgers (DSL) .		13	47	15	17	7	0	4	16	11	13	1-...	.362	...	.766	...	...
1997—	Savannah (S.Atl.)	1B	127	460	63	106	24	2	25	83	48	155	2-2	.230	.306	.454	15	.977
—	Vero Beach (FSL)	1B	2	7	2	3	0	0	1	3	0	4	0-0	.429	.500	.857	0	1.000
1998—	Vero Beach (FSL)	1B	67	250	33	73	12	1	17	51	21	52	1-2	.292	.353	.552	7	.986
—	San Antonio (Texas)...	1B	56	188	26	50	13	0	13	30	15	45	0-0	.266	.327	.543	15	.963
1999—	San Antonio (Texas)...	1B	66	254	42	77	21	1	9	52	26	77	0-0	.303	.369	.500	15	.963
2000—	Sarasota (FSL)■	1B	14	51	7	14	2	1	4	12	4	15	0-0	.275	.333	.588	1	.992
—	Trenton (East.)	1B	50	198	36	62	14	1	17	53	10	56	0-0	.313	.343	.652	8	.973
—	Pawtucket (I.L.)..........	1B	13	43	11	12	0	0	7	17	6	9	1-0	.279	.353	.767	2	.980
2001—	Pawtucket (I.L.)..........	1B	74	279	45	75	17	1	20	51	17	85	0-0	.269	.323	.552	•10	.970
2002—	Pawtucket (I.L.)..........	1B	104	389	47	101	14	0	20	53	24	105	0-0	.260	.305	.450	6	.986
—	Boston (A.L.)..............	DH-1B	4	7	2	2	1	0	1	2	1	2	0-0	.286	.375	.857	0	1.000
Major League totals (1 year)			4	7	2	2	1	0	1	2	1	2	0-0	.286	.375	.857	0	1.000

DIFELICE, MIKE — C

PERSONAL: Born May 28, 1969, in Philadelphia. ... 6-2/205. ... Bats right, throws right. ... Full name: Michael William Difelice. ... Name pronounced DEE-fah-lease.

HIGH SCHOOL: Bearden (Knoxville, Tenn.).

COLLEGE: Tennessee.

TRANSACTIONS/CAREER NOTES: Selected by St. Louis Cardinals organization in 11th round of free-agent draft (June 3, 1991). ... Selected by Tampa Bay Devil Rays in first round (20th pick overall) of expansion draft (November 18, 1997). ... Traded by Devil Rays with P Albie Lopez to Arizona Diamondbacks for OF Jason Conti and P Nick Bierbrodt (July 25, 2001). ... Released by Diamondbacks (September 4, 2001). ... Signed by Cardinals (November 20, 2001). ... Granted free agency (November 1, 2002).

RECORDS: Shares major league single-season record for fewest double plays by catcher for leader—8 (1998).

STATISTICAL NOTES: Tied for N.L. lead in passed balls with 12 in 1997. ... Tied for A.L. lead in double plays by catcher with eight in 1998.

2002 GAMES PLAYED BY POSITION (MLB): C—61.

Year	Team (League)	Pos.	G	AB	R	H	2B	3B	HR	RBI	BB	SO	SB-CS	Avg.	OBP	SLG	E	Avg.
			BATTING														FIELDING	
1991—	Hamilton (NY-Penn) ...	C	43	157	10	33	5	0	4	15	9	40	1-5	.210	.257	.318	9	.974
1992—	Hamilton (NY-Penn) ...	C-1B	18	58	11	20	3	0	2	9	4	7	2-0	.345	.397	.500	5	.969
—	St. Petersburg (FSL) ..	C	17	53	0	12	3	0	0	4	3	11	0-0	.226	.259	.283	2	.977
1993—	Springfield (Midw.)	C	8	20	5	7	1	0	0	3	2	3	0-1	.350	.435	.400	0	1.000
—	St. Petersburg (FSL) ..	C	30	97	5	22	2	0	0	8	11	13	1-0	.227	.306	.247	7	.964
1994—	Arkansas (Texas)........	C	71	200	19	50	11	2	2	15	12	48	0-1	.250	.296	.355	6	.987
1995—	Arkansas (Texas)........	C	62	176	14	47	10	1	1	24	23	29	0-2	.267	.360	.352	6	.984
—	Louisville (A.A.)..........	C	21	63	8	17	4	0	0	3	5	11	1-0	.270	.324	.333	2	.984
1996—	Louisville (A.A.)..........	C	79	246	25	70	13	0	9	33	20	43	0-3	.285	.338	.447	8	.984
—	St. Louis (N.L.)...........	C	4	7	0	2	1	0	0	2	0	1	0-0	.286	.286	.429	0	1.000
1997—	Arkansas (Texas)........	C	1	3	0	1	1	0	0	0	1	0	0-0	.333	.500	.667	0	1.000
—	St. Louis (N.L.)...........	C-1B	93	260	16	62	10	1	4	30	19	61	1-1	.238	.297	.331	6	.991
—	Louisville (A.A.)..........	C	1	4	1	1	0	0	1	1	0	1	0-0	.250	.250	1.000	0	1.000
1998—	Tampa Bay (A.L.)■.....	C	84	248	17	57	12	3	3	23	15	56	0-0	.230	.274	.339	4	.993
1999—	Tampa Bay (A.L.)........	C	51	179	21	55	11	0	6	27	8	23	0-0	.307	.346	.469	5	.987
2000—	Tampa Bay (A.L.)........	C	60	204	23	49	13	1	6	19	12	40	0-0	.240	.280	.402	8	.980
2001—	Tampa Bay (A.L.)........	C	48	149	13	31	5	1	2	9	8	39	1-1	.208	.259	.295	6	.982
—	Arizona (N.L.)■..........	C	12	21	1	1	0	0	0	1	0	10	0-0	.048	.091	.048	1	.982
—	Tucson (PCL)	C-1B	7	26	6	9	0	0	1	2	3	6	0-0	.346	.414	.462	3	.940
2002—	St. Louis (N.L.)■	C	70	174	17	40	11	0	4	19	17	42	0-0	.230	.297	.362	3	.991
American League totals (4 years)			243	780	74	192	41	5	17	78	43	158	1-1	.246	.289	.377	23	.986
National League totals (4 years)			179	462	34	105	22	1	8	52	36	114	1-1	.227	.288	.331	10	.991
Major League totals (7 years)			422	1242	108	297	63	6	25	130	79	272	2-2	.239	.289	.360	33	.988

CHAMPIONSHIP SERIES RECORD

Year	Team (League)	Pos.	G	AB	R	H	2B	3B	HR	RBI	BB	SO	SB-CS	Avg.	OBP	SLG	E	Avg.
			BATTING														FIELDING	
2002—	St. Louis (N.L.)...........	PH	1	1	0	0	0	0	0	0	0	0	0-0	.000	.000	.000	...	...

DIGGINS, BEN — P — BREWERS

PERSONAL: Born June 13, 1979, in Leota, Kan. ... 6-7/230. ... Throws right, bats right. ... Full name: Benjamin H. Diggins.

HIGH SCHOOL: Bradshaw Mountain (Dewey, Ariz.).

COLLEGE: Arizona.

TRANSACTIONS/CAREER NOTES: Selected by St. Louis Cardinals organization in first round (32nd pick overall) of free-agent draft (June 2, 1998); did not sign. ... Selected by Los Angeles Dodgers organization in first round (17th pick overall) of free-agent draft (June 5, 2000). ... Traded by Dodgers with P Shane Nance to Milwaukee Brewers for 3B Tyler Houston and a player to be named later (July 23, 2002); Dodgers acquired P Brian Mallette to complete deal (October 16, 2002).

CAREER HITTING (MLB): 1-for-7 (.143), 0 R, 0 2B, 0 3B, 0 HR, 0 RBI.

Year	League	W	L	Pct.	ERA	G	GS	CG	ShO	Sv.-Opp.	IP	H	R	ER	HR	BB-IBB	SO
2001—	Wilmington (S.Atl.)	7	6	.538	3.58	21	21	0	0	0-...	105.2	88	49	42	5	48-0	79
2002—	Vero Beach (FSL)	6	10	.375	3.63	20	19	0	0	0-...	114.0	103	54	46	8	41-1	101
—	Huntsville (Sou.)■	2	1	.667	1.91	7	7	0	0	0-...	37.2	26	13	8	0	15-0	34
—	Milwaukee (N.L.)	0	4	.000	8.63	5	5	0	0	0-0	24.0	28	24	23	4	18-1	15
Major League totals (1 year).......		0	4	.000	8.63	5	5	0	0	0-0	24.0	28	24	23	4	18-1	15

DONNELLY, BRENDAN — P — ANGELS

PERSONAL: Born July 4, 1971, in Washington, D.C. ... 6-3/205. ... Throws right, bats right. ... Full name: Brendan Kevin Donnelly.

HIGH SCHOOL: Sandia (Albuquerque, N.M.).

JUNIOR COLLEGE: Mesa (Colo.).

TRANSACTIONS/CAREER NOTES: Selected by Chicago White Sox organization in 27th round of free-agent draft (June 1, 1992). ... Released by White Sox (April 16, 1993). ... Signed by Chicago Cubs organization (June 16, 1993). ... Released by Cubs (March 29, 1994). ... Signed by Ohio Valley, Frontier League (July 1994). ... Signed by Cincinnati Reds organization (March 4, 1995). ... Granted free agency (October 16, 1998). ... Signed by Reds organization (March 15, 1999). ... Released by Reds (April 3, 1999). ... Signed by Nashua, Atlantic League (May 1999). ... Sold by Nashua to Tampa Bay Devil Rays organization (May 15, 1999). ... Released by Devil Rays (August 12, 1999). ... Signed by Pittsburgh Pirates organization (August 18, 1999). ... Released by Pirates (August 25, 1999). ... Signed by Toronto Blue Jays organization (August 26, 1999). ... Released by Blue Jays (July 28, 2000). ... Signed by Cubs organization (August 10, 2000). ... Granted free agency (October 15, 2000). ... Signed by Anaheim Angels organization (January 9, 2001).

CAREER HITTING (MLB): 0-for-0 (.000), 0 R, 0 2B, 0 3B, 0 HR, 0 RBI.

Year	League	W	L	Pct.	ERA	G	GS	CG	ShO	Sv.-Opp.	IP	H	R	ER	HR	BB-IBB	SO
1992—	GC White Sox (GCL)	0	3	.000	3.67	9	7	0	0	1-...	41.2	41	25	17	0	21-0	31
1993—	Geneva (NY-Penn)■	4	0	1.000	6.28	21	3	0	0	1-...	43.0	39	34	30	4	29-0	29
1994—	Ohio Valley (Fron.)■	1	1	.500	2.57	10	0	0	0	0-...	14.0	13	5	4	1	4-0	20
1995—	Charl., W.Va. (S.Atl.)■	1	1	.500	1.19	24	0	0	0	12-...	30.1	14	4	4	0	7-1	33
—	Winston-Salem (Caro.)	1	2	.333	1.02	23	0	0	0	2-...	35.1	20	6	4	1	14-2	32
—	Indianapolis (A.A.)	1	1	.500	23.63	3	0	0	0	0-...	2.2	7	8	7	2	2-0	1
1996—	Chattanooga (Sou.)	1	2	.333	5.52	22	0	0	0	0-...	29.1	27	21	18	4	17-2	22
1997—	Chattanooga (Sou.)	6	4	.600	3.27	62	0	0	0	6-...	82.2	71	43	30	6	37-4	64
1998—	Chattanooga (Sou.)	2	5	.286	2.98	38	0	0	0	13-...	45.1	43	16	15	4	24-5	47
—	Indianapolis (I.L.)	4	1	.800	2.65	19	1	0	0	0-...	37.1	29	16	11	3	16-3	39
1999—	Nashua (Atl.)■	0	0	...	3.00	3	0	0	0	0-...	3.0	1	1	1	...	3-...	4
—	Durham (I.L.)■	5	5	.500	3.05	37	1	0	0	2-...	62.0	53	23	21	5	18-1	61
—	Altoona (East.)■	0	0	...	7.71	2	0	0	0	1-...	2.1	4	2	2	0	2-0	0
—	Syracuse (I.L.)■	0	1	.000	2.89	5	0	0	0	0-...	9.1	8	4	3	1	4-1	9
2000—	Syracuse (I.L.)	4	6	.400	5.48	37	0	0	0	0-...	42.2	47	34	26	5	27-2	34
—	Iowa (PCL)■	0	3	.000	7.56	9	0	0	0	1-...	16.2	25	19	14	3	6-1	14
2001—	Arkansas (Texas)■	4	1	.800	2.48	27	0	0	0	12-...	29.0	21	8	8	2	13-1	37
—	Salt Lake (PCL)	5	1	.833	2.40	29	0	0	0	1-...	41.1	38	11	11	4	8-0	50
2002—	Salt Lake (PCL)	4	0	1.000	3.48	25	0	0	0	6-...	33.2	27	13	13	5	11-0	42
—	Anaheim (A.L.)	1	1	.500	2.17	46	0	0	0	1-3	49.2	32	13	12	2	19-3	54
Major League totals (1 year)		1	1	.500	2.17	46	0	0	0	1-3	49.2	32	13	12	2	19-3	54

DIVISION SERIES RECORD

Year	League	W	L	Pct.	ERA	G	GS	CG	ShO	Sv.-Opp.	IP	H	R	ER	HR	BB-IBB	SO
2002—	Anaheim (A.L.)	0	0	...	13.50	3	0	0	0	0-0	2.0	3	3	3	2	1-0	2

CHAMPIONSHIP SERIES RECORD

Year	League	W	L	Pct.	ERA	G	GS	CG	ShO	Sv.-Opp.	IP	H	R	ER	HR	BB-IBB	SO
2002—	Anaheim (A.L.)	0	0	...	8.10	3	0	0	0	0-0	3.1	3	3	3	0	0-0	5

WORLD SERIES RECORD

NOTES: Member of World Series championship team (2002).

Year	League	W	L	Pct.	ERA	G	GS	CG	ShO	Sv.-Opp.	IP	H	R	ER	HR	BB-IBB	SO
2002—	Anaheim (A.L.)	1	0	1.000	0.00	5	0	0	0	0-0	7.2	1	0	0	0	4-0	6

DONNELS, CHRIS — IF

PERSONAL: Born April 21, 1966, in Los Angeles. ... 6-0/185. ... Bats left, throws right. ... Full name: Chris Barton Donnels. ... Name pronounced DON-uls.

HIGH SCHOOL: South Torrance (Calif.).

COLLEGE: Loyola Marymount.

TRANSACTIONS/CAREER NOTES: Selected by New York Mets organization in first round (24th pick overall) of free-agent draft (June 2, 1987). ... On Tidewater disabled list (June 20-28, 1991). ... Selected by Florida Marlins in third round (67th pick overall) of expansion draft (November 17, 1992). ... Claimed on waivers by Houston Astros (December 18, 1992). ... On Houston disabled list (April 23-May 12, 1995); included rehabilitation assignment to Jackson (May 8-12). ... Traded by Astros to Boston Red Sox for a player to be named later (June 10, 1995). ... Released by Red Sox (October 26, 1995). ... Signed by Kintetsu Buffaloes, Japan Pacific League (1996). ... Signed by Red Sox (December 20, 1996). ... Released by Red Sox (March 26, 1997). ... Played with Orix Blue Wave of Japan Pacific League (1997-99). ... Signed by Los Angeles Dodgers organization (February 8, 2000). ... On Los Angeles disabled list (August 2-September 1, 2000); included rehabilitation assignment to Albuquerque (August 12-31). ... On Los Angeles disabled list (May 19-June 4, 2001); included rehabilitation assignment to Las Vegas (May 31-June 4). ... Granted free agency (October 16, 2001). ... Signed by Arizona Diamondbacks organization (January 11, 2002). ... On Arizona disabled list (July 31-September 1, 2002); included rehabilitation assignment to Tucson (August 26-September 1). ... Granted free agency (October 28, 2002).

HONORS: Named Florida State League Most Valuable Player (1989).

STATISTICAL NOTES: Led Florida State League with 15 intentional bases on balls received in 1989. ... Led Florida State League third basemen with 93 putouts, 202 assists and 320 total chances in 1989. ... Led Texas League third basemen with 79 putouts, 242 assists, 31 errors, 352 total chances and 24 double plays in 1990.

2002 GAMES PLAYED BY POSITION (MLB): 3B—26; 1B—1.

			BATTING														FIELDING	
Year	Team (League)	Pos.	G	AB	R	H	2B	3B	HR	RBI	BB	SO	SB-CS	Avg.	OBP	SLG	E	Avg.
1987—	Kingsport (Appl.)	3B	26	86	18	26	4	0	3	16	17	17	4-1	.302	.415	.453	6	.909
—	Columbia (S.Atl.)	3B	41	136	20	35	7	0	2	17	24	27	3-1	.257	.370	.353	10	.922
1988—	St. Lucie (FSL)	3B	65	198	25	43	14	2	3	22	32	53	4-3	.217	.330	.354	15	.912
—	Columbia (S.Atl.)	3B	42	133	19	32	6	0	2	13	30	25	5-0	.241	.382	.331	7	.942
1989—	St. Lucie (FSL)	3B-1B	117	386	70	121	23	1	17	*78	83	65	18-4	.313	.439	*.510	28	.942
1990—	Jackson (Texas)	3B-1B-2B	130	419	66	114	24	0	12	63	*111	81	11-8	.272	.420	.415	†32	.914
1991—	Tidewater (I.L.)	3B-2B	84	287	45	87	19	2	8	56	62	56	1-4	.303	.425	.467	14	.952
—	New York (N.L.)	1B-3B	37	89	7	20	2	0	0	5	14	19	1-1	.225	.330	.247	2	.988

Year	Team (League)	Pos.	G	AB	R	H	2B	3B	HR	RBI	BB	SO	SB-CS	Avg.	OBP	SLG	E	Avg.
			BATTING														FIELDING	
1992—	Tidewater (I.L.)	3B-1B-2B	81	279	35	84	15	3	5	32	58	45	12-1	.301	.419	.430	16	.952
—	New York (N.L.)	3B-2B	45	121	8	21	4	0	0	6	17	25	1-0	.174	.275	.207	5	.957
1993—	Houston (N.L.)■	3B-1B-2B	88	179	18	46	14	2	2	24	19	33	2-0	.257	.327	.391	8	.965
1994—	Houston (N.L.)	3B-1B-2B	54	86	12	23	5	0	3	5	13	18	1-0	.267	.364	.430	0	1.000
1995—	Jackson (Texas)	3B	4	12	1	2	1	0	0	1	4	4	0-0	.167	.375	.250	1	.929
—	Houston (N.L.)	3B-2B	19	30	4	9	0	0	0	2	3	6	0-0	.300	.364	.300	2	.833
—	Boston (A.L.)■	3B-1B-2B	40	91	13	23	2	2	2	11	9	18	0-0	.253	.317	.385	4	.960
—	Pawtucket (I.L.)	3B-DH	4	15	1	6	0	0	1	4	1	3	0-0	.400	.438	.600	1	.833
1996—	Kintetsu (Jap. Pac.)■		108	324	50	91	20	2	20	53	54	86	3-...	.281	...	.540	...	...
1997—	Orix (Jap. Pac.)■		112	384	55	116	25	1	17	67	84	80	0-...	.302	...	.505	...	...
1998—	Orix (Jp. West.)		8	20	4	10	4	0	1	4	7	2	0-...	.500	...	.850	...	...
—	Orix (Jap. Pac.)		44	140	17	37	9	0	5	22	23	44	1-...	.264	...	.436	...	...
1999—	Orix (Jap. Pac.)		36	90	10	22	5	0	2	13	14	15	0-...	.244	...	.367	...	...
2000—	Albuquerque (PCL)■	1B-3B-2B-C	105	332	79	109	27	1	27	84	66	52	6-1	.328	.440	*.660	9	.985
—	Los Angeles (N.L.)	OF-1B-3B-2B	27	34	8	10	3	0	4	9	6	7	0-0	.294	.390	.735	1	.968
2001—	Los Angeles (N.L.)	3B-1B-P	66	88	8	15	2	0	3	8	12	25	0-0	.170	.277	.295	3	.958
—	Las Vegas (PCL)	1B-3B	39	137	17	32	5	0	7	25	21	24	0-1	.234	.333	.423	2	.991
2002—	Arizona (N.L.)	3B-1B	74	80	5	19	4	1	3	16	10	14	0-0	.238	.312	.425	0	1.000
—	Tucson (PCL)	3B	4	10	3	3	1	0	0	0	2	3	0-0	.300	.500	.400	0	1.000
American League totals (1 year)			40	91	13	23	2	2	2	11	9	18	0-0	.253	.317	.385	4	.960
National League totals (8 years)			410	707	70	163	34	3	15	75	94	147	5-1	.231	.320	.351	21	.971
Major League totals (8 years)			450	798	83	186	36	5	17	86	103	165	5-1	.233	.319	.355	25	.970

DIVISION SERIES RECORD

Year	Team (League)	Pos.	G	AB	R	H	2B	3B	HR	RBI	BB	SO	SB-CS	Avg.	OBP	SLG	E	Avg.
			BATTING														FIELDING	
2002—	Arizona (N.L.)	PH	3	2	0	0	0	0	0	0	1	0	0-0	.000	.333	.000	0	...

RECORD AS PITCHER

Year	League	W	L	Pct.	ERA	G	GS	CG	ShO	Sv.	IP	H	R	ER	BB	SO
2001—	Los Angeles (N.L.)	0	0	...	0.00	1	0	0	0	0	.1	0	0	0	0	0

DOTEL, OCTAVIO — P — ASTROS

PERSONAL: Born November 25, 1973, in Santo Domingo, Dominican Republic. ... 6-0/200. ... Throws right, bats right. ... Full name: Octavio Eduardo Dotel. ... Brother of Angel Dotel, third baseman in Los Angeles Dodgers organization (1991-93).

HIGH SCHOOL: Liceo Eansino Afuera (Dominican Republic).

TRANSACTIONS/CAREER NOTES: Signed as non-drafted free agent by New York Mets organization (March 20, 1993). ... On disabled list (July 18-August 16, 1996). ... On Binghamton disabled list (June 3-24, 1997). ... On Norfolk disabled list (May 7-17, 1999). ... Traded by Mets with OF Roger Cedeno and P Kyle Kessel to Houston Astros for P Mike Hampton and OF Derek Bell (December 23, 1999).

CAREER HITTING (MLB): 5-for-68 (.074), 3 R, 0 2B, 0 3B, 0 HR, 1 RBI.

Year	League	W	L	Pct.	ERA	G	GS	CG	ShO	Sv.-Opp.	IP	H	R	ER	HR	BB-IBB	SO
1993—	Dominican Mets (DSL)	6	2	.750	4.10	15	11	0	0	0-...	59.1	46	30	27	...	38-...	48
1994—	Dominican Mets (DSL)	5	0	1.000	4.32	15	14	1	0	0-...	81.1	84	53	39	...	31-...	95
1995—	Gulf Coast Mets (GCL)	•7	4	.636	2.18	13	12	2	0	0-...	*74.1	48	23	18	0	17-1	*86
—	St. Lucie (FSL)	1	0	1.000	5.63	3	0	0	0	0-...	8.0	10	5	5	1	4-0	9
1996—	Capital City (S.Atl.)	11	3	.786	3.59	22	19	0	0	0-...	115.1	89	49	46	7	49-0	142
1997—	St. Lucie (FSL)	5	2	.714	2.52	9	8	1	1	0-...	50.0	44	18	14	2	23-0	39
—	Binghamton (East.)	3	4	.429	5.98	12	12	0	0	0-...	55.2	66	50	37	5	38-1	40
—	Gulf Coast Mets (GCL)	0	0	...	0.96	3	2	0	0	1-...	9.1	9	1	1	0	2-0	7
1998—	Binghamton (East.)	4	2	.667	1.97	10	10	2	1	0-...	68.2	41	19	15	4	24-1	82
—	Norfolk (I.L.)	8	6	.571	3.45	17	16	1	0	0-...	99.0	82	47	38	9	43-1	118
1999—	Norfolk (I.L.)	5	2	.714	3.84	13	13	1	0	0-...	70.1	52	33	30	9	34-1	90
—	New York (N.L.)	8	3	.727	5.38	19	14	0	0	0-0	85.1	69	52	51	12	49-1	85
2000—	Houston (N.L.)■	3	7	.300	5.40	50	16	0	0	16-23	125.0	127	80	75	26	61-3	142
2001—	Houston (N.L.)	7	5	.583	2.66	61	4	0	0	2-4	105.0	79	35	31	5	47-2	145
2002—	Houston (N.L.)	6	4	.600	1.85	83	0	0	0	6-10	97.1	58	21	20	7	27-2	118
Major League totals (4 years)		24	19	.558	3.86	213	34	0	0	24-37	412.2	333	188	177	50	184-8	490

DIVISION SERIES RECORD

Year	League	W	L	Pct.	ERA	G	GS	CG	ShO	Sv.-Opp.	IP	H	R	ER	HR	BB-IBB	SO
1999—	New York (N.L.)	0	0	...	54.00	1	0	0	0	0-0	.1	1	2	2	0	2-0	0
2001—	Houston (N.L.)	0	0	...	5.40	2	0	0	0	0-0	3.1	5	2	2	1	0-0	5
Division series totals (2 years)		0	0	...	9.82	3	0	0	0	0-0	3.2	6	4	4	1	2-0	5

CHAMPIONSHIP SERIES RECORD

Year	League	W	L	Pct.	ERA	G	GS	CG	ShO	Sv.-Opp.	IP	H	R	ER	HR	BB-IBB	SO
1999—	New York (N.L.)	1	0	1.000	3.00	1	0	0	0	0-0	3.0	4	1	1	0	2-1	5

DOUGLASS, SEAN — P — ORIOLES

PERSONAL: Born April 28, 1979, in Lancaster, Calif. ... 6-6/198. ... Throws right, bats right. ... Full name: Sean R. Douglass.

HIGH SCHOOL: Antelope Valley (Lancaster, Calif.).

TRANSACTIONS/CAREER NOTES: Selected by Baltimore Orioles organization in second round of free-agent draft (June 3, 1997).

CAREER HITTING (MLB): 0-for-0 (.000), 0 R, 0 2B, 0 3B, 0 HR, 0 RBI.

Year	League	W	L	Pct.	ERA	G	GS	CG	ShO	Sv.-Opp.	IP	H	R	ER	HR	BB-IBB	SO
1997—	Gulf Coast Orioles (GCL)	1	3	.250	6.11	9	1	0	0	0-...	17.2	20	14	12	2	9-0	10
1998—	Bluefield (Appl.)	2	2	.500	3.23	10	0	0	0	0-...	53.0	45	20	19	6	14-0	62
1999—	Frederick (Caro.)	5	6	.455	3.32	16	16	1	0	0-...	97.2	101	48	36	9	58-0	161
2000—	Bowie (East.)	9	8	.529	4.02	27	27	2	0	0-...	159.0	174	88	71	17	34-1	105
2001—	Rochester (I.L.)	8	9	.471	3.49	27	27	0	0	0-...	162.1	160	79	63	13	61-0	156
—	Baltimore (A.L.)	2	1	.667	5.31	4	4	0	0	0-0	20.1	21	12	12	3	11-0	17
2002—	Rochester (I.L.)	4	6	.400	4.72	14	13	0	0	0-...	66.2	66	39	35	4	35-0	71
—	Baltimore (A.L.)	0	5	.000	6.07	15	8	0	0	0-0	53.1	58	41	36	10	35-2	44
Major League totals (2 years)		2	6	.250	5.86	19	12	0	0	0-0	73.2	79	53	48	13	46-2	61

DREIFORT, DARREN P DODGERS

PERSONAL: Born May 3, 1972, in Wichita, Kan. ... 6-2/211. ... Throws right, bats right. ... Full name: Darren John Dreifort. ... Name pronounced DRY-fert.

HIGH SCHOOL: Wichita (Kan.) Heights.

COLLEGE: Wichita State.

TRANSACTIONS/CAREER NOTES: Selected by New York Mets organization in 11th round of free-agent draft (June 4, 1990); did not sign. ... Selected by Los Angeles Dodgers organization in first round (second pick overall) of free-agent draft (June 3, 1993). ... On San Antonio disabled list (July 7-28, 1994). ... On Albuquerque disabled list (August 27, 1994-remainder of season). ... On disabled list (April 23, 1995-entire season). ... On Los Angeles disabled list (March 25-May 16, 1996); included rehabilitation assignment to Albuquerque (April 18-May 15). ... On Los Angeles disabled list (May 12-June 17, 1997); included rehabilitation assignment to Albuquerque (June 11-17). ... Granted free agency (October 30, 2000). ... Re-signed by Dodgers (December 11, 2000). ... On disabled list (June 30, 2001-remainder of season; and March 19, 2002-entire season).

HONORS: Named righthanded pitcher on The Sporting News college All-America team (1992-93). ... Named Golden Spikes Award winner by USA Baseball (1993).

STATISTICAL NOTES: Tied for N.L. lead with four balks in 1999.

MISCELLANEOUS: Member of 1992 U.S. Olympic baseball team. ... Singled with an RBI in one game as pinch hitter with Los Angeles (1994). ... Made an out in only appearance as pinch hitter with Los Angeles (1996). ... Received a base on balls in only appearance as pinch hitter (1998).

CAREER HITTING (MLB): 42-for-223 (.188), 26 R, 9 2B, 0 3B, 6 HR, 22 RBI.

Year	League	W	L	Pct.	ERA	G	GS	CG	ShO	Sv.-Opp.	IP	H	R	ER	HR	BB-IBB	SO
1994	—Los Angeles (N.L.)	0	5	.000	6.21	27	0	0	0	6-9	29.0	45	21	20	0	15-3	22
	—San Antonio (Texas)	3	1	.750	2.80	8	8	0	0	0-...	35.1	36	14	11	0	13-0	32
	—Albuquerque (PCL)	1	0	1.000	5.68	1	1	0	0	0-...	6.1	8	4	4	1	3-0	3
1995	—Los Angeles (N.L.)									Did not play.							
1996	—Albuquerque (PCL)	5	6	.455	4.17	18	18	0	0	0-...	86.1	88	49	40	6	52-3	75
	—Los Angeles (N.L.)	1	4	.200	4.94	19	0	0	0	0-2	23.2	23	13	13	2	12-4	24
1997	—Los Angeles (N.L.)	5	2	.714	2.86	48	0	0	0	4-7	63.0	45	21	20	3	34-2	63
	—Albuquerque (PCL)	0	0	...	1.59	2	2	0	0	0-...	5.2	2	1	1	1	1-2	3
1998	—Los Angeles (N.L.)	8	12	.400	4.00	32	26	1	1	0-0	180.0	171	84	80	12	57-2	168
1999	—Los Angeles (N.L.)	13	13	.500	4.79	30	29	1	1	0-0	178.2	177	105	95	20	76-1	140
2000	—Los Angeles (N.L.)	12	9	.571	4.16	32	32	1	1	0-0	192.2	175	105	89	31	87-0	164
2001	—Los Angeles (N.L.)	4	7	.364	5.13	16	16	0	0	0-0	94.2	89	62	54	11	47-0	91
2002	—Los Angeles (N.L.)									Did not play.							
Major League totals (7 years)		43	52	.453	4.38	204	103	3	3	10-18	761.2	725	411	371	79	328-14	672

DIVISION SERIES RECORD

Year	League	W	L	Pct.	ERA	G	GS	CG	ShO	Sv.-Opp.	IP	H	R	ER	HR	BB-IBB	SO
1996	—Los Angeles (N.L.)	0	0	...	0.00	1	0	0	0	0-0	.2	0	0	0	0	0-0	0

DRESE, RYAN P INDIANS

PERSONAL: Born April 5, 1976, in San Francisco. ... 6-3/220. ... Throws right, bats right. ... Full name: Ryan T. Drese.

HIGH SCHOOL: Bishop O'Dowd (Oakland).

COLLEGE: California.

TRANSACTIONS/CAREER NOTES: Selected by Oakland Athletics organization in fifth round of free-agent draft (June 2, 1994); did not sign. ... Selected by Cleveland Indians organization in fifth round of free-agent draft (June 2, 1998). ... On disabled list (April 10-June 20, 2000).

CAREER HITTING (MLB): 0-for-3 (.000), 0 R, 0 2B, 0 3B, 0 HR, 0 RBI.

Year	League	W	L	Pct.	ERA	G	GS	CG	ShO	Sv.-Opp.	IP	H	R	ER	HR	BB-IBB	SO
1998	—Watertown (NY-Penn)	2	5	.286	4.07	9	9	0	0	0-...	42.0	40	21	19	1	14-0	40
1999	—Kinston (Caro.)	5	4	.556	4.93	15	15	1	0	0-...	69.1	46	47	38	2	52-0	81
	—Mahoning Valley (NY-P)	0	2	.000	2.65	5	5	0	0	0-...	17.0	8	6	5	1	7-0	26
	—Columbia (S.Atl.)	0	2	.000	4.50	2	2	0	0	0-...	12.0	9	6	6	2	4-0	15
2000	—Kinston (Caro.)	0	1	.000	3.86	1	1	0	0	0-...	2.1	2	1	1	0	1-0	4
2001	—Akron (East.)	5	7	.417	3.35	14	13	1	1	0-...	86.0	64	34	32	4	29-0	73
	—Buffalo (I.L.)	5	1	.833	4.01	11	10	0	0	0-...	60.2	60	28	27	7	17-0	52
	—Cleveland (A.L.)	1	2	.333	3.44	9	4	0	0	0-0	36.2	32	15	14	2	15-2	24
2002	—Cleveland (A.L.)	10	9	.526	6.55	26	26	1	0	0-0	137.1	176	104	100	15	62-1	102
	—Buffalo (I.L.)	1	0	1.000	1.64	3	3	0	0	0-...	22.0	16	4	4	1	4-0	16
Major League totals (2 years)		11	11	.500	5.90	35	30	1	0	0-0	174.0	208	119	114	17	77-3	126

DREW, J.D. OF CARDINALS

PERSONAL: Born November 20, 1975, in Valdosta, Ga. ... 6-1/195. ... Bats left, throws right. ... Full name: David Jonathan Drew. ... Brother of Tim Drew, pitcher, Montreal Expos.

HIGH SCHOOL: Lowndes County (Hahira, Ga.).

COLLEGE: Florida State.

TRANSACTIONS/CAREER NOTES: Selected by San Francisco Giants organization in 20th round of free-agent draft (June 2, 1994); did not sign. ... Selected by Philadelphia Phillies organization in first round (second pick overall) of free-agent draft (June 3, 1997); did not sign. ... Selected by St. Louis Cardinals organization in first round (fifth pick overall) of free-agent draft (June 2, 1998). ... On Arkansas disabled list (July 21-August 6, 1998). ... On St. Louis disabled list (May 16-June 17, 1999); included rehabilitation assignment to Memphis (May 28-June 17). ... On disabled list (July 8-27, 2000). ... On St. Louis disabled list (June 18-July 31, 2001); included rehabilitation assignment to Peoria (July 26-31). ... On disabled list (June 28-July 13, 2002).

HONORS: Named Golden Spikes Award winner by USA Baseball (1997). ... Named college Player of the Year by The Sporting News (1997). ... Named outfielder on The Sporting News college All-America team (1997).

STATISTICAL NOTES: Led N.L. outfielders with six double plays in 1999. ... Career major league grand slams: 1.

2002 GAMES PLAYED BY POSITION (MLB): OF—120.

Year	Team (League)	Pos.	G	AB	R	H	2B	3B	HR	RBI	BB	SO	SB-CS	Avg.	OBP	SLG	E	Avg.
			BATTING														FIELDING	
1997—	St. Paul (Nor.)	OF	44	170	51	58	6	1	18	50	30	40	5-3	.341	.443	.706	...	...
1998—	St. Paul (Nor.)	OF	30	114	27	44	11	2	9	33	21	32	8-1	.386	.504	.754	...	...
	—Arkansas (Texas)■	OF	19	67	18	22	3	1	5	11	13	15	2-1	.328	.444	.627	1	.980
	—Memphis (PCL)	OF	26	79	15	25	8	1	2	13	22	18	1-3	.316	.471	.519	2	.966
	—St. Louis (N.L.)	OF	14	36	9	15	3	1	5	13	4	10	0-0	.417	.463	.972	0	1.000
1999—	St. Louis (N.L.)	OF	104	368	72	89	16	6	13	39	50	77	19-3	.242	.340	.424	7	.972
	—Memphis (PCL)	OF	25	87	11	26	5	1	2	15	8	20	6-1	.299	.371	.448	0	1.000
2000—	St. Louis (N.L.)	OF	135	407	73	120	17	2	18	57	67	99	17-9	.295	.401	.479	9	.966
2001—	St. Louis (N.L.)	OF	109	375	80	121	18	5	27	73	57	75	13-3	.323	.414	.613	6	.973
	—Peoria (Midw.)	OF	3	11	3	6	2	0	0	0	1	0	0-0	.545	.583	.727	0	1.000
2002—	St. Louis (N.L.)	OF	135	424	61	107	19	1	18	56	57	104	8-2	.252	.349	.429	3	.987
Major League totals (5 years)			497	1610	295	452	73	15	81	238	235	365	57-17	.281	.378	.496	25	.975

DIVISION SERIES RECORD

Year	Team (League)	Pos.	G	AB	R	H	2B	3B	HR	RBI	BB	SO	SB-CS	Avg.	OBP	SLG	E	Avg.
			BATTING														FIELDING	
2000—	St. Louis (N.L.)	OF	2	6	1	1	0	0	0	0	2	1	2-0	.167	.375	.167	0	1.000
2001—	St. Louis (N.L.)	OF	5	13	1	2	0	0	1	2	3	1	0-0	.154	.313	.385	0	1.000
2002—	St. Louis (N.L.)	OF	2	9	1	2	0	0	1	1	1	2	0-0	.222	.300	.556	0	1.000
Division series totals (3 years)			9	28	3	5	0	0	2	3	6	4	2-0	.179	.324	.393	0	1.000

CHAMPIONSHIP SERIES RECORD

Year	Team (League)	Pos.	G	AB	R	H	2B	3B	HR	RBI	BB	SO	SB-CS	Avg.	OBP	SLG	E	Avg.
			BATTING														FIELDING	
2000—	St. Louis (N.L.)	OF-PH	5	12	2	4	1	0	0	1	0	3	0-0	.333	.333	.417	0	1.000
2002—	St. Louis (N.L.)	OF	5	13	1	5	0	0	1	1	1	2	0-0	.385	.429	.615	0	1.000
Championship series totals (2 years)			10	25	3	9	1	0	1	2	1	5	0-0	.360	.385	.520	0	1.000

DREW, TIM — P — EXPOS

PERSONAL: Born August 31, 1978, in Valdosta, Ga. ... 6-1/195. ... Throws right, bats right. ... Full name: Timothy Andrew Drew. ... Brother of J.D. Drew, outfielder, St. Louis Cardinals.

HIGH SCHOOL: Lowndes County (Hahira, Ga.).

TRANSACTIONS/CAREER NOTES: Selected by Cleveland Indians organization in first round (28th pick overall) of free-agent draft (June 3, 1997). ... On Buffalo disabled list (June 18-26, 2001). ... Traded by Indians to Montreal Expos (June 28, 2002), completing deal in which Indians traded P Bartolo Colon with future considerations to Expos for 1B Lee Stevens, SS Brandon Phillips, P Cliff Lee and OF Grady Sizemore (June 27, 2002).

STATISTICAL NOTES: Led International League with 181 innings pitched and tied for lead with 10 sacrifice hits allowed in 2002.

CAREER HITTING (MLB): 0-for-4 (.000), 0 R, 0 2B, 0 3B, 0 HR, 0 RBI.

Year	League	W	L	Pct.	ERA	G	GS	CG	ShO	Sv.-Opp.	IP	H	R	ER	HR	BB-IBB	SO
1997—	Burlington (Appl.)	0	1	.000	6.17	4	4	0	0	0-...	11.2	16	15	8	0	4-0	14
	—Watertown (NY-Penn)	0	0	...	1.93	1	1	0	0	0-...	4.2	4	1	1	0	3-0	9
1998—	Columbus (S.Atl.)	4	3	.571	3.79	13	13	0	0	0-...	71.1	68	43	30	5	26-0	64
	—Kinston (Caro.)	3	8	.273	5.20	15	15	0	0	0-...	90.0	105	58	52	9	31-1	67
1999—	Kinston (Caro.)	*13	5	*.722	3.73	28	*28	2	0	0-...	169.0	154	79	70	12	60-0	125
2000—	Akron (East.)	3	2	.600	2.42	9	9	0	0	0-...	52.0	41	19	14	1	15-0	22
	—Cleveland (A.L.)	1	0	1.000	10.00	3	3	0	0	0-0	9.0	17	12	10	1	8-0	5
	—Buffalo (I.L.)	7	8	.467	5.87	16	16	2	0	0-...	95.0	122	69	62	12	31-0	53
2001—	Cleveland (A.L.)	0	2	.000	7.97	8	6	0	0	0-0	35.0	51	39	31	9	16-0	15
	—Buffalo (I.L.)	8	6	.571	3.92	18	18	1	1	0-...	108.0	115	54	47	13	27-1	75
2002—	Buffalo (I.L.)	8	4	.667	3.27	15	15	2	2	0-...	96.1	96	43	35	6	23-1	43
	—Ottawa (I.L.)■	6	3	.667	2.87	13	13	0	0	0-...	§84.2	77	31	27	5	24-2	29
	—Montreal (N.L.)	1	0	1.000	2.81	7	1	0	0	2-3	16.0	12	8	5	1	2-0	10
A.L. totals (2 years)		1	2	.333	8.39	11	9	0	0	0-0	44.0	68	51	41	10	24-0	20
N.L. totals (1 year)		1	0	1.000	2.81	7	1	0	0	2-3	16.0	12	8	5	1	2-0	10
Major League totals (3 years)		2	2	.500	6.90	18	10	0	0	2-3	60.0	80	59	46	11	26-0	30

DRISKILL, TRAVIS — P — ORIOLES

PERSONAL: Born August 1, 1971, in Omaha, Neb. ... 6-0/225. ... Throws right, bats right. ... Full name: Travis Corey Driskill.

HIGH SCHOOL: L.C. Anderson (Austin, Texas).

COLLEGE: Texas Tech.

TRANSACTIONS/CAREER NOTES: Selected by Houston Astros organization in 76th round of free-agent draft (June 4, 1990); did not sign. ... Selected by Cleveland Indians organization in fourth round of free-agent draft (June 3, 1993). ... Contract sold by Indians to Yakult Swallows of Japan Central League (January 6, 1998). ... Signed by Indians organization (August 3, 1998). ... Granted free agency (October 15, 1999). ... Signed by Astros organization (January 3, 2000). ... Granted free agency (October 15, 2001). ... Signed by Baltimore Orioles organization (November 16, 2001).

CAREER HITTING (MLB): 0-for-3 (.000), 1 R, 0 2B, 0 3B, 0 HR, 0 RBI.

Year	League	W	L	Pct.	ERA	G	GS	CG	ShO	Sv.-Opp.	IP	H	R	ER	HR	BB-IBB	SO
1993—	Watertown (NY-Penn)	5	4	.556	4.14	21	8	0	0	3-...	63.0	62	38	29	4	21-0	53
1994—	Columbus (S.Atl.)	5	5	.500	2.52	62	0	0	0	35-...	64.1	51	25	18	2	30-4	88
1995—	Kinston (Caro.)	0	2	.000	2.74	15	0	0	0	0-...	23.0	17	7	7	2	5-1	24
	—Canton/Akron (East.)	3	4	.429	4.66	33	0	0	0	4-...	46.1	46	24	24	3	19-1	39
1996—	Canton/Akron (East.)	13	7	.650	3.61	29	24	4	2	0-...	172.0	169	89	69	8	63-0	148
1997—	Buffalo (A.A.)	8	7	.533	4.65	29	24	1	0	0-...	147.0	159	86	76	22	60-0	102
1998—	Yakult (Jap. East)■	1	6	.142	6.13	12	5	0	0	0-...	40	46	29	27	...	19-...	25
	—Yakult (Jap. Cen.)	0	1	.000	4.80	7	3	0	0	0-...	15	21	9	8	...	6-...	7
	—Akron (East.)■	3	0	1.000	3.42	5	4	0	0	0-...	26.1	27	12	10	4	7-0	16
	—Buffalo (I.L.)	0	0	...	9.00	1	1	0	0	0-...	6.0	9	6	6	0	1-0	5

Year	League	W	L	Pct.	ERA	G	GS	CG	ShO	Sv.-Opp.	IP	H	R	ER	HR	BB-IBB	SO
1999—	Buffalo (I.L.)	9	8	.529	4.83	31	18	0	0	0-...	132.1	146	78	71	21	32-2	90
2000—	New Orleans (PCL)■	12	11	.522	4.01	28	28	2	1	0-...	*179.1	201	101	80	15	45-0	113
2001—	New Orleans (PCL)	11	5	.688	3.78	28	28	1	0	0-...	*178.2	175	83	75	21	33-2	145
2002—	Rochester (I.L.)■	2	2	.500	1.64	4	4	1	1	0-...	22.0	17	8	4	1	1-0	15
—	Baltimore (A.L.)	8	8	.500	4.95	29	19	0	0	0-0	132.2	150	78	73	21	48-1	78
Major League totals (1 year)		8	8	.500	4.95	29	19	0	0	0-0	132.2	150	78	73	21	48-1	78

DuBOSE, ERIC — P — ORIOLES

PERSONAL: Born May 15, 1976, in Bradenton, Fla. ... 6-3/231. ... Throws left, bats left. ... Full name: Eric Ladell DuBose.
HIGH SCHOOL: Patrician Academy (Butler, Ala.).
COLLEGE: Mississippi State.
TRANSACTIONS/CAREER NOTES: Selected by Oakland Athletics organization in first round (21st pick overall) of free-agent draft (June 3, 1997); pick received as compensation for Baltimore Orioles signing SS Mike Bordick. ... On Midland disabled list (June 18-July 23, 1999). ... On Midland disabled list (April 14-June 13, 2000). ... Claimed on waivers by Cleveland Indians (September 8, 2000). ... Claimed on waivers by Detroit Tigers (September 22, 2000). ... Released by Tigers (March 31, 2001). ... Signed by Baltimore Orioles organization (February 4, 2002). ... On Rochester disabled list (April 4-May 1, 2002).
CAREER HITTING (MLB): 0-for-0 (.000), 0 R, 0 2B, 0 3B, 0 HR, 0 RBI.

Year	League	W	L	Pct.	ERA	G	GS	CG	ShO	Sv.-Opp.	IP	H	R	ER	HR	BB-IBB	SO
1997—	S. Oregon (N'West)	1	0	1.000	0.00	3	1	0	0	0-...	10.0	5	0	0	0	6-0	15
—	Visalia (Calif.)	1	3	.250	7.04	10	9	0	0	0-...	38.1	43	37	30	4	28-0	39
1998—	Visalia (Calif.)	6	1	.857	3.38	17	10	0	0	1-...	72.0	56	34	27	5	25-0	85
—	Huntsville (Sou.)	7	6	.538	2.70	14	14	1	1	0-...	83.1	86	37	25	2	34-1	66
1999—	Midland (Texas)	4	2	.667	5.49	21	14	0	0	1-...	77.0	89	57	47	10	44-1	68
2000—	Midland (Texas)	5	1	.833	4.13	18	0	0	0	0-...	28.1	25	16	13	1	18-2	20
—	Visalia (Calif.)	0	1	.000	1.69	5	0	0	0	1-...	10.2	8	2	2	0	5-1	12
2001—										Did not play.							
2002—	Rochester (I.L.)■	0	0	...	27.00	1	0	0	0	0-...	.1	1	2	1	0	2-0	0
—	Bowie (East.)	5	3	.625	2.51	41	0	0	0	3-...	64.2	46	21	18	2	21-0	66
—	Baltimore (A.L.)	0	0	...	3.00	4	0	0	0	0-0	6.0	7	2	2	1	1-0	4
Major League totals (1 year)		0	0	...	3.00	4	0	0	0	0-0	6.0	7	2	2	1	1-0	4

DUCKWORTH, BRANDON — P — PHILLIES

PERSONAL: Born January 23, 1976, in Salt Lake City. ... 6-2/185. ... Throws right, bats right. ... Full name: Brandon J. Duckworth.
HIGH SCHOOL: Kearns (Utah).
JUNIOR COLLEGE: Southern Idaho.
COLLEGE: Cal State-Fullerton.
TRANSACTIONS/CAREER NOTES: Selected by Toronto Blue Jays organization in 30th round of free-agent draft (June 1, 1995); did not sign. ... Selected by Arizona Diamondbacks organization in 61st round of free-agent draft (June 4, 1996); did not sign. ... Signed by Philadelphia Phillies organization as non-drafted free agent (August 13, 1997).
HONORS: Named International League Most Valuable Pitcher (2001).
CAREER HITTING (MLB): 14-for-70 (.200), 4 R, 2 2B, 0 3B, 0 HR, 5 RBI.

Year	League	W	L	Pct.	ERA	G	GS	CG	ShO	Sv.-Opp.	IP	H	R	ER	HR	BB-IBB	SO
1998—	Piedmont (S.Atl.)	9	8	.529	2.80	21	21	•5	•3	0-...	147.2	116	58	46	10	24-0	119
—	Clearwater (FSL)	6	2	.750	3.74	9	9	1	1	0-...	53.0	64	25	22	2	22-0	46
1999—	Clearwater (FSL)	11	5	.688	4.84	27	17	0	0	1-...	132.0	164	84	71	13	40-0	101
2000—	Reading (East.)	13	7	.650	3.16	27	27	1	0	0-...	165.0	145	70	58	17	52-0	*178
2001—	Scranton/W.B. (I.L.)	*13	2	*.867	2.63	22	20	2	1	0-...	147.0	122	46	43	14	36-2	150
—	Philadelphia (N.L.)	3	2	.600	3.52	11	11	0	0	0-0	69.0	57	29	27	2	29-5	40
2002—	Philadelphia (N.L.)	8	9	.471	5.41	30	29	0	0	0-0	163.0	167	103	98	26	69-5	167
Major League totals (2 years)		11	11	.500	4.85	41	40	0	0	0-0	232.0	224	132	125	28	98-10	207

DUFF, MATT — P — CARDINALS

PERSONAL: Born October 6, 1974, in Clarksdale, Miss. ... 6-1/192. ... Throws right, bats right. ... Full name: Matthew Clark Duff.
COLLEGE: Mississippi.
TRANSACTIONS/CAREER NOTES: Signed by Springfield of the Frontier League (1997). ... Contract purchased by Pittsburgh Pirates organization from Springfield (August 25, 1997). ... Released by Pirates (March 30, 2001). ... Signed by St. Paul, Northern League (May 2001). ... Signed by Sioux Falls, Northern League (July 2001). ... Signed by Florida Marlins organization (November 13, 2001). ... Released by Marlins (March 30, 2002). ... Signed by St. Louis Cardinals organization (April 1, 2002).
CAREER HITTING (MLB): 0-for-0 (.000), 0 R, 0 2B, 0 3B, 0 HR, 0 RBI.

Year	League	W	L	Pct.	ERA	G	GS	CG	ShO	Sv.-Opp.	IP	H	R	ER	HR	BB-IBB	SO
1997—	Springfield (Fron.)	7	4	.636	2.70	14	12	2	...	0-...	80.0	70	33	24	3	27-1	76
—	Augusta (S.Atl.)■	0	1	.000	1.50	2	1	0	0	0-...	6.0	6	1	1	0	2-0	6
1998—	Augusta (S.Atl.)	1	0	1.000	3.00	10	0	0	0	3-...	9.0	8	3	3	1	4-0	12
—	Lynchburg (Caro.)	4	5	.444	3.30	40	0	0	0	10-...	62.2	52	26	23	4	20-2	61
1999—	Lynchburg (Caro.)	2	3	.400	4.99	7	7	0	0	0-...	39.2	41	22	22	6	13-0	40
—	Altoona (East.)	2	4	.333	2.81	44	0	0	0	12-...	57.2	43	19	18	5	35-4	59
2000—	Altoona (East.)	0	4	.000	3.93	47	0	0	0	6-...	55.0	50	31	24	1	36-9	61
2001—	St. Paul (Nor.)■	0	3	.000	4.78	22	0	0	0	3-...	32.0	38	23	17	...	11-...	41
—	Sioux Falls (Nor.)■	4	0	1.000	1.71	17	0	0	0	7-...	21.0	16	5	4	...	6-...	29
2002—	Potomac (Caro.)■	0	0	...	0.00	4	0	0	0	4-...	4.1	4	0	0	0	1-0	7
—	New Haven (East.)	11	1	*.917	1.38	47	0	0	0	4-...	65.0	38	12	10	3	21-2	91
—	St. Louis (N.L.)	0	0	...	4.76	7	0	0	0	0-0	5.2	3	3	3	0	8-2	4
—	Memphis (PCL)	0	0	...	1.93	4	0	0	0	1-...	4.2	2	1	1	1	4-0	3
Major League totals (1 year)		0	0	...	4.76	7	0	0	0	0-0	5.2	3	3	3	0	8-2	4

DUNCAN, COURTNEY — P — CUBS

PERSONAL: Born October 9, 1974, in Mobile, Ala. ... 6-0/190. ... Throws right, bats left. ... Full name: Courtney Demond Duncan.
HIGH SCHOOL: Daphne (Ala.).
COLLEGE: Grambling State.
TRANSACTIONS/CAREER NOTES: Selected by Chicago Cubs organization in 20th round of free-agent draft (June 2, 1996). ... On West Tenn disabled list (June 10-24, 1999). ... On Chicago disabled list (June 29-July 16 and July 20-September 1, 2001); included rehabilitation assignment to Iowa (August 14-September 1).
CAREER HITTING (MLB): 0-for-3 (.000), 1 R, 0 2B, 0 3B, 0 HR, 1 RBI.

Year League	W	L	Pct.	ERA	G	GS	CG	ShO	Sv.-Opp.	IP	H	R	ER	HR	BB-IBB	SO
1996— Williamsport (NY-Penn) ...	*11	1	*.917	2.19	15	•15	1	0	0-...	90.1	58	28	22	6	34-0	91
1997— Daytona (FSL)	8	4	.667	*1.63	19	19	1	0	0-...	121.2	90	35	22	3	35-0	120
— Orlando (Sou.)	2	2	.500	3.40	8	8	0	0	0-...	45.0	37	28	17	2	29-5	45
1998— West Tenn (Sou.)	7	9	.438	4.26	29	•29	0	0	0-...	162.2	141	89	77	7	*108-5	157
1999— West Tenn (Sou.)	1	7	.125	7.13	11	8	0	0	0-...	41.2	44	42	33	3	42-4	42
— Daytona (FSL)	4	5	.444	5.54	15	11	1	1	1-...	65.0	70	60	40	6	34-1	48
2000— West Tenn (Sou.)	5	4	.556	3.07	61	0	0	0	25-...	73.1	57	32	25	2	33-2	72
2001— Chicago (N.L.)	3	3	.500	5.06	36	0	0	0	0-2	42.2	42	24	24	5	25-3	49
— Iowa (PCL)	1	0	1.000	3.24	7	0	0	0	0-...	8.1	7	3	3	1	5-1	15
2002— Iowa (PCL)	3	5	.375	3.99	55	0	0	0	6-...	67.2	67	35	30	6	33-1	64
— Chicago (N.L.)	0	0	...	0.00	2	0	0	0	0-0	2.1	2	0	0	0	1-0	1
Major League totals (2 years).....	3	3	.500	4.80	38	0	0	0	0-2	45.0	44	24	24	5	26-3	50

DUNN, ADAM — OF — REDS

PERSONAL: Born November 9, 1979, in Houston. ... 6-6/240. ... Bats left, throws right. ... Full name: Adam Troy Dunn.
HIGH SCHOOL: New Caney (Texas).
COLLEGE: Texas.
TRANSACTIONS/CAREER NOTES: Selected by Cincinnati Reds organization in second round of free-agent draft (June 2, 1998). ... On Clinton disabled list (June 8-25, 2000).
RECORDS: Shares major league single-game record for most strikeouts (nine-inning game)—5 (August 20, 2002).
STATISTICAL NOTES: Career major league grand slams: 1.
2002 GAMES PLAYED BY POSITION (MLB): OF—119; 1B—44; DH—1.

		BATTING														FIELDING	
Year Team (League)	Pos.	G	AB	R	H	2B	3B	HR	RBI	BB	SO	SB-CS	Avg.	OBP	SLG	E	Avg.
1998— Billings (Pio.)	OF	34	125	26	36	3	1	4	13	22	33	4-2	.288	.404	.424	6	.860
1999— Rockford (Midw.)	OF	93	313	62	96	16	2	11	44	46	64	21-9	.307	.409	.476	8	.918
2000— Dayton (Midw.)	OF	122	420	101	118	29	1	16	79	100	101	24-5	.281	*.428	.469	9	.958
2001— Chattanooga (Sou.)	OF	39	140	30	48	9	0	12	31	24	31	6-3	.343	.449	.664	3	.961
— Louisville (I.L.)	OF	55	210	44	69	13	0	20	53	38	51	5-1	.329	.441	.676	5	.954
— Cincinnati (N.L.)	OF	66	244	54	64	18	1	19	43	38	74	4-2	.262	.371	.578	2	.986
2002— Cincinnati (N.L.)	OF-1B-DH	158	535	84	133	28	2	26	71	128	170	19-9	.249	.400	.454	15	.975
Major League totals (2 years)		224	779	138	197	46	3	45	114	166	244	23-11	.253	.391	.493	17	.977

ALL-STAR GAME RECORD

	AB	R	H	2B	3B	HR	RBI	BB	SO	SB-CS	Avg.	OBP	SLG	E	Avg.
All-Star Game totals (1 year)	1	0	0	0	0	0	0	1	0	0-0	.000	.500	.000	0	...

DUNSTON, SHAWON — OF/IF

PERSONAL: Born March 21, 1963, in Brooklyn, N.Y. ... 6-1/180. ... Bats right, throws right. ... Full name: Shawon Donnell Dunston.
HIGH SCHOOL: Thomas Jefferson (Brooklyn, N.Y.).
TRANSACTIONS/CAREER NOTES: Selected by Chicago Cubs organization in first round (first pick overall) of free-agent draft (June 7, 1982). ... On disabled list (May 31-June 10, 1983). ... On Chicago disabled list (June 16-August 21, 1987); included rehabilitation assignment to Iowa (August 14-21). ... On disabled list (May 5, 1992-remainder of season and March 27-September 1, 1993). ... On suspended list (September 8-12, 1995). ... Granted free agency (October 31, 1995). ... Signed by San Francisco Giants (January 9, 1996). ... On disabled list (April 24-May 13 and August 5-October 1, 1996). ... Granted free agency (November 18, 1996). ... Signed by Cubs (December 7, 1996). ... On Chicago disabled list (June 9-24, 1997). ... Traded by Cubs to Pittsburgh Pirates for a player to be named later (August 31, 1997). ... Granted free agency (October 28, 1997). ... Signed by Cleveland Indians (February 16, 1998). ... Traded by Indians with P Jose Mesa and P Alvin Morman to Giants for P Steve Reed and OF Jacob Cruz (July 23, 1998). ... Granted free agency (October 23, 1998). ... Signed by St. Louis Cardinals (February 16, 1999). ... On suspended list (June 17-20, 1999). ... On St. Louis disabled list (June 23-July 9, 1999). ... Traded by Cardinals to New York Mets for IF Craig Paquette (July 31, 1999). ... Granted free agency (October 29, 1999). ... Signed by Cardinals organization (February 3, 2000). ... Granted free agency (October 27, 2000). ... Signed by Giants (December 8, 2000). ... On disabled list (August 4-19, 2001). ... On disabled list (May 7-21 and August 9-September 1, 2002). ... Granted free agency (October 28, 2002).
RECORDS: Shares modern major league single-game record for most triples—3 (July 28, 1990).
HONORS: Named shortstop on The Sporting News N.L. All-Star team (1989).
STATISTICAL NOTES: Led N.L. shortstops with 320 putouts, 465 assists and 817 total chances and tied for lead in double plays with 96 in 1986. ... Led N.L. shortstops with 257 putouts in 1988 and 261 in 1991. ... Career major league grand slams: 5.
2002 GAMES PLAYED BY POSITION (MLB): OF—49; DH—3; 1B—1; SS—1.

		BATTING														FIELDING	
Year Team (League)	Pos.	G	AB	R	H	2B	3B	HR	RBI	BB	SO	SB-CS	Avg.	OBP	SLG	E	Avg.
1982— GC Cubs (GCL)	SS-3B	53	190	27	61	11	0	2	28	11	22	32-24	.321	.354	.411	24	.888
1983— Quad Cities (Midw.)	SS	117	455	65	141	17	8	4	62	7	51	58-23	.310	.332	.409	47	.914
1984— Midland (Texas)	SS	73	298	44	98	13	3	3	34	11	38	11-8	.329	.354	.423	32	.920
— Iowa (A.A.)	SS	61	210	25	49	11	1	7	27	4	40	9-3	.233	.247	.395	26	.907
1985— Chicago (N.L.)	SS	74	250	40	65	12	4	4	18	19	42	11-3	.260	.310	.388	17	.958
— Iowa (A.A.)	SS	73	272	24	73	9	6	2	28	5	48	17-12	.268	.283	.368	12	.963
1986— Chicago (N.L.)	SS	150	581	66	145	37	3	17	68	21	114	13-11	.250	.278	.411	*32	.961
1987— Chicago (N.L.)	SS	95	346	40	85	18	3	5	22	10	68	12-3	.246	.267	.358	14	.969
— Iowa (A.A.)	SS	5	19	1	8	1	0	0	2	0	3	1-1	.421	.421	.474	1	.947
1988— Chicago (N.L.)	SS	155	575	69	143	23	6	9	56	16	108	30-9	.249	.271	.357	20	.973

Year	Team (League)	Pos.	G	AB	R	H	2B	3B	HR	RBI	BB	SO	SB-CS	Avg.	OBP	SLG	E	Avg.
			BATTING														FIELDING	
1989—	Chicago (N.L.)	SS	138	471	52	131	20	6	9	60	30	86	19-11	.278	.320	.403	17	.972
1990—	Chicago (N.L.)	SS	146	545	73	143	22	8	17	66	15	87	25-5	.262	.283	.426	20	.970
1991—	Chicago (N.L.)	SS	142	492	59	128	22	7	12	50	23	64	21-6	.260	.292	.407	21	.968
1992—	Chicago (N.L.)	SS	18	73	8	23	3	1	0	2	3	13	2-3	.315	.342	.384	1	.986
1993—	Chicago (N.L.)	SS	7	10	3	4	2	0	0	2	0	1	0-0	.400	.400	.600	0	1.000
1994—	Chicago (N.L.)	SS	88	331	38	92	19	0	11	35	16	48	3-8	.278	.313	.435	12	.966
1995—	Chicago (N.L.)	SS	127	477	58	141	30	6	14	69	10	75	10-5	.296	.317	.472	17	.969
1996—	San Fran. (N.L.)■	SS	82	287	27	86	12	2	5	25	13	40	8-0	.300	.331	.408	15	.957
1997—	Chicago (N.L.)■	SS-OF	114	419	57	119	18	4	9	41	8	64	29-7	.284	.300	.411	12	.971
—	Pittsburgh (N.L.)■	SS	18	71	14	28	4	1	5	16	0	11	3-1	.394	.389	.690	3	.965
1998—	Cleveland (A.L.)■	2-S-O-DH	62	156	26	37	11	3	3	12	6	18	9-2	.237	.265	.404	4	.972
—	San Fran. (N.L.)■	SS-OF-2B	36	51	10	9	2	0	3	8	0	10	0-2	.176	.222	.392	2	.926
1999—	St. Louis (N.L.)■	0-1-S-3-DH	62	150	23	46	5	2	5	25	2	23	6-3	.307	.327	.467	2	.981
—	New York (N.L.)■	OF-3B	42	93	12	32	6	1	0	16	0	16	4-1	.344	.354	.430	1	.979
2000—	St. Louis (N.L.)■	O-S-1-3-DH	98	216	28	54	11	2	12	43	6	47	3-1	.250	.278	.486	2	.984
2001—	San Fran. (N.L.)■	OF-1B-DH	88	186	26	52	10	3	9	25	2	32	3-1	.280	.293	.511	3	.966
2002—	San Francisco (N.L.)	OF-DH-1B-SS	72	147	7	34	5	0	1	9	3	33	1-0	.231	.250	.286	0	1.000
American League totals (1 year)			62	156	26	37	11	3	3	12	6	18	9-2	.237	.265	.404	4	.972
National League totals (18 years)			1752	5771	710	1560	281	59	147	656	197	982	203-80	.270	.297	.416	211	.968
Major League totals (18 years)			1814	5927	736	1597	292	62	150	668	203	1000	212-82	.269	.296	.416	215	.968

DIVISION SERIES RECORD

Year	Team (League)	Pos.	G	AB	R	H	2B	3B	HR	RBI	BB	SO	SB-CS	Avg.	OBP	SLG	E	Avg.
			BATTING														FIELDING	
1999—	New York (N.L.)	OF-PH-PR	4	6	0	1	0	0	0	0	0	1	0-0	.167	.167	.167	0	1.000
2000—	St. Louis (N.L.)	PH	1	1	0	1	0	0	0	0	0	0	0-0	1.000	1.000	1.000	...	...
2002—	San Francisco (N.L.)	PH	2	1	0	0	0	0	0	0	0	1	0-0	.000	.000	.000	0	...
Division series totals (3 years)			7	8	0	2	0	0	0	0	0	2	0-0	.250	.250	.250	0	1.000

CHAMPIONSHIP SERIES RECORD

Year	Team (League)	Pos.	G	AB	R	H	2B	3B	HR	RBI	BB	SO	SB-CS	Avg.	OBP	SLG	E	Avg.
			BATTING														FIELDING	
1989—	Chicago (N.L.)	SS	5	19	2	6	0	0	0	0	1	1	1-0	.316	.350	.316	1	.960
1999—	New York (N.L.)	PH-OF	5	7	2	1	0	0	0	0	0	2	1-1	.143	.143	.143	0	...
2000—	St. Louis (N.L.)	PH-OF	4	6	1	2	1	0	0	0	0	0	0-0	.333	.333	.500	0	1.000
2002—	San Francisco (N.L.)	OF	2	2	0	1	0	0	0	0	0	1	0-0	.500	.500	.500	0	...
Championship series totals (4 years)			16	34	5	10	1	0	0	0	1	4	2-1	.294	.314	.324	1	.962

WORLD SERIES RECORD

Year	Team (League)	Pos.	G	AB	R	H	2B	3B	HR	RBI	BB	SO	SB-CS	Avg.	OBP	SLG	E	Avg.
			BATTING														FIELDING	
2002—	San Francisco (N.L.)	DH	4	9	1	2	0	0	1	3	0	1	0-0	.222	.222	.556	0	...

ALL-STAR GAME RECORD

	AB	R	H	2B	3B	HR	RBI	BB	SO	SB-CS	Avg.	OBP	SLG	E	Avg.
All-Star Game totals (1 year)	2	0	0	0	0	0	0	0	0	0-0	.000	.000	.000	0	...

DUNWOODY, TODD OF

PERSONAL: Born April 11, 1975, in Lafayette, Ind. ... 6-1/205. ... Bats left, throws left. ... Full name: Todd Franklin Dunwoody.

HIGH SCHOOL: West Lafayette (Ind.) Harrison.

TRANSACTIONS/CAREER NOTES: Selected by Florida Marlins organization in seventh round of free-agent draft (June 3, 1993). ... On Charlotte disabled list (April 11-18, 1998). ... Traded by Marlins to Kansas City Royals for IF Sean McNally (December 15, 1999). ... On Kansas City disabled list (March 24-June 3, 2000); included rehabilitation assignments to Omaha (May 13-20 and June 1-3). ... Granted free agency (December 21, 2000). ... Signed by Chicago Cubs organization (January 9, 2001). ... Granted free agency (October 15, 2001). ... Signed by Cleveland Indians organization (November 6, 2001). ... On Cleveland disabled list (June 22-July 30, 2002); included rehabilitation assignment to Buffalo (July 11-30). ... Released by Indians (October 1, 2002).

STATISTICAL NOTES: Tied for Midwest League lead in intentional bases on balls received with seven in 1995. ... Led Eastern League with 267 total bases in 1996.

2002 GAMES PLAYED BY POSITION (MLB): OF—2.

Year	Team (League)	Pos.	G	AB	R	H	2B	3B	HR	RBI	BB	SO	SB-CS	Avg.	OBP	SLG	E	Avg.
			BATTING														FIELDING	
1993—	GC Marlins (GCL)	OF	31	109	13	21	2	2	0	7	7	28	5-0	.193	.252	.248	1	.979
1994—	Kane County (Midw.)	OF	15	45	7	5	0	0	1	1	5	17	1-0	.111	.200	.178	0	1.000
—	GC Marlins (GCL)	OF	46	169	32	44	6	6	1	25	21	28	11-3	.260	.354	.385	1	.989
1995—	Kane County (Midw.)	OF	132	494	89	140	20	8	14	89	52	105	39-11	.283	.355	.441	5	.983
1996—	Portland (East.)	OF	138	*552	88	153	30	6	24	93	45	*149	24-19	.277	.337	.484	1	*.996
1997—	Charlotte (I.L.)	OF-DH	107	401	74	105	16	7	23	62	39	129	25-3	.262	.331	.509	2	.992
—	Florida (N.L.)	OF	19	50	7	13	2	2	2	7	7	21	2-0	.260	.362	.500	2	.929
1998—	Charlotte (I.L.)	OF	28	102	20	31	6	3	6	22	12	28	4-2	.304	.398	.598	1	.987
—	Florida (N.L.)	OF	116	434	53	109	27	7	5	28	21	113	5-1	.251	.292	.380	3	.989
1999—	Florida (N.L.)	OF	64	186	20	41	6	3	2	20	12	41	3-4	.220	.270	.317	2	.981
—	Calgary (PCL)	OF-DH	65	246	35	67	16	7	9	36	10	56	7-8	.272	.304	.504	4	.977
2000—	Omaha (PCL)■	OF	9	31	5	10	1	0	1	5	4	8	1-2	.323	.405	.452	0	1.000
—	Kansas City (A.L.)	OF-DH	61	178	12	37	9	0	1	23	8	42	3-0	.208	.238	.275	2	.976
2001—	Iowa (PCL)	OF	75	251	31	71	18	3	8	32	17	75	6-4	.283	.331	.474	3	.974
—	Chicago (N.L.)	OF	33	61	6	13	4	0	1	3	3	14	0-1	.213	.250	.328	1	.973
2002—	Buffalo (I.L.)■	OF	102	363	57	97	31	4	7	29	12	62	8-3	.267	.298	.433	3	.983
—	Cleveland (A.L.)	OF	2	6	0	0	0	0	0	0	0	3	0-0	.000	.000	.000	0	1.000
American League totals (2 years)			63	184	12	37	9	0	1	23	8	45	3-0	.201	.231	.266	2	.976
National League totals (4 years)			232	731	86	176	39	12	10	58	43	189	10-6	.241	.288	.368	8	.982
Major League totals (6 years)			295	915	98	213	48	12	11	81	51	234	13-6	.233	.277	.348	10	.982

DURAZO, ERUBIEL — 1B — DIAMONDBACKS

PERSONAL: Born January 23, 1974, in Hermosillo, Mexico. ... 6-3/240. ... Bats left, throws left. ... Full name: Erubiel Durazo Cardenas.
HIGH SCHOOL: Amphitheater (Tucson, Ariz.).
JUNIOR COLLEGE: Pima Community College (Ariz.).
TRANSACTIONS/CAREER NOTES: Signed by Monterrey, Mexican League (1997). ... Contract sold by Monterrey to Arizona Diamondbacks organization (December 16, 1998). ... On Arizona disabled list (May 30-June 24, June 27-July 13 and August 20, 2000-remainder of season); included rehabilitation assignments to Tuscon (June 20-24 and July 8-9) and Arizona League Diamondbacks (July 9-13). ... On Arizona disabled list (August 15-September 1, 2001); included rehabilitation assignment to Tucson (August 28-September 1). ... On Arizona disabled list (March 22-May 16 and June 30-July 27, 2002); included rehabilitation assignments to Tucson (May 10-16) and El Paso (July 20-27).
STATISTICAL NOTES: Led Southern League with a .569 slugging percentage in 1999. ... Hit three home runs in one game (May 17, 2002). ... Career major league grand slams: 1.
2002 GAMES PLAYED BY POSITION (MLB): 1B—56; DH—6; OF—2.

			BATTING														FIELDING	
Year	Team (League)	Pos.	G	AB	R	H	2B	3B	HR	RBI	BB	SO	SB-CS	Avg.	OBP	SLG	E	Avg.
1997—	Monterrey (Mex.)	1B-OF	110	358	47	101	21	10	8	61	52	43	3-7	.282	.371	.464	3	.994
1998—	Monterrey (Mex.)	OF-1B	119	420	84	147	32	2	19	98	99	71	4-3	.350	.477	.571	0	1.000
1999—	El Paso (Texas)■	1B	64	226	53	91	18	3	14	55	44	37	2-1	.403	.498	.695	10	.982
	—Tucson (PCL)	1B-DH	30	118	27	48	7	0	10	28	14	18	1-0	.407	.470	.720	1	.996
	—Arizona (N.L.)	1B	52	155	31	51	4	2	11	30	26	43	1-1	.329	.422	.594	0	1.000
2000—	Arizona (N.L.)	1B	67	196	35	52	11	0	8	33	34	43	1-0	.265	.373	.444	5	.989
	—Tucson (PCL)	1B	13	43	9	18	6	0	3	10	6	7	0-0	.419	.490	.767	3	.957
	—Ariz. D-backs (Ariz.)	1B	2	5	2	3	0	0	1	2	1	0	0-0	.600	.667	1.200	0	1.000
2001—	Arizona (N.L.)	1B-DH-OF	92	175	34	47	11	0	12	38	28	49	0-0	.269	.372	.537	2	.993
	—Tucson (PCL)	1B	3	11	3	3	0	0	1	1	1	3	0-0	.273	.333	.545	0	1.000
2002—	Tucson (PCL)	1B	7	22	5	7	2	1	1	3	0	2	0-0	.318	.348	.636	1	.971
	—Arizona (N.L.)	1B-DH-OF	76	222	46	58	12	2	16	48	49	60	0-1	.261	.395	.550	7	.984
	—El Paso (Texas)	1B	5	14	5	7	3	0	2	7	4	1	0-0	.500	.611	1.143	0	1.000
Major League totals (4 years)			287	748	146	208	38	4	47	149	137	195	2-2	.278	.390	.528	14	.991

DIVISION SERIES RECORD

			BATTING														FIELDING	
Year	Team (League)	Pos.	G	AB	R	H	2B	3B	HR	RBI	BB	SO	SB-CS	Avg.	OBP	SLG	E	Avg.
1999—	Arizona (N.L.)	1B	2	7	1	1	0	0	1	1	1	0	0-0	.143	.250	.571	0	1.000
2001—	Arizona (N.L.)	PH	1	1	0	0	0	0	0	0	0	0	0-0	.000	.000	.000	...	...
2002—	Arizona (N.L.)	1B	2	4	0	0	0	0	0	0	1	1	0-0	.000	.200	.000	0	1.000
Division series totals (3 years)			5	12	1	1	0	0	1	1	2	1	0-0	.083	.214	.333	0	1.000

CHAMPIONSHIP SERIES RECORD

			BATTING														FIELDING	
Year	Team (League)	Pos.	G	AB	R	H	2B	3B	HR	RBI	BB	SO	SB-CS	Avg.	OBP	SLG	E	Avg.
2001—	Arizona (N.L.)	PH-1B	2	3	1	1	0	0	1	2	0	1	0-0	.333	.333	1.333	0	1.000

WORLD SERIES RECORD

NOTES: Member of World Series championship team (2001).

			BATTING														FIELDING	
Year	Team (League)	Pos.	G	AB	R	H	2B	3B	HR	RBI	BB	SO	SB-CS	Avg.	OBP	SLG	E	Avg.
2001—	Arizona (N.L.)	DH-PH	4	11	0	4	1	0	0	1	3	4	0-0	.364	.500	.455	...	...

DURBIN, CHAD — P — ROYALS

PERSONAL: Born December 3, 1977, in Spring Valley, Ill. ... 6-2/200. ... Throws right, bats right. ... Full name: Chad Griffin Durbin.
HIGH SCHOOL: Woodlawn (Shreveport, La.).
TRANSACTIONS/CAREER NOTES: Selected by Kansas City Royals organization in third round of free-agent draft (June 4, 1996). ... On Omaha disabled list (April 17-August 12, 2002). ... On Wichita disabled list (August 22, 2002-remainder of season).
CAREER HITTING (MLB): 0-for-1 (.000), 0 R, 0 2B, 0 3B, 0 HR, 0 RBI.

Year	League	W	L	Pct.	ERA	G	GS	CG	ShO	Sv.-Opp.	IP	H	R	ER	HR	BB-IBB	SO
1996—	Gulf Coast Royals (GCL)	3	2	.600	4.26	11	8	1	1	0-...	44.1	34	22	21	3	25-0	43
1997—	Lansing (Midw.)	5	8	.385	4.79	26	26	0	0	0-...	144.2	157	85	77	15	53-0	116
1998—	Wilmington (Caro.)	10	7	.588	2.93	26	26	0	0	0-...	147.2	126	57	48	10	59-3	162
1999—	Wichita (Texas)	8	10	.444	4.64	28	27	1	•1	0-...	157.0	154	88	81	20	49-1	122
	—Kansas City (A.L.)	0	0	...	0.00	1	0	0	0	0-0	2.1	1	0	0	0	1-0	3
2000—	Kansas City (A.L.)	2	5	.286	8.21	16	16	0	0	0-0	72.1	91	71	66	14	43-1	37
	—Omaha (PCL)	4	4	.500	4.46	12	12	0	0	0-...	72.2	75	37	36	10	22-0	53
2001—	Omaha (PCL)	2	2	.500	3.33	5	5	0	0	0-...	27.0	22	11	10	4	6-0	35
	—Kansas City (A.L.)	9	16	.360	4.93	29	29	2	0	0-0	179.0	201	109	98	26	58-0	95
2002—	Kansas City (A.L.)	0	1	.000	11.88	2	2	0	0	0-0	8.1	13	11	11	3	4-0	5
	—Omaha (PCL)	0	1	.000	10.80	1	1	0	0	0-...	1.2	4	2	2	0	0-0	2
	—Gulf Coast Royals (GCL)	0	0	...	0.00	3	3	0	0	0-...	6.0	4	0	0	0	1-0	5
	—Wichita (Texas)	0	0	...	5.06	3	1	0	0	0-...	5.1	5	4	3	1	4-0	6
Major League totals (4 years)		11	22	.333	6.01	48	47	2	0	0-0	262.0	306	191	175	43	106-1	140

DURHAM, RAY — 2B

PERSONAL: Born November 30, 1971, in Charlotte. ... 5-8/180. ... Bats both, throws right.
HIGH SCHOOL: Harding (Charlotte).
TRANSACTIONS/CAREER NOTES: Selected by Chicago White Sox organization in fifth round of free-agent draft (June 4, 1990). ... On Utica suspended list (April 1-May 22, 1992). ... On Sarasota disabled list (June 16-July 9, 1992). ... Traded by White Sox to Oakland Athletics for P Jon Adkins (July 25, 2002). ... Granted free agency (November 1, 2002).

RECORDS: Holds major league single-season record for fewest putouts by second baseman (150 or more games)—236 (1996).
STATISTICAL NOTES: Led Southern League in caught stealing with 25 in 1993. ... Led Southern League second basemen with 541 total chances in 1993. ... Led American Association with 261 total bases in 1994. ... Led American Association second basemen with 254 putouts, 429 assists, 702 total chances and 92 double plays in 1994. ... Led A.L. second basemen with 738 total chances and 128 double plays in 1998. ... Led A.L. second basemen with 126 double plays in 2000. ... Career major league grand slams: 3.
2002 GAMES PLAYED BY POSITION (MLB): 2B—103; DH—43.

			BATTING														FIELDING	
Year Team (League)	Pos.	G	AB	R	H	2B	3B	HR	RBI	BB	SO	SB-CS	Avg.	OBP	SLG	E	Avg.
1990—GC White Sox (GCL) ..	2B-SS	35	116	18	32	3	3	0	13	15	36	23-9	.276	.375	.353	15	.907
1991—Utica (NY-Penn)	2B	39	142	29	36	2	7	0	17	25	44	12-1	.254	.371	.366	12	.928
—GC White Sox (GCL) ..	2B	6	23	3	7	1	0	0	4	3	5	5-1	.304	.385	.348	0	1.000
1992—Sarasota (FSL)	2B	57	202	37	55	6	3	0	7	32	36	28-8	.272	.398	.332	10	.945
—GC White Sox (GCL) ..	2B	5	13	3	7	2	0	0	2	3	1	1-0	.538	.625	.692	0	1.000
1993—Birmingham (Sou.).....	2B	137	528	83	143	22	*10	3	37	42	100	39-*25	.271	.338	.367	*30	.945
1994—Nashville (A.A.)	2B	133	527	89	156	33	•12	16	66	46	91	34-11	.296	.363	.495	*19	*.973
1995—Chicago (A.L.)	2B-DH	125	471	68	121	27	6	7	51	31	83	18-5	.257	.309	.384	15	.973
1996—Chicago (A.L.)	2B-DH	156	557	79	153	33	5	10	65	58	95	30-4	.275	.350	.406	11	.984
1997—Chicago (A.L.)	2B-DH	155	634	106	172	27	5	11	53	61	96	33-16	.271	.337	.382	*18	.974
1998—Chicago (A.L.)	2B	158	635	126	181	35	8	19	67	73	105	36-9	.285	.363	.455	18	.976
1999—Chicago (A.L.)	2B-DH	153	612	109	181	30	8	13	60	73	105	34-11	.296	.373	.435	19	.974
2000—Chicago (A.L.)	2B	151	614	121	172	35	9	17	75	75	105	25-13	.280	.361	.450	15	.980
2001—Chicago (A.L.)	2B-DH	152	611	104	163	42	10	20	65	64	110	23-10	.267	.337	.466	10	.986
2002—Chicago (A.L.)	2B	96	345	71	103	20	2	9	48	49	59	20-5	.299	.390	.446	15	.968
—Oakland (A.L.)■	DH-2B	54	219	43	60	14	4	6	22	24	34	6-2	.274	.350	.457	2	.967
Major League totals (8 years)		1200	4698	827	1306	263	57	112	506	508	792	225-75	.278	.352	.430	123	.977

DIVISION SERIES RECORD

			BATTING														FIELDING	
Year Team (League)	Pos.	G	AB	R	H	2B	3B	HR	RBI	BB	SO	SB-CS	Avg.	OBP	SLG	E	Avg.
2000—Chicago (A.L.)	2B	3	10	2	2	1	0	1	1	3	3	0-0	.200	.385	.600	0	1.000
2002—Oakland (A.L.)	DH	5	21	7	7	3	0	2	2	2	4	1-0	.333	.417	.762	0	...
Division series totals (2 years)		8	31	9	9	4	0	3	3	5	7	1-0	.290	.405	.710	0	1.000

ALL-STAR GAME RECORD

	AB	R	H	2B	3B	HR	RBI	BB	SO	SB-CS	Avg.	OBP	SLG	E	Avg.
All-Star Game totals (2 years)	3	2	2	0	0	0	1	0	0	0-0	.667	.667	.667	0	1.000

DUROCHER, JAYSON P BREWERS

PERSONAL: Born August 18, 1974, in Hartford. ... 6-3/195. ... Throws right, bats right. ... Full name: Jayson Paul Durocher.
HIGH SCHOOL: Horizon (Scottsdale, Ariz.).
TRANSACTIONS/CAREER NOTES: Selected by Montreal Expos organization in ninth round of free-agent draft (June 3, 1993). ... Selected by Chicago White Sox from Expos organization in Rule 5 major league draft (December 9, 1996). ... Returned by White Sox to Expos organization (March 31, 1997). ... On disabled list (April 3-20, 1997). ... On Harrisburg disabled list (April 3-May 21, 1998). ... Granted free agency (October 15, 1999). ... Signed by San Diego Padres organization (November 22, 1999). ... Granted free agency (October 18, 2000). ... Signed by Texas Rangers organization (November 13, 2000). ... On disabled list (July 4-15, 2001). ... Granted free agency (October 15, 2001). ... Signed by Milwaukee Brewers organization (November 20, 2001). ... On Indianapolis disabled list (May 23-30, 2002).
CAREER HITTING (MLB): 0-for-2 (.000), 0 R, 0 2B, 0 3B, 0 HR, 0 RBI.

Year League	W	L	Pct.	ERA	G	GS	CG	ShO	Sv.-Opp.	IP	H	R	ER	HR	BB-IBB	SO
1993—Gulf Coast Expos (GCL) ...	2	3	.400	3.46	7	7	3	2	0-...	39.0	32	23	15	0	13-0	21
1994—Vermont (NY-Penn)..........	•9	2	.818	3.09	15	•15	•3	1	0-...	•99.0	92	40	34	0	44-1	74
1995—Albany (S.Atl.)	3	7	.300	3.91	24	22	1	0	0-...	122.0	105	67	53	5	56-1	88
1996—West Palm Beach (FSL) ...	7	6	.538	3.34	23	23	1	1	0-...	129.1	118	65	48	5	44-0	101
1997—West Palm Beach (FSL) ...	6	4	.600	3.83	25	17	0	0	0-...	87.0	84	58	37	6	39-0	71
1998—Jupiter (FSL)	2	1	.667	4.21	23	0	0	0	5-...	36.1	47	21	17	3	8-0	27
—Harrisburg (East.)............	0	1	.000	3.97	10	0	0	0	1-...	11.1	10	8	5	0	6-0	12
1999—Harrisburg (East.)............	1	3	.250	3.48	29	1	0	0	4-...	51.2	44	29	20	5	25-1	36
—Ottawa (I.L.)	1	3	.250	1.51	17	0	0	0	4-...	35.2	17	12	6	2	20-2	22
2000—Las Vegas (PCL)■	3	5	.375	4.95	31	0	0	0	7-...	40.0	44	25	22	2	25-3	38
—Mobile (Sou.)	1	1	.500	2.08	27	0	0	0	14-...	30.1	26	7	7	4	12-1	43
2001—Tulsa (Texas)	0	0	...	0.00	3	0	0	0	0-...	3.2	0	0	0	0	3-0	4
—Oklahoma (PCL)	4	1	.800	4.99	31	0	0	0	6-...	39.2	34	25	22	5	23-1	52
2002—Indianapolis (I.L.)■..........	1	0	1.000	2.73	20	0	0	0	2-...	26.1	19	9	8	3	15-0	39
—Milwaukee (N.L.)	1	1	.500	1.88	39	0	0	0	0-1	48.0	27	13	10	3	21-2	44
Major League totals (1 year).......	1	1	.500	1.88	39	0	0	0	0-1	48.0	27	13	10	3	21-2	44

DUVALL, MIKE P

PERSONAL: Born October 11, 1974, in Warrenton, Va. ... 6-0/200. ... Throws left, bats right. ... Full name: Michael Alan Duvall.
HIGH SCHOOL: Fauquier (Warrenton, Va.).
JUNIOR COLLEGE: Potomac State College (W.Va.).
TRANSACTIONS/CAREER NOTES: Selected by Florida Marlins organization in 19th round of free-agent draft (June 1, 1995). ... Selected by Tampa Bay Devil Rays in second round (32nd pick overall) of expansion draft (November 18, 1997). ... On Durham disabled list (April 9-May 13, 1998). ... On Tampa Bay disabled list (June 9-July 6, 1999). ... On Durham disabled list (April 6-20 and August 19-September 1, 2000). ... Released by Devil Rays (March 22, 2001). ... Signed by Minnesota Twins organization (September 19, 2001). ... On disabled list (March 28, 2002-entire season). ... Released by Twins (October 21, 2002).
CAREER HITTING (MLB): 0-for-0 (.000), 0 R, 0 2B, 0 3B, 0 HR, 0 RBI.

Year League	W	L	Pct.	ERA	G	GS	CG	ShO	Sv.-Opp.	IP	H	R	ER	HR	BB-IBB	SO
1995— Gulf Coast Marlins (GCL).	5	0	1.000	2.22	16	1	0	0	1-...	28.1	15	8	7	1	12-1	34
1996— Kane County (Midw.)........	4	1	.800	2.06	41	0	0	0	8-...	48.0	43	20	11	0	21-2	46
1997— Brevard County (FSL).......	1	0	1.000	0.73	11	0	0	0	6-...	12.1	7	1	1	0	3-1	9
— Portland (East.)...............	4	6	.400	1.84	45	0	0	0	18-...	68.1	63	20	14	4	20-2	49
1998— St. Petersburg (FSL)■.....	0	0	...	2.70	2	0	0	0	0-...	3.1	4	1	1	0	2-0	3
— Durham (I.L.)..................	5	3	.625	3.22	32	9	1	0	0-...	72.2	74	31	26	3	32-3	55
— Tampa Bay (A.L.).............	0	0	...	6.75	3	0	0	0	0-0	4.0	4	3	3	0	2-0	1
1999— Tampa Bay (A.L.)............	1	1	.500	4.05	40	0	0	0	0-1	40.0	46	21	18	5	27-1	18
— Durham (I.L.)..................	2	2	.500	5.40	19	1	0	0	2-...	30.0	32	20	18	4	12-1	27
2000— Durham (I.L.)..................	6	2	.750	4.59	30	8	0	0	0-...	80.1	85	47	41	8	44-0	49
— Tampa Bay (A.L.).............	0	0	...	7.71	2	0	0	0	0-0	2.1	5	2	2	0	1-0	0
2001— Edmonton (PCL).............	2	2	.500	4.45	55	0	0	0	3-...	62.2	73	32	31	7	21-1	63
— Minnesota (A.L.).............	0	0	...	7.71	8	0	0	0	0-1	4.2	7	4	4	1	2-0	4
2002— Minnesota (A.L.)...............									Did not play.							
Major League totals (4 years).....	1	1	.500	4.76	53	0	0	0	0-2	51.0	62	30	27	6	32-1	23

DYE, JERMAINE — OF — ATHLETICS

PERSONAL: Born January 28, 1974, in Vacaville, Calif. ... 6-5/220. ... Bats right, throws right. ... Full name: Jermaine Trevell Dye.

HIGH SCHOOL: Will C. Wood (Vacaville, Calif.).

JUNIOR COLLEGE: Cosumnes River (Calif.) College.

TRANSACTIONS/CAREER NOTES: Selected by Atlanta Braves organization in 17th round of free-agent draft (June 3, 1993). ... On disabled list (July 13-August 9, 1995). ... Traded by Braves with P Jamie Walker to Kansas City Royals for OF Michael Tucker and IF Keith Lockhart (March 27, 1997). ... On Kansas City disabled list (April 17-May 3, 1997); included rehabilitation assignment to Omaha (May 1-3). ... On Kansas City disabled list (July 10-August 13, 1997); included rehabilitation assignment to Omaha (July 27-August 13). ... On Kansas City disabled list (March 23-May 8 and September 1, 1998-remainder of season); included rehabilitation assignment to Omaha (April 21-May 8). ... Traded by Royals to Colorado Rockies for SS Neifi Perez (July 25, 2001). ... Traded by Rockies to Oakland Athletics for OF Mario Encarnacion, 2B/SS Jose Ortiz and P Todd Belitz (July 25, 2001). ... On Oakland disabled list (March 22-April 26, 2002); included rehabilitation assignments to Sacramento (April 16-23) and Modesto (April 23-26).

HONORS: Won A.L. Gold Glove as outfielder (2000).

STATISTICAL NOTES: Led South Atlantic League outfielders with 22 assists and six double plays in 1994. ... Led Southern League outfielders with 22 assists in 1995. ... Led A.L. outfielders with six double plays and tied for league lead with 17 assists in 1999. ... Had 16-game hitting streak (August 25-September 18, 2001). ... Career major league grand slams: 4.

MISCELLANEOUS: Hit home run in first major league at-bat (May 17, 1996).

2002 GAMES PLAYED BY POSITION (MLB): OF—111; DH—19.

		BATTING														FIELDING	
Year Team (League)	Pos.	G	AB	R	H	2B	3B	HR	RBI	BB	SO	SB-CS	Avg.	OBP	SLG	E	Avg.
1993— GC Braves (GCL)........	OF-3B	31	124	17	43	14	0	0	27	5	13	5-0	.347	.393	.460	3	.948
— Danville (Appl.)...........	OF	25	94	6	26	6	1	2	12	8	10	19-1	.277	.327	.426	2	.963
1994— Macon (S.Atl.)............	OF	135	506	73	151	*41	1	15	98	33	82	19-10	.298	.346	.472	9	.969
1995— Greenville (Sou.)........	OF	104	403	50	115	26	4	15	71	27	74	4-8	.285	.329	.481	5	.981
1996— Richmond (I.L.)..........	OF	36	142	25	33	7	1	6	19	5	25	3-0	.232	.264	.423	4	.955
— Atlanta (N.L.).............	OF	98	292	32	82	16	0	12	37	8	67	1-4	.281	.304	.459	8	.950
1997— Kansas City (A.L.)■...	OF	75	263	26	62	14	0	7	22	17	51	2-1	.236	.284	.369	6	.966
— Omaha (A.A.)..............	OF-DH	39	144	21	44	6	0	10	25	9	25	0-2	.306	.348	.556	0	1.000
1998— Omaha (PCL)............	OF-1B-DH	41	157	29	47	6	0	12	35	19	29	7-0	.299	.374	.567	1	.992
— Kansas City (A.L.)......	OF	60	214	24	50	5	1	5	23	11	46	2-2	.234	.270	.336	2	.987
1999— Kansas City (A.L.)......	OF-DH	158	608	96	179	44	8	27	119	58	119	2-3	.294	.354	.526	6	.984
2000— Kansas City (A.L.)......	OF-DH	157	601	107	193	41	2	33	118	69	99	0-1	.321	.390	.561	7	.976
2001— Kansas City (A.L.)......	OF-DH	97	367	50	100	14	0	13	47	30	68	7-1	.272	.333	.417	3	.984
— Oakland (A.L.)■.........	OF	61	232	41	69	17	1	13	59	27	44	2-0	.297	.366	.547	3	.971
2002— Sacramento (PCL)......	DH	4	16	3	3	2	0	0	1	2	2	0-0	.188	.278	.313	...	...
— Modesto (Calif.).........	OF	2	8	1	4	3	0	0	2	0	0	0-0	.500	.500	.875	0	1.000
— Oakland (A.L.)...........	OF-DH	131	488	74	123	27	1	24	86	52	108	2-0	.252	.333	.459	5	.972
American League totals (6 years)		739	2773	418	776	162	13	122	474	264	535	17-8	.280	.344	.480	32	.978
National League totals (1 year)		98	292	32	82	16	0	12	37	8	67	1-4	.281	.304	.459	8	.950
Major League totals (7 years)		837	3065	450	858	178	13	134	511	272	602	18-12	.280	.340	.478	40	.976

DIVISION SERIES RECORD

		BATTING														FIELDING	
Year Team (League)	Pos.	G	AB	R	H	2B	3B	HR	RBI	BB	SO	SB-CS	Avg.	OBP	SLG	E	Avg.
1996— Atlanta (N.L.).............	OF	3	11	1	2	0	0	1	1	0	6	1-0	.182	.182	.455	0	1.000
2001— Oakland (A.L.)...........	OF	4	13	0	3	2	0	0	0	2	2	0-0	.231	.333	.385	0	1.000
2002— Oakland (A.L.)...........	OF	5	20	3	8	2	0	1	1	1	5	0-0	.400	.429	.650	0	1.000
Division series totals (3 years)		12	44	4	13	4	0	2	2	3	13	1-0	.295	.340	.523	0	1.000

CHAMPIONSHIP SERIES RECORD

RECORDS: Shares N.L. single-game record for most at-bats—6 (October 14, 1996).

		BATTING														FIELDING	
Year Team (League)	Pos.	G	AB	R	H	2B	3B	HR	RBI	BB	SO	SB-CS	Avg.	OBP	SLG	E	Avg.
1996— Atlanta (N.L.).............	OF	7	28	2	6	1	0	0	4	1	7	0-1	.214	.226	.250	0	1.000

WORLD SERIES RECORD

		BATTING														FIELDING	
Year Team (League)	Pos.	G	AB	R	H	2B	3B	HR	RBI	BB	SO	SB-CS	Avg.	OBP	SLG	E	Avg.
1996— Atlanta (N.L.).............	OF	5	17	0	2	0	0	0	1	1	1	0-0	.118	.167	.118	1	.938

ALL-STAR GAME RECORD

	AB	R	H	2B	3B	HR	RBI	BB	SO	SB-CS	Avg.	OBP	SLG	E	Avg.
All-Star Game totals (1 year)	2	1	0	0	0	0	0	1	1	0-0	.000	.333	.000	0	1.000

EASLEY, DAMION — 2B — TIGERS

PERSONAL: Born November 11, 1969, in New York. ... 5-11/187. ... Bats right, throws right. ... Full name: Jacinto Damion Easley.
HIGH SCHOOL: Lakewood (Calif.).
JUNIOR COLLEGE: Long Beach (Calif.) City College.
COLLEGE: Long Beach State.
TRANSACTIONS/CAREER NOTES: Selected by California Angels organization in 30th round of free-agent draft (June 1, 1988). ... On disabled list (June 19-July 4 and July 28, 1993-remainder of season; and May 30-June 17, 1994). ... On California disabled list (April 1-May 10, 1996); included rehabilitation assignment to Vancouver (April 30-May 10). ... Traded by Angels to Detroit Tigers for P Greg Gohr (July 31, 1996). ... On Detroit disabled list (April 10-25 and May 9-June 2, 2000); included rehabilitation assignments to Toledo (April 24-25 and May 29-June 2). ... On Detroit disabled list (April 17-June 1, 2002) included rehabilitation assignment to Toledo (May 23-June 1).
RECORDS: Holds major league single-season record for fewest putouts by second baseman for leader—285 (1998). ... Shares major league single-game record for most times hit by pitch—3 (May 31, 1999).
HONORS: Named second baseman on THE SPORTING NEWS A.L. Silver Slugger team (1998).
STATISTICAL NOTES: Led A.L. second basemen with 285 putouts and .985 fielding percentage in 1998. ... Had 19-game hitting streak (May 10-30 and July 3-23, 1998). ... Hit for the cycle (June 8, 2001). ... Collected six hits in one game (August 8, 2001). ... Career major league grand slams: 1.
2002 GAMES PLAYED BY POSITION (MLB): 2B—84; DH—1.

		BATTING														FIELDING	
Year Team (League)	Pos.	G	AB	R	H	2B	3B	HR	RBI	BB	SO	SB-CS	Avg.	OBP	SLG	E	Avg.
1989—Bend (N'West)	2B	36	131	34	39	5	1	4	21	25	21	9-4	.298	.425	.443	22	.863
1990—Quad City (Midw.)	SS	103	365	59	100	19	3	10	56	41	60	25-8	.274	.358	.425	41	.893
1991—Midland (Texas)	SS	127	452	73	115	24	5	6	57	58	67	23-9	.254	.347	.369	*47	.924
1992—Edmonton (PCL)	SS-3B	108	429	61	124	18	3	3	44	31	44	26-10	.289	.340	.366	30	.943
—California (A.L.)	3B-SS	47	151	14	39	5	0	1	12	8	26	9-5	.258	.307	.311	5	.964
1993—California (A.L.)	2B-3B-DH	73	230	33	72	13	2	2	22	28	35	6-6	.313	.392	.413	6	.978
1994—California (A.L.)	3B-2B	88	316	41	68	16	1	6	30	29	48	4-5	.215	.288	.329	7	.977
1995—California (A.L.)	2B-SS	114	357	35	77	14	2	4	35	32	47	5-2	.216	.288	.300	10	.979
1996—Vancouver (PCL)	SS-2B-3B	12	48	13	15	2	1	2	8	9	6	4-1	.313	.424	.521	2	.958
—Midland (Texas)	3B-SS	4	14	1	6	2	0	0	2	0	0	1-0	.429	.429	.571	1	.944
—California (A.L.)	S-2-3-DH-O	28	45	4	7	1	0	2	7	6	12	0-0	.156	.255	.311	3	.954
—Detroit (A.L.)■	2-S-3-DH	21	67	10	23	1	0	2	10	4	13	3-1	.343	.384	.448	3	.958
1997—Detroit (A.L.)	2B-SS-DH	151	527	97	139	37	3	22	72	68	102	28-13	.264	.362	.471	12	.982
1998—Detroit (A.L.)	2B-SS-DH	153	594	84	161	38	2	27	100	39	112	15-5	.271	.332	.478	12	†.985
1999—Detroit (A.L.)	2B-SS	151	549	83	146	30	1	20	65	51	124	11-3	.266	.346	.434	8	.990
2000—Detroit (A.L.)	2B	126	464	76	120	27	2	14	58	55	79	13-4	.259	.350	.416	6	*.990
—Toledo (I.L.)	2B	4	13	3	3	1	0	1	4	4	2	0-0	.231	.474	.538	0	1.000
2001—Detroit (A.L.)	2B	154	585	77	146	27	7	11	65	52	90	10-5	.250	.323	.376	14	.982
2002—Detroit (A.L.)	2B-DH	85	304	29	68	14	1	8	30	27	43	1-3	.224	.307	.355	9	.980
—Toledo (I.L.)	2B	8	26	5	3	1	0	0	0	5	0	0-2	.115	.281	.154	2	.949
Major League totals (11 years)		1191	4189	583	1066	223	21	119	506	399	731	105-52	.254	.332	.403	95	.982

ALL-STAR GAME RECORD

	AB	R	H	2B	3B	HR	RBI	BB	SO	SB-CS	Avg.	OBP	SLG	E	Avg.
All-Star Game totals (1 year)	1	1	1	0	0	0	0	0	0	0-0	1.000	1.000	1.000	0	...

EATON, ADAM — P — PADRES

PERSONAL: Born November 23, 1977, in Seattle. ... 6-2/190. ... Throws right, bats right. ... Full name: Adam Thomas Eaton.
HIGH SCHOOL: Snohomish (Wash.).
TRANSACTIONS/CAREER NOTES: Selected by Philadelphia Phillies organization in first round (11th pick overall) of free-agent draft (June 4, 1996). ... Traded by Phillies with P Carlton Loewer and P Steve Montgomery to San Diego Padres for P Andy Ashby (November 10, 1999). ... On disabled list (July 6, 2001-remainder of season). ... On San Diego disabled list (March 27-September 1, 2002); included rehabilitation assignments to Lake Elsinore (August 7-21) and Portland (August 22-29).
STATISTICAL NOTES: Pitched 1-0 no-hit loss for Reading against Norwich (June 22, 1999).
MISCELLANEOUS: Appeared in one game as pinch runner (2000). ... Appeared in five games as pinch runner (2001). ... Appeared in one game as pinch hitter (2001).
CAREER HITTING (MLB): 16-for-85 (.188), 9 R, 3 2B, 0 3B, 0 HR, 6 RBI.

Year League	W	L	Pct.	ERA	G	GS	CG	ShO	Sv.-Opp.	IP	H	R	ER	HR	BB-IBB	SO
1997—Piedmont (S.Atl.)	5	6	.455	4.16	14	14	0	0	0-...	71.1	81	38	33	2	30-0	57
1998—Clearwater (FSL)	9	8	.529	4.44	24	23	1	0	0-...	131.2	152	68	65	9	47-1	89
1999—Clearwater (FSL)	5	5	.500	3.91	13	13	0	0	0-...	69.0	81	39	30	2	24-0	50
—Reading (East.)	5	4	.556	2.92	12	12	2	0	0-...	77.0	60	30	25	9	28-1	67
—Scranton/W.B. (I.L.)	1	1	.500	3.00	3	3	0	0	0-...	21.0	17	10	7	1	6-0	10
2000—Mobile (Sou.)■	4	1	.800	2.68	10	10	1	1	0-...	57.0	47	20	17	3	18-0	58
—San Diego (N.L.)	7	4	.636	4.13	22	22	0	0	0-0	135.0	134	63	62	14	61-3	90
2001—San Diego (N.L.)	8	5	.615	4.32	17	17	2	0	0-0	116.2	108	61	56	20	40-3	109
2002—Lake Elsinore (Calif.)	0	0	...	2.70	3	3	0	0	0-...	13.1	10	7	4	0	3-0	19
—Portland (PCL)	1	1	.500	2.92	2	2	0	0	0-...	12.1	9	9	4	3	3-0	6
—San Diego (N.L.)	1	1	.500	5.40	6	6	0	0	0-0	33.1	28	20	20	5	17-0	25
Major League totals (3 years)	16	10	.615	4.36	45	45	2	0	0-0	285.0	270	144	138	39	118-6	224

ECHEVARRIA, ANGEL — OF — CUBS

PERSONAL: Born May 25, 1971, in Bridgeport, Conn. ... 6-4/235. ... Bats right, throws right. ... Full name: Angel Santos Echevarria.
HIGH SCHOOL: Bassick (Bridgeport, Conn.).
COLLEGE: Rutgers.

TRANSACTIONS/CAREER NOTES: Selected by Colorado Rockies organization in 17th round of free-agent draft (June 1, 1992). ... On Colorado disabled list (April 29-June 4 and July 29-August 16, 1997). ... Claimed on waivers by Milwaukee Brewers (July 19, 2000). ... Granted free agency (October 9, 2001). ... Signed by Chicago Cubs organization (December 14, 2001).
STATISTICAL NOTES: Led Eastern League outfielders with 20 assists in 1995.
2002 GAMES PLAYED BY POSITION (MLB): OF—19; 1B—13.

						BATTING										FIELDING	
Year Team (League)	**Pos.**	**G**	**AB**	**R**	**H**	**2B**	**3B**	**HR**	**RBI**	**BB**	**SO**	**SB-CS**	**Avg.**	**OBP**	**SLG**	**E**	**Avg.**
1992— Bend (N'West)	OF	57	205	24	46	4	1	5	30	19	54	8-1	.224	.296	.327	0	1.000
1993— Central Valley (Calif.)	OF	104	358	45	97	16	2	6	52	44	74	6-5	.271	.356	.377	6	.961
1994— Central Valley (Calif.)	OF	50	192	25	58	8	1	6	35	9	25	2-2	.302	.341	.448	1	.982
— New Haven (East.)	OF	58	205	25	52	6	0	6	32	15	46	2-4	.254	.308	.371	2	.980
1995— New Haven (East.)	OF	124	453	78	136	30	1	21	100	56	93	8-3	.300	.382	.510	5	.978
1996— Colo. Springs (PCL)	OF-DH	110	415	67	140	19	2	16	74	38	81	4-3	.337	.393	.508	4	.978
— Colorado (N.L.)	OF	26	21	2	6	0	0	0	6	2	5	0-0	.286	.346	.286	0	1.000
1997— Colo. Springs (PCL)	OF-DH-1B	77	295	59	95	24	0	13	80	28	47	6-2	.322	.387	.536	1	.993
— Colorado (N.L.)	OF	15	20	4	5	2	0	0	0	2	5	0-0	.250	.318	.350	0	1.000
1998— Colo. Springs (PCL)	1B-OF-DH	85	301	50	98	21	2	15	60	14	47	0-1	.326	.359	.558	7	.984
— Colorado (N.L.)	1B-OF	19	29	7	11	3	0	1	9	2	3	0-0	.379	.455	.586	0	1.000
1999— Colorado (N.L.)	OF-1B	102	191	28	56	7	0	11	35	17	34	1-3	.293	.360	.503	1	.992
2000— Colo. Springs (PCL)	OF-1B	74	284	46	95	23	2	7	50	26	44	1-1	.335	.395	.504	4	.981
— Colorado (N.L.)	1B-OF	10	9	0	1	0	0	0	2	0	2	0-0	.111	.111	.111	0	1.000
— Milwaukee (N.L.)■	1B-OF	31	42	3	9	2	0	1	4	7	9	0-0	.214	.327	.333	0	1.000
2001— Milwaukee (N.L.)	OF-1B-DH	75	133	12	34	11	0	5	13	8	29	0-1	.256	.310	.451	2	.974
2002— Iowa (PCL)■	OF-1B	63	217	40	64	12	3	13	45	17	48	0-0	.295	.357	.558	0	1.000
— Chicago (N.L.)	OF-1B	50	98	14	30	7	0	3	21	8	17	0-0	.306	.351	.469	2	.980
Major League totals (7 years)		328	543	70	152	32	0	21	90	46	104	1-4	.280	.343	.455	5	.987

ECKENSTAHLER, ERIC — P — TIGERS

PERSONAL: Born December 17, 1976, in Waukegan, Ill. ... 6-7/220. ... Throws left, bats left. ... Full name: Eric R. Eckenstahler.
HIGH SCHOOL: Antioch (Lindenhurst, Ill.).
COLLEGE: Illinois State.
TRANSACTIONS/CAREER NOTES: Selected by Houston Astros organization in 35th round of free-agent draft (June 1, 1995); did not sign. ... Selected by New York Yankees organization in 36th round of free-agent draft (June 2, 1998); did not sign. ... Selected by Detroit Tigers organization in 32nd round of free-agent draft (June 2, 1999).
CAREER HITTING (MLB): 0-for-0 (.000), 0 R, 0 2B, 0 3B, 0 HR, 0 RBI.

Year League	**W**	**L**	**Pct.**	**ERA**	**G**	**GS**	**CG**	**ShO**	**Sv.-Opp.**	**IP**	**H**	**R**	**ER**	**HR**	**BB-IBB**	**SO**
2000— Oneonta (NY-Penn)	0	0	...	1.64	8	0	0	0	0-...	11.0	7	3	2	0	3-0	13
— West Michigan (Midw.)	0	2	.000	5.79	10	3	0	0	1-...	18.2	21	15	12	4	11-0	22
2001— Lakeland (FSL)	1	0	1.000	1.50	4	0	0	0	1-...	6.0	3	1	1	0	2-0	7
— Erie (East.)	4	2	.667	3.90	46	0	0	0	4-...	64.2	65	32	28	7	31-4	73
2002— Toledo (I.L.)	2	4	.333	4.43	52	0	0	0	0-...	67.0	57	37	33	8	35-1	69
— Detroit (A.L.)	1	0	1.000	5.63	7	0	0	0	0-0	8.0	14	5	5	1	2-0	13
Major League totals (1 year)	1	0	1.000	5.63	7	0	0	0	0-0	8.0	14	5	5	1	2-0	13

ECKSTEIN, DAVID — 2B — ANGELS

PERSONAL: Born January 20, 1975, in Sanford, Fla. ... 5-8/170. ... Bats right, throws right. ... Full name: David Mark Eckstein.
HIGH SCHOOL: Seminole (Sanford, Fla.).
COLLEGE: Florida.
TRANSACTIONS/CAREER NOTES: Selected by Boston Red Sox organization in 19th round of free-agent draft (June 3, 1997). ... Claimed on waivers by Anaheim Angels (August 16, 2000).
RECORDS: Shares major league record for most grand slams in two consecutive games—2 (April 27 and 28, 2002).
STATISTICAL NOTES: Tied for New York-Pennsylvania League lead in sacrifice hits with eight in 1997. ... Led Florida State League in being hit by pitch with 22 in 1998. ... Led Florida State League second basemen in fielding percentage with .989 in 1998. ... Tied for Eastern League lead with 87 double plays by second baseman in 1999. ... Led International League in being hit by pitch with 20 in 2000. ... Led International League second basemen with .992 fielding percentage in 2000. ... Led A.L. with 16 sacrifice hits in 2001 and with 14 in 2002. ... Led A.L. in being hit by pitch with 21 in 2001 and with 27 in 2002. ... Had 15-game hitting streak (August 24-September 8, 2002). ... Career major league grand slams: 3.
2002 GAMES PLAYED BY POSITION (MLB): SS—147; DH—3.

						BATTING										FIELDING	
Year Team (League)	**Pos.**	**G**	**AB**	**R**	**H**	**2B**	**3B**	**HR**	**RBI**	**BB**	**SO**	**SB-CS**	**Avg.**	**OBP**	**SLG**	**E**	**Avg.**
1997— Lowell (NY-Penn)	2B	68	249	43	75	11	4	4	39	33	29	21-5	.301	.407	.426	9	*.971
1998— Sarasota (FSL)	2B-SS	135	503	99	154	29	4	3	58	87	51	45-16	.306	.428	.398	8	†.986
1999— Trenton (East.)	2B-DH	131	483	109	151	22	5	6	52	89	48	32-13	.313	.440	.416	9	*.985
2000— Pawtucket (I.L.)	2B-SS	119	422	77	104	20	0	1	31	60	45	11-8	.246	.364	.301	4	†.992
— Edmonton (PCL)■	2B	15	52	17	18	8	0	3	8	9	1	5-3	.346	.485	.673	0	1.000
2001— Anaheim (A.L.)	SS-2B-DH	153	582	82	166	26	2	4	41	43	60	29-4	.285	.355	.357	18	.969
2002— Anaheim (A.L.)	SS-DH	152	608	107	178	22	6	8	63	45	44	21-13	.293	.363	.388	14	.977
Major League totals (2 years)		305	1190	189	344	48	8	12	104	88	104	50-17	.289	.359	.373	32	.973

DIVISION SERIES RECORD

						BATTING										FIELDING	
Year Team (League)	**Pos.**	**G**	**AB**	**R**	**H**	**2B**	**3B**	**HR**	**RBI**	**BB**	**SO**	**SB-CS**	**Avg.**	**OBP**	**SLG**	**E**	**Avg.**
2002— Anaheim (A.L.)	SS	4	18	2	5	0	0	0	1	0	0	1-0	.278	.316	.278	0	1.000

CHAMPIONSHIP SERIES RECORD

Year	Team (League)	Pos.	G	AB	R	H	2B	3B	HR	RBI	BB	SO	SB-CS	Avg.	OBP	SLG	E	Avg.
			BATTING														FIELDING	
2002—	Anaheim (A.L.)	SS	5	21	1	6	0	0	0	2	0	2	0-0	.286	.318	.286	1	.944

WORLD SERIES RECORD

NOTES: Member of World Series championship team (2002).

Year	Team (League)	Pos.	G	AB	R	H	2B	3B	HR	RBI	BB	SO	SB-CS	Avg.	OBP	SLG	E	Avg.
			BATTING														FIELDING	
2002—	Anaheim (A.L.)	SS	7	29	6	9	0	0	0	3	3	2	1-0	.310	.364	.310	0	1.000

EDMONDS, JIM — OF — CARDINALS

PERSONAL: Born June 27, 1970, in Fullerton, Calif. ... 6-1/212. ... Bats left, throws left. ... Full name: James Patrick Edmonds. ... Name pronounced ED-muns.

HIGH SCHOOL: Diamond Bar (Calif.).

TRANSACTIONS/CAREER NOTES: Selected by California Angels organization in seventh round of free-agent draft (June 1, 1988). ... On disabled list (June 19-September 2, 1989; April 10-May 7 and May 23, 1991-remainder of season). ... On Vancouver disabled list (June 29-July 19, 1993). ... On California disabled list (May 26-June 10 and June 12-July 18, 1996); included rehabilitation assignment to Lake Elsinore (July 13-18). ... Angels franchise renamed Anaheim Angels for 1997 season. ... On disabled list (August 1-16, 1997). ... On Anaheim disabled list (March 30-August 2, 1999): included rehabilitation assignment to Lake Elsinore (July 26-August 2). ... Traded by Angels to St. Louis Cardinals for 2B/SS Adam Kennedy and P Kent Bottenfield (March 23, 2000). ... On disabled list (June 1-16, 2002).

RECORDS: Holds N.L. single-season record for most strikeouts by lefthander—167 (2000).

HONORS: Named outfielder on The Sporting News A.L. All-Star team (1995). ... Won A.L. Gold Glove as outfielder (1997-98). ... Won N.L. Gold Glove as outfielder (2000-02).

STATISTICAL NOTES: Had 23-game hitting streak (June 4-29, 1995). ... Career major league grand slams: 4.

2002 GAMES PLAYED BY POSITION (MLB): OF—139.

Year	Team (League)	Pos.	G	AB	R	H	2B	3B	HR	RBI	BB	SO	SB-CS	Avg.	OBP	SLG	E	Avg.
			BATTING														FIELDING	
1988—	Bend (N'West)	OF	35	122	23	27	4	0	0	13	20	44	4-0	.221	.329	.254	1	.984
1989—	Quad City (Midw.)	OF	31	92	11	24	4	0	1	4	7	34	1-0	.261	.313	.337	3	.942
1990—	Palm Springs (Calif.)	OF	91	314	36	92	18	6	3	56	27	75	5-2	.293	.351	.417	10	.954
1991—	Palm Springs (Calif.)	OF-1B-P	60	187	28	55	15	1	2	27	40	57	2-2	.294	.417	.417	0	1.000
1992—	Midland (Texas)	OF	70	246	42	77	15	2	8	32	41	83	3-4	.313	.413	.488	5	.967
—	Edmonton (PCL)	OF	50	194	37	58	15	2	6	36	14	55	3-1	.299	.343	.490	1	.988
1993—	Vancouver (PCL)	OF	95	356	59	112	28	4	9	74	41	81	6-8	.315	.382	.492	3	.983
—	California (A.L.)	OF	18	61	5	15	4	1	0	4	2	16	0-2	.246	.270	.344	1	.981
1994—	California (A.L.)	OF-1B	94	289	35	79	13	1	5	37	30	72	4-2	.273	.343	.377	3	.991
1995—	California (A.L.)	OF	141	558	120	162	30	4	33	107	51	130	1-4	.290	.352	.536	1	.998
1996—	California (A.L.)	OF-DH	114	431	73	131	28	3	27	66	46	101	4-0	.304	.375	.571	1	.997
—	Lake Elsinore (Calif.)	OF-DH	5	15	4	6	2	0	1	4	1	1	0-0	.400	.471	.733	0	1.000
1997—	Anaheim (A.L.)	OF-1B-DH	133	502	82	146	27	0	26	80	60	80	5-7	.291	.368	.500	5	.988
1998—	Anaheim (A.L.)	OF	154	599	115	184	42	1	25	91	57	114	7-5	.307	.368	.506	5	.988
1999—	Lake Elsinore (Calif.)	DH	5	19	4	8	2	0	0	3	4	2	2-0	.421	.522	.526	0	...
—	Anaheim (A.L.)	OF-DH-1B	55	204	34	51	17	2	5	23	28	45	5-4	.250	.339	.426	1	.993
2000—	St. Louis (N.L.)■	OF-1B	152	525	129	155	25	0	42	108	103	167	10-3	.295	.411	.583	4	.990
2001—	St. Louis (N.L.)	OF-1B	150	500	95	152	38	1	30	110	93	136	5-5	.304	.410	.564	6	.983
2002—	St. Louis (N.L.)	OF	144	476	96	148	31	2	28	83	86	134	4-3	.311	.420	.561	5	.986
American League totals (7 years)			709	2644	464	768	161	12	121	408	274	558	26-24	.290	.359	.498	17	.992
National League totals (3 years)			446	1501	320	455	94	3	100	301	282	437	19-11	.303	.414	.570	15	.987
Major League totals (10 years)			1155	4145	784	1223	255	15	221	709	556	995	45-35	.295	.380	.524	32	.990

DIVISION SERIES RECORD

RECORDS: Holds N.L. career records for most doubles—5; and extra-base hits—10.

Year	Team (League)	Pos.	G	AB	R	H	2B	3B	HR	RBI	BB	SO	SB-CS	Avg.	OBP	SLG	E	Avg.
			BATTING														FIELDING	
2000—	St. Louis (N.L.)	OF	3	14	5	8	4	0	2	7	1	2	1-0	.571	.600	1.286	0	1.000
2001—	St. Louis (N.L.)	OF	5	17	3	4	1	0	2	3	3	6	0-0	.235	.350	.647	0	1.000
2002—	St. Louis (N.L.)	OF	3	11	1	3	0	0	1	2	2	4	0-1	.273	.385	.545	0	1.000
Division series totals (3 years)			11	42	9	15	5	0	5	12	6	12	1-1	.357	.438	.833	0	1.000

CHAMPIONSHIP SERIES RECORD

Year	Team (League)	Pos.	G	AB	R	H	2B	3B	HR	RBI	BB	SO	SB-CS	Avg.	OBP	SLG	E	Avg.
			BATTING														FIELDING	
2000—	St. Louis (N.L.)	OF	5	22	1	5	1	0	1	5	1	9	0-0	.227	.261	.409	1	.933
2002—	St. Louis (N.L.)	OF	5	20	2	8	2	0	1	4	2	5	0-0	.400	.455	.650	0	1.000
Championship series totals (2 years)			10	42	3	13	3	0	2	9	3	14	0-0	.310	.356	.524	1	.962

ALL-STAR GAME RECORD

	AB	R	H	2B	3B	HR	RBI	BB	SO	SB-CS	Avg.	OBP	SLG	E	Avg.
All-Star Game totals (2 years)	3	0	1	0	0	0	0	0	1	0-0	.333	.333	.333	0	1.000

RECORD AS PITCHER

Year	League	W	L	Pct.	ERA	G	GS	CG	ShO	Sv.-Opp.	IP	H	R	ER	HR	BB-IBB	SO
1991—	Palm Springs (Calif.)	0	0	...	0.00	1	0	0	0	0-...	2.0	1	0	0	0	3-0	2

EISCHEN, JOEY — P — EXPOS

PERSONAL: Born May 25, 1970, in West Covina, Calif. ... 6-0/210. ... Throws left, bats left. ... Full name: Joseph Raymond Eischen. ... Name pronounced EYE-shen.

HIGH SCHOOL: West Covina (Calif.).

JUNIOR COLLEGE: Pasadena (Calif.) City College.

E

TRANSACTIONS/CAREER NOTES: Selected by Chicago White Sox organization in fifth round of free-agent draft (June 1, 1988); did not sign. ... Selected by Texas Rangers in fourth round of free-agent draft (June 5, 1989). ... Traded by Rangers with P Jonathan Hurst and a player to be named later to Montreal Expos for P Oil Can Boyd (July 21, 1991); Expos acquired P Travis Buckley to complete deal (September 1, 1991). ... Traded by Expos with OF Roberto Kelly to Los Angeles Dodgers for OF Henry Rodriguez and IF Jeff Treadway (May 23, 1995). ... Traded by Dodgers with P John Cummings to Detroit Tigers for OF Chad Curtis (July 31, 1996). ... Traded by Tigers with P Cam Smith to San Diego Padres for C Brian Johnson and P Willie Blair (December 17, 1996). ... Traded by Padres to Cincinnati Reds for a player to be named later (March 16, 1997); Padres acquired IF Ray Brown to complete deal (March 19, 1997). ... On Cincinnati disabled list (March 25-April 26 and April 29-July 18, 1997); included rehabilitation assignment to Indianapolis (April 13-26). ... Granted free agency (December 21, 1997). ... Signed by New York Yankees organization (February 3, 1998). ... Released by Yankees (March 11, 1998). ... Signed by Reds (March 19, 1998). ... Released by Reds (March 12, 1999). ... Signed by Arizona Diamondbacks organization (March 18, 1999). ... Released by Diamondbacks (July 1, 1999). ... Signed by Adirondack, Northern League (July 1999). ... Signed by Cleveland Indians organization (December 23, 1999). ... Released by Indians (April 29, 2000). ... Signed by Adirondack, Northern League (May 2000). ... Signed by Expos organization (July 12, 2000). ... Granted free agency (October 12, 2001). ... Re-signed by Expos organization (October 22, 2001).

HONORS: Named Eastern League Pitcher of the Year (1993).

STATISTICAL NOTES: Led Pioneer League with 11 balks in 1989. ... Led Florida State League with 86 runs allowed in 1991. ... Pitched 5-0 no-hit victory against Vero Beach (June 16, 1992, first game).

CAREER HITTING (MLB): 1-for-16 (.063), 1 R, 1 2B, 0 3B, 0 HR, 0 RBI.

Year League	W	L	Pct.	ERA	G	GS	CG	ShO	Sv.-Opp.	IP	H	R	ER	HR	BB-IBB	SO
1989— Butte (Pio.)	3	7	.300	5.30	12	12	0	0	0-...	52.2	50	45	31	4	38-0	57
1990— Gastonia (S.Atl.)	3	7	.300	2.70	17	14	0	0	0-...	73.1	51	36	22	0	40-0	69
1991— Charlotte (FSL)	4	10	.286	3.41	18	18	1	0	0-...	108.1	99	59	41	5	55-1	80
— West Palm Beach (FSL)■	4	2	.667	5.17	8	8	1	0	0-...	38.1	35	§27	22	3	24-0	26
1992— West Palm Beach (FSL)	9	8	.529	3.08	27	26	3	2	0-...	169.2	128	68	58	5	*83-2	167
1993— Harrisburg (East.)	*14	4	*.778	3.62	20	20	0	0	0-...	119.1	122	62	48	11	60-0	110
— Ottawa (I.L.)	2	2	.500	3.54	6	6	0	0	0-...	40.2	34	18	16	3	15-0	29
1994— Ottawa (I.L.)	2	6	.250	4.94	48	2	0	0	2-...	62.0	54	38	34	7	40-4	57
— Montreal (N.L.)	0	0	...	54.00	1	0	0	0	0-0	.2	4	4	4	0	0-0	1
1995— Ottawa (I.L.)	2	1	.667	1.72	11	0	0	0	0-...	15.2	9	4	3	0	8-1	13
— Los Angeles (N.L.)■	0	0	...	3.10	17	0	0	0	0-0	20.1	19	9	7	1	11-1	15
— Albuquerque (PCL)	3	0	1.000	0.00	13	0	0	0	2-...	16.1	8	0	0	0	3-0	14
1996— Los Angeles (N.L.)	0	1	.000	4.78	28	0	0	0	0-0	43.1	48	25	23	4	20-4	36
— Detroit (A.L.)■	1	1	.500	3.24	24	0	0	0	0-2	25.0	27	11	9	3	14-3	15
1997— Indianapolis (A.A.)■	1	0	1.000	1.27	26	5	0	0	2-...	42.2	41	7	6	1	13-1	26
— Cincinnati (N.L.)	0	0	...	6.75	1	0	0	0	0-0	1.1	2	2	1	0	1-0	2
1998— Indianapolis (I.L.)	2	5	.286	4.54	61	0	0	0	2-...	73.1	73	42	37	9	29-3	60
1999— Tucson (PCL)■	1	3	.250	9.07	27	1	0	0	1-...	41.2	63	47	42	7	26-3	36
— Adirondack (Nor.)■	4	2	.667	3.75	7	7	1	0	0-...	48.0	52	22	20	1	11-...	49
2000— Buffalo (I.L.)■	0	0	...	40.50	1	0	0	0	0-...	.2	4	3	3	0	0-0	0
— Adirondack (Nor.)■	7	1	.875	1.80	10	10	0	0	0-...	65.0	55	25	13	...	24-...	57
— Ottawa (I.L.)■	0	4	.000	3.64	10	9	0	0	0-...	59.1	55	31	24	8	22-0	34
2001— Ottawa (I.L.)	2	3	.400	2.24	34	1	0	0	7-...	52.1	42	16	13	6	11-0	54
— Montreal (N.L.)	0	1	.000	4.85	24	0	0	0	0-2	29.2	29	17	16	4	16-1	19
2002— Ottawa (I.L.)	1	0	1.000	0.00	11	0	0	0	4-...	14.0	8	4	0	0	3-0	15
— Montreal (N.L.)	6	1	.857	1.34	59	0	0	0	2-3	53.2	43	11	8	1	18-5	51
A.L. totals (1 year)	1	1	.500	3.24	24	0	0	0	0-2	25.0	27	11	9	3	14-3	15
N.L. totals (6 years)	6	3	.667	3.56	130	0	0	0	2-5	149.0	145	68	59	10	66-11	124
Major League totals (6 years)	7	4	.636	3.52	154	0	0	0	2-7	174.0	172	79	68	13	80-14	139

ELARTON, SCOTT P ROCKIES

PERSONAL: Born February 23, 1976, in Lamar, Colo. ... 6-7/240. ... Throws right, bats right. ... Full name: Vincent Scott Elarton.

HIGH SCHOOL: Lamar (Colo.).

TRANSACTIONS/CAREER NOTES: Selected by Houston Astros organization in first round (25th pick overall) of free-agent draft (June 2, 1994). ... On Houston disabled list (March 29-April 23, 2000); included rehabilitation assignments to New Orleans (April 6-11) and Round Rock (April 18). ... On Houston disabled list (July 17-31, 2001). ... Traded by Astros with a player to be named later to Colorado Rockies for P Pedro Astacio (July 31, 2001). ... On Colorado disabled list (July 31-September 4, 2001); included rehabilitation assignment to Colorado Springs (August 29-September 4). ... On disabled list (March 8, 2002-entire season).

STATISTICAL NOTES: Tied for Florida State League lead with 13 home runs allowed in 1996.

MISCELLANEOUS: Appeared in one game as outfielder with no chances (1999).

CAREER HITTING (MLB): 18-for-134 (.134), 8 R, 2 2B, 0 3B, 0 HR, 3 RBI.

Year League	W	L	Pct.	ERA	G	GS	CG	ShO	Sv.-Opp.	IP	H	R	ER	HR	BB-IBB	SO
1994— Gulf Coast Astros (GCL)	4	0	1.000	0.00	5	5	0	0	0-...	28.0	9	0	0	0	5-0	28
— Quad City (Midw.)	4	1	.800	3.29	9	9	0	0	0-...	54.2	42	23	20	4	18-0	42
1995— Quad City (Midw.)	13	7	.650	4.45	26	26	0	0	0-...	149.2	149	86	74	12	71-2	112
1996— Kissimmee (FSL)	12	7	.632	2.92	27	27	3	1	0-...	172.1	154	67	56	13	54-0	130
1997— Jackson (Texas)	7	4	.636	3.24	20	20	2	0	0-...	133.1	103	57	48	6	47-3	141
— New Orleans (A.A.)	4	4	.500	5.33	9	9	0	0	0-...	54.0	51	36	32	5	17-1	50
1998— New Orleans (PCL)	9	4	.692	4.01	14	14	2	1	0-...	92.0	71	42	41	6	41-3	100
— Houston (N.L.)	2	1	.667	3.32	28	2	0	0	2-3	57.0	40	21	21	5	20-0	56
1999— Houston (N.L.)	9	5	.643	3.48	42	15	0	0	1-4	124.0	111	55	48	8	43-0	121
2000— New Orleans (PCL)	1	0	1.000	0.75	2	2	0	0	0-...	12.0	3	1	1	0	4-0	12
— Round Rock (Texas)	1	0	1.000	2.84	1	1	0	0	0-...	6.1	7	2	2	1	0-0	7
— Houston (N.L.)	17	7	.708	4.81	30	30	2	0	0-0	192.2	198	117	103	29	84-1	131
2001— Houston (N.L.)	4	8	.333	7.14	20	20	0	0	0-0	109.2	126	88	87	26	49-1	76
— Colo. Springs (PCL)■	0	1	.000	7.04	2	2	0	0	0-...	7.2	14	6	6	2	0-0	8
— Colorado (N.L.)	0	2	.000	6.65	4	4	0	0	0-0	23.0	20	17	17	8	10-1	11
2002— Colorado (N.L.)									Did not play.							
Major League totals (4 years)	32	23	.582	4.91	124	71	2	0	3-7	506.1	495	298	276	76	206-3	395

DIVISION SERIES RECORD

Year League	W	L	Pct.	ERA	G	GS	CG	ShO	Sv.-Opp.	IP	H	R	ER	HR	BB-IBB	SO
1998— Houston (N.L.)	0	1	.000	4.50	1	0	0	0	0-0	2.0	1	1	1	1	1-0	3
1999— Houston (N.L.)	0	0	...	3.86	2	0	0	0	0-0	2.1	4	1	1	0	1-0	3
Division series totals (2 years)	0	1	.000	4.15	3	0	0	0	0-0	4.1	5	2	2	1	2-0	6

ELDER, DAVID — P — INDIANS

PERSONAL: Born September 23, 1975, in Atlanta. ... 6-0/180. ... Throws right, bats right. ... Full name: David Matthew Elder.
HIGH SCHOOL: Booker T. Washington (Pensacola, Fla.).
COLLEGE: Georgia Tech.
TRANSACTIONS/CAREER NOTES: Selected by Texas Rangers organization in fourth round of free-agent draft (June 3, 1997). ... On disabled list (April 7, 1998-entire season). ... On Charlotte disabled list (May 8-19, 1999). ... Traded by Rangers to Cleveland Indians for P John Rocker (December 18, 2001).
CAREER HITTING (MLB): 0-for-0 (.000), 0 R, 0 2B, 0 3B, 0 HR, 0 RBI.

Year League	W	L	Pct.	ERA	G	GS	CG	ShO	Sv.-Opp.	IP	H	R	ER	HR	BB-IBB	SO
1997—Pulaski (Appl.)	2	2	.500	1.95	20	0	0	0	6-...	32.1	18	8	7	2	12-0	57
1998—Pulaski (Appl.)									Did not play.							
1999—Charlotte (FSL)	4	2	.667	2.84	24	1	0	0	4-...	44.1	33	15	14	2	25-0	42
—Tulsa (Texas)	1	0	1.000	8.10	3	0	0	0	0-...	6.2	8	7	6	0	6-1	7
2000—Tulsa (Texas)	7	6	.538	4.94	33	21	0	0	3-...	116.2	121	80	64	9	*88-0	104
2001—Tulsa (Texas)	4	6	.400	3.00	13	13	0	0	0-...	72.0	64	28	24	1	43-0	78
—Oklahoma (PCL)	5	4	.556	4.99	15	8	0	0	0-...	57.2	54	36	32	4	43-0	56
2002—Akron (East.)■	2	1	.667	2.00	23	1	0	0	9-...	36.0	19	8	8	1	18-2	42
—Buffalo (I.L.)	3	1	.750	2.65	22	1	0	0	5-...	34.0	32	11	10	1	14-0	42
—Cleveland (A.L.)	0	2	.000	3.13	15	0	0	0	0-0	23.0	18	10	8	1	14-3	23
Major League totals (1 year)	0	2	.000	3.13	15	0	0	0	0-0	23.0	18	10	8	1	14-3	23

ELLIS, MARK — SS/2B — ATHLETICS

PERSONAL: Born June 6, 1977, in Rapid City, S.D. ... 5-11/180. ... Bats right, throws right. ... Full name: Mark William Ellis.
HIGH SCHOOL: Stevens (Rapid City, S.D.).
COLLEGE: Florida.
TRANSACTIONS/CAREER NOTES: Selected by Kansas City Royals organization in ninth round of free-agent draft (June 2, 1999). ... Traded by Royals with OF Johnny Damon and player to be named later to Oakland Athletics as part of three-way deal in which Royals received P Roberto Hernandez from Tampa Bay Devil Rays, A's received P Cory Lidle from Devil Rays, Royals received C A.J. Hinch, IF Angel Berroa and cash from A's and Devil Rays received OF Ben Grieve and player to be named later or cash from A's (January 8, 2001). ... On Sacramento disabled list (May 12-29, 2002).
STATISTICAL NOTES: Led Northwest League shortstops with 138 putouts and 384 total chances in 1999. ... Led Carolina League shortstops with 219 putouts, 31 errors and 78 double plays in 2000.
2002 GAMES PLAYED BY POSITION (MLB): 2B—85; SS—8; 3B—7; DH—1.

		BATTING													FIELDING	
Year Team (League)	Pos.	G	AB	R	H	2B	3B	HR	RBI	BB	SO	SB-CS	Avg.	OBP	SLG	E	Avg.
1999—Spokane (N'West)	SS	71	281	67	92	14	0	7	47	47	40	21-7	.327	.424	.452	16	*.958
2000—Wilmington (Caro.)	SS-2B	132	484	83	*146	27	4	6	62	78	72	25-7	.302	*.404	.411	†31	.954
—Wichita (Texas)	2B	7	22	4	7	1	0	0	4	5	5	1-0	.318	.444	.364	0	1.000
2001—Sacramento (PCL)■	SS	132	472	71	129	38	0	10	53	54	78	21-7	.273	.351	.417	19	.968
2002—Sacramento (PCL)	SS	21	84	14	25	10	1	0	5	6	13	4-0	.298	.372	.440	3	.974
—Oakland (A.L.)	2B-SS-3B-DH	98	345	58	94	16	4	6	35	44	54	4-2	.272	.359	.394	11	.976
Major League totals (1 year)		98	345	58	94	16	4	6	35	44	54	4-2	.272	.359	.394	11	.976

DIVISION SERIES RECORD

		BATTING													FIELDING	
Year Team (League)	Pos.	G	AB	R	H	2B	3B	HR	RBI	BB	SO	SB-CS	Avg.	OBP	SLG	E	Avg.
2002—Oakland (A.L.)	2B	5	19	1	7	2	0	1	4	1	2	0-0	.368	.400	.632	1	.960

ELLIS, ROBERT — P — RANGERS

PERSONAL: Born December 15, 1970, in Baton Rouge, La. ... 6-5/220. ... Throws right, bats right. ... Full name: Robert Randolph Ellis.
HIGH SCHOOL: Belaire (Baton Rouge, La.).
JUNIOR COLLEGE: Panola Junior College (Texas).
COLLEGE: Northwestern State (La.).
TRANSACTIONS/CAREER NOTES: Selected by Chicago White Sox organization in third round of free-agent draft (June 4, 1990). ... On South Bend disabled list (May 20-July 1, 1992). ... On disabled list (July 25, 1994-remainder of season; and May 17, 1995-remainder of season). ... Traded by White Sox to California Angels for C Pat Borders (July 27, 1996). ... Angels franchise renamed Anaheim Angels for 1997 season. ... Granted free agency (October 15, 1997). ... Signed by Detroit Tigers organization (November 10, 1997). ... Released by Tigers (March 3, 1998). ... Signed by Milwaukee Brewers organization (March 4, 1998). ... On Louisville disabled list (May 23-30, 1998). ... Granted free agency (October 16, 1998). ... Signed by Houston Astros organization (January 15, 1999). ... Granted free agency (October 15, 1999). ... Signed by Toronto Blue Jays organization (January 6, 2000). ... Released by Blue Jays (May 23, 2000). ... Signed by Monterrey, Mexican League (June 2000). ... Signed by Arizona Diamondbacks organization (October 10, 2000). ... On Arizona disabled list (July 23-September 25, 2001); included rehabilitation assignment to Tucson (August 4-16). ... Granted free agency (December 21, 2001). ... Signed by Los Angeles Dodgers organization (January 14, 2002). ... Released by Dodgers (October 7, 2002). ... Signed by Texas Rangers organization (November 13, 2002).
STATISTICAL NOTES: Led Pacific Coast League with 12 sacrifice hits allowed in 2002.
CAREER HITTING (MLB): 4-for-26 (.154), 2 R, 0 2B, 0 3B, 0 HR, 1 RBI.

Year League	W	L	Pct.	ERA	G	GS	CG	ShO	Sv.-Opp.	IP	H	R	ER	HR	BB-IBB	SO
1991—Utica (NY-Penn)	3	•9	.250	4.62	15	15	1	1	0-...	87.2	86	*66	45	4	61-0	66
1992—South Bend (Midw.)	6	5	.545	2.34	18	18	1	1	0-...	123.0	90	46	32	3	35-0	97
—GC White Sox (GCL)	1	0	1.000	10.80	1	1	0	0	0-...	5.0	10	6	6	0	1-0	4
1993—Sarasota (FSL)	7	8	.467	2.51	15	15	*8	2	0-...	104.0	81	37	29	3	31-1	79
—Birmingham (Sou.)	6	3	.667	3.10	12	12	2	1	0-...	81.1	68	33	28	2	21-0	77
1994—Nashville (A.A.)	4	10	.286	6.09	19	19	1	0	0-...	105.0	126	77	71	19	55-1	76
1995—Nashville (A.A.)	1	1	.500	2.18	4	4	0	0	0-...	20.2	16	7	5	2	10-0	9
1996—Nashville (A.A.)	3	8	.273	6.01	19	13	1	0	0-...	70.1	78	49	47	6	45-3	35
—Birmingham (Sou.)	0	1	.000	11.05	2	2	0	0	0-...	7.1	6	9	9	1	8-0	8
—Vancouver (PCL)■	2	3	.400	3.25	7	7	1	0	0-...	44.1	30	19	16	2	28-0	29
—California (A.L.)	0	0	...	0.00	3	0	0	0	0-0	5.0	0	0	0	0	4-0	5

Year League	W	L	Pct.	ERA	G	GS	CG	ShO	Sv.-Opp.	IP	H	R	ER	HR	BB-IBB	SO
1997— Vancouver (PCL)	9	10	.474	5.92	29	23	3	0	0-...	149.0	185	108	98	15	83-1	70
1998— Louisville (I.L.)■	10	10	.500	5.63	30	28	0	0	0-...	150.1	171	103	94	21	78-1	79
1999— New Orleans (PCL)■	7	12	.368	5.43	27	27	1	0	0-...	155.2	176	106	94	20	51-1	105
2000— Syracuse (I.L.)■	1	1	.500	4.50	16	0	0	0	2-...	18.0	17	10	9	2	15-1	18
— Monterrey (Mex.)■	8	5	.615	3.51	15	14	3	0	0-...	92.1	78	39	36	8	32-0	70
2001— Tucson (PCL)■	1	1	.500	3.08	5	5	0	0	0-...	26.1	25	12	9	2	5-0	13
— Arizona (N.L.)	6	5	.545	5.77	19	17	0	0	0-0	92.0	106	61	59	12	34-2	41
2002— Las Vegas (PCL)■	9	7	.563	4.17	29	•28	1	0	0-...	172.2	195	100	80	17	37-0	110
— Los Angeles (N.L.)	0	1	.000	10.13	3	0	0	0	0-0	2.2	6	3	3	1	0-0	0
A.L. totals (1 year)	0	0	...	0.00	3	0	0	0	0-0	5.0	0	0	0	0	4-0	5
N.L. totals (2 years)	6	6	.500	5.89	22	17	0	0	0-0	94.2	112	64	62	13	34-2	41
Major League totals (3 years)	6	6	.500	5.60	25	17	0	0	0-0	99.2	112	64	62	13	38-2	46

EMBREE, ALAN — P — RED SOX

PERSONAL: Born January 23, 1970, in Vancouver, Wash. ... 6-2/190. ... Throws left, bats left. ... Full name: Alan Duane Embree.

HIGH SCHOOL: Prairie (Vancouver, Wash.).

TRANSACTIONS/CAREER NOTES: Selected by Cleveland Indians organization in fifth round of free-agent draft (June 5, 1989). ... On Cleveland disabled list (April 1-June 2 and June 2, 1993-remainder of season); included rehabilitation assignment to Canton/Akron (June 2-15). ... On Cleveland disabled list (August 1-September 7, 1996); included rehabilitation assignment to Buffalo (August 6-September 4). ... Traded by Indians with OF Kenny Lofton to Atlanta Braves for OF Marquis Grissom and OF Dave Justice (March 25, 1997). ... Traded by Braves to Arizona Diamondbacks for P Russ Springer (June 23, 1998). ... Traded by Diamondbacks to San Francisco Giants for OF Dante Powell (November 10, 1998). ... On San Francisco disabled list (May 23-June 12, 2001); included rehabilitation assignment to Fresno (May 28-June 12). ... Traded by Giants to Chicago White Sox for P Derek Hasselhoff (June 29, 2001). ... Granted free agency (November 6, 2001). ... Signed by San Diego Padres (January 3, 2002). ... Traded by Padres with P Andy Shibilo to Boston Red Sox for P Brad Baker and P Dan Giese (June 26, 2002). ... On Boston disabled list (July 14-29, 2002).

RECORDS: Shares major league record for most home runs allowed in one inning—4 (May 20, 2001, seventh inning).

CAREER HITTING (MLB): 0-for-2 (.000), 0 R, 0 2B, 0 3B, 0 HR, 0 RBI.

Year League	W	L	Pct.	ERA	G	GS	CG	ShO	Sv.-Opp.	IP	H	R	ER	HR	BB-IBB	SO
1990— Burlington (Appl.)	4	4	.500	2.64	15	•15	0	0	0-...	81.2	87	36	24	3	30-0	58
1991— Columbus (S.Atl.)	10	8	.556	3.59	27	26	3	1	0-...	155.1	126	80	62	4	77-1	137
1992— Kinston (Caro.)	10	5	.667	3.30	15	15	1	0	0-...	101.0	89	48	37	10	32-0	115
— Canton/Akron (East.)	7	2	.778	2.28	12	12	0	0	0-...	79.0	61	24	20	2	28-1	56
— Cleveland (A.L.)	0	2	.000	7.00	4	4	0	0	0-0	18.0	19	14	14	3	8-0	12
1993— Canton/Akron (East.)	0	0	...	3.38	1	1	0	0	0-...	5.1	3	2	2	0	3-0	4
1994— Canton/Akron (East.)	9	•16	.360	5.50	30	27	2	1	0-...	157.0	183	106	96	15	64-3	81
1995— Buffalo (A.A.)	3	4	.429	0.89	30	0	0	0	5-...	40.2	31	10	4	0	19-2	56
— Cleveland (A.L.)	3	2	.600	5.11	23	0	0	0	1-1	24.2	23	16	14	2	16-0	23
1996— Cleveland (A.L.)	1	1	.500	6.39	24	0	0	0	0-0	31.0	30	26	22	10	21-3	33
— Buffalo (A.A.)	4	1	.800	3.93	20	0	0	0	5-...	34.1	26	16	15	1	14-0	46
1997— Atlanta (N.L.)■	3	1	.750	2.54	66	0	0	0	0-0	46.0	36	13	13	1	20-2	45
1998— Atlanta (N.L.)	1	0	1.000	4.34	20	0	0	0	0-1	18.2	23	14	9	2	10-0	19
— Arizona (N.L.)■	3	2	.600	4.11	35	0	0	0	1-2	35.0	33	18	16	5	13-0	24
1999— San Francisco (N.L.)■	3	2	.600	3.38	68	0	0	0	0-3	58.2	42	22	22	6	26-2	53
2000— San Francisco (N.L.)	3	5	.375	4.95	63	0	0	0	2-5	60.0	62	34	33	4	25-2	49
2001— San Francisco (N.L.)	0	2	.000	11.25	22	0	0	0	0-1	20.0	34	26	25	7	10-2	25
— Fresno (PCL)	1	0	1.000	1.13	7	0	0	0	1-...	8.0	5	3	1	0	1-0	6
— Chicago (A.L.)■	1	2	.333	5.03	39	0	0	0	0-2	34.0	31	21	19	7	7-0	34
2002— San Diego (N.L.)■	3	4	.429	0.94	36	0	0	0	0-2	28.2	23	7	3	2	9-2	38
— Boston (A.L.)■	1	2	.333	2.97	32	0	0	0	2-5	33.1	24	12	11	4	11-1	43
A.L. totals (5 years)	6	9	.400	5.11	122	4	0	0	3-8	141.0	127	89	80	26	63-4	145
N.L. totals (6 years)	16	16	.500	4.08	310	0	0	0	3-14	267.0	253	134	121	27	113-10	253
Major League totals (9 years)	22	25	.468	4.43	432	4	0	0	6-22	408.0	380	223	201	53	176-14	398

DIVISION SERIES RECORD

Year League	W	L	Pct.	ERA	G	GS	CG	ShO	Sv.-Opp.	IP	H	R	ER	HR	BB-IBB	SO
1996— Cleveland (A.L.)	0	0	...	9.00	3	0	0	0	0-0	1.0	0	1	1	0	0-0	1
2000— San Francisco (N.L.)	0	0	...	0.00	2	0	0	0	0-0	1.2	0	0	0	0	0-0	0
Division series totals (2 years)	0	0	...	3.38	5	0	0	0	0-0	2.2	0	1	1	0	0-0	1

CHAMPIONSHIP SERIES RECORD

Year League	W	L	Pct.	ERA	G	GS	CG	ShO	Sv.-Opp.	IP	H	R	ER	HR	BB-IBB	SO
1995— Cleveland (A.L.)	0	0	...	0.00	1	0	0	0	0-0	.1	0	0	0	0	0-0	1
1997— Atlanta (N.L.)	0	0	...	0.00	1	0	0	0	0-0	1.0	0	0	0	0	1-0	1
Champ. series totals (2 years)	0	0	...	0.00	2	0	0	0	0-0	1.1	0	0	0	0	1-0	2

WORLD SERIES RECORD

Year League	W	L	Pct.	ERA	G	GS	CG	ShO	Sv.-Opp.	IP	H	R	ER	HR	BB-IBB	SO
1995— Cleveland (A.L.)	0	0	...	2.70	4	0	0	0	0-0	3.1	2	1	1	0	2-1	2

ENCARNACION, JUAN — OF — MARLINS

PERSONAL: Born March 8, 1976, in Las Matas de Faran, Dominican Republic. ... 6-3/215. ... Bats right, throws right. ... Full name: Juan de Dios Encarnacion. ... Name pronounced en-car-nah-CION.

HIGH SCHOOL: Liceo Mercedes Maria Mateo (Las Matas de Faran, Dominican Republic).

TRANSACTIONS/CAREER NOTES: Signed as non-drafted free agent by Detroit Tigers organization (December 27, 1992). ... On Detroit disabled list (March 20-April 29, 1998); included rehabilitation assignment to Lakeland (April 24-29). ... On suspended list (May 27-29, 2000). ... Traded by Tigers with P Luis Pineda to Cincinnati Reds for OF Dmitri Young (December 11, 2001). ... Traded by Reds with OF/2B Wilton Guerrero and P Ryan Snare to Florida Marlins for P Ryan Dempster (July 11, 2002).

STATISTICAL NOTES: Led Appalachian League outfielders with nine assists in 1994. ... Tied for Florida State League lead in double plays by outfielder with four in 1996. ... Led Southern League in being hit by pitch with 19 in 1997. ... Tied for International League lead in double plays by outfielder with three in 1998. ... Had 19-game hitting streak (April 16-May 7, 2000). ... Led N.L. outfielders with six double plays in 2002. ... Career major league grand slams: 1.

2002 GAMES PLAYED BY POSITION (MLB): OF—149.

		BATTING														FIELDING	
Year Team (League)	Pos.	G	AB	R	H	2B	3B	HR	RBI	BB	SO	SB-CS	Avg.	OBP	SLG	E	Avg.
1993—Dom. Tigers (DSL)	OF	72	251	36	63	13	4	13	49	15	65	6-...	.251	...	.490	17	.879
1994—Bristol (Appl.)	OF	54	197	16	49	7	1	4	31	13	54	9-2	.249	.310	.355	3	.968
—Fayetteville (S.Atl.)	OF	24	83	6	16	1	1	1	4	8	36	1-1	.193	.272	.265	2	.920
—Lakeland (FSL)	OF	3	6	1	2	0	0	0	0	0	3	0-0	.333	.429	.333	0	...
1995—Fayetteville (S.Atl.)	OF	124	457	62	129	31	7	16	72	30	113	30-6	.282	.336	.486	7	.956
1996—Lakeland (FSL)	OF	131	499	54	120	31	2	15	58	24	104	11-5	.240	.290	.401	6	.976
1997—Jacksonville (Sou.)	OF	131	493	91	159	31	4	26	90	43	86	17-3	.323	.394	.560	3	.987
—Detroit (A.L.)	OF	11	33	3	7	1	1	1	5	3	12	3-1	.212	.316	.394	0	1.000
1998—Lakeland (FSL)	OF	4	16	4	4	0	1	0	4	2	4	4-0	.250	.368	.375	0	1.000
—Toledo (I.L.)	OF	92	356	55	102	17	3	8	41	29	85	24-4	.287	.353	.419	5	.973
—Detroit (A.L.)	OF-DH	40	164	30	54	9	4	7	21	7	31	7-4	.329	.354	.561	1	.985
1999—Detroit (A.L.)	OF	132	509	62	130	30	6	19	74	14	113	33-12	.255	.287	.450	9	.968
2000—Detroit (A.L.)	OF	141	547	75	158	25	6	14	72	29	90	16-4	.289	.330	.433	5	.987
2001—Detroit (A.L.)	OF-DH	120	417	52	101	19	7	12	52	25	93	9-5	.242	.292	.408	6	.977
2002—Cincinnati (N.L.)■	OF	83	321	43	89	11	2	16	51	26	63	9-4	.277	.330	.474	5	.977
—Florida (N.L.)■	OF	69	263	34	69	11	3	8	34	20	50	12-5	.262	.317	.418	1	.993
American League totals (5 years)		444	1670	222	450	84	24	53	224	78	339	68-26	.269	.310	.444	21	.979
National League totals (1 year)		152	584	77	158	22	5	24	85	46	113	21-9	.271	.324	.449	6	.983
Major League totals (6 years)		596	2254	299	608	106	29	77	309	124	452	89-35	.270	.314	.445	27	.980

ENCARNACION, MARIO — OF

PERSONAL: Born September 24, 1975, in Bani, Dominican Republic. ... 6-2/210. ... Bats right, throws right. ... Full name: Mario Gonzalez Encarnacion.

TRANSACTIONS/CAREER NOTES: Signed as non-drafted free agent by Oakland Athletics organization (July 11, 1994). ... On Sacramento disabled list (May 25-July 7, 2000). ... On Sacramento disabled list (April 5-July 5, 2001). ... Traded by A's with 2B/SS Jose Ortiz and P Todd Belitz to Colorado Rockies for OF Jermaine Dye (July 25, 2001). ... On Colorado Springs disabled list (August 10-21, 2001). ... Claimed on waivers by Chicago Cubs (April 4, 2002). ... On Iowa disabled list (May 31-August 2, 2002). ... Granted free agency (October 15, 2002).

2002 GAMES PLAYED BY POSITION (MLB): OF—2.

		BATTING														FIELDING	
Year Team (League)	Pos.	G	AB	R	H	2B	3B	HR	RBI	BB	SO	SB-CS	Avg.	OBP	SLG	E	Avg.
1995—Dom. Athletics (DSL)	OF	64	229	56	79	11	5	8	44	40	36	17-...	.345	...	.541	7	.945
1996—West Mich. (Midw.)	OF	118	401	55	92	14	3	7	43	49	131	23-8	.229	.321	.332	11	.949
1997—Modesto (Calif.)	OF	111	364	70	108	17	9	18	78	42	121	14-11	.297	.378	.541	12	.927
1998—Huntsville (Sou.)	OF	110	357	70	97	15	2	15	61	60	123	11-8	.272	.382	.451	6	.969
1999—Midland (Texas)	OF-DH	94	353	69	109	21	4	18	71	47	86	9-9	.309	.390	.544	9	.936
—Vancouver (PCL)	OF-DH	39	145	18	35	5	0	3	17	6	44	5-4	.241	.277	.338	4	.960
2000—Sacramento (PCL)	OF	81	301	51	81	16	3	13	61	36	95	15-7	.269	.348	.472	5	.972
—Modesto (Calif.)	OF	5	15	1	3	0	0	0	1	1	4	0-0	.200	.250	.200	0	1.000
2001—Sacramento (PCL)	OF	51	186	29	53	8	2	12	33	17	61	4-3	.285	.356	.543	4	.947
—Colo. Springs (PCL)■	OF	16	45	8	17	5	0	2	10	4	8	0-1	.378	.440	.622	0	1.000
—Colorado (N.L.)	OF	20	62	3	14	1	0	0	3	5	14	2-1	.226	.284	.242	0	1.000
2002—Chicago (N.L.)■	OF	3	7	0	0	0	0	0	0	2	3	0-0	.000	.222	.000	0	1.000
—Iowa (PCL)	OF-3B	61	200	24	56	9	0	7	28	17	61	0-2	.280	.342	.430	3	.969
Major League totals (2 years)		23	69	3	14	1	0	0	3	7	17	2-1	.203	.276	.217	0	1.000

ENNIS, JOHN — P — BRAVES

PERSONAL: Born October 17, 1979, in Montrose, Colo. ... 6-5/220. ... Throws right, bats right. ... Full name: John Wayne Ennis.

HIGH SCHOOL: Monroe (Panorama City, Calif.).

TRANSACTIONS/CAREER NOTES: Selected by Atlanta Braves organization in 14th round of free-agent draft (June 2, 1998). ... On disabled list (May 15-30, 2001).

STATISTICAL NOTES: Tied for Southern League lead with 11 sacrifice hits allowed in 2002.

CAREER HITTING (MLB): 0-for-1 (.000), 0 R, 0 2B, 0 3B, 0 HR, 0 RBI.

Year League	W	L	Pct.	ERA	G	GS	CG	ShO	Sv.-Opp.	IP	H	R	ER	HR	BB-IBB	SO
1998—Gulf Coast Braves (GCL)	0	3	.000	4.62	8	2	0	0	0-...	25.1	30	16	13	0	6-1	18
1999—Danville (Appl.)	4	3	.571	5.07	13	13	13	0	0-...	65.2	71	46	37	7	21-0	60
2000—Macon (S.Atl.)	7	4	.636	2.55	18	16	0	0	0-...	98.2	77	37	28	5	25-0	105
2001—Myrtle Beach (Caro.)	6	8	.429	3.58	25	25	1	0	0-...	138.1	111	63	55	12	45-0	144
2002—Greenville (Sou.)	9	9	.500	4.18	26	26	0	0	0-...	148.2	131	79	69	7	62-0	103
—Atlanta (N.L.)	0	0	...	4.50	1	1	0	0	0-0	4.0	5	2	2	0	3-0	1
Major League totals (1 year)	0	0	...	4.50	1	1	0	0	0-0	4.0	5	2	2	0	3-0	1

ENSBERG, MORGAN — 3B — ASTROS

PERSONAL: Born August 26, 1975, in Redondo Beach, Calif. ... 6-2/210. ... Bats right, throws right. ... Full name: Morgan P. Ensberg.

HIGH SCHOOL: Redondo Union (Redondo Beach, Calif.).

COLLEGE: Southern California.

TRANSACTIONS/CAREER NOTES: Selected by Houston Astros organization in ninth round of free-agent draft (June 2, 1998). ... On disabled list (June 22-August 10, 2001).

STATISTICAL NOTES: Led New York-Pennsylvania League third baseman with .926 fielding percentage in 1998. ... Led Texas League with 307 assists and 415 total chances and tied for league lead with 84 putouts in 2000.

2002 GAMES PLAYED BY POSITION (MLB): 3B—43.

Year	Team (League)	Pos.	G	AB	R	H	2B	3B	HR	RBI	BB	SO	SB-CS	Avg.	OBP	SLG	E	Avg.
			BATTING														FIELDING	
1998—	Auburn (NY-Penn)	3B-SS	59	196	39	45	10	1	5	31	46	51	15-3	.230	.388	.367	11	†.927
1999—	Kissimmee (FSL)	3B-SS-1B	123	427	72	102	25	2	15	69	68	90	17-6	.239	.353	.412	35	.900
2000—	Round Rock (Texas)	3B	137	483	95	145	34	0	28	90	92	107	9-12	.300	.416	.545	24	*.942
—	Houston (N.L.)	3B	4	7	0	2	0	0	0	0	0	1	0-0	.286	.286	.286	1	.667
2001—	New Orleans (PCL)	3B-SS	87	316	65	98	20	0	23	61	45	60	6-3	.310	.397	.592	17	.929
2002—	Houston (N.L.)	3B	49	132	14	32	7	2	3	19	18	25	2-0	.242	.346	.394	8	.929
—	New Orleans (PCL)	3B-1B	83	292	50	84	12	3	7	37	50	56	9-5	.288	.401	.421	19	.926
Major League totals (2 years)			53	139	14	34	7	2	3	19	18	26	2-0	.245	.344	.388	9	.922

ERICKSON, SCOTT — P — ORIOLES

PERSONAL: Born February 2, 1968, in Long Beach, Calif. ... 6-4/230. ... Throws right, bats right. ... Full name: Scott Gavin Erickson.
HIGH SCHOOL: Homestead (Cupertino, Calif.).
JUNIOR COLLEGE: San Jose City College.
COLLEGE: Arizona.
TRANSACTIONS/CAREER NOTES: Selected by New York Mets organization in 36th round of free-agent draft (June 2, 1986); did not sign. ... Selected by Houston Astros organization in 34th round of free-agent draft (June 2, 1987); did not sign. ... Selected by Toronto Blue Jays organization in 44th round of free-agent draft (June 1, 1988); did not sign. ... Selected by Minnesota Twins organization in fourth round of free-agent draft (June 5, 1989). ... On disabled list (June 30-July 15, 1991; April 3-18, 1993 and May 15-31, 1994). ... Traded by Twins to Baltimore Orioles for P Scott Klingenbeck and a player to be named later (July 7, 1995); Twins acquired OF Kimera Bartee to complete deal (September 18, 1995). ... On Baltimore disabled list (March 28-May 4 and July 28, 2000-remainder of season); included rehabilitation assignments to Frederick (April 25) and Bowie (April 30). ... On disabled list (April 1, 2001-entire season).
STATISTICAL NOTES: Pitched 5-0 one-hit, complete-game victory against Boston (July 24, 1992, first game). ... Pitched 6-0 no-hit victory against Milwaukee (April 27, 1994). ... Tied for A.L. lead with nine hit batsmen in 1994.
MISCELLANEOUS: Appeared in one game as pinch runner (2000).
CAREER HITTING (MLB): 2-for-19 (.105), 4 R, 1 2B, 0 3B, 0 HR, 1 RBI.

Year	League	W	L	Pct.	ERA	G	GS	CG	ShO	Sv.-Opp.	IP	H	R	ER	HR	BB-IBB	SO
1989—	Visalia (Calif.)	3	4	.429	2.97	12	12	2	0	0-...	78.2	79	29	26	3	22-0	59
1990—	Orlando (Sou.)	8	3	.727	3.03	15	15	3	1	0-...	101.0	75	38	34	3	24-0	69
—	Minnesota (A.L.)	8	4	.667	2.87	19	17	1	0	0-0	113.0	108	49	36	9	51-4	53
1991—	Minnesota (A.L.)	•20	8	.714	3.18	32	32	5	3	0-0	204.0	189	80	72	13	71-3	108
1992—	Minnesota (A.L.)	13	12	.520	3.40	32	32	5	3	0-0	212.0	197	86	80	18	83-3	101
1993—	Minnesota (A.L.)	8	*19	.296	5.19	34	34	1	0	0-0	218.2	*266	*138	126	17	71-1	116
1994—	Minnesota (A.L.)	8	11	.421	5.44	23	23	2	1	0-0	144.0	173	95	87	15	59-0	104
1995—	Minnesota (A.L.)	4	6	.400	5.95	15	15	0	0	0-0	87.2	102	61	58	11	32-0	45
—	Baltimore (A.L.)■	9	4	.692	3.89	17	16	7	2	0-0	108.2	111	47	47	7	35-0	61
1996—	Baltimore (A.L.)	13	12	.520	5.02	34	34	6	0	0-0	222.1	262	137	124	21	66-4	100
1997—	Baltimore (A.L.)	16	7	.696	3.69	34	33	3	2	0-0	221.2	218	100	91	16	61-5	131
1998—	Baltimore (A.L.)	16	13	.552	4.01	36	*36	*11	2	0-0	*251.1	*284	125	112	23	69-4	186
1999—	Baltimore (A.L.)	15	12	.556	4.81	34	34	6	*3	0-0	230.1	244	127	123	27	*99-4	106
2000—	Frederick (Caro.)	0	0	...	2.70	1	1	0	0	0-...	6.2	3	2	2	0	1-0	5
—	Bowie (East.)	0	0	...	0.00	1	1	0	0	0-...	7.0	4	0	0	0	0-0	5
—	Baltimore (A.L.)	5	8	.385	7.87	16	16	1	0	0-0	92.2	127	81	81	14	48-0	41
2001—	Baltimore (A.L.)									Did not play.							
2002—	Baltimore (A.L.)	5	12	.294	5.55	29	28	3	1	0-0	160.2	192	109	99	20	68-2	74
Major League totals (12 years)		140	128	.522	4.51	355	350	51	17	0-0	2267.0	2473	1235	1136	211	813-30	1226

DIVISION SERIES RECORD

Year	League	W	L	Pct.	ERA	G	GS	CG	ShO	Sv.-Opp.	IP	H	R	ER	HR	BB-IBB	SO
1996—	Baltimore (A.L.)	0	0	...	4.05	1	1	0	0	0-0	6.2	6	3	3	1	2-0	6
1997—	Baltimore (A.L.)	1	0	1.000	4.05	1	1	0	0	0-0	6.2	7	3	3	0	2-0	6
Division series totals (2 years)		1	0	1.000	4.05	2	2	0	0	0-0	13.1	13	6	6	1	4-0	12

CHAMPIONSHIP SERIES RECORD

RECORDS: Shares A.L. record for most runs allowed in one inning—6 (October 13, 1996, third inning). ... Holds record for most home runs allowed in one inning—3 (October 13, 1996, third inning).

Year	League	W	L	Pct.	ERA	G	GS	CG	ShO	Sv.-Opp.	IP	H	R	ER	HR	BB-IBB	SO
1991—	Minnesota (A.L.)	0	0	...	4.50	1	1	0	0	0-0	4.0	3	2	2	1	5-0	2
1996—	Baltimore (A.L.)	0	1	.000	2.38	2	2	0	0	0-0	11.1	14	9	3	3	4-0	8
1997—	Baltimore (A.L.)	1	0	1.000	4.26	2	2	0	0	0-0	12.2	15	7	6	2	1-0	6
Champ. series totals (3 years)		1	1	.500	3.54	5	5	0	0	0-0	28.0	32	18	11	6	10-0	16

WORLD SERIES RECORD

NOTES: Member of World Series championship team (1991).

Year	League	W	L	Pct.	ERA	G	GS	CG	ShO	Sv.-Opp.	IP	H	R	ER	HR	BB-IBB	SO
1991—	Minnesota (A.L.)	0	0	...	5.06	2	2	0	0	0-0	10.2	10	7	6	3	4-0	5

ERSTAD, DARIN — OF — ANGELS

PERSONAL: Born June 4, 1974, in Jamestown, N.D. ... 6-2/220. ... Bats left, throws left. ... Full name: Darin Charles Erstad.
HIGH SCHOOL: Jamestown (N.D.).
COLLEGE: Nebraska.
TRANSACTIONS/CAREER NOTES: Selected by New York Mets organization in 13th round of free-agent draft (June 1, 1992); did not sign. ... Selected by California Angels organization in first round (first pick overall) of free-agent draft (June 1, 1995). ... Angels franchise renamed Anaheim Angels for 1997 season. ... On disabled list (August 4-19, 1998; and August 11-26, 1999).
HONORS: Won A.L. Gold Glove as outfielder (2000 and 2002). ... Named outfielder on The Sporting News A.L. All-Star team (2000). ... Named outfielder on The Sporting News A.L. Silver Slugger team (2000).
STATISTICAL NOTES: Had 15-game hitting streak (April 1-18, 1998). ... Had 15-game hitting streak (May 19-June 5, 2001). ... Led A.L. outfielders with 452 putouts and 464 total chances in 2002. ... Career major league grand slams: 1.
2002 GAMES PLAYED BY POSITION (MLB): OF—143; 1B—5; DH—4.

Year	Team (League)	Pos.	G	AB	R	H	2B	3B	HR	RBI	BB	SO	SB-CS	Avg.	OBP	SLG	E	Avg.
			BATTING														FIELDING	
1995—	Arizona Angels (Ariz.).	OF	4	18	2	10	1	0	0	1	1	1	1-0	.556	.579	.611	0	1.000
—	Lake Elsinore (Calif.)..	OF	25	113	24	41	7	2	5	24	6	22	3-0	.363	.392	.593	1	.985
1996—	Vancouver (PCL)........	OF-1B	85	351	63	107	22	5	6	41	44	53	11-6	.305	.385	.447	1	.995
—	California (A.L.)..........	OF	57	208	34	59	5	1	4	20	17	29	3-3	.284	.333	.375	3	.976
1997—	Anaheim (A.L.)...........	1B-DH-OF	139	539	99	161	34	4	16	77	51	86	23-8	.299	.360	.466	11	.990
1998—	Anaheim (A.L.)...........	OF-1B-DH	133	537	84	159	39	3	19	82	43	77	20-6	.296	.353	.486	3	.995
1999—	Anaheim (A.L.)...........	1B-OF-DH	142	585	84	148	22	5	13	53	47	101	13-7	.253	.308	.374	1	.999
2000—	Anaheim (A.L.)...........	OF-DH-1B	157	*676	121	*240	39	6	25	100	64	82	28-8	.355	.409	.541	3	.992
2001—	Anaheim (A.L.)...........	OF-1B-DH	157	631	89	163	35	1	9	63	62	113	24-10	.258	.331	.360	1	.998
2002—	Anaheim (A.L.)...........	OF-1B-DH	150	625	99	177	28	4	10	73	27	67	23-3	.283	.313	.389	1	.998
Major League totals (7 years)			935	3801	610	1107	202	24	96	468	311	555	134-45	.291	.346	.433	23	.994

DIVISION SERIES RECORD

Year	Team (League)	Pos.	G	AB	R	H	2B	3B	HR	RBI	BB	SO	SB-CS	Avg.	OBP	SLG	E	Avg.
			BATTING														FIELDING	
2002—	Anaheim (A.L.)...........	OF	4	19	4	8	2	0	0	2	0	1	1-0	.421	.421	.526	0	1.000

CHAMPIONSHIP SERIES RECORD

Year	Team (League)	Pos.	G	AB	R	H	2B	3B	HR	RBI	BB	SO	SB-CS	Avg.	OBP	SLG	E	Avg.
			BATTING														FIELDING	
2002—	Anaheim (A.L.)...........	OF	5	22	4	8	0	0	1	2	0	3	1-0	.364	.364	.500	0	1.000

WORLD SERIES RECORD

NOTES: Member of World Series championship team (2002).

Year	Team (League)	Pos.	G	AB	R	H	2B	3B	HR	RBI	BB	SO	SB-CS	Avg.	OBP	SLG	E	Avg.
			BATTING														FIELDING	
2002—	Anaheim (A.L.)...........	OF	7	30	6	9	3	0	1	3	1	4	1-0	.300	.313	.500	1	.955

ALL-STAR GAME RECORD

	AB	R	H	2B	3B	HR	RBI	BB	SO	SB-CS	Avg.	OBP	SLG	E	Avg.
All-Star Game totals (2 years)	4	1	0	0	0	0	1	0	0	0-0	.000	.000	.000	0	1.000

ESCALONA, FELIX — SS — DEVIL RAYS

PERSONAL: Born March 12, 1979, in Puerto Cabello, Venezuela. ... 6-0/196. ... Bats right, throws right. ... Full name: Felix Eduardo Escalona.
TRANSACTIONS/CAREER NOTES: Signed as non-drafted free agent by Houston Astros organization (September 20, 1995). ... Selected by San Francisco Giants from Astros organization in Rule 5 major league draft (December 13, 2001). ... Claimed on waivers by Tampa Bay Devil Rays (March 27, 2002).
STATISTICAL NOTES: Led Gulf Coast League with 127 assists and 37 double plays in 1997.
2002 GAMES PLAYED BY POSITION (MLB): SS—26; 2B—25; 3B—4; DH—1.

Year	Team (League)	Pos.	G	AB	R	H	2B	3B	HR	RBI	BB	SO	SB-CS	Avg.	OBP	SLG	E	Avg.
			BATTING														FIELDING	
1996—	GC Astros (GCL)........	3B-2B	28	75	8	11	2	0	1	9	8	31	1-2	.147	.261	.213	6	.924
1997—	GC Astros (GCL)........	2B	51	189	27	39	9	0	1	9	20	49	11-3	.206	.292	.270	7	.969
—	Kissimmee (FSL)........	2B	3	9	6	2	0	0	0	0	1	2	0-0	.222	.462	.222	3	.833
1998—	Kissimmee (FSL)........	3B	3	4	0	0	0	0	0	0	0	1	0-0	.000	.000	.000	0	1.000
—	Auburn (NY-Penn)......	SS-2B-3B	51	149	22	31	5	0	1	17	11	33	4-2	.208	.282	.262	14	.933
1999—	Michigan (Midw.).......	2B-SS-3B	116	396	78	114	29	4	6	47	29	60	7-7	.288	.360	.427	21	.955
2000—	Michigan (Midw.).......	2B-SS	64	251	42	65	14	1	6	35	22	49	7-0	.259	.326	.394	14	.953
—	Kissimmee (FSL)........	SS-2B-3B	42	143	19	36	5	1	0	8	9	21	5-3	.252	.321	.301	7	.955
2001—	Lexington (S.Atl.).......	2B-SS	130	536	92	155	42	2	16	64	30	85	46-12	.289	.342	.465	23	.963
2002—	Tampa Bay (A.L.)■.....	SS-2B-3B-DH	59	157	17	34	8	2	0	9	3	44	7-2	.217	.262	.293	11	.949
Major League totals (1 year)			59	157	17	34	8	2	0	9	3	44	7-2	.217	.262	.293	11	.949

ESCOBAR, ALEX — OF — INDIANS

PERSONAL: Born September 6, 1978, in Valencia, Venezuela. ... 6-1/180. ... Bats right, throws right. ... Full name: Alexander Jose Escobar.
HIGH SCHOOL: El Santuario (Valencia, Venezuela).
TRANSACTIONS/CAREER NOTES: Signed as non-drafted free agent by New York Mets organization (July 1, 1995). ... On St. Lucie disabled list (April 14-June 21 and July 8, 1999-remainder of season). ... Traded by Mets with OF Matt Lawton, P Jerrod Riggan and two players to be named later to Cleveland Indians for 2B Roberto Alomar, P Mike Bacsik and OF Danny Peoples (December 11, 2001); Indians acquired P Billy Traber and 1B Earl Snyder to complete deal (December 13, 2001). ... On disabled list (March 30, 2002-entire season).

Year	Team (League)	Pos.	G	AB	R	H	2B	3B	HR	RBI	BB	SO	SB-CS	Avg.	OBP	SLG	E	Avg.
			BATTING														FIELDING	
1996—	GC Mets (GCL)...........	OF-SS	24	75	15	27	4	0	0	10	4	9	7-1	.360	.410	.413	3	.936
1997—	Kingsport (Appl.)........	OF	10	36	6	7	3	0	0	3	3	8	1-0	.194	.250	.278	2	.905
—	GC Mets (GCL)...........	OF	26	73	12	18	4	1	1	11	10	17	0-0	.247	.341	.370	1	.966
1998—	Capital City (S.Atl.).....	OF	112	416	90	129	23	5	27	91	54	133	49-7	.310	.393	.584	12	.941
1999—	GC Mets (GCL)...........	DH-OF	2	8	1	3	2	0	0	1	1	2	0-0	.375	.444	.625	0	1.000
—	St. Lucie (FSL)...........	OF	1	3	1	2	0	0	1	3	1	1	1-1	.667	.600	1.667	0	1.000
2000—	Binghamton (East.).....	OF	122	437	79	126	25	7	16	67	57	114	24-5	.288	.375	.487	5	.983
2001—	Norfolk (I.L.)..............	OF	111	397	55	106	21	4	12	52	35	146	18-3	.267	.327	.431	5	.980
—	New York (N.L.)..........	OF	18	50	3	10	1	0	3	8	3	19	1-0	.200	.245	.400	2	.935
2002—	Cleveland (A.L.)■......								Did not play.									
Major League totals (1 year)			18	50	3	10	1	0	3	8	3	19	1-0	.200	.245	.400	2	.935

ESCOBAR, KELVIM — P — BLUE JAYS

PERSONAL: Born April 11, 1976, in La Guaria, Venezuela. ... 6-1/210. ... Throws right, bats right. ... Full name: Kelvim Jose Bolivar Escobar.
TRANSACTIONS/CAREER NOTES: Signed as non-drafted free agent by Toronto Blue Jays organization (July 9, 1992). ... On Toronto disabled list (April 16-May 6, 1998); included rehabilitation assignment to Syracuse (May 2-6).
STATISTICAL NOTES: Pitched 2-0 no-hit victory against Ogden (July 20, 1995, first game).
CAREER HITTING (MLB): 0-for-8 (.000), 0 R, 0 2B, 0 3B, 0 HR, 0 RBI.

Year League	W	L	Pct.	ERA	G	GS	CG	ShO	Sv.-Opp.	IP	H	R	ER	HR	BB-IBB	SO
1993— Dom. Blue Jays (DSL)	2	1	.667	4.13	8	7	0	0	0-...	32.2	34	17	15	...	25-...	31
1994— GC Blue Jays (GCL)	4	4	.500	2.35	11	10	1	0	1-...	65.0	56	23	17	0	18-0	64
1995— Dom. Blue Jays (DSL)	0	1	.000	1.72	3	2	0	0	0-...	15.2	14	3	3	...	5-...	20
— Medicine Hat (Pio.)	3	3	.500	5.71	14	14	1	•1	0-...	69.1	66	47	44	6	33-0	75
1996— Dunedin (FSL)	9	5	.643	2.69	18	18	1	0	0-...	110.1	101	44	33	5	33-0	113
— Knoxville (Sou.)	3	4	.429	5.33	10	10	0	0	0-...	54.0	61	36	32	7	24-0	44
1997— Dunedin (FSL)	0	1	.000	3.75	3	2	0	0	0-...	12.0	16	9	5	0	3-0	16
— Knoxville (Sou.)	2	1	.667	3.70	5	5	1	0	0-...	24.1	20	13	10	1	16-0	31
— Toronto (A.L.)	3	2	.600	2.90	27	0	0	0	14-17	31.0	28	12	10	1	19-2	36
1998— Toronto (A.L.)	7	3	.700	3.73	22	10	0	0	0-1	79.2	72	37	33	5	35-0	72
— Syracuse (I.L.)	2	2	.500	3.77	13	10	0	0	1-...	59.2	51	26	25	7	24-0	64
1999— Toronto (A.L.)	14	11	.560	5.69	33	30	1	0	0-0	174.0	203	118	110	19	81-2	129
2000— Toronto (A.L.)	10	15	.400	5.35	43	24	3	1	2-3	180.0	186	118	107	26	85-3	142
2001— Toronto (A.L.)	6	8	.429	3.50	59	11	1	1	0-0	126.0	93	51	49	8	52-5	121
2002— Toronto (A.L.)	5	7	.417	4.27	76	0	0	0	38-46	78.0	75	39	37	10	44-6	85
Major League totals (6 years)	45	46	.495	4.66	260	75	5	2	54-67	668.2	657	375	346	69	316-18	585

ESPINOSA, DAVID — SS — TIGERS

PERSONAL: Born December 16, 1981, in Miami, Fla. ... 6-1/170. ... Bats both, throws right.
TRANSACTIONS/CAREER NOTES: Selected by Cincinnati Reds organization in first round (23rd pick overall) of free-agent draft (June 5, 2000). ... Traded by Reds with two players to be named later to Detroit Tigers for P Brian Moehler and IF Matt Boone (July 23, 2002); Tigers acquired OF Gary Varner (August 30, 2002) and P Jorge Cordova to complete deal (September 24, 2002). ... On Lakeland disabled list (August 1, 2002-remainder of season).

		BATTING														FIELDING	
Year Team (League)	Pos.	G	AB	R	H	2B	3B	HR	RBI	BB	SO	SB-CS	Avg.	OBP	SLG	E	Avg.
2001— Dayton (Midw.)	SS	122	493	88	129	29	8	7	37	55	120	15-10	.262	.340	.396	*48	.909
2002— Stockton (Calif.)	2B	95	367	71	90	13	7	7	44	62	104	26-17	.245	.356	.376	26	.942

ESTALELLA, BOBBY — C — ROCKIES

PERSONAL: Born August 23, 1974, in Hialeah, Fla. ... 6-1/213. ... Bats right, throws right. ... Full name: Robert M. Estalella. ... Grandson of Bobby Estalella, outfielder with Washington Senators (1935-36, 1939 and 1942), St. Louis Browns (1941), and Philadelphia Athletics (1943-45 and 1949).
HIGH SCHOOL: Cooper City (Fla.).
JUNIOR COLLEGE: Miami-Dade (South) Community College.
TRANSACTIONS/CAREER NOTES: Selected by Philadelphia Phillies organization in 23rd round of free-agent draft (June 1, 1992). ... On Philadelphia disabled list (March 27-April 29, 1999); included rehabilitation assignments to Clearwater (April 9-17) and to Scranton/Wilkes-Barre (April 19-29). ... Traded by Phillies to San Francisco Giants for P Chris Brock (December 12, 1999). ... Traded by Giants with P Joe Smith to New York Yankees for P Brian Boehringer (July 5, 2001). ... Released by Yankees (March 27, 2002). ... Signed by Colorado Rockies organization (March 31, 2002). ... On Colorado disabled list (July 8, 2002-remainder of season).
STATISTICAL NOTES: Tied for South Atlantic League lead in double plays by catcher with eight in 1994. ... Led Florida State League catchers with 771 putouts and 864 total chances in 1995. ... Led International League with 844 putouts and 928 total chances and tied for league lead in double plays by catcher with nine in 1997. ... Hit three home runs in one game (September 4, 1997). ... Led International League catchers with 10 double plays in 1999. ... Led N.L. catchers with 14 double plays in 2000. ... Career major league grand slams: 2.
2002 GAMES PLAYED BY POSITION (MLB): C—38.

		BATTING														FIELDING	
Year Team (League)	Pos.	G	AB	R	H	2B	3B	HR	RBI	BB	SO	SB-CS	Avg.	OBP	SLG	E	Avg.
1993— Martinsville (Appl.)	C	35	122	14	36	11	0	3	19	14	24	0-1	.295	.377	.459	6	.975
— Clearwater (FSL)	C	11	35	4	8	0	0	0	4	2	3	0-0	.229	.270	.229	0	1.000
1994— Spartanburg (S.Atl.)	C	86	299	34	65	19	1	9	41	31	85	0-1	.217	.290	.378	10	.985
— Clearwater (FSL)	C	13	46	3	12	1	0	2	9	3	17	0-0	.261	.300	.413	1	.990
1995— Clearwater (FSL)	C	117	404	61	105	24	1	15	58	56	76	0-3	.260	.350	.436	11	.987
— Reading (East.)	C	10	34	5	8	1	0	2	9	4	7	0-0	.235	.333	.441	1	.986
1996— Reading (East.)	C	111	365	48	89	14	2	23	72	67	104	2-4	.244	.365	.482	14	.984
— Scranton/W.B. (I.L.)	C	11	36	7	9	3	0	3	8	5	10	0-0	.250	.341	.583	2	.968
— Philadelphia (N.L.)	C	7	17	5	6	0	0	2	4	1	6	1-0	.353	.389	.706	0	1.000
1997— Scranton/W.B. (I.L.)	C-DH	123	433	63	101	32	0	16	65	56	109	3-0	.233	.332	.418	13	.986
— Philadelphia (N.L.)	C	13	29	9	10	1	0	4	9	7	7	0-0	.345	.472	.793	0	1.000
1998— Scranton/W.B. (I.L.)	C-DH	76	242	49	68	14	1	17	49	66	49	0-0	.281	.436	.558	5	.990
— Philadelphia (N.L.)	C	47	165	16	31	6	1	8	20	13	49	0-0	.188	.247	.382	4	.988
1999— Clearwater (FSL)	C-DH	8	26	3	11	3	0	1	8	3	3	0-0	.423	.483	.654	1	.976
— Scranton/W.B. (I.L.)	C-DH	110	386	58	89	23	2	15	62	55	100	4-1	.231	.330	.417	5	.993
— Philadelphia (N.L.)	C	9	18	2	3	0	0	0	1	4	7	0-1	.167	.318	.167	1	.976
2000— San Fran. (N.L.)■	C	106	299	45	70	22	3	14	53	57	92	3-0	.234	.357	.468	5	.993
2001— San Francisco (N.L.)	C	29	93	11	19	5	1	3	10	11	28	0-0	.204	.295	.376	0	1.000
— Fresno (PCL)	1B-C	6	22	3	7	1	0	1	4	1	9	0-0	.318	.348	.500	0	1.000
— Columbus (I.L.)■	C-1B	48	171	26	44	10	1	10	38	21	45	0-2	.257	.340	.503	2	.993
— New York (A.L.)	C	3	4	1	0	0	0	0	0	1	2	0-0	.000	.333	.000	0	1.000

Year	Team (League)	Pos.	G	AB	R	H	2B	3B	HR	RBI	BB	SO	SB-CS	Avg.	OBP	SLG	E	Avg.
								BATTING									FIELDING	
2002	—Colo. Springs (PCL)■	C	23	79	16	23	9	0	6	20	11	20	0-0	.291	.374	.633	1	.995
	—Colorado (N.L.)	C	38	112	17	23	8	0	8	25	14	33	0-1	.205	.285	.491	1	.995
American League totals (1 year)			3	4	1	0	0	0	0	0	1	2	0-0	.000	.333	.000	0	1.000
National League totals (7 years)			249	733	105	162	42	5	39	122	107	222	4-2	.221	.320	.452	11	.993
Major League totals (7 years)			252	737	106	162	42	5	39	122	108	224	4-2	.220	.320	.449	11	.993

DIVISION SERIES RECORD

Year	Team (League)	Pos.	G	AB	R	H	2B	3B	HR	RBI	BB	SO	SB-CS	Avg.	OBP	SLG	E	Avg.
								BATTING									FIELDING	
2000	—San Francisco (N.L.) ..	C	4	12	1	1	0	0	0	1	0	2	0-0	.083	.083	.083	0	1.000

ESTES, SHAWN — P

PERSONAL: Born February 18, 1973, in San Francisco. ... 6-2/200. ... Throws left, bats right. ... Full name: Aaron Shawn Estes. ... Name pronounced EST-us.

HIGH SCHOOL: Douglas (Minden, Nev.).

TRANSACTIONS/CAREER NOTES: Selected by Seattle Mariners organization in first round (11th pick overall) of free-agent draft (June 3, 1991). ... On disabled list (August 19, 1993-remainder of season). ... On Appleton disabled list (April 8-July 19 and July 25-August 15, 1994). ... Traded by Mariners with IF Wilson Delgado to San Francisco Giants for P Salomon Torres (May 21, 1995). ... On disabled list (March 23-April 6, 1997). ... On San Francisco disabled list (July 11-September 4, 1998); included rehabilitation assignments to Bakersfield (August 26-29) and Fresno (August 30-September 4). ... On San Francisco disabled list (March 29-April 17, 2000); included rehabilitation assignments to Fresno (April 7-12) and San Jose (April 13-17). ... On disabled list (May 9-24 and August 23, 2001-remainder of season). ... Traded by Giants to New York Mets for OF Tsuyoshi Shinjo and SS Desi Relaford (December 16, 2001). ... Traded by Mets with cash to Cincinnati Reds for P Pedro Feliciano, OF Elvin Andujar and two players to be named later (August 15, 2002); Mets acquired OF Raul Gonzalez (August 20, 2002) and OF Brady Clark to complete deal (September 9, 2002). ... Granted free agency (October 28, 2002).

STATISTICAL NOTES: Tied for N.L. lead with 15 wild pitches in 1999. ... Pitched 1-0 one-hit, complete-game victory against Milwaukee (April 26, 2002). ... Career major league grand slams: 1.

MISCELLANEOUS: Appeared in four games as pinch runner with San Francisco (1996). ... Appeared in four games as pinch runner (1997). ... Scored two runs in two games as pinch runner with San Francisco (1998). ... Struck out in both appearances as pinch hitter and scored two runs in eight appearances as pinch runner (1999). ... Appeared in two games as pinch runner (2000).

CAREER HITTING (MLB): 51-for-348 (.147), 30 R, 10 2B, 0 3B, 3 HR, 23 RBI.

Year	League	W	L	Pct.	ERA	G	GS	CG	ShO	Sv.-Opp.	IP	H	R	ER	HR	BB-IBB	SO
1991	—Bellingham (N'West)	1	3	.250	6.88	9	9	0	0	0-...	34.0	27	33	26	2	55-0	35
1992	—Bellingham (N'West)	3	3	.500	4.32	15	15	0	0	0-...	77.0	84	55	37	6	45-0	77
1993	—Appleton (Midw.)..............	5	9	.357	7.24	19	18	0	0	0-...	83.1	108	85	67	3	52-1	65
1994	—Arizona Mariners (Ariz.) ...	0	3	.000	3.15	5	5	0	0	0-...	20.0	16	9	7	0	6-0	31
	—Appleton (Midw.)..............	0	2	.000	4.58	5	4	0	0	0-...	19.2	19	13	10	1	17-0	28
1995	—Wisconsin (Midw.)...........	0	0	...	0.90	2	2	0	0	0-...	10.0	5	1	1	0	5-0	11
	—Burlington (Midw.)■........	0	0	...	4.11	4	4	0	0	0-...	15.1	13	8	7	2	12-0	22
	—San Jose (Calif.)..............	5	2	.714	2.17	9	8	0	0	0-...	49.2	32	13	12	1	17-0	61
	—Shreveport (Texas)...........	2	0	1.000	2.01	4	4	0	0	0-...	22.1	14	5	5	1	10-0	18
	—San Francisco (N.L.)	0	3	.000	6.75	3	3	0	0	0-0	17.1	16	14	13	2	5-0	14
1996	—Phoenix (PCL)..................	9	3	.750	3.43	18	18	0	0	0-...	110.1	92	43	42	7	38-1	95
	—San Francisco (N.L.)	3	5	.375	3.60	11	11	0	0	0-0	70.0	63	30	28	3	39-3	60
1997	—San Francisco (N.L.)	19	5	.792	3.18	32	32	3	2	0-0	201.0	162	80	71	12	*100-2	181
1998	—San Francisco (N.L.)	7	12	.368	5.06	25	25	1	1	0-0	149.1	150	89	84	14	80-6	136
	—Bakersfield (Calif.)...........	0	0	...	0.00	1	1	0	0	0-...	4.1	3	0	0	0	1-0	5
	—Fresno (PCL)....................	1	0	1.000	1.80	1	1	0	0	0-...	5.0	3	1	1	1	3-0	6
1999	—San Francisco (N.L.)	11	11	.500	4.92	32	32	1	1	0-0	203.0	209	121	111	21	112-2	159
2000	—Fresno (PCL)....................	0	1	.000	9.00	1	1	0	0	0-...	3.0	5	9	3	2	2-0	2
	—San Jose (Calif.)..............	1	0	1.000	0.00	1	1	0	0	0-...	7.0	2	0	0	0	1-0	11
	—San Francisco (N.L.)	15	6	.714	4.26	30	30	4	2	0-0	190.1	194	99	90	11	108-1	136
2001	—San Francisco (N.L.)	9	8	.529	4.02	27	27	0	0	0-0	159.0	151	78	71	11	77-7	109
2002	—New York (N.L.)■	4	9	.308	4.55	23	23	1	1	0-0	132.2	133	70	67	12	66-9	92
	—Cincinnati (N.L.)■............	1	3	.250	7.71	6	6	0	0	0-0	28.0	38	24	24	1	17-0	17
Major League totals (8 years).....		69	62	.527	4.37	189	189	10	7	0-0	1150.2	1116	605	559	87	604-30	904

DIVISION SERIES RECORD

Year	League	W	L	Pct.	ERA	G	GS	CG	ShO	Sv.-Opp.	IP	H	R	ER	HR	BB-IBB	SO
1997	—San Francisco (N.L.)	0	0	...	15.00	1	1	0	0	0-0	3.0	5	5	5	1	4-0	3
2000	—San Francisco (N.L.)	0	0	...	6.00	1	1	0	0	0-0	3.0	3	2	2	0	3-0	3
Division series totals (2 years)...		0	0	...	10.50	2	2	0	0	0-0	6.0	8	7	7	1	7-0	6

ALL-STAR GAME RECORD

	W	L	Pct.	ERA	GS	CG	ShO	Sv.-Opp.	IP	H	R	ER	HR	BB-IBB	SO
All-Star Game totals (1 year)........	0	1	.000	18.00	0	0	0	0-0	1.0	1	2	2	1	1-0	1

ESTRADA, JOHNNY — C — PHILLIES

PERSONAL: Born June 27, 1976, in Hayward, Calif. ... 5-11/209. ... Bats both, throws right. ... Full name: Johnny P. Estrada III.

HIGH SCHOOL: Roosevelt (Fresno, Calif.).

JUNIOR COLLEGE: Fresno City, then Sequoias.

TRANSACTIONS/CAREER NOTES: Selected by Houston Astros organization in 71st round of free-agent draft (June 2, 1994); did not sign. ... Selected by Philadelphia Phillies organization in 17th round of free-agent draft (June 3, 1997).

STATISTICAL NOTES: Led New York-Pennsylvania League catchers with 391 putouts, 434 total chances and 1.000 fielding percentage in 1997. ... Tied for South Atlantic League lead in double plays by catcher with six in 1998. ... Led International League lead with 19 grounded into double plays and tied for lead with seven intentional bases on balls received in 2002. ... Led International League catchers with 745 putouts and 795 total chances in 2002.

2002 GAMES PLAYED BY POSITION (MLB): C—10.

Year	Team (League)	Pos.	BATTING G	AB	R	H	2B	3B	HR	RBI	BB	SO	SB-CS	Avg.	OBP	SLG	FIELDING E	Avg.
1997—	Batavia (NY-Penn)	C-1B	58	223	28	70	17	2	6	43	9	15	0-0	.314	.336	.489	0	†1.000
1998—	Piedmont (S.Atl.)	C	77	303	33	94	14	2	7	44	6	19	0-1	.310	.331	.439	6	.990
—	Clearwater (FSL)	C	37	117	8	26	8	0	0	13	5	7	0-0	.222	.250	.291	5	.979
1999—	Clearwater (FSL)	C	98	346	35	96	15	0	9	52	14	26	1-0	.277	.303	.399	5	.989
2000—	Reading (East.)	C	95	356	42	105	18	0	12	42	10	20	1-0	.295	.322	.447	7	.990
2001—	Scranton/W.B. (I.L.)	C	32	131	13	38	13	0	0	16	5	6	0-0	.290	.319	.389	0	1.000
—	Philadelphia (N.L.)	C	89	298	26	68	15	0	8	37	16	32	0-0	.228	.273	.359	4	.993
2002—	Scranton/W.B. (I.L.)	C	118	434	49	121	27	0	11	67	26	53	1-0	.279	.322	.417	4	.995
—	Philadelphia (N.L.)	C	10	17	0	2	1	0	0	2	2	2	0-0	.118	.211	.176	0	1.000
Major League totals (2 years)			99	315	26	70	16	0	8	39	18	34	0-0	.222	.270	.349	4	.993

ETHERTON, SETH — P — REDS

PERSONAL: Born October 17, 1976, in Laguna Beach, Calif. ... 6-1/200. ... Throws right, bats right. ... Full name: Seth Michael Etherton.
HIGH SCHOOL: Dana Hills (Dana Point, Calif.).
COLLEGE: Southern California.
TRANSACTIONS/CAREER NOTES: Selected by St. Louis Cardinals organization in ninth-round of free-agent draft (June 3, 1997); did not sign. ... Selected by Anaheim Angels organization in first round (18th pick overall) of free-agent draft (June 2, 1998). ... On Anaheim disabled list (August 5, 2000-remainder of season) ... Traded by Angels to Cincinnati Reds for SS Wilmy Caceres (December 10, 2000). ... On disabled list (March 22, 2001-entire season). ... On Cincinnati disabled list (March 21-July 11 and July 23, 2002-remainder of season); included rehabilitation assignment to Dayton (May 17-20), Chattanooga (May 21-June 6) and Louisville (June 13-July 9). ... Claimed on waivers by New York Yankees (July 11, 2002). ... Waiver claim voided by commissioner's office (July 23, 2002).

Year	League	W	L	Pct.	ERA	G	GS	CG	ShO	Sv.-Opp.	IP	H	R	ER	HR	BB-IBB	SO
1998—	Midland (Texas)	1	5	.167	6.14	9	7	1	0	0-...	48.1	57	36	33	9	12-0	35
1999—	Erie (East.)	10	10	.500	3.27	24	24	4	1	0-...	167.2	153	72	61	14	43-0	153
—	Edmonton (PCL)	0	2	.000	5.48	4	4	0	0	0-...	21.1	25	13	13	7	6-0	19
2000—	Edmonton (PCL)	3	2	.600	4.01	9	9	0	0	0-...	58.1	60	30	26	6	19-0	50
—	Anaheim (A.L.)	5	1	.833	5.52	11	11	0	0	0-0	60.1	68	38	37	16	22-0	32
2001—	Cincinnati (N.L.)■									Did not play.							
2002—	Dayton (Midw.)	0	0	...	0.00	1	1	0	0	0-...	1.0	1	0	0	0	0-0	2
—	Chattanooga (Sou.)	0	1	.000	0.96	3	3	0	0	0-...	9.1	5	1	1	0	2-0	4
—	Louisville (I.L.)	0	1	.000	8.22	5	5	0	0	0-...	15.1	21	16	14	4	6-0	10
—	Norwich (East.)■	0	0	...	0.00	1	1	0	0	0-...	2.0	1	1	0	0	1-0	2
Major League totals (1 year)		5	1	.833	5.52	11	11	0	0	0-0	60.1	68	38	37	16	22-0	32

EVERETT, ADAM — SS — ASTROS

PERSONAL: Born February 2, 1977, in Austell, Ga. ... 6-0/160. ... Bats right, throws right.
HIGH SCHOOL: Harrison (Kennesaw, Ga.).
COLLEGE: North Carolina State, then South Carolina.
TRANSACTIONS/CAREER NOTES: Selected by Boston Red Sox organization in first round (12th pick overall) of free-agent draft (June 2, 1998). ... Traded by Red Sox with P Greg Miller to Houston Astros for OF Carl Everett (December 14, 1999).
STATISTICAL NOTES: Led Pacific Coast League shortstops with 410 assists in 2000.
MISCELLANEOUS: Member of 2000 U.S. Olympic baseball team.
2002 GAMES PLAYED BY POSITION (MLB): SS—34.

Year	Team (League)	Pos.	BATTING G	AB	R	H	2B	3B	HR	RBI	BB	SO	SB-CS	Avg.	OBP	SLG	FIELDING E	Avg.
1998—	Lowell (NY-Penn)	SS	21	71	11	21	6	2	0	9	11	13	2-1	.296	.407	.437	9	.918
1999—	Trenton (East.)	SS	98	338	56	89	11	0	10	44	41	64	21-5	.263	.356	.385	18	.959
2000—	New Orleans (PCL)■	SS	126	453	82	111	25	2	5	37	75	100	13-4	.245	.363	.342	25	.959
2001—	New Orleans (PCL)	SS	114	441	69	110	20	8	5	40	39	74	24-5	.249	.330	.365	24	.956
—	Houston (N.L.)	SS	9	3	1	0	0	0	0	0	0	1	1-0	.000	.000	.000	2	.667
2002—	Houston (N.L.)	SS	40	88	11	17	3	0	0	4	12	19	3-0	.193	.297	.227	5	.962
—	New Orleans (PCL)	SS	88	345	51	95	16	7	2	25	24	59	12-3	.275	.331	.380	7	.984
Major League totals (2 years)			49	91	12	17	3	0	0	4	12	20	4-0	.187	.288	.220	7	.949

EVERETT, CARL — OF — RANGERS

PERSONAL: Born June 3, 1971, in Tampa. ... 6-0/215. ... Bats both, throws right. ... Full name: Carl Edward Everett.
HIGH SCHOOL: Hillsborough (Tampa).
TRANSACTIONS/CAREER NOTES: Selected by New York Yankees organization in first round (10th pick overall) of free-agent draft (June 4, 1990). ... On Fort Lauderdale disabled list (July 7-August 15, 1992). ... Selected by Florida Marlins in second round (27th pick overall) of expansion draft (November 17, 1992). ... On High Desert disabled list (April 8-13, 1993). ... On Florida disabled list (July 23-August 10, 1994). ... On Edmonton suspended list (August 29, 1994-remainder of season). ... Traded by Marlins to New York Mets for 2B Quilvio Veras (November 29, 1994). ... On disabled list (April 12-27, 1996). ... Traded by Mets to Houston Astros for P John Hudek (December 22, 1997). ... On disabled list (July 16-August 6, 1999). ... Traded by Astros to Boston Red Sox for SS Adam Everett and P Greg Miller (December 14, 1999). ... On suspended list (July 24-August 5, 2000; and March 29-30, 2001). ... On Boston disabled list (June 22-July 28, 2001); included rehabilitation assignments to Sarasota (July 21-24) and Gulf Coast Red Sox (July 25-28). ... Traded by Red Sox to Texas Rangers for P Darren Oliver (December 13, 2001). ... On Texas disabled list (May 5-21 and June 3-July 2, 2002); included rehabilitation assignment to Charlotte (May 19-21).
RECORDS: Shares major league single-game record for most home runs in one inning—2 (July 26, 2002, seventh inning).
STATISTICAL NOTES: Led South Atlantic League in being hit by pitch with 23 in 1991. ... Switch-hit home runs in one game five times (April 20, 1997, first game; April 24, 1998; August 7, 1999; April 11 and August 29, 2000). ... Career major league grand slams: 8.
2002 GAMES PLAYED BY POSITION (MLB): OF—83; DH—18.

Year	Team (League)	Pos.	G	AB	R	H	2B	3B	HR	RBI	BB	SO	SB-CS	Avg.	OBP	SLG	E	Avg.
			BATTING														FIELDING	
1990—	GC Yankees (GCL)	OF	48	185	28	48	8	5	1	14	15	38	15-2	.259	.333	.373	5	.932
1991—	Greensboro (S.Atl.)	OF	123	468	96	127	18	0	4	40	57	122	28-19	.271	.376	.335	7	.974
1992—	Fort Lauderdale (FSL)	OF	46	183	30	42	8	2	2	9	12	40	11-3	.230	.291	.328	3	.975
—	Prince William (Caro.)	OF	6	22	7	7	0	0	4	9	5	7	1-0	.318	.444	.864	0	1.000
1993—	High Desert (Calif.)■	OF	59	253	48	73	12	6	10	52	22	73	24-9	.289	.358	.502	2	.985
—	Florida (N.L.)	OF	11	19	0	2	0	0	0	0	1	9	1-0	.105	.150	.105	1	.857
—	Edmonton (PCL)	OF-DH	35	136	28	42	13	4	6	16	19	45	12-1	.309	.401	.596	2	.976
1994—	Edmonton (PCL)	OF-DH	78	321	63	108	17	2	11	47	19	65	16-13	.336	.380	.505	2	.989
—	Florida (N.L.)	OF	16	51	7	11	1	0	2	6	3	15	4-0	.216	.259	.353	0	1.000
1995—	New York (N.L.)■	OF	79	289	48	75	13	1	12	54	39	67	2-5	.260	.352	.436	3	.981
—	Norfolk (I.L.)	OF-DH-SS	67	260	52	78	16	4	6	35	20	47	12-6	.300	.358	.462	0	1.000
1996—	New York (N.L.)	OF	101	192	29	46	8	1	1	16	21	53	6-0	.240	.326	.307	7	.935
1997—	New York (N.L.)	OF	142	443	58	110	28	3	14	57	32	102	17-9	.248	.308	.420	7	.971
1998—	Houston (N.L.)■	OF	133	467	72	138	34	4	15	76	44	102	14-12	.296	.359	.482	4	.987
1999—	Houston (N.L.)	OF-DH	123	464	86	151	33	3	25	108	50	94	27-7	.325	.398	.571	6	.978
2000—	Boston (A.L.)■	OF-DH	137	496	82	149	32	4	34	108	52	113	11-4	.300	.373	.587	6	.980
2001—	Boston (A.L.)	OF-DH	102	409	61	105	24	4	14	58	27	104	9-2	.257	.323	.438	5	.974
—	Sarasota (FSL)	DH	2	7	0	3	0	0	0	0	2	0	0-0	.429	.556	.429	...	...
—	GC Red Sox (GCL)	OF	3	10	2	2	0	0	2	2	1	3	0-0	.200	.273	.800	0	1.000
2002—	Texas (A.L.)■	OF-DH	105	374	47	100	16	0	16	62	33	77	2-3	.267	.333	.439	5	.969
—	Charlotte (FSL)	OF	1	4	1	2	0	1	0	1	0	1	0-0	.500	.500	1.000	0	1.000
American League totals (3 years)			344	1279	190	354	72	8	64	228	112	294	22-9	.277	.345	.496	16	.975
National League totals (7 years)			605	1925	300	533	117	12	69	317	190	442	71-33	.277	.348	.458	28	.975
Major League totals (10 years)			949	3204	490	887	189	20	133	545	302	736	93-42	.277	.347	.473	44	.975

DIVISION SERIES RECORD

Year	Team (League)	Pos.	G	AB	R	H	2B	3B	HR	RBI	BB	SO	SB-CS	Avg.	OBP	SLG	E	Avg.
			BATTING														FIELDING	
1998—	Houston (N.L.)	OF-PH	4	13	1	2	0	0	0	0	0	4	0-0	.154	.154	.154	0	1.000
1999—	Houston (N.L.)	OF	4	15	2	2	0	0	0	1	2	8	1-0	.133	.263	.133	0	1.000
Division series totals (2 years)			8	28	3	4	0	0	0	1	2	12	1-0	.143	.219	.143	0	1.000

ALL-STAR GAME RECORD

	AB	R	H	2B	3B	HR	RBI	BB	SO	SB-CS	Avg.	OBP	SLG	E	Avg.
All-Star Game totals (1 year)	2	0	0	0	0	0	1	1	0	0-0	.000	.333	.000	0	1.000

EYRE, SCOTT — P — GIANTS

PERSONAL: Born May 30, 1972, in Inglewood, Calif. ... 6-1/210. ... Throws left, bats left. ... Full name: Scott Alan Eyre.

HIGH SCHOOL: Cyprus (Magna, Utah).

JUNIOR COLLEGE: College of Southern Idaho.

TRANSACTIONS/CAREER NOTES: Selected by Texas Rangers organization in ninth round of free-agent draft (June 3, 1991). ... Traded by Rangers to Chicago White Sox for SS Esteban Beltre (March 28, 1994). ... On disabled list (April 8-27, 1994). ... On Prince William disabled list (April 6-September 7, 1995). ... On Charlotte disabled list (June 2-13, 1999). ... On Chicago disabled list (August 31-September 26, 1999); included rehabilitation assignment to Charlotte (September 8-26). ... Traded by White Sox to Toronto Blue Jays for P Gary Glover (November 7, 2000). ... Claimed on waivers by San Francisco Giants (August 8, 2002).

HONORS: Named Southern League Most Outstanding Pitcher (1997).

CAREER HITTING (MLB): 1-for-5 (.200), 0 R, 0 2B, 0 3B, 0 HR, 0 RBI.

Year	League	W	L	Pct.	ERA	G	GS	CG	ShO	Sv.-Opp.	IP	H	R	ER	HR	BB-IBB	SO
1992—	Butte (Pio.)	7	3	.700	2.90	15	14	2	1	0-...	80.2	71	30	26	6	39-0	94
1993—	Charleston, S.C. (S.Atl.)	11	7	.611	3.45	26	26	0	0	0-...	143.2	115	74	55	6	59-1	154
1994—	South Bend (Midw.)■	8	4	.667	3.47	19	18	2	0	0-...	111.2	108	56	43	7	37-0	111
1995—	GC White Sox (GCL)	0	2	.000	2.30	9	9	0	0	0-...	27.1	16	7	7	0	12-0	40
1996—	Birmingham (Sou.)	12	7	.632	4.38	27	27	0	0	0-...	158.1	170	90	77	12	79-3	137
1997—	Birmingham (Sou.)	•13	5	.722	3.84	22	22	0	0	0-...	126.2	110	61	54	14	55-2	127
—	Chicago (A.L.)	4	4	.500	5.04	11	11	0	0	0-0	60.2	62	36	34	11	31-1	36
1998—	Chicago (A.L.)	3	8	.273	5.38	33	17	0	0	0-0	107.0	114	78	64	24	64-0	73
1999—	Charlotte (I.L.)	6	4	.600	3.82	12	11	0	0	0-...	68.1	75	32	29	3	23-1	63
—	Chicago (A.L.)	1	1	.500	7.56	21	0	0	0	0-0	25.0	38	22	21	6	15-2	17
2000—	Chicago (A.L.)	1	1	.500	6.63	13	1	0	0	0-0	19.0	29	15	14	3	12-0	16
—	Charlotte (I.L.)	3	2	.600	3.00	47	0	0	0	12-...	48.0	33	18	16	1	20-3	46
2001—	Syracuse (I.L.)■	4	6	.400	3.18	62	2	0	0	0-...	79.1	67	30	28	8	26-4	96
—	Toronto (A.L.)	1	2	.333	3.45	17	0	0	0	2-3	15.2	15	6	6	1	7-2	16
2002—	Toronto (A.L.)	2	4	.333	4.97	49	3	0	0	0-1	63.1	69	37	35	4	29-7	51
—	San Francisco (N.L.)■	0	0	...	1.59	21	0	0	0	0-0	11.1	11	4	2	0	7-1	7
A.L. totals (6 years)		12	20	.375	5.39	144	32	0	0	2-4	290.2	327	194	174	49	158-12	209
N.L. totals (1 year)		0	0	...	1.59	21	0	0	0	0-0	11.1	11	4	2	0	7-1	7
Major League totals (6 years)		12	20	.375	5.25	165	32	0	0	2-4	302.0	338	198	176	49	165-13	216

DIVISION SERIES RECORD

Year	League	W	L	Pct.	ERA	G	GS	CG	ShO	Sv.-Opp.	IP	H	R	ER	HR	BB-IBB	SO
2002—	San Francisco (N.L.)	0	0	...	0.00	3	0	0	0	0-0	1.1	1	0	0	0	0-0	0

CHAMPIONSHIP SERIES RECORD

Year	League	W	L	Pct.	ERA	G	GS	CG	ShO	Sv.-Opp.	IP	H	R	ER	HR	BB-IBB	SO
2002—	San Francisco (N.L.)	0	0	...	0.00	4	0	0	0	0-0	1.2	2	0	0	0	0-0	0

WORLD SERIES RECORD

Year	League	W	L	Pct.	ERA	G	GS	CG	ShO	Sv.-Opp.	IP	H	R	ER	HR	BB-IBB	SO
2002—	San Francisco (N.L.)	0	0	...	0.00	3	0	0	0	0-0	3.0	5	1	0	0	1-1	2

FABREGAS, JORGE C

PERSONAL: Born March 13, 1970, in Miami. ... 6-3/220. ... Bats left, throws right. ... Name pronounced FAB-ruh-gas.
HIGH SCHOOL: Christopher Columbus (Miami).
COLLEGE: Miami (Fla.).
TRANSACTIONS/CAREER NOTES: Selected by Cleveland Indians organization in 11th round of free-agent draft (June 1, 1988); did not sign. ... Selected by California Angels organization in supplemental round ("sandwich pick" between first and second round, 34th pick overall) of free-agent draft (June 3, 1991); pick received as part of compensation for Minnesota Twins signing Type A free-agent OF/DH Chili Davis. ... On disabled list (April 12-May 4 and July 28-September 5, 1992). ... Angels franchise renamed Anaheim Angels for 1997 season. ... Traded by Angels with P Chuck McElroy to Chicago White Sox for OF Tony Phillips and C Chad Kreuter (May 18, 1997). ... Selected by Arizona Diamondbacks in first round (seventh pick overall) of expansion draft (November 18, 1997). ... On Arizona disabled list (May 31-June 30, 1998); included rehabilitation assignment to Tucson (June 22-30). ... Traded by Diamondbacks with P Willie Blair and cash considerations to New York Mets for OF Bernard Gilkey, P Nelson Figueroa and cash (July 31, 1998). ... Traded by Mets to Florida Marlins for P Oscar Henriquez (November 20, 1998). ... Released by Marlins (August 26, 1999). ... Signed by Atlanta Braves (August 31, 1999). ... Released by Braves (November 5, 1999). ... Signed by Kansas City Royals organization (January 12, 2000). ... On Kansas City disabled list (July 19-September 1, 2000); included rehabilitation assignment to Omaha (July 31-August 9 and August 24-September 1). ... Granted free agency (November 1, 2000). ... Signed by Angels (November 20, 2000). ... On disabled list (May 6-22, 2001). ... Granted free agency (November 5, 2001). ... Re-signed by Angels (November 19, 2001). ... Traded by Angels with two players to be named later to Milwaukee Brewers for OF Alex Ochoa and C Sal Fasano (July 31, 2002); Brewers acquired IF Johnny Raburn (August 14, 2002) and P Pedro Liriano to complete deal (September 20, 2002). ... Granted free agency (October 29, 2002).
STATISTICAL NOTES: Led Texas League with 17 passed balls in 1993. ... Career major league grand slams: 1.
2002 GAMES PLAYED BY POSITION (MLB): C—52.

			BATTING														FIELDING	
Year	**Team (League)**	**Pos.**	**G**	**AB**	**R**	**H**	**2B**	**3B**	**HR**	**RBI**	**BB**	**SO**	**SB-CS**	**Avg.**	**OBP**	**SLG**	**E**	**Avg.**
1992—	Palm Springs (Calif.)	C	70	258	35	73	13	0	0	40	30	27	0-4	.283	.356	.333	*17	.967
1993—	Midland (Texas)	C	113	409	63	118	26	3	6	56	31	60	1-1	.289	.338	.411	•11	.985
—	Vancouver (PCL)	C	4	13	1	3	1	0	0	1	1	3	0-0	.231	.286	.308	0	1.000
1994—	Vancouver (PCL)	C-DH	66	211	17	47	6	1	1	24	12	25	1-1	.223	.264	.275	4	.990
—	California (A.L.)	C	43	127	12	36	3	0	0	16	7	18	2-1	.283	.321	.307	3	.987
1995—	California (A.L.)	C	73	227	24	56	10	0	1	22	17	28	0-2	.247	.298	.304	6	.986
—	Vancouver (PCL)	C	21	73	9	18	3	0	4	10	9	12	0-0	.247	.325	.452	4	.969
1996—	California (A.L.)	C-DH	90	254	18	73	6	0	2	26	17	27	0-1	.287	.326	.335	6	.989
—	Vancouver (PCL)	DH-C-1B	10	37	4	11	3	0	0	5	4	4	0-0	.297	.381	.378	0	1.000
1997—	Anaheim (A.L.)	C	21	38	2	3	1	0	0	3	3	3	0-0	.079	.146	.105	1	.989
—	Chicago (A.L.)■	C-1B	100	322	31	90	10	1	7	48	11	43	1-1	.280	.302	.382	7	.988
1998—	Arizona (N.L.)■	C	50	151	8	30	4	0	1	15	13	26	0-0	.199	.263	.245	1	.996
—	Tucson (PCL)	C-DH	6	20	2	5	1	0	0	3	3	1	0-0	.250	.348	.300	0	1.000
—	New York (N.L.)■	C	20	32	3	6	0	0	1	5	1	6	0-0	.188	.212	.281	2	.971
1999—	Florida (N.L.)■	C	82	223	20	46	10	2	3	21	26	27	0-0	.206	.289	.309	5	.989
—	Atlanta (N.L.)■	C-1B	6	8	0	0	0	0	0	0	0	0	0-0	.000	.000	.000	0	1.000
2000—	Omaha (PCL)■	C-1B	37	129	8	32	5	1	1	18	12	9	1-1	.248	.310	.326	3	.985
—	Kansas City (A.L.)	C-DH	43	142	13	40	4	0	3	17	8	11	1-0	.282	.320	.373	2	.992
2001—	Anaheim (A.L.)■	C	53	148	9	33	4	2	2	16	3	15	0-0	.223	.235	.318	3	.990
2002—	Anaheim (A.L.)	C	35	88	8	17	1	0	0	8	6	6	0-0	.193	.245	.205	1	.994
—	Milwaukee (N.L.)■	C	30	67	5	11	3	0	3	14	2	7	0-0	.164	.178	.343	1	.992
American League totals (7 years)			458	1346	117	348	39	3	15	156	72	151	4-5	.259	.294	.325	29	.989
National League totals (3 years)			188	481	36	93	17	2	8	55	42	66	0-0	.193	.257	.287	9	.990
Major League totals (9 years)			646	1827	153	441	56	5	23	211	114	217	4-5	.241	.284	.315	38	.989

DIVISION SERIES RECORD

			BATTING														FIELDING	
Year	**Team (League)**	**Pos.**	**G**	**AB**	**R**	**H**	**2B**	**3B**	**HR**	**RBI**	**BB**	**SO**	**SB-CS**	**Avg.**	**OBP**	**SLG**	**E**	**Avg.**
1999—	Atlanta (N.L.)								Did not play.									

CHAMPIONSHIP SERIES RECORD

			BATTING														FIELDING	
Year	**Team (League)**	**Pos.**	**G**	**AB**	**R**	**H**	**2B**	**3B**	**HR**	**RBI**	**BB**	**SO**	**SB-CS**	**Avg.**	**OBP**	**SLG**	**E**	**Avg.**
1999—	Atlanta (N.L.)	PH	2	2	0	0	0	0	0	0	0	1	0-0	.000	.000	.000	...	...

WORLD SERIES RECORD

			BATTING														FIELDING	
Year	**Team (League)**	**Pos.**	**G**	**AB**	**R**	**H**	**2B**	**3B**	**HR**	**RBI**	**BB**	**SO**	**SB-CS**	**Avg.**	**OBP**	**SLG**	**E**	**Avg.**
1999—	Atlanta (N.L.)	PH	1	1	0	0	0	0	0	0	0	1	0-0	.000	.000	.000	...	...

FARNSWORTH, JEFF P TIGERS

PERSONAL: Born October 6, 1975, in Wichita, Kan. ... 6-2/190. ... Throws right, bats right. ... Full name: Jeffrey Ellis Farnsworth.
HIGH SCHOOL: Pensacola Catholic (Pensacola, Fla.).
JUNIOR COLLEGE: Okaloosa-Walton (Fla.).
COLLEGE: West Florida.
TRANSACTIONS/CAREER NOTES: Selected by Seattle Mariners organization in second round of free-agent draft (June 4, 1996). ... On disabled list (May 13, 1997-remainder of season; and April 2, 1998-entire season). ... On disabled list (May 22-June 1, 2001). ... Selected by Detroit Tigers from Mariners organization in Rule 5 major league draft (December 13, 2001).
CAREER HITTING (MLB): 0-for-0 (.000), 0 R, 0 2B, 0 3B, 0 HR, 0 RBI.

Year	**League**	**W**	**L**	**Pct.**	**ERA**	**G**	**GS**	**CG**	**ShO**	**Sv.-Opp.**	**IP**	**H**	**R**	**ER**	**HR**	**BB-IBB**	**SO**
1996—	Everett (N'West)	3	3	.500	4.12	10	7	0	0	0-...	39.1	33	19	18	4	13-0	42
1997—	Lancaster (Calif.)	1	1	.500	6.97	5	5	0	0	0-...	20.2	24	20	16	2	8-0	18
1998—	Lancaster (Calif.)									Did not play.							
1999—	Lancaster (Calif.)	3	6	.333	6.50	26	9	0	0	3-...	72.0	91	61	52	7	43-1	43
2000—	New Haven (East.)	9	3	.750	3.46	39	8	0	0	2-...	101.1	91	40	39	6	25-1	70
2001—	San Antonio (Texas)	11	10	.524	4.35	27	27	0	0	0-...	155.1	182	92	75	10	47-0	113
2002—	Detroit (A.L.)■	2	3	.400	5.79	44	0	0	0	0-1	70.0	100	47	45	6	29-8	28
Major League totals (1 year)		2	3	.400	5.79	44	0	0	0	0-1	70.0	100	47	45	6	29-8	28

FARNSWORTH, KYLE — P — CUBS

PERSONAL: Born April 14, 1976, in Wichita, Kan. ... 6-4/235. ... Throws right, bats right. ... Full name: Kyle Lynn Farnsworth.

HIGH SCHOOL: Milton (Alpharetta, Ga.).

JUNIOR COLLEGE: Abraham Baldwin Agricultural College (Ga.).

TRANSACTIONS/CAREER NOTES: Selected by Chicago Cubs organization in 47th round of free-agent draft (June 2, 1994). ... On Chicago disabled list (April 10-June 4, 2002); included rehabilitation assignment to Iowa (May 31-June 3).

RECORDS: Shares N.L. single-inning record for most consecutive home runs allowed—3 (April 6, 2000, third inning).

CAREER HITTING (MLB): 4-for-52 (.077), 3 R, 1 2B, 0 3B, 0 HR, 3 RBI.

Year	League	W	L	Pct.	ERA	G	GS	CG	ShO	Sv.-Opp.	IP	H	R	ER	HR	BB-IBB	SO
1995—	Gulf Coast Cubs (GCL)	3	2	.600	0.87	16	0	0	0	1-...	31.0	22	8	3	0	11-0	18
1996—	Rockford (Midw.)	9	6	.600	3.70	20	20	1	0	0-...	112.0	122	62	46	7	35-0	82
1997—	Daytona (FSL)	10	10	.500	4.09	27	27	2	0	0-...	156.1	178	91	71	13	47-1	105
1998—	West Tenn (Sou.)	8	2	.800	2.77	13	13	0	0	0-...	81.1	70	32	25	6	21-0	73
—	Iowa (PCL)	5	9	.357	6.93	18	18	0	0	0-...	102.2	129	88	79	18	36-0	79
1999—	Iowa (PCL)	2	2	.500	3.20	6	6	0	0	0-...	39.1	38	16	14	5	9-0	29
—	Chicago (N.L.)	5	9	.357	5.05	27	21	1	1	0-0	130.0	140	80	73	28	52-1	70
2000—	Chicago (N.L.)	2	9	.182	6.43	46	5	0	0	1-6	77.0	90	58	55	14	50-8	74
—	Iowa (PCL)	0	2	.000	3.20	22	0	0	0	9-...	25.1	24	10	9	1	18-2	22
2001—	Chicago (N.L.)	4	6	.400	2.74	76	0	0	0	2-3	82.0	65	26	25	8	29-2	107
2002—	Chicago (N.L.)	4	6	.400	7.33	45	0	0	0	1-7	46.2	53	47	38	9	24-7	46
—	Iowa (PCL)	0	1	.000	6.00	2	0	0	0	0-...	3.0	3	2	2	1	0-0	2
Major League totals (4 years)		15	30	.333	5.12	194	26	1	1	4-16	335.2	348	211	191	59	155-18	297

FASANO, SAL — C

PERSONAL: Born August 10, 1971, in Chicago. ... 6-2/254. ... Bats right, throws right. ... Full name: Salvatore Frank Fasano.

HIGH SCHOOL: Hoffman Estates (Ill.).

COLLEGE: Evansville.

TRANSACTIONS/CAREER NOTES: Selected by Kansas City Royals organization in 37th round of free-agent draft (June 3, 1993). ... On Kansas City disabled list (April 20-May 9 and August 30, 1998-remainder of season); included rehabilitation assignment to Omaha (May 5-9). ... On Omaha disabled list (August 1-26, 1999). ... Traded by Royals to Oakland Athletics for cash (March 30, 2000). ... Contract purchased by Royals from A's (May 22, 2001). ... Traded by Royals with P Mac Suzuki to Colorado Rockies for C Brent Mayne (June 24, 2001). ... Granted free agency (December 21, 2001). ... Signed by Tampa Bay Devil Rays organization (January 28, 2002). ... Released by Devil Rays (June 1, 2002). ... Signed by Milwaukee Brewers organization (June 6, 2002). ... Traded by Brewers with OF Alex Ochoa to Anaheim Angels for C Jorge Fabregas and two players to be named later (July 31, 2002); Brewers acquired IF Johnny Raburn (August 14, 2002) and P Pedro Liriano to complete deal (September 20, 2002). ... Released by Angels (November 5, 2002).

STATISTICAL NOTES: Led Northwest League catchers with seven double plays in 1993. ... Led Pacific Coast League in being hit by pitch with 26 in 1999. ... Tied for Pacific Coast League lead with 12 errors by catcher in 1999. ... Career major league grand slams: 1.

2002 GAMES PLAYED BY POSITION (MLB): C—2.

			BATTING														FIELDING	
Year	Team (League)	Pos.	G	AB	R	H	2B	3B	HR	RBI	BB	SO	SB-CS	Avg.	OBP	SLG	E	Avg.
1993—	Eugene (N'West)	C	49	176	25	47	11	1	10	36	19	49	4-3	.267	.355	.511	1	.997
1994—	Rockford (Midw.)	C-1B	97	345	61	97	16	1	25	81	33	66	8-3	.281	.366	.551	12	.981
—	Wilmington (Caro.)	C-1B	23	90	15	29	7	0	7	32	13	24	0-0	.322	.408	.633	4	.957
1995—	Wilmington (Caro.)	C-1B	23	88	12	20	2	1	2	7	5	16	0-0	.227	.277	.341	0	1.000
—	Wichita (Texas)	C-1B	87	317	60	92	19	2	20	66	27	61	3-6	.290	.373	.552	14	.979
1996—	Kansas City (A.L.)	C	51	143	20	29	2	0	6	19	14	25	1-1	.203	.283	.343	5	.984
—	Omaha (A.A.)	C-1B-3B	29	104	12	24	4	0	4	15	6	21	0-1	.231	.277	.385	4	.982
1997—	Omaha (A.A.)	C-DH	49	152	17	25	7	0	4	14	12	53	0-0	.164	.247	.289	4	.988
—	Kansas City (A.L.)	C-DH	13	38	4	8	2	0	1	1	1	12	0-0	.211	.231	.342	1	.982
—	Wichita (Texas)	C-1B	40	131	27	31	5	0	13	27	20	35	0-2	.237	.360	.573	4	.984
1998—	Kansas City (A.L.)	C-1B-3B	74	216	21	49	10	0	8	31	10	56	1-0	.227	.307	.384	2	.996
—	Omaha (PCL)	C	4	14	1	3	1	0	1	2	1	4	0-1	.214	.267	.500	0	1.000
1999—	Omaha (PCL)	C-DH-1B	88	280	63	77	15	0	21	49	42	69	4-2	.275	.415	.554	‡12	.981
—	Kansas City (A.L.)	C	23	60	11	14	2	0	5	16	7	17	0-1	.233	.373	.517	0	1.000
2000—	Oakland (A.L.)■	C	52	126	21	27	6	0	7	19	14	47	0-0	.214	.306	.429	5	.981
2001—	Oakland (A.L.)	C-DH	11	21	2	1	0	0	0	0	1	12	0-0	.048	.130	.048	2	.952
—	Kansas City (A.L.)■	C	3	1	0	0	0	0	0	0	0	0	0-0	.000	.000	.000	0	1.000
—	Omaha (PCL)	C-1B	13	46	6	11	1	0	2	7	4	11	0-0	.239	.364	.391	3	.966
—	Colo. Springs (PCL)■	C	26	82	16	25	4	0	7	23	9	26	0-0	.305	.396	.610	3	.984
—	Colorado (N.L.)	C	25	63	10	16	5	0	3	9	4	19	0-0	.254	.329	.476	3	.982
2002—	Durham (I.L.)■	C	31	101	11	26	6	0	6	9	12	29	0-1	.257	.385	.495	4	.984
—	Indianapolis (I.L.)■	C-1B	34	97	5	20	9	0	1	11	3	24	0-0	.206	.271	.330	3	.984
—	Salt Lake (PCL)■	C	22	76	13	21	3	0	5	10	7	24	1-0	.276	.349	.513	4	.978
—	Anaheim (A.L.)	C	2	1	0	0	0	0	0	0	0	1	0-0	.000	.000	.000	0	1.000
American League totals (7 years)			229	606	79	128	22	0	27	86	47	170	2-2	.211	.297	.381	15	.988
National League totals (1 year)			25	63	10	16	5	0	3	9	4	19	0-0	.254	.329	.476	3	.982
Major League totals (7 years)			254	669	89	144	27	0	30	95	51	189	2-2	.215	.300	.390	18	.988

DIVISION SERIES RECORD

			BATTING														FIELDING	
Year	Team (League)	Pos.	G	AB	R	H	2B	3B	HR	RBI	BB	SO	SB-CS	Avg.	OBP	SLG	E	Avg.
2000—	Oakland (A.L.)	C	1	0	0	0	0	0	0	0	0	0	0-0	...	...	...	0	1.000

F

FASSERO, JEFF — P

PERSONAL: Born January 5, 1963, in Springfield, Ill. ... 6-1/200. ... Throws left, bats left. ... Full name: Jeffrey Joseph Fassero. ... Name pronounced fuh-SAIR-oh.

HIGH SCHOOL: Griffin (Springfield, Ill.).

JUNIOR COLLEGE: Lincoln Land Community College (Ill.).

COLLEGE: Mississippi.

TRANSACTIONS/CAREER NOTES: Selected by St. Louis Cardinals organization in 22nd round of free-agent draft (June 4, 1984). ... Selected by Chicago White Sox organization from Cardinals organization in Rule 5 minor league draft (December 5, 1989). ... Released by White Sox (April 3, 1990). ... Signed by Cleveland Indians organization (April 9, 1990). ... Granted free agency (October 15, 1990). ... Signed by Montreal Expos organization (January 3, 1991). ... On disabled list (July 24-August 11, 1994). ... Traded by Expos with P Alex Pacheco to Seattle Mariners for C Chris Widger, P Trey Moore and P Matt Wagner (October 29, 1996). ... On disabled list (March 22-April 12, 1998). ... Traded by Mariners to Texas Rangers for a player to named later (August 27, 1999); Mariners acquired OF Adrian Myers to complete deal (September 22, 1999). ... Granted free agency (October 28, 1999). ... Signed by Boston Red Sox (December 22, 1999). ... On disabled list (June 19-July 5, 2000). ... Granted free agency (November 1, 2000). ... Signed by Chicago Cubs (December 8, 2000). ... Traded by Cubs with cash to Cardinals for two players to be named later (August 24, 2002); Cubs acquired P Jason Karnuth and P Jared Blasdell to complete deal (September 24, 2002). ... Granted free agency (November 1, 2002).

STATISTICAL NOTES: Pitched 5-0 no-hit victory for Arkansas against Jackson (June 12, 1989).

CAREER HITTING (MLB): 18-for-229 (.079), 16 R, 2 2B, 1 3B, 0 HR, 5 RBI.

Year League	W	L	Pct.	ERA	G	GS	CG	ShO	Sv.-Opp.	IP	H	R	ER	HR	BB-IBB	SO
1984— Johnson City (Appl.)	4	7	.364	4.59	13	11	2	0	1-...	66.2	65	42	34	2	39-0	59
1985— Springfield (Midw.)	4	8	.333	4.01	29	15	1	0	1-...	119.0	125	78	53	11	45-3	65
1986— St. Petersburg (FSL)	13	7	.650	2.45	26	•26	6	1	0-...	*176.0	156	63	48	5	56-4	112
1987— Arkansas (Texas)	10	7	.588	4.10	28	27	2	1	0-...	151.1	168	90	69	16	67-7	118
1988— Arkansas (Texas)	5	5	.500	3.58	70	1	0	0	17-...	78.0	97	48	31	1	41-13	72
1989— Louisville (A.A.)	3	10	.231	5.22	22	19	0	0	0-...	112.0	136	79	65	13	47-1	73
— Arkansas (Texas)	4	1	.800	1.64	6	6	2	1	0-...	44.0	32	11	8	1	12-0	38
1990— Canton/Akron (East.)■	5	4	.556	2.80	*61	0	0	0	6-...	64.1	66	24	20	5	24-6	61
1991— Indianapolis (A.A.)■	3	0	1.000	1.47	18	0	0	0	4-...	18.1	11	3	3	1	7-3	12
— Montreal (N.L.)	2	5	.286	2.44	51	0	0	0	8-11	55.1	39	17	15	1	17-1	42
1992— Montreal (N.L.)	8	7	.533	2.84	70	0	0	0	1-7	85.2	81	35	27	1	34-6	63
1993— Montreal (N.L.)	12	5	.706	2.29	56	15	1	0	1-3	149.2	119	50	38	7	54-0	140
1994— Montreal (N.L.)	8	6	.571	2.99	21	21	1	0	0-0	138.2	119	54	46	13	40-4	119
1995— Montreal (N.L.)	13	14	.481	4.33	30	30	1	0	0-0	189.0	207	102	91	15	74-3	164
1996— Montreal (N.L.)	15	11	.577	3.30	34	34	5	1	0-0	231.2	217	95	85	20	55-3	222
1997— Seattle (A.L.)■	16	9	.640	3.61	35	•35	2	1	0-0	234.1	226	108	94	21	84-6	189
1998— Seattle (A.L.)	13	12	.520	3.97	32	32	7	0	0-0	224.2	223	115	99	33	66-2	176
1999— Seattle (A.L.)	4	14	.222	7.38	30	24	0	0	0-0	139.0	188	123	114	34	73-3	101
— Texas (A.L.)■	1	0	1.000	5.71	7	3	0	0	0-0	17.1	20	12	11	1	10-0	13
2000— Boston (A.L.)■	8	8	.500	4.78	38	23	0	0	0-0	130.0	153	72	69	16	50-2	97
2001— Chicago (N.L.)■	4	4	.500	3.42	82	0	0	0	12-17	73.2	66	31	28	6	23-5	79
2002— Chicago (N.L.)	5	6	.455	6.18	57	0	0	0	0-1	51.0	65	37	35	5	22-5	44
— St. Louis (N.L.)■	3	0	1.000	3.00	16	0	0	0	0-2	18.0	16	6	6	4	5-0	12
A.L. totals (4 years)	42	43	.494	4.67	142	117	9	1	0-0	745.1	810	430	387	105	283-13	576
N.L. totals (8 years)	70	58	.547	3.36	417	100	8	1	22-41	992.2	929	427	371	72	324-27	885
Major League totals (12 years)	112	101	.526	3.93	559	217	17	2	22-41	1738.0	1739	857	758	177	607-40	1461

DIVISION SERIES RECORD

Year League	W	L	Pct.	ERA	G	GS	CG	ShO	Sv.-Opp.	IP	H	R	ER	HR	BB-IBB	SO
1997— Seattle (A.L.)	1	0	1.000	1.13	1	1	0	0	0-0	8.0	3	1	1	0	4-0	3
1999— Texas (A.L.)	0	0	...	9.00	1	0	0	0	0-0	1.0	2	1	1	0	1-0	1
2002— St. Louis (N.L.)	2	0	1.000	0.00	3	0	0	0	0-0	2.2	3	0	0	0	0-0	2
Division series totals (3 years)	3	0	1.000	1.54	5	1	0	0	0-0	11.2	8	2	2	0	5-0	6

CHAMPIONSHIP SERIES RECORD

Year League	W	L	Pct.	ERA	G	GS	CG	ShO	Sv.-Opp.	IP	H	R	ER	HR	BB-IBB	SO
2002— St. Louis (N.L.)	0	0	...	0.00	1	0	0	0	0-0	.2	0	0	0	0	0-0	1

F

FEBLES, CARLOS — 2B — ROYALS

PERSONAL: Born May 24, 1976, in El Seybo, Dominican Republic. ... 5-11/185. ... Bats right, throws right. ... Full name: Carlos Manuel Febles.

HIGH SCHOOL: Sagrado Corazon de Jesus (Dominican Republic).

TRANSACTIONS/CAREER NOTES: Signed as non-drafted free agent by Kansas City Royals (November 2, 1993). ... On disabled list (August 24-September 17, 1999). ... On Kansas City disabled list (June 5-July 18 and August 14-September 2, 2000); included rehabilitation assignments to Gulf Coast Royals (June 29-30), Wichita (July 1-4) and Omaha (July 10-18). ... On Kansas City disabled list (April 20-June 8, 2001); included rehabilitation assignment to Omaha (June 4-8).

STATISTICAL NOTES: Led Gulf Coast League second basemen with 117 putouts, 230 total chances and 39 double plays in 1995. ... Led Carolina League second basemen with 355 assists, 590 total chances and 85 double plays in 1997. ... Had 15-game hitting streak (April 6-21, 2000).

2002 GAMES PLAYED BY POSITION (MLB): 2B—116; SS—1.

		BATTING														FIELDING	
Year Team (League)	Pos.	G	AB	R	H	2B	3B	HR	RBI	BB	SO	SB-CS	Avg.	OBP	SLG	E	Avg.
1994— Dom. Royals (DSL)	2B	56	184	38	61	9	3	2	37	38	27	12-...	.332	...	.446	16	.934
1995— GC Royals (GCL)	2B	54	188	40	53	13	5	3	20	26	30	16-8	.282	.381	.452	12	.948
1996— Lansing (Midw.)	2B-SS	102	363	84	107	23	5	5	43	66	64	30-14	.295	.414	.427	19	.963
1997— Wilmington (Caro.)	2B	122	438	78	104	27	6	3	29	51	95	49-11	.237	.333	.347	*23	.961
1998— Wichita (Texas)	2B	126	432	110	141	28	9	14	52	80	70	*51-16	.326	*.441	.530	19	.968
— Kansas City (A.L.)	2B	11	25	5	10	1	2	0	2	4	7	2-1	.400	.483	.600	0	1.000
1999— Kansas City (A.L.)	2B	123	453	71	116	22	9	10	53	47	91	20-4	.256	.336	.411	14	.979

Year	Team (League)	Pos.	G	AB	R	H	2B	3B	HR	RBI	BB	SO	SB-CS	Avg.	OBP	SLG	E	Avg.
			BATTING														FIELDING	
2000—	Kansas City (A.L.)	2B	100	339	59	87	12	1	2	29	36	48	17-6	.257	.345	.316	10	.978
—	GC Royals (GCL)	2B	1	3	0	1	1	0	0	0	1	0	1-0	.333	.500	.667	0	1.000
—	Wichita (Texas)	2B	4	15	2	2	0	0	0	1	2	4	2-0	.133	.263	.133	0	1.000
—	Omaha (PCL)	2B	11	42	6	9	4	0	1	5	7	10	3-3	.214	.340	.381	1	.983
2001—	Kansas City (A.L.)	2B	79	292	45	69	9	2	8	25	22	58	5-2	.236	.291	.363	7	.981
—	Omaha (PCL)	2B	25	98	23	33	7	1	2	9	9	14	6-2	.337	.414	.490	0	1.000
2002—	Kansas City (A.L.)	2B-SS	119	351	44	86	16	4	4	26	41	63	16-5	.245	.336	.348	15	.971
—	Omaha (PCL)	2B	13	54	10	12	2	1	1	5	4	5	2-1	.222	.283	.352	1	.982
Major League totals (5 years)			432	1460	224	368	60	18	24	135	150	267	60-18	.252	.332	.367	46	.977

FELICIANO, PEDRO — P — TIGERS

PERSONAL: Born August 25, 1976, in Rio Piedras, Puerto Rico. ... 5-10/185. ... Throws left, bats left. ... Full name: Pedro Juan Molina Feliciano.

HIGH SCHOOL: Jose S. Alegria (Dorado, Puerto Rico).

TRANSACTIONS/CAREER NOTES: Selected by Los Angeles Dodgers organization in 31st round of free-agent draft (June 1, 1995). ... On disabled list (April 8, 1999-entire season). ... Granted free agency (October 15, 2001). ... Signed by Cincinnati Reds organization (November 19, 2001). ... Traded by Reds with OF Elvin Andujar and two players to be named later to New York Mets for P Shawn Estes and cash (August 15, 2002); Mets acquired OF Raul Gonzalez (August 20, 2002) and OF Brady Clark to complete deal (September 9, 2002). ... Claimed on waivers by Detroit Tigers (October 11, 2002).

CAREER HITTING (MLB): 0-for-0 (.000), 0 R, 0 2B, 0 3B, 0 HR, 0 RBI.

Year	League	W	L	Pct.	ERA	G	GS	CG	ShO	Sv.-Opp.	IP	H	R	ER	HR	BB-IBB	SO
1995—	Great Falls (Pio.)	0	0	...	13.50	6	0	0	0	0-...	6.2	12	12	10	0	7-1	9
1996—	Great Falls (Pio.)	2	3	.400	5.71	22	1	0	0	3-...	41.0	50	36	26	1	26-2	39
1997—	Savannah (S.Atl.)	3	7	.300	2.64	36	9	1	0	4-...	105.2	90	45	31	11	39-0	94
—	Vero Beach (FSL)	0	0	...	4.50	1	0	0	0	0-...	2.0	3	1	1	1	0-0	1
1998—	Vero Beach (FSL)	2	5	.286	4.61	22	10	0	0	2-...	68.1	68	44	35	8	30-1	51
1999—											Did not play.						
2000—	Vero Beach (FSL)	4	5	.444	3.82	25	2	0	0	0-...	61.1	76	31	26	4	24-1	48
—	San Antonio (Texas)	0	0	...	1.93	9	0	0	0	2-...	9.1	7	2	2	0	4-1	11
—	Albuquerque (PCL)	0	0	...	18.00	1	0	0	0	0-...	1.0	3	3	2	2	1-0	2
2001—	Jacksonville (Sou.)	5	4	.556	1.94	54	0	0	0	17-...	60.1	41	14	13	3	11-1	55
—	Las Vegas (PCL)	0	1	.000	7.27	6	0	0	0	0-...	8.2	16	11	7	2	5-1	5
2002—	Chattanooga (Sou.)■	2	1	.667	2.56	28	0	0	0	4-...	38.2	33	14	11	1	11-1	26
—	Louisville (I.L.)	1	1	.500	3.04	20	0	0	0	0-...	26.2	35	10	9	3	4-0	19
—	Norfolk (I.L.)■	0	0	...	7.00	5	0	0	0	2-...	9.0	14	7	7	1	1-0	11
—	New York (N.L.)	0	0	...	7.50	6	0	0	0	0-0	6.0	9	5	5	0	1-0	4
Major League totals (1 year)		0	0	...	7.50	6	0	0	0	0-0	6.0	9	5	5	0	1-0	4

FELIZ, PEDRO — 3B — GIANTS

PERSONAL: Born April 27, 1977, in Azua, Dominican Republic. ... 6-1/205. ... Bats right, throws right. ... Full name: Pedro Julio Feliz.

HIGH SCHOOL: Augustine de Chequer (Dominican Republic).

TRANSACTIONS/CAREER NOTES: Signed as non-drafted free agent by San Francisco Giants organization (February 7, 1994).

STATISTICAL NOTES: Led California League third basemen with 112 putouts, 322 assists, 457 total chances and 39 double plays in 1997. ... Led Texas League third basemen with 71 putouts and 31 double plays in 1998. ... Led Texas League in grounding into double plays with 18 in 1999. ... Led Texas League third baseman with 304 assists and 407 total chances in 1999. ... Led Pacific Coast League third basemen with 287 assists, 24 errors and 394 total chances in 2000.

2002 GAMES PLAYED BY POSITION (MLB): 3B—44; SS—1; OF—1.

Year	Team (League)	Pos.	G	AB	R	H	2B	3B	HR	RBI	BB	SO	SB-CS	Avg.	OBP	SLG	E	Avg.
			BATTING														FIELDING	
1994—	Arizona Giants (Ariz.)	3B	38	119	7	23	0	0	0	3	2	20	2-3	.193	.220	.193	5	.953
1995—	Bellingham (N'West)	3B-1B	43	113	14	31	2	1	0	16	7	33	1-1	.274	.311	.310	2	.971
1996—	Burlington (Midw.)	3B-1B	93	321	36	85	12	2	5	36	18	65	5-2	.265	.303	.361	17	.937
1997—	Bakersfield (Calif.)	3B	135	515	59	140	25	4	14	56	23	90	5-7	.272	.310	.417	23	*.950
1998—	Shreveport (Texas)	3B	100	364	39	96	23	2	12	50	9	62	0-1	.264	.282	.437	22	*.926
—	Fresno (PCL)	3B	3	7	1	3	1	0	1	3	1	0	0-0	.429	.500	1.000	0	1.000
1999—	Shreveport (Texas)	3B	131	491	52	124	24	6	13	77	19	90	4-2	.253	.282	.405	27	.934
2000—	Fresno (PCL)	3B-SS	128	503	85	150	34	2	33	105	30	94	1-1	.298	.337	.571	†24	.939
—	San Francisco (N.L.)	3B	8	7	1	2	0	0	0	0	0	1	0-0	.286	.286	.286	0	...
2001—	San Francisco (N.L.)	3B-DH	94	220	23	50	9	1	7	22	10	50	2-1	.227	.264	.373	12	.908
2002—	San Francisco (N.L.)	3B-SS-OF	67	146	14	37	4	1	2	13	6	27	0-0	.253	.281	.336	3	.966
Major League totals (3 years)			169	373	38	89	13	2	9	35	16	78	2-1	.239	.271	.357	15	.932

DIVISION SERIES RECORD

Year	Team (League)	Pos.	G	AB	R	H	2B	3B	HR	RBI	BB	SO	SB-CS	Avg.	OBP	SLG	E	Avg.
			BATTING														FIELDING	
2002—	San Francisco (N.L.)	PH	1	1	0	0	0	0	0	0	0	1	0-0	.000	.000	.000	...	...

CHAMPIONSHIP SERIES RECORD

Year	Team (League)	Pos.	G	AB	R	H	2B	3B	HR	RBI	BB	SO	SB-CS	Avg.	OBP	SLG	E	Avg.
			BATTING														FIELDING	
2002—	San Francisco (N.L.)	PH	1	1	0	0	0	0	0	0	0	0	0-0	.000	.000	.000	...	...

WORLD SERIES RECORD

Year	Team (League)	Pos.	G	AB	R	H	2B	3B	HR	RBI	BB	SO	SB-CS	Avg.	OBP	SLG	E	Avg.
			BATTING														FIELDING	
2002—	San Francisco (N.L.)	DH	3	5	0	0	0	0	0	0	0	2	0-0	.000	.000	.000	...	...

FERNANDEZ, JARED P REDS

PERSONAL: Born February 2, 1972, in Salt Lake City, Utah. ... 6-1/225. ... Throws right, bats right. ... Full name: Jared Wade Fernandez.
HIGH SCHOOL: Kearns (Utah).
JUNIOR COLLEGE: Eastern Utah.
COLLEGE: Fresno State.
TRANSACTIONS/CAREER NOTES: Signed as non-drafted free agent by Boston Red Sox organization (June 23, 1994). ... On disabled list (July 30, 2000-remainder of season). ... Granted free agency (October 15, 2000). ... Signed by Cincinnati Reds organization (December 15, 2000).
STATISTICAL NOTES: Led Eastern League pitchers with 798 nine sacrifice flies allowed in 1996. ... Led International League pitchers with 20 wild pitches in 2001.
CAREER HITTING (MLB): 2-for-12 (.167), 2 R, 0 2B, 0 3B, 0 HR, 1 RBI.

Year League	W	L	Pct.	ERA	G	GS	CG	ShO	Sv.-Opp.	IP	H	R	ER	HR	BB-IBB	SO
1994— Utica (NY-Penn)	1	1	.500	3.60	21	1	0	0	4-...	30.0	43	18	12	4	8-2	24
1995— Utica (NY-Penn)	3	2	.600	1.89	5	5	1	0	0-...	38.0	30	11	8	2	9-1	23
— Trenton (East.)	5	4	.556	3.90	11	10	1	0	0-...	67.0	64	32	29	4	28-1	40
1996— Trenton (East.)	9	9	.500	5.08	30	*29	3	0	0-...	179.0	185	•115	*101	19	83-5	94
1997— Trenton (East.)	4	6	.400	5.41	21	16	1	0	0-...	121.1	138	90	73	12	66-0	73
— Pawtucket (I.L.)	0	3	.000	5.79	11	11	0	0	0-...	60.2	76	45	39	7	28-1	33
1998— Trenton (East.)	3	7	.300	5.25	36	7	0	0	1-...	118.1	132	80	69	8	51-3	70
— Pawtucket (I.L.)	1	1	.500	4.74	5	2	0	0	0-...	24.2	26	16	13	5	7-0	15
1999— Trenton (East.)	3	0	1.000	3.38	7	0	0	0	1-...	18.2	18	9	7	4	8-0	10
— Pawtucket (I.L.)	12	9	.571	4.25	27	20	3	0	0-...	163.0	172	88	77	20	39-0	76
2000— Pawtucket (I.L.)	10	4	.714	3.02	31	9	2	0	4-...	113.1	103	51	38	10	36-0	65
2001— Louisville (I.L.)■	10	9	.526	4.13	33	28	4	1	0-...	*196.1	*218	105	90	24	54-0	118
— Cincinnati (N.L.)	0	1	.000	4.38	5	2	0	0	0-0	12.1	13	9	6	1	6-0	5
2002— Louisville (I.L.)	12	5	.706	3.93	26	18	1	0	1-...	128.1	151	63	56	14	31-1	80
— Cincinnati (N.L.)	1	3	.250	4.44	14	8	0	0	0-0	50.2	59	31	25	5	24-1	36
Major League totals (2 years)	1	4	.200	4.43	19	10	0	0	0-0	63.0	72	40	31	6	30-1	41

FETTERS, MIKE P

PERSONAL: Born December 19, 1964, in Van Nuys, Calif. ... 6-4/239. ... Throws right, bats right. ... Full name: Michael Lee Fetters.
HIGH SCHOOL: Iolani (Honolulu, Hawaii).
COLLEGE: Pepperdine.
TRANSACTIONS/CAREER NOTES: Selected by Los Angeles Dodgers organization in 22nd round of free-agent draft (June 6, 1983); did not sign. ... Selected by California Angels organization in supplemental round ("sandwich pick" between first and second round, 27th pick overall) of free-agent draft (June 2, 1986); pick received as compensation for Baltimore Orioles signing Type A free-agent OF/IF Juan Beniquez. ... Traded by Angels with P Glenn Carter to Milwaukee Brewers for P Chuck Crim (December 10, 1991). ... On disabled list (May 3-19, 1992; and May 25-June 9, 1995). ... On Milwaukee disabled list (April 4-May 5, 1997); included rehabilitation assignment to Tucson (April 30-May 5). ... Traded by Brewers with P Ben McDonald and P Ron Villone to Cleveland Indians for OF Marquis Grissom and P Jeff Juden (December 8, 1997). ... Traded by Indians to Oakland Athletics for P Steve Karsay (December 8, 1997). ... On Oakland disabled list (April 6-26, 1998). ... Traded by A's to Anaheim Angels for a player to be named later and cash (August 10, 1998). ... Granted free agency (October 26, 1998). ... Signed by Baltimore Orioles organization (February 4, 1999). ... On Baltimore disabled list (June 7-September 1, 1999); included rehabilitation assignment to Rochester (August 23-31). ... Granted free agency (November 1, 1999). ... Signed by Dodgers organization (December 15, 1999). ... On disabled list (May 4-26, 2000). ... On suspened list (July 21-22, 2000). ... On Los Angeles disabled list (June 20-July 5, 2001). ... Traded by Dodgers with P Adrian Burnside to Pittsburgh Pirates for P Terry Mulholland (July 31, 2001). ... Traded by Pirates to Arizona Diamondbacks for P Duaner Sanchez (July 6, 2002). ... Granted free agency (November 11, 2002).
CAREER HITTING (MLB): 0-for-0 (.000), 0 R, 0 2B, 0 3B, 0 HR, 0 RBI.

Year League	W	L	Pct.	ERA	G	GS	CG	ShO	Sv.-Opp.	IP	H	R	ER	HR	BB-IBB	SO
1986— Salem (N'West)	4	2	.667	3.38	12	12	1	0	0-...	72.0	60	39	27	4	51-0	72
1987— Palm Springs (Calif.)	9	7	.563	3.57	19	19	2	0	0-...	116.0	106	62	46	2	73-0	105
1988— Midland (Texas)	8	8	.500	5.92	20	20	2	0	0-...	114.0	116	78	75	10	67-3	101
— Edmonton (PCL)	2	0	1.000	1.93	2	2	1	0	0-...	14.0	8	3	3	0	10-0	11
1989— Edmonton (PCL)	12	8	.600	3.80	26	26	•6	2	0-...	168.0	160	80	71	11	72-2	*144
— California (A.L.)	0	0	...	8.10	1	0	0	0	0-0	3.1	5	4	3	1	1-0	4
1990— Edmonton (PCL)	1	1	.500	0.99	5	5	1	1	0-...	27.1	22	9	3	0	13-0	26
— California (A.L.)	1	1	.500	4.12	26	2	0	0	1-1	67.2	77	33	31	9	20-0	35
1991— Edmonton (PCL)	2	7	.222	4.87	11	11	1	0	0-...	61.0	65	39	33	5	26-0	43
— California (A.L.)	2	5	.286	4.84	19	4	0	0	0-1	44.2	53	29	24	4	28-2	24
1992— Milwaukee (A.L.)■	5	1	.833	1.87	50	0	0	0	2-5	62.2	38	15	13	3	24-2	43
1993— Milwaukee (A.L.)	3	3	.500	3.34	45	0	0	0	0-0	59.1	59	29	22	4	22-4	23
1994— Milwaukee (A.L.)	1	4	.200	2.54	42	0	0	0	17-20	46.0	41	16	13	0	27-5	31
1995— Milwaukee (A.L.)	0	3	.000	3.38	40	0	0	0	22-27	34.2	40	16	13	3	20-4	33
1996— Milwaukee (A.L.)	3	3	.500	3.38	61	0	0	0	32-38	61.1	65	28	23	4	26-4	53
1997— Tucson (PCL)	0	0	...	10.80	2	0	0	0	0-...	1.2	1	2	2	0	1-0	0
— Milwaukee (A.L.)	1	5	.167	3.45	51	0	0	0	6-11	70.1	62	30	27	4	33-3	62
1998— Oakland (A.L.)■	1	6	.143	3.99	48	0	0	0	5-8	47.1	48	26	21	3	21-2	34
— Anaheim (A.L.)■	1	2	.333	5.56	12	0	0	0	0-1	11.1	14	8	7	2	4-0	9
1999— Baltimore (A.L.)■	1	0	1.000	5.81	27	0	0	0	0-3	31.0	35	23	20	5	22-2	22
— Rochester (I.L.)	0	0	...	0.00	4	0	0	0	0-...	3.2	0	0	0	0	2-0	6
2000— Los Angeles (N.L.)■	6	2	.750	3.24	51	0	0	0	5-7	50.0	35	18	18	7	25-2	40
2001— Los Angeles (N.L.)	2	1	.667	6.07	34	0	0	0	1-3	29.2	33	23	20	6	13-0	26
— Pittsburgh (N.L.)■	1	1	.500	4.58	20	0	0	0	8-9	17.2	16	9	9	1	13-1	11
2002— Pittsburgh (N.L.)	1	0	1.000	3.26	32	0	0	0	0-1	30.1	25	13	11	3	18-1	29
— Arizona (N.L.)■	2	3	.400	5.11	33	0	0	0	0-1	24.2	28	18	14	1	19-5	24
A.L. totals (11 years)	19	33	.365	3.62	422	6	0	0	85-115	539.2	537	257	217	42	248-28	373
N.L. totals (3 years)	12	7	.632	4.25	170	0	0	0	14-21	152.1	137	81	72	18	88-9	130
Major League totals (14 years)	31	40	.437	3.76	592	6	0	0	99-136	692.0	674	338	289	60	336-37	503

DIVISION SERIES RECORD

Year League	W	L	Pct.	ERA	G	GS	CG	ShO	Sv.-Opp.	IP	H	R	ER	HR	BB-IBB	SO
2002— Arizona (N.L.)	0	0	...	0.00	1	0	0	0	0-0	.2	1	0	0	0	1-0	1

FICK, ROBERT — OF — TIGERS

PERSONAL: Born March 15, 1974, in Torrance, Calif. ... 6-1/200. ... Bats left, throws right. ... Full name: Robert Charles John Fick. ... Brother of Chris Fick, former outfielder/first baseman in St. Louis Cardinals and Arizona Diamondbacks organizations; and brother of Chuck Fick, St. Louis Cardinals scout and former catcher in Montreal Expos and Oakland Athletics organization.

HIGH SCHOOL: Newbury Park (Calif.).

JUNIOR COLLEGE: Ventura (Calif.) College.

COLLEGE: Cal State-Northridge.

TRANSACTIONS/CAREER NOTES: Selected by Oakland Athletics organization in 45th round of free-agent draft (June 1, 1992); did not sign. ... Selected by Detroit Tigers organization in 43rd round of free-agent draft (June 1, 1995); did not sign. ... Selected by Tigers organization in fifth round of free-agent draft (June 4, 1996). ... On Detroit disabled list (March 31-September 7, 1999); included rehabilitation assignments to Gulf Coast Tigers (August 18-20), West Michigan (August 21-23) and Toledo (August 24-September 6). ... On suspended list (May 23-26, 2000). ... On Detroit disabled list (July 6-September 1, 2000); included rehabilitation assignment to Toledo (August 13-September 1). ... On suspended list (September 22-27, 2001).

RECORDS: Shares major league single-inning record for most doubles—2 (May 29, 2002, seventh inning).

HONORS: Named Midwest League Most Valuable Player (1996).

STATISTICAL NOTES: Led Midwest League with 262 total bases in 1997. ... Had 18-game hitting streak (May 29-June 16, 2002). ... Led A.L. outfielders with 21 assists and tied for lead with five double plays in 2002. ... Career major league grand slams: 1.

2002 GAMES PLAYED BY POSITION (MLB): OF—140; DH—6.

			BATTING														FIELDING	
Year	Team (League)	Pos.	G	AB	R	H	2B	3B	HR	RBI	BB	SO	SB-CS	Avg.	OBP	SLG	E	Avg.
1996—	Jamestown (NY-P)	C	43	133	18	33	6	0	1	14	12	25	3-1	.248	.306	.316	3	.982
1997—	West Mich. (Midw.)	1B-C-3B	122	463	100	*158	*50	3	16	90	75	74	13-4	*.341	.429	*.566	12	.989
1998—	Jacksonville (Sou.)	C-1B-OF	130	515	101	164	•47	6	18	114	71	83	8-4	.318	.401	.538	9	.985
	—Detroit (A.L.)	C-DH-1B	7	22	6	8	1	0	3	7	2	7	1-0	.364	.417	.818	1	.966
1999—	GC Tigers (GCL)	DH-C-1B	3	9	2	3	1	0	0	2	2	0	1-0	.333	.455	.444	0	1.000
	—West Mich. (Midw.)	DH-C-1B	3	11	2	3	0	0	0	0	2	0	1-0	.273	.385	.273	2	.913
	—Toledo (I.L.)	1B-C-DH-3B	14	48	11	15	0	1	2	8	8	5	1-0	.313	.414	.479	5	.944
	—Detroit (A.L.)	DH-C	15	41	6	9	0	0	3	10	7	6	1-0	.220	.327	.439	0	1.000
2000—	Detroit (A.L.)	1B-C-DH	66	163	18	41	7	2	3	22	22	39	2-1	.252	.340	.374	5	.983
	—Toledo (I.L.)	1B	17	68	5	10	5	0	1	7	6	13	1-0	.147	.234	.265	0	1.000
2001—	Detroit (A.L.)	C-1B-OF-DH	124	401	62	109	21	2	19	61	39	62	0-3	.272	.339	.476	7	.989
2002—	Detroit (A.L.)	OF-DH	148	556	66	150	36	2	17	63	46	90	0-1	.270	.331	.433	*12	.963
Major League totals (5 years)			360	1183	158	317	65	6	45	163	116	204	4-5	.268	.336	.447	25	.981

ALL-STAR GAME RECORD

	AB	R	H	2B	3B	HR	RBI	BB	SO	SB-CS	Avg.	OBP	SLG	E	Avg.
All-Star Game totals (1 year)	2	1	1	0	0	0	0	0	0	1-0	.500	.500	.500	0	1.000

FIELD, NATE — P

PERSONAL: Born December 11, 1975, in Denver. ... 6-2/200. ... Throws right, bats right. ... Full name: Nathan Patrick Field.

COLLEGE: Fort Hays State.

TRANSACTIONS/CAREER NOTES: Signed as non-drafted free agent by Montreal Expos organization (June 11, 1998). ... Released by Expos (March 29, 2000). ... Signed by Sioux City, Northern League (May 2000). ... Contract purchased by Kansas City Royals organization from Sioux City (June 29, 2000). ... Claimed on waivers by New York Yankees (June 12, 2002). ... On Columbus disabled list (July 30-August 11, 2002). ... Granted free agency (October 15, 2002).

CAREER HITTING (MLB): 0-for-0 (.000), 0 R, 0 2B, 0 3B, 0 HR, 0 RBI.

Year	League	W	L	Pct.	ERA	G	GS	CG	ShO	Sv.-Opp.	IP	H	R	ER	HR	BB-IBB	SO
1998—	Vermont (NY-Penn)	3	1	.750	3.09	25	0	0	0	2-...	35.0	32	16	12	1	11-0	39
1999—	Cape Fear (S.Atl.)	4	8	.333	5.40	42	0	0	0	2-...	65.0	75	49	39	8	22-2	55
	—Ottawa (I.L.)	0	0	...	3.00	2	0	0	0	0-...	3.0	4	1	1	0	4-0	4
2000—	Sioux City (Nor.)■	3	0	1.000	1.93	11	0	0	0	0-...	23.1	17	10	5	...	15-...	19
	—Charl., W.Va. (S.Atl.)■	1	2	.333	2.23	17	0	0	0	0-...	36.1	28	10	9	2	15-0	31
2001—	Wichita (Texas)	4	2	.667	1.48	52	0	0	0	19-...	73.0	61	16	12	3	18-3	67
2002—	Omaha (PCL)	0	1	.000	3.31	18	0	0	0	7-...	16.1	22	10	6	0	8-0	13
	—Kansas City (A.L.)	0	0	...	9.00	5	0	0	0	0-0	5.0	8	5	5	2	3-1	3
	—Columbus (I.L.)■	2	1	.667	6.75	21	2	0	0	0-...	38.2	46	30	29	6	21-1	25
Major League totals (1 year)		0	0	...	9.00	5	0	0	0	0-0	5.0	8	5	5	2	3-1	3

FIGGINS, CHONE — 2B — ANGELS

PERSONAL: Born January 22, 1978, in Leary, Ga. ... 5-9/155. ... Bats both, throws right. ... Full name: Desmond DeChone Figgins.

HIGH SCHOOL: Brandon (Fla.).

TRANSACTIONS/CAREER NOTES: Selected by Colorado Rockies organization in fourth round of free-agent draft (June 3, 1997). ... Traded by Rockies to Anaheim Angels for OF Kimera Bartee (July 13, 2001).

STATISTICAL NOTES: Led Pacific Coast League second basemen with 380 assists, 21 errors and 81 double plays in 2002.

2002 GAMES PLAYED BY POSITION (MLB): 2B—8.

			BATTING														FIELDING	
Year	Team (League)	Pos.	G	AB	R	H	2B	3B	HR	RBI	BB	SO	SB-CS	Avg.	OBP	SLG	E	Avg.
1997—	Ariz. Rockies (Ariz.)	SS	54	214	41	60	5	6	1	23	35	51	30-12	.280	.386	.374	40	.865
1998—	Portland (N'West)	SS	69	269	41	76	9	3	1	26	24	56	25-4	.283	.345	.349	16	.947
1999—	Salem (Caro.)	SS	123	444	65	106	12	3	0	22	41	86	27-13	.239	.306	.279	45	.925
2000—	Salem (Caro.)	2B	134	522	92	145	26	14	3	48	67	107	37-19	.278	.358	.398	28	.955
2001—	Carolina (Sou.)	2B-SS	86	332	41	73	14	5	2	25	40	73	27-8	.220	.306	.310	16	.963
	—Arkansas (Texas)	2B-SS-3B	39	138	21	37	12	2	0	12	14	26	7-2	.268	.329	.384	10	.945
2002—	Salt Lake (PCL)	2B-SS	125	511	100	156	25	18	7	62	53	83	39-8	.305	.364	.466	†23	.964
	—Anaheim (A.L.)	2B	15	12	6	2	1	0	0	1	0	5	2-1	.167	.167	.250	1	.941
Major League totals (1 year)			15	12	6	2	1	0	0	1	0	5	2-1	.167	.167	.250	1	.941

DIVISION SERIES RECORD

Year	Team (League)	Pos.	G	AB	R	H	2B	3B	HR	RBI	BB	SO	SB-CS	Avg.	OBP	SLG	E	Avg.
			BATTING														FIELDING	
2002—	Anaheim (A.L.)	DH	1	0	1	0	0	0	0	0	0	0	1-0	...	...	...	...	...

CHAMPIONSHIP SERIES RECORD

RECORDS: Shares A.L. single-inning record for most runs—2 (October 13, 2002, seventh inning).

Year	Team (League)	Pos.	G	AB	R	H	2B	3B	HR	RBI	BB	SO	SB-CS	Avg.	OBP	SLG	E	Avg.
			BATTING														FIELDING	
2002—	Anaheim (A.L.)	PH	3	1	2	1	0	0	0	0	0	0	0-0	1.000	1.000	1.000	...	...

WORLD SERIES RECORD

NOTES: Member of World Series championship team (2002).

Year	Team (League)	Pos.	G	AB	R	H	2B	3B	HR	RBI	BB	SO	SB-CS	Avg.	OBP	SLG	E	Avg.
			BATTING														FIELDING	
2002—	Anaheim (A.L.)	PH	2	0	1	0	0	0	0	0	0	0	0-0	...	...	...	...	...

FIGUEROA, NELSON P

PERSONAL: Born May 18, 1974, in Brooklyn, N.Y. ... 6-1/155. ... Throws right, bats right. ... Full name: Nelson Walter Figueroa Jr.

HIGH SCHOOL: Abraham Lincoln (Brooklyn, N.Y.).

COLLEGE: Brandeis (Mass.).

TRANSACTIONS/CAREER NOTES: Selected by New York Mets organization in 30th round of free-agent draft (June 1, 1995). ... Traded by Mets with OF Bernard Gilkey and cash to Arizona Diamondbacks for P Willie Blair, C Jorge Fabregas and cash considerations (July 31, 1998). ... On Tucson disabled list (June 12-23 and July 6-30, 1999). ... Traded by Diamondbacks with OF Travis Lee, P Omar Daal and P Vicente Padilla to Philadelphia Phillies for P Curt Schilling (July 26, 2000). ... Claimed on waivers by Milwaukee Brewers (April 3, 2002). ... On Milwaukee disabled list (May 8-21, 2002). ... Released by Brewers (October 11, 2002).

HONORS: Named South Atlantic League Most Outstanding Pitcher (1996).

CAREER HITTING (MLB): 9-for-42 (.214), 5 R, 1 2B, 0 3B, 0 HR, 4 RBI.

Year	League	W	L	Pct.	ERA	G	GS	CG	ShO	Sv.-Opp.	IP	H	R	ER	HR	BB-IBB	SO
1995—	Kingsport (Appl.)	7	3	.700	3.07	12	12	2	*2	0-...	76.1	57	31	26	3	22-1	79
1996—	Capital City (S.Atl.)	14	7	.667	*2.04	26	25	*8	*4	0-...	*185.1	119	55	42	10	58-1	*200
1997—	Binghamton (East.)	5	11	.313	4.34	33	22	0	0	0-...	143.0	137	76	69	14	68-1	116
1998—	Binghamton (East.)	12	3	.800	4.66	21	21	3	2	0-...	123.2	133	73	64	19	44-2	116
—	Tucson (PCL)■	2	2	.500	3.70	7	7	0	0	0-...	41.1	46	22	17	8	16-1	29
1999—	Tucson (PCL)	11	6	.647	3.94	24	21	1	1	0-...	128.0	128	59	56	16	41-0	106
—	Ariz. D-backs (Ariz.)	0	1	.000	0.00	1	1	0	0	0-...	3.0	3	1	0	0	0-0	2
2000—	Tucson (PCL)	9	4	.692	2.81	17	16	1	0	0-...	112.0	101	41	35	9	28-2	78
—	Arizona (N.L.)	0	1	.000	7.47	3	3	0	0	0-0	15.2	17	13	13	4	5-0	7
—	Scranton/W.B. (I.L.)■	4	3	.571	3.78	8	8	1	0	0-...	50.0	50	28	21	9	11-0	35
2001—	Scranton/W.B. (I.L.)	4	2	.667	2.47	13	12	3	0	0-...	87.1	74	33	24	6	18-2	74
—	Philadelphia (N.L.)	4	5	.444	3.94	19	13	0	0	0-0	89.0	95	40	39	8	37-3	61
2002—	Milwaukee (N.L.)■	1	7	.125	5.03	30	11	0	0	0-0	93.0	96	59	52	18	37-6	51
—	Indianapolis (I.L.)	5	0	1.000	3.63	6	6	0	0	0-...	39.2	39	18	16	2	13-0	25
Major League totals (3 years)		5	13	.278	4.74	52	27	0	0	0-0	197.2	208	112	104	30	79-9	119

FIKAC, JEREMY P PADRES

PERSONAL: Born April 8, 1975, in Shine, Texas. ... 6-2/185. ... Throws right, bats right. ... Full name: Jeremy Joseph Fikac.

HIGH SCHOOL: Somerville (Texas).

COLLEGE: Southwest Texas State.

TRANSACTIONS/CAREER NOTES: Selected by San Diego Padres organization in 19th round of free-agent draft (June 2, 1998).

CAREER HITTING (MLB): 0-for-2 (.000), 0 R, 0 2B, 0 3B, 0 HR, 0 RBI.

Year	League	W	L	Pct.	ERA	G	GS	CG	ShO	Sv.-Opp.	IP	H	R	ER	HR	BB-IBB	SO
1998—	Idaho Falls (Pio.)	2	0	1.000	2.25	12	0	0	0	1-...	20.0	11	6	5	0	8-1	19
1999—	Rancho Cuca. (Calif.)	8	3	.727	5.08	40	6	0	0	0-...	85.0	94	50	48	7	43-0	75
2000—	Rancho Cuca. (Calif.)	5	3	.625	1.80	61	0	0	0	20-...	75.0	46	19	15	2	24-0	101
2001—	Mobile (Sou.)	6	0	1.000	1.97	53	0	0	0	18-...	68.2	54	16	15	3	20-4	75
—	Portland (PCL)	0	0	...	3.00	1	0	0	0	0-...	3.0	3	1	1	0	0-0	3
—	San Diego (N.L.)	2	0	1.000	1.37	23	0	0	0	0-2	26.1	15	6	4	2	5-1	19
2002—	San Diego (N.L.)	4	7	.364	5.48	65	0	0	0	0-6	69.0	74	50	42	13	34-8	66
—	Mobile (Sou.)	1	0	1.000	3.00	3	0	0	0	1-...	3.0	5	1	1	0	0-0	0
Major League totals (2 years)		6	7	.462	4.34	88	0	0	0	0-8	95.1	89	56	46	15	39-9	85

FILE, BOB P BLUE JAYS

PERSONAL: Born January 28, 1977, in Philadelphia. ... 6-4/215. ... Throws right, bats right. ... Full name: Robert Michael File.

HIGH SCHOOL: Father Judge (Philadelphia).

COLLEGE: Philadelphia College of Textiles and Science.

TRANSACTIONS/CAREER NOTES: Selected by Toronto Blue Jays organization in 19th round of free-agent draft (June 2, 1998). ... On Toronto disabled list (March 27-April 16 and April 24-May 22, 2002); included rehabilitation assignments to Dunedin (April 14-16 and May 15-22). ... On Syracuse disabled list (May 24-June 6 and July 3-17, 2002).

CAREER HITTING (MLB): 0-for-0 (.000), 0 R, 0 2B, 0 3B, 0 HR, 0 RBI.

Year League	W	L	Pct.	ERA	G	GS	CG	ShO	Sv.-Opp.	IP	H	R	ER	HR	BB-IBB	SO
1998—Medicine Hat (Pio.)	2	1	.667	1.41	28	0	0	0	•16-...	32.0	24	7	5	1	5-0	28
1999—Dunedin (FSL)	4	1	.800	1.70	47	0	0	0	26-...	53.0	30	13	10	2	14-0	48
2000—Tennessee (Sou.)	4	3	.571	3.12	36	0	0	0	20-...	34.2	29	20	12	1	13-0	40
—Syracuse (I.L.)	2	0	1.000	0.93	20	0	0	0	8-...	19.1	14	2	2	1	2-0	10
2001—Tennessee (Sou.)	0	0	...	3.00	3	0	0	0	1-...	3.0	3	1	1	1	0-0	2
—Toronto (A.L.)	5	3	.625	3.27	60	0	0	0	0-2	74.1	57	28	27	6	29-8	38
—Syracuse (I.L.)	0	0	...	0.00	2	0	0	0	0-...	4.0	1	0	0	0	0-0	3
2002—Dunedin (FSL)	0	2	.000	11.12	4	3	0	0	0-...	5.2	13	9	7	0	3-0	1
—Toronto (A.L.)	0	1	.000	18.90	5	0	0	0	0-0	3.1	8	7	7	0	2-0	2
—Syracuse (I.L.)	0	0	...	5.94	33	0	0	0	2-...	36.1	39	29	24	2	15-1	23
Major League totals (2 years)	5	4	.556	3.94	65	0	0	0	0-2	77.2	65	35	34	6	31-8	40

FINLEY, CHUCK P

PERSONAL: Born November 26, 1962, in Monroe, La. ... 6-6/226. ... Throws left, bats left. ... Full name: Charles Edward Finley.

HIGH SCHOOL: West Monroe (La.).

COLLEGE: Northeast Louisiana.

TRANSACTIONS/CAREER NOTES: Selected by California Angels organization in 15th round of free-agent draft (June 4, 1984); did not sign. ... Selected by Angels organization in secondary phase of free-agent draft (January 9, 1985). ... On disabled list (August 22-September 15, 1989 and April 6-22, 1992). ... Granted free agency (November 7, 1995). ... Re-signed by Angels (January 4, 1996). ... Angels franchise renamed Anaheim Angels for 1997 season. ... On Anaheim disabled list (March 23-April 15 and August 20, 1997-remainder of season); included rehabilitation assignment to Lake Elsinore (April 5-10). ... Granted free agency (November 2, 1999). ... Signed by Cleveland Indians (December 16, 1999). ... On Cleveland disabled list (May 29-June 20 and June 26-August 9, 2001); included rehabilitation assignments to Akron (July 15 and August 1-9). ... Traded by Indians to St. Louis Cardinals for 1B Luis Garcia and a player to be named later (July 19, 2002); Indians acquired OF Covelli Crisp to complete deal (August 6, 2002). ... Granted free agency (November 11, 2002).

RECORDS: Shares major league single-inning record for most strikeouts—4 (May 12, 1999, third inning; August 15, 1999, first inning; and April 16, 2000, third inning).

HONORS: Named lefthanded pitcher on The Sporting News A.L. All-Star team (1989-90).

STATISTICAL NOTES: Pitched 5-0 one-hit, complete-game victory against Boston (May 26, 1989). ... Struck out 15 batters in one game (June 24, 1989; and May 23, 1995). ... Led A.L. with 17 wild pitches in 1996 and 15 wild pitches in 1999.

MISCELLANEOUS: Holds Anaheim Angels franchise all-time records for most wins (165) and innings pitched (2,675).

CAREER HITTING (MLB): 3-for-53 (.057), 3 R, 1 2B, 0 3B, 0 HR, 1 RBI.

Year League	W	L	Pct.	ERA	G	GS	CG	ShO	Sv.-Opp.	IP	H	R	ER	HR	BB-IBB	SO
1985—Salem (N'West)	3	1	.750	4.66	18	0	0	0	5-...	29.0	34	21	15	1	10-0	32
1986—Quad Cities (Midw.)	1	0	1.000	0.00	10	0	0	0	6-...	12.0	4	0	0	0	3-0	16
—California (A.L.)	3	1	.750	3.30	25	0	0	0	0-0	46.1	40	17	17	2	23-1	37
1987—California (A.L.)	2	7	.222	4.67	35	3	0	0	0-2	90.2	102	54	47	7	43-3	63
1988—California (A.L.)	9	15	.375	4.17	31	31	2	0	0-0	194.1	191	95	90	15	82-7	111
1989—California (A.L.)	16	9	.640	2.57	29	29	9	1	0-0	199.2	171	64	57	13	82-0	156
1990—California (A.L.)	18	9	.667	2.40	32	32	7	2	0-0	236.0	210	77	63	17	81-3	177
1991—California (A.L.)	18	9	.667	3.80	34	34	4	2	0-0	227.1	205	102	96	23	101-1	171
1992—California (A.L.)	7	12	.368	3.96	31	31	4	1	0-0	204.1	212	99	90	24	98-2	124
1993—California (A.L.)	16	14	.533	3.15	35	35	*13	2	0-0	251.1	243	108	88	22	82-1	187
1994—California (A.L.)	10	10	.500	4.32	25	•25	7	2	0-0	*183.1	178	95	88	21	71-0	148
1995—California (A.L.)	15	12	.556	4.21	32	32	2	1	0-0	203.0	192	106	95	20	93-1	195
1996—California (A.L.)	15	16	.484	4.16	35	35	4	1	0-0	238.0	241	124	110	27	94-5	215
1997—Lake Elsinore (Calif.)	0	0	...	2.00	2	2	0	0	0-...	9.0	5	3	2	0	4-0	12
—Anaheim (A.L.)	13	6	.684	4.23	25	25	3	1	0-0	164.0	152	79	77	20	65-0	155
1998—Anaheim (A.L.)	11	9	.550	3.39	34	34	1	1	0-0	223.1	210	97	84	20	109-1	212
1999—Anaheim (A.L.)	12	11	.522	4.43	33	33	1	0	0-0	213.1	197	117	105	23	94-2	200
2000—Cleveland (A.L.)■	16	11	.593	4.17	34	34	3	0	0-0	218.0	211	108	101	23	101-3	189
2001—Cleveland (A.L.)	8	7	.533	5.54	22	22	1	0	0-0	113.2	131	78	70	14	35-0	96
—Akron (East.)	1	1	.500	0.82	2	2	0	0	0-...	11.0	7	3	1	0	2-0	11
2002—Cleveland (A.L.)	4	11	.267	4.44	18	18	1	0	0-0	105.1	114	56	52	6	48-3	91
—St. Louis (N.L.)■	7	4	.636	3.80	14	14	1	1	0-0	85.1	69	41	36	7	30-3	83
A.L. totals (17 years)	193	169	.533	3.85	510	453	62	14	0-2	3112.0	3000	1476	1330	297	1302-33	2527
N.L. totals (1 year)	7	4	.636	3.80	14	14	1	1	0-0	85.1	69	41	36	7	30-3	83
Major League totals (17 years)	200	173	.536	3.85	524	467	63	15	0-2	3197.1	3069	1517	1366	304	1332-36	2610

DIVISION SERIES RECORD

Year League	W	L	Pct.	ERA	G	GS	CG	ShO	Sv.-Opp.	IP	H	R	ER	HR	BB-IBB	SO
2001—Cleveland (A.L.)	0	2	.000	7.27	2	2	0	0	0-0	8.2	9	7	7	3	6-0	10
2002—St. Louis (N.L.)	0	0	...	0.00	1	1	0	0	0-0	6.1	4	0	0	0	2-0	7
Division series totals (2 years)	0	2	.000	4.20	3	3	0	0	0-0	15.0	13	7	7	3	8-0	17

CHAMPIONSHIP SERIES RECORD

Year League	W	L	Pct.	ERA	G	GS	CG	ShO	Sv.-Opp.	IP	H	R	ER	HR	BB-IBB	SO
1986—California (A.L.)	0	0	...	0.00	3	0	0	0	0-0	2.0	1	0	0	0	0-0	1
2002—St. Louis (N.L.)	1	0	1.000	7.20	1	1	0	0	0-0	5.0	7	4	4	1	3-0	1
Champ. series totals (2 years)	1	0	1.000	5.14	4	1	0	0	0-0	7.0	8	4	4	1	3-0	2

ALL-STAR GAME RECORD

	W	L	Pct.	ERA	GS	CG	ShO	Sv.-Opp.	IP	H	R	ER	HR	BB-IBB	SO
All-Star Game totals (2 years)	0	0	...	3.00	0	0	0	0-0	3.0	3	1	1	0	1-0	5

FINLEY, STEVE OF

PERSONAL: Born March 12, 1965, in Union City, Tenn. ... 6-2/195. ... Bats left, throws left. ... Full name: Steven Allen Finley.

HIGH SCHOOL: Paducah (Ky.) Tilghman.

COLLEGE: Southern Illinois.

TRANSACTIONS/CAREER NOTES: Selected by Atlanta Braves organization in 11th round of free-agent draft (June 2, 1986); did not sign. ... Selected by Baltimore Orioles organization in 13th round of free-agent draft (June 2, 1987). ... On Baltimore disabled list (April 4-22, 1989). ... On Baltimore disabled list (July 29-September 1, 1989); included rehabilitation assignment to Hagerstown (August 21-23). ... Traded by Orioles with P Pete Harnisch and P Curt Schilling to Houston Astros for 1B Glenn Davis (January 10, 1991). ... On disabled list (April 25-May 14, 1993). ... On Houston disabled list (June 13-July 3, 1994); included rehabilitation assignment to Jackson (June 28-July 3). ... Traded by Astros with 3B Ken Caminiti, SS Andujar Cedeno, 1B Roberto Petagine, P Brian Williams and a player to be named later to San Diego Padres for OF Phil Plantier, OF Derek Bell, P Pedro Martinez, P Doug Brocail, IF Craig Shipley and SS Ricky Gutierrez (December 28, 1994); Padres acquired P Sean Fesh to complete deal (May 1, 1995). ... On San Diego disabled list (April 20-May 6, 1997); included rehabilitation assignment to Rancho Cucamonga (April 25-May 6). ... Granted free agency (October 26, 1998). ... Signed by Arizona Diamondbacks (December 18, 1998). ... Granted free agency (October 29, 2002).

RECORDS: Shares major league single-season record for fewest double plays by outfielder (150 or more games)—0 (1999).

HONORS: Won N.L. Gold Glove as outfielder (1995, 1996, 1999 and 2000).

STATISTICAL NOTES: Led International League outfielders with 289 putouts and 315 total chances in 1988. ... Had 21-game hitting streak (June 20-July 14, 1996). ... Hit three home runs in one game (May 19 and June 23, 1997; and September 8, 1999). ... Tied for N.L. lead with six double plays by outfielder in 1998. ... Career major league grand slams: 8.

2002 GAMES PLAYED BY POSITION (MLB): OF—144.

								BATTING								FIELDING	
Year Team (League)	**Pos.**	**G**	**AB**	**R**	**H**	**2B**	**3B**	**HR**	**RBI**	**BB**	**SO**	**SB-CS**	**Avg.**	**OBP**	**SLG**	**E**	**Avg.**
1987—Newark (NY-Penn)	OF	54	222	40	65	13	2	3	33	22	24	26-5	.293	.359	.410	4	.970
—Hagerstown (Caro.)	OF	15	65	9	22	3	2	1	5	1	6	7-2	.338	.348	.492	0	1.000
1988—Hagerstown (Caro.)	OF	8	28	2	6	2	0	0	3	4	3	4-0	.214	.313	.286	0	1.000
—Charlotte (Sou.)	OF	10	40	7	12	4	2	1	6	4	3	2-0	.300	.378	.575	0	1.000
—Rochester (I.L.)	OF	120	456	61	*143	19	7	5	54	28	55	20-11	*.314	.352	.419	*12	.962
1989—Baltimore (A.L.)	OF-DH	81	217	35	54	5	2	2	25	15	30	17-3	.249	.298	.318	2	.986
—Rochester (I.L.)	OF	7	25	2	4	0	0	0	2	1	5	3-0	.160	.192	.160	0	1.000
—Hagerstown (East.)	OF	11	48	11	20	3	1	0	7	4	3	4-0	.417	.453	.521	3	.925
1990—Baltimore (A.L.)	OF-DH	142	464	46	119	16	4	3	37	32	53	22-9	.256	.304	.328	7	.977
1991—Houston (N.L.)■	OF	159	596	84	170	28	10	8	54	42	65	34-18	.285	.331	.406	5	.985
1992—Houston (N.L.)	OF	•162	607	84	177	29	13	5	55	58	63	44-9	.292	.355	.407	3	.993
1993—Houston (N.L.)	OF	142	545	69	145	15	*13	8	44	28	65	19-6	.266	.304	.385	4	.988
1994—Houston (N.L.)	OF	94	373	64	103	16	5	11	33	28	52	13-7	.276	.329	.434	4	.982
—Jackson (Texas)	OF-DH	5	13	3	4	0	0	0	0	4	0	1-0	.308	.471	.308	0	1.000
1995—San Diego (N.L.)■	OF	139	562	104	167	23	8	10	44	59	62	36-12	.297	.366	.420	7	.977
1996—San Diego (N.L.)	OF	161	655	126	195	45	9	30	95	56	87	22-8	.298	.354	.531	7	.982
1997—San Diego (N.L.)	OF	143	560	101	146	26	5	28	92	43	92	15-3	.261	.313	.475	4	.989
—Mobile (Sou.)	DH	1	4	1	2	0	0	1	2	1	2	0-0	.500	.600	1.250	...	...
—Rancho Cuca. (Calif.)	DH-OF	4	14	3	4	0	0	2	3	3	2	1-0	.286	.444	.714	0	...
1998—San Diego (N.L.)	OF	159	619	92	154	40	6	14	67	45	103	12-3	.249	.301	.401	7	.981
1999—Arizona (N.L.)■	OF-DH	156	590	100	156	32	10	34	103	63	94	8-4	.264	.336	.525	2	.995
2000—Arizona (N.L.)	OF-DH	152	539	100	151	27	5	35	96	65	87	12-6	.280	.361	.544	3	.992
2001—Arizona (N.L.)	OF-P	140	495	66	136	27	4	14	73	47	67	11-7	.275	.337	.430	2	.994
2002—Arizona (N.L.)	OF	150	505	82	145	24	4	25	89	65	73	16-4	.287	.370	.499	2	.994
American League totals (2 years)		223	681	81	173	21	6	5	62	47	83	39-12	.254	.302	.325	9	.980
National League totals (12 years)		1757	6646	1072	1845	332	92	222	845	599	910	242-87	.278	.338	.455	50	.988
Major League totals (14 years)		1980	7327	1153	2018	353	98	227	907	646	993	281-99	.275	.335	.443	59	.987

DIVISION SERIES RECORD

RECORDS: Shares N.L. single-game record for most runs batted in—5 (October 6, 1999).

								BATTING								FIELDING	
Year Team (League)	**Pos.**	**G**	**AB**	**R**	**H**	**2B**	**3B**	**HR**	**RBI**	**BB**	**SO**	**SB-CS**	**Avg.**	**OBP**	**SLG**	**E**	**Avg.**
1996—San Diego (N.L.)	OF	3	12	0	1	0	0	0	1	0	4	1-0	.083	.154	.083	0	1.000
1998—San Diego (N.L.)	OF-PR	4	10	2	1	1	0	0	1	1	4	0-0	.100	.182	.200	0	1.000
1999—Arizona (N.L.)	OF	4	13	0	5	1	0	0	5	3	1	0-0	.385	.500	.462	0	1.000
2001—Arizona (N.L.)	OF	5	19	1	8	1	0	0	2	0	2	0-0	.421	.421	.474	0	1.000
2002—Arizona (N.L.)	OF	3	9	1	2	0	0	0	1	2	2	1-0	.222	.333	.222	0	1.000
Division series totals (5 years)		19	63	4	17	3	0	0	10	6	13	2-0	.270	.338	.317	0	1.000

CHAMPIONSHIP SERIES RECORD

								BATTING								FIELDING	
Year Team (League)	**Pos.**	**G**	**AB**	**R**	**H**	**2B**	**3B**	**HR**	**RBI**	**BB**	**SO**	**SB-CS**	**Avg.**	**OBP**	**SLG**	**E**	**Avg.**
1998—San Diego (N.L.)	OF	6	21	3	7	1	0	0	2	6	2	1-0	.333	.481	.381	0	1.000
2001—Arizona (N.L.)	OF	5	14	1	4	1	0	0	4	3	1	1-0	.286	.412	.357	0	1.000
Championship series totals (2 years)		11	35	4	11	2	0	0	6	9	3	2-0	.314	.455	.371	0	1.000

WORLD SERIES RECORD

NOTES: Member of World Series championship team (2001).

								BATTING								FIELDING	
Year Team (League)	**Pos.**	**G**	**AB**	**R**	**H**	**2B**	**3B**	**HR**	**RBI**	**BB**	**SO**	**SB-CS**	**Avg.**	**OBP**	**SLG**	**E**	**Avg.**
1998—San Diego (N.L.)	OF	3	12	0	1	1	0	0	0	0	2	1-0	.083	.083	.167	0	1.000
2001—Arizona (N.L.)	OF-PH	7	19	5	7	0	0	1	2	4	5	0-1	.368	.478	.526	0	1.000
World Series totals (2 years)		10	31	5	8	1	0	1	2	4	7	1-1	.258	.343	.387	0	1.000

ALL-STAR GAME RECORD

	AB	**R**	**H**	**2B**	**3B**	**HR**	**RBI**	**BB**	**SO**	**SB-CS**	**Avg.**	**OBP**	**SLG**	**E**	**Avg.**
All-Star Game totals (2 years)	2	0	1	0	0	0	1	0	1	0-0	.500	.500	.500	0	1.000

RECORD AS PITCHER

Year League	**W**	**L**	**Pct.**	**ERA**	**G**	**GS**	**CG**	**ShO**	**Sv.-Opp.**	**IP**	**H**	**R**	**ER**	**HR**	**BB-IBB**	**SO**
2001—Arizona (N.L.)	0	0	...	0.00	1	0	0	0	0-0	1.0	0	0	0	0	1-0	0

FIORE, TONY — P — TWINS

PERSONAL: Born October 12, 1971, in Oak Park, Ill. ... 6-4/210. ... Throws right, bats right. ... Full name: Anthony James Fiore.

HIGH SCHOOL: Holy Cross (River Grove, Ill.).

JUNIOR COLLEGE: Triton College (Ill.).

TRANSACTIONS/CAREER NOTES: Selected by Philadelphia Phillies organization in 28th round of free-agent draft (June 1, 1992). ... On disabled list (April 2-20, 1995). ... Granted free agency (October 15, 1998). ... Re-signed by Phillies organization (November 28, 1998). ... Released by Phillies (May 19, 1999). ... Signed by Minnesota Twins organization (June 3, 1999). ... Granted free agency (October 15, 1999). ... Signed by Tampa Bay Devil Rays organization (January 14, 2000). ... On suspended list (September 22-24, 2000). ... Released by Devil Rays (May 25, 2001). ... Signed by Twins organization (May 30, 2001).

CAREER HITTING (MLB): 0-for-3 (.000), 0 R, 0 2B, 0 3B, 0 HR, 0 RBI.

Year	League	W	L	Pct.	ERA	G	GS	CG	ShO	Sv.-Opp.	IP	H	R	ER	HR	BB-IBB	SO
1992—	Martinsville (Appl.)	2	3	.400	4.18	17	2	0	0	0-...	32.1	32	20	15	0	31-1	30
1993—	Batavia (NY-Penn)	2	•8	.200	3.05	16	•16	1	0	0-...	97.1	82	51	33	1	40-0	55
1994—	Spartanburg (S.Atl.)	12	13	.480	4.10	28	•28	*9	1	0-...	166.2	162	94	76	10	77-1	113
1995—	Clearwater (FSL)	6	2	.750	3.71	24	10	0	0	0-...	70.1	70	41	29	4	44-2	45
1996—	Clearwater (FSL)	8	4	.667	3.16	22	22	3	1	0-...	128.0	102	61	45	4	56-1	80
	—Reading (East.)	1	2	.333	4.35	5	5	0	0	0-...	31.0	32	21	15	2	18-0	19
1997—	Reading (East.)	8	3	.727	3.01	17	16	0	0	0-...	104.2	89	47	35	6	40-0	64
	—Scranton/W.B. (I.L.)	3	5	.375	3.86	9	9	1	0	0-...	60.2	60	34	26	3	26-1	56
1998—	Scranton/W.B. (I.L.)	4	7	.364	4.45	41	7	0	0	1-...	95.0	92	53	47	4	52-1	71
1999—	Scranton/W.B. (I.L.)	0	0	...	6.64	13	0	0	0	0-...	20.1	28	19	15	0	15-1	13
	—Salt Lake (PCL)■	2	1	.667	3.47	40	0	0	0	19-...	46.2	45	21	18	1	26-3	38
2000—	Durham (I.L.)■	8	5	.615	2.28	53	1	0	0	8-...	75.0	62	22	19	3	38-6	39
	—Tampa Bay (A.L.)	1	1	.500	8.40	11	0	0	0	0-1	15.0	21	16	14	3	9-2	8
2001—	Durham (I.L.)	1	0	1.000	0.00	15	0	0	0	3-...	20.1	7	0	0	0	8-0	11
	—Tampa Bay (A.L.)	0	0	...	5.40	3	0	0	0	0-0	3.1	4	2	2	0	1-0	3
	—Edmonton (PCL)■	5	0	1.000	3.68	32	6	0	0	1-...	80.2	85	35	33	4	25-0	58
	—Minnesota (A.L.)	0	1	.000	5.68	4	0	0	0	0-0	6.1	5	4	4	0	2-0	5
2002—	Edmonton (PCL)	2	0	1.000	4.15	2	2	0	0	0-...	13.0	15	6	6	2	2-0	6
	—Minnesota (A.L.)	10	3	.769	3.16	48	2	0	0	0-0	91.0	74	32	32	10	43-4	55
Major League totals (3 years)		11	5	.688	4.05	66	2	0	0	0-1	115.2	104	54	52	13	55-6	71

DIVISION SERIES RECORD

Year	League	W	L	Pct.	ERA	G	GS	CG	ShO	Sv.-Opp.	IP	H	R	ER	HR	BB-IBB	SO
2002—	Minnesota (A.L.)	0	0	...	20.25	1	0	0	0	0-0	1.1	4	3	3	0	2-0	0

FITZGERALD, BRIAN — P

PERSONAL: Born December 26, 1974, in Woodbridge, Va. ... 5-11/175. ... Throws left, bats left. ... Full name: Brian Michael Fitzgerald.

HIGH SCHOOL: Potomac (Va.).

COLLEGE: Virginia Tech.

TRANSACTIONS/CAREER NOTES: Selected by Seattle Mariners organization in 20th round of free-agent draft (June 4, 1996). ... Claimed on waivers by Colorado Rockies (August 12, 2002). ... Granted free agency (October 15, 2002).

CAREER HITTING (MLB): 0-for-0 (.000), 0 R, 0 2B, 0 3B, 0 HR, 0 RBI.

Year	League	W	L	Pct.	ERA	G	GS	CG	ShO	Sv.-Opp.	IP	H	R	ER	HR	BB-IBB	SO
1996—	Everett (N'West)	1	2	.333	6.46	21	1	0	0	1-...	39.0	56	36	28	2	8-0	31
1997—	Wisconsin (Midw.)	3	1	.750	1.94	41	0	0	0	10-...	69.2	63	16	15	4	19-2	68
1998—	Lancaster (Calif.)	1	2	.333	4.20	41	0	0	0	1-...	70.2	79	39	33	5	24-2	48
	—Orlando (Sou.)	0	0	...	2.08	2	0	0	0	1-...	4.1	5	1	1	0	1-0	4
1999—	Lancaster (Calif.)	1	3	.250	7.15	6	6	0	0	0-...	34.0	50	35	27	3	4-0	23
	—New Haven (East.)	2	2	.500	3.83	29	1	0	0	3-...	54.0	58	24	23	2	18-0	37
2000—	New Haven (East.)	6	4	.600	3.53	44	2	0	0	4-...	79.0	84	33	31	7	19-0	62
2001—	San Antonio (Texas)	4	1	.800	1.96	30	0	0	0	1-...	41.1	33	10	9	0	16-4	26
	—Tacoma (PCL)	2	1	.667	3.89	20	1	0	0	0-...	34.2	40	19	15	5	11-0	26
2002—	Tacoma (PCL)	2	3	.400	5.59	29	0	0	0	2-...	48.1	57	36	30	4	23-1	37
	—Seattle (A.L.)	0	0	...	8.53	6	0	0	0	0-0	6.1	11	8	6	2	2-0	3
	—Colorado Springs (PCL)■	1	1	.500	4.00	7	0	0	0	0-...	9.0	8	4	4	1	3-0	4
Major League totals (1 year)		0	0	...	8.53	6	0	0	0	0-0	6.1	11	8	6	2	2-0	3

FLAHERTY, JOHN — C

PERSONAL: Born October 21, 1967, in New York. ... 6-1/196. ... Bats right, throws right. ... Full name: John Timothy Flaherty.

HIGH SCHOOL: St. Joseph's Regional (Montvale, N.J.).

COLLEGE: George Washington.

TRANSACTIONS/CAREER NOTES: Selected by Boston Red Sox organization in 25th round of free-agent draft (June 1, 1988). ... Traded by Red Sox to Detroit Tigers for C Rich Rowland (April 1, 1994). ... Traded by Tigers with SS Chris Gomez to San Diego Padres for C Brad Ausmus, SS Andujar Cedeno and P Russ Spear (June 18, 1996). ... Traded by Padres to Tampa Bay Devil Rays for P Brian Boehringer and IF Andy Sheets (November 18, 1997). ... On Tampa Bay disabled list (May 26-June 20, 1998); included rehabilitation assignment to Durham (June 14-20). ... Granted free agency (October 28, 2002).

STATISTICAL NOTES: Tied for Florida State League lead with 19 passed balls in 1989. ... Had 27-game hitting streak (June 21-July 27, 1996). ... Career major league grand slams: 2.

2002 GAMES PLAYED BY POSITION (MLB): C—75.

			BATTING														FIELDING	
Year	Team (League)	Pos.	G	AB	R	H	2B	3B	HR	RBI	BB	SO	SB-CS	Avg.	OBP	SLG	E	Avg.
1988—	Elmira (NY-Penn)	C	46	162	17	38	3	0	3	16	12	23	2-1	.235	.294	.309	7	.975
1989—	Winter Haven (FSL)	C-1B	95	334	31	87	14	2	4	28	20	44	1-0	.260	.306	.350	9	.979
1990—	Pawtucket (I.L.)	C-3B	99	317	35	72	18	0	4	32	24	43	1-1	.227	.284	.322	10	.983
	—Lynchburg (Caro.)	C	1	4	0	0	0	0	0	1	0	1	0-0	.000	.000	.000	0	1.000
1991—	New Britain (East.)	C	67	225	27	65	9	0	3	18	31	22	0-2	.289	.375	.369	9	.977
	—Pawtucket (I.L.)	C	45	156	18	29	7	0	3	13	15	14	0-1	.186	.257	.288	•9	.970
1992—	Boston (A.L.)	C	35	66	3	13	2	0	0	2	3	7	0-0	.197	.229	.227	2	.982
	—Pawtucket (I.L.)	C	31	104	11	26	3	0	0	7	5	8	0-0	.250	.291	.279	4	.978
1993—	Pawtucket (I.L.)	C	105	365	29	99	22	0	6	35	26	41	0-2	.271	.327	.381	10	.986
	—Boston (A.L.)	C	13	25	3	3	2	0	0	2	2	6	0-0	.120	.214	.200	0	1.000

			BATTING														FIELDING	
Year	Team (League)	Pos.	G	AB	R	H	2B	3B	HR	RBI	BB	SO	SB-CS	Avg.	OBP	SLG	E	Avg.
1994—	Toledo (I.L.)■	C-DH	44	151	20	39	10	2	7	17	6	21	3-1	.258	.285	.490	2	.994
—	Detroit (A.L.)	C-DH	34	40	2	6	1	0	0	4	1	11	0-1	.150	.167	.175	0	1.000
1995—	Detroit (A.L.)	C	112	354	39	86	22	1	11	40	18	47	0-0	.243	.284	.404	*11	.982
1996—	Detroit (A.L.)	C	47	152	18	38	12	0	4	23	8	25	1-0	.250	.290	.408	5	.981
—	San Diego (N.L.)■	C	72	264	22	80	12	0	9	41	9	36	2-3	.303	.327	.451	5	.990
1997—	San Diego (N.L.)	C	129	439	38	120	21	1	9	46	33	62	4-4	.273	.323	.387	11	.987
1998—	Tampa Bay (A.L.)■	C	91	304	21	63	11	0	3	24	22	46	0-5	.207	.261	.273	4	.993
—	Durham (I.L.)	DH-C	6	23	1	3	1	0	0	2	1	5	0-0	.130	.160	.174	0	1.000
1999—	Tampa Bay (A.L.)	C-DH	117	446	53	124	19	0	14	71	19	64	0-2	.278	.310	.415	6	.993
2000—	Tampa Bay (A.L.)	C	109	394	36	103	15	0	10	39	20	57	0-0	.261	.296	.376	5	.993
2001—	Tampa Bay (A.L.)	C	78	248	20	59	17	1	4	29	10	33	1-0	.238	.269	.363	7	.986
2002—	Tampa Bay (A.L.)	C	76	281	27	73	20	0	4	33	15	50	2-2	.260	.296	.374	4	.992
American League totals (10 years)			712	2310	222	568	121	2	50	267	118	346	4-10	.246	.284	.365	44	.989
National League totals (2 years)			201	703	60	200	33	1	18	87	42	98	6-7	.284	.324	.411	16	.988
Major League totals (11 years)			913	3013	282	768	154	3	68	354	160	444	10-17	.255	.293	.376	60	.989

DIVISION SERIES RECORD

			BATTING														FIELDING	
Year	Team (League)	Pos.	G	AB	R	H	2B	3B	HR	RBI	BB	SO	SB-CS	Avg.	OBP	SLG	E	Avg.
1996—	San Diego (N.L.)	C	2	4	0	0	0	0	0	0	0	1	0-0	.000	.000	.000	0	1.000

FLETCHER, DARRIN C

PERSONAL: Born October 3, 1966, in Elmhurst, Ill. ... 6-2/210. ... Bats left, throws right. ... Full name: Darrin Glen Fletcher. ... Son of Tom Fletcher, pitcher with Detroit Tigers (1962); and grandson of Glen Fletcher, pitcher in Philadelphia Phillies organization (1938-48).

HIGH SCHOOL: Oakwood (Ill.).

COLLEGE: Illinois.

TRANSACTIONS/CAREER NOTES: Selected by Los Angeles Dodgers organization in sixth round of free-agent draft (June 2, 1987). ... Traded by Dodgers to Philadelphia Phillies for P Dennis Cook (September 13, 1990). ... Traded by Phillies with cash to Montreal Expos for P Barry Jones (December 9, 1991). ... On Montreal disabled list (May 12-June 15, 1992); included rehabilitation assignment to Indianapolis (May 31-June 14). ... On disabled list (June 18-July 3, 1997). ... Granted free agency (October 27, 1997). ... Signed by Toronto Blue Jays (November 26, 1997). ... On disabled list (May 30-June 14, 1998). ... On Toronto disabled list (May 1-June 1, 1999); included rehabilitation assignment to Syracuse (May 24-27). ... On disabled list (June 11-July 4, 2000; and May 6-21, 2002). ... Announced retirement (July 26, 2002).

STATISTICAL NOTES: Tied for Texas League lead in double plays by catcher with nine in 1988. ... Led Pacific Coast League catchers with 715 putouts and 787 total chances in 1990. ... Led N.L. with 12 sacrifice flies in 1994. ... Hit three home runs in one game (August 27, 2000). ... Career major league grand slams: 6.

2002 GAMES PLAYED BY POSITION (MLB): C—36; DH—4.

			BATTING														FIELDING	
Year	Team (League)	Pos.	G	AB	R	H	2B	3B	HR	RBI	BB	SO	SB-CS	Avg.	OBP	SLG	E	Avg.
1987—	Vero Beach (FSL)	C	43	124	13	33	7	0	0	15	22	12	0-2	.266	.371	.323	3	.988
1988—	San Antonio (Texas)	C	89	279	19	58	8	0	1	20	17	42	2-6	.208	.259	.247	5	*.992
1989—	Albuquerque (PCL)	C	100	315	34	86	16	1	5	44	30	38	1-5	.273	.334	.378	9	.987
—	Los Angeles (N.L.)	C	5	8	1	4	0	0	1	2	1	0	0-0	.500	.556	.875	0	1.000
1990—	Albuquerque (PCL)	C	105	350	58	102	23	1	13	65	40	37	1-1	.291	.367	.474	8	.990
—	Los Angeles (N.L.)	C	2	1	0	0	0	0	0	0	0	1	0-0	.000	.000	.000	0	...
—	Philadelphia (N.L.)■	C	9	22	3	3	1	0	0	1	1	5	0-0	.136	.174	.182	0	1.000
1991—	Scranton/W.B. (I.L.)	C-1B	90	306	39	87	13	1	8	50	23	29	1-2	.284	.334	.412	5	.991
—	Philadelphia (N.L.)	C	46	136	5	31	8	0	1	12	5	15	0-1	.228	.255	.309	2	.992
1992—	Montreal (N.L.)■	C	83	222	13	54	10	2	2	26	14	28	0-2	.243	.289	.333	2	.995
—	Indianapolis (A.A.)	C	13	51	2	13	2	0	1	9	2	10	0-0	.255	.283	.353	1	.986
1993—	Montreal (N.L.)	C	133	396	33	101	20	1	9	60	34	40	0-0	.255	.320	.379	8	.988
1994—	Montreal (N.L.)	C	94	285	28	74	18	1	10	57	25	23	0-0	.260	.314	.435	2	.996
1995—	Montreal (N.L.)	C	110	350	42	100	21	1	11	45	32	23	0-1	.286	.351	.446	4	.994
1996—	Montreal (N.L.)	C	127	394	41	105	22	0	12	57	27	42	0-0	.266	.321	.414	6	.992
1997—	Montreal (N.L.)	C	96	310	39	86	20	1	17	55	17	35	1-1	.277	.323	.513	4	.994
1998—	Toronto (A.L.)■	C-DH	124	407	37	115	23	1	9	52	25	39	0-0	.283	.328	.410	8	.991
1999—	Toronto (A.L.)	C	115	412	48	120	26	0	18	80	26	47	0-0	.291	.339	.485	2	.997
—	Syracuse (I.L.)	C-DH	4	15	0	4	0	0	0	0	1	1	0-0	.267	.313	.267	0	1.000
2000—	Toronto (A.L.)	C	122	416	43	133	19	1	20	58	20	45	1-0	.320	.355	.514	4	.994
2001—	Toronto (A.L.)	C-DH	134	416	36	94	20	0	11	56	24	43	0-1	.226	.274	.353	4	.995
2002—	Toronto (A.L.)	C-DH	45	127	8	28	6	0	3	22	4	13	0-0	.220	.239	.339	1	.995
American League totals (5 years)			540	1778	172	490	94	2	61	268	99	187	1-1	.276	.318	.434	19	.994
National League totals (9 years)			705	2124	205	558	120	6	63	315	156	212	1-5	.263	.317	.414	28	.993
Major League totals (14 years)			1245	3902	377	1048	214	8	124	583	255	399	2-6	.269	.318	.423	47	.993

ALL-STAR GAME RECORD

	AB	R	H	2B	3B	HR	RBI	BB	SO	SB-CS	Avg.	OBP	SLG	E	Avg.
All-Star Game totals (1 year)	0	0	0	0	0	0	0	0	0	0-0	...	...	...	0	1.000

FLORES, JOSE SS ATHLETICS

PERSONAL: Born June 28, 1973, in New York. ... 5-11/180. ... Bats right, throws right. ... Full name: Jose Carlos Flores.

HIGH SCHOOL: Louis D. Brandeis (N.Y.).

COLLEGE: Texas.

TRANSACTIONS/CAREER NOTES: Selected by Philadelphia Phillies organization in 34th round of free-agent draft (June 2, 1994). ... Traded by Phillies to Seattle Mariners for SS Domingo Cedeno (July 7, 1999). ... Granted free agency (October 15, 2000). ... Signed by Milwaukee Brewers organization (January 8, 2001). ... Traded by Brewers with P Kane Davis and P Juan Acevedo to Colorado Rockies for P Mark Leiter, P Mike DeJean and SS Elvis Pena (April 4, 2001). ... Granted free agency (October 15, 2001). ... Signed by Oakland Athletics organization (October 26, 2001). ... On Sacramento disabled list (May 28-June 11, 2002).

2002 GAMES PLAYED BY POSITION (MLB): 2B—2; DH—1; SS—1.

									BATTING								FIELDING	
Year	Team (League)	Pos.	G	AB	R	H	2B	3B	HR	RBI	BB	SO	SB-CS	Avg.	OBP	SLG	E	Avg.
1994—	Batavia (NY-Penn)	SS-2B	68	229	41	58	7	3	0	16	41	31	23-8	.253	.378	.310	20	.935
1995—	Clearwater (FSL)	3B-SS-2B	49	185	25	41	4	3	1	19	15	27	12-5	.222	.293	.292	12	.938
—	Piedmont (S.Atl.)	3B-2B-SS	61	186	22	49	7	0	0	19	24	29	11-8	.263	.350	.301	12	.937
1996—	Clearwater (FSL)	SS-2B-3B	84	281	39	64	6	5	1	39	34	42	15-2	.228	.317	.295	22	.948
—	Scranton/W.B. (I.L.)	2B-SS	26	70	10	18	1	0	0	3	12	10	0-1	.257	.376	.271	4	.955
1997—	Scranton/W.B. (I.L.)	2B-3B-SS	71	204	32	51	14	1	1	18	28	51	3-1	.250	.343	.343	11	.957
1998—	Scranton/W.B. (I.L.)	SS-3B-2B	98	345	53	104	18	2	6	34	49	45	12-6	.301	.389	.417	14	.964
1999—	Scranton/W.B. (I.L.)	SS	64	228	35	56	6	2	0	18	37	43	13-3	.246	.368	.289	11	.960
—	Tacoma (PCL)■	SS-3B	42	143	33	44	6	1	3	15	37	23	4-3	.308	.460	.427	11	.947
2000—	Tacoma (PCL)	SS-3B-2B	91	328	53	93	14	4	3	30	53	44	19-7	.284	.388	.378	23	.930
—	New Haven (East.)	SS	12	38	5	7	3	0	0	1	7	5	0-0	.184	.340	.263	2	.960
2001—	Colo. Springs (PCL)■	S-3-2-O-1	100	316	61	93	21	5	2	36	48	57	8-2	.294	.391	.411	18	.950
2002—	Sacramento (PCL)■	SS-OF-2B-3B	95	363	64	111	19	1	2	38	56	53	16-4	.306	.397	.380	15	.959
—	Oakland (A.L.)	2B-DH-SS	7	3	2	0	0	0	0	0	1	0	1-1	.000	.400	.000	0	1.000
Major League totals (1 year)			7	3	2	0	0	0	0	0	1	0	1-1	.000	.400	.000	0	1.000

FLORES, RANDY — P — RANGERS

PERSONAL: Born July 31, 1975, in Bellflower, Calif. ... 6-0/180. ... Throws left, bats left. ... Full name: Randy Alan Flores.
HIGH SCHOOL: El Rancho (Pico Rivera, Calif.).
COLLEGE: Southern California.
TRANSACTIONS/CAREER NOTES: Selected by New York Yankees organization in ninth round of free-agent draft (June 3, 1997). ... Traded by Yankees with P Rosman Garcia to Texas Rangers (October 11, 2001), completing deal in which Rangers traded 2B Randy Velarde to Yankees for two players to be named later (August 31, 2001). ... Claimed on waivers by Colorado Rockies (July 18, 2002).
CAREER HITTING (MLB): 0-for-4 (.000), 0 R, 0 2B, 0 3B, 0 HR, 0 RBI.

Year	League	W	L	Pct.	ERA	G	GS	CG	ShO	Sv.-Opp.	IP	H	R	ER	HR	BB-IBB	SO
1997—	Oneonta (NY-Penn)	4	4	.500	3.25	13	13	2	1	0-...	74.2	64	32	27	3	23-1	70
1998—	Tampa (FSL)	1	2	.333	6.46	5	5	0	0	0-...	23.2	28	23	17	2	16-2	15
—	Greensboro (S.Atl.)	12	7	.632	2.62	21	20	2	1	0-...	130.2	119	48	38	6	33-0	139
1999—	Tampa (FSL)	11	4	.733	2.87	21	20	1	1	0-...	135.0	118	56	43	4	38-0	99
—	Norwich (East.)	0	1	.000	6.48	4	4	0	0	0-...	25.0	32	20	18	0	11-1	19
2000—	Norwich (East.)	10	9	.526	2.94	31	20	3	0	1-...	141.0	138	64	46	8	58-1	97
—	Columbus (I.L.)	1	2	.333	7.33	4	4	0	0	0-...	23.1	43	21	19	3	7-0	16
2001—	Columbus (I.L.)	0	1	.000	4.76	3	0	0	0	0-...	5.2	5	4	3	2	2-0	4
—	Norwich (East.)	14	6	.700	2.78	25	25	3	2	0-...	158.2	156	64	49	13	63-0	115
2002—	Oklahoma (PCL)■	1	1	.500	5.75	15	0	0	0	1-...	20.1	22	13	13	1	5-1	16
—	Texas (A.L.)	0	0	...	4.50	20	0	0	0	1-2	12.0	11	7	6	2	8-2	7
—	Colorado Springs (PCL)■	2	2	.500	3.28	7	7	0	0	0-...	35.2	36	15	13	1	18-0	27
—	Colorado (N.L.)	0	2	.000	9.53	8	2	0	0	0-0	17.0	29	19	18	5	8-1	7
A.L. totals (1 year)		0	0	...	4.50	20	0	0	0	1-2	12.0	11	7	6	2	8-2	7
N.L. totals (1 year)		0	2	.000	9.53	8	2	0	0	0-0	17.0	29	19	18	5	8-1	7
Major League totals (1 year)		0	2	.000	7.45	28	2	0	0	1-2	29.0	40	26	24	7	16-3	14

FLOYD, CLIFF — OF

PERSONAL: Born December 5, 1972, in Chicago. ... 6-4/260. ... Bats left, throws right. ... Full name: Cornelius Clifford Floyd.
HIGH SCHOOL: Thornwood (South Holland, Ill.).
TRANSACTIONS/CAREER NOTES: Selected by Montreal Expos organization in first round (14th pick overall) of free-agent draft (June 3, 1991). ... On disabled list (May 16-September 11, 1995). ... Traded by Expos to Florida Marlins for OF Joe Orsulak and P Dustin Hermanson (March 26, 1997). ... On Florida disabled list (May 9-24 and June 21-September 1, 1997); included rehabilitation assignment to Charlotte (July 20-September 1). ... On Florida disabled list (March 30-April 27 and June 20-September 7, 1999); included rehabilitation assigment to Calgary (August 28-September 7). ... On disabled list (July 29-August 29, 2000). ... Traded by Marlins with P Claudio Vargas, OF/2B Wilton Guerrero, cash considerations and a player to be named later to Expos for P Carl Pavano, P Graeme Lloyd, IF Mike Mordecai and P Justin Wayne (July 11, 2002); Expos acquired P Don Levinski to complete deal (August 5, 2002). ... Traded by Expos to Boston Red Sox for P Seung Song, P Sun-Woo Kim and a player to be named later (July 30, 2002). ... Granted free agency (October 28, 2002).
HONORS: Named Minor League Player of the Year by The Sporting News (1993). ... Named Eastern League Most Valuable Player (1993).
STATISTICAL NOTES: Led South Atlantic League with 261 total bases and nine intentional bases on balls received in 1992. ... Led Eastern League with .600 slugging percentage and 12 intentional bases on balls received in 1993. ... Had 18-game hitting streak (June 5-24, 2001). ... Career major league grand slams: 2.
MISCELLANEOUS: Holds Florida Marlins all-time record for most doubles (167).
2002 GAMES PLAYED BY POSITION (MLB): OF—119; DH—20.

									BATTING								FIELDING	
Year	Team (League)	Pos.	G	AB	R	H	2B	3B	HR	RBI	BB	SO	SB-CS	Avg.	OBP	SLG	E	Avg.
1991—	GC Expos (GCL)	1B	56	214	35	56	9	3	6	30	19	37	13-3	.262	.335	.416	15	.970
1992—	Albany (S.Atl.)	OF-1B	134	516	83	157	24	*16	16	*97	45	75	32-11	.304	.368	.506	17	.964
—	W. Palm Beach (FSL)	OF	1	4	0	0	0	0	0	1	0	1	0-0	.000	.000	.000	0	1.000
1993—	Harrisburg (East.)	1B-OF	101	380	82	125	17	4	•26	*101	54	71	31-10	.329	.417	.600	19	.969
—	Ottawa (I.L.)	1B	32	125	12	30	2	2	2	18	16	34	2-2	.240	.329	.336	5	.983
—	Montreal (N.L.)	1B	10	31	3	7	0	0	1	2	0	9	0-0	.226	.226	.323	0	1.000
1994—	Montreal (N.L.)	1B-OF	100	334	43	94	19	4	4	41	24	63	10-3	.281	.332	.398	6	.990
1995—	Montreal (N.L.)	1B-OF	29	69	6	9	1	0	1	8	7	22	3-0	.130	.221	.188	3	.981
1996—	Ottawa (I.L.)	OF-DH-3B	20	76	7	23	3	1	1	8	7	20	2-2	.303	.369	.408	2	.951
—	Montreal (N.L.)	OF-1B	117	227	29	55	15	4	6	26	30	52	7-1	.242	.340	.423	5	.957
1997—	Florida (N.L.)■	OF-1B	61	137	23	32	9	1	6	19	24	33	6-2	.234	.354	.445	3	.971
—	Charlotte (I.L.)	OF-1B	39	131	27	48	10	0	9	33	10	29	7-2	.366	.415	.649	1	.988
1998—	Florida (N.L.)	OF-DH	153	588	85	166	45	3	22	90	47	112	27-14	.282	.337	.481	7	.974
1999—	Florida (N.L.)	OF-DH	69	251	37	76	19	1	11	49	30	47	5-6	.303	.379	.518	6	.952
—	Calgary (PCL)	OF	9	31	6	12	1	0	3	8	2	8	0-1	.387	.424	.710	0	1.000

F

Year	Team (League)	Pos.	G	AB	R	H	2B	3B	HR	RBI	BB	SO	SB-CS	Avg.	OBP	SLG	E	Avg.
			BATTING														FIELDING	
2000—	Florida (N.L.)	OF-DH	121	420	75	126	30	0	22	91	50	82	24-3	.300	.378	.529	9	.951
2001—	Florida (N.L.)	OF-DH	149	555	123	176	44	4	31	103	59	101	18-3	.317	.390	.578	8	.972
2002—	Florida (N.L.)	OF-DH	84	296	49	85	20	0	18	57	58	68	10-5	.287	.414	.537	3	.983
—	Montreal (N.L.)■	OF	15	53	7	11	2	0	3	4	3	10	1-0	.208	.263	.415	1	.941
—	Boston (A.L.)■	OF-DH	47	171	30	54	21	0	7	18	15	28	4-0	.316	.374	.561	1	.977
American League totals (1 year)			47	171	30	54	21	0	7	18	15	28	4-0	.316	.374	.561	1	.977
National League totals (10 years)			908	2961	480	837	204	17	125	490	332	599	111-37	.283	.360	.490	51	.976
Major League totals (10 years)			955	3132	510	891	225	17	132	508	347	627	115-37	.284	.361	.494	52	.976

DIVISION SERIES RECORD

Year	Team (League)	Pos.	G	AB	R	H	2B	3B	HR	RBI	BB	SO	SB-CS	Avg.	OBP	SLG	E	Avg.
			BATTING														FIELDING	
1997—	Florida (N.L.)		Did not play.															

CHAMPIONSHIP SERIES RECORD

Year	Team (League)	Pos.	G	AB	R	H	2B	3B	HR	RBI	BB	SO	SB-CS	Avg.	OBP	SLG	E	Avg.
			BATTING														FIELDING	
1997—	Florida (N.L.)		Did not play.															

WORLD SERIES RECORD

NOTES: Member of World Series championship team (1997).

Year	Team (League)	Pos.	G	AB	R	H	2B	3B	HR	RBI	BB	SO	SB-CS	Avg.	OBP	SLG	E	Avg.
			BATTING														FIELDING	
1997—	Florida (N.L.)	PH-DH	4	2	1	0	0	0	0	0	1	1	0-0	.000	.333	.000	...	...

ALL-STAR GAME RECORD

	AB	R	H	2B	3B	HR	RBI	BB	SO	SB-CS	Avg.	OBP	SLG	E	Avg.
All-Star Game totals (1 year)	2	0	0	0	0	0	0	0	0	0-0	.000	.000	.000	0	...

FOGG, JOSH — P — PIRATES

PERSONAL: Born December 13, 1976, in Lynn, Mass. ... 6-0/202. ... Throws right, bats right. ... Full name: Joshua Smith Fogg.
HIGH SCHOOL: Cadinal Gibbons (Fort Lauderdale, Fla.).
COLLEGE: Florida.
TRANSACTIONS/CAREER NOTES: Selected by Chicago White Sox organization in third round of free-agent draft (June 2, 1998). ... Traded by White Sox with P Kip Wells and P Sean Lowe to Pittsburgh Pirates for P Todd Ritchie and C Lee Evans (December 13, 2001).
CAREER HITTING (MLB): 7-for-58 (.121), 2 R, 0 2B, 0 3B, 0 HR, 1 RBI.

Year	League	W	L	Pct.	ERA	G	GS	CG	ShO	Sv.-Opp.	IP	H	R	ER	HR	BB-IBB	SO
1998—	Arizona White Sox (Ariz.)	1	0	1.000	0.00	2	0	0	0	0-...	4.0	0	0	0	0	1-0	5
—	Hickory (S.Atl.)	1	3	.250	2.18	8	8	0	0	0-...	41.1	36	17	10	4	13-0	29
—	Winston-Salem (Caro.)	0	1	.000	0.00	1	0	0	0	0-...	1.0	2	2	0	0	0-0	2
1999—	Winston-Salem (Caro.)	10	5	.667	2.96	17	17	1	1	0-...	103.1	93	44	34	3	33-0	109
—	Birmingham (Sou.)	3	2	.600	5.89	10	10	0	0	0-...	55.0	66	37	36	8	18-0	40
2000—	Birmingham (Sou.)	11	7	.611	2.57	27	27	2	0	0-...	192.1	190	68	55	7	44-2	136
2001—	Charlotte (I.L.)	4	7	.364	4.79	40	16	0	0	4-...	114.2	129	68	61	19	30-1	89
—	Chicago (A.L.)	0	0	...	2.03	11	0	0	0	0-0	13.1	10	3	3	0	3-1	17
2002—	Pittsburgh (N.L.)■	12	12	.500	4.35	33	33	0	0	0-0	194.1	199	102	94	28	69-12	113
A.L. totals (1 year)		0	0	...	2.03	11	0	0	0	0-0	13.1	10	3	3	0	3-1	17
N.L. totals (1 year)		12	12	.500	4.35	33	33	0	0	0-0	194.1	199	102	94	28	69-12	113
Major League totals (2 years)		12	12	.500	4.20	44	33	0	0	0-0	207.2	209	105	97	28	72-13	130

FOPPERT, JESSE — P — GIANTS

PERSONAL: Born July 10, 1980, in Reading, Pa. ... 6-6/210. ... Throws right, bats right. ... Full name: Jesse W. Foppert.
COLLEGE: University of San Francisco.
TRANSACTIONS/CAREER NOTES: Selected by San Francisco Giants organization in second round of free-agent draft (June 5, 2001).

Year	League	W	L	Pct.	ERA	G	GS	CG	ShO	Sv.-Opp.	IP	H	R	ER	HR	BB-IBB	SO
2001—	Salem-Kaizer (N'West)	8	1	.889	*1.93	14	14	0	0	0-...	70.0	35	18	15	7	23-0	88
2002—	Shreveport (Texas)	3	3	.500	2.79	11	11	1	0	0-...	61.1	44	22	19	3	21-0	74
—	Fresno (PCL)	3	6	.333	3.99	14	14	0	0	0-...	79.0	71	37	35	12	35-0	109

F

FORDYCE, BROOK — C — ORIOLES

PERSONAL: Born May 7, 1970, in New London, Conn. ... 6-0/190. ... Bats right, throws right. ... Full name: Brook Alexander Fordyce. ... Name pronounced FOR-dice.
HIGH SCHOOL: St. Bernard (Uncasville, Conn.).
TRANSACTIONS/CAREER NOTES: Selected by New York Mets organization in third round of free-agent draft (June 5, 1989). ... On disabled list (June 19-July 2 and July 18-August 30, 1994). ... On suspended list (August 30-September 1, 1994). ... Claimed on waivers by Cleveland Indians (May 15, 1995). ... Granted free agency (October 16, 1995). ... Signed by Cincinnati Reds organization (December 7, 1995). ... On disabled list (July 16-August 5, 1997); included rehabilitation assignment to Indianapolis (July 21-August 5). ... On Cincinnati disabled list (July 13-August 12, 1998); included rehabilitation assignment to Indianapolis (August 4-12). ... Traded by Reds to Chicago White Sox for P Jake Meyer (March 25, 1999). ... On Chicago disabled list (March 25-May 23, 2000); included rehabilitation assignment to Charlotte (May 5-23). ... Traded by White Sox with P Miguel Felix, P Juan Figueroa and P Jason Lakman to Baltimore Orioles for C Charles Johnson and DH Harold Baines (July 29, 2000).
STATISTICAL NOTES: Led Appalachian League catchers with .991 fielding percentage in 1989. ... Tied for South Atlantic League lead in grounding into double plays with 18 in 1990. ... Led South Atlantic League with 30 passed balls in 1990. ... Led Eastern League catchers with 713 putouts, 79 assists and 795 total chances in 1992. ... Led International League catchers with 735 putouts and 810 total chances and tied for lead in double plays by catcher with 11 in 1993. ... Tied for International League lead in double plays by catcher with nine in 1996.
2002 GAMES PLAYED BY POSITION (MLB): C—55.

Year	Team (League)	Pos.	G	AB	R	H	2B	3B	HR	RBI	BB	SO	SB-CS	Avg.	OBP	SLG	E	Avg.
			BATTING														FIELDING	
1989—	Kingsport (Appl.)	C-OF-3B	69	226	45	74	15	0	9	38	30	26	10-6	.327	.405	.513	4	†.988
1990—	Columbia (S.Atl.)	C	104	372	45	117	29	1	10	54	39	42	4-1	.315	.378	*.478	15	.977
1991—	St. Lucie (FSL)	C	115	406	42	97	19	3	7	55	37	50	4-5	.239	.305	.352	13	.982
1992—	Binghamton (East.)	C	118	425	59	118	30	0	11	61	37	78	1-2	.278	.337	.426	3	*.996
1993—	Norfolk (I.L.)	C	116	409	33	106	21	2	2	41	26	62	2-2	.259	.307	.335	8	.990
1994—	Norfolk (I.L.)	C-DH	66	229	26	60	13	3	3	32	19	26	1-0	.262	.320	.384	7	.981
1995—	New York (N.L.)	PH-PR	4	2	1	1	1	0	0	0	1	0	0-0	.500	.667	1.000	...	...
—	Buffalo (A.A.)■	C-OF-DH	58	176	18	44	13	0	0	9	14	20	1-0	.250	.313	.324	3	.991
1996—	Indianapolis (A.A.)■	C-DH-1B	107	374	48	103	20	3	16	64	25	56	2-1	.275	.319	.473	4	†.994
—	Cincinnati (N.L.)	C	4	7	0	2	1	0	0	1	3	1	0-0	.286	.500	.429	0	1.000
1997—	Cincinnati (N.L.)	C-DH	47	96	7	20	5	0	1	8	8	15	2-0	.208	.267	.292	3	.983
—	Indianapolis (A.A.)	C-DH	12	47	7	11	2	0	2	6	5	6	1-1	.234	.321	.404	0	1.000
1998—	Cincinnati (N.L.)	C	57	146	8	37	9	0	3	14	11	28	0-1	.253	.306	.377	7	.978
—	Indianapolis (I.L.)	C	6	24	4	6	1	0	2	3	1	2	0-0	.250	.280	.542	0	1.000
1999—	Chicago (A.L.)■	C	105	333	36	99	25	1	9	49	21	48	2-0	.297	.343	.459	8	.987
2000—	Charlotte (I.L.)	C	17	67	9	16	5	0	2	12	8	13	0-1	.239	.316	.403	0	1.000
—	Chicago (A.L.)	C	40	125	18	34	7	1	5	21	6	23	0-0	.272	.313	.464	0	1.000
—	Baltimore (A.L.)■	C	53	177	23	57	11	0	9	28	11	27	0-0	.322	.361	.537	4	.988
2001—	Baltimore (A.L.)	C	95	292	30	61	18	0	5	19	21	56	1-2	.209	.268	.322	10	.983
2002—	Baltimore (A.L.)	C	56	130	7	30	8	0	1	8	9	19	1-0	.231	.301	.315	4	.986
American League totals (4 years)			349	1057	114	281	69	2	29	125	68	173	4-2	.266	.316	.417	26	.987
National League totals (4 years)			112	251	16	60	16	0	4	23	23	44	2-1	.239	.302	.351	10	.980
Major League totals (8 years)			461	1308	130	341	85	2	33	148	91	217	6-3	.261	.314	.404	36	.986

FOSSUM, CASEY — P — RED SOX

PERSONAL: Born January 6, 1978, in Cherry Hill, N.J. ... 6-1/165. ... Throws left, bats both. ... Full name: Casey Paul Fossum.
HIGH SCHOOL: Midway (Waco, Texas).
COLLEGE: Texas A&M.
TRANSACTIONS/CAREER NOTES: Selected by Arizona Diamondbacks organization in sixth round of free-agent draft (June 4, 1996); did not sign. ... Selected by Boston Red Sox organization as "sandwich pick" between first and second round of free-agent draft (June 2, 1999); pick received as part of compensation for Arizona Diamondbacks signing Type A free agent P Greg Swindell.
CAREER HITTING (MLB): 0-for-0 (.000), 0 R, 0 2B, 0 3B, 0 HR, 0 RBI.

Year	League	W	L	Pct.	ERA	G	GS	CG	ShO	Sv.-Opp.	IP	H	R	ER	HR	BB-IBB	SO
1999—	Lowell (NY-Penn)	0	1	.000	1.26	5	5	0	0	0-...	14.1	6	2	2	1	5-0	16
2000—	Sarasota (FSL)	9	10	.474	3.44	27	27	3	*3	0-...	149.1	147	71	57	7	36-0	143
2001—	Trenton (East.)	3	7	.300	2.83	20	20	0	0	0-...	117.2	102	47	37	5	28-0	130
—	Boston (A.L.)	3	2	.600	4.87	13	7	0	0	0-0	44.1	44	26	24	4	20-1	26
2002—	Boston (A.L.)	5	4	.556	3.46	43	12	0	0	1-1	106.2	113	56	41	12	30-0	101
—	Pawtucket (I.L.)	0	3	.000	3.96	5	3	1	0	0-...	25.0	34	15	11	1	6-0	28
Major League totals (2 years)		8	6	.571	3.87	56	19	0	0	1-1	151.0	157	82	65	16	50-1	127

FOSTER, JOHN — P — BRAVES

PERSONAL: Born May 17, 1978, in Stockton, Calif. ... 6-0/200. ... Throws left, bats left. ... Full name: John Norman Foster.
COLLEGE: Lewis-Clark State (Idaho).
TRANSACTIONS/CAREER NOTES: Selected by Atlanta Braves organization in 25th round of free-agent draft (June 2, 1999). ... On Atlanta disabled list (August 18, 2002-remainder of season); included rehabilitation assignment to Richmond (August 28-September 3).
STATISTICAL NOTES: Tied for Southern League lead with 11 sacrifice hits allowed and seven intentional bases on balls allowed in 2001. ... Led International League with eight intentional bases on balls issued in 2002.
CAREER HITTING (MLB): 0-for-0 (.000), 0 R, 0 2B, 0 3B, 0 HR, 0 RBI.

Year	League	W	L	Pct.	ERA	G	GS	CG	ShO	Sv.-Opp.	IP	H	R	ER	HR	BB-IBB	SO
1999—	Danville (Appl.)	4	1	.800	1.38	18	0	0	0	1-...	39.0	28	10	6	0	6-0	36
2000—	Myrtle Beach (Caro.)	2	1	.667	1.85	38	0	0	0	3-...	48.2	48	13	10	2	14-4	46
2001—	Greenville (Sou.)	8	7	.533	3.01	50	0	0	0	7-...	68.2	71	30	23	6	33-7	63
2002—	Richmond (I.L.)	8	4	.667	4.21	55	0	0	0	8-...	62.0	67	30	29	5	28-8	48
—	Atlanta (N.L.)	1	0	1.000	10.80	5	0	0	0	0-0	5.0	6	6	6	3	6-0	6
Major League totals (1 year)		1	0	1.000	10.80	5	0	0	0	0-0	5.0	6	6	6	3	6-0	6

FOULKE, KEITH — P — WHITE SOX

PERSONAL: Born October 19, 1972, in San Diego. ... 6-0/210. ... Throws right, bats right. ... Full name: Keith Charles Foulke.
HIGH SCHOOL: Hargrove (Huffman, Texas).
JUNIOR COLLEGE: Galveston (Texas) College.
COLLEGE: Lewis-Clark State (Idaho).
TRANSACTIONS/CAREER NOTES: Selected by San Francisco Giants organization in ninth round of free-agent draft (June 2, 1994). ... Traded by Giants with SS Mike Caruso, OF Brian Manning, P Lorenzo Barcelo, P Bobby Howry and P Ken Vining to Chicago White Sox for P Wilson Alvarez, P Danny Darwin and P Roberto Hernandez (July 31, 1997). ... On disabled list (August 28, 1998-remainder of season). ... On suspended list (May 5-7, 2000).
CAREER HITTING (MLB): 2-for-16 (.125), 0 R, 0 2B, 0 3B, 0 HR, 0 RBI.

Year	League	W	L	Pct.	ERA	G	GS	CG	ShO	Sv.-Opp.	IP	H	R	ER	HR	BB-IBB	SO
1994—	Everett (N'West)	2	0	1.000	0.93	4	4	0	0	0-...	19.1	17	4	2	0	3-0	22
1995—	San Jose (Calif.)	13	6	.684	3.50	28	26	2	1	0-...	177.1	166	85	69	16	32-0	168
1996—	Shreveport (Texas)	12	7	.632	*2.76	27	27	4	2	0-...	*182.2	149	61	56	16	35-0	129
1997—	Phoenix (PCL)	5	4	.556	4.50	12	12	0	0	0-...	76.0	79	38	38	11	15-0	54
—	San Francisco (N.L.)	1	5	.167	8.26	11	8	0	0	0-1	44.2	60	41	41	9	18-1	33
—	Nashville (A.A.)■	0	0	...	5.79	1	1	0	0	0-...	4.2	8	3	3	1	0-0	4
—	Chicago (A.L.)	3	0	1.000	3.45	16	0	0	0	3-5	28.2	28	11	11	4	5-1	21

Year	League	W	L	Pct.	ERA	G	GS	CG	ShO	Sv.-Opp.	IP	H	R	ER	HR	BB-IBB	SO
1998—	Chicago (A.L.)	3	2	.600	4.13	54	0	0	0	1-2	65.1	51	31	30	9	20-3	57
1999—	Chicago (A.L.)	3	3	.500	2.22	67	0	0	0	9-13	105.1	72	28	26	11	21-4	123
2000—	Chicago (A.L.)	3	1	.750	2.97	72	0	0	0	34-39	88.0	66	31	29	9	22-2	91
2001—	Chicago (A.L.)	4	9	.308	2.33	72	0	0	0	42-45	81.0	57	21	21	3	22-1	75
2002—	Chicago (A.L.)	2	4	.333	2.90	65	0	0	0	11-14	77.2	65	26	25	7	13-2	58
A.L. totals (6 years)		18	19	.486	2.87	346	0	0	0	100-118	446.0	339	148	142	43	103-13	425
N.L. totals (1 year)		1	5	.167	8.26	11	8	0	0	0-1	44.2	60	41	41	9	18-1	33
Major League totals (6 years)		19	24	.442	3.36	357	8	0	0	100-119	490.2	399	189	183	52	121-14	458

DIVISION SERIES RECORD

Year	League	W	L	Pct.	ERA	G	GS	CG	ShO	Sv.-Opp.	IP	H	R	ER	HR	BB-IBB	SO
2000—	Chicago (A.L.)	0	1	.000	11.57	2	0	0	0	0-0	2.1	4	3	3	2	2-0	2

FOX, ANDY — IF — MARLINS

PERSONAL: Born January 12, 1971, in Sacramento. ... 6-4/202. ... Bats left, throws right. ... Full name: Andrew Junipero Fox.
HIGH SCHOOL: Christian Brothers (Sacramento).
TRANSACTIONS/CAREER NOTES: Selected by New York Yankees organization in second round of free-agent draft (June 5, 1989). ... On disabled list (June 11-21, 1991; April 9-22, 1992 and June 10-August 1, 1993). ... On Columbus disabled list (August 5-19, 1997). ... Traded by Yankees to Arizona Diamondbacks for P Marty Janzen and P Todd Erdos (March 8, 1998). ... On disabled list (August 28-September 11, 1999). ... On Arizona disabled list (March 23-April 17, 2000); included rehabilitation assignments to El Paso (April 10-14) and Tucson (April 15-17). ... Traded by Diamondbacks to Florida Marlins for OF Danny Bautista (June 9, 2000). ... On Florida disabled list (April 11-July 12, 2001); included rehabilitation assignments to Calgary (June 5-15 and July 2-9).
STATISTICAL NOTES: Led Carolina League third basemen with 96 putouts in 1992. ... Led Eastern League third basemen with 30 errors in 1994. ... Led International League third basemen with 22 double plays in 1995.
2002 GAMES PLAYED BY POSITION (MLB): SS—112; 2B—7; 3B—4; OF—1.

			BATTING														FIELDING	
Year	Team (League)	Pos.	G	AB	R	H	2B	3B	HR	RBI	BB	SO	SB-CS	Avg.	OBP	SLG	E	Avg.
1989—	GC Yankees (GCL)	3B	40	141	26	35	9	2	3	25	31	29	6-1	.248	.386	.404	10	.920
1990—	Greensboro (S.Atl.)	3B	134	455	68	99	19	4	9	55	92	132	26-5	.218	.353	.336	*45	.880
1991—	Prince William (Caro.)	3B	126	417	60	96	22	2	10	46	81	104	15-13	.230	.357	.365	*29	.920
1992—	Prince William (Caro.)	3B-SS	125	473	75	113	18	3	7	42	54	81	28-14	.239	.325	.334	27	.937
1993—	Albany/Colonie (East.)	3B	65	236	44	65	16	1	3	24	32	54	12-6	.275	.362	.390	19	.917
1994—	Albany/Colonie (East.)	3B-SS-2B	121	472	75	105	20	3	11	43	62	102	22-13	.222	.315	.347	†34	.916
1995—	Norwich (East.)	SS	44	175	23	36	3	5	5	17	19	36	8-1	.206	.282	.366	9	.958
—	Columbus (I.L.)	3B-SS-OF-2B	82	302	61	105	16	6	9	37	43	41	22-4	.348	.432	.530	9	.970
1996—	New York (A.L.)	2-3-S-DH-O	113	189	26	37	4	0	3	13	20	28	11-3	.196	.276	.265	12	.955
1997—	Columbus (I.L.)	3-2-S-O-DH	95	318	66	87	11	4	6	33	54	64	28-11	.274	.380	.390	14	.959
—	New York (A.L.)	3-2-DH-S-O	22	31	13	7	1	0	0	1	7	9	2-1	.226	.368	.258	1	.980
1998—	Arizona (N.L.)■	2-O-3-1	139	502	67	139	21	6	9	44	43	97	14-7	.277	.355	.396	8	.984
1999—	Arizona (N.L.)	SS-3B	99	274	34	70	12	2	6	33	33	61	4-1	.255	.351	.380	14	.955
2000—	El Paso (Texas)	3B-SS-OF	4	15	3	6	2	0	0	4	2	2	1-1	.400	.471	.533	2	.714
—	Tucson (PCL)	2B-3B-SS	3	13	1	3	0	1	0	3	0	1	0-1	.231	.231	.385	1	.917
—	Arizona (N.L.)	3B-OF-1B	31	86	10	18	4	0	1	10	4	16	2-1	.209	.244	.291	2	.962
—	Florida (N.L.)■	SS-OF-3B-2B	69	164	19	40	4	2	3	10	18	37	8-3	.244	.330	.348	11	.938
2001—	Florida (N.L.)	SS-3B-2B-OF	54	81	8	15	0	1	3	7	15	17	1-0	.185	.327	.321	3	.957
—	Calgary (PCL)	2-S-O-1-3	11	42	10	18	2	1	2	8	3	2	1-1	.429	.478	.667	1	.971
2002—	Florida (N.L.)	S-2-3-O	133	435	55	109	14	5	4	41	49	94	31-7	.251	.338	.333	18	.966
American League totals (2 years)			135	220	39	44	5	0	3	14	27	37	13-4	.200	.290	.264	13	.959
National League totals (5 years)			525	1542	193	391	55	16	26	145	162	322	60-19	.254	.339	.361	56	.966
Major League totals (7 years)			660	1762	232	435	60	16	29	159	189	359	73-23	.247	.333	.348	69	.964

DIVISION SERIES RECORD

			BATTING														FIELDING	
Year	Team (League)	Pos.	G	AB	R	H	2B	3B	HR	RBI	BB	SO	SB-CS	Avg.	OBP	SLG	E	Avg.
1996—	New York (A.L.)	DH-PR	2	0	0	0	0	0	0	0	0	0	0-0	...	...	...	...	...
1997—	New York (A.L.)	2B-PR	2	0	0	0	0	0	0	0	0	0	0-0	...	...	...	0	...
1999—	Arizona (N.L.)	SS	1	3	0	0	0	0	0	0	0	1	0-0	.000	.000	.000	1	.750
Division series totals (3 years)			5	3	0	0	0	0	0	0	0	1	0-0	.000	.000	.000	1	.750

CHAMPIONSHIP SERIES RECORD

			BATTING														FIELDING	
Year	Team (League)	Pos.	G	AB	R	H	2B	3B	HR	RBI	BB	SO	SB-CS	Avg.	OBP	SLG	E	Avg.
1996—	New York (A.L.)	DH-PR	2	0	0	0	0	0	0	0	0	0	0-0	...	...	...	...	...

WORLD SERIES RECORD

NOTES: Member of World Series championship team (1996).

			BATTING														FIELDING	
Year	Team (League)	Pos.	G	AB	R	H	2B	3B	HR	RBI	BB	SO	SB-CS	Avg.	OBP	SLG	E	Avg.
1996—	New York (A.L.)	2B-PR-3B	4	0	1	0	0	0	0	0	0	0	0-0	...	...	...	0	1.000

FOX, CHAD — P

PERSONAL: Born September 3, 1970, in Coronado, Calif. ... 6-3/206. ... Throws right, bats right. ... Full name: Chad Douglas Fox.
HIGH SCHOOL: Westfield (Houston).
JUNIOR COLLEGE: Blinn College (Texas).
COLLEGE: Tarleton State (Texas).
TRANSACTIONS/CAREER NOTES: Selected by Cincinnati Reds organization in 23rd round of free-agent draft (June 1, 1992). ... Traded by Reds with a player to be named later to Atlanta Braves for OF Mike Kelly (January 9, 1996); Braves acquired P Ray King to complete deal (June

F

11, 1996). ... On disabled list (July 16-September 3, 1996). ... Traded by Braves to Milwaukee Brewers for OF Gerald Williams (December 11, 1997). ... On Milwaukee disabled list (May 11-June 30, 1998); included rehabilitation assignment to Beloit (June 25-July 1). ... On disabled list (April 21, 1999-remainder of season; and March 28, 2000-entire season). ... On Milwaukee disabled list (March 30-May 31 and June 8, 2002-remainder of season); included rehabilitation assignment to Huntsville (May 25-31). ... Released by Brewers (October 15, 2002).

STATISTICAL NOTES: Led Carolina League with 20 wild pitches in 1994.

CAREER HITTING (MLB): 0-for-7 (.000), 0 R, 0 2B, 0 3B, 0 HR, 0 RBI.

Year League	W	L	Pct.	ERA	G	GS	CG	ShO	Sv.-Opp.	IP	H	R	ER	HR	BB-IBB	SO
1992— Princeton (Appl.)	4	2	.667	4.74	15	8	0	0	0-...	49.1	55	43	26	2	34-1	37
1993— Charleston, W.Va. (S.Atl.)	9	12	.429	5.37	27	26	0	0	0-...	135.2	138	100	81	7	97-0	81
1994— Winston-Salem (Caro.)	12	5	.706	3.86	25	25	1	0	0-...	156.1	121	77	67	18	*94-0	137
1995— Chattanooga (Sou.)	4	5	.444	5.06	20	17	0	0	0-...	80.0	76	49	45	2	52-1	56
1996— Richmond (I.L.)■	3	10	.231	4.72	18	18	1	0	0-...	93.1	91	57	49	9	49-1	87
1997— Richmond (I.L.)	1	0	1.000	3.70	13	0	0	0	0-...	24.1	24	10	10	1	14-0	25
— Atlanta (N.L.)	0	1	.000	3.29	30	0	0	0	0-1	27.1	24	12	10	4	16-0	28
1998— Milwaukee (N.L.)■	1	4	.200	3.95	49	0	0	0	0-2	57.0	56	27	25	4	20-0	64
— Beloit (Midw.)	0	1	.000	4.50	2	1	0	0	0-...	2.0	1	1	1	0	0-0	3
1999— Milwaukee (N.L.)	0	0	...	10.80	6	0	0	0	0-0	6.2	11	8	8	1	4-0	12
2000— Milwaukee (N.L.)									Did not play.							
2001— Indianapolis (I.L.)	3	0	1.000	1.50	4	0	0	0	0-...	6.0	4	1	1	0	3-0	8
— Milwaukee (N.L.)	5	2	.714	1.89	65	0	0	0	2-4	66.2	44	16	14	6	36-7	80
2002— Huntsville (Sou.)	0	1	.000	0.00	3	0	0	0	0-...	5.1	5	1	0	0	2-0	7
— Milwaukee (N.L.)	1	0	1.000	5.79	3	0	0	0	0-0	4.2	6	3	3	0	5-1	3
Major League totals (5 years)	7	7	.500	3.33	153	0	0	0	2-7	162.1	141	66	60	15	81-8	187

FRANCO, JOHN P METS

PERSONAL: Born September 17, 1960, in Brooklyn, N.Y. ... 5-10/185. ... Throws left, bats left. ... Full name: John Anthony Franco.

HIGH SCHOOL: Lafayette (Brooklyn, N.Y.).

COLLEGE: St. John's.

TRANSACTIONS/CAREER NOTES: Selected by Los Angeles Dodgers organization in fifth round of free-agent draft (June 8, 1981). ... Traded by Dodgers with P Brett Wise to Cincinnati Reds for IF Rafael Landestoy (May 9, 1983). ... Traded by Reds with OF Don Brown to New York Mets for P Randy Myers and P Kip Gross (December 6, 1989). ... On disabled list (June 30-August 1 and August 26, 1992-remainder of season; April 17-May 7 and August 3-26, 1993). ... Granted free agency (October 18, 1994). ... Re-signed by Mets (April 5, 1995). ... On New York disabled list (July 3-September 4, 1999); included rehabilitation assignment to Binghamton (September 3-4). ... Granted free agency (October 31, 2000). ... Re-signed by Mets (November 25, 2000). ... On disabled list (March 21, 2002-entire season).

RECORDS: Holds N.L. career record for most saves—422.

HONORS: Named N.L. Fireman of the Year by The Sporting News (1988, 1990 and 1994).

STATISTICAL NOTES: Led N.L. with 42 save opportunities in 1988, 39 in 1990 and 36 in 1994.

MISCELLANEOUS: Holds Cincinnati Reds all-time record for most saves (148). ... Holds New York Mets all-time records for most saves (274) and games pitched (605).

CAREER HITTING (MLB): 3-for-34 (.088), 2 R, 0 2B, 0 3B, 0 HR, 1 RBI.

Year League	W	L	Pct.	ERA	G	GS	CG	ShO	Sv.-Opp.	IP	H	R	ER	HR	BB-IBB	SO
1981— Vero Beach (FSL)	7	4	.636	3.53	13	11	3	0	0-...	79.0	78	41	31	1	41-2	60
1982— Albuquerque (PCL)	1	2	.333	7.24	5	5	0	0	0-...	27.1	41	22	22	3	15-1	24
— San Antonio (Texas)	10	5	.667	4.96	17	17	3	0	0-...	105.1	137	70	58	11	46-1	76
1983— Albuquerque (PCL)	0	0	...	5.40	11	0	0	0	0-...	15.0	10	11	9	3	11-2	8
— Indianapolis (A.A.)■	6	10	.375	4.85	23	18	2	0	2-...	115.0	148	69	62	10	42-3	54
1984— Wichita (A.A.)	1	0	1.000	5.79	6	0	0	0	0-...	9.1	8	6	6	1	4-0	11
— Cincinnati (N.L.)	6	2	.750	2.61	54	0	0	0	4-9	79.1	74	28	23	3	36-4	55
1985— Cincinnati (N.L.)	12	3	.800	2.18	67	0	0	0	12-15	99.0	83	27	24	5	40-8	61
1986— Cincinnati (N.L.)	6	6	.500	2.94	74	0	0	0	29-38	101.0	90	40	33	7	44-12	84
1987— Cincinnati (N.L.)	8	5	.615	2.52	68	0	0	0	32-41	82.0	76	26	23	6	27-6	61
1988— Cincinnati (N.L.)	6	6	.500	1.57	70	0	0	0	*39-42	86.0	60	18	15	3	27-3	46
1989— Cincinnati (N.L.)	4	8	.333	3.12	60	0	0	0	32-39	80.2	77	35	28	3	36-8	60
1990— New York (N.L.)■	5	3	.625	2.53	55	0	0	0	*33-39	67.2	66	22	19	4	21-2	56
1991— New York (N.L.)	5	9	.357	2.93	52	0	0	0	30-35	55.1	61	27	18	2	18-4	45
1992— New York (N.L.)	6	2	.750	1.64	31	0	0	0	15-17	33.0	24	6	6	1	11-2	20
1993— New York (N.L.)	4	3	.571	5.20	35	0	0	0	10-17	36.1	46	24	21	6	19-3	29
1994— New York (N.L.)	1	4	.200	2.70	47	0	0	0	*30-36	50.0	47	20	15	2	19-0	42
1995— New York (N.L.)	5	3	.625	2.44	48	0	0	0	29-36	51.2	48	17	14	4	17-2	41
1996— New York (N.L.)	4	3	.571	1.83	51	0	0	0	28-36	54.0	54	15	11	2	21-0	48
1997— New York (N.L.)	5	3	.625	2.55	59	0	0	0	36-42	60.0	49	18	17	3	20-2	53
1998— New York (N.L.)	0	8	.000	3.62	61	0	0	0	38-46	64.2	66	28	26	4	29-7	59
1999— New York (N.L.)	0	2	.000	2.88	46	0	0	0	19-21	40.2	40	14	13	1	19-1	41
— Binghamton (East.)	0	0	...	0.00	1	1	0	0	0-...	1.1	0	0	0	0	0-0	1
2000— New York (N.L.)	5	4	.556	3.40	62	0	0	0	4-4	55.2	46	24	21	6	26-6	56
2001— New York (N.L.)	6	2	.750	4.05	58	0	0	0	2-7	53.1	55	25	24	8	19-2	50
2002— New York (N.L.)									Did not play.							
Major League totals (18 years)	88	76	.537	2.75	998	0	0	0	422-520	1150.1	1062	414	351	70	449-72	907

DIVISION SERIES RECORD

Year League	W	L	Pct.	ERA	G	GS	CG	ShO	Sv.-Opp.	IP	H	R	ER	HR	BB-IBB	SO
1999— New York (N.L.)	1	0	1.000	0.00	3	0	0	0	0-0	3.2	1	0	0	0	0-0	2
2000— New York (N.L.)	0	0	...	0.00	2	0	0	0	1-1	2.0	1	0	0	0	0-0	2
Division series totals (2 years)	1	0	1.000	0.00	5	0	0	0	1-1	5.2	2	0	0	0	0-0	4

CHAMPIONSHIP SERIES RECORD

Year League	W	L	Pct.	ERA	G	GS	CG	ShO	Sv.-Opp.	IP	H	R	ER	HR	BB-IBB	SO
1999— New York (N.L.)	0	0	...	3.38	3	0	0	0	0-1	2.2	3	1	1	0	1-0	3
2000— New York (N.L.)	0	0	...	6.75	3	0	0	0	0-0	2.2	3	2	2	0	2-0	2
Champ. series totals (2 years)	0	0	...	5.06	6	0	0	0	0-1	5.1	6	3	3	0	3-0	5

WORLD SERIES RECORD

Year	League	W	L	Pct.	ERA	G	GS	CG	ShO	Sv.-Opp.	IP	H	R	ER	HR	BB-IBB	SO
2000—	New York (N.L.)...............	1	0	1.000	0.00	4	0	0	0	0-0	3.1	3	0	0	0	0-0	1

ALL-STAR GAME RECORD

	W	L	Pct.	ERA	GS	CG	ShO	Sv.-Opp.	IP	H	R	ER	HR	BB-IBB	SO
All-Star Game totals (2 years)	0	0	...	0.00	0	0	0	0-0	1.2	0	0	0	0	0-0	0

FRANCO, JULIO 1B/DH

PERSONAL: Born August 23, 1958, in San Pedro de Macoris, Dominican Republic. ... 6-1/188. ... Bats right, throws right. ... Full name: Julio Cesar Franco.

HIGH SCHOOL: Divine Providence (San Pedro de Macoris, Dominican Republic).

TRANSACTIONS/CAREER NOTES: Signed as non-drafted free agent by Philadelphia Phillies organization (June 23, 1978). ... Traded by Phillies with 2B Manny Trillo, OF George Vukovich, P Jay Baller and C Jerry Willard to Cleveland Indians for OF Von Hayes (December 9, 1982). ... On disabled list (July 13-August 8, 1987). ... Traded by Indians to Texas Rangers for 1B Pete O'Brien, OF Oddibe McDowell and 2B Jerry Browne (December 6, 1988). ... On disabled list (March 28-April 19, May 4-June 1 and July 9, 1992-remainder of season). ... Granted free agency (October 27, 1993). ... Signed by Chicago White Sox (December 15, 1993). ... Granted free agency (October 21, 1994). ... Signed by Chiba Lotte Marines of Japan Pacific League (December 28, 1994). ... Signed by Indians (December 7, 1995). ... On disabled list (July 7-25 and August 4-30, 1996). ... Released by Indians (August 13, 1997). ... Signed by Milwaukee Brewers (August 13, 1997). ... Granted free agency (October 28, 1997). ... Played for Chiba Lotte Marines of Japan Pacific League (1998). ... Signed by Tampa Bay Devil Rays organization (February 19, 1999). ... Loaned by Devil Rays organization to Mexico City Tigres, Mexican League (March 29-September 18, 1999). ... Granted free agency (October 13, 1999). ... Contract purchased by Atlanta Braves organization from Mexico City, Mexican League (August 31, 2001). ... Granted free agency (November 5, 2001). ... Re-signed by Braves organization (December 17, 2001). ... Granted free agency (October 28, 2002).

HONORS: Named Carolina League Most Valuable Player (1980). ... Named second baseman on The Sporting News A.L. Silver Slugger team (1988-91). ... Named second baseman on The Sporting News A.L. All-Star team (1989-91). ... Named designated hitter on The Sporting News A.L. Silver Slugger team (1994).

STATISTICAL NOTES: Led Northwest League with 153 total bases in 1979. ... Led Northwest League shortstops with 256 assists, 390 total chances and 45 double plays in 1979. ... Led Carolina League shortstops with 412 assists and 73 double plays in 1980. ... Led American Association shortstops with 42 errors in 1982. ... Led A.L. shortstops with 35 errors in 1985. ... Led A.L. in grounding into double plays with 28 in 1986 and 27 in 1989. ... Had 21-game hitting streak (May 11-June 3, 1988). ... Had 22-game hitting streak (July 3-27, 1988). ... Led Mexican League with 276 total bases in 2001. ... Career major league grand slams: 6.

2002 GAMES PLAYED BY POSITION (MLB): 1B—95; DH—2.

			BATTING														FIELDING	
Year	Team (League)	Pos.	G	AB	R	H	2B	3B	HR	RBI	BB	SO	SB-CS	Avg.	OBP	SLG	E	Avg.
1978—	Butte (Pio.)................	SS	47	141	34	43	5	2	3	28	17	30	4-3	.305	.381	.433	25	.781
1979—	Central Oregon (NW)..	SS	•71	299	57	*98	15	5	•10	45	24	59	22-9	.328	.381	.512	31	.921
1980—	Peninsula (Caro.)	SS	•140	*555	105	178	25	6	11	*99	33	66	44-12	.321	.361	.447	42	.934
1981—	Reading (East.)..........	SS	*139	*532	70	160	17	3	8	74	52	60	27-14	.301	.365	.389	30	.958
1982—	Oklahoma City (A.A.)..	SS-3B	120	463	80	139	19	5	21	66	39	56	33-11	.300	.357	.499	†42	.930
—	Philadelphia (N.L.)......	SS-3B	16	29	3	8	1	0	0	3	2	4	0-2	.276	.323	.310	0	1.000
1983—	Cleveland (A.L.)■.......	SS	149	560	68	153	24	8	8	80	27	50	32-12	.273	.306	.388	28	.961
1984—	Cleveland (A.L.)..........	SS-DH	160	*658	82	188	22	5	3	79	43	68	19-10	.286	.331	.348	*36	.955
1985—	Cleveland (A.L.)..........	SS-2B-DH	160	636	97	183	33	4	6	90	54	74	13-9	.288	.343	.381	†36	.950
1986—	Cleveland (A.L.)..........	SS-2B-DH	149	599	80	183	30	5	10	74	32	66	10-7	.306	.338	.422	19	.972
1987—	Cleveland (A.L.)..........	SS-2B-DH	128	495	86	158	24	3	8	52	57	56	32-9	.319	.389	.428	18	.964
1988—	Cleveland (A.L.)..........	2B-DH	152	613	88	186	23	6	10	54	56	72	25-11	.303	.361	.409	14	.982
1989—	Texas (A.L.)■............	2B-DH	150	548	80	173	31	5	13	92	66	69	21-3	.316	.386	.462	13	.980
1990—	Texas (A.L.)...............	2B-DH	157	582	96	172	27	1	11	69	82	83	31-10	.296	.383	.402	•19	.975
1991—	Texas (A.L.)...............	2B	146	589	108	201	27	3	15	78	65	78	36-9	*.341	.408	.474	14	.979
1992—	Texas (A.L.)...............	DH-2B-OF	35	107	19	25	7	0	2	8	15	17	1-1	.234	.328	.355	3	.927
1993—	Texas (A.L.)...............	DH	144	532	85	154	31	3	14	84	62	95	9-3	.289	.360	.438	...	...
1994—	Chicago (A.L.)■.........	DH-1B	112	433	72	138	19	2	20	98	62	75	8-1	.319	.406	.510	3	.969
1995—	Chiba Lotte (Jp. Pc.)■	1B	127	474	60	145	25	3	10	58	...	...	11-...	.306	...	.435	...	...
1996—	Cleveland (A.L.)■.......	1B-DH	112	432	72	139	20	1	14	76	61	82	8-8	.322	.407	.470	9	.990
1997—	Cleveland (A.L.)..........	DH-2B-1B	78	289	46	82	13	1	3	25	38	75	8-5	.284	.367	.367	3	.983
—	Milwaukee (A.L.)■.....	DH-1B	42	141	22	34	3	0	4	19	31	41	7-1	.241	.373	.348	1	.992
1998—	Chiba Lotte (Jp. Pc.)■		131	487	78	141	27	2	18	77	...	...	7-...	.290	...	.464	...	...
1999—	Tigres (Mex.)■..........	1B	93	326	90	138	22	6	14	77	80	44	9-...	*.423	*.541	*.656	2	.993
—	Tampa Bay (A.L.)■.....	1B	1	1	0	0	0	0	0	0	0	1	0-0	.000	.000	.000	0	1.000
2000—	Samsung (Korean)■..		132	477	...	156	...	...	22	110	...	...	...-...	.327	...	.465	...	...
2001—	Tigres (Mex.)■..........	1B-DH-OF	110	407	90	*178	34	5	18	90	50	56	15-...	*.437	*.497	*.678	5	.991
—	Atlanta (N.L.)■..........	1B	25	90	13	27	4	0	3	11	10	20	0-0	.300	.376	.444	1	.995
2002—	Atlanta (N.L.).............	1B-DH	125	338	51	96	13	1	6	30	39	75	5-1	.284	.357	.382	8	.990
American League totals (15 years)			1875	7215	1101	2169	334	47	141	978	751	1002	260-99	.301	.366	.419	216	.972
National League totals (3 years)			166	457	67	131	18	1	9	44	51	99	5-3	.287	.359	.389	9	.991
Major League totals (18 years)			2041	7672	1168	2300	352	48	150	1022	802	1101	265-102	.300	.366	.417	225	.974

DIVISION SERIES RECORD

			BATTING														FIELDING	
Year	Team (League)	Pos.	G	AB	R	H	2B	3B	HR	RBI	BB	SO	SB-CS	Avg.	OBP	SLG	E	Avg.
1996—	Cleveland (A.L.)..........	1B-DH	4	15	1	2	0	0	0	1	1	6	0-0	.133	.176	.133	0	1.000
2001—	Atlanta (N.L.)............	1B	3	13	3	4	0	0	1	1	0	1	0-1	.308	.308	.538	0	1.000
2002—	Atlanta (N.L.)............	1B	5	22	2	4	0	0	0	1	2	3	1-0	.182	.250	.182	0	1.000
Division series totals (3 years)			12	50	6	10	0	0	1	3	3	10	1-1	.200	.241	.260	0	1.000

CHAMPIONSHIP SERIES RECORD

			BATTING														FIELDING	
Year	Team (League)	Pos.	G	AB	R	H	2B	3B	HR	RBI	BB	SO	SB-CS	Avg.	OBP	SLG	E	Avg.
2001—	Atlanta (N.L.)............	1B	5	23	2	6	0	0	1	2	0	2	0-0	.261	.261	.391	0	1.000

ALL-STAR GAME RECORD

NOTES: Named Most Valuable Player (1990).

	AB	R	H	2B	3B	HR	RBI	BB	SO	SB-CS	Avg.	OBP	SLG	E	Avg.
All-Star Game totals (2 years)	6	0	2	1	0	0	2	0	0	0-0	.333	.333	.500	0	1.000

F

FRANCO, MATT — IF/OF — BRAVES

PERSONAL: Born August 19, 1969, in Santa Monica, Calif. ... 6-1/210. ... Bats left, throws right. ... Full name: Matthew Neil Franco. ... Nephew of actor Kurt Russell.

HIGH SCHOOL: Westlake (Calif.).

TRANSACTIONS/CAREER NOTES: Selected by Chicago Cubs organization in seventh round of free-agent draft (June 2, 1987). ... On disabled list (May 6-13, 1994). ... Traded by Cubs to New York Mets organization for a player to be named later (April 8, 1996); Cubs acquired P Chris DeWitt to complete deal (June 11, 1996). ... On Norfolk disabled list (April 8-11, 1996). ... Granted free agency (October 15, 1996). ... Re-signed by Mets organization (November 21, 1996). ... On New York disabled list (June 29-July 14, 1998); included rehabilitation assignment to Norfolk (July 9-14). ... Granted free agency (December 21, 2000). ... Re-signed by Mets organization (February 1, 2001). ... Granted free agency (October 15, 2001). ... Signed by Atlanta Braves organization (November 8, 2001).

RECORDS: Holds major league single-season record for most bases on balls by pinch hitter—20 (1999).

STATISTICAL NOTES: Led Midwest League in grounding into double plays with 19 in 1990. ... Career major league grand slams: 1.

2002 GAMES PLAYED BY POSITION (MLB): 1B—51; OF—4.

			BATTING														FIELDING	
Year	Team (League)	Pos.	G	AB	R	H	2B	3B	HR	RBI	BB	SO	SB-CS	Avg.	OBP	SLG	E	Avg.
1987—	Wytheville (Appl.)	3B-1B-2B	62	202	25	50	10	1	1	21	26	41	4-1	.248	.333	.322	23	.888
1988—	Wytheville (Appl.)	3B-1B	20	79	14	31	9	1	0	16	7	5	0-1	.392	.442	.532	6	.902
—	Geneva (NY-Penn)	3B-1B	44	164	19	42	2	0	3	21	19	13	2-0	.256	.332	.323	14	.943
1989—	Charl., W.Va. (S.Atl.)	3-1-0-S	109	377	42	102	16	1	5	48	57	40	2-2	.271	.363	.358	22	.932
—	Peoria (Midw.)	3B	16	58	4	13	4	0	0	9	5	5	0-1	.224	.292	.293	6	.878
1990—	Peoria (Midw.)	1B-3B	123	443	52	125	*33	2	6	65	43	39	4-4	.282	.346	.406	18	.980
1991—	Win.-Salem (Caro.)	1B-3B-SS	104	307	47	66	12	1	4	41	46	42	4-1	.215	.316	.300	11	.986
1992—	Charlotte (Sou.)	3B-1B-OF	108	343	35	97	18	3	2	31	26	46	3-3	.283	.332	.370	13	.961
1993—	Orlando (Sou.)	1B-3B	68	237	31	75	20	1	7	37	29	30	3-6	.316	.393	.498	4	.992
—	Iowa (A.A.)	1-DH-0-2-P	62	199	24	58	17	4	5	29	16	30	4-1	.291	.342	.492	2	.996
1994—	Iowa (A.A.)	1-DH-3-0	128	437	63	121	32	4	11	71	52	66	3-3	.277	.353	.444	7	.993
1995—	Iowa (A.A.)	3-1-DH-P-C	121	455	51	128	28	5	6	58	37	44	1-1	.281	.331	.404	19	.960
—	Chicago (N.L.)	2B-1B-3B	16	17	3	5	1	0	0	1	0	4	0-0	.294	.294	.353	0	1.000
1996—	Norfolk (I.L.)■	3B-1B-DH	133	508	74	*164	*40	2	7	81	36	55	5-2	.323	.365	.451	22	.962
—	New York (N.L.)	3B-1B	14	31	3	6	1	0	1	2	1	5	0-0	.194	.235	.323	3	.900
1997—	Norfolk (I.L.)	OF-DH-1B-3B	7	26	5	7	2	0	0	0	2	2	0-0	.269	.345	.346	0	1.000
—	New York (N.L.)	3-1-DH-0	112	163	21	45	5	0	5	21	13	23	1-0	.276	.330	.399	4	.966
1998—	New York (N.L.)	3-0-1-DH	103	161	20	44	7	2	1	13	23	26	0-1	.273	.366	.360	1	.991
—	Norfolk (I.L.)	3B-OF-1B	5	19	2	7	1	0	0	1	3	1	2-0	.368	.455	.421	2	.909
1999—	New York (N.L.)	1-0-3-DH-P	122	132	18	31	5	0	4	21	28	21	0-0	.235	.366	.364	1	.987
2000—	New York (N.L.)	1-3-0-DH-2	101	134	9	32	4	0	2	14	21	22	0-0	.239	.340	.313	4	.969
—	Norfolk (I.L.)	3B-OF-1B	14	51	3	7	1	0	0	1	3	10	0-0	.137	.185	.157	2	.933
2001—	Norfolk (I.L.)	3B-1B-OF	124	433	49	106	25	1	8	47	52	72	5-2	.245	.325	.363	14	.973
2002—	Richmond (I.L.)	1B-3B	47	173	24	50	11	0	6	28	14	19	1-0	.289	.349	.457	2	.993
—	Atlanta (N.L.)	1B-OF	81	205	25	65	15	4	6	30	27	31	1-0	.317	.395	.517	4	.990
Major League totals (7 years)			549	843	99	228	38	6	19	102	113	132	2-1	.270	.356	.397	17	.980

DIVISION SERIES RECORD

			BATTING														FIELDING	
Year	Team (League)	Pos.	G	AB	R	H	2B	3B	HR	RBI	BB	SO	SB-CS	Avg.	OBP	SLG	E	Avg.
1999—	New York (N.L.)	PH	1	0	0	0	0	0	0	0	1	0	0-0	...	1.000	...	...	...
2000—	New York (N.L.)								Did not play.									
2002—	Atlanta (N.L.)	PH	4	2	0	0	0	0	0	0	0	0	0-0	.000	.000	.000	0	...
Division series totals (2 years)			5	2	0	0	0	0	0	0	1	0	0-0	.000	.333	.000	0	...

CHAMPIONSHIP SERIES RECORD

			BATTING														FIELDING	
Year	Team (League)	Pos.	G	AB	R	H	2B	3B	HR	RBI	BB	SO	SB-CS	Avg.	OBP	SLG	E	Avg.
1999—	New York (N.L.)	PH	5	2	1	1	1	0	0	0	1	0	0-0	.500	.667	1.000	...	...
2000—	New York (N.L.)	PH-1B	2	3	0	0	0	0	0	0	0	1	0-0	.000	.000	.000	0	1.000
Championship series totals (2 years)			7	5	1	1	1	0	0	0	1	1	0-0	.200	.333	.400	0	1.000

WORLD SERIES RECORD

			BATTING														FIELDING	
Year	Team (League)	Pos.	G	AB	R	H	2B	3B	HR	RBI	BB	SO	SB-CS	Avg.	OBP	SLG	E	Avg.
2000—	New York (N.L.)	1B	1	1	0	0	0	0	0	0	0	1	0-0	.000	.000	.000	0	1.000

RECORD AS PITCHER

Year	League	W	L	Pct.	ERA	G	GS	CG	ShO	Sv.-Opp.	IP	H	R	ER	HR	BB-IBB	SO
1993—	Iowa (A.A.)	0	0	...	36.00	1	0	0	0	0-...	1.0	5	4	4	2	1-0	1
1995—	Iowa (A.A.)	0	0	...	0.00	1	0	0	0	0-...	1.0	1	0	0	0	1-0	1
1999—	New York (N.L.)	0	0	...	13.50	2	0	0	0	0-...	1.1	3	2	2	1	3-0	2

FRANKLIN, RYAN — P — MARINERS

PERSONAL: Born March 5, 1973, in Fort Smith, Ark. ... 6-3/165. ... Throws right, bats right. ... Full name: Ryan Ray Franklin.

HIGH SCHOOL: Spiro (Okla.).

JUNIOR COLLEGE: Seminole (Okla.) State College.

TRANSACTIONS/CAREER NOTES: Selected by Toronto Blue Jays organization in 25th round of free-agent draft (June 3, 1991); did not sign. ... Selected by Seattle Mariners organization in 23rd round of free-agent draft (June 1, 1992). ... On Seattle disabled list (June 28-July 15, 2002); included rehabilitation assignment to Everett (July 10-15).

STATISTICAL NOTES: Led Southern League with 16 hit batsmen in 1996. ... Pitched 6-0 no-hit victory against Carolina (April 21, 1997, first game).

MISCELLANEOUS: Member of 2000 U.S. Olympic baseball team.

CAREER HITTING (MLB): 0-for-0 (.000), 0 R, 0 2B, 0 3B, 0 HR, 0 RBI.

Year League	W	L	Pct.	ERA	G	GS	CG	ShO	Sv.-Opp.	IP	H	R	ER	HR	BB-IBB	SO
1993— Bellingham (N'West)	5	3	.625	2.92	15	14	1	1	0-...	74.0	72	38	24	2	27-0	55
1994— Appleton (Midw.)	9	6	.600	3.13	18	18	5	1	0-...	118.0	105	60	41	6	23-0	102
— Riverside (Calif.)	4	2	.667	3.06	8	8	1	1	0-...	61.2	61	26	21	5	8-0	35
— Calgary (PCL)	0	0	...	7.94	1	1	0	0	0-...	5.2	9	6	5	2	1-0	2
1995— Port City (Sou.)	6	10	.375	4.32	31	20	1	1	0-...	146.0	153	84	70	13	43-4	102
1996— Port City (Sou.)	6	12	.333	4.01	28	27	2	0	0-...	182.0	186	99	81	23	37-0	127
1997— Memphis (Sou.)	4	2	.667	3.03	11	8	2	•2	0-...	59.1	45	22	20	4	14-1	49
— Tacoma (PCL)	5	5	.500	4.18	14	14	0	0	0-...	90.1	97	48	42	11	24-1	59
1998— Tacoma (PCL)	5	6	.455	4.51	34	16	1	0	1-...	127.2	148	75	64	18	32-2	90
1999— Tacoma (PCL)	6	9	.400	4.71	29	19	2	1	2-...	135.2	142	81	71	17	33-1	94
— Seattle (A.L.)	0	0	...	4.76	6	0	0	0	0-0	11.1	10	6	6	2	8-1	6
2000— Tacoma (PCL)	11	5	.688	3.90	31	22	4	0	0-...	164.0	147	85	71	*28	35-1	142
2001— Seattle (A.L.)	5	1	.833	3.56	38	0	0	0	0-1	78.1	76	32	31	13	24-4	60
— Tacoma (PCL)	0	0	...	0.00	1	0	0	0	0-...	3.2	2	0	0	0	0-0	3
2002— Seattle (A.L.)	7	5	.583	4.02	41	12	0	0	0-1	118.2	117	62	53	14	22-1	65
— Everett (N'West)	0	0	...	0.00	1	1	0	0	0-...	2.2	2	1	0	0	0-0	1
Major League totals (3 years)	12	6	.667	3.89	85	12	0	0	0-2	208.1	203	100	90	29	54-6	131

FRANKLIN, WAYNE — P — BREWERS

PERSONAL: Born March 9, 1974, in Wilmington, Del. ... 6-2/205. ... Throws left, bats left. ... Full name: Gary Wayne Franklin Jr.
HIGH SCHOOL: Northeast (Md.).
COLLEGE: Maryland-Baltimore County.
TRANSACTIONS/CAREER NOTES: Selected by Los Angeles Dodgers organization in 36th round of free-agent draft (June 4, 1996). ... Selected by Houston Astros organization from Dodgers organization in Rule 5 minor league draft (December 14, 1998). ... Traded by Astros to Milwaukee Brewers (September 3, 2002), as partial completion of deal in which Brewers traded IF Mark Loretta to Astros for two players to be named later (August 31, 2002); Brewers acquired 2B Keith Ginter to complete deal (September 5, 2002).
CAREER HITTING (MLB): 0-for-8 (.000), 0 R, 0 2B, 0 3B, 0 HR, 0 RBI.

Year League	W	L	Pct.	ERA	G	GS	CG	ShO	Sv.-Opp.	IP	H	R	ER	HR	BB-IBB	SO
1996— Yakima (N'West)	1	0	1.000	2.52	20	0	0	0	1-...	25.0	32	10	7	2	12-3	22
1997— Savannah (S.Atl.)	5	3	.625	3.18	28	7	1	0	2-...	82.0	79	41	29	10	35-0	58
— San Bernardino (Calif.)	0	0	...	0.00	1	0	0	0	0-...	2.0	2	0	0	0	0-0	1
1998— Vero Beach (FSL)	9	3	.750	3.53	48	0	0	0	10-...	86.2	81	43	34	7	26-0	78
1999— Kissimmee (FSL)■	3	0	1.000	1.53	12	0	0	0	1-...	17.2	11	4	3	0	6-0	22
— Jackson (Texas)	3	1	.750	1.61	46	0	0	0	20-...	50.1	31	11	9	3	16-3	40
2000— New Orleans (PCL)	3	3	.500	3.63	48	0	0	0	4-...	44.2	51	29	18	4	19-3	37
— Houston (N.L.)	0	0	...	5.48	25	0	0	0	0-0	21.1	24	14	13	2	12-1	21
2001— Houston (N.L.)	0	0	...	6.75	11	0	0	0	0-0	12.0	17	9	9	4	9-0	9
— New Orleans (PCL)	2	1	.667	3.81	41	0	0	0	0-...	49.2	47	28	21	6	18-2	51
2002— New Orleans (PCL)	13	9	.591	3.12	29	27	1	0	0-...	179.0	153	68	62	14	59-2	*141
— Milwaukee (N.L.)■	2	1	.667	2.63	4	4	0	0	0-0	24.0	16	8	7	1	17-1	17
Major League totals (3 years)	2	1	.667	4.55	40	4	0	0	0-0	57.1	57	31	29	7	38-2	47

FREDERICK, KEVIN — P — TWINS

PERSONAL: Born November 4, 1976, in Evanston, Ill. ... 6-1/208. ... Throws right, bats left. ... Full name: Kevin Albert Francis Frederick.
HIGH SCHOOL: Adlai E. Stevenson (Lincolnshire, Ill.).
COLLEGE: Creighton.
TRANSACTIONS/CAREER NOTES: Selected by Minnesota Twins organization in 34th round of free-agent draft (June 2, 1998). ... On disabled list (July 6-August 19, 1999). ... On Edmonton disabled list (May 12-22, 2002).
CAREER HITTING (MLB): 0-for-0 (.000), 0 R, 0 2B, 0 3B, 0 HR, 0 RBI.

Year League	W	L	Pct.	ERA	G	GS	CG	ShO	Sv.-Opp.	IP	H	R	ER	HR	BB-IBB	SO
1998— Elizabethton (Appl.)	1	4	.200	4.25	17	0	0	0	1-...	29.2	28	21	14	4	10-1	46
1999— Gulf Coast Twins (GCL)	0	0	...	15.43	2	0	0	0	0-...	2.1	6	5	4	0	1-0	3
2000— Quad City (Midw.)	5	0	1.000	2.35	27	0	0	0	4-...	46.0	34	17	12	1	23-4	51
— Fort Myers (FSL)	2	1	.667	2.70	19	0	0	0	3-...	30.0	20	11	9	0	14-1	37
2001— Fort Myers (FSL)	2	0	1.000	1.00	9	0	0	0	1-...	18.0	9	2	2	1	3-1	19
— New Britain (East.)	6	2	.750	1.63	44	0	0	0	7-...	82.2	56	17	15	5	28-7	109
2002— Edmonton (PCL)	3	6	.333	4.58	46	2	0	0	22-...	55.0	63	31	28	8	21-1	47
— Minnesota (A.L.)	0	0	...	10.03	8	0	0	0	0-0	11.2	13	13	13	3	10-0	5
Major League totals (1 year)	0	0	...	10.03	8	0	0	0	0-0	11.2	13	13	13	3	10-0	5

FRYMAN, TRAVIS — 3B — INDIANS

PERSONAL: Born March 25, 1969, in Lexington, Ky. ... 6-1/195. ... Bats right, throws right. ... Full name: David Travis Fryman.
HIGH SCHOOL: Tate (Gonzalez, Fla.).
TRANSACTIONS/CAREER NOTES: Selected by Detroit Tigers organization in supplemental round ("sandwich pick" between first and second round, 30th pick overall) of free-agent draft (June 2, 1987); pick received as compensation for Philadelphia Phillies signing Type A free-agent C Lance Parrish. ... Traded by Tigers to Arizona Diamondbacks for 3B Joe Randa, P Matt Drews and 3B Gabe Alvarez (November 18, 1997). ... Traded by Diamondbacks with P Tom Martin and cash to Cleveland Indians for 3B Matt Williams (December 1, 1997). ... On Cleveland disabled list (June 6-25 and July 4-September 2, 1999); included rehabilitation assignments to Akron (August 24-30) and Buffalo (August 31-September 2). ... On Cleveland disabled list (March 23-June 2, 2001); included rehabilitation assignments to Buffalo (April 5-7) and Akron (May 14-June 2). ... On disabled list (July 17-August 1, 2002).
RECORDS: Holds A.L. single-season record for fewest putouts by third baseman (150 or more games)—79 (2000).
HONORS: Named shortstop on The Sporting News A.L. All-Star team (1992). ... Named shortstop on The Sporting News A.L. Silver Slugger team (1992). ... Named third baseman on The Sporting News A.L. All-Star team (1993 and 2000). ... Won A.L. Gold Glove as third baseman (2000).

F

STATISTICAL NOTES: Led Appalachian League shortstops with 103 putouts and 313 total chances in 1987. ... Hit for the cycle (July 28, 1993). ... Tied for A.L. lead with 13 sacrifice flies in 1994. ... Led A.L. third basemen with 221 assists in 1994 and 337 in 1995. ... Led A.L. third basemen with 313 total chances in 1994 and 458 in 1995. ... Led A.L. third basemen with 38 double plays in 1995. ... Led A.L. third basemen with 271 assists and .979 fielding percentage in 1996. ... Tied for A.L. lead with 126 putouts by third basemen in 1997. ... Led A.L. third basemen with .978 fielding percentage in 2000. ... Career major league grand slams: 7.

2002 GAMES PLAYED BY POSITION (MLB): 3B—113.

		BATTING														FIELDING	
Year Team (League)	**Pos.**	**G**	**AB**	**R**	**H**	**2B**	**3B**	**HR**	**RBI**	**BB**	**SO**	**SB-CS**	**Avg.**	**OBP**	**SLG**	**E**	**Avg.**
1987—Bristol (Appl.)	SS	67	248	25	58	9	0	2	20	22	39	6-2	.234	.297	.294	•23	.927
1988—Fayetteville (S.Atl.)	SS-2B	123	411	44	96	17	4	0	47	24	83	16-5	.234	.289	.294	32	.946
1989—London (East.)	SS	118	426	52	113	*30	1	9	56	19	78	5-3	.265	.306	.404	*27	.952
1990—Toledo (I.L.)	SS	87	327	38	84	22	2	10	53	17	59	4-7	.257	.295	.428	26	.940
—Detroit (A.L.)	3B-SS-DH	66	232	32	69	11	1	9	27	17	51	3-3	.297	.348	.470	14	.932
1991—Detroit (A.L.)	3B-SS	149	557	65	144	36	3	21	91	40	149	12-5	.259	.309	.447	23	.957
1992—Detroit (A.L.)	SS-3B	161	*659	87	175	31	4	20	96	45	144	8-4	.266	.316	.416	22	.970
1993—Detroit (A.L.)	SS-3B-DH	151	607	98	182	37	5	22	97	77	128	9-4	.300	.379	.486	23	.960
1994—Detroit (A.L.)	3B	114	*464	66	122	34	5	18	85	45	*128	2-2	.263	.326	.474	14	.955
1995—Detroit (A.L.)	3B	144	567	79	156	21	5	15	81	63	100	4-2	.275	.347	.409	14	.969
1996—Detroit (A.L.)	3B-SS	157	616	90	165	32	3	22	100	57	118	4-3	.268	.329	.437	10	†.981
1997—Detroit (A.L.)	3B	154	595	90	163	27	3	22	102	46	113	16-3	.274	.326	.440	10	*.978
1998—Cleveland (A.L.)■	3B-SS-DH	146	557	74	160	33	2	28	96	44	125	10-8	.287	.340	.504	13	.963
1999—Cleveland (A.L.)	3B	85	322	45	82	16	2	10	48	25	57	2-1	.255	.309	.410	6	.969
—Akron (East.)	DH-3B	4	12	4	3	0	0	1	4	2	4	0-0	.250	.333	.500	0	1.000
—Buffalo (I.L.)	3B-DH	3	11	1	2	0	0	1	2	0	3	0-0	.182	.182	.455	1	.750
2000—Cleveland (A.L.)	3B-DH-1B	155	574	93	184	38	4	22	106	73	111	1-1	.321	.392	.516	8	†.978
2001—Buffalo (I.L.)	3B	8	27	9	13	1	0	2	8	5	6	1-0	.481	.545	.741	0	1.000
—Akron (East.)	DH	6	25	3	9	2	0	1	3	2	5	0-0	.360	.407	.560	...	...
—Cleveland (A.L.)	3B-DH-SS	98	334	34	88	15	0	3	38	30	63	1-2	.263	.327	.335	12	.945
2002—Cleveland (A.L.)	3B	118	397	42	86	14	3	11	55	40	82	0-0	.217	.292	.350	10	.960
Major League totals (13 years)		1698	6481	895	1776	345	40	223	1022	602	1369	72-38	.274	.336	.443	179	.965

DIVISION SERIES RECORD

		BATTING														FIELDING	
Year Team (League)	**Pos.**	**G**	**AB**	**R**	**H**	**2B**	**3B**	**HR**	**RBI**	**BB**	**SO**	**SB-CS**	**Avg.**	**OBP**	**SLG**	**E**	**Avg.**
1998—Cleveland (A.L.)	3B	4	13	1	2	1	0	0	0	3	4	1-1	.154	.313	.231	0	1.000
1999—Cleveland (A.L.)	3B	5	15	2	4	0	0	1	4	3	2	1-0	.267	.400	.467	0	1.000
2001—Cleveland (A.L.)	3B	5	17	4	3	1	0	0	2	2	7	0-0	.176	.263	.235	0	1.000
Division series totals (3 years)		14	45	7	9	2	0	1	6	8	13	2-1	.200	.327	.311	0	1.000

CHAMPIONSHIP SERIES RECORD

		BATTING														FIELDING	
Year Team (League)	**Pos.**	**G**	**AB**	**R**	**H**	**2B**	**3B**	**HR**	**RBI**	**BB**	**SO**	**SB-CS**	**Avg.**	**OBP**	**SLG**	**E**	**Avg.**
1998—Cleveland (A.L.)	3B	6	23	2	4	0	0	0	0	1	5	1-0	.174	.240	.174	1	.889

ALL-STAR GAME RECORD

	AB	**R**	**H**	**2B**	**3B**	**HR**	**RBI**	**BB**	**SO**	**SB-CS**	**Avg.**	**OBP**	**SLG**	**E**	**Avg.**
All-Star Game totals (5 years)	6	2	2	0	0	0	1	1	2	0-0	.333	.429	.333	0	1.000

FUENTES, BRIAN P ROCKIES

PERSONAL: Born August 9, 1975, in Merced, Calif. ... 6-4/220. ... Throws left, bats left. ... Full name: Brian Christopher Fuentes.

HIGH SCHOOL: Merced (Calif.).

JUNIOR COLLEGE: Merced (Calif.) Junior College.

TRANSACTIONS/CAREER NOTES: Selected by Seattle Mariners organization in 25th round of free-agent draft (June 1, 1995). ... On disabled list (April 2-20, 1998). ... On disabled list (June 9-August 22, 1999). ... On Tacoma disabled list (August 26, 2001-remainder of season). ... Traded by Mariners with P Jose Paniagua and P Dennis Stark to Colorado Rockies for 3B Jeff Cirillo (December 15, 2001).

STATISTICAL NOTES: Tied for Eastern League lead with 14 wild pitches in 2000.

CAREER HITTING (MLB): 0-for-0 (.000), 0 R, 0 2B, 0 3B, 0 HR, 0 RBI.

Year League	**W**	**L**	**Pct.**	**ERA**	**G**	**GS**	**CG**	**ShO**	**Sv.-Opp.**	**IP**	**H**	**R**	**ER**	**HR**	**BB-IBB**	**SO**
1996—Everett (N'West)	0	1	.000	4.39	13	2	0	0	0-...	26.2	23	14	13	2	13-0	26
1997—Wisconsin (Midw.)	6	7	.462	3.56	22	22	0	0	0-...	118.2	84	52	47	6	59-0	153
1998—Lancaster (Calif.)	7	7	.500	4.17	24	22	0	0	0-...	118.2	121	73	55	8	81-0	137
1999—New Haven (East.)	3	3	.500	4.95	15	14	0	0	0-...	60.0	53	36	33	5	46-0	66
2000—New Haven (East.)	7	12	.368	4.51	26	26	1	0	0-...	139.2	127	80	70	7	70-0	152
2001—Tacoma (PCL)	3	2	.600	2.94	35	0	0	0	6-...	52.0	35	19	17	4	25-0	70
—Seattle (A.L.)	1	1	.500	4.63	10	0	0	0	0-1	11.2	6	6	6	2	8-0	10
2002—Colo. Springs (PCL)■	3	3	.500	3.70	41	0	0	0	1-...	48.2	44	25	20	0	32-1	61
—Colorado (N.L.)	2	0	1.000	4.72	31	0	0	0	0-0	26.2	25	14	14	4	13-0	38
A.L. totals (1 year)	1	1	.500	4.63	10	0	0	0	0-1	11.2	6	6	6	2	8-0	10
N.L. totals (1 year)	2	0	1.000	4.72	31	0	0	0	0-0	26.2	25	14	14	4	13-0	38
Major League totals (2 years)	3	1	.750	4.70	41	0	0	0	0-1	38.1	31	20	20	6	21-0	48

FULLMER, BRAD DH/1B ANGELS

PERSONAL: Born January 17, 1975, in Chatsworth, Calif. ... 6-0/220. ... Bats left, throws right. ... Full name: Bradley Ryan Fullmer.

HIGH SCHOOL: Montclair Prep (Van Nuys, Calif.).

TRANSACTIONS/CAREER NOTES: Selected by Montreal Expos organization in second round of free-agent draft (June 3, 1993). ... On disabled list (June 20, 1994-entire season). ... Traded by Expos to Toronto Blue Jays as part of three-way deal in which Blue Jays sent 1B/DH David Segui and cash to Texas Rangers and Rangers sent 1B Lee Stevens to Expos (March 16, 2000). ... Traded by Blye Jays to Anaheim Angels for P Brian Cooper (January 17, 2002).

STATISTICAL NOTES: Hit home run in first major league at-bat (September 2, 1997). ... Had 16-game hitting streak (August 7-22, 1999). ... Career major league grand slams: 4.

2002 GAMES PLAYED BY POSITION (MLB): DH—94; 1B—29.

		BATTING														FIELDING	
Year Team (League)	**Pos.**	**G**	**AB**	**R**	**H**	**2B**	**3B**	**HR**	**RBI**	**BB**	**SO**	**SB-CS**	**Avg.**	**OBP**	**SLG**	**E**	**Avg.**
1994—								Did not play.									
1995—Albany (S.Atl.)	3B-1B	123	468	69	•151	38	4	8	67	36	33	10-10	.323	.387	.472	30	.918
1996—W. Palm Beach (FSL) .	OF-1B	102	380	52	115	29	1	5	63	32	43	4-6	.303	.367	.424	7	.967
—Harrisburg (East.)	OF-1B	24	98	11	27	4	1	4	14	3	8	0-0	.276	.311	.459	2	.957
1997—Harrisburg (East.)	1B-OF-DH	94	357	60	111	24	2	19	62	30	25	6-4	.311	.372	.549	6	.990
—Ottawa (I.L.)	1B-DH-OF	24	91	13	27	7	0	3	17	3	10	1-1	.297	.317	.473	1	.995
—Montreal (N.L.)	1B-OF	19	40	4	12	2	0	3	8	2	7	0-0	.300	.349	.575	2	.966
1998—Montreal (N.L.)	1B	140	505	58	138	44	2	13	73	39	70	6-6	.273	.327	.446	*17	.985
1999—Montreal (N.L.)	1B	100	347	38	96	34	2	9	47	22	35	2-3	.277	.321	.464	7	.991
—Ottawa (I.L.)	1B-DH	39	142	31	45	9	0	11	32	12	16	2-2	.317	.380	.613	2	.990
2000—Toronto (A.L.)■	DH-1B	133	482	76	142	29	1	32	104	30	68	3-1	.295	.340	.558	0	1.000
2001—Toronto (A.L.)	DH-1B	146	522	71	143	31	2	18	83	38	88	5-2	.274	.326	.444	0	1.000
2002—Anaheim (A.L.)■	DH-1B	130	429	75	124	35	6	19	59	32	44	10-3	.289	.357	.531	1	.995
American League totals (3 years)		409	1433	222	409	95	9	69	246	100	200	18-6	.285	.340	.509	1	.995
National League totals (3 years)		259	892	100	246	80	4	25	128	63	112	8-9	.276	.326	.459	26	.987
Major League totals (6 years)		668	2325	322	655	175	13	94	374	163	312	26-15	.282	.335	.489	27	.988

DIVISION SERIES RECORD

		BATTING														FIELDING	
Year Team (League)	**Pos.**	**G**	**AB**	**R**	**H**	**2B**	**3B**	**HR**	**RBI**	**BB**	**SO**	**SB-CS**	**Avg.**	**OBP**	**SLG**	**E**	**Avg.**
2002—Anaheim (A.L.)	DH	3	7	1	2	1	0	0	0	1	1	0-0	.286	.375	.429	0	...

CHAMPIONSHIP SERIES RECORD

		BATTING														FIELDING	
Year Team (League)	**Pos.**	**G**	**AB**	**R**	**H**	**2B**	**3B**	**HR**	**RBI**	**BB**	**SO**	**SB-CS**	**Avg.**	**OBP**	**SLG**	**E**	**Avg.**
2002—Anaheim (A.L.)	DH	4	12	2	4	2	0	1	4	0	2	0-0	.333	.333	.750	0	...

WORLD SERIES RECORD

NOTES: Member of World Series championship team (2002).

		BATTING														FIELDING	
Year Team (League)	**Pos.**	**G**	**AB**	**R**	**H**	**2B**	**3B**	**HR**	**RBI**	**BB**	**SO**	**SB-CS**	**Avg.**	**OBP**	**SLG**	**E**	**Avg.**
2002—Anaheim (A.L.)	DH	5	15	3	4	0	0	0	1	2	2	2-0	.267	.353	.267	0	...

FULTZ, AARON — P — GIANTS

PERSONAL: Born September 4, 1973, in Memphis, Tenn. ... 6-0/200. ... Throws left, bats left. ... Full name: Richard Aaron Fultz.

HIGH SCHOOL: Munford (Tenn.).

JUNIOR COLLEGE: North Florida Junior College.

TRANSACTIONS/CAREER NOTES: Selected by San Francisco Giants organization in sixth round of free-agent draft (June 1, 1992). ... Traded by Giants with SS Andres Duncan and P Greg Brummett to Minnesota Twins for P Jim Deshaies (August 28, 1993). ... Released by Twins (April 1, 1996). ... Signed by Giants organization (April 4, 1996). ... Granted free agency (October 16, 1998). ... Re-signed by Giants organization (October 23, 1998).

CAREER HITTING (MLB): 4-for-12 (.333), 1 R, 0 2B, 0 3B, 0 HR, 0 RBI.

Year League	**W**	**L**	**Pct.**	**ERA**	**G**	**GS**	**CG**	**ShO**	**Sv.-Opp.**	**IP**	**H**	**R**	**ER**	**HR**	**BB-IBB**	**SO**
1992—Arizona Giants (Ariz.)	3	2	.600	2.13	14	•14	0	0	0-...	67.2	51	24	16	0	33-0	72
1993—Clinton (Midw.)	14	8	.636	3.41	26	25	2	1	0-...	148.0	132	63	56	8	64-2	144
—Fort Wayne (Midw.)■	0	0	...	9.00	1	1	0	0	0-...	4.0	10	4	4	0	0-0	3
1994—Fort Myers (FSL)	9	10	.474	4.33	28	28	3	0	0-...	168.1	193	95	*81	9	60-5	132
1995—New Britain (East.)	0	2	.000	6.60	3	3	0	0	0-...	15.0	11	12	11	1	9-0	12
—Fort Myers (FSL)	3	6	.333	3.25	21	21	2	2	0-...	122.0	115	52	44	10	41-1	127
1996—San Jose (Calif.)■	9	5	.643	3.96	36	12	0	0	1-...	104.2	101	52	46	7	54-2	103
1997—Shreveport (Texas)	6	3	.667	2.83	49	0	0	0	1-...	70.0	65	30	22	6	19-0	60
1998—Shreveport (Texas)	5	7	.417	3.77	54	0	0	0	15-...	62.0	58	40	26	4	29-10	61
—Fresno (PCL)	0	0	...	5.06	10	0	0	0	0-...	16.0	22	10	9	2	2-1	13
1999—Fresno (PCL)	9	8	.529	4.98	37	20	1	0	0-...	137.1	141	87	76	32	51-1	151
2000—San Francisco (N.L.)	5	2	.714	4.67	58	0	0	0	1-3	69.1	67	38	36	8	28-0	62
2001—San Francisco (N.L.)	3	1	.750	4.56	66	0	0	0	1-2	71.0	70	40	36	9	21-3	67
2002—San Francisco (N.L.)	2	2	.500	4.79	43	0	0	0	0-1	41.1	47	22	22	4	19-3	31
—Fresno (PCL)	1	3	.250	3.18	17	0	0	0	4-...	22.2	18	8	8	1	11-2	22
Major League totals (3 years)	10	5	.667	4.66	167	0	0	0	2-6	181.2	184	100	94	21	68-6	160

DIVISION SERIES RECORD

Year League	**W**	**L**	**Pct.**	**ERA**	**G**	**GS**	**CG**	**ShO**	**Sv.-Opp.**	**IP**	**H**	**R**	**ER**	**HR**	**BB-IBB**	**SO**
2000—San Francisco (N.L.)	0	1	.000	6.75	1	0	0	0	0-0	1.1	3	1	1	1	0-0	0
2002—San Francisco (N.L.)	0	0	...	...	2	0	0	0	0-0	.0	2	1	1	0	0-0	0
Division series totals (2 years) ...	0	1	.000	13.50	3	0	0	0	0-0	1.1	5	2	2	1	0-0	0

CHAMPIONSHIP SERIES RECORD

Year League	**W**	**L**	**Pct.**	**ERA**	**G**	**GS**	**CG**	**ShO**	**Sv.-Opp.**	**IP**	**H**	**R**	**ER**	**HR**	**BB-IBB**	**SO**
2002—San Francisco (N.L.)	0	0	...	0.00	1	0	0	0	0-0	.1	0	0	0	0	0-0	0

WORLD SERIES RECORD

Year League	**W**	**L**	**Pct.**	**ERA**	**G**	**GS**	**CG**	**ShO**	**Sv.-Opp.**	**IP**	**H**	**R**	**ER**	**HR**	**BB-IBB**	**SO**
2002—San Francisco (N.L.)	0	0	...	3.86	2	0	0	0	0-1	2.1	4	1	1	0	1-0	0

FURCAL, RAFAEL — SS/2B — BRAVES

PERSONAL: Born August 24, 1977, in Loma De Cabrera, Dominican Republic. ... 5-10/165. ... Bats both, throws right. ... Full name: Rafael Antoni Furcal.

HIGH SCHOOL: Jose Cabrera (Loma De Cabrera, Dominican Republic).

TRANSACTIONS/CAREER NOTES: Signed as non-drafted free agent by Atlanta Braves organization (November 9, 1996). ... On Atlanta disabled list (June 13-29, 2000). ... On disabled list (July 7, 2001-remainder of season).

RECORDS: Shares major league single-game record for most triples—4 (April 21, 2002).

HONORS: Named N.L. Rookie Player of the Year by The Sporting News (2000). ... Named N.L. Rookie of the Year by Baseball Writers' Association of America (2000).

STATISTICAL NOTES: Led Gulf Coast League second basemen with 122 putouts and 257 total chances in 1997. ... Led Appalachian League in caught stealing with 15 in 1998. ... Led Appalachian League second basemen with 183 putouts, 395 total chances and 51 double plays in 1998. ... Had 15-game hitting streak (June 21-July 6, 2002).

2002 GAMES PLAYED BY POSITION (MLB): SS—150; 2B—4.

		BATTING														FIELDING	
Year Team (League)	**Pos.**	**G**	**AB**	**R**	**H**	**2B**	**3B**	**HR**	**RBI**	**BB**	**SO**	**SB-CS**	**Avg.**	**OBP**	**SLG**	**E**	**Avg.**
1997—GC Braves (GCL)	2B-OF	50	190	31	49	5	4	1	9	20	21	15-2	.258	.335	.342	10	.961
1998—Danville (Appl.)	2B	66	268	56	88	15	4	0	23	36	29	*60-15	.328	.412	.414	14	.965
1999—Macon (S.Atl.)	SS	83	335	73	113	15	1	1	29	41	36	*73-22	*.337	*.417	.397	30	.912
—Myrtle Beach (Caro.)	SS	43	184	32	54	9	3	0	12	14	42	23-8	.293	.343	.375	4	.975
2000—Greenville (Sou.)	SS	3	10	1	2	0	0	1	3	1	0	0-0	.200	.273	.500	1	.889
—Atlanta (N.L.)	SS-2B	131	455	87	134	20	4	4	37	73	80	40-14	.295	.394	.382	24	.958
2001—Atlanta (N.L.)	SS	79	324	39	89	19	0	4	30	24	56	22-6	.275	.321	.370	11	.970
2002—Atlanta (N.L.)	SS-2B	154	636	95	175	31	8	8	47	43	114	27-15	.275	.323	.387	27	.964
Major League totals (3 years)		364	1415	221	398	70	12	16	114	140	250	89-35	.281	.347	.382	62	.963

DIVISION SERIES RECORD

		BATTING														FIELDING	
Year Team (League)	**Pos.**	**G**	**AB**	**R**	**H**	**2B**	**3B**	**HR**	**RBI**	**BB**	**SO**	**SB-CS**	**Avg.**	**OBP**	**SLG**	**E**	**Avg.**
2000—Atlanta (N.L.)	2B-SS	3	11	2	1	0	0	0	0	3	0	1-1	.091	.286	.091	1	.933
2002—Atlanta (N.L.)	SS	5	24	2	6	1	1	0	2	0	5	1-1	.250	.250	.375	0	1.000
Division series totals (2 years)		8	35	4	7	1	1	0	2	3	5	2-2	.200	.263	.286	1	.970

FYHRIE, MICHAEL — P — ATHLETICS

PERSONAL: Born December 9, 1969, in Westminster, Calif. ... 6-2/205. ... Throws right, bats right. ... Full name: Michael Edwin Fyhrie. ... Name pronounced Feery.

HIGH SCHOOL: Ocean View (Huntington Beach, Calif.).

COLLEGE: UCLA.

TRANSACTIONS/CAREER NOTES: Selected by Kansas City Royals organization in 12th round of free-agent draft (June 3, 1991). ... Traded by Royals to New York Mets for a player to be named later (March 23, 1996). ... Contract sold by Mets to Chiba Lotte of Japan Pacific League (November 25, 1996). ... Re-signed by Mets organization (December 6, 1997). ... On disabled list (August 2, 1998-remainder of season). ... Granted free agency (October 15, 1998). ... Signed by Anaheim Angels organization (November 18, 1998). ... On Anaheim disabled list (August 12-September 4, 2000). ... Traded by Angels with a player to be named later to Chicago Cubs for SS/2B Jose Nieves (March 25, 2001). ... On Chicago disabled list (May 2-July 14, 2001); included rehabilitation assignments to Arizona League Cubs (July 2-7) and Iowa (July 7-14). ... Traded by Cubs to Oakland Athletics for OF Michael Wenner (September 4, 2001).

HONORS: Named International League Most Valuable Pitcher in 1996.

CAREER HITTING (MLB): 0-for-2 (.000), 0 R, 0 2B, 0 3B, 0 HR, 0 RBI.

Year League	**W**	**L**	**Pct.**	**ERA**	**G**	**GS**	**CG**	**ShO**	**Sv.-Opp.**	**IP**	**H**	**R**	**ER**	**HR**	**BB-IBB**	**SO**
1991—Eugene (N'West)	2	1	.667	2.52	21	0	0	0	5-...	39.1	42	17	11	0	19-1	45
1992—Baseball City (FSL)	7	13	.350	2.50	26	26	0	0	0-...	162.0	148	65	45	6	37-1	92
1993—Wilmington (Caro.)	3	2	.600	3.68	5	5	0	0	0-...	29.1	32	15	12	3	8-0	19
—Memphis (Sou.)	11	4	.733	3.56	22	22	3	0	0-...	131.1	143	59	52	11	59-0	59
1994—Omaha (A.A.)	6	5	.545	5.72	18	16	0	0	0-...	85.0	100	57	54	13	33-1	37
—Memphis (Sou.)	2	5	.286	3.22	11	11	0	0	0-...	67.0	67	29	24	4	17-1	38
1995—Wichita (Texas)	3	2	.600	3.04	17	9	0	0	1-...	74.0	76	31	25	4	23-0	41
—Omaha (A.A.)	3	4	.429	4.45	14	11	0	0	0-...	60.2	71	34	30	7	14-0	39
1996—Norfolk (I.L.)■	*15	6	.714	3.04	27	27	2	•2	0-...	169.0	150	61	57	16	33-1	103
—New York (N.L.)	0	1	.000	15.43	2	0	0	0	0-0	2.1	4	4	4	0	3-0	0
1997—Chiba Lotte (Jap. Pac.)■	3	4	.429	5.86	8	8	0	0	0-...	43.0	54	29	28	...	15-...	15
—Chiba (Jp. East.)	4	2	.667	3.09	15	11	1	...	1-...	70.0	77	25	24	...	24-...	33
1998—Norfolk (I.L.)■	3	7	.300	6.64	24	17	0	0	0-...	100.1	115	83	74	12	45-1	60
1999—Edmonton (PCL)■	9	5	.643	3.47	19	18	0	0	0-...	114.0	90	47	44	8	40-0	113
—Anaheim (A.L.)	0	4	.000	5.05	16	7	0	0	0-0	51.2	61	32	29	8	21-1	26
2000—Anaheim (A.L.)	0	0	...	2.39	32	0	0	0	0-0	52.2	54	14	14	4	15-4	43
—Edmonton (PCL)	2	1	.667	2.30	9	0	0	0	1-...	15.2	6	4	4	1	12-0	9
2001—Chicago (N.L.)■	0	2	.000	4.20	15	0	0	0	0-0	15.0	16	7	7	1	7-0	6
—Arizona Cubs (Ariz.)	0	0	...	0.00	2	2	0	0	0-...	2.0	1	0	0	0	0-0	4
—Iowa (PCL)	1	0	1.000	4.80	13	0	0	0	2-...	15.0	14	8	8	1	8-0	15
—Oakland (A.L.)■	0	0	...	0.00	3	0	0	0	0-0	5.0	2	0	0	0	1-0	5
2002—Sacramento (PCL)■	7	2	.778	2.33	13	13	0	0	0-...	77.1	61	22	20	4	23-0	68
—Oakland (A.L.)	2	4	.333	4.44	16	4	0	0	0-0	48.2	46	25	24	3	20-1	29
A.L. totals (4 years)	2	8	.200	3.82	67	11	0	0	0-0	158.0	163	71	67	15	57-6	103
N.L. totals (2 years)	0	3	.000	5.71	17	0	0	0	0-0	17.1	20	11	11	1	10-0	6
Major League totals (5 years)	2	11	.154	4.00	84	11	0	0	0-0	175.1	183	82	78	16	67-6	109

GAGNE, ERIC — P — DODGERS

PERSONAL: Born January 7, 1976, in Montreal. ... 6-2/195. ... Throws right, bats right. ... Full name: Eric Serge Gagne. ... Name pronounced GAHN-yay.

HIGH SCHOOL: Polyvalente Edouard Montpetit (Montreal).

JUNIOR COLLEGE: Seminole State Junior College (Okla.).

TRANSACTIONS/CAREER NOTES: Signed as non-drafted free agent by Los Angeles Dodgers organization (July 26, 1995). ... On disabled list entire 1997 season. ... On San Antonio suspended list (April 26-29, 1999).

HONORS: Named Texas League Pitcher of the Year (1999).

CAREER HITTING (MLB): 12-for-83 (.145), 5 R, 2 2B, 1 3B, 1 HR, 3 RBI.

Year	League	W	L	Pct.	ERA	G	GS	CG	ShO	Sv.-Opp.	IP	H	R	ER	HR	BB-IBB	SO
1996—	Savannah (S.Atl.)	7	6	.538	3.28	23	21	1	1	0-...	115.1	94	48	42	11	43-1	131
1997—										Did not play.							
1998—	Vero Beach (FSL)	9	7	.563	3.74	25	25	3	1	0-...	139.2	118	69	58	16	48-0	144
1999—	San Antonio (Texas)	12	4	.750	2.63	26	26	0	0	0-...	167.2	122	55	49	17	64-0	185
—	Los Angeles (N.L.)	1	1	.500	2.10	5	5	0	0	0-0	30.0	18	8	7	3	15-0	30
2000—	Albuquerque (PCL)	5	1	.833	3.88	9	9	0	0	0-...	55.2	56	30	24	8	15-0	59
—	Los Angeles (N.L.)	4	6	.400	5.15	20	19	0	0	0-0	101.1	106	62	58	20	60-1	79
2001—	Los Angeles (N.L.)	6	7	.462	4.75	33	24	0	0	0-0	151.2	144	90	80	24	46-1	130
—	Las Vegas (PCL)	3	0	1.000	1.52	4	4	0	0	0-...	23.2	15	4	4	2	8-0	31
2002—	Los Angeles (N.L.)	4	1	.800	1.97	77	0	0	0	52-56	82.1	55	18	18	6	16-4	114
Major League totals (4 years)		15	15	.500	4.02	135	48	0	0	52-56	365.1	323	178	163	53	137-6	353

ALL-STAR GAME RECORD

	W	L	Pct.	ERA	GS	CG	ShO	Sv.-Opp.	IP	H	R	ER	HR	BB-IBB	SO
All-Star Game totals (1 year)	0	0	...	9.00	0	0	0	0-0	1.0	2	1	1	1	0-0	1

GALARRAGA, ANDRES — 1B

PERSONAL: Born June 18, 1961, in Caracas, Venezuela. ... 6-3/250. ... Bats right, throws right. ... Full name: Andres Jose Galarraga. ... Name pronounced GAHL-ah-RAH-guh.

HIGH SCHOOL: Enrique Felmi (Caracas, Venezuela).

TRANSACTIONS/CAREER NOTES: Signed as non-drafted free agent by Montreal Expos organization (January 19, 1979). ... On disabled list (July 10-August 19 and August 20-September 4, 1986; and May 26-July 4, 1991). ... Traded by Expos to St. Louis Cardinals for P Ken Hill (November 25, 1991). ... On St. Louis disabled list (April 8-May 22, 1992); included rehabilitation assignment to Louisville (May 13-22). ... Granted free agency (October 27, 1992). ... Signed by Colorado Rockies (November 16, 1992). ... On disabled list (May 10-27 and July 25-August 21, 1993). ... Granted free agency (October 25, 1993). ... Re-signed by Rockies (December 6, 1993). ... On disabled list (July 29, 1994-remainder of season). ... On suspended list (August 3-5, 1997). ... Granted free agency (October 27, 1997). ... Signed by Atlanta Braves (November 20, 1997). ... On suspended list (September 2-5, 1998). ... On Atlanta disabled list (April 3, 1999-entire season). ... On suspended list (September 7-10, 2000). ... Granted free agency (October 30, 2000). ... Signed by Texas Rangers (December 8, 2000). ... Traded by Rangers to San Francisco Giants for P Erasma Ramirez, IF Chris Magruder and P Todd Ozias (July 24, 2001). ... Granted free agency (November 7, 2001). ... Signed by Expos (March 7, 2002). ... On disabled list (May 3-26, 2002). ... Granted free agency (October 28, 2002).

RECORDS: Shares major league single-inning record for most times hit by pitch—2 (July 12, 1996, seventh inning).

HONORS: Named Southern League Most Valuable Player (1984). ... Named first baseman on The Sporting News N.L. Silver Slugger team (1988 and 1996). ... Won N.L. Gold Glove at first base (1989-90). ... Named N.L. Comeback Player of the Year by The Sporting News (1993 and 2000).

STATISTICAL NOTES: Led Southern League with 271 total bases and 10 intentional bases on balls received and tied for lead in being hit by pitch with nine in 1984. ... Led Southern League first basemen with 1,302 putouts, 110 assists, 1,428 total chances and 130 double plays in 1984. ... Led N.L. first basemen with 1,302 putouts in 1987. ... Led N.L. in being hit by pitch with 10 in 1987 and tied for lead with 13 in 1989. ... Led N.L. with 329 total bases in 1988. ... Hit three home runs in one game (June 25, 1995). ... Collected six hits in one game (July 3, 1995). ... Led N.L. first basemen with 1,299 putouts, 1,432 total chances and 129 double plays in 1995. ... Led N.L. first basemen with 1,528 putouts, 1,658 total chances and 154 double plays in 1996. ... Led N.L. first basemen with 1,458 putouts, 1,590 total chances and 176 double plays in 1997. ... Had 15-game hitting streak (April 23-May 8, 1998). ... Career major league grand slams: 10.

2002 GAMES PLAYED BY POSITION (MLB): 1B—89.

			BATTING															FIELDING	
Year	Team (League)	Pos.	G	AB	R	H	2B	3B	HR	RBI	BB	SO	SB-CS	Avg.	OBP	SLG	E	Avg.
1979—	W. Palm Beach (FSL)	1B	7	23	3	3	0	0	0	1	2	11	0-0	.130	.231	.130	0	1.000
—	Calgary (Pio.)	1B-3B-C	42	112	14	24	3	1	4	16	9	42	1-1	.214	.299	.366	5	.977
1980—	Calgary (Pio.)	1B-3B-C-OF	59	190	27	50	11	4	4	22	7	55	3-0	.263	.307	.426	21	.942
1981—	Jamestown (NY-P)	C-1B-OF-3B	47	154	24	40	5	4	6	26	15	44	0-0	.260	.339	.461	0	1.000
1982—	W. Palm Beach (FSL)	1B-OF	105	338	39	95	20	2	14	51	34	77	2-1	.281	.360	.476	9	.982
1983—	W. Palm Beach (FSL)	1B-OF-3B	104	401	55	116	18	3	10	66	33	68	7-5	.289	.353	.424	13	.986
1984—	Jacksonville (Sou.)	1B	143	533	81	154	28	4	27	87	59	122	2-8	.289	.367	*.508	16	.989
1985—	Indianapolis (A.A.)	1B-OF	121	439	*75	118	15	8	25	87	45	103	3-0	.269	.344	.510	14	.986
—	Montreal (N.L.)	1B	24	75	9	14	1	0	2	4	3	18	1-2	.187	.228	.280	1	.995
1986—	Montreal (N.L.)	1B	105	321	39	87	13	0	10	42	30	79	6-5	.271	.338	.405	4	.995
1987—	Montreal (N.L.)	1B	147	551	72	168	40	3	13	90	41	127	7-10	.305	.361	.459	10	.993
1988—	Montreal (N.L.)	1B	157	609	99	*184	*42	8	29	92	39	*153	13-4	.302	.352	.540	15	.991
1989—	Montreal (N.L.)	1B	152	572	76	147	30	1	23	85	48	*158	12-5	.257	.327	.434	11	.992
1990—	Montreal (N.L.)	1B	155	579	65	148	29	0	20	87	40	*169	10-1	.256	.306	.409	10	.993
1991—	Montreal (N.L.)	1B	107	375	34	82	13	2	9	33	23	86	5-6	.219	.268	.336	9	.991
1992—	St. Louis (N.L.)■	1B	95	325	38	79	14	2	10	39	11	69	5-4	.243	.282	.391	8	.991
—	Louisville (A.A.)	1B	11	34	3	6	0	1	2	3	0	8	1-0	.176	.200	.412	2	.971
1993—	Colorado (N.L.)■	1B	120	470	71	174	35	4	22	98	24	73	2-4	*.370	.403	.602	11	.990
1994—	Colorado (N.L.)	1B	103	417	77	133	21	0	31	85	19	93	8-3	.319	.356	.592	8	.992
1995—	Colorado (N.L.)	1B	143	554	89	155	29	3	31	106	32	*146	12-2	.280	.331	.511	*13	.991
1996—	Colorado (N.L.)	1B-3B	159	626	119	190	39	3	*47	*150	40	157	18-8	.304	.357	.601	14	.992
1997—	Colorado (N.L.)	1B	154	600	120	191	31	3	41	*140	54	141	15-8	.318	.389	.585	*15	.991
1998—	Atlanta (N.L.)■	1B-DH	153	555	103	169	27	1	44	121	63	146	7-6	.305	.397	.595	11	.992
1999—	Atlanta (N.L.)								Did not play.									

Year Team (League)	Pos.	G	AB	R	H	2B	3B	HR	RBI	BB	SO	SB-CS	Avg.	OBP	SLG	E	Avg.
		BATTING														FIELDING	
2000—Atlanta (N.L.)	1B-DH	141	494	67	149	25	1	28	100	36	126	3-5	.302	.369	.526	14	.988
2001—Texas (A.L.)■	DH-1B	72	243	33	57	16	0	10	34	18	68	1-0	.235	.310	.424	1	.995
—San Fran. (N.L.)■	1B	49	156	17	45	12	1	7	35	13	49	0-3	.288	.351	.513	5	.984
2002—Montreal (N.L.)■	1B	104	292	30	76	12	0	9	40	30	81	2-2	.260	.344	.394	13	.981
American League totals (1 year)		72	243	33	57	16	0	10	34	18	68	1-0	.235	.310	.424	1	.995
National League totals (17 years)		2068	7571	1125	2191	413	32	376	1347	546	1871	126-78	.289	.348	.501	172	.991
Major League totals (17 years)		2140	7814	1158	2248	429	32	386	1381	564	1939	127-78	.288	.347	.499	173	.991

DIVISION SERIES RECORD

Year Team (League)	Pos.	G	AB	R	H	2B	3B	HR	RBI	BB	SO	SB-CS	Avg.	OBP	SLG	E	Avg.
		BATTING														FIELDING	
1995—Colorado (N.L.)	1B	4	18	1	5	1	0	0	2	0	6	0-0	.278	.278	.333	0	1.000
1998—Atlanta (N.L.)	1B	3	12	1	3	0	0	0	0	1	3	0-0	.250	.308	.250	0	1.000
2000—Atlanta (N.L.)	1B	3	10	1	2	1	0	0	1	2	4	0-0	.200	.385	.300	0	1.000
Division series totals (3 years)		10	40	3	10	2	0	0	3	3	13	0-0	.250	.318	.300	0	1.000

CHAMPIONSHIP SERIES RECORD

RECORDS: Shares single-inning record for most runs batted in—4 (October 11, 1998, seventh inning).

Year Team (League)	Pos.	G	AB	R	H	2B	3B	HR	RBI	BB	SO	SB-CS	Avg.	OBP	SLG	E	Avg.
		BATTING														FIELDING	
1998—Atlanta (N.L.)	1B	6	21	1	2	0	0	1	4	6	6	0-0	.095	.296	.238	4	.949

ALL-STAR GAME RECORD

	AB	R	H	2B	3B	HR	RBI	BB	SO	SB-CS	Avg.	OBP	SLG	E	Avg.
All-Star Game totals (5 years)	8	0	1	0	0	0	0	0	2	0-0	.125	.125	.125	0	1.000

GANT, RON OF

PERSONAL: Born March 2, 1965, in Victoria, Texas. ... 6-0/195. ... Bats right, throws right. ... Full name: Ronald Edwin Gant.

HIGH SCHOOL: Victoria (Texas).

TRANSACTIONS/CAREER NOTES: Selected by Atlanta Braves organization in fourth round of free-agent draft (June 6, 1983). ... On suspended list (July 31, 1991). ... Released by Braves (March 15, 1994). ... Signed by Cincinnati Reds (June 21, 1994). ... On disabled list (June 21, 1994-remainder of season). ... On suspended list (September 11-15, 1995). ... Granted free agency (October 30, 1995). ... Signed by St. Louis Cardinals (December 23, 1995). ... On disabled list (May 11-June 14, 1996; and June 21-July 11, 1998). ... Traded by Cardinals with P Jeff Brantley and P Cliff Politte to Philadelphia Phillies for P Ricky Bottalico and P Garrett Stephenson (November 19, 1998). ... Traded by Phillies to Anaheim Angels for P Kent Bottenfield (July 30, 2000). ... Granted free agency (October 30, 2000). ... Signed by Colorado Rockies (December 10, 2000). ... Traded by Rockies to Oakland Athletics for OF Robin Jennings (July 3, 2001). ... Granted free agency (November 5, 2001). ... Signed by San Diego Padres organization (January 18, 2002). ... On disabled list (April 24-May 21, 2002). ... Granted free agency (October 28, 2002).

HONORS: Named outfielder on The Sporting News N.L. All-Star team (1991). ... Named outfielder on The Sporting News N.L. Silver Slugger team (1991). ... Named N.L. Comeback Player of the Year by The Sporting News (1995).

STATISTICAL NOTES: Led Carolina League with 271 total bases in 1986. ... Led Southern League second basemen with 328 putouts, 434 assists, 783 total chances and 108 double plays in 1987. ... Led N.L. second basemen with 26 errors in 1988. ... Career major league grand slams: 5.

2002 GAMES PLAYED BY POSITION (MLB): OF—80; DH—4.

Year Team (League)	Pos.	G	AB	R	H	2B	3B	HR	RBI	BB	SO	SB-CS	Avg.	OBP	SLG	E	Avg.
		BATTING														FIELDING	
1983—GC Braves (GCL)	SS	56	193	32	45	2	2	1	14	41	34	4-6	.233	.366	.280	22	.902
1984—Anderson (S.Atl.)	2B	105	359	44	85	14	6	3	38	29	65	13-5	.237	.291	.334	31	.943
1985—Sumter (S.Atl.)	2B-SS-OF	102	305	46	78	14	4	7	37	33	59	19-10	.256	.332	.397	10	.973
1986—Durham (Caro.)	2B	137	512	108	142	31	10	*26	102	78	85	35-9	.277	.372	.529	26	.960
1987—Greenville (Sou.)	2B	140	527	78	130	27	3	14	82	59	91	24-4	.247	.321	.389	21	*.973
—Atlanta (N.L.)	2B	21	83	9	22	4	0	2	9	1	11	4-2	.265	.271	.386	3	.972
1988—Richmond (I.L.)	2B	12	45	3	14	2	2	0	4	2	10	1-1	.311	.333	.444	5	.900
—Atlanta (N.L.)	2B-3B	146	563	85	146	28	8	19	60	46	118	19-10	.259	.317	.439	†31	.959
1989—Atlanta (N.L.)	3B-OF	75	260	26	46	8	3	9	25	20	63	9-6	.177	.237	.335	17	.911
—Sumter (S.Atl.)	OF	12	39	13	15	4	1	1	5	11	3	4-2	.385	.520	.615	2	.909
—Richmond (I.L.)	OF-3B	63	225	42	59	13	2	11	27	29	42	6-2	.262	.345	.484	5	.962
1990—Atlanta (N.L.)	OF	152	575	107	174	34	3	32	84	50	86	33-16	.303	.357	.539	8	.978
1991—Atlanta (N.L.)	OF	154	561	101	141	35	3	32	105	71	104	34-15	.251	.338	.496	6	.983
1992—Atlanta (N.L.)	OF	153	544	74	141	22	6	17	80	45	101	32-10	.259	.321	.415	4	.986
1993—Atlanta (N.L.)	OF	157	606	113	166	27	4	36	117	67	117	26-9	.274	.345	.510	*11	.962
1994—Cincinnati (N.L.)■								Did not play.									
1995—Cincinnati (N.L.)	OF	119	410	79	113	19	4	29	88	74	108	23-8	.276	.386	.554	3	.985
1996—St. Louis (N.L.)■	OF	122	419	74	103	14	2	30	82	73	98	13-4	.246	.359	.504	5	.978
1997—St. Louis (N.L.)	OF-DH	139	502	68	115	21	4	17	62	58	162	14-6	.229	.310	.388	6	.977
1998—St. Louis (N.L.)	OF	121	383	60	92	17	1	26	67	51	92	8-0	.240	.331	.493	5	.971
1999—Philadelphia (N.L.)■	OF-DH	138	516	107	134	27	5	17	77	85	112	13-3	.260	.364	.430	2	.993
2000—Philadelphia (N.L.)	OF	89	343	54	87	16	2	20	38	36	73	5-4	.254	.324	.487	6	.968
—Anaheim (A.L.)■	OF-DH	34	82	15	19	3	1	6	16	20	18	1-2	.232	.379	.512	1	.977
2001—Colorado (N.L.)■	OF	59	171	31	44	8	2	8	22	24	56	3-1	.257	.345	.468	3	.965
—Oakland (A.L.)■	DH-OF	34	81	15	21	5	1	2	13	11	24	2-0	.259	.344	.420	0	1.000
2002—San Diego (N.L.)■	OF-DH	102	309	58	81	14	1	18	59	36	59	4-6	.262	.338	.489	3	.980
American League totals (2 years)		68	163	30	40	8	2	8	29	31	42	3-2	.245	.362	.466	1	.979
National League totals (15 years)		1747	6245	1046	1605	294	48	312	975	737	1360	240-100	.257	.336	.469	113	.971
Major League totals (15 years)		1815	6408	1076	1645	302	50	320	1004	768	1402	243-102	.257	.337	.469	114	.971

DIVISION SERIES RECORD

Year	Team (League)	Pos.	G	AB	R	H	2B	3B	HR	RBI	BB	SO	SB-CS	Avg.	OBP	SLG	E	Avg.
			BATTING														FIELDING	
1995—	Cincinnati (N.L.)	OF	3	13	3	3	0	0	1	2	0	3	0-0	.231	.231	.462	0	1.000
1996—	St. Louis (N.L.)	OF	3	10	3	4	1	0	1	4	2	0	2-0	.400	.538	.800	0	1.000
2001—	Oakland (A.L.)	PH-DH-OF	4	11	1	2	0	0	1	1	0	3	0-0	.182	.182	.455	0	1.000
Division series totals (3 years)			10	34	7	9	1	0	3	7	2	6	2-0	.265	.324	.559	0	1.000

CHAMPIONSHIP SERIES RECORD

RECORDS: Shares single-game record for most grand slams—1 (October 7, 1992). ... Shares single-inning records for most runs batted in—4 (October 7, 1992, fifth inning); and most stolen bases—2 (October 10, 1991, third inning). ... Holds N.L. career record for most strikeouts—26. ... Holds N.L. single-series record for most stolen bases—7 (1991). ... Shares N.L. single-game record for most stolen bases—3 (October 10, 1991).

Year	Team (League)	Pos.	G	AB	R	H	2B	3B	HR	RBI	BB	SO	SB-CS	Avg.	OBP	SLG	E	Avg.
			BATTING														FIELDING	
1991—	Atlanta (N.L.)	OF	7	27	4	7	1	0	1	3	2	4	7-0	.259	.323	.407	0	1.000
1992—	Atlanta (N.L.)	OF	7	22	5	4	0	0	2	6	4	4	1-0	.182	.296	.455	0	1.000
1993—	Atlanta (N.L.)	OF	6	27	4	5	3	0	0	3	2	9	0-1	.185	.241	.296	1	.917
1995—	Cincinnati (N.L.)	OF	4	16	1	3	0	0	0	1	0	3	0-0	.188	.235	.188	0	1.000
1996—	St. Louis (N.L.)	OF	7	25	3	6	1	0	2	4	2	6	0-0	.240	.296	.520	0	1.000
Championship series totals (5 years)			31	117	17	25	5	0	5	17	10	26	8-1	.214	.282	.385	1	.985

WORLD SERIES RECORD

Year	Team (League)	Pos.	G	AB	R	H	2B	3B	HR	RBI	BB	SO	SB-CS	Avg.	OBP	SLG	E	Avg.
			BATTING														FIELDING	
1991—	Atlanta (N.L.)	OF	7	30	3	8	0	1	0	4	2	3	1-0	.267	.313	.333	0	1.000
1992—	Atlanta (N.L.)	OF-PR-PH	4	8	2	1	1	0	0	0	1	2	2-0	.125	.222	.250	0	1.000
World Series totals (2 years)			11	38	5	9	1	1	0	4	3	5	3-0	.237	.293	.316	0	1.000

ALL-STAR GAME RECORD

	AB	R	H	2B	3B	HR	RBI	BB	SO	SB-CS	Avg.	OBP	SLG	E	Avg.
All-Star Game totals (2 years)	4	0	0	0	0	0	0	0	1	0-0	.000	.000	.000	0	1.000

GARCES, RICH — P

PERSONAL: Born May 18, 1971, in Maracay, Venezuela. ... 6-0/250. ... Throws right, bats right. ... Full name: Richard Aron Garces Jr. ... Name pronounced gar-SESS.

HIGH SCHOOL: Jose Felix Rivas (Maracay, Venezuela).

COLLEGE: Venezuela Universidad.

TRANSACTIONS/CAREER NOTES: Signed as non-drafted free agent by Minnesota Twins organization (December 29, 1987). ... On Portland suspended list (May 17-September 16, 1991). ... On Portland disabled list (July 28, 1991-remainder of season). ... Granted free agency (October 15, 1994). ... Signed by Chicago Cubs organization (January 30, 1995). ... Claimed on waivers by Florida Marlins (August 9, 1995). ... Granted free agency (October 16, 1995). ... Signed by Boston Red Sox (April 25, 1996). ... On Boston disabled list (July 25-August 20 and August 24, 1996-remainder of season); included rehabilitation assignment to Pawtucket (August 9-20). ... On Boston disabled list (March 27-April 27 and June 2-23, 1997); included rehabilitation assignments to Pawtucket (April 18-21, April 25-27 and June 12-23). ... On Boston disabled list (April 11-May 7, July 1-17 and August 3, 1998-remainder of season); included rehabilitation assignments to Pawtucket (April 21-May 7 and August 30-September 3) and Gulf Coast Red Sox (August 12-29). ... Released by Red Sox (November 23, 1998). ... Re-signed by Red Sox organization (January 26, 1999). ... On Pawtucket disabled list (April 8-22 and May 15-31, 1999). ... On Boston disabled list (June 26-July 12, 2001); included rehabilitation assignment to Lowell (July 8-12). ... On Boston disabled list (June 2-25, 2002); included rehabilitation assignment to Gulf Coast Red Sox (June 19-25). ... Released by Red Sox (August 1, 2002).

CAREER HITTING (MLB): 0-for-3 (.000), 0 R, 0 2B, 0 3B, 0 HR, 0 RBI.

Year	League	W	L	Pct.	ERA	G	GS	CG	ShO	Sv.-Opp.	IP	H	R	ER	HR	BB-IBB	SO
1988—	Elizabethton (Appl.)	5	4	.556	2.29	17	3	1	0	5-...	59.0	51	22	15	1	27-2	69
1989—	Kenosha (Midw.)	9	10	.474	3.41	24	24	4	1	0-...	142.2	117	70	54	5	62-1	84
1990—	Visalia (Calif.)	2	2	.500	1.81	47	0	0	0	*28-...	54.2	33	14	11	2	16-0	75
—	Orlando (Sou.)	2	1	.667	2.08	15	0	0	0	8-...	17.1	17	4	4	0	14-2	22
—	Minnesota (A.L.)	0	0	...	1.59	5	0	0	0	2-2	5.2	4	2	1	0	4-0	1
1991—	Portland (PCL)	0	1	.000	4.85	10	0	0	0	3-...	13.0	10	7	7	1	8-1	13
—	Orlando (Sou.)	2	1	.667	3.31	10	0	0	0	0-...	16.1	12	6	6	0	14-2	17
1992—	Orlando (Sou.)	3	3	.500	4.54	58	0	0	0	13-...	73.1	76	46	37	6	39-1	72
1993—	Portland (PCL)	1	3	.250	8.33	35	7	0	0	0-...	54.0	70	55	50	4	64-0	48
—	Minnesota (A.L.)	0	0	...	0.00	3	0	0	0	0-0	4.0	4	2	0	0	2-0	3
1994—	Nashville (Sou.)	4	5	.444	3.72	40	1	0	0	3-...	77.1	70	40	32	5	31-0	76
1995—	Iowa (A.A.)■	0	2	.000	2.86	23	0	0	0	7-...	28.1	25	10	9	3	8-1	36
—	Chicago (N.L.)	0	0	...	3.27	7	0	0	0	0-0	11.0	11	6	4	0	3-0	6
—	Florida (N.L.)■	0	2	.000	5.40	11	0	0	0	0-1	13.1	14	9	8	1	8-2	16
1996—	Pawtucket (I.L.)■	4	0	1.000	2.30	10	0	0	0	0-...	15.2	10	4	4	2	5-0	13
—	Boston (A.L.)	3	2	.600	4.91	37	0	0	0	0-2	44.0	42	26	24	5	33-5	55
1997—	Boston (A.L.)	0	1	.000	4.61	12	0	0	0	0-2	13.2	14	9	7	2	9-0	12
—	Pawtucket (I.L.)	2	1	.667	1.45	26	0	0	0	5-...	31.0	24	5	5	0	13-3	42
1998—	Boston (A.L.)	1	1	.500	3.33	30	0	0	0	1-3	46.0	36	19	17	6	27-3	34
—	Pawtucket (I.L.)	0	1	.000	5.40	7	0	0	0	3-...	8.1	6	5	5	1	2-1	10
—	Gulf Coast Red Sox (GCL)	0	0	...	3.27	7	7	0	0	0-...	11.0	11	4	4	0	0-0	8
1999—	Pawtucket (I.L.)	1	0	1.000	3.25	21	0	0	0	7-...	27.2	24	11	10	5	10-0	24
—	Boston (A.L.)	5	1	.833	1.55	30	0	0	0	2-3	40.2	25	9	7	1	18-1	33
2000—	Boston (A.L.)	8	1	.889	3.25	64	0	0	0	1-5	74.2	64	28	27	7	23-5	69
2001—	Boston (A.L.)	6	1	.857	3.90	62	0	0	0	1-2	67.0	55	32	29	6	25-1	51
—	Lowell (NY-Penn)	0	0	...	0.00	2	2	0	0	0-...	2.0	1	0	0	0	0-0	1
2002—	Boston (A.L.)	0	1	.000	7.59	26	0	0	0	0-0	21.1	21	20	18	4	12-2	16
—	Gulf Coast Red Sox (GCL)	0	0	...	0.00	2	2	0	0	0-...	4.0	1	1	0	0	0-0	5
A.L. totals (9 years)		23	8	.742	3.69	269	0	0	0	7-19	317.0	265	147	130	31	153-17	274
N.L. totals (1 year)		0	2	.000	4.44	18	0	0	0	0-1	24.1	25	15	12	1	11-2	22
Major League totals (10 years)		23	10	.697	3.74	287	0	0	0	7-20	341.1	290	162	142	32	164-19	296

DIVISION SERIES RECORD

Year	League	W	L	Pct.	ERA	G	GS	CG	ShO	Sv.-Opp.	IP	H	R	ER	HR	BB-IBB	SO
1999—	Boston (A.L.)	1	0	1.000	3.86	2	0	0	0	0-0	2.1	2	1	1	0	3-0	2

CHAMPIONSHIP SERIES RECORD

Year	League	W	L	Pct.	ERA	G	GS	CG	ShO	Sv.-Opp.	IP	H	R	ER	HR	BB-IBB	SO
1999—	Boston (A.L.)	0	0	...	12.00	2	0	0	0	0-0	3.0	3	5	4	0	1-1	2

GARCIA, FREDDY P MARINERS

PERSONAL: Born June 10, 1976, in Caracas, Venezuela. ... 6-4/235. ... Throws right, bats right. ... Full name: Freddy Antonio Garcia.

TRANSACTIONS/CAREER NOTES: Signed as non-drafted free agent by Houston Astros organization (October 21, 1993). ... Traded by Astros with SS Carlos Guillen and a player to be named later to Seattle Mariners for P Randy Johnson (July 31, 1998); Mariners acquired P John Halama to complete deal (October 1, 1998). ... On Seattle disabled list (April 22-July 7, 2000); included rehabilitation assignments to Tacoma (June 15-20) and Everett (June 21-July 7).

STATISTICAL NOTES: Tied for A.L. lead with three balks in 1999.

MISCELLANEOUS: Struck out in only appearance as pinch hitter (1999).

CAREER HITTING (MLB): 6-for-20 (.300), 0 R, 1 2B, 0 3B, 0 HR, 1 RBI.

Year	League	W	L	Pct.	ERA	G	GS	CG	ShO	Sv.-Opp.	IP	H	R	ER	HR	BB-IBB	SO
1994—	Dominican Astros (DSL)	4	6	.400	5.29	16	15	0	0	0-...	85.0	80	61	50	...	38-...	68
1995—	Gulf Coast Astros (GCL)	6	3	.667	4.47	11	11	0	0	0-...	58.1	60	32	29	2	14-0	58
1996—	Quad City (Midw.)	5	4	.556	3.12	13	13	0	0	0-...	60.2	57	27	21	3	27-0	50
1997—	Kissimmee (FSL)	10	8	.556	2.56	27	27	5	•2	0-...	179.0	165	63	51	6	49-3	131
1998—	Jackson (Texas)	6	7	.462	3.24	19	19	2	0	0-...	119.1	94	48	43	8	58-0	115
—	New Orleans (PCL)	1	0	1.000	3.14	2	2	0	0	0-...	14.1	14	5	5	2	1-0	13
—	Tacoma (PCL)■	3	1	.750	3.86	5	5	0	0	0-...	32.2	30	14	14	6	13-0	30
1999—	Seattle (A.L.)	17	8	.680	4.07	33	33	2	1	0-0	201.1	205	96	91	18	90-4	170
2000—	Seattle (A.L.)	9	5	.643	3.91	21	20	0	0	0-0	124.1	112	62	54	16	64-4	79
—	Everett (N'West)	0	0	...	4.50	2	2	0	0	0-...	10.0	11	5	5	1	2-0	15
—	Tacoma (PCL)	1	0	1.000	2.57	1	1	0	0	0-...	7.0	5	2	2	2	2-0	11
2001—	Seattle (A.L.)	18	6	.750	3.05	34	34	4	3	0-0	*238.2	199	88	81	16	69-6	163
2002—	Seattle (A.L.)	16	10	.615	4.39	34	34	1	0	0-0	223.2	227	110	109	30	63-3	181
Major League totals (4 years)		60	29	.674	3.83	122	121	7	4	0-0	788.0	743	356	335	80	286-17	593

DIVISION SERIES RECORD

Year	League	W	L	Pct.	ERA	G	GS	CG	ShO	Sv.-Opp.	IP	H	R	ER	HR	BB-IBB	SO
2000—	Seattle (A.L.)	0	0	...	10.80	1	1	0	0	0-0	3.1	6	4	4	1	3-0	2
2001—	Seattle (A.L.)	1	1	.500	3.86	2	2	0	0	0-0	11.2	13	6	5	1	3-0	13
Division series totals (2 years)		1	1	.500	5.40	3	3	0	0	0-0	15.0	19	10	9	2	6-0	15

CHAMPIONSHIP SERIES RECORD

Year	League	W	L	Pct.	ERA	G	GS	CG	ShO	Sv.-Opp.	IP	H	R	ER	HR	BB-IBB	SO
2000—	Seattle (A.L.)	2	0	1.000	1.54	2	2	0	0	0-0	11.2	10	2	2	0	4-0	11
2001—	Seattle (A.L.)	0	1	.000	3.68	1	1	0	0	0-0	7.1	7	3	3	0	4-0	6
Champ. series totals (2 years)		2	1	.667	2.37	3	3	0	0	0-0	19.0	17	5	5	0	8-0	17

ALL-STAR GAME RECORD

	W	L	Pct.	ERA	GS	CG	ShO	Sv.-Opp.	IP	H	R	ER	HR	BB-IBB	SO
All-Star Game totals (2 years)	1	0	1.000	0.00	0	0	0	0-0	3.0	2	0	0	0	0-0	3

GARCIA, JESSE SS/2B BRAVES

PERSONAL: Born September 24, 1973, in Corpus Christi, Texas. ... 5-10/171. ... Bats right, throws right. ... Full name: Jesus Jesse Garcia Jr.

HIGH SCHOOL: Robstown (Texas).

JUNIOR COLLEGE: Lee College (Texas).

TRANSACTIONS/CAREER NOTES: Selected by Baltimore Orioles organization in 26th round of free-agent draft (June 3, 1993). ... On disabled list (June 19, 1994-entire season). ... Granted free agency (December 21, 1998). ... Re-signed by Orioles organization (December 21, 1998). ... On Rochester disabled list (May 25-July 18, 1999). ... Traded by Orioles for Atlanta Braves for IF Steve Sisco (December 18, 2000).

STATISTICAL NOTES: Led California League with 20 sacrifice hits in 1996. ... Led California League second basemen with 263 putouts, 409 assists, .968 fielding percentage, 694 total chances and 81 double plays in 1996; tied for lead in errors with 22. ... Led Eastern League with 24 sacrifice hits in 1997. ... Led Eastern League second basemen with .985 fielding percentage in 1997. ... Tied for International League lead with 16 sacrifice hits in 2000. ... Tied for International League lead with 21 sacrifice hits in 2001.

2002 GAMES PLAYED BY POSITION (MLB): 2B—21; SS—5; OF—4.

			BATTING													FIELDING	
Year	Team (League)	Pos.	G	AB	R	H	2B	3B	HR	RBI	BB	SO	SB-CS	Avg.	OBP	SLG	E	Avg.
1993—	GC Orioles (GCL)	2B-SS-3B	48	156	20	37	4	0	0	16	21	32	14-6	.237	.326	.263	14	.934
1994—	Bluefield (Appl.)								Did not play.									
1995—	Frederick (Caro.)	2B	124	365	52	82	11	3	3	27	49	75	5-10	.225	.329	.296	28	.952
1996—	High Desert (Calif.)	2B-SS	137	459	94	122	21	5	10	66	57	81	25-7	.266	.354	.399	‡22	†.968
1997—	Bowie (East.)	2B-SS-3B	*141	437	52	103	18	1	5	42	38	71	7-7	.236	.304	.316	13	†.981
1998—	Bowie (East.)	2B-SS-OF	86	258	46	73	13	1	2	20	34	37	12-3	.283	.369	.364	9	.973
—	Rochester (I.L.)	2B	44	160	20	47	6	4	0	18	7	22	7-5	.294	.329	.381	8	.969
1999—	Baltimore (A.L.)	SS-2B-3B-DH	17	29	6	6	0	0	2	2	2	3	0-0	.207	.258	.414	0	1.000
—	Rochester (I.L.)	SS-2B	62	220	25	56	10	2	2	23	11	21	9-6	.255	.289	.345	15	.944
2000—	Baltimore (A.L.)	2B-SS	14	17	2	1	0	0	0	0	2	2	0-0	.059	.158	.059	0	1.000
—	Rochester (I.L.)	SS-2B-3B	106	372	44	90	12	2	1	23	27	60	9-4	.242	.300	.293	18	.963
2001—	Richmond (I.L.)■	SS-2B-3B	105	375	50	100	22	3	2	22	22	54	18-6	.267	.313	.357	20	.955
—	Atlanta (N.L.)	2B-SS	22	5	3	1	0	0	0	0	0	1	6-2	.200	.200	.200	0	1.000
2002—	Richmond (I.L.)	2B-SS-3B-OF	58	230	29	69	12	1	6	17	16	32	9-5	.300	.349	.439	9	.966
—	Atlanta (N.L.)	2B-SS-OF	39	61	6	12	1	0	0	5	0	14	0-1	.197	.197	.213	1	.989
American League totals (2 years)			31	46	8	7	0	0	2	2	4	5	0-0	.152	.220	.283	0	1.000
National League totals (2 years)			61	66	9	13	1	0	0	5	0	15	6-3	.197	.197	.212	1	.989
Major League totals (4 years)			92	112	17	20	1	0	2	7	4	20	6-3	.179	.207	.241	1	.994

GARCIA, KARIM — OF — INDIANS

PERSONAL: Born October 29, 1975, in Ciudad Obregon, Mexico. ... 6-0/195. ... Bats left, throws left. ... Full name: Gustavo Karim Garcia.
HIGH SCHOOL: Preparatoria Abierta (Ciudad Obregon, Mexico).
TRANSACTIONS/CAREER NOTES: Signed as non-drafted free agent by Los Angeles Dodgers organization (July 16, 1992). ... On Los Angeles disabled list (September 1, 1997-remainder of season). ... Selected by Arizona Diamondbacks in first round (ninth pick overall) of expansion draft (November 18, 1997). ... Traded by Diamondbacks to Detroit Tigers for OF Luis Gonzalez (December 28, 1998). ... Traded by Tigers to Baltimore Orioles for future considerations (June 12, 2000). ... On suspended list (September 1-4, 2000). ... Released by Orioles (October 17, 2000). ... Signed by Cleveland Indians organization (December 22, 2000). ... Released by Indians (March 27, 2002). ... Signed by New York Yankees organization (April 2, 2002). ... Released by Yankees (July 2, 2002). ... Signed by Indians organization (July 12, 2002).
HONORS: Named Minor League Player of the Year by The Sporting News (1995).
STATISTICAL NOTES: Led Pacific Coast League with 257 total bases in 1995. ... Career major league grand slams: 3.
2002 GAMES PLAYED BY POSITION (MLB): OF—53.

		BATTING														FIELDING	
Year Team (League)	Pos.	G	AB	R	H	2B	3B	HR	RBI	BB	SO	SB-CS	Avg.	OBP	SLG	E	Avg.
1993—Bakersfield (Calif.)	OF	123	460	61	111	20	9	19	54	37	109	5-3	.241	.299	.448	*13	.940
1994—Vero Beach (FSL)	OF	121	452	72	120	28	10	*21	84	37	112	8-3	.265	.319	.511	5	.980
1995—Albuquerque (PCL)	OF-DH	124	474	88	151	26	10	20	•91	38	102	12-6	.319	.369	.542	*14	.932
—Los Angeles (N.L.)	OF	13	20	1	4	0	0	0	0	0	4	0-0	.200	.200	.200	0	1.000
1996—Albuquerque (PCL)	OF-DH	84	327	54	97	17	10	13	58	29	67	6-4	.297	.353	.529	13	.921
—San Antonio (Texas)	OF	35	129	21	32	6	1	5	22	9	38	1-1	.248	.297	.426	2	.971
—Los Angeles (N.L.)	OF	1	1	0	0	0	0	0	0	0	1	0-0	.000	.000	.000	0	...
1997—Albuquerque (PCL)	OF-DH	71	262	53	80	17	6	20	66	23	70	11-5	.305	.361	.645	5	.952
—Los Angeles (N.L.)	OF	15	39	5	5	0	0	1	8	6	14	0-0	.128	.239	.205	0	1.000
1998—Arizona (N.L.)■	OF	113	333	39	74	10	8	9	43	18	78	5-4	.222	.260	.381	5	.975
—Tucson (PCL)	OF	27	106	21	33	4	2	10	27	15	24	5-1	.311	.393	.670	3	.958
1999—Detroit (A.L.)■	OF-DH	96	288	38	69	10	3	14	32	20	67	2-4	.240	.288	.441	7	.958
2000—Detroit (A.L.)	OF-DH	8	17	1	3	0	0	0	0	0	4	0-0	.176	.176	.176	0	1.000
—Toledo (I.L.)	OF	40	155	31	46	6	2	15	38	11	32	2-1	.297	.349	.652	4	.956
—Rochester (I.L.)■	OF	76	270	38	75	17	1	13	54	34	70	3-3	.278	.358	.493	3	.977
—Baltimore (A.L.)	DH-OF	8	16	0	0	0	0	0	0	0	6	0-0	.000	.000	.000	0	1.000
2001—Buffalo (I.L.)■	OF-1B	125	462	73	122	16	4	31	85	44	106	4-4	.264	.326	.517	7	.973
—Cleveland (A.L.)	OF-1B	20	45	8	14	3	0	5	9	3	13	0-0	.311	.360	.711	2	.917
2002—Columbus (I.L.)■	OF-1B	74	288	44	78	16	3	12	49	20	48	1-5	.271	.316	.472	2	.987
—New York (A.L.)	OF	2	5	1	1	0	0	0	0	0	1	0-0	.200	.200	.200	0	1.000
—Buffalo (I.L.)■	OF	23	91	16	36	7	2	3	22	9	14	0-1	.396	.450	.615	0	1.000
—Cleveland (A.L.)	OF	51	197	29	59	8	0	16	52	6	40	0-3	.299	.317	.584	1	.990
American League totals (4 years)		185	568	77	146	21	3	35	93	29	131	2-7	.257	.292	.489	10	.967
National League totals (4 years)		142	393	45	83	10	8	10	51	24	97	5-4	.211	.254	.354	5	.977
Major League totals (8 years)		327	961	122	229	31	11	45	144	53	228	7-11	.238	.277	.434	15	.971

GARCIA, LUIS — OF

PERSONAL: Born September 22, 1975, in Hermosillo, Mexico. ... 6-3/208. ... Bats right, throws right. ... Full name: Luis Carlos Garcia.
HIGH SCHOOL: Miami.
TRANSACTIONS/CAREER NOTES: Selected by Chicago White Sox organization in 19th round of free-agent draft (June 2, 1994). ... Selected by Tampa Bay Devil Rays from White Sox organization in Rule 5 minor league draft (December 14, 1998). ... Loaned by Devil Rays to Mexico City Tigres, Mexican League (March 22-September 20, 1999; April 3-September 6, 2000; and March 21-September 13, 2001). ... Granted free agency (October 15, 2001). ... Signed by Baltimore Orioles organization (November 12, 2001). ... Granted free agency (October 15, 2002).
2002 GAMES PLAYED BY POSITION (MLB): OF—2.

		BATTING														FIELDING	
Year Team (League)	Pos.	G	AB	R	H	2B	3B	HR	RBI	BB	SO	SB-CS	Avg.	OBP	SLG	E	Avg.
1995—GC White Sox (GCL)	OF	45	161	33	37	5	2	0	12	20	29	9-3	.230	.310	.286	3	.958
1996—Hickory (SAL)	OF	76	289	31	79	18	3	3	38	14	41	9-6	.273	.311	.388	3	.968
—South Bend (Midw.)	OF	58	221	23	48	9	1	1	16	9	29	3-4	.217	.250	.281	3	.975
1997—Win.-Salem (Caro.)	OF	130	498	55	128	29	7	13	81	16	93	4-8	.257	.277	.422	3	.984
1998—Win.-Salem (Caro.)	OF	106	389	49	105	29	1	10	58	13	63	8-5	.270	.295	.427	3	.983
1999—MC Tigres (Mex.)■	OF	56	239	38	88	18	3	8	54	13	22	13-5	.368	.353	.569	0	1.000
2000—MC Tigres (Mex.)■	OF	120	477	86	169	27	2	22	81	39	91	33-9	.354	.399	.558	4	...
2001—MC Tigres (Mex.)■	OF	98	368	73	122	25	5	19	82	38	51	16-6	.332	.396	.582	4	.581
2002—Rochester (I.L.)	OF	89	339	23	82	14	2	4	31	7	45	1-1	.242	.260	.330	2	.991
—Baltimore (A.L.)	OF	6	3	0	1	0	0	0	0	0	1	0-0	.333	.333	.333	0	1.000
Major League totals (1 year)		6	3	0	1	0	0	0	0	0	1	0-0	.333	.333	.333	0	1.000

GARCIA, REYNALDO — P — RANGERS

PERSONAL: Born April 15, 1974, in Nagua, Dominican Republic. ... 6-3/170. ... Throws right, bats right.
TRANSACTIONS/CAREER NOTES: Signed as non-drafted free agent by Texas Rangers organization (December 16, 1996).
CAREER HITTING (MLB): 0-for-0 (.000), 0 R, 0 2B, 0 3B, 0 HR, 0 RBI.

Year League	W	L	Pct.	ERA	G	GS	CG	ShO	Sv.-Opp.	IP	H	R	ER	HR	BB-IBB	SO
1997—Dom. Rangers (DSL)	1	3	.250	6.81	16	1	0	0	5-...	37.0	39	34	28	...	22-...	27
1998—Dom. Rangers (DSL)	3	8	.273	4.56	13	13	1	...	0-...	73.0	88	50	37	...	27-...	36
1999—Gulf Coast Rangers (GCL)	4	4	.500	3.23	12	11	0	0	0-...	64.0	55	30	23	3	26-0	42
2000—Savannah (S.Atl.)	6	7	.462	2.69	49	2	1	0	14-...	97.0	87	37	29	6	33-1	82
2001—Charlotte (FSL)	5	10	.333	3.56	35	16	0	0	4-...	116.1	107	62	46	7	45-3	111
2002—Tulsa (Texas)	5	1	.833	3.69	18	9	0	0	0-...	68.1	63	36	28	11	30-1	54
—Oklahoma (PCL)	2	2	.500	2.84	25	0	0	0	4-...	31.2	23	12	10	2	14-1	33
—Texas (A.L.)	0	0	...	31.50	3	0	0	0	0-0	2.0	7	7	7	3	1-0	2
Major League totals (1 year)	0	0	...	31.50	3	0	0	0	0-0	2.0	7	7	7	3	1-0	2

GARCIAPARRA, NOMAR SS RED SOX

PERSONAL: Born July 23, 1973, in Whittier, Calif. ... 6-0/190. ... Bats right, throws right. ... Full name: Anthony Nomar Garciaparra. ... Brother of Michael Garciaparra, shortstop, Seattle Mariners organization.

HIGH SCHOOL: St. John Bosco (Bellflower, Calif.).

COLLEGE: Georgia Tech.

TRANSACTIONS/CAREER NOTES: Selected by Milwaukee Brewers organization in fifth round of free-agent draft (June 3, 1991); did not sign. ... Selected by Boston Red Sox organization in first round (12th pick overall) of free-agent draft (June 2, 1994). ... On Pawtucket disabled list (April 4-15 and April 19-July 11, 1996). ... On disabled list (May 9-28, 1998; and May 12-27, 2000). ... On Boston disabled list (March 21-July 29 and August 27, 2001-remainder of season); included rehabilitation assignment to Pawtucket (July 24-29).

RECORDS: Shares major league career record for most home runs in two consecutive games—5 (July 21 [2] and 23, a.m. game [3], 2002). ... Shares major league single-game records for most grand slams—2 (May 10, 1999); and for most home runs in one inning—2 (July 23, 2002, third inning). ... Holds A.L. rookie-season record for most consecutive games batted safely—30 (1997).

HONORS: Named A.L. Rookie Player of the Year by The Sporting News (1997). ... Named shortstop on The Sporting News A.L. All-Star team (1997 and 1999). ... Named shortstop on The Sporting News A.L. Silver Slugger team (1997). ... Named A.L. Rookie of the Year by Baseball Writers' Association of America (1997).

STATISTICAL NOTES: Led Eastern League shortstops with 396 assists and 624 total chances in 1995. ... Had 30-game hitting streak (July 26-August 29, 1997). ... Led A.L. shortstops with 249 putouts, 720 total chances and double plays with 113 in 1997. ... Had 16-game hitting streak (April 2-19, 1998). ... Had 24-game hitting streak (June 7-July 3, 1998). ... Had 16-game hitting streak (April 26-May 14, 1999). ... Hit three home runs in one game (May 10, 1999; and July 23, 2002). ... Had 17-game hitting streak (June 13-July 2, 1999). ... Had 20-game hitting streak (September 10-29, 2000). ... Led A.L. with 20 intentional bases on balls received in 2000. ... Had 15-game hitting streak (April 13-May 1, 2002). ... Career major league grand slams: 4.

MISCELLANEOUS: Member of 1992 U.S. Olympic baseball team.

2002 GAMES PLAYED BY POSITION (MLB): SS—154.

			BATTING													FIELDING	
Year	Team (League)	Pos.	G	AB	R	H	2B	3B	HR	RBI	BB	SO	SB-CS	Avg.	OBP	SLG	E	Avg.
1994—	Sarasota (FSL)	SS	28	105	20	31	8	1	1	16	10	6	5-2	.295	.356	.419	3	.974
1995—	Trenton (East.)	SS	125	513	77	137	20	8	8	47	50	42	35-12	.267	.338	.384	23	.963
1996—	Pawtucket (I.L.)	SS	43	172	40	59	15	2	16	46	14	21	3-1	.343	.387	.733	5	.973
	—GC Red Sox (GCL)	SS	5	14	4	4	2	1	0	5	1	0	0-0	.286	.375	.571	1	.950
	—Boston (A.L.)	SS-DH-2B	24	87	11	21	2	3	4	16	4	14	5-0	.241	.272	.471	1	.989
1997—	Boston (A.L.)	SS	153	*684	122	*209	44	*11	30	98	35	92	22-9	.306	.342	.534	21	.971
1998—	Boston (A.L.)	SS	143	604	111	195	37	8	35	122	33	62	12-6	.323	.362	.584	25	.962
1999—	Boston (A.L.)	SS	135	532	103	190	42	4	27	104	51	39	14-3	*.357	.418	.603	17	.972
2000—	Boston (A.L.)	SS-DH	140	529	104	197	51	3	21	96	61	50	5-2	*.372	.434	.599	18	.971
2001—	Pawtucket (I.L.)	SS	4	16	3	7	2	0	1	4	1	2	0-0	.438	.500	.750	1	.941
	—Boston (A.L.)	SS	21	83	13	24	3	0	4	8	7	9	0-1	.289	.352	.470	3	.968
2002—	Boston (A.L.)	SS	156	635	101	197	56	5	24	120	41	63	5-2	.310	.352	.528	*25	.965
Major League totals (7 years)			772	3154	565	1033	235	34	145	564	232	329	63-23	.328	.375	.562	110	.969

DIVISION SERIES RECORD

			BATTING													FIELDING	
Year	Team (League)	Pos.	G	AB	R	H	2B	3B	HR	RBI	BB	SO	SB-CS	Avg.	OBP	SLG	E	Avg.
1998—	Boston (A.L.)	SS	4	15	4	5	1	0	3	11	1	0	0-0	.333	.333	1.000	0	1.000
1999—	Boston (A.L.)	SS	4	12	6	5	2	0	2	4	3	3	0-0	.417	.563	1.083	0	1.000
Division series totals (2 years)			8	27	10	10	3	0	5	15	4	3	0-0	.370	.441	1.037	0	1.000

CHAMPIONSHIP SERIES RECORD

			BATTING													FIELDING	
Year	Team (League)	Pos.	G	AB	R	H	2B	3B	HR	RBI	BB	SO	SB-CS	Avg.	OBP	SLG	E	Avg.
1999—	Boston (A.L.)	SS	5	20	2	8	2	0	2	5	2	2	1-0	.400	.455	.800	4	.833

ALL-STAR GAME RECORD

	AB	R	H	2B	3B	HR	RBI	BB	SO	SB-CS	Avg.	OBP	SLG	E	Avg.
All-Star Game totals (4 years)	6	1	1	0	0	0	0	0	0	0-0	.167	.167	.167	2	.714

GARDNER, LEE P

PERSONAL: Born January 16, 1975, in Hartland, Mich. ... 6-0/219. ... Throws right, bats right. ... Full name: Terrence Lee Gardner.

COLLEGE: Central Michigan.

TRANSACTIONS/CAREER NOTES: Signed as non-drafted free agent by Tampa Bay Devil Rays organization (May 19, 1998). ... Released by Devil Rays (September 30, 2002).

CAREER HITTING (MLB): 0-for-0 (.000), 0 R, 0 2B, 0 3B, 0 HR, 0 RBI.

Year	League	W	L	Pct.	ERA	G	GS	CG	ShO	Sv.-Opp.	IP	H	R	ER	HR	BB-IBB	SO
1998—	St. Petersburg (FSL)	0	0	...	0.00	3	0	0	0	0-...	4.0	3	0	0	0	1-0	2
	—Charleston, S.C. (S.Atl.)	0	3	.000	4.04	28	0	0	0	3-...	35.2	38	18	16	3	4-0	55
1999—	Orlando (Sou.)	0	0	...	9.00	1	0	0	0	0-...	2.0	3	2	2	0	1-0	1
	—St. Petersburg (FSL)	2	0	1.000	1.96	20	0	0	0	7-...	23.0	20	7	5	1	5-0	22
2000—	Orlando (Sou.)	3	2	.600	3.40	36	0	0	0	12-...	45.0	34	19	17	0	14-1	48
	—Durham (I.L.)	1	0	1.000	3.38	21	0	0	0	5-...	18.2	12	7	7	1	9-1	8
2001—	Durham (I.L.)	5	2	.714	2.72	56	0	0	0	2-...	76.0	76	27	23	10	23-2	55
	—Orlando (Sou.)	0	0	...	0.00	1	0	0	0	0-...	1.2	0	0	0	0	0-0	0
2002—	Durham (I.L.)	2	1	.667	2.36	45	0	0	0	25-...	49.2	50	14	13	1	15-3	52
	—Tampa Bay (A.L.)	1	1	.500	4.05	12	0	0	0	0-2	13.1	12	11	6	3	8-0	8
Major League totals (1 year)		1	1	.500	4.05	12	0	0	0	0-2	13.1	12	11	6	3	8-0	8

GARLAND, JON P WHITE SOX

PERSONAL: Born September 27, 1979, in Valencia, Calif. ... 6-6/205. ... Throws right, bats right. ... Full name: Jon Steven Garland.

HIGH SCHOOL: John F. Kennedy (Granada Hills, Calif.).

TRANSACTIONS/CAREER NOTES: Selected by Chicago Cubs organization in first round (10th pick overall) of free-agent draft (June 3, 1997). ... Traded by Cubs to Chicago White Sox for P Matt Karchner (July 29, 1998). ... On Chicago disabled list (August 19-September 3, 2000); included rehabilitation assignment to Birmingham (August 30-September 3).
HONORS: Named International League Most Valuable Pitcher (2000).
CAREER HITTING (MLB): 0-for-4 (.000), 0 R, 0 2B, 0 3B, 0 HR, 0 RBI.

Year	League	W	L	Pct.	ERA	G	GS	CG	ShO	Sv.-Opp.	IP	H	R	ER	HR	BB-IBB	SO
1997—	Arizona Cubs (Ariz.)	3	2	.600	2.70	10	7	0	0	0-...	40.0	37	14	12	3	10-0	39
1998—	Rockford (Midw.)	4	7	.364	5.03	19	19	1	0	0-...	107.1	124	69	60	11	45-0	70
—	Hickory (S.Atl.)■	1	4	.200	5.40	5	5	0	0	0-...	26.2	36	20	16	2	13-0	19
1999—	Winston-Salem (Caro.)	5	7	.417	3.33	19	19	2	1	0-...	119.0	109	57	44	7	39-2	84
—	Birmingham (Sou.)	3	1	.750	4.38	7	7	0	0	0-...	39.0	39	22	19	4	18-0	27
2000—	Charlotte (I.L.)	9	2	.818	2.26	16	16	2	1	0-...	103.2	99	28	26	3	32-2	63
—	Chicago (A.L.)	4	8	.333	6.46	15	13	0	0	0-0	69.2	82	55	50	10	40-0	42
—	Birmingham (Sou.)	0	0	...	0.00	1	1	0	0	0-...	6.0	4	0	0	0	1-0	10
2001—	Charlotte (I.L.)	0	3	.000	2.73	5	5	1	0	0-...	33.0	31	10	10	1	11-1	26
—	Chicago (A.L.)	6	7	.462	3.69	35	16	0	0	1-1	117.0	123	59	48	16	55-2	61
2002—	Chicago (A.L.)	12	12	.500	4.58	33	33	1	1	0-0	192.2	188	109	98	23	83-1	112
Major League totals (3 years)		22	27	.449	4.65	83	62	1	1	1-1	379.1	393	223	196	49	178-3	215

GEORGE, CHRIS — P — ROYALS

PERSONAL: Born September 16, 1979, in Houston. ... 6-2/200. ... Throws left, bats left. ... Full name: Christopher Coleman George.
HIGH SCHOOL: Klein (Texas).
TRANSACTIONS/CAREER NOTES: Selected by Kansas City Royals organization as "sandwich pick" between first and second round of free-agent draft (June 2, 1998); pick received as part of compensation for Arizona Diamondbacks signing Type A free agent IF Jay Bell. ... On Kansas City disabled list (May 18-June 18, 2002); included rehabiltiation assignment to Omaha (May 30-June 18).
MISCELLANEOUS: Member of 2000 U.S. Olympic baseball team.
CAREER HITTING (MLB): 0-for-0 (.000), 0 R, 0 2B, 0 3B, 0 HR, 0 RBI.

Year	League	W	L	Pct.	ERA	G	GS	CG	ShO	Sv.-Opp.	IP	H	R	ER	HR	BB-IBB	SO
1998—	Gulf Coast Royals (GCL)	0	1	.000	2.87	5	4	0	0	0-...	15.2	14	9	5	1	4-0	10
1999—	Wilmington (Caro.)	9	7	.563	3.60	27	27	0	0	0-...	145.0	142	65	58	8	53-0	142
2000—	Wichita (Texas)	8	5	.615	3.14	18	18	0	0	0-...	97.1	92	41	34	5	51-1	80
—	Omaha (PCL)	3	2	.600	4.84	8	8	0	0	0-...	44.2	47	29	24	8	20-0	27
2001—	Omaha (PCL)	11	3	.786	3.53	20	20	0	0	0-...	117.1	103	54	46	14	51-0	84
—	Kansas City (A.L.)	4	8	.333	5.59	13	13	1	0	0-0	74.0	83	48	46	14	18-0	32
2002—	Omaha (PCL)	6	12	.333	5.87	22	21	1	0	0-...	127.1	145	86	83	15	65-0	94
—	Kansas City (A.L.)	0	4	.000	5.60	6	6	0	0	0-0	27.1	37	17	17	2	8-0	13
Major League totals (2 years)		4	12	.250	5.60	19	19	1	0	0-0	101.1	120	65	63	16	26-0	45

GERMAN, ESTEBAN — 2B — ATHLETICS

PERSONAL: Born January 26, 1978, in Santo Domingo, Dominican Republic. ... 5-9/165. ... Bats right, throws right. ... Full name: Esteban German Guridi.
TRANSACTIONS/CAREER NOTES: Signed as non-drafted free agent by Oakland Athletics organization (July 4, 1996).
STATISTICAL NOTES: Led Arizona League second basemen with 82 putouts, 116 assists and 216 total chances in 1998. ... Led California League second basemen with 21 errors in 2000.
2002 GAMES PLAYED BY POSITION (MLB): 2B—8.

			BATTING														FIELDING	
Year	Team (League)	Pos.	G	AB	R	H	2B	3B	HR	RBI	BB	SO	SB-CS	Avg.	OBP	SLG	E	Avg.
1997—	Dom. Athletics (DSL)		69	249	69	79	17	1	2	29	73	30	58-...	.317	...	.418	...	...
1998—	Dom. Athletics (DSL)		10	32	9	10	1	1	0	4	7	2	1-...	.313	...	.406	...	...
—	Ariz. Athletics (Ariz.)	2B	•55	202	*52	62	3	*10	2	28	33	43	*40-8	.307	.413	.450	*13	.940
1999—	Modesto (Calif.)	2B	128	501	107	156	16	12	4	52	*102	128	40-16	.311	.428	.415	*38	.932
2000—	Midland (Texas)	2B	24	75	13	16	1	0	1	6	18	21	5-3	.213	.379	.267	5	.951
—	Visalia (Calif.)	2B-SS	109	428	82	113	14	10	2	35	61	86	*78-8	.264	.361	.357	†25	.953
2001—	Midland (Texas)	2B	92	335	79	95	20	3	6	30	63	66	31-11	.284	.415	.415	16	.963
—	Sacramento (PCL)	2B	38	150	40	56	8	0	4	14	18	20	17-2	.373	.457	.507	7	.962
2002—	Sacramento (PCL)	2B	121	458	72	126	16	4	2	43	78	66	26-14	.275	.390	.341	8	.986
—	Oakland (A.L.)	2B	9	35	4	7	0	0	0	0	4	11	1-0	.200	.300	.200	1	.978
Major League totals (1 year)			9	35	4	7	0	0	0	0	4	11	1-0	.200	.300	.200	1	.978

GERMAN, FRANKLYN — P — TIGERS

PERSONAL: Born January 20, 1980, in San Cristobal, Dominican Republic. ... 6-4/170. ... Throws right, bats right. ... Full name: Franklyn Miguel Made German.
TRANSACTIONS/CAREER NOTES: Signed as non-drafted free agent by Oakland Athletics organization (July 2, 1996). ... Traded by A's to Detroit Tigers with 1B Carlos Pena and a player to be named later as part of three-way deal in which New York Yankees acquired P Jeff Weaver from Tigers and A's acquired P Ted Lilly, OF John-Ford Griffin and P Jason Arnold from Yankees (July 5, 2002); Tigers acquired P Jeremy Bonderman to complete deal (August 22, 2002).
CAREER HITTING (MLB): 0-for-0 (.000), 0 R, 0 2B, 0 3B, 0 HR, 0 RBI.

Year	League	W	L	Pct.	ERA	G	GS	CG	ShO	Sv.-Opp.	IP	H	R	ER	HR	BB-IBB	SO
1997—	Dom. Athletics (DSL)	8	3	.727	2.33	13	13	5	...	0-...	89.0	66	33	23	...	31-...	80
1998—	Arizona Athletics (Ariz.)	2	1	.667	6.13	14	12	0	0	0-...	54.1	69	43	37	5	18-0	48
1999—	S. Oregon (N'West)	3	5	.375	5.99	15	15	0	0	0-...	73.2	89	52	49	10	45-1	58
2000—	Modesto (Calif.)	5	5	.500	5.50	17	14	0	0	0-...	72.0	88	55	44	4	37-0	52
—	Vancouver (N'West)	1	0	1.000	1.77	9	2	0	0	0-...	20.1	13	4	4	0	10-0	20
2001—	Visalia (Calif.)	2	4	.333	3.98	53	0	0	0	19-...	63.1	67	34	28	7	31-1	93
2002—	Midland (Texas)	1	1	.500	3.05	37	0	0	0	16-...	41.1	28	14	14	0	27-2	59
—	Toledo (I.L.)■	1	1	.500	1.59	23	0	0	0	13-...	22.2	15	4	4	0	7-0	31
—	Detroit (A.L.)	1	0	1.000	0.00	7	0	0	0	1-1	6.2	3	0	0	0	2-1	6
Major League totals (1 year)		1	0	1.000	0.00	7	0	0	0	1-1	6.2	3	0	0	0	2-1	6

GIAMBI, JASON — 1B — YANKEES

PERSONAL: Born January 8, 1971, in West Covina, Calif. ... 6-3/235. ... Bats left, throws right. ... Full name: Jason Gilbert Giambi. ... Brother of Jeremy Giambi, first baseman/outfielder, Philadelphia Phillies. ... Name pronounced GEE-om-bee.

HIGH SCHOOL: South Hills (West Covina, Calif.).

COLLEGE: Long Beach State.

TRANSACTIONS/CAREER NOTES: Selected by Milwaukee Brewers organization in 43rd round of free-agent draft (June 5, 1989); did not sign. ... Selected by Oakland Athletics organization in second round of free-agent draft (June 1, 1992). ... On disabled list (July 27-August 28, 1993). ... On Huntsville disabled list (April 7-14, 1994). ... Granted free agency (November 5, 2001). ... Signed by New York Yankees (December 18, 2001).

RECORDS: Shares major league single-game record for most unassisted double plays by first baseman—2 (August 2, 2000).

HONORS: Named A.L. Most Valuable Player by Baseball Writers' Association of America (2000). ... Named first baseman on A.L. Silver Slugger team (2001 and 2002). ... Named first baseman on The Sporting News A.L. All-Star team (2002).

STATISTICAL NOTES: Had 25-game hitting streak (May 12-June 23, 1997). ... Had 17-game hitting streak (July 16-August 2, 1998). ... Had 16-game hitting streak (September 5-24, 1998). ... Had 18-game hitting streak (July 23-August 10, 1999). ... Career major league grand slams: 9.

MISCELLANEOUS: Member of 1992 U.S. Olympic baseball team. ... Holds Oakland Athletics all-time record for highest career batting average (.308).

2002 GAMES PLAYED BY POSITION (MLB): 1B—92; DH—63.

			BATTING														FIELDING	
Year	Team (League)	Pos.	G	AB	R	H	2B	3B	HR	RBI	BB	SO	SB-CS	Avg.	OBP	SLG	E	Avg.
1992—	S. Oregon (N'West)	3B	13	41	9	13	3	0	3	13	9	6	1-1	.317	.440	.610	1	.962
1993—	Modesto (Calif.)	3B	89	313	72	91	16	2	12	60	73	47	2-3	.291	.436	.470	19	.911
1994—	Huntsville (Sou.)	3B-1B	56	193	31	43	9	0	6	30	27	31	0-0	.223	.319	.363	11	.945
—	Tacoma (PCL)	3B-SS	52	176	28	56	20	0	4	38	25	32	1-0	.318	.388	.500	8	.949
1995—	Edmonton (PCL)	3B-DH-1B	55	190	34	65	26	1	3	41	34	26	0-0	.342	.441	.537	9	.938
—	Oakland (A.L.)	3B-1B-DH	54	176	27	45	7	0	6	25	28	31	2-1	.256	.364	.398	4	.984
1996—	Oakland (A.L.)	1-O-3-DH	140	536	84	156	40	1	20	79	51	95	0-1	.291	.355	.481	11	.982
1997—	Oakland (A.L.)	OF-1B-DH	142	519	66	152	41	2	20	81	55	89	0-1	.293	.362	.495	7	.987
1998—	Oakland (A.L.)	1B-DH	153	562	92	166	28	0	27	110	81	102	2-2	.295	.384	.489	*14	.990
1999—	Oakland (A.L.)	1B-DH-3B	158	575	115	181	36	1	33	123	105	106	1-1	.315	.422	.553	7	.995
2000—	Oakland (A.L.)	1B-DH	152	510	108	170	29	1	43	137	*137	96	2-0	.333	*.476	.647	6	.995
2001—	Oakland (A.L.)	1B-DH	154	520	109	178	*47	2	38	120	*129	83	2-0	.342	*.477	*.660	11	.992
2002—	New York (A.L.)■	1B-DH	155	560	120	176	34	1	41	122	109	112	2-2	.314	.435	.598	4	.995
Major League totals (8 years)			1108	3958	721	1224	262	8	228	797	695	714	11-8	.309	.416	.552	64	.991

DIVISION SERIES RECORD

			BATTING														FIELDING	
Year	Team (League)	Pos.	G	AB	R	H	2B	3B	HR	RBI	BB	SO	SB-CS	Avg.	OBP	SLG	E	Avg.
2000—	Oakland (A.L.)	1B	5	14	2	4	0	0	0	1	7	2	1-0	.286	.500	.286	1	.976
2001—	Oakland (A.L.)	1B	5	17	2	6	0	0	1	4	4	2	0-0	.353	.455	.529	1	.982
2002—	New York (A.L.)	1B-DH	4	14	5	5	0	0	1	3	4	1	0-0	.357	.526	.571	0	1.000
Division series totals (3 years)			14	45	9	15	0	0	2	8	15	5	1-0	.333	.492	.467	2	.984

ALL-STAR GAME RECORD

	AB	R	H	2B	3B	HR	RBI	BB	SO	SB-CS	Avg.	OBP	SLG	E	Avg.
All-Star Game totals (3 years)	5	2	1	0	0	0	0	1	3	0-0	.200	.333	.200	0	1.000

GIAMBI, JEREMY — 1B/OF — PHILLIES

PERSONAL: Born September 30, 1974, in San Jose, Calif. ... 5-11/216. ... Bats left, throws left. ... Full name: Jeremy Dean Giambi. ... Brother of Jason Giambi, first baseman, New York Yankees.

HIGH SCHOOL: South Hills (West Covina, Calif.).

COLLEGE: Cal State-Fullerton.

TRANSACTIONS/CAREER NOTES: Selected by Detroit Tigers organization in 44th round of free-agent draft (June 1, 1995); did not sign. ... Selected by Kansas City Royals organization in sixth round of free-agent draft (June 4, 1996). ... On Omaha disabled list (July 12-August 2, 1998). ... On Kansas City disabled list (March 27-May 15, 1999); included rehabilitation assignment to Omaha (April 28-May 15). ... Traded by Royals to Oakland Athletics for P Brett Laxton (February 18, 2000). ... On Oakland disabled list (August 22-September 8, 2000); included rehabilitation assignment to Sacramento (September 6-8). ... On Oakland disabled list (May 16-June 9, 2001); included rehabilitation assignment to Sacramento (May 25-June 9). ... Traded by A's to Philadelphia Phillies for OF/3B John Mabry (May 22, 2002).

STATISTICAL NOTES: Career major league grand slams: 1.

2002 GAMES PLAYED BY POSITION (MLB): OF—60; 1B—21; DH—10.

			BATTING														FIELDING	
Year	Team (League)	Pos.	G	AB	R	H	2B	3B	HR	RBI	BB	SO	SB-CS	Avg.	OBP	SLG	E	Avg.
1996—	Spokane (N'West)	OF	67	231	•58	63	17	0	6	39	*61	32	22-5	.273	*.440	.424	*11	.901
1997—	Lansing (Midw.)	OF	31	116	33	39	11	1	5	21	23	16	5-1	.336	.451	.578	0	1.000
—	Wichita (Texas)	OF-1B	74	268	50	86	15	1	11	52	44	47	4-4	.321	.422	.507	3	.975
1998—	Omaha (PCL)	OF-1B	96	325	68	121	21	2	20	66	57	64	8-5	*.372	*.469	.634	3	.976
—	Kansas City (A.L.)	OF-DH	18	58	6	13	4	0	2	8	11	9	0-1	.224	.343	.397	0	1.000
1999—	Omaha (PCL)	OF-1B-DH	35	127	31	44	5	1	12	28	31	30	1-1	.346	.472	.685	2	.988
—	Kansas City (A.L.)	DH-1B-OF	90	288	34	82	13	1	3	34	40	67	0-0	.285	.373	.368	2	.991
2000—	Sacramento (PCL)■	OF-1B	8	31	8	11	2	0	2	8	8	7	1-1	.355	.487	.613	1	.960
—	Oakland (A.L.)	OF-DH-1B	104	260	42	66	10	2	10	50	32	61	0-0	.254	.338	.423	3	.980
2001—	Oakland (A.L.)	DH-OF-1B	124	371	64	105	26	0	12	57	63	83	0-1	.283	.391	.450	5	.962
—	Sacramento (PCL)	OF	9	27	1	9	1	0	0	1	1	6	0-0	.333	.357	.370	0	1.000
2002—	Oakland (A.L.)	OF-DH	42	157	26	43	7	0	8	17	27	40	0-0	.274	.390	.471	1	.984
—	Philadelphia (N.L.)■	1B-OF-DH	82	156	32	38	10	0	12	28	52	54	0-1	.244	.435	.538	4	.981
American League totals (5 years)			378	1134	172	309	60	3	35	166	173	260	0-2	.272	.372	.423	11	.981
National League totals (1 year)			82	156	32	38	10	0	12	28	52	54	0-1	.244	.435	.538	4	.981
Major League totals (5 years)			460	1290	204	347	70	3	47	194	225	314	0-3	.269	.381	.437	15	.981

DIVISION SERIES RECORD

			BATTING														FIELDING	
Year	Team (League)	Pos.	G	AB	R	H	2B	3B	HR	RBI	BB	SO	SB-CS	Avg.	OBP	SLG	E	Avg.
2000—	Oakland (A.L.)	DH-OF-PH	4	9	1	3	0	0	0	1	2	2	0-0	.333	.455	.333	0	1.000
2001—	Oakland (A.L.)	DH-PH	5	13	0	4	1	0	0	2	1	0	1-0	.308	.357	.385	...	...
Division series totals (2 years)			9	22	1	7	1	0	0	3	3	2	1-0	.318	.400	.364	0	1.000

GIBBONS, JAY — OF/1B — ORIOLES

PERSONAL: Born March 2, 1977, in Rochester, Mich. ... 6-0/200. ... Bats left, throws left. ... Full name: Jay Jonathan Gibbons.
HIGH SCHOOL: Mayfair (Lakewood, Calif.).
COLLEGE: Cal State Los Angeles.
TRANSACTIONS/CAREER NOTES: Selected by Toronto Blue Jays organization in 14th round of free-agent draft (June 4, 1998). ... Selected by Baltimore Orioles from Blue Jays organization in Rule 5 major league draft (December 11, 2000). ... On disabled list (August 5, 2001-remainder of season).
HONORS: Named Pioneer League Most Valuable Player (1998).
STATISTICAL NOTES: Led Pioneer League with 203 total bases and nine sacrifice flies in 1998.
2002 GAMES PLAYED BY POSITION (MLB): OF—92; 1B—30; DH—12.

			BATTING														FIELDING	
Year	Team (League)	Pos.	G	AB	R	H	2B	3B	HR	RBI	BB	SO	SB-CS	Avg.	OBP	SLG	E	Avg.
1998—	Medicine Hat (Pio.)	1B	73	290	66	*115	*29	1	*19	*98	37	25	2-1	*.397	.457	*.700	6	.983
1999—	Hagerstown (S.Atl.)	1B-OF	71	292	53	89	20	2	16	69	32	56	3-0	.305	.370	.551	6	.975
—	Dunedin (FSL)	1B	60	212	34	66	14	0	9	39	25	38	2-1	.311	.382	.505	5	.991
2000—	Tennessee (Sou.)	1B-OF	132	474	85	152	38	1	19	75	61	67	3-1	.321	.404	.525	8	.991
2001—	Baltimore (A.L.)■	OF-DH-1B	73	225	27	53	10	0	15	36	17	39	0-1	.236	.301	.480	0	1.000
2002—	Baltimore (A.L.)	OF-1B-DH	136	490	71	121	29	1	28	69	45	66	1-3	.247	.311	.482	2	.995
Major League totals (2 years)			209	715	98	174	39	1	43	105	62	105	1-4	.243	.307	.481	2	.996

GIL, BENJI — SS — ANGELS

PERSONAL: Born October 6, 1972, in Tijuana, Mexico. ... 6-2/210. ... Bats right, throws right. ... Full name: Romas Benjamin Gil.
HIGH SCHOOL: Castle Park (Chula Vista, Calif.).
TRANSACTIONS/CAREER NOTES: Selected by Texas Rangers organization in first round (19th pick overall) of free-agent draft (June 3, 1991). ... On Texas disabled list (March 22-May 22, 1996); included rehabilitation assigments to Charlotte (May 2-17) and Oklahoma City (May 17-21). ... Traded by Rangers to Chicago White Sox for P Al Levine and P Larry Thomas (December 19, 1997). ... On disabled list (August 12-20, 1998). ... Selected by Florida Marlins organization from White Sox organization in Rule 5 minor league draft (December 15, 1998). ... Granted free agency (October 15, 1999). ... Signed by Anaheim Angels organization (February 1, 2000). ... On Anaheim disabled list (April 5-May 30, 2002); included rehabilitation assignment to Salt Lake (May 24-30).
STATISTICAL NOTES: Led American Association shortstops with 222 putouts, 401 assists, 660 total chances and 85 double plays in 1994. ... Career major league grand slams: 1.
2002 GAMES PLAYED BY POSITION (MLB): 2B—26; SS—14; 1B—10; DH—10.

			BATTING														FIELDING	
Year	Team (League)	Pos.	G	AB	R	H	2B	3B	HR	RBI	BB	SO	SB-CS	Avg.	OBP	SLG	E	Avg.
1991—	Butte (Pio.)	SS	32	129	25	37	4	3	2	15	14	36	9-3	.287	.354	.411	14	.914
1992—	Gastonia (S.Atl.)	SS	132	482	75	132	21	1	9	55	50	106	26-13	.274	.343	.378	45	.931
1993—	Texas (A.L.)	SS	22	57	3	7	0	0	0	2	5	22	1-2	.123	.194	.123	5	.954
—	Tulsa (Texas)	SS	101	342	45	94	9	1	17	59	35	89	20-12	.275	.351	.456	19	.959
1994—	Oklahoma City (A.A.)	SS	*139	487	62	121	20	6	10	55	33	120	14-8	.248	.298	.376	*37	.944
1995—	Texas (A.L.)	SS	130	415	36	91	20	3	9	46	26	147	2-4	.219	.266	.347	17	.974
1996—	Charlotte (FSL)	SS-DH	11	31	2	8	6	0	1	7	3	7	0-0	.258	.324	.548	2	.931
—	Oklahoma City (A.A.)	SS	84	292	32	65	15	1	6	28	21	90	4-6	.223	.277	.342	21	.949
—	Texas (A.L.)	SS	5	5	0	2	0	0	0	1	1	1	0-1	.400	.500	.400	1	.923
1997—	Texas (A.L.)	SS-DH	110	317	35	71	13	2	5	31	17	96	1-2	.224	.263	.325	19	.963
1998—	Calgary (PCL)■	SS-DH-OF	128	460	80	114	24	5	14	69	41	90	11-4	.248	.311	.413	30	.941
1999—	Calgary (PCL)■	SS-OF	116	412	74	115	29	1	17	64	27	101	17-5	.279	.332	.478	29	.944
2000—	Anaheim (A.L.)■	S-2-DH-1	110	301	28	72	14	1	6	23	30	59	10-6	.239	.317	.352	18	.961
2001—	Anaheim (A.L.)	S-2-1-DH-O	104	260	33	77	15	4	8	39	14	57	3-4	.296	.330	.477	14	.961
2002—	Anaheim (A.L.)	2B-SS-1B-DH	61	130	11	37	8	1	3	20	5	33	2-1	.285	.307	.431	4	.979
—	Salt Lake (PCL)	2B-SS-1B	6	24	4	10	5	1	2	6	1	4	0-2	.417	.440	.958	1	.969
Major League totals (7 years)			542	1485	146	357	70	11	31	162	98	415	19-20	.240	.288	.365	78	.966

DIVISION SERIES RECORD

			BATTING														FIELDING	
Year	Team (League)	Pos.	G	AB	R	H	2B	3B	HR	RBI	BB	SO	SB-CS	Avg.	OBP	SLG	E	Avg.
2002—	Anaheim (A.L.)	2B	2	5	1	4	0	0	0	1	0	0	0-0	.800	.800	.800	1	.875

CHAMPIONSHIP SERIES RECORD

			BATTING														FIELDING	
Year	Team (League)	Pos.	G	AB	R	H	2B	3B	HR	RBI	BB	SO	SB-CS	Avg.	OBP	SLG	E	Avg.
2002—	Anaheim (A.L.)	2B	1	2	0	0	0	0	0	0	0	1	0-0	.000	.000	.000	1	.750

WORLD SERIES RECORD

NOTES: Member of World Series championship team (2002).

			BATTING														FIELDING	
Year	Team (League)	Pos.	G	AB	R	H	2B	3B	HR	RBI	BB	SO	SB-CS	Avg.	OBP	SLG	E	Avg.
2002—	Anaheim (A.L.)	2B	3	5	1	4	1	0	0	0	0	1	0-0	.800	.800	1.000	0	1.000

GIL, GERONIMO — C/IF — ORIOLES

PERSONAL: Born August 7, 1975, in Oaxaca, Mexico. ... 6-2/195. ... Bats right, throws right.

TRANSACTIONS/CAREER NOTES: Signed by Mexico City Red Devils, Mexican League (1993). ... Contract sold by Mexico City to Los Angeles Dodgers organization (February 15, 1996). ... Traded by Dodgers with P Kris Foster to Baltimore Orioles for P Mike Trombley (July 31, 2001).
STATISTICAL NOTES: Led Texas League catchers with 10 double plays in 2000. ... Led A.L. catchers with 14 double plays and 19 passed balls in 2002.
2002 GAMES PLAYED BY POSITION (MLB): C—125.

		BATTING														FIELDING	
Year Team (League)	**Pos.**	**G**	**AB**	**R**	**H**	**2B**	**3B**	**HR**	**RBI**	**BB**	**SO**	**SB-CS**	**Avg.**	**OBP**	**SLG**	**E**	**Avg.**
1993—MC Red Devils (Mex.)	DH	1	1	0	0	0	0	0	0	0	1	0-0	.000	.000	.000	...	...
1994—								Did not play.									
1995—MC Red Devils (Mex.)	OF	4	7	1	2	0	0	0	0	0	1	0-0	.286	.286	.286	0	1.000
1996—Savannah (S.Atl.)■	C	79	276	29	67	13	1	7	38	8	69	0-2	.243	.274	.373	10	.983
1997—Vero Beach (FSL)	C	66	213	30	53	13	1	6	24	15	41	3-0	.249	.310	.404	13	.975
1998—San Antonio (Texas)	C-OF-1B	75	241	27	70	17	3	6	29	15	43	2-1	.290	.329	.461	9	.972
1999—San Antonio (Texas)	C-OF-1B-3B	106	343	47	97	26	1	15	59	49	58	2-0	.283	.372	.496	9	.986
2000—San Antonio (Texas)	C-OF-1B-3B	100	352	42	100	19	1	11	58	33	65	3-2	.284	.351	.438	8	.988
—Albuquerque (PCL)	C-OF-3B	15	50	9	19	5	0	2	22	5	8	0-1	.380	.421	.600	3	.959
2001—Las Vegas (PCL)	C-1B-SS	82	281	40	83	15	0	9	40	16	56	0-1	.295	.334	.445	3	.995
—Rochester (I.L.)■	C	23	82	7	22	6	1	2	14	0	23	0-0	.268	.271	.439	3	.986
—Baltimore (A.L.)	C	17	58	3	17	2	0	0	6	5	7	0-0	.293	.369	.328	2	.985
2002—Baltimore (A.L.)	C	125	422	33	98	19	0	12	45	21	88	2-2	.232	.270	.363	4	.995
Major League totals (2 years)		142	480	36	115	21	0	12	51	26	95	2-2	.240	.282	.358	6	.994

GILES, BRIAN — OF — PIRATES

PERSONAL: Born January 20, 1971, in El Cajon, Calif. ... 5-10/202. ... Bats left, throws left. ... Full name: Brian Stephen Giles. ... Brother of Marcus Giles, second baseman, Atlanta Braves. ... Name pronounced JYLES.
HIGH SCHOOL: Granite Hills (El Cajon, Calif.).
TRANSACTIONS/CAREER NOTES: Selected by Cleveland Indians organization in 17th round of free-agent draft (June 5, 1989). ... On Canton/Akron disabled list (May 15-July 7, 1992). ... On Cleveland disabled list (June 1-July 7, 1998); included rehabilitation assignment to Buffalo (June 23-July 7). ... Traded by Indians to Pittsburgh Pirates for P Ricardo Rincon (November 18, 1998).
STATISTICAL NOTES: Led International League with 10 intentional bases on balls received in 1994. ... Led International League outfielders with five double plays in 1994. ... Career major league grand slams: 4.
2002 GAMES PLAYED BY POSITION (MLB): OF—151.

		BATTING														FIELDING	
Year Team (League)	**Pos.**	**G**	**AB**	**R**	**H**	**2B**	**3B**	**HR**	**RBI**	**BB**	**SO**	**SB-CS**	**Avg.**	**OBP**	**SLG**	**E**	**Avg.**
1989—Burlington (Appl.)	OF	36	129	18	40	7	0	0	20	11	19	6-3	.310	.366	.364	1	.982
1990—Watertown (NY-Penn)	OF	70	246	44	71	15	2	1	23	48	23	11-8	.289	.403	.378	1	.991
1991—Kinston (Caro.)	OF	125	394	71	122	14	0	4	47	68	70	19-7	.310	.411	.376	5	.975
1992—Canton/Akron (East.)	OF	23	74	6	16	4	0	0	3	10	10	3-1	.216	.310	.270	0	1.000
—Kinston (Caro.)	OF	42	140	28	37	5	1	3	18	30	21	3-5	.264	.398	.379	1	.987
1993—Canton/Akron (East.)	OF	123	425	64	139	17	6	6	64	57	43	18-12	.327	.409	.438	5	.974
1994—Charlotte (I.L.)	OF	128	434	74	136	18	3	16	58	55	61	8-5	.313	.390	.479	4	.984
1995—Buffalo (A.A.)	OF-DH	123	413	67	128	18	•8	15	67	54	40	7-3	.310	.395	.501	5	.981
—Cleveland (A.L.)	OF-DH	6	9	6	5	0	0	1	3	0	1	0-0	.556	.556	.889	0	1.000
1996—Buffalo (A.A.)	OF	83	318	65	100	17	6	20	64	42	29	1-0	.314	.395	.594	2	.986
—Cleveland (A.L.)	DH-OF	51	121	26	43	14	1	5	27	19	13	3-0	.355	.434	.612	0	1.000
1997—Cleveland (A.L.)	OF-DH	130	377	62	101	15	3	17	61	63	50	13-3	.268	.368	.459	6	.972
1998—Cleveland (A.L.)	OF-DH	112	350	56	94	19	0	16	66	73	75	10-5	.269	.396	.460	5	.978
—Buffalo (I.L.)	OF-DH	13	46	5	11	2	0	2	7	6	8	0-0	.239	.327	.413	1	.947
1999—Pittsburgh (N.L.)■	OF-DH	141	521	109	164	33	3	39	115	95	80	6-2	.315	.418	.614	3	.990
2000—Pittsburgh (N.L.)	OF	156	559	111	176	37	7	35	123	114	69	6-0	.315	.432	.594	6	.982
2001—Pittsburgh (N.L.)	OF	160	576	116	178	37	7	37	95	90	67	13-6	.309	.404	.590	10	.969
2002—Pittsburgh (N.L.)	OF	153	497	95	148	37	5	38	103	135	74	15-6	.298	.450	.622	7	.973
American League totals (4 years)		299	857	150	243	48	4	39	157	155	139	26-8	.284	.391	.485	11	.976
National League totals (4 years)		610	2153	431	666	144	22	149	436	434	290	40-14	.309	.426	.604	26	.979
Major League totals (8 years)		909	3010	581	909	192	26	188	593	589	429	66-22	.302	.416	.570	37	.978

DIVISION SERIES RECORD

		BATTING														FIELDING	
Year Team (League)	**Pos.**	**G**	**AB**	**R**	**H**	**2B**	**3B**	**HR**	**RBI**	**BB**	**SO**	**SB-CS**	**Avg.**	**OBP**	**SLG**	**E**	**Avg.**
1996—Cleveland (A.L.)	PH	1	1	0	0	0	0	0	0	0	1	0-0	.000	.000	.000	...	...
1997—Cleveland (A.L.)	OF	3	7	0	1	0	0	0	0	0	1	0-0	.143	.143	.143	0	1.000
1998—Cleveland (A.L.)	OF-DH	3	10	1	2	1	0	0	0	1	4	0-0	.200	.333	.300	0	1.000
Division series totals (3 years)		7	18	1	3	1	0	0	0	1	6	0-0	.167	.250	.222	0	1.000

CHAMPIONSHIP SERIES RECORD

		BATTING														FIELDING	
Year Team (League)	**Pos.**	**G**	**AB**	**R**	**H**	**2B**	**3B**	**HR**	**RBI**	**BB**	**SO**	**SB-CS**	**Avg.**	**OBP**	**SLG**	**E**	**Avg.**
1997—Cleveland (A.L.)	OF	6	16	1	3	3	0	0	0	2	6	0-0	.188	.278	.375	0	1.000
1998—Cleveland (A.L.)	OF-PH	4	12	0	1	0	0	0	0	1	3	0-0	.083	.154	.083	1	.875
Championship series totals (2 years)		10	28	1	4	3	0	0	0	3	9	0-0	.143	.226	.250	1	.941

WORLD SERIES RECORD

		BATTING														FIELDING	
Year Team (League)	**Pos.**	**G**	**AB**	**R**	**H**	**2B**	**3B**	**HR**	**RBI**	**BB**	**SO**	**SB-CS**	**Avg.**	**OBP**	**SLG**	**E**	**Avg.**
1997—Cleveland (A.L.)	PH-OF	5	4	1	2	1	0	0	2	4	1	0-1	.500	.750	.750	0	1.000

ALL-STAR GAME RECORD

	AB	**R**	**H**	**2B**	**3B**	**HR**	**RBI**	**BB**	**SO**	**SB-CS**	**Avg.**	**OBP**	**SLG**	**E**	**Avg.**
All-Star Game totals (2 years)	3	0	0	0	0	0	0	0	0	0-0	.000	.000	.000	0	...

GILES, MARCUS — 2B — BRAVES

PERSONAL: Born May 18, 1978, in San Diego, Calif. ... 5-8/180. ... Bats right, throws right. ... Full name: Marcus William Giles. ... Brother of Brian Giles, outfielder, Pittsburgh Pirates. ... Name pronounced JYLES.
HIGH SCHOOL: Granite Hills (Calif.).
JUNIOR COLLEGE: Grossmont (Calif.).
TRANSACTIONS/CAREER NOTES: Selected by Atlanta Braves organization in 53rd round of free-agent draft (June 4, 1996). ... On Atlanta disabled list (May 29-July 16, 2002); included rehabilitation assignment to Richmond (June 28-July 16).
HONORS: Named South Atlantic League Most Valuable Player (1998). ... Named Carolina League Most Valuable Player (1999).
STATISTICAL NOTES: Led South Atlantic League with 321 total bases in 1998. ... Led Southern League second basemen with 304 putouts, 333 assists, 655 total chances and 70 double plays in 2000. ... Career major league grand slams: 1.
2002 GAMES PLAYED BY POSITION (MLB): 2B—52; 3B—8.

			BATTING														FIELDING	
Year	Team (League)	Pos.	G	AB	R	H	2B	3B	HR	RBI	BB	SO	SB-CS	Avg.	OBP	SLG	E	Avg.
1997—	Danville (Appl.)	2B	55	207	53	72	13	3	8	45	32	47	5-2	.348	.437	.556	7	.962
1998—	Macon (S.Atl.)	2B	135	505	*111	166	38	3	*37	*108	*85	103	12-5	.329	.433	*.636	25	.954
1999—	Myrtle Beach (Caro.)	2B	126	497	80	*162	*40	7	13	73	54	89	9-6	*.326	.393	.513	8	*.985
2000—	Greenville (Sou.)	2B	132	458	73	133	28	2	17	62	72	71	25-5	.290	.388	.472	18	*.973
2001—	Richmond (I.L.)	2B-SS-3B-OF	67	252	48	84	19	1	6	44	22	48	13-5	.333	.387	.488	8	.975
	—Atlanta (N.L.)	2B	68	244	36	64	10	2	9	31	28	37	2-5	.262	.338	.430	6	.978
2002—	Atlanta (N.L.)	2B-3B	68	213	27	49	10	1	8	23	25	41	1-1	.230	.315	.399	8	.972
	—Richmond (I.L.)	2B-3B	31	115	25	37	6	0	3	16	13	15	3-0	.322	.385	.452	3	.970
Major League totals (2 years)			136	457	63	113	20	3	17	54	53	78	3-6	.247	.327	.416	14	.975

DIVISION SERIES RECORD

			BATTING														FIELDING	
Year	Team (League)	Pos.	G	AB	R	H	2B	3B	HR	RBI	BB	SO	SB-CS	Avg.	OBP	SLG	E	Avg.
2001—	Atlanta (N.L.)	2B	3	12	2	3	1	0	0	1	0	3	0-0	.250	.250	.333	0	1.000
2002—	Atlanta (N.L.)	PH	3	2	0	1	0	0	0	0	0	0	0-0	.500	.500	.500	0	...
Division series totals (2 years)			6	14	2	4	1	0	0	1	0	3	0-0	.286	.286	.357	0	1.000

CHAMPIONSHIP SERIES RECORD

			BATTING														FIELDING	
Year	Team (League)	Pos.	G	AB	R	H	2B	3B	HR	RBI	BB	SO	SB-CS	Avg.	OBP	SLG	E	Avg.
2001—	Atlanta (N.L.)	2B	5	20	4	4	1	0	1	1	3	4	0-0	.200	.304	.400	2	.917

GINTER, KEITH — 2B — BREWERS

PERSONAL: Born May 5, 1976, in Norwalk, Conn. ... 5-10/190. ... Bats right, throws right. ... Full name: Keith Michael Ginter.
HIGH SCHOOL: Fullerton Union (Fullerton, Calif.).
JUNIOR COLLEGE: Cypress (Calif.) College.
COLLEGE: Texas Tech.
TRANSACTIONS/CAREER NOTES: Selected by Houston Astros organization in 10th round of free-agent draft (June 2, 1998). ... Traded by Astros to Milwaukee Brewers (September 5, 2002), completing deal in which Brewers traded IF Mark Loretta to Astros for two players to be named later (August 31, 2002); Brewers acquired P Wayne Franklin as partial completion (September 3, 2002).
HONORS: Named Texas League Most Valuable Player (2000).
STATISTICAL NOTES: Led Texas League in being hit by pitch with 24 in 2000. ... Led Texas League second basemen with 338 assists in 2000. ... Tied second basemen for Pacific Coast League lead with 236 assists in 2001.
2002 GAMES PLAYED BY POSITION (MLB): 3B—25; SS—1.

			BATTING														FIELDING	
Year	Team (League)	Pos.	G	AB	R	H	2B	3B	HR	RBI	BB	SO	SB-CS	Avg.	OBP	SLG	E	Avg.
1998—	Auburn (NY-Penn)	2B	71	241	•55	76	22	1	8	41	*60	68	10-7	.315	.461	.515	8	*.971
1999—	Kissimmee (FSL)	2B	103	376	66	99	15	4	13	46	61	90	9-10	.263	.381	.428	21	.959
	—Jackson (Texas)	2B	9	34	9	13	1	0	1	6	4	6	0-0	.382	.463	.500	2	.956
2000—	Round Rock (Texas)	2B	125	462	108	154	30	3	26	92	82	127	24-11	.333	*.457	.580	17	.972
	—Houston (N.L.)	2B	5	8	3	2	0	0	1	3	1	3	0-0	.250	.300	.625	0	1.000
2001—	New Orleans (PCL)	2B-OF-3B	132	457	76	123	31	5	16	70	61	147	8-6	.269	.380	.464	12	.975
	—Houston (N.L.)	PH	1	1	0	0	0	0	0	0	0	0	0-0	.000	.000	.000	...	...
2002—	New Orleans (PCL)	2B-3B-OF	121	435	70	115	28	1	12	54	56	97	3-4	.264	.362	.416	22	.952
	—Houston (N.L.)	3B-SS	7	5	1	1	1	0	0	0	2	1	0-0	.200	.500	.400	1	.909
	—Milwaukee (N.L.)■	3B	21	76	6	18	8	0	1	8	15	14	0-0	.237	.363	.382	2	.961
Major League totals (3 years)			34	90	10	21	9	0	2	11	18	18	0-0	.233	.364	.400	3	.958

GINTER, MATT — P — WHITE SOX

PERSONAL: Born December 24, 1977, in Lexington, Ky. ... 6-1/220. ... Throws right, bats right. ... Full name: Matthew Shane Ginter.
HIGH SCHOOL: George Rogers Clark (Winchester, Ky.).
COLLEGE: Mississippi State.
TRANSACTIONS/CAREER NOTES: Selected by New York Yankees organization in 17th round of free-agent draft (June 4, 1996); did not sign. ... Selected by Chicago White Sox organization in first round (22nd pick overall) of free-agent draft (June 2, 1999); pick received from New York Mets as compensation for signing Type A free agent 3B Robin Ventura.
CAREER HITTING (MLB): 0-for-0 (.000), 0 R, 0 2B, 0 3B, 0 HR, 0 RBI.

Year	League	W	L	Pct.	ERA	G	GS	CG	ShO	Sv.-Opp.	IP	H	R	ER	HR	BB-IBB	SO
1999—	Arizona White Sox (Ariz.)	1	0	1.000	3.24	3	0	0	0	1-...	8.1	5	4	3	0	3-0	10
	—Burlington (Midw.)	4	2	.667	4.05	9	9	0	0	0-...	40.0	38	20	18	3	19-0	29
2000—	Birmingham (Sou.)	11	8	.579	2.25	27	26	0	0	0-...	179.2	153	72	45	6	60-2	126
	—Chicago (A.L.)	1	0	1.000	13.50	7	0	0	0	0-1	9.1	18	14	14	5	7-0	6
2001—	Charlotte (I.L.)	2	3	.400	2.59	22	10	0	0	0-...	76.1	62	26	22	3	24-4	67
	—Chicago (A.L.)	1	0	1.000	5.22	20	0	0	0	0-0	39.2	34	23	23	2	14-2	24
2002—	Charlotte (I.L.)	1	0	1.000	3.94	13	0	0	0	0-...	16.0	20	8	7	3	10-1	9
	—Chicago (A.L.)	1	0	1.000	4.47	33	0	0	0	1-1	54.1	59	34	27	6	21-0	37
Major League totals (3 years)		3	0	1.000	5.57	60	0	0	0	1-2	103.1	111	71	64	13	42-2	67

GIPSON, CHARLES — OF/IF — MARINERS

PERSONAL: Born December 16, 1972, in Orange, Calif. ... 6-1/195. ... Bats right, throws right. ... Full name: Charles Wells Gipson Jr.
HIGH SCHOOL: Loara (Anaheim, Calif.).
JUNIOR COLLEGE: Cypress (Calif.) College.
TRANSACTIONS/CAREER NOTES: Selected by Seattle Mariners organization in 63rd round of free-agent draft (June 3, 1991). ... On disabled list (May 4-19, 1993). ... On Seattle disabled list (July 11-September 1, 1999); included rehabilitation assignments to New Haven (August 14-21) and Everett (August 22-September 1).
STATISTICAL NOTES: Led Midwest League in being hit by pitch with 27 in 1993. ... Tied for Southern League lead in caught stealing with 15 in 1996.
2002 GAMES PLAYED BY POSITION (MLB): OF—73; 3B—4; DH—3.

				BATTING													FIELDING	
Year	Team (League)	Pos.	G	AB	R	H	2B	3B	HR	RBI	BB	SO	SB-CS	Avg.	OBP	SLG	E	Avg.
1992—	Ariz. Mariners (Ariz.)..	SS	39	124	30	29	2	0	0	14	13	19	11-5	.234	.333	.250	•23	.876
1993—	Appleton (Midw.)........	2B-OF-SS	109	348	53	89	13	1	0	20	61	76	21-15	.256	.405	.299	28	.933
1994—	Riverside (Calif.).........	OF	128	481	*102	141	12	3	1	41	76	67	34-15	.293	.401	.337	9	.972
1995—	Port City (Sou.)..........	OF-2B	112	391	36	87	11	2	0	29	30	66	10-12	.223	.291	.261	6	.977
1996—	Port City (Sou.)..........	OF-SS	119	407	54	109	12	3	1	30	41	62	15-15	.268	.345	.319	15	.961
1997—	Memphis (Sou.).........	SS-3B-2B-OF	88	320	56	79	9	4	1	28	34	71	31-6	.247	.342	.309	23	.939
	—Tacoma (PCL)............	3B-OF-2B-SS	11	35	5	11	2	0	0	5	4	3	0-1	.314	.400	.371	3	.912
1998—	Seattle (A.L.).............	OF-3B-DH	44	51	11	12	1	0	0	2	5	9	2-1	.235	.316	.255	2	.957
	—Tacoma (PCL)............	OF-SS-2B-3B	75	278	39	67	16	2	0	11	27	50	14-11	.241	.322	.313	11	.954
1999—	Seattle (A.L.).............	O-3-DH-2-S	55	80	16	18	5	2	0	9	6	13	3-4	.225	.287	.338	3	.967
	—Tacoma (PCL)............	S-O-3-2-DH	47	174	26	52	6	3	0	21	14	24	18-4	.299	.361	.368	9	.940
	—New Haven (East.)......	2-DH-3-S-O	5	18	2	0	0	0	0	0	3	2	1-0	.000	.143	.000	1	.944
	—Everett (N'West).........	SS	1	2	0	1	0	1	0	1	2	0	1-0	.500	.750	1.500	0	1.000
2000—	Seattle (A.L.).............	OF-3B-SS-DH	59	29	7	9	1	1	0	3	4	9	2-3	.310	.394	.414	0	1.000
	—Tacoma (PCL)............	OF-3B-SS-2B	67	214	27	53	6	6	1	22	31	38	16-7	.248	.347	.346	6	.971
2001—	Seattle (A.L.).............	O-DH-3-S-2	94	64	16	14	2	2	0	5	4	20	1-1	.219	.282	.313	2	.972
2002—	Seattle (A.L.).............	OF-3B-DH	79	72	22	17	5	2	0	8	9	14	4-0	.236	.329	.361	2	.972
Major League totals (5 years)			331	296	72	70	14	7	0	27	28	65	12-9	.236	.312	.331	9	.971

DIVISION SERIES RECORD

				BATTING													FIELDING	
Year	Team (League)	Pos.	G	AB	R	H	2B	3B	HR	RBI	BB	SO	SB-CS	Avg.	OBP	SLG	E	Avg.
2000—	Seattle (A.L.).............								Did not play.									
2001—	Seattle (A.L.).............	PH	1	1	0	0	0	0	0	0	0	0	0-0	.000	.000	.000	...	...

CHAMPIONSHIP SERIES RECORD

				BATTING													FIELDING	
Year	Team (League)	Pos.	G	AB	R	H	2B	3B	HR	RBI	BB	SO	SB-CS	Avg.	OBP	SLG	E	Avg.
2000—	Seattle (A.L.).............	OF	2	0	0	0	0	0	0	0	0	0	0-0	...	...	...	0	...
2001—	Seattle (A.L.).............	PR-DH-OF	2	1	1	0	0	0	0	0	0	0	0-0	.000	.000	.000	0	...
Championship series totals (2 years)			4	1	1	0	0	0	0	0	0	0	0-0	.000	.000	.000	0	...

GIRARDI, JOE — C

PERSONAL: Born October 14, 1964, in Peoria, Ill. ... 5-11/200. ... Bats right, throws right. ... Full name: Joseph Elliott Girardi. ... Name pronounced jeh-RAR-dee.
HIGH SCHOOL: Spalding Institute (Peoria, Ill.).
COLLEGE: Northwestern.
TRANSACTIONS/CAREER NOTES: Selected by Chicago Cubs organization in fifth round of free-agent draft (June 2, 1986). ... On disabled list (August 27, 1986-remainder of season; and August 7, 1988-remainder of season). ... On Chicago disabled list (April 17-August 6, 1991); included rehabilitation assignment to Iowa (July 23-August 6). ... Selected by Colorado Rockies in first round (19th pick overall) of expansion draft (November 17, 1992). ... On Colorado disabled list (June 5-August 11, 1993); included rehabilitation assignment to Colorado Springs (August 1-11). ... On disabled list (July 11-26, 1994). ... Traded by Rockies to New York Yankees for P Mike DeJean and a player to be named later (November 20, 1995); Rockies acquired P Steve Shoemaker to complete deal (December 6, 1995). ... Granted free agency (November 5, 1996). ... Re-signed by Yankees (December 3, 1996). ... Granted free agency (November 5, 1999). ... Signed by Cubs (December 15, 1999). ... On disabled list (July 17-August 1, 2002). ... Granted free agency (October 28, 2002).
STATISTICAL NOTES: Led Carolina League catchers with 569 putouts, 74 assists, 661 total chances and tied for lead with 17 passed balls in 1987. ... Led Eastern League catchers with .992 fielding percentage, 448 putouts, 76 assists and 528 total chances and tied for lead with five double plays in 1988. ... Tied for N.L. lead with 16 passed balls in 1990.
2002 GAMES PLAYED BY POSITION (MLB): C—88.

				BATTING													FIELDING	
Year	Team (League)	Pos.	G	AB	R	H	2B	3B	HR	RBI	BB	SO	SB-CS	Avg.	OBP	SLG	E	Avg.
1986—	Peoria (Midw.)............	C	68	230	36	71	13	1	3	28	17	36	6-3	.309	.360	.413	5	.989
1987—	Win.-Salem (Caro.)	C	99	364	51	102	9	8	8	46	33	64	9-2	.280	.343	.415	18	.973
1988—	Pittsfield (East.)..........	C-OF	104	357	44	97	14	1	7	41	29	51	7-4	.272	.330	.375	6	†.989
1989—	Chicago (N.L.)............	C	59	157	15	39	10	0	1	14	11	26	2-1	.248	.304	.331	7	.981
	—Iowa (A.A.).................	C	32	110	12	27	4	2	2	11	5	19	3-1	.245	.278	.373	1	.995
1990—	Chicago (N.L.)............	C	133	419	36	113	24	2	1	38	17	50	8-3	.270	.300	.344	11	.985
1991—	Chicago (N.L.)............	C	21	47	3	9	2	0	0	6	6	6	0-0	.191	.283	.234	3	.972
	—Iowa (A.A.).................	C	12	36	3	8	1	0	0	4	4	8	2-0	.222	.300	.250	3	.957
1992—	Chicago (N.L.)............	C	91	270	19	73	3	1	1	12	19	38	0-2	.270	.320	.300	4	.991
1993—	Colorado (N.L.)■.......	C	86	310	35	90	14	5	3	31	24	41	6-6	.290	.346	.397	6	.989
	—Colo. Springs (PCL)...	C	8	31	6	15	1	1	1	6	0	3	1-0	.484	.484	.677	1	.977
1994—	Colorado (N.L.)..........	C	93	330	47	91	9	4	4	34	21	48	3-3	.276	.321	.364	5	.992
1995—	Colorado (N.L.)..........	C	125	462	63	121	17	2	8	55	29	76	3-3	.262	.308	.359	10	.988
1996—	New York (A.L.)■.......	C-DH	124	422	55	124	22	3	2	45	30	55	13-4	.294	.346	.374	3	.996
1997—	New York (A.L.)..........	C	112	398	38	105	23	1	1	50	26	53	2-3	.264	.311	.334	5	.994
1998—	New York (A.L.)..........	C	78	254	31	70	11	4	3	31	14	38	2-4	.276	.317	.386	3	.995

Year	Team (League)	Pos.	BATTING G	AB	R	H	2B	3B	HR	RBI	BB	SO	SB-CS	Avg.	OBP	SLG	FIELDING E	Avg.
1999—	New York (A.L.)	C	65	209	23	50	16	1	2	27	10	26	3-1	.239	.271	.354	8	.984
2000—	Chicago (N.L.)■	C	106	363	47	101	15	1	6	40	32	61	1-0	.278	.339	.375	5	.993
2001—	Chicago (N.L.)	C	78	229	22	58	10	1	3	25	21	50	0-1	.253	.315	.345	0	1.000
2002—	Chicago (N.L.)	C	90	234	19	53	10	1	1	13	16	35	1-0	.226	.275	.291	6	.990
American League totals (4 years)			379	1283	147	349	72	9	8	153	80	172	20-12	.272	.317	.361	19	.993
National League totals (10 years)			882	2821	306	748	114	17	28	268	196	431	24-19	.265	.315	.347	57	.990
Major League totals (14 years)			1261	4104	453	1097	186	26	36	421	276	603	44-31	.267	.316	.352	76	.991

DIVISION SERIES RECORD

Year	Team (League)	Pos.	BATTING G	AB	R	H	2B	3B	HR	RBI	BB	SO	SB-CS	Avg.	OBP	SLG	FIELDING E	Avg.
1995—	Colorado (N.L.)	C	4	16	0	2	0	0	0	0	0	2	0-0	.125	.125	.125	1	.966
1996—	New York (A.L.)	C-PR	4	9	1	2	0	0	0	0	4	1	0-0	.222	.462	.222	1	.967
1997—	New York (A.L.)	C	5	15	2	2	0	0	0	0	1	3	0-0	.133	.188	.133	0	1.000
1998—	New York (A.L.)	C	2	7	0	3	0	0	0	0	0	1	0-0	.429	.429	.429	0	1.000
1999—	New York (A.L.)	C	2	6	0	0	0	0	0	0	0	1	0-0	.000	.000	.000	0	1.000
Division series totals (5 years)			17	53	3	9	0	0	0	0	5	8	0-0	.170	.241	.170	2	.982

CHAMPIONSHIP SERIES RECORD

Year	Team (League)	Pos.	BATTING G	AB	R	H	2B	3B	HR	RBI	BB	SO	SB-CS	Avg.	OBP	SLG	FIELDING E	Avg.
1989—	Chicago (N.L.)	C	4	10	1	1	0	0	0	0	1	2	0-0	.100	.182	.100	0	1.000
1996—	New York (A.L.)	C-PH	4	12	1	3	0	1	0	0	1	3	0-0	.250	.308	.417	0	1.000
1998—	New York (A.L.)	C	3	8	2	2	0	0	0	0	1	0	0-0	.250	.333	.250	0	1.000
1999—	New York (A.L.)	C	3	8	0	2	0	0	0	0	0	2	0-0	.250	.250	.250	0	1.000
Championship series totals (4 years)			14	38	4	8	0	1	0	0	3	7	0-0	.211	.268	.263	0	1.000

WORLD SERIES RECORD

NOTES: Member of World Series championship team (1996, 1998 and 1999).

Year	Team (League)	Pos.	BATTING G	AB	R	H	2B	3B	HR	RBI	BB	SO	SB-CS	Avg.	OBP	SLG	FIELDING E	Avg.
1996—	New York (A.L.)	C	4	10	1	2	0	1	0	1	1	2	0-0	.200	.273	.400	0	1.000
1998—	New York (A.L.)	C	2	6	0	0	0	0	0	0	0	2	0-0	.000	.000	.000	0	1.000
1999—	New York (A.L.)	C	2	7	1	2	0	0	0	0	0	1	0-0	.286	.286	.286	0	1.000
World Series totals (3 years)			8	23	2	4	0	1	0	1	1	5	0-0	.174	.208	.261	0	1.000

ALL-STAR GAME RECORD

	AB	R	H	2B	3B	HR	RBI	BB	SO	SB-CS	Avg.	OBP	SLG	E	Avg.
All-Star Game totals (1 year)	2000—Selected, did not play.														

GLANVILLE, DOUG — OF

PERSONAL: Born August 25, 1970, in Hackensack, N.J. ... 6-2/174. ... Bats right, throws right. ... Full name: Douglas Metunwa Glanville.
HIGH SCHOOL: Teaneck (N.J.).
COLLEGE: Pennsylvania.
TRANSACTIONS/CAREER NOTES: Selected by Chicago Cubs organization in first round (12th pick overall) of free-agent draft (June 3, 1991). ... Traded by Cubs to Philadelphia Phillies for 2B Mickey Morandini (December 23, 1997). ... Granted free agency (October 29, 2002).
STATISTICAL NOTES: Led Carolina League outfielders with 293 putouts and 312 total chances in 1992. ... Led Southern League in caught stealing with 20 in 1994. ... Led Southern League outfielders with 322 putouts and 339 total chances in 1994. ... Had 18-game hitting streak (May 1-20, 1998). ... Had 17-game hitting streak (May 30-June 17, 1998). ... Tied N.L. outfielders for lead in double plays with four in 2000. ... Had 15-game hitting streaks (May 3-19, 2001 and May 27-June 12, 2001).
2002 GAMES PLAYED BY POSITION (MLB): OF—117.

Year	Team (League)	Pos.	BATTING G	AB	R	H	2B	3B	HR	RBI	BB	SO	SB-CS	Avg.	OBP	SLG	FIELDING E	Avg.
1991—	Geneva (NY-Penn)	OF	36	152	29	46	8	0	2	12	11	25	17-3	.303	.352	.395	0	1.000
1992—	Win.-Salem (Caro.)	OF	120	485	72	125	18	4	4	36	40	78	32-9	.258	.318	.336	7	.978
1993—	Daytona (FSL)	OF	61	239	47	70	10	1	2	21	28	24	18-15	.293	.374	.368	7	.950
—	Orlando (Sou.)	OF	73	296	42	78	14	4	9	40	12	41	15-7	.264	.292	.429	5	.972
1994—	Orlando (Sou.)	OF	130	483	53	127	22	2	5	52	24	49	26-20	.263	.301	.348	3	.991
1995—	Iowa (A.A.)	OF-DH	112	419	48	113	16	2	4	37	16	64	13-9	.270	.299	.346	4	.982
1996—	Iowa (A.A.)	OF-DH	90	373	53	115	23	3	3	34	12	35	15-10	.308	.331	.410	3	.987
—	Chicago (N.L.)	OF	49	83	10	20	5	1	1	10	3	11	2-0	.241	.264	.361	1	.973
1997—	Chicago (N.L.)	OF	146	474	79	142	22	5	4	35	24	46	19-11	.300	.333	.392	3	.989
1998—	Philadelphia (N.L.)■	OF	158	*678	106	189	28	7	8	49	42	89	23-6	.279	.325	.376	2	.995
1999—	Philadelphia (N.L.)	OF	150	628	101	204	38	6	11	73	48	82	34-2	.325	.376	.457	8	.980
2000—	Philadelphia (N.L.)	OF	154	637	89	175	27	6	8	52	31	76	31-8	.275	.307	.374	4	.990
2001—	Philadelphia (N.L.)	OF	153	634	74	166	24	3	14	55	19	91	28-6	.262	.285	.375	4	.991
2002—	Philadelphia (N.L.)	OF	138	422	49	105	16	3	6	29	25	57	19-2	.249	.292	.344	0	•1.000
Major League totals (7 years)			948	3556	508	1001	160	31	52	303	192	452	156-35	.281	.320	.388	22	.990

GLAUS, TROY — 3B — ANGELS

PERSONAL: Born August 3, 1976, in Tarzana, Calif. ... 6-5/245. ... Bats right, throws right. ... Full name: Troy Edward Glaus. ... Name pronounced GLOSS.
HIGH SCHOOL: Carlsbad (Calif.).
COLLEGE: UCLA.
TRANSACTIONS/CAREER NOTES: Selected by San Diego Padres organization in second round of free-agent draft (June 2, 1994); did not sign. ... Selected by Anaheim Angels organization in first round (third pick overall) of free-agent draft (June 3, 1997).

RECORDS: Shares major league record for most consecutive home runs—4 (September 15 [3], 16 [1], 2002). ... Hold A.L. single-season record for most home runs by third baseman—46 (2000).

HONORS: Named third baseman on The Sporting News A.L. Silver Slugger team (2000). ... Named third baseman on A.L. Silver Slugger team (2001). ... Named third baseman on The Sporting News A.L. All-Star team (2001).

STATISTICAL NOTES: Led A.L. third basemen with 349 assists and 493 total chances in 2000. ... Tied for A.L. lead with 33 errors by third baseman in 2000. ... Hit three home runs in one game (September 15, 2002). ... Career major league grand slams: 2.

MISCELLANEOUS: Member of 1996 U.S. Olympic baseball team.

2002 GAMES PLAYED BY POSITION (MLB): 3B—156; SS—2.

Year	Team (League)	Pos.	G	AB	R	H	2B	3B	HR	RBI	BB	SO	SB-CS	Avg.	OBP	SLG	E	Avg.
			BATTING														FIELDING	
1998—	Midland (Texas)..........	3B	50	188	51	58	11	2	19	51	39	41	4-2	.309	.430	.691	11	.925
	—Vancouver (PCL)........	3B	59	219	33	67	16	0	16	42	21	55	3-2	.306	.374	.598	13	.932
	—Anaheim (A.L.)...........	3B	48	165	19	36	9	0	1	23	15	51	1-0	.218	.280	.291	7	.941
1999—	Anaheim (A.L.)...........	3B-DH	154	551	85	132	29	0	29	79	71	143	5-1	.240	.331	.450	19	.954
2000—	Anaheim (A.L.)...........	3B-SS-DH	159	563	120	160	37	1	*47	102	112	163	14-11	.284	.404	.604	†33	.934
2001—	Anaheim (A.L.)...........	3B-SS-DH	161	588	100	147	38	2	41	108	107	158	10-3	.250	.367	.531	19	.954
2002—	Anaheim (A.L.)...........	3B-SS	156	569	99	142	24	1	30	111	88	144	10-3	.250	.352	.453	20	.950
Major League totals (5 years)			678	2436	423	617	137	4	148	423	393	659	40-18	.253	.359	.495	98	.947

DIVISION SERIES RECORD

RECORDS: Shares single-game record for most home runs—2 (October 1, 2002).

Year	Team (League)	Pos.	G	AB	R	H	2B	3B	HR	RBI	BB	SO	SB-CS	Avg.	OBP	SLG	E	Avg.
			BATTING														FIELDING	
2002—	Anaheim (A.L.)...........	3B	4	16	4	5	0	0	3	3	1	3	0-0	.313	.389	.875	1	.929

CHAMPIONSHIP SERIES RECORD

Year	Team (League)	Pos.	G	AB	R	H	2B	3B	HR	RBI	BB	SO	SB-CS	Avg.	OBP	SLG	E	Avg.
			BATTING														FIELDING	
2002—	Anaheim (A.L.)...........	3B	5	19	4	6	0	1	1	2	2	5	0-0	.316	.381	.579	0	1.000

WORLD SERIES RECORD

NOTES: Hit home run in first at-bat (October 19, 2002). ... Member of World Series championship team (2002). ... Named Most Valuable Player (2002).

Year	Team (League)	Pos.	G	AB	R	H	2B	3B	HR	RBI	BB	SO	SB-CS	Avg.	OBP	SLG	E	Avg.
			BATTING														FIELDING	
2002—	Anaheim (A.L.)...........	3B	7	26	7	10	3	0	3	8	4	6	0-0	.385	.467	.846	1	.938

ALL-STAR GAME RECORD

	AB	R	H	2B	3B	HR	RBI	BB	SO	SB-CS	Avg.	OBP	SLG	E	Avg.
All-Star Game totals (2 years)	2	0	0	0	0	0	0	0	0	0-0	.000	.000	.000	0	1.000

GLAVINE, TOM — P

PERSONAL: Born March 25, 1966, in Concord, Mass. ... 6-0/185. ... Throws left, bats left. ... Full name: Thomas Michael Glavine. ... Brother of Mike Glavine, first baseman, Cleveland Indians organization (1995-98) and Atlanta Braves organization (1999-2001). ... Name pronounced GLAV-in.

HIGH SCHOOL: Billerica (Mass.).

TRANSACTIONS/CAREER NOTES: Selected by Atlanta Braves organization in second round of free-agent draft (June 4, 1984). ... Granted free agency (October 28, 2002).

RECORDS: Shsares major league record for most years leading league in games started—6 (1993, 1996 and 1999-2002).

HONORS: Named N.L. Pitcher of the Year by The Sporting News (1991 and 2000). ... Named lefthanded pitcher on The Sporting News N.L. All-Star team (1991-92, 1998 and 2000). ... Named pitcher on The Sporting News N.L. Silver Slugger team (1991, 1995, 1996 and 1998). ... Named N.L. Cy Young Award winner by Baseball Writers' Association of America (1991 and 1998).

STATISTICAL NOTES: Led Gulf Coast League with 12 wild pitches in 1984. ... Tied for N.L. lead with 17 sacrifice hits in 2001.

MISCELLANEOUS: Selected by Los Angeles Kings in fourth round (69th pick overall) of NHL entry draft (June 9, 1984). ... Appeared in eight games as pinch runner (1988). ... Appeared in one game as pinch runner (1989). ... Appeared in one game as pinch runner (1990). ... Received a base on balls and scored once in one game as pinch hitter and appeared in one game as pinch runner (1991). ... Singled and struck out in two appearances as pinch hitter (1992). ... Struck out in only appearance as pinch hitter (1994). ... Singled and struck out in three appearances as pinch hitter (1996). ... Had a sacrifice hit in only appearance as pinch hitter (1999). ... Grounded out twice in two appearances as pinch hitter (2000).

CAREER HITTING (MLB): 191-for-1024 (.187), 71 R, 20 2B, 2 3B, 1 HR, 69 RBI.

Year	League	W	L	Pct.	ERA	G	GS	CG	ShO	Sv.-Opp.	IP	H	R	ER	HR	BB-IBB	SO
1984—	Gulf Coast Braves (GCL) ..	2	3	.400	3.34	8	7	0	0	0-...	32.1	29	17	12	0	13-0	34
1985—	Sumter (S.Atl.).................	9	6	.600	*2.35	26	26	2	1	0-...	168.2	114	58	44	6	73-0	174
1986—	Greenville (Sou.).............	11	6	.647	3.41	22	22	2	1	0-...	145.1	129	62	55	14	70-3	114
	—Richmond (I.L.)...............	1	5	.167	5.63	7	7	1	1	0-...	40.0	40	29	25	4	27-0	12
1987—	Richmond (I.L.)...............	6	12	.333	3.35	22	22	4	1	0-...	150.1	142	70	56	15	56-3	91
	—Atlanta (N.L.)...................	2	4	.333	5.54	9	9	0	0	0-0	50.1	55	34	31	5	33-4	20
1988—	Atlanta (N.L.)...................	7	*17	.292	4.56	34	34	1	0	0-0	195.1	201	111	99	12	63-7	84
1989—	Atlanta (N.L.)...................	14	8	.636	3.68	29	29	6	4	0-0	186.0	172	88	76	20	40-3	90
1990—	Atlanta (N.L.)...................	10	12	.455	4.28	33	33	1	0	0-0	214.1	232	111	102	18	78-10	129
1991—	Atlanta (N.L.)...................	•20	11	.645	2.55	34	34	•9	1	0-0	246.2	201	83	70	17	69-6	192
1992—	Atlanta (N.L.)...................	•20	8	.714	2.76	33	33	7	•5	0-0	225.0	197	81	69	6	70-7	129
1993—	Atlanta (N.L.)...................	•22	6	.786	3.20	36	•36	4	2	0-0	239.1	236	91	85	16	90-7	120
1994—	Atlanta (N.L.)...................	13	9	.591	3.97	25	25	2	0	0-0	165.1	173	76	73	10	70-10	140
1995—	Atlanta (N.L.)...................	16	7	.696	3.08	29	29	3	1	0-0	198.2	182	76	68	9	66-0	127
1996—	Atlanta (N.L.)...................	15	10	.600	2.98	36	*36	1	0	0-0	235.1	222	91	78	14	85-7	181
1997—	Atlanta (N.L.)...................	14	7	.667	2.96	33	33	5	2	0-0	240.0	197	86	79	20	79-9	152
1998—	Atlanta (N.L.)...................	*20	6	.769	2.47	33	33	4	3	0-0	229.1	202	67	63	13	74-2	157
1999—	Atlanta (N.L.)...................	14	11	.560	4.12	35	•35	2	0	0-0	234.0	*259	115	107	18	83-14	138
2000—	Atlanta (N.L.)...................	*21	9	.700	3.40	35	•35	4	2	0-0	241.0	222	101	91	24	65-6	152
2001—	Atlanta (N.L.)...................	16	7	.696	3.57	35	•35	1	1	0-0	219.1	213	92	87	24	97-10	116
2002—	Atlanta (N.L.)...................	18	11	.621	2.96	36	*36	2	1	0-0	224.2	210	85	74	21	78-8	127
Major League totals (16 years)...		242	143	.629	3.37	505	505	52	22	0-0	3344.2	3174	1388	1252	247	1140-110	2054

DIVISION SERIES RECORD

RECORDS: Holds N.L. career records for most runs allowed—30; earned runs allowed—29; and bases on balls allowed—23.

Year	League	W	L	Pct.	ERA	G	GS	CG	ShO	Sv.-Opp.	IP	H	R	ER	HR	BB-IBB	SO
1995—	Atlanta (N.L.)	0	0	...	2.57	1	1	0	0	0-0	7.0	5	3	2	1	1-0	3
1996—	Atlanta (N.L.)	1	0	1.000	1.35	1	1	0	0	0-0	6.2	5	1	1	0	3-0	7
1997—	Atlanta (N.L.)	1	0	1.000	4.50	1	1	0	0	0-0	6.0	5	3	3	0	5-0	4
1998—	Atlanta (N.L.)	0	0	...	1.29	1	1	0	0	0-0	7.0	3	1	1	0	1-0	8
1999—	Atlanta (N.L.)	0	0	...	3.00	1	1	0	0	0-0	6.0	5	2	2	0	3-0	6
2000—	Atlanta (N.L.)	0	1	.000	27.00	1	1	0	0	0-0	2.1	6	7	7	2	1-0	2
2001—	Atlanta (N.L.)	1	0	1.000	0.00	1	1	0	0	0-0	8.0	6	0	0	0	2-0	3
2002—	Atlanta (N.L.)	0	2	.000	15.26	2	2	0	0	0-0	7.2	17	13	13	1	7-3	4
Division series totals (8 years)		3	3	.500	5.15	9	9	0	0	0-0	50.2	52	30	29	4	23-3	37

CHAMPIONSHIP SERIES RECORD

RECORDS: Holds career records for most losses—9; games started—15; hits allowed—91; and bases on balls allowed—37. ... Shares N.L. career record for home runs allowed—8; and hit batsmen—5. ... Holds single-inning records for most runs allowed—8 (October 13, 1992, second inning); and most earned runs allowed—7 (October 13, 1992, second inning). ... Shares single-game record for most earned runs allowed—7 (October 13, 1992 and October 14, 1997). ... Shares single-inning record for most hits allowed—6 (October 13, 1992, second inning).

NOTES: Received a base on balls in only appearance as pinch hitter (1998).

Year	League	W	L	Pct.	ERA	G	GS	CG	ShO	Sv.-Opp.	IP	H	R	ER	HR	BB-IBB	SO
1991—	Atlanta (N.L.)	0	2	.000	3.21	2	2	0	0	0-0	14.0	12	5	5	1	6-2	11
1992—	Atlanta (N.L.)	0	2	.000	12.27	2	2	0	0	0-0	7.1	13	11	10	3	3-1	2
1993—	Atlanta (N.L.)	1	0	1.000	2.57	1	1	0	0	0-0	7.0	6	2	2	1	0-0	5
1995—	Atlanta (N.L.)	0	0	...	1.29	1	1	0	0	0-0	7.0	7	1	1	0	2-1	5
1996—	Atlanta (N.L.)	1	1	.500	2.08	2	2	0	0	0-0	13.0	10	3	3	2	0-0	9
1997—	Atlanta (N.L.)	1	1	.500	5.40	2	2	0	0	0-0	13.1	13	8	8	0	11-3	9
1998—	Atlanta (N.L.)	0	2	.000	2.31	2	2	0	0	0-0	11.2	13	6	3	0	9-0	8
1999—	Atlanta (N.L.)	1	0	1.000	0.00	1	1	0	0	0-0	7.0	7	0	0	0	1-0	8
2001—	Atlanta (N.L.)	1	1	.500	1.50	2	2	0	0	0-0	12.0	10	4	2	1	5-0	5
Champ. series totals (9 years)		5	9	.357	3.31	15	15	0	0	0-0	92.1	91	40	34	8	37-7	62

WORLD SERIES RECORD

RECORDS: Shares single-inning records for most bases on balls allowed—4 (October 24, 1991, sixth inning); and most consecutive bases on balls allowed—3 (October 24, 1991, sixth inning).

NOTES: Named Most Valuable Player (1995). ... Member of World Series championship team (1995).

Year	League	W	L	Pct.	ERA	G	GS	CG	ShO	Sv.-Opp.	IP	H	R	ER	HR	BB-IBB	SO
1991—	Atlanta (N.L.)	1	1	.500	2.70	2	2	1	0	0-0	13.1	8	6	4	2	7-0	8
1992—	Atlanta (N.L.)	1	1	.500	1.59	2	2	2	0	0-0	17.0	10	3	3	2	4-0	8
1995—	Atlanta (N.L.)	2	0	1.000	1.29	2	2	0	0	0-0	14.0	4	2	2	1	6-0	11
1996—	Atlanta (N.L.)	0	1	.000	1.29	1	1	0	0	0-0	7.0	4	2	1	0	3-0	8
1999—	Atlanta (N.L.)	0	0	...	5.14	1	1	0	0	0-0	7.0	7	5	4	3	0-0	3
World Series totals (5 years)		4	3	.571	2.16	8	8	3	0	0-0	58.1	33	18	14	8	20-0	38

ALL-STAR GAME RECORD

RECORDS: Holds single-game record for most hits allowed—9 (July 14, 1992). ... Holds single-inning record for most hits allowed—7 (July 14, 1992, first inning).

	W	L	Pct.	ERA	GS	CG	ShO	Sv.-Opp.	IP	H	R	ER	HR	BB-IBB	SO
All-Star Game totals (5 years)	0	1	.000	11.57	2	0	0	0-0	7.0	15	9	9	0	4-0	7

GLOAD, ROSS — 1B/OF — ROCKIES

PERSONAL: Born April 5, 1976, in Brooklyn, N.Y. ... 6-0/185. ... Bats left, throws left. ... Full name: Ross Peter Gload.

HIGH SCHOOL: East Hampton (N.Y.).

COLLEGE: South Florida.

TRANSACTIONS/CAREER NOTES: Selected by Florida Marlins organization in 13th round of free-agent draft (June 3, 1997). ... Traded by Marlins with P David Noyce to Chicago Cubs for OF Henry Rodriguez (July 31, 2000). ... Claimed on waivers by Colorado Rockies (September 12, 2001). ... Traded by Rockies to New York Mets as part of three-way deal in which Mets traded P Glendon Rusch to Milwaukee Brewers, Rockies traded P Craig House to Mets, Brewers traded P Jeff D'Amico, OF Jeromy Burnitz, IF Lou Collier, OF/1B Mark Sweeney and cash to Mets, Mets traded 1B/3B Todd Zeile, OF Benny Agbayani, IF/OF Lenny Harris and cash to Rockies and Rockies traded OF Alex Ochoa to Brewers (January 21, 2002). ... Traded by Mets to Rockies for cash (January 27, 2002). ... On Colorado Springs disabled list (April 4-25, 2002).

STATISTICAL NOTES: Led New York Pennsylvania League first basemen with 546 putouts and 599 total chances in 1997. ... Led Midwest League with seven intentional bases on balls received in 1998.

2002 GAMES PLAYED BY POSITION (MLB): 1B—4; OF—2.

			BATTING													FIELDING	
Year	Team (League)	Pos.	G	AB	R	H	2B	3B	HR	RBI	BB	SO	SB-CS	Avg.	OBP	SLG	E	Avg.
1997—	Utica (NY-Penn)	1B	68	245	28	64	15	2	3	43	28	57	1-1	.261	.336	.376	*16	.973
1998—	Kane County (Midw.)	1B	132	501	77	157	*41	3	12	92	58	84	7-6	.313	.386	.479	14	.989
1999—	Brevard County (FSL)	1B	133	490	80	146	26	3	10	74	53	76	3-1	.298	.369	.424	9	.993
2000—	Portland (East.)	OF-1B	100	401	60	114	28	4	16	65	29	53	4-1	.284	.333	.494	7	.986
—	Iowa (PCL)■	OF	28	104	24	42	10	2	14	39	9	13	1-1	.404	.452	.942	4	.917
—	Chicago (N.L.)	OF-1B	18	31	4	6	0	1	1	3	3	10	0-0	.194	.257	.355	0	1.000
2001—	Iowa (PCL)	1B-OF	133	475	70	141	32	*10	15	93	35	88	9-7	.297	.344	.501	3	.994
2002—	Colo. Springs (PCL)■	1B-OF	104	442	69	139	28	6	16	71	18	59	9-4	.314	.338	.514	11	.987
—	Colorado (N.L.)	1B-OF	26	31	4	8	1	0	1	4	3	7	0-0	.258	.324	.387	0	1.000
Major League totals (2 years)			44	62	8	14	1	1	2	7	6	17	0-0	.226	.290	.371	0	1.000

GLOVER, GARY — P — WHITE SOX

PERSONAL: Born December 3, 1976, in Cleveland. ... 6-5/205. ... Throws right, bats right. ... Full name: John Gary Glover II.

HIGH SCHOOL: Deland (Fla.).

G

TRANSACTIONS/CAREER NOTES: Selected by Toronto Blue Jays organization in 15th round of free-agent draft (June 2, 1994). ... On disabled list (August 10-September 8, 1994). ... Traded by Blue Jays to Chicago White Sox for P Scott Eyre (November 7, 2000).

CAREER HITTING (MLB): 0-for-1 (.000), 0 R, 0 2B, 0 3B, 0 HR, 0 RBI.

Year	League	W	L	Pct.	ERA	G	GS	CG	ShO	Sv.-Opp.	IP	H	R	ER	HR	BB-IBB	SO
1994—	GC Blue Jays (GCL)	0	0	...	47.25	2	0	0	0	0-...	1.1	4	8	7	1	4-0	2
1995—	GC Blue Jays (GCL)	3	7	.300	4.91	12	10	2	0	0-...	62.1	62	48	34	4	26-0	46
1996—	Medicine Hat (Pio.)	3	*12	.200	7.75	15	•15	*2	0	0-...	83.2	*119	*94	*72	14	29-1	54
1997—	Hagerstown (S.Atl.)	6	*17	.261	3.73	28	28	3	0	0-...	173.2	165	94	72	9	58-1	155
1998—	Knoxville (Sou.)	0	5	.000	6.75	8	8	0	0	0-...	37.1	41	36	28	2	28-0	14
	—Dunedin (FSL)	7	6	.538	4.28	19	18	0	0	0-...	109.1	117	66	52	8	36-0	88
1999—	Knoxville (Sou.)	8	2	.800	3.56	13	13	1	0	0-...	86.0	70	39	34	5	27-0	77
	—Syracuse (I.L.)	4	6	.400	5.19	14	14	0	0	0-...	76.1	93	50	44	10	35-0	57
	—Toronto (A.L.)	0	0	...	0.00	1	0	0	0	0-0	1.0	0	0	0	0	1-0	0
2000—	Syracuse (I.L.)	9	9	.500	5.02	27	27	1	0	0-...	166.2	181	104	93	21	62-0	119
2001—	Chicago (A.L.)■	5	5	.500	4.93	46	11	0	0	0-1	100.1	98	61	55	16	32-3	63
	—Charlotte (I.L.)	2	1	.667	1.88	6	6	1	1	0-...	38.1	21	8	8	3	5-0	29
2002—	Chicago (A.L.)	7	8	.467	5.20	41	22	0	0	1-1	138.1	136	86	80	21	52-1	70
Major League totals (3 years)		12	13	.480	5.07	88	33	0	0	1-2	239.2	234	147	135	37	85-4	133

GOMES, WAYNE — P — RED SOX

PERSONAL: Born January 15, 1973, in Hampton, Va. ... 6-2/225. ... Throws right, bats right. ... Full name: Wayne Maurice Gomes.

HIGH SCHOOL: Phoebus (Hampton, Va.).

COLLEGE: Old Dominion.

TRANSACTIONS/CAREER NOTES: Selected by Philadelphia Phillies organization in first round (fourth pick overall) of free-agent draft (June 3, 1993). ... On disabled list (May 12-June 23, 1995). ... On Philadelphia disabled list (July 7-August 8, 2000); included rehabilitation assignment to Scranton/Wilkes-Barre (August 1-8). ... On Philadelphia disabled list (May 30-June 19, 2001); included rehabilitation assignment to Lakewood (June 16-19). ... Traded by Phillies to San Francisco Giants for IF/OF Felipe Crespo (July 27, 2001). ... On San Francisco disabled list (August 19-September 3, 2001). ... Released by Giants (November 28, 2001). ... Signed by Pittsburgh Pirates organization (January 25, 2002). ... Released by Pirates (April 26, 2002). ... Signed by Boston Red Sox organization (April 28, 2002).

STATISTICAL NOTES: Led Florida State League with 27 wild pitches in 1994. ... Tied for Eastern League lead with six balks in 1995.

CAREER HITTING (MLB): 1-for-6 (.167), 0 R, 0 2B, 0 3B, 0 HR, 1 RBI.

Year	League	W	L	Pct.	ERA	G	GS	CG	ShO	Sv.-Opp.	IP	H	R	ER	HR	BB-IBB	SO
1993—	Batavia (NY-Penn)	1	0	1.000	1.23	5	0	0	0	0-...	7.1	1	1	1	0	8-0	11
	—Clearwater (FSL)	0	0	...	1.17	9	0	0	0	4-...	7.2	4	1	1	0	9-0	13
1994—	Clearwater (FSL)	6	8	.429	4.74	23	21	1	1	0-...	104.1	85	63	55	5	82-2	102
1995—	Reading (East.)	7	4	.636	3.96	22	22	1	1	0-...	104.2	89	54	46	8	70-0	102
1996—	Reading (East.)	0	4	.000	4.48	*67	0	0	0	24-...	64.1	53	35	32	7	48-3	79
1997—	Scranton/W.B. (I.L.)	3	1	.750	2.37	26	0	0	0	7-...	38.0	31	11	10	2	24-2	36
	—Philadelphia (N.L.)	5	1	.833	5.27	37	0	0	0	0-1	42.2	45	26	25	4	24-0	24
1998—	Philadelphia (N.L.)	9	6	.600	4.24	71	0	0	0	1-8	93.1	94	48	44	9	35-4	86
1999—	Philadelphia (N.L.)	5	5	.500	4.26	73	0	0	0	19-24	74.0	70	38	35	5	56-2	58
2000—	Philadelphia (N.L.)	4	6	.400	4.40	65	0	0	0	7-11	73.2	72	41	36	6	35-3	49
	—Scranton/W.B. (I.L.)	0	0	...	2.25	3	0	0	0	0-...	4.0	3	1	1	0	1-0	1
2001—	Philadelphia (N.L.)	4	3	.571	4.31	42	0	0	0	1-5	48.0	51	23	23	4	22-4	35
	—Lakewood (S.Atl.)	0	0	...	3.00	2	2	0	0	0-...	3.0	2	1	1	0	3-0	3
	—San Francisco (N.L.)■	2	0	1.000	8.40	13	0	0	0	0-0	15.0	21	14	14	3	7-2	17
2002—	Nashville (PCL)■	0	2	.000	15.43	6	1	0	0	0-...	9.1	21	16	16	1	12-1	7
	—Pawtucket (I.L.)■	5	2	.714	2.64	42	0	0	0	4-...	71.2	61	30	21	8	28-2	54
	—Boston (A.L.)	1	2	.333	4.64	20	0	0	0	1-1	21.1	20	11	11	2	12-2	15
A.L. totals (1 year)		1	2	.333	4.64	20	0	0	0	1-1	21.1	20	11	11	2	12-2	15
N.L. totals (5 years)		29	21	.580	4.60	301	0	0	0	28-49	346.2	353	190	177	31	179-15	269
Major League totals (6 years)		30	23	.566	4.60	321	0	0	0	29-50	368.0	373	201	188	33	191-17	284

GOMEZ, ALEXIS — OF — ROYALS

PERSONAL: Born August 6, 1980, in Loma de Cabrera, Dominican Republic. ... 6-2/180. ... Bats left, throws left. ... Full name: Alexis De Jesus Gomez.

HIGH SCHOOL: Liceo General Jose Cabrera (Loma de Cabrera, Dominican Republic).

TRANSACTIONS/CAREER NOTES: Signed as non-drafted free agent by Kansas City Royals organization (February 21, 1997). ... On Wichita disabled list (April 29-May 10, 2002).

STATISTICAL NOTES: Led Gulf Coast League outfielders with 131 putouts and 140 total chances in 1999. ... Led Texas League with 24 caught stealing in 2002.

2002 GAMES PLAYED BY POSITION (MLB): OF—2.

			BATTING														FIELDING	
Year	Team (League)	Pos.	G	AB	R	H	2B	3B	HR	RBI	BB	SO	SB-CS	Avg.	OBP	SLG	E	Avg.
1997—	Dom. Royals (DSL)		64	248	51	87	12	9	0	42	33	52	9-...	.351	...	.472	...	...
1998—	Dom. Royals (DSL)		67	233	51	66	11	3	1	34	50	46	17-...	.283	...	.369	...	...
1999—	GC Royals (GCL)	OF	56	214	44	59	12	1	5	31	32	48	13-5	.276	.371	.411	2	.986
2000—	Wilmington (Caro.)	OF	121	461	63	117	13	4	1	33	45	121	21-10	.254	.322	.306	14	.950
2001—	Wilmington (Caro.)	OF	48	169	29	51	8	2	1	9	11	43	7-3	.302	.348	.391	5	.957
	—Wichita (Texas)	OF	83	342	55	96	15	6	4	34	27	70	16-10	.281	.337	.395	6	.971
2002—	Wichita (Texas)	OF	114	461	72	136	21	8	14	75	45	84	36-24	.295	.359	.466	•8	.967
	—Kansas City (A.L.)	OF	5	10	0	2	0	0	0	0	0	2	0-0	.200	.200	.200	0	1.000
Major League totals (1 year)			5	10	0	2	0	0	0	0	0	2	0-0	.200	.200	.200	0	1.000

GOMEZ, CHRIS — SS

PERSONAL: Born June 16, 1971, in Los Angeles. ... 6-1/185. ... Bats right, throws right. ... Full name: Christopher Cory Gomez.
HIGH SCHOOL: Lakewood (Calif.).
COLLEGE: Loyola Marymount, then Long Beach State.
TRANSACTIONS/CAREER NOTES: Selected by California Angels organization in 37th round of free-agent draft (June 5, 1989); did not sign. ... Selected by Detroit Tigers organization in third round of free-agent draft (June 1, 1992). ... Traded by Tigers with C John Flaherty to San Diego Padres for C Brad Ausmus, SS Andujar Cedeno and P Russ Spear (June 18, 1996). ... On San Diego disabled list (June 2-July 31, 1999); included rehabilitation assignment to Las Vegas (July 15-30). ... On disabled list (June 22, 2000-remainder of season). ... Released by Padres (June 22, 2001). ... Signed by Tampa Bay Devil Rays organization (June 27, 2001). ... Granted free agency (November 5, 2001). ... Re-signed by Devil Rays (December 7, 2001). ... Released by Devil Rays (September 30, 2002).
2002 GAMES PLAYED BY POSITION (MLB): SS—130.

			BATTING														FIELDING	
Year	Team (League)	Pos.	G	AB	R	H	2B	3B	HR	RBI	BB	SO	SB-CS	Avg.	OBP	SLG	E	Avg.
1992	London (East.)	SS	64	220	20	59	13	2	1	19	20	34	1-3	.268	.337	.359	14	.951
1993	Toledo (I.L.)	SS	87	277	29	68	12	2	0	20	23	37	6-2	.245	.308	.303	16	.961
	Detroit (A.L.)	SS-2B-DH	46	128	11	32	7	1	0	11	9	17	2-2	.250	.304	.320	5	.974
1994	Detroit (A.L.)	SS-2B	84	296	32	76	19	0	8	53	33	64	5-3	.257	.336	.402	8	.978
1995	Detroit (A.L.)	SS-2B-DH	123	431	49	96	20	2	11	50	41	96	4-1	.223	.292	.355	15	.974
1996	Detroit (A.L.)	SS	48	128	21	31	5	0	1	16	18	20	1-1	.242	.340	.305	6	.970
	San Diego (N.L.)■	SS	89	328	32	86	16	1	3	29	39	64	2-2	.262	.349	.345	13	.967
1997	San Diego (N.L.)	SS	150	522	62	132	19	2	5	54	53	114	5-8	.253	.326	.326	15	.978
1998	San Diego (N.L.)	SS	145	449	55	120	32	3	4	39	51	87	1-3	.267	.346	.379	12	*.980
1999	San Diego (N.L.)	SS	76	234	20	59	8	1	1	15	27	49	1-2	.252	.331	.308	12	.961
	Las Vegas (PCL)	SS	10	27	3	9	1	0	0	4	2	6	0-0	.333	.400	.370	2	.933
2000	San Diego (N.L.)	SS-2B	33	54	4	12	0	0	0	3	7	5	0-0	.222	.306	.222	5	.933
2001	San Diego (N.L.)	SS-2B	40	112	6	21	3	0	0	7	9	14	1-0	.188	.244	.214	6	.948
	Portland (PCL)	SS-2B	11	40	5	12	3	0	1	5	2	4	1-0	.300	.333	.450	2	.959
	Durham (I.L.)■	SS	23	93	16	28	5	1	4	17	11	5	1-1	.301	.375	.505	2	.978
	Tampa Bay (A.L.)	SS	58	189	31	57	16	0	8	36	8	24	3-0	.302	.332	.513	7	.968
2002	Tampa Bay (A.L.)	SS	130	461	51	122	31	3	10	46	21	58	1-3	.265	.305	.410	12	.980
American League totals (6 years)			489	1633	195	414	98	6	38	212	130	279	16-10	.254	.313	.391	53	.975
National League totals (6 years)			533	1699	179	430	78	7	13	147	186	333	10-15	.253	.331	.330	63	.971
Major League totals (10 years)			1022	3332	374	844	176	13	51	359	316	612	26-25	.253	.322	.360	116	.973

DIVISION SERIES RECORD

			BATTING														FIELDING	
Year	Team (League)	Pos.	G	AB	R	H	2B	3B	HR	RBI	BB	SO	SB-CS	Avg.	OBP	SLG	E	Avg.
1996	San Diego (N.L.)	SS	3	12	0	2	0	0	0	1	0	4	0-0	.167	.167	.167	0	1.000
1998	San Diego (N.L.)	SS	4	11	1	3	0	0	0	0	4	1	0-0	.273	.467	.273	1	.938
Division series totals (2 years)			7	23	1	5	0	0	0	1	4	5	0-0	.217	.333	.217	1	.966

CHAMPIONSHIP SERIES RECORD

			BATTING														FIELDING	
Year	Team (League)	Pos.	G	AB	R	H	2B	3B	HR	RBI	BB	SO	SB-CS	Avg.	OBP	SLG	E	Avg.
1998	San Diego (N.L.)	SS	6	20	2	3	0	0	0	0	2	5	0-0	.150	.227	.200	1	.950

WORLD SERIES RECORD

			BATTING														FIELDING	
Year	Team (League)	Pos.	G	AB	R	H	2B	3B	HR	RBI	BB	SO	SB-CS	Avg.	OBP	SLG	E	Avg.
1998	San Diego (N.L.)	SS	4	11	2	4	0	1	0	0	1	1	0-0	.364	.417	.545	0	1.000

GONZALEZ, ALEX — SS — CUBS

PERSONAL: Born April 8, 1973, in Miami. ... 6-0/200. ... Bats right, throws right. ... Full name: Alexander Scott Gonzalez.
HIGH SCHOOL: Miami Killian.
TRANSACTIONS/CAREER NOTES: Selected by Toronto Blue Jays organization in 14th round of free-agent draft (June 3, 1991). ... On Toronto disabled list (April 29-May 27, 1994); included rehabilitation assignment to Syracuse (May 14-27). ... On disabled list (August 13-September 14, 1997; and May 17, 1999-remainder of season). ... On Toronto disabled list (July 7-22, 2000); included rehabilitation assignment to Syracuse (July 21). ... Granted free agency (October 30, 2000). ... Re-signed by Blue Jays (December 10, 2000). ... Traded by Blue Jays to Chicago Cubs for P Felix Heredia and a player to be named later (December 10, 2001); Blue Jays acquired IF James Deschaine to complete deal (December 13, 2001). ... On disabled list (May 10-25, 2002).
RECORDS: Shares major league single-game record for most strikeouts—6 (September 9, 1998, 13 innings). ... Shares A.L. record for most assists by shortstop (nine-inning game)—13 (April 26, 1996).
STATISTICAL NOTES: Led Gulf Coast League shortstops with 160 assists and 247 total chances in 1991. ... Led South Atlantic League shortstops with 248 putouts, 406 assists and 702 total chances in 1992. ... Led Southern League with 253 total bases in 1993. ... Led Southern League shortstops with 224 putouts, 428 assists, 682 total chances and 92 double plays in 1993. ... Led International League shortstops with 163 putouts, 348 assists and 542 total chances in 1994. ... Led A.L. shortstops with 765 total chances and 122 double plays in 1996. ... Had 15-game hitting streak (August 2-18, 2000). ... Led A.L. with 16 sacrifice hits in 2000. ... Had 15-game hitting streak (August 6-21, 2002).
2002 GAMES PLAYED BY POSITION (MLB): SS—142.

			BATTING														FIELDING	
Year	Team (League)	Pos.	G	AB	R	H	2B	3B	HR	RBI	BB	SO	SB-CS	Avg.	OBP	SLG	E	Avg.
1991	GC Blue Jays (GCL)	SS	53	191	29	40	5	4	0	10	12	41	7-2	.209	.267	.277	21	.915
1992	Myrtle Beach (S.Atl.)	SS	134	535	83	145	22	9	10	62	38	119	26-14	.271	.322	.402	48	.932
1993	Knoxville (Sou.)	SS	*142	561	*93	162	29	7	16	69	39	110	38-13	.289	.339	.451	30	*.956
1994	Toronto (A.L.)	SS	15	53	7	8	3	1	0	1	4	17	3-0	.151	.224	.245	6	.918
	Syracuse (I.L.)	SS-DH	110	437	69	124	22	4	12	57	53	92	23-6	.284	.361	.435	*31	.943
1995	Toronto (A.L.)	SS-3B-DH	111	367	51	89	19	4	10	42	44	114	4-4	.243	.322	.398	19	.954
1996	Toronto (A.L.)	SS	147	527	64	124	30	5	14	64	45	127	16-6	.235	.300	.391	21	.973
1997	Toronto (A.L.)	SS	126	426	46	102	23	2	12	35	34	94	15-6	.239	.302	.387	8	*.986

Year Team (League)	Pos.	G	AB	R	H	2B	3B	HR	RBI	BB	SO	SB-CS	Avg.	OBP	SLG	E	Avg.
						BATTING										FIELDING	
1998—Toronto (A.L.)............	SS	158	568	70	136	28	1	13	51	28	121	21-6	.239	.281	.361	17	.976
1999—Toronto (A.L.)............	SS-DH	38	154	22	45	13	0	2	12	16	23	4-2	.292	.370	.416	4	.980
2000—Toronto (A.L.)............	SS	141	527	68	133	31	2	15	69	43	113	4-4	.252	.313	.404	16	.975
—Syracuse (I.L.)...........	SS	1	5	0	0	0	0	0	0	0	2	0-0	.000	.000	.000	0	1.000
2001—Toronto (A.L.)............	SS	154	636	79	161	25	5	17	76	43	149	18-11	.253	.303	.388	10	.987
2002—Chicago (N.L.)■.........	SS	142	513	58	127	27	5	18	61	46	136	5-3	.248	.312	.425	21	.965
American League totals (8 years)		890	3258	407	798	172	20	83	350	257	758	85-39	.245	.304	.386	101	.975
National League totals (1 year)		142	513	58	127	27	5	18	61	46	136	5-3	.248	.312	.425	21	.965
Major League totals (9 years)		1032	3771	465	925	199	25	101	411	303	894	90-42	.245	.306	.392	122	.974

GONZALEZ, ALEX — SS — MARLINS

PERSONAL: Born February 15, 1977, in Cagua, Venezuela. ... 6-0/200. ... Bats right, throws right. ... Full name: Alexander Gonzalez.
HIGH SCHOOL: Liceo Ramon Bastidas (Venezuela).
TRANSACTIONS/CAREER NOTES: Signed as non-drafted free agent by Florida Marlins organization (April 18, 1994). ... On Kane County disabled list (April 5-August 17, 1996). ... On Portland disabled list (September 7, 1996-remainder of season). ... On Florida disabled list (July 28-September 1, 2000); included rehabilitation assignment to Brevard County (August 26-31). ... On Florida disabled list (May 19, 2002-remainder of season); included rehabilitation assignments to Gulf Coast Marlins (July 3-5 and July 15-19).
2002 GAMES PLAYED BY POSITION (MLB): SS—42.

Year Team (League)	Pos.	G	AB	R	H	2B	3B	HR	RBI	BB	SO	SB-CS	Avg.	OBP	SLG	E	Avg.
						BATTING										FIELDING	
1994—Dom. Marlins (DSL)...	SS	54	239	30	54	7	3	3	31	15	36	4-...	.226	...	.318	34	.914
1995—Brevard County (FSL).	SS	17	59	6	12	2	1	0	8	1	14	1-1	.203	.230	.271	8	.906
—GC Marlins (GCL).......	SS	53	187	30	55	7	4	2	30	19	27	11-2	.294	.358	.406	17	.932
1996—GC Marlins (GCL).......	SS	10	41	6	16	3	0	0	6	2	4	1-0	.390	.419	.463	5	.898
—Kane County (Midw.)..	SS	4	10	2	2	0	0	0	0	2	4	0-0	.200	.385	.200	0	1.000
—Portland (East.)..........	SS	11	34	4	8	0	1	0	1	2	10	0-0	.235	.297	.294	7	.887
1997—Portland (East.)..........	SS	133	449	69	114	16	4	19	65	27	83	4-7	.254	.305	.434	37	.943
1998—Charlotte (I.L.)...........	SS	108	422	71	117	20	10	10	51	28	80	4-7	.277	.330	.443	20	.960
—Florida (N.L.).............	SS	25	86	11	13	2	0	3	7	9	30	0-0	.151	.240	.279	2	.978
1999—Florida (N.L.).............	SS	136	560	81	155	28	8	14	59	15	113	3-5	.277	.308	.430	27	.955
2000—Florida (N.L.).............	SS	109	385	35	77	17	4	7	42	13	77	7-1	.200	.229	.319	19	.957
—Brevard County (FSL).	SS	4	17	1	2	0	0	0	2	1	3	1-0	.118	.167	.118	0	1.000
2001—Florida (N.L.).............	SS-C	145	515	57	129	36	1	9	48	30	107	2-2	.250	.303	.377	26	.960
2002—Florida (N.L.).............	SS	42	151	15	34	7	1	2	18	12	32	3-1	.225	.296	.325	3	.984
—GC Marlins (GCL).......	SS	5	12	0	2	1	0	0	1	0	5	0-0	.167	.154	.250	1	.923
Major League totals (5 years)		457	1697	199	408	90	14	35	174	79	359	15-9	.240	.284	.372	77	.961

ALL-STAR GAME RECORD

	AB	R	H	2B	3B	HR	RBI	BB	SO	SB-CS	Avg.	OBP	SLG	E	Avg.
All-Star Game totals (1 year)	1	0	0	0	0	0	0	0	0	0-0	.000	.000	.000	0	1.000

GONZALEZ, JUAN — OF — RANGERS

PERSONAL: Born October 16, 1969, in Vega Baja, Puerto Rico. ... 6-3/220. ... Bats right, throws right. ... Full name: Juan Alberto Vazquez Gonzalez.
HIGH SCHOOL: Vega Baja (Puerto Rico).
TRANSACTIONS/CAREER NOTES: Signed as non-drafted free agent by Texas Rangers organization (May 30, 1986). ... On disabled list (April 27-June 17, 1988; March 30-April 26, 1991; April 16-June 1 and July 27-August 16, 1995; May 8-June 1, 1996; and March 24-May 2, 1997). ... Traded by Rangers with P Danny Patterson and C Gregg Zaun to Detroit Tigers for P Justin Thompson, P Francisco Cordero, OF Gabe Kapler, C Bill Haselman, 2B Frank Catalanotto and P Alan Webb (November 2, 1999). ... On disabled list (July 8-26, 2000). ... Granted free agency (November 1, 2000). ... Signed by Cleveland Indians (January 9, 2001). ... Granted free agency (November 5, 2001). ... Signed by Rangers (January 8, 2002). ... On disabled list (April 9-May 17 and July 31, 2002-remainder of season).
RECORDS: Shares major league single-game record for most sacrifice flies—3 (July 3, 1999). ... Holds A.L. single-season record for most major league ballparks, one or more home runs—16 (1999).
HONORS: Named American Association Most Valuable Player (1990). ... Named outfielder on The Sporting News A.L. Silver Slugger team (1992-93 and 1996-98). ... Named outfielder on The Sporting News A.L. All-Star team (1993, 1996, 1998 and 2001). ... Named A.L. Most Valuable Player by Baseball Writers' Association of America (1996 and 1998). ... Named outfielder on A.L. Silver Slugger team (2001).
STATISTICAL NOTES: Led Texas League with 254 total bases in 1989. ... Led American Association with 252 total bases in 1990. ... Hit three home runs in one game (June 7, 1992; August 28, 1993; and September 24, 1999). ... Had 21-game hitting streak (June 25-July 19 and August 8-31, 1996). ... Had 20-game hitting streak (August 20-September 9, 1998). ... Had 15-game hitting streak (August 29-September 19, 2001). ... Led A.L. with 16 sacrifice flies in 2001. ... Career major league grand slams: 8.
MISCELLANEOUS: Holds Texas Rangers franchise all-time records for most home runs (348) and most runs batted in (1,110).
2002 GAMES PLAYED BY POSITION (MLB): OF—62; DH—8.

Year Team (League)	Pos.	G	AB	R	H	2B	3B	HR	RBI	BB	SO	SB-CS	Avg.	OBP	SLG	E	Avg.
						BATTING										FIELDING	
1986—GC Rangers (GCL)......	OF	60	*233	24	56	4	1	0	36	21	57	7-5	.240	.302	.266	•6	.941
1987—Gastonia (S.Atl.).........	OF	127	509	69	135	21	2	14	74	30	92	9-4	.265	.310	.397	12	.953
1988—Charlotte (FSL)...........	OF	77	277	25	71	14	3	8	43	25	64	5-2	.256	.325	.415	4	.973
1989—Tulsa (Texas).............	OF	133	502	73	147	30	7	21	85	31	98	1-8	.293	.342	.506	9	.972
—Texas (A.L.)...............	OF	24	60	6	9	3	0	1	7	6	17	0-0	.150	.227	.250	2	.964
1990—Oklahoma City (A.A.)..	OF	128	496	78	128	29	4	*29	*101	32	109	2-2	.258	.300	.508	8	.966
—Texas (A.L.)...............	OF-DH	25	90	11	26	7	1	4	12	2	18	0-1	.289	.316	.522	0	1.000
1991—Texas (A.L.)...............	OF-DH	142	545	78	144	34	1	27	102	42	118	4-4	.264	.321	.479	6	.981
1992—Texas (A.L.)...............	OF-DH	155	584	77	152	24	2	*43	109	35	143	0-1	.260	.304	.529	10	.975
1993—Texas (A.L.)...............	OF-DH	140	536	105	166	33	1	*46	118	37	99	4-1	.310	.368	*.632	4	.985
1994—Texas (A.L.)...............	OF	107	422	57	116	18	4	19	85	30	66	6-4	.275	.330	.472	2	.991
1995—Texas (A.L.)...............	DH-OF	90	352	57	104	20	2	27	82	17	66	0-0	.295	.324	.594	0	1.000
1996—Texas (A.L.)...............	OF-DH	134	541	89	170	33	2	47	144	45	82	2-0	.314	.368	.643	2	.988

								BATTING								FIELDING	
Year Team (League)	Pos.	G	AB	R	H	2B	3B	HR	RBI	BB	SO	SB-CS	Avg.	OBP	SLG	E	Avg.
1997—Texas (A.L.)	DH-OF	133	533	87	158	24	3	42	131	33	107	0-0	.296	.335	.589	4	.971
1998—Texas (A.L.)	OF-DH	154	606	110	193	*50	2	45	*157	46	126	2-1	.318	.366	.630	4	.982
1999—Texas (A.L.)	OF-DH	144	562	114	183	36	1	39	128	51	105	3-3	.326	.378	.601	4	.983
2000—Detroit (A.L.)■	OF-DH	115	461	69	133	30	2	22	67	32	84	1-2	.289	.337	.505	1	.992
2001—Cleveland (A.L.)■	OF-DH	140	532	97	173	34	1	35	140	41	94	1-0	.325	.370	.590	3	.987
2002—Texas (A.L.)■	OF-DH	70	277	38	78	21	1	8	35	17	56	2-0	.282	.324	.451	1	.992
Major League totals (14 years)		1573	6101	995	1805	367	23	405	1317	434	1181	25-17	.296	.344	.563	43	.983

DIVISION SERIES RECORD

RECORDS: Shares A.L. career record for most home runs—8. ... Shares single-series record for most home runs—5 (1996). ... Shares single-game record for most home runs—2 (October 2, 1996). ... Shares single-game record for most at-bats (nine-inning game)—6 (October 13, 2001).

NOTES: Shares postseason single-series record for most home runs—5 (1996).

								BATTING								FIELDING	
Year Team (League)	Pos.	G	AB	R	H	2B	3B	HR	RBI	BB	SO	SB-CS	Avg.	OBP	SLG	E	Avg.
1996—Texas (A.L.)	OF	4	16	5	7	0	0	5	9	3	2	0-0	.438	.526	1.375	0	1.000
1998—Texas (A.L.)	OF	3	12	1	1	1	0	0	0	0	3	0-0	.083	.083	.167	0	1.000
1999—Texas (A.L.)	OF	3	11	1	2	0	0	1	1	1	3	0-0	.182	.250	.455	0	1.000
2001—Cleveland (A.L.)	OF	5	23	4	8	3	0	2	5	0	7	0-0	.348	.348	.739	0	1.000
Division series totals (4 years)		15	62	11	18	4	0	8	15	4	15	0-0	.290	.333	.742	0	1.000

ALL-STAR GAME RECORD

	AB	R	H	2B	3B	HR	RBI	BB	SO	SB-CS	Avg.	OBP	SLG	E	Avg.
All-Star Game totals (3 years)	5	0	0	0	0	0	1	1	2	0-0	.000	.125	.000	0	1.000

GONZALEZ, LUIS OF DIAMONDBACKS

PERSONAL: Born September 3, 1967, in Tampa. ... 6-2/195. ... Bats left, throws right. ... Full name: Luis Emilio Gonzalez.

HIGH SCHOOL: Jefferson (Tampa).

COLLEGE: South Alabama.

TRANSACTIONS/CAREER NOTES: Selected by Houston Astros organization in fourth round of free-agent draft (June 1, 1988). ... On disabled list (May 26-July 5, 1989 and August 29-September 13, 1991). ... On Houston disabled list (July 21-August 5, 1992). ... Traded by Astros with C Scott Servais to Chicago Cubs for C Rick Wilkins (June 28, 1995). ... Granted free agency (December 7, 1996). ... Signed by Astros (December 19, 1996). ... Granted free agency (October 28, 1997). ... Signed by Detroit Tigers (December 9, 1997). ... Traded by Tigers to Arizona Diamondbacks for OF Karim Garcia (December 28, 1998).

RECORDS: Shares major league single-month record for most home runs—13 (April 2001). ... Shares major league single-season record for highest fielding percentage by outfielder (150 or more games)—1.000 (2001); and fewest errors by outfielder—0 (2001). ... Shares N.L. single-season record for most consecutive errorless games by outfielder—161 (April 3 through October 7, 2001).

HONORS: Named outfielder on N.L. Silver Slugger team (2001). ... Named outfielder on The Sporting News N.L. All-Star team (2001).

STATISTICAL NOTES: Tied for Southern League lead with 12 sacrifice flies and nine intentional bases on balls received in 1990. ... Led N.L. with 10 sacrifice flies in 1993. ... Had 23-game hitting streak (May 26-June 20, 1997). ... Had 30-game hitting streak (April 11-May 18, 1999). ... Had 16-game hitting streak (August 16-September 1, 1999). ... Hit for the cycle (July 5, 2000). ... Hit three home runs in one game (June 8, 2001). ... Career major league grand slams: 3.

MISCELLANEOUS: Holds Arizona Diamondbacks all-time record for most hits (747), most runs (436), doubles (147), home runs (142) and runs batted in (470).

2002 GAMES PLAYED BY POSITION (MLB): OF—146.

								BATTING								FIELDING	
Year Team (League)	Pos.	G	AB	R	H	2B	3B	HR	RBI	BB	SO	SB-CS	Avg.	OBP	SLG	E	Avg.
1988—Asheville (S.Atl.)	3B	31	115	13	29	7	1	2	14	12	17	2-2	.252	.333	.383	6	.931
—Auburn (NY-Penn)	3B-SS-1B	39	157	32	49	10	3	5	27	12	19	2-0	.312	.354	.510	13	.902
1989—Osceola (FSL)	DH	86	287	46	82	16	7	6	38	37	49	2-1	.286	.370	.453	...	...
1990—Columbus (Sou.)	1B-3B	138	495	86	131	30	6	•24	89	54	100	27-9	.265	.337	.495	23	.980
—Houston (N.L.)	3B-1B	12	21	1	4	2	0	0	0	2	5	0-0	.190	.261	.286	0	1.000
1991—Houston (N.L.)	OF	137	473	51	120	28	9	13	69	40	101	10-7	.254	.320	.433	5	.984
1992—Houston (N.L.)	OF	122	387	40	94	19	3	10	55	24	52	7-7	.243	.289	.385	2	.993
—Tucson (PCL)	OF	13	44	11	19	4	2	1	9	5	7	4-1	.432	.490	.682	1	.963
1993—Houston (N.L.)	OF	154	540	82	162	34	3	15	72	47	83	20-9	.300	.361	.457	8	.978
1994—Houston (N.L.)	OF	112	392	57	107	29	4	8	67	49	57	15-13	.273	.353	.429	2	.991
1995—Houston (N.L.)	OF	56	209	35	54	10	4	6	35	18	30	1-3	.258	.322	.431	2	.980
—Chicago (N.L.)■	OF	77	262	34	76	19	4	7	34	39	33	5-5	.290	.384	.473	4	.978
1996—Chicago (N.L.)	OF-1B	146	483	70	131	30	4	15	79	61	49	9-6	.271	.354	.443	3	.988
1997—Houston (N.L.)■	OF-1B	152	550	78	142	31	2	10	68	71	67	10-7	.258	.345	.376	5	.982
1998—Detroit (A.L.)■	OF-DH	154	547	84	146	35	5	23	71	57	62	12-7	.267	.340	.475	3	.988
1999—Arizona (N.L.)■	OF-DH	153	614	112	*206	45	4	26	111	66	63	9-5	.336	.403	.549	5	.983
2000—Arizona (N.L.)	OF	•162	618	106	192	47	2	31	114	78	85	2-4	.311	.392	.544	3	.990
2001—Arizona (N.L.)	OF	•162	609	128	198	36	7	57	142	100	83	1-1	.325	.429	.688	0	1.000
2002—Arizona (N.L.)	OF	148	524	90	151	19	3	28	103	97	76	9-2	.288	.400	.496	4	.985
American League totals (1 year)		154	547	84	146	35	5	23	71	57	62	12-7	.267	.340	.475	3	.988
National League totals (12 years)		1593	5682	884	1637	349	49	226	949	692	784	98-69	.288	.369	.486	43	.986
Major League totals (13 years)		1747	6229	968	1783	384	54	249	1020	749	846	110-76	.286	.366	.485	46	.986

DIVISION SERIES RECORD

								BATTING								FIELDING	
Year Team (League)	Pos.	G	AB	R	H	2B	3B	HR	RBI	BB	SO	SB-CS	Avg.	OBP	SLG	E	Avg.
1997—Houston (N.L.)	OF	3	12	0	4	0	0	0	0	0	1	0-0	.333	.333	.333	1	.933
1999—Arizona (N.L.)	OF	4	10	3	2	1	0	1	2	5	1	0-0	.200	.500	.600	0	1.000
2001—Arizona (N.L.)	OF	5	19	1	5	0	0	1	1	2	4	0-0	.263	.333	.421	0	1.000
Division series totals (3 years)		12	41	4	11	1	0	2	3	7	6	0-0	.268	.388	.439	1	.958

CHAMPIONSHIP SERIES RECORD

Year	Team (League)	Pos.	G	AB	R	H	2B	3B	HR	RBI	BB	SO	SB-CS	Avg.	OBP	SLG	E	Avg.
			BATTING														FIELDING	
2001	—Arizona (N.L.)	OF	5	19	4	4	0	0	1	4	3	3	0-0	.211	.348	.368	0	1.000

WORLD SERIES RECORD

NOTES: Member of World Series championship team (2001).

Year	Team (League)	Pos.	G	AB	R	H	2B	3B	HR	RBI	BB	SO	SB-CS	Avg.	OBP	SLG	E	Avg.
			BATTING														FIELDING	
2001	—Arizona (N.L.)	OF	7	27	4	7	2	0	1	5	1	11	0-0	.259	.333	.444	0	1.000

ALL-STAR GAME RECORD

	AB	R	H	2B	3B	HR	RBI	BB	SO	SB-CS	Avg.	OBP	SLG	E	Avg.
All-Star Game totals (3 years)	5	0	2	1	0	0	0	0	0	0-0	.400	.400	.600	0	...

GONZALEZ, RAUL — OF — METS

PERSONAL: Born December 27, 1973, in Santurce, Puerto Rico. ... 5-9/190. ... Bats right, throws right. ... Full name: Victor Raul Gonzalez.
HIGH SCHOOL: Gilberto Concepcion (Carolina, Puerto Rico).
TRANSACTIONS/CAREER NOTES: Selected by Kansas City Royals organization in 17th round free-agent draft (June 4, 1990). ... On disabled list (April 28-September 19, 1996). ... Granted free agency (October 17, 1997). ... Re-signed by Royals organization (November 27, 1997). ... Granted free agency (October 16, 1998). ... Signed by Boston Red Sox organization (November 18, 1998). ... Granted free agency (October 15, 1999). ... Signed by Chicago Cubs organization (November 18, 1999). ... On Iowa disabled list (July 8-26 and August 2-September 5, 2000). ... Granted free agency (October 18, 2000). ... Signed by Cincinnati Reds organization (December 21, 2000). ... Traded by Reds to New York Mets (August 20, 2002), as partial completion of deal in which Mets traded P Shawn Estes and cash to Reds for P Pedro Feliciano, OF Elvin Andujar and two players to be named later (August 15, 2002); Mets acquired OF Brady Clark to complete deal (September 9, 2002).
HONORS: Named International League Most Valuable Player (2002).
2002 GAMES PLAYED BY POSITION (MLB): OF—30.

Year	Team (League)	Pos.	G	AB	R	H	2B	3B	HR	RBI	BB	SO	SB-CS	Avg.	OBP	SLG	E	Avg.
			BATTING														FIELDING	
1991	—GC Royals (GCL)	OF	47	160	24	47	5	3	0	17	19	21	3-4	.294	.365	.363	4	.941
1992	—Appleton (Midw.)	OF	119	449	82	115	32	1	9	51	57	58	13-5	.256	.339	.392	5	.981
1993	—Wilmington (Caro.)	OF	127	461	59	124	30	3	11	55	54	58	13-5	.269	.348	.419	8	.969
1994	—Wilmington (Caro.)	OF	115	414	60	108	19	8	9	51	45	50	0-4	.261	.333	.411	10	.941
1995	—Wichita (Texas)	OF	22	79	14	23	3	2	2	11	8	13	4-0	.291	.356	.456	2	.957
	—Wilmington (Caro.)	OF	86	308	36	90	19	3	11	49	14	34	6-4	.292	.320	.481	5	.966
1996	—Wichita (Texas)	OF	23	84	17	24	5	1	1	9	5	12	1-2	.286	.333	.405	1	.969
1997	—Wichita (Texas)	OF	129	452	66	129	30	4	13	74	36	52	12-8	.285	.335	.456	*14	.926
1998	—Wichita (Texas)	OF	118	455	84	148	31	1	17	86	58	53	12-8	.325	.401	.510	9	.957
1999	—Trenton (East.)■	OF	127	505	80	*169	33	4	18	103	51	71	12-3	.335	.394	.523	2	.993
2000	—Iowa (PCL)■	OF	69	241	35	64	13	1	4	33	21	20	5-5	.266	.328	.378	3	.974
	—Chicago (N.L.)	OF	3	2	0	0	0	0	0	0	0	2	0-0	.000	.000	.000	0	...
2001	—Louisville (I.L.)■	OF	*142	539	*90	*161	*39	1	11	66	64	70	6-8	.299	.371	.436	9	.973
	—Cincinnati (N.L.)	OF	11	14	0	3	0	0	0	0	1	3	0-0	.214	.267	.214	0	1.000
2002	—Louisville (I.L.)	OF	114	432	91	144	27	2	13	69	61	59	9-8	.333	*.416	.495	8	.970
	—Cincinnati (N.L.)	OF	10	23	4	6	1	0	0	1	2	5	2-0	.261	.320	.304	0	1.000
	—New York (N.L.)■	OF	30	81	9	21	2	0	3	11	4	17	2-2	.259	.291	.395	0	1.000
Major League totals (3 years)			54	120	13	30	3	0	3	12	7	27	4-2	.250	.289	.350	0	1.000

GONZALEZ, WIKI — C — PADRES

PERSONAL: Born May 17, 1974, in Aragua, Venezuela. ... 5-11/203. ... Bats right, throws right. ... Full name: Wiklenman Vicente Gonzalez.
TRANSACTIONS/CAREER NOTES: Signed as non-drafted free agent by Pittsburgh Pirates organization (February 12, 1992). ... Selected by San Diego Padres organization from Pirates organization in Rule 5 minor league draft (December 9, 1996). ... Granted free agency (October 16, 1998). ... Re-signed by Padres organization (October 23, 1998). ... On Mobile disabled list (May 24-June 6, 1999). ... On San Diego disabled list (June 3-July 3, 2001); included rehabilitation assignment to Lake Elsinore (June 28-July 3). ... On San Diego disabled list (April 5-May 15 and July 18-August 24, 2002); included rehabilitation assignment to Lake Elsinore (August 5-21).
2002 GAMES PLAYED BY POSITION (MLB): C—54.

Year	Team (League)	Pos.	G	AB	R	H	2B	3B	HR	RBI	BB	SO	SB-CS	Avg.	OBP	SLG	E	Avg.
			BATTING														FIELDING	
1992	—Dom. Pirates (DSL)	C	63	190	20	48	6	1	3	33	22	12	4-...	.253	...	.342	9	.969
1993	—Dom. Pirates (DSL)	C-IF	69	244	47	73	10	3	7	47	40	15	24-...	.299	...	.451	8	.986
1994	—GC Pirates (GCL)	C-1B	41	143	25	48	8	2	4	26	13	13	2-4	.336	.400	.503	12	.961
1995	—Augusta (S.Atl.)	C	84	278	41	67	17	0	3	36	26	32	5-4	.241	.305	.335	6	.985
1996	—Augusta (S.Atl.)	C	118	419	52	106	21	3	4	62	58	41	4-6	.253	.350	.346	*23	.976
1997	—Rancho Cuca. (Calif.)■	C	33	110	18	33	9	1	5	26	7	25	1-1	.300	.339	.536	2	.985
	—Mobile (Sou.)	C	47	143	15	39	7	1	4	25	10	12	1-1	.273	.327	.420	3	.989
1998	—Rancho Cuca. (Calif.)	C	75	292	51	84	24	2	10	59	26	54	0-0	.288	.346	.486	3	.993
	—Mobile (Sou.)	C	22	67	20	26	9	0	4	26	14	4	0-0	.388	.494	.701	0	1.000
1999	—Mobile (Sou.)	C-DH	61	225	38	76	16	2	10	49	29	28	0-0	.338	.424	.560	7	.982
	—Las Vegas (PCL)	C-DH	24	92	13	25	6	0	6	12	5	10	0-0	.272	.330	.533	3	.984
	—San Diego (N.L.)	C	30	83	7	21	2	1	3	12	1	8	0-0	.253	.271	.410	1	.992
2000	—San Diego (N.L.)	C	95	284	25	66	15	1	5	30	30	31	1-2	.232	.311	.345	5	.991
2001	—San Diego (N.L.)	C-DH	64	160	16	44	6	0	8	27	11	28	2-0	.275	.335	.463	3	.989
	—Lake Elsinore (Calif.)	C	4	13	1	2	0	0	0	1	2	4	0-0	.154	.250	.154	1	.973
2002	—San Diego (N.L.)	C	56	164	16	36	8	1	1	20	27	24	0-0	.220	.330	.299	6	.985
	—Lake Elsinore (Calif.)	C	19	53	10	18	8	0	1	6	12	3	0-0	.340	.486	.547	2	.983
Major League totals (4 years)			245	691	64	167	31	3	17	89	69	91	3-2	.242	.317	.369	15	.989

GOODWIN, TOM OF

PERSONAL: Born July 27, 1968, in Fresno, Calif. ... 6-1/175. ... Bats left, throws right. ... Full name: Thomas Jones Goodwin.
HIGH SCHOOL: Central (Fresno, Calif.).
COLLEGE: Fresno State.
TRANSACTIONS/CAREER NOTES: Selected by Pittsburgh Pirates organization in sixth round of free-agent draft (June 2, 1986); did not sign. ... Selected by Los Angeles Dodgers organization in first round (22nd pick overall) of free-agent draft (June 5, 1989). ... Claimed on waivers by Kansas City Royals (January 6, 1994). ... Traded by Royals to Texas Rangers for 3B Dean Palmer (July 25, 1997). ... On Texas disabled list (June 11-27 and June 28-August 6, 1999); included rehabilitation assignment to Charlotte (August 2-6). ... Granted free agency (October 28, 1999). ... Signed by Colorado Rockies (December 9, 1999). ... Traded by Rockies with cash to Dodgers for OF Todd Hollandsworth, OF Kevin Gibbs and P Randey Dorame (July 31, 2000). ... On Los Angeles disabled list (July 21-August 9, 2001); included rehabilitation assignment to Wilmington (August 7-9). ... Released by Dodgers (April 8, 2002). ... Signed by San Francisco Giants organization (April 17, 2002). ... Granted free agency (November 7, 2002).
HONORS: Named outfielder on The Sporting News college All-America team (1989).
STATISTICAL NOTES: Tied for Pacific Coast League lead in caught stealing with 23 in 1991. ... Led American Association in caught stealing with 20 in 1994. ... Led A.L. in sacrifice hits with 14 in 1995 and 21 in 1996. ... Led A.L. in caught stealing with 22 in 1996 and 20 in 1998. ... Career major league grand slams: 2.
MISCELLANEOUS: Member of 1988 U.S. Olympic baseball team.
2002 GAMES PLAYED BY POSITION (MLB): OF—53.

		BATTING														FIELDING	
Year Team (League)	Pos.	G	AB	R	H	2B	3B	HR	RBI	BB	SO	SB-CS	Avg.	OBP	SLG	E	Avg.
1989—Great Falls (Pio.)	OF	63	240	*55	74	12	3	2	33	28	30	*60-8	.308	.382	.408	1	.986
1990—Bakersfield (Calif.)	OF	32	134	24	39	6	2	0	13	11	22	22-4	.291	.345	.366	0	1.000
—San Antonio (Texas)	OF	102	428	76	119	15	4	0	28	38	72	*60-11	.278	.336	.332	3	*.989
1991—Albuquerque (PCL)	OF	132	509	84	139	19	4	1	45	59	83	48-23	.273	.349	.332	3	.990
—Los Angeles (N.L.)	OF	16	7	3	1	0	0	0	0	0	0	1-1	.143	.143	.143	0	1.000
1992—Albuquerque (PCL)	OF	82	319	48	96	10	4	2	28	37	47	27-10	.301	.372	.376	1	.995
—Los Angeles (N.L.)	OF	57	73	15	17	1	1	0	3	6	10	7-3	.233	.291	.274	0	1.000
1993—Los Angeles (N.L.)	OF	30	17	6	5	1	0	0	1	1	4	1-2	.294	.333	.353	0	1.000
—Albuquerque (PCL)	OF	85	289	48	75	5	5	1	28	30	51	21-5	.260	.329	.322	2	.986
1994—Kansas City (A.L.)■	DH-OF	2	2	0	0	0	0	0	0	0	1	0-0	.000	.000	.000	0	1.000
—Omaha (A.A.)	OF	113	429	67	132	17	7	2	34	23	60	*50-20	.308	.346	.394	2	.993
1995—Kansas City (A.L.)	OF-DH	133	480	72	138	16	3	4	28	38	72	50-18	.288	.346	.358	3	.990
1996—Kansas City (A.L.)	OF-DH	143	524	80	148	14	4	1	35	39	79	66-22	.282	.334	.330	5	.984
1997—Kansas City (A.L.)	OF	97	367	51	100	13	4	2	22	19	51	34-10	.272	.311	.346	1	.996
—Texas (A.L.)■	OF	53	207	39	49	13	2	0	17	25	37	16-6	.237	.319	.319	2	.986
1998—Texas (A.L.)	OF-DH	154	520	102	151	13	3	2	33	73	90	38-20	.290	.378	.338	3	.992
1999—Texas (A.L.)	OF	109	405	63	105	12	6	3	33	40	61	39-11	.259	.324	.341	3	.989
—Charlotte (FSL)	OF	3	11	2	4	1	0	0	0	1	4	0-0	.364	.417	.455	0	1.000
2000—Colorado (N.L.)■	OF	91	317	65	86	8	8	5	47	50	76	39-7	.271	.368	.394	3	.986
—Los Angeles (N.L.)■	OF	56	211	29	53	3	1	1	11	18	41	16-3	.251	.310	.289	0	1.000
2001—Los Angeles (N.L.)	OF	105	286	51	66	8	5	4	22	23	58	22-8	.231	.286	.336	1	.994
—Wilmington (S.Atl.)	OF	2	5	2	2	0	1	0	1	1	0	0-0	.400	.429	.800	0	1.000
2002—Fresno (PCL)■	OF	17	62	11	14	3	1	0	7	8	8	3-2	.226	.314	.306	0	1.000
—San Francisco (N.L.)	OF	78	154	23	40	5	2	1	17	14	25	16-2	.260	.321	.338	1	.990
American League totals (6 years)		691	2505	407	691	81	22	12	168	234	391	243-87	.276	.339	.340	17	.990
National League totals (6 years)		433	1065	192	268	26	17	11	101	112	214	102-26	.252	.322	.339	5	.993
Major League totals (12 years)		1124	3570	599	959	107	39	23	269	346	605	345-113	.269	.334	.340	22	.990

DIVISION SERIES RECORD

		BATTING														FIELDING	
Year Team (League)	Pos.	G	AB	R	H	2B	3B	HR	RBI	BB	SO	SB-CS	Avg.	OBP	SLG	E	Avg.
1998—Texas (A.L.)	OF	2	4	0	1	0	0	0	0	0	1	0-0	.250	.250	.250	0	1.000
1999—Texas (A.L.)	OF	3	7	0	1	0	0	0	0	0	1	0-0	.143	.143	.143	0	1.000
2002—San Francisco (N.L.)	PH	2	2	0	0	0	0	0	0	0	2	0-0	.000	.000	.000	0	...
Division series totals (3 years)		7	13	0	2	0	0	0	0	0	4	0-0	.154	.154	.154	0	1.000

CHAMPIONSHIP SERIES RECORD

		BATTING														FIELDING	
Year Team (League)	Pos.	G	AB	R	H	2B	3B	HR	RBI	BB	SO	SB-CS	Avg.	OBP	SLG	E	Avg.
2002—San Francisco (N.L.)	OF	2	3	0	0	0	0	0	0	0	2	0-0	.000	.000	.000	0	1.000

WORLD SERIES RECORD

		BATTING														FIELDING	
Year Team (League)	Pos.	G	AB	R	H	2B	3B	HR	RBI	BB	SO	SB-CS	Avg.	OBP	SLG	E	Avg.
2002—San Francisco (N.L.)	DH-OF	5	4	0	0	0	0	0	0	1	2	1-0	.000	.200	.000	0	1.000

GORDON, TOM P

PERSONAL: Born November 18, 1967, in Sebring, Fla. ... 5-10/190. ... Throws right, bats right. ... Full name: Thomas Gordon.
HIGH SCHOOL: Avon Park (Fla.).
TRANSACTIONS/CAREER NOTES: Selected by Kansas City Royals organization in sixth round of free-agent draft (June 2, 1986). ... On disabled list (August 12-September 1, 1992; and May 8-24, 1995). ... Granted free agency (October 30, 1995). ... Signed by Boston Red Sox (December 21, 1995). ... On Boston disabled list (April 18-May 10 and June 12-September 27, 1999); included rehabilitation assignments to Trenton (September 11-13) and Augusta (September 14-25). ... On disabled list (April 2, 2000-entire season). ... Granted free agency (November 1, 2000). ... Signed by Chicago Cubs (December 14, 2000). ... On Chicago disabled list (March 23-May 1, 2001); included rehabilitation assignments to Daytona (April 23-27) and Iowa (April 28-May 1). ... On Chicago disabled list (March 28-July 2, 2002); included rehabilitation assignments to Daytona (June 21-27) and Iowa (June 28-July 1). ... Traded by Cubs to Houston Astros for P Russ Rohlicek and two players to be named later (August 22, 2002); Cubs acquired P Travis Anderson and P Mike Nannini to complete deal (September 11, 2002). ... Granted free agency (October 29, 2002).
HONORS: Named A.L. Rookie Pitcher of the Year by The Sporting News (1989). ... Named A.L. Fireman of the Year by The Sporting News (1998).

STATISTICAL NOTES: Tied for Northwest League lead with four balks in 1987.
MISCELLANEOUS: Appeared in one game as pinch runner (1991). ... Appeared in one game as pinch runner (1995).
CAREER HITTING (MLB): 0-for-1 (.000), 0 R, 0 2B, 0 3B, 0 HR, 0 RBI.

Year	League	W	L	Pct.	ERA	G	GS	CG	ShO	Sv.-Opp.	IP	H	R	ER	HR	BB-IBB	SO
1986—	Gulf Coast Royals (GCL)	3	1	.750	1.02	9	7	2	1	0-...	44.0	31	12	5	0	23-1	47
	—Omaha (A.A.)	0	0	...	47.25	1	0	0	0	0-...	1.1	6	7	7	0	2-0	3
1987—	Eugene (N'West)	•9	0	•1.000	2.86	15	13	0	0	1-...	72.1	48	33	23	2	47-0	91
	—Fort Myers (FSL)	1	0	1.000	2.63	3	3	0	0	0-...	13.2	5	4	4	0	17-0	11
1988—	Appleton (Midw.)	7	5	.583	2.06	17	17	5	1	0-...	118.0	69	30	27	3	43-1	*172
	—Memphis (Sou.)	6	0	1.000	0.38	6	6	2	2	0-...	47.1	16	3	2	1	17-0	62
	—Omaha (A.A.)	3	0	1.000	1.33	3	3	0	0	0-...	20.1	11	3	3	0	15-0	29
	—Kansas City (A.L.)	0	2	.000	5.17	5	2	0	0	0-0	15.2	16	9	9	1	7-0	18
1989—	Kansas City (A.L.)	17	9	.654	3.64	49	16	1	1	1-7	163.0	122	67	66	10	86-4	153
1990—	Kansas City (A.L.)	12	11	.522	3.73	32	32	6	1	0-0	195.1	192	99	81	17	99-1	175
1991—	Kansas City (A.L.)	9	14	.391	3.87	45	14	1	0	1-4	158.0	129	76	68	16	87-6	167
1992—	Kansas City (A.L.)	6	10	.375	4.59	40	11	0	0	0-2	117.2	116	67	60	9	55-4	98
1993—	Kansas City (A.L.)	12	6	.667	3.58	48	14	2	0	1-6	155.2	125	65	62	11	77-5	143
1994—	Kansas City (A.L.)	11	7	.611	4.35	24	24	0	0	0-0	155.1	136	79	75	15	87-3	126
1995—	Kansas City (A.L.)	12	12	.500	4.43	31	31	2	0	0-0	189.0	204	110	93	12	89-4	119
1996—	Boston (A.L.)■	12	9	.571	5.59	34	34	4	1	0-0	215.2	249	143	*134	28	105-5	171
1997—	Boston (A.L.)	6	10	.375	3.74	42	25	2	1	11-13	182.2	155	85	76	10	78-1	159
1998—	Boston (A.L.)	7	4	.636	2.72	73	0	0	0	*46-47	79.1	55	24	24	2	25-1	78
1999—	Boston (A.L.)	0	2	.000	5.60	21	0	0	0	11-13	17.2	17	11	11	2	12-2	24
2000—	Boston (A.L.)									Did not play.							
2001—	Daytona (FSL)■	0	0	...	0.00	2	2	0	0	0-...	2.0	0	0	0	0	0-0	3
	—Iowa (PCL)	0	0	...	0.00	2	0	0	0	0-...	2.0	1	0	0	0	1-0	2
	—Chicago (N.L.)	1	2	.333	3.38	47	0	0	0	27-31	45.1	32	18	17	4	16-1	67
2002—	Daytona (FSL)	0	0	...	3.38	2	2	0	0	0-...	2.2	1	1	1	0	2-0	3
	—Iowa (PCL)	0	0	...	16.20	2	0	0	0	1-...	1.2	1	4	3	0	3-0	0
	—Chicago (N.L.)	1	1	.500	3.42	19	0	0	0	0-0	23.2	27	12	9	1	10-1	31
	—Houston (N.L.)■	0	2	.000	3.32	15	0	0	0	0-0	19.0	15	7	7	2	6-2	17
A.L. totals (12 years)		104	96	.520	4.15	444	203	18	4	71-92	1645.0	1516	835	759	133	807-36	1431
N.L. totals (2 years)		2	5	.286	3.38	81	0	0	0	27-31	88.0	74	37	33	7	32-4	115
Major League totals (14 years)		106	101	.512	4.11	525	203	18	4	98-123	1733.0	1590	872	792	140	839-40	1546

DIVISION SERIES RECORD

Year	League	W	L	Pct.	ERA	G	GS	CG	ShO	Sv.-Opp.	IP	H	R	ER	HR	BB-IBB	SO
1998—	Boston (A.L.)	0	1	.000	9.00	2	0	0	0	0-1	3.0	4	3	3	0	4-0	1
1999—	Boston (A.L.)	0	0	...	4.50	2	0	0	0	0-0	2.0	1	1	1	1	1-0	3
Division series totals (2 years)		0	1	.000	7.20	4	0	0	0	0-1	5.0	5	4	4	1	5-0	4

CHAMPIONSHIP SERIES RECORD

Year	League	W	L	Pct.	ERA	G	GS	CG	ShO	Sv.-Opp.	IP	H	R	ER	HR	BB-IBB	SO
1999—	Boston (A.L.)	0	0	...	13.50	3	0	0	0	0-0	2.0	3	3	3	2	1-0	3

ALL-STAR GAME RECORD

	W	L	Pct.	ERA	GS	CG	ShO	Sv.-Opp.	IP	H	R	ER	HR	BB-IBB	SO
All-Star Game totals (1 year)	0	0	...	18.00	0	0	0	0-0	1.0	3	2	2	0	1-0	0

GRABOWSKI, JASON 3B

PERSONAL: Born May 24, 1976, in New Haven, Conn. ... 6-3/200. ... Bats left, throws right. ... Full name: Jason William Grabowski.
HIGH SCHOOL: The Morgan School (Clinton, Conn.).
COLLEGE: Connecticut.
TRANSACTIONS/CAREER NOTES: Selected by New York Yankees organization in 17th round of free-agent draft (June 2, 1994); did not sign. ... Selected by Texas Rangers organization in second round of free-agent draft (June 3, 1997). ... Claimed on waivers by Seattle Mariners (December 18, 2000). ... On disabled list (June 22-July 2, 2001). ... Selected by Oakland Athletics from Mariners organization in Rule 5 major league draft (December 13, 2001). ... On Sacramento disabled list (April 18-May 29 and June 29-July 19, 2002).
STATISTICAL NOTES: Tied for Texas League lead with 84 putouts by third basemen in 2000.
2002 GAMES PLAYED BY POSITION (MLB): OF—4.

			BATTING														FIELDING	
Year	Team (League)	Pos.	G	AB	R	H	2B	3B	HR	RBI	BB	SO	SB-CS	Avg.	OBP	SLG	E	Avg.
1997—	Pulaski (Appl.)	C	50	174	36	51	14	0	4	24	40	32	6-1	.293	.423	.443	8	.982
1998—	Savannah (S.Atl.)	C-1B	104	352	63	95	13	6	14	52	57	93	16-9	.270	.372	.460	6	.990
1999—	Charlotte (FSL)	3B-1B	123	434	68	136	31	6	12	87	65	66	13-10	.313	.407	.495	27	.917
	—Tulsa (Texas)	DH	2	6	1	1	0	0	0	0	2	2	0-0	.167	.375	.167	...	...
2000—	Tulsa (Texas)	3B	135	493	93	135	33	5	19	90	88	106	8-7	.274	.383	.477	*40	.898
2001—	Tacoma (PCL)■	3B-OF-1B-SS	114	394	60	117	32	3	9	58	61	94	7-4	.297	.390	.462	21	.942
2002—	Sacramento (PCL)■	OF-C-3B-1B	73	265	50	78	22	3	12	52	39	56	6-4	.294	.387	.536	8	.962
	—Oakland (A.L.)	OF	4	8	3	3	1	1	0	1	3	1	0-0	.375	.545	.750	0	1.000
Major League totals (1 year)			4	8	3	3	1	1	0	1	3	1	0-0	.375	.545	.750	0	1.000

GRACE, MARK 1B

PERSONAL: Born June 28, 1964, in Winston-Salem, N.C. ... 6-2/200. ... Bats left, throws left. ... Full name: Mark Eugene Grace.
HIGH SCHOOL: Tustin (Calif.).
JUNIOR COLLEGE: Saddleback Community College (Calif.).
COLLEGE: San Diego State.
TRANSACTIONS/CAREER NOTES: Selected by Minnesota Twins organization in 15th round of free-agent draft (January 17, 1984); did not sign. ... Selected by Chicago Cubs organization in 24th round of free-agent draft (June 3, 1985). ... On disabled list (June 5-23, 1989). ... Granted free agency (October 15, 1994). ... Re-signed by Cubs (April 7, 1995). ... Granted free agency (November 3, 1995). ... Re-signed by

Cubs (December 19, 1995). ... On disabled list (June 11-28, 1996; April 4-19, 1997; and May 11-31, 2000). ... Granted free agency (October 30, 2000). ... Signed by Arizona Diamondbacks (December 8, 2000). ... Granted free agency (November 1, 2002).

RECORDS: Holds major league single-season record for fewest double plays by first baseman (150 or more games)—82 (1998). ... Shares major league record for most assists by first baseman in one inning—3 (May 23, 1990, fourth inning). ... Holds N.L. single-season record for most assists by first baseman—180 (1990).

HONORS: Named Eastern League Most Valuable Player (1987). ... Named N.L. Rookie Player of the Year by The Sporting News (1988). ... Won N.L. Gold Glove at first base (1992-93 and 1995-96).

STATISTICAL NOTES: Led Midwest League first basemen with 103 double plays in 1986. ... Led Eastern League first baseman with 96 assists in 1987. ... Led N.L. first basemen with 1,520 putouts in 1991, 1,580 in 1992, 1,580 in 1993 and 1,456 in 1994. ... Led N.L. first basemen with 180 assists in 1990, 167 in 1991 and 141 in 1992. ... Led N.L. first basemen with 1,695 total chances in 1991, 1,725 in 1992 and 1,573 in 1993. ... Tied for N.L. lead in grounding into double plays with 25 in 1993. ... Led N.L. first basemen with 134 double plays in 1993. ... Hit for the cycle (May 9, 1993). ... Tied for N.L. lead with 10 sacrifice flies in 1999. ... Had 18-game hitting streak (May 18-June 10, 2001). ... Career major league grand slams: 3.

2002 GAMES PLAYED BY POSITION (MLB): 1B—98.

								BATTING								FIELDING	
Year Team (League)	Pos.	G	AB	R	H	2B	3B	HR	RBI	BB	SO	SB-CS	Avg.	OBP	SLG	E	Avg.
1986— Peoria (Midw.)	1B-OF	126	465	81	159	30	4	15	95	60	28	6-5	*.342	.417	.520	13	.989
1987— Pittsfield (East.)	1B	123	453	81	151	29	8	17	*101	48	24	5-5	.333	.394	*.545	6	*.995
1988— Iowa (A.A.)	1B	21	67	11	17	4	0	0	14	13	4	1-0	.254	.361	.313	1	.995
— Chicago (N.L.)	1B	134	486	65	144	23	4	7	57	60	43	3-3	.296	.371	.403	•17	.987
1989— Chicago (N.L.)	1B	142	510	74	160	28	3	13	79	80	42	14-7	.314	.405	.457	6	.996
1990— Chicago (N.L.)	1B	157	589	72	182	32	1	9	82	59	54	15-6	.309	.372	.413	12	.992
1991— Chicago (N.L.)	1B	160	*619	87	169	28	5	8	58	70	53	3-4	.273	.346	.373	8	.995
1992— Chicago (N.L.)	1B	158	603	72	185	37	5	9	79	72	36	6-1	.307	.380	.430	4	.998
1993— Chicago (N.L.)	1B	155	594	86	193	39	4	14	98	71	32	8-4	.325	.393	.475	5	.997
1994— Chicago (N.L.)	1B	106	403	55	120	23	3	6	44	48	41	0-1	.298	.370	.414	7	.993
1995— Chicago (N.L.)	1B	143	552	97	180	*51	3	16	92	65	46	6-2	.326	.395	.516	7	.995
1996— Chicago (N.L.)	1B	142	547	88	181	39	1	9	75	62	41	2-3	.331	.396	.455	4	.997
1997— Chicago (N.L.)	1B	151	555	87	177	32	5	13	78	88	45	2-4	.319	.409	.465	6	.995
1998— Chicago (N.L.)	1B	158	595	92	184	39	3	17	89	93	56	4-7	.309	.401	.471	8	.994
1999— Chicago (N.L.)	1B	161	593	107	183	44	5	16	91	83	44	3-4	.309	.390	.481	8	.994
2000— Chicago (N.L.)	1B	143	510	75	143	41	1	11	82	95	28	1-2	.280	.394	.429	4	*.997
2001— Arizona (N.L.)■	1B	145	476	66	142	31	2	15	78	67	36	1-0	.298	.386	.466	5	.995
2002— Arizona (N.L.)	1B-P	124	298	43	75	19	0	7	48	46	30	2-0	.252	.351	.386	7	.990
Major League totals (15 years)		2179	7930	1166	2418	506	45	170	1130	1059	627	70-48	.305	.385	.444	108	.995

DIVISION SERIES RECORD

								BATTING								FIELDING	
Year Team (League)	Pos.	G	AB	R	H	2B	3B	HR	RBI	BB	SO	SB-CS	Avg.	OBP	SLG	E	Avg.
1998— Chicago (N.L.)	1B	3	12	0	1	0	0	0	1	0	2	0-0	.083	.083	.083	0	1.000
2001— Arizona (N.L.)	1B	4	14	0	3	1	0	0	0	2	3	0-0	.214	.313	.286	0	1.000
2002— Arizona (N.L.)	1B	2	4	0	1	0	0	0	0	1	0	0-0	.250	.400	.250	0	1.000
Division series totals (3 years)		9	30	0	5	1	0	0	1	3	5	0-0	.167	.242	.200	0	1.000

CHAMPIONSHIP SERIES RECORD

NOTES: Hit home run in first at-bat (October 4, 1989).

								BATTING								FIELDING	
Year Team (League)	Pos.	G	AB	R	H	2B	3B	HR	RBI	BB	SO	SB-CS	Avg.	OBP	SLG	E	Avg.
1989— Chicago (N.L.)	1B	5	17	3	11	3	1	1	8	4	1	1-0	.647	.682	1.118	0	1.000
2001— Arizona (N.L.)	1B	5	16	1	6	0	0	0	1	2	1	0-0	.375	.444	.375	0	1.000
Championship series totals (2 years)		10	33	4	17	3	1	1	9	6	2	1-0	.515	.575	.758	0	1.000

WORLD SERIES RECORD

NOTES: Member of World Series championship team (2001).

								BATTING								FIELDING	
Year Team (League)	Pos.	G	AB	R	H	2B	3B	HR	RBI	BB	SO	SB-CS	Avg.	OBP	SLG	E	Avg.
2001— Arizona (N.L.)	1B	6	19	1	5	1	0	1	3	4	1	0-0	.263	.391	.474	1	.982

ALL-STAR GAME RECORD

	AB	R	H	2B	3B	HR	RBI	BB	SO	SB-CS	Avg.	OBP	SLG	E	Avg.
All-Star Game totals (3 years)	4	0	0	0	0	0	0	0	0	0-0	.000	.000	.000	0	1.000

RECORD AS PITCHER

Year League	W	L	Pct.	ERA	G	GS	CG	ShO	Sv.-Opp.	IP	H	R	ER	HR	BB-IBB	SO
2002— Arizona (N.L.)	0	0	...	9.00	1	0	0	0	0-0	1.0	1	1	1	1	0-0	0

GRAFFANINO, TONY — SS/2B — WHITE SOX

G

PERSONAL: Born June 6, 1972, in Amityville, N.Y. ... 6-1/190. ... Bats right, throws right. ... Full name: Anthony Joseph Graffanino. ... Name pronounced GRAF-uh-NEE-noh.

HIGH SCHOOL: East Islip (Islip Terrace, N.Y.).

TRANSACTIONS/CAREER NOTES: Selected by Atlanta Braves organization in 10th round of free-agent draft (June 4, 1990). ... On disabled list (July 3, 1995-remainder of season). ... Released by Braves (April 2, 1999). ... Signed by Tampa Bay Devil Rays organization (April 9, 1999). ... Traded by Devil Rays to Chicago White Sox for P Tanyon Sturtze (May 31, 2000). ... On disabled list (August 26-September 30, 2002).

STATISTICAL NOTES: Led Pioneer League shortstops with 41 double plays in 1991. ... Led Carolina League second basemen with .968 fielding percentage in 1993. ... Led International League second basemen with 215 putouts and 441 total chances in 1996. ... Career major league grand slams: 1.

2002 GAMES PLAYED BY POSITION (MLB): 3B—35; 2B—25; SS—8.

								BATTING								FIELDING	
Year Team (League)	Pos.	G	AB	R	H	2B	3B	HR	RBI	BB	SO	SB-CS	Avg.	OBP	SLG	E	Avg.
1990— Pulaski (Appl.)	SS	42	131	23	27	5	1	0	11	26	17	6-3	.206	.344	.260	24	.873
1991— Idaho Falls (Pio.)	SS	66	274	53	95	16	4	4	56	27	37	19-4	.347	.408	.478	*29	.912
1992— Macon (S.Atl.)	2B	112	400	50	96	15	5	10	31	50	84	9-6	.240	.333	.378	17	.961
1993— Durham (Caro.)	2B-DH-SS	123	459	78	126	30	5	15	69	45	78	24-11	.275	.342	.460	15	†.968

Year	Team (League)	Pos.	G	AB	R	H	2B	3B	HR	RBI	BB	SO	SB-CS	Avg.	OBP	SLG	E	Avg.
								BATTING									FIELDING	
1994—	Greenville (Sou.)	2B-DH	124	440	66	132	28	3	7	52	50	53	29-7	.300	.372	.425	14	.976
1995—	Richmond (I.L.)	2B	50	179	20	34	6	0	4	17	15	49	2-2	.190	.254	.291	4	.983
1996—	Richmond (I.L.)	2B	96	353	57	100	29	2	7	33	34	72	11-7	.283	.350	.436	10	.977
	— Atlanta (N.L.)	2B	22	46	7	8	1	1	0	2	4	13	0-0	.174	.250	.239	2	.969
1997—	Atlanta (N.L.)	2-3-S-1	104	186	33	48	9	1	8	20	26	46	6-4	.258	.344	.446	5	.982
1998—	Atlanta (N.L.)	2B-SS-3B	105	289	32	61	14	1	5	22	24	68	1-4	.211	.275	.318	11	.971
1999—	Durham (I.L.)■	2B-DH-3B	87	345	66	108	25	6	9	58	37	46	16-9	.313	.379	.499	1	.998
	— Tampa Bay (A.L.)	2B-SS-DH-3B	39	130	20	41	9	4	2	19	9	22	3-2	.315	.364	.492	5	.973
2000—	Tampa Bay (A.L.)	2B-3B-SS	13	20	8	6	1	0	0	1	1	2	0-0	.300	.364	.350	0	1.000
	— Durham (I.L.)	SS-2B-1B-3B	10	35	9	10	3	0	2	6	7	8	2-0	.286	.405	.543	0	1.000
	— Chicago (A.L.)■	SS-2B-3B-DH	57	148	25	40	5	1	2	16	21	25	7-4	.270	.363	.358	6	.968
2001—	Chicago (A.L.)	3-2-S-O-DH-1	74	145	23	44	9	0	2	15	16	29	4-1	.303	.370	.407	7	.957
2002—	Chicago (A.L.)	3B-2B-SS	70	229	35	60	12	4	6	31	22	38	2-1	.262	.329	.428	10	.953
American League totals (4 years)			253	672	111	191	36	9	12	82	69	116	16-8	.284	.353	.418	28	.964
National League totals (3 years)			231	521	72	117	24	3	13	44	54	127	7-8	.225	.299	.357	18	.975
Major League totals (7 years)			484	1193	183	308	60	12	25	126	123	243	23-16	.258	.329	.391	46	.969

DIVISION SERIES RECORD

Year	Team (League)	Pos.	G	AB	R	H	2B	3B	HR	RBI	BB	SO	SB-CS	Avg.	OBP	SLG	E	Avg.
								BATTING									FIELDING	
1997—	Atlanta (N.L.)	2B	3	3	0	0	0	0	0	0	2	1	0-0	.000	.400	.000	0	1.000
1998—	Atlanta (N.L.)	PH	1	0	0	0	0	0	0	0	0	0	0-0	...	...	...	...	...
2000—	Chicago (A.L.)	PR-3B	1	0	0	0	0	0	0	0	0	0	0-0	...	...	...	0	1.000
Division series totals (3 years)			5	3	0	0	0	0	0	0	2	1	0-0	.000	.400	.000	0	1.000

CHAMPIONSHIP SERIES RECORD

Year	Team (League)	Pos.	G	AB	R	H	2B	3B	HR	RBI	BB	SO	SB-CS	Avg.	OBP	SLG	E	Avg.
								BATTING									FIELDING	
1997—	Atlanta (N.L.)	2B	3	8	1	2	1	0	0	0	0	3	0-0	.250	.250	.375	0	1.000
1998—	Atlanta (N.L.)	PH-2B	4	3	2	1	1	0	0	1	2	1	0-0	.333	.600	.667	0	1.000
Championship series totals (2 years)			7	11	3	3	2	0	0	1	2	4	0-0	.273	.385	.455	0	1.000

GRAMAN, ALEX — P — YANKEES

PERSONAL: Born November 17, 1977, in Huntingburg, Ind. ... 6-4/200. ... Throws left, bats left. ... Full name: Alex J. Graman.
HIGH SCHOOL: Southridge (Huntingburg, Ind.).
COLLEGE: Indiana State.
TRANSACTIONS/CAREER NOTES: Selected by New York Yankees organization in third round of free-agent draft (June 2, 1999).

Year	League	W	L	Pct.	ERA	G	GS	CG	ShO	Sv.-Opp.	IP	H	R	ER	HR	BB-IBB	SO
1999—	Staten Island (NY-Penn)	6	3	.667	2.99	14	14	0	0	0-...	81.1	74	30	27	7	16-0	85
2000—	Tampa (FSL)	8	9	.471	3.65	28	•28	3	1	0-...	143.0	120	64	58	6	58-1	111
	— Norwich (East.)	0	1	.000	11.81	1	1	0	0	0-...	5.1	6	7	7	3	4-0	3
2001—	Norwich (East.)	12	9	.571	3.52	28	28	1	0	0-...	166.1	174	83	65	10	60-0	138
2002—	Norwich (East.)	5	2	.714	2.88	8	8	2	1	0-...	50.0	46	19	16	2	13-0	31
	— Columbus (I.L.)	6	9	.400	4.65	20	20	1	0	0-...	124.0	141	74	64	11	37-3	98

GRAVES, DANNY — P — REDS

PERSONAL: Born August 7, 1973, in Saigon, Vietnam. ... 6-0/185. ... Throws right, bats right. ... Full name: Daniel Peter Graves.
HIGH SCHOOL: Brandon (Fla.).
COLLEGE: Miami (Fla.).
TRANSACTIONS/CAREER NOTES: Selected by Cleveland Indians organization in fourth round of free-agent draft (June 2, 1994). ... Traded by Indians with P Jim Crowell, P Scott Winchester and IF Damian Jackson to Cincinnati Reds for P John Smiley and IF Jeff Branson (July 31, 1997).
CAREER HITTING (MLB): 2-for-22 (.091), 3 R, 0 2B, 0 3B, 2 HR, 3 RBI.

Year	League	W	L	Pct.	ERA	G	GS	CG	ShO	Sv.-Opp.	IP	H	R	ER	HR	BB-IBB	SO
1995—	Kinston (Caro.)	3	1	.750	0.82	38	0	0	0	21-...	44.0	30	11	4	0	12-2	46
	— Canton/Akron (East.)	1	0	1.000	0.00	17	0	0	0	10-...	23.1	10	1	0	0	2-0	11
	— Buffalo (A.A.)	0	0	...	3.00	3	0	0	0	0-...	3.0	5	4	1	0	1-0	2
1996—	Buffalo (A.A.)	4	3	.571	1.48	43	0	0	0	19-...	79.0	57	14	13	1	24-2	46
	— Cleveland (A.L.)	2	0	1.000	4.55	15	0	0	0	0-1	29.2	29	18	15	2	10-0	22
1997—	Buffalo (A.A.)	2	3	.400	4.19	19	3	0	0	2-...	43.0	45	21	20	3	11-0	21
	— Cleveland (A.L.)	0	0	...	4.76	5	0	0	0	0-0	11.1	15	8	6	2	9-0	4
	— Indianapolis (A.A.)■	1	0	1.000	3.09	11	0	0	0	5-...	11.2	7	4	4	1	5-0	5
	— Cincinnati (N.L.)	0	0	...	6.14	10	0	0	0	0-0	14.2	26	14	10	0	11-1	7
1998—	Indianapolis (I.L.)	1	0	1.000	1.93	13	0	0	0	0-...	14.0	15	3	3	0	3-0	11
	— Cincinnati (N.L.)	2	1	.667	3.32	62	0	0	0	8-8	81.1	76	31	30	6	28-4	44
1999—	Cincinnati (N.L.)	8	7	.533	3.08	75	0	0	0	27-36	111.0	90	42	38	10	49-4	69
2000—	Cincinnati (N.L.)	10	5	.667	2.56	66	0	0	0	30-35	91.1	81	31	26	8	42-7	53
2001—	Cincinnati (N.L.)	6	5	.545	4.15	66	0	0	0	32-39	80.1	83	41	37	7	18-6	49
2002—	Cincinnati (N.L.)	7	3	.700	3.19	68	4	0	0	32-39	98.2	99	37	35	7	25-9	58
A.L. totals (2 years)		2	0	1.000	4.61	20	0	0	0	0-1	41.0	44	26	21	4	19-0	26
N.L. totals (6 years)		33	21	.611	3.32	347	4	0	0	129-157	477.1	455	196	176	38	173-31	280
Major League totals (7 years)		35	21	.625	3.42	367	4	0	0	129-158	518.1	499	222	197	42	192-31	306

ALL-STAR GAME RECORD

	W	L	Pct.	ERA	GS	CG	ShO	Sv.-Opp.	IP	H	R	ER	HR	BB-IBB	SO
All-Star Game totals (1 year)	0	0	...	0.00	0	0	0	0-0	1.0	1	0	0	0	0-0	1

GREEN, SHAWN — OF — DODGERS

PERSONAL: Born November 10, 1972, in Des Plaines, Ill. ... 6-4/200. ... Bats left, throws left. ... Full name: Shawn David Green.

HIGH SCHOOL: Tustin (Calif.).

TRANSACTIONS/CAREER NOTES: Selected by Toronto Blue Jays organization in first round (16th pick overall) of free-agent draft (June 3, 1991); pick received as compensation for San Francisco Giants signing Type A free-agent P Bud Black. ... On disabled list (June 30-July 23, 1992). ... On Knoxville disabled list (June 11-July 24, 1993). ... Traded by Blue Jays with 2B Jorge Nunez to Los Angeles Dodgers for OF Raul Mondesi and P Pedro Borbon (November 8, 1999).

RECORDS: Holds major league career record for most home runs in three straight games—7 (May 23 [4], 24 [1] and 25 [2], 2002). ... Holds major league single-game record for most total bases in one game—19 (May 23, 2002; four home runs, one single and one double). ... Shares major league record for most consecutive home runs—4 (June 14 [2], 15 [2], 2002); for most home runs in two consecutive games—5 (June 14 [4] and 15 [1], 2002); and most total bases in two consecutive games— 25 (May 23 and 24, 2002). ... Shares major league single-season record for fewest double plays by outfielder (150 or more games)—0 (2001). ... Shares major league single-game records for most runs scored—6 (May 23, 2002); most home runs in one game—4 (May 23, 2002); and most extra-base hits in one game—5 (May 23, 2002; one double, four home runs). ... Holds N.L. record for most home runs in one week (Sunday through Saturday)—9 (May 19-25, 2002).

HONORS: Won A.L. Gold Glove as outfielder (1999). ... Named outfielder on The Sporting News A.L. All-Star team (1999). ... Named outfielder on The Sporting News A.L. Silver Slugger team (1999).

STATISTICAL NOTES: Tied for Florida State League lead with eight sacrifice flies in 1992. ... Had 28-game hitting streak (June 29-July 31, 1999). ... Led A.L. with 361 total bases in 1999. ... Hit three home runs in one game (August 15, 2001; and May 23, 2002). ... Collected six hits in one game (May 23, 2002). ... Career major league grand slams: 5.

2002 GAMES PLAYED BY POSITION (MLB): OF—156; DH—1.

		BATTING														FIELDING	
Year Team (League)	Pos.	G	AB	R	H	2B	3B	HR	RBI	BB	SO	SB-CS	Avg.	OBP	SLG	E	Avg.
1992—Dunedin (FSL)	OF	114	417	44	114	21	3	1	49	28	66	22-9	.273	.319	.345	5	.974
1993—Knoxville (Sou.)	OF	99	360	40	102	14	2	4	34	26	72	4-9	.283	.339	.367	8	.956
—Toronto (A.L.)	OF-DH	3	6	0	0	0	0	0	0	0	1	0-0	.000	.000	.000	0	1.000
1994—Syracuse (I.L.)	OF-DH	109	433	82	149	27	3	13	61	40	54	19-7	*.344	.401	.510	1	*.996
—Toronto (A.L.)	OF	14	33	1	3	1	0	0	1	1	8	1-0	.091	.118	.121	0	1.000
1995—Toronto (A.L.)	OF	121	379	52	109	31	4	15	54	20	68	1-2	.288	.326	.509	6	.973
1996—Toronto (A.L.)	OF-DH	132	422	52	118	32	3	11	45	33	75	5-1	.280	.342	.448	2	.992
1997—Toronto (A.L.)	OF-DH	135	429	57	123	22	4	16	53	36	99	14-3	.287	.340	.469	3	.984
1998—Toronto (A.L.)	OF	158	630	106	175	33	4	35	100	50	142	35-12	.278	.334	.510	7	.979
1999—Toronto (A.L.)	OF	153	614	134	190	*45	0	42	123	66	117	20-7	.309	.384	.588	1	.997
2000—Los Angeles (N.L.)■	OF	•162	610	98	164	44	4	24	99	90	121	24-5	.269	.367	.472	6	.980
2001—Los Angeles (N.L.)	OF-1B	161	619	121	184	31	4	49	125	72	107	20-4	.297	.372	.598	6	.982
2002—Los Angeles (N.L.)	OF-DH	158	582	110	166	31	1	42	114	93	112	8-5	.285	.385	.558	2	.994
American League totals (7 years)		716	2513	402	718	164	15	119	376	206	510	76-25	.286	.344	.505	19	.986
National League totals (3 years)		481	1811	329	514	106	9	115	338	255	340	52-14	.284	.375	.543	14	.986
Major League totals (10 years)		1197	4324	731	1232	270	24	234	714	461	850	128-39	.285	.358	.521	33	.986

ALL-STAR GAME RECORD

	AB	R	H	2B	3B	HR	RBI	BB	SO	SB-CS	Avg.	OBP	SLG	E	Avg.
All-Star Game totals (2 years)	4	0	2	0	0	0	0	0	1	1-0	.500	.500	.500	0	1.000

GREEN, STEVE — P — ANGELS

PERSONAL: Born January 26, 1978, in Greenfield Park, Que. ... 6-2/195. ... Throws right, bats right.

HIGH SCHOOL: Polyvalente Edouard Montpetit (Montreal).

JUNIOR COLLEGE: Fort Scott (Kan.) Community College.

TRANSACTIONS/CAREER NOTES: Selected by Anaheim Angels organization in 10th round of free-agent draft (June 3, 1997). ... On Edmonton disabled list (July 16-28 and August 21-September 29, 2000). ... On Salt Lake disabled list (June 2, 2001-remainder of season). ... On disabled list (March 11, 2002-entire season).

CAREER HITTING (MLB): 0-for-0 (.000), 0 R, 0 2B, 0 3B, 0 HR, 0 RBI.

Year League	W	L	Pct.	ERA	G	GS	CG	ShO	Sv.-Opp.	IP	H	R	ER	HR	BB-IBB	SO
1998—Cedar Rapids (Midw.)	2	6	.250	4.54	18	10	1	0	0-...	83.1	86	49	42	9	25-0	61
1999—Lake Elsinore (Calif.)	7	6	.538	3.95	19	19	4	*4	0-...	120.2	130	70	53	9	37-2	91
—Erie (East.)	3	1	.750	3.32	6	6	1	0	0-...	40.2	34	25	15	4	19-0	32
2000—Erie (East.)	7	4	.636	3.40	13	13	0	0	0-...	79.1	71	34	30	7	34-0	66
—Edmonton (PCL)	0	4	.000	7.29	8	8	0	0	0-...	42.0	55	35	34	4	27-1	24
2001—Anaheim (A.L.)	0	0	...	3.00	1	1	0	0	0-0	6.0	4	2	2	0	6-0	4
—Salt Lake (PCL)	6	2	.750	3.66	10	10	1	0	0-...	59.0	59	30	24	3	13-0	40
2002—Anaheim (A.L.)	Did not play.															
Major League totals (1 year)	0	0	...	3.00	1	1	0	0	0-0	6.0	4	2	2	0	6-0	4

GREENE, TODD — C/DH — RANGERS

PERSONAL: Born May 8, 1971, in Augusta, Ga. ... 5-10/208. ... Bats right, throws right. ... Full name: Todd Anthony Greene.

HIGH SCHOOL: Evans (Ga.).

COLLEGE: Georgia Southern.

TRANSACTIONS/CAREER NOTES: Selected by Atlanta Braves organization in 27th round of free-agent draft (June 5, 1989); did not sign. ... Selected by California Angels organization in 12th round of free-agent draft (June 3, 1993). ... On Vancouver disabled list (April 11-May 25, 1996). ... Angels franchise renamed Anaheim Angels for 1997 season. ... On Anaheim disabled list (August 20, 1997-remainder of season). ... On Anaheim disabled list (March 19-August 5, 1998); included rehabilitation assignments to Lake Elsinore (April 14-May 16, May 21 and May 27-31) and Vancouver (May 17-20, May 22-26, June 1-2 and July 17-August 5). ... On suspended list (May 13-16, 1999). ... Released by Angels (March 29, 2000). ... Signed by Toronto Blue Jays organization (April 10, 2000). ... On Toronto disabled list (June 7-23, 2000); included rehabilitation assignment to Dunedin (June 20-22). ... Released by Blue Jays (March 28, 2001). ... Signed by New York Yankees organization (April 5, 2001). ... Released by Yankees (March 26, 2002). ... Signed by Los Angeles Dodgers organization (April 2, 2002). ... Released by Dodgers (May 15, 2002). ... Signed by Texas Rangers (May 16, 2002).

HONORS: Named California League Most Valuable Player (1994).

STATISTICAL NOTES: Led California League with 306 total bases and 12 intentional bases on balls received in 1994. ... Led California League catchers with 15 errors, 13 double plays and 44 passed balls in 1994. ... Career major league grand slams: 1.

2002 GAMES PLAYED BY POSITION (MLB): C—15; 1B—15; DH—4; OF—1.

			BATTING														FIELDING	
Year	**Team (League)**	**Pos.**	**G**	**AB**	**R**	**H**	**2B**	**3B**	**HR**	**RBI**	**BB**	**SO**	**SB-CS**	**Avg.**	**OBP**	**SLG**	**E**	**Avg.**
1993—	Boise (N'West)	OF	•76	*305	55	82	15	3	*15	*71	34	44	4-3	.269	.356	.485	3	.979
1994—	Lake Elsinore (Calif.)	C-OF-1B	133	524	98	158	39	2	35	124	64	96	10-3	.302	.378	*.584	15	.979
1995—	Midland (Texas)	C-DH-1B	82	318	59	104	19	1	26	57	17	55	3-5	.327	.365	.638	3	.992
—	Vancouver (PCL)	C-DH	43	168	28	42	3	1	14	35	11	36	1-0	.250	.308	.530	1	.995
1996—	Vancouver (PCL)	C-DH	60	223	27	68	18	0	5	33	16	36	0-2	.305	.347	.453	3	.988
—	California (A.L.)	C-DH	29	79	9	15	1	0	2	9	4	11	2-0	.190	.238	.278	0	1.000
1997—	Anaheim (A.L.)	C-DH	34	124	24	36	6	0	9	24	7	25	2-0	.290	.328	.556	0	1.000
—	Vancouver (PCL)	C-DH-1B-OF	64	260	51	92	22	0	25	75	20	31	5-1	.354	.408	.727	3	.992
1998—	Lake Elsinore (Calif.)	DH-1B	12	44	9	10	2	0	1	6	4	7	1-0	.227	.286	.341	2	.833
—	Vancouver (PCL)	DH-1B-C-OF	30	108	16	30	12	0	7	20	12	17	1-0	.278	.360	.583	1	.990
—	Anaheim (A.L.)	OF-DH-1B	29	71	3	18	4	0	1	7	2	20	0-0	.254	.274	.352	0	1.000
1999—	Anaheim (A.L.)	DH-OF-C	97	321	36	78	20	0	14	42	12	63	1-4	.243	.275	.436	2	.980
—	Edmonton (PCL)	OF-DH	19	74	10	18	6	0	5	14	0	12	0-0	.243	.253	.527	0	1.000
2000—	Syracuse (I.L.)■	OF-C	24	91	14	27	3	0	7	14	6	16	1-0	.297	.337	.560	1	.970
—	Toronto (A.L.)	DH-C-OF	34	85	11	20	2	0	5	10	5	18	0-0	.235	.278	.435	0	1.000
—	Dunedin (FSL)	OF	5	20	2	4	1	0	1	4	2	4	0-0	.200	.304	.400	0	1.000
2001—	Columbus (I.L.)■	C-OF	34	131	16	33	8	0	6	17	4	19	3-2	.252	.279	.450	4	.982
—	New York (A.L.)	C-DH	35	96	9	20	4	0	1	11	3	21	0-0	.208	.240	.281	0	1.000
2002—	Las Vegas (PCL)■	C-1B-OF	32	125	27	44	12	0	11	41	3	21	0-0	.352	.373	.712	2	.989
—	Texas (A.L.)■	C-1B-DH-OF	42	112	15	30	5	0	10	19	2	23	0-0	.268	.282	.580	3	.985
—	Oklahoma (PCL)	C-OF-1B	39	152	21	46	9	0	6	29	9	27	2-0	.303	.339	.480	2	.991
Major League totals (7 years)			300	888	107	217	42	0	42	122	35	181	5-4	.244	.277	.434	5	.994

DIVISION SERIES RECORD

			BATTING														FIELDING	
Year	**Team (League)**	**Pos.**	**G**	**AB**	**R**	**H**	**2B**	**3B**	**HR**	**RBI**	**BB**	**SO**	**SB-CS**	**Avg.**	**OBP**	**SLG**	**E**	**Avg.**
2001—	New York (A.L.)								Did not play.									

CHAMPIONSHIP SERIES RECORD

			BATTING														FIELDING	
Year	**Team (League)**	**Pos.**	**G**	**AB**	**R**	**H**	**2B**	**3B**	**HR**	**RBI**	**BB**	**SO**	**SB-CS**	**Avg.**	**OBP**	**SLG**	**E**	**Avg.**
2001—	New York (A.L.)	C	1	1	0	0	0	0	0	0	0	0	0-0	.000	.000	.000	0	1.000

WORLD SERIES RECORD

			BATTING														FIELDING	
Year	**Team (League)**	**Pos.**	**G**	**AB**	**R**	**H**	**2B**	**3B**	**HR**	**RBI**	**BB**	**SO**	**SB-CS**	**Avg.**	**OBP**	**SLG**	**E**	**Avg.**
2001—	New York (A.L.)	C	2	2	1	1	1	0	0	0	0	0	0-0	.500	.500	1.000	0	1.000

GREER, RUSTY — OF — RANGERS

PERSONAL: Born January 21, 1969, in Fort Rucker, Ala. ... 6-0/195. ... Bats left, throws left. ... Full name: Thurman Clyde Greer III.

HIGH SCHOOL: Albertville (Ala.).

COLLEGE: Montevallo (Ala.).

TRANSACTIONS/CAREER NOTES: Selected by Texas Rangers organization in 10th round of free-agent draft (June 4, 1990). ... On disabled list (July 31-August 22, 1992). ... On Texas disabled list (April 15-May 27, 2000); included rehabilitation assignment to Tulsa (May 15-27). ... On Texas disabled list (June 12, 2001-remainder of season); included rehabilitation assignment to Tulsa (July 18-23). ... On Texas disabled list (June 4-July 11 and July 12, 2002-remainder of season); included rehabilitation assignment to Tulsa (July 1-11).

RECORDS: Shares major league record for fewest double plays by outfielder (150 or more games)—0 (1997 and 1998).

STATISTICAL NOTES: Led Florida State League with .395 on-base percentage in 1991. ... Career major league grand slams: 6.

2002 GAMES PLAYED BY POSITION (MLB): OF—26; DH—22; 1B—1.

			BATTING														FIELDING	
Year	**Team (League)**	**Pos.**	**G**	**AB**	**R**	**H**	**2B**	**3B**	**HR**	**RBI**	**BB**	**SO**	**SB-CS**	**Avg.**	**OBP**	**SLG**	**E**	**Avg.**
1990—	Butte (Pio.)	OF	62	226	48	78	12	6	10	50	41	23	9-7	.345	.444	.584	*8	.918
1991—	Charlotte (FSL)	OF-1B	111	388	52	114	25	1	5	48	66	48	12-6	.294	*.395	.402	7	.970
—	Tulsa (Texas)	OF	20	64	12	19	3	2	3	12	17	6	2-0	.297	.451	.547	0	1.000
1992—	Tulsa (Texas)	1B-OF	106	359	47	96	22	4	5	37	60	63	2-2	.267	.376	.393	11	.987
1993—	Tulsa (Texas)	1B	129	474	76	138	25	6	15	59	53	79	10-5	.291	.365	.464	8	.993
—	Oklahoma City (A.A.)	OF	8	27	6	6	2	0	1	4	6	7	0-0	.222	.364	.407	0	1.000
1994—	Oklahoma City (A.A.)	OF-DH-1B	31	111	18	35	12	1	3	13	18	24	1-1	.315	.412	.523	3	.948
—	Texas (A.L.)	OF-1B	80	277	36	87	16	1	10	46	46	46	0-0	.314	.410	.487	6	.973
1995—	Texas (A.L.)	OF-1B	131	417	58	113	21	2	13	61	55	66	3-1	.271	.355	.424	6	.976
1996—	Texas (A.L.)	OF-DH-1B	139	542	96	180	41	6	18	100	62	86	9-0	.332	.397	.530	5	.984
1997—	Texas (A.L.)	OF-DH	157	601	112	193	42	3	26	87	83	87	9-5	.321	.405	.531	*12	.965
1998—	Texas (A.L.)	OF	155	598	107	183	31	5	16	108	80	93	2-4	.306	.386	.455	3	.990
1999—	Texas (A.L.)	OF-DH	147	556	107	167	41	3	20	101	96	67	2-2	.300	.405	.493	5	.983
2000—	Texas (A.L.)	OF-DH	105	394	65	117	34	3	8	65	51	61	4-1	.297	.377	.459	3	.985
—	Tulsa (Texas)	OF	2	7	0	1	0	0	0	1	1	3	0-0	.143	.250	.143	0	1.000
2001—	Texas (A.L.)	OF-DH	62	245	38	67	23	0	7	29	27	32	1-2	.273	.342	.453	5	.962
—	Tulsa (Texas)	DH	1	3	1	0	0	0	0	0	1	1	0-0	.000	.250	.000	...	...
2002—	Texas (A.L.)	OF-DH-1B	51	199	24	59	9	2	1	17	19	17	1-0	.296	.356	.377	2	.957
—	Tulsa (Texas)	OF	6	17	4	7	2	0	0	1	5	3	0-0	.412	.545	.529	0	1.000
Major League totals (9 years)			1027	3829	643	1166	258	25	119	614	519	555	31-15	.305	.387	.478	47	.978

DIVISION SERIES RECORD

Year	Team (League)	Pos.	G	AB	R	H	2B	3B	HR	RBI	BB	SO	SB-CS	Avg.	OBP	SLG	E	Avg.
			BATTING														FIELDING	
1996—	Texas (A.L.)	OF	4	16	2	2	0	0	0	0	3	3	0-0	.125	.263	.125	0	1.000
1998—	Texas (A.L.)	OF	3	11	0	1	0	0	0	0	1	2	0-0	.091	.167	.091	0	1.000
1999—	Texas (A.L.)	OF	3	9	0	1	0	0	0	0	3	1	0-0	.111	.333	.111	0	1.000
Division series totals (3 years)			10	36	2	4	0	0	0	0	7	6	0-0	.111	.256	.111	0	1.000

GREISINGER, SETH — P

PERSONAL: Born July 29, 1975, in Kansas City, Kan. ... 6-3/200. ... Throws right, bats right. ... Full name: Seth Adam Greisinger.
HIGH SCHOOL: McLean (Va.).
COLLEGE: Virginia.
TRANSACTIONS/CAREER NOTES: Selected by Cleveland Indians organization in seventh round of free-agent draft (June 3, 1993); did not sign. ... Selected by Detroit Tigers organization in first round (sixth pick overall) of free-agent draft (June 4, 1996). ... On Detroit disabled list (March 26, 1999-entire season); included rehabilitation assignments to Lakeland (May 12-25) and Toledo (June 1-30). ... On disabled list (March 13, 2000-entire season; and March 30, 2001-entire sesaon). ... On Toledo disabled list (June 18-July 1 and July 11, 2002-remainder of season). ... Released by Tigers (October 7, 2002).
STATISTICAL NOTES: Led Southern League in home runs allowed with 29 in 1997.
MISCELLANEOUS: Member of 1996 U.S. Olympic baseball team.
CAREER HITTING (MLB): 1-for-4 (.250), 0 R, 0 2B, 0 3B, 0 HR, 1 RBI.

Year	League	W	L	Pct.	ERA	G	GS	CG	ShO	Sv.-Opp.	IP	H	R	ER	HR	BB-IBB	SO
1997—	Jacksonville (Sou.)	10	6	.625	5.20	28	*28	1	0	0-...	159.1	194	103	92	29	53-0	105
1998—	Toledo (I.L.)	3	4	.429	2.91	10	10	0	0	0-...	58.2	50	21	19	5	22-0	37
	—Detroit (A.L.)	6	9	.400	5.12	21	21	0	0	0-0	130.0	142	79	74	17	48-2	66
1999—	Lakeland (FSL)	0	0	...	3.86	1	1	0	0	0-...	4.2	2	2	2	1	1-0	2
	—Toledo (I.L.)	0	1	.000	5.87	2	2	0	0	0-...	7.2	9	5	5	0	3-0	4
2000—	Detroit (A.L.)									Did not play.							
2001—	Detroit (A.L.)									Did not play.							
2002—	Erie (East.)	2	0	1.000	1.29	4	4	0	0	0-...	21.0	12	4	3	1	9-0	21
	—Detroit (A.L.)	2	2	.500	6.21	8	8	0	0	0-0	37.2	46	26	26	4	13-2	14
	—Toledo (I.L.)	1	1	.500	4.11	3	3	0	0	0-...	15.1	15	8	7	0	7-0	11
Major League totals (2 years)		8	11	.421	5.37	29	29	0	0	0-0	167.2	188	105	100	21	61-4	80

GRIEVE, BEN — OF — DEVIL RAYS

PERSONAL: Born May 4, 1976, in Arlington, Texas. ... 6-4/216. ... Bats left, throws right. ... Full name: Benjamin Grieve. ... Son of Tom Grieve, outfielder with four major league teams (1970-79); first father/son combination to be selected in first round of free-agent draft.
HIGH SCHOOL: James W. Martin (Arlington, Texas).
TRANSACTIONS/CAREER NOTES: Selected by Oakland Athletics organization in first round (second pick overall) of free-agent draft (June 2, 1994). ... Traded by A's with a player to be named later or cash to Tampa Bay Devil Rays as part of three-way deal in which Kansas City Royals received P Roberto Hernandez from Devil Rays, A's received P Cory Lidle from Devil Rays, A's received OF Johnny Damon, IF Mark Ellis and a player to be named later from Royals and Royals received C A.J. Hinch, IF Angel Berroa and cash from A's (January 8, 2001).
RECORDS: Shares major league record for fewest double plays by outfielder (150 or more games)—0 (1998).
HONORS: Named Minor League Player of the Year by The Sporting News (1997). ... Named Southern League Most Valuable Player (1997). ... Named A.L. Rookie Player of the Year by The Sporting News (1998). ... Named A.L. Rookie of the Year by Baseball Writers' Association of America (1998).
STATISTICAL NOTES: Tied for Northwest League lead with seven intentional bases on balls received in 1994. ... Led A.L. in grounding into double plays with 32 in 2000. ... Career major league grand slams: 5.
2002 GAMES PLAYED BY POSITION (MLB): OF—118; DH—16.

Year	Team (League)	Pos.	G	AB	R	H	2B	3B	HR	RBI	BB	SO	SB-CS	Avg.	OBP	SLG	E	Avg.
			BATTING														FIELDING	
1994—	S. Oregon (N'West)	OF	72	252	44	83	13	0	7	50	51	48	2-2	.329	.456	.464	6	.959
1995—	West Mich. (Midw.)	OF	102	371	53	97	16	1	4	62	60	75	11-3	.261	.371	.342	8	.942
	—Modesto (Calif.)	OF	28	107	17	28	5	0	2	14	14	15	2-0	.262	.341	.364	2	.951
1996—	Modesto (Calif.)	OF-DH	72	281	61	100	20	1	11	51	38	52	8-7	.356	.430	.552	5	.956
	—Huntsville (Sou.)	OF-DH	63	232	34	55	8	1	8	32	35	53	0-3	.237	.338	.384	4	.953
1997—	Huntsville (Sou.)	OF-DH	100	372	100	122	29	2	24	108	81	75	5-1	.328	*.455	.610	•8	.961
	—Edmonton (PCL)	OF	27	108	27	46	11	1	7	28	12	16	0-1	.426	.484	.741	2	.964
	—Oakland (A.L.)	OF	24	93	12	29	6	0	3	24	13	25	0-0	.312	.402	.473	0	1.000
1998—	Oakland (A.L.)	OF-DH	155	583	94	168	41	2	18	89	85	123	2-2	.288	.386	.458	2	.993
1999—	Oakland (A.L.)	OF-DH	148	486	80	129	21	0	28	86	63	108	4-0	.265	.358	.481	3	.988
2000—	Oakland (A.L.)	OF-DH	158	594	92	166	40	1	27	104	73	130	3-0	.279	.359	.487	3	.988
2001—	Tampa Bay (A.L.)■	OF-DH	154	542	72	143	30	2	11	72	87	159	7-1	.264	.372	.387	4	.984
2002—	Tampa Bay (A.L.)	OF-DH	136	482	62	121	30	0	19	64	69	121	8-2	.251	.353	.432	3	.988
Major League totals (6 years)			775	2780	412	756	168	5	106	439	390	666	24-5	.272	.368	.450	15	.988

DIVISION SERIES RECORD

Year	Team (League)	Pos.	G	AB	R	H	2B	3B	HR	RBI	BB	SO	SB-CS	Avg.	OBP	SLG	E	Avg.
			BATTING														FIELDING	
2000—	Oakland (A.L.)	OF	5	17	1	2	0	0	0	2	3	7	0-0	.118	.250	.118	0	1.000

ALL-STAR GAME RECORD

	AB	R	H	2B	3B	HR	RBI	BB	SO	SB-CS	Avg.	OBP	SLG	E	Avg.
All-Star Game totals (1 year)	0	0	0	0	0	0	0	1	0	0-0	...	1.000	...	0	...

GRIFFEY, KEN — OF — REDS

PERSONAL: Born November 21, 1969, in Donora, Pa. ... 6-3/205. ... Bats left, throws left. ... Full name: George Kenneth Griffey Jr. ... Son of Ken Griffey Sr., special consultant to general manager, Cincinnati Reds, and major league outfielder with four teams (1973-91); and brother of Craig Griffey, outfielder in Seattle Mariners and Cincinnati Reds organizations (1991-97).

HIGH SCHOOL: Moeller (Cincinnati).

TRANSACTIONS/CAREER NOTES: Selected by Seattle Mariners organization in first round (first pick overall) of free-agent draft (June 2, 1987). ... On San Bernardino disabled list (June 9-August 15, 1988). ... On disabled list (July 24-August 20, 1989; June 9-25, 1992; and June 20-July 13, 1996). ... On Seattle disabled list (May 27-August 15, 1995); included rehabilitation assignment to Tacoma (August 13-15). ... Traded by Mariners to Cincinnati Reds for P Brett Tomko, OF Mike Cameron, IF Antonio Perez and P Jake Meyer (February 10, 2000). ... On disabled list (April 29-June 15, 2001; April 7-May 24 and June 24-July 22, 2002).

RECORDS: Shares major league record for most consecutive games with one or more home runs—8 (July 20 through July 28, 1993). ... Holds A.L. single-season record for most major league ballparks, one or more home runs—16 (1998).

HONORS: Won A.L. Gold Glove as outfielder (1990-99). ... Named outfielder on The Sporting News A.L. All-Star team (1991, 1993-94 and 1996-99). ... Named outfielder on The Sporting News A.L. Silver Slugger team (1991, 1993-94 and 1996-99). ... Named Major League Player of the Year by The Sporting News (1997). ... Named A.L. Most Valuable Player by Baseball Writers' Association of America (1997).

STATISTICAL NOTES: Led A.L. outfielders with six double plays in 1989. ... Led A.L. with 359 total bases in 1993 and 393 in 1997. ... Hit three home runs in one game (May 24, 1996 and April 25, 1997). ... Led A.L. with 23 intentional bases on balls received in 1997. ... Led A.L. outfielders with 409 putouts and 425 total chances in 1998. ... Had 16-game hitting streak (May 10-28, 1999). ... Tied for A.L. lead with 17 intentional bases on balls received in 1999. ... Career major league grand slams: 14.

MISCELLANEOUS: Holds Seattle Mariners franchise all-time records for most home runs (398) and most runs batted in (1,152).

2002 GAMES PLAYED BY POSITION (MLB): OF—55.

			BATTING													FIELDING	
Year	Team (League)	Pos.	G	AB	R	H	2B	3B	HR	RBI	BB	SO	SB-CS	Avg.	OBP	SLG	E	Avg.
1987	Bellingham (N'West)	OF	54	182	43	57	9	1	14	40	44	42	13-6	.313	.445	.604	1	*.992
1988	San Bern. (Calif.)	OF	58	219	50	74	13	3	11	42	34	39	32-9	.338	.431	.575	2	.987
—	Vermont (East.)	OF	17	61	10	17	5	1	2	10	5	12	4-2	.279	.353	.492	1	.977
1989	Seattle (A.L.)	OF-DH	127	455	61	120	23	0	16	61	44	83	16-7	.264	.329	.420	•10	.969
1990	Seattle (A.L.)	OF	155	597	91	179	28	7	22	80	63	81	16-11	.300	.366	.481	7	.980
1991	Seattle (A.L.)	OF-DH	154	548	76	179	42	1	22	100	71	82	18-6	.327	.399	.527	4	.989
1992	Seattle (A.L.)	OF-DH	142	565	83	174	39	4	27	103	44	67	10-5	.308	.361	.535	1	.997
1993	Seattle (A.L.)	OF-DH-1B	156	582	113	180	38	3	45	109	96	91	17-9	.309	.408	.617	3	.991
1994	Seattle (A.L.)	OF-DH	111	433	94	140	24	4	*40	90	56	73	11-3	.323	.402	.674	4	.983
1995	Seattle (A.L.)	OF-DH	72	260	52	67	7	0	17	42	52	53	4-2	.258	.379	.481	2	.990
—	Tacoma (PCL)	DH	1	3	0	0	0	0	0	0	0	1	0-0	.000	.000	.000	...	...
1996	Seattle (A.L.)	OF-DH	140	545	125	165	26	2	49	140	78	104	16-1	.303	.392	.628	4	.990
1997	Seattle (A.L.)	OF-DH	157	608	*125	185	34	3	*56	*147	76	121	15-4	.304	.382	*.646	6	.985
1998	Seattle (A.L.)	OF-DH-1B	161	633	120	180	33	3	*56	146	76	121	20-5	.284	.365	.611	5	.988
1999	Seattle (A.L.)	OF-DH	160	606	123	173	26	3	*48	134	91	108	24-7	.285	.384	.576	9	.978
2000	Cincinnati (N.L.)■	OF	145	520	100	141	22	3	40	118	94	117	6-4	.271	.387	.556	5	.987
2001	Cincinnati (N.L.)	OF-DH	111	364	57	104	20	2	22	65	44	72	2-0	.286	.365	.533	3	.985
2002	Cincinnati (N.L.)	OF	70	197	17	52	8	0	8	23	28	39	1-2	.264	.358	.426	3	.971
American League totals (11 years)			1535	5832	1063	1742	320	30	398	1152	747	984	167-60	.299	.380	.569	55	.986
National League totals (3 years)			326	1081	174	297	50	5	70	206	166	228	9-6	.275	.375	.525	11	.984
Major League totals (14 years)			1861	6913	1237	2039	370	35	468	1358	913	1212	176-66	.295	.379	.562	66	.985

DIVISION SERIES RECORD

RECORDS: Holds single-series record for most runs scored—9 (1995). ... Shares single-game record for most home runs—2 (October 3, 1995). ... Shares single-series record for most home runs—5 (1996).

NOTES: Shares postseason single-series record for most home runs—5 (1995).

			BATTING													FIELDING	
Year	Team (League)	Pos.	G	AB	R	H	2B	3B	HR	RBI	BB	SO	SB-CS	Avg.	OBP	SLG	E	Avg.
1995	Seattle (A.L.)	OF	5	23	9	9	0	0	5	7	2	4	1-0	.391	.444	1.043	0	1.000
1997	Seattle (A.L.)	OF	4	15	0	2	0	0	0	2	1	3	2-0	.133	.188	.133	0	1.000
Division series totals (2 years)			9	38	9	11	0	0	5	9	3	7	3-0	.289	.349	.684	0	1.000

CHAMPIONSHIP SERIES RECORD

			BATTING													FIELDING	
Year	Team (League)	Pos.	G	AB	R	H	2B	3B	HR	RBI	BB	SO	SB-CS	Avg.	OBP	SLG	E	Avg.
1995	Seattle (A.L.)	OF	6	21	2	7	2	0	1	2	4	4	2-1	.333	.440	.571	1	.929

ALL-STAR GAME RECORD

NOTES: Named Most Valuable Player (1992).

	AB	R	H	2B	3B	HR	RBI	BB	SO	SB-CS	Avg.	OBP	SLG	E	Avg.
All-Star Game totals (8 years)	23	4	10	2	0	1	5	2	4	1-0	.435	.480	.652	1	.900

G

GRIMSLEY, JASON — P — ROYALS

PERSONAL: Born August 7, 1967, in Cleveland, Texas. ... 6-3/205. ... Throws right, bats right. ... Full name: Jason Alan Grimsley.

HIGH SCHOOL: Tarkington (Cleveland, Texas).

TRANSACTIONS/CAREER NOTES: Selected by Philadelphia Phillies organization in 10th round of free-agent draft (June 3, 1985). ... On Clearwater disabled list (April 8-May 10, 1988). ... On Philadelphia disabled list (June 6-August 22, 1991); included rehabilitation assignments to Scranton/Wilkes-Barre (June 15-30 and August 7-21). ... Traded by Phillies to Houston Astros for P Curt Schilling (April 2, 1992). ... On disabled list (May 14-June 14, 1992). ... Released by Astros (March 30, 1993). ... Signed by Cleveland Indians organization (April 7, 1993). ... On Charlotte disabled list (April 15-26, 1993). ... Traded by Indians with P Pep Harris to California Angels for P Brian Anderson (February 15, 1996). ... Granted free agency (October 8, 1996). ... Signed by Detroit Tigers organization (January 17, 1997). ... Released by Tigers (March 20, 1997). ... Signed by Milwaukee Brewers (April 3, 1997). ... Traded by Brewers to Kansas City Royals for P Jamie Brewington (July 29, 1997). ... Granted free agency (October 15, 1997). ... Signed by Indians organization (January 8, 1998). ... Granted free agency (October 15, 1998). ... Signed by New York Yankees organization (January 26, 1999). ... On suspended list (August 11-15, 1999). ... Released by

Yankees (November 20, 2000). ... Signed by Royals (January 19, 2001). ... On Kansas City disabled list (June 4-22, 2002); included rehabilitation assignment to Wichita (June 20-22).

STATISTICAL NOTES: Led New York-Pennsylvania League with 11 hit batsmen and 18 wild pitches in 1986. ... Pitched 3-0 no-hit victory for Reading against Harrisburg (May 3, 1989, first game). ... Led International League with 18 wild pitches in 1990. ... Tied for A.L. lead with 13 hit batsmen in 1996. ... Led Pacific Coast League with 20 wild pitches in 1997.

MISCELLANEOUS: Appeared in one game as pinch runner with Philadelphia (1990).

CAREER HITTING (MLB): 4-for-39 (.103), 3 R, 0 2B, 0 3B, 0 HR, 2 RBI.

Year League	W	L	Pct.	ERA	G	GS	CG	ShO	Sv.-Opp.	IP	H	R	ER	HR	BB-IBB	SO
1985— Bend (N'West)	0	1	.000	13.50	6	1	0	0	0-...	11.1	12	21	17	0	25-0	10
1986— Utica (NY-Penn)	1	•10	.091	6.40	14	14	3	0	0-...	64.2	63	61	46	3	*77-0	46
1987— Spartanburg (S.Atl.)	7	4	.636	3.16	23	9	3	0	0-...	88.1	59	48	31	4	54-2	98
1988— Clearwater (FSL)	4	7	.364	3.73	16	15	2	0	0-...	101.1	80	48	42	2	37-1	90
— Reading (East.)	1	3	.250	7.17	5	4	0	0	0-...	21.1	20	19	17	1	13-1	14
1989— Reading (East.)	11	8	.579	2.98	26	26	8	2	0-...	172.0	121	65	57	13	*109-4	134
— Philadelphia (N.L.)	1	3	.250	5.89	4	4	0	0	0-0	18.1	19	13	12	2	19-1	7
1990— Scranton/W.B. (I.L.)	8	5	.615	3.93	22	22	0	0	0-...	128.1	111	68	56	7	78-1	99
— Philadelphia (N.L.)	3	2	.600	3.30	11	11	0	0	0-0	57.1	47	21	21	1	43-0	41
1991— Philadelphia (N.L.)	1	7	.125	4.87	12	12	0	0	0-0	61.0	54	34	33	4	41-3	42
— Scranton/W.B. (I.L.)	2	3	.400	4.35	9	9	0	0	0-...	51.2	48	28	25	3	37-2	43
1992— Tucson (PCL)■	8	7	.533	5.05	26	20	0	0	0-...	124.2	152	79	70	4	55-0	90
1993— Charlotte (I.L.)■	6	6	.500	3.39	28	19	3	1	0-...	135.1	138	64	51	10	49-1	102
— Cleveland (A.L.)	3	4	.429	5.31	10	6	0	0	0-0	42.1	52	26	25	3	20-1	27
1994— Charlotte (I.L.)	7	0	1.000	3.42	10	10	2	0	0-...	71.0	58	36	27	10	17-0	60
— Cleveland (A.L.)	5	2	.714	4.57	14	13	1	0	0-0	82.2	91	47	42	7	34-1	59
1995— Cleveland (A.L.)	0	0		6.09	15	2	0	0	1-1	34.0	37	24	23	4	32-1	25
— Buffalo (A.A.)	5	3	.625	2.91	10	10	2	0	0-...	68.0	61	26	22	4	19-0	40
1996— Vancouver (PCL)■	2	0	1.000	1.20	2	2	1	0	0-...	15.0	8	2	2	0	3-0	11
— California (A.L.)	5	7	.417	6.84	35	20	2	1	0-0	130.1	150	110	99	14	74-5	82
1997— Tucson (PCL)■	5	10	.333	5.70	36	10	0	0	4-...	85.1	96	70	54	6	43-2	65
— Omaha (A.A.)■	1	5	.167	6.68	7	6	0	0	0-...	31.0	36	26	23	3	29-0	22
1998— Buffalo (I.L.)■	6	3	.667	3.76	52	0	0	0	0-...	88.2	76	40	37	10	57-3	68
1999— New York (A.L.)■	7	2	.778	3.60	55	0	0	0	1-4	75.0	66	39	30	7	40-5	49
2000— New York (A.L.)	3	2	.600	5.04	63	4	0	0	1-4	96.1	100	58	54	10	42-1	53
2001— Kansas City (A.L.)■	1	5	.167	3.02	73	0	0	0	0-7	80.1	71	32	27	8	28-5	61
2002— Kansas City (A.L.)	4	7	.364	3.91	70	0	0	0	1-3	71.1	64	32	31	4	37-8	59
— Wichita (Texas)	0	0	...	9.00	1	1	0	0	0-...	1.0	1	1	1	0	1-0	0
A.L. totals (8 years)	28	29	.491	4.86	335	45	3	1	4-19	612.1	631	368	331	57	307-27	415
N.L. totals (3 years)	5	12	.294	4.35	27	27	0	0	0-0	136.2	120	68	66	7	103-4	90
Major League totals (11 years)	33	41	.446	4.77	362	72	3	1	4-19	749.0	751	436	397	64	410-31	505

DIVISION SERIES RECORD

Year League	W	L	Pct.	ERA	G	GS	CG	ShO	Sv.-Opp.	IP	H	R	ER	HR	BB-IBB	SO
1999— New York (A.L.)									Did not play.							
2000— New York (A.L.)									Did not play.							

CHAMPIONSHIP SERIES RECORD

Year League	W	L	Pct.	ERA	G	GS	CG	ShO	Sv.-Opp.	IP	H	R	ER	HR	BB-IBB	SO
1999— New York (A.L.)									Did not play.							
2000— New York (A.L.)	0	0	...	0.00	2	0	0	0	0-0	1.0	2	0	0	0	3-0	1

WORLD SERIES RECORD

NOTES: Member of World Series championship team (1999 and 2000).

Year League	W	L	Pct.	ERA	G	GS	CG	ShO	Sv.-Opp.	IP	H	R	ER	HR	BB-IBB	SO
1999— New York (A.L.)	0	0	...	0.00	1	0	0	0	0-0	2.1	2	0	0	0	2-0	0
2000— New York (A.L.)									Did not play.							

GRISSOM, MARQUIS OF

PERSONAL: Born April 17, 1967, in Atlanta. ... 5-11/188. ... Bats right, throws right. ... Full name: Marquis Deon Grissom. ... Brother of Antonio Grissom, outfielder in Philadelphia Phillies (1990-91) and Montreal Expos organizations (1992-94). ... Name pronounced mar-KEESE.

HIGH SCHOOL: Lakeshore (College Park, Ga.).

COLLEGE: Florida A&M.

TRANSACTIONS/CAREER NOTES: Selected by Montreal Expos organization in third round of free-agent draft (June 1, 1988). ... On Montreal disabled list (May 29-June 30, 1990); included rehabilitation assignment to Indianapolis (June 25-30). ... Traded by Expos to Atlanta Braves for OF Roberto Kelly, OF Tony Tarasco and P Esteban Yan (April 6, 1995). ... Traded by Braves with OF Dave Justice to Cleveland Indians for OF Kenny Lofton and P Alan Embree (March 25, 1997). ... On disabled list (April 22-May 5, 1997). ... Traded by Indians with P Jeff Juden to Milwaukee Brewers for P Ben McDonald, P Mike Fetters and P Ron Villone (December 8, 1997). ... Traded by Brewers with a player to be named later to Los Angeles Dodgers for OF Devon White (February 25, 2001); Dodgers acquired P Rudy Lugo to complete deal (June 1, 2001). ... On suspended list (July 18-24, 2001). ... Granted free agency (October 28, 2002).

HONORS: Won N.L. Gold Glove as outfielder (1993-96).

STATISTICAL NOTES: Led New York-Pennsylvania League with 146 total bases in 1988. ... Tied for New York-Pennsylvania League lead with 11 assists by outfielder in 1988. ... Tied for N.L. lead with 15 assists by outfielder in 1991. ... Led N.L. outfielders with 321 putouts and 333 total chances in 1994. ... Had 28-game hitting streak (July 25-August 24, 1996). ... Career major league grand slams: 3.

2002 GAMES PLAYED BY POSITION (MLB): OF—102.

		BATTING														FIELDING	
Year Team (League)	Pos.	G	AB	R	H	2B	3B	HR	RBI	BB	SO	SB-CS	Avg.	OBP	SLG	E	Avg.
1988— Jamestown (NY-P)	OF	74	*291	*69	94	14	7	8	39	35	39	23-7	.323	.393	.502	3	.978
1989— Jacksonville (Sou.)	OF	78	278	43	83	15	4	3	31	24	31	24-6	.299	.365	.414	3	.980
— Indianapolis (A.A.)	OF	49	187	28	52	10	4	2	21	14	23	16-4	.278	.327	.406	0	1.000
— Montreal (N.L.)	OF	26	74	16	19	2	0	1	2	12	21	1-0	.257	.360	.324	2	.943
1990— Montreal (N.L.)	OF	98	288	42	74	14	2	3	29	27	40	22-2	.257	.320	.351	2	.988
— Indianapolis (A.A.)	OF	5	22	3	4	0	0	2	3	0	5	1-0	.182	.182	.455	0	1.000
1991— Montreal (N.L.)	OF	148	558	73	149	23	9	6	39	34	89	*76-17	.267	.310	.373	6	.984

Year Team (League)	Pos.	G	AB	R	H	2B	3B	HR	RBI	BB	SO	SB-CS	Avg.	OBP	SLG	E	Avg.
		BATTING														FIELDING	
1992—Montreal (N.L.)	OF	159	*653	99	180	39	6	14	66	42	81	*78-13	.276	.322	.418	7	.983
1993—Montreal (N.L.)	OF	157	630	104	188	27	2	19	95	52	76	53-10	.298	.351	.438	7	.984
1994—Montreal (N.L.)	OF	110	475	96	137	25	4	11	45	41	66	36-6	.288	.344	.427	5	.985
1995—Atlanta (N.L.)■	OF	139	551	80	142	23	3	12	42	47	61	29-9	.258	.317	.376	2	.994
1996—Atlanta (N.L.)	OF	158	671	106	207	32	10	23	74	41	73	28-11	.308	.349	.489	1	.997
1997—Cleveland (A.L.)■	OF	144	558	74	146	27	6	12	66	43	89	22-13	.262	.317	.396	3	.992
1998—Milwaukee (N.L.)■	OF	142	542	57	147	28	1	10	60	24	78	13-8	.271	.304	.382	3	.991
1999—Milwaukee (N.L.)	OF	154	603	92	161	27	1	20	83	49	109	24-6	.267	.320	.415	5	.987
2000—Milwaukee (N.L.)	OF	146	595	67	145	18	2	14	62	39	99	20-10	.244	.288	.351	3	.992
2001—Los Angeles (N.L.)■	OF-DH	135	448	56	99	17	1	21	60	16	107	7-5	.221	.250	.404	0	1.000
2002—Los Angeles (N.L.)	OF	111	343	57	95	21	4	17	60	22	68	5-1	.277	.321	.510	4	.978
American League totals (1 year)		144	558	74	146	27	6	12	66	43	89	22-13	.262	.317	.396	3	.992
National League totals (13 years)		1683	6431	945	1743	296	45	171	717	446	968	392-98	.271	.319	.411	47	.988
Major League totals (14 years)		1827	6989	1019	1889	323	51	183	783	489	1057	414-111	.270	.318	.410	50	.988

DIVISION SERIES RECORD

RECORDS: Holds single-game record for most hits—5 (October 7, 1995). ... Holds N.L. single-series record for most hits—11 (1995). ... Shares single-game records for most at-bats (nine-inning game)—6 (October 4, 1995); and most home runs—2 (October 4, 1995).

Year Team (League)	Pos.	G	AB	R	H	2B	3B	HR	RBI	BB	SO	SB-CS	Avg.	OBP	SLG	E	Avg.
		BATTING														FIELDING	
1995—Atlanta (N.L.)	OF	4	21	5	11	2	0	3	4	0	3	2-1	.524	.524	1.048	0	1.000
1996—Atlanta (N.L.)	OF	3	12	2	1	0	0	0	0	1	2	1-0	.083	.154	.083	1	.800
1997—Cleveland (A.L.)	OF	5	17	3	4	0	1	0	0	1	2	0-1	.235	.278	.353	0	1.000
Division series totals (3 years)		12	50	10	16	2	1	3	4	2	7	3-2	.320	.346	.580	1	.964

CHAMPIONSHIP SERIES RECORD

RECORDS: Holds single-series record for most at-bats—35 (1996). ... Shares single-game record for most strikeouts—4 (October 11 [12 innings] and 15 [11 innings], 1997). ... Shares N.L. single-game record for most at-bats—6 (October 14 and 17, 1996).
NOTES: Named A.L. Championship Series Most Valuable Player (1997).

Year Team (League)	Pos.	G	AB	R	H	2B	3B	HR	RBI	BB	SO	SB-CS	Avg.	OBP	SLG	E	Avg.
		BATTING														FIELDING	
1995—Atlanta (N.L.)	OF	4	19	2	5	0	1	0	0	1	4	0-0	.263	.300	.368	1	.889
1996—Atlanta (N.L.)	OF	7	35	7	10	1	0	1	3	0	8	2-0	.286	.286	.400	1	.944
1997—Cleveland (A.L.)	OF	6	23	2	6	0	0	1	4	1	9	3-0	.261	.292	.391	0	1.000
Championship series totals (3 years)		17	77	11	21	1	1	2	7	2	21	5-0	.273	.291	.390	2	.951

WORLD SERIES RECORD

NOTES: Member of World Series championship team (1995).

Year Team (League)	Pos.	G	AB	R	H	2B	3B	HR	RBI	BB	SO	SB-CS	Avg.	OBP	SLG	E	Avg.
		BATTING														FIELDING	
1995—Atlanta (N.L.)	OF	6	25	3	9	1	0	0	1	1	3	3-1	.360	.407	.400	0	1.000
1996—Atlanta (N.L.)	OF	6	27	4	12	2	1	0	5	1	2	1-0	.444	.464	.593	1	.875
1997—Cleveland (A.L.)	OF	7	25	5	9	1	0	0	2	4	4	0-0	.360	.448	.400	1	.950
World Series totals (3 years)		19	77	12	30	4	1	0	8	6	9	4-1	.390	.440	.468	2	.951

ALL-STAR GAME RECORD

	AB	R	H	2B	3B	HR	RBI	BB	SO	SB-CS	Avg.	OBP	SLG	E	Avg.
All-Star Game totals (2 years)	4	1	1	0	0	1	1	1	1	0-0	.250	.400	1.000	0	1.000

GROOM, BUDDY — P — ORIOLES

PERSONAL: Born July 10, 1965, in Dallas. ... 6-2/207. ... Throws left, bats left. ... Full name: Wedsel Gary Groom Jr.
HIGH SCHOOL: Red Oak (Texas).
COLLEGE: Mary Hardin-Baylor (Texas).
TRANSACTIONS/CAREER NOTES: Selected by Chicago White Sox organization in 12th round of free-agent draft (June 2, 1987). ... Selected by Detroit Tigers organization from White Sox organization in Rule 5 minor league draft (December 3, 1990). ... Traded by Tigers to Florida Marlins for a player to be named later (August 7, 1995); Tigers acquired P Mike Myers to complete deal (August 9, 1995). ... Granted free agency (October 16, 1995). ... Signed by Oakland Athletics organization (November 27, 1995). ... Granted free agency (November 1, 1999). ... Signed by Baltimore Orioles (December 21, 1999).
CAREER HITTING (MLB): 0-for-0 (.000), 0 R, 0 2B, 0 3B, 0 HR, 0 RBI.

Year League	W	L	Pct.	ERA	G	GS	CG	ShO	Sv.-Opp.	IP	H	R	ER	HR	BB-IBB	SO
1987—GC White Sox (GCL)	1	0	1.000	0.75	4	1	0	0	1-...	12.0	12	1	1	0	2-0	8
—Daytona Beach (FSL)	7	2	.778	3.59	11	10	2	0	0-...	67.2	60	30	27	4	33-1	29
1988—Tampa (FSL)	13	10	.565	2.54	27	27	8	0	0-...	*195.0	181	69	55	7	51-1	118
1989—Birmingham (Sou.)	13	8	.619	4.52	26	26	3	1	0-...	167.1	172	101	84	13	78-1	94
1990—Birmingham (Sou.)	6	8	.429	5.07	20	20	0	0	0-...	115.1	135	81	65	10	48-1	66
1991—Toledo (I.L.)■	2	5	.286	4.32	24	6	0	0	1-...	75.0	75	39	36	7	25-2	49
—London (East.)	7	1	.875	3.48	11	7	0	0	0-...	51.2	51	20	20	7	12-1	39
1992—Toledo (I.L.)	7	7	.500	2.80	16	16	1	0	0-...	109.1	102	41	34	8	23-1	71
—Detroit (A.L.)	0	5	.000	5.82	12	7	0	0	1-2	38.2	48	28	25	4	22-4	15
1993—Toledo (I.L.)	9	3	.750	2.74	16	15	0	0	0-...	102.0	98	34	31	5	30-1	78
—Detroit (A.L.)	0	2	.000	6.14	19	3	0	0	0-0	36.2	48	25	25	4	13-5	15
1994—Toledo (I.L.)	0	0	...	2.25	5	0	0	0	0-...	4.0	2	1	1	0	0-0	6
—Detroit (A.L.)	0	1	.000	3.94	40	0	0	0	1-1	32.0	31	14	14	4	13-2	27
1995—Detroit (A.L.)	1	3	.250	7.52	23	4	0	0	1-3	40.2	55	35	34	6	26-4	23
—Toledo (I.L.)	2	3	.400	1.91	6	5	1	0	0-...	33.0	31	14	7	4	4-0	24
—Florida (N.L.)■	1	2	.333	7.20	14	0	0	0	0-0	15.0	26	12	12	2	6-0	12
1996—Oakland (A.L.)■	5	0	1.000	3.84	72	1	0	0	2-4	77.1	85	37	33	8	34-3	57
1997—Oakland (A.L.)	2	2	.500	5.15	78	0	0	0	3-5	64.2	75	38	37	9	24-1	45
1998—Oakland (A.L.)	3	1	.750	4.24	75	0	0	0	0-6	57.1	62	30	27	4	20-1	36
1999—Oakland (A.L.)	3	2	.600	5.09	•76	0	0	0	0-3	46.0	48	29	26	1	18-5	32
2000—Baltimore (A.L.)■	6	3	.667	4.85	70	0	0	0	4-11	59.1	63	37	32	5	21-2	44

Year League	W	L	Pct.	ERA	G	GS	CG	ShO	Sv.-Opp.	IP	H	R	ER	HR	BB-IBB	SO
2001— Baltimore (A.L.)	1	4	.200	3.55	70	0	0	0	11-13	66.0	64	28	26	4	9-0	54
2002— Baltimore (A.L.)	3	2	.600	1.60	70	0	0	0	2-4	62.0	44	11	11	4	12-3	48
A.L. totals (11 years)	24	25	.490	4.49	605	15	0	0	25-52	580.2	623	312	290	53	212-30	396
N.L. totals (1 year)	1	2	.333	7.20	14	0	0	0	0-0	15.0	26	12	12	2	6-0	12
Major League totals (11 years)	25	27	.481	4.56	619	15	0	0	25-52	595.2	649	324	302	55	218-30	408

GRUDZIELANEK, MARK — 2B — DODGERS

PERSONAL: Born June 30, 1970, in Milwaukee. ... 6-1/185. ... Bats right, throws right. ... Full name: Mark James Grudzielanek. ... Name pronounced gress-UH-lawn-ick.

HIGH SCHOOL: J.M. Hanks (El Paso, Texas).

JUNIOR COLLEGE: Trinidad (Colo.) State Junior College.

COLLEGE: Oklahoma State.

TRANSACTIONS/CAREER NOTES: Selected by New York Mets organization in 17th round of free-agent draft (June 5, 1989); did not sign. ... Selected by Montreal Expos organization in 11th round of free-agent draft (June 3, 1991). ... On disabled list (July 13-August 9, 1993 and May 12-19, 1994). ... Traded by Expos with P Carlos Perez and OF Hiram Bocachica to Los Angeles Dodgers for 2B Wilton Guerrero, P Ted Lilly, OF Peter Bergeron and 1B Jonathan Tucker (July 31, 1998). ... On Los Angeles disabled list (June 12-July 6, 1999); included rehabilitation assignment to San Bernadino (July 2-6). ... On disabled list (June 12-28, 2001).

RECORDS: Holds major league single-season record for fewest chances accepted by shortstop who led league in chances accepted—683 (1997). ... Shares major league single-season record for fewest putouts by shortstop (150 or more games)—180 (1996).

HONORS: Named Eastern League Most Valuable Player (1994).

STATISTICAL NOTES: Led Eastern League shortstops with .959 fielding percentage in 1994. ... Led N.L. shortstops with 715 total chances and 99 double plays in 1997. ... Led N.L. shortstops with 33 errors in 1998. ... Career major league grand slams: 1.

2002 GAMES PLAYED BY POSITION (MLB): 2B—147; DH—1.

		BATTING														FIELDING	
Year Team (League)	Pos.	G	AB	R	H	2B	3B	HR	RBI	BB	SO	SB-CS	Avg.	OBP	SLG	E	Avg.
1991— Jamestown (NY-P)	SS	72	275	44	72	9	3	2	32	18	43	14-4	.262	.311	.338	23	.933
1992— Rockford (Midw.)	SS	128	496	64	122	12	5	5	54	22	59	25-4	.246	.285	.321	41	.919
1993— W. Palm Beach (FSL)	2B-SS-OF-3B	86	300	41	80	11	6	1	34	14	42	17-10	.267	.315	.353	13	.949
1994— Harrisburg (East.)	SS-3B	122	488	92	157	•37	3	11	66	43	66	32-10	.322	.382	.477	23	†.958
1995— Montreal (N.L.)	SS-3B-2B	78	269	27	66	12	2	1	20	14	47	8-3	.245	.300	.316	10	.967
— Ottawa (I.L.)	SS	49	181	26	54	9	1	1	22	10	17	12-1	.298	.342	.376	14	.939
1996— Montreal (N.L.)	SS	153	657	99	201	34	4	6	49	26	83	33-7	.306	.340	.397	27	.959
1997— Montreal (N.L.)	SS	156	*649	76	177	*54	3	4	51	23	76	25-9	.273	.307	.384	*32	.955
1998— Montreal (N.L.)	SS	105	396	51	109	15	1	8	41	21	50	11-5	.275	.323	.379	23	.950
— Los Angeles (N.L.)■	SS	51	193	11	51	6	0	2	21	5	23	7-0	.264	.286	.326	§10	.962
1999— Los Angeles (N.L.)	SS	123	488	72	159	23	5	7	46	31	65	6-6	.326	.376	.436	13	.973
— San Bern. (Calif.)	SS	4	16	2	4	0	0	0	0	0	1	0-2	.250	.250	.250	0	1.000
2000— Los Angeles (N.L.)	2B-SS	148	617	101	172	35	6	7	49	45	81	12-3	.279	.335	.389	17	.976
2001— Los Angeles (N.L.)	2B	133	539	83	146	21	3	13	55	28	83	4-4	.271	.317	.393	10	.984
2002— Los Angeles (N.L.)	2B-DH	150	536	56	145	23	0	9	50	22	89	4-1	.271	.301	.364	7	.989
Major League totals (8 years)		1097	4344	576	1226	223	24	57	382	215	597	110-38	.282	.324	.384	149	.969

ALL-STAR GAME RECORD

	AB	R	H	2B	3B	HR	RBI	BB	SO	SB-CS	Avg.	OBP	SLG	E	Avg.
All-Star Game totals (1 year)	1	0	0	0	0	0	0	0	0	0-0	.000	.000	.000	0	...

GRYBOSKI, KEVIN — P — BRAVES

PERSONAL: Born November 15, 1973, in Wilkes-Barre, Pa. ... 6-5/235. ... Throws right, bats right. ... Full name: Kevin John Gryboski.

COLLEGE: Wilkes.

TRANSACTIONS/CAREER NOTES: Selected by Seattle Mariners organization in 16th round of free-agent draft (June 1, 1995). ... On disabled list (May 11-June 14 and July 31-August 12, 1997). ... On Lancaster disabled list (May 3-10, 1998). ... On Tacoma disabled list (July 24-31, 2000). ... Traded by Mariners to Atlanta Braves for P Elvis Perez (January 18, 2002). ... On Atlanta disabled list (July 24-August 20, 2002); included rehabilitation assignment to Macon (August 16-20).

CAREER HITTING (MLB): 0-for-0 (.000), 0 R, 0 2B, 0 3B, 0 HR, 0 RBI.

Year League	W	L	Pct.	ERA	G	GS	CG	ShO	Sv.-Opp.	IP	H	R	ER	HR	BB-IBB	SO
1995— Everett (N'West)	1	5	.167	3.50	25	0	0	0	2-...	36.0	27	18	14	2	18-2	25
1996— Wisconsin (Midw.)	10	5	.667	4.74	32	21	3	0	1-...	138.2	146	90	73	7	62-2	100
1997— Lancaster (Calif.)	0	7	.000	9.89	21	15	0	0	0-...	67.1	113	82	74	13	26-0	41
1998— Lancaster (Calif.)	5	5	.500	2.65	37	3	0	0	8-...	85.0	75	35	25	4	31-1	73
— Orlando (Sou.)	0	0	...	9.00	2	0	0	0	0-...	5.0	8	5	5	1	1-0	4
1999— New Haven (East.)	2	5	.286	2.89	47	0	0	0	10-...	62.1	67	27	20	5	20-4	41
2000— New Haven (East.)	2	2	.500	2.50	16	0	0	0	9-...	18.0	15	5	5	0	8-1	20
— Tacoma (PCL)	2	2	.500	4.83	31	0	0	0	2-...	41.0	45	23	22	3	23-4	35
2001— Tacoma (PCL)	2	5	.286	3.90	58	0	0	0	22-...	60.0	64	29	26	8	19-2	50
2002— Richmond (I.L.)■	1	0	1.000	1.29	7	0	0	0	3-...	7.0	7	1	1	0	1-0	5
— Atlanta (N.L.)	2	1	.667	3.48	57	0	0	0	0-2	51.2	50	20	20	6	37-5	33
— Macon (S.Atl.)	0	0	...	0.00	2	1	0	0	0-...	2.0	1	0	0	0	1-0	2
Major League totals (1 year)	2	1	.667	3.48	57	0	0	0	0-2	51.2	50	20	20	6	37-5	33

DIVISION SERIES RECORD

Year League	W	L	Pct.	ERA	G	GS	CG	ShO	Sv.-Opp.	IP	H	R	ER	HR	BB-IBB	SO
2002— Atlanta (N.L.)	0	0	...	0.00	3	0	0	0	0-0	3.2	2	0	0	0	2-1	3

GUARDADO, EDDIE P TWINS

PERSONAL: Born October 2, 1970, in Stockton, Calif. ... 6-0/194. ... Throws left, bats right. ... Full name: Edward Adrian Guardado. ... Name pronounced gwar-DAH-doh.

HIGH SCHOOL: Franklin (Stockton, Calif.).

JUNIOR COLLEGE: San Joaquin Delta College (Calif.).

TRANSACTIONS/CAREER NOTES: Selected by Minnesota Twins organization in 21st round of free-agent draft (June 4, 1990). ... On Minnesota disabled list (May 22-June 28, 1999); included rehabilitation assignment to New Britain (June 22-28). ... On disabled list (June 5-20, 2001).

STATISTICAL NOTES: Pitched 5-0 no-hit victory against Pulaski (August 26, 1991). ... Led A.L. with 51 save opportunities in 2002.

CAREER HITTING (MLB): 0-for-0 (.000), 0 R, 0 2B, 0 3B, 0 HR, 0 RBI.

Year League	W	L	Pct.	ERA	G	GS	CG	ShO	Sv.-Opp.	IP	H	R	ER	HR	BB-IBB	SO
1991— Elizabethton (Appl.)	8	4	.667	1.86	14	13	3	•1	0-...	92.0	67	30	19	5	31-0	*106
1992— Kenosha (Midw.)	5	10	.333	4.37	18	18	2	1	0-...	101.0	106	57	49	5	30-0	103
— Visalia (Calif.)	7	0	1.000	1.64	7	7	1	1	0-...	49.1	47	13	9	1	10-0	39
1993— Nashville (Sou.)	4	0	1.000	1.24	10	10	2	2	0-...	65.1	53	10	9	1	10-0	57
— Minnesota (A.L.)	3	8	.273	6.18	19	16	0	0	0-0	94.2	123	68	65	13	36-2	46
1994— Salt Lake (PCL)	12	7	.632	4.83	24	24	2	0	0-...	151.0	171	90	81	23	51-0	87
— Minnesota (A.L.)	0	2	.000	8.47	4	4	0	0	0-0	17.0	26	16	16	3	4-0	8
1995— Minnesota (A.L.)	4	9	.308	5.12	51	5	0	0	2-5	91.1	99	54	52	13	45-2	71
1996— Minnesota (A.L.)	6	5	.545	5.25	•83	0	0	0	4-7	73.2	61	45	43	12	33-4	74
1997— Minnesota (A.L.)	0	4	.000	3.91	69	0	0	0	1-1	46.0	45	23	20	7	17-2	54
1998— Minnesota (A.L.)	3	1	.750	4.52	79	0	0	0	0-4	65.2	66	34	33	10	28-6	53
1999— Minnesota (A.L.)	2	5	.286	4.50	63	0	0	0	2-4	48.0	37	24	24	6	25-4	50
— New Britain (East.)	0	0	...	1.93	3	0	0	0	0-...	4.2	3	1	1	0	0-0	5
2000— Minnesota (A.L.)	7	4	.636	3.94	70	0	0	0	9-11	61.2	55	27	27	14	25-3	52
2001— Minnesota (A.L.)	7	1	.875	3.51	67	0	0	0	12-14	66.2	47	27	26	5	23-4	67
2002— Minnesota (A.L.)	1	3	.250	2.93	68	0	0	0	*45-51	67.2	53	22	22	9	18-2	70
Major League totals (10 years)	33	42	.440	4.67	573	25	0	0	75-97	632.1	612	340	328	92	254-29	545

DIVISION SERIES RECORD

Year League	W	L	Pct.	ERA	G	GS	CG	ShO	Sv.-Opp.	IP	H	R	ER	HR	BB-IBB	SO
2002— Minnesota (A.L.)	0	0	...	13.50	2	0	0	0	1-1	2.0	5	3	3	1	1-0	1

CHAMPIONSHIP SERIES RECORD

Year League	W	L	Pct.	ERA	G	GS	CG	ShO	Sv.-Opp.	IP	H	R	ER	HR	BB-IBB	SO
2002— Minnesota (A.L.)	0	0	...	0.00	1	0	0	0	1-1	1.0	0	0	0	0	1-0	2

ALL-STAR GAME RECORD

	W	L	Pct.	ERA	GS	CG	ShO	Sv.-Opp.	IP	H	R	ER	HR	BB-IBB	SO
All-Star Game totals (1 year)	0	0	...	0.00	0	0	0	0-0	.2	0	0	0	0	0-0	2

GUERRERO, VLADIMIR OF EXPOS

PERSONAL: Born February 9, 1976, in Nizao Bani, Dominican Republic. ... 6-3/210. ... Bats right, throws right. ... Full name: Vladimir Alvino Guerrero. ... Brother of Wilton Guerrero, outfielder/second baseman with Los Angeles Dodgers (1996-98), Montreal Expos (1998-2000 and 2002) and Cincinnati Reds (2001 and 2002).

TRANSACTIONS/CAREER NOTES: Signed as non-drafted free agent by Montreal Expos organization (March 1, 1993). ... On Montreal disabled list (March 30-May 2, June 5-21 and July 12-27, 1997); included rehabilitation assignment to West Palm Beach (April 29-May 2).

RECORDS: Shares major league single-season record for fewest assists by outfielder who led league in assists—14 (2002).

HONORS: Named Eastern League Most Valuable Player (1996). ... Named Minor League Player of the Year by The Sporting News (1996). ... Named outfielder on The Sporting News N.L. All-Star team (1999, 2000 and 2002). ... Named outfielder on The Sporting News N.L. Silver Slugger team (1999 and 2000). ... Named outfielder on N.L. Silver Slugger team (2002).

STATISTICAL NOTES: Led Eastern League with 13 intentional bases on balls received in 1996. ... Had 31-game hitting streak (July 27-August 26, 1999). ... Led N.L. with 23 intentional bases on balls received in 2000. ... Led N.L. in grounding into double plays with 24 in 2001. ... Had 26-game hitting streak (June 3-July 3, 2002). ... Led N.L. with 364 total bases in 2002. ... Tied for N.L. lead with 14 assists by outfielder in 2002. ... Career major league grand slams: 1.

MISCELLANEOUS: Holds Montreal Expos all-time record for highest career batting average (.322).

2002 GAMES PLAYED BY POSITION (MLB): OF—161.

					BATTING											FIELDING	
Year Team (League)	Pos.	G	AB	R	H	2B	3B	HR	RBI	BB	SO	SB-CS	Avg.	OBP	SLG	E	Avg.
1993— Dom. Expos (DSL)	OF-IF-P	34	105	19	35	4	0	1	14	8	13	4-...	.333	...	.400	5	.943
1994— Dom. Expos (DSL)	OF	25	92	34	39	11	0	12	35	21	6	5-...	.424	...	.935	2	.957
— GC Expos (GCL)	OF	37	137	24	43	13	3	5	25	11	18	0-7	.314	.366	.562	1	.986
1995— Albany (S.Atl.)	OF	110	421	77	140	21	10	16	63	30	45	12-7	*.333	.383	.544	11	.953
1996— W. Palm Beach (FSL)	OF	20	80	16	29	8	0	5	18	3	10	2-2	.363	.388	.650	3	.917
— Harrisburg (East.)	OF	118	417	84	150	32	8	19	78	51	42	17-10	*.360	*.438	.612	8	.961
— Montreal (N.L.)	OF	9	27	2	5	0	0	1	1	0	3	0-0	.185	.185	.296	0	1.000
1997— W. Palm Beach (FSL)	OF	3	10	0	4	2	0	0	2	1	0	1-0	.400	.455	.600	0	1.000
— Montreal (N.L.)	OF	90	325	44	98	22	2	11	40	19	39	3-4	.302	.350	.483	*12	.929
1998— Montreal (N.L.)	OF	159	623	108	202	37	7	38	109	42	95	11-9	.324	.371	.589	*17	.951
1999— Montreal (N.L.)	OF	160	610	102	193	37	5	42	131	55	62	14-7	.316	.378	.600	*19	.948
2000— Montreal (N.L.)	OF-DH	154	571	101	197	28	11	44	123	58	74	9-10	.345	.410	.664	•10	.969
2001— Montreal (N.L.)	OF	159	599	107	184	45	4	34	108	60	88	37-16	.307	.377	.566	12	.965
2002— Montreal (N.L.)	OF	161	614	106	*206	37	2	39	111	84	70	40-*20	.336	.417	.593	*10	.969
Major League totals (7 years)		892	3369	570	1085	206	31	209	623	318	431	114-66	.322	.386	.588	80	.958

ALL-STAR GAME RECORD

	AB	R	H	2B	3B	HR	RBI	BB	SO	SB-CS	Avg.	OBP	SLG	E	Avg.
All-Star Game totals (4 years)	6	1	2	0	0	0	0	0	1	0-0	.333	.333	.333	0	1.000

RECORD AS PITCHER

Year League	W	L	Pct.	ERA	G	GS	CG	ShO	Sv.-Opp.	IP	H	R	ER	HR	BB-IBB	SO
1993— Dominican Expos (DSL)	0	0	...	2.25	3	0	0	0	0-...	8.0	10	3	2	...	4-...	6

GUERRERO, WILTON — OF/2B

PERSONAL: Born October 24, 1974, in Don Gregorio, Dominican Republic. ... 6-0/175. ... Bats both, throws right. ... Full name: Wilton Alvaro Guerrero. ... Brother of Vladimir Guerrero, outfielder, Montreal Expos.

HIGH SCHOOL: Escuela Primaria Don Gregorio (Dominican Republic).

TRANSACTIONS/CAREER NOTES: Signed as non-drafted free agent by Los Angeles Dodgers organization (October 8, 1991). ... On Albuquerque disabled list (June 26-July 5 and July 26-August 23, 1996). ... On suspended list (June 2-9, 1997). ... Traded by Dodgers with P Ted Lilly, OF Peter Bergeron and 1B Jonathan Tucker to Montreal Expos for P Carlos Perez, SS Mark Grudzielanek and OF Hiram Bocachica (July 31, 1998). ... Granted free agency (December 21, 2000). ... Signed by Cincinnati Reds (January 9, 2001). ... On Louisville disabled list (May 14-21, 2001). ... Traded by Reds with OF Juan Encarnacion and P Ryan Snare to Florida Marlins for P Ryan Dempster (July 11, 2002). ... Traded by Marlins with OF Cliff Floyd, P Claudio Vargas, cash considerations and a player to be named later to Expos for P Carl Pavano, P Graeme Lloyd, IF Mike Mordecai and P Justin Wayne (July 11, 2002); Expos acquired P Don Levinski to complete deal (August 6, 2002). ... Released by Expos (October 10, 2002).

STATISTICAL NOTES: Led Florida State League in caught stealing with 20 in 1994. ... Led Texas League in caught stealing with 22 in 1995. ... Career major league grand slams: 1.

2002 GAMES PLAYED BY POSITION (MLB): 2B—17; OF—12; SS—7; 3B—5.

							BATTING									FIELDING	
Year	Team (League)	Pos.	G	AB	R	H	2B	3B	HR	RBI	BB	SO	SB-CS	Avg.	OBP	SLG	E	Avg.
1992—	Dom. Dodgers (DSL)	SS	61	225	52	87	7	4	0	38	34	21	15-...	.387	...	.453	21	.938
1993—	Great Falls (Pio.)	SS	66	256	44	76	5	1	0	21	24	33	20-8	.297	.364	.324	21	.925
—	Dom. Dodgers (DSL)	SS	8	31	6	11	0	1	0	4	4	3	2-...	.355	...	.419	1	.971
1994—	Vero Beach (FSL)	SS	110	402	55	118	11	4	1	32	29	71	23-20	.294	.341	.348	17	.960
1995—	San Antonio (Texas)	SS	95	382	53	133	13	6	0	26	26	63	21-22	*.348	.390	.414	19	.953
—	Albuquerque (PCL)	SS-OF	14	49	10	16	1	1	0	2	1	7	2-3	.327	.340	.388	9	.852
1996—	Albuquerque (PCL)	2B-SS	98	425	79	146	17	12	2	38	26	48	26-15	.344	.383	.454	19	.963
—	Los Angeles (N.L.)	OF	5	2	1	0	0	0	0	0	0	2	0-0	.000	.000	.000	0	...
1997—	Los Angeles (N.L.)	2B-SS	111	357	39	104	10	9	4	32	8	52	6-5	.291	.305	.403	4	.990
—	Albuquerque (PCL)	SS-2B	10	45	9	18	0	1	0	5	2	3	3-0	.400	.417	.444	5	.915
1998—	Los Angeles (N.L.)	2B-SS-OF	64	180	21	51	4	3	0	7	4	33	5-2	.283	.299	.339	7	.959
—	Albuquerque (PCL)	2B-OF-DH	30	121	15	36	3	2	1	10	9	12	11-3	.298	.351	.380	1	.990
—	Montreal (N.L.)■	2B	52	222	29	63	10	6	2	20	10	30	3-0	.284	.313	.410	6	.975
1999—	Montreal (N.L.)	2B-OF-DH	132	315	42	92	15	7	2	31	13	38	7-6	.292	.324	.403	12	.939
2000—	Montreal (N.L.)	OF-DH-2B	127	288	30	77	7	2	2	23	19	41	8-1	.267	.312	.326	4	.967
2001—	Cincinnati (N.L.)■	S-2-O-3-DH	60	142	16	48	5	1	1	8	3	17	5-2	.338	.352	.408	5	.956
—	Louisville (I.L.)	2B-SS-OF	54	227	23	69	14	2	0	28	12	30	12-5	.304	.342	.383	8	.963
2002—	Cincinnati (N.L.)	2B-SS-3B	59	78	9	19	1	1	0	4	6	13	2-1	.244	.298	.282	2	.962
—	Montreal (N.L.)■	OF-2B-3B	44	62	3	12	1	0	0	1	1	19	5-0	.194	.206	.210	1	.974
Major League totals (7 years)			654	1646	190	466	53	29	11	126	64	245	41-17	.283	.310	.371	41	.969

GUIEL, AARON — OF — ROYALS

PERSONAL: Born October 5, 1972, in Vancouver. ... 5-10/200. ... Bats left, throws right. ... Full name: Aaron Colin Guiel.

HIGH SCHOOL: Woodlands Senior (B.C.).

COLLEGE: Kwantlen College (B.C.).

TRANSACTIONS/CAREER NOTES: Selected by California Angels organization in 21st round of free-agent draft (June 1, 1992). ... Traded by Angels to San Diego Padres for C Angelo Encarnacion (August 25, 1997). ... Granted free agency (October 15, 1999). ... Signed by Oakland Athletics organization (March 18, 2000). ... Released by A's (March 30, 2000). ... Signed by Oaxaca of Mexican League (April 2000). ... Signed by Kansas City Royals organization (June 13, 2000). ... Granted free agency (October 15, 2001). ... Re-signed by Royals organization (October 31, 2001). ... On Omaha disabled list (May 25-June 3, 2002).

2002 GAMES PLAYED BY POSITION (MLB): OF—61; DH—2.

							BATTING									FIELDING	
Year	Team (League)	Pos.	G	AB	R	H	2B	3B	HR	RBI	BB	SO	SB-CS	Avg.	OBP	SLG	E	Avg.
1993—	Boise (N'West)	2B-OF	35	104	24	31	6	4	2	12	26	21	3-0	.298	.455	.490	12	.874
1994—	Cedar Rapids (Midw.)	2B	127	454	84	122	30	1	18	82	64	93	21-7	.269	.364	.458	32	.944
1995—	Lake Elsinore (Calif.)	2B	113	409	73	110	25	7	7	58	69	96	7-6	.269	.380	.416	22	.958
1996—	Midland (Texas)	3B-2B-OF	129	439	72	118	29	7	10	48	56	71	11-7	.269	.364	.435	28	.933
1997—	Midland (Texas)	OF-3B-2B	116	419	91	138	37	7	22	85	59	94	14-10	.329	.431	.609	8	.953
—	Mobile (Sou.)	OF	8	26	9	10	2	0	1	9	5	4	1-0	.385	.500	.577	0	1.000
1998—	Las Vegas (PCL)	OF-3B	60	183	33	57	15	4	5	31	28	51	5-1	.311	.410	.519	4	.947
—	Arizona Padres (Ariz.)	OF	8	16	8	8	3	1	1	6	5	5	1-1	.500	.667	1.000	0	1.000
1999—	Las Vegas (PCL)	OF	84	257	46	63	25	2	12	39	44	86	5-4	.245	.362	.498	5	.944
2000—	Oaxaca (Mex.)■	OF	56	192	55	70	11	1	22	62	52	35	7-5	.365	.502	.776	4	...
—	Omaha (PCL)■	OF	73	258	47	74	15	2	13	40	35	54	6-0	.287	.389	.512	4	.977
2001—	Omaha (PCL)	OF	121	442	78	118	27	3	21	73	51	92	6-4	.267	.355	.484	6	.973
2002—	Omaha (PCL)	OF	61	215	44	76	11	1	9	50	29	34	8-1	.353	.443	.540	3	.977
—	Kansas City (A.L.)	OF-DH	70	240	30	56	13	0	4	38	19	61	1-5	.233	.296	.338	6	.952
Major League totals (1 year)			70	240	30	56	13	0	4	38	19	61	1-5	.233	.296	.338	6	.952

GUILLEN, CARLOS — SS — MARINERS

PERSONAL: Born September 30, 1975, in Maracay, Venezuela. ... 6-1/202. ... Bats both, throws right. ... Full name: Carlos Alfonso Guillen.

TRANSACTIONS/CAREER NOTES: Signed as non-drafted free agent by Houston Astros organization (September 19, 1992). ... On disabled list (June 1, 1994-entire season). ... On disabled list (May 2, 1996-remainder of season). ... Traded by Astros with P Freddy Garcia and a player to be named later to Seattle Mariners for P Randy Johnson (July 31, 1998); Mariners acquired P John Halama to complete deal (October 1, 1998). ... On disabled list (April 7, 1999-remainder of season). ... On Seattle disabled list (April 13-28, 2000); included rehabilitation assignment to Tacoma (April 22-28).

STATISTICAL NOTES: Career major league grand slams: 1.

2002 GAMES PLAYED BY POSITION (MLB): SS—130; DH—3.

		BATTING														FIELDING	
Year Team (League)	Pos.	G	AB	R	H	2B	3B	HR	RBI	BB	SO	SB-CS	Avg.	OBP	SLG	E	Avg.
1993— Dom. Astros (DSL).....	IF	18	56	12	14	4	2	0	8	8	12	0-...	.250	...	.393	2	.956
1994—								Did not play.									
1995— GC Astros (GCL)........		30	105	17	31	4	2	2	15	9	17	17-1	.295	.350	.429	...	...
1996— Quad City (Midw.)......	SS	29	112	23	37	7	1	3	17	16	25	13-6	.330	.405	.491	9	.929
1997— Jackson (Texas).........	SS-DH	115	390	47	99	16	1	10	39	38	78	6-5	.254	.322	.377	35	.932
— New Orleans (A.A.).....	SS	3	13	3	4	1	0	0	0	0	4	0-0	.308	.308	.385	0	1.000
1998— New Orleans (PCL).....	SS	100	374	67	109	18	4	12	51	31	61	3-4	.291	.350	.457	26	.943
— Tacoma (PCL)■.........	2B	24	92	8	21	1	1	1	4	9	17	1-2	.228	.297	.293	2	.982
— Seattle (A.L.)............	2B	10	39	9	13	1	1	0	5	3	9	2-0	.333	.381	.410	0	1.000
1999— Seattle (A.L.).............	SS-2B	5	19	2	3	0	0	1	3	1	6	0-0	.158	.200	.316	1	.964
2000— Seattle (A.L.).............	3B-SS	90	288	45	74	15	2	7	42	28	53	1-3	.257	.324	.396	21	.921
— Tacoma (PCL)...........	3B-SS	24	87	19	26	4	1	2	11	12	17	4-1	.299	.386	.437	6	.926
2001— Seattle (A.L.).............	SS-DH	140	456	72	118	21	4	5	53	53	89	4-1	.259	.333	.355	10	.980
2002— Seattle (A.L.).............	SS-DH	134	475	73	124	24	6	9	56	46	91	4-5	.261	.326	.394	18	.966
Major League totals (5 years)		379	1277	201	332	61	13	22	159	131	248	11-9	.260	.328	.380	50	.964

DIVISION SERIES RECORD

		BATTING														FIELDING	
Year Team (League)	Pos.	G	AB	R	H	2B	3B	HR	RBI	BB	SO	SB-CS	Avg.	OBP	SLG	E	Avg.
2000— Seattle (A.L.).............	PH	1	1	0	1	0	0	0	1	0	0	0-0	1.000	1.000	1.000	...	...
2001— Seattle (A.L.).............								Did not play.									

CHAMPIONSHIP SERIES RECORD

		BATTING														FIELDING	
Year Team (League)	Pos.	G	AB	R	H	2B	3B	HR	RBI	BB	SO	SB-CS	Avg.	OBP	SLG	E	Avg.
2000— Seattle (A.L.).............	3B	2	5	1	1	0	0	1	2	2	2	0-1	.200	.429	.800	0	1.000
2001— Seattle (A.L.).............	SS-PH	3	8	1	2	0	0	0	0	0	1	0-0	.250	.250	.250	0	1.000
Championship series totals (2 years)		5	13	2	3	0	0	1	2	2	3	0-1	.231	.333	.462	0	1.000

GUILLEN, JOSE OF REDS

PERSONAL: Born May 17, 1976, in San Cristobal, Dominican Republic. ... 5-11/195. ... Bats right, throws right. ... Full name: Jose Manuel Guillen.

TRANSACTIONS/CAREER NOTES: Signed as non-drafted free agent by Pittsburgh Pirates organization (August 19, 1992). ... Traded by Pirates with P Jeff Sparks to Tampa Bay Devil Rays for C Joe Oliver and C Humberto Cota (July 23, 1999). ... On Durham disabled list (July 23-30, 1999). ... On Tampa Bay disabled list (March 28-April 12, 2000). ... On Tampa Bay disabled list (May 17-June 24 and June 25-July 30, 2001); included rehabilitation assignments to Durham (June 10-24 and July 14-30). ... On Durham disabled list (August 7-24, 2001). ... Released by Devil Rays (November 27, 2001). ... Signed by Arizona Diamondbacks (December 18, 2001). ... Released by Diamondbacks (July 22, 2002). ... Signed by Colorado Rockies organization (July 29, 2002). ... Released by Rockies (August 1, 2002). ... Signed by Cincinnati Reds organization (August 20, 2002).

RECORDS: Shares major league single-inning record for most doubles—2 (May 16, 1999, fourth inning; and May 28, 2000, eighth inning).

HONORS: Named Carolina League Most Valuable Player (1996).

STATISTICAL NOTES: Led Carolina League with 263 total bases and grounding into double plays with 16 in 1996. ... Led Carolina League outfielders with six double plays in 1996. ... Career major league grand slams: 3.

2002 GAMES PLAYED BY POSITION (MLB): OF—64.

		BATTING														FIELDING	
Year Team (League)	Pos.	G	AB	R	H	2B	3B	HR	RBI	BB	SO	SB-CS	Avg.	OBP	SLG	E	Avg.
1993— Dom. Pirates (DSL)....	OF	63	234	39	53	3	4	11	41	21	55	10-...	.226	...	.415	7	.947
1994— GC Pirates (GCL)........	OF	30	110	17	29	4	1	4	11	7	15	2-1	.264	.341	.427	2	.970
1995— Erie (NY-Penn)..........	OF	66	258	41	81	17	1	*12	46	10	44	1-5	.314	.367	.527	13	.900
— Augusta (S.Atl.)..........	OF	10	34	6	8	1	1	2	6	2	9	0-0	.235	.316	.500	0	1.000
1996— Lynchburg (Caro.)......	OF-DH	136	*528	78	*170	30	0	•21	94	20	73	24-13	.322	.357	.498	*13	.949
1997— Pittsburgh (N.L.)........	OF	143	498	58	133	20	5	14	70	17	88	1-2	.267	.300	.412	9	.963
1998— Pittsburgh (N.L.)........	OF	153	573	60	153	38	2	14	84	21	100	3-5	.267	.298	.414	10	.968
1999— Pittsburgh (N.L.)........	OF	40	120	18	32	6	0	1	18	10	21	1-0	.267	.321	.342	3	.952
— Nashville (PCL)..........	OF-DH	35	132	28	44	10	0	5	22	8	21	0-1	.333	.378	.523	4	.939
— Durham (I.L.)■..........	OF	9	34	8	13	1	0	3	12	7	7	0-1	.382	.476	.676	0	1.000
— Tampa Bay (A.L.)........	OF	47	168	24	41	10	0	2	13	10	36	0-0	.244	.312	.339	3	.966
2000— Durham (I.L.)............	OF	19	78	20	33	8	2	9	31	8	11	0-1	.423	.477	.923	3	.912
— Tampa Bay (A.L.)........	OF	105	316	40	80	16	5	10	41	18	65	3-1	.253	.320	.430	4	.978
2001— Tampa Bay (A.L.)........	OF-DH	41	135	14	37	5	0	3	11	6	26	2-3	.274	.317	.378	3	.969
— Durham (I.L.)............	OF	33	119	18	35	9	0	7	29	3	28	0-0	.294	.306	.546	1	.982
2002— Arizona (N.L.)■..........	OF-DH	54	131	13	30	4	0	4	15	7	25	3-4	.229	.277	.351	0	1.000
— Colo. Springs (PCL)■	OF	5	17	2	7	3	0	0	5	1	2	0-1	.412	.474	.588	0	1.000
— Louisville (I.L.)■........	OF	8	29	4	9	4	0	2	8	0	5	0-0	.310	.310	.655	0	1.000
— Cincinnati (N.L.)........	OF	31	109	12	27	3	0	4	16	7	18	1-1	.248	.299	.385	1	.979
American League totals (3 years)		193	619	78	158	31	5	15	65	34	127	5-4	.255	.317	.394	10	.973
National League totals (4 years)		421	1431	161	375	71	7	37	203	62	252	9-12	.262	.299	.399	23	.968
Major League totals (6 years)		614	2050	239	533	102	12	52	268	96	379	14-16	.260	.305	.398	33	.970

GUTHRIE, MARK P

PERSONAL: Born September 22, 1965, in Buffalo. ... 6-4/215. ... Throws left, bats right. ... Full name: Mark Andrew Guthrie.

HIGH SCHOOL: Venice (Fla.).

COLLEGE: Louisiana State.

TRANSACTIONS/CAREER NOTES: Selected by St. Louis Cardinals organization in fourth round of free-agent draft (June 2, 1986); did not sign. ... Selected by Minnesota Twins organization in seventh round of free-agent draft (June 2, 1987). ... On disabled list (May 29, 1993-remainder of season). ... Traded by Twins with P Kevin Tapani to Los Angeles Dodgers for 1B/3B Ron Coomer, P Greg Hansell, P Jose Parra and a player to be named later (July 31, 1995); Twins acquired OF Chris Latham to complete deal (October 30, 1995). ... Granted free agency (October 29, 1996). ... Re-signed by Dodgers (November 6, 1996). ... Granted free agency (October 26, 1998). ... Signed by Boston Red Sox (December 19, 1998). ... On Boston disabled list (July 5-24, 1999); included rehabilitation assignment to Pawtucket (July 22-23). ... Traded by Red Sox with a player to named later to Chicago Cubs for P Rod Beck (August 31, 1999); Cubs acquired 3B Cole Liniak to complete deal (September 1, 1999). ... Traded by Cubs to Tampa Bay Devil Rays for OF Dave Martinez (May 12, 2000). ... Traded by Devil Rays with P Steve Trachsel to Toronto Blue Jays for 2B Brent Abernathy and a player to be named later (July 31, 2000). ... Granted free agency (October 31, 2000). ... Signed by Oakland Athletics (January 5, 2001). ... Traded by A's with P Tyler Yates to New York Mets for OF David Justice (December 14, 2001). ... Granted free agency (October 29, 2002).

MISCELLANEOUS: Appeared in one game as pinch runner (1991).

CAREER HITTING (MLB): 1-for-13 (.077), 0 R, 0 2B, 0 3B, 0 HR, 0 RBI.

Year League	W	L	Pct.	ERA	G	GS	CG	ShO	Sv.-Opp.	IP	H	R	ER	HR	BB-IBB	SO
1987— Visalia (Calif.)	2	1	.667	4.50	4	1	0	0	0-...	12.0	10	7	6	0	5-1	9
1988— Visalia (Calif.)	12	9	.571	3.31	25	25	4	1	0-...	171.1	169	81	63	6	86-1	182
1989— Orlando (Sou.)	8	3	.727	1.97	14	14	0	0	0-...	96.0	75	32	21	4	38-0	103
— Portland (PCL)	3	4	.429	3.65	7	7	1	0	0-...	44.1	45	21	18	4	16-0	35
— Minnesota (A.L.)	2	4	.333	4.55	13	8	0	0	0-0	57.1	66	32	29	7	21-1	38
1990— Minnesota (A.L.)	7	9	.438	3.79	24	21	3	1	0-0	144.2	154	65	61	8	39-3	101
— Portland (PCL)	1	3	.250	2.98	9	8	1	0	0-...	42.1	47	19	14	1	12-0	39
1991— Minnesota (A.L.)	7	5	.583	4.32	41	12	0	0	2-2	98.0	116	52	47	11	41-2	72
1992— Minnesota (A.L.)	2	3	.400	2.88	54	0	0	0	5-7	75.0	59	27	24	7	23-7	76
1993— Minnesota (A.L.)	2	1	.667	4.71	22	0	0	0	0-1	21.0	20	11	11	2	16-2	15
1994— Minnesota (A.L.)	4	2	.667	6.14	50	2	0	0	1-3	51.1	65	43	35	8	18-2	38
1995— Minnesota (A.L.)	5	3	.625	4.46	36	0	0	0	0-2	42.1	47	22	21	5	16-3	48
— Los Angeles (N.L.)■	0	2	.000	3.66	24	0	0	0	0-0	19.2	19	11	8	1	9-2	19
1996— Los Angeles (N.L.)	2	3	.400	2.22	66	0	0	0	1-3	73.0	65	21	18	3	22-2	56
1997— Los Angeles (N.L.)	1	4	.200	5.32	62	0	0	0	1-4	69.1	71	44	41	12	30-6	42
1998— Los Angeles (N.L.)	2	1	.667	3.50	53	0	0	0	0-1	54.0	56	26	21	3	24-1	45
1999— Boston (A.L.)■	1	1	.500	5.83	46	0	0	0	2-2	46.1	50	32	30	9	20-3	36
— Pawtucket (I.L.)	0	0	...	0.00	1	1	0	0	0-...	1.0	0	0	0	0	0-0	1
— Chicago (N.L.)■	0	2	.000	3.65	11	0	0	0	0-0	12.1	7	6	5	1	4-2	9
2000— Chicago (N.L.)	2	3	.400	4.82	19	0	0	0	0-0	18.2	17	11	10	1	10-4	17
— Tampa Bay (A.L.)■	1	1	.500	4.50	34	0	0	0	0-3	32.0	33	18	16	4	18-5	26
— Toronto (A.L.)■	0	2	.000	4.79	23	0	0	0	0-1	20.2	20	12	11	3	9-0	20
2001— Oakland (A.L.)■	6	2	.750	4.47	54	0	0	0	1-3	52.1	49	29	26	7	20-1	52
2002— New York (N.L.)■	5	3	.625	2.44	68	0	0	0	1-2	48.0	35	13	13	3	19-3	44
A.L. totals (10 years)	37	33	.529	4.37	397	43	3	1	11-24	641.0	679	343	311	71	241-29	522
N.L. totals (7 years)	12	18	.400	3.54	303	0	0	0	3-10	295.0	270	132	116	24	118-20	232
Major League totals (14 years)	49	51	.490	4.11	700	43	3	1	14-34	936.0	949	475	427	95	359-49	754

DIVISION SERIES RECORD

Year League	W	L	Pct.	ERA	G	GS	CG	ShO	Sv.-Opp.	IP	H	R	ER	HR	BB-IBB	SO
1995— Los Angeles (N.L.)	0	0	...	6.75	3	0	0	0	0-0	1.1	2	1	1	1	1-0	1
1996— Los Angeles (N.L.)	0	0	...	0.00	1	0	0	0	0-0	.1	0	0	0	0	1-0	1
2001— Oakland (A.L.)	0	0	...	0.00	2	0	0	0	0-0	3.0	0	0	0	0	0-0	2
Division series totals (3 years)	0	0	...	1.93	6	0	0	0	0-0	4.2	2	1	1	1	2-0	4

CHAMPIONSHIP SERIES RECORD

Year League	W	L	Pct.	ERA	G	GS	CG	ShO	Sv.-Opp.	IP	H	R	ER	HR	BB-IBB	SO
1991— Minnesota (A.L.)	1	0	1.000	0.00	2	0	0	0	0-0	2.2	0	0	0	0	0-0	0

WORLD SERIES RECORD

NOTES: Member of World Series championship team (1991).

Year League	W	L	Pct.	ERA	G	GS	CG	ShO	Sv.-Opp.	IP	H	R	ER	HR	BB-IBB	SO
1991— Minnesota (A.L.)	0	1	.000	2.25	4	0	0	0	0-0	4.0	3	1	1	0	4-1	3

GUTIERREZ, RICKY — 2B — INDIANS

PERSONAL: Born May 23, 1970, in Miami. ... 6-1/190. ... Bats right, throws right. ... Full name: Ricardo Gutierrez.

HIGH SCHOOL: American (Hialeah, Fla.).

TRANSACTIONS/CAREER NOTES: Selected by Baltimore Orioles organization in supplemental round ("sandwich pick" between first and second round, 28th pick overall) of free-agent draft (June 1, 1988); pick received as compensation for Orioles failing to sign 1987 No. 1 pick P Brad DuVall. ... Traded by Orioles to San Diego Padres (September 4, 1992), completing deal in which Padres traded P Craig Lefferts to Orioles for P Erik Schullstrom and a player to be named later (August 31, 1992). ... Traded by Padres with OF Phil Plantier, OF Derek Bell, P Pedro Martinez, P Doug Brocail and IF Craig Shipley to Houston Astros for 3B Ken Caminiti, OF Steve Finley, SS Andujar Cedeno, 1B Robert Petagine, P Brian Williams and a player to be named later (December 28, 1994); Padres acquired P Sean Fesh to complete deal (May 1, 1995). ... On Houston disabled list (March 31-May 6, 1997); included rehabilitation assignment to New Orleans (April 29-May 6). ... On Houston disabled list (April 28-June 7 and July 10-August 9, 1999); included rehabilitation assignments to Jackson (June 3-7) and New Orleans (August 5-9). ... Granted free agency (October 28, 1999). ... Signed by Chicago Cubs (December 20, 1999). ... On Chicago disabled list (May 25-June 23, 2000); included rehabilitation assignment to Daytona (June 19-23). ... Granted free agency (November 5, 2001). ... Signed by Cleveland Indians (December 19, 2001). ... On disabled list (June 14-July 2 and August 15, 2002-remainder of season).

STATISTICAL NOTES: Led Appalachian League shortstops with 100 putouts and 309 total chances in 1988. ... Led N.L. with 16 sacrifice hits in 2000. ... Tied for N.L. lead with 17 sacrifice hits in 2001. ... Career major league grand slams: 1.

2002 GAMES PLAYED BY POSITION (MLB): 2B—93; DH—1.

							BATTING									FIELDING	
Year Team (League)	Pos.	G	AB	R	H	2B	3B	HR	RBI	BB	SO	SB-CS	Avg.	OBP	SLG	E	Avg.
1988— Bluefield (Appl.)	SS	62	208	35	51	8	2	2	19	44	40	5-3	.245	.383	.332	34	.890
1989— Frederick (Caro.)	SS	127	456	48	106	16	2	3	41	39	89	15-10	.232	.294	.296	34	*.943
1990— Frederick (Caro.)	SS	112	425	54	117	16	4	1	46	38	59	12-6	.275	.341	.339	26	.948
— Hagerstown (East.)	SS	20	64	4	15	0	1	0	6	3	8	2-0	.234	.265	.266	4	.944
1991— Hagerstown (East.)	SS	84	292	47	69	6	4	0	30	57	52	11-0	.236	.363	.284	22	.941
— Rochester (I.L.)	SS-3B	49	157	23	48	5	3	0	15	24	27	4-1	.306	.396	.376	8	.960

			BATTING															FIELDING	
Year	Team (League)	Pos.	G	AB	R	H	2B	3B	HR	RBI	BB	SO	SB-CS	Avg.	OBP	SLG	E	Avg.
1992—	Rochester (I.L.)	2B-SS	125	431	54	109	9	3	0	41	53	77	14-12	.253	.331	.288	15	.973
—	Las Vegas (PCL)■	SS	3	6	0	1	0	0	0	1	1	3	0-0	.167	.250	.167	0	1.000
1993—	Las Vegas (PCL)	2B-SS	5	24	4	10	4	0	0	4	0	4	4-0	.417	.417	.583	2	.926
—	San Diego (N.L.)	SS-2B-OF-3B	133	438	76	110	10	5	5	26	50	97	4-3	.251	.334	.331	14	.973
1994—	San Diego (N.L.)	SS-2B	90	275	27	66	11	2	1	28	32	54	2-6	.240	.321	.305	22	.931
1995—	Houston (N.L.)■	SS-3B	52	156	22	43	6	0	0	12	10	33	5-0	.276	.321	.314	8	.956
—	Tucson (PCL)	SS-DH	64	236	46	71	12	4	1	26	28	28	9-7	.301	.379	.398	6	.977
1996—	Houston (N.L.)	SS-3B-2B	89	218	28	62	8	1	1	15	23	42	6-1	.284	.359	.344	12	.951
1997—	New Orleans (A.A.)	SS	7	27	2	5	1	0	0	4	2	4	0-1	.185	.233	.222	1	.971
—	Houston (N.L.)	SS-3B-2B	102	303	33	79	14	4	3	34	21	50	5-2	.261	.315	.363	8	.974
1998—	Houston (N.L.)	SS	141	491	55	128	24	3	2	46	54	84	13-7	.261	.337	.334	15	.976
1999—	Houston (N.L.)	SS-3B	85	268	33	70	7	5	1	25	37	45	2-5	.261	.354	.336	9	.971
—	Jackson (Texas)	SS-DH	4	12	4	4	1	0	0	1	4	3	0-1	.333	.500	.417	0	1.000
—	New Orleans (PCL)	SS	4	14	0	3	0	0	0	1	2	3	0-0	.214	.313	.214	3	.875
2000—	Chicago (N.L.)■	SS	125	449	73	124	19	2	11	56	66	58	8-2	.276	.375	.401	7	*.986
—	Daytona (FSL)	SS	4	10	0	4	1	0	0	1	2	2	1-0	.400	.500	.500	3	.727
2001—	Chicago (N.L.)	SS	147	528	76	153	23	3	10	66	40	56	4-3	.290	.345	.402	16	.971
2002—	Cleveland (A.L.)■	2B-DH	94	353	38	97	13	0	4	38	20	48	0-1	.275	.325	.346	11	.976
American League totals (1 year)			94	353	38	97	13	0	4	38	20	48	0-1	.275	.325	.346	11	.976
National League totals (9 years)			964	3126	423	835	122	25	34	308	333	519	49-29	.267	.342	.355	111	.969
Major League totals (10 years)			1058	3479	461	932	135	25	38	346	353	567	49-30	.268	.341	.354	122	.969

DIVISION SERIES RECORD

			BATTING															FIELDING	
Year	Team (League)	Pos.	G	AB	R	H	2B	3B	HR	RBI	BB	SO	SB-CS	Avg.	OBP	SLG	E	Avg.
1997—	Houston (N.L.)	SS	3	8	0	1	0	0	0	0	2	1	0-0	.125	.300	.125	0	1.000
1998—	Houston (N.L.)	SS	4	10	1	3	0	0	0	0	3	7	1-0	.300	.500	.300	0	1.000
1999—	Houston (N.L.)	SS	3	10	0	0	0	0	0	0	2	5	0-0	.000	.167	.000	1	.952
Division series totals (3 years)			10	28	1	4	0	0	0	0	7	13	1-0	.143	.333	.143	1	.980

GUZMAN, CRISTIAN — SS — TWINS

PERSONAL: Born March 21, 1978, in Santo Domingo, Dominican Republic. ... 6-0/195. ... Bats both, throws right. ... Full name: Cristian Antonio Guzman.

TRANSACTIONS/CAREER NOTES: Signed as non-drafted free agent by New York Yankees organization (August 24, 1994). ... Traded by Yankees with P Eric Milton, P Danny Mota, OF Brian Buchanan and cash to Minnesota Twins for 2B Chuck Knoblauch (February 6, 1998). ... On disabled list (May 27-June 11, 1999). ... On suspended list (September 10-13, 1999). ... On Minnesota disabled list (July 13-August 17, 2001); included rehabilitation assignment to Gulf Coast Twins (August 13-17).

RECORDS: Shares major league record for fewest errors for leader by shortstop—21 (2001).

STATISTICAL NOTES: Led South Atlantic League shortstops with 68 double plays in 1997. ... Led Eastern League with 17 sacrifice hits in 1998. ... Led Eastern League shortstops with 426 assists and 95 double plays in 1998. ... Had 17-game hitting streak (June 8-26, 2001). ... Had 23-game hitting streak (August 1-25, 2002). ... Career major league grand slams: 1.

2002 GAMES PLAYED BY POSITION (MLB): SS—147; DH—1.

			BATTING															FIELDING	
Year	Team (League)	Pos.	G	AB	R	H	2B	3B	HR	RBI	BB	SO	SB-CS	Avg.	OBP	SLG	E	Avg.
1995—	Dom. Yankees (DSL)	SS	46	160	24	43	6	5	3	20	12	23	11-...	.269	...	.425	13	.935
1996—	GC Yankees (GCL)	SS	42	170	37	50	8	2	1	21	10	31	7-6	.294	.341	.382	20	.890
1997—	Greensboro (S.Atl.)	SS	124	495	68	135	21	4	4	52	17	105	23-12	.273	.309	.356	37	.936
—	Tampa (FSL)	SS	4	14	4	4	0	0	0	1	1	1	0-1	.286	.333	.286	2	.889
1998—	New Britain (East.)■	SS	•140	566	68	157	29	5	1	40	21	111	23-14	.277	.304	.352	*32	.952
1999—	Minnesota (A.L.)	SS	131	420	47	95	12	3	1	26	22	90	9-7	.226	.267	.276	24	.959
2000—	Minnesota (A.L.)	SS-DH	156	631	89	156	25	*20	8	54	46	101	28-10	.247	.299	.388	22	.967
2001—	Minnesota (A.L.)	SS	118	493	80	149	28	*14	10	51	21	78	25-8	.302	.337	.477	*21	.959
—	GC Twins (GCL)	SS	5	16	4	4	0	1	0	0	2	4	0-1	.250	.368	.375	0	1.000
2002—	Minnesota (A.L.)	SS-DH	148	623	80	170	31	6	9	59	17	79	12-13	.273	.292	.385	12	.981
Major League totals (4 years)			553	2167	296	570	96	43	28	190	106	348	74-38	.263	.299	.386	79	.967

DIVISION SERIES RECORD

			BATTING															FIELDING	
Year	Team (League)	Pos.	G	AB	R	H	2B	3B	HR	RBI	BB	SO	SB-CS	Avg.	OBP	SLG	E	Avg.
2002—	Minnesota (A.L.)	SS	5	21	5	6	2	0	1	2	2	4	2-0	.286	.348	.524	1	.923

CHAMPIONSHIP SERIES RECORD

			BATTING															FIELDING	
Year	Team (League)	Pos.	G	AB	R	H	2B	3B	HR	RBI	BB	SO	SB-CS	Avg.	OBP	SLG	E	Avg.
2002—	Minnesota (A.L.)	SS	5	18	1	3	1	0	0	0	0	3	0-0	.167	.211	.222	1	.962

ALL-STAR GAME RECORD

	AB	R	H	2B	3B	HR	RBI	BB	SO	SB-CS	Avg.	OBP	SLG	E	Avg.
All-Star Game totals (1 year)	1	0	0	0	0	0	0	0	1	0-0	.000	.000	.000	0	...

HACKMAN, LUTHER — P — CARDINALS

PERSONAL: Born October 10, 1974, in Columbus, Miss. ... 6-4/195. ... Throws right, bats right. ... Full name: Luther Gean Hackman.

HIGH SCHOOL: Columbus (Miss.).

TRANSACTIONS/CAREER NOTES: Selected by Colorado Rockies organization in sixth round of free-agent draft (June 2, 1994). ... On disabled list (June 1-July 10, 1996). ... Traded by Rockies with P Darryl Kile and P Dave Veres to St. Louis Cardinals for P Jose Jimenez,

P Manny Aybar, P Rick Croushore and SS Brent Butler (November 16, 1999). ... On Memphis disabled list (June 3-July 4, 2000). ... On St. Louis disabled list (March 23-May 9, 2001); included rehabilitation assignment to New Haven (May 1-9).
STATISTICAL NOTES: Led South Atlantic League in balks with seven in 1995.
CAREER HITTING (MLB): 2-for-22 (.091), 1 R, 0 2B, 0 3B, 0 HR, 0 RBI.

Year	League	W	L	Pct.	ERA	G	GS	CG	ShO	Sv.-Opp.	IP	H	R	ER	HR	BB-IBB	SO
1994—	Arizona Rockies (Ariz.)	1	3	.250	2.10	12	12	0	0	0-...	55.2	50	21	13	1	16-0	63
1995—	Asheville (S.Atl.)	11	11	.500	4.64	28	28	2	0	0-...	165.0	162	*95	*85	11	65-0	108
1996—	Salem (Caro.)	5	7	.417	4.24	21	21	1	0	0-...	110.1	93	60	52	2	69-1	83
1997—	New Haven (East.)	0	6	.000	7.82	10	10	0	0	0-...	50.2	58	49	44	11	34-1	34
	—Salem (Caro.)	1	4	.200	5.80	15	15	2	0	0-...	80.2	99	60	52	14	37-0	59
1998—	New Haven (East.)	3	12	.200	5.44	28	23	1	0	0-...	139.0	169	•102	84	18	54-1	90
1999—	Carolina (Sou.)	4	3	.571	4.04	11	10	0	0	0-...	62.1	53	33	28	4	28-0	50
	—Colorado Springs (PCL)	7	6	.538	3.74	15	15	1	1	0-...	101.0	106	49	42	7	44-2	88
	—Colorado (N.L.)	1	2	.333	10.69	5	3	0	0	0-0	16.0	26	19	19	5	12-0	10
2000—	Memphis (PCL)■	8	9	.471	4.74	21	21	0	0	0-...	119.2	134	71	63	11	36-1	66
	—St. Louis (N.L.)	0	0	...	10.13	1	0	0	0	0-0	2.2	4	3	3	0	4-1	0
2001—	New Haven (East.)	0	0	...	2.25	3	1	0	0	0-...	4.0	2	2	1	0	1-0	5
	—Memphis (PCL)	0	2	.000	2.78	16	0	0	0	0-...	22.2	21	7	7	2	1-0	12
	—St. Louis (N.L.)	1	2	.333	4.29	35	0	0	0	1-3	35.2	28	18	17	7	14-0	24
2002—	St. Louis (N.L.)	5	4	.556	4.11	43	6	0	0	0-1	81.0	90	42	37	7	39-3	46
Major League totals (4 years)		7	8	.467	5.05	84	9	0	0	1-4	135.1	148	82	76	19	69-4	80

HAFNER, TRAVIS — 1B — RANGERS

PERSONAL: Born June 3, 1977, in Jamestown, N.D. ... 6-3/240. ... Bats left, throws right. ... Full name: Travis Lee Hafner.
JUNIOR COLLEGE: Cowley County Community College (Kan.).
TRANSACTIONS/CAREER NOTES: Selected by Texas Rangers organization in 31st round of free-agent draft (June 4, 1996). ... On disabled list (August 6-22, 2000). ... On disabled list (April 5-May 11, 2001).
2002 GAMES PLAYED BY POSITION (MLB): DH—13; 1B—3.

			BATTING														FIELDING	
Year	Team (League)	Pos.	G	AB	R	H	2B	3B	HR	RBI	BB	SO	SB-CS	Avg.	OBP	SLG	E	Avg.
1997—	GC Rangers (GCL)	1B-OF	55	189	38	54	14	0	5	24	24	45	7-2	.286	.375	.439	3	.991
1998—	Savannah (S.Atl.)	1B-3B-OF	123	405	62	96	15	4	16	84	68	139	7-3	.237	.351	.412	12	.980
1999—	Savannah (S.Atl.)	1B-3B	134	480	94	140	30	4	•28	*111	67	151	5-4	.292	.387	*.546	15	.984
2000—	Charlotte (FSL)	1B-3B	122	436	90	151	34	1	22	109	67	86	0-4	.346	*.447	.580	13	.978
2001—	Tulsa (Texas)	1B	88	323	59	91	25	0	20	74	59	82	3-1	.282	.396	.545	5	.993
2002—	Oklahoma (PCL)	1B	110	401	79	137	22	1	21	77	79	76	2-1	.342	*.463	.559	4	.993
	—Texas (A.L.)	DH-1B	23	62	6	15	4	1	1	6	8	15	0-1	.242	.329	.387	1	.909
Major League totals (1 year)			23	62	6	15	4	1	1	6	8	15	0-1	.242	.329	.387	1	.909

HAIRSTON, JERRY — 2B — ORIOLES

PERSONAL: Born May 29, 1976, in Des Moines, Iowa. ... 5-10/175. ... Bats right, throws right. ... Full name: Jerry W. Hairston Jr. ... Grandson of Sam Hairston, catcher with Chicago White Sox (1951) and Cincinnati and Indianapolis of Negro American League (1945-49); son of Jerry Hairston, outfielder with Chicago White Sox (1973-77 and 1981-89) and Pittsburgh Pirates (1977); nephew of John Hairston, catcher/outfielder with Chicago Cubs (1969); and nephew of Sam Hairston Jr., former minor league player in Chicago White Sox organization (1966 and 1969).
HIGH SCHOOL: Naperville (Ill.) North.
COLLEGE: Southern Illinois-Carbondale.
TRANSACTIONS/CAREER NOTES: Selected by Baltimore Orioles organization in 42nd round of free-agent draft (June 1, 1995); did not sign. ... Selected by Orioles organization in 11th round of free-agent draft (June 3, 1997). ... On Rochester disabled list (May 16-July 4, 2000).
STATISTICAL NOTES: Tied for Appalachian League lead in caught stealing with nine in 1997.
2002 GAMES PLAYED BY POSITION (MLB): 2B—119.

			BATTING														FIELDING	
Year	Team (League)	Pos.	G	AB	R	H	2B	3B	HR	RBI	BB	SO	SB-CS	Avg.	OBP	SLG	E	Avg.
1997—	Bluefield (Appl.)	SS	59	221	44	73	13	4	2	36	21	29	13-9	.330	.409	.452	14	*.949
1998—	Frederick (Caro.)	SS-2B	80	293	56	83	22	3	5	33	28	32	13-7	.283	.366	.430	24	.943
	—Bowie (East.)	2B-SS	55	221	42	72	12	3	5	37	20	25	6-4	.326	.393	.475	5	.980
	—Baltimore (A.L.)	2B	6	7	2	0	0	0	0	0	0	1	0-0	.000	.000	.000	2	.750
1999—	Rochester (I.L.)	2B-SS	107	413	65	120	24	5	7	48	30	50	19-10	.291	.363	.424	16	.968
	—Baltimore (A.L.)	2B	50	175	26	47	12	1	4	17	11	24	9-4	.269	.323	.417	0	1.000
2000—	Baltimore (A.L.)	2B	49	180	27	46	5	0	5	19	21	22	8-5	.256	.353	.367	5	.981
	—Rochester (I.L.)	2B-SS	58	201	43	59	15	1	4	21	29	32	6-4	.294	.392	.438	11	.963
	—GC Orioles (GCL)	2B	4	10	3	3	2	0	0	3	3	2	4-0	.300	.500	.500	0	1.000
	—Frederick (Caro.)	2B	2	8	1	3	2	0	0	1	1	0	0-0	.375	.444	.625	0	1.000
2001—	Baltimore (A.L.)	2B	159	532	63	124	25	5	8	47	44	73	29-11	.233	.305	.344	19	.976
2002—	Baltimore (A.L.)	2B	122	426	55	114	25	3	5	32	34	55	21-6	.268	.329	.376	11	.982
Major League totals (5 years)			386	1320	173	331	67	9	22	115	110	175	67-26	.251	.320	.365	37	.981

HALAMA, JOHN — P — MARINERS

PERSONAL: Born February 22, 1972, in Brooklyn, N.Y. ... 6-5/210. ... Throws left, bats left. ... Full name: John Thadeuz Halama. ... Name pronounced ha-LA-ma.
HIGH SCHOOL: Bishop Ford (Brooklyn, N.Y.).
COLLEGE: St. Francis (N.Y.).

TRANSACTIONS/CAREER NOTES: Selected by Houston Astros organization in 23rd round of free-agent draft (June 3, 1994). ... On New Orleans disabled list (July 2-August 6, 1998). ... Traded by Astros to Seattle Mariners (October 1, 1998), completing deal in which Mariners traded P Randy Johnson to Astros for SS Carlos Guillen, P Freddy Garcia and a player to be named later (July 31, 1998).
CAREER HITTING (MLB): 2-for-18 (.111), 2 R, 1 2B, 0 3B, 0 HR, 0 RBI.

Year League	W	L	Pct.	ERA	G	GS	CG	ShO	Sv.-Opp.	IP	H	R	ER	HR	BB-IBB	SO
1994—Auburn (NY-Penn)	4	1	.800	1.29	6	3	0	0	1-...	28.0	18	5	4	1	5-0	27
—Quad City (Midw.)	3	4	.429	4.56	9	9	1	1	0-...	51.1	63	31	26	2	18-1	37
1995—Quad City (Midw.)	1	2	.333	2.02	55	0	0	0	2-...	62.1	48	16	14	7	22-1	56
1996—Jackson (Texas)	9	10	.474	3.21	27	27	0	0	0-...	162.2	151	77	58	10	59-0	110
1997—New Orleans (A.A.)	13	3	*.813	*2.58	26	24	1	0	0-...	171.0	150	57	49	9	32-1	126
1998—Houston (N.L.)	1	1	.500	5.85	6	6	0	0	0-0	32.1	37	21	21	0	13-0	21
—New Orleans (PCL)	12	3	.800	3.20	17	17	4	1	0-...	121.0	118	48	43	11	16-1	86
1999—Seattle (A.L.)■	11	10	.524	4.22	38	24	1	1	0-0	179.0	193	88	84	20	56-3	105
2000—Seattle (A.L.)	14	9	.609	5.08	30	30	1	1	0-0	166.2	206	108	94	19	56-0	87
2001—Seattle (A.L.)	10	7	.588	4.73	31	17	0	0	0-0	110.1	132	69	58	18	26-0	50
—Tacoma (PCL)	2	0	1.000	0.47	3	3	1	1	0-...	19.0	9	2	1	1	0-0	22
2002—Seattle (A.L.)	6	5	.545	3.56	31	10	0	0	0-0	101.0	112	45	40	9	33-5	70
—Tacoma (PCL)	0	1	.000	6.14	2	2	0	0	0-...	14.2	19	11	10	0	1-1	9
A.L. totals (4 years)	41	31	.569	4.46	130	81	2	2	0-0	557.0	643	310	276	66	171-8	312
N.L. totals (1 year)	1	1	.500	5.85	6	6	0	0	0-0	32.1	37	21	21	0	13-0	21
Major League totals (5 years)	42	32	.568	4.54	136	87	2	2	0-0	589.1	680	331	297	66	184-8	333

DIVISION SERIES RECORD

Year League	W	L	Pct.	ERA	G	GS	CG	ShO	Sv.-Opp.	IP	H	R	ER	HR	BB-IBB	SO
2000—Seattle (A.L.)									Did not play.							
2001—Seattle (A.L.)	0	0	...	0.00	2	0	0	0	0-0	3.0	3	0	0	0	0-0	3

CHAMPIONSHIP SERIES RECORD

Year League	W	L	Pct.	ERA	G	GS	CG	ShO	Sv.-Opp.	IP	H	R	ER	HR	BB-IBB	SO
2000—Seattle (A.L.)	0	0	...	2.89	2	2	0	0	0-0	9.1	10	3	3	0	5-0	3
2001—Seattle (A.L.)	0	0	...	13.50	2	0	0	0	0-0	2.0	3	3	3	0	0-0	0
Champ. series totals (2 years)	0	0	...	4.76	4	2	0	0	0-0	11.1	13	6	6	0	5-0	3

HALL, BILL — SS — BREWERS

PERSONAL: Born December 28, 1979, in Nettleton, Miss. ... 6-0/175. ... Bats right, throws right. ... Full name: William Hall.
HIGH SCHOOL: Nettleton (Miss.).
TRANSACTIONS/CAREER NOTES: Selected by Milwaukee Brewers organization in sixth round of free-agent draft (June 2, 1998).
STATISTICAL NOTES: Led Pioneer League shortstops with 115 putouts, 204 assists, 357 total chances and 48 double plays in 1999. ... Led Midwest League shortstops with 397 assists and 651 total chances in 2000. ... Led International League shortstops with 207 putouts in 2002.
2002 GAMES PLAYED BY POSITION (MLB): SS—13; 3B—2.

								BATTING								FIELDING	
Year Team (League)	Pos.	G	AB	R	H	2B	3B	HR	RBI	BB	SO	SB-CS	Avg.	OBP	SLG	E	Avg.
1998—Helena (Pio.)	SS	29	85	11	15	3	0	0	5	9	27	5-5	.176	.263	.212	16	.876
1999—Ogden (Pio.)	SS	69	280	41	81	15	2	6	31	15	61	19-8	.289	.329	.421	*38	.894
2000—Beloit (Midw.)	SS	130	470	57	123	30	6	3	41	18	127	10-11	.262	.287	.370	*40	.939
2001—High Desert (Calif.)	SS	89	346	61	105	21	6	15	51	22	78	18-9	.303	.348	.529	30	.929
—Huntsville (Sou.)	SS	41	160	14	41	8	1	3	14	5	46	5-3	.256	.279	.375	15	.925
2002—Indianapolis (I.L.)	SS	134	465	35	106	20	1	4	31	25	105	17-10	.228	.272	.301	*41	.934
—Milwaukee (N.L.)	SS-3B	19	36	3	7	1	1	1	5	3	13	0-1	.194	.256	.361	2	.951
Major League totals (1 year)		19	36	3	7	1	1	1	5	3	13	0-1	.194	.256	.361	2	.951

HALL, TOBY — C — DEVIL RAYS

PERSONAL: Born October 21, 1975, in Tacoma, Wash. ... 6-3/240. ... Bats right, throws right. ... Full name: Toby Jason Hall.
HIGH SCHOOL: El Dorado (Placentia, Calif.).
COLLEGE: UNLV.
TRANSACTIONS/CAREER NOTES: Selected by Tampa Bay Devil Rays organization in ninth round of free-agent draft (June 3, 1997).
HONORS: Named International League Most Valuable Player (2001).
2002 GAMES PLAYED BY POSITION (MLB): C—83.

								BATTING								FIELDING	
Year Team (League)	Pos.	G	AB	R	H	2B	3B	HR	RBI	BB	SO	SB-CS	Avg.	OBP	SLG	E	Avg.
1997—Hudson Valley (NY-P)	C	55	200	25	50	3	0	1	27	13	33	0-0	.250	.295	.280	3	.989
1998—Charl., S.C. (S.Atl.)	C	105	377	59	121	25	1	6	50	39	32	3-7	.321	.386	.440	18	.979
1999—Orlando (Sou.)	C	46	173	20	44	7	0	9	34	4	10	1-1	.254	.269	.451	4	.986
—St. Petersburg (FSL)	C	56	212	24	63	13	1	4	36	17	9	0-2	.297	.350	.425	4	.980
2000—Orlando (Sou.)	C	68	271	37	93	14	0	9	50	17	24	3-2	.343	.378	.494	7	.984
—Durham (I.L.)	C	47	184	21	56	15	0	7	35	3	19	0-0	.304	.314	.500	2	.993
—Tampa Bay (A.L.)	C	4	12	1	2	0	0	1	1	1	0	0-0	.167	.231	.417	0	1.000
2001—Durham (I.L.)	C	94	373	59	125	28	1	19	72	29	22	1-3	.335	.385	.568	6	.987
—Tampa Bay (A.L.)	C	49	188	28	56	16	0	4	30	4	16	2-2	.298	.321	.447	5	.986
2002—Tampa Bay (A.L.)	C	85	330	37	85	19	1	6	42	17	27	0-1	.258	.293	.376	6	.989
—Durham (I.L.)	C	22	92	13	32	4	0	2	20	3	10	0-0	.348	.382	.457	1	.993
Major League totals (3 years)		138	530	66	143	35	1	11	73	22	43	2-3	.270	.302	.402	11	.988

HALLADAY, ROY — P — BLUE JAYS

PERSONAL: Born May 14, 1977, in Denver. ... 6-6/230. ... Throws right, bats right. ... Full name: Harry Leroy Halladay III.
HIGH SCHOOL: Arvada (Colo.) West.

TRANSACTIONS/CAREER NOTES: Selected by Toronto Blue Jays organization in first round (17th pick overall) of free-agent draft (June 1, 1995). ... On Syracuse disabled list (May 15-June 17, 1998). ... On Tennessee disabled list (May 16-23, 2001).
STATISTICAL NOTES: Pitched 2-1 one-hit, complete-game victory against Detroit (September 27, 1998).
CAREER HITTING (MLB): 0-for-9 (.000), 0 R, 0 2B, 0 3B, 0 HR, 0 RBI.

Year League	W	L	Pct.	ERA	G	GS	CG	ShO	Sv.-Opp.	IP	H	R	ER	HR	BB-IBB	SO
1995—GC Blue Jays (GCL)	3	5	.375	3.40	10	8	0	0	0-...	50.1	35	25	19	4	16-0	48
1996—Dunedin (FSL)	15	7	.682	2.73	27	27	2	•2	0-...	164.2	158	75	50	7	46-0	109
1997—Knoxville (Sou.)	2	3	.400	5.40	7	7	0	0	0-...	36.2	46	26	22	4	11-0	30
—Syracuse (I.L.)	7	10	.412	4.58	22	22	2	2	0-...	125.2	132	74	64	13	53-1	64
1998—Syracuse (I.L.)	9	5	.643	3.79	21	21	1	1	0-...	116.1	107	52	49	11	53-3	71
—Toronto (A.L.)	1	0	1.000	1.93	2	2	1	0	0-0	14.0	9	4	3	2	2-0	13
1999—Toronto (A.L.)	8	7	.533	3.92	36	18	1	1	1-1	149.1	156	76	65	19	79-1	82
2000—Toronto (A.L.)	4	7	.364	10.64	19	13	0	0	0-0	67.2	107	87	80	14	42-0	44
—Syracuse (I.L.)	2	3	.400	5.50	11	11	3	0	0-...	73.2	85	46	45	10	21-0	38
2001—Dunedin (FSL)	0	1	.000	3.97	13	0	0	0	2-...	22.2	28	12	10	1	3-0	15
—Tennessee (Sou.)	2	1	.667	2.12	5	5	3	0	0-...	34.0	25	9	8	2	6-0	29
—Syracuse (I.L.)	1	0	1.000	3.21	2	2	0	0	0-...	14.0	12	5	5	2	0-0	13
—Toronto (A.L.)	5	3	.625	3.16	17	16	1	1	0-0	105.1	97	41	37	3	25-0	96
2002—Toronto (A.L.)	19	7	.731	2.93	34	34	2	1	0-0	*239.1	223	93	78	10	62-6	168
Major League totals (5 years)	37	24	.607	4.11	108	83	5	3	1-1	575.2	592	301	263	48	210-7	403

ALL-STAR GAME RECORD

	W	L	Pct.	ERA	GS	CG	ShO	Sv.-Opp.	IP	H	R	ER	HR	BB-IBB	SO
All-Star Game totals (1 year)	0	0	...	27.00	0	0	0	0-0	1.0	3	3	3	1	0-0	1

HALTER, SHANE — IF — TIGERS

PERSONAL: Born November 8, 1969, in La Plata, Md. ... 6-0/180. ... Bats right, throws right. ... Full name: Shane David Halter.
HIGH SCHOOL: Hooks (Texas).
JUNIOR COLLEGE: Seminole (Okla.) Junior College.
COLLEGE: Texas.
TRANSACTIONS/CAREER NOTES: Selected by Cincinnati Reds organization in 16th round of free-agent draft (June 4, 1990); did not sign. ... Selected by Kansas City Royals organization in fifth round of free-agent draft (June 3, 1991). ... Loaned by Royals organization to Charlotte, Florida Marlins organization (April 11-May 7, 1996). ... Traded by Royals to New York Mets for OF Jonathan Guzman (March 23, 1999). ... Claimed on waivers by Detroit Tigers (March 13, 2000).
STATISTICAL NOTES: Led Northwest League shortstops with 118 putouts in 1991. ... Led Midwest League shortstops with 64 double plays in 1992. ... Led American Association with 19 sacrifice hits in 1995. ... Led International League with 17 sacrifice hits and in caught stealing with 18 in 1999. ... Career major league grand slams: 1.
2002 GAMES PLAYED BY POSITION (MLB): SS—81; 3B—30; OF—8; 2B—4; DH—2; 1B—1.

								BATTING								FIELDING	
Year Team (League)	Pos.	G	AB	R	H	2B	3B	HR	RBI	BB	SO	SB-CS	Avg.	OBP	SLG	E	Avg.
1991—Eugene (N'West)	SS	64	236	41	55	9	1	1	18	49	60	12-6	.233	.370	.292	21	.928
1992—Appleton (Midw.)	SS	80	313	50	83	22	3	3	33	41	54	21-6	.265	.349	.383	16	.959
—Baseball City (FSL)	SS	44	117	11	28	1	0	1	14	24	31	5-5	.239	.359	.274	6	.969
1993—Wilmington (Caro.)	SS	54	211	44	63	8	5	5	32	27	55	5-4	.299	.377	.455	15	.939
—Memphis (Sou.)	SS	81	306	50	79	7	0	4	20	30	74	4-7	.258	.326	.320	16	.959
1994—Memphis (Sou.)	SS	129	494	61	111	23	1	6	35	39	102	10-14	.225	.282	.312	29	.950
1995—Omaha (A.A.)	SS-2B	124	392	42	90	19	3	8	39	40	97	2-3	.230	.300	.355	19	.968
1996—Omaha (A.A.)	0-3-S-2-P	93	299	43	77	24	0	3	33	31	49	7-2	.258	.330	.368	13	.940
—Charlotte (I.L.)	0-2-DH-3-1	16	41	3	12	1	0	0	4	2	8	0-0	.293	.311	.317	1	.962
1997—Omaha (A.A.)	3B-OF-2B-SS	14	49	10	13	1	1	2	9	6	10	0-0	.265	.345	.449	2	.947
—Kansas City (A.L.)	0-2-3-S-DH	74	123	16	34	5	1	2	10	10	28	4-3	.276	.341	.382	1	.990
1998—Kansas City (A.L.)	S-0-3-2-P-1	86	204	17	45	12	0	2	13	12	38	2-5	.221	.265	.309	10	.964
—Omaha (PCL)	S-1-2-3-0	22	97	15	30	6	1	1	13	6	15	4-1	.309	.350	.423	3	.973
1999—Norfolk (I.L.)■	S-0-2-3-C	127	474	77	130	22	3	6	35	60	90	19-17	.274	.354	.371	20	.955
—New York (N.L.)	OF-SS	7	0	0	0	0	0	0	0	0	0	0-0	...	...	...	0	...
2000—Detroit (A.L.)■	IF-OF-C-P	105	238	26	62	12	2	3	27	14	49	5-2	.261	.302	.366	8	.979
2001—Detroit (A.L.)	3-S-1-DH	136	450	53	128	32	7	12	65	37	100	3-3	.284	.344	.467	26	.955
2002—Detroit (A.L.)	S-3-0-2-D-1	122	410	46	98	22	6	10	39	39	92	0-4	.239	.309	.395	21	.958
American League totals (5 years)		523	1425	158	367	83	16	29	154	112	307	14-17	.258	.315	.399	66	.964
National League totals (1 year)		7	0	0	0	0	0	0	0	0	0	0-0	...	...	...	0	...
Major League totals (6 years)		530	1425	158	367	83	16	29	154	112	307	14-17	.258	.315	.399	66	.964

RECORD AS PITCHER

Year League	W	L	Pct.	ERA	G	GS	CG	ShO	Sv.-Opp.	IP	H	R	ER	HR	BB-IBB	SO
1998—Kansas City (A.L.)	0	0	...	0.00	1	0	0	0	0-0	1.0	1	0	0	0	0-0	0
2000—Detroit (A.L.)	0	0	...	...	1	0	0	0	0-0	.0	0	0	0	0	1-0	0
Major League totals (2 years)	0	0	...	0.00	2	0	0	0	0-0	1.0	1	0	0	0	1-0	0

HAMILTON, JOEY — P

PERSONAL: Born September 9, 1970, in Statesboro, Ga. ... 6-4/240. ... Throws right, bats right. ... Full name: Johns Joseph Hamilton.
HIGH SCHOOL: Statesboro (Ga.).
COLLEGE: Georgia Southern.
TRANSACTIONS/CAREER NOTES: Selected by Baltimore Orioles organization in 28th round of free-agent draft (June 1, 1988); did not sign. ... Selected by San Diego Padres organization in first round (eighth pick overall) of free-agent draft (June 3, 1991). ... On Rancho Cucamonga disabled list (April 5-20, 1993). ... On disabled list (April 24-May 17, 1997). ... Traded by Padres to Toronto Blue Jays for P Woody Williams, P Carlos Almanzar and OF Peter Tucci (December 13, 1998). ... On Toronto disabled list (April 14-May 24, 1999); included rehabilitation assignment to Syracuse (May 10-24). ... On Toronto disabled list (March 21-August 19, 2000); included rehabilitation assignment to Syracuse (July 17-August 15). ... Released by Blue Jays (August 3, 2001). ... Signed by Cincinnati Reds organization (August 17, 2001). ... Granted free

agency (November 5, 2001). ... Re-signed by Reds organization (January 7, 2002). ... On Cincinnati disabled list (May 7-22 and July 8-August 6, 2002); included rehabilitation assignment to Louisville (July 24-August 6). ... Granted free agency (October 30, 2002).
HONORS: Named righthanded pitcher on The Sporting News college All-America second team (1990).
MISCELLANEOUS: Made an out in only appearance as pinch hitter (1998).
CAREER HITTING (MLB): 43-for-336 (.128), 19 R, 8 2B, 1 3B, 4 HR, 22 RBI.

Year League	W	L	Pct.	ERA	G	GS	CG	ShO	Sv.-Opp.	IP	H	R	ER	HR	BB-IBB	SO
1992—Charleston, S.C. (S.Atl.)	2	2	.500	3.38	7	7	0	0	0-...	34.2	37	24	13	2	4-0	35
—High Desert (Calif.)	4	3	.571	2.74	9	8	0	0	0-...	49.1	46	20	15	0	18-0	43
—Wichita (Texas)	3	0	1.000	2.86	6	6	0	0	0-...	34.2	33	12	11	2	11-1	26
1993—Rancho Cuca. (Calif.)	1	0	1.000	4.09	2	2	0	0	0-...	11.0	11	5	5	0	2-0	6
—Wichita (Texas)	4	9	.308	3.97	15	15	0	0	0-...	90.2	101	55	40	3	36-2	50
—Las Vegas (PCL)	3	2	.600	4.40	8	8	0	0	0-...	47.0	49	25	23	0	22-1	33
1994—Las Vegas (PCL)	3	5	.375	2.73	9	9	1	1	0-...	59.1	69	25	18	2	22-0	32
—San Diego (N.L.)	9	6	.600	2.98	16	16	1	1	0-0	108.2	98	40	36	7	29-3	61
1995—San Diego (N.L.)	6	9	.400	3.08	31	30	2	2	0-0	204.1	189	89	70	17	56-5	123
1996—San Diego (N.L.)	15	9	.625	4.17	34	33	3	1	0-0	211.2	206	100	98	19	83-3	184
1997—San Diego (N.L.)	12	7	.632	4.25	31	29	1	0	0-0	192.2	199	100	91	22	69-2	124
1998—San Diego (N.L.)	13	13	.500	4.27	34	34	0	0	0-0	217.1	220	113	103	15	*106-10	147
1999—Toronto (A.L.)■	7	8	.467	6.52	22	18	0	0	0-0	98.0	118	73	71	13	39-0	56
—Syracuse (I.L.)	0	1	.000	5.11	3	3	0	0	0-...	12.1	15	8	7	2	5-0	9
2000—Syracuse (I.L.)	3	2	.600	3.66	6	6	1	0	0-...	39.1	41	18	16	1	12-0	17
—Toronto (A.L.)	2	1	.667	3.55	6	6	0	0	0-0	33.0	28	13	13	3	12-0	15
2001—Toronto (A.L.)	5	8	.385	5.89	22	22	0	0	0-0	122.1	170	88	80	17	38-1	82
—Louisville (I.L.)■	1	0	1.000	5.40	1	1	0	0	0-...	5.0	4	3	3	1	1-0	1
—Cincinnati (N.L.)	1	2	.333	6.23	4	4	0	0	0-0	17.1	23	12	12	3	6-0	10
2002—Cincinnati (N.L.)	4	10	.286	5.27	39	17	0	0	1-2	124.2	136	78	73	11	50-2	85
—Louisville (I.L.)	1	0	1.000	2.57	3	3	0	0	0-...	14.0	10	4	4	2	6-0	10
A.L. totals (3 years)	14	17	.452	5.83	50	46	0	0	0-0	253.1	316	174	164	33	89-1	153
N.L. totals (7 years)	60	56	.517	4.04	189	163	7	4	1-2	1076.2	1071	532	483	94	399-25	734
Major League totals (9 years)	74	73	.503	4.38	239	209	7	4	1-2	1330.0	1387	706	647	127	488-26	887

DIVISION SERIES RECORD

Year League	W	L	Pct.	ERA	G	GS	CG	ShO	Sv.-Opp.	IP	H	R	ER	HR	BB-IBB	SO
1996—San Diego (N.L.)	0	1	.000	4.50	1	1	0	0	0-0	6.0	5	3	3	1	0-0	6
1998—San Diego (N.L.)	0	0	...	0.00	2	0	0	0	0-0	3.1	1	0	0	0	2-1	3
Division series totals (2 years)	0	1	.000	2.89	3	1	0	0	0-0	9.1	6	3	3	1	2-1	9

CHAMPIONSHIP SERIES RECORD

Year League	W	L	Pct.	ERA	G	GS	CG	ShO	Sv.-Opp.	IP	H	R	ER	HR	BB-IBB	SO
1998—San Diego (N.L.)	0	1	.000	4.91	2	1	0	0	0-0	7.1	7	4	4	1	3-0	6

WORLD SERIES RECORD

Year League	W	L	Pct.	ERA	G	GS	CG	ShO	Sv.-Opp.	IP	H	R	ER	HR	BB-IBB	SO
1998—San Diego (N.L.)	0	0	...	0.00	1	0	0	0	0-0	1.0	0	0	0	0	1-0	1

HAMMOND, CHRIS P

PERSONAL: Born January 21, 1966, in Atlanta. ... 6-1/195. ... Throws left, bats left. ... Full name: Christopher Andrew Hammond. ... Brother of Steve Hammond, outfielder with Kansas City Royals (1982).
HIGH SCHOOL: Vestavia Hills (Birmingham, Ala.).
JUNIOR COLLEGE: Gulf Coast Community College (Fla.).
COLLEGE: Alabama-Birmingham.
TRANSACTIONS/CAREER NOTES: Selected by Cincinnati Reds organization in sixth round of free-agent draft (January 14, 1986). ... On disabled list (July 27-September 1, 1991). ... Traded by Reds to Florida Marlins for 3B Gary Scott and a player to be named later (March 27, 1993); Reds acquired P Hector Carrasco to complete deal (September 10, 1993). ... On Florida disabled list (June 11-August 3, 1994); included rehabilitation assignments to Portland (June 24-25) and Brevard County (July 25-30). ... On Florida disabled list (April 16-May 13 and August 3-19, 1995); included rehabilitation assignments to Brevard County (May 4-9) and Charlotte (May 9-13). ... On Florida disabled list (June 9-July 14, 1996); included rehabilitation assignments to Brevard County (July 1-5) and Charlotte (July 5-14). ... Granted free agency (October 4, 1996). ... Signed by Boston Red Sox (December 17, 1996). ... On disabled list (June 30, 1997-remainder of season). ... Granted free agency (October 30, 1997). ... Signed by Kansas City Royals organization (January 12, 1998). ... Released by Royals (March 23, 1998). ... Signed by Marlins organization (March 27, 1998). ... Released by Marlins (June 2, 1998). ... Signed by Cleveland Indians organization (March 30, 2001). ... Released by Indians (July 3, 2001). ... Signed by Atlanta Braves organization (July 17, 2001). ... Granted free agency (October 15, 2001). ... Re-signed by Braves organization (November 19, 2001). ... On suspended list (September 13-16, 2002). ... Granted free agency (October 28, 2002).
HONORS: Named American Association Pitcher of the Year (1990).
STATISTICAL NOTES: Career major league grand slams: 1.
MISCELLANEOUS: Appeared in two games as pinch runner (1992). ... Struck out in only appearance as pinch hitter (1993).
CAREER HITTING (MLB): 48-for-235 (.204), 30 R, 7 2B, 1 3B, 4 HR, 14 RBI.

Year League	W	L	Pct.	ERA	G	GS	CG	ShO	Sv.-Opp.	IP	H	R	ER	HR	BB-IBB	SO
1986—Gulf Coast Reds (GCL)	3	2	.600	2.81	7	7	1	0	0-...	41.2	27	21	13	0	17-1	53
—Tampa (FSL)	0	2	.000	3.32	5	5	0	0	0-...	21.2	25	8	8	0	13-1	5
1987—Tampa (FSL)	11	11	.500	3.55	25	24	6	0	0-...	170.0	174	81	67	10	60-1	126
1988—Chattanooga (Sou.)	*16	5	.762	*1.72	26	26	4	2	0-...	182.2	127	48	35	2	77-3	127
1989—Nashville (A.A.)	11	7	.611	3.38	24	24	3	1	0-...	157.1	144	69	59	7	96-1	142
1990—Nashville (A.A.)	*15	1	*.938	*2.17	24	24	5	*3	0-...	149.0	118	43	36	7	63-1	*149
—Cincinnati (N.L.)	0	2	.000	6.35	3	3	0	0	0-0	11.1	13	9	8	2	12-1	4
1991—Cincinnati (N.L.)	7	7	.500	4.06	20	18	0	0	0-0	99.2	92	51	45	4	48-3	50
1992—Cincinnati (N.L.)	7	10	.412	4.21	28	26	0	0	0-0	147.1	149	75	69	13	55-6	79
1993—Florida (N.L.)■	11	12	.478	4.66	32	32	1	0	0-0	191.0	207	106	99	18	66-2	108
1994—Florida (N.L.)	4	4	.500	3.07	13	13	1	1	0-0	73.1	79	30	25	5	23-1	40
—Portland (East.)	0	0	...	0.00	1	1	0	0	0-...	2.0	0	0	0	0	0-0	2
—Brevard County (FSL)	0	0	...	1.23	2	2	0	0	0-...	7.1	4	3	1	0	3-0	5

Year	League	W	L	Pct.	ERA	G	GS	CG	ShO	Sv.-Opp.	IP	H	R	ER	HR	BB-IBB	SO
1995—	Brevard County (FSL)	0	0	...	0.00	1	1	0	0	0-...	4.0	3	1	0	0	0-0	4
	—Charlotte (I.L.)	0	0	...	0.00	1	1	0	0	0-...	4.0	3	1	0	0	2-0	3
	—Florida (N.L.)	9	6	.600	3.80	25	24	3	2	0-0	161.0	157	73	68	17	47-2	126
1996—	Florida (N.L.)	5	8	.385	6.56	38	9	0	0	0-0	81.0	104	65	59	14	27-3	50
	—Brevard County (FSL)	0	0	...	0.00	1	1	0	0	0-...	4.0	3	0	0	0	0-0	8
	—Charlotte (I.L.)	1	0	1.000	7.20	1	1	0	0	0-...	5.0	5	4	4	0	0-0	3
1997—	Boston (A.L.)■	3	4	.429	5.92	29	8	0	0	1-2	65.1	81	45	43	5	27-4	48
1998—	Charlotte (I.L.)■	1	3	.250	4.82	5	5	0	0	0-...	28.0	35	17	15	2	14-2	22
	—Florida (N.L.)	0	2	.000	6.59	3	3	0	0	0-0	13.2	20	11	10	3	8-0	8
1999—										Did not play.							
2000—										Did not play.							
2001—	Buffalo (I.L.)■	7	3	.700	3.31	28	4	0	0	0-...	51.2	53	22	19	5	20-1	54
	—Richmond (I.L.)■	3	1	.750	2.35	21	0	0	0	1-...	30.2	32	9	8	0	4-0	29
2002—	Atlanta (N.L.)	7	2	.778	0.95	63	0	0	0	0-2	76.0	53	15	8	1	31-9	63
A.L. totals (1 year)		3	4	.429	5.92	29	8	0	0	1-2	65.1	81	45	43	5	27-4	48
N.L. totals (9 years)		50	53	.485	4.12	225	128	5	3	0-2	854.1	874	435	391	77	317-27	528
Major League totals (10 years)		53	57	.482	4.25	254	136	5	3	1-4	919.2	955	480	434	82	344-31	576

DIVISION SERIES RECORD

Year	League	W	L	Pct.	ERA	G	GS	CG	ShO	Sv.-Opp.	IP	H	R	ER	HR	BB-IBB	SO
2002—	Atlanta (N.L.)	0	0	...	6.75	3	0	0	0	0-0	2.2	2	2	2	0	3-1	2

HAMMONDS, JEFFREY — OF — BREWERS

PERSONAL: Born March 5, 1971, in Scotch Plains, N.J. ... 6-0/200. ... Bats right, throws right. ... Full name: Jeffrey Bryan Hammonds. ... Brother of Reggie Hammonds, outfielder with Pittsburgh Pirates organization (1984-86).

HIGH SCHOOL: Scotch Plains (N.J.)-Fanwood.

COLLEGE: Stanford.

TRANSACTIONS/CAREER NOTES: Selected by Toronto Blue Jays organization in ninth round of free-agent draft (June 5, 1989); did not sign. ... Selected by Baltimore Orioles organization in first round (fourth pick overall) of free-agent draft (June 1, 1992). ... On Rochester disabled list (May 17-28, 1993). ... On Baltimore disabled list (August 8-September 1 and September 28, 1993-remainder of season); included rehabilitation assignment to Bowie (August 28-September 1). ... On Baltimore disabled list (May 4-June 16, 1994; July 18-September 3, 1995; and August 17-September 22, 1996). ... On Baltimore disabled list (June 3-July 11, 1998); included rehabilitation assignment to Bowie (July 9-11). ... Traded by Orioles to Cincinnati Reds for 3B/OF Willie Greene (August 10, 1998). ... Traded by Reds with P Stan Belinda to Colorado Rockies for OF Dante Bichette and cash (October 30, 1999). ... On disabled list (April 4-22, 2000). ... Granted free agency (October 27, 2000). ... Signed by Milwaukee Brewers (December 22, 2000). ... On Milwaukee disabled list (June 7, 2001-remainder of season); included rehabilitation assignment to Arizona League Brewers (July 15-18).

HONORS: Named outfielder on The Sporting News college All-America team (1990 and 1992).

STATISTICAL NOTES: Hit three home runs in one game (May 19, 1999). ... Had 18-game hitting streak (May 29-June 21, 2000). ... Career major league grand slams: 2.

MISCELLANEOUS: Member of 1992 U.S. Olympic baseball team.

2002 GAMES PLAYED BY POSITION (MLB): OF—125.

			BATTING														FIELDING	
Year	Team (League)	Pos.	G	AB	R	H	2B	3B	HR	RBI	BB	SO	SB-CS	Avg.	OBP	SLG	E	Avg.
1992—	Hagerstown (East.)								Did not play.									
1993—	Bowie (East.)	OF	24	92	13	26	3	0	3	10	9	18	4-3	.283	.356	.413	0	1.000
	—Rochester (I.L.)	OF	36	151	25	47	9	1	5	23	5	27	6-3	.311	.338	.483	0	1.000
	—Baltimore (A.L.)	OF-DH	33	105	10	32	8	0	3	19	2	16	4-0	.305	.312	.467	2	.961
1994—	Baltimore (A.L.)	OF	68	250	45	74	18	2	8	31	17	39	5-0	.296	.339	.480	6	.962
1995—	Baltimore (A.L.)	OF-DH	57	178	18	43	9	1	4	23	9	30	4-2	.242	.279	.371	1	.989
	—Bowie (East.)	OF-DH	9	31	7	12	3	1	1	11	10	7	3-0	.387	.524	.645	1	.923
1996—	Baltimore (A.L.)	OF-DH	71	248	38	56	10	1	9	27	23	53	3-3	.226	.301	.383	3	.980
	—Rochester (I.L.)	OF-DH	34	125	24	34	4	2	3	19	19	19	3-1	.272	.365	.408	1	.987
1997—	Baltimore (A.L.)	OF-DH	118	397	71	105	19	3	21	55	32	73	15-1	.264	.323	.486	5	.980
1998—	Baltimore (A.L.)	OF-DH	63	171	36	46	12	1	6	28	26	38	7-2	.269	.369	.456	2	.980
	—Bowie (East.)	OF	3	6	4	2	0	0	0	0	2	2	3-1	.333	.556	.333	0	1.000
	—Cincinnati (N.L.)■	OF	26	86	14	26	4	1	0	11	13	18	1-1	.302	.390	.372	1	.985
1999—	Cincinnati (N.L.)	OF	123	262	43	73	13	0	17	41	27	64	3-6	.279	.347	.523	0	1.000
2000—	Colorado (N.L.)■	OF	122	454	94	152	24	2	20	106	44	83	14-7	.335	.395	.529	2	.991
2001—	Milwaukee (N.L.)■	OF	49	174	20	43	11	1	6	21	14	42	5-3	.247	.314	.425	2	.982
	—Ariz. Brewers (Ariz.)	OF	1	3	0	1	0	0	0	0	0	0	0-0	.333	.333	.333	0	...
2002—	Milwaukee (N.L.)	OF	128	448	47	115	26	5	9	41	52	86	4-5	.257	.332	.397	2	.992
American League totals (6 years)			410	1349	218	356	76	8	51	183	109	249	38-8	.264	.322	.446	19	.976
National League totals (5 years)			448	1424	218	409	78	9	52	220	150	293	27-22	.287	.356	.464	7	.991
Major League totals (10 years)			858	2773	436	765	154	17	103	403	259	542	65-30	.276	.340	.455	26	.984

DIVISION SERIES RECORD

			BATTING														FIELDING	
Year	Team (League)	Pos.	G	AB	R	H	2B	3B	HR	RBI	BB	SO	SB-CS	Avg.	OBP	SLG	E	Avg.
1997—	Baltimore (A.L.)	OF-PR	4	10	3	1	1	0	0	2	2	2	1-0	.100	.250	.200	0	1.000

CHAMPIONSHIP SERIES RECORD

			BATTING														FIELDING	
Year	Team (League)	Pos.	G	AB	R	H	2B	3B	HR	RBI	BB	SO	SB-CS	Avg.	OBP	SLG	E	Avg.
1997—	Baltimore (A.L.)	PH-OF-PR	5	3	0	0	0	0	0	0	1	2	1-0	.000	.250	.000	0	1.000

ALL-STAR GAME RECORD

	AB	R	H	2B	3B	HR	RBI	BB	SO	SB-CS	Avg.	OBP	SLG	E	Avg.
All-Star Game totals (1 year)	1	0	0	0	0	0	0	0	0	0-0	.000	.000	.000	0	...

HAMPTON, MIKE — P — ROCKIES

PERSONAL: Born September 9, 1972, in Brooksville, Fla. ... 5-10/180. ... Throws left, bats right. ... Full name: Michael William Hampton.
HIGH SCHOOL: Crystal River (Fla.).
TRANSACTIONS/CAREER NOTES: Selected by Seattle Mariners organization in sixth round of free-agent draft (June 4, 1990). ... Traded by Mariners with OF Mike Felder to Houston Astros for OF Eric Anthony (December 10, 1993). ... On disabled list (May 15-June 13, 1995; June 16-July 4, 1998). ... Traded by Astros with OF Derek Bell to New York Mets for OF Roger Cedeno, P Octavio Dotel and P Kyle Kessel (December 23, 1999). ... Granted free agency (November 4, 2000). ... Signed by Colorado Rockies (December 9, 2000). ... On suspended list (October 3-8, 2001).
RECORDS: Shares N.L. single-season record for most home runs by pitcher—7 (2001).
HONORS: Named N.L. Pitcher of the Year by The Sporting News (1999). ... Named lefthanded pitcher on The Sporting News N.L. All-Star team (1999). ... Named pitcher on The Sporting News N.L. Silver Slugger team (1999 and 2000). ... Named pitcher on N.L. Silver Slugger team (2001 and 2002).
STATISTICAL NOTES: Led Arizona League with 10 wild pitches in 1990. ... Pitched 6-0 no-hit victory for San Bernardino against Visalia (May 31, 1991).
MISCELLANEOUS: Appeared in two games as pinch runner (1996). ... Scored run in only appearance as pinch runner (2000). ... Struck out in only appearance as pinch hitter (2000). ... Appeared in eight games as pinch runner (2001). ... Appeared in three games as pinch hitter (2001).
CAREER HITTING (MLB): 131-for-515 (.254), 71 R, 13 2B, 4 3B, 10 HR, 52 RBI.

Year League	W	L	Pct.	ERA	G	GS	CG	ShO	Sv.-Opp.	IP	H	R	ER	HR	BB-IBB	SO
1990— Arizona Mariners (Ariz.)	•7	2	.778	2.66	14	•13	0	0	0-...	64.1	52	32	19	0	40-0	59
1991— San Bernardino (Calif.)	1	7	.125	5.25	18	15	1	1	0-...	73.2	71	58	43	3	47-1	57
— Bellingham (N'West)	5	2	.714	1.58	9	9	0	0	0-...	57.0	32	15	10	0	26-0	65
1992— San Bernardino (Calif.)	13	8	.619	3.12	25	25	6	•2	0-...	170.0	163	75	59	8	66-1	132
— Jacksonville (Sou.)	0	1	.000	4.35	2	2	1	0	0-...	10.1	13	5	5	0	1-0	6
1993— Seattle (A.L.)	1	3	.250	9.53	13	3	0	0	1-1	17.0	28	20	18	3	17-3	8
— Jacksonville (Sou.)	6	4	.600	3.71	15	14	1	0	0-...	87.1	71	43	36	3	33-1	84
1994— Houston (N.L.)■	2	1	.667	3.70	44	0	0	0	0-1	41.1	46	19	17	4	16-1	24
1995— Houston (N.L.)	9	8	.529	3.35	24	24	0	0	0-0	150.2	141	73	56	13	49-3	115
1996— Houston (N.L.)	10	10	.500	3.59	27	27	2	1	0-0	160.1	175	79	64	12	49-1	101
1997— Houston (N.L.)	15	10	.600	3.83	34	34	7	2	0-0	223.0	217	105	95	16	77-2	139
1998— Houston (N.L.)	11	7	.611	3.36	32	32	1	1	0-0	211.2	227	92	79	18	81-1	137
1999— Houston (N.L.)	*22	4	*.846	2.90	34	34	3	2	0-0	239.0	206	86	77	12	101-2	177
2000— New York (N.L.)■	15	10	.600	3.14	33	33	3	1	0-0	217.2	194	89	76	10	99-5	151
2001— Colorado (N.L.)■	14	13	.519	5.41	32	32	2	1	0-0	203.0	236	138	122	31	85-7	122
2002— Colorado (N.L.)	7	15	.318	6.15	30	30	0	0	0-0	178.2	228	*135	122	24	91-4	74
A.L. totals (1 year)	1	3	.250	9.53	13	3	0	0	1-1	17.0	28	20	18	3	17-3	8
N.L. totals (9 years)	105	78	.574	3.92	290	246	18	8	0-1	1625.1	1670	816	708	140	648-26	1040
Major League totals (10 years)	106	81	.567	3.98	303	249	18	8	1-2	1642.1	1698	836	726	143	665-29	1048

DIVISION SERIES RECORD

Year League	W	L	Pct.	ERA	G	GS	CG	ShO	Sv.-Opp.	IP	H	R	ER	HR	BB-IBB	SO
1997— Houston (N.L.)	0	1	.000	11.57	1	1	0	0	0-0	4.2	2	6	6	1	8-0	2
1998— Houston (N.L.)	0	0	...	1.50	1	1	0	0	0-0	6.0	2	1	1	0	1-0	2
1999— Houston (N.L.)	0	0	...	3.86	1	1	0	0	0-0	7.0	6	3	3	1	1-0	9
2000— New York (N.L.)	0	1	.000	8.44	1	1	0	0	0-0	5.1	6	5	5	1	3-1	2
Division series totals (4 years)	0	2	.000	5.87	4	4	0	0	0-0	23.0	16	15	15	3	13-1	15

CHAMPIONSHIP SERIES RECORD

NOTES: Named Most Valuable Player (2000).

Year League	W	L	Pct.	ERA	G	GS	CG	ShO	Sv.-Opp.	IP	H	R	ER	HR	BB-IBB	SO
2000— New York (N.L.)	2	0	1.000	0.00	2	2	1	1	0-0	16.0	9	0	0	0	4-0	12

WORLD SERIES RECORD

Year League	W	L	Pct.	ERA	G	GS	CG	ShO	Sv.-Opp.	IP	H	R	ER	HR	BB-IBB	SO
2000— New York (N.L.)	0	1	.000	6.00	1	1	0	0	0-0	6.0	8	4	4	1	5-1	4

ALL-STAR GAME RECORD

	W	L	Pct.	ERA	GS	CG	ShO	Sv.-Opp.	IP	H	R	ER	HR	BB-IBB	SO
All-Star Game totals (2 years)	0	0	...	0.00	0	0	0	0-0	1.2	1	1	0	0	0-0	0

HANCOCK, JOSH — P — RED SOX

PERSONAL: Born April 11, 1978, in Cleveland, Miss. ... 6-3/217. ... Throws right, bats right. ... Full name: Joshua Morgan Hancock.
HIGH SCHOOL: Vestavia Hills (Ala.).
COLLEGE: Auburn.
TRANSACTIONS/CAREER NOTES: Selected by Boston Red Sox organization in fifth round of free-agent draft (June 2, 1998). ... On disabled list (July 18-30 and August 26, 2001-remainder of season). ... On Trenton disabled list (June 4-July 3, 2002).
CAREER HITTING (MLB): 0-for-0 (.000), 0 R, 0 2B, 0 3B, 0 HR, 0 RBI.

Year League	W	L	Pct.	ERA	G	GS	CG	ShO	Sv.-Opp.	IP	H	R	ER	HR	BB-IBB	SO
1998— Gulf Coast Red Sox (GCL)	1	1	.500	3.38	5	1	0	0	0-...	13.1	9	5	5	1	3-0	21
— Lowell (NY-Penn)	0	1	.000	2.25	1	1	0	0	0-...	4.0	5	2	1	0	4-0	4
1999— Augusta (S.Atl.)	6	8	.429	3.80	25	25	0	0	0-...	139.2	154	79	59	12	46-0	106
2000— Sarasota (FSL)	5	10	.333	4.45	26	24	1	0	0-...	143.2	164	89	71	9	37-0	95
2001— Trenton (East.)	8	6	.571	3.65	24	24	0	0	0-...	130.2	138	60	53	8	37-0	119
2002— Trenton (East.)	3	4	.429	3.61	15	14	2	0	1-...	84.2	82	40	34	9	18-0	69
— Pawtucket (I.L.)	4	2	.667	3.45	8	8	0	0	0-...	44.1	39	20	17	2	26-0	29
— Boston (A.L.)	0	1	.000	3.68	3	1	0	0	0-0	7.1	5	3	3	1	2-0	6
Major League totals (1 year)	0	1	.000	3.68	3	1	0	0	0-0	7.1	5	3	3	1	2-0	6

HANEY, CHRIS — P

PERSONAL: Born November 16, 1968, in Baltimore. ... 6-3/210. ... Throws left, bats left. ... Full name: Christopher Deane Haney. ... Son of Larry Haney, catcher with five major league teams (1966-70 and 1972-78), and coach, Milwaukee Brewers (1978-91).

HIGH SCHOOL: Orange County (Va.).

COLLEGE: UNC Charlotte.

TRANSACTIONS/CAREER NOTES: Selected by Milwaukee Brewers organization in 25th round of free-agent draft (June 2, 1987); did not sign. ... Selected by Montreal Expos organization in second round of free-agent draft (June 4, 1990). ... On Indianapolis disabled list (June 17-25, 1992). ... Traded by Expos with P Bill Sampen to Kansas City Royals for 3B Sean Berry and P Archie Corbin (August 29, 1992). ... On disabled list (July 13, 1995-remainder of season). ... On Kansas City disabled list (April 15-June 17 and June 27-September 3, 1997); included rehabilitation assignments to Omaha (May 31-June 13) and Wichita (August 25-29). ... On Kansas City disabled list (June 8-24, 1998); included rehabilitation assignment to Gulf Coast Royals (June 22). ... Contract sold by Royals to Chicago Cubs (September 12, 1998). ... Granted free agency (October 27, 1998). ... Signed by Los Angeles Dodgers organization (January 22, 1999). ... Released by Dodgers (April 1, 1999). ... Signed by Cleveland Indians organzation (April 6, 1999). ... On Buffalo disabled list (May 3-June 11, 1999). ... Granted free agency (October 28, 1999). ... Re-signed by Indians organization (January 8, 2000). ... On Buffalo disabled list (April 6-June 22, 2000). ... Released by Indians (October 6, 2000). ... Signed by Texas Rangers organization (January 10, 2001). ... Released by Rangers (March 26, 2001). ... Signed by Boston Red Sox organization (March 30, 2002). ... Released by Red Sox (August 29, 2002).

MISCELLANEOUS: Appeared in one game as pinch runner with Montreal (1992).

CAREER HITTING (MLB): 4-for-36 (.111), 2 R, 0 2B, 0 3B, 0 HR, 4 RBI.

Year	League	W	L	Pct.	ERA	G	GS	CG	ShO	Sv.-Opp.	IP	H	R	ER	HR	BB-IBB	SO
1990	—Jamestown (NY-Penn)	3	0	1.000	0.96	6	5	0	0	1-...	28.0	17	3	3	1	10-0	26
	—Rockford (Midw.)	2	4	.333	2.21	8	8	3	0	0-...	53.0	40	15	13	1	6-0	45
	—Jacksonville (Sou.)	1	0	1.000	0.00	1	1	0	0	0-...	6.0	6	0	0	0	3-0	6
1991	—Harrisburg (East.)	5	3	.625	2.16	12	12	3	0	0-...	83.1	65	21	20	4	31-1	68
	—Montreal (N.L.)	3	7	.300	4.04	16	16	0	0	0-0	84.2	94	49	38	6	43-1	51
	—Indianapolis (A.A.)	1	1	.500	4.35	2	2	0	0	0-...	10.1	14	10	5	2	6-0	8
1992	—Montreal (N.L.)	2	3	.400	5.45	9	6	1	1	0-0	38.0	40	25	23	6	10-0	27
	—Indianapolis (A.A.)	5	2	.714	5.14	15	15	0	0	0-...	84.0	88	50	48	4	42-0	61
	—Kansas City (A.L.)■	2	3	.400	3.86	7	7	1	1	0-0	42.0	35	18	18	5	16-2	27
1993	—Omaha (A.A.)	6	1	.857	2.27	8	7	2	0	0-...	47.2	43	13	12	2	14-0	32
	—Kansas City (A.L.)	9	9	.500	6.02	23	23	1	1	0-0	124.0	141	87	83	13	53-2	65
1994	—Kansas City (A.L.)	2	2	.500	7.31	6	6	0	0	0-0	28.1	36	25	23	2	11-1	18
	—Omaha (A.A.)	8	7	.533	5.25	18	18	1	0	0-...	104.2	125	77	61	11	37-0	78
1995	—Kansas City (A.L.)	3	4	.429	3.65	16	13	1	0	0-0	81.1	78	35	33	7	33-0	31
1996	—Kansas City (A.L.)	10	14	.417	4.70	35	35	4	1	0-0	228.0	*267	136	119	29	51-0	115
1997	—Kansas City (A.L.)	1	2	.333	4.38	8	3	0	0	0-0	24.2	29	16	12	1	5-2	16
	—Omaha (A.A.)	1	0	1.000	3.79	4	3	0	0	0-...	19.0	16	12	8	3	6-0	7
	—Wichita (Texas)	0	1	.000	2.70	2	2	0	0	0-...	6.2	5	3	2	1	0-0	2
1998	—Kansas City (A.L.)	6	6	.500	7.03	33	12	0	0	0-1	97.1	125	78	76	18	36-0	51
	—Gulf Coast Royals (GCL)	0	1	.000	0.00	1	1	0	0	0-...	2.1	2	2	0	0	0-0	1
	—Chicago (N.L.)■	0	0	...	7.20	5	0	0	0	0-0	5.0	3	4	4	2	1-0	4
1999	—Buffalo (I.L.)■	2	5	.286	3.22	13	10	0	0	0-...	58.2	50	25	21	4	22-1	37
	—Cleveland (A.L.)	0	2	.000	4.69	13	4	0	0	0-0	40.1	43	22	21	3	16-0	22
2000	—Buffalo (I.L.)	8	3	.727	2.44	15	13	1	1	0-...	92.1	87	27	25	8	17-0	70
	—Cleveland (A.L.)	0	0	...	9.00	1	0	0	0	0-0	1.0	1	1	1	0	1-0	0
2002	—Pawtucket (I.L.)■	2	0	1.000	2.79	25	0	0	0	4-...	29.0	27	10	9	1	10-0	31
	—Boston (A.L.)	0	0	...	4.20	24	0	0	0	1-1	30.0	32	14	14	2	10-2	15
A.L. totals (10 years)		33	42	.440	5.16	166	103	7	3	1-2	697.0	787	432	400	80	232-9	360
N.L. totals (3 years)		5	10	.333	4.58	30	22	1	1	0-0	127.2	137	78	65	14	54-1	82
Major League totals (11 years)		38	52	.422	5.07	196	125	8	4	1-2	824.2	924	510	465	94	286-10	442

HANSEN, DAVE — 1B/3B

PERSONAL: Born November 24, 1968, in Long Beach, Calif. ... 6-0/195. ... Bats left, throws right. ... Full name: David Andrew Hansen.

HIGH SCHOOL: Rowland (Long Beach, Calif.).

TRANSACTIONS/CAREER NOTES: Selected by Los Angeles Dodgers organization in second round of free-agent draft (June 2, 1986). ... On disabled list (May 9-28, 1994). ... Granted free agency (November 27, 1996). ... Signed by Chicago Cubs organization (January 22, 1997). ... Granted free agency (October 27, 1997). ... Signed by Hanshin Tigers of Japan Central League (November 7, 1997). ... Signed by Dodgers (January 11, 1999). ... On Los Angeles disabled list (March 23-April 26, 2001); included rehabilitation assignment to Vero Beach (April 21-27). ... Granted free agency (October 29, 2002).

RECORDS: Shares major league single-season record for most home runs by pinch-hitter—7 (2000).

STATISTICAL NOTES: Led California League third basemen with 45 errors in 1987. ... Led Florida State League with 210 total bases and tied for lead with nine sacrifice flies in 1988. ... Led Florida State League third basemen with 102 putouts, 263 assists, 383 total chances and 24 double plays in 1988. ... Led Texas League third basemen with 92 putouts in 1989. ... Led Pacific Coast League third basemen with .926 fielding percentage, 254 assists, 349 total chances and 25 double plays in 1990. ... Career major league grand slams: 1.

2002 GAMES PLAYED BY POSITION (MLB): 1B—27; 3B—11; DH—4.

					BATTING												FIELDING	
Year	Team (League)	Pos.	G	AB	R	H	2B	3B	HR	RBI	BB	SO	SB-CS	Avg.	OBP	SLG	E	Avg.
1986	—Great Falls (Pio.)	OF-3B-C-2B	61	204	39	61	7	3	1	36	27	28	9-3	.299	.381	.377	7	.901
1987	—Bakersfield (Calif.)	3B-OF	132	432	68	113	22	1	3	38	65	61	4-2	.262	.363	.338	†45	.860
1988	—Vero Beach (FSL)	3B	135	512	68	*149	•28	6	7	*81	56	46	2-2	.291	.360	.410	18	*.953
1989	—San Antonio (Texas)	3B	121	464	72	138	21	4	6	52	50	44	3-2	.297	.365	.399	16	*.949
	—Albuquerque (PCL)	3B	6	30	6	8	1	0	2	10	2	3	0-0	.267	.313	.500	3	.786
1990	—Albuquerque (PCL)	3B-OF-SS	135	487	90	154	20	3	11	92	*90	54	9-4	.316	.419	.437	26	†.926
	—Los Angeles (N.L.)	3B	5	7	0	1	0	0	0	1	0	3	0-0	.143	.143	.143	1	.500
1991	—Albuquerque (PCL)	3B-SS	68	254	42	77	11	1	5	40	49	33	4-3	.303	.406	.413	6	.966
	—Los Angeles (N.L.)	3B-SS	53	56	3	15	4	0	1	5	2	12	1-0	.268	.293	.393	0	1.000
1992	—Los Angeles (N.L.)	3B	132	341	30	73	11	0	6	22	34	49	0-2	.214	.286	.299	8	*.968
1993	—Los Angeles (N.L.)	3B	84	105	13	38	3	0	4	30	21	13	0-1	.362	.465	.505	3	.927
1994	—Los Angeles (N.L.)	3B	40	44	3	15	3	0	0	5	5	5	0-0	.341	.408	.409	1	.857
1995	—Los Angeles (N.L.)	3B	100	181	19	52	10	0	1	14	28	28	0-0	.287	.384	.359	7	.933
1996	—Los Angeles (N.L.)	3B-1B	80	104	7	23	1	0	0	6	11	22	0-0	.221	.293	.231	1	.988

Year	Team (League)	Pos.	G	AB	R	H	2B	3B	HR	RBI	BB	SO	SB-CS	Avg.	OBP	SLG	E	Avg.
			BATTING														FIELDING	
1997—	Chicago (N.L.)■	3B-1B-2B	90	151	19	47	8	2	3	21	31	32	1-2	.311	.429	.450	7	.929
1998—	Hanshin (Jap. Cen.)■	3B	121	400	42	101	13	1	11	55	42	89	0-...	.253	...	.373	...	...
1999—	Los Angeles (N.L.)■	1-3-DH-0	100	107	14	27	8	1	2	17	26	20	0-0	.252	.404	.402	3	.962
2000—	Los Angeles (N.L.)	1-3-DH-0	102	121	18	35	6	2	8	26	26	32	0-1	.289	.415	.570	2	.973
2001—	Vero Beach (FSL)	3B	3	9	1	0	0	0	0	0	1	2	0-0	.000	.100	.000	0	1.000
	—Los Angeles (N.L.)	1B-3B-SS-DH	92	140	13	33	10	0	2	20	32	29	0-1	.236	.371	.350	6	.973
2002—	Los Angeles (N.L.)	1B-3B-DH	96	120	15	35	6	0	2	17	14	22	1-0	.292	.363	.392	2	.980
Major League totals (12 years)			974	1477	154	394	70	5	29	184	230	267	3-7	.267	.365	.380	41	.962

DIVISION SERIES RECORD

Year	Team (League)	Pos.	G	AB	R	H	2B	3B	HR	RBI	BB	SO	SB-CS	Avg.	OBP	SLG	E	Avg.
			BATTING														FIELDING	
1995—	Los Angeles (N.L.)	PH	3	3	0	2	0	0	0	0	0	0	0-0	.667	.667	.667	...	...
1996—	Los Angeles (N.L.)	PH-3B	2	2	0	0	0	0	0	0	0	0	0-0	.000	.000	.000	0	1.000
Division series totals (2 years)			5	5	0	2	0	0	0	0	0	0	0-0	.400	.400	.400	0	1.000

HARANG, AARON — P — ATHLETICS

PERSONAL: Born May 9, 1978, in San Diego. ... 6-7/240. ... Throws right, bats right. ... Full name: Aaron Michael Harang.

HIGH SCHOOL: Patrick Henry (San Diego).

COLLEGE: San Diego State.

TRANSACTIONS/CAREER NOTES: Selected by Texas Rangers organization in sixth round of free-agent draft (June 2, 1999). ... Traded by Rangers with P Ryan Cullen to Oakland Athletics for 2B Randy Velarde (December 12, 2000).

CAREER HITTING (MLB): 0-for-3 (.000), 0 R, 0 2B, 0 3B, 0 HR, 0 RBI.

Year	League	W	L	Pct.	ERA	G	GS	CG	ShO	Sv.-Opp.	IP	H	R	ER	HR	BB-IBB	SO
1999—	Pulaski (Appl.)	9	2	.818	2.30	16	10	1	1	1-...	78.1	64	22	20	5	17-1	87
2000—	Charlotte (FSL)	13	5	.722	3.32	28	27	3	2	0-...	157.0	128	68	58	10	50-0	136
2001—	Midland (Texas)■	10	8	.556	4.14	27	27	0	0	0-...	150.0	173	81	69	9	37-1	112
2002—	Midland (Texas)	2	0	1.000	1.08	3	3	0	0	0-...	16.2	12	3	2	0	7-0	21
	—Sacramento (PCL)	3	3	.500	3.26	8	8	0	0	0-...	38.2	41	17	14	1	9-0	39
	—Oakland (A.L.)	5	4	.556	4.83	16	15	0	0	0-0	78.1	78	44	42	7	45-2	64
Major League totals (1 year)		5	4	.556	4.83	16	15	0	0	0-0	78.1	78	44	42	7	45-2	64

HARNISCH, PETE — P

PERSONAL: Born September 23, 1966, in Huntington, N.Y. ... 6-0/228. ... Throws right, bats right. ... Full name: Peter Thomas Harnisch.

HIGH SCHOOL: Commack (N.Y.).

COLLEGE: Fordham.

TRANSACTIONS/CAREER NOTES: Selected by Baltimore Orioles organization in supplemental round ("sandwich pick" between first and second round, 27th pick overall) of free-agent draft (June 2, 1987); pick received as compensation for Cleveland Indians signing Type A free-agent C Rick Dempsey. ... Traded by Orioles with P Curt Schilling and OF Steve Finley to Houston Astros for 1B Glenn Davis (January 10, 1991). ... On suspended list (July 7-9, 1992). ... On Houston disabled list (May 23-June 30, 1994); included rehabilitation assignment to Tucson (June 25-26). ... Traded by Astros to New York Mets for two players to be named later (November 28, 1994); Astros acquired P Andy Beckerman (December 6, 1994) and P Juan Castillo (April 12, 1995) to complete deal. ... Granted free agency (December 23, 1994). ... Re-signed by Mets (April 7, 1995). ... On disabled list (August 2, 1995-remainder of season). ... On New York disabled list (March 26-April 14, 1996); included rehabilitation assignment to St. Lucie (March 30-April 14). ... On New York suspended list (May 22-31, 1996). ... On New York disabled list (April 2-August 5, 1997); included rehabilitation assignments to Gulf Coast Mets (July 7-10), St. Lucie (July 11-19) and Norfolk (July 20-August 5). ... Traded by Mets to Milwaukee Brewers for OF Donny Moore (August 31, 1997). ... Granted free agency (October 27, 1997). ... Signed by Cincinnati Reds (January 21, 1998). ... On Cincinnati disabled list (May 5-June 29, 2000); included rehabilitation assignment to Louisville (June 25-29). ... On Cincinnati disabled list (May 8, 2001-remainder of season); included rehabilitation assignment to Louisville (June 9-14). ... Granted free agency (November 5, 2001). ... Signed by Colorado Rockies (February 25, 2002). ... On disabled list (March 22, 2002-entire season). ... Granted free agency (October 28, 2002).

RECORDS: Shares major league record for striking out side on nine pitches (September 6, 1991, seventh inning). ... Shares N.L. record for most consecutive home runs allowed in one inning—4 (July 23, 1996, first inning).

STATISTICAL NOTES: Pitched 4-0 one-hit, complete-game victory against Chicago (July 10, 1993). ... Pitched 3-0 one-hit, complete-game victory against San Diego (September 17, 1993).

MISCELLANEOUS: Appeared in one game as pinch runner with Houston (1994). ... Appeared in one game as pinch runner with New York (1996). ... Appeared in two games as pinch runner (2000). ... Appeared in one game as pinch runner (2001).

CAREER HITTING (MLB): 66-for-513 (.129), 40 R, 19 2B, 0 3B, 2 HR, 29 RBI.

Year	League	W	L	Pct.	ERA	G	GS	CG	ShO	Sv.-Opp.	IP	H	R	ER	HR	BB-IBB	SO
1987—	Bluefield (Appl.)	3	1	.750	2.56	9	9	0	0	0-...	52.2	38	19	15	0	26-1	64
	—Hagerstown (Caro.)	1	2	.333	2.25	4	4	0	0	0-...	20.0	17	7	5	0	14-0	18
1988—	Charlotte (Sou.)	7	6	.538	2.58	20	20	4	2	0-...	132.1	113	55	38	6	52-4	141
	—Rochester (I.L.)	4	1	.800	2.16	7	7	3	2	0-...	58.1	44	16	14	2	14-1	43
	—Baltimore (A.L.)	0	2	.000	5.54	2	2	0	0	0-0	13.0	13	8	8	1	9-1	10
1989—	Baltimore (A.L.)	5	9	.357	4.62	18	17	2	0	0-0	103.1	97	55	53	10	64-3	70
	—Rochester (I.L.)	5	5	.500	2.58	12	12	3	1	0-...	87.1	60	27	25	7	35-0	59
1990—	Baltimore (A.L.)	11	11	.500	4.34	31	31	3	0	0-0	188.2	189	96	91	17	86-5	122
1991—	Houston (N.L.)■	12	9	.571	2.70	33	33	4	2	0-0	216.2	169	71	65	14	83-3	172
1992—	Houston (N.L.)	9	10	.474	3.70	34	34	0	0	0-0	206.2	182	92	85	18	64-3	164
1993—	Houston (N.L.)	16	9	.640	2.98	33	33	5	*4	0-0	217.2	171	84	72	20	79-5	185
1994—	Houston (N.L.)	8	5	.615	5.40	17	17	1	0	0-0	95.0	100	59	57	13	39-1	62
	—Tucson (PCL)	0	0	...	0.00	1	1	0	0	0-...	5.0	2	0	0	0	1-0	1
1995—	New York (N.L.)■	2	8	.200	3.68	18	18	0	0	0-0	110.0	111	55	45	13	24-4	82
1996—	St. Lucie (FSL)	1	0	1.000	2.77	2	2	0	0	0-...	13.0	11	4	4	1	0-0	12
	—New York (N.L.)	8	12	.400	4.21	31	31	2	1	0-0	194.2	195	103	91	30	61-5	114
1997—	New York (N.L.)	0	1	.000	8.06	6	5	0	0	0-0	25.2	35	24	23	5	11-1	12
	—Gulf Coast Mets (GCL)	0	0	...	12.00	1	1	0	0	0-...	3.0	7	4	4	1	0-0	5
	—St. Lucie (FSL)	1	0	1.000	3.00	2	2	0	0	0-...	12.0	5	5	4	1	4-0	7
	—Norfolk (I.L.)	1	1	.500	5.40	3	3	0	0	0-...	16.2	16	12	10	4	10-0	16
	—Milwaukee (A.L.)■	1	1	.500	5.14	4	3	0	0	0-0	14.0	13	9	8	1	12-0	10

Year	League	W	L	Pct.	ERA	G	GS	CG	ShO	Sv.-Opp.	IP	H	R	ER	HR	BB-IBB	SO
1998—	Cincinnati (N.L.)■	14	7	.667	3.14	32	32	2	1	0-0	209.0	176	79	73	24	64-4	157
1999—	Cincinnati (N.L.)	16	10	.615	3.68	33	33	2	2	0-0	198.1	190	86	81	25	57-2	120
2000—	Cincinnati (N.L.)	8	6	.571	4.74	22	22	3	1	0-0	131.0	133	76	69	23	46-1	71
	—Louisville (I.L.)	0	0	...	3.18	1	1	0	0	0-...	5.2	6	6	2	1	0-0	6
2001—	Cincinnati (N.L.)	1	3	.250	6.37	7	7	0	0	0-1	35.1	48	29	25	9	17-0	17
	—Louisville (I.L.)	0	1	.000	54.00	1	1	0	0	0-...	.1	3	3	2	0	0-0	0
2002—	Colorado (N.L.)■									Did not play.							
A.L. totals (4 years)		17	23	.425	4.51	55	53	5	0	0-0	319.0	312	168	160	29	171-9	212
N.L. totals (11 years)		94	80	.540	3.76	266	265	19	11	0-0	1640.0	1510	758	686	194	545-29	1156
Major League totals (14 years)		111	103	.519	3.89	321	318	24	11	0-0	1959.0	1822	926	846	223	716-38	1368

ALL-STAR GAME RECORD

	W	L	Pct.	ERA	GS	CG	ShO	Sv.-Opp.	IP	H	R	ER	HR	BB-IBB	SO
All-Star Game totals (1 year)	0	0	...	0.00	0	0	0	0-0	1.0	2	0	0	0	0-0	1

HARPER, TRAVIS — P — DEVIL RAYS

PERSONAL: Born May 21, 1976, in Harrisonburg, Va. ... 6-4/192. ... Throws right, bats right. ... Full name: Travis Boyd Harper.
HIGH SCHOOL: Circleville (W. Va.).
COLLEGE: James Madison.
TRANSACTIONS/CAREER NOTES: Selected by New York Mets organization in 14th round of free-agent draft (June 2, 1994); did not sign. ... Selected by Boston Red Sox organization in third round of free-agent draft (June 3, 1997). ... Contract with Red Sox voided due to pre-existing injury (October 29, 1997). ... Signed by Tampa Bay Devil Rays organization (June 29, 1998).
CAREER HITTING (MLB): 0-for-0 (.000), 0 R, 0 2B, 0 3B, 0 HR, 0 RBI.

Year	League	W	L	Pct.	ERA	G	GS	CG	ShO	Sv.-Opp.	IP	H	R	ER	HR	BB-IBB	SO
1998—	Hudson Valley (NY-Penn)	6	2	.750	1.92	13	10	0	0	0-...	56.1	38	14	12	2	20-0	81
1999—	St. Petersburg (FSL)	5	4	.556	3.43	14	14	0	0	0-...	81.1	82	36	31	4	23-0	79
	—Orlando (Sou.)	6	3	.667	5.38	14	14	1	1	0-...	72.0	73	45	43	10	26-0	68
2000—	Orlando (Sou.)	3	1	.750	2.63	9	9	0	0	0-...	51.1	49	19	15	1	11-0	33
	—Durham (I.L.)	7	4	.636	4.24	17	17	0	0	0-...	104.0	98	53	49	15	26-1	48
	—Tampa Bay (A.L.)	1	2	.333	4.78	6	5	1	1	0-0	32.0	30	17	17	5	15-0	14
2001—	Tampa Bay (A.L.)	0	2	.000	7.71	2	2	0	0	0-0	7.0	15	11	6	5	3-0	2
	—Durham (I.L.)	12	6	.667	3.70	25	25	1	1	0-...	155.2	140	70	64	25	38-0	115
2002—	Durham (I.L.)	1	2	.333	6.98	4	4	0	0	0-...	19.1	31	15	15	5	3-0	17
	—Tampa Bay (A.L.)	5	9	.357	5.46	37	7	0	0	1-2	85.2	101	54	52	14	27-3	60
Major League totals (3 years)		6	13	.316	5.41	45	14	1	1	1-2	124.2	146	82	75	24	45-3	76

HARRIS, LENNY — IF/OF

PERSONAL: Born October 28, 1964, in Miami. ... 5-10/220. ... Bats left, throws right. ... Full name: Leonard Anthony Harris.
HIGH SCHOOL: Jackson (Miami).
JUNIOR COLLEGE: Miami-Dade (North) Community College.
TRANSACTIONS/CAREER NOTES: Selected by Cincinnati Reds organization in fifth round of free-agent draft (June 6, 1983). ... Loaned by Reds organization to Glens Falls, Detroit Tigers organization (May 6-28, 1988). ... Traded by Reds with OF Kal Daniels to Los Angeles Dodgers for P Tim Leary and SS Mariano Duncan (July 18, 1989). ... Granted free agency (October 8, 1993). ... Signed by Reds (December 1, 1993). ... Granted free agency (October 31, 1996). ... Re-signed by Reds (November 13, 1996). ... Traded by Reds to New York Mets for P John Hudek (July 3, 1998). ... Granted free agency (October 27, 1998). ... Signed by Colorado Rockies (November 9, 1998). ... Traded by Rockies to Arizona Diamondbacks for IF Belvani Martinez (August 31, 1999). ... Traded by Diamondbacks to Mets for P Bill Pulsipher (June 2, 2000). ... Granted free agency (October 28, 2002).
RECORDS: Holds major league career record for most pinch hits—173. ... Holds major league single-season records for most games by pinch hitter—95 and at bats by pinch hitter—83 (2001).
STATISTICAL NOTES: Led Florida State League third basemen with 277 assists and 34 double plays in 1985. ... Led Eastern League third basemen with 116 putouts, 28 errors and 360 total chances in 1986. ... Led American Association in caught stealing with 22 in 1988. ... Led American Association second basemen with 23 errors in 1988. ... Career major league grand slams: 3.
2002 GAMES PLAYED BY POSITION (MLB): OF—16; 3B—14; 1B—12; DH—2.

				BATTING													FIELDING	
Year	Team (League)	Pos.	G	AB	R	H	2B	3B	HR	RBI	BB	SO	SB-CS	Avg.	OBP	SLG	E	Avg.
1983—	Billings (Pio.)	3B	56	224	37	63	8	1	1	26	13	35	7-1	.281	.322	.339	22	.854
1984—	Cedar Rapids (Midw.)	3B	132	468	52	115	15	3	6	53	42	59	31-10	.246	.308	.329	*34	.903
1985—	Tampa (FSL)	3B	132	499	66	129	11	8	3	51	37	57	15-8	.259	.307	.331	*35	.913
1986—	Vermont (East.)	3B-SS	119	450	68	114	17	2	10	52	29	38	36-10	.253	.303	.367	†28	.924
1987—	Nashville (A.A.)	SS-3B	120	403	45	100	12	3	2	31	27	43	30-12	.248	.302	.308	34	.908
1988—	Nashville (A.A.)■	2B-SS-3B	107	422	46	117	20	2	0	35	22	36	*45-*22	.277	.313	.334	†25	.947
	—Glens Falls (East.)■	2B	17	65	9	22	5	1	1	7	9	6	6-2	.338	.419	.492	5	.947
	—Cincinnati (N.L.)■	3B-2B	16	43	7	16	1	0	0	8	5	4	4-1	.372	.420	.395	1	.979
1989—	Cincinnati (N.L.)	2B-SS-3B	61	188	17	42	4	0	2	11	9	20	10-6	.223	.263	.277	13	.946
	—Nashville (A.A.)	2B	8	34	6	9	2	0	3	6	0	5	0-2	.265	.265	.588	0	1.000
	—Los Angeles (N.L.)■	OF-2B-3B-SS	54	147	19	37	6	1	1	15	11	13	4-3	.252	.308	.327	2	.978
1990—	Los Angeles (N.L.)	3B-2B-OF-SS	137	431	61	131	16	4	2	29	29	31	15-10	.304	.348	.374	11	.969
1991—	Los Angeles (N.L.)	3B-2B-SS-OF	145	429	59	123	16	1	3	38	37	32	12-3	.287	.349	.350	20	.949
1992—	Los Angeles (N.L.)	2B-3B-OF-SS	135	347	28	94	11	0	0	30	24	24	19-7	.271	.318	.303	27	.943
1993—	Los Angeles (N.L.)	2B-3B-SS-OF	107	160	20	38	6	1	2	11	15	15	3-1	.238	.303	.325	3	.982
1994—	Cincinnati (N.L.)■	3B-1B-OF-2B	66	100	13	31	3	1	0	14	5	13	7-2	.310	.340	.360	6	.903
1995—	Cincinnati (N.L.)	3B-1B-OF-2B	101	197	32	41	8	3	2	16	14	20	10-1	.208	.259	.310	4	.982
1996—	Cincinnati (N.L.)	OF-3B-1B-2B	125	302	33	86	17	2	5	32	21	31	14-6	.285	.330	.404	6	.978
1997—	Cincinnati (N.L.)	OF-2B-3B-1B	120	238	32	65	13	1	3	28	18	18	4-3	.273	.327	.374	3	.983
1998—	Cincinnati (N.L.)	OF-DH-P	57	122	12	36	8	0	0	10	8	9	1-3	.295	.338	.361	3	.929
	—New York (N.L.)■	OF-3B-2B-1B	75	168	18	39	7	0	6	17	9	12	5-2	.232	.272	.381	2	.980
1999—	Colorado (N.L.)■	2-O-DH-3	91	158	15	47	12	0	0	13	6	6	1-1	.297	.323	.373	9	.926
	—Arizona (N.L.)■	3B-OF	19	29	2	11	1	0	1	7	0	1	1-0	.379	.367	.517	0	1.000

H

			BATTING														FIELDING	
Year	Team (League)	Pos.	G	AB	R	H	2B	3B	HR	RBI	BB	SO	SB-CS	Avg.	OBP	SLG	E	Avg.
2000—	Arizona (N.L.)	3B-OF	36	85	9	16	1	1	1	13	3	5	5-0	.188	.209	.259	4	.909
—	New York (N.L.)■	IF-OF-DH	76	138	22	42	6	3	3	13	17	17	8-1	.304	.381	.457	11	.904
2001—	New York (N.L.)	3-O-1-DH-2	110	135	12	30	5	1	0	9	8	9	3-2	.222	.266	.274	3	.943
2002—	Milwaukee (N.L.)■	OF-3B-1B-DH	122	197	23	60	8	2	3	17	14	17	4-1	.305	.355	.411	0	1.000
Major League totals (15 years)			1653	3614	434	985	149	21	34	331	253	297	130-53	.273	.321	.354	128	.959

DIVISION SERIES RECORD

			BATTING														FIELDING	
Year	Team (League)	Pos.	G	AB	R	H	2B	3B	HR	RBI	BB	SO	SB-CS	Avg.	OBP	SLG	E	Avg.
1999—	Arizona (N.L.)	PH-3B	2	2	0	0	0	0	0	0	0	0	0-0	.000	.000	.000	0	...
2000—	New York (N.L.)	PH	2	2	1	0	0	0	0	0	0	0	1-0	.000	.000	.000	...	...
Division series totals (2 years)			4	4	1	0	0	0	0	0	0	0	1-0	.000	.000	.000	0	...

CHAMPIONSHIP SERIES RECORD

			BATTING														FIELDING	
Year	Team (League)	Pos.	G	AB	R	H	2B	3B	HR	RBI	BB	SO	SB-CS	Avg.	OBP	SLG	E	Avg.
1995—	Cincinnati (N.L.)	PH	3	2	0	2	0	0	0	1	0	0	1-0	1.000	1.000	1.000	...	...
2000—	New York (N.L.)	PH	2	1	0	0	0	0	0	0	0	1	0-0	.000	.000	.000	...	...
Championship series totals (2 years)			5	3	0	2	0	0	0	1	0	1	1-0	.667	.667	.667	...	...

WORLD SERIES RECORD

			BATTING														FIELDING	
Year	Team (League)	Pos.	G	AB	R	H	2B	3B	HR	RBI	BB	SO	SB-CS	Avg.	OBP	SLG	E	Avg.
2000—	New York (N.L.)	DH-PH	3	4	1	0	0	0	0	0	1	1	0-0	.000	.200	.000	...	...

RECORD AS PITCHER

Year	League	W	L	Pct.	ERA	G	GS	CG	ShO	Sv.-Opp.	IP	H	R	ER	HR	BB-IBB	SO
1998—	Cincinnati (N.L.)	0	0	...	0.00	1	0	0	0	0-0	1.0	0	0	0	0	0-0	1

HARRIS, WILLIE — 2B/OF — WHITE SOX

PERSONAL: Born June 22, 1978, in Cairo, Ga. ... 5-9/175. ... Bats left, throws right. ... Full name: William Charles Harris. ... Nephew of Ernest Riles, infielder with Milwaukee Brewers, San Francisco Giants, Oakland Athletics, Houston Astros and Boston Red Sox (1985-1993).

HIGH SCHOOL: Cairo (Ga.).

JUNIOR COLLEGE: Middle Georgia.

COLLEGE: Kennesaw State.

TRANSACTIONS/CAREER NOTES: Selected by Pittsburgh Pirates organization in 28th round of free-agent draft (June 4, 1996); did not sign. ... Selected by Baltimore Orioles organization in 24th round of free-agent draft (June 2, 1999). ... Traded by Orioles to Chicago White Sox for OF Chris Singleton (January 29, 2002).

2002 GAMES PLAYED BY POSITION (MLB): 2B—38; OF—6.

			BATTING														FIELDING	
Year	Team (League)	Pos.	G	AB	R	H	2B	3B	HR	RBI	BB	SO	SB-CS	Avg.	OBP	SLG	E	Avg.
1999—	Bluefield (Appl.)	2B	5	22	3	6	1	0	0	3	4	2	1-0	.273	.370	.318	1	.966
—	Delmarva (S.Atl.)	2B-OF	66	272	42	72	13	3	2	32	20	41	11-11	.265	.313	.357	11	.965
2000—	Delmarva (S.Atl.)	2B-OF-SS	133	474	106	130	27	10	6	60	89	89	38-15	.274	.396	.411	19	.968
2001—	Bowie (East.)	2B-OF	133	525	83	160	27	4	9	49	46	71	54-16	.305	.364	.423	14	.974
—	Baltimore (A.L.)	OF	9	24	3	3	1	0	0	0	0	7	0-0	.125	.125	.167	0	1.000
2002—	Charlotte (I.L.)■	2B-OF	89	360	54	102	16	5	5	33	33	61	32-14	.283	.345	.397	6	.986
—	Chicago (A.L.)	2B-OF	49	163	14	38	4	0	2	12	9	21	8-0	.233	.270	.294	3	.986
Major League totals (2 years)			58	187	17	41	5	0	2	12	9	28	8-0	.219	.253	.278	3	.987

HART, JASON — 1B — RANGERS

PERSONAL: Born September 5, 1977, in Walnut Creek, Calif. ... 6-4/240. ... Bats right, throws right. ... Full name: Jason Wyatt Hart.

HIGH SCHOOL: Fair Grove (Mo.).

COLLEGE: Southwest Missouri.

TRANSACTIONS/CAREER NOTES: Selected by Oakland Athletics organization in fifth round of free-agent draft (June 2, 1998). ... Traded by A's with P Mario Ramos, C Gerald Laird and OF Ryan Ludwick to Texas Rangers for 1B Carlos Pena and P Mike Venafro (January 14, 2002).

HONORS: Named Northwest League Most Valuable Player (1998).

STATISTICAL NOTES: Led Northwest League with 157 total bases and eight sacrifice flies in 1998. ... Led Northwest League first basemen with 622 putouts, 12 errors, 679 total chances and 45 double plays in 1998. ... Led California League first basemen with 1,148 putouts and 1,237 total chances in 1999. ... Led Texas League with 318 total bases in 2000. ... Led Texas League first basemen with 1,184 putouts, 1,261 total chances and 117 double plays in 2000. ... Led Pacific Coast League first basemen with 1,130 putouts and 1,208 total chances in 2001.

2002 GAMES PLAYED BY POSITION (MLB): OF—7; 1B—2.

			BATTING														FIELDING	
Year	Team (League)	Pos.	G	AB	R	H	2B	3B	HR	RBI	BB	SO	SB-CS	Avg.	OBP	SLG	E	Avg.
1998—	S. Oregon (N'West)	1B-3B	•75	295	58	76	19	1	*20	69	36	67	0-1	.258	.336	.532	*12	.982
1999—	Modesto (Calif.)	1B	135	*550	96	168	*48	2	19	•123	56	105	2-5	.305	.370	.504	13	.989
2000—	Midland (Texas)	1B	135	*546	98	*178	44	3	30	*121	67	112	4-0	.326	.401	.582	11	*.991
—	Sacramento (PCL)	1B	5	18	4	5	1	0	1	4	3	7	0-0	.278	.381	.500	0	1.000
2001—	Sacramento (PCL)	1B	134	494	71	122	26	1	19	75	57	102	3-3	.247	.325	.419	•15	.988
2002—	Oklahoma (PCL)■	1B-OF	134	514	78	135	32	1	25	83	68	122	1-0	.263	.356	.475	8	.987
—	Texas (A.L.)	OF-1B	10	15	2	4	3	0	0	0	2	7	0-0	.267	.353	.467	0	1.000
Major League totals (1 year)			10	15	2	4	3	0	0	0	2	7	0-0	.267	.353	.467	0	1.000

HARVEY, KEN — 1B — ROYALS

PERSONAL: Born March 1, 1978, in Los Angeles. ... 6-2/240. ... Bats right, throws right. ... Full name: Kenneth Eugene Harvey.
HIGH SCHOOL: Beverly Hills (Calif.).
COLLEGE: Nebraska.
TRANSACTIONS/CAREER NOTES: Selected by Kansas City Royals organization in fifth round of free-agent draft (June 2, 1999).
STATISTICAL NOTES: Tied for Northwest League lead with four intentional bases on balls received in 1999. ... Tied for Texas League lead with eight sacrifice flies in 2001. ... Led Pacific Coast League with 22 grounded into double plays in 2002.

		BATTING														FIELDING	
Year Team (League)	Pos.	G	AB	R	H	2B	3B	HR	RBI	BB	SO	SB-CS	Avg.	OBP	SLG	E	Avg.
1999—Spokane (N'West)	1B	56	204	49	81	17	0	8	41	23	30	7-3	*.397	*.477	*.598	5	.984
2000—Wilmington (Caro.)	1B	46	164	20	55	10	0	4	25	14	29	0-2	.335	.411	.470	3	.983
2001—Wilmington (Caro.)	1B	35	137	22	52	9	1	6	27	13	21	3-1	.380	.455	.591	3	.984
—Wichita (Texas)	1B-OF	79	314	54	106	20	3	9	63	18	60	3-0	.338	.372	.506	5	.990
—Kansas City (A.L.)	1B-DH	4	12	1	3	1	0	0	2	0	4	0-1	.250	.250	.333	0	1.000
2002—Omaha (PCL)	1B	128	488	75	135	30	1	20	75	42	87	8-3	.277	.342	.465	*15	.984
Major League totals (1 year)		4	12	1	3	1	0	0	2	0	4	0-1	.250	.250	.333	0	1.000

HARVILLE, CHAD — P — ATHLETICS

PERSONAL: Born September 16, 1976, in Selmer, Tenn. ... 5-9/180. ... Throws right, bats right. ... Full name: Chad Ashley Harville.
HIGH SCHOOL: Hardin County (Savannah, Tenn.).
COLLEGE: Memphis.
TRANSACTIONS/CAREER NOTES: Selected by Oakland Athletics organization in second round of free-agent draft (June 3, 1997). ... On Oakland disabled list (March 31-June 9, 2001); included rehabilitation assignments to Visalia (June 3-5) and Modesto (June 5-9). ... On Sacramento disabled list (May 20-August 7, 2002).
CAREER HITTING (MLB): 0-for-0 (.000), 0 R, 0 2B, 0 3B, 0 HR, 0 RBI.

Year League	W	L	Pct.	ERA	G	GS	CG	ShO	Sv.-Opp.	IP	H	R	ER	HR	BB-IBB	SO
1997—S. Oregon (N'West)	1	0	1.000	0.00	3	0	0	0	0-...	5.0	3	0	0	0	3-0	6
—Visalia (Calif.)	0	0	...	5.79	14	0	0	0	0-...	18.2	25	14	12	2	13-1	24
1998—Visalia (Calif.)	4	3	.571	3.00	24	7	0	0	4-...	69.0	59	25	23	0	31-0	76
—Huntsville (Sou.)	0	0	...	2.45	12	0	0	0	8-...	14.2	6	4	4	0	13-1	24
1999—Midland (Texas)	2	0	1.000	2.01	17	0	0	0	7-...	22.1	13	6	5	1	9-0	35
—Vancouver (PCL)	1	0	1.000	1.75	22	0	0	0	11-...	25.2	24	5	5	0	11-1	36
—Oakland (A.L.)	0	2	.000	6.91	15	0	0	0	0-0	14.1	18	11	11	2	10-1	15
2000—Sacramento (PCL)	5	3	.625	4.50	53	0	0	0	9-...	64.0	53	35	32	8	35-0	77
2001—Modesto (Calif.)	0	0	...	3.00	2	1	0	0	0-...	3.0	2	2	1	0	0-0	3
—Visalia (Calif.)	0	0	...	0.00	1	1	0	0	0-...	3.0	3	0	0	0	0-0	3
—Sacramento (PCL)	5	2	.714	3.98	33	0	0	0	8-...	40.2	35	20	18	5	12-0	55
—Oakland (A.L.)	0	0	...	0.00	3	0	0	0	0-0	3.0	2	0	0	0	0-0	2
2002—Sacramento (PCL)	1	2	.333	5.40	24	0	0	0	5-...	30.0	32	19	18	5	13-1	26
Major League totals (2 years)	0	2	.000	5.71	18	0	0	0	0-0	17.1	20	11	11	2	10-1	17

HASEGAWA, SHIGETOSHI — P — MARINERS

PERSONAL: Born August 1, 1968, in Kobe, Japan ... 5-11/178. ... Throws right, bats right. ... Name pronounced SHE-geh-TOE-she HAH-seh-GAH-wah.
COLLEGE: Ritsumeikan University (Kyoto, Japan).
TRANSACTIONS/CAREER NOTES: Played for Orix Blue Wave of Japan Pacific League (1991-96). ... Signed as non-drafted free agent by Anaheim Angels (January 9, 1997). ... On Anaheim disabled list (May 20-June 29, 2001); included rehabilitation assignment to Rancho Cucamonga (June 25-29). ... Granted free agency (December 21, 2001). ... Signed by Seattle Mariners (January 23, 2002).
CAREER HITTING (MLB): 0-for-1 (.000), 0 R, 0 2B, 0 3B, 0 HR, 0 RBI.

Year League	W	L	Pct.	ERA	G	GS	CG	ShO	Sv.-Opp.	IP	H	R	ER	HR	BB-IBB	SO
1991—Orix (Jap. Pac.)	12	9	.571	3.55	28	25	11	3	1-...	185.0	184	76	73	...	50-...	111
1992—Orix (Jap. Pac.)	6	8	.429	3.27	24	19	4	0	1-...	143.1	138	60	52	...	51-...	86
1993—Orix (Jap. Pac.)	12	6	.667	2.71	23	22	9	3	0-...	159.2	146	61	48	...	48-...	86
1994—Orix (Jap. Pac.)	11	9	.550	3.11	25	22	8	3	1-...	156.1	169	61	54	...	46-...	86
1995—Orix (Jap. Pac.)	12	7	.632	2.89	24	23	9	4	0-...	171.0	167	62	55	...	51-...	91
1996—Orix (Jap. Pac.)	4	6	.400	5.34	18	16	2	0	1-...	87.2	109	60	52	...	40-...	55
1997—Anaheim (A.L.)■	3	7	.300	3.93	50	7	0	0	0-1	116.2	118	60	51	14	46-6	83
1998—Anaheim (A.L.)	8	3	.727	3.14	61	0	0	0	5-7	97.1	86	37	34	14	32-2	73
1999—Anaheim (A.L.)	4	6	.400	4.91	64	1	0	0	2-5	77.0	80	45	42	14	34-2	44
2000—Anaheim (A.L.)	10	5	.667	3.48	66	0	0	0	9-18	95.2	100	42	37	11	38-6	59
2001—Anaheim (A.L.)	5	6	.455	4.04	46	0	0	0	0-6	55.2	52	28	25	5	20-5	41
—Rancho Cuca. (Calif.)	0	0	...	0.00	2	2	0	0	0-...	2.0	3	1	0	0	0-0	1
2002—Seattle (A.L.)■	8	3	.727	3.20	53	0	0	0	1-5	70.1	60	26	25	4	30-8	39
Major League totals (6 years)	38	30	.559	3.76	340	8	0	0	17-42	512.2	496	238	214	62	200-29	339

HASELMAN, BILL — C

PERSONAL: Born May 25, 1966, in Long Branch, N.J. ... 6-3/225. ... Bats right, throws right. ... Full name: William Joseph Haselman.
HIGH SCHOOL: Saratoga (Calif.).
COLLEGE: UCLA.
TRANSACTIONS/CAREER NOTES: Selected by Texas Rangers organization in first round (23rd pick overall) of free-agent draft (June 2, 1987); pick received as compensation for New York Yankees signing Type A free-agent OF Gary Ward. ... On Oklahoma City disabled list (March 28-May 4, 1992). ... Claimed on waivers by Seattle Mariners (May 29, 1992). ... On suspended list (July 22-25, 1993). ... Granted free agency (October 15, 1994). ... Signed by Boston Red Sox (November 7, 1994). ... On Boston disabled list (June 30-August 8, 1997); included rehabilitation assignment to Gulf Coast Red Sox (July 29-August 1) and Trenton (August 1-8). ... Traded by Red Sox with P Aaron Sele and P Mark Brandenburg to Rangers for C Jim Leyritz and OF Damon Buford (November 6, 1997). ... Granted free agency (October 23, 1998). ...

Signed by Detroit Tigers (December 14, 1998). ... Traded by Tigers with P Justin Thompson, P Francisco Cordero, OF Gabe Kapler, 2B Frank Catalanotto and P Alan Webb to Rangers for OF Juan Gonzalez, P Danny Patterson and C Gregg Zaun (November 2, 1999). ... On Texas disabled list (March 31-June 22, 2001); included rehabilitation assignment to Oklahoma (June 13-22). ... Granted free agency (October 30, 2002).
RECORDS: Holds major league record for most chances accepted in consecutive nine-inning games—37 (April 29 and 30, 1996). ... Shares A.L. single-game record for most chances accepted by catcher (nine-inning game)—20 (September 18, 1996).
STATISTICAL NOTES: Led Texas League with 12 passed balls in 1989. ... Led Texas League catchers with 676 putouts, 90 assists, 20 errors, 786 total chances and 20 passed balls in 1990. ... Led American Association catchers with 673 putouts and 751 total chances in 1991. ... Tied for A.L. lead in passed balls with 17 in 1997. ... Career major league grand slams: 1.
2002 GAMES PLAYED BY POSITION (MLB): C—67; DH—2.

			BATTING														FIELDING	
Year	**Team (League)**	**Pos.**	**G**	**AB**	**R**	**H**	**2B**	**3B**	**HR**	**RBI**	**BB**	**SO**	**SB-CS**	**Avg.**	**OBP**	**SLG**	**E**	**Avg.**
1987—	Gastonia (S.Atl.)	C	61	235	35	72	13	1	8	33	19	46	1-2	.306	.359	.472	2	.933
1988—	Charlotte (FSL)	C	122	453	56	111	17	2	10	54	45	99	8-5	.245	.316	.358	6	.979
1989—	Tulsa (Texas)	C	107	352	38	95	17	2	7	36	40	88	5-10	.270	.348	.389	9	.984
1990—	Tulsa (Texas)	C-1B-OF-3B	120	430	68	137	39	2	18	80	43	96	3-7	.319	.386	.544	†20	.976
	—Texas (A.L.)	DH-C	7	13	0	2	0	0	0	3	1	5	0-0	.154	.214	.154	0	1.000
1991—	Oklahoma City (A.A.)	C-OF-1B-3B	126	442	57	113	22	2	9	60	61	89	10-6	.256	.344	.376	11	.986
1992—	Oklahoma City (A.A.)	OF-C	17	58	8	14	5	0	1	9	13	12	1-0	.241	.380	.379	3	.945
	—Calgary (PCL)■	C-OF	88	302	49	77	14	2	19	53	41	89	3-3	.255	.345	.503	6	.977
	—Seattle (A.L.)	C-OF	8	19	1	5	0	0	0	0	0	7	0-0	.263	.263	.263	0	1.000
1993—	Seattle (A.L.)	C-DH-OF	58	137	21	35	8	0	5	16	12	19	2-1	.255	.316	.423	2	.992
1994—	Seattle (A.L.)	C-DH-OF	38	83	11	16	7	1	1	8	3	11	1-0	.193	.230	.337	3	.982
	—Calgary (PCL)	C-DH-1B	44	163	44	54	10	0	15	46	30	33	1-0	.331	.436	.669	5	.979
1995—	Boston (A.L.)■	C-DH-1B-3B	64	152	22	37	6	1	5	23	17	30	0-2	.243	.322	.395	3	.989
1996—	Boston (A.L.)	C-DH-1B	77	237	33	65	13	1	8	34	19	52	4-2	.274	.331	.439	3	.994
1997—	Boston (A.L.)	C	67	212	22	50	15	0	6	26	15	44	0-2	.236	.290	.392	7	.983
	—GC Red Sox (GCL)	DH	4	16	2	2	0	0	0	1	0	1	1-0	.125	.125	.125	0	...
	—Trenton (East.)	C-DH	7	26	3	6	1	0	2	3	2	2	0-0	.231	.286	.500	0	1.000
1998—	Texas (A.L.)■	C-DH	40	105	11	33	6	0	6	17	3	17	0-0	.314	.327	.543	1	.995
1999—	Detroit (A.L.)■	C-DH	48	143	13	39	8	0	4	14	10	26	2-0	.273	.320	.413	1	.996
2000—	Texas (A.L.)■	C	62	193	23	53	18	0	6	26	15	36	0-1	.275	.329	.461	4	.989
2001—	Oklahoma (PCL)	C	8	28	2	4	0	0	0	1	1	10	0-0	.143	.194	.143	1	.957
	—Texas (A.L.)	C	47	130	12	37	6	0	3	25	8	27	0-1	.285	.331	.400	0	1.000
2002—	Texas (A.L.)	C-DH	69	179	16	44	7	0	3	18	11	25	0-0	.246	.297	.335	3	.991
Major League totals (12 years)			585	1603	185	416	94	3	47	210	114	299	9-9	.260	.311	.410	27	.991

DIVISION SERIES RECORD

			BATTING														FIELDING	
Year	**Team (League)**	**Pos.**	**G**	**AB**	**R**	**H**	**2B**	**3B**	**HR**	**RBI**	**BB**	**SO**	**SB-CS**	**Avg.**	**OBP**	**SLG**	**E**	**Avg.**
1995—	Boston (A.L.)	C	1	2	0	0	0	0	0	0	0	0	0-0	.000	.000	.000	0	1.000

HATTEBERG, SCOTT — 1B — ATHLETICS

PERSONAL: Born December 14, 1969, in Salem, Ore. ... 6-1/210. ... Bats left, throws right. ... Full name: Scott Allen Hatteberg. ... Name pronounced HAT-ee-berg.
HIGH SCHOOL: Eisenhower (Yakima, Wash.).
COLLEGE: Washington State.
TRANSACTIONS/CAREER NOTES: Selected by Philadelphia Phillies organization in 12th round of free-agent draft (June 1, 1988); did not sign. ... Selected by Boston Red Sox organization in supplemental round ("sandwich pick" between first and second round, 43rd pick overall) of free-agent draft (June 3, 1991); pick received as part of compensation for Kansas City signing Type A free-agent P Mike Boddicker. ... On disabled list (July 27-August 3, 1992). ... On Boston disabled list (April 15-May 7 and May 17-August 16, 1999); included rehabilitation assignments to Pawtucket (May 4-7 and August 3-13), Gulf Coast Red Sox (July 24-31) and Sarasota (August 1-2). ... Traded by Red Sox to Colorado Rockies for 2B Pokey Reese (December 19, 2001). ... Granted free agency (December 21, 2001). ... Signed by Oakland Athletics (January 2, 2002).
STATISTICAL NOTES: Tied for A.L. lead in double plays by catcher with 13 and passed balls with 17 in 1997. ... Career major league grand slams: 2.
2002 GAMES PLAYED BY POSITION (MLB): 1B—91; DH—42.

			BATTING														FIELDING	
Year	**Team (League)**	**Pos.**	**G**	**AB**	**R**	**H**	**2B**	**3B**	**HR**	**RBI**	**BB**	**SO**	**SB-CS**	**Avg.**	**OBP**	**SLG**	**E**	**Avg.**
1991—	Winter Haven (FSL)	C	56	191	21	53	7	3	1	25	22	22	1-2	.277	.349	.361	5	.983
	—Lynchburg (Caro.)	C	8	25	4	5	1	0	0	2	7	6	0-0	.200	.375	.240	0	1.000
1992—	New Britain (East.)	C	103	297	28	69	13	2	1	30	41	49	1-3	.232	.327	.300	11	.979
1993—	New Britain (East.)	C	68	227	35	63	10	2	7	28	42	38	1-3	.278	.393	.432	10	.978
	—Pawtucket (I.L.)	C	18	53	6	10	0	0	1	2	6	12	0-0	.189	.283	.245	5	.964
1994—	New Britain (East.)	C	20	68	6	18	4	1	1	9	7	9	0-2	.265	.329	.397	1	.993
	—Pawtucket (I.L.)	C	78	238	26	56	14	0	7	19	32	49	2-1	.235	.332	.382	7	.986
1995—	Pawtucket (I.L.)	C-DH	85	251	36	68	15	1	7	27	40	39	2-0	.271	.376	.422	•8	.984
	—Boston (A.L.)	C	2	2	1	1	0	0	0	0	0	0	0-0	.500	.500	.500	0	1.000
1996—	Pawtucket (I.L.)	C-DH	90	287	52	77	16	0	12	49	58	66	1-1	.268	.391	.449	6	.990
	—Boston (A.L.)	C	10	11	3	2	1	0	0	0	3	2	0-0	.182	.357	.273	0	1.000
1997—	Boston (A.L.)	C-DH	114	350	46	97	23	1	10	44	40	70	0-1	.277	.354	.434	11	.983
1998—	Boston (A.L.)	C	112	359	46	99	23	1	12	43	43	58	0-0	.276	.359	.446	5	.993
1999—	Boston (A.L.)	C-DH	30	80	12	22	5	0	1	11	18	14	0-0	.275	.410	.375	1	.993
	—Pawtucket (I.L.)	C-DH	10	34	3	6	2	0	0	4	4	6	0-0	.176	.263	.235	0	1.000
	—GC Red Sox (GCL)	C-DH	6	15	4	6	2	0	1	6	7	1	0-0	.400	.591	.733	0	1.000
	—Sarasota (FSL)	C	1	1	0	1	0	0	0	1	0	0	0-0	1.000	1.000	1.000	0	1.000
2000—	Boston (A.L.)	C-DH-3B	92	230	21	61	15	0	8	36	38	39	0-1	.265	.367	.435	6	.981
2001—	Boston (A.L.)	C-DH	94	278	34	68	19	0	3	25	33	26	1-1	.245	.332	.345	4	.992
2002—	Oakland (A.L.)■	1B-DH	136	492	58	138	22	4	15	61	68	56	0-0	.280	.374	.433	5	.994
Major League totals (8 years)			590	1802	221	488	108	6	49	220	243	265	1-3	.271	.361	.419	32	.990

DIVISION SERIES RECORD

		BATTING														FIELDING	
Year Team (League)	Pos.	G	AB	R	H	2B	3B	HR	RBI	BB	SO	SB-CS	Avg.	OBP	SLG	E	Avg.
1998—Boston (A.L.)	C	3	9	0	1	0	0	0	0	3	1	0-0	.111	.333	.111	0	1.000
1999—Boston (A.L.)	C	1	1	1	1	0	0	0	1	0	0	0-0	1.000	1.000	1.000	0	1.000
2002—Oakland (A.L.)	1B	5	14	5	7	2	0	1	3	3	0	0-0	.500	.588	.857	1	.973
Division series totals (3 years)		9	24	6	9	2	0	1	4	6	1	0-0	.375	.500	.583	1	.983

CHAMPIONSHIP SERIES RECORD

		BATTING														FIELDING	
Year Team (League)	Pos.	G	AB	R	H	2B	3B	HR	RBI	BB	SO	SB-CS	Avg.	OBP	SLG	E	Avg.
1999—Boston (A.L.)	PH-C	3	1	0	0	0	0	0	0	0	1	0-0	.000	.000	.000	0	...

HAWKINS, LaTROY — P — TWINS

PERSONAL: Born December 21, 1972, in Gary, Ind. ... 6-5/204. ... Throws right, bats right.
HIGH SCHOOL: West Side (Gary, Ind.).
TRANSACTIONS/CAREER NOTES: Selected by Minnesota Twins organization in seventh round of free-agent draft (June 3, 1991).
STATISTICAL NOTES: Tied for A.L. lead with three balks in 1997.
CAREER HITTING (MLB): 0-for-5 (.000), 0 R, 0 2B, 0 3B, 0 HR, 0 RBI.

Year League	W	L	Pct.	ERA	G	GS	CG	ShO	Sv.-Opp.	IP	H	R	ER	HR	BB-IBB	SO
1991—Gulf Coast Twins (GCL)	4	3	.571	4.75	11	11	0	0	0-...	55.0	62	34	29	2	26-0	47
1992—Gulf Coast Twins (GCL)	3	2	.600	3.22	6	6	1	0	0-...	36.1	36	19	13	1	10-0	35
—Elizabethton (Appl.)	0	1	.000	3.38	5	5	1	0	0-...	26.2	21	12	10	2	11-0	36
1993—Fort Wayne (Midw.)	•15	5	.750	*2.06	26	23	4	•3	0-...	157.1	110	53	36	5	41-0	*179
1994—Fort Myers (FSL)	4	0	1.000	2.33	6	6	1	1	0-...	38.2	32	10	10	1	6-0	36
—Nashville (Sou.)	9	2	•.818	2.33	11	11	1	0	0-...	73.1	50	23	19	2	28-0	53
—Salt Lake (PCL)	5	4	.556	4.08	12	12	1	0	0-...	81.2	92	42	37	8	33-0	37
1995—Minnesota (A.L.)	2	3	.400	8.67	6	6	1	0	0-0	27.0	39	29	26	3	12-0	9
—Salt Lake (PCL)	9	7	.563	3.55	22	22	4	1	0-...	144.1	150	63	57	7	40-1	74
1996—Minnesota (A.L.)	1	1	.500	8.20	7	6	0	0	0-0	26.1	42	24	24	8	9-0	24
—Salt Lake (PCL)	9	8	.529	3.92	20	20	4	1	0-...	137.2	138	66	60	11	31-3	99
1997—Salt Lake (PCL)	9	4	.692	5.45	14	13	2	1	0-...	76.0	100	53	46	4	16-1	53
—Minnesota (A.L.)	6	12	.333	5.84	20	20	0	0	0-0	103.1	134	71	67	19	47-0	58
1998—Minnesota (A.L.)	7	14	.333	5.25	33	33	0	0	0-0	190.1	227	126	111	27	61-1	105
1999—Minnesota (A.L.)	10	14	.417	6.66	33	33	1	0	0-0	174.1	238	*136	*129	29	60-2	103
2000—Minnesota (A.L.)	2	5	.286	3.39	66	0	0	0	14-14	87.2	85	34	33	7	32-1	59
2001—Minnesota (A.L.)	1	5	.167	5.96	62	0	0	0	28-37	51.1	59	34	34	3	39-3	36
2002—Minnesota (A.L.)	6	0	1.000	2.13	65	0	0	0	0-3	80.1	63	23	19	5	15-1	63
Major League totals (8 years)	35	54	.393	5.38	292	98	2	0	42-54	740.2	887	477	443	101	275-8	457

DIVISION SERIES RECORD

Year League	W	L	Pct.	ERA	G	GS	CG	ShO	Sv.-Opp.	IP	H	R	ER	HR	BB-IBB	SO
2002—Minnesota (A.L.)	0	0	...	0.00	3	0	0	0	0-0	2.1	0	0	0	0	0-0	5

CHAMPIONSHIP SERIES RECORD

Year League	W	L	Pct.	ERA	G	GS	CG	ShO	Sv.-Opp.	IP	H	R	ER	HR	BB-IBB	SO
2002—Minnesota (A.L.)	0	0	...	20.25	4	0	0	0	0-0	1.1	4	3	3	0	1-0	1

HAYNES, JIMMY — P

PERSONAL: Born September 5, 1972, in La Grange, Ga. ... 6-4/219. ... Throws right, bats right. ... Full name: Jimmy Wayne Haynes.
HIGH SCHOOL: Troup (La Grange, Ga.).
TRANSACTIONS/CAREER NOTES: Selected by Baltimore Orioles organization in seventh round of free-agent draft (June 3, 1991). ... Traded by Orioles with a player to be named later to Oakland Athletics for OF Geronimo Berroa (June 27, 1997); A's acquired P Mark Seaver to complete deal (September 2, 1997). ... Traded by A's to Milwaukee Brewers as part of three-way deal in which A's received P Justin Miller and cash from Colorado Rockies, Brewers received P Jamey Wright and C Henry Blanco from Rockies and Rockies received 3B Jeff Cirillo, P Scott Karl and cash from Brewers (December 13, 1999). ... On disabled list (August 24-September 26, 2001). ... Granted free agency (December 21, 2001). ... Signed by Cincinnati Reds organization (January 11, 2002). ... Granted free agency (October 31, 2002).
RECORDS: Shares N.L. single-inning record for most consecutive home runs allowed—3 (July 12, 2001, third inning).
STATISTICAL NOTES: Led N.L. with 17 intentional bases on balls issued in 2001.
MISCELLANEOUS: Appeared in one game as pinch runner (2001).
CAREER HITTING (MLB): 26-for-186 (.140), 14 R, 8 2B, 0 3B, 0 HR, 10 RBI.

Year League	W	L	Pct.	ERA	G	GS	CG	ShO	Sv.-Opp.	IP	H	R	ER	HR	BB-IBB	SO
1991—Gulf Coast Orioles (GCL)	3	2	.600	1.60	14	8	1	0	2-...	62.0	44	27	11	0	21-0	67
1992—Kane County (Midw.)	7	11	.389	2.56	24	24	4	0	0-...	144.0	131	66	41	2	45-0	141
1993—Frederick (Caro.)	12	8	.600	3.03	27	27	2	1	0-...	172.1	139	73	58	13	61-1	174
1994—Bowie (East.)	13	8	.619	2.90	25	25	5	1	0-...	173.2	154	67	56	16	46-1	*177
—Rochester (I.L.)	1	0	1.000	6.75	3	3	0	0	0-...	13.1	20	12	10	3	6-0	14
1995—Rochester (I.L.)	•12	8	.600	3.29	26	25	3	1	0-...	167.0	162	77	61	16	49-0	*140
—Baltimore (A.L.)	2	1	.667	2.25	4	3	0	0	0-0	24.0	11	6	6	2	12-1	22
1996—Baltimore (A.L.)	3	6	.333	8.29	26	11	0	0	1-1	89.0	122	84	82	14	58-1	65
—Rochester (I.L.)	1	1	.500	5.65	5	5	0	0	0-...	28.2	31	19	18	5	18-0	24
1997—Rochester (I.L.)	5	4	.556	3.44	16	16	2	1	0-...	102.0	89	49	39	9	55-0	113
—Edmonton (PCL)■	0	2	.000	4.85	5	5	0	0	0-...	29.2	36	22	16	4	11-0	24
—Oakland (A.L.)	3	6	.333	4.42	13	13	0	0	0-0	73.1	74	38	36	7	40-1	65
1998—Oakland (A.L.)	11	9	.550	5.09	33	33	1	1	0-0	194.1	229	124	110	25	88-4	134
1999—Oakland (A.L.)	7	12	.368	6.34	30	25	0	0	0-0	142.0	158	112	100	21	80-3	93
2000—Milwaukee (N.L.)■	12	13	.480	5.33	33	33	0	0	0-0	199.1	228	128	118	21	100-7	88
2001—Milwaukee (N.L.)	8	17	.320	4.85	31	29	0	0	0-0	172.2	182	98	93	20	78-17	112
2002—Cincinnati (N.L.)■	15	10	.600	4.12	34	34	0	0	0-0	196.2	210	97	90	21	81-4	126
A.L. totals (5 years)	26	34	.433	5.75	106	85	1	1	1-1	522.2	594	364	334	69	278-10	379
N.L. totals (3 years)	35	40	.467	4.76	98	96	0	0	0-0	568.2	620	323	301	62	259-28	326
Major League totals (8 years)	61	74	.452	5.24	204	181	1	1	1-1	1091.1	1214	687	635	131	537-38	705

HAYNES, NATHAN — OF — ANGELS

PERSONAL: Born September 7, 1979, in Oakland. ... 5-9/170. ... Bats left, throws left. ... Full name: Nathan Raymond Quinn Haynes.
HIGH SCHOOL: Pinole Valley (Pinole, Calif.).
TRANSACTIONS/CAREER NOTES: Selected by Oakland Athletics organization in supplemental round ("sandwich pick" between first and second round, 32nd pick overall) of free-agent draft (June 3, 1997); pick received as part of compensation for Baltimore Orioles signing service-time free agent SS Mike Bordick. ... Traded by A's with OF Jeff DaVanon and P Elvin Nina to Anaheim Angels for P Omar Olivares and 2B Randy Velarde (July 29, 1999). ... On Erie disabled list (June 4-13, 2000). ... On disabled list (April 30-June 22, 2001). ... On Salt Lake disabled list (April 4-June 1, 2002).
STATISTICAL NOTES: Tied for Texas League lead with 15 caught stealing in 2001.

			BATTING													FIELDING	
Year	Team (League)	Pos.	G	AB	R	H	2B	3B	HR	RBI	BB	SO	SB-CS	Avg.	OBP	SLG	E	Avg.
1997—	Ariz. Athletics (Ariz.)	OF	17	54	8	15	1	0	0	6	7	9	5-1	.278	.381	.296	1	.955
	—S. Oregon (N'West)	OF	24	82	18	23	1	1	0	9	26	21	19-3	.280	.459	.317	1	.970
1998—	Modesto (Calif.)	OF	125	507	89	128	13	7	1	41	54	139	42-18	.252	.328	.312	•14	.939
1999—	Visalia (Calif.)	OF	35	145	28	45	7	1	1	14	17	27	12-10	.310	.392	.393	2	.972
	—Lake Elsinore (Cal.)■	OF	26	110	19	36	5	5	1	15	12	19	10-5	.327	.395	.491	2	.967
	—Erie (East.)	OF	5	19	3	3	1	0	0	0	5	5	0-0	.158	.360	.211	0	1.000
2000—	Erie (East.)	OF	118	457	56	116	16	4	6	43	33	107	37-20	.254	.315	.346	9	.965
2001—	Arkansas (Texas)	OF	79	316	49	98	11	5	5	23	32	65	33-15	.310	.379	.424	3	.985
2002—	Rancho Cuca. (Calif.)	OF	11	50	6	14	0	0	0	2	4	8	6-2	.280	.345	.280	1	.955
	—Salt Lake (PCL)	OF	67	283	37	80	14	6	2	12	12	53	10-10	.283	.313	.396	4	.974

HELLING, RICK — P

PERSONAL: Born December 15, 1970, in Devils Lake, N.D. ... 6-3/220. ... Throws right, bats right. ... Full name: Ricky Allen Helling.
HIGH SCHOOL: Lakota (Fargo, N.D.), then Shanley (Fargo, N.D.).
JUNIOR COLLEGE: Kishwaukee College (Ill.).
COLLEGE: North Dakota, then Stanford.
TRANSACTIONS/CAREER NOTES: Selected by New York Mets organization in 50th round of free-agent draft (June 4, 1990); did not sign. ... Selected by Texas Rangers organization in first round (22nd pick overall) of free-agent draft (June 1, 1992). ... Traded by Rangers to Florida Marlins (September 3, 1996), completing deal in which Marlins traded P John Burkett to Rangers for P Ryan Dempster and a player to be named later (August 8, 1996). ... Traded by Marlins to Rangers for P Ed Vosberg (August 12, 1997). ... Granted free agency (December 21, 2001). ... Signed by Arizona Diamondbacks (January 19, 2002). ... On Arizona disabled list (July 16-August 7, 2002); included rehabilitation assignment to Tucson (August 2-7). ... Granted free agency (October 28, 2002).
STATISTICAL NOTES: Pitched 4-0 no-hit victory against Nashville (August 13, 1996).
MISCELLANEOUS: Member of 1992 U.S. Olympic baseball team.
CAREER HITTING (MLB): 5-for-85 (.059), 4 R, 0 2B, 0 3B, 0 HR, 1 RBI.

Year	League	W	L	Pct.	ERA	G	GS	CG	ShO	Sv.-Opp.	IP	H	R	ER	HR	BB-IBB	SO
1992—	Charlotte (FSL)	1	1	.500	2.29	3	3	0	0	0-...	19.2	13	5	5	1	4-0	20
1993—	Tulsa (Texas)	12	8	.600	3.60	26	26	2	•2	0-...	177.1	150	76	71	14	46-1	*188
	—Oklahoma City (A.A.)	1	1	.500	1.64	2	2	1	0	0-...	11.0	5	3	2	0	3-0	17
1994—	Texas (A.L.)	3	2	.600	5.88	9	9	1	1	0-0	52.0	62	34	34	14	18-0	25
	—Oklahoma City (A.A.)	4	12	.250	5.78	20	20	2	0	0-...	132.1	153	93	85	17	43-2	85
1995—	Texas (A.L.)	0	2	.000	6.57	3	3	0	0	0-0	12.1	17	11	9	2	8-0	5
	—Oklahoma City (A.A.)	4	8	.333	5.33	20	20	3	0	0-...	109.2	132	73	65	13	41-1	80
1996—	Oklahoma City (A.A.)	12	4	.750	2.96	23	22	2	1	0-...	140.0	124	54	46	10	38-1	157
	—Texas (A.L.)	1	2	.333	7.52	6	2	0	0	0-0	20.1	23	17	17	7	9-0	16
	—Florida (N.L.)■	2	1	.667	1.95	5	4	0	0	0-0	27.2	14	6	6	2	7-0	26
1997—	Florida (N.L.)	2	6	.250	4.38	31	8	0	0	0-1	76.0	61	38	37	12	48-2	53
	—Texas (A.L.)■	3	3	.500	4.58	10	8	0	0	0-0	55.0	47	29	28	5	21-0	46
1998—	Texas (A.L.)	•20	7	.741	4.41	33	33	4	2	0-0	216.1	209	109	106	27	78-6	164
1999—	Texas (A.L.)	13	11	.542	4.84	35	*35	3	0	0-0	219.1	228	127	118	*41	85-5	131
2000—	Texas (A.L.)	16	13	.552	4.48	35	•35	0	0	0-0	217.0	212	122	108	29	99-2	146
2001—	Texas (A.L.)	12	11	.522	5.17	34	34	2	1	0-0	215.2	*256	*134	*124	*38	63-2	154
2002—	Arizona (N.L.)■	10	12	.455	4.51	30	30	0	0	0-0	175.2	180	94	88	31	48-6	120
	—Tucson (PCL)	1	0	1.000	1.29	1	1	0	0	0-...	7.0	4	1	1	0	1-0	7
A.L. totals (8 years)		68	51	.571	4.86	165	159	10	4	0-0	1008.0	1054	583	544	163	381-15	687
N.L. totals (3 years)		14	19	.424	4.22	66	42	0	0	0-1	279.1	255	138	131	45	103-8	199
Major League totals (9 years)		82	70	.539	4.72	231	201	10	4	0-1	1287.1	1309	721	675	208	484-23	886

DIVISION SERIES RECORD

Year	League	W	L	Pct.	ERA	G	GS	CG	ShO	Sv.-Opp.	IP	H	R	ER	HR	BB-IBB	SO
1998—	Texas (A.L.)	0	1	.000	4.50	1	1	0	0	0-0	6.0	8	3	3	2	1-0	9
1999—	Texas (A.L.)	0	1	.000	2.84	1	1	0	0	0-0	6.1	5	2	2	0	1-0	8
2002—	Arizona (N.L.)	0	0	...	0.00	2	0	0	0	0-0	4.0	1	0	0	0	0-0	2
Division series totals (3 years)		0	2	.000	2.76	4	2	0	0	0-0	16.1	14	5	5	2	2-0	19

HELMS, WES — 3B — BRAVES

PERSONAL: Born May 12, 1976, in Gastonia, N.C. ... 6-4/230. ... Bats right, throws right. ... Full name: Wesley Ray Helms.
HIGH SCHOOL: Ashbrook (Gastonia, N.C.).
TRANSACTIONS/CAREER NOTES: Selected by Atlanta Braves organization in 10th round of free-agent draft (June 2, 1994). ... On Atlanta disabled list (April 3-July 15 and September 5, 1999-remainder of season); included rehabilitation assignment to Gulf Coast Braves (June 22-July 11). ... On Greenville disabled list (August 15-September 4, 1999). ... On disabled list (August 10-September 10, 2002).
STATISTICAL NOTES: Tied for Gulf Coast League lead with 47 putouts by third basemen in 1994. ... Led South Atlantic League third basemen with 269 assists, 400 total chances and 25 double plays in 1995. ... Led International League third basemen with 24 double plays in 1998. ... Led International League third basemen with 341 total chances and 28 double plays in 2000. ... Career major league grand slams: 1.
2002 GAMES PLAYED BY POSITION (MLB): 1B—45; 3B—24; OF—9.

Year	Team (League)	Pos.	G	AB	R	H	2B	3B	HR	RBI	BB	SO	SB-CS	Avg.	OBP	SLG	E	Avg.
								BATTING									FIELDING	
1994—	GC Braves (GCL)	3B	56	184	22	49	15	1	4	29	22	36	6-1	.266	.355	.424	20	.875
1995—	Macon (S.Atl.)	3B	136	*539	89	149	32	1	11	85	50	107	2-2	.276	.347	.401	40	.900
1996—	Durham (Caro.)	3B	67	258	40	83	19	2	13	54	12	51	1-1	.322	.367	.562	15	.920
—	Greenville (Sou.)	3B	64	231	24	59	13	2	4	22	13	48	2-1	.255	.306	.381	12	.924
1997—	Richmond (I.L.)	3B	32	110	11	21	4	0	3	15	10	34	1-1	.191	.286	.309	9	.902
—	Greenville (Sou.)	3B	86	314	50	93	14	1	11	44	33	50	3-4	.296	.371	.452	11	.950
1998—	Richmond (I.L.)	3B-DH	125	451	56	124	27	1	13	75	35	103	6-2	.275	.342	.426	15	.952
—	Atlanta (N.L.)	3B	7	13	2	4	1	0	1	2	0	4	0-0	.308	.308	.615	1	.750
1999—	GC Braves (GCL)	DH-1B	9	33	1	15	2	0	0	10	5	4	0-1	.455	.538	.515	0	1.000
—	Greenville (Sou.)	1B	30	113	15	34	6	0	8	26	7	34	1-0	.301	.347	.566	4	.984
2000—	Richmond (I.L.)	3B	136	539	74	155	27	7	20	88	27	92	0-6	.288	.325	.475	23	.933
—	Atlanta (N.L.)	3B	6	5	0	1	0	0	0	0	0	2	0-0	.200	.200	.200	1	.833
2001—	Atlanta (N.L.)	1B-3B-OF	100	216	28	48	10	3	10	36	21	56	1-1	.222	.293	.435	4	.992
2002—	Atlanta (N.L.)	1B-3B-OF	85	210	20	51	16	0	6	22	11	57	1-1	.243	.283	.405	5	.986
Major League totals (4 years)			198	444	50	104	27	3	17	60	32	119	2-2	.234	.287	.423	11	.987

DIVISION SERIES RECORD

Year	Team (League)	Pos.	G	AB	R	H	2B	3B	HR	RBI	BB	SO	SB-CS	Avg.	OBP	SLG	E	Avg.
								BATTING									FIELDING	
2002—	Atlanta (N.L.)	1B	1	0	0	0	0	0	0	0	0	0	0-0	...	...	...	0	...

HELTON, TODD — 1B — ROCKIES

PERSONAL: Born August 20, 1973, in Knoxville, Tenn. ... 6-2/204. ... Bats left, throws left. ... Full name: Todd Lynn Helton.

HIGH SCHOOL: Knoxville (Tenn.) Central.

COLLEGE: Tennessee.

TRANSACTIONS/CAREER NOTES: Selected by San Diego Padres organization in second round of free-agent draft (June 1, 1992); did not sign. ... Selected by Colorado Rockies organization in first round (eighth pick overall) of free-agent draft (June 3, 1995). ... On New Haven disabled list (June 15-24, 1996).

HONORS: Named N.L. Rookie Player of the Year by The Sporting News (1998). ... Named first baseman on The Sporting News N.L. All-Star team (2000-02). ... Named first baseman on The Sporting News N.L. Silver Slugger team (2000). ... Named first baseman on N.L. Silver Slugger team (2001 and 2002). ... Won N.L. Gold Glove at first base (2001-02).

STATISTICAL NOTES: Led N.L. first basemen with 146 assists in 1998 and 148 in 2000. ... Led N.L. first basemen in double plays with 156 in 1998, 152 in 1999 and 143 in 2000. ... Hit for the cycle (June 19, 1999). ... Led N.L. first basemen with 1,328 putouts and 1,482 total chances in 2000. ... Hit three home runs in one game (May 1, 2000). ... Led N.L. with 405 total bases in 2000. ... Led N.L. first basemen with 1,358 putouts, 1,477 total chances and 138 double plays in 2002. ... Career major league grand slams: 2.

2002 GAMES PLAYED BY POSITION (MLB): 1B—156.

Year	Team (League)	Pos.	G	AB	R	H	2B	3B	HR	RBI	BB	SO	SB-CS	Avg.	OBP	SLG	E	Avg.
								BATTING									FIELDING	
1995—	Asheville (S.Atl.)	1B-DH	54	201	24	51	11	1	1	15	25	32	1-1	.254	.339	.333	4	.990
1996—	New Haven (East.)	1B-DH	93	319	46	106	24	2	7	51	51	37	2-5	.332	.425	.486	5	.994
—	Colo. Springs (PCL)	1B-OF	21	71	13	25	4	1	2	13	11	12	0-0	.352	.439	.521	2	.988
1997—	Colo. Springs (PCL)	1B-OF-DH	99	392	87	138	31	2	16	88	61	68	3-1	.352	.434	.564	9	.987
—	Colorado (N.L.)	OF-1B	35	93	13	26	2	1	5	11	8	11	0-1	.280	.337	.484	0	1.000
1998—	Colorado (N.L.)	1B	152	530	78	167	37	1	25	97	53	54	3-3	.315	.380	.530	7	.995
1999—	Colorado (N.L.)	1B	159	578	114	185	39	5	35	113	68	77	7-6	.320	.395	.587	9	.993
2000—	Colorado (N.L.)	1B	160	580	138	*216	*59	2	42	*147	103	61	5-3	*.372	*.463	*.698	7	.995
2001—	Colorado (N.L.)	1B	159	587	132	197	54	2	49	146	98	104	7-5	.336	.432	.685	2	.999
2002—	Colorado (N.L.)	1B	156	553	107	182	39	4	30	109	99	91	5-1	.329	.429	.577	7	.995
Major League totals (6 years)			821	2921	582	973	230	15	186	623	429	398	27-19	.333	.419	.613	32	.996

ALL-STAR GAME RECORD

	AB	R	H	2B	3B	HR	RBI	BB	SO	SB-CS	Avg.	OBP	SLG	E	Avg.
All-Star Game totals (3 years)	6	1	1	0	0	0	1	0	1	0-0	.167	.167	.167	0	1.000

HENDERSON, RICKEY — OF — RED SOX

PERSONAL: Born December 25, 1958, in Chicago. ... 5-10/190. ... Bats right, throws left. ... Full name: Rickey Henley Henderson.

HIGH SCHOOL: Technical (Oakland).

TRANSACTIONS/CAREER NOTES: Selected by Oakland Athletics organization in fourth round of free-agent draft (June 8, 1976). ... Traded by A's with P Bert Bradley and cash to New York Yankees for OF Stan Javier, P Jay Howell, P Jose Rijo, P Eric Plunk and P Tim Birtsas (December 5, 1984). ... On New York disabled list (March 30-April 22, 1985); included rehabilitation assignment to Fort Lauderdale (April 19-22). ... On disabled list (June 5-29 and July 26-September 1, 1987). ... Traded by Yankees to A's for P Greg Cadaret, P Eric Plunk and OF Luis Polonia (June 21, 1989). ... Granted free agency (November 13, 1989). ... Re-signed by A's (November 28, 1989). ... On disabled list (April 12-27, 1991; May 28-June 17 and June 30-July 16, 1992). ... Traded by A's to Toronto Blue Jays for P Steve Karsay and a player to be named later (July 31, 1993); A's acquired OF Jose Herrera to complete deal (August 6, 1993). ... Granted free agency (October 29, 1993). ... Signed by A's (December 17, 1993). ... On disabled list (May 11-27, 1994). ... Granted free agency (October 30, 1995). ... Signed by San Diego Padres (December 29, 1995). ... On San Diago disabled list (May 9-24, 1997). ... Traded by Padres to Anaheim Angels for P Ryan Hancock, P Stevenson Agosto and a player to be named later (August 13, 1997); Padres acquired 3B George Arias to complete deal (August 19, 1997). ... Granted free agency (October 27, 1997). ... Signed by A's (January 22, 1998). ... Granted free agency (October 26, 1998). ... Signed by New York Mets (December 16, 1998). ... On disabled list (May 3-22, 1999). ... Released by Mets (May 13, 2000). ... Signed by Seattle Mariners (May 19, 2000). ... Granted free agency (November 3, 2000). ... Signed by Padres organization (March 19, 2001). ... Granted free agency (November 5, 2001). ... Signed by Boston Red Sox organization (February 13, 2002).

RECORDS: Holds major league career records for most stolen bases—1,403; most bases on balls—2,179; most times caught stealing—335; most runs—2,288; and most home runs leading off game—80. ... Holds major league single-season records for most stolen bases—130 (1982); and most times caught stealing—42 (1982). ... Holds major league record for most seasons leading league in stolen bases—12; and most years with 50 or more stolen bases—13. ... Holds A.L. career records for most stolen bases—1,270; most home runs leading off game—72; and most times caught stealing—293. ... Holds A.L. record for most consecutive years with 50 or more stolen bases—7 (1980-86).

... Shares major league career record for most years by outfielder—24 (1979-2002). ... Shares A.L. single-season record for fewest times caught stealing (50 or more stolen bases)—8 (1993). ... Shares A.L. record for most stolen bases in two consecutive games—7 (July 3 [4], 15 innings, and 4 [3], 1983; and August 11 [4], 11 innings and 12 [3], 1988).

HONORS: Named outfielder on The Sporting News A.L. All-Star team (1981, 1985 and 1990). ... Named outfielder on The Sporting News A.L. Silver Slugger team (1981, 1985 and 1990). ... Won A.L. Gold Glove as outfielder (1981). ... Won The Sporting News Silver Shoe Award (1982). ... Won The Sporting News Golden Shoe Award (1983). ... Named A.L. Most Valuable Player by Baseball Writers' Association of America (1990). ... Named N.L. Comeback Player of the Year by The Sporting News (1999).

STATISTICAL NOTES: Led California League in caught stealing with 22 in 1977. ... Led Eastern League in caught stealing with 28 in 1978. ... Led Eastern League outfielders with four double plays and tied for league lead with 15 assists in 1978. ... Led A.L. in caught stealing with 26 in 1980, 22 in 1981, 42 in 1982, 19 in 1983 and tied for lead with 18 in 1986. ... Led A.L. outfielders with 327 putouts and 341 total chances in 1981. ... Tied for A.L. lead in double plays by outfielder with five in 1988. ... Led A.L. with 77 stolen bases and 126 bases on balls in 1989. ... Tied for A.L. lead with 113 runs scored in 1989. ... Career major league grand slams: 3.

MISCELLANEOUS: Holds Oakland Athletics franchise all-time records for most runs (1,270) and most stolen bases (867). ... Holds New York Yankees all-time record for most stolen bases (326).

2002 GAMES PLAYED BY POSITION (MLB): OF—54; DH—5.

			BATTING														FIELDING	
Year	Team (League)	Pos.	G	AB	R	H	2B	3B	HR	RBI	BB	SO	SB-CS	Avg.	OBP	SLG	E	Avg.
1976—	Boise (N'West)	OF	46	140	34	47	13	2	3	23	33	32	29-7	.336	.463	.521	*12	.895
1977—	Modesto (Calif.)	OF	134	481	120	166	18	4	11	69	104	67	*95-22	.345	.466	.468	*20	.936
1978—	Jersey City (East.)	OF	133	455	81	141	14	4	0	34	83	67	*81-28	.310	.417	.358	7	.979
1979—	Ogden (PCL)	OF	71	259	66	80	11	8	3	26	53	41	44-9	.309	.430	.448	6	.963
—	Oakland (A.L.)	OF	89	351	49	96	13	3	1	26	34	39	33-11	.274	.338	.336	6	.973
1980—	Oakland (A.L.)	OF-DH	158	591	111	179	22	4	9	53	117	54	*100-26	.303	.420	.399	7	.984
1981—	Oakland (A.L.)	OF	108	423	*89	*135	18	7	6	35	64	68	*56-22	.319	.408	.437	7	.979
1982—	Oakland (A.L.)	OF-DH	149	536	119	143	24	4	10	51	*116	94	*130-42	.267	.398	.382	9	.977
1983—	Oakland (A.L.)	OF-DH	145	513	105	150	25	7	9	48	*103	80	*108-19	.292	.414	.421	3	.992
1984—	Oakland (A.L.)	OF	142	502	113	147	27	4	16	58	86	81	*66-18	.293	.399	.458	11	.969
1985—	Fort Laud. (FSL)■	OF	3	6	5	1	0	1	0	3	5	2	1-1	.167	.545	.500	0	1.000
—	New York (A.L.)	OF-DH	143	547	*146	172	28	5	24	72	99	65	*80-10	.314	.419	.516	9	.980
1986—	New York (A.L.)	OF-DH	153	608	*130	160	31	5	28	74	89	81	*87-18	.263	.358	.469	6	.986
1987—	New York (A.L.)	OF-DH	95	358	78	104	17	3	17	37	80	52	41-8	.291	.423	.497	4	.980
1988—	New York (A.L.)	OF-DH	140	554	118	169	30	2	6	50	82	54	*93-13	.305	.394	.399	12	.965
1989—	New York (A.L.)	OF	65	235	41	58	13	1	3	22	56	29	25-8	.247	.392	.349	1	.993
—	Oakland (A.L.)■	OF-DH	85	306	§72	90	13	2	9	35	§70	39	§52-6	.294	.425	.438	3	.985
1990—	Oakland (A.L.)	OF-DH	136	489	*119	159	33	3	28	61	97	60	*65-10	.325	*.439	.577	5	.983
1991—	Oakland (A.L.)	OF-DH	134	470	105	126	17	1	18	57	98	73	*58-18	.268	.400	.423	8	.970
1992—	Oakland (A.L.)	OF-DH	117	396	77	112	18	3	15	46	95	56	48-11	.283	.426	.457	4	.984
1993—	Oakland (A.L.)	OF-DH	90	318	77	104	19	1	17	47	85	46	31-6	.327	.469	.553	5	.974
—	Toronto (A.L.)■	OF	44	163	37	35	3	1	4	12	35	19	22-2	.215	.356	.319	2	.975
1994—	Oakland (A.L.)■	OF-DH	87	296	66	77	13	0	6	20	72	45	22-7	.260	.411	.365	4	.977
1995—	Oakland (A.L.)	OF-DH	112	407	67	122	31	1	9	54	72	66	32-10	.300	.407	.447	2	.988
1996—	San Diego (N.L.)■	OF	148	465	110	112	17	2	9	29	125	90	37-15	.241	.410	.344	6	.975
1997—	San Diego (N.L.)	OF-DH	88	288	63	79	11	0	6	27	71	62	29-4	.274	.422	.375	7	.959
—	Anaheim (A.L.)■	DH-OF	32	115	21	21	3	0	2	7	26	23	16-4	.183	.343	.261	0	1.000
1998—	Oakland (A.L.)■	OF	152	542	101	128	16	1	14	57	*118	114	*66-13	.236	.376	.347	4	.988
1999—	New York (N.L.)■	OF-DH	121	438	89	138	30	0	12	42	82	82	37-14	.315	.423	.466	2	.988
2000—	New York (N.L.)	OF	31	96	17	21	1	0	0	2	25	20	5-2	.219	.387	.229	2	.946
—	Seattle (A.L.)■	OF-DH	92	324	58	77	13	2	4	30	63	55	31-9	.238	.362	.327	3	.984
2001—	Portland (PCL)■	OF	9	40	5	11	3	0	0	2	1	9	1-0	.275	.293	.350	1	.933
—	San Diego (N.L.)	OF-DH	123	379	70	86	17	3	8	42	81	84	25-7	.227	.366	.351	3	.982
2002—	Boston (A.L.)■	OF-DH	72	179	40	40	6	1	5	16	38	47	8-2	.223	.369	.352	5	.946
American League totals (21 years)			2540	9223	1939	2604	433	61	260	968	1795	1340	1270-293	.282	.401	.427	120	.980
National League totals (5 years)			511	1666	349	436	76	5	35	142	384	338	133-42	.262	.404	.376	20	.974
Major League totals (24 years)			3051	10889	2288	3040	509	66	295	1110	2179	1678	1403-335	.279	.402	.419	140	.979

DIVISION SERIES RECORD

RECORDS: Shares career record for most stolen bases—9.

			BATTING														FIELDING	
Year	Team (League)	Pos.	G	AB	R	H	2B	3B	HR	RBI	BB	SO	SB-CS	Avg.	OBP	SLG	E	Avg.
1981—	Oakland (A.L.)	OF	3	11	3	2	0	0	0	0	2	0	2-0	.182	.308	.182	0	1.000
1996—	San Diego (N.L.)	OF	3	12	2	4	0	0	1	1	2	3	0-0	.333	.429	.583	0	1.000
1999—	New York (N.L.)	OF	4	15	5	6	0	0	0	1	3	1	6-0	.400	.500	.400	0	1.000
2000—	Seattle (A.L.)	OF-PR	3	5	3	2	0	0	0	0	1	0	1-0	.400	.500	.400	0	1.000
Division series totals (4 years)			13	43	13	14	0	0	1	2	8	4	9-0	.326	.431	.395	0	1.000

CHAMPIONSHIP SERIES RECORD

RECORDS: Holds career records for most stolen bases—17. ... Holds single-series record for most stolen bases—8 (1989). ... Holds single-game record for most stolen bases—4 (October 4, 1989). ... Shares career record for most doubles—7. ... Shares single inning records for most at-bats in—2; most hits in—2; most singles in—2 (October 6, 1990, ninth inning); and most stolen bases in—2 (October 4, 1989, fourth and seventh innings). ... Shares single-series record for most runs—8 (1989). ... Shares A.L. single-game record for most at-bats—6 (October 5, 1993).

NOTES: Named Most Valuable Player (1989).

			BATTING														FIELDING	
Year	Team (League)	Pos.	G	AB	R	H	2B	3B	HR	RBI	BB	SO	SB-CS	Avg.	OBP	SLG	E	Avg.
1981—	Oakland (A.L.)	OF	3	11	0	4	2	1	0	1	1	2	2-0	.364	.417	.727	1	.857
1989—	Oakland (A.L.)	OF	5	15	8	6	1	1	2	5	7	0	8-1	.400	.609	1.000	1	.929
1990—	Oakland (A.L.)	OF	4	17	1	5	0	0	0	3	1	2	2-1	.294	.316	.294	0	1.000
1992—	Oakland (A.L.)	OF	6	23	5	6	0	0	0	1	4	4	2-0	.261	.370	.261	3	.833
1993—	Toronto (A.L.)	OF	6	25	4	3	2	0	0	0	4	5	2-1	.120	.241	.200	1	.900
1999—	New York (N.L.)	OF	6	23	2	4	1	0	0	1	0	5	1-0	.174	.174	.217	1	.900
2000—	Seattle (A.L.)	OF	3	9	2	2	1	0	0	1	2	2	0-1	.222	.364	.333	0	1.000
Championship series totals (7 years)			33	123	22	30	7	2	2	12	19	20	17-4	.244	.347	.382	7	.901

WORLD SERIES RECORD

RECORDS: Shares single-game record for most at-bats—6 (October 28, 1989).

NOTES: Member of World Series championship team (1989 and 1993).

		BATTING														FIELDING	
Year Team (League)	**Pos.**	**G**	**AB**	**R**	**H**	**2B**	**3B**	**HR**	**RBI**	**BB**	**SO**	**SB-CS**	**Avg.**	**OBP**	**SLG**	**E**	**Avg.**
1989— Oakland (A.L.)	OF	4	19	4	9	1	2	1	3	2	2	3-1	.474	.524	.895	0	1.000
1990— Oakland (A.L.)	OF	4	15	2	5	2	0	1	1	3	4	3-0	.333	.444	.667	0	1.000
1993— Toronto (A.L.)	OF	6	22	6	5	2	0	0	2	5	2	1-1	.227	.393	.318	0	1.000
World Series totals (3 years)		14	56	12	19	5	2	2	6	10	8	7-2	.339	.448	.607	0	1.000

ALL-STAR GAME RECORD

RECORDS: Shares single-game record for most singles—3 (July 13, 1982).

	AB	**R**	**H**	**2B**	**3B**	**HR**	**RBI**	**BB**	**SO**	**SB-CS**	**Avg.**	**OBP**	**SLG**	**E**	**Avg.**
All-Star Game totals (10 years)	24	3	7	0	0	0	1	1	4	2-0	.292	.320	.292	1	.900

HENDRICKSON, MARK — P — BLUE JAYS

PERSONAL: Born June 23, 1974, in Mount Vernon, Wash. ... 6-9/230. ... Throws left, bats left. ... Full name: Mark A. Hendrickson.

COLLEGE: Washington State.

TRANSACTIONS/CAREER NOTES: Selected by Toronto Blue Jays organization in 20th round of free-agent draft (June 3, 1997). ... On Syracuse disabled list (June 18-July 12, 2002).

CAREER HITTING (MLB): 0-for-0 (.000), 0 R, 0 2B, 0 3B, 0 HR, 0 RBI.

Year League	**W**	**L**	**Pct.**	**ERA**	**G**	**GS**	**CG**	**ShO**	**Sv.-Opp.**	**IP**	**H**	**R**	**ER**	**HR**	**BB-IBB**	**SO**
1998— Dunedin (FSL)	4	3	.571	2.37	16	5	0	0	1-...	49.1	44	16	13	2	26-1	38
1999— Knoxville (Sou.)	2	7	.222	6.63	12	11	0	0	0-...	55.2	73	46	41	4	21-0	39
2000— Dunedin (FSL)	2	2	.500	5.61	12	12	1	0	0-...	51.1	63	34	32	7	29-0	38
— Tennessee (Sou.)	3	1	.750	3.63	6	6	0	0	0-...	39.2	32	17	16	5	12-0	29
2001— Syracuse (I.L.)	2	9	.182	4.66	38	6	0	0	0-...	73.1	80	43	38	13	18-1	33
2002— Syracuse (I.L.)	7	5	.583	3.52	19	14	0	0	0-...	92.0	90	38	36	12	22-0	68
— Toronto (A.L.)	3	0	1.000	2.45	16	4	0	0	0-1	36.2	25	11	10	1	12-3	21
Major League totals (1 year)	3	0	1.000	2.45	16	4	0	0	0-1	36.2	25	11	10	1	12-3	21

HENRIQUEZ, OSCAR — P — TIGERS

PERSONAL: Born January 28, 1974, in LaGuaira, Venezuela. ... 6-6/220. ... Throws right, bats right. ... Full name: Oscar Eduardo Henriquez.

TRANSACTIONS/CAREER NOTES: Signed as non-drafted free agent by Houston Astros organization (May 20, 1991). ... On disabled list (June 15, 1994-remainder of season). ... Traded by Astros with P Manuel Barrios and a player to be named later to Florida Marlins for OF Moises Alou (November 11, 1997). ... On Charlotte disabled list (July 14-31, 1998). ... Traded by Marlins to New York Mets for C Jorge Fabregas (November 20, 1998). ... Released by Mets (March 17, 1999). ... Re-signed by Mets organization (March 22, 1999). ... Granted free agency (October 15, 1999). ... Signed by San Diego Padres organization (November 4, 1999). ... Released by Padres (March 29, 2000). ... Signed by Mexico City Red Devils, Mexican League (April 2000). ... Contract purchased by Mets organization from Mexico City (July 12, 2000). ... Granted free agency (October 18, 2000). ... Re-signed by Mets organization (December 23, 2000). ... Contract sold by Mets to Hyundai, Korean League (July 16, 2001). ... Signed by Detroit Tigers organization (December 19, 2001). ... On Detroit disabled list (September 20, 2002-remainder of season).

CAREER HITTING (MLB): 0-for-1 (.000), 0 R, 0 2B, 0 3B, 0 HR, 0 RBI.

Year League	**W**	**L**	**Pct.**	**ERA**	**G**	**GS**	**CG**	**ShO**	**Sv.-Opp.**	**IP**	**H**	**R**	**ER**	**HR**	**BB-IBB**	**SO**
1991— Dominican Astros (DSL)	1	5	.167	7.50	9	9	0	0	0-...	24.0	29	31	20	...	24-...	6
1992—	Dominican League statistics unavailable.															
1993— Asheville (S.Atl.)	9	10	.474	4.44	27	26	2	1	0-...	150.0	154	95	74	12	70-2	117
1994—	Did not play.															
1995— Kissimmee (FSL)	3	4	.429	5.04	20	0	0	0	1-...	44.2	40	29	25	2	30-0	36
1996— Kissimmee (FSL)	0	4	.000	3.97	37	0	0	0	15-...	34.0	28	18	15	0	29-2	40
1997— New Orleans (A.A.)	4	5	.444	2.80	*60	0	0	0	12-...	74.0	65	28	23	4	27-3	80
— Houston (N.L.)	0	1	.000	4.50	4	0	0	0	0-0	4.0	2	2	2	0	3-0	3
1998— Florida (N.L.)■	0	0	...	8.55	15	0	0	0	0-0	20.0	26	22	19	4	12-0	19
— Charlotte (I.L.)	1	0	1.000	2.56	26	0	0	0	11-...	31.2	29	12	9	3	12-0	37
1999— Norfolk (I.L.)■	3	4	.429	4.00	53	0	0	0	23-...	54.0	54	31	24	8	38-4	65
2000— MC Red Devils (Mex.)■	7	2	.778	3.83	36	0	0	0	0-...	47.0	38	26	20	...	23-...	65
— Norfolk (I.L.)■	0	1	.000	6.43	16	0	0	0	4-...	14.0	12	10	10	2	11-1	14
2001— Norfolk (I.L.)	2	4	.333	2.82	39	0	0	0	19-...	38.1	30	13	12	1	19-0	44
— Hyundai (Kor.)■	Statistics unavailable.															
2002— Toledo (I.L.)■	2	1	.667	3.31	33	0	0	0	17-...	32.2	30	13	12	4	14-0	39
— Detroit (A.L.)	1	1	.500	4.50	30	0	0	0	2-2	28.0	19	14	14	5	15-4	23
A.L. totals (1 year)	1	1	.500	4.50	30	0	0	0	2-2	28.0	19	14	14	5	15-4	23
N.L. totals (2 years)	0	1	.000	7.88	19	0	0	0	0-0	24.0	28	24	21	4	15-0	22
Major League totals (3 years)	1	2	.333	6.06	49	0	0	0	2-2	52.0	47	38	35	9	30-4	45

HENSON, DREW — 3B — YANKEES

PERSONAL: Born February 13, 1980, in San Diego. ... 6-5/222. ... Bats right, throws right. ... Full name: Drew Daniel Henson.

HIGH SCHOOL: Brighton (Mich.).

COLLEGE: Michigan.

TRANSACTIONS/CAREER NOTES: Selected by New York Yankees organization in third round of free-agent draft (June 2, 1998). ... Traded by Yankees with OF Jackson Melian, P Ed Yarnall and P Brian Reith to Cincinnati Reds for P Denny Neagle and OF Mike Frank (July 12, 2000). ... Traded by Reds with OF Michael Coleman to Yankees for OF Wily Mo Pena (March 20, 2001).

2002 GAMES PLAYED BY POSITION (MLB): DH—2.

Year	Team (League)	Pos.	G	AB	R	H	2B	3B	HR	RBI	BB	SO	SB-CS	Avg.	OBP	SLG	E	Avg.
			BATTING														FIELDING	
1998—	GC Yankees (GCL)	3B	10	38	5	12	3	0	1	2	3	9	0-0	.316	.366	.474	2	.951
1999—	Tampa (FSL)	3B	69	254	37	71	12	0	13	37	26	71	3-1	.280	.345	.480	17	.864
2000—	Tampa (FSL)	3B	5	21	4	7	2	0	1	1	1	7	0-1	.333	.364	.571	0	1.000
	—Norwich (East.)	3B	59	223	39	64	9	2	7	39	20	75	0-5	.287	.347	.439	9	.917
	—Chattanooga (Sou.)■	3B	16	64	7	11	8	0	1	9	4	25	2-0	.172	.221	.344	3	.933
2001—	Tampa (FSL)	3B	5	14	2	2	0	0	1	3	2	7	1-0	.143	.316	.357	1	.929
	—Norwich (East.)	3B	5	19	2	7	1	0	0	2	1	4	0-1	.368	.429	.421	3	.842
	—Columbus (I.L.)	3B	71	270	29	60	6	0	11	38	10	85	2-1	.222	.249	.367	16	.912
2002—	Columbus (I.L.)	3B	128	471	68	113	30	4	18	65	37	151	2-1	.240	.301	.435	*35	.893
	—New York (A.L.)	DH	3	1	1	0	0	0	0	0	0	1	0-0	.000	.000	.000	...	...
Major League totals (1 year)			3	1	1	0	0	0	0	0	0	1	0-0	.000	.000	.000	0	...

HENTGEN, PAT — P — ORIOLES

PERSONAL: Born November 13, 1968, in Detroit. ... 6-2/195. ... Throws right, bats right. ... Full name: Patrick George Hentgen.

HIGH SCHOOL: Fraser (Mich.).

TRANSACTIONS/CAREER NOTES: Selected by Toronto Blue Jays organization in fifth round of free-agent draft (June 2, 1986). ... On Toronto disabled list (August 13-September 29, 1992); included rehabilitation assignment to Syracuse (September 1-8). ... Traded by Blue Jays with P Paul Spoljaric to St. Louis Cardinals for P Lance Painter, C Alberto Castillo and P Matt DeWitt (November 11, 1999). ... Granted free agency (October 31, 2000). ... Signed by Baltimore Orioles (December 19, 2000). ... On disabled list (May 17, 2001-remainder of season). ... On Baltimore disabled list (March 31-September 8, 2002); included rehabilitation assignments to Gulf Coast Orioles (August 5-9), Delmarva (August 10-15), Aberdeen (August 16-27 and September), Bowie (August 28-September 1) and Frederick (September 3).

HONORS: Named A.L. Pitcher of the Year by The Sporting News (1996). ... Named righthanded pitcher on The Sporting News A.L. All-Star team (1996). ... Named A.L. Cy Young Award winner by Baseball Writers' Association of America (1996).

STATISTICAL NOTES: Combined with relievers Willie Blair and Enrique Burgos in 2-1 no-hit victory against Osceola (May 10, 1988).

CAREER HITTING (MLB): 9-for-78 (.115), 4 R, 0 2B, 0 3B, 0 HR, 0 RBI.

Year	League	W	L	Pct.	ERA	G	GS	CG	ShO	Sv.-Opp.	IP	H	R	ER	HR	BB-IBB	SO
1986—	St. Catharines (NY-Penn)	0	4	.000	4.50	13	11	0	0	1-...	40.0	38	27	20	3	30-1	30
1987—	Myrtle Beach (S.Atl.)	11	5	.688	2.35	32	*31	2	2	0-...	*188.0	145	62	49	5	60-0	131
1988—	Dunedin (FSL)	3	12	.200	3.45	31	*30	0	0	0-...	151.1	139	80	58	10	65-1	125
1989—	Dunedin (FSL)	9	8	.529	2.68	29	28	0	0	0-...	151.1	123	53	45	5	71-1	148
1990—	Knoxville (Sou.)	9	5	.643	3.05	28	26	0	0	0-...	153.1	121	57	52	10	68-0	142
1991—	Syracuse (I.L.)	8	9	.471	4.47	31	•28	1	0	0-...	171.0	146	91	85	17	*90-1	*155
	—Toronto (A.L.)	0	0	...	2.45	3	1	0	0	0-0	7.1	5	2	2	1	3-0	3
1992—	Toronto (A.L.)	5	2	.714	5.36	28	2	0	0	0-1	50.1	49	30	30	7	32-5	39
	—Syracuse (I.L.)	1	2	.333	2.66	4	4	0	0	0-...	20.1	15	6	6	1	8-0	17
1993—	Toronto (A.L.)	19	9	.679	3.87	34	32	3	0	0-0	216.1	215	103	93	27	74-0	122
1994—	Toronto (A.L.)	13	8	.619	3.40	24	24	6	3	0-0	174.2	158	74	66	21	59-1	147
1995—	Toronto (A.L.)	10	14	.417	5.11	30	30	2	0	0-0	200.2	*236	*129	*114	24	90-6	135
1996—	Toronto (A.L.)	20	10	.667	3.22	35	35	*10	•3	0-0	*265.2	238	105	95	20	94-3	177
1997—	Toronto (A.L.)	15	10	.600	3.68	35	•35	•9	•3	0-0	•264.0	253	116	108	31	71-2	160
1998—	Toronto (A.L.)	12	11	.522	5.17	29	29	0	0	0-0	177.2	208	109	102	28	69-1	94
1999—	Toronto (A.L.)	11	12	.478	4.79	34	34	1	0	0-0	199.0	225	115	106	32	65-1	118
2000—	St. Louis (N.L.)■	15	12	.556	4.72	33	33	1	1	0-0	194.1	202	107	102	24	89-4	118
2001—	Baltimore (A.L.)■	2	3	.400	3.47	9	9	1	0	0-0	62.1	51	25	24	7	19-3	33
2002—	Gulf Coast Orioles (GCL)	0	0	...	0.00	1	1	0	0	0-...	3.0	2	0	0	0	0-0	3
	—Delmarva (S.Atl.)	0	1	.000	1.80	1	1	0	0	0-...	5.0	4	1	1	0	1-0	4
	—Aberdeen (NY-Penn)	1	1	.500	3.09	2	2	0	0	0-...	11.2	16	8	4	1	0-0	10
	—Bowie (East.)	0	0	...	1.50	1	1	0	0	0-...	6.0	5	2	1	1	2-0	3
	—Frederick (Caro.)	1	0	1.000	2.57	1	1	1	0	0-...	7.0	5	2	2	0	2-0	5
	—Baltimore (A.L.)	0	4	.000	7.77	4	4	0	0	0-0	22.0	31	20	19	6	10-0	11
A.L. totals (11 years)		107	83	.563	4.17	265	235	32	9	0-1	1640.0	1669	828	759	204	586-22	1039
N.L. totals (1 year)		15	12	.556	4.72	33	33	1	1	0-0	194.1	202	107	102	24	89-4	118
Major League totals (12 years)		122	95	.562	4.22	298	268	33	10	0-1	1834.1	1871	935	861	228	675-26	1157

DIVISION SERIES RECORD

Year	League	W	L	Pct.	ERA	G	GS	CG	ShO	Sv.-Opp.	IP	H	R	ER	HR	BB-IBB	SO
2000—	St. Louis (N.L.)									Did not play.							

CHAMPIONSHIP SERIES RECORD

Year	League	W	L	Pct.	ERA	G	GS	CG	ShO	Sv.-Opp.	IP	H	R	ER	HR	BB-IBB	SO
1993—	Toronto (A.L.)	0	1	.000	18.00	1	1	0	0	0-0	3.0	9	6	6	0	2-0	3
2000—	St. Louis (N.L.)	0	1	.000	14.73	1	1	0	0	0-0	3.2	7	6	6	0	5-0	2
Champ. series totals (2 years)		0	2	.000	16.20	2	2	0	0	0-0	6.2	16	12	12	0	7-0	5

WORLD SERIES RECORD

NOTES: Member of World Series championship team (1993).

Year	League	W	L	Pct.	ERA	G	GS	CG	ShO	Sv.-Opp.	IP	H	R	ER	HR	BB-IBB	SO
1993—	Toronto (A.L.)	1	0	1.000	1.50	1	1	0	0	0-0	6.0	5	1	1	0	3-0	6

ALL-STAR GAME RECORD

	W	L	Pct.	ERA	GS	CG	ShO	Sv.-Opp.	IP	H	R	ER	HR	BB-IBB	SO
All-Star Game totals (2 years)	0	0	...	0.00	0	0	0	0-0	2.0	1	0	0	0	0-0	0

HEREDIA, FELIX — P

PERSONAL: Born June 18, 1975, in Barahona, Dominican Republic. ... 6-0/190. ... Throws left, bats left. ... Full name: Felix Perez Heredia. ... Name pronounced heh-RAY-dee-ah.

HIGH SCHOOL: Escuela Dominical (Barahona, Dominican Republic).

TRANSACTIONS/CAREER NOTES: Signed as non-drafted free agent by Florida Marlins organization (November 22, 1992). ... Traded by Marlins with P Steve Hoff to Chicago Cubs for 3B Kevin Orie, P Todd Noel and P Justin Speier (July 31, 1998). ... On disabled list (August 21-September 5 and September 18-October 3, 2001). ... Traded by Cubs with a player to be named later to Toronto Blue Jays for SS Alex Gonzalez (December 10, 2001); Blue Jays acquired IF James Deschaine to complete deal (December 13, 2001). ... Granted free agency (October 28, 2002).
CAREER HITTING (MLB): 3-for-12 (.250), 0 R, 0 2B, 0 3B, 0 HR, 1 RBI.

Year League	W	L	Pct.	ERA	G	GS	CG	ShO	Sv.-Opp.	IP	H	R	ER	HR	BB-IBB	SO
1993— Gulf Coast Marlins (GCL)	5	1	.833	2.47	12	•12	0	0	0-...	62.0	50	18	17	0	11-0	53
1994— Kane County (Midw.)	4	5	.444	5.69	24	8	1	0	3-...	68.0	86	55	43	7	14-0	65
1995— Brevard County (FSL)	6	4	.600	3.57	34	8	0	0	1-...	95.2	101	52	38	6	36-1	76
1996— Portland (East.)	8	1	.889	1.50	55	0	0	0	5-...	60.0	48	11	10	3	15-2	42
— Florida (N.L.)	1	1	.500	4.32	21	0	0	0	0-0	16.2	21	8	8	1	10-1	10
1997— Florida (N.L.)	5	3	.625	4.29	56	0	0	0	0-1	56.2	53	30	27	3	30-1	54
1998— Florida (N.L.)	0	3	.000	5.49	41	2	0	0	2-3	41.0	38	30	25	1	32-2	38
— Chicago (N.L.)■	3	0	1.000	4.08	30	0	0	0	0-2	17.2	19	9	8	1	6-1	16
1999— Chicago (N.L.)	3	1	.750	4.85	69	0	0	0	1-7	52.0	56	35	28	7	25-2	50
2000— Chicago (N.L.)	7	3	.700	4.76	74	0	0	0	2-5	58.2	46	31	31	6	33-4	52
2001— Chicago (N.L.)	2	2	.500	6.17	48	0	0	0	0-3	35.0	45	27	24	6	16-1	28
2002— Toronto (A.L.)	1	2	.333	3.61	53	0	0	0	0-2	52.1	51	29	21	5	26-3	31
A.L. totals (1 year)	1	2	.333	3.61	53	0	0	0	0-2	52.1	51	29	21	5	26-3	31
N.L. totals (6 years)	21	13	.618	4.89	339	2	0	0	5-21	277.2	278	170	151	25	152-12	248
Major League totals (7 years)	22	15	.595	4.69	392	2	0	0	5-23	330.0	329	199	172	30	178-15	279

DIVISION SERIES RECORD

Year League	W	L	Pct.	ERA	G	GS	CG	ShO	Sv.-Opp.	IP	H	R	ER	HR	BB-IBB	SO
1997— Florida (N.L.)									Did not play.							
1998— Chicago (N.L.)	0	0	...	54.00	1	0	0	0	0-0	.1	0	2	2	0	2-0	0

CHAMPIONSHIP SERIES RECORD

Year League	W	L	Pct.	ERA	G	GS	CG	ShO	Sv.-Opp.	IP	H	R	ER	HR	BB-IBB	SO
1997— Florida (N.L.)	0	0	...	5.40	2	0	0	0	0-0	3.1	3	2	2	0	2-0	4

WORLD SERIES RECORD

NOTES: Member of World Series championship team (1997).

Year League	W	L	Pct.	ERA	G	GS	CG	ShO	Sv.-Opp.	IP	H	R	ER	HR	BB-IBB	SO
1997— Florida (N.L.)	0	0	...	0.00	4	0	0	0	0-0	5.1	2	0	0	0	1-0	5

HERGES, MATT — P — EXPOS

PERSONAL: Born April 1, 1970, in Champaign, Ill. ... 6-0/200. ... Throws right, bats left. ... Full name: Matthew Tyler Herges.
HIGH SCHOOL: Centennial (Champaign, Ill.).
COLLEGE: Illinois State.
TRANSACTIONS/CAREER NOTES: Signed as non-drafted free agent by Los Angeles Dodgers organization (June 13, 1992). ... Granted free agency (October 15, 1998). ... Re-signed by Dodgers organization (January 1, 1999). ... Traded by Dodgers with IF Jorge Nunez to Montreal Expos for P Guillermo Mota and OF Wilkin Ruan (March 24, 2002).
CAREER HITTING (MLB): 5-for-24 (.208), 0 R, 0 2B, 0 3B, 0 HR, 1 RBI.

Year League	W	L	Pct.	ERA	G	GS	CG	ShO	Sv.-Opp.	IP	H	R	ER	HR	BB-IBB	SO
1992— Yakima (N'West)	2	3	.400	3.22	27	0	0	0	9-...	44.2	33	21	16	2	24-1	57
1993— Bakersfield (Calif.)	2	6	.250	3.69	51	0	0	0	2-...	90.1	70	49	37	6	56-6	84
1994— Vero Beach (FSL)	8	9	.471	3.32	48	3	1	0	3-...	111.0	115	45	41	8	33-3	61
1995— San Antonio (Texas)	0	3	.000	4.88	19	0	0	0	8-...	27.2	34	16	15	2	16-1	18
— San Bernardino (Calif.)	5	2	.714	3.66	22	2	0	0	1-...	51.2	58	29	21	3	15-0	35
1996— San Antonio (Texas)	3	2	.600	2.71	30	6	0	0	3-...	83.0	83	38	25	3	28-0	45
— Albuquerque (PCL)	4	1	.800	2.60	10	4	2	1	0-...	34.2	33	11	10	2	14-0	15
1997— Albuquerque (PCL)	0	8	.000	8.89	31	12	0	0	0-...	85.0	120	92	84	13	46-1	61
— San Antonio (Texas)	0	1	.000	8.80	4	3	0	0	0-...	15.1	22	15	15	2	10-0	12
1998— Albuquerque (PCL)	3	5	.375	5.71	34	8	0	0	0-...	88.1	115	64	56	9	37-1	75
— San Antonio (Texas)	0	0	...	0.00	3	0	0	0	0-...	6.0	3	0	0	0	2-0	3
1999— Albuquerque (PCL)	8	3	.727	4.73	21	21	2	0	0-...	131.1	135	82	69	17	47-0	88
— Los Angeles (N.L.)	0	2	.000	4.07	17	0	0	0	0-2	24.1	24	13	11	5	8-0	18
2000— Los Angeles (N.L.)	11	3	.786	3.17	59	4	0	0	1-3	110.2	100	43	39	7	40-5	75
2001— Los Angeles (N.L.)	9	8	.529	3.44	75	0	0	0	1-8	99.1	97	39	38	8	46-12	76
2002— Montreal (N.L.)■	2	5	.286	4.04	62	0	0	0	6-14	64.2	80	33	29	10	26-8	50
Major League totals (4 years)	22	18	.550	3.52	213	4	0	0	8-27	299.0	301	128	117	30	120-25	219

HERMANSEN, CHAD — OF — CUBS

PERSONAL: Born September 10, 1977, in Salt Lake City. ... 6-2/192. ... Bats right, throws right. ... Full name: Chad B. Hermansen.
HIGH SCHOOL: Green Valley (Henderson, Nev.).
TRANSACTIONS/CAREER NOTES: Selected by Pittsburgh Pirates organization in first round (10th pick overall) of free-agent draft (June 1, 1995). ... On Pittsburgh disabled list (March 27-May 10, 2002); included rehabilitation assignment to Nashville (April 22-May 11). ... Traded by Pirates to Chicago Cubs for OF Darren Lewis (July 31, 2002).
STATISTICAL NOTES: Tied for Southern League lead in errors by outfielder with eight in 1997.
2002 GAMES PLAYED BY POSITION (MLB): OF—81.

		BATTING														FIELDING	
Year Team (League)	Pos.	G	AB	R	H	2B	3B	HR	RBI	BB	SO	SB-CS	Avg.	OBP	SLG	E	Avg.
1995— GC Pirates (GCL)	SS	24	92	14	28	10	1	3	17	9	19	0-0	.304	.363	.533	10	.884
— Erie (NY-Penn)	SS	44	165	30	45	8	3	6	25	18	39	4-2	.273	.354	.467	30	.839
1996— Augusta (S.Atl.)	SS-DH	62	226	41	57	11	3	14	41	38	65	11-3	.252	.377	.513	25	.892
— Lynchburg (Caro.)	SS-DH	66	251	40	69	11	3	10	46	29	56	5-1	.275	.352	.462	28	.897
1997— Carolina (Sou.)	OF-S-2-DH	129	487	87	134	31	4	20	70	69	*136	18-6	.275	.373	.478	‡39	.891

Year	Team (League)	Pos.	BATTING														FIELDING	
			G	AB	R	H	2B	3B	HR	RBI	BB	SO	SB-CS	Avg.	OBP	SLG	E	Avg.
1998—	Nashville (PCL)	OF-2B	126	458	81	118	26	5	28	78	50	152	21-4	.258	.334	.520	14	.942
1999—	Nashville (PCL)	OF-DH	125	496	89	134	27	3	32	97	35	119	19-9	.270	.321	.530	3	.989
—	Pittsburgh (N.L.)	OF	19	60	5	14	3	0	1	1	7	19	2-2	.233	.324	.333	0	1.000
2000—	Pittsburgh (N.L.)	OF	33	108	12	20	4	1	2	8	6	37	0-0	.185	.226	.296	1	.979
—	Nashville (PCL)	OF	78	294	47	66	12	1	11	38	25	89	16-4	.224	.304	.384	4	.975
2001—	Nashville (PCL)	OF	123	447	75	110	22	6	17	64	41	154	22-5	.246	.315	.436	4	.984
—	Pittsburgh (N.L.)	OF	22	55	5	9	1	0	2	5	1	18	0-1	.164	.179	.291	0	1.000
2002—	Nashville (PCL)	OF	16	56	11	11	2	0	4	9	8	23	1-0	.196	.318	.446	0	1.000
—	Pittsburgh (N.L.)	OF	65	194	22	40	11	1	7	15	17	68	7-5	.206	.272	.381	2	.982
—	Chicago (N.L.)■	OF	35	43	3	9	3	0	1	3	5	14	0-0	.209	.292	.349	2	.895
Major League totals (4 years)			174	460	47	92	22	2	13	32	36	156	9-8	.200	.260	.341	5	.979

HERMANSON, DUSTIN P

PERSONAL: Born December 21, 1972, in Springfield, Ohio. ... 6-2/200. ... Throws right, bats right. ... Full name: Dustin Michael Hermanson.
HIGH SCHOOL: Kenton Ridge (Springfield, Ohio).
COLLEGE: Kent.
TRANSACTIONS/CAREER NOTES: Selected by Pittsburgh Pirates organization in 39th round of free-agent draft (June 3, 1991); did not sign. ... Selected by San Diego Padres organization in first round (third pick overall) of free-agent draft (June 2, 1994). ... Traded by Padres to Florida Marlins for 2B Quilvio Veras (November 21, 1996). ... Traded by Marlins with OF Joe Orsulak to Montreal Expos for OF/1B Cliff Floyd (March 26, 1997). ... On disabled list (May 15-30, 1998). ... Traded by Expos with P Steve Kline to St. Louis Cardinals for 3B Fernando Tatis and P Britt Reames (December 14, 2000). ... Traded by Cardinals to Boston Red Sox for OF Rick Asadoorian, 1B Luis Garcia and 1B Dustin Brisson (December 15, 2001). ... On Boston disabled list (April 4-July 20 and July 21-August 22, 2002); included rehabiliation assignments to Pawtucket (July 13-20 and August 14-20) and Gulf Coast Red Sox (August 9-13). ... Granted free agency (November 1, 2002).
RECORDS: Shares major league single-inning record for most doubles allowed—6 (July 22, 1999, second inning).
STATISTICAL NOTES: Hit home run in first major league at-bat (April 16, 1997).
MISCELLANEOUS: Appeared in one game as pinch runner (2001).
CAREER HITTING (MLB): 27-for-281 (.096), 12 R, 5 2B, 0 3B, 2 HR, 9 RBI.

Year	League	W	L	Pct.	ERA	G	GS	CG	ShO	Sv.-Opp.	IP	H	R	ER	HR	BB-IBB	SO
1994—	Wichita (Texas)	1	0	1.000	0.43	16	0	0	0	8-...	21.0	13	1	1	0	6-2	30
—	Las Vegas (PCL)	0	0	...	6.14	7	0	0	0	3-...	7.1	6	5	5	1	5-0	6
1995—	Las Vegas (PCL)	0	1	.000	3.50	31	0	0	0	11-...	36.0	35	23	14	5	29-0	42
—	San Diego (N.L.)	3	1	.750	6.82	26	0	0	0	0-0	31.2	35	26	24	8	22-1	19
1996—	Las Vegas (PCL)	1	4	.200	3.13	42	0	0	0	21-...	46.0	41	20	16	3	27-7	54
—	San Diego (N.L.)	1	0	1.000	8.56	8	0	0	0	0-0	13.2	18	15	13	3	4-0	11
1997—	Montreal (N.L.)■	8	8	.500	3.69	32	28	1	1	0-0	158.1	134	68	65	15	66-2	136
1998—	Montreal (N.L.)	14	11	.560	3.13	32	30	1	0	0-0	187.0	163	80	65	21	56-3	154
1999—	Montreal (N.L.)	9	14	.391	4.20	34	34	0	0	0-0	216.1	225	110	101	20	69-4	145
2000—	Montreal (N.L.)	12	14	.462	4.77	38	30	2	1	4-7	198.0	226	128	105	26	75-5	94
2001—	St. Louis (N.L.)■	14	13	.519	4.45	33	33	0	0	0-0	192.1	195	106	95	34	73-3	123
2002—	Boston (A.L.)■	1	1	.500	7.77	12	1	0	0	0-1	22.0	35	19	19	3	7-0	13
—	Pawtucket (I.L.)	0	1	.000	2.63	5	3	0	0	0-...	13.2	9	5	4	0	7-0	11
—	Gulf Coast Red Sox (GCL)	0	0	...	9.00	1	1	0	0	0-...	2.0	5	3	2	0	0-0	1
A.L. totals (1 year)		1	1	.500	7.77	12	1	0	0	0-1	22.0	35	19	19	3	7-0	13
N.L. totals (7 years)		61	61	.500	4.22	203	155	4	2	4-7	997.1	996	533	468	127	365-18	682
Major League totals (8 years)		62	62	.500	4.30	215	156	4	2	4-8	1019.1	1031	552	487	130	372-18	695

DIVISION SERIES RECORD

Year	League	W	L	Pct.	ERA	G	GS	CG	ShO	Sv.-Opp.	IP	H	R	ER	HR	BB-IBB	SO
2001—	St. Louis (N.L.)	0	0	...	0.00	1	0	0	0	0-0	3.0	0	0	0	0	0-0	0

HERNANDEZ, ADRIAN P YANKEES

PERSONAL: Born March 25, 1975, in Ciudad Havana, Cuba. ... 6-1/185. ... Throws right, bats right.
TRANSACTIONS/CAREER NOTES: Signed as non-drafted free agent by New York Yankees organization (June 2, 2000). ... On Columbus disabled list (August 1, 2000-remainder of season). ... On Columbus disabled list (June 1-10 and July 4-21, 2001; and May 27-June 10, 2002).
STATISTICAL NOTES: Tied for International League lead with five balks in 2001. ... Led International League with five balks in 2002.
CAREER HITTING (MLB): 0-for-0 (.000), 0 R, 0 2B, 0 3B, 0 HR, 0 RBI.

Year	League	W	L	Pct.	ERA	G	GS	CG	ShO	Sv.-Opp.	IP	H	R	ER	HR	BB-IBB	SO
2000—	Tampa (FSL)	1	0	1.000	1.35	1	1	0	0	0-...	6.2	3	1	1	0	1-0	13
—	Norwich (East.)	5	1	.833	4.04	6	6	1	0	0-...	35.2	34	17	16	1	18-0	44
—	Columbus (I.L.)	2	1	.667	4.40	5	5	2	1	0-...	30.2	24	18	15	2	18-0	29
2001—	Columbus (I.L.)	8	7	.533	5.51	21	21	0	0	0-...	117.2	116	75	72	13	60-1	97
—	New York (A.L.)	0	3	.000	3.68	6	3	0	0	0-0	22.0	15	10	9	7	10-1	10
2002—	Columbus (I.L.)	6	7	.462	5.25	20	20	0	0	0-...	109.2	114	67	64	9	45-1	109
—	New York (A.L.)	0	1	.000	12.00	2	1	0	0	0-0	6.0	10	8	8	2	6-0	9
Major League totals (2 years)		0	4	.000	5.46	8	4	0	0	0-0	28.0	25	18	17	9	16-1	19

HERNANDEZ, CARLOS P ASTROS

PERSONAL: Born April 22, 1980, in Guacara, Venezuela. ... 5-10/185. ... Throws left, bats both. ... Full name: Carlos E. Hernandez.
TRANSACTIONS/CAREER NOTES: Signed as non-drafted free agent by Houston Astros organization (April 23, 1997). ... On Houston disabled list (July 2-August 18, 2002); included rehabilitation assignments to New Orleans (August 2-4) and Round Rock (August 5-18).
STATISTICAL NOTES: Pitched 2-0 no-hit victory for Michigan against West Michigan (May 28, 2000; second game).
CAREER HITTING (MLB): 7-for-40 (.175), 3 R, 0 2B, 0 3B, 0 HR, 1 RBI.

Year	League	W	L	Pct.	ERA	G	GS	CG	ShO	Sv.-Opp.	IP	H	R	ER	HR	BB-IBB	SO
1997—	VSL Astros (VSL)............	5	1	.833	2.54	22	0	0	0	3-...	46.0	47	20	13	...	21-...	53
1998—	Dominican Astros (DSL)..	2	0	1.000	1.46	17	0	0	0	9-...	24.2	16	4	4	...	12-...	33
1999—	Martinsville (Appl.)...........	5	1	.833	1.79	13	9	0	0	0-...	55.1	36	21	11	2	23-0	82
2000—	Michigan (Midw.)............	6	6	.500	3.82	22	22	2	1	0-...	110.2	92	57	47	8	63-0	115
2001—	Round Rock (Texas).........	12	3	.800	3.69	24	23	0	0	0-...	139.0	115	60	57	11	69-0	167
—	Houston (N.L.)................	1	0	1.000	1.02	3	3	0	0	0-0	17.2	11	2	2	1	7-0	17
2002—	Houston (N.L.)................	7	5	.583	4.38	23	21	0	0	0-0	111.0	112	56	54	11	61-5	93
—	New Orleans (PCL)...........	0	0	...	0.00	1	1	0	0	0-...	3.0	1	0	0	0	1-0	2
—	Round Rock (Texas).........	0	0	...	4.15	2	2	0	0	0-...	8.2	4	4	4	1	4-0	10
Major League totals (2 years).....		8	5	.615	3.92	26	24	0	0	0-0	128.2	123	58	56	12	68-5	110

HERNANDEZ, JOSE — SS

PERSONAL: Born July 14, 1969, in Vega Alta, Puerto Rico. ... 6-1/188. ... Bats right, throws right. ... Full name: Jose Antonio Hernandez.

HIGH SCHOOL: Maestro Ladi (Vega Alta, Puerto Rico).

COLLEGE: Interamerican (Puerto Rico).

TRANSACTIONS/CAREER NOTES: Signed as non-drafted free agent by Texas Rangers organization (January 13, 1987). ... Claimed on waivers by Cleveland Indians (April 3, 1992). ... Traded by Indians to Chicago Cubs for P Heathcliff Slocumb (June 1, 1993). ... Traded by Cubs with P Terry Mulholland to Atlanta Braves for P Micah Bowie, P Ruben Quevado and a player to be named later (July 31, 1999); Cubs acquired P Joey Nation to complete deal (August 24, 1999). ... Granted free agency (November 5, 1999). ... Signed by Milwaukee Brewers (December 16, 1999). ... On Milwaukee disabled list (August 10-September 1, 2000); included rehabilitation assignment to Indianapolis (August 29-31). ... Granted free agency (October 28, 2002).

STATISTICAL NOTES: Led Gulf Coast League third basemen with .950 fielding percentage, 47 putouts and 11 double plays in 1988. ... Led Florida State League shortstops with .959 fielding percentage in 1990. ... Led Eastern League shortstops with 226 putouts and 586 total chances in 1992. ... Career major league grand slams: 4.

2002 GAMES PLAYED BY POSITION (MLB): SS—149.

			BATTING														FIELDING	
Year	Team (League)	Pos.	G	AB	R	H	2B	3B	HR	RBI	BB	SO	SB-CS	Avg.	OBP	SLG	E	Avg.
1987—	GC Rangers (GCL)......	SS	24	52	5	9	1	1	0	2	9	25	2-1	.173	.306	.231	5	.932
1988—	GC Rangers (GCL)......	3-2-S-1-O	55	162	19	26	7	1	1	13	12	36	4-1	.160	.217	.235	8	†.958
1989—	Gastonia (S.Atl.).........	3B-SS-2B-OF	91	215	35	47	7	6	1	16	33	67	9-2	.219	.323	.321	17	.941
1990—	Charlotte (FSL)..........	SS-OF	121	388	43	99	14	7	1	44	50	122	11-8	.255	.345	.335	25	†.958
1991—	Tulsa (Texas).............	SS	91	301	36	72	17	4	1	20	26	75	4-3	.239	.298	.332	15	*.968
—	Oklahoma City (A.A.)..	SS	14	46	6	14	1	1	1	3	4	10	0-0	.304	.353	.435	3	.962
—	Texas (A.L.)...............	SS-3B	45	98	8	18	2	1	0	4	3	31	0-1	.184	.208	.224	4	.976
1992—	Cant./Akron (East.)■..	SS	130	404	56	103	16	4	3	46	37	108	7-2	.255	.315	.337	*40	.932
—	Cleveland (A.L.)..........	SS	3	4	0	0	0	0	0	0	0	2	0-0	.000	.000	.000	1	.857
1993—	Canton/Akron (East.)..	SS-3B	45	150	19	30	6	0	2	17	10	39	9-2	.200	.250	.280	7	.968
—	Orlando (Sou.)■........	SS	71	263	42	80	8	3	8	33	20	60	8-4	.304	.352	.449	14	.961
—	Iowa (A.A.)................	SS	6	24	3	6	1	0	0	3	0	2	0-0	.250	.280	.292	1	.976
1994—	Chicago (N.L.)...........	3B-SS-2B-OF	56	132	18	32	2	3	1	9	8	29	2-2	.242	.291	.326	4	.971
1995—	Chicago (N.L.)...........	SS-2B-3B	93	245	37	60	11	4	13	40	13	69	1-0	.245	.281	.482	9	.971
1996—	Chicago (N.L.)...........	SS-3B-2B-OF	131	331	52	80	14	1	10	41	24	97	4-0	.242	.293	.381	20	.952
1997—	Chicago (N.L.)...........	IF-OF-DH	121	183	33	50	8	5	7	26	14	42	2-5	.273	.323	.486	8	.955
1998—	Chicago (N.L.)...........	3-OF-S-1-2	149	488	76	124	23	7	23	75	40	140	4-6	.254	.311	.471	13	.970
1999—	Chicago (N.L.)...........	SS-OF-1B	99	342	57	93	12	2	15	43	40	101	7-2	.272	.357	.450	11	.973
—	Atlanta (N.L.)■..........	SS-1B-OF	48	166	22	42	8	0	4	19	12	44	4-1	.253	.302	.373	6	.966
2000—	Milwaukee (N.L.)■.....	3B-SS-OF	124	446	51	109	22	1	11	59	41	125	3-7	.244	.315	.372	19	.955
—	Indianapolis (I.L.).......	3B	2	9	2	3	0	0	2	3	1	3	0-0	.333	.400	1.000	0	1.000
2001—	Milwaukee (N.L.)........	SS-OF	152	542	67	135	26	2	25	78	39	*185	5-4	.249	.300	.443	18	.972
2002—	Milwaukee (N.L.)........	SS	152	525	72	151	24	2	24	73	52	*188	3-5	.288	.356	.478	19	.973
American League totals (2 years)			48	102	8	18	2	1	0	4	3	33	0-1	.176	.200	.216	5	.971
National League totals (9 years)			1125	3400	485	876	150	27	133	463	283	1020	35-32	.258	.317	.435	127	.967
Major League totals (11 years)			1173	3502	493	894	152	28	133	467	286	1053	35-33	.255	.314	.429	132	.967

DIVISION SERIES RECORD

			BATTING														FIELDING	
Year	Team (League)	Pos.	G	AB	R	H	2B	3B	HR	RBI	BB	SO	SB-CS	Avg.	OBP	SLG	E	Avg.
1998—	Chicago (N.L.)...........	SS	2	7	1	2	0	0	0	0	0	2	0-0	.286	.286	.286	2	.750
1999—	Atlanta (N.L.)............	SS	4	11	1	1	0	0	0	0	1	3	1-0	.091	.167	.091	1	.938
Division series totals (2 years)			6	18	2	3	0	0	0	0	1	5	1-0	.167	.211	.167	3	.875

CHAMPIONSHIP SERIES RECORD

			BATTING														FIELDING	
Year	Team (League)	Pos.	G	AB	R	H	2B	3B	HR	RBI	BB	SO	SB-CS	Avg.	OBP	SLG	E	Avg.
1999—	Atlanta (N.L.)............	PH	2	2	0	1	0	0	0	2	0	1	0-0	.500	.500	.500	...	...

WORLD SERIES RECORD

			BATTING														FIELDING	
Year	Team (League)	Pos.	G	AB	R	H	2B	3B	HR	RBI	BB	SO	SB-CS	Avg.	OBP	SLG	E	Avg.
1999—	Atlanta (N.L.)............	PH-SS-DH	2	5	0	1	1	0	0	2	0	2	1-0	.200	.200	.400	0	1.000

ALL-STAR GAME RECORD

	AB	R	H	2B	3B	HR	RBI	BB	SO	SB-CS	Avg.	OBP	SLG	E	Avg.
All-Star Game totals (1 year)	3	0	0	0	0	0	0	0	2	0-0	.000	.000	.000	0	1.000

H

HERNANDEZ, LIVAN — P — GIANTS

PERSONAL: Born February 20, 1975, in Villa Clara, Cuba. ... 6-2/240. ... Throws right, bats right. ... Full name: Eisler Livan Hernandez. ... Half-brother of Orlando Hernandez, pitcher, New York Yankees. ... Name pronounced lee-VAHN.

TRANSACTIONS/CAREER NOTES: Signed as non-drafted free agent by Florida Marlins orgaization (January 13, 1996). ... Traded by Marlins to San Francisco Giants for P Jason Grilli and P Nathan Bump (July 24, 1999).

STATISTICAL NOTES: Led International League with four balks in 1996.

MISCELLANEOUS: Member of Cuban national baseball team (1994-95). ... Struck out once in two appearances as pinch hitter (1998). ... Struck out in only appearance as pinch hitter with Giants (1999). ... Struck out in only appearance as pinch hitter (2000). ... Appeared one game as pinch hitter (2001).

CAREER HITTING (MLB): 99-for-409 (.242), 31 R, 18 2B, 1 3B, 4 HR, 39 RBI.

Year League	W	L	Pct.	ERA	G	GS	CG	ShO	Sv.-Opp.	IP	H	R	ER	HR	BB-IBB	SO
1996— Charlotte (I.L.)	2	4	.333	5.14	10	10	0	0	0-...	49.0	61	32	28	3	34-1	45
— Portland (East.)	9	2	.818	4.34	15	15	0	0	0-...	93.1	81	48	45	14	34-1	95
— Florida (N.L.)	0	0	...	0.00	1	0	0	0	0-0	3.0	3	0	0	0	2-0	2
1997— Charlotte (I.L.)	5	3	.625	3.98	14	14	0	0	0-...	81.1	76	39	36	5	38-2	58
— Florida (N.L.)	9	3	.750	3.18	17	17	0	0	0-0	96.1	81	39	34	5	38-1	72
— Portland (East.)	0	0	...	2.25	1	1	0	0	0-...	4.0	2	1	1	0	7-0	2
1998— Florida (N.L.)	10	12	.455	4.72	33	33	9	0	0-0	234.1	*265	133	123	37	104-8	162
1999— Florida (N.L.)	5	9	.357	4.76	20	20	2	0	0-0	136.0	161	78	72	17	55-3	97
— San Francisco (N.L.)■	3	3	.500	4.38	10	10	0	0	0-0	63.2	66	32	31	6	21-2	47
2000— San Francisco (N.L.)	17	11	.607	3.75	33	33	5	2	0-0	240.0	*254	114	100	22	73-3	165
2001— San Francisco (N.L.)	13	15	.464	5.24	34	34	2	0	0-0	226.2	*266	*143	*132	24	85-7	138
2002— San Francisco (N.L.)	12	•16	.429	4.38	33	33	5	3	0-0	216.0	233	113	105	19	71-5	134
Major League totals (7 years)	69	69	.500	4.42	181	180	23	5	0-0	1216.0	1329	652	597	130	449-29	817

DIVISION SERIES RECORD

Year League	W	L	Pct.	ERA	G	GS	CG	ShO	Sv.-Opp.	IP	H	R	ER	HR	BB-IBB	SO
1997— Florida (N.L.)	0	0	...	2.25	1	0	0	0	0-0	4.0	3	1	1	0	0-0	3
2000— San Francisco (N.L.)	1	0	1.000	1.17	1	1	0	0	0-0	7.2	5	1	1	0	5-0	5
2002— San Francisco (N.L.)	1	0	1.000	3.24	1	1	0	0	0-0	8.1	8	3	3	0	2-0	6
Division series totals (3 years)	2	0	1.000	2.25	3	2	0	0	0-0	20.0	16	5	5	0	7-0	14

CHAMPIONSHIP SERIES RECORD

NOTES: Named N.L. Championship Series Most Valuable Player (1997).

Year League	W	L	Pct.	ERA	G	GS	CG	ShO	Sv.-Opp.	IP	H	R	ER	HR	BB-IBB	SO
1997— Florida (N.L.)	2	0	1.000	0.84	2	1	1	0	0-0	10.2	5	1	1	1	2-0	16
2002— San Francisco (N.L.)	0	0	...	2.84	1	1	0	0	0-0	6.1	9	2	2	0	1-0	0
Champ. series totals (2 years)	2	0	1.000	1.59	3	2	1	0	0-0	17.0	14	3	3	1	3-0	16

WORLD SERIES RECORD

NOTES: Named Most Valuable Player (1997). ... Member of World Series championship team (1997).

Year League	W	L	Pct.	ERA	G	GS	CG	ShO	Sv.-Opp.	IP	H	R	ER	HR	BB-IBB	SO
1997— Florida (N.L.)	2	0	1.000	5.27	2	2	0	0	0-0	13.2	15	9	8	3	10-0	7
2002— San Francisco (N.L.)	0	2	.000	14.29	2	2	0	0	0-0	5.2	9	10	9	0	9-3	4
World Series totals (2 years)	2	2	.500	7.91	4	4	0	0	0-0	19.1	24	19	17	3	19-3	11

HERNANDEZ, ORLANDO — P — YANKEES

PERSONAL: Born October 11, 1969, in Villa Clara, Cuba. ... 6-2/220. ... Throws right, bats right. ... Full name: Orlando P. Hernandez. ... Nickname: El Duque. ... Half-brother of Livan Hernandez, pitcher, San Francisco Giants.

TRANSACTIONS/CAREER NOTES: Signed as non-drafted free agent by New York Yankees (March 23, 1998). ... On New York disabled list (July 18-August 6, 2000); included rehabilitation assignment to Tampa (August 1-3). ... On New York disabled list (June 1-August 21, 2001); included rehabilitation assignments to Tampa (August 6-16) and Staten Island (August 17-20). ... On New York disabled list (May 16-June 27, 2002); included rehabilitation assignment to Columbus (June 22-27). ... On suspended list (July 21-28, 2002).

MISCELLANEOUS: Member of Cuban national baseball team.

CAREER HITTING (MLB): 1-for-19 (.053), 1 R, 0 2B, 0 3B, 0 HR, 0 RBI.

Year League	W	L	Pct.	ERA	G	GS	CG	ShO	Sv.-Opp.	IP	H	R	ER	HR	BB-IBB	SO
1998— Tampa (FSL)	1	1	.500	1.00	2	2	0	0	0-...	9.0	3	2	1	0	3-0	15
— Columbus (I.L.)	6	0	1.000	3.83	7	7	0	0	0-...	42.1	41	19	18	2	17-0	59
— New York (A.L.)	12	4	.750	3.13	21	21	3	1	0-0	141.0	113	53	49	11	52-1	131
1999— New York (A.L.)	17	9	.654	4.12	33	33	2	1	0-0	214.1	187	108	98	24	87-2	157
2000— New York (A.L.)	12	13	.480	4.51	29	29	3	0	0-0	195.2	186	104	98	34	51-2	141
— Tampa (FSL)	0	0	...	0.00	1	0	0	0	0-...	4.0	1	0	0	0	1-0	5
2001— New York (A.L.)	4	7	.364	4.85	17	16	0	0	0-0	94.2	90	51	51	19	42-1	77
— Tampa (FSL)	0	0	...	0.00	2	2	0	0	0-...	7.0	6	2	0	0	1-0	8
— Staten Island (NY-Penn)	1	0	1.000	0.00	1	1	0	0	0-...	6.0	2	0	0	0	1-0	11
2002— New York (A.L.)	8	5	.615	3.64	24	22	0	0	1-1	146.0	131	63	59	17	36-2	113
— Columbus (I.L.)	1	0	1.000	1.59	1	1	0	0	0-...	5.2	7	2	1	0	1-0	5
Major League totals (5 years)	53	38	.582	4.04	124	121	8	2	1-1	791.2	707	379	355	105	268-8	619

DIVISION SERIES RECORD

Year League	W	L	Pct.	ERA	G	GS	CG	ShO	Sv.-Opp.	IP	H	R	ER	HR	BB-IBB	SO
1998— New York (A.L.)									Did not play.							
1999— New York (A.L.)	1	0	1.000	0.00	1	1	0	0	0-0	8.0	2	0	0	0	6-0	4
2000— New York (A.L.)	1	0	1.000	2.45	2	1	0	0	0-0	7.1	5	2	2	1	5-0	5
2001— New York (A.L.)	1	0	1.000	3.18	1	1	0	0	0-0	5.2	8	2	2	0	2-0	5
2002— New York (A.L.)	0	1	.000	2.84	2	0	0	0	0-0	6.1	5	2	2	2	0-0	7
Division series totals (4 years)	3	1	.750	1.98	6	3	0	0	0-0	27.1	20	6	6	3	13-0	21

CHAMPIONSHIP SERIES RECORD

NOTES: Named A.L. Championship Series Most Valuable Player (1999).

Year League	W	L	Pct.	ERA	G	GS	CG	ShO	Sv.-Opp.	IP	H	R	ER	HR	BB-IBB	SO
1998— New York (A.L.)	1	0	1.000	0.00	1	1	0	0	0-0	7.0	3	0	0	0	2-0	6
1999— New York (A.L.)	1	0	1.000	1.80	2	2	0	0	0-0	15.0	12	4	3	1	6-0	13
2000— New York (A.L.)	2	0	1.000	4.20	2	2	0	0	0-0	15.0	13	7	7	2	8-2	14
2001— New York (A.L.)	0	1	.000	7.20	1	1	0	0	0-0	5.0	5	5	4	1	5-0	7
Champ. series totals (4 years)	4	1	.800	3.00	6	6	0	0	0-0	42.0	33	16	14	4	21-2	40

WORLD SERIES RECORD

NOTES: Member of World Series championship team (1998, 1999 and 2000).

Year League	W	L	Pct.	ERA	G	GS	CG	ShO	Sv.-Opp.	IP	H	R	ER	HR	BB-IBB	SO
1998— New York (A.L.)	1	0	1.000	1.29	1	1	0	0	0-0	7.0	6	1	1	0	3-0	7
1999— New York (A.L.)	1	0	1.000	1.29	1	1	0	0	0-0	7.0	1	1	1	1	2-0	10
2000— New York (A.L.)	0	1	.000	4.91	1	1	0	0	0-0	7.1	9	4	4	1	3-0	12
2001— New York (A.L.)	0	0	...	1.42	1	1	0	0	0-0	6.1	4	1	1	1	4-0	5
World Series totals (4 years)	2	1	.667	2.28	4	4	0	0	0-0	27.2	20	7	7	3	12-0	34

HERNANDEZ, RAMON — C — ATHLETICS

PERSONAL: Born May 20, 1976, in Caracas, Venezuela. ... 6-0/210. ... Bats right, throws right. ... Full name: Ramon Jose Marin Hernandez.
TRANSACTIONS/CAREER NOTES: Signed as non-drafted free agent by Oakland Athletics organization (February 18, 1994). ... On Oakland disabled list (July 26-August 27, 1999); included rehabilitation assignment to Vancouver (August 13-27).
HONORS: Named Arizona League Most Valuable Player (1995).
STATISTICAL NOTES: Led Arizona League in being hit by pitch with eight in 1992. ... Led Arizona League catchers with a .982 fielding percentage in 1995. ... Led Midwest League catchers with 877 putouts and 981 totals chances and tied for lead with 20 errors in 1996. ... Led California League catchers with 16 errors in 1997. ... Led Southern League in being hit by pitch with 19 in 1998. ... Career major league grand slams: 1.
2002 GAMES PLAYED BY POSITION (MLB): C—135.

		BATTING														FIELDING	
Year Team (League)	Pos.	G	AB	R	H	2B	3B	HR	RBI	BB	SO	SB-CS	Avg.	OBP	SLG	E	Avg.
1994— Dom. Athletics (DSL)	C	42	134	24	33	2	0	2	18	18	10	1-5	.246	.342	.306	2	.991
1995— Ariz. Athletics (Ariz.)	C-1B-3B	48	143	37	52	9	6	4	•37	*39	16	6-2	*.364	*.510	*.594	12	†.972
1996— West Mich. (Midw.)	C-DH-1B	123	447	62	114	26	2	12	68	69	62	2-3	.255	.355	.403	‡20	.980
1997— Visalia (Calif.)	C-DH-1B	86	332	57	120	21	2	15	85	35	47	2-4	*.361	*.427	.572	†16	.976
— Huntsville (Sou.)	C-DH-1B-3B	44	161	27	31	3	0	4	24	18	23	0-0	.193	.281	.286	1	.997
1998— Huntsville (Sou.)	DH-C-1B	127	479	83	142	24	1	15	98	57	61	4-5	.296	.389	.445	11	.981
1999— Vancouver (PCL)	C-DH-3B-1B	77	291	38	76	11	3	13	55	23	37	1-2	.261	.326	.454	5	.987
— Oakland (A.L.)	C	40	136	13	38	7	0	3	21	18	11	1-0	.279	.363	.397	6	.980
2000— Oakland (A.L.)	C	143	419	52	101	19	0	14	62	38	64	1-0	.241	.311	.387	*13	.984
2001— Oakland (A.L.)	C-1B	136	453	55	115	25	0	15	60	37	68	1-1	.254	.316	.408	12	.988
2002— Oakland (A.L.)	C	136	403	51	94	20	0	7	42	43	64	0-0	.233	.313	.335	7	.992
Major League totals (4 years)		455	1411	171	348	71	0	39	185	136	207	3-1	.247	.318	.380	38	.987

DIVISION SERIES RECORD

		BATTING														FIELDING	
Year Team (League)	Pos.	G	AB	R	H	2B	3B	HR	RBI	BB	SO	SB-CS	Avg.	OBP	SLG	E	Avg.
2000— Oakland (A.L.)	C	5	16	3	6	2	0	0	3	0	3	0-0	.375	.412	.500	1	.974
2001— Oakland (A.L.)	C-PH	5	10	0	0	0	0	0	0	1	4	0-0	.000	.167	.000	0	1.000
2002— Oakland (A.L.)	C	5	17	0	1	0	0	0	0	0	4	0-0	.059	.059	.059	0	1.000
Division series totals (3 years)		15	43	3	7	2	0	0	3	1	11	0-0	.163	.217	.209	1	.990

HERNANDEZ, ROBERTO — P

PERSONAL: Born November 11, 1964, in Santurce, Puerto Rico. ... 6-4/250. ... Throws right, bats right. ... Full name: Roberto Manuel Hernandez.
HIGH SCHOOL: New Hampton (N.H.) Prep.
COLLEGE: South Carolina-Aiken.
TRANSACTIONS/CAREER NOTES: Selected by California Angels organization in first round (16th pick overall) of free-agent draft (June 2, 1986); pick received as compensation for Baltimore Orioles signing Type A free-agent OF/IF Juan Beniquez. ... On disabled list (May 6-21 and June 4-August 14, 1987). ... Traded by Angels with OF Mark Doran to Chicago White Sox organization for OF Mark Davis (August 2, 1989). ... On Vancouver disabled list (May 17-August 10, 1991). ... Traded by White Sox with P Wilson Alvarez and P Danny Darwin to San Francisco Giants for SS Mike Caruso, OF Brian Manning, P Lorenzo Barcelo, P Keith Foulke, P Bobby Howry and P Ken Vining (July 31, 1997). ... Granted free agency (October 30, 1997). ... Signed by Tampa Bay Devil Rays (November 18, 1997). ... Traded by Devil Rays to Kansas City Royals as part of three-way deal in which Devil Rays received OF Ben Grieve and a player to be named later or cash from the Oakland Athletics, A's received P Cory Lidle from Devil Rays, A's received OF Johnny Damon, IF Mark Ellis and a player to be named later from Royals and Royals received C A.J. Hinch, IF Angel Berroa and cash from A's (January 8, 2001). ... On Kansas City disabled list (March 22-May 2, 2002); included rehabilitation assignment to Omaha (April 4-8). ... Granted free agency (October 28, 2002).
MISCELLANEOUS: Holds Tampa Bay Devil Rays all-time records for most saves (101) and lowest career earned-run average (3.43).
CAREER HITTING (MLB): 1-for-2 (.500), 0 R, 0 2B, 0 3B, 0 HR, 0 RBI.

Year League	W	L	Pct.	ERA	G	GS	CG	ShO	Sv.-Opp.	IP	H	R	ER	HR	BB-IBB	SO
1986— Salem (N'West)	2	2	.500	4.58	10	10	0	0	0-...	55.0	57	37	28	3	42-1	38
1987— Quad City (Midw.)	2	3	.400	6.86	7	6	0	0	1-...	21.0	24	21	16	2	12-0	21
1988— Quad City (Midw.)	9	10	.474	3.17	24	24	6	1	0-...	164.2	157	70	58	8	48-0	114
— Midland (Texas)	0	2	.000	6.57	3	3	0	0	0-...	12.1	16	13	9	0	8-0	7
1989— Midland (Texas)	2	7	.222	6.89	12	12	0	0	0-...	64.0	94	57	49	4	30-0	42
— Palm Springs (Calif.)	1	4	.200	4.64	7	7	0	0	0-...	42.2	49	27	22	2	16-0	33
— South Bend (Midw.)■	1	1	.500	3.33	4	4	0	0	0-...	24.1	19	9	9	1	7-0	17
1990— Birmingham (Sou.)	8	5	.615	3.67	17	17	1	0	0-...	108.0	103	57	44	6	43-2	62
— Vancouver (PCL)	3	5	.375	2.84	11	11	3	1	0-...	79.1	73	33	25	4	26-0	49
1991— Vancouver (PCL)	4	1	.800	3.22	7	7	0	0	0-...	44.2	41	17	16	2	23-0	40
— GC White Sox (GCL)	0	0	...	0.00	1	1	0	0	0-...	6.0	2	0	0	0	0-0	7
— Birmingham (Sou.)	2	1	.667	1.99	4	4	0	0	0-...	22.2	11	5	5	2	6-0	25
— Chicago (A.L.)	1	0	1.000	7.80	9	3	0	0	0-0	15.0	18	15	13	1	7-0	6
1992— Chicago (A.L.)	7	3	.700	1.65	43	0	0	0	12-16	71.0	45	15	13	4	20-1	68

Year	League	W	L	Pct.	ERA	G	GS	CG	ShO	Sv.-Opp.	IP	H	R	ER	HR	BB-IBB	SO
	—Vancouver (PCL)	3	3	.500	2.61	9	0	0	0	2-...	20.2	13	9	6	0	11-1	23
1993—	Chicago (A.L.)	3	4	.429	2.29	70	0	0	0	38-44	78.2	66	21	20	6	20-1	71
1994—	Chicago (A.L.)	4	4	.500	4.91	45	0	0	0	14-20	47.2	44	29	26	5	19-1	50
1995—	Chicago (A.L.)	3	7	.300	3.92	60	0	0	0	32-42	59.2	63	30	26	9	28-4	84
1996—	Chicago (A.L.)	6	5	.545	1.91	72	0	0	0	38-46	84.2	65	21	18	2	38-5	85
1997—	Chicago (A.L.)	5	1	.833	2.44	46	0	0	0	27-31	48.0	38	15	13	5	24-4	47
	—San Francisco (N.L.)■	5	2	.714	2.48	28	0	0	0	4-8	32.2	29	9	9	2	14-1	35
1998—	Tampa Bay (A.L.)■	2	6	.250	4.04	67	0	0	0	26-35	71.1	55	33	32	5	41-4	55
1999—	Tampa Bay (A.L.)	2	3	.400	3.07	72	0	0	0	43-47	73.1	68	27	25	1	33-1	69
2000—	Tampa Bay (A.L.)	4	7	.364	3.19	68	0	0	0	32-40	73.1	76	33	26	9	23-1	61
2001—	Kansas City (A.L.)■	5	6	.455	4.12	63	0	0	0	28-34	67.2	69	34	31	7	26-3	46
2002—	Omaha (PCL)	0	0	...	0.00	2	0	0	0	0-...	2.0	0	1	0	0	3-0	3
	—Kansas City (A.L.)	1	3	.250	4.33	53	0	0	0	26-33	52.0	62	29	25	6	12-2	39
A.L. totals (12 years)		43	49	.467	3.25	668	3	0	0	316-388	742.1	669	302	268	60	291-27	681
N.L. totals (1 year)		5	2	.714	2.48	28	0	0	0	4-8	32.2	29	9	9	2	14-1	35
Major League totals (12 years)		48	51	.485	3.22	696	3	0	0	320-396	775.0	698	311	277	62	305-28	716

DIVISION SERIES RECORD

Year	League	W	L	Pct.	ERA	G	GS	CG	ShO	Sv.-Opp.	IP	H	R	ER	HR	BB-IBB	SO
1997—	San Francisco (N.L.)	0	1	.000	20.25	3	0	0	0	0-0	1.1	5	3	3	0	3-1	1

CHAMPIONSHIP SERIES RECORD

Year	League	W	L	Pct.	ERA	G	GS	CG	ShO	Sv.-Opp.	IP	H	R	ER	HR	BB-IBB	SO
1993—	Chicago (A.L.)	0	0	...	0.00	4	0	0	0	1-1	4.0	4	0	0	0	0-0	1

ALL-STAR GAME RECORD

	W	L	Pct.	ERA	GS	CG	ShO	Sv.-Opp.	IP	H	R	ER	HR	BB-IBB	SO
All-Star Game totals (2 years)	0	0	...	0.00	0	0	0	0-0	2.0	1	0	0	0	0-0	0

HERNANDEZ, RUNELVYS — P — ROYALS

PERSONAL: Born April 27, 1978, in Santo Domingo, Dominican Republic. ... 6-1/205. ... Throws right, bats right. ... Full name: Runelvys Antonio Hernandez.

TRANSACTIONS/CAREER NOTES: Signed as non-drafted free agent by Kansas City Royals organization (December 16, 1997).

CAREER HITTING (MLB): 0-for-0 (.000), 0 R, 0 2B, 0 3B, 0 HR, 0 RBI.

Year	League	W	L	Pct.	ERA	G	GS	CG	ShO	Sv.-Opp.	IP	H	R	ER	HR	BB-IBB	SO
1998—	Dominican Royals (DSL)	0	2	.000	5.34	19	2	0	0	0-...	32.0	31	26	19	...	29-...	27
1999—	Dominican Royals (DSL)	2	2	.500	3.09	16	2	0	0	5-...	32.0	23	19	11	...	17-...	36
2000—	Dominican Royals (DSL)	7	3	.700	2.25	14	10	0	0	1-...	72.0	57	25	18	...	18-...	70
2001—	Burlington (Midw.)	7	5	.583	3.40	17	17	0	0	0-...	100.2	94	46	38	5	29-0	100
2002—	Wilmington (Caro.)	1	1	.500	3.75	2	2	0	0	0-...	12.0	12	6	5	0	1-0	9
	—Wichita (Texas)	8	3	.727	2.71	16	14	2	0	0-...	106.1	96	38	32	3	24-1	86
	—Kansas City (A.L.)	4	4	.500	4.36	12	12	0	0	0-0	74.1	79	36	36	8	22-0	45
Major League totals (1 year)		4	4	.500	4.36	12	12	0	0	0-0	74.1	79	36	36	8	22-0	45

HERRERA, ALEX — P — INDIANS

PERSONAL: Born November 5, 1976, in Maracaibo, Venezuela. ... 5-11/175. ... Throws left, bats left. ... Full name: Alexander J. Herrera.

TRANSACTIONS/CAREER NOTES: Signed as non-drafted free agent by Cleveland Indians organization (July 4, 1997).

CAREER HITTING (MLB): 0-for-0 (.000), 0 R, 0 2B, 0 3B, 0 HR, 0 RBI.

Year	League	W	L	Pct.	ERA	G	GS	CG	ShO	Sv.-Opp.	IP	H	R	ER	HR	BB-IBB	SO
1998—	Guacara 2 (VSL)	7	4	.636	2.30	18	11	0	0	3-...	74.1	70	34	19	...	17-...	68
1999—	San Felipe (VSL)	3	2	.600	1.28	16	9	0	0	5-...	56.1	42	19	8	...	20-...	74
2000—	Columbus (S.Atl.)	4	3	.571	3.43	20	0	0	0	0-...	42.0	41	25	16	1	21-1	41
	—Kinston (Caro.)	0	1	.000	2.32	17	0	0	0	1-...	31.0	28	11	8	1	19-0	40
	—Akron (East.)	0	0	...	0.00	2	0	0	0	0-...	1.1	2	1	0	0	1-0	1
2001—	Kinston (Caro.)	4	0	1.000	0.60	28	0	0	0	3-...	59.2	36	6	4	1	18-0	83
	—Akron (East.)	3	0	1.000	2.83	15	0	0	0	2-...	28.2	24	9	9	1	9-0	22
2002—	Akron (East.)	0	2	.000	3.38	30	0	0	0	5-...	61.1	47	24	23	8	30-1	65
	—Cleveland (A.L.)	0	0	...	0.00	5	0	0	0	0-0	5.1	3	0	0	0	1-0	5
	—Buffalo (I.L.)	0	1	.000	11.57	5	0	0	0	0-...	7.0	10	9	9	0	8-0	5
Major League totals (1 year)		0	0	...	0.00	5	0	0	0	0-0	5.1	3	0	0	0	1-0	5

HIDALGO, RICHARD — OF — ASTROS

PERSONAL: Born July 2, 1975, in Caracas, Venezuela. ... 6-3/220. ... Bats right, throws right. ... Full name: Richard Jose Hidalgo.

TRANSACTIONS/CAREER NOTES: Signed as non-drafted free agent by Houston Astros organization (July 2, 1991). ... On Houston disabled list (May 30-July 21, 1998); included rehabilitation assignment to New Orleans (July 11-21). ... On disabled list (August 9, 1999-remainder of season). ... On disabled list (August 23-September 9, 2002).

RECORDS: Shares major league single-game record for most times hit by pitch—3 (April 19, 2000).

STATISTICAL NOTES: Led South Atlantic League outfielders with 30 assists in 1993. ... Led Midwest League outfielders with 23 assists in 1994. ... Led Texas League in grounding into double plays with 24 in 1996. ... Led Texas League outfielders with six double plays in 1996. ... Led American Association outfielders with 15 assists in 1997. ... Had 15-game hitting streak (August 28-September 13, 2000). ... Career major league grand slams: 1.

2002 GAMES PLAYED BY POSITION (MLB): OF—110.

			BATTING														FIELDING	
Year	Team (League)	Pos.	G	AB	R	H	2B	3B	HR	RBI	BB	SO	SB-CS	Avg.	OBP	SLG	E	Avg.
1992—	GC Astros (GCL)	OF	51	184	20	57	7	3	1	27	13	27	14-5	.310	.360	.397	0	1.000
1993—	Asheville (S.Atl.)	OF	111	403	49	109	23	3	10	55	30	76	21-13	.270	.324	.417	6	.974
1994—	Quad City (Midw.)	OF	124	476	68	139	*47	6	12	76	23	80	12-12	.292	.331	.492	11	.953
1995—	Jackson (Texas)	OF	133	489	59	130	28	6	14	59	32	76	8-9	.266	.309	.434	5	.981

Year	Team (League)	Pos.	BATTING G	AB	R	H	2B	3B	HR	RBI	BB	SO	SB-CS	Avg.	OBP	SLG	FIELDING E	Avg.
1996—	Jackson (Texas)	OF-DH	130	513	66	151	34	2	14	78	29	55	11-7	.294	.341	.450	6	.981
1997—	New Orleans (A.A.)	OF-DH	134	526	74	147	*37	5	11	78	35	57	6-10	.279	.330	.432	9	.968
	—Houston (N.L.)	OF	19	62	8	19	5	0	2	6	4	18	1-0	.306	.358	.484	0	1.000
1998—	Houston (N.L.)	OF	74	211	31	64	15	0	7	35	17	37	3-3	.303	.355	.474	3	.978
	—New Orleans (PCL)	OF	10	24	0	4	2	0	0	1	3	2	0-0	.167	.259	.250	0	1.000
1999—	Houston (N.L.)	OF	108	383	49	87	25	2	15	56	56	73	8-5	.227	.328	.420	2	.991
2000—	Houston (N.L.)	OF	153	558	118	175	42	3	44	122	56	110	13-6	.314	.391	.636	7	.984
2001—	Houston (N.L.)	OF	146	512	70	141	29	3	19	80	54	107	3-5	.275	.356	.455	3	.991
2002—	Houston (N.L.)	OF	114	388	54	91	17	4	15	48	43	85	6-2	.235	.319	.415	1	.995
Major League totals (6 years)			614	2114	330	577	133	12	102	347	230	430	34-21	.273	.353	.492	16	.989

DIVISION SERIES RECORD

Year	Team (League)	Pos.	BATTING G	AB	R	H	2B	3B	HR	RBI	BB	SO	SB-CS	Avg.	OBP	SLG	FIELDING E	Avg.
1997—	Houston (N.L.)	OF	2	5	1	0	0	0	0	0	1	2	0-0	.000	.167	.000	0	1.000
1998—	Houston (N.L.)	OF	1	4	0	1	0	0	0	0	0	1	0-0	.250	.250	.250	0	1.000
1999—	Houston (N.L.)								Did not play.									
2001—	Houston (N.L.)	OF	3	8	1	1	0	0	0	0	3	2	0-0	.125	.364	.125	0	1.000
Division series totals (3 years)			6	17	2	2	0	0	0	0	4	5	0-0	.118	.286	.118	0	1.000

HIGGINSON, BOBBY — OF — TIGERS

PERSONAL: Born August 18, 1970, in Philadelphia. ... 5-11/202. ... Bats left, throws right. ... Full name: Robert Leigh Higginson.
HIGH SCHOOL: Frankford (Philadelphia).
COLLEGE: Temple.
TRANSACTIONS/CAREER NOTES: Selected by Detroit Tigers organization in 12th round of free-agent draft (June 1, 1992). ... On Detroit disabled list (May 11-June 7, 1996); included rehabilitation assignment to Toledo (June 4-7). ... On disabled list (June 15-26, 1997). ... On suspended list (September 26, 1997). ... On disabled list (July 24-August 24, 1999). ... On suspended list (May 10-16, 2000). ... On disabled list (May 20-June 5, 2001; and June 9-July 11, 2002).
RECORDS: Shares major league record for most consecutive home runs—4 (June 30 [3], July 1 [1], 1997).
STATISTICAL NOTES: Led A.L. outfielders with 13 assists in 1995, 20 in 1997 and 19 in 2000. ... Hit three home runs in one game (June 30, 1997; and June 24, 2000). ... Tied for A.L. lead in double plays by outfielder with five in 1997. ... Career major league grand slams: 4.
2002 GAMES PLAYED BY POSITION (MLB): OF—117; DH—1.

Year	Team (League)	Pos.	BATTING G	AB	R	H	2B	3B	HR	RBI	BB	SO	SB-CS	Avg.	OBP	SLG	FIELDING E	Avg.
1992—	Niagara Falls (NY-P)	OF	70	232	35	68	17	4	2	37	33	47	12-8	.293	.383	.427	2	.983
1993—	Lakeland (FSL)	OF	61	223	42	67	11	7	3	25	40	31	8-3	.300	.406	.453	2	.979
	—London (East.)	OF	63	224	25	69	15	4	4	35	19	37	3-4	.308	.358	.464	2	.982
1994—	Toledo (I.L.)	OF	137	476	81	131	28	3	23	67	46	99	16-8	.275	.343	.492	8	.973
1995—	Detroit (A.L.)	OF-DH	131	410	61	92	17	5	14	43	62	107	6-4	.224	.329	.393	4	.985
1996—	Detroit (A.L.)	OF-DH	130	440	75	141	35	0	26	81	65	66	6-3	.320	.404	.577	9	.963
	—Toledo (I.L.)	OF	3	13	4	4	0	1	0	1	3	0	0-0	.308	.438	.462	0	1.000
1997—	Detroit (A.L.)	OF-DH	146	546	94	163	30	5	27	101	70	85	12-7	.299	.379	.520	9	.972
1998—	Detroit (A.L.)	OF-DH	157	612	92	174	37	4	25	85	63	101	3-3	.284	.355	.480	6	.982
1999—	Detroit (A.L.)	OF-DH	107	377	51	90	18	0	12	46	64	66	4-6	.239	.351	.382	3	.983
2000—	Detroit (A.L.)	OF-DH	154	597	104	179	44	4	30	102	74	99	15-3	.300	.377	.538	7	.979
2001—	Detroit (A.L.)	OF-DH	147	541	84	150	28	6	17	71	80	65	20-12	.277	.367	.445	8	.976
2002—	Detroit (A.L.)	OF-DH	119	444	50	125	24	3	10	63	41	45	12-5	.282	.345	.417	7	.973
Major League totals (8 years)			1091	3967	611	1114	233	27	161	592	519	634	78-43	.281	.364	.475	53	.977

HILJUS, ERIK — P — ATHLETICS

PERSONAL: Born December 25, 1972, in Panorama City, Calif. ... 6-6/222. ... Throws right, bats right. ... Full name: Erik Kristian Hiljus.
HIGH SCHOOL: Canyon (Anaheim).
TRANSACTIONS/CAREER NOTES: Selected by New York Mets organization in fourth round of free-agent draft (June 3, 1991). ... Traded by Mets with P Eric Ludwick and OF Yudith Ozono to St. Louis Cardinals for OF Bernard Gilkey (January 23, 1996). ... On disabled list (April 4-July 14, 1996). ... On disabled list (April 3-August 20, 1997). ... Released by Cardinals (August 20, 1997). ... Signed by Detroit Tigers organization (March 9, 1998). ... On Toledo disabled list (April 8-19, 1999). ... Released by Tigers (November 27, 2000). ... Signed by Oakland Athletics organization (December 6, 2000). ... On Sacramento disabled list (July 12-August 22, 2002).
RECORDS: Shares major league single-inning record for most strikeouts—4 (June 30, 2001).
STATISTICAL NOTES: Tied for Florida State League lead with eight balks in 1994.
CAREER HITTING (MLB): 0-for-0 (.000), 0 R, 0 2B, 0 3B, 0 HR, 0 RBI.

Year	League	W	L	Pct.	ERA	G	GS	CG	ShO	Sv.-Opp.	IP	H	R	ER	HR	BB-IBB	SO
1991—	Gulf Coast Mets (GCL)	2	3	.400	4.26	9	9	1	•1	0-...	38.0	31	27	18	1	37-0	38
1992—	Kingsport (Appl.)	3	6	.333	5.09	12	11	0	0	0-...	70.2	66	49	40	5	40-0	63
1993—	Capital City (S.Atl.)	7	10	.412	4.32	27	27	1	0	0-...	145.2	114	76	70	8	*111-1	157
1994—	St. Lucie (FSL)	11	10	.524	3.98	26	26	3	1	0-...	160.2	159	85	71	8	*90-3	140
1995—	St. Lucie (FSL)	8	4	.667	2.99	17	17	0	0	0-...	111.1	85	46	37	4	50-2	98
	—Binghamton (East.)	2	4	.333	5.86	10	10	0	0	0-...	55.1	60	38	36	8	32-1	40
1996—	Arkansas (Texas)■	3	5	.375	6.11	10	10	0	0	0-...	45.2	62	37	31	6	30-1	21
1997—										Did not play.							
1998—	Jacksonville (Sou.)■	2	3	.400	3.70	42	0	0	0	2-...	65.2	49	31	27	7	35-0	85
1999—	Lakeland (FSL)	0	0	...	2.25	3	0	0	0	0-...	4.0	4	1	1	0	0-0	9
	—Jacksonville (Sou.)	1	0	1.000	1.04	10	0	0	0	0-...	17.1	5	4	2	1	5-0	28
	—Toledo (I.L.)	2	3	.400	4.40	33	0	0	0	5-...	59.1	49	31	29	5	16-0	73
	—Detroit (A.L.)	0	0	...	5.19	6	0	0	0	0-0	8.2	7	5	5	2	5-0	1
2000—	Toledo (I.L.)	5	3	.625	3.44	46	0	0	0	2-...	70.2	67	33	27	3	20-1	81
	—Detroit (A.L.)	0	0	...	7.36	3	0	0	0	0-0	3.2	5	3	3	1	1-0	2

Year	League	W	L	Pct.	ERA	G	GS	CG	ShO	Sv.-Opp.	IP	H	R	ER	HR	BB-IBB	SO
2001—	Sacramento (PCL)■	8	5	.615	3.63	15	15	3	1	0-...	101.2	79	46	41	18	26-1	108
	— Oakland (A.L.)	5	0	1.000	3.41	16	11	0	0	0-0	66.0	70	29	25	7	21-1	67
2002—	Oakland (A.L.)	3	3	.500	6.50	9	9	0	0	0-0	45.2	52	36	33	11	21-1	29
	— Sacramento (PCL)	1	3	.250	7.65	9	6	0	0	0-...	37.2	54	32	32	3	15-0	30
Major League totals (4 years)		8	3	.727	4.79	34	20	0	0	0-0	124.0	134	73	66	21	48-2	99

DIVISION SERIES RECORD

Year	League	W	L	Pct.	ERA	G	GS	CG	ShO	Sv.-Opp.	IP	H	R	ER	HR	BB-IBB	SO
2001—	Oakland (A.L.)	0	0	...	27.00	1	0	0	0	0-0	.1	0	1	1	0	2-0	0

HILL, BOBBY — 2B — CUBS

PERSONAL: Born April 3, 1978, in San Jose, Calif. ... 5-10/190. ... Bats both, throws right. ... Full name: William Robert Hill.
HIGH SCHOOL: Leland (Calif.).
COLLEGE: Miami (Fla.).
TRANSACTIONS/CAREER NOTES: Selected by California Angels organization in fifth round of free-agent draft (June 4, 1996); did not sign. ... Selected by Chicago White Sox organization in second round of free-agent draft (June 2, 1999); did not sign. ... Selected by Chicago Cubs organization in second round of free-agent draft (June 5, 2000). ... Played with Newark, Atlantic League (2000). ... On West Tenn disabled list (May 4-19 and June 13-August 8, 2001).
2002 GAMES PLAYED BY POSITION (MLB): 2B—55; SS—1.

			BATTING													FIELDING	
Year	Team (League)	Pos.	G	AB	R	H	2B	3B	HR	RBI	BB	SO	SB-CS	Avg.	OBP	SLG	E	Avg.
2000—	Newark (Atl.)	SS	132	481	109	157	22	9	13	82	101	57	81-15	.326	.442	.491	...	...
2001—	West Tenn (Sou.)■	2B-SS	57	209	30	63	8	1	3	21	32	39	20-8	.301	.396	.392	6	.973
	— Arizona Cubs (Ariz.)	2B	3	9	1	2	0	0	0	1	2	3	1-0	.222	.364	.222	0	1.000
2002—	Iowa (PCL)	2B	92	354	80	99	23	3	8	39	49	66	29-5	.280	.382	.429	6	.986
	— Chicago (N.L.)	2B-SS	59	190	26	48	7	2	4	20	17	42	6-1	.253	.327	.374	3	.986
Major League totals (1 year)			59	190	26	48	7	2	4	20	17	42	6-1	.253	.327	.374	3	.986

HILL, JEREMY — P — ROYALS

PERSONAL: Born August 8, 1977, in Dallas. ... 5-10/185. ... Throws right, bats right. ... Full name: Jeremy Dee Hill.
HIGH SCHOOL: W.T. White (Dallas).
TRANSACTIONS/CAREER NOTES: Selected by Kansas City Royals organization in fifth round of free-agent draft (June 4, 1996).
CAREER HITTING (MLB): 0-for-0 (.000), 0 R, 0 2B, 0 3B, 0 HR, 0 RBI.

Year	League	W	L	Pct.	ERA	G	GS	CG	ShO	Sv.-Opp.	IP	H	R	ER	HR	BB-IBB	SO
2001—	Burlington (Midw.)	0	2	.000	1.51	40	0	0	0	12-...	47.2	22	11	8	2	25-0	66
	— Wilmington (Caro.)	4	0	1.000	0.73	9	0	0	0	2-...	12.1	10	2	1	0	8-1	13
2002—	Wichita (Texas)	4	7	.364	2.36	56	0	0	0	19-...	76.1	61	26	20	4	32-5	80
	— Kansas City (A.L.)	0	1	.000	3.86	10	0	0	0	0-0	9.1	8	4	4	1	8-1	7
Major League totals (1 year)		0	1	.000	3.86	10	0	0	0	0-0	9.1	8	4	4	1	8-1	7

RECORD AS POSITION PLAYER

			BATTING													FIELDING	
Year	Team (League)	Pos.	G	AB	R	H	2B	3B	HR	RBI	BB	SO	SB-CS	Avg.	OBP	SLG	E	Avg.
1996—	GC Royals (GCL)	C	31	90	4	16	6	0	0	4	12	17	0-0	.178	.286	.244	9	.961
1997—	Spokane (N'West)	C	60	187	35	53	12	1	3	29	25	53	1-0	.283	.366	.406	8	.985
1998—	Lansing (Midw.)	C	86	288	25	69	12	1	4	37	15	75	4-1	.240	.285	.330	9	.986
1999—	Wilmington (Caro.)	C	92	304	37	71	12	1	4	27	38	75	2-0	.234	.329	.319	7	.991
2000—	Wilmington (Caro.)	C	99	299	33	59	12	2	3	26	33	84	1-2	.197	.281	.281	14	.980

HILLENBRAND, SHEA — 3B — RED SOX

PERSONAL: Born July 27, 1975, in Mesa, Ariz. ... 6-1/211. ... Bats right, throws right. ... Full name: Shea Matthew Hillenbrand.
HIGH SCHOOL: Mountain View (Mesa, Ariz.).
JUNIOR COLLEGE: Mesa (Ariz.) Community College.
TRANSACTIONS/CAREER NOTES: Selected by Boston Red Sox organization in 10th round of free-agent draft (June 4, 1996). ... On Trenton disabled list (July 5-August 31, 1999). ... On Boston disabled list (August 31, 1999-remainder of season). ... Granted free agency (December 21, 1999). ... Re-signed by Red Sox organization (January 29, 2000).
STATISTICAL NOTES: Led New York-Penn League first beasmen with 17 errors in 1996. ... Led Midwest League with 272 total bases and .546 slugging percentage in 1998. ... Led Midwest League with 20 passed balls in 1998. ... Led Eastern League with seven double plays by catchers in 1999. ... Career major league grand slams: 1.
2002 GAMES PLAYED BY POSITION (MLB): 3B—156.

			BATTING													FIELDING	
Year	Team (League)	Pos.	G	AB	R	H	2B	3B	HR	RBI	BB	SO	SB-CS	Avg.	OBP	SLG	E	Avg.
1996—	Lowell (NY-Penn)	1B-SS-3B	72	279	33	88	18	2	2	38	18	32	4-3	.315	.371	.416	†33	.938
1997—	Michigan (Midw.)	1B-3B	64	224	28	65	13	3	3	39	9	20	1-3	.290	.315	.415	8	.950
	— Sarasota (FSL)	1B-3B	57	220	25	65	12	0	2	28	7	29	9-8	.295	.320	.377	20	.926
1998—	Michigan (Midw.)	C-1B-3B	129	498	80	174	33	4	19	93	19	49	13-7	.349	.383	.546	14	.982
1999—	Trenton (East.)	C-DH	69	282	41	73	15	0	7	36	14	27	6-5	.259	.298	.387	5	.987
2000—	Trenton (East.)	1B-3B	135	529	77	*171	35	3	11	79	19	39	3-3	.323	.355	.463	15	.979
2001—	Boston (A.L.)	3B-1B-DH	139	468	52	123	20	2	12	49	13	61	3-4	.263	.291	.391	18	.950
2002—	Boston (A.L.)	3B	156	634	94	186	43	4	18	83	25	95	4-2	.293	.330	.459	*23	.943
Major League totals (2 years)			295	1102	146	309	63	6	30	132	38	156	7-6	.280	.313	.430	41	.946

ALL-STAR GAME RECORD

	AB	R	H	2B	3B	HR	RBI	BB	SO	SB-CS	Avg.	OBP	SLG	E	Avg.
All-Star Game totals (1 year)	2	0	0	0	0	0	0	0	1	0-0	.000	.000	.000	0	1.000

HINCH, A.J. — C

PERSONAL: Born May 15, 1974, in Waverly, Iowa. ... 6-1/205. ... Bats right, throws right. ... Full name: Andrew Jay Hinch.
HIGH SCHOOL: Midwest City (Okla.).
COLLEGE: Stanford.
TRANSACTIONS/CAREER NOTES: Selected by Chicago White Sox organization in second round of free-agent draft (June 2, 1992); did not sign. ... Selected by Minnesota Twins organization in third round of free-agent draft (June 1, 1995); did not sign. ... Selected by Oakland Athletics organization in third round of free-agent draft (June 4, 1996). ... On Modesto suspended list (June 7-9, 1997). ... Traded by A's with IF Angel Berroa and cash to Kansas City Royals as part of three-way deal in which Royals received P Roberto Hernandez from Tampa Bay Devil Rays, A's received P Cory Lidle from Devil Rays, A's received OF Johnny Damon, IF Mark Ellis and a player to be named later from Royals and Devil Rays received OF Ben Grieve and a player to be named later or cash from A's (January 8, 2001). ... Released by Royals (October 15, 2002).
RECORDS: Shares major league single-season record for fewest double plays by catcher for leader—8 (1998).
STATISTICAL NOTES: Led California League catchers with .996 fielding percentage in 1997. ... Tied for A.L. lead in double plays by catcher with eight in 1998. ... Led Pacific Coast League catchers with .994 fielding percentage in 2000. ... Career major league grand slams: 1.
MISCELLANEOUS: Member of 1996 U.S. Olympic baseball team.
2002 GAMES PLAYED BY POSITION (MLB): C—68.

			BATTING														FIELDING	
Year	Team (League)	Pos.	G	AB	R	H	2B	3B	HR	RBI	BB	SO	SB-CS	Avg.	OBP	SLG	E	Avg.
1997	—Modesto (Calif.)	C-DH-1B	95	333	70	103	25	3	20	73	42	68	8-3	.309	.400	.583	3	†.996
	—Edmonton (PCL)	C-DH-OF	39	125	23	47	7	0	4	24	20	13	2-0	.376	.473	.528	3	.986
1998	—Oakland (A.L.)	C	120	337	34	78	10	0	9	35	30	89	3-0	.231	.296	.341	•9	.986
1999	—Oakland (A.L.)	C	76	205	26	44	4	1	7	24	11	41	6-2	.215	.260	.346	5	.987
	—Vancouver (PCL)	C-DH	15	61	9	23	3	0	2	7	3	12	1-1	.377	.415	.525	1	.989
2000	—Sacramento (PCL)	C-1B	109	417	65	111	23	2	6	47	45	67	5-5	.266	.344	.374	4	†.994
	—Oakland (A.L.)	C-DH	6	8	1	2	0	0	0	0	1	1	0-0	.250	.333	.250	1	.900
2001	—Kansas City (A.L.)■	C-DH	45	121	10	19	3	0	6	15	8	26	1-1	.157	.226	.331	3	.987
	—Omaha (PCL)	C-OF	45	168	28	54	14	0	10	33	11	33	1-0	.321	.365	.583	1	.995
2002	—Kansas City (A.L.)	C	72	197	25	49	7	1	7	27	18	35	3-3	.249	.321	.401	4	.989
Major League totals (5 years)			319	868	96	192	24	2	29	101	68	192	13-6	.221	.284	.354	22	.987

HINSKE, ERIC — 3B — BLUE JAYS

PERSONAL: Born August 5, 1977, in Menasha, Wisc. ... 6-2/225. ... Bats left, throws right. ... Full name: Eric Scott Hinske. ... Name pronounced hin-SKEE.
HIGH SCHOOL: Menasha (Wisc.).
COLLEGE: Arkansas.
TRANSACTIONS/CAREER NOTES: Selected by Chicago Cubs organization in 17th round of free-agent draft (June 2, 1998). ... Traded by Cubs to Oakland Athletics for 2B Miguel Cairo (March 28, 2001). ... On disabled list (May 1-12, 2001). ... Traded by A's with P Justin Miller to Toronto Blue Jays for P Billy Koch (December 7, 2001).
HONORS: Named A.L. Rookie of the Year by The Sporting News (2002). ... Named A.L. Rookie of the Year by Baseball Writers' Association of America (2002).
STATISTICAL NOTES: Led New York-Pennsylvania League first basemen with 561 putouts, 49 assists, 51 double plays and 612 total chances in 1998.
2002 GAMES PLAYED BY POSITION (MLB): 3B—148.

			BATTING														FIELDING	
Year	Team (League)	Pos.	G	AB	R	H	2B	3B	HR	RBI	BB	SO	SB-CS	Avg.	OBP	SLG	E	Avg.
1998	—Williamsport (NY-P)	1B	68	248	46	74	20	0	9	57	35	61	19-3	.298	.384	.488	2	*.997
	—Rockford (Midw.)	1B	6	20	8	9	4	0	1	4	5	6	1-0	.450	.538	.800	0	1.000
1999	—Daytona (FSL)	3B-1B-OF	130	445	76	132	28	6	19	79	62	90	16-10	.297	.385	.515	22	.965
	—Iowa (PCL)	1B-3B	4	15	3	4	0	1	1	2	1	4	0-0	.267	.313	.600	1	.952
2000	—West Tenn (Sou.)	3B-1B-OF	131	436	76	113	21	9	20	73	78	133	14-5	.259	.373	.486	28	.916
2001	—Sacramento (PCL)■	3B-2B	121	436	71	123	27	1	25	79	54	113	20-7	.282	.373	.521	17	.941
2002	—Toronto (A.L.)■	3B	151	566	99	158	38	2	24	84	77	138	13-1	.279	.365	.481	20	.946
Major League totals (1 year)			151	566	99	158	38	2	24	84	77	138	13-1	.279	.365	.481	20	.946

HITCHCOCK, STERLING — P — YANKEES

PERSONAL: Born April 29, 1971, in Fayetteville, N.C. ... 6-0/205. ... Throws left, bats left. ... Full name: Sterling Alex Hitchcock.
HIGH SCHOOL: Armwood (Seffner, Fla.).
TRANSACTIONS/CAREER NOTES: Selected by New York Yankees organization in ninth round of free-agent draft (June 5, 1989). ... On disabled list (June 26-August 14, 1991). ... On Columbus disabled list (May 23-July 21, 1993). ... Traded by Yankees with 3B Russ Davis to Seattle Mariners for 1B Tino Martinez, P Jeff Nelson and P Jim Mecir (December 7, 1995). ... Traded by Mariners to San Diego Padres for P Scott Sanders (December 6, 1996). ... On disabled list (June 6-July 3, 1997; and May 27, 2000-remainder of season). ... On San Diego disabled list (March 27-July 4, 2001); included rehabilitation assignments to Lake Elsinore (April 5-27 and June 14-18) and Portland (June 19-July 4). ... Traded by Padres to Yankees for P Brett Jodie and OF Darren Blakely (July 30, 2001). ... Granted free agency (November 6, 2001). ... Re-signed by Yankees (December 19, 2001). ... On New York disabled list (March 22-May 8 and June 28-July 28, 2002); included rehabilitation assignments to Tampa (April 25-29), Columbus (April 30-May 8) and Gulf Coast Yankees (July 25-28).
STATISTICAL NOTES: Pitched 1-0 no-hit victory against Sumter (July 16, 1990). ... Struck out 15 batters in one game (August 29, 1998). ... Tied for N.L. lead with 15 wild pitches in 1999.
CAREER HITTING (MLB): 18-for-191 (.094), 14 R, 0 2B, 0 3B, 0 HR, 5 RBI.

Year	League	W	L	Pct.	ERA	G	GS	CG	ShO	Sv.-Opp.	IP	H	R	ER	HR	BB-IBB	SO
1989	—Gulf Coast Yankees (GCL)	*9	1	.900	1.64	13	•13	0	0	0-...	76.2	48	16	14	1	27-0	*98
1990	—Greensboro (S.Atl.)	12	12	.500	2.91	27	27	6	*5	0-...	173.1	122	68	56	7	60-1	*171
1991	—Prince William (Caro.)	7	7	.500	2.64	19	19	2	0	0-...	119.1	111	49	35	2	26-0	101
1992	—Albany/Colonie (East.)	6	9	.400	2.58	24	24	2	0	0-...	146.2	116	51	42	6	42-0	*155
	—New York (A.L.)	0	2	.000	8.31	3	3	0	0	0-0	13.0	23	12	12	2	6-0	6
1993	—Columbus (I.L.)	3	5	.375	4.81	16	16	0	0	0-...	76.2	80	43	41	8	28-0	85
	—Oneonta (NY-Penn)	0	0	...	0.00	1	0	0	0	0-...	1.0	0	0	0	0	0-0	0
	—New York (A.L.)	1	2	.333	4.65	6	6	0	0	0-0	31.0	32	18	16	4	14-1	26
1994	—New York (A.L.)	4	1	.800	4.20	23	5	1	0	2-2	49.1	48	24	23	3	29-1	37
	—Columbus (I.L.)	3	4	.429	4.32	10	9	1	0	0-...	50.0	53	30	24	4	18-0	47
	—Albany/Colonie (East.)	1	0	1.000	1.80	1	1	0	0	0-...	5.0	4	1	1	0	0-0	7
1995	—New York (A.L.)	11	10	.524	4.70	27	27	4	1	0-0	168.1	155	91	88	22	68-1	121
1996	—Seattle (A.L.)■	13	9	.591	5.35	35	35	0	0	0-0	196.2	245	131	117	27	73-4	132
1997	—San Diego (N.L.)■	10	11	.476	5.20	32	28	1	0	0-0	161.0	172	102	93	24	55-2	106
1998	—San Diego (N.L.)	9	7	.563	3.93	39	27	2	1	1-2	176.1	169	83	77	29	48-2	158
1999	—San Diego (N.L.)	12	14	.462	4.11	33	33	1	0	0-0	205.2	202	99	94	29	76-6	194
2000	—San Diego (N.L.)	1	6	.143	4.93	11	11	0	0	0-0	65.2	69	38	36	12	26-1	61
2001	—Lake Elsinore (Calif.)	0	2	.000	4.10	6	6	0	0	0-...	26.1	33	18	12	3	1-0	31
	—Portland (PCL)	2	0	1.000	3.71	3	3	0	0	0-...	17.0	20	7	7	1	2-0	11
	—San Diego (N.L.)	2	1	.667	3.32	3	3	0	0	0-0	19.0	22	9	7	1	3-0	15
	—New York (A.L.)■	4	4	.500	6.49	10	9	1	0	0-0	51.1	67	37	37	5	18-0	28
2002	—Tampa (FSL)	0	0	...	1.50	1	1	0	0	0-...	6.0	3	1	1	0	0-0	3
	—Columbus (I.L.)	0	0	...	13.50	2	2	0	0	0-...	7.1	19	11	11	2	3-0	3
	—New York (A.L.)	1	2	.333	5.49	20	2	0	0	0-0	39.1	57	29	24	4	15-3	31
	—Gulf Coast Yankees (GCL)	0	0	...	0.00	2	2	0	0	0-...	3.0	0	0	0	0	0-0	6
A.L. totals (7 years)		34	30	.531	5.20	124	87	6	1	2-2	549.0	627	342	317	67	223-10	381
N.L. totals (5 years)		34	39	.466	4.40	118	102	4	1	1-2	627.2	634	331	307	95	208-11	534
Major League totals (11 years)		68	69	.496	4.77	242	189	10	2	3-4	1176.2	1261	673	624	162	431-21	915

DIVISION SERIES RECORD

Year	League	W	L	Pct.	ERA	G	GS	CG	ShO	Sv.-Opp.	IP	H	R	ER	HR	BB-IBB	SO
1995	—New York (A.L.)	0	0	...	5.40	2	0	0	0	0-0	1.2	2	2	1	1	2-1	1
1998	—San Diego (N.L.)	1	0	1.000	1.50	1	1	0	0	0-0	6.0	3	1	1	0	0-0	11
2001	—New York (A.L.)	0	0	...	6.00	1	0	0	0	0-0	3.0	5	2	2	2	0-0	2
Division series totals (3 years)		1	0	1.000	3.38	4	1	0	0	0-0	10.2	10	5	4	3	2-1	14

CHAMPIONSHIP SERIES RECORD

RECORDS: Shares single-inning record for most wild pitches—2 (October 14, 1998, second inning).
NOTES: Named N.L. Championship Series Most Valuable Player (1998).

Year	League	W	L	Pct.	ERA	G	GS	CG	ShO	Sv.-Opp.	IP	H	R	ER	HR	BB-IBB	SO
1998	—San Diego (N.L.)	2	0	1.000	0.90	2	2	0	0	0-0	10.0	5	1	1	0	8-1	14
2001	—New York (A.L.)									Did not play.							

WORLD SERIES RECORD

Year	League	W	L	Pct.	ERA	G	GS	CG	ShO	Sv.-Opp.	IP	H	R	ER	HR	BB-IBB	SO
1998	—San Diego (N.L.)	0	0	...	1.50	1	1	0	0	0-0	6.0	7	2	1	1	1-0	7
2001	—New York (A.L.)	1	0	1.000	0.00	2	0	0	0	0-0	4.0	1	0	0	0	0-0	6
World Series totals (2 years)		1	0	1.000	0.90	3	1	0	0	0-0	10.0	8	2	1	1	1-0	13

HOCKING, DENNY — IF — TWINS

PERSONAL: Born April 2, 1970, in Torrance, Calif. ... 5-10/183. ... Bats both, throws right. ... Full name: Dennis Lee Hocking.
HIGH SCHOOL: West Torrance (Calif.).
COLLEGE: El Camino College (Calif.).
TRANSACTIONS/CAREER NOTES: Selected by Minnesota Twins organization in 52nd round of free-agent draft (June 5, 1989). ... On Nashville disabled list (April 8-29, 1993). ... On Minnesota disabled list (March 22-April 30, May 30-June 29 and July 31-September 8, 1996); included rehabilitation assignments to Salt Lake (April 4-30, June 21-29 and August 24-September 8).
STATISTICAL NOTES: Led California League shortstops with 469 assists and 721 total chances in 1992. ... Led Pacific Coast League shortstops with .966 fielding percentage and 390 assists in 1995. ... Career major league grand slams: 1.
2002 GAMES PLAYED BY POSITION (MLB): 2B—56; SS—25; 3B—16; 1B—6; OF—5.

			BATTING													FIELDING	
Year	Team (League)	Pos.	G	AB	R	H	2B	3B	HR	RBI	BB	SO	SB-CS	Avg.	OBP	SLG	E	Avg.
1990	—Elizabethton (Appl.)	SS-2B-3B	54	201	45	59	6	2	6	30	40	26	14-4	.294	.422	.433	20	.928
1991	—Kenosha (Midw.)	SS	125	432	72	110	17	8	2	36	77	69	22-10	.255	.372	.345	42	.923
1992	—Visalia (Calif.)	SS	135	*550	117	*182	34	9	7	81	72	77	38-18	.331	.415	.464	38	.947
1993	—Nashville (Sou.)	SS-DH-2B	107	409	54	109	9	4	8	50	34	66	15-5	.267	.327	.367	30	.937
	—Minnesota (A.L.)	SS-2B	15	36	7	5	1	0	0	0	6	8	1-0	.139	.262	.167	1	.977
1994	—Salt Lake (PCL)	SS	112	394	61	110	14	6	5	57	28	57	13-7	.279	.327	.383	26	.949
	—Minnesota (A.L.)	SS	11	31	3	10	3	0	0	2	0	4	2-0	.323	.323	.419	0	1.000
1995	—Salt Lake (PCL)	SS-DH-2B	117	397	51	112	24	2	8	75	25	41	12-8	.282	.324	.413	20	†.966
	—Minnesota (A.L.)	SS	9	25	4	5	0	2	0	3	2	2	1-0	.200	.259	.360	1	.971
1996	—Salt Lake (PCL)	S-O-DH-1-2-3	37	130	18	36	6	2	3	22	10	17	2-2	.277	.333	.423	3	.976
	—Minnesota (A.L.)	O-S-2-DH-1	49	127	16	25	6	0	1	10	8	24	3-3	.197	.243	.268	1	.987
1997	—Minnesota (A.L.)	IF-OF-DH	115	253	28	65	12	4	2	25	18	51	3-5	.257	.308	.360	4	.985
1998	—Minnesota (A.L.)	IF-OF-DH	110	198	32	40	6	1	3	15	16	44	2-1	.202	.259	.288	4	.982
1999	—Minnesota (A.L.)	S-2-O-3-1	136	386	47	103	18	2	7	41	22	54	11-7	.267	.307	.378	3	.992
2000	—Minnesota (A.L.)	OF-IF-DH	134	373	52	111	24	4	4	47	48	77	7-5	.298	.373	.416	5	.985
2001	—Minnesota (A.L.)■	S-2-1-DH-3	112	327	34	82	16	2	3	25	29	67	6-1	.251	.315	.339	5	.984
2002	—Minnesota (A.L.)	2-S-3-1-O	102	260	28	65	13	0	2	25	24	44	0-2	.250	.310	.323	10	.968
Major League totals (10 years)			793	2016	251	511	99	15	22	193	173	375	36-24	.253	.312	.350	34	.983

DIVISION SERIES RECORD

			BATTING													FIELDING	
Year	Team (League)	Pos.	G	AB	R	H	2B	3B	HR	RBI	BB	SO	SB-CS	Avg.	OBP	SLG	E	Avg.
2002	—Minnesota (A.L.)	OF-2B	3	6	0	3	1	0	0	1	0	1	0-0	.500	.500	.667	0	1.000

HODGES, TREY — P — BRAVES

PERSONAL: Born June 29, 1978, in Houston. ... 6-3/187. ... Throws right, bats right. ... Full name: Trey Alan Hodges.
COLLEGE: Louisiana State.
TRANSACTIONS/CAREER NOTES: Selected by Atlanta Braves organization in 17th round of free-agent draft (June 5, 2000).
HONORS: Shared Carolina League Pitcher of the Year (2001).
CAREER HITTING (MLB): 0-for-3 (.000), 0 R, 0 2B, 0 3B, 0 HR, 0 RBI.

Year League	W	L	Pct.	ERA	G	GS	CG	ShO	Sv.-Opp.	IP	H	R	ER	HR	BB-IBB	SO
2000—Jamestown (NY-Penn)	0	2	.000	5.95	13	2	0	0	0-...	19.2	22	14	13	3	12-0	13
2001—Myrtle Beach (Caro.)	*15	8	.652	2.76	26	26	1	0	0-...	*173.0	156	64	53	13	18-0	139
2002—Richmond (I.L.)	*15	9	.625	3.19	28	28	1	1	0-...	172.1	158	66	61	9	56-1	116
—Atlanta (N.L.)	2	0	1.000	5.40	4	0	0	0	0-0	11.2	16	7	7	2	2-0	6
Major League totals (1 year).......	2	0	1.000	5.40	4	0	0	0	0-0	11.2	16	7	7	2	2-0	6

HOFFMAN, TREVOR — P — PADRES

PERSONAL: Born October 13, 1967, in Bellflower, Calif. ... 6-0/205. ... Throws right, bats right. ... Full name: Trevor William Hoffman. ... Brother of Glenn Hoffman, assistant coach, Los Angeles Dodgers; and infielder with Boston Red Sox (1980-87), Los Angeles Dodgers (1987) and California Angels (1989).
HIGH SCHOOL: Savanna (Anaheim).
JUNIOR COLLEGE: Cypress (Calif.) College.
COLLEGE: Arizona.
TRANSACTIONS/CAREER NOTES: Selected by Cincinnati Reds organization in 11th round of free-agent draft (June 5, 1989). ... Selected by Florida Marlins in first round (eighth pick overall) of expansion draft (November 17, 1992). ... Traded by Marlins with P Jose Martinez and P Andres Berumen to San Diego Padres for 3B Gary Sheffield and P Rich Rodriguez (June 24, 1993).
HONORS: Named N.L. Fireman of the Year by The Sporting News (1996 and 1998).
STATISTICAL NOTES: Tied for N.L. lead with 13 intentional bases on balls issued in 1993. ... Led N.L. with 50 save opportunities in 2000.
MISCELLANEOUS: Holds San Diego Padres all-time record for most games pitched (604), saves (350) and lowest career earned-run average (2.76).
CAREER HITTING (MLB): 4-for-33 (.121), 1 R, 2 2B, 0 3B, 0 HR, 5 RBI.

Year League	W	L	Pct.	ERA	G	GS	CG	ShO	Sv.-Opp.	IP	H	R	ER	HR	BB-IBB	SO
1991—Cedar Rapids (Midw.)	1	1	.500	1.87	27	0	0	0	12-...	33.2	22	8	7	0	13-0	52
—Chattanooga (Sou.)	1	0	1.000	1.93	14	0	0	0	8-...	14.0	10	4	3	0	7-0	23
1992—Chattanooga (Sou.)	3	0	1.000	1.52	6	6	0	0	0-...	29.2	22	6	5	1	11-1	31
—Nashville (A.A.)	4	6	.400	4.27	42	5	0	0	6-...	65.1	57	32	31	6	32-3	63
1993—Florida (N.L.)■.................	2	2	.500	3.28	28	0	0	0	2-3	35.2	24	13	13	5	19-7	26
—San Diego (N.L.)■...........	2	4	.333	4.31	39	0	0	0	3-5	54.1	56	30	26	5	20-6	53
1994—San Diego (N.L.)	4	4	.500	2.57	47	0	0	0	20-23	56.0	39	16	16	4	20-6	68
1995—San Diego (N.L.)	7	4	.636	3.88	55	0	0	0	31-38	53.1	48	25	23	10	14-3	52
1996—San Diego (N.L.)	9	5	.643	2.25	70	0	0	0	42-49	88.0	50	23	22	6	31-5	111
1997—San Diego (N.L.)	6	4	.600	2.66	70	0	0	0	37-44	81.1	59	25	24	9	24-4	111
1998—San Diego (N.L.)	4	2	.667	1.48	66	0	0	0	*53-54	73.0	41	12	12	2	21-2	86
1999—San Diego (N.L.)	2	3	.400	2.14	64	0	0	0	40-43	67.1	48	23	16	5	15-2	73
2000—San Diego (N.L.)	4	7	.364	2.99	70	0	0	0	43-50	72.1	61	29	24	7	11-4	85
2001—San Diego (N.L.)	3	4	.429	3.43	62	0	0	0	43-46	60.1	48	25	23	10	21-2	63
2002—San Diego (N.L.)	2	5	.286	2.73	61	0	0	0	38-41	59.1	52	20	18	2	18-2	69
Major League totals (10 years)...	45	44	.506	2.79	632	0	0	0	352-396	701.0	526	241	217	65	214-43	797

DIVISION SERIES RECORD

Year League	W	L	Pct.	ERA	G	GS	CG	ShO	Sv.-Opp.	IP	H	R	ER	HR	BB-IBB	SO
1996—San Diego (N.L.)	0	1	.000	10.80	2	0	0	0	0-0	1.2	3	2	2	1	1-0	2
1998—San Diego (N.L.)	0	0	...	0.00	4	0	0	0	2-2	3.0	3	1	0	0	1-1	4
Division series totals (2 years) ...	0	1	.000	3.86	6	0	0	0	2-2	4.2	6	3	2	1	2-1	6

CHAMPIONSHIP SERIES RECORD

Year League	W	L	Pct.	ERA	G	GS	CG	ShO	Sv.-Opp.	IP	H	R	ER	HR	BB-IBB	SO
1998—San Diego (N.L.)	1	0	1.000	2.08	3	0	0	0	1-2	4.1	2	1	1	0	2-0	7

WORLD SERIES RECORD

Year League	W	L	Pct.	ERA	G	GS	CG	ShO	Sv.-Opp.	IP	H	R	ER	HR	BB-IBB	SO
1998—San Diego (N.L.)	0	1	.000	9.00	1	0	0	0	0-1	2.0	2	2	2	1	1-0	0

ALL-STAR GAME RECORD

	W	L	Pct.	ERA	GS	CG	ShO	Sv.-Opp.	IP	H	R	ER	HR	BB-IBB	SO
All-Star Game totals (4 years)	0	0	...	10.80	0	0	0	0-0	3.1	5	4	4	2	0-0	5

RECORD AS POSITION PLAYER

		BATTING														FIELDING	
Year Team (League)	Pos.	G	AB	R	H	2B	3B	HR	RBI	BB	SO	SB-CS	Avg.	OBP	SLG	E	Avg.
1989—Billings (Pio.)	SS	61	201	22	50	5	0	1	20	19	40	1-6	.249	.319	.289	•25	.911
1990—Charl., W.Va. (S.Atl.) ..	SS-3B	103	278	41	59	10	1	2	23	38	53	3-3	.212	.311	.277	30	.915

HOLLANDSWORTH, TODD — OF

PERSONAL: Born April 20, 1973, in Dayton, Ohio. ... 6-2/207. ... Bats left, throws left. ... Full name: Todd Mathew Hollandsworth.
HIGH SCHOOL: Newport (Bellevue, Wash.).
TRANSACTIONS/CAREER NOTES: Selected by Los Angeles Dodgers organization in third round of free-agent draft (June 3, 1991); pick received as part of compensation for Kansas City Royals signing Type B free-agent OF/DH Kirk Gibson. ... On Los Angeles disabled list (May 3-July 7 and August 9-September 12, 1995); included rehabilitation assignments to San Bernardino (June 6-7) and Albuquerque (June 27-July 7). ... On Los Angeles disabled list (August 2-16 and August 17-September 6, 1997); included rehabilitation assignment to San Bernardino

(August 15-17). ... On disabled list (June 5, 1998-remainder of season). ... On Los Angeles disabled list (April 3-23 and June 4-19, 1999); included rehabilitation assignments to San Bernardino (April 20-23 and June 18-19). ... Traded by Dodgers with OF Kevin Gibbs and P Randey Dorame to Colorado Rockies for OF Tom Goodwin and cash (July 31, 2000). ... Granted free agency (October 27, 2000). ... Re-signed by Rockies (November 16, 2000). ... On disabled list (May 12, 2001-remainder of season). ... Traded by Rockies with P Dennys Reyes to Texas Rangers for OF Gabe Kapler and 2B Jason Romano (July 31, 2002). ... On Texas disabled list (August 4-20, 2002). ... Granted free agency (October 28, 2002).

HONORS: Named N.L. Rookie of the Year by Baseball Writers' Association of America (1996).

STATISTICAL NOTES: Had 16-game hitting streak (April 14-May 3, 2001). ... Hit three home runs in one game (April 15, 2001). ... Career major league grand slams: 2.

2002 GAMES PLAYED BY POSITION (MLB): OF—128.

		BATTING														FIELDING	
Year Team (League)	**Pos.**	**G**	**AB**	**R**	**H**	**2B**	**3B**	**HR**	**RBI**	**BB**	**SO**	**SB-CS**	**Avg.**	**OBP**	**SLG**	**E**	**Avg.**
1991—GC Dodgers (GCL)	OF	6	16	1	5	0	0	0	0	0	6	0-0	.313	.313	.313	0	1.000
—Yakima (N'West)	OF	56	203	34	48	5	1	8	33	27	57	11-1	.236	.338	.389	7	.939
1992—Bakersfield (Calif.)	OF	119	430	70	111	23	5	13	58	50	113	27-13	.258	.338	.426	6	.975
1993—San Antonio (Texas)	OF	126	474	57	119	24	9	17	63	29	101	24-12	.251	.298	.447	12	.956
1994—Albuquerque (PCL)	OF	132	505	80	144	31	5	19	91	46	96	15-9	.285	.343	.479	13	.949
1995—Los Angeles (N.L.)	OF	41	103	16	24	2	0	5	13	10	29	2-1	.233	.304	.398	4	.938
—San Bern. (Calif.)	OF	1	2	0	1	0	0	0	0	0	1	0-1	.500	.500	.500	0	...
—Albuquerque (PCL)	OF	10	38	9	9	2	0	2	4	6	8	1-0	.237	.356	.447	0	1.000
1996—Los Angeles (N.L.)	OF	149	478	64	139	26	4	12	59	41	93	21-6	.291	.348	.437	5	.978
1997—Los Angeles (N.L.)	OF	106	296	39	73	20	2	4	31	17	60	5-5	.247	.286	.368	3	.984
—Albuquerque (PCL)	OF	13	56	13	24	4	3	1	14	4	4	2-3	.429	.467	.661	0	1.000
—San Bern. (Calif.)	OF	2	8	1	2	0	1	0	2	1	2	0-0	.250	.333	.500	0	1.000
1998—Los Angeles (N.L.)	OF	55	175	23	47	6	4	3	20	9	42	4-3	.269	.308	.400	4	.957
1999—San Bern. (Calif.)	OF	4	13	3	5	2	0	0	3	2	4	0-1	.385	.500	.538	0	1.000
—Los Angeles (N.L.)	OF-1B	92	261	39	74	12	2	9	32	24	61	5-2	.284	.345	.448	3	.987
2000—Los Angeles (N.L.)	OF	81	261	42	61	12	0	8	24	30	61	11-4	.234	.314	.372	2	.987
—Colorado (N.L.)■	OF	56	167	39	54	8	0	11	23	11	38	7-3	.323	.365	.569	1	.988
2001—Colorado (N.L.)	OF	33	117	21	43	15	1	6	19	8	20	5-0	.368	.408	.667	1	.981
2002—Colorado (N.L.)	OF	95	298	39	88	21	1	11	48	26	71	7-8	.295	.352	.483	4	.973
—Texas (A.L.)■	OF	39	132	16	34	6	0	5	19	14	27	1-0	.258	.327	.417	0	1.000
American League totals (1 year)		39	132	16	34	6	0	5	19	14	27	1-0	.258	.327	.417	0	1.000
National League totals (8 years)		708	2156	322	603	122	14	69	269	176	475	67-32	.280	.335	.445	27	.978
Major League totals (8 years)		747	2288	338	637	128	14	74	288	190	502	68-32	.278	.334	.444	27	.979

DIVISION SERIES RECORD

		BATTING														FIELDING	
Year Team (League)	**Pos.**	**G**	**AB**	**R**	**H**	**2B**	**3B**	**HR**	**RBI**	**BB**	**SO**	**SB-CS**	**Avg.**	**OBP**	**SLG**	**E**	**Avg.**
1995—Los Angeles (N.L.)	OF-PH	2	2	0	0	0	0	0	0	0	0	0-0	.000	.000	.000	0	...
1996—Los Angeles (N.L.)	OF	3	12	1	4	3	0	0	1	0	3	0-0	.333	.333	.583	0	1.000
Division series totals (2 years)		5	14	1	4	3	0	0	1	0	3	0-0	.286	.286	.500	0	1.000

HOLLINS, DAVE 3B/1B

PERSONAL: Born May 25, 1966, in Orchard Park, NY. ... 6-1/232. ... Bats both, throws right. ... Full name: David Michael Hollins.

HIGH SCHOOL: Orchard Park (N.Y.).

COLLEGE: South Carolina.

TRANSACTIONS/CAREER NOTES: Selected by San Diego Padres organization in sixth round of free-agent draft (June 2, 1987). ... Selected by Philadelphia Phillies from Padres organization in Rule 5 major league draft (December 4, 1989). ... On Philadelphia disabled list (August 16-September 6, 1991); included rehabilitation assignment to Scranton/Wilkes-Barre (September 2-5). ... On suspended list (September 29-October 3, 1992). ... On disabled list (June 11-28, 1993). ... On Philadelphia disabled list (May 23-July 23 and July 25, 1994-remainder of season); included rehabilitation assignment to Scranton/Wilkes-Barre (July 16-23). ... On Philadelphia disabled list (June 12-27, 1995). ... Traded by Phillies to Boston Red Sox for OF Mark Whiten (July 24, 1995). ... On Boston disabled list (August 9, 1995-remainder of season). ... Granted free agency (December 21, 1995). ... Signed by Minnesota Twins (December 23, 1995). ... Traded by Twins to Seattle Mariners for a player to be named later (August 29, 1996); Twins acquired 1B David Arias to complete deal (September 13, 1996). ... Granted free agency (October 31, 1996). ... Signed by Anaheim Angels (November 20, 1996). ... On disabled list (August 10, 1998-remainder of season). ... Traded by Angels with cash to Toronto Blue Jays for SS Tomas Perez (March 30, 1999). ... On Toronto disabled list (April 18-May 21, 1999); included rehabilitation assignment to Syracuse (May 10-13). ... Released by Blue Jays (June 21, 1999). ... Signed by Chicago White Sox organization (July 1, 1999). ... Granted free agency (October 15, 1999). ... Signed by Tampa Bay Devil Rays organization (January 14, 2000). ... On Durham disabled list (April 24-May 21, 2000). ... Released by Devils Rays (May 21, 2000). ... Signed by Baltimore Orioles organization (July 13, 2000). ... Released by Orioles (August 3, 2000). ... Signed by Cleveland Indians organization (August 3, 2000). ... On Buffalo disabled list (August 20-September 10, 2000). ... Granted free agency (October 18, 2000). ... Re-signed by Indians organization (December 20, 2000). ... On Buffalo disabled list (April 30-May 13, 2001). ... Granted free agency (October 8, 2001). ... On Philadelphia disabled list (April 12-September 1, 2002); included rehabilitation assignments to Scranton/Wilkes-Barre (May 28-June 4, July 4-17 and August 27-September 1). ... Granted free agency (October 29, 2002).

STATISTICAL NOTES: Led Northwest League with seven intentional bases on balls received in 1987. ... Led Northwest League third basemen with 59 putouts, 167 assists and 241 total chances in 1987. ... Led Texas League with 10 sacrifice flies in 1989. ... Led N.L. in being hit by pitch with 19 in 1992. ... Led A.L. third basemen with 29 errors in 1997. ... Tied for International League lead with eight intentional bases on balls received in 2001. ... Career major league grand slams: 3.

2002 GAMES PLAYED BY POSITION (MLB): 1B—5.

		BATTING														FIELDING	
Year Team (League)	**Pos.**	**G**	**AB**	**R**	**H**	**2B**	**3B**	**HR**	**RBI**	**BB**	**SO**	**SB-CS**	**Avg.**	**OBP**	**SLG**	**E**	**Avg.**
1987—Spokane (N'West)	3B	75	278	52	86	14	4	2	44	53	36	20-5	.309	.418	.410	15	*.938
1988—Riverside (Calif.)	3B-1B-SS	139	516	90	157	32	1	9	92	82	67	13-11	.304	.395	.422	29	.923
1989—Wichita (Texas)	3B	131	459	69	126	29	4	9	79	63	88	8-3	.275	.361	.414	25	.920
1990—Philadelphia (N.L.)■	3B-1B	72	114	14	21	0	0	5	15	10	28	0-0	.184	.252	.316	4	.941
1991—Philadelphia (N.L.)	3B-1B	56	151	18	45	10	2	6	21	17	26	1-1	.298	.378	.510	8	.942
—Scranton/W.B. (I.L.)	3B-1B	72	229	37	61	11	6	8	35	43	43	4-1	.266	.388	.472	10	.945
1992—Philadelphia (N.L.)	3B-1B	156	586	104	158	28	4	27	93	76	110	9-6	.270	.369	.469	18	.954

Year	Team (League)	Pos.	G	AB	R	H	2B	3B	HR	RBI	BB	SO	SB-CS	Avg.	OBP	SLG	E	Avg.
			BATTING														FIELDING	
1993—	Philadelphia (N.L.)	3B	143	543	104	148	30	4	18	93	85	109	2-3	.273	.372	.442	27	.914
1994—	Philadelphia (N.L.)	3B-OF	44	162	28	36	7	1	4	26	23	32	1-0	.222	.328	.352	11	.888
—	Scranton/W.B. (I.L.)	OF	6	19	6	4	0	0	1	3	5	4	0-0	.211	.375	.368	2	.867
1995—	Philadelphia (N.L.)	1B	65	205	46	47	12	2	7	25	53	38	1-1	.229	.393	.410	7	.988
—	Boston (A.L.)■	DH-OF	5	13	2	2	0	0	0	1	4	7	0-0	.154	.353	.154	0	1.000
1996—	Minnesota (A.L.)■	3B-DH-SS	121	422	71	102	26	0	13	53	71	102	6-4	.242	.364	.396	15	.950
—	Seattle (A.L.)■	3B-1B	28	94	17	33	3	0	3	25	13	15	0-2	.351	.438	.479	3	.961
1997—	Anaheim (A.L.)■	3B-1B	149	572	101	165	29	2	16	85	62	124	16-6	.288	.363	.430	†29	.940
1998—	Anaheim (A.L.)	3B-1B-DH	101	363	60	88	16	2	11	39	44	69	11-3	.242	.334	.388	17	.938
1999—	Toronto (A.L.)■	DH	27	99	12	22	5	0	2	6	5	22	0-0	.222	.260	.333	...	...
—	Syracuse (I.L.)	DH	4	15	2	3	1	0	0	1	1	5	0-0	.200	.294	.267	...	...
—	Charlotte (I.L.)■	3B-1B-DH	63	199	49	63	18	0	8	33	33	37	5-1	.317	.438	.528	10	.938
2000—	Durham (I.L.)■	1B	11	27	4	5	2	0	1	3	10	6	1-0	.185	.450	.370	0	1.000
—	Rochester (I.L.)■	3B	20	70	8	19	2	0	0	8	9	12	1-0	.271	.358	.300	2	.935
—	Buffalo (I.L.)■	3B	5	13	0	1	1	0	0	2	2	6	0-0	.077	.200	.154	2	.833
2001—	Buffalo (I.L.)	1B-OF-3B	89	316	50	86	25	2	16	67	45	79	0-0	.272	.373	.516	3	.980
—	Cleveland (A.L.)	DH	2	5	0	1	0	0	0	0	1	2	0-0	.200	.333	.200	...	...
2002—	Philadelphia (N.L.)■	1B	14	17	1	2	0	0	0	0	0	3	0-1	.118	.167	.118	0	1.000
—	Scranton/W.B. (I.L.)	1B	14	38	8	9	1	0	2	7	11	9	0-1	.237	.463	.421	1	.990
American League totals (6 years)			433	1568	263	413	79	4	45	209	200	341	33-15	.263	.355	.405	64	.944
National League totals (7 years)			550	1778	315	457	87	13	67	273	264	346	14-12	.257	.361	.434	75	.954
Major League totals (12 years)			983	3346	578	870	166	17	112	482	464	687	47-27	.260	.358	.420	139	.950

CHAMPIONSHIP SERIES RECORD

Year	Team (League)	Pos.	G	AB	R	H	2B	3B	HR	RBI	BB	SO	SB-CS	Avg.	OBP	SLG	E	Avg.
			BATTING														FIELDING	
1993—	Philadelphia (N.L.)	3B	6	20	2	4	1	0	2	4	5	4	1-0	.200	.360	.550	0	1.000

WORLD SERIES RECORD

Year	Team (League)	Pos.	G	AB	R	H	2B	3B	HR	RBI	BB	SO	SB-CS	Avg.	OBP	SLG	E	Avg.
			BATTING														FIELDING	
1993—	Philadelphia (N.L.)	3B	6	23	5	6	1	0	0	2	6	5	0-0	.261	.414	.304	0	1.000

ALL-STAR GAME RECORD

	AB	R	H	2B	3B	HR	RBI	BB	SO	SB-CS	Avg.	OBP	SLG	E	Avg.
All-Star Game totals (1 year)	1	0	1	1	0	0	0	0	0	0-0	1.000	1.000	2.000	0	1.000

HOLMES, DARREN P

PERSONAL: Born April 25, 1966, in Asheville, N.C. ... 6-0/202. ... Throws right, bats right. ... Full name: Darren Lee Holmes.

HIGH SCHOOL: T.C. Roberson (Asheville, N.C.).

TRANSACTIONS/CAREER NOTES: Selected by Los Angeles Dodgers organization in 16th round of free-agent draft (June 4, 1984). ... On disabled list (June 5, 1986-remainder of season). ... Loaned by Dodgers organization to San Luis Potosi, Mexican League (1988). ... Traded by Dodgers to Milwaukee Brewers for C Bert Heffernan (December 20, 1990). ... On Milwaukee disabled list (July 3-18, 1991); included rehabilitation assignment to Beloit (July 13-18). ... Selected by Colorado Rockies in first round (fifth pick overall) of expansion draft (November 17, 1992). ... On Colorado disabled list (May 30-June 24 and July 21-August 11, 1994); included rehabilitation assignments to Asheville (June 14-19) and Colorado Springs (June 20). ... On disabled list (April 30-May 15, 1997). ... Granted free agency (October 27, 1997). ... Signed by New York Yankees (December 22, 1997). ... On New York disabled list (July 30-September 4, 1998); included rehabilitation assignment to Tampa (August 31-September 4). ... Traded by Yankees with cash to Arizona Diamondbacks for C Izzy Molina and P Ben Ford (March 30, 1999). ... On Arizona disabled list (June 24-July 15 and July 18-August 11, 1999); included rehabilitation assignments to Arizona League Diamondbacks (August 3-8) and Tucson (August 9-11). ... Released by Diamondbacks (April 28, 2000) ... Signed by St. Louis Cardinals organization (May 4, 2000). ... Traded by Cardinals to Baltimore Orioles for future considerations (June 28, 2000). ... Released by Orioles (July 19, 2000). ... Signed by Diamondbacks organization (August 11, 2000). ... Granted free agency (October 13, 2000). ... Signed by Atlanta Braves organization (January 28, 2002). ... On disabled list (July 7-27, 2002). ... Granted free agency (November 4, 2002).

CAREER HITTING (MLB): 3-for-28 (.107), 2 R, 0 2B, 0 3B, 1 HR, 2 RBI.

Year	League	W	L	Pct.	ERA	G	GS	CG	ShO	Sv.-Opp.	IP	H	R	ER	HR	BB-IBB	SO
1984—	Great Falls (Pio.)	2	5	.286	6.65	18	6	1	0	0-...	44.2	53	41	33	5	30-1	29
1985—	Vero Beach (FSL)	4	3	.571	3.11	33	0	0	0	2-...	63.2	57	31	22	0	35-2	46
1986—	Vero Beach (FSL)	3	6	.333	2.92	11	10	0	0	0-...	64.2	55	30	21	0	39-2	59
1987—	Vero Beach (FSL)	6	4	.600	4.52	19	19	1	0	0-...	99.2	111	60	50	4	53-0	46
1988—	San Luis Potosi (Mex.)■	9	9	.500	4.64	23	23	7	1	0-...	139.2	151	88	72	5	92-5	110
—	Albuquerque (PCL)■	0	1	.000	5.06	2	1	0	0	0-...	5.1	6	3	3	0	1-0	1
1989—	San Antonio (Texas)	5	8	.385	3.83	17	16	3	2	1-...	110.1	102	59	47	5	44-2	81
—	Albuquerque (PCL)	1	4	.200	7.45	9	8	0	0	0-...	38.2	50	32	32	8	18-1	31
1990—	Albuquerque (PCL)	12	2	*.857	3.11	56	0	0	0	13-...	92.2	78	34	32	3	39-2	99
—	Los Angeles (N.L.)	0	1	.000	5.19	14	0	0	0	0-0	17.1	15	10	10	1	11-3	19
1991—	Denver (A.A.)■	0	0	...	9.00	1	0	0	0	0-...	1.0	1	1	1	0	2-0	2
—	Milwaukee (A.L.)	1	4	.200	4.72	40	0	0	0	3-6	76.1	90	43	40	6	27-1	59
—	Beloit (Midw.)	0	0	...	0.00	2	0	0	0	2-...	2.0	0	0	0	0	0-0	3
1992—	Denver (A.A.)	0	0	...	1.38	12	0	0	0	7-...	13.0	7	2	2	1	1-0	12
—	Milwaukee (A.L.)	4	4	.500	2.55	41	0	0	0	6-8	42.1	35	12	12	1	11-4	31
1993—	Colorado (N.L.)■	3	3	.500	4.05	62	0	0	0	25-29	66.2	56	31	30	6	20-1	60
—	Colorado Springs (PCL)	1	0	1.000	0.00	3	2	0	0	0-...	8.2	1	1	0	0	1-0	9
1994—	Colorado (N.L.)	0	3	.000	6.35	29	0	0	0	3-8	28.1	35	25	20	5	24-4	33
—	Colorado Springs (PCL)	0	1	.000	8.22	4	2	0	0	0-...	7.2	11	7	7	1	3-0	12
—	Asheville (S.Atl.)	0	0	...	0.00	2	1	0	0	0-...	3.0	1	0	0	0	0-0	7
1995—	Colorado (N.L.)	6	1	.857	3.24	68	0	0	0	14-18	66.2	59	26	24	3	28-3	61
1996—	Colorado (N.L.)	5	4	.556	3.97	62	0	0	0	1-8	77.0	78	41	34	8	28-2	73
1997—	Colorado (N.L.)	9	2	.818	5.34	42	6	0	0	3-4	89.1	113	58	53	12	36-3	70
1998—	New York (A.L.)■	0	3	.000	3.33	34	0	0	0	2-3	51.1	53	19	19	4	14-3	31
—	Tampa (FSL)	0	1	.000	4.50	2	1	0	0	0-...	2.0	4	2	1	0	0-0	6

H

Year League	W	L	Pct.	ERA	G	GS	CG	ShO	Sv.-Opp.	IP	H	R	ER	HR	BB-IBB	SO
1999— Arizona (N.L.)■	4	3	.571	3.70	44	0	0	0	0-2	48.2	50	21	20	3	25-8	35
— Ariz. D-backs (Ariz.)	0	0	...	0.00	2	2	0	0	0-...	2.2	1	0	0	0	0-0	4
— Tucson (PCL)	0	0	...	0.00	1	1	0	0	0-...	1.0	0	0	0	0	1-0	0
2000— Arizona (N.L.)	0	0	...	8.53	8	0	0	0	1-1	6.1	12	6	6	1	1-0	5
— Tucson (PCL)	1	1	.500	2.08	3	0	0	0	1-...	4.1	4	1	1	0	4-1	2
— St. Louis (N.L.)■	0	1	.000	9.72	5	0	0	0	0-1	8.1	12	9	9	2	3-0	5
— Memphis (PCL)	0	0	...	2.45	9	0	0	0	0-...	14.2	10	4	4	0	3-0	8
— Baltimore (A.L.)■	0	0	...	25.07	5	0	0	0	0-0	4.2	13	13	13	3	5-0	6
2001—								Did not play.								
2002— Atlanta (N.L.)■	2	2	.500	1.81	55	0	0	0	1-2	54.2	41	12	11	3	12-4	47
A.L. totals (4 years)	5	11	.313	4.33	120	0	0	0	11-17	174.2	191	87	84	14	57-8	127
N.L. totals (9 years)	29	20	.592	4.22	389	6	0	0	48-73	463.1	471	239	217	44	188-28	408
Major League totals (12 years)	34	31	.523	4.25	509	6	0	0	59-90	638.0	662	326	301	58	245-36	535

DIVISION SERIES RECORD

Year League	W	L	Pct.	ERA	G	GS	CG	ShO	Sv.-Opp.	IP	H	R	ER	HR	BB-IBB	SO
1995— Colorado (N.L.)	1	0	1.000	0.00	3	0	0	0	0-1	1.2	6	2	0	0	9-0	2
1998— New York (A.L.)									Did not play.							
1999— Arizona (N.L.)	0	0	...	27.00	1	0	0	0	0-0	1.1	1	4	4	0	3-1	0
2002— Atlanta (N.L.)	0	0	...	0.00	3	0	0	0	0-0	2.2	1	0	0	0	0-0	5
Division series totals (3 years)	1	0	1.000	6.35	7	0	0	0	0-1	5.2	8	6	4	0	12-1	7

CHAMPIONSHIP SERIES RECORD

Year League	W	L	Pct.	ERA	G	GS	CG	ShO	Sv.-Opp.	IP	H	R	ER	HR	BB-IBB	SO
1998— New York (A.L.)									Did not play.							

WORLD SERIES RECORD

NOTES: Member of World Series championship team (1998).

Year League	W	L	Pct.	ERA	G	GS	CG	ShO	Sv.-Opp.	IP	H	R	ER	HR	BB-IBB	SO
1998— New York (A.L.)									Did not play.							

HOLTZ, MIKE P

PERSONAL: Born October 10, 1972, in Arlington, Va. ... 5-9/185. ... Throws left, bats left. ... Full name: Michael James Holtz.

HIGH SCHOOL: Central Cambria (Ebensburg, Pa.).

COLLEGE: Clemson.

TRANSACTIONS/CAREER NOTES: Selected by California Angels organization in 17th round of free-agent draft (June 2, 1994). ... Angels franchise renamed Anaheim Angels for 1997 season. ... On suspended list (June 18-20, 1998). ... On Anaheim disabled list (August 25-September 10, 1999). ... On Anaheim disabled list (May 11-30, 2001); included rehabilitation assignment to Rancho Cucamonga (May 26-30). ... Granted free agency (December 21, 2001). ... Signed by Oakland Athletics (January 2, 2002). ... Released by A's (June 5, 2002). ... Signed by San Diego Padres (July 2, 2002). ... Released by Padres (October 2, 2002).

CAREER HITTING (MLB): 0-for-3 (.000), 0 R, 0 2B, 0 3B, 0 HR, 0 RBI.

Year League	W	L	Pct.	ERA	G	GS	CG	ShO	Sv.-Opp.	IP	H	R	ER	HR	BB-IBB	SO
1994— Boise (N'West)	0	0	...	0.51	22	0	0	0	11-...	35.0	22	4	2	0	11-2	59
1995— Lake Elsinore (Calif.)	4	4	.500	2.29	56	0	0	0	3-...	82.2	70	26	21	7	23-3	101
1996— Midland (Texas)	1	2	.333	4.17	33	0	0	0	2-...	41.0	52	34	19	6	9-1	41
— California (A.L.)	3	3	.500	2.45	30	0	0	0	0-0	29.1	21	11	8	1	19-2	31
1997— Anaheim (A.L.)	3	4	.429	3.32	66	0	0	0	2-8	43.1	38	21	16	7	15-4	40
1998— Anaheim (A.L.)	2	2	.500	4.75	53	0	0	0	1-2	30.1	38	16	16	0	15-1	29
— Vancouver (PCL)	0	0	...	1.74	10	0	0	0	2-...	10.1	10	4	2	1	6-0	18
1999— Anaheim (A.L.)	2	3	.400	8.06	28	0	0	0	0-0	22.1	26	20	20	3	15-1	17
— Edmonton (PCL)	2	1	.667	2.30	20	0	0	0	1-...	27.1	20	7	7	4	11-1	39
2000— Edmonton (PCL)	0	1	.000	10.80	6	0	0	0	0-...	5.0	5	6	6	1	1-0	1
— Anaheim (A.L.)	3	4	.429	5.05	61	0	0	0	0-0	41.0	37	26	23	4	18-2	40
2001— Anaheim (A.L.)	1	2	.333	4.86	63	0	0	0	0-1	37.0	40	24	20	5	15-4	38
— Rancho Cuca. (Calif.)	0	0	...	9.00	2	2	0	0	0-...	2.0	3	2	2	1	1-0	3
2002— Oakland (A.L.)■	0	0	...	6.43	16	0	0	0	0-1	14.0	24	11	10	3	9-0	7
— San Diego (N.L.)■	2	2	.500	4.71	33	0	0	0	0-3	21.0	18	14	11	2	21-3	19
A.L. totals (7 years)	14	18	.438	4.68	317	0	0	0	3-12	217.1	224	129	113	23	106-14	202
N.L. totals (1 year)	2	2	.500	4.71	33	0	0	0	0-3	21.0	18	14	11	2	21-3	19
Major League totals (7 years)	16	20	.444	4.68	350	0	0	0	3-15	238.1	242	143	124	25	127-17	221

HOOVER, PAUL C/IF

PERSONAL: Born April 14, 1976, in Columbus, Ohio. ... 6-1/211. ... Bats right, throws right. ... Full name: Paul Chester Hoover.

HIGH SCHOOL: Steubenville (Ohio).

COLLEGE: Kent State.

TRANSACTIONS/CAREER NOTES: Selected by Houston Astros organization in 64th round of free-agent draft (June 2, 1994); did not sign. ... Selected by Tampa Bay Devil Rays organization in 23rd round of free-agent draft (June 3, 1997). ... On Durham disabled list (April 4-11, 2002). ... Released by Devil Rays (October 14, 2002).

STATISTICAL NOTES: Led Appalachian League shortstops with 111 putouts, 199 assists, 343 total chances and 35 double plays in 1997.

2002 GAMES PLAYED BY POSITION (MLB): C—4.

		BATTING														FIELDING	
Year Team (League)	Pos.	G	AB	R	H	2B	3B	HR	RBI	BB	SO	SB-CS	Avg.	OBP	SLG	E	Avg.
1997— Princeton (Appl.)	SS	66	251	55	76	16	4	4	37	20	37	7-4	.303	.363	.446	•33	.904
1998— Charl., S.C. (S.Atl.)	C-3B-SS-1B	40	124	24	36	10	1	3	19	22	29	2-1	.290	.417	.460	8	.969
— Hudson Valley (NY-P)	C-3B	73	269	51	76	20	1	4	37	39	44	26-3	.283	.388	.409	5	.990
1999— St. Petersburg (FSL)	C-1B-3B	118	408	66	111	13	6	8	54	54	81	23-7	.272	.376	.392	5	.992
2000— Orlando (Sou.)	C-3-O-S-1-2	106	360	54	90	20	4	3	44	67	66	9-8	.250	.382	.353	18	.961
— Durham (I.L.)	C-3B-OF	4	10	0	3	0	0	0	0	0	5	1-0	.300	.364	.300	0	1.000

			BATTING														FIELDING	
Year	Team (League)	Pos.	G	AB	R	H	2B	3B	HR	RBI	BB	SO	SB-CS	Avg.	OBP	SLG	E	Avg.
2001	—Durham (I.L.)	C-3-O-1-S-2	89	293	37	63	18	4	3	21	11	66	5-3	.215	.260	.334	6	.987
	—Tampa Bay (A.L.)	C	3	4	1	1	0	0	0	0	0	1	0-0	.250	.250	.250	0	1.000
2002	—Durham (I.L.)	C-1B-3B-OF	69	227	27	50	12	3	5	20	18	67	3-3	.220	.285	.366	5	.989
	—Tampa Bay (A.L.)	C	5	17	1	3	0	0	0	2	0	5	0-0	.176	.176	.176	0	1.000
Major League totals (2 years)			8	21	2	4	0	0	0	2	0	6	0-0	.190	.190	.190	0	1.000

HOUSE, J.R. — C — PIRATES

PERSONAL: Born November 11, 1979, in Charleston, W.Va. ... 6-1/202. ... Bats right, throws right. ... Full name: James Rodger House.

HIGH SCHOOL: Seabreeze (Daytona Beach, Fla.).

TRANSACTIONS/CAREER NOTES: Selected by Pittsburgh Pirates organization in fifth round of free-agent draft (June 2, 1999). ... On disabled list (April 24-May 1 and May 8-22, 2001). ... On Altoona disabled list (April 19-August 9, 2002).

HONORS: Shared South Atlantic League Most Valuable Player (2000).

			BATTING														FIELDING	
Year	Team (League)	Pos.	G	AB	R	H	2B	3B	HR	RBI	BB	SO	SB-CS	Avg.	OBP	SLG	E	Avg.
1999	—GC Pirates (GCL)	1B-C-3B	33	113	13	37	9	3	5	23	11	23	1-0	.327	.394	.593	3	.987
	—Williamsport (NY-P)	C-1B	26	100	11	30	6	0	1	13	9	21	0-1	.300	.358	.390	3	.985
	—Hickory (S.Atl.)	3B	4	11	1	3	0	0	0	0	0	3	0-0	.273	.273	.273	0	.000
2000	—Hickory (S.Atl.)	C-1B	110	420	78	146	29	1	23	90	46	91	1-2	.348	.414	.586	8	.990
2001	—Altoona (East.)	C-1B	112	426	51	110	25	1	11	56	37	103	1-1	.258	.323	.399	7	.991
2002	—Altoona (East.)	C	30	91	9	24	6	0	2	11	13	21	0-0	.264	.349	.396	1	.994
	—GC Pirates (GCL)	C-1B	5	16	3	5	2	0	1	2	3	1	0-0	.313	.421	.625	0	1.000

HOUSTON, TYLER — 3B

PERSONAL: Born January 17, 1971, in Long Beach, Calif. ... 6-1/218. ... Bats left, throws right. ... Full name: Tyler Sam Houston.

HIGH SCHOOL: Valley (Las Vegas).

TRANSACTIONS/CAREER NOTES: Selected by Atlanta Braves organization in first round (second pick overall) of free-agent draft (June 5, 1989). ... On Greenville disabled list (June 25-July 5, 1993). ... Traded by Braves to Chicago Cubs for P Ismael Villegas (June 27, 1996). ... On Chicago disabled list (May 3-19, 1997); included rehabilitation assignment to Iowa (May 14-19, 1997). ... On Chicago disabled list (June 11-July 11, 1997); included rehabilitation assignment to Rockford (July 9-11). ... On suspended list (September 16, 1997). ... On disabled list (May 26-June 24, 1998). ... Traded by Cubs to Cleveland Indians for P Richard Negrette (August 31, 1999). ... Granted free agency (December 21, 1999). ... Signed by Milwaukee Brewers (January 17, 2000). ... On disabled list (May 19-June 2, 2000). ... On Milwaukee disabled list (July 14-September 1 and September 8, 2001-remainder of season); included rehabilitation assignment to Beloit (August 29-September 1). ... Traded by Brewers with a player to be named later to Los Angeles Dodgers for P Ben Diggins and P Shane Nance (July 23, 2002); Dodgers acquired P Brian Mallette to complete deal (October 16, 2002). ... Granted free agency (October 28, 2002).

STATISTICAL NOTES: Led Pioneer League with 14 passed balls in 1989. ... Hit three home runs in one game (July 9, 2000). ... Career major league grand slams: 1.

2002 GAMES PLAYED BY POSITION (MLB): 3B—74; 1B—14.

			BATTING														FIELDING	
Year	Team (League)	Pos.	G	AB	R	H	2B	3B	HR	RBI	BB	SO	SB-CS	Avg.	OBP	SLG	E	Avg.
1989	—Idaho Falls (Pio.)	C	50	176	30	43	11	0	4	24	25	41	4-0	.244	.342	.375	5	.970
1990	—Sumter (S.Atl.)	C	117	442	58	93	14	3	13	56	49	101	6-2	.210	.288	.344	*18	.968
1991	—Macon (S.Atl.)	C	107	351	41	81	16	3	8	47	39	70	10-2	.231	.307	.362	10	.985
1992	—Durham (Caro.)	C-3B-1B	117	402	39	91	17	1	7	38	20	89	5-6	.226	.262	.326	15	.974
1993	—Greenville (Sou.)	C-OF	84	262	27	73	14	1	5	33	13	50	5-3	.279	.313	.397	9	.980
	—Richmond (I.L.)	C-DH	13	36	4	5	1	1	1	3	1	8	0-0	.139	.162	.306	3	.959
1994	—Richmond (I.L.)	1B-C-DH-OF	97	312	33	76	15	2	4	33	16	44	3-3	.244	.276	.343	7	.990
1995	—Richmond (I.L.)	1-C-O-3-DH	103	349	41	89	10	3	12	42	18	62	3-5	.255	.298	.404	11	.983
1996	—Atlanta (N.L.)	1B-OF	33	27	3	6	2	1	1	8	1	9	0-0	.222	.250	.481	0	1.000
	—Chicago (N.L.)■	C-3B-2B-1B	46	115	18	39	7	0	2	19	8	18	3-2	.339	.382	.452	3	.982
1997	—Chicago (N.L.)	C-3-1-2-S	72	196	15	51	10	0	2	28	9	35	1-0	.260	.290	.342	5	.984
	—Iowa (A.A.)	3B-DH-C	6	23	0	5	2	0	0	4	0	2	0-0	.217	.217	.304	2	.882
	—Rockford (Midw.)	C-3B	2	6	1	3	1	0	0	1	0	0	0-0	.500	.500	.667	0	1.000
1998	—Chicago (N.L.)	C-3B-1B	95	255	26	65	7	1	9	33	13	53	2-2	.255	.290	.396	5	.990
1999	—Chicago (N.L.)	3B-C-1B-OF	100	249	26	58	9	1	9	27	28	67	1-1	.233	.309	.386	17	.921
	—Cleveland (A.L.)■	3B-C	13	27	2	4	1	0	1	3	3	11	0-0	.148	.233	.296	0	1.000
2000	—Milwaukee (N.L.)■	1B-3B-C	101	284	30	71	15	0	18	43	17	72	2-1	.250	.292	.493	13	.974
2001	—Milwaukee (N.L.)	3B-1B	75	235	36	68	7	0	12	38	18	62	0-0	.289	.343	.472	10	.934
	—Beloit (Midw.)	3B	1	3	0	0	0	0	0	0	0	1	0-0	.000	.000	.000	1	.500
2002	—Milwaukee (N.L.)	3B-1B	76	255	25	77	15	2	7	33	14	41	1-0	.302	.347	.459	8	.949
	—Los Angeles (N.L.)■	1B-3B	35	65	9	13	5	1	0	7	2	21	0-0	.200	.224	.308	3	.972
American League totals (1 year)			13	27	2	4	1	0	1	3	3	11	0-0	.148	.233	.296	0	1.000
National League totals (7 years)			633	1681	188	448	77	6	60	236	110	378	10-6	.267	.313	.427	64	.970
Major League totals (7 years)			646	1708	190	452	78	6	61	239	113	389	10-6	.265	.311	.424	64	.970

DIVISION SERIES RECORD

			BATTING														FIELDING	
Year	Team (League)	Pos.	G	AB	R	H	2B	3B	HR	RBI	BB	SO	SB-CS	Avg.	OBP	SLG	E	Avg.
1998	—Chicago (N.L.)	C	3	6	1	1	0	0	1	1	0	3	0-0	.167	.167	.667	0	1.000
1999	—Cleveland (A.L.)								Did not play.									

HOWARD, BEN — P — PADRES

PERSONAL: Born January 15, 1979, in Danville, Ill. ... 6-2/190. ... Throws right, bats right. ... Full name: Benjamin Richard Howard.
HIGH SCHOOL: Jackson-Central Merry (Jackson, Tenn.).
TRANSACTIONS/CAREER NOTES: Selected by San Diego Padres organization in second round of free-agent draft (June 3, 1997). ... On Portland disabled list (June 19-August 18, 2002).
STATISTICAL NOTES: Tied for Arizona League lead in wild pitches with 19 in 1997. ... Led Pioneer League with 17 wild pitches and six balks in 1998.
CAREER HITTING (MLB): 0-for-4 (.000), 0 R, 0 2B, 0 3B, 0 HR, 0 RBI.

Year League	W	L	Pct.	ERA	G	GS	CG	ShO	Sv.-Opp.	IP	H	R	ER	HR	BB-IBB	SO
1997— Arizona Padres (Ariz.)	1	4	.200	7.45	13	12	0	0	0-...	54.1	54	53	*45	3	*63-0	59
1998— Idaho Falls (Pio.)	4	5	.444	6.03	15	15	0	0	0-...	68.2	67	61	46	2	*87-0	79
1999— Fort Wayne (Midw.)	6	10	.375	4.73	28	28	0	0	0-...	144.2	123	100	76	17	*110-0	131
2000— Rancho Cuca. (Calif.)	5	11	.313	6.37	32	19	0	0	0-...	107.1	88	87	76	8	*111-1	150
2001— Lake Elsinore (Calif.)	8	2	.800	2.83	18	18	0	0	0-...	101.2	86	37	32	4	32-0	107
— Mobile (Sou.)	2	0	1.000	2.40	7	5	0	0	0-...	30.0	17	9	8	3	15-0	29
2002— Mobile (Sou.)	3	1	.750	2.18	6	6	0	0	0-...	33.0	26	10	8	2	16-0	30
— San Diego (N.L.)	0	1	.000	9.28	3	2	0	0	0-0	10.2	13	11	11	4	14-1	10
— Portland (PCL)	0	4	.000	6.20	11	7	0	0	0-...	45.0	47	34	31	10	15-0	25
Major League totals (1 year)	0	1	.000	9.28	3	2	0	0	0-0	10.2	13	11	11	4	14-1	10

HOWRY, BOBBY — P — RED SOX

PERSONAL: Born August 4, 1973, in Phoenix. ... 6-5/220. ... Throws right, bats left. ... Full name: Bobby Dean Howry.
HIGH SCHOOL: Deer Valley (Phoenix).
JUNIOR COLLEGE: Yavapai College (Ariz.).
COLLEGE: McNeese State.
TRANSACTIONS/CAREER NOTES: Selected by San Francisco Giants organization in fifth round of free-agent draft (June 2, 1994). ... Traded by Giants with SS Mike Caruso, OF Brian Manning, P Keith Foulke, P Lorenzo Barcelo and P Ken Vining to Chicago White Sox for P Wilson Alvarez, P Danny Darwin and P Roberto Hernandez (July 31, 1997). ... On suspended list (April 28-May 30, 2000). ... Traded by White Sox to Boston Red Sox for P Franklin Francisco and P Byeong An (July 31, 2002).
CAREER HITTING (MLB): 0-for-0 (.000), 0 R, 0 2B, 0 3B, 0 HR, 0 RBI.

Year League	W	L	Pct.	ERA	G	GS	CG	ShO	Sv.-Opp.	IP	H	R	ER	HR	BB-IBB	SO
1994— Everett (N'West)	0	4	.000	4.74	5	5	0	0	0-...	19.0	29	15	10	3	10-2	16
— Clinton (Midw.)	1	3	.250	4.20	9	8	0	0	0-...	49.1	61	29	23	1	16-0	22
1995— San Jose (Calif.)	12	10	.545	3.54	27	25	1	0	0-...	165.1	171	79	65	6	54-0	107
1996— Shreveport (Texas)	12	10	.545	4.65	27	27	0	0	0-...	156.2	163	90	81	17	56-3	57
1997— Shreveport (Texas)	6	3	.667	4.91	48	0	0	0	*22-...	55.0	58	35	30	6	21-0	43
— Birmingham (Sou.)■	0	0	...	2.84	12	0	0	0	0-...	12.2	16	4	4	1	3-0	3
1998— Calgary (PCL)	1	2	.333	3.41	23	0	0	0	5-...	31.2	25	12	12	2	10-3	22
— Chicago (A.L.)	0	3	.000	3.15	44	0	0	0	9-11	54.1	37	20	19	7	19-2	51
1999— Chicago (A.L.)	5	3	.625	3.59	69	0	0	0	28-34	67.2	58	34	27	8	38-3	80
2000— Chicago (A.L.)	2	4	.333	3.17	65	0	0	0	7-12	71.0	54	26	25	6	29-2	60
2001— Chicago (A.L.)	4	5	.444	4.69	69	0	0	0	5-11	78.2	85	41	41	11	30-9	64
2002— Chicago (A.L.)	2	2	.500	3.91	47	0	0	0	0-0	50.2	45	22	22	7	17-2	31
— Boston (A.L.)■	1	3	.250	5.00	20	0	0	0	0-1	18.0	22	15	10	2	4-2	14
Major League totals (5 years)	14	20	.412	3.81	314	0	0	0	49-69	340.1	301	158	144	41	137-20	300

DIVISION SERIES RECORD

Year League	W	L	Pct.	ERA	G	GS	CG	ShO	Sv.-Opp.	IP	H	R	ER	HR	BB-IBB	SO
2000— Chicago (A.L.)	0	0	...	3.38	2	0	0	0	0-0	2.2	2	1	1	0	2-0	4

HUBBARD, TRENIDAD — OF

PERSONAL: Born May 11, 1966, in Chicago. ... 5-9/203. ... Bats right, throws right. ... Full name: Trenidad Aviel Hubbard. ... Cousin of Joe Cribbs, running back with Buffalo Bills (1980-83 and 1985).
HIGH SCHOOL: South Shore (Chicago).
COLLEGE: Southern (La.).
TRANSACTIONS/CAREER NOTES: Selected by Houston Astros organization in 12th round of free-agent draft (June 2, 1986). ... Granted free agency (October 15, 1992). ... Signed by Colorado Rockies organization (October 30, 1992). ... On disabled list (June 15-24, 1993). ... Granted free agency (October 15, 1993). ... Re-signed by Rockies organization (December 3, 1993). ... Granted free agency (October 15, 1994). ... Re-signed by Rockies organization (November 14, 1994). ... Claimed on waivers by San Francisco Giants (August 21, 1996). ... On San Francisco disabled list (September 13, 1996-remainder of season). ... Traded by Giants to Cleveland Indians for P Joe Roa (December 16, 1996), completing deal in which Indians traded IF Jeff Kent, IF Jose Vizcaino, P Julian Tavarez and a player to be named later to Giants for 3B Matt Williams and a player to be named later (November 13, 1996). ... Granted free agency (October 8, 1997). ... Signed by Los Angeles Dodgers (December 3, 1997). ... On Los Angeles disabled list (May 14-June 22, 1998); included rehabilitation assignment to Albuquerque (June 9-22). ... Granted free agency (January 19, 2000). ... Signed by Atlanta Braves organization (January 20, 2000). ... Traded by Braves with P Luis Rivera and C Fernando Rivera to Baltimore Orioles for OF B.J. Surhoff and P Gabe Molina (July 31, 2000). ... Released by Orioles (October 5, 2000). ... Signed by Toronto Blue Jays organization (December 21, 2000). ... Released by Blue Jays (March 17, 2001). ... Signed by Kansas City Royals organization (March 23, 2001). ... Released by Royals (May 23, 2001). ... Signed by Chicago Cubs organization (July 4, 2001). ... Released by Cubs (September 10, 2001). ... Signed by San Diego Padres organization (February 24, 2002). ... Released by Padres (September 4, 2002).
STATISTICAL NOTES: Led Texas League second basemen with 296 putouts, 653 total chances and 81 double plays in 1991. ... Tied for Pacific Coast League lead in caught stealing with 18 in 1993. ... Tied for Pacific Coast League lead in caught stealing with 10 in 2001.
MISCELLANEOUS: Batted lefthanded on occasion though not a switch hitter (1986-91).
2002 GAMES PLAYED BY POSITION (MLB): OF—57; 3B—6; 2B—4; DH—1.

									BATTING								FIELDING	
Year	Team (League)	Pos.	G	AB	R	H	2B	3B	HR	RBI	BB	SO	SB-CS	Avg.	OBP	SLG	E	Avg.
1986—	Auburn (NY-Penn)	2B-OF	70	242	42	75	12	1	1	32	28	42	35-5	.310	.381	.380	18	.931
1987—	Asheville (S.Atl.)	2-O-C-3-P	101	284	39	67	8	1	1	35	28	42	28-13	.236	.298	.282	14	.943
1988—	Osceola (FSL)	2-C-O-3-1	130	446	68	116	15	11	3	65	61	72	44-18	.260	.351	.363	12	.972
1989—	Columbus (Sou.)	2B-C-OF-3B	104	348	55	92	7	8	3	37	43	53	28-6	.264	.347	.356	15	.967
	—Tucson (PCL)	OF-3B-C	21	50	3	11	2	0	0	2	1	10	3-3	.220	.250	.260	1	.967
1990—	Columbus (Sou.)	2B-OF-C-3B	95	335	39	84	14	4	4	35	32	51	17-8	.251	.320	.352	11	.968
	—Tucson (PCL)	2B-3B-C	12	27	5	6	2	2	0	2	3	6	1-1	.222	.300	.444	3	.933
1991—	Jackson (Texas)	2B-OF-1B-P	126	455	78	135	21	3	2	41	65	81	39-17	.297	.394	.369	21	.968
	—Tucson (PCL)	2B	2	4	0	0	0	0	0	0	0	0	0-0	.000	.000	.000	0	1.000
1992—	Tucson (PCL)	2B-3B	115	420	69	130	16	4	2	33	45	68	34-10	.310	.380	.381	18	.970
1993—	Colo. Springs (PCL)■	O-2-3-DH-S	117	439	83	138	24	8	7	56	47	57	33-•18	.314	.387	.453	6	.975
1994—	Colo. Springs (PCL)	OF	79	320	78	116	22	5	8	38	44	40	28-10	.363	.441	.538	7	.964
	—Colorado (N.L.)	OF	18	25	3	7	1	1	1	3	3	4	0-0	.280	.357	.520	0	1.000
1995—	Colo. Springs (PCL)	OF	123	480	*102	163	29	7	12	66	61	59	*37-14	.340	*.416	.504	6	.980
	—Colorado (N.L.)	OF	24	58	13	18	4	0	3	9	8	6	2-1	.310	.394	.534	0	1.000
1996—	Colorado (N.L.)	OF	45	60	12	13	5	1	1	12	9	22	2-0	.217	.329	.383	0	1.000
	—Colo. Springs (PCL)	OF-2B-3B-C	50	188	41	59	15	5	6	16	28	14	6-8	.314	.406	.543	4	.973
	—San Fran. (N.L.)■	OF	10	29	3	6	0	1	1	2	2	5	0-0	.207	.258	.379	0	1.000
1997—	Buffalo (A.A.)■	OF-3B-DH	103	375	71	117	22	1	16	60	57	52	26-10	.312	*.401	.504	2	.992
	—Cleveland (A.L.)	OF	7	12	3	3	1	0	0	0	1	3	2-0	.250	.308	.333	0	1.000
1998—	Los Angeles (N.L.)■	OF-3B	94	208	29	62	9	1	7	18	18	46	9-5	.298	.358	.452	1	.991
	—Albuquerque (PCL)	OF-DH	11	30	6	9	0	0	3	5	5	5	2-1	.300	.417	.600	0	1.000
1999—	Albuquerque (PCL)	OF-DH	32	123	24	41	8	2	5	24	16	27	16-3	.333	.401	.553	2	.974
	—Los Angeles (N.L.)	OF-C-2B	82	105	23	33	5	0	1	13	13	24	4-3	.314	.387	.390	1	.981
2000—	Atlanta (N.L.)■	OF	61	81	15	15	2	1	1	6	11	20	2-1	.185	.290	.272	0	1.000
	—Baltimore (A.L.)■	OF-DH	31	27	3	5	0	1	0	0	0	3	2-1	.185	.185	.259	1	.929
2001—	Omaha (PCL)■	OF	49	175	35	50	9	1	10	28	30	34	8-5	.286	.392	.520	0	1.000
	—Kansas City (A.L.)	OF	5	12	2	3	0	1	0	0	0	2	0-0	.250	.250	.417	0	1.000
	—Iowa (PCL)■	OF-3B	49	171	38	54	11	3	6	31	37	27	17-5	.316	.439	.520	1	.989
2002—	San Diego (N.L.)■	OF-3B-2B-DH	89	129	16	27	5	0	1	7	14	28	9-6	.209	.285	.271	2	.970
	—Portland (PCL)	OF	8	29	9	11	2	0	3	6	2	3	2-2	.379	.406	.759	0	1.000
American League totals (3 years)			43	51	8	11	1	2	0	0	1	8	4-1	.216	.231	.314	1	.947
National League totals (7 years)			423	695	114	181	31	5	16	70	78	155	28-16	.260	.337	.388	4	.988
Major League totals (9 years)			466	746	122	192	32	7	16	70	79	163	32-17	.257	.331	.383	5	.986

DIVISION SERIES RECORD

									BATTING								FIELDING	
Year	Team (League)	Pos.	G	AB	R	H	2B	3B	HR	RBI	BB	SO	SB-CS	Avg.	OBP	SLG	E	Avg.
1995—	Colorado (N.L.)	PH	3	2	0	0	0	0	0	0	0	0	0-0	.000	.000	.000	...	...

RECORD AS PITCHER

Year	League	W	L	Pct.	ERA	G	GS	CG	ShO	Sv.-Opp.	IP	H	R	ER	HR	BB-IBB	SO
1987—	Asheville (S.Atl.)	0	0	...	0.00	1	0	0	0	0-...	1.0	1	0	0	0	1-0	0
1991—	Jackson (Texas)	0	0	...	0.00	1	0	0	0	0-...	1.0	0	0	0	0	2-0	0

HUCKABY, KEN — C — BLUE JAYS

PERSONAL: Born January 27, 1971, in San Leandro, Calif. ... 6-1/205. ... Bats right, throws right. ... Full name: Kenneth Paul Huckaby.
HIGH SCHOOL: Manteca (Calif.).
JUNIOR COLLEGE: San Joaquin Delta (Calif.).
TRANSACTIONS/CAREER NOTES: Selected by Los Angeles Dodgers organization in 22nd round of free-agent draft (June 3, 1991). ... On disabled list (May 26-June 5 and July 2-21, 1992). ... On San Antonio disabled list (May 4-13, 1994). ... Granted free agency (October 15, 1997). ... Signed by Seattle Mariners organization (December 3, 1997). ... On Tacoma disabled list (April 7-May 3, 1998). ... Released by Mariners (June 13, 1998). ... Signed by New York Yankees organization (June 28, 1998). ... Granted free agency (October 16, 1998). ... Signed by Arizona Diamondbacks organization (January 22, 1999). ... Granted free agency (October 15, 1999). ... Re-signed by Diamondbacks organization (November 15, 1999). ... Granted free agency (October 18, 2000). ... Re-signed by Diamondbacks organization (November 2, 2000). ... Released by Diamondbacks (October 29, 2001). ... Signed by Toronto Blue Jays organization (February 10, 2002).
STATISTICAL NOTES: Led Florida State League catchers with 99 assists and 14 double plays in 1993. ... Led Pacific Coast League catchers with 592 total chances in 1995. ... Led Pacific Coast League catchers with 11 double plays in 1996. ... Led Pacific Coast League catchers with 695 putouts and 756 total chances in 1999.
2002 GAMES PLAYED BY POSITION (MLB): C—88.

									BATTING								FIELDING	
Year	Team (League)	Pos.	G	AB	R	H	2B	3B	HR	RBI	BB	SO	SB-CS	Avg.	OBP	SLG	E	Avg.
1991—	Great Falls (Pio.)	C	57	213	39	55	16	0	3	37	17	38	3-2	.258	.321	.376	*12	.977
1992—	Vero Beach (FSL)	C	73	261	14	63	9	0	0	21	7	42	1-1	.241	.262	.276	9	.982
1993—	Vero Beach (FSL)	C	79	281	22	75	14	1	4	41	11	35	2-1	.267	.297	.367	12	.980
	—San Antonio (Texas)	C	28	82	4	18	1	0	0	5	2	7	0-0	.220	.253	.232	4	.978
1994—	San Antonio (Texas)	C	11	41	3	11	1	0	1	9	1	1	1-0	.268	.286	.366	6	.931
	—Bakersfield (Calif.)	C	77	270	29	81	18	1	2	30	10	37	2-3	.300	.329	.396	10	.986
1995—	Albuquerque (PCL)	C-1B	89	278	30	90	16	2	1	40	12	26	3-1	.324	.359	.406	16	.973
1996—	Albuquerque (PCL)	C	103	287	37	79	16	2	3	41	17	35	0-0	.275	.319	.376	6	.990
1997—	Albuquerque (PCL)	C-DH	69	201	14	40	5	1	0	18	9	36	1-0	.199	.231	.234	10	.975
1998—	Tacoma (PCL)■	C-1B	16	49	4	11	2	0	0	1	5	6	0-0	.224	.296	.265	0	1.000
	—Columbus (I.L.)■	C	36	101	13	21	3	1	1	10	11	14	0-2	.208	.286	.287	5	.978
1999—	Tucson (PCL)■	C-3B-DH-1B	107	355	44	107	20	1	2	42	13	33	0-0	.301	.325	.380	10	.987
2000—	Tucson (PCL)	C-3B-OF-1B	76	243	31	67	11	1	4	33	10	30	2-2	.276	.306	.379	8	.982
2001—	El Paso (Texas)	1B-C	30	104	14	36	4	0	2	14	3	16	0-0	.346	.368	.442	4	.983
	—Tucson (PCL)	C-1B-3B-2B	78	262	31	76	15	1	2	34	7	62	1-3	.290	.313	.378	14	.972
	—Arizona (N.L.)	C	1	1	0	0	0	0	0	0	0	1	0-0	.000	.000	.000	0	1.000
2002—	Syracuse (I.L.)■	C-1B	21	81	7	22	2	0	0	9	2	15	0-2	.272	.286	.296	3	.981
	—Toronto (A.L.)	C	88	273	29	67	6	1	3	22	9	44	0-0	.245	.270	.308	6	.989
American League totals (1 year)			88	273	29	67	6	1	3	22	9	44	0-0	.245	.270	.308	6	.989
National League totals (1 year)			1	1	0	0	0	0	0	0	0	1	0-0	.000	.000	.000	0	1.000
Major League totals (2 years)			89	274	29	67	6	1	3	22	9	45	0-0	.245	.269	.307	6	.989

HUDSON, LUKE P REDS

PERSONAL: Born May 2, 1977, in Fountain Valley, Calif. ... 6-3/195. ... Throws right, bats right. ... Full name: Luke Stephen Hudson.
HIGH SCHOOL: Fountain Valley (Calif.).
COLLEGE: Tennessee.
TRANSACTIONS/CAREER NOTES: Selected by Colorado Rockies organization in fourth round of free-agent draft (June 2, 1998). ... On Carolina disabled list (July 7-August 19, 2000). ... Traded by Rockies with P Gabe White to Cincinnati Reds for 2B Pokey Reese and P Dennys Reyes (December 18, 2001).
STATISTICAL NOTES: Led Southern League with 18 wild pitches in 2001. ... Led International League with 16 hit batsmen in 2002.
CAREER HITTING (MLB): 0-for-0 (.000), 0 R, 0 2B, 0 3B, 0 HR, 0 RBI.

Year League	W	L	Pct.	ERA	G	GS	CG	ShO	Sv.-Opp.	IP	H	R	ER	HR	BB-IBB	SO
1998—Portland (N'West)	3	6	.333	4.74	15	15	0	0	0-...	79.2	68	46	42	8	51-0	82
1999—Asheville (S.Atl.)	6	5	.545	4.30	21	20	1	0	0-...	88.0	89	47	42	10	24-0	96
2000—Salem (Caro.)	5	8	.385	3.27	19	19	2	2	0-...	110.0	101	47	40	9	34-0	80
2001—Carolina (Sou.)	7	12	.368	4.20	29	•28	1	0	0-...	165.0	159	90	77	19	68-0	145
2002—Louisville (I.L.)■	5	9	.357	4.51	30	17	0	0	3-...	117.2	102	64	59	6	57-1	129
—Cincinnati (N.L.)	0	0	...	4.50	3	0	0	0	0-0	6.0	5	5	3	1	6-0	7
Major League totals (1 year)	0	0	...	4.50	3	0	0	0	0-0	6.0	5	5	3	1	6-0	7

HUDSON, ORLANDO 2B BLUE JAYS

PERSONAL: Born December 12, 1977, in Darlington, S.C. ... 6-0/185. ... Bats both, throws right. ... Full name: Orlando Thill Hudson.
HIGH SCHOOL: Darlington (S.C.).
JUNIOR COLLEGE: Spartanburg Methodist (S.C.).
TRANSACTIONS/CAREER NOTES: Selected by Toronto Blue Jays organization in 43rd round of free-agent draft (June 3, 1997).
STATISTICAL NOTES: Led South Atlantic League third basemen in fielding with .940 percentage in 1999. ... Led International League second basemen with 225 putouts, 312 assists and 547 total chances in 2002.
2002 GAMES PLAYED BY POSITION (MLB): 2B—52.

					BATTING											FIELDING	
Year Team (League)	Pos.	G	AB	R	H	2B	3B	HR	RBI	BB	SO	SB-CS	Avg.	OBP	SLG	E	Avg.
1998—Medicine Hat (Pio.)	2B	65	242	50	71	18	1	8	42	22	36	6-5	.293	.366	.475	13	.959
1999—Hagerstown (S.Atl.)	3B-OF-2B	132	513	66	137	36	6	7	74	42	85	8-6	.267	.322	.402	21	†.946
2000—Dunedin (FSL)	3B-2B-SS	96	358	54	102	16	2	7	48	37	42	9-5	.285	.354	.399	19	.941
—Tennessee (Sou.)	3B	39	134	17	32	4	3	2	15	15	18	3-2	.239	.320	.358	11	.921
2001—Tennessee (Sou.)	2B-3B	84	306	51	94	22	8	4	52	37	42	8-3	.307	.385	.471	8	.979
—Syracuse (I.L.)	2B-3B	55	194	31	59	14	3	4	27	23	34	11-3	.304	.378	.469	4	.986
2002—Syracuse (I.L.)	2B	100	417	63	127	27	3	10	37	35	54	8-5	.305	.363	.456	10	.982
—Toronto (A.L.)	2B	54	192	20	53	10	5	4	23	11	27	0-1	.276	.319	.443	4	.986
Major League totals (1 year)		54	192	20	53	10	5	4	23	11	27	0-1	.276	.319	.443	4	.986

HUDSON, TIM P ATHLETICS

PERSONAL: Born July 14, 1975, in Columbus, Ga. ... 6-1/164. ... Throws right, bats right. ... Full name: Timothy Adam Hudson.
HIGH SCHOOL: Glenwood (Phenix City, Ala.).
COLLEGE: Auburn.
TRANSACTIONS/CAREER NOTES: Selected by Oakland Athletics organization in sixth-round of free-agent draft (June 3, 1997).
HONORS: Named A.L. Rookie Pitcher of the Year by The Sporting News (1999).
STATISTICAL NOTES: Pitched 3-0 one-hit, complete-game victory against Chicago White Sox (August 28, 2000).
MISCELLANEOUS: Appeared in three games as pinch runner (1999). ... Appeared in one game as pinch runner (2000). ... Appeared in one game as pinch runner (2001).
CAREER HITTING (MLB): 2-for-20 (.100), 2 R, 1 2B, 0 3B, 0 HR, 0 RBI.

Year League	W	L	Pct.	ERA	G	GS	CG	ShO	Sv.-Opp.	IP	H	R	ER	HR	BB-IBB	SO
1997—S. Oregon (N'West)	3	1	.750	2.51	8	4	0	0	0-...	28.2	12	8	8	0	15-2	37
1998—Modesto (Calif.)	4	0	1.000	1.67	8	5	0	0	0-...	37.2	19	10	7	0	18-0	48
—Huntsville (Sou.)	10	9	.526	4.54	22	22	2	0	0-...	134.2	136	84	68	13	71-2	104
1999—Midland (Texas)	3	0	1.000	0.50	3	3	0	0	0-...	18.0	9	1	1	0	3-0	18
—Vancouver (PCL)	4	0	1.000	2.20	8	8	0	0	0-...	49.0	38	16	12	2	21-0	61
—Oakland (A.L.)	11	2	.846	3.23	21	21	1	0	0-0	136.1	121	56	49	8	62-2	132
2000—Oakland (A.L.)	•20	6	*.769	4.14	32	32	2	2	0-0	202.1	169	100	93	24	82-5	169
2001—Oakland (A.L.)	18	9	.667	3.37	35	•35	3	0	0-0	235.0	216	100	88	20	71-5	181
2002—Oakland (A.L.)	15	9	.625	2.98	34	34	4	2	0-0	238.1	237	87	79	19	62-9	152
Major League totals (4 years)	64	26	.711	3.42	122	122	10	4	0-0	812.0	743	343	309	71	277-21	634

DIVISION SERIES RECORD

Year League	W	L	Pct.	ERA	G	GS	CG	ShO	Sv.-Opp.	IP	H	R	ER	HR	BB-IBB	SO
2000—Oakland (A.L.)	0	1	.000	3.38	1	1	1	0	0-0	8.0	6	4	3	0	4-0	5
2001—Oakland (A.L.)	1	0	1.000	0.93	2	1	0	0	0-0	9.2	8	1	1	1	1-0	5
2002—Oakland (A.L.)	0	1	.000	6.23	2	2	0	0	0-0	8.2	13	11	6	2	4-0	8
Division series totals (3 years)	1	2	.333	3.42	5	4	1	0	0-0	26.1	27	16	10	3	9-0	18

ALL-STAR GAME RECORD

	W	L	Pct.	ERA	GS	CG	ShO	Sv.-Opp.	IP	H	R	ER	HR	BB-IBB	SO
All-Star Game totals (1 year)	0	0	...	0.00	0	0	0	0-0	1.0	0	0	0	0	0-0	1

H

HUFF, AUBREY — 3B — DEVIL RAYS

PERSONAL: Born December 20, 1976, in Marion, Ohio. ... 6-4/231. ... Bats left, throws right. ... Full name: Aubrey L. Huff.
HIGH SCHOOL: Brewer (Fort Worth, Texas).
JUNIOR COLLEGE: Vernon Regional (Texas).
COLLEGE: Miami (Fla.).
TRANSACTIONS/CAREER NOTES: Selected by Tampa Bay Devil Rays organization in fifth round of free-agent draft (June 2, 1998). ... On Durham disabled list (April 4-24, 2002).
STATISTICAL NOTES: Led Southern League third baseman with 395 total chances in 1999. ... Had 17-game hitting streak (August 23-September 10, 2002).
2002 GAMES PLAYED BY POSITION (MLB): DH—53; 1B—45; 3B—14.

			BATTING														FIELDING	
Year	Team (League)	Pos.	G	AB	R	H	2B	3B	HR	RBI	BB	SO	SB-CS	Avg.	OBP	SLG	E	Avg.
1998—	Charl., S.C. (S.Atl.)	3B	69	265	38	85	19	1	13	54	24	40	3-1	.321	.371	.547	8	.957
1999—	Orlando (Sou.)	3B	133	491	85	148	40	3	22	78	64	77	2-3	.301	.385	.530	29	.927
2000—	Durham (I.L.)	3B-1B	108	408	73	129	36	3	20	76	51	72	2-3	.316	.394	.566	21	.915
	—Tampa Bay (A.L.)	3B	39	122	12	35	7	0	4	14	5	18	0-0	.287	.318	.443	5	.939
2001—	Durham (I.L.)	3B	17	66	14	19	6	0	3	10	5	7	0-0	.288	.338	.515	4	.929
	—Tampa Bay (A.L.)	3B-DH-1B	111	411	42	102	25	1	8	45	23	72	1-3	.248	.288	.372	20	.940
2002—	Durham (I.L.)	1B	32	126	18	41	9	0	3	20	12	13	0-0	.325	.386	.468	0	1.000
	—Tampa Bay (A.L.)	DH-1B-3B	113	454	67	142	25	0	23	59	37	55	4-1	.313	.364	.520	8	.981
Major League totals (3 years)			263	987	121	279	57	1	35	118	65	145	5-4	.283	.327	.449	33	.960

HUNDLEY, TODD — C — CUBS

PERSONAL: Born May 27, 1969, in Martinsville, Va. ... 5-11/200. ... Bats both, throws right. ... Full name: Todd Randolph Hundley. ... Son of Randy Hundley, catcher with four major league teams (1964-77).
HIGH SCHOOL: William Fremd (Palatine, Ill.).
COLLEGE: William Rainey Harper College (Ill.).
TRANSACTIONS/CAREER NOTES: Selected by New York Mets organization in second round of free-agent draft (June 2, 1987); pick received as compensation for Baltimore Orioles signing Type B free-agent 3B/1B Ray Knight. ... On Tidewater disabled list (June 29-July 6, 1991). ... On disabled list (July 23, 1995-remainder of season). ... On New York disabled list (March 21-July 11 and August 28-September 12, 1998); included rehabilitation assignments to St. Lucie (June 24-July 6 and July 9), Gulf Coast Mets (July 7-8) and Norfolk (July 10-11 and August 31-September 8). ... Traded by Mets with P Arnold Gooch to Los Angeles Dodgers for C Charles Johnson and OF Roger Cedeno (December 1, 1998). ... On suspended list (July 22-24, 1999). ... On Los Angeles disabled list (May 31-June 26 and July 9-27, 2000); included rehabilitation assignment to Albuquerque (June 23-26). ... Granted free agency (October 27, 2000). ... Signed by Chicago Cubs (December 13, 2000). ... On Chicago disabled list (June 19-July 26, 2001); included rehabilitation assignment to West Tenn (June 29-July 2) and Iowa (July 7-25). ... On Chicago disabled list (May 6-29, 2002); included rehabilitation assignment to Iowa (May 25-28).
RECORDS: Holds major league single-season record for most home runs by catcher—41 (1996). ... Holds N.L. single-season record for most strikeouts by switch hitter—146 (1996).
STATISTICAL NOTES: Led South Atlantic League in intentional bases on balls received with 10 and in grounding into double plays with 20 in 1989. ... Led South Atlantic League catchers with 826 putouts and 930 total chances in 1989. ... Tied for International League lead in errors by catcher with nine and double plays with 12 in 1991. ... Switch-hit home runs in one game five times (June 18, 1994; May 18; June 10, 1996; May 5 and July 20, 1997). ... Career major league grand slams: 7.
2002 GAMES PLAYED BY POSITION (MLB): C—79; DH—1.

			BATTING														FIELDING	
Year	Team (League)	Pos.	G	AB	R	H	2B	3B	HR	RBI	BB	SO	SB-CS	Avg.	OBP	SLG	E	Avg.
1987—	Little Falls (NY-Penn)	C	34	103	12	15	4	0	1	10	12	27	0-0	.146	.254	.214	7	.967
1988—	Little Falls (NY-Penn)	C	52	176	23	33	8	0	2	18	16	31	1-1	.188	.269	.267	8	.980
	—St. Lucie (FSL)	C	1	1	0	0	0	0	0	0	2	1	0-0	.000	.667	.000	1	.800
1989—	Columbia (S.Atl.)	C-OF	125	439	67	118	23	4	11	66	54	67	6-3	.269	.356	.415	13	.986
1990—	Jackson (Texas)	C-3B	81	279	27	74	12	2	1	35	34	44	5-3	.265	.344	.333	9	.984
	—New York (N.L.)	C	36	67	8	14	6	0	0	2	6	18	0-0	.209	.274	.299	2	.988
1991—	Tidewater (I.L.)	C-1B	125	454	62	124	24	4	14	66	51	95	1-2	.273	.344	.436	‡9	.986
	—New York (N.L.)	C	21	60	5	8	0	1	1	7	6	14	0-0	.133	.221	.217	0	1.000
1992—	New York (N.L.)	C	123	358	32	75	17	0	7	32	19	76	3-0	.209	.256	.316	3	.996
1993—	New York (N.L.)	C	130	417	40	95	17	2	11	53	23	62	1-1	.228	.269	.357	8	.988
1994—	New York (N.L.)	C	91	291	45	69	10	1	16	42	25	73	2-1	.237	.303	.443	5	.990
1995—	New York (N.L.)	C	90	275	39	77	11	0	15	51	42	64	1-0	.280	.382	.484	7	.987
1996—	New York (N.L.)	C	153	540	85	140	32	1	41	112	79	146	1-3	.259	.356	.550	8	.992
1997—	New York (N.L.)	C-DH	132	417	78	114	21	2	30	86	83	116	2-3	.273	.394	.549	10	.987
1998—	St. Lucie (FSL)	OF-DH	12	42	4	9	2	0	1	6	12	8	0-1	.214	.389	.333	2	.900
	—GC Mets (GCL)	OF	1	2	0	0	0	0	0	0	2	1	0-0	.000	.500	.000	0	1.000
	—Norfolk (I.L.)	OF-DH-C	10	30	9	13	1	0	4	15	14	10	0-0	.433	.614	.867	1	.960
	—New York (N.L.)	OF-C	53	124	8	20	4	0	3	12	16	55	1-1	.161	.261	.266	5	.928
1999—	Los Angeles (N.L.)■	C	114	376	49	78	14	0	24	55	44	113	3-0	.207	.295	.436	*16	.979
2000—	Los Angeles (N.L.)	C-DH	90	299	49	85	16	0	24	70	45	69	0-1	.284	.375	.579	*13	.979
	—Albuquerque (PCL)	C	3	9	2	5	0	0	1	5	1	0	0-0	.556	.600	.889	0	1.000
2001—	Chicago (N.L.)■	C	79	246	23	46	10	0	12	31	25	89	0-0	.187	.268	.374	4	.993
	—West Tenn (Sou.)	C	4	12	1	4	2	0	0	1	1	3	0-0	.333	.385	.500	0	1.000
	—Iowa (PCL)	C	15	51	7	10	1	0	3	8	4	23	0-0	.196	.263	.392	0	1.000
2002—	Chicago (N.L.)	C-DH	92	266	32	56	8	0	16	35	32	80	0-0	.211	.301	.421	11	.984
	—Iowa (PCL)	C	3	9	1	2	0	0	1	4	1	2	0-0	.222	.300	.556	0	1.000
Major League totals (13 years)			1204	3736	493	877	166	7	200	588	445	975	14-10	.235	.319	.444	92	.987

ALL-STAR GAME RECORD

	AB	R	H	2B	3B	HR	RBI	BB	SO	SB-CS	Avg.	OBP	SLG	E	Avg.
All-Star Game totals (1 year)	1	0	0	0	0	0	0	0	0	0-0	.000	.000	.000	0	1.000

HUNTER, BRIAN — OF — ASTROS

PERSONAL: Born March 25, 1971, in Portland, Ore. ... 6-3/180. ... Bats right, throws right. ... Full name: Brian Lee Hunter.
HIGH SCHOOL: Fort Vancouver (Vancouver, Wash.).
TRANSACTIONS/CAREER NOTES: Selected by Houston Astros organization in second round of free-agent draft (June 5, 1989); pick received as part of compensation for Texas Rangers signing Type A free-agent P Nolan Ryan. ... On Houston disabled list (July 5-23, 1995); included rehabilitation assignment to Jackson (July 21-23). ... On Houston disabled list (June 29-July 27, 1996); included rehabilitation assignment to Tucson (July 23-27). ... Traded by Astros with IF Orlando Miller, P Doug Brocail, P Todd Jones and cash to Detroit Tigers for C Brad Ausmus, P Jose Lima, P C.J. Nitkowski, P Trever Miller and IF Daryle Ward (December 10, 1996). ... Traded by Tigers to Seattle Mariners for two players to be named later (April 29, 1999); Tigers acquired P Andrew Vanhekken (June 27, 1999) and OF Jerry Amador (August 26, 1999) to complete deal. ... On Seattle disabled list (July 12-27, 1999). ... Released by Mariners (March 27, 2000). ... Signed by Colorado Rockies (March 31, 2000). ... Traded by Rockies from Cincinnati Reds for P Robert Averette (August 6, 2000). ... On suspended list (August 14-17, 2000). ... Released by Reds (November 27, 2000). ... Signed by Philadelphia Phillies (January 10, 2001). ... On Philadelphia disabled list (April 4-22, 2001); included rehabilitation assignment to Scranton/Wilkes-Barre (April 20-22). ... Granted free agency (November 5, 2001). ... Signed by Astros (December 3, 2001). ... On Houston disabled list (July 14-August 20, 2002); included rehabilitation assignment to New Orleans (August 14-20).
RECORDS: Holds major league record for most at-bats with no hits in doubleheader (more than 18 innings)—13 (June 20, 1998, 26 innings). ... Shares major league single season record for fewest double plays by outfielder (150 or more games)—0 (1997).
STATISTICAL NOTES: Led A.L. in caught stealing with 18 in 1997. ... Led A.L. outfielders with 408 putouts and 420 total chances in 1997. ... Led A.L. with 44 stolen bases in 1999. ... Career major league grand slams: 1.
2002 GAMES PLAYED BY POSITION (MLB): OF—88.

		BATTING														FIELDING	
Year Team (League)	Pos.	G	AB	R	H	2B	3B	HR	RBI	BB	SO	SB-CS	Avg.	OBP	SLG	E	Avg.
1989—GC Astros (GCL)	OF	51	206	15	35	2	0	0	13	7	42	12-6	.170	.201	.180	2	.980
1990—Asheville (S.Atl.)	OF	127	444	84	111	14	6	0	16	60	72	45-13	.250	.349	.309	11	.955
1991—Osceola (FSL)	OF	118	392	51	94	15	3	1	30	45	75	32-9	.240	.316	.301	9	.966
1992—Osceola (FSL)	OF	131	489	62	146	18	9	1	62	31	76	39-19	.299	.344	.378	9	.971
1993—Jackson (Texas)	OF-DH	133	523	84	154	22	5	10	52	34	85	*35-18	.294	.338	.413	*14	.953
1994—Tucson (PCL)	OF-DH	128	513	*113	*191	28	9	10	51	52	52	*49-14	*.372	.432	.520	5	.981
—Houston (N.L.)	OF	6	24	2	6	1	0	0	0	1	6	2-1	.250	.280	.292	1	.938
1995—Tucson (PCL)	OF	38	155	28	51	5	1	1	16	17	13	11-3	.329	.395	.394	0	1.000
—Houston (N.L.)	OF	78	321	52	97	14	5	2	28	21	52	24-7	.302	.346	.396	9	.955
—Jackson (Texas)	OF	2	6	1	3	0	0	0	0	1	0	0-0	.500	.571	.500	0	1.000
1996—Houston (N.L.)	OF	132	526	74	145	27	2	5	35	17	92	35-9	.276	.297	.363	•12	.960
—Tucson (PCL)	OF	3	14	3	5	0	1	0	1	0	2	3-0	.357	.333	.500	0	1.000
1997—Detroit (A.L.)■	OF	•162	658	112	177	29	7	4	45	66	121	*74-18	.269	.334	.353	4	.990
1998—Detroit (A.L.)	OF	142	595	67	151	29	3	4	36	36	94	42-12	.254	.298	.333	5	.988
1999—Detroit (A.L.)	OF	18	55	8	13	2	1	0	0	5	11	0-3	.236	.311	.309	0	1.000
—Seattle (A.L.)■	OF	121	484	71	112	11	5	4	34	32	80	§44-5	.231	.277	.300	4	.985
2000—Colorado (N.L.)■	OF	72	200	36	55	4	1	1	13	21	31	15-3	.275	.347	.320	2	.981
—Cincinnati (N.L.)■	OF	32	40	11	9	1	0	0	1	6	9	5-0	.225	.319	.250	1	.971
2001—Philadelphia (N.L.)■	OF-DH	83	145	22	40	6	0	2	16	16	25	14-3	.276	.344	.359	0	1.000
—Scranton/W.B. (I.L.)	OF	2	9	1	1	0	0	0	0	1	3	0-0	.111	.200	.111	1	.833
2002—Houston (N.L.)■	OF	98	201	32	54	16	3	3	20	16	39	5-0	.269	.329	.423	0	1.000
—New Orleans (PCL)	OF	5	19	4	3	0	1	0	0	2	7	2-0	.158	.238	.263	0	1.000
American League totals (3 years)		443	1792	258	453	71	16	12	115	139	306	160-38	.253	.306	.330	13	.989
National League totals (6 years)		501	1457	229	406	69	11	13	113	98	254	100-23	.279	.324	.368	25	.971
Major League totals (9 years)		944	3249	487	859	140	27	25	228	237	560	260-61	.264	.314	.347	38	.981

HUNTER, TORII — OF — TWINS

PERSONAL: Born July 18, 1975, in Pine Bluff, Ark. ... 6-2/205. ... Bats right, throws right. ... Full name: Torii Kedar Hunter. ... Name pronounced TORE-ee.
HIGH SCHOOL: Pine Bluff (Ark.).
TRANSACTIONS/CAREER NOTES: Selected by Minnesota Twins organization in first round (20th pick overall) of free-agent draft (June 3, 1993); pick recieved as part of compensation for Cincinnati Reds signing Type A free-agent P John Smiley. ... On New Britain disabled list (April 4-May 10, 1996). ... On Salt Lake disabled list (July 28-August 11, 1998). ... On disabled list (April 6-21, 2001). ... On suspended list (July 20-23, 2002).
HONORS: Won A.L. Gold Glove as outfielder (2001-02). ... Named outfielder on The Sporting News A.L. All-Star team (2002).
STATISTICAL NOTES: Led Florida State League outfielders with seven double plays in 1995. ... Tied for Eastern League lead for double plays by an outfielder with four in 1997. ... Career major league grand slams: 3.
2002 GAMES PLAYED BY POSITION (MLB): OF—146; DH—1.

		BATTING														FIELDING	
Year Team (League)	Pos.	G	AB	R	H	2B	3B	HR	RBI	BB	SO	SB-CS	Avg.	OBP	SLG	E	Avg.
1993—GC Twins (GCL)	OF	28	100	6	19	3	0	0	8	4	23	4-2	.190	.283	.220	•6	.895
1994—Fort Wayne (Midw.)	OF	91	335	57	98	17	1	10	50	25	80	8-10	.293	.358	.439	7	.971
1995—Fort Myers (FSL)	OF	113	391	64	96	15	2	7	36	38	77	7-4	.246	.330	.348	7	.973
1996—Fort Myers (FSL)	OF	4	16	1	3	0	0	0	1	2	5	1-1	.188	.278	.188	0	1.000
—New Britain (East.)	OF	99	342	49	90	20	3	7	33	28	60	7-7	.263	.331	.401	4	.982
1997—New Britain (East.)	OF-DH	127	471	57	109	22	2	8	56	47	94	8-8	.231	.305	.338	7	.974
—Minnesota (A.L.)	PR	1	0	0	0	0	0	0	0	0	0	0-0	...	...	...	...	...
1998—New Britain (East.)	OF	82	308	42	87	24	3	6	32	19	64	11-9	.282	.329	.438	2	.989
—Minnesota (A.L.)	OF	6	17	0	4	1	0	0	2	2	6	0-1	.235	.316	.294	0	1.000
—Salt Lake (PCL)	OF-DH	26	92	15	31	7	0	4	20	1	13	2-2	.337	.347	.543	2	.966
1999—Minnesota (A.L.)	OF	135	384	52	98	17	2	9	35	26	72	10-6	.255	.309	.380	1	.997
2000—Minnesota (A.L.)	OF	99	336	44	94	14	7	5	44	18	68	4-3	.280	.318	.408	3	.989
—Salt Lake (PCL)		55	209	58	77	17	2	18	61	11	28	11-3	.368	.403	.727	3	.973
2001—Minnesota (A.L.)	OF	148	564	82	147	32	5	27	92	29	125	9-6	.261	.306	.479	4	.992
2002—Minnesota (A.L.)	OF-DH	148	561	89	162	37	4	29	94	35	118	23-8	.289	.334	.524	3	.992
Major League totals (6 years)		537	1862	267	505	101	18	70	267	110	389	46-24	.271	.317	.458	11	.992

H I

DIVISION SERIES RECORD

RECORDS: Shares single-series record for most doubles—4 (2002).

Year	Team (League)	Pos.	G	AB	R	H	2B	3B	HR	RBI	BB	SO	SB-CS	Avg.	OBP	SLG	E	Avg.
			BATTING														FIELDING	
2002—	Minnesota (A.L.)	OF	5	20	4	6	4	0	0	2	1	4	0-0	.300	.333	.500	0	1.000

CHAMPIONSHIP SERIES RECORD

Year	Team (League)	Pos.	G	AB	R	H	2B	3B	HR	RBI	BB	SO	SB-CS	Avg.	OBP	SLG	E	Avg.
			BATTING														FIELDING	
2002—	Minnesota (A.L.)	OF	5	18	2	3	2	0	0	0	1	3	0-0	.167	.211	.278	0	1.000

ALL-STAR GAME RECORD

	AB	R	H	2B	3B	HR	RBI	BB	SO	SB-CS	Avg.	OBP	SLG	E	Avg.
All-Star Game totals (1 year)	2	0	0	0	0	0	0	0	0	0-0	.000	.000	.000	0	1.000

HYZDU, ADAM — OF — PIRATES

PERSONAL: Born December 6, 1971, in San Jose, Calif. ... 6-2/220. ... Bats right, throws right. ... Full name: Adam Davis Hyzdu. ... Name pronounced HIZE-doo.

HIGH SCHOOL: Moeller (Cincinnati).

COLLEGE: Xavier.

TRANSACTIONS/CAREER NOTES: Selected by San Francisco Giants organization in first round (15th pick overall) of free-agent draft (June 4, 1990); pick received as compensation for Houston Astros signing Type B free-agent IF Ken Oberkfell. ... Selected by Cincinnati Reds from Giants organization in Rule 5 major league draft (December 13, 1993). ... Released by Reds (March 23, 1996). ... Signed by Boston Red Sox organization (April 26, 1996). ... Signed by Arizona Diamondbacks organization (January 2, 1998). ... Loaned by Diamondbacks organization to Monterrey, Mexican League (April 7-May 17, 1998). ... On disabled list (June 30-August 23, 1998). ... Granted free agency (October 15, 1998). ... Signed by Pittsburgh Pirates organization (May 10, 1999). ... Granted free agency (October 15, 1999). ... Re-signed by Pirates organization (October 30, 1999). ... Granted free agency (October 18, 2000). ... Re-signed by Pirates organization (October 24, 2000).

HONORS: Named Eastern League Most Valuable Player (2000).

STATISTICAL NOTES: Led Eastern League with 285 total bases in 2000. ... Tied for Eastern League lead with seven intentional bases on balls received in 2000. ... Career major league grand slams: 2.

2002 GAMES PLAYED BY POSITION (MLB): OF—50; 1B—1.

Year	Team (League)	Pos.	G	AB	R	H	2B	3B	HR	RBI	BB	SO	SB-CS	Avg.	OBP	SLG	E	Avg.
			BATTING														FIELDING	
1990—	Everett (N'West)	OF	69	253	31	62	16	1	6	34	28	78	2-4	.245	.319	.387	5	.963
1991—	Clinton (Midw.)	OF	124	410	47	96	13	5	5	50	64	131	4-5	.234	.340	.327	9	.955
1992—	San Jose (Calif.)	OF	128	457	60	127	25	5	9	60	55	134	10-5	.278	.351	.414	5	.976
1993—	San Jose (Calif.)	OF	44	165	35	48	11	3	13	38	29	53	1-1	.291	.393	.630	3	.963
—	Shreveport (Texas)	OF	86	302	30	61	17	0	6	25	20	82	0-5	.202	.253	.318	4	.973
1994—	Chattanooga (Sou.)■	OF-DH-1B	38	133	17	35	10	0	3	9	8	21	0-2	.263	.310	.406	4	.949
—	Win.-Salem (Caro.)	OF-DH	55	210	30	58	11	1	15	39	18	33	1-5	.276	.336	.552	4	.945
—	Indianapolis (A.A.)	OF	12	25	3	3	2	0	0	3	1	5	0-0	.120	.143	.200	1	.917
1995—	Chattanooga (Sou.)	OF	102	312	55	82	14	1	13	48	45	56	3-2	.263	.362	.439	1	*.995
1996—	Trenton (East.)■	OF-DH-C	109	374	71	126	24	3	25	80	56	75	1-8	.337	.424	*.618	3	.980
1997—	Pawtucket (I.L.)	OF-DH	119	413	77	114	21	1	23	84	72	113	10-6	.276	.387	.499	4	.978
1998—	Monterrey (Mex.)■	OF	29	110	20	36	3	0	5	22	14	17	7-1	.327	.402	.491	0	1.000
—	Tucson (PCL)■	OF-DH-P	34	100	21	34	7	1	4	14	15	23	0-1	.340	.419	.550	1	.974
1999—	Pawtucket (I.L.)■	OF-DH	12	35	4	8	0	0	1	6	4	13	0-0	.229	.308	.314	0	1.000
—	Altoona (East.)■	OF-1B-3B-DH	91	345	64	109	26	2	24	78	40	62	8-4	.316	.392	.612	11	.965
—	Nashville (PCL)	OF	14	44	6	11	1	0	5	13	4	11	0-0	.250	.313	.614	0	1.000
2000—	Altoona (East.)	OF-1B	*142	514	•96	149	39	2	*31	*106	94	102	3-7	.290	.405	.554	1	.996
—	Pittsburgh (N.L.)	OF	12	18	2	7	2	0	1	4	0	4	0-0	.389	.389	.667	0	1.000
2001—	Nashville (PCL)	OF-1B-3B	69	261	38	76	17	2	11	39	17	68	1-3	.291	.332	.498	1	.994
—	Pittsburgh (N.L.)	OF-1B	51	72	7	15	1	0	5	9	4	18	0-1	.208	.260	.431	0	1.000
2002—	Nashville (PCL)	OF-1B	65	243	33	59	17	0	10	50	29	59	1-2	.243	.318	.436	3	.980
—	Pittsburgh (N.L.)	OF-1B	59	155	24	36	6	0	11	34	21	44	0-0	.232	.324	.484	0	1.000
Major League totals (3 years)			122	245	33	58	9	0	17	47	25	66	0-1	.237	.310	.482	0	1.000

RECORD AS PITCHER

Year	League	W	L	Pct.	ERA	G	GS	CG	ShO	Sv.-Opp.	IP	H	R	ER	HR	BB-IBB	SO
1998—	Tucson (PCL)	0	0	...	0.00	1	0	0	0	0-...	1.0	0	0	0	0	0-0	1

IBANEZ, RAUL — OF — ROYALS

PERSONAL: Born June 2, 1972, in Manhattan, N.Y. ... 6-2/200. ... Bats left, throws right. ... Full name: Raul Javier Ibanez.

HIGH SCHOOL: Sunset (Miami).

JUNIOR COLLEGE: Miami-Dade (South) Community College.

TRANSACTIONS/CAREER NOTES: Selected by Seattle Mariners organization in 36th round of free-agent draft (June 1, 1992). ... On disabled list (June 4-July 16, 1994). ... On Seattle disabled list (March 30-June 29, 1998); included rehabilitation assignment to Tacoma (May 30-June 28). ... On Tacoma disabled list (July 7-14, 1998). ... On Seattle disabled list (May 18-June 3, 1999); included rehabilitation assignment to Tacoma (May 26-June 3). ... On Seattle disabled list (August 7-22, 2000); included rehabilitation assignment to Tacoma (August 11-22). ... Granted free agency (December 21, 2000). ... Signed by Kansas City Royals organization (January 22, 2001).

STATISTICAL NOTES: Led California League with 25 passed balls in 1995. ... Career major league grand slams: 2.

2002 GAMES PLAYED BY POSITION (MLB): OF—55; 1B—49; DH—36.

Year	Team (League)	Pos.	BATTING G	AB	R	H	2B	3B	HR	RBI	BB	SO	SB-CS	Avg.	OBP	SLG	FIELDING E	Avg.
1992—	Ariz. Mariners (Ariz.)	1B-C-OF	33	120	25	37	8	2	1	16	9	18	1-2	.308	.366	.433	4	.931
1993—	Appleton (Midw.)	1B-C-OF	52	157	26	43	9	0	5	21	24	31	0-2	.274	.370	.427	2	.980
—	Bellingham (N'West)	C	43	134	16	38	5	2	0	15	21	23	0-3	.284	.378	.351	1	.993
1994—	Appleton (Midw.)	C-1B-OF	91	327	55	102	30	3	7	59	32	37	10-5	.312	.375	.486	10	.971
1995—	Riverside (Calif.)	C-1B	95	361	59	120	23	9	20	108	41	49	4-3	.332	.395	*.612	12	.977
1996—	Tacoma (PCL)	OF-1B-DH	111	405	59	115	20	3	11	47	44	56	7-7	.284	.353	.430	11	.951
—	Port City (Sou.)	OF-DH-C-1B	19	76	12	28	8	1	1	13	8	7	3-2	.368	.424	.539	4	.905
—	Seattle (A.L.)	DH	4	5	0	0	0	0	0	0	0	1	0-0	.000	.167	.000	0	...
1997—	Tacoma (PCL)	OF	111	438	84	133	30	5	15	84	32	75	7-5	.304	.349	.498	5	.976
—	Seattle (A.L.)	OF-DH	11	26	3	4	0	1	1	4	0	6	0-0	.154	.154	.346	0	1.000
1998—	Tacoma (PCL)	OF-DH	52	190	24	41	8	1	6	25	24	47	1-1	.216	.301	.363	1	.988
—	Seattle (A.L.)	OF-1B-DH	37	98	12	25	7	1	2	12	5	22	0-0	.255	.291	.408	1	.991
1999—	Seattle (A.L.)	OF-1B-DH-C	87	209	23	54	7	0	9	27	17	32	5-1	.258	.313	.421	3	.988
—	Tacoma (PCL)	OF-DH-1B	8	31	6	11	1	0	3	5	1	7	1-0	.355	.375	.677	0	1.000
2000—	Seattle (A.L.)	OF-DH-1B	92	140	21	32	8	0	2	15	14	25	2-0	.229	.301	.329	2	.980
—	Tacoma (PCL)	OF	10	40	3	10	4	0	0	6	1	3	0-0	.250	.268	.350	0	1.000
2001—	Kansas City (A.L.)■	O-D-1-3	104	279	44	78	11	5	13	54	32	51	0-2	.280	.353	.495	5	.962
—	Omaha (PCL)	OF-SS	8	27	3	4	1	0	2	5	1	10	0-0	.148	.179	.407	1	.857
2002—	Kansas City (A.L.)	OF-1B-DH	137	497	70	146	37	6	24	103	40	76	5-3	.294	.346	.537	3	.994
Major League totals (7 years)			472	1254	173	339	70	13	51	215	108	213	12-6	.270	.328	.469	14	.987

DIVISION SERIES RECORD

Year	Team (League)	Pos.	BATTING G	AB	R	H	2B	3B	HR	RBI	BB	SO	SB-CS	Avg.	OBP	SLG	FIELDING E	Avg.
2000—	Seattle (A.L.)	PR-OF	3	8	2	3	0	0	0	0	0	0	0-0	.375	.375	.375	0	1.000

CHAMPIONSHIP SERIES RECORD

Year	Team (League)	Pos.	BATTING G	AB	R	H	2B	3B	HR	RBI	BB	SO	SB-CS	Avg.	OBP	SLG	FIELDING E	Avg.
2000—	Seattle (A.L.)	OF-PH	6	9	0	0	0	0	0	0	0	2	0-0	.000	.000	.000	0	1.000

INFANTE, OMAR — SS — TIGERS

PERSONAL: Born December 26, 1981, in Puerto la Cruz, Venezuela. ... 5-9/150. ... Bats right, throws right. ... Full name: Omar R. Infante.
TRANSACTIONS/CAREER NOTES: Signed as non-drafted free agent by Detroit Tigers organization (April 28, 1999).
STATISTICAL NOTES: Led International League with 15 caught stealing in 2002. ... Led International League shortstops with 416 assists and 633 total chances in 2002.
2002 GAMES PLAYED BY POSITION (MLB): SS—16; 2B—2.

Year	Team (League)	Pos.	BATTING G	AB	R	H	2B	3B	HR	RBI	BB	SO	SB-CS	Avg.	OBP	SLG	FIELDING E	Avg.
1999—	GC Tigers (GCL)	SS	25	97	11	26	4	0	0	7	4	11	4-0	.268	.294	.309	8	.932
2000—	Lakeland (FSL)	SS	79	259	35	71	11	0	2	24	20	29	11-5	.274	.324	.340	19	.951
—	West Mich. (Midw.)	SS	12	48	7	11	0	0	0	5	5	7	1-0	.229	.327	.229	1	.983
2001—	Erie (East.)	SS	132	540	86	163	21	4	2	62	46	87	27-12	.302	.355	.367	27	.955
2002—	Toledo (I.L.)	SS	120	436	49	117	16	8	4	51	28	49	19-15	.268	.309	.369	26	.959
—	Detroit (A.L.)	SS-2B	18	72	4	24	3	0	1	6	3	10	0-1	.333	.360	.417	5	.945
Major League totals (1 year)			18	72	4	24	3	0	1	6	3	10	0-1	.333	.360	.417	5	.945

INGE, BRANDON — C — TIGERS

PERSONAL: Born May 19, 1977, in Lynchburg, Va. ... 5-11/189. ... Bats right, throws right. ... Full name: Charles Brandon Inge.
HIGH SCHOOL: Brookville (Lynchburg, Va.).
COLLEGE: Virginia Commonwealth.
TRANSACTIONS/CAREER NOTES: Selected by Detroit Tigers organization in second round of free-agent draft (June 2, 1998). ... On Detroit disabled list (June 25-August 6, 2001); included rehabilitation assignments to Gulf Coast Tigers (July 25-29), West Michigan (July 30-August 2) and Toledo (August 3-6). ... On Detroit disabled list (May 12-May 27, 2002); included rehabilitation assignment to Toledo (May 17-27).
STATISTICAL NOTES: Led Midwest League with 114 assists in 1999. ... Led Southern League catchers with .990 fielding percentage in 2000.
2002 GAMES PLAYED BY POSITION (MLB): C—94; DH—1.

Year	Team (League)	Pos.	BATTING G	AB	R	H	2B	3B	HR	RBI	BB	SO	SB-CS	Avg.	OBP	SLG	FIELDING E	Avg.
1998—	Jamestown (NY-P)	C	51	191	24	44	10	1	8	29	17	53	8-8	.230	.312	.419	6	.981
1999—	West Mich. (Midw.)	C	100	352	54	86	25	2	9	46	39	87	15-3	.244	.320	.403	8	.990
2000—	Jacksonville (Sou.)	C-OF	78	298	39	77	25	1	6	53	26	73	10-3	.258	.313	.409	5	†.990
—	Toledo (I.L.)	C	55	190	24	42	9	3	5	20	15	51	2-1	.221	.280	.379	3	.991
2001—	Detroit (A.L.)	C	79	189	13	34	11	0	0	15	9	41	1-4	.180	.215	.238	4	.989
—	GC Tigers (GCL)	C	3	10	1	1	0	0	1	2	2	2	0-0	.100	.250	.400	0	1.000
—	West Mich. (Midw.)	C	4	16	3	3	1	0	0	2	2	5	0-0	.188	.316	.250	0	1.000
—	Toledo (I.L.)	C	27	90	11	26	11	1	2	15	7	24	1-0	.289	.337	.500	2	.989
2002—	Toledo (I.L.)	C	21	65	10	17	2	4	3	13	11	16	1-3	.262	.380	.554	4	.978
—	Detroit (A.L.)	C-DH	95	321	27	65	15	3	7	24	24	101	1-3	.202	.266	.333	1	.998
Major League totals (2 years)			174	510	40	99	26	3	7	39	33	142	2-7	.194	.247	.298	5	.994

IRABU, HIDEKI — P

PERSONAL: Born May 5, 1969, in Hyogo, Japan. ... 6-4/250. ... Throws right, bats right.
HIGH SCHOOL: Jinsei.

TRANSACTIONS/CAREER NOTES: Rights acquired by San Diego Padres from Chiba Lotte Marines of Japan Pacific League (January 13, 1997). ... Rights traded by Padres with 2B Homer Bush, OF Gordon Amerson and a player to be named later to New York Yankees for OF Ruben Rivera, P Rafael Medina and cash (April 22, 1997); Padres traded OF Vernon Maxwell to Yankees to complete deal (June 9, 1997). ... Signed by Yankees (May 29, 1997). ... Traded by Yankees to Montreal Expos for P Jake Westbrook and two players to be named (December 22, 1999); Yankees acquired P Ted Lilly (March 17, 2000) and P Christian Parker (March 22, 2000) to complete deal. ... On Montreal disabled list (May 27-July 26 and July 28, 2000-remainder of season); included rehabilitation assignments to Jupiter (July 8-18) and Ottawa (July 19-20). ... On Montreal disabled list (March 23-May 31, 2001 and June 14-September 6, 2001); included rehabilitation assignments to Jupiter (April 26-May 31) and Ottawa (August 22-30). ... Released by Expos (September 6, 2001). ... Signed by Texas Rangers organization (December 27, 2001). ... On disabled list (July 13, 2002-remainder of season). ... Released by Rangers (November 13, 2002).

STATISTICAL NOTES: Tied for A.L. lead with three balks in 1997.

CAREER HITTING (MLB): 3-for-28 (.107), 1 R, 0 2B, 0 3B, 0 HR, 1 RBI.

Year League	W	L	Pct.	ERA	G	GS	CG	ShO	Sv.-Opp.	IP	H	R	ER	HR	BB-IBB	SO
1988—Lotte Orions (Jp. East.)....	2	5	.286	3.89	14	6	...	...	1-...	39.1	30	19	17	...	15-...	21
1989—Lotte Orions (Jp. East.)....	0	2	.000	3.53	33	2	...	...	9-...	51.0	37	20	20	...	27-...	50
1990—Lotte Orions (Jp. East.)....	8	5	.615	3.78	34	7	...	...	0-...	123.2	110	56	52	...	72-...	102
1991—Lotte Orions (Jp. East.)....	3	8	.273	6.88	24	14	...	...	0-...	100.2	110	78	77	...	70-...	78
1992—Chiba Lotte (Jap. Pac.).....	0	5	.000	3.86	28	4	...	...	0-...	77.0	38	33	33	...	37-...	55
1993—Chiba Lotte (Jap. Pac.).....	8	7	.533	3.10	32	8	...	...	1-...	142.1	125	59	49	...	58-...	160
1994—Chiba Lotte (Jap. Pac.).....	*15	10	.600	3.04	27	20	...	...	0-...	207.1	170	77	70	...	94-...	*239
1995—Chiba Lotte (Jap. Pac.).....	11	11	.500	*2.53	28	18	...	...	0-...	203.0	158	70	57	...	72-...	*239
1996—Chiba Lotte (Jap. Pac.).....	12	6	.667	*2.40	23	20	3	...	0-...	157.1	108	57	42	...	59-...	167
1997—Tampa (FSL)■................	1	0	1.000	0.00	2	2	0	0	0-...	9.0	4	0	0	0	0-0	12
—Norwich (East.)................	1	1	.500	4.50	2	2	0	0	0-...	10.0	13	5	5	1	0-0	9
—Columbus (I.L.)................	2	0	1.000	1.67	4	4	1	1	0-...	27.0	19	7	5	1	5-0	28
—New York (A.L.)................	5	4	.556	7.09	13	9	0	0	0-0	53.1	69	47	42	15	20-0	56
1998—New York (A.L.)................	13	9	.591	4.06	29	28	2	1	0-0	173.0	148	79	78	27	76-1	126
1999—New York (A.L.)................	11	7	.611	4.84	32	27	2	1	0-0	169.1	180	98	91	26	46-0	133
2000—Montreal (N.L.)■..............	2	5	.286	7.24	11	11	0	0	0-0	54.2	77	45	44	9	14-0	42
—Jupiter (FSL)....................	1	0	1.000	1.04	2	2	0	0	0-...	8.2	7	1	1	1	1-0	9
—Ottawa (I.L.)....................	0	1	.000	3.18	1	1	0	0	0-...	5.2	5	2	2	1	2-0	6
2001—Jupiter (FSL)....................	0	0	...	3.00	3	3	0	0	0-...	9.0	5	3	3	1	4-0	9
—Ottawa (I.L.)....................	1	2	.333	4.43	4	4	0	0	0-...	22.1	22	12	11	2	6-0	21
—Montreal (N.L.)..................	0	2	.000	4.86	3	3	0	0	0-0	16.2	22	9	9	3	3-0	18
2002—Texas (A.L.)■..................	3	8	.273	5.74	38	2	0	0	16-20	47.0	51	30	30	11	16-2	30
A.L. totals (4 years).....................	32	28	.533	4.90	112	66	4	2	16-20	442.2	448	254	241	79	158-3	345
N.L. totals (2 years).....................	2	7	.222	6.69	14	14	0	0	0-0	71.1	99	54	53	12	17-0	60
Major League totals (6 years).....	34	35	.493	5.15	126	80	4	2	16-20	514.0	547	308	294	91	175-3	405

DIVISION SERIES RECORD

Year League	W	L	Pct.	ERA	G	GS	CG	ShO	Sv.-Opp.	IP	H	R	ER	HR	BB-IBB	SO
1998—New York (A.L.)..................									Did not play.							
1999—New York (A.L.)..................									Did not play.							

CHAMPIONSHIP SERIES RECORD

Year League	W	L	Pct.	ERA	G	GS	CG	ShO	Sv.-Opp.	IP	H	R	ER	HR	BB-IBB	SO
1998—New York (A.L.)..................									Did not play.							
1999—New York (A.L.)................	0	0	...	13.50	1	0	0	0	0-0	4.2	13	8	7	2	0-0	3

WORLD SERIES RECORD

NOTES: Member of World Series championship team (1998 and 1999).

Year League	W	L	Pct.	ERA	G	GS	CG	ShO	Sv.-Opp.	IP	H	R	ER	HR	BB-IBB	SO
1998—New York (A.L.)..................									Did not play.							
1999—New York (A.L.)..................									Did not play.							

ISHII, KAZ — P — DODGERS

PERSONAL: Born September 9, 1973, in Chiba, Japan. ... 6-0/190. ... Throws left, bats left. ... Full name: Kazuhisa Ishii. ... Name pronounced E-shee-ee.

TRANSACTIONS/CAREER NOTES: Played with Yakult Swallows of Japan Central League (1992-2001). ... Signed as non-drafted free agent by Los Angeles Dodgers (February 8, 2002). ... On disabled list (September 9, 2002-remainder of season).

CAREER HITTING (MLB): 5-for-50 (.100), 1 R, 0 2B, 0 3B, 0 HR, 2 RBI.

Year League	W	L	Pct.	ERA	G	GS	CG	ShO	Sv.-Opp.	IP	H	R	ER	HR	BB-IBB	SO
1992—Yakult (Jap. Cen.)............	0	0	...	4.18	12	...	0	0	0-...	28.0	23	13	13	...	17-...	22
1993—Yakult (Jap. Cen.)............	3	1	.750	4.70	19	...	1	0	0-...	59.1	48	32	31	...	38-...	66
1994—Yakult (Jap. Cen.)............	7	5	.583	4.08	54	...	2	2	0-...	108.0	92	56	49	...	77-...	98
1995—Yakult (Jap. Cen.)............	13	4	.765	2.76	26	...	3	0	1-...	153.0	112	49	47	...	77-...	159
1996—Yakult (Jap. Cen.)............	1	5	.167	5.23	8	...	0	0	0-...	31.0	28	19	18	...	22-...	26
1997—Yakult (Jap. Cen.)............	10	4	.714	1.91	18	...	2	2	0-...	117.2	73	28	25	...	50-...	120
1998—Yakult (Jap. Cen.)............	14	6	.700	3.30	28	...	6	0	0-...	196.1	149	78	72	...	105-...	241
1999—Yakult (Jap. Cen.)............	8	6	.571	4.80	23	...	2	1	0-...	133.0	123	75	71	...	71-...	162
2000—Yakult (Jap. Cen.)............	10	9	.526	2.61	29	...	3	1	0-...	183.0	137	54	53	...	73-...	210
2001—Yakult (Jap. Cen.)............	12	6	.667	3.39	27	...	0	0	0-...	175.0	135	74	66	...	73-...	173
2002—Los Angeles (N.L.)■........	14	10	.583	4.27	28	28	0	0	0-0	154.0	137	82	73	20	*106-3	143
Major League totals (1 year).......	14	10	.583	4.27	28	28	0	0	0-0	154.0	137	82	73	20	106-3	143

ISRINGHAUSEN, JASON — P — CARDINALS

PERSONAL: Born September 7, 1972, in Brighton, Ill. ... 6-3/230. ... Throws right, bats right. ... Full name: Jason Derik Isringhausen. ... Name pronounced IS-ring-how-zin.

HIGH SCHOOL: Southwestern (Brighton, Ill.).

JUNIOR COLLEGE: Lewis & Clark Community College (Ill.).

TRANSACTIONS/CAREER NOTES: Selected by New York Mets organization in 44th round of free-agent draft (June 3, 1991). ... On disabled list (August 13-September 1, 1996). ... On disabled list (March 24-August 27, 1997); included rehabilitation assignments to Norfolk (April 6-11 and August 22-27), Gulf Coast Mets (August 6-11) and St. Lucie (August 11-22). ... On disabled list (March 21, 1998-entire season). ... Traded by Mets with P Greg McMichael to Oakland Athletics for P Billy Taylor (July 31, 1999). ... Granted free agency (November 5, 2001). ... Signed by St. Louis Cardinals (December 11, 2001).

RECORDS: Shares major league record for striking out side on nine pitches (April 13, 2002, ninth inning).

HONORS: Named International League Most Valuable Pitcher (1995).

CAREER HITTING (MLB): 19-for-97 (.196), 10 R, 4 2B, 0 3B, 2 HR, 11 RBI.

Year League	W	L	Pct.	ERA	G	GS	CG	ShO	Sv.-Opp.	IP	H	R	ER	HR	BB-IBB	SO
1992— Gulf Coast Mets (GCL)	2	4	.333	4.34	6	6	0	0	0-...	29.0	26	19	14	0	17-1	25
— Kingsport (Appl.)	4	1	.800	3.25	7	6	1	1	0-...	36.0	32	22	13	2	12-1	24
1993— Pittsfield (NY-Penn)	7	4	.636	3.29	15	15	2	0	0-...	90.1	68	45	33	7	28-0	*104
1994— St. Lucie (FSL)	6	4	.600	2.23	14	14	•6	•3	0-...	101.0	76	31	25	2	27-2	59
— Binghamton (East.)	5	4	.556	3.02	14	14	2	0	0-...	92.1	78	35	31	6	23-0	69
1995— Binghamton (East.)	2	1	.667	2.85	6	6	1	0	0-...	41.0	26	15	13	1	12-0	59
— Norfolk (I.L.)	9	1	*.900	1.55	12	12	3	*3	0-...	87.0	64	17	15	2	24-0	75
— New York (N.L.)	9	2	.818	2.81	14	14	1	0	0-0	93.0	88	29	29	6	31-2	55
1996— New York (N.L.)	6	14	.300	4.77	27	27	2	1	0-0	171.2	190	103	91	13	73-5	114
1997— Norfolk (I.L.)	0	2	.000	4.05	3	3	0	0	0-...	20.0	20	10	9	4	8-0	17
— Gulf Coast Mets (GCL)	1	0	1.000	1.93	1	0	0	0	0-...	4.2	2	1	1	0	1-0	7
— St. Lucie (FSL)	1	0	1.000	0.00	2	2	0	0	0-...	12.0	8	1	0	0	5-0	15
— New York (N.L.)	2	2	.500	7.58	6	6	0	0	0-0	29.2	40	27	25	3	22-0	25
1998— New York (N.L.)									Did not play.							
1999— Norfolk (I.L.)	3	1	.750	2.29	12	8	0	0	0-...	51.0	33	18	13	4	20-0	51
— New York (N.L.)	1	3	.250	6.41	13	5	0	0	1-1	39.1	43	29	28	7	22-2	31
— Oakland (A.L.)■	0	1	.000	2.13	20	0	0	0	8-8	25.1	21	6	6	2	12-2	20
2000— Oakland (A.L.)	6	4	.600	3.78	66	0	0	0	33-40	69.0	67	34	29	6	32-5	57
2001— Oakland (A.L.)	4	3	.571	2.65	65	0	0	0	34-43	71.1	54	24	21	5	23-5	74
2002— St. Louis (N.L.)■	3	2	.600	2.48	60	0	0	0	32-37	65.1	46	22	18	0	18-1	68
A.L. totals (3 years)	10	8	.556	3.04	151	0	0	0	75-91	165.2	142	64	56	13	67-12	151
N.L. totals (5 years)	21	23	.477	4.31	120	52	3	1	33-38	399.0	407	210	191	29	166-10	293
Major League totals (7 years)	31	31	.500	3.94	271	52	3	1	108-129	564.2	549	274	247	42	233-22	444

DIVISION SERIES RECORD

Year League	W	L	Pct.	ERA	G	GS	CG	ShO	Sv.-Opp.	IP	H	R	ER	HR	BB-IBB	SO
2000— Oakland (A.L.)	0	0	...	0.00	2	0	0	0	1-1	2.0	1	0	0	0	0-0	3
2001— Oakland (A.L.)	0	0	...	0.00	2	0	0	0	2-2	2.0	1	0	0	0	1-0	3
2002— St. Louis (N.L.)	0	0	...	0.00	2	0	0	0	2-2	2.0	0	0	0	0	0-0	1
Division series totals (3 years)	0	0	...	0.00	6	0	0	0	5-5	6.0	2	0	0	0	1-0	7

CHAMPIONSHIP SERIES RECORD

Year League	W	L	Pct.	ERA	G	GS	CG	ShO	Sv.-Opp.	IP	H	R	ER	HR	BB-IBB	SO
2002— St. Louis (N.L.)	0	0	...	4.50	2	0	0	0	1-1	2.0	1	1	1	0	3-2	3

ALL-STAR GAME RECORD

	W	L	Pct.	ERA	GS	CG	ShO	Sv.-Opp.	IP	H	R	ER	HR	BB-IBB	SO
All-Star Game totals (1 year)	0	0	...	9.00	0	0	0	0-0	1.0	2	1	1	0	1-0	0

IZQUIERDO, HANSEL — P — RED SOX

PERSONAL: Born January 2, 1977, in Havana, Cuba. ... 6-2/205. ... Throws right, bats right.

HIGH SCHOOL: Southwest (Miami, Fla.).

TRANSACTIONS/CAREER NOTES: Selected by Florida Marlins organization in seventh round of free-agent draft (June 1, 1995). ... Released by Marlins (June 3, 1997). ... Signed by Chicago White Sox organization (June 20, 1997). ... Granted free agency (October 17, 1997). ... Re-signed by White Sox organization (November 4, 1997). ... Released by White Sox (May 4, 2000). ... Signed by Cleveland Indians organization (May 30, 2000). ... Released by Indians (July 21, 2000). ... Signed by Sonoma County, Western League (August, 2000). ... Signed by Marlins organization (November 10, 2000). ... On Calgary disabled list (July 22-August 6, 2002). ... Released by Marlins (October 3, 2002). ... Signed by Boston Red Sox organization (October 17, 2002).

STATISTICAL NOTES: Led South Atlantic League with 22 hit batsmen in 1998.

CAREER HITTING (MLB): 0-for-2 (.000), 0 R, 0 2B, 0 3B, 0 HR, 0 RBI.

Year League	W	L	Pct.	ERA	G	GS	CG	ShO	Sv.-Opp.	IP	H	R	ER	HR	BB-IBB	SO
1995— Gulf Coast Marlins (GCL)	0	0	...	0.00	1	0	0	0	0-...	2.0	3	3	0	0	2-0	0
1996— Gulf Coast Marlins (GCL)	0	1	.000	2.70	12	0	0	0	3-...	13.1	7	4	4	0	5-0	17
1997— GC White Sox (GCL)■	0	0	...	3.48	5	0	0	0	0-...	10.1	9	4	4	0	8-0	15
— Bristol (Appl.)	2	2	.500	4.30	9	2	0	0	0-...	23.0	25	14	11	5	8-0	24
1998— Hickory (S.Atl.)	9	11	.450	4.37	28	27	2	1	0-...	175.0	159	*104	85	14	*76-0	186
— Winston-Salem (Caro.)	0	0	...	0.00	1	0	0	0	1-...	2.0	1	0	0	0	1-0	2
1999— Winston-Salem (Caro.)	3	5	.375	4.14	18	13	0	0	0-...	82.2	76	46	38	5	46-1	72
2000— Birmingham (Sou.)	1	2	.333	7.50	8	0	0	0	0-...	12.0	12	11	10	2	5-1	5
— Kinston (Caro.)■	1	3	.250	4.79	10	5	0	0	1-...	41.1	39	29	22	4	13-0	34
— Sonoma County (West.)■	0	1	.000	9.69	4	3	0	0	0-...	13.0	16	14	14	0	17-1	10
2001— Kane County (Midw.)■	7	1	.875	1.32	24	2	0	0	2-...	47.2	27	8	7	1	13-0	42
— Brevard County (FSL)	2	0	1.000	2.70	4	4	0	0	0-...	26.2	15	8	8	3	6-0	22
— Portland (East.)	7	2	.778	3.81	10	9	1	1	0-...	56.2	47	24	24	10	10-0	45
2002— Portland (East.)	0	1	.000	1.29	1	1	0	0	0-...	7.0	5	2	1	0	1-0	4
— Florida (N.L.)	2	0	1.000	4.55	20	2	0	0	0-0	29.2	33	17	15	2	21-3	20
— Calgary (PCL)	4	5	.444	5.32	13	13	0	0	0-...	71.0	90	55	42	11	23-0	36
Major League totals (1 year)	2	0	1.000	4.55	20	2	0	0	0-0	29.2	33	17	15	2	21-3	20

IZTURIS, CESAR — SS — DODGERS

PERSONAL: Born February 10, 1980, in Lara, Venezuela. ... 5-9/175. ... Bats both, throws right. ... Full name: Cesar D. Izturis.

TRANSACTIONS/CAREER NOTES: Signed as non-drafted free agent by Toronto Blue Jays organization (July 11, 1996). ... Traded by Blue Jays with P Paul Quantrill to Los Angeles Dodgers for P Luke Prokopec and P Chad Ricketts (December 13, 2001).

STATISTICAL NOTES: Led South Atlantic League shortstops with 183 assists and .951 fielding percentage in 1998. ... Led International League shortstops with 231 putouts, 638 total chances and 87 double plays in 2000.

2002 GAMES PLAYED BY POSITION (MLB): SS—128; 2B—1; DH—1.

		BATTING														FIELDING	
Year Team (League)	Pos.	G	AB	R	H	2B	3B	HR	RBI	BB	SO	SB-CS	Avg.	OBP	SLG	E	Avg.
1997—St. Catharines (NY-P)	2B-SS	70	231	32	44	3	0	1	11	15	27	6-3	.190	.241	.216	16	.951
1998—Hagerstown (S.Atl.)	SS-2B-3B	130	413	56	108	13	1	1	38	20	43	20-9	.262	.297	.305	29	•.952
1999—Dunedin (FSL)	SS-2B-3B	131	536	77	165	28	12	3	77	22	58	32-16	.308	.337	.422	21	.969
2000—Syracuse (I.L.)	SS	132	435	54	95	16	5	0	27	20	44	21-11	.218	.253	.278	12	*.981
2001—Syracuse (I.L.)	SS-2B	87	342	32	100	16	3	2	35	10	22	24-9	.292	.310	.374	16	.962
—Toronto (A.L.)	2B-SS	46	134	19	36	6	2	2	9	2	15	8-1	.269	.279	.388	3	.985
2002—Los Angeles (N.L.)■	SS-2B-DH	135	439	43	102	24	2	1	31	14	39	7-7	.232	.253	.303	10	.979
American League totals (1 year)		46	134	19	36	6	2	2	9	2	15	8-1	.269	.279	.388	3	.985
National League totals (1 year)		135	439	43	102	24	2	1	31	14	39	7-7	.232	.253	.303	10	.979
Major League totals (2 years)		181	573	62	138	30	4	3	40	16	54	15-8	.241	.259	.323	13	.981

JACKSON, DAMIAN — SS — TIGERS

PERSONAL: Born August 16, 1973, in Los Angeles. ... 5-11/185. ... Bats right, throws right. ... Full name: Damian Jacques Jackson.

HIGH SCHOOL: Ygnacio Valley (Concord, Calif.).

JUNIOR COLLEGE: Laney (Calif.).

TRANSACTIONS/CAREER NOTES: Selected by Cleveland Indians organization in 44th round of free-agent draft (June 3, 1991). ... Traded by Indians with P Danny Graves, P Jim Crowell and P Scott Winchester to Cincinnati Reds for P John Smiley and IF Jeff Branson (July 31, 1997). ... Traded by Reds with OF Reggie Sanders and P Josh Harris to San Diego Padres for OF Greg Vaughn and OF/1B Mark Sweeney (February 2, 1999). ... On San Diego disabled list (May 13-June 22, 2001); included rehabilitation assignment to Portland (June 18-21). ... Traded by Padres with C Matt Walbeck to Detroit Tigers for C Javier Cardona and OF Rich Gomez (March 24, 2002). ... On disabled list (April 7-22, 2002).

STATISTICAL NOTES: Led Appalachian League shortstops with 102 putouts, 217 assists, 342 total chances and 45 double plays in 1992. ... Led Eastern League shortstops with 241 putouts, 446 assists, 54 errors, 741 total chances and 85 double plays in 1994. ... Led Eastern League in caught stealing with 22 in 1995. ... Led Eastern League shortstops in putouts with 220 and tied for league lead in double plays with 80 in 1995. ... Led American Association shortstops with 203 putouts, 403 assists, 635 total chances and 84 double plays in 1996. ... Led International League shortstops with 227 putouts, 434 assists, 44 errors, 705 total chances and 101 double plays in 1998. ... Career major league grand slams: 2.

2002 GAMES PLAYED BY POSITION (MLB): 2B—56; OF—6; SS—6; DH—5; 3B—2.

		BATTING														FIELDING	
Year Team (League)	Pos.	G	AB	R	H	2B	3B	HR	RBI	BB	SO	SB-CS	Avg.	OBP	SLG	E	Avg.
1992—Burlington (Appl.)	SS	62	226	32	56	12	1	0	23	32	31	29-5	.248	.352	.310	23	*.933
1993—Columbus (S.Atl.)	SS	108	350	70	94	19	3	6	45	41	61	26-7	.269	.353	.391	52	.908
1994—Canton/Akron (East.)	SS-OF	138	531	85	143	29	5	5	60	60	121	37-16	.269	.346	.371	†54	.927
1995—Canton/Akron (East.)	SS	131	484	67	120	20	2	3	34	65	103	40-22	.248	.348	.316	*36	.939
1996—Buffalo (A.A.)	SS	133	452	77	116	15	1	12	49	48	78	24-7	.257	.333	.374	29	.954
—Cleveland (A.L.)	SS	5	10	2	3	2	0	0	1	1	4	0-0	.300	.364	.500	0	1.000
1997—Buffalo (A.A.)	SS-2B-OF	73	266	51	78	12	0	4	13	37	45	20-8	.293	.383	.383	23	.942
—Cleveland (A.L.)	SS-2B	8	9	2	1	0	0	0	0	0	1	1-0	.111	.200	.111	0	1.000
—Indianapolis (A.A.)■	2B-SS	19	71	12	19	6	1	0	7	10	17	4-1	.268	.361	.380	5	.948
—Cincinnati (N.L.)	SS-2B	12	27	6	6	2	1	1	2	4	7	1-1	.222	.323	.481	1	.971
1998—Cincinnati (N.L.)	SS-OF	13	38	4	12	5	0	0	7	6	4	2-0	.316	.400	.447	1	.976
—Indianapolis (I.L.)	SS-OF	131	517	102	135	36	10	6	49	62	125	25-10	.261	.349	.404	†44	.938
1999—San Diego (N.L.)■	SS-2B-OF	133	388	56	87	20	2	9	39	53	105	34-10	.224	.320	.356	26	.948
2000—San Diego (N.L.)	SS-2B-OF	138	470	68	120	27	6	6	37	62	108	28-6	.255	.345	.377	25	.960
2001—San Diego (N.L.)	2B-SS-OF	122	440	67	106	21	6	4	38	44	128	23-6	.241	.316	.343	8	.986
—Portland (PCL)	SS	3	10	4	3	3	0	0	0	3	1	0-1	.300	.462	.600	0	1.000
2002—Detroit (A.L.)■	2-O-S-D-3	81	245	31	63	20	1	1	25	21	36	12-3	.257	.320	.359	8	.972
American League totals (3 years)		94	264	35	67	22	1	1	26	22	41	13-3	.254	.317	.356	8	.975
National League totals (5 years)		418	1363	201	331	75	15	20	123	169	352	88-23	.243	.330	.364	61	.966
Major League totals (7 years)		512	1627	236	398	97	16	21	149	191	393	101-26	.245	.328	.363	69	.967

JACKSON, MIKE — P

PERSONAL: Born December 22, 1964, in Houston. ... 6-2/215. ... Throws right, bats right. ... Full name: Michael Ray Jackson.

HIGH SCHOOL: Forest Brook (Houston).

JUNIOR COLLEGE: Hill Junior College (Texas).

TRANSACTIONS/CAREER NOTES: Selected by Philadelphia Phillies organization in 29th round of free-agent draft (June 6, 1983); did not sign. ... Selected by Phillies organization in secondary phase of free-agent draft (January 17, 1984). ... On Philadelphia disabled list (August 6-21, 1987). ... Traded by Phillies with OF Glenn Wilson and OF Dave Brundage to Seattle Mariners for OF Phil Bradley and P Tim Fortugno (December 9, 1987). ... Traded by Mariners with P Bill Swift and P Dave Burba to San Francisco Giants for OF Kevin Mitchell and P Mike Remlinger (December 11, 1991). ... On disabled list (July 24-August 9, 1993; June 17-July 2 and July 7, 1994-remainder of season). ... Granted free agency (October 17, 1994). ... Signed by Cincinnati Reds (April 8, 1995). ... On Cincinnati disabled list (April 20-June 5, 1995); included rehabilitation assignments to Chattanooga (May 21-30) and Indianapolis (May 30-June 5). ... Granted free agency (November 3, 1995). ... Signed by Mariners (February 2, 1996). ... Granted free agency (October 30, 1996). ... Signed by Cleveland Indians (December 12, 1996). ... Granted free agency (October 28, 1999). ... Signed by Phillies (December 7, 1999). ... On disabled list (March 31, 2000-entire season). ... Granted free agency (October 14, 2000). ... Signed by Houston Astros (December 14, 2000). ... Granted free agency (November 5, 2001). ... Signed by Minnesota Twins organization (January 23, 2002). ... On disabled list (July 23-August 15, 2002). ... Granted free agency (October 28, 2002).

STATISTICAL NOTES: Led Carolina League with seven balks in 1985. ... Tied for N.L. lead with eight balks in 1987. ... Led A.L. with 10 intentional bases on balls issued in 1988. ... Tied for A.L. lead with three balks in 1998.
CAREER HITTING (MLB): 5-for-28 (.179), 3 R, 2 2B, 0 3B, 0 HR, 1 RBI.

Year	League	W	L	Pct.	ERA	G	GS	CG	ShO	Sv.-Opp.	IP	H	R	ER	HR	BB-IBB	SO
1984—	Spartanburg (S.Atl.)	7	2	.778	2.68	14	0	0	0	0-...	80.2	53	35	24	8	50-0	77
1985—	Peninsula (Caro.)	7	9	.438	4.60	31	18	0	0	1-...	125.1	127	71	64	11	53-1	96
1986—	Reading (East.)	2	3	.400	1.66	30	0	0	0	6-...	43.1	25	9	8	1	22-2	42
	—Portland (PCL)	3	1	.750	3.18	17	0	0	0	3-...	22.2	18	8	8	2	13-4	23
	—Philadelphia (N.L.)	0	0	...	3.38	9	0	0	0	0-1	13.1	12	5	5	2	4-1	3
1987—	Philadelphia (N.L.)	3	10	.231	4.20	55	7	0	0	1-2	109.1	88	55	51	16	56-6	93
	—Maine (I.L.)	1	0	1.000	0.82	2	2	0	0	0-...	11.0	9	2	1	0	5-1	13
1988—	Seattle (A.L.)■	6	5	.545	2.63	62	0	0	0	4-11	99.1	74	37	29	10	43-10	76
1989—	Seattle (A.L.)	4	6	.400	3.17	65	0	0	0	7-10	99.1	81	43	35	8	54-6	94
1990—	Seattle (A.L.)	5	7	.417	4.54	63	0	0	0	3-12	77.1	64	42	39	8	44-12	69
1991—	Seattle (A.L.)	7	7	.500	3.25	72	0	0	0	14-22	88.2	64	35	32	5	34-11	74
1992—	San Francisco (N.L.)■	6	6	.500	3.73	67	0	0	0	2-3	82.0	76	35	34	7	33-10	80
1993—	San Francisco (N.L.)	6	6	.500	3.03	*81	0	0	0	1-6	77.1	58	28	26	7	24-6	70
1994—	San Francisco (N.L.)	3	2	.600	1.49	36	0	0	0	4-6	42.1	23	8	7	4	11-0	51
1995—	Chattanooga (Sou.)■	0	0	...	0.00	3	2	0	0	0-...	3.0	2	0	0	0	0-0	2
	—Indianapolis (A.A.)	0	0	...	0.00	2	1	0	0	0-...	2.0	0	0	0	0	0-0	1
	—Cincinnati (N.L.)	6	1	.857	2.39	40	0	0	0	2-4	49.0	38	13	13	5	19-1	41
1996—	Seattle (A.L.)■	1	1	.500	3.63	73	0	0	0	6-8	72.0	61	32	29	11	24-3	70
1997—	Cleveland (A.L.)■	2	5	.286	3.24	71	0	0	0	15-17	75.0	59	33	27	3	29-5	74
1998—	Cleveland (A.L.)	1	1	.500	1.55	69	0	0	0	40-45	64.0	43	11	11	4	13-0	55
1999—	Cleveland (A.L.)	3	4	.429	4.06	72	0	0	0	39-43	68.2	60	32	31	11	26-1	55
2000—	Philadelphia (N.L.)■									Did not play.							
2001—	Houston (N.L.)■	5	3	.625	4.70	67	0	0	0	4-9	69.0	68	36	36	14	22-3	46
2002—	Minnesota (A.L.)■	2	3	.400	3.27	58	0	0	0	0-2	55.0	59	20	20	5	13-3	29
A.L. totals (9 years)		31	39	.443	3.26	605	0	0	0	128-170	699.1	565	285	253	65	280-51	596
N.L. totals (7 years)		29	28	.509	3.50	355	7	0	0	14-31	442.1	363	180	172	55	169-27	384
Major League totals (16 years)		60	67	.472	3.35	960	7	0	0	142-201	1141.2	928	465	425	120	449-78	980

DIVISION SERIES RECORD

NOTES: Shares A.L. single-series record for most saves—3.

Year	League	W	L	Pct.	ERA	G	GS	CG	ShO	Sv.-Opp.	IP	H	R	ER	HR	BB-IBB	SO
1995—	Cincinnati (N.L.)	0	0	...	0.00	3	0	0	0	0-0	3.2	4	0	0	0	0-0	1
1997—	Cleveland (A.L.)	1	0	1.000	0.00	4	0	0	0	0-0	4.1	3	0	0	0	1-0	5
1998—	Cleveland (A.L.)	0	0	...	4.50	3	0	0	0	3-3	4.0	3	2	2	1	1-0	1
1999—	Cleveland (A.L.)	0	0	...	4.50	2	0	0	0	0-0	2.0	2	1	1	0	1-1	1
2001—	Houston (N.L.)	0	1	.000	27.00	2	0	0	0	0-1	.2	3	3	2	0	0-0	1
2002—	Minnesota (A.L.)	0	0	...	0.00	1	0	0	0	0-0	.2	1	0	0	0	0-0	0
Division series totals (6 years)		1	1	.500	2.93	15	0	0	0	3-4	15.1	16	6	5	1	3-1	9

CHAMPIONSHIP SERIES RECORD

Year	League	W	L	Pct.	ERA	G	GS	CG	ShO	Sv.-Opp.	IP	H	R	ER	HR	BB-IBB	SO
1995—	Cincinnati (N.L.)	0	1	.000	23.14	3	0	0	0	0-0	2.1	5	6	6	1	4-2	1
1997—	Cleveland (A.L.)	0	0	...	0.00	5	0	0	0	0-0	4.1	1	0	0	0	1-0	7
1998—	Cleveland (A.L.)	0	0	...	0.00	1	0	0	0	1-1	1.0	0	0	0	0	0-0	2
2002—	Minnesota (A.L.)	0	0	...	27.00	3	0	0	0	0-0	1.0	5	3	3	0	2-1	2
Champ. series totals (4 years)		0	1	.000	9.35	12	0	0	0	1-1	8.2	11	9	9	1	7-3	12

WORLD SERIES RECORD

Year	League	W	L	Pct.	ERA	G	GS	CG	ShO	Sv.-Opp.	IP	H	R	ER	HR	BB-IBB	SO
1997—	Cleveland (A.L.)	0	0	...	1.93	4	0	0	0	0-1	4.2	5	1	1	0	3-1	4

JACKSON, RYAN 1B/OF

PERSONAL: Born November 15, 1971, in Orlando, Fla. ... 6-2/200. ... Bats left, throws left. ... Full name: Ryan DeWitte Jackson.
HIGH SCHOOL: Cardinal Mooney (Sarasota, Fla.).
COLLEGE: Duke.
TRANSACTIONS/CAREER NOTES: Selected by Florida Marlins organization in seventh round of free-agent draft (June 2, 1994). ... On Kane County disabled list (April 5-August 1, 1996). ... On Portland disabled list (August 1-26, 1996). ... Claimed on waivers by Seattle Mariners (April 2, 1999). ... Released by Mariners (December 21, 1999). ... Signed by Tampa Bay Devil Rays organization (January 14, 2000). ... Granted free agency (October 18, 2000). ... Signed by Detroit Tigers organization (January 18, 2001). ... Granted free agency (October 15, 2001). ... Re-signed by Tigers organization (December 16, 2001). ... On Toledo disabled list (April 18-28, 2002). ... Released by Tigers (September 30, 2002).
STATISTICAL NOTES: Tied for Midwest League lead with seven intentional bases on balls received in 1995. ... Led International League first basemen with 1,195 putouts, 96 assists, 1,303 total chances and 112 double plays in 2000. ... Career major league grand slams: 1.
2002 GAMES PLAYED BY POSITION (MLB): OF—3.

			BATTING														FIELDING	
Year	Team (League)	Pos.	G	AB	R	H	2B	3B	HR	RBI	BB	SO	SB-CS	Avg.	OBP	SLG	E	Avg.
1994—	Elmira (NY-Penn)	OF-1B	72	276	46	80	18	1	6	41	22	40	4-3	.290	.338	.428	7	.965
1995—	Kane County (Midw.)	OF-1B	132	471	78	138	*39	6	10	82	67	74	13-8	.293	.382	.465	7	.989
1996—	GC Marlins (GCL)	1B-OF	8	26	5	9	0	0	0	7	1	3	2-0	.346	.393	.346	0	1.000
	—Brevard County (FSL)	1B	6	26	4	8	2	0	1	4	1	7	1-0	.308	.333	.500	2	.938
1997—	Portland (East.)	OF-1B	134	491	87	153	28	4	26	98	51	85	2-5	.312	.380	.544	5	.979
1998—	Florida (N.L.)	1B-OF-DH	111	260	26	65	15	1	5	31	20	73	1-1	.250	.305	.373	10	.973
	—Charlotte (I.L.)	1B-OF	13	50	5	19	4	0	2	11	4	14	2-0	.380	.426	.580	0	1.000
1999—	Tacoma (PCL)■	1B-DH-OF	105	409	57	126	25	2	8	62	36	64	12-3	.308	.360	.438	9	.988
	—Seattle (A.L.)	1B-OF	32	68	4	16	3	0	0	10	6	19	3-3	.235	.299	.279	2	.989
2000—	Durham (I.L.)■	1B	139	502	69	156	38	2	18	85	50	112	6-4	.311	.368	.502	12	.991
2001—	Detroit (A.L.)■	1B-OF-DH	79	118	19	25	4	2	2	11	5	26	3-1	.212	.250	.331	2	.988
	—Toledo (I.L.)	OF-1B	9	35	2	10	1	0	1	9	5	6	0-0	.286	.375	.400	1	.955
2002—	Toledo (I.L.)	OF-1B	104	420	40	114	35	1	8	50	13	84	5-3	.271	.297	.417	2	.993
	—Detroit (A.L.)	OF	4	6	0	2	1	1	0	0	1	2	0-0	.333	.429	.833	0	1.000
American League totals (3 years)			115	192	23	43	8	3	2	21	12	47	6-4	.224	.274	.328	4	.989
National League totals (1 year)			111	260	26	65	15	1	5	31	20	73	1-1	.250	.305	.373	10	.973
Major League totals (4 years)			226	452	49	108	23	4	7	52	32	120	7-5	.239	.292	.354	14	.981

JAMES, DELVIN — P — DEVIL RAYS

PERSONAL: Born January 3, 1978, in Nacogdoches, Texas. ... 6-4/240. ... Throws right, bats right. ... Full name: Delvin Dewayne James.
HIGH SCHOOL: Nacogdoches (Texas).
TRANSACTIONS/CAREER NOTES: Selected by Tampa Bay Devil Rays organization in 14th round of free-agent draft (June 4, 1996). ... On Tampa Bay disabled list (May 9-June 13, 2002). ... On Orlando disabled list (June 26-July 30, 2002). ... On Durham disabled list (Spetember 3-10, 2002).
CAREER HITTING (MLB): 0-for-0 (.000), 0 R, 0 2B, 0 3B, 0 HR, 0 RBI.

Year League	W	L	Pct.	ERA	G	GS	CG	ShO	Sv.-Opp.	IP	H	R	ER	HR	BB-IBB	SO
1996—GC Devil Rays (GCL)	2	8	.200	8.87	11	11	1	0	0-...	47.2	64	52	47	0	21-0	40
1997—Princeton (Appl.)	4	4	.500	4.94	20	5	0	0	0-...	58.1	71	57	32	11	24-1	46
1998—St. Petersburg (FSL)	0	0	...	10.80	1	0	0	0	0-...	1.2	2	2	2	0	0-0	0
—Charleston, S.C. (S.Atl.)	2	0	1.000	5.40	7	0	0	0	0-...	8.1	12	5	5	0	2-0	8
—Hudson Valley (NY-Penn)	7	4	.636	2.98	15	15	0	0	0-...	81.2	71	39	27	2	32-0	64
1999—Charleston, S.C. (S.Atl.)	8	8	.500	3.64	25	25	1	0	0-...	158.1	142	76	64	13	33-1	106
—St. Petersburg (FSL)	3	0	1.000	3.18	3	2	0	0	0-...	17.0	18	6	6	0	4-0	6
2000—St. Petersburg (FSL)	7	9	.438	4.26	22	22	3	1	0-...	137.1	142	74	65	10	27-2	74
—Orlando (Sou.)	1	3	.250	2.92	6	6	1	0	0-...	37.0	31	15	12	3	7-0	26
2001—Orlando (Sou.)	2	0	1.000	1.65	7	7	0	0	0-...	43.2	25	8	8	1	9-0	31
—Durham (I.L.)	3	7	.300	4.80	31	9	1	0	0-...	84.1	99	51	45	8	27-1	51
2002—Durham (I.L.)	2	1	.667	3.93	7	7	0	0	0-...	34.1	41	15	15	4	4-0	26
—Tampa Bay (A.L.)	0	3	.000	6.55	8	6	0	0	0-0	34.1	40	25	25	5	15-1	17
—Orlando (Sou.)	1	2	.333	3.55	3	1	0	0	0-...	12.2	12	7	5	2	2-0	13
Major League totals (1 year)	0	3	.000	6.55	8	6	0	0	0-0	34.1	40	25	25	5	15-1	17

JAMES, MIKE — P — DEVIL RAYS

PERSONAL: Born August 15, 1967, in Fort Walton Beach, Fla. ... 6-3/205. ... Throws right, bats right. ... Full name: Michael Elmo James.
HIGH SCHOOL: Fort Walton Beach (Fla.).
JUNIOR COLLEGE: Lurleen B. Wallace State Junior College (Ala.).
TRANSACTIONS/CAREER NOTES: Selected by Los Angeles Dodgers organization in 43rd round of free-agent draft (June 2, 1987). ... On Albuquerque disabled list (July 12-August 26, 1992). ... On Vero Beach disabled list (July 2-9, 1993). ... Traded by Dodgers to California Angels for OF Reggie Williams (October 26, 1993). ... On California disabled list (May 11-June 1, 1995); included rehabilitation assignment to Lake Elsinore (May 25-June 1). ... Angels franchise renamed Anaheim Angels for 1997 season. ... On disabled list (July 3-27, 1997 and May 5, 1998-remainder of season). ... On Anaheim disabled list (March 24-September 7, 1999); included rehabilitation assignment to Lake Elsinore (July 31-September 3). ... Released by Angels (September 7, 1999). ... Signed by St. Louis Cardinals organization (October 15, 1999). ... On St. Louis disabled list (May 26-June 20, 2000); included rehabilitation assignment to Memphis (June 18-20). ... On St. Louis disabled list (July 7-September 1, 2001); included rehabilitation assignment to Memphis (August 8-September 1). ... Granted free agency (November 5, 2001). ... Signed by Colorado Rockies organization (January 30, 2002). ... Released by Rockies (July 21, 2002). ... Signed by Tampa Bay Devil Rays organization (November 6, 2002).
MISCELLANEOUS: Scored run in only appearance as pinch runner (2000).
CAREER HITTING (MLB): 0-for-2 (.000), 1 R, 0 2B, 0 3B, 0 HR, 0 RBI.

Year League	W	L	Pct.	ERA	G	GS	CG	ShO	Sv.-Opp.	IP	H	R	ER	HR	BB-IBB	SO
1988—Great Falls (Pio.)	7	1	*.875	3.76	14	12	0	0	0-...	67.0	61	36	28	7	41-0	59
1989—Bakersfield (Calif.)	11	8	.579	3.78	27	27	1	1	0-...	159.2	144	82	67	11	78-1	127
1990—San Antonio (Texas)	11	4	.733	3.32	26	26	3	0	0-...	157.0	144	73	58	14	78-1	97
1991—San Antonio (Texas)	9	5	.643	4.53	15	15	2	1	0-...	89.1	88	54	45	10	51-1	74
—Albuquerque (PCL)	1	3	.250	6.60	13	8	0	0	0-...	45.0	51	36	33	7	30-0	39
1992—Albuquerque (PCL)	2	1	.667	5.59	18	6	0	0	1-...	46.2	55	35	29	4	22-0	33
—San Antonio (Texas)	2	1	.667	2.67	8	8	0	0	0-...	54.0	39	16	16	3	20-0	52
1993—Albuquerque (PCL)	1	0	1.000	7.47	16	0	0	0	2-...	31.1	38	28	26	5	19-3	32
—Vero Beach (FSL)	2	3	.400	4.92	30	1	0	0	5-...	60.1	54	37	33	2	33-5	60
1994—Vancouver (PCL)■	5	3	.625	5.22	37	10	0	0	8-...	91.1	101	56	53	15	34-1	66
1995—California (A.L.)	3	0	1.000	3.88	46	0	0	0	1-2	55.2	49	27	24	6	26-2	36
—Lake Elsinore (Calif.)	0	0	...	9.53	5	1	0	0	0-...	5.2	9	6	6	1	3-0	8
1996—California (A.L.)	5	5	.500	2.67	69	0	0	0	1-6	81.0	62	27	24	7	42-7	65
1997—Anaheim (A.L.)	5	5	.500	4.31	58	0	0	0	7-13	62.2	69	32	30	3	28-4	57
1998—Anaheim (A.L.)	0	0	...	1.93	11	0	0	0	0-0	14.0	10	3	3	0	7-0	12
1999—Lake Elsinore (Calif.)	0	0	...	5.79	3	3	0	0	0-...	9.1	12	6	6	0	0-0	6
—Edmonton (PCL)	1	2	.333	8.64	8	1	0	0	0-...	8.1	16	14	8	3	2-0	3
2000—Memphis (PCL)■	2	1	.667	0.93	8	0	0	0	1-...	9.2	6	3	1	1	4-0	8
—St. Louis (N.L.)	2	2	.500	3.16	51	0	0	0	2-5	51.1	40	22	18	7	24-2	41
2001—St. Louis (N.L.)	1	2	.333	5.21	40	0	0	0	0-0	38.0	43	24	22	5	17-2	26
—Memphis (PCL)	0	2	.000	4.00	10	0	0	0	0-...	9.0	10	6	4	1	4-1	9
2002—Colo. Springs (PCL)■	1	1	.500	8.13	24	0	0	0	1-...	31.0	38	31	28	5	16-0	25
—Colorado (N.L.)	0	0	...	5.56	13	0	0	0	0-0	11.1	12	9	7	2	5-0	10
A.L. totals (4 years)	13	10	.565	3.42	184	0	0	0	9-21	213.1	190	89	81	16	103-13	170
N.L. totals (3 years)	3	4	.429	4.20	104	0	0	0	2-5	100.2	95	55	47	14	46-4	77
Major League totals (7 years)	16	14	.533	3.67	288	0	0	0	11-26	314.0	285	144	128	30	149-17	247

DIVISION SERIES RECORD

Year League	W	L	Pct.	ERA	G	GS	CG	ShO	Sv.-Opp.	IP	H	R	ER	HR	BB-IBB	SO
2000—St. Louis (N.L.)	1	0	1.000	0.00	2	0	0	0	0-0	4.1	1	0	0	0	1-0	1

CHAMPIONSHIP SERIES RECORD

Year League	W	L	Pct.	ERA	G	GS	CG	ShO	Sv.-Opp.	IP	H	R	ER	HR	BB-IBB	SO
2000—St. Louis (N.L.)	0	0	...	15.43	4	0	0	0	0-0	2.1	5	4	4	3	1-0	0

JARVIS, KEVIN P PADRES

PERSONAL: Born August 1, 1969, in Lexington, Ky. ... 6-2/200. ... Throws right, bats left. ... Full name: Kevin Thomas Jarvis.
HIGH SCHOOL: Tates Creek (Lexington, Ky.).
COLLEGE: Wake Forest.
TRANSACTIONS/CAREER NOTES: Selected by Cincinnati Reds organization in 21st round of free-agent draft (June 3, 1991). ... Claimed on waivers by Detroit Tigers (May 2, 1997). ... Claimed on waivers by Minnesota Twins (May 9, 1997). ... Claimed on waivers by Tigers (June 17, 1997). ... On Detroit disabled list (June 25-July 14, 1997); included rehabilitation assignment to Toledo (July 4-14). ... Released by Tigers (December 12, 1997). ... Signed by Chunichi Dragons of the Japan Central League (January 23, 1998). ... Signed by Reds organization (August 27, 1998). ... Released by Reds (September 9, 1998). ... Signed by Oakland Athletics organization (January 4, 1999). ... On Oakland disabled list (April 19-June 4, 1999); included rehabilitation assignment to Modesto (May 28-June 4). ... Granted free agency (October 8, 1999). ... Signed by Colorado Rockies organization (December 1, 1999). ... On Colorado disabled list (July 28-September 1, 2000); included rehabilitation assignment to Colorado Springs (August 12-September 1). ... Granted free agency (December 21, 2000). ... Signed by San Diego Padres (January 5, 2001). ... On San Diego disabled list (April 18-May 5, May 10-June 27 and July 12, 2002-remainder of season); included rehabilitation assignments to Mobile (June 17-22) and Lake Elsinore (June 23-25).
RECORDS: Shares N.L. single-inning record for most consecutive home runs allowed—3 (August 3, 2001, sixth inning; and July 2, 2002, second inning).
MISCELLANEOUS: Appeared in one game as pinch runner (2000). ... Appeared in two games as pinch hitter (2001).
CAREER HITTING (MLB): 27-for-166 (.163), 16 R, 6 2B, 0 3B, 1 HR, 12 RBI.

Year League	W	L	Pct.	ERA	G	GS	CG	ShO	Sv.-Opp.	IP	H	R	ER	HR	BB-IBB	SO
1991—Princeton (Appl.)	5	6	.455	2.42	13	13	4	•1	0-...	85.2	73	34	23	6	29-3	79
1992—Cedar Rapids (Midw.)	0	0	...	0.00	1	0	0	0	0-...	1.0	1	0	0	0	0-0	0
—Charleston, W.Va. (S.Atl.)	6	8	.429	3.11	28	18	2	1	0-...	133.0	123	59	46	3	37-1	131
1993—Winston-Salem (Caro.)	8	7	.533	3.41	21	20	2	1	0-...	145.0	133	68	55	13	48-2	101
—Chattanooga (Sou.)	3	1	.750	1.69	7	3	2	0	0-...	37.1	26	7	7	0	11-0	18
1994—Cincinnati (N.L.)	1	1	.500	7.13	6	3	0	0	0-0	17.2	22	14	14	4	5-0	10
—Indianapolis (A.A.)	10	2	•.833	3.54	21	20	2	0	0-...	132.1	136	55	52	13	34-2	90
1995—Indianapolis (A.A.)	4	2	.667	4.45	10	10	2	1	0-...	60.2	62	33	30	2	18-1	37
—Cincinnati (N.L.)	3	4	.429	5.70	19	11	1	1	0-0	79.0	91	56	50	13	32-2	33
1996—Indianapolis (A.A.)	4	3	.571	5.06	8	8	0	0	0-...	42.2	45	27	24	3	12-0	32
—Cincinnati (N.L.)	8	9	.471	5.98	24	20	2	1	0-0	120.1	152	93	80	17	43-5	63
1997—Cincinnati (N.L.)	0	1	.000	10.13	9	0	0	0	1-1	13.1	21	16	15	4	7-0	12
—Minnesota (A.L.)■	0	0	...	12.46	6	2	0	0	0-0	13.0	23	18	18	4	8-0	9
—Detroit (A.L.)■	0	3	.000	5.40	17	3	0	0	0-0	41.2	55	28	25	9	14-0	27
—Toledo (I.L.)	0	1	.000	6.75	2	2	0	0	0-...	8.0	7	6	6	0	4-0	5
1998—Chunichi (Jap. Cen.)■	1	2	.333	4.41	4	3	0	0	0-...	16.1	18	8	8	...	5-...	7
—Indianapolis (I.L.)■	1	0	1.000	9.00	2	2	0	0	0-...	7.0	10	7	7	3	1-0	5
1999—Oakland (A.L.)■	0	1	.000	11.57	4	1	0	0	0-0	14.0	28	19	18	6	6-0	11
—Modesto (Calif.)	0	0	...	1.29	2	2	0	0	0-...	7.0	4	1	1	0	1-0	10
—Vancouver (PCL)	10	2	.833	3.41	17	16	2	1	0-...	103.0	110	47	39	14	26-0	64
2000—Colorado Springs (PCL)■	3	2	.600	0.69	7	7	0	0	0-...	39.0	18	6	3	1	13-0	18
—Colorado (N.L.)	3	4	.429	5.95	24	19	0	0	0-0	115.0	138	83	76	26	33-3	60
2001—San Diego (N.L.)■	12	11	.522	4.79	32	32	1	1	0-0	193.1	189	107	103	•37	49-4	133
2002—San Diego (N.L.)	2	4	.333	4.37	7	7	0	0	0-0	35.0	36	19	17	5	10-1	24
—Mobile (Sou.)	0	0	...	0.00	1	1	0	0	0-...	3.0	2	0	0	0	0-0	3
—Lake Elsinore (Calif.)	1	0	1.000	0.00	1	1	0	0	0-...	5.0	2	0	0	0	1-0	1
A.L. totals (2 years)	0	4	.000	8.00	27	6	0	0	0-0	68.2	106	65	61	19	28-0	47
N.L. totals (7 years)	29	34	.460	5.57	121	92	4	3	1-1	573.2	649	388	355	106	179-15	335
Major League totals (8 years)	29	38	.433	5.83	148	98	4	3	1-1	642.1	755	453	416	125	207-15	382

JENKINS, GEOFF OF BREWERS

PERSONAL: Born July 21, 1974, in Olympia, Wash. ... 6-1/213. ... Bats left, throws right. ... Full name: Geoffrey Scott Jenkins.
HIGH SCHOOL: Cordova Senior (Rancho Cordova, Calif.).
COLLEGE: Southern California.
TRANSACTIONS/CAREER NOTES: Selected by Milwaukee Brewers organization in first round (ninth pick overall) of free-agent draft (June 1, 1995). ... On El Paso disabled list (May 8-July 23, 1996). ... On disabled list (July 4-August 11, 1997). ... On disabled list (May 7-29, 2000). ... On Milwaukee disabled list (May 2-19 and July 29-August 28, 2001); included rehabilitation assignment to Beloit (August 27-28). ... On disabled list (June 18, 2002-remainder of season).
RECORDS: Shares major league record for most home runs in two consecutive games—5 (April 28 [3] and 29 [2], 2001).
STATISTICAL NOTES: Hit three home runs in one game (April 28, 2001). ... Career major league grand slams: 1.
2002 GAMES PLAYED BY POSITION (MLB): OF—66.

		BATTING														FIELDING	
Year Team (League)	Pos.	G	AB	R	H	2B	3B	HR	RBI	BB	SO	SB-CS	Avg.	OBP	SLG	E	Avg.
1995—Helena (Pio.)	OF	7	28	2	9	0	1	0	9	3	11	0-2	.321	.375	.393	0	1.000
—Stockton (Calif.)	OF	13	47	13	12	2	0	3	12	10	12	2-0	.255	.373	.489	2	.895
—El Paso (Texas)	OF	22	79	12	22	4	2	1	13	8	23	3-1	.278	.341	.418	7	.857
1996—El Paso (Texas)	DH	22	77	17	22	5	4	1	11	12	21	1-2	.286	.391	.494	...	...
—Stockton (Calif.)	DH-OF	37	138	27	48	8	4	3	25	20	32	3-3	.348	.433	.529	0	1.000
1997—Tucson (PCL)	OF-SS	93	347	44	82	24	3	10	56	33	87	0-2	.236	.308	.409	5	.961
1998—Louisville (I.L.)	OF	55	215	38	71	10	4	7	52	14	39	1-1	.330	.381	.512	2	.979
—Milwaukee (N.L.)	OF	84	262	33	60	12	1	9	28	20	61	1-3	.229	.288	.385	4	.968
1999—Milwaukee (N.L.)	OF	135	447	70	140	43	3	21	82	35	87	5-1	.313	.371	.564	7	.974
2000—Milwaukee (N.L.)	OF	135	512	100	155	36	4	34	94	33	135	11-1	.303	.360	.588	7	.975
2001—Milwaukee (N.L.)	OF	105	397	60	105	21	1	20	63	36	120	4-2	.264	.334	.474	3	.986
—Beloit (Midw.)	OF	1	3	1	1	1	0	0	1	1	1	0-0	.333	.500	.667	0	...
2002—Milwaukee (N.L.)	OF	67	243	35	59	17	1	10	29	22	60	1-2	.243	.320	.444	1	.992
Major League totals (5 years)		526	1861	298	519	129	10	94	296	146	463	22-9	.279	.342	.510	22	.979

JENNINGS, JASON — P — ROCKIES

PERSONAL: Born July 17, 1978, in Dallas. ... 6-2/242. ... Throws right, bats left. ... Full name: Jason Ryan Jennings. ... Son of Jim Jennings, member of Texas Rangers organization.
HIGH SCHOOL: Dr. Ralph H. Poteet (Mesquite, Texas).
COLLEGE: Baylor.
TRANSACTIONS/CAREER NOTES: Selected by Colorado Rockies organization in first round (16th pick overall) of free-agent draft (June 2, 1999).
HONORS: Named N.L. Rookie Pitcher of the Year by The Sporting News (2002). ... Named N.L. Rookie of the Year by Baseball Writers' Association of America (2002).
STATISTICAL NOTES: Pitched shutout in first major league game (August 23, 2001).
CAREER HITTING (MLB): 23-for-77 (.299), 8 R, 5 2B, 0 3B, 1 HR, 13 RBI.

Year League	W	L	Pct.	ERA	G	GS	CG	ShO	Sv.-Opp.	IP	H	R	ER	HR	BB-IBB	SO
1999—Portland (N'West)	1	0	1.000	1.00	2	2	0	0	0-...	9.0	5	1	1	0	2-0	11
—Asheville (S.Atl.)	2	2	.500	3.70	12	12	0	0	0-...	58.1	55	27	24	3	8-0	69
2000—Salem (Caro.)	7	10	.412	3.47	22	22	3	1	0-...	150.1	136	66	58	6	42-0	133
—Carolina (Sou.)	1	3	.250	3.44	6	6	0	0	0-...	36.2	32	19	14	4	11-0	33
2001—Carolina (Sou.)	2	0	1.000	2.88	4	4	0	0	0-...	25.0	25	9	8	1	8-0	24
—Colorado Springs (PCL)	7	8	.467	4.72	22	22	4	0	0-...	131.2	145	80	69	9	41-0	110
—Colorado (N.L.)	4	1	.800	4.58	7	7	1	1	0-0	39.1	42	21	20	2	19-0	26
2002—Colorado (N.L.)	16	8	.667	4.52	32	32	0	0	0-0	185.1	201	102	93	26	70-2	127
Major League totals (2 years)	20	9	.690	4.53	39	39	1	1	0-0	224.2	243	123	113	28	89-2	153

JENSEN, MARCUS — C

PERSONAL: Born December 14, 1972, in Oakland. ... 6-4/204. ... Bats both, throws right. ... Full name: Marcus C. Jensen.
HIGH SCHOOL: Skyline (Oakland).
TRANSACTIONS/CAREER NOTES: Selected by San Francisco Giants organization in supplemental round ("sandwich pick" between first and second round, 33rd pick overall) of free-agent draft (June 4, 1990); pick received as part of compensation for San Diego Padres signing Type A free-agent P Craig Lefferts. ... On disabled list (June 1-14, 1993). ... Traded by Giants to Detroit Tigers for C Brian Johnson (July 16, 1997). ... Granted free agency (July 22, 1997). ... Re-signed by Tigers (July 26, 1997). ... Released by Tigers (March 25, 1998). ... Signed by Milwaukee Brewers organization (April 5, 1998). ... On Louisville disabled list (April 9-21, 1998). ... Released by Brewers (September 29, 1998). ... Signed by St. Louis Cardinals organization (January 13, 1999). ... Granted free agency (October 15, 1999). ... Signed by Minnesota Twins organization (January 4, 2000). ... Granted free agency (October 2, 2000). ... Signed by Boston Red Sox organization (May 2, 2001). ... Claimed on waivers by Texas Rangers (June 15, 2001). ... Granted free agency (October 11, 2001). ... Signed by Brewers organization (January 18, 2002). ... Released by Brewers (October 1, 2002).
STATISTICAL NOTES: Tied for Arizona League lead with three intentional bases on balls received in 1991. ... Led California League catchers with 627 putouts and 722 total chances in 1994. ... Led Texas League catchers with 471 putouts and 546 total chances in 1995.
MISCELLANEOUS: Member of 2000 U.S. Olympic baseball team.
2002 GAMES PLAYED BY POSITION (MLB): C—15.

		BATTING														FIELDING	
Year Team (League)	Pos.	G	AB	R	H	2B	3B	HR	RBI	BB	SO	SB-CS	Avg.	OBP	SLG	E	Avg.
1990—Everett (N'West)	C	51	171	21	29	3	0	2	12	24	60	0-1	.170	.290	.222	3	.986
1991—Arizona Giants (Ariz.)	C-1B	48	155	28	44	8	3	2	30	34	22	4-2	.284	.419	.413	7	.973
1992—Clinton (Midw.)	C-1B	86	264	35	62	14	0	4	33	54	87	4-2	.235	.370	.333	10	.982
1993—Clinton (Midw.)	C	104	324	53	85	24	2	11	56	66	98	1-2	.262	.389	.451	7	.990
1994—San Jose (Calif.)	C-DH	118	418	56	101	18	0	7	47	61	100	1-1	.242	.345	.335	9	.988
1995—Shreveport (Texas)	C-DH	95	321	55	91	22	8	4	45	41	68	0-0	.283	.362	.439	5	.991
1996—Phoenix (PCL)	C-DH	120	405	41	107	22	4	5	53	44	95	1-1	.264	.338	.375	8	.988
—San Francisco (N.L.)	C	9	19	4	4	1	0	0	4	8	7	0-0	.211	.444	.263	2	.955
1997—San Francisco (N.L.)	C	30	74	5	11	2	0	1	3	7	23	0-0	.149	.222	.216	2	.983
—Toledo (I.L.)■	C-DH	24	80	5	14	5	0	0	9	9	25	0-0	.175	.258	.238	1	.994
—Detroit (A.L.)	C	8	11	1	2	0	0	0	1	1	5	0-0	.182	.250	.182	1	.964
1998—Louisville (I.L.)■	C-1B	74	230	29	52	13	0	10	33	33	64	0-3	.226	.326	.413	3	.994
—Milwaukee (N.L.)	C	2	2	0	0	0	0	0	0	0	2	0-0	.000	.000	.000	0	1.000
1999—Memphis (PCL)■	C-DH	72	237	38	69	19	4	8	44	30	59	0-0	.291	.379	.506	2	.995
—St. Louis (N.L.)	C	16	34	5	8	5	0	1	1	6	12	0-0	.235	.350	.471	1	.988
2000—Minnesota (A.L.)■	C-DH	52	139	16	29	7	1	3	14	24	36	0-1	.209	.325	.338	2	.993
—Salt Lake (PCL)	C	15	55	10	16	4	0	1	12	11	10	0-2	.291	.420	.418	2	.974
2001—Pawtucket (I.L.)■	C	27	102	11	24	7	2	4	12	6	27	0-0	.235	.278	.461	1	.994
—Boston (A.L.)	C	1	4	0	1	0	0	0	0	0	1	0-0	.250	.250	.250	0	1.000
—Texas (A.L.)■	C	11	25	0	4	1	0	0	2	0	9	0-0	.160	.160	.200	0	1.000
—Oklahoma (PCL)	C	53	188	42	56	10	1	8	25	46	46	0-0	.298	.438	.489	0	1.000
2002—Indianapolis (I.L.)■	C	70	183	24	42	7	0	4	25	33	39	0-0	.230	.347	.333	6	.986
—Milwaukee (N.L.)	C	16	35	2	4	0	0	1	4	4	11	0-0	.114	.200	.200	2	.976
American League totals (3 years)		72	179	17	36	8	1	3	17	25	51	0-1	.201	.299	.307	3	.992
National League totals (5 years)		73	164	16	27	8	0	3	12	25	55	0-0	.165	.274	.268	7	.979
Major League totals (7 years)		145	343	33	63	16	1	6	29	50	106	0-1	.184	.287	.289	10	.985

JENSEN, RYAN — P — GIANTS

PERSONAL: Born September 17, 1975, in Salt Lake City. ... 6-0/205. ... Throws right, bats right. ... Full name: Larry Ryan Jensen.
HIGH SCHOOL: Cottonwood (Salt Lake City).
COLLEGE: Southern Utah.
TRANSACTIONS/CAREER NOTES: Selected by San Francisco Giants organization in eighth round of free-agent draft (June 4, 1996). ... On disabled list (June 21-30, 1999).
CAREER HITTING (MLB): 8-for-68 (.118), 5 R, 2 2B, 0 3B, 0 HR, 4 RBI.

Year	League	W	L	Pct.	ERA	G	GS	CG	ShO	Sv.-Opp.	IP	H	R	ER	HR	BB-IBB	SO
1996—	Bellingham (N'West)	2	4	.333	4.98	13	11	0	0	0-...	47.0	35	30	26	4	38-0	31
1997—	Bakersfield (Calif.)	0	0	...	13.50	1	1	0	0	0-...	1.1	3	2	2	1	0-0	2
	—Salem-Kaizer (N'West)	7	3	.700	5.15	16	•16	0	0	0-...	80.1	87	55	46	•10	32-0	67
1998—	Bakersfield (Calif.)	11	12	.478	3.37	29	27	0	0	0-...	168.1	162	89	63	14	61-3	164
	—Fresno (PCL)	0	0	...	4.76	2	1	0	0	0-...	5.2	4	5	3	2	4-0	6
1999—	Fresno (PCL)	11	10	.524	5.12	27	27	0	0	0-...	156.1	160	96	89	17	68-1	150
2000—	Fresno (PCL)	5	8	.385	5.79	26	26	1	0	0-...	135.1	167	106	87	18	63-0	114
2001—	Fresno (PCL)	11	2	.846	3.48	20	17	1	1	0-...	106.0	97	43	41	11	34-0	95
	—San Francisco (N.L.)	1	2	.333	4.25	10	7	0	0	0-0	42.1	44	21	20	5	25-0	26
2002—	San Francisco (N.L.)	13	8	.619	4.51	32	30	1	0	0-0	171.2	183	93	86	21	66-4	105
Major League totals (2 years)		14	10	.583	4.46	42	37	1	0	0-0	214.0	227	114	106	26	91-4	131

JETER, DEREK — SS — YANKEES

PERSONAL: Born June 26, 1974, in Pequannock, N.J. ... 6-3/195. ... Bats right, throws right. ... Full name: Derek Sanderson Jeter.
HIGH SCHOOL: Central (Kalamazoo, Mich.).
COLLEGE: Michigan.
TRANSACTIONS/CAREER NOTES: Selected by New York Yankees organization in first round (sixth pick overall) of free-agent draft (June 1, 1992). ... On New York disabled list (June 3-19, 1998); included rehabilitation assignment to Columbus (June 18-19). ... On New York disabled list (May 12-27, 2000); included rehabilitation assignment to Tampa (May 26-27). ... On disabled list (March 23-April 7, 2001).
RECORDS: Shares major league single-season record for most games with at least one hit—135 (1999). ... Shares A.L. single-season record for fewest putouts by shortstop (150 or more games)—212 (2001). ... Holds A.L. single-season record for fewest assists by shortstop (150 or more games)—343 (2001); and fewest chances accepted by shortstop (150 or more games)—555 (2001).
HONORS: Named Minor League Player of the Year by The Sporting News (1994). ... Named A.L. Rookie Player of the Year by The Sporting News (1996). ... Named A.L. Rookie of the Year by Baseball Writers' Association of America (1996).
STATISTICAL NOTES: Led A.L. shortstops with 457 assists in 1997. ... Had 15-game hitting streak (May 2-20, 1998). ... Had 16-game hitting streak (May 4-22, 1999). ... Had 16-game hitting streak (May 9-25, 2002).
2002 GAMES PLAYED BY POSITION (MLB): SS—156; DH—1.

			BATTING														FIELDING	
Year	Team (League)	Pos.	G	AB	R	H	2B	3B	HR	RBI	BB	SO	SB-CS	Avg.	OBP	SLG	E	Avg.
1992—	GC Yankees (GCL)	SS	47	173	19	35	10	0	3	25	19	36	2-2	.202	.296	.312	12	.943
	—Greensboro (S.Atl.)	SS	11	37	4	9	0	0	1	4	7	16	0-1	.243	.378	.324	9	.813
1993—	Greensboro (S.Atl.)	SS	128	515	85	152	14	11	5	71	56	95	18-9	.295	.374	.394	56	.889
1994—	Tampa (FSL)	SS	69	292	61	96	13	8	0	39	23	30	28-2	.329	.380	.428	12	.961
	—Albany/Colonie (East.)	SS	34	122	17	46	7	2	2	13	15	16	12-2	.377	.446	.516	6	.961
	—Columbus (I.L.)	SS	35	126	25	44	7	1	3	16	20	15	10-4	.349	.439	.492	7	.955
1995—	Columbus (I.L.)	SS	123	486	*96	154	27	9	2	45	61	56	20-12	.317	.394	.422	*29	.953
	—New York (A.L.)	SS	15	48	5	12	4	1	0	7	3	11	0-0	.250	.294	.375	2	.962
1996—	New York (A.L.)	SS	157	582	104	183	25	6	10	78	48	102	14-7	.314	.370	.430	22	.969
1997—	New York (A.L.)	SS	159	654	116	190	31	7	10	70	74	125	23-12	.291	.370	.405	18	.975
1998—	New York (A.L.)	SS	149	626	*127	203	25	8	19	84	57	119	30-6	.324	.384	.481	9	.986
	—Columbus (I.L.)	SS	1	5	2	2	2	0	0	0	0	2	0-0	.400	.400	.800	1	.875
1999—	New York (A.L.)	SS	158	627	134	*219	37	9	24	102	91	116	19-8	.349	.438	.552	14	.978
2000—	New York (A.L.)	SS	148	593	119	201	31	4	15	73	68	99	22-4	.339	.416	.481	24	.961
	—Tampa (FSL)	SS	1	3	2	2	1	0	0	0	0	0	0-0	.667	.667	1.000	0	1.000
2001—	New York (A.L.)	SS	150	614	110	191	35	3	21	74	56	99	27-3	.311	.377	.480	15	.974
2002—	New York (A.L.)	SS-DH	157	644	124	191	26	0	18	75	73	114	32-3	.297	.373	.421	14	.977
Major League totals (8 years)			1093	4388	839	1390	214	38	117	563	470	785	167-43	.317	.389	.463	118	.974

DIVISION SERIES RECORD

RECORDS: Holds A.L. career record for most hits—40.

			BATTING														FIELDING	
Year	Team (League)	Pos.	G	AB	R	H	2B	3B	HR	RBI	BB	SO	SB-CS	Avg.	OBP	SLG	E	Avg.
1996—	New York (A.L.)	SS	4	17	2	7	1	0	0	1	0	2	0-0	.412	.412	.471	1	.947
1997—	New York (A.L.)	SS	5	21	6	7	1	0	2	2	3	5	1-0	.333	.417	.667	0	1.000
1998—	New York (A.L.)	SS	3	9	0	1	0	0	0	0	2	2	0-0	.111	.273	.111	0	1.000
1999—	New York (A.L.)	SS	3	11	3	5	1	1	0	0	2	3	0-0	.455	.538	.727	0	1.000
2000—	New York (A.L.)	SS	5	19	1	4	0	0	0	2	2	3	0-1	.211	.318	.211	0	1.000
2001—	New York (A.L.)	SS	5	18	2	8	1	0	0	1	1	0	0-1	.444	.476	.500	0	1.000
2002—	New York (A.L.)	SS	4	16	6	8	0	0	2	3	2	3	0-0	.500	.526	.875	1	.944
Division series totals (7 years)			29	111	20	40	4	1	4	9	12	18	1-2	.360	.425	.523	2	.984

CHAMPIONSHIP SERIES RECORD

			BATTING														FIELDING	
Year	Team (League)	Pos.	G	AB	R	H	2B	3B	HR	RBI	BB	SO	SB-CS	Avg.	OBP	SLG	E	Avg.
1996—	New York (A.L.)	SS	5	24	5	10	2	0	1	1	0	5	2-0	.417	.417	.625	0	1.000
1998—	New York (A.L.)	SS	6	25	3	5	1	1	0	2	2	5	3-0	.200	.259	.320	0	1.000
1999—	New York (A.L.)	SS	5	20	3	7	1	0	1	3	2	3	0-0	.350	.409	.550	2	.909
2000—	New York (A.L.)	SS	6	22	6	7	0	0	2	5	6	7	1-0	.318	.464	.591	0	1.000
2001—	New York (A.L.)	SS	5	17	0	2	0	0	0	2	2	2	0-0	.118	.200	.118	0	1.000
Championship series totals (5 years)			27	108	17	31	4	1	4	13	12	22	6-0	.287	.355	.454	2	.981

WORLD SERIES RECORD

NOTES: Named Most Valuable Player (2000). ... Member of World Series championship team (1996, 1998, 1999 and 2000).

			BATTING														FIELDING	
Year	Team (League)	Pos.	G	AB	R	H	2B	3B	HR	RBI	BB	SO	SB-CS	Avg.	OBP	SLG	E	Avg.
1996—	New York (A.L.)	SS	6	20	5	5	0	0	0	1	4	6	1-0	.250	.400	.250	2	.949
1998—	New York (A.L.)	SS	4	17	4	6	0	0	0	1	3	3	0-0	.353	.450	.353	0	1.000
1999—	New York (A.L.)	SS	4	17	4	6	1	0	0	1	1	3	3-1	.353	.389	.412	0	1.000
2000—	New York (A.L.)	SS	5	22	6	9	2	1	2	2	3	8	0-0	.409	.480	.864	0	1.000
2001—	New York (A.L.)	SS	7	27	3	4	0	0	1	1	0	6	0-0	.148	.179	.259	0	1.000
World Series totals (5 years)			26	103	22	30	3	1	3	6	11	26	4-1	.291	.371	.427	2	.983

ALL-STAR GAME RECORD

RECORDS: Holds record for highest career batting average—.571 (1998 through 2002, five games, seven at-bats).

NOTES: Named Most Valuable Player (2000).

	AB	R	H	2B	3B	HR	RBI	BB	SO	SB-CS	Avg.	OBP	SLG	E	Avg.
All-Star Game totals (5 years)	7	2	4	1	0	1	3	0	3	0-0	.571	.571	1.143	0	1.000

JIMENEZ, D'ANGELO — SS — WHITE SOX

PERSONAL: Born December 21, 1977, in Santo Domingo, Dominican Republic. ... 6-0/194. ... Bats both, throws right.

TRANSACTIONS/CAREER NOTES: Signed as non-drafted free agent by New York Yankees organization (August 1, 1994). ... On Columbus disabled list (August 6-19, 1999). ... On New York disabled list (March 23-August 24, 2000); included rehabilitation assignments to Gulf Coast Yankees (July 26-31), Tampa (August 1-14) and Columbus (August 15-24). ... Traded by Yankees to San Diego Padres for P Jay Witasick (June 23, 2001). ... Traded by Padres to Chicago White Sox for OF Alex Fernandez and C Humberto Quintero (July 12, 2002).

STATISTICAL NOTES: Led Gulf Coast League shortstops with 95 putouts, 173 assists, 289 total chances and 31 double plays in 1995. ... Led South Atlantic League shortstops with 400 assists and 640 total chances in 1996. ... Led International League shortstops with 188 putouts in 1999.

2002 GAMES PLAYED BY POSITION (MLB): 2B—71; 3B—33; SS—10.

							BATTING										FIELDING	
Year	**Team (League)**	**Pos.**	**G**	**AB**	**R**	**H**	**2B**	**3B**	**HR**	**RBI**	**BB**	**SO**	**SB-CS**	**Avg.**	**OBP**	**SLG**	**E**	**Avg.**
1995—	GC Yankees (GCL)	SS	57	214	41	60	14	*8	2	28	23	31	6-3	.280	.347	.449	21	.927
1996—	Greensboro (S.Atl.)	SS	138	*537	68	131	25	5	6	48	56	113	15-17	.244	.317	.343	*50	.922
1997—	Tampa (FSL)	SS	94	352	52	99	14	6	6	48	50	50	8-14	.281	.368	.406	21	.953
—	Columbus (I.L.)	SS	2	7	1	1	0	0	0	1	0	1	0-0	.143	.125	.143	2	.833
1998—	Norwich (East.)	SS	40	152	21	41	6	2	2	21	25	26	5-5	.270	.378	.375	12	.938
—	Columbus (I.L.)	SS-2B	91	344	55	88	19	4	8	51	46	67	6-6	.256	.341	.404	26	.946
1999—	Columbus (I.L.)	SS-3B-2B	126	526	97	172	32	5	15	88	59	75	26-14	.327	.392	.492	26	.957
—	New York (A.L.)	3B-2B	7	20	3	8	2	0	0	4	3	4	0-0	.400	.478	.500	0	1.000
2000—	GC Yankees (GCL)	2B-SS	4	10	2	1	0	0	0	0	5	1	0-0	.100	.400	.100	2	.900
—	Tampa (FSL)	SS-2B	12	41	8	8	1	1	1	2	8	7	0-0	.195	.320	.341	7	.875
—	Columbus (I.L.)	2B-3B-SS	21	73	11	17	3	1	1	5	7	12	2-0	.233	.309	.342	4	.944
2001—	Columbus (I.L.)	2B-SS-3B	56	214	33	56	11	1	5	19	24	31	5-6	.262	.333	.393	7	.965
—	San Diego (N.L.)■	SS	86	308	45	85	19	0	3	33	39	68	2-3	.276	.355	.367	21	.948
2002—	San Diego (N.L.)	2B-3B-P	87	321	39	77	11	4	3	33	34	63	4-2	.240	.311	.327	12	.968
—	Charlotte (I.L.)■	SS	42	157	24	44	11	1	6	18	24	14	6-2	.280	.372	.478	6	.966
—	Chicago (A.L.)	2B-SS-3B	27	108	22	31	4	3	1	11	16	10	2-1	.287	.384	.407	2	.985
American League totals (2 years)			34	128	25	39	6	3	1	15	19	14	2-1	.305	.399	.422	2	.986
National League totals (2 years)			173	629	84	162	30	4	6	66	73	131	6-5	.258	.333	.347	33	.958
Major League totals (3 years)			207	757	109	201	36	7	7	81	92	145	8-6	.266	.344	.359	35	.962

RECORD AS PITCHER

Year	League	W	L	Pct.	ERA	G	GS	CG	ShO	Sv.-Opp.	IP	H	R	ER	HR	BB-IBB	SO
2002—	San Diego (N.L.)	0	0	...	0.00	1	0	0	0	0-0	1.1	0	0	0	0	0-0	0

JIMENEZ, JASON — P — TIGERS

PERSONAL: Born January 10, 1976, in Modesto, Calif. ... 6-2/208. ... Throws left, bats right. ... Full name: Jason Jon Jimenez.

COLLEGE: San Jose State.

TRANSACTIONS/CAREER NOTES: Selected by Tampa Bay Devil Rays organization in 28th round of free-agent draft (June 3, 1997). ... Claimed on waivers by Detroit Tigers (September 24, 2002).

CAREER HITTING (MLB): 0-for-0 (.000), 0 R, 0 2B, 0 3B, 0 HR, 0 RBI.

Year	League	W	L	Pct.	ERA	G	GS	CG	ShO	Sv.-Opp.	IP	H	R	ER	HR	BB-IBB	SO
1997—	Hudson Valley (NY-Penn)	3	0	1.000	0.28	19	0	0	0	0-...	31.2	16	5	1	1	10-0	31
1998—	St. Petersburg (FSL)	0	2	.000	8.53	13	0	0	0	0-...	19.0	24	20	18	3	10-2	15
—	Hudson Valley (NY-Penn)	5	2	.714	1.60	29	0	0	0	4-...	39.1	20	13	7	1	13-1	55
1999—	St. Petersburg (FSL)	4	4	.500	2.38	41	1	0	0	5-...	56.2	46	23	15	2	21-2	47
2000—	Orlando (Sou.)	5	1	.833	1.94	30	1	0	0	0-...	46.1	29	13	10	4	12-0	53
—	Durham (I.L.)	1	1	.500	4.83	19	1	0	0	0-...	31.2	33	17	17	4	25-0	28
2001—	Orlando (Sou.)	3	3	.500	3.18	35	4	0	0	10-...	51.0	46	20	18	2	24-1	46
—	Durham (I.L.)	0	1	.000	4.70	15	0	0	0	1-...	23.0	23	12	12	4	14-0	25
2002—	Durham (I.L.)	2	2	.500	2.63	44	0	0	0	3-...	51.1	47	21	15	3	16-1	55
—	Tampa Bay (A.L.)	0	0	...	5.40	5	0	0	0	0-0	6.2	9	4	4	2	1-0	5
—	Detroit (A.L.)■	0	0	...	27.00	1	0	0	0	0-0	.2	3	4	2	0	1-0	0
Major League totals (1 year)		0	0	...	7.36	6	0	0	0	0-0	7.1	12	8	6	2	2-0	5

JIMENEZ, JOSE — P — ROCKIES

PERSONAL: Born July 7, 1973, in San Pedro de Macoris, Dominican Republic ... 6-3/228. ... Throws right, bats right. ... Name pronounced he-MEN-ez.

TRANSACTIONS/CAREER NOTES: Signed as non-drafted free agent by St. Louis Cardinals organization (October 21, 1991). ... Traded by Cardinals with P Manny Aybar, P Rick Croushore and SS Brent Butler to Colorado Rockies for P Darryl Kile, P Dave Veres and P Luther Hackman (November 16, 1999). ... On disabled list (July 8-23 and August 20-September 17, 2001).

HONORS: Named Texas League Pitcher of the Year (1998).

STATISTICAL NOTES: Pitched 6-0 no-hit victory for Arkansas against Shreveport (August 27, 1998). ... Pitched 1-0 no-hit victory against Arizona (June 25, 1999).

MISCELLANEOUS: Holds Colorado Rockies all-time record for most saves (82). ... Scored one run in two appearances as pinch runner (1999).

CAREER HITTING (MLB): 7-for-64 (.109), 5 R, 0 2B, 1 3B, 0 HR, 4 RBI.

Year	League	W	L	Pct.	ERA	G	GS	CG	ShO	Sv.-Opp.	IP	H	R	ER	HR	BB-IBB	SO
1992—	Dom. Cardinals (DSL)	3	2	.600	6.10	18	2	0	0	0-...	48.2	68	43	33	...	23-...	21
1993—	Dom. Cardinals (DSL)	3	5	.375	3.51	12	12	0	0	0-...	56.1	61	47	22	...	35-...	30
1994—	Dom. Cardinals (DSL)	3	9	.250	2.77	19	9	0	0	3-...	68.1	54	43	21	...	30-...	54
1995—	Johnson City (Appl.)	5	7	.417	3.49	14	•14	1	1	0-...	*90.1	81	48	35	3	25-0	85
1996—	Peoria (Midw.)	12	9	.571	2.92	28	27	3	1	0-...	172.1	158	75	56	6	53-0	129

Year League	W	L	Pct.	ERA	G	GS	CG	ShO	Sv.-Opp.	IP	H	R	ER	HR	BB-IBB	SO
1997— Prince William (Caro.)	9	7	.563	3.09	24	24	2	0	0-...	145.2	128	73	50	12	42-2	81
1998— Arkansas (Texas)	*15	6	.714	3.11	26	26	1	•1	0-...	*179.2	156	71	62	9	68-1	88
— St. Louis (N.L.)	3	0	1.000	2.95	4	3	0	0	0-0	21.1	22	8	7	0	8-0	12
1999— St. Louis (N.L.)	5	14	.263	5.85	29	28	2	2	0-1	163.0	173	114	106	16	71-2	113
— Memphis (PCL)	2	2	.500	3.04	4	4	0	0	0-...	26.2	30	10	9	0	9-0	18
2000— Colorado (N.L.)■	5	2	.714	3.18	72	0	0	0	24-30	70.2	63	27	25	4	28-6	44
2001— Colorado (N.L.)	6	1	.857	4.09	56	0	0	0	17-22	55.0	56	27	25	6	22-4	37
2002— Colorado (N.L.)	2	10	.167	3.56	74	0	0	0	41-47	73.1	76	34	29	7	11-4	47
Major League totals (5 years)	21	27	.438	4.51	235	31	2	2	82-100	383.1	390	210	192	33	140-16	253

JOHNSON, ADAM — P — TWINS

PERSONAL: Born July 12, 1979, in San Jose, Calif. ... 6-2/210. ... Throws right, bats right. ... Full name: Adam Bryant Johnson.
HIGH SCHOOL: Torrey Pines (Del Mar, Calif.).
COLLEGE: California State-Fullerton.
TRANSACTIONS/CAREER NOTES: Selected by Minnesota Twins organization in first round (second pick overall) of free-agent draft (June 5, 2000).
CAREER HITTING (MLB): 0-for-2 (.000), 0 R, 0 2B, 0 3B, 0 HR, 0 RBI.

Year League	W	L	Pct.	ERA	G	GS	CG	ShO	Sv.-Opp.	IP	H	R	ER	HR	BB-IBB	SO
2000— Fort Myers (FSL)	5	4	.556	2.47	13	12	1	1	0-...	69.1	45	21	19	2	20-1	92
2001— New Britain (East.)	5	6	.455	3.82	18	18	0	0	0-...	113.0	105	53	48	10	39-2	110
— Minnesota (A.L.)	1	2	.333	8.28	7	4	0	0	0-0	25.0	32	25	23	6	13-0	17
— Edmonton (PCL)	1	1	.500	5.70	4	4	0	0	0-...	23.2	19	15	15	0	10-0	25
2002— Edmonton (PCL)	13	8	.619	5.47	27	27	1	1	0-...	151.1	182	96	92	25	55-0	112
Major League totals (1 year)	1	2	.333	8.28	7	4	0	0	0-0	25.0	32	25	23	6	13-0	17

JOHNSON, CHARLES — C — MARLINS

PERSONAL: Born July 20, 1971, in Fort Pierce, Fla. ... 6-3/250. ... Bats right, throws right. ... Full name: Charles Edward Johnson Jr. ... Nephew of Fred McGriff, first baseman with five major league teams (1986-2002).
HIGH SCHOOL: Westwood (Fort Pierce, Fla.).
COLLEGE: Miami (Fla.).
TRANSACTIONS/CAREER NOTES: Selected by Montreal Expos organization in first round (10th pick overall) of free-agent draft (June 5, 1989); did not sign. ... Selected by Florida Marlins organization in first round (28th pick overall) of free-agent draft (June 1, 1992). ... On Florida disabled list (August 9-September 1, 1995); included rehabilitation assignment to Portland (August 30-September 1). ... On disabled list (July 28-September 1, 1996). ... Traded by Marlins with OF Gary Sheffield, 3B Bobby Bonilla, OF Jim Eisenreich and P Manuel Barrios to Los Angeles Dodgers for C Mike Piazza and 3B Todd Zeile (May 15, 1998). ... Traded by Dodgers with OF Roger Cedeno to New York Mets for C Todd Hundley and P Arnold Gooch; then traded by Mets to Baltimore Orioles for P Armando Benitez (December 1, 1998). ... Traded by Orioles with DH Harold Baines to Chicago White Sox for C Brook Fordyce, P Miguel Felix, P Juan Figueroa and P Jason Lakman (July 29, 2000). ... Granted free agency (October 30, 2000). ... Signed by Marlins (December 18, 2000). ... On Florida disabled list (March 22-April 8 and July 28-August 16, 2002); included rehabilitation assignment to Jupiter (August 13-16).
RECORDS: Holds major league career records for most consecutive errorless games by catcher—159 (June 24, 1996-September 28, 1997); and most consecutive chances accepted by catcher without an error—1,294 (June 23, 1996-September 28, 1997). ... Holds major league single-season records for most consecutive errorless games by catcher—123 (April 1 through September 28, 1997); and most chances accepted without an error by catcher—973 (April 1 through September 28, 1997). ... Shares major league single-season records for highest fielding average by catcher (100 or more games)—1.000 (1997); and fewest errors (100 or more games)—0 (1997).
HONORS: Named catcher on The Sporting News college All-America team (1992). ... Won N.L. Gold Glove at catcher (1995-98).
STATISTICAL NOTES: Led Midwest League with 230 total bases in 1993. ... Led Midwest League catchers with 852 putouts, 140 assists and 1,004 total chances in 1993. ... Led Eastern League catchers with 84 assists in 1994. ... Tied for N.L. lead with 63 assists by catcher in 1995. ... Led N.L. catchers with 12 double plays in 1996. ... Led A.L. catchers with 14 double plays in 1999. ... Career major league grand slams: 1.
MISCELLANEOUS: Member of 1992 U.S. Olympic baseball team.
2002 GAMES PLAYED BY POSITION (MLB): C—82.

		BATTING														FIELDING	
Year Team (League)	Pos.	G	AB	R	H	2B	3B	HR	RBI	BB	SO	SB-CS	Avg.	OBP	SLG	E	Avg.
1993— Kane County (Midw.)	C	•135	488	74	134	29	5	19	*94	62	111	9-1	.275	.356	.471	12	.988
1994— Portland (East.)	C-DH	132	443	64	117	29	1	*28	80	*74	97	4-5	.264	.371	.524	7	.991
— Florida (N.L.)	C	4	11	5	5	1	0	1	4	1	4	0-0	.455	.462	.818	0	1.000
1995— Florida (N.L.)	C	97	315	40	79	15	1	11	39	46	71	0-2	.251	.351	.410	6	.992
— Portland (East.)	C	2	7	0	0	0	0	0	0	1	3	0-0	.000	.125	.000	1	.958
1996— Florida (N.L.)	C	120	386	34	84	13	1	13	37	40	91	1-0	.218	.292	.358	4	*.995
1997— Florida (N.L.)	C	124	416	43	104	26	1	19	63	60	109	0-2	.250	.347	.454	0	*1.000
1998— Florida (N.L.)	C	31	113	13	25	5	0	7	23	16	30	0-1	.221	.315	.451	2	.990
— Los Angeles (N.L.)■	C	102	346	31	75	13	0	12	35	29	99	0-1	.217	.279	.358	6	.992
1999— Baltimore (A.L.)■	C	135	426	58	107	19	1	16	54	55	107	0-0	.251	.340	.413	5	.994
2000— Baltimore (A.L.)	C-DH	84	286	52	84	16	0	21	55	32	69	2-0	.294	.364	.570	3	.994
— Chicago (A.L.)■	C	44	135	24	44	8	0	10	36	20	37	0-0	.326	.411	.607	3	.987
2001— Florida (N.L.)■	C	128	451	51	117	32	0	18	75	38	133	0-0	.259	.321	.450	4	.996
2002— Florida (N.L.)	C	83	244	18	53	19	0	6	36	31	61	0-0	.217	.301	.369	3	.994
American League totals (2 years)		263	847	134	235	43	1	47	145	107	213	2-0	.277	.360	.497	11	.993
National League totals (7 years)		689	2282	235	542	124	3	87	312	261	598	1-6	.238	.317	.409	25	.995
Major League totals (9 years)		952	3129	369	777	167	4	134	457	368	811	3-6	.248	.329	.433	36	.995

DIVISION SERIES RECORD

		BATTING														FIELDING	
Year Team (League)	Pos.	G	AB	R	H	2B	3B	HR	RBI	BB	SO	SB-CS	Avg.	OBP	SLG	E	Avg.
1997— Florida (N.L.)	C	3	8	5	2	1	0	1	2	3	2	0-0	.250	.500	.750	0	1.000
2000— Chicago (A.L.)	C	3	9	0	3	0	0	0	0	1	1	0-0	.333	.455	.333	0	1.000
Division series totals (2 years)		6	17	5	5	1	0	1	2	4	3	0-0	.294	.478	.529	0	1.000

CHAMPIONSHIP SERIES RECORD

			BATTING													FIELDING	
Year	Team (League)	Pos.	G	AB	R	H	2B	3B	HR	RBI	BB	SO	SB-CS	Avg.	OBP	SLG	E	Avg.
1997—	Florida (N.L.)	C	6	17	1	2	2	0	0	5	3	8	0-1	.118	.286	.235	2	.965

WORLD SERIES RECORD

NOTES: Member of World Series championship team (1997).

			BATTING													FIELDING	
Year	Team (League)	Pos.	G	AB	R	H	2B	3B	HR	RBI	BB	SO	SB-CS	Avg.	OBP	SLG	E	Avg.
1997—	Florida (N.L.)	C	7	28	4	10	0	0	1	3	1	6	0-0	.357	.379	.464	0	1.000

ALL-STAR GAME RECORD

	AB	R	H	2B	3B	HR	RBI	BB	SO	SB-CS	Avg.	OBP	SLG	E	Avg.
All-Star Game totals (2 years)	2	0	0	0	0	0	0	0	1	0-0	.000	.000	.000	0	1.000

JOHNSON, JASON — P — ORIOLES

PERSONAL: Born October 27, 1973, in Santa Barbara, Calif. ... 6-6/235. ... Throws right, bats right. ... Full name: Jason Michael Johnson.
HIGH SCHOOL: Conner (Hebron, Ky.).
TRANSACTIONS/CAREER NOTES: Signed as non-drafted free agent by Pittsburgh Pirates organization (July 21, 1992). ... Selected by Tampa Bay Devil Rays in first round (14th pick overall) of expansion draft (November 18, 1997). ... On Tampa Bay disabled list (July 4, 1998-remainder of season). ... Traded by Devil Rays to Baltimore Orioles for OF Danny Clyburn and a player to be named later (March 29, 1999); Devil Rays acquired SS Bolivar Voquez to complete deal (April 22, 1999). ... On Baltimore disabled list (April 25-June 7 and July 23-August 9, 2002); included rehabilitation assignment to Bowie (June 1-7).
CAREER HITTING (MLB): 1-for-14 (.071), 0 R, 0 2B, 0 3B, 0 HR, 0 RBI.

Year	League	W	L	Pct.	ERA	G	GS	CG	ShO	Sv.-Opp.	IP	H	R	ER	HR	BB-IBB	SO
1992—	Gulf Coast Pirates (GCL)	2	0	1.000	3.68	5	0	0	0	0-...	7.1	6	3	3	0	6-0	3
1993—	Gulf Coast Pirates (GCL)	1	4	.200	2.33	9	9	0	0	0-...	54.0	48	22	14	0	14-0	39
—	Welland (NY-Penn)	1	5	.167	4.63	6	6	1	0	0-...	35.0	33	24	18	0	9-0	19
1994—	Augusta (S.Atl.)	2	12	.143	4.03	20	19	1	0	0-...	102.2	119	67	46	5	32-0	69
1995—	Augusta (S.Atl.)	3	5	.375	4.36	11	11	1	0	0-...	53.2	57	32	26	2	17-0	42
—	Lynchburg (Caro.)	1	2	.333	2.05	5	4	0	0	0-...	22.0	23	6	5	9	5-0	9
1996—	Lynchburg (Caro.)	1	4	.200	6.50	15	5	0	0	0-...	44.1	56	37	32	6	12-0	27
—	Augusta (S.Atl.)	4	4	.500	3.11	14	14	1	1	0-...	84.0	82	40	29	2	25-0	83
1997—	Lynchburg (Caro.)	8	4	.667	3.71	17	17	0	0	0-...	99.1	98	43	41	4	30-1	92
—	Carolina (Sou.)	3	3	.500	4.08	9	9	1	0	0-...	57.1	56	31	26	6	16-0	63
—	Pittsburgh (N.L.)	0	0	...	6.00	3	0	0	0	0-0	6.0	10	4	4	2	1-0	3
1998—	Durham (I.L.)■	1	0	1.000	2.92	2	2	0	0	0-...	12.1	6	4	4	2	2-0	14
—	Tampa Bay (A.L.)	2	5	.286	5.70	13	13	0	0	0-0	60.0	74	38	38	9	27-0	36
1999—	Rochester (I.L.)■	4	2	.667	3.65	8	8	0	0	0-...	44.1	35	19	18	6	27-0	47
—	Baltimore (A.L.)	8	7	.533	5.46	22	21	0	0	0-0	115.1	120	74	70	16	55-0	71
2000—	Rochester (I.L.)	3	1	.750	1.47	8	8	1	1	0-...	55.0	32	12	9	2	21-0	56
—	Baltimore (A.L.)	1	10	.091	7.02	25	13	0	0	0-0	107.2	119	95	84	21	61-2	79
2001—	Baltimore (A.L.)	10	12	.455	4.09	32	32	2	0	0-0	196.0	194	109	89	28	77-3	114
2002—	Baltimore (A.L.)	5	14	.263	4.59	22	22	1	0	0-0	131.1	141	68	67	19	41-2	97
—	Bowie (East.)	1	0	1.000	0.00	1	1	0	0	0-...	5.0	4	0	0	0	1-0	6
A.L. totals (5 years)		26	48	.351	5.13	114	101	3	0	0-0	610.1	648	384	348	93	261-7	397
N.L. totals (1 year)		0	0	...	6.00	3	0	0	0	0-0	6.0	10	4	4	2	1-0	3
Major League totals (6 years)		26	48	.351	5.14	117	101	3	0	0-0	616.1	658	388	352	95	262-7	400

JOHNSON, JONATHAN — P — ASTROS

PERSONAL: Born July 16, 1974, in La Grange, Ga. ... 6-0/180. ... Throws right, bats right. ... Full name: Jonathan Kent Johnson.
HIGH SCHOOL: Forest (Ocala, Fla.).
COLLEGE: Florida State.
TRANSACTIONS/CAREER NOTES: Selected by Texas Rangers organization in first round (seventh pick overall) of free-agent draft (June 1, 1995). ... On Oklahoma disabled list (May 1-17, 1998; and May 13-July 5, 1999). ... Traded by Rangers to Arizona Diamondback for cash considerations (April 27, 2001). ... On Tucson disabled list (July 21, 2001-remainder of season). ... Granted free agency (October 15, 2001). ... Re-signed by Diamondbacks organization (December 26, 2001). ... On Tucson disabled list (May 15-June 4, 2002). ... Released by Diamondbacks (June 30, 2002). ... Signed by San Diego Padres organization (July 18, 2002). ... Released by Padres (October 7, 2002). ... Signed by Houston Astros organization (November 1, 2002).
CAREER HITTING (MLB): 0-for-0 (.000), 0 R, 0 2B, 0 3B, 0 HR, 0 RBI.

Year	League	W	L	Pct.	ERA	G	GS	CG	ShO	Sv.-Opp.	IP	H	R	ER	HR	BB-IBB	SO
1995—	Charlotte (FSL)	1	5	.167	2.70	8	7	1	0	0-...	43.1	34	14	13	2	16-0	25
1996—	Tulsa (Texas)	*13	10	.565	3.56	26	25	*6	0	0-...	174.1	176	86	69	15	41-1	97
—	Oklahoma City (A.A.)	1	0	1.000	0.00	1	1	1	1	0-...	9.0	2	0	0	0	1-0	6
1997—	Oklahoma City (A.A.)	1	8	.111	7.29	13	12	1	0	1-...	58.0	83	54	47	6	29-3	33
—	Tulsa (Texas)	5	4	.556	3.52	10	10	4	0	0-...	71.2	70	35	28	3	15-0	47
1998—	Oklahoma (PCL)	6	6	.500	4.90	19	18	1	0	1-...	112.0	109	66	61	15	32-0	94
—	Charlotte (FSL)	0	2	.000	4.63	3	3	0	0	0-...	11.2	10	6	6	2	4-0	11
—	Texas (A.L.)	0	0	...	8.31	1	1	0	0	0-0	4.1	5	4	4	0	5-0	3
1999—	Oklahoma (PCL)	8	4	.667	6.25	21	8	0	0	2-...	67.2	91	53	47	9	23-0	38
—	Gulf Coast Rangers (GCL)	0	0	...	1.80	1	1	0	0	0-...	5.0	3	1	1	0	0-0	5
—	Tulsa (Texas)	0	0	...	9.53	1	1	0	0	0-...	5.2	12	6	6	3	0-0	4
—	Texas (A.L.)	0	0	...	15.00	1	0	0	0	0-0	3.0	9	5	5	0	2-0	3
2000—	Oklahoma (PCL)	4	7	.364	5.08	36	2	0	0	5-...	56.2	55	38	32	8	26-2	63
—	Texas (A.L.)	1	1	.500	6.21	15	0	0	0	0-0	29.0	34	23	20	3	19-2	23
2001—	Texas (A.L.)	0	0	...	9.58	5	0	0	0	0-0	10.1	13	11	11	2	7-1	11
—	Tucson (PCL)■	4	4	.500	5.25	15	12	0	0	0-...	73.2	63	48	43	7	42-0	51
2002—	El Paso (Texas)	0	1	.000	5.56	3	1	0	0	0-...	11.1	14	7	7	1	3-0	9
—	Tucson (PCL)	0	3	.000	9.41	14	5	0	0	0-...	36.1	48	41	38	6	14-0	27
—	Portland (PCL)■	0	0	...	2.41	12	0	0	0	1-...	18.2	14	5	5	2	2-0	17
—	San Diego (N.L.)	1	2	.333	4.11	16	0	0	0	0-0	15.1	15	8	7	2	5-1	21
A.L. totals (4 years)		1	1	.500	7.71	22	1	0	0	0-0	46.2	61	43	40	5	33-3	40
N.L. totals (1 year)		1	2	.333	4.11	16	0	0	0	0-0	15.1	15	8	7	2	5-1	21
Major League totals (5 years)		2	3	.400	6.82	38	1	0	0	0-0	62.0	76	51	47	7	38-4	61

JOHNSON, MARK — 1B

PERSONAL: Born October 17, 1967, in Worcester, Mass. ... 6-4/230. ... Bats left, throws left. ... Full name: Mark Patrick Johnson.
HIGH SCHOOL: Holy Name (Worcester, Mass.).
COLLEGE: Dartmouth.
TRANSACTIONS/CAREER NOTES: Selected by Pittsburgh Pirates organization in 42nd round of free-agent draft (June 5, 1989); did not sign. ... Selected by Pirates organization in 20th round of free-agent draft (June 4, 1990). ... On Calgary disabled list (August 26-September 8, 1995). ... Claimed on waivers by Cincinnati Reds (August 29, 1997). ... Traded by Reds to Anaheim Angels for a player to be named later (September 11, 1998). ... Released by Angels (December 22, 1998). ... Signed by Hanshin Tigers of Japan Central League (December 22, 1998). ... Signed by New York Mets organization (February 22, 2000). ... Granted free agency (October 18, 2000). ... Re-signed by Mets (May 29, 2001). ... Granted free agency (October 15, 2001). ... Re-signed by Mets organization (December 19, 2001). ... Released by Mets (October 10, 2002).
HONORS: Named Southern League Most Valuable Player (1994).
STATISTICAL NOTES: Led Southern League with 11 intentional bases on balls received in 1994. ... Career major league grand slams: 1.
2002 GAMES PLAYED BY POSITION (MLB): 1B—15; OF—1.

			BATTING														FIELDING	
Year	Team (League)	Pos.	G	AB	R	H	2B	3B	HR	RBI	BB	SO	SB-CS	Avg.	OBP	SLG	E	Avg.
1990—	Welland (NY-Penn)	1B	5	8	2	4	1	0	0	2	2	0	0-0	.500	.600	.625	0	1.000
—	Augusta (S.Atl.)	1B	43	144	12	36	7	0	0	19	24	18	4-2	.250	.353	.299	5	.981
1991—	Augusta (S.Atl.)	1B	49	139	23	36	7	4	2	25	29	1	15-2	.259	.382	.410	9	.975
—	Salem (Caro.)	1B-OF-3B	37	103	12	26	2	0	2	13	18	25	0-2	.252	.369	.330	3	.952
1992—	Carolina (Sou.)	1B	122	383	40	89	16	1	7	45	55	94	16-11	.232	.333	.334	8	.988
1993—	Carolina (Sou.)	1B-OF	125	399	48	93	18	4	14	52	66	93	6-2	.233	.344	.404	4	.993
1994—	Carolina (Sou.)	1B-OF	111	388	69	107	20	2	*23	85	67	89	6-6	.276	.384	.515	6	.990
1995—	Pittsburgh (N.L.)	1B	79	221	32	46	6	1	13	28	37	66	5-2	.208	.326	.421	8	.986
—	Calgary (PCL)	1B	9	23	7	7	4	0	2	8	6	4	1-0	.304	.467	.739	2	.972
1996—	Pittsburgh (N.L.)	1B-OF	127	343	55	94	24	0	13	47	44	64	6-4	.274	.361	.458	6	.993
1997—	Pittsburgh (N.L.)	1B-DH	78	219	30	47	10	0	4	29	43	78	1-1	.215	.345	.315	5	.992
—	Calgary (PCL)	1B-DH-OF	34	115	28	39	11	1	6	16	22	28	4-2	.339	.446	.609	0	1.000
—	Indianapolis (A.A.)■	1B	3	4	0	0	0	0	0	0	2	2	0-1	.000	.333	.000	0	1.000
1998—	Indianapolis (I.L.)	1B-OF-DH	116	357	65	107	33	1	22	75	68	82	2-2	.300	.409	.583	5	.990
—	Anaheim (A.L.)■	1B-DH	10	14	1	1	0	0	0	0	0	6	0-0	.071	.071	.071	0	1.000
1999—	Hanshin (Jap. Cen.)■	IF	125	438	52	95	23	1	20	66	53	78	1-...	.217	...	.411	...	...
2000—	Norfolk (I.L.)■	1B-OF	94	315	49	85	21	1	17	60	67	54	14-2	.270	.405	.505	3	.993
—	New York (N.L.)	1B-DH-OF	21	22	2	4	0	0	1	6	5	9	0-0	.182	.333	.318	0	1.000
2001—	Norfolk (I.L.)	1B-OF	42	152	27	48	15	0	8	25	22	20	2-1	.316	.407	.572	1	.998
—	New York (N.L.)	1B-OF-DH	71	118	17	30	6	1	6	23	16	31	0-2	.254	.338	.475	1	.992
2002—	Norfolk (I.L.)	1B-OF	77	270	45	70	17	1	14	37	32	53	1-0	.259	.343	.485	1	.998
—	New York (N.L.)	1B-OF	42	51	5	7	4	0	1	4	9	18	0-0	.137	.267	.275	1	.989
American League totals (1 year)			10	14	1	1	0	0	0	0	0	6	0-0	.071	.071	.071	0	1.000
National League totals (6 years)			418	974	141	228	50	2	38	137	154	266	12-9	.234	.341	.407	21	.991
Major League totals (7 years)			428	988	142	229	50	2	38	137	154	272	12-9	.232	.338	.402	21	.991

JOHNSON, MARK — C — WHITE SOX

PERSONAL: Born September 12, 1975, in Wheatridge, Colo. ... 6-0/185. ... Bats left, throws right. ... Full name: Mark Landon Johnson.
HIGH SCHOOL: Warner Robins (Ga.).
TRANSACTIONS/CAREER NOTES: Selected by Chicago White Sox organization in first round (26th pick overall) of free-agent draft (June 2, 1994).
STATISTICAL NOTES: Led Carolina League catchers with 899 putouts and 1,000 total chances and tied for league lead with eight double plays in 1997.
2002 GAMES PLAYED BY POSITION (MLB): C—85.

			BATTING														FIELDING	
Year	Team (League)	Pos.	G	AB	R	H	2B	3B	HR	RBI	BB	SO	SB-CS	Avg.	OBP	SLG	E	Avg.
1994—	GC White Sox (GCL)	C	32	87	10	21	5	0	0	14	14	15	1-1	.241	.365	.299	3	.986
1995—	Hickory (S.Atl.)	C	107	319	31	58	9	0	2	17	59	52	3-5	.182	.313	.229	11	.986
1996—	South Bend (Midw.)	C	67	214	29	55	14	3	2	27	39	25	3-3	.257	.368	.379	9	.980
—	Prince William (Caro.)	C	18	58	9	14	3	0	0	3	13	6	0-0	.241	.389	.293	1	.992
1997—	Win.-Salem (Caro.)	C	120	375	59	95	27	4	4	46	*106	85	4-2	.253	*.420	.379	11	*.989
1998—	Birmingham (Sou.)	C-1B	117	382	68	108	17	3	9	59	*105	72	0-1	.283	*.443	.414	8	.990
—	Chicago (A.L.)	C	7	23	2	2	0	2	0	1	1	8	0-0	.087	.125	.261	0	1.000
1999—	Chicago (A.L.)	C-DH	73	207	27	47	11	0	4	16	36	58	3-1	.227	.344	.338	3	.993
2000—	Chicago (A.L.)	C-DH	75	213	29	48	11	0	3	23	27	40	3-2	.225	.315	.319	4	.992
2001—	Charlotte (I.L.)	C-1B	55	196	24	53	5	2	4	24	29	34	2-1	.270	.363	.378	4	.991
—	Chicago (A.L.)	C	61	173	21	43	6	1	5	18	23	31	2-1	.249	.338	.382	3	.992
2002—	Chicago (A.L.)	C	86	263	31	55	8	1	4	18	30	52	0-0	.209	.297	.293	3	.994
Major League totals (5 years)			302	879	110	195	36	4	16	76	117	189	8-4	.222	.317	.327	13	.993

JOHNSON, NICK — 1B — YANKEES

PERSONAL: Born September 19, 1978, in Sacramento. ... 6-3/224. ... Bats left, throws left. ... Full name: Nicholas Robert Johnson. ... Nephew of Larry Bowa, manager, Philadelphia Phillies and shortstop with Phillies (1970-81) and Chicago Cubs (1982-85).
HIGH SCHOOL: McClatchy (Sacramento).
TRANSACTIONS/CAREER NOTES: Selected by New York Yankees organization in third round of free-agent draft (June 4, 1996). ... On disabled list (April 2, 2000-entire season). ... On Columbus disabled list (May 18-June 3, 2001). ... On New York disabled list (August 8-September 3, 2002); included rehabilitation assignment to Columbus (August 31-September 3).
STATISTICAL NOTES: Led South Atlantic League first basemen with 1,176 putouts and 99 double plays in 1997. ... Led Eastern League in being hit by pitch with 37 in 1999. ... Led International League in being hit by pitch with 14 in 2001.
2002 GAMES PLAYED BY POSITION (MLB): 1B—78; DH—50; OF—2.

Year	Team (League)	Pos.	G	AB	R	H	2B	3B	HR	RBI	BB	SO	SB-CS	Avg.	OBP	SLG	E	Avg.
						BATTING											FIELDING	
1996—	GC Yankees (GCL)	1B	47	157	31	45	11	1	2	33	30	35	0-0	.287	*.422	.408	3	.991
1997—	Greensboro (S.Atl.)	1B	127	433	77	118	23	1	16	75	76	99	16-3	.273	.398	.441	16	.987
1998—	Tampa (FSL)	1B	92	303	69	96	14	1	17	58	68	76	1-4	.317	*.466	.538	12	.986
1999—	Norwich (East.)	1B	132	420	*114	145	33	5	14	87	*123	88	8-6	*.345	*.525	.548	*20	.983
2000—	New York (A.L.)								Did not play.									
2001—	Columbus (I.L.)	1B	110	359	68	92	20	0	18	49	81	105	9-2	.256	*.407	.462	•10	.989
—	New York (A.L.)	1B-DH	23	67	6	13	2	0	2	8	7	15	0-0	.194	.308	.313	0	1.000
2002—	New York (A.L.)	1B-DH-OF	129	378	56	92	15	0	15	58	48	98	1-3	.243	.347	.402	7	.988
—	Columbus (I.L.)	1B	3	11	1	1	0	0	0	0	1	4	0-0	.091	.167	.091	0	1.000
Major League totals (2 years)			152	445	62	105	17	0	17	66	55	113	1-3	.236	.341	.389	7	.990

DIVISION SERIES RECORD

Year	Team (League)	Pos.	G	AB	R	H	2B	3B	HR	RBI	BB	SO	SB-CS	Avg.	OBP	SLG	E	Avg.
						BATTING											FIELDING	
2002—	New York (A.L.)	DH-1B	3	11	1	2	0	0	0	1	1	5	0-0	.182	.250	.182	0	1.000

JOHNSON, RANDY — P — DIAMONDBACKS

PERSONAL: Born September 10, 1963, in Walnut Grove, Calif. ... 6-10/232. ... Throws left, bats right. ... Full name: Randall David Johnson.

HIGH SCHOOL: Livermore (Calif.).

COLLEGE: Southern California.

TRANSACTIONS/CAREER NOTES: Selected by Atlanta Braves organization in third round of free-agent draft (June 7, 1982); did not sign. ... Selected by Montreal Expos organization in second round of free-agent draft (June 3, 1985). ... Traded by Expos with P Brian Holman and P Gene Harris to Seattle Mariners for P Mark Langston and a player to be named later (May 25, 1989); Expos acquired P Mike Campbell to complete deal (July 31, 1989). ... On disabled list (June 11-27, 1992). ... On Seattle disabled list (May 15-August 6 and August 27, 1996-remainder of season); included rehabilitation assignment to Everett (August 3-6). ... On suspended list (April 24-27, 1998). ... Traded by Mariners to Houston Astros for SS Carlos Guillen, P Freddy Garcia and a player to be named later (July 31, 1998); Mariners acquired P John Halama to complete deal (October 1, 1998). ... Granted free agency (October 28, 1998). ... Signed by Arizona Diamondbacks (December 10, 1998).

RECORDS: Shares major league career record for most years with 300 or more strikeouts—6 (1993 and 1998-2002). ... Shares major league single-game record for most strikeouts by lefthander—19 (June 24 and August 8, 1997). ... Shares major league record for striking out side on nine pitches (August 23, 2001, sixth inning). ... Holds N.L. career record for most years with 300 or more strikeouts—4 (1999-2002). ... Holds N.L. single-season record for most games with 10 or more strikeouts—23 (1999). ... Shares A.L. record for most strikeouts in two consecutive games—32 (August 8 [19] and 15 [13], 1997, 17 innings). ... Shares N.L. record for most strikeouts in three consecutive games—43 (June 25 [14] and 30 [17] and July 5 [12], 1999; April 28 [12], May 3 [11] and 8 [20], 2001; May 3 [11], 8 [20] and 13 [12], 2001); and most years with 300 or more strikeouts—3 (1999-2001). ... Shares N.L. single-game record for most strikeouts (extra-inning game)—20 (May 8, 2001). ... Holds N.L. single-game record for most strikeouts by relief pitcher—16 (July 18, 2001); and most consecutive strikeouts by relief pitcher—7 (July 19, 2001).

HONORS: Named A.L. Pitcher of the Year by The Sporting News (1995). ... Named lefthanded pitcher on The Sporting News A.L. All-Star team (1995 and 1997). ... Named A.L. Cy Young Award winner by Baseball Writers' Association of America (1995). ... Named N.L. Cy Young Award winner by Baseball Writers' Association of America (1999, 2000, 2001 and 2002). ... Named lefthanded pitcher on The Sporting News N.L. All-Star team (2001 and 2002).

STATISTICAL NOTES: Led American Association with 20 balks in 1988. ... Pitched 2-0 no-hit victory against Detroit (June 2, 1990). ... Pitched 4-0 one-hit, complete-game victory against Oakland (August 14, 1991). ... Struck out 15 batters in one game (September 16, 1992; June 14 and September 16, 1993; June 4 and August 11, 1994; June 24 and September 23, 1995; May 28 and June 8, 1997; April 10, May 24 and July 11, 1998; April 10, 1999; and July 31, 2002). ... Struck out 18 batters in one game (September 27, 1992). ... Led A.L. with 18 hit batsmen in 1992 and 16 in 1993. ... Pitched 7-0 one-hit, complete-game victory against Oakland (May 16, 1993). ... Struck out 16 batters in one game (July 15, 1995; July 18, 1997; August 28, 1998; July 18, August 23 and Septmeber 27, 2001; and August 25, 2002). ... Struck out 19 batters in one game (June 24 and August 8, 1997). ... Pitched 3-0 one-hit, complete-game victory against Minnesota (July 16, 1998). ... Struck out 17 batters in one game (June 30, 1999; April 21 and September 14, 2002). ... Struck out 20 batters in one game (May 8, 2001).

MISCELLANEOUS: Holds Seattle Mariners all-time records for most wins (130), most innings pitched (1,838$^{1}/_{3}$), most strikeouts (2,162), most shutouts (19) and lowest earned-run average (3.42). ... Holds Arizona Diamondbacks all-time records for most wins (81), most innings pitched (1,030), most strikeouts (1,417), most shutouts (11) and lowest earned-run average (2.48). ... Appeared in one game as outfielder with no chances (1993).

CAREER HITTING (MLB): 50-for-404 (.124), 14 R, 10 2B, 0 3B, 0 HR, 26 RBI.

Year	League	W	L	Pct.	ERA	G	GS	CG	ShO	Sv.-Opp.	IP	H	R	ER	HR	BB-IBB	SO
1985—	Jamestown (NY-Penn)	0	3	.000	5.93	8	8	0	0	0-...	27.1	29	22	18	2	24-0	21
1986—	West Palm Beach (FSL)	8	7	.533	3.16	26	•26	2	1	0-...	119.2	89	49	42	3	*94-0	133
1987—	Jacksonville (Sou.)	11	8	.579	3.73	25	24	0	0	0-...	140.0	100	63	58	10	128-0	*163
1988—	Indianapolis (A.A.)	8	7	.533	3.26	20	19	0	0	0-...	113.1	85	52	41	6	72-0	111
—	Montreal (N.L.)	3	0	1.000	2.42	4	4	1	0	0-0	26.0	23	8	7	3	7-0	25
1989—	Montreal (N.L.)	0	4	.000	6.67	7	6	0	0	0-0	29.2	29	25	22	2	26-1	26
—	Indianapolis (A.A.)	1	1	.500	2.00	3	3	0	0	0-...	18.0	13	5	4	0	9-0	17
—	Seattle (A.L.)■	7	9	.438	4.40	22	22	2	0	0-0	131.0	118	75	64	11	70-1	104
1990—	Seattle (A.L.)	14	11	.560	3.65	33	33	5	2	0-0	219.2	174	103	89	26	*120-2	194
1991—	Seattle (A.L.)	13	10	.565	3.98	33	33	2	1	0-0	201.1	151	96	89	15	*152-0	228
1992—	Seattle (A.L.)	12	14	.462	3.77	31	31	6	2	0-0	210.1	154	104	88	13	*144-1	*241
1993—	Seattle (A.L.)	19	8	.704	3.24	35	34	10	3	1-1	255.1	185	97	92	22	99-1	*308
1994—	Seattle (A.L.)	13	6	.684	3.19	23	23	*9	*4	0-0	172.0	132	65	61	14	72-2	*204
1995—	Seattle (A.L.)	18	2	*.900	*2.48	30	30	6	3	0-0	214.1	159	65	59	12	65-1	*294
1996—	Seattle (A.L.)	5	0	1.000	3.67	14	8	0	0	1-2	61.1	48	27	25	8	25-0	85
—	Everett (N'West)	0	0	...	0.00	1	1	0	0	0-...	2.0	0	0	0	0	0-0	5
1997—	Seattle (A.L.)	20	4	*.833	2.28	30	29	5	2	0-0	213.0	147	60	54	20	77-2	291
1998—	Seattle (A.L.)	9	10	.474	4.33	23	23	6	2	0-0	160.0	146	90	77	19	60-0	213
—	Houston (N.L.)■	10	1	.909	1.28	11	11	4	4	0-0	84.1	57	12	12	4	26-1	116
1999—	Arizona (N.L.)■	17	9	.654	*2.48	35	•35	*12	2	0-0	*271.2	207	86	75	30	70-3	*364
2000—	Arizona (N.L.)	19	7	*.731	2.64	35	•35	•8	•3	0-0	248.2	202	89	73	23	76-1	*347
2001—	Arizona (N.L.)	21	6	.778	*2.49	35	34	3	2	0-0	249.2	181	74	69	19	71-2	*372
2002—	Arizona (N.L.)	*24	5	*.828	*2.32	35	35	*8	4	0-0	*260.0	197	78	67	26	71-1	*334
A.L. totals (10 years)		130	74	.637	3.42	274	266	51	19	2-3	1838.1	1414	782	698	160	884-10	2162
N.L. totals (7 years)		94	32	.746	2.50	162	160	36	15	0-0	1170.0	896	372	325	107	347-9	1584
Major League totals (15 years)		224	106	.679	3.06	436	426	87	34	2-3	3008.1	2310	1154	1023	267	1231-19	3746

DIVISION SERIES RECORD

RECORDS: Holds career records for most losses—7; and strikeouts—73. ... Shares career record for runs allowed—31. ... Holds N.L. career record for most games lost—5. ... Holds A.L. single-game record for most strikeouts—13 (October 5, 1997).

Year	League	W	L	Pct.	ERA	G	GS	CG	ShO	Sv.-Opp.	IP	H	R	ER	HR	BB-IBB	SO
1995—	Seattle (A.L.)	2	0	1.000	2.70	2	1	0	0	0-0	10.0	5	3	3	1	6-1	16
1997—	Seattle (A.L.)	0	2	.000	5.54	2	2	1	0	0-0	13.0	14	8	8	3	6-0	16
1998—	Houston (N.L.)	0	2	.000	1.93	2	2	0	0	0-0	14.0	12	4	3	2	2-0	17
1999—	Arizona (N.L.)	0	1	.000	7.56	1	1	0	0	0-0	8.1	8	7	7	2	3-0	11
2001—	Arizona (N.L.)	0	1	.000	3.38	1	1	0	0	0-0	8.0	6	3	3	1	2-0	9
2002—	Arizona (N.L.)	0	1	.000	7.50	1	1	0	0	0-0	6.0	10	6	5	2	2-1	4
Division series totals (6 years)		2	7	.222	4.40	9	8	1	0	0-0	59.1	55	31	29	11	21-2	73

CHAMPIONSHIP SERIES RECORD

Year	League	W	L	Pct.	ERA	G	GS	CG	ShO	Sv.-Opp.	IP	H	R	ER	HR	BB-IBB	SO
1995—	Seattle (A.L.)	0	1	.000	2.35	2	2	0	0	0-0	15.1	12	6	4	1	2-0	13
2001—	Arizona (N.L.)	2	0	1.000	1.13	2	2	1	1	0-0	16.0	10	2	2	1	3-0	19
Champ. series totals (2 years)		2	1	.667	1.72	4	4	1	1	0-0	31.1	22	8	6	2	5-0	32

WORLD SERIES RECORD

RECORDS: Shares single-series record for most games won—3 (2001).
NOTES: Named co-Most Valuable Player (2001). ... Member of World Series championship team (2001).

Year	League	W	L	Pct.	ERA	G	GS	CG	ShO	Sv.-Opp.	IP	H	R	ER	HR	BB-IBB	SO
2001—	Arizona (N.L.)	3	0	1.000	1.04	3	2	1	1	0-0	17.1	9	2	2	0	3-0	19

ALL-STAR GAME RECORD

	W	L	Pct.	ERA	GS	CG	ShO	Sv.-Opp.	IP	H	R	ER	HR	BB-IBB	SO
All-Star Game totals (7 years)	0	0	...	0.82	4	0	0	0-0	11.0	4	1	1	1	2-0	11

JOHNSON, RUSS — IF — DEVIL RAYS

PERSONAL: Born February 22, 1973, in Baton Rouge, La. ... 5-10/198. ... Bats right, throws right. ... Full name: William Russell Johnson.
HIGH SCHOOL: Denham Springs (La.).
COLLEGE: Louisiana State.
TRANSACTIONS/CAREER NOTES: Selected by Houston Astros organization in supplemental round ("sandwich pick" between first and second round, 30th pick overall) of free-agent draft (June 2, 1994); pick received as part of compensation for San Francisco Giants signing Type A free-agent P Mark Portugal. ... Traded by Astros to Tampa Bay Devil Rays for P Marc Valdes (May 27, 2000). ... On Tampa Bay disabled list (May 16-31, 2001); included rehabilitation assignment to Orlando (May 28-31). ... On Tampa Bay disabled list (March 28-April 15 and August 1-September 7, 2002); included rehabilitation assignments to Orlando (April 7-10 and August 19-28) and Durham (April 11-12 and August 29-September 7).
STATISTICAL NOTES: Led Texas League shortstops with 664 total chances and 87 double plays and tied for league lead with 219 putouts in 1996. ... Led Pacific Coast League third basemen with .962 fielding percentage in 1998.
2002 GAMES PLAYED BY POSITION (MLB): 3B—27; DH—5; SS—2; 2B—1.

			BATTING														FIELDING	
Year	Team (League)	Pos.	G	AB	R	H	2B	3B	HR	RBI	BB	SO	SB-CS	Avg.	OBP	SLG	E	Avg.
1995—	Jackson (Texas)	SS	132	475	65	118	16	2	9	53	50	60	10-5	.248	.327	.347	13	*.978
1996—	Jackson (Texas)	SS	132	496	86	154	24	5	15	74	56	50	9-4	.310	.382	.470	34	.949
1997—	New Orleans (A.A.)	3B-SS-DH	122	445	72	123	16	6	4	49	66	78	7-4	.276	.370	.366	21	.944
—	Houston (N.L.)	3B-2B	21	60	7	18	1	0	2	9	6	14	1-1	.300	.364	.417	1	.974
1998—	New Orleans (PCL)	3-2-S-DH	122	453	*95	140	28	2	7	52	*90	64	11-11	.309	.424	.426	11	†.966
—	Houston (N.L.)	3B-2B	8	13	2	3	1	0	0	0	1	5	1-0	.231	.333	.308	0	1.000
1999—	New Orleans (PCL)	2B-SS-OF	22	77	17	27	6	0	1	12	16	13	1-3	.351	.468	.468	3	.968
—	Houston (N.L.)	3B-2B-SS	83	156	24	44	10	0	5	23	20	31	2-3	.282	.358	.442	7	.945
2000—	Houston (N.L.)	SS-3B-2B	26	45	4	8	0	0	0	3	2	10	1-1	.178	.213	.178	1	.962
—	Tampa Bay (A.L.)■	3B-2B-SS	74	185	28	47	8	0	2	17	25	30	4-1	.254	.344	.330	5	.974
2001—	Tampa Bay (A.L.)	3B-2B-SS-DH	85	248	32	73	19	2	4	33	34	57	2-2	.294	.380	.435	7	.969
—	Orlando (Sou.)	2B	1	3	0	2	0	0	0	0	1	0	0-0	.667	.750	.667	2	.818
2002—	Orlando (Sou.)	3B-2B-OF	12	43	10	12	5	0	0	3	8	7	1-0	.279	.392	.395	3	.885
—	Durham (I.L.)	3B	10	33	9	9	0	1	2	5	4	5	1-0	.273	.351	.515	3	.903
—	Tampa Bay (A.L.)	3B-DH-SS-2B	45	111	15	24	5	0	1	12	16	22	5-2	.216	.320	.288	1	.984
American League totals (3 years)			204	544	75	144	32	2	7	62	75	109	11-5	.265	.356	.369	13	.973
National League totals (4 years)			138	274	37	73	12	0	7	35	29	60	5-5	.266	.336	.387	9	.956
Major League totals (6 years)			342	818	112	217	44	2	14	97	104	169	16-10	.265	.349	.375	22	.968

DIVISION SERIES RECORD

			BATTING														FIELDING	
Year	Team (League)	Pos.	G	AB	R	H	2B	3B	HR	RBI	BB	SO	SB-CS	Avg.	OBP	SLG	E	Avg.
1997—	Houston (N.L.)	PH	1	1	0	0	0	0	0	0	0	1	0-0	.000	.000	.000	...	...
1999—	Houston (N.L.)	PH	2	1	0	1	1	0	0	0	1	0	0-0	1.000	1.000	2.000	...	...
Division series totals (2 years)			3	2	0	1	1	0	0	0	1	1	0-0	.500	.667	1.000	0	...

JONES, ANDRUW — OF — BRAVES

PERSONAL: Born April 23, 1977, in Willemstad, Curacao. ... 6-1/210. ... Bats right, throws right. ... Full name: Andruw Rudolf Jones.
HIGH SCHOOL: St. Paulus (Willemstad, Curacao).
TRANSACTIONS/CAREER NOTES: Signed as non-drafted free agent by Atlanta Braves organization (July 1, 1993).
RECORDS: Shares major league record for most consecutive home runs—4 (September 7 [2], 8 [2], 2002). ... Holds N.L. single-season record for fewest singles (150 or more games)—55 (1997).
HONORS: Named South Atlantic League Most Valuable Player (1995). ... Won N.L. Gold Glove as outfielder (1998-2002).
STATISTICAL NOTES: Led South Atlantic League with nine sacrifice flies in 1995. ... Led South Atlantic League outfielders with 332 putouts and 346 total chances in 1995. ... Led N.L. outfielders with 435 total chances and tied for lead with 20 assists and six double plays in 1998. ... Led N.L. outfielders with 413 putouts in 1998, 492 in 1999 and 438 in 2000. ... Led N.L. outfielders in total chances with 515 in 1999 and

449 in 2000. ... Hit three home runs in one game (September 25, 2002). ... Led N.L. outfielders with 404 putouts and 412 total chances in 2002. ... Career major league grand slams: 1.

2002 GAMES PLAYED BY POSITION (MLB): OF—154; DH—1.

			BATTING														FIELDING	
Year	**Team (League)**	**Pos.**	**G**	**AB**	**R**	**H**	**2B**	**3B**	**HR**	**RBI**	**BB**	**SO**	**SB-CS**	**Avg.**	**OBP**	**SLG**	**E**	**Avg.**
1994—	GC Braves (GCL)	OF	27	95	22	21	5	1	2	10	16	19	5-2	.221	.345	.358	3	.968
—	Danville (Appl.)	OF	36	143	20	48	9	2	1	16	9	25	16-9	.336	.385	.448	2	.977
1995—	Macon (S.Atl.)	OF	•139	537	*104	149	41	5	25	100	70	122	*56-11	.277	.372	.512	4	.988
1996—	Durham (Caro.)	OF	66	243	65	76	14	3	17	43	42	54	16-4	.313	.419	.605	7	.963
—	Greenville (Sou.)	OF	38	157	39	58	10	1	12	37	17	34	12-4	.369	.432	.675	1	.993
—	Richmond (I.L.)	OF	12	45	11	17	3	1	5	12	1	9	2-2	.378	.391	.822	1	.972
—	Atlanta (N.L.)	OF	31	106	11	23	7	1	5	13	7	29	3-0	.217	.265	.443	2	.975
1997—	Atlanta (N.L.)	OF	153	399	60	92	18	1	18	70	56	107	20-11	.231	.329	.416	7	.977
1998—	Atlanta (N.L.)	OF	159	582	89	158	33	8	31	90	40	129	27-4	.271	.321	.515	2	.995
1999—	Atlanta (N.L.)	OF	•162	592	97	163	35	5	26	84	76	103	24-12	.275	.365	.483	10	.981
2000—	Atlanta (N.L.)	OF	161	*656	122	199	36	6	36	104	59	100	21-6	.303	.366	.541	2	.996
2001—	Atlanta (N.L.)	OF	161	625	104	157	25	2	34	104	56	142	11-4	.251	.312	.461	6	.987
2002—	Atlanta (N.L.)	OF-DH	154	560	91	148	34	0	35	94	83	135	8-3	.264	.366	.513	3	.993
Major League totals (7 years)			981	3520	574	940	188	23	185	559	377	745	114-40	.267	.342	.491	32	.988

DIVISION SERIES RECORD

			BATTING														FIELDING	
Year	**Team (League)**	**Pos.**	**G**	**AB**	**R**	**H**	**2B**	**3B**	**HR**	**RBI**	**BB**	**SO**	**SB-CS**	**Avg.**	**OBP**	**SLG**	**E**	**Avg.**
1996—	Atlanta (N.L.)	OF-PR	3	0	0	0	0	0	0	0	1	0	0-0	...	1.000	...	0	1.000
1997—	Atlanta (N.L.)	OF	3	5	1	0	0	0	0	1	1	1	0-0	.000	.167	.000	0	1.000
1998—	Atlanta (N.L.)	OF	3	9	2	0	0	0	0	1	3	2	2-0	.000	.231	.000	0	1.000
1999—	Atlanta (N.L.)	OF	4	18	1	4	1	0	0	2	1	3	0-0	.222	.263	.278	0	1.000
2000—	Atlanta (N.L.)	OF	3	9	3	1	0	0	1	1	4	1	0-1	.111	.385	.444	0	1.000
2001—	Atlanta (N.L.)	OF	3	12	2	6	0	0	1	1	0	3	0-0	.500	.500	.750	0	1.000
2002—	Atlanta (N.L.)	OF	5	19	4	6	1	0	0	2	2	3	0-0	.316	.381	.368	0	1.000
Division series totals (7 years)			24	72	13	17	2	0	2	8	12	13	2-1	.236	.341	.347	0	1.000

CHAMPIONSHIP SERIES RECORD

			BATTING														FIELDING	
Year	**Team (League)**	**Pos.**	**G**	**AB**	**R**	**H**	**2B**	**3B**	**HR**	**RBI**	**BB**	**SO**	**SB-CS**	**Avg.**	**OBP**	**SLG**	**E**	**Avg.**
1996—	Atlanta (N.L.)	OF-PR-PH	5	9	3	2	0	0	1	3	3	2	0-0	.222	.417	.556	0	1.000
1997—	Atlanta (N.L.)	OF-PH	5	9	0	4	0	0	0	1	1	1	0-0	.444	.500	.444	0	1.000
1998—	Atlanta (N.L.)	OF	6	22	3	6	0	0	1	2	1	4	1-1	.273	.292	.409	0	1.000
1999—	Atlanta (N.L.)	OF	6	23	5	5	0	0	0	1	4	3	0-1	.217	.333	.217	0	1.000
2001—	Atlanta (N.L.)	OF	5	17	4	3	0	0	1	1	1	5	0-0	.176	.222	.353	0	1.000
Championship series totals (5 years)			27	80	15	20	0	0	3	8	10	15	1-2	.250	.330	.363	0	1.000

WORLD SERIES RECORD

RECORDS: Shares record for most home runs in two consecutive innings—2 (October 20, 1996, second and third innings). ... Shares single-inning record for most putouts by outfielder—3 (October 24, 1999, seventh inning).

NOTES: Hit home runs in first two at-bats (October 20, 1996, second and third innings).

			BATTING														FIELDING	
Year	**Team (League)**	**Pos.**	**G**	**AB**	**R**	**H**	**2B**	**3B**	**HR**	**RBI**	**BB**	**SO**	**SB-CS**	**Avg.**	**OBP**	**SLG**	**E**	**Avg.**
1996—	Atlanta (N.L.)	OF	6	20	4	8	1	0	2	6	3	6	1-2	.400	.500	.750	0	1.000
1999—	Atlanta (N.L.)	OF	4	13	1	1	0	0	0	0	1	3	0-0	.077	.143	.077	0	1.000
World Series totals (2 years)			10	33	5	9	1	0	2	6	4	9	1-2	.273	.368	.485	0	1.000

ALL-STAR GAME RECORD

	AB	**R**	**H**	**2B**	**3B**	**HR**	**RBI**	**BB**	**SO**	**SB-CS**	**Avg.**	**OBP**	**SLG**	**E**	**Avg.**
All-Star Game totals (2 years)	5	0	1	0	0	0	1	0	3	0-0	.200	.200	.200	0	1.000

JONES, BOBBY — P

PERSONAL: Born February 10, 1970, in Fresno, Calif. ... 6-4/225. ... Throws right, bats right. ... Full name: Robert Joseph Jones.

HIGH SCHOOL: Fresno (Calif.).

COLLEGE: Fresno State.

TRANSACTIONS/CAREER NOTES: Selected by New York Mets organization in supplemental round ("sandwich pick" between first and second round, 36th pick overall) of free-agent draft (June 3, 1991); pick received as part of compensation for Los Angeles Dodgers signing Type A free-agent OF Darryl Strawberry. ... On New York disabled list (May 24-September 10, 1999); included rehabilitation assignments to Binghamton (August 7-17 and September 5-10) and Norfolk (August 18-25). ... On New York disabled list (April 17-May 18, 2000); included rehabilitation assignment to Norfolk (May 7-18). ... Granted free agency (November 4, 2000). ... Signed by San Diego Padres (February 15, 2001). ... On disabled list (May 13-30, June 16-July 12 and August 17-September 2, 2002). ... Released by Padres (September 4, 2002).

HONORS: Named Eastern League Pitcher of the Year (1992).

STATISTICAL NOTES: Led International League with 11 hit batsmen in 1993. ... Led N.L. with 18 sacrifice hits in 1995.

CAREER HITTING (MLB): 59-for-442 (.133), 29 R, 8 2B, 0 3B, 1 HR, 17 RBI.

Year	**League**	**W**	**L**	**Pct.**	**ERA**	**G**	**GS**	**CG**	**ShO**	**Sv.-Opp.**	**IP**	**H**	**R**	**ER**	**HR**	**BB-IBB**	**SO**
1991—	Columbia (S.Atl.)	3	1	.750	1.85	5	5	0	0	0-...	24.1	20	5	5	2	3-0	35
1992—	Binghamton (East.)	12	4	.750	*1.88	24	24	4	*4	0-...	158.0	118	40	33	5	43-0	143
1993—	Norfolk (I.L.)	12	10	.545	3.63	24	24	6	*3	0-...	166.0	149	72	67	9	32-2	126
—	New York (N.L.)	2	4	.333	3.65	9	9	0	0	0-0	61.2	61	35	25	6	22-3	35
1994—	New York (N.L.)	12	7	.632	3.15	24	24	1	1	0-0	160.0	157	75	56	10	56-9	80
1995—	New York (N.L.)	10	10	.500	4.19	30	30	3	1	0-0	195.2	209	107	91	20	53-6	127
1996—	New York (N.L.)	12	8	.600	4.42	31	31	3	1	0-0	195.2	219	102	96	26	46-6	116
1997—	New York (N.L.)	15	9	.625	3.63	30	30	2	1	0-0	193.1	177	88	78	24	63-3	125
1998—	New York (N.L.)	9	9	.500	4.05	30	30	0	0	0-0	195.1	192	94	88	23	53-2	115

Year	League	W	L	Pct.	ERA	G	GS	CG	ShO	Sv.-Opp.	IP	H	R	ER	HR	BB-IBB	SO
1999—	New York (N.L.)...............	3	3	.500	5.61	12	9	0	0	0-0	59.1	69	37	37	3	11-0	31
	—Binghamton (East.).........	1	2	.333	3.86	3	3	0	0	0-...	11.2	11	5	5	3	5-0	12
	—Norfolk (I.L.)..................	2	0	1.000	2.45	2	2	0	0	0-...	11.0	11	3	3	2	3-0	8
2000—	New York (N.L.)...............	11	6	.647	5.06	27	27	1	0	0-0	154.2	171	90	87	25	49-3	85
	—Norfolk (I.L.)..................	2	0	1.000	5.32	4	4	0	0	0-...	23.2	31	14	14	5	4-0	19
2001—	San Diego (N.L.)■..........	8	*19	.296	5.12	33	33	1	0	0-0	195.0	250	137	111	•37	38-6	113
2002—	San Diego (N.L.).............	7	8	.467	5.50	19	18	0	0	0-0	108.0	134	68	66	20	21-1	60
Major League totals (10 years)...		89	83	.517	4.36	245	241	11	4	0-0	1518.2	1639	833	735	194	412-39	887

DIVISION SERIES RECORD

RECORDS: Shares career record for most shutouts—1.

Year	League	W	L	Pct.	ERA	G	GS	CG	ShO	Sv.-Opp.	IP	H	R	ER	HR	BB-IBB	SO
1999—	New York (N.L.)...............									Did not play.							
2000—	New York (N.L.)...............	1	0	1.000	0.00	1	1	1	1	0-0	9.0	1	0	0	0	2-0	5

CHAMPIONSHIP SERIES RECORD

Year	League	W	L	Pct.	ERA	G	GS	CG	ShO	Sv.-Opp.	IP	H	R	ER	HR	BB-IBB	SO
1999—	New York (N.L.)...............									Did not play.							
2000—	New York (N.L.)...............	0	0	...	13.50	1	1	0	0	0-0	4.0	6	6	6	2	0-0	2

WORLD SERIES RECORD

Year	League	W	L	Pct.	ERA	G	GS	CG	ShO	Sv.-Opp.	IP	H	R	ER	HR	BB-IBB	SO
2000—	New York (N.L.)...............	0	1	.000	5.40	1	1	0	0	0-0	5.0	4	3	3	1	3-2	3

ALL-STAR GAME RECORD

	W	L	Pct.	ERA	GS	CG	ShO	Sv.-Opp.	IP	H	R	ER	HR	BB-IBB	SO
All-Star Game totals (1 year)........	0	0	...	0.00	0	0	0	0-0	1.0	1	0	0	0	0-0	2

JONES, BOBBY — P

PERSONAL: Born April 11, 1972, in Orange, N.J. ... 6-0/178. ... Throws left, bats right. ... Full name: Robert Mitchell Jones.

HIGH SCHOOL: Rutherford (N.J.).

JUNIOR COLLEGE: Chipola Junior College (Fla.).

TRANSACTIONS/CAREER NOTES: Selected by Milwaukee Brewers organization in 44th round of free-agent draft (June 3, 1991). ... Selected by Colorado Rockies organization from Brewers organization in Rule 5 minor league draft (December 5, 1994). ... Traded by Rockies with P Lariel Gonzalez to New York Mets for P Masato Yoshii (January 14, 2000). ... On New York disabled list (March 20, 2001-entire season); included rehabilitation assignments to St. Lucie (May 11-27), Binghamton (June 25-30) and Norfolk (July 1-4). ... Granted free agency (October 15, 2001). ... Re-signed by Mets organization (December 19, 2001). ... Traded by Mets with P Josh Reynolds and OF Jay Bay to San Diego Padres for P Steve Reed and P Jason Middlebrook (July 31, 2002). ... Released by Padres (September 3, 2002).

STATISTICAL NOTES: Tied for Pacific Coast League lead with 12 hit batsmen in 1997.

CAREER HITTING (MLB): 14-for-81 (.173), 7 R, 2 2B, 0 3B, 0 HR, 8 RBI.

Year	League	W	L	Pct.	ERA	G	GS	CG	ShO	Sv.-Opp.	IP	H	R	ER	HR	BB-IBB	SO
1992—	Helena (Pio.).....................	5	4	.556	4.36	14	13	1	0	0-...	76.1	93	51	37	7	23-0	53
1993—	Beloit (Midw.)...................	10	10	.500	4.11	25	25	4	0	0-...	144.2	159	82	66	9	65-1	115
1994—	Stockton (Calif.)...............	6	12	.333	4.21	26	26	2	0	0-...	147.2	131	90	69	12	64-0	147
1995—	New Haven (East.)■.........	5	2	.714	2.58	27	8	0	0	3-...	73.1	61	27	21	4	36-2	70
	—Colorado Springs (PCL)...	1	2	.333	7.30	11	8	0	0	0-...	40.2	50	38	33	5	33-1	48
1996—	Colorado Springs (PCL)...	2	8	.200	4.97	57	0	0	0	3-...	88.2	88	54	49	8	63-4	78
1997—	Colorado Springs (PCL)...	7	11	.389	5.14	25	21	0	0	0-...	133.0	135	89	76	16	71-2	104
	—Colorado (N.L.)...............	1	1	.500	8.38	4	4	0	0	0-0	19.1	30	18	18	2	12-0	5
1998—	Colorado (N.L.)...............	7	8	.467	5.22	35	20	1	0	0-0	141.1	153	87	82	12	66-0	109
1999—	Colorado (N.L.)...............	6	10	.375	6.33	30	20	0	0	0-0	112.1	132	91	79	24	77-0	74
	—Colorado Springs (PCL)...	2	1	.667	5.40	3	3	0	0	0-...	16.2	17	13	10	1	15-0	14
2000—	Norfolk (I.L.)■................	10	8	.556	4.32	22	21	4	1	0-...	133.1	122	66	64	13	58-4	100
	—New York (N.L.)...............	0	1	.000	4.15	11	1	0	0	0-0	21.2	18	11	10	2	14-1	20
2001—	St. Lucie (FSL)................	0	1	.000	0.93	4	4	0	0	0-...	9.2	6	2	1	0	4-0	9
	—Binghamton (East.)..........	0	0	...	0.00	2	1	0	0	0-...	5.0	0	0	0	0	0-0	6
	—Norfolk (I.L.)..................	0	0	...	0.00	1	1	0	0	0-...	2.0	0	0	0	0	0-0	0
2002—	Norfolk (I.L.)..................	1	4	.200	4.02	13	6	0	0	0-...	40.1	42	25	18	4	15-0	35
	—New York (N.L.)...............	0	0	...	5.29	12	0	0	0	0-0	17.0	20	11	10	3	11-2	11
	—San Diego (N.L.)■..........	0	0	...	6.52	4	2	0	0	0-0	9.2	10	7	7	1	7-0	7
Major League totals (5 years).....		14	20	.412	5.77	96	47	1	0	0-0	321.1	363	225	206	44	187-3	226

JONES, CHIPPER — OF — BRAVES

PERSONAL: Born April 24, 1972, in De Land, Fla. ... 6-4/210. ... Bats both, throws right. ... Full name: Larry Wayne Jones Jr.

HIGH SCHOOL: The Bolles School (Jacksonville).

TRANSACTIONS/CAREER NOTES: Selected by Atlanta Braves organization in first round (first pick overall) of free-agent draft (June 4, 1990). ... On disabled list (March 20, 1994-entire season; and March 22-April 16, 1996).

RECORDS: Holds major league single-season records for fewest putouts by third baseman (150 or more games)—77 (1997); and fewest chances accepted by third baseman (150 or more games)—318. ... Shares major league single-season record for fewest double plays by third baseman (150 or more games)—10 (1999); and fewest double plays by outfielder (150 or more games)—0 (2002). ... Holds N.L. career record for most home runs by switch hitter—253. ... Holds N.L. record for most home runs by switch hitter in two consecutive seasons—81 (1999-2000). ... Holds N.L. single-season records for most home runs by switch hitter—45 (1999); most home runs hit at home by switch hitter—25 (1999); highest slugging average by switch hitter—.633 (1999); most bases on balls by switch-hitter—126 (1999); fewest putouts by third baseman (150 or more games)—77 (1997); fewest assists by third baseman (150 or more games)—238 (1999); and fewest chances by third baseman (150 or more games)—318 (1997).

HONORS: Named N.L. Rookie Player of the Year by The Sporting News (1995). ... Named N.L. Most Valuable Player by Baseball Writers' Association of America (1999). ... Named third baseman on The Sporting News N.L. All-Star team (1999 and 2000-01). ... Named third baseman on The Sporting News N.L. Silver Slugger team (1999 and 2000).

STATISTICAL NOTES: Led South Atlantic League with 10 sacrifice flies in 1991. ... Led South Atlantic League shortstops with 217 putouts, 419 assists, 692 total chances and 71 double plays in 1991. ... Led International League with 268 total bases in 1993. ... Led International League shortstops with 619 total chances in 1993. ... Switch-hit home runs in one game five times (May 1, August 1 and September 21, 1999; and May 14 and July 5, 2000). ... Had 19-game hitting streak (June 1-21, 2000). ... Career major league grand slams: 6.

2002 GAMES PLAYED BY POSITION (MLB): OF—152.

		BATTING														FIELDING	
Year Team (League)	**Pos.**	**G**	**AB**	**R**	**H**	**2B**	**3B**	**HR**	**RBI**	**BB**	**SO**	**SB-CS**	**Avg.**	**OBP**	**SLG**	**E**	**Avg.**
1990—GC Braves (GCL)	SS	44	140	20	32	1	1	1	18	14	25	5-3	.229	.321	.271	18	.919
1991—Macon (S.Atl.)	SS	136	473	*104	154	24	11	15	98	69	70	40-11	.326	.407	.518	56	.919
1992—Durham (Caro.)	SS	70	264	43	73	22	1	4	31	31	34	10-8	.277	.353	.413	14	.956
—Greenville (Sou.)	SS	67	266	43	92	17	11	9	42	11	32	14-1	.346	.367	.594	18	.945
1993—Richmond (I.L.)	SS	139	536	*97	*174	31	*12	13	89	57	70	23-7	.325	.387	.500	*43	.931
—Atlanta (N.L.)	SS	8	3	2	2	1	0	0	0	1	1	0-0	.667	.750	1.000	0	1.000
1994—Atlanta (N.L.)								Did not play.									
1995—Atlanta (N.L.)	3B-OF	140	524	87	139	22	3	23	86	73	99	8-4	.265	.353	.450	25	.935
1996—Atlanta (N.L.)	3B-SS-OF	157	598	114	185	32	5	30	110	87	88	14-1	.309	.393	.530	17	.958
1997—Atlanta (N.L.)	3B-OF	157	597	100	176	41	3	21	111	76	88	20-5	.295	.371	.479	15	.956
1998—Atlanta (N.L.)	3B	160	601	123	188	29	5	34	107	96	93	16-6	.313	.404	.547	12	.971
1999—Atlanta (N.L.)	3B-SS	157	567	116	181	41	1	45	110	126	94	25-3	.319	.441	.633	17	.951
2000—Atlanta (N.L.)	3B-SS	156	579	118	180	38	1	36	111	95	64	14-7	.311	.404	.566	25	.941
2001—Atlanta (N.L.)	3B-OF-DH	159	572	113	189	33	5	38	102	98	82	9-10	.330	.427	.605	18	.947
2002—Atlanta (N.L.)	OF	158	548	90	179	35	1	26	100	107	89	8-2	.327	.435	.536	7	.975
Major League totals (9 years)		1252	4589	863	1419	272	24	253	837	759	698	114-38	.309	.404	.544	136	.954

DIVISION SERIES RECORD

RECORDS: Holds N.L. career records for most games—28; at-bats—96; runs—20; hits—31; runs batted in—18; total bases—52; and bases on balls—26. ... Shares N.L. career record for most home runs—6. ... Shares single-game record for most home runs—2 (October 3, 1995).

		BATTING														FIELDING	
Year Team (League)	**Pos.**	**G**	**AB**	**R**	**H**	**2B**	**3B**	**HR**	**RBI**	**BB**	**SO**	**SB-CS**	**Avg.**	**OBP**	**SLG**	**E**	**Avg.**
1995—Atlanta (N.L.)	3B	4	18	4	7	2	0	2	4	2	2	0-0	.389	.450	.833	0	1.000
1996—Atlanta (N.L.)	3B	3	9	2	2	0	0	1	2	3	4	1-1	.222	.417	.556	0	1.000
1997—Atlanta (N.L.)	3B	3	8	3	4	0	0	1	2	3	2	1-0	.500	.583	.875	1	.833
1998—Atlanta (N.L.)	3B	3	10	2	2	0	0	0	1	4	3	0-0	.200	.429	.200	0	1.000
1999—Atlanta (N.L.)	3B	4	13	2	3	0	0	0	1	5	2	0-0	.231	.421	.231	1	.875
2000—Atlanta (N.L.)	3B	3	12	2	4	1	0	0	1	1	4	0-0	.333	.385	.417	2	.800
2001—Atlanta (N.L.)	3B	3	9	2	4	0	0	2	5	3	1	0-1	.444	.583	1.111	0	1.000
2002—Atlanta (N.L.)	OF	5	17	3	5	0	0	0	2	5	2	0-0	.294	.455	.294	0	1.000
Division series totals (8 years)		28	96	20	31	3	0	6	18	26	20	2-2	.323	.460	.542	4	.929

CHAMPIONSHIP SERIES RECORD

RECORDS: Shares career record for most bases on balls—24. ... Holds N.L. career record for most runs scored—20. ... Shares N.L. career record for most doubles—7. ... Shares N.L. single-series record for most singles—9 (1996). ... Shares single-game record for most singles—4 (October 9, 1996).

		BATTING														FIELDING	
Year Team (League)	**Pos.**	**G**	**AB**	**R**	**H**	**2B**	**3B**	**HR**	**RBI**	**BB**	**SO**	**SB-CS**	**Avg.**	**OBP**	**SLG**	**E**	**Avg.**
1995—Atlanta (N.L.)	3B	4	16	3	7	0	0	1	3	3	1	1-0	.438	.526	.625	0	1.000
1996—Atlanta (N.L.)	3B	7	25	6	11	2	0	0	4	3	1	1-0	.440	.483	.520	1	.923
1997—Atlanta (N.L.)	3B	6	24	5	7	1	0	2	4	2	3	0-0	.292	.346	.583	0	1.000
1998—Atlanta (N.L.)	3B	6	24	2	5	1	0	0	1	4	5	0-0	.208	.321	.250	0	1.000
1999—Atlanta (N.L.)	3B	6	19	3	5	2	0	0	1	9	7	3-0	.263	.517	.368	2	.867
2001—Atlanta (N.L.)	3B	5	19	1	5	1	0	0	2	3	6	0-0	.263	.364	.316	1	.923
Championship series totals (6 years)		34	127	20	40	7	0	3	15	24	23	5-0	.315	.425	.441	4	.950

WORLD SERIES RECORD

NOTES: Member of World Series championship team (1995).

		BATTING														FIELDING	
Year Team (League)	**Pos.**	**G**	**AB**	**R**	**H**	**2B**	**3B**	**HR**	**RBI**	**BB**	**SO**	**SB-CS**	**Avg.**	**OBP**	**SLG**	**E**	**Avg.**
1995—Atlanta (N.L.)	3B	6	21	3	6	3	0	0	1	4	3	0-0	.286	.385	.429	1	.947
1996—Atlanta (N.L.)	3B-SS	6	21	3	6	3	0	0	3	4	2	1-0	.286	.385	.429	0	1.000
1999—Atlanta (N.L.)	3B	4	13	2	3	0	0	1	2	4	2	0-1	.231	.412	.462	0	1.000
World Series totals (3 years)		16	55	8	15	6	0	1	6	12	7	1-1	.273	.391	.436	1	.972

ALL-STAR GAME RECORD

	AB	**R**	**H**	**2B**	**3B**	**HR**	**RBI**	**BB**	**SO**	**SB-CS**	**Avg.**	**OBP**	**SLG**	**E**	**Avg.**
All-Star Game totals (5 years)	10	3	4	0	0	1	1	1	0	0-0	.400	.455	.700	0	1.000

JONES, JACQUE — OF — TWINS

PERSONAL: Born April 25, 1975, in San Diego. ... 5-10/176. ... Bats left, throws left. ... Full name: Jacque Dewayne Jones.

HIGH SCHOOL: San Diego High.

COLLEGE: Southern California.

TRANSACTIONS/CAREER NOTES: Selected by Minnesota Twins organization in second round of free-agent draft (June 2, 1996).

STATISTICAL NOTES: Career major league grand slams: 2.

MISCELLANEOUS: Member of 1996 U.S. Olympic baseball team.

2002 GAMES PLAYED BY POSITION (MLB): OF—143; DH—3.

Year Team (League)	Pos.	G	AB	R	H	2B	3B	HR	RBI	BB	SO	SB-CS	Avg.	OBP	SLG	E	Avg.
							BATTING									FIELDING	
1996—Fort Myers (FSL)	OF	1	3	0	2	1	0	0	1	0	0	0-1	.667	.667	1.000	0	...
1997—Fort Myers (FSL)	OF	131	539	84	*160	33	6	15	82	33	110	24-12	.297	.340	.464	7	.979
1998—New Britain (East.)	OF-DH	134	518	78	155	39	3	21	85	37	134	18-11	.299	.349	.508	10	.968
1999—Salt Lake (PCL)	OF	52	198	32	59	13	2	4	26	9	36	9-2	.298	.325	.444	2	.987
—Minnesota (A.L.)	OF	95	322	54	93	24	2	9	44	17	63	3-4	.289	.329	.460	5	.980
2000—Minnesota (A.L.)	OF	154	523	66	149	26	5	19	76	26	111	7-5	.285	.319	.463	2	.994
2001—Minnesota (A.L.)	OF-DH	149	475	57	131	25	0	14	49	39	92	12-9	.276	.335	.417	5	.983
2002—Minnesota (A.L.)	OF-DH	149	577	96	173	37	2	27	85	37	129	6-7	.300	.341	.511	5	.986
Major League totals (4 years)		547	1897	273	546	112	9	69	254	119	395	28-25	.288	.331	.465	17	.986

DIVISION SERIES RECORD

Year Team (League)	Pos.	G	AB	R	H	2B	3B	HR	RBI	BB	SO	SB-CS	Avg.	OBP	SLG	E	Avg.
							BATTING									FIELDING	
2002—Minnesota (A.L.)	OF	5	20	3	5	3	0	0	1	1	8	0-0	.250	.318	.400	1	.952

CHAMPIONSHIP SERIES RECORD

Year Team (League)	Pos.	G	AB	R	H	2B	3B	HR	RBI	BB	SO	SB-CS	Avg.	OBP	SLG	E	Avg.
							BATTING									FIELDING	
2002—Minnesota (A.L.)	OF	5	20	0	2	1	0	0	2	0	4	0-0	.100	.095	.150	0	1.000

JONES, TODD — P — ROCKIES

PERSONAL: Born April 24, 1968, in Marietta, Ga. ... 6-3/230. ... Throws right, bats both. ... Full name: Todd Barton Jones.
HIGH SCHOOL: Osborne (Ga.).
COLLEGE: Jacksonville (Ala.) State.
TRANSACTIONS/CAREER NOTES: Selected by New York Mets organization in 41st round of free-agent draft (June 2, 1986); did not sign. ... Selected by Houston Astros organization in supplemental round ("sandwich pick" between first and second round, 27th pick overall) of free-agent draft (June 5, 1989); pick received as part of compensation for Texas Rangers signing Type A free-agent P Nolan Ryan. ... On suspended list (September 14-16, 1993). ... On Houston disabled list (July 19-August 12 and August 18-September 12, 1996); included rehabilitation assignment to Tucson (August 9-12). ... Traded by Astros with OF Brian Hunter, IF Orlando Miller, P Doug Brocail and cash to Detroit Tigers for C Brad Ausmus, P Jose Lima, P C.J. Nitkowski, P Trever Miller and IF Daryle Ward (December 10, 1996). ... Traded by Tigers to Minnesota Twins for P Mark Redman (July 28, 2001). ... Granted free agency (November 5, 2001). ... Signed by Colorado Rockies (January 15, 2002).
RECORDS: Shares N.L. single-inning record for most consecutive home runs allowed—3 (September 19, 2002, eighth inning).
HONORS: Named A.L. Fireman of the Year by THE SPORTING NEWS (2000).
CAREER HITTING (MLB): 3-for-14 (.214), 1 R, 1 2B, 0 3B, 0 HR, 0 RBI.

Year League	W	L	Pct.	ERA	G	GS	CG	ShO	Sv.-Opp.	IP	H	R	ER	HR	BB-IBB	SO
1989—Auburn (NY-Penn)	2	3	.400	5.44	11	9	1	0	0-...	49.2	47	39	30	2	42-1	71
1990—Osceola (FSL)	12	10	.545	3.51	27	•27	1	0	0-...	151.1	124	81	59	2	*109-1	106
1991—Osceola (FSL)	4	4	.500	4.35	14	14	0	0	0-...	72.1	69	38	35	2	35-0	51
—Jackson (Texas)	4	3	.571	4.88	10	10	0	0	0-...	55.1	51	37	30	2	39-1	37
1992—Jackson (Texas)	3	7	.300	3.14	*61	0	0	0	25-...	66.0	52	28	23	3	44-3	60
—Tucson (PCL)	0	1	.000	4.50	3	0	0	0	0-...	4.0	1	2	2	0	10-1	4
1993—Tucson (PCL)	4	2	.667	4.44	41	0	0	0	12-...	48.2	49	26	24	5	31-2	45
—Houston (N.L.)	1	2	.333	3.13	27	0	0	0	2-3	37.1	28	14	13	4	15-2	25
1994—Houston (N.L.)	5	2	.714	2.72	48	0	0	0	5-9	72.2	52	23	22	3	26-4	63
1995—Houston (N.L.)	6	5	.545	3.07	68	0	0	0	15-20	99.2	89	38	34	8	52-17	96
1996—Houston (N.L.)	6	3	.667	4.40	51	0	0	0	17-23	57.1	61	30	28	5	32-6	44
—Tucson (PCL)	0	0	...	0.00	1	0	0	0	0-...	2.0	1	1	0	0	2-0	0
1997—Detroit (A.L.)■	5	4	.556	3.09	68	0	0	0	31-36	70.0	60	29	24	3	35-2	70
1998—Detroit (A.L.)	1	4	.200	4.97	65	0	0	0	28-32	63.1	58	38	35	7	36-4	57
1999—Detroit (A.L.)	4	4	.500	3.80	65	0	0	0	30-35	66.1	64	30	28	7	35-1	64
2000—Detroit (A.L.)	2	4	.333	3.52	67	0	0	0	•42-46	64.0	67	28	25	6	25-1	67
2001—Detroit (A.L.)	4	5	.444	4.62	45	0	0	0	11-17	48.2	60	31	25	6	22-1	39
—Minnesota (A.L.)■	1	0	1.000	3.26	24	0	0	0	2-4	19.1	27	8	7	3	7-0	15
2002—Colorado (N.L.)■	1	4	.200	4.70	79	0	0	0	1-3	82.1	84	43	43	10	28-3	73
A.L. totals (5 years)	17	21	.447	3.91	334	0	0	0	144-170	331.2	336	164	144	32	160-9	312
N.L. totals (5 years)	19	16	.543	3.61	273	0	0	0	40-58	349.1	314	148	140	30	153-32	301
Major League totals (10 years)	36	37	.493	3.75	607	0	0	0	184-228	681.0	650	312	284	62	313-41	613

ALL-STAR GAME RECORD

	W	L	Pct.	ERA	GS	CG	ShO	Sv.-Opp.	IP	H	R	ER	HR	BB-IBB	SO
All-Star Game totals (1 year)	0	0	...	0.00	0	0	0	0-0	1.0	0	0	0	0	0-0	1

JORDAN, BRIAN — OF — DODGERS

PERSONAL: Born March 29, 1967, in Baltimore. ... 6-1/205. ... Bats right, throws right. ... Full name: Brian O'Neal Jordan.
HIGH SCHOOL: Milford (Baltimore).
COLLEGE: Richmond.
TRANSACTIONS/CAREER NOTES: Selected by Cleveland Indians organization in 20th round of free-agent draft (June 3, 1985); did not sign. ... Selected by St. Louis Cardinals organization in supplemental round ("sandwich pick" between first and second round, 30th pick overall) of free-agent draft (June 1, 1988); pick received as part of compensation for New York Yankees signing Type A free-agent 1B/OF Jack Clark. ... On disabled list (May 1-8 and June 3-10, 1991). ... On temporarily inactive list (July 3, 1991-remainder of season). ... On St. Louis disabled list (May 23-June 22, 1992); included rehabilitation assignment to Louisville (June 10-22). ... On Louisville disabled list (June 7-14, 1993). ... On disabled list (July 10, 1994-remainder of season; and March 31-April 15, 1996). ... On St. Louis disabled list (May 6-June 13, June 26-August 10 and August 25, 1997-remainder of season); included rehabilitation assignment to Louisville (June 5-13). ... Granted free agency (October 22, 1998). ... Signed by Atlanta Braves (November 23, 1998). ... On disabled list (April 4-19, 2000). ... Traded by Braves with P Odalis Perez and P Andrew Brown to Los Angeles Dodgers for OF Gary Sheffield (January 15, 2002). ... On disabled list (August 17-September 1, 2002).
STATISTICAL NOTES: Tied for N.L. lead with six double plays by outfielder in 1998. ... Career major league grand slams: 6.
2002 GAMES PLAYED BY POSITION (MLB): OF—125; DH—3.

Year Team (League)	Pos.	BATTING														FIELDING	
		G	AB	R	H	2B	3B	HR	RBI	BB	SO	SB-CS	Avg.	OBP	SLG	E	Avg.
1988— Hamilton (NY-Penn)...	OF	19	71	12	22	3	1	4	12	6	15	3-3	.310	.388	.549	1	.971
1989— St. Petersburg (FSL)..	OF	11	43	7	15	4	1	2	11	0	8	0-2	.349	.378	.628	0	1.000
1990— Arkansas (Texas)........	OF	16	50	4	8	1	0	0	0	0	11	0-0	.160	.176	.180	2	.933
— St. Petersburg (FSL)..	OF	9	30	3	5	0	1	0	1	2	11	0-2	.167	.219	.233	0	1.000
1991— Louisville (A.A.)..........	OF	61	212	35	56	11	4	4	24	17	41	10-4	.264	.342	.410	2	.987
1992— St. Louis (N.L.)..........	OF	55	193	17	40	9	4	5	22	10	48	7-2	.207	.250	.373	1	.991
— Louisville (A.A.)..........	OF	43	155	23	45	3	1	4	16	8	21	13-2	.290	.337	.400	1	.989
1993— St. Louis (N.L.)..........	OF	67	223	33	69	10	6	10	44	12	35	6-6	.309	.351	.543	4	.973
— Louisville (A.A.)..........	OF	38	144	24	54	13	2	5	35	16	17	9-4	.375	.442	.597	0	1.000
1994— St. Louis (N.L.)..........	OF-1B	53	178	14	46	8	2	5	15	16	40	4-3	.258	.320	.410	1	.991
1995— St. Louis (N.L.)..........	OF	131	490	83	145	20	4	22	81	22	79	24-9	.296	.339	.488	1	.996
1996— St. Louis (N.L.)..........	OF-1B	140	513	82	159	36	1	17	104	29	84	22-5	.310	.349	.483	2	.994
1997— St. Louis (N.L.)..........	OF	47	145	17	34	5	0	0	10	10	21	6-1	.234	.311	.269	0	1.000
— Louisville (A.A.)..........	OF-DH	6	20	1	3	0	0	0	2	1	2	0-1	.150	.227	.150	0	1.000
1998— St. Louis (N.L.)..........	OF-DH-3B	150	564	100	178	34	7	25	91	40	66	17-5	.316	.368	.534	9	.970
1999— Atlanta (N.L.)■..........	OF	153	576	100	163	28	4	23	115	51	81	13-8	.283	.346	.465	3	.990
2000— Atlanta (N.L.)............	OF	133	489	71	129	26	0	17	77	38	80	10-2	.264	.320	.421	3	.990
2001— Atlanta (N.L.)............	OF-DH	148	560	82	165	32	3	25	97	31	88	3-2	.295	.334	.496	3	.991
2002— Los Angeles (N.L.)■..	OF-DH	128	471	65	134	27	3	18	80	34	86	2-2	.285	.338	.469	4	.982
Major League totals (11 years)		1205	4402	664	1262	235	34	167	736	293	708	114-45	.287	.337	.469	31	.988

DIVISION SERIES RECORD

RECORDS: Holds N.L. career records for highest batting average (50 or more at-bats)—.353; and highest slugging percentage (50 or more at-bats)—.569. ... Shares N.L. single-game record for most runs batted in—5 (October 8, 1999). ... Shares single-inning record for most at-bats—2 (October 9, 1999, sixth inning).

Year Team (League)	Pos.	BATTING														FIELDING	
		G	AB	R	H	2B	3B	HR	RBI	BB	SO	SB-CS	Avg.	OBP	SLG	E	Avg.
1996— St. Louis (N.L.)..........	OF	3	12	4	4	0	0	1	3	1	3	1-0	.333	.385	.583	0	1.000
1999— Atlanta (N.L.)............	OF	4	17	2	8	1	0	1	7	1	2	0-1	.471	.474	.706	0	1.000
2000— Atlanta (N.L.)............	OF	3	11	1	4	1	0	0	4	1	1	0-0	.364	.417	.455	0	1.000
2001— Atlanta (N.L.)............	OF	3	11	1	2	0	0	1	2	0	5	0-1	.182	.167	.455	0	1.000
Division series totals (4 years)		13	51	8	18	2	0	3	16	3	11	1-2	.353	.375	.569	0	1.000

CHAMPIONSHIP SERIES RECORD

Year Team (League)	Pos.	BATTING														FIELDING	
		G	AB	R	H	2B	3B	HR	RBI	BB	SO	SB-CS	Avg.	OBP	SLG	E	Avg.
1996— St. Louis (N.L.)..........	OF	7	25	3	6	1	1	1	2	1	3	0-0	.240	.269	.480	0	1.000
1999— Atlanta (N.L.)............	OF	6	25	3	5	0	0	2	5	3	5	0-0	.200	.310	.440	0	1.000
2001— Atlanta (N.L.)............	OF	5	21	1	4	2	0	0	3	0	6	0-0	.190	.190	.286	0	1.000
Championship series totals (3 years)		18	71	7	15	3	1	3	10	4	14	0-0	.211	.263	.408	0	1.000

WORLD SERIES RECORD

Year Team (League)	Pos.	BATTING														FIELDING	
		G	AB	R	H	2B	3B	HR	RBI	BB	SO	SB-CS	Avg.	OBP	SLG	E	Avg.
1999— Atlanta (N.L.)............	OF	4	13	1	1	0	0	0	1	4	2	0-0	.077	.294	.077	1	.889

ALL-STAR GAME RECORD

	AB	R	H	2B	3B	HR	RBI	BB	SO	SB-CS	Avg.	OBP	SLG	E	Avg.
All-Star Game totals (1 year)	1	0	1	0	0	0	0	1	0	0-1	1.000	1.000	1.000	0	...

RECORD AS FOOTBALL PLAYER

TRANSACTIONS/CAREER NOTES: Selected by Buffalo Bills in seventh round (173rd pick overall) of 1989 NFL draft. ... Signed by Bills (July 17, 1989). ... Claimed on waivers by Atlanta Falcons (September 5, 1989). ... On injured reserve with ankle injury (September 9-October 22, 1989). ... On developmental squad (October 23-December 2, 1989). ... Granted free agency (February 1, 1992).

PRO STATISTICS: 1989—Recovered two fumbles. 1990—Recovered one fumble. 1991—Credited with two safeties and recovered one fumble.

MISCELLANEOUS: Played safety. ... Named alternate for 1992 Pro Bowl.

Year Team	G	INTERCEPTIONS				SACKS	PUNT RETURNS				KICKOFF RETURNS				TOTAL		
		No.	Yds.	Avg.	TD	No.	No.	Yds.	Avg.	TD	No.	Yds.	Avg.	TD	TD	Pts.	Fum.
1989— Atlanta NFL................	4	0	0	...	0	0.0	4	34	8.5	0	3	27	9.0	0	0	0	1
1990— Atlanta NFL................	16	3	14	4.7	0	0.0	2	19	9.5	0	0	0	...	0	0	0	0
1991— Atlanta NFL................	16	2	3	1.5	0	4.0	14	116	8.3	0	5	100	20.0	0	0	4	0
Pro totals (3 years)...............	36	5	17	3.4	0	4.0	20	169	8.5	0	8	127	15.9	0	0	4	1

JOSE, FELIX — OF — DIAMONDBACKS

PERSONAL: Born May 8, 1965, in Santo Domingo, Dominican Republic. ... 6-1/220. ... Bats both, throws right. ... Full name: Domingo Felix Jose.

HIGH SCHOOL: Eldo Foreda Reyez de Munoz (Santo Domingo, Dominican Republic).

TRANSACTIONS/CAREER NOTES: Signed as non-drafted free agent by Oakland Athletics organization (January 3, 1984). ... Traded by A's with 3B Stan Royer and P Daryl Green to St. Louis Cardinals for OF Willie McGee (August 29, 1990). ... On St. Louis disabled list (March 28-April 29, 1992); included rehabilitation assignments to Louisville (April 17-22) and St. Petersburg (April 22-29). ... Traded by Cardinals with IF/OF Craig Wilson to Kansas City Royals for 3B Gregg Jefferies and OF Ed Gerald (February 12, 1993). ... On Kansas City disabled list (March 25-April 15, 1994); included rehabilitation assignment to Memphis (April 7-13). ... Granted free agency (December 12, 1994). ... Re-signed by Royals organization (April 19, 1995). ... Released by Royals (May 14, 1995). ... Signed by Chicago Cubs organization (May 24, 1995). ... Released by Cubs (June 1, 1995). ... Signed by Boston Red Sox organization (February 15, 1996). ... On Pawtucket disabled list (April 4-20, 1996). ... Released by Red Sox (May 12, 1996). ... Signed by Toronto Blue Jays organization (May 24, 1996). ... Granted free agency (October 15, 1996). ... Signed by New York Yankees organization (April 2, 2000). ... On New York disabled list (April 30-May 30, 2000); included rehabilitation assignment to Columbus (May 19-29). ... Granted free agency (October 2, 2000). ... Contract purchased by Arizona Diamondbacks organization from Mexico City Reds, Mexican League (September 4, 2002).

STATISTICAL NOTES: Tied for N.L. lead with 15 assists by outfielder in 1991. ... Career major league grand slams: 2.
2002 GAMES PLAYED BY POSITION (MLB): OF—5.

			BATTING														FIELDING	
Year	Team (League)	Pos.	G	AB	R	H	2B	3B	HR	RBI	BB	SO	SB-CS	Avg.	OBP	SLG	E	Avg.
1984—	Idaho Falls (Pio.)	OF	45	152	16	33	6	0	1	18	18	37	5-1	.217	.301	.276	1	.982
1985—	Madison (Midw.)	OF	117	409	46	89	13	3	3	33	32	82	6-6	.218	.281	.286	12	.942
1986—	Modesto (Calif.)	OF	127	516	77	147	22	8	14	77	36	89	14-9	.285	.333	.440	14	.942
1987—	Huntsville (Sou.)	OF	91	296	29	67	11	1	5	42	28	61	9-3	.226	.295	.321	8	.945
1988—	Tacoma (PCL)	OF	134	508	72	161	29	5	12	83	53	75	16-8	.317	.380	.465	8	.971
—	Oakland (A.L.)	OF	8	6	2	2	1	0	0	1	0	1	1-0	.333	.333	.500	0	1.000
1989—	Oakland (A.L.)	OF	20	57	3	11	2	0	0	5	4	13	0-1	.193	.246	.228	1	.974
—	Tacoma (PCL)	OF	104	387	59	111	26	0	14	63	41	82	11-7	.287	.358	.463	*10	.951
1990—	Oakland (A.L.)	OF-DH	101	341	42	90	12	0	8	39	16	65	8-2	.264	.306	.370	5	.977
—	St. Louis (N.L.)■	OF	25	85	12	23	4	1	3	13	8	16	4-4	.271	.333	.447	0	1.000
1991—	St. Louis (N.L.)	OF	154	568	69	173	40	6	8	77	50	113	20-12	.305	.360	.438	3	.990
1992—	Louisville (A.A.)	OF	2	7	0	1	0	0	0	0	1	0	0-0	.143	.250	.143	0	1.000
—	St. Petersburg (FSL)	OF	6	18	2	8	1	1	0	2	1	2	1-0	.444	.474	.611	0	1.000
—	St. Louis (N.L.)	OF	131	509	62	150	22	3	14	75	40	100	28-12	.295	.347	.432	6	.979
1993—	Kansas City (A.L.)■	OF-DH	149	499	64	126	24	3	6	43	36	95	31-13	.253	.303	.349	7	.972
1994—	Memphis (Sou.)	OF	6	21	3	7	2	0	0	6	5	6	1-1	.333	.462	.429	0	1.000
—	Kansas City (A.L.)	OF	99	366	56	111	28	1	11	55	35	75	10-12	.303	.362	.475	4	.980
1995—	Kansas City (A.L.)	OF	9	30	2	4	1	0	0	1	2	9	0-0	.133	.188	.167	0	1.000
—	Iowa (A.A.)■	OF-DH	10	37	2	5	3	0	0	1	1	6	0-0	.135	.179	.216	0	1.000
1996—	Pawtucket (I.L.)■	DH-OF	11	32	3	7	3	0	2	5	3	10	0-0	.219	.286	.500	1	.889
—	Syracuse (I.L.)■	DH-OF	88	327	47	84	14	2	16	61	32	63	3-0	.257	.321	.459	1	.923
1997—	Monc.-Tab. (Mex.)■		92	308	54	83	16	1	10	41	61	60	8-5	.269	.370	.425	2	.977
1998—	Tabasco (Mex.)		26	91	15	25	6	0	2	13	18	11	0-...	.275	...	.407	...	...
—	Nashua (Atl.)■	OF-DH	98	327	72	112	19	1	26	86	78	55	8-9	.343	.469	.645	3	.975
1999—	Lotte (KBO)■		...	462	93	151	...	...	36	122	...	...	12-...	.327	...	...	...	...
2000—	Columbus (I.L.)■	OF	59	210	31	65	17	2	11	38	23	60	4-3	.310	.379	.567	1	.970
—	New York (A.L.)	OF-DH	20	29	4	7	0	0	1	5	2	9	0-1	.241	.281	.345	1	.929
2002—	MC Reds (Mex.)■	OF	85	324	88	124	21	2	27	102	62	56	4-1	.383	.477	.710	2	.969
—	Arizona (N.L.)■	OF	13	19	5	5	0	0	2	4	4	8	0-0	.263	.360	.579	0	1.000
American League totals (7 years)			406	1328	173	351	68	4	26	149	95	267	50-29	.264	.315	.380	18	.976
National League totals (4 years)			323	1181	148	351	66	10	27	169	102	237	52-28	.297	.352	.439	9	.986
Major League totals (10 years)			729	2509	321	702	134	14	53	318	197	504	102-57	.280	.333	.408	27	.980

ALL-STAR GAME RECORD

	AB	R	H	2B	3B	HR	RBI	BB	SO	SB-CS	Avg.	OBP	SLG	E	Avg.
All-Star Game totals (1 year)	2	0	1	0	0	0	0	0	0	0-0	.500	.500	.500	0	1.000

JOSEPH, KEVIN — P — CARDINALS

PERSONAL: Born August 1, 1976, in Camp Hill, Pa. ... 6-4/200. ... Throws right, bats right. ... Full name: Kevin John Joseph.
HIGH SCHOOL: Trinity Christian (Addison, Texas).
COLLEGE: Rice.
TRANSACTIONS/CAREER NOTES: Selected by San Francisco Giants organization in sixth round of free-agent draft (June 3, 1997). ... On Shreveport disabled list (May 11-June 9, 2000). ... Traded by Giants with a player to be named later or cash to St. Louis Cardinals for P Jason Christiansen (July 31, 2001). ... On Memphis disabled list (April 22-June 9, 2002).
CAREER HITTING (MLB): 0-for-0 (.000), 0 R, 0 2B, 0 3B, 0 HR, 0 RBI.

Year	League	W	L	Pct.	ERA	G	GS	CG	ShO	Sv.-Opp.	IP	H	R	ER	HR	BB-IBB	SO
1997—	Salem-Kaizer (N'West)	3	5	.375	5.40	17	6	0	0	1-...	45.0	44	35	27	4	26-0	45
1998—	Bakersfield (Calif.)	0	4	.000	8.14	6	6	0	0	0-...	21.0	35	26	19	3	20-0	17
—	Salem-Kaizer (N'West)	1	1	.500	4.36	23	0	0	0	0-...	43.1	36	25	21	3	27-0	37
1999—	San Jose (Calif.)	1	2	.333	2.35	20	0	0	0	2-...	30.2	17	9	8	1	13-0	30
—	Shreveport (Texas)	0	2	.000	1.42	7	0	0	0	0-...	12.2	8	4	2	0	5-0	16
2000—	Shreveport (Texas)	3	11	.214	5.17	27	16	0	0	1-...	102.2	116	60	59	8	48-1	71
2001—	Shreveport (Texas)	2	1	.667	2.43	24	0	0	0	1-...	33.1	31	9	9	1	13-3	27
—	San Jose (Calif.)	0	0	...	3.38	9	0	0	0	3-...	13.1	12	6	5	0	1-0	15
—	Fresno (PCL)	0	1	.000	7.56	5	0	0	0	0-...	8.1	9	7	7	0	4-1	2
—	Memphis (PCL)■	0	2	.000	6.75	12	0	0	0	0-...	12.0	8	9	9	2	11-1	6
2002—	Memphis (PCL)	1	1	.500	1.77	31	0	0	0	2-...	35.2	37	10	7	2	11-0	14
—	St. Louis (N.L.)	0	1	.000	4.91	11	0	0	0	0-0	11.0	16	7	6	1	6-0	2
Major League totals (1 year)		0	1	.000	4.91	11	0	0	0	0-0	11.0	16	7	6	1	6-0	2

JOURNELL, JIMMY — P — CARDINALS

PERSONAL: Born December 29, 1977, in Springfield, Ohio. ... 6-4/205. ... Throws right, bats right. ... Full name: James R. Journell.
HIGH SCHOOL: Springfield North (Springfield, Ohio).
COLLEGE: Illinois.
TRANSACTIONS/CAREER NOTES: Selected by St. Louis Cardinals organization in fourth round of free-agent draft (June 2, 1999). ... On New Haven disabled list (April 15-29, 2002). ... On Memphis disabled list (July 3-August 6, 2002).
HONORS: Shared Carolina League Pitcher of the Year (2001).

Year	League	W	L	Pct.	ERA	G	GS	CG	ShO	Sv.-Opp.	IP	H	R	ER	HR	BB-IBB	SO
1999—	Johnson City (Appl.)	Did not play.															
2000—	New Jersey (NY-Penn)	1	0	1.000	1.97	13	1	0	0	0-...	32.0	12	12	7	0	24-0	39
2001—	Potomac (Caro.)	14	6	.700	2.50	26	26	0	0	0-...	151.0	121	54	42	8	42-0	156
—	New Haven (East.)	1	0	1.000	0.00	1	1	1	1	0-...	7.0	0	0	0	0	3-0	6
2002—	New Haven (East.)	3	3	.500	2.70	10	10	2	0	0-...	66.2	50	22	20	3	18-0	66
—	Memphis (PCL)	2	4	.333	3.68	7	7	0	0	0-...	36.2	38	16	15	3	18-0	32

JULIO, JORGE — P — ORIOLES

PERSONAL: Born March 3, 1979, in Caracas, Venezuela. ... 6-1/190. ... Throws right, bats right. ... Full name: Jorge Dandys Julio.
HIGH SCHOOL: Fundacion Bolivariana (Caracas, Venezuela).
TRANSACTIONS/CAREER NOTES: Signed as non-drafted free agent by Montreal Expos organization (February 14, 1996). ... Traded by Expos to Baltimore Orioles for 3B Ryan Minor (December 22, 2000).
CAREER HITTING (MLB): 0-for-0 (.000), 0 R, 0 2B, 0 3B, 0 HR, 0 RBI.

Year League	W	L	Pct.	ERA	G	GS	CG	ShO	Sv.-Opp.	IP	H	R	ER	HR	BB-IBB	SO
1996— Dominican Expos (DSL)...	1	1	.500	6.06	10	0	0	0	0-...	16.1	13	12	11	...	11-...	21
1997— Gulf Coast Expos (GCL) ...	5	6	.455	3.58	15	8	0	0	1-...	55.1	57	25	22	0	21-0	42
— West Palm Beach (FSL) ...	0	0	...	...	1	0	0	0	0-...	.0	2	1	1	0	0-0	0
1998— Vermont (NY-Penn)..........	3	1	.750	2.57	7	7	0	0	0-...	42.0	30	12	12	1	15-0	52
— Cape Fear (S.Atl.)............	2	2	.500	5.68	6	6	0	0	0-...	31.2	33	20	20	4	12-0	20
1999— Jupiter (FSL)....................	4	8	.333	3.92	23	22	0	0	0-...	114.2	116	62	50	6	34-0	80
2000— Jupiter (FSL)....................	2	10	.167	5.90	21	15	0	0	1-...	79.1	93	60	52	4	35-0	67
2001— Bowie (East.)■..................	0	0	...	0.73	12	0	0	0	7-...	12.1	5	1	1	0	2-1	14
— Baltimore (A.L.)...............	1	1	.500	3.80	18	0	0	0	0-1	21.1	25	13	9	2	9-0	22
— Rochester (I.L.)...............	1	2	.333	3.74	34	0	0	0	12-...	43.1	39	27	18	4	19-3	48
2002— Baltimore (A.L.)................	5	6	.455	1.99	67	0	0	0	25-31	68.0	55	22	15	5	27-3	55
Major League totals (2 years).....	6	7	.462	2.42	85	0	0	0	25-32	89.1	80	35	24	7	36-3	77

J

JUNGE, ERIC — P — PHILLIES

PERSONAL: Born January 5, 1977, in Manhasset, N.Y. ... 6-5/215. ... Throws right, bats right. ... Full name: Eric DeBari Junge.
HIGH SCHOOL: Rye (N.Y.).
COLLEGE: Bucknell.
TRANSACTIONS/CAREER NOTES: Selected by Los Angeles Dodgers organization in 11th round of free-agent draft (June 2, 1999). ... Traded with P Jesus Cordero to Philadelphia Phillies for P Omar Daal (November 9, 2001).
CAREER HITTING (MLB): 0-for-3 (.000), 0 R, 0 2B, 0 3B, 0 HR, 0 RBI.

Year League	W	L	Pct.	ERA	G	GS	CG	ShO	Sv.-Opp.	IP	H	R	ER	HR	BB-IBB	SO
1999— Yakima (N'West)..............	5	7	.417	5.82	15	15	0	0	0-...	82.0	98	60	53	10	31-0	55
2000— San Bernardino (Calif.).....	8	1	.889	3.36	29	24	0	0	1-...	158.0	159	69	59	8	53-0	116
2001— Jacksonville (Sou.)...........	10	11	.476	3.46	27	27	1	1	0-...	164.0	143	72	63	19	56-2	116
2002— Scranton/W.B. (I.L.)■......	12	6	.667	3.54	29	•29	1	0	0-...	180.2	170	77	71	16	67-1	126
— Philadelphia (N.L.)...........	2	0	1.000	1.42	4	1	0	0	0-0	12.2	14	3	2	0	5-0	11
Major League totals (1 year).......	2	0	1.000	1.42	4	1	0	0	0-0	12.2	14	3	2	0	5-0	11

JUSTICE, DAVID — OF/DH

PERSONAL: Born April 14, 1966, in Cincinnati. ... 6-3/215. ... Bats left, throws left. ... Full name: David Christopher Justice.
HIGH SCHOOL: Covington (Ky.) Latin.
COLLEGE: Thomas More College (Ky.).
TRANSACTIONS/CAREER NOTES: Selected by Atlanta Braves organization in fourth round of free-agent draft (June 3, 1985). ... On Atlanta disabled list (June 27-August 20, 1991); included rehabilitation assignment to Macon (August 16-20). ... On disabled list (April 12-27, 1992; June 2-17, 1995 and May 16, 1996-remainder of season). ... Traded by Braves with OF Marquis Grissom to Cleveland Indians for OF Kenny Lofton and P Alan Embree (March 25, 1997). ... On disabled list (June 24-July 10, 1997). ... Traded by Indians to New York Yankees for OF Ricky Ledee and two players to be named later (June 29, 2000); Indians acquired P Jake Westbrook and P Zach Day to complete deal (July 25, 2000). ... On New York disabled list (June 15-30 and July 2-August 2, 2001); included rehabilitation assignment to Norwich (July 31-August 2). ... Traded by Yankees to New York Mets for 3B Robin Ventura (December 7, 2001). ... Traded by Mets to Oakland Athletics for P Mark Guthrie and P Tyler Yates (December 14, 2001). ... On disabled list (May 8-June 4, 2002). ... Granted free agency (October 28, 2002).
RECORDS: Holds major league single-season record for fewest errors by outfielder who led league in errors—8 (1992).
HONORS: Named N.L. Rookie Player of the Year by The Sporting News (1990). ... Named N.L. Rookie of the Year by Baseball Writers' Association of America (1990). ... Named outfielder on The Sporting News N.L. All-Star team (1993). ... Named outfielder on The Sporting News N.L. Silver Slugger team (1993). ... Named outfielder on The Sporting News A.L. Silver Slugger team (1997). ... Named A.L. Comeback Player of the Year by The Sporting News (1997). ... Named outfielder on The Sporting News A.L. All-Star team (1997).
STATISTICAL NOTES: Tied for Appalachian League lead with five sacrifice flies in 1985. ... Career major league grand slams: 5.
2002 GAMES PLAYED BY POSITION (MLB): OF—75; DH—37.

							BATTING									FIELDING	
Year Team (League)	Pos.	G	AB	R	H	2B	3B	HR	RBI	BB	SO	SB-CS	Avg.	OBP	SLG	E	Avg.
1985— Pulaski (Appl.)............	OF	66	204	39	50	8	0	•10	46	40	30	0-1	.245	.361	.431	4	.957
1986— Sumter (S.Atl.)...........	OF	61	220	48	66	16	0	10	61	48	28	10-2	.300	.425	.509	4	.970
— Durham (Caro.)..........	OF-1B	67	229	47	64	9	1	12	44	46	24	2-4	.279	.413	.485	1	.994
1987— Greenville (Sou.)........	OF	93	348	38	79	12	4	6	40	53	48	3-2	.227	.327	.336	8	.962
1988— Richmond (I.L.)..........	OF	70	227	27	46	9	1	8	28	39	55	4-3	.203	.311	.357	4	.972
— Greenville (Sou.)........	OF	58	198	34	55	13	1	9	37	37	41	6-2	.278	.395	.490	5	.954
1989— Richmond (I.L.)..........	OF-1B	115	391	47	102	24	3	12	58	59	66	12-8	.261	.360	.430	6	.975
— Atlanta (N.L.).............	OF	16	51	7	12	3	0	1	3	3	9	2-1	.235	.291	.353	0	1.000
1990— Richmond (I.L.)..........	OF-1B	12	45	7	16	5	1	2	7	7	6	0-0	.356	.442	.644	2	.931
— Atlanta (N.L.).............	1B-OF	127	439	76	124	23	2	28	78	64	92	11-6	.282	.373	.535	14	.979
1991— Atlanta (N.L.).............	OF	109	396	67	109	25	1	21	87	65	81	8-8	.275	.377	.503	7	.968
— Macon (S.Atl.)...........	OF	3	10	2	2	0	0	2	5	2	1	0-0	.200	.308	.800	0	1.000
1992— Atlanta (N.L.).............	OF	144	484	78	124	19	5	21	72	79	85	2-4	.256	.359	.446	*8	.976
1993— Atlanta (N.L.).............	OF	157	585	90	158	15	4	40	120	78	90	3-5	.270	.357	.515	5	.985
1994— Atlanta (N.L.).............	OF	104	352	61	110	16	2	19	59	69	45	2-4	.313	.427	.531	*11	.947
1995— Atlanta (N.L.).............	OF	120	411	73	104	17	2	24	78	73	68	4-2	.253	.365	.479	4	.984
1996— Atlanta (N.L.).............	OF	40	140	23	45	9	0	6	25	21	22	1-1	.321	.409	.514	0	1.000

Year Team (League)	Pos.	BATTING														FIELDING	
		G	AB	R	H	2B	3B	HR	RBI	BB	SO	SB-CS	Avg.	OBP	SLG	E	Avg.
1997—Cleveland (A.L.)■	OF-DH	139	495	84	163	31	1	33	101	80	79	3-5	.329	.418	.596	2	.984
1998—Cleveland (A.L.)	DH-OF	146	540	94	151	39	2	21	88	76	98	9-3	.280	.363	.476	0	1.000
1999—Cleveland (A.L.)	OF-DH	133	429	75	123	18	0	21	88	94	90	1-3	.287	.413	.476	4	.977
2000—Cleveland (A.L.)	OF-DH	68	249	46	66	14	1	21	58	38	49	1-1	.265	.361	.582	2	.977
—New York (A.L.)■	OF-DH	78	275	43	84	17	0	20	60	39	42	1-0	.305	.391	.585	2	.985
2001—New York (A.L.)	DH-OF	111	381	58	92	16	1	18	51	54	83	1-2	.241	.333	.430	1	.981
—Norwich (East.)	DH	2	8	0	0	0	0	0	0	0	1	0-0	.000	.000	.000	...	...
2002—Oakland (A.L.)■	OF-DH	118	398	54	106	18	3	11	49	70	66	4-1	.266	.376	.410	2	.985
American League totals (6 years)		793	2767	454	785	153	8	145	495	451	507	20-15	.284	.381	.502	13	.982
National League totals (8 years)		817	2858	475	786	127	16	160	522	452	492	33-31	.275	.374	.499	49	.977
Major League totals (14 years)		1610	5625	929	1571	280	24	305	1017	903	999	53-46	.279	.378	.500	62	.978

DIVISION SERIES RECORD

RECORDS: Shares A.L. career record for most triples—2. ... Shares single-series record for most doubles—4 (1998).

Year Team (League)	Pos.	BATTING														FIELDING	
		G	AB	R	H	2B	3B	HR	RBI	BB	SO	SB-CS	Avg.	OBP	SLG	E	Avg.
1995—Atlanta (N.L.)	OF	4	13	2	3	0	0	0	0	5	2	0-0	.231	.444	.231	1	.857
1997—Cleveland (A.L.)	DH	5	19	3	5	2	0	1	2	2	3	0-0	.263	.333	.526	...	...
1998—Cleveland (A.L.)	DH-OF	4	16	2	5	4	0	1	6	0	1	0-0	.313	.294	.750	0	1.000
1999—Cleveland (A.L.)	OF	3	8	0	0	0	0	0	1	2	2	0-0	.000	.182	.000	0	1.000
2000—New York (A.L.)	OF	5	18	2	4	0	0	1	1	3	4	0-0	.222	.333	.389	0	1.000
2001—New York (A.L.)	OF-DH-PH	4	13	3	3	0	1	1	1	2	5	0-0	.231	.333	.615	0	1.000
2002—Oakland (A.L.)	OF	5	21	2	5	1	1	0	4	0	4	0-0	.238	.238	.381	0	1.000
Division series totals (7 years)		30	108	14	25	7	2	4	15	14	21	0-0	.231	.315	.444	1	.976

CHAMPIONSHIP SERIES RECORD

RECORDS: Holds career records for most games—46; runs—24; runs batted in—27; and at-bats—166. ... Shares career records for most doubles—7; bases on balls—24; and times grounded into double play—5.

NOTES: Named Most Valuable Player (2000).

Year Team (League)	Pos.	BATTING														FIELDING	
		G	AB	R	H	2B	3B	HR	RBI	BB	SO	SB-CS	Avg.	OBP	SLG	E	Avg.
1991—Atlanta (N.L.)	OF	7	25	4	5	1	0	1	2	3	7	0-1	.200	.286	.360	1	.944
1992—Atlanta (N.L.)	OF	7	25	5	7	1	0	2	6	6	2	0-0	.280	.419	.560	0	1.000
1993—Atlanta (N.L.)	OF	6	21	2	3	1	0	0	4	3	3	0-0	.143	.231	.190	1	.933
1995—Atlanta (N.L.)	OF	3	11	1	3	0	0	0	1	2	1	0-0	.273	.385	.273	0	1.000
1997—Cleveland (A.L.)	DH	6	21	3	7	1	0	0	0	2	4	0-0	.333	.417	.381	...	...
1998—Cleveland (A.L.)	OF-DH-PH	6	19	2	3	0	0	1	2	3	3	0-0	.158	.304	.316	0	1.000
2000—New York (A.L.)	OF	6	26	4	6	2	0	2	8	2	7	0-0	.231	.286	.538	0	1.000
2001—New York (A.L.)	DH	5	18	3	5	1	0	0	4	3	1	0-0	.278	.409	.333	...	...
Championship series totals (8 years)		46	166	24	39	7	0	6	27	24	28	0-1	.235	.338	.386	2	.972

WORLD SERIES RECORD

RECORDS: Shares record for most consecutive strikeouts in one series—5 (October 30 [2] and 31 [3], 2001).

NOTES: Member of World Series championship team (1995 and 2000).

Year Team (League)	Pos.	BATTING														FIELDING	
		G	AB	R	H	2B	3B	HR	RBI	BB	SO	SB-CS	Avg.	OBP	SLG	E	Avg.
1991—Atlanta (N.L.)	OF	7	27	5	7	0	0	2	6	5	5	2-0	.259	.375	.481	1	.957
1992—Atlanta (N.L.)	OF	6	19	4	3	0	0	1	3	6	5	1-0	.158	.360	.316	1	.938
1995—Atlanta (N.L.)	OF	6	20	3	5	1	0	1	5	5	1	0-0	.250	.400	.450	0	1.000
1997—Cleveland (A.L.)	OF-DH	7	27	4	5	0	0	0	4	6	8	0-1	.185	.333	.185	0	1.000
2000—New York (A.L.)	OF	5	19	1	3	2	0	0	3	3	2	0-0	.158	.333	.263	0	1.000
2001—New York (A.L.)	OF-PH-DH	5	12	0	2	0	0	0	0	1	9	0-0	.167	.231	.167	1	.500
World Series totals (6 years)		36	124	17	25	3	0	4	21	26	30	3-1	.202	.349	.323	3	.960

ALL-STAR GAME RECORD

	AB	R	H	2B	3B	HR	RBI	BB	SO	SB-CS	Avg.	OBP	SLG	E	Avg.
All-Star Game totals (2 years)	5	0	1	0	0	0	0	0	0	0-0	.200	.200	.200	1	.667

KAPLER, GABE — OF — ROCKIES

PERSONAL: Born August 31, 1975, in Hollywood, Calif. ... 6-2/208. ... Bats right, throws right. ... Full name: Gabriel Stefan Kapler.

HIGH SCHOOL: Taft (Woodland Hills, Calif.).

JUNIOR COLLEGE: Moorpark (Calif.) College.

TRANSACTIONS/CAREER NOTES: Selected by Detroit Tigers organization in 57th round of free-agent draft (June 1, 1995). ... Traded by Tigers with P Justin Thompson, P Francisco Cordero, C Bill Haselman, 2B Frank Catalanotto and P Alan Webb to Texas Rangers for OF Juan Gonzalez, P Danny Patterson and C Gregg Zaun (November 2, 1999). ... On Texas disabled list (May 4-June 9, 2000); included rehabilitation assignments to Oklahoma (May 20-24) and Tulsa (June 5-9). ... On Texas disabled list (March 23-April 22, 2001); included rehabilitation assignment to Tulsa (April 17-22). ... On Texas disabled list (June 24-July 16, 2002); included rehabilitation assignment to Oklahoma (July 11-16). ... Traded by Rangers with 2B Jason Romano to Colorado Rockies for OF Todd Hollandsworth and P Dennys Reyes (July 31, 2002).

HONORS: Named Minor League Player of the Year by The Sporting News (1998). ... Named Southern League Most Valuable Player (1998).

STATISTICAL NOTES: Led South Atlantic League with 280 total bases in 1996. ... Led Florida State League with 262 total bases in 1997. ... Led Southern League with 319 total bases and 11 sacrifice flies in 1998. ... Had 28-game hitting streak (July 17-August 15, 2000). ... Career major league grand slams: 1.

2002 GAMES PLAYED BY POSITION (MLB): OF—102; DH—1; 1B—1.

			BATTING														FIELDING	
Year	Team (League)	Pos.	G	AB	R	H	2B	3B	HR	RBI	BB	SO	SB-CS	Avg.	OBP	SLG	E	Avg.
1995—	Jamestown (NY-P)	OF	63	236	38	68	19	4	4	34	23	37	1-2	.288	.351	.453	9	.926
1996—	Fayetteville (S.Atl.)	OF-3B	138	524	81	*157	*45	0	26	99	62	73	14-4	.300	.378	.534	7	.968
1997—	Lakeland (FSL)	OF	137	519	87	153	*40	6	19	87	54	68	8-6	.295	.361	.505	6	.978
1998—	Jacksonville (Sou.)	OF-1B	•139	547	*113	*176	•47	6	*28	*146	66	93	6-4	.322	.393	.583	5	.984
	—Detroit (A.L.)	OF-DH	7	25	3	5	0	1	0	0	1	4	2-0	.200	.231	.280	0	1.000
1999—	Detroit (A.L.)	OF-DH	130	416	60	102	22	4	18	49	42	74	11-5	.245	.315	.447	6	.981
	—Toledo (I.L.)	OF	14	54	11	17	6	2	3	14	9	10	0-1	.315	.400	.667	0	1.000
2000—	Texas (A.L.)■	OF	116	444	59	134	32	1	14	66	42	57	8-4	.302	.360	.473	•10	.969
	—Oklahoma (PCL)	OF	3	9	3	3	0	0	0	0	3	2	0-0	.333	.500	.333	0	1.000
	—Tulsa (Texas)	OF	3	12	3	7	0	0	1	4	1	2	0-0	.583	.615	.833	0	1.000
2001—	Tulsa (Texas)	OF	5	15	2	5	1	0	0	0	6	1	0-1	.333	.524	.400	0	1.000
	—Texas (A.L.)	OF-DH	134	483	77	129	29	1	17	72	61	70	23-6	.267	.348	.437	1	.997
2002—	Texas (A.L.)	OF-DH-1B	72	196	25	51	12	1	0	17	8	30	5-2	.260	.285	.332	3	.977
	—Oklahoma (PCL)	OF	5	17	6	8	2	0	1	5	3	2	1-0	.471	.550	.765	0	1.000
	—Colorado (N.L.)■	OF	40	119	12	37	4	3	2	17	8	23	6-2	.311	.359	.445	0	1.000
American League totals (5 years)			459	1564	224	421	95	8	49	204	154	235	49-17	.269	.333	.434	20	.982
National League totals (1 year)			40	119	12	37	4	3	2	17	8	23	6-2	.311	.359	.445	0	1.000
Major League totals (5 years)			499	1683	236	458	99	11	51	221	162	258	55-19	.272	.335	.435	20	.983

KARROS, ERIC — 1B — DODGERS

PERSONAL: Born November 4, 1967, in Hackensack, N.J. ... 6-4/226. ... Bats right, throws right. ... Full name: Eric Peter Karros. ... Name pronounced CARE-ose.

HIGH SCHOOL: Patrick Henry (San Diego).

COLLEGE: UCLA.

TRANSACTIONS/CAREER NOTES: Selected by Los Angeles Dodgers organization in sixth round of free-agent draft (June 1, 1988). ... On Los Angeles disabled list (March 29-April 24, 1998); included rehabilitation assignment to San Bernardino (April 19-25). ... On disabled list (May 22-June 15, 2001).

RECORDS: Shares major league single-inning record for most home runs—2 (August 22, 2000, sixth inning).

HONORS: Named N.L. Rookie Player of the Year by The Sporting News (1992). ... Named N.L. Rookie of the Year by Baseball Writers' Association of America (1992). ... Named first baseman on The Sporting News N.L. All-Star team (1995). ... Named first baseman on The Sporting News N.L. Silver Slugger team (1995).

STATISTICAL NOTES: Tied for Pioneer League lead in errors by first baseman with 14 in 1988. ... Led California League first basemen with 1,232 putouts, 110 assists and 1,358 total chances in 1989. ... Led Texas League with 282 total bases in 1990. ... Led Texas League first basemen with 1,223 putouts, 106 assists, 1,337 total chances and 129 double plays in 1990. ... Led Pacific Coast League with 269 total bases in 1991. ... Tied for Pacific Coast League lead with eight intentional bases on balls received in 1991. ... Led Pacific Coast League first basemen with 1,095 putouts, 109 assists and 1,215 total chances in 1991. ... Led N.L. first basemen with 147 assists in 1993 and 126 in 1999. ... Led N.L. in grounding into double plays with 27 in 1996. ... Career major league grand slams: 2.

2002 GAMES PLAYED BY POSITION (MLB): 1B—142.

			BATTING														FIELDING	
Year	Team (League)	Pos.	G	AB	R	H	2B	3B	HR	RBI	BB	SO	SB-CS	Avg.	OBP	SLG	E	Avg.
1988—	Great Falls (Pio.)	1B-3B	66	268	68	98	12	1	12	55	32	35	8-2	.366	.433	.552	‡19	.966
1989—	Bakersfield (Calif.)	1B-3B	*142	545	86	*165	*40	1	15	86	63	99	18-7	.303	.375	.462	19	.986
1990—	San Antonio (Texas)	1B	•131	509	91	*179	*45	2	18	78	57	79	8-10	*.352	.419	.554	8	*.994
1991—	Albuquerque (PCL)	1B-3B	132	488	88	154	33	8	22	101	58	80	3-2	.316	.391	.551	11	.991
	—Los Angeles (N.L.)	1B	14	14	0	1	1	0	0	1	1	6	0-0	.071	.133	.143	0	1.000
1992—	Los Angeles (N.L.)	1B	149	545	63	140	30	1	20	88	37	103	2-4	.257	.304	.426	9	.993
1993—	Los Angeles (N.L.)	1B	158	619	74	153	27	2	23	80	34	82	0-1	.247	.287	.409	12	.992
1994—	Los Angeles (N.L.)	1B	111	406	51	108	21	1	14	46	29	53	2-0	.266	.310	.426	•9	.991
1995—	Los Angeles (N.L.)	1B	143	551	83	164	29	3	32	105	61	115	4-4	.298	.369	.535	7	.995
1996—	Los Angeles (N.L.)	1B	154	608	84	158	29	1	34	111	53	121	8-0	.260	.316	.479	15	.990
1997—	Los Angeles (N.L.)	1B	•162	628	86	167	28	0	31	104	61	116	15-7	.266	.329	.459	11	.992
1998—	San Bern. (Calif.)	1B	4	15	3	4	1	0	0	1	0	2	0-0	.267	.267	.333	0	1.000
	—Los Angeles (N.L.)	1B-DH	139	507	59	150	20	1	23	87	47	93	7-2	.296	.355	.475	12	.991
1999—	Los Angeles (N.L.)	1B	153	578	74	176	40	0	34	112	53	119	8-5	.304	.362	.550	13	.991
2000—	Los Angeles (N.L.)	1B-DH	155	584	84	146	29	0	31	106	63	122	4-3	.250	.321	.459	7	.995
2001—	Los Angeles (N.L.)	1B	121	438	42	103	22	0	15	63	41	101	3-1	.235	.303	.388	4	.996
2002—	Los Angeles (N.L.)	1B	142	524	52	142	26	1	13	73	37	74	4-2	.271	.323	.399	4	*.997
Major League totals (12 years)			1601	6002	752	1608	302	10	270	976	517	1105	57-29	.268	.325	.457	103	.993

DIVISION SERIES RECORD

RECORDS: Shares single-game record for most home runs—2 (October 4, 1995).

			BATTING														FIELDING	
Year	Team (League)	Pos.	G	AB	R	H	2B	3B	HR	RBI	BB	SO	SB-CS	Avg.	OBP	SLG	E	Avg.
1995—	Los Angeles (N.L.)	1B	3	12	3	6	1	0	2	4	1	0	0-0	.500	.538	1.083	0	1.000
1996—	Los Angeles (N.L.)	1B	3	9	0	0	0	0	0	0	2	3	0-0	.000	.182	.000	0	1.000
Division series totals (2 years)			6	21	3	6	1	0	2	4	3	3	0-0	.286	.375	.619	0	1.000

KARSAY, STEVE — P — YANKEES

PERSONAL: Born March 24, 1972, in Flushing, N.Y. ... 6-3/215. ... Throws right, bats right. ... Full name: Stefan Andrew Karsay. ... Name pronounced CAR-say.

HIGH SCHOOL: Christ the King (Queens, N.Y.).

TRANSACTIONS/CAREER NOTES: Selected by Toronto Blue Jays organization in first round (22nd pick overall) of free-agent draft (June 4, 1990). ... On Knoxville disabled list (July 3-16, 1993). ... Traded by Blue Jays with a player to be named later to Oakland Athletics for OF Rickey Henderson (July 31, 1993); A's acquired OF Jose Herrera to complete deal (August 6, 1993). ... On disabled list (April 26, 1994-remainder of

season; April 24, 1995-entire season; and August 6, 1997-remainder of season). ... Traded by A's to Cleveland Indians for P Mike Fetters (December 8, 1997). ... On Buffalo disabled list (May 14-25 and June 12-July 15, 1998). ... On disabled list (July 2-26 and August 25-September 22, 1999). ... Traded by Indians with P Steve Reed to Atlanta Braves for P John Rocker and 3B Troy Cameron (June 22, 2001). ... Granted free agency (November 5, 2001). ... Signed by New York Yankees (December 7, 2001).
STATISTICAL NOTES: Led A.L. with 14 intentional bases on balls issued in 2002.
MISCELLANEOUS: Appeared in one game as pinch runner (1997).
CAREER HITTING (MLB): 0-for-4 (.000), 1 R, 0 2B, 0 3B, 0 HR, 0 RBI.

Year League	W	L	Pct.	ERA	G	GS	CG	ShO	Sv.-Opp.	IP	H	R	ER	HR	BB-IBB	SO
1990— St. Catharines (NY-Penn)	1	1	.500	0.79	5	5	0	0	0-...	22.2	11	4	2	0	12-0	25
1991— Myrtle Beach (S.Atl.)	4	9	.308	3.58	20	20	1	0	0-...	110.2	96	58	44	7	48-0	100
1992— Dunedin (FSL)	6	3	.667	2.73	16	16	3	2	0-...	85.2	56	32	26	6	29-0	87
1993— Knoxville (Sou.)	8	4	.667	3.38	19	18	1	0	0-...	104.0	98	42	39	9	32-1	100
— Huntsville (Sou.)■	0	0	...	5.14	2	2	0	0	0-...	14.0	13	8	8	2	3-0	22
— Oakland (A.L.)	3	3	.500	4.04	8	8	0	0	0-0	49.0	49	23	22	4	16-1	33
1994— Oakland (A.L.)	1	1	.500	2.57	4	4	1	0	0-0	28.0	26	8	8	1	8-0	15
1995— Oakland (A.L.)									Did not play.							
1996— Modesto (Calif.)	0	1	.000	2.65	14	14	0	0	0-...	34.0	35	16	10	2	1-0	31
1997— Oakland (A.L.)	3	12	.200	5.77	24	24	0	0	0-0	132.2	166	92	85	20	47-3	92
1998— Buffalo (I.L.)■	6	4	.600	3.76	16	14	0	0	0-...	79.0	89	39	33	5	15-0	63
— Cleveland (A.L.)	0	2	.000	5.92	11	1	0	0	0-0	24.1	31	16	16	3	6-1	13
1999— Cleveland (A.L.)	10	2	.833	2.97	50	3	0	0	1-3	78.2	71	29	26	6	30-3	68
2000— Cleveland (A.L.)	5	9	.357	3.76	72	0	0	0	20-29	76.2	79	33	32	5	25-4	66
2001— Cleveland (A.L.)	0	1	.000	1.25	31	0	0	0	1-1	43.1	29	6	6	1	8-2	44
— Atlanta (N.L.)■	3	4	.429	3.43	43	0	0	0	7-11	44.2	44	21	17	4	17-8	39
2002— New York (A.L.)■	6	4	.600	3.26	78	0	0	0	12-16	88.1	87	33	32	7	30-14	65
A.L. totals (8 years)	28	34	.452	3.92	278	40	1	0	34-49	521.0	538	240	227	47	170-28	396
N.L. totals (1 year)	3	4	.429	3.43	43	0	0	0	7-11	44.2	44	21	17	4	17-8	39
Major League totals (8 years)	31	38	.449	3.88	321	40	1	0	41-60	565.2	582	261	244	51	187-36	435

DIVISION SERIES RECORD

Year League	W	L	Pct.	ERA	G	GS	CG	ShO	Sv.-Opp.	IP	H	R	ER	HR	BB-IBB	SO
1999— Cleveland (A.L.)	0	0	...	9.00	2	0	0	0	0-0	3.0	5	3	3	1	1-0	3
2001— Atlanta (N.L.)	0	0	...	0.00	1	0	0	0	0-0	1.0	0	0	0	0	0-0	1
2002— New York (A.L.)	1	0	1.000	6.75	4	0	0	0	0-0	2.2	3	2	2	1	0-0	1
Division series totals (3 years)	1	0	1.000	6.75	7	0	0	0	0-0	6.2	8	5	5	2	1-0	5

CHAMPIONSHIP SERIES RECORD

Year League	W	L	Pct.	ERA	G	GS	CG	ShO	Sv.-Opp.	IP	H	R	ER	HR	BB-IBB	SO
2001— Atlanta (N.L.)	0	0	...	2.08	4	0	0	0	0-0	4.1	3	1	1	0	1-1	6

KAYE, JUSTIN P

PERSONAL: Born June 9, 1976, in Fort Lauderdale, Fla. ... 6-4/195. ... Throws right, bats right. ... Full name: Justin Malcolm Kaye.
HIGH SCHOOL: Bishop Gorman (Las Vegas, Nev.).
TRANSACTIONS/CAREER NOTES: Selected by Seattle Mariners organization in 19th round of free-agent draft (June 1, 1995). ... Granted free agency (October 15, 2002).
CAREER HITTING (MLB): 0-for-0 (.000), 0 R, 0 2B, 0 3B, 0 HR, 0 RBI.

Year League	W	L	Pct.	ERA	G	GS	CG	ShO	Sv.-Opp.	IP	H	R	ER	HR	BB-IBB	SO
1995— Arizona Mariners (Ariz.)	0	1	.000	10.71	12	0	0	0	0-...	19.1	33	28	23	1	19-0	13
1996— Arizona Mariners (Ariz.)	1	0	1.000	3.62	20	0	0	0	3-...	32.1	34	23	13	4	19-1	36
1997— Wisconsin (Midw.)	8	12	.400	7.30	26	26	0	0	0-...	127.0	129	113	103	13	104-0	115
1998— Wisconsin (Midw.)	6	2	.750	1.71	28	0	0	0	9-...	47.1	25	11	9	2	30-4	79
— Lancaster (Calif.)	1	2	.333	6.82	16	0	0	0	0-...	30.1	37	24	23	4	13-2	34
1999— Lancaster (Calif.)	3	5	.375	5.75	53	0	0	0	14-...	61.0	68	42	39	4	40-1	66
2000— New Haven (East.)	2	5	.286	2.67	50	0	0	0	8-...	84.1	80	32	25	3	36-4	109
2001— Tacoma (PCL)	3	2	.600	2.92	56	0	0	0	4-...	77.0	51	27	25	5	46-2	107
2002— Tacoma (PCL)	3	7	.300	4.04	47	0	0	0	6-...	62.1	54	32	28	2	42-1	65
— Seattle (A.L.)	0	0	...	12.00	3	0	0	0	0-0	3.0	6	4	4	0	1-0	3
Major League totals (1 year)	0	0	...	12.00	3	0	0	0	0-0	3.0	6	4	4	0	1-0	3

KEARNS, AUSTIN OF REDS

PERSONAL: Born May 20, 1980, in Lexington, Ky. ... 6-3/220. ... Bats right, throws right. ... Full name: Austin Ryan Kearns.
HIGH SCHOOL: Lafayette (Lexington, Ky.).
TRANSACTIONS/CAREER NOTES: Selected by Cincinnati Reds organization in first round (seventh pick overall) of free-agent draft (June 2, 1998). ... On Chattanooga disabled list (May 27-August 13, 2001). ... On Cincinnati disabled list (August 27, 2002-remainder of season).
STATISTICAL NOTES: Led Midwest League with 270 total bases in 2000. ... Led Midwest League outfielders with 23 assists and tied for league lead with five double plays in 2000. ... Career major league grand slams: 1.
2002 GAMES PLAYED BY POSITION (MLB): OF—103.

		BATTING														FIELDING	
Year Team (League)	Pos.	G	AB	R	H	2B	3B	HR	RBI	BB	SO	SB-CS	Avg.	OBP	SLG	E	Avg.
1998— Billings (Pio.)	OF	30	108	17	34	9	0	1	14	23	22	1-1	.315	.433	.426	4	.905
1999— Rockford (Midw.)	OF	124	426	72	110	36	5	13	48	50	120	21-8	.258	.346	.458	13	.939
2000— Dayton (Midw.)	OF	*136	484	*110	148	37	2	*27	•104	90	93	18-5	.306	.415	.558	12	.955
2001— Chattanooga (Sou.)	OF	59	205	30	55	11	2	6	36	26	43	7-5	.268	.364	.429	2	.979
— GC Reds (GCL)	OF	6	17	2	3	2	0	0	4	2	7	0-0	.176	.227	.294	0	1.000
2002— Chattanooga (Sou.)	OF	12	41	10	11	2	0	5	13	9	9	1-0	.268	.434	.683	0	1.000
— Cincinnati (N.L.)	OF	107	372	66	117	24	3	13	56	54	81	6-3	.315	.407	.500	4	.983
— Louisville (I.L.)	OF	1	4	3	3	2	0	0	2	1	0	0-0	.750	.800	1.250	0	1.000
Major League totals (1 year)		107	372	66	117	24	3	13	56	54	81	6-3	.315	.407	.500	4	.983

KEISLER, RANDY — P — YANKEES

PERSONAL: Born February 24, 1976, in Richards, Texas. ... 6-3/190. ... Throws left, bats left. ... Full name: Randy Dean Keisler.
HIGH SCHOOL: Navasota (Texas), then Palmer (Texas).
JUNIOR COLLEGE: Navarro College (Texas).
COLLEGE: Louisiana State.
TRANSACTIONS/CAREER NOTES: Selected by Cleveland Indians organization in 40th round of free-agent draft (June 1, 1995); did not sign. ... Selected by Indians organization in 57th round of free-agent draft (June 4, 1996); did not sign. ... Selected by New York Yankees organization in second round of free-agent draft (June 2, 1998). ... On disabled list (March 31, 2002-entire season).
CAREER HITTING (MLB): 0-for-2 (.000), 0 R, 0 2B, 0 3B, 0 HR, 0 RBI.

Year	League	W	L	Pct.	ERA	G	GS	CG	ShO	Sv.-Opp.	IP	H	R	ER	HR	BB-IBB	SO
1998—	Oneonta (NY-Penn)	1	1	.500	7.45	6	2	0	0	1-...	9.2	14	10	8	0	7-1	11
1999—	Greensboro (S.Atl.)	1	1	.500	2.38	4	4	0	0	0-...	22.2	12	6	6	1	10-0	42
	—Tampa (FSL)	10	3	.769	3.30	15	15	1	0	0-...	90.0	67	43	33	2	40-0	77
	—Norwich (East.)	3	4	.429	4.57	8	8	0	0	0-...	43.1	45	24	22	2	17-0	33
2000—	Norwich (East.)	6	2	.750	2.60	11	11	1	0	0-...	72.2	63	29	21	4	34-1	70
	—Columbus (I.L.)	8	3	.727	3.02	17	17	1	1	0-...	113.1	104	44	38	9	42-1	86
	—New York (A.L.)	1	0	1.000	11.81	4	1	0	0	0-0	10.2	16	14	14	1	8-0	6
2001—	Columbus (I.L.)	5	7	.417	5.18	18	18	3	1	0-...	97.1	111	67	56	10	39-0	88
	—New York (A.L.)	1	2	.333	6.22	10	10	0	0	0-0	50.2	52	36	35	12	34-0	36
2002—	New York (A.L.)	Did not play.															
Major League totals (2 years)		2	2	.500	7.19	14	11	0	0	0-0	61.1	68	50	49	13	42-0	42

KELLER, KRIS — P

PERSONAL: Born March 1, 1978, in Williamsport, Pa. ... 6-2/225. ... Throws right, bats right. ... Full name: Kristopher Shane Keller.
HIGH SCHOOL: Fletcher (Neptune Beach, Fla.).
TRANSACTIONS/CAREER NOTES: Selected by Detroit Tigers organization in fourth round of free-agent draft (June 4, 1996). ... On Detroit disabled list (May 25-June 19, 2002). ... Traded by Tigers to Atlanta Braves for OF George Lombard (June 19, 2002). ... On Atlanta disabled list (June 19-23, 2002). ... Granted free agency (October 15, 2002).
CAREER HITTING (MLB): 0-for-0 (.000), 0 R, 0 2B, 0 3B, 0 HR, 0 RBI.

Year	League	W	L	Pct.	ERA	G	GS	CG	ShO	Sv.-Opp.	IP	H	R	ER	HR	BB-IBB	SO
1996—	Gulf Coast Tigers (GCL)	1	1	.500	2.38	8	6	0	0	0-...	34.0	23	12	9	0	21-0	23
1997—	Jamestown (NY-Penn)	0	2	.000	8.67	16	0	0	0	0-...	27.0	37	33	26	3	20-0	18
1998—	Jamestown (NY-Penn)	1	3	.250	3.27	27	0	0	0	8-...	33.0	29	12	12	3	16-0	41
1999—	West Michigan (Midw.)	5	3	.625	2.92	49	0	0	0	8-...	77.0	63	28	25	6	36-1	87
2000—	Jacksonville (Sou.)	2	3	.400	2.91	62	0	0	0	*26-...	68.0	58	24	22	0	44-3	60
2001—	Toledo (I.L.)	5	2	.714	4.48	52	0	0	0	4-...	68.1	64	42	34	10	38-3	60
2002—	Toledo (I.L.)	2	0	1.000	2.08	17	0	0	0	0-...	26.0	20	10	6	1	17-1	20
	—Detroit (A.L.)	0	0	...	27.00	1	0	0	0	0-0	1.0	2	3	3	1	3-0	1
	—Richmond (I.L.)■	1	0	1.000	3.60	29	0	0	0	2-...	35.0	26	16	14	4	13-2	20
Major League totals (1 year)		0	0	...	27.00	1	0	0	0	0-0	1.0	2	3	3	1	3-0	1

KELLY, KENNY — OF — MARINERS

PERSONAL: Born January 26, 1979, in Plant City, Fla. ... 6-2/180. ... Bats right, throws right. ... Full name: Kenneth Alphonso Kelly.
HIGH SCHOOL: Tampa Catholic.
COLLEGE: Miami (Fla.).
TRANSACTIONS/CAREER NOTES: Selected by Tampa Bay Devil Rays organization in second round of free-agent draft (June 3, 1997). ... Traded by Devil Rays to Seattle Mariners for cash considerations (April 4, 2001). ... On disabled list (June 3-10, 2001). ... On Seattle disabled list (September 4, 2002-remainder of season).
STATISTICAL NOTES: Led Southern League with 21 caught stealing in 2000. ... Tied outfielders for Texas League lead with three double plays in 2001.

			BATTING														FIELDING	
Year	Team (League)	Pos.	G	AB	R	H	2B	3B	HR	RBI	BB	SO	SB-CS	Avg.	OBP	SLG	E	Avg.
1997—	GC Devil Rays (GCL)	OF	27	99	21	21	2	1	2	7	11	24	6-3	.212	.304	.313	2	.958
1998—	Charl., S.C. (S.Atl.)	OF	54	218	46	61	7	5	3	17	19	52	19-4	.280	.347	.399	5	.964
1999—	St. Petersburg (FSL)	OF	51	206	39	57	10	4	3	21	18	46	14-5	.277	.346	.408	4	.970
2000—	Orlando (Sou.)	OF	124	489	73	123	17	8	3	29	59	119	31-21	.252	.338	.337	8	.974
	—Tampa Bay (A.L.)	DH	2	1	0	0	0	0	0	0	0	0	0-0	.000	.000	.000	...	...
2001—	San Antonio (Texas)■	OF	121	478	72	125	20	5	11	46	45	111	18-12	.262	.326	.393	5	.981
2002—	Tacoma (PCL)	OF	122	391	51	97	13	10	11	53	26	93	11-3	.248	.296	.417	8	.972
Major League totals (1 year)			2	1	0	0	0	0	0	0	0	0	0-0	.000	.000	.000	0	...

KELTON, DAVE — 3B — CUBS

PERSONAL: Born December 17, 1979, in Dothan, Ala. ... 6-3/205. ... Bats right, throws right. ... Full name: David Wayne Kelton.
HIGH SCHOOL: Troup County (La Grange, Ga.).
TRANSACTIONS/CAREER NOTES: Selected by Chicago Cubs organization in second round of free-agent draft (June 2, 1998). ... On disabled list (June 16, 2001-remainder of season). ... On West Tenn disabled list (April 4-13, 2002).
STATISTICAL NOTES: Led Arizona League third basemen with 138 total chances and nine double plays in 1998.

			BATTING														FIELDING	
Year	Team (League)	Pos.	G	AB	R	H	2B	3B	HR	RBI	BB	SO	SB-CS	Avg.	OBP	SLG	E	Avg.
1998—	Arizona Cubs (Ariz.)	3B	50	181	39	48	7	5	•6	29	23	58	16-3	.265	.353	.459	15	.891
1999—	Lansing (Midw.)	3B	124	509	75	137	17	4	13	68	39	121	22-9	.269	.322	.395	32	.893
2000—	Daytona (FSL)	3B	132	523	75	140	30	7	18	84	38	120	7-8	.268	.317	.455	26	.896
2001—	West Tenn (Sou.)	3B	58	224	33	70	9	4	12	45	24	55	1-3	.313	.378	.549	15	.883
2002—	West Tenn (Sou.)	1B-3B-OF	129	498	68	130	28	6	•20	*79	52	129	12-6	.261	.332	.462	13	.988

KENDALL, JASON C PIRATES

PERSONAL: Born June 26, 1974, in San Diego. ... 6-0/195. ... Bats right, throws right. ... Full name: Jason Daniel Kendall. ... Son of Fred Kendall, coach, Colorado Rockies; and catcher/first baseman with three major league teams (1969-80).
HIGH SCHOOL: Torrance (Calif.).
TRANSACTIONS/CAREER NOTES: Selected by Pittsburgh Pirates organization in first round (23rd pick overall) of free-agent draft (June 1, 1992). ... On suspended list (July 21-23, 1998). ... On disabled list (July 5, 1999-remainder of season). ... On suspended list (September 19-20, 2001).
HONORS: Named Southern League Most Valuable Player (1995). ... Named N.L. Rookie Player of the Year by THE SPORTING NEWS (1996).
STATISTICAL NOTES: Led Gulf Coast League with 13 passed balls in 1992. ... Led Southern League catchers with 692 putouts and 754 total chances in 1995. ... Led N.L. catchers with 103 assists and 20 double plays in 1997. ... Led N.L. in being hit by pitch with 31 in 1998. ... Led N.L. catchers with 1,015 putouts in 1998. ... Led N.L. catchers in total chances with 1,082 in 1998 and 1,081 in 2000. ... Had 16-game hitting streak (May 20-June 7, 1999). ... Led N.L. catchers with 13 double plays in 1999. ... Led N.L. catchers with 990 putouts 81 assists and 11 passed balls in 2000. ... Hit for the cycle (May 19, 2000). ... Led N.L. catchers with 13 double plays in 2002.
2002 GAMES PLAYED BY POSITION (MLB): C—143.

		BATTING														FIELDING	
Year Team (League)	Pos.	G	AB	R	H	2B	3B	HR	RBI	BB	SO	SB-CS	Avg.	OBP	SLG	E	Avg.
1992—GC Pirates (GCL)	C	33	111	7	29	2	0	0	10	8	9	2-2	.261	.317	.279	5	.978
1993—Augusta (S.Atl.)	C	102	366	43	101	17	4	1	40	22	30	8-5	.276	.325	.352	20	.964
1994—Salem (Caro.)	C	101	371	68	118	19	2	7	66	47	21	14-3	.318	.406	.437	9	.980
—Carolina (Sou.)	C	13	47	6	11	2	0	0	6	2	3	0-0	.234	.294	.277	2	.969
1995—Carolina (Sou.)	C	117	429	87	140	26	1	8	71	56	22	10-7	.326	*.414	.448	8	.989
1996—Pittsburgh (N.L.)	C	130	414	54	124	23	5	3	42	35	30	5-2	.300	.372	.401	*18	.980
1997—Pittsburgh (N.L.)	C	144	486	71	143	36	4	8	49	49	53	18-6	.294	.391	.434	11	.990
1998—Pittsburgh (N.L.)	C	149	535	95	175	36	3	12	75	51	51	26-5	.327	.411	.473	9	.992
1999—Pittsburgh (N.L.)	C	78	280	61	93	20	3	8	41	38	32	22-3	.332	.428	.511	7	.988
2000—Pittsburgh (N.L.)	C	152	579	112	185	33	6	14	58	79	79	22-12	.320	.412	.470	10	.991
2001—Pittsburgh (N.L.)	C-OF	157	606	84	161	22	2	10	53	44	48	13-14	.266	.335	.358	17	.980
2002—Pittsburgh (N.L.)	C	145	545	59	154	25	3	3	44	49	29	15-8	.283	.350	.356	9	.990
Major League totals (7 years)		955	3445	536	1035	195	26	58	362	345	322	121-50	.300	.383	.423	81	.987

ALL-STAR GAME RECORD

	AB	R	H	2B	3B	HR	RBI	BB	SO	SB-CS	Avg.	OBP	SLG	E	Avg.
All-Star Game totals (3 years)	3	0	1	0	0	0	0	0	1	0-0	.333	.333	.333	0	1.000

KENNEDY, ADAM 2B ANGELS

PERSONAL: Born January 10, 1976, in Riverside, Calif. ... 6-1/192. ... Bats left, throws right. ... Full name: Adam Thomas Kennedy.
HIGH SCHOOL: J.W. North (Riverside, Calif.).
COLLEGE: Cal State-Northridge.
TRANSACTIONS/CAREER NOTES: Selected by St. Louis Cardinals organization in first round (20th pick overall) of free-agent draft (June 3, 1997). ... On Memphis disabled list (June 9-19, 1999). ... Traded by Cardinals with P Kent Bottenfield to Anaheim Angels for OF Jim Edmonds (March 23, 2000). ... On Anaheim disabled list (March 23-April 13, 2001); included rehabilitation assignment to Rancho Cucamonga (April 9-13).
STATISTICAL NOTES: Led A.L. second basemen with 337 putouts and 781 total chances in 2000. ... Career major league grand slams: 1.
2002 GAMES PLAYED BY POSITION (MLB): 2B—139; OF—1; DH—1.

		BATTING														FIELDING	
Year Team (League)	Pos.	G	AB	R	H	2B	3B	HR	RBI	BB	SO	SB-CS	Avg.	OBP	SLG	E	Avg.
1997—New Jersey (NY-P)	SS	29	114	20	39	6	3	0	19	13	10	9-1	.342	.412	.447	7	.951
—Prince William (Caro.)	SS	35	154	24	48	9	3	1	27	6	17	4-3	.312	.346	.429	10	.939
1998—Prince William (Caro.)	2B-SS	17	69	9	18	6	0	0	7	5	12	5-2	.261	.307	.348	5	.938
—Arkansas (Texas)	SS-2B	52	205	35	57	11	2	6	24	8	21	6-2	.278	.307	.439	15	.940
—Memphis (PCL)	SS-2B	74	305	36	93	22	7	4	41	12	42	15-4	.305	.331	.462	10	.972
1999—Memphis (PCL)	2-S-O-3-DH	91	367	69	120	22	4	10	63	29	36	20-6	.327	.378	.490	18	.953
—St. Louis (N.L.)	2B	33	102	12	26	10	1	1	16	3	8	0-1	.255	.284	.402	4	.971
2000—Anaheim (A.L.)■	2B	156	598	82	159	33	11	9	72	28	73	22-8	.266	.300	.403	*19	.976
2001—Rancho Cuca. (Calif.)	2B	3	8	3	3	2	0	0	1	2	1	3-0	.375	.545	.625	0	1.000
—Anaheim (A.L.)	2B-DH	137	478	48	129	25	3	6	40	27	71	12-7	.270	.318	.372	10	.984
2002—Anaheim (A.L.)	2B-OF-DH	144	474	65	148	32	6	7	52	19	80	17-4	.312	.345	.449	11	.983
American League totals (3 years)		437	1550	195	436	90	20	22	164	74	224	51-19	.281	.319	.408	40	.981
National League totals (1 year)		33	102	12	26	10	1	1	16	3	8	0-1	.255	.284	.402	4	.971
Major League totals (4 years)		470	1652	207	462	100	21	23	180	77	232	51-20	.280	.317	.407	44	.980

DIVISION SERIES RECORD

		BATTING														FIELDING	
Year Team (League)	Pos.	G	AB	R	H	2B	3B	HR	RBI	BB	SO	SB-CS	Avg.	OBP	SLG	E	Avg.
2002—Anaheim (A.L.)	2B	4	8	4	4	1	0	1	3	1	2	1-0	.500	.455	1.000	0	1.000

CHAMPIONSHIP SERIES RECORD

RECORDS: Shares single-game records for most home runs—3 (October 13, 2002); and total bases—13 (October 13, 2002). ... Shares single-inning records for most hits—2 (October 13, 2002, seventh inning); and total bases—5 (October 13, 2002, seventh inning, one home run and one single). ... Shares A.L. single-game records for most extra-base hits—3 (October 13, 2002); and most runs batted in—5 (October 13, 2002).
NOTES: Named Most Valuable Player (2002).

		BATTING														FIELDING	
Year Team (League)	Pos.	G	AB	R	H	2B	3B	HR	RBI	BB	SO	SB-CS	Avg.	OBP	SLG	E	Avg.
2002—Anaheim (A.L.)	2B	4	14	5	5	0	0	3	5	0	2	1-0	.357	.357	1.000	0	1.000

WORLD SERIES RECORD

NOTES: Member of World Series championship team (2002).

		BATTING														FIELDING	
Year Team (League)	Pos.	G	AB	R	H	2B	3B	HR	RBI	BB	SO	SB-CS	Avg.	OBP	SLG	E	Avg.
2002—Anaheim (A.L.)	2B	7	25	1	7	2	0	0	2	0	7	0-0	.280	.308	.360	0	1.000

K

KENNEDY, JOE — P — DEVIL RAYS

PERSONAL: Born May 24, 1979, in La Mesa, Calif. ... 6-4/237. ... Throws left, bats right. ... Full name: Joseph Darley Kennedy.

HIGH SCHOOL: El Cajon Valley (El Cajon, Calif.).

JUNIOR COLLEGE: Grossmont (Calif.).

TRANSACTIONS/CAREER NOTES: Selected by Tampa Bay Devil Rays organization in eighth round of free-agent draft (June 2, 1998). ... On suspended list (July 12-19, 2002).

CAREER HITTING (MLB): 4-for-11 (.364), 2 R, 0 2B, 0 3B, 0 HR, 1 RBI.

Year	League	W	L	Pct.	ERA	G	GS	CG	ShO	Sv.-Opp.	IP	H	R	ER	HR	BB-IBB	SO
1998—	Princeton (Appl.)	6	4	.600	3.74	13	13	0	0	0-...	67.1	66	37	28	5	26-0	44
1999—	Hudson Valley (NY-Penn)	6	5	.545	2.65	16	*16	1	1	0-...	*95.0	78	33	28	2	26-0	*101
2000—	Charleston, S.C. (S.Atl.)	11	6	.647	3.30	22	22	3	2	0-...	136.1	122	59	50	6	29-1	142
2001—	Orlando (Sou.)	4	0	1.000	0.19	7	7	0	0	0-...	47.0	29	3	1	0	3-0	52
—	Durham (I.L.)	2	0	1.000	2.42	4	4	0	0	0-...	26.0	22	8	7	2	9-0	23
—	Tampa Bay (A.L.)	7	8	.467	4.44	20	20	0	0	0-0	117.2	122	63	58	16	34-0	78
2002—	Tampa Bay (A.L.)	8	11	.421	4.53	30	30	5	1	0-0	196.2	204	114	99	23	55-0	109
Major League totals (2 years)		15	19	.441	4.50	50	50	5	1	0-0	314.1	326	177	157	39	89-0	187

KENT, JEFF — 2B

PERSONAL: Born March 7, 1968, in Bellflower, Calif. ... 6-1/220. ... Bats right, throws right. ... Full name: Jeffrey Franklin Kent.

HIGH SCHOOL: Edison (Huntington Beach, Calif.).

COLLEGE: California.

TRANSACTIONS/CAREER NOTES: Selected by Toronto Blue Jays organization in 20th round of free-agent draft (June 5, 1989). ... Traded by Blue Jays with a player to be named later to New York Mets for P David Cone (August 27, 1992); Mets acquired OF Ryan Thompson to complete deal (September 1, 1992). ... On disabled list (July 6-21, 1995). ... Traded by New York Mets with IF Jose Vizcaino to Cleveland Indians for 2B Carlos Baerga and IF Alvaro Espinoza (July 29, 1996). ... Traded by Indians with IF Jose Vizcaino, P Julian Tavarez and a player to be named later to San Francisco Giants for 3B Matt Williams and a player to be named later (November 13, 1996); Indians traded P Joe Roa to Giants for OF Trenidad Hubbard to complete deal (December 16, 1996). ... On suspended list (August 22-25, 1997). ... On disabled list (June 10-July 10, 1998; and August 3-21, 1999). ... On disabled list (March 21-April 6, 2002). ... Granted free agency (October 29, 2002).

RECORDS: Shares major league single-inning record for most doubles—2 (May 10, 2001, sixth inning).

HONORS: Named second baseman on The Sporting News N.L. All-Star team (2000 and 2002). ... Named second baseman on The Sporting News N.L. Silver Slugger team (2000). ... Named N.L. Most Valuable Player by Baseball Writers' Association of America (2000). ... Named second baseman on N.L. Silver Slugger team (2001 and 2002).

STATISTICAL NOTES: Led Florida State League second basemen with 261 putouts, 404 assists, 680 total chances and 83 double plays in 1990. ... Led Southern League second basemen with 395 assists, 673 total chances and 96 double plays in 1991. ... Led N.L. second basemen in errors with 18 in 1993 and 20 in 1998. ... Tied for N.L. lead with 10 sacrifice flies in 1998. ... Hit for the cycle (May 3, 1999). ... Led N.L. with 13 sacrifice flies in 2001. ... Led N.L. second basemen with 113 double plays in 2002. ... Career major league grand slams: 9.

2002 GAMES PLAYED BY POSITION (MLB): 2B—149; 1B—9.

			BATTING														FIELDING	
Year	Team (League)	Pos.	G	AB	R	H	2B	3B	HR	RBI	BB	SO	SB-CS	Avg.	OBP	SLG	E	Avg.
1989—	St. Catharines (NY-P)	SS-3B	73	268	34	60	14	1	*13	37	33	81	5-1	.224	.318	.429	29	.906
1990—	Dunedin (FSL)	2B	132	447	72	124	32	2	16	60	53	98	17-7	.277	.360	.465	15	.978
1991—	Knoxville (Sou.)	2B	•139	445	68	114	*34	1	2	61	80	104	25-6	.256	.379	.351	*29	.957
1992—	Toronto (A.L.)	3B-2B-1B	65	192	36	46	13	1	8	35	20	47	2-1	.240	.324	.443	11	.941
—	New York (N.L.)■	2B-SS-3B	37	113	16	27	8	1	3	15	7	29	0-2	.239	.289	.407	3	.981
1993—	New York (N.L.)	2B-3B-SS	140	496	65	134	24	0	21	80	30	88	4-4	.270	.320	.446	†22	.965
1994—	New York (N.L.)	2B	107	415	53	121	24	5	14	68	23	84	1-4	.292	.341	.475	•14	.976
1995—	New York (N.L.)	2B	125	472	65	131	22	3	20	65	29	89	3-3	.278	.327	.464	10	.984
1996—	New York (N.L.)	3B	89	335	45	97	20	1	9	39	21	56	4-3	.290	.331	.436	21	.925
—	Cleveland (A.L.)■	1B-2B-3B-DH	39	102	16	27	7	0	3	16	10	22	2-1	.265	.328	.422	1	.994
1997—	San Fran. (N.L.)■	2B-1B	155	580	90	145	38	2	29	121	48	133	11-3	.250	.316	.472	16	.981
1998—	San Francisco (N.L.)	2B-1B	137	526	94	156	37	3	31	128	48	110	9-4	.297	.359	.555	†20	.972
1999—	San Francisco (N.L.)	2B-1B	138	511	86	148	40	2	23	101	61	112	13-6	.290	.366	.511	10	.984
2000—	San Francisco (N.L.)	2B-1B	159	587	114	196	41	7	33	125	90	107	12-9	.334	.424	.596	12	.985
2001—	San Francisco (N.L.)	2B-1B	159	607	84	181	49	6	22	106	65	96	7-6	.298	.369	.507	11	.987
2002—	San Francisco (N.L.)	2B-1B	152	623	102	195	42	2	37	108	52	101	5-1	.313	.368	.565	16	.979
American League totals (2 years)			104	294	52	73	20	1	11	51	30	69	4-2	.248	.325	.435	12	.966
National League totals (11 years)			1398	5265	814	1531	345	32	242	956	474	1005	69-45	.291	.354	.506	155	.977
Major League totals (11 years)			1502	5559	866	1604	365	33	253	1007	504	1074	73-47	.289	.353	.503	167	.977

DIVISION SERIES RECORD

RECORDS: Shares single-game record for most home runs—2 (October 3, 1997).

			BATTING														FIELDING	
Year	Team (League)	Pos.	G	AB	R	H	2B	3B	HR	RBI	BB	SO	SB-CS	Avg.	OBP	SLG	E	Avg.
1996—	Cleveland (A.L.)	2B-1B-PR-3B	4	8	2	1	1	0	0	0	0	0	0-0	.125	.125	.250	0	1.000
1997—	San Francisco (N.L.)	2B-1B	3	10	2	3	0	0	2	2	2	1	0-0	.300	.417	.900	0	1.000
2000—	San Francisco (N.L.)	2B-1B	4	16	3	6	1	0	0	1	1	3	1-0	.375	.412	.438	0	1.000
2002—	San Francisco (N.L.)	2B	5	19	1	5	2	0	0	1	2	7	0-0	.263	.364	.368	1	.960
Division series totals (4 years)			16	53	8	15	4	0	2	4	5	11	1-0	.283	.356	.472	1	.987

CHAMPIONSHIP SERIES RECORD

			BATTING														FIELDING	
Year	Team (League)	Pos.	G	AB	R	H	2B	3B	HR	RBI	BB	SO	SB-CS	Avg.	OBP	SLG	E	Avg.
2002—	San Francisco (N.L.)	2B	5	19	3	5	0	0	0	0	2	4	0-0	.263	.364	.263	0	1.000

WORLD SERIES RECORD

RECORDS: Shares single-game record for most runs—4 (October 24, 2002). ... Shares record for most home runs in two consecutive innings—2 (October 24, 2002, sixth and seventh innings).

		BATTING														FIELDING	
Year	**Team (League)**	**Pos.**	**G**	**AB**	**R**	**H**	**2B**	**3B**	**HR**	**RBI**	**BB**	**SO**	**SB-CS**	**Avg.**	**OBP**	**SLG**	**E**	**Avg.**
2002—	San Francisco (N.L.) ..	2B	7	29	6	8	1	0	3	7	1	7	0-0	.276	.290	.621	0	1.000

ALL-STAR GAME RECORD

	AB	R	H	2B	3B	HR	RBI	BB	SO	SB-CS	Avg.	OBP	SLG	E	Avg.
All-Star Game totals (3 years)	5	1	1	1	0	0	0	1	0	0-0	.200	.333	.400	1	.875

KENT, STEVE — P — DEVIL RAYS

PERSONAL: Born October 3, 1978, in Frankfurt, Germany. ... 5-11/170. ... Throws left, bats both. ... Full name: Steven Patrick Kent.
HIGH SCHOOL: C.E. Ellison (Killeen, Texas).
JUNIOR COLLEGE: Odessa (Texas).
COLLEGE: Florida International.
TRANSACTIONS/CAREER NOTES: Selected by Seattle Mariners organization in ninth round of free-agent draft (June 2, 1999). ... Selected by Anaheim Angels from Mariners organization in Rule 5 major league draft (December 13, 2001). ... Traded by Angels to Tampa Bay Devil Rays for cash considerations (December 17, 2001).
STATISTICAL NOTES: Tied for A.L. lead with three balks in 2002.
CAREER HITTING (MLB): 0-for-0 (.000), 0 R, 0 2B, 0 3B, 0 HR, 0 RBI.

Year	**League**	**W**	**L**	**Pct.**	**ERA**	**G**	**GS**	**CG**	**ShO**	**Sv.-Opp.**	**IP**	**H**	**R**	**ER**	**HR**	**BB-IBB**	**SO**
1999—	Everett (N'West)	3	2	.600	5.35	21	0	0	0	4-...	37.0	31	24	22	2	26-1	43
2000—	Everett (N'West)	4	1	.800	2.56	24	3	0	0	0-...	52.2	38	16	15	5	23-1	61
2001—	San Bernardino (Calif.)	0	3	.000	2.20	51	0	0	0	1-...	65.1	50	21	16	2	34-0	73
2002—	Tampa Bay (A.L.)■	0	2	.000	5.65	34	0	0	0	1-2	57.1	67	41	36	6	38-0	41
Major League totals (1 year)		0	2	.000	5.65	34	0	0	0	1-2	57.1	67	41	36	6	38-0	41

KERSHNER, JASON — P — BLUE JAYS

PERSONAL: Born December 19, 1976, in Scottsdale, Ariz. ... 6-2/165. ... Throws left, bats left. ... Full name: Jason Ashley Kershner.
HIGH SCHOOL: Saguaro (Scottsdale, Ariz.).
TRANSACTIONS/CAREER NOTES: Selected by Philadelphia Phillies organization in 12th round of free-agent draft (June 1, 1995). ... Granted free agency (October 15, 2001). ... Signed by San Diego Padres organization (November 20, 2001). ... Claimed on waivers by Toronto Blue Jays (August 30, 2002).
CAREER HITTING (MLB): 0-for-0 (.000), 0 R, 0 2B, 0 3B, 0 HR, 0 RBI.

Year	**League**	**W**	**L**	**Pct.**	**ERA**	**G**	**GS**	**CG**	**ShO**	**Sv.-Opp.**	**IP**	**H**	**R**	**ER**	**HR**	**BB-IBB**	**SO**
1995—	Martinsville (Appl.)	4	2	.667	5.14	13	13	0	0	0-...	63.0	67	42	36	10	29-0	64
1996—	Piedmont (S.Atl.)	11	9	.550	3.75	28	28	2	1	0-...	168.0	154	81	70	12	59-0	156
1997—	Clearwater (FSL)	5	10	.333	3.90	22	16	0	0	1-...	99.1	113	49	43	9	21-0	51
1998—	Clearwater (FSL)	3	3	.500	4.01	41	8	0	0	3-...	94.1	108	57	42	8	25-0	65
1999—	Reading (East.)	4	4	.500	5.73	57	2	0	0	8-...	92.2	99	67	59	14	40-3	86
2000—	Reading (East.)	9	2	.818	3.63	27	19	0	0	1-...	119.0	125	49	48	15	25-0	80
—	Clearwater (FSL)	1	0	1.000	0.64	2	2	0	0	0-...	14.0	7	1	1	1	5-0	15
2001—	Reading (East.)	5	9	.357	4.80	26	19	0	0	0-...	123.2	147	75	66	18	26-1	70
—	Scranton/W.B. (I.L.)	1	1	.500	3.60	6	1	0	0	0-...	15.0	12	8	6	3	3-0	7
2002—	Portland (PCL)■	7	2	.778	3.03	31	12	0	0	0-...	86.0	65	30	29	8	26-0	83
—	San Diego (N.L.)	0	1	.000	5.79	15	0	0	0	0-0	18.2	15	14	12	2	10-0	11
—	Toronto (A.L.)■	0	0	...	1.69	10	0	0	0	1-2	5.1	5	2	1	1	4-1	7
A.L. totals (1 year)		0	0	...	1.69	10	0	0	0	1-2	5.1	5	2	1	1	4-1	7
N.L. totals (1 year)		0	1	.000	5.79	15	0	0	0	0-0	18.2	15	14	12	2	10-0	11
Major League totals (1 year)		0	1	.000	4.88	25	0	0	0	1-2	24.0	20	16	13	3	14-1	18

KIELTY, BOBBY — OF — TWINS

PERSONAL: Born August 5, 1976, in Fontana, Calif. ... 6-1/215. ... Bats both, throws right. ... Full name: Robert Michael Kielty.
HIGH SCHOOL: Canyon Springs (Moreno Valley, Calif.).
JUNIOR COLLEGE: Riverside.
COLLEGE: Southern California, then Mississippi.
TRANSACTIONS/CAREER NOTES: Signed as non-drafted free agent by Minnesota Twins organization (February 16, 1999). ... On disabled list (May 21-June 24 and August 25-September 3, 1999). ... On Edmonton disabled list (May 4-18, 2001).
RECORDS: Shares major league single-inning record for most doubles—2 (June 4, 2002, seventh inning).
2002 GAMES PLAYED BY POSITION (MLB): OF—82; DH—11; 1B—5.

			BATTING														FIELDING	
Year	**Team (League)**	**Pos.**	**G**	**AB**	**R**	**H**	**2B**	**3B**	**HR**	**RBI**	**BB**	**SO**	**SB-CS**	**Avg.**	**OBP**	**SLG**	**E**	**Avg.**
1999—	Quad City (Midw.)	OF	69	245	52	72	13	1	13	43	43	56	12-3	.294	.401	.514	3	.977
2000—	New Britain (East.)	OF	129	451	79	118	30	3	14	65	98	109	6-4	.262	.396	.435	3	.988
—	Salt Lake (PCL)	OF	9	33	8	8	4	0	0	2	7	10	0-0	.242	.375	.364	1	.957
2001—	Edmonton (PCL)	OF	94	341	58	98	25	2	12	50	53	76	5-0	.287	.391	.478	2	.991
—	Minnesota (A.L.)	OF-DH	37	104	8	26	8	0	2	14	8	25	3-0	.250	.297	.385	3	.956
2002—	Edmonton (PCL)	OF	2	7	0	3	1	0	0	0	1	1	0-0	.429	.500	.571	0	1.000
—	Minnesota (A.L.)	OF-DH-1B	112	289	49	84	14	3	12	46	52	66	4-1	.291	.405	.484	0	1.000
Major League totals (2 years)			149	393	57	110	22	3	14	60	60	91	7-1	.280	.378	.458	3	.988

DIVISION SERIES RECORD

Year	Team (League)	Pos.	G	AB	R	H	2B	3B	HR	RBI	BB	SO	SB-CS	Avg.	OBP	SLG	E	Avg.
			BATTING														FIELDING	
2002—	Minnesota (A.L.)	OF-DH	3	4	0	0	0	0	0	0	0	1	0-0	.000	.000	.000	0	1.000

CHAMPIONSHIP SERIES RECORD

Year	Team (League)	Pos.	G	AB	R	H	2B	3B	HR	RBI	BB	SO	SB-CS	Avg.	OBP	SLG	E	Avg.
			BATTING														FIELDING	
2002—	Minnesota (A.L.)	DH-OF	4	3	0	0	0	0	0	1	1	2	0-0	.000	.250	.000	0	...

IN MEMORIAM—DARRYL KILE

PERSONAL: Born December 2, 1968, in Garden Grove, Calif. ... 6-5/212. ... Throws right, bats right. ... Full name: Darryl Andrew Kile. ... Died June 22, 2002.

HIGH SCHOOL: Norco Senior (Calif.).

JUNIOR COLLEGE: Chaffey College (Calif.).

TRANSACTIONS/CAREER NOTES: Selected by Houston Astros organization in 30th round of free-agent draft (June 2, 1987). ... On Tucson disabled list (June 25-July 5, 1992). ... Granted free agency (October 28, 1997). ... Signed by Colorado Rockies (December 4, 1997). ... Traded by Rockies with P Dave Veres and P Luther Hackman to St. Louis Cardinals for P Jose Jimenez, P Manny Aybar, P Rick Croushore and SS Brent Butler (November 16, 1999).

RECORDS: Shares modern N.L. record for most hit batsmen (nine-inning game)—4 (June 2, 1996).

STATISTICAL NOTES: Led N.L. with 15 hit batsmen in 1993. ... Pitched 7-1 no-hit victory against New York (September 8, 1993). ... Tied for N.L. lead with 10 wild pitches in 1994. ... Tied for N.L. lead with 16 hit batsmen in 1996.

MISCELLANEOUS: Appeared in two games as pinch runner (1996). ... Had one sacrifice hit in two appearances as pinch hitter and appeared in one game as pinch runner (1998).

CAREER HITTING (MLB): 87-for-657 (.132), 38 R, 23 2B, 0 3B, 2 HR, 40 RBI.

Year	League	W	L	Pct.	ERA	G	GS	CG	ShO	Sv.-Opp.	IP	H	R	ER	HR	BB-IBB	SO
1988—	Gulf Coast Astros (GCL)	5	3	.625	3.17	12	12	0	0	0-...	59.2	48	34	21	1	33-0	54
1989—	Columbus (Sou.)	11	6	.647	2.58	20	20	6	•2	0-...	125.2	74	47	36	5	68-1	108
—	Tucson (PCL)	2	1	.667	5.96	6	6	1	1	0-...	25.2	33	20	17	1	13-0	18
1990—	Tucson (PCL)	5	10	.333	6.64	26	23	1	0	0-...	123.1	147	97	91	16	68-1	77
1991—	Houston (N.L.)	7	11	.389	3.69	37	22	0	0	0-1	153.2	144	81	63	16	84-4	100
1992—	Houston (N.L.)	5	10	.333	3.95	22	22	2	0	0-0	125.1	124	61	55	8	63-4	90
—	Tucson (PCL)	4	1	.800	3.99	9	9	0	0	0-...	56.1	50	31	25	3	32-0	43
1993—	Houston (N.L.)	15	8	.652	3.51	32	26	4	2	0-0	171.2	152	73	67	12	69-1	141
1994—	Houston (N.L.)	9	6	.600	4.57	24	24	0	0	0-0	147.2	153	84	75	13	*82-6	105
1995—	Houston (N.L.)	4	12	.250	4.96	25	21	0	0	0-0	127.0	114	81	70	5	73-2	113
—	Tucson (PCL)	2	1	.667	8.51	4	4	0	0	0-...	24.1	29	23	23	0	12-0	15
1996—	Houston (N.L.)	12	11	.522	4.19	35	33	4	0	0-0	219.0	233	113	102	16	97-8	219
1997—	Houston (N.L.)	19	7	.731	2.57	34	34	6	4	0-0	255.2	208	87	73	19	94-2	205
1998—	Colorado (N.L.)■	13	*17	.433	5.20	36	•35	4	1	0-0	230.1	257	141	133	28	96-4	158
1999—	Colorado (N.L.)	8	13	.381	6.61	32	32	1	0	0-0	190.2	225	*150	*140	33	109-5	116
2000—	St. Louis (N.L.)■	20	9	.690	3.91	34	34	5	1	0-0	232.1	215	109	101	33	58-1	192
2001—	St. Louis (N.L.)	16	11	.593	3.09	34	34	2	1	0-0	227.1	228	83	78	22	65-3	179
2002—	St. Louis (N.L.)	5	4	.556	3.72	14	14	0	0	0-0	84.2	82	36	35	9	28-1	50
Major League totals (12 years)		133	119	.528	4.12	359	331	28	9	0-1	2165.1	2135	1099	992	214	918-41	1668

DIVISION SERIES RECORD

Year	League	W	L	Pct.	ERA	G	GS	CG	ShO	Sv.-Opp.	IP	H	R	ER	HR	BB-IBB	SO
1997—	Houston (N.L.)	0	1	.000	2.57	1	1	0	0	0-0	7.0	2	2	2	1	2-0	4
2000—	St. Louis (N.L.)	1	0	1.000	2.57	1	1	0	0	0-0	7.0	4	2	2	0	2-0	6
2001—	St. Louis (N.L.)	0	0	...	3.00	1	1	0	0	0-0	6.0	3	2	2	1	5-0	5
Division series totals (3 years)		1	1	.500	2.70	3	3	0	0	0-0	20.0	9	6	6	2	9-0	15

CHAMPIONSHIP SERIES RECORD

RECORDS: Shares single-game record for most earned runs allowed—7 (October 15, 2000).

Year	League	W	L	Pct.	ERA	G	GS	CG	ShO	Sv.-Opp.	IP	H	R	ER	HR	BB-IBB	SO
2000—	St. Louis (N.L.)	0	2	.000	9.00	2	2	0	0	0-0	10.0	13	10	10	0	5-1	3

ALL-STAR GAME RECORD

	W	L	Pct.	ERA	GS	CG	ShO	Sv.-Opp.	IP	H	R	ER	HR	BB-IBB	SO
All-Star Game totals (1 year)	0	0	...	0.00	0	0	0	0-0	2.0	2	0	0	0	0-0	0

KIM, BYUNG-HYUN — P — DIAMONDBACKS

PERSONAL: Born January 19, 1979, in Kwangsan-ku Songjunsdon, Korea. ... 5-11/177. ... Throws right, bats right.

HIGH SCHOOL: Kwang-ju (Korea).

TRANSACTIONS/CAREER NOTES: Signed as non-drafted free agent by Arizona Diamondbacks organization (February 19, 1999). ... On Arizona disabled list (July 28-September 7, 2000).

RECORDS: Shares major league record for striking out side on nine pitches (May 11, 2002, eighth inning).

MISCELLANEOUS: Member of Korean National Team (1997-98). ... Holds Arizona Diamondbacks all-time records for most saves (70).

CAREER HITTING (MLB): 2-for-12 (.167), 0 R, 0 2B, 0 3B, 0 HR, 2 RBI.

Year	League	W	L	Pct.	ERA	G	GS	CG	ShO	Sv.-Opp.	IP	H	R	ER	HR	BB-IBB	SO
1999—	El Paso (Texas)	2	0	1.000	2.11	10	0	0	0	0-...	21.1	6	5	5	0	9-0	32
—	Tucson (PCL)	4	0	1.000	2.40	11	3	0	0	1-...	30.0	21	9	8	2	15-1	40
—	Arizona (N.L.)	1	2	.333	4.61	25	0	0	0	1-4	27.1	20	15	14	2	20-2	31
—	Ariz. D-backs (Ariz.)	0	0	...	0.00	1	1	0	0	0-...	2.0	1	0	0	0	1-0	2
2000—	Arizona (N.L.)	6	6	.500	4.46	61	1	0	0	14-20	70.2	52	39	35	9	46-5	111
—	Tucson (PCL)	0	0	...	0.00	2	2	0	0	0-...	8.1	1	0	0	0	4-0	13
2001—	Arizona (N.L.)	5	6	.455	2.94	78	0	0	0	19-23	98.0	58	32	32	10	44-3	113
2002—	Arizona (N.L.)	8	3	.727	2.04	72	0	0	0	36-42	84.0	64	20	19	5	26-2	92
Major League totals (4 years)		20	17	.541	3.21	236	1	0	0	70-89	280.0	194	106	100	26	136-12	347

DIVISION SERIES RECORD

Year League	W	L	Pct.	ERA	G	GS	CG	ShO	Sv.-Opp.	IP	H	R	ER	HR	BB-IBB	SO
2001—Arizona (N.L.)	0	0	...	0.00	1	0	0	0	1-1	1.1	1	0	0	0	2-0	1
2002—Arizona (N.L.)	0	0	...	18.00	1	0	0	0	0-0	1.0	2	2	2	0	3-1	0
Division series totals (2 years)	0	0	...	7.71	2	0	0	0	1-1	2.1	3	2	2	0	5-1	1

CHAMPIONSHIP SERIES RECORD

Year League	W	L	Pct.	ERA	G	GS	CG	ShO	Sv.-Opp.	IP	H	R	ER	HR	BB-IBB	SO
2001—Arizona (N.L.)	0	0	...	0.00	3	0	0	0	2-2	5.0	0	0	0	0	1-0	3

WORLD SERIES RECORD

NOTES: Member of World Series championship team (2001).

Year League	W	L	Pct.	ERA	G	GS	CG	ShO	Sv.-Opp.	IP	H	R	ER	HR	BB-IBB	SO
2001—Arizona (N.L.)	0	1	.000	13.50	2	0	0	0	0-2	3.1	6	5	5	3	1-0	6

ALL-STAR GAME RECORD

	W	L	Pct.	ERA	GS	CG	ShO	Sv.-Opp.	IP	H	R	ER	HR	BB-IBB	SO
All-Star Game totals (1 year)	0	0	...	54.00	0	0	0	0-0	.1	3	2	2	0	0-0	0

KIM, SUN-WOO — P — EXPOS

PERSONAL: Born September 4, 1977, in Inchon, Korea. ... 6-2/188. ... Throws right, bats right.
COLLEGE: Korea University.
TRANSACTIONS/CAREER NOTES: Signed as non-drafted free agent by Boston Red Sox organization (November 21, 1997). ... Traded by Red Sox with P Seung Song and a player to be named later to Montreal Expos for OF Cliff Floyd (July 30, 2002).
CAREER HITTING (MLB): 2-for-8 (.250), 2 R, 0 2B, 0 3B, 0 HR, 0 RBI.

Year League	W	L	Pct.	ERA	G	GS	CG	ShO	Sv.-Opp.	IP	H	R	ER	HR	BB-IBB	SO
1998—Sarasota (FSL)	12	8	.600	4.82	26	24	•5	0	0-...	153.0	159	88	82	18	40-1	132
1999—Trenton (East.)	9	8	.529	4.89	26	26	1	1	0-...	149.0	160	86	81	16	44-2	130
2000—Pawtucket (I.L.)	11	7	.611	6.03	26	25	0	0	0-...	134.1	170	98	90	17	42-1	116
2001—Pawtucket (I.L.)	6	7	.462	5.36	19	14	0	0	0-...	89.0	93	55	53	10	27-1	79
—Boston (A.L.)	0	2	.000	5.83	20	2	0	0	0-0	41.2	54	27	27	1	21-5	27
2002—Pawtucket (I.L.)	4	2	.667	3.18	8	8	1	0	0-...	45.1	34	18	16	4	16-0	37
—Boston (A.L.)	2	0	1.000	7.45	15	2	0	0	0-0	29.0	34	24	24	5	7-0	18
—Ottawa (I.L.)■	3	0	1.000	1.24	7	7	1	1	0-...	43.2	29	11	6	2	16-0	28
—Montreal (N.L.)	1	0	1.000	0.89	4	3	0	0	0-0	20.1	18	2	2	0	7-2	11
A.L. totals (2 years)	2	2	.500	6.50	35	4	0	0	0-0	70.2	88	51	51	6	28-5	45
N.L. totals (1 year)	1	0	1.000	0.89	4	3	0	0	0-0	20.1	18	2	2	0	7-2	11
Major League totals (2 years)	3	2	.600	5.24	39	7	0	0	0-0	91.0	106	53	53	6	35-7	56

KING, RAY — P — BREWERS

PERSONAL: Born January 15, 1974, in Chicago. ... 6-1/242. ... Throws left, bats left. ... Full name: Raymond Keith King.
HIGH SCHOOL: Ripley (Tenn.).
COLLEGE: Lambuth (Tenn.).
TRANSACTIONS/CAREER NOTES: Selected by Cincinnati Red organization in eighth round of free-agent draft (June 1, 1995). ... Loaned by Reds organization to Macon, Atlanta Braves organization (March 22-June 11, 1996). ... Traded by Reds to Braves (June 11, 1996), completing deal in which Braves traded OF Mike Kelly to Reds for P Chad Fox and a player to be named later (January 9, 1996). ... Traded by Braves to Chicago Cubs for P Jon Ratliff (January 20, 1998). ... Traded by Cubs to Milwaukee Brewers for P Doug Johnston (April 14, 2000). ... On Milwaukee disabled list (April 5-19, 2002); included rehabilitation assignment to Indianapolis (April 17-18).
CAREER HITTING (MLB): 0-for-3 (.000), 0 R, 0 2B, 0 3B, 0 HR, 0 RBI.

Year League	W	L	Pct.	ERA	G	GS	CG	ShO	Sv.-Opp.	IP	H	R	ER	HR	BB-IBB	SO
1995—Billings (Pio.)	3	0	1.000	1.67	28	0	0	0	5-...	43.0	31	11	8	1	15-3	43
1996—Macon (S.Atl.)■	3	5	.375	2.80	18	10	1	0	0-...	70.2	63	34	22	4	20-0	63
—Durham (Caro.)■	3	6	.333	4.46	14	14	2	0	0-...	82.2	104	54	41	3	15-2	52
1997—Greenville (Sou.)	5	5	.500	6.85	12	9	0	0	0-...	65.2	85	53	50	9	24-2	42
—Durham (Caro.)	6	9	.400	5.40	24	6	0	0	3-...	71.2	89	54	43	6	26-4	60
1998—West Tenn (Sou.)■	1	2	.333	2.43	25	0	0	0	3-...	29.2	23	9	8	1	10-0	26
—Iowa (PCL)	1	3	.250	5.01	37	0	0	0	2-...	32.1	36	20	18	4	15-1	26
1999—Iowa (PCL)	4	4	.500	1.88	37	0	0	0	2-...	43.0	31	11	9	1	22-3	41
—Chicago (N.L.)	0	0	...	5.91	10	0	0	0	0-0	10.2	11	8	7	2	10-0	5
2000—Iowa (PCL)	1	0	1.000	0.00	1	0	0	0	0-...	1.1	1	0	0	0	0-0	1
—Indianapolis (I.L.)■	0	3	.000	3.51	29	0	0	0	1-...	25.2	26	15	10	1	12-0	20
—Milwaukee (N.L.)	3	2	.600	1.26	36	0	0	0	0-1	28.2	18	7	4	1	10-1	19
2001—Milwaukee (N.L.)	0	4	.000	3.60	82	0	0	0	1-4	55.0	49	22	22	5	25-7	49
2002—Milwaukee (N.L.)	3	2	.600	3.05	76	0	0	0	0-1	65.0	61	24	22	5	24-6	50
—Indianapolis (I.L.)	0	0	...	0.00	1	1	0	0	0-...	1.0	1	0	0	0	1-0	1
Major League totals (4 years)	6	8	.429	3.11	204	0	0	0	1-6	159.1	139	61	55	13	69-14	123

KINGSALE, GENE — OF — PADRES

PERSONAL: Born August 20, 1976, in Oranjestad, Aruba. ... 6-3/190. ... Bats both, throws right. ... Full name: Eugene Humphrey Kingsale.
HIGH SCHOOL: John F. Kennedy Technical School (Oranjestad, Aruba).
TRANSACTIONS/CAREER NOTES: Signed as non-drafted free agent by Baltimore Orioles organization (June 19, 1993). ... On Frederick disabled list (May 29-August 31, 1996). ... On Bowie disabled list (April 8-August 8, 1997). ... On Baltimore disabled list (March 29-August 27, 2000); included rehabilitation assignments Gulf Coast Orioles (August 8-18), Frederick (August 19-25) and Bowie (August 26-27). ... Claimed on waivers by Seattle Mariners (July 10, 2001). ... Claimed on waivers by San Diego Padres (June 14, 2002).
STATISTICAL NOTES: Tied for Gulf Coast League lead in double plays by outfielder with two in 1994.
2002 GAMES PLAYED BY POSITION (MLB): OF—84.

Year Team (League)	Pos.	G	AB	R	H	2B	3B	HR	RBI	BB	SO	SB-CS	Avg.	OBP	SLG	E	Avg.
		BATTING														FIELDING	
1994—GC Orioles (GCL)........	OF-2B	50	168	26	52	2	3	0	9	18	24	15-8	.310	.381	.357	3	.971
1995—Bluefield (Appl.)	OF	47	171	45	54	11	2	0	16	27	31	20-8	.316	.420	.404	*11	.899
1996—Frederick (Caro.)	OF	49	166	26	45	6	4	0	9	19	32	23-4	.271	.363	.355	4	.962
—Baltimore (A.L.)..........	OF	3	0	0	0	0	0	0	0	0	0	0-0	...	...	...	0	1.000
1997—Bowie (East.).............	OF	13	46	8	19	6	0	0	4	5	4	5-1	.413	.481	.543	1	.958
—GC Orioles (GCL)........	OF	6	17	2	5	0	0	0	0	2	2	1-0	.294	.400	.294	1	.941
1998—Bowie (East.).............	OF	111	427	69	112	11	5	1	34	48	79	29-12	.262	.350	.319	6	.980
—Rochester (I.L.)..........	OF-DH	18	55	3	12	1	1	0	2	4	8	3-3	.218	.283	.273	0	1.000
—Baltimore (A.L.)..........	OF-DH	11	2	1	0	0	0	0	0	0	1	0-0	.000	.000	.000	0	1.000
1999—Bowie (East.).............	OF	67	268	43	63	11	4	3	23	33	46	13-7	.235	.319	.340	4	.978
—Rochester (I.L.)..........	OF	48	191	31	59	9	0	2	20	13	23	10-9	.309	.361	.387	3	.975
—Baltimore (A.L.)..........	OF-DH	28	85	9	21	2	0	0	7	5	13	1-3	.247	.301	.271	1	.980
2000—GC Orioles (GCL)........	OF	5	16	7	5	0	0	0	4	4	0	2-0	.313	.429	.313	0	1.000
—Frederick (Caro.)	OF	6	25	8	11	3	0	1	3	1	6	2-1	.440	.462	.680	0	1.000
—Bowie (East.).............	OF	3	11	5	4	2	0	1	5	3	0	1-0	.364	.500	.818	0	1.000
—Rochester (I.L.)..........	OF	2	10	2	4	1	0	0	1	0	0	1-1	.400	.400	.500	0	1.000
—Baltimore (A.L.)..........	OF-DH	26	88	13	21	2	1	0	9	2	14	1-2	.239	.253	.284	3	.954
2001—Rochester (I.L.)..........	OF	64	244	31	49	12	2	0	15	26	44	16-2	.201	.283	.266	5	.965
—Baltimore (A.L.)..........	OF	3	4	0	0	0	0	0	0	0	2	1-1	.000	.000	.000	0	1.000
—Tacoma (PCL)■	OF	51	215	30	63	14	4	3	24	8	25	12-4	.293	.327	.437	3	.976
—Seattle (A.L.)	OF	10	15	4	5	0	0	0	1	2	2	2-0	.333	.444	.333	0	1.000
2002—Tacoma (PCL)	OF	49	188	25	49	15	3	6	26	15	30	10-3	.261	.317	.468	0	1.000
—Seattle (A.L.)	OF	2	3	0	2	0	0	0	0	0	0	0-0	.667	.667	.667	0	1.000
—San Diego (N.L.)■	OF	89	216	27	60	10	3	2	28	20	47	9-2	.278	.346	.380	2	.985
American League totals (6 years)		83	197	27	49	4	1	0	17	9	32	5-6	.249	.289	.279	4	.971
National League totals (1 year)		89	216	27	60	10	3	2	28	20	47	9-2	.278	.346	.380	2	.985
Major League totals (6 years)		172	413	54	109	14	4	2	45	29	79	14-8	.264	.319	.332	6	.978

KINKADE, MIKE — 3B — DODGERS

PERSONAL: Born May 6, 1973, in Livonia, Mich. ... 6-1/210. ... Bats right, throws right. ... Full name: Michael A. Kinkade.
HIGH SCHOOL: Tigard (Ore.).
COLLEGE: Washington State.
TRANSACTIONS/CAREER NOTES: Selected by Milwaukee Brewers organization in ninth round of free-agent draft (June 1, 1995). ... On Louisville disabled list (April 20-May 14, 1998). ... Traded by Brewers to New York Mets for P Bill Pulsipher (July 31, 1998). ... Traded by Mets with OF Melvin Mora, P Leslie Brea and P Pat Gorman to Baltimore Orioles for SS Mike Bordick (July 28, 2000). ... On disabled list (August 24-September 18 and October 3, 2001-remainder of season). ... Released by Orioles (November 19, 2001). ... Signed by Los Angeles Dodgers organization (January 10, 2002). ... On Las Vegas disabled list (May 17-June 4 and June 16-23, 2002).
HONORS: Named Texas League Player of the Year (1997).
STATISTICAL NOTES: Led Midwest league in being hit by pitch with 32 in 1996. ... Tied for Texas League lead with 275 total bases in 1997. ... Led Texas League third basemen with 79 putouts and 288 total chances in 1997. ... Led Eastern League with .434 on-base percentage and .561 slugging percentage in 2000.
MISCELLANEOUS: Member of 2000 U.S. Olympic baseball team.
2002 GAMES PLAYED BY POSITION (MLB): 1B—11; OF—8.

Year Team (League)	Pos.	G	AB	R	H	2B	3B	HR	RBI	BB	SO	SB-CS	Avg.	OBP	SLG	E	Avg.
		BATTING														FIELDING	
1995—Helena (Pio.)	3B-1B-C	69	266	76	94	19	1	4	39	43	38	26-9	.353	.452	.477	10	.974
1996—Beloit (Midw.).............	3B-C-1B	•135	499	*104	151	33	4	15	100	47	69	23-12	.303	.394	.475	39	.922
1997—El Paso (Texas)...........	3B-DH	125	468	•112	*180	35	12	12	*109	52	66	17-4	*.385	*.455	.588	*60	.845
1998—Louisville (I.L.)	3B-1B-DH	80	291	57	90	24	6	7	46	36	52	10-2	.309	.394	.505	15	.953
—Norfolk (I.L.)■	3B-1B	30	125	12	35	5	0	1	18	3	24	6-1	.280	.319	.344	5	.949
—New York (N.L.)..........	3B	3	2	2	0	0	0	0	0	0	0	0-0	.000	.000	.000	0	...
1999—New York (N.L.)..........	OF-3B-C-1B	28	46	3	9	2	1	2	6	3	9	1-0	.196	.275	.413	0	1.000
—Norfolk (I.L.)	3-C-1-O-DH	84	312	53	96	20	2	7	49	21	31	7-1	.308	.359	.452	10	.967
2000—Binghamton (East.)	C-3B-OF	90	317	66	116	24	3	10	67	35	39	18-7	.366	.440	.555	9	.985
—New York (N.L.)..........	OF	2	2	0	0	0	0	0	0	0	1	0-0	.000	.000	.000	0	...
—Bowie (East.)■...........	C-3B	8	27	4	7	1	0	3	5	3	7	0-0	.259	§.375	§.630	0	1.000
—Rochester (I.L.)..........	C-1B-3B	15	55	10	20	5	0	1	10	11	11	0-1	.364	.471	.509	4	.953
—Baltimore (A.L.)..........	DH-1B	3	7	0	3	1	0	0	1	0	0	0-0	.429	.500	.571	0	1.000
2001—Baltimore (A.L.)■.......	0-3-DH-1-C	61	160	19	44	5	0	4	16	14	31	2-1	.275	.345	.381	2	.977
2002—Las Vegas (PCL)■	OF-3B-1B-C	74	287	63	98	22	6	11	50	29	49	6-2	.341	.433	.575	5	.976
—Los Angeles (N.L.)	1B-OF	37	50	7	19	5	0	2	11	4	10	1-0	.380	.483	.600	0	1.000
American League totals (2 years)		64	167	19	47	6	0	4	17	14	31	2-1	.281	.351	.389	2	.977
National League totals (4 years)		70	100	12	28	7	1	4	17	7	20	2-0	.280	.374	.490	0	1.000
Major League totals (5 years)		134	267	31	75	13	1	8	34	21	51	4-1	.281	.360	.427	2	.987

DIVISION SERIES RECORD

Year Team (League)	Pos.	G	AB	R	H	2B	3B	HR	RBI	BB	SO	SB-CS	Avg.	OBP	SLG	E	Avg.
		BATTING														FIELDING	
1999— New York (N.L.)								Did not play.									

CHAMPIONSHIP SERIES RECORD

Year Team (League)	Pos.	G	AB	R	H	2B	3B	HR	RBI	BB	SO	SB-CS	Avg.	OBP	SLG	E	Avg.
		BATTING														FIELDING	
1999— New York (N.L.)								Did not play.									

KINNEY, MATT — P — TWINS

PERSONAL: Born December 16, 1976, in Bangor, Maine. ... 6-5/220. ... Throws right, bats right. ... Full name: Matthew John Kinney.

HIGH SCHOOL: Bangor (Maine).

TRANSACTIONS/CAREER NOTES: Selected by Boston Red Sox organization in sixth round of free-agent draft (June 1, 1995). ... Traded by Red Sox with P Joe Thomas and OF John Barnes to Minnesota Twins for P Greg Swindell and 1B Orlando Merced (July 31, 1998). ... On New Britain disabled list (June 7-August 16, 1999). ... On disabled list (April 23-May 3, 2001). ... On Minnesota disabled list (June 30-August 19, 2002); included rehabilitation assignments to Gulf Coast Twins (July 27-August 10), Fort Myers (August 11-13) and New Britain (August 14-19).

STATISTICAL NOTES: Led Florida State League with 93 bases on balls and 25 wild pitches in 1998.

CAREER HITTING (MLB): 0-for-2 (.000), 0 R, 0 2B, 0 3B, 0 HR, 0 RBI.

Year League	W	L	Pct.	ERA	G	GS	CG	ShO	Sv.-Opp.	IP	H	R	ER	HR	BB-IBB	SO
1995— Gulf Coast Red Sox (GCL)	1	3	.250	2.93	8	2	0	0	2-...	27.2	29	13	9	0	10-0	11
1996— Lowell (NY-Penn)	3	9	.250	2.68	15	•15	0	0	0-...	87.1	68	51	26	0	44-2	72
1997— Michigan (Midw.)	8	5	.615	3.53	22	22	2	1	0-...	117.1	93	59	46	4	78-2	123
1998— Sarasota (FSL)	9	6	.600	4.01	22	20	2	1	1-...	121.1	109	70	54	5	*75-3	96
— Fort Myers (FSL)■	3	2	.600	3.13	7	7	0	0	0-...	37.1	31	18	13	0	§18-0	39
1999— New Britain (East.)	4	7	.364	7.12	14	13	0	0	0-...	60.2	69	54	48	8	36-0	50
— Gulf Coast Twins (GCL)	0	1	.000	4.76	3	3	0	0	0-...	5.2	6	4	3	0	3-0	8
2000— New Britain (East.)	6	1	.857	2.71	15	15	0	0	0-...	86.1	74	31	26	7	35-0	93
— Salt Lake (PCL)	5	2	.714	4.25	9	9	0	0	0-...	55.0	42	26	26	5	26-0	59
— Minnesota (A.L.)	2	2	.500	5.10	8	8	0	0	0-0	42.1	41	26	24	7	25-1	24
2001— Edmonton (PCL)	6	11	.353	5.07	29	•29	2	0	0-...	161.2	178	101	91	25	74-0	146
2002— Edmonton (PCL)	2	1	.667	8.89	5	5	0	0	0-...	27.1	42	27	27	9	4-0	21
— Minnesota (A.L.)	2	7	.222	4.64	14	12	0	0	0-0	66.0	78	39	34	13	33-0	45
— Gulf Coast Twins (GCL)	0	0	...	3.00	2	2	0	0	0-...	6.0	2	2	2	1	4-0	7
— Fort Myers (FSL)	0	0	...	0.00	1	1	0	0	0-...	5.0	4	2	0	0	3-0	5
— New Britain (East.)	0	0	...	6.75	1	1	0	0	0-...	4.0	4	4	3	1	1-0	3
Major League totals (2 years)	4	9	.308	4.82	22	20	0	0	0-0	108.1	119	65	58	20	58-1	69

KLASSEN, DANNY — SS/2B

PERSONAL: Born September 22, 1975, in Learington, Ont. ... 6-0/190. ... Bats right, throws right. ... Full name: Daniel Victor Klassen.

HIGH SCHOOL: John Carroll (Fort Pierce, Fla.).

TRANSACTIONS/CAREER NOTES: Selected by Milwaukee Brewers organization in second round of free-agent draft (June 3, 1993). ... On disabled list (April 7-June 23, 1995 and April 11-22, 1996). ... Selected by Arizona Diamondbacks in second round (37th pick overall) of expansion draft (November 18, 1997). ... On Tucson disabled list (August 13-September 8, 1998; and June 11-August 26, 1999). ... On Arizona disabled list (July 8-September 1, 2000). ... On Arizona disabled list (April 3, 2001-entire season); included rehabilitation assignment to Tucson (June 18-30). ... On Arizona disabled list (April 10-May 3, 2002); included rehabilitation assignment to El Paso (April 12-May 1). ... Granted free agency (October 15, 2002).

STATISTICAL NOTES: Tied for Arizona League lead in intentional bases on balls received with three in 1993.

2002 GAMES PLAYED BY POSITION (MLB): 3B—2; SS—1.

		BATTING													FIELDING	
Year Team (League)	Pos.	G	AB	R	H	2B	3B	HR	RBI	BB	SO	SB-CS	Avg.	OBP	SLG	E	Avg.
1993— Ariz. Brewers (Ariz.)	SS	38	117	26	26	5	0	2	20	24	28	14-3	.222	.379	.316	12	.922
— Helena (Pio.)	SS	18	45	8	9	1	0	0	3	7	11	2-1	.200	.333	.222	7	.905
1994— Beloit (Midw.)	SS	133	458	61	119	20	3	6	54	58	123	28-14	.260	.356	.356	40	.927
1995— Beloit (Midw.)	SS-3B	59	218	27	60	15	2	2	25	16	43	12-4	.275	.332	.390	18	.920
1996— Stockton (Calif.)	SS	118	432	58	116	22	4	2	46	34	77	14-8	.269	.335	.352	*33	.944
1997— El Paso (Texas)	SS	135	519	112	172	30	6	14	81	48	104	16-9	.331	.396	.493	*50	.920
1998— Tucson (PCL)■	SS-2B	73	281	47	82	25	2	10	47	19	54	6-2	.292	.344	.502	8	.976
— Arizona (N.L.)	2B	29	108	12	21	2	1	3	8	9	33	1-1	.194	.263	.315	5	.964
1999— Tucson (PCL)	SS-DH-2B	64	245	38	66	16	3	6	33	20	51	5-3	.269	.325	.433	9	.969
— Ariz. D-backs (Ariz.)	SS	6	17	2	4	1	0	0	1	1	4	0-0	.235	.278	.294	1	.962
— Arizona (N.L.)	PH	1	1	0	1	0	0	0	0	0	0	0-0	1.000	1.000	1.000	...	...
2000— Arizona (N.L.)	3B-SS	29	76	13	18	3	0	2	8	8	24	1-1	.237	.318	.355	2	.966
— Tucson (PCL)	SS-2B-3B	28	97	25	31	7	2	2	14	19	23	1-2	.320	.436	.495	8	.946
2001— Tucson (PCL)	3B-2B-SS	7	18	5	4	0	0	1	3	2	3	0-0	.222	.333	.389	1	.952
2002— Arizona (N.L.)	3B-SS	4	3	0	1	0	0	0	0	0	1	0-0	.333	.333	.333	0	1.000
— El Paso (Texas)	SS-3B-2B	18	65	11	15	4	0	2	7	7	24	0-0	.231	.306	.385	7	.923
— Tucson (PCL)	SS-3B-2B	103	361	41	83	20	5	2	42	22	106	6-1	.230	.277	.330	11	.974
Major League totals (4 years)		63	188	25	41	5	1	5	16	17	58	2-2	.218	.290	.335	7	.965

KLESKO, RYAN — 1B — PADRES

PERSONAL: Born June 12, 1971, in Westminster, Calif. ... 6-3/220. ... Bats left, throws left. ... Full name: Ryan Anthony Klesko.

HIGH SCHOOL: Westminster (Calif.).

TRANSACTIONS/CAREER NOTES: Selected by Atlanta Braves organization in fifth round of free-agent draft (June 5, 1989). ... On Atlanta disabled list (May 3-18, 1995); included rehabilitation assignment to Greenville (May 13-17). ... Traded by Braves with 2B Bret Boone and P Jason Shiell to San Diego Padres for 2B Quilvio Veras, 1B Wally Joyner and OF Reggie Sanders (December 22, 1999).

HONORS: Named Southern League Most Valuable Player (1991).

STATISTICAL NOTES: Had 16-game hitting streak (April 9-28, 2002). ... Career major league grand slams: 8.

2002 GAMES PLAYED BY POSITION (MLB): 1B—112; OF—31; DH—1.

			BATTING														FIELDING	
Year	Team (League)	Pos.	G	AB	R	H	2B	3B	HR	RBI	BB	SO	SB-CS	Avg.	OBP	SLG	E	Avg.
1989—	GC Braves (GCL)	DH	17	57	14	23	5	4	1	16	6	6	4-3	.404	.453	.684	...	...
—	Sumter (S.Atl.)	1B	25	90	17	26	6	0	1	12	11	14	1-0	.289	.363	.389	4	.979
1990—	Sumter (S.Atl.)	1B	63	231	41	85	15	1	10	38	31	30	13-1	.368	.437	.571	14	.978
—	Durham (Caro.)	1B	77	292	40	80	16	1	7	47	32	53	10-5	.274	.343	.408	13	.976
1991—	Greenville (Sou.)	1B	126	419	64	122	22	3	14	67	75	60	14-17	.291	.404	.458	*17	.985
1992—	Richmond (I.L.)	1B	123	418	63	105	22	2	17	59	41	72	3-5	.251	.323	.435	*11	.989
—	Atlanta (N.L.)	1B	13	14	0	0	0	0	0	1	0	5	0-0	.000	.067	.000	0	1.000
1993—	Richmond (I.L.)	1B-OF	98	343	59	94	14	2	22	74	47	69	4-3	.274	.361	.519	12	.981
—	Atlanta (N.L.)	1B-OF	22	17	3	6	1	0	2	5	3	4	0-0	.353	.450	.765	0	1.000
1994—	Atlanta (N.L.)	OF-1B	92	245	42	68	13	3	17	47	26	48	1-0	.278	.344	.563	7	.929
1995—	Atlanta (N.L.)	OF-1B	107	329	48	102	25	2	23	70	47	72	5-4	.310	.396	.608	8	.944
—	Greenville (Sou.)	DH-OF	4	13	1	3	0	0	1	4	2	1	0-0	.231	.333	.462	0	1.000
1996—	Atlanta (N.L.)	OF-1B	153	528	90	149	21	4	34	93	68	129	6-3	.282	.364	.530	5	.977
1997—	Atlanta (N.L.)	OF-1B	143	467	67	122	23	6	24	84	48	130	4-4	.261	.334	.490	6	.977
1998—	Atlanta (N.L.)	OF-1B	129	427	69	117	29	1	18	70	56	66	5-3	.274	.359	.473	2	.990
1999—	Atlanta (N.L.)	1B-OF-DH	133	404	55	120	28	2	21	80	53	69	5-2	.297	.376	.532	6	.990
2000—	San Diego (N.L.)■	1B-OF	145	494	88	140	33	2	26	92	91	81	23-7	.283	.393	.516	9	.992
2001—	San Diego (N.L.)	1B	146	538	105	154	34	6	30	113	88	89	23-4	.286	.384	.539	11	.991
2002—	San Diego (N.L.)	1B-OF-DH	146	540	90	162	39	1	29	95	76	86	6-2	.300	.388	.537	7	.993
Major League totals (11 years)			1229	4003	657	1140	246	27	224	750	556	779	78-29	.285	.372	.528	61	.988

DIVISION SERIES RECORD

RECORDS: Shares career record for most grand slams—1 (September 30, 1998). ... Shares single-inning record for most runs batted in—4 (September 30, 1998).

			BATTING														FIELDING	
Year	Team (League)	Pos.	G	AB	R	H	2B	3B	HR	RBI	BB	SO	SB-CS	Avg.	OBP	SLG	E	Avg.
1995—	Atlanta (N.L.)	OF	4	15	5	7	1	0	0	1	0	3	0-0	.467	.467	.533	0	1.000
1996—	Atlanta (N.L.)	OF	3	8	1	1	0	0	1	1	3	4	1-0	.125	.364	.500	1	.667
1997—	Atlanta (N.L.)	OF	3	8	2	2	1	0	1	1	0	2	0-0	.250	.250	.750	1	.750
1998—	Atlanta (N.L.)	OF	3	11	1	3	0	0	1	4	0	3	0-0	.273	.273	.545	0	1.000
1999—	Atlanta (N.L.)	1B-PH	4	12	3	4	0	0	0	1	1	4	0-0	.333	.385	.333	0	1.000
Division series totals (5 years)			17	54	12	17	2	0	3	8	4	16	1-0	.315	.362	.519	2	.949

CHAMPIONSHIP SERIES RECORD

			BATTING														FIELDING	
Year	Team (League)	Pos.	G	AB	R	H	2B	3B	HR	RBI	BB	SO	SB-CS	Avg.	OBP	SLG	E	Avg.
1995—	Atlanta (N.L.)	OF-PH	4	7	0	0	0	0	0	0	3	4	0-1	.000	.300	.000	0	1.000
1996—	Atlanta (N.L.)	OF	6	16	1	4	0	0	1	3	2	6	0-0	.250	.333	.438	0	1.000
1997—	Atlanta (N.L.)	OF	5	17	2	4	0	0	2	4	2	3	0-0	.235	.316	.588	0	1.000
1998—	Atlanta (N.L.)	OF-PH	5	12	2	1	0	0	0	1	6	3	0-0	.083	.389	.083	1	.750
1999—	Atlanta (N.L.)	1B-PH	4	8	1	1	0	0	1	1	2	1	0-0	.125	.300	.500	2	.935
Championship series totals (5 years)			24	60	6	10	0	0	4	9	15	17	0-1	.167	.333	.367	3	.944

WORLD SERIES RECORD

NOTES: Member of World Series championship team (1995).

			BATTING														FIELDING	
Year	Team (League)	Pos.	G	AB	R	H	2B	3B	HR	RBI	BB	SO	SB-CS	Avg.	OBP	SLG	E	Avg.
1995—	Atlanta (N.L.)	OF-DH	6	16	4	5	0	0	3	4	3	4	0-0	.313	.421	.875	0	1.000
1996—	Atlanta (N.L.)	DH-OF-1B-PH	5	10	2	1	0	0	0	1	2	4	0-0	.100	.250	.100	1	.500
1999—	Atlanta (N.L.)	1B-PH	4	12	0	2	0	0	0	0	0	1	0-0	.167	.167	.167	0	1.000
World Series totals (3 years)			15	38	6	8	0	0	3	5	5	9	0-0	.211	.302	.447	1	.958

ALL-STAR GAME RECORD

	AB	R	H	2B	3B	HR	RBI	BB	SO	SB-CS	Avg.	OBP	SLG	E	Avg.
All-Star Game totals (1 year)	1	0	0	0	0	0	1	0	1	0-0	.000	.000	.000	0	1.000

KLINE, STEVE — P — CARDINALS

PERSONAL: Born August 22, 1972, in Sunbury, Pa. ... 6-1/215. ... Throws left, bats both. ... Full name: Steven James Kline.
HIGH SCHOOL: Lewisburg (Pa.).
COLLEGE: West Virginia.
TRANSACTIONS/CAREER NOTES: Selected by Cleveland Indians organization in eighth round of free-agent draft (June 3, 1993). ... On disabled list (May 23-August 5, 1995). ... On temporarily inactive list (April 5-20, 1996). ... Traded by Indians to Montreal Expos for P Jeff Juden (July 31, 1997). ... On disabled list (April 11-27, 1999). ... Traded by Expos with P Dustin Hermanson to St. Louis Cardinals for 3B Fernando Tatis and P Britt Reames (December 14, 2000). ... On St. Louis disabled list (April 29-May 31, 2002); included rehabilitation assignments to Peoria (May 24-28) and New Haven (May 29-31).
RECORDS: Shares major league single-inning record for most strikeouts—4 (August 17, 2000, seventh inning).
CAREER HITTING (MLB): 1-for-11 (.091), 0 R, 0 2B, 0 3B, 0 HR, 0 RBI.

Year	League	W	L	Pct.	ERA	G	GS	CG	ShO	Sv.-Opp.	IP	H	R	ER	HR	BB-IBB	SO
1993—	Burlington (Appl.)	1	1	.500	4.91	2	1	0	0	0-...	7.1	11	4	4	0	2-1	4
—	Watertown (NY-Penn)	5	4	.556	3.19	13	13	2	1	0-...	79.0	77	36	28	3	12-0	45
1994—	Columbus (S.Atl.)	*18	5	.783	3.01	28	•28	2	1	0-...	*185.2	175	67	62	14	36-0	*174
1995—	Canton/Akron (East.)	2	3	.400	2.42	14	14	0	0	0-...	89.1	86	34	24	6	30-3	45
1996—	Canton/Akron (East.)	8	12	.400	5.46	25	24	0	0	0-...	146.2	168	98	89	16	55-2	107
1997—	Cleveland (A.L.)	3	1	.750	5.81	20	1	0	0	0-2	26.1	42	19	17	6	13-1	17
—	Buffalo (A.A.)	3	3	.500	4.03	20	4	0	0	1-...	51.1	53	26	23	4	13-1	41
—	Montreal (N.L.)■	1	3	.250	6.15	26	0	0	0	0-1	26.1	31	18	18	4	10-3	20

Year League	W	L	Pct.	ERA	G	GS	CG	ShO	Sv.-Opp.	IP	H	R	ER	HR	BB-IBB	SO
1998—Ottawa (I.L.)	0	0	...	0.00	2	0	0	0	0-...	2.2	1	0	0	0	0-0	1
—Montreal (N.L.)	3	6	.333	2.76	78	0	0	0	1-2	71.2	62	25	22	4	41-7	76
1999—Montreal (N.L.)	7	4	.636	3.75	*82	0	0	0	0-2	69.2	56	32	29	8	33-6	69
2000—Montreal (N.L.)	1	5	.167	3.50	*83	0	0	0	14-18	82.1	88	36	32	8	27-2	64
2001—St. Louis (N.L.)■	3	3	.500	1.80	*89	0	0	0	9-10	75.0	53	16	15	3	29-7	54
2002—St. Louis (N.L.)	2	1	.667	3.39	66	0	0	0	6-8	58.1	54	23	22	3	21-2	41
—Peoria (Midw.)	0	0	...	0.00	2	1	0	0	0-...	2.1	1	0	0	0	1-0	5
—New Haven (East.)	0	0	...	0.00	1	1	0	0	0-...	2.0	0	0	0	0	1-0	2
A.L. totals (1 year)	3	1	.750	5.81	20	1	0	0	0-2	26.1	42	19	17	6	13-1	17
N.L. totals (6 years)	17	22	.436	3.24	424	0	0	0	30-41	383.1	344	150	138	30	161-27	324
Major League totals (6 years)	20	23	.465	3.41	444	1	0	0	30-43	409.2	386	169	155	36	174-28	341

DIVISION SERIES RECORD

Year League	W	L	Pct.	ERA	G	GS	CG	ShO	Sv.-Opp.	IP	H	R	ER	HR	BB-IBB	SO
2001—St. Louis (N.L.)	0	1	.000	2.08	4	0	0	0	2-2	4.1	4	1	1	0	2-1	0
2002—St. Louis (N.L.)	0	0	...	0.00	2	0	0	0	0-0	1.1	1	0	0	0	1-0	0
Division series totals (2 years)	0	1	.000	1.59	6	0	0	0	2-2	5.2	5	1	1	0	3-1	0

CHAMPIONSHIP SERIES RECORD

Year League	W	L	Pct.	ERA	G	GS	CG	ShO	Sv.-Opp.	IP	H	R	ER	HR	BB-IBB	SO
2002—St. Louis (N.L.)	0	0	...	0.00	4	0	0	0	0-0	2.1	2	0	0	0	0-0	1

KNIGHT, BRANDON P YANKEES

PERSONAL: Born October 1, 1975, in Oxnard, Calif. ... 6-0/170. ... Throws right, bats left. ... Full name: Brandon Michael Knight.

HIGH SCHOOL: Buena (Ventura, Calif.).

JUNIOR COLLEGE: Ventura (Calif.) College.

TRANSACTIONS/CAREER NOTES: Selected by Texas Rangers organization in 14th round of free-agent draft (June 1, 1995). ... Traded by Rangers with P Sam Marsonek to New York Yankees for OF Chad Curtis (December 13, 1999). ... Selected by Minnesota Twins from Yankees organization in Rule 5 major league draft (December 11, 2000). ... Returned to Yankees organization (March 28, 2001). ... Released by Yankees (March 30, 2001). ... Re-signed by Yankees organization (April 1, 2001).

CAREER HITTING (MLB): 0-for-0 (.000), 0 R, 0 2B, 0 3B, 0 HR, 0 RBI.

Year League	W	L	Pct.	ERA	G	GS	CG	ShO	Sv.-Opp.	IP	H	R	ER	HR	BB-IBB	SO
1995—Gulf Coast Rangers (GCL)	2	1	.667	5.25	3	2	0	0	0-...	12.0	12	7	7	0	6-0	11
—Charleston, S.C. (S.Atl.)	4	2	.667	3.13	9	9	0	0	0-...	54.2	37	22	19	5	21-0	52
1996—Charlotte (FSL)	4	10	.286	5.12	19	17	2	0	0-...	102.0	118	65	58	9	45-0	74
—Hudson Valley (NY-Penn).	2	2	.500	4.42	9	9	0	0	0-...	53.0	59	29	26	1	21-0	52
1997—Charlotte (FSL)	7	4	.636	2.23	14	12	3	1	0-...	92.2	82	33	23	9	22-0	91
—Tulsa (Texas)	6	4	.600	4.50	14	14	2	•1	0-...	90.0	83	52	45	12	35-0	84
1998—Tulsa (Texas)	6	6	.500	5.11	14	14	0	0	0-...	86.1	94	54	49	11	37-0	87
—Oklahoma City (PCL)	0	7	.000	9.74	16	12	0	0	0-...	64.2	100	75	70	16	29-0	52
1999—Oklahoma (PCL)	9	8	.529	4.91	27	26	*5	0	0-...	163.0	173	96	89	23	47-2	97
2000—Columbus (I.L.)■	10	12	.455	4.44	28	•28	*8	1	0-...	*184.2	172	105	91	21	61-3	*128
2001—Columbus (I.L.)	12	7	.632	3.66	25	25	3	0	0-...	162.1	174	77	66	16	45-0	173
—New York (A.L.)	0	0	...	10.13	4	0	0	0	0-0	10.2	18	12	12	5	3-0	7
2002—Columbus (I.L.)	2	7	.222	3.90	36	7	1	0	12-...	80.2	67	40	35	6	37-1	81
—New York (A.L.)	0	0	...	11.42	7	0	0	0	0-0	8.2	11	12	11	2	5-0	7
Major League totals (2 years)	0	0	...	10.71	11	0	0	0	0-0	19.1	29	24	23	7	8-0	14

KNOBLAUCH, CHUCK OF

PERSONAL: Born July 7, 1968, in Houston. ... 5-9/175. ... Bats right, throws right. ... Full name: Edward Charles Knoblauch. ... Son of Ray Knoblauch, minor league pitcher (1947-56); and nephew of Ed Knoblauch, minor league outfielder (1938-42 and 1947-55). ... Name pronounced NOB-lock.

HIGH SCHOOL: Bellaire (Houston).

COLLEGE: Texas A&M.

TRANSACTIONS/CAREER NOTES: Selected by Philadelphia Phillies organization in 18th round of free-agent draft (June 2, 1986); did not sign. ... Selected by Minnesota Twins organization in first round (25th pick overall) of free-agent draft (June 5, 1989). ... Traded by Twins to New York Yankees for P Eric Milton, P Danny Mota, OF Brian Buchanan, SS Cristian Guzman and cash (February 6, 1998). ... On New York disabled list (August 3-September 1, 2000); included rehabilitation assignment to Tampa (August 25-September 1). ... Granted free agency (November 5, 2001). ... Signed by Kansas City Royals (December 18, 2001). ... On Kansas City disabled list (June 6-July 20, 2002); included rehabilitation assignment to Wichita (July 15-20). ... Granted free agency (October 28, 2002).

HONORS: Named A.L. Rookie Player of the Year by The Sporting News (1991). ... Named A.L. Rookie of the Year by Baseball Writers' Association of America (1991). ... Named second baseman on The Sporting News A.L. All-Star team (1994 and 1997). ... Named second baseman on The Sporting News A.L. Silver Slugger team (1995 and 1997). ... Won A.L. Gold Glove at second base (1997).

STATISTICAL NOTES: Had 20-game hitting streak (September 2-25, 1991). ... Led A.L. second basemen with 424 assists, 101 double plays and 718 total chances in 1997. ... Led A.L. in being hit by pitch with 18 in 1998. ... Career major league grand slams: 4.

MISCELLANEOUS: Holds Minnesota Twins all-time record for most stolen bases (276).

2002 GAMES PLAYED BY POSITION (MLB): OF—74; DH—2.

							BATTING									FIELDING	
Year Team (League)	Pos.	G	AB	R	H	2B	3B	HR	RBI	BB	SO	SB-CS	Avg.	OBP	SLG	E	Avg.
1989—Kenosha (Midw.)	SS	51	196	29	56	13	1	2	19	32	23	9-7	.286	.387	.393	21	.898
—Visalia (Calif.)	SS	18	77	20	28	10	0	0	21	6	11	4-0	.364	.412	.494	10	.882
1990—Orlando (Sou.)	2B	118	432	74	125	23	6	2	53	63	31	23-7	.289	.389	.384	20	.966
1991—Minnesota (A.L.)	2B	151	565	78	159	24	6	1	50	59	40	25-5	.281	.351	.350	18	.975
1992—Minnesota (A.L.)	2B-DH-SS	155	600	104	178	19	6	2	56	88	60	34-13	.297	.384	.358	6	.992
1993—Minnesota (A.L.)	2B-SS-OF	153	602	82	167	27	4	2	41	65	44	29-11	.277	.354	.346	9	.988
1994—Minnesota (A.L.)	2B-SS	109	445	85	139	*45	3	5	51	41	56	35-6	.312	.381	.461	3	.994
1995—Minnesota (A.L.)	2B-SS	136	538	107	179	34	8	11	63	78	95	46-18	.333	.424	.487	10	.985

Year	Team (League)	Pos.	G	AB	R	H	2B	3B	HR	RBI	BB	SO	SB-CS	Avg.	OBP	SLG	E	Avg.
			BATTING														FIELDING	
1996—	Minnesota (A.L.)	2B-DH	153	578	140	197	35	*14	13	72	98	74	45-14	.341	.448	.517	8	*.988
1997—	Minnesota (A.L.)	2B-DH-SS	156	611	117	178	26	10	9	58	84	84	62-10	.291	.390	.411	12	.983
1998—	New York (A.L.)■	2B-DH	150	603	117	160	25	4	17	64	76	70	31-12	.265	.361	.405	13	.981
1999—	New York (A.L.)	2B	150	603	120	176	36	4	18	68	83	57	28-9	.292	.393	.454	*26	.963
2000—	New York (A.L.)	2B-DH	102	400	75	113	22	2	5	26	46	45	15-7	.283	.366	.385	15	.958
—	Tampa (FSL)	2B	1	1	0	0	0	0	0	0	0	1	0-0	.000	.500	.000	0	1.000
2001—	New York (A.L.)	OF-DH	137	521	66	130	20	3	9	44	58	73	38-9	.250	.339	.351	2	.989
2002—	Kansas City (A.L.)■	OF-DH	80	300	41	63	9	0	6	22	28	32	19-3	.210	.284	.300	3	.980
—	Wichita (Texas)	OF	5	16	3	5	2	0	0	0	6	4	1-0	.313	.500	.438	0	1.000
Major League totals (12 years)			1632	6366	1132	1839	322	64	98	615	804	730	407-117	.289	.378	.406	125	.982

DIVISION SERIES RECORD

Year	Team (League)	Pos.	G	AB	R	H	2B	3B	HR	RBI	BB	SO	SB-CS	Avg.	OBP	SLG	E	Avg.
			BATTING														FIELDING	
1998—	New York (A.L.)	2B	3	11	0	1	0	0	0	0	0	4	0-0	.091	.167	.091	1	.933
1999—	New York (A.L.)	2B	3	12	1	2	0	0	0	0	1	3	0-0	.167	.231	.167	1	.929
2000—	New York (A.L.)	DH-PR	3	9	1	3	0	0	0	1	0	2	1-0	.333	.333	.333	...	...
2001—	New York (A.L.)	OF	5	22	1	6	1	0	0	1	0	0	1-1	.273	.273	.318	1	.923
Division series totals (4 years)			14	54	3	12	1	0	0	2	1	9	2-1	.222	.250	.241	3	.929

CHAMPIONSHIP SERIES RECORD

RECORDS: Shares A.L. career record for most doubles—7.

Year	Team (League)	Pos.	G	AB	R	H	2B	3B	HR	RBI	BB	SO	SB-CS	Avg.	OBP	SLG	E	Avg.
			BATTING														FIELDING	
1991—	Minnesota (A.L.)	2B	5	20	5	7	2	0	0	3	3	3	2-1	.350	.435	.450	0	1.000
1998—	New York (A.L.)	2B	6	25	4	5	1	0	0	0	4	2	0-0	.200	.333	.240	0	1.000
1999—	New York (A.L.)	2B	5	18	3	6	1	0	0	1	3	0	1-0	.333	.429	.389	1	.947
2000—	New York (A.L.)	DH	6	23	3	6	2	0	0	2	3	4	0-0	.261	.370	.348	...	...
2001—	New York (A.L.)	OF	5	18	0	6	1	0	0	3	2	3	0-1	.333	.400	.389	0	1.000
Championship series totals (5 years)			27	104	15	30	7	0	0	9	15	12	3-2	.288	.388	.356	1	.988

WORLD SERIES RECORD

NOTES: Member of World Series championship team (1991, 1998, 1999 and 2000).

Year	Team (League)	Pos.	G	AB	R	H	2B	3B	HR	RBI	BB	SO	SB-CS	Avg.	OBP	SLG	E	Avg.
			BATTING														FIELDING	
1991—	Minnesota (A.L.)	2B	7	26	3	8	1	0	0	2	4	2	4-0	.308	.387	.346	1	.967
1998—	New York (A.L.)	2B	4	16	3	6	0	0	1	3	3	2	1-0	.375	.500	.563	1	.944
1999—	New York (A.L.)	2B	4	16	5	5	1	0	1	3	1	3	1-0	.313	.353	.563	0	1.000
2000—	New York (A.L.)	DH-PR	4	10	1	1	0	0	0	1	2	1	0-1	.100	.231	.100	...	...
2001—	New York (A.L.)	OF-DH-PR-PH	6	18	1	1	0	0	0	0	1	2	0-0	.056	.105	.056	0	1.000
World Series totals (5 years)			25	86	13	21	2	0	2	9	11	10	6-1	.244	.330	.337	2	.971

ALL-STAR GAME RECORD

	AB	R	H	2B	3B	HR	RBI	BB	SO	SB-CS	Avg.	OBP	SLG	E	Avg.
All-Star Game totals (4 years)	5	1	1	0	0	0	0	1	2	0-0	.200	.333	.200	0	1.000

KNOTTS, GARY — P — MARLINS

PERSONAL: Born February 12, 1977, in Decatur, Ala. ... 6-3/230. ... Throws right, bats right. ... Full name: Gary E. Knotts.
HIGH SCHOOL: Brewer (Somerville, Ala.).
JUNIOR COLLEGE: Northwest Shoals Community College (Ala.).
TRANSACTIONS/CAREER NOTES: Selected by Florida Marlins organization in 11th round of free agent draft (June 1, 1995). ... Granted free agency (December 21, 1999). ... Re-signed by Marlins organization (December 22, 1999). ... On Calgary disabled list (August 21, 2001-remainder of season).
CAREER HITTING (MLB): 1-for-3 (.333), 0 R, 0 2B, 0 3B, 0 HR, 0 RBI.

Year	League	W	L	Pct.	ERA	G	GS	CG	ShO	Sv.-Opp.	IP	H	R	ER	HR	BB-IBB	SO
1996—	Gulf Coast Marlins (GCL)	4	2	.667	2.04	12	9	1	1	0-...	57.1	35	16	13	0	17-0	48
1997—	Kane County (Midw.)	1	5	.167	13.05	7	7	0	0	0-...	20.0	33	34	29	2	17-0	19
—	Utica (NY-Penn)	3	5	.375	3.62	12	12	1	0	0-...	69.2	70	34	28	3	27-1	65
1998—	Kane County (Midw.)	8	8	.500	3.87	27	27	3	0	0-...	158.1	144	84	68	11	66-1	148
1999—	Brevard County (FSL)	9	6	.600	4.60	16	16	3	2	0-...	94.0	101	52	48	7	29-0	65
—	Portland (East.)	6	3	.667	3.75	12	12	1	1	0-...	81.2	79	39	34	12	33-0	63
2000—	Portland (East.)	9	8	.529	4.66	27	27	2	0	0-...	156.1	161	102	81	15	63-1	113
2001—	Calgary (PCL)	6	7	.462	5.46	21	21	1	1	0-...	118.2	136	77	72	16	43-0	104
—	Florida (N.L.)	0	1	.000	6.00	2	1	0	0	0-0	6.0	7	4	4	1	1-0	9
2002—	Florida (N.L.)	3	1	.750	4.40	28	0	0	0	0-1	30.2	21	15	15	6	16-0	21
—	Calgary (PCL)	5	3	.625	4.25	42	0	0	0	3-...	53.0	53	29	25	4	32-2	44
Major League totals (2 years)		3	2	.600	4.66	30	1	0	0	0-1	36.2	28	19	19	7	17-0	30

KOCH, BILLY — P — ATHLETICS

PERSONAL: Born December 14, 1974, in Rockville Center, N.Y. ... 6-3/215. ... Throws right, bats right. ... Full name: William Christopher Koch.
HIGH SCHOOL: West Babylon (N.Y.).
COLLEGE: Clemson.
TRANSACTIONS/CAREER NOTES: Selected by Toronto Blue Jays organization in first round (fourth pick overall) of free-agent draft (June 4, 1996). ... On disabled list (April 14, 1997-remainder of season). ... Traded by Blue Jays to Oakland Athletics for P Justin Miller and 3B Eric Hinske (December 7, 2001).
HONORS: Named A.L. Relief Pitcher of the Year by The Sporting News (2002).
MISCELLANEOUS: Member of 1996 U.S. Olympic baseball team.
CAREER HITTING (MLB): 0-for-2 (.000), 0 R, 0 2B, 0 3B, 0 HR, 0 RBI.

Year	League	W	L	Pct.	ERA	G	GS	CG	ShO	Sv.-Opp.	IP	H	R	ER	HR	BB-IBB	SO
1997—	Dunedin (FSL)	0	1	.000	2.49	3	3	0	0	0-...	21.2	27	10	6	1	3-0	20
1998—	Dunedin (FSL)	•14	7	.667	3.75	25	25	0	0	0-...	124.2	120	65	52	8	41-0	108
	—Syracuse (I.L.)	0	1	.000	14.29	2	2	0	0	0-...	5.2	9	9	9	1	5-0	9
1999—	Syracuse (I.L.)	3	0	1.000	3.86	5	5	0	0	0-...	25.2	27	11	11	3	10-0	22
	—Toronto (A.L.)	0	5	.000	3.39	56	0	0	0	31-35	63.2	55	26	24	5	30-5	57
2000—	Toronto (A.L.)	9	3	.750	2.63	68	0	0	0	33-38	78.2	78	28	23	6	18-4	60
2001—	Toronto (A.L.)	2	5	.286	4.80	69	0	0	0	36-44	69.1	69	39	37	7	33-7	55
2002—	Oakland (A.L.)■	11	4	.733	3.27	*84	0	0	0	44-50	93.2	73	38	34	7	46-6	93
Major League totals (4 years)		22	17	.564	3.48	277	0	0	0	144-167	305.1	275	131	118	25	127-22	265

DIVISION SERIES RECORD

Year	League	W	L	Pct.	ERA	G	GS	CG	ShO	Sv.-Opp.	IP	H	R	ER	HR	BB-IBB	SO
2002—	Oakland (A.L.)	0	0	...	9.00	3	0	0	0	1-1	3.0	5	3	3	1	2-0	3

KOLB, DANNY — P — RANGERS

PERSONAL: Born March 29, 1975, in Sterling, Ill. ... 6-4/215. ... Throws right, bats right. ... Full name: Daniel Lee Kolb. ... Cousin of Gary Kolb, outfielder with four major league teams (1960-69).
HIGH SCHOOL: Walnut (Ill.).
JUNIOR COLLEGE: Sauk Valley Community College (Ill.).
COLLEGE: Illinois State.
TRANSACTIONS/CAREER NOTES: Selected by Minnesota Twins organization in 17th round of free-agent draft (June 3, 1993); did not sign. ... Selected by Texas Rangers organization in sixth round of free-agent draft (June 3, 1995). ... On Texas disabled list (October 3, 1999-remainder of season). ... On Texas disabled list (May 29, 2000-remainder of season). ... On Texas disabled list (March 23-July 11, 2001); included rehabilitation assignments to Charlotte (June 11-July 3) and Tulsa (July 4-10). ... On Texas disabled list (March 28-July 16, 2002); included rehabilitation assignments to Charlotte (June 25-July 1) and Tulsa (July 2-16).
STATISTICAL NOTES: Pitched six-inning, 3-0 no-hit victory against Columbus (June 12, 1996). ... Tied for Appalachian League lead with 22 hit batsmen in 1996.
CAREER HITTING (MLB): 0-for-0 (.000), 0 R, 0 2B, 0 3B, 0 HR, 0 RBI.

Year	League	W	L	Pct.	ERA	G	GS	CG	ShO	Sv.-Opp.	IP	H	R	ER	HR	BB-IBB	SO
1995—	Gulf Coast Rangers (GCL)	1	7	.125	2.21	12	11	0	0	0-...	53.0	38	22	13	0	28-0	46
1996—	Charleston, S.C. (S.Atl.)	8	6	.571	2.57	20	20	4	2	0-...	126.0	80	50	36	5	60-2	127
	—Charlotte (FSL)	2	2	.500	4.26	6	6	0	0	0-...	38.0	38	18	18	1	14-0	28
	—Tulsa (Texas)	1	0	1.000	0.77	2	2	0	0	0-...	11.2	5	1	1	0	8-0	7
1997—	Charlotte (FSL)	4	10	.286	4.87	24	23	3	0	0-...	133.0	146	91	72	10	62-1	83
	—Tulsa (Texas)	0	2	.000	4.76	2	2	0	0	0-...	11.1	7	7	6	1	11-0	6
1998—	Tulsa (Texas)	12	11	.522	4.82	28	28	2	0	0-...	162.1	187	104	87	11	76-1	83
	—Oklahoma (PCL)	0	0	...	0.00	1	0	0	0	0-...	1.0	1	0	0	0	1-0	0
1999—	Tulsa (Texas)	1	2	.333	2.79	7	7	1	1	0-...	38.2	38	16	12	0	18-0	32
	—Oklahoma (PCL)	5	3	.625	5.10	11	8	0	0	0-...	60.0	74	35	34	4	27-0	21
	—Texas (A.L.)	2	1	.667	4.65	16	0	0	0	0-0	31.0	33	18	16	2	15-0	15
2000—	Oklahoma (PCL)	4	1	.800	0.98	13	0	0	0	4-...	18.1	11	6	2	0	8-1	18
	—Texas (A.L.)	0	0	...	67.50	1	0	0	0	0-0	.2	5	5	5	0	2-0	0
2001—	Charlotte (FSL)	1	2	.333	3.86	7	3	0	0	0-...	18.2	21	8	8	1	2-0	16
	—Tulsa (Texas)	1	0	1.000	0.00	1	0	0	0	0-...	2.0	0	0	0	0	1-0	0
	—Oklahoma (PCL)	0	1	.000	1.42	12	0	0	0	3-...	19.0	13	3	3	1	4-0	21
	—Texas (A.L.)	0	0	...	4.70	17	0	0	0	0-0	15.1	15	8	8	2	10-1	15
2002—	Charlotte (FSL)	1	0	1.000	1.50	4	0	0	0	0-...	6.0	5	1	1	0	4-0	2
	—Tulsa (Texas)	0	1	.000	2.16	5	1	0	0	0-...	8.1	9	2	2	0	3-0	4
	—Texas (A.L.)	3	6	.333	4.22	34	0	0	0	1-4	32.0	27	17	15	1	22-2	20
Major League totals (4 years)		5	7	.417	5.01	68	0	0	0	1-4	79.0	80	48	44	5	49-3	50

KOMIYAMA, SATORU — P

PERSONAL: Born September 15, 1965, in Chiba, Japan. ... 6-2/195. ... Throws right, bats right.
TRANSACTIONS/CAREER NOTES: Played with Chiba Lotte Marines of Japan Pacific League (1990-99). ... Played with Yokohama BayStars of Japan Central League (2000 and 2001). ... Signed as non-drafted free agent by New York Mets organization (December 3, 2001). ... On New York disabled list (April 14-29, 2002); included rehabilitation assignment to Norfolk (April 25-29). ... Released by Mets (October 8, 2002).
CAREER HITTING (MLB): 0-for-1 (.000), 0 R, 0 2B, 0 3B, 0 HR, 0 RBI.

Year	League	W	L	Pct.	ERA	G	GS	CG	ShO	Sv.-Opp.	IP	H	R	ER	HR	BB-IBB	SO
1990—	Chiba Lotte (Jap. Pac.)	6	10	.375	3.27	30	22	6	2	2-...	170.2	159	...	...	...	63-...	126
1991—	Chiba Lotte (Jap. Pac.)	10	16	.385	3.95	29	28	15	1	0-...	212.0	219	...	...	...	80-...	130
1992—	Chiba Lotte (Jap. Pac.)	8	15	.348	3.96	29	25	9	1	0-...	172.2	187	...	...	...	64-...	124
1993—	Chiba Lotte (Jap. Pac.)	12	14	.462	3.44	27	27	14	0	0-...	204.1	193	...	...	...	71-...	160
1994—	Chiba Lotte (Jap. Pac.)	3	9	.250	4.24	14	14	3	2	0-...	85.0	81	...	...	...	28-...	67
1995—	Chiba Lotte (Jap. Pac.)	11	4	.733	2.60	25	25	6	1	0-...	187.0	150	...	...	...	53-...	169
1996—	Chiba Lotte (Jap. Pac.)	8	13	.381	4.54	25	25	2	0	0-...	154.2	192	...	...	...	39-...	90
1997—	Chiba Lotte (Jap. Pac.)	11	9	.550	2.49	27	27	3	2	0-...	187.2	186	...	...	...	30-...	130
1998—	Chiba Lotte (Jap. Pac.)	11	12	.478	3.57	27	27	10	2	0-...	201.2	224	...	...	...	27-...	126
1999—	Chiba Lotte (Jap. Pac.)	7	10	.412	4.07	21	21	4	0	0-...	141.2	158	...	...	...	15-...	96
2000—	Yokohama (Jap. Cen.)■	8	11	.421	3.96	26	24	5	3	0-...	161.2	166	...	...	...	37-...	108
2001—	Yokohama (Jap. Cen.)	12	9	.571	3.03	24	24	6	3	0-...	148.2	150	...	...	...	30-...	74
2002—	New York (N.L.)■	0	3	.000	5.61	25	0	0	0	0-0	43.1	53	29	27	7	12-4	33
	—Norfolk (I.L.)	3	1	.750	1.42	17	6	1	0	0-...	44.1	27	8	7	4	9-2	43
Major League totals (1 year)		0	3	.000	5.61	25	0	0	0	0-0	43.1	53	29	27	7	12-4	33

KONERKO, PAUL — 1B — WHITE SOX

PERSONAL: Born March 5, 1976, in Providence, R.I. ... 6-2/215. ... Bats right, throws right. ... Full name: Paul Henry Konerko.
HIGH SCHOOL: Chaparral (Scottsdale, Ariz.).

TRANSACTIONS/CAREER NOTES: Selected by Los Angeles Dodgers organization in first round (13th pick overall) of free-agent draft (June 2, 1994). ... Traded by Dodgers with P Dennis Reyes to Cincinnati Reds for P Jeff Shaw (July 4, 1998). ... Traded by Reds to Chicago White Sox for OF Mike Cameron (November 11, 1998).
HONORS: Named Pacific Coast League Most Valuable Player (1997).
STATISTICAL NOTES: Led Northwest League with seven sacrifice flies in 1994. ... Led Pacific Coast League with 300 total bases in 1997. ... Had 18-game hitting streak (April 13-May 1, 2002). ... Career major league grand slams: 4.
2002 GAMES PLAYED BY POSITION (MLB): 1B—140; DH—7.

		BATTING														FIELDING	
Year Team (League)	**Pos.**	**G**	**AB**	**R**	**H**	**2B**	**3B**	**HR**	**RBI**	**BB**	**SO**	**SB-CS**	**Avg.**	**OBP**	**SLG**	**E**	**Avg.**
1994—Yakima (N'West)	C-DH	67	257	25	74	15	2	6	*58	36	52	1-0	.288	.379	.432	5	.984
1995—San Bern. (Calif.)	C-DH	118	448	7	124	21	1	19	77	59	88	3-1	.277	.362	.455	11	.985
1996—San Antonio (Texas)	1B-DH	133	470	78	141	23	2	29	86	72	85	1-3	.300	.397	.543	14	.989
—Albuquerque (PCL)	1B	4	14	2	6	0	0	1	2	1	2	0-1	.429	.467	.643	0	1.000
1997—Albuquerque (PCL)	3-1-DH-2	130	483	97	156	31	1	*37	*127	64	61	2-3	.323	.407	*.621	24	.952
—Los Angeles (N.L.)	1B-3B	6	7	0	1	0	0	0	0	1	2	0-0	.143	.250	.143	0	1.000
1998—Los Angeles (N.L.)	1B-3B-OF-DH	49	144	14	31	1	0	4	16	10	30	0-1	.215	.272	.306	2	.991
—Albuquerque (PCL)	OF-1B-3B	24	87	16	33	10	0	6	26	11	12	0-0	.379	.436	.701	3	.955
—Cincinnati (N.L.)■	3B-1B-OF	26	73	7	16	3	0	3	13	6	10	0-0	.219	.284	.384	0	1.000
—Indianapolis (I.L.)	3B	39	150	25	49	8	0	8	39	19	18	1-0	.327	.402	.540	4	.957
1999—Chicago (A.L.)■	1B-DH-3B	142	513	71	151	31	4	24	81	45	68	1-0	.294	.352	.511	4	.995
2000—Chicago (A.L.)	1B-DH-3B	143	524	84	156	31	1	21	97	47	72	1-0	.298	.363	.481	11	.990
2001—Chicago (A.L.)	1B-DH	156	582	92	164	35	0	32	99	54	89	1-0	.282	.349	.507	8	.994
2002—Chicago (A.L.)	1B-DH	151	570	81	173	30	0	27	104	44	72	0-0	.304	.359	.498	8	.993
American League totals (4 years)		592	2189	328	644	127	5	104	381	190	301	3-0	.294	.356	.499	31	.993
National League totals (2 years)		81	224	21	48	4	0	7	29	17	42	0-1	.214	.275	.326	2	.993
Major League totals (6 years)		673	2413	349	692	131	5	111	410	207	343	3-1	.287	.348	.483	33	.993

DIVISION SERIES RECORD

		BATTING														FIELDING	
Year Team (League)	**Pos.**	**G**	**AB**	**R**	**H**	**2B**	**3B**	**HR**	**RBI**	**BB**	**SO**	**SB-CS**	**Avg.**	**OBP**	**SLG**	**E**	**Avg.**
2000—Chicago (A.L.)	1B-PH	3	9	1	0	0	0	0	0	1	1	0-0	.000	.100	.000	0	1.000

ALL-STAR GAME RECORD

RECORDS: Holds single-game record for most doubles—2 (July 9, 2002).

	AB	**R**	**H**	**2B**	**3B**	**HR**	**RBI**	**BB**	**SO**	**SB-CS**	**Avg.**	**OBP**	**SLG**	**E**	**Avg.**
All-Star Game totals (1 year)	2	0	2	2	0	0	2	0	0	0-0	1.000	1.000	2.000	0	1.000

KOPLOVE, MIKE — P — DIAMONDBACKS

PERSONAL: Born August 30, 1976, in Philadelphia. ... 6-0/170. ... Throws right, bats right. ... Full name: Michael Paul Koplove.
HIGH SCHOOL: Chestnut Hill Academy (Philadelphia).
COLLEGE: Delaware.
TRANSACTIONS/CAREER NOTES: Selected by Arizona Diamondbacks organization in 29th round of free-agent draft (June 2, 1998). ... On El Paso disabled list (April 7-29, 2001).
CAREER HITTING (MLB): 0-for-2 (.000), 0 R, 0 2B, 0 3B, 0 HR, 0 RBI.

Year League	**W**	**L**	**Pct.**	**ERA**	**G**	**GS**	**CG**	**ShO**	**Sv.-Opp.**	**IP**	**H**	**R**	**ER**	**HR**	**BB-IBB**	**SO**
1998—Ariz. D-backs (Ariz.)	0	0	...	9.00	2	0	0	0	0-...	4.0	4	4	4	0	2-0	5
—Lethbridge (Pio.)	1	2	.333	3.54	12	1	0	0	2-...	28.0	23	12	11	2	3-0	22
1999—South Bend (Midw.)	5	2	.714	2.04	45	45	0	0	7-...	84.0	70	23	19	5	29-0	98
2000—High Desert (Calif.)	2	0	1.000	1.42	20	0	0	0	8-...	25.1	14	4	4	0	10-0	31
—El Paso (Texas)	4	3	.571	4.46	35	0	0	0	6-...	40.1	38	28	20	2	19-1	47
2001—El Paso (Texas)	3	2	.600	2.66	34	0	0	0	4-...	44.0	44	18	13	3	19-3	43
—Tucson (PCL)	4	1	.800	2.82	17	0	0	0	9-...	22.1	17	7	7	1	10-1	22
—Arizona (N.L.)	0	1	.000	3.60	9	0	0	0	0-0	10.0	8	7	4	1	9-1	14
2002—Tucson (PCL)	1	2	.333	1.17	23	0	0	0	3-...	30.2	21	5	4	1	4-0	31
—Arizona (N.L.)	6	1	.857	3.36	55	0	0	0	0-0	61.2	47	24	23	2	23-4	46
Major League totals (2 years)	6	2	.750	3.39	64	0	0	0	0-0	71.2	55	31	27	3	32-5	60

DIVISION SERIES RECORD

Year League	**W**	**L**	**Pct.**	**ERA**	**G**	**GS**	**CG**	**ShO**	**Sv.-Opp.**	**IP**	**H**	**R**	**ER**	**HR**	**BB-IBB**	**SO**
2002—Arizona (N.L.)	0	1	.000	6.75	1	0	0	0	0-0	1.1	2	1	1	0	0-0	1

KOSKIE, COREY — 3B — TWINS

PERSONAL: Born June 28, 1973, in Anola, Man. ... 6-3/217. ... Bats left, throws right. ... Full name: Cordel Leonard Koskie.
HIGH SCHOOL: Springfield Collegiate (Oakbank, Man.).
JUNIOR COLLEGE: Des Moines (Iowa) Area Community College.
COLLEGE: Manitoba, then Kwantlen (B.C.).
TRANSACTIONS/CAREER NOTES: Selected by Minnesota Twins organization in 26th round of free-agent draft (June 2, 1994). ... On disabled list (May 10-28 and June 25-July 4, 1996). ... On disabled list (May 8-24, 2002).
STATISTICAL NOTES: Tied for Eastern League lead with 10 intentional bases on balls received in 1997. ... Career major league grand slams: 2.
2002 GAMES PLAYED BY POSITION (MLB): 3B—138; DH—1.

		BATTING														FIELDING	
Year Team (League)	**Pos.**	**G**	**AB**	**R**	**H**	**2B**	**3B**	**HR**	**RBI**	**BB**	**SO**	**SB-CS**	**Avg.**	**OBP**	**SLG**	**E**	**Avg.**
1994—Elizabethton (Appl.)	3B	34	107	13	25	2	1	3	10	18	27	0-0	.234	.354	.355	8	.930
1995—Fort Wayne (Midw.)	3B	123	462	64	143	37	5	16	78	38	79	2-4	.310	.370	.515	36	.900
1996—Fort Myers (FSL)	3B	95	338	43	88	19	4	9	55	40	76	1-1	.260	.338	.420	19	.926
1997—New Britain (East.)	3B-DH	131	437	88	125	26	6	23	79	90	106	9-5	.286	.414	.531	22	.933
1998—Salt Lake (PCL)	3B-DH	135	505	91	152	32	5	26	105	51	104	15-7	.301	.368	.539	23	.935
—Minnesota (A.L.)	3B	11	29	2	4	0	0	1	2	2	10	0-0	.138	.194	.241	1	.941

Year	Team (League)	Pos.	G	AB	R	H	2B	3B	HR	RBI	BB	SO	SB-CS	Avg.	OBP	SLG	E	Avg.
								BATTING									FIELDING	
1999—	Minnesota (A.L.)	3B-OF-DH	117	342	42	106	21	0	11	58	40	72	4-4	.310	.387	.468	8	.962
2000—	Minnesota (A.L.)	3B-DH	146	474	79	142	32	4	9	65	77	104	5-4	.300	.400	.441	12	.966
2001—	Minnesota (A.L.)	3B-DH	153	562	100	155	37	2	26	103	68	118	27-6	.276	.362	.488	15	.964
2002—	Minnesota (A.L.)	3B-DH	140	490	71	131	37	3	15	69	72	127	10-11	.267	.368	.447	12	.969
Major League totals (5 years)			567	1897	294	538	127	9	62	297	259	431	46-25	.284	.375	.458	48	.965

DIVISION SERIES RECORD

Year	Team (League)	Pos.	G	AB	R	H	2B	3B	HR	RBI	BB	SO	SB-CS	Avg.	OBP	SLG	E	Avg.
								BATTING									FIELDING	
2002—	Minnesota (A.L.)	3B	5	21	3	3	0	1	1	5	2	6	0-0	.143	.250	.381	1	.923

CHAMPIONSHIP SERIES RECORD

RECORDS: Shares single-game record for most strikeouts—4 (October 11, 2002).

Year	Team (League)	Pos.	G	AB	R	H	2B	3B	HR	RBI	BB	SO	SB-CS	Avg.	OBP	SLG	E	Avg.
								BATTING									FIELDING	
2002—	Minnesota (A.L.)	3B	5	18	3	5	2	0	0	2	2	8	0-0	.278	.350	.389	0	1.000

KOTSAY, MARK — OF — PADRES

PERSONAL: Born December 2, 1975, in Whittier, Calif. ... 6-0/201. ... Bats left, throws left. ... Full name: Mark Steven Kotsay.

HIGH SCHOOL: Santa Fe Springs (Calif.).

COLLEGE: Cal State Fullerton.

TRANSACTIONS/CAREER NOTES: Selected by Florida Marlins organization in first round (ninth pick overall) of free-agent draft (June 4, 1996). ... Traded by Marlins with OF Cesar Crespo to San Diego Padres for OF Eric Owens, P Matt Clement and P Omar Ortiz (March 28, 2001). ... On disabled list (April 16-May 1, 2001).

HONORS: Named Golden Spikes Award winner by USA Baseball (1995). ... Named Most Outstanding Player of College World Series (1995).

STATISTICAL NOTES: Tied for Eastern League lead in double plays by outfielder with four in 1997. ... Tied for N.L. lead with 20 assists by outfielder in 1998. ... Led N.L. outfielders with 19 assists in 1999. ... Had 16-game hitting streak (May 24-June 9, 2002). ... Career major league grand slams: 3.

MISCELLANEOUS: Member of 1996 U.S. Olympic baseball team.

2002 GAMES PLAYED BY POSITION (MLB): OF—147.

Year	Team (League)	Pos.	G	AB	R	H	2B	3B	HR	RBI	BB	SO	SB-CS	Avg.	OBP	SLG	E	Avg.
								BATTING									FIELDING	
1996—	Kane County (Midw.)	OF	17	60	16	17	5	0	2	8	16	8	3-0	.283	.436	.467	0	1.000
1997—	Portland (East.)	OF-DH	114	438	103	134	27	2	20	77	75	65	17-5	.306	.405	.514	2	.992
—	Florida (N.L.)	OF	14	52	5	10	1	1	0	4	4	7	3-0	.192	.250	.250	0	1.000
1998—	Florida (N.L.)	OF-1B	154	578	72	161	25	7	11	68	34	61	10-5	.279	.318	.403	6	.984
1999—	Florida (N.L.)	OF-1B	148	495	57	134	23	9	8	50	29	50	7-6	.271	.306	.402	5	.987
2000—	Florida (N.L.)	OF-1B	152	530	87	158	31	5	12	57	42	46	19-9	.298	.347	.443	3	.990
2001—	San Diego (N.L.)■	OF	119	406	67	118	29	1	10	58	48	58	13-5	.291	.366	.441	4	.986
2002—	San Diego (N.L.)	OF	153	578	82	169	27	7	17	61	59	89	11-9	.292	.359	.452	4	.989
Major League totals (6 years)			740	2639	370	750	136	30	58	298	216	311	63-34	.284	.337	.424	22	.987

KOZLOWSKI, BEN — P — RANGERS

PERSONAL: Born August 16, 1980, in St. Petersburg, Fla. ... 6-6/220. ... Throws left, bats left. ... Full name: Benjamin Anthony Kozlowski.

JUNIOR COLLEGE: Santa Fe Community College (Fla.).

TRANSACTIONS/CAREER NOTES: Selected by Atlanta Braves organization in 12th round of free-agent draft (June 2, 1999). ... Traded by Braves to Texas Rangers for P Andy Pratt (April 9, 2002).

CAREER HITTING (MLB): 0-for-0 (.000), 0 R, 0 2B, 0 3B, 0 HR, 0 RBI.

Year	League	W	L	Pct.	ERA	G	GS	CG	ShO	Sv.-Opp.	IP	H	R	ER	HR	BB-IBB	SO
1999—	Gulf Coast Braves (GCL)	1	1	.500	1.87	15	0	0	0	3-...	33.2	28	9	7	0	6-0	29
2000—	Macon (S.Atl.)	3	8	.273	4.21	15	14	0	0	0-...	77.0	76	53	36	6	39-0	67
2001—	Macon (S.Atl.)	10	7	.588	2.48	26	23	1	1	0-...	145.1	134	60	40	8	27-0	147
—	Myrtle Beach (Caro.)	0	2	.000	3.77	2	2	0	0	0-...	14.1	15	7	6	1	3-1	13
2002—	Myrtle Beach (Caro.)	0	1	.000	4.50	1	1	0	0	0-...	4.0	4	5	2	0	3-0	3
—	Charlotte (FSL)■	4	4	.500	2.05	21	12	0	0	0-...	79.0	63	31	18	2	25-0	76
—	Tulsa (Texas)	4	2	.667	1.90	8	8	0	0	0-...	52.0	28	12	11	3	22-0	41
—	Texas (A.L.)	0	0	...	6.30	2	2	0	0	0-0	10.0	11	7	7	3	11-0	6
Major League totals (1 year)		0	0	...	6.30	2	2	0	0	0-0	10.0	11	7	7	3	11-0	6

KREUTER, CHAD — C

PERSONAL: Born August 26, 1964, in Greenbrae, Calif. ... 6-2/200. ... Bats both, throws right. ... Full name: Chad Michael Kreuter. ... Name pronounced CREW-ter.

HIGH SCHOOL: Redwood (Calif.).

COLLEGE: Pepperdine.

TRANSACTIONS/CAREER NOTES: Selected by Texas Rangers organization in fifth round of free-agent draft (June 3, 1985). ... Granted free agency (October 15, 1991). ... Signed by Detroit Tigers organization (January 2, 1992). ... Granted free agency (December 23, 1994). ... Signed by Seattle Mariners (April 8, 1995). ... On Seattle disabled list (June 19-July 6, 1995). ... On Tacoma disabled list (August 4-25, 1995). ... Granted free agency (October 16, 1995). ... Signed by Chicago White Sox organization (December 11, 1995). ... On disabled list (July 20, 1996-remainder of season). ... Granted free agency (October 14, 1996). ... Re-signed by White Sox organization (January 29, 1997). ... Traded by White Sox with OF Tony Phillips to Anaheim Angels for P Chuck McElroy and C Jorge Fabregas (May 18, 1997). ... Granted free agency (November 7, 1997). ... Signed by White Sox (December 10, 1997). ... Traded by White Sox to Angels for cash considerations (September 18, 1998). ... Granted free agency (October 26, 1998). ... Signed by Kansas City Royals (December 15, 1998). ... Granted free agency (October 29, 1999). ... Signed by Los Angeles Dodgers organization (January 20, 2000). ... On disabled list (June 25-July 12, 2002). ... Granted free agency (November 11, 2002).

RECORDS: Shares major league single-game record for most sacrifice flies—3 (July 30, 1994). ... Shares major league record for most hits in one inning in first major league game—2 (September 14, 1988, fifth inning).

STATISTICAL NOTES: Led Carolina League catchers with 21 errors and 17 double plays and tied for lead with 113 assists in 1986. ... Tied for Texas League lead in double plays by catcher with nine in 1988. ... Led A.L. with 21 passed balls in 1989. ... Switch-hit home runs in one game (September 7, 1993). ... Career major league grand slams: 1.
MISCELLANEOUS: Batted righthanded only (1985 and 1990).
2002 GAMES PLAYED BY POSITION (MLB): C—41.

		BATTING														FIELDING	
Year Team (League)	**Pos.**	**G**	**AB**	**R**	**H**	**2B**	**3B**	**HR**	**RBI**	**BB**	**SO**	**SB-CS**	**Avg.**	**OBP**	**SLG**	**E**	**Avg.**
1985—Burlington (Midw.)	C	69	199	25	53	9	0	4	26	38	48	3-2	.266	.382	.372	8	.980
1986—Salem (Caro.)	C-OF-3B	125	387	55	85	21	2	6	49	67	82	5-5	.220	.336	.331	†21	.972
1987—Charlotte (FSL)	C-OF-3B	85	281	36	61	18	1	9	40	31	32	1-1	.217	.296	.384	8	.982
1988—Tulsa (Texas)	C	108	358	46	95	24	6	3	51	55	66	2-2	.265	.362	.391	•13	.981
—Texas (A.L.)	C	16	51	3	14	2	1	1	5	7	13	0-0	.275	.362	.412	1	.990
1989—Texas (A.L.)	C	87	158	16	24	3	0	5	9	27	40	0-1	.152	.274	.266	4	.992
—Oklahoma City (A.A.)	C	26	87	10	22	3	0	0	6	13	11	1-1	.253	.347	.287	2	.988
1990—Texas (A.L.)	C	22	22	2	1	1	0	0	2	8	9	0-0	.045	.290	.091	1	.977
—Oklahoma City (A.A.)	C	92	291	41	65	17	1	7	35	52	80	0-3	.223	.345	.361	10	.984
1991—Texas (A.L.)	C	3	4	0	0	0	0	0	0	0	1	0-0	.000	.000	.000	0	1.000
—Oklahoma City (A.A.)	C	24	70	14	19	6	0	1	12	18	16	2-0	.271	.416	.400	7	.960
—Tulsa (Texas)	C	42	128	23	30	5	1	2	10	29	23	1-0	.234	.380	.336	4	.987
1992—Detroit (A.L.)■	C-DH	67	190	22	48	9	0	2	16	20	38	0-1	.253	.321	.332	5	.983
1993—Detroit (A.L.)	C-DH-1B	119	374	59	107	23	3	15	51	49	92	2-1	.286	.371	.484	7	.988
1994—Detroit (A.L.)	C-1B-OF	65	170	17	38	8	0	1	19	28	36	0-1	.224	.327	.288	4	.987
1995—Seattle (A.L.)■	C	26	75	12	17	5	0	1	8	5	22	0-0	.227	.293	.333	4	.976
—Tacoma (PCL)	C-DH	15	48	6	14	5	0	1	11	8	11	0-0	.292	.393	.458	1	.988
1996—Chicago (A.L.)■	C-1B-DH	46	114	14	25	8	0	3	18	13	29	0-0	.219	.308	.368	2	.990
1997—Chicago (A.L.)	C-1B	19	37	6	8	2	1	1	3	8	9	0-1	.216	.356	.405	2	.969
—Anaheim (A.L.)■	C-DH	70	218	19	51	7	1	4	18	21	57	0-2	.234	.301	.330	3	.994
1998—Chicago (A.L.)■	C	93	245	26	62	9	1	2	33	32	45	1-0	.253	.345	.322	7	.985
—Anaheim (A.L.)■	C	3	7	1	1	1	0	0	0	1	4	0-0	.143	.250	.286	§2	.882
1999—Kansas City (A.L.)■	C-DH	107	324	31	73	15	0	5	35	34	65	0-0	.225	.309	.318	3	.994
2000—Los Angeles (N.L.)■	C	80	212	32	56	13	0	6	28	54	48	1-0	.264	.416	.410	3	.994
2001—Los Angeles (N.L.)	C-DH	73	191	21	41	11	1	6	17	41	52	0-0	.215	.355	.377	0	1.000
2002—Los Angeles (N.L.)	C	41	95	8	25	5	0	2	12	10	31	1-0	.263	.333	.379	3	.986
American League totals (12 years)		743	1989	228	469	93	7	40	217	253	460	3-7	.236	.325	.350	45	.988
National League totals (3 years)		194	498	61	122	29	1	14	57	105	131	2-0	.245	.378	.392	6	.995
Major League totals (15 years)		937	2487	289	591	122	8	54	274	358	591	5-7	.238	.336	.358	51	.990

LACKEY, JOHN — P — ANGELS

PERSONAL: Born October 23, 1978, in Abilene, Texas. ... 6-6/205. ... Throws right, bats right. ... Full name: John Derran Lackey.
HIGH SCHOOL: Abilene (Texas).
JUNIOR COLLEGE: Grayson County (Texas).
TRANSACTIONS/CAREER NOTES: Selected by Anaheim Angels organization in second round of free-agent draft (June 2, 1999).
CAREER HITTING (MLB): 0-for-0 (.000), 0 R, 0 2B, 0 3B, 0 HR, 0 RBI.

Year League	**W**	**L**	**Pct.**	**ERA**	**G**	**GS**	**CG**	**ShO**	**Sv.-Opp.**	**IP**	**H**	**R**	**ER**	**HR**	**BB-IBB**	**SO**
1999—Boise (N'West)	6	2	.750	4.98	15	15	1	0	0-...	81.1	81	59	45	7	50-1	77
2000—Cedar Rapids (Midw.)	3	2	.600	2.08	5	5	0	0	0-...	30.1	20	7	7	1	5-0	21
—Lake Elsinore (Calif.)	6	6	.500	3.40	15	15	2	•1	0-...	100.2	94	56	38	9	42-0	74
—Erie (East.)	6	1	.857	3.30	8	8	2	0	0-...	57.1	58	23	21	6	9-0	43
2001—Arkansas (Texas)	9	7	.563	3.46	18	18	3	2	0-...	127.1	106	55	49	11	29-0	94
—Salt Lake (PCL)	3	4	.429	6.71	10	10	1	0	0-...	57.2	75	44	43	5	16-0	42
2002—Salt Lake (PCL)	8	2	.800	2.57	16	16	2	1	0-...	101.2	89	35	29	5	28-0	82
—Anaheim (A.L.)	9	4	.692	3.66	18	18	1	0	0-0	108.1	113	52	44	10	33-0	69
Major League totals (1 year)	9	4	.692	3.66	18	18	1	0	0-0	108.1	113	52	44	10	33-0	69

DIVISION SERIES RECORD

Year League	**W**	**L**	**Pct.**	**ERA**	**G**	**GS**	**CG**	**ShO**	**Sv.-Opp.**	**IP**	**H**	**R**	**ER**	**HR**	**BB-IBB**	**SO**
2002—Anaheim (A.L.)	0	0	...	0.00	1	0	0	0	0-0	3.0	3	0	0	0	1-0	3

CHAMPIONSHIP SERIES RECORD

Year League	**W**	**L**	**Pct.**	**ERA**	**G**	**GS**	**CG**	**ShO**	**Sv.-Opp.**	**IP**	**H**	**R**	**ER**	**HR**	**BB-IBB**	**SO**
2002—Anaheim (A.L.)	1	0	1.000	0.00	1	1	0	0	0-0	7.0	3	0	0	0	0-0	7

WORLD SERIES RECORD

NOTES: Member of World Series championship team (2002).

Year League	**W**	**L**	**Pct.**	**ERA**	**G**	**GS**	**CG**	**ShO**	**Sv.-Opp.**	**IP**	**H**	**R**	**ER**	**HR**	**BB-IBB**	**SO**
2002—Anaheim (A.L.)	1	0	1.000	4.38	3	2	0	0	0-0	12.1	15	6	6	0	5-4	7

LAMB, DAVID — SS/2B — TWINS

PERSONAL: Born June 6, 1975, in West Hills, Cailf. ... 6-2/165. ... Bats both, throws right. ... Full name: David Christian Lamb.
HIGH SCHOOL: Newbury Park (Calif.).
TRANSACTIONS/CAREER NOTES: Selected by Baltimore Orioles organization in second round of free-agent draft (June 3, 1993). ... Selected by Tampa Bay Devil Rays from Orioles organization in Rule 5 major league draft (December 14, 1998). ... On Tampa Bay disabled list (August 14-September 1, 1999); included rehabilitation assignment to Durham (August 24-31). ... Claimed on waivers by New York Mets (February 7, 2000). ... Granted free agency (October 3, 2000). ... Signed by Anaheim Angels organization (November 8, 2000). ... Released by Angels (March 29, 2001). ... Signed by Colorado Rockies organization (April 9, 2001). ... On Colorado Springs disabled list (July 26-August 2, 2001). ... Released by Rockies (August 8, 2001). ... Signed by Florida Marlins organization (August 8, 2001). ... Granted free agency (October 15, 2001). ... Signed by Minnesota Twins organization (November 7, 2001). ... Released by Twins (November 1, 2002). ... Re-signed by Twins organization (November 8, 2002).
2002 GAMES PLAYED BY POSITION (MLB): SS—4; 2B—2; 3B—1.

Year	Team (League)	Pos.	G	AB	R	H	2B	3B	HR	RBI	BB	SO	SB-CS	Avg.	OBP	SLG	E	Avg.
			BATTING														FIELDING	
1993—	GC Orioles (GCL)	SS	16	56	4	10	1	0	0	6	10	8	2-0	.179	.303	.196	3	.927
1994—	Albany (S.Atl.)	SS	92	308	37	74	9	2	0	29	32	40	4-1	.240	.316	.282	22	.941
1995—	Frederick (Caro.)	SS-2B	124	436	39	97	14	2	2	34	38	81	6-7	.222	.297	.278	24	.954
	— Bowie (East.)	SS	1	4	0	1	0	0	0	1	0	1	0-0	.250	.250	.250	1	.800
1996—	High Desert (Calif.)	SS	116	460	63	118	24	3	3	55	50	68	5-6	.257	.341	.341	18	.969
1997—	Frederick (Caro.)	2B-SS-3B	70	249	30	65	21	1	2	39	25	32	3-1	.261	.339	.378	9	.971
	— Bowie (East.)	SS-3B-2B	73	269	46	89	20	2	4	38	34	35	0-0	.331	.408	.465	11	.956
1998—	Bowie (East.)	SS	66	241	29	73	10	1	2	25	27	33	1-3	.303	.374	.378	14	.946
	— Rochester (I.L.)	SS-3B-2B	48	178	24	53	7	1	1	16	17	25	1-5	.298	.365	.365	7	.964
1999—	Tampa Bay (A.L.)■	SS-2B-DH	55	124	18	28	5	1	1	13	10	18	0-1	.226	.284	.306	9	.946
	— Durham (I.L.)	SS-2B	7	30	7	7	3	0	0	7	2	4	0-1	.233	.273	.333	3	.923
2000—	Norfolk (I.L.)■	SS-3B-2B	109	356	45	80	23	1	2	35	40	49	8-3	.225	.312	.312	9	.977
	— New York (N.L.)	3B-2B-SS	7	5	1	1	0	0	0	0	1	1	0-0	.200	.333	.200	0	1.000
2001—	Carolina (Sou.)■	SS-2B-3B	82	287	32	78	16	0	5	32	37	39	2-3	.272	.361	.380	13	.965
	— Colo. Springs (PCL)	SS-2B	5	9	1	2	0	0	0	0	0	4	0-0	.222	.222	.222	1	.889
	— Calgary (PCL)■	22-SS-3B	23	67	15	20	6	0	1	6	11	11	0-0	.299	.413	.433	3	.967
2002—	Edmonton (PCL)■	SS-2B	123	440	72	136	25	3	10	72	45	57	2-6	.309	.377	.448	18	.964■
	— Minnesota (A.L.)	SS-2B-3B	7	10	0	1	0	0	0	0	0	2	0-0	.100	.100	.100	0	1.000
American League totals (2 years)			62	134	18	29	5	1	1	13	10	20	0-1	.216	.271	.291	9	.950
National League totals (1 year)			7	5	1	1	0	0	0	0	1	1	0-0	.200	.333	.200	0	1.000
Major League totals (3 years)			69	139	19	30	5	1	1	13	11	21	0-1	.216	.273	.288	9	.951

CHAMPIONSHIP SERIES RECORD

Year	Team (League)	Pos.	G	AB	R	H	2B	3B	HR	RBI	BB	SO	SB-CS	Avg.	OBP	SLG	E	Avg.
			BATTING														FIELDING	
2002—	Minnesota (A.L.)	2B	2	0	0	0	0	0	0	0	0	0	0-0	...	...	...	0	...

LAMB, MIKE — 3B — RANGERS

PERSONAL: Born August 9, 1975, in West Covina, Calif. ... 6-1/195. ... Bats left, throws right. ... Full name: Michael Robert Lamb.
HIGH SCHOOL: Bishop Amat (La Puente, Calif.).
COLLEGE: Cal State Fullerton.
TRANSACTIONS/CAREER NOTES: Selected by Texas Rangers organization in seventh round of free-agent draft (June 3, 1997).
STATISTICAL NOTES: Led Florida State League third basemen with 98 putouts, 304 assists, 432 total chances, 19 double plays and .931 fielding percentage in 1998.
2002 GAMES PLAYED BY POSITION (MLB): 1B—52; DH—21; OF—16; 3B—14; C—3; 2B—1.

Year	Team (League)	Pos.	G	AB	R	H	2B	3B	HR	RBI	BB	SO	SB-CS	Avg.	OBP	SLG	E	Avg.
			BATTING														FIELDING	
1997—	Pulaski (Appl.)	3B	60	233	59	78	19	3	9	47	31	18	7-2	.335	.412	.558	25	.862
1998—	Charlotte (FSL)	3B-1B	135	536	83	162	35	3	9	93	45	63	18-7	.302	.356	.429	31	†.933
1999—	Tulsa (Texas)	3B-C	137	*544	98	*176	*51	5	21	100	53	65	4-3	.324	.386	.551	28	.930
	— Oklahoma (PCL)	3B	2	2	0	1	0	0	0	0	1	0	0-1	.500	.750	.500	0	...
2000—	Oklahoma (PCL)	3B	14	55	8	14	5	1	2	5	5	6	2-1	.255	.317	.491	7	.806
	— Texas (A.L.)	3B-DH	138	493	65	137	25	2	6	47	34	60	0-2	.278	.328	.373	•33	.913
2001—	Oklahoma (PCL)	3B	69	273	35	81	19	3	8	40	13	31	0-2	.297	.331	.476	15	.908
	— Texas (A.L.)	3B	76	284	42	87	18	0	4	35	14	27	2-1	.306	.348	.412	18	.914
2002—	Oklahoma (PCL)	C-3B	6	28	3	11	1	0	0	4	1	4	0-0	.393	.414	.429	3	.893
	— Texas (A.L.)	1-D-O-3-C-2	115	314	54	89	13	0	9	33	33	48	0-0	.283	.354	.411	9	.980
Major League totals (3 years)			329	1091	161	313	56	2	19	115	81	135	2-3	.287	.341	.394	60	.942

LAMPKIN, TOM — C

PERSONAL: Born March 4, 1964, in Cincinnati. ... 5-11/198. ... Bats left, throws right. ... Full name: Thomas Michael Lampkin.
HIGH SCHOOL: Blanchet (Seattle).
JUNIOR COLLEGE: Edmonds College (Wash.).
COLLEGE: Portland.
TRANSACTIONS/CAREER NOTES: Selected by Cleveland Indians organization in 11th round of free-agent draft (June 2, 1986). ... On disabled list (July 6, 1989-remainder of season). ... Traded by Indians to San Diego Padres for OF Alex Cole (July 11, 1990). ... Traded by Padres to Milwaukee Brewers for cash (March 25, 1993). ... Granted free agency (December 20, 1993). ... Signed by San Francisco Giants organization (January 5, 1994). ... On San Francisco disabled list (March 31-April 24 and August 26, 1996-remainder of season); included rehabilitation assignment to San Jose (April 22-24). ... Traded by Giants to St. Louis Cardinals for a player to be named later or cash (December 19, 1996); Giants acquired P Rene Arocha to complete deal (February 12, 1997). ... Granted free agency (October 23, 1998). ... Signed by Seattle Mariners (December 14, 1998). ... On Seattle disabled list (March 25-April 13 and June 28, 2000-remainder of season); included rehabilitation assignment to Tacoma (April 8-13). ... Granted free agency (October 27, 2000). ... Re-signed by Mariners (December 22, 2000). ... Traded by Mariners with P Brett Tomko and SS Ramon Vazquez to San Diego Padres for C Ben Davis, P Wascar Serrano and SS Alex Arias (December 11, 2001). ... Granted free agency (October 28, 2002).
STATISTICAL NOTES: Led Midwest League catchers with 100 assists in 1987. ... Led Pacific Coast League catchers with 64 assists and 11 double plays in 1992. ... Led Pacific Coast League catchers with 595 putouts in 1994. ... Career major league grand slams: 1.
2002 GAMES PLAYED BY POSITION (MLB): C—94.

Year	Team (League)	Pos.	G	AB	R	H	2B	3B	HR	RBI	BB	SO	SB-CS	Avg.	OBP	SLG	E	Avg.
			BATTING														FIELDING	
1986—	Batavia (NY-Penn)	C	63	190	24	49	5	1	1	20	31	14	4-3	.258	.360	.311	8	.978
1987—	Waterloo (Midw.)	C	118	398	49	106	19	2	7	55	34	41	5-0	.266	.323	.377	15	.981
1988—	Williamsport (East.)	C	80	263	38	71	10	0	3	23	25	20	1-2	.270	.340	.342	9	.982
	— Colo. Springs (PCL)	C	34	107	14	30	5	0	0	7	9	2	0-0	.280	.347	.327	5	.975
	— Cleveland (A.L.)	C	4	4	0	0	0	0	0	0	1	0	0-0	.000	.200	.000	0	1.000

Year Team (League)	Pos.	G	AB	R	H	2B	3B	HR	RBI	BB	SO	SB-CS	Avg.	OBP	SLG	E	Avg.
		BATTING														FIELDING	
1989— Colo. Springs (PCL) ...	C	63	209	26	67	10	3	4	32	10	18	4-2	.321	.356	.455	8	.976
1990— Colo. Springs (PCL) ...	C-2B	69	199	32	44	7	5	1	18	19	19	7-2	.221	.294	.322	12	.967
— San Diego (N.L.)■	C	26	63	4	14	0	1	1	4	4	9	0-1	.222	.269	.302	3	.971
— Las Vegas (PCL)	C	1	2	0	1	0	0	0	0	0	1	0-0	.500	.500	.500	0	1.000
1991— San Diego (N.L.)	C	38	58	4	11	3	1	0	3	3	9	0-0	.190	.230	.276	0	1.000
— Las Vegas (PCL)	C-1B-OF	45	164	25	52	11	1	2	29	10	19	2-1	.317	.362	.433	6	.975
1992— Las Vegas (PCL)	C	108	340	45	104	17	4	3	48	53	27	15-8	.306	.405	.406	12	.979
— San Diego (N.L.)	C-OF	9	17	3	4	0	0	0	0	6	1	2-0	.235	.458	.235	0	1.000
1993— New Orleans (A.A.)■..	C-OF	25	80	18	26	5	0	2	10	18	4	5-4	.325	.465	.463	3	.982
— Milwaukee (A.L.)	C-OF-DH	73	162	22	32	8	0	4	25	20	26	7-3	.198	.280	.321	6	.978
1994— Phoenix (PCL)■.........	C-DH-OF	118	453	76	136	32	8	8	70	42	49	8-7	.300	.370	.459	10	.985
1995— San Francisco (N.L.) ..	C-OF	65	76	8	21	2	0	1	9	9	8	2-0	.276	.360	.342	0	1.000
1996— San Jose (Calif.).........	C	2	7	2	2	0	1	0	2	1	2	0-0	.286	.375	.571	0	1.000
— San Francisco (N.L.) ..	C	66	177	26	41	8	0	6	29	20	22	1-5	.232	.324	.379	3	.992
1997— St. Louis (N.L.)■	C	108	229	28	56	8	1	7	22	28	30	2-1	.245	.335	.380	5	.989
1998— St. Louis (N.L.)...........	C-OF-1B	93	216	25	50	12	1	6	28	24	32	3-2	.231	.328	.380	5	.986
1999— Seattle (A.L.)■...........	C-DH-OF	76	206	29	60	11	2	9	34	13	32	1-3	.291	.345	.495	5	.985
2000— Tacoma (PCL)	C	3	8	1	2	1	0	0	0	3	2	0-0	.250	.455	.375	0	1.000
— Seattle (A.L.)	C-DH	36	103	15	26	6	1	7	23	9	17	0-0	.252	.325	.534	2	.987
2001— Seattle (A.L.)	C-OF-DH	79	204	28	46	10	0	5	22	18	41	1-0	.225	.309	.348	2	.995
2002— San Diego (N.L.)■	C	104	281	32	61	10	1	10	37	38	59	4-2	.217	.313	.367	5	.992
American League totals (5 years)		268	679	94	164	35	3	25	104	61	116	9-6	.242	.314	.412	15	.987
National League totals (8 years)		509	1117	130	258	43	5	31	132	132	170	14-11	.231	.322	.362	21	.990
Major League totals (13 years)		777	1796	224	422	78	8	56	236	193	286	23-17	.235	.319	.381	36	.989

DIVISION SERIES RECORD

Year Team (League)	Pos.	G	AB	R	H	2B	3B	HR	RBI	BB	SO	SB-CS	Avg.	OBP	SLG	E	Avg.
		BATTING														FIELDING	
2001— Seattle (A.L.)	PH-C	2	2	0	0	0	0	0	0	0	2	0-0	.000	.000	.000	0	1.000

CHAMPIONSHIP SERIES RECORD

Year Team (League)	Pos.	G	AB	R	H	2B	3B	HR	RBI	BB	SO	SB-CS	Avg.	OBP	SLG	E	Avg.
		BATTING														FIELDING	
2001— Seattle (A.L.)	C	2	4	0	1	0	0	0	0	1	2	0-0	.250	.400	.250	0	1.000

LANE, JASON — OF — ASTROS

PERSONAL: Born December 22, 1976, in Santa Rosa, Calif. ... 6-2/215. ... Bats right, throws left. ... Full name: Jason Dean Lane.
HIGH SCHOOL: Santa Rosa (Calif.).
JUNIOR COLLEGE: El Molino (Forestville, Calif.).
COLLEGE: Southern California.
TRANSACTIONS/CAREER NOTES: Selected by Houston Astros organization in sixth round of free-agent draft (June 2, 1999).
HONORS: Named Texas League Most Valuable Player (2001).
STATISTICAL NOTES: Led Midwest League with 13 sacrifice flies in 2000. ... Led Texas League with 320 total bases in 2001. ... Tied for Texas League lead with 11 intentional bases on balls received in 2001.
2002 GAMES PLAYED BY POSITION (MLB): OF—38.

Year Team (League)	Pos.	G	AB	R	H	2B	3B	HR	RBI	BB	SO	SB-CS	Avg.	OBP	SLG	E	Avg.
		BATTING														FIELDING	
1999— Auburn (NY-Penn)......	1B-P	74	283	46	79	18	5	13	*59	38	46	6-4	.279	.366	.516	9	.986
2000— Michigan (Midw.)	OF-1B	133	511	98	153	38	0	23	•104	62	91	20-7	.299	.375	.509	5	.986
2001— Round Rock (Texas)...	OF	137	526	*103	166	36	2	38	*124	61	98	14-2	.316	.407	.608	2	.992
2002— New Orleans (PCL).....	OF-1B	111	426	65	116	36	2	15	83	31	90	13-3	.272	.328	.472	2	.993
— Houston (N.L.)	OF	44	69	12	20	3	1	4	10	10	12	1-1	.290	.375	.536	1	.980
Major League totals (1 year)		44	69	12	20	3	1	4	10	10	12	1-1	.290	.375	.536	1	.980

RECORD AS PITCHER

Year League	W	L	Pct.	ERA	G	GS	CG	ShO	Sv.	IP	H	R	ER	BB	SO
1999— Auburn (NY-Penn).............	0	0	...	0.00	1	0	0	0	0	1	0	0	0	0	1

LANGERHANS, RYAN — OF — BRAVES

PERSONAL: Born February 20, 1980, in San Antonio. ... 6-3/195. ... Bats left, throws left. ... Full name: Ryan David Langerhans.
HIGH SCHOOL: Round Rock (Texas).
TRANSACTIONS/CAREER NOTES: Selected by Atlanta Braves organization in third round of free-agent draft (June 2, 1998). ... On Greenville disabled list (May 24-June 17, 2002).
2002 GAMES PLAYED BY POSITION (MLB): OF—1.

Year Team (League)	Pos.	G	AB	R	H	2B	3B	HR	RBI	BB	SO	SB-CS	Avg.	OBP	SLG	E	Avg.
		BATTING														FIELDING	
1998— GC Braves (GCL)........	OF	43	148	15	41	10	4	2	19	19	38	2-5	.277	.357	.439	2	.975
1999— Macon (S.Atl.)...........	OF	121	448	66	120	30	1	9	49	52	99	19-11	.268	.352	.400	5	.977
2000— Myrtle Beach (Caro.)..	OF	116	392	55	83	14	7	6	37	32	104	25-11	.212	.286	.329	6	.961
2001— Myrtle Beach (Caro.)..	OF	125	450	66	186	30	3	7	48	55	104	22-13	.413	.485	.540	7	.972
2002— Greenville (Sou.)	OF	109	391	57	98	23	2	9	62	68	83	10-5	.251	.366	.389	2	.992
— Atlanta (N.L.).............	OF	1	1	0	0	0	0	0	0	0	0	0-0	.000	.000	.000	0	...
Major League totals (1 year)		1	1	0	0	0	0	0	0	0	0	0-0	.000	.000	.000	0	...

LANKFORD, RAY OF

PERSONAL: Born June 5, 1967, in Los Angeles, Calif. ... 5-11/200. ... Bats left, throws left. ... Full name: Raymond Lewis Lankford. ... Nephew of Carl Nichols, catcher with Baltimore Orioles (1986-88) and Houston Astros (1989-91).

HIGH SCHOOL: Grace Davis (Modesto, Calif.).

JUNIOR COLLEGE: Modesto (Calif.) Junior College.

TRANSACTIONS/CAREER NOTES: Selected by Chicago Cubs organization in third round of free-agent draft (January 14, 1986); did not sign. ... Selected by St. Louis Cardinals organization in third round of free-agent draft (June 2, 1987). ... On disabled list (June 24-July 9, 1993). ... On St. Louis disabled list (March 27-April 22, 1997); included rehabilitation assignment to Prince William (April 14-22). ... On disabled list (March 26-April 24, 1999). ... Traded by Cardinals with cash to San Diego Padres for P Woody Williams (August 2, 2001). ... On disabled list (July 4-September 10, 2002). ... Granted free agency (October 28, 2002).

RECORDS: Shares major league single-season record for fewest double plays by outfielder (150 or more games)—0 (1992).

HONORS: Named Texas League Most Valuable Player (1989).

STATISTICAL NOTES: Led Appalachian League outfielders with 143 putouts and 155 total chances in 1987. ... Led Appalachian League in caught stealing with 11 in 1987. ... Led Midwest League with 242 total bases in 1988. ... Led Texas League outfielders with 367 putouts and 387 total chances in 1989. ... Led American Association outfielders with 333 putouts and 352 total chances in 1990. ... Tied for American Association lead with nine intentional bases on balls received in 1990. ... Hit for the cycle (September 15, 1991). ... Led N.L. in caught stealing with 24 in 1992. ... Led N.L. outfielders with 438 putouts in 1992. ... Career major league grand slams: 6.

2002 GAMES PLAYED BY POSITION (MLB): OF—59; DH—1.

		BATTING														FIELDING	
Year Team (League)	Pos.	G	AB	R	H	2B	3B	HR	RBI	BB	SO	SB-CS	Avg.	OBP	SLG	E	Avg.
1987—Johnson City (Appl.) ..	OF	66	253	45	78	17	4	3	32	19	43	14-*11	.308	.367	.443	5	.968
1988—Springfield (Midw.)	OF	135	532	90	151	26	*16	11	66	60	92	33-17	.284	.366	.455	7	.976
1989—Arkansas (Texas)........	OF	*134	498	98	*158	28	*12	11	98	65	57	38-10	.317	.395	.488	11	.972
1990—Louisville (A.A.)..........	OF	132	473	61	123	25	8	10	72	72	81	30-7	.260	.362	.410	•11	.969
—St. Louis (N.L.)...........	OF	39	126	12	36	10	1	3	12	13	27	8-2	.286	.353	.452	1	.989
1991—St. Louis (N.L.)...........	OF	151	566	83	142	23	*15	9	69	41	114	44-20	.251	.301	.392	6	.984
1992—St. Louis (N.L.)...........	OF	153	598	87	175	40	6	20	86	72	*147	42-24	.293	.371	.480	2	.996
1993—St. Louis (N.L.)...........	OF	127	407	64	97	17	3	7	45	81	111	14-14	.238	.366	.346	7	.978
1994—St. Louis (N.L.)...........	OF	109	416	89	111	25	5	19	57	58	113	11-10	.267	.359	.488	6	.978
1995—St. Louis (N.L.)...........	OF	132	483	81	134	35	2	25	82	63	110	24-8	.277	.360	.513	3	.990
1996—St. Louis (N.L.)...........	OF	149	545	100	150	36	8	21	86	79	133	35-7	.275	.366	.486	1	*.997
1997—Prince William (Caro.)	DH-OF	4	13	3	4	1	0	0	4	4	5	1-1	.308	.444	.385	0	1.000
—St. Louis (N.L.)...........	OF	133	465	94	137	36	3	31	98	95	125	21-11	.295	.411	.585	9	.971
1998—St. Louis (N.L.)...........	OF-DH	154	533	94	156	37	1	31	105	86	151	26-5	.293	.391	.540	5	.986
1999—St. Louis (N.L.)...........	OF-DH	122	422	77	129	32	1	15	63	49	110	14-4	.306	.380	.493	3	.987
2000—St. Louis (N.L.)...........	OF-DH	128	392	73	99	16	3	26	65	70	148	5-6	.253	.367	.508	5	.973
2001—St. Louis (N.L.)...........	OF	91	264	38	62	18	3	15	39	44	105	4-2	.235	.345	.496	5	.966
—San Diego (N.L.)■	OF	40	125	20	36	10	1	4	19	18	40	6-0	.288	.386	.480	1	.985
2002—San Diego (N.L.)	OF-DH	81	205	20	46	7	1	6	26	30	61	2-2	.224	.326	.356	5	.953
Major League totals (13 years)		1609	5547	932	1510	342	53	232	852	799	1495	256-115	.272	.364	.478	59	.983

DIVISION SERIES RECORD

		BATTING														FIELDING	
Year Team (League)	Pos.	G	AB	R	H	2B	3B	HR	RBI	BB	SO	SB-CS	Avg.	OBP	SLG	E	Avg.
1996—St. Louis (N.L.)...........	OF-PH	1	2	1	1	0	0	0	0	1	0	0-0	.500	.667	.500	0	1.000
2000—St. Louis (N.L.)...........	OF	3	10	2	2	1	0	0	3	2	5	0-0	.200	.333	.300	0	1.000
Division series totals (2 years)		4	12	3	3	1	0	0	3	3	5	0-0	.250	.400	.333	0	1.000

CHAMPIONSHIP SERIES RECORD

		BATTING														FIELDING	
Year Team (League)	Pos.	G	AB	R	H	2B	3B	HR	RBI	BB	SO	SB-CS	Avg.	OBP	SLG	E	Avg.
1996—St. Louis (N.L.)...........	OF-PH	5	13	1	0	0	0	0	1	1	4	0-0	.000	.067	.000	0	1.000
2000—St. Louis (N.L.)...........	PH-OF	5	12	1	4	1	0	0	1	1	5	0-0	.333	.385	.417	0	1.000
Championship series totals (2 years)		10	25	2	4	1	0	0	2	2	9	0-0	.160	.214	.200	0	1.000

ALL-STAR GAME RECORD

	AB	R	H	2B	3B	HR	RBI	BB	SO	SB-CS	Avg.	OBP	SLG	E	Avg.
All-Star Game totals (1 year)	2	0	0	0	0	0	0	1	1	0-0	.000	.333	.000	0	...

LARKIN, BARRY SS REDS

PERSONAL: Born April 28, 1964, in Cincinnati. ... 6-0/185. ... Bats right, throws right. ... Full name: Barry Louis Larkin. ... Brother of Steve Larkin, minor league outfielder/first baseman (1994-2000); and cousin of Nathan Davis, defensive tackle with Atlanta Falcons (1997) and Dallas Cowboys (1998-99).

HIGH SCHOOL: Moeller (Cincinnati).

COLLEGE: Michigan.

TRANSACTIONS/CAREER NOTES: Selected by Cincinnati Reds organization in second round of free-agent draft (June 7, 1982); did not sign. ... Selected by Reds organization in first round (fourth pick overall) of free-agent draft (June 3, 1985). ... On disabled list (April 13-May 2, 1987). ... On Cincinnati disabled list (July 11-September 1, 1989); included rehabilitation assignment to Nashville (August 27-September 1). ... On disabled list (May 18-June 4, 1991; April 19-May 8, 1992; and August 5, 1993-remainder of season). ... On disabled list (June 17-August 2 and September 1, 1997-remainder of season; March 12-April 7, 1998; April 22-May16, 2000; May 17-June 15 and June 29, 2001-remainder of season).

RECORDS: Holds major league single-season record for fewest putouts by shortstop for leader—230 (1996). ... Shares major league record for most home runs in two consecutive games—5 (June 27 [2] and 28 [3], 1991).

HONORS: Named shortstop on The Sporting News college All-America team (1985). ... Named American Association Most Valuable Player (1986). ... Named shortstop on The Sporting News N.L. All-Star team (1988-92, 1994-96, 1998 and 1999). ... Named shortstop on The Sporting

News N.L. Silver Slugger team (1988-92, 1995-96, 1998 and 1999). ... Won N.L. Gold Glove at shortstop (1994-96). ... Named N.L. Most Valuable Player by Baseball Writers' Association of America (1995).

STATISTICAL NOTES: Had 21-game hitting streak (September 10-October 2, 1988). ... Led N.L. shortstopts with 469 assists and tied for league lead with 86 double plays in 1990. ... Hit three home runs in one game (June 28, 1991). ... Led N.L. shortstops with 178 putouts in 1994 and 230 in 1996. ... Had 16-game hitting streak (June 20-July 6, 1999). ... Career major league grand slams: 1.

MISCELLANEOUS: Member of 1984 U.S. Olympic baseball team.

2002 GAMES PLAYED BY POSITION (MLB): SS—135.

			BATTING													FIELDING	
Year	Team (League)	Pos.	G	AB	R	H	2B	3B	HR	RBI	BB	SO	SB-CS	Avg.	OBP	SLG	E	Avg.
1985	—Vermont (East.)	SS	72	255	42	68	13	2	1	31	23	21	12-1	.267	.331	.345	17	.942
1986	—Denver (A.A.)	SS-2B	103	413	67	136	31	10	10	51	31	43	19-6	.329	.373	*.525	18	.962
	—Cincinnati (N.L.)	SS-2B	41	159	27	45	4	3	3	19	9	21	8-0	.283	.320	.403	4	.978
1987	—Cincinnati (N.L.)	SS	125	439	64	107	16	2	12	43	36	52	21-6	.244	.306	.371	19	.965
1988	—Cincinnati (N.L.)	SS	151	588	91	174	32	5	12	56	41	24	40-7	.296	.347	.429	•29	.960
1989	—Cincinnati (N.L.)	SS	97	325	47	111	14	4	4	36	20	23	10-5	.342	.375	.446	10	.976
	—Nashville (A.A.)	SS	2	5	2	5	1	0	0	0	0	0	0-0	1.000	1.000	1.200	0	1.000
1990	—Cincinnati (N.L.)	SS	158	614	85	185	25	6	7	67	49	49	30-5	.301	.358	.396	17	.977
1991	—Cincinnati (N.L.)	SS	123	464	88	140	27	4	20	69	55	64	24-6	.302	.378	.506	15	.976
1992	—Cincinnati (N.L.)	SS	140	533	76	162	32	6	12	78	63	58	15-4	.304	.377	.454	11	.983
1993	—Cincinnati (N.L.)	SS	100	384	57	121	20	3	8	51	51	33	14-1	.315	.394	.445	16	.965
1994	—Cincinnati (N.L.)	SS	110	427	78	119	23	5	9	52	64	58	26-2	.279	.369	.419	10	.980
1995	—Cincinnati (N.L.)	SS	131	496	98	158	29	6	15	66	61	49	51-5	.319	.394	.492	11	.980
1996	—Cincinnati (N.L.)	SS	152	517	117	154	32	4	33	89	96	52	36-10	.298	.410	.567	17	.975
1997	—Cincinnati (N.L.)	SS-DH	73	224	34	71	17	3	4	20	47	24	14-3	.317	.440	.473	5	.980
1998	—Cincinnati (N.L.)	SS	145	538	93	166	34	10	17	72	79	69	26-3	.309	.397	.504	12	.979
1999	—Cincinnati (N.L.)	SS	161	583	108	171	30	4	12	75	93	57	30-8	.293	.390	.420	14	.978
2000	—Cincinnati (N.L.)	SS-DH	102	396	71	124	26	5	11	41	48	31	14-6	.313	.389	.487	11	.973
2001	—Cincinnati (N.L.)	SS	45	156	29	40	12	0	2	17	27	25	3-2	.256	.373	.372	9	.951
2002	—Cincinnati (N.L.)	SS	145	507	72	124	37	2	7	47	44	57	13-4	.245	.305	.367	12	.979
Major League totals (17 years)			1999	7350	1235	2172	410	72	188	898	883	746	375-77	.296	.372	.448	222	.974

DIVISION SERIES RECORD

			BATTING													FIELDING	
Year	Team (League)	Pos.	G	AB	R	H	2B	3B	HR	RBI	BB	SO	SB-CS	Avg.	OBP	SLG	E	Avg.
1995	—Cincinnati (N.L.)	SS	3	13	2	5	0	0	0	1	1	2	4-0	.385	.429	.385	0	1.000

CHAMPIONSHIP SERIES RECORD

			BATTING													FIELDING	
Year	Team (League)	Pos.	G	AB	R	H	2B	3B	HR	RBI	BB	SO	SB-CS	Avg.	OBP	SLG	E	Avg.
1990	—Cincinnati (N.L.)	SS	6	23	5	6	2	0	0	1	3	1	3-0	.261	.346	.348	1	.973
1995	—Cincinnati (N.L.)	SS	4	18	1	7	2	1	0	0	1	1	1-1	.389	.421	.611	1	.962
Championship series totals (2 years)			10	41	6	13	4	1	0	1	4	2	4-1	.317	.378	.463	2	.968

WORLD SERIES RECORD

RECORDS: Shares single-inning record for most at-bats—2 (October 19, 1990, third inning).

NOTES: Member of World Series championship team (1990).

			BATTING													FIELDING	
Year	Team (League)	Pos.	G	AB	R	H	2B	3B	HR	RBI	BB	SO	SB-CS	Avg.	OBP	SLG	E	Avg.
1990	—Cincinnati (N.L.)	SS	4	17	3	6	1	1	0	1	2	0	0-0	.353	.421	.529	0	1.000

ALL-STAR GAME RECORD

	AB	R	H	2B	3B	HR	RBI	BB	SO	SB-CS	Avg.	OBP	SLG	E	Avg.
All-Star Game totals (8 years)	17	1	2	0	0	0	2	0	3	1-0	.118	.111	.118	1	.952

LaROCCA, GREG — IF — INDIANS

PERSONAL: Born November 10, 1972, in Oswego, N.Y. ... 5-11/185. ... Bats right, throws right. ... Full name: Gregory Mark LaRocca.

HIGH SCHOOL: West (Manchester, N.H.).

COLLEGE: Massachusetts.

TRANSACTIONS/CAREER NOTES: Selected by San Diego Padres organization in 10th round of free-agent draft (June 2, 1994). ... On disabled list (April 22, 1999-remainder of season). ... Released by Padres (March 28, 2001). ... Signed by Cleveland Indians organization (May 7, 2001). ... On Buffalo disabled list (June 13-21, 2002).

STATISTICAL NOTES: Led International League in with 23 being hit by pitch in 2002.

2002 GAMES PLAYED BY POSITION (MLB): 3B—15; 2B—3; DH—1.

			BATTING													FIELDING	
Year	Team (League)	Pos.	G	AB	R	H	2B	3B	HR	RBI	BB	SO	SB-CS	Avg.	OBP	SLG	E	Avg.
1994	—Spokane (N'West)	SS-2B	42	158	20	46	9	2	0	14	14	18	7-2	.291	.356	.373	8	.961
	—Rancho Cuca. (Calif.)	SS	28	85	7	14	5	1	1	8	7	11	3-1	.165	.242	.282	10	.921
1995	—Rancho Cuca. (Calif.)	SS-2B-3B	125	466	77	150	36	5	8	74	44	77	15-4	.322	.393	.472	36	.931
	—Memphis (Sou.)	SS	2	7	0	1	0	0	0	0	0	1	0-1	.143	.143	.143	1	.889
1996	—Memphis (Sou.)	2B-SS	128	445	66	122	22	5	6	42	51	58	5-9	.274	.358	.387	24	.955
1997	—Mobile (Sou.)	2B-SS-3B	76	300	44	80	16	2	3	31	26	46	8-3	.267	.336	.363	4	.988
1998	—Las Vegas (PCL)	3B-2B-SS-OF	95	304	55	94	22	5	8	39	19	48	7-4	.309	.371	.493	12	.953
1999	—Las Vegas (PCL)	3B-SS-2B	14	51	3	14	2	0	0	2	2	10	2-2	.275	.345	.314	3	.939
2000	—Las Vegas (PCL)	C	*137	482	90	142	*42	7	9	80	54	62	13-4	.295	.378	.467	25	.940
	—San Diego (N.L.)	3B-SS-2B	13	27	1	6	2	0	0	2	1	4	0-0	.222	.250	.296	2	.917
2001	—Akron (East.)■	SS-3B-2B	31	104	16	33	9	0	3	19	18	11	0-2	.317	.421	.490	8	.942
	—Buffalo (I.L.)	3B-SS-2B	61	216	39	67	12	1	12	37	12	35	2-1	.310	.362	.542	6	.967
2002	—Buffalo (I.L.)	3B-2B-OF-SS	107	382	70	112	28	2	7	41	48	48	17-4	.293	.402	.432	10	.966
	—Cleveland (A.L.)	3B-2B-DH	21	52	12	14	3	1	0	4	6	6	1-0	.269	.367	.365	6	.838
American League totals (1 year)			21	52	12	14	3	1	0	4	6	6	1-0	.269	.367	.365	6	.838
National League totals (1 year)			13	27	1	6	2	0	0	2	1	4	0-0	.222	.250	.296	2	.917
Major League totals (2 years)			34	79	13	20	5	1	0	6	7	10	1-0	.253	.330	.342	8	.869

LARSON, BRANDON 3B REDS

PERSONAL: Born May 24, 1976, in San Angelo, Texas. ... 6-0/210. ... Bats right, throws right. ... Full name: Brandon John Larson.
HIGH SCHOOL: Holmes (San Antonio, Texas).
JUNIOR COLLEGE: Blinn College (Texas).
COLLEGE: Louisiana State.
TRANSACTIONS/CAREER NOTES: Selected by Pittsburgh Pirates organization in 46th round of free-agent draft (June 2, 1994); did not sign. ... Selected by Pittsburgh Pirates organization in 38th round of free-agent draft (June 1, 1995); did not sign. ... Selected by San Francisco Giants organization in 44th round of free-agent draft (June 4, 1996); did not sign. ... Selected by Cincinnati Reds organization in first round (14th pick overall) of free-agent draft (June 3, 1997). ... On Chattanooga disabled list (July 3-18, 1999). ... On Cincinnati disabled list (August 16-August 31 and September 4, 2002-remainder of season); included rehabilitation assignment to Louisville (August 28-31).
2002 GAMES PLAYED BY POSITION (MLB): OF—9; 3B—5; 1B—2.

			BATTING														FIELDING	
Year	Team (League)	Pos.	G	AB	R	H	2B	3B	HR	RBI	BB	SO	SB-CS	Avg.	OBP	SLG	E	Avg.
1997—	Chattanooga (Sou.)	SS	11	41	4	11	5	1	0	6	1	10	0-0	.268	.279	.439	5	.891
1998—	Burlington (Midw.)	3B	18	68	5	15	3	0	2	9	4	16	2-1	.221	.264	.353	0	1.000
1999—	Rockford (Midw.)	3B	69	250	38	75	18	1	13	52	25	67	12-2	.300	.367	.536	18	.912
	—Chattanooga (Sou.)	3B	43	172	28	49	10	0	12	42	10	51	4-5	.285	.332	.552	15	.885
2000—	Chattanooga (Sou.)	3B	111	427	61	116	26	0	20	64	31	122	15-5	.272	.330	.473	24	.917
	—Louisville (I.L.)	3B	17	63	11	18	7	1	2	4	4	16	0-0	.286	.328	.524	4	.929
2001—	Louisville (I.L.)	3B-SS-1B	115	424	61	108	22	2	14	55	24	123	5-6	.255	.312	.415	20	.949
	—Cincinnati (N.L.)	3B	14	33	2	4	2	0	0	1	2	10	0-0	.121	.171	.182	2	.939
2002—	Louisville (I.L.)	3B-OF	80	297	47	101	20	1	25	69	24	70	1-1	.340	.393	.667	17	.917
	—Cincinnati (N.L.)	OF-3B-1B	23	51	8	14	2	0	4	13	6	10	1-0	.275	.362	.549	0	1.000
Major League totals (2 years)			37	84	10	18	4	0	4	14	8	20	1-0	.214	.290	.405	2	.968

LaRUE, JASON C REDS

PERSONAL: Born March 19, 1974, in Houston. ... 5-11/200. ... Bats right, throws right. ... Full name: Michael Jason LaRue.
HIGH SCHOOL: Spring Valley (Spring Branch, Texas).
COLLEGE: Dallas Baptist.
TRANSACTIONS/CAREER NOTES: Selected by Cincinnati Reds organization in fifth round of free-agent draft (June 1, 1995). ... On disabled list (June 30-September 13, 1996). ... On disabled list (September 23, 2002-remainder of season).
STATISTICAL NOTES: Tied for Pioneer League lead in being hit by pitch with 12 in 1995. ... Led Pioneer League catchers with seven double plays in 1995. ... Tied for Southern League lead with 21 passed balls in 1998. ... Led N.L. catchers with 20 passed balls in 2002. ... Career major league grand slams: 3.
2002 GAMES PLAYED BY POSITION (MLB): C—110.

			BATTING														FIELDING	
Year	Team (League)	Pos.	G	AB	R	H	2B	3B	HR	RBI	BB	SO	SB-CS	Avg.	OBP	SLG	E	Avg.
1995—	Billings (Pio.)	C	58	183	35	50	8	1	5	31	16	28	3-5	.273	.366	.410	8	.980
1996—	Charl., W.Va. (S.Atl.)	C-1B	37	123	17	26	8	0	2	14	11	28	3-0	.211	.287	.325	6	.979
1997—	Charl., W.Va. (S.Atl.)	C-1B-3B-OF	132	473	78	149	50	3	8	81	47	90	14-4	.315	.377	.484	19	.977
1998—	Chattanooga (Sou.)	C-3B-1B	105	386	71	141	39	8	14	82	40	60	4-3	*.365	.429	*.617	10	.985
	—Indianapolis (I.L.)	C	15	51	5	12	4	0	0	5	4	8	0-1	.235	.286	.314	0	1.000
1999—	Indianapolis (I.L.)	C-DH	70	263	42	66	12	2	12	37	15	52	0-3	.251	.299	.449	7	.984
	—Cincinnati (N.L.)	C	36	90	12	19	7	0	3	10	11	32	4-1	.211	.311	.389	2	.990
2000—	Louisville (I.L.)	C	82	307	54	78	22	1	14	48	22	52	3-2	.254	.320	.469	8	.984
	—Cincinnati (N.L.)	C	31	98	12	23	3	0	5	12	5	19	0-0	.235	.299	.418	2	.991
2001—	Cincinnati (N.L.)	C-3B-OF-1B	121	364	39	86	21	2	12	43	27	106	3-3	.236	.303	.404	7	.990
2002—	Cincinnati (N.L.)	C	113	353	42	88	17	1	12	52	27	117	1-2	.249	.324	.405	4	.994
Major League totals (4 years)			301	905	105	216	48	3	32	117	70	274	8-6	.239	.312	.404	15	.991

LAWRENCE, BRIAN P PADRES

PERSONAL: Born May 14, 1976, in Fort Collins, Colo. ... 6-0/195. ... Throws right, bats right. ... Full name: Brian Michael Lawrence.
HIGH SCHOOL: Carthage (Texas).
COLLEGE: Northwestern State (La.).
TRANSACTIONS/CAREER NOTES: Selected by San Diego Padres organization in 17th round of free-agent draft (June 2, 1998).
RECORDS: Shares major league record for striking out side on nine pitches (June 12, 2002, third inning).
STATISTICAL NOTES: Tied for California League lead with five balks in 1999.
CAREER HITTING (MLB): 9-for-89 (.101), 1 R, 4 2B, 0 3B, 0 HR, 9 RBI.

Year	League	W	L	Pct.	ERA	G	GS	CG	ShO	Sv.-Opp.	IP	H	R	ER	HR	BB-IBB	SO
1998—	Idaho Falls (Pio.)	3	0	1.000	2.45	4	4	2	•1	0-...	22.0	22	7	6	1	5-0	21
	—Clinton (Midw.)	5	3	.625	2.80	12	12	2	0	0-...	80.1	67	34	25	5	13-0	79
1999—	Rancho Cuca. (Calif.)	12	8	.600	3.39	27	27	4	3	0-...	175.1	178	72	66	6	30-1	166
2000—	Mobile (Sou.)	7	6	.538	2.42	21	21	0	0	0-...	126.2	99	40	34	6	28-0	119
	—Las Vegas (PCL)	4	0	1.000	1.93	8	8	0	0	0-...	46.2	48	13	10	6	7-0	46
2001—	Portland (PCL)	1	3	.250	3.80	9	8	0	0	1-...	45.0	42	22	19	3	17-2	42
	—San Diego (N.L.)	5	5	.500	3.45	27	15	1	0	0-0	114.2	107	53	44	10	34-5	84
2002—	San Diego (N.L.)	12	12	.500	3.69	35	31	2	2	0-0	210.0	230	97	86	16	52-6	149
Major League totals (2 years)		17	17	.500	3.60	62	46	3	2	0-0	324.2	337	150	130	26	86-11	233

LAWRENCE, JOE C/IF

PERSONAL: Born February 13, 1977, in Lake Charles, La. ... 6-2/200. ... Bats right, throws right. ... Full name: Joseph Dudley Lawrence.
HIGH SCHOOL: Barbe (Lake Charles, La.).

TRANSACTIONS/CAREER NOTES: Selected by Toronto Blue Jays organization in first round (16th pick overall) of free-agent draft (June 4, 1996); pick received as compensation for Baltimore Orioles signing Type A free-agent 2B Roberto Alomar. ... On disabled list (June 30, 1999-remainder of season). ... On disabled list (June 4-12, 2001). ... Granted free agency (October 15, 2002).
2002 GAMES PLAYED BY POSITION (MLB): 2B—49; DH—1.

			BATTING														FIELDING	
Year	Team (League)	Pos.	G	AB	R	H	2B	3B	HR	RBI	BB	SO	SB-CS	Avg.	OBP	SLG	E	Avg.
1996—	St. Catharines (NY-P)	SS-3B	29	98	23	22	7	2	0	11	14	17	1-1	.224	.325	.337	11	.899
1997—	Hagerstown (S.Atl.)	SS	116	446	63	102	24	1	8	38	49	107	10-12	.229	.311	.341	33	.926
1998—	Dunedin (FSL)	SS-3B	125	454	102	140	31	6	11	44	*105	88	15-12	.308	.441	.476	48	.914
1999—	Knoxville (Sou.)	3B-DH-SS	70	250	52	66	16	2	7	24	56	48	7-6	.264	.402	.428	14	.911
2000—	Dunedin (FSL)	OF	101	375	69	113	32	1	13	67	69	74	21-7	.301	.414	.496	11	.978
—	Tennessee (Sou.)	C	39	133	22	35	9	0	0	9	30	27	7-1	.263	.407	.331	5	.978
2001—	Syracuse (I.L.)	C-3B-1B-SS	93	318	27	70	11	4	1	26	36	62	6-9	.220	.310	.289	5	.991
2002—	Toronto (A.L.)	2B-DH	55	150	16	27	4	0	2	15	16	38	2-1	.180	.262	.247	7	.967
—	Syracuse (I.L.)	2B	29	108	13	18	4	1	2	12	14	23	3-0	.167	.262	.278	8	.944
Major League totals (1 year)			55	150	16	27	4	0	2	15	16	38	2-1	.180	.262	.247	7	.967

LAWTON, MATT — OF — INDIANS

PERSONAL: Born November 3, 1971, in Gulfport, Miss. ... 5-10/186. ... Bats left, throws right. ... Full name: Matthew Lawton III. ... Brother of Marcus Lawton, outfielder with New York Yankees (1989).
HIGH SCHOOL: Harrison Central (Gulfport, Miss.).
JUNIOR COLLEGE: Gulf Coast Community College (Fla.).
TRANSACTIONS/CAREER NOTES: Selected by Minnesota Twins organization in 13th round of free-agent draft (June 3, 1991). ... On Minnesota disabled list (June 9-July 18, 1999); included rehabilitation assignments to Fort Myers (July 12-16) and Gulf Coast Twins (July 17-18). ... Traded by Twins to New York Mets for P Rick Reed (July 30, 2001). ... Traded by Mets with OF Alex Escobar, P Jerrod Riggan and two players to be named later to Cleveland Indians for 2B Roberto Alomar, P Mike Bacsik and OF Danny Peoples (December 11, 2001); Indians acquired P Billy Traber and 1B Earl Snyder to complete deal (December 13, 2001). ... On Cleveland disabled list (July 12-July 27 and September 4, 2002-remainder of season); included rehabilitation assignment to Akron (July 23-27).
STATISTICAL NOTES: Led Florida State League with .407 on-base percentage in 1994. ... Had 16-game hitting streak (April 13-30, 2000). ... Career major league grand slams: 3.
2002 GAMES PLAYED BY POSITION (MLB): OF—108; DH—3.

			BATTING														FIELDING	
Year	Team (League)	Pos.	G	AB	R	H	2B	3B	HR	RBI	BB	SO	SB-CS	Avg.	OBP	SLG	E	Avg.
1992—	GC Twins (GCL)	2B	53	173	39	45	8	3	2	26	27	27	20-1	.260	.375	.376	12	.958
1993—	Fort Wayne (Midw.)	OF	111	340	50	97	21	3	9	38	65	42	23-15	.285	.410	.444	3	.959
1994—	Fort Myers (FSL)	OF	122	446	79	134	30	1	7	51	80	64	42-19	.300	*.407	.419	6	.971
1995—	New Britain (East.)	OF-DH	114	412	75	111	19	5	13	54	56	70	26-9	.269	.371	.434	2	*.991
—	Minnesota (A.L.)	OF-DH	21	60	11	19	4	1	1	12	7	11	1-1	.317	.414	.467	1	.972
1996—	Minnesota (A.L.)	OF-DH	79	252	34	65	7	1	6	42	28	28	4-4	.258	.339	.365	3	.985
—	Salt Lake (PCL)	OF-DH	53	212	40	63	16	1	7	33	26	34	2-4	.297	.379	.481	6	.936
1997—	Minnesota (A.L.)	OF	142	460	74	114	29	3	14	60	76	81	7-4	.248	.366	.415	7	.976
1998—	Minnesota (A.L.)	OF	152	557	91	155	36	6	21	77	86	64	16-8	.278	.387	.478	4	.990
1999—	Minnesota (A.L.)	OF-DH	118	406	58	105	18	0	7	54	57	42	26-4	.259	.353	.355	4	.982
—	Fort Myers (FSL)	OF	4	14	3	8	1	0	0	2	3	1	1-0	.571	.647	.643	0	1.000
—	GC Twins (GCL)	OF	1	4	0	1	0	0	0	1	0	2	0-0	.250	.250	.250	0	1.000
2000—	Minnesota (A.L.)	OF-DH	156	561	84	171	44	2	13	88	91	63	23-7	.305	.405	.460	5	.983
2001—	Minnesota (A.L.)	OF-DH	103	376	71	110	25	0	10	51	63	46	19-6	.293	.396	.439	4	.980
—	New York (N.L.)■	OF	48	183	24	45	11	1	3	13	22	34	10-2	.246	.352	.366	0	1.000
2002—	Cleveland (A.L.)■	OF-DH	114	416	71	98	19	2	15	57	59	34	8-9	.236	.342	.399	6	.975
—	Akron (East.)	OF	3	10	1	0	0	0	0	0	3	1	0-0	.000	.231	.000	0	1.000
American League totals (8 years)			885	3088	494	837	182	15	87	441	467	369	104-43	.271	.374	.424	34	.982
National League totals (1 year)			48	183	24	45	11	1	3	13	22	34	10-2	.246	.352	.366	0	1.000
Major League totals (8 years)			933	3271	518	882	193	16	90	454	489	403	114-45	.270	.373	.421	34	.983

ALL-STAR GAME RECORD

	AB	R	H	2B	3B	HR	RBI	BB	SO	SB-CS	Avg.	OBP	SLG	E	Avg.
All-Star Game totals (1 year)	2	1	1	0	0	0	1	0	0	1-0	.500	.500	.500	0	...

LeCROY, MATT — C — TWINS

PERSONAL: Born December 13, 1975, in Belton, S.C. ... 6-2/225. ... Bats right, throws right. ... Full name: Matthew Hanks LeCroy.
HIGH SCHOOL: Belton-Honea Path (S.C.).
COLLEGE: Clemson.
TRANSACTIONS/CAREER NOTES: Selected by Minnesota Twins organization in supplemental round ("sandwich pick" between first and second round, 50th pick overall) of free-agent draft (June 3, 1997); pick received as compensation for failure to sign 1996 first-round pick Travis Lee. ... On Salt Lake disabled list (September 10, 1999-remainder of season). ... On Edmonton disabled list (May 25-June 4 and June 5-23, 2001).
MISCELLANEOUS: Member of 1996 U.S. Olympic baseball team.
2002 GAMES PLAYED BY POSITION (MLB): DH—41; 1B—8; C—6.

			BATTING														FIELDING	
Year	Team (League)	Pos.	G	AB	R	H	2B	3B	HR	RBI	BB	SO	SB-CS	Avg.	OBP	SLG	E	Avg.
1998—	Fort Wayne (Midw.)	C	64	225	33	62	17	1	9	40	34	45	0-0	.276	.387	.480	1	.997
—	Fort Myers (FSL)	C	51	200	32	61	9	1	12	51	21	35	2-1	.305	.372	.540	3	.991
—	Salt Lake (PCL)	C	3	13	2	4	1	0	2	4	0	7	0-0	.308	.308	.846	0	1.000
1999—	Fort Myers (FSL)	C	89	333	54	93	20	1	20	69	42	51	0-0	.279	.364	.526	8	.983
—	Salt Lake (PCL)	C	29	119	23	36	4	1	10	30	5	22	0-1	.303	.331	.605	0	1.000

Year Team (League)	Pos.	G	AB	R	H	2B	3B	HR	RBI	BB	SO	SB-CS	Avg.	OBP	SLG	E	Avg.
		BATTING														FIELDING	
2000—Minnesota (A.L.)	C-DH-1B	56	167	18	29	10	0	5	17	17	38	0-0	.174	.254	.323	4	.989
—New Britain (East.)	C	54	195	33	55	12	1	10	38	29	34	0-0	.282	.391	.508	10	.970
—Salt Lake (PCL)	C	16	65	15	20	5	0	5	15	4	11	0-0	.308	.348	.615	0	1.000
2001—Edmonton (PCL)	C-1B	101	396	53	130	17	0	20	80	36	95	0-2	.328	.390	.523	5	.980
—Minnesota (A.L.)	DH-C-1B	15	40	6	17	5	0	3	12	0	8	0-1	.425	.429	.775	0	1.000
2002—Edmonton (PCL)	C-1B	46	174	36	61	7	1	12	50	17	34	2-0	.351	.412	.609	1	.993
—Minnesota (A.L.)	DH-1B-C	63	181	19	47	11	1	7	27	13	38	0-2	.260	.306	.448	1	.984
Major League totals (3 years)		134	388	43	93	26	1	15	56	30	84	0-3	.240	.295	.428	5	.988

DIVISION SERIES RECORD

Year Team (League)	Pos.	G	AB	R	H	2B	3B	HR	RBI	BB	SO	SB-CS	Avg.	OBP	SLG	E	Avg.
		BATTING														FIELDING	
2002—Minnesota (A.L.)	DH	3	9	1	4	0	0	0	1	0	3	0-0	.444	.444	.444	0	...

CHAMPIONSHIP SERIES RECORD

Year Team (League)	Pos.	G	AB	R	H	2B	3B	HR	RBI	BB	SO	SB-CS	Avg.	OBP	SLG	E	Avg.
		BATTING														FIELDING	
2002—Minnesota (A.L.)	DH	1	3	0	1	0	0	0	0	0	1	0-0	.333	.333	.333	0	...

LEDEE, RICKY — OF — PHILLIES

PERSONAL: Born November 22, 1973, in Ponce, Puerto Rico. ... 6-1/190. ... Bats left, throws left. ... Full name: Ricardo Alberto Ledee. ... Name pronounced le-DAY.

HIGH SCHOOL: Colonel Nuestra Sonora de Valvanera (Coano, Puerto Rico).

TRANSACTIONS/CAREER NOTES: Selected by New York Yankees organization in 16th round of free-agent draft (June 3, 1990). ... On Tampa disabled list (April 6-May 27, 1996). ... On Columbus disabled list (May 5-16 and May 22-August 4, 1997; and May 25-June 3, 1999). ... Traded by Yankees with two players to be named later to Cleveland Indians for OF David Justice (June 29, 2000); Indians acquired P Jake Westbrook and P Zach Day to complete deal (July 24, 2000). ... Traded by Indians to Texas Rangers for 1B/DH David Segui (July 28, 2000). ... On Texas disabled list (March 23-June 13, 2001); included rehabilitation assignment to Oklahoma (June 9-13). ... Granted free agency (December 21, 2001). ... Signed by Philadelphia Phillies (January 29, 2002).

STATISTICAL NOTES: Career major league grand slams: 2.

2002 GAMES PLAYED BY POSITION (MLB): OF—51.

Year Team (League)	Pos.	G	AB	R	H	2B	3B	HR	RBI	BB	SO	SB-CS	Avg.	OBP	SLG	E	Avg.
		BATTING														FIELDING	
1990—GC Yankees (GCL)......	OF	19	37	5	4	2	0	0	1	6	18	2-0	.108	.233	.162	0	1.000
1991—GC Yankees (GCL)......	OF	47	165	22	44	6	2	0	18	22	40	3-1	.267	.351	.327	6	.934
1992—GC Yankees (GCL)......	OF	52	179	25	41	9	2	2	23	24	47	1-4	.229	.322	.335	2	.971
1993—Oneonta (NY-Penn)	OF	52	192	32	49	7	6	8	20	25	46	7-5	.255	.347	.479	3	.970
1994—Greensboro (S.Atl.)	OF	134	484	87	121	23	9	22	71	91	126	10-11	.250	.369	.471	5	.973
1995—Greensboro (S.Atl.)	OF	89	335	65	90	16	6	14	49	51	66	10-4	.269	.368	.478	3	.982
1996—Norwich (East.)	OF	39	137	27	50	11	1	8	37	16	25	2-2	.365	.421	.635	1	.980
—Columbus (I.L.)	OF	96	358	79	101	22	6	21	64	44	95	6-3	.282	.360	.553	5	.952
1997—Columbus (I.L.)	OF-DH	43	170	38	52	12	1	10	39	21	49	4-0	.306	.385	.565	2	.966
—GC Yankees (GCL)......	DH-OF	7	21	3	7	1	0	0	2	2	4	0-0	.333	.417	.381	0	1.000
1998—Columbus (I.L.)	OF-DH	96	360	70	102	21	1	19	41	54	108	7-2	.283	.378	.506	4	.971
—New York (A.L.)	OF	42	79	13	19	5	2	1	12	7	29	3-1	.241	.299	.392	1	.981
1999—New York (A.L.)	OF-DH	88	250	45	69	13	5	9	40	28	73	4-3	.276	.346	.476	9	.942
—Columbus (I.L.)	OF	30	115	18	29	7	1	4	15	17	29	4-2	.252	.346	.435	3	.953
2000—New York (A.L.)	OF-DH	62	191	23	46	11	1	7	31	26	39	7-3	.241	.332	.419	2	.979
—Cleveland (A.L.)■	OF	17	63	13	14	2	1	2	8	8	9	0-0	.222	.310	.381	0	1.000
—Texas (A.L.)■	OF	58	213	23	50	6	3	4	38	25	50	6-3	.235	.317	.347	3	.977
2001—Oklahoma (PCL)	OF	4	16	4	8	1	0	1	3	1	1	0-0	.500	.529	.750	0	1.000
—Texas (A.L.)	OF	78	242	33	56	21	1	2	36	23	58	3-3	.231	.303	.351	3	.979
2002—Philadelphia (N.L.)■ ..	OF	96	203	33	46	13	1	8	23	35	50	1-2	.227	.342	.419	0	1.000
American League totals (4 years)		345	1038	150	254	58	13	25	165	117	258	23-13	.245	.322	.398	18	.971
National League totals (1 year)		96	203	33	46	13	1	8	23	35	50	1-2	.227	.342	.419	0	1.000
Major League totals (5 years)		441	1241	183	300	71	14	33	188	152	308	24-15	.242	.325	.401	18	.975

DIVISION SERIES RECORD

Year Team (League)	Pos.	G	AB	R	H	2B	3B	HR	RBI	BB	SO	SB-CS	Avg.	OBP	SLG	E	Avg.
		BATTING														FIELDING	
1998—New York (A.L.)								Did not play.									
1999—New York (A.L.)..........	OF	3	11	1	3	2	0	0	2	1	5	0-0	.273	.333	.455	0	1.000

CHAMPIONSHIP SERIES RECORD

RECORDS: Shares single-game record for most grand slams—1 (October 17, 1999). ... Shares single-inning record for most runs batted in—4 (October 17, 1999, ninth inning).

Year Team (League)	Pos.	G	AB	R	H	2B	3B	HR	RBI	BB	SO	SB-CS	Avg.	OBP	SLG	E	Avg.
		BATTING														FIELDING	
1998—New York (A.L.)..........	PH-OF-PR-DH	3	5	0	0	0	0	0	0	0	0	0-0	.000	.000	.000	0	1.000
1999—New York (A.L.)..........	OF-PH-DH	3	8	2	2	0	0	1	4	1	4	0-1	.250	.333	.625	1	.750
Championship series totals (2 years)		6	13	2	2	0	0	1	4	1	4	0-1	.154	.214	.385	1	.857

WORLD SERIES RECORD

NOTES: Member of World Series championship team (1998 and 1999).

Year Team (League)	Pos.	G	AB	R	H	2B	3B	HR	RBI	BB	SO	SB-CS	Avg.	OBP	SLG	E	Avg.
		BATTING														FIELDING	
1998—New York (A.L.)..........	OF-PH	4	10	1	6	3	0	0	4	2	1	0-1	.600	.615	.900	0	1.000
1999—New York (A.L.)..........	OF	3	10	0	2	1	0	0	1	1	4	0-0	.200	.273	.300	0	1.000
World Series totals (2 years)		7	20	1	8	4	0	0	5	3	5	0-1	.400	.458	.600	0	1.000

LEE, CARLOS — OF — WHITE SOX

PERSONAL: Born June 20, 1976, in Aguadulce, Panama. ... 6-2/235. ... Bats right, throws right. ... Full name: Carlos Noriel Lee.
TRANSACTIONS/CAREER NOTES: Signed as non-drafted free agent by Chicago White Sox organization (February 8, 1994). ... On suspended list (April 28-May 1, 2000).
STATISTICAL NOTES: Led Appalachian League with 133 total bases and tied for league lead with three intentional bases on balls received in 1995. ... Led Appalachian League third basemen with 58 putouts and 10 double plays in 1995. ... Led South Atlantic League with 11 sacrifice flies in 1996. ... Led Carolina League with 282 total bases in 1997. ... Led Carolina League third basemen with 93 putouts in 1997. ... Led Southern League in grounding into double plays with 32 in 1998. ... Led Southern League third basemen with 99 putouts in 1998. ... Hit home run in first major league at-bat (May 7, 1999). ... Had 15-game hitting streak (August 23-September 6, 1999). ... Career major league grand slams: 5.
2002 GAMES PLAYED BY POSITION (MLB): OF—137; DH—2.

							BATTING									FIELDING	
Year Team (League)	Pos.	G	AB	R	H	2B	3B	HR	RBI	BB	SO	SB-CS	Avg.	OBP	SLG	E	Avg.
1994—GC White Sox (GCL)...	3B	29	56	6	7	1	0	0	1	4	8	0-1	.125	.183	.143	2	.959
1995—Hickory (S.Atl.)...........	3B	63	218	18	54	9	1	4	30	8	34	1-5	.248	.278	.353	19	.848
—Bristol (Appl.)............	3B-1B	•67	*269	43	*93	17	1	7	45	8	34	17-7	.346	.365	.494	18	.914
1996—Hickory (S.Atl.)...........	3B-1B	119	480	65	150	23	6	8	70	23	50	18-13	.313	.337	.435	32	.923
1997—Win.-Salem (Caro.)	3B-DH	*139	*546	81	*173	*50	4	17	82	36	65	11-5	.317	.357	.516	34	.906
1998—Birmingham (Sou.).....	3B-DH	138	*549	77	166	33	2	21	106	39	55	11-5	.302	.350	.485	*35	.902
1999—Charlotte (I.L.)............	3B-OF-1B-DH	25	94	16	33	5	0	4	20	8	14	2-1	.351	.396	.532	4	.951
—Chicago (A.L.)...........	OF-DH-1B	127	492	66	144	32	2	16	84	13	72	4-2	.293	.312	.463	5	.979
2000—Chicago (A.L.)...........	OF-DH	152	572	107	172	29	2	24	92	38	94	13-4	.301	.345	.484	3	.990
2001—Chicago (A.L.)...........	OF-DH	150	558	75	150	33	3	24	84	38	85	17-7	.269	.321	.468	8	.969
2002—Chicago (A.L.)...........	OF-DH	140	492	82	130	26	2	26	80	75	73	1-4	.264	.359	.484	1	.996
Major League totals (4 years)		569	2114	330	596	120	9	90	340	164	324	35-17	.282	.335	.475	17	.984

DIVISION SERIES RECORD

							BATTING									FIELDING	
Year Team (League)	Pos.	G	AB	R	H	2B	3B	HR	RBI	BB	SO	SB-CS	Avg.	OBP	SLG	E	Avg.
2000—Chicago (A.L.)...........	OF	3	11	0	1	1	0	0	1	0	2	0-0	.091	.083	.182	0	1.000

LEE, CLIFF — P — INDIANS

PERSONAL: Born August 30, 1978, in Benton, Ark. ... 6-3/190. ... Throws left, bats left. ... Full name: Clifton Phifer Lee.
HIGH SCHOOL: Benton (Ark.).
COLLEGE: Arkansas.
TRANSACTIONS/CAREER NOTES: Selected by Montreal Expos organization in fourth round of free-agent draft (June 5, 2000). ... Traded by Expos with 1B Lee Stevens, SS Brandon Phillips and OF Grady Sizemore to Cleveland Indians for P Bartolo Colon and future considerations (June 27, 2002); Expos acquired P Tim Drew to complete deal (June 28, 2002).
CAREER HITTING (MLB): 0-for-0 (.000), 0 R, 0 2B, 0 3B, 0 HR, 0 RBI.

Year League	W	L	Pct.	ERA	G	GS	CG	ShO	Sv.-Opp.	IP	H	R	ER	HR	BB-IBB	SO
2000—Cape Fear (S.Atl.)............	1	4	.200	5.24	11	11	0	0	0-...	44.2	50	39	26	1	36-0	63
2001—Jupiter (FSL)....................	6	7	.462	2.79	21	20	0	0	0-...	109.2	78	43	34	13	46-0	129
2002—Harrisburg (East.)............	7	2	.778	3.23	15	15	0	0	0-...	86.1	61	31	31	12	23-0	105
—Akron (East.)■................	2	1	.667	5.40	3	3	0	0	0-...	16.2	11	11	10	1	10-0	18
—Buffalo (I.L.)....................	3	2	.600	3.77	8	8	0	0	0-...	43.0	36	18	18	7	22-0	30
—Cleveland (A.L.)................	0	1	.000	1.74	2	2	0	0	0-0	10.1	6	2	2	0	8-1	6
Major League totals (1 year).......	0	1	.000	1.74	2	2	0	0	0-0	10.1	6	2	2	0	8-1	6

LEE, DERREK — 1B — MARLINS

PERSONAL: Born September 6, 1975, in Sacramento. ... 6-5/248. ... Bats right, throws right. ... Full name: Derrek Leon Lee. ... Son of Leon Lee, infielder in St. Louis Cardinals organization (1969-71) and Lotte Orions (1978-82), Taiyo Whales (1983-85) and Yakult Swallows (1986-87) of Japan League; and nephew of Leron Lee, outfielder with four major league teams (1969-76) and Lotte Orions (1977-87) of Japan League.
HIGH SCHOOL: El Camino (Sacramento).
TRANSACTIONS/CAREER NOTES: Selected by San Diego Padres in first round (14th pick overall) of free-agent draft (June 1, 1993). ... Traded by Padres with P Rafael Medina and P Steve Hoff to Florida Marlins for P Kevin Brown (December 15, 1997).
RECORDS: Shares major league single-inning record for most assists by first baseman—3 (June 2, 1999, second inning).
HONORS: Named Southern League Most Valuable Player (1996).
STATISTICAL NOTES: Led Southern League with 285 total bases in 1996. ... Led Southern League first basemen 1,121 putouts in 1996. ... Led Pacific Coast League first basemen with 1,069 putouts, 111 assists, 1,189 total chances and 108 double plays in 1997. ... Led N.L. first basemen with 121 assists and and tied for lead with 138 double plays in 2002. ... Career major league grand slams: 4.
2002 GAMES PLAYED BY POSITION (MLB): 1B—162.

							BATTING									FIELDING	
Year Team (League)	Pos.	G	AB	R	H	2B	3B	HR	RBI	BB	SO	SB-CS	Avg.	OBP	SLG	E	Avg.
1993—Arizona Padres (Ariz.)	1B	15	52	11	17	1	1	2	5	6	7	4-0	.327	.397	.500	2	.985
—Rancho Cuca. (Calif.) .	1B-DH	20	73	13	20	5	1	1	10	10	20	0-2	.274	.369	.411	5	.960
1994—Rancho Cuca. (Calif.) .	DH-1B	126	442	66	118	19	2	8	53	42	95	18-14	.267	.336	.373	4	.988
1995—Rancho Cuca. (Calif.) .	1B	128	502	82	151	25	2	23	95	49	130	14-7	.301	.366	.496	*18	.983
—Memphis (Sou.).........	1B	2	9	0	1	0	0	0	1	0	2	0-0	.111	.111	.111	0	1.000
1996—Memphis (Sou.).........	1B-DH-3B	134	500	98	140	39	2	34	*104	65	*170	13-6	.280	.360	.570	11	.991
1997—Las Vegas (PCL)........	1B	125	472	86	153	29	2	13	64	60	116	17-3	.324	.399	.477	9	*.992
—San Diego (N.L.)........	1B	22	54	9	14	3	0	1	4	9	24	0-0	.259	.365	.370	0	1.000
1998—Florida (N.L.)■..........	1B	141	454	62	106	29	1	17	74	47	120	5-2	.233	.318	.414	8	.993
1999—Florida (N.L.).............	1B	70	218	21	45	9	1	5	20	17	70	2-1	.206	.263	.326	3	.994
—Calgary (PCL)............	1B-DH	89	339	60	96	20	1	19	73	30	90	3-4	.283	.345	.516	14	.983
2000—Florida (N.L.).............	1B	158	477	70	134	18	3	28	70	63	123	0-3	.281	.368	.507	8	.993
2001—Florida (N.L.).............	1B	158	561	83	158	37	4	21	75	50	126	4-2	.282	.346	.474	8	.994
2002—Florida (N.L.).............	1B	•162	581	95	157	35	7	27	86	98	164	19-9	.270	.378	.494	12	.992
Major League totals (6 years)		711	2345	340	614	131	16	99	329	284	627	30-17	.262	.346	.458	39	.993

LEE, TRAVIS — 1B — PHILLIES

PERSONAL: Born May 26, 1975, in San Diego. ... 6-3/210. ... Bats left, throws left. ... Full name: Travis Reynolds Lee.
HIGH SCHOOL: Olympia (Wash.).
COLLEGE: San Diego State.
TRANSACTIONS/CAREER NOTES: Selected by Minnesota Twins organization in first round (second pick overall) of free-agent draft (June 4, 1996). ... Granted free agency (June 19, 1996). ... Signed by Arizona Diamondbacks organization (October 15, 1996). ... Loaned by Diamondbacks organization to Tucson, Milwaukee Brewers organization (June 5, 1997-remainder of season). ... On disabled list (July 25-August 9, 1998; and August 16-September 9, 1999). ... On Arizona disabled list (May 25-June 9, 2000); included rehabilitation assignment to El Paso (June 5-9). ... Traded by Diamondbacks with P Vicente Padilla, P Omar Daal and P Nelson Figueroa to Philadelphia Phillies for P Curt Schilling (July 26, 2000).
HONORS: Named Golden Spikes Award winner by USA Baseball (1996).
STATISTICAL NOTES: Led N.L. first basemen with .997 fielding percentage in 1999. ... Career major league grand slams: 3.
MISCELLANEOUS: Member of 1996 U.S. Olympic baseball team.
2002 GAMES PLAYED BY POSITION (MLB): 1B—148.

			BATTING														FIELDING	
Year	Team (League)	Pos.	G	AB	R	H	2B	3B	HR	RBI	BB	SO	SB-CS	Avg.	OBP	SLG	E	Avg.
1997—	High Desert (Calif.)	1B-DH	61	226	63	82	18	1	18	63	47	36	5-1	.363	.473	.690	1	.998
—	Tucson (PCL)■	1B-DH-OF	59	227	42	68	16	2	14	46	31	46	2-0	.300	.387	.573	3	.993
1998—	Arizona (N.L.)■	1B	146	562	71	151	20	2	22	72	67	123	8-1	.269	.346	.429	3	.998
1999—	Arizona (N.L.)	1B-OF	120	375	57	89	16	2	9	50	58	50	17-3	.237	.337	.363	3	†.997
2000—	Arizona (N.L.)	OF-1B	72	224	34	52	13	0	8	40	25	46	5-1	.232	.308	.397	4	.983
—	El Paso (Texas)	C	3	10	0	2	0	0	0	0	2	1	0-0	.200	.333	.200	0	1.000
—	Tucson (PCL)	1B-OF	7	30	4	11	4	0	0	3	1	6	1-0	.367	.387	.500	0	1.000
—	Philadelphia (N.L.)■	1B-OF	56	180	19	43	11	1	1	14	40	33	3-0	.239	.381	.328	0	1.000
2001—	Philadelphia (N.L.)	1B	157	555	75	143	34	2	20	90	71	109	3-4	.258	.341	.434	6	.996
2002—	Philadelphia (N.L.)	1B	153	536	55	142	26	2	13	70	54	104	5-3	.265	.331	.394	6	.996
Major League totals (5 years)			704	2432	311	620	120	9	73	336	315	465	41-12	.255	.340	.402	22	.996

LEITER, AL — P — METS

PERSONAL: Born October 23, 1965, in Toms River, N.J. ... 6-3/220. ... Throws left, bats left. ... Full name: Alois Terry Leiter. ... Brother of Mark Leiter, pitcher with eight teams (1990-99 and 2001); and brother of Kurt Leiter, minor league pitcher (1982-84 and 1986). ... Name pronounced LIE-ter.
HIGH SCHOOL: Central Regional (Bayville, N.J.).
TRANSACTIONS/CAREER NOTES: Selected by New York Yankees organization in second round of free-agent draft (June 4, 1984). ... On New York disabled list (June 22-July 26, 1988); included rehabilitation assignment to Columbus (July 17-25). ... Traded by Yankees to Toronto Blue Jays for OF Jesse Barfield (April 30, 1989). ... On Toronto disabled list (May 11, 1989-remainder of season); included rehabilitation assignment to Dunedin (August 12-29). ... On Syracuse disabled list (May 20-June 13, 1990). ... On Toronto disabled list (April 27, 1991-remainder of season); included rehabilitation assignments to Dunedin (May 20-28 and July 19-August 7). ... On disabled list (April 24-May 9, 1993; and June 9-24, 1994). ... Granted free agency (November 6, 1995). ... Signed by Florida Marlins (December 14, 1995). ... On disabled list (May 1-20 and August 13-29, 1997). ... Traded by Marlins with 2B Ralph Milliard to New York Mets for P Jesus Sanchez, P A.J. Burnett and OF Robert Stratton (February 6, 1998). ... On disabled list (June 27-July 18, 1998; and April 21-May 18, 2001).
HONORS: Named lefthanded pitcher on The Sporting News N.L. All-Star team (1996).
STATISTICAL NOTES: Tied for A.L. lead with five balks in 1994. ... Led A.L. with 14 wild pitches in 1995. ... Pitched 11-0 no-hit victory against Colorado (May 11, 1996). ... Struck out 15 batters in one game (August 1, 1999).
CAREER HITTING (MLB): 39-for-405 (.096), 13 R, 6 2B, 1 3B, 0 HR, 16 RBI.

Year	League	W	L	Pct.	ERA	G	GS	CG	ShO	Sv.-Opp.	IP	H	R	ER	HR	BB-IBB	SO
1984—	Oneonta (NY-Penn)	3	2	.600	3.63	10	10	0	0	0-...	57.0	52	32	23	1	26-0	48
1985—	Fort Lauderdale (FSL)	1	6	.143	6.48	17	17	1	0	0-...	82.0	87	70	59	3	57-1	44
—	Oneonta (NY-Penn)	3	2	.600	2.37	6	6	2	0	0-...	38.0	27	14	10	0	25-0	34
1986—	Fort Lauderdale (FSL)	4	8	.333	4.05	22	21	1	1	0-...	117.2	96	64	53	2	90-1	101
1987—	Columbus (I.L.)	1	4	.200	6.17	5	5	0	0	0-...	23.1	21	18	16	1	15-0	23
—	Albany/Colonie (East.)	3	3	.500	3.35	15	14	2	0	0-...	78.0	64	34	29	4	37-0	71
—	New York (A.L.)	2	2	.500	6.35	4	4	0	0	0-0	22.2	24	16	16	2	15-0	28
1988—	New York (A.L.)	4	4	.500	3.92	14	14	0	0	0-0	57.1	49	27	25	7	33-0	60
—	Columbus (I.L.)	0	2	.000	3.46	4	4	0	0	0-...	13.0	5	7	5	0	14-0	12
1989—	New York (A.L.)	1	2	.333	6.07	4	4	0	0	0-0	26.2	23	20	18	1	21-0	22
—	Toronto (A.L.)■	0	0	...	4.05	1	1	0	0	0-0	6.2	9	3	3	1	2-0	4
—	Dunedin (FSL)	0	2	.000	5.63	3	3	0	0	0-...	8.0	11	5	5	0	5-0	4
1990—	Dunedin (FSL)	0	0	...	2.63	6	6	0	0	0-...	24.0	18	8	7	1	12-0	14
—	Syracuse (I.L.)	3	8	.273	4.62	15	14	1	1	0-...	78.0	59	43	40	4	68-0	69
—	Toronto (A.L.)	0	0	...	0.00	4	0	0	0	0-0	6.1	1	0	0	0	2-0	5
1991—	Toronto (A.L.)	0	0	...	27.00	3	0	0	0	0-0	1.2	3	5	5	0	5-0	1
—	Dunedin (FSL)	0	0	...	1.86	4	3	0	0	0-...	9.2	5	2	2	0	7-0	5
1992—	Syracuse (I.L.)	8	9	.471	3.86	27	27	2	0	0-...	163.1	159	82	70	9	64-0	108
—	Toronto (A.L.)	0	0	...	9.00	1	0	0	0	0-0	1.0	1	1	1	0	2-0	0
1993—	Toronto (A.L.)	9	6	.600	4.11	34	12	1	1	2-3	105.0	93	52	48	8	56-2	66
1994—	Toronto (A.L.)	6	7	.462	5.08	20	20	1	0	0-0	111.2	125	68	63	6	65-3	100
1995—	Toronto (A.L.)	11	11	.500	3.64	28	28	2	1	0-0	183.0	162	80	74	15	*108-1	153
1996—	Florida (N.L.)■	16	12	.571	2.93	33	33	2	1	0-0	215.1	153	74	70	14	*119-3	200
1997—	Florida (N.L.)	11	9	.550	4.34	27	27	0	0	0-0	151.1	133	78	73	13	91-4	132
1998—	New York (N.L.)■	17	6	.739	2.47	28	28	4	2	0-0	193.0	151	55	53	8	71-2	174
1999—	New York (N.L.)	13	12	.520	4.23	32	32	1	1	0-0	213.0	209	107	100	19	93-8	162
2000—	New York (N.L.)	16	8	.667	3.20	31	31	2	1	0-0	208.0	176	84	74	19	76-1	200
2001—	New York (N.L.)	11	11	.500	3.31	29	29	0	0	0-0	187.1	178	81	69	18	46-3	142
2002—	New York (N.L.)	13	13	.500	3.48	33	33	2	2	0-0	204.1	194	99	79	23	69-5	172
A.L. totals (9 years)		33	32	.508	4.36	113	83	4	2	2-3	522.0	490	272	253	40	309-6	439
N.L. totals (7 years)		97	71	.577	3.40	213	213	11	7	0-0	1372.1	1194	578	518	114	565-26	1182
Major League totals (16 years)		130	103	.558	3.66	326	296	15	9	2-3	1894.1	1684	850	771	154	874-32	1621

DIVISION SERIES RECORD

Year League	W	L	Pct.	ERA	G	GS	CG	ShO	Sv.-Opp.	IP	H	R	ER	HR	BB-IBB	SO
1997— Florida (N.L.)	0	0	...	9.00	1	1	0	0	0-0	4.0	7	4	4	1	3-0	3
1999— New York (N.L.)	0	0	...	3.52	1	1	0	0	0-0	7.2	3	3	3	1	3-0	4
2000— New York (N.L.)	0	0	...	2.25	1	1	0	0	0-0	8.0	5	2	2	0	3-0	6
Division series totals (3 years)	0	0	...	4.12	3	3	0	0	0-0	19.2	15	9	9	2	9-0	13

CHAMPIONSHIP SERIES RECORD

Year League	W	L	Pct.	ERA	G	GS	CG	ShO	Sv.-Opp.	IP	H	R	ER	HR	BB-IBB	SO
1993— Toronto (A.L.)	0	0	...	3.38	2	0	0	0	0-0	2.2	4	1	1	0	2-1	2
1997— Florida (N.L.)	0	1	.000	4.32	2	1	0	0	0-0	8.1	13	4	4	1	2-0	6
1999— New York (N.L.)	0	1	.000	6.43	2	2	0	0	0-0	7.0	5	6	5	0	4-0	5
2000— New York (N.L.)	0	0	...	3.86	1	1	0	0	0-0	7.0	8	3	3	0	0-0	9
Champ. series totals (4 years)	0	2	.000	4.68	7	4	0	0	0-0	25.0	30	14	13	1	8-1	22

WORLD SERIES RECORD

RECORDS: Shares single-inning record for most bases on balls allowed—4 (October 21, 1997, fourth inning).
NOTES: Member of World Series championship team (1993 and 1997).

Year League	W	L	Pct.	ERA	G	GS	CG	ShO	Sv.-Opp.	IP	H	R	ER	HR	BB-IBB	SO
1993— Toronto (A.L.)	1	0	1.000	7.71	3	0	0	0	0-0	7.0	12	6	6	2	2-0	5
1997— Florida (N.L.)	0	0	...	5.06	2	2	0	0	0-0	10.2	10	9	6	1	10-1	10
2000— New York (N.L.)	0	1	.000	2.87	2	2	0	0	0-0	15.2	12	6	5	2	6-1	16
World Series totals (3 years)	1	1	.500	4.59	7	4	0	0	0-0	33.1	34	21	17	5	18-2	31

ALL-STAR GAME RECORD

	W	L	Pct.	ERA	GS	CG	ShO	Sv.-Opp.	IP	H	R	ER	HR	BB-IBB	SO
All-Star Game totals (2 years)	0	1	.000	6.75	0	0	0	0-0	1.1	2	2	1	0	1-0	1

LEON, JOSE — 3B — ORIOLES

PERSONAL: Born December 8, 1976, in Caguas, Puerto Rico. ... 6-0/175. ... Bats right, throws right. ... Full name: Jose Geraldo Leon.
HIGH SCHOOL: Tecnico de Portiro (Cayey, Puerto Rico).
TRANSACTIONS/CAREER NOTES: Selected by St. Louis Cardinals organization in 22nd round of free-agent draft (June 2, 1994). ... Traded by Cardinals to Baltimore Orioles for 1B Will Clark and cash (July 31, 2000).
2002 GAMES PLAYED BY POSITION (MLB): 1B—17; 3B—12; DH—2; OF—2.

		BATTING														FIELDING	
Year Team (League)	Pos.	G	AB	R	H	2B	3B	HR	RBI	BB	SO	SB-CS	Avg.	OBP	SLG	E	Avg.
1994—Ariz. Cardinals (Ariz.)	3B-2B	46	161	16	37	3	2	0	17	11	51	1-4	.230	.285	.273	11	.922
1995—Savannah (S.Atl.)	3B-OF	41	133	15	22	4	1	0	11	10	46	0-1	.165	.229	.211	8	.814
1996—Johnson City (Appl.)	3B-1B	59	222	29	55	9	3	10	36	17	92	5-3	.248	.306	.450	11	.960
—New Jersey (NY-P)	3B	7	28	4	8	3	1	1	3	0	7	0-0	.286	.333	.571	3	.833
1997—Peoria (Midw.)	3B-OF-1B	118	399	50	92	21	2	20	54	32	122	6-5	.231	.301	.444	25	.903
1998—Prince William (Caro.)	3B-1B	124	436	77	127	31	3	21	74	53	137	5-3	.291	.376	.521	25	.935
1999—Arkansas (Texas)	3B-OF	112	335	37	78	17	0	18	54	25	114	3-3	.233	.297	.445	22	.900
2000—Arkansas (Texas)	3B-1B-OF	90	297	41	80	16	3	14	41	16	66	2-1	.269	.318	.485	14	.951
—Bowie (East.)	3B	18	68	7	17	1	0	1	6	4	13	5-2	.250	.311	.309	2	.955
2001—Bowie (East.)	3B	26	95	18	34	9	1	4	20	8	21	1-1	.358	.413	.600	7	.879
—Rochester (I.L.)	3B	109	416	54	116	20	4	12	53	25	96	7-3	.279	.325	.433	21	.933
2002—Rochester (I.L.)	3B	83	312	39	87	16	1	8	40	18	54	0-0	.279	.319	.413	10	.957
—Baltimore (A.L.)	1B-3B-DH-OF	36	89	8	22	2	0	3	10	3	20	1-0	.247	.280	.371	1	.994
Major League totals (1 year)		36	89	8	22	2	0	3	10	3	20	1-0	.247	.280	.371	1	.994

LESHER, BRIAN — OF

PERSONAL: Born March 5, 1971, in Antwerp, Belgium. ... 6-5/222. ... Bats right, throws left. ... Full name: Brian Herbert Lesher.
HIGH SCHOOL: Newark (Del.).
COLLEGE: Delaware.
TRANSACTIONS/CAREER NOTES: Selected by Oakland Athletics organization in 25th round of free-agent draft (June 1, 1992). ... On Oakland disabled list (March 22-May 11, 1998); included rehabilitation assignment to Edmonton (May 2-11). ... On Modesto disabled list (August 5, 1999-remainder of season). ... Granted free agency (October 15, 1999). ... Signed by Seattle Mariners organization (January 14, 2000). ... Released by Mariners (November 16, 2000). ... Signed by Milwaukee Brewers organization (December 20, 2000). ... On disabled list (July 22-September 4, 2001). ... Granted free agency (October 15, 2001). ... Signed by Toronto Blue Jays organization (December 18, 2001). ... Granted free agency (October 15, 2002).
STATISTICAL NOTES: Led Pacific Coast League first basemen with 85 assists in 2000.
2002 GAMES PLAYED BY POSITION (MLB): 1B—12; OF—5; DH—3.

		BATTING														FIELDING	
Year Team (League)	Pos.	G	AB	R	H	2B	3B	HR	RBI	BB	SO	SB-CS	Avg.	OBP	SLG	E	Avg.
1992—S. Oregon (N'West)	OF-1B	46	136	21	26	7	1	3	18	12	35	3-7	.191	.265	.324	4	.943
1993—Madison (Midw.)	OF	119	394	63	108	13	5	5	47	46	102	20-9	.274	.358	.371	5	.976
1994—Modesto (Calif.)	OF-1B	117	393	76	114	21	0	14	68	81	84	11-11	.290	.414	.450	11	.970
1995—Huntsville (Sou.)	OF-1B	127	471	78	123	23	2	19	71	64	110	7-8	.261	.351	.439	6	.972
1996—Edmonton (PCL)	1B-OF-DH	109	414	57	119	29	2	18	75	36	108	6-5	.287	.352	.498	9	.988
—Oakland (A.L.)	OF-1B	26	82	11	19	3	0	5	16	5	17	0-0	.232	.281	.451	1	.980
1997—Edmonton (PCL)	OF-1B-DH	110	415	85	134	27	5	21	78	64	86	14-3	.323	.415	.564	6	.974
—Oakland (A.L.)	OF-DH-1B	46	131	17	30	4	1	4	16	9	30	4-1	.229	.275	.366	3	.968
1998—Edmonton (PCL)	OF-1B-DH	99	360	62	108	31	1	11	60	46	96	3-4	.300	.380	.483	5	.979
—Oakland (A.L.)	OF-1B	7	7	0	1	1	0	0	1	0	3	0-0	.143	.143	.286	1	.857
1999—Vancouver (PCL)	1B-OF-DH	103	387	66	113	29	2	14	64	41	71	8-2	.292	.364	.486	4	.994
2000—Tacoma (PCL)■	1B-OF	132	489	77	141	33	3	25	92	70	104	4-4	.288	.377	.521	6	.995
—Seattle (A.L.)	1B-DH	5	5	1	4	1	1	0	3	1	0	1-0	.800	.833	1.400	0	1.000
2001—Indianapolis (I.L.)■	OF-1B	93	346	51	98	17	4	7	63	40	78	1-1	.283	.356	.416	4	.978
2002—Toronto (A.L.)■	1B-OF-DH	24	38	2	5	1	0	0	2	4	15	0-0	.132	.209	.158	0	1.000
—Syracuse (I.L.)	OF-1B	66	248	34	65	13	1	7	28	20	55	6-1	.262	.315	.407	4	.975
Major League totals (5 years)		108	263	31	59	10	2	9	38	19	65	5-1	.224	.275	.380	5	.976

LESKANIC, CURTIS — P — BREWERS

PERSONAL: Born April 2, 1968, in Homestead, Pa. ... 6-0/196. ... Throws right, bats right. ... Full name: Curtis John Leskanic. ... Name pronounced less-CAN-ik.

HIGH SCHOOL: Steel Valley (Munhall, Pa.).

COLLEGE: Louisiana State.

TRANSACTIONS/CAREER NOTES: Selected by Cleveland Indians organization in eighth round of free-agent draft (June 5, 1989). ... On disabled list (April 23-June 25, 1990). ... Traded by Indians with P Oscar Munoz to Minnesota Twins for 1B Paul Sorrento (March 28, 1992). ... Selected by Colorado Rockies in third round (66th pick overall) of expansion draft (November 17, 1992). ... Loaned by Rockies organization to Wichita, San Diego Padres organization (April 7-May 20, 1993). ... On Colorado disabled list (May 30-June 28, 1996); included rehabilitation assignment to Colorado Springs (June 22-27). ... On Colorado disabled list (March 23-April 12, 1997); included rehabilitation assignment to Salem (April 6-8). ... Traded by Rockies to Milwaukee Brewers for P Mike Myers (November 17, 1999). ... On disabled list (May 17-30, 2000). ... On Milwaukee disabled list (March 30, 2002-entire season); included rehabilitation assignments to Indianapolis (May 10-24) and Huntsville (May 25-29).

MISCELLANEOUS: Holds Colorado Rockies all-time record for most games pitched (356). ... Had a sacrifice hit in only appearance as pinch hitter (1998).

CAREER HITTING (MLB): 7-for-39 (.179), 4 R, 3 2B, 0 3B, 1 HR, 7 RBI.

Year League	W	L	Pct.	ERA	G	GS	CG	ShO	Sv.-Opp.	IP	H	R	ER	HR	BB-IBB	SO
1990— Kinston (Caro.)	6	5	.545	3.68	14	14	2	0	0-...	73.1	61	34	30	6	30-1	71
1991— Kinston (Caro.)	•15	8	.652	2.79	28	28	0	0	0-...	174.1	143	63	54	10	91-0	*163
1992— Orlando (Sou.)■	9	11	.450	4.30	26	23	3	0	0-...	152.2	158	84	73	15	64-0	126
— Portland (PCL)	1	2	.333	9.98	5	3	0	0	0-...	15.1	16	17	17	1	8-0	14
1993— Wichita (Texas)■	3	2	.600	3.45	7	7	0	0	0-...	44.1	37	20	17	3	17-0	42
— Colorado Springs (PCL)■	4	3	.571	4.47	9	7	1	1	0-...	44.1	39	24	22	3	26-0	38
— Colorado (N.L.)	1	5	.167	5.37	18	8	0	0	0-0	57.0	59	40	34	7	27-1	30
1994— Colorado Springs (PCL)	5	7	.417	3.31	21	21	2	0	0-...	130.1	129	60	48	7	54-2	98
— Colorado (N.L.)	1	1	.500	5.64	8	3	0	0	0-0	22.1	27	14	14	2	10-0	17
1995— Colorado (N.L.)	6	3	.667	3.40	*76	0	0	0	10-16	98.0	83	38	37	7	33-1	107
1996— Colorado (N.L.)	7	5	.583	6.23	70	0	0	0	6-10	73.2	82	51	51	12	38-1	76
— Colorado Springs (PCL)	0	0	...	3.00	3	0	0	0	0-...	3.0	5	1	1	0	1-0	2
1997— Salem (Caro.)	0	0	...	3.86	2	1	0	0	0-...	2.1	5	2	1	0	1-0	3
— Colorado (N.L.)	4	0	1.000	5.55	55	0	0	0	2-4	58.1	59	36	36	8	24-0	53
— Colorado Springs (PCL)	0	0	...	3.79	10	3	0	0	2-...	19.0	11	9	8	1	18-0	20
1998— Colorado (N.L.)	6	4	.600	4.40	66	0	0	0	2-5	75.2	75	37	37	9	40-2	55
1999— Colorado (N.L.)	6	2	.750	5.08	63	0	0	0	0-3	85.0	87	54	48	7	49-4	77
2000— Milwaukee (N.L.)■	9	3	.750	2.56	73	0	0	0	12-13	77.1	58	23	22	7	51-5	75
2001— Milwaukee (N.L.)	2	6	.250	3.63	70	0	0	0	17-24	69.1	63	30	28	11	31-5	64
2002— Indianapolis (I.L.)	0	0	...	1.35	5	1	0	0	0-...	6.2	5	1	1	0	1-0	7
— Huntsville (Sou.)	0	0	...	3.00	3	0	0	0	0-...	3.0	4	2	1	0	2-0	2
Major League totals (9 years)	42	29	.592	4.48	499	11	0	0	49-75	616.2	593	323	307	70	303-19	554

DIVISION SERIES RECORD

Year League	W	L	Pct.	ERA	G	GS	CG	ShO	Sv.-Opp.	IP	H	R	ER	HR	BB-IBB	SO
1995— Colorado (N.L.)	0	1	.000	6.00	3	0	0	0	0-0	3.0	3	2	2	1	0-0	4

LEVINE, AL — P — ANGELS

PERSONAL: Born May 22, 1968, in Park Ridge, Ill. ... 6-3/190. ... Throws right, bats left. ... Full name: Alan Brian Levine.

HIGH SCHOOL: Hoffman Estates (Ill.).

JUNIOR COLLEGE: Harper Junior College (Ill.).

COLLEGE: Southern Illinois-Carbondale.

TRANSACTIONS/CAREER NOTES: Selected by Chicago White Sox in 11th round of free-agent draft (June 3, 1991). ... Traded by White Sox with P Larry Thomas to Texas Rangers for SS Benji Gil (December 19, 1997). ... Claimed on waivers by Anaheim Angels (April 2, 1999). ... On Anaheim disabled list (July 31-August 19, 2000); included rehabilitation assignment to Erie (August 17). ... On Anaheim disabled list (June 27-July 20, 2002); included rehabilitation assignment to Salt Lake (July 16-20).

CAREER HITTING (MLB): 0-for-0 (.000), 0 R, 0 2B, 0 3B, 0 HR, 0 RBI.

Year League	W	L	Pct.	ERA	G	GS	CG	ShO	Sv.-Opp.	IP	H	R	ER	HR	BB-IBB	SO
1991— Utica (NY-Penn)	6	4	.600	3.18	16	12	2	1	1-...	85.0	75	45	30	2	26-0	83
1992— South Bend (Midw.)	9	5	.643	2.81	23	23	2	0	0-...	156.2	151	67	49	6	36-1	131
— Sarasota (FSL)	0	2	.000	4.02	3	2	0	0	0-...	15.2	17	11	7	1	5-1	11
1993— Sarasota (FSL)	11	8	.579	3.68	27	26	5	1	0-...	161.1	169	87	66	6	50-3	*129
1994— Birmingham (Sou.)	5	9	.357	3.31	18	18	1	0	0-...	114.1	117	50	42	7	44-1	94
— Nashville (A.A.)	0	2	.000	7.88	8	4	0	0	0-...	24.0	34	23	21	2	11-0	24
1995— Nashville (A.A.)	0	2	.000	5.14	3	3	0	0	0-...	14.0	20	10	8	1	7-0	14
— Birmingham (Sou.)	4	3	.571	2.34	43	1	0	0	7-...	73.0	61	22	19	2	25-5	68
1996— Nashville (A.A.)	4	5	.444	3.65	43	0	0	0	12-...	61.2	58	27	25	4	24-6	45
— Chicago (A.L.)	0	1	.000	5.40	16	0	0	0	0-1	18.1	22	14	11	1	7-1	12
1997— Chicago (A.L.)	2	2	.500	6.91	25	0	0	0	0-1	27.1	35	22	21	4	16-1	22
— Nashville (A.A.)	1	1	.500	7.13	26	0	0	0	2-...	35.1	58	32	28	3	11-1	29
1998— Oklahoma (PCL)■	1	3	.250	4.72	12	7	0	0	1-...	53.1	51	33	28	7	17-0	30
— Texas (A.L.)	0	1	.000	4.50	30	0	0	0	0-0	58.0	68	30	29	6	16-1	19
1999— Anaheim (A.L.)■	1	1	.500	3.39	50	1	0	0	0-1	85.0	76	40	32	13	29-2	37
2000— Anaheim (A.L.)	3	4	.429	3.87	51	5	0	0	2-2	95.1	98	44	41	10	49-5	42
— Erie (East.)	0	0	...	0.00	1	1	0	0	0-...	2.0	3	2	0	0	0-0	0
2001— Anaheim (A.L.)	8	10	.444	2.38	64	1	0	0	2-6	75.2	71	25	20	7	28-4	40
2002— Anaheim (A.L.)	4	4	.500	4.24	52	0	0	0	5-7	63.2	61	35	30	8	34-3	40
— Salt Lake (PCL)	0	0	...	3.00	2	0	0	0	0-...	3.0	5	1	1	0	0-0	0
Major League totals (7 years)	18	23	.439	3.91	288	7	0	0	9-18	423.1	431	210	184	49	179-17	212

LEWIS, COLBY — P — RANGERS

PERSONAL: Born August 2, 1979, in Bakersfield, Calif. ... 6-4/215. ... Throws right, bats right. ... Full name: Colby Preston Lewis.
HIGH SCHOOL: North (Bakersfield, Calif.).
JUNIOR COLLEGE: Bakersfield (Calif.).
TRANSACTIONS/CAREER NOTES: Selected by Texas Rangers organization in supplemental round ("sandwich pick" between first and second round, 38th pick overall) of free-agent draft (June 2, 1999); pick received as part of compensation for Arizona Diamondbacks signing Type A free agent P Todd Stottlemyre.
STATISTICAL NOTES: Led Texas League with 16 hit batsmen and 16 wild pitches in 2001.
CAREER HITTING (MLB): 0-for-0 (.000), 0 R, 0 2B, 0 3B, 0 HR, 0 RBI.

Year League	W	L	Pct.	ERA	G	GS	CG	ShO	Sv.-Opp.	IP	H	R	ER	HR	BB-IBB	SO
1999— Pulaski (Appl.)	7	3	.700	1.95	14	11	1	1	0-...	64.2	46	24	14	3	27-0	84
2000— Charlotte (FSL)	11	10	.524	4.07	28	27	3	1	0-...	163.2	169	83	74	11	45-0	153
2001— Charlotte (FSL)	1	0	1.000	0.00	1	0	0	0	0-...	4.1	0	0	0	0	0-0	8
— Tulsa (Texas)	10	10	.500	4.50	25	25	1	0	0-...	156.0	150	85	78	15	62-2	162
2002— Texas (A.L.)	1	3	.250	6.29	15	4	0	0	0-2	34.1	42	26	24	4	26-2	28
— Oklahoma (PCL)	5	6	.455	3.63	20	20	0	0	0-...	106.2	100	49	43	4	28-0	99
Major League totals (1 year)	1	3	.250	6.29	15	4	0	0	0-2	34.1	42	26	24	4	26-2	28

LEWIS, DARREN — OF

PERSONAL: Born August 28, 1967, in Berkeley, Calif. ... 6-0/200. ... Bats right, throws right. ... Full name: Darren Joel Lewis.
HIGH SCHOOL: Moreau (Hayward, Calif.).
JUNIOR COLLEGE: Chabot College (Calif.).
COLLEGE: California.
TRANSACTIONS/CAREER NOTES: Selected by Los Angeles Dodgers organization in sixth round of free-agent draft (January 14, 1986); did not sign. ... Selected by Toronto Blue Jays organization in 45th round of free-agent draft (June 2, 1987); did not sign. ... Selected by Oakland Athletics organization in 18th round of free-agent draft (June 1, 1988). ... Traded by A's with a player to be named later to San Francisco Giants for IF Ernest Riles (December 4, 1990); Giants acquired P Pedro Pena to complete deal (December 17, 1990). ... On disabled list (August 20-September 4, 1993). ... Traded by Giants with P Mark Portugal and P Dave Burba to Cincinnati Reds for OF Deion Sanders, P John Roper, P Ricky Pickett, P Scott Service and IF Dave McCarty (July 21, 1995). ... Released by Reds (December 1, 1995). ... Signed by Chicago White Sox (December 14, 1995). ... Traded by White Sox to Dodgers for a player to be named later (August 27, 1997); White Sox acquired IF Chad Fonville to complete deal (September 2, 1997). ... Granted free agency (October 27, 1997). ... Signed by Boston Red Sox (December 23, 1997). ... Granted free agency (November 3, 1998). ... Re-signed by Red Sox (November 5, 1998). ... On Boston disabled list (July 1-14, 2000); included rehabilitation assignment to Gulf Coast Red Sox (July 11-13). ... Granted free agency (November 5, 2001). ... Signed by Chicago Cubs (January 14, 2002). ... Traded by Cubs to Pittsburgh Pirates for OF Chad Hermansen (July 31, 2002). ... Announced retirement (August 1, 2002). ... Granted free agency (November 1, 2002).
RECORDS: Holds major league records for most consecutive errorless games by outfielder—392 (August 21, 1990-June 29, 1994); and most consecutive chances accepted without an error by outfielder—938 (August 21, 1990-June 29, 1994). ... Shares major league record for fewest double plays by outfielder (150 or more games)—0 (1998). ... Holds N.L. records for most consecutive errorless games by outfielder—369 (July 13, 1991-June 29, 1994); and most consecutive chances accepted without an error by outfielder—905 (July 13, 1991-June 29, 1994).
HONORS: Won N.L. Gold Glove as outfielder (1994).
STATISTICAL NOTES: Led California League outfielders with 311 putouts and 324 total chances in 1989. ... Career major league grand slams: 1.

		BATTING														FIELDING	
Year Team (League)	Pos.	G	AB	R	H	2B	3B	HR	RBI	BB	SO	SB-CS	Avg.	OBP	SLG	E	Avg.
1988— Ariz. Athletics (Ariz.)	OF	5	15	8	5	3	0	0	4	6	5	4-0	.333	.522	.533	0	1.000
— Madison (Midw.)	OF-2B	60	199	38	49	4	1	0	11	46	37	31-10	.246	.393	.276	4	.980
1989— Modesto (Calif.)	OF	129	503	74	150	23	5	4	39	59	84	27-22	.298	.381	.388	5	.985
— Huntsville (Sou.)	OF	9	31	7	10	1	1	1	7	2	6	0-1	.323	.382	.516	0	1.000
1990— Huntsville (Sou.)	OF	71	284	52	84	11	3	3	23	36	28	21-7	.296	.385	.387	0	1.000
— Tacoma (PCL)	OF	60	247	32	72	5	2	2	26	16	35	16-6	.291	.335	.352	2	.986
— Oakland (A.L.)	OF-DH	25	35	4	8	0	0	0	1	7	4	2-0	.229	.372	.229	0	1.000
1991— Phoenix (PCL)■	OF	81	315	63	107	12	10	2	52	41	36	32-10	.340	.413	.460	2	.992
— San Francisco (N.L.)	OF	72	222	41	55	5	3	1	15	36	30	13-7	.248	.358	.311	0	1.000
1992— San Francisco (N.L.)	OF	100	320	38	74	8	1	1	18	29	46	28-8	.231	.295	.272	0	1.000
— Phoenix (PCL)	OF	42	158	22	36	5	2	0	6	11	15	9-6	.228	.287	.285	0	1.000
1993— San Francisco (N.L.)	OF	136	522	84	132	17	7	2	48	30	40	46-15	.253	.302	.324	0	•1.000
1994— San Francisco (N.L.)	OF	114	451	70	116	15	•9	4	29	53	50	30-13	.257	.340	.357	2	.993
1995— San Francisco (N.L.)	OF	74	309	47	78	10	3	1	16	17	37	21-7	.252	.303	.314	1	.995
— Cincinnati (N.L.)■	OF	58	163	19	40	3	0	0	8	17	20	11-11	.245	.324	.264	1	.992
1996— Chicago (A.L.)■	OF	141	337	55	77	12	2	4	53	45	40	21-5	.228	.321	.312	3	.990
1997— Chicago (A.L.)	OF-DH	81	77	15	18	1	0	0	5	11	14	11-4	.234	.330	.247	0	1.000
— Los Angeles (N.L.)■	OF	26	77	7	23	3	1	1	10	6	17	3-2	.299	.349	.403	1	.980
1998— Boston (A.L.)■	OF-DH	155	585	95	157	25	3	8	63	70	94	29-12	.268	.352	.362	3	.992
1999— Boston (A.L.)	OF-DH	135	470	63	113	14	6	2	40	45	52	16-10	.240	.311	.309	2	.994
2000— Boston (A.L.)	OF-DH	97	270	44	65	12	0	2	17	22	34	10-5	.241	.305	.307	3	.981
— GC Red Sox (GCL)	OF	2	6	0	1	0	0	0	1	1	0	1-0	.167	.286	.167	0	1.000
2001— Boston (A.L.)	OF-DH	82	164	18	46	9	1	1	12	8	25	5-5	.280	.326	.366	0	1.000
2002— Chicago (N.L.)■	OF	58	79	7	19	3	1	0	7	7	11	1-3	.241	.326	.304	0	1.000
— Pittsburgh (N.L.)■									Did not play.								
American League totals (7 years)		716	1938	294	484	73	12	17	191	208	263	94-41	.250	.328	.326	11	.992
National League totals (7 years)		638	2143	313	537	64	25	10	151	195	251	153-66	.251	.320	.318	5	.997
Major League totals (13 years)		1354	4081	607	1021	137	37	27	342	403	514	247-107	.250	.323	.322	16	.994

DIVISION SERIES RECORD

Year	Team (League)	Pos.	BATTING G	AB	R	H	2B	3B	HR	RBI	BB	SO	SB-CS	Avg.	OBP	SLG	FIELDING E	Avg.
1995—	Cincinnati (N.L.)	OF-PH	3	3	0	0	0	0	0	0	0	1	0-0	.000	.000	.000	0	1.000
1998—	Boston (A.L.)	OF	4	14	4	5	2	0	0	0	1	3	1-0	.357	.438	.500	0	1.000
1999—	Boston (A.L.)	OF	4	16	5	6	1	0	0	2	0	2	1-0	.375	.412	.438	0	1.000
Division series totals (3 years)			11	33	9	11	3	0	0	2	1	6	2-0	.333	.389	.424	0	1.000

CHAMPIONSHIP SERIES RECORD

Year	Team (League)	Pos.	BATTING G	AB	R	H	2B	3B	HR	RBI	BB	SO	SB-CS	Avg.	OBP	SLG	FIELDING E	Avg.
1995—	Cincinnati (N.L.)	OF-PR	2	1	0	0	0	0	0	0	0	0	0-0	.000	.000	.000	0	1.000
1999—	Boston (A.L.)	OF	5	17	2	2	1	0	0	1	1	3	1-1	.118	.167	.176	1	.875
Championship series totals (2 years)			7	18	2	2	1	0	0	1	1	3	1-1	.111	.158	.167	1	.900

LIDGE, BRAD — P — ASTROS

PERSONAL: Born December 23, 1976, in Sacramento, Calif. ... 6-5/200. ... Throws right, bats right. ... Full name: Bradley Thomas Lidge.
COLLEGE: Notre Dame.
TRANSACTIONS/CAREER NOTES: Selected by Houston Astros in first round (17th pick overall) of free-agent draft (June 2, 1998); pick received from Colorado Rockies as part of compensation for signing Type A free agent Darryl Kile. ... On disabled list (August 18, 1998-remainder of season). ... On disabled list (April 1-June and July 10, 1999-remainder of season). ... On disabled list (April 24-June 13 and July 1, 2000-remainder of season). ... On disabled list (May 5, 2001-remainder of season).
CAREER HITTING (MLB): 2-for-2 (1.000), 0 R, 1 2B, 0 3B, 0 HR, 2 RBI.

Year	League	W	L	Pct.	ERA	G	GS	CG	ShO	Sv.-Opp.	IP	H	R	ER	HR	BB-IBB	SO
1998—	Quad City (Midw.)	0	1	.000	3.27	4	4	0	0	0-...	11.0	10	5	4	0	5-0	6
1999—	Kissimmee (FSL)	0	2	.000	3.38	6	6	0	0	0-...	21.1	13	8	8	0	11-0	19
2000—	Kissimmee (FSL)	2	1	.667	2.81	8	8	0	0	0-...	41.2	28	14	13	3	15-0	46
2001—	Round Rock (Texas)	2	0	1.000	1.73	5	5	0	0	0-...	26.0	21	5	5	1	7-0	42
2002—	Round Rock (Texas)	1	1	.500	2.45	5	0	0	0	0-...	11.0	9	4	3	0	3-0	18
—	Houston (N.L.)	1	0	1.000	6.23	6	1	0	0	0-0	8.2	12	6	6	0	9-1	12
—	New Orleans (PCL)	5	5	.500	3.39	24	19	0	0	0-...	111.2	83	47	42	9	47-0	110
Major League totals (1 year)		1	0	1.000	6.23	6	1	0	0	0-0	8.2	12	6	6	0	9-1	12

LIDLE, CORY — P — ATHLETICS

PERSONAL: Born March 22, 1972, in Hollywood, Calif. ... 5-11/192. ... Throws right, bats right. ... Full name: Cory Fulton Lidle. ... Twin brother of Kevin Lidle, catcher, California Angels organization.
HIGH SCHOOL: South Hills (Covina, Calif.).
TRANSACTIONS/CAREER NOTES: Signed as non-drafted free agent by Minnesota Twins organization (August 25, 1990). ... Released by Twins (April 1, 1993). ... Signed by Pocatello, Pioneer League (May 28, 1993). ... Contract sold by Pocatello to Milwaukee Brewers organization (September 17, 1993). ... Traded by Brewers to New York Mets for C Kelly Stinnett (January 17, 1996). ... Selected by Arizona Diamondbacks in first round (13th pick overall) of expansion draft (November 18, 1997). ... On Arizona disabled list (March 31, 1998-entire season); included rehabilitation assignments to High Desert (April 20-28) and Tucson (September 3-7). ... Claimed on waivers by Tampa Bay Devil Rays (October 7, 1998). ... On Tampa Bay disabled list (March 23-September 18, 1999); included rehabilitation assignments to St. Petersburg (August 20-28) and Durham (August 29-September 18). ... On suspended list (September 5-8, 2000). ... Traded by Devil Rays to Oakland Athletics as part of three-way deal in which Devil Rays received OF Ben Grieve and a player to be named later or cash from the A's, Royals received P Roberto Hernandez from Devil Rays, A's received OF Johnny Damon, IF Mark Ellis and a player to be named later from Royals and Royals received C A.J. Hinch, IF Angel Berroa and cash from A's (January 8, 2001). ... On Oakland disabled list (May 13-30, 2002); included rehabilitation assignment to Sacramento (May 26-30).
STATISTICAL NOTES: Pitched 10-0 one-hit, complete-game victory against Texas (July 19, 2002). ... Pitched 6-0 one-hit, complete-game victory against Cleveland (August 21, 2002).
CAREER HITTING (MLB): 0-for-10 (.000), 1 R, 0 2B, 0 3B, 0 HR, 0 RBI.

Year	League	W	L	Pct.	ERA	G	GS	CG	ShO	Sv.-Opp.	IP	H	R	ER	HR	BB-IBB	SO
1991—	Gulf Coast Twins (GCL)	1	1	.500	5.79	4	0	0	0	0-...	4.2	5	3	3	0	0-0	5
1992—	Elizabethton (Appl.)	2	1	.667	3.71	19	2	0	0	6-...	43.2	40	29	18	2	21-0	32
1993—	Pocatello (Pio.)■	•8	4	.667	4.13	17	16	3	0	1-...	106.2	104	59	49	6	54-0	91
1994—	Stockton (Calif.)■	1	2	.333	4.43	25	1	0	0	4-...	42.2	60	32	21	2	13-1	38
—	Beloit (Midw.)	3	4	.429	2.61	13	9	1	1	0-...	69.0	65	24	20	4	11-0	62
1995—	El Paso (Texas)	5	4	.556	3.36	45	9	0	0	2-...	109.2	126	52	41	6	36-3	78
1996—	Binghamton (East.)■	14	10	.583	3.31	27	27	•6	1	0-...	*190.1	186	78	70	13	49-4	141
1997—	Norfolk (I.L.)	4	2	.667	3.64	7	7	1	0	0-...	42.0	46	20	17	1	10-0	34
—	New York (N.L.)	7	2	.778	3.53	54	2	0	0	2-3	81.2	86	38	32	7	20-4	54
1998—	High Desert (Calif.)■	0	0	...	0.00	1	1	0	0	0-...	2.2	2	1	0	0	2-0	6
—	Tucson (PCL)	0	0	...	0.00	1	1	0	0	0-...	4.2	2	0	0	0	2-0	2
1999—	St. Petersburg (FSL)■	0	0	...	0.00	2	2	0	0	0-...	5.0	2	0	0	0	2-0	0
—	Durham (I.L.)	0	0	...	4.76	3	2	0	0	0-...	5.2	9	3	3	0	1-0	6
—	Tampa Bay (A.L.)	1	0	1.000	7.20	5	1	0	0	0-0	5.0	8	4	4	0	2-0	4
2000—	Durham (I.L.)	6	2	.750	2.52	9	9	0	0	0-...	50.0	52	15	14	3	8-0	44
—	Tampa Bay (A.L.)	4	6	.400	5.03	31	11	0	0	0-0	96.2	114	61	54	13	29-3	62
2001—	Sacramento (PCL)■	1	0	1.000	3.00	1	1	0	0	0-...	6.0	6	2	2	0	3-0	2
—	Oakland (A.L.)	13	6	.684	3.59	29	29	1	0	0-0	188.0	170	84	75	23	47-7	118
2002—	Oakland (A.L.)	8	10	.444	3.89	31	30	2	2	0-0	192.0	191	90	83	17	39-3	111
—	Sacramento (PCL)	0	0	...	2.25	1	1	0	0	0-...	4.0	2	1	1	0	3-0	3
A.L. totals (4 years)		26	22	.542	4.04	96	71	3	2	0-0	481.2	483	239	216	53	117-13	295
N.L. totals (1 year)		7	2	.778	3.53	54	2	0	0	2-3	81.2	86	38	32	7	20-4	54
Major League totals (5 years)		33	24	.579	3.96	150	73	3	2	2-3	563.1	569	277	248	60	137-17	349

DIVISION SERIES RECORD

Year	League	W	L	Pct.	ERA	G	GS	CG	ShO	Sv.-Opp.	IP	H	R	ER	HR	BB-IBB	SO
2001—	Oakland (A.L.)	0	1	.000	10.80	1	1	0	0	0-0	3.1	5	6	4	0	3-0	0
2002—	Oakland (A.L.)	0	0	...	9.00	1	0	0	0	0-0	1.0	2	1	1	0	0-0	0
Division series totals (2 years)		0	1	.000	10.38	2	1	0	0	0-0	4.1	7	7	5	0	3-0	0

LIEBER, JON — P

PERSONAL: Born April 2, 1970, in Council Bluffs, Iowa. ... 6-2/230. ... Throws right, bats left. ... Full name: Jonathan Ray Lieber. ... Name pronounced LEE-ber.

HIGH SCHOOL: Abraham Lincoln (Council Bluffs, Iowa.).

JUNIOR COLLEGE: Iowa Western Community College-Council Bluffs.

COLLEGE: South Alabama.

TRANSACTIONS/CAREER NOTES: Selected by Chicago Cubs organization in ninth round of free-agent draft (June 3, 1991); did not sign. ... Selected by Kansas City Royals organization in second round of free-agent draft (June 1, 1992); pick received as part of compensation for New York Yankees signing Type A free-agent OF Danny Tartabull. ... Traded by Royals with P Dan Miceli to Pittsburgh Pirates for P Stan Belinda (July 31, 1993). ... On disabled list (August 21-September 15, 1998). ... Traded by Pirates to Chicago Cubs for OF Brant Brown (December 14, 1998). ... On disabled list (April 21-May 8, 1999; and August 2, 2002-remainder of season). ... Granted free agency (November 1, 2002).

STATISTICAL NOTES: Pitched 3-0 one-hit, complete-game victory against Cincinnati (May 24, 2001).

MISCELLANEOUS: Walked in only appearance as pinch hitter (2000). ... Appeared in one game as pinch hitter (2001).

CAREER HITTING (MLB): 71-for-461 (.154), 27 R, 15 2B, 0 3B, 0 HR, 20 RBI.

Year League	W	L	Pct.	ERA	G	GS	CG	ShO	Sv.-Opp.	IP	H	R	ER	HR	BB-IBB	SO
1992— Eugene (N'West)	3	0	1.000	1.16	5	5	0	0	0-...	31.0	26	6	4	1	2-0	23
— Baseball City (FSL)	3	3	.500	4.65	7	6	0	0	0-...	31.0	45	20	16	2	8-0	19
1993— Wilmington (Caro.)	9	3	.750	2.67	17	16	2	0	0-...	114.2	125	47	34	4	9-1	89
— Memphis (Sou.)	2	1	.667	6.86	4	4	0	0	0-...	21.0	32	16	16	4	6-0	17
— Carolina (Sou.)■	4	2	.667	3.97	6	6	0	0	0-...	34.0	39	15	15	3	10-0	28
1994— Carolina (Sou.)	2	0	1.000	1.29	3	3	1	1	0-...	21.0	13	4	3	0	2-0	21
— Buffalo (A.A.)	1	1	.500	1.69	3	3	0	0	0-...	21.1	16	4	4	1	1-0	21
— Pittsburgh (N.L.)	6	7	.462	3.73	17	17	1	0	0-0	108.2	116	62	45	12	25-3	71
1995— Pittsburgh (N.L.)	4	7	.364	6.32	21	12	0	0	0-1	72.2	103	56	51	7	14-0	45
— Calgary (PCL)	1	5	.167	7.01	14	14	0	0	0-...	77.0	122	69	60	6	19-0	34
1996— Pittsburgh (N.L.)	9	5	.643	3.99	51	15	0	0	1-4	142.0	156	70	63	19	28-2	94
1997— Pittsburgh (N.L.)	11	14	.440	4.49	33	32	1	0	0-0	188.1	193	102	94	23	51-8	160
1998— Pittsburgh (N.L.)	8	14	.364	4.11	29	28	2	0	1-1	171.0	182	93	78	23	40-4	138
1999— Chicago (N.L.)■	10	11	.476	4.07	31	31	3	1	0-0	203.1	226	107	92	28	46-6	186
2000— Chicago (N.L.)	12	11	.522	4.41	35	•35	6	1	0-0	*251.0	248	130	123	36	54-3	192
2001— Chicago (N.L.)	20	6	.769	3.80	34	34	5	1	0-0	232.1	226	104	98	25	41-4	148
2002— Chicago (N.L.)	6	8	.429	3.70	21	21	3	0	0-0	141.0	153	64	58	15	12-2	87
Major League totals (9 years)	86	83	.509	4.18	272	225	21	3	2-6	1510.1	1603	788	702	188	311-32	1121

ALL-STAR GAME RECORD

RECORDS: Shares record for most home runs allowed in one inning—2 (July 10, 2001, sixth inning).

	W	L	Pct.	ERA	GS	CG	ShO	Sv.-Opp.	IP	H	R	ER	HR	BB-IBB	SO
All-Star Game totals (1 year)	0	0	...	18.00	0	0	0	0-0	1.0	3	2	2	2	0-0	1

LIEBERTHAL, MIKE — C — PHILLIES

PERSONAL: Born January 18, 1972, in Glendale, Calif. ... 6-0/190. ... Bats right, throws right. ... Full name: Michael Scott Lieberthal. ... Name pronounced LEE-ber-thal.

HIGH SCHOOL: Westlake (Westlake Village, Calif.).

TRANSACTIONS/CAREER NOTES: Selected by Philadelphia Phillies organization in first round (third pick overall) of free-agent draft (June 4, 1990). ... On Scranton/Wilkes-Barre disabled list (August 31, 1992-remainder of season). ... On disabled list (August 22, 1996-remainder of season; July 24-September 2, 1998; July 18-August 4 and September 11, 2000-remainder of season; and May 13, 2001-remainder of season).

HONORS: Won N.L. Gold Glove at catcher (1999). ... Named N.L. Comeback Player of the Year by The Sporting News (2002).

STATISTICAL NOTES: Led Appalachian League with 52 assists in 1990. ... Tied for N.L. lead with 12 passed balls in 1997. ... Led N.L. catchers with 62 assists and tied league lead with 11 passed balls in 1999. ... Hit three home runs in one game (August 10, 2002). ... Career major league grand slams: 2.

2002 GAMES PLAYED BY POSITION (MLB): C—129.

		BATTING														FIELDING	
Year Team (League)	Pos.	G	AB	R	H	2B	3B	HR	RBI	BB	SO	SB-CS	Avg.	OBP	SLG	E	Avg.
1990— Martinsville (Appl.)	C	49	184	26	42	9	0	4	22	11	40	2-0	.228	.279	.342	5	*.990
1991— Spartanburg (S.Atl.)	C	72	243	34	74	17	0	0	31	23	25	1-2	.305	.372	.374	10	.984
— Clearwater (FSL)	C	16	52	7	15	2	0	0	7	3	12	0-0	.288	.333	.327	1	.993
1992— Reading (East.)	C	86	309	30	88	16	1	2	37	19	26	4-1	.285	.342	.362	7	.988
— Scranton/W.B. (I.L.)	C	16	45	4	9	1	0	0	4	2	5	0-0	.200	.245	.222	1	.989
1993— Scranton/W.B. (I.L.)	C	112	382	35	100	17	0	7	40	24	32	2-0	.262	.313	.361	•11	.985
1994— Scranton/W.B. (I.L.)	C-DH	84	296	23	69	16	0	1	32	21	29	1-1	.233	.286	.297	9	.983
— Philadelphia (N.L.)	C	24	79	6	21	3	1	1	5	3	5	0-0	.266	.301	.367	4	.969
1995— Philadelphia (N.L.)	C	16	47	1	12	2	0	0	4	5	5	0-0	.255	.327	.298	1	.991
— Scranton/W.B. (I.L.)	C-DH-3B	85	278	44	78	20	2	6	42	44	26	1-4	.281	.388	.432	5	.991
1996— Philadelphia (N.L.)	C	50	166	21	42	8	0	7	23	10	30	0-0	.253	.297	.428	3	.990
1997— Philadelphia (N.L.)	C-DH	134	455	59	112	27	1	20	77	44	76	3-4	.246	.314	.442	12	.988
1998— Philadelphia (N.L.)	C	86	313	39	80	15	3	8	45	17	44	2-1	.256	.304	.399	8	.988
1999— Philadelphia (N.L.)	C	145	510	84	153	33	1	31	96	44	86	0-0	.300	.363	.551	3	*.997
2000— Philadelphia (N.L.)	C	108	389	55	108	30	0	15	71	40	53	2-0	.278	.352	.470	5	.993
2001— Philadelphia (N.L.)	C	34	121	21	28	8	0	2	11	12	21	0-0	.231	.316	.347	2	.992
2002— Philadelphia (N.L.)	C	130	476	46	133	29	2	15	52	38	58	0-1	.279	.349	.443	6	.993
Major League totals (9 years)		727	2556	332	689	155	8	99	384	213	378	7-6	.270	.334	.453	44	.991

ALL-STAR GAME RECORD

	AB	R	H	2B	3B	HR	RBI	BB	SO	SB-CS	Avg.	OBP	SLG	E	Avg.
All-Star Game totals (2 years)	3	1	1	0	0	0	0	0	0	0-0	.333	.333	.333	0	1.000

LIEFER, JEFF — OF/3B — WHITE SOX

PERSONAL: Born August 17, 1974, in Fontana, Calif. ... 6-3/210. ... Bats left, throws right. ... Full name: Jeffrey David Liefer.
HIGH SCHOOL: Upland (Calif.).
COLLEGE: Long Beach State.
TRANSACTIONS/CAREER NOTES: Selected by Cleveland Indians organization in sixth round of free-agent draft (June 1, 1992); did not sign. ... Selected by Chicago White Sox organization in first round (25th pick overall) of free-agent draft (June 1, 1995). ... On Charlotte disabled list (August 30, 1999-remainder of season). ... On Chicago disabled list (March 25-April 17, 2000).
STATISTICAL NOTES: Career major league grand slams: 1.
2002 GAMES PLAYED BY POSITION (MLB): OF—36; 1B—31; DH—6.

			BATTING													FIELDING	
Year	Team (League)	Pos.	G	AB	R	H	2B	3B	HR	RBI	BB	SO	SB-CS	Avg.	OBP	SLG	E	Avg.
1996—	South Bend (Midw.)	DH-3B	74	277	60	90	14	0	15	58	30	62	6-5	.325	.396	.538	23	.802
—	Prince William (Caro.)	DH	37	147	17	33	6	0	1	13	11	27	0-0	.224	.277	.286	0	...
1997—	Birmingham (Sou.)	OF-DH	119	474	67	113	24	9	15	71	38	115	2-0	.238	.302	.422	•8	.955
1998—	Birmingham (Sou.)	1B-DH-OF	127	471	84	137	33	6	21	89	60	125	1-2	.291	.381	.520	11	.987
—	Calgary (PCL)	OF-DH-1B	8	31	3	8	3	0	1	10	2	12	0-0	.258	.303	.452	0	1.000
1999—	Chicago (A.L.)	OF-1B-DH	45	113	8	28	7	1	0	14	8	28	2-0	.248	.295	.327	0	1.000
—	Charlotte (I.L.)	1B-OF-3B	46	171	36	58	17	1	9	34	21	26	2-1	.339	.412	.608	3	.988
2000—	Charlotte (I.L.)	1B-OF-3B	120	445	75	125	29	1	32	91	53	107	2-3	.281	.356	.566	9	.987
—	Chicago (A.L.)	OF-1B	5	11	0	2	0	0	0	0	0	4	0-0	.182	.182	.182	1	.900
2001—	Charlotte (I.L.)	1B-3B	32	119	23	34	7	0	6	21	15	41	3-1	.286	.381	.496	3	.989
—	Chicago (A.L.)	OF-1B-3B-DH	83	254	36	65	13	0	18	39	20	69	0-1	.256	.313	.520	7	.964
2002—	Chicago (A.L.)	OF-1B-DH	76	204	28	47	8	0	7	26	19	60	0-0	.230	.295	.373	2	.992
Major League totals (4 years)			209	582	72	142	28	1	25	79	47	161	2-1	.244	.301	.424	10	.983

LIGTENBERG, KERRY — P — BRAVES

PERSONAL: Born May 11, 1971, in Rapid City, S.D. ... 6-2/215. ... Throws right, bats right. ... Full name: Kerry Dale Ligtenberg. ... Name pronounced Light-en-berg.
HIGH SCHOOL: Park (Cottage Grove, Minn.).
COLLEGE: Minnesota-Morris, then Minnesota.
TRANSACTIONS/CAREER NOTES: Signed by Minneapolis, North Central League (1994). ... Contract sold by Minneapolis to Seattle Mariners organization (March 28, 1995). ... Released by Mariners (April 2, 1995). ... Signed by Minneapolis, Prairie League (1995). ... Contract sold by Minneapolis to Atlanta Braves organization (January 27, 1996). ... On disabled list (April 3, 1999-entire season).
CAREER HITTING (MLB): 0-for-0 (.000), 0 R, 0 2B, 0 3B, 0 HR, 0 RBI.

Year	League	W	L	Pct.	ERA	G	GS	CG	ShO	Sv.-Opp.	IP	H	R	ER	HR	BB-IBB	SO
1994—	Minneapolis (NCL)■	5	5	.500	3.31	19	19	2	...	0-...	114.1	103	47	42	11	44-4	94
1995—	Minneapolis (PRA)■	11	2	.846	2.73	17	15	4	...	0-...	108.2	101	41	33	...	26-...	100
1996—	Durham (Caro.)■	7	4	.636	2.41	49	0	0	0	20-...	59.2	58	20	16	3	16-3	76
1997—	Greenville (Sou.)	3	1	.750	2.04	31	0	0	0	16-...	35.1	20	8	8	3	14-1	43
—	Richmond (I.L.)	0	3	.000	4.32	14	0	0	0	1-...	25.0	21	13	12	3	2-0	35
—	Atlanta (N.L.)	1	0	1.000	3.00	15	0	0	0	1-1	15.0	12	5	5	4	4-2	19
1998—	Atlanta (N.L.)	3	2	.600	2.71	75	0	0	0	30-34	73.0	51	24	22	6	24-1	79
1999—	Atlanta (N.L.)									Did not play.							
2000—	Atlanta (N.L.)	2	3	.400	3.61	59	0	0	0	12-14	52.1	43	21	21	7	24-5	51
—	Richmond (I.L.)	0	0	...	0.00	5	0	0	0	1-...	5.2	0	0	0	0	4-0	7
2001—	Atlanta (N.L.)	3	3	.500	3.02	53	0	0	0	1-2	59.2	50	22	20	4	30-8	56
—	Richmond (I.L.)	0	0	...	0.00	1	0	0	0	0-...	1.0	0	0	0	0	1-0	2
2002—	Atlanta (N.L.)	3	4	.429	2.97	52	0	0	0	0-0	66.2	52	23	22	6	33-3	51
Major League totals (5 years)		12	12	.500	3.04	254	0	0	0	44-51	266.2	208	95	90	27	115-19	256

DIVISION SERIES RECORD

Year	League	W	L	Pct.	ERA	G	GS	CG	ShO	Sv.-Opp.	IP	H	R	ER	HR	BB-IBB	SO
1998—	Atlanta (N.L.)	0	0	...	0.00	3	0	0	0	0-0	3.1	1	0	0	0	4-1	3
2000—	Atlanta (N.L.)	0	0	...	5.40	3	0	0	0	0-0	1.2	0	1	1	0	1-1	3
2001—	Atlanta (N.L.)									Did not play.							
2002—	Atlanta (N.L.)	0	0	...	0.00	1	0	0	0	0-0	2.0	0	0	0	0	0-0	1
Division series totals (3 years)		0	0	...	1.29	7	0	0	0	0-0	7.0	1	1	1	0	5-2	7

CHAMPIONSHIP SERIES RECORD

Year	League	W	L	Pct.	ERA	G	GS	CG	ShO	Sv.-Opp.	IP	H	R	ER	HR	BB-IBB	SO
1997—	Atlanta (N.L.)	0	0	...	0.00	2	0	0	0	0-0	3.0	1	0	0	0	0-0	4
1998—	Atlanta (N.L.)	0	1	.000	7.36	4	0	0	0	0-0	3.2	3	3	3	2	2-0	5
2001—	Atlanta (N.L.)	0	0	...	0.00	2	0	0	0	0-0	3.0	0	0	0	0	1-0	2
Champ. series totals (3 years)		0	1	.000	2.79	8	0	0	0	0-0	9.2	4	3	3	2	3-0	11

LILLY, TED — P — ATHLETICS

PERSONAL: Born January 4, 1976, in Lameta, Calif. ... 6-0/185. ... Throws left, bats left. ... Full name: Theodore Roosevelt Lilly.
HIGH SCHOOL: Yosemite (Oakhurst, Calif.).
JUNIOR COLLEGE: Fresno (Calif.) City College.
TRANSACTIONS/CAREER NOTES: Selected by Los Angeles Dodgers in 23rd round of free-agent draft (June 4, 1996). ... Traded by Dodgers with 2B Wilton Guerrero, OF Peter Bergeron and 1B Jonathan Tucker to Montreal Expos for P Carlos Perez, SS Mark Grudzielanek and IF Hiram Bocachica (July 31, 1998). ... On Ottawa disabled list (June 21, 1999-remainder of season). ... Traded by Expos to New York Yankees (March 17, 2000), as part of deal in which Yankees traded P Hideki Irabu to Expos for P Jake Westbrook and two players to be named later (December 29, 1999); Yankees acquired P Christian Parker to complete deal (March 22, 2000). ... On New York disabled list (April 2-May 23, 2000);

included rehabilitation assignments to Tampa (April 27-May 1) and Columbus (May 2-6 and May 20-23). ... On suspended list (August 11-17, 2001). ... Traded by Yankees with OF John-Ford Griffin and P Jason Arnold to Oakland Athletics as part of three-way deal in which Tigers acquired 1B Carlos Pena, P Franklyn German and a player to be named later from A's and Yankees acquired P Jeff Weaver from Tigers (July 5, 2002); Tigers acquired P Jeremy Bonderman to complete deal (August 22, 2002). ... On Oakland disabled list (July 23-September 10, 2002).
HONORS: Named California League Pitcher of the Year (1997).
STATISTICAL NOTES: Pitched 8-0 no-hit victory against Lake Elsinore (May 10, 1997). ... Tied for International League lead with four balks in 2000. ... Pitched 1-0 one-hit, complete-game loss against Seattle (April 27, 2002).
CAREER HITTING (MLB): 1-for-9 (.111), 0 R, 0 2B, 0 3B, 0 HR, 0 RBI.

Year League	W	L	Pct.	ERA	G	GS	CG	ShO	Sv.-Opp.	IP	H	R	ER	HR	BB-IBB	SO
1996—Yakima (N'West)	4	0	1.000	0.84	13	8	0	0	0-...	53.2	25	9	5	0	14-1	75
1997—San Bernardino (Calif.)	7	8	.467	*2.81	23	21	2	1	0-...	134.2	116	52	42	9	32-0	158
1998—San Antonio (Texas)	8	4	.667	3.30	17	17	0	0	0-...	111.2	114	50	41	8	37-0	96
—Albuquerque (PCL)	1	3	.250	4.94	5	5	0	0	0-...	31.0	39	20	17	3	9-0	25
—Ottawa (I.L.)■	2	2	.500	4.85	7	7	0	0	0-...	39.0	45	28	21	8	19-0	49
1999—Ottawa (I.L.)	8	5	.615	3.84	16	16	0	0	0-...	89.0	81	40	38	12	23-0	78
—Montreal (N.L.)	0	1	.000	7.61	9	3	0	0	0-0	23.2	30	20	20	7	9-0	28
2000—Tampa (FSL)■	0	0	...	1.35	1	1	0	0	0-...	6.2	5	3	1	0	1-0	6
—Columbus (I.L.)	8	11	.421	4.19	22	22	3	1	0-...	137.1	157	77	64	14	48-0	127
—New York (A.L.)	0	0	...	5.63	7	0	0	0	0-0	8.0	8	6	5	1	5-0	11
2001—Columbus (I.L.)	0	0	...	2.84	5	5	0	0	0-...	25.1	16	10	8	2	8-0	30
—New York (A.L.)	5	6	.455	5.37	26	21	0	0	0-0	120.2	126	81	72	20	51-1	112
2002—New York (A.L.)	3	6	.333	3.40	16	11	2	1	0-0	76.2	57	31	29	10	24-3	59
—Oakland (A.L.)■	2	1	.667	4.63	6	5	0	0	0-0	23.1	23	12	12	5	7-0	18
A.L. totals (3 years)	10	13	.435	4.64	55	37	2	1	0-0	228.2	214	130	118	36	87-4	200
N.L. totals (1 year)	0	1	.000	7.61	9	3	0	0	0-0	23.2	30	20	20	7	9-0	28
Major League totals (4 years)	10	14	.417	4.92	64	40	2	1	0-0	252.1	244	150	138	43	96-4	228

DIVISION SERIES RECORD

Year League	W	L	Pct.	ERA	G	GS	CG	ShO	Sv.-Opp.	IP	H	R	ER	HR	BB-IBB	SO
2002—Oakland (A.L.)	0	1	.000	13.50	2	0	0	0	0-1	4.0	10	6	6	1	1-0	3

LIMA, JOSE P

PERSONAL: Born September 30, 1972, in Santiago, Dominican Republic. ... 6-2/205. ... Throws right, bats right. ... Full name: Jose D. Lima. ... Name pronounced LEE-mah.
HIGH SCHOOL: Escuela Primaria Las Charcas (Santiago, Dominican Republic).
TRANSACTIONS/CAREER NOTES: Signed as non-drafted free agent by Detroit Tigers organization (July 5, 1989). ... Traded by Tigers with C Brad Ausmus, P C.J. Nitkowski, P Trever Miller and IF Daryle Ward to Houston Astros for OF Brian Hunter, IF Orlando Miller, P Doug Brocail, P Todd Jones and cash (December 10, 1996). ... On suspended list (May 9-15, 2001). ... Traded by Astros to Detroit Tigers for P Dave Mlicki (June 23, 2001). ... Released by Tigers (September 7, 2002).
RECORDS: Shares major league record for most home runs allowed in one inning—4 (April 27, 2000, first inning). ... Holds N.L. single-season record for most home runs allowed—48 (2000). ... Shares N.L. single-inning record for most consecutive home runs allowed—3 (September 17, 1999, fourth inning).
HONORS: Named righthanded pitcher on The Sporting News N.L. All-Star team (1999).
STATISTICAL NOTES: Led Eastern League with 13 balks in 1993. ... Pitched 3-0 no-hit victory for Toledo against Pawtucket (August 17, 1994).
MISCELLANEOUS: Appeared in one game as third baseman with no chances (1999).
CAREER HITTING (MLB): 27-for-234 (.115), 16 R, 4 2B, 0 3B, 0 HR, 8 RBI.

Year League	W	L	Pct.	ERA	G	GS	CG	ShO	Sv.-Opp.	IP	H	R	ER	HR	BB-IBB	SO
1990—Bristol (Appl.)	3	8	.273	5.02	14	12	1	0	1-...	75.1	89	49	42	9	22-3	64
1991—Lakeland (FSL)	0	1	.000	10.38	4	1	0	0	0-...	8.2	16	10	10	1	2-0	5
—Fayetteville (S.Atl.)	1	3	.250	4.97	18	7	0	0	0-...	58.0	53	38	32	4	25-0	60
1992—Lakeland (FSL)	5	11	.313	3.16	25	25	5	2	0-...	151.0	132	57	53	*14	21-2	137
1993—London (East.)	8	•13	.381	4.07	27	27	2	0	0-...	177.0	160	96	80	19	59-4	138
1994—Toledo (I.L.)	7	9	.438	3.60	23	22	3	2	0-...	142.1	124	70	57	16	48-1	117
—Detroit (A.L.)	0	1	.000	13.50	3	1	0	0	0-0	6.2	11	10	10	2	3-1	7
1995—Lakeland (FSL)	3	1	.750	2.57	4	4	0	0	0-...	21.0	23	11	6	2	0-0	20
—Toledo (I.L.)	5	3	.625	3.01	11	11	1	0	0-...	74.2	69	26	25	9	14-2	40
—Detroit (A.L.)	3	9	.250	6.11	15	15	0	0	0-0	73.2	85	52	50	10	18-4	37
1996—Toledo (I.L.)	5	4	.556	6.78	12	12	0	0	0-...	69.0	93	53	52	11	12-0	57
—Detroit (A.L.)	5	6	.455	5.70	39	4	0	0	3-7	72.2	87	48	46	13	22-4	59
1997—Houston (N.L.)■	1	6	.143	5.28	52	1	0	0	2-2	75.0	79	45	44	9	16-2	63
1998—Houston (N.L.)	16	8	.667	3.70	33	33	3	1	0-0	233.1	229	100	96	34	32-1	169
1999—Houston (N.L.)	21	10	.677	3.58	35	•35	3	0	0-0	246.1	256	108	98	30	44-2	187
2000—Houston (N.L.)	7	16	.304	6.65	33	33	0	0	0-0	196.1	251	*152	*145	*48	68-3	124
2001—Houston (N.L.)	1	2	.333	7.30	14	9	0	0	0-0	53.0	77	48	43	12	16-1	41
—Detroit (A.L.)■	5	10	.333	4.71	18	18	2	0	0-0	112.2	120	66	59	23	22-2	43
2002—Detroit (A.L.)	4	6	.400	7.77	20	12	0	0	0-0	68.1	86	60	59	12	21-0	33
A.L. totals (5 years)	17	32	.347	6.04	95	50	2	0	3-7	334.0	389	236	224	60	86-11	179
N.L. totals (5 years)	46	42	.523	4.77	167	111	6	1	2-2	804.0	892	453	426	133	176-9	584
Major League totals (9 years)	63	74	.460	5.14	262	161	8	1	5-9	1138.0	1281	689	650	193	262-20	763

DIVISION SERIES RECORD

Year League	W	L	Pct.	ERA	G	GS	CG	ShO	Sv.-Opp.	IP	H	R	ER	HR	BB-IBB	SO
1997—Houston (N.L.)	0	0	...	0.00	1	0	0	0	0-0	1.0	0	0	0	0	1-0	1
1998—Houston (N.L.)									Did not play.							
1999—Houston (N.L.)	0	1	.000	5.40	1	1	0	0	0-0	6.2	9	4	4	0	2-2	4
Division series totals (2 years)	0	1	.000	4.70	2	1	0	0	0-0	7.2	9	4	4	0	3-2	5

ALL-STAR GAME RECORD

	W	L	Pct.	ERA	GS	CG	ShO	Sv.-Opp.	IP	H	R	ER	HR	BB-IBB	SO
All-Star Game totals (1 year)	0	0	...	0.00	0	0	0	0-0	1.0	1	0	0	0	0-0	0

LINCOLN, MIKE — P — PIRATES

PERSONAL: Born April 10, 1975, in Carmichael, Calif. ... 6-2/203. ... Throws right, bats right. ... Full name: Michael George Lincoln.
HIGH SCHOOL: Casa Roble (Orangevale, Calif.).
JUNIOR COLLEGE: American River College (Calif.).
COLLEGE: Tennessee.
TRANSACTIONS/CAREER NOTES: Selected by Minnesota Twins organization in 13th round of free-agent draft (June 4, 1996). ... On Minnesota disabled list (July 23, 2000-remainder of season). ... Released by Twins (January 15, 2001). ... Signed by Pittsburgh Pirates organization (February 17, 2001). ... On Pittsburgh disabled list (August 13-28, 2001).
CAREER HITTING (MLB): 1-for-10 (.100), 0 R, 0 2B, 0 3B, 0 HR, 0 RBI.

Year League	W	L	Pct.	ERA	G	GS	CG	ShO	Sv.-Opp.	IP	H	R	ER	HR	BB-IBB	SO
1996— Fort Myers (FSL)	5	2	.714	4.07	12	11	0	0	0-...	59.2	64	31	27	5	25-0	24
1997— Fort Myers (FSL)	13	4	.765	2.28	20	20	1	1	0-...	134.0	130	41	34	4	25-0	75
1998— New Britain (East.)	*15	7	.682	3.22	26	26	1	0	0-...	173.1	180	80	62	13	35-0	109
1999— Minnesota (A.L.)	3	10	.231	6.84	18	15	0	0	0-0	76.1	102	59	58	11	26-0	27
— Salt Lake (PCL)	5	2	.714	7.78	9	9	0	0	0-...	59.0	82	52	51	12	21-0	39
2000— Salt Lake (PCL)	4	1	.800	3.87	12	12	2	1	0-...	74.1	72	35	32	4	16-1	37
— Minnesota (A.L.)	0	3	.000	10.89	8	4	0	0	0-0	20.2	36	25	25	10	13-0	15
2001— Nashville (PCL)■	5	4	.556	3.44	18	13	1	0	0-...	91.2	90	39	35	10	25-0	71
— Pittsburgh (N.L.)	2	1	.667	2.68	31	0	0	0	0-2	40.1	34	16	12	3	11-0	24
2002— Pittsburgh (N.L.)	2	4	.333	3.11	55	0	0	0	0-3	72.1	80	28	25	7	27-8	50
— Nashville (PCL)	0	0	...	1.23	10	0	0	0	2-...	14.2	14	2	2	0	2-0	15
A.L. totals (2 years)	3	13	.188	7.70	26	19	0	0	0-0	97.0	138	84	83	21	39-0	42
N.L. totals (2 years)	4	5	.444	2.96	86	0	0	0	0-5	112.2	114	44	37	10	38-8	74
Major League totals (4 years)	7	18	.280	5.15	112	19	0	0	0-5	209.2	252	128	120	31	77-8	116

LINEBRINK, SCOTT — P — ASTROS

PERSONAL: Born August 4, 1976, in Austin, Texas. ... 6-2/200. ... Throws right, bats right. ... Full name: Scott Cameron Linebrink.
HIGH SCHOOL: McNeil (Austin, Texas).
COLLEGE: Concordia, then Southwest Texas State.
TRANSACTIONS/CAREER NOTES: Selected by San Francisco Giants organization in second round of free-agent draft (June 3, 1997). ... On disabled list (April 8-July 17, 1999). ... Traded by Giants to Houston Astros for P Doug Henry (July 30, 2000). ... On Houston disabled list (May 20-June 17, 2002); included rehabilitation assignment to New Orleans (June 11-14) and Round Rock (June 15-17).
CAREER HITTING (MLB): 1-for-1 (1.000), 0 R, 0 2B, 0 3B, 0 HR, 0 RBI.

Year League	W	L	Pct.	ERA	G	GS	CG	ShO	Sv.-Opp.	IP	H	R	ER	HR	BB-IBB	SO
1997— Salem-Kaizer (N'West)	0	0	...	4.50	3	3	0	0	0-...	10.0	7	5	5	1	6-0	6
— San Jose (Calif.)	2	1	.667	3.18	6	6	0	0	0-...	28.1	29	11	10	2	10-0	40
1998— Shreveport (Texas)	10	8	.556	5.02	21	21	0	0	0-...	113.0	101	66	63	12	58-1	128
1999— Shreveport (Texas)	1	8	.111	6.44	10	10	0	0	0-...	43.1	48	31	31	7	14-0	33
2000— Fresno (PCL)	1	4	.200	5.23	28	7	0	0	4-...	62.0	54	42	36	10	12-0	49
— San Francisco (N.L.)	0	0	...	11.57	3	0	0	0	0-0	2.1	7	3	3	1	2-0	0
— Houston (N.L.)■	0	0	...	4.66	8	0	0	0	0-0	9.2	11	5	5	3	6-0	6
— New Orleans (PCL)	2	0	1.000	1.80	11	0	0	0	1-...	15.0	15	4	3	0	7-0	22
2001— Houston (N.L.)	0	0	...	2.61	9	0	0	0	0-0	10.1	6	4	3	0	6-0	9
— New Orleans (PCL)	7	6	.538	3.50	50	0	0	0	8-...	72.0	52	28	28	4	24-6	72
2002— Houston (N.L.)	0	0	...	7.03	22	0	0	0	0-0	24.1	31	21	19	2	13-4	24
— New Orleans (PCL)	1	1	.500	6.00	13	0	0	0	0-...	15.0	17	11	10	1	11-3	16
— Round Rock (Texas)	0	0	...	0.00	2	2	0	0	0-...	2.0	2	0	0	0	2-0	1
Major League totals (3 years)	0	0	...	5.79	42	0	0	0	0-0	46.2	55	33	30	6	27-4	39

LITTLE, MARK — OF — DIAMONDBACKS

PERSONAL: Born July 11, 1972, in Edwardsville, Ill. ... 6-0/195. ... Bats right, throws right. ... Full name: Mark Travis Little.
HIGH SCHOOL: Edwardsville (Ill.).
COLLEGE: Memphis.
TRANSACTIONS/CAREER NOTES: Selected by Texas Rangers organization in eighth round of free-agent draft (June 2, 1994). ... On disabled list (August 5-September 5, 1996). ... On Oklahoma disabled list (June 23-July 25, 1998). ... Traded by Rangers to St. Louis Cardinals (August 9, 1998), completing deal in which Cardinals traded P Todd Stottlemyre and SS Royce Clayton to Rangers for P Darren Oliver, 3B Fernando Tatis and a player to be named later (July 31, 1998). ... On Memphis disabled list (April 8-June 9 and June 19-29, 1999). ... On Memphis disabled ist (May 18-June 14, 2000). ... Granted free agency (October 18, 2000). ... Signed by Colorado Rockies organization (November 21, 2000). ... On Colorado disabled list (May 29-August 5 and August 25, 2001-remainder of season); included rehabilitation assignment to Colorado Springs (July 24-August 5). ... Traded by Rockies with P John Thomson to New York Mets for OF Jay Payton, P Mark Corey and OF Robert Stratton (July 31, 2002). ... Traded by Mets to Arizona Diamondbacks for a player to be named later (August 16, 2002); Mets acquired P P.J. Bevis to complete deal (August 20, 2002).
STATISTICAL NOTES: Led American Association outfielders with 280 putouts and 297 total chances in 1997.
2002 GAMES PLAYED BY POSITION (MLB): OF—49.

		BATTING														FIELDING	
Year Team (League)	Pos.	G	AB	R	H	2B	3B	HR	RBI	BB	SO	SB-CS	Avg.	OBP	SLG	E	Avg.
1994— Hudson Valley (NY-P)	OF	54	208	33	61	15	5	3	27	22	38	14-5	.293	.357	.457	6	.959
1995— Charlotte (FSL)	OF	115	438	75	112	31	8	9	50	51	108	20-14	.256	.350	.425	10	.966
1996— Tulsa (Texas)	OF	101	409	69	119	24	2	13	50	48	88	22-10	.291	.377	.455	9	.968
1997— Oklahoma City (A.A.)	OF-DH-1B	121	415	72	109	23	4	15	45	39	100	21-9	.263	.338	.446	8	.973
1998— Oklahoma (PCL)	OF-DH	69	274	58	81	20	4	8	46	16	60	9-6	.296	.351	.485	1	.994
— Memphis (PCL)■	OF	19	63	9	17	3	3	0	6	6	10	0-3	.270	.342	.413	1	.971
— St. Louis (N.L.)	OF	7	12	0	1	0	0	0	0	2	5	1-0	.083	.214	.083	0	1.000
1999— Memphis (PCL)	OF	51	196	40	58	11	5	3	22	10	48	12-4	.296	.347	.449	5	.960

Year	Team (League)	Pos.	G	AB	R	H	2B	3B	HR	RBI	BB	SO	SB-CS	Avg.	OBP	SLG	E	Avg.
							BATTING										FIELDING	
2000—	Memphis (PCL)	OF	107	424	70	120	29	7	15	64	51	98	22-11	.283	.373	.491	7	.974
2001—	Colorado (N.L.)■	OF	51	85	18	29	6	0	3	13	1	20	5-2	.341	.378	.518	0	1.000
—	Colo. Springs (PCL)	OF	9	40	6	15	2	0	0	4	3	9	0-2	.375	.432	.425	0	1.000
2002—	Colorado (N.L.)	OF	61	105	20	21	5	2	0	5	13	28	2-1	.200	.311	.286	2	.970
—	New York (N.L.)■	OF	3	3	0	0	0	0	0	0	0	1	0-1	.000	.000	.000	0	...
—	Norfolk (I.L.)	OF	2	10	1	5	0	0	0	2	1	3	0-0	.500	.545	.500	0	1.000
—	Tucson (PCL)■	OF	13	54	6	17	3	1	2	8	0	11	2-1	.315	.304	.519	1	.976
—	Arizona (N.L.)	OF	15	22	8	6	0	1	0	2	2	5	0-0	.273	.429	.364	0	1.000
Major League totals (3 years)			137	227	46	57	11	3	3	20	18	59	8-4	.251	.339	.366	2	.985

DIVISION SERIES RECORD

Year	Team (League)	Pos.	G	AB	R	H	2B	3B	HR	RBI	BB	SO	SB-CS	Avg.	OBP	SLG	E	Avg.
							BATTING										FIELDING	
2002—	Arizona (N.L.)	OF	2	4	0	0	0	0	0	0	0	2	0-0	.000	.000	.000	0	1.000

LLOYD, GRAEME — P

PERSONAL: Born April 9, 1967, in Geelong, Victoria, Australia. ... 6-7/225. ... Throws left, bats left. ... Full name: Graeme John Lloyd. ... Name pronounced GRAM.

HIGH SCHOOL: Geelong Technical School (Victoria, Australia).

COLLEGE: Geelong Tech.

TRANSACTIONS/CAREER NOTES: Signed as non-drafted free agent by Toronto Blue Jays organization (January 26, 1988). ... On Myrtle Beach disabled list (June 29-September 1, 1989). ... Selected by Philadelphia Phillies from Blue Jays organization in Rule 5 major league draft (December 7, 1992). ... Traded by Phillies to Milwaukee Brewers for P John Trisler (December 8, 1992). ... On disabled list (August 20-September 4, 1993; and July 25-September 10, 1995). ... On suspended list (September 5-9, 1993). ... Traded by Brewers with OF Pat Listach to New York Yankees for OF Gerald Williams and P Bob Wickman (August 23, 1996). ... On disabled list (April 22-May 8, 1998). ... On suspended list (May 25-27, 1998). ... Traded by Yankees with P David Wells and 2B Homer Bush to Toronto Blue Jays for P Roger Clemens (February 18, 1999). ... Granted free agency (October 29, 1999). ... Signed by Montreal Expos (December 20, 1999). ... On disabled list (March 29, 2000-entire season). ... Traded by Expos with P Carl Pavano, IF Mike Mordecai and P Justin Wayne to Florida Marlins for OF Cliff Floyd, P Claudio Vargas, 2B/OF Wilton Guerrero, cash considerations and a player to be named later (July 11, 2002); Expos acquired P Don Levinski to complete deal (August 6, 2002). ... Granted free agency (October 30, 2002).

CAREER HITTING (MLB): 0-for-6 (.000), 0 R, 0 2B, 0 3B, 0 HR, 0 RBI.

Year	League	W	L	Pct.	ERA	G	GS	CG	ShO	Sv.-Opp.	IP	H	R	ER	HR	BB-IBB	SO
1988—	Myrtle Beach (S.Atl.)	3	2	.600	3.62	41	0	0	0	2-...	59.2	71	33	24	2	30-5	43
1989—	Dunedin (FSL)	0	0	...	10.13	2	0	0	0	0-...	2.2	6	3	3	0	1-0	0
—	Myrtle Beach (S.Atl.)	0	0	...	5.40	1	1	0	0	0-...	5.0	5	4	3	1	0-0	3
1990—	Myrtle Beach (S.Atl.)	5	2	.714	2.72	19	6	0	0	6-...	49.2	51	20	15	3	16-1	42
1991—	Dunedin (FSL)	2	5	.286	2.24	50	0	0	0	24-...	60.1	54	17	15	1	25-2	39
—	Knoxville (Sou.)	0	0	...	0.00	2	0	0	0	0-...	1.2	1	0	0	0	1-0	2
1992—	Knoxville (Sou.)	4	8	.333	1.96	49	7	1	0	14-...	92.0	79	30	20	2	25-2	65
1993—	Milwaukee (A.L.)■	3	4	.429	2.83	55	0	0	0	0-4	63.2	64	24	20	5	13-3	31
1994—	Milwaukee (A.L.)	2	3	.400	5.17	43	0	0	0	3-6	47.0	49	28	27	4	15-6	31
1995—	Milwaukee (A.L.)	0	5	.000	4.50	33	0	0	0	4-6	32.0	28	16	16	4	8-2	13
1996—	Milwaukee (A.L.)	2	4	.333	2.82	52	0	0	0	0-3	51.0	49	19	16	3	17-3	24
—	New York (A.L.)■	0	2	.000	17.47	13	0	0	0	0-2	5.2	12	11	11	1	5-1	6
1997—	New York (A.L.)	1	1	.500	3.31	46	0	0	0	1-1	49.0	55	24	18	6	20-7	26
1998—	New York (A.L.)	3	0	1.000	1.67	50	0	0	0	0-2	37.2	26	10	7	3	6-2	20
1999—	Toronto (A.L.)■	5	3	.625	3.63	74	0	0	0	3-9	72.0	68	36	29	11	23-4	47
2000—	Montreal (N.L.)■									Did not play.							
2001—	Montreal (N.L.)	9	5	.643	4.35	84	0	0	0	1-3	70.1	74	38	34	6	21-2	44
2002—	Montreal (N.L.)	2	3	.400	5.87	41	0	0	0	5-7	30.2	41	21	20	5	8-3	17
—	Florida (N.L.)■	2	2	.500	4.44	25	0	0	0	0-1	26.1	26	13	13	1	11-1	20
A.L. totals (7 years)		16	22	.421	3.62	366	0	0	0	11-33	358.0	351	168	144	37	107-28	198
N.L. totals (2 years)		13	10	.565	4.74	150	0	0	0	6-11	127.1	141	72	67	12	40-6	81
Major League totals (9 years)		29	32	.475	3.91	516	0	0	0	17-44	485.1	492	240	211	49	147-34	279

DIVISION SERIES RECORD

Year	League	W	L	Pct.	ERA	G	GS	CG	ShO	Sv.-Opp.	IP	H	R	ER	HR	BB-IBB	SO
1996—	New York (A.L.)	0	0	...	0.00	2	0	0	0	0-0	1.0	1	0	0	0	0-0	0
1997—	New York (A.L.)	0	0	...	0.00	2	0	0	0	0-0	1.1	0	0	0	0	0-0	1
1998—	New York (A.L.)	0	0	...	0.00	1	0	0	0	0-0	.1	0	0	0	0	0-0	0
Division series totals (3 years)		0	0	...	0.00	5	0	0	0	0-0	2.2	1	0	0	0	0-0	1

CHAMPIONSHIP SERIES RECORD

Year	League	W	L	Pct.	ERA	G	GS	CG	ShO	Sv.-Opp.	IP	H	R	ER	HR	BB-IBB	SO
1996—	New York (A.L.)	0	0	...	0.00	2	0	0	0	0-0	1.2	0	0	0	0	0-0	1
1998—	New York (A.L.)	0	0	...	0.00	1	0	0	0	0-0	.2	1	0	0	0	0-0	0
Champ. series totals (2 years)		0	0	...	0.00	3	0	0	0	0-0	2.1	1	0	0	0	0-0	1

WORLD SERIES RECORD

NOTES: Member of World Series championship team (1996 and 1998).

Year	League	W	L	Pct.	ERA	G	GS	CG	ShO	Sv.-Opp.	IP	H	R	ER	HR	BB-IBB	SO
1996—	New York (A.L.)	1	0	1.000	0.00	4	0	0	0	0-0	2.2	0	0	0	0	0-0	4
1998—	New York (A.L.)	0	0	...	0.00	1	0	0	0	0-0	.1	0	0	0	0	0-0	0
World Series totals (2 years)		1	0	1.000	0.00	5	0	0	0	0-0	3.0	0	0	0	0	0-0	4

LOAIZA, ESTEBAN — P

PERSONAL: Born December 31, 1971, in Tijuana, Mexico. ... 6-3/205. ... Throws right, bats right. ... Full name: Esteban Antonio Veyna Loaiza. ... Name pronounced low-EYE-zah.

HIGH SCHOOL: Mar Vista (Imperial Beach, Calif.).

TRANSACTIONS/CAREER NOTES: Signed as non-drafted free agent by Pittsburgh Pirates organization (March 21, 1991). ... Loaned by Pirates organization to Mexico City Red Devils, Mexican League (May 7-28, 1993). ... On disabled list (April 7-28 and July 7-14, 1994). ... Loaned to Red Devils, Mexican League (June 19-August 14, 1996). ... Traded by Pirates to Texas Rangers for P Todd Van Poppel and 2B Warren Morris (July 17, 1998). ... On Texas disabled list (May 12-July 5, 1999); included rehabilitation assignment to Oklahoma City (June 26-July 5). ... Traded by Rangers to Toronto Blue Jays for P Darwin Cubillan and 2B/SS Mike Young (July 19, 2000). ... On Toronto disabled list (March 22-May 14, 2002); included rehabilitation assignment to Dunedin (April 19-28), Syracuse (April 29-May 3) and Tennessee (May 4-14). ... Granted free agency (October 29, 2002).
MISCELLANEOUS: Made an out in only appearance as pinch hitter (1995). ... Had a sacrifice hit in only appearance as pinch hitter (1996).
CAREER HITTING (MLB): 30-for-169 (.178), 11 R, 2 2B, 1 3B, 0 HR, 11 RBI.

Year League	W	L	Pct.	ERA	G	GS	CG	ShO	Sv.-Opp.	IP	H	R	ER	HR	BB-IBB	SO
1991—Gulf Coast Pirates (GCL)..	5	1	.833	2.26	11	11	1	•1	0-...	51.2	48	17	13	0	14-0	41
1992—Augusta (S.Atl.)...............	10	8	.556	3.89	26	25	3	0	0-...	143.1	134	72	62	7	60-0	123
1993—Salem (Caro.)..................	6	7	.462	3.39	17	17	3	0	0-...	109.0	113	53	41	7	30-0	61
—MC Red Devils (Mex.)■...	1	1	.500	5.18	4	3	0	0	0-...	24.1	32	18	14	3	4-1	15
—Carolina (Sou.)■............	2	1	.667	3.77	7	7	1	0	0-...	43.0	39	18	18	5	12-1	40
1994—Carolina (Sou.)................	10	5	.667	3.79	24	24	3	0	0-...	154.1	169	69	65	15	30-0	115
1995—Pittsburgh (N.L.).............	8	9	.471	5.16	32	•31	1	0	0-0	172.2	205	*115	*99	21	55-3	85
1996—Calgary (PCL)..................	3	4	.429	4.02	12	11	1	1	0-...	69.1	61	34	31	5	25-2	38
—Pittsburgh (N.L.).............	2	3	.400	4.96	10	10	1	1	0-0	52.2	65	32	29	11	19-2	32
—MC Red Devils (Mex.)■...	2	0	1.000	2.43	5	5	0	0	0-...	33.1	28	12	9	1	14-0	16
1997—Pittsburgh (N.L.)■..........	11	11	.500	4.13	33	32	1	0	0-0	196.1	214	99	90	17	56-9	122
1998—Pittsburgh (N.L.).............	6	5	.545	4.52	21	14	0	0	0-1	91.2	96	50	46	13	30-1	53
—Texas (A.L.)■..................	3	6	.333	5.90	14	14	1	0	0-0	79.1	103	57	52	15	22-3	55
1999—Texas (A.L.).....................	9	5	.643	4.56	30	15	0	0	0-0	120.1	128	65	61	10	40-2	77
—Oklahoma (PCL)..............	0	0	...	0.00	2	2	0	0	0-...	4.1	3	0	0	0	3-0	6
2000—Texas (A.L.).....................	5	6	.455	5.37	20	17	0	0	1-1	107.1	133	67	64	21	31-1	75
—Toronto (A.L.)■...............	5	7	.417	3.62	14	14	1	1	0-0	92.0	95	45	37	8	26-0	62
2001—Toronto (A.L.)..................	11	11	.500	5.02	36	30	1	1	0-0	190.0	239	113	106	27	40-1	110
2002—Dunedin (FSL)..................	0	0	...	0.00	2	2	0	0	0-...	5.0	2	0	0	0	2-0	2
—Syracuse (I.L.).................	0	0	...	2.08	1	1	0	0	0-...	4.1	4	1	1	0	0-0	4
—Tennessee (Sou.)............	2	0	1.000	1.88	2	2	0	0	0-...	14.1	10	3	3	0	1-0	13
—Toronto (A.L.)..................	9	10	.474	5.71	25	25	3	1	0-0	151.1	192	102	96	18	38-3	87
A.L. totals (5 years)..................	42	45	.483	5.06	139	115	6	3	1-1	740.1	890	449	416	99	197-10	466
N.L. totals (4 years)..................	27	28	.491	4.63	96	87	3	1	0-1	513.1	580	296	264	62	160-15	292
Major League totals (8 years).....	69	73	.486	4.88	235	202	9	4	1-2	1253.2	1470	745	680	161	357-25	758

DIVISION SERIES RECORD

Year League	W	L	Pct.	ERA	G	GS	CG	ShO	Sv.-Opp.	IP	H	R	ER	HR	BB-IBB	SO
1998—Texas (A.L.).......................									Did not play.							
1999—Texas (A.L.).......................	0	1	.000	3.86	1	1	0	0	0-0	7.0	5	3	3	1	1-0	4

LOCKHART, KEITH — 2B

PERSONAL: Born November 10, 1964, in Whittier, Calif. ... 5-10/170. ... Bats left, throws right. ... Full name: Keith Virgil Lockhart.
HIGH SCHOOL: Northview (Covina, Calif.).
JUNIOR COLLEGE: Mount San Antonio College (Calif.).
COLLEGE: Oral Roberts.
TRANSACTIONS/CAREER NOTES: Selected by Cincinnati Reds organization in 11th round of free-agent draft (June 2, 1986). ... Contract sold by Reds to Oakland Athletics organization (February 4, 1992). ... Granted free agency (October 15, 1992). ... Signed by St. Louis Cardinals organization (December 12, 1992). ... Granted free agency (October 15, 1993). ... Signed by San Diego Padres organization (January 7, 1994). ... Granted free agency (October 15, 1994). ... Signed by Kansas City Royals organization (November 14, 1994). ... Traded by Royals with OF Michael Tucker to Atlanta Braves for OF Jermaine Dye and P Jamie Walker (March 27, 1997). ... On disabled list (August 6-22, 1997). ... Granted free agency (November 5, 2001). ... Re-signed by Braves organization (January 8, 2002). ... Granted free agency (October 30, 2002).
STATISTICAL NOTES: Led Midwest League third basemen with 33 double plays in 1987. ... Led Southern League with 11 sacrifice flies in 1988. ... Led American Association second basemen with 279 putouts, 335 assists and 631 total chances in 1989. ... Career major league grand slams: 1.
2002 GAMES PLAYED BY POSITION (MLB): 2B—89; 3B—1.

					BATTING											FIELDING	
Year Team (League)	Pos.	G	AB	R	H	2B	3B	HR	RBI	BB	SO	SB-CS	Avg.	OBP	SLG	E	Avg.
1986—Billings (Pio.)............	2B-3B	53	202	51	70	11	3	7	31	35	22	4-2	.347	.447	.535	17	.931
—Cedar Rapids (Midw.)	2B-3B	13	42	4	8	2	0	0	1	6	6	1-1	.190	.306	.238	0	1.000
1987—Cedar Rapids (Midw.)	3B-2B	*140	511	101	160	37	5	23	84	86	70	20-8	.313	.420	.540	28	.931
1988—Chattanooga (Sou.)....	3B-2B	139	515	74	137	27	3	12	67	61	59	7-5	.266	.343	.400	36	.922
1989—Nashville (A.A.)..........	2B	131	479	77	128	21	6	14	58	61	41	4-3	.267	.355	.424	17	.973
1990—Nashville (A.A.)..........	2B-3B-OF	126	431	48	112	25	4	9	63	51	74	8-7	.260	.342	.399	9	.979
1991—Nashville (A.A.)..........	3B-2B-OF	116	411	53	107	25	3	8	36	24	64	3-7	.260	.304	.394	13	.968
1992—Tacoma (PCL)■..........	2B-3B-SS	107	363	44	101	25	3	5	37	29	21	5-3	.278	.334	.405	11	.976
1993—Louisville (A.A.)■.......3B-2B-OF-1B		132	467	66	140	24	3	13	68	60	43	3-3	.300	.383	.448	12	.971
1994—San Diego (N.L.)■.....3B-2B-SS-OF		27	43	4	9	0	0	2	6	4	10	1-0	.209	.286	.349	1	.969
—Las Vegas (PCL)........O-S-2-3-P-C		89	331	61	106	15	5	7	43	26	37	3-4	.320	.369	.459	10	.962
1995—Omaha (A.A.)■..........	3B-DH	44	148	24	56	7	1	5	19	16	10	1-3	.378	.442	.541	8	.928
—Kansas City (A.L.)......	2B-3B-DH	94	274	41	88	19	3	6	33	14	21	8-1	.321	.355	.478	8	.973
1996—Kansas City (A.L.)......	2B-3B-DH	138	433	49	118	33	3	7	55	30	40	11-6	.273	.319	.411	13	.970
1997—Atlanta (N.L.)■..........	2B-3B-DH	96	147	25	41	5	3	6	32	14	17	0-0	.279	.337	.476	3	.960
1998—Atlanta (N.L.).............	2B-DH-3B	109	366	50	94	21	0	9	37	29	37	2-2	.257	.311	.388	6	.984
1999—Atlanta (N.L.).............	2B-3B-DH	108	161	20	42	3	1	1	21	19	21	3-1	.261	.337	.311	1	.989
2000—Atlanta (N.L.).............	2B-3B	113	275	32	73	12	3	2	32	29	31	4-1	.265	.331	.353	8	.975
2001—Atlanta (N.L.).............	2B-3B	104	178	17	39	6	0	3	12	16	22	1-2	.219	.289	.303	0	1.000
2002—Atlanta (N.L.).............	2B-3B	128	296	34	64	13	3	5	32	27	50	0-1	.216	.282	.331	8	.979
American League totals (2 years)		232	707	90	206	52	6	13	88	44	61	19-7	.291	.333	.437	21	.971
National League totals (7 years)		685	1466	182	362	60	10	28	172	138	188	11-7	.247	.311	.359	27	.981
Major League totals (9 years)		917	2173	272	568	112	16	41	260	182	249	30-14	.261	.318	.384	48	.978

DIVISION SERIES RECORD

			BATTING														FIELDING	
Year	Team (League)	Pos.	G	AB	R	H	2B	3B	HR	RBI	BB	SO	SB-CS	Avg.	OBP	SLG	E	Avg.
1997—	Atlanta (N.L.).............	2B	2	6	0	0	0	0	0	0	0	1	0-0	.000	.000	.000	1	.900
1998—	Atlanta (N.L.).............	2B	3	12	2	4	0	0	0	0	1	0	0-0	.333	.385	.333	0	1.000
1999—	Atlanta (N.L.).............	PH-2B	3	1	0	0	0	0	0	0	0	1	0-0	.000	.000	.000	0	...
2000—	Atlanta (N.L.).............	2B	3	8	0	1	0	0	0	0	0	1	0-0	.125	.125	.125	0	1.000
2001—	Atlanta (N.L.).............	PH-2B	1	2	1	1	1	0	0	0	0	0	0-0	.500	.500	1.000	0	1.000
2002—	Atlanta (N.L.).............	2B	5	12	1	4	0	0	1	4	2	4	0-0	.333	.467	.583	0	1.000
Division series totals (6 years)			17	41	4	10	1	0	1	4	3	7	0-0	.244	.311	.341	1	.981

CHAMPIONSHIP SERIES RECORD

			BATTING														FIELDING	
Year	Team (League)	Pos.	G	AB	R	H	2B	3B	HR	RBI	BB	SO	SB-CS	Avg.	OBP	SLG	E	Avg.
1997—	Atlanta (N.L.).............	2B-PH	5	16	4	8	1	1	0	3	1	1	0-0	.500	.556	.688	0	1.000
1998—	Atlanta (N.L.).............	2B-PH	6	17	2	4	1	1	0	0	0	4	0-0	.235	.235	.412	0	1.000
1999—	Atlanta (N.L.).............	PH-2B	3	5	0	2	0	1	0	1	0	2	0-0	.400	.400	.800	0	1.000
2001—	Atlanta (N.L.).............	PH	2	1	0	0	0	0	0	0	1	0	0-0	.000	.500	.000	...	...
Championship series totals (4 years)			16	39	6	14	2	3	0	4	2	7	0-0	.359	.405	.564	0	1.000

WORLD SERIES RECORD

			BATTING														FIELDING	
Year	Team (League)	Pos.	G	AB	R	H	2B	3B	HR	RBI	BB	SO	SB-CS	Avg.	OBP	SLG	E	Avg.
1999—	Atlanta (N.L.).............	PH-2B-DH	4	7	1	1	0	0	0	0	2	0	0-0	.143	.333	.143	0	1.000

RECORD AS PITCHER

Year	League	W	L	Pct.	ERA	G	GS	CG	ShO	Sv.-Opp.	IP	H	R	ER	HR	BB-IBB	SO
1994—	Las Vegas (PCL)	0	0	...	0.00	1	1	0	0	0-...	1.0	0	0	0	0	0-0	0

LoDUCA, PAUL — C — DODGERS

PERSONAL: Born April 12, 1972, in Brooklyn, N.Y. ... 5-10/185. ... Bats right, throws right. ... Full name: Paul Anthony LoDuca.
HIGH SCHOOL: Apollo (Phoenix).
JUNIOR COLLEGE: Glendale (Ariz.) Community College.
COLLEGE: Arizona State.
TRANSACTIONS/CAREER NOTES: Selected by Los Angeles Dodgers organization in 25th round of free-agent draft (June 3, 1993). ... On Albuquerque disabled list (June 4-July 20, 1999). ... On Los Angeles disabled list (April 29-May 21, 2001); included rehabilitation assignment to Las Vegas (May 18-21).
STATISTICAL NOTES: Led Florida State League catchers with 17 errors in 1996. ... Led Texas League catchers with .990 fielding percentage, 84 assists and 667 total chances in 1997. ... Led Pacific Coast League in grounding into double plays with 20 in 1998. ... Collected six hits in one game (May 28, 2001). ... Led N.L. catchers with 965 putouts, 76 assists and 1,049 total chances in 2002.
2002 GAMES PLAYED BY POSITION (MLB): C—137; 1B—18; OF—9.

			BATTING														FIELDING	
Year	Team (League)	Pos.	G	AB	R	H	2B	3B	HR	RBI	BB	SO	SB-CS	Avg.	OBP	SLG	E	Avg.
1993—	Vero Beach (FSL).......	C	39	134	17	42	6	0	0	13	13	22	0-0	.313	.380	.358	2	.992
1994—	Bakersfield (Calif.)......	1B-C	123	455	65	144	32	1	6	68	52	49	16-9	.316	.387	.431	5	.993
1995—	San Antonio (Texas)...	C-1B-3B	61	199	27	49	8	0	1	8	26	25	5-5	.246	.339	.302	11	.973
1996—	Vero Beach (FSL).......	C-1B-3B	124	439	54	134	22	0	3	66	70	38	8-2	.305	*.400	.376	†18	.980
1997—	San Antonio (Texas)...	C-1B	105	385	63	126	28	2	7	69	46	27	16-8	.327	.399	.465	7	†.990
1998—	Albuquerque (PCL).....	C-1B-3B	126	451	69	144	30	3	8	58	59	40	19-7	.319	.399	.452	17	.980
—	Los Angeles (N.L.).....	C	6	14	2	4	1	0	0	1	0	1	0-0	.286	.286	.357	0	1.000
1999—	Los Angeles (N.L.).....	C	36	95	11	22	1	0	3	11	10	9	1-2	.232	.312	.337	2	.990
—	Albuquerque (PCL).....	C-DH-1B	26	76	17	28	9	0	1	8	10	1	1-1	.368	.478	.526	4	.978
2000—	Albuquerque (PCL).....	C-O-1-3-2	78	279	47	98	27	3	4	54	33	14	8-5	.351	.421	.513	9	.979
—	Los Angeles (N.L.).....	C-OF-3B	34	65	6	16	2	0	2	8	6	8	0-2	.246	.301	.369	1	.993
2001—	Los Angeles (N.L.).....	C-1B-OF-DH	125	460	71	147	28	0	25	90	39	30	2-4	.320	.374	.543	9	.990
—	Las Vegas (PCL)........	C-1B	3	9	3	3	2	0	0	3	1	0	0-0	.333	.400	.556	1	.950
2002—	Los Angeles (N.L.).....	C-1B-OF	149	580	74	163	38	1	10	64	34	31	3-1	.281	.330	.402	9	.992
Major League totals (5 years)			350	1214	164	352	70	1	40	174	89	79	6-9	.290	.343	.448	21	.991

LOFTON, KENNY — OF

PERSONAL: Born May 31, 1967, in East Chicago, Ind. ... 6-0/180. ... Bats left, throws left. ... Full name: Kenneth Lofton.
HIGH SCHOOL: Washington (East Chicago, Ind.).
COLLEGE: Arizona.
TRANSACTIONS/CAREER NOTES: Selected by Houston Astros organization in 17th round of free-agent draft (June 1, 1988). ... Traded by Astros with IF Dave Rohde to Cleveland Indians for P Willie Blair and C Eddie Taubensee (December 10, 1991). ... On disabled list (July 17-August 1, 1995). ... Traded by Indians with P Alan Embree to Atlanta Braves for OF Marquis Grissom and OF Dave Justice (March 25, 1997). ... On disabled list (June 18-July 5 and July 6-28, 1997). ... Granted free agency (October 28, 1997). ... Signed by Indians (December 8, 1997). ... On disabled list (July 28-August 14 and August 17-September 1, 1999; April 30-May 12, 2000; and May 16-June 1, 2001). ... Granted free agency (November 5, 2001). ... Signed by Chicago White Sox (February 1, 2002). ... Traded by White Sox to San Francisco Giants for P Felix Diaz and P Ryan Meaux (July 28, 2002). ... Granted free agency (November 4, 2002).
RECORDS: Holds A.L. rookie-season record for most stolen bases—66 (1992). ... Shares A.L. single-season record for fewest errors by outfielder who led league in errors—8 (1998). ... Shares A.L. record for most consecutive games scoring one or more runs—18 (26 runs, August 15-September 3, 2000).
HONORS: Won A.L. Gold Glove as outfielder (1993-96).
STATISTICAL NOTES: Tied for Pacific Coast League lead in caught stealing with 23 in 1991. ... Led Pacific Coast League outfielders with 308 putouts, 27 assists and 344 total chances in 1991. ... Tied for A.L. lead 13 assists by outfielder in 1994. ... Led N.L. in caught stealing with 20 in 1997. ... Led A.L. outfielders with 19 assists in 1998. ... Career major league grand slams: 2.
MISCELLANEOUS: Holds Cleveland Indians all-time record for most stolen bases (450).
2002 GAMES PLAYED BY POSITION (MLB): OF—136.

						BATTING										FIELDING	
Year Team (League)	Pos.	G	AB	R	H	2B	3B	HR	RBI	BB	SO	SB-CS	Avg.	OBP	SLG	E	Avg.
1988—Auburn (NY-Penn)......	OF	48	187	23	40	6	1	1	14	19	51	26-4	.214	.286	.273	4	.961
1989—Auburn (NY-Penn)......	OF	34	110	21	29	3	1	0	8	14	30	26-5	.264	.336	.309	8	.837
—Asheville (S.Atl.).........	OF	22	82	14	27	2	0	1	9	12	10	14-6	.329	.421	.390	2	.951
1990—Osceola (FSL)............	OF	124	481	98	*159	15	5	2	35	61	77	62-16	.331	.407	.395	7	.974
1991—Tucson (PCL)............	OF	130	*545	93	*168	19	*17	2	50	52	95	40-23	.308	.367	.417	9	.974
—Houston (N.L.)............	OF	20	74	9	15	1	0	0	0	5	19	2-1	.203	.253	.216	1	.977
1992—Cleveland (A.L.)■.......	OF	148	576	96	164	15	8	5	42	68	54	*66-12	.285	.362	.365	8	.982
1993—Cleveland (A.L.)..........	OF	148	569	116	185	28	8	1	42	81	83	*70-14	.325	.408	.408	•9	.979
1994—Cleveland (A.L.)..........	OF	112	459	105	*160	32	9	12	57	52	56	*60-12	.349	.412	.536	2	.993
1995—Cleveland (A.L.)..........	OF-DH	118	481	93	149	22	*13	7	53	40	49	*54-15	.310	.362	.453	•8	.970
1996—Cleveland (A.L.)..........	OF	154	*662	132	210	35	4	14	67	61	82	*75-17	.317	.372	.446	10	.975
1997—Atlanta (N.L.)■..........	OF	122	493	90	164	20	6	5	48	64	83	27-20	.333	.409	.428	5	.983
1998—Cleveland (A.L.)■.......	OF	154	600	101	169	31	6	12	64	87	80	54-10	.282	.371	.413	•8	.978
1999—Cleveland (A.L.)..........	OF-DH	120	465	110	140	28	6	7	39	79	84	25-6	.301	.405	.432	3	.989
2000—Cleveland (A.L.)..........	OF-DH	137	543	107	151	23	5	15	73	79	72	30-7	.278	.369	.422	4	.989
2001—Cleveland (A.L.)..........	OF	133	517	91	135	21	4	14	66	47	69	16-8	.261	.322	.398	6	.981
2002—Chicago (A.L.)■.........	OF	93	352	68	91	20	6	8	42	49	51	22-8	.259	.348	.418	0	1.000
—San Fran. (N.L.)■.......	OF	46	180	30	48	10	3	3	9	23	22	7-3	.267	.353	.406	0	1.000
American League totals (10 years)		1317	5224	1019	1554	255	69	95	545	643	680	472-109	.297	.374	.427	58	.983
National League totals (3 years)		188	747	129	227	31	9	8	57	92	124	36-24	.304	.381	.402	6	.987
Major League totals (12 years)		1505	5971	1148	1781	286	78	103	602	735	804	508-133	.298	.375	.424	64	.983

DIVISION SERIES RECORD

RECORDS: Shares career record for most stolen bases—10.

						BATTING										FIELDING	
Year Team (League)	Pos.	G	AB	R	H	2B	3B	HR	RBI	BB	SO	SB-CS	Avg.	OBP	SLG	E	Avg.
1995—Cleveland (A.L.)..........	OF	3	13	1	2	0	0	0	0	1	3	0-0	.154	.267	.154	2	.818
1996—Cleveland (A.L.)..........	OF	4	18	3	3	0	0	0	1	2	3	5-0	.167	.250	.167	0	1.000
1997—Atlanta (N.L.)..............	OF	3	13	2	2	1	0	0	0	1	2	0-1	.154	.214	.231	0	1.000
1998—Cleveland (A.L.)..........	OF	4	16	5	6	1	0	2	4	1	1	2-0	.375	.412	.813	0	1.000
1999—Cleveland (A.L.)..........	OF	5	16	5	2	1	0	0	1	5	6	2-0	.125	.333	.188	1	.933
2001—Cleveland (A.L.)..........	OF	5	19	2	2	0	0	1	3	3	5	0-0	.105	.217	.263	0	1.000
2002—San Francisco (N.L.) ..	OF	5	20	5	7	1	0	0	2	2	3	1-0	.350	.391	.400	0	1.000
Division series totals (7 years)		29	115	23	24	4	0	3	11	15	23	10-1	.209	.301	.322	3	.959

CHAMPIONSHIP SERIES RECORD

						BATTING										FIELDING	
Year Team (League)	Pos.	G	AB	R	H	2B	3B	HR	RBI	BB	SO	SB-CS	Avg.	OBP	SLG	E	Avg.
1995—Cleveland (A.L.)..........	OF	6	24	4	11	0	2	0	3	4	6	5-0	.458	.517	.625	0	1.000
1997—Atlanta (N.L.)..............	OF	6	27	3	5	0	1	0	1	1	7	1-1	.185	.214	.259	2	.833
1998—Cleveland (A.L.)..........	OF	6	27	2	5	1	0	1	3	1	7	1-0	.185	.214	.333	1	.889
2002—San Francisco (N.L.) ..	OF	5	21	4	5	0	0	1	2	2	4	1-0	.238	.333	.381	0	1.000
Championship series totals (4 years)		23	99	13	26	1	3	2	9	8	24	8-1	.263	.321	.394	3	.941

WORLD SERIES RECORD

RECORDS: Shares single-inning record for most stolen bases—2 (October 21, 1995, first inning). ... Shares single-game record for most at-bats—6 (October 24, 2002).

						BATTING										FIELDING	
Year Team (League)	Pos.	G	AB	R	H	2B	3B	HR	RBI	BB	SO	SB-CS	Avg.	OBP	SLG	E	Avg.
1995—Cleveland (A.L.)..........	OF	6	25	6	5	1	0	0	0	3	1	6-1	.200	.286	.240	0	1.000
2002—San Francisco (N.L.) ..	OF	7	31	7	9	1	1	0	2	2	2	3-0	.290	.333	.387	1	.962
World Series totals (2 years)		13	56	13	14	2	1	0	2	5	3	9-1	.250	.311	.321	1	.974

ALL-STAR GAME RECORD

RECORDS: Shares single-game record for most stolen bases—2 (July 9, 1996).

	AB	R	H	2B	3B	HR	RBI	BB	SO	SB-CS	Avg.	OBP	SLG	E	Avg.
All-Star Game totals (5 years)	14	1	5	0	0	0	2	1	3	5-0	.357	.400	.357	0	1.000

LOHSE, KYLE P TWINS

PERSONAL: Born October 4, 1978, in Chico, Calif. ... 6-2/190. ... Throws right, bats right. ... Full name: Kyle Matthew Lohse.

HIGH SCHOOL: Hamilton Union (Hamilton City, Calif.).

COLLEGE: Butte (Calif.).

TRANSACTIONS/CAREER NOTES: Selected by Chicago Cubs organization in 29th round of free-agent draft (June 4, 1996). ... Traded with P Jason Ryan by Cubs to Minnesota Twins for P Rick Aguilera and P Scott Downs (May 21, 1999).

CAREER HITTING (MLB): 3-for-9 (.333), 0 R, 1 2B, 0 3B, 0 HR, 1 RBI.

Year League	W	L	Pct.	ERA	G	GS	CG	ShO	Sv.-Opp.	IP	H	R	ER	HR	BB-IBB	SO
1997—Arizona Cubs (Ariz.).........	2	2	.500	3.02	12	11	0	0	0-...	47.2	46	22	16	0	22-0	49
1998—Rockford (Midw.).............	13	8	.619	3.22	28	26	3	1	0-...	170.2	158	76	61	8	45-1	121
1999—Daytona (FSL).................	5	3	.625	2.89	9	9	1	1	0-...	53.0	48	21	17	4	16-0	41
—Fort Myers (FSL)■...........	2	3	.400	5.18	7	7	0	0	0-...	41.2	47	28	24	5	9-0	33
—New Britain (East.)...........	3	4	.429	5.89	11	11	1	0	0-...	70.1	87	49	46	9	23-0	41
2000—New Britain (East.)...........	3	*18	.143	6.04	28	28	0	0	0-...	167.0	•196	*123	*112	23	55-0	124
2001—New Britain (East.)...........	3	1	.750	2.37	6	6	0	0	0-...	38.0	32	10	10	5	4-0	32
—Edmonton (PCL).............	4	2	.667	3.12	8	8	1	1	0-...	49.0	50	21	17	3	13-0	48
—Minnesota (A.L.).............	4	7	.364	5.68	19	16	0	0	0-0	90.1	102	60	57	16	29-0	64
2002—Minnesota (A.L.).............	13	8	.619	4.23	32	31	1	1	0-1	180.2	181	92	85	26	70-2	124
Major League totals (2 years).....	17	15	.531	4.72	51	47	1	1	0-1	271.0	283	152	142	42	99-2	188

DIVISION SERIES RECORD

Year League	W	L	Pct.	ERA	G	GS	CG	ShO	Sv.-Opp.	IP	H	R	ER	HR	BB-IBB	SO
2002— Minnesota (A.L.)	0	0	...	0.00	2	0	0	0	0-0	4.0	2	0	0	0	0-0	5

CHAMPIONSHIP SERIES RECORD

Year League	W	L	Pct.	ERA	G	GS	CG	ShO	Sv.-Opp.	IP	H	R	ER	HR	BB-IBB	SO
2002— Minnesota (A.L.)	0	0	...	0.00	1	0	0	0	0-0	1.0	0	0	0	0	0-0	1

LOMBARD, GEORGE OF TIGERS

PERSONAL: Born September 14, 1975, in Atlanta. ... 6-0/212. ... Bats left, throws right. ... Full name: George Paul Lombard.
HIGH SCHOOL: Lovett (Atlanta).
TRANSACTIONS/CAREER NOTES: Selected by Atlanta Braves organization in second round of free-agent draft (June 2, 1994). ... On disabled list (August 16, 1996-remainder of season). ... On Richmond disabled list (May 29-June 22 and July 2-August 11, 1999). ... On Atlanta disabled list (March 28, 2001-entire season); included rehabilitation assignments to Richmond (June 2-9 and June 11-19). ... On Atlanta disabled list (March 22-June 19, 2002); included rehabilitation assignment to Greenville (May 28-June 7) and Richmond (June 8-16). ... Traded by Braves to Detroit Tigers for P Kris Keller (June 19, 2002).
STATISTICAL NOTES: Tied for South Atlantic League lead in caught stealing with 13 in 1995. ... Led Carolina League outfielders with 270 putouts and 284 total chances in 1997. ... Led Southern League with 10 intentional bases on balls in 1998.
2002 GAMES PLAYED BY POSITION (MLB): OF—69; DH—2.

		BATTING														FIELDING	
Year Team (League)	Pos.	G	AB	R	H	2B	3B	HR	RBI	BB	SO	SB-CS	Avg.	OBP	SLG	E	Avg.
1994— GC Braves (GCL)	OF	40	129	10	18	2	0	0	5	18	47	10-4	.140	.260	.155	2	.944
1995— Macon (S.Atl.)	OF	49	180	32	37	6	1	3	16	27	44	16-4	.206	.325	.300	2	.958
— Eugene (N'West)	OF	68	262	38	66	5	3	5	19	23	91	35-13	.252	.323	.351	3	.962
1996— Macon (S.Atl.)	OF-DH	116	444	76	109	16	8	15	51	36	122	24-17	.245	.311	.419	7	.971
1997— Durham (Caro.)	OF-DH	131	462	65	122	25	7	14	72	66	145	35-7	.264	.365	.439	9	.968
1998— Greenville (Sou.)	OF	122	422	84	130	25	4	22	65	71	140	35-5	.308	.410	.543	10	.947
— Atlanta (N.L.)	OF	6	6	2	2	0	0	1	1	0	1	1-0	.333	.333	.833	0	1.000
1999— Richmond (I.L.)	OF-DH	74	233	25	48	11	3	7	29	35	98	21-6	.206	.317	.369	3	.974
— Atlanta (N.L.)	OF	6	6	1	2	0	0	0	0	1	2	2-0	.333	.429	.333	0	1.000
2000— Richmond (I.L.)	OF	112	424	72	117	25	7	10	48	55	130	32-9	.276	.365	.439	6	.972
— Atlanta (N.L.)	OF	27	39	8	4	0	0	0	2	1	14	4-0	.103	.146	.103	0	1.000
2001— Richmond (I.L.)	OF	13	44	7	14	2	1	4	8	6	14	3-2	.318	.423	.682	0	1.000
2002— Greenville (Sou.)	OF	8	25	4	7	0	0	3	5	5	6	2-0	.280	.419	.640	0	1.000
— Richmond (I.L.)	OF	11	39	10	12	4	1	1	5	5	12	2-0	.308	.400	.538	0	1.000
— Detroit (A.L.)■	OF-DH	72	241	34	58	11	3	5	13	20	78	13-2	.241	.300	.373	3	.982
American League totals (1 year)		72	241	34	58	11	3	5	13	20	78	13-2	.241	.300	.373	3	.982
National League totals (3 years)		39	51	11	8	0	0	1	3	2	17	7-0	.157	.204	.216	0	1.000
Major League totals (4 years)		111	292	45	66	11	3	6	16	22	95	20-2	.226	.284	.346	3	.984

LONG, TERRENCE OF ATHLETICS

PERSONAL: Born February 29, 1976, in Montgomery, Ala. ... 6-1/202. ... Bats left, throws left. ... Full name: Terrence Deon Long.
HIGH SCHOOL: Stanhope Elmore (Millbrook, Ala.).
TRANSACTIONS/CAREER NOTES: Selected by New York Mets organization in first round (20th pick overall) of free-agent draft (June 2, 1994); pick received as compensation for Baltimore Orioles signing Type A free-agent P Sid Fernandez. ... On disabled list (May 15-27, 1996). ... Traded by Mets with P Leo Vasquez to Oakland Athletics for P Kenny Rogers (July 23, 1999).
STATISTICAL NOTES: Had 17-game hitting streak (June 10-29, 2000). ... Career major league grand slams: 1.
2002 GAMES PLAYED BY POSITION (MLB): OF—162.

		BATTING														FIELDING	
Year Team (League)	Pos.	G	AB	R	H	2B	3B	HR	RBI	BB	SO	SB-CS	Avg.	OBP	SLG	E	Avg.
1994— Kingsport (Appl.)	OF-1B	60	215	39	50	9	2	12	39	32	52	9-3	.233	.340	.460	5	.980
1995— Capital City (S.Atl.)	OF	55	178	27	35	1	2	2	13	28	43	8-5	.197	.309	.258	5	.937
— Pittsfield (NY-Penn)	OF	51	187	24	48	9	4	4	31	18	36	11-4	.257	.324	.412	1	*.991
1996— Capital City (S.Atl.)	OF-DH	123	473	66	136	26	9	12	78	36	120	32-7	.288	.342	.457	5	.981
1997— St. Lucie (FSL)	OF-DH	126	470	52	118	29	7	8	61	40	102	24-8	.251	.310	.394	7	.972
1998— Binghamton (East.)	OF-DH	130	455	69	135	20	*10	16	58	62	105	23-11	.297	.380	.490	10	.958
1999— Norfolk (I.L.)	OF	78	304	41	99	20	4	7	47	23	41	14-6	.326	.374	.487	4	.980
— New York (N.L.)	PH	3	3	0	0	0	0	0	0	0	2	0-0	.000	.000	.000	...	...
— Vancouver (PCL)■	OF-DH	40	154	16	38	6	2	2	21	10	29	7-5	.247	.297	.351	4	.961
2000— Sacramento (PCL)	OF	15	60	11	24	6	0	3	15	4	4	0-3	.400	.431	.650	3	.903
— Oakland (A.L.)	OF	138	584	104	168	34	4	18	80	43	77	5-0	.288	.336	.452	•10	.971
2001— Oakland (A.L.)	OF	•162	629	90	178	37	4	12	85	52	103	9-3	.283	.335	.412	7	.980
2002— Oakland (A.L.)	OF	•162	587	71	141	32	4	16	67	48	96	3-6	.240	.298	.390	8	.980
American League totals (3 years)		462	1800	265	487	103	12	46	232	143	276	17-9	.271	.323	.418	25	.977
National League totals (1 year)		3	3	0	0	0	0	0	0	0	2	0-0	.000	.000	.000	0	...
Major League totals (4 years)		465	1803	265	487	103	12	46	232	143	278	17-9	.270	.323	.417	25	.977

DIVISION SERIES RECORD

RECORDS: Shares single-game record for most home runs—2 (October 10, 2001).

		BATTING														FIELDING	
Year Team (League)	Pos.	G	AB	R	H	2B	3B	HR	RBI	BB	SO	SB-CS	Avg.	OBP	SLG	E	Avg.
2000— Oakland (A.L.)	OF	5	19	2	3	0	0	1	1	3	2	0-0	.158	.273	.316	1	.923
2001— Oakland (A.L.)	OF	5	18	3	7	3	0	2	3	1	2	0-0	.389	.421	.889	0	1.000
2002— Oakland (A.L.)	OF	5	18	1	3	0	0	1	1	1	2	0-0	.167	.211	.333	0	1.000
Division series totals (3 years)		15	55	6	13	3	0	4	5	5	6	0-0	.236	.300	.509	1	.970

LOOPER, BRADEN P MARLINS

PERSONAL: Born October 28, 1974, in Weatherford, Okla. ... 6-3/220. ... Throws right, bats right. ... Full name: Braden LaVern Looper. ... Name pronounced BRAY-dun.

HIGH SCHOOL: Mangum (Okla.).

COLLEGE: Wichita State.

TRANSACTIONS/CAREER NOTES: Selected by St. Louis Cardinals organization in first round (third pick overall) of free-agent draft (June 2, 1996). ... On Memphis disabled list (May 6-June 21, 1998). ... Traded by Cardinals with P Armando Almanza and SS Pablo Ozuna to Florida Marlins for SS Edgar Renteria (December 14, 1998).

MISCELLANEOUS: Member of 1996 U.S. Olympic baseball team. ... Holds Florida Marlins all-time record for most game pitched (294).

CAREER HITTING (MLB): 0-for-5 (.000), 0 R, 0 2B, 0 3B, 0 HR, 0 RBI.

Year League	W	L	Pct.	ERA	G	GS	CG	ShO	Sv.-Opp.	IP	H	R	ER	HR	BB-IBB	SO
1997— Prince William (Caro.)	3	6	.333	4.48	12	12	0	0	0-...	64.1	71	38	32	6	25-0	58
— Arkansas (Texas)	1	4	.200	5.91	19	0	0	0	5-...	21.1	24	14	14	2	7-2	20
1998— St. Louis (N.L.)	0	1	.000	5.40	4	0	0	0	0-2	3.1	5	4	2	1	1-0	4
— Memphis (PCL)	2	3	.400	3.10	40	0	0	0	20-...	40.2	43	16	14	3	13-1	43
1999— Florida (N.L.)■	3	3	.500	3.80	72	0	0	0	0-4	83.0	96	43	35	7	31-6	50
2000— Florida (N.L.)	5	1	.833	4.41	73	0	0	0	2-5	67.1	71	41	33	3	36-6	29
2001— Florida (N.L.)	3	3	.500	3.55	71	0	0	0	3-6	71.0	63	28	28	8	30-3	52
2002— Florida (N.L.)	2	5	.286	3.14	78	0	0	0	13-16	86.0	73	31	30	8	28-3	55
Major League totals (5 years)	13	13	.500	3.71	298	0	0	0	18-33	310.2	308	147	128	27	126-18	190

LOPEZ, ALBIE P

PERSONAL: Born August 18, 1971, in Mesa, Ariz. ... 6-2/240. ... Throws right, bats right. ... Full name: Albert Anthony Lopez.

HIGH SCHOOL: Westwood (Mesa, Ariz.).

JUNIOR COLLEGE: Mesa (Ariz.) Community College.

TRANSACTIONS/CAREER NOTES: Selected by San Francisco Giants organization in 46th round of free-agent draft (June 5, 1989); did not sign. ... Selected by Seattle Mariners organization in 19th round of free-agent draft (June 4, 1990); did not sign. ... Selected by Cleveland Indians organization in 20th round of free-agent draft (June 3, 1991). ... On Cleveland disabled list (July 2-28 and August 13-September 1, 1997). ... Selected by Tampa Bay Devil Rays in second round (48th pick overall) of expansion draft (November 18, 1997). ... On Tampa Bay disabled list (August 1-26, 1998); included rehabilitation assignments to Durham (August 15-18) and St. Petersburg (August 25-26). ... On Tampa Bay disabled list (May 12-June 20, 1999); included rehabilitation assignment to St. Petersburg (June 14-20). ... Traded by Devil Rays with C Mike Difelice to Arizona Diamondbacks for OF Jason Conti and P Nick Bierbrodt (July 25, 2001). ... Granted free agency (November 6, 2001). ... Signed by Atlanta Braves (December 20, 2001). ... On Atlanta disabled list (April 9-28 and June 26-July 13, 2002); included rehabilitation assignments to Greenville (April 25-28) and Macon (July 13). ... Granted free agency (October 28, 2002).

STATISTICAL NOTES: Led American Association with 10 hit batsmen and tied for lead with three balks in 1996.

MISCELLANEOUS: Shares Tampa Bay Devil Rays all-time records for most wins (26) and most shutouts (2).

CAREER HITTING (MLB): 2-for-46 (.043), 0 R, 0 2B, 0 3B, 0 HR, 0 RBI.

Year League	W	L	Pct.	ERA	G	GS	CG	ShO	Sv.-Opp.	IP	H	R	ER	HR	BB-IBB	SO
1991— Burlington (Appl.)	4	5	.444	3.44	13	13	0	0	0-...	73.1	61	33	28	4	23-0	81
1992— Columbus (S.Atl.)	7	2	.778	2.88	16	16	1	0	0-...	97.0	80	41	31	4	33-0	117
— Kinston (Caro.)	5	2	.714	3.52	10	10	1	1	0-...	64.0	56	28	25	5	26-1	44
1993— Canton/Akron (East.)	9	4	.692	3.11	16	16	2	0	0-...	110.0	79	44	38	10	47-0	80
— Cleveland (A.L.)	3	1	.750	5.98	9	9	0	0	0-0	49.2	49	34	33	7	32-1	25
— Charlotte (I.L.)	1	0	1.000	2.25	3	2	0	0	0-...	12.0	8	3	3	1	2-0	7
1994— Charlotte (I.L.)	13	3	.813	3.94	22	22	3	0	0-...	144.0	136	68	63	20	42-0	105
— Cleveland (A.L.)	1	2	.333	4.24	4	4	1	1	0-0	17.0	20	11	8	3	6-0	18
1995— Buffalo (A.A.)	5	10	.333	4.44	18	18	1	1	0-...	101.1	101	57	50	10	51-0	82
— Cleveland (A.L.)	0	0	...	3.13	6	2	0	0	0-0	23.0	17	8	8	4	7-1	22
1996— Buffalo (A.A.)	10	2	*.833	3.87	17	17	2	0	0-...	104.2	90	54	45	13	40-0	89
— Cleveland (A.L.)	5	4	.556	6.39	13	10	0	0	0-0	62.0	80	47	44	14	22-1	45
1997— Cleveland (A.L.)	3	7	.300	6.93	37	6	0	0	0-1	76.2	101	61	59	11	40-9	63
— Akron (East.)	0	0	...	0.00	1	0	0	0	0-...	1.0	2	0	0	0	0-0	2
— Buffalo (A.A.)	1	0	1.000	0.00	7	0	0	0	1-...	11.1	6	0	0	0	2-0	13
1998— Tampa Bay (A.L.)■	7	4	.636	2.60	54	0	0	0	1-5	79.2	73	31	23	7	32-4	62
— Durham (I.L.)	0	0	...	0.00	2	0	0	0	0-...	3.0	4	0	0	0	1-0	2
— St. Petersburg (FSL)	0	1	.000	18.00	1	1	0	0	0-...	1.0	2	2	2	1	0-0	1
1999— Tampa Bay (A.L.)	3	2	.600	4.64	51	0	0	0	1-3	64.0	66	40	33	8	24-2	37
— St. Petersburg (FSL)	0	0	...	5.40	2	1	0	0	0-...	3.1	7	5	2	0	0-0	3
2000— Tampa Bay (A.L.)	11	13	.458	4.13	45	24	4	1	2-4	185.1	199	95	85	24	70-3	96
— Princeton (Appl.)	0	0	...	0.00	1	0	0	0	0-...	.2	0	0	0	0	0-0	1
2001— Tampa Bay (A.L.)	5	12	.294	5.34	20	20	1	1	0-0	124.2	152	87	74	16	51-1	67
— Arizona (N.L.)■	4	7	.364	4.00	13	13	2	2	0-0	81.0	74	36	36	10	24-2	69
2002— Atlanta (N.L.)■	1	4	.200	4.37	30	4	0	0	0-0	55.2	66	29	27	1	18-3	39
— Greenville (Sou.)	0	0	...	4.50	1	1	0	0	0-...	4.0	2	2	2	0	4-0	4
A.L. totals (9 years)	38	45	.458	4.84	239	75	6	3	4-13	682.0	757	414	367	94	284-22	435
N.L. totals (2 years)	5	11	.313	4.15	43	17	2	2	0-0	136.2	140	65	63	11	42-5	108
Major League totals (10 years)	43	56	.434	4.73	282	92	8	5	4-13	818.2	897	479	430	105	326-27	543

DIVISION SERIES RECORD

Year League	W	L	Pct.	ERA	G	GS	CG	ShO	Sv.-Opp.	IP	H	R	ER	HR	BB-IBB	SO
2001— Arizona (N.L.)	0	1	.000	12.00	1	1	0	0	0-0	3.0	4	4	4	2	3-0	0

CHAMPIONSHIP SERIES RECORD

Year League	W	L	Pct.	ERA	G	GS	CG	ShO	Sv.-Opp.	IP	H	R	ER	HR	BB-IBB	SO
2001— Arizona (N.L.)	0	0	...	6.00	1	1	0	0	0-0	3.0	5	2	2	1	1-0	1

WORLD SERIES RECORD

NOTES: Member of World Series championship team (2001).

Year League	W	L	Pct.	ERA	G	GS	CG	ShO	Sv.-Opp.	IP	H	R	ER	HR	BB-IBB	SO
2001— Arizona (N.L.)	0	1	.000	27.00	1	0	0	0	0-0	.1	2	1	1	0	0-0	0

LOPEZ, FELIPE — SS — BLUE JAYS

PERSONAL: Born May 12, 1980, in Bayamon, Puerto Rico. ... 6-0/185. ... Bats both, throws right.
HIGH SCHOOL: Lake Brantley (Altamonte Springs, Fla.).
TRANSACTIONS/CAREER NOTES: Selected by Toronto Blue Jays organization in first round (eighth pick overall) of free-agent draft (June 2, 1998).
2002 GAMES PLAYED BY POSITION (MLB): SS—79; 3B—2; DH—1.

			BATTING														FIELDING	
Year	Team (League)	Pos.	G	AB	R	H	2B	3B	HR	RBI	BB	SO	SB-CS	Avg.	OBP	SLG	E	Avg.
1998—	St. Catharines (NY-P)	SS	19	83	14	31	5	2	1	11	3	14	4-2	.373	.395	.518	9	.895
—	Dunedin (FSL)	SS	4	13	3	5	0	1	1	1	0	3	0-0	.385	.385	.769	4	.692
1999—	Hagerstown (S.Atl.)	SS	134	537	87	149	27	4	14	80	61	157	21-14	.277	.351	.421	22	.960
2000—	Tennessee (Sou.)	SS	127	463	52	119	18	4	9	41	31	110	12-11	.257	.303	.371	*44	.923
2001—	Tennessee (Sou.)	SS-2B	19	72	12	16	2	1	2	4	9	23	4-4	.222	.309	.361	8	.904
—	Syracuse (I.L.)	SS-2B-3B	89	358	65	100	19	7	16	44	30	94	13-5	.279	.337	.506	19	.950
—	Toronto (A.L.)	3B-SS	49	177	21	46	5	4	5	23	12	39	4-3	.260	.304	.418	9	.938
2002—	Toronto (A.L.)	SS-3B-DH	85	282	35	64	15	3	8	34	23	90	5-4	.227	.287	.387	8	.975
—	Syracuse (I.L.)	SS	43	173	35	55	11	2	3	16	29	37	13-0	.318	.419	.457	16	.934
Major League totals (2 years)			134	459	56	110	20	7	13	57	35	129	9-7	.240	.293	.399	17	.964

LOPEZ, JAVY — C — BRAVES

PERSONAL: Born November 5, 1970, in Ponce, Puerto Rico. ... 6-3/225. ... Bats right, throws right. ... Full name: Javier Torres Lopez.
HIGH SCHOOL: Academia Cristo Rey (Urb la Ramble Ponce, Puerto Rico).
TRANSACTIONS/CAREER NOTES: Signed as non-drafted free agent by Atlanta Braves organization (November 6, 1987). ... On Greenville disabled list (July 18-August 2, 1992). ... On Atlanta disabled list (July 6-22, 1997; and June 21-July 15 and July 25, 1999-remainder of season). ... Granted free agency (November 5, 2001). ... Re-signed by Braves (December 7, 2001). ... On disabled list (August 1-16, 2002).
HONORS: Named Southern League Most Valuable Player (1992).
STATISTICAL NOTES: Led Midwest League catchers with 11 double plays and 31 passed balls in 1990. ... Led Carolina League catchers with 610 putouts, 701 total chances and 14 double plays in 1991. ... Led Southern League catchers with 680 putouts, 763 total chances and 19 passed balls in 1992. ... Led International League catchers with 15 passed balls in 1993. ... Tied for N.L. lead with 10 passed balls in 1994. ... Career major league grand slams: 6.
2002 GAMES PLAYED BY POSITION (MLB): C—103.

			BATTING														FIELDING	
Year	Team (League)	Pos.	G	AB	R	H	2B	3B	HR	RBI	BB	SO	SB-CS	Avg.	OBP	SLG	E	Avg.
1988—	GC Braves (GCL)	C	31	94	8	18	4	0	1	9	3	19	1-0	.191	.214	.266	7	.958
1989—	Pulaski (Appl.)	C	51	153	27	40	8	1	3	27	5	35	3-2	.261	.284	.386	5	.983
1990—	Burlington (Midw.)	C	116	422	48	112	17	3	11	55	14	84	0-2	.265	.297	.398	11	.986
1991—	Durham (Caro.)	C	113	384	43	94	14	2	11	51	25	88	10-3	.245	.294	.378	6	.991
1992—	Greenville (Sou.)	C	115	442	63	142	28	3	16	60	24	47	7-3	.321	.362	.507	8	.990
—	Atlanta (N.L.)	C	9	16	3	6	2	0	0	2	0	1	0-0	.375	.375	.500	0	1.000
1993—	Richmond (I.L.)	C-DH	100	380	56	116	23	2	17	74	12	53	1-6	.305	.334	.511	10	.987
—	Atlanta (N.L.)	C	8	16	1	6	1	1	1	2	0	2	0-0	.375	.412	.750	1	.975
1994—	Atlanta (N.L.)	C	80	277	27	68	9	0	13	35	17	61	0-2	.245	.299	.419	3	.995
1995—	Atlanta (N.L.)	C	100	333	37	105	11	4	14	51	14	57	0-1	.315	.344	.498	8	.988
1996—	Atlanta (N.L.)	C	138	489	56	138	19	1	23	69	28	84	1-6	.282	.322	.466	6	.994
1997—	Atlanta (N.L.)	C	123	414	52	122	28	1	23	68	40	82	1-1	.295	.361	.534	6	.993
1998—	Atlanta (N.L.)	C-DH	133	489	73	139	21	1	34	106	30	85	5-3	.284	.328	.540	5	*.995
1999—	Atlanta (N.L.)	C-DH	65	246	34	78	18	1	11	45	20	41	0-3	.317	.375	.533	4	.991
2000—	Atlanta (N.L.)	C	134	481	60	138	21	1	24	89	35	80	0-0	.287	.337	.484	6	.993
2001—	Atlanta (N.L.)	C	128	438	45	117	16	1	17	66	28	82	1-0	.267	.322	.425	10	.989
2002—	Atlanta (N.L.)	C	109	347	31	81	15	0	11	52	26	63	0-1	.233	.299	.372	10	.986
Major League totals (11 years)			1027	3546	419	998	161	11	171	585	238	638	8-17	.281	.332	.478	59	.992

DIVISION SERIES RECORD

			BATTING														FIELDING	
Year	Team (League)	Pos.	G	AB	R	H	2B	3B	HR	RBI	BB	SO	SB-CS	Avg.	OBP	SLG	E	Avg.
1995—	Atlanta (N.L.)	C	3	9	0	4	0	0	0	3	0	3	0-1	.444	.400	.444	0	1.000
1996—	Atlanta (N.L.)	C	2	7	1	2	0	0	1	1	1	0	1-0	.286	.375	.714	1	.958
1997—	Atlanta (N.L.)	C	2	7	3	2	2	0	0	1	2	1	0-0	.286	.444	.571	0	1.000
1998—	Atlanta (N.L.)	C	2	7	1	2	0	0	1	1	1	1	0-0	.286	.375	.714	0	1.000
2000—	Atlanta (N.L.)	PH-C	3	11	0	1	0	0	0	0	0	1	0-1	.091	.091	.091	0	1.000
2002—	Atlanta (N.L.)	C	4	15	4	5	1	0	2	4	1	3	0-0	.333	.375	.800	0	1.000
Division series totals (6 years)			16	56	9	16	3	0	4	10	5	9	1-2	.286	.339	.554	1	.993

CHAMPIONSHIP SERIES RECORD

RECORDS: Shares career record for most doubles—7; and extra base hits—12. ... Shares single-game record for most runs—4 (October 14, 1996). ... Holds single-series records for most doubles—5 (1996); extra base hits—7 (1996); and hits—13 (1996). ... Shares single-series record for most total bases—24 (1996). ... Shares N.L. single-series records for most runs—8 (1996); and most consecutive hits—5 (1996).
NOTES: Named N.L. Championship Series Most Valuable Player (1996).

			BATTING														FIELDING	
Year	Team (League)	Pos.	G	AB	R	H	2B	3B	HR	RBI	BB	SO	SB-CS	Avg.	OBP	SLG	E	Avg.
1992—	Atlanta (N.L.)	C	1	1	0	0	0	0	0	0	0	0	0-0	.000	.000	.000	0	1.000
1995—	Atlanta (N.L.)	C	3	14	2	5	1	0	1	3	0	1	0-0	.357	.357	.643	0	1.000
1996—	Atlanta (N.L.)	C	7	24	8	13	5	0	2	6	3	1	1-0	.542	.607	1.000	0	1.000
1997—	Atlanta (N.L.)	C-PH	5	17	0	1	1	0	0	2	1	7	0-0	.059	.100	.118	0	1.000
1998—	Atlanta (N.L.)	C-PH	6	20	2	6	0	0	1	1	0	7	0-0	.300	.300	.450	1	.978
2001—	Atlanta (N.L.)	PH-C	5	14	1	2	0	0	1	2	1	4	0-0	.143	.200	.357	1	.957
Championship series totals (6 years)			27	90	13	27	7	0	5	14	5	20	1-0	.300	.337	.544	2	.990

WORLD SERIES RECORD

NOTES: Member of World Series championship team (1995).

Year	Team (League)	Pos.	G	AB	R	H	2B	3B	HR	RBI	BB	SO	SB-CS	Avg.	OBP	SLG	E	Avg.
			BATTING														FIELDING	
1992—	Atlanta (N.L.)								Did not play.									
1995—	Atlanta (N.L.)	C-PH	6	17	1	3	2	0	1	3	1	1	0-0	.176	.263	.471	0	1.000
1996—	Atlanta (N.L.)	C	6	21	3	4	0	0	0	1	3	4	0-0	.190	.280	.190	0	1.000
World Series totals (2 years)			12	38	4	7	2	0	1	4	4	5	0-0	.184	.273	.316	0	1.000

ALL-STAR GAME RECORD

RECORDS: Hit home run in first at-bat (July 8, 1997).

	AB	R	H	2B	3B	HR	RBI	BB	SO	SB-CS	Avg.	OBP	SLG	E	Avg.
All-Star Game totals (2 years)	2	1	1	0	0	1	1	0	1	0-0	.500	.500	2.000	0	1.000

LOPEZ, LUIS IF

PERSONAL: Born September 4, 1970, in Cidra, Puerto Rico. ... 5-11/175. ... Bats both, throws right. ... Full name: Luis Manuel Lopez.

HIGH SCHOOL: San Jose (Caguas, Puerto Rico).

TRANSACTIONS/CAREER NOTES: Signed as non-drafted free agent by San Diego Padres organization (September 9, 1987). ... On Las Vegas disabled list (July 3-14, 1994). ... Granted free agency (October 15, 1994). ... Re-signed by Padres (April 20, 1995). ... On disabled list (April 24, 1995-entire season). ... On San Diego disabled list (March 29-April 18 and July 31-September 1, 1996); included rehabilitation assignments to Las Vegas (March 30-April 18 and August 17-September 1). ... Traded by Padres to Houston Astros for P Sean Runyan (March 15, 1997). ... Traded by Astros to New York Mets for IF Tim Bogar (March 31, 1997). ... Traded by Mets to Milwaukee Brewers for P Bill Pulsipher (January 21, 2000). ... On Milwaukee disabled list (March 30-May 19, 2002); included rehabilitation assignment to Indianapolis (April 29-May 6). ... Released by Brewers (June 6, 2002). ... Signed by Baltimore Orioles organization (June 18, 2002). ... Released by Orioles (October 1, 2002).

STATISTICAL NOTES: Led Northwest League shortstops with 118 putouts and 382 total chances in 1988. ... Led South Atlantic League shortstops with 256 putouts, 373 assists, 703 total chances and 78 double plays in 1989. ... Led Pacific Coast League shortstops with 30 errors in 1992. ... Tied for Pacific Coast League lead with 13 sacrifice hits in 1993. ... Career major league grand slams: 2.

2002 GAMES PLAYED BY POSITION (MLB): SS—26; 2B—12; DH—1; 1B—1.

Year	Team (League)	Pos.	G	AB	R	H	2B	3B	HR	RBI	BB	SO	SB-CS	Avg.	OBP	SLG	E	Avg.
			BATTING														FIELDING	
1988—	Spokane (N'West)	SS	70	312	50	95	13	1	0	35	18	59	14-5	.304	.348	.353	*47	.877
1989—	Charl., S.C. (S.Atl.)	SS	127	460	50	102	15	1	1	29	17	85	12-9	.222	.251	.265	*74	.895
1990—	Riverside (Calif.)	SS	14	46	5	17	3	1	1	4	3	3	4-2	.370	.408	.543	6	.903
1991—	Wichita (Texas)	2B-SS	125	452	43	121	17	1	1	41	18	70	6-7	.268	.305	.316	26	.959
1992—	Las Vegas (PCL)	SS-OF	120	395	44	92	8	8	1	31	19	65	6-4	.233	.271	.301	†30	.949
1993—	Las Vegas (PCL)	SS-2B-DH	131	491	52	150	36	6	6	58	27	62	8-0	.305	.346	.440	29	.955
	—San Diego (N.L.)	2B	17	43	1	5	1	0	0	1	0	8	0-0	.116	.114	.140	1	.983
1994—	Las Vegas (PCL)	2B	12	49	2	10	2	2	0	6	1	5	0-0	.204	.216	.327	2	.973
	—San Diego (N.L.)	SS-2B-3B	77	235	29	65	16	1	2	20	15	39	3-2	.277	.325	.379	14	.952
1995—	San Diego (N.L.)								Did not play.									
1996—	Las Vegas (PCL)	2B-SS	18	68	4	14	3	0	1	12	2	15	0-0	.206	.229	.294	2	.976
	—San Diego (N.L.)	SS-2B-3B	63	139	10	25	3	0	2	11	9	35	0-0	.180	.233	.245	4	.975
1997—	Norfolk (I.L.)■	SS-2B-DH	48	203	32	67	12	1	4	19	9	29	2-6	.330	.358	.458	14	.935
	—New York (N.L.)	SS-2B-3B	78	178	19	48	12	1	1	19	12	42	2-4	.270	.330	.365	9	.963
1998—	New York (N.L.)	2-S-3-O	117	266	37	67	13	2	2	22	20	60	2-2	.252	.312	.338	11	.960
1999—	New York (N.L.)	SS-2B-3B	68	104	11	22	4	0	2	13	12	33	1-1	.212	.308	.308	4	.962
2000—	Milwaukee (N.L.)■	SS-2B-3B	78	201	24	53	14	0	6	27	9	35	1-2	.264	.309	.423	8	.969
2001—	Milwaukee (N.L.)	3B-SS-2B	92	222	22	60	8	3	4	18	14	44	0-1	.270	.326	.387	8	.959
2002—	Indianapolis (I.L.)	2B-SS-3B	6	22	2	5	0	0	0	0	0	4	0-0	.227	.261	.227	0	1.000
	—Milwaukee (N.L.)	SS	6	8	1	0	0	0	0	1	2	1	0-0	.000	.200	.000	0	1.000
	—Rochester (I.L.)■	2B-SS	17	68	12	22	6	0	3	8	3	11	0-0	.324	.361	.544	1	.988
	—Baltimore (A.L.)	SS-2B-DH-1B	52	109	10	23	6	0	2	9	3	20	1-0	.211	.232	.321	3	.969
American League totals (1 year)			52	109	10	23	6	0	2	9	3	20	1-0	.211	.232	.321	3	.969
National League totals (9 years)			596	1396	154	345	71	7	19	132	93	297	9-12	.247	.304	.349	59	.963
Major League totals (9 years)			648	1505	164	368	77	7	21	141	96	317	10-12	.245	.299	.347	62	.963

DIVISION SERIES RECORD

Year	Team (League)	Pos.	G	AB	R	H	2B	3B	HR	RBI	BB	SO	SB-CS	Avg.	OBP	SLG	E	Avg.
			BATTING														FIELDING	
1996—	San Diego (N.L.)	PR	1	0	0	0	0	0	0	0	0	0	0-0	...	...	...	...	...
1999—	New York (N.L.)								Did not play.									

CHAMPIONSHIP SERIES RECORD

Year	Team (League)	Pos.	G	AB	R	H	2B	3B	HR	RBI	BB	SO	SB-CS	Avg.	OBP	SLG	E	Avg.
			BATTING														FIELDING	
1999—	New York (N.L.)								Did not play.									

LOPEZ, MENDY IF

PERSONAL: Born October 15, 1974, in Santo Domingo, Dominican Republic. ... 6-2/200. ... Bats right, throws right. ... Full name: Mendy Aude Lopez.

HIGH SCHOOL: Liceo Los Trinitanos (Santo Domingo, Dominican Republic).

TRANSACTIONS/CAREER NOTES: Signed as non-drafted free agent by Kansas City Royals organization (February 26, 1992). ... On Omaha disabled list (May 28-July 7, 1999). ... Released by Royals (December 13, 1999). ... Signed by Florida Marlins organization (January 12, 2000). ... On Calgary disabled list (April 6-June 23, 2000). ... Granted free agency (October 2, 2000). ... Signed by Houston Astros organization (January 8, 2001). ... Claimed on waivers by Pittsburgh Pirates (August 13, 2001). ... Granted free agency (October 15, 2001). ... On Nashville disabled list (April 4-24, 2002). ... Released by Pirates (October 11, 2002).

STATISTICAL NOTES: Led Gulf Coast League shortstops with .971 fielding percentage, 80 putouts, 154 assists, 241 total chances and 39 double plays in 1994. ... Tied for Texas League lead with 28 double plays by third baseman in 1996.

									BATTING								FIELDING	
Year	Team (League)	Pos.	G	AB	R	H	2B	3B	HR	RBI	BB	SO	SB-CS	Avg.	OBP	SLG	E	Avg.
1992—	Dom. Royals (DSL)	SS	49	145	22	40	1	0	1	23	22	15	7-...	.276	...	.303	26	.901
1993—	Dom. Royals (DSL)	IF	28	98	15	27	5	2	0	20	11	5	2-...	.276	...	.367	15	.894
1994—	GC Royals (GCL)	SS-3B-2B	59	*235	56	85	*19	3	5	*50	22	27	10-2	.362	.415	.532	12	†.959
1995—	Wilmington (Caro.)	3B-SS	130	428	42	116	29	3	2	36	28	73	18-10	.271	.322	.367	25	.944
1996—	Wichita (Texas)	3B-SS	93	327	47	92	20	5	6	32	26	67	14-4	.281	.341	.428	24	.935
1997—	Omaha (A.A.)	3B	17	52	6	12	2	0	1	6	8	21	0-0	.231	.333	.327	6	.898
	—Wichita (Texas)	SS	101	357	56	83	16	3	5	42	36	70	7-5	.232	.304	.336	20	.961
1998—	Omaha (PCL)	SS-3B	60	195	18	35	6	1	3	14	18	44	2-3	.179	.252	.267	10	.960
	—Kansas City (A.L.)	SS-3B	74	206	18	50	10	2	1	15	12	40	5-2	.243	.286	.325	15	.956
1999—	Omaha (PCL)	SS-2B-3B-DH	61	222	41	69	8	0	12	40	18	41	2-2	.311	.361	.509	8	.971
	—GC Royals (GCL)	SS-DH	3	5	0	1	1	0	0	2	3	1	0-0	.200	.500	.400	0	1.000
	—Kansas City (A.L.)	2B-SS	7	20	2	8	0	1	0	3	0	5	0-0	.400	.429	.500	0	1.000
2000—	Calgary (PCL)■	SS-2B-3B	56	225	34	73	20	1	7	29	13	38	1-1	.324	.361	.516	12	.955
	—Florida (N.L.)	PH	4	3	0	0	0	0	0	0	1	1	0-0	.000	.250	.000	...	...
2001—	New Orleans (PCL)■	2-S-1-0-3	63	208	37	58	11	1	14	36	18	49	2-2	.279	.343	.543	3	.990
	—Houston (N.L.)	2B-3B	10	15	3	4	0	0	1	3	2	4	0-0	.267	.389	.467	0	1.000
	—Pittsburgh (N.L.)■	2B-SS-3B	22	43	5	10	3	1	0	4	4	16	0-0	.233	.292	.349	1	.983
2002—	Nashville (PCL)	SS-3B-2B	101	385	60	97	26	0	11	72	34	99	4-1	.252	.309	.405	9	.977
	—Pittsburgh (N.L.)	PH	3	3	0	0	0	0	0	0	0	3	0-0	.000	.000	.000	...	...
American League totals (2 years)			81	226	20	58	10	3	1	18	12	45	5-2	.257	.299	.341	15	.959
National League totals (3 years)			39	64	8	14	3	1	1	7	7	24	0-0	.219	.301	.344	1	.985
Major League totals (5 years)			120	290	28	72	13	4	2	25	19	69	5-2	.248	.299	.341	16	.963

LOPEZ, RODRIGO P ORIOLES

PERSONAL: Born December 14, 1975, in Mexico City, Mexico. ... 6-1/180. ... Throws right, bats right. ... Full name: Rodrigo Munoz Lopez.
TRANSACTIONS/CAREER NOTES: Signed by Aguila of Mexican League (1994). ... Contract sold by Aguila to San Diego Padres organization (March 21, 1995). ... Loaned by Padres to Mexico City Red Devils, Mexican League (March 13-August 19, 1998). ... On Portland disabled list (April 5-June 13, 2001). ... Granted free agency (October 15, 2001). ... Signed by Baltimore Orioles organization (February 4, 2002).
HONORS: Named A.L. Rookie Pitcher of the Year by The Sporting News (2002).
CAREER HITTING (MLB): 1-for-12 (.083), 1 R, 0 2B, 0 3B, 0 HR, 0 RBI.

Year	League	W	L	Pct.	ERA	G	GS	CG	ShO	Sv.-Opp.	IP	H	R	ER	HR	BB-IBB	SO
1993—	Aguila (Mex.)	0	0	.000	36.00	2	0	0	0	0-...	1.0	3	4	4	0	3-0	0
1994—	Aguila (Mex.)	0	0	...	4.97	10	0	0	0	0-...	12.2	15	7	7	2	3-0	5
1995—	Arizona Padres (Ariz.)■	1	1	.500	5.45	11	7	0	0	1-...	34.2	41	29	21	0	14-0	33
1996—	Poza Rica (Mex.)■	1	1	.500	3.54	7	3	0	0	1-...	20.1	15	8	8	2	16-3	22
	—Idaho Falls (Pio.)■	4	4	.500	5.70	15	14	0	0	1-...	71.0	76	52	45	3	34-0	72
1997—	Clinton (Midw.)	6	8	.429	3.18	37	14	2	0	9-...	121.2	103	49	43	6	42-1	123
1998—	MC Red Devils (Mex.)■	10	6	.625	3.35	26	26	1	0	0-...	163.2	165	73	61	9	79-0	95
	—Mobile (Sou.)■	3	0	1.000	1.40	4	4	2	1	0-...	25.2	21	11	4	1	4-0	20
1999—	Mobile (Sou.)	10	8	.556	4.41	28	•28	2	1	0-...	169.1	187	91	83	14	58-3	138
2000—	Las Vegas (PCL)	8	7	.533	4.69	20	20	1	0	0-...	109.1	123	66	57	9	45-1	100
	—San Diego (N.L.)	0	3	.000	8.76	6	6	0	0	0-0	24.2	40	24	24	5	13-0	17
2001—	Lake Elsinore (Calif.)	0	1	.000	0.69	9	0	0	0	0-...	13.0	15	7	1	1	4-0	9
	—Portland (PCL)	2	2	.500	3.44	11	8	0	0	0-...	52.1	45	22	20	7	15-0	37
2002—	Baltimore (A.L.)■	15	9	.625	3.57	33	28	1	0	0-0	196.2	172	83	78	23	62-4	136
A.L. totals (1 year)		15	9	.625	3.57	33	28	1	0	0-0	196.2	172	83	78	23	62-4	136
N.L. totals (1 year)		0	3	.000	8.76	6	6	0	0	0-0	24.2	40	24	24	5	13-0	17
Major League totals (2 years)		15	12	.556	4.15	39	34	1	0	0-0	221.1	212	107	102	28	75-4	153

LORETTA, MARK IF

PERSONAL: Born August 14, 1971, in Santa Monica, Calif. ... 6-0/186. ... Bats right, throws right. ... Full name: Mark David Loretta.
HIGH SCHOOL: St. Francis (La Canada, Calif.).
COLLEGE: Northwestern.
TRANSACTIONS/CAREER NOTES: Selected by Milwaukee Brewers organization in seventh round of free-agent draft (June 3, 1993). ... On New Orleans suspended list (May 17-20, 1996). ... On Milwaukee disabled list (June 3-August 16, 2000); included rehabilitation assignment to Indianapolis (August 3-16). ... On Milwaukee disabled list (March 27-May 19, 2001); included rehabilitation assignment to Indianapolis (May 9-17). ... Traded by Brewers to Houston Astros from two players to be named later (August 31, 2002); Brewers acquired P Wayne Franklin (September 3, 2002) and 2B Keith Ginter (September 5, 2002) to complete deal. ... Granted free agency (October 28, 2002).
STATISTICAL NOTES: Led American Association shortstops with 200 putouts and 591 total chances in 1995. ... Had 16-game hitting streak (May 20-June 9, 2001). ... Career major league grand slams: 1.
2002 GAMES PLAYED BY POSITION (MLB): 3B—57; SS—18; 2B—6; 1B—5; DH—1.

									BATTING								FIELDING	
Year	Team (League)	Pos.	G	AB	R	H	2B	3B	HR	RBI	BB	SO	SB-CS	Avg.	OBP	SLG	E	Avg.
1993—	Helena (Pio.)	SS	6	28	5	9	1	0	1	8	1	4	0-0	.321	.367	.464	0	1.000
	—Stockton (Calif.)	SS-3B	53	201	36	73	4	1	4	31	22	17	8-2	.363	.427	.453	15	.943
1994—	El Paso (Texas)	SS-P	77	302	50	95	13	6	0	38	27	33	8-5	.315	.369	.397	11	.973
	—New Orleans (A.A.)	SS-2B	43	138	16	29	7	0	1	14	12	13	2-1	.210	.282	.283	11	.945
1995—	New Orleans (A.A.)	S-3-DH-2	127	479	48	137	22	5	7	79	34	47	8-9	.286	.340	.397	25	.959
	—Milwaukee (A.L.)	SS-2B-DH	19	50	13	13	3	0	1	3	4	7	1-1	.260	.327	.380	1	.984
1996—	New Orleans (A.A.)	SS	19	71	10	18	5	1	0	11	9	8	1-1	.254	.345	.352	5	.948
	—Milwaukee (A.L.)	2B-3B-SS	73	154	20	43	3	0	1	13	14	15	2-1	.279	.339	.318	2	.989
1997—	Milwaukee (A.L.)	2-S-1-3-DH	132	418	56	120	17	5	5	47	47	60	5-5	.287	.354	.388	15	.976
1998—	Milwaukee (N.L.)	1-S-3-2-0	140	434	55	137	29	0	6	54	42	47	9-6	.316	.382	.424	6	.991
1999—	Milwaukee (N.L.)	SS-1B-2B-3B	153	587	93	170	34	5	5	67	52	59	4-1	.290	.354	.390	13	.986
2000—	Milwaukee (N.L.)	SS-2B	91	352	49	99	21	1	7	40	37	38	0-3	.281	.350	.406	2	.995
	—Indianapolis (I.L.)	SS	10	25	6	6	1	0	0	5	2	4	0-0	.240	.310	.280	0	1.000

Year	Team (League)	Pos.	G	AB	R	H	2B	3B	HR	RBI	BB	SO	SB-CS	Avg.	OBP	SLG	E	Avg.
			BATTING														FIELDING	
2001—	Indianapolis (I.L.)	SS-2B-3B	8	31	4	3	0	0	0	1	2	4	0-0	.097	.152	.097	3	.850
—	Milwaukee (N.L.)	2-3-S-DH-P	102	384	40	111	14	2	2	29	28	46	1-2	.289	.346	.352	8	.978
2002—	Milwaukee (N.L.)	3-S-1-2-D	86	217	23	58	14	0	2	19	23	32	0-0	.267	.350	.359	3	.982
—	Houston (N.L.)■	3B-SS-2B	21	66	10	28	4	0	2	8	9	5	1-1	.424	.481	.576	2	.964
American League totals (3 years)			224	622	89	176	23	5	7	63	65	82	8-7	.283	.349	.370	18	.979
National League totals (5 years)			593	2040	270	603	116	8	24	217	191	227	15-13	.296	.362	.396	34	.987
Major League totals (8 years)			817	2662	359	779	139	13	31	280	256	309	23-20	.293	.359	.390	52	.985

RECORD AS PITCHER

Year	League	W	L	Pct.	ERA	G	GS	CG	ShO	Sv.-Opp.	IP	H	R	ER	HR	BB-IBB	SO
1994—	El Paso (Texas)	0	0	...	...	1	0	0	0	0-...	.0	0	1	1	0	1-1	0

LORRAINE, ANDREW P

PERSONAL: Born August 11, 1972, in Los Angeles. ... 6-3/200. ... Throws left, bats left. ... Full name: Andrew Jason Lorraine.

HIGH SCHOOL: William S. Hart (Newhall, Calif.).

COLLEGE: Stanford.

TRANSACTIONS/CAREER NOTES: Selected by New York Mets organization in 38th round of free-agent draft (June 4, 1990); did not sign. ... Selected by California Angels organization in fourth round of free-agent draft (June 3, 1993). ... Traded by Angels with OF McKay Christensen, P Bill Simas and P John Snyder to Chicago White Sox for P Jim Abbott and P Tim Fortugno (July 27, 1995). ... Traded by White Sox with OF Charles Poe to Oakland Athletics for OF/DH Danny Tartabull (January 22, 1996). ... Released by A's (October 16, 1997). ... Signed by Seattle Mariners organization (October 17, 1997). ... Granted free agency (October 3, 1998). ... Signed by Chicago Cubs organization (November 13, 1998). ... Released by Cubs (May 21, 2000). ... Signed by Cleveland Indians organization (May 22, 2000). ... Granted free agency (October 5, 2000). ... Signed by Florida Marlins organization (February 12, 2001). ... Released by Marlins (September 2, 2001). ... Signed by Philadelphia Phillies organization (September 3, 2001). ... Granted free agency (October 15, 2001). ... Signed by Milwaukee Brewers organization (December 20, 2001). ... Released by Brewers (October 12, 2002).

STATISTICAL NOTES: Tied for International League lead with 10 sacrifice hits allowed in 2002.

MISCELLANEOUS: Scored a run in only appearance as pinch runner (1999).

CAREER HITTING (MLB): 3-for-24 (.125), 3 R, 1 2B, 0 3B, 0 HR, 0 RBI.

Year	League	W	L	Pct.	ERA	G	GS	CG	ShO	Sv.-Opp.	IP	H	R	ER	HR	BB-IBB	SO
1993—	Boise (N'West)	4	1	.800	1.29	6	6	3	1	0-...	42.0	33	6	6	3	6-0	39
1994—	Vancouver (PCL)	12	4	.750	3.42	22	22	•4	•2	0-...	142.0	156	63	54	13	34-1	90
—	California (A.L.)	0	2	.000	10.61	4	3	0	0	0-0	18.2	30	23	22	7	11-0	10
1995—	Vancouver (PCL)	6	6	.500	3.96	18	18	4	1	0-...	97.2	105	49	43	7	30-0	51
—	Nashville (A.A.)■	4	1	.800	6.00	7	7	0	0	0-...	39.0	51	29	26	4	12-0	26
—	Chicago (A.L.)	0	0	...	3.38	5	0	0	0	0-0	8.0	3	3	3	0	2-0	5
1996—	Edmonton (PCL)■	8	10	.444	5.68	30	25	0	0	0-...	141.0	181	95	89	19	46-2	73
1997—	Edmonton (PCL)	8	6	.571	4.74	23	20	2	2	0-...	117.2	143	72	62	12	34-1	75
—	Oakland (A.L.)	3	1	.750	6.37	12	6	0	0	0-0	29.2	45	22	21	2	15-0	18
1998—	Tacoma (PCL)■	7	4	.636	4.82	52	4	0	0	2-...	80.1	93	44	43	10	36-2	70
—	Seattle (A.L.)	0	0	...	2.45	4	0	0	0	0-0	3.2	3	1	1	0	4-0	0
1999—	Iowa (PCL)■	9	8	.529	3.71	22	21	1	0	0-...	143.0	149	67	59	16	34-0	96
—	Chicago (N.L.)	2	5	.286	5.55	11	11	2	1	0-0	61.2	71	42	38	9	22-3	40
2000—	Chicago (N.L.)	1	2	.333	6.47	8	5	0	0	0-1	32.0	36	25	23	5	18-1	25
—	Buffalo (I.L.)■	8	3	.727	3.47	14	13	0	0	0-...	90.2	97	37	35	8	24-0	51
—	Cleveland (A.L.)	0	0	...	3.86	10	0	0	0	0-0	9.1	8	4	4	1	5-0	5
2001—	Calgary (PCL)■	9	5	.643	5.40	30	25	1	1	0-...	150.0	209	100	90	19	36-4	101
2002—	Indianapolis (I.L.)■	7	11	.389	3.05	25	24	2	0	0-...	165.0	157	65	56	14	42-7	86
—	Milwaukee (N.L.)	0	1	.000	11.25	5	1	0	0	0-0	12.0	22	18	15	7	6-0	10
A.L. totals (5 years)		3	3	.500	6.62	35	9	0	0	0-0	69.1	89	53	51	10	37-0	38
N.L. totals (3 years)		3	8	.273	6.47	24	17	2	1	0-1	105.2	129	85	76	21	46-4	75
Major League totals (7 years)		6	11	.353	6.53	59	26	2	1	0-1	175.0	218	138	127	31	83-4	113

LOUX, SHANE P TIGERS

PERSONAL: Born August 31, 1979, in Rapid City, S.D. ... 6-2/205. ... Throws right, bats right. ... Full name: Shane A. Loux.

HIGH SCHOOL: Highland (Gilbert, Ariz.).

TRANSACTIONS/CAREER NOTES: Selected by Detroit Tigers organization in second round of free-agent draft (June 3, 1997). ... On Toledo disabled list (July 18-26, 2002).

STATISTICAL NOTES: Tied for International League lead with 10 sacrifice flies allowed and 15 hit batsmen in 2001.

CAREER HITTING (MLB): 0-for-0 (.000), 0 R, 0 2B, 0 3B, 0 HR, 0 RBI.

Year	League	W	L	Pct.	ERA	G	GS	CG	ShO	Sv.-Opp.	IP	H	R	ER	HR	BB-IBB	SO
1997—	Gulf Coast Tigers (GCL)	4	1	.800	0.84	10	9	1	1	0-...	43.0	19	7	4	0	10-0	33
1998—	West Michigan (Midw.)	7	13	.350	4.64	28	•28	2	1	0-...	157.0	184	96	81	13	52-0	88
1999—	West Michigan (Midw.)	1	3	.250	6.27	8	8	0	0	0-...	47.1	55	39	33	5	16-1	43
—	Lakeland (FSL)	6	5	.545	4.05	17	17	0	0	0-...	91.0	92	48	41	8	47-0	52
2000—	Lakeland (FSL)	0	1	.000	1.80	1	1	0	0	0-...	5.0	2	1	1	0	3-0	6
—	Jacksonville (Sou.)	12	9	.571	3.82	26	26	2	0	0-...	157.2	150	78	67	12	55-0	130
2001—	Toledo (I.L.)	10	11	.476	5.78	28	27	2	0	0-...	151.0	203	111	*97	22	73-0	72
2002—	Toledo (I.L.)	11	10	.524	4.72	26	26	*5	*3	0-...	158.1	196	94	83	11	38-1	87
—	Detroit (A.L.)	0	3	.000	9.00	3	3	0	0	0-0	14.0	19	16	14	4	3-0	7
Major League totals (1 year)		0	3	.000	9.00	3	3	0	0	0-0	14.0	19	16	14	4	3-0	7

LOWE, DEREK P RED SOX

PERSONAL: Born June 1, 1973, in Dearborn, Mich. ... 6-6/214. ... Throws right, bats right. ... Full name: Derek Christopher Lowe.

HIGH SCHOOL: Edsel Ford (Dearborn, Mich.).

TRANSACTIONS/CAREER NOTES: Selected by Seattle Mariners organization in eighth round of free-agent draft (June 3, 1991). ... Traded by Mariners with C Jason Varitek to Boston Red Sox for P Heathcliff Slocumb (July 31, 1997). ... On suspended list (September 15-20, 2002).
HONORS: Named righthanded pitcher on THE SPORTING NEWS A.L. All-Star team (2002).
STATISTICAL NOTES: Led Southern League with seven balks in 1994. ... Led A.L. with 47 save opportunities in 2000. ... Led A.L. with nine intentional bases on balls issued in 2001. ... Pitched 10-0 no-hit victory against Tampa Bay (April 27, 2002).
MISCELLANEOUS: Struck out in only appearance as pinch hitter (2000).
CAREER HITTING (MLB): 1-for-12 (.083), 0 R, 0 2B, 0 3B, 0 HR, 0 RBI.

Year League	W	L	Pct.	ERA	G	GS	CG	ShO	Sv.-Opp.	IP	H	R	ER	HR	BB-IBB	SO
1991— Arizona Mariners (Ariz.)	5	3	.625	2.41	12	12	0	0	0-...	71.0	58	26	19	2	21-0	60
1992— Bellingham (N'West)	7	3	.700	2.42	14	13	2	•1	0-...	85.2	69	34	23	2	22-0	66
1993— Riverside (Calif.)	12	9	.571	5.26	27	26	3	2	0-...	154.0	189	104	90	9	60-0	80
1994— Jacksonville (Sou.)	7	10	.412	4.94	26	26	2	0	0-...	151.1	177	92	83	7	50-1	75
1995— Arizona Mariners (Ariz.)	1	0	1.000	0.93	2	2	0	0	0-...	9.2	5	1	1	0	2-0	11
— Port City (Sou.)	1	6	.143	6.07	10	10	1	0	0-...	53.1	70	41	36	8	22-1	30
1996— Port City (Sou.)	5	3	.625	3.05	10	10	0	0	0-...	65.0	56	27	22	7	17-0	33
— Tacoma (PCL)	6	9	.400	4.54	17	16	1	1	0-...	105.0	118	64	53	7	37-1	54
1997— Tacoma (PCL)	3	4	.429	3.45	10	9	1	0	0-...	57.1	53	26	22	3	20-0	49
— Seattle (A.L.)	2	4	.333	6.96	12	9	0	0	0-0	53.0	59	43	41	11	20-2	39
— Pawtucket (I.L.)■	4	0	1.000	2.37	6	5	0	0	0-...	30.1	23	8	8	3	11-0	21
— Boston (A.L.)	0	2	.000	3.38	8	0	0	0	0-2	16.0	15	6	6	0	3-1	13
1998— Boston (A.L.)	3	9	.250	4.02	63	10	0	0	4-9	123.0	126	65	55	5	42-5	77
1999— Boston (A.L.)	6	3	.667	2.63	74	0	0	0	15-20	109.1	84	35	32	7	25-1	80
2000— Boston (A.L.)	4	4	.500	2.56	74	0	0	0	•42-47	91.1	90	27	26	6	22-5	79
2001— Boston (A.L.)	5	10	.333	3.53	67	3	0	0	24-30	91.2	103	39	36	7	29-9	82
2002— Boston (A.L.)	21	8	.724	2.58	32	32	1	1	0-0	219.2	166	65	63	12	48-0	127
Major League totals (6 years)	41	40	.506	3.31	330	54	1	1	85-108	704.0	643	280	259	48	189-23	497

DIVISION SERIES RECORD

Year League	W	L	Pct.	ERA	G	GS	CG	ShO	Sv.-Opp.	IP	H	R	ER	HR	BB-IBB	SO
1998— Boston (A.L.)	0	0	...	2.08	2	0	0	0	0-0	4.1	3	1	1	0	1-1	2
1999— Boston (A.L.)	1	1	.500	4.32	3	0	0	0	0-0	8.1	6	7	4	2	1-0	7
Division series totals (2 years)	1	1	.500	3.55	5	0	0	0	0-0	12.2	9	8	5	2	2-1	9

CHAMPIONSHIP SERIES RECORD

Year League	W	L	Pct.	ERA	G	GS	CG	ShO	Sv.-Opp.	IP	H	R	ER	HR	BB-IBB	SO
1999— Boston (A.L.)	0	0	...	1.42	3	0	0	0	0-1	6.1	6	3	1	0	2-0	7

ALL-STAR GAME RECORD

	W	L	Pct.	ERA	GS	CG	ShO	Sv.-Opp.	IP	H	R	ER	HR	BB-IBB	SO
All-Star Game totals (2 years)	0	0	...	3.00	1	0	0	0-0	3.0	2	1	1	0	0-0	0

LOWE, SEAN — P — ROCKIES

PERSONAL: Born March 29, 1971, in Dallas. ... 6-2/225. ... Throws right, bats right. ... Full name: Jonathan Sean Lowe.
HIGH SCHOOL: Mesquite (Texas).
JUNIOR COLLEGE: McLennan Community College (Texas).
COLLEGE: Arizona State.
TRANSACTIONS/CAREER NOTES: Selected by Cincinnati Reds organization in 43rd round of free-agent draft (June 5, 1989); did not sign. ... Selected by Oakland Athletics organization in 43rd round of free-agent draft (June 4, 1990); did not sign. ... Selected by St. Louis Cardinals organization in first round (15th pick overall) of free-agent draft (June 1, 1992). ... On St. Petersburg disabled list (July 19-August 8, 1994). ... On Arkansas disabled list (May 28-June 4, 1996). ... On Louisville disabled list (April 9-18, 1997). ... Traded by Cardinals to Chicago White Sox for P John Ambrose (February 9, 1999). ... On Chicago disabled list (July 29-August 23, 2000); included rehabilitation assignment to Charlotte (August 8-23). ... Traded by White Sox with P Kip Wells and P Josh Fogg to Pittsburgh Pirates for P Todd Ritchie and C Lee Evans (December 13, 2001). ... Released by Pirates (September 8, 2002). ... Signed by Colorado Rockies (September 12, 2002).
STATISTICAL NOTES: Tied for American Association lead with 10 hit batsmen in 1997.
CAREER HITTING (MLB): 3-for-22 (.136), 0 R, 0 2B, 0 3B, 0 HR, 0 RBI.

Year League	W	L	Pct.	ERA	G	GS	CG	ShO	Sv.-Opp.	IP	H	R	ER	HR	BB-IBB	SO
1992— Hamilton (NY-Penn)	2	0	1.000	1.61	5	5	0	0	0-...	28.0	14	8	5	0	14-0	22
1993— St. Petersburg (FSL)	6	11	.353	4.27	25	25	0	0	0-...	132.2	152	80	63	6	62-1	87
1994— St. Petersburg (FSL)	5	6	.455	3.47	21	21	0	0	0-...	114.0	119	51	44	6	37-0	92
— Arkansas (Texas)	2	1	.667	1.40	3	3	0	0	0-...	19.1	13	3	3	0	8-0	11
1995— Arkansas (Texas)	9	8	.529	4.88	24	24	0	0	0-...	129.0	143	84	70	2	64-0	77
1996— Louisville (A.A.)	8	9	.471	4.70	25	18	0	0	0-...	115.0	127	72	60	7	51-7	76
— Arkansas (Texas)	2	3	.400	6.00	6	6	0	0	0-...	33.0	32	24	22	2	15-1	25
1997— Louisville (A.A.)	6	10	.375	4.37	26	23	1	0	1-...	131.2	142	74	64	13	53-4	117
— St. Louis (N.L.)	0	2	.000	9.35	6	4	0	0	0-0	17.1	27	21	18	2	10-0	8
1998— Memphis (PCL)	12	8	.600	3.18	25	21	0	0	0-...	153.0	147	57	54	17	61-1	114
— St. Louis (N.L.)	0	3	.000	15.19	4	1	0	0	0-0	5.1	11	9	9	1	5-0	2
1999— Chicago (A.L.)■	4	1	.800	3.67	64	0	0	0	0-3	95.2	90	39	39	10	46-1	62
2000— Chicago (A.L.)	4	1	.800	5.48	50	5	0	0	0-0	70.2	78	47	43	10	39-3	53
— Charlotte (I.L.)	0	0	...	3.00	2	1	0	0	0-...	3.0	5	1	1	1	1-0	1
2001— Chicago (A.L.)	9	4	.692	3.61	45	11	0	0	3-3	127.0	123	55	51	12	32-2	71
— Charlotte (I.L.)	1	1	.500	4.50	2	2	0	0	0-...	10.0	9	6	5	0	2-0	8
2002— Pittsburgh (N.L.)■	4	2	.667	5.35	43	1	0	0	0-2	69.0	85	45	41	8	34-6	57
— Nashville (PCL)	1	1	.500	5.73	5	5	0	0	0-...	22.0	29	14	14	0	3-0	21
— Colorado (N.L.)■	1	1	.500	8.71	8	0	0	0	0-0	10.1	16	13	10	1	7-0	7
A.L. totals (3 years)	17	6	.739	4.08	159	16	0	0	3-6	293.1	291	141	133	32	117-6	186
N.L. totals (3 years)	5	8	.385	6.88	61	6	0	0	0-2	102.0	139	88	78	12	56-6	74
Major League totals (6 years)	22	14	.611	4.80	220	22	0	0	3-8	395.1	430	229	211	44	173-12	260

LOWELL, MIKE — 3B — MARLINS

PERSONAL: Born February 24, 1974, in San Juan, Puerto Rico. ... 6-3/217. ... Bats right, throws right. ... Full name: Michael Averett Lowell.
HIGH SCHOOL: Coral Gables (Fla.).
COLLEGE: Florida International.
TRANSACTIONS/CAREER NOTES: Selected by New York Yankees organization in 20th round of free-agent draft (June 1, 1995). ... Traded by Yankees to Florida Marlins for P Ed Yarnall, P Mark Johnson and P Todd Noel (February 1, 1999). ... On Florida disabled list (March 26-May 29, 1999); included rehabilitation assignments to Calgary (April 8-13 and May 6-29). ... On disabled list (May 13-29, 2000).
RECORDS: Holds major league single-season record for fewest putouts by third baseman for leader—107 (2001).
STATISTICAL NOTES: Led New York-Pennsylvania League third basemen with 271 total chances in 1995. ... Led South Atlantic League third basemen with 301 putouts, 421 total chances and .926 fielding percentage in 1996. ... Tied for International League lead with 20 errors by third baseman in 1998. ... Had 16-game hitting streak (August 18-September 5, 2000). ... Had 16-game hitting streak (September 3-18, 2002). ... Tied for N.L. lead with 11 sacrifice flies in 2002. ... Led N.L. third basemen with 150 putouts in 2002. ... Career major league grand slams: 3.
2002 GAMES PLAYED BY POSITION (MLB): 3B—159.

		BATTING														FIELDING	
Year Team (League)	Pos.	G	AB	R	H	2B	3B	HR	RBI	BB	SO	SB-CS	Avg.	OBP	SLG	E	Avg.
1995—Oneonta (NY-Penn)	3B	72	281	36	73	18	0	1	27	23	34	3-1	.260	.316	.335	24	.911
1996—Greensboro (S.Atl.)	3B-SS	113	433	58	122	33	0	8	64	46	43	10-3	.282	.355	.413	32	.925
—Tampa (FSL)	3B	24	78	8	22	5	0	0	11	3	13	1-1	.282	.298	.346	3	.954
1997—Norwich (East.)	3B-SS	78	285	60	98	17	0	15	47	48	30	2-1	.344	.439	.561	15	.927
—Columbus (I.L.)	3B-SS	57	210	36	58	13	1	15	45	23	34	2-4	.276	.347	.562	5	.954
1998—Columbus (I.L.)	3B-1B-SS	126	510	79	155	34	3	26	99	37	85	4-0	.304	.355	.535	‡21	.950
—New York (A.L.)	3B-DH	8	15	1	4	0	0	0	0	0	1	0-0	.267	.267	.267	0	1.000
1999—Calgary (PCL)■	3B	24	83	11	26	3	0	2	9	8	19	0-0	.313	.374	.422	4	.939
—Florida (N.L.)	3B	97	308	32	78	15	0	12	47	26	69	0-0	.253	.317	.419	4	.981
2000—Florida (N.L.)	3B	140	508	73	137	38	0	22	91	54	75	4-0	.270	.344	.474	12	.968
2001—Florida (N.L.)	3B	146	551	65	156	37	0	18	100	43	79	1-2	.283	.340	.448	9	.976
2002—Florida (N.L.)	3B	160	597	88	165	44	0	24	92	65	92	4-3	.276	.346	.471	14	.969
American League totals (1 year)		8	15	1	4	0	0	0	0	0	1	0-0	.267	.267	.267	0	1.000
National League totals (4 years)		543	1964	258	536	134	0	76	330	188	315	9-5	.273	.339	.457	39	.972
Major League totals (5 years)		551	1979	259	540	134	0	76	330	188	316	9-5	.273	.339	.456	39	.972

ALL-STAR GAME RECORD

	AB	R	H	2B	3B	HR	RBI	BB	SO	SB-CS	Avg.	OBP	SLG	E	Avg.
All-Star Game totals (1 year)	3	1	2	0	0	0	0	0	0	0-0	.667	.667	.667	0	...

LUDWICK, RYAN — OF — RANGERS

PERSONAL: Born July 13, 1978, in Sattelite Beach, Fla. ... 6-3/203. ... Bats right, throws left. ... Full name: Ryan Andrew Ludwick.
HIGH SCHOOL: Durango (Las Vegas, Nev.).
COLLEGE: Nevada-Las Vegas.
TRANSACTIONS/CAREER NOTES: Selected by Oakland Athletics organization in second round of free-agent draft (June 2, 1999). ... Traded by A's with 1B Jason Hart, P Mario Ramos and C Gerald Laird to Texas Rangers for 1B Carlos Pena and P Mike Venafro (January 14, 2002). ... On Oklahoma disabled list (August 3, 2002-remainder of season).
2002 GAMES PLAYED BY POSITION (MLB): OF—22.

		BATTING														FIELDING	
Year Team (League)	Pos.	G	AB	R	H	2B	3B	HR	RBI	BB	SO	SB-CS	Avg.	OBP	SLG	E	Avg.
1999—Modesto (Calif.)	OF	43	171	28	47	11	3	4	34	19	45	2-1	.275	.348	.444	0	1.000
2000—Modesto (Calif.)	OF	129	493	86	130	26	3	29	102	68	128	10-6	.264	.359	.505	5	.983
2001—Midland (Texas)	OF	119	443	82	119	23	3	25	96	53	113	9-10	.269	.352	.503	6	.977
—Sacramento (PCL)	OF	17	57	10	13	3	0	1	7	2	16	2-0	.228	.246	.333	1	.981
2002—Oklahoma (PCL)■	OF	78	305	62	87	27	4	15	52	38	76	2-2	.285	.370	.548	5	.973
—Texas (A.L.)	OF	23	81	10	19	6	0	1	9	7	24	2-1	.235	.295	.346	0	1.000
Major League totals (1 year)		23	81	10	19	6	0	1	9	7	24	2-1	.235	.295	.346	0	1.000

LUGO, JULIO — SS — ASTROS

PERSONAL: Born November 16, 1975, in Barahona, Dominican Republic. ... 6-1/170. ... Bats right, throws right. ... Full name: Julio Cesar Lugo.
JUNIOR COLLEGE: Connors State College (Okla.).
TRANSACTIONS/CAREER NOTES: Selected by Houston Astros organization in 43rd round of free-agent draft (June 2, 1994). ... On disabled list (July 21-29, 1999). ... On disabled list (August 13, 2002-remainder of season).
STATISTICAL NOTES: Led Florida State League shortstops with 40 errors in 1997. ... Career major league grand slams: 1.
2002 GAMES PLAYED BY POSITION (MLB): SS—84.

		BATTING														FIELDING	
Year Team (League)	Pos.	G	AB	R	H	2B	3B	HR	RBI	BB	SO	SB-CS	Avg.	OBP	SLG	E	Avg.
1995—Auburn (NY-Penn)	2B-SS-OF	59	230	36	67	6	3	1	16	26	31	17-7	.291	.368	.357	12	.944
1996—Quad City (Midw.)	SS-2B-3B	101	393	60	116	18	2	10	50	32	75	24-11	.295	.350	.427	29	.934
1997—Kissimmee (FSL)	SS-2B-3B	125	505	89	135	22	*14	7	61	46	99	35-8	.267	.329	.408	†41	.938
1998—Kissimmee (FSL)	SS	128	509	81	154	20	*14	7	62	49	72	51-18	.303	.367	.438	42	.921
1999—Jackson (Texas)	SS-2B-DH	116	445	77	142	24	5	10	42	44	53	25-11	.319	.381	.463	29	.946
2000—New Orleans (PCL)	2B-SS	24	101	22	33	4	1	3	12	11	20	12-7	.327	.393	.475	4	.964
—Houston (N.L.)	SS-2B-OF	116	420	78	119	22	5	10	40	37	93	22-9	.283	.346	.431	17	.963
2001—Houston (N.L.)	SS-OF-2B	140	513	93	135	20	3	10	37	46	116	12-11	.263	.326	.372	22	.964
2002—Houston (N.L.)	SS	88	322	45	84	15	1	8	35	28	74	9-3	.261	.322	.388	8	.976
Major League totals (3 years)		344	1255	216	338	57	9	28	112	111	283	43-23	.269	.332	.396	47	.966

DIVISION SERIES RECORD

		BATTING														FIELDING	
Year Team (League)	Pos.	G	AB	R	H	2B	3B	HR	RBI	BB	SO	SB-CS	Avg.	OBP	SLG	E	Avg.
2001—Houston (N.L.)	SS-PH	3	8	1	0	0	0	0	0	0	2	0-0	.000	.000	.000	3	.786

LUKASIEWICZ, MARK — P — ANGELS

PERSONAL: Born March 8, 1973, in Jersey City, N.J. ... 6-5/240. ... Throws left, bats left. ... Full name: Mark Francis Lukasiewicz.
HIGH SCHOOL: Secaucus (N.J.).
JUNIOR COLLEGE: Brevard.
COLLEGE: Oklahoma State.
TRANSACTIONS/CAREER NOTES: Selected by Toronto Blue Jays organization in supplemental round ("sandwich pick" between first and second round, 41st pick overall) of free-agent draft (June 3, 1993); pick received as partial compensation for New York Yankees signing Type A free agent P Jimmy Key. ... Loaned by Blue Jays organization to Bakersfield, California League (June 19-July 12, 1996). ... Claimed on waivers by Anaheim Angels (October 10, 2000).
CAREER HITTING (MLB): 0-for-0 (.000), 0 R, 0 2B, 0 3B, 0 HR, 0 RBI.

Year League	W	L	Pct.	ERA	G	GS	CG	ShO	Sv.-Opp.	IP	H	R	ER	HR	BB-IBB	SO
1994—Hagerstown (S.Atl.)	3	6	.333	4.78	29	17	0	0	0-...	98.0	108	70	52	8	21-0	84
1995—Dunedin (FSL)	3	6	.333	5.73	31	13	0	0	1-...	86.1	80	62	55	13	42-0	71
1996—Dunedin (FSL)	2	1	.667	4.60	23	0	0	0	1-...	31.1	28	20	16	1	22-1	31
—Bakersfield (Calif.)■	0	2	.000	9.24	7	0	0	0	0-...	12.2	17	14	13	2	11-0	9
—Hagerstown (S.Atl.)■	2	0	1.000	2.30	9	1	0	0	0-...	15.2	8	5	4	0	7-0	20
1997—Knoxville (Sou.)	2	0	1.000	3.65	27	0	0	0	7-...	37.0	26	17	15	2	14-1	43
—Syracuse (I.L.)	2	3	.400	5.17	30	0	0	0	0-...	31.1	37	22	18	7	13-1	31
1998—Syracuse (I.L.)	2	2	.500	3.40	22	4	0	0	1-...	47.2	38	18	18	8	24-1	30
—Knoxville (Sou.)	0	0	...	1.93	5	0	0	0	1-...	9.1	6	2	2	0	1-0	16
—Dunedin (FSL)	1	1	.500	0.84	9	0	0	0	0-...	10.2	7	2	1	0	4-0	8
1999—Syracuse (I.L.)	4	4	.500	5.34	37	9	1	0	3-...	97.2	109	59	58	20	40-1	77
2000—Syracuse (I.L.)	2	1	.667	3.48	42	0	0	0	0-...	41.1	34	17	16	7	25-1	52
—Tennessee (Sou.)	0	0	...	5.79	3	0	0	0	0-...	4.2	4	3	3	1	4-0	6
2001—Salt Lake (PCL)■	3	0	1.000	1.48	20	0	0	0	2-...	30.1	12	5	5	4	2-0	41
—Anaheim (A.L.)	0	2	.000	6.04	24	0	0	0	0-0	22.1	21	17	15	6	9-2	25
2002—Anaheim (A.L.)	2	0	1.000	3.86	17	0	0	0	0-0	14.0	17	6	6	0	9-0	15
—Salt Lake (PCL)	3	2	.600	3.98	35	0	0	0	0-...	43.0	46	26	19	6	17-0	48
Major League totals (2 years)	2	2	.500	5.20	41	0	0	0	0-0	36.1	38	23	21	6	18-2	40

LUNAR, FERNANDO — C — RANGERS

PERSONAL: Born May 25, 1977, in Cantanura, Venezuela. ... 6-1/190. ... Bats right, throws right. ... Full name: Fernando Jose Lunar.
HIGH SCHOOL: Liceo Anaco Venezuela (Anzoategui, El Salvador).
TRANSACTIONS/CAREER NOTES: Signed as non-drafted free agent by Atlanta Braves organization (March 15, 1994). ... On disabled list (April 16-24, 1995). ... Traded by Braves with OF Trenidad Hubbard and P Luis Rivera to Baltimore Orioles for OF B.J. Surhoff and P Gabe Molina (July 31, 2000). ... On Rochester disabled list (June 21-July 11 and August 3, 2002-remainder of season). ... Released by Orioles (September 30, 2002). ... Signed by Texas Rangers organization (November 13, 2002).
STATISTICAL NOTES: Tied for Gulf Coast League lead in double plays by catcher with three in 1994. ... Led South Atlantic League catchers with 11 double plays in 1996. ... Led South Atlantic League catchers with 888 putouts, 135 assists and 1,036 total chances in 1997. ... Led Carolina League catchers with nine double plays in 1998. ... Led Southern League catchers with 88 assists and 12 double plays in 1999.
2002 GAMES PLAYED BY POSITION (MLB): C—2.

		BATTING														FIELDING	
Year Team (League)	Pos.	G	AB	R	H	2B	3B	HR	RBI	BB	SO	SB-CS	Avg.	OBP	SLG	E	Avg.
1994—GC Braves (GCL)	C	33	100	9	24	5	0	2	12	1	13	0-0	.240	.267	.350	7	.971
1995—Eugene (N'West)	C	39	131	13	32	6	0	2	16	9	28	0-1	.244	.293	.336	8	.977
—Macon (S.Atl.)	C	39	134	13	24	2	0	0	9	10	38	1-0	.179	.252	.194	10	.967
1996—Macon (S.Atl.)	C	104	343	33	63	9	0	7	33	20	65	3-2	.184	.252	.271	12	.984
1997—Macon (S.Atl.)	C	105	380	41	99	26	2	7	37	18	42	0-1	.261	.302	.395	13	.987
1998—Danville (Caro.)	C	91	286	19	63	9	0	3	28	6	52	1-1	.220	.266	.283	8	.990
1999—Greenville (Sou.)	C-DH	105	343	33	77	15	1	3	35	12	64	0-1	.224	.275	.300	10	.986
2000—Greenville (Sou.)	C	31	102	6	17	3	0	0	4	8	15	0-0	.167	.227	.196	3	.989
—Atlanta (N.L.)	C	22	54	5	10	1	0	0	5	3	15	0-2	.185	.267	.204	1	.993
—Bowie (East.)■	C	22	80	12	23	7	1	0	8	6	8	0-0	.288	.360	.400	2	.989
—Baltimore (A.L.)	C	9	16	0	2	0	0	0	1	0	4	0-0	.125	.176	.125	0	1.000
2001—Baltimore (A.L.)	C	64	167	8	41	7	0	0	16	7	32	0-0	.246	.287	.287	4	.987
2002—Baltimore (A.L.)	C	2	0	0	0	0	0	0	0	0	0	0-0	...	...	...	0	1.000
—Rochester (I.L.)	C	42	145	7	28	1	0	2	8	4	27	1-0	.193	.234	.241	5	.982
American League totals (3 years)		75	183	8	43	7	0	0	17	7	36	0-0	.235	.277	.273	4	.989
National League totals (1 year)		22	54	5	10	1	0	0	5	3	15	0-2	.185	.267	.204	1	.993
Major League totals (3 years)		97	237	13	53	8	0	0	22	10	51	0-2	.224	.275	.257	5	.990

LUNDQUIST, DAVID — P

PERSONAL: Born June 4, 1973, in Beverly, Mass. ... 6-2/200. ... Throws right, bats right. ... Full name: David Bruce Lundquist Jr.
HIGH SCHOOL: Carson City (Nev.).
JUNIOR COLLEGE: Cochise County Community College (Ariz.).
COLLEGE: UNLV.
TRANSACTIONS/CAREER NOTES: Selected by Chicago White Sox organization in fifth round of free-agent draft (June 3, 1993). ... On Prince William disabled list (April 5-June 5 and June 19, 1996-remainder of season). ... On Charlotte disabled list (July 1, 1999-remainder of season). ... Claimed on waivers by Kansas City Royals (October 15, 1999). ... Released by Royals (March 29, 2000). ... Played with Aberdeen, Northern League (2000). ... Signed by San Diego Padres organization (February 6, 2001). ... Granted free agency (October 15, 2001). ... Re-signed by Padres organization (December 6, 2001). ... On San Diego disabled list (June 29-July 15, 2002). ... Released by Padres (July 15, 2002).
CAREER HITTING (MLB): 0-for-0 (.000), 0 R, 0 2B, 0 3B, 0 HR, 0 RBI.

Year League	W	L	Pct.	ERA	G	GS	CG	ShO	Sv.-Opp.	IP	H	R	ER	HR	BB-IBB	SO
1993—GC White Sox (GCL)	5	3	.625	3.14	11	10	0	0	0-...	63.0	70	26	22	0	15-0	40
1994—Hickory (S.Atl.)	13	10	.565	3.48	27	27	3	2	0-...	178.2	170	88	69	15	43-0	133
1995—South Bend (Midw.)	8	4	.667	3.58	18	18	5	1	0-...	118.0	107	54	47	4	38-0	60
1996—GC White Sox (GCL)	1	1	.500	2.63	3	3	0	0	0-...	13.2	8	4	4	1	2-0	16
—Prince William (Caro.)	0	2	.000	5.67	5	5	0	0	0-...	27.0	31	17	17	2	14-1	23
1997—Winston-Salem (Caro.)	3	1	.750	6.75	20	6	0	0	0-...	48.0	65	41	36	7	23-3	39
—Birmingham (Sou.)	0	0	...	8.77	7	0	0	0	0-...	13.1	26	20	13	3	5-0	15
1998—Winston-Salem (Caro.)	1	0	1.000	2.53	6	0	0	0	0-...	10.2	9	4	3	0	3-0	9
—Birmingham (Sou.)	1	1	.500	3.29	33	0	0	0	10-...	41.0	28	15	15	1	15-1	41
—Calgary (PCL)	3	0	1.000	3.60	12	0	0	0	2-...	15.0	12	6	6	0	7-0	12
1999—Chicago (A.L.)	1	1	.500	8.59	17	0	0	0	0-0	22.0	28	21	21	3	12-0	18
—Charlotte (I.L.)	0	0	...	0.00	3	0	0	0	0-...	3.2	3	0	0	0	1-0	4
2000—Aberdeen (Nor.)■	4	3	.571	9.07	21	0	0	0	0-...	41.2	69	49	42	11	17-3	32
2001—Portland (PCL)■	4	7	.364	3.11	50	0	0	0	7-...	63.2	59	25	22	6	20-0	67
—San Diego (N.L.)	0	1	.000	5.95	17	0	0	0	0-1	19.2	20	13	13	1	7-1	19
2002—Portland (PCL)	1	4	.200	5.63	30	0	0	0	21-...	32.0	28	21	20	6	15-1	31
—San Diego (N.L.)	0	0	...	16.88	3	0	0	0	0-1	2.2	8	5	5	0	5-2	0
A.L. totals (1 year)	1	1	.500	8.59	17	0	0	0	0-0	22.0	28	21	21	3	12-0	18
N.L. totals (2 years)	0	1	.000	7.25	20	0	0	0	0-2	22.1	28	18	18	1	12-3	19
Major League totals (3 years)	1	2	.333	7.92	37	0	0	0	0-2	44.1	56	39	39	4	24-3	37

LUNSFORD, TREY — C — GIANTS

PERSONAL: Born May 25, 1979, in Odessa, Texas. ... 6-1/195. ... Bats right, throws right. ... Full name: James L. Lunsford.
HIGH SCHOOL: Central (San Angelo, Texas).
JUNIOR COLLEGE: Grayson County Junior College (Texas).
COLLEGE: Texas Tech.
TRANSACTIONS/CAREER NOTES: Selected by San Francisco Giants organization in 33rd round of free-agent draft (June 5, 2000). ... On San Jose disabled list (April 4-28, 2002).
2002 GAMES PLAYED BY POSITION (MLB): C—3.

		BATTING													FIELDING	
Year Team (League)	Pos.	G	AB	R	H	2B	3B	HR	RBI	BB	SO	SB-CS	Avg.	OBP	SLG	E	Avg.
2000—Salem-Kaizer (NW)	C	59	215	23	58	9	0	3	30	30	40	1-0	.270	.378	.353	7	.987
2001—Hagerstown (S.Atl.)	C-1B	114	396	53	94	19	0	5	50	45	89	10-5	.237	.320	.323	14	.986
2002—San Jose (Calif.)	C	16	51	7	13	3	0	1	5	3	5	2-0	.255	.321	.373	1	.991
—Shreveport (Texas)	C-1B	66	210	26	59	13	0	1	20	29	42	5-2	.281	.379	.357	5	.987
—Fresno (PCL)	C	19	57	3	10	0	0	2	9	6	15	0-0	.175	.258	.281	2	.987
—San Francisco (N.L.)	C	3	3	0	2	1	0	0	1	0	1	0-0	.667	.667	1.000	1	.800
Major League totals (1 year)		3	3	0	2	1	0	0	1	0	1	0-0	.667	.667	1.000	1	.800

LYON, BRANDON — P — RED SOX

PERSONAL: Born August 10, 1979, in Salt Lake City. ... 6-1/185. ... Throws right, bats right. ... Full name: Brandon J. Lyon.
HIGH SCHOOL: Taylorsville (Salt Lake City).
JUNIOR COLLEGE: Dixie (Utah).
TRANSACTIONS/CAREER NOTES: Selected by Toronto Blue Jays organization in 14th round of free-agent draft (June 2, 1999). ... Claimed on waivers by Boston Red Sox (October 9, 2002).
CAREER HITTING (MLB): 0-for-0 (.000), 0 R, 0 2B, 0 3B, 0 HR, 0 RBI.

Year League	W	L	Pct.	ERA	G	GS	CG	ShO	Sv.-Opp.	IP	H	R	ER	HR	BB-IBB	SO
2000—Queens (NY-Penn)	5	3	.625	2.39	15	13	0	0	0-...	60.1	43	20	16	1	6-0	55
2001—Tennessee (Sou.)	5	0	1.000	3.68	9	9	0	0	0-...	58.2	57	25	24	7	9-0	45
—Syracuse (I.L.)	5	3	.625	3.69	11	11	2	1	0-...	68.1	68	33	28	7	10-0	53
—Toronto (A.L.)	5	4	.556	4.29	11	11	0	0	0-0	63.0	63	31	30	6	15-0	35
2002—Toronto (A.L.)	1	4	.200	6.53	15	10	0	0	0-1	62.0	78	47	45	14	19-2	30
—Syracuse (I.L.)	4	9	.308	5.11	14	14	0	0	0-...	75.2	99	54	43	4	19-0	35
Major League totals (2 years)	6	8	.429	5.40	26	21	0	0	0-1	125.0	141	78	75	20	34-2	65

MABRY, JOHN — OF/3B

PERSONAL: Born October 17, 1970, in Wilmington, Del. ... 6-4/210. ... Bats left, throws right. ... Full name: John Steven Mabry. ... Name pronounced MAY-bree.
HIGH SCHOOL: Bohemia Manor (Chesapeake City, Md.).
COLLEGE: West Chester (Pa.) University.
TRANSACTIONS/CAREER NOTES: Selected by St. Louis Cardinals organization in sixth round of free-agent draft (June 3, 1991). ... On disabled list (April 22-30 and May 6-18, 1992). ... On disabled list (August 20-September 24, 1997). ... Granted free agency (December 21, 1998). ... Signed by Seattle Mariners (December 30, 1998). ... On disabled list (August 14, 1999-remainder of season). ... On Seattle disabled list (April 22-May 12, 2000); included rehabilitation assignment to Tacoma (May 8-12). ... Traded by Mariners with P Tom Davey to San Diego Padres for OF Al Martin (July 31, 2000). ... Granted free agency (October 30, 2000). ... Signed by Cardinals organization (January 5, 2001). ... Traded by Cardinals to Florida Marlins for cash considerations (April 9, 2001). ... On Florida disabled list (April 16-May 20, 2001); included rehabilitation assignment to Brevard County (May 16-20). ... Granted free agency (November 5, 2001). ... Signed by Philadelphia Phillies organization (January 28, 2002). ... Traded by Phillies to Oakland Athletics for 1B/OF Jeremy Giambi (May 22, 2002). ... Granted free agency (November 4, 2002).
STATISTICAL NOTES: Led New York-Pennsylvania League outfielders with 10 assists in 1991. ... Led Texas League in grounding into double plays with 17 in 1993. ... Led Texas League outfielders with six double plays in 1993. ... Hit for the cycle (May 18, 1996). ... Had 20-game hitting streak (May 19-June 9, 1997).
2002 GAMES PLAYED BY POSITION (MLB): OF—54; 1B—51.

Year	Team (League)	Pos.	G	AB	R	H	2B	3B	HR	RBI	BB	SO	SB-CS	Avg.	OBP	SLG	E	Avg.
			BATTING														FIELDING	
1991—	Hamilton (NY-Penn) ...	OF	49	187	25	58	11	0	1	31	17	18	9-3	.310	.370	.385	5	.943
—	Savannah (S.Atl.)	OF	22	86	10	20	6	1	0	8	7	12	1-0	.233	.284	.326	1	.974
1992—	Springfield (Midw.)	OF	115	438	63	115	13	6	11	57	24	39	2-8	.263	.300	.395	6	.969
1993—	Arkansas (Texas)........	OF	*136	528	68	153	32	2	16	72	27	68	7-15	.290	.326	.449	3	*.989
—	Louisville (A.A.)..........	OF	4	7	0	1	0	0	0	1	0	1	0-0	.143	.143	.143	0	1.000
1994—	Louisville (A.A.)..........	OF	122	477	76	125	30	1	15	68	32	67	2-6	.262	.311	.423	2	.992
—	St. Louis (N.L.)...........	OF	6	23	2	7	3	0	0	3	2	4	0-0	.304	.360	.435	0	1.000
1995—	St. Louis (N.L.)...........	1B-OF	129	388	35	119	21	1	5	41	24	45	0-3	.307	.347	.405	4	.994
—	Louisville (A.A.)..........	OF	4	12	0	1	0	0	0	0	0	0	0-0	.083	.083	.083	1	.889
1996—	St. Louis (N.L.)...........	1B-OF	151	543	63	161	30	2	13	74	37	84	3-2	.297	.342	.431	8	.994
1997—	St. Louis (N.L.)...........	OF-1B-3B	116	388	40	110	19	0	5	36	39	77	0-1	.284	.352	.371	1	.998
1998—	St. Louis (N.L.)...........	OF-3B-1B	142	377	41	94	22	0	9	46	30	76	0-2	.249	.305	.379	9	.968
1999—	Seattle (A.L.)■...........	OF-3B-1B-DH	87	262	34	64	14	0	9	33	20	60	2-1	.244	.297	.401	10	.964
2000—	Seattle (A.L.)	3-O-D-1-P	48	103	18	25	5	0	1	7	10	31	0-1	.243	.322	.320	4	.934
—	Tacoma (PCL)	1B-3B	4	14	1	3	1	0	0	1	0	4	0-0	.214	.214	.286	1	.800
—	San Diego (N.L.)■.....	OF-1B	48	123	17	28	8	0	7	25	5	38	0-0	.228	.256	.463	1	.983
2001—	St. Louis (N.L.)■.......	1B-OF	5	7	0	0	0	0	0	0	0	2	0-0	.000	.000	.000	0	1.000
—	Florida (N.L.)■...........	OF-1B-DH-P	82	147	14	32	7	0	6	20	13	44	1-0	.218	.299	.388	2	.964
—	Brevard County (FSL).	OF	4	13	0	2	0	0	0	4	2	1	0-0	.154	.250	.154	0	1.000
2002—	Philadelphia (N.L.)■..	OF-1B	21	21	1	6	0	0	0	3	1	5	0-0	.286	.304	.286	0	1.000
—	Oakland (A.L.)■.........	OF-1B	89	193	27	53	13	1	11	40	14	37	1-1	.275	.322	.523	2	.992
American League totals (3 years)			224	558	79	142	32	1	21	80	44	128	3-3	.254	.310	.428	16	.973
National League totals (8 years)			700	2017	213	557	110	3	45	248	151	375	4-8	.276	.328	.401	25	.991
Major League totals (9 years)			924	2575	292	699	142	4	66	328	195	503	7-11	.271	.324	.407	41	.988

DIVISION SERIES RECORD

RECORDS: Shares career record for most triples—1.

Year	Team (League)	Pos.	G	AB	R	H	2B	3B	HR	RBI	BB	SO	SB-CS	Avg.	OBP	SLG	E	Avg.
			BATTING														FIELDING	
1996—	St. Louis (N.L.)...........	1B	3	10	1	3	0	1	0	1	1	1	0-0	.300	.364	.500	0	1.000
2002—	Oakland (A.L.)	1B-OF	2	2	0	0	0	0	0	0	0	1	0-0	.000	.000	.000	0	1.000
Division series totals (2 years)			5	12	1	3	0	1	0	1	1	2	0-0	.250	.308	.417	0	1.000

CHAMPIONSHIP SERIES RECORD

Year	Team (League)	Pos.	G	AB	R	H	2B	3B	HR	RBI	BB	SO	SB-CS	Avg.	OBP	SLG	E	Avg.
			BATTING														FIELDING	
1996—	St. Louis (N.L.)...........	1B-OF	7	23	1	6	0	0	0	0	0	6	0-0	.261	.292	.261	0	1.000

RECORD AS PITCHER

Year	League	W	L	Pct.	ERA	G	GS	CG	ShO	Sv.-Opp.	IP	H	R	ER	HR	BB-IBB	SO
2000—	Seattle (N.L.)	0	0	...	27.27	1	0	0	0	0-0	0.2	3	2	2	0	1-0	0
2001—	Florida (N.L.)......................	0	0	...	135.00	1	0	0	0	0-0	0.1	3	5	5	0	3-0	0
Major League totals (2 years).....		0	0	...	63.00	2	0	0	0	0-0	1.0	6	7	7	0	4-0	0

MacDOUGAL, MIKE — P — ROYALS

PERSONAL: Born March 5, 1977, in Las Vegas, Nev. ... 6-4/195. ... Throws right, bats both. ... Full name: Robert Meiklejohn MacDougal.

HIGH SCHOOL: Mesa (Ariz.).

COLLEGE: Wake Forest.

TRANSACTIONS/CAREER NOTES: Selected by Baltimore Orioles organization in 22nd round of free-agent draft (June 4, 1996); did not sign. ... Selected by Baltimore Orioles organization in 17th round of free-agent draft (June 2, 1998); did not sign. ... Selected by Kansas City Royals organization in first round (25th pick overall) of free-agent draft (June 2, 1999); pick received from Boston Red Sox as part of compensation for signing Type A free agent 2B Jose Offerman. ... On Wichita disabled list (July 1-August 20, 2002).

CAREER HITTING (MLB): 0-for-0 (.000), 0 R, 0 2B, 0 3B, 0 HR, 0 RBI.

Year	League	W	L	Pct.	ERA	G	GS	CG	ShO	Sv.-Opp.	IP	H	R	ER	HR	BB-IBB	SO
1999—	Spokane (N'West)	2	2	.500	4.47	11	11	0	0	0-...	46.1	43	25	23	3	17-0	57
2000—	Wilmington (Caro.)...........	9	7	.563	3.92	26	25	0	0	1-...	144.2	115	79	63	5	76-0	129
—	Wichita (Texas)	0	1	.000	7.71	2	2	0	0	0-...	11.2	16	10	10	0	7-0	9
2001—	Omaha (PCL).....................	8	8	.500	4.68	28	27	1	0	0-...	144.1	144	90	75	13	76-0	110
—	Kansas City (A.L.)	1	1	.500	4.70	3	3	0	0	0-0	15.1	18	10	8	2	4-0	7
2002—	Omaha (PCL).....................	3	5	.375	5.60	12	10	0	0	0-...	53.0	52	42	33	4	55-0	30
—	Wichita (Texas)	1	1	.500	3.06	4	4	1	0	0-...	17.2	11	12	6	1	24-0	14
—	Gulf Coast Royals (GCL)..	0	0	...	3.00	1	1	0	0	0-...	3.0	3	1	1	0	0-0	3
—	Wilmington (Caro.)...........	0	1	.000	1.08	5	0	0	0	2-...	8.1	3	4	1	1	5-0	10
—	Kansas City (A.L.)	0	1	.000	5.00	6	0	0	0	0-0	9.0	5	5	5	0	7-1	10
Major League totals (2 years).....		1	2	.333	4.81	9	3	0	0	0-0	24.1	23	15	13	2	11-1	17

MACHADO, ANDERSON — SS — PHILLIES

PERSONAL: Born January 25, 1981, in Caracas, Venezuela. ... 5-11/165. ... Bats both, throws right. ... Full name: Anderson Javier Machado.

HIGH SCHOOL: Liceo De Aplicacion (Caracas, Venezuela).

TRANSACTIONS/CAREER NOTES: Signed as non-drafted free agent by Philadelphia Phillies organization (January 14, 1998). ... On Reading disabled list (May 22-June 2, 2002).

STATISTICAL NOTES: Tied for Gulf Coast League lead with seven sacrifice hits in 1999. ... Led Florida State League shortstops with 210 putouts in 2000. ... Led Eastern League shortstops with 391 assists, 614 total chances and 79 double plays in 2002.

									BATTING								FIELDING	
Year	Team (League)	Pos.	G	AB	R	H	2B	3B	HR	RBI	BB	SO	SB-CS	Avg.	OBP	SLG	E	Avg.
1998—	Dom. Phillies (DSL) ...		68	219	26	44	7	0	0	17	30	44	4-...	.201	...	.233	...	...
1999—	GC Phillies (GCL)	2B-SS-3B	43	143	26	37	6	3	2	12	15	38	6-3	.259	.335	.385	8	.958
	—Clearwater (FSL)	SS	1	2	0	0	0	0	0	0	0	1	0-0	.000	.000	.000	0	...
	—Piedmont (S.Atl.)........	SS	20	60	7	14	4	2	0	7	7	20	2-1	.233	.324	.367	8	.910
2000—	Clearwater (FSL)	SS	117	417	55	102	19	7	1	35	54	103	32-18	.245	.330	.331	43	.934
	—Reading (East.)...........	SS	3	11	2	4	1	0	1	2	0	4	0-0	.364	.364	.727	1	.929
2001—	Clearwater (FSL)	SS	82	272	49	71	5	8	5	36	31	66	23-9	.261	.242	.393	16	.962
	—Reading (East.)...........	SS	31	101	13	15	2	0	1	8	12	25	5-2	.149	.237	.198	9	.941
2002—	Reading (East.)...........	SS	126	450	71	113	24	3	12	77	72	118	40-11	.251	.353	.398	•28	.954

MACHADO, ROBERT C BREWERS

PERSONAL: Born June 3, 1973, in Caracas, Venezuela. ... 6-1/210. ... Bats right, throws right. ... Full name: Robert Alexis Machado.

TRANSACTIONS/CAREER NOTES: Signed as non-drafted free agent by Chicago White Sox organization (August 10, 1989). ... Released by White Sox (May 19, 1999). ... Signed by Montreal Expos organization (May 21, 1999). ... Granted free agency (October 15, 1999). ... Signed by Seattle Mariners organization (November 17, 1999). ... Granted free agency (October 2, 2000). ... Signed by Chicago Cubs organization (December 13, 2000). ... Traded by Cubs to Milwaukee Brewers for OF Jackson Melian (June 8, 2002).

STATISTICAL NOTES: Led Gulf Coast League catchers with 287 putouts, 54 assists and 349 total chances in 1991. ... Tied for Southern League lead in double plays by catcher with 10 in 1996. ... Tied for American Association lead in passed balls with nine in 1997.

2002 GAMES PLAYED BY POSITION (MLB): C—69; 1B—3.

									BATTING								FIELDING	
Year	Team (League)	Pos.	G	AB	R	H	2B	3B	HR	RBI	BB	SO	SB-CS	Avg.	OBP	SLG	E	Avg.
1990—	Dom. Orioles/WS (DSL)		55	191	28	53	9	0	5	20	14	32	2-...	.277	...	.403	...	...
1991—	GC White Sox (GCL) ..	C	38	126	11	31	4	1	0	15	6	21	2-1	.246	.309	.294	8	.977
1992—	Utica (NY-Penn)	C	45	161	16	44	13	1	2	20	5	26	1-5	.273	.293	.404	12	.963
1993—	South Bend (Midw.) ...	C	75	281	34	86	14	3	2	33	19	59	1-2	.306	.354	.399	12	.979
1994—	Prince William (Caro.)	C	93	312	45	81	17	1	11	47	27	68	0-1	.260	.326	.426	*16	.975
1995—	Nashville (A.A.)	C	16	49	7	7	3	0	1	5	7	12	0-1	.143	.250	.265	3	.972
	—Prince William (Caro.)	C	83	272	37	69	14	0	6	31	40	47	0-0	.254	.363	.371	5	.992
1996—	Birmingham (Sou.).....	C-DH	87	309	35	74	16	0	6	28	20	56	1-4	.239	.291	.350	5	.991
	—Chicago (A.L.)	C	4	6	1	4	1	0	0	2	0	0	0-0	.667	.667	.833	0	1.000
1997—	Nashville (A.A.)	C-DH	84	308	43	83	18	0	8	30	12	61	5-0	.269	.297	.406	6	.988
	—Chicago (A.L.)	C	10	15	1	3	0	1	0	2	1	6	0-0	.200	.250	.333	0	1.000
1998—	Calgary (PCL).............	C-DH	66	239	31	63	19	0	4	27	20	33	2-2	.264	.326	.393	6	.987
	—Chicago (A.L.)	C	34	111	14	23	6	0	3	15	7	22	0-0	.207	.254	.342	4	.981
1999—	Charlotte (I.L.)............	C	16	54	4	11	3	0	2	7	4	13	0-0	.204	.283	.370	3	.976
	—Ottawa (I.L.)■	C-DH	21	75	6	17	5	0	0	3	0	13	0-1	.227	.266	.293	3	.981
	—Montreal (N.L.)...........	C	17	22	3	4	1	0	0	0	2	6	0-0	.182	.250	.227	0	1.000
2000—	Tacoma (PCL)■	C	92	330	41	99	20	0	9	58	28	43	1-5	.300	.357	.442	•11	.980
	—Seattle (A.L.)	C	8	14	2	3	0	0	1	1	1	4	0-0	.214	.267	.429	0	1.000
2001—	Iowa (PCL)■	C	53	180	20	51	11	0	8	30	11	36	0-0	.283	.332	.478	5	.988
	—Chicago (N.L.)	C	52	135	13	30	10	0	2	13	7	26	0-0	.222	.266	.341	1	.997
2002—	Chicago (N.L.)............	C-1B	22	58	5	16	4	0	1	5	5	11	0-0	.276	.333	.397	2	.985
	—Milwaukee (N.L.)■.....	C-1B	51	153	14	39	10	1	2	17	12	30	0-0	.255	.310	.373	4	.988
American League totals (4 years)			56	146	18	33	7	1	4	20	9	32	0-0	.226	.271	.370	4	.986
National League totals (3 years)			142	368	35	89	25	1	5	35	26	73	0-0	.242	.294	.356	7	.992
Major League totals (7 years)			198	514	53	122	32	2	9	55	35	105	0-0	.237	.288	.360	11	.990

M

MACIAS, JOSE OF/IF EXPOS

PERSONAL: Born January 25, 1972, in Panama City, Panama. ... 5-10/189. ... Bats both, throws right. ... Full name: Jose Prade Macias.

HIGH SCHOOL: Instituto Technologico (Panama City, Panama).

TRANSACTIONS/CAREER NOTES: Signed as non-drafted free agent by Montreal Expos organization (February 14, 1992). ... Selected by Detroit Tigers organization from Expos organization in Rule 5 minor league draft (December 9, 1996). ... Traded by Tigers to Montreal Expos for 3B Chris Truby (May 16, 2002). ... On Montreal disabled list (September 10, 2002-remainder of season).

STATISTICAL NOTES: Led Florida State League second basemen with 255 putouts, 349 assists, 611 total chances and .989 fielding percentage in 1997. ... Tied for International League lead with 16 errors by second baseman in 1999. ... Career major league grand slams: 1.

2002 GAMES PLAYED BY POSITION (MLB): OF—59; 3B—30; 2B—23; SS—4.

									BATTING								FIELDING	
Year	Team (League)	Pos.	G	AB	R	H	2B	3B	HR	RBI	BB	SO	SB-CS	Avg.	OBP	SLG	E	Avg.
1992—	Dom. Expos (DSL)	OF	61	198	58	58	5	1	2	23	60	11	41-...	.293	...	.359	7	.942
1993—	Dom. Expos (DSL)	OF	64	211	60	66	12	1	4	26	59	26	38-...	.313	...	.436	7	.954
1994—	GC Expos (GCL)	OF-2B-3B	31	104	23	28	8	2	1	6	14	15	4-1	.269	.356	.413	4	.937
1995—	Vermont (NY-Penn)....	OF-2B-3B	53	176	24	42	4	2	0	9	19	19	11-7	.239	.320	.284	9	.949
1996—	Delmarva (S.Atl.)........	OF-2B-3B	116	369	64	91	13	4	1	33	56	48	38-15	.247	.353	.312	8	.970
1997—	Lakeland (FSL)■........	2B-OF	122	424	54	113	18	2	2	52	52	33	10-14	.267	.348	.333	7	†.989
1998—	Jacksonville (Sou.).....	2B	128	511	82	156	28	10	12	71	52	46	6-9	.305	.372	.470	14	*.977
1999—	Toledo (I.L.)...............	2B-OF-SS	112	438	44	107	18	8	2	36	36	60	10-5	.244	.306	.336	‡18	.969
	—Detroit (A.L.)	2B	5	4	2	1	0	0	1	2	0	1	0-0	.250	.250	1.000	0	1.000
2000—	Toledo (I.L.)..............	OF-SS-2B	33	130	19	30	5	0	0	8	17	17	2-3	.231	.322	.269	6	.940
	—Detroit (A.L.)	2-3-O-DH-S	73	173	25	44	3	5	2	24	18	24	2-0	.254	.328	.364	4	.977
2001—	Detroit (A.L.)	3B-OF-2B-DH	137	488	62	131	24	6	8	51	32	54	21-6	.268	.316	.391	12	.970
2002—	Detroit (A.L.)	2B-OF-3B	33	107	10	25	4	0	0	6	8	13	3-2	.234	.291	.271	5	.959
	—Montreal (N.L.)■........	OF-3B-2B-SS	90	231	33	59	17	1	7	33	13	44	5-6	.255	.294	.429	6	.968
American League totals (4 years)			248	772	99	201	31	11	11	83	58	92	26-8	.260	.315	.372	21	.970
National League totals (1 year)			90	231	33	59	17	1	7	33	13	44	5-6	.255	.294	.429	6	.968
Major League totals (4 years)			338	1003	132	260	48	12	18	116	71	136	31-14	.259	.310	.385	27	.969

RECORD AS PITCHER

Year	League	W	L	Pct.	ERA	G	GS	CG	ShO	Sv.-Opp.	IP	H	R	ER	HR	BB-IBB	SO
1994—	GC Expos (GCL)...............	0	0	...	0.00	1	0	0	0	0-...	1.0	0	0	0	0	0-0	0

MACKOWIAK, ROB — IF/OF — PIRATES

PERSONAL: Born June 20, 1976, in Oak Lawn, Ill. ... 5-10/190. ... Bats left, throws right. ... Full name: Robert William Mackowiak.
HIGH SCHOOL: Oak Lawn (Ill.), then Lake Central (Schererville, Ind.).
JUNIOR COLLEGE: South Suburban (Ill.).
TRANSACTIONS/CAREER NOTES: Selected by Pittsburgh Pirates organization in 53rd round of free-agent draft (June 4, 1996). ... On Pittsburgh disabled list (July 20-August 18, 2001); included rehabilitation assignment to Nashville (August 9-18).
2002 GAMES PLAYED BY POSITION (MLB): OF—106; 3B—26; 2B—3.

		BATTING														FIELDING	
Year Team (League)	Pos.	G	AB	R	H	2B	3B	HR	RBI	BB	SO	SB-CS	Avg.	OBP	SLG	E	Avg.
1996—GC Pirates (GCL)	OF-SS	27	86	8	23	6	1	0	14	13	11	3-1	.267	.366	.360	10	.796
1997—Erie (NY-Penn)	OF-3B-1B-C-P	61	203	26	58	14	2	1	25	21	47	1-7	.286	.371	.389	6	.949
1998—Augusta (S.Atl.)	OF-1B	25	70	16	17	4	0	1	8	13	19	4-2	.243	.369	.343	2	.941
—Lynchburg (Caro.)	3B-2B-OF	86	292	30	80	24	6	3	31	17	65	6-3	.274	.321	.428	18	.916
1999—Lynchburg (Caro.)	2B-OF	74	263	51	80	7	4	7	30	18	57	9-3	.304	.362	.441	1	.996
—Altoona (East.)	1B-OF	53	195	21	51	15	3	3	27	8	34	0-2	.262	.308	.415	8	.971
2000—Altoona (East.)	2B-OF-3B-SS	134	526	82	156	33	4	13	87	22	96	18-5	.297	.332	.449	17	.965
2001—Nashville (PCL)	OF-2B-3B	32	118	14	31	5	0	4	14	7	39	1-1	.263	.302	.407	7	.940
—Pittsburgh (N.L.)	OF-2B-3B-1B	83	214	30	57	15	2	4	21	15	52	4-3	.266	.319	.411	6	.965
2002—Pittsburgh (N.L.)	OF-3B-2B	136	385	57	94	22	0	16	48	42	120	9-3	.244	.328	.426	6	.974
Major League totals (2 years)		219	599	87	151	37	2	20	69	57	172	13-6	.252	.325	.421	12	.970

RECORD AS PITCHER

Year League	W	L	Pct.	ERA	G	GS	CG	ShO	Sv.-Opp.	IP	H	R	ER	HR	BB-IBB	SO
1997—Erie (NY-Penn)	0	0	...	0.00	1	0	0	0	0-...	1.1	1	0	0	0	0-0	1

MADDUX, GREG — P

PERSONAL: Born April 14, 1966, in San Angelo, Texas. ... 6-0/185. ... Throws right, bats right. ... Full name: Gregory Alan Maddux. ... Brother of Mike Maddux, pitcher with nine major league teams (1986-2000).
HIGH SCHOOL: Valley (Las Vegas).
TRANSACTIONS/CAREER NOTES: Selected by Chicago Cubs organization in second round of free-agent draft (June 4, 1984). ... Granted free agency (October 26, 1992). ... Signed by Atlanta Braves (December 9, 1992). ... On disabled list (March 23-April 12, 2002). ... Granted free agency (October 29, 2002).
RECORDS: Holds major league career records for most years leading league in putouts by pitcher—7; most years leading league in chances accepted by pitcher—12; most putouts by pitcher—443; and most years leading league in assists by pitcher—8. ... Shares major league career records for most years leading league in double plays by pitcher—5; and most years leading league in assists by pitcher—7. ... Shares major league single-season record for fewest complete games for leader—8 (1993). ... Shares major league single-game record for most putouts by pitcher—7 (April 29, 1990). ... Holds N.L. single season record for most consecutive innings with no bases on balls—72$^{1}/_{3}$ (June 20 through August 12, 2001).
HONORS: Won N.L. Gold Glove at pitcher (1990-2002). ... Named righthanded pitcher on The Sporting News N.L. All-Star team (1992-95 and 2000). ... Named N.L. Cy Young Award winner by Baseball Writers' Association of America (1992-95). ... Named N.L. Pitcher of the Year by The Sporting News (1993-95).
STATISTICAL NOTES: Led Appalachian League with eight hit batsmen in 1984. ... Led American Association with 12 hit batsmen in 1986. ... Led N.L. with 16 intentional bases on balls issued in 1988. ... Led N.L. with 14 hit batsmen in 1992. ... Pitched 3-1 one-hit, complete-game victory against Houston (May 28, 1995). ... Pitched 2-0 one-hit, complete-game victory against San Diego (April 27, 1997).
MISCELLANEOUS: Appeared in three games as pinch runner (1988). ... Singled and scored and struck out in two appearances as pinch hitter (1991). ... Appeared in one game as pinch hitter (2001).
CAREER HITTING (MLB): 214-for-1193 (.179), 86 R, 28 2B, 2 3B, 4 HR, 62 RBI.

Year League	W	L	Pct.	ERA	G	GS	CG	ShO	Sv.-Opp.	IP	H	R	ER	HR	BB-IBB	SO
1984—Pikeville (Appl.)	6	2	.750	2.63	14	12	2	•2	0-...	85.2	63	35	25	2	41-2	62
1985—Peoria (Midw.)	13	9	.591	3.19	27	27	6	0	0-...	186.0	176	86	66	9	52-0	125
1986—Pittsfield (East.)	4	3	.571	2.73	8	8	4	2	0-...	62.2	49	22	19	1	15-0	35
—Iowa (A.A.)	10	1	*.909	3.02	18	18	5	•2	0-...	128.1	127	49	43	3	30-3	65
—Chicago (N.L.)	2	4	.333	5.52	6	5	1	0	0-0	31.0	44	20	19	3	11-2	20
1987—Chicago (N.L.)	6	14	.300	5.61	30	27	1	1	0-0	155.2	181	111	97	17	74-13	101
—Iowa (A.A.)	3	0	1.000	0.98	4	4	2	•2	0-...	27.2	17	3	3	1	12-0	22
1988—Chicago (N.L.)	18	8	.692	3.18	34	34	9	3	0-0	249.0	230	97	88	13	81-16	140
1989—Chicago (N.L.)	19	12	.613	2.95	35	35	7	1	0-0	238.1	222	90	78	13	82-13	135
1990—Chicago (N.L.)	15	15	.500	3.46	35	•35	8	2	0-0	237.0	*242	*116	91	11	71-10	144
1991—Chicago (N.L.)	15	11	.577	3.35	37	*37	7	2	0-0	*263.0	232	113	98	18	66-9	198
1992—Chicago (N.L.)	•20	11	.645	2.18	35	•35	9	4	0-0	*268.0	201	68	65	7	70-7	199
1993—Atlanta (N.L.)■	20	10	.667	*2.36	36	•36	*8	1	0-0	*267.0	228	85	70	14	52-7	197
1994—Atlanta (N.L.)	•16	6	.727	*1.56	25	25	*10	•3	0-0	*202.0	150	44	35	4	31-3	156
1995—Atlanta (N.L.)	*19	2	*.905	*1.63	28	28	*10	•3	0-0	•209.2	147	39	38	8	23-3	181
1996—Atlanta (N.L.)	15	11	.577	2.72	35	35	5	1	0-0	245.0	225	85	74	11	28-11	172
1997—Atlanta (N.L.)	19	4	*.826	2.20	33	33	5	2	0-0	232.2	200	58	57	9	20-6	177
1998—Atlanta (N.L.)	18	9	.667	*2.22	34	34	9	*5	0-0	251.0	201	75	62	13	45-10	204
1999—Atlanta (N.L.)	19	9	.679	3.57	33	33	4	0	0-0	219.1	258	103	87	16	37-8	136
2000—Atlanta (N.L.)	19	9	.679	3.00	35	•35	6	•3	0-0	249.1	225	91	83	19	42-12	190
2001—Atlanta (N.L.)	17	11	.607	3.05	34	34	3	•3	0-0	233.0	220	86	79	20	27-10	173
2002—Atlanta (N.L.)	16	6	.727	2.62	34	34	0	0	0-0	199.1	194	67	58	14	45-7	118
Major League totals (17 years)	273	152	.642	2.83	539	535	102	34	0-0	3750.1	3400	1348	1179	210	805-147	2641

DIVISION SERIES RECORD

RECORDS: Holds N.L. career records for most wins—5; games started—9; runs allowed—24; hits allowed—64; and earned runs allowed—19. ... Shares N.L. career records for most games pitched— 10; and strikeouts—56. ... Shares career record for most innings pitched—60.
NOTES: Appeared in one game as pinch runner (2000).

Year League	W	L	Pct.	ERA	G	GS	CG	ShO	Sv.-Opp.	IP	H	R	ER	HR	BB-IBB	SO
1995— Atlanta (N.L.)	1	0	1.000	4.50	2	2	0	0	0-0	14.0	19	7	7	3	2-1	7
1996— Atlanta (N.L.)	1	0	1.000	0.00	1	1	0	0	0-0	7.0	3	2	0	0	0-0	7
1997— Atlanta (N.L.)	1	0	1.000	1.00	1	1	1	0	0-0	9.0	7	1	1	0	1-0	6
1998— Atlanta (N.L.)	1	0	1.000	2.57	1	1	0	0	0-0	7.0	7	2	2	0	0-0	4
1999— Atlanta (N.L.)	0	1	.000	2.57	2	1	0	0	0-0	7.0	10	2	2	1	5-2	5
2000— Atlanta (N.L.)	0	1	.000	11.25	1	1	0	0	0-0	4.0	9	7	5	1	3-2	2
2001— Atlanta (N.L.)	0	0	...	3.00	1	1	0	0	0-0	6.0	4	3	2	1	3-0	5
2002— Atlanta (N.L.)	1	0	1.000	3.00	1	1	0	0	0-0	6.0	5	2	2	1	1-1	3
Division series totals (8 years)	5	2	.714	3.15	10	9	1	0	0-0	60.0	64	26	21	7	15-6	39

CHAMPIONSHIP SERIES RECORD

RECORDS: Holds career records for most runs allowed—50; earned runs allowed—36; and sacrifice hits—6. ... Shares career record for hit batsmen—5. ... Shares single-series record for most earned runs allowed—11 (1989). ... Holds N.L. single-series record for most runs allowed—12 (1989).

NOTES: Scored in only appearance as pinch runner (1989).

Year League	W	L	Pct.	ERA	G	GS	CG	ShO	Sv.-Opp.	IP	H	R	ER	HR	BB-IBB	SO
1989— Chicago (N.L.)	0	1	.000	13.50	2	2	0	0	0-0	7.1	13	12	11	2	4-2	5
1993— Atlanta (N.L.)	1	1	.500	4.97	2	2	0	0	0-0	12.2	11	8	7	2	7-1	11
1995— Atlanta (N.L.)	1	0	1.000	1.13	1	1	0	0	0-0	8.0	7	1	1	0	2-0	4
1996— Atlanta (N.L.)	1	1	.500	2.51	2	2	0	0	0-0	14.1	15	9	4	1	2-1	10
1997— Atlanta (N.L.)	0	2	.000	1.38	2	2	0	0	0-0	13.0	9	7	2	0	4-1	16
1998— Atlanta (N.L.)	0	1	.000	3.00	2	1	0	0	1-1	6.0	5	2	2	0	3-1	4
1999— Atlanta (N.L.)	1	0	1.000	1.93	2	2	0	0	0-0	14.0	12	3	3	1	1-0	7
2001— Atlanta (N.L.)	0	2	.000	5.40	2	2	0	0	0-0	10.0	14	8	6	0	2-1	7
Champ. series totals (8 years)	4	8	.333	3.80	15	14	0	0	1-1	85.1	86	50	36	6	25-7	64

WORLD SERIES RECORD

NOTES: Member of World Series championship team (1995).

Year League	W	L	Pct.	ERA	G	GS	CG	ShO	Sv.-Opp.	IP	H	R	ER	HR	BB-IBB	SO
1995— Atlanta (N.L.)	1	1	.500	2.25	2	2	1	0	0-0	16.0	9	6	4	1	3-1	8
1996— Atlanta (N.L.)	1	1	.500	1.72	2	2	0	0	0-0	15.2	14	3	3	0	1-0	5
1999— Atlanta (N.L.)	0	1	.000	2.57	1	1	0	0	0-0	7.0	5	4	2	0	3-0	5
World Series totals (3 years)	2	3	.400	2.09	5	5	1	0	0-0	38.2	28	13	9	1	7-1	18

ALL-STAR GAME RECORD

	W	L	Pct.	ERA	GS	CG	ShO	Sv.-Opp.	IP	H	R	ER	HR	BB-IBB	SO
All-Star Game totals (4 years)	0	0	...	3.24	3	0	0	0-0	8.1	9	3	3	2	1-0	3

MADURO, CALVIN P

PERSONAL: Born September 5, 1974, in Santa Cruz, Aruba. ... 6-0/180. ... Throws right, bats right. ... Full name: Calvin Gregory Maduro.
HIGH SCHOOL: Tourist Economy School (Santa Cruz, Aruba).
COLLEGE: St. Antonius College (Aruba).
TRANSACTIONS/CAREER NOTES: Signed as non-drafted free agent by Baltimore Orioles organization (September 9, 1991). ... Traded by Orioles with P Garrett Stephenson to Philadelphia Phillies (September 4, 1996), completing deal in which Phillies traded 3B Todd Zeile and OF Pete Incaviglia to Orioles for two players to be named later (August 29, 1996). ... Released by Phillies (November 19, 1998). ... Signed by Orioles organization (February 5, 1999). ... On Baltimore disabled list (May 14-June 20 and June 22, 2000-remainder of season); included rehabilitation assignments to Rochester (June 10-16) and Frederick (June 17). ... Granted free agency (December 21, 2000). ... Re-signed by Orioles (February 16, 2001). ... On disabled list (March 22-April 7 and June 7, 2002-remainder of season). ... Released by Orioles (October 7, 2002).
STATISTICAL NOTES: Pitched 5-0 no-hit victory for Bowie against Portland (May 28, 1996, first game).
MISCELLANEOUS: Appeared in one game as pinch runner with Philadelphia (1997).
CAREER HITTING (MLB): 1-for-24 (.042), 1 R, 0 2B, 0 3B, 0 HR, 0 RBI.

Year League	W	L	Pct.	ERA	G	GS	CG	ShO	Sv.-Opp.	IP	H	R	ER	HR	BB-IBB	SO
1992— Gulf Coast Orioles (GCL)	1	4	.200	2.27	13	•12	1	1	0-...	71.1	56	29	18	2	26-0	66
1993— Bluefield (Appl.)	•9	4	.692	3.96	14	•14	*3	0	0-...	*91.0	90	46	40	4	17-0	*83
1994— Frederick (Caro.)	9	8	.529	4.25	27	26	0	0	0-...	152.1	132	86	72	18	59-0	137
1995— Bowie (East.)	0	6	.000	5.09	7	7	0	0	0-...	35.1	39	28	20	3	27-0	26
— Frederick (Caro.)	8	5	.615	2.94	20	20	2	2	0-...	122.1	109	43	40	16	34-0	120
1996— Bowie (East.)	9	7	.563	3.26	19	19	4	*3	0-...	124.1	116	50	45	8	36-0	87
— Rochester (I.L.)	3	5	.375	4.74	8	8	0	0	0-...	43.2	49	25	23	8	18-0	40
— Philadelphia (N.L.)■	0	1	.000	3.52	4	2	0	0	0-0	15.1	13	6	6	1	3-0	11
1997— Philadelphia (N.L.)	3	7	.300	7.23	15	13	0	0	0-0	71.0	83	59	57	12	41-5	31
— Scranton/W.B. (I.L.)	6	4	.600	4.99	13	13	2	0	0-...	79.1	71	48	44	10	57-1	53
1998— Scranton/W.B. (I.L.)	12	9	.571	5.98	28	27	4	1	0-...	177.2	*211	123	118	28	68-1	120
1999— Rochester (I.L.)■	11	11	.500	3.99	29	•28	2	1	0-...	169.0	179	88	75	23	60-0	149
2000— Baltimore (A.L.)	0	0	...	9.64	15	2	0	0	0-0	23.1	29	25	25	8	16-1	18
— Rochester (I.L.)	1	0	1.000	0.00	4	1	0	0	0-...	4.0	1	1	0	1	4-0	6
— Frederick (Caro.)	0	0	...	0.00	1	1	0	0	0-...	2.0	1	0	0	0	0-0	6
2001— Baltimore (A.L.)	5	6	.455	4.23	22	12	0	0	0-0	93.2	83	44	44	10	36-0	51
— Rochester (I.L.)	2	7	.222	4.03	12	11	1	1	0-...	67.0	61	37	30	9	22-0	48
2002— Baltimore (A.L.)	2	5	.286	5.56	12	10	0	0	0-0	56.2	64	37	35	12	22-1	29
A.L. totals (3 years)	7	11	.389	5.39	49	24	0	0	0-0	173.2	176	106	104	30	74-2	98
N.L. totals (2 years)	3	8	.273	6.57	19	15	0	0	0-0	86.1	96	65	63	13	44-5	42
Major League totals (5 years)	10	19	.345	5.78	68	39	0	0	0-0	260.0	272	171	167	43	118-7	140

MAGEE, WENDELL OF

PERSONAL: Born August 3, 1972, in Hattiesburg, Miss. ... 6-0/227. ... Bats right, throws right. ... Full name: Wendell Errol Magee Jr.
HIGH SCHOOL: Hattiesburg (Miss.).
JUNIOR COLLEGE: Pearl River Community College (Miss.).
COLLEGE: Samford.

TRANSACTIONS/CAREER NOTES: Selected by Philadelphia Phillies organization in 12th round of free-agent draft (June 2, 1994). ... Traded by Phillies to Detroit Tigers for P Bobby Sismondo (March 10, 2000). ... On Detroit disabled list (May 7-29, 2000); included rehabilitation assignment to Toledo (May 27-29). ... On Detriot disabled list (April 28-May 22, 2001); included rehabilitation assignment to Toledo (May 20-22). ... Released by Tigers (October 2, 2002).
STATISTICAL NOTES: Led International League outfielders with 302 putouts and 320 total chances in 1998. ... Led International League outfielders with 310 putouts and 325 total chances in 1999.
2002 GAMES PLAYED BY POSITION (MLB): OF—91; DH—4.

		BATTING														FIELDING	
Year Team (League)	**Pos.**	**G**	**AB**	**R**	**H**	**2B**	**3B**	**HR**	**RBI**	**BB**	**SO**	**SB-CS**	**Avg.**	**OBP**	**SLG**	**E**	**Avg.**
1994—Batavia (NY-Penn)......	OF	63	229	42	64	12	4	2	35	16	24	10-2	.279	.335	.393	6	.953
1995—Clearwater (FSL)........	OF	96	388	67	137	24	5	6	46	33	40	7-10	*.353	.405	.487	5	.973
—Reading (East.)...........	OF	39	136	17	40	9	1	3	21	21	17	3-4	.294	.379	.441	5	.932
1996—Reading (East.)...........	OF	71	270	38	79	15	5	6	30	24	40	10-6	.293	.353	.452	3	.973
—Scranton/W.B. (I.L.) ...	OF	44	155	31	44	9	2	10	32	21	31	3-1	.284	.365	.561	4	.959
—Philadelphia (N.L.)......	OF	38	142	9	29	7	0	2	14	9	33	0-0	.204	.252	.296	2	.978
1997—Philadelphia (N.L.)......	OF	38	115	7	23	4	0	1	9	9	20	1-4	.200	.254	.261	4	.960
—Scranton/W.B. (I.L.) ...	OF	83	294	39	72	20	1	10	39	30	56	4-7	.245	.310	.422	3	.983
1998—Scranton/W.B. (I.L.) ...	OF	126	507	86	147	30	7	24	72	46	102	7-7	.290	.349	.519	•11	.966
—Philadelphia (N.L.)......	OF	20	75	9	22	6	1	1	11	7	11	0-0	.293	.354	.440	2	.941
1999—Scranton/W.B. (I.L.) ...	OF	*142	*566	95	160	34	2	20	79	55	124	10-8	.283	.346	.456	*8	.975
—Philadelphia (N.L.)......	OF	12	14	4	5	1	0	2	5	1	4	0-0	.357	.400	.857	0	1.000
2000—Detroit (A.L.)■..........	OF-DH	91	186	31	51	4	2	7	31	10	28	1-0	.274	.310	.430	0	1.000
—Toledo (I.L.)................	OF	2	7	1	4	1	0	0	1	1	1	0-1	.571	.625	.714	0	1.000
2001—Detroit (A.L.).............	OF-DH	90	207	26	44	11	4	5	17	23	44	3-0	.213	.293	.377	1	.992
—Toledo (I.L.)................	OF	2	9	0	4	0	0	0	1	0	0	0-0	.444	.444	.444	0	1.000
2002—Detroit (A.L.).............	OF-DH	97	347	34	94	19	1	6	35	10	64	2-4	.271	.289	.383	5	.982
American League totals (3 years)		278	740	91	189	34	7	18	83	43	136	6-4	.255	.295	.393	6	.988
National League totals (4 years)		108	346	29	79	18	1	6	39	26	68	1-4	.228	.281	.338	8	.966
Major League totals (7 years)		386	1086	120	268	52	8	24	122	69	204	7-8	.247	.291	.376	14	.981

MAGNANTE, MIKE P DODGERS

PERSONAL: Born June 17, 1965, in Glendale, Calif. ... 6-2/212. ... Throws left, bats left. ... Full name: Michael Anthony Magnante. ... Name pronounced mag-NAN-tee.
HIGH SCHOOL: John Burroughs (Burbank, Calif.).
COLLEGE: UCLA.
TRANSACTIONS/CAREER NOTES: Selected by Kansas City Royals organization in 11th round of free-agent draft (June 1, 1988). ... On disabled list (June 17, 1990-remainder of season; July 2-20, 1992; and July 16-31, 1994). ... On Kansas City disabled list (May 19-June 13, 1996); included rehabilitation assignment to Omaha (June 8-13). ... Released by Royals (October 2, 1996). ... Signed by Houston Astros organization (December 19, 1996). ... On disabled list (May 10-25, 1998). ... Granted free agency (October 23, 1998). ... Signed by Anaheim Angels (January 27, 1999). ... Granted free agency (October 29, 1999). ... Signed by Oakland Athletics (November 19, 1999). ... On Oakland disabled list (May 27-June 27, 2000); included rehabilitation assignments to Sacramento (June 8-14 and June 23-27). ... Released by A's (August 6, 2002). ... Signed by Los Angeles Dodgers organization (August 16, 2002).
RECORDS: Shares major league record for striking out side on nine pitches (August 22, 1997, ninth inning).
CAREER HITTING (MLB): 2-for-6 (.333), 0 R, 0 2B, 0 3B, 0 HR, 1 RBI.

Year League	**W**	**L**	**Pct.**	**ERA**	**G**	**GS**	**CG**	**ShO**	**Sv.-Opp.**	**IP**	**H**	**R**	**ER**	**HR**	**BB-IBB**	**SO**
1988—Eugene (N'West).............	1	1	.500	0.56	3	3	0	0	0-...	16.0	10	6	1	0	2-0	26
—Appleton (Midw.).............	3	2	.600	3.21	9	8	0	0	0-...	47.2	48	20	17	3	15-0	40
—Baseball City (FSL)..........	1	1	.500	4.13	4	4	1	0	0-...	24.0	19	12	11	1	8-0	19
1989—Memphis (Sou.)...............	8	9	.471	3.66	26	26	4	1	0-...	157.1	137	70	64	10	53-3	118
1990—Omaha (A.A.)..................	2	5	.286	4.11	13	13	2	0	0-...	76.2	72	39	35	6	25-0	56
1991—Omaha (A.A.)..................	6	1	.857	3.02	10	10	2	0	0-...	65.2	53	23	22	2	23-0	50
—Kansas City (A.L.)	0	1	.000	2.45	38	0	0	0	0-0	55.0	55	19	15	3	23-3	42
1992—Kansas City (A.L.)	4	9	.308	4.94	44	12	0	0	0-3	89.1	115	53	49	5	35-5	31
1993—Omaha (A.A.)..................	2	6	.250	3.67	33	13	0	0	2-...	105.1	97	46	43	7	29-2	74
—Kansas City (A.L.)	1	2	.333	4.08	7	6	0	0	0-0	35.1	37	16	16	3	11-1	16
1994—Kansas City (A.L.)	2	3	.400	4.60	36	1	0	0	0-0	47.0	55	27	24	5	16-1	21
1995—Omaha (A.A.)..................	5	1	.833	2.84	15	8	0	0	0-...	57.0	55	23	18	3	13-0	38
—Kansas City (A.L.)	1	1	.500	4.23	28	0	0	0	0-1	44.2	45	23	21	6	16-1	28
1996—Kansas City (A.L.)	2	2	.500	5.67	38	0	0	0	0-1	54.0	58	38	34	5	24-1	32
—Omaha (A.A.)..................	1	0	1.000	0.00	1	0	0	0	0-...	3.0	3	1	0	0	0-0	6
1997—New Orleans (A.A.)■........	2	3	.400	4.50	17	0	0	0	1-...	24.0	31	14	12	0	5-0	23
—Houston (N.L.)	3	1	.750	2.27	40	0	0	0	1-5	47.2	39	16	12	2	11-2	43
1998—Houston (N.L.)	4	7	.364	4.88	48	0	0	0	2-4	51.2	56	28	28	2	26-4	39
1999—Anaheim (A.L.)■..............	5	2	.714	3.38	53	0	0	0	0-3	69.1	68	30	26	2	29-4	44
2000—Oakland (A.L.)■..............	1	1	.500	4.31	55	0	0	0	0-3	39.2	50	22	19	3	19-7	17
—Sacramento (PCL)............	0	0	...	4.05	5	2	0	0	0-...	6.2	6	3	3	2	1-0	4
2001—Oakland (A.L.)	3	1	.750	2.77	65	0	0	0	0-1	55.1	50	23	17	7	13-3	23
2002—Oakland (A.L.)	0	2	.000	5.97	32	0	0	0	0-1	28.2	38	22	19	2	11-1	11
—Las Vegas (PCL)■	1	0	1.000	3.00	7	0	0	0	0-...	6.0	5	3	2	1	2-0	4
A.L. totals (10 years)	19	24	.442	4.17	396	19	0	0	0-13	518.1	571	273	240	41	197-27	265
N.L. totals (2 years)	7	8	.467	3.62	88	0	0	0	3-9	99.1	95	44	40	4	37-6	82
Major League totals (12 years)...	26	32	.448	4.08	484	19	0	0	3-22	617.2	666	317	280	45	234-33	347

DIVISION SERIES RECORD

Year League	**W**	**L**	**Pct.**	**ERA**	**G**	**GS**	**CG**	**ShO**	**Sv.-Opp.**	**IP**	**H**	**R**	**ER**	**HR**	**BB-IBB**	**SO**
1997—Houston (N.L.)	0	0	...	4.50	2	0	0	0	0-0	2.0	4	3	1	0	0-0	2
1998—Houston (N.L.)									Did not play.							
2000—Oakland (A.L.)	0	0	...	0.00	2	0	0	0	0-0	3.0	1	0	0	0	0-0	2
2001—Oakland (A.L.)	0	0	...	0.00	1	0	0	0	0-0	1.1	3	0	0	0	1-0	1
Division series totals (3 years)...	0	0	...	1.42	5	0	0	0	0-0	6.1	8	3	1	0	1-0	5

MAGRUDER, CHRIS OF INDIANS

PERSONAL: Born April 26, 1977, in Tacoma, Wash. ... 5-11/200. ... Bats both, throws right. ... Full name: Christopher James Magruder.
HIGH SCHOOL: West Valley (Yakima, Wash.).
COLLEGE: Washington.
TRANSACTIONS/CAREER NOTES: Selected by San Francisco Giants in second round of free agent draft (June 2, 1998); choice received from Tampa Bay Devil Rays as part of compensation for signing of Type A free agent P Wilson Alvarez. ... Traded with P Todd Ozias and P Erasmo Ramirez to Texas Rangers for 1B Andres Galarraga (July 24, 2001). ... Traded by Rangers to Cleveland Indians for OF Rashad Eldridge (April 4, 2002).
2002 GAMES PLAYED BY POSITION (MLB): OF—83.

		BATTING														FIELDING	
Year Team (League)	Pos.	G	AB	R	H	2B	3B	HR	RBI	BB	SO	SB-CS	Avg.	OBP	SLG	E	Avg.
1998—Salem-Kaizer (NW).....	OF	47	177	43	59	8	5	3	18	37	21	14-7	.333	.464	.486	2	.976
—Bakersfield (Calif.)......	OF	22	92	21	28	7	0	1	4	13	16	3-0	.304	.390	.413	0	1.000
1999—Shreveport (Texas).....	OF	133	476	78	122	21	4	6	60	69	85	17-12	.256	.358	.355	3	*.988
2000—Shreveport (Texas).....	OF	134	496	85	140	33	3	4	39	67	75	18-10	.282	.375	.385	5	.983
2001—Fresno (PCL).............	OF	54	214	37	60	7	1	10	30	18	45	3-1	.280	.354	.463	1	.992
—Shreveport (Texas).....	OF	40	149	22	38	6	3	2	11	15	27	5-3	.255	.335	.376	2	.979
—Oklahoma (PCL)■......	OF	33	127	28	46	14	4	5	21	21	19	1-2	.362	.464	.654	1	.986
—Texas (A.L.)...............	OF	17	29	3	5	0	0	0	1	1	5	0-0	.172	.226	.172	0	1.000
2002—Cleveland (A.L.)■.......	OF	87	258	34	56	15	1	6	29	15	55	2-0	.217	.261	.353	2	.987
—Buffalo (I.L.)..............	OF	54	191	28	51	10	2	5	16	26	34	3-2	.267	.364	.419	1	.991
Major League totals (2 years)		104	287	37	61	15	1	6	30	16	60	2-0	.213	.257	.334	2	.988

MAHAY, RON P RANGERS

PERSONAL: Born June 28, 1971, in Crestwood, Ill. ... 6-2/190. ... Throws left, bats left. ... Full name: Ronald Matthew Mahay.
HIGH SCHOOL: Alan B. Shepard (Palos Heights, Ill.).
JUNIOR COLLEGE: South Suburban College (Ill.).
TRANSACTIONS/CAREER NOTES: Selected by Boston Red Sox organization in 18th round of free-agent draft (June 3, 1991). ... On disabled list (May 5, 1992-remainder of season). ... On Lynchburg disabled list (August 6-September 9, 1993). ... On disabled list (August 23-September 1, 1994). ... On Pawtucket temporarily inactive list (April 19-25, 1995). ... On Sarasota disabled list (April 4-25, 1996). ... Claimed on waivers by Oakland Athletics (March 30, 1999). ... Traded by Athletics to Florida Marlins for cash (May 11, 2000). ... Granted free agency (October 2, 2000). ... Signed by San Diego Padres organization (November 20, 2000). ... On Portland disabled list (April 12-24, 2001). ... Released by Padres (May 15, 2001). ... Signed by Chicago Cubs organization (May 19, 2001). ... On Chicago disabled list (May 24-June 13, 2002); included rehabilitation assignment to Iowa (June 7-13). ... Released by Cubs (September 30, 2002). ... Signed by Texas Rangers organization (November 13, 2002).
MISCELLANEOUS: Played outfield (1991-95). ... Appeared in one game as pinch runner with Oakland (2000).
CAREER HITTING (MLB): 6-for-26 (.231), 3 R, 3 2B, 0 3B, 1 HR, 3 RBI.

Year League	W	L	Pct.	ERA	G	GS	CG	ShO	Sv.-Opp.	IP	H	R	ER	HR	BB-IBB	SO
1996—Sarasota (FSL)................	2	2	.500	3.82	31	4	0	0	2-...	70.2	61	33	30	5	35-0	68
—Trenton (East.)................	0	1	.000	29.45	1	1	0	0	0-...	3.2	12	13	12	1	6-0	0
1997—Trenton (East.)................	3	3	.500	3.10	17	4	0	0	5-...	40.2	29	16	14	0	13-0	47
—Pawtucket (I.L.)................	1	0	1.000	0.00	2	0	0	0	0-...	4.2	3	0	0	0	1-0	6
—Boston (A.L.)..................	3	0	1.000	2.52	28	0	0	0	0-2	25.0	19	7	7	3	11-0	22
1998—Pawtucket (I.L.)................	3	1	.750	4.17	23	1	0	0	3-...	41.0	37	20	19	8	19-2	41
—Boston (A.L.)..................	1	1	.500	3.46	29	0	0	0	1-2	26.0	26	16	10	2	15-1	14
1999—Vancouver (PCL)■..........	7	2	.778	4.29	32	15	0	0	0-...	107.0	116	57	51	12	45-0	73
—Oakland (A.L.)................	2	0	1.000	1.86	6	1	0	0	1-1	19.1	8	4	4	2	3-0	15
2000—Oakland (A.L.)................	0	1	.000	9.00	5	2	0	0	0-0	16.0	26	18	16	4	9-0	5
—Florida (N.L.)■................	1	0	1.000	6.04	18	0	0	0	0-0	25.1	31	17	17	6	16-1	27
—Calgary (PCL)................	0	1	.000	4.85	8	0	0	0	0-...	13.0	7	7	7	1	7-1	15
2001—Portland (PCL)■............	1	2	.333	3.78	14	0	0	0	0-...	16.2	13	9	7	2	5-0	18
—Iowa (PCL)■..................	3	1	.750	2.31	36	0	0	0	14-...	46.2	29	12	12	5	10-1	52
—Chicago (N.L.)................	0	0	...	2.61	17	0	0	0	0-0	20.2	14	6	6	4	15-1	24
2002—Iowa (PCL)......................	0	1	.000	1.93	39	1	0	0	2-...	46.2	32	11	10	3	15-1	50
—Chicago (N.L.)................	2	0	1.000	8.59	11	0	0	0	0-0	14.2	13	14	14	6	8-0	14
A.L. totals (5 years)................	6	2	.750	3.86	73	3	0	0	2-5	86.1	79	45	37	11	38-1	56
N.L. totals (3 years)................	3	0	1.000	5.49	46	0	0	0	0-0	60.2	58	37	37	16	39-2	65
Major League totals (7 years).....	9	2	.818	4.53	119	3	0	0	2-5	147.0	137	82	74	27	77-3	121

RECORD AS POSITION PLAYER

		BATTING														FIELDING	
Year Team (League)	Pos.	G	AB	R	H	2B	3B	HR	RBI	BB	SO	SB-CS	Avg.	OBP	SLG	E	Avg.
1991—GC Red Sox (GCL).....	OF	54	187	30	51	6	5	1	29	33	40	2-0	.273	.389	.374	3	.971
1992—Winter Haven (FSL)....	OF	19	63	6	16	2	1	0	4	2	19	0-1	.254	.277	.317	1	.972
1993—Lynchburg (Caro.)......	OF-C	73	254	28	54	8	1	5	23	11	63	2-2	.213	.258	.311	5	.973
—New Britain (East.).....	OF	8	25	2	3	0	0	1	2	1	6	1-0	.120	.154	.240	2	.889
1994—Sarasota (FSL)...........	OF	105	367	43	102	18	0	4	46	39	67	3-5	.278	.347	.360	4	.981
1995—Pawtucket (I.L.)..........	OF	11	44	5	14	4	0	0	3	4	9	1-0	.318	.375	.409	0	1.000
—Trenton (East.)...........	OF	93	310	37	73	12	3	5	28	44	90	5-6	.235	.332	.342	6	.970
—Boston (A.L.).............	OF	5	20	3	4	2	0	1	3	1	6	0-0	.200	.273	.450	0	1.000

MAHOMES, PAT P

PERSONAL: Born August 9, 1970, in Bryan, Texas. ... 6-4/212. ... Throws right, bats right. ... Full name: Patrick Lavon Mahomes. ... Name pronounced muh-HOMES.
HIGH SCHOOL: Lindale (Texas).

TRANSACTIONS/CAREER NOTES: Selected by Minnesota Twins organization in eighth round of free-agent draft (June 1, 1988). ... On disabled list (July 6-23, 1994). ... Traded by Twins to Boston Red Sox for a player to be named later (August 26, 1996); Twins acquired P Brian Looney to complete deal (December 17, 1996). ... Contract sold by Red Sox to Yokohoma BayStars of Japan Central League (1997). ... Signed by New York Mets (December 21, 1998). ... Granted free agency (December 21, 2000). ... Signed by Texas Rangers organization (January 11, 2001). ... Granted free agency (November 5, 2001). ... Signed by Chicago Cubs organization (January 30, 2002). ... Granted free agency (October 30, 2002).
RECORDS: Shares major league record for most home runs allowed in one inning—4 (August 17, 2001, sixth inning).
STATISTICAL NOTES: Led A.L. with nine intentional bases on balls issued in 2001.
MISCELLANEOUS: Appeared in one game as pinch runner (1994). ... Struck out in only appearance as pinch hitter and appeared in one game as pinch runner (1999).
CAREER HITTING (MLB): 10-for-39 (.256), 6 R, 4 2B, 0 3B, 0 HR, 4 RBI.

Year League	W	L	Pct.	ERA	G	GS	CG	ShO	Sv.-Opp.	IP	H	R	ER	HR	BB-IBB	SO
1988—Elizabethton (Appl.)	6	3	.667	3.69	13	13	3	0	0-...	78.0	66	45	32	4	51-0	93
1989—Kenosha (Midw.)	13	7	.650	3.28	25	25	3	1	0-...	156.1	120	66	57	4	•100-3	167
1990—Visalia (Calif.)	11	11	.500	3.30	28	*28	5	1	0-...	•185.1	136	77	68	14	*118-1	178
1991—Orlando (Sou.)	8	5	.615	*1.78	18	17	2	0	0-...	116.0	77	30	23	5	57-0	136
—Portland (PCL)	3	5	.375	3.44	9	9	2	0	0-...	55.0	50	26	21	2	36-1	41
1992—Minnesota (A.L.)	3	4	.429	5.04	14	13	0	0	0-0	69.2	73	41	39	5	37-0	44
—Portland (PCL)	9	5	.643	3.41	17	16	3	*3	1-...	111.0	97	43	42	7	43-1	87
1993—Minnesota (A.L.)	1	5	.167	7.71	12	5	0	0	0-0	37.1	47	34	32	8	16-0	23
—Portland (PCL)	11	4	•.733	*3.03	17	16	3	1	0-...	115.2	89	47	39	11	54-1	94
1994—Minnesota (A.L.)	9	5	.643	4.72	21	21	0	0	0-0	120.0	121	68	63	22	62-1	53
1995—Minnesota (A.L.)	4	10	.286	6.37	47	7	0	0	3-7	94.2	100	74	67	22	47-1	67
1996—Minnesota (A.L.)	1	4	.200	7.20	20	5	0	0	0-0	45.0	63	38	36	10	27-0	30
—Salt Lake (PCL)	3	1	.750	3.74	22	2	0	0	7-...	33.2	32	14	14	0	12-0	41
—Boston (A.L.)■	2	0	1.000	5.84	11	0	0	0	2-2	12.1	9	8	8	3	6-0	6
1997—Boston (A.L.)	1	0	1.000	8.10	10	0	0	0	0-0	10.0	15	10	9	2	10-1	5
—Pawtucket (I.L.)	5	1	.833	2.84	18	1	0	0	7-...	31.2	22	11	10	2	17-0	40
—Yokohama (Jap. Cen.)■	3	4	.429	4.82	11	9	0	0	0-...	52.1	54	30	28	...	25-...	42
1998—Yokohama (Jp. East.)	2	5	.286	4.68	19	5	0	0	5-...	50.0	38	30	26	...	36-...	50
—Yokohama (Jap. Cen.)	0	4	.000	5.98	10	8	0	0	0-...	43.2	61	30	29	...	29-...	24
1999—Norfolk (I.L.)■	4	1	.800	3.49	6	6	0	0	0-...	38.2	38	17	15	6	12-1	24
—New York (N.L.)	8	0	1.000	3.68	39	0	0	0	0-1	63.2	44	26	26	7	37-5	51
2000—New York (N.L.)	5	3	.625	5.46	53	5	0	0	0-1	94.0	96	63	57	15	66-4	76
2001—Texas (A.L.)■	7	6	.538	5.70	56	4	0	0	0-1	107.1	115	71	68	17	55-9	61
2002—Iowa (PCL)■	4	5	.444	3.48	44	5	0	0	14-...	72.1	57	30	28	11	20-1	70
—Chicago (N.L.)	1	1	.500	3.86	16	2	0	0	0-1	32.2	36	15	14	3	17-3	23
A.L. totals (7 years)	28	34	.452	5.84	191	55	0	0	5-10	496.1	543	344	322	89	260-12	289
N.L. totals (3 years)	14	4	.778	4.59	108	7	0	0	0-3	190.1	176	104	97	25	120-12	150
Major League totals (10 years)	42	38	.525	5.49	299	62	0	0	5-13	686.2	719	448	419	114	380-24	439

DIVISION SERIES RECORD

Year League	W	L	Pct.	ERA	G	GS	CG	ShO	Sv.-Opp.	IP	H	R	ER	HR	BB-IBB	SO
1999—New York (N.L.)	0	0	...	5.40	1	0	0	0	0-0	1.2	3	1	1	0	0-0	1
2000—New York (N.L.)									Did not play.							

CHAMPIONSHIP SERIES RECORD

Year League	W	L	Pct.	ERA	G	GS	CG	ShO	Sv.-Opp.	IP	H	R	ER	HR	BB-IBB	SO
1999—New York (N.L.)	0	0	...	1.42	3	0	0	0	0-0	6.1	4	1	1	1	3-1	3
2000—New York (N.L.)									Did not play.							

WORLD SERIES RECORD

Year League	W	L	Pct.	ERA	G	GS	CG	ShO	Sv.-Opp.	IP	H	R	ER	HR	BB-IBB	SO
2000—New York (N.L.)									Did not play.							

MAHONEY, MIKE — C — CUBS

PERSONAL: Born December 5, 1972, in Des Moines, Iowa. ... 6-1/200. ... Bats right, throws right. ... Full name: Michael John Mahoney.
HIGH SCHOOL: Dowling (West Des Moines, Iowa).
COLLEGE: Creighton.
TRANSACTIONS/CAREER NOTES: Selected by Atlanta Braves organization in 39th round of free-agent draft (June 1, 1995). ... On disabled list (April 26-May 5, 1997). ... Released by Braves (October 7, 1999). ... Signed by Chicago Cubs organization (October 27, 1999). ... Granted free agency (October 18, 2000). ... Re-signed by Cubs organization (November 2, 2000).
STATISTICAL NOTES: Led Carolina League catchers with 674 putouts and 765 total chances in 1996. ... Led Southern League catchers with 589 putouts and 657 total chances in 1997. ... Tied for Pacific Coast League lead in double plays by catcher with 10 in 2001.
2002 GAMES PLAYED BY POSITION (MLB): C—16.

		BATTING														FIELDING	
Year Team (League)	Pos.	G	AB	R	H	2B	3B	HR	RBI	BB	SO	SB-CS	Avg.	OBP	SLG	E	Avg.
1995—Eugene (N'West)	C	43	112	14	27	6	0	1	15	15	17	6-2	.241	.344	.321	6	.981
1996—Durham (Caro.)	C	101	363	52	94	24	2	9	46	23	64	4-3	.259	.312	.410	8	.990
1997—Greenville (Sou.)	C	87	298	46	68	17	0	8	46	28	75	1-0	.228	.299	.366	•10	.985
1998—Greenville (Sou.)	C	20	74	3	16	5	0	1	6	1	20	1-1	.216	.241	.324	2	.987
—Richmond (I.L.)	C	71	208	26	44	10	0	5	28	24	49	1-1	.212	.302	.332	7	.984
1999—Richmond (I.L.)	C	55	145	10	33	7	0	2	20	6	25	0-1	.228	.258	.317	3	.989
2000—West Tenn (Sou.)■	C	24	76	12	23	7	0	0	7	7	16	0-0	.303	.372	.395	1	.995
—Iowa (PCL)	C-1B-2B	63	181	29	55	14	0	6	28	16	28	2-1	.304	.374	.481	4	.988
—Chicago (N.L.)	C	4	7	1	2	1	0	0	1	1	0	0-0	.286	.444	.429	0	...
2001—Iowa (PCL)	C-1B-3B	95	289	22	65	14	1	3	27	22	63	1-3	.225	.287	.311	3	.996
2002—Iowa (PCL)	C	78	223	33	57	12	1	2	18	17	44	1-1	.256	.311	.345	*12	.978
—Chicago (N.L.)	C	16	29	2	6	3	0	0	3	1	10	0-0	.207	.233	.310	0	1.000
Major League totals (2 years)		20	36	3	8	4	0	0	4	2	10	0-0	.222	.282	.333	0	1.000

MAIRENA, OSWALDO P MARLINS

PERSONAL: Born June 30, 1974, in Chinandega, Nicaragua. ... 5-11/165. ... Throws left, bats left. ... Full name: Oswaldo Antonio Mairena.
COLLEGE: Universidad Unan (Chinandega, Nicaragua).
TRANSACTIONS/CAREER NOTES: Signed as non-drafted free agent by New York Yankees organization (August 2, 1996). ... Traded by Yankees with P Ben Ford to Chicago Cubs for OF Glenallen Hill (July 21, 2000). ... On Iowa disabled list (August 25-September 1, 2000). ... Traded by Cubs to Florida Marlins for P Manny Aybar (March 30, 2001). ... On Florida disabled list (June 16-30, 2002); included rehabilitation assignment to Gulf Coast Marlins (June 27-30).
CAREER HITTING (MLB): 0-for-0 (.000), 0 R, 0 2B, 0 3B, 0 HR, 0 RBI.

Year	League	W	L	Pct.	ERA	G	GS	CG	ShO	Sv.-Opp.	IP	H	R	ER	HR	BB-IBB	SO
1997—	Greensboro (S.Atl.)	6	1	.857	2.54	49	0	0	0	8-...	60.1	43	24	17	2	16-3	75
—	Tampa (FSL)	0	0	...	4.15	3	0	0	0	0-...	4.1	6	2	2	1	0-0	6
1998—	Tampa (FSL)	1	5	.167	3.17	52	0	0	0	0-...	54.0	53	24	19	5	23-3	50
1999—	Norwich (East.)	4	3	.571	2.67	49	0	0	0	2-...	57.1	48	24	17	3	27-4	47
2000—	Norwich (East.)	0	4	.000	2.78	35	0	0	0	0-...	32.1	29	16	10	0	11-3	30
—	Columbus (I.L.)	1	1	.500	3.00	5	1	0	0	0-...	9.0	12	3	3	2	5-1	4
—	West Tenn (Sou.)■	0	1	.000	0.00	2	0	0	0	0-...	2.0	3	1	0	0	1-1	0
—	Iowa (PCL)	1	0	1.000	4.91	11	0	0	0	0-...	14.2	13	9	8	1	2-0	4
—	Chicago (N.L.)	0	0	...	18.00	2	0	0	0	0-0	2.0	7	4	4	1	2-0	0
2001—	Portland (East.)■	4	2	.667	1.57	22	0	0	0	3-...	34.1	27	12	6	3	8-0	27
—	Calgary (PCL)	3	2	.600	7.55	31	0	0	0	0-...	39.1	52	33	33	4	13-5	44
2002—	Calgary (PCL)	3	0	1.000	4.97	25	0	0	0	1-...	29.0	39	20	16	2	13-0	19
—	Florida (N.L.)	2	3	.400	5.35	31	0	0	0	0-0	33.2	38	21	20	7	12-0	21
—	Gulf Coast Marlins (GCL)	0	0	...	0.00	1	1	0	0	0-...	1.1	1	0	0	0	0-0	1
Major League totals (2 years)		2	3	.400	6.06	33	0	0	0	0-0	35.2	45	25	24	8	14-0	21

MALLETTE, BRIAN P DODGERS

PERSONAL: Born January 19, 1975, in Dublin, Ga. ... 6-0/185. ... Throws right, bats right. ... Full name: Brian Drew Mallette.
COLLEGE: Columbus State (Ga.).
TRANSACTIONS/CAREER NOTES: Selected by Milwaukee Brewers organization in 27th round of free-agent draft (June 3, 1997). ... Traded by Brewers to Los Angeles Dodgers (October 16, 2002), completing deal in which Brewers traded 3B Tyler Houston and a player to be named later to Dodgers for P Ben Diggins and P Shane Nance (July 23, 2002).
CAREER HITTING (MLB): 0-for-0 (.000), 0 R, 0 2B, 0 3B, 0 HR, 0 RBI.

Year	League	W	L	Pct.	ERA	G	GS	CG	ShO	Sv.-Opp.	IP	H	R	ER	HR	BB-IBB	SO
1997—	Helena (Pio.)	6	2	.750	4.33	23	0	0	0	5-...	35.1	33	19	17	1	20-2	58
1998—	Beloit (Midw.)	2	1	.667	3.09	50	0	0	0	23-...	55.1	40	23	19	2	29-2	76
1999—	Stockton (Calif.)	2	0	1.000	1.50	28	0	0	0	4-...	36.0	38	16	6	1	16-1	34
2000—	Mudville (Calif.)	4	4	.500	3.30	50	0	0	0	2-...	71.0	52	35	26	6	52-1	94
2001—	Huntsville (Sou.)	7	2	.778	1.96	44	0	0	0	17-...	55.0	43	13	12	4	23-4	71
—	Indianapolis (I.L.)	0	1	.000	1.06	12	0	0	0	2-...	17.0	10	4	2	2	8-0	23
2002—	Indianapolis (I.L.)	3	2	.600	2.78	45	0	0	0	25-...	45.1	39	15	14	4	17-1	50
—	Milwaukee (N.L.)	0	0	...	10.80	5	0	0	0	0-0	5.0	7	6	6	3	3-1	5
Major League totals (1 year)		0	0	...	10.80	5	0	0	0	0-0	5.0	7	6	6	3	3-1	5

MALLOY, MARTY 2B

PERSONAL: Born July 6, 1972, in Gainesville, Fla. ... 5-10/165. ... Bats left, throws right. ... Full name: Marty Thomas Malloy.
HIGH SCHOOL: Trenton (Fla.).
JUNIOR COLLEGE: Santa Fe Community College (Fla.).
TRANSACTIONS/CAREER NOTES: Signed as non-drafted free agent by Atlanta Braves organization (June 26, 1992). ... Granted free agency (October 4, 1999). ... Signed by Detroit Tigers organization (December 20, 1999). ... On Toledo disabled list (April 6-July 3, 2000). ... Granted free agency (October 18, 2000). ... Signed by Cincinnati Reds organization (January 24, 2001). ... Granted free agency (October 15, 2001). ... Signed by Florida Marlins organization (December 14, 2001). ... Released by Marlins (June 10, 2002). ... Signed by Reds organization (June 11, 2002). ... Granted free agency (October 15, 2002).
STATISTICAL NOTES: Led International League second basemen with 195 putouts in 1997.
2002 GAMES PLAYED BY POSITION (MLB): 2B—3; 3B—2.

			BATTING														FIELDING	
Year	Team (League)	Pos.	G	AB	R	H	2B	3B	HR	RBI	BB	SO	SB-CS	Avg.	OBP	SLG	E	Avg.
1992—	Idaho Falls (Pio.)	2B-SS	62	251	45	79	18	1	2	28	11	43	8-4	.315	.347	.418	17	.941
1993—	Macon (S.Atl.)	2B-SS-OF	109	376	55	110	19	3	2	36	39	70	24-8	.293	.360	.375	19	.960
1994—	Durham (Caro.)	2B-SS	118	428	53	113	22	1	6	35	52	69	18-12	.264	.344	.362	19	.964
1995—	Greenville (Sou.)	2B	124	461	73	128	20	3	10	59	39	58	11-12	.278	.329	.399	16	.973
1996—	Greenville (Sou.)	2B	111	429	82	134	27	2	4	36	54	50	11-10	.312	.393	.413	14	.972
—	Richmond (I.L.)	2B-SS	18	64	7	13	2	1	0	8	5	7	3-0	.203	.257	.266	2	.974
1997—	Richmond (I.L.)	2B-DH	108	414	66	118	19	5	2	25	41	61	17-7	.285	.351	.370	•12	.975
1998—	Richmond (I.L.)	2B	124	483	75	140	25	3	7	54	51	65	20-7	.290	.361	.398	13	.977
—	Atlanta (N.L.)	2B	11	28	3	5	1	0	1	1	2	2	0-0	.179	.233	.321	0	1.000
1999—	Richmond (I.L.)	2-3-S-D-O	114	407	58	119	23	1	7	36	53	52	19-15	.292	.374	.405	11	.973
2000—	Toledo (I.L.)■	2B	30	115	16	27	8	0	4	16	7	18	0-0	.235	.276	.409	0	1.000
—	GC Tigers (GCL)	2B-SS	2	1	0	1	0	0	0	1	2	0	0-0	1.000	1.000	1.000	0	1.000
—	Lakeland (FSL)	SS	7	26	4	6	1	0	1	4	1	1	1-0	.231	.286	.385	2	.920
2001—	Louisville (I.L.)■	2B-SS-3B	126	468	69	142	36	4	6	49	27	51	8-7	.303	.340	.436	22	.953
2002—	Florida (N.L.)■	2B-3B	24	25	1	3	0	0	0	1	2	8	0-0	.120	.185	.120	0	1.000
—	Louisville (I.L.)■	2B-SS-3B	56	180	25	44	7	1	4	16	21	24	7-4	.244	.330	.361	6	.968
Major League totals (2 years)			35	53	4	8	1	0	1	2	4	10	0-0	.151	.211	.226	0	1.000

CHAMPIONSHIP SERIES RECORD

			BATTING														FIELDING	
Year	Team (League)	Pos.	G	AB	R	H	2B	3B	HR	RBI	BB	SO	SB-CS	Avg.	OBP	SLG	E	Avg.
1998—	Atlanta (N.L.)	PR-2B	1	1	1	0	0	0	0	0	0	1	0-0	.000	.000	.000	0	1.000

MANN, JIM — P — PIRATES

PERSONAL: Born November 17, 1974, in Brockton, Mass. ... 6-3/225. ... Throws right, bats right. ... Full name: James Joseph Mann.
HIGH SCHOOL: Holbrook (Mass.).
JUNIOR COLLEGE: Massasoit Community College (Mass.).
TRANSACTIONS/CAREER NOTES: Selected by Toronto Blue Jays organization in 54th round of free-agent draft (June 3, 1993). ... Selected by New York Mets from Blue Jays organization in Rule 5 major league draft (December 13, 1999); Blue Jays acquired IF Jersen Perez as compensation for Mets keeping Mann (March 22, 2000). ... Granted free agency (October 18, 2000). ... Signed by Houston Astros organization (January 3, 2001). ... Claimed on waivers by Pittsburgh Pirates (October 10, 2002).
CAREER HITTING (MLB): 0-for-1 (.000), 0 R, 0 2B, 0 3B, 0 HR, 0 RBI.

Year League	W	L	Pct.	ERA	G	GS	CG	ShO	Sv.-Opp.	IP	H	R	ER	HR	BB-IBB	SO
1994— GC Blue Jays (GCL)	3	2	.600	3.74	11	9	0	0	0-...	53.0	54	28	22	1	26-1	41
1995— Medicine Hat (Pio.)	5	4	.556	4.29	14	14	1	•1	0-...	77.2	78	47	37	5	37-0	66
1996— St. Catharines (NY-Penn)	2	1	.667	3.62	26	0	0	0	17-...	27.1	22	12	11	3	10-1	37
1997— Hagerstown (S.Atl.)	0	1	.000	5.06	19	0	0	0	4-...	26.2	35	18	15	4	11-0	30
— Dunedin (FSL)	1	0	1.000	6.00	12	0	0	0	0-...	18.0	27	12	12	2	6-1	13
1998— Dunedin (FSL)	0	2	.000	3.04	51	0	0	0	25-...	50.1	31	19	17	4	24-1	59
1999— Knoxville (Sou.)	1	2	.333	0.93	6	0	0	0	0-...	9.2	6	2	1	1	1-0	12
— Syracuse (I.L.)	6	5	.545	4.64	47	0	0	0	5-...	66.0	53	35	34	11	39-1	72
2000— Norfolk (I.L.)■	3	4	.429	2.98	49	0	0	0	3-...	81.2	61	27	27	8	33-3	74
— New York (N.L.)	0	0	...	10.13	2	0	0	0	0-0	2.2	6	3	3	1	1-0	0
2001— New Orleans (PCL)■	6	3	.667	2.51	53	0	0	0	27-...	68.0	52	21	19	7	17-2	81
— Houston (N.L.)	0	0	...	3.38	4	0	0	0	0-0	5.1	3	2	2	0	4-0	5
2002— New Orleans (PCL)	0	3	.000	4.15	33	0	0	0	22-...	34.2	33	20	16	6	8-1	29
— Houston (N.L.)	0	1	.000	4.09	17	0	0	0	0-0	22.0	19	10	10	3	7-1	19
— Round Rock (Texas)	0	0	...	4.50	1	0	0	0	0-...	2.0	1	1	1	1	0-0	2
Major League totals (3 years)	0	1	.000	4.50	23	0	0	0	0-0	30.0	28	15	15	4	12-1	24

MANTEI, MATT — P — DIAMONDBACKS

PERSONAL: Born July 7, 1973, in Tampa. ... 6-1/200. ... Throws right, bats right. ... Full name: Matthew Bruce Mantei. ... Name pronounced MAN-tay.
HIGH SCHOOL: River Valley (Three Oaks, Mich.).
TRANSACTIONS/CAREER NOTES: Selected by Seattle Mariners organization in 25th round of free-agent draft (June 3, 1991). ... Selected by Florida Marlins from Mariners organization in Rule 5 major league draft (December 5, 1994). ... On Florida disabled list (April 20-June 18 and July 29-September 1, 1995); included rehabilitation assignments to Portland and Charlotte (May 13-June 18). ... On Florida disabled list (June 19, 1996-remainder of season). ... On Florida disabled list (March 31, 1997-entire season). ... Granted free agency (December 21, 1997). ... Re-signed by Marlins organization (December 21, 1997). ... On Florida disabled list (August 19-September 4, 1998). ... Traded by Marlins to Arizona Diamondbacks for P Vladimir Nunez, P Brad Penny and a player to be named later (July 9, 1999); Marlins acquired OF Abraham Nunez to complete deal (December 13, 1999). ... On Arizona disabled list (April 2-21 and May 5-21, 2000); included rehabilitation assignment to Tuscon (April 14-21). ... On disabled list (April 25, 2001-remainder of season). ... On Arizona disabled list (March 22-June 27, 2002); included rehabilitation assignments to El Paso (May 10-20) and Tucson (May 21-25 and June 14-27).
STATISTICAL NOTES: Tied for Arizona League lead with eight balks in 1991.
CAREER HITTING (MLB): 1-for-5 (.200), 0 R, 0 2B, 0 3B, 0 HR, 0 RBI.

Year League	W	L	Pct.	ERA	G	GS	CG	ShO	Sv.-Opp.	IP	H	R	ER	HR	BB-IBB	SO
1991— Arizona Mariners (Ariz.)	1	4	.200	6.69	17	5	0	0	0-...	40.1	54	40	30	0	28-2	29
1992— Arizona Mariners (Ariz.)	1	1	.500	5.63	3	3	0	0	0-...	16.0	18	10	10	1	5-0	19
1993— Bellingham (N'West)	1	1	.500	5.96	26	0	0	0	*12-...	25.2	26	19	17	2	15-0	34
1994— Appleton (Midw.)	5	1	.833	2.06	48	0	0	0	26-...	48.0	42	14	11	2	21-3	70
1995— Portland (East.)■	1	0	1.000	2.38	8	0	0	0	1-...	11.1	10	3	3	0	5-0	15
— Charlotte (I.L.)	0	1	.000	2.57	6	0	0	0	0-...	7.0	1	3	2	1	5-0	10
— Florida (N.L.)	0	1	.000	4.72	12	0	0	0	0-0	13.1	12	8	7	1	13-0	15
1996— Florida (N.L.)	1	0	1.000	6.38	14	0	0	0	0-1	18.1	13	13	13	2	21-1	25
— Charlotte (I.L.)	0	2	.000	4.70	7	0	0	0	2-...	7.2	6	4	4	1	7-0	8
1997— Brevard County (FSL)	0	0	...	6.00	4	0	0	0	0-...	6.0	4	4	4	1	6-0	11
— Portland (East.)	1	0	1.000	6.75	5	0	0	0	0-...	4.0	1	3	3	0	8-0	7
1998— Charlotte (I.L.)	1	2	.333	5.51	16	0	0	0	3-...	16.1	11	10	10	2	18-1	25
— Florida (N.L.)	3	4	.429	2.96	42	0	0	0	9-12	54.2	38	19	18	1	23-3	63
1999— Florida (N.L.)	1	2	.333	2.72	35	0	0	0	10-12	36.1	24	11	11	4	25-1	50
— Arizona (N.L.)■	0	1	.000	2.79	30	0	0	0	22-25	29.0	20	10	9	1	19-0	49
2000— Tucson (PCL)	0	0	...	2.45	4	2	0	0	0-...	3.2	1	1	1	0	3-0	2
— Arizona (N.L.)	1	1	.500	4.57	47	0	0	0	17-20	45.1	31	24	23	4	35-1	53
2001— Arizona (N.L.)	0	0	...	2.57	8	0	0	0	2-2	7.0	6	2	2	2	4-0	12
2002— El Paso (Texas)	0	1	.000	2.25	4	3	0	0	0-...	4.0	3	3	1	0	1-0	5
— Tucson (PCL)	1	0	1.000	0.00	9	1	0	0	0-...	10.0	8	1	0	0	4-0	9
— Arizona (N.L.)	2	2	.500	4.72	31	0	0	0	0-1	26.2	28	15	14	3	12-0	26
Major League totals (7 years)	8	11	.421	3.78	219	0	0	0	60-73	230.2	172	102	97	18	152-6	293

DIVISION SERIES RECORD

Year League	W	L	Pct.	ERA	G	GS	CG	ShO	Sv.-Opp.	IP	H	R	ER	HR	BB-IBB	SO
1999— Arizona (N.L.)	0	1	.000	4.50	1	0	0	0	0-0	2.0	1	1	1	1	3-1	1
2002— Arizona (N.L.)	0	0	...	54.00	1	0	0	0	0-0	.1	1	2	2	0	1-0	0
Division series totals (2 years)	0	1	.000	11.57	2	0	0	0	0-0	2.1	2	3	3	1	4-1	1

MANZANILLO, JOSIAS — P

PERSONAL: Born October 16, 1967, in San Pedro de Macoris, Dominican Republic. ... 6-0/205. ... Throws right, bats right. ... Brother of Ravelo Manzanillo, pitcher with Chicago White Sox (1988) and Pittsburgh Pirates (1994-95). ... Name pronounced hose-EYE-ess MAN-zan-EE-oh..
TRANSACTIONS/CAREER NOTES: Signed as non-drafted free agent by Boston Red Sox organization (January 10, 1983). ... On disabled list (June 8, 1987-remainder of season; and April 8, 1988-entire season). ... Granted free agency (March 24, 1992). ... Signed by Kansas City

Royals organization (April 3, 1992). ... Granted free agency (October 15, 1992). ... Signed by Milwaukee Brewers (November 20, 1992). ... Traded by Brewers to New York Mets for OF Wayne Housie (June 12, 1993). ... On New York disabled list (July 27, 1994-remainder of season). ... Claimed on waivers by New York Yankees (June 5, 1995). ... On New York disabled list (July 6, 1995-remainder of season). ... Granted free agency (October 16, 1995). ... Played in Taiwan for 1996 season. ... Signed by Seattle Mariners organization (December 21, 1996). ... On Seattle disabled list (April 9-May 6 and May 25-July 1, 1997); included rehabilitation assignments to Memphis (May 1-6) and Tacoma (May 25-July 1). ... Released by Mariners (July 17, 1997). ... Signed by Houston Astros organization (July 27, 1997). ... Granted free agency (October 15, 1997). ... Signed by Tampa Bay Devil Rays organization (December 18, 1997). ... Released by Devil Rays (July 1, 1998). ... Signed by Mets organization (July 3, 1998). ... Granted free agency (October 15, 1998). ... Re-signed by Mets organization (December 18, 1998). ... On Norfolk disabled list (June 21, 1999-remainder of season). ... Granted free agency (October 4, 1999). ... Signed by Pittsburgh Pirates organization (February 9, 2000). ... Granted free agency (November 5, 2001). ... Re-signed by Pirates organization (February 27, 2002). ... On Pittsburgh disabled list (May 4-July 13, 2002); included rehabilitation assignments to Nashville (June 25-July 10) and Hickory (July 11-13). ... Released by Pirates (August 15, 2002).

MISCELLANEOUS: Appeared in one game as pinch runner (1999).

CAREER HITTING (MLB): 1-for-11 (.091), 0 R, 0 2B, 0 3B, 0 HR, 0 RBI.

Year	League	W	L	Pct.	ERA	G	GS	CG	ShO	Sv.-Opp.	IP	H	R	ER	HR	BB-IBB	SO
1983—	Elmira (NY-Penn)	1	5	.167	7.98	12	4	0	0	0-...	38.1	52	44	34	7	20-1	19
1984—	Elmira (NY-Penn)	2	3	.400	5.26	14	0	0	0	1-...	25.2	27	24	15	1	26-1	15
1985—	Greensboro (S.Atl.)	1	1	.500	9.75	7	0	0	0	0-...	12.0	12	13	13	1	18-0	10
—	Elmira (NY-Penn)	2	4	.333	3.86	19	4	0	0	1-...	39.2	36	19	17	1	36-4	43
1986—	Winter Haven (FSL)	13	5	.722	2.27	23	21	3	2	0-...	142.2	110	51	36	3	81-0	102
1987—	New Britain (East.)	2	0	1.000	4.50	2	2	0	0	0-...	10.0	8	5	5	1	8-0	12
1988—	New Britain (East.)									Did not play.							
1989—	New Britain (East.)	9	10	.474	3.66	26	•26	3	1	0-...	147.2	129	78	60	11	85-7	93
1990—	New Britain (East.)	4	4	.500	3.41	12	12	2	1	0-...	74.0	66	34	28	3	37-1	51
—	Pawtucket (I.L.)	4	7	.364	5.55	15	15	5	0	0-...	82.2	75	57	51	9	45-0	77
1991—	Pawtucket (I.L.)	5	5	.500	5.61	20	16	0	0	0-...	102.2	109	69	64	12	53-0	65
—	New Britain (East.)	2	2	.500	2.90	7	7	0	0	0-...	49.2	37	25	16	0	28-1	35
—	Boston (A.L.)	0	0	...	18.00	1	0	0	0	0-0	1.0	2	2	2	0	3-0	1
1992—	Omaha (A.A.)■	7	10	.412	4.36	26	21	0	0	0-...	136.1	138	76	66	12	71-0	114
—	Memphis (Sou.)	0	2	.000	7.36	2	0	0	0	0-...	7.1	6	6	6	0	6-0	8
1993—	Milwaukee (A.L.)■	1	1	.500	9.53	10	1	0	0	1-2	17.0	22	20	18	1	10-3	10
—	New Orleans (A.A.)	0	1	.000	9.00	1	0	0	0	0-...	1.0	1	1	1	1	0-0	3
—	Norfolk (I.L.)■	1	5	.167	3.11	14	12	2	1	0-...	84.0	82	40	29	3	25-1	79
—	New York (N.L.)	0	0	...	3.00	6	0	0	0	0-0	12.0	8	7	4	1	9-0	11
1994—	Norfolk (I.L.)	0	1	.000	4.38	8	0	0	0	3-...	12.1	12	6	6	1	6-1	10
—	New York (N.L.)	3	2	.600	2.66	37	0	0	0	2-5	47.1	34	15	14	4	13-2	48
1995—	New York (N.L.)	1	2	.333	7.88	12	0	0	0	0-0	16.0	18	15	14	3	6-2	14
—	New York (A.L.)■	0	0	...	2.08	11	0	0	0	0-0	17.1	19	4	4	1	9-2	11
1996—										Statistics unavailable.							
1997—	Seattle (A.L.)■	0	1	.000	5.40	16	0	0	0	0-1	18.1	19	13	11	3	17-1	18
—	Memphis (Sou.)	0	0	...	3.00	2	0	0	0	0-...	3.0	1	1	1	1	0-0	6
—	Tacoma (PCL)	0	0	...	6.43	11	0	0	0	1-...	14.0	16	10	10	4	8-0	15
—	New Orleans (A.A.)■	0	0	...	4.40	11	0	0	0	0-...	14.1	17	7	7	3	6-0	11
1998—	Durham (I.L.)■	7	6	.538	4.64	19	14	0	0	1-...	85.1	93	57	44	12	30-0	61
—	Norfolk (I.L.)■	4	4	.500	3.24	13	12	1	0	1-...	77.2	77	35	28	5	31-0	72
1999—	New York (N.L.)	0	0	...	5.79	12	0	0	0	0-0	18.2	19	12	12	5	4-1	25
2000—	Nashville (PCL)■	0	2	.000	2.70	15	0	0	0	3-...	23.1	19	8	7	0	6-1	23
—	Pittsburgh (N.L.)	2	2	.500	3.38	43	0	0	0	0-2	58.2	50	23	22	6	32-4	39
2001—	Pittsburgh (N.L.)	3	2	.600	3.39	71	0	0	0	2-7	79.2	60	32	30	4	26-3	80
2002—	Nashville (PCL)	1	0	1.000	2.66	15	1	0	0	1-...	20.1	18	6	6	3	2-1	14
—	Pittsburgh (N.L.)	0	0	...	7.62	13	0	0	0	0-1	13.0	20	11	11	5	5-0	4
—	Hickory (S.Atl.)	0	0	...	9.00	1	0	0	0	0-...	2.0	5	3	2	1	0-0	1
A.L. totals (4 years)		1	2	.333	5.87	38	1	0	0	1-3	53.2	62	39	35	5	39-6	40
N.L. totals (7 years)		9	8	.529	3.93	194	0	0	0	4-15	245.1	209	115	107	28	95-12	221
Major League totals (9 years)		10	10	.500	4.27	232	1	0	0	5-18	299.0	271	154	142	33	134-18	261

MAROTH, MIKE — P — TIGERS

PERSONAL: Born August 17, 1977, in Orlando, Fla. ... 6-0/180. ... Throws left, bats left. ... Full name: Michael Warren Maroth.

HIGH SCHOOL: William R. Boone (Orlando, Fla.).

COLLEGE: Central Florida.

TRANSACTIONS/CAREER NOTES: Selected by Boston Red Sox organization in third round of free-agent draft (June 2, 1998). ... Traded by Red Sox to Detroit Tigers for P Bryce Florie (July 31, 1999). ... On disabled list (July 31-August 22, 2001).

CAREER HITTING (MLB): 1-for-6 (.167), 1 R, 0 2B, 0 3B, 0 HR, 0 RBI.

Year	League	W	L	Pct.	ERA	G	GS	CG	ShO	Sv.-Opp.	IP	H	R	ER	HR	BB-IBB	SO
1998—	Gulf Coast Red Sox (GCL)	1	1	.500	0.00	4	2	0	0	0-...	12.2	9	3	0	0	2-0	14
—	Lowell (NY-Penn)	2	3	.400	2.90	6	6	0	0	0-...	31.0	22	13	10	1	13-0	34
1999—	Sarasota (FSL)	11	6	.647	4.04	20	19	0	0	0-...	111.1	124	65	50	3	35-1	64
—	Lakeland (FSL)■	2	1	.667	3.24	3	3	0	0	0-...	16.2	18	7	6	1	7-0	11
—	Jacksonville (Sou.)	1	2	.333	4.79	4	4	0	0	0-...	20.2	27	15	11	2	7-0	10
2000—	Jacksonville (Sou.)	9	14	.391	3.94	27	26	2	1	0-...	164.1	176	79	72	14	58-0	85
2001—	Toledo (I.L.)	7	10	.412	4.65	24	23	0	0	0-...	131.2	158	80	68	11	50-1	63
2002—	Toledo (I.L.)	8	1	.889	2.82	11	11	1	0	0-...	73.1	53	25	23	7	22-0	51
—	Detroit (A.L.)	6	10	.375	4.48	21	21	0	0	0-0	128.2	136	68	64	7	36-1	58
Major League totals (1 year)		6	10	.375	4.48	21	21	0	0	0-0	128.2	136	68	64	7	36-1	58

MARQUIS, JASON — P — BRAVES

PERSONAL: Born August 21, 1978, in Manhasset, N.Y. ... 6-1/210. ... Throws right, bats left. ... Full name: Jason Scott Marquis.

HIGH SCHOOL: Tottenville (Staten Island, N.Y.).

TRANSACTIONS/CAREER NOTES: Selected by Atlanta Braves organization as "sandwich" pick between first and second round of free-agent draft (June 4, 1996); pick received as supplemental pick for failure to signed 1995 first-round choice. ... On Greenville disabled list (July 5-31, 1999). ... On disabled list (April 22-May 12, 2002).

MISCELLANEOUS: Appeared in two games as pinch runner (2001).

CAREER HITTING (MLB): 6-for-71 (.085), 9 R, 0 2B, 0 3B, 1 HR, 1 RBI.

Year League	W	L	Pct.	ERA	G	GS	CG	ShO	Sv.-Opp.	IP	H	R	ER	HR	BB-IBB	SO
1996—Danville (Appl.)	1	1	.500	4.63	7	4	0	0	0-...	23.1	30	18	12	0	7-0	24
1997—Macon (S.Atl.)	•14	10	.583	4.38	28	28	0	0	0-...	141.2	156	78	69	10	55-1	121
1998—Danville (Caro.)	2	12	.143	4.87	22	22	1	0	0-...	114.2	120	65	62	3	41-0	135
1999—Myrtle Beach (Caro.)	3	0	1.000	0.28	6	6	0	0	0-...	32.0	22	2	1	0	17-0	41
—Greenville (Sou.)	3	4	.429	4.58	12	12	1	0	0-...	55.0	52	33	28	7	29-0	35
2000—Greenville (Sou.)	4	2	.667	3.57	11	11	0	0	0-...	68.0	68	35	27	10	23-0	49
—Atlanta (N.L.)	1	0	1.000	5.01	15	0	0	0	0-1	23.1	23	16	13	4	12-1	17
—Richmond (I.L.)	0	3	.000	9.00	6	6	0	0	0-...	20.0	26	21	20	2	13-0	18
2001—Atlanta (N.L.)	5	6	.455	3.48	38	16	0	0	0-2	129.1	113	62	50	14	59-4	98
2002—Atlanta (N.L.)	8	9	.471	5.04	22	22	0	0	0-0	114.1	127	66	64	19	49-3	84
Major League totals (3 years)	14	15	.483	4.28	75	38	0	0	0-3	267.0	263	144	127	37	120-8	199

DIVISION SERIES RECORD

Year League	W	L	Pct.	ERA	G	GS	CG	ShO	Sv.-Opp.	IP	H	R	ER	HR	BB-IBB	SO
2001—Atlanta (N.L.)									Did not play.							

CHAMPIONSHIP SERIES RECORD

Year League	W	L	Pct.	ERA	G	GS	CG	ShO	Sv.-Opp.	IP	H	R	ER	HR	BB-IBB	SO
2001—Atlanta (N.L.)	0	0	...	0.00	4	0	0	0	0-0	2.0	2	4	0	1	2-0	3

MARRERO, ELI — OF/C — CARDINALS

PERSONAL: Born November 17, 1973, in Havana, Cuba. ... 6-1/180. ... Bats right, throws right. ... Full name: Elieser Marrero.

HIGH SCHOOL: Coral Gables (Fla.).

TRANSACTIONS/CAREER NOTES: Selected by St. Louis Cardinals organization in third round of free-agent draft (June 3, 1993). ... On St. Louis disabled list (March 22-April 13, 1998). ... On St. Louis disabled list (July 2-September 1, 2000); included rehabilitation assignment to Memphis (August 24-September 1).

STATISTICAL NOTES: Led Texas League catchers with 676 putouts and 746 total chances in 1996. ... Led American Association catchers with 675 putouts, 68 assists and 750 total chances in 1997. ... Career major league grand slams: 2.

2002 GAMES PLAYED BY POSITION (MLB): OF—106; C—44; 1B—4.

		BATTING														FIELDING	
Year Team (League)	Pos.	G	AB	R	H	2B	3B	HR	RBI	BB	SO	SB-CS	Avg.	OBP	SLG	E	Avg.
1993—Johnson City (Appl.)	C	18	61	10	22	8	0	2	14	12	9	2-2	.361	.467	.590	1	.994
1994—Savannah (S.Atl.)	C	116	421	71	110	16	3	21	79	39	92	5-4	.261	.328	.463	•15	.984
1995—St. Petersburg (FSL)	C	107	383	43	81	16	1	10	55	23	55	9-4	.211	.254	.337	10	.984
1996—Arkansas (Texas)	C-DH	116	374	65	101	17	3	19	65	32	55	9-6	.270	.336	.484	3	*.996
1997—Louisville (A.A.)	C-DH	112	395	60	108	21	7	20	68	25	53	4-4	.273	.318	.514	7	.991
—St. Louis (N.L.)	C	17	45	4	11	2	0	2	7	2	13	4-0	.244	.271	.422	3	.969
1998—St. Louis (N.L.)	C-1B	83	254	28	62	18	1	4	20	28	42	6-2	.244	.318	.370	4	.991
—Memphis (PCL)	C-DH	32	130	22	31	5	0	7	21	13	23	5-4	.238	.306	.438	2	.991
1999—St. Louis (N.L.)	C-1B	114	317	32	61	13	1	6	34	18	56	11-2	.192	.236	.297	7	.988
2000—St. Louis (N.L.)	C-1B	53	102	21	23	3	1	5	17	9	16	5-0	.225	.302	.422	0	1.000
—Memphis (PCL)	C	6	15	1	1	0	0	0	0	0	2	0-0	.067	.067	.067	0	1.000
2001—St. Louis (N.L.)	C-OF-1B	86	203	37	54	11	3	6	23	15	36	6-3	.266	.312	.438	7	.983
2002—St. Louis (N.L.)	OF-C-1B	131	397	63	104	19	1	18	66	40	72	14-2	.262	.327	.451	7	.981
Major League totals (6 years)		484	1318	185	315	66	7	41	167	112	235	46-9	.239	.298	.393	28	.987

DIVISION SERIES RECORD

		BATTING														FIELDING	
Year Team (League)	Pos.	G	AB	R	H	2B	3B	HR	RBI	BB	SO	SB-CS	Avg.	OBP	SLG	E	Avg.
2000—St. Louis (N.L.)									Did not play.								
2001—St. Louis (N.L.)	PH-C	3	7	0	0	0	0	0	0	0	0	0-0	.000	.000	.000	0	1.000
2002—St. Louis (N.L.)	OF	2	6	0	0	0	0	0	1	0	1	0-0	.000	.000	.000	0	1.000
Division series totals (2 years)		5	13	0	0	0	0	0	1	0	1	0-0	.000	.000	.000	0	1.000

CHAMPIONSHIP SERIES RECORD

		BATTING														FIELDING	
Year Team (League)	Pos.	G	AB	R	H	2B	3B	HR	RBI	BB	SO	SB-CS	Avg.	OBP	SLG	E	Avg.
2000—St. Louis (N.L.)	PR-C	4	4	0	0	0	0	0	1	0	1	0-0	.000	.000	.000	0	1.000
2002—St. Louis (N.L.)	OF	4	16	1	3	1	0	1	1	1	1	0-0	.188	.235	.438	0	1.000
Championship series totals (2 years)		8	20	1	3	1	0	1	2	1	2	0-0	.150	.190	.350	0	1.000

MARTE, DAMASO — P — WHITE SOX

PERSONAL: Born February 14, 1975, in Santo Domingo, Dominican Republic. ... 6-2/200. ... Throws left, bats left. ... Full name: Damaso Sabinon Marte.

TRANSACTIONS/CAREER NOTES: Signed as non-drafted free agent by Seattle Mariners organization (October 28, 1992). ... On disabled list (April 3-17, 1997). ... On disabled list (April 2-May 3 and September 2, 1998-remainder of season). ... On New Haven disabled list (April 7-August 22, 2000). ... Granted free agency (October 18, 2000). ... Signed by New York Yankees organization (November 16, 2000). ... Traded by Yankees to Pittsburgh Pirates for IF Enrique Wilson (June 13, 2001). ... Traded by Pirates with IF Edwin Yan to Chicago White Sox for P Matt Guerrier (March 27, 2002).

CAREER HITTING (MLB): 0-for-5 (.000), 0 R, 0 2B, 0 3B, 0 HR, 0 RBI.

Year	League	W	L	Pct.	ERA	G	GS	CG	ShO	Sv.-Opp.	IP	H	R	ER	HR	BB-IBB	SO
1993—	Dom. Mariners (DSL)	2	5	.286	6.55	17	15	2	0	0-...	56.1	62	48	41	...	50-...	29
1994—	Dom. Mariners (DSL)	7	0	1.000	3.86	17	13	0	0	0-...	65.1	53	41	28	...	48-...	80
1995—	Everett (N'West)	2	2	.500	2.21	11	11	5	0	0-...	36.2	25	11	9	2	10-0	39
1996—	Wisconsin (Midw.)	8	6	.571	4.49	26	26	2	1	0-...	142.1	134	82	71	8	75-5	115
1997—	Lancaster (Calif.)	8	8	.500	4.13	25	25	2	1	0-...	139.1	144	75	64	15	62-1	127
1998—	Orlando (Sou.)	7	6	.538	5.27	22	20	0	0	0-...	121.1	136	82	71	14	47-0	99
1999—	Tacoma (PCL)	3	3	.500	5.13	31	11	0	0	0-...	73.2	79	43	42	13	40-1	59
—	Seattle (A.L.)	0	1	.000	9.35	5	0	0	0	0-0	8.2	16	9	9	3	6-0	3
2000—	Arizona Mariners (Ariz.)	0	0	...	0.00	2	2	0	0	0-...	5.0	1	0	0	0	0-0	6
—	New Haven (East.)	0	0	...	1.59	4	0	0	0	0-...	5.2	6	1	1	1	2-0	4
2001—	Norwich (East.)■	3	1	.750	3.50	23	0	0	0	1-...	36.0	29	16	14	3	7-0	36
—	Nashville (PCL)■	0	0	...	3.38	4	0	0	0	0-...	5.1	3	2	2	2	0-0	4
—	Pittsburgh (N.L.)	0	1	.000	4.71	23	0	0	0	0-0	36.1	34	21	19	5	12-3	39
2002—	Chicago (A.L.)■	1	1	.500	2.83	68	0	0	0	10-12	60.1	44	19	19	5	18-2	72
A.L. totals (2 years)		1	2	.333	3.65	73	0	0	0	10-12	69.0	60	28	28	8	24-2	75
N.L. totals (1 year)		0	1	.000	4.71	23	0	0	0	0-0	36.1	34	21	19	5	12-3	39
Major League totals (3 years)		1	3	.250	4.02	96	0	0	0	10-12	105.1	94	49	47	13	36-5	114

MARTIN, TOM — P

PERSONAL: Born May 21, 1970, in Charleston, S.C. ... 6-1/206. ... Throws left, bats left. ... Full name: Thomas Edgar Martin.

HIGH SCHOOL: Bay (Panama City, Fla.).

TRANSACTIONS/CAREER NOTES: Selected by Baltimore Orioles organization in sixth round of free-agent draft (June 1, 1988). ... Traded by Orioles with 3B Craig Worthington to San Diego Padres for P Jim Lewis and OF Steve Martin (February 17, 1992). ... Selected by Atlanta Braves organization from Padres organization in Rule 5 minor league draft (December 13, 1993). ... Loaned by Braves organization to Mexico City Tigres, Mexican League (May 1-7, 1995). ... Released by Braves (January 25, 1996). ... Signed by Houston Astros organization (February 21, 1996). ... On disabled list (May 30-June 15, 1997). ... Selected by Arizona Diamondbacks in second round (29th pick overall) of expansion draft (November 18, 1997). ... Traded by Diamondbacks with 3B Travis Fryman and cash to Cleveland Indians for 3B Matt Williams (December 1, 1997). ... On Cleveland disabled list (April 30-May 18 and August 31-September 19, 1998); included rehabilitation assignments to Buffalo (May 13-18 and September 3-19). ... On Cleveland disabled list (April 4-August 9, 1999); included rehabilitation assignment to Akron (July 27-August 9). ... On Cleveland disabled list (June 13-August 4, 2000); included rehabilitation assignment to Buffalo (July 28-August 4). ... Traded by Indians to New York Mets for C Javier Ochoa (January 11, 2001). ... On New York disabled list (May 13-August 16, 2001); included rehabilitation assignments to Brooklyn (July 27-30) and Norfolk (July 31-August 16). ... Released by Mets (October 11, 2001). ... Signed by Tampa Bay Devils Rays organization (January 28, 2002). ... On disabled list (April 23-September 30, 2002). ... Released by Devil Rays (September 30, 2002).

CAREER HITTING (MLB): 0-for-6 (.000), 0 R, 0 2B, 0 3B, 0 HR, 0 RBI.

Year	League	W	L	Pct.	ERA	G	GS	CG	ShO	Sv.-Opp.	IP	H	R	ER	HR	BB-IBB	SO
1989—	Bluefield (Appl.)	3	3	.500	4.62	8	8	0	0	0-...	39.0	36	28	20	3	25-0	31
—	Erie (NY-Penn)	0	5	.000	6.64	7	7	0	0	0-...	40.2	42	39	30	2	25-0	44
1990—	Wausau (Midw.)	2	3	.400	2.47	9	9	0	0	0-...	40.0	31	25	11	1	27-0	45
1991—	Kane County (Midw.)	4	10	.286	3.64	38	10	0	0	6-...	99.0	92	50	40	4	56-3	106
1992—	High Desert (Calif.)■	0	2	.000	9.37	11	0	0	0	0-...	16.1	23	19	17	4	16-0	10
—	Waterloo (Midw.)	2	6	.250	4.25	39	2	0	0	3-...	55.0	62	38	26	3	22-4	57
1993—	Rancho Cuca. (Calif.)	1	4	.200	5.61	47	1	0	0	0-...	59.1	72	41	37	4	39-2	53
1994—	Greenville (Sou.)■	5	6	.455	4.62	36	6	0	0	0-...	74.0	82	40	38	6	27-3	51
1995—	Richmond (I.L.)	0	0	...	9.00	7	0	0	0	0-...	9.0	10	9	9	4	10-2	3
—	MC Tigres (Mex.)■	0	1	.000	27.00	1	1	0	0	0-...	1.1	5	5	4	0	1-0	0
1996—	Tucson (PCL)■	0	0	...	0.00	5	0	0	0	0-...	6.0	6	0	0	0	2-2	1
—	Jackson (Texas)	6	2	.750	3.24	57	0	0	0	3-...	75.0	71	35	27	8	42-4	58
1997—	Houston (N.L.)	5	3	.625	2.09	55	0	0	0	2-3	56.0	52	13	13	2	23-2	36
1998—	Cleveland (A.L.)■	1	1	.500	12.89	14	0	0	0	0-0	14.2	29	21	21	3	12-0	9
—	Buffalo (I.L.)	3	1	.750	6.00	41	0	0	0	0-...	36.0	46	25	24	4	13-0	35
1999—	Akron (East.)	0	0	...	1.00	3	3	0	0	0-...	9.0	4	1	1	0	3-0	9
—	Cleveland (A.L.)	0	1	.000	8.68	6	0	0	0	0-0	9.1	13	9	9	2	3-1	8
—	Buffalo (I.L.)	1	0	1.000	3.00	5	0	0	0	0-...	6.0	5	2	2	1	1-0	6
2000—	Cleveland (A.L.)	1	0	1.000	4.05	31	0	0	0	0-0	33.1	32	16	15	3	15-2	21
—	Buffalo (I.L.)	0	1	.000	3.60	9	3	0	0	0-...	10.0	12	4	4	1	1-0	4
2001—	Norfolk (I.L.)■	2	1	.667	6.26	23	0	0	0	1-...	23.0	31	17	16	4	10-0	24
—	New York (N.L.)	1	0	1.000	10.06	14	0	0	0	0-0	17.0	23	22	19	4	10-2	12
—	Brooklyn (NY-Penn)	0	0	...	0.00	1	1	0	0	0-...	1.0	2	0	0	0	0-0	0
2002—	Durham (I.L.)■	0	0	...	0.00	4	0	0	0	2-...	3.1	3	0	0	0	1-0	6
—	Tampa Bay (A.L.)	0	0	...	16.20	2	0	0	0	0-0	1.2	5	3	3	0	1-0	1
A.L. totals (4 years)		2	2	.500	7.32	53	0	0	0	0-0	59.0	79	49	48	8	31-3	39
N.L. totals (2 years)		6	3	.667	3.95	69	0	0	0	2-3	73.0	75	35	32	6	33-4	48
Major League totals (6 years)		8	5	.615	5.45	122	0	0	0	2-3	132.0	154	84	80	14	64-7	87

DIVISION SERIES RECORD

Year	League	W	L	Pct.	ERA	G	GS	CG	ShO	Sv.-Opp.	IP	H	R	ER	HR	BB-IBB	SO
1997—	Houston (N.L.)	0	0	...	0.00	2	0	0	0	0-0	.2	1	1	0	0	1-0	0

MARTINEZ, DAVE — OF

PERSONAL: Born September 26, 1964, in Brooklyn, N.Y. ... 5-10/175. ... Bats left, throws left. ... Full name: David Martinez.

HIGH SCHOOL: Lake Howell (Casselberry, Fla.).

JUNIOR COLLEGE: Valencia Community College (Fla.).

TRANSACTIONS/CAREER NOTES: Selected by Texas Rangers organization in 40th round of free-agent draft (June 7, 1982); did not sign. ... Selected by Chicago Cubs organization in secondary phase of free-agent draft (January 11, 1983). ... On disabled list (April 27, 1984-remainder of season). ... Traded by Cubs to Montreal Expos for OF Mitch Webster (July 14, 1988). ... On disqualified list (October 4-5, 1991). ... Traded by Expos with P Scott Ruskin and SS Willie Greene to Cincinnati Reds for P John Wetteland and P Bill Risley (December 11, 1991). ... Granted free agency (October 27, 1992). ... Signed by San Francisco Giants (December 9, 1992). ... On San Francisco disabled list (April

30-June 4, 1993); included rehabilitation assignment to Phoenix (June 1-4). ... Granted free agency (October 14, 1994). ... Signed by Chicago White Sox (April 5, 1995). ... Granted free agency (November 3, 1995). ... Re-signed by White Sox (November 14, 1995). ... Granted free agency (October 27, 1997). ... Signed by Tampa Bay Devil Rays (December 4, 1997). ... On disabled list (July 22, 1998-remainder of season). ... Traded by Devil Rays to Cubs for P Mark Guthrie (May 12, 2000). ... Traded by Cubs to Rangers for IF/OF Brant Brown (June 9, 2000). ... Traded by Rangers to Toronto Blue Jays for a player to be named later (August 4, 2000); Rangers acquired P Peter Munro to complete deal (August 8, 2000). ... Granted free agency (October 31, 2000). ... Signed by Atlanta Braves (December 10, 2000). ... On disabled list (March 30, 2002-entire season). ... Granted free agency (October 28, 2002).

RECORDS: Shares major league single-game record for most unassisted double plays by first baseman—2 (June 21, 1997). ... Shares major league record for most clubs played for in one season—4 (2000).

STATISTICAL NOTES: Had 21-game hitting streak (August 6-September 1, 2000). ... Career major league grand slams: 2.

			BATTING														FIELDING	
Year	Team (League)	Pos.	G	AB	R	H	2B	3B	HR	RBI	BB	SO	SB-CS	Avg.	OBP	SLG	E	Avg.
1983—	Quad Cities (Midw.)	OF	44	119	17	29	6	2	0	10	26	30	10-8	.244	.378	.328	1	.982
—	Geneva (NY-Penn)	OF	64	241	35	63	15	2	5	33	40	52	16-6	.261	.363	.402	8	.945
1984—	Quad Cities (Midw.)	OF	12	41	6	9	2	2	0	5	9	13	3-4	.220	.373	.366	1	.938
1985—	Win.-Salem (Caro.)	OF	115	386	52	132	14	4	5	54	62	35	38-14	*.342	.434	.438	7	.969
1986—	Iowa (A.A.)	OF	83	318	52	92	11	5	5	32	36	34	42-5	.289	.356	.403	2	.991
—	Chicago (N.L.)	OF	53	108	13	15	1	1	1	7	6	22	4-2	.139	.190	.194	1	.988
1987—	Chicago (N.L.)	OF	142	459	70	134	18	8	8	36	57	96	16-8	.292	.372	.418	6	.980
1988—	Chicago (N.L.)	OF	75	256	27	65	10	1	4	34	21	46	7-3	.254	.311	.348	5	.970
—	Montreal (N.L.)■	OF	63	191	24	49	3	5	2	12	17	48	16-6	.257	.316	.356	1	.992
1989—	Montreal (N.L.)	OF	126	361	41	99	16	7	3	27	27	57	23-4	.274	.324	.382	7	.967
1990—	Montreal (N.L.)	OF-P	118	391	60	109	13	5	11	39	24	48	13-11	.279	.321	.422	3	.989
1991—	Montreal (N.L.)	OF	124	396	47	117	18	5	7	42	20	54	16-7	.295	.332	.419	4	.982
1992—	Cincinnati (N.L.)■	OF-1B	135	393	47	100	20	5	3	31	42	54	12-8	.254	.323	.354	6	.985
1993—	San Fran. (N.L.)■	OF	91	241	28	58	12	1	5	27	27	39	6-3	.241	.317	.361	1	.993
—	Phoenix (PCL)	OF	3	15	4	7	0	0	0	2	1	1	1-0	.467	.314	.467	0	1.000
1994—	San Francisco (N.L.)	OF-1B	97	235	23	58	9	3	4	27	21	22	3-4	.247	.371	.362	3	.989
1995—	Chicago (A.L.)■	OF-1B-DH-P	119	303	49	93	16	4	5	37	32	41	8-2	.307	.348	.436	3	.993
1996—	Chicago (A.L.)	OF-1B	146	440	85	140	20	8	10	53	52	52	15-7	.318	.393	.468	6	.985
1997—	Chicago (A.L.)	OF-1B-DH	145	504	78	144	16	6	12	55	55	69	12-6	.286	.356	.413	7	.987
1998—	Tampa Bay (A.L.)■	OF-DH-1B	90	309	31	79	11	0	3	20	35	52	8-7	.256	.334	.320	1	.994
1999—	Tampa Bay (A.L.)	OF	143	514	79	146	25	5	6	66	60	76	13-6	.284	.361	.387	4	.985
2000—	Tampa Bay (A.L.)	OF	29	104	12	27	4	2	1	12	10	17	1-4	.260	.319	.365	0	1.000
—	Chicago (N.L.)■	OF-1B	18	54	5	10	1	1	0	1	2	8	1-0	.185	.214	.241	1	.988
—	Texas (A.L.)■	OF-1B	38	119	14	32	4	1	2	12	14	20	2-1	.269	.351	.370	0	1.000
—	Toronto (A.L.)■	OF	47	180	29	56	10	1	2	22	24	28	4-2	.311	.393	.411	2	.982
2001—	Atlanta (N.L.)■	OF-1B-DH	120	237	33	68	11	3	2	20	21	44	3-3	.287	.347	.384	0	1.000
2002—	Atlanta (N.L.)								Did not play.									
American League totals (6 years)			757	2473	377	717	106	27	41	277	282	355	63-35	.290	.360	.404	23	.989
National League totals (11 years)			1162	3322	418	882	132	45	50	303	285	538	120-59	.266	.322	.377	38	.984
Major League totals (16 years)			1919	5795	795	1599	238	72	91	580	567	893	183-94	.276	.341	.389	61	.986

DIVISION SERIES RECORD

			BATTING														FIELDING	
Year	Team (League)	Pos.	G	AB	R	H	2B	3B	HR	RBI	BB	SO	SB-CS	Avg.	OBP	SLG	E	Avg.
2001—	Atlanta (N.L.)	PH	1	1	0	0	0	0	0	0	0	0	0-0	.000	.000	.000	...	...

CHAMPIONSHIP SERIES RECORD

			BATTING														FIELDING	
Year	Team (League)	Pos.	G	AB	R	H	2B	3B	HR	RBI	BB	SO	SB-CS	Avg.	OBP	SLG	E	Avg.
2001—	Atlanta (N.L.)	PH-OF	4	5	0	1	0	0	0	0	0	1	0-0	.200	.200	.200	0	1.000

RECORD AS PITCHER

Year	League	W	L	Pct.	ERA	G	GS	CG	ShO	Sv.-Opp.	IP	H	R	ER	HR	BB-IBB	SO
1990—	Montreal (N.L.)	0	0	...	54.00	1	0	0	0	0-0	.1	2	2	2	0	2-0	0
1995—	Chicago (A.L.)■	0	0	...	0.00	1	0	0	0	0-0	1.0	0	0	0	0	2-0	0
Major League totals (2 years)		0	0	...	13.50	2	0	0	0	0-0	1.1	2	2	2	0	4-0	0

MARTINEZ, EDGAR — DH — MARINERS

PERSONAL: Born January 2, 1963, in New York. ... 5-11/210. ... Bats right, throws right. ... Cousin of Carmelo Martinez, first baseman/outfielder with six major league teams (1983-91).

HIGH SCHOOL: Dorado (Puerto Rico).

COLLEGE: American College (Puerto Rico).

TRANSACTIONS/CAREER NOTES: Signed as non-drafted free agent by Seattle Mariners organization (December 19, 1982). ... On Seattle disabled list (April 4-May 17, June 15-July 21 and August 17, 1993-remainder of season); included rehabilitation assignment to Jacksonville (July 17-21). ... On disabled list (April 16-May 6, 1994; July 21-August 12, 1996; and July 17-August 3, 2001). ... On suspended list (October 3-5, 2001). ... On disabled list (April 12-June 14, 2002).

RECORDS: Shares major league single-game record for most sacrifice flies—3 (August 3, 2002). ... Shares A.L. single-game record for most errors by third baseman—4 (May 6, 1990).

HONORS: Named third baseman on The Sporting News A.L. All-Star team (1992). ... Named third baseman on The Sporting News A.L. Silver Slugger team (1992). ... Named designated hitter on The Sporting News A.L. All-Star team (1995, 1997 and 2001). ... Named designated hitter on The Sporting News A.L. Silver Slugger team (1995 and 1997). ... Named designated hitter on A.L. Silver Slugger team (2001).

STATISTICAL NOTES: Led Southern League third basemen with 94 putouts, 247 assists, 360 total chances and 34 double plays in 1985. ... Led Southern League with 12 sacrifice flies in 1985. ... Led Southern League third basemen with .960 fielding percentage in 1986. ... Led Pacific Coast League third basemen with 91 putouts, 278 assists, 389 total chances and 31 double plays in 1987. ... Hit three home runs in one game (July 6, 1996 and May 18, 1999). ... Career major league grand slams: 9.

MISCELLANEOUS: Holds Seattle Mariners franchise all-time records for most hits (1,973), most runs (1,102), most doubles (466) and highest batting average (.317).

2002 GAMES PLAYED BY POSITION (MLB): DH—91.

Year	Team (League)	Pos.	BATTING														FIELDING	
			G	AB	R	H	2B	3B	HR	RBI	BB	SO	SB-CS	Avg.	OBP	SLG	E	Avg.
1983—	Bellingham (N'West) ..	3B	32	104	14	18	1	1	0	5	18	24	1-3	.173	.304	.202	6	.930
1984—	Wausau (Midw.)	3B	126	433	72	131	32	2	15	66	84	57	11-9	.303	.414	.490	25	.930
1985—	Chattanooga (Sou.)	3B	111	357	43	92	15	5	3	47	71	30	1-3	.258	.378	.353	19	*.947
—	Calgary (PCL)	3B-2B	20	68	8	24	7	1	0	14	12	7	1-0	.353	.450	.485	4	.937
1986—	Chattanooga (Sou.)	3B-2B	132	451	71	119	29	5	6	74	89	35	2-5	.264	.383	.390	15	†.960
1987—	Calgary (PCL)	3B	129	438	75	144	31	1	10	66	82	47	3-5	.329	.434	.473	20	.949
—	Seattle (A.L.)	3B-DH	13	43	6	16	5	2	0	5	2	5	0-0	.372	.413	.581	0	1.000
1988—	Calgary (PCL)	3B-2B	95	331	63	120	19	4	8	64	66	40	9-1	*.363	.467	.517	20	.921
—	Seattle (A.L.)	3B	14	32	0	9	4	0	0	5	4	7	0-0	.281	.351	.406	1	.929
1989—	Seattle (A.L.)	3B	65	171	20	41	5	0	2	20	17	26	2-1	.240	.314	.304	6	.949
—	Calgary (PCL)	3B-2B	32	113	30	39	11	0	3	23	22	13	2-2	.345	.457	.522	12	.867
1990—	Seattle (A.L.)	3B-DH	144	487	71	147	27	2	11	49	74	62	1-4	.302	.397	.433	*27	.928
1991—	Seattle (A.L.)	3B-DH	150	544	98	167	35	1	14	52	84	72	0-3	.307	.405	.452	15	.962
1992—	Seattle (A.L.)	3B-DH-1B	135	528	100	181	•46	3	18	73	54	61	14-4	*.343	.404	.544	17	.946
1993—	Seattle (A.L.)	DH-3B	42	135	20	32	7	0	4	13	28	19	0-0	.237	.366	.378	2	.889
—	Jacksonville (Sou.)	DH	4	14	2	5	0	0	1	3	2	0	0-0	.357	.438	.571	...	...
1994—	Seattle (A.L.)	3B-DH	89	326	47	93	23	1	13	51	53	42	6-2	.285	.387	.482	9	.950
1995—	Seattle (A.L.)	DH-3B-1B	•145	511	•121	182	•52	0	29	113	116	87	4-3	*.356	*.479	.628	2	.944
1996—	Seattle (A.L.)	DH-1-3-0	139	499	121	163	52	2	26	103	123	84	3-3	.327	.464	.595	1	.968
1997—	Seattle (A.L.)	DH-1B-3B	155	542	104	179	35	1	28	108	119	86	2-4	.330	.456	.554	1	.986
1998—	Seattle (A.L.)	DH-1B	154	556	86	179	46	1	29	102	106	96	1-1	.322	*.429	.565	0	1.000
1999—	Seattle (A.L.)	DH-1B	142	502	86	169	35	1	24	86	97	99	7-2	.337	*.447	.554	0	1.000
2000—	Seattle (A.L.)	DH-1B	153	556	100	180	31	0	37	*145	96	95	3-0	.324	.423	.579	0	1.000
2001—	Seattle (A.L.)	DH-1B	132	470	80	144	40	1	23	116	93	90	4-1	.306	.423	.543	0	1.000
2002—	Seattle (A.L.)	DH	97	328	42	91	23	0	15	59	67	69	1-1	.277	.403	.485	...	...
Major League totals (16 years)			1769	6230	1102	1973	466	15	273	1100	1133	1000	48-29	.317	.424	.528	81	.952

DIVISION SERIES RECORD

RECORDS: Holds A.L. career record for highest slugging percentage (50 or more at-bats)—.781. ... Shares single-series record for most hits—12 (1995). ... Shares single-game records for most runs batted in—7; and most home runs—2 (October 7, 1995).

NOTES: Shares postseason single-game record for most RBIs—7 (October 7, 1995).

Year	Team (League)	Pos.	BATTING														FIELDING	
			G	AB	R	H	2B	3B	HR	RBI	BB	SO	SB-CS	Avg.	OBP	SLG	E	Avg.
1995—	Seattle (A.L.)	DH	5	21	6	12	3	0	2	10	6	2	0-0	.571	.667	1.000	...	...
1997—	Seattle (A.L.)	DH	4	16	2	3	0	0	2	3	0	3	0-0	.188	.188	.563	...	...
2000—	Seattle (A.L.)	DH	3	11	2	4	1	0	1	2	2	1	0-0	.364	.462	.727	...	...
2001—	Seattle (A.L.)	DH	5	16	3	5	1	0	2	5	5	2	1-0	.313	.476	.750	...	...
Division series totals (4 years)			17	64	13	24	5	0	7	20	13	8	1-0	.375	.481	.781	0	...

CHAMPIONSHIP SERIES RECORD

Year	Team (League)	Pos.	BATTING														FIELDING	
			G	AB	R	H	2B	3B	HR	RBI	BB	SO	SB-CS	Avg.	OBP	SLG	E	Avg.
1995—	Seattle (A.L.)	DH	6	23	0	2	0	0	0	0	2	5	1-1	.087	.192	.087	...	...
2000—	Seattle (A.L.)	DH	6	21	2	5	1	0	1	4	3	5	0-0	.238	.333	.429	...	...
2001—	Seattle (A.L.)	DH	5	20	1	3	1	0	0	0	1	6	0-0	.150	.190	.200	...	...
Championship series totals (3 years)			17	64	3	10	2	0	1	4	6	16	1-1	.156	.239	.234	0	...

ALL-STAR GAME RECORD

	AB	R	H	2B	3B	HR	RBI	BB	SO	SB-CS	Avg.	OBP	SLG	E	Avg.
All-Star Game totals (6 years)	10	1	2	0	0	1	1	0	2	0-1	.200	.200	.500	0	...

MARTINEZ, PEDRO — P — RED SOX

PERSONAL: Born October 25, 1971, in Manoguayabo, Dominican Republic. ... 5-11/180. ... Throws right, bats right. ... Full name: Pedro Jaime Martinez. ... Brother of Ramon J. Martinez, pitcher with three teams (1988-2001); and brother of Jesus Martinez, pitcher in Los Angeles Dodgers (1991-97) and Cincinnati Reds (1998) organizations.

COLLEGE: Ohio Dominican College (Dominican Republic).

TRANSACTIONS/CAREER NOTES: Signed as non-drafted free agent by Los Angeles Dodgers organization (June 18, 1988). ... On Albuquerque disabled list (June 20-July 2 and July 13-August 25, 1992). ... Traded by Dodgers to Montreal Expos for 2B Delino DeShields (November 19, 1993). ... On suspended list (April 1-9, 1997). ... Traded by Expos to Boston Red Sox for P Carl Pavano and a player to be named later (November 18, 1997); Expos acquired P Tony Armas Jr. to complete deal (December 18, 1997). ... On disabled list (July 19-August 3, 1999; June 29-July 13, 2000; June 27-August 26 and September 8, 2001-remainder of season).

RECORDS: Shares major league record for striking out side on nine pitches (May 18, 2002, first inning). ... Shares A.L. record for most strikeouts in two consecutive games—32 (May 6 [17] and 12 [15], 2000, 18 innings).

HONORS: Named Minor League Player of the Year by The Sporting News (1991). ... Named N.L. Pitcher of the Year by The Sporting News (1997). ... Named righthanded pitcher on The Sporting News N.L. All-Star team (1997). ... Named N.L. Cy Young Award winner by Baseball Writers' Association of America (1997). ... Named righthanded pitcher on The Sporting News A.L. All-Star team (1998, 1999 and 2000). ... Named A.L. Pitcher of the Year by The Sporting News (1999 and 2000). ... Named A.L. Cy Young Award winner by Baseball Writers' Association of America (1999 and 2000).

STATISTICAL NOTES: Led N.L. with 11 hit batsmen in 1994. ... Pitched nine perfect innings against San Diego, before being relieved after yielding leadoff double in 10th inning (June 3, 1995). ... Tied for N.L. lead with 16 sacrifice hits in 1996. ... Pitched 2-0 one-hit, complete-game victory against Cincinnati (July 13, 1997). ... Struck out 15 batters in one game (May 7, May 12, August 24 and September 4, 1999; May 12 and July 23, 2000). ... Struck out 16 batters in one game (June 4, 1999; and April 8, 2001). ... Struck out 17 batters in one game (September 10, 1999; and May 6, 2000). ... Pitched 3-1 one-hit, complete-game victory against New York Yankees (September 10, 1999). ... Pitched 8-0 one-hit, complete-game victory against Tampa Bay (August 29, 2000).

CAREER HITTING (MLB): 25-for-260 (.096), 14 R, 3 2B, 2 3B, 0 HR, 11 RBI.

Year	League	W	L	Pct.	ERA	G	GS	CG	ShO	Sv.-Opp.	IP	H	R	ER	HR	BB-IBB	SO
1988—	Dom. Dodgers (DSL)	5	1	.833	3.10	8	7	1	0	0-...	49.1	45	25	17	...	16-...	28
1989—	Dom. Dodgers (DSL)	7	2	.778	2.73	13	7	2	3	1-...	85.2	59	30	26	...	25-...	63
1990—	Great Falls (Pio.)	8	3	.727	3.62	14	•14	0	0	0-...	77.0	74	39	31	5	40-1	82
1991—	Bakersfield (Calif.)	8	0	1.000	2.05	10	10	0	0	0-...	61.1	41	17	14	3	19-0	83
	—San Antonio (Texas)	7	5	.583	1.76	12	12	4	•3	0-...	76.2	57	21	15	1	31-1	74
	—Albuquerque (PCL)	3	3	.500	3.66	6	6	0	0	0-...	39.1	28	17	16	3	16-0	35
1992—	Albuquerque (PCL)	7	6	.538	3.81	20	20	3	1	0-...	125.1	104	57	53	10	57-0	124
	—Los Angeles (N.L.)	0	1	.000	2.25	2	1	0	0	0-0	8.0	6	2	2	0	1-0	8
1993—	Albuquerque (PCL)	0	0	...	3.00	1	1	0	0	0-...	3.0	1	1	1	0	1-0	4
	—Los Angeles (N.L.)	10	5	.667	2.61	65	2	0	0	2-3	107.0	76	34	31	5	57-4	119
1994—	Montreal (N.L.)■	11	5	.688	3.42	24	23	1	1	1-1	144.2	115	58	55	11	45-3	142
1995—	Montreal (N.L.)	14	10	.583	3.51	30	30	2	2	0-0	194.2	158	79	76	21	66-1	174
1996—	Montreal (N.L.)	13	10	.565	3.70	33	33	4	1	0-0	216.2	189	100	89	19	70-3	222
1997—	Montreal (N.L.)	17	8	.680	*1.90	31	31	*13	4	0-0	241.1	158	65	51	16	67-5	305
1998—	Boston (A.L.)■	19	7	.731	2.89	33	33	3	2	0-0	233.2	188	82	75	26	67-3	251
1999—	Boston (A.L.)	*23	4	*.852	*2.07	31	29	5	1	0-0	213.1	160	56	49	9	37-1	*313
2000—	Boston (A.L.)	18	6	.750	*1.74	29	29	7	*4	0-0	217.0	128	44	42	17	32-0	*284
2001—	Boston (A.L.)	7	3	.700	2.39	18	18	1	0	0-0	116.2	84	33	31	5	25-0	163
2002—	Boston (A.L.)	20	4	*.833	*2.26	30	30	2	0	0-0	199.1	144	62	50	13	40-1	*239
A.L. totals (5 years)		87	24	.784	2.27	141	139	18	7	0-0	980.0	704	277	247	70	201-5	1250
N.L. totals (6 years)		65	39	.625	3.00	185	120	20	8	3-4	912.1	702	338	304	72	306-16	970
Major League totals (11 years)		152	63	.707	2.62	326	259	38	15	3-4	1892.1	1406	615	551	142	507-21	2220

DIVISION SERIES RECORD

Year	League	W	L	Pct.	ERA	G	GS	CG	ShO	Sv.-Opp.	IP	H	R	ER	HR	BB-IBB	SO
1998—	Boston (A.L.)	1	0	1.000	3.86	1	1	0	0	0-0	7.0	6	3	3	2	0-0	8
1999—	Boston (A.L.)	1	0	1.000	0.00	2	1	0	0	0-0	10.0	3	0	0	0	4-0	11
Division series totals (2 years)		2	0	1.000	1.59	3	2	0	0	0-0	17.0	9	3	3	2	4-0	19

CHAMPIONSHIP SERIES RECORD

Year	League	W	L	Pct.	ERA	G	GS	CG	ShO	Sv.-Opp.	IP	H	R	ER	HR	BB-IBB	SO
1999—	Boston (A.L.)	1	0	1.000	0.00	1	1	0	0	0-0	7.0	2	0	0	0	2-0	12

ALL-STAR GAME RECORD

RECORDS: Holds record for most consecutive strikeouts from start of game—4 (1999).
NOTES: Named Most Valuable Player (1999).

	W	L	Pct.	ERA	GS	CG	ShO	Sv.-Opp.	IP	H	R	ER	HR	BB-IBB	SO
All-Star Game totals (3 years)	1	0	1.000	0.00	1	0	0	0-0	4.0	2	0	0	0	0-0	8

MARTINEZ, RAMON 2B/SS GIANTS

PERSONAL: Born October 10, 1972, in Philadelphia. ... 6-1/183. ... Bats right, throws right. ... Full name: Ramon E. Martinez.
HIGH SCHOOL: Escuela Superior Catholica (Bayamon, Puerto Rico).
JUNIOR COLLEGE: Vernon (Texas) Regional Junior College.
TRANSACTIONS/CAREER NOTES: Signed as non-drafted free agent by Kansas City Royals organization (January 15, 1993). ... Traded by Royals to San Francisco Giants (December 9, 1996), completing deal in which Giants traded P Jamie Brewington to Royals for a player to be named later (November 26, 1996). ... On Fresno disabled list (June 10-23, 1999). ... On San Francisco disabled list (August 21-September 5, 1999). ... On disabled list (June 1-16, 2002).
STATISTICAL NOTES: Led Texas League with 18 sacrifice hits and nine sacrifice flies in 1995. ... Led Texas League second basemen with .984 fielding percentage in 1995. ... Led American Association with 13 sacrifice hits in 1996.
2002 GAMES PLAYED BY POSITION (MLB): SS—40; 2B—17; 1B—4; OF—3; 3B—2.

			BATTING														FIELDING	
Year	Team (League)	Pos.	G	AB	R	H	2B	3B	HR	RBI	BB	SO	SB-CS	Avg.	OBP	SLG	E	Avg.
1993—	GC Royals (GCL)	2B	37	97	16	23	5	0	0	9	8	6	3-0	.237	.303	.289	5	.973
	—Wilmington (Caro.)	2B-SS	24	75	8	19	4	0	0	6	11	9	1-4	.253	.352	.307	6	.954
1994—	Wilmington (Caro.)	2B	90	325	40	87	13	2	2	35	35	25	6-3	.268	.341	.338	16	.964
	—Rockford (Midw.)	2B	6	18	3	5	0	0	0	3	4	2	1-0	.278	.409	.278	1	.955
1995—	Wichita (Texas)	2B-SS	103	393	58	108	20	2	3	51	42	50	11-8	.275	.344	.359	9	†.982
1996—	Omaha (A.A.)	2B	85	320	35	81	12	3	6	41	21	34	3-2	.253	.305	.366	12	.969
	—Wichita (Texas)	2B	26	93	16	32	4	1	1	8	7	8	4-1	.344	.390	.441	6	.956
1997—	Shreveport (Texas)■	SS	105	404	72	129	32	4	5	54	40	48	4-5	.319	.382	.455	18	.968
	—Phoenix (PCL)	2B-SS	18	57	6	16	2	0	1	7	5	9	1-0	.281	.333	.368	3	.959
1998—	Fresno (PCL)	2B-SS	98	364	58	114	21	2	14	59	38	42	0-3	.313	.375	.497	10	.980
	—San Francisco (N.L.)	2B	19	19	4	6	1	0	0	0	4	2	0-0	.316	.435	.368	0	1.000
1999—	San Francisco (N.L.)	2B-SS-3B-DH	61	144	21	38	6	0	5	19	14	17	1-2	.264	.327	.410	6	.966
	—Fresno (PCL)	SS-DH-3B	29	114	13	37	7	1	2	17	10	17	2-0	.325	.376	.456	5	.951
2000—	San Francisco (N.L.)	SS-2B-1B-3B	88	189	30	57	13	2	6	25	15	22	3-2	.302	.354	.487	1	.995
2001—	San Francisco (N.L.)	3B-2B-SS	128	391	48	99	18	3	5	37	38	52	1-2	.253	.323	.353	8	.980
2002—	San Francisco (N.L.)	S-2-1-O-3	72	181	26	49	10	2	4	25	14	26	2-0	.271	.335	.414	8	.965
Major League totals (5 years)			368	924	129	249	48	7	20	106	85	119	7-6	.269	.335	.402	23	.978

DIVISION SERIES RECORD

			BATTING														FIELDING	
Year	Team (League)	Pos.	G	AB	R	H	2B	3B	HR	RBI	BB	SO	SB-CS	Avg.	OBP	SLG	E	Avg.
2000—	San Francisco (N.L.)	2B-SS	2	6	0	2	0	0	0	0	0	2	0-0	.333	.333	.333	0	1.000
2002—	San Francisco (N.L.)	PH	1	0	0	0	0	0	0	0	1	0	0-0	...	1.000	...	0	...
Division series totals (2 years)			3	6	0	2	0	0	0	0	1	2	0-0	.333	.429	.333	0	1.000

CHAMPIONSHIP SERIES RECORD

			BATTING														FIELDING	
Year	Team (League)	Pos.	G	AB	R	H	2B	3B	HR	RBI	BB	SO	SB-CS	Avg.	OBP	SLG	E	Avg.
2002—	San Francisco (N.L.)	SS	2	1	0	0	0	0	0	1	0	0	0-0	.000	.000	.000	0	1.000

WORLD SERIES RECORD

			BATTING														FIELDING	
Year	Team (League)	Pos.	G	AB	R	H	2B	3B	HR	RBI	BB	SO	SB-CS	Avg.	OBP	SLG	E	Avg.
2002—	San Francisco (N.L.)	PH	2	2	0	0	0	0	0	0	0	2	0-0	.000	.000	.000	0	...

MARTINEZ, TINO 1B CARDINALS

PERSONAL: Born December 7, 1967, in Tampa. ... 6-2/210. ... Bats left, throws right. ... Full name: Constantino Martinez.
HIGH SCHOOL: Tampa Catholic.
COLLEGE: Tampa (Fla.).
TRANSACTIONS/CAREER NOTES: Selected by Boston Red Sox organization in third round of free-agent draft (June 3, 1985); did not sign. ... Selected by Seattle Mariners organization in first round (14th pick overall) of free-agent draft (June 1, 1988). ... On disabled list (August 10, 1993-remainder of season). ... Traded by Mariners with P Jeff Nelson and P Jim Mecir to New York Yankees for P Sterling Hitchcock and 3B Russ Davis (December 7, 1995). ... Granted free agency (November 5, 2001). ... Signed by St. Louis Cardinals (December 19, 2001).
RECORDS: Holds A.L. single-season record for fewest putouts by first baseman (150 or more games)—1,154 (2000); and fewest chances accepted by first baseman (150 or more games)—1,242 (2000).
HONORS: Named first baseman on The Sporting News college All-America team (1988). ... Named Pacific Coast League Most Valuable Player (1991). ... Named first baseman on The Sporting News A.L. All-Star team (1997). ... Named first baseman on The Sporting News A.L. Silver Slugger team (1997).
STATISTICAL NOTES: Led Eastern League with 13 intentional bases on balls received in 1989. ... Led Eastern League first basemen with 1,260 putouts, 81 assists, 1,348 total chances and 106 double plays in 1989. ... Tied for Pacific Coast League lead with 11 intentional bases on balls received in 1990. ... Led Pacific Coast League first basemen with .991 fielding percentage, 1,051 putouts, 98 assists, 1,159 total chances and 117 double plays in 1990. ... Led Pacific Coast League first basemen with .992 fielding percentage and 122 double plays in 1991. ... Hit three home runs in one game (April 2, 1997). ... Led A.L. with 13 sacrifice flies in 1997. ... Led A.L. first baseman with 106 assists and 1,410 total chances in 1999. ... Career major league grand slams: 10.
MISCELLANEOUS: Member of 1988 U.S. Olympic baseball team.
2002 GAMES PLAYED BY POSITION (MLB): 1B—149.

							BATTING									FIELDING	
Year Team (League)	Pos.	G	AB	R	H	2B	3B	HR	RBI	BB	SO	SB-CS	Avg.	OBP	SLG	E	Avg.
1989—Williamsport (East.)	1B	*137	*509	51	131	29	2	13	64	59	54	7-1	.257	.330	.399	7	*.995
1990—Calgary (PCL)	1B-3B	128	453	83	145	28	1	17	93	74	37	8-5	.320	.413	.499	10	†.991
—Seattle (A.L.)	1B	24	68	4	15	4	0	0	5	9	9	0-0	.221	.308	.279	0	1.000
1991—Calgary (PCL)	1B-3B	122	442	94	144	34	5	18	86	82	44	3-3	.326	.428	.548	9	†.992
—Seattle (A.L.)	1B-DH	36	112	11	23	2	0	4	9	11	24	0-0	.205	.272	.330	2	.993
1992—Seattle (A.L.)	1B-DH	136	460	53	118	19	2	16	66	42	77	2-1	.257	.316	.411	4	.995
1993—Seattle (A.L.)	1B-DH	109	408	48	108	25	1	17	60	45	56	0-3	.265	.343	.456	3	.997
1994—Seattle (A.L.)	1B-DH	97	329	42	86	21	0	20	61	29	52	1-2	.261	.320	.508	2	.997
1995—Seattle (A.L.)	1B-DH	141	519	92	152	35	3	31	111	62	91	0-0	.293	.369	.551	8	.993
1996—New York (A.L.)■	1B-DH	155	595	82	174	28	0	25	117	68	85	2-1	.292	.364	.466	5	*.996
1997—New York (A.L.)	1B-DH	158	594	96	176	31	2	44	141	75	75	3-1	.296	.371	.577	8	.994
1998—New York (A.L.)	1B	142	531	92	149	33	1	28	123	61	83	2-1	.281	.355	.505	10	.992
1999—New York (A.L.)	1B	159	589	95	155	27	2	28	105	69	86	3-4	.263	.341	.458	7	.995
2000—New York (A.L.)	1B	155	569	69	147	37	4	16	91	52	74	4-1	.258	.328	.422	7	.994
2001—New York (A.L.)	1B-DH	154	589	89	165	24	2	34	113	42	89	1-2	.280	.329	.501	5	.996
2002—St. Louis (N.L.)■	1B	150	511	63	134	25	1	21	75	58	71	3-2	.262	.337	.438	5	.996
American League totals (12 years)		1466	5363	773	1468	286	17	263	1002	565	801	18-16	.274	.343	.481	61	.995
National League totals (1 year)		150	511	63	134	25	1	21	75	58	71	3-2	.262	.337	.438	5	.996
Major League totals (13 years)		1616	5874	836	1602	311	18	284	1077	623	872	21-18	.273	.343	.477	66	.995

DIVISION SERIES RECORD

RECORDS: Shares single-game record for most at-bats—7 (October 4, 1995).

							BATTING									FIELDING	
Year Team (League)	Pos.	G	AB	R	H	2B	3B	HR	RBI	BB	SO	SB-CS	Avg.	OBP	SLG	E	Avg.
1995—Seattle (A.L.)	1B	5	22	4	9	1	0	1	5	3	4	0-1	.409	.480	.591	0	1.000
1996—New York (A.L.)	1B	4	15	3	4	2	0	0	0	3	1	0-0	.267	.389	.400	0	1.000
1997—New York (A.L.)	1B	5	18	1	4	1	0	1	4	2	4	0-0	.222	.333	.444	0	1.000
1998—New York (A.L.)	1B	3	11	1	3	2	0	0	0	0	2	0-0	.273	.273	.455	0	1.000
1999—New York (A.L.)	1B	3	11	2	2	0	0	0	0	2	2	0-0	.182	.308	.182	1	.968
2000—New York (A.L.)	1B	5	19	2	8	2	0	0	4	1	3	0-0	.421	.429	.526	1	.980
2001—New York (A.L.)	1B	5	18	1	2	0	0	1	2	1	6	0-0	.111	.238	.278	0	1.000
2002—St. Louis (N.L.)	1B	3	11	2	0	0	0	0	0	2	1	0-0	.000	.154	.000	0	1.000
Division series totals (8 years)		33	125	16	32	8	0	3	15	14	23	0-1	.256	.343	.392	2	.994

CHAMPIONSHIP SERIES RECORD

RECORDS: Shares A.L. career record for most times hit by pitch—3.

							BATTING									FIELDING	
Year Team (League)	Pos.	G	AB	R	H	2B	3B	HR	RBI	BB	SO	SB-CS	Avg.	OBP	SLG	E	Avg.
1995—Seattle (A.L.)	1B	6	22	1	3	0	0	0	0	3	7	0-0	.136	.240	.136	1	.980
1996—New York (A.L.)	1B	5	22	3	4	1	0	0	0	0	2	0-0	.182	.217	.227	0	1.000
1998—New York (A.L.)	1B	6	19	1	2	1	0	0	1	6	8	2-0	.105	.333	.158	1	.981
1999—New York (A.L.)	1B	5	19	3	5	1	0	1	3	2	4	0-0	.263	.364	.474	0	1.000
2000—New York (A.L.)	1B	6	25	5	8	2	0	1	1	2	4	0-0	.320	.370	.520	0	1.000
2001—New York (A.L.)	1B	5	20	3	5	1	0	1	3	0	4	0-1	.250	.250	.450	0	1.000
2002—St. Louis (N.L.)	1B	4	14	1	2	0	0	0	1	2	1	1-0	.143	.250	.143	0	1.000
Championship series totals (7 years)		37	141	17	29	6	0	3	9	15	30	3-1	.206	.294	.312	2	.994

WORLD SERIES RECORD

RECORDS: Shares single-game record for most grand slams—1 (October 17, 1998). ... Shares single-inning record for most runs batted in—4 (October 17, 1998, seventh inning).
NOTES: Member of World Series championship team (1996, 1998, 1999 and 2000).

							BATTING									FIELDING	
Year Team (League)	Pos.	G	AB	R	H	2B	3B	HR	RBI	BB	SO	SB-CS	Avg.	OBP	SLG	E	Avg.
1996—New York (A.L.)	1B-PH	6	11	0	1	0	0	0	0	2	5	0-0	.091	.231	.091	0	1.000
1998—New York (A.L.)	1B	4	13	4	5	0	0	1	4	4	2	0-0	.385	.529	.615	0	1.000
1999—New York (A.L.)	1B	4	15	3	4	0	0	1	5	2	4	0-0	.267	.353	.467	0	1.000
2000—New York (A.L.)	1B	5	22	3	8	1	0	0	2	1	4	0-0	.364	.391	.409	0	1.000
2001—New York (A.L.)	1B	6	21	1	4	0	0	1	3	2	2	0-0	.190	.261	.333	0	1.000
World Series totals (5 years)		25	82	11	22	1	0	3	14	11	17	0-0	.268	.355	.390	0	1.000

ALL-STAR GAME RECORD

	AB	R	H	2B	3B	HR	RBI	BB	SO	SB-CS	Avg.	OBP	SLG	E	Avg.
All-Star Game totals (2 years)	3	0	1	0	0	0	0	0	0	0-0	.333	.333	.333	0	1.000

MARTINEZ, VICTOR C INDIANS

PERSONAL: Born December 23, 1978, in Ciudad Bolivar, Venezuela. ... 6-2/170. ... Bats both, throws right. ... Full name: Victor Jesus Martinez.
TRANSACTIONS/CAREER NOTES: Signed as non-drafted free agent by Cleveland Indians organization (July 15, 1996). ... On Kinston disabled list (May 25-July 19, 2000).
HONORS: Named Carolina League Most Valuable Player (2001). ... Named Eastern League Most Valuable Player (2002).
STATISTICAL NOTES: Led New York-Pennsylvania League catchers with 56 assists in 1999. ... Led Carolina League catchers with 967 putouts and 1,061 total chances in 2001. ... Led Eastern League catchers with 770 putouts and 846 total chances in 2002.
2002 GAMES PLAYED BY POSITION (MLB): C—9; DH—1.

		BATTING														FIELDING	
Year Team (League)	Pos.	G	AB	R	H	2B	3B	HR	RBI	BB	SO	SB-CS	Avg.	OBP	SLG	E	Avg.
1997—Maracay 1 (VSL)		53	122	21	42	12	0	0	26	32	11	6-...	.344	...	.443	...	...
1998—Guacara 2 (VSL)		55	160	28	43	13	0	1	27	32	14	8-...	.269	...	.369	...	...
1999—Mahoning Val. (NY-P)	C	64	235	37	65	9	0	4	36	27	31	0-1	.277	.346	.366	8	.984
2000—Kinston (Caro.)	C	26	83	9	18	7	0	0	8	11	5	1-1	.217	.313	.301	5	.980
—Columbus (S.Atl.)	C	21	70	11	26	9	1	2	12	11	6	0-0	.371	.452	.614	2	.988
2001—Kinston (Caro.)	C	114	420	59	138	33	2	10	57	39	60	3-3	.329	.394	*.488	*16	.985
2002—Akron (East.)	C	121	443	*84	149	40	0	22	85	58	62	3-3	*.336	.417	.576	10	.988
—Cleveland (A.L.)	C-DH	12	32	2	9	1	0	1	5	3	2	0-0	.281	.333	.406	1	.983
Major League totals (1 year)		12	32	2	9	1	0	1	5	3	2	0-0	.281	.333	.406	1	.983

MATEO, HENRY 2B EXPOS

PERSONAL: Born October 14, 1976, in Santo Domingo, Dominican Republic. ... 5-11/180. ... Bats both, throws right. ... Full name: Henry Valera Mateo.
HIGH SCHOOL: Centro Estudios Libres (Santurce, Puerto Rico).
TRANSACTIONS/CAREER NOTES: Selected by Montreal Expos organization in second round of free-agent draft (June 1, 1995).
STATISTICAL NOTES: Tied for Florida State League lead with 17 sacrifice hits in 1999. ... Led International League second basemen with 251 putouts and 601 total chances and tied for lead with 328 assists in 2001.
2002 GAMES PLAYED BY POSITION (MLB): 2B—3; SS—2.

		BATTING														FIELDING	
Year Team (League)	Pos.	G	AB	R	H	2B	3B	HR	RBI	BB	SO	SB-CS	Avg.	OBP	SLG	E	Avg.
1995—GC Expos (GCL)	2B-SS	38	122	11	18	0	0	0	6	14	47	2-7	.148	.261	.148	9	.951
1996—GC Expos (GCL)	2B	14	44	8	11	3	0	0	3	5	11	5-1	.250	.365	.318	7	.901
1997—Vermont (NY-Penn)	2B	67	228	32	56	9	3	1	31	30	44	21-11	.246	.348	.325	14	.956
1998—Cape Fear (S.Atl.)	2B	114	416	72	115	20	5	4	41	40	111	22-16	.276	.355	.377	15	.971
—Jupiter (FSL)	2B	12	43	11	12	3	1	0	6	2	6	3-0	.279	.333	.395	0	1.000
1999—Jupiter (FSL)	2B	118	447	69	116	27	7	4	58	44	112	32-16	.260	.335	.378	17	.962
2000—Harrisburg (East.)	2B	140	530	91	152	25	11	5	63	58	97	48-16	.287	.362	.404	24	.962
2001—Ottawa (I.L.)	2B	118	500	71	134	14	*12	5	43	33	89	*47-14	.268	.322	.374	22	.963
—Montreal (N.L.)	2B	5	9	1	3	1	0	0	0	0	1	0-0	.333	.333	.444	2	.818
2002—Ottawa (I.L.)	2B-SS	74	285	35	73	10	6	5	25	18	53	15-6	.256	.306	.386	12	.970
—Montreal (N.L.)	2B-SS	22	23	1	4	0	1	0	0	2	6	2-0	.174	.240	.261	1	.950
Major League totals (2 years)		27	32	2	7	1	1	0	0	2	7	2-0	.219	.265	.313	3	.903

MATEO, JULIO P MARINERS

PERSONAL: Born August 2, 1977, in Bani, Dominican Republic. ... 6-0/177. ... Throws right, bats right. ... Full name: Julio Cesar Mateo.
TRANSACTIONS/CAREER NOTES: Signed as non-drafted free agent by Seattle Mariners organization (May 15, 1996).
CAREER HITTING (MLB): 0-for-0 (.000), 0 R, 0 2B, 0 3B, 0 HR, 0 RBI.

Year League	W	L	Pct.	ERA	G	GS	CG	ShO	Sv.-Opp.	IP	H	R	ER	HR	BB-IBB	SO
1996—Dom. Mariners (DSL)	4	2	.667	1.74	14	5	2	1	1-...	51.2	42	14	10	...	19-...	23
1997—Arizona Mariners (Ariz.)	3	1	.750	3.30	13	6	0	0	1-...	60.0	45	32	22	1	23-0	54
1998—Lancaster (Calif.)	0	0	...	6.75	1	0	0	0	0-...	1.1	1	1	1	1	1-0	1
—Everett (N'West)	3	3	.500	4.70	28	0	0	0	4-...	38.1	40	25	20	6	17-1	37
1999—Wisconsin (Midw.)	1	3	.250	4.34	20	0	0	0	4-...	29.0	31	18	14	2	8-2	27
2000—Wisconsin (Midw.)	4	8	.333	4.19	36	1	0	0	4-...	68.2	63	38	32	12	23-1	73
2001—San Bernardino (Calif.)	5	4	.556	2.86	56	0	0	0	26-...	66.0	58	28	21	5	16-5	79
2002—San Antonio (Texas)	1	0	1.000	0.52	12	0	0	0	0-...	17.1	7	3	1	2	3-0	18
—Tacoma (PCL)	4	2	.667	4.06	20	0	0	0	6-...	31.0	39	15	14	2	7-1	23
—Seattle (A.L.)	0	0	...	4.29	12	0	0	0	0-0	21.0	20	10	10	2	12-0	15
Major League totals (1 year)	0	0	...	4.29	12	0	0	0	0-0	21.0	20	10	10	2	12-0	15

MATEO, RUBEN OF REDS

PERSONAL: Born February 10, 1978, in San Cristobal, Dominican Republic. ... 6-0/185. ... Bats right, throws right. ... Full name: Ruben Amaurys Mateo.
HIGH SCHOOL: Liceo Jose Manuel Maria Balance (San Cristobal, Dominican Republic).
TRANSACTIONS/CAREER NOTES: Signed as non-drafted free agent by Texas Rangers organization (October 24, 1994). ... On Tulsa disabled list (April 13-May 13, 1998). ... On Texas disabled list (June 23-July 9 and August 5, 1999-remainder of season); included rehabilitation assignment to Oklahoma (July 6-9). ... On disabled list (June 3, 2000-remainder of season). ... Traded by Rangers with 3B Edwin Encarnacion

to Cincinnati Reds for P Rob Bell (June 15, 2001). ... On Louisville disabled list (September 11-13, 2001). ... On Louisville disabled list (July 4-24 and July 25-August 3, 2002).

2002 GAMES PLAYED BY POSITION (MLB): OF—24.

								BATTING								FIELDING	
Year Team (League)	Pos.	G	AB	R	H	2B	3B	HR	RBI	BB	SO	SB-CS	Avg.	OBP	SLG	E	Avg.
1995—Dom. Rangers (DSL)..	OF	48	176	30	53	9	3	4	42	20	23	1-2	.301	...	.455	1	.982
1996—Charl., S.C. (S.Atl.).....	OF-DH	134	496	65	129	30	8	8	58	26	78	30-9	.260	.309	.401	7	.970
1997—Charlotte (FSL)..........	OF-DH	99	385	63	121	23	8	12	67	22	55	20-5	.314	.359	.509	8	.958
1998—Tulsa (Texas)............	OF	107	433	79	134	32	3	18	75	30	56	18-8	.309	.371	.522	7	.970
—Charlotte (FSL)..........	OF	1	4	0	0	0	0	0	1	0	1	0-0	.000	.000	.000	0	1.000
1999—Texas (A.L.)...............	OF-DH	32	122	16	29	9	1	5	18	4	28	3-0	.238	.268	.451	0	1.000
—Oklahoma (PCL)........	OF-DH	63	253	53	85	12	0	18	62	14	36	6-3	.336	.385	.597	5	.963
2000—Texas (A.L.)...............	OF	52	206	32	60	11	0	7	19	10	34	6-0	.291	.339	.447	3	.980
2001—Texas (A.L.)...............	OF	40	129	18	32	5	2	1	13	9	28	1-0	.248	.322	.341	1	.986
—Oklahoma (PCL)........	OF	14	51	3	11	3	0	1	8	2	8	1-2	.216	.241	.333	1	.957
—Louisville (I.L.)■.......	OF	65	251	35	63	16	4	2	25	13	45	2-0	.251	.307	.371	5	.954
2002—Louisville (I.L.)..........	OF	52	209	37	63	14	0	9	23	11	40	6-2	.301	.342	.498	3	.967
—Cincinnati (N.L.)........	OF	46	86	11	22	6	0	2	7	6	20	0-0	.256	.319	.395	0	1.000
American League totals (3 years)		124	457	66	121	25	3	13	50	23	90	10-0	.265	.316	.418	4	.986
National League totals (1 year)		46	86	11	22	6	0	2	7	6	20	0-0	.256	.319	.395	0	1.000
Major League totals (4 years)		170	543	77	143	31	3	15	57	29	110	10-0	.263	.316	.414	4	.987

MATHENY, MIKE C CARDINALS

PERSONAL: Born September 22, 1970, in Reynoldsburg, Ohio. ... 6-3/205. ... Bats right, throws right. ... Full name: Michael Scott Matheny.

HIGH SCHOOL: Reynoldsburg (Ohio).

COLLEGE: Michigan.

TRANSACTIONS/CAREER NOTES: Selected by Toronto Blue Jays organization in 31st round of free-agent draft (June 1, 1988); did not sign. ... Selected by Milwaukee Brewers organization in eighth round of free-agent draft (June 3, 1991). ... On Milwaukee suspended list (June 20-23, 1996). ... On Milwaukee disabled list (June 15-July 12, 1998); included rehabilitation assignment to Beloit (July 11-13). ... Granted free agency (December 21, 1998). ... Signed by Blue Jays (December 23, 1998). ... Released by Blue Jays (November 16, 1999). ... Signed by St. Louis Cardinals (December 15, 1999).

HONORS: Won N.L. Gold Glove as catcher (2000).

STATISTICAL NOTES: Led California League catchers with 20 double plays in 1992. ... Led Texas League catchers with 100 assists and 18 double plays in 1993. ... Career major league grand slams: 2.

2002 GAMES PLAYED BY POSITION (MLB): C—106; 1B—1.

								BATTING								FIELDING	
Year Team (League)	Pos.	G	AB	R	H	2B	3B	HR	RBI	BB	SO	SB-CS	Avg.	OBP	SLG	E	Avg.
1991—Helena (Pio.).............	C	64	253	35	72	14	0	2	34	19	52	2-4	.285	.348	.364	5	*.991
1992—Stockton (Calif.).........	C	106	333	42	73	13	2	6	46	35	81	2-2	.219	.297	.324	8	*.989
1993—El Paso (Texas)...........	C	107	339	39	86	21	2	2	28	17	73	1-4	.254	.292	.345	9	.986
1994—Milwaukee (A.L.)........	C	28	53	3	12	3	0	1	2	3	13	0-1	.226	.293	.340	1	.989
—New Orleans (A.A.).....	C-DH-1B	57	177	20	39	10	1	4	21	16	39	1-1	.220	.299	.356	5	.987
1995—Milwaukee (A.L.)........	C	80	166	13	41	9	1	0	21	12	28	2-1	.247	.306	.313	4	.986
—New Orleans (A.A.).....	C	6	17	3	6	2	0	3	4	0	5	0-0	.353	.450	1.000	0	1.000
1996—Milwaukee (A.L.)........	C-DH	106	313	31	64	15	2	8	46	14	80	3-2	.204	.243	.342	8	.985
—New Orleans (A.A.).....	C-DH	20	66	3	15	4	0	1	6	2	17	1-0	.227	.246	.333	0	1.000
1997—Milwaukee (A.L.)........	C-1B	123	320	29	78	16	1	4	32	17	68	0-1	.244	.294	.338	5	.993
1998—Milwaukee (N.L.)........	C	108	320	24	76	13	0	6	27	11	63	1-0	.238	.278	.334	8	.987
—Beloit (Midw.)............	DH-C	2	8	1	2	1	0	0	2	1	3	0-0	.250	.333	.375	0	1.000
1999—Toronto (A.L.)■..........	C	57	163	16	35	6	0	3	17	12	37	0-0	.215	.271	.307	2	.995
2000—St. Louis (N.L.)■	C-1B	128	417	43	109	22	1	6	47	32	96	0-0	.261	.317	.362	5	.994
2001—St. Louis (N.L.)..........	C-1B	121	381	40	83	12	0	7	42	28	76	0-1	.218	.276	.304	4	.995
2002—St. Louis (N.L.)..........	C-1B	110	315	31	77	12	1	3	35	32	49	1-3	.244	.313	.317	4	.994
American League totals (5 years)		394	1015	92	230	49	4	16	118	58	226	5-5	.227	.276	.330	20	.990
National League totals (4 years)		467	1433	138	345	59	2	22	151	103	284	2-4	.241	.297	.331	21	.993
Major League totals (9 years)		861	2448	230	575	108	6	38	269	161	510	7-9	.235	.289	.330	41	.992

DIVISION SERIES RECORD

								BATTING								FIELDING	
Year Team (League)	Pos.	G	AB	R	H	2B	3B	HR	RBI	BB	SO	SB-CS	Avg.	OBP	SLG	E	Avg.
2000— St. Louis (N.L.)..........								Did not play.									
2001—St. Louis (N.L.)..........	C	4	10	0	2	0	0	0	0	0	3	0-0	.200	.200	.200	0	1.000
2002—St. Louis (N.L.)..........	C	3	9	3	4	1	0	0	2	2	1	0-0	.444	.545	.556	0	1.000
Division series totals (2 years)		7	19	3	6	1	0	0	2	2	4	0-0	.316	.381	.368	0	1.000

CHAMPIONSHIP SERIES RECORD

								BATTING								FIELDING	
Year Team (League)	Pos.	G	AB	R	H	2B	3B	HR	RBI	BB	SO	SB-CS	Avg.	OBP	SLG	E	Avg.
2000— St. Louis (N.L.)..........								Did not play.									
2002—St. Louis (N.L.)..........	C	5	19	2	6	2	0	1	1	0	2	0-0	.316	.316	.579	0	1.000

MATHEWS, T.J. P

PERSONAL: Born January 19, 1970, in Belleville, Ill. ... 6-1/225. ... Throws right, bats right. ... Full name: Timothy Jay Mathews. ... Son of Nelson Mathews, outfielder with Chicago Cubs (1960-63) and Kansas City Athletics (1964-65).

HIGH SCHOOL: Columbia (Ill.).

JUNIOR COLLEGE: Meramec Community College (Mo.).

COLLEGE: UNLV.

TRANSACTIONS/CAREER NOTES: Selected by St. Louis Cardinals organization in 36th round of free-agent draft (June 1, 1992). ... On Louisville disabled list (May 30-June 6, 1995). ... On suspended list (April 1-7, 1997). ... Traded by Cardinals with P Eric Ludwick and P Blake Stein to Oakland Athletics for 1B Mark McGwire (July 31, 1997). ... On Oakland disabled list (July 1-24, 1999); included rehabilitation assignment to Vancouver (July 21-24). ... On Oakland disabled list (August 11-September 1, 2000); included rehabilitation assignment to Sacramento (August 27-September 1). ... Released by A's (June 22, 2001). ... Signed by Cardinals organization (August 7, 2001). ... Granted free agency (November 5, 2001). ... Signed by Houston Astros organization (January 7, 2002). ... On Houston disabled list (May 3-July 17, 2002); included rehabilitation assignments to New Orleans (July 4-15) and Round Rock (July 16-17). ... Released by Astros (July 29, 2002). ... Signed by Cardinals organization (August 21, 2002). ... Granted free agency (October 15, 2002).

STATISTICAL NOTES: Pitched 4-0 no-hit victory against Burlington (August 13, 1993).

CAREER HITTING (MLB): 0-for-11 (.000), 0 R, 0 2B, 0 3B, 0 HR, 0 RBI.

Year League	W	L	Pct.	ERA	G	GS	CG	ShO	Sv.-Opp.	IP	H	R	ER	HR	BB-IBB	SO
1992—Hamilton (NY-Penn)	10	1	*.909	2.18	14	14	1	0	0-...	86.2	70	25	21	4	30-0	89
1993—Springfield (Midw.)	12	9	.571	2.71	25	25	5	2	0-...	159.1	121	59	48	7	29-0	144
1994—St. Petersburg (FSL)	5	5	.500	2.44	11	11	1	0	0-...	66.1	52	22	18	1	23-0	62
—Arkansas (Texas)	5	5	.500	3.15	16	16	1	0	0-...	97.0	83	37	34	8	24-1	93
1995—Louisville (A.A.)	9	4	.692	2.70	32	7	0	0	1-...	66.2	60	35	20	2	27-2	50
—St. Louis (N.L.)	1	1	.500	1.52	23	0	0	0	2-2	29.2	21	7	5	1	11-1	28
1996—St. Louis (N.L.)	2	6	.250	3.01	67	0	0	0	6-11	83.2	62	32	28	8	32-4	80
1997—St. Louis (N.L.)	4	4	.500	2.15	40	0	0	0	0-3	46.0	41	14	11	4	18-3	46
—Oakland (A.L.)■	6	2	.750	4.40	24	0	0	0	3-6	28.2	34	18	14	5	12-1	24
1998—Oakland (A.L.)	7	4	.636	4.58	66	0	0	0	1-4	72.2	71	44	37	6	29-3	53
1999—Oakland (A.L.)	9	5	.643	3.81	50	0	0	0	3-5	59.0	46	28	25	9	20-4	42
—Vancouver (PCL)	0	0	...	9.00	1	1	0	0	0-...	1.0	1	1	1	0	0-0	0
2000—Oakland (A.L.)	2	3	.400	6.03	50	0	0	0	0-1	59.2	73	40	40	10	25-5	42
—Sacramento (PCL)	0	0	...	0.00	3	1	0	0	0-...	3.2	2	1	0	0	1-0	5
2001—Oakland (A.L.)	0	1	.000	5.09	20	0	0	0	1-1	23.0	28	14	13	2	11-3	19
—Memphis (PCL)■	1	1	.500	1.80	15	0	0	0	4-...	15.0	16	4	3	0	1-0	14
—St. Louis (N.L.)	1	0	1.000	3.07	10	0	0	0	0-0	14.2	11	6	5	2	1-0	10
2002—Houston (N.L.)■	0	0	...	3.44	12	0	0	0	0-0	18.1	19	7	7	2	5-3	13
—New Orleans (PCL)	0	0	...	1.80	4	0	0	0	0-...	5.0	3	1	1	0	1-0	3
—Round Rock (Texas)	0	0	...	0.00	1	0	0	0	0-...	1.0	1	0	0	0	0-0	1
—Memphis (PCL)■	0	0	...	4.50	4	0	0	0	0-...	4.0	3	2	2	1	2-0	3
A.L. totals (5 years)	24	15	.615	4.78	210	0	0	0	8-17	243.0	252	144	129	32	97-16	180
N.L. totals (5 years)	8	11	.421	2.62	152	0	0	0	8-16	192.1	154	66	56	17	67-11	177
Major League totals (8 years)	32	26	.552	3.82	362	0	0	0	16-33	435.1	406	210	185	49	164-27	357

DIVISION SERIES RECORD

Year League	W	L	Pct.	ERA	G	GS	CG	ShO	Sv.-Opp.	IP	H	R	ER	HR	BB-IBB	SO
1996—St. Louis (N.L.)	1	0	1.000	0.00	1	0	0	0	0-0	1.0	1	0	0	0	0-0	2

CHAMPIONSHIP SERIES RECORD

Year League	W	L	Pct.	ERA	G	GS	CG	ShO	Sv.-Opp.	IP	H	R	ER	HR	BB-IBB	SO
1996—St. Louis (N.L.)	0	0	...	0.00	2	0	0	0	0-0	.2	2	0	0	0	1-1	2

MATOS ULIUS SS

M

PERSONAL: Born December 12, 1974, in New York. ... 5-11/175. ... Bats right, throws right.

HIGH SCHOOL: William Horlick (Wis.).

JUNIOR COLLEGE: South Suburban Junior College (Ill.).

TRANSACTIONS/CAREER NOTES: Selected by Cleveland Indians organization in 16th round of free-agent draft (June 2, 1994). ... Released by Indians (March 28, 1996). ... Signed by Thunder Bay of Northern League (May 1996). ... Signed by Sioux City of Northern League (May 1997). ... Contract purchased by Arizona Diamondbacks organization from Sioux City (September 8, 1997). ... Selected by San Diego Padres from Diamondbacks organization in Rule 5 minor league draft (December 13, 1999). ... Granted free agency (October 15, 2001). ... Re-signed by Padres organization (December 6, 2001). ... Granted free agency (October 15, 2002).

2002 GAMES PLAYED BY POSITION (MLB): 2B—49; 3B—17; SS—4; OF—3; 1B—2; DH—1.

					BATTING												FIELDING	
Year	Team (League)	Pos.	G	AB	R	H	2B	3B	HR	RBI	BB	SO	SB-CS	Avg.	OBP	SLG	E	Avg.
1994—	Watertown (NY-Penn)	SS-2B	43	138	13	34	2	2	0	18	13	33	3-2	.246	.307	.290	19	.912
1995—	Columbus (S.Atl.)	SS-OF-2B-3B	52	155	16	38	7	3	0	13	11	21	2-2	.245	.308	.329	14	.929
1996—	Thunder Bay (Nor.)■		82	295	33	81	13	0	3	32	14	48	8-7	.275	.311	.349	...	...
1997—	Sioux City (Nor.)■	SS	83	353	64	94	12	3	6	44	20	38	8-7	.266	.311	.368	24	.943
1998—	High Desert (Calif.)■	SS	111	439	70	132	27	4	4	60	23	40	19-13	.301	.333	.408	33	.941
1999—	El Paso (Texas)	SS-2B	120	425	54	119	17	5	5	41	13	37	5-2	.280	.301	.379	27	.954
2000—	Mobile (Sou.)	SS-2B	135	546	61	144	30	0	5	35	31	57	11-9	.264	.306	.346	29	.954
2001—	Mobile (Sou.)	SS-2B	19	67	13	22	6	0	0	2	1	5	1-2	.328	.343	.418	5	.941
	—Portland (PCL)	SS-2B	106	383	40	107	12	2	7	34	15	48	6-8	.279	.314	.376	14	.970
2002—	Portland (PCL)	SS-2B	50	186	20	58	17	0	4	26	9	20	1-2	.312	.345	.468	8	.961
	—San Diego (N.L.)	IF-OF-DH	76	185	19	44	3	0	2	19	9	33	1-1	.238	.279	.286	9	.961
Major League totals (1 year)			76	185	19	44	3	0	2	19	9	33	1-1	.238	.279	.286	9	.961

MATOS LUIS OF ORIOLES

PERSONAL: Born October 30, 1978, in Bayamon, Puerto Rico. ... 6-0/179. ... Bats right, throws right. ... Full name: Luis D. Matos.

HIGH SCHOOL: Disciple of Christ Academy (Bayamon, Puerto Rico).

TRANSACTIONS/CAREER NOTES: Selected by Baltimore Orioles organization in 10th round of free-agent draft (June 4, 1996). ... On Baltimore disabled list (March 30-August 24, 2001); included rehabilitation assignments to Gulf Coast Orioles (August 7-10), Frederick (August 11-13) and Bowie (August 14-24). ... On Baltimore disabled list (March 29-June 6, 2002); included rehabilitation assignment to Frederick (June 3-6).

2002 GAMES PLAYED BY POSITION (MLB): OF—14; DH—1.

									BATTING								FIELDING	
Year	Team (League)	Pos.	G	AB	R	H	2B	3B	HR	RBI	BB	SO	SB-CS	Avg.	OBP	SLG	E	Avg.
1996—	GC Orioles (GCL)........	OF	43	130	21	38	2	0	0	13	15	18	12-7	.292	.374	.308	1	.983
1997—	Delmarva (S.Atl.)........	OF	36	119	10	25	1	2	0	13	9	21	8-5	.210	.275	.252	2	.972
	—Bluefield (Appl.)	OF	61	240	37	66	7	3	2	35	20	36	26-4	.275	.340	.354	3	.977
1998—	Delmarva (S.Atl.)........	OF	133	503	73	137	26	6	7	32	38	90	42-14	.272	.328	.390	10	.964
	—Bowie (East.).............	OF	5	19	2	5	0	0	1	3	1	1	1-1	.263	.300	.421	1	.833
1999—	Frederick (Caro.)	OF-DH	68	273	40	81	15	1	7	41	20	35	27-6	.297	.343	.436	2	.987
	—Bowie (East.).............	OF	66	283	41	67	11	1	9	36	15	39	14-4	.237	.272	.378	3	.982
2000—	Rochester (I.L.)		11	35	2	6	1	0	0	0	3	8	2-0	.171	.256	.200	0	1.000
	—Bowie (East.).............	OF	50	181	26	49	7	5	2	33	17	23	8-8	.271	.345	.398	2	.984
	—Baltimore (A.L.)..........	OF-DH	72	182	21	41	6	3	1	17	12	30	13-4	.225	.281	.308	2	.988
2001—	GC Orioles (GCL)........	DH	3	14	1	4	2	0	0	2	0	3	0-0	.286	.286	.429	...	...
	—Frederick (Caro.)	DH	2	7	3	3	0	0	1	2	1	3	0-0	.429	.500	.857	...	...
	—Bowie (East.).............	OF	13	46	6	14	5	0	1	8	5	7	0-1	.304	.385	.478	1	.955
	—Baltimore (A.L.)..........	OF	31	98	16	21	7	0	4	12	11	30	7-0	.214	.300	.408	1	.985
2002—	Frederick (Caro.)	OF	3	12	2	4	1	0	0	1	2	3	0-0	.333	.429	.417	0	1.000
	—Bowie (East.).............	OF	62	218	34	60	14	2	9	40	32	45	14-4	.275	.370	.482	1	.992
	—Baltimore (A.L.)..........	OF-DH	17	31	0	4	1	0	0	1	1	6	1-0	.129	.156	.161	0	1.000
Major League totals (3 years)			120	311	37	66	14	3	5	30	24	66	21-4	.212	.276	.325	3	.988

MATTHEWS, GARY — OF — ORIOLES

PERSONAL: Born August 25, 1974, in San Francisco. ... 6-3/210. ... Bats both, throws right. ... Full name: Gary Nathaniel Matthews Jr. ... Son of Gary Matthews, hitting coach with Toronto Blue Jays (1997-99) and outfielder with five major league teams (1972-87).
HIGH SCHOOL: Granada Hills (Calif.).
JUNIOR COLLEGE: Mission College (Calif.).
TRANSACTIONS/CAREER NOTES: Selected by San Diego Padres organization in 13th round of free-agent draft (June 3, 1993). ... Traded by Padres to Chicago Cubs for P Rodney Myers (March 23, 2000). ... Claimed on waivers by Pittsburgh Pirates (August 10, 2001). ... Traded by Pirates to New York Mets for cash (December 28, 2001). ... Traded by Mets to Baltimore Orioles for P John Bale (April 3, 2002). ... On Baltimore disabled list (August 25-September 11, 2002).
2002 GAMES PLAYED BY POSITION (MLB): OF—100; DH—2.

									BATTING								FIELDING	
Year	Team (League)	Pos.	G	AB	R	H	2B	3B	HR	RBI	BB	SO	SB-CS	Avg.	OBP	SLG	E	Avg.
1994—	Spokane (N'West)	OF-2B	52	191	23	40	6	1	0	18	19	58	3-5	.209	.286	.251	4	.961
1995—	Clinton (Midw.)	OF	128	421	57	100	18	4	2	40	68	109	28-8	.238	.349	.314	9	.966
1996—	Rancho Cuca. (Calif.) .	OF	123	435	65	118	21	11	7	54	60	102	7-8	.271	.366	.418	16	.934
1997—	Rancho Cuca. (Calif.) .	OF	69	268	66	81	15	4	8	40	49	57	10-4	.302	.416	.478	5	.959
	—Mobile (Sou.)	OF	28	90	14	22	4	1	2	12	15	29	3-1	.244	.352	.378	2	.960
1998—	Mobile (Sou.)	OF	72	254	62	78	15	4	7	51	55	50	11-1	.307	.428	.480	1	.995
1999—	Las Vegas (PCL)	OF	121	422	57	108	22	3	9	52	58	104	17-6	.256	.352	.386	7	.976
	—San Diego (N.L.)	OF	23	36	4	8	0	0	0	7	9	9	2-0	.222	.378	.222	0	1.000
2000—	Iowa (PCL)■	OF	60	211	27	51	11	3	5	22	18	41	6-1	.242	.300	.393	4	.970
	—Chicago (N.L.)	OF	80	158	24	30	1	2	4	14	15	28	3-0	.190	.264	.297	2	.978
2001—	Chicago (N.L.)	OF	106	258	41	56	9	1	9	30	38	55	5-3	.217	.320	.364	4	.976
	—Pittsburgh (N.L.)■	OF	46	147	22	36	6	1	5	14	22	45	3-2	.245	.341	.401	3	.971
2002—	New York (N.L.)■	PH	2	1	0	0	0	0	0	0	0	0	0-0	.000	.000	.000	...	...
	—Baltimore (A.L.)■.......	OF-DH	109	344	54	95	25	3	7	38	43	69	15-5	.276	.355	.427	6	.969
American League totals (1 year)			109	344	54	95	25	3	7	38	43	69	15-5	.276	.355	.427	6	.969
National League totals (4 years)			257	600	91	130	16	4	18	65	84	137	13-5	.217	.314	.347	9	.976
Major League totals (4 years)			366	944	145	225	41	7	25	103	127	206	28-10	.238	.329	.376	15	.974

MATTHEWS, MIKE — P — BREWERS

PERSONAL: Born October 24, 1973, in Fredericksburg, Va. ... 6-2/175. ... Throws left, bats left. ... Full name: Michael Scott Matthews.
HIGH SCHOOL: Woodbridge Senior (Va.).
JUNIOR COLLEGE: Montgomery-Rockville College (Md.).
TRANSACTIONS/CAREER NOTES: Selected by Cleveland Indians organization in second round of free-agent draft (June 1, 1992). ... On Watertown disabled list (June 17, 1993-entire season). ... On disabled list (June 7-28, 1995). ... On disabled list (June 8-July 1, 1998). ... Traded by Indians to Boston Red Sox for IF Jose Olmeda (August 4, 1999). ... Traded by Red Sox with C David Menham to St. Louis Cardinals for P Kent Mercker (August 24, 1999). ... On St. Louis disabled list (July 16, 2000-remainder of season). ... On St. Louis disabled list (August 21-September 11, 2002). ... Traded by Cardinals to Milwaukee Brewers (September 11, 2002), completing deal in which Brewers traded P Jamey Wright and cash to Cardinals for OF Chris Morris and a player to be named later (August 29, 2002).
STATISTICAL NOTES: Tied for Eastern League lead with four balks in 1997.
MISCELLANEOUS: Appeared in one game as pinch runner (2001).
CAREER HITTING (MLB): 3-for-23 (.130), 2 R, 0 2B, 0 3B, 1 HR, 1 RBI.

Year	League	W	L	Pct.	ERA	G	GS	CG	ShO	Sv.-Opp.	IP	H	R	ER	HR	BB-IBB	SO
1992—	Burlington (Appl.)............	7	0	•1.000	*1.01	10	10	0	0	0-...	62.1	33	13	7	1	27-0	55
	—Watertown (NY-Penn)	1	0	1.000	3.27	2	2	2	0	0-...	11.0	10	4	4	0	8-0	5
1993—	....									Did not play.							
1994—	Columbus (S.Atl.)............	6	8	.429	3.08	23	23	0	0	0-...	119.2	120	53	41	8	44-1	99
1995—	Canton/Akron (East.)........	5	8	.385	5.93	15	15	1	0	0-...	74.1	82	62	49	6	43-1	37
1996—	Canton/Akron (East.)........	9	11	.450	4.66	27	27	3	0	0-...	162.1	178	96	84	13	74-3	112
1997—	Buffalo (A.A.)....................	0	2	.000	7.71	5	5	0	0	0-...	21.0	32	19	18	7	10-0	17
	—Akron (East.).................	6	8	.429	3.82	19	19	3	1	0-...	113.0	116	62	48	13	57-0	69
1998—	Buffalo (I.L.)....................	9	6	.600	4.63	24	23	0	0	0-...	130.1	137	79	67	19	68-1	86
1999—	Buffalo (I.L.)....................	1	2	.333	7.59	25	0	0	0	0-...	21.1	23	18	18	3	18-0	16
	—Akron (East.).................	0	5	.000	8.77	6	6	0	0	0-...	25.2	36	30	25	7	15-0	10
	—Trenton (East.)■	0	0	...	4.63	3	3	0	0	0-...	11.2	11	7	6	1	9-0	8
	—Arkansas (Texas)■...........	2	0	1.000	0.00	2	2	1	1	0-...	12.0	3	0	0	0	1-0	10

Year League	W	L	Pct.	ERA	G	GS	CG	ShO	Sv.-Opp.	IP	H	R	ER	HR	BB-IBB	SO
2000— Memphis (PCL)	3	1	.750	3.12	9	9	0	0	0-...	52.0	33	19	18	4	32-1	50
— St. Louis (N.L.)	0	0	...	11.57	14	0	0	0	0-0	9.1	15	12	12	2	10-2	8
2001— St. Louis (N.L.)	3	4	.429	3.24	51	10	0	0	1-3	89.0	74	32	32	11	33-4	72
2002— St. Louis (N.L.)	2	1	.667	3.89	43	0	0	0	0-2	41.2	40	21	18	5	22-2	32
— Milwaukee (N.L.)■	0	0	...	4.50	4	0	0	0	0-0	4.0	3	2	2	0	7-1	2
Major League totals (3 years)	5	5	.500	4.00	112	10	0	0	1-5	144.0	132	67	64	18	72-9	114

DIVISION SERIES RECORD

Year League	W	L	Pct.	ERA	G	GS	CG	ShO	Sv.-Opp.	IP	H	R	ER	HR	BB-IBB	SO
2001— St. Louis (N.L.)	0	1	.000	40.50	1	0	0	0	0-1	.2	4	3	3	1	0-0	0

MAURER, DAVID — P

PERSONAL: Born February 23, 1975, in Minneapolis. ... 6-2/205. ... Throws left, bats right. ... Full name: David Charles Maurer. ... Brother of Mike Maurer, pitcher, Oakland Athletics organization; son of Thomas Maurer, pitcher in Minnesota Twins organization.

HIGH SCHOOL: Apple Valley (Minn.).

COLLEGE: Oklahoma State.

TRANSACTIONS/CAREER NOTES: Selected by San Diego Padres organization in 11th round of free-agent draft (June 3, 1997). ... Selected by San Francisco Giants from Padres organization in Rule 5 major league draft (December 13, 1999). ... Returned to Padres (March 20, 2000). ... Released by Padres (June 1, 2001). ... Signed by Cincinnati Reds organization (June 1, 2001). ... Released by Reds (July 26, 2001). ... Signed by Oakland Athletics organization (July 29, 2001). ... Granted free agency (October 15, 2001). ... Signed by Cleveland Indians organization (December 18, 2001). ... On Buffalo disabled list (July 15-23, 2002). ... Granted free agency (October 15, 2002).

CAREER HITTING (MLB): 0-for-1 (.000), 0 R, 0 2B, 0 3B, 0 HR, 0 RBI.

Year League	W	L	Pct.	ERA	G	GS	CG	ShO	Sv.-Opp.	IP	H	R	ER	HR	BB-IBB	SO
1997— Clinton (Midw.)	0	4	.000	2.88	25	0	0	0	3-...	34.1	24	15	11	1	15-0	43
1998— Rancho Cuca. (Calif.)	5	2	.714	2.70	48	0	0	0	5-...	83.1	56	27	25	1	46-1	93
1999— Mobile (Sou.)	4	4	.500	3.63	54	0	0	0	3-...	72.0	59	30	29	7	26-5	59
2000— Mobile (Sou.)	1	2	.333	2.70	24	0	0	0	0-...	26.2	15	8	8	2	3-1	28
— Las Vegas (PCL)	4	1	.800	3.25	35	0	0	0	0-...	44.1	47	19	16	5	15-1	44
— San Diego (N.L.)	1	0	1.000	3.68	14	0	0	0	0-1	14.2	15	8	6	2	5-1	13
2001— San Diego (N.L.)	0	0	...	10.80	3	0	0	0	0-0	5.0	8	6	6	1	4-0	4
— Portland (PCL)	0	0	...	4.34	17	0	0	0	1-...	18.2	11	9	9	4	9-2	21
— Louisville (I.L.)■	0	1	.000	4.15	18	0	0	0	1-...	21.2	18	11	10	4	7-0	23
— Sacramento (PCL)■	0	0	...	5.54	11	0	0	0	0-...	13.0	14	9	8	2	8-0	21
2002— Buffalo (I.L.)■	5	1	.833	2.90	36	3	0	0	5-...	68.1	50	27	22	6	24-0	73
— Cleveland (A.L.)	0	1	.000	13.50	2	0	0	0	0-0	1.1	3	2	2	1	0-0	0
A.L. totals (1 year)	0	1	.000	13.50	2	0	0	0	0-0	1.1	3	2	2	1	0-0	0
N.L. totals (2 years)	1	0	1.000	5.49	17	0	0	0	0-1	19.2	23	14	12	3	9-1	17
Major League totals (3 years)	1	1	.500	6.00	19	0	0	0	0-1	21.0	26	16	14	4	9-1	17

MAY, DARRELL — P — ROYALS

PERSONAL: Born June 13, 1972, in San Bernardino, Calif. ... 6-2/184. ... Throws left, bats left. ... Full name: Darrell Kevin May.

HIGH SCHOOL: Rogue River (Ore.).

JUNIOR COLLEGE: Sacramento City College.

TRANSACTIONS/CAREER NOTES: Selected by Atlanta Braves organization in 46th round of free-agent draft (June 1, 1992). ... Claimed on waivers by Pittsburgh Pirates (April 4, 1996). ... Claimed on waivers by California Angels (September 6, 1996). ... Angels franchise renamed Anaheim Angels for 1997 season. ... Released by Angels (March 27, 1998). ... Played with Hanshin Tigers of Japan Central League (1998-99). ... Played with Yomiuri Giants of Japan Central League (2000-01). ... Signed by Kansas City Royals organization (December 17, 2001). ... On Kansas City disabled list (March 27-April 13 and April 14-May 18, 2002) included rehabilitation assignments to Omaha (April 8-9 and May 14-18) and Wichita (May 8-13).

STATISTICAL NOTES: Pitched 4-0 no-hit victory against Colorado Springs (April 30, 1997, second game).

CAREER HITTING (MLB): 1-for-9 (.111), 1 R, 0 2B, 0 3B, 0 HR, 0 RBI.

Year League	W	L	Pct.	ERA	G	GS	CG	ShO	Sv.-Opp.	IP	H	R	ER	HR	BB-IBB	SO
1992— Gulf Coast Braves (GCL)	4	3	.571	1.36	12	7	0	0	1-...	53.0	34	13	8	0	13-0	61
1993— Macon (S.Atl.)	10	4	.714	2.24	17	17	0	0	0-...	104.1	81	29	26	6	22-1	111
— Durham (Caro.)	5	2	.714	2.09	9	9	0	0	0-...	51.2	44	18	12	4	16-0	47
1994— Durham (Caro.)	8	2	*.800	3.01	12	12	1	0	0-...	74.2	74	29	25	6	17-1	73
— Greenville (Sou.)	5	3	.625	3.11	11	11	1	0	0-...	63.2	61	25	22	4	17-0	42
1995— Greenville (Sou.)	2	8	.200	3.55	15	15	0	0	0-...	91.1	81	44	36	18	20-0	79
— Richmond (I.L.)	4	2	.667	3.71	9	9	0	0	0-...	51.0	53	21	21	1	16-1	42
— Atlanta (N.L.)	0	0	...	11.25	2	0	0	0	0-0	4.0	10	5	5	0	0-0	1
1996— Calgary (PCL)■	7	6	.538	4.10	23	22	1	1	0-...	131.2	146	64	60	17	36-6	75
— Pittsburgh (N.L.)	0	1	.000	9.35	5	2	0	0	0-0	8.2	15	10	9	5	4-0	5
— California (A.L.)■	0	0	...	10.13	5	0	0	0	0-0	2.2	3	3	3	1	2-0	1
1997— Vancouver (PCL)	7	5	.583	3.26	13	12	2	2	0-...	80.0	65	31	29	10	31-0	62
— Anaheim (A.L.)	2	1	.667	5.23	29	2	0	0	0-1	51.2	56	31	30	6	25-2	42
1998— Hanshin (Jap. Cen.)■	4	9	.308	3.47	21	21	1	1	0-...	129.2	122	55	50	...	55-...	94
— Hanshin (Jp. West.)	1	2	.333	5.82	5	3	0	0	0-...	17.0	19	11	11	...	2-...	11
1999— Hanshin (Jap. Cen.)	6	7	.462	4.25	18	18	0	0	0-...	112.1	101	56	53	...	38-...	113
— Hanshin (Jp. West.)	1	0	1.000	0.00	2	2	0	0	0-...	10.0	4	1	0	...	2-...	12
2000— Yomiuri (Jap. Cen.)■	12	7	.632	2.95	24	24	3	3	0-...	155.1	123	52	51	...	40-...	165
— Yomiuri (Jp. East.)	0	0	...	0.00	1	0	0	0	0-...	4.0	2	0	0	...	1-...	4
2001— Yomiuri (Jap. Cen.)	10	8	.556	4.13	26	26	1	0	0-...	159.0	160	74	73	...	45-...	168
2002— Omaha (PCL)■	1	0	1.000	0.75	2	2	0	0	0-...	12.0	8	1	1	0	0-0	9
— Kansas City (A.L.)	4	10	.286	5.35	30	21	2	1	0-1	131.1	144	83	78	28	50-3	95
— Wichita (Texas)	0	0	...	2.08	1	1	0	0	0-...	4.1	4	1	1	0	1-0	5
A.L. totals (3 years)	6	11	.353	5.38	64	23	2	1	0-2	185.2	203	117	111	35	77-5	138
N.L. totals (2 years)	0	1	.000	9.95	7	2	0	0	0-0	12.2	25	15	14	5	4-0	6
Major League totals (4 years)	6	12	.333	5.67	71	25	2	1	0-2	198.1	228	132	125	40	81-5	144

MAYNE, BRENT C ROYALS

PERSONAL: Born April 19, 1968, in Loma Linda, Calif. ... 6-1/190. ... Bats left, throws right. ... Full name: Brent Danem Mayne.
HIGH SCHOOL: Costa Mesa (Calif.).
JUNIOR COLLEGE: Orange Coast College (Calif.).
COLLEGE: Cal State Fullerton.
TRANSACTIONS/CAREER NOTES: Selected by Kansas City Royals organization in first round (13th pick overall) of free-agent draft (June 5, 1989). ... On disabled list (July 24, 1989-remainder of season). ... Traded by Royals to New York Mets for OF Al Shirley (December 19, 1995). ... Granted free agency (December 7, 1996). ... Signed by Seattle Mariners organization (January 10, 1997). ... Released by Mariners (March 28, 1997). ... Signed by Oakland Athletics organization (April 8, 1997). ... Granted free agency (October 30, 1997). ... Signed by San Francisco Giants (November 21, 1997). ... Granted free agency (October 28, 1999). ... Signed by Colorado Rockies (December 9, 1999). ... Traded by Rockies to Royals for P Mac Suzuki and C Sal Fasano (June 24, 2001). ... On Kansas City disabled list (April 30-May 28, 2002); included rehabilitation assignment to Wichita (May 24-28). ... On suspended list (September 25-27, 2002).
STATISTICAL NOTES: Led A.L. catchers with 11 double plays in 1995. ... Career major league grand slams: 2.
2002 GAMES PLAYED BY POSITION (MLB): C—99.

		BATTING														FIELDING	
Year Team (League)	Pos.	G	AB	R	H	2B	3B	HR	RBI	BB	SO	SB-CS	Avg.	OBP	SLG	E	Avg.
1989—Baseball City (FSL)	C	7	24	5	13	3	1	0	8	0	3	0-1	.542	.542	.750	0	1.000
1990—Memphis (Sou.)	C	115	412	48	110	16	3	2	61	52	51	5-2	.267	.346	.335	11	.983
—Kansas City (A.L.)	C	5	13	2	3	0	0	0	1	3	3	0-1	.231	.375	.231	1	.970
1991—Kansas City (A.L.)	C-DH	85	231	22	58	8	0	3	31	23	42	2-4	.251	.315	.325	6	.987
1992—Kansas City (A.L.)	C-3B-DH	82	213	16	48	10	0	0	18	11	26	0-4	.225	.260	.272	3	.991
1993—Kansas City (A.L.)	C-DH	71	205	22	52	9	1	2	22	18	31	3-2	.254	.317	.337	2	.995
1994—Kansas City (A.L.)	C-DH	46	144	19	37	5	1	2	20	14	27	1-0	.257	.323	.347	1	.996
1995—Kansas City (A.L.)	C	110	307	23	77	18	1	1	27	25	41	0-1	.251	.313	.326	3	.995
1996—New York (N.L.)■	C	70	99	9	26	6	0	1	6	12	22	0-1	.263	.342	.354	0	1.000
1997—Edmonton (PCL)■	C	2	3	0	0	0	0	0	0	0	1	0-0	.000	.000	.000	0	1.000
—Oakland (A.L.)	C	85	256	29	74	12	0	6	22	18	33	1-0	.289	.343	.406	2	.996
1998—San Fran. (N.L.)■	C	94	275	26	75	15	0	3	32	37	47	2-1	.273	.359	.360	5	.991
1999—San Francisco (N.L.)	C	117	322	39	97	32	0	2	39	43	65	2-2	.301	.389	.419	3	.995
2000—Colorado (N.L.)■	C-P	117	335	36	101	21	0	6	64	47	48	1-3	.301	.381	.418	6	.990
2001—Colorado (N.L.)	C-1B	49	160	15	53	7	0	0	20	16	24	0-0	.331	.385	.375	1	.997
—Kansas City (A.L.)■	C	51	166	13	40	4	1	2	20	10	17	1-2	.241	.283	.313	2	.993
2002—Kansas City (A.L.)	C	101	326	35	77	8	2	4	30	34	54	4-4	.236	.309	.310	4	.993
—Wichita (Texas)	C	2	4	0	2	0	0	0	1	1	0	0-0	.500	.600	.500	0	1.000
American League totals (9 years)		636	1861	181	466	74	6	20	191	156	274	12-18	.250	.310	.329	24	.993
National League totals (5 years)		447	1191	125	352	81	0	12	161	155	206	5-7	.296	.375	.394	15	.993
Major League totals (13 years)		1083	3052	306	818	155	6	32	352	311	480	17-25	.268	.336	.354	39	.993

RECORD AS PITCHER

Year League	W	L	Pct.	ERA	G	GS	CG	ShO	Sv.-Opp.	IP	H	R	ER	HR	BB-IBB	SO
2000—Colorado (N.L.)■	1	0	1.000	0.00	1	0	0	0	0-0	1.0	1	0	0	0	1-0	0

MAYS, JOE P TWINS

PERSONAL: Born December 10, 1975, in Flint, Mich. ... 6-1/185. ... Throws right, bats both. ... Full name: Joseph E. Mays.
HIGH SCHOOL: Southeast (Bradenton, Fla.).
JUNIOR COLLEGE: Manatee.
TRANSACTIONS/CAREER NOTES: Selected by Seattle Mariners organization in sixth round of free-agent draft (June 2, 1994). ... Traded by Mariners to Minnesota Twins (October 8, 1997), completing deal in which Twins traded OF Roberto Kelly to Mariners for P Jeromy Palki and a player to be named later (August 20, 1997). ... On Minnesota disabled list (April 15-July 20, 2002); included rehabilitation assignments to Fort Myers (July 2-14) and New Britain (July 15-17).
CAREER HITTING (MLB): 2-for-9 (.222), 1 R, 1 2B, 0 3B, 0 HR, 0 RBI.

Year League	W	L	Pct.	ERA	G	GS	CG	ShO	Sv.-Opp.	IP	H	R	ER	HR	BB-IBB	SO
1995—Arizona Mariners (Ariz.)	2	3	.400	3.25	10	10	0	0	0-...	44.1	41	24	16	0	18-0	44
1996—Everett (N'West)	4	4	.500	3.08	13	10	0	0	0-...	64.1	55	33	22	3	22-0	56
1997—Wisconsin (Midw.)	9	3	.750	2.09	13	13	1	0	0-...	81.2	62	20	19	3	23-1	79
—Lancaster (Calif.)	7	4	.636	4.86	15	15	1	0	0-...	96.1	108	55	52	9	34-0	82
1998—Fort Myers (FSL)■	7	2	.778	3.04	16	15	0	0	0-...	94.2	101	45	32	7	23-0	83
—New Britain (East.)	5	3	.625	4.99	11	10	0	0	0-...	57.2	63	40	32	4	21-0	45
1999—Minnesota (A.L.)	6	11	.353	4.37	49	20	2	1	0-0	171.0	179	92	83	24	67-2	115
2000—Minnesota (A.L.)	7	15	.318	5.56	31	28	2	1	0-0	160.1	193	105	99	20	67-1	102
—Salt Lake (PCL)	2	0	1.000	1.72	3	3	0	0	0-...	15.2	16	4	3	0	2-0	18
2001—Minnesota (A.L.)	17	13	.567	3.16	34	34	4	2	0-0	233.2	205	87	82	25	64-2	123
2002—Minnesota (A.L.)	4	8	.333	5.38	17	17	1	1	0-0	95.1	113	60	57	14	25-0	38
—Fort Myers (FSL)	0	1	.000	2.08	3	3	0	0	0-...	8.2	9	2	2	0	3-0	7
—New Britain (East.)	1	0	1.000	1.29	1	1	0	0	0-...	7.0	2	1	1	1	1-0	5
Major League totals (4 years)	34	47	.420	4.38	131	99	9	5	0-0	660.1	690	344	321	83	223-5	378

DIVISION SERIES RECORD

Year League	W	L	Pct.	ERA	G	GS	CG	ShO	Sv.-Opp.	IP	H	R	ER	HR	BB-IBB	SO
2002—Minnesota (A.L.)	0	1	.000	14.73	1	1	0	0	0-0	3.2	9	6	6	1	2-1	1

CHAMPIONSHIP SERIES RECORD

Year League	W	L	Pct.	ERA	G	GS	CG	ShO	Sv.-Opp.	IP	H	R	ER	HR	BB-IBB	SO
2002—Minnesota (A.L.)	1	0	1.000	2.03	2	2	0	0	0-0	13.1	12	4	3	3	0-0	3

ALL-STAR GAME RECORD

	W	L	Pct.	ERA	GS	CG	ShO	Sv.-Opp.	IP	H	R	ER	HR	BB-IBB	SO
All-Star Game totals (1 year)	0	0	...	0.00	0	0	0	0-0	1.0	0	0	0	0	0-0	0

McCARTY, DAVE 1B/OF

PERSONAL: Born November 23, 1969, in Houston. ... 6-5/215. ... Bats right, throws left. ... Full name: David Andrew McCarty.
HIGH SCHOOL: Sharpstown (Houston).
COLLEGE: Stanford.
TRANSACTIONS/CAREER NOTES: Selected by Minnesota Twins organization in first round (third pick overall) of free-agent draft (June 3, 1991). ... Traded by Twins to Cincinnati Reds for P John Courtright (June 8, 1995). ... Traded by Reds with OF Deion Sanders, P Ricky Pickett, P Scott Service and P John Roper to San Francisco Giants for OF Darren Lewis, P Mark Portugal and P Dave Burba (July 21, 1995). ... On San Francisco disabled list (June 6-27, 1996); included rehabilitation assignment to Phoenix (June 20-27). ... Traded by Giants to Seattle Mariners for OF Jay Leach and OF Scott Smith (January 30, 1998). ... Granted free agency (September 30, 1998). ... Signed by Detroit Tigers organization (December 18, 1998). ... Granted free agency (October 15, 1999). ... Signed by Oakland Athletics organization (November 23, 1999). ... Traded by A's to Kansas City Royals for cash (March 24, 2000). ... Released by Royals (May 15, 2002). ... Signed by Tampa Bay Devil Rays organization (May 21, 2002). ... Released by Devil Rays (August 7, 2002).
STATISTICAL NOTES: Led International League first basemen with 104 assists and .999 fielding percentage in 1999. ... Career major league grand slams: 1.
2002 GAMES PLAYED BY POSITION (MLB): OF—11; 1B—9; DH—2.

			BATTING														FIELDING	
Year	Team (League)	Pos.	G	AB	R	H	2B	3B	HR	RBI	BB	SO	SB-CS	Avg.	OBP	SLG	E	Avg.
1991—	Visalia (Calif.)	OF	15	50	16	19	3	0	3	8	13	7	3-1	.380	.530	.620	0	1.000
—	Orlando (Sou.)	OF	28	88	18	23	4	0	3	11	10	20	0-1	.261	.350	.409	1	.977
1992—	Orlando (Sou.)	OF-1B	129	456	75	124	16	2	18	79	55	89	6-6	.272	.356	.434	9	.977
—	Portland (PCL)	OF-1B	7	26	7	13	2	0	1	8	5	3	1-0	.500	.594	.692	1	.977
1993—	Portland (PCL)	OF-1B	40	143	42	55	11	0	8	31	27	25	5-2	.385	.477	.629	2	.990
—	Minnesota (A.L.)	OF-1B-DH	98	350	36	75	15	2	2	21	19	80	2-6	.214	.257	.286	8	.983
1994—	Minnesota (A.L.)	1B-OF	44	131	21	34	8	2	1	12	7	32	2-1	.260	.322	.374	5	.982
—	Salt Lake (PCL)	OF-1B	55	186	32	47	9	3	3	19	35	34	1-3	.253	.379	.382	5	.976
1995—	Minnesota (A.L.)	1B-OF	25	55	10	12	3	1	0	4	4	18	0-1	.218	.279	.309	1	.993
—	Indianapolis (A.A.)■	1B	37	140	31	47	10	1	8	32	15	30	0-0	.336	.401	.593	2	.994
—	Phoenix (PCL)■	1B-OF-DH	37	151	31	53	19	2	4	19	17	27	1-1	.351	.434	.583	2	.995
—	San Francisco (N.L.)	OF-1B	12	20	1	5	1	0	0	2	2	4	1-0	.250	.318	.300	1	.950
1996—	San Francisco (N.L.)	1B-OF	91	175	16	38	3	0	6	24	18	43	2-1	.217	.294	.337	3	.990
—	Phoenix (PCL)	OF-1B	6	25	4	10	1	1	1	7	2	4	0-0	.400	.429	.640	0	1.000
1997—	Phoenix (PCL)	1B-DH-OF	121	434	85	153	27	5	22	92	49	75	9-4	.353	.419	.590	3	.995
1998—	Tacoma (PCL)■	OF-1B-DH	108	398	73	126	30	2	11	52	59	85	9-6	.317	.411	.485	2	.996
—	Seattle (A.L.)	OF-1B	8	18	1	5	0	0	1	2	5	4	1-0	.278	.435	.444	0	1.000
1999—	Toledo (I.L.)■	1B-OF-P-DH	132	466	85	125	24	3	31	77	70	110	6-6	.268	.366	.532	2	†.998
2000—	Kansas City (A.L.)■	1B-OF-DH	103	270	34	75	14	2	12	53	22	68	0-0	.278	.329	.478	5	.991
2001—	Kansas City (A.L.)	1B-OF-DH	98	200	26	50	10	0	7	26	24	45	0-0	.250	.328	.405	8	.984
2002—	Kansas City (A.L.)	1B-DH	13	32	3	3	1	0	1	2	2	10	0-0	.094	.147	.219	0	1.000
—	Durham (I.L.)■	1B-OF	29	114	25	37	7	1	8	22	14	33	0-1	.325	.398	.614	2	.992
—	Tampa Bay (A.L.)	OF	12	34	2	6	0	0	1	2	4	9	0-0	.176	.300	.265	0	1.000
American League totals (7 years)			401	1090	133	260	51	7	25	122	87	266	5-8	.239	.299	.367	27	.987
National League totals (2 years)			103	195	17	43	4	0	6	26	20	47	3-1	.221	.297	.333	4	.988
Major League totals (8 years)			504	1285	150	303	55	7	31	148	107	313	8-9	.236	.298	.362	31	.987

RECORD AS PITCHER

Year	League	W	L	Pct.	ERA	G	GS	CG	ShO	Sv.-Opp.	IP	H	R	ER	HR	BB-IBB	SO
1999—	Toledo (I.L.)	0	0	...	4.50	2	0	0	0	0-...	2.0	1	1	1	0	1-0	0

McCRACKEN, QUINTON OF

PERSONAL: Born March 16, 1970, in Wilmington, N.C. ... 5-7/173. ... Bats both, throws right. ... Full name: Quinton Antoine McCracken.
HIGH SCHOOL: South Brunswick (Southport, N.C.).
COLLEGE: Duke.
TRANSACTIONS/CAREER NOTES: Selected by Colorado Rockies organization in 25th round of free-agent draft (June 1, 1992). ... Selected by Tampa Bay Devil Rays in first round (fourth pick overall) of expansion draft (November 18, 1997). ... On disabled list (May 25, 1999-remainder of season). ... Released by Devil Rays (November 27, 2000). ... Signed by St. Louis Cardinals (December 22, 2000). ... Released by Cardinals (March 28, 2001). ... Signed by Minnesota Twins organization (April 13, 2001). ... Granted free agency (October 8, 2001).
STATISTICAL NOTES: Tied for Northwest League lead with 17 errors by second basemen in 1992. ... Led California League with 12 sacrifice hits in 1993. ... Led Eastern League in caught stealing with 19 in 1994. ... Had 18-game hitting streak (August 18-September 9, 1998). ... Tied for Pacific Coast League lead in caught stealing with 10 in 2001.
2002 GAMES PLAYED BY POSITION (MLB): OF—97.

			BATTING														FIELDING	
Year	Team (League)	Pos.	G	AB	R	H	2B	3B	HR	RBI	BB	SO	SB-CS	Avg.	OBP	SLG	E	Avg.
1992—	Bend (N'West)	2B-OF	67	232	37	65	13	2	0	27	25	39	18-6	.280	.347	.353	‡17	.930
1993—	Central Valley (Calif.)	OF-2B	127	483	94	141	17	7	2	58	78	90	60-19	.292	.390	.369	13	.946
1994—	New Haven (East.)	OF	136	544	94	151	27	4	5	39	48	72	36-19	.278	.338	.369	8	.972
1995—	New Haven (East.)	OF-DH	55	221	33	79	11	4	1	26	21	32	26-8	.357	.419	.457	3	.971
—	Colo. Springs (PCL)	OF-DH	61	244	55	88	14	6	3	28	23	30	17-6	.361	.418	.504	1	.991
—	Colorado (N.L.)	OF	3	1	0	0	0	0	0	0	0	1	0-0	.000	.000	.000	0	...
1996—	Colorado (N.L.)	OF	124	283	50	82	13	6	3	40	32	62	17-6	.290	.363	.410	6	.957
1997—	Colorado (N.L.)	OF	147	325	69	95	11	1	3	36	42	62	28-11	.292	.374	.360	4	.980
1998—	Tampa Bay (A.L.)■	OF	155	614	77	179	38	7	7	59	41	107	19-10	.292	.335	.410	3	.992
1999—	Tampa Bay (A.L.)	OF	40	148	20	37	6	1	1	18	14	23	6-5	.250	.317	.324	1	.988
2000—	Tampa Bay (A.L.)	OF	15	31	5	4	0	0	0	2	6	4	0-1	.129	.270	.129	0	1.000
—	Durham (I.L.)	OF	85	334	54	87	18	2	2	28	34	57	13-7	.260	.332	.344	4	.977
2001—	Edmonton (PCL)■	OF	81	361	53	122	27	4	4	45	21	54	8-10	.338	.374	.468	5	.971
—	Minnesota (A.L.)	OF-DH	24	64	7	14	2	2	0	3	5	13	0-1	.219	.275	.313	0	1.000
2002—	Arizona (N.L.)■	OF	123	349	60	108	27	8	3	40	32	68	5-4	.309	.367	.458	1	.995
American League totals (4 years)			234	857	109	234	46	10	8	82	66	147	25-17	.273	.325	.378	4	.992
National League totals (4 years)			397	958	179	285	51	15	9	116	106	193	50-21	.297	.368	.410	11	.979
Major League totals (8 years)			631	1815	288	519	97	25	17	198	172	340	75-38	.286	.348	.395	15	.985

DIVISION SERIES RECORD

			BATTING														FIELDING	
Year	Team (League)	Pos.	G	AB	R	H	2B	3B	HR	RBI	BB	SO	SB-CS	Avg.	OBP	SLG	E	Avg.
2002—	Arizona (N.L.)	OF	3	11	1	4	1	0	0	2	1	2	0-0	.364	.417	.455	0	1.000

McDONALD, DONZELL OF

PERSONAL: Born February 20, 1975, in Long Beach, Calif. ... 5-11/180. ... Bats both, throws right. ... Brother of Darnell McDonald, outfielder, Baltimore Orioles organization.

HIGH SCHOOL: Cherry Creek (Colo.).

JUNIOR COLLEGE: Yavapai College (Ariz).

TRANSACTIONS/CAREER NOTES: Selected by New York Yankees organization in 22nd round of free-agent draft (June 1, 1995). ... On disabled list (July 3-August 6, 1997). ... On Columbus disabled list (May 10-July 21, 2000). ... Granted free agency (October 15, 2001). ... Signed by Cleveland Indians organization (November 2, 2001). ... Traded by Indians to Kansas City Royals for player to be named later (March 28, 2002). ... On Omaha disabled list (April 24-May 3, 2002). ... Released by Royals (October 14, 2002).

STATISTICAL NOTES: Led New York-Pennsylvania League outfielders with 169 putouts and 179 total chances in 1996. ... Led Eastern League in caught stealing with 22 in 1998. ... Led Eastern League outfielders with 312 putouts and 328 total chances in 1998.

2002 GAMES PLAYED BY POSITION (MLB): OF—7.

		BATTING														FIELDING	
Year Team (League)	Pos.	G	AB	R	H	2B	3B	HR	RBI	BB	SO	SB-CS	Avg.	OBP	SLG	E	Avg.
1995—GC Yankees (GCL)	OF	28	110	23	26	5	1	0	9	16	24	11-2	.236	.341	.300	3	.936
1996—Oneonta (NY-Penn)	OF	74	282	57	78	8	*10	2	30	43	62	*54-4	.277	.374	.397	6	.966
1997—Tampa (FSL)	OF	77	297	69	88	23	8	3	23	48	75	39-18	.296	.400	.458	4	.978
1998—Norwich (East.)	OF	134	495	80	125	20	7	6	36	55	127	35-22	.253	.330	.358	8	.976
—Tampa (FSL)	OF	5	18	6	6	1	2	0	2	2	7	2-0	.333	.429	.611	0	1.000
1999—Norwich (East.)	OF-DH	137	533	95	145	19	10	4	33	90	110	54-20	.272	.383	.368	9	.973
2000—Columbus (I.L.)	OF	24	77	17	19	4	4	1	6	23	11	12-0	.247	.431	.442	0	1.000
—Norwich (East.)	OF	44	170	23	41	7	2	2	10	35	36	13-7	.241	.371	.341	2	.980
2001—Columbus (I.L.)	OF	105	374	59	96	11	9	8	36	42	79	20-4	.257	.342	.398	5	.979
—New York (A.L.)	OF	5	3	0	1	0	0	0	0	0	2	0-0	.333	.333	.333	0	1.000
2002—Omaha (PCL)■	OF	112	452	63	118	15	15	7	35	56	102	30-6	.261	.346	.407	6	.979
—Kansas City (A.L.)	OF	10	22	3	4	2	0	0	1	4	5	1-0	.182	.296	.273	0	1.000
Major League totals (2 years)		15	25	3	5	2	0	0	1	4	7	1-0	.200	.300	.280	0	1.000

McDONALD, JOHN SS/2B INDIANS

PERSONAL: Born September 24, 1974, in New London, Conn. ... 5-11/175. ... Bats right, throws right. ... Full name: John J. McDonald.

HIGH SCHOOL: East Lyme (Conn.).

JUNIOR COLLEGE: Connecticut-Avery Point.

COLLEGE: Providence.

TRANSACTIONS/CAREER NOTES: Selected by Cleveland Indians organization in 12th round of free-agent draft (June 4, 1996). ... On Buffalo disabled list (April 27-May 9 and May 10-June 22, 2000). ... On Buffalo disabled list (May 10-17, 2001).

STATISTICAL NOTES: Led Carolina League shortstops with 209 putouts, 413 assists, 647 total chances and 105 double plays in 1997. ... Led Eastern League shortstops with 242 putouts and 672 total chances in 1998.

2002 GAMES PLAYED BY POSITION (MLB): 2B—64; SS—21; 3B—10; DH—1.

		BATTING														FIELDING	
Year Team (League)	Pos.	G	AB	R	H	2B	3B	HR	RBI	BB	SO	SB-CS	Avg.	OBP	SLG	E	Avg.
1996—Watertown (NY-Penn)	SS	75	278	48	75	11	0	2	26	32	49	11-1	.270	.354	.331	18	.946
1997—Kinston (Caro.)	SS	130	541	77	140	27	3	5	53	51	75	6-5	.259	.324	.348	25	*.961
1998—Akron (East.)	SS	132	514	68	118	18	2	2	43	43	61	17-6	.230	.293	.284	23	.966
1999—Akron (East.)	SS-2B	55	226	31	67	12	0	1	26	19	26	7-3	.296	.351	.363	8	.970
—Buffalo (I.L.)	SS-3B-2B	66	237	30	75	12	1	0	25	11	23	6-3	.316	.349	.376	13	.956
—Cleveland (A.L.)	2B-SS	18	21	2	7	0	0	0	0	0	3	0-1	.333	.333	.333	1	.967
2000—Buffalo (I.L.)	SS-2B-3B	75	286	37	77	17	2	1	36	21	29	4-3	.269	.315	.353	8	.975
—Mahoning Val. (NY-P)	SS	5	17	0	2	1	0	0	1	2	3	0-0	.118	.211	.176	0	1.000
—Cleveland (A.L.)	SS-2B	9	9	0	4	0	0	0	0	0	1	0-0	.444	.444	.444	0	1.000
—Kinston (Caro.)	SS	1	3	0	1	0	0	0	0	0	0	0-0	.333	.333	.333	0	1.000
2001—Cleveland (A.L.)	SS-2B-3B	17	22	1	2	1	0	0	0	1	7	0-0	.091	.167	.136	1	.964
—Buffalo (I.L.)	SS-2B-3B	116	410	52	100	17	1	2	33	33	72	17-10	.244	.305	.305	23	.957
2002—Cleveland (A.L.)	2B-SS-3B-DH	93	264	35	66	11	3	1	12	10	50	3-0	.250	.288	.326	8	.979
Major League totals (4 years)		137	316	38	79	12	3	1	12	11	61	3-1	.250	.287	.316	10	.978

McEWING, JOE OF/IF METS

PERSONAL: Born October 19, 1972, in Bristol, Pa. ... 5-11/170. ... Bats right, throws right. ... Full name: Joseph Earl McEwing.

HIGH SCHOOL: Bishop Egan (Fairless Hills, Pa.).

JUNIOR COLLEGE: County College of Morris (N.J.).

TRANSACTIONS/CAREER NOTES: Selected by St. Louis Cardinals organization in 28th round of free-agent draft (June 1, 1992). ... Traded by Cardinals to New York Mets for P Jesse Orosco (March 18, 2000). ... On New York disabled list (July 14-31, 2002); included rehabilitation assignments to Brooklyn (July 29-30) and Binghamton (July 31).

STATISTICAL NOTES: Led Arizona League outfielders with 94 putouts, 11 assists, four double plays, 106 total chances and .991 fielding percentage in 1992. ... Led South Atlantic League with 15 sacrifice hits in 1993. ... Led Texas League outfielders with .993 fielding percentage in 1996. ... Tied for Pacific Coast League lead with three double plays by outfielder in 1998. ... Had 25-game hitting streak (June 8-July 4, 1999).

2002 GAMES PLAYED BY POSITION (MLB): OF—35; SS—21; 1B—20; 2B—13; 3B—10.

		BATTING														FIELDING	
Year Team (League)	Pos.	G	AB	R	H	2B	3B	HR	RBI	BB	SO	SB-CS	Avg.	OBP	SLG	E	Avg.
1992—Ariz. Cardinals (Ariz.)	OF-SS	55	211	*55	71	4	2	0	13	24	18	23-7	.336	.415	.374	1	†.991
1993—Savannah (S.Atl.)	OF	138	511	*94	127	35	1	0	43	89	73	22-9	.249	.362	.321	5	.982
1994—Madison (Midw.)	OF	90	346	58	112	24	2	4	47	32	53	18-15	.324	.380	.439	5	.974
—St. Petersburg (FSL)	OF-2B	50	197	22	49	7	0	1	20	19	32	8-4	.249	.314	.299	2	.985

Year Team (League)	Pos.	BATTING G	AB	R	H	2B	3B	HR	RBI	BB	SO	SB-CS	Avg.	OBP	SLG	FIELDING E	Avg.
1995— St. Petersburg (FSL) ..	2B-OF	75	281	33	64	13	0	1	23	25	49	2-3	.228	.289	.285	15	.955
— Arkansas (Texas)	OF-2B	42	121	16	30	4	0	2	12	9	13	3-2	.248	.305	.331	0	1.000
1996— Arkansas (Texas)	OF-2B	106	216	27	45	7	3	2	14	13	32	2-4	.208	.252	.296	2	†.987
1997— Arkansas (Texas)	O-2-1-3-P	103	263	33	68	6	3	4	35	19	39	2-4	.259	.309	.350	2	.988
1998— Arkansas (Texas)	OF-SS-P	60	223	45	79	21	4	9	46	21	18	4-2	.354	.409	.605	1	.994
— Memphis (PCL)	OF-3B-SS-2B	78	329	52	110	30	7	6	46	21	39	11-10	.334	.379	.523	3	.982
— St. Louis (N.L.)	2B-OF	10	20	5	4	1	0	0	1	1	3	0-1	.200	.273	.250	0	1.000
1999— St. Louis (N.L.)	2-O-3-1-S	152	513	65	141	28	4	9	44	41	87	7-4	.275	.333	.398	11	.981
2000— Norfolk (I.L.)■	OF-2B-3B-SS	43	171	28	44	10	2	5	18	16	34	7-3	.257	.319	.427	4	.973
— New York (N.L.)	OF-3B-2B-SS	87	153	20	34	14	1	2	19	5	29	3-1	.222	.248	.366	5	.957
2001— New York (N.L.)	O-3-S-2-1-D	116	283	41	80	17	3	8	30	17	57	8-5	.283	.342	.449	3	.981
2002— New York (N.L.)	O-S-1-2-3	105	196	22	39	8	1	3	26	9	50	4-4	.199	.242	.296	7	.967
— Brooklyn (NY-Penn) ...	DH	1	4	0	1	0	0	0	1	0	0	0-0	.250	.250	.250	...	...
— Binghamton (East.)	2B-3B	1	5	0	0	0	0	0	0	0	1	0-0	.000	.000	.000	0	1.000
Major League totals (5 years)		470	1165	153	298	68	9	22	120	73	226	22-15	.256	.308	.386	26	.976

DIVISION SERIES RECORD

Year Team (League)	Pos.	BATTING G	AB	R	H	2B	3B	HR	RBI	BB	SO	SB-CS	Avg.	OBP	SLG	FIELDING E	Avg.
2000— New York (N.L.)	OF-PR-3B	4	1	0	1	0	0	0	0	0	0	0-0	1.000	1.000	1.000	0	...

CHAMPIONSHIP SERIES RECORD

Year Team (League)	Pos.	BATTING G	AB	R	H	2B	3B	HR	RBI	BB	SO	SB-CS	Avg.	OBP	SLG	FIELDING E	Avg.
2000— New York (N.L.)	PR-OF-3B	4	0	2	0	0	0	0	0	0	0	0-0	...	...	...	0	1.000

WORLD SERIES RECORD

Year Team (League)	Pos.	BATTING G	AB	R	H	2B	3B	HR	RBI	BB	SO	SB-CS	Avg.	OBP	SLG	FIELDING E	Avg.
2000— New York (N.L.)	OF-PR	3	1	1	0	0	0	0	0	0	0	0-0	.000	.000	.000	0	1.000

RECORD AS PITCHER

Year League	W	L	Pct.	ERA	G	GS	CG	ShO	Sv.-Opp.	IP	H	R	ER	HR	BB-IBB	SO
1997— Arkansas (Texas)	0	0	...	27.00	1	0	0	0	0-...	.1	1	1	1	1	0-0	0
1998— Arkansas (Texas)	0	0	...	27.00	1	0	0	0	0-...	1.0	3	3	3	0	1-0	1

McGRIFF, FRED — 1B

PERSONAL: Born October 31, 1963, in Tampa. ... 6-3/225. ... Bats left, throws left. ... Full name: Frederick Stanley McGriff. ... Cousin of Terry McGriff, catcher with four major league teams (1987-90, 1993 and 1994); and uncle of Charles Johnson, catcher, Florida Marlins.

HIGH SCHOOL: Jefferson (Tampa).

TRANSACTIONS/CAREER NOTES: Selected by New York Yankees organization in ninth round of free-agent draft (June 8, 1981). ... Traded by Yankees with OF Dave Collins, P Mike Morgan and cash to Toronto Blue Jays for OF/C Tom Dodd and P Dale Murray (December 9, 1982). ... On disabled list (June 5-August 14, 1985). ... Traded by Blue Jays with SS Tony Fernandez to San Diego Padres for OF Joe Carter and 2B Roberto Alomar (December 5, 1990). ... On suspended list (June 23-26, 1992). ... Traded by Padres to Atlanta Braves for OF Melvin Nieves, P Donnie Elliott and OF Vince Moore (July 18, 1993). ... Granted free agency (November 6, 1995). ... Re-signed by Braves (December 2, 1995). ... Traded by Braves to Tampa Bay Devil Rays for a player to be named later or cash (November 18, 1997); Braves received an undisclosed amount of cash to complete deal (April 1, 1998). ... Traded by Devil Rays to Chicago Cubs for P Manny Aybar and a player to be named later (July 27, 2001); Devil Rays acquired SS Jason Smith to complete deal (August 5, 2001). ... Granted free agency (November 1, 2002).

RECORDS: Holds major league career record for most major league ballparks, one or more home runs (since 1900)—42. ... Shares major league record for most grand slams in two consecutive games—2 (August 13 and 14, 1991). ... Shares N.L. single-season record for fewest errors by first baseman who led league in errors—12 (1992).

HONORS: Named first baseman on The Sporting News A.L. All-Star team (1989). ... Named first baseman on The Sporting News A.L. Silver Slugger team (1989). ... Named first baseman on The Sporting News N.L. All-Star team (1992-93). ... Named first baseman on The Sporting News N.L. Silver Slugger team (1992-93).

STATISTICAL NOTES: Led International League first basemen with .992 fielding percentage, 1,219 putouts, 85 assists, 1,314 total chances and 108 double plays in 1986. ... Tied for International League lead in intentional bases on balls received with eight and in grounding into double plays with 16 in 1986. ... Led A.L. first basemen with 1,592 total chances and 148 double plays in 1989. ... Led N.L. with 26 intentional base on balls received in 1991. ... Led N.L. first basemen with 1,004 putouts and 1,077 total chances in 1994. ... Led N.L. in grounding into double plays with 22 in 1997. ... Led A.L. first basemen with 140 double plays in 1998. ... Career major league grand slams: 8.

MISCELLANEOUS: Holds Tampa Bay Devil Rays all-time records for most hits (590), most runs (270), most doubles (99), most home runs (97), most runs batted in (352) and highest career batting average (.295).

2002 GAMES PLAYED BY POSITION (MLB): 1B—137; DH—2.

Year Team (League)	Pos.	BATTING G	AB	R	H	2B	3B	HR	RBI	BB	SO	SB-CS	Avg.	OBP	SLG	FIELDING E	Avg.
1981— GC Yankees (GCL)	1B	29	81	6	12	2	0	0	9	11	20	0-0	.148	.239	.173	7	.963
1982— GC Yankees (GCL)	1B	62	217	38	59	11	1	*9	•41	*48	63	6-6	.272	.413	.456	8	.986
1983— Florence (S.Atl.)■	1B	33	119	26	37	3	1	7	26	20	35	3-0	.311	.414	.529	6	.978
— Kinston (Caro.)	1B	94	350	53	85	14	1	21	57	55	112	3-2	.243	.356	.469	10	.988
1984— Knoxville (Sou.)	1B	56	189	29	47	13	2	9	25	29	55	0-2	.249	.347	.481	10	.981
— Syracuse (I.L.)	1B	70	238	28	56	10	1	13	28	26	89	0-1	.235	.309	.450	3	.996
1985— Syracuse (I.L.)	1B	51	176	19	40	8	2	5	20	23	53	0-0	.227	.330	.381	5	.989
1986— Syracuse (I.L.)	1B-OF	133	468	69	121	23	4	19	74	83	119	0-3	.259	.369	.447	10	†.992
— Toronto (A.L.)	DH-1B	3	5	1	1	0	0	0	0	0	2	0-0	.200	.200	.200	0	1.000
1987— Toronto (A.L.)	DH-1B	107	295	58	73	16	0	20	43	60	104	3-2	.247	.376	.505	2	.983
1988— Toronto (A.L.)	1B	154	536	100	151	35	4	34	82	79	149	6-1	.282	.376	.552	5	*.997
1989— Toronto (A.L.)	1B-DH	161	551	98	148	27	3	*36	92	119	132	7-4	.269	.399	.525	*17	.989
1990— Toronto (A.L.)	1B-DH	153	557	91	167	21	1	35	88	94	108	5-3	.300	.400	.530	6	.996
1991— San Diego (N.L.)■	1B	153	528	84	147	19	1	31	106	105	135	4-1	.278	.396	.494	14	.990
1992— San Diego (N.L.)	1B	152	531	79	152	30	4	*35	104	96	108	8-6	.286	.394	.556	•12	.991

			BATTING														FIELDING	
Year	Team (League)	Pos.	G	AB	R	H	2B	3B	HR	RBI	BB	SO	SB-CS	Avg.	OBP	SLG	E	Avg.
1993—	San Diego (N.L.)	1B	83	302	52	83	11	1	18	46	42	55	4-3	.275	.361	.497	12	.983
—	Atlanta (N.L.)■	1B	68	255	59	79	18	1	19	55	34	51	1-0	.310	.392	.612	5	.992
1994—	Atlanta (N.L.)	1B	113	424	81	135	25	1	34	94	50	76	7-3	.318	.389	.623	7	.994
1995—	Atlanta (N.L.)	1B	•144	528	85	148	27	1	27	93	65	99	3-6	.280	.361	.489	5	.996
1996—	Atlanta (N.L.)	1B	159	617	81	182	37	1	28	107	68	116	7-3	.295	.365	.494	12	.992
1997—	Atlanta (N.L.)	1B	152	564	77	156	25	1	22	97	68	112	5-0	.277	.356	.441	13	.990
1998—	Tampa Bay (A.L.)■	1B-DH	151	564	73	160	33	0	19	81	79	118	7-2	.284	.371	.443	6	.995
1999—	Tampa Bay (A.L.)	1B-DH	144	529	75	164	30	1	32	104	86	107	1-0	.310	.405	.552	13	.989
2000—	Tampa Bay (A.L.)	1B-DH	158	566	82	157	18	0	27	106	91	120	2-0	.277	.373	.452	10	.993
2001—	Tampa Bay (A.L.)	1B-DH	97	343	40	109	18	0	19	61	40	69	1-1	.318	.387	.536	9	.986
—	Chicago (N.L.)■	1B	49	170	27	48	7	2	12	41	26	37	0-1	.282	.383	.559	4	.990
2002—	Chicago (N.L.)	1B-DH	146	523	67	143	27	2	30	103	63	99	1-2	.273	.353	.505	7	.993
American League totals (9 years)			1128	3946	618	1130	198	9	222	657	648	909	32-13	.286	.386	.510	68	.992
National League totals (9 years)			1219	4442	692	1273	226	15	256	846	617	888	40-25	.287	.374	.517	91	.992
Major League totals (17 years)			2347	8388	1310	2403	424	24	478	1503	1265	1797	72-38	.286	.380	.514	159	.992

DIVISION SERIES RECORD

RECORDS: Holds N.L. single-game record for most runs batted in—5 (October 7, 1995). ... Shares single-game record for most home runs—2 (October 7, 1995).

			BATTING														FIELDING	
Year	Team (League)	Pos.	G	AB	R	H	2B	3B	HR	RBI	BB	SO	SB-CS	Avg.	OBP	SLG	E	Avg.
1995—	Atlanta (N.L.)	1B	4	18	4	6	0	0	2	6	2	3	0-0	.333	.400	.667	0	1.000
1996—	Atlanta (N.L.)	1B	3	9	1	3	1	0	1	3	2	1	0-1	.333	.417	.778	0	1.000
1997—	Atlanta (N.L.)	1B	3	9	4	2	0	0	0	1	3	2	0-0	.222	.417	.222	0	1.000
Division series totals (3 years)			10	36	9	11	1	0	3	10	7	6	0-1	.306	.409	.583	0	1.000

CHAMPIONSHIP SERIES RECORD

RECORDS: Holds single-game record for most doubles—3 (October 11, 1995). ... Shares N.L. single-game records for most at-bats—6 (October 14, 1996); and most runs—4 (October 17, 1996). ... Shares career record for most doubles—7.

			BATTING														FIELDING	
Year	Team (League)	Pos.	G	AB	R	H	2B	3B	HR	RBI	BB	SO	SB-CS	Avg.	OBP	SLG	E	Avg.
1989—	Toronto (A.L.)	1B	5	21	1	3	0	0	0	3	0	4	0-0	.143	.143	.143	1	.974
1993—	Atlanta (N.L.)	1B	6	23	6	10	2	0	1	4	4	7	0-0	.435	.519	.652	0	1.000
1995—	Atlanta (N.L.)	1B	4	16	5	7	4	0	0	0	3	0	0-0	.438	.526	.688	0	1.000
1996—	Atlanta (N.L.)	1B	7	28	6	7	0	1	2	7	3	5	0-0	.250	.323	.536	1	.982
1997—	Atlanta (N.L.)	1B	6	21	0	7	1	0	0	4	2	7	0-0	.333	.375	.381	1	.977
Championship series totals (5 years)			28	109	18	34	7	1	3	18	12	23	0-0	.312	.377	.477	3	.987

WORLD SERIES RECORD

RECORDS: Holds single game record for chances accepted, nine inning game—20 (October 21, 1995). ... Shares single-game record for most putouts by first baseman—19 (October 21, 1995).

NOTES: Hit home run in first at-bat (October 21, 1995). ... Member of World Series championship team (1995).

			BATTING														FIELDING	
Year	Team (League)	Pos.	G	AB	R	H	2B	3B	HR	RBI	BB	SO	SB-CS	Avg.	OBP	SLG	E	Avg.
1995—	Atlanta (N.L.)	1B	6	23	5	6	2	0	2	3	3	7	1-0	.261	.346	.609	1	.986
1996—	Atlanta (N.L.)	1B	6	20	4	6	0	0	2	6	5	4	0-0	.300	.423	.600	0	1.000
World Series totals (2 years)			12	43	9	12	2	0	4	9	8	11	1-0	.279	.385	.605	1	.993

ALL-STAR GAME RECORD

NOTES: Named Most Valuable Player (1994).

	AB	R	H	2B	3B	HR	RBI	BB	SO	SB-CS	Avg.	OBP	SLG	E	Avg.
All-Star Game totals (5 years)	11	1	3	0	0	1	3	0	5	0-0	.273	.273	.545	0	1.000

McGUIRE, RYAN 1B

PERSONAL: Born November 23, 1971, in Bellflower, Calif. ... 6-0/215. ... Bats left, throws left. ... Full name: Ryan Byron McGuire.

HIGH SCHOOL: El Camino Real (Woodland Hills, Calif.).

COLLEGE: UCLA.

TRANSACTIONS/CAREER NOTES: Selected by Boston Red Sox organization in third round of free-agent draft (June 3, 1993). ... Traded by Red Sox with P Rheal Cormier and P Shayne Bennett to Montreal Expos for SS Wil Cordero and P Bryan Eversgerd (January 10, 1996). ... Granted free agency (November 19, 1999). ... Signed by New York Mets organization (December 13, 1999). ... Granted free agency (October 3, 2000). ... Signed by Florida Marlins organization (November 3, 2000). ... Granted free agency (October 8, 2001). ... Signed by Baltimore Orioles organization (November 16, 2001). ... Released by Orioles (September 30, 2002).

STATISTICAL NOTES: Led Carolina League first basemen with 1,165 putouts, 129 assists and 1,312 total chances in 1994. ... Tied for Carolina League lead with 19 grounded into double plays in 1994. ... Career major league grand slams: 1.

2002 GAMES PLAYED BY POSITION (MLB): 1B—7; DH—1.

			BATTING														FIELDING	
Year	Team (League)	Pos.	G	AB	R	H	2B	3B	HR	RBI	BB	SO	SB-CS	Avg.	OBP	SLG	E	Avg.
1993—	Fort Lauderdale (FSL)	1B	56	213	23	69	12	2	4	38	27	34	2-4	.324	.400	.455	5	.991
1994—	Lynchburg (Caro.)	1B	*137	489	70	133	29	0	10	73	79	77	10-9	.272	.371	.393	18	.986
1995—	Trenton (East.)	1B	109	414	59	138	29	1	7	59	58	51	11-8	.333	.414	.459	10	.987
1996—	Ottawa (I.L.)■	1B-DH-OF	134	451	62	116	21	2	12	60	59	80	11-4	.257	.344	.392	8	.993
1997—	Ottawa (I.L.)	1B	50	184	37	55	11	1	3	15	36	29	5-2	.299	.410	.418	2	.996
—	Montreal (N.L.)	OF-1B-DH	84	199	22	51	15	2	3	17	19	34	1-4	.256	.320	.397	3	.988
1998—	Montreal (N.L.)	1B-OF	130	210	17	39	9	0	1	10	32	55	0-0	.186	.292	.243	7	.981
1999—	Ottawa (I.L.)	1B-OF-DH	53	183	23	46	6	1	4	27	35	37	1-3	.251	.367	.361	1	.997
—	Montreal (N.L.)	1B-OF	88	140	17	31	7	2	2	18	27	33	1-1	.221	.347	.343	2	.994
2000—	Norfolk (I.L.)■	OF-1B	122	392	63	117	23	1	10	62	*87	84	6-3	.298	.422	.439	1	.998
—	New York (N.L.)	OF	1	2	0	0	0	0	0	0	1	0	0-0	.000	.333	.000	0	1.000

Year	Team (League)	Pos.	G	AB	R	H	2B	3B	HR	RBI	BB	SO	SB-CS	Avg.	OBP	SLG	E	Avg.
			BATTING														FIELDING	
2001—	Calgary (PCL)■	OF-1B	62	239	45	72	14	2	8	42	26	49	0-1	.301	.369	.477	3	.991
—	Florida (N.L.)	OF-1B	48	54	8	10	2	0	1	8	7	15	1-0	.185	.270	.278	0	1.000
2002—	Rochester (I.L.)■	1B-OF	81	315	44	90	15	2	11	46	29	69	0-1	.286	.343	.451	4	.991
—	Baltimore (A.L.)	1B-DH	17	26	0	2	1	0	0	2	2	7	0-0	.077	.143	.115	0	1.000
American League totals (1 year)			17	26	0	2	1	0	0	2	2	7	0-0	.077	.143	.115	0	1.000
National League totals (5 years)			351	605	64	131	33	4	7	53	86	137	3-5	.217	.312	.319	12	.988
Major League totals (6 years)			368	631	64	133	34	4	7	55	88	144	3-5	.211	.306	.311	12	.988

McKAY, CODY C

PERSONAL: Born January 11, 1974, in Vancouver. ... 6-0/208. ... Bats left, throws right. ... Full name: Cody Dean McKay. ... Son of Dave McKay, coach, St. Louis Cardinals.

HIGH SCHOOL: Horizon (Scottsdale, Ariz.).

COLLEGE: Arizona State.

TRANSACTIONS/CAREER NOTES: Selected by Oakland Athletics organization in ninth round of free-agent draft (June 4, 1996). ... Granted free agency (October 15, 2002).

2002 GAMES PLAYED BY POSITION (MLB): C—1.

Year	Team (League)	Pos.	G	AB	R	H	2B	3B	HR	RBI	BB	SO	SB-CS	Avg.	OBP	SLG	E	Avg.
			BATTING														FIELDING	
1996—	S. Oregon (N'West)	C-3B	69	254	33	68	13	0	3	30	25	42	0-5	.268	.344	.354	12	.971
1997—	Modesto (Calif.)	3B-C	125	390	47	97	20	1	7	50	46	69	4-2	.249	.349	.359	20	.966
1998—	Modesto (Calif.)	C-3B-1B	107	402	59	114	25	1	6	58	40	62	2-4	.284	.370	.396	13	.986
—	Huntsville (Sou.)	1-3-C-S-O	9	21	5	6	0	0	1	1	6	5	0-0	.286	.483	.429	0	1.000
—	Edmonton (PCL)	C-3B	19	57	6	13	3	0	0	5	7	5	1-0	.228	.343	.281	0	1.000
1999—	Midland (Texas)	C-3B-1B	94	333	59	98	21	1	6	43	38	40	1-2	.294	.375	.417	14	.975
2000—	Midland (Texas)	C-3B-1B	115	427	70	136	35	2	5	89	67	54	1-5	.319	.414	.445	14	.980
—	Sacramento (PCL)	C-1B	16	58	8	13	4	0	1	7	5	14	0-0	.224	.297	.345	1	.989
2001—	Sacramento (PCL)	C-3B-OF	99	350	36	92	19	0	6	41	27	64	1-0	.263	.324	.369	6	.991
2002—	Sacramento (PCL)	C-3B-1B-OF	108	378	55	109	16	1	13	57	21	59	2-1	.288	.337	.439	5	.991
—	Oakland (A.L.)	C	2	3	0	2	0	0	0	2	0	1	0-0	.667	.500	.667	0	1.000
Major League totals (1 year)			2	3	0	2	0	0	0	2	0	1	0-0	.667	.500	.667	0	1.000

McKEEL, WALT C

PERSONAL: Born January 17, 1972, in Wilson, N.C. ... 6-0/200. ... Bats right, throws right. ... Full name: Walter Thomas McKeel.

HIGH SCHOOL: Greene Central (Snow Hill, N.C.).

TRANSACTIONS/CAREER NOTES: Selected by Boston Red Sox organization in third round of free-agent draft (June 4, 1990). ... On Pawtucket disabled list (May 19-July 29, 1998). ... Granted free agency (October 15, 1998). ... Signed by Toronto Blue Jays organization (January 4, 1999). ... Released by Blue Jays (April 1, 1999). ... Signed by Detroit Tigers organization (April 10, 1999). ... Released by Tigers (August 19, 1999). ... Signed by Sonoma County, Western League (September 1999). ... Signed by Colorado Rockies organization (February 15, 2000). ... Granted free agency (October 15, 2000). ... Re-signed by Rockies organization (January 8, 2001). ... On Colorado Springs disabled list (April 5-13, 2001). ... On Carolina disabled list (July 28, 2001-remainder of season). ... Granted free agency (October 15, 2001). ... Re-signed by Rockies organization (December 1, 2001). ... Released by Rockies (October 3, 2002).

STATISTICAL NOTES: Led Carolina League with 22 passed balls in 1992. ... Led Eastern League with 17 passed balls and tied for lead with 11 double plays in 1996. ... Led International League with 10 passed balls in 1997.

2002 GAMES PLAYED BY POSITION (MLB): C—5.

Year	Team (League)	Pos.	G	AB	R	H	2B	3B	HR	RBI	BB	SO	SB-CS	Avg.	OBP	SLG	E	Avg.
			BATTING														FIELDING	
1990—	GC Red Sox (GCL)	C	13	44	2	11	3	0	0	6	3	8	0-2	.250	.292	.318	2	.959
1991—	GC Red Sox (GCL)	C-1B	35	113	10	15	0	1	2	12	17	20	0-0	.133	.244	.204	4	.981
1992—	Lynchburg (Caro.)	C	96	288	33	64	11	0	12	33	22	77	2-1	.222	.283	.385	17	.973
1993—	Lynchburg (Caro.)	C	80	247	28	59	17	2	5	32	26	40	0-1	.239	.315	.385	8	.982
1994—	Sarasota (FSL)	C	37	137	15	38	8	1	2	15	8	19	1-0	.277	.322	.394	8	.971
—	New Britain (East.)	C	50	164	10	30	6	1	1	17	7	35	0-0	.183	.227	.250	12	.965
1995—	Trenton (East.)	C-1B	29	84	11	20	3	1	2	11	8	15	2-1	.238	.298	.369	2	.980
—	Sarasota (FSL)	C	62	198	26	66	14	0	8	35	25	28	6-3	.333	.407	.525	9	.977
1996—	Trenton (East.)	C-1B-3B-DH	128	464	86	140	19	1	16	78	60	52	2-4	.302	.385	.450	10	.989
—	Boston (A.L.)	C	1	0	0	0	0	0	0	0	0	0	0-0	...	...	...	0	...
1997—	Pawtucket (I.L.)	C-1B	66	237	34	60	15	0	6	30	34	39	0-1	.253	.347	.392	6	.988
—	Boston (A.L.)	C-1B	5	3	0	0	0	0	0	0	0	1	0-0	.000	.000	.000	0	1.000
—	Trenton (East.)	DH-C-1B	7	25	0	4	2	0	0	4	1	2	0-0	.160	.192	.240	0	1.000
1998—	Pawtucket (I.L.)	C-1B-3B	48	170	26	49	10	1	4	26	21	27	1-2	.288	.370	.429	6	.982
—	GC Red Sox (GCL)	DH-C-1B	13	36	1	9	2	0	1	4	4	8	0-0	.250	.317	.389	0	1.000
1999—	Toledo (I.L.)■	C-D-O-1-3	67	215	21	52	9	1	7	37	26	32	2-2	.242	.332	.391	7	.979
—	Sonoma Co. (West.)■	C	2	9	1	4	0	0	1	1	0	3	0-0	.444	...	.778	0	1.000
2000—	Carolina (Sou.)■	C-1B	72	227	29	51	15	0	8	26	31	45	3-3	.225	.336	.396	6	.988
2001—	Colo. Springs (PCL)	C-1B	28	79	13	19	4	1	1	4	6	22	0-0	.241	.294	.354	0	1.000
—	Carolina (Sou.)	C-1B	24	68	11	15	2	0	3	9	14	14	0-0	.221	.384	.382	5	.972
2002—	Colo. Springs (PCL)	C-1B	49	130	10	32	7	0	2	11	16	27	0-0	.246	.327	.346	3	.989
—	Colorado (N.L.)	C	5	13	1	4	0	0	0	0	0	3	0-0	.308	.308	.308	0	1.000
American League totals (2 years)			6	3	0	0	0	0	0	0	0	1	0-0	.000	.000	.000	0	1.000
National League totals (1 year)			5	13	1	4	0	0	0	0	0	3	0-0	.308	.308	.308	0	1.000
Major League totals (3 years)			11	16	1	4	0	0	0	0	0	4	0-0	.250	.250	.250	0	1.000

McLEMORE, MARK OF/IF MARINERS

PERSONAL: Born October 4, 1964, in San Diego. ... 5-11/207. ... Bats both, throws right. ... Full name: Mark Tremell McLemore.

HIGH SCHOOL: Samuel F.B. Morse (San Diego).

TRANSACTIONS/CAREER NOTES: Selected by California Angels organization in ninth round of free-agent draft (June 7, 1982). ... On disabled list (May 15-27, 1985). ... On California disabled list (May 24-August 2, 1988); included rehabilitation assignments to Palm Springs (July 7-21) and Edmonton (July 22-27). ... On California disabled list (May 17-August 17, 1990); included rehabilitation assignments to Edmonton (May 24-June 6) and Palm Springs (August 9-13). ... Traded by Angels to Cleveland Indians (August 17, 1990), completing deal in which Indians traded C Ron Tingley to Angels for a player to be named later (September 6, 1989). ... Released by Indians (December 13, 1990). ... Signed by Houston Astros organization (March 6, 1991). ... On Houston disabled list (May 9-June 25, 1991); included rehabilitation assignments to Tucson (May 24-29) and Jackson (June 14-22). ... Released by Astros (June 25, 1991). ... Signed by Baltimore Orioles organization (July 5, 1991). ... Granted free agency (October 15, 1991). ... Re-signed by Orioles organization (February 5, 1992). ... Granted free agency (December 19, 1992). ... Re-signed by Orioles organization (January 6, 1993). ... Granted free agency (October 18, 1994). ... Signed by Texas Rangers (December 13, 1994). ... Granted free agency (December 7, 1996). ... Re-signed by Rangers (December 13, 1996). ... On Texas disabled list (May 15-June 12 and August 19-September 28, 1997); included rehabilitation assignments to Charlotte (June 7-8) and Oklahoma City (June 9-12). ... On disabled list (June 7-22, 1998). ... Granted free agency (October 29, 1999). ... Signed by Seattle Mariners (December 20, 1999). ... On suspended list (June 20-24, 2000). ... Granted free agency (November 5, 2001). ... Re-signed by Mariners (December 7, 2001).

STATISTICAL NOTES: Led California League second basemen with 400 assists and 84 double plays in 1984. ... Led Pacific Coast League second basemen with 264 putouts, 597 total chances and 95 double plays in 1989. ... Led A.L. second basemen with 473 assists and 798 total chances in 1996. ... Led A.L. in caught stealing with 14 in 2000. ... Career major league grand slams: 1.

2002 GAMES PLAYED BY POSITION (MLB): OF—88; 3B—14; DH—4; 2B—2; SS—1.

			BATTING														FIELDING	
Year	Team (League)	Pos.	G	AB	R	H	2B	3B	HR	RBI	BB	SO	SB-CS	Avg.	OBP	SLG	E	Avg.
1982—	Salem (N'West)	2B-SS	55	165	42	49	6	2	0	25	39	38	14-6	.297	.431	.358	11	.949
1983—	Peoria (Midw.)	2B-SS	95	329	42	79	7	3	0	18	53	64	15-11	.240	.346	.280	24	.946
1984—	Redwood (Calif.)	2B-SS	134	482	102	142	8	3	0	45	106	75	59-15	.295	.421	.324	25	.966
1985—	Midland (Texas)	2B-SS	117	458	80	124	17	6	2	46	66	59	31-16	.271	.362	.347	19	.971
1986—	Midland (Texas)	2B	63	237	54	75	9	1	1	29	48	18	38-8	.316	.428	.376	13	.964
—	Edmonton (PCL)	2B	73	286	41	79	13	1	0	23	39	30	29-9	.276	.359	.329	7	.982
—	California (A.L.)	2B	5	4	0	0	0	0	0	0	1	2	0-1	.000	.200	.000	0	1.000
1987—	California (A.L.)	2B-SS-DH	138	433	61	102	13	3	3	41	48	72	25-8	.236	.310	.300	17	.975
1988—	California (A.L.)	2B-3B-DH	77	233	38	56	11	2	2	16	25	28	13-7	.240	.312	.330	6	.979
—	Palm Springs (Calif.)	2B	11	44	9	15	3	1	0	6	11	7	7-3	.341	.474	.455	1	.977
—	Edmonton (PCL)	2B	12	45	7	12	3	0	0	6	4	4	7-1	.267	.327	.333	1	.986
1989—	Edmonton (PCL)	2B	114	430	60	105	13	2	2	34	49	67	26-11	.244	.321	.298	10	*.983
—	California (A.L.)	2B-DH	32	103	12	25	3	1	0	14	7	19	6-1	.243	.295	.291	5	.966
1990—	California (A.L.)	2B	20	48	4	7	2	0	0	2	4	9	1-0	.146	.212	.188	0	1.000
—	Edmonton (PCL)	2B-SS	9	39	4	10	2	0	0	3	6	10	0-3	.256	.356	.308	4	.933
—	Palm Springs (Calif.)	2B	6	22	3	6	0	0	0	2	3	7	0-2	.273	.360	.273	0	1.000
—	Colo. Springs (PCL)■	2B-3B-SS	14	54	11	15	2	0	1	7	11	8	5-0	.278	.400	.370	2	.969
—	Cleveland (A.L.)	SS-3B-2B	8	12	2	2	0	0	0	0	0	6	0-0	.167	.167	.167	4	.922
1991—	Houston (N.L.)■	2B	21	61	6	9	1	0	0	2	6	13	0-1	.148	.221	.164	2	.975
—	Tucson (PCL)	2B	4	14	2	5	1	0	0	0	2	1	0-0	.357	.438	.429	0	1.000
—	Jackson (Texas)	2B	7	22	6	5	3	0	1	4	6	3	1-0	.227	.393	.500	0	1.000
—	Rochester (I.L.)■	2B	57	228	32	64	11	4	1	28	27	29	12-5	.281	.354	.377	5	.984
1992—	Baltimore (A.L.)	2B-DH	101	228	40	56	7	2	0	27	21	26	11-5	.246	.308	.294	7	.978
1993—	Baltimore (A.L.)	0-2-3-DH	148	581	81	165	27	5	4	72	64	92	21-15	.284	.353	.368	6	.986
1994—	Baltimore (A.L.)	2B-OF-DH	104	343	44	88	11	1	3	29	51	50	20-5	.257	.354	.321	9	.982
1995—	Texas (A.L.)■	OF-2B-DH	129	467	73	122	20	5	5	41	59	71	21-11	.261	.346	.358	4	.991
1996—	Texas (A.L.)	2B-OF	147	517	84	150	23	4	5	46	87	69	27-10	.290	.389	.379	12	.985
1997—	Texas (A.L.)	2B-OF	89	349	47	91	17	2	1	25	40	54	7-5	.261	.338	.330	8	.980
—	Charlotte (FSL)	2B	2	7	1	4	1	0	0	3	2	1	1-1	.571	.667	.714	0	1.000
—	Oklahoma City (A.A.)	2B-DH	3	10	0	1	0	0	0	1	1	1	1-0	.100	.167	.100	0	1.000
1998—	Texas (A.L.)	2B-DH	126	461	79	114	15	1	5	53	89	64	12-4	.247	.369	.317	15	.975
1999—	Texas (A.L.)	2B-OF-DH	144	566	105	155	20	7	6	45	83	79	16-8	.274	.363	.366	12	.983
2000—	Seattle (A.L.)■	2B-OF	138	481	72	118	23	1	3	46	81	78	30-14	.245	.353	.316	8	.988
2001—	Seattle (A.L.)	O-3-S-2-DH	125	409	78	117	16	9	5	57	69	84	39-7	.286	.384	.406	12	.963
2002—	Seattle (A.L.)	O-3-D-2-S	104	337	54	91	17	2	7	41	61	63	18-10	.270	.380	.395	7	.966
American League totals (16 years)			1635	5572	874	1459	225	45	49	555	790	866	267-111	.262	.352	.345	132	.980
National League totals (1 year)			21	61	6	9	1	0	0	2	6	13	0-1	.148	.221	.164	2	.975
Major League totals (17 years)			1656	5633	880	1468	226	45	49	557	796	879	267-112	.261	.351	.343	134	.980

DIVISION SERIES RECORD

			BATTING														FIELDING	
Year	Team (League)	Pos.	G	AB	R	H	2B	3B	HR	RBI	BB	SO	SB-CS	Avg.	OBP	SLG	E	Avg.
1996—	Texas (A.L.)	2B	4	15	1	2	0	0	0	2	0	4	0-1	.133	.133	.133	0	1.000
1998—	Texas (A.L.)	2B	3	10	0	1	1	0	0	0	2	3	0-0	.100	.250	.200	0	1.000
1999—	Texas (A.L.)	2B	3	10	0	1	0	0	0	0	1	3	0-0	.100	.182	.100	0	1.000
2000—	Seattle (A.L.)	2B	3	9	1	1	0	0	0	0	2	1	0-0	.111	.273	.111	0	1.000
2001—	Seattle (A.L.)	SS-OF	5	18	0	3	0	0	0	3	1	8	0-0	.167	.211	.167	1	.957
Division series totals (5 years)			18	62	2	8	1	0	0	5	6	19	0-1	.129	.206	.145	1	.989

CHAMPIONSHIP SERIES RECORD

			BATTING														FIELDING	
Year	Team (League)	Pos.	G	AB	R	H	2B	3B	HR	RBI	BB	SO	SB-CS	Avg.	OBP	SLG	E	Avg.
2000—	Seattle (A.L.)	2B	5	16	2	4	3	0	0	2	2	1	0-0	.250	.333	.438	2	.923
2001—	Seattle (A.L.)	PH-SS-OF-2B	5	14	1	2	0	1	0	3	2	2	0-0	.143	.250	.286	0	1.000
Championship series totals (2 years)			10	30	3	6	3	1	0	5	4	3	0-0	.200	.294	.367	2	.939

MEADOWS, BRIAN — P — PIRATES

PERSONAL: Born November 21, 1975, in Montgomery, Ala. ... 6-4/220. ... Throws right, bats right. ... Full name: Matthew Brian Meadows.
HIGH SCHOOL: Charles Henderson (Troy, Ala.).
TRANSACTIONS/CAREER NOTES: Selected by Florida Marlins organization in third round of free-agent draft (June 2, 1994); pick received as compensation for Colorado Rockies signing Type B free-agent SS Walt Weiss. ... On disabled list (July 28-August 13, 1998). ... Traded by Marlins to San Diego Padres for P Dan Miceli (November 15, 1999). ... Traded by Padres to Kansas City Royals for P Jay Witasick (July 31, 2000). ... Granted free agency (October 8, 2001). ... Signed by Minnesota Twins organization (January 15, 2002). ... Released by Twins (March 30, 2002). ... Signed by Pittsburgh Pirates organization (April 5, 2002).
RECORDS: Shares major league single-inning record for most putouts by pitcher—3 (June 2, 1998, second inning).
CAREER HITTING (MLB): 20-for-162 (.123), 12 R, 3 2B, 0 3B, 0 HR, 7 RBI.

Year League	W	L	Pct.	ERA	G	GS	CG	ShO	Sv.-Opp.	IP	H	R	ER	HR	BB-IBB	SO
1994—Gulf Coast Marlins (GCL)	3	0	1.000	1.95	8	7	0	0	0-...	37.0	34	9	8	1	6-0	33
1995—Kane County (Midw.)	9	9	.500	4.22	26	26	1	1	0-...	147.0	163	90	69	11	41-0	103
1996—Brevard County (FSL)	8	7	.533	3.58	24	23	3	1	0-...	146.0	129	73	58	13	25-1	69
—Portland (East.)	0	1	.000	4.33	4	4	1	0	0-...	27.0	26	15	•13	1	4-0	13
1997—Portland (East.)	9	7	.563	4.61	29	29	4	0	0-...	175.2	204	99	90	23	48-4	115
1998—Florida (N.L.)	11	13	.458	5.21	31	31	1	0	0-0	174.1	222	106	101	20	46-3	88
1999—Florida (N.L.)	11	15	.423	5.60	31	31	0	0	0-0	178.1	214	117	111	31	57-5	72
2000—San Diego (N.L.)■	7	8	.467	5.34	22	22	0	0	0-0	124.2	150	80	74	24	50-6	53
—Kansas City (A.L.)■	6	2	.750	4.77	11	10	2	0	0-0	71.2	84	39	38	8	14-0	26
2001—Kansas City (A.L.)	1	6	.143	6.97	10	10	0	0	0-0	50.1	73	41	39	12	12-2	21
—Omaha (PCL)	6	5	.545	6.17	18	18	0	0	0-...	105.0	143	73	72	21	20-1	74
2002—Nashville (PCL)■	9	8	.529	4.27	23	22	1	1	0-...	126.1	132	69	60	15	26-1	98
—Pittsburgh (N.L.)	1	6	.143	3.88	11	11	0	0	0-0	62.2	62	29	27	7	14-8	31
A.L. totals (2 years)	7	8	.467	5.68	21	20	2	0	0-0	122.0	157	80	77	20	26-2	47
N.L. totals (4 years)	30	42	.417	5.22	95	95	1	0	0-0	540.0	648	332	313	82	167-22	244
Major League totals (5 years)	37	50	.425	5.30	116	115	3	0	0-0	662.0	805	412	390	102	193-24	291

MEARES, PAT — SS — PIRATES

PERSONAL: Born September 6, 1968, in Salina, Kan. ... 6-0/187. ... Bats right, throws right. ... Full name: Patrick James Meares.
HIGH SCHOOL: Sacred Heart (Salina, Kan.).
COLLEGE: Wichita State.
TRANSACTIONS/CAREER NOTES: Selected by Minnesota Twins organization in 12th round of free-agent draft (June 4, 1990). ... On disabled list (June 22-July 7, 1994; and August 11-26, 1997). ... Granted free agency (December 21, 1998). ... Signed by Pittsburgh Pirates (February 20, 1999). ... On Pittsburgh disabled list (April 2-23 and May 12-September 21, 1999); included rehabilitation assignment to Nashville (August 26-September 3). ... On disabled list (June 27-July 23, 2001; and March 29, 2002).
STATISTICAL NOTES: Tied for A.L. lead with 18 errors by shortstops in 1995. ... Career major league grand slams: 1.

		BATTING														FIELDING	
Year Team (League)	Pos.	G	AB	R	H	2B	3B	HR	RBI	BB	SO	SB-CS	Avg.	OBP	SLG	E	Avg.
1990—Kenosha (Midw.)	3B-2B	52	197	26	47	10	2	4	22	25	45	2-1	.239	.335	.371	16	.890
1991—Visalia (Calif.)	2B-3B-OF	89	360	53	109	21	4	6	44	24	63	15-5	.303	.351	.433	26	.936
1992—Orlando (Sou.)	SS	81	300	42	76	19	0	3	23	11	57	5-5	.253	.294	.347	35	.889
1993—Portland (PCL)	SS	18	54	6	16	5	0	0	3	3	11	0-0	.296	.345	.389	5	.938
—Minnesota (A.L.)	SS	111	346	33	87	14	3	0	33	7	52	4-5	.251	.266	.309	19	.961
1994—Minnesota (A.L.)	SS	80	229	29	61	12	1	2	24	14	50	5-1	.266	.310	.354	13	.963
1995—Minnesota (A.L.)	SS-OF	116	390	57	105	19	4	12	49	15	68	10-4	.269	.311	.431	‡18	.966
1996—Minnesota (A.L.)	SS-OF	152	517	66	138	26	7	8	67	17	90	9-4	.267	.298	.391	22	.965
1997—Minnesota (A.L.)	SS	134	439	63	121	23	3	10	60	18	86	7-7	.276	.323	.410	20	.969
1998—Minnesota (A.L.)	SS	149	543	56	141	26	3	9	70	24	86	7-4	.260	.296	.368	24	.966
1999—Pittsburgh (N.L.)■	SS	21	91	15	28	4	0	0	7	9	20	0-0	.308	.382	.352	6	.939
—Nashville (PCL)	SS	5	18	3	3	0	0	0	0	1	3	1-0	.167	.250	.167	2	.800
2000—Pittsburgh (N.L.)	SS	132	462	55	111	22	2	13	47	36	91	1-0	.240	.305	.381	20	.967
2001—Pittsburgh (N.L.)	2B	87	270	27	57	11	1	4	25	10	45	0-2	.211	.244	.304	10	.973
2002—Pittsburgh (N.L.)		Did not play.															
American League totals (6 years)		742	2464	304	653	120	21	41	303	95	432	42-25	.265	.301	.381	116	.965
National League totals (3 years)		240	823	97	196	37	3	17	79	55	156	1-2	.238	.294	.352	36	.967
Major League totals (9 years)		982	3287	401	849	157	24	58	382	150	588	43-27	.258	.299	.374	152	.966

MECIR, JIM — P — ATHLETICS

PERSONAL: Born May 16, 1970, in Queens, N.Y. ... 6-1/230. ... Throws right, bats both. ... Full name: James Jason Mecir. ... Name pronounced ma-SEER.
HIGH SCHOOL: Smithtown East (St. James, N.Y.).
COLLEGE: Eckerd (Fla.).
TRANSACTIONS/CAREER NOTES: Selected by Seattle Mariners organization in third round of free-agent draft (June 3, 1991). ... On disabled list (June 25-August 25, 1992). ... Traded by Mariners with 1B Tino Martinez and P Jeff Nelson to New York Yankees for P Sterling Hitchcock and 3B Russ Davis (December 7, 1995). ... Traded by Yankees to Boston Red Sox (September 29, 1997), completing deal in which Yankees traded P Tony Armas Jr. and a player to be named later to Red Sox for C Mike Stanley and IF Randy Brown (August 13, 1997). ... Selected by Tampa Bay Devil Rays in second round (36th pick overall) of expansion draft (November 18, 1997). ... On disabled list (May 12, 1999-remainder of season). ... On Tampa Bay disabled list (April 27-May 23, 2000). ... Traded by Devil Rays with P Todd Belitz to Oakland Athletics for P Jesus Colome and a player to be named later (July 28, 2000). ... On Oakland disabled list (August 2-September 5, 2001); included rehabilitation assignment to Sacramento (September 3-5). ... On suspended list (September 2-7, 2002).
STATISTICAL NOTES: Led California League with 15 hit batsmen in 1993.
CAREER HITTING (MLB): 0-for-1 (.000), 0 R, 0 2B, 0 3B, 0 HR, 0 RBI.

Year League	W	L	Pct.	ERA	G	GS	CG	ShO	Sv.-Opp.	IP	H	R	ER	HR	BB-IBB	SO
1991—San Bernardino (Calif.)	3	5	.375	4.22	14	12	0	0	1-...	70.1	72	40	33	3	37-0	48

1992—San Bernardino (Calif.).....	4	5	.444	4.67	14	11	0	0	0-...	61.2	72	40	32	8	26-0	53
1993—Riverside (Calif.)...............	9	11	.450	4.33	26	26	1	0	0-...	145.1	160	89	70	3	58-2	85
1994—Jacksonville (Sou.)...........	6	5	.545	2.69	46	0	0	0	13-...	80.1	73	28	24	5	35-3	53
1995—Tacoma (PCL)	1	4	.200	3.10	40	0	0	0	8-...	69.2	63	29	24	3	28-7	46
—Seattle (A.L.)	0	0	...	0.00	2	0	0	0	0-0	4.2	5	1	0	0	2-0	3
1996—Columbus (I.L.)■............	3	3	.500	2.27	33	0	0	0	7-...	47.2	37	14	12	2	15-2	52
—New York (A.L.)................	1	1	.500	5.13	26	0	0	0	0-0	40.1	42	24	23	6	23-4	38
1997—Columbus (I.L.)	1	1	.500	1.00	24	0	0	0	11-...	27.0	14	4	3	0	6-0	34
—New York (A.L.)................	0	4	.000	5.88	25	0	0	0	0-1	33.2	36	23	22	5	10-1	25
1998—Tampa Bay (A.L.)■..........	7	2	.778	3.11	68	0	0	0	0-3	84.0	68	30	29	6	33-5	77
1999—Tampa Bay (A.L.).............	0	1	.000	2.61	17	0	0	0	0-2	20.2	15	7	6	0	14-0	15
2000—Tampa Bay (A.L.).............	7	2	.778	3.08	38	0	0	0	1-4	49.2	35	17	17	2	22-0	33
—Oakland (A.L.)■	3	1	.750	2.80	25	0	0	0	4-9	35.1	35	14	11	2	14-2	37
2001—Oakland (A.L.)	2	8	.200	3.43	54	0	0	0	3-8	63.0	54	25	24	4	26-7	61
—Sacramento (PCL)............	0	0	...	0.00	1	1	0	0	0-...	1.0	1	0	0	0	0-0	0
2002—Oakland (A.L.)	6	4	.600	4.26	61	0	0	0	1-6	67.2	68	36	32	5	29-4	53
Major League totals (8 years).....	26	23	.531	3.70	316	0	0	0	9-33	399.0	358	177	164	30	173-23	342

DIVISION SERIES RECORD

Year League	W	L	Pct.	ERA	G	GS	CG	ShO	Sv.-Opp.	IP	H	R	ER	HR	BB-IBB	SO
2000—Oakland (A.L.)	0	0	...	0.00	3	0	0	0	0-0	5.1	1	0	0	0	0-0	2
2001—Oakland (A.L.)	0	0	...	5.40	2	0	0	0	0-0	3.1	4	2	2	1	0-0	4
2002—Oakland (A.L.)	0	0	...	0.00	1	0	0	0	0-0	1.0	0	0	0	0	0-0	2
Division series totals (3 years)...	0	0	...	1.86	6	0	0	0	0-0	9.2	5	2	2	1	0-0	8

MELUSKEY, MITCH C

PERSONAL: Born September 18, 1973, in Yakima, Wash. ... 6-0/185. ... Bats both, throws right. ... Full name: Mitchell Wade Meluskey.
HIGH SCHOOL: Eisenhower (Yakima, Wash.).
TRANSACTIONS/CAREER NOTES: Selected by Cleveland Indians organization in 12th round of free-agent draft (June 1, 1992). ... Traded by Indians to Houston Astros for OF Buck McNabb (April 27, 1995). ... On disabled list (April 26, 1999-remainder of season; and July 31-August 18, 2000). ... Traded by Astros with P Chris Holt and OF Roger Cedeno to Detroit Tigers for C Brad Ausmus, P Doug Brocail and P Nelson Cruz (December 11, 2000). ... On disabled list (March 23, 2001-entire season; and April 21, 2002-remainder of season). ... Released by Tigers (October 2, 2002).
STATISTICAL NOTES: Led South Atlantic catchers with nine double plays in 1993. ... Tied for Texas League lead with four intentional bases on balls received in 1997. ... Led Pacific Coast League with 10 intentional bases on balls received in 1998.
2002 GAMES PLAYED BY POSITION (MLB): C—8.

		BATTING														FIELDING	
Year Team (League)	Pos.	G	AB	R	H	2B	3B	HR	RBI	BB	SO	SB-CS	Avg.	OBP	SLG	E	Avg.
1992—Burlington (Appl.).......	C	43	126	23	29	7	0	3	16	29	36	3-0	.230	.369	.357	4	.985
1993—Columbus (S.Atl.).......	C	101	342	36	84	18	3	3	47	35	69	1-1	.246	.317	.342	7	.990
1994—Kinston (Caro.)...........	C	100	319	36	77	16	1	3	41	49	62	3-4	.241	.342	.326	6	.988
1995—Kinston (Caro.)...........	C	8	29	5	7	5	0	0	2	2	9	0-0	.241	.290	.414	1	.985
—Kissimmee (FSL)■.....	C	78	261	23	56	18	1	3	31	27	33	3-0	.215	.287	.326	10	.980
1996—Kissimmee (FSL)........	C	74	231	29	77	19	0	1	31	29	26	1-1	.333	.402	.429	9	.974
—Jackson (Texas)	C	38	134	18	42	11	0	0	21	18	24	0-0	.313	.396	.396	5	.978
1997—Jackson (Texas)	C	73	241	49	82	18	0	14	46	31	39	1-3	.340	.417	.589	6	.985
—New Orleans (A.A.).....	C	51	172	22	43	7	0	3	21	25	38	0-0	.250	.347	.343	4	.989
1998—New Orleans (PCL).....	C-OF	121	397	76	140	41	0	17	71	85	59	2-0	.353	.465	.584	10	.987
—Houston (N.L.)	C	8	8	1	2	1	0	0	0	1	4	0-0	.250	.333	.375	0	1.000
1999—Houston (N.L.)	C	10	33	4	7	1	0	1	3	5	6	1-0	.212	.316	.333	0	1.000
2000—Houston (N.L.)	C-3B	117	337	47	101	21	0	14	69	55	74	1-0	.300	.401	.487	13	.981
2001— Detroit (A.L.)■...........								Did not play.									
2002—Detroit (A.L.)	C	8	27	3	6	0	0	0	1	5	3	0-0	.222	.353	.222	0	1.000
American League totals (1 year)		8	27	3	6	0	0	0	1	5	3	0-0	.222	.353	.222	0	1.000
National League totals (3 years)		135	378	52	110	23	0	15	72	61	84	2-0	.291	.392	.471	13	.983
Major League totals (4 years)		143	405	55	116	23	0	15	73	66	87	2-0	.286	.390	.454	13	.983

MENCH, KEVIN OF RANGERS

PERSONAL: Born January 7, 1978, in Wilmington, Del. ... 6-0/215. ... Bats right, throws right. ... Full name: Kevin Ford Mench.
HIGH SCHOOL: St. Mark's (Wilmington, Del.).
COLLEGE: Delaware.
TRANSACTIONS/CAREER NOTES: Selected by Texas Rangers organization in fourth round of free-agent draft (June 2, 1999); pick received as part of compensation for Arizona Diamondbacks signing Type A free agent P Todd Stottlemyre. ... On disabled list (June 10-30, 2001).
HONORS: Named Florida State League Most Valuable Player (2000).
STATISTICAL NOTES: Led Florida State League with 302 total bases in 2000. ... Tied outfielders for Texas League lead with three double plays in 2001.
2002 GAMES PLAYED BY POSITION (MLB): OF—106; DH—3.

		BATTING														FIELDING	
Year Team (League)	Pos.	G	AB	R	H	2B	3B	HR	RBI	BB	SO	SB-CS	Avg.	OBP	SLG	E	Avg.
1999—Pulaski (Appl.)............	OF	65	260	36	94	22	1	*16	60	28	48	12-2	.362	.420	.638	1	*.989
—Savannah (S.Atl.)	OF	6	23	4	7	1	1	2	8	2	4	0-0	.304	.360	.696	2	.900
2000—Charlotte (FSL)...........	OF	132	491	*118	*164	*39	9	27	*121	78	72	19-7	.334	.427	*.615	1	*.996
2001—Tulsa (Texas)..............	OF	120	475	78	126	34	2	26	83	34	76	4-6	.265	.319	.509	4	.983
2002—Oklahoma (PCL)..........	OF	26	98	17	21	8	0	6	15	17	33	0-0	.214	.342	.480	2	.965
—Texas (A.L.)	OF-DH	110	366	52	95	20	2	15	60	31	83	1-1	.260	.327	.448	2	.990
Major League totals (1 year)		110	366	52	95	20	2	15	60	31	83	1-1	.260	.327	.448	2	.990

MENDOZA, RAMIRO — P

PERSONAL: Born June 15, 1972, in Los Santos, Panama. ... 6-2/195. ... Throws right, bats right.
TRANSACTIONS/CAREER NOTES: Signed as non-drafted free agent by New York Yankees organization (November 13, 1991). ... On New York disabled list (June 28-July 28 and August 4, 2000-remainder of season); included rehabilitation assignment to Tampa (July 19-27). ... On disabled list (March 26-April 10, 2001). ... On disabled list (March 24-April 7, 2002). ... Granted free agency (October 28, 2002).
CAREER HITTING (MLB): 0-for-3 (.000), 0 R, 0 2B, 0 3B, 0 HR, 0 RBI.

Year	League	W	L	Pct.	ERA	G	GS	CG	ShO	Sv.-Opp.	IP	H	R	ER	HR	BB-IBB	SO
1992	Dominican Yankees (DSL)	10	2	.833	2.13	15	15	5	0	0-...	109.2	93	37	26	...	28-...	79
1993	Gulf Coast Yankees (GCL)	4	5	.444	2.79	15	9	0	0	1-...	67.2	59	26	21	3	7-0	61
—	Greensboro (S.Atl.)	0	1	.000	2.45	2	0	0	0	0-...	3.2	3	1	1	0	5-0	3
1994	Tampa (FSL)	12	6	.667	3.01	22	21	1	0	0-...	134.1	133	54	45	7	35-1	110
1995	Norwich (East.)	5	6	.455	3.21	19	19	2	1	0-...	89.2	87	39	32	4	33-0	68
—	Columbus (I.L.)	1	0	1.000	2.57	2	2	0	0	0-...	14.0	10	4	4	0	2-0	13
1996	Columbus (I.L.)	6	2	.750	2.51	15	15	0	0	0-...	97.0	96	30	27	2	19-0	61
—	New York (A.L.)	4	5	.444	6.79	12	11	0	0	0-0	53.0	80	43	40	5	10-1	34
1997	Columbus (I.L.)	0	0	...	5.68	1	1	0	0	0-...	6.1	7	6	4	1	1-0	4
—	New York (A.L.)	8	6	.571	4.24	39	15	0	0	2-4	133.2	157	67	63	15	28-2	82
1998	New York (A.L.)	10	2	.833	3.25	41	14	1	1	1-4	130.1	131	50	47	9	30-6	56
1999	New York (A.L.)	9	9	.500	4.29	53	6	0	0	3-6	123.2	141	68	59	13	27-3	80
2000	New York (A.L.)	7	4	.636	4.25	14	9	1	1	0-1	65.2	66	32	31	9	20-1	30
—	Tampa (FSL)	0	2	.000	7.20	2	2	0	0	0-...	5.0	9	4	4	0	0-0	7
2001	New York (A.L.)	8	4	.667	3.75	56	2	0	0	6-8	100.2	89	44	42	9	23-3	70
2002	New York (A.L.)	8	4	.667	3.44	62	0	0	0	4-8	91.2	102	43	35	8	16-2	61
Major League totals (7 years)		54	34	.614	4.08	277	57	2	2	16-31	698.2	766	347	317	68	154-18	413

DIVISION SERIES RECORD

Year	League	W	L	Pct.	ERA	G	GS	CG	ShO	Sv.-Opp.	IP	H	R	ER	HR	BB-IBB	SO
1997	New York (A.L.)	1	1	.500	2.45	2	0	0	0	0-0	3.2	3	1	1	0	0-0	2
1998	New York (A.L.)									Did not play.							
1999	New York (A.L.)									Did not play.							
2001	New York (A.L.)	0	0	...	0.00	3	0	0	0	0-0	4.1	2	0	0	0	1-1	5
2002	New York (A.L.)	0	0	...	13.50	2	0	0	0	0-0	1.1	5	2	2	1	0-0	0
Division series totals (3 years)		1	1	.500	2.89	7	0	0	0	0-0	9.1	10	3	3	1	1-1	7

CHAMPIONSHIP SERIES RECORD

Year	League	W	L	Pct.	ERA	G	GS	CG	ShO	Sv.-Opp.	IP	H	R	ER	HR	BB-IBB	SO
1998	New York (A.L.)	0	0	...	0.00	2	0	0	0	0-0	4.1	4	0	0	0	0-0	1
1999	New York (A.L.)	0	0	...	0.00	2	0	0	0	1-1	2.1	0	0	0	0	0-0	2
2001	New York (A.L.)	0	0	...	1.69	3	0	0	0	0-0	5.1	3	1	1	1	2-1	4
Champ. series totals (3 years)		0	0	...	0.75	7	0	0	0	1-1	12.0	7	1	1	1	2-1	7

WORLD SERIES RECORD

NOTES: Member of World Series championship team (1998 and 1999).

Year	League	W	L	Pct.	ERA	G	GS	CG	ShO	Sv.-Opp.	IP	H	R	ER	HR	BB-IBB	SO
1998	New York (A.L.)	1	0	1.000	9.00	1	0	0	0	0-0	1.0	2	1	1	0	0-0	1
1999	New York (A.L.)	0	0	...	10.80	1	0	0	0	0-0	1.2	3	2	2	0	1-0	0
2001	New York (A.L.)	0	0	...	0.00	2	0	0	0	0-0	2.2	1	0	0	0	0-0	1
World Series totals (3 years)		1	0	1.000	5.06	4	0	0	0	0-0	5.1	6	3	3	0	1-0	2

M

MENECHINO, FRANK — IF — ATHLETICS

PERSONAL: Born January 7, 1971, in Staten Island, N.Y. ... 5-8/198. ... Bats right, throws right.
HIGH SCHOOL: Susan E. Wagner (Staten Island, N.Y.).
JUNIOR COLLEGE: Gulf Coast Community College (Fla.).
COLLEGE: Alabama.
TRANSACTIONS/CAREER NOTES: Selected by Chicago White Sox organization in 45th round of free-agent draft (June 3, 1993). ... Selected by Oakland Athletics organization from White Sox organization in Rule 5 minor league draft (December 15, 1997).
STATISTICAL NOTES: Led Carolina League second basemen with 293 putouts and 603 total chances in 1995. ... Led Southern League second basemen with 273 putouts in 196. ... Led Pacific Coast League with seven intentional bases on balls received in 1999.
2002 GAMES PLAYED BY POSITION (MLB): 2B—32; 3B—4; SS—2; DH—1.

			BATTING														FIELDING	
Year	Team (League)	Pos.	G	AB	R	H	2B	3B	HR	RBI	BB	SO	SB-CS	Avg.	OBP	SLG	E	Avg.
1993	GC White Sox (GCL)	2B	17	45	10	11	4	1	1	9	12	4	3-1	.244	.443	.444	1	.979
—	Hickory (S.Atl.)	2B	50	178	35	50	6	3	4	19	33	28	11-2	.281	.403	.416	6	.977
1994	South Bend (Midw.)	2B	106	379	77	113	21	5	5	48	78	70	15-8	.298	.427	.420	10	*.979
1995	Prince William (Caro.)	2B	*137	476	65	124	31	3	6	58	96	75	6-2	.261	.391	.376	15	.975
1996	Birmingham (Sou.)	2B	125	415	77	121	25	3	12	62	64	84	7-9	.292	.391	.453	13	*.978
1997	Nashville (A.A.)	2B-3B-OF	37	113	20	26	4	0	4	11	26	31	3-2	.230	.397	.372	9	.948
—	Birmingham (Sou.)	2B-3B	90	318	78	95	28	4	12	60	79	77	7-3	.299	.447	.525	11	.974
1998	Edmonton (PCL)■	2B	106	378	72	105	11	7	10	40	70	75	9-10	.278	.403	.423	7	.979
1999	Vancouver (PCL)	3-S-2-DH	130	501	103	155	31	•9	15	88	73	97	4-5	.309	.403	.497	10	.980
—	Oakland (A.L.)	SS-DH-3B	9	9	0	2	0	0	0	0	0	4	0-0	.222	.222	.222	0	1.000
2000	Oakland (A.L.)	2-S-DH-3-P	66	145	31	37	9	1	6	26	20	45	1-4	.255	.345	.455	6	.974
—	Sacramento (PCL)	SS-3B	9	38	8	12	2	0	2	2	5	4	1-0	.316	.395	.526	0	1.000
2001	Oakland (A.L.)	2-S-3-DH	139	471	82	114	22	2	12	60	79	97	2-3	.242	.369	.374	16	.976
2002	Oakland (A.L.)	2B-3B-SS-DH	38	132	22	27	7	0	3	15	20	32	0-0	.205	.312	.326	2	.986
—	Sacramento (PCL)	SS-2B-3B	84	314	50	78	12	0	6	50	46	58	10-3	.248	.356	.344	22	.941
Major League totals (4 years)			252	757	135	180	38	3	21	101	119	178	3-7	.238	.353	.379	24	.977

DIVISION SERIES RECORD

Year	Team (League)	Pos.	G	AB	R	H	2B	3B	HR	RBI	BB	SO	SB-CS	Avg.	OBP	SLG	E	Avg.
			BATTING														FIELDING	
2000—	Oakland (A.L.)	2B	1	0	0	0	0	0	0	0	0	0	0-0	...	...	...	0	1.000
2001—	Oakland (A.L.)	2B	4	12	2	1	0	0	0	0	1	4	0-0	.083	.154	.083	1	.957
Division series totals (2 years)			5	12	2	1	0	0	0	0	1	4	0-0	.083	.154	.083	1	.960

RECORD AS PITCHER

Year	League	W	L	Pct.	ERA	G	GS	CG	ShO	Sv.-Opp.	IP	H	R	ER	HR	BB-IBB	SO
2000—	Oakland (A.L.)	0	0	...	36.00	1	0	0	0	0-0	1.0	1	6	4	4	0-0	0

MERCADO, HECTOR — P — PHILLIES

PERSONAL: Born April 29, 1974, in Catano, Puerto Rico. ... 6-3/235. ... Throws left, bats left. ... Full name: Hector Luis Mercado.
HIGH SCHOOL: Jose S. Alegria (Dorado, Puerto Rico).
TRANSACTIONS/CAREER NOTES: Selected by Houston Astros organization in 13th round of free-agent draft (June 1, 1992). ... Selected by Florida Marlins organization from Astros organization in Rule 5 minor league draft (December 9, 1996). ... Selected by Philadelphia Phillies from Marlins organization in Rule 5 major league draft (December 15, 1997). ... Traded by Phillies to New York Mets for P Mike Welch (December 15, 1997). ... On disabled list (March 21, 1998-entire season). ... On disabled list (April 8-18 and April 24, 1999-remainder of season). ... Released by Mets (August 4, 1999). ... Signed by Cincinnati Reds organization (December 16, 1999). ... Traded by Reds to Philadelphia Phillies (March 30, 2002), completing deal in which Phillies traded OF Reggie Taylor to Reds for a player to be named (March 28, 2002).
CAREER HITTING (MLB): 1-for-7 (.143), 0 R, 0 2B, 0 3B, 0 HR, 0 RBI.

Year	League	W	L	Pct.	ERA	G	GS	CG	ShO	Sv.-Opp.	IP	H	R	ER	HR	BB-IBB	SO
1992—	Gulf Coast Astros (GCL)	1	2	.333	4.20	13	3	0	0	0-...	30.0	22	17	14	0	25-0	36
1993—	Gulf Coast Astros (GCL)	5	4	.556	2.42	11	11	1	1	0-...	67.0	49	26	18	1	29-0	59
—	Osceola (FSL)	1	1	.500	5.19	2	2	0	0	0-...	8.2	9	7	5	0	6-1	5
1994—	Osceola (FSL)	6	•13	.316	3.95	25	25	1	1	0-...	136.2	123	75	60	5	79-4	88
1995—	Jackson (Texas)	1	4	.200	7.80	8	7	0	0	0-...	30.0	36	33	26	5	32-1	20
—	Kissimmee (FSL)	6	8	.429	3.46	19	17	2	0	0-...	104.0	96	50	40	2	37-0	75
1996—	Kissimmee (FSL)	3	5	.375	4.16	56	0	0	0	3-...	80.0	78	43	37	4	48-1	68
1997—	Portland (East.)■	11	3	.786	3.96	31	17	1	1	0-...	129.2	129	66	57	10	54-5	125
—	Charlotte (I.L.)	0	1	.000	9.00	1	1	0	0	0-...	5.0	5	5	5	2	5-0	1
1998—	New York (N.L.)■									Did not play.							
1999—	Norfolk (I.L.)	0	0	...	1.50	2	2	0	0	0-...	6.0	3	1	1	1	1-0	2
2000—	Cincinnati (N.L.)■	0	0	...	4.50	12	0	0	0	0-0	14.0	12	7	7	2	8-0	13
—	Louisville (I.L.)	1	5	.167	3.04	47	5	0	0	2-...	77.0	69	26	26	2	48-2	67
2001—	Louisville (I.L.)	1	0	1.000	1.35	12	0	0	0	1-...	13.1	12	2	2	0	6-1	13
—	Cincinnati (N.L.)	3	2	.600	4.08	56	0	0	0	0-2	53.0	55	27	24	6	30-1	59
2002—	Scranton/W.B. (I.L.)■	3	1	.750	1.62	26	0	0	0	3-...	33.1	22	6	6	2	12-1	43
—	Philadelphia (N.L.)	2	2	.500	4.62	31	3	0	0	0-0	39.0	32	21	20	2	25-2	40
Major League totals (3 years)		5	4	.556	4.33	99	3	0	0	0-2	106.0	99	55	51	10	63-3	112

MERCED, ORLANDO — OF/1B — ASTROS

PERSONAL: Born November 2, 1966, in San Juan, Puerto Rico. ... 6-1/195. ... Bats left, throws right. ... Full name: Orlando Luis Merced. ... Name pronounced mer-SED.
HIGH SCHOOL: University Garden (San Juan, Puerto Rico).
TRANSACTIONS/CAREER NOTES: Signed as non-drafted free agent by Pittsburgh Pirates organization (February 22, 1985). ... On Macon disabled list (April 18-28, 1987). ... On Watertown disabled list (June 23, 1987-remainder of season). ... On disabled list (May 1-18, August 1-16 and August 22-September 6, 1996). ... Traded by Pirates with IF Carlos Garcia and P Dan Plesac to Toronto Blue Jays for P Jose Silva, P Jose Pett, IF Brandon Cromer and three players to be named later (November 14, 1996); Pirates acquired P Mike Halperin, IF Abraham Nunez and C/OF Craig Wilson to complete deal (December 11, 1996). ... On disabled list (July 29-September 28, 1997). ... Granted free agency (October 27, 1997). ... Signed by Minnesota Twins organization (January 12, 1998). ... Traded by Twins with P Greg Swindell to Boston Red Sox for P Matt Kinney, P Joe Thomas and P John Barnes (July 31, 1998). ... Released by Red Sox (August 31, 1998). ... Signed by Chicago Cubs (September 5, 1998). ... Granted free agency (October 28, 1998). ... Signed by Montreal Expos organization (January 28, 1999). ... On disabled list (July 1-28, 1999). ... Granted free agency (October 15, 1999). ... Played with Orix Blue Wave of Japan Pacific League (2000). ... Signed by Houston Astros organization (August 16, 2000). ... Granted free agency (October 18, 2000). ... Re-signed by Astros organization (January 8, 2001). ... On disabled list (June 23-July 12, 2001). ... Granted free agency (November 5, 2001). ... Re-signed by Astros (December 7, 2001).
STATISTICAL NOTES: Led N.L. outfielders in double plays with five in 1993 and five in 1996. ... Career major league grand slams: 3.
MISCELLANEOUS: Batted as switch hitter (1985-92).
2002 GAMES PLAYED BY POSITION (MLB): OF—56; 1B—7; 3B—1; DH—1.

Year	Team (League)	Pos.	G	AB	R	H	2B	3B	HR	RBI	BB	SO	SB-CS	Avg.	OBP	SLG	E	Avg.
			BATTING														FIELDING	
1985—	GC Pirates (GCL)	SS-3B-1B	40	136	16	31	6	0	1	13	9	9	3-1	.228	.281	.294	28	.816
1986—	Macon (S.Atl.)	OF-3B	65	173	20	34	4	1	2	24	12	38	5-3	.197	.250	.266	13	.840
—	Watertown (NY-Penn)	3B-1B-OF	27	89	12	16	0	1	3	9	14	21	6-2	.180	.302	.303	10	.885
1987—	Macon (S.Atl.)	OF	4	4	1	0	0	0	0	0	1	3	0-0	.000	.200	.000	0	1.000
—	Watertown (NY-Penn)	2B	4	12	4	5	0	1	0	3	1	1	1-0	.417	.500	.583	2	.900
1988—	Augusta (S.Atl.)	2B-3B-SS	37	136	19	36	6	3	1	17	7	20	2-0	.265	.308	.375	7	.914
—	Salem (Caro.)	3B-2B-OF-SS	80	298	47	87	12	7	7	42	27	64	13-3	.292	.347	.450	31	.893
1989—	Harrisburg (East.)	1B-OF-3B	95	341	43	82	16	4	6	48	32	66	13-3	.240	.306	.364	10	.979
—	Buffalo (A.A.)	1B-OF-3B	35	129	18	44	5	3	1	16	7	26	0-1	.341	.372	.450	3	.984
1990—	Buffalo (A.A.)	1B-3B-OF	101	378	52	99	12	6	9	55	46	63	14-5	.262	.341	.397	20	.975
—	Pittsburgh (N.L.)	OF-C	25	24	3	5	1	0	0	0	1	9	0-0	.208	.240	.250	0	...
1991—	Buffalo (A.A.)	1B	3	12	1	2	0	0	0	0	1	4	1-1	.167	.231	.167	0	1.000
—	Pittsburgh (N.L.)	1B-OF	120	411	83	113	17	2	10	50	64	81	8-4	.275	.373	.399	12	.988
1992—	Pittsburgh (N.L.)	1B-OF	134	405	50	100	28	5	6	60	52	63	5-4	.247	.332	.385	5	.995
1993—	Pittsburgh (N.L.)	OF-1B	137	447	68	140	26	4	8	70	77	64	3-3	.313	.414	.443	10	.981

Year	Team (League)	Pos.	G	AB	R	H	2B	3B	HR	RBI	BB	SO	SB-CS	Avg.	OBP	SLG	E	Avg.
								BATTING									FIELDING	
1994—	Pittsburgh (N.L.)	OF-1B	108	386	48	105	21	3	9	51	42	58	4-1	.272	.343	.412	5	.991
1995—	Pittsburgh (N.L.)	OF-1B	132	487	75	146	29	4	15	83	52	74	7-2	.300	.365	.468	6	.985
1996—	Pittsburgh (N.L.)	OF-1B	120	453	69	130	24	1	17	80	51	74	8-4	.287	.357	.457	3	.988
1997—	Toronto (A.L.)■	OF-DH-1B	98	368	45	98	23	2	9	40	47	62	7-3	.266	.352	.413	3	.985
1998—	Minnesota (A.L.)■	1B-OF-DH	63	204	22	59	12	0	5	33	17	29	1-4	.289	.345	.422	6	.983
	—Boston (A.L.)■	DH-OF	9	9	0	0	0	0	0	2	2	3	0-0	.000	.167	.000	0	1.000
	—Chicago (N.L.)■	OF	12	10	2	3	0	0	1	5	1	2	0-0	.300	.333	.600	0	1.000
1999—	Montreal (N.L.)■	OF-1B-DH	93	194	25	52	12	1	8	26	26	27	2-1	.268	.353	.464	5	.952
2000—	Orix (Jap. Pac.)■		23	80	9	18	2	1	2	15	4	14	0-...	.225	...	.350	...	...
	—New Orleans (PCL)■	OF-3B-1B	17	67	8	18	4	0	1	14	2	4	0-1	.269	.290	.373	1	.981
2001—	Houston (N.L.)	OF-3B-1B	94	137	19	36	6	1	6	29	14	32	5-1	.263	.333	.453	1	.976
2002—	Houston (N.L.)	O-1-3-DH	123	251	35	72	13	3	6	30	26	50	4-0	.287	.350	.434	2	.987
American League totals (2 years)			170	581	67	157	35	2	14	75	66	94	8-7	.270	.347	.410	9	.984
National League totals (11 years)			1098	3205	477	902	177	24	86	484	406	534	46-20	.281	.361	.432	49	.988
Major League totals (12 years)			1268	3786	544	1059	212	26	100	559	472	628	54-27	.280	.359	.429	58	.987

DIVISION SERIES RECORD

Year	Team (League)	Pos.	G	AB	R	H	2B	3B	HR	RBI	BB	SO	SB-CS	Avg.	OBP	SLG	E	Avg.
								BATTING									FIELDING	
1998—	Chicago (N.L.)								Did not play.									
2001—	Houston (N.L.)	PH	1	1	0	0	0	0	0	0	0	0	0-0	.000	.000	.000	...	...

CHAMPIONSHIP SERIES RECORD

NOTES: Hit home run in first at-bat (October 12, 1991).

Year	Team (League)	Pos.	G	AB	R	H	2B	3B	HR	RBI	BB	SO	SB-CS	Avg.	OBP	SLG	E	Avg.
								BATTING									FIELDING	
1991—	Pittsburgh (N.L.)	1B-PH	3	9	1	2	0	0	1	1	0	1	0-0	.222	.222	.556	1	.929
1992—	Pittsburgh (N.L.)	1B-PH	4	10	0	1	1	0	0	2	2	4	0-1	.100	.231	.200	1	.967
Championship series totals (2 years)			7	19	1	3	1	0	1	3	2	5	0-1	.158	.227	.368	2	.955

MERCKER, KENT — P

PERSONAL: Born February 1, 1968, in Dublin, Ohio. ... 6-2/195. ... Throws left, bats left. ... Full name: Kent Franklin Mercker.

HIGH SCHOOL: Dublin (Ohio).

TRANSACTIONS/CAREER NOTES: Selected by Atlanta Braves organization in first round (fifth pick overall) of free-agent draft (June 2, 1986). ... On Richmond disabled list (March 30-May 6, 1990). ... On disabled list (August 9-24, 1991). ... Traded by Braves to Baltimore Orioles for P Joe Borowski and P Rachaad Stewart (December 17, 1995). ... Traded by Orioles to Cleveland Indians for 1B Eddie Murray (July 21, 1996). ... Granted free agency (November 4, 1996). ... Signed by Cincinnati Reds (December 10, 1996). ... On disabled list (August 17-September 2, 1997). ... Granted free agency (October 27, 1997). ... Signed by St. Louis Cardinals (December 16, 1997). ... On disabled list (June 14-July 1, 1998). ... Traded by Cardinals to Boston Red Sox for P Mike Matthews and C David Benham (August 24, 1999). ... On Boston disabled list (September 7-23, 1999). ... Granted free agency (November 8, 1999). ... Signed by Anaheim Angels organization (January 26, 2000). ... On Anaheim disabled list (May 12-August 12, 2000); included rehabilitation assignment to Lake Elsinore (August 4-8). ... Granted free agency (November 8, 2000). ... Signed by Red Sox organization (January 5, 2001). ... Released by Red Sox (March 29, 2001). ... Signed by Colorado Rockies organization (January 31, 2002). ... On Colorado disabled list (June 6-July 30, 2002); included rehabilitation assignment to Colorado Springs (July 24-30). ... On suspended list (September 20-23, 2002). ... Granted free agency (November 1, 2002).

HONORS: Named Carolina League co-Pitcher of the Year (1988).

STATISTICAL NOTES: Pitched six innings, combining with Mark Wohlers (two innings) and Alejandro Pena (one inning) in 1-0 no-hit victory against San Diego (September 11, 1991). ... Pitched 6-0 no-hit victory against Los Angeles (April 8, 1994).

MISCELLANEOUS: Had a sacrifice hit and received a base on balls in two games as pinch hitter (1991). ... Appeared in one game as pinch runner (1997). ... Appeared in one game as pinch runner (1998). ... Scored a run in only appearance as pinch runner with Cardinals (1999).

CAREER HITTING (MLB): 28-for-245 (.114), 12 R, 5 2B, 2 3B, 1 HR, 18 RBI.

Year	League	W	L	Pct.	ERA	G	GS	CG	ShO	Sv.-Opp.	IP	H	R	ER	HR	BB-IBB	SO
1986—	Gulf Coast Braves (GCL)	4	3	.571	2.47	9	8	0	0	0-...	47.1	37	21	13	1	16-1	42
1987—	Durham (Caro.)	0	1	.000	5.40	3	3	0	0	0-...	11.2	11	8	7	1	6-0	14
1988—	Durham (Caro.)	11	4	.733	*2.75	19	19	5	0	0-...	127.2	102	44	39	5	47-0	159
	—Greenville (Sou.)	3	1	.750	3.35	9	9	0	0	0-...	48.1	36	20	18	2	26-1	60
1989—	Richmond (I.L.)	9	12	.429	3.20	27	•27	4	0	0-...	168.2	107	66	60	17	*95-4	*144
	—Atlanta (N.L.)	0	0	...	12.46	2	1	0	0	0-0	4.1	8	6	6	0	6-0	4
1990—	Richmond (I.L.)	5	4	.556	3.55	12	10	0	0	1-...	58.1	60	30	23	1	27-1	69
	—Atlanta (N.L.)	4	7	.364	3.17	36	0	0	0	7-10	48.1	43	22	17	6	24-3	39
1991—	Atlanta (N.L.)	5	3	.625	2.58	50	4	0	0	6-8	73.1	56	23	21	5	35-3	62
1992—	Atlanta (N.L.)	3	2	.600	3.42	53	0	0	0	6-9	68.1	51	27	26	4	35-1	49
1993—	Atlanta (N.L.)	3	1	.750	2.86	43	6	0	0	0-3	66.0	52	24	21	2	36-3	59
1994—	Atlanta (N.L.)	9	4	.692	3.45	20	17	2	1	0-0	112.1	90	46	43	16	45-3	111
1995—	Atlanta (N.L.)	7	8	.467	4.15	29	26	0	0	0-0	143.0	140	73	66	16	61-2	102
1996—	Baltimore (A.L.)■	3	6	.333	7.76	14	12	0	0	0-0	58.0	73	56	50	12	35-1	22
	—Buffalo (A.A.)■	0	2	.000	3.94	3	3	0	0	0-...	16.0	11	7	7	3	9-0	11
	—Cleveland (A.L.)	1	0	1.000	3.09	10	0	0	0	0-0	11.2	10	4	4	1	3-1	7
1997—	Cincinnati (N.L.)■	8	11	.421	3.92	28	25	0	0	0-0	144.2	135	65	63	16	62-6	75
1998—	St. Louis (N.L.)■	11	11	.500	5.07	30	29	0	0	0-0	161.2	199	99	91	11	53-4	72
1999—	St. Louis (N.L.)	6	5	.545	5.12	25	18	0	0	0-0	103.2	125	73	59	16	51-3	64
	—Boston (A.L.)■	2	0	1.000	3.51	5	5	0	0	0-0	25.2	23	12	10	0	13-0	17
2000—	Anaheim (A.L.)■	1	3	.250	6.52	21	7	0	0	0-0	48.1	57	35	35	12	29-3	30
	—Lake Elsinore (Calif.)	0	0	...	0.00	1	1	0	0	0-...	4.0	0	0	0	0	0-0	3
2001—										Did not play.							
2002—	Colorado (N.L.)■	3	1	.750	6.14	58	0	0	0	0-3	44.0	55	33	30	12	22-2	37
	—Colorado Springs (PCL)	0	0	...	21.60	2	0	0	0	0-...	1.2	3	4	4	2	2-0	0
A.L. totals (3 years)		7	9	.438	6.20	50	24	0	0	0-0	143.2	163	107	99	25	80-5	76
N.L. totals (11 years)		59	53	.527	4.11	374	126	2	1	19-33	969.2	954	491	443	104	430-30	674
Major League totals (13 years)		66	62	.516	4.38	424	150	2	1	19-33	1113.1	1117	598	542	129	510-35	750

DIVISION SERIES RECORD

Year	League	W	L	Pct.	ERA	G	GS	CG	ShO	Sv.-Opp.	IP	H	R	ER	HR	BB-IBB	SO
1995—	Atlanta (N.L.)	0	0	...	0.00	1	0	0	0	0-0	.1	0	0	0	0	0-0	0
1999—	Boston (A.L.)	0	0	...	10.80	1	1	0	0	0-0	1.2	3	2	2	0	3-0	1
Division series totals (2 years)		0	0	...	9.00	2	1	0	0	0-0	2.0	3	2	2	0	3-0	1

CHAMPIONSHIP SERIES RECORD

Year	League	W	L	Pct.	ERA	G	GS	CG	ShO	Sv.-Opp.	IP	H	R	ER	HR	BB-IBB	SO
1991—	Atlanta (N.L.)	0	1	.000	13.50	1	0	0	0	0-0	.2	0	1	1	0	2-0	0
1992—	Atlanta (N.L.)	0	0	...	0.00	2	0	0	0	0-0	3.0	1	0	0	0	1-0	1
1993—	Atlanta (N.L.)	0	0	...	1.80	5	0	0	0	0-0	5.0	3	1	1	0	2-0	4
1999—	Boston (A.L.)	0	1	.000	4.70	2	2	0	0	0-0	7.2	12	4	4	2	4-0	5
Champ. series totals (4 years)		0	2	.000	3.31	10	2	0	0	0-0	16.1	16	6	6	2	9-0	10

WORLD SERIES RECORD

NOTES: Member of World Series championship team (1995).

Year	League	W	L	Pct.	ERA	G	GS	CG	ShO	Sv.-Opp.	IP	H	R	ER	HR	BB-IBB	SO
1991—	Atlanta (N.L.)	0	0	...	0.00	2	0	0	0	0-0	1.0	0	0	0	0	0-0	1
1995—	Atlanta (N.L.)	0	0	...	4.50	1	0	0	0	0-0	2.0	1	1	1	0	2-0	2
World Series totals (2 years)		0	0	...	3.00	3	0	0	0	0-0	3.0	1	1	1	0	2-0	3

MERLONI, LOU — IF — RED SOX

PERSONAL: Born April 6, 1971, in Framingham, Mass. ... 5-10/201. ... Bats right, throws right. ... Full name: Louis William Merloni.
HIGH SCHOOL: Framingham (Mass.) South.
COLLEGE: Providence.
TRANSACTIONS/CAREER NOTES: Selected by Boston Red Sox organization in 10th round of free-agent draft (June 3, 1993). ... On Boston disabled list (June 29-September 12, 1998); included rehabilitation assignment to Gulf Coast Red Sox (August 8-20). ... Contract sold by Red Sox to Yokohama BayStars of Japan Central League (November 22, 1999). ... Re-signed by Red Sox organization (July 28, 2000). ... On Boston disabled list (June 6-21, 2001); included rehabilitation assignment to Pawtucket (June 10-21).
2002 GAMES PLAYED BY POSITION (MLB): 2B—66; 3B—8; SS—5; 1B—3; OF—2.

			BATTING														FIELDING	
Year	Team (League)	Pos.	G	AB	R	H	2B	3B	HR	RBI	BB	SO	SB-CS	Avg.	OBP	SLG	E	Avg.
1993—	GC Red Sox (GCL)	SS	4	14	4	5	1	0	0	1	1	1	1-1	.357	.438	.429	1	.952
—	Fort Lauderdale (FSL)	3B-SS	44	156	14	38	1	1	2	21	13	26	1-1	.244	.299	.301	8	.951
1994—	Sarasota (FSL)	2B-3B-SS	113	419	59	120	16	2	1	63	36	57	5-2	.286	.345	.341	18	.965
1995—	Trenton (East.)	2B-3B-SS	93	318	42	88	16	1	1	30	39	50	7-7	.277	.373	.343	20	.951
1996—	Trenton (East.)	3B-2B-SS-1B	28	95	11	22	6	1	3	16	9	18	0-2	.232	.330	.411	8	.930
—	GC Red Sox (GCL)	2B	1	4	1	1	0	0	0	1	0	0	0-0	.250	.200	.250	0	1.000
—	Pawtucket (I.L.)	3B-2B-SS	38	115	19	29	6	0	1	12	10	20	0-1	.252	.328	.330	8	.945
1997—	Trenton (East.)	3B-2B-SS	69	255	49	79	17	4	5	37	30	43	3-2	.310	.402	.467	9	.957
—	Pawtucket (I.L.)	2B-3B-SS	49	165	24	49	10	0	5	24	15	20	0-2	.297	.368	.448	4	.979
1998—	Pawtucket (I.L.)	SS-2B-3B	27	88	17	34	3	1	8	22	16	13	2-2	.386	.518	.716	2	.976
—	Boston (A.L.)	2B-3B-SS	39	96	10	27	6	0	1	15	7	20	1-0	.281	.343	.375	5	.962
—	GC Red Sox (GCL)	2B	1	1	0	0	0	0	0	0	0	0	0-0	.000	.000	.000	0	...
1999—	Boston (A.L.)	S-3-2-DH-1-O	43	126	18	32	7	0	1	13	8	16	0-0	.254	.307	.333	10	.940
—	Pawtucket (I.L.)	S-3-DH-1-2	66	229	45	64	14	1	7	36	30	38	1-1	.279	.383	.441	12	.945
2000—	Pawtucket (I.L.)	SS-1B-2B-3B	11	39	6	16	2	0	1	5	3	3	0-1	.410	.452	.538	4	.897
—	Yokohama (Jp.Cn.)■		42	94	10	20	4	0	1	3	7	15	0-...	.213	...	.287	...	...
—	Boston (A.L.)	3B	40	128	10	41	11	2	0	18	4	22	1-0	.320	.341	.438	7	.928
2001—	Pawtucket (I.L.)	SS-2B-3B-1B	52	195	30	51	12	0	4	20	15	37	2-0	.262	.330	.385	10	.954
—	Boston (A.L.)	SS-2B-3B	52	146	21	39	10	0	3	13	6	31	2-1	.267	.306	.397	3	.983
2002—	Boston (A.L.)	2-3-S-1-O	84	194	28	48	12	2	4	18	20	35	1-2	.247	.332	.392	5	.982
—	Pawtucket (I.L.)	3B-SS-OF	8	25	1	5	2	0	0	2	1	3	0-0	.200	.250	.280	0	1.000
Major League totals (5 years)			258	690	87	187	46	4	9	77	45	124	5-3	.271	.325	.388	30	.965

DIVISION SERIES RECORD

			BATTING														FIELDING	
Year	Team (League)	Pos.	G	AB	R	H	2B	3B	HR	RBI	BB	SO	SB-CS	Avg.	OBP	SLG	E	Avg.
1999—	Boston (A.L.)	SS-PH	3	6	1	2	0	0	0	1	1	1	0-0	.333	.429	.333	1	.833

CHAMPIONSHIP SERIES RECORD

			BATTING														FIELDING	
Year	Team (League)	Pos.	G	AB	R	H	2B	3B	HR	RBI	BB	SO	SB-CS	Avg.	OBP	SLG	E	Avg.
1999—	Boston (A.L.)	PH	1	0	0	0	0	0	0	0	1	0	0-0	...	1.000	...	...	...

MESA, JOSE — P — PHILLIES

PERSONAL: Born May 22, 1966, in Azua, Dominican Republic. ... 6-3/225. ... Throws right, bats right. ... Full name: Jose Ramon Mesa.
HIGH SCHOOL: Santa School (Azua, Dominican Republic).
TRANSACTIONS/CAREER NOTES: Signed as non-drafted free agent by Toronto Blue Jays organization (October 31, 1981). ... On Kinston disabled list (August 27, 1984-remainder of season). ... Traded by Blue Jays to Baltimore Orioles (September 4, 1987), completing deal in which Orioles traded P Mike Flanagan to Blue Jays for P Oswald Peraza and a player to be named later (August 31, 1987). ... On Rochester disabled list (April 18-May 16 and June 30, 1988-remainder of season; May 27, 1989-remainder of season; and August 21-September 5, 1991). ... Traded by Orioles to Cleveland Indians for OF Kyle Washington (July 14, 1992). ... On suspended list (April 5-8, 1993). ... Traded by Indians with IF Shawon Dunston and P Alvin Morman to San Francisco Giants for P Steve Reed and OF Jacob Cruz (July 23, 1998). ... Granted free agency (October 23, 1998). ... Signed by Seattle Mariners (November 13, 1998). ... Granted free agency (November 6, 2000). ... Signed by Philadelphia Phillies (November 17, 2000). ... On suspended list (August 28-30, 2001).
HONORS: Named A.L. Fireman of the Year by The Sporting News (1995).
STATISTICAL NOTES: Tied for Carolina League lead with nine hit batsmen in 1985. ... Led A.L. with 48 save opportunities in 1995.

MISCELLANEOUS: Appeared in one game as pinch runner for Baltimore (1991).
CAREER HITTING (MLB): 0-for-0 (.000), 1 R, 0 2B, 0 3B, 0 HR, 0 RBI.

Year League	W	L	Pct.	ERA	G	GS	CG	ShO	Sv.-Opp.	IP	H	R	ER	HR	BB-IBB	SO
1982—GC Blue Jays (GCL)	6	4	.600	2.70	13	12	6	*3	1-...	83.1	58	34	25	1	20-0	40
1983—Florence (S.Atl.)	6	12	.333	5.48	28	27	1	0	0-...	141.1	153	*116	86	14	93-0	91
1984—Florence (S.Atl.)	4	3	.571	3.76	7	7	0	0	0-...	38.1	38	24	16	3	25-0	35
—Kinston (Caro.)	5	2	.714	3.91	10	9	0	0	0-...	50.2	51	23	22	2	28-0	24
1985—Kinston (Caro.)	5	10	.333	6.16	30	20	0	0	1-...	106.2	110	89	73	11	79-2	71
1986—Ventura County (Calif.)	10	6	.625	3.86	24	24	2	1	0-...	142.1	141	71	61	6	58-0	113
—Knoxville (Sou.)	2	2	.500	4.35	9	8	2	1	0-...	41.1	40	32	20	6	23-0	30
1987—Knoxville (Sou.)	10	•13	.435	5.21	35	*35	4	2	0-...	*193.1	*206	*131	*112	19	104-0	115
—Baltimore (A.L.)■	1	3	.250	6.03	6	5	0	0	0-0	31.1	38	23	21	7	15-0	17
1988—Rochester (I.L.)	0	3	.000	8.62	11	2	0	0	0-...	15.2	21	20	15	2	14-0	15
1989—Rochester (I.L.)	0	2	.000	5.40	7	1	0	0	0-...	10.0	10	6	6	2	6-0	3
—Hagerstown (East.)	0	0	...	1.38	3	3	0	0	0-...	13.0	9	2	2	0	4-0	12
1990—Hagerstown (East.)	5	5	.500	3.42	15	15	3	1	0-...	79.0	77	35	30	4	30-0	72
—Rochester (I.L.)	1	2	.333	2.42	4	4	0	0	0-...	26.0	21	11	7	2	12-0	23
—Baltimore (A.L.)	3	2	.600	3.86	7	7	0	0	0-0	46.2	37	20	20	2	27-2	24
1991—Baltimore (A.L.)	6	11	.353	5.97	23	23	2	1	0-0	123.2	151	86	82	11	62-2	64
—Rochester (I.L.)	3	3	.500	3.86	8	8	1	1	0-...	51.1	37	25	22	4	30-0	48
1992—Baltimore (A.L.)	3	8	.273	5.19	13	12	0	0	0-0	67.2	77	41	39	9	27-1	22
—Cleveland (A.L.)■	4	4	.500	4.16	15	15	1	1	0-0	93.0	92	45	43	5	43-0	40
1993—Cleveland (A.L.)	10	12	.455	4.92	34	33	3	0	0-0	208.2	232	122	114	21	62-2	118
1994—Cleveland (A.L.)	7	5	.583	3.82	51	0	0	0	2-6	73.0	71	33	31	3	26-7	63
1995—Cleveland (A.L.)	3	0	1.000	1.13	62	0	0	0	*46-48	64.0	49	9	8	3	17-2	58
1996—Cleveland (A.L.)	2	7	.222	3.73	69	0	0	0	39-44	72.1	69	32	30	6	28-4	64
1997—Cleveland (A.L.)	4	4	.500	2.40	66	0	0	0	16-21	82.1	83	28	22	7	28-3	69
1998—Cleveland (A.L.)	3	4	.429	5.17	44	0	0	0	1-3	54.0	61	36	31	7	20-3	35
—San Francisco (N.L.)■	5	3	.625	3.52	32	0	0	0	0-1	30.2	30	14	12	1	18-2	28
1999—Seattle (A.L.)■	3	6	.333	4.98	68	0	0	0	33-38	68.2	84	42	38	11	40-4	42
2000—Seattle (A.L.)	4	6	.400	5.36	66	0	0	0	1-3	80.2	89	48	48	11	41-0	84
2001—Philadelphia (N.L.)■	3	3	.500	2.34	71	0	0	0	42-46	69.1	65	26	18	4	20-2	59
2002—Philadelphia (N.L.)	4	6	.400	2.97	74	0	0	0	45-54	75.2	65	26	25	5	39-7	64
A.L. totals (12 years)	53	72	.424	4.45	524	95	6	2	138-163	1066.0	1133	565	527	103	436-30	700
N.L. totals (3 years)	12	12	.500	2.82	177	0	0	0	87-101	175.2	160	66	55	10	77-11	151
Major League totals (14 years)	65	84	.436	4.22	701	95	6	2	225-264	1241.2	1293	631	582	113	513-41	851

DIVISION SERIES RECORD

Year League	W	L	Pct.	ERA	G	GS	CG	ShO	Sv.-Opp.	IP	H	R	ER	HR	BB-IBB	SO
1995—Cleveland (A.L.)	0	0	...	0.00	2	0	0	0	0-0	2.0	0	0	0	0	2-0	0
1996—Cleveland (A.L.)	0	1	.000	3.86	2	0	0	0	0-1	4.2	8	2	2	1	0-0	7
1997—Cleveland (A.L.)	0	0	...	2.70	2	0	0	0	1-1	3.1	5	1	1	1	1-0	2
2000—Seattle (A.L.)	1	0	1.000	0.00	2	0	0	0	0-0	2.0	0	0	0	0	1-1	2
Division series totals (4 years)	1	1	.500	2.25	8	0	0	0	1-2	12.0	13	3	3	2	4-1	11

CHAMPIONSHIP SERIES RECORD

Year League	W	L	Pct.	ERA	G	GS	CG	ShO	Sv.-Opp.	IP	H	R	ER	HR	BB-IBB	SO
1995—Cleveland (A.L.)	0	0	...	2.25	4	0	0	0	1-1	4.0	3	1	1	1	1-0	1
1997—Cleveland (A.L.)	1	0	1.000	3.38	4	0	0	0	2-4	5.1	5	2	2	0	3-1	5
2000—Seattle (A.L.)	0	0	...	12.46	3	0	0	0	0-0	4.1	5	6	6	2	3-0	3
Champ. series totals (3 years)	1	0	1.000	5.93	11	0	0	0	3-5	13.2	13	9	9	3	7-1	9

WORLD SERIES RECORD

Year League	W	L	Pct.	ERA	G	GS	CG	ShO	Sv.-Opp.	IP	H	R	ER	HR	BB-IBB	SO
1995—Cleveland (A.L.)	1	0	1.000	4.50	2	0	0	0	1-1	4.0	5	2	2	1	1-0	4
1997—Cleveland (A.L.)	0	0	...	5.40	5	0	0	0	1-2	5.0	10	3	3	0	1-0	5
World Series totals (2 years)	1	0	1.000	5.00	7	0	0	0	2-3	9.0	15	5	5	1	2-0	9

ALL-STAR GAME RECORD

	W	L	Pct.	ERA	GS	CG	ShO	Sv.-Opp.	IP	H	R	ER	HR	BB-IBB	SO
All-Star Game totals (1 year)	0	0	...	0.00	0	0	0	0-0	1.0	0	0	0	0	0-0	1

MICELI, DAN — P

PERSONAL: Born September 9, 1970, in Newark, N.J. ... 6-0/216. ... Throws right, bats right. ... Full name: Daniel Miceli.
HIGH SCHOOL: Dr. Phillips (Orlando).
TRANSACTIONS/CAREER NOTES: Signed as non-drafted free agent by Kansas City Royals organization (March 7, 1990). ... Traded by Royals with P Jon Lieber to Pittsburgh Pirates for P Stan Belinda (July 31, 1993). ... Traded by Pirates to Detroit Tigers for P Clint Sodowsky (November 1, 1996). ... Traded by Tigers with P Donne Wall and 3B Ryan Balfe to San Diego Padres for P Tim Worrell and OF Trey Beamon (November 19, 1997). ... Traded by Padres to Florida Marlins for P Brian Meadows (November 15, 1999). ... On Florida disabled list (May 30-July 19, 2000); included rehabilitation assignments to Gulf Coast Marlins (July 4-8) and Brevard County (July 9-19). ... Released by Marlins (June 25, 2001). ... Signed by Colorado Rockies organization (July 2, 2001). ... Granted free agency (November 5, 2001). ... Signed by Texas Rangers organization (January 29, 2002). ... Released by Rangers (May 6, 2002).
CAREER HITTING (MLB): 1-for-19 (.053), 0 R, 0 2B, 0 3B, 0 HR, 0 RBI.

Year League	W	L	Pct.	ERA	G	GS	CG	ShO	Sv.-Opp.	IP	H	R	ER	HR	BB-IBB	SO
1990—Gulf Coast Royals (GCL)	3	4	.429	3.91	*27	0	0	0	4-...	53.0	45	27	23	0	29-5	48
1991—Eugene (N'West)	0	1	.000	2.14	25	0	0	0	10-...	33.2	18	8	8	1	18-0	43
1992—Appleton (Midw.)	1	1	.500	1.93	23	0	0	0	9-...	23.1	12	6	5	0	4-1	44
—Memphis (Sou.)	3	0	1.000	1.91	32	0	0	0	4-...	37.2	20	10	8	5	13-0	46
1993—Memphis (Sou.)	6	4	.600	4.60	40	0	0	0	7-...	58.2	54	30	30	7	39-3	68
—Carolina (Sou.)■	0	2	.000	5.11	13	0	0	0	10-...	12.1	11	8	7	2	4-1	19
—Pittsburgh (N.L.)	0	0	...	5.06	9	0	0	0	0-0	5.1	6	3	3	0	3-0	4
1994—Buffalo (A.A.)	1	1	.500	1.88	19	0	0	0	2-...	24.0	15	5	5	2	6-0	31
—Pittsburgh (N.L.)	2	1	.667	5.93	28	0	0	0	2-3	27.1	28	19	18	5	11-2	27

Year	League	W	L	Pct.	ERA	G	GS	CG	ShO	Sv.-Opp.	IP	H	R	ER	HR	BB-IBB	SO
1995	—Pittsburgh (N.L.)	4	4	.500	4.66	58	0	0	0	21-27	58.0	61	30	30	7	28-5	56
1996	—Pittsburgh (N.L.)	2	10	.167	5.78	44	9	0	0	1-1	85.2	99	65	55	15	45-5	66
	—Carolina (Sou.)	1	0	1.000	1.00	3	0	0	0	1-...	9.0	4	1	1	0	1-0	17
1997	—Detroit (A.L.)■	3	2	.600	5.01	71	0	0	0	3-8	82.2	77	49	46	13	38-4	79
1998	—San Diego (N.L.)■	10	5	.667	3.22	67	0	0	0	2-8	72.2	64	28	26	6	27-4	70
1999	—San Diego (N.L.)	4	5	.444	4.46	66	0	0	0	2-4	68.2	67	39	34	7	36-5	59
2000	—Florida (N.L.)■	6	4	.600	4.25	45	0	0	0	0-3	48.2	45	23	23	4	18-2	40
	—Gulf Coast Marlins (GCL)	0	0	...	0.00	2	2	0	0	0-...	3.0	0	0	0	0	1-0	3
	—Brevard County (FSL)	1	0	1.000	3.00	5	4	0	0	0-...	6.0	3	2	2	1	0-0	7
2001	—Florida (N.L.)	0	5	.000	6.93	29	0	0	0	0-3	24.2	29	21	19	5	11-2	31
	—Colorado Springs (PCL)■	0	2	.000	6.00	4	0	0	0	0-...	3.0	2	2	2	0	1-1	4
	—Colorado (N.L.)	2	0	1.000	2.21	22	0	0	0	1-1	20.1	18	8	5	2	5-0	17
2002	—Texas (A.L.)■	0	2	.000	8.64	9	0	0	0	0-1	8.1	13	8	8	1	3-0	5
A.L. totals (2 years)		3	4	.429	5.34	80	0	0	0	3-9	91.0	90	57	54	14	41-4	84
N.L. totals (8 years)		30	34	.469	4.66	368	9	0	0	29-50	411.1	417	236	213	51	184-25	370
Major League totals (10 years)		33	38	.465	4.78	448	9	0	0	32-59	502.1	507	293	267	65	225-29	454

DIVISION SERIES RECORD

Year	League	W	L	Pct.	ERA	G	GS	CG	ShO	Sv.-Opp.	IP	H	R	ER	HR	BB-IBB	SO
1998	—San Diego (N.L.)	1	1	.500	2.70	3	0	0	0	0-0	3.1	2	1	1	0	0-0	4

CHAMPIONSHIP SERIES RECORD

Year	League	W	L	Pct.	ERA	G	GS	CG	ShO	Sv.-Opp.	IP	H	R	ER	HR	BB-IBB	SO
1998	—San Diego (N.L.)	0	0	...	13.50	3	0	0	0	0-0	.2	4	1	1	1	0-0	1

WORLD SERIES RECORD

Year	League	W	L	Pct.	ERA	G	GS	CG	ShO	Sv.-Opp.	IP	H	R	ER	HR	BB-IBB	SO
1998	—San Diego (N.L.)	0	0	...	0.00	2	0	0	0	0-0	1.2	2	0	0	0	2-0	1

MICHAELS, JASON OF PHILLIES

PERSONAL: Born May 4, 1976, in Tampa, Fla. ... 6-0/204. ... Bats right, throws right. ... Full name: Jason Drew Michaels. ... Grandson of John Michaels, pitcher with Boston Red Sox (1932).

HIGH SCHOOL: Jesuit (Tampa, Fla.).

JUNIOR COLLEGE: Okaloosa-Walton.

COLLEGE: Miami (Fla.).

TRANSACTIONS/CAREER NOTES: Selected by San Diego Padres organization in 49th round of free-agent draft (June 2, 1994); did not sign. ... Selected by Tampa Bay Devil Rays organization in 44th round of free-agent draft (June 4, 1996); did not sign. ... Selected by St. Louis Cardinals organization in 15th round of free-agent draft (June 3, 1997); did not sign. ... Selected by Philadelphia Phillies organization in fourth round of free-agent draft (June 2, 1998). ... On Scranton/Wilkes-Barre disabled list (May 1-10, 2001).

2002 GAMES PLAYED BY POSITION (MLB): OF—26; DH—2; 3B—1.

			BATTING														FIELDING	
Year	Team (League)	Pos.	G	AB	R	H	2B	3B	HR	RBI	BB	SO	SB-CS	Avg.	OBP	SLG	E	Avg.
1998	—Batavia (NY-Penn)	OF	67	235	45	63	14	3	11	49	40	69	4-2	.268	.381	.494	5	.949
1999	—Clearwater (FSL)	OF	122	451	91	138	31	6	14	65	68	103	10-7	.306	.396	.494	1	.996
2000	—Reading (East.)	OF	113	437	71	129	30	4	10	74	28	87	7-4	.295	.337	.451	6	.977
2001	—Scranton/W.B. (I.L.)	OF	109	418	58	109	19	3	17	69	37	126	11-3	.261	.332	.443	0	1.000
	—Philadelphia (N.L.)	OF	6	6	0	1	0	0	0	1	0	2	0-0	.167	.167	.167	0	...
2002	—Scranton/W.B. (I.L.)	OF	9	32	3	9	2	0	0	7	5	5	1-3	.281	.359	.344	0	1.000
	—Philadelphia (N.L.)	OF-DH-3B	81	105	16	28	10	3	2	11	13	33	1-1	.267	.347	.476	2	.923
Major League totals (2 years)			87	111	16	29	10	3	2	12	13	35	1-1	.261	.339	.459	2	.923

MICHALAK, CHRIS P

PERSONAL: Born January 4, 1971, in Joliet, Ill. ... 6-2/195. ... Throws left, bats left. ... Full name: Christian Matthew Michalak.

HIGH SCHOOL: Joliet (Ill.) Catholic.

COLLEGE: Notre Dame.

TRANSACTIONS/CAREER NOTES: Selected by Oakland Athletics organization in 12th round of free-agent draft (June 3, 1993). ... Released by A's (April 1, 1997). ... Signed by Arizona Diamondbacks organization (April 8, 1997). ... Loaned to Tulsa, Texas Rangers organization by Diamondbacks (March 24-May 6, 1998). ... Granted free agency (October 17, 1998). ... Signed by Anaheim Angels organization (January 25, 1999). ... Released by Angels (June 19, 1999). ... Signed by Diamondbacks organization (June 23, 1999). ... Granted free agency (October 15, 1999). ... Signed by Tampa Bay Devil Rays organization (January 9, 2000). ... Released by Devil Rays (April 25, 2000). ... Signed by Los Angeles Dodgers organization (May 6, 2000). ... Granted free agency (October 18, 2000). ... Signed by Toronto Blue Jays organization (December 13, 2000). ... Claimed on waivers by Rangers (August 22, 2001). ... Released by Rangers (May 31, 2002). ... Signed by Boston Red Sox organization (June 6, 2002). ... Granted free agency (October 15, 2002).

STATISTICAL NOTES: Led A.L. with six balks in 2001.

CAREER HITTING (MLB): 1-for-3 (.333), 0 R, 0 2B, 1 3B, 0 HR, 0 RBI.

Year	League	W	L	Pct.	ERA	G	GS	CG	ShO	Sv.-Opp.	IP	H	R	ER	HR	BB-IBB	SO
1993	—S. Oregon (N'West)	7	3	.700	2.85	16	15	0	0	0-...	79.0	77	41	25	2	36-0	57
1994	—West Michigan (Midw.)	5	3	.625	3.90	15	10	0	0	0-...	67.0	66	32	29	3	28-0	38
	—Modesto (Calif.)	5	3	.625	2.91	17	10	1	0	2-...	77.1	67	28	25	13	20-1	46
1995	—Huntsville (Sou.)	1	1	.500	11.12	7	0	0	0	1-...	5.2	10	7	7	1	5-0	4
	—Modesto (Calif.)	3	2	.600	2.62	44	0	0	0	2-...	65.1	56	26	19	3	27-1	49
1996	—Modesto (Calif.)	2	2	.500	3.03	21	0	0	0	4-...	38.2	37	21	13	4	17-0	39
	—Huntsville (Sou.)	4	0	1.000	7.71	21	0	0	0	0-...	23.1	32	29	20	2	26-4	15
1997	—High Desert (Calif.)■	3	7	.300	2.65	49	0	0	0	4-...	85.0	76	36	25	4	31-1	74
1998	—Tulsa (Texas)■	1	2	.333	1.83	10	0	0	0	0-...	19.2	10	4	4	2	2-0	15
	—Tucson (PCL)■	3	8	.273	5.03	29	9	0	0	0-...	73.1	91	47	41	11	29-3	50
	—Arizona (N.L.)	0	0	...	11.81	5	0	0	0	0-0	5.1	9	7	7	1	4-0	5

Year League	W	L	Pct.	ERA	G	GS	CG	ShO	Sv.-Opp.	IP	H	R	ER	HR	BB-IBB	SO
1999—Edmonton (PCL)■	1	0	1.000	5.72	24	0	0	0	0-...	28.1	28	20	18	3	14-0	25
—Tucson (PCL)■	5	0	1.000	3.66	21	6	0	0	3-...	64.0	64	30	26	6	26-2	41
2000—Durham (I.L.)■	0	0	...	5.68	6	0	0	0	0-...	6.1	6	4	4	1	1-0	7
—Albuquerque (PCL)■	11	3	.786	4.26	23	21	1	0	0-...	133.0	166	72	63	18	55-0	83
2001—Toronto (A.L.)■	6	7	.462	4.62	24	18	0	0	0-0	115.0	133	66	59	14	49-5	57
—Texas (A.L.)■	2	2	.500	3.32	11	0	0	0	1-2	21.2	24	8	8	5	6-0	10
2002—Oklahoma (PCL)	0	0	...	0.00	1	0	0	0	0-...	1.0	0	0	0	0	0-0	1
—Texas (A.L.)	0	2	.000	4.40	13	0	0	0	0-0	14.1	20	7	7	1	10-2	5
—Pawtucket (I.L.)■	5	9	.357	5.77	17	16	0	0	0-...	93.2	125	68	60	15	31-0	52
A.L. totals (2 years)	8	11	.421	4.41	48	18	0	0	1-2	151.0	177	81	74	20	65-7	72
N.L. totals (1 year)	0	0	...	11.81	5	0	0	0	0-0	5.1	9	7	7	1	4-0	5
Major League totals (3 years)	8	11	.421	4.66	53	18	0	0	1-2	156.1	186	88	81	21	69-7	77

MIDDLEBROOK, JASON — P — METS

PERSONAL: Born June 26, 1975, in Jackson, Mich. ... 6-3/215. ... Throws right, bats right. ... Full name: Jason Douglas Middlebrook.
HIGH SCHOOL: Grass Lake (Mich.).
COLLEGE: Stanford.
TRANSACTIONS/CAREER NOTES: Selected by New York Mets organization in 18th round of free-agent draft (June 3, 1993); did not sign. ... Selected by San Diego Padres organization in ninth round of free-agent draft (June 4, 1996). ... On Rancho Cucamonga disabled list (April 8-June 25, 1999). ... On Mobile disabled list (May 8-June 2, 2000). ... Claimed on waivers by Mets (October 5, 2000). ... Claimed on waivers by Padres (November 22, 2000). ... On Mobile disabled list (May 22-June 1, 2001). ... On San Diego disabled list (July 1-31, 2002); included rehabilitation assignment to Portland (July 22-31). ... Traded by Padres with P Steve Reed to New York Mets for P Bobby M. Jones, P Josh Reynolds and OF Jay Bay (July 31, 2002). ... On New York disabled list (July 31-August 18, 2002); included rehabilitation assignment to Norfolk (August 6-18).
CAREER HITTING (MLB): 3-for-18 (.167), 2 R, 0 2B, 0 3B, 0 HR, 1 RBI.

Year League	W	L	Pct.	ERA	G	GS	CG	ShO	Sv.-Opp.	IP	H	R	ER	HR	BB-IBB	SO
1997—Rancho Cuca. (Calif.)	0	2	.000	4.03	6	6	0	0	0-...	22.1	29	15	10	1	12-1	18
—Clinton (Midw.)	6	4	.600	3.98	14	14	2	1	0-...	81.1	76	46	36	4	39-0	86
1998—Rancho Cuca. (Calif.)	10	12	.455	4.92	28	•28	0	0	0-...	150.0	162	99	82	10	63-0	132
1999—Arizona Padres (Ariz.)	1	0	1.000	7.20	1	1	0	0	0-...	5.0	9	5	4	0	1-0	3
—Mobile (Sou.)	4	6	.400	8.06	13	13	0	0	0-...	63.2	78	59	57	9	30-1	38
2000—Mobile (Sou.)	5	13	.278	6.15	24	24	0	0	0-...	120.0	133	89	82	15	52-0	75
—Las Vegas (PCL)	0	1	.000	216.00	1	1	0	0	0-...	.1	8	8	8	1	0-0	0
2001—Mobile (Sou.)	3	0	1.000	1.20	10	9	0	0	0-...	52.2	36	10	7	1	9-0	51
—Portland (PCL)	7	4	.636	3.29	15	15	0	0	0-...	90.1	86	34	33	5	23-1	66
—San Diego (N.L.)	2	1	.667	5.12	4	3	0	0	0-0	19.1	18	11	11	6	10-1	10
2002—Portland (PCL)	2	5	.286	5.65	10	7	0	0	0-...	36.2	42	27	23	6	13-0	32
—San Diego (N.L.)	1	3	.250	5.09	12	2	0	0	0-0	35.1	31	20	20	1	15-2	28
—Norfolk (I.L.)■	2	1	.667	2.66	5	5	0	0	0-...	23.2	13	7	7	1	1-0	22
—New York (N.L.)	1	0	1.000	3.94	3	3	0	0	0-0	16.0	13	7	7	1	7-0	14
Major League totals (2 years)	4	4	.500	4.84	19	8	0	0	0-0	70.2	62	38	38	8	32-3	52

MIENTKIEWICZ, DOUG — 1B — TWINS

PERSONAL: Born June 19, 1974, in Toledo, Ohio. ... 6-2/200. ... Bats left, throws right. ... Full name: Douglas Andrew Mientkiewicz. ... Name pronounced mint-KAY-vich.
HIGH SCHOOL: Westminster Christian (Miami).
COLLEGE: Florida State.
TRANSACTIONS/CAREER NOTES: Selected by Minnesota Twins organization in fifth round of free-agent draft (June 1, 1995).
HONORS: Won A.L. Gold Glove at first base (2001).
STATISTICAL NOTES: Led Florida State League first basemen with 1,183 putouts, 1,271 total chances and 113 double plays in 1996. ... Led Eastern League first basemen with .995 fielding percentage in 1997. ... Had 15-game hitting streak (April 16-May 2, 2001).
MISCELLANEOUS: Member of 2000 U.S. Olympic baseball team.
2002 GAMES PLAYED BY POSITION (MLB): 1B—143.

		BATTING														FIELDING	
Year Team (League)	Pos.	G	AB	R	H	2B	3B	HR	RBI	BB	SO	SB-CS	Avg.	OBP	SLG	E	Avg.
1995—Fort Myers (FSL)	1B	38	110	9	27	6	1	1	15	18	19	2-2	.245	.357	.345	1	.994
1996—Fort Myers (FSL)	1B	133	492	69	143	•36	4	5	79	66	47	12-2	.291	.374	.411	3	*.998
1997—New Britain (East.)	1B-OF	132	467	87	119	28	2	15	61	*98	67	21-8	.255	.390	.420	5	†.995
1998—New Britain (East.)	1B-OF	139	502	*96	162	*45	0	16	88	96	58	11-4	*.323	.432	.508	12	.991
—Minnesota (A.L.)	1B	8	25	1	5	1	0	0	2	4	3	1-1	.200	.310	.240	0	1.000
1999—Minnesota (A.L.)	1B	118	327	34	75	21	3	2	32	43	51	1-1	.229	.324	.330	3	*.997
2000—Salt Lake (PCL)	1B-3B-2B-OF	130	485	96	162	32	3	18	96	61	68	9-5	.334	.406	.524	10	.989
—Minnesota (A.L.)	1B	3	14	0	6	0	0	0	4	0	0	0-0	.429	.400	.429	0	1.000
2001—Minnesota (A.L.)	1B-DH	151	543	77	166	39	1	15	74	67	92	2-6	.306	.387	.464	4	.997
2002—Minnesota (A.L.)	1B	143	467	60	122	29	1	10	64	74	69	1-2	.261	.365	.392	5	.996
Major League totals (5 years)		423	1376	172	374	90	5	27	176	188	215	5-10	.272	.363	.403	12	.997

DIVISION SERIES RECORD

		BATTING														FIELDING	
Year Team (League)	Pos.	G	AB	R	H	2B	3B	HR	RBI	BB	SO	SB-CS	Avg.	OBP	SLG	E	Avg.
2002—Minnesota (A.L.)	1B	5	20	3	5	0	0	2	4	1	1	0-0	.250	.286	.550	0	1.000

CHAMPIONSHIP SERIES RECORD

		BATTING														FIELDING	
Year Team (League)	Pos.	G	AB	R	H	2B	3B	HR	RBI	BB	SO	SB-CS	Avg.	OBP	SLG	E	Avg.
2002—Minnesota (A.L.)	1B	5	18	1	5	1	0	0	2	1	2	0-0	.278	.316	.333	0	1.000

MILLAR, KEVIN — OF/1B — MARLINS

PERSONAL: Born September 24, 1971, in Los Angeles. ... 6-0/210. ... Bats right, throws right. ... Full name: Kevin Charles Millar. ... Nephew of Wayne Nordhagen, outfielder with four major league teams (1976-83). ... Name pronounced mi-LAR.

HIGH SCHOOL: University (Los Angeles).

JUNIOR COLLEGE: Los Angeles Community College.

COLLEGE: Lamar.

TRANSACTIONS/CAREER NOTES: Contract sold by St. Paul, Northern League to Florida Marlins organization (September 20, 1993). ... Granted free agency (December 21, 1997). ... Re-signed by Marlins (December 21, 1997). ... On Florida disabled list (April 19, 1998-remainder of season); included rehabilitation assignment to Charlotte (June 14-29). ... On Florida disabled list (May 4-28, 2002); included rehabilitation assignment to Portland (May 25-28).

HONORS: Named Eastern League Player of the Year (1997).

STATISTICAL NOTES: Led Midwest League with 240 total bases in 1994. ... Led Florida State League with 10 sacrifice flies in 1995. ... Led Florida State League first basemen with 1,213 putouts, 1,320 total chances and 134 double plays in 1995. ... Led Eastern League with 309 total bases and tied for league lead with seven sacrifice flies in 1997. ... Led Eastern League first basemen with 93 assists and 116 double plays in 1997. ... Had 18-game hitting streak (April 20-June 7, 2002). ... Had 25-game hitting streak (August 24-September 19, 2002). ... Career major league grand slams: 2.

MISCELLANEOUS: Holds Florida Marlins all-time record for highest career batting average (.296).

2002 GAMES PLAYED BY POSITION (MLB): OF—108; DH—6; 1B—2; 3B—2.

			BATTING														FIELDING	
Year	Team (League)	Pos.	G	AB	R	H	2B	3B	HR	RBI	BB	SO	SB-CS	Avg.	OBP	SLG	E	Avg.
1993—	St. Paul (Nor.)	3B-2B	63	227	33	59	11	1	5	30	24	27	2-...	.260	...	.383	18	.911
1994—	Kane Co. (Midw.)■	1B	135	477	75	144	35	2	19	93	74	88	3-3	.302	.405	.503	11	.990
1995—	Brevard County (FSL)	1B	129	459	53	132	32	2	13	68	70	66	4-4	.288	.388	.451	12	.991
1996—	Portland (East.)	1B-3B	130	472	69	150	32	0	18	86	37	53	6-5	.318	.375	.500	15	.983
1997—	Portland (East.)	1B-3B	135	511	94	175	34	2	32	131	66	53	2-3	.342	*.423	.605	17	.987
1998—	Florida (N.L.)	3B	2	2	1	1	0	0	0	0	1	0	0-0	.500	.667	.500	1	.833
—	Charlotte (I.L.)	3B-1B	14	46	14	15	3	0	4	15	9	7	1-0	.326	.448	.652	4	.930
1999—	Calgary (PCL)	OF-3B-1B	36	143	24	43	11	1	7	26	11	19	2-0	.301	.348	.538	2	.973
—	Florida (N.L.)	1B-3B-OF	105	351	48	100	17	4	9	67	40	64	1-0	.285	.362	.433	4	.995
2000—	Florida (N.L.)	1-O-3-D	123	259	36	67	14	3	14	42	36	47	0-0	.259	.364	.498	5	.985
2001—	Florida (N.L.)	O-1-3-D	144	449	62	141	39	5	20	85	39	70	0-0	.314	.374	.557	2	.993
2002—	Florida (N.L.)	O-D-1-3	126	438	58	134	41	0	16	57	40	74	0-2	.306	.366	.509	4	.981
Major League totals (5 years)			500	1499	205	443	111	12	59	251	156	255	1-2	.296	.367	.504	16	.990

MILLER, CORKY — C — REDS

PERSONAL: Born March 18, 1976, in Yucaipa, Calif. ... 6-1/225. ... Bats right, throws right. ... Full name: Abraham Philip Miller.

HIGH SCHOOL: Yucaipa (Calif.).

JUNIOR COLLEGE: San Bernardino Valley.

COLLEGE: Nevada-Reno.

TRANSACTIONS/CAREER NOTES: Signed as non-drafted free agent by Cincinnati Reds organization (June 5, 1998).

STATISTICAL NOTES: Led Pioneer League catchers with six double plays in 1998. ... Led Midwest League catchers with six double plays in 1999. ... Tied for Midwest League lead in hit by pitch with 20 in 1999. ... Led Southern League catchers with 732 putouts and 851 total chances in 2000. ... Tied for Southern League lead in passed balls with 11 in 2000. ... Led Southern League in being hit by pitch with 30 in 2000.

2002 GAMES PLAYED BY POSITION (MLB): C—38.

			BATTING														FIELDING	
Year	Team (League)	Pos.	G	AB	R	H	2B	3B	HR	RBI	BB	SO	SB-CS	Avg.	OBP	SLG	E	Avg.
1998—	Billings (Pio.)	C	45	129	28	35	8	0	5	24	24	24	1-4	.271	.455	.450	*14	.963
1999—	Rockford (Midw.)	C	66	195	43	56	10	1	10	40	33	42	3-6	.287	.438	.503	*14	.975
—	Chattanooga (Sou.)	C	33	104	20	23	10	0	4	16	11	30	0-0	.221	.354	.433	3	.989
2000—	Chattanooga (Sou.)	C	103	317	40	74	18	0	9	44	41	51	5-8	.233	.373	.375	*16	.981
2001—	Chattanooga (Sou.)	C	59	170	25	47	12	0	9	42	25	32	1-2	.276	.425	.506	7	.985
—	Louisville (I.L.)	C	44	144	30	50	11	0	7	28	10	19	2-0	.347	.431	.569	2	.994
—	Cincinnati (N.L.)	C	17	49	5	9	2	0	3	7	4	16	1-0	.184	.263	.408	1	.991
2002—	Louisville (I.L.)	C	43	134	14	31	5	0	6	21	16	21	1-2	.231	.340	.403	2	.993
—	Cincinnati (N.L.)	C	39	114	9	29	10	0	3	15	9	20	0-0	.254	.328	.421	2	.992
Major League totals (2 years)			56	163	14	38	12	0	6	22	13	36	1-0	.233	.308	.417	3	.992

MILLER, DAMIAN — C — CUBS

PERSONAL: Born October 13, 1969, in La Crosse, Wis. ... 6-2/218. ... Bats right, throws right. ... Full name: Damian Donald Miller.

HIGH SCHOOL: West Salem (Wis.).

COLLEGE: Viterbo (Wis.).

TRANSACTIONS/CAREER NOTES: Selected by Minnesota Twins organization in 20th round of free-agent draft (June 4, 1990). ... Selected by Arizona Diamondbacks in second round (47th pick overall) of expansion draft (November 18, 1997). ... On Arizona disabled list (July 24-August 14, 2002); included rehabilitation assignment to Tucson (August 9-14). ... Traded by Diamondbacks to Chicago Cubs for P David Noyce and OF Gary Johnson (November 13, 2002).

RECORDS: Shares major league single-game records for most double plays (nine-inning game)—3 (May 25, 1999); and most double plays started (nine-inning game)—3 (May 25, 1999).

STATISTICAL NOTES: Led Pacific Coast League catchers with .998 fielding percentage in 1995. ... Led Pacific Coast League catchers with 70 assists and 695 total chances in 1996. ... Tied for N.L. lead with 11 passed balls in 1999. ... Career major league grand slams: 4.

2002 GAMES PLAYED BY POSITION (MLB): C—100.

Year	Team (League)	Pos.	G	AB	R	H	2B	3B	HR	RBI	BB	SO	SB-CS	Avg.	OBP	SLG	E	Avg.
							BATTING										FIELDING	
1990—	Elizabethton (Appl.)	C	14	45	7	10	1	0	1	6	9	3	1-0	.222	.352	.311	2	.982
1991—	Kenosha (Midw.)	C-1B-OF	80	267	28	62	11	1	3	34	24	53	3-2	.232	.297	.315	4	.990
1992—	Kenosha (Midw.)	C	115	377	53	110	27	2	5	56	53	66	6-1	.292	.385	.414	9	.989
1993—	Fort Myers (FSL)	C	87	325	31	69	12	1	1	26	31	44	6-3	.212	.281	.265	8	.985
	—Nashville (Sou.)	C	4	13	0	3	0	0	0	0	2	4	0-0	.231	.333	.231	0	1.000
1994—	Nashville (Sou.)	C	103	328	36	88	10	0	8	35	35	51	4-6	.268	.336	.372	8	.989
1995—	Salt Lake (PCL)	C-OF	83	295	39	84	23	1	3	41	15	39	2-4	.285	.324	.400	1	†.998
1996—	Salt Lake (PCL)	C-1B	104	385	54	110	27	1	7	55	25	58	1-4	.286	.336	.416	6	.992
1997—	Salt Lake (PCL)	C-DH	85	314	48	106	19	3	11	82	29	62	6-1	.338	.395	.522	6	.988
	—Minnesota (A.L.)	C-DH	25	66	5	18	1	0	2	13	2	12	0-0	.273	.282	.379	0	1.000
1998—	Tucson (PCL)■	C	18	63	14	22	7	1	0	11	9	9	0-0	.349	.434	.492	3	.973
	—Arizona (N.L.)	C-DH-OF-1B	57	168	17	48	14	2	3	14	11	43	1-0	.286	.337	.446	4	.986
1999—	Arizona (N.L.)	C	86	296	35	80	19	0	11	47	19	78	0-0	.270	.316	.446	6	.991
2000—	Arizona (N.L.)	C-1B	100	324	43	89	24	0	10	44	36	74	2-2	.275	.347	.441	7	.991
2001—	Arizona (N.L.)	C	123	380	45	103	19	0	13	47	35	80	0-1	.271	.337	.424	7	.993
2002—	Arizona (N.L.)	C	101	297	40	74	22	0	11	42	38	88	0-0	.249	.340	.434	2	*.997
	—Tucson (PCL)	C	3	9	1	3	1	0	0	0	0	1	0-0	.333	.333	.444	0	1.000
American League totals (1 year)			25	66	5	18	1	0	2	13	2	12	0-0	.273	.282	.379	0	1.000
National League totals (5 years)			467	1465	180	394	98	2	48	194	139	363	3-3	.269	.336	.437	26	.993
Major League totals (6 years)			492	1531	185	412	99	2	50	207	141	375	3-3	.269	.334	.434	26	.993

DIVISION SERIES RECORD

Year	Team (League)	Pos.	G	AB	R	H	2B	3B	HR	RBI	BB	SO	SB-CS	Avg.	OBP	SLG	E	Avg.
							BATTING										FIELDING	
2001—	Arizona (N.L.)	C	5	15	1	4	0	0	0	0	1	3	0-0	.267	.353	.267	0	1.000
2002—	Arizona (N.L.)	C	1	2	0	1	1	0	0	0	2	0	0-0	.500	.750	1.000	0	1.000
Division series totals (2 years)			6	17	1	5	1	0	0	0	3	3	0-0	.294	.429	.353	0	1.000

CHAMPIONSHIP SERIES RECORD

Year	Team (League)	Pos.	G	AB	R	H	2B	3B	HR	RBI	BB	SO	SB-CS	Avg.	OBP	SLG	E	Avg.
							BATTING										FIELDING	
2001—	Arizona (N.L.)	C	5	17	0	3	0	0	0	0	2	5	0-0	.176	.263	.176	0	1.000

WORLD SERIES RECORD

RECORDS: Shares record for most consecutive strikeouts in one series—5 (November 3 [2] and 4 [3], 2001).
NOTES: Member of World Series championship team (2001).

Year	Team (League)	Pos.	G	AB	R	H	2B	3B	HR	RBI	BB	SO	SB-CS	Avg.	OBP	SLG	E	Avg.
							BATTING										FIELDING	
2001—	Arizona (N.L.)	C	6	21	3	4	2	0	0	2	1	11	0-0	.190	.261	.286	1	.982

ALL-STAR GAME RECORD

RECORDS: Holds single-game record for most doubles—2 (July 9, 2002).

	AB	R	H	2B	3B	HR	RBI	BB	SO	SB-CS	Avg.	OBP	SLG	E	Avg.
All-Star Game totals (1 year)	3	1	2	2	0	0	1	0	0	0-0	.667	.667	1.333	0	1.000

MILLER, JUSTIN — P — BLUE JAYS

PERSONAL: Born August 27, 1977, in Torrance, Calif. ... 6-2/195. ... Throws right, bats right. ... Full name: Justin Mark Miller.
HIGH SCHOOL: Torrance (Calif.).
JUNIOR COLLEGE: Los Angeles Harbor College.
TRANSACTIONS/CAREER NOTES: Selected by San Francisco Giants organization in 34th round of free-agent draft (June 1, 1995); did not sign. ... Selected by Colorado Rockies organization in fifth round of free-agent draft (June 3, 1997). ... On Salem disabled list (May 5-June 18, 1999). ... Traded by Rockies with cash to Oakland Athletics as part of three-way deal in which Brewers received P Jimmy Haynes from A's, Rockies received 3B Jeff Cirillo, P Scott Karl and cash from Brewers and Brewers received P Jamey Wright and C Henry Blanco from Rockies (December 13, 1999). ... On Midland disabled list (June 8-17 and June 22-30, 2000). ... Traded by A's with 3B Eric Hinske to Toronto Blue Jays for P Billy Koch (December 7, 2001).
STATISTICAL NOTES: Led Pacific Coast League with 16 hit batsmen in 2001.
CAREER HITTING (MLB): 0-for-2 (.000), 0 R, 0 2B, 0 3B, 0 HR, 0 RBI.

Year	League	W	L	Pct.	ERA	G	GS	CG	ShO	Sv.-Opp.	IP	H	R	ER	HR	BB-IBB	SO
1997—	Portland (N'West)	4	2	.667	*2.14	14	11	0	0	0-...	67.1	68	26	16	3	20-0	54
1998—	Asheville (S.Atl.)	13	8	.619	3.69	27	27	3	1	0-...	163.1	177	89	67	14	40-0	142
1999—	Salem (Caro.)	1	2	.333	4.14	8	8	0	0	0-...	37.0	35	18	17	3	11-0	35
2000—	Midland (Texas)■	5	4	.556	4.55	18	18	0	0	0-...	87.0	74	49	44	8	41-1	82
	—Sacramento (PCL)	4	1	.800	2.47	9	9	0	0	0-...	54.2	42	18	15	3	13-0	34
2001—	Sacramento (PCL)	7	10	.412	4.75	29	28	1	0	0-...	165.0	174	94	87	26	64-1	134
2002—	Syracuse (I.L.)■	3	2	.600	1.61	8	8	0	0	0-...	44.2	34	11	8	0	16-0	29
	—Toronto (A.L.)	9	5	.643	5.54	25	18	0	0	0-0	102.1	103	70	63	12	66-2	68
Major League totals (1 year)		9	5	.643	5.54	25	18	0	0	0-0	102.1	103	70	63	12	66-2	68

MILLER, MATT — P

PERSONAL: Born August 2, 1974, in Lubbock, Texas. ... 6-3/190. ... Throws left, bats left. ... Full name: Matthew Lincoln Miller.
HIGH SCHOOL: Monterey (Lubbock, Texas).
COLLEGE: Texas Tech.
TRANSACTIONS/CAREER NOTES: Selected by Detroit Tigers organization in second round of free-agent draft (June 4, 1996). ... On disabled list (April 3, 1997-entire season). ... On disabled list (April 25-June 3, 2000). ... On Toledo disabled list (May 31-June 18, 2001). ... Granted free agency (October 15, 2001). ... Re-signed by Tigers (March 11, 2002). ... On disabled list (April 5, 2002-remainder of season). ... Granted free agency (October 15, 2002).
CAREER HITTING (MLB): 0-for-0 (.000), 0 R, 0 2B, 0 3B, 0 HR, 0 RBI.

Year	League	W	L	Pct.	ERA	G	GS	CG	ShO	Sv.-Opp.	IP	H	R	ER	HR	BB-IBB	SO
1996—	Jamestown (NY-Penn)	1	3	.250	4.62	6	6	0	0	0-...	25.1	33	16	13	0	13-0	21
1997—										Did not play.							
1998—	West Michigan (Midw.)	7	4	.636	1.52	14	14	3	0	0-...	95.0	59	20	16	1	26-0	102
	—Jacksonville (Sou.)	3	7	.300	7.04	13	13	0	0	0-...	61.1	70	49	48	6	50-1	49
1999—	Lakeland (FSL)	4	9	.308	4.15	19	19	1	0	0-...	108.1	108	58	50	9	45-0	82
	—Jacksonville (Sou.)	4	1	.800	4.43	7	7	0	0	0-...	40.2	43	23	20	3	12-0	25
2000—	Jacksonville (Sou.)	8	5	.615	3.18	20	20	1	0	0-...	121.2	126	50	43	10	32-1	99
2001—	Toledo (I.L.)	1	2	.333	2.87	50	0	0	0	4-...	62.2	60	26	20	3	18-3	49
	—Detroit (A.L.)	0	0	...	7.45	13	0	0	0	0-0	9.2	16	8	8	0	4-0	6
2002—	Detroit (A.L.)	0	0	...	13.50	2	0	0	0	0-1	.2	4	2	1	1	1-0	1
Major League totals (2 years)		0	0	...	7.84	15	0	0	0	0-1	10.1	20	10	9	1	5-0	7

MILLER, TRAVIS — P

PERSONAL: Born November 2, 1972, in Dayton, Ohio. ... 6-3/215. ... Throws left, bats right. ... Full name: Travis Eugene Miller.
HIGH SCHOOL: National Trail (New Paris, Ohio).
COLLEGE: Kent.
TRANSACTIONS/CAREER NOTES: Selected by Minnesota Twins organization in supplemental round ("sandwich pick" between first and second round, 34th pick overall) of free-agent draft (June 2, 1994); pick received as compensation for Twins failing to sign 1993 first-round pick C Jason Varitek. ... On Salt Lake disabled list (April 20-May 3, 1998). ... Released by Twins (June 26, 2002). ... Signed by Chicago Cubs organization (June 30, 2002). ... Released by Cubs (July 30, 2002). ... Signed by Cleveland Indians organization (August 7, 2002). ... On Buffalo disabled list (August 12-19, 2002). ... Granted free agency (October 15, 2002).
CAREER HITTING (MLB): 0-for-0 (.000), 0 R, 0 2B, 0 3B, 0 HR, 0 RBI.

Year	League	W	L	Pct.	ERA	G	GS	CG	ShO	Sv.-Opp.	IP	H	R	ER	HR	BB-IBB	SO
1994—	Fort Wayne (Midw.)	4	1	.800	2.60	11	9	1	0	0-...	55.1	52	17	16	2	12-0	50
	—Nashville (Sou.)	0	0	...	2.84	1	1	0	0	0-...	6.1	3	3	2	0	2-0	4
1995—	New Britain (East.)	7	9	.438	4.37	28	27	1	1	0-...	162.2	*172	93	79	17	65-2	151
1996—	Salt Lake (PCL)	8	10	.444	4.83	27	27	1	0	0-...	160.1	187	97	86	17	57-1	*143
	—Minnesota (A.L.)	1	2	.333	9.23	7	7	0	0	0-0	26.1	45	29	27	7	9-0	15
1997—	Salt Lake (PCL)	10	6	.625	4.73	21	21	0	0	0-...	125.2	140	73	66	11	57-0	86
	—Minnesota (A.L.)	1	5	.167	7.63	13	7	0	0	0-0	48.1	64	49	41	8	23-2	26
1998—	Salt Lake (PCL)	3	4	.429	4.84	34	2	0	0	9-...	57.2	60	33	31	3	31-1	65
	—Minnesota (A.L.)	0	2	.000	3.86	14	0	0	0	0-0	23.1	25	10	10	0	11-1	23
1999—	Salt Lake (PCL)	1	2	.333	2.50	16	0	0	0	1-...	18.0	16	7	5	1	6-0	19
	—Minnesota (A.L.)	2	2	.500	2.72	52	0	0	0	0-2	49.2	55	19	15	3	16-3	40
2000—	Minnesota (A.L.)	2	3	.400	3.90	67	0	0	0	1-4	67.0	83	35	29	4	32-2	62
2001—	Minnesota (A.L.)	1	4	.200	4.81	45	0	0	0	0-0	48.2	54	30	26	5	20-1	30
2002—	Edmonton (PCL)	0	1	.000	3.99	24	0	0	0	1-...	29.1	35	15	13	3	5-0	24
	—Minnesota (A.L.)	0	0	...	4.50	5	0	0	0	0-0	4.0	5	2	2	0	2-2	3
	—Iowa (PCL)■	0	1	.000	6.17	9	0	0	0	0-...	11.2	13	8	8	1	5-1	8
	—Buffalo (I.L.)■	1	1	.500	2.45	7	0	0	0	0-...	14.2	15	9	4	1	8-3	5
Major League totals (7 years)		7	18	.280	5.05	203	14	0	0	1-6	267.1	331	174	150	27	113-11	199

MILLER, WADE — P — ASTROS

PERSONAL: Born September 13, 1976, in Reading, Pa. ... 6-2/210. ... Throws right, bats right. ... Full name: Wade T. Miller.
HIGH SCHOOL: Brandywine Heights (Pa.).
COLLEGE: Alvernia (Pa.) College.
TRANSACTIONS/CAREER NOTES: Selected by Houston Astros organization in 20th round of free-agent draft (June 4, 1996). ... On disabled list (June 1, 1998-remainder of season). ... On New Orleans disabled list (May 16-25, 2000). ... On Houston disabled list (April 15-May 29, 2002); included rehabilitation assignment to New Orleans (May 17-24).
CAREER HITTING (MLB): 26-for-169 (.154), 14 R, 6 2B, 0 3B, 0 HR, 8 RBI.

Year	League	W	L	Pct.	ERA	G	GS	CG	ShO	Sv.-Opp.	IP	H	R	ER	HR	BB-IBB	SO
1996—	Gulf Coast Astros (GCL)	3	4	.429	3.79	11	10	0	0	0-...	57.0	49	26	24	1	12-0	53
	—Auburn (NY-Penn)	1	1	.500	5.00	2	2	0	0	0-...	9.0	8	9	5	0	4-0	11
1997—	Quad City (Midw.)	5	3	.625	3.36	10	8	2	0	0-...	59.0	45	27	22	7	10-0	50
	—Kissimmee (FSL)	10	2	.833	1.80	14	14	4	1	0-...	100.0	79	28	20	3	14-1	76
1998—	Jackson (Texas)	5	0	1.000	2.32	10	10	0	0	0-...	62.0	49	23	16	7	27-2	48
1999—	New Orleans (PCL)	11	9	.550	4.38	26	26	2	0	0-...	162.1	156	85	79	16	64-0	135
	—Houston (N.L.)	0	1	.000	9.58	5	1	0	0	0-0	10.1	17	11	11	4	5-0	8
2000—	New Orleans (PCL)	4	5	.444	3.67	16	15	0	0	0-...	105.1	95	46	43	6	38-1	81
	—Houston (N.L.)	6	6	.500	5.14	16	16	2	0	0-0	105.0	104	66	60	14	42-1	89
2001—	Houston (N.L.)	16	8	.667	3.40	32	32	1	0	0-0	212.0	183	91	80	31	76-3	183
2002—	Houston (N.L.)	15	4	.789	3.28	26	26	1	1	0-0	164.2	151	63	60	14	62-9	144
	—New Orleans (PCL)	0	0	...	2.25	2	2	0	0	0-...	8.0	10	4	2	0	1-0	9
Major League totals (4 years)		37	19	.661	3.86	79	75	4	1	0-0	492.0	455	231	211	63	185-13	424

DIVISION SERIES RECORD

Year	League	W	L	Pct.	ERA	G	GS	CG	ShO	Sv.-Opp.	IP	H	R	ER	HR	BB-IBB	SO
2001—	Houston (N.L.)	0	0	...	2.57	1	1	0	0	0-0	7.0	7	2	2	1	0-0	6

MILLWOOD, KEVIN — P — BRAVES

PERSONAL: Born December 24, 1974, in Gastonia, N.C. ... 6-4/220. ... Throws right, bats right. ... Full name: Kevin Austin Millwood.
HIGH SCHOOL: Bessemer City (N.C.).
TRANSACTIONS/CAREER NOTES: Selected by Atlanta Braves organization in 11th round of free-agent draft (June 3, 1993). ... On Atlanta disabled list (May 7-July 20, 2001); included rehabilitation assignments to Macon (July 4-9) and Greenville (July 10-20).
STATISTICAL NOTES: Pitched 6-0 one-hit, complete-game victory against Pittsburgh (April 14, 1998).
CAREER HITTING (MLB): 41-for-312 (.131), 14 R, 10 2B, 0 3B, 2 HR, 22 RBI.

Year League	W	L	Pct.	ERA	G	GS	CG	ShO	Sv.-Opp.	IP	H	R	ER	HR	BB-IBB	SO
1993— Gulf Coast Braves (GCL) ..	3	3	.500	3.06	12	9	0	0	0-...	50.0	36	27	17	3	28-0	49
1994— Danville (Appl.)	3	3	.500	3.72	13	5	0	0	1-...	46.0	42	25	19	4	34-2	56
— Macon (S.Atl.)	0	5	.000	5.79	12	4	0	0	1-...	32.2	31	31	21	4	32-1	24
1995— Macon (S.Atl.)	5	6	.455	4.63	29	12	0	0	0-...	103.0	86	65	53	10	57-0	89
1996— Durham (Caro.)	6	9	.400	4.28	33	20	1	0	1-...	149.1	138	77	71	17	58-0	139
1997— Greenville (Sou.)	3	5	.375	4.11	11	11	0	0	0-...	61.1	59	37	28	8	24-0	61
— Richmond (I.L.)	7	0	1.000	1.93	9	9	1	0	0-...	60.2	38	13	13	2	16-0	46
— Atlanta (N.L.)	5	3	.625	4.03	12	8	0	0	0-0	51.1	55	26	23	1	21-1	42
1998— Atlanta (N.L.)	17	8	.680	4.08	31	29	3	1	0-0	174.1	175	86	79	18	56-3	163
1999— Atlanta (N.L.)	18	7	.720	2.68	33	33	2	0	0-0	228.0	168	80	68	24	59-2	205
2000— Atlanta (N.L.)	10	13	.435	4.66	36	•35	0	0	0-0	212.2	213	115	110	26	62-2	168
2001— Atlanta (N.L.)	7	7	.500	4.31	21	21	0	0	0-0	121.0	121	66	58	20	40-6	84
— Macon (S.Atl.)	0	0	...	0.00	1	1	0	0	0-...	3.0	0	0	0	0	0-0	5
— Greenville (Sou.)	0	1	.000	4.50	2	2	0	0	0-...	10.0	9	6	5	2	3-0	10
2002— Atlanta (N.L.)	18	8	.692	3.24	35	34	1	1	0-0	217.0	186	83	78	16	65-7	178
Major League totals (6 years)	75	46	.620	3.73	168	160	6	2	0-0	1004.1	918	456	416	105	303-21	840

DIVISION SERIES RECORD

Year League	W	L	Pct.	ERA	G	GS	CG	ShO	Sv.-Opp.	IP	H	R	ER	HR	BB-IBB	SO
1999— Atlanta (N.L.)	1	0	1.000	0.90	2	1	1	0	1-1	10.0	1	1	1	1	0-0	9
2000— Atlanta (N.L.)	0	1	.000	7.71	1	1	0	0	0-0	4.2	4	4	4	2	3-0	3
2001— Atlanta (N.L.)	Did not play.															
2002— Atlanta (N.L.)	1	1	.500	3.27	2	2	0	0	0-0	11.0	7	4	4	3	0-0	14
Division series totals (3 years)	2	2	.500	3.16	5	4	1	0	1-1	25.2	12	9	9	6	3-0	26

CHAMPIONSHIP SERIES RECORD

Year League	W	L	Pct.	ERA	G	GS	CG	ShO	Sv.-Opp.	IP	H	R	ER	HR	BB-IBB	SO
1999— Atlanta (N.L.)	1	0	1.000	3.55	2	2	0	0	0-0	12.2	13	6	5	1	1-0	9
2001— Atlanta (N.L.)	0	0	...	0.00	1	0	0	0	0-0	1.0	0	0	0	0	0-0	1
Champ. series totals (2 years)	1	0	1.000	3.29	3	2	0	0	0-0	13.2	13	6	5	1	1-0	10

WORLD SERIES RECORD

Year League	W	L	Pct.	ERA	G	GS	CG	ShO	Sv.-Opp.	IP	H	R	ER	HR	BB-IBB	SO
1999— Atlanta (N.L.)	0	1	.000	18.00	1	1	0	0	0-0	2.0	8	5	4	0	2-0	2

ALL-STAR GAME RECORD

	W	L	Pct.	ERA	GS	CG	ShO	Sv.-Opp.	IP	H	R	ER	HR	BB-IBB	SO
All-Star Game totals (1 year)	0	0	...	0.00	0	0	0	0-0	1.0	1	0	0	0	0-0	1

MILTON, ERIC — P — TWINS

PERSONAL: Born August 4, 1975, in State College, Pa. ... 6-3/220. ... Throws left, bats left. ... Full name: Eric Robert Milton.

HIGH SCHOOL: Bellefonte (Pa.).

COLLEGE: Maryland.

TRANSACTIONS/CAREER NOTES: Selected by New York Yankees organization in first round (20th pick overall) of free-agent draft (June 2, 1996). ... Traded by Yankees with P Danny Mota, OF Brian Buchanan, SS Cristian Guzman and cash to Minnesota Twins for 2B Chuck Knoblauch (February 6, 1998). ... On disabled list (August 7-September 2, 2002).

STATISTICAL NOTES: Tied for Eastern League lead with four balks in 1997. ... Pitched 7-0 no-hit victory against Anaheim (September 11, 1999).

CAREER HITTING (MLB): 6-for-20 (.300), 1 R, 0 2B, 0 3B, 0 HR, 2 RBI.

Year League	W	L	Pct.	ERA	G	GS	CG	ShO	Sv.-Opp.	IP	H	R	ER	HR	BB-IBB	SO
1997— Tampa (FSL)	8	3	.727	3.09	14	14	1	0	0-...	93.1	78	35	32	8	14-0	95
— Norwich (East.)	6	3	.667	3.13	14	14	1	0	0-...	77.2	59	29	27	2	36-0	67
1998— Minnesota (A.L.)■	8	14	.364	5.64	32	32	1	0	0-0	172.1	195	113	108	25	70-0	107
1999— Minnesota (A.L.)	7	11	.389	4.49	34	34	5	2	0-0	206.1	190	111	103	28	63-2	163
2000— Minnesota (A.L.)	13	10	.565	4.86	33	33	0	0	0-0	200.0	205	123	108	35	44-0	160
2001— Minnesota (A.L.)	15	7	.682	4.32	35	34	2	1	0-0	220.2	222	109	106	35	61-0	157
2002— Minnesota (A.L.)	13	9	.591	4.84	29	29	2	1	0-0	171.0	173	96	92	24	30-0	121
Major League totals (5 years)	56	51	.523	4.80	163	162	10	4	0-0	970.1	985	552	517	147	268-2	708

DIVISION SERIES RECORD

Year League	W	L	Pct.	ERA	G	GS	CG	ShO	Sv.-Opp.	IP	H	R	ER	HR	BB-IBB	SO
2002— Minnesota (A.L.)	1	0	1.000	2.57	1	1	0	0	0-0	7.0	6	2	2	1	1-0	3

CHAMPIONSHIP SERIES RECORD

Year League	W	L	Pct.	ERA	G	GS	CG	ShO	Sv.-Opp.	IP	H	R	ER	HR	BB-IBB	SO
2002— Minnesota (A.L.)	0	0	...	1.50	1	1	0	0	0-0	6.0	5	1	1	1	2-0	4

ALL-STAR GAME RECORD

	W	L	Pct.	ERA	GS	CG	ShO	Sv.-Opp.	IP	H	R	ER	HR	BB-IBB	SO
All-Star Game totals (1 year)	2001—Selected, did not play.														

MINOR, DAMON — 1B — GIANTS

PERSONAL: Born January 5, 1974, in Canton, Ohio. ... 6-7/230. ... Bats left, throws left. ... Full name: Damon Reed Minor. ... Brother of Ryan Minor, third baseman, Seattle Mariners.

HIGH SCHOOL: Hammon (Okla.).

COLLEGE: Oklahoma.

TRANSACTIONS/CAREER NOTES: Selected by New York Mets organization in 19th round of free-agent draft (June 1, 1995); did not sign. ... Selected by San Francisco Giants organization in 12th round of free-agent draft (June 4, 1996). ... On San Francisco disabled list (March 23-April 10, 2001). ... On San Francisco disabled list (April 7-23, 2002); included rehabiliation assignment to Fresno (April 12-23).

STATISTICAL NOTES: Tied for Northwest League lead in intentional bases on balls received with four in 1996. ... Led Northwest League first basemen with 650 putouts, 693 total chances and 56 double plays in 1996. ... Led California League with eight intentional bases in balls received in 1997. ... Led California League first basemen with 1,261 putouts, 88 assists, 1,371 total chances and 127 double plays in 1997. ... Led Texas League first baseman with 1,160 putouts, 104 assists and 1,273 total chances in 1999. ... Led Pacific Coast League with 1,134 putouts, 1,205 total chances and 115 double plays in 2000.

2002 GAMES PLAYED BY POSITION (MLB): 1B—44; DH—3.

			BATTING														FIELDING	
Year	Team (League)	Pos.	G	AB	R	H	2B	3B	HR	RBI	BB	SO	SB-CS	Avg.	OBP	SLG	E	Avg.
1996—	Bellingham (N'West) ..	1B	75	269	44	65	11	1	12	55	47	86	0-2	.242	.363	.424	5	.993
1997—	Bakersfield (Calif.)	1B	*140	532	98	154	34	1	31	99	87	143	2-1	.289	.391	.532	*22	.984
1998—	Shreveport (Texas)	1B	81	289	39	69	11	1	14	52	30	51	1-0	.239	.321	.429	8	.988
—	San Jose (Calif.)	1B	48	176	26	50	10	1	7	36	28	40	0-1	.284	.386	.472	6	.987
1999—	Shreveport (Texas)	1B-DH	136	473	76	129	33	4	20	82	80	115	1-0	.273	.385	.486	9	*.993
2000—	Fresno (PCL)	1B	133	482	84	140	27	1	30	106	87	97	0-0	.290	.394	.537	11	.991
—	San Francisco (N.L.) ..	1B-2B	10	9	3	4	0	0	3	6	2	1	0-0	.444	.545	1.444	0	1.000
2001—	Fresno (PCL)	1B-OF	112	406	74	125	22	3	24	71	44	83	1-1	.308	.380	.554	11	.988
—	San Francisco (N.L.) ..	1B	19	45	3	7	1	0	0	3	3	8	0-0	.156	.208	.178	1	.989
2002—	San Francisco (N.L.) ..	1B-DH	83	173	21	41	6	0	10	24	24	34	0-0	.237	.333	.445	1	.997
—	Fresno (PCL)	1B	9	29	8	15	6	1	0	5	5	5	0-0	.517	.588	.793	2	.972
Major League totals (3 years)			112	227	27	52	7	0	13	33	29	43	0-0	.229	.319	.432	2	.995

MIRABELLI, DOUG C RED SOX

PERSONAL: Born October 18, 1970, in Kingman, Ariz. ... 6-1/227. ... Bats right, throws right. ... Full name: Douglas Anthony Mirabelli. ... Name pronounced mirr-uh-BEL-ee.

HIGH SCHOOL: Valley (Las Vegas).

COLLEGE: Wichita State.

TRANSACTIONS/CAREER NOTES: Selected by Detroit Tigers organization in sixth round of free-agent draft (June 5, 1989); did not sign. ... Selected by San Francisco Giants organization in fifth round of free-agent draft (June 1, 1992). ... On Phoenix disabled list (May 16-23, 1995). ... Contract purchased by Texas Rangers from Giants (March 27, 2001). ... Traded by Rangers to Boston Red Sox for P Justin Duchscherer (June 12, 2001).

STATISTICAL NOTES: Led Pacific Coast League catchers with 629 putouts and 680 total chances in 1997. ... Career major league grand slams: 1.

2002 GAMES PLAYED BY POSITION (MLB): C—50; DH—4.

			BATTING														FIELDING	
Year	Team (League)	Pos.	G	AB	R	H	2B	3B	HR	RBI	BB	SO	SB-CS	Avg.	OBP	SLG	E	Avg.
1992—	San Jose (Calif.)	C	53	177	30	41	11	1	0	21	24	18	1-3	.232	.333	.305	10	.973
1993—	San Jose (Calif.)	C	113	371	58	100	19	2	1	48	72	55	0-4	.270	.390	.340	9	.989
1994—	Shreveport (Texas)	C-1B	85	255	23	56	8	0	4	24	36	48	3-1	.220	.316	.298	3	.993
1995—	Phoenix (PCL)	C	23	66	3	11	0	1	0	7	12	10	1-0	.167	.296	.197	2	.985
—	Shreveport (Texas)	C-1B	40	126	14	38	13	0	0	16	20	14	1-0	.302	.397	.405	3	.986
1996—	Shreveport (Texas)	C-DH-1B	115	380	60	112	23	0	21	70	76	49	0-1	.295	*.419	.521	7	.989
—	Phoenix (PCL)	C	14	47	10	14	7	0	0	7	4	7	0-0	.298	.365	.447	2	.982
—	San Francisco (N.L.) ..	C	9	18	2	4	1	0	0	1	3	4	0-0	.222	.333	.278	0	1.000
1997—	Phoenix (PCL)	C-DH	100	332	49	88	23	2	8	48	58	69	1-2	.265	.384	.419	4	.994
—	San Francisco (N.L.) ..	C	6	7	0	1	0	0	0	0	1	3	0-0	.143	.250	.143	0	1.000
1998—	Fresno (PCL)	C-DH	85	265	45	69	12	2	13	53	52	55	2-0	.260	.386	.468	3	*.995
—	San Francisco (N.L.) ..	C	10	17	2	4	2	0	1	4	2	6	0-0	.235	.316	.529	1	.974
1999—	Fresno (PCL)	C-1B-DH	86	320	63	100	24	1	14	51	48	56	8-2	.313	.398	.525	5	.993
—	San Francisco (N.L.) ..	C	33	87	10	22	6	0	1	10	9	25	0-0	.253	.327	.356	0	1.000
2000—	San Francisco (N.L.) ..	C	82	230	23	53	10	2	6	28	36	57	1-0	.230	.337	.370	7	.985
2001—	Texas (A.L.)■	C-DH	23	49	4	5	2	0	2	3	10	21	0-0	.102	.254	.265	1	.990
—	Boston (A.L.)■	C-DH	54	141	16	38	8	0	9	26	17	36	0-0	.270	.360	.518	2	.995
2002—	Boston (A.L.)	C-DH	57	151	17	34	7	0	7	25	17	33	0-0	.225	.312	.411	0	1.000
American League totals (2 years)			134	341	37	77	17	0	18	54	44	90	0-0	.226	.323	.434	3	.996
National League totals (5 years)			140	359	37	84	19	2	8	43	51	95	1-0	.234	.332	.365	8	.989
Major League totals (7 years)			274	700	74	161	36	2	26	97	95	185	1-0	.230	.328	.399	11	.993

DIVISION SERIES RECORD

			BATTING														FIELDING	
Year	Team (League)	Pos.	G	AB	R	H	2B	3B	HR	RBI	BB	SO	SB-CS	Avg.	OBP	SLG	E	Avg.
2000—	San Francisco (N.L.) ..	C	2	2	0	0	0	0	0	0	1	1	0-0	.000	.333	.000	0	1.000

MLICKI, DAVE P

PERSONAL: Born June 8, 1968, in Cleveland. ... 6-4/200. ... Throws right, bats right. ... Full name: David John Mlicki. ... Brother of Doug Mlicki, minor league pitcher (1992-99). ... Name pronounced muh-LICK-ee.

HIGH SCHOOL: Cheyenne Mountain (Colorado Springs, Colo.).

COLLEGE: Oklahoma State.

TRANSACTIONS/CAREER NOTES: Selected by Seattle Mariners organization in 23rd round of free-agent draft (June 5, 1989); did not sign. ... Selected by Cleveland Indians organization in 17th round of free-agent draft (June 4, 1990). ... On Cleveland disabled list (April 4-August 4, 1993); included rehabilitation assignment to Canton/Akron (July 19-August 4). ... Traded by Indians with P Jerry DiPoto, P Paul Byrd and a player to be named later to New York Mets for OF Jeromy Burnitz and P Joe Roa (November 18, 1994); Mets acquired 2B Jesus Azuaje to complete deal (December 6, 1994). ... Traded by Mets with P Greg McMichael to Los Angeles Dodgers for P Hideo Nomo and P Brad Clontz (June 5, 1998). ... Traded by Dodgers with P Mel Rojas and cash considerations to Detroit Tigers for P Robinson Checo, P Apostol Garcia and P Rick Roberts (April 16, 1999). ... On Detroit disabled list (July 23-September 5, 2000); included rehabilitation assignment to West Michigan (August 25-31) and Toledo (August 31-September 5). ... Traded by Tigers to Houston Astros for P Jose Lima (June 23, 2001). ... On Houston disabled list (May 26-July 26, 2002); included rehabilitation assignments to New Orleans (July 11-16) and Round Rock (July 17-26). ... Granted free agency (October 28, 2002).

RECORDS: Shares N.L. single-inning record for most consecutive home runs allowed—3 (September 29, 2001).
MISCELLANEOUS: Struck out in only appearance as pinch hitter (1996). ... Appeared in one game as pinch runner (1997).
CAREER HITTING (MLB): 26-for-208 (.125), 13 R, 5 2B, 0 3B, 0 HR, 6 RBI.

Year League	W	L	Pct.	ERA	G	GS	CG	ShO	Sv.-Opp.	IP	H	R	ER	HR	BB-IBB	SO
1990—Burlington (Appl.)	3	1	.750	3.50	8	1	0	0	0-...	18.0	16	11	7	1	6-0	17
—Watertown (NY-Penn)	3	0	1.000	3.38	7	4	0	0	0-...	32.0	33	15	12	3	11-0	28
1991—Columbus (S.Atl.)	8	6	.571	4.20	22	19	2	0	0-...	115.2	101	70	54	3	70-1	136
1992—Canton/Akron (East.)	11	9	.550	3.60	27	*27	2	0	0-...	172.2	143	77	69	8	•80-3	146
—Cleveland (A.L.)	0	2	.000	4.98	4	4	0	0	0-0	21.2	23	14	12	3	16-0	16
1993—Canton/Akron (East.)	2	1	.667	0.39	6	6	0	0	0-...	23.0	15	2	1	0	8-0	21
—Cleveland (A.L.)	0	0	...	3.38	3	3	0	0	0-0	13.1	11	6	5	2	6-0	7
1994—Charlotte (I.L.)	6	10	.375	4.25	28	28	0	0	0-...	165.1	179	85	78	*26	64-1	152
1995—New York (N.L.)■	9	7	.563	4.26	29	25	0	0	0-0	160.2	160	82	76	23	54-2	123
1996—New York (N.L.)	6	7	.462	3.30	51	2	0	0	1-3	90.0	95	46	33	9	33-8	83
1997—New York (N.L.)	8	12	.400	4.00	32	32	1	1	0-0	193.2	194	89	86	21	76-7	157
1998—New York (N.L.)	1	4	.200	5.68	10	10	1	0	0-0	57.0	68	38	36	8	25-4	39
—Los Angeles (N.L.)■	7	3	.700	4.05	20	20	2	1	0-0	124.1	120	64	56	15	38-1	78
1999—Los Angeles (N.L.)	0	1	.000	4.91	2	0	0	0	0-0	7.1	10	4	4	1	2-0	1
—Detroit (A.L.)■	14	12	.538	4.60	31	31	2	0	0-0	191.2	209	108	98	24	70-1	119
2000—Detroit (A.L.)	6	11	.353	5.58	24	21	0	0	0-0	119.1	143	79	74	17	44-1	57
—West Michigan (Midw.)	1	0	1.000	0.00	1	1	0	0	0-...	6.0	1	0	0	0	1-0	6
—Toledo (I.L.)	0	1	.000	7.94	1	1	0	0	0-...	5.2	11	5	5	0	0-0	3
2001—Detroit (A.L.)	4	8	.333	7.33	15	15	0	0	0-0	81.0	118	69	66	19	41-2	48
—Houston (N.L.)■	7	3	.700	5.09	19	14	0	0	0-0	86.2	85	53	49	18	33-1	49
2002—Houston (N.L.)	4	10	.286	5.34	22	16	0	0	0-0	86.0	101	57	51	11	34-5	57
—New Orleans (PCL)	0	0	...	0.00	1	1	0	0	0-...	3.0	2	0	0	0	1-0	2
—Round Rock (Texas)	1	1	.500	3.00	2	2	0	0	0-...	9.0	8	3	3	0	2-0	7
A.L. totals (5 years)	24	33	.421	5.37	77	74	2	0	0-0	427.0	504	276	255	65	177-4	247
N.L. totals (7 years)	42	47	.472	4.37	185	119	4	2	1-3	805.2	833	433	391	106	295-28	587
Major League totals (10 years)	66	80	.452	4.72	262	193	6	2	1-3	1232.2	1337	709	646	171	472-32	834

DIVISION SERIES RECORD

Year League	W	L	Pct.	ERA	G	GS	CG	ShO	Sv.-Opp.	IP	H	R	ER	HR	BB-IBB	SO
2001—Houston (N.L.)	0	1	.000	0.00	1	1	0	0	0-0	5.0	4	1	0	0	2-0	0

MOEHLER, BRIAN P

PERSONAL: Born December 31, 1971, in Rockingham, N.C. ... 6-3/235. ... Throws right, bats right. ... Full name: Brian Merritt Moehler.
HIGH SCHOOL: Richmond (N.C.) South.
COLLEGE: UNC Greensboro.
TRANSACTIONS/CAREER NOTES: Selected by Detroit Tigers organization in sixth round of free-agent draft (June 3, 1993). ... On disabled list (August 9-22, 1997). ... On suspended list (May 3-13, 1999). ... On Detroit disabled list (April 17-May 19, 2000); included rehabilitation assignment to West Michigan (May 12-19). ... On Detroit disabled list (April 7, 2001-remainder of season); included rehabilitation assignment to Toledo (May 20-June 1). ... On Detroit disabled list (March 22-July 3, 2002); included rehabilitation assignment to Lakeland (June 1-10) and Toledo (June 11-27). ... Traded by Tigers with IF Matt Boone to Cincinnati Reds for SS David Espinosa and two players to be named later (July 23, 2002); Tigers acquired OF Gary Varner (August 30, 2002) and P Jorge Cordova (September 24, 2002) to complete deal. ... On Cincinnati disabled list (August 28-September 13, 2002). ... Granted free agency (October 28, 2002).
CAREER HITTING (MLB): 0-for-26 (.000), 1 R, 0 2B, 0 3B, 0 HR, 0 RBI.

Year League	W	L	Pct.	ERA	G	GS	CG	ShO	Sv.-Opp.	IP	H	R	ER	HR	BB-IBB	SO
1993—Niagara Falls (NY-Penn)	6	5	.545	3.22	12	11	0	0	0-...	58.2	51	33	21	3	27-0	38
1994—Lakeland (FSL)	12	12	.500	3.01	26	25	5	2	0-...	164.2	153	66	55	3	65-0	92
1995—Jacksonville (Sou.)	8	10	.444	4.82	28	27	0	0	0-...	162.1	176	94	87	14	52-1	89
1996—Jacksonville (Sou.)	*15	6	.714	3.48	28	28	1	0	0-...	173.1	186	80	67	9	50-2	120
—Detroit (A.L.)	0	1	.000	4.35	2	2	0	0	0-0	10.1	11	10	5	1	8-1	2
1997—Detroit (A.L.)	11	12	.478	4.67	31	31	2	1	0-0	175.1	198	97	91	22	61-1	97
1998—Detroit (A.L.)	14	13	.519	3.90	33	33	4	3	0-0	221.1	220	103	96	30	56-1	123
1999—Detroit (A.L.)	10	*16	.385	5.04	32	32	2	2	0-0	196.1	229	116	110	22	59-5	106
2000—Detroit (A.L.)	12	9	.571	4.50	29	29	2	0	0-0	178.0	222	99	89	20	40-0	103
—West Michigan (Midw.)	0	1	.000	4.26	1	1	0	0	0-...	6.1	5	3	3	1	1-0	4
2001—Detroit (A.L.)	0	0	...	3.38	1	1	0	0	0-0	8.0	6	3	3	0	1-0	2
—Toledo (I.L.)	0	2	.000	4.35	2	2	0	0	0-...	10.1	12	6	5	2	2-0	6
2002—Lakeland (FSL)	1	1	.500	2.92	2	2	0	0	0-...	12.1	10	9	4	2	1-0	7
—Toledo (I.L.)	2	1	.667	4.88	4	4	0	0	0-...	24.0	28	15	13	3	3-0	7
—Detroit (A.L.)	1	1	.500	2.29	3	3	0	0	0-0	19.2	17	5	5	3	2-0	13
—Cincinnati (N.L.)■	2	4	.333	6.02	10	9	0	0	0-0	43.1	61	34	29	8	11-0	18
A.L. totals (7 years)	48	52	.480	4.44	131	131	10	6	0-0	809.0	903	433	399	98	227-8	446
N.L. totals (1 year)	2	4	.333	6.02	10	9	0	0	0-0	43.1	61	34	29	8	11-0	18
Major League totals (7 years)	50	56	.472	4.52	141	140	10	6	0-0	852.1	964	467	428	106	238-8	464

MOELLER, CHAD C DIAMONDBACKS

PERSONAL: Born February 18, 1975, in Upland, Calif. ... 6-3/210. ... Bats right, throws right. ... Full name: Chad Edward Moeller.
HIGH SCHOOL: Upland (Calif.).
COLLEGE: Southern California.
TRANSACTIONS/CAREER NOTES: Selected by New York Yankees organization in 25th round of free-agent draft (June 3, 1993); did not sign. ... Selected by Minnesota Twins organization in seventh round of free-agent draft (June 4, 1996). ... On disabled list (July 12, 1996-remainder of season). ... On Minnesota disabled list (August 12-30, 2000). ... Traded by Twins to Arizona Diamondbacks for SS Hanley Frias (March 28, 2001).
2002 GAMES PLAYED BY POSITION (MLB): C—35.

Year	Team (League)	Pos.	BATTING														FIELDING	
			G	AB	R	H	2B	3B	HR	RBI	BB	SO	SB-CS	Avg.	OBP	SLG	E	Avg.
1996	— Elizabethton (Appl.)	C	17	59	17	21	4	0	4	13	18	9	1-2	.356	.519	.627	1	.991
1997	— Fort Wayne (Midw.)	C	108	384	58	111	18	3	9	39	48	76	11-8	.289	.386	.422	*15	.984
1998	— Fort Myers (FSL)	C	66	254	37	83	24	1	6	39	31	37	2-3	.327	.406	.500	9	.980
	— New Britain (East.)	C	58	187	21	44	10	0	6	23	24	41	2-1	.235	.332	.385	6	.987
1999	— New Britain (East.)	C	89	250	29	62	11	3	4	24	21	44	0-0	.248	.317	.364	10	.984
2000	— Salt Lake (PCL)	C	47	167	30	48	13	1	5	20	9	45	0-1	.287	.322	.467	2	.993
	— Minnesota (A.L.)	C	48	128	13	27	3	1	1	9	9	33	1-0	.211	.261	.273	6	.979
2001	— Tucson (PCL)■	C	78	274	41	75	20	0	8	36	25	54	1-4	.274	.337	.434	5	.989
	— Arizona (N.L.)	C	25	56	8	13	0	1	1	2	6	12	0-0	.232	.306	.321	0	1.000
2002	— Tucson (PCL)	C	60	211	37	67	8	2	10	48	29	46	1-0	.318	.401	.517	3	.994
	— Arizona (N.L.)	C	37	105	10	30	11	1	2	16	17	23	0-1	.286	.385	.467	1	.997
American League totals (1 year)			48	128	13	27	3	1	1	9	9	33	1-0	.211	.261	.273	6	.979
National League totals (2 years)			62	161	18	43	11	2	3	18	23	35	0-1	.267	.359	.416	1	.998
Major League totals (3 years)			110	289	31	70	14	3	4	27	32	68	1-1	.242	.317	.353	7	.990

DIVISION SERIES RECORD

Year	Team (League)	Pos.	BATTING														FIELDING	
			G	AB	R	H	2B	3B	HR	RBI	BB	SO	SB-CS	Avg.	OBP	SLG	E	Avg.
2002	— Arizona (N.L.)	C	3	5	0	2	0	0	0	0	0	1	0-0	.400	.400	.400	0	1.000

MOHR, DUSTAN — OF — TWINS

PERSONAL: Born June 19, 1976, in Hattiesburg, Miss. ... 6-0/210. ... Bats right, throws right. ... Full name: Dustan Kyle Mohr.

HIGH SCHOOL: Oak Grove (Miss.).

COLLEGE: Alabama.

TRANSACTIONS/CAREER NOTES: Selected by California Angels organization in 20th round of free-agent draft (June 2, 1994); did not sign. ... Selected by Cleveland Indians organization in ninth round of free-agent draft (June 3, 1997). ... Released by Indians (March 31, 2000). ... Signed by Minnesota Twins organization (April 1, 2000). ... On disabled list (August 24-31, 2000).

STATISTICAL NOTES: Led New York-Pennsylvania League outfielders with 140 putouts and 152 total chances in 1997. ... Tied for New York-Pennsylvania League lead in double plays by outfielder with 11 in 1997. ... Tied for Carolina League lead in double plays by outfielder with four in 1999.

2002 GAMES PLAYED BY POSITION (MLB): OF—113; DH—3.

Year	Team (League)	Pos.	BATTING														FIELDING	
			G	AB	R	H	2B	3B	HR	RBI	BB	SO	SB-CS	Avg.	OBP	SLG	E	Avg.
1997	— Watertown (NY-Penn)	OF	74	275	52	80	20	2	7	53	31	76	3-6	.291	.366	.455	1	*.993
1998	— Kinston (Caro.)	OF	134	491	60	119	23	9	19	65	39	146	8-4	.242	.309	.442	7	.968
1999	— Akron (East.)	OF	12	42	3	7	2	1	0	2	5	7	0-1	.167	.255	.262	0	1.000
	— Kinston (Caro.)	OF	112	429	46	120	29	3	8	60	26	104	6-6	.280	.322	.417	6	.973
2000	— Fort Myers (FSL)■	OF	101	370	58	98	19	2	11	75	35	65	7-4	.265	.338	.416	4	.978
2001	— New Britain (East.)	OF	135	518	90	174	41	3	24	91	49	111	9-9	.336	.395	.566	6	.978
	— Minnesota (A.L.)	OF-DH	20	51	6	12	2	0	0	4	5	17	1-1	.235	.298	.275	0	1.000
2002	— Minnesota (A.L.)	OF-DH	120	383	55	103	23	2	12	45	31	86	6-3	.269	.325	.433	2	.992
Major League totals (2 years)			140	434	61	115	25	2	12	49	36	103	7-4	.265	.322	.415	2	.993

DIVISION SERIES RECORD

Year	Team (League)	Pos.	BATTING														FIELDING	
			G	AB	R	H	2B	3B	HR	RBI	BB	SO	SB-CS	Avg.	OBP	SLG	E	Avg.
2002	— Minnesota (A.L.)	OF	4	2	1	2	1	0	0	0	1	0	0-0	1.000	1.000	1.500	0	1.000

CHAMPIONSHIP SERIES RECORD

Year	Team (League)	Pos.	BATTING														FIELDING	
			G	AB	R	H	2B	3B	HR	RBI	BB	SO	SB-CS	Avg.	OBP	SLG	E	Avg.
2002	— Minnesota (A.L.)	OF	5	12	3	5	1	0	0	0	0	4	1-0	.417	.417	.500	0	1.000

MOLINA, BENGIE — C — ANGELS

PERSONAL: Born July 20, 1974, in Rio Pedras, Puerto Rico. ... 5-11/210. ... Bats right, throws right. ... Full name: Benjamin Jose Molina. ... Brother of Jose Molina, catcher, Anaheim Angels.

HIGH SCHOOL: Maestra Ladi (Puerto Rico).

JUNIOR COLLEGE: Arizona Western.

TRANSACTIONS/CAREER NOTES: Signed as non-drafted free agent by California Angels organization (May 23, 1993). ... Angels franchise renamed Anaheim Angels for 1997 season. ... On Vancouver disabled list (May 13-22, 1998). ... On Edmonton disabled list (June 4-14, 1999). ... On Anaheim disabled list (May 5-June 27, 2001); included rehabilitation assignments to Rancho Cucamonga (June 9-11, June 17-18 and June 26-27) and Salt Lake (June 19-26). ... On Anaheim disabled list (July 17-August 1, 2002); included rehabilitation assignment to Rancho Cucamonga (July 30-August 1).

HONORS: Won A.L. Gold Glove as catcher (2002).

STATISTICAL NOTES: Led Texas League catchers with 81 assists and nine double plays in 1996. ... Career major league grand slams: 1.

2002 GAMES PLAYED BY POSITION (MLB): C—121.

Year	Team (League)	Pos.	BATTING														FIELDING	
			G	AB	R	H	2B	3B	HR	RBI	BB	SO	SB-CS	Avg.	OBP	SLG	E	Avg.
1993	— Arizona Angels (Ariz.)	C	27	80	9	21	6	2	0	10	10	4	0-2	.263	.348	.388	0	1.000
1994	— Cedar Rapids (Midw.)	C	48	171	14	48	8	0	3	16	8	12	1-2	.281	.324	.380	10	.975
1995	— Vancouver (PCL)		2	2	0	0	0	0	0	0	0	1	0-0	.000	.000	.000	0	1.000
	— Cedar Rapids (Midw.)	C	39	133	15	39	9	0	4	17	15	11	1-1	.293	.367	.451	7	.978
	— Lake Elsinore (Calif.)	C	27	96	21	37	7	2	2	12	8	7	0-0	.385	.450	.563	1	.995
1996	— Midland (Texas)	C	108	365	45	100	21	2	8	54	25	25	0-1	.274	.327	.408	7	.990
1997	— Lake Elsinore (Calif.)	C	36	149	18	42	10	2	4	33	7	9	0-1	.282	.308	.456	1	.996
	— Midland (Texas)	C	29	106	18	35	8	0	6	30	10	7	0-0	.330	.381	.575	2	.978

Year	Team (League)	Pos.	BATTING														FIELDING	
			G	AB	R	H	2B	3B	HR	RBI	BB	SO	SB-CS	Avg.	OBP	SLG	E	Avg.
1998—	Vancouver (PCL)	C	49	184	13	54	9	1	1	22	5	14	1-1	.293	.311	.370	5	.986
	—Midland (Texas)	C	41	154	28	55	8	0	9	39	14	7	0-1	.357	.419	.584	3	.988
	—Anaheim (A.L.)	C	2	1	0	0	0	0	0	0	0	0	0-0	.000	.000	.000	0	1.000
1999—	Edmonton (PCL)	C-DH	65	241	28	69	16	0	7	41	15	17	1-2	.286	.338	.440	3	.993
	—Anaheim (A.L.)	C	31	101	8	26	5	0	1	10	6	6	0-1	.257	.312	.337	2	.991
2000—	Anaheim (A.L.)	C-DH	130	473	59	133	20	2	14	71	23	33	1-0	.281	.318	.421	7	.991
2001—	Anaheim (A.L.)	C-DH	96	325	31	85	11	0	6	40	16	51	0-1	.262	.309	.351	5	.991
	—Rancho Cuca. (Calif.)	C	3	11	1	6	1	0	0	2	0	1	0-0	.545	.545	.636	0	1.000
	—Salt Lake (PCL)	C	5	18	2	5	1	0	0	3	2	3	0-0	.278	.350	.333	0	1.000
2002—	Anaheim (A.L.)	C	122	428	34	105	18	0	5	47	15	34	0-0	.245	.274	.322	1	*.999
	—Rancho Cuca. (Calif.)	C	1	2	0	1	0	0	0	0	1	0	0-0	.500	.750	.500	0	1.000
Major League totals (5 years)			381	1328	132	349	54	2	26	168	60	124	1-2	.263	.301	.365	15	.993

DIVISION SERIES RECORD

Year	Team (League)	Pos.	BATTING														FIELDING	
			G	AB	R	H	2B	3B	HR	RBI	BB	SO	SB-CS	Avg.	OBP	SLG	E	Avg.
2002—	Anaheim (A.L.)	C	4	15	0	4	2	0	0	2	0	1	0-0	.267	.267	.400	0	1.000

CHAMPIONSHIP SERIES RECORD

Year	Team (League)	Pos.	BATTING														FIELDING	
			G	AB	R	H	2B	3B	HR	RBI	BB	SO	SB-CS	Avg.	OBP	SLG	E	Avg.
2002—	Anaheim (A.L.)	C	5	14	0	3	0	1	0	2	1	2	0-0	.214	.313	.357	0	1.000

WORLD SERIES RECORD

NOTES: Member of World Series championship team (2002).

Year	Team (League)	Pos.	BATTING														FIELDING	
			G	AB	R	H	2B	3B	HR	RBI	BB	SO	SB-CS	Avg.	OBP	SLG	E	Avg.
2002—	Anaheim (A.L.)	C	7	21	2	6	2	0	0	2	3	1	0-0	.286	.375	.381	1	.979

MOLINA, GABE — P — CARDINALS

PERSONAL: Born May 3, 1975, in Denver. ... 6-1/220. ... Throws right, bats right. ... Full name: Cruz Gabriel Molina.

HIGH SCHOOL: John F. Kennedy (Denver).

COLLEGE: Arizona State.

TRANSACTIONS/CAREER NOTES: Selected by Baltimore Orioles organization in 21st round of free-agent draft (June 4, 1996). ... Traded by Orioles with OF B.J. Surhoff to Atlanta Braves for OF Trenidad Hubbard, C Fernando Lunar and P Luis Rivera (July 31, 2000). ... Granted free agency (December 21, 2000). ... Signed by Florida Marlins organization (January 10, 2001). ... Granted free agency (October 15, 2001). ... Signed by St. Louis Cardinals organization (November 21, 2001).

CAREER HITTING (MLB): 0-for-0 (.000), 0 R, 0 2B, 0 3B, 0 HR, 0 RBI.

Year	League	W	L	Pct.	ERA	G	GS	CG	ShO	Sv.-Opp.	IP	H	R	ER	HR	BB-IBB	SO
1996—	Bluefield (Appl.)	4	0	1.000	3.60	23	0	0	0	7-...	30.0	29	12	12	1	13-1	33
1997—	Delmarva (S.Atl.)	8	6	.571	2.18	46	0	0	0	7-...	91.0	59	24	22	3	32-5	119
1998—	Bowie (East.)	3	2	.600	3.36	47	0	0	0	24-...	61.2	48	24	23	5	27-0	75
1999—	Rochester (I.L.)	2	2	.500	3.14	45	0	0	0	18-...	57.1	45	22	20	3	23-1	58
	—Baltimore (A.L.)	1	2	.333	6.65	20	0	0	0	0-1	23.0	22	19	17	4	16-1	14
2000—	Baltimore (A.L.)	0	0	...	9.00	9	0	0	0	0-0	13.0	25	14	13	2	9-0	8
	—Rochester (I.L.)	1	2	.333	4.94	18	4	0	0	5-...	27.1	30	16	15	3	10-0	26
	—Richmond (I.L.)■	1	0	1.000	3.60	9	0	0	0	3-...	10.0	7	5	4	2	3-0	9
	—Atlanta (N.L.)	0	0	...	9.00	2	0	0	0	0-0	2.0	3	4	2	1	1-0	1
2001—	Calgary (PCL)■	5	9	.357	5.89	40	16	0	0	0-...	107.0	126	75	70	14	39-1	105
2002—	Memphis (PCL)■	5	4	.556	2.15	56	0	0	0	12-...	71.0	59	21	17	7	24-1	54
	—St. Louis (N.L.)	1	0	1.000	1.59	12	0	0	0	0-0	11.1	6	2	2	1	6-0	4
A.L. totals (2 years)		1	2	.333	7.50	29	0	0	0	0-1	36.0	47	33	30	6	25-1	22
N.L. totals (2 years)		1	0	1.000	2.70	14	0	0	0	0-0	13.1	9	6	4	2	7-0	5
Major League totals (3 years)		2	2	.500	6.20	43	0	0	0	0-1	49.1	56	39	34	8	32-1	27

MOLINA, IZZY — C — ORIOLES

PERSONAL: Born June 3, 1971, in New York. ... 6-1/224. ... Bats right, throws right. ... Full name: Islay Molina.

HIGH SCHOOL: Columbus (Miami).

TRANSACTIONS/CAREER NOTES: Selected by Oakland Athletics organization in 22nd round of free-agent draft (June 4, 1990). ... Granted free agency (December 21, 1997). ... Re-signed by A's organization (December 22, 1997). ... Granted free agency (October 15, 1998). ... Signed by Arizona Diamondbacks organization (December 17, 1998). ... Traded by Diamondbacks with P Ben Ford to New York Yankees for P Darren Holmes and cash (March 30, 1999). ... Granted free agency (October 15, 1999). ... Signed by Kansas City Royals organization (November 16, 1999). ... On Omaha disabled list (April 6-13, 2000). ... Granted free agency (October 18, 2000). ... Signed by Toronto Blue Jays organization (December 13, 2000). ... Granted free agency (October 15, 2001). ... Signed by Baltimore Orioles organization (February 4, 2002).

STATISTICAL NOTES: Tied for Arizona League lead in errors by catcher with six in 1990. ... Tied for Midwest League lead in double plays by catcher with eight in 1991. ... Tied for California League lead in grounding into double plays with 20 in 1992. ... Led California League catchers with 716 putouts, 139 assists, 871 total chances and 28 passed balls in 1992. ... Led California League catchers with 740 putouts, 119 assists, 15 errors, 874 total chances, 11 double plays and 20 passed balls in 1993. ... Led Southern League catchers with 831 total chances and 14 passed balls in 1994. ... Led Southern League catchers with 74 assists and 11 double plays in 1995.

2002 GAMES PLAYED BY POSITION (MLB): C—1.

Year	Team (League)	Pos.	BATTING														FIELDING	
			G	AB	R	H	2B	3B	HR	RBI	BB	SO	SB-CS	Avg.	OBP	SLG	E	Avg.
1990—	Ariz. Athletics (Ariz.)	C-1B	39	127	20	43	12	2	0	18	9	22	5-0	.339	.383	.465	‡6	.979
1991—	Madison (Midw.)	C	95	316	35	89	16	1	3	45	15	38	6-4	.282	.323	.367	8	.987
1992—	Reno (Calif.)	C	116	436	71	113	17	2	10	75	39	57	8-7	.259	.326	.376	16	.982
	—Tacoma (PCL)	C	10	36	3	7	0	1	0	5	2	6	1-0	.194	.237	.250	0	1.000
1993—	Modesto (Calif.)	C-OF	125	444	61	116	26	5	6	69	44	85	2-8	.261	.325	.383	†15	.983

Year	Team (League)	Pos.	G	AB	R	H	2B	3B	HR	RBI	BB	SO	SB-CS	Avg.	OBP	SLG	E	Avg.
									BATTING								FIELDING	
1994—	Huntsville (Sou.)	C	116	388	31	84	17	2	8	50	16	47	5-1	.216	.252	.332	12	.986
1995—	Edmonton (PCL)	C	2	6	0	1	0	0	0	0	0	2	0-0	.167	.167	.167	0	1.000
—	Huntsville (Sou.)	C-DH-1B	83	301	38	78	16	1	8	26	26	62	3-4	.259	.332	.399	12	.978
1996—	Edmonton (PCL)	C-1B	98	342	45	90	12	3	12	56	25	55	2-5	.263	.317	.421	7	.989
—	Oakland (A.L.)	C-DH	14	25	0	5	2	0	0	1	1	3	0-0	.200	.231	.280	0	1.000
1997—	Oakland (A.L.)	C	48	111	6	22	3	1	3	7	3	17	0-0	.198	.219	.324	2	.992
—	Edmonton (PCL)	C-DH-P	1	218	33	57	11	3	6	34	12	27	2-0	.261	.300	.422	2	.995
1998—	Edmonton (PCL)	C-D-1-P-O	86	303	29	73	15	2	8	38	17	60	3-0	.241	.287	.383	12	.980
—	Oakland (A.L.)	C-DH	6	2	1	1	0	0	0	0	0	0	0-0	.500	.500	.500	0	1.000
1999—	Columbus (I.L.)■	C-DH	97	338	44	83	16	1	4	51	18	47	4-2	.246	.281	.334	10	.985
2000—	Omaha (PCL)	C	90	311	39	73	9	1	10	36	14	55	5-4	.235	.268	.367	8	.980
2001—	Syracuse (I.L.)■	C	73	256	34	78	20	1	16	38	18	52	1-0	.305	.353	.578	6	.987
2002—	Rochester (I.L.)■	C	42	146	11	25	4	0	2	15	9	24	1-1	.171	.231	.240	6	.978
—	Baltimore (A.L.)	C	1	3	1	1	0	0	0	0	0	0	0-0	.333	.333	.333	0	1.000
—	Bowie (East.)	C	57	196	23	51	7	0	5	18	19	34	1-0	.260	.327	.372	5	.988
Major League totals (4 years)			69	141	8	29	5	1	3	8	4	20	0-0	.206	.228	.319	2	.993

RECORD AS PITCHER

Year	League	W	L	Pct.	ERA	G	GS	CG	ShO	Sv.-Opp.	IP	H	R	ER	HR	BB-IBB	SO
1997—	Edmonton (PCL)	0	0	...	0.00	1	0	0	0	0-...	.1	0	0	0	0	0-0	0
1998—	Edmonton (PCL)	0	0	...	27.00	1	0	0	0	0-...	1.0	2	3	3	1	2-0	0

MOLINA, JOSE — C — ANGELS

PERSONAL: Born June 3, 1975, in Bayamon, Puerto Rico. ... 6-1/215. ... Bats right, throws right. ... Full name: Jose Benjamin Molina Matta. ... Brother of Bengie Molina, catcher, Anaheim Angels.

HIGH SCHOOL: Maestro Ladi (Vega Alta, Puerto Rico).

TRANSACTIONS/CAREER NOTES: Selected by Chicago Cubs organization in 14th round of free-agent draft (June 3, 1993). ... On Iowa disabled list (July 31-August 10, 1999). ... On disabled list (August 4-September 5, 2000). ... Released by Cubs (November 27, 2000). ... Signed by Anaheim Angels organization (May 17, 2001). ... On Anaheim disabled list (May 21-July 1, 2001); included rehabilitation assignment to Salt Lake (June 26-July 1).

STATISTICAL NOTES: Led Southern League catchers with 108 assists and tied for lead with 21 passed balls in 1998. ... Tied for Pacific Coast League lead in errors by catcher with 11 in 2000.

2002 GAMES PLAYED BY POSITION (MLB): C—29.

Year	Team (League)	Pos.	G	AB	R	H	2B	3B	HR	RBI	BB	SO	SB-CS	Avg.	OBP	SLG	E	Avg.
									BATTING								FIELDING	
1993—	GC Cubs (GCL)	C-1B	33	78	5	17	2	0	0	4	12	12	3-2	.218	.322	.244	7	.960
—	Daytona (FSL)	C	3	7	0	1	0	0	0	1	2	0	0-1	.143	.333	.143	0	1.000
1994—	Peoria (Midw.)	C	78	253	31	58	13	1	1	33	24	61	4-3	.229	.302	.300	13	.980
1995—	Daytona (FSL)	C	82	233	27	55	9	1	1	19	29	53	1-0	.236	.336	.296	8	.987
1996—	Rockford (Midw.)	C	96	305	35	69	10	1	2	27	36	71	2-4	.226	.310	.285	11	.985
1997—	Daytona (FSL)	C	55	179	17	45	9	1	0	23	14	25	4-0	.251	.306	.313	8	.981
—	Iowa (A.A.)	C	1	3	0	1	0	0	0	0	1	1	0-0	.333	.500	.333	0	1.000
—	Orlando (Sou.)	C	37	99	10	17	3	0	1	15	12	28	0-1	.172	.267	.232	2	.993
1998—	West Tenn (Sou.)	C-1B	109	320	33	71	10	1	2	28	32	74	1-5	.222	.296	.278	8	.991
1999—	West Tenn (Sou.)	C	14	35	2	6	3	0	0	5	2	14	0-0	.171	.211	.257	2	.982
—	Iowa (PCL)	C	74	240	24	63	11	1	4	26	20	54	0-1	.263	.327	.367	7	.987
—	Chicago (N.L.)	C	10	19	3	5	1	0	0	1	2	4	0-0	.263	.333	.316	0	1.000
2000—	Iowa (PCL)	C-1B	76	248	22	58	9	0	1	17	23	61	1-4	.234	.296	.282	†11	.981
2001—	Salt Lake (PCL)■	C	61	213	29	64	11	1	5	31	14	49	1-2	.300	.349	.432	2	.996
—	Anaheim (A.L.)	C	15	37	8	10	3	0	2	4	3	8	0-0	.270	.325	.514	0	1.000
2002—	Salt Lake (PCL)	C	79	290	30	89	14	2	4	43	12	60	0-3	.307	.341	.410	4	.994
—	Anaheim (A.L.)	C	29	70	5	19	3	0	0	5	5	15	0-2	.271	.312	.314	3	.983
American League totals (2 years)			44	107	13	29	6	0	2	9	8	23	0-2	.271	.316	.383	3	.988
National League totals (1 year)			10	19	3	5	1	0	0	1	2	4	0-0	.263	.333	.316	0	1.000
Major League totals (3 years)			54	126	16	34	7	0	2	10	10	27	0-2	.270	.319	.373	3	.990

CHAMPIONSHIP SERIES RECORD

Year	Team (League)	Pos.	G	AB	R	H	2B	3B	HR	RBI	BB	SO	SB-CS	Avg.	OBP	SLG	E	Avg.
									BATTING								FIELDING	
2002—	Anaheim (A.L.)	C	3	1	0	0	0	0	0	0	0	0	0-0	.000	.000	.000	0	1.000

WORLD SERIES RECORD

NOTES: Member of World Series championship team (2002).

Year	Team (League)	Pos.	G	AB	R	H	2B	3B	HR	RBI	BB	SO	SB-CS	Avg.	OBP	SLG	E	Avg.
									BATTING								FIELDING	
2002—	Anaheim (A.L.)	C	3	0	0	0	0	0	0	0	0	0	0-0	...	...	...	0	1.000

MONDESI, RAUL — OF — YANKEES

PERSONAL: Born March 12, 1971, in San Cristobal, Dominican Republic. ... 5-11/230. ... Bats right, throws right. ... Name pronounced MON-de-see.

HIGH SCHOOL: Liceo Manuel Maria Valencia (Dominican Republic).

TRANSACTIONS/CAREER NOTES: Signed as non-drafted free agent by Los Angeles Dodgers organization (June 6, 1988). ... On Bakersfield disabled list (May 8-July 5, 1991). ... On Albuquerque disabled list (May 8-16, 1992). ... On San Antonio disabled list (June 2-16, June 24-August 10 and August 24, 1992-remainder of season). ... Traded by Dodgers with P Pedro Borbon to Toronto Blue Jays for OF Shawn Green and 2B Jorge Nunez (November 8, 1999). ... On disabled list (July 22-September 20, 2000). ... Traded by Blue Jays to New York Yankees for P Scott Wiggins (July 1, 2002).

RECORDS: Shares major league single-season record for fewest double plays by outfielder, 150 or more games—0 (1997).
HONORS: Named N.L. Rookie Player of the Year by The Sporting News (1994). ... Named N.L. Rookie of the Year by Baseball Writers' Association of America (1994). ... Won N.L. Gold Glove as outfielder (1995 and 1997).
STATISTICAL NOTES: Led N.L. outfielders with 16 assists in 1994 and 16 in 1995. ... Career major league grand slams: 4.
2002 GAMES PLAYED BY POSITION (MLB): OF—132; DH—14.

			BATTING														FIELDING	
Year	Team (League)	Pos.	G	AB	R	H	2B	3B	HR	RBI	BB	SO	SB-CS	Avg.	OBP	SLG	E	Avg.
1988—	Dom. Dodgers (DSL)	OF	36	117	21	26	10	1	2	44	23	36	4-0	.222	...	.376	...	...
1989—	Dom. Dodgers (DSL)	OF	46	156	32	43	15	3	2	27	16	26	8-0	.276	...	.449	...	...
1990—	Great Falls (Pio.)	OF	44	175	35	53	10	4	8	31	11	30	30-6	.303	.349	.543	1	.986
1991—	Bakersfield (Calif.)	OF	28	106	23	30	7	2	3	13	5	21	9-4	.283	.330	.472	3	.940
—	San Antonio (Texas)	OF	53	213	32	58	11	5	5	26	8	47	8-3	.272	.307	.441	4	.964
—	Albuquerque (PCL)	OF	2	9	3	3	0	1	0	0	0	1	1-0	.333	.333	.556	1	.000
1992—	Albuquerque (PCL)	OF	35	138	23	43	4	7	4	15	9	35	2-3	.312	.358	.529	7	.933
—	San Antonio (Texas)	OF	18	68	8	18	2	2	2	14	1	24	3-2	.265	.264	.441	1	.974
1993—	Albuquerque (PCL)	OF	110	425	65	119	22	7	12	65	18	85	13-10	.280	.309	.449	10	.957
—	Los Angeles (N.L.)	OF	42	86	13	25	3	1	4	10	4	16	4-1	.291	.322	.488	3	.951
1994—	Los Angeles (N.L.)	OF	112	434	63	133	27	8	16	56	16	78	11-8	.306	.333	.516	8	.965
1995—	Los Angeles (N.L.)	OF	139	536	91	153	23	6	26	88	33	96	27-4	.285	.328	.496	6	.980
1996—	Los Angeles (N.L.)	OF	157	634	98	188	40	7	24	88	32	122	14-7	.297	.334	.495	•12	.967
1997—	Los Angeles (N.L.)	OF	159	616	95	191	42	5	30	87	44	105	32-15	.310	.360	.541	4	.989
1998—	Los Angeles (N.L.)	OF	148	580	85	162	26	5	30	90	30	112	16-10	.279	.316	.497	6	.980
1999—	Los Angeles (N.L.)	OF	159	601	98	152	29	5	33	99	71	134	36-9	.253	.332	.483	6	.982
2000—	Toronto (A.L.)■	OF	96	388	78	105	22	2	24	67	32	73	22-6	.271	.329	.523	7	.967
2001—	Toronto (A.L.)	OF	149	572	88	144	26	4	27	84	73	128	30-11	.252	.342	.453	8	.972
2002—	Toronto (A.L.)	OF-DH	75	299	51	67	16	1	15	45	31	57	9-2	.224	.301	.435	2	.984
—	New York (A.L.)■	OF-DH	71	270	39	65	18	0	11	43	28	46	6-4	.241	.315	.430	4	.969
American League totals (3 years)			391	1529	256	381	82	7	77	239	164	304	67-23	.249	.326	.463	21	.972
National League totals (7 years)			916	3487	543	1004	190	37	163	518	230	663	140-54	.288	.334	.504	45	.977
Major League totals (10 years)			1307	5016	799	1385	272	44	240	757	394	967	207-77	.276	.331	.491	66	.975

DIVISION SERIES RECORD

			BATTING														FIELDING	
Year	Team (League)	Pos.	G	AB	R	H	2B	3B	HR	RBI	BB	SO	SB-CS	Avg.	OBP	SLG	E	Avg.
1995—	Los Angeles (N.L.)	OF	3	9	0	2	0	0	0	1	0	2	0-0	.222	.300	.222	0	1.000
1996—	Los Angeles (N.L.)	OF	3	11	0	2	2	0	0	1	0	4	0-0	.182	.182	.364	0	1.000
2002—	New York (A.L.)	OF	4	12	1	3	0	0	0	1	3	1	0-0	.250	.471	.250	0	1.000
Division series totals (3 years)			10	32	1	7	2	0	0	3	3	7	0-0	.219	.342	.281	0	1.000

ALL-STAR GAME RECORD

	AB	R	H	2B	3B	HR	RBI	BB	SO	SB-CS	Avg.	OBP	SLG	E	Avg.
All-Star Game totals (1 year)	1	0	0	0	0	0	0	0	0	0-0	.000	.000	.000	0	1.000

MONROE, CRAIG — OF — TIGERS

PERSONAL: Born February 27, 1977, in Texarkana, Texas. ... 6-1/195. ... Bats right, throws right. ... Full name: Craig Keystone Monroe.
HIGH SCHOOL: Texas (Texarkana, Texas).
TRANSACTIONS/CAREER NOTES: Selected by Texas Rangers organization in eighth round of free-agent draft (June 1, 1995). ... Claimed on waivers by Detroit Tigers (February 1, 2002).
STATISTICAL NOTES: Tied for Florida State League lead with 17 assists by outfielder in 1998. ... Led Florida State League outfielders with 326 putouts and 346 total chances in 1999.
2002 GAMES PLAYED BY POSITION (MLB): OF—9; DH—3.

			BATTING														FIELDING	
Year	Team (League)	Pos.	G	AB	R	H	2B	3B	HR	RBI	BB	SO	SB-CS	Avg.	OBP	SLG	E	Avg.
1995—	GC Rangers (GCL)	OF	54	193	22	48	6	2	0	33	18	25	13-2	.249	.316	.301	4	.962
1996—	Charl., S.C. (S.Atl.)	OF	49	153	11	23	11	1	0	9	18	48	2-2	.150	.253	.235	4	.954
—	Hudson Valley (NY-P)	OF	67	268	53	74	16	6	5	29	23	63	21-7	.276	.336	.437	6	.938
1997—	Charlotte (FSL)	OF	92	328	54	77	23	1	7	41	44	80	24-1	.235	.320	.375	7	.959
1998—	Charlotte (FSL)	OF	132	472	73	114	26	7	17	76	66	102	50-13	.242	.334	.434	11	.951
1999—	Charlotte (FSL)	OF	130	480	77	125	21	1	17	81	42	102	40-15	.260	.321	.415	7	.980
—	Oklahoma (PCL)	OF	6	16	2	4	1	0	0	1	1	4	0-0	.250	.294	.313	0	1.000
2000—	Tulsa (Texas)	OF	120	464	89	131	34	5	20	89	64	91	12-13	.282	.366	.506	*12	.948
2001—	Oklahoma (PCL)	OF	114	410	60	115	25	5	20	75	46	85	10-8	.280	.358	.512	5	.975
—	Texas (A.L.)	OF-DH	27	52	8	11	1	0	2	5	6	18	2-0	.212	.293	.346	0	1.000
2002—	Toledo (I.L.)■	OF	99	358	61	115	30	4	10	49	35	57	7-3	.321	.379	.511	3	.983
—	Detroit (A.L.)	OF-DH	13	25	3	3	1	0	1	1	0	5	0-2	.120	.154	.280	1	.950
Major League totals (2 years)			40	77	11	14	2	0	3	6	6	23	2-2	.182	.250	.325	1	.985

MORA, MELVIN — OF — ORIOLES

PERSONAL: Born February 2, 1972, in Aqua Negar, Venezuela. ... 5-10/180. ... Bats right, throws right.
HIGH SCHOOL: Libertador (Venezuela).
TRANSACTIONS/CAREER NOTES: Signed as non-drafted free agent by Houston Astros organization (March 30, 1991). ... Granted free agency (October 17, 1997). ... Played in Taiwan (1998). ... Signed by New York Mets organization (July 24, 1998). ... Granted free agency (October 16, 1998). ... Re-signed by Mets organization (February 5, 1999). ... On New York disabled list (May 13-30, 2000); included rehabilitation assignment to Norfolk (May 22-30). ... Traded by Mets with 3B Mike Kinkade, P Leslie Brea and P Pat Gorman to Baltimore Orioles for SS Mike Bordick (July 28, 2000). ... On suspended list (September 13-16, 2002).
STATISTICAL NOTES: Tied for Texas League lead in double plays by outfielder with six in 1995. ... Tied for A.L. lead with five double plays by outfielder in 2002.
2002 GAMES PLAYED BY POSITION (MLB): OF—104; SS—41; 2B—12; DH—3.

Year Team (League)	Pos.	BATTING														FIELDING	
		G	AB	R	H	2B	3B	HR	RBI	BB	SO	SB-CS	Avg.	OBP	SLG	E	Avg.
1991—Dom. Astros (DSL).....		58	211	38	63	18	1	0	20	19	22	21-...	.299	...	.393	...	...
1992—GC Astros (GCL)........	OF-2B-3B	49	144	28	32	3	0	0	8	18	16	16-3	.222	.327	.243	4	.961
1993—Asheville (S.Atl.).........	2-O-3-S	108	365	66	104	22	2	2	31	36	46	20-13	.285	.356	.373	17	.936
1994—Osceola (FSL)............	OF-3B	118	425	57	120	29	4	8	46	37	60	24-16	.282	.352	.426	15	.947
1995—Jackson (Texas).........	OF-3B-2B	123	467	63	139	32	0	3	45	32	57	22-11	.298	.350	.385	6	.977
—Tucson (PCL)............	OF	2	5	3	3	0	1	0	1	2	0	1-0	.600	.714	1.000	0	1.000
1996—Jackson (Texas).........OF-2B-SS-3B		70	255	36	73	6	1	5	23	14	23	4-7	.286	.336	.376	7	.959
—Tucson (PCL)............	3B-OF-2B	62	228	35	64	11	2	3	26	17	27	3-5	.281	.328	.386	14	.912
1997—New Orleans (A.A.).....	O-3-2-S	119	370	55	95	15	3	2	38	47	52	7-7	.257	.356	.330	11	.956
1998—Mercury (Taiwan)■....		...	164	34	55	11	2	3	11	...	...	...-...	.335	...	.482	...	...
—St. Lucie (FSL)■........	2B-SS-OF	17	55	5	15	0	0	0	8	5	9	1-1	.273	.328	.273	1	.985
—Norfolk (I.L.)...........	3B-OF-2B	11	28	5	5	1	0	0	2	5	7	0-0	.179	.303	.214	2	.875
1999—Norfolk (I.L.).............SS-OF-2B-3B		82	304	55	92	17	2	8	36	41	54	18-8	.303	.393	.451	16	.942
—New York (N.L.).........OF-2B-3B-SS		66	31	6	5	0	0	0	1	4	7	2-1	.161	.278	.161	0	1.000
2000—New York (N.L.).........SS-OF-2B-3B		79	215	35	56	13	2	6	30	18	48	7-3	.260	.317	.423	8	.962
—Norfolk (I.L.).............	OF-2B-SS	8	27	7	9	2	0	0	7	7	3	2-0	.333	.471	.407	0	1.000
—Baltimore (A.L.)■.......	SS-2B	53	199	25	58	9	3	2	17	17	32	5-8	.291	.359	.397	12	.953
2001—Baltimore (A.L.).........	OF-SS-2B	128	436	49	109	28	0	7	48	41	91	11-4	.250	.329	.362	11	.974
2002—Baltimore (A.L.).........	O-S-2-D	149	557	86	130	30	4	19	64	70	108	16-10	.233	.338	.404	12	.976
American League totals (3 years)		330	1192	160	297	67	7	28	129	128	231	32-22	.249	.338	.388	35	.970
National League totals (2 years)		145	246	41	61	13	2	6	31	22	55	9-4	.248	.312	.390	8	.967
Major League totals (4 years)		475	1438	201	358	80	9	34	160	150	286	41-26	.249	.334	.388	43	.970

DIVISION SERIES RECORD

Year Team (League)	Pos.	BATTING														FIELDING	
		G	AB	R	H	2B	3B	HR	RBI	BB	SO	SB-CS	Avg.	OBP	SLG	E	Avg.
1999—New York (N.L.).........	OF	3	1	1	0	0	0	0	0	1	0	0-0	.000	.500	.000	0	1.000

CHAMPIONSHIP SERIES RECORD

Year Team (League)	Pos.	BATTING														FIELDING	
		G	AB	R	H	2B	3B	HR	RBI	BB	SO	SB-CS	Avg.	OBP	SLG	E	Avg.
1999—New York (N.L.)..........	PH-OF	6	14	3	6	0	0	1	2	2	2	2-0	.429	.500	.643	0	1.000

RECORD AS PITCHER

Year League	W	L	Pct.	ERA	G	GS	CG	ShO	Sv.	IP	H	R	ER	BB	SO
1993—Asheville (SAL)..................	0	0	...	0.00	1	0	0	0	0	.2	1	0	0	0	0
1997—New Orleans (A.A.)............	0	0	...	0.00	1	0	0	0	0	1	2	1	1	1	0

MORDECAI, MIKE IF MARLINS

PERSONAL: Born December 13, 1967, in Birmingham, Ala. ... 5-10/185. ... Bats right, throws right. ... Full name: Michael Howard Mordecai.
HIGH SCHOOL: Hewitt Trussville (Ala.).
COLLEGE: Southern Alabama.
TRANSACTIONS/CAREER NOTES: Selected by Pittsburgh Pirates organization in 33rd round of free-agent draft (June 2, 1986); did not sign. ... Selected by Atlanta Braves organization in sixth round of free-agent draft (June 5, 1989). ... On disabled list (April 8-29, 1993). ... On Atlanta disabled list (April 19-May 11, 1996); included rehabilitation assignment to Richmond (May 8-11). ... Granted free agency (December 21, 1997). ... Signed by Montreal Expos organization (March 27, 1998). ... On Montreal disabled list (June 24-July 24, 1998); included rehabilitation assignments to Jupiter (July 16-19) and Ottawa (July 19-24). ... Traded by Expos with P Carl Pavano, P Graeme Lloyd and P Justin Wayne to Florida Marlins for OF Cliff Floyd, P Claudio Vargas, 2B/OF Wilton Guerrero, cash considerations and a player to be named later (July 11, 2002); Expos acquired P Don Levinski to complete deal (August 6, 2002).
2002 GAMES PLAYED BY POSITION (MLB): 3B—35; SS—27; 2B—4; 1B—4; OF—1.

Year Team (League)	Pos.	BATTING														FIELDING	
		G	AB	R	H	2B	3B	HR	RBI	BB	SO	SB-CS	Avg.	OBP	SLG	E	Avg.
1989—Burlington (Midw.).....	SS-3B	65	241	39	61	11	1	1	22	33	43	12-5	.253	.352	.320	21	.920
—Greenville (Sou.)........	3B-2B	4	8	0	3	0	0	0	1	1	1	0-0	.375	.444	.375	0	1.000
1990—Durham (Caro.)..........	SS	72	271	42	76	11	7	3	36	42	45	10-6	.280	.379	.406	29	.920
1991—Durham (Caro.)..........	SS	109	397	52	104	15	2	4	42	40	58	30-16	.262	.330	.340	27	.945
1992—Greenville (Sou.)........	SS	65	222	31	58	13	1	4	31	29	31	9-6	.261	.344	.383	11	.964
—Richmond (I.L.)..........	SS-2B-3B	36	118	12	29	3	0	1	6	5	19	0-4	.246	.272	.297	10	.937
1993—Richmond (I.L.)..........2-S-3-O-C-1		72	205	29	55	8	1	2	14	14	33	10-2	.268	.318	.346	9	.964
1994—Richmond (I.L.)..........SS-1B-DH-3B		99	382	67	107	25	1	14	57	35	50	14-7	.280	.340	.461	22	.947
—Atlanta (N.L.).............	SS	4	4	1	1	0	0	1	3	1	0	0-0	.250	.400	1.000	0	1.000
1995—Atlanta (N.L.)............	2-1-3-S-O	69	75	10	21	6	0	3	11	9	16	0-0	.280	.353	.480	0	1.000
1996—Atlanta (N.L.)..............2B-3B-SS-1B		66	108	12	26	5	0	2	8	9	24	1-0	.241	.297	.343	2	.977
—Richmond (I.L.)..........	SS	3	11	2	2	0	0	1	2	0	3	0-0	.182	.167	.455	0	1.000
1997—Atlanta (N.L.).............3-2-S-1-DH-O		61	81	8	14	2	1	0	3	6	16	0-1	.173	.227	.222	0	1.000
—Richmond (I.L.).........2B-3B-DH-SS		31	122	23	38	10	0	3	15	9	17	0-1	.311	.361	.467	1	.989
1998—Montreal (N.L.)■........SS-2B-3B-1B		73	119	12	24	4	2	3	10	9	20	1-0	.202	.258	.345	5	.960
—Jupiter (FSL)............	2B-SS	2	8	0	0	0	0	0	0	1	3	0-0	.000	.111	.000	0	1.000
—Ottawa (I.L.)..............	SS-2B	6	22	2	5	2	0	0	1	3	3	0-0	.227	.320	.318	1	.969
1999—Montreal (N.L.)..........	2-S-3-1	109	226	29	53	10	2	5	25	20	31	2-5	.235	.297	.363	7	.970
2000—Montreal (N.L.)...........3B-SS-2B-1B		86	169	20	48	16	0	4	16	12	34	2-2	.284	.335	.450	8	.942
2001—Montreal (N.L.)...........3-2-S-C-1-O-D		96	254	28	71	17	2	3	32	19	53	2-2	.280	.330	.398	3	.985
2002—Montreal (N.L.)..........	3-2-S-1-O	55	74	9	15	4	0	0	4	8	14	1-1	.203	.289	.257	4	.948
—Florida (N.L.)■..........	SS-3B-1B	38	77	10	22	4	0	0	7	5	13	1-1	.286	.337	.338	1	.989
Major League totals (9 years)		657	1187	139	295	68	7	21	119	98	221	10-12	.249	.307	.371	30	.972

DIVISION SERIES RECORD

Year	Team (League)	Pos.	G	AB	R	H	2B	3B	HR	RBI	BB	SO	SB-CS	Avg.	OBP	SLG	E	Avg.
			BATTING														FIELDING	
1995—	Atlanta (N.L.)	PH-SS	2	3	1	2	1	0	0	2	0	0	0-0	.667	.667	1.000	0	1.000
1996—	Atlanta (N.L.)		Did not play.															

CHAMPIONSHIP SERIES RECORD

Year	Team (League)	Pos.	G	AB	R	H	2B	3B	HR	RBI	BB	SO	SB-CS	Avg.	OBP	SLG	E	Avg.
			BATTING														FIELDING	
1995—	Atlanta (N.L.)	PH-SS	2	2	0	0	0	0	0	0	0	1	0-0	.000	.000	.000	0	...
1996—	Atlanta (N.L.)	3B-PH-2B	4	4	1	1	0	0	0	0	0	1	0-0	.250	.250	.250	0	1.000
Championship series totals (2 years)			6	6	1	1	0	0	0	0	0	2	0-0	.167	.167	.167	0	1.000

WORLD SERIES RECORD

NOTES: Member of World Series championship team (1995).

Year	Team (League)	Pos.	G	AB	R	H	2B	3B	HR	RBI	BB	SO	SB-CS	Avg.	OBP	SLG	E	Avg.
			BATTING														FIELDING	
1995—	Atlanta (N.L.)	SS-DH	3	3	0	1	0	0	0	0	0	1	0-0	.333	.333	.333	0	1.000
1996—	Atlanta (N.L.)	PH	1	1	0	0	0	0	0	0	0	0	0-0	.000	.000	.000	...	...
World Series totals (2 years)			4	4	0	1	0	0	0	0	0	1	0-0	.250	.250	.250	0	1.000

MORENO, JUAN P

PERSONAL: Born February 28, 1975, in Maiquetia, Venezuela. ... 6-1/205. ... Throws left, bats left. ... Full name: Juan Carlos Moreno.
HIGH SCHOOL: Josefina Crespo (Venezuela).
TRANSACTIONS/CAREER NOTES: Signed as non-drafted free agent by Oakland Athletics organization (April 14, 1993). ... Released by Athletics (February 4, 1997). ... Missed entire 1997 season due to injury. ... Missed entire 1998 season due to injury. ... Signed by Texas Rangers organization (November 24, 1998). ... On Tulsa disabled list (April 6-May 28 and June 20-September 13, 2000). ... Granted free agency (October 18, 2000). ... Re-signed by Rangers (December 1, 2000). ... Traded by Rangers to San Diego Padres for SS Jason Moore (April 3, 2002). ... Traded by Padres to Boston Red Sox for P Andrew Hazlett (April 23, 2002). ... On Pawtucket disabled list (April 28-August 28, 2002). ... Released by Red Sox (September 10, 2002).
CAREER HITTING (MLB): 0-for-0 (.000), 0 R, 0 2B, 0 3B, 0 HR, 0 RBI.

Year	League	W	L	Pct.	ERA	G	GS	CG	ShO	Sv.-Opp.	IP	H	R	ER	HR	BB-IBB	SO
1993—	Dom. Athletics (DSL)	3	1	.750	3.33	13	3	0	0	1-...	48.2	47	25	18	...	35-...	36
1994—	Dom. Athletics (DSL)	3	1	.750	4.23	17	4	0	0	3-...	38.1	26	27	18	...	44-...	41
1995—	Arizona Athletics (Ariz.)	6	2	.750	1.21	20	0	0	0	0-...	44.2	36	10	6	1	20-0	49
1996—	West Michigan (Midw.)	4	6	.400	4.37	38	11	0	0	0-...	107.0	98	60	52	6	69-5	97
1997—		Did not play.															
1998—		Did not play.															
1999—	Tulsa (Texas)■	4	3	.571	2.30	42	0	0	0	3-...	62.2	33	20	16	5	32-2	83
2000—	Charlotte (FSL)	0	0	...	0.00	1	1	0	0	0-...	2.0	0	0	0	0	1-0	0
—	Tulsa (Texas)	0	0	...	5.40	5	0	0	0	1-...	6.2	6	4	4	0	5-0	12
2001—	Tulsa (Texas)	1	1	.500	0.00	6	0	0	0	1-...	8.2	6	1	0	0	3-0	10
—	Oklahoma (PCL)	0	0	...	1.86	7	0	0	0	0-...	9.2	4	2	2	1	2-0	13
—	Texas (A.L.)	3	3	.500	3.92	45	0	0	0	0-2	41.1	22	21	18	6	28-2	36
2002—	San Diego (N.L.)	0	0	...	7.50	4	0	0	0	0-0	6.0	6	6	5	1	10-1	3
—	Pawtucket (I.L.)■	0	0	...	10.13	3	0	0	0	0-...	2.2	2	4	3	1	3-0	1
—	Gulf Coast Red Sox (GCL)	0	1	.000	1.80	3	3	0	0	0-...	5.0	4	2	1	0	0-0	10
A.L. totals (1 year)		3	3	.500	3.92	45	0	0	0	0-2	41.1	22	21	18	6	28-2	36
N.L. totals (1 year)		0	0	...	7.50	4	0	0	0	0-0	6.0	6	6	5	1	10-1	3
Major League totals (2 years)		3	3	.500	4.37	49	0	0	0	0-2	47.1	28	27	23	7	38-3	39

MORGAN, MIKE P

PERSONAL: Born October 8, 1959, in Tulare, Calif. ... 6-2/226. ... Throws right, bats right. ... Full name: Michael Thomas Morgan.
HIGH SCHOOL: Valley (Las Vegas).
TRANSACTIONS/CAREER NOTES: Selected by Oakland Athletics organization in first round (fourth pick overall) of free-agent draft (June 6, 1978). ... On disabled list (May 14-June 27, 1980). ... Traded by A's to New York Yankees for SS Fred Stanley and a player to be named later (November 3, 1980); A's acquired 2B Brian Doyle to complete deal (November 17, 1980). ... On disabled list (April 9-22, 1981). ... Traded by Yankees with OF/1B Dave Collins, 1B Fred McGriff and cash to Toronto Blue Jays for P Dale Murray and OF/C Tom Dodd (December 9, 1982). ... On Toronto disabled list (July 2-August 23, 1983); included rehabilitation assignment to Syracuse (August 1-18). ... Selected by Seattle Mariners from Blue Jays organization in Rule 5 major league draft (December 3, 1984). ... On Seattle disabled list (April 17, 1985-remainder of season); included rehabilitation assignment to Calgary (July 19-22). ... Traded by Mariners to Baltimore Orioles for P Ken Dixon (December 9, 1987). ... On Baltimore disabled list (June 9-July 19, 1988); included rehabilitation assignment to Rochester (June 30-July 17). ... On Baltimore disabled list (August 12, 1988-remainder of season). ... Traded by Orioles to Los Angeles Dodgers for OF Mike Devereaux (March 12, 1989). ... Granted free agency (October 28, 1991). ... Signed by Chicago Cubs (December 3, 1991). ... On disabled list (June 14-29, 1993; May 9-27, June 2-22 and July 28, 1994-remainder of season). ... On Chicago disabled list (April 24-May 25, 1995); included rehabilitation assignment to Orlando (May 15-25). ... Traded by Cubs with 3B/OF Paul Torres and C Francisco Morales to St. Louis Cardinals for 3B Todd Zeile and cash (June 16, 1995). ... On St. Louis disabled list (July 4-24, 1995). ... Granted free agency (November 6, 1995). ... Re-signed by Cardinals (December 7, 1995). ... On St. Louis disabled list (March 22-May 18, 1996); included rehabilitation assignment to St. Petersburg (April 20-May 15). ... Released by Cardinals (August 28, 1996). ... Signed by Cincinnati Reds (September 4, 1996). ... On disabled list (June 8-24, 1997). ... Granted free agency (October 28, 1997). ... Signed by Minnesota Twins (December 16, 1997). ... On Minnesota disabled list (June 27-July 13 and July 15-August 16, 1998). ... Traded by Twins to Cubs for cash and a player to be named later (August 25, 1998); Twins acquired P Scott Downs to complete deal (November 3, 1998). ... Granted free agency (October 30, 1998). ... Signed by Texas Rangers organization (January 26, 1999). ... On disabled list (May 25-June 9, 1999). ... Granted free agency (November 8, 1999). ... Signed by Arizona Diamondbacks organization (January 14, 2000). ... On Arizona disabled list (April 15-July 23, 2001); included rehabilitation assignment to Tucson (July 16-23). ... Granted free agency (November 19, 2001). ... Re-signed by Diamondbacks (January 8, 2002). ... On Arizona disabled list (June 24-September 1, 2002); included rehabilitation assignment to Tucson (August 30-September 1). ... Granted free agency (November 4, 2002).
RECORDS: Holds major league record for most clubs played and pitched for in career (since 1900)—12.
CAREER HITTING (MLB): 54-for-497 (.109), 13 R, 3 2B, 1 3B, 0 HR, 15 RBI.

Year	League	W	L	Pct.	ERA	G	GS	CG	ShO	Sv.-Opp.	IP	H	R	ER	HR	BB-IBB	SO
1978—	Oakland (A.L.)	0	3	.000	7.30	3	3	1	0	0-0	12.1	19	12	10	1	8-0	0
—	Vancouver (PCL)	5	6	.455	5.58	14	14	5	1	0-...	92.0	109	67	57	5	54-2	31
1979—	Ogden (PCL)	5	5	.500	3.48	13	13	6	0	0-...	101.0	93	48	39	11	49-2	42
—	Oakland (A.L.)	2	10	.167	5.94	13	13	2	0	0-0	77.1	102	57	51	7	50-0	17
1980—	Ogden (PCL)	6	9	.400	5.40	20	20	3	0	0-...	115.0	135	79	69	7	77-4	46
1981—	Nashville (Sou.)■	8	7	.533	4.42	26	26	7	0	0-...	169.0	164	97	83	16	83-0	100
1982—	New York (A.L.)	7	11	.389	4.37	30	23	2	0	0-0	150.1	167	77	73	15	67-5	71
1983—	Toronto (A.L.)■	0	3	.000	5.16	16	4	0	0	0-0	45.1	48	26	26	6	21-0	22
—	Syracuse (I.L.)	0	3	.000	5.59	5	4	0	0	1-...	19.1	20	12	12	1	13-0	17
1984—	Syracuse (I.L.)	13	11	.542	4.07	34	28	10	•4	1-...	*185.2	167	•101	84	11	•100-3	105
1985—	Seattle (A.L.)■	1	1	.500	12.00	2	2	0	0	0-0	6.0	11	8	8	2	5-0	2
—	Calgary (PCL)	0	0	...	4.50	1	1	0	0	0-...	2.0	3	1	1	0	0-0	0
1986—	Seattle (A.L.)	11	•17	.393	4.53	37	33	9	1	1-1	216.1	243	122	109	24	86-3	116
1987—	Seattle (A.L.)	12	17	.414	4.65	34	31	8	2	0-0	207.0	245	117	107	25	53-3	85
1988—	Baltimore (A.L.)■	1	6	.143	5.43	22	10	2	0	1-1	71.1	70	45	43	6	23-1	29
—	Rochester (I.L.)	0	2	.000	4.76	3	3	0	0	0-...	17.0	19	10	9	1	6-0	7
1989—	Los Angeles (N.L.)■	8	11	.421	2.53	40	19	0	0	0-1	152.2	130	51	43	6	33-8	72
1990—	Los Angeles (N.L.)	11	15	.423	3.75	33	33	6	•4	0-0	211.0	216	100	88	19	60-5	106
1991—	Los Angeles (N.L.)	14	10	.583	2.78	34	33	5	1	1-1	236.1	197	85	73	12	61-10	140
1992—	Chicago (N.L.)■	16	8	.667	2.55	34	34	6	1	0-0	240.0	203	80	68	14	79-10	123
1993—	Chicago (N.L.)	10	15	.400	4.03	32	32	1	1	0-0	207.2	206	100	93	15	74-8	111
1994—	Chicago (N.L.)	2	10	.167	6.69	15	15	1	0	0-0	80.2	111	65	60	12	35-2	57
1995—	Orlando (Sou.)	0	2	.000	7.59	2	2	0	0	0-...	10.2	13	9	9	1	7-0	5
—	Chicago (N.L.)	2	1	.667	2.19	4	4	0	0	0-0	24.2	19	8	6	2	9-1	15
—	St. Louis (N.L.)■	5	6	.455	3.88	17	17	1	0	0-0	106.2	114	48	46	10	25-1	46
1996—	St. Petersburg (FSL)	1	0	1.000	0.00	1	1	0	0	0-...	5.2	4	0	0	0	1-0	4
—	Louisville (A.A.)	1	3	.250	7.04	4	4	1	0	0-...	23.0	29	18	18	2	11-1	10
—	St. Louis (N.L.)	4	8	.333	5.24	18	18	0	0	0-0	103.0	118	63	60	14	40-0	55
—	Cincinnati (N.L.)■	2	3	.400	2.30	5	5	0	0	0-0	27.1	28	9	7	2	7-0	19
1997—	Cincinnati (N.L.)	9	12	.429	4.78	31	30	1	0	0-0	162.0	165	91	86	13	49-6	103
1998—	Minnesota (A.L.)■	4	2	.667	3.49	18	17	0	0	0-0	98.0	108	41	38	13	24-1	50
—	Chicago (N.L.)■	0	1	.000	7.15	5	5	0	0	0-0	22.2	30	21	18	8	15-1	10
1999—	Texas (A.L.)■	13	10	.565	6.24	34	25	1	0	0-1	140.0	184	108	97	25	48-2	61
2000—	Arizona (N.L.)■	5	5	.500	4.87	60	4	0	0	5-6	101.2	123	55	55	10	40-5	56
2001—	Arizona (N.L.)	1	0	1.000	4.26	31	1	0	0	0-1	38.0	45	20	18	2	17-4	24
—	Tucson (PCL)	0	0	...	3.00	2	2	0	0	0-...	3.0	5	1	1	0	0-0	4
2002—	Arizona (N.L.)	1	1	.500	5.29	29	0	0	0	0-1	34.0	41	22	20	7	9-1	13
—	Tucson (PCL)	0	0	...	0.00	2	0	0	0	0-...	3.0	3	1	0	0	0-0	2
A.L. totals (10 years)		51	80	.389	4.94	209	161	25	3	2-3	1024.0	1197	613	562	124	385-15	453
N.L. totals (13 years)		90	106	.459	3.81	388	250	21	7	6-10	1748.1	1746	818	741	146	553-62	950
Major League totals (22 years)		141	186	.431	4.23	597	411	46	10	8-13	2772.1	2943	1431	1303	270	938-77	1403

DIVISION SERIES RECORD

Year	League	W	L	Pct.	ERA	G	GS	CG	ShO	Sv.-Opp.	IP	H	R	ER	HR	BB-IBB	SO
1998—	Chicago (N.L.)	0	0	...	0.00	2	0	0	0	0-0	1.1	0	0	0	0	0-0	1
2001—	Arizona (N.L.)	0	0	...	6.75	3	0	0	0	0-0	1.1	2	1	1	0	2-0	1
Division series totals (2 years)		0	0	...	3.38	5	0	0	0	0-0	2.2	2	1	1	0	2-0	2

CHAMPIONSHIP SERIES RECORD

Year	League	W	L	Pct.	ERA	G	GS	CG	ShO	Sv.-Opp.	IP	H	R	ER	HR	BB-IBB	SO
2001—	Arizona (N.L.)	0	0	...	27.00	2	0	0	0	0-0	1.0	3	3	3	0	1-0	1

WORLD SERIES RECORD

NOTES: Member of World Series championship team (2001).

Year	League	W	L	Pct.	ERA	G	GS	CG	ShO	Sv.-Opp.	IP	H	R	ER	HR	BB-IBB	SO
2001—	Arizona (N.L.)	0	0	...	0.00	3	0	0	0	0-0	4.2	1	0	0	0	0-0	1

ALL-STAR GAME RECORD

	W	L	Pct.	ERA	GS	CG	ShO	Sv.-Opp.	IP	H	R	ER	HR	BB-IBB	SO
All-Star Game totals (1 year)	0	0	...	0.00	0	0	0	0-0	1.0	0	0	0	0	0-0	1

MORIARTY, MIKE — SS — BLUE JAYS

PERSONAL: Born March 8, 1974, in Camden, N.J. ... 6-0/188. ... Bats right, throws right. ... Full name: Michael Thomas Moriarty.
HIGH SCHOOL: Bishop Eustace Prep (Pennsauken, N.J.).
COLLEGE: Seton Hall.
TRANSACTIONS/CAREER NOTES: Selected by Minnesota Twins in seventh round of free-agent draft (June 1, 1995). ... Granted free agency (October 15, 2001). ... Signed by Baltimore Orioles organization (November 5, 2001). ... Granted free agency (October 15, 2002). ... Signed by Toronto Blue Jays organization (November 1, 2002).
2002 GAMES PLAYED BY POSITION (MLB): SS—4; 2B—2; 3B—1.

			BATTING														FIELDING	
Year	Team (League)	Pos.	G	AB	R	H	2B	3B	HR	RBI	BB	SO	SB-CS	Avg.	OBP	SLG	E	Avg.
1995—	Fort Wayne (Midw.)	SS	62	203	26	46	6	3	4	26	27	44	8-0	.227	.319	.345	12	.956
1996—	Fort Myers (FSL)	SS	133	428	76	107	18	2	3	39	59	67	14-15	.250	.349	.322	24	.967
1997—	New Britain (East.)	SS	135	421	60	93	22	5	6	48	53	68	12-5	.221	.309	.340	19	.973
1998—	New Britain (East.)	3B-2B-SS	38	112	22	32	8	0	4	15	17	16	0-4	.286	.391	.464	9	.929
—	Salt Lake (PCL)	2B-SS-3B	64	161	21	36	8	2	3	19	22	39	2-1	.224	.319	.354	14	.950
1999—	Salt Lake (PCL)	SS-3B	128	380	63	98	21	7	4	51	56	62	6-4	.258	.358	.382	30	.953
2000—	Salt Lake (PCL)	SS	127	390	73	97	23	4	13	55	63	58	1-2	.249	.357	.428	20	.968
2001—	Edmonton (PCL)	SS-3B-2B-P	131	404	66	98	17	2	13	50	58	94	5-4	.243	.354	.391	20	.966
2002—	Rochester (I.L.)■	SS-3B-2B	90	311	48	86	18	1	4	26	37	50	4-1	.277	.357	.379	15	.956
—	Baltimore (A.L.)	SS-2B-3B	8	16	0	3	1	0	0	3	0	2	0-1	.188	.188	.250	0	1.000
Major League totals (1 year)			8	16	0	3	1	0	0	3	0	2	0-1	.188	.188	.250	0	1.000

RECORD AS PITCHER

Year	League	W	L	Pct.	ERA	G	GS	CG	ShO	Sv.-Opp.	IP	H	R	ER	HR	BB-IBB	SO
2001—	Edmonton (PCL)	0	0	...	18.00	1	0	0	0	0-...	1.0	2	2	2	1	0-0	0

MORRIS, MATT — P — CARDINALS

PERSONAL: Born August 9, 1974, in Middletown, N.Y. ... 6-5/210. ... Throws right, bats right. ... Full name: Matthew Christian Morris.
HIGH SCHOOL: Valley Central (Montgomery, N.Y.).
COLLEGE: Seton Hall.
TRANSACTIONS/CAREER NOTES: Selected by Milwaukee Brewers organization in 25th round of free-agent draft (June 1, 1992); did not sign. ... Selected by St. Louis Cardinals organization in first round (12th pick overall) of free-agent draft (June 1, 1995). ... On St. Louis disabled list (March 24-April 11 and April 12-July 10, 1998); included rehabilitation assignments to Arkansas (April 6-11) and Memphis (June 21-July 10). ... On disabled list (March 26, 1999-entire season). ... On St. Louis disabled list (April 2-May 28, 2000); included rehabilitation assignments to Arkansas (May 2-11) and Memphis (May 12-May 28). ... On disabled list (August 24-September 10, 2002).
HONORS: Named N.L. Rookie Pitcher of the Year by THE SPORTING NEWS (1997). ... Named N.L. Comeback Player of the Year by THE SPORTING NEWS (2001).
MISCELLANEOUS: Struck out in only appearance as pinch hitter (1997). ... Appeared in one game as pinch runner (2000).
CAREER HITTING (MLB): 40-for-248 (.161), 14 R, 8 2B, 0 3B, 0 HR, 17 RBI.

Year League	W	L	Pct.	ERA	G	GS	CG	ShO	Sv.-Opp.	IP	H	R	ER	HR	BB-IBB	SO
1995— New Jersey (NY-Penn)	2	0	1.000	1.64	2	2	0	0	0-...	11.0	12	3	2	1	3-0	13
— St. Petersburg (FSL)	3	2	.600	2.38	6	6	1	1	0-...	34.0	22	16	9	1	11-0	31
1996— Arkansas (Texas)	12	12	.500	3.88	27	27	4	*4	0-...	167.0	178	79	72	14	48-1	120
— Louisville (A.A.)	0	1	.000	3.38	1	1	0	0	0-...	8.0	8	3	3	0	1-0	9
1997— St. Louis (N.L.)	12	9	.571	3.19	33	33	3	0	0-0	217.0	208	88	77	12	69-2	149
1998— Arkansas (Texas)	0	0	...	0.00	1	0	0	0	1-...	4.0	4	0	0	0	0-0	2
— St. Louis (N.L.)	7	5	.583	2.53	17	17	2	1	0-0	113.2	101	37	32	8	42-6	79
— Memphis (PCL)	1	0	1.000	4.50	4	4	0	0	0-...	14.0	16	8	7	1	4-0	21
1999— St. Louis (N.L.)									Did not play.							
2000— Arkansas (Texas)	0	0	...	6.43	2	2	0	0	0-...	7.0	8	5	5	0	4-0	7
— Memphis (PCL)	1	2	.333	7.98	3	3	0	0	0-...	14.2	20	13	13	2	6-1	8
— St. Louis (N.L.)	3	3	.500	3.57	31	0	0	0	4-7	53.0	53	22	21	3	17-1	34
2001— St. Louis (N.L.)	•22	8	.733	3.16	34	34	2	1	0-0	216.1	218	86	76	13	54-3	185
2002— St. Louis (N.L.)	17	9	.654	3.42	32	32	1	1	0-0	210.1	210	86	80	16	64-3	171
Major League totals (5 years)	61	34	.642	3.18	147	116	8	3	4-7	810.1	790	319	286	52	246-15	618

DIVISION SERIES RECORD

Year League	W	L	Pct.	ERA	G	GS	CG	ShO	Sv.-Opp.	IP	H	R	ER	HR	BB-IBB	SO
2000— St. Louis (N.L.)	0	0	...	0.00	2	0	0	0	0-0	2.0	0	0	0	0	1-0	0
2001— St. Louis (N.L.)	0	1	.000	1.20	2	2	0	0	0-0	15.0	13	2	2	1	5-0	12
2002— St. Louis (N.L.)	1	0	1.000	1.29	1	1	0	0	0-0	7.0	7	2	1	0	2-0	3
Division series totals (3 years)	1	1	.500	1.13	5	3	0	0	0-0	24.0	20	4	3	1	8-0	15

CHAMPIONSHIP SERIES RECORD

RECORDS: Shares single-series record for most hit batsmen—3 (2002). ... Shares single-game records for most earned runs allowed—7 (October 9, 2002); and hit batsmen—3 (October 14, 2002). ... Shares single-inning record for most hits allowed—6 (October 9, 2002, second inning). ... Shares career record for most consecutive hits allowed in one inning—6 (October 9, 2002, second inning).

Year League	W	L	Pct.	ERA	G	GS	CG	ShO	Sv.-Opp.	IP	H	R	ER	HR	BB-IBB	SO
2000— St. Louis (N.L.)	0	0	...	4.91	2	0	0	0	0-0	3.2	3	2	2	0	2-1	2
2002— St. Louis (N.L.)	0	2	.000	6.23	2	2	0	0	0-0	13.0	16	9	9	2	6-1	6
Champ. series totals (2 years)	0	2	.000	5.94	4	2	0	0	0-0	16.2	19	11	11	2	8-2	8

ALL-STAR GAME RECORD

	W	L	Pct.	ERA	GS	CG	ShO	Sv.-Opp.	IP	H	R	ER	HR	BB-IBB	SO
All-Star Game totals (1 year)	0	0	...	0.00	0	0	0	0-0	1.0	1	0	0	0	0-0	1

MORRIS, WARREN — 2B

PERSONAL: Born January 11, 1974, in Alexandria, La. ... 5-11/188. ... Bats left, throws right. ... Full name: Warren Randall Morris.
HIGH SCHOOL: Bolton (Alexandria, La.).
COLLEGE: Louisiana State.
TRANSACTIONS/CAREER NOTES: Selected by Texas Rangers organization in fifth round of free-agent draft (June 2, 1996). ... Traded by Rangers with P Todd Van Poppel to Pittsburgh Pirates for P Esteban Loaiza (July 17, 1998). ... On Nashville disabled list (July 1-12, 2001). ... On Pittsburgh disabled list (August 14-September 1, 2001). ... Released by Pirates (March 13, 2002). ... Signed by Minnesota Twins organization (March 15, 2002). ... On Edmonton disabled list (May 22-June 10, 2002). ... Traded by Twins to St. Louis Cardinals for a player to be named later (June 11, 2002); Twins acquired SS Seth Davidson to complete deal (June 20). ... Claimed on waivers by Boston Red Sox (July 16, 2002). ... Granted free agency (October 15, 2002).
MISCELLANEOUS: Member of 1996 U.S. Olympic baseball team.
2002 GAMES PLAYED BY POSITION (MLB): 2B—4.

		BATTING														FIELDING	
Year Team (League)	Pos.	G	AB	R	H	2B	3B	HR	RBI	BB	SO	SB-CS	Avg.	OBP	SLG	E	Avg.
1997— Charlotte (FSL)	2B-3B	128	494	78	151	27	9	12	75	62	100	16-5	.306	.390	.470	18	.961
— Oklahoma City (A.A.)	2B	8	32	3	7	1	0	1	3	3	5	0-0	.219	.286	.344	0	1.000
1998— Tulsa (Texas)	2B	95	390	59	129	22	5	14	73	43	63	12-7	.331	.401	.521	17	.964
— Carolina (Sou.)■	2B	44	151	28	50	8	3	5	30	24	34	5-2	.331	.419	.523	7	.964
1999— Pittsburgh (N.L.)	2B	147	511	65	147	20	3	15	73	59	88	3-7	.288	.360	.427	14	.979
2000— Pittsburgh (N.L.)	2B	144	528	68	137	31	2	3	43	65	78	7-10	.259	.341	.343	15	.979
2001— Nashville (PCL)	2B-3B	57	223	26	68	16	2	5	40	12	21	3-4	.305	.342	.462	9	.966
— Pittsburgh (N.L.)	2B-3B	48	103	6	21	6	0	2	11	3	9	2-3	.204	.239	.320	4	.965
2002— Minnesota (A.L.)■	2B	4	7	0	0	0	0	0	0	0	1	0-0	.000	.000	.000	0	1.000
— Edmonton (PCL)	2B-3B-SS	27	92	15	24	6	2	2	10	3	16	2-1	.261	.281	.435	6	.942
— Memphis (PCL)■	2B-3B	29	100	16	26	4	1	2	14	8	12	0-1	.260	.306	.380	4	.966
— Pawtucket (I.L.)■	2B-OF	43	164	21	50	11	2	3	21	11	22	2-1	.305	.352	.451	1	.991
American League totals (1 year)		4	7	0	0	0	0	0	0	0	1	0-0	.000	.000	.000	0	1.000
National League totals (3 years)		339	1142	139	305	57	5	20	127	127	175	12-20	.267	.341	.378	33	.978
Major League totals (4 years)		343	1149	139	305	57	5	20	127	127	176	12-20	.265	.339	.376	33	.978

MOSS, DAMIAN — P — BRAVES

PERSONAL: Born November 24, 1976, in Darlinghurst, Australia. ... 6-0/187. ... Throws left, bats right. ... Full name: Damian Joseph Moss.

HIGH SCHOOL: Liverpool Boys (Australia).

TRANSACTIONS/CAREER NOTES: Signed as non-drafted free agent by Atlanta Braves organization (July 1, 1993). ... On disabled list (March 27, 1998-entire season). ... On Atlanta disabled list (April 3-June 1, 1999). ... On Atlanta disabled list (May 11-June 18, 2001); included rehabilitation assignment to Greenville (June 8-18). ... On Richmond disabled list (August 3-12, 2001).

STATISTICAL NOTES: Pitched 6-0 no-hit victory vs. Bluefield (June 26, 1994; second game). ... Led Appalachian League with 14 hit batsmen in 1994.

CAREER HITTING (MLB): 5-for-51 (.098), 2 R, 1 2B, 0 3B, 0 HR, 2 RBI.

Year League	W	L	Pct.	ERA	G	GS	CG	ShO	Sv.-Opp.	IP	H	R	ER	HR	BB-IBB	SO
1994—Danville (Appl.)	2	5	.286	3.58	12	12	1	1	0-...	60.1	30	28	24	1	55-0	77
1995—Macon (S.Atl.)	9	10	.474	3.56	27	27	0	0	0-...	149.1	134	73	59	13	70-0	•177
1996—Durham (Caro.)	9	1	*.900	2.25	14	14	0	0	0-...	84.0	52	25	21	9	40-0	89
—Greenville (Sou.)	2	5	.286	4.97	11	10	0	0	0-...	58.0	57	41	32	5	35-0	48
1997—Greenville (Sou.)	6	8	.429	5.35	21	19	1	0	0-...	112.2	111	73	67	13	58-0	116
1998—Greenville (Sou.)									Did not play.							
1999—Macon (S.Atl.)	0	3	.000	4.32	12	12	0	0	0-...	41.2	33	20	20	8	15-0	49
—Greenville (Sou.)	1	3	.250	8.54	7	7	0	0	0-...	32.2	50	33	31	6	21-0	22
2000—Richmond (I.L.)	9	6	.600	3.14	29	•28	0	0	0-...	160.2	130	67	56	14	*106-0	123
2001—Richmond (I.L.)	5	4	.556	3.15	17	16	0	0	0-...	88.2	75	34	31	10	38-1	94
—Atlanta (N.L.)	0	0	...	3.00	5	1	0	0	0-0	9.0	3	3	3	1	9-0	8
—Greenville (Sou.)	0	1	.000	3.00	3	2	0	0	0-...	9.0	7	3	3	3	0-0	10
2002—Atlanta (N.L.)	12	6	.667	3.42	33	29	0	0	0-0	179.0	140	80	68	20	89-5	111
Major League totals (2 years)	12	6	.667	3.40	38	30	0	0	0-0	188.0	143	83	71	21	98-5	119

DIVISION SERIES RECORD

Year League	W	L	Pct.	ERA	G	GS	CG	ShO	Sv.-Opp.	IP	H	R	ER	HR	BB-IBB	SO
2002—Atlanta (N.L.)	0	0	...	3.00	2	0	0	0	0-0	3.0	2	1	1	0	1-0	3

MOTA, GUILLERMO — P — DODGERS

PERSONAL: Born July 25, 1973, in San Pedro de Macoris, Dominican Republic. ... 6-4/205. ... Throws right, bats right. ... Full name: Guillermo Reynoso Mota.

HIGH SCHOOL: Jose Joaquin Perez (San Pedro de Macoris, Dominican Republic).

TRANSACTIONS/CAREER NOTES: Signed as non-drafted free agent by New York Mets organization (September 7, 1990). ... Selected by Montreal Expos organization from Mets organization in Rule 5 minor league draft (December 9, 1996). ... Re-signed by Expos organization (March 20, 1999). ... On Montreal disabled list (July 13-September 1, 2001); included rehabilitation assignment to Ottawa (August 24-31). ... Traded by Expos with OF Wilkin Ruan to Los Angeles Dodgers for P Matt Herges and IF Jorge Nunez (March 24, 2002).

STATISTICAL NOTES: Led Gulf Coast League third basemen with .943 fielding percentage and tied for lead with 40 putouts and 11 double plays in 1993.. ... Led Appalachian League third basemen with 44 putouts, 157 assists, 214 total chances, 12 double plays and .939 fielding percentage in 1994. ... Led South Atlantic League shortstops with 615 total chances and 66 double plays in 1995. ... Hit home run in first major league at-bat (June 9, 1999).

CAREER HITTING (MLB): 3-for-9 (.333), 2 R, 0 2B, 0 3B, 1 HR, 3 RBI.

Year League	W	L	Pct.	ERA	G	GS	CG	ShO	Sv.-Opp.	IP	H	R	ER	HR	BB-IBB	SO
1997—Cape Fear (S.Atl.)■	5	10	.333	4.36	25	23	0	0	0-...	126.0	135	65	61	8	33-0	112
1998—Jupiter (FSL)	3	2	.600	0.66	20	0	0	0	2-...	41.0	18	6	3	0	6-0	27
—Harrisburg (East.)	2	0	1.000	1.06	12	0	0	0	4-...	17.0	10	2	2	0	2-0	19
1999—Ottawa (I.L.)	2	0	1.000	1.89	14	0	0	0	5-...	19.0	16	6	4	0	5-0	17
—Montreal (N.L.)	2	4	.333	2.93	51	0	0	0	0-1	55.1	54	24	18	5	25-3	27
2000—Ottawa (I.L.)	4	5	.444	2.29	35	0	0	0	7-...	63.0	49	16	16	4	31-3	35
—Montreal (N.L.)	1	1	.500	6.00	29	0	0	0	0-0	30.0	27	21	20	3	12-0	24
2001—Montreal (N.L.)	1	3	.250	5.26	53	0	0	0	0-3	49.2	51	30	29	9	18-1	31
—Ottawa (I.L.)	0	0	...	2.25	4	0	0	0	0-...	4.0	1	1	1	1	0-0	4
2002—Las Vegas (PCL)■	1	3	.250	2.95	20	0	0	0	1-...	36.2	34	13	12	1	8-1	38
—Los Angeles (N.L.)	1	3	.250	4.15	43	0	0	0	0-1	60.2	45	30	28	4	27-6	49
Major League totals (4 years)	5	11	.313	4.37	176	0	0	0	0-5	195.2	177	105	95	21	82-10	131

RECORD AS POSITION PLAYER

		BATTING														FIELDING	
Year Team (League)	Pos.	G	AB	R	H	2B	3B	HR	RBI	BB	SO	SB-CS	Avg.	OBP	SLG	E	Avg.
1991—Dom. Mets (DSL)		32	90	4	22	2	0	0	12	9	19	0-...	.244	...	.267	...	...
1992—Dom. Mets (DSL)	IF	70	228	49	68	10	3	6	40	28	40	10-...	.298	...	.447	24	.927
1993—GC Mets (GCL)	3B-SS	43	169	23	42	7	2	1	22	7	37	1-0	.249	.289	.331	8	†.945
1994—St. Lucie (FSL)	3B	1	4	1	0	0	0	0	0	0	0	0-0	.000	.000	.000	1	.857
—Kingsport (Appl.)	3B-SS	65	245	40	60	10	2	9	37	20	78	5-4	.245	.312	.412	16	†.935
1995—Capital City (S.Atl.)	SS-2B	123	400	45	97	24	3	4	45	32	127	8-3	.243	.304	.348	40	.935
1996—St. Lucie (FSL)	SS-3B	102	304	34	71	10	3	1	21	34	90	8-8	.234	.311	.296	21	.952

MOYER, JAMIE — P

PERSONAL: Born November 18, 1962, in Sellersville, Pa. ... 6-0/175. ... Throws left, bats left. ... Son-in-law of Digger Phelps, ESPN college basketball analyst, and Notre Dame basketball coach (1971-72 through 1990-91).

HIGH SCHOOL: Souderton (Pa.) Area.

COLLEGE: St. Joseph's (Pa.).

TRANSACTIONS/CAREER NOTES: Selected by Chicago Cubs organization in sixth round of free-agent draft (June 4, 1984). ... Traded by Cubs with OF Rafael Palmeiro and P Drew Hall to Texas Rangers for P Mitch Williams, P Paul Kilgus, P Steve Wilson, IF Curtis Wilkerson, IF Luis Benitez and OF Pablo Delgado (December 5, 1988). ... On Texas disabled list (May 31-September 1, 1989); included rehabilitation assignments to Gulf Coast Rangers (August 5-14) and Tulsa (August 15-24). ... Released by Rangers (November 13, 1990). ... Signed by St. Louis Cardinals organization (January 9, 1991). ... Released by Cardinals (October 14, 1991). ... Signed by Cubs organization (January 8, 1992). ... Released by Cubs (March 30, 1992). ... Signed by Detroit Tigers organization (May 24, 1992). ... Granted free agency (December 8, 1992). ... Signed by Baltimore Orioles organization (December 14, 1992). ... Granted free agency (November 1, 1995). ... Signed by Boston Red Sox (January 2, 1996). ... Traded by Red Sox to Seattle Mariners for OF Darren Bragg (July 30, 1996). ... Granted free agency (October 29, 1996). ... Re-signed by Mariners (November 20, 1996). ... On Seattle disabled list (March 23-April 29, 1997); included rehabilitation assignment to Tacoma (April 24-29). ... On disabled list (April 15-June 2, 2000). ... Granted free agency (October 28, 2002).

HONORS: Named lefthanded pitcher on The Sporting News A.L. All-Star team (1999).

STATISTICAL NOTES: Led A.L. with .813 winning percentage in 1996.

CAREER HITTING (MLB): 24-for-166 (.145), 10 R, 2 2B, 0 3B, 0 HR, 4 RBI.

Year League	W	L	Pct.	ERA	G	GS	CG	ShO	Sv.-Opp.	IP	H	R	ER	HR	BB-IBB	SO
1984— Geneva (NY-Penn)	•9	3	.750	1.89	14	14	5	2	0-...	*104.2	59	27	22	5	31-0	*120
1985— Winston-Salem (Caro.)	8	2	.800	2.30	12	12	6	2	0-...	94.0	82	36	24	1	22-3	94
— Pittsfield (East.)	7	6	.538	3.72	15	15	3	0	0-...	96.2	99	49	40	4	32-1	51
1986— Pittsfield (East.)	3	1	.750	0.88	6	6	0	0	0-...	41.0	27	10	4	2	16-0	42
— Iowa (A.A.)	3	2	.600	2.55	6	6	2	0	0-...	42.1	25	14	12	2	11-0	25
— Chicago (N.L.)	7	4	.636	5.05	16	16	1	1	0-0	87.1	107	52	49	10	42-1	45
1987— Chicago (N.L.)	12	15	.444	5.10	35	33	1	0	0-0	201.0	210	127	*114	28	97-9	147
1988— Chicago (N.L.)	9	15	.375	3.48	34	30	3	1	0-2	202.0	212	84	78	20	55-7	121
1989— Texas (A.L.)■	4	9	.308	4.86	15	15	1	0	0-0	76.0	84	51	41	10	33-0	44
— Gulf Coast Rangers (GCL)	1	0	1.000	1.64	3	3	0	0	0-...	11.0	8	4	2	0	1-0	18
— Tulsa (Texas)	1	1	.500	5.11	2	2	1	1	0-...	12.1	16	8	7	1	3-0	9
1990— Texas (A.L.)	2	6	.250	4.66	33	10	1	0	0-0	102.1	115	59	53	6	39-4	58
1991— St. Louis (N.L.)■	0	5	.000	5.74	8	7	0	0	0-0	31.1	38	21	20	5	16-0	20
— Louisville (A.A.)	5	10	.333	3.80	20	20	1	0	0-...	125.2	125	64	53	*16	43-4	69
1992— Toledo (I.L.)■	10	8	.556	2.86	21	20	5	0	0-...	138.2	128	48	44	8	37-3	80
1993— Rochester (I.L.)■	6	0	1.000	1.67	8	8	1	1	0-...	54.0	42	13	10	2	13-0	41
— Baltimore (A.L.)	12	9	.571	3.43	25	25	3	1	0-0	152.0	154	63	58	11	38-2	90
1994— Baltimore (A.L.)	5	7	.417	4.77	23	23	0	0	0-0	149.0	158	81	79	23	38-3	87
1995— Baltimore (A.L.)	8	6	.571	5.21	27	18	0	0	0-0	115.2	117	70	67	18	30-0	65
1996— Boston (A.L.)■	7	1	.875	4.50	23	10	0	0	0-0	90.0	111	50	45	14	27-2	50
— Seattle (A.L.)■	6	2	§.750	3.31	11	11	0	0	0-0	70.2	66	36	26	9	19-3	29
1997— Tacoma (PCL)	1	0	1.000	0.00	1	1	0	0	0-...	5.0	1	0	0	0	0-0	6
— Seattle (A.L.)	17	5	.773	3.86	30	30	2	0	0-0	188.2	187	82	81	21	43-2	113
1998— Seattle (A.L.)	15	9	.625	3.53	34	34	4	3	0-0	234.1	234	99	92	23	42-2	158
1999— Seattle (A.L.)	14	8	.636	3.87	32	32	4	0	0-0	228.0	235	108	98	23	48-1	137
2000— Seattle (A.L.)	13	10	.565	5.49	26	26	0	0	0-0	154.0	173	103	94	22	53-2	98
2001— Seattle (A.L.)	20	6	.769	3.43	33	33	1	0	0-0	209.2	187	84	80	24	44-4	119
2002— Seattle (A.L.)	13	8	.619	3.32	34	34	4	2	0-0	230.2	198	89	85	28	50-4	147
A.L. totals (12 years)	136	86	.613	4.04	346	301	20	6	0-0	2001.0	2019	975	899	232	504-29	1195
N.L. totals (4 years)	28	39	.418	4.50	93	86	5	2	0-2	521.2	567	284	261	63	210-17	333
Major League totals (16 years)	164	125	.567	4.14	439	387	25	8	0-2	2522.2	2586	1259	1160	295	714-46	1528

DIVISION SERIES RECORD

Year League	W	L	Pct.	ERA	G	GS	CG	ShO	Sv.-Opp.	IP	H	R	ER	HR	BB-IBB	SO
1997— Seattle (A.L.)	0	1	.000	5.79	1	1	0	0	0-0	4.2	5	3	3	1	1-0	2
2001— Seattle (A.L.)	2	0	1.000	1.50	2	2	0	0	0-0	12.0	8	2	2	0	2-0	10
Division series totals (2 years)	2	1	.667	2.70	3	3	0	0	0-0	16.2	13	5	5	1	3-0	12

CHAMPIONSHIP SERIES RECORD

Year League	W	L	Pct.	ERA	G	GS	CG	ShO	Sv.-Opp.	IP	H	R	ER	HR	BB-IBB	SO
2001— Seattle (A.L.)	1	0	1.000	2.57	1	1	0	0	0-0	7.0	4	2	2	1	1-0	5

MUELLER, BILL — 3B

PERSONAL: Born March 17, 1971, in Maryland Heights, Mo. ... 5-10/180. ... Bats both, throws right. ... Full name: William Richard Mueller. ... Name pronounced MILL-er.

HIGH SCHOOL: DeSmet (Creve Coeur, Mo.).

COLLEGE: Southwest Missouri State.

TRANSACTIONS/CAREER NOTES: Selected by San Francisco Giants organization in 15th round of free-agent draft (June 3, 1993). ... On disabled list (July 1-16, 1997). ... On San Francisco disabled list (April 6-May 17, 1999); included rehabilitation assignment to Fresno (May 11-17). ... Traded by Giants to Chicago Cubs for P Tim Worrell (November 19, 2000). ... On Chicago disabled list (May 14-August 13, 2001); included rehabilitation assignment to Iowa (August 2-13). ... On Chicago disabled list (March 28-May 6, 2002); included rehabilitation assignment to Iowa (April 29-May 6). ... Traded by Cubs with cash to Giants for P Jeff Verplancke (September 3, 2002). ... Granted free agency (October 28, 2002).

STATISTICAL NOTES: Led Pacific Coast League third basemen with 25 double plays in 1996. ... Had 17-game hitting streak (April 24-May 14, 1998). ... Had 15-game hitting streak (May 1-19, 2000). ... Led N.L. third basemen with .974 fielding percentage in 2000. ... Career major league grand slams: 2.

2002 GAMES PLAYED BY POSITION (MLB): 3B—104.

		BATTING													FIELDING	
Year Team (League)	Pos.	G	AB	R	H	2B	3B	HR	RBI	BB	SO	SB-CS	Avg.	OBP	SLG	E	Avg.
1993— Everett (N'West)	2B	58	200	31	60	8	2	1	24	42	17	13-6	.300	.425	.375	8	.966
1994— San Jose (Calif.)	3B-2B-SS	120	431	79	130	20	•9	5	72	*103	47	4-8	.302	*.435	.425	29	.925
1995— Shreveport (Texas)	3B-2B	88	330	56	102	16	2	1	39	53	36	6-5	.309	.406	.379	5	.978
— Phoenix (PCL)	3B-2B	41	172	23	51	13	6	2	19	19	31	0-0	.297	.365	.477	7	.941
1996— Phoenix (PCL)	3-S-2-DH	106	440	73	133	14	6	4	36	44	40	2-5	.302	.365	.389	11	.969
— San Francisco (N.L.)	3B-2B	55	200	31	66	15	1	0	19	24	26	0-0	.330	.401	.415	6	.962
1997— San Francisco (N.L.)	3B	128	390	51	114	26	3	7	44	48	71	4-3	.292	.369	.428	14	.956
1998— San Francisco (N.L.)	3B-2B	145	534	93	157	27	0	9	59	79	83	3-3	.294	.383	.395	19	.953
1999— San Francisco (N.L.)	3B-2B	116	414	61	120	24	0	2	36	65	52	4-2	.290	.388	.362	12	.959
— Fresno (PCL)	3B	3	12	3	5	0	1	0	6	0	0	0-0	.417	.385	.583	3	.800
2000— San Francisco (N.L.)	3B-2B	153	560	97	150	29	4	10	55	52	62	4-2	.268	.333	.388	9	†.975

Year Team (League)	Pos.	G	AB	R	H	2B	3B	HR	RBI	BB	SO	SB-CS	Avg.	OBP	SLG	E	Avg.
		BATTING														FIELDING	
2001—Chicago (N.L.)	3B-2B	70	210	38	62	12	1	6	23	37	19	1-1	.295	.403	.448	8	.942
—Iowa (PCL)	3B	8	26	3	11	3	0	0	4	1	2	0-0	.423	.444	.538	0	1.000
2002—Iowa (PCL)	3B	6	16	2	6	1	0	1	5	3	1	0-1	.375	.474	.625	1	.909
—Chicago (N.L.)	3B	103	353	51	94	19	4	7	37	51	41	0-0	.266	.355	.402	6	.973
—San Fran. (N.L.)■	3B	8	13	0	2	0	0	0	1	1	1	0-0	.154	.214	.154	0	1.000
Major League totals (7 years)		778	2674	422	765	152	13	41	274	357	355	16-11	.286	.370	.399	74	.961

DIVISION SERIES RECORD

Year Team (League)	Pos.	G	AB	R	H	2B	3B	HR	RBI	BB	SO	SB-CS	Avg.	OBP	SLG	E	Avg.
		BATTING														FIELDING	
1997—San Francisco (N.L.)	3B	3	12	1	3	0	0	1	1	0	0	0-1	.250	.250	.500	0	1.000
2000—San Francisco (N.L.)	3B	4	20	2	5	2	0	0	0	0	4	0-0	.250	.250	.350	0	1.000
Division series totals (2 years)		7	32	3	8	2	0	1	1	0	4	0-1	.250	.250	.406	0	1.000

MULDER, MARK P ATHLETICS

PERSONAL: Born August 5, 1977, in South Holland, Ill. ... 6-6/215. ... Throws left, bats left. ... Full name: Mark Alan Mulder.

HIGH SCHOOL: Thornwood (South Holland, Ill.).

COLLEGE: Michigan State.

TRANSACTIONS/CAREER NOTES: Selected by Detroit Tigers organization in 55th round of free-agent draft (June 1, 1995); did not sign. ... Selected by Oakland Athletics organization in first round (second pick overall) of free-agent draft (June 2, 1998). ... On disabled list (April 12-May 10, 2002).

HONORS: Named lefthanded pitcher on The Sporting News A.L. All-Star team (2001).

STATISTICAL NOTES: Pitched 3-0 one-hit, complete-game victory against Arizona (July 6, 2001).

CAREER HITTING (MLB): 1-for-14 (.071), 0 R, 0 2B, 0 3B, 0 HR, 0 RBI.

Year League	W	L	Pct.	ERA	G	GS	CG	ShO	Sv.-Opp.	IP	H	R	ER	HR	BB-IBB	SO
1999—Vancouver (PCL)	6	7	.462	4.06	22	22	1	0	0-...	128.2	152	69	58	13	31-0	81
2000—Sacramento (PCL)	1	1	.500	5.40	2	2	0	0	0-...	8.1	15	11	5	1	4-0	6
—Oakland (A.L.)	9	10	.474	5.44	27	27	0	0	0-0	154.0	191	106	93	22	69-3	88
2001—Oakland (A.L.)	*21	8	.724	3.45	34	34	6	*4	0-0	229.1	214	92	88	16	51-4	153
2002—Oakland (A.L.)	19	7	.731	3.47	30	30	2	1	0-0	207.1	182	88	80	21	55-3	159
Major League totals (3 years)	49	25	.662	3.98	91	91	8	5	0-0	590.2	587	286	261	59	175-10	400

DIVISION SERIES RECORD

Year League	W	L	Pct.	ERA	G	GS	CG	ShO	Sv.-Opp.	IP	H	R	ER	HR	BB-IBB	SO
2000—Oakland (A.L.)									Did not play.							
2001—Oakland (A.L.)	1	1	.500	2.45	2	2	0	0	0-0	11.0	14	5	3	0	2-0	7
2002—Oakland (A.L.)	1	1	.500	2.08	2	2	0	0	0-0	13.0	14	3	3	1	3-1	12
Division series totals (2 years)	2	2	.500	2.25	4	4	0	0	0-0	24.0	28	8	6	1	5-1	19

MULHOLLAND, TERRY P

PERSONAL: Born March 9, 1963, in Uniontown, Pa. ... 6-3/220. ... Throws left, bats right. ... Full name: Terence John Mulholland.

HIGH SCHOOL: Laurel Highlands (Uniontown, Pa.).

COLLEGE: Marietta College (Ohio).

TRANSACTIONS/CAREER NOTES: Selected by San Francisco Giants organization in first round (24th pick overall) of free-agent draft (June 4, 1984); pick received as compensation for Detroit Tigers signing free-agent IF Darrell Evans. ... On San Francisco disabled list (August 1, 1988-remainder of season). ... Traded by Giants with P Dennis Cook and 3B Charlie Hayes to Philadelphia Phillies for P Steve Bedrosian and a player to be named later (June 18, 1989); Giants acquired IF Rick Parker to complete deal (August 7, 1989). ... On Philadelphia disabled list (June 12-28, 1990); included rehabilitation assignment to Scranton/Wilkes-Barre (June 23-24). ... Traded by Phillies with a player to be named later to New York Yankees for P Bobby Munoz, 2B Kevin Jordan and P Ryan Karp (February 9, 1994); Yankees acquired P Jeff Patterson to complete deal (November 8, 1994). ... Granted free agency (October 17, 1994). ... Signed by Giants (April 8, 1995). ... On San Francisco disabled list (June 6-July 4, 1995); included rehabilitation assignment to Phoenix (June 23-July 4). ... Granted free agency (November 3, 1995). ... Signed by Phillies organization (February 17, 1996). ... Traded by Phillies to Seattle Mariners for IF Desi Relaford (July 31, 1996). ... Granted free agency (October 28, 1996). ... Signed by Chicago Cubs (December 10, 1996). ... Claimed on waivers by Giants (August 8, 1997). ... Granted free agency (October 27, 1997). ... Signed by Cubs (February 2, 1998). ... Granted free agency (October 28, 1998). ... Re-signed by Cubs (November 6, 1998). ... Traded by Cubs with IF Jose Hernandez to Atlanta Braves for P Micah Bowie, P Ruben Quevado and a player to be named later (July 31, 1999); Cubs acquired P Joey Nation to complete deal (August 24, 1999). ... Granted free agency (October 31, 2000). ... Signed by Pittsburgh Pirates (December 10, 2000). ... On Pittsburgh disabled list (April 6-20 and June 12-August 1, 2001); included rehabilitation assignment to Altoona (July 27-29). ... Traded by Pirates to Los Angeles Dodgers for P Mike Fetters and P Adrian Burnside (July 31, 2001). ... On Los Angeles disabled list (May 3-June 4, 2002). ... Traded by Dodgers with P Ricardo Rodriguez and P Francisco Cruceta to Cleveland Indians for P Paul Shuey (July 28, 2002). ... Granted free agency (October 31, 2002).

STATISTICAL NOTES: Pitched 6-0 no-hit victory for Philadelphia against San Francisco (August 15, 1990).

MISCELLANEOUS: Appeared in one game as pinch runner (1991). ... Appeared in one game as pinch runner with San Francisco (1995).

CAREER HITTING (MLB): 69-for-616 (.112), 26 R, 13 2B, 1 3B, 2 HR, 23 RBI.

Year League	W	L	Pct.	ERA	G	GS	CG	ShO	Sv.-Opp.	IP	H	R	ER	HR	BB-IBB	SO
1984—Everett (N'West)	1	0	1.000	0.00	3	3	0	0	0-...	19.0	10	2	0	0	4-0	15
—Fresno (Calif.)	5	2	.714	2.95	9	9	0	0	0-...	42.2	32	17	14	1	36-0	39
1985—Shreveport (Texas)	9	8	.529	2.90	26	26	8	*3	0-...	176.2	166	79	57	9	87-2	122
1986—Phoenix (PCL)	8	5	.615	4.46	17	17	3	0	0-...	111.0	112	60	55	6	56-4	77
—San Francisco (N.L.)	1	7	.125	4.94	15	10	0	0	0-0	54.2	51	33	30	3	35-2	27
1987—Phoenix (PCL)	7	12	.368	5.07	37	*29	3	1	1-...	172.1	200	*124	•97	7	90-0	94
1988—Phoenix (PCL)	7	3	.700	3.58	19	14	3	2	0-...	100.2	116	45	40	2	44-0	57
—San Francisco (N.L.)	2	1	.667	3.72	9	6	2	1	0-0	46.0	50	20	19	3	7-0	18
1989—Phoenix (PCL)	4	5	.444	2.99	13	10	3	0	0-...	78.1	67	30	26	3	26-2	61
—San Francisco (N.L.)	0	0	...	4.09	5	1	0	0	0-0	11.0	15	5	5	0	4-0	6
—Philadelphia (N.L.)■	4	7	.364	5.00	20	17	2	1	0-0	104.1	122	61	58	8	32-3	60

Year League	W	L	Pct.	ERA	G	GS	CG	ShO	Sv.-Opp.	IP	H	R	ER	HR	BB-IBB	SO
1990— Philadelphia (N.L.)	9	10	.474	3.34	33	26	6	1	0-1	180.2	172	78	67	15	42-7	75
— Scranton/W.B. (I.L.)	0	1	.000	3.00	1	1	0	0	0-...	6.0	9	4	2	0	2-0	2
1991— Philadelphia (N.L.)	16	13	.552	3.61	34	34	8	3	0-0	232.0	231	100	93	15	49-2	142
1992— Philadelphia (N.L.)	13	11	.542	3.81	32	32	*12	2	0-0	229.0	227	101	97	14	46-3	125
1993— Philadelphia (N.L.)	12	9	.571	3.25	29	28	7	2	0-0	191.0	177	80	69	20	40-2	116
1994— New York (A.L.)■	6	7	.462	6.49	24	19	2	0	0-0	120.2	150	94	87	24	37-1	72
1995— San Francisco (N.L.)■	5	13	.278	5.80	29	24	2	0	0-0	149.0	190	112	96	25	38-1	65
— Phoenix (PCL)	0	0	...	2.25	1	1	0	0	0-...	4.0	4	3	1	0	1-0	4
1996— Philadelphia (N.L.)■	8	7	.533	4.66	21	21	3	0	0-0	133.1	157	74	69	17	21-1	52
— Seattle (A.L.)■	5	4	.556	4.67	12	12	0	0	0-0	69.1	75	38	36	5	28-3	34
1997— Chicago (N.L.)■	6	12	.333	4.07	25	25	1	0	0-0	157.0	162	79	71	20	45-2	74
— San Francisco (N.L.)■	0	1	.000	5.16	15	2	0	0	0-0	29.2	28	21	17	4	6-1	25
1998— Chicago (N.L.)■	6	5	.545	2.89	70	6	0	0	3-5	112.0	100	49	36	7	39-7	72
1999— Chicago (N.L.)	6	6	.500	5.15	26	16	0	0	0-0	110.0	137	71	63	16	32-4	44
— Atlanta (N.L.)■	4	2	.667	2.98	16	8	0	0	1-1	60.1	64	24	20	5	13-2	39
2000— Atlanta (N.L.)	9	9	.500	5.11	54	20	1	0	1-3	156.2	198	96	89	24	41-7	78
2001— Pittsburgh (N.L.)■	0	0	...	3.72	22	1	0	0	0-0	36.1	38	15	15	5	10-1	17
— Altoona (East.)	0	2	.000	3.86	2	2	0	0	0-...	2.1	5	3	1	0	1-0	3
— Los Angeles (N.L.)■	1	1	.500	5.83	19	3	0	0	0-0	29.1	40	20	19	7	7-0	25
2002— Los Angeles (N.L.)	0	0	...	7.31	21	0	0	0	0-0	32.0	45	29	26	10	7-0	17
— Cleveland (A.L.)■	3	2	.600	4.60	16	3	0	0	0-0	47.0	56	27	24	5	14-3	21
A.L. totals (3 years)	14	13	.519	5.58	52	34	2	0	0-0	237.0	281	159	147	34	79-7	127
N.L. totals (15 years)	102	114	.472	4.20	495	280	44	10	5-10	2054.1	2204	1068	959	218	514-45	1077
Major League totals (16 years)	116	127	.477	4.34	547	314	46	10	5-10	2291.1	2485	1227	1106	252	593-52	1204

DIVISION SERIES RECORD

Year League	W	L	Pct.	ERA	G	GS	CG	ShO	Sv.-Opp.	IP	H	R	ER	HR	BB-IBB	SO
1998— Chicago (N.L.)	0	1	.000	11.57	2	0	0	0	0-0	2.1	2	3	3	0	2-0	2
1999— Atlanta (N.L.)	0	0	...	27.00	2	0	0	0	0-0	.2	3	2	2	0	0-0	0
2000— Atlanta (N.L.)	0	0	...	5.40	3	0	0	0	0-0	3.1	1	2	2	0	2-0	1
Division series totals (3 years)	0	1	.000	9.95	7	0	0	0	0-0	6.1	6	7	7	0	4-0	3

CHAMPIONSHIP SERIES RECORD

Year League	W	L	Pct.	ERA	G	GS	CG	ShO	Sv.-Opp.	IP	H	R	ER	HR	BB-IBB	SO
1993— Philadelphia (N.L.)	0	1	.000	7.20	1	1	0	0	0-0	5.0	9	5	4	0	1-0	2
1999— Atlanta (N.L.)	0	0	...	0.00	2	0	0	0	0-0	2.2	1	0	0	0	1-0	2
Champ. series totals (2 years)	0	1	.000	4.70	3	1	0	0	0-0	7.2	10	5	4	0	2-0	4

WORLD SERIES RECORD

Year League	W	L	Pct.	ERA	G	GS	CG	ShO	Sv.-Opp.	IP	H	R	ER	HR	BB-IBB	SO
1993— Philadelphia (N.L.)	1	0	1.000	6.75	2	2	0	0	0-0	10.2	14	8	8	2	3-0	5
1999— Atlanta (N.L.)	0	0	...	7.36	2	0	0	0	0-0	3.2	5	3	3	1	1-1	3
World Series totals (2 years)	1	0	1.000	6.91	4	2	0	0	0-0	14.1	19	11	11	3	4-1	8

ALL-STAR GAME RECORD

	W	L	Pct.	ERA	GS	CG	ShO	Sv.-Opp.	IP	H	R	ER	HR	BB-IBB	SO
All-Star Game totals (1 year)	0	0	...	4.50	1	0	0	0-0	2.0	1	1	1	1	2-0	0

MULLEN, SCOTT — P — ROYALS

PERSONAL: Born January 17, 1975, in San Benito, Texas. ... 6-2/195. ... Throws left, bats right. ... Full name: Kenneth Scott Mullen.
HIGH SCHOOL: Beaufort (S.C.).
COLLEGE: Dallas Baptist.
TRANSACTIONS/CAREER NOTES: Selected by Kansas City Royals organization in seventh round of free-agent draft (June 4, 1996). ... On Kansas City disabled list (March 31-May 4, 2001); included rehabilitation assignment to Omaha (April 5-May 4). ... On Omaha disabled list (April 4-11, 2002).
CAREER HITTING (MLB): 0-for-0 (.000), 0 R, 0 2B, 0 3B, 0 HR, 0 RBI.

Year League	W	L	Pct.	ERA	G	GS	CG	ShO	Sv.-Opp.	IP	H	R	ER	HR	BB-IBB	SO
1996— Spokane (N'West)	5	6	.455	3.92	15	15	0	0	0-...	80.1	78	45	35	6	29-0	78
1997— Lansing (Midw.)	5	2	.714	3.70	16	16	0	0	0-...	92.1	90	46	38	14	31-0	78
— Wilmington (Caro.)	4	4	.500	4.55	11	11	0	0	0-...	59.1	64	35	30	5	26-4	43
1998— Wilmington (Caro.)	8	4	.667	2.21	14	14	1	1	0-...	85.2	68	28	21	4	25-0	56
— Wichita (Texas)	8	2	.800	4.11	12	12	0	0	0-...	70.0	66	34	32	7	26-0	42
1999— Wichita (Texas)	4	3	.571	4.01	9	9	0	0	0-...	49.1	47	28	22	2	18-1	30
— Omaha (PCL)	6	7	.462	6.26	20	20	0	0	0-...	119.1	150	91	83	24	53-2	87
2000— Wichita (Texas)	3	2	.600	3.19	33	1	0	0	7-...	73.1	65	27	26	5	26-1	61
— Omaha (PCL)	2	1	.667	3.05	16	0	0	0	0-...	20.2	15	10	7	1	8-0	21
— Kansas City (A.L.)	0	0	...	4.35	11	0	0	0	0-0	10.1	10	5	5	2	3-0	7
2001— Omaha (PCL)	5	4	.556	6.62	48	0	0	0	5-...	53.0	66	39	39	8	22-2	38
— Kansas City (A.L.)	0	0	...	4.50	17	0	0	0	0-0	10.0	13	6	5	0	9-0	3
2002— Omaha (PCL)	1	2	.333	2.61	19	1	0	0	0-...	31.0	32	12	9	0	9-3	21
— Kansas City (A.L.)	4	5	.444	3.15	44	0	0	0	0-2	40.0	40	16	14	5	13-2	21
Major League totals (3 years)	4	5	.444	3.58	72	0	0	0	0-2	60.1	63	27	24	7	25-2	31

MUNRO, PETER — P — ASTROS

PERSONAL: Born June 14, 1975, in Flushing, N.Y. ... 6-3/210. ... Throws right, bats right. ... Full name: Peter Daniel Munro.
HIGH SCHOOL: Benjamin Cardozo (Bayside, N.Y.).
JUNIOR COLLEGE: Okaloosa-Walton Community College (Fla.).
TRANSACTIONS/CAREER NOTES: Selected by Boston Red Sox organization in sixth round of free-agent draft (June 3, 1993). ... On disabled list (June 28, 1994-entire season). ... On Pawtucket disabled list (May 24-June 8, 1998). ... Traded by Red Sox with P Jay Yennaco to Toronto Blue Jays for 1B/DH Mike Stanley (July 30, 1998). ... On Toronto disabled list (June 4-July 3, 2000); included rehabilitation assignments to

Dunedin (June 12-July 1) and Syracuse (July 2-3). ... Traded by Blue Jays to Texas Rangers (August 8, 2000); completing deal in which Rangers traded OF Dave Martinez to Blue Jays for a player to be named later (August 4, 2000). ... Granted free agency (December 21, 2000). ... Re-signed by Rangers organization (January 2, 2001). ... Granted free agency (October 15, 2001). ... Signed by Houston Astros organization (January 17, 2002).

CAREER HITTING (MLB): 3-for-23 (.130), 1 R, 0 2B, 0 3B, 0 HR, 2 RBI.

Year League	W	L	Pct.	ERA	G	GS	CG	ShO	Sv.-Opp.	IP	H	R	ER	HR	BB-IBB	SO
1994—									Did not play.							
1995—Utica (NY-Penn)	5	4	.556	2.60	14	14	0	0	0-...	90.0	79	38	26	3	33-1	74
1996—Sarasota (FSL)	11	6	.647	3.60	27	25	2	•2	1-...	155.0	153	76	62	4	62-1	115
1997—Trenton (East.)	7	10	.412	4.95	22	22	1	0	0-...	116.1	113	76	64	12	47-0	109
1998—Pawtucket (I.L.)	5	4	.556	4.05	18	17	0	0	0-...	106.2	111	49	48	10	35-2	75
—Syracuse (I.L.)■	2	5	.286	7.46	8	8	0	0	0-...	44.2	58	42	37	7	23-2	42
1999—Toronto (A.L.)	0	2	.000	6.02	31	2	0	0	0-1	55.1	70	38	37	6	23-0	38
—Syracuse (I.L.)	6	1	.857	3.10	18	11	0	0	0-...	69.2	70	29	24	6	33-1	68
2000—Syracuse (I.L.)	4	3	.571	2.48	10	10	2	0	0-...	61.2	52	20	17	1	25-0	45
—Dunedin (FSL)	0	1	.000	5.56	3	3	0	0	0-...	11.1	11	7	7	0	4-0	12
—Toronto (A.L.)	1	1	.500	5.96	9	3	0	0	0-0	25.2	38	22	17	1	16-0	16
—Oklahoma (PCL)■	1	2	.333	4.65	5	5	1	1	0-...	31.0	27	17	16	3	14-0	15
2001—Oklahoma (PCL)	8	6	.571	4.67	33	8	0	0	0-...	88.2	89	50	46	12	43-1	73
2002—New Orleans (PCL)■	7	1	.875	2.39	19	13	1	1	0-...	94.1	68	30	25	3	15-1	73
—Houston (N.L.)	5	5	.500	3.57	19	14	0	0	0-0	80.2	89	37	32	5	23-3	45
A.L. totals (2 years)	1	3	.250	6.00	40	5	0	0	0-1	81.0	108	60	54	7	39-0	54
N.L. totals (1 year)	5	5	.500	3.57	19	14	0	0	0-0	80.2	89	37	32	5	23-3	45
Major League totals (3 years)	6	8	.429	4.79	59	19	0	0	0-1	161.2	197	97	86	12	62-3	99

MUNSON, ERIC — 1B — TIGERS

PERSONAL: Born October 3, 1977, in San Diego, Calif. ... 6-3/228. ... Bats left, throws right. ... Full name: Eric Walter Munson.
HIGH SCHOOL: Mount Carmel (San Diego).
COLLEGE: Southern California.
TRANSACTIONS/CAREER NOTES: Selected by Atlanta Braves organization in second round of free-agent draft (June 4, 1996); did not sign. ... Selected by Detroit Tigers organization in first round (third pick overall) of free-agent draft (June 2, 1999). ... On Jacksonville disabled list (August 28-September 18, 2000).
STATISTICAL NOTES: Led Eastern League first basemen with 1,031 putouts, 93 assists, 1,141 total chances and 94 double plays in 2001. ... Led International League first basemen with 1,159 putouts and 1,260 total chances in 2002.
2002 GAMES PLAYED BY POSITION (MLB): DH—14; 1B—4.

		BATTING														FIELDING	
Year Team (League)	Pos.	G	AB	R	H	2B	3B	HR	RBI	BB	SO	SB-CS	Avg.	OBP	SLG	E	Avg.
1999—Lakeland (FSL)	DH	2	6	0	2	0	0	0	1	1	1	0-0	.333	.429	.333	...	...
—West Mich. (Midw.)	1B-C	67	252	42	67	16	1	14	44	37	47	3-1	.266	.378	.504	3	.991
2000—Jacksonville (Sou.)	1B	98	365	52	92	21	4	15	68	39	96	5-2	.252	.348	.455	8	.989
—Detroit (A.L.)	1B	3	5	0	0	0	0	0	1	0	1	0-0	.000	.000	.000	1	.941
2001—Erie (East.)	1B	*142	519	88	135	35	1	26	*102	*84	141	0-3	.260	.371	.482	*17	.985
—Detroit (A.L.)	1B	17	66	4	10	3	1	1	6	3	21	0-1	.152	.188	.273	1	.994
2002—Toledo (I.L.)	1B	136	477	77	125	30	4	24	84	77	114	1-3	.262	.367	.493	•12	.990
—Detroit (A.L.)	DH-1B	18	59	3	11	0	0	2	5	6	11	0-0	.186	.269	.288	1	.970
Major League totals (3 years)		38	130	7	21	3	1	3	12	9	33	0-1	.162	.220	.269	3	.986

MURRAY, CALVIN — OF

PERSONAL: Born July 30, 1971, in Dallas. ... 5-11/184. ... Bats right, throws right. ... Full name: Calvin Duane Murray.
HIGH SCHOOL: Warren Travis White (Dallas).
COLLEGE: Texas.
TRANSACTIONS/CAREER NOTES: Selected by San Francisco Giants organization in first round (seventh pick overall) of free-agent draft (June 1, 1992). ... Traded by Giants to Texas Rangers for cash (April 22, 2002). ... On Oklahoma disabled list (July 25, 2002-remainder of season). ... Granted free agency (October 15, 2002).
HONORS: Named Pacific Coast League Most Valuable Player (1999).
STATISTICAL NOTES: Led Pacific Coast League with 297 total bases in 1999. ... Career major league grand slams: 1.
MISCELLANEOUS: Member of 1992 U.S. Olympic Baseball team.
2002 GAMES PLAYED BY POSITION (MLB): OF—44; DH—2.

		BATTING														FIELDING	
Year Team (League)	Pos.	G	AB	R	H	2B	3B	HR	RBI	BB	SO	SB-CS	Avg.	OBP	SLG	E	Avg.
1993—Shreveport (Texas)	OF	37	138	15	26	6	0	0	6	14	29	12-6	.188	.271	.232	2	.976
—San Jose (Calif.)	OF	85	345	61	97	24	1	9	42	40	63	42-10	.281	.362	.435	2	.991
—Phoenix (PCL)	OF	5	19	4	6	1	1	0	0	2	5	1-1	.316	.381	.474	2	.867
1994—Shreveport (Texas)	OF	480	480	67	111	19	5	2	35	47	81	33-13	.231	.304	.304	3	.989
1995—Phoenix (PCL)	OF	13	50	8	9	1	0	4	10	4	6	2-2	.180	.236	.440	0	1.000
—Shreveport (Texas)	OF	110	441	77	104	17	3	2	29	59	70	26-10	.236	.329	.302	2	.993
1996—Shreveport (Texas)	OF	50	169	32	44	7	0	7	24	25	33	6-5	.260	.352	.426	3	.969
—Phoenix (PCL)	OF	83	311	50	76	16	6	3	28	43	60	12-6	.244	.341	.363	2	.991
1997—Shreveport (Texas)	OF	122	419	83	114	25	3	10	56	66	73	*52-6	.272	.375	.418	5	.978
1998—Fresno (PCL)	OF	33	90	16	21	3	1	3	5	12	18	3-1	.233	.324	.389	0	1.000
—Shreveport (Texas)	OF	88	337	63	104	22	5	8	39	58	45	34-15	.309	.418	.475	7	.966
1999—Fresno (PCL)	OF-DH	130	*548	*122	*183	31	7	23	73	49	88	*42-14	.334	.389	.542	6	.980
—San Francisco (N.L.)	OF	15	19	1	5	2	0	0	5	2	4	1-0	.263	.333	.368	0	1.000
2000—San Francisco (N.L.)	OF	108	194	35	47	12	1	2	22	29	33	9-3	.242	.348	.345	3	.980
2001—San Francisco (N.L.)	OF	106	326	54	80	14	2	6	25	32	57	8-8	.245	.319	.356	5	.979
—Fresno (PCL)	OF	35	138	17	36	6	1	4	12	12	33	3-3	.261	.322	.406	2	.978

Year	Team (League)	Pos.	G	AB	R	H	2B	3B	HR	RBI	BB	SO	SB-CS	Avg.	OBP	SLG	E	Avg.
			BATTING														FIELDING	
2002—	San Francisco (N.L.) ..	OF	11	12	0	0	0	0	0	0	1	2	0-0	.000	.077	.000	1	.917
	—Texas (A.L.)■	OF-DH	37	77	16	13	5	1	0	1	6	15	4-0	.169	.238	.260	0	1.000
	—Oklahoma (PCL)	OF	33	139	23	37	7	1	2	14	11	20	4-0	.266	.318	.374	0	1.000
American League totals (1 year)			37	77	16	13	5	1	0	1	6	15	4-0	.169	.238	.260	0	1.000
National League totals (4 years)			240	551	90	132	28	3	8	52	64	96	18-11	.240	.325	.345	9	.978
Major League totals (4 years)			277	628	106	145	33	4	8	53	70	111	22-11	.231	.314	.334	9	.981

DIVISION SERIES RECORD

Year	Team (League)	Pos.	G	AB	R	H	2B	3B	HR	RBI	BB	SO	SB-CS	Avg.	OBP	SLG	E	Avg.
			BATTING														FIELDING	
2000—	San Francisco (N.L.) ..	OF	3	5	0	1	0	0	0	0	0	3	0-0	.200	.200	.200	0	1.000

MURRAY, HEATH P

PERSONAL: Born April 19, 1973, in Troy, Ohio. ... 6-4/210. ... Throws left, bats left. ... Full name: Heath Robertson Murray.
HIGH SCHOOL: Troy (Ohio).
COLLEGE: Michigan.
TRANSACTIONS/CAREER NOTES: Selected by San Diego Padres organization in third round of free-agent draft (June 2, 1994). ... On San Diego disabled list (June 23-July 10, 1997). ... On San Diego disabled list (September 19, 1998-remainder of season). ... Claimed on waivers by Cincinnati Reds (October 6, 1999). ... Released by Reds (March 29, 2000). ... Signed by Los Angeles Dodgers organization (April 5, 2000). ... Granted free agency (October 18, 2000). ... Signed by Detroit Tigers organization (January 18, 2001). ... Released by Tigers (November 20, 2001). ... Signed by Cleveland Indians organization (December 18, 2001). ... On Cleveland disabled list (July 22, 2002-remainder of season); included rehabilitation assignment to Buffalo (August 15-17). ... Released by Indians (October 2, 2002).
STATISTICAL NOTES: Tied for Pacific Coast League lead with four double plays by pitcher in 1999.
CAREER HITTING (MLB): 2-for-19 (.105), 1 R, 0 2B, 0 3B, 0 HR, 0 RBI.

Year	League	W	L	Pct.	ERA	G	GS	CG	ShO	Sv.-Opp.	IP	H	R	ER	HR	BB-IBB	SO
1994—	Spokane (N'West)	5	6	.455	2.90	15	15	•2	•1	0-...	*99.1	101	46	32	6	18-0	78
1995—	Rancho Cuca. (Calif.)	9	4	.692	3.12	14	14	4	•2	0-...	92.1	80	37	32	5	38-1	81
	—Memphis (Sou.)	5	4	.556	3.38	14	14	0	0	0-...	77.1	83	36	29	1	42-1	71
1996—	Memphis (Sou.)	13	9	.591	3.21	27	27	1	1	0-...	174.0	154	83	62	13	60-2	156
1997—	Las Vegas (PCL)	6	8	.429	5.45	19	19	2	1	0-...	109.0	142	72	66	10	41-1	99
	—San Diego (N.L.)	1	2	.333	6.75	17	3	0	0	0-0	33.1	50	25	25	3	21-3	16
1998—	Las Vegas (PCL)	9	11	.450	4.99	27	27	3	0	0-...	162.1	191	103	90	13	62-3	121
1999—	Las Vegas (PCL)	5	4	.556	4.26	15	15	1	1	0-...	82.1	99	45	39	5	32-0	65
	—San Diego (N.L.)	0	4	.000	5.76	22	8	0	0	0-0	50.0	60	33	32	7	26-4	25
2000—	Albuquerque (PCL)■	7	10	.412	4.73	29	24	3	1	0-...	156.0	184	96	82	8	66-5	110
2001—	Toledo (I.L.)■	1	1	.500	2.00	11	3	0	0	1-...	36.0	22	9	8	5	2-0	44
	—Detroit (A.L.)	1	7	.125	6.54	40	4	0	0	0-2	63.1	82	48	46	11	40-5	42
2002—	Buffalo (I.L.)■	1	2	.333	3.03	21	2	0	0	5-...	29.2	23	10	10	2	6-0	32
	—Cleveland (A.L.)	0	2	.000	7.50	9	0	0	0	0-0	12.0	12	10	10	3	7-0	11
A.L. totals (2 years)		1	9	.100	6.69	49	4	0	0	0-2	75.1	94	58	56	14	47-5	53
N.L. totals (2 years)		1	6	.143	6.16	39	11	0	0	0-0	83.1	110	58	57	10	47-7	41
Major League totals (4 years)		2	15	.118	6.41	88	15	0	0	0-2	158.2	204	116	113	24	94-12	94

MUSSINA, MIKE P YANKEES

PERSONAL: Born December 8, 1968, in Williamsport, Pa. ... 6-2/185. ... Throws right, bats left. ... Full name: Michael Cole Mussina. ... Name pronounced myoo-SEEN-uh.
HIGH SCHOOL: Montoursville (Pa.).
COLLEGE: Stanford.
TRANSACTIONS/CAREER NOTES: Selected by Baltimore Orioles organization in 11th round of free-agent draft (June 2, 1987); did not sign. ... Selected by Orioles organization in first round (20th pick overall) of free-agent draft (June 4, 1990). ... On Rochester disabled list (May 5-12, 1991). ... On Baltimore disabled list (July 22-August 20, 1993); included rehabilitation assignment to Bowie (August 9-20). ... On disabled list (April 17-May 3 and May 15-June 6, 1998). ... Granted free agency (October 27, 2000). ... Signed by New York Yankees (November 30, 2000).
RECORDS: Shares major league single-inning record for most doubles allowed—6 (July 31, 2002, second inning).
HONORS: Named International League Most Valuable Pitcher (1991). ... Named righthanded pitcher on The Sporting News A.L. All-Star team (1995). ... Won A.L. Gold Glove at pitcher (1996-99 and 2001).
STATISTICAL NOTES: Pitched 8-0 one-hit, complete-game victory against Texas (July 17, 1992). ... Pitched 3-0 one-hit, complete-game victory against Cleveland (May 30, 1997). ... Struck out 15 batters in one game (August 1 and September 24, 2000). ... Pitched 10-0 one-hit, complete-game victory against Minnesota (August 1, 2000). ... Pitched 1-0 one-hit, complete-game victory against Boston (September 2, 2001).
CAREER HITTING (MLB): 8-for-35 (.229), 3 R, 1 2B, 0 3B, 0 HR, 5 RBI.

Year	League	W	L	Pct.	ERA	G	GS	CG	ShO	Sv.-Opp.	IP	H	R	ER	HR	BB-IBB	SO
1990—	Hagerstown (East.)	3	0	1.000	1.49	7	7	2	1	0-...	42.1	34	10	7	1	7-0	40
	—Rochester (I.L.)	0	0	...	1.35	2	2	0	0	0-...	13.1	8	2	2	2	4-0	15
1991—	Rochester (I.L.)	10	4	.714	2.87	19	19	3	1	0-...	122.1	108	42	39	9	31-0	107
	—Baltimore (A.L.)	4	5	.444	2.87	12	12	2	0	0-0	87.2	77	31	28	7	21-0	52
1992—	Baltimore (A.L.)	18	5	*.783	2.54	32	32	8	4	0-0	241.0	212	70	68	16	48-2	130
1993—	Baltimore (A.L.)	14	6	.700	4.46	25	25	3	2	0-0	167.2	163	84	83	20	44-2	117
	—Bowie (East.)	1	0	1.000	2.25	2	2	0	0	0-...	8.0	5	2	2	0	1-0	10
1994—	Baltimore (A.L.)	16	5	.762	3.06	24	24	3	0	0-0	176.1	163	63	60	19	42-1	99
1995—	Baltimore (A.L.)	*19	9	.679	3.29	32	32	7	*4	0-0	221.2	187	86	81	24	50-4	158
1996—	Baltimore (A.L.)	19	11	.633	4.81	36	*36	4	1	0-0	243.1	264	137	130	31	69-0	204
1997—	Baltimore (A.L.)	15	8	.652	3.20	33	33	4	1	0-0	224.2	197	87	80	27	54-3	218
1998—	Baltimore (A.L.)	13	10	.565	3.49	29	29	4	2	0-0	206.1	189	85	80	22	41-3	175
1999—	Baltimore (A.L.)	18	7	.720	3.50	31	31	4	0	0-0	203.1	207	88	79	16	52-0	172
2000—	Baltimore (A.L.)	11	15	.423	3.79	34	34	6	1	0-0	*237.2	236	105	100	28	46-0	210
2001—	New York (A.L.)■	17	11	.607	3.15	34	34	4	3	0-0	228.2	202	87	80	20	42-2	214
2002—	New York (A.L.)	18	10	.643	4.05	33	33	2	2	0-0	215.2	208	103	97	27	48-1	182
Major League totals (12 years)		182	102	.641	3.54	355	355	51	20	0-0	2454.0	2305	1026	966	257	557-18	1931

DIVISION SERIES RECORD

RECORDS: Shares A.L. career record for most wins—3.

Year League	W	L	Pct.	ERA	G	GS	CG	ShO	Sv.-Opp.	IP	H	R	ER	HR	BB-IBB	SO
1996—Baltimore (A.L.)	0	0	...	4.50	1	1	0	0	0-0	6.0	7	4	3	1	2-0	6
1997—Baltimore (A.L.)	2	0	1.000	1.93	2	2	0	0	0-0	14.0	7	3	3	3	3-0	16
2001—New York (A.L.)	1	0	1.000	0.00	1	1	0	0	0-0	7.0	4	0	0	0	1-0	4
2002—New York (A.L.)	0	0	...	9.00	1	1	0	0	0-0	4.0	6	4	4	1	0-0	2
Division series totals (4 years)	3	0	1.000	2.90	5	5	0	0	0-0	31.0	24	11	10	5	6-0	28

CHAMPIONSHIP SERIES RECORD

Year League	W	L	Pct.	ERA	G	GS	CG	ShO	Sv.-Opp.	IP	H	R	ER	HR	BB-IBB	SO
1996—Baltimore (A.L.)	0	1	.000	5.87	1	1	0	0	0-0	7.2	8	5	5	1	2-0	6
1997—Baltimore (A.L.)	0	0	...	0.60	2	2	0	0	0-0	15.0	4	1	1	0	4-0	25
2001—New York (A.L.)	1	0	1.000	3.00	1	1	0	0	0-0	6.0	4	2	2	1	1-0	3
Champ. series totals (3 years)	1	1	.500	2.51	4	4	0	0	0-0	28.2	16	8	8	2	7-0	34

WORLD SERIES RECORD

Year League	W	L	Pct.	ERA	G	GS	CG	ShO	Sv.-Opp.	IP	H	R	ER	HR	BB-IBB	SO
2001—New York (A.L.)	0	1	.000	4.09	2	2	0	0	0-0	11.0	11	7	5	4	4-3	14

ALL-STAR GAME RECORD

	W	L	Pct.	ERA	GS	CG	ShO	Sv.-Opp.	IP	H	R	ER	HR	BB-IBB	SO
All-Star Game totals (3 years)	0	0	...	0.00	0	0	0	0-0	3.0	2	0	0	0	1-0	3

MYERS, BRETT P PHILLIES

PERSONAL: Born August 17, 1980, in Jacksonville, Fla. ... 6-4/215. ... Throws right, bats right. ... Full name: Brett Allen Myers.

HIGH SCHOOL: Englewood (Jacksonville, Fla.).

TRANSACTIONS/CAREER NOTES: Selected by Philadelphia Phillies organization in first round (12th pick overall) of free-agent draft (June 2, 1999).

CAREER HITTING (MLB): 3-for-23 (.130), 0 R, 1 2B, 0 3B, 0 HR, 1 RBI.

Year League	W	L	Pct.	ERA	G	GS	CG	ShO	Sv.-Opp.	IP	H	R	ER	HR	BB-IBB	SO
1999—Gulf Coast Phillies (GCL)	2	1	.667	2.33	7	5	0	0	0-...	27.0	17	8	7	0	7-0	30
2000—Piedmont (S.Atl.)	13	7	.650	3.18	27	27	2	1	0-...	175.1	165	78	62	7	69-0	140
2001—Reading (East.)	13	4	.765	3.87	26	23	1	1	0-...	156.0	156	71	67	21	43-1	130
2002—Scranton/W.B. (I.L.)	9	6	.600	3.59	19	19	4	1	0-...	128.0	121	54	51	9	20-0	97
—Philadelphia (N.L.)	4	5	.444	4.25	12	12	1	0	0-0	72.0	73	38	34	11	29-1	34
Major League totals (1 year)	4	5	.444	4.25	12	12	1	0	0-0	72.0	73	38	34	11	29-1	34

MYERS, GREG C

PERSONAL: Born April 14, 1966, in Riverside, Calif. ... 6-2/225. ... Bats left, throws right. ... Full name: Gregory Richard Myers.

HIGH SCHOOL: Riverside (Calif.) Polytechnical.

TRANSACTIONS/CAREER NOTES: Selected by Toronto Blue Jays organization in third round of free-agent draft (June 4, 1984). ... On disabled list (June 17, 1988-remainder of season). ... On Toronto disabled list (March 26-June 5, 1989); included rehabilitation assignment to Knoxville (May 17-June 5). ... On Toronto disabled list (May 5-25, 1990); included rehabilitation assignment to Syracuse (May 21-24). ... Traded by Blue Jays with OF Rob Ducey to California Angels for P Mark Eichhorn (July 30, 1992). ... On California disabled list (August 27, 1992-remainder of season). ... On California disabled list (April 24-June 21, 1994); included rehabilitation assignments to Lake Elsinore (May 20-June 6 and June 13-21). ... On disabled list (April 21-May 6, June 1-21 and September 30, 1995-remainder of season). ... Granted free agency (November 3, 1995). ... Signed by Minnesota Twins (December 8, 1995). ... On disabled list (July 14-August 2, 1996). ... On Minnesota disabled list (August 9-24, 1997). ... Traded by Twins to Atlanta Braves for a player to be named later (September 5, 1997); Twins acquired 1B Steve Hacker to complete deal (December 18, 1997). ... Granted free agency (October 28, 1997). ... Signed by San Diego Padres (November 25, 1997). ... On San Diego disabled list (June 4-July 24, 1998); included rehabilitation assignments to Rancho Cucamonga (July 17-19) and Las Vegas (July 21-23). ... On San Diego disabled list (June 29-July 26, 1999); included rehabilitation assignment to Rancho Cucamonga (July 20-26). ... Traded by Padres to Braves for P Doug Dent (July 26, 1999). ... Granted free agency (November 1, 1999). ... Signed by Baltimore Orioles (December 17, 1999). ... On disabled list (April 2-17, 2000). ... Released by Orioles (June 14, 2001). ... Signed by Oakland Athletics (June 23, 2001). ... Granted free agency (November 5, 2001). ... Re-signed by A's (November 15, 2001). ... Granted free agency (October 29, 2002).

STATISTICAL NOTES: Led California League catchers with 849 putouts and 967 total chances in 1986. ... Led International League catchers with 637 putouts and 698 total chances in 1987.

2002 GAMES PLAYED BY POSITION (MLB): C—53; DH—1.

		BATTING													FIELDING	
Year Team (League)	Pos.	G	AB	R	H	2B	3B	HR	RBI	BB	SO	SB-CS	Avg.	OBP	SLG	E	Avg.
1984—Medicine Hat (Pio.)	C	38	133	20	42	9	0	2	20	16	6	0-0	.316	.387	.429	4	.984
1985—Florence (S.Atl.)	C	134	489	52	109	19	2	5	62	39	54	0-0	.223	.279	.301	7	*.989
1986—Ventura (Calif.)	C	124	451	65	133	23	4	20	79	43	46	9-4	.295	.355	.497	19	.980
1987—Syracuse (I.L.)	C	107	342	35	84	19	1	10	47	22	46	3-3	.246	.292	.395	11	.984
—Toronto (A.L.)	C	7	9	1	1	0	0	0	0	0	3	0-0	.111	.111	.111	0	1.000
1988—Syracuse (I.L.)	C	34	120	18	34	7	1	7	21	8	24	1-0	.283	.328	.533	1	.986
1989—Knoxville (Sou.)	C	29	90	11	30	10	0	5	19	3	16	1-0	.333	.351	.611	1	.993
—Toronto (A.L.)	C-DH	17	44	0	5	2	0	0	1	2	9	0-1	.114	.152	.159	0	1.000
—Syracuse (I.L.)	C	24	89	8	24	6	0	1	11	4	9	0-0	.270	.301	.371	1	.985
1990—Toronto (A.L.)	C	87	250	33	59	7	1	5	22	22	33	0-1	.236	.293	.332	3	.993
—Syracuse (I.L.)	C	3	11	0	2	1	0	0	2	1	1	0-0	.182	.231	.273	0	1.000
1991—Toronto (A.L.)	C	107	309	25	81	22	0	8	36	21	45	0-0	.262	.306	.411	11	.979
1992—Toronto (A.L.)	C	22	61	4	14	6	0	1	13	5	5	0-0	.230	.279	.377	1	.991
—California (A.L.)■	C-DH	8	17	0	4	1	0	0	0	0	6	0-0	.235	.235	.294	0	1.000
1993—California (A.L.)	C-DH	108	290	27	74	10	0	7	40	17	47	3-3	.255	.298	.362	6	.986
1994—California (A.L.)	C-DH	45	126	10	31	6	0	2	8	10	27	0-2	.246	.299	.341	2	.991
—Lake Elsinore (Calif.)	C-DH	10	32	4	8	2	0	0	5	2	6	0-0	.250	.286	.313	0	1.000
1995—California (A.L.)	C-DH	85	273	35	71	12	2	9	38	17	49	0-1	.260	.304	.418	4	.989
1996—Minnesota (A.L.)■	C	97	329	37	94	22	3	6	47	19	52	0-0	.286	.320	.426	8	.985

Year	Team (League)	Pos.	G	AB	R	H	2B	3B	HR	RBI	BB	SO	SB-CS	Avg.	OBP	SLG	E	Avg.
			BATTING														FIELDING	
1997—	Minnesota (A.L.)	C-DH	62	165	24	44	11	1	5	28	16	29	0-0	.267	.328	.436	3	.986
	— Atlanta (N.L.)■	C	9	9	0	1	0	0	0	1	1	3	0-0	.111	.200	.111	0	1.000
1998—	San Diego (N.L.)■	C	69	171	19	42	10	0	4	20	17	36	0-1	.246	.312	.374	4	.987
	— Rancho Cuca. (Calif.)	C-DH	3	9	1	0	0	0	0	0	2	1	0-0	.000	.182	.000	0	1.000
	— Las Vegas (PCL)	C	3	9	0	5	0	0	0	1	0	0	0-0	.556	.556	.556	0	1.000
1999—	San Diego (N.L.)	C	50	128	9	37	4	0	3	15	13	14	0-0	.289	.355	.391	3	.986
	— Rancho Cuca. (Calif.)	C-DH	3	3	0	0	0	0	0	0	1	1	0-0	.000	.250	.000	0	1.000
	— Atlanta (N.L.)■	C	34	72	10	16	2	0	2	9	13	16	0-0	.222	.337	.333	1	.994
2000—	Baltimore (A.L.)■	C-DH	43	125	9	28	6	0	3	12	8	29	0-0	.224	.271	.344	0	1.000
2001—	Baltimore (A.L.)	DH-C	25	74	11	20	2	0	4	18	8	17	0-0	.270	.341	.459	0	1.000
	— Sacramento (PCL)■	C	2	5	0	0	0	0	0	1	3	2	0-0	.000	.375	.000	0	1.000
	— Oakland (A.L.)	C-DH	33	87	13	16	1	0	7	13	13	21	0-0	.184	.290	.437	0	1.000
2002—	Oakland (A.L.)	C-DH	65	144	15	32	5	0	6	21	26	36	0-0	.222	.341	.382	1	.997
American League totals (13 years)			811	2303	244	574	113	7	63	297	184	408	3-8	.249	.303	.386	39	.989
National League totals (3 years)			162	380	38	96	16	0	9	45	44	69	0-1	.253	.329	.366	8	.989
Major League totals (15 years)			973	2683	282	670	129	7	72	342	228	477	3-9	.250	.307	.384	47	.989

DIVISION SERIES RECORD

Year	Team (League)	Pos.	G	AB	R	H	2B	3B	HR	RBI	BB	SO	SB-CS	Avg.	OBP	SLG	E	Avg.
			BATTING														FIELDING	
1998—	San Diego (N.L.)	C	1	0	0	0	0	0	0	0	0	0	0-0	...	...	...	0	...
1999—	Atlanta (N.L.)								Did not play.									
2001—	Oakland (A.L.)	PH-C	3	7	0	1	0	0	0	0	0	3	0-0	.143	.143	.143	1	.929
2002—	Oakland (A.L.)	C	2	1	0	0	0	0	0	0	0	1	0-0	.000	.000	.000	0	1.000
Division series totals (3 years)			6	8	0	1	0	0	0	0	0	4	0-0	.125	.125	.125	1	.944

CHAMPIONSHIP SERIES RECORD

Year	Team (League)	Pos.	G	AB	R	H	2B	3B	HR	RBI	BB	SO	SB-CS	Avg.	OBP	SLG	E	Avg.
			BATTING														FIELDING	
1991—	Toronto (A.L.)								Did not play.									
1998—	San Diego (N.L.)	PH	2	1	1	1	0	0	1	2	1	0	0-0	1.000	1.000	4.000	...	...
1999—	Atlanta (N.L.)	C	2	2	0	0	0	0	0	0	1	1	0-0	.000	.333	.000	0	1.000
Championship series totals (2 years)			4	3	1	1	0	0	1	2	2	1	0-0	.333	.600	1.333	0	1.000

WORLD SERIES RECORD

Year	Team (League)	Pos.	G	AB	R	H	2B	3B	HR	RBI	BB	SO	SB-CS	Avg.	OBP	SLG	E	Avg.
			BATTING														FIELDING	
1998—	San Diego (N.L.)	PH-C	2	4	0	0	0	0	0	0	0	2	0-0	.000	.000	.000	0	1.000
1999—	Atlanta (N.L.)	PH-C	4	6	0	2	0	0	0	1	1	0	0-0	.333	.429	.333	0	1.000
World Series totals (2 years)			6	10	0	2	0	0	0	1	1	2	0-0	.200	.273	.200	0	1.000

MYERS, MIKE — P — DIAMONDBACKS

M

PERSONAL: Born June 26, 1969, in Arlington Heights, Ill. ... 6-4/212. ... Throws left, bats left. ... Full name: Michael Stanley Myers.

HIGH SCHOOL: Crystal Lake (Ill.) Central.

COLLEGE: Iowa State.

TRANSACTIONS/CAREER NOTES: Selected by San Francisco Giants organization in fourth round of free-agent draft (June 4, 1990). ... On Clinton disabled list (June 3-September 16, 1991; April 9-June 2 and June 21-July 6, 1992). ... Selected by Florida Marlins from Giants organization in Rule 5 major league draft (December 7, 1992). ... On Edmonton disabled list (April 13-June 7, 1994). ... On Florida disabled list (June 7-August 5, 1994); included rehabilitation assignment to Brevard County (June 23-July 11). ... Traded by Marlins to Detroit Tigers (August 9, 1995), completing deal in which Marlins acquired P Buddy Groom for a player to be named later (August 7, 1995). ... Traded by Tigers with P Rick Greene and SS Santiago Perez to Milwaukee Brewers for P Bryce Florie and a player to be named later (November 20, 1997). ... Traded by Brewers to Colorado Rockies for P Curtis Leskanic (November 17, 1999). ... Traded by Rockies to Arizona Diamondbacks for OF Jack Cust and C J.D. Closser (January 7, 2002).

STATISTICAL NOTES: Led Pacific Coast League with 10 hit batsmen in 1993.

CAREER HITTING (MLB): 0-for-1 (.000), 0 R, 0 2B, 0 3B, 0 HR, 0 RBI.

Year	League	W	L	Pct.	ERA	G	GS	CG	ShO	Sv.-Opp.	IP	H	R	ER	HR	BB-IBB	SO
1990—	Everett (N'West)	4	5	.444	3.90	15	14	1	0	0-...	85.1	91	43	37	9	30-0	73
1991—	Clinton (Midw.)	5	3	.625	2.62	11	11	1	0	0-...	65.1	61	23	19	3	18-0	59
	— Arizona Giants (Ariz.)	0	1	.000	12.00	1	0	0	0	0-...	3.0	5	5	4	0	2-0	2
1992—	San Jose (Calif.)	5	1	.833	2.30	8	8	0	0	0-...	54.2	43	20	14	1	17-0	40
	— Clinton (Midw.)	1	2	.333	1.19	7	7	0	0	0-...	37.2	28	11	5	0	8-0	32
1993—	Edmonton (PCL)■	7	14	.333	5.18	27	27	3	0	0-...	161.2	195	109	93	20	52-1	112
1994—	Edmonton (PCL)	1	5	.167	5.55	12	11	0	0	0-...	60.0	78	42	37	9	21-0	55
	— Brevard County (FSL)	0	0	...	0.79	3	2	0	0	0-...	11.1	7	1	1	1	4-0	15
1995—	Florida (N.L.)	0	0	...	0.00	2	0	0	0	0-0	2.0	1	0	0	0	3-0	0
	— Charlotte (I.L.)	0	5	.000	5.65	37	0	0	0	0-...	36.2	41	25	23	6	15-1	24
	— Toledo (I.L.)■	0	0	...	4.32	6	0	0	0	0-...	8.1	6	4	4	1	3-0	8
	— Detroit (A.L.)	1	0	1.000	9.95	11	0	0	0	0-1	6.1	10	7	7	1	4-0	4
1996—	Detroit (A.L.)	1	5	.167	5.01	•83	0	0	0	6-8	64.2	70	41	36	6	34-8	69
1997—	Detroit (A.L.)	0	4	.000	5.70	*88	0	0	0	2-5	53.2	58	36	34	12	25-2	50
1998—	Milwaukee (N.L.)■	2	2	.500	2.70	70	0	0	0	1-3	50.0	44	19	15	5	22-1	40
1999—	Milwaukee (N.L.)	2	1	.667	5.23	71	0	0	0	0-3	41.1	46	24	24	7	13-1	35
2000—	Colorado (N.L.)■	0	1	.000	1.99	78	0	0	0	1-2	45.1	24	10	10	2	24-3	41
2001—	Colorado (N.L.)	2	3	.400	3.60	73	0	0	0	0-2	40.0	32	17	16	2	24-7	36
2002—	Arizona (N.L.)■	4	3	.571	4.38	69	0	0	0	4-9	37.0	39	18	18	2	17-0	31
A.L. totals (3 years)		2	9	.182	5.56	182	0	0	0	8-14	124.2	138	84	77	19	63-10	123
N.L. totals (6 years)		10	10	.500	3.46	363	0	0	0	6-19	215.2	186	88	83	18	103-12	183
Major League totals (8 years)		12	19	.387	4.23	545	0	0	0	14-33	340.1	324	172	160	37	166-22	306

DIVISION SERIES RECORD

Year	League	W	L	Pct.	ERA	G	GS	CG	ShO	Sv.-Opp.	IP	H	R	ER	HR	BB-IBB	SO
2002—	Arizona (N.L.)	0	0	...	0.00	2	0	0	0	0-0	1.2	2	0	0	0	0-0	1

MYERS, RODNEY — P

PERSONAL: Born June 26, 1969, in Rockford, Ill. ... 6-1/215. ... Throws right, bats right. ... Full name: Rodney Luther Myers.
HIGH SCHOOL: Rockford (Ill.) East.
COLLEGE: Wisconsin.
TRANSACTIONS/CAREER NOTES: Selected by Kansas City Royals organization in 12th round of free-agent draft (June 4, 1990). ... On disabled list (May 17-June 3 and June 21-September 15, 1994; and June 30-July 21, 1995). ... Selected by Chicago Cubs from Royals organization in Rule 5 major league draft (December 4, 1995). ... On Iowa disabled list (June 7-15, 1998). ... Traded by Cubs to San Diego Padres for OF Gary Matthews Jr. (March 23, 2000). ... On San Diego disabled list (March 29-May 5 and May 12, 2000-remainder of season); included rehabilitation assignment to Rancho Cucamonga (April 30-May 5). ... On San Diego disabled list (May 20-June 19, 2001); included rehabilitation assignment to Portland (June 14-19). ... Granted free agency (October 8, 2001). ... Re-signed by Padres organization (March 11, 2002). ... Granted free agency (October 15, 2002).
MISCELLANEOUS: Doubled in only appearance as pinch hitter (1999).
CAREER HITTING (MLB): 3-for-16 (.188), 2 R, 1 2B, 0 3B, 0 HR, 1 RBI.

Year	League	W	L	Pct.	ERA	G	GS	CG	ShO	Sv.-Opp.	IP	H	R	ER	HR	BB-IBB	SO
1990—	Eugene (N'West)	0	2	.000	1.19	6	4	0	0	0-...	22.2	19	9	3	2	13-0	17
1991—	Appleton (Midw.)	1	1	.500	2.60	9	4	0	0	0-...	27.2	22	9	8	0	26-0	29
1992—	Lethbridge (Pio.)	5	•8	.385	4.01	15	15	*5	0	0-...	*103.1	93	57	46	3	61-1	76
1993—	Rockford (Midw.)	7	3	.700	1.79	12	12	5	2	0-...	85.1	65	22	17	3	18-0	65
	—Memphis (Sou.)	3	6	.333	5.62	12	12	1	1	0-...	65.2	73	46	41	8	32-0	42
1994—	Wilmington (Caro.)	1	1	.500	4.82	4	0	0	0	1-...	9.1	9	6	5	1	1-0	9
	—Memphis (Sou.)	5	1	.833	1.03	42	0	0	0	9-...	69.2	45	20	8	3	29-2	53
1995—	Omaha (A.A.)	4	5	.444	4.10	38	0	0	0	2-...	48.1	52	26	22	5	19-1	38
1996—	Chicago (N.L.)■	2	1	.667	4.68	45	0	0	0	0-0	67.1	61	38	35	6	38-3	50
1997—	Iowa (A.A.)	7	8	.467	4.09	24	23	1	0	0-...	140.2	140	76	64	18	38-1	79
	—Chicago (N.L.)	0	0	...	6.00	5	1	0	0	0-0	9.0	12	6	6	1	7-1	6
1998—	Iowa (PCL)	7	5	.583	3.91	33	13	2	1	11-...	101.1	84	47	44	10	45-1	86
	—Chicago (N.L.)	0	0	...	7.00	12	0	0	0	0-1	18.0	26	14	14	3	6-0	15
1999—	Iowa (PCL)	2	4	.333	4.06	20	1	0	0	2-...	31.0	29	18	14	3	11-3	24
	—Chicago (N.L.)	3	1	.750	4.38	46	0	0	0	0-1	63.2	71	34	31	10	25-2	41
2000—	Rancho Cuca. (Calif.)■	0	0	...	0.00	3	2	0	0	0-...	4.0	2	0	0	0	0-0	4
	—San Diego (N.L.)	0	0	...	4.50	3	0	0	0	0-0	2.0	2	1	1	0	0-0	3
2001—	San Diego (N.L.)	1	2	.333	5.32	37	0	0	0	1-2	47.1	53	31	28	6	20-0	29
	—Portland (PCL)	1	1	.500	3.00	8	1	0	0	0-...	15.0	13	5	5	1	5-0	14
2002—	Portland (PCL)	5	2	.714	3.70	42	0	0	0	4-...	48.2	48	23	20	2	13-1	35
	—San Diego (N.L.)	1	1	.500	5.91	14	0	0	0	0-0	21.1	29	20	14	1	10-0	11
Major League totals (7 years)		7	5	.583	5.08	162	1	0	0	1-4	228.2	254	144	129	27	106-6	155

MYETTE, AARON — P — RANGERS

PERSONAL: Born September 26, 1977, in New Westminster, B.C. ... 6-4/210. ... Throws right, bats right. ... Full name: Aaron Kenneth Myette. ... Son of Kenneth Myette, pitcher with Cincinnati Reds organization (1969).
HIGH SCHOOL: Johnston Heights Sectional (Surrey, B.C.).
JUNIOR COLLEGE: Central Arizona College.
TRANSACTIONS/CAREER NOTES: Selected by Seattle Mariners organization in 17th round of free-agent draft (June 1, 1995); did not sign. ... Selected by Chicago White Sox organization in supplemental round ("sandwich pick" between first and second round, 43rd pick overall) of free-agent draft (June 3, 1997); pick received as part of compensation for Florida Marlins signing P Alex Fernandez. ... On Hickory disabled list (April 2-May 2, 1998). ... On Birmingham disabled list (July 25-August 2, 1999). ... On Chicago disabled list (March 25-May 9, 2000). ... Traded by White Sox with P Brian Schmack to Texas Rangers for SS Royce Clayton (December 14, 2000).
STATISTICAL NOTES: Led Southern League with 15 hit batsmen in 1999.
CAREER HITTING (MLB): 0-for-0 (.000), 0 R, 0 2B, 0 3B, 0 HR, 0 RBI.

Year	League	W	L	Pct.	ERA	G	GS	CG	ShO	Sv.-Opp.	IP	H	R	ER	HR	BB-IBB	SO
1997—	Bristol (Appl.)	4	3	.571	3.61	9	8	1	0	0-...	47.1	39	28	19	9	20-0	50
	—Hickory (S.Atl.)	3	1	.750	1.14	5	5	0	0	0-...	31.2	19	6	4	1	11-0	27
1998—	Hickory (S.Atl.)	9	4	.692	2.47	17	17	0	0	0-...	102.0	84	43	28	4	30-0	103
	—Winston-Salem (Caro.)	4	2	.667	2.01	6	6	1	1	0-...	44.2	32	14	10	4	14-0	54
1999—	Birmingham (Sou.)	12	7	.632	3.66	28	•28	0	0	0-...	164.2	138	76	67	19	77-0	135
	—Chicago (A.L.)	0	2	.000	6.32	4	3	0	0	0-0	15.2	17	11	11	2	14-1	11
2000—	Birmingham (Sou.)	2	0	1.000	3.52	3	3	0	0	0-...	15.1	11	7	6	1	8-0	21
	—Charlotte (I.L.)	5	5	.500	4.35	19	18	0	0	0-...	111.2	103	58	54	18	56-0	85
	—Chicago (A.L.)	0	0	...	0.00	2	0	0	0	0-0	2.2	0	0	0	0	4-0	1
2001—	Oklahoma (PCL)■	4	3	.571	3.73	12	12	2	0	0-...	70.0	64	32	29	5	30-0	76
	—Texas (A.L.)	4	5	.444	7.14	19	15	0	0	0-0	80.2	94	65	64	12	37-0	67
	—Tulsa (Texas)	1	0	1.000	0.00	1	1	0	0	0-...	6.0	3	0	0	0	1-0	2
2002—	Oklahoma (PCL)	7	4	.636	3.14	16	16	2	1	0-...	106.0	86	41	37	5	44-0	106
	—Texas (A.L.)	2	5	.286	10.06	15	12	0	0	0-0	48.1	64	57	54	11	41-0	48
Major League totals (4 years)		6	12	.333	7.88	40	30	0	0	0-0	147.1	175	133	129	25	96-1	127

NADY, XAVIER — 1B — PADRES

PERSONAL: Born November 14, 1978, in Carmel, Calif. ... 6-2/205. ... Bats right, throws right. ... Full name: Xavier Clifford Nady.
HIGH SCHOOL: Salinas (Calif.).
COLLEGE: California.
TRANSACTIONS/CAREER NOTES: Selected by San Diego Padres organization in second round of free-agent draft (June 5, 2000).
HONORS: Named California League Most Valuable Player (2001).
STATISTICAL NOTES: Led California League with 276 total bases in 2001.

Year	Team (League)	Pos.	G	AB	R	H	2B	3B	HR	RBI	BB	SO	SB-CS	Avg.	OBP	SLG	E	Avg.
			BATTING														FIELDING	
2000—	San Diego (N.L.)	PH	1	1	1	1	0	0	0	0	0	0	0-0	1.000	1.000	1.000	...	...
2001—	Lake Elsinore (Calif.)	1B	137	524	96	158	38	1	26	100	62	109	6-0	.302	.381	.527	10	*.989
2002—	Lake Elsinore (Calif.)	OF	45	169	41	47	6	3	13	37	28	40	2-0	.278	.382	.580	0	1.000
—	Portland (PCL)	OF	85	315	46	89	12	1	10	43	20	60	0-1	.283	.329	.422	2	.981
Major League totals (1 year)			1	1	1	1	0	0	0	0	0	0	0-0	1.000	1.000	1.000	...	...

NAGY, CHARLES P

PERSONAL: Born May 5, 1967, in Fairfield, Conn. ... 6-3/200. ... Throws right, bats left. ... Full name: Charles Harrison Nagy. ... Name pronounced NAG-ee.

HIGH SCHOOL: Roger Ludlowe (Fairfield, Conn.).

COLLEGE: Connecticut.

TRANSACTIONS/CAREER NOTES: Selected by Cleveland Indians organization in first round (17th pick overall) of free-agent draft (June 1, 1988); pick received as part of compensation for San Francisco Giants signing Type A free-agent OF Brett Butler. ... On Cleveland disabled list (May 16-October 1, 1993); included rehabilitation assignment to Canton/Akron (June 10-24). ... On Cleveland disabled list (May 17-September 14 and September 25, 2000-remainder of season); included rehabilitation assignments to Buffalo (June 19-July 12 and September 3-14) and Akron (July 13 and August 28-September 2). ... On Cleveland disabled list (March 31-June 1 and August 24, 2001-remainder of season); included rehabilitation assignment to Buffalo (April 30-May 29). ... On Cleveland disabled list (June 5-July 20, 2002); included rehabilitation assignment to Buffalo (June 19-July 18). ... Granted free agency (October 28, 2002).

HONORS: Named Carolina League Pitcher of the Year (1989).

STATISTICAL NOTES: Pitched 6-0 one-hit, complete-game victory against Baltimore (August 8, 1992).

MISCELLANEOUS: Member of 1988 U.S. Olympic baseball team. ... Struck out once in two appearances as designated hitter and appeared in one game as pinch runner (1999).

CAREER HITTING (MLB): 2-for-17 (.118), 3 R, 0 2B, 0 3B, 0 HR, 0 RBI.

Year	League	W	L	Pct.	ERA	G	GS	CG	ShO	Sv.-Opp.	IP	H	R	ER	HR	BB-IBB	SO
1989—	Kinston (Caro.)	8	4	.667	1.51	13	13	6	*4	0-...	95.1	69	22	16	0	24-0	99
—	Canton/Akron (East.)	4	5	.444	3.35	15	14	2	0	0-...	94.0	102	44	35	4	32-0	65
1990—	Canton/Akron (East.)	13	8	.619	2.52	23	23	•9	0	0-...	175.0	132	62	49	9	39-0	99
—	Cleveland (A.L.)	2	4	.333	5.91	9	8	0	0	0-0	45.2	58	31	30	7	21-1	26
1991—	Cleveland (A.L.)	10	15	.400	4.13	33	33	6	1	0-0	211.1	228	103	97	15	66-7	109
1992—	Cleveland (A.L.)	17	10	.630	2.96	33	33	10	3	0-0	252.0	245	91	83	11	57-1	169
1993—	Cleveland (A.L.)	2	6	.250	6.29	9	9	1	0	0-0	48.2	66	38	34	6	13-1	30
—	Canton/Akron (East.)	0	0	...	1.13	2	2	0	0	0-...	8.0	8	1	1	0	2-0	4
1994—	Cleveland (A.L.)	10	8	.556	3.45	23	23	3	0	0-0	169.1	175	76	65	15	48-1	108
1995—	Cleveland (A.L.)	16	6	.727	4.55	29	29	2	1	0-0	178.0	194	95	90	20	61-0	139
1996—	Cleveland (A.L.)	17	5	.773	3.41	32	32	5	0	0-0	222.0	217	89	84	21	61-2	167
1997—	Cleveland (A.L.)	15	11	.577	4.28	34	34	1	1	0-0	227.0	253	115	108	27	77-4	149
1998—	Cleveland (A.L.)	15	10	.600	5.22	33	33	2	0	0-0	210.1	250	*139	122	34	66-12	120
1999—	Cleveland (A.L.)	17	11	.607	4.95	33	32	1	0	0-0	202.0	238	120	111	26	59-4	126
2000—	Cleveland (A.L.)	2	7	.222	8.21	11	11	0	0	0-0	57.0	71	53	52	15	21-2	41
—	Buffalo (I.L.)	1	1	.500	4.30	3	3	0	0	0-...	14.2	12	7	7	2	4-0	5
—	Akron (East.)	1	0	1.000	1.00	2	2	0	0	0-...	9.0	4	1	1	0	2-0	10
2001—	Buffalo (I.L.)	5	1	.833	2.56	6	6	0	0	0-...	38.2	40	12	11	0	9-0	18
—	Cleveland (A.L.)	5	6	.455	6.40	15	13	0	0	0-0	70.1	102	53	50	10	20-1	29
2002—	Cleveland (A.L.)	1	4	.200	8.88	19	7	0	0	0-0	48.2	76	51	48	10	13-1	22
—	Buffalo (I.L.)	1	2	.333	3.19	5	5	2	0	0-...	36.2	38	18	13	6	4-0	18
Major League totals (13 years)		129	103	.556	4.51	313	297	31	6	0-0	1942.1	2173	1054	974	217	583-37	1235

DIVISION SERIES RECORD

RECORDS: Holds career record for most earned runs allowed—23; and bases on balls allowed—18. ... Shares A.L. career record for most wins—3.

Year	League	W	L	Pct.	ERA	G	GS	CG	ShO	Sv.-Opp.	IP	H	R	ER	HR	BB-IBB	SO
1995—	Cleveland (A.L.)	1	0	1.000	1.29	1	1	0	0	0-0	7.0	4	1	1	0	5-0	6
1996—	Cleveland (A.L.)	0	1	.000	7.15	2	2	0	0	0-0	11.1	15	9	9	4	5-0	13
1997—	Cleveland (A.L.)	0	1	.000	9.82	1	1	0	0	0-0	3.2	2	5	4	0	6-1	1
1998—	Cleveland (A.L.)	1	0	1.000	1.13	1	1	0	0	0-0	8.0	4	1	1	0	0-0	3
1999—	Cleveland (A.L.)	1	0	1.000	7.20	2	2	0	0	0-0	10.0	11	9	8	2	2-1	6
Division series totals (5 years)		3	2	.600	5.18	7	7	0	0	0-0	40.0	36	25	23	6	18-2	29

CHAMPIONSHIP SERIES RECORD

RECORDS: Shares A.L. single-game record for most consecutive strikeouts—4 (October 13, 1995).

Year	League	W	L	Pct.	ERA	G	GS	CG	ShO	Sv.-Opp.	IP	H	R	ER	HR	BB-IBB	SO
1995—	Cleveland (A.L.)	0	0	...	1.13	1	1	0	0	0-0	8.0	5	2	1	1	0-0	6
1997—	Cleveland (A.L.)	0	0	...	2.77	2	2	0	0	0-0	13.0	17	4	4	1	5-0	5
1998—	Cleveland (A.L.)	0	1	.000	3.72	2	2	0	0	0-0	9.2	13	7	4	1	1-0	6
Champ. series totals (3 years)		0	1	.000	2.64	5	5	0	0	0-0	30.2	35	13	9	3	6-0	17

WORLD SERIES RECORD

RECORDS: Shares single-inning record for most consecutive bases on balls allowed—3 (October 21, 1997, third inning).

Year	League	W	L	Pct.	ERA	G	GS	CG	ShO	Sv.-Opp.	IP	H	R	ER	HR	BB-IBB	SO
1995—	Cleveland (A.L.)	0	0	...	6.43	1	1	0	0	0-0	7.0	8	5	5	2	1-0	4
1997—	Cleveland (A.L.)	0	1	.000	6.43	2	1	0	0	0-0	7.0	8	6	5	3	5-1	5
World Series totals (2 years)		0	1	.000	6.43	3	2	0	0	0-0	14.0	16	11	10	5	6-1	9

ALL-STAR GAME RECORD

	W	L	Pct.	ERA	GS	CG	ShO	Sv.-Opp.	IP	H	R	ER	HR	BB-IBB	SO
All-Star Game totals (2 years)	0	1	.000	9.00	1	0	0	0-0	3.0	4	3	3	1	0-0	2

NANCE, SHANE — P — BREWERS

PERSONAL: Born September 7, 1977, in Pasadena, Calif. ... 5-8/180. ... Throws left, bats left. ... Full name: Joseph Shane Nance.
HIGH SCHOOL: Dobie (Texas).
COLLEGE: Houston.
TRANSACTIONS/CAREER NOTES: Selected by Los Angeles Dodgers organization in 11th round of free-agent draft (June 5, 2000). ... Traded by Dodgers with P Ben Diggins to Milwaukee Brewers for 3B Tyler Houston and a player to be named later (July 23, 2002); Dodgers acquired P Brian Mallette to complete deal (October 16, 2002). ... On Milwaukee disabled list (September 1, 2002-remainder of season).
CAREER HITTING (MLB): 1-for-3 (.333), 0 R, 0 2B, 0 3B, 0 HR, 1 RBI.

Year League	W	L	Pct.	ERA	G	GS	CG	ShO	Sv.-Opp.	IP	H	R	ER	HR	BB-IBB	SO
2000— Yakima (N'West)	2	4	.333	2.48	12	9	0	0	0-...	58.0	41	19	16	1	22-0	66
2001— Vero Beach (FSL)	6	3	.667	2.63	21	0	0	0	4-...	48.0	28	15	14	3	21-1	63
— Jacksonville (Sou.)	7	0	1.000	1.59	28	0	0	0	1-...	45.1	31	11	8	4	17-1	44
2002— Las Vegas (PCL)	11	3	.786	4.17	37	0	0	0	1-...	58.1	58	32	27	5	26-1	53
— Indianapolis (I.L.)■	3	0	1.000	0.00	9	0	0	0	0-...	16.2	12	0	0	0	6-0	10
— Milwaukee (N.L.)	0	0	...	4.26	4	0	0	0	0-0	6.1	4	3	3	1	4-0	5
Major League totals (1 year)	0	0	...	4.26	4	0	0	0	0-0	6.1	4	3	3	1	4-0	5

NATHAN, JOE — P — GIANTS

PERSONAL: Born November 22, 1974, in Houston. ... 6-4/195. ... Throws right, bats right. ... Full name: Joseph Michael Nathan.
HIGH SCHOOL: Pine Bush (N.Y.).
COLLEGE: New York-Stony Brook.
TRANSACTIONS/CAREER NOTES: Selected by San Francisco Giants organization in sixth round of free-agent draft (June 1, 1995). ... On San Francisco disabled list (May 13-June 6 and July 14-August 19, 2000); included rehabilitation assignments to San Jose (May 26-31), Bakersfield (May 31-June 6) and Fresno (August 2-19).
CAREER HITTING (MLB): 10-for-60 (.167), 4 R, 3 2B, 0 3B, 2 HR, 4 RBI.

Year League	W	L	Pct.	ERA	G	GS	CG	ShO	Sv.-Opp.	IP	H	R	ER	HR	BB-IBB	SO
1996—	Did not play-attended New York-Stony Brook.															
1997— Salem-Kaizer (N'West)	2	1	.667	2.47	18	5	0	0	2-...	62.0	53	22	17	7	26-0	44
1998— San Jose (Calif.)	8	6	.571	3.32	22	22	0	0	0-...	122.0	100	51	45	13	48-0	118
— Shreveport (Texas)	1	3	.250	8.80	4	4	0	0	0-...	15.1	20	15	15	4	9-0	10
1999— Shreveport (Texas)	0	1	.000	3.12	2	2	0	0	0-...	8.2	5	4	3	0	7-0	7
— San Francisco (N.L.)	7	4	.636	4.18	19	14	0	0	1-1	90.1	84	45	42	17	46-0	54
— Fresno (PCL)	6	4	.600	4.46	13	13	1	0	0-...	74.2	68	44	37	11	36-0	82
2000— San Francisco (N.L.)	5	2	.714	5.21	20	15	0	0	0-1	93.1	89	63	54	12	63-4	61
— San Jose (Calif.)	0	1	.000	3.60	1	1	0	0	0-...	5.0	4	2	2	1	1-0	2
— Bakersfield (Calif.)	1	0	1.000	5.06	1	1	0	0	0-...	5.1	2	3	3	0	7-0	6
— Fresno (PCL)	0	2	.000	4.40	3	3	0	0	0-...	14.1	15	8	7	4	7-0	9
2001— Fresno (PCL)	0	5	.000	7.77	10	10	0	0	0-...	46.1	63	47	40	13	33-0	21
— Shreveport (Texas)	3	6	.333	6.93	21	7	0	0	0-...	62.1	73	49	48	11	37-5	33
2002— Fresno (PCL)	6	12	.333	5.60	31	25	1	0	0-...	146.1	167	97	91	20	74-0	117
— San Francisco (N.L.)	0	0	...	0.00	4	0	0	0	0-0	3.2	1	0	0	0	0-0	2
Major League totals (3 years)	12	6	.667	4.61	43	29	0	0	1-2	187.1	174	108	96	29	109-4	117

RECORD AS POSITION PLAYER

		BATTING													FIELDING	
Year Team (League)	Pos.	G	AB	R	H	2B	3B	HR	RBI	BB	SO	SB-CS	Avg.	OBP	SLG	E	Avg.
1995— Bellingham (N'West)	SS	56	177	23	41	7	2	3	20	22	48	3-2	.232	.320	.345	26	.897

NEAGLE, DENNY — P — ROCKIES

PERSONAL: Born September 13, 1968, in Gambrills, Md. ... 6-3/225. ... Throws left, bats left. ... Full name: Dennis Edward Neagle Jr. ... Name pronounced NAY-ghul.
HIGH SCHOOL: Arundel (Gambrills, Md.).
COLLEGE: Minnesota.
TRANSACTIONS/CAREER NOTES: Selected by Minnesota Twins organization in third round of free-agent draft (June 5, 1989). ... On Portland disabled list (April 5-23, 1991). ... On Minnesota disabled list (July 28-August 12, 1991). ... Traded by Twins with OF Midre Cummings to Pittsburgh Pirates for P John Smiley (March 17, 1992). ... Traded by Pirates to Atlanta Braves for 1B Ron Wright and a player to be named later (August 28, 1996); Pirates acquired P Jason Schmidt to complete deal (August 30, 1996). ... Traded by Braves with OF Michael Tucker and P Rob Bell to Cincinnati Reds for 2B Bret Boone and P Mike Remlinger (November 10, 1998). ... On Cincinnati disabled list (March 24-April 21 and May 24-July 29, 1999); included rehabilitation assignment to Indianapolis (April 8-21 and July 23-29). ... Traded by Reds with OF Mike Frank to New York Yankees for 3B Drew Henson, OF Jackson Melian, P Brian Reith and P Ed Yarnall (July 12, 2000). ... Granted free agency (October 31, 2000). ... Signed by Colorado Rockies (December 4, 2000). ... On disabled list (June 9-24, 2001).
HONORS: Named lefthanded pitcher on The Sporting News N.L. All-Star team (1997).
STATISTICAL NOTES: Tied for N.L. lead with 16 sacrifice hits in 1996. ... Career major league grand slams: 2.
MISCELLANEOUS: Appeared in one game as pinch runner (1992). ... Appeared in one game as pinch runner (1995). ... Doubled and had a sacrifice hit in three appearances as pinch hitter with Pittsburgh (1996). ... Struck out in only appearance as pinch hitter with Cincinnati (2000).
CAREER HITTING (MLB): 87-for-520 (.167), 31 R, 17 2B, 0 3B, 5 HR, 44 RBI.

Year League	W	L	Pct.	ERA	G	GS	CG	ShO	Sv.-Opp.	IP	H	R	ER	HR	BB-IBB	SO
1989— Elizabethton (Appl.)	1	2	.333	4.50	6	3	0	0	1-...	22.0	20	11	11	1	8-0	32
— Kenosha (Midw.)	2	1	.667	1.65	6	6	1	1	0-...	43.2	25	9	8	3	16-0	40
1990— Visalia (Calif.)	8	0	1.000	1.43	10	10	0	0	0-...	63.0	39	13	10	2	16-0	92
— Orlando (Sou.)	12	3	.800	2.45	17	17	4	1	0-...	121.1	94	40	33	11	31-0	94
1991— Portland (PCL)	9	4	.692	3.27	19	17	1	1	0-...	104.2	101	41	38	6	32-1	94
— Minnesota (A.L.)	0	1	.000	4.05	7	3	0	0	0-0	20.0	28	9	9	3	7-2	14
1992— Pittsburgh (N.L.)■	4	6	.400	4.48	55	6	0	0	2-4	86.1	81	46	43	9	43-8	77
1993— Pittsburgh (N.L.)	3	5	.375	5.31	50	7	0	0	1-1	81.1	82	49	48	10	37-3	73
— Buffalo (A.A.)	0	0	...	0.00	3	0	0	0	0-...	3.1	3	0	0	0	2-0	6

Year	League	W	L	Pct.	ERA	G	GS	CG	ShO	Sv.-Opp.	IP	H	R	ER	HR	BB-IBB	SO
1994—	Pittsburgh (N.L.)	9	10	.474	5.12	24	24	2	0	0-0	137.0	135	80	78	18	49-3	122
1995—	Pittsburgh (N.L.)	13	8	.619	3.43	31	•31	5	1	0-0	•209.2	*221	91	80	20	45-3	150
1996—	Pittsburgh (N.L.)	14	6	.700	3.05	27	27	1	0	0-0	182.2	186	67	62	21	34-2	131
—	Atlanta (N.L.)■	2	3	.400	5.59	6	6	1	0	0-0	38.2	40	26	24	5	14-0	18
1997—	Atlanta (N.L.)	*20	5	.800	2.97	34	34	4	4	0-0	233.1	204	87	77	18	49-5	172
1998—	Atlanta (N.L.)	16	11	.593	3.55	32	31	5	2	0-0	210.1	196	91	83	25	60-3	165
1999—	Indianapolis (I.L.)■	2	0	1.000	4.67	3	3	0	0	0-...	17.1	11	9	9	2	2-0	9
—	Cincinnati (N.L.)	9	5	.643	4.27	20	19	0	0	0-0	111.2	95	54	53	23	40-3	76
2000—	Cincinnati (N.L.)	8	2	.800	3.52	18	18	0	0	0-0	117.2	111	48	46	15	50-3	88
—	New York (A.L.)■	7	7	.500	5.81	16	15	1	0	0-0	91.1	99	61	59	16	31-1	58
2001—	Colorado (N.L.)■	9	8	.529	5.38	30	30	0	0	0-0	170.2	192	107	102	29	60-3	139
2002—	Colorado (N.L.)	8	11	.421	5.26	35	28	1	0	0-0	164.1	170	101	96	26	63-5	111
A.L. totals (2 years)		7	8	.467	5.50	23	18	1	0	0-0	111.1	127	70	68	19	38-3	72
N.L. totals (11 years)		115	80	.590	4.09	362	261	19	7	3-5	1743.2	1713	847	792	219	544-41	1322
Major League totals (12 years)		122	88	.581	4.17	385	279	20	7	3-5	1855.0	1840	917	860	238	582-44	1394

DIVISION SERIES RECORD

Year	League	W	L	Pct.	ERA	G	GS	CG	ShO	Sv.-Opp.	IP	H	R	ER	HR	BB-IBB	SO
1998—	Atlanta (N.L.)									Did not play.							
2000—	New York (A.L.)									Did not play.							

CHAMPIONSHIP SERIES RECORD

Year	League	W	L	Pct.	ERA	G	GS	CG	ShO	Sv.-Opp.	IP	H	R	ER	HR	BB-IBB	SO
1992—	Pittsburgh (N.L.)	0	0	...	27.00	2	0	0	0	0-0	1.2	4	5	5	0	3-1	0
1996—	Atlanta (N.L.)	0	0	...	2.35	2	1	0	0	0-0	7.2	2	2	2	0	3-0	8
1997—	Atlanta (N.L.)	1	0	1.000	0.00	2	1	1	1	0-0	12.0	5	0	0	0	1-0	9
1998—	Atlanta (N.L.)	0	0	...	3.52	2	1	0	0	0-0	7.2	8	3	3	1	2-0	9
2000—	New York (A.L.)	0	2	.000	4.50	2	2	0	0	0-0	10.0	6	5	5	1	7-0	7
Champ. series totals (5 years)		1	2	.333	3.46	10	5	1	1	0-0	39.0	25	15	15	2	16-1	33

WORLD SERIES RECORD

NOTES: Member of World Series championship team (2000).

Year	League	W	L	Pct.	ERA	G	GS	CG	ShO	Sv.-Opp.	IP	H	R	ER	HR	BB-IBB	SO
1996—	Atlanta (N.L.)	0	0	...	3.00	2	1	0	0	0-0	6.0	5	3	2	0	4-0	3
2000—	New York (A.L.)	0	0	...	3.86	1	1	0	0	0-0	4.2	4	2	2	1	2-0	3
World Series totals (2 years)		0	0	...	3.38	3	2	0	0	0-0	10.2	9	5	4	1	6-0	6

ALL-STAR GAME RECORD

	W	L	Pct.	ERA	GS	CG	ShO	Sv.-Opp.	IP	H	R	ER	HR	BB-IBB	SO
All-Star Game totals (1 year)	0	0	...	0.00	0	0	0	0-0	1.0	1	0	0	0	0-0	1

NEAL, BLAINE — P — MARLINS

PERSONAL: Born April 6, 1978, in Marlton, N.J. ... 6-5/240. ... Throws right, bats left.
HIGH SCHOOL: Bishop Eustace Prep (Pennsauken, N.J.).
TRANSACTIONS/CAREER NOTES: Selected by Florida Marlins organization in fourth round of free-agent draft (June 4, 1996).
CAREER HITTING (MLB): 0-for-0 (.000), 0 R, 0 2B, 0 3B, 0 HR, 0 RBI.

Year	League	W	L	Pct.	ERA	G	GS	CG	ShO	Sv.-Opp.	IP	H	R	ER	HR	BB-IBB	SO
1996—	Gulf Coast Marlins (GCL)	1	1	.500	4.60	7	5	0	0	1-...	29.1	32	18	15	1	6-0	15
1997—	Gulf Coast Marlins (GCL)	4	1	.800	3.63	10	0	0	0	1-...	22.1	24	11	9	1	11-0	19
1999—	Kane County (Midw.)	4	2	.667	2.32	26	0	0	0	6-...	31.0	21	8	8	2	10-0	31
2000—	Brevard County (FSL)	2	2	.500	2.15	41	0	0	0	11-...	54.1	40	27	13	1	24-3	65
2001—	Portland (East.)	2	3	.400	2.36	54	0	0	0	21-...	53.1	43	17	14	1	21-3	45
—	Florida (N.L.)	0	0	...	6.75	4	0	0	0	0-0	5.1	7	4	4	0	5-0	3
2002—	Calgary (PCL)	3	1	.750	2.90	29	0	0	0	11-...	31.0	27	11	10	2	15-1	26
—	Florida (N.L.)	3	0	1.000	2.73	32	0	0	0	0-0	33.0	32	12	10	1	14-2	33
Major League totals (2 years)		3	0	1.000	3.29	36	0	0	0	0-0	38.1	39	16	14	1	19-2	36

RECORD AS POSITION PLAYER

			BATTING													FIELDING	
Year	Team (League)	Pos.	G	AB	R	H	2B	3B	HR	RBI	BB	SO	SB-CS	Avg.	OBP	SLG	E	Avg.
1998—	Utica (NY-Penn)	1B-OF	53	121	13	23	4	0	0	13	23	32	2-1	.190	.329	.223	5	.982

NELSON, BRY — OF

PERSONAL: Born January 27, 1974, in Crossett, Ark. ... 5-10/205. ... Bats both, throws right. ... Full name: Bryant Lawrence Nelson.
HIGH SCHOOL: Crossett (Ark.).
JUNIOR COLLEGE: Texarkana Junior College (Texas).
TRANSACTIONS/CAREER NOTES: Selected by Houston Astros organization in 44th round of free-agent draft (June 2, 1993). ... Released by Astros (March 21, 1997). ... Signed by Chicago Cubs organization (March 30, 1997). ... Granted free agency (October 17, 1997). ... Re-signed by Cubs organization (December 30, 1997). ... Granted free agency (October 16, 1998). ... Re-signed by Cubs organization (January 11, 1999). ... Granted free agency (October 15, 1999). ... Signed by Arizona Diamondbacks organization (November 18, 1999). ... Loaned by Diamondbacks to Monterrey, Mexican League (April 19-June 26, 2000). ... Traded by Diamondbacks to Pittsburgh Pirates for 2B Chris Petersen (July 11, 2001). ... Granted free agency (October 15, 2001). ... Signed by Boston Red Sox organization (December 14, 2001). ... Granted free agency (October 15, 2002).
2002 GAMES PLAYED BY POSITION (MLB): OF—11; 2B—11; DH—1.

			BATTING													FIELDING	
Year	Team (League)	Pos.	G	AB	R	H	2B	3B	HR	RBI	BB	SO	SB-CS	Avg.	OBP	SLG	E	Avg.
1994—	Quad City (Midw.)	2B-SS-OF	45	156	20	38	6	0	1	6	11	15	3-5	.244	.293	.301	5	.956
—	Auburn (NY-Penn)	SS-2B	65	261	53	84	16	7	6	35	11	13	2-1	.322	.350	.506	17	.922

Year	Team (League)	Pos.	G	AB	R	H	2B	3B	HR	RBI	BB	SO	SB-CS	Avg.	OBP	SLG	E	Avg.
			BATTING														FIELDING	
1995—	Kissimmee (FSL)	S-0-2-3	105	395	47	129	34	5	3	52	20	37	14-10	.327	.355	.461	27	.925
—	Quad City (Midw.)	OF-3B-SS	6	26	1	1	1	0	0	2	0	3	0-0	.038	.038	.077	2	.882
1996—	Kissimmee (FSL)	3B-SS	89	345	38	87	21	6	3	52	19	27	8-2	.252	.290	.374	28	.889
1997—	Orlando (Sou.)■	3B-SS	110	382	51	110	33	2	8	58	45	43	5-7	.288	.359	.448	33	.885
1998—	West Tenn (Sou.)	3B-SS-OF	32	102	10	29	6	2	2	18	12	12	4-2	.284	.357	.441	8	.905
1999—	West Tenn (Sou.)	3-2-0-S	129	471	66	126	24	5	16	78	42	52	10-7	.268	.328	.442	22	.932
2000—	Tucson (PCL)	1B-2B-3B-OF	69	261	34	81	21	0	5	31	16	20	4-2	.310	.348	.448	14	.910
—	Monterrey (Mex.)■	OF-3B	59	227	51	79	18	0	20	72	22	23	8-6	.348	.404	.692	4	...
2001—	Tucson (PCL)■	3B-2B-OF-1B	85	326	37	98	15	0	6	41	16	20	9-5	.301	.332	.402	16	.939
—	Nashville (PCL)■	2B-3B	49	185	23	58	7	0	5	15	10	16	3-3	.314	.348	.432	7	.970
2002—	Pawtucket (I.L.)■	OF-2B-3B-SS	60	223	25	66	8	3	8	24	14	19	1-5	.296	.340	.466	13	.934
—	Boston (A.L.)	OF-2B-DH	25	34	6	9	3	0	0	2	4	1	1-1	.265	.342	.353	1	.977
Major League totals (1 year)			25	34	6	9	3	0	0	2	4	1	1-1	.265	.342	.353	1	.977

NELSON, JEFF P MARINERS

PERSONAL: Born November 17, 1966, in Baltimore. ... 6-8/235. ... Throws right, bats right. ... Full name: Jeffrey Allan Nelson. ... Nephew of Cole Nelson, who played in the Washington Senators organization.

HIGH SCHOOL: Catonsville (Md.).

JUNIOR COLLEGE: Catonsville (Md.) Community College.

TRANSACTIONS/CAREER NOTES: Selected by Los Angeles Dodgers organization in 22nd round of free-agent draft (June 4, 1984). ... On Great Falls disabled list (April 10-June 4, 1986). ... Selected by Seattle Mariners organization from Dodgers organization in Rule 5 minor league draft (December 9, 1986). ... On disabled list (July 16, 1989-remainder of season). ... Traded by Mariners with 1B Tino Martinez and P Jim Mecir to New York Yankees for P Sterling Hitchcock and 3B Russ Davis (December 7, 1995). ... On suspended list (September 3-5, 1996). ... On suspended list (May 28-29, 1998). ... On New York disabled list (June 26-September 4, 1998); included rehabilitation assignment to Tampa (August 31-September 4). ... On New York disabled list (May 3-20 and June 3-August 11, 1999); included rehabilitation assignments to Gulf Coast Yankees (August 2-4 and August 9-10) and Tampa (August 5-8). ... Granted free agency (October 31, 2000). ... Signed by Mariners (December 4, 2000). ... On Seattle disabled list (May 8-June 27, 2002); included rehabilitation assignment to Everett (June 25-27).

STATISTICAL NOTES: Led A.L. with 12 intentional bases on balls issued in 1992.

MISCELLANEOUS: Holds Seattle Mariners all-time record for most games pitched (337). ... Appeared in one game as outfielder with no chances for Seattle (1993).

CAREER HITTING (MLB): 0-for-2 (.000), 0 R, 0 2B, 0 3B, 0 HR, 0 RBI.

Year	League	W	L	Pct.	ERA	G	GS	CG	ShO	Sv.-Opp.	IP	H	R	ER	HR	BB-IBB	SO
1984—	Great Falls (Pio.)	0	0	...	54.00	1	0	0	0	0-...	.2	3	4	4	1	3-0	1
—	Gulf Coast Dodgers (GCL)	0	0	...	1.35	9	0	0	0	0-...	13.1	6	3	2	0	6-0	7
1985—	Gulf Coast Dodgers (GCL)	0	5	.000	5.51	14	7	0	0	0-...	47.1	72	50	29	1	32-0	31
1986—	Bakersfield (Calif.)	0	7	.000	6.69	24	11	0	0	0-...	71.1	79	83	53	9	84-1	37
—	Great Falls (Pio.)	0	0	...	13.50	3	0	0	0	0-...	2.0	5	3	3	0	3-2	1
1987—	Salinas (Calif.)■	3	7	.300	5.74	17	16	1	0	0-...	80.0	80	61	51	2	71-0	43
1988—	San Bernardino (Calif.)	8	9	.471	5.54	27	27	1	1	0-...	149.1	163	115	92	9	91-2	94
1989—	Williamsport (East.)	7	5	.583	3.31	15	15	2	0	0-...	92.1	72	41	34	2	53-1	61
1990—	Williamsport (East.)	1	4	.200	6.44	10	10	0	0	0-...	43.1	65	35	31	2	18-1	14
—	Peninsula (Caro.)	2	2	.500	3.15	18	7	1	1	6-...	60.0	47	21	21	5	25-1	49
1991—	Jacksonville (Sou.)	4	0	1.000	1.27	21	0	0	0	12-...	28.1	23	5	4	0	9-0	34
—	Calgary (PCL)	3	4	.429	3.90	28	0	0	0	21-...	32.1	39	19	14	1	15-3	26
1992—	Calgary (PCL)	1	0	1.000	0.00	2	0	0	0	0-...	3.2	0	0	0	0	1-0	0
—	Seattle (A.L.)	1	7	.125	3.44	66	0	0	0	6-14	81.0	71	34	31	7	44-12	46
1993—	Calgary (PCL)	1	0	1.000	1.17	5	0	0	0	1-...	7.2	6	1	1	0	2-0	6
—	Seattle (A.L.)	5	3	.625	4.35	71	0	0	0	1-11	60.0	57	30	29	5	34-10	61
1994—	Seattle (A.L.)	0	0	...	2.76	28	0	0	0	0-0	42.1	35	18	13	3	20-4	44
—	Calgary (PCL)	1	4	.200	2.84	18	0	0	0	8-...	25.1	21	9	8	1	7-1	30
1995—	Seattle (A.L.)	7	3	.700	2.17	62	0	0	0	2-4	78.2	58	21	19	4	27-5	96
1996—	New York (A.L.)■	4	4	.500	4.36	73	0	0	0	2-4	74.1	75	38	36	6	36-1	91
1997—	New York (A.L.)	3	7	.300	2.86	77	0	0	0	2-8	78.2	53	32	25	7	37-12	81
1998—	New York (A.L.)	5	3	.625	3.79	45	0	0	0	3-6	40.1	44	18	17	1	22-4	35
—	Tampa (FSL)	0	0	...	0.00	2	1	0	0	0-...	2.0	1	1	0	0	1-0	4
1999—	New York (A.L.)	2	1	.667	4.15	39	0	0	0	1-2	30.1	27	14	14	2	22-2	35
—	Gulf Coast Yankees (GCL)	0	0	...	0.00	2	2	0	0	0-...	2.0	1	0	0	0	1-...	3
—	Tampa (FSL)	0	0	...	0.00	3	3	0	0	0-...	3.0	1	0	0	0	2-0	5
2000—	New York (A.L.)	8	4	.667	2.45	73	0	0	0	0-4	69.2	44	24	19	2	45-1	71
2001—	Seattle (A.L.)■	4	3	.571	2.76	69	0	0	0	4-5	65.1	30	21	20	3	44-1	88
2002—	Seattle (A.L.)	3	2	.600	3.94	41	0	0	0	2-4	45.2	36	20	20	4	27-3	55
—	Everett (N'West)	0	1	.000	0.00	1	1	0	0	0-...	1.1	1	1	0	0	0-0	4
Major League totals (11 years)		42	37	.532	3.28	644	0	0	0	23-62	666.1	530	270	243	44	358-55	703

DIVISION SERIES RECORD

RECORDS: Shares A.L. career record for most games pitched—19.

Year	League	W	L	Pct.	ERA	G	GS	CG	ShO	Sv.-Opp.	IP	H	R	ER	HR	BB-IBB	SO
1995—	Seattle (A.L.)	0	1	.000	3.18	3	0	0	0	0-0	5.2	7	2	2	0	3-0	7
1996—	New York (A.L.)	1	0	1.000	0.00	2	0	0	0	0-0	3.2	2	0	0	0	2-1	5
1997—	New York (A.L.)	0	0	...	0.00	4	0	0	0	0-0	4.0	4	0	0	0	2-0	0
1998—	New York (A.L.)	0	0	...	0.00	2	0	0	0	0-0	2.2	2	0	0	0	1-0	2
1999—	New York (A.L.)	0	0	...	0.00	3	0	0	0	0-0	1.2	1	0	0	0	1-0	3
2000—	New York (A.L.)	0	0	...	0.00	2	0	0	0	0-0	2.0	0	0	0	0	0-0	2
2001—	Seattle (A.L.)	0	0	...	0.00	3	0	0	0	0-0	3.0	1	0	0	0	1-0	5
Division series totals (7 years)		1	1	.500	0.79	19	0	0	0	0-0	22.2	17	2	2	0	10-1	24

CHAMPIONSHIP SERIES RECORD

Year	League	W	L	Pct.	ERA	G	GS	CG	ShO	Sv.-Opp.	IP	H	R	ER	HR	BB-IBB	SO
1995—	Seattle (A.L.)	0	0	...	0.00	3	0	0	0	0-0	3.0	3	0	0	0	5-1	3
1996—	New York (A.L.)	0	1	.000	11.57	2	0	0	0	0-0	2.1	5	3	3	1	0-0	2
1998—	New York (A.L.)	0	1	.000	20.25	3	0	0	0	0-0	1.1	3	3	3	0	1-0	3

Year League	W	L	Pct.	ERA	G	GS	CG	ShO	Sv.-Opp.	IP	H	R	ER	HR	BB-IBB	SO
1999— New York (A.L.)	0	0	...	0.00	2	0	0	0	0-0	.2	0	0	0	0	0-0	0
2000— New York (A.L.)	0	0	...	9.00	3	0	0	0	0-0	3.0	5	3	3	2	0-0	6
2001— Seattle (A.L.)	0	0	...	0.00	2	0	0	0	0-0	2.1	1	0	0	0	1-0	3
Champ. series totals (6 years)	0	2	.000	6.39	15	0	0	0	0-0	12.2	17	9	9	3	7-1	17

WORLD SERIES RECORD

NOTES: Member of World Series championship team (1996, 1998, 1999 and 2000).

Year League	W	L	Pct.	ERA	G	GS	CG	ShO	Sv.-Opp.	IP	H	R	ER	HR	BB-IBB	SO
1996— New York (A.L.)	0	0	...	0.00	3	0	0	0	0-0	4.1	1	0	0	0	1-0	5
1998— New York (A.L.)	0	0	...	0.00	3	0	0	0	0-0	2.1	2	1	0	0	1-0	4
1999— New York (A.L.)	0	0	...	0.00	4	0	0	0	0-0	2.2	2	0	0	0	1-0	3
2000— New York (A.L.)	1	0	1.000	10.13	3	0	0	0	0-0	2.2	5	3	3	1	1-0	1
World Series totals (4 years)	1	0	1.000	2.25	13	0	0	0	0-0	12.0	10	4	3	1	4-0	13

ALL-STAR GAME RECORD

	W	L	Pct.	ERA	GS	CG	ShO	Sv.-Opp.	IP	H	R	ER	HR	BB-IBB	SO
All-Star Game totals (1 year)	0	0	...	0.00	0	0	0	0-0	1.0	0	0	0	0	1-0	1

NEN, ROBB P GIANTS

PERSONAL: Born November 28, 1969, in San Pedro, Calif. ... 6-5/222. ... Throws right, bats right. ... Full name: Robert Allen Nen. ... Son of Dick Nen, first baseman with three major league teams (1963, 1965-68 and 1970).

HIGH SCHOOL: Los Alamitos (Calif.).

TRANSACTIONS/CAREER NOTES: Selected by Texas Rangers organization in 32nd round of free-agent draft (June 2, 1987). ... On Charlotte disabled list (April 6-26 and May 6-24, 1990). ... On disabled list (April 23-June 10, June 28-July 8 and July 11-September 3, 1991; and May 7-September 9, 1992). ... On Texas disabled list (June 12-July 17, 1993); included rehabilitation assignment to Oklahoma City (June 21-July 17). ... Traded by Rangers with P Kurt Miller to Florida Marlins for P Cris Carpenter (July 17, 1993). ... Traded by Marlins to San Francisco Giants for P Mike Villano, P Joe Fontenot and P Mick Pageler (November 18, 1997).

HONORS: Named N.L. co-Reliever of the Year by THE SPORTING NEWS (2001).

STATISTICAL NOTES: Tied for N.L. lead with 52 save opportunities in 2001.

MISCELLANEOUS: Holds Florida Marlins all-time record for most saves (108). ... Holds San Francisco Giants all-time record for most saves (206).

CAREER HITTING (MLB): 1-for-15 (.067), 0 R, 0 2B, 0 3B, 0 HR, 0 RBI.

Year League	W	L	Pct.	ERA	G	GS	CG	ShO	Sv.-Opp.	IP	H	R	ER	HR	BB-IBB	SO
1987— Gulf Coast Rangers (GCL)	0	0	...	7.71	2	0	0	0	0-...	2.1	4	2	2	0	3-1	4
1988— Gastonia (S.Atl.)	0	5	.000	7.45	14	10	0	0	0-...	48.1	69	57	40	5	45-0	36
— Butte (Pio.)	4	5	.444	8.75	14	13	0	0	0-...	48.1	65	55	47	4	45-0	30
1989— Gastonia (S.Atl.)	7	4	.636	2.41	24	24	1	1	0-...	138.1	96	47	37	7	76-0	146
1990— Charlotte (FSL)	1	4	.200	3.69	11	11	1	0	0-...	53.2	44	28	22	1	36-0	38
— Tulsa (Texas)	0	5	.000	5.06	7	7	0	0	0-...	26.2	23	20	15	1	21-0	21
1991— Tulsa (Texas)	0	2	.000	5.79	6	6	0	0	0-...	28.0	24	21	18	6	20-0	23
1992— Tulsa (Texas)	1	1	.500	2.16	4	4	1	0	0-...	25.0	21	7	6	1	2-0	20
1993— Texas (A.L.)	1	1	.500	6.35	9	3	0	0	0-0	22.2	28	17	16	1	26-0	12
— Oklahoma City (A.A.)	0	2	.000	6.67	6	5	0	0	0-...	28.1	45	22	21	3	18-0	12
— Florida (N.L.)■	1	0	1.000	7.02	15	1	0	0	0-0	33.1	35	28	26	5	20-0	27
1994— Florida (N.L.)	5	5	.500	2.95	44	0	0	0	15-15	58.0	46	20	19	6	17-2	60
1995— Florida (N.L.)	0	7	.000	3.29	62	0	0	0	23-29	65.2	62	26	24	6	23-3	68
1996— Florida (N.L.)	5	1	.833	1.95	75	0	0	0	35-42	83.0	67	21	18	2	21-6	92
1997— Florida (N.L.)	9	3	.750	3.89	73	0	0	0	35-42	74.0	72	35	32	7	40-7	81
1998— San Francisco (N.L.)■	7	7	.500	1.52	78	0	0	0	40-45	88.2	59	21	15	4	25-5	110
1999— San Francisco (N.L.)	3	8	.273	3.98	72	0	0	0	37-46	72.1	79	36	32	8	27-3	77
2000— San Francisco (N.L.)	4	3	.571	1.50	68	0	0	0	41-46	66.0	37	15	11	4	19-1	92
2001— San Francisco (N.L.)	4	5	.444	3.01	79	0	0	0	*45-52	77.2	58	28	26	6	22-6	93
2002— San Francisco (N.L.)	6	2	.750	2.20	68	0	0	0	43-51	73.2	64	19	18	2	20-8	81
A.L. totals (1 year)	1	1	.500	6.35	9	3	0	0	0-0	22.2	28	17	16	1	26-0	12
N.L. totals (10 years)	44	41	.518	2.87	634	1	0	0	314-368	692.1	579	249	221	50	234-41	781
Major League totals (10 years)	45	42	.517	2.98	643	4	0	0	314-368	715.0	607	266	237	51	260-41	793

DIVISION SERIES RECORD

Year League	W	L	Pct.	ERA	G	GS	CG	ShO	Sv.-Opp.	IP	H	R	ER	HR	BB-IBB	SO
1997— Florida (N.L.)	1	0	1.000	0.00	2	0	0	0	0-1	2.0	1	1	0	0	2-0	2
2000— San Francisco (N.L.)	0	0	...	0.00	2	0	0	0	0-1	2.1	2	0	0	0	1-0	3
2002— San Francisco (N.L.)	0	0	...	0.00	4	0	0	0	2-2	2.2	4	0	0	0	1-0	1
Division series totals (3 years)	1	0	1.000	0.00	8	0	0	0	2-4	7.0	7	1	0	0	4-0	6

CHAMPIONSHIP SERIES RECORD

Year League	W	L	Pct.	ERA	G	GS	CG	ShO	Sv.-Opp.	IP	H	R	ER	HR	BB-IBB	SO
1997— Florida (N.L.)	0	0	...	0.00	2	0	0	0	2-2	2.0	0	0	0	0	0-0	0
2002— San Francisco (N.L.)	0	0	...	2.70	3	0	0	0	3-3	3.1	3	1	1	0	1-0	4
Champ. series totals (2 years)	0	0	...	1.69	5	0	0	0	5-5	5.1	3	1	1	0	1-0	4

WORLD SERIES RECORD

NOTES: Member of World Series championship team (1997).

Year League	W	L	Pct.	ERA	G	GS	CG	ShO	Sv.-Opp.	IP	H	R	ER	HR	BB-IBB	SO
1997— Florida (N.L.)	0	0	...	7.71	4	0	0	0	2-2	4.2	8	5	4	0	2-0	7
2002— San Francisco (N.L.)	0	0	...	0.00	3	0	0	0	2-3	3.0	2	0	0	0	1-1	3
World Series totals (2 years)	0	0	...	4.70	7	0	0	0	4-5	7.2	10	5	4	0	3-1	10

ALL-STAR GAME RECORD

	W	L	Pct.	ERA	GS	CG	ShO	Sv.-Opp.	IP	H	R	ER	HR	BB-IBB	SO
All-Star Game totals (2 years)	0	0	...	9.00	0	0	0	0-1	2.0	5	4	2	0	0-0	2

NEUGEBAUER, NICK — P — BREWERS

PERSONAL: Born July 15, 1980, in Riverside, Calif. ... 6-3/235. ... Throws right, bats right. ... Full name: Nickolas D. Neugebauer.
HIGH SCHOOL: Arlington (Riverside, Calif.).
TRANSACTIONS/CAREER NOTES: Selected by Milwaukee Brewers organization in second round of free-agent draft (June 2, 1998). ... On Milwaukee disabled list (August 25, 2001-remainder of season). ... On Milwaukee disabled list (May 11-September 1, 2002); included rehabilitation assignment to Indianapolis (August 2-28).
CAREER HITTING (MLB): 2-for-22 (.091), 0 R, 1 2B, 0 3B, 0 HR, 1 RBI.

Year League	W	L	Pct.	ERA	G	GS	CG	ShO	Sv.-Opp.	IP	H	R	ER	HR	BB-IBB	SO
1999— Beloit (Midw.)	7	5	.583	3.90	18	18	0	0	0-...	80.2	50	41	35	4	80-0	125
2000— Mudville (Calif.)	4	4	.500	4.19	18	18	0	0	0-...	77.1	43	40	36	0	87-0	117
— Huntsville (Sou.)	1	3	.250	3.73	10	10	0	0	0-...	50.2	35	28	21	2	47-0	57
2001— Huntsville (Sou.)	5	6	.455	3.46	21	21	1	1	0-...	106.2	94	46	41	6	52-0	*149
— Indianapolis (I.L.)	2	1	.667	1.50	4	4	0	0	0-...	24.0	10	5	4	1	9-0	26
— Milwaukee (N.L.)	1	1	.500	7.50	2	2	0	0	0-0	6.0	6	5	5	1	6-0	11
2002— Milwaukee (N.L.)	1	7	.125	4.72	12	12	0	0	0-0	55.1	56	33	29	10	44-3	47
— Indianapolis (I.L.)	0	3	.000	5.12	5	5	0	0	0-...	19.1	20	13	11	4	12-0	18
Major League totals (2 years)	2	8	.200	4.99	14	14	0	0	0-0	61.1	62	38	34	11	50-3	58

NEVIN, PHIL — 3B — PADRES

PERSONAL: Born January 19, 1971, in Fullerton, Calif. ... 6-2/231. ... Bats right, throws right. ... Full name: Phillip Joseph Nevin.
HIGH SCHOOL: El Dorado (Placentia, Calif.).
COLLEGE: Cal State-Fullerton.
TRANSACTIONS/CAREER NOTES: Selected by Los Angeles Dodgers organization in third round of free-agent draft (June 5, 1989); did not sign. ... Selected by Houston Astros organization in first round (first pick overall) of free-agent draft (June 1, 1992). ... On Tucson disabled list (July 12-30, 1995). ... Traded by Astros to Detroit Tigers (August 15, 1995), completing deal in which Tigers traded P Mike Henneman to Astros for a player to be named later (August 10, 1995). ... On Detroit disabled list (March 21-April 16, 1997); included rehabilitation assignment to Lakeland (April 8-16). ... Traded by Tigers with C Matt Walbeck to Anaheim Angels for P Nick Skuse (November 20, 1997). ... On suspended list (June 12-15, 1998). ... Traded by Angels with P Keith Volkman to San Diego Padres for INF Andy Sheets and OF Gus Kennedy (March 29, 1999). ... On San Diego disabled list (April 1-16, 1999); included rehabilitaion assignment to Las Vegas (April 12-15). ... On San Diego disabled list (May 12-27 and May 30-July 12, 2002); included rehabilitation assignment to Lake Elsinore (July 9-12).
HONORS: Named Golden Spikes Award winner by USA Baseball (1992). ... Named third baseman on The Sporting News college All-America team (1992). ... Named Most Outstanding Player of College World Series (1992).
STATISTICAL NOTES: Led Pacific Coast League third basemen with .891 fielding percentage in 1993. ... Led Pacific Coast League in grounding into double plays with 21 in 1994. ... Led Pacific Coast League third basemen with 31 errors and 32 double plays in 1994. ... Led A.L. catchers with 20 passed balls in 1998. ... Hit three home runs in one game (October 6, 2001). ... Career major league grand slams: 5.
MISCELLANEOUS: Member of 1992 U.S. Olympic baseball team.
2002 GAMES PLAYED BY POSITION (MLB): 3B—71; 1B—36.

		BATTING														FIELDING	
Year Team (League)	Pos.	G	AB	R	H	2B	3B	HR	RBI	BB	SO	SB-CS	Avg.	OBP	SLG	E	Avg.
1993— Tucson (PCL)	3B-OF	123	448	67	128	21	3	10	93	52	99	8-1	.286	.359	.413	29	†.898
1994— Tucson (PCL)	3B-OF	118	445	67	117	20	1	12	79	55	101	3-2	.263	.343	.393	†32	.907
1995— Tucson (PCL)	3B-DH	62	223	31	65	16	0	7	41	27	39	2-3	.291	.371	.457	14	.923
— Houston (N.L.)	3B	18	60	4	7	1	0	0	1	7	13	1-0	.117	.221	.133	3	.933
— Toledo (I.L.)■	OF-DH	7	23	3	7	2	0	1	3	1	5	0-0	.304	.333	.522	0	1.000
— Detroit (A.L.)	OF-DH	29	96	9	21	3	1	2	12	11	27	0-0	.219	.318	.333	2	.963
1996— Jacksonville (Sou.)	C-DH-3-O-1	98	344	77	101	18	1	24	69	60	83	6-2	.294	.397	.561	11	.977
— Detroit (A.L.)	3B-OF-C-DH	38	120	15	35	5	0	8	19	8	39	1-0	.292	.338	.533	5	.950
1997— Lakeland (FSL)	DH-1B-3B	3	9	3	5	1	0	1	4	3	2	0-0	.556	.667	1.000	1	.929
— Toledo (I.L.)	1B-DH-3B	5	19	1	3	0	0	1	3	2	9	0-0	.158	.238	.316	0	1.000
— Detroit (A.L.)	O-DH-3-1-C	93	251	32	59	16	1	9	35	25	68	0-1	.235	.306	.414	2	.982
1998— Anaheim (A.L.)■	C-DH-1B	75	237	27	54	8	1	8	27	17	67	0-0	.228	.291	.371	5	.989
1999— Las Vegas (PCL)■	C-1B-3B	3	10	2	2	0	0	2	2	0	2	0-0	.200	.200	.800	0	1.000
— San Diego (N.L.)	3-C-O-1-DH	128	383	52	103	27	0	24	85	51	82	1-0	.269	.352	.527	5	.989
2000— San Diego (N.L.)	3B	143	538	87	163	34	1	31	107	59	121	2-0	.303	.374	.543	*26	.929
2001— San Diego (N.L.)	3B-DH	149	546	97	167	31	0	41	126	71	147	4-4	.306	.388	.588	27	.930
2002— San Diego (N.L.)	3B-1B	107	407	53	116	16	0	12	57	38	87	4-0	.285	.344	.413	18	.963
— Lake Elsinore (Calif.)	3B	2	6	2	2	1	0	1	6	1	2	0-0	.333	.375	1.000	2	.000
American League totals (4 years)		235	704	83	169	32	3	27	93	61	201	1-1	.240	.308	.409	14	.980
National League totals (5 years)		545	1934	293	556	109	1	108	376	226	450	12-4	.287	.363	.512	79	.954
Major League totals (8 years)		780	2638	376	725	141	4	135	469	287	651	13-5	.275	.348	.485	93	.962

ALL-STAR GAME RECORD

	AB	R	H	2B	3B	HR	RBI	BB	SO	SB-CS	Avg.	OBP	SLG	E	Avg.
All-Star Game totals (1 year)	1	0	0	0	0	0	0	0	0	0-0	.000	.000	.000	0	...

NICHTING, CHRIS — P

PERSONAL: Born May 13, 1966, in Cincinnati. ... 6-2/220. ... Throws right, bats right. ... Full name: Christopher Thomas Nichting. ... Name pronounced NICK-ting.
HIGH SCHOOL: Elder (Cincinnati).
COLLEGE: Northwestern.
TRANSACTIONS/CAREER NOTES: Selected by Los Angeles Dodgers organization in third round of free-agent draft (June 2, 1987). ... On disabled list (April 10, 1990-entire season). ... On disabled list (June 17, 1991-entire season). ... On San Antonio disabled list (August 12, 1992-remainder of season). ... On Albuquerque disabled list (April 8-July 2, 1993). ... On Vero Beach disabled list (July 15-26 and July 28, 1993-remainder of season). ... On San Antonio disabled list (April 7-23, 1994). ... Granted free agency (October 15, 1994). ... Signed by Texas Rangers (November 18, 1994). ... On Oklahoma City suspended list (June 8-10, 1995). ... On Texas disabled list (March 22-September 3,

1996); included rehabilitation assignment to Oklahoma City (August 19-September 3). ... Granted free agency (October 15, 1996). ... Signed by Oakland Athletics organization (November 19, 1996). ... Granted free agency (October 15, 1997). ... Signed by Cleveland Indians organization (February 26, 1998). ... Granted free agency (October 15, 1998). ... Signed by New York Yankees organization (December 15, 1998). ... On Columbus disabled list (July 7-15, 1999). ... Granted free agency (October 15, 1999). ... Signed by Indians organization (February 8, 2000). ... Granted free agency (October 18, 2000). ... Signed by Cincinnati Reds organization (January 1, 2001). ... Released by Reds (September 18, 2001). ... Signed by Colorado Rockies organization (September 19, 2001). ... Released by Rockies (October 19, 2001).

CAREER HITTING (MLB): 1-for-4 (.250), 2 R, 0 2B, 0 3B, 0 HR, 0 RBI.

Year League	W	L	Pct.	ERA	G	GS	CG	ShO	Sv.-Opp.	IP	H	R	ER	HR	BB-IBB	SO
1988—Vero Beach (FSL)	11	4	.733	2.09	21	19	5	1	1-...	138.0	90	40	32	7	51-0	*151
1989—San Antonio (Texas)	4	*14	.222	5.03	26	26	2	0	0-...	154.0	160	96	86	13	*101-6	*136
1990—San Antonio (Texas)									Did not play.							
1991—Yakima (N'West)									Did not play.							
1992—San Antonio (Texas)	4	5	.444	2.52	13	13	0	0	0-...	78.2	58	25	22	3	37-0	81
—Albuquerque (PCL)	1	3	.250	7.93	10	9	0	0	0-...	42.0	64	42	37	2	23-1	25
1993—Vero Beach (FSL)	0	1	.000	4.15	4	4	0	0	0-...	17.1	18	9	8	2	6-0	18
1994—San Antonio (Texas)	3	4	.429	1.64	21	8	0	0	1-...	65.2	47	21	12	1	34-1	74
—Albuquerque (PCL)	2	2	.500	7.40	10	7	0	0	0-...	41.1	61	39	34	5	28-1	25
1995—Oklahoma City (A.A.)■	5	5	.500	2.13	23	7	3	•2	1-...	67.2	58	19	16	4	19-0	72
—Texas (A.L.)	0	0	...	7.03	13	0	0	0	0-0	24.1	36	19	19	1	13-1	6
1996—Oklahoma City (A.A.)	1	0	1.000	1.00	4	1	0	0	0-...	9.0	9	1	1	0	3-0	7
1997—Edmonton (PCL)■	7	13	.350	7.76	33	24	3	0	1-...	131.0	170	120	*113	21	46-2	90
1998—Buffalo (I.L.)■	8	6	.571	4.39	43	5	0	0	1-...	96.1	104	54	47	9	37-4	97
1999—Columbus (I.L.)■	8	5	.615	5.29	25	21	2	0	0-...	127.2	135	80	75	22	47-0	110
2000—Buffalo (I.L.)■	2	3	.400	4.23	47	3	0	0	26-...	66.0	65	31	31	6	16-1	60
—Cleveland (A.L.)	0	0	...	7.00	7	0	0	0	0-1	9.0	13	7	7	0	5-1	7
2001—Louisville (I.L.)■	2	1	.667	2.97	27	0	0	0	17-...	33.1	24	11	11	5	10-0	45
—Cincinnati (N.L.)	0	3	.000	4.46	36	0	0	0	1-3	36.1	46	24	18	6	8-1	33
—Colorado (N.L.)■	0	0	...	4.50	7	0	0	0	0-0	6.0	9	3	3	2	0-0	7
2002—Colorado Springs (PCL)	1	4	.200	10.19	23	0	0	0	1-...	32.2	53	40	37	7	22-1	23
—Colorado (N.L.)	1	1	.500	4.46	29	0	0	0	0-0	36.1	40	18	18	7	5-0	25
A.L. totals (2 years)	0	0	...	7.02	20	0	0	0	0-1	33.1	49	26	26	1	18-2	13
N.L. totals (2 years)	1	4	.200	4.46	72	0	0	0	1-3	78.2	95	45	39	15	13-1	65
Major League totals (4 years)	1	4	.200	5.22	92	0	0	0	1-4	112.0	144	71	65	16	31-3	78

NICKLE, DOUG — P — METS

PERSONAL: Born October 2, 1974, in Sonoma, Calif. ... 6-4/230. ... Throws right, bats right. ... Full name: Douglas A. Nickle.

HIGH SCHOOL: Sonoma Valley (Sonoma, Calif.).

COLLEGE: California.

TRANSACTIONS/CAREER NOTES: Selected by Anaheim Angels organization in 13th round of free-agent draft (June 3, 1997). ... Traded by Angels to Philadelphia Phillies (September 10, 1998), completing deal in which Phillies traded OF Gregg Jefferies for a player to be named later (August 26, 1998). ... On Reading disabled list (May 3-26, 2000). ... Traded by Phillies with 3B Scott Rolen to St. Louis Cardinals for IF/OF Placido Polanco, P Bud Smith and P Mike Timlin (July 29, 2002). ... Claimed on waivers by San Diego Padres (August 28, 2002). ... Claimed on waivers by New York Mets (October 2, 2002).

STATISTICAL NOTES: Led International League with seven intentional bases on balls issued in 2001.

CAREER HITTING (MLB): 0-for-1 (.000), 0 R, 0 2B, 0 3B, 0 HR, 0 RBI.

Year League	W	L	Pct.	ERA	G	GS	CG	ShO	Sv.-Opp.	IP	H	R	ER	HR	BB-IBB	SO
1997—Boise (N'West)	0	1	.000	6.41	17	2	0	0	0-...	19.2	27	17	14	3	8-1	22
1998—Cedar Rapids (Midw.)	8	4	.667	3.78	20	7	1	1	0-...	69.0	66	30	29	2	20-0	59
—Lake Elsinore (Calif.)	3	4	.429	4.48	11	10	1	0	0-...	66.1	68	40	33	3	25-0	69
1999—Clearwater (FSL)■	2	4	.333	2.29	*60	0	0	0	28-...	70.2	60	25	18	1	23-3	70
2000—Reading (East.)	8	3	.727	2.44	49	0	0	0	16-...	77.1	55	25	21	4	22-2	58
—Philadelphia (N.L.)	0	0	...	13.50	4	0	0	0	0-0	2.2	5	4	4	0	2-0	0
2001—Scranton/W.B. (I.L.)	9	3	.750	1.68	47	1	0	0	7-...	85.2	62	19	16	2	37-7	60
—Philadelphia (N.L.)	0	0	...	0.00	2	0	0	0	0-0	2.0	1	0	0	0	0-0	1
2002—Scranton/W.B. (I.L.)	3	5	.375	2.97	34	1	0	0	7-...	60.2	58	24	20	4	16-4	37
—Philadelphia (N.L.)	0	0	...	6.23	4	0	0	0	0-0	4.1	6	3	3	2	4-0	2
—Memphis (PCL)■	3	1	.750	4.60	14	0	0	0	3-...	15.2	13	8	8	3	7-0	10
—San Diego (N.L.)■	1	0	1.000	8.49	10	0	0	0	0-0	11.2	20	13	11	1	9-0	7
Major League totals (3 years)	1	0	1.000	7.84	20	0	0	0	0-0	20.2	32	20	18	3	15-0	10

NIEVES, JOSE — SS/2B

PERSONAL: Born June 16, 1975, in Guacara, Venezuela. ... 6-0/180. ... Bats right, throws right. ... Full name: Jose Miguel Nieves Pinto. ... Brother of Juan Nieves, former outfielder with Toronto Blue Jays organization. ... Name pronounced nee-A-vez.

HIGH SCHOOL: Enrique Delgado Palacios (Carabobo, Venezuela).

TRANSACTIONS/CAREER NOTES: Signed as non-drafted free agent by Milwaukee Brewers organization (June 10, 1992). ... Released by Brewers (October 19, 1993). ... Signed by Chicago Cubs organization (June 30, 1994). ... On disabled list (May 29-June 12, 1997). ... On Chicago disabled list (May 31-June 18, 2000); included rehabilitation assignments to Daytona (June 14-16) and West Tenn (June 16-18). ... Traded by Cubs to Anaheim Angels for P Mike Fyhrie and a player to be named later (March 25, 2001). ... On Anaheim disabled list (August 9-28, 2001). ... On Salt Lake disabled list (August 29, 2002-remainder of season). ... Granted free agency (October 15, 2002).

2002 GAMES PLAYED BY POSITION (MLB): 2B—18; SS—13; 3B—5; 1B—3; OF—2; DH—2.

						BATTING									FIELDING	
Year Team (League)	Pos.	G	AB	R	H	2B	3B	HR	RBI	BB	SO	SB-CS	Avg.	OBP	SLG	E	Avg.
1992—Dom. Brewers (DSL)	IF	8	15	2	5	0	0	1	3	4	4	0-...	.333	...	.533	5	.815
1993—Dom. Brewers (DSL)	IF	54	144	21	29	4	3	2	14	22	25	6-...	.201	...	.313	19	.864
1994—Dom. Cubs (DSL)■	2B	37	137	21	39	6	1	4	24	13	23	5-...	.285	...	.431	9	.933
1995—Williamsport (NY-P)	SS-2B	69	276	46	59	13	1	4	44	21	39	11-10	.214	.281	.312	33	.894
1996—Rockford (Midw.)	SS-2B-3B	113	396	55	96	20	4	5	57	33	59	17-9	.242	.307	.351	37	.928
1997—Daytona (FSL)	SS-2B	85	331	51	91	20	1	4	42	17	55	16-6	.275	.313	.378	27	.932

N

Year	Team (League)	Pos.	G	AB	R	H	2B	3B	HR	RBI	BB	SO	SB-CS	Avg.	OBP	SLG	E	Avg.
			BATTING														FIELDING	
1998	—West Tenn (Sou.)	SS-2B	82	314	42	91	27	5	8	39	18	55	17-10	.290	.327	.484	24	.934
	—Chicago (N.L.)	SS	2	1	0	0	0	0	0	0	0	0	0-0	.000	.000	.000	0	...
	—Iowa (PCL)	SS	19	75	7	19	4	0	0	4	2	11	1-1	.253	.273	.307	4	.960
1999	—Iowa (PCL)	SS-2B	104	392	55	105	25	3	11	59	24	65	11-8	.268	.314	.431	19	.958
	—Chicago (N.L.)	SS	54	181	16	45	9	1	2	18	8	25	0-2	.249	.291	.343	16	.935
2000	—Chicago (N.L.)	SS	82	198	17	42	6	3	5	24	11	43	1-1	.212	.251	.348	5	.968
	—Daytona (FSL)	3B-SS	2	6	2	1	0	0	0	0	1	0	0-0	.167	.286	.167	0	1.000
	—West Tenn (Sou.)	3B-SS	2	7	2	4	0	0	2	2	0	0	0-0	.571	.571	1.429	0	1.000
	—Iowa (PCL)	3B-SS-2B	7	32	7	9	4	1	1	7	2	5	1-0	.281	.324	.563	1	.947
2001	—Anaheim (A.L.)■	2-S-DH-3-1	29	53	5	13	3	1	2	3	2	20	0-1	.245	.298	.453	1	.988
	—Salt Lake (PCL)	2B-SS-3B	61	258	50	85	15	4	11	37	8	36	8-7	.329	.354	.547	13	.955
2002	—Anaheim (A.L.)	IF-OF-DH	45	97	17	28	2	0	0	6	2	14	1-1	.289	.303	.309	7	.943
	—Salt Lake (PCL)	3-2-0-S-1	15	63	12	18	3	1	4	13	4	6	2-1	.286	.328	.556	4	.905
American League totals (2 years)			74	150	22	41	5	1	2	9	4	34	1-2	.273	.301	.360	8	.960
National League totals (3 years)			138	380	33	87	15	4	7	42	19	68	1-3	.229	.270	.345	21	.947
Major League totals (5 years)			212	530	55	128	20	5	9	51	23	102	2-5	.242	.278	.349	29	.952

NIEVES, WIL — C — PADRES

PERSONAL: Born September 25, 1977, in San Juan, Puerto Rico. ... 5-11/190. ... Bats right, throws right. ... Full name: Wilbert Nieves. ... Brother of Melvin Nieves, outfielder with four major league teams (1992-98).

TRANSACTIONS/CAREER NOTES: Selected by San Diego Padres organization in 47th round of free-agent draft (June 1, 1995).

2002 GAMES PLAYED BY POSITION (MLB): C—27.

Year	Team (League)	Pos.	G	AB	R	H	2B	3B	HR	RBI	BB	SO	SB-CS	Avg.	OBP	SLG	E	Avg.
			BATTING														FIELDING	
1996	—Arizona Padres (Ariz.)	C-3B-OF	43	113	23	39	5	0	2	22	13	19	3-4	.345	.413	.442	10	.960
1997	—Clinton (Midw.)	C	18	55	6	12	1	1	1	7	6	10	2-1	.218	.290	.327	7	.952
	—Arizona Padres (Ariz.)	OF	8	27	2	8	2	0	0	2	5	5	1-0	.296	.406	.370	0	1.000
1998	—Clinton (Midw.)	C	115	380	47	97	22	0	3	55	47	69	7-9	.255	.343	.337	14	.982
1999	—Rancho Cuca. (Calif.)	C	120	427	58	140	26	2	7	61	40	54	2-7	.328	.389	.447	5	.995
2000	—Las Vegas (PCL)	PH	1	1	0	0	0	0	0	0	0	0	0-0	.000	.000	.000	...	...
	—Mobile (Sou.)	C-1B-2B	68	214	18	57	4	0	4	30	16	22	1-1	.266	.319	.341	4	.991
	—Rancho Cuca. (Calif.)	C	31	101	16	26	5	0	0	9	15	17	2-0	.257	.350	.307	5	.984
2001	—Mobile (Sou.)	C	95	330	28	99	24	0	3	41	18	40	1-0	.300	.336	.400	3	.996
2002	—Portland (PCL)	C-1B	70	237	24	73	20	2	7	29	5	40	0-0	.308	.321	.498	3	.993
	—San Diego (N.L.)	C	28	72	2	13	3	1	0	3	4	15	1-0	.181	.224	.250	5	.971
Major League totals (1 year)			28	72	2	13	3	1	0	3	4	15	1-0	.181	.224	.250	5	.971

NITKOWSKI, C.J. — P

PERSONAL: Born March 9, 1973, in Suffern, N.Y. ... 6-3/205. ... Throws left, bats left. ... Full name: Christopher John Nitkowski.

HIGH SCHOOL: Don Bosco (N.J.).

COLLEGE: St. John's.

TRANSACTIONS/CAREER NOTES: Selected by Cincinnati Reds organization in first round (ninth pick overall) of free-agent draft (June 2, 1994). ... Traded by Reds with P David Tuttle and a player to be named later to Detroit Tigers for P David Wells (July 31, 1995); Tigers acquired IF Mark Lewis to complete deal (November 16, 1995). ... On Detroit disabled list (August 11-29, 1996). ... Traded by Tigers with C Brad Ausmus, P Jose Lima, P Trever Miller and IF Daryle Ward to Houston Astros for OF Brian Hunter, IF Orlando Miller, P Doug Brocail, P Todd Jones and cash (December 10, 1996). ... Traded by Astros with C Brad Ausmus to Tigers for C Paul Bako, P Dean Crow, P Mark Persails, P Brian Powell and 3B Carlos Villalobos (January 14, 1999). ... On suspended list (May 28-30, 1999). ... Traded by Tigers with cash to New York Mets for a player to be named later (September 1, 2001); Tigers acquired P Kyle Kessel to complete deal (December 13, 2001). ... Granted free agency (October 15, 2001). ... Signed by Astros organization (December 21, 2001). ... Released by Astros (March 25, 2002). ... Re-signed by Astros organization (March 28, 2002). ... Released by Astros (June 6, 2002). ... Signed by St. Louis Cardinals organization (June 6, 2002). ... Released by Cardinals (July 21, 2002). ... Signed by Texas Rangers organization (July 29, 2002). ... Released by Rangers (September 30, 2002).

RECORDS: Shares major league record for most hit batsmen in one inning—3 (August 3, 1998, eighth inning).

STATISTICAL NOTES: Tied for A.L. lead with three balks in 1999.

MISCELLANEOUS: Struck out in only appearance as pinch hitter and appeared in one game as pinch runner (1999).

CAREER HITTING (MLB): 2-for-15 (.133), 1 R, 0 2B, 0 3B, 0 HR, 1 RBI.

Year	League	W	L	Pct.	ERA	G	GS	CG	ShO	Sv.-Opp.	IP	H	R	ER	HR	BB-IBB	SO
1994	—Chattanooga (Sou.)	6	3	.667	3.50	14	14	0	0	0-...	74.2	61	30	29	4	40-0	60
1995	—Chattanooga (Sou.)	4	2	.667	2.50	8	8	0	0	0-...	50.1	39	20	14	1	20-0	52
	—Indianapolis (A.A.)	0	2	.000	5.20	6	6	0	0	0-...	27.2	28	16	16	3	10-0	21
	—Cincinnati (N.L.)	1	3	.250	6.12	9	7	0	0	0-1	32.1	41	25	22	4	15-1	18
	—Detroit (A.L.)■	1	4	.200	7.09	11	11	0	0	0-0	39.1	53	32	31	7	20-2	13
1996	—Toledo (I.L.)	4	6	.400	4.46	19	19	1	0	0-...	111.0	104	60	55	13	53-1	103
	—Detroit (A.L.)	2	3	.400	8.08	11	8	0	0	0-0	45.2	62	44	41	7	38-1	36
1997	—New Orleans (A.A.)■	8	10	.444	3.98	28	28	1	0	0-...	174.1	183	82	77	10	56-2	*141
1998	—Houston (N.L.)	3	3	.500	3.77	43	0	0	0	3-5	59.2	49	27	25	4	23-2	44
	—New Orleans (PCL)	0	1	.000	6.00	5	3	0	0	1-...	15.0	22	12	10	1	7-0	18
1999	—Detroit (A.L.)■	4	5	.444	4.30	68	7	0	0	0-0	81.2	63	44	39	11	45-3	66
2000	—Detroit (A.L.)	4	9	.308	5.25	67	11	0	0	0-2	109.2	124	79	64	13	49-3	81
2001	—Detroit (A.L.)	0	3	.000	5.56	56	0	0	0	0-6	45.1	51	30	28	7	31-7	38
	—Toledo (I.L.)	0	0	...	0.00	1	0	0	0	0-...	1.0	1	0	0	0	0-0	1
	—New York (N.L.)■	1	0	1.000	0.00	5	0	0	0	0-0	5.2	3	0	0	0	3-1	4
2002	—New Orleans (PCL)■	1	2	.333	2.78	24	0	0	0	2-...	22.2	21	7	7	1	7-1	20
	—Memphis (PCL)■	1	2	.333	9.82	16	1	0	0	0-...	14.2	24	18	16	3	9-0	12
	—Oklahoma (PCL)■	1	1	.500	1.80	9	0	0	0	0-...	10.0	8	3	2	0	4-0	11
	—Texas (A.L.)	0	1	.000	2.63	12	0	0	0	0-0	13.2	11	4	4	0	13-0	14
A.L. totals (6 years)		11	25	.306	5.56	225	37	0	0	0-8	335.1	364	233	207	45	196-16	248
N.L. totals (3 years)		5	6	.455	4.33	57	7	0	0	3-6	97.2	93	52	47	8	41-4	66
Major League totals (7 years)		16	31	.340	5.28	282	44	0	0	3-14	433.0	457	285	254	53	237-20	314

NIXON, TROT — OF — RED SOX

PERSONAL: Born April 11, 1974, in Durham, N.C. ... 6-2/211. ... Bats left, throws left. ... Full name: Christopher Trotman Nixon.

HIGH SCHOOL: New Hanover (Wilmington, N.C.).

TRANSACTIONS/CAREER NOTES: Selected by Boston Red Sox organization in first round (seventh pick overall) of free-agent draft (June 3, 1993). ... On disabled list (July 12, 1994-remainder of season). ... On Boston disabled list (June 27-July 25, 2000); included rehabilitation assignment to Gulf Coast Red Sox (July 8-9 and July 20-23).

STATISTICAL NOTES: Led Eastern League outfielders with 14 assists and tied for lead with four double plays in 1996. ... Tied for International League lead with 11 errors and three double plays by outfielder in 1998. ... Hit three home runs in one game (July 24, 1999). ... Had 16-game hitting streak (July 16-31, 2002). ... Career major league grand slams: 5.

2002 GAMES PLAYED BY POSITION (MLB): OF—152.

		BATTING														FIELDING	
Year Team (League)	Pos.	G	AB	R	H	2B	3B	HR	RBI	BB	SO	SB-CS	Avg.	OBP	SLG	E	Avg.
1994—Lynchburg (Caro.)	OF	71	264	33	65	12	0	12	43	44	53	10-3	.246	.357	.428	4	.974
1995—Sarasota (FSL)	OF	73	264	43	80	11	4	5	39	45	46	7-5	.303	.404	.432	2	.986
—Trenton (East.)	OF	25	94	9	15	3	1	2	8	7	20	2-1	.160	.214	.277	0	1.000
1996—Trenton (East.)	OF-DH	123	438	55	110	11	4	11	63	50	65	7-9	.251	.329	.370	5	.979
—Boston (A.L.)	OF	2	4	2	2	1	0	0	0	0	1	1-0	.500	.500	.750	0	1.000
1997—Pawtucket (I.L.)	OF	130	475	80	116	18	3	20	61	63	86	11-4	.244	.331	.421	4	.986
1998—Pawtucket (I.L.)	OF-DH-1B	135	509	97	158	26	4	23	74	76	81	26-13	.310	.400	.513	‡11	.957
—Boston (A.L.)	OF-DH	13	27	3	7	1	0	0	0	1	3	0-0	.259	.286	.296	0	1.000
1999—Boston (A.L.)	OF	124	381	67	103	22	5	15	52	53	75	3-1	.270	.357	.472	7	.968
2000—Boston (A.L.)	OF-DH	123	427	66	118	27	8	12	60	63	85	8-1	.276	.368	.461	2	.991
—GC Red Sox (GCL)	OF	3	10	3	4	0	0	1	5	2	0	0-0	.400	.538	.700	0	1.000
2001—Boston (A.L.)	OF-DH	148	535	100	150	31	4	27	88	79	113	7-4	.280	.376	.505	8	.973
2002—Boston (A.L.)	OF	152	532	81	136	36	3	24	94	65	109	4-2	.256	.338	.470	5	.984
Major League totals (6 years)		562	1906	319	516	118	20	78	294	261	386	23-8	.271	.359	.476	22	.979

DIVISION SERIES RECORD

		BATTING														FIELDING	
Year Team (League)	Pos.	G	AB	R	H	2B	3B	HR	RBI	BB	SO	SB-CS	Avg.	OBP	SLG	E	Avg.
1998—Boston (A.L.)	OF	2	3	0	1	0	0	0	0	1	0	0-0	.333	.500	.333	0	1.000
1999—Boston (A.L.)	OF	5	14	5	3	3	0	0	6	4	5	0-0	.214	.350	.429	0	1.000
Division series totals (2 years)		7	17	5	4	3	0	0	6	5	5	0-0	.235	.375	.412	0	1.000

CHAMPIONSHIP SERIES RECORD

		BATTING														FIELDING	
Year Team (League)	Pos.	G	AB	R	H	2B	3B	HR	RBI	BB	SO	SB-CS	Avg.	OBP	SLG	E	Avg.
1999—Boston (A.L.)	OF	4	14	2	4	2	0	0	0	1	5	0-0	.286	.333	.429	0	1.000

NOMO, HIDEO — P — DODGERS

PERSONAL: Born August 31, 1968, in Osaka, Japan. ... 6-2/210. ... Throws right, bats right.

HIGH SCHOOL: Seijyo Kogyo (Japan).

TRANSACTIONS/CAREER NOTES: Selected by Kintetsu Buffaloes in first round of 1989 Japanese free-agent draft. ... Signed as free agent by Los Angeles Dodgers organization (February 8, 1995). ... On Albuquerque temporarily inactive list (April 3-27, 1995). ... Traded by Dodgers with P Brad Clontz to New York Mets for P Dave Mlicki and P Greg McMichael (June 4, 1998). ... Released by Mets (March 26, 1999). ... Signed by Chicago Cubs organization (April 2, 1999). ... Released by Cubs (April 23, 1999). ... Signed by Milwaukee Brewers (April 29, 1999). ... Claimed on waivers by Philadelphia Phillies (October 28, 1999). ... Granted free agency (October 29, 1999). ... Signed by Detroit Tigers organization (January 21, 2000). ... On disabled list (July 30-August 18, 2000). ... Released by Tigers (November 2, 2000). ... Signed by Boston Red Sox (December 15, 2000). ... Granted free agency (November 5, 2001). ... Signed by Dodgers (December 21, 2001).

HONORS: Named N.L. Rookie Pitcher of the Year by The Sporting News (1995). ... Named N.L. Rookie of the Year by Baseball Writers' Association of America (1995).

STATISTICAL NOTES: Struck out 16 batters in one game (June 14, 1995). ... Pitched 3-0 one-hit, complete-game victory against San Francisco (August 5, 1995). ... Led N.L. with 19 wild pitches in 1995. ... Led N.L. with five balks in 1995 and four in 1997. ... Struck out 17 batters in one game (April 13, 1996). ... Pitched 9-0 no-hit victory against Colorado (September 17, 1996). ... Pitched 3-0 no-hit victory against Baltimore (April 4, 2001). ... Pitched 4-0 one-hit, complete-game victory against Toronto (May 25, 2001).

MISCELLANEOUS: Member of 1988 Japanese Olympic baseball team. ... Appeared in one game as pinch runner (1999).

CAREER HITTING (MLB): 53-for-390 (.136), 16 R, 13 2B, 1 3B, 2 HR, 22 RBI.

Year League	W	L	Pct.	ERA	G	GS	CG	ShO	Sv.-Opp.	IP	H	R	ER	HR	BB-IBB	SO
1990—Kintetsu (Jap. Pac.)	*18	8	.692	*2.91	29	27	21	2	0-...	235.0	167	...	76	...	*109-...	*287
1991—Kintetsu (Jap. Pac.)	*17	11	.607	3.05	31	29	22	*4	1-...	242.1	183	...	82	...	*128-...	*287
1992—Kintetsu (Jap. Pac.)	*18	8	.692	2.66	30	29	17	*5	0-...	216.2	150	...	64	...	*117-...	*228
1993—Kintetsu (Jap. Pac.)	*17	12	.586	3.70	32	32	14	2	0-...	243.1	*201	...	100	...	*148-...	*276
1994—Kintetsu (Jap. Pac.)	8	7	.533	3.63	17	17	6	0	0-...	114.0	...	...	46	...	86-...	126
1995—Bakersfield (Calif.)■	0	1	.000	3.38	1	1	0	0	0-...	5.1	6	2	2	0	1-0	6
—Los Angeles (N.L.)	13	6	.684	2.54	28	28	4	•3	0-0	191.1	124	63	54	14	78-2	*236
1996—Los Angeles (N.L.)	16	11	.593	3.19	33	33	3	2	0-0	228.1	180	93	81	23	85-6	234
1997—Los Angeles (N.L.)	14	12	.538	4.25	33	33	1	0	0-0	207.1	193	104	98	23	92-2	233
1998—Los Angeles (N.L.)	2	7	.222	5.05	12	12	2	0	0-0	67.2	57	39	38	8	38-0	73
—New York (N.L.)■	4	5	.444	4.82	17	16	1	0	0-0	89.2	73	49	48	11	56-2	94
1999—Iowa (PCL)■	1	1	.500	3.71	3	3	0	0	0-...	17.0	12	7	7	1	12-0	18
—Huntsville (Sou.)■	1	0	1.000	0.00	1	1	0	0	0-...	7.0	5	0	0	0	1-0	7
—Milwaukee (N.L.)	12	8	.600	4.54	28	28	0	0	0-0	176.1	173	96	89	27	78-2	161
2000—Detroit (A.L.)■	8	12	.400	4.74	32	31	1	0	0-0	190.0	191	102	100	31	89-1	181
2001—Boston (A.L.)■	13	10	.565	4.50	33	33	2	2	0-0	198.0	171	105	99	26	*96-2	*220
2002—Los Angeles (N.L.)■	16	6	.727	3.39	34	34	0	0	0-0	220.1	189	92	83	26	101-5	193
A.L. totals (2 years)	21	22	.488	4.62	65	64	3	2	0-0	388.0	362	207	199	57	185-3	401
N.L. totals (6 years)	77	55	.583	3.74	185	184	11	5	0-0	1181.0	989	536	491	132	528-19	1224
Major League totals (8 years)	98	77	.560	3.96	250	248	14	7	0-0	1569.0	1351	743	690	189	713-22	1625

DIVISION SERIES RECORD

Year	League	W	L	Pct.	ERA	G	GS	CG	ShO	Sv.-Opp.	IP	H	R	ER	HR	BB-IBB	SO
1995—	Los Angeles (N.L.)	0	1	.000	9.00	1	1	0	0	0-0	5.0	7	5	5	2	2-1	6
1996—	Los Angeles (N.L.)	0	1	.000	12.27	1	1	0	0	0-0	3.2	5	5	5	1	5-0	3
Division series totals (2 years)		0	2	.000	10.38	2	2	0	0	0-0	8.2	12	10	10	3	7-1	9

ALL-STAR GAME RECORD

	W	L	Pct.	ERA	GS	CG	ShO	Sv.-Opp.	IP	H	R	ER	HR	BB-IBB	SO
All-Star Game totals (1 year)	0	0	...	0.00	1	0	0	0-0	2.0	1	0	0	0	0-0	3

NOMURA, TAKAHITO — P

PERSONAL: Born January 10, 1969, in Kouci, Japan. ... 5-7/175. ... Throws left, bats left.

HIGH SCHOOL: Takaoka (Japan).

TRANSACTIONS/CAREER NOTES: Played with Orix Blue Wave in Japan Pacific League (1992-97). ... Played with Yomiuri Giants of Japan Central League (1998-2001). ... Signed as non-drafted free agent by Milwaukee Brewers organization (January 29, 2002). ... Granted free agency (October 15, 2002).

CAREER HITTING (MLB): 0-for-0 (.000), 0 R, 0 2B, 0 3B, 0 HR, 0 RBI.

Year	League	W	L	Pct.	ERA	G	GS	CG	ShO	Sv.-Opp.	IP	H	R	ER	HR	BB-IBB	SO
1992—	Orix (Jap. Pac.)	1	2	.333	2.53	27	...	0	0	5-...	46.1	51	15	13	2	15-...	35
1993—	Orix (Jap. Pac.)	3	3	.500	1.53	36	...	0	0	8-...	70.2	46	14	12	1	12-...	83
1994—	Orix (Jap. Pac.)	3	4	.429	4.34	29	...	0	0	6-...	47.2	49	29	23	4	25-...	58
1995—	Orix (Jap. Pac.)	3	1	.750	0.98	37	...	0	0	2-...	36.2	21	5	4	0	11-...	43
1996—	Orix (Jap. Pac.)	4	1	.800	2.86	54	...	0	0	5-...	69.1	55	28	22	2	28-...	84
1997—	Orix (Jap. Pac.)	4	5	.444	3.60	52	...	0	0	8-...	65.0	60	30	26	4	31-...	76
1998—	Yomiuri (Jap. Cen.)■	1	4	.200	5.03	24	...	0	0	4-...	19.2	19	11	11	2	18-...	23
1999—	Yomiuri (Jap. Cen.)	2	0	1.000	1.32	15	...	0	0	0-...	13.2	9	2	2	1	4-...	16
2000—	Yomiuri (Jap. Cen.)	1	1	.500	6.75	24	...	0	0	1-...	20.0	18	18	15	5	8-...	21
2001—	Yomiuri (Jap. Cen.)	2	1	.667	4.62	40	...	0	0	0-...	37.0	47	19	19	4	12-...	34
2002—	Milwaukee (N.L.)■	0	0	...	8.56	21	0	0	0	0-1	13.2	11	14	13	2	18-4	9
—	Indianapolis (I.L.)	1	2	.333	5.73	31	0	0	0	0-...	33.0	38	24	21	4	11-1	23
Major League totals (1 year)		0	0	...	8.56	21	0	0	0	0-1	13.2	11	14	13	2	18-4	9

NORTON, GREG — IF — ROCKIES

PERSONAL: Born July 6, 1972, in San Leandro, Calif. ... 6-1/200. ... Bats both, throws right. ... Full name: Gregory Blakemoor Norton. ... Son of Jerry Norton, outfielder with Pittsburgh Pirates organization.

HIGH SCHOOL: Bishop O'Dowd (Oakland).

COLLEGE: Oklahoma.

TRANSACTIONS/CAREER NOTES: Selected by San Francisco Giants organization in seventh round of free-agent draft (June 4, 1990); did not sign. ... Selected by Chicago White Sox organization in second round of free-agent draft (June 3, 1993). ... Granted free agency (December 21, 2000). ... Signed by Colorado Rockies (January 5, 2001). ... On Colorado disabled list (June 30-July 18, 2002); included rehabilitation assignment to Colorado Springs (July 15-18).

STATISTICAL NOTES: Led Midwest League third basemen with 265 assists and 387 total chances in 1994. ... Led American Association with .534 slugging percentage in 1997. ... Led American Association third basemen with 29 errors in 1997. ... Tied for A.L. third baseman lead with 25 errors in 1999. ... Career major league grand slams: 2.

2002 GAMES PLAYED BY POSITION (MLB): 3B—22; 1B—15; OF—2; DH—1.

			BATTING														FIELDING	
Year	Team (League)	Pos.	G	AB	R	H	2B	3B	HR	RBI	BB	SO	SB-CS	Avg.	OBP	SLG	E	Avg.
1993—	GC White Sox (GCL)	3B	3	9	1	2	0	0	0	2	1	1	0-0	.222	.300	.222	0	1.000
—	Hickory (S.Atl.)	3B-SS	71	254	36	62	12	2	4	36	41	44	0-2	.244	.347	.354	17	.928
1994—	South Bend (Midw.)	3B	127	477	73	137	22	2	6	64	62	71	5-3	.287	.369	.379	30	.922
1995—	Birmingham (Sou.)	3B	133	469	65	117	23	2	6	60	64	90	19-12	.249	.339	.345	25	*.938
1996—	Birmingham (Sou.)	SS	76	287	40	81	14	3	8	44	33	55	5-5	.282	.357	.436	17	.949
—	Nashville (A.A.)	SS-DH-3B	43	164	28	47	14	2	7	26	17	42	2-3	.287	.350	.524	13	.914
—	Chicago (A.L.)	SS-3B-DH	11	23	4	5	0	0	2	3	4	6	0-1	.217	.333	.478	2	.867
1997—	Nashville (A.A.)	3-S-2-DH	114	414	82	114	27	1	26	76	57	101	3-5	.275	.366	.534	†38	.897
—	Chicago (A.L.)	3B-DH	18	34	5	9	2	2	0	1	2	8	0-0	.265	.306	.441	3	.864
1998—	Chicago (A.L.)	1-3-DH-2	105	299	38	71	17	2	9	36	26	77	3-3	.237	.301	.398	6	.991
1999—	Chicago (A.L.)	3B-1B-DH	132	436	62	111	26	0	16	50	69	93	4-4	.255	.358	.424	‡27	.931
2000—	Chicago (A.L.)	3B-1B-DH	71	201	25	49	6	1	6	28	26	47	1-0	.244	.333	.373	8	.960
—	Charlotte (I.L.)	3B-SS-1B	29	97	18	28	4	0	5	17	24	23	1-0	.289	.435	.485	1	.991
2001—	Colorado (N.L.)■	0-3-1-D	117	225	30	60	13	2	13	40	19	65	1-0	.267	.321	.516	4	.968
2002—	Colorado (N.L.)	3-1-0-D	113	168	19	37	8	1	7	37	24	52	2-3	.220	.314	.405	5	.955
—	Colo. Springs (PCL)	1B-3B	3	12	2	1	0	0	0	0	3	5	0-0	.083	.267	.083	0	1.000
American League totals (5 years)			337	993	134	245	51	5	33	118	127	231	8-8	.247	.334	.408	46	.965
National League totals (2 years)			230	393	49	97	21	3	20	77	43	117	3-3	.247	.318	.468	9	.962
Major League totals (7 years)			567	1386	183	342	72	8	53	195	170	348	11-11	.247	.330	.425	55	.965

NUNEZ, ABRAHAM — SS — PIRATES

PERSONAL: Born March 16, 1976, in Santo Domingo, Dominican Republic. ... 5-11/190. ... Bats both, throws right. ... Full name: Abraham Orlando Nunez Adames.

HIGH SCHOOL: Emmanuel (Santo Domingo, Dominican Republic).

TRANSACTIONS/CAREER NOTES: Signed as non-drafted free agent by Toronto Blue Jays organization (May 5, 1994). ... Traded by Blue Jays with P Mike Halperin and C/OF Craig Wilson to Pittsburgh Pirates (December 11, 1996), completing deal in which Blue Jays traded P Jose Silva, P Jose Pett, IF Brandon Cromer and three players to be named later to Pirates for OF/1B Orlando Merced, IF Carlos Garcia, and P Dan Plesac (November 14, 1996).

STATISTICAL NOTES: Tied for New York-Pennsylvania League lead in caught stealing with 14 in 1996. ... Led New York-Pennsylvania League shortstops with .953 fielding percentage in 1996.
2002 GAMES PLAYED BY POSITION (MLB): 2B—46; SS—24; DH—1.

			BATTING														FIELDING	
Year	Team (League)	Pos.	G	AB	R	H	2B	3B	HR	RBI	BB	SO	SB-CS	Avg.	OBP	SLG	E	Avg.
1994—	Dom. Blue Jays (DSL)	2B	59	188	31	47	5	0	0	15	42	37	22-...	.250	...	.277	12	.938
1995—	Dom. Blue Jays (DSL)	2B	54	186	49	56	10	3	4	25	30	27	24-...	.301	...	.452	7	.962
1996—	St. Catharines (NY-P)	SS-2B	75	*297	43	83	6	4	3	26	31	43	37-14	.279	.353	.357	15	‡.962
1997—	Lynchburg (Caro.)■	SS	78	304	45	79	9	4	3	32	23	47	29-14	.260	.313	.345	15	.955
—	Carolina (Sou.)	SS	47	198	31	65	6	1	1	14	20	28	10-5	.328	.385	.384	11	.949
—	Pittsburgh (N.L.)	SS-2B	19	40	3	9	2	2	0	6	3	10	1-0	.225	.289	.375	0	1.000
1998—	Nashville (PCL)	SS	94	366	50	91	12	3	3	32	39	73	16-8	.249	.328	.322	21	.953
—	Lynchburg (Caro.)	SS-2B	5	18	2	4	1	0	0	2	3	1	1-0	.222	.333	.278	1	.960
—	Pittsburgh (N.L.)	SS	24	52	6	10	2	0	1	2	12	14	4-2	.192	.344	.288	7	.930
1999—	Pittsburgh (N.L.)	SS-2B	90	259	25	57	8	0	0	17	28	54	9-1	.220	.299	.251	14	.959
—	Nashville (PCL)	SS	15	58	12	18	0	0	0	3	5	8	1-0	.310	.365	.310	2	.971
2000—	Pittsburgh (N.L.)	SS-2B	40	91	10	20	1	0	1	8	8	14	0-0	.220	.283	.264	2	.982
2001—	Pittsburgh (N.L.)	2B-SS-3B-OF	115	301	30	79	11	4	1	21	28	53	8-2	.262	.326	.336	4	.990
2002—	Pittsburgh (N.L.)	2B-SS-DH	112	253	28	59	14	1	2	15	27	44	3-4	.233	.311	.320	7	.977
—	Nashville (PCL)	SS-2B-OF	5	18	3	4	0	0	0	0	2	7	4-1	.222	.300	.222	0	1.000
Major League totals (6 years)			400	996	102	234	38	7	5	69	106	189	25-9	.235	.311	.302	34	.974

NUNEZ, ABRAHAM — OF — MARLINS

PERSONAL: Born February 5, 1977, in Haina, Dominican Republic. ... 6-2/186. ... Bats both, throws right.
TRANSACTIONS/CAREER NOTES: Signed as non-drafted free agent by Arizona Diamondbacks organization (September 17, 1996). ... On disabled list (June 30-July 16, 1998). ... On disabled list (April 13-20, 1999). ... Traded by Diamondbacks to Florida Marlins (December 13, 1999), completing deal in which Diamondbacks traded P Vladamir Nunez, P Brad Penny and a player to be named to Marlins for P Matt Mantei (July 9, 1999). ... On Portland disabled list (April 7-14 and June 24-July 14, 2000).
STATISTICAL NOTES: Led Arizona League outfielders with 94 putouts and 103 total chances and tied for lead with eight assists in 1997.
2002 GAMES PLAYED BY POSITION (MLB): OF—15.

			BATTING														FIELDING	
Year	Team (League)	Pos.	G	AB	R	H	2B	3B	HR	RBI	BB	SO	SB-CS	Avg.	OBP	SLG	E	Avg.
1997—	Ariz. D-backs (Ariz.)	OF	54	213	52	65	17	4	0	21	26	40	3-3	.305	.384	.423	1	*.990
—	Lethbridge (Pio.)	OF	2	6	2	1	0	0	0	1	1	0	0-0	.167	.286	.167	0	1.000
1998—	South Bend (Midw.)	OF	110	364	44	93	14	2	9	47	67	81	12-14	.255	.371	.379	*14	.944
1999—	High Desert (Calif.)	OF	130	488	106	133	29	6	22	93	86	122	40-13	.273	.378	.492	*14	.951
2000—	Portland (East.)■	OF	74	221	39	61	17	3	6	42	44	64	8-6	.276	.392	.462	0	1.000
—	Brevard County (FSL)	DH	31	103	17	20	4	0	1	9	28	34	11-3	.194	.376	.262	...	...
2001—	Portland (East.)	OF	136	467	75	112	14	*9	17	53	83	155	26-19	.240	.357	.418	8	.976
2002—	Calgary (PCL)	OF	129	428	68	107	24	5	21	60	51	112	31-6	.250	.329	.477	7	.978
—	Florida (N.L.)	OF	19	17	2	2	0	0	0	1	0	5	0-1	.118	.118	.118	0	1.000
Major League totals (1 year)			19	17	2	2	0	0	0	1	0	5	0-1	.118	.118	.118	0	1.000

NUNEZ, JOSE — P — PADRES

PERSONAL: Born March 14, 1979, in Montecristi, Dominican Republic. ... 6-2/173. ... Throws left, bats left. ... Full name: Jose Antonio Nunez.
HIGH SCHOOL: Liceo Cristo Liberador.
TRANSACTIONS/CAREER NOTES: Signed as non-drafted free agent by New York Mets organization (February 21, 1996). ... Selected by Los Angeles Dodgers from Mets organization in Rule 5 major league draft (December 11, 2000). ... Claimed on waivers by San Diego Padres (May 11, 2001). ... On disabled list (April 2, 2002-remainder of season).
CAREER HITTING (MLB): 0-for-3 (.000), 0 R, 0 2B, 0 3B, 0 HR, 0 RBI.

Year	League	W	L	Pct.	ERA	G	GS	CG	ShO	Sv.-Opp.	IP	H	R	ER	HR	BB-IBB	SO
1997—	Dominican Mets (DSL)	2	2	.500	2.93	18	6	0	0	0-...	46.0	43	21	15	...	15-...	37
1998—	Gulf Coast Mets (GCL)	3	4	.429	2.38	13	11	1	0	0-...	68.0	60	26	18	6	12-0	69
1999—	Kingsport (Appl.)	3	4	.429	3.75	13	13	0	0	0-...	69.2	75	36	29	6	15-0	63
2000—	Capital City (S.Atl.)	3	4	.429	3.82	34	5	0	0	8-...	75.1	82	36	32	6	23-0	112
2001—	Los Angeles (N.L.)■	0	1	.000	13.50	6	0	0	0	0-1	7.1	14	15	11	4	5-0	11
—	San Diego (N.L.)■	4	1	.800	3.31	56	0	0	0	0-1	51.2	48	20	19	3	20-3	49
2002—	San Diego (N.L.)	0	0	...	0.00	1	0	0	0	0-0	1.0	0	0	0	0	1-0	0
Major League totals (2 years)		4	2	.667	4.50	63	0	0	0	0-2	60.0	62	35	30	7	26-3	60

NUNEZ, VLADIMIR — P — MARLINS

PERSONAL: Born March 15, 1975, in Havana, Cuba. ... 6-4/240. ... Throws right, bats right. ... Full name: Vladimir Nunez Zarabaza.
TRANSACTIONS/CAREER NOTES: Signed as non-drafted free agent by Arizona Diamondbacks organization (February 1, 1996). ... On Tucson disabled list (April 7-24, 1998). ... Traded by Diamondbacks with P Brad Penny and a player to be named later to Florida Marlins for P Matt Mantei (July 9, 1999); Marlins acquired OF Abraham Nunez to complete deal (December 13, 1999). ... On Florida disabled list (July 19-August 3, 2001); included rehabilitation assignment to Kane County (August 1-2).
CAREER HITTING (MLB): 8-for-59 (.136), 3 R, 0 2B, 0 3B, 1 HR, 5 RBI.

Year	League	W	L	Pct.	ERA	G	GS	CG	ShO	Sv.-Opp.	IP	H	R	ER	HR	BB-IBB	SO
1996—	Visalia (Calif.)	1	6	.143	5.43	12	10	0	0	0-...	53.0	64	45	32	10	17-0	37
—	Lethbridge (Pio.)	*10	0	*1.000	*2.22	14	13	0	0	0-...	85.0	78	25	21	4	10-0	*93
1997—	High Desert (Calif.)	8	5	.615	5.17	28	28	1	1	0-...	158.1	169	102	91	*36	40-1	142
1998—	Tucson (PCL)	4	4	.500	4.91	31	13	1	0	2-...	95.1	103	58	52	12	37-0	78
—	Arizona (N.L.)	0	0	...	10.13	4	0	0	0	0-0	5.1	7	6	6	0	2-0	2
1999—	Tucson (PCL)	1	0	1.000	6.75	3	0	0	0	0-...	2.2	5	2	2	0	0-0	3
—	Arizona (N.L.)	3	2	.600	2.91	27	0	0	0	1-2	34.0	29	15	11	2	20-5	28
—	Florida (N.L.)■	4	8	.333	4.58	17	12	0	0	0-1	74.2	66	48	38	9	34-1	58

Year	League	W	L	Pct.	ERA	G	GS	CG	ShO	Sv.-Opp.	IP	H	R	ER	HR	BB-IBB	SO
2000—	Florida (N.L.)	0	6	.000	7.90	17	12	0	0	0-0	68.1	88	63	60	12	34-2	45
—	Calgary (PCL)	6	7	.462	4.12	15	15	1	0	0-...	89.2	92	43	41	9	38-1	95
2001—	Florida (N.L.)	4	5	.444	2.74	52	3	0	0	0-1	92.0	79	33	28	9	30-5	64
—	Kane County (Midw.)	0	0	...	9.00	1	1	0	0	0-...	1.0	3	1	1	0	0-0	0
2002—	Florida (N.L.)	6	5	.545	3.41	77	0	0	0	20-28	97.2	80	38	37	8	37-1	73
Major League totals (5 years)		17	26	.395	4.35	194	27	0	0	21-32	372.0	349	203	180	40	157-14	270

OBERMUELLER, WES — P — ROYALS

PERSONAL: Born December 22, 1976, in Cedar Rapids, Iowa. ... 6-2/195. ... Throws right, bats right. ... Full name: Wesley Mitchell Obermueller.

HIGH SCHOOL: Washington (Vinton, Iowa).

COLLEGE: Iowa.

TRANSACTIONS/CAREER NOTES: Selected by Kansas City Royals organization in second round of free-agent draft (June 2, 1999).

CAREER HITTING (MLB): 0-for-0 (.000), 0 R, 0 2B, 0 3B, 0 HR, 0 RBI.

Year	League	W	L	Pct.	ERA	G	GS	CG	ShO	Sv.-Opp.	IP	H	R	ER	HR	BB-IBB	SO
1999—	Gulf Coast Royals (GCL)	2	1	.667	2.58	11	7	0	0	0-...	38.1	33	16	11	2	12-1	39
2000—	Charleston, W.Va. (S.Atl.)	3	0	1.000	1.14	8	7	0	0	0-...	31.2	19	6	4	0	5-0	29
2001—	Wilmington (Caro.)	0	2	.000	3.08	20	6	0	0	0-...	38.0	38	15	13	3	16-1	28
2002—	Wilmington (Caro.)	5	0	1.000	2.76	8	4	0	0	0-...	45.2	38	14	14	1	14-0	44
—	Wichita (Texas)	9	5	.643	2.90	17	17	0	0	0-...	105.2	98	39	34	6	40-3	65
—	Kansas City (A.L.)	0	2	.000	11.74	2	2	0	0	0-0	7.2	14	10	10	3	2-0	5
Major League totals (1 year)		0	2	.000	11.74	2	2	0	0	0-0	7.2	14	10	10	3	2-0	5

OCHOA, ALEX — OF

PERSONAL: Born March 29, 1972, in Miami Lakes, Fla. ... 6-0/200. ... Bats right, throws right.

HIGH SCHOOL: Hialeah (Fla.) Miami Lakes.

TRANSACTIONS/CAREER NOTES: Selected by Baltimore Orioles organization in third round of free-agent draft (June 3, 1991). ... Traded by Orioles with OF Damon Buford to New York Mets for 3B/OF Bobby Bonilla and a player to be named later (July 28, 1995); Orioles acquired P Jimmy Williams to complete deal (August 17, 1995). ... Traded by Mets to Minnesota Twins for OF Rich Becker (December 12, 1997). ... Traded by Twins to Milwaukee Brewers for a player to be named later (December 14, 1998); Twins acquired OF Darrell Nicholas to complete deal (December 15, 1998). ... Traded by Brewers to Cincinnati Reds for OF/1B Mark Sweeney and a player to be named later (January 14, 2000); Brewers acquired P Gene Altman to complete deal (May 15, 2000). ... On Cincinnati disabled list (May 31-June 16, 2000); included rehabilitation assignment to Chattanooga (June 11-16). ... Traded by Reds to Colorado Rockies for 2B Todd Walker and OF Robin Jennings (July 19, 2001). ... Traded by Rockies to Milwaukee Brewers as part of three-way deal in which New York Mets traded P Glendon Rusch to Brewers, Rockies traded 1B/OF Ross Gload and P Craig House to Mets, Brewers traded P Jeff D'Amico, OF Jeromy Burnitz, IF Lou Collier, OF/1B Mark Sweeney and cash to Mets and Mets traded 1B/3B Todd Zeile, OF, Benny Agbayani, IF/OF Lenny Harris and cash to Rockies (January 21, 2002). ... Traded by Brewers with C Sal Fasano to Anaheim Angels for C Jorge Fabregas and two players to be named later (July 31, 2002); Brewers acquired IF Johnny Raburn (August 14, 2002) and P Pedro Liriano to complete deal (September 20, 2002). ... Granted free agency (October 31, 2002).

STATISTICAL NOTES: Tied for Midwest League lead with 17 assists by outfielder in 1992. ... Led Carolina League in grounding into double plays with 15 in 1993. ... Led Eastern League with 12 sacrifice flies in 1994. ... Led Eastern League outfielders with 22 assists and tied for league lead with five double plays in 1994. ... Led International League outfielders with 249 putouts and 266 total chances in 1995. ... Hit for the cycle (July 3, 1996). ... Tied for International League lead in double plays by outfielder with three in 1996. ... Career major league grand slams: 1.

2002 GAMES PLAYED BY POSITION (MLB): OF—108.

			BATTING															FIELDING	
Year	Team (League)	Pos.	G	AB	R	H	2B	3B	HR	RBI	BB	SO	SB-CS	Avg.	OBP	SLG	E	Avg.
1991—	GC Orioles (GCL)	OF	53	179	26	55	8	3	1	30	16	14	11-6	.307	.365	.402	2	.960
1992—	Kane County (Midw.)	OF	133	499	65	147	22	7	1	59	58	55	31-17	.295	.371	.373	•12	.953
1993—	Frederick (Caro.)	OF	137	532	84	147	29	5	13	90	46	67	34-13	.276	.341	.423	11	.943
1994—	Bowie (East.)	OF	134	519	77	156	25	2	14	82	49	67	28-15	.301	.355	.437	6	.977
1995—	Rochester (I.L.)	OF	91	336	41	92	18	2	8	46	26	50	17-7	.274	.328	.411	5	.975
—	Norfolk (I.L.)■	OF-DH	34	123	17	38	6	2	2	15	14	12	7-3	.309	.377	.439	2	.971
—	New York (N.L.)	OF	11	37	7	11	1	0	0	0	2	10	1-0	.297	.333	.324	0	1.000
1996—	Norfolk (I.L.)	OF-DH	67	233	45	79	12	4	8	39	32	22	5-11	.339	.420	.528	5	.960
—	New York (N.L.)	OF	82	282	37	83	19	3	4	33	17	30	4-3	.294	.336	.426	5	.966
1997—	New York (N.L.)	OF-DH	113	238	31	58	14	1	3	22	18	32	3-4	.244	.300	.349	2	.982
1998—	Minnesota (A.L.)■	OF-DH	94	249	35	64	14	2	2	25	10	35	6-3	.257	.288	.353	4	.969
1999—	Milwaukee (N.L.)■	OF-DH	119	277	47	83	16	3	8	40	45	43	6-4	.300	.404	.466	3	.979
2000—	Cincinnati (N.L.)■	OF	118	244	50	77	21	3	13	58	24	27	9-4	.316	.378	.586	3	.977
—	Chattanooga (Sou.)	OF	4	16	3	3	2	0	1	2	2	1	1-0	.188	.316	.500	0	1.000
2001—	Cincinnati (N.L.)	OF-DH	90	349	48	101	20	4	7	35	24	53	12-9	.289	.337	.430	2	.989
—	Colorado (N.L.)■	OF	58	187	25	47	10	3	1	17	21	23	5-4	.251	.330	.353	1	.990
2002—	Milwaukee (N.L.)	OF	85	215	32	55	9	0	6	21	32	30	8-5	.256	.357	.381	1	.993
—	Anaheim (A.L.)■	OF	37	65	8	18	7	0	2	10	10	5	2-2	.277	.373	.477	1	.975
American League totals (2 years)			131	314	43	82	21	2	4	35	20	40	8-5	.261	.307	.379	5	.970
National League totals (7 years)			676	1829	277	515	110	17	42	226	183	248	48-33	.282	.350	.429	17	.983
Major League totals (8 years)			807	2143	320	597	131	19	46	261	203	288	56-38	.279	.344	.422	22	.981

DIVISION SERIES RECORD

			BATTING														FIELDING	
Year	Team (League)	Pos.	G	AB	R	H	2B	3B	HR	RBI	BB	SO	SB-CS	Avg.	OBP	SLG	E	Avg.
2002—	Anaheim (A.L.)	OF	3	0	0	0	0	0	0	0	0	0	0-0	...	...	...	0	...

CHAMPIONSHIP SERIES RECORD

Year	Team (League)	Pos.	G	AB	R	H	2B	3B	HR	RBI	BB	SO	SB-CS	Avg.	OBP	SLG	E	Avg.
				BATTING													FIELDING	
2002—	Anaheim (A.L.)	OF	4	4	2	0	0	0	0	0	0	3	0-0	.000	.000	.000	0	1.000

WORLD SERIES RECORD

NOTES: Member of World Series championship team (2002).

Year	Team (League)	Pos.	G	AB	R	H	2B	3B	HR	RBI	BB	SO	SB-CS	Avg.	OBP	SLG	E	Avg.
				BATTING													FIELDING	
2002—	Anaheim (A.L.)	OF	5	1	0	0	0	0	0	0	0	0	0-0	.000	.000	.000	0	1.000

OFFERMAN, JOSE 2B/1B

PERSONAL: Born November 11, 1968, in San Pedro de Macoris, Dominican Republic. ... 6-0/192. ... Bats both, throws right. ... Full name: Jose Antonio Dono Offerman.

HIGH SCHOOL: Colegio Biblico Cristiano (Dominican Republic).

TRANSACTIONS/CAREER NOTES: Signed as non-drafted free agent by Los Angeles Dodgers organization (July 24, 1986). ... Traded by Dodgers to Kansas City Royals for P Billy Brewer (December 17, 1995). ... On Kansas City disabled list (April 6-29, July 10-22 and August 14-September 6, 1997). ... Granted free agency (October 23, 1998). ... Signed by Boston Red Sox (November 16, 1998). ... On disabled list (May 27-June 10 and July 30-August 16, 2000). ... Traded by Red Sox to Seattle Mariners for cash considerations (August 8, 2002). ... Granted free agency (October 30, 2002).

RECORDS: Holds A.L. single-season record for most consecutive games batted safely by switch hitter—27 (1998).

HONORS: Named Minor League Player of the Year by The Sporting News (1990). ... Named Pacific Coast League Player of the Year (1990).

STATISTICAL NOTES: Tied for Pioneer League lead in caught stealing with 10 in 1988. ... Tied for Pacific Coast League lead in caught stealing with 19 in 1990. ... Led Pacific Coast League shortstops with 36 errors in 1990. ... Hit home run in first major league at-bat (August 19, 1990). ... Led N.L. with 25 sacrifice hits in 1993. ... Had 27-game hitting streak (July 11-August 7, 1998). ... Career major league grand slams: 1.

2002 GAMES PLAYED BY POSITION (MLB): 1B—52; DH—28; OF—8; 2B—1.

Year	Team (League)	Pos.	G	AB	R	H	2B	3B	HR	RBI	BB	SO	SB-CS	Avg.	OBP	SLG	E	Avg.
				BATTING													FIELDING	
1987—						Dominican Summer League statistics unavailable.												
1988—	Vero Beach (FSL)	SS	4	14	4	4	2	0	0	2	2	0	0-0	.286	.375	.429	5	.643
	—Great Falls (Pio.)	SS	60	251	75	83	11	5	2	28	38	42	*57-10	.331	.421	.438	18	*.926
1989—	Bakersfield (Calif.)	SS	62	245	53	75	9	4	2	22	35	48	37-13	.306	.396	.400	30	.901
	—San Antonio (Texas)	SS	68	278	47	80	6	3	2	22	40	39	32-13	.288	.379	.353	20	.932
1990—	Albuquerque (PCL)	SS-2B	117	454	104	148	16	11	0	56	71	81	*60-19	.326	.416	.410	†36	.937
	—Los Angeles (N.L.)	SS	29	58	7	9	0	0	1	7	4	14	1-0	.155	.210	.207	4	.946
1991—	Albuquerque (PCL)	SS	79	289	58	86	8	4	0	29	47	58	32-15	.298	.396	.353	17	.956
	—Los Angeles (N.L.)	SS	52	113	10	22	2	0	0	3	25	32	3-2	.195	.345	.212	10	.945
1992—	Los Angeles (N.L.)	SS	149	534	67	139	20	8	1	30	57	98	23-16	.260	.331	.333	*42	.935
1993—	Los Angeles (N.L.)	SS	158	590	77	159	21	6	1	62	71	75	30-13	.269	.346	.331	*37	.950
1994—	Los Angeles (N.L.)	SS	72	243	27	51	8	4	1	25	38	38	2-1	.210	.314	.288	11	.967
	—Albuquerque (PCL)	SS	56	224	43	74	7	5	1	31	37	48	9-4	.330	.419	.420	13	.957
1995—	Los Angeles (N.L.)	SS	119	429	69	123	14	6	4	33	69	67	2-7	.287	.389	.375	*35	.932
1996—	Kansas City (A.L.)■	1B-2B-SS-OF	151	561	85	170	33	8	5	47	74	98	24-10	.303	.384	.417	16	.986
1997—	Kansas City (A.L.)	2B-DH	106	424	59	126	23	6	2	39	41	64	9-10	.297	.359	.394	9	.981
1998—	Kansas City (A.L.)	2B-DH	158	607	102	191	28	*13	7	66	89	96	45-12	.315	.403	.438	19	.974
1999—	Boston (A.L.)■	2B-DH-1B	149	586	107	172	37	*11	8	69	96	79	18-12	.294	.391	.435	14	.977
2000—	Boston (A.L.)	2B-1B-DH	116	451	73	115	14	3	9	41	70	70	0-8	.255	.354	.359	11	.983
2001—	Boston (A.L.)	2B-1B	128	524	76	140	23	3	9	49	61	97	5-2	.267	.342	.374	14	.982
2002—	Boston (A.L.)	1B-DH-OF	72	237	39	55	10	0	4	27	33	29	8-5	.232	.325	.325	3	.991
	—Seattle (A.L.)■	1B-OF-DH-2B	29	47	9	11	2	1	1	4	4	9	1-1	.234	.294	.383	0	1.000
American League totals (7 years)			909	3437	550	980	170	45	45	342	468	542	110-60	.285	.370	.400	86	.982
National League totals (6 years)			579	1967	257	503	65	24	8	160	264	324	61-39	.256	.344	.325	139	.944
Major League totals (13 years)			1488	5404	807	1483	235	69	53	502	732	866	171-99	.274	.361	.373	225	.969

DIVISION SERIES RECORD

Year	Team (League)	Pos.	G	AB	R	H	2B	3B	HR	RBI	BB	SO	SB-CS	Avg.	OBP	SLG	E	Avg.
				BATTING													FIELDING	
1995—	Los Angeles (N.L.)	PR	1	0	0	0	0	0	0	0	0	0	0-0	...	...	...	...	...
1999—	Boston (A.L.)	2B	5	18	4	7	1	0	1	6	7	0	0-1	.389	.560	.611	0	1.000
Division series totals (2 years)			6	18	4	7	1	0	1	6	7	0	0-1	.389	.560	.611	0	1.000

CHAMPIONSHIP SERIES RECORD

RECORDS: Shares single-game record for most at-bats (nine-inning game)—6 (October 16, 1999).

Year	Team (League)	Pos.	G	AB	R	H	2B	3B	HR	RBI	BB	SO	SB-CS	Avg.	OBP	SLG	E	Avg.
				BATTING													FIELDING	
1999—	Boston (A.L.)	2B	5	24	4	11	0	1	0	2	1	3	1-0	.458	.480	.542	2	.917

ALL-STAR GAME RECORD

	AB	R	H	2B	3B	HR	RBI	BB	SO	SB-CS	Avg.	OBP	SLG	E	Avg.
All-Star Game totals (2 years)	1	0	0	0	0	0	0	0	0	0-0	.000	.000	.000	1	.750

OHKA, TOMO P EXPOS

PERSONAL: Born March 18, 1976, in Kyoto, Japan. ... 6-1/180. ... Throws right, bats right. ... Full name: Tomokazu Ohka.

HIGH SCHOOL: Kyoto Siesio (Kyoto, Japan).

TRANSACTIONS/CAREER NOTES: Contract purchased by Boston Red Sox from Yokohama BayStars of Japan Central League (November 20, 1998). ... Traded by Red Sox with P Rich Rundles to Montreal Expos for P Ugueth Urbina (July 31, 2001). ... On suspended list (September 24-30, 2002).

STATISTICAL NOTES: Pitched 2-0 no-hit victory for Pawtucket against Charlotte (June 1, 2000).
CAREER HITTING (MLB): 10-for-73 (.137), 4 R, 1 2B, 0 3B, 0 HR, 3 RBI.

Year League	W	L	Pct.	ERA	G	GS	CG	ShO	Sv.-Opp.	IP	H	R	ER	HR	BB-IBB	SO
1994— Yokohama (Jap. Cen.)	1	1	.500	4.18	15	2	0	0	0-...	28.0	29	13	13	...	18-...	18
1995— Yokohama (Jap. Cen.)	0	0	...	1.93	3	1	0	0	0-...	9.1	3	2	2	...	13-...	6
1996— Yokohama (Jap. Cen.)	0	1	.000	9.50	14	1	0	0	0-...	18.0	27	19	19	...	14-...	11
1997—	Japan minor league statistics unavailable.															
1998— Yokohama (Jap. Cen.)■	0	0	...	9.00	2	0	0	0	0-...	2.0	2	2	2	...	2-...	1
1999— Trenton (East.)■	8	0	1.000	3.00	12	12	0	0	0-...	72.0	63	26	24	9	25-0	53
— Pawtucket (I.L.)	7	0	1.000	1.58	12	12	1	1	0-...	68.1	60	17	12	5	11-0	63
— Boston (A.L.)	1	2	.333	6.23	8	2	0	0	0-0	13.0	21	12	9	2	6-0	8
2000— Pawtucket (I.L.)	9	6	.600	2.96	19	19	3	•2	0-...	130.2	111	52	43	15	23-1	78
— Boston (A.L.)	3	6	.333	3.12	13	12	0	0	0-0	69.1	70	25	24	7	26-0	40
2001— Boston (A.L.)	2	5	.286	6.19	12	11	0	0	0-0	52.1	69	40	36	7	19-0	37
— Pawtucket (I.L.)	2	5	.286	5.57	8	8	1	0	0-...	42.0	55	35	26	5	9-0	33
— Montreal (N.L.)■	1	4	.200	4.77	10	10	0	0	0-0	54.2	65	30	29	8	10-0	31
2002— Montreal (N.L.)	13	8	.619	3.18	32	31	2	0	0-0	192.2	194	83	68	19	45-7	118
A.L. totals (3 years)	6	13	.316	4.61	33	25	0	0	0-0	134.2	160	77	69	16	51-0	85
N.L. totals (2 years)	14	12	.538	3.53	42	41	2	0	0-0	247.1	259	113	97	27	55-7	149
Major League totals (4 years)	20	25	.444	3.91	75	66	2	0	0-0	382.0	419	190	166	43	106-7	234

OHMAN, WILL — P — CUBS

PERSONAL: Born August 13, 1977, in Frankfurt, West Germany. ... 6-2/195. ... Throws left, bats left. ... Full name: William McDaniel Ohman.
HIGH SCHOOL: Ponderos (Parker, Colo.).
COLLEGE: Pepperdine.
TRANSACTIONS/CAREER NOTES: Selected by Chicago Cubs organization in eighth round of free-agent draft (June 2, 1998). ... On disabled list (March 15, 2002-entire season).
CAREER HITTING (MLB): 0-for-2 (.000), 0 R, 0 2B, 0 3B, 0 HR, 0 RBI.

Year League	W	L	Pct.	ERA	G	GS	CG	ShO	Sv.-Opp.	IP	H	R	ER	HR	BB-IBB	SO
1998— Williamsport (NY-Penn)	4	4	.500	8.77	10	7	0	0	0-...	39.0	39	32	38	6	13-0	35
— Rockford (Midw.)	1	1	.500	4.44	4	4	0	0	0-...	24.1	25	13	12	3	7-0	21
1999— Daytona (FSL)	4	7	.364	3.46	31	15	2	•2	5-...	106.2	102	59	41	11	41-1	97
2000— West Tenn (Sou.)	6	4	.600	1.89	59	0	0	0	3-...	71.1	53	20	15	3	36-5	85
— Chicago (N.L.)	1	0	1.000	8.10	6	0	0	0	0-0	3.1	4	3	3	0	4-1	2
2001— Iowa (PCL)	5	2	.714	4.06	40	1	0	0	4-...	51.0	51	24	23	9	18-3	66
— Chicago (N.L.)	0	1	.000	7.71	11	0	0	0	0-0	11.2	14	10	10	2	6-0	12
2002— Chicago (N.L.)	Did not play.															
Major League totals (2 years)	1	1	.500	7.80	17	0	0	0	0-0	15.0	18	13	13	2	10-1	14

OJEDA, AUGIE — SS — CUBS

PERSONAL: Born December 20, 1974, in Eldorado Culican, Mexico. ... 5-8/170. ... Bats both, throws right. ... Full name: Octavio Augie Ojeda.
HIGH SCHOOL: Pius X (Downey, Calif.).
JUNIOR COLLEGE: Cypress (Calif.) College.
COLLEGE: Tennessee.
TRANSACTIONS/CAREER NOTES: Selected by Baltimore Orioles organization in 13th round of free-agent draft (June 4, 1996). ... Traded by Orioles to Chicago Cubs for P Richard Negrette (December 13, 1999).
STATISTICAL NOTES: Led Eastern League with 25 sacrifice hits in 1999. ... Led Eastern League shortstops with .969 fielding percentage in 1999. ... Led Pacific Coast League shortstops with .976 fielding percentage in 2000.
MISCELLANEOUS: Member of 1996 U.S. Olympic baseball team.
2002 GAMES PLAYED BY POSITION (MLB): SS—16; 2B—10; 3B—5.

		BATTING														FIELDING	
Year Team (League)	Pos.	G	AB	R	H	2B	3B	HR	RBI	BB	SO	SB-CS	Avg.	OBP	SLG	E	Avg.
1997— Bowie (East.)	SS	58	204	33	60	9	1	2	23	31	17	7-0	.294	.390	.377	9	.967
— Frederick (Caro.)	SS	34	128	25	44	11	1	1	20	18	18	2-5	.344	.429	.469	5	.966
— Rochester (I.L.)	SS	15	47	5	11	3	1	0	6	8	4	1-2	.234	.345	.340	5	.922
1998— GC Orioles (GCL)	SS	4	15	6	6	2	0	0	2	3	1	3-0	.400	.550	.533	0	1.000
— Bowie (East.)	SS-3B	73	254	36	65	10	2	1	19	36	30	0-3	.256	.354	.323	11	.964
1999— Rochester (I.L.)	SS	1	1	0	0	0	0	0	0	0	0	0-0	.000	.000	.000	0	...
— Bowie (East.)	SS-3B	134	460	73	123	18	4	10	60	57	47	6-2	.267	.359	.389	19	†.969
2000— Iowa (PCL)■	SS-2B	113	396	56	111	23	2	8	43	33	27	16-6	.280	.343	.409	11	†.976
— Chicago (N.L.)	SS-2B	28	77	10	17	3	1	2	8	10	9	0-1	.221	.307	.364	1	.990
2001— Chicago (N.L.)	3B-SS-2B	78	144	16	29	5	1	1	12	12	20	1-0	.201	.269	.271	6	.962
2002— Chicago (N.L.)	SS-2B-3B	30	70	4	13	4	0	0	4	5	5	1-0	.186	.247	.243	3	.969
— Iowa (PCL)	SS-3B	73	291	54	67	20	4	1	27	31	30	5-3	.230	.318	.337	5	.984
Major League totals (3 years)		136	291	30	59	12	2	3	24	27	34	2-1	.203	.274	.289	10	.972

O'LEARY, TROY — OF

PERSONAL: Born August 4, 1969, in Compton, Calif. ... 6-0/208. ... Bats left, throws left. ... Full name: Troy Franklin O'Leary.
HIGH SCHOOL: Cypress (Calif.).
JUNIOR COLLEGE: Chaffey College (Calif.).
TRANSACTIONS/CAREER NOTES: Selected by Milwaukee Brewers organization in 13th round of free-agent draft (June 2, 1987). ... Claimed on waivers by Boston Red Sox (April 14, 1995). ... On Boston disabled list (June 19-July 3, 2000); included rehabilitation assignment to Gulf Coast Red Sox (June 30-July 3). ... Granted free agency (November 5, 2001). ... Signed by Tampa Bay Devil Rays organization (January 29, 2002). ... Released by Devil Rays (March 25, 2002). ... Signed by Montreal Expos organization (March 28, 2002). ... Granted free agency (October 29, 2002).

HONORS: Named Texas League Most Valuable Player (1992).
STATISTICAL NOTES: Led Pioneer League with 144 total bases in 1989. ... Led Texas League with 227 total bases in 1992. ... Led Texas League outfielders with 220 putouts and 242 total chances in 1992. ... Had 15-game hitting streak (July 30-August 14, 1999). ... Career major league grand slams: 2.
2002 GAMES PLAYED BY POSITION (MLB): OF—70; DH—3.

		BATTING														FIELDING	
Year Team (League)	**Pos.**	**G**	**AB**	**R**	**H**	**2B**	**3B**	**HR**	**RBI**	**BB**	**SO**	**SB-CS**	**Avg.**	**OBP**	**SLG**	**E**	**Avg.**
1987—Helena (Pio.)	OF	3	5	0	2	0	0	0	1	0	0	0-0	.400	.400	.400	0	...
1988—Helena (Pio.)	OF	67	203	40	70	11	1	0	27	30	32	10-8	.345	.425	.409	3	.958
1989—Beloit (Midw.)	OF	42	115	7	21	4	0	0	8	15	20	1-7	.183	.277	.217	1	.982
—Helena (Pio.)	OF	•68	263	54	*89	16	3	11	*56	28	43	9-8	.338	.402	.548	3	.970
1990—Beloit (Midw.)	OF	118	436	73	130	29	1	6	62	41	90	12-12	.298	.356	.411	8	.961
—Stockton (Calif.)	OF	2	6	1	3	1	0	0	0	2	1	0-0	.500	.625	.667	1	.750
1991—Stockton (Calif.)	OF	126	418	63	110	20	4	5	46	73	96	4-9	.263	.377	.366	3	.982
1992—El Paso (Texas)	OF	*135	*506	*92	*169	27	8	5	79	59	87	28-16	*.334	*.399	.449	*11	.955
1993—New Orleans (A.A.)	OF-1B	111	388	65	106	32	1	7	59	43	61	6-3	.273	.345	.415	6	.970
—Milwaukee (A.L.)	OF	19	41	3	12	3	0	0	3	5	9	0-0	.293	.370	.366	0	1.000
1994—New Orleans (A.A.)	OF-DH-1B	63	225	44	74	18	5	8	43	32	37	10-2	.329	.411	.560	2	.982
—Milwaukee (A.L.)	OF-DH	27	66	9	18	1	1	2	7	5	12	1-1	.273	.329	.409	0	1.000
1995—Boston (A.L.)■	OF-DH	112	399	60	123	31	6	10	49	29	64	5-3	.308	.355	.491	5	.976
1996—Boston (A.L.)	OF	149	497	68	129	28	5	15	81	47	80	3-2	.260	.327	.427	7	.971
1997—Boston (A.L.)	OF-DH	146	499	65	154	32	4	15	80	39	70	0-5	.309	.358	.479	6	.979
1998—Boston (A.L.)	OF	156	611	95	165	36	8	23	83	36	108	2-2	.270	.314	.468	3	.990
1999—Boston (A.L.)	OF	157	596	84	167	36	4	28	103	56	91	1-2	.280	.343	.495	2	.993
2000—Boston (A.L.)	OF	138	513	68	134	30	4	13	70	44	76	0-2	.261	.320	.411	3	.988
—GC Red Sox (GCL)	DH	3	8	3	6	1	0	0	1	3	1	0-0	.750	.818	.875	...	...
2001—Boston (A.L.)	OF-DH	104	341	50	82	16	6	13	50	25	73	1-3	.240	.298	.437	1	.994
2002—Ottawa (I.L.)■	OF	23	86	11	29	6	0	3	16	7	15	0-1	.337	.387	.512	1	.974
—Montreal (N.L.)	OF-DH	97	273	27	78	12	2	3	37	34	47	1-2	.286	.371	.377	3	.977
American League totals (9 years)		1008	3563	502	984	213	38	119	526	286	583	13-20	.276	.332	.457	27	.985
National League totals (1 year)		97	273	27	78	12	2	3	37	34	47	1-2	.286	.371	.377	3	.977
Major League totals (10 years)		1105	3836	529	1062	225	40	122	563	320	630	14-22	.277	.335	.452	30	.985

DIVISION SERIES RECORD

RECORDS: Shares single-game record for most home runs—2; grand slams—1; and runs batted in—7 (October 11, 1999). ... Shares single-inning record for most runs batted in—4 (October 11, 1999, third inning).

		BATTING														FIELDING	
Year Team (League)	**Pos.**	**G**	**AB**	**R**	**H**	**2B**	**3B**	**HR**	**RBI**	**BB**	**SO**	**SB-CS**	**Avg.**	**OBP**	**SLG**	**E**	**Avg.**
1998—Boston (A.L.)	OF	4	16	0	1	0	0	0	0	1	4	0-0	.063	.118	.063	0	1.000
1999—Boston (A.L.)	OF	5	20	4	4	0	0	2	7	2	3	0-0	.200	.273	.500	0	1.000
Division series totals (2 years)		9	36	4	5	0	0	2	7	3	7	0-0	.139	.205	.306	0	1.000

CHAMPIONSHIP SERIES RECORD

		BATTING														FIELDING	
Year Team (League)	**Pos.**	**G**	**AB**	**R**	**H**	**2B**	**3B**	**HR**	**RBI**	**BB**	**SO**	**SB-CS**	**Avg.**	**OBP**	**SLG**	**E**	**Avg.**
1999—Boston (A.L.)	OF	5	20	2	7	3	0	0	1	2	5	0-0	.350	.409	.500	0	1.000

OLERUD, JOHN 1B

PERSONAL: Born August 5, 1968, in Seattle. ... 6-5/220. ... Bats left, throws left. ... Full name: John Garrett Olerud. ... Son of John E. Olerud, minor league catcher (1965-70); and cousin of Dale Sveum, infielder with seven major league teams (1986-99). ... Name pronounced OH-luh-rude.
HIGH SCHOOL: Interlake (Bellevue, Wash.).
COLLEGE: Washington State.
TRANSACTIONS/CAREER NOTES: Selected by New York Mets organization in 27th round of free-agent draft (June 2, 1986); did not sign. ... Selected by Toronto Blue Jays organization in third round of free-agent draft (June 5, 1989). ... Traded by Blue Jays with cash to Mets for P Robert Person (December 20, 1996). ... Granted free agency (October 27, 1997). ... Re-signed by Mets (November 24, 1997). ... Granted free agency (October 29, 1999). ... Signed by Seattle Mariners (December 15, 1999). ... Granted free agency (October 29, 2002).
RECORDS: Shares A.L. single-season records for most intentional bases on balls received—33 (1993); most intentional bases on balls received by lefthanded hitter—33 (1993); and most years without a stolen base (150 games or more per year)—4. ... Shares N.L. single-season record for most consecutive times reached base safely—15 (September 16 [1], 18 [5], 20 [4], 22 [1], 1998; 6 singles, 1 double, 2 home runs, 6 bases on balls).
HONORS: Won A.L. Gold Glove as first baseman (2000 and 2002).
STATISTICAL NOTES: Tied for A.L. lead with 10 sacrifice flies in 1991. ... Had 26-game hitting streak (May 26-June 22, 1993). ... Led A.L. with 33 intentional bases on balls received in 1993. ... Hit for the cycle (September 11, 1997; and June 16, 2001). ... Had 23-game hitting streak (July 19-August 9, 1998). ... Led A.L. first basemen with 132 assists in 2000. ... Led A.L. in grounding into double plays with 21 in 2001. ... Had 16-game hitting streak (May 30-June 15, 2002). ... Led A.L. with 12 sacrifice flies in 2002. ... Led A.L. first basemen with 122 double plays in 2002. ... Career major league grand slams: 6.
2002 GAMES PLAYED BY POSITION (MLB): 1B—152; DH—2.

		BATTING														FIELDING	
Year Team (League)	**Pos.**	**G**	**AB**	**R**	**H**	**2B**	**3B**	**HR**	**RBI**	**BB**	**SO**	**SB-CS**	**Avg.**	**OBP**	**SLG**	**E**	**Avg.**
1989—Toronto (A.L.)	1B-DH	6	8	2	3	0	0	0	0	0	1	0-0	.375	.375	.375	0	1.000
1990—Toronto (A.L.)	DH-1B	111	358	43	95	15	1	14	48	57	75	0-2	.265	.364	.430	2	.986
1991—Toronto (A.L.)	1B-DH	139	454	64	116	30	1	17	68	68	84	0-2	.256	.353	.438	5	.996
1992—Toronto (A.L.)	1B-DH	138	458	68	130	28	0	16	66	70	61	1-0	.284	.375	.450	7	.994
1993—Toronto (A.L.)	1B-DH	158	551	109	200	*54	2	24	107	114	65	0-2	*.363	*.473	.599	10	.992
1994—Toronto (A.L.)	1B-DH	108	384	47	114	29	2	12	67	61	53	1-2	.297	.393	.477	6	.993
1995—Toronto (A.L.)	1B	135	492	72	143	32	0	8	54	84	54	0-0	.291	.398	.404	4	.997
1996—Toronto (A.L.)	1B-DH	125	398	59	109	25	0	18	61	60	37	1-0	.274	.382	.472	2	.998
1997—New York (N.L.)■	1B	154	524	90	154	34	1	22	102	85	67	0-0	.294	.400	.489	7	.995
1998—New York (N.L.)	1B	160	557	91	197	36	4	22	93	96	73	2-2	.354	.447	.551	5	.996

			BATTING														FIELDING	
Year	Team (League)	Pos.	G	AB	R	H	2B	3B	HR	RBI	BB	SO	SB-CS	Avg.	OBP	SLG	E	Avg.
1999—	New York (N.L.)	1B	•162	581	107	173	39	0	19	96	125	66	3-0	.298	.427	.463	9	.994
2000—	Seattle (A.L.)■	1B	159	565	84	161	45	0	14	103	102	96	0-2	.285	.392	.439	5	*.996
2001—	Seattle (A.L.)	1B	159	572	91	173	32	1	21	95	94	70	3-1	.302	.401	.472	9	.993
2002—	Seattle (A.L.)	1B-DH	154	553	85	166	39	0	22	102	98	66	0-0	.300	.403	.490	5	.996
American League totals (11 years)			1392	4793	724	1410	329	7	166	771	808	662	6-11	.294	.396	.470	55	.995
National League totals (3 years)			476	1662	288	524	109	5	63	291	306	206	5-2	.315	.425	.501	21	.995
Major League totals (14 years)			1868	6455	1012	1934	438	12	229	1062	1114	868	11-13	.300	.404	.478	76	.995

DIVISION SERIES RECORD

			BATTING														FIELDING	
Year	Team (League)	Pos.	G	AB	R	H	2B	3B	HR	RBI	BB	SO	SB-CS	Avg.	OBP	SLG	E	Avg.
1999—	New York (N.L.)	1B	4	16	3	7	0	0	1	6	3	2	0-0	.438	.526	.625	0	1.000
2000—	Seattle (A.L.)	1B	3	10	2	3	0	0	1	2	2	1	0-0	.300	.462	.600	0	1.000
2001—	Seattle (A.L.)	1B	5	17	1	3	0	0	0	1	3	5	0-0	.176	.300	.176	0	1.000
Division series totals (3 years)			12	43	6	13	0	0	2	9	8	8	0-0	.302	.423	.442	0	1.000

CHAMPIONSHIP SERIES RECORD

			BATTING														FIELDING	
Year	Team (League)	Pos.	G	AB	R	H	2B	3B	HR	RBI	BB	SO	SB-CS	Avg.	OBP	SLG	E	Avg.
1991—	Toronto (A.L.)	1B	5	19	1	3	0	0	0	3	3	1	0-0	.158	.273	.158	0	1.000
1992—	Toronto (A.L.)	1B	6	23	4	8	2	0	1	4	2	5	0-0	.348	.400	.565	0	1.000
1993—	Toronto (A.L.)	1B	6	23	5	8	1	0	0	3	4	1	0-0	.348	.464	.391	1	.983
1999—	New York (N.L.)	1B	6	27	4	8	0	0	2	6	2	3	0-0	.296	.345	.519	2	.969
2000—	Seattle (A.L.)	1B	6	20	3	7	3	0	1	2	2	2	1-0	.350	.391	.650	0	1.000
2001—	Seattle (A.L.)	1B	5	19	2	4	0	0	1	3	2	4	0-0	.211	.286	.368	0	1.000
Championship series totals (6 years)			34	131	19	38	6	0	5	21	15	16	1-0	.290	.365	.450	3	.991

WORLD SERIES RECORD

NOTES: Member of World Series championship team (1992 and 1993).

			BATTING														FIELDING	
Year	Team (League)	Pos.	G	AB	R	H	2B	3B	HR	RBI	BB	SO	SB-CS	Avg.	OBP	SLG	E	Avg.
1992—	Toronto (A.L.)	1B	4	13	2	4	0	0	0	0	0	4	0-0	.308	.308	.308	0	1.000
1993—	Toronto (A.L.)	1B	5	17	5	4	1	0	1	2	4	1	0-0	.235	.364	.471	0	1.000
World Series totals (2 years)			9	30	7	8	1	0	1	2	4	5	0-0	.267	.343	.400	0	1.000

ALL-STAR GAME RECORD

	AB	R	H	2B	3B	HR	RBI	BB	SO	SB-CS	Avg.	OBP	SLG	E	Avg.
All-Star Game totals (2 years)	4	0	0	0	0	0	0	0	0	0-0	.000	.000	.000	0	1.000

OLIVER, DARREN — P — CARDINALS

PERSONAL: Born October 6, 1970, in Kansas City, Mo. ... 6-2/220. ... Throws left, bats right. ... Full name: Darren Christopher Oliver. ... Son of Bob Oliver, first baseman/outfielder with five major league teams (1965 and 1969-1975).

HIGH SCHOOL: Rio Linda (Calif.) Senior.

TRANSACTIONS/CAREER NOTES: Selected by Texas Rangers organization in third round of free-agent draft (June 1, 1988). ... On Gulf Coast Rangers disabled list (April 6-August 9, 1990). ... On disabled list (May 1, 1991-remainder of season). ... On Tulsa disabled list (July 1, 1992-remainder of season). ... On disabled list (June 27, 1995-remainder of season). ... On Texas disabled list (June 11-26, 1998); included rehabilitation assignment to Oklahoma City (June 21-26). ... Traded by Rangers with 3B Fernando Tatis and a player to be named later to St. Louis Cardinals for P Todd Stottlemyre and SS Royce Clayton (July 31, 1998); Cardinals acquired OF Mark Little to complete deal (August 9, 1998). ... Granted free agency (October 29, 1999). ... Signed by Rangers (January 27, 2000). ... On Texas disabled list (June 21-July 20 and August 1-September 1, 2000); included rehabilitation assignments to Oklahoma (July 5-20 and August 12-26) and Tulsa (August 27-31). ... On Texas disabled list (May 8-June 6, 2001); included rehabilitation assignments to Oklahoma (May 27-31) and Tulsa (June 1-6). ... Traded by Rangers to Boston Red Sox for OF Carl Everett (December 13, 2001). ... Released by Red Sox (July 2, 2002). ... Signed by Cardinals organization (July 19, 2002).

MISCELLANEOUS: Made an out in only appearance as pinch hitter with St. Louis (1998). ... Had one sacrifice hit and struck out once in five appearances as pinch hitter (1999).

CAREER HITTING (MLB): 26-for-113 (.230), 9 R, 7 2B, 0 3B, 0 HR, 9 RBI.

Year	League	W	L	Pct.	ERA	G	GS	CG	ShO	Sv.-Opp.	IP	H	R	ER	HR	BB-IBB	SO
1988—	Gulf Coast Rangers (GCL)	5	1	.833	2.15	12	9	0	0	0-...	54.1	39	16	13	0	18-0	59
1989—	Gastonia (S.Atl.)	8	7	.533	3.16	24	23	2	1	0-...	122.1	86	54	43	4	82-1	108
1990—	Gulf Coast Rangers (GCL)	0	0	...	0.00	3	3	0	0	0-...	6.0	1	1	0	0	1-0	7
—	Gastonia (S.Atl.)	0	0	...	13.50	1	1	0	0	0-...	2.0	1	3	3	0	4-0	2
1991—	Charlotte (FSL)	0	1	.000	4.50	2	2	0	0	0-...	8.0	6	4	4	1	3-0	12
1992—	Charlotte (FSL)	1	0	1.000	0.72	8	2	1	1	2-...	25.0	11	2	2	0	10-2	33
—	Tulsa (Texas)	0	1	.000	3.14	3	3	0	0	0-...	14.1	15	9	5	1	4-0	14
1993—	Tulsa (Texas)	7	5	.583	1.96	46	0	0	0	6-...	73.1	51	18	16	1	41-5	77
—	Texas (A.L.)	0	0	...	2.70	2	0	0	0	0-0	3.1	2	1	1	1	1-1	4
1994—	Texas (A.L.)	4	0	1.000	3.42	43	0	0	0	2-3	50.0	40	24	19	4	35-4	50
—	Oklahoma City (A.A.)	0	0	...	0.00	6	0	0	0	1-...	7.1	1	0	0	0	3-2	6
1995—	Texas (A.L.)	4	2	.667	4.22	17	7	0	0	0-0	49.0	47	25	23	3	32-1	39
1996—	Charlotte (FSL)	0	1	.000	3.00	2	1	0	0	0-...	12.0	8	4	4	1	3-0	9
—	Texas (A.L.)	14	6	.700	4.66	30	30	1	1	0-0	173.2	190	97	90	20	76-3	112
1997—	Texas (A.L.)	13	12	.520	4.20	32	32	3	1	0-0	201.1	213	111	94	29	82-3	104
1998—	Texas (A.L.)	6	7	.462	6.53	19	19	2	0	0-0	103.1	140	84	75	11	43-1	58
—	Oklahoma (PCL)	0	0	...	0.00	1	1	0	0	0-...	5.0	2	0	0	0	1-0	1
—	St. Louis (N.L.)■	4	4	.500	4.26	10	10	0	0	0-0	57.0	64	31	27	7	23-1	29
1999—	St. Louis (N.L.)	9	9	.500	4.26	30	30	2	1	0-0	196.1	197	96	93	16	74-4	119
2000—	Texas (A.L.)■	2	9	.182	7.42	21	21	0	0	0-0	108.0	151	95	89	16	42-3	49
—	Oklahoma (PCL)	2	1	.667	1.97	7	7	1	1	0-...	32.0	22	11	7	2	14-0	28
—	Tulsa (Texas)	0	1	.000	11.57	1	1	0	0	0-...	4.2	10	7	6	0	2-0	5

Year	League	W	L	Pct.	ERA	G	GS	CG	ShO	Sv.-Opp.	IP	H	R	ER	HR	BB-IBB	SO
2001—	Texas (A.L.)	11	11	.500	6.02	28	28	1	0	0-0	154.0	189	109	103	23	65-0	104
	—Oklahoma (PCL)	0	0	...	0.00	1	1	0	0	0-...	3.0	3	0	0	0	0-0	3
	—Tulsa (Texas)	0	1	.000	5.40	1	1	0	0	0-...	5.0	4	3	3	1	2-0	5
2002—	Boston (A.L.)■	4	5	.444	4.66	14	9	1	1	0-0	58.0	70	30	30	7	27-0	32
	—Memphis (PCL)■	0	2	.000	7.88	5	5	0	0	0-...	16.0	17	16	14	1	17-0	9
A.L. totals (9 years)		58	52	.527	5.24	206	146	8	3	2-3	900.2	1042	576	524	114	403-16	552
N.L. totals (2 years)		13	13	.500	4.26	40	40	2	1	0-0	253.1	261	127	120	23	97-5	148
Major League totals (10 years)		71	65	.522	5.02	246	186	10	4	2-3	1154.0	1303	703	644	137	500-21	700

DIVISION SERIES RECORD

Year	League	W	L	Pct.	ERA	G	GS	CG	ShO	Sv.-Opp.	IP	H	R	ER	HR	BB-IBB	SO
1996—	Texas (A.L.)	0	1	.000	3.38	1	1	0	0	0-0	8.0	6	3	3	1	2-0	3

OLIVO, MIGUEL — C — WHITE SOX

PERSONAL: Born July 15, 1978, in Villa Vasquez, Dominican Republic. ... 6-0/180. ... Bats right, throws right. ... Full name: Miguel Eduardo Olivo.

TRANSACTIONS/CAREER NOTES: Signed as non-drafted free agent by Oakland Athletics organization (September 30, 1996). ... On Midland inactive list (July 8-10, 2000). ... On Modesto suspended list (July 13-23, 2000). ... On Modesto disabled list (August 8, 2000-remainder of season). ... Traded by A's to Chicago White Sox (December 12, 2000); completing deal in which White Sox traded P Chad Bradford to A's for player to be named later (December 7, 2000). ... On disabled list (April 22-May 2, 2001). ... On Birmingham disabled list (June 4-11, 2002).

STATISTICAL NOTES: Led Arizona League catchers with 44 assists and 22 passed balls in 1998. ... Led Southern League catchers with 78 assists and 19 passed balls in 2001. ... Hit home run in first major league at-bat (September 15, 2002).

2002 GAMES PLAYED BY POSITION (MLB): C—6.

			BATTING														FIELDING	
Year	Team (League)	Pos.	G	AB	R	H	2B	3B	HR	RBI	BB	SO	SB-CS	Avg.	OBP	SLG	E	Avg.
1997—	Dom. Athletics (DSL)		63	221	37	60	11	4	6	57	34	36	6-...	.271	...	.439	...	...
1998—	Ariz. Athletics (Ariz.)	C-OF	46	164	30	51	11	3	2	23	8	43	2-2	.311	.356	.451	8	.977
1999—	Modesto (Calif.)	C	73	243	46	74	13	6	9	42	21	60	4-5	.305	.363	.519	15	.974
2000—	Modesto (Calif.)	C	58	227	40	64	11	5	5	35	16	53	5-2	.282	.332	.441	*19	.959
	—Midland (Texas)	C	19	59	8	14	2	0	1	9	5	15	0-0	.237	.297	.322	2	.980
2001—	Birmingham (Sou.)■	C	93	316	45	82	23	1	14	55	37	62	6-3	.259	.347	.472	9	.988
2002—	Birmingham (Sou.)	C	106	359	51	110	24	*10	6	49	40	66	29-13	.306	.381	.479	13	.983
	—Chicago (A.L.)	C	6	19	2	4	1	0	1	5	2	5	0-0	.211	.286	.421	0	1.000
Major League totals (1 year)			6	19	2	4	1	0	1	5	2	5	0-0	.211	.286	.421	0	1.000

OLSEN, KEVIN — P — MARLINS

PERSONAL: Born July 26, 1976, in Covina, Calif. ... 6-2/196. ... Throws right, bats right. ... Full name: Kevin Gary Olsen.

HIGH SCHOOL: Norco (Calif.).

JUNIOR COLLEGE: Riverside (Calif.).

COLLEGE: Oklahoma.

TRANSACTIONS/CAREER NOTES: Selected by Florida Marlins organization in 26th round of free-agent draft (June 2, 1998). ... On Calgary disabled list (August 16, 2002-remainder of season).

CAREER HITTING (MLB): 1-for-15 (.067), 0 R, 0 2B, 0 3B, 0 HR, 0 RBI.

Year	League	W	L	Pct.	ERA	G	GS	CG	ShO	Sv.-Opp.	IP	H	R	ER	HR	BB-IBB	SO
1998—	Utica (NY-Penn)	4	3	.571	2.60	21	4	0	0	2-...	45.0	37	21	13	3	10-1	56
1999—	Brevard County (FSL)	2	5	.286	5.05	11	11	0	0	0-...	57.0	70	37	32	8	13-0	45
	—Kane County (Midw.)	5	2	.714	3.38	10	9	0	0	0-...	61.1	65	25	23	3	16-0	52
2000—	Brevard County (FSL)	4	8	.333	2.86	18	18	1	0	0-...	110.0	93	40	35	2	25-2	77
	—Portland (East.)	3	4	.429	4.83	9	9	0	0	0-...	54.0	54	30	29	8	21-0	47
2001—	Portland (East.)	10	3	.769	2.68	26	26	2	1	0-...	154.2	123	56	46	11	21-1	144
	—Florida (N.L.)	0	0	...	1.20	4	2	0	0	0-0	15.0	11	2	2	0	2-1	13
2002—	Florida (N.L.)	0	5	.000	4.53	17	8	0	0	0-0	55.2	57	31	28	5	31-1	38
	—Calgary (PCL)	2	5	.286	3.86	8	8	1	1	0-...	49.0	45	22	21	6	14-0	25
Major League totals (2 years)		0	5	.000	3.82	21	10	0	0	0-0	70.2	68	33	30	5	33-2	51

ORDAZ, LUIS — SS/2B

PERSONAL: Born August 12, 1975, in Maracaibo, Venezuela. ... 5-11/170. ... Bats right, throws right. ... Full name: Luis Javier Ordaz.

HIGH SCHOOL: Santa Maria Gorette (Maracaibo, Venezuela).

TRANSACTIONS/CAREER NOTES: Signed as non-drafted free agent by Cincinnati Reds organization (January 27, 1993). ... Traded by Reds to St. Louis Cardinals as part of three-team deal in which Reds sent P Mike Remlinger to Kansas City Royals, Cardinals sent OF Andre King to Reds and Royals sent OF Miguel Mejia to Cardinals (December 4, 1995). ... On Memphis disabled list (April 7-16, 1998). ... Traded by Cardinals to Arizona Diamondbacks for OF Dante Powell (December 15, 1999). ... Claimed on waivers by Kansas City Royals (April 5, 2000). ... On Kansas City disabled list (May 18-July 1, 2001); included rehabilitation assignment to Omaha (June 20-July 1). ... Granted free agency (October 15, 2001). ... Signed by Chicago Cubs organization (December 7, 2001). ... Released by Cubs (July 1, 2002). ... Signed by Royals organization (July 1, 2002). ... Granted free agency (October 15, 2002).

STATISTICAL NOTES: Led Appalachian League shortstops with 277 total chances and 24 errors and tied for lead with 173 assists in 1994. ... Led Texas League in grounding into double plays with 19 in 1997.

2002 GAMES PLAYED BY POSITION (MLB): 2B—28; 3B—6; SS—2.

			BATTING														FIELDING	
Year	Team (League)	Pos.	G	AB	R	H	2B	3B	HR	RBI	BB	SO	SB-CS	Avg.	OBP	SLG	E	Avg.
1993—	Princeton (Appl.)	3B-SS-2B	57	217	28	65	9	7	2	39	7	32	3-1	.300	.320	.433	13	.931
1994—	Charl., W.Va. (S.Atl.)	SS	9	31	3	7	0	0	0	0	1	4	1-0	.226	.273	.226	7	.829
	—Princeton (Appl.)	SS-2B	60	211	33	52	12	3	0	12	10	27	7-5	.246	.286	.332	†24	.914
1995—	Charl., W.Va. (S.Atl.)	SS	112	359	43	83	14	7	2	42	13	47	12-5	.231	.267	.326	22	.954

Year	Team (League)	Pos.	G	AB	R	H	2B	3B	HR	RBI	BB	SO	SB-CS	Avg.	OBP	SLG	E	Avg.
			BATTING														FIELDING	
1996—	St. Pete. (FSL)■	SS	126	423	46	115	13	3	3	49	30	53	10-5	.272	.317	.338	21	.963
1997—	Arkansas (Texas)	SS-DH	115	390	44	112	20	6	4	58	22	39	11-10	.287	.324	.400	33	.935
—	St. Louis (N.L.)	SS	12	22	3	6	1	0	0	1	1	2	3-0	.273	.304	.318	1	.963
1998—	Memphis (PCL)	SS-2B	59	214	29	62	9	2	6	35	16	20	3-3	.290	.341	.435	14	.952
—	St. Louis (N.L.)	SS-3B-2B	57	153	9	31	5	0	0	8	12	18	2-0	.203	.261	.235	13	.946
1999—	St. Louis (N.L.)	SS-2B-3B	10	9	3	1	0	0	0	2	1	2	1-0	.111	.200	.111	3	.800
—	Memphis (PCL)	SS	107	362	31	103	25	4	1	45	24	40	3-4	.285	.328	.384	23	.956
2000—	Kansas City (A.L.)■	SS-2B	65	104	17	23	2	0	0	11	5	10	4-2	.221	.257	.240	1	.992
2001—	Kansas City (A.L.)	2B-SS-3B-DH	28	56	8	14	3	0	0	4	3	8	0-0	.250	.295	.304	3	.969
—	Omaha (PCL)	SS-2B-3B	14	52	5	16	1	0	1	4	2	10	3-0	.308	.368	.385	2	.947
2002—	Iowa (PCL)■	SS-2B	61	194	22	53	10	0	1	14	9	21	5-2	.273	.309	.340	12	.948
—	Omaha (PCL)■	2B-SS	35	136	25	42	11	4	2	19	9	16	4-1	.309	.351	.493	3	.983
—	Kansas City (A.L.)	2B-3B-SS	33	94	11	21	2	0	0	4	12	13	2-3	.223	.308	.245	2	.984
American League totals (3 years)			126	254	36	58	7	0	0	19	20	31	6-5	.228	.285	.256	6	.983
National League totals (3 years)			79	184	15	38	6	0	0	11	14	22	6-0	.207	.263	.239	17	.940
Major League totals (6 years)			205	438	51	96	13	0	0	30	34	53	12-5	.219	.276	.249	23	.964

ORDONEZ, MAGGLIO — OF — WHITE SOX

PERSONAL: Born January 28, 1974, in Caracas, Venezuela. ... 6-0/210. ... Bats right, throws right.

TRANSACTIONS/CAREER NOTES: Signed as non-drafted free agent by Chicago White Sox organization (May 18, 1991). ... On suspended list (May 1-6, 2000).

RECORDS: Shares major league single-season record for fewest double plays by outfielder (150 or more games)—0 (2001 and 2002).

HONORS: Named American Association Most Valuable Player (1997). ... Named outfielder on The Sporting News A.L. All-Star team (2000). ... Named outfielder on The Sporting News A.L. Silver Slugger team (2000). ... Named outfielder on A.L. Silver Slugger team (2002).

STATISTICAL NOTES: Led American Association with nine sacrifice flies and tied for league lead with 249 total bases in 1997. ... Led A.L. with 15 sacrifice flies in 2000. ... Had 17-game hitting streak (August 2-21, 2002). ... Career major league grand slams: 6.

2002 GAMES PLAYED BY POSITION (MLB): OF—150; DH—1.

Year	Team (League)	Pos.	G	AB	R	H	2B	3B	HR	RBI	BB	SO	SB-CS	Avg.	OBP	SLG	E	Avg.
			BATTING														FIELDING	
1991—	Dom. Orioles/WS (DSL)		25	94	17	28	3	1	0	8	6	12	4-...	.298	...	.351	...	...
1992—	GC White Sox (GCL)	OF	38	111	17	20	10	2	1	14	13	26	6-4	.180	.276	.333	0	1.000
1993—	Hickory (S.Atl.)	OF	84	273	32	59	14	4	3	20	26	66	5-5	.216	.284	.330	6	.959
1994—	Hickory (S.Atl.)	OF	132	490	86	144	24	5	11	69	45	57	16-7	.294	.353	.431	6	.980
1995—	Prince William (Caro.)	OF	131	487	61	116	24	2	12	65	41	71	11-5	.238	.299	.370	6	.978
1996—	Birmingham (Sou.)	OF	130	479	66	126	41	0	18	67	39	74	9-10	.263	.330	.461	6	.976
1997—	Nashville (A.A.)	OF-DH	135	523	65	*172	29	3	14	90	32	61	14-10	*.329	.364	.476	5	.983
—	Chicago (A.L.)	OF	21	69	12	22	6	0	4	11	2	8	1-2	.319	.338	.580	0	1.000
1998—	Chicago (A.L.)	OF	145	535	70	151	25	2	14	65	28	53	9-7	.282	.326	.415	5	.985
1999—	Chicago (A.L.)	OF-DH	157	624	100	188	34	3	30	117	47	64	13-6	.301	.349	.510	3	.991
2000—	Chicago (A.L.)	OF	153	588	102	185	34	3	32	126	60	64	18-4	.315	.371	.546	5	.983
2001—	Chicago (A.L.)	OF-DH	160	593	97	181	40	1	31	113	70	70	25-7	.305	.382	.533	5	.983
2002—	Chicago (A.L.)	OF-DH	153	590	116	189	47	1	38	135	53	77	7-5	.320	.381	.597	4	.986
Major League totals (6 years)			789	2999	497	916	186	10	149	567	260	336	73-31	.305	.362	.523	22	.986

DIVISION SERIES RECORD

Year	Team (League)	Pos.	G	AB	R	H	2B	3B	HR	RBI	BB	SO	SB-CS	Avg.	OBP	SLG	E	Avg.
			BATTING														FIELDING	
2000—	Chicago (A.L.)	OF	3	11	0	2	0	1	0	1	2	2	1-0	.182	.308	.364	0	1.000

ALL-STAR GAME RECORD

	AB	R	H	2B	3B	HR	RBI	BB	SO	SB-CS	Avg.	OBP	SLG	E	Avg.
All-Star Game totals (3 years)	5	1	3	1	0	1	2	0	0	0-0	.600	.500	1.400	0	1.000

ORDONEZ, REY — SS — METS

PERSONAL: Born January 11, 1971, in Havana, Cuba. ... 5-9/159. ... Bats right, throws right. ... Full name: Reynaldo Ordonez.

HIGH SCHOOL: Espa (Havana, Cuba).

COLLEGE: Fajardo College (Havana, Cuba).

TRANSACTIONS/CAREER NOTES: Played with St. Paul Saints of Northern League (1993). ... Rights acquired by New York Mets organization in lottery of Cuban defectors (October 29, 1993). ... Signed by Mets organization (February 8, 1994). ... On disabled list (June 2-July 11, 1997; and May 30, 2000-remainder of season).

RECORDS: Holds major league career record for most consecutive errorless games by shortstop—100 (June 14-October 4, 1999). ... Holds N.L. career record for most consecutive chances accepted without an error by shorstop—412 (June 13-October 4, 1999). ... Holds N.L. single-season records for highest fielding average by shortstop (150 or more games)—.994 (1999); fewest errors by shortstop (150 or more games—4 (1999); most consecutive errorless games by shortstop—100 (June 14-October 4, 1999); and most consecutive chances accepted without an error by shortstop—412 (June 13-October 4, 1999).

HONORS: Won N.L. Gold Glove at shortstop (1997-99).

STATISTICAL NOTES: Led International League shortstops with 436 assists and 645 total chances in 1995. ... Led N.L. shortstops with 705 total chances and 102 double plays in 1996. ... Career major league grand slams: 1.

2002 GAMES PLAYED BY POSITION (MLB): SS—142.

Year	Team (League)	Pos.	G	AB	R	H	2B	3B	HR	RBI	BB	SO	SB-CS	Avg.	OBP	SLG	E	Avg.
			BATTING														FIELDING	
1993—	St. Paul (Nor.)	SS-2B	15	60	10	17	4	0	0	7	3	9	3-...	.283	...	.350	2	.971
1994—	St. Lucie (FSL)■	SS	79	314	47	97	21	2	2	40	14	28	11-6	.309	.336	.408	15	.966
—	Binghamton (East.)	SS	48	191	22	50	10	2	1	20	4	18	4-3	.262	.279	.351	8	.961
1995—	Norfolk (I.L.)	SS	125	439	49	94	21	4	2	50	27	50	11-13	.214	.261	.294	21	.967

								BATTING									FIELDING	
Year	Team (League)	Pos.	G	AB	R	H	2B	3B	HR	RBI	BB	SO	SB-CS	Avg.	OBP	SLG	E	Avg.
1996—	New York (N.L.)..........	SS	151	502	51	129	12	4	1	30	22	53	1-3	.257	.289	.303	27	.962
1997—	New York (N.L.)..........	SS	120	356	35	77	5	3	1	33	18	36	11-5	.216	.255	.256	9	*.983
1998—	New York (N.L.)..........	SS	153	505	46	124	20	2	1	42	23	60	3-6	.246	.278	.299	17	.975
1999—	New York (N.L.)..........	SS	154	520	49	134	24	2	1	60	49	59	8-4	.258	.319	.317	4	*.994
2000—	New York (N.L.)..........	SS	45	133	10	25	5	0	0	9	17	16	0-0	.188	.278	.226	6	.965
2001—	New York (N.L.)..........	SS	149	461	31	114	24	4	3	44	34	43	3-2	.247	.299	.336	12	.980
2002—	New York (N.L.)..........	SS	144	460	53	117	25	2	1	42	24	46	2-2	.254	.292	.324	19	.969
Major League totals (7 years)			916	2937	275	720	115	17	8	260	187	313	28-22	.245	.290	.304	94	.976

DIVISION SERIES RECORD

								BATTING									FIELDING	
Year	Team (League)	Pos.	G	AB	R	H	2B	3B	HR	RBI	BB	SO	SB-CS	Avg.	OBP	SLG	E	Avg.
1999—	New York (N.L.)..........	SS	4	14	1	4	1	0	0	2	0	5	1-0	.286	.286	.357	0	1.000

CHAMPIONSHIP SERIES RECORD

								BATTING									FIELDING	
Year	Team (League)	Pos.	G	AB	R	H	2B	3B	HR	RBI	BB	SO	SB-CS	Avg.	OBP	SLG	E	Avg.
1999—	New York (N.L.)..........	SS	6	24	0	1	0	0	0	0	0	2	0-0	.042	.042	.042	0	1.000

ORIE, KEVIN — 3B — CUBS

PERSONAL: Born September 1, 1972, in West Chester, Pa. ... 6-4/215. ... Bats right, throws right. ... Full name: Kevin Leonard Orie.

HIGH SCHOOL: Upper St. Clair (Pa.).

COLLEGE: Indiana.

TRANSACTIONS/CAREER NOTES: Selected by Chicago Cubs organization in supplemental round ("sandwich pick" between first and second round, 29th pick overall) of free-agent draft (June 3, 1993); pick received as part of compensation for Atlanta Braves signing Type A free-agent P Greg Maddux. ... On disabled list (May 3, 1994-remainder of season). ... On Iowa disabled list (July 27-August 19, 1996). ... On Chicago disabled list (April 30-May 30, 1997); included rehabilitation assignments to Orlando (May 16-20) and Iowa (May 20-30). ... Traded by Cubs with P Todd Noel and P Justin Speier to Florida Marlins for P Felix Heredia and P Steve Hoff (July 31, 1998). ... On Florida disabled list (May 23-June 8 and July 1-September 6, 1999); included rehabilitation assignments to Calgary (July 28-August 3 and August 17-September 6). ... Traded by Marlins to Los Angeles Dodgers for a player to be named later (November 12, 1999); Marlins received cash to complete deal (March 28, 2000). ... Released by Dodgers (March 29, 2000). ... Signed by Kansas City Royals organization (April 3, 2000). ... Released by Royals (June 15, 2000). ... Signed by New York Yankees organization (June 17, 2000). ... On Columbus disabled list (August 1, 2000-remainder of season). ... Granted free agency (October 18, 2000). ... Signed by Philadelphia Phillies organization (December 20, 2000). ... Granted free agency (October 15, 2001). ... Signed by Cubs organization (November 19, 2001). ... On Iowa disabled list (April 23-June 2, 2002).

2002 GAMES PLAYED BY POSITION (MLB): 3B—12.

								BATTING									FIELDING	
Year	Team (League)	Pos.	G	AB	R	H	2B	3B	HR	RBI	BB	SO	SB-CS	Avg.	OBP	SLG	E	Avg.
1993—	Peoria (Midw.)...........	SS-OF	65	238	28	64	17	1	7	45	21	51	3-5	.269	.351	.437	12	.950
1994—	Daytona (FSL)...........	DH	6	17	4	7	3	1	1	5	8	4	0-1	.412	.615	.882	...	...
1995—	Daytona (FSL)...........	3B	119	409	54	100	17	4	9	51	42	71	5-4	.244	.333	.372	26	.916
1996—	Orlando (Sou.)...........	3B-DH	82	296	42	93	25	0	8	58	48	52	2-0	.314	.403	.480	14	.936
—	Iowa (A.A.)................	3B	14	48	5	10	1	0	2	6	6	10	0-0	.208	.296	.354	1	.974
1997—	Chicago (N.L.)...........	3B-SS	114	364	40	100	23	5	8	44	39	57	2-2	.275	.350	.431	9	.971
—	Orlando (Sou.)...........	DH	3	13	3	5	2	0	2	6	2	1	0-0	.385	.467	1.000	...	...
—	Iowa (A.A.)................	3B-DH	9	32	7	12	4	0	1	8	5	5	0-0	.375	.459	.594	1	.938
1998—	Chicago (N.L.)...........	3B	64	204	24	37	14	0	2	21	18	35	1-1	.181	.253	.279	5	.966
—	Iowa (PCL)................	3B	24	92	27	34	8	0	9	24	12	15	1-0	.370	.453	.750	2	.960
—	Florida (N.L.)■..........	3B	48	175	23	46	8	1	6	17	14	24	1-0	.263	.335	.423	10	.939
1999—	Florida (N.L.).............	3B-1B	77	240	26	61	16	0	6	29	22	43	1-0	.254	.322	.396	7	.961
—	Calgary (PCL)............	3B-DH	23	72	10	23	9	0	3	8	13	7	0-0	.319	.430	.569	6	.875
2000—	Omaha (PCL)..............	3B	54	175	30	49	11	2	5	23	28	24	3-3	.280	.390	.451	7	.951
—	Columbus (I.L.)■.......	3B	41	149	19	43	13	0	4	19	12	28	1-0	.289	.354	.456	8	.925
2001—	Scranton/W.B. (I.L.)■	3B	134	509	77	149	34	2	13	45	77	63	11-6	.293	.394	.444	13	.965
2002—	Iowa (PCL)■..............	3B	86	294	51	88	16	3	20	63	25	40	0-1	.299	.358	.578	9	.954
—	Chicago (N.L.)...........	3B	13	32	4	9	3	0	0	5	1	4	0-0	.281	.306	.375	2	.895
Major League totals (4 years)			316	1015	117	253	64	6	22	116	94	163	5-3	.249	.320	.389	33	.960

OROPESA, EDDIE — P — DIAMONDBACKS

PERSONAL: Born November 23, 1971, in Colon, Cuba. ... 6-3/215. ... Throws left, bats left. ... Full name: Edilberto Oropesa.

COLLEGE: Mantazas (Cuba).

TRANSACTIONS/CAREER NOTES: Signed by St. Paul of Northern League (August 1993). ... Selected by Los Angeles Dodgers organization in 14th round of free-agent draft (June 2, 1994). ... Selected by San Francisco Giants organization from Dodgers organization in Rule 5 minor league draft (December 9, 1996). ... Loaned by Giants organization to Reynosa, Mexican League (July 8-August 5, 1999). ... Granted free agency (October 15, 2000). ... Signed by Philadelphia Phillies organization (November 15, 2000). ... On Philadelphia disabled list (June 13-July 5, 2001); included rehabilitation assignment to Scranton/Wilkes-Barre (June 29-July 5). ... Granted free agency (October 15, 2001). ... Signed by Arizona Diamondbacks organization (November 20, 2001).

STATISTICAL NOTES: Tied for Texas League lead with 15 wild pitches in 1998. ... Tied for Pacific Coast League lead with four balks in 1999.

CAREER HITTING (MLB): 0-for-0 (.000), 0 R, 0 2B, 0 3B, 0 HR, 0 RBI.

Year	League	W	L	Pct.	ERA	G	GS	CG	ShO	Sv.-Opp.	IP	H	R	ER	HR	BB-IBB	SO
1993—	St. Paul (Nor.)..................	3	1	.750	1.93	4	3	0	0	0-...	18.2	6	4	4	...	9-...	19
1994—	Vero Beach (FSL)■..........	4	3	.571	2.13	19	10	1	1	0-...	72.0	54	24	17	2	25-2	67
1995—	San Antonio (Texas).........	1	1	.500	3.12	16	0	0	0	1-...	17.1	22	8	6	2	12-1	16
—	Vero Beach (FSL)............	3	1	.750	3.81	19	1	0	0	1-...	28.1	25	12	12	0	10-0	23
—	San Bernardino (Calif.).....	0	0	...	0.00	1	0	0	0	1-...	1.0	0	0	0	0	0-0	0
1996—	San Bernardino (Calif.).....	11	6	.647	3.34	33	19	0	0	1-...	156.1	133	74	58	8	77-1	133
1997—	Shreveport (Texas)■........	7	7	.500	3.92	43	9	1	0	0-...	124.0	122	58	54	7	64-0	65

Year	League	W	L	Pct.	ERA	G	GS	CG	ShO	Sv.-Opp.	IP	H	R	ER	HR	BB-IBB	SO
1998—	Shreveport (Texas)	7	11	.389	3.78	32	20	2	0	0-...	143.0	143	71	60	6	67-3	104
—	President (Taiwan)■	0	2	.000	6.43	8	0	0	0	1-...	14.0	...	...	10	...	11-...	6
1999—	Fresno (PCL)■	6	5	.545	4.85	21	18	1	0	0-...	102.0	113	69	55	15	49-0	61
—	Bakersfield (Calif.)	2	0	1.000	3.60	2	1	0	0	0-...	10.0	13	5	4	2	1-0	10
—	Reynosa (Mex.)■	0	4	.000	7.06	7	3	0	0	0-...	21.2	32	19	17	3	16-2	8
2000—	Shreveport (Texas)■	2	4	.333	3.07	59	2	0	0	4-...	76.1	70	38	26	6	40-6	76
2001—	Philadelphia (N.L.)■	1	0	1.000	4.74	30	0	0	0	0-1	19.0	16	10	10	1	17-6	15
—	Scranton/W.B. (I.L.)	1	1	.500	2.35	14	1	0	0	0-...	15.1	14	5	4	1	4-1	11
—	Clearwater (FSL)	0	0	...	0.00	2	0	0	0	0-...	2.0	2	0	0	0	1-0	3
2002—	Arizona (N.L.)■	2	0	1.000	10.30	32	0	0	0	0-1	25.1	39	30	29	6	15-0	18
—	Tucson (PCL)	1	0	1.000	3.86	29	0	0	0	0-...	25.2	23	11	11	2	13-2	26
Major League totals (2 years)		3	0	1.000	7.92	62	0	0	0	0-2	44.1	55	40	39	7	32-6	33

OROSCO, JESSE P

PERSONAL: Born April 21, 1957, in Santa Barbara, Calif. ... 6-2/205. ... Throws left, bats right. ... Full name: Jesse Russell Orosco. ... Name pronounced oh-ROSS-koh.

HIGH SCHOOL: Santa Barbara (Calif.).

JUNIOR COLLEGE: Santa Barbara (Calif.) City College.

TRANSACTIONS/CAREER NOTES: Selected by St. Louis Cardinals organization in seventh round of free-agent draft (January 11, 1977); did not sign. ... Selected by Minnesota Twins organization in second round of free-agent draft (January 10, 1978). ... Traded by Twins to New York Mets (February 7, 1979), completing deal in which Twins traded P Greg Field and a player to be named later to Mets for P Jerry Koosman (December 8, 1978). ... Traded by Mets as part of an eight-player, three-team deal in which Mets sent Orosco to Oakland Athletics (December 11, 1987); A's then traded Orosco, SS Alfredo Griffin and P Jay Howell to Los Angeles Dodgers for P Bob Welch, P Matt Young and P Jack Savage; A's then traded Savage, P Wally Whitehurst and P Kevin Tapani to Mets. ... Granted free agency (November 4, 1988). ... Signed by Cleveland Indians (December 3, 1988). ... Traded by Indians to Milwaukee Brewers for a player to be named later (December 6, 1991); deal settled in cash. ... Granted free agency (November 5, 1992). ... Re-signed by Brewers (December 4, 1992). ... Granted free agency (October 15, 1994). ... Signed by Baltimore Orioles (April 9, 1995). ... Granted free agency (October 27, 1996). ... Re-signed by Orioles (November 15, 1996). ... Traded by Orioles to Mets for P Chuck McElroy (December 10, 1999). ... Traded by Mets to Cardinals for 2B/OF Joe McEwing (March 18, 2000). ... On St. Louis disabled list (April 9-June 9 and June 22, 2000-remainder of season); included rehabilitation assignments to Peoria (May 30-June 5) and Memphis (June 6-9). ... Granted free agency (October 30, 2000). ... Signed by Los Angeles Dodgers organization (February 8, 2001). ... Released by Dodgers (March 30, 2001). ... Re-signed by Dodgers organization (April 24, 2001). ... On Los Angeles disabled list (August 13-September 1, 2001). ... Granted free agency (November 5, 2001). ... Re-signed by Dodgers organization (December 7, 2001). ... On disabled list (May 14-29, 2002). ... Granted free agency (October 28, 2002).

RECORDS: Holds major league career records for most games pitched—1,187; and most games as relief pitcher—1,183.

MISCELLANEOUS: Appeared in one game as outfielder with one putout (1986). ... Struck out in only plate appearance (1993).

CAREER HITTING (MLB): 10-for-59 (.169), 3 R, 0 2B, 0 3B, 0 HR, 4 RBI.

Year	League	W	L	Pct.	ERA	G	GS	CG	ShO	Sv.-Opp.	IP	H	R	ER	HR	BB-IBB	SO
1978—	Elizabethton (Appl.)	4	4	.500	1.13	20	0	0	0	6-...	40.0	29	7	5	0	20-5	48
1979—	Tidewater (I.L.)■	4	4	.500	3.89	16	15	1	0	0-...	81.0	82	45	35	2	43-4	55
—	New York (N.L.)	1	2	.333	4.89	18	2	0	0	0-0	35.0	33	20	19	4	22-0	22
1980—	Jackson (Texas)	4	4	.500	3.68	37	1	0	0	3-...	71.0	52	36	29	3	62-4	85
1981—	Tidewater (I.L.)	9	5	.643	3.31	46	10	0	0	8-...	87.0	80	39	32	7	32-4	81
—	New York (N.L.)	0	1	.000	1.56	8	0	0	0	1-1	17.1	13	4	3	2	6-2	18
1982—	New York (N.L.)	4	10	.286	2.72	54	2	0	0	4-5	109.1	92	37	33	7	40-2	89
1983—	New York (N.L.)	13	7	.650	1.47	62	0	0	0	17-22	110.0	76	27	18	3	38-7	84
1984—	New York (N.L.)	10	6	.625	2.59	60	0	0	0	31-39	87.0	58	29	25	7	34-6	85
1985—	New York (N.L.)	8	6	.571	2.73	54	0	0	0	17-25	79.0	66	26	24	6	34-7	68
1986—	New York (N.L.)	8	6	.571	2.33	58	0	0	0	21-29	81.0	64	23	21	6	35-3	62
1987—	New York (N.L.)	3	9	.250	4.44	58	0	0	0	16-22	77.0	78	41	38	5	31-9	78
1988—	Los Angeles (N.L.)■	3	2	.600	2.72	55	0	0	0	9-15	53.0	41	18	16	4	30-3	43
1989—	Cleveland (A.L.)■	3	4	.429	2.08	69	0	0	0	3-7	78.0	54	20	18	7	26-4	79
1990—	Cleveland (A.L.)	5	4	.556	3.90	55	0	0	0	2-3	64.2	58	35	28	9	38-7	55
1991—	Cleveland (A.L.)	2	0	1.000	3.74	47	0	0	0	0-0	45.2	52	20	19	4	15-8	36
1992—	Milwaukee (A.L.)■	3	1	.750	3.23	59	0	0	0	1-2	39.0	33	15	14	5	13-1	40
1993—	Milwaukee (A.L.)	3	5	.375	3.18	57	0	0	0	8-13	56.2	47	25	20	2	17-3	67
1994—	Milwaukee (A.L.)	3	1	.750	5.08	40	0	0	0	0-4	39.0	32	26	22	4	26-2	36
1995—	Baltimore (A.L.)■	2	4	.333	3.26	*65	0	0	0	3-6	49.2	28	19	18	4	27-7	58
1996—	Baltimore (A.L.)	3	1	.750	3.40	66	0	0	0	0-3	55.2	42	22	21	5	28-4	52
1997—	Baltimore (A.L.)	6	3	.667	2.32	71	0	0	0	0-4	50.1	29	13	13	6	30-0	46
1998—	Baltimore (A.L.)	4	1	.800	3.18	69	0	0	0	7-9	56.2	46	20	20	6	28-1	50
1999—	Baltimore (A.L.)	0	2	.000	5.34	65	0	0	0	1-4	32.0	28	21	19	5	20-3	35
2000—	St. Louis (N.L.)■	0	0	...	3.86	6	0	0	0	0-0	2.1	3	3	1	1	3-2	4
—	Peoria (Midw.)	0	0	...	0.00	2	2	0	0	0-...	1.2	0	0	0	0	0-0	1
—	Memphis (PCL)	0	1	.000	9.00	2	1	0	0	0-...	1.0	1	1	1	0	0-0	0
2001—	Las Vegas (PCL)■	1	0	1.000	0.00	10	0	0	0	0-...	7.1	4	0	0	0	2-0	11
—	Los Angeles (N.L.)	0	1	.000	3.94	35	0	0	0	0-2	16.0	17	7	7	3	7-1	21
2002—	Los Angeles (N.L.)	1	2	.333	3.00	56	0	0	0	1-1	27.0	24	10	9	4	12-1	22
A.L. totals (11 years)		34	26	.567	3.36	663	0	0	0	25-55	567.1	449	236	212	57	268-40	554
N.L. totals (12 years)		51	52	.495	2.78	524	4	0	0	117-161	694.0	565	245	214	52	292-43	596
Major League totals (23 years)		85	78	.521	3.04	1187	4	0	0	142-216	1261.1	1014	481	426	109	560-83	1150

DIVISION SERIES RECORD

Year	League	W	L	Pct.	ERA	G	GS	CG	ShO	Sv.-Opp.	IP	H	R	ER	HR	BB-IBB	SO
1996—	Baltimore (A.L.)	0	1	.000	36.00	4	0	0	0	0-0	1.0	2	4	4	0	3-0	2
1997—	Baltimore (A.L.)	0	0	...	0.00	2	0	0	0	0-0	1.1	1	0	0	0	0-0	1
Division series totals (2 years)		0	1	.000	15.43	6	0	0	0	0-0	2.1	3	4	4	0	3-0	3

CHAMPIONSHIP SERIES RECORD

RECORDS: Holds single-series record for most games won—3 (1986).

Year	League	W	L	Pct.	ERA	G	GS	CG	ShO	Sv.-Opp.	IP	H	R	ER	HR	BB-IBB	SO
1986—	New York (N.L.)	3	0	1.000	3.38	4	0	0	0	0-1	8.0	5	3	3	1	2-0	10
1988—	Los Angeles (N.L.)	0	0	...	7.71	4	0	0	0	0-0	2.1	4	2	2	0	3-1	0
1996—	Baltimore (A.L.)	0	0	...	4.50	4	0	0	0	0-0	2.0	2	1	1	0	1-1	2
1997—	Baltimore (A.L.)	0	0	...	0.00	2	0	0	0	0-0	1.1	0	0	0	0	1-0	1
Champ. series totals (4 years)		3	0	1.000	3.95	14	0	0	0	0-1	13.2	11	6	6	1	7-2	13

WORLD SERIES RECORD

NOTES: Member of World Series championship team (1986 and 1988).

Year	League	W	L	Pct.	ERA	G	GS	CG	ShO	Sv.-Opp.	IP	H	R	ER	HR	BB-IBB	SO
1986—	New York (N.L.)................	0	0	...	0.00	4	0	0	0	2-2	5.2	2	0	0	0	0-0	6
1988—	Los Angeles (N.L.)............									Did not play.							

ALL-STAR GAME RECORD

	W	L	Pct.	ERA	GS	CG	ShO	Sv.-Opp.	IP	H	R	ER	HR	BB-IBB	SO
All-Star Game totals (1 year)........	0	0	...	0.00	0	0	0	0-0	.1	0	0	0	0	0-0	1

ORTIZ, DAVID — DH/1B — TWINS

PERSONAL: Born November 18, 1975, in Santo Domingo, Dominican Republic. ... 6-4/230. ... Bats left, throws left. ... Full name: David Americo Ortiz. ... Formerly known as David Arias.

HIGH SCHOOL: Estudia Espallat (Dominican Republic).

TRANSACTIONS/CAREER NOTES: Signed as non-drafted free agent by Seattle Mariners organization (November 28, 1992). ... Traded by Mariners to Minnesota Twins (September 13, 1996), completing deal in which Twins traded 3B Dave Hollins to Mariners for a player to be named later (August 29, 1996). ... On Minnesota disabled list (May 10-July 9, 1998); included rehabilitation assignment to Salt Lake (June 25-July 9). ... On Minnesota disabled list (May 5-July 21, 2001); included rehabilitation assignments to Gulf Coast Twins (July 5-11), Fort Myers (July 11-12) and New Britain (July 12-21). ... On disabled list (April 19-May 12, 2002).

STATISTICAL NOTES: Led Arizona League first basemen with 372 putouts and 393 total chances in 1994. ... Led Arizona League first basemen with 27 assists in 1995. ... Tied for Arizona League lead with 99 total bases in 1995. ... Had 19-game hitting streak (July 17-August 6, 2002). ... Career major league grand slams: 1.

2002 GAMES PLAYED BY POSITION (MLB): DH—95; 1B—15.

			BATTING														FIELDING	
Year	Team (League)	Pos.	G	AB	R	H	2B	3B	HR	RBI	BB	SO	SB-CS	Avg.	OBP	SLG	E	Avg.
1993—	Dom. Mariners (DSL).		61	201	61	53	17	1	7	31	34	44	1-...	.264	...	.463	...	...
1994—	Ariz. Mariners (Ariz.)..	1B	53	167	14	41	10	1	2	20	14	46	1-4	.246	.305	.353	6	.985
1995—	Ariz. Mariners (Ariz.)..	1B	48	184	30	61	*18	4	4	•37	23	52	2-0	.332	.403	.538	5	*.989
1996—	Wisconsin (Midw.).....	1B-DH-3B	129	485	89	156	34	2	18	93	52	108	3-4	.322	.390	.511	13	.989
1997—	Fort Myers (FSL)■.....	1B-DH	61	239	45	79	15	0	13	58	22	53	2-1	.331	.385	.556	9	.984
—	New Britain (East.).....	DH-1B	69	258	40	83	22	2	14	56	21	78	2-6	.322	.379	.585	3	.990
—	Salt Lake (PCL)..........	1B-DH	10	42	5	9	1	0	4	10	2	11	0-1	.214	.250	.524	0	1.000
—	Minnesota (A.L.)........	1B-DH	15	49	10	16	3	0	1	6	2	19	0-0	.327	.353	.449	1	.989
1998—	Minnesota (A.L.)........	1B-DH	86	278	47	77	20	0	9	46	39	72	1-0	.277	.371	.446	6	.989
—	Salt Lake (PCL)..........	1B-DH	11	37	5	9	3	0	2	6	3	9	0-0	.243	.300	.486	3	.966
1999—	Salt Lake (PCL)..........	1B-DH	130	476	85	150	35	3	30	*110	79	105	2-2	.315	.412	.590	•20	.980
—	Minnesota (A.L.)........	DH-1B	10	20	1	0	0	0	0	0	5	12	0-0	.000	.200	.000	0	1.000
2000—	Minnesota (A.L.)........	DH-1B	130	415	59	117	36	1	10	63	57	81	1-0	.282	.364	.446	1	.996
2001—	Minnesota (A.L.)........	DH-1B	89	303	46	71	17	1	18	48	40	68	1-0	.234	.324	.475	0	1.000
—	GC Twins (GCL)..........	DH	4	10	3	4	0	0	0	1	3	1	1-0	.400	.538	.400	...	...
—	Fort Myers (FSL)........	1B	1	3	0	0	0	0	0	0	1	0	0-0	.000	.250	.000	0	1.000
—	New Britain (East.).....	1B	9	37	3	9	4	0	0	1	3	9	0-0	.243	.293	.351	0	1.000
2002—	Minnesota (A.L.)........	DH-1B	125	412	52	112	32	1	20	75	43	87	1-2	.272	.339	.500	1	.990
Major League totals (6 years)			455	1477	215	393	108	3	58	238	186	339	4-2	.266	.348	.461	9	.991

DIVISION SERIES RECORD

			BATTING														FIELDING	
Year	Team (League)	Pos.	G	AB	R	H	2B	3B	HR	RBI	BB	SO	SB-CS	Avg.	OBP	SLG	E	Avg.
2002—	Minnesota (A.L.)........	DH	4	13	0	3	2	0	0	2	0	5	0-0	.231	.231	.385	...	...

CHAMPIONSHIP SERIES RECORD

			BATTING														FIELDING	
Year	Team (League)	Pos.	G	AB	R	H	2B	3B	HR	RBI	BB	SO	SB-CS	Avg.	OBP	SLG	E	Avg.
2002—	Minnesota (A.L.)........	DH	5	16	0	5	1	0	0	2	0	5	0-0	.313	.313	.375	...	...

ORTIZ, HECTOR — C

PERSONAL: Born October 14, 1969, in Rio Piedras, Puerto Rico. ... 6-0/205. ... Bats right, throws right. ... Full name: Hector Ortiz Jr.

HIGH SCHOOL: Luis Hernaiz Verone (Canovanas, Puerto Rico).

JUNIOR COLLEGE: Ranger (Texas) College.

TRANSACTIONS/CAREER NOTES: Selected by Los Angeles Dodgers organization in 35th round of free-agent draft (June 1, 1988). ... Granted free agency (October 17, 1994). ... Signed by Chicago Cubs organization (January 22, 1995). ... Granted free agency (October 15, 1996). ... Signed by Kansas City Royals organization (January 29, 1997). ... On Omaha disabled list (May 19-June 6, 1998). ... Granted free agency (October 15, 1998). ... Signed by Dodgers organization (January 18, 1999). ... Granted free agency (October 15, 1999). ... Signed by Royals organization (November 30, 1999). ... Granted free agency (October 15, 2001). ... Re-signed by Royals organization (November 20, 2001). ... Contract purchased by Texas Rangers organization from Royals (April 26, 2002). ... Granted free agency (October 15, 2002).

STATISTICAL NOTES: Led Northwest League catchers with 392 putouts, 62 assists and 461 total chances in 1990. ... Tied for Northwest League lead in double plays by catcher with five in 1990.

2002 GAMES PLAYED BY POSITION (MLB): C—7.

			BATTING														FIELDING	
Year	Team (League)	Pos.	G	AB	R	H	2B	3B	HR	RBI	BB	SO	SB-CS	Avg.	OBP	SLG	E	Avg.
1988—	Salem (N'West)..........	C-3B	32	77	5	11	1	0	0	4	5	16	0-2	.143	.205	.156	7	.962
1989—	Vero Beach (FSL).......	C	42	85	5	12	0	1	0	4	6	15	0-0	.141	.215	.165	6	.970
—	Salem (N'West)..........	C	44	140	13	32	3	1	0	12	4	24	2-1	.229	.255	.264	*12	.961
1990—	Yakima (N'West)........	C	52	173	16	47	3	1	0	12	5	15	1-1	.272	.296	.301	7	.985
1991—	Vero Beach (FSL).......	C	42	123	3	28	2	0	0	8	5	8	0-0	.228	.275	.244	7	.974
1992—	Bakersfield (Calif.)......	C	63	206	19	58	8	1	1	31	21	16	2-3	.282	.359	.345	3	.994
—	San Antonio (Texas)...	C	26	59	1	12	1	0	0	5	11	13	0-0	.203	.338	.220	3	.982
1993—	San Antonio (Texas)...	C-3B	49	131	6	28	5	0	1	6	9	17	0-2	.214	.264	.275	8	.978
—	Albuquerque (PCL).....	C	18	44	0	8	1	1	0	3	0	6	0-0	.182	.200	.250	2	.978

Year	Team (League)	Pos.	G	AB	R	H	2B	3B	HR	RBI	BB	SO	SB-CS	Avg.	OBP	SLG	E	Avg.
			BATTING														FIELDING	
1994—	Albuquerque (PCL).....	C	34	93	7	28	1	1	0	10	3	12	0-0	.301	.320	.333	4	.976
	—San Antonio (Texas)...	C-P	24	75	4	9	0	0	0	4	2	7	0-0	.120	.150	.120	2	.990
1995—	Orlando (Sou.)■	C	96	299	13	70	12	0	0	18	20	39	0-5	.234	.281	.274	6	.991
1996—	Orlando (Sou.)	C	78	216	16	47	8	0	0	15	26	23	1-2	.218	.298	.255	6	.988
	—Iowa (A.A.)	C	27	79	6	19	2	0	0	3	3	16	0-0	.241	.265	.266	2	.987
1997—	Omaha (A.A.)■	C	21	63	7	12	3	0	0	3	13	15	0-0	.190	.329	.238	3	.978
	—Wichita (Texas)	C	59	180	20	45	3	0	1	25	21	15	1-2	.250	.332	.283	*15	.962
1998—	Wichita (Texas)	C	4	13	1	2	0	0	0	0	2	1	0-1	.154	.267	.154	1	.968
	—Omaha (PCL).............	C	63	191	17	43	7	0	0	12	9	26	0-0	.225	.264	.262	8	.978
	—Kansas City (A.L.)	C-1B	4	4	1	0	0	0	0	0	0	0	0-0	.000	.000	.000	0	1.000
1999—	San Antonio (Texas)■	C	40	121	10	29	4	0	0	13	10	17	0-1	.240	.291	.273	6	.978
	—Albuquerque (PCL).....	C-1B	55	164	21	50	9	0	6	20	7	27	2-3	.305	.331	.470	10	.972
2000—	Omaha (PCL)■	C	68	227	30	73	12	0	6	24	22	18	4-3	.322	.382	.454	6	.982
	—Kansas City (A.L.)	C	26	88	15	34	6	0	0	5	8	8	0-0	.386	.443	.455	1	.993
2001—	Kansas City (A.L.)	C-DH	56	154	12	38	6	1	0	11	9	24	1-3	.247	.293	.299	3	.990
	—Omaha (PCL).............	C	42	150	19	39	7	0	2	15	15	26	0-3	.260	.320	.347	2	.991
2002—	Omaha (PCL).............	C	35	99	10	25	5	0	1	5	11	15	1-0	.253	.339	.333	5	.979
	—Oklahoma (PCL)■......	C-3B	25	82	3	17	2	0	0	7	11	16	0-1	.207	.298	.232	2	.990
	—Texas (A.L.)	C	7	14	1	3	1	0	1	2	1	1	0-0	.214	.267	.500	1	.957
Major League totals (4 years)			93	260	29	75	13	1	1	18	18	33	1-3	.288	.339	.358	5	.990

RECORD AS PITCHER

Year	League	W	L	Pct.	ERA	G	GS	CG	ShO	Sv.-Opp.	IP	H	R	ER	HR	BB-IBB	SO
1994—	San Antonio (Texas).........	0	0	...	0.00	1	0	0	0	0-...	1.0	0	0	0	0	1-0	1

ORTIZ, JOSE — 2B/SS — ROCKIES

PERSONAL: Born June 13, 1977, in Santo Domingo, Dominican Republic. ... 5-10/182. ... Bats right, throws right. ... Full name: Jose Daniel Ortiz Santos.

TRANSACTIONS/CAREER NOTES: Signed as non-drafted free agent by Oakland Athletics organization (November 8, 1994). ... On disabled list (May 10-June 30, 1998). ... On disabled list (June 15-25, 1999). ... On Oakland disabled list (April 15-May 16, 2001); included rehabilitation assignment to Sacramento (May 8-16). ... Traded by A's with OF Mario Encarnacion and P Todd Belitz to Colorado Rockies for OF Jermaine Dye (July 25, 2001). ... On Colorado disabled list (June 16-September 1, 2002); included rehabilitation assignments to Colorado Springs (July 4-7, July 11-21 and August 19-September 1).

HONORS: Named Pacific Coast League Most Valuable Player (2000).

STATISTICAL NOTES: Led Arizona League shortstops with 93 putouts, 165 assists, 279 total chances and 42 double plays in 1996. ... Led California League shortstops with 53 errors and 80 double plays in 1997. ... Hit three home runs in one game (August 17, 2001).

2002 GAMES PLAYED BY POSITION (MLB): 2B—53; 3B—1.

Year	Team (League)	Pos.	G	AB	R	H	2B	3B	HR	RBI	BB	SO	SB-CS	Avg.	OBP	SLG	E	Avg.
			BATTING														FIELDING	
1995—	Dom. Athletics (DSL) .	SS	61	217	45	65	12	2	9	41	32	22	14-...	.300	...	.498	17	.928
1996—	Ariz. Athletics (Ariz.) ..	SS	52	200	*43	66	12	8	4	25	20	34	16-5	.330	.392	*.530	21	.925
	—Modesto (Calif.)	2B	1	4	0	1	0	0	0	0	0	1	0-0	.250	.250	.250	0	1.000
1997—	Modesto (Calif.)	SS-2B	128	497	92	122	25	7	16	58	60	107	22-14	.245	.332	.421	†53	.913
1998—	Huntsville (Sou.)	2B-SS-OF	94	354	70	98	24	2	6	55	48	63	22-8	.277	.369	.407	27	.941
1999—	Vancouver (PCL)........	SS-2B	107	377	66	107	29	2	9	45	29	50	13-4	.284	.346	.443	28	.944
2000—	Sacramento (PCL)......	2B-SS-3B	131	*518	107	*182	34	5	24	108	47	64	22-9	.351	.408	.575	32	.949
	—Oakland (A.L.)	DH-2B	7	11	4	2	0	0	0	1	2	3	0-0	.182	.308	.182	1	.857
2001—	Oakland (A.L.)	2B-DH	11	42	4	7	0	0	0	3	3	5	1-0	.167	.217	.167	2	.951
	—Sacramento (PCL)......	2B-SS	65	256	41	70	16	4	7	39	25	50	7-4	.273	.345	.449	10	.964
	—Colorado (N.L.)■	2B	53	204	38	52	8	1	13	35	14	36	3-1	.255	.314	.495	8	.965
2002—	Colorado (N.L.)	2B-3B	65	192	22	48	7	1	1	12	16	30	2-0	.250	.315	.313	3	.988
	—Colo. Springs (PCL) ...	SS-3B-2B	26	111	23	37	9	2	6	18	4	13	1-1	.333	.353	.613	4	.969
American League totals (2 years)			18	53	8	9	0	0	0	4	5	8	1-0	.170	.237	.170	3	.938
National League totals (2 years)			118	396	60	100	15	2	14	47	30	66	5-1	.253	.314	.407	11	.977
Major League totals (3 years)			136	449	68	109	15	2	14	51	35	74	6-1	.243	.305	.379	14	.973

ORTIZ, RAMON — P — ANGELS

PERSONAL: Born March 23, 1973, in Cotui, Dominican Republic. ... 6-0/170. ... Throws right, bats right. ... Full name: Diogenes Ramon Ortiz.

HIGH SCHOOL: 8th Intermedian (Dominican Republic).

TRANSACTIONS/CAREER NOTES: Signed as non-drafted free agent by California Angels organization (June 20, 1995). ... Angels franchise renamed Anaheim Angels for 1997 season. ... On disabled list (May 9, 1998-remainder of season). ... On Anaheim disabled list (March 20-April 11, 2000); included rehabilitation assignment to Lake Elsinore (April 6).

STATISTICAL NOTES: Pitched 12-0 no-hit victory against Quad City (August 7, 1997). ... Tied for A.L. lead with three balks in 2002.

CAREER HITTING (MLB): 0-for-14 (.000), 0 R, 0 2B, 0 3B, 0 HR, 0 RBI.

Year	League	W	L	Pct.	ERA	G	GS	CG	ShO	Sv.-Opp.	IP	H	R	ER	HR	BB-IBB	SO
1995—	Dominican Angels (DSL)..	8	6	.571	2.23	16	16	7	0	0-...	97.0	79	44	24	...	54-...	100
1996—	Arizona Angels (Ariz.).......	5	4	.556	2.12	16	8	•2	*2	1-...	68.0	55	28	16	5	27-0	78
	—Boise (N'West)	1	1	.500	3.66	3	3	0	0	0-...	19.2	21	10	8	3	6-0	18
1997—	Cedar Rapids (Midw.)	11	10	.524	3.58	27	•27	*8	*4	0-...	181.0	156	78	72	22	53-0	*225
1998—	Midland (Texas)...............	2	1	.667	5.55	7	7	0	0	0-...	47.0	50	31	29	10	16-0	53
1999—	Erie (East.)	9	4	.692	2.82	15	15	2	•2	0-...	102.0	88	38	32	12	40-0	86
	—Edmonton (PCL)	5	3	.625	4.05	9	9	0	0	0-...	53.1	46	26	24	7	19-0	64
	—Anaheim (A.L.)	2	3	.400	6.52	9	9	0	0	0-0	48.1	50	35	35	7	25-0	44
2000—	Lake Elsinore (Calif.)	1	0	1.000	3.00	1	1	0	0	0-...	6.0	8	2	2	0	2-0	7
	—Anaheim (A.L.)	8	6	.571	5.09	18	18	2	0	0-0	111.1	96	69	63	18	55-0	73
	—Edmonton (PCL)	6	6	.500	4.55	15	15	1	0	0-...	89.0	74	49	45	7	37-0	76
2001—	Anaheim (A.L.)	13	11	.542	4.36	32	32	2	0	0-0	208.2	223	114	101	25	76-6	135
2002—	Anaheim (A.L.)	15	9	.625	3.77	32	32	4	1	0-0	217.1	188	97	91	*40	68-0	162
Major League totals (4 years).....		38	29	.567	4.46	91	91	8	1	0-0	585.2	557	315	290	90	224-6	414

O

DIVISION SERIES RECORD

Year	League	W	L	Pct.	ERA	G	GS	CG	ShO	Sv.-Opp.	IP	H	R	ER	HR	BB-IBB	SO
2002—	Anaheim (A.L.)	0	0	...	20.25	1	1	0	0	0-0	2.2	3	6	6	0	4-0	1

CHAMPIONSHIP SERIES RECORD

Year	League	W	L	Pct.	ERA	G	GS	CG	ShO	Sv.-Opp.	IP	H	R	ER	HR	BB-IBB	SO
2002—	Anaheim (A.L.)	1	0	1.000	5.06	1	1	0	0	0-0	5.1	10	3	3	0	1-0	3

WORLD SERIES RECORD

NOTES: Member of World Series championship team (2002).

Year	League	W	L	Pct.	ERA	G	GS	CG	ShO	Sv.-Opp.	IP	H	R	ER	HR	BB-IBB	SO
2002—	Anaheim (A.L.)	1	0	1.000	7.20	1	1	0	0	0-0	5.0	5	4	4	2	4-1	3

ORTIZ, RUSS — P — GIANTS

PERSONAL: Born June 5, 1974, in Encino, Calif. ... 6-1/208. ... Throws right, bats right. ... Full name: Russell Reid Ortiz.
HIGH SCHOOL: Montclair Prep (Van Nuys, Calif.).
COLLEGE: Oklahoma.
TRANSACTIONS/CAREER NOTES: Selected by San Francisco Giants organization in fourth round of free-agent draft (June 1, 1995).
RECORDS: Shares N.L. single-inning record for most consecutive home runs allowed—3 (August 10, 1998, fifth inning).
CAREER HITTING (MLB): 63-for-293 (.215), 34 R, 15 2B, 0 3B, 4 HR, 30 RBI.

Year	League	W	L	Pct.	ERA	G	GS	CG	ShO	Sv.-Opp.	IP	H	R	ER	HR	BB-IBB	SO
1995—	Bellingham (N'West)	2	0	1.000	0.52	25	0	0	0	11-...	34.1	19	4	2	1	13-0	55
—	San Jose (Calif.)	0	1	.000	1.50	5	0	0	0	0-...	6.0	4	1	1	0	2-0	7
1996—	San Jose (Calif.)	0	0	...	0.25	34	0	0	0	23-...	36.2	16	2	1	0	20-0	63
—	Shreveport (Texas)	1	2	.333	4.05	26	0	0	0	13-...	26.2	22	14	12	0	21-3	29
1997—	Shreveport (Texas)	2	3	.400	4.13	12	12	0	0	0-...	56.2	52	28	26	3	37-0	50
—	Phoenix (PCL)	4	3	.571	5.51	14	14	0	0	0-...	85.0	96	57	52	11	34-0	70
1998—	San Francisco (N.L.)	4	4	.500	4.99	22	13	0	0	0-0	88.1	90	51	49	11	46-1	75
—	Fresno (PCL)	3	1	.750	1.60	10	10	0	0	0-...	50.2	35	10	9	3	22-0	59
1999—	San Francisco (N.L.)	18	9	.667	3.81	33	33	3	0	0-0	207.2	189	109	88	24	*125-5	164
2000—	San Francisco (N.L.)	14	12	.538	5.01	33	32	0	0	0-0	195.2	192	117	109	28	112-1	167
2001—	San Francisco (N.L.)	17	9	.654	3.29	33	33	1	1	0-0	218.2	187	90	80	13	91-3	169
2002—	San Francisco (N.L.)	14	10	.583	3.61	33	33	2	0	0-0	214.1	191	89	86	15	94-5	137
Major League totals (5 years)		67	44	.604	4.01	154	144	6	1	0-0	924.2	849	456	412	91	468-15	712

DIVISION SERIES RECORD

Year	League	W	L	Pct.	ERA	G	GS	CG	ShO	Sv.-Opp.	IP	H	R	ER	HR	BB-IBB	SO
2000—	San Francisco (N.L.)	0	0	...	1.69	1	1	0	0	0-0	5.1	2	1	1	0	4-1	4
2002—	San Francisco (N.L.)	2	0	1.000	2.19	2	2	0	0	0-0	12.1	9	3	3	0	8-1	8
Division series totals (2 years)		2	0	1.000	2.04	3	3	0	0	0-0	17.2	11	4	4	0	12-2	12

CHAMPIONSHIP SERIES RECORD

Year	League	W	L	Pct.	ERA	G	GS	CG	ShO	Sv.-Opp.	IP	H	R	ER	HR	BB-IBB	SO
2002—	San Francisco (N.L.)	0	0	...	7.71	1	1	0	0	0-0	4.2	5	4	4	2	3-0	3

WORLD SERIES RECORD

Year	League	W	L	Pct.	ERA	G	GS	CG	ShO	Sv.-Opp.	IP	H	R	ER	HR	BB-IBB	SO
2002—	San Francisco (N.L.)	0	0	...	10.13	2	2	0	0	0-0	8.0	13	9	9	1	2-0	2

OSBORNE, DONOVAN — P

PERSONAL: Born June 21, 1969, in Roseville, Calif. ... 6-2/210. ... Throws left, bats left. ... Full name: Donovan Alan Osborne.
HIGH SCHOOL: Carson City (Nev.).
COLLEGE: UNLV.
TRANSACTIONS/CAREER NOTES: Selected by Montreal Expos organization in ninth round of free-agent draft (June 2, 1987); did not sign. ... Selected by St. Louis Cardinals organization in first round (13th pick overall) of free-agent draft (June 4, 1990). ... On St. Louis disabled list (April 2, 1994-entire season). ... On St. Louis disabled list (May 15-July 14, 1995); included rehabilitation assignments to Arkansas and Louisville (June 28-July 14). ... On St. Louis disabled list (March 25-April 17, 1996); included rehabilitation assignments to St. Petersburg (April 7-12) and Louisville (April 12-17). ... On St. Louis disabled list (May 3-July 29, 1997). ... On St. Louis disabled list (March 22-April 16 and May 8-August 8, 1998); included rehabilitation assignments to Arkansas (April 6-10, April 12-16 and July 17-August 1) and Memphis (April 11). ... On disabled list (May 7, 1999-remainder of season). ... Granted free agency (November 3, 1999). ... Signed by Chicago Cubs organization (February 5, 2002). ... On disabled list (May 8-September 2, 2002). ... Released by Cubs (September 2, 2002).
HONORS: Named lefthanded pitcher on The Sporting News college All-America team (1989).
STATISTICAL NOTES: Career major league grand slams: 1.
MISCELLANEOUS: Appeared in three games as pinch runner (1993).
CAREER HITTING (MLB): 42-for-259 (.162), 18 R, 10 2B, 1 3B, 1 HR, 19 RBI.

Year	League	W	L	Pct.	ERA	G	GS	CG	ShO	Sv.-Opp.	IP	H	R	ER	HR	BB-IBB	SO
1990—	Hamilton (NY-Penn)	0	2	.000	3.60	4	4	0	0	0-...	20.0	21	8	8	0	5-1	14
—	Savannah (S.Atl.)	2	2	.500	2.61	6	6	1	0	0-...	41.1	40	20	12	2	7-0	28
1991—	Arkansas (Texas)	8	12	.400	3.63	26	26	3	0	0-...	166.0	178	82	67	6	43-3	130
1992—	St. Louis (N.L.)	11	9	.550	3.77	34	29	0	0	0-0	179.0	193	91	75	14	38-2	104
1993—	St. Louis (N.L.)	10	7	.588	3.76	26	26	1	0	0-0	155.2	153	73	65	18	47-4	83
1994—	St. Louis (N.L.)									Did not play.							
1995—	St. Louis (N.L.)	4	6	.400	3.81	19	19	0	0	0-0	113.1	112	58	48	17	34-2	82
—	Arkansas (Texas)	0	1	.000	2.45	2	2	0	0	0-...	11.0	12	4	3	0	2-0	6
—	Louisville (A.A.)	0	1	.000	3.86	1	1	0	0	0-...	7.0	8	3	3	0	0-0	3
1996—	St. Petersburg (FSL)	1	0	1.000	0.00	1	1	0	0	0-...	6.0	2	0	0	0	0-0	2
—	Louisville (A.A.)	1	0	1.000	2.57	1	1	0	0	0-...	7.0	6	2	2	1	2-0	3
—	St. Louis (N.L.)	13	9	.591	3.53	30	30	2	1	0-0	198.2	191	87	78	22	57-5	134
1997—	St. Louis (N.L.)	3	7	.300	4.93	14	14	0	0	0-0	80.1	84	46	44	10	23-2	51
—	Louisville (A.A.)	0	1	.000	4.72	3	3	0	0	0-...	13.1	13	7	7	2	5-1	13

Year	League	W	L	Pct.	ERA	G	GS	CG	ShO	Sv.-Opp.	IP	H	R	ER	HR	BB-IBB	SO
1998—	Arkansas (Texas)	2	0	1.000	4.26	5	5	0	0	0-...	19.0	16	9	9	2	3-0	21
—	Memphis (PCL)	0	0	...	6.23	1	1	0	0	0-...	4.1	5	4	3	2	0-0	6
—	St. Louis (N.L.)	5	4	.556	4.09	14	14	1	1	0-0	83.2	84	42	38	11	22-2	60
1999—	St. Louis (N.L.)	1	3	.250	5.52	6	6	0	0	0-0	29.1	34	18	18	4	10-0	21
2000—										Did not play.							
2001—										Did not play.							
2002—	Chicago (N.L.)■	0	1	.000	6.19	11	0	0	0	0-0	16.0	19	11	11	1	10-2	13
Major League totals (8 years)		47	46	.505	3.96	154	138	4	2	0-0	856.0	870	426	377	97	241-19	548

DIVISION SERIES RECORD

Year	League	W	L	Pct.	ERA	G	GS	CG	ShO	Sv.-Opp.	IP	H	R	ER	HR	BB-IBB	SO
1996—	St. Louis (N.L.)	0	0	...	9.00	1	1	0	0	0-0	4.0	7	4	4	1	0-0	5

CHAMPIONSHIP SERIES RECORD

Year	League	W	L	Pct.	ERA	G	GS	CG	ShO	Sv.-Opp.	IP	H	R	ER	HR	BB-IBB	SO
1996—	St. Louis (N.L.)	1	1	.500	9.39	2	2	0	0	0-0	7.2	12	8	8	0	4-0	6

OSIK, KEITH — C

PERSONAL: Born October 22, 1968, in Port Jefferson, N.Y. ... 6-0/200. ... Bats right, throws right. ... Full name: Keith Richard Osik. ... Name pronounced OH-sik.

HIGH SCHOOL: Shoreham (N.Y.)-Wading River.

COLLEGE: Louisiana State.

TRANSACTIONS/CAREER NOTES: Selected by Texas Rangers organization in 47th round of free-agent draft (June 2, 1987); did not sign. ... Selected by Pittsburgh Pirates organization in 24th round of free-agent draft (June 4, 1990). ... On Pittsburgh disabled list (July 16-August 13, 1996); included rehabilitation assignment to Erie (August 10-13). ... On Pittsburgh disabled list (July 21-August 13, 1999); included rehabilitation assignment to Nashville (August 9-13). ... On disabled list (April 30-May 15, 2001). ... Granted free agency (October 28, 2002).

2002 GAMES PLAYED BY POSITION (MLB): C—27; 3B—4; 1B—3; 2B—1; OF—1.

			BATTING													FIELDING	
Year	Team (League)	Pos.	G	AB	R	H	2B	3B	HR	RBI	BB	SO	SB-CS	Avg.	OBP	SLG	E	Avg.
1990—	Welland (NY-Penn)	3-C-1-2-S	29	97	13	27	4	0	1	20	11	12	2-6	.278	.354	.351	2	.978
1991—	Salem (Caro.)	C-3B-2B	87	300	31	81	12	1	6	35	38	48	2-3	.270	.356	.377	12	.970
—	Carolina (Sou.)	C-3B	17	43	9	13	3	1	0	5	5	5	0-0	.302	.375	.419	2	.980
1992—	Carolina (Sou.)	3B-C-2B-P	129	425	41	110	17	1	5	45	52	69	2-9	.259	.357	.339	19	.956
1993—	Carolina (Sou.)	C-3B-DH	103	371	47	104	21	2	10	47	30	46	0-2	.280	.348	.429	6	.992
1994—	Buffalo (A.A.)	C-O-1-DH-P-2	83	260	27	55	16	0	5	33	28	41	0-1	.212	.294	.331	8	.983
1995—	Calgary (PCL)	C-1B-OF-P-3B	90	301	40	101	25	1	10	59	21	42	2-2	.336	.384	.525	4	.992
1996—	Pittsburgh (N.L.)	C-3B-OF	48	140	18	41	14	1	1	14	14	22	1-0	.293	.361	.429	6	.978
—	Erie (NY-Penn)	C	3	10	1	3	1	0	0	2	1	2	0-0	.300	.417	.400	0	1.000
1997—	Pittsburgh (N.L.)	C-2B-1B-3B	49	105	10	27	9	1	0	7	9	21	0-1	.257	.322	.362	2	.989
1998—	Pittsburgh (N.L.)	C-3B	39	98	8	21	4	0	0	7	13	16	1-2	.214	.316	.255	1	.995
1999—	Pittsburgh (N.L.)	C-P	66	167	12	31	3	1	2	13	11	30	0-0	.186	.239	.251	1	.997
—	Nashville (PCL)	C-OF	4	11	0	1	0	0	0	0	0	1	0-0	.091	.167	.091	0	1.000
2000—	Pittsburgh (N.L.)	C-3B-1B-DH-P	46	123	11	36	6	1	4	22	14	11	3-0	.293	.387	.455	2	.989
2001—	Pittsburgh (N.L.)	C-1-3-2-O	56	120	9	25	4	0	2	13	13	24	1-0	.208	.299	.292	1	.996
2002—	Pittsburgh (N.L.)	C-3-1-2-O	55	100	6	16	3	0	2	11	6	25	0-0	.160	.211	.250	1	.994
Major League totals (7 years)			359	853	74	197	43	4	11	87	80	149	6-3	.231	.306	.329	14	.991

RECORD AS PITCHER

Year	League	W	L	Pct.	ERA	G	GS	CG	ShO	Sv.-Opp.	IP	H	R	ER	HR	BB-IBB	SO
1992—	Carolina (Sou.)	0	0	...	0.00	2	0	0	0	0-...	2.2	2	0	0	0	0-0	3
1994—	Buffalo (A.A.)	0	1	.000	13.50	1	0	0	0	0-...	.2	2	1	1	0	0-0	1
1995—	Calgary (PCL)	0	0	...	4.50	2	0	0	0	0-...	2.0	1	1	1	1	1-0	3
1999—	Pittsburgh (N.L.)	0	0	...	36.00	1	0	0	0	0-0	1.0	2	4	4	0	2-0	1
2000—	Pittsburgh (N.L.)	0	0	...	45.00	1	0	0	0	0-0	1.0	5	5	5	1	0-0	1
Major League totals (2 years)		0	0	...	40.50	2	0	0	0	0-0	2.0	7	9	9	1	2-0	2

OSTING, JIMMY — P

PERSONAL: Born April 7, 1977, in Louisville, Ky. ... 6-5/190. ... Throws left, bats right. ... Full name: James Michael Osting.

HIGH SCHOOL: Trinity (Louisville, Ky.).

TRANSACTIONS/CAREER NOTES: Selected by Atlanta Braves in fourth round of free-agent draft (June 1, 1995). ... On disabled list (April 2, 1998-entire season). ... Traded by Braves with P Bruce Chen to Philadelphia Phillies for P Andy Ashby (July 12, 2000). ... Claimed on waivers by Colorado Rockies (April 4, 2001). ... Claimed on waivers by San Diego Padres (April 11, 2001). ... Granted free agency (October 15, 2001). ... Signed by Milwaukee Brewers organization (November 20, 2001). ... On Milwaukee disabled list (July 24-August 16, 2002); included rehabilitation assignment to Indianapolis (August 14-15). ... Released by Brewers (September 30, 2002).

CAREER HITTING (MLB): 0-for-3 (.000), 0 R, 0 2B, 0 3B, 0 HR, 0 RBI.

Year	League	W	L	Pct.	ERA	G	GS	CG	ShO	Sv.-Opp.	IP	H	R	ER	HR	BB-IBB	SO
1995—	Danville (Appl.)	2	7	.222	7.15	11	10	0	0	0-...	39.0	46	34	31	1	25-0	43
1996—	Eugene (N'West)	2	1	.667	2.59	5	5	0	0	0-...	24.1	14	11	7	1	13-0	35
1997—	Macon (S.Atl.)	2	3	.400	3.28	15	15	0	0	0-...	57.2	54	28	21	3	29-0	62
1998—										Did not play.							
1999—	Macon (S.Atl.)	*14	4	.778	2.88	27	22	0	0	2-...	147.0	130	52	47	13	30-0	131
2000—	Myrtle Beach (Caro.)	2	2	.500	3.13	4	4	0	0	0-...	23.0	25	8	8	0	5-0	17
—	Greenville (Sou.)	2	6	.250	2.65	11	11	0	0	0-...	71.1	67	30	21	6	29-1	52
—	Richmond (I.L.)	0	2	.000	11.57	3	3	0	0	0-...	9.1	15	12	12	2	11-1	2
—	Reading (East.)■	4	2	.667	2.38	10	9	1	1	0-...	56.2	53	17	15	1	26-2	31
2001—	Carolina (Sou.)■	1	0	1.000	1.80	1	1	0	0	0-...	5.0	3	1	1	1	3-0	3
—	Mobile (Sou.)■	9	4	.692	3.59	18	18	0	0	0-...	97.2	85	41	39	6	42-1	69
—	San Diego (N.L.)	0	0	...	0.00	3	0	0	0	0-0	2.0	1	0	0	0	2-1	3
—	Portland (PCL)	1	4	.200	9.59	5	5	0	0	0-...	25.1	41	27	27	5	10-0	15
2002—	Indianapolis (I.L.)■	5	7	.417	3.48	22	22	3	1	0-...	126.2	115	52	49	7	38-1	112
—	Milwaukee (N.L.)	0	2	.000	7.50	3	3	0	0	0-0	12.0	18	11	10	3	10-0	7
Major League totals (2 years)		0	2	.000	6.43	6	3	0	0	0-0	14.0	19	11	10	3	12-1	10

OSUNA, ANTONIO — P — WHITE SOX

PERSONAL: Born April 12, 1973, in Sinaloa, Mexico. ... 5-11/205. ... Throws right, bats right. ... Full name: Antonio Pedro Osuna.
HIGH SCHOOL: Secondaria Federal (Mexico).
TRANSACTIONS/CAREER NOTES: Signed as non-drafted free agent by Los Angeles Dodgers organization (June 12, 1991). ... Loaned by Dodgers to Mexico City Tigres, Mexican League (March 6-September 25, 1992). ... On suspended list (April 8-July 17, 1993). ... On San Antonio disabled list (April 8-June 6, 1994). ... On Los Angeles disabled list (May 19-June 16, 1995); included rehabilitation assignment to San Bernardino (June 6-16). ... On disabled list (September 9, 1998-remainder of season). ... On Los Angeles disabled list (March 25-April 16, April 18-May 3 and May 19, 1999-remainder of season); included rehabilitation assignments to San Bernardino (April 10-16, April 25-May 3, July 7-15 and September 1-29). ... On Los Angeles disabled list (March 31-May 5, 2000); included rehabilitation assignment to San Bernardino (April 8-May 5). ... Traded by Dodgers with P Carlos Ortega to Chicago White Sox for P Gary Majewski, P Andre Simpson and P Orlando Rodriguez (March 17, 2001). ... On disabled list (April 12, 2001-remainder of season).
CAREER HITTING (MLB): 1-for-9 (.111), 0 R, 0 2B, 0 3B, 0 HR, 1 RBI.

Year League	W	L	Pct.	ERA	G	GS	CG	ShO	Sv.-Opp.	IP	H	R	ER	HR	BB-IBB	SO
1991— Gulf Coast Dodgers (GCL)	0	0	...	0.82	8	0	0	0	4-...	11.0	8	5	1	0	0-0	13
— Yakima (N'West)	0	0	...	3.20	13	0	0	0	5-...	25.1	18	10	9	1	8-0	39
1992— MC Tigres (Mex.)■	13	7	.650	4.05	28	26	3	1	0-...	166.2	181	80	75	16	74-2	129
1993— Bakersfield (Calif.)■	0	2	.000	4.91	14	2	0	0	2-...	18.1	19	10	10	2	5-0	20
1994— San Antonio (Texas)	1	2	.333	0.98	35	0	0	0	19-...	46.0	19	6	5	0	18-1	53
— Albuquerque (PCL)	0	0	...	0.00	6	0	0	0	4-...	6.0	5	1	0	0	1-0	8
1995— Los Angeles (N.L.)	2	4	.333	4.43	39	0	0	0	0-2	44.2	39	22	22	5	20-2	46
— San Bernardino (Calif.)	0	0	...	1.29	5	0	0	0	0-...	7.0	3	1	1	1	5-0	11
— Albuquerque (PCL)	0	1	.000	4.42	19	0	0	0	11-...	18.1	15	9	9	2	9-0	19
1996— Albuquerque (PCL)	0	0	...	0.00	1	0	0	0	0-...	1.0	2	0	0	0	0-0	1
— Los Angeles (N.L.)	9	6	.600	3.00	73	0	0	0	4-9	84.0	65	33	28	6	32-12	85
1997— Albuquerque (PCL)	1	1	.500	1.93	13	0	0	0	6-...	14.0	9	3	3	0	4-0	26
— Los Angeles (N.L.)	3	4	.429	2.19	48	0	0	0	0-0	61.2	46	15	15	6	19-2	68
1998— Los Angeles (N.L.)	7	1	.875	3.06	54	0	0	0	6-11	64.2	50	26	22	8	32-0	72
1999— San Bernardino (Calif.)	0	0	...	2.33	13	4	0	0	0-...	19.1	19	6	5	0	6-0	27
— Los Angeles (N.L.)	0	0	...	7.71	5	0	0	0	0-0	4.2	4	5	4	0	3-0	5
2000— San Bernardino (Calif.)	0	2	.000	4.91	3	3	0	0	0-...	7.1	4	4	4	2	3-0	11
— Albuquerque (PCL)	0	0	...	0.00	3	1	0	0	0-...	5.2	2	2	0	0	5-0	7
— Los Angeles (N.L.)	3	6	.333	3.74	46	0	0	0	0-3	67.1	57	30	28	7	35-2	70
2001— Chicago (A.L.)■	0	0	...	20.77	4	0	0	0	0-1	4.1	8	10	10	3	2-1	6
2002— Chicago (A.L.)	8	2	.800	3.86	59	0	0	0	11-14	67.2	64	32	29	1	28-4	66
A.L. totals (2 years)	8	2	.800	4.88	63	0	0	0	11-15	72.0	72	42	39	4	30-5	72
N.L. totals (6 years)	24	21	.533	3.28	265	0	0	0	10-25	327.0	261	131	119	32	141-18	346
Major League totals (8 years)	32	23	.582	3.56	328	0	0	0	21-40	399.0	333	173	158	36	171-23	418

DIVISION SERIES RECORD

Year League	W	L	Pct.	ERA	G	GS	CG	ShO	Sv.-Opp.	IP	H	R	ER	HR	BB-IBB	SO
1995— Los Angeles (N.L.)	0	1	.000	2.70	3	0	0	0	0-0	3.1	3	1	1	0	1-1	3
1996— Los Angeles (N.L.)	0	1	.000	4.50	2	0	0	0	0-0	2.0	3	1	1	1	1-0	4
Division series totals (2 years)	0	2	.000	3.38	5	0	0	0	0-0	5.1	6	2	2	1	2-1	7

OSWALT, ROY — P — ASTROS

PERSONAL: Born August 29, 1977, in Kosciusko, Miss. ... 6-0/175. ... Throws right, bats right. ... Full name: Roy Edward Oswalt. ... Name pronounced OZE-walt.
HIGH SCHOOL: Weir (Miss.).
JUNIOR COLLEGE: Holmes Community College (Miss.).
TRANSACTIONS/CAREER NOTES: Selected by Houston Astros organization in 23rd round of free-agent draft (June 4, 1996). ... On suspended list (August 29-September 3, 2002).
HONORS: Named N.L. Rookie Pitcher of the Year by The Sporting News (2001).
MISCELLANEOUS: Member of 2000 U.S. Olympic baseball team.
CAREER HITTING (MLB): 19-for-124 (.153), 8 R, 3 2B, 0 3B, 0 HR, 7 RBI.

Year League	W	L	Pct.	ERA	G	GS	CG	ShO	Sv.-Opp.	IP	H	R	ER	HR	BB-IBB	SO
1997— Gulf Coast Astros (GCL)	1	1	.500	0.64	5	5	0	0	0-...	28.1	25	7	2	2	7-0	28
— Auburn (NY-Penn)	2	4	.333	4.53	9	9	1	1	0-...	51.2	50	29	26	1	15-1	44
1998— Gulf Coast Astros (GCL)	1	1	.500	2.25	4	4	0	0	0-...	16.0	10	6	4	2	1-0	27
— Auburn (NY-Penn)	4	5	.444	2.18	11	11	0	0	0-...	70.1	49	24	17	3	31-0	67
1999— Michigan (Midw.)	13	4	.765	4.46	22	22	2	0	0-...	151.1	144	78	75	8	54-0	143
2000— Kissimmee (FSL)	4	3	.571	2.98	8	8	0	0	0-...	45.1	52	15	15	1	11-0	47
— Round Rock (Texas)	11	4	.733	1.94	19	18	2	2	0-...	129.2	106	37	28	5	22-1	141
2001— New Orleans (PCL)	2	3	.400	4.35	5	5	0	0	0-...	31.0	32	16	15	4	6-0	34
— Houston (N.L.)	14	3	.824	2.73	28	20	3	1	0-0	141.2	126	48	43	13	24-2	144
2002— Houston (N.L.)	19	9	.679	3.01	35	34	0	0	0-0	233.0	215	86	78	17	62-4	208
Major League totals (2 years)	33	12	.733	2.91	63	54	3	1	0-0	374.2	341	134	121	30	86-6	352

OVERBAY, LYLE — 1B — DIAMONDBACKS

PERSONAL: Born January 28, 1977, in Centralia, Wash. ... 6-2/215. ... Bats left, throws left. ... Full name: Lyle Stefan Overbay.
COLLEGE: Nevada.
TRANSACTIONS/CAREER NOTES: Selected by Arizona Diamondbacks organization in 18th round of free-agent draft (June 2, 1999).
HONORS: Named Pioneer League Most Valuable Player (1999).
STATISTICAL NOTES: Led Pioneer League with 180 total bases and grounding into double plays with 14 in 1999. ... Led Pioneer League first baseman with 697 total chances, 641 putouts and .986 fielding percentage in 1999. ... Tied for Texas League lead with eight sacrifice flies and 11 intentional bases on balls received in 2001. ... Led Pacific Coast League first basemen with 87 assists in 2002.

			BATTING														FIELDING	
Year	Team (League)	Pos.	G	AB	R	H	2B	3B	HR	RBI	BB	SO	SB-CS	Avg.	OBP	SLG	E	Avg.
1999	Missoula (Pio.)	1B-OF	75	*306	66	*105	25	7	12	*101	40	53	10-3	.343	.418	.588	10	†.986
2000	South Bend (Midw.)	1B	71	259	47	86	19	3	6	47	27	36	9-2	.332	.397	.498	11	.983
	El Paso (Texas)	1B	62	244	43	86	16	2	8	49	28	39	3-2	.352	.420	.533	12	.979
2001	El Paso (Texas)	1B-OF	*138	*532	82	*187	*49	3	13	100	67	92	5-4	*.352	*.423	.528	13	.987
	Arizona (N.L.)	PH	2	2	0	1	0	0	0	0	0	1	0-0	.500	.500	.500	...	...
2002	Tucson (PCL)	1B	134	525	83	180	*40	0	19	109	42	86	0-0	.343	.396	.528	10	.991
	Arizona (N.L.)	PH	10	10	0	1	0	0	0	1	0	5	0-0	.100	.100	.100	0	...
Major League totals (2 years)			12	12	0	2	0	0	0	1	0	6	0-0	.167	.167	.167	0	...

OWENS, ERIC — OF — MARLINS

PERSONAL: Born February 3, 1971, in Danville, Va. ... 6-0/208. ... Bats right, throws right. ... Full name: Eric Blake Owens.

HIGH SCHOOL: Tunstall (Dry Fork, Va.).

COLLEGE: Ferrum (Va.).

TRANSACTIONS/CAREER NOTES: Selected by Cincinnati Reds organization in fourth round of free-agent draft (June 1, 1992). ... On Indianapolis disabled list (August 20-September 11, 1995). ... Traded by Reds to Florida Marlins for a player to be named later (March 21, 1998); Reds acquired P Jesus Martinez to complete deal (March 26, 1998). ... Contract sold by Marlins to Milwaukee Brewers (March 25, 1998). ... Granted free agency (October 15, 1998). ... Signed by San Diego Padres organization (December 10, 1998). ... Traded by Padres with P Matt Clement and P Omar Ortiz to Marlins for OF Mark Kotsay and OF Cesar Crespo (March 28, 2001). ... On Florida disabled list (August 2-22, 2001); included rehabilitation assignment to Calgary (August 19-22).

HONORS: Named American Association Most Valuable Player (1995).

STATISTICAL NOTES: Tied for Pioneer League lead in errors by shortstops with 28 in 1992. ... Led Carolina League shortstops with 215 putouts in 1993. ... Tied for American Association lead in errors by second baseman with 17 in 1997. ... Had 18-game hitting streak (June 17-July 6, 1999). ... Led N.L. outfielders with 1.000 fielding percentage in 2000.

2002 GAMES PLAYED BY POSITION (MLB): OF—121.

			BATTING														FIELDING	
Year	Team (League)	Pos.	G	AB	R	H	2B	3B	HR	RBI	BB	SO	SB-CS	Avg.	OBP	SLG	E	Avg.
1992	Billings (Pio.)	SS-3B	67	239	41	72	10	3	3	26	23	22	15-4	.301	.363	.406	‡29	.895
1993	Win.-Salem (Caro.)	SS	122	487	74	132	25	4	10	63	53	69	21-12	.271	.343	.400	34	.943
1994	Chattanooga (Sou.)	3B-2B	134	523	73	133	17	3	3	36	54	86	38-14	.254	.325	.315	40	.912
1995	Indianapolis (A.A.)	2B	108	427	*86	134	24	•8	12	63	52	61	*33-12	.314	.388	.492	*17	.967
	Cincinnati (N.L.)	3B	2	2	0	2	0	0	0	1	0	0	0-0	1.000	1.000	1.000	0	...
1996	Cincinnati (N.L.)	OF-2B-3B	88	205	26	41	6	0	0	9	23	38	16-2	.200	.281	.229	2	.978
	Indianapolis (A.A.)	SS-3B-2B-OF	33	128	24	41	8	2	4	14	11	16	6-3	.320	.379	.508	6	.947
1997	Cincinnati (N.L.)	OF-2B	27	57	8	15	0	0	0	3	4	11	3-2	.263	.311	.263	1	.938
	Indianapolis (A.A.)	2-S-O-3	104	391	56	112	15	4	11	44	42	55	23-10	.286	.357	.430	‡27	.940
1998	Milwaukee (N.L.)■	OF-2B	34	40	5	5	2	0	1	4	2	6	0-0	.125	.167	.250	1	.941
	Louisville (I.L.)	OF-3B-DH	77	254	48	85	11	4	5	40	34	30	21-6	.335	.408	.469	8	.947
1999	San Diego (N.L.)■	OF-1B-3B-2B	149	440	55	117	22	3	9	61	38	50	33-7	.266	.327	.391	4	.986
2000	San Diego (N.L.)	OF-2B	145	583	87	171	19	7	6	51	45	63	29-14	.293	.346	.381	0	†1.000
2001	Florida (N.L.)■	OF-DH	119	400	51	101	16	1	5	28	29	59	8-6	.253	.302	.335	3	.984
	Calgary (PCL)	OF	3	15	2	4	2	0	0	2	0	2	1-0	.267	.267	.400	1	.667
2002	Florida (N.L.)	OF	131	385	44	104	15	5	4	37	31	33	26-9	.270	.324	.366	6	.975
Major League totals (8 years)			695	2112	276	556	80	16	25	194	172	260	115-40	.263	.320	.352	17	.985

OZUNA, PABLO — SS — MARLINS

PERSONAL: Born August 25, 1974, in Santo Domingo, Dominican Republic. ... 6-0/160. ... Bats right, throws right. ... Full name: Pablo Jose Ozuna.

TRANSACTIONS/CAREER NOTES: Signed as non-drafted free agent by St. Louis Cardinals orgnaization (April 8, 1996). ... Traded by Cardinals with P Braden Looper and P Armando Almanza to Florida Marlins for SS Edgar Renteria (December 14, 1998). ... On disabled list (March 23, 2001-entire season).

HONORS: Named Midwest League Most Valuable Player (1998).

STATISTICAL NOTES: Tied for Appalachian League lead in sacrifice hits with six in 1997. ... Led Midwest League with 26 caught stealing. ... Led Midwest League shortstops with 395 assists and tied for league lead with 80 double plays in 1998. ... Led Eastern League with 24 caught stealing in 2000. ... Led Eastern League second basemen with 242 putouts in 2000.

2002 GAMES PLAYED BY POSITION (MLB): 2B—10; OF—1.

			BATTING														FIELDING	
Year	Team (League)	Pos.	G	AB	R	H	2B	3B	HR	RBI	BB	SO	SB-CS	Avg.	OBP	SLG	E	Avg.
1996	Dom. Cardinals (DSL)	SS	74	295	57	107	12	4	6	60	23	19	19-...	.363	...	.492	32	.915
1997	Johnson City (Appl.)	SS	56	232	40	75	13	1	5	24	10	24	23-5	.323	.351	.453	25	.898
1998	Peoria (Midw.)	SS	133	538	*122	*192	27	10	9	62	29	56	62-26	*.357	.400	.494	45	.929
1999	Portland (East.)■	SS	117	502	62	141	25	7	7	46	13	50	31-15	.281	.315	.400	28	.946
2000	Portland (East.)	2B	118	464	74	143	25	6	7	59	40	55	35-24	.308	.368	.433	*25	.956
	Florida (N.L.)	2B	14	24	2	8	1	0	0	0	0	2	1-0	.333	.333	.375	1	.967
2001	Florida (N.L.)		Did not play.															
2002	Calgary (PCL)	2B-OF	77	261	37	85	16	1	7	33	17	37	16-3	.326	.371	.475	9	.961
	Florida (N.L.)	2B-OF	34	47	4	13	2	2	0	3	1	3	1-1	.277	.300	.404	1	.967
Major League totals (2 years)			48	71	6	21	3	2	0	3	1	5	2-1	.296	.311	.394	2	.967

PADILLA, JORGE — OF — PHILLIES

PERSONAL: Born August 11, 1979, in Rio Piedras, Puerto Rico. ... 6-2/200. ... Bats right, throws right. ... Full name: Jorge R. Padilla.

HIGH SCHOOL: Florida Air Academy (Melbourne, Fla.).

TRANSACTIONS/CAREER NOTES: Selected by Philadelphia Phillies organization in third round of free-agent draft (June 2, 1998). ... On disabled list (August 6-21, 2000). ... On disabled list (April 30-May 19 and June 8-23, 2001).
STATISTICAL NOTES: Tied for New York-Pennsylvania League lead in double plays by outfielder with three in 1999.

			BATTING														FIELDING	
Year	Team (League)	Pos.	G	AB	R	H	2B	3B	HR	RBI	BB	SO	SB-CS	Avg.	OBP	SLG	E	Avg.
1998—	Martinsville (Appl.)	OF	23	90	10	32	3	0	5	25	4	24	2-0	.356	.378	.556	2	.955
1999—	Piedmont (S.Atl.)	OF	44	168	13	35	10	1	3	17	5	44	0-0	.208	.247	.333	3	.963
—	Batavia (NY-Penn)	OF	65	238	28	60	10	1	3	30	22	79	2-1	.252	.331	.340	6	.955
2000—	Piedmont (S.Atl.)	OF	108	413	62	126	24	8	11	67	26	89	8-4	.305	.346	.482	5	.976
2001—	Clearwater (FSL)	OF	100	358	62	93	13	2	16	66	40	73	23-6	.260	.343	.441	3	.983
2002—	Reading (East.)	OF	127	484	71	124	30	2	7	65	40	77	32-11	.256	.322	.370	8	.971

PADILLA, VICENTE — P — PHILLIES

PERSONAL: Born September 27, 1977, in Chinandoga, Nicaragua. ... 6-2/200. ... Throws right, bats right. ... Full name: Vicente D. Padilla.
HIGH SCHOOL: Ruben Dario (Nicaragua).
TRANSACTIONS/CAREER NOTES: Signed as non-drafted free agent by Arizona Diamondbacks organization (August 31, 1998). ... Traded by Diamondbacks with OF Travis Lee, P Omar Daal and P Nelson Figueroa to Philadelphia Phillies for P Curt Schilling (July 26, 2000). ... On Philadelphia disabled list (May 4-30, 2001); included rehabilitation assignment to Scranton/Wilkes-Barre (May 22-30).
CAREER HITTING (MLB): 5-for-62 (.081), 2 R, 2 2B, 0 3B, 0 HR, 5 RBI.

Year	League	W	L	Pct.	ERA	G	GS	CG	ShO	Sv.-Opp.	IP	H	R	ER	HR	BB-IBB	SO
1999—	High Desert (Calif.)	4	1	.800	3.73	9	9	0	0	0-...	50.2	50	27	21	3	17-0	55
—	Tucson (PCL)	7	4	.636	3.75	18	14	0	0	0-...	93.2	107	47	39	6	24-7	58
—	Arizona (N.L.)	0	1	.000	16.88	5	0	0	0	0-1	2.2	7	5	5	1	3-0	0
2000—	Tucson (PCL)	0	1	.000	4.42	12	3	0	0	1-...	18.1	22	9	9	2	8-0	22
—	Arizona (N.L.)	2	1	.667	2.31	27	0	0	0	0-1	35.0	32	10	9	0	10-2	30
—	Philadelphia (N.L.)■	2	6	.250	5.34	28	0	0	0	2-6	30.1	40	23	18	3	18-5	21
2001—	Philadelphia (N.L.)	3	1	.750	4.24	23	0	0	0	0-3	34.0	36	18	16	1	12-0	29
—	Scranton/W.B. (I.L.)	7	0	1.000	2.42	16	16	0	0	0-...	81.2	64	24	22	8	11-0	75
2002—	Philadelphia (N.L.)	14	11	.560	3.28	32	32	1	1	0-0	206.0	198	83	75	16	53-5	128
Major League totals (4 years)		21	20	.512	3.59	115	32	1	1	2-11	308.0	313	139	123	21	96-12	208

ALL-STAR GAME RECORD

	W	L	Pct.	ERA	GS	CG	ShO	Sv.-Opp.	IP	H	R	ER	HR	BB-IBB	SO
All-Star Game totals (1 year)	0	0	...	0.00	0	0	0	0-0	2.0	0	0	0	0	1-0	0

PALMEIRO, ORLANDO — OF

PERSONAL: Born January 19, 1969, in Hoboken, N.J. ... 5-10/182. ... Bats left, throws left. ... Cousin of Rafael Palmeiro, first baseman, Texas Rangers. ... Name pronounced pal-MAIR-oh.
HIGH SCHOOL: Southridge (Miami).
JUNIOR COLLEGE: Miami-Dade (South) Community College.
COLLEGE: Miami (Fla.).
TRANSACTIONS/CAREER NOTES: Selected by California Angels organization in 33rd round of free-agent draft (June 3, 1991). ... On disabled list (September 1-26, 1994). ... Angels franchise renamed Anaheim Angels for 1997 season. ... On disabled list (August 23-September 7, 1997). ... Granted free agency (October 30, 2002).
STATISTICAL NOTES: Led Texas League with 18 sacrifice hits in 1993. ... Led Texas League outfielders with 307 putouts and 328 total chances in 1993. ... Led Pacific Coast League in caught stealing with 16 in 1994. ... Led Pacific Coast League with 11 sacrifice hits in 1995.
2002 GAMES PLAYED BY POSITION (MLB): OF—86; DH—8.

			BATTING														FIELDING	
Year	Team (League)	Pos.	G	AB	R	H	2B	3B	HR	RBI	BB	SO	SB-CS	Avg.	OBP	SLG	E	Avg.
1991—	Boise (N'West)	OF	70	277	56	77	11	2	1	24	33	22	8-8	.278	.358	.343	2	*.986
1992—	Quad City (Midw.)	OF	127	451	83	143	22	4	0	41	56	41	31-13	*.317	.393	.384	6	.973
1993—	Midland (Texas)	OF	131	*535	85	163	19	5	0	64	42	35	18-14	.305	.356	.359	9	.973
1994—	Vancouver (PCL)	OF	117	458	79	150	28	4	1	47	58	46	21-16	.328	.402	.413	1	.996
1995—	Vancouver (PCL)	OF-DH	107	398	66	122	21	4	0	47	41	34	16-7	.307	.371	.379	1	*.995
—	California (A.L.)	OF-DH	15	20	3	7	0	0	0	1	1	1	0-0	.350	.381	.350	0	1.000
1996—	Vancouver (PCL)	OF	62	245	40	75	13	4	0	33	30	19	7-3	.306	.384	.392	5	.959
—	California (A.L.)	OF-DH	50	87	6	25	6	1	0	6	8	13	0-1	.287	.361	.379	0	1.000
1997—	Anaheim (A.L.)	OF-DH	74	134	19	29	2	2	0	8	17	11	2-2	.216	.307	.261	2	.975
1998—	Vancouver (PCL)	OF	43	140	21	42	13	3	1	29	16	10	3-1	.300	.363	.457	0	1.000
—	Anaheim (A.L.)	OF-DH	75	165	28	53	7	2	0	21	20	11	5-4	.321	.395	.388	0	1.000
1999—	Anaheim (A.L.)	OF-DH	109	317	46	88	12	1	1	23	39	30	5-5	.278	.364	.331	1	.994
2000—	Anaheim (A.L.)	OF-DH	108	243	38	73	20	2	0	25	38	20	4-1	.300	.395	.399	2	.984
2001—	Anaheim (A.L.)	OF-DH	104	230	29	56	10	1	2	23	25	24	6-6	.243	.319	.322	1	.989
2002—	Anaheim (A.L.)	OF-DH	110	263	35	79	12	1	0	31	30	22	7-2	.300	.368	.354	1	.993
Major League totals (8 years)			645	1459	204	410	69	10	3	138	178	132	29-21	.281	.361	.348	7	.991

CHAMPIONSHIP SERIES RECORD

			BATTING														FIELDING	
Year	Team (League)	Pos.	G	AB	R	H	2B	3B	HR	RBI	BB	SO	SB-CS	Avg.	OBP	SLG	E	Avg.
2002—	Anaheim (A.L.)	OF	2	2	0	0	0	0	0	0	0	1	0-0	.000	.000	.000	0	...

WORLD SERIES RECORD

NOTES: Member of World Series championship team (2002).

			BATTING														FIELDING	
Year	Team (League)	Pos.	G	AB	R	H	2B	3B	HR	RBI	BB	SO	SB-CS	Avg.	OBP	SLG	E	Avg.
2002—	Anaheim (A.L.)	PH	4	4	1	1	1	0	0	0	0	2	0-0	.250	.250	.500	0	...

PALMEIRO, RAFAEL 1B RANGERS

PERSONAL: Born September 24, 1964, in Havana, Cuba. ... 6-0/190. ... Bats left, throws left. ... Full name: Rafael Corrales Palmeiro. ... Cousin of Orlando Palmeiro, outfielder with Anaheim Angels (1995-2002). ... Name pronounced pal-MAIR-oh.

HIGH SCHOOL: Jackson (Miami).

COLLEGE: Mississippi State.

TRANSACTIONS/CAREER NOTES: Selected by New York Mets organization in eighth round of free-agent draft (June 7, 1982); did not sign. ... Selected by Chicago Cubs organization in first round (22nd pick overall) of free-agent draft (June 3, 1985); pick received as compensation for San Diego Padres signing Type A free-agent P Tim Stoddard. ... Traded by Cubs with P Jamie Moyer and P Drew Hall to Texas Rangers for P Mitch Williams, P Paul Kilgus, P Steve Wilson, IF Curtis Wilkerson, IF Luis Benitez and OF Pablo Delgado (December 5, 1988). ... Granted free agency (October 25, 1993). ... Signed by Baltimore Orioles (December 12, 1993). ... Granted free agency (October 23, 1998). ... Signed by Rangers (December 4, 1998).

RECORDS: Shares A.L. record for most seasons leading league in assists by first baseman—6.

HONORS: Named outfielder on The Sporting News college All-America team (1985). ... Named Eastern League Most Valuable Player (1986). ... Won A.L. Gold Glove at first base (1997-99). ... Named first baseman on The Sporting News A.L. All-Star team (1998 and 1999). ... Named first baseman on The Sporting News A.L. Silver Slugger team (1998). ... Named Major League Player of the Year by The Sporting News (1999). ... Named designated hitter on The Sporting News A.L. Silver Slugger team (1999).

STATISTICAL NOTES: Led Eastern League with 225 total bases, 13 sacrifice flies and 13 intentional bases on balls received in 1986. ... Had 20-game hitting streak (July 18-August 11, 1988). ... Led A.L. first basemen with 119 assists in 1989, 143 in 1992, 147 in 1993, 119 in 1995, 119 in 1996 and 124 in 1998. ... Led A.L. first basemen with 1,388 putouts in 1993, 1,383 in 1996 and 1,435 in 1998. ... Led A.L. first basemen in total chances with 1,540 in 1993 and 1,510 in 1996. ... Led A.L. first basemen in double plays with 133 in 1993 and 157 in 1996. ... Led A.L. first basemen with 1,568 total chances in 1998. ... Had 24-game hitting streak (April 23-May 22, 1994). ... Career major league grand slams: 10.

MISCELLANEOUS: Holds Texas Rangers franchise all-time record for most runs (866).

2002 GAMES PLAYED BY POSITION (MLB): 1B—97; DH—55.

		BATTING														FIELDING	
Year Team (League)	Pos.	G	AB	R	H	2B	3B	HR	RBI	BB	SO	SB-CS	Avg.	OBP	SLG	E	Avg.
1985— Peoria (Midw.)	OF	73	279	34	83	22	4	5	51	31	34	9-3	.297	.369	.459	1	.992
1986— Pittsfield (East.)	OF	•140	509	66	*156	29	2	12	*95	54	32	15-7	.306	.367	.442	3	*.988
— Chicago (N.L.)	OF	22	73	9	18	4	0	3	12	4	6	1-1	.247	.295	.425	4	.900
1987— Iowa (A.A.)	OF-1B	57	214	36	64	14	3	11	41	22	22	4-3	.299	.366	.547	2	.988
— Chicago (N.L.)	OF-1B	84	221	32	61	15	1	14	30	20	26	2-2	.276	.336	.543	1	.995
1988— Chicago (N.L.)	OF-1B	152	580	75	178	41	5	8	53	38	34	12-2	.307	.349	.436	5	.985
1989— Texas (A.L.)■	1B-DH	156	559	76	154	23	4	8	64	63	48	4-3	.275	.354	.374	12	.991
1990— Texas (A.L.)	1B-DH	154	598	72	*191	35	6	14	89	40	59	3-3	.319	.361	.468	7	.995
1991— Texas (A.L.)	1B-DH	159	631	115	203	*49	3	26	88	68	72	4-3	.322	.389	.532	*12	.992
1992— Texas (A.L.)	1B-DH	159	608	84	163	27	4	22	85	72	83	2-3	.268	.352	.434	7	.995
1993— Texas (A.L.)	1B	160	597	*124	176	40	2	37	105	73	85	22-3	.295	.371	.554	5	.997
1994— Baltimore (A.L.)■	1B	111	436	82	139	32	0	23	76	54	63	7-3	.319	.392	.550	4	.996
1995— Baltimore (A.L.)	1B	143	554	89	172	30	2	39	104	62	65	3-1	.310	.380	.583	4	.997
1996— Baltimore (A.L.)	1B-DH	162	626	110	181	40	2	39	142	95	96	8-0	.289	.381	.546	8	.995
1997— Baltimore (A.L.)	1B-DH	158	614	95	156	24	2	38	110	67	109	5-2	.254	.329	.485	10	.993
1998— Baltimore (A.L.)	1B-DH	162	619	98	183	36	1	43	121	79	91	11-7	.296	.379	.565	9	.994
1999— Texas (A.L.)■	DH-1B	158	565	96	183	30	1	47	148	97	69	2-4	.324	.420	.630	1	.996
2000— Texas (A.L.)	1B-DH	158	565	102	163	29	3	39	120	103	77	2-1	.288	.397	.558	4	.995
2001— Texas (A.L.)	1B-DH	160	600	98	164	33	0	47	123	101	90	1-1	.273	.381	.563	8	.992
2002— Texas (A.L.)	1B-DH	155	546	99	149	34	0	43	105	104	94	2-0	.273	.391	.571	5	.994
American League totals (14 years)		2155	8118	1340	2377	462	30	465	1480	1078	1101	76-34	.293	.377	.529	96	.994
National League totals (3 years)		258	874	116	257	60	6	25	95	62	66	15-5	.294	.341	.462	10	.982
Major League totals (17 years)		2413	8992	1456	2634	522	36	490	1575	1140	1167	91-39	.293	.373	.522	106	.994

DIVISION SERIES RECORD

		BATTING														FIELDING	
Year Team (League)	Pos.	G	AB	R	H	2B	3B	HR	RBI	BB	SO	SB-CS	Avg.	OBP	SLG	E	Avg.
1996— Baltimore (A.L.)	1B	4	17	4	3	1	0	1	2	1	6	0-0	.176	.263	.412	1	.973
1997— Baltimore (A.L.)	1B	4	12	2	3	2	0	0	0	0	2	0-0	.250	.250	.417	0	1.000
1999— Texas (A.L.)	DH	3	11	0	3	0	0	0	0	1	1	0-0	.273	.333	.273	...	...
Division series totals (3 years)		11	40	6	9	3	0	1	2	2	9	0-0	.225	.279	.375	1	.985

CHAMPIONSHIP SERIES RECORD

NOTES: Hit home run in first at-bat (October 9, 1996).

		BATTING														FIELDING	
Year Team (League)	Pos.	G	AB	R	H	2B	3B	HR	RBI	BB	SO	SB-CS	Avg.	OBP	SLG	E	Avg.
1996— Baltimore (A.L.)	1B	5	17	4	4	0	0	2	4	4	4	0-0	.235	.364	.588	0	1.000
1997— Baltimore (A.L.)	1B	6	25	3	7	2	0	1	2	0	10	0-0	.280	.308	.480	0	1.000
Championship series totals (2 years)		11	42	7	11	2	0	3	6	4	14	0-0	.262	.333	.524	0	1.000

ALL-STAR GAME RECORD

	AB	R	H	2B	3B	HR	RBI	BB	SO	SB-CS	Avg.	OBP	SLG	E	Avg.
All-Star Game totals (4 years)	4	1	3	0	0	0	2	2	0	0-0	.750	.833	.750	0	1.000

PALMER, DEAN DH TIGERS

PERSONAL: Born December 27, 1968, in Tallahassee, Fla. ... 6-1/219. ... Bats right, throws right. ... Full name: Dean William Palmer.

HIGH SCHOOL: Florida (Tallahassee, Fla.).

TRANSACTIONS/CAREER NOTES: Selected by Texas Rangers organization in third round of free-agent draft (June 2, 1986). ... On disabled list (July 19, 1988-remainder of season; April 28-May 13, 1994; and June 4-September 22, 1995). ... Traded by Rangers to Kansas City Royals for OF Tom Goodwin (July 25, 1997). ... Granted free agency (October 27, 1997). ... Re-signed by Royals (December 15, 1997). ... Granted free agency (October 23, 1998). ... Signed by Detroit Tigers (November 13, 1998). ... On suspended list (April 28-May 5 and June 15-18, 2000).

... On Detroit disabled list (March 23-April 7, April 13-29 and July 3, 2001-remainder of season); included rehabilitation assignment to Toledo (April 28-29). ... On suspended list (June 15-18, 2001). ... On disabled list (March 22-April 7 and April 14, 2002-remainder of season).

RECORDS: Shares major league single-season record for fewest assists by third baseman (150 or more games)—221 (1996). ... Holds A.L. single-season record for fewest chances accepted by third baseman (150 or more games)—326 (1996). ... Shares A.L. single-season record for fewest double plays by third baseman (150 or more games)—17 (1996).

HONORS: Named third baseman on The Sporting News A.L. Silver Slugger team (1998 and 1999). ... Named third baseman on The Sporting News A.L. All-Star team (1999).

STATISTICAL NOTES: Led Texas League third basemen with 30 errors in 1989. ... Led A.L. third basemen with 29 errors in 1993. ... Career major league grand slams: 8.

2002 GAMES PLAYED BY POSITION (MLB): DH—4.

			BATTING														FIELDING	
Year	**Team (League)**	**Pos.**	**G**	**AB**	**R**	**H**	**2B**	**3B**	**HR**	**RBI**	**BB**	**SO**	**SB-CS**	**Avg.**	**OBP**	**SLG**	**E**	**Avg.**
1986—	GC Rangers (GCL)	3B	50	163	19	34	7	1	0	12	22	34	6-3	.209	.318	.264	13	.885
1987—	Gastonia (S.Atl.)	3B	128	484	51	104	16	0	9	54	36	126	5-4	.215	.277	.304	*59	.819
1988—	Charlotte (FSL)	3B	74	305	38	81	12	1	4	35	15	69	0-0	.266	.299	.351	28	.873
1989—	Tulsa (Texas)	3B-SS	133	498	82	125	32	5	*25	90	41	*152	15-5	.251	.311	.486	†31	.906
—	Texas (A.L.)	3B-DH-SS-OF	16	19	0	2	2	0	0	1	0	12	0-0	.105	.100	.211	2	.778
1990—	Tulsa (Texas)	3B	7	24	4	7	0	1	3	9	4	10	0-1	.292	.414	.750	3	.833
—	Oklahoma City (A.A.)	3B-1B	88	316	33	69	17	4	12	39	20	106	1-1	.218	.271	.411	21	.938
1991—	Oklahoma City (A.A.)	3B-OF	60	234	45	70	11	2	*22	59	20	61	4-5	.299	.357	.645	11	.933
—	Texas (A.L.)	3B-OF-DH	81	268	38	50	9	2	15	37	32	98	0-2	.187	.281	.403	9	.941
1992—	Texas (A.L.)	3B	152	541	74	124	25	0	26	72	62	*154	10-4	.229	.311	.420	22	.945
1993—	Texas (A.L.)	3B-SS	148	519	88	127	31	2	33	96	53	154	11-10	.245	.321	.503	†29	.922
1994—	Texas (A.L.)	3B	93	342	50	84	14	2	19	59	26	89	3-4	.246	.302	.465	*22	.912
1995—	Texas (A.L.)	3B	36	119	30	40	6	0	9	24	21	21	1-1	.336	.448	.613	5	.948
1996—	Texas (A.L.)	3B-DH	154	582	98	163	26	2	38	107	59	145	2-0	.280	.348	.527	16	.953
1997—	Texas (A.L.)	3B	94	355	47	87	21	0	14	55	26	84	1-0	.245	.296	.423	10	.959
—	Kansas City (A.L.)■	3B-DH	49	187	23	52	10	1	9	31	15	50	1-2	.278	.335	.487	9	.924
1998—	Kansas City (A.L.)	3B-DH	152	572	84	159	27	2	34	119	48	134	8-2	.278	.333	.510	22	.921
1999—	Detroit (A.L.)■	3B-DH	150	560	92	147	25	2	38	100	57	153	3-3	.263	.339	.518	19	.945
2000—	Detroit (A.L.)	3B-1B-DH	145	524	73	134	22	2	29	102	66	146	4-2	.256	.338	.471	25	.937
2001—	Toledo (I.L.)	DH	1	2	0	1	0	0	0	0	2	0	0-0	.500	.750	.500	...	...
—	Detroit (A.L.)	DH	57	216	34	48	11	0	11	40	27	59	4-1	.222	.317	.426	...	...
2002—	Detroit (A.L.)	DH	4	12	0	0	0	0	0	0	1	5	0-0	.000	.077	.000	...	...
Major League totals (13 years)			1331	4816	731	1217	229	15	275	843	493	1304	48-31	.253	.326	.478	190	.937

DIVISION SERIES RECORD

			BATTING														FIELDING	
Year	**Team (League)**	**Pos.**	**G**	**AB**	**R**	**H**	**2B**	**3B**	**HR**	**RBI**	**BB**	**SO**	**SB-CS**	**Avg.**	**OBP**	**SLG**	**E**	**Avg.**
1996—	Texas (A.L.)	3B	4	19	3	4	1	0	1	2	0	5	0-0	.211	.211	.421	1	.929

ALL-STAR GAME RECORD

	AB	**R**	**H**	**2B**	**3B**	**HR**	**RBI**	**BB**	**SO**	**SB-CS**	**Avg.**	**OBP**	**SLG**	**E**	**Avg.**
All-Star Game totals (1 year)	1	0	0	0	0	0	0	0	0	0-0	.000	.000	.000	0	...

PANIAGUA, JOSE P

PERSONAL: Born August 20, 1973, in San Jose de Ocoa, Dominican Republic. ... 6-2/195. ... Throws right, bats right. ... Full name: Jose Luis Sanchez Paniagua.

HIGH SCHOOL: Liceo Nuestra Senora del Altagracia (Santo Domingo, Dominican Republic).

TRANSACTIONS/CAREER NOTES: Signed as non-drafted free agent by Montreal Expos organization (September 17, 1990). ... On Montreal disabled list (May 25-June 11, 1996). ... On Ottawa disabled list (July 16-August 2, 1996). ... Selected by Tampa Bay Devil Rays in second round (50th pick overall) of expansion draft (November 18, 1997). ... Claimed on waivers by Seattle Mariners (March 26, 1998). ... On suspended list (August 10-16, 1999; and August 22-24, 2001). ... Traded by Mariners with P Dennis Stark and P Brian Fuentes to Colorado Rockies for 3B Jeff Cirillo (December 15, 2001). ... Traded by Rockies to Detriot Tigers for P Victor Santos and IF Ronnie Merrill (March 25, 2002). ... Released by Tigers (September 7, 2002).

CAREER HITTING (MLB): 0-for-18 (.000), 1 R, 0 2B, 0 3B, 0 HR, 0 RBI.

Year	**League**	**W**	**L**	**Pct.**	**ERA**	**G**	**GS**	**CG**	**ShO**	**Sv.-Opp.**	**IP**	**H**	**R**	**ER**	**HR**	**BB-IBB**	**SO**
1991—	Dominican Expos (DSL)	2	2	.500	2.18	13	2	0	0	0-...	33.0	24	16	8	...	17-...	19
1992—	Dominican Expos (DSL)	3	7	.300	4.15	13	13	3	1	0-...	73.2	69	50	34	...	46-...	60
1993—	Gulf Coast Expos (GCL)	3	0	1.000	0.67	4	4	1	0	0-...	27.0	13	2	2	0	5-0	25
1994—	West Palm Beach (FSL)	9	9	.500	3.64	26	26	1	0	0-...	141.0	131	82	57	6	54-2	110
1995—	Harrisburg (East.)	7	•12	.368	5.34	25	25	2	1	0-...	126.1	140	84	75	9	62-0	89
1996—	Montreal (N.L.)	2	4	.333	3.53	13	11	0	0	0-0	51.0	55	24	20	7	23-0	27
—	Harrisburg (East.)	3	0	1.000	0.00	3	3	0	0	0-...	18.0	12	1	0	0	2-0	16
—	Ottawa (I.L.)	9	5	.643	3.18	15	14	2	1	0-...	85.0	72	39	30	7	23-0	61
1997—	West Palm Beach (FSL)	1	0	1.000	0.00	2	2	0	0	0-...	10.0	5	0	0	0	2-0	11
—	Ottawa (I.L.)	8	10	.444	4.64	22	22	1	0	0-...	137.2	164	79	71	13	44-1	87
—	Montreal (N.L.)	1	2	.333	12.00	9	3	0	0	0-0	18.0	29	24	24	2	16-1	8
1998—	Tacoma (PCL)■	3	1	.750	2.77	44	0	0	0	5-...	68.1	66	25	21	2	22-1	61
—	Seattle (A.L.)	2	0	1.000	2.05	18	0	0	0	1-2	22.0	15	5	5	3	5-0	16
1999—	Seattle (A.L.)	6	11	.353	4.06	59	0	0	0	3-12	77.2	75	37	35	5	52-4	74
2000—	Seattle (A.L.)	3	0	1.000	3.47	69	0	0	0	5-8	80.1	68	31	31	6	38-3	71
2001—	Seattle (A.L.)	4	3	.571	4.36	60	0	0	0	3-4	66.0	59	35	32	7	38-2	46
2002—	Detroit (A.L.)■	0	1	.000	5.83	41	0	0	0	1-2	41.2	50	30	27	10	15-1	34
—	Toledo (I.L.)	2	0	1.000	1.15	12	0	0	0	1-...	15.2	10	2	2	1	4-1	13
A.L. totals (5 years)		15	15	.500	4.07	247	0	0	0	13-28	287.2	267	138	130	31	148-10	241
N.L. totals (2 years)		3	6	.333	5.74	22	14	0	0	0-0	69.0	84	48	44	9	39-1	35
Major League totals (7 years)		18	21	.462	4.39	269	14	0	0	13-28	356.2	351	186	174	40	187-11	276

DIVISION SERIES RECORD

Year League	W	L	Pct.	ERA	G	GS	CG	ShO	Sv.-Opp.	IP	H	R	ER	HR	BB-IBB	SO
2000—Seattle (A.L.)	1	0	1.000	0.00	2	0	0	0	0-0	2.1	1	0	0	0	2-0	3
2001—Seattle (A.L.)	0	0	...	27.00	2	0	0	0	0-0	2.0	4	6	6	1	2-0	1
Division series totals (2 years)	1	0	1.000	12.46	4	0	0	0	0-0	4.1	5	6	6	1	4-0	4

CHAMPIONSHIP SERIES RECORD

Year League	W	L	Pct.	ERA	G	GS	CG	ShO	Sv.-Opp.	IP	H	R	ER	HR	BB-IBB	SO
2000—Seattle (A.L.)	0	1	.000	4.15	5	0	0	0	0-0	4.1	4	2	2	0	1-0	4
2001—Seattle (A.L.)	0	0	...	12.27	3	0	0	0	0-0	3.2	7	5	5	1	1-0	1
Champ. series totals (2 years)	0	1	.000	7.88	8	0	0	0	0-0	8.0	11	7	7	1	2-0	5

PAQUETTE, CRAIG 3B/OF TIGERS

PERSONAL: Born March 28, 1969, in Long Beach, Calif. ... 6-0/190. ... Bats right, throws right. ... Full name: Craig Howard Paquette.
HIGH SCHOOL: Ranchos Alamitos (Garden Grove, Calif.).
JUNIOR COLLEGE: Golden West College (Calif.).
TRANSACTIONS/CAREER NOTES: Selected by Minnesota Twins organization in 36th round of free-agent draft (June 2, 1987); did not sign. ... Selected by Oakland Athletics organization in eighth round of free-agent draft (June 5, 1989). ... On Modesto disabled list (April 10-May 5, 1991). ... On Huntsville disabled list (June 1-11, 1991). ... On Tacoma disabled list (July 18, 1994-remainder of season). ... Released by A's (March 26, 1996). ... Signed by Kansas City Royals organization (April 3, 1996). ... Granted free agency (October 15, 1997). ... Signed by New York Mets organization (December 23, 1997). ... On New York disabled list (May 7, 1998-remainder of season). ... Granted free agency (October 15, 1998). ... Re-signed by Mets organization (December 18, 1998). ... On Norfolk disabled list (April 22-May 1, 1999). ... Traded by Mets to St. Louis Cardinals for IF/OF Shawon Dunston (July 31, 1999). ... Granted free agency (November 5, 2001). ... Signed by Detroit Tigers (December 17, 2001).
STATISTICAL NOTES: Tied for Northwest League lead with 163 total bases in 1989. ... Led Northwest League third basemen with .936 fielding percentage and 12 double plays in 1989. ... Led California League third basemen with 88 putouts in 1990. ... Led Southern League third basemen with 248 assists and 349 total chances in 1992. ... Career major league grand slams: 2.
2002 GAMES PLAYED BY POSITION (MLB): 3B—49; 1B—14; OF—8; DH—5.

			BATTING													FIELDING	
Year Team (League)	Pos.	G	AB	R	H	2B	3B	HR	RBI	BB	SO	SB-CS	Avg.	OBP	SLG	E	Avg.
1989—S. Oregon (N'West)	3B-SS-2B	71	277	53	93	*22	3	14	56	30	46	9-4	.336	.403	.588	15	†.935
1990—Modesto (Calif.)	3B	130	495	65	118	23	4	15	59	47	123	8-5	.238	.306	.392	26	*.922
1991—Huntsville (Sou.)	3B-1B	102	378	50	99	18	1	8	60	28	87	0-5	.262	.314	.378	16	.920
1992—Huntsville (Sou.)	3B	115	450	59	116	25	4	17	71	29	118	13-10	.258	.304	.444	*32	.908
—Tacoma (PCL)	3B	17	66	10	18	7	0	2	11	2	16	3-1	.273	.294	.470	3	.940
1993—Tacoma (PCL)	3B-SS-2B	50	183	29	49	8	0	8	29	14	54	3-3	.268	.320	.443	15	.908
—Oakland (A.L.)	3B-DH-OF	105	393	35	86	20	4	12	46	14	108	4-2	.219	.245	.382	13	.950
1994—Tacoma (PCL)	3B	65	245	39	70	12	3	17	48	14	48	3-3	.286	.326	.567	14	.936
—Oakland (A.L.)	3B	14	49	0	7	2	0	0	0	0	14	1-0	.143	.143	.184	0	1.000
1995—Oakland (A.L.)	3-O-S-1	105	283	42	64	13	1	13	49	12	88	5-2	.226	.256	.417	8	.953
1996—Omaha (A.A.)■	DH-3B-1B-OF	18	63	9	21	3	0	4	13	8	14	1-0	.333	.403	.571	3	.917
—Kansas City (A.L.)	3-O-1-S-DH	118	429	61	111	15	1	22	67	23	101	5-3	.259	.296	.452	14	.963
1997—Kansas City (A.L.)	3B-OF	77	252	26	58	15	1	8	33	10	57	2-2	.230	.263	.393	12	.938
—Omaha (A.A.)	3B-DH	23	91	9	28	6	0	3	20	6	26	0-2	.308	.343	.473	2	.953
1998—Norfolk (I.L.)■	3B-SS-OF	15	61	11	17	1	1	3	14	1	13	2-1	.279	.286	.475	4	.923
—New York (N.L.)	3B-1B-OF	7	19	3	5	2	0	0	0	0	6	1-0	.263	.263	.368	0	1.000
1999—Norfolk (I.L.)	3B-OF-1B-SS	70	283	40	77	20	3	15	54	10	47	3-0	.272	.298	.523	8	.969
—St. Louis (N.L.)■	OF-3B-2B-1B	48	157	21	45	6	0	10	37	6	38	1-0	.287	.309	.516	3	.975
2000—St. Louis (N.L.)	3B-OF-1B-2B	134	384	47	94	24	2	15	61	27	83	4-3	.245	.294	.435	15	.958
2001—St. Louis (N.L.)	OF-3B-1B-2B	123	340	47	96	17	0	15	64	18	67	3-1	.282	.326	.465	5	.982
2002—Detroit (A.L.)■	3B-1B-OF-DH	72	252	20	49	14	1	4	20	10	53	1-0	.194	.223	.306	9	.963
American League totals (6 years)		491	1658	184	375	79	8	59	215	69	421	18-9	.226	.257	.390	56	.956
National League totals (4 years)		312	900	118	240	49	2	40	162	51	194	9-4	.267	.308	.459	23	.970
Major League totals (10 years)		803	2558	302	615	128	10	99	377	120	615	27-13	.240	.275	.414	79	.961

DIVISION SERIES RECORD

			BATTING													FIELDING	
Year Team (League)	Pos.	G	AB	R	H	2B	3B	HR	RBI	BB	SO	SB-CS	Avg.	OBP	SLG	E	Avg.
2000—St. Louis (N.L.)	OF-3B	2	2	0	0	0	0	0	0	0	0	0-0	.000	.000	.000	0	1.000
2001—St. Louis (N.L.)	OF-3B	2	7	0	1	0	0	0	0	0	5	0-0	.143	.143	.143	0	1.000
Division series totals (2 years)		4	9	0	1	0	0	0	0	0	5	0-0	.111	.111	.111	0	1.000

CHAMPIONSHIP SERIES RECORD

			BATTING													FIELDING	
Year Team (League)	Pos.	G	AB	R	H	2B	3B	HR	RBI	BB	SO	SB-CS	Avg.	OBP	SLG	E	Avg.
2000—St. Louis (N.L.)	3B-OF-PH	4	6	0	1	0	0	0	0	0	2	0-0	.167	.167	.167	0	1.000

PARK, CHAN HO P RANGERS

PERSONAL: Born June 30, 1973, in Kong Ju City, Korea. ... 6-2/204. ... Throws right, bats right. ... Full name: Chan Ho Park.
HIGH SCHOOL: Kong Ju (Kong Ju City, Korea).
COLLEGE: Hanyang University (Seoul, Korea).
TRANSACTIONS/CAREER NOTES: Signed as non-drafted free agent by Los Angeles Dodgers organization (January 14, 1994). ... On Albuquerque disabled list (July 16-29, 1995). ... On suspended list (June 8-17, 1999). ... Granted free agency (November 5, 2001). ... Signed by Texas Rangers (December 23, 2001). ... On Texas disabled list (April 2-May 12 and August 7-23, 2002); included rehabilitation assignment to Oklahoma (August 18-23).
RECORDS: Shares major league single-season record for most grand slams allowed—4 (1999).
STATISTICAL NOTES: Tied for N.L. lead with 20 hit batsmen and three balks in 2001. ... Led A.L. with 17 hit batsmen in 2002.
CAREER HITTING (MLB): 58-for-345 (.168), 23 R, 15 2B, 1 3B, 2 HR, 23 RBI.

Year League	W	L	Pct.	ERA	G	GS	CG	ShO	Sv.-Opp.	IP	H	R	ER	HR	BB-IBB	SO
1994— Los Angeles (N.L.)	0	0	...	11.25	2	0	0	0	0-0	4.0	5	5	5	1	5-0	6
— San Antonio (Texas)	5	7	.417	3.55	20	20	0	0	0-...	101.1	91	52	40	4	57-0	100
1995— Albuquerque (PCL)	6	7	.462	4.91	23	22	0	0	0-...	110.0	93	64	60	10	76-2	101
— Los Angeles (N.L.)	0	0	...	4.50	2	1	0	0	0-0	4.0	2	2	2	1	2-0	7
1996— Los Angeles (N.L.)	5	5	.500	3.64	48	10	0	0	0-0	108.2	82	48	44	7	71-3	119
1997— Los Angeles (N.L.)	14	8	.636	3.38	32	29	2	0	0-0	192.0	149	80	72	24	70-1	166
1998— Los Angeles (N.L.)	15	9	.625	3.71	34	34	2	0	0-0	220.2	199	101	91	16	97-1	191
1999— Los Angeles (N.L.)	13	11	.542	5.23	33	33	0	0	0-0	194.1	208	120	113	31	100-4	174
2000— Los Angeles (N.L.)	18	10	.643	3.27	34	34	3	1	0-0	226.0	173	92	82	21	124-4	217
2001— Los Angeles (N.L.)	15	11	.577	3.50	36	•35	2	1	0-0	234.0	183	98	91	23	91-1	218
2002— Texas (A.L.)■	9	8	.529	5.75	25	25	0	0	0-0	145.2	154	95	93	20	78-2	121
— Oklahoma (PCL)	0	1	.000	27.00	1	1	0	0	0-...	3.0	9	9	9	0	3-0	3
A.L. totals (1 year)	9	8	.529	5.75	25	25	0	0	0-0	145.2	154	95	93	20	78-2	121
N.L. totals (8 years)	80	54	.597	3.80	221	176	9	2	0-0	1183.2	1001	546	500	124	560-14	1098
Major League totals (9 years)	89	62	.589	4.01	246	201	9	2	0-0	1329.1	1155	641	593	144	638-16	1219

ALL-STAR GAME RECORD

	W	L	Pct.	ERA	GS	CG	ShO	Sv.-Opp.	IP	H	R	ER	HR	BB-IBB	SO
All-Star Game totals (1 year)	0	1	.000	9.00	0	0	0	0-0	1.0	1	1	1	1	0-0	1

PARKER, CHRISTIAN — P — YANKEES

PERSONAL: Born July 3, 1975, in Albuquerque, N.M. ... 6-1/200. ... Throws right, bats right. ... Full name: Christian Michael Parker.
HIGH SCHOOL: Eldorado (Albuquerque, N.M.).
COLLEGE: Notre Dame.
TRANSACTIONS/CAREER NOTES: Selected by Montreal Expos organization in fourth round of free-agent draft (June 4, 1996). ... Traded by Expos to New York Yankees (March 22, 2000), completing deal in which Yankees traded P Hideki Irabu to Expos for P Jake Westbrook and two players to be named later (December 22, 1999). ... On disabled list (April 10, 2001-remainder of season; and March 31, 2002-entire season).
CAREER HITTING (MLB): 0-for-0 (.000), 0 R, 0 2B, 0 3B, 0 HR, 0 RBI.

Year League	W	L	Pct.	ERA	G	GS	CG	ShO	Sv.-Opp.	IP	H	R	ER	HR	BB-IBB	SO
1996— Vermont (NY-Penn)	7	1	.875	2.47	14	14	2	1	0-...	80.0	63	26	22	1	22-0	61
1997— Cape Fear (S.Atl.)	11	10	.524	3.12	25	25	0	0	0-...	153.0	146	72	53	5	49-0	106
— West Palm Beach (FSL)	0	1	.000	3.32	3	3	0	0	0-...	19.0	22	7	7	0	5-0	10
1998— Harrisburg (East.)	6	6	.500	3.48	36	16	0	0	5-...	126.2	124	66	49	9	47-3	73
1999— Ottawa (I.L.)	0	1	.000	7.59	7	0	0	0	0-...	10.2	10	9	9	0	7-0	5
— Harrisburg (East.)	8	5	.615	3.65	36	6	0	0	3-...	88.2	86	39	36	11	37-2	45
2000— Norwich (East.)■	14	6	.700	3.13	28	28	4	0	0-...	204.0	196	86	71	8	58-5	147
2001— New York (A.L.)	0	1	.000	21.00	1	1	0	0	0-0	3.0	8	7	7	2	1-0	1
2002— New York (A.L.)									Did not play.							
Major League totals (1 year)	0	1	.000	21.00	1	1	0	0	0-0	3.0	8	7	7	2	1-0	1

PARONTO, CHAD — P — INDIANS

PERSONAL: Born July 28, 1975, in Woodsville, N.H. ... 6-5/250. ... Throws right, bats right. ... Full name: Chad Michael Paronto. ... Nephew of Dennis Paronto, pitcher with Atlanta Braves organization.
HIGH SCHOOL: Woodsville (N.H.).
COLLEGE: Massachusetts.
TRANSACTIONS/CAREER NOTES: Selected by Baltimore Orioles organization in eighth round of free-agent draft (June 4, 1996). ... On Bowie disabled list (April 7-June 2, 2000). ... Claimed on waivers by Cleveland Indians (November 19, 2001). ... On Cleveland disabled list (July 29, 2002-remainder of season); included rehabilitation assignment to Akron (August 12-30).
CAREER HITTING (MLB): 0-for-0 (.000), 0 R, 0 2B, 0 3B, 0 HR, 0 RBI.

Year League	W	L	Pct.	ERA	G	GS	CG	ShO	Sv.-Opp.	IP	H	R	ER	HR	BB-IBB	SO
1996— Bluefield (Appl.)	1	1	.500	1.69	9	2	0	0	1-...	21.1	16	4	4	0	5-0	24
— Frederick (Caro.)	0	1	.000	4.80	8	1	0	0	0-...	15.0	11	9	8	0	8-0	6
1997— Delmarva (S.Atl.)	6	9	.400	4.74	28	23	0	0	0-...	127.1	133	95	67	9	56-1	93
1998— Frederick (Caro.)	7	6	.538	3.13	18	18	0	0	0-...	103.2	116	44	36	4	39-0	87
— Bowie (East.)	1	3	.250	5.80	8	7	0	0	1-...	35.2	38	30	23	1	23-0	28
1999— Bowie (East.)	0	4	.000	8.12	15	9	0	0	0-...	41.0	59	39	37	3	32-1	27
— Frederick (Caro.)	3	5	.375	4.73	13	13	1	0	0-...	72.1	81	46	38	7	26-1	55
2000— Rochester (I.L.)	1	1	.500	5.75	12	6	0	0	0-...	36.0	40	26	23	5	15-0	18
— Bowie (East.)	4	2	.667	2.87	8	8	1	0	0-...	47.0	29	19	15	2	16-0	31
2001— Rochester (I.L.)	3	3	.500	4.57	33	0	0	0	1-...	43.1	44	28	22	5	24-4	39
— Baltimore (A.L.)	1	3	.250	5.00	24	0	0	0	0-1	27.0	33	24	15	5	11-0	16
2002— Buffalo (I.L.)■	0	0	...	0.00	8	0	0	0	1-...	13.0	10	0	0	0	1-1	7
— Cleveland (A.L.)	0	2	.000	4.04	29	0	0	0	0-0	35.2	34	19	16	3	11-1	23
— Akron (East.)	0	0	...	27.00	1	1	0	0	0-...	.1	1	1	1	0	1-0	0
Major League totals (2 years)	1	5	.167	4.45	53	0	0	0	0-1	62.2	67	43	31	8	22-1	39

PARQUE, JIM — P — WHITE SOX

PERSONAL: Born February 8, 1976, in Norwalk, Calif. ... 5-11/170. ... Throws left, bats left. ... Full name: James Vo Parque.
HIGH SCHOOL: Crescenta Valley (Calif.).
COLLEGE: UCLA.
TRANSACTIONS/CAREER NOTES: Selected by Chicago White Sox organization in second round of free-agent draft (June 3, 1997). ... On suspended list (May 7-9, 2000). ... On disabled list (April 27, 2001-remainder of season).
STATISTICAL NOTES: Tied for A.L. lead with three balks in 1998. ... Led A.L. with five balks in 2000.
MISCELLANEOUS: Member of 1996 U.S. Olympic baseball team.
CAREER HITTING (MLB): 2-for-10 (.200), 0 R, 0 2B, 0 3B, 0 HR, 0 RBI.

Year	League	W	L	Pct.	ERA	G	GS	CG	ShO	Sv.-Opp.	IP	H	R	ER	HR	BB-IBB	SO
1997—	Winston-Salem (Caro.)	7	2	.778	2.77	11	11	0	0	0-...	61.2	29	19	19	3	23-0	76
—	Nashville (PCL)	1	0	1.000	4.22	2	2	0	0	0-...	10.2	9	5	5	0	9-0	5
1998—	Calgary (PCL)	2	3	.400	3.94	8	8	0	0	0-...	48.0	49	26	21	7	25-0	31
—	Chicago (A.L.)	7	5	.583	5.10	21	21	0	0	0-0	113.0	135	72	64	14	49-0	77
1999—	Chicago (A.L.)	9	15	.375	5.13	31	30	1	0	0-0	173.2	210	111	99	23	79-2	111
2000—	Chicago (A.L.)	13	6	.684	4.28	33	32	0	0	0-0	187.0	208	105	89	21	71-1	111
2001—	Chicago (A.L.)	0	3	.000	8.04	5	5	1	0	0-0	28.0	36	26	25	7	10-1	15
2002—	Charlotte (I.L.)	7	9	.438	6.47	20	20	0	0	0-...	105.2	131	80	76	21	38-0	63
—	Chicago (A.L.)	1	4	.200	9.95	8	4	0	0	0-0	25.1	34	29	28	11	16-0	13
Major League totals (5 years)		30	33	.476	5.21	98	92	2	0	0-0	527.0	623	343	305	76	225-4	327

DIVISION SERIES RECORD

Year	League	W	L	Pct.	ERA	G	GS	CG	ShO	Sv.-Opp.	IP	H	R	ER	HR	BB-IBB	SO
2000—	Chicago (A.L.)	0	0	...	4.50	1	1	0	0	0-0	6.0	6	3	3	1	1-0	2

PARRA, JOSE — P

PERSONAL: Born November 28, 1972, in Jacagua, Dominican Republic. ... 5-11/175. ... Throws right, bats right. ... Full name: Jose Miguel Parra.

HIGH SCHOOL: Liceo Evangelico Jacagua (Dominican Republic).

TRANSACTIONS/CAREER NOTES: Signed as non-drafted free agent by Los Angeles Dodgers organization (December 7, 1989). ... On disabled list (May 15-June 17 and August 13, 1993-remainder of season). ... Traded by Dodgers with 3B/1B Ron Coomer, P Greg Hansell and a player to be named later to Minnesota Twins for P Kevin Tapani and P Mark Guthrie (July 31, 1995); Twins acquired OF Chris Latham to complete deal (October 30, 1995). ... Granted free agency (October 17, 1997). ... Signed by Samsung, Korean League (February 3, 1998). ... Signed by Yomiuri Giants of Japan Central League (January 13, 1999). ... Signed by Pittsbugh Pirates organization (January 14, 2000). ... On Nashville disabled list (June 3-10, 2000). ... Granted free agency (October 2, 2000). ... Re-signed by Pirates organization (February 2, 2001). ... Loaned by Pirates to Mexico City Red Devils, Mexican League (March 12-July 31, 2001). ... Released by Pirates (July 31, 2001). ... Signed by Oaxaca, Mexican League (2001). ... Signed by President, Taiwan League (2001). ... Signed by Arizona Diamondbacks organization (November 20, 2001). ... Released by Diamondbacks (June 5, 2002).

STATISTICAL NOTES: Led Pacific Coast League with 14 wild pitches in 2000.

CAREER HITTING (MLB): 0-for-0 (.000), 0 R, 0 2B, 0 3B, 0 HR, 0 RBI.

Year	League	W	L	Pct.	ERA	G	GS	CG	ShO	Sv.-Opp.	IP	H	R	ER	HR	BB-IBB	SO
1989—	Dom. Dodgers (DSL)	8	1	.889	1.87	13	11	4	3	2-...	67.1	60	21	14	...	20-...	51
1990—	Gulf Coast Dodgers (GCL)	5	3	.625	2.67	10	10	1	0	0-...	57.1	50	22	17	1	18-0	50
1991—	Great Falls (Pio.)	4	6	.400	6.16	14	14	1	1	0-...	64.1	86	58	44	5	18-0	55
1992—	Bakersfield (Calif.)	7	8	.467	3.59	24	23	3	0	0-...	143.0	151	73	57	5	47-4	107
—	San Antonio (Texas)	2	0	1.000	6.14	3	3	0	0	0-...	14.2	22	12	10	0	7-0	7
1993—	San Antonio (Texas)	1	8	.111	3.15	17	17	0	0	0-...	111.1	103	46	39	10	12-2	87
1994—	Albuquerque (PCL)	10	10	.500	4.78	27	27	1	0	0-...	145.0	190	92	77	10	38-2	90
1995—	Albuquerque (PCL)	3	2	.600	5.13	12	10	1	1	1-...	52.2	62	33	30	7	17-3	33
—	Los Angeles (N.L.)	0	0	...	4.35	8	0	0	0	0-0	10.1	10	8	5	2	6-1	7
—	Minnesota (A.L.)■	1	5	.167	7.59	12	12	0	0	0-0	61.2	83	59	52	11	22-0	29
1996—	Salt Lake (PCL)	5	3	.625	5.11	23	1	0	0	8-...	44.0	51	25	25	2	13-2	26
—	Minnesota (A.L.)	5	5	.500	6.04	27	5	0	0	0-1	70.0	88	48	47	15	27-0	50
1997—	Salt Lake (PCL)	2	8	.200	6.03	50	4	0	0	8-...	94.0	126	73	63	8	30-7	61
1998—	Samsung (Korean)■	7	8	.467	3.67	60	4	0	0	19-...	95.2	79	45	39	...	40-...	55
1999—	Yomiuri (Jap. East.)■	4	3	.571	2.75	13	11	0	0	0-...	59.0	63	26	18	...	16-...	48
—	Yomiuri (Jap. Cen.)	2	3	.400	5.32	12	9	0	0	0-...	47.1	43	29	28	5	23-...	25
2000—	Nashville (PCL)■	6	5	.545	5.22	23	21	0	0	1-...	101.2	106	66	59	7	65-0	68
—	Pittsburgh (N.L.)	0	1	.000	6.94	6	2	0	0	0-0	11.2	17	9	9	3	7-0	9
2001—	MC Red Devils (Mex.)■	4	5	.444	3.20	45	0	0	0	24-...	50.2	44	20	18	3	23-2	47
—	Oaxaca (Mex.)■	1	0	1.000	0.71	12	0	0	0	9-...	12.2	6	4	1	0	7-0	16
—	President (Taiwan)■	0	2	.000	0.64	10	...	...	...	0-...	14.0	9	...	...	...	4-...	10
2002—	Tucson (PCL)■	0	0	...	0.00	7	0	0	0	1-...	9.1	3	0	0	0	2-0	10
—	Arizona (N.L.)	0	1	.000	3.21	16	0	0	0	0-0	14.0	13	5	5	0	11-2	8
A.L. totals (2 years)		6	10	.375	6.77	39	17	0	0	0-1	131.2	171	107	99	26	49-0	79
N.L. totals (3 years)		0	2	.000	4.75	30	2	0	0	0-0	36.0	40	22	19	5	24-3	24
Major League totals (4 years)		6	12	.333	6.33	69	19	0	0	0-1	167.2	211	129	118	31	73-3	103

PARRIS, STEVE — P

PERSONAL: Born December 17, 1967, in Joliet, Ill. ... 6-0/195. ... Throws right, bats right. ... Full name: Steven Michael Parris.

HIGH SCHOOL: Joliet (Ill.) West.

COLLEGE: College of St. Francis (Ill.).

TRANSACTIONS/CAREER NOTES: Selected by Philadelphia Phillies organization in fifth round of free-agent draft (June 5, 1989). ... Claimed on waivers by Los Angeles Dodgers (April 19, 1993). ... Claimed on waivers by Seattle Mariners (April 26, 1993). ... On Jacksonville disabled list (May 12-June 23 and July 17-31, 1993). ... Released by Mariners (July 31, 1993). ... Signed by Pittsburgh Pirates organization (June 24, 1994). ... On Pittsburgh disabled list (March 6-July 11 and August 18-September 10, 1996); included rehabilitation assignments to Augusta (June 12-13) and Carolina (June 13-July 11). ... Released by Pirates (March 13, 1997). ... Signed by Cincinnati Reds organization (May 6, 1997). ... Granted free agency (October 15, 1997). ... Re-signed by Reds organization (October 27, 1997). ... On Cincinnati disabled list (July 31-September 1, 1999); included rehabilitation assignment to Indianapolis (August 22-30). ... Traded by Reds to Toronto Blue Jays for P Clayton Andrews and P Leo Estrella (November 22, 2000). ... On Toronto disabled list (July 24, 2001-remainder of season); included rehabilitation assignments to Tennessee (August 24-29) and Syracuse (August 30-September 4). ... On Toronto disabled list (March 23-June 16, 2002); included rehabilitation assignment to Dunedin (May 16-31), Tennessee (June 1-6) and Syracuse (June 7-14). ... Granted free agency (October 28, 2002).

MISCELLANEOUS: Scored one run in two appearances as pinch runner (2000).

CAREER HITTING (MLB): 25-for-161 (.155), 8 R, 4 2B, 0 3B, 0 HR, 15 RBI.

Year	League	W	L	Pct.	ERA	G	GS	CG	ShO	Sv.-Opp.	IP	H	R	ER	HR	BB-IBB	SO
1989—	Batavia (NY-Penn)	3	5	.375	3.91	13	10	1	0	0-...	66.2	69	38	29	6	20-1	46
1990—	Batavia (NY-Penn)	7	1	*.875	2.64	14	14	0	0	0-...	81.2	70	34	24	1	22-2	50

Year	League	W	L	Pct.	ERA	G	GS	CG	ShO	Sv.-Opp.	IP	H	R	ER	HR	BB-IBB	SO
1991—	Clearwater (FSL)	7	5	.583	3.39	43	6	0	0	1-...	93.0	101	43	35	1	25-4	59
1992—	Reading (East.)	5	7	.417	4.64	18	14	0	0	0-...	85.1	94	55	44	9	21-1	60
—	Scranton/W.B. (I.L.)	3	3	.500	4.03	11	6	0	0	1-...	51.1	57	25	23	1	17-1	29
1993—	Scranton/W.B. (I.L.)	0	0	...	12.71	3	0	0	0	0-...	5.2	9	9	8	3	3-0	4
—	Jacksonville (Sou.)■	0	1	.000	5.93	7	1	0	0	0-...	13.2	15	9	9	3	6-0	5
1994—	Salem (Caro.)■	3	3	.500	3.63	17	7	0	0	0-...	57.0	58	24	23	7	21-1	48
1995—	Carolina (Sou.)	9	1	.900	2.51	14	14	2	2	0-...	89.2	61	25	25	2	16-1	86
—	Pittsburgh (N.L.)	6	6	.500	5.38	15	15	1	1	0-0	82.0	89	49	49	12	33-1	61
1996—	Augusta (S.Atl.)	0	0	...	0.00	1	1	0	0	0-...	5.0	1	0	0	0	1-0	6
—	Carolina (Sou.)	2	0	1.000	3.04	5	5	0	0	0-...	26.2	24	11	9	1	6-0	22
—	Pittsburgh (N.L.)	0	3	.000	7.18	8	4	0	0	0-0	26.1	35	22	21	4	11-0	27
1997—	Chattanooga (Sou.)■	6	2	.750	4.13	14	14	0	0	0-...	80.2	78	44	37	9	29-0	68
—	Indianapolis (A.A.)	2	3	.400	3.57	5	5	1	1	0-...	35.1	26	15	14	4	11-1	27
1998—	Indianapolis (I.L.)	6	1	.857	3.84	13	13	1	1	0-...	84.1	74	38	36	8	26-1	102
—	Cincinnati (N.L.)	6	5	.545	3.73	18	16	1	1	0-0	99.0	89	44	41	9	32-3	77
1999—	Indianapolis (I.L.)	0	2	.000	4.04	6	6	0	0	0-...	35.2	39	16	16	5	9-1	31
—	Cincinnati (N.L.)	11	4	.733	3.50	22	21	2	1	0-0	128.2	124	59	50	16	52-4	86
2000—	Cincinnati (N.L.)	12	17	.414	4.81	33	33	0	0	0-0	192.2	227	109	103	30	71-5	117
2001—	Toronto (A.L.)■	4	6	.400	4.60	19	19	1	0	0-0	105.2	126	60	54	18	41-4	49
—	Tennessee (Sou.)	0	0	...	0.00	1	1	0	0	0-...	3.0	2	0	0	0	1-0	2
—	Syracuse (I.L.)	0	0	...	4.70	2	2	0	0	0-...	7.2	6	4	4	1	2-0	8
2002—	Toronto (A.L.)	5	5	.500	5.97	14	14	0	0	0-0	75.1	96	50	50	13	35-5	48
—	Dunedin (FSL)	0	1	.000	4.41	3	3	0	0	0-...	16.1	19	10	8	1	1-0	8
—	Tennessee (Sou.)	0	0	...	3.00	1	1	0	0	0-...	6.0	7	2	2	0	2-0	5
—	Syracuse (I.L.)	1	1	.500	1.29	2	2	0	0	0-...	14.0	10	6	2	0	2-0	5
A.L. totals (2 years)		9	11	.450	5.17	33	33	1	0	0-0	181.0	222	110	104	31	76-9	97
N.L. totals (5 years)		35	35	.500	4.49	96	89	4	3	0-0	528.2	564	283	264	71	199-13	368
Major League totals (7 years)		44	46	.489	4.67	129	122	5	3	0-0	709.2	786	393	368	102	275-22	465

PARRISH, JOHN — P — ORIOLES

PERSONAL: Born November 26, 1977, in Lancaster, Pa. ... 5-11/180. ... Throws left, bats left. ... Full name: John Henry Parrish Jr.
HIGH SCHOOL: J.P. McCaskey (Lancaster, Pa.).
TRANSACTIONS/CAREER NOTES: Selected by Baltimore Orioles organization in 25th round of free-agent draft (June 4, 1996). ... On disabled list (March 30, 2002-entire season).
CAREER HITTING (MLB): 0-for-0 (.000), 0 R, 0 2B, 0 3B, 0 HR, 0 RBI.

Year	League	W	L	Pct.	ERA	G	GS	CG	ShO	Sv.-Opp.	IP	H	R	ER	HR	BB-IBB	SO
1996—	Gulf Coast Orioles (GCL)	2	0	1.000	1.86	11	0	0	0	2-...	19.1	13	5	4	0	11-0	33
—	Bluefield (Appl.)	2	1	.667	2.70	8	0	0	0	1-...	13.1	11	6	4	0	9-1	18
1997—	Delmarva (S.Atl.)	3	3	.500	3.84	23	10	0	0	1-...	72.2	69	39	31	7	32-3	76
—	Bowie (East.)	1	0	1.000	1.80	1	1	0	0	0-...	5.0	3	1	1	0	2-0	3
—	Frederick (Caro.)	1	3	.250	6.04	5	5	0	0	0-...	22.1	23	18	15	3	16-0	17
1998—	Frederick (Caro.)	4	4	.500	3.27	16	16	1	0	0-...	82.2	77	39	30	5	27-1	81
1999—	Delmarva (S.Atl.)	0	1	.000	7.20	4	0	0	0	0-...	10.0	9	8	8	1	6-1	10
—	Frederick (Caro.)	2	2	.500	4.17	6	6	0	0	0-...	36.2	34	17	17	4	12-0	44
—	Bowie (East.)	0	2	.000	4.04	12	10	0	0	0-...	55.2	49	28	25	4	43-1	42
2000—	Bowie (East.)	2	0	1.000	1.69	3	3	0	0	0-...	16.0	12	3	3	0	7-0	16
—	Rochester (I.L.)	6	7	.462	4.24	18	18	0	0	0-...	104.0	85	54	49	10	56-1	87
—	Baltimore (A.L.)	2	4	.333	7.18	8	8	0	0	0-0	36.1	40	32	29	6	35-0	28
2001—	Rochester (I.L.)	7	7	.500	3.52	26	19	1	0	0-...	133.0	115	68	52	11	51-4	126
—	Baltimore (A.L.)	1	2	.333	6.14	16	1	0	0	0-0	22.0	22	17	15	5	17-1	20
2002—	Baltimore (A.L.)	Did not play.															
Major League totals (2 years)		3	6	.333	6.79	24	9	0	0	0-0	58.1	62	49	44	11	52-1	48

PASCUCCI, VAL — OF/1B — EXPOS

PERSONAL: Born November 17, 1978, in Bellflower, Calif. ... 6-6/235. ... Bats right, throws right. ... Full name: Valentino Martin Pascucci.
HIGH SCHOOL: Richard Gahr (Cerritos, Calif.).
COLLEGE: Oklahoma.
TRANSACTIONS/CAREER NOTES: Selected by Montreal Expos organization in 15th round of free-agent draft (June 2, 1999).
STATISTICAL NOTES: Tied for New York-Pennsylvania League lead with three intentional bases on balls received in 1999.

				BATTING													FIELDING	
Year	Team (League)	Pos.	G	AB	R	H	2B	3B	HR	RBI	BB	SO	SB-CS	Avg.	OBP	SLG	E	Avg.
1999—	Vermont (NY-Penn)	OF	72	259	*62	91	26	1	7	48	53	46	17-2	.351	.482	.541	6	.956
2000—	Cape Fear (S.Atl.)	OF	20	69	17	22	4	0	3	10	16	15	5-0	.319	.442	.507	1	.975
—	Jupiter (FSL)	OF-1B	113	405	70	115	30	2	14	66	66	98	14-6	.284	.394	.472	7	.975
2001—	Harrisburg (East.)	OF-1B	138	476	79	116	17	1	21	67	65	114	8-8	.244	.344	.416	6	.983
2002—	Harrisburg (East.)	OF-1B-3B	137	459	73	108	14	1	*27	82	*93	115	2-0	.235	.374	.447	9	.976

PATTERSON, COREY — OF — CUBS

PERSONAL: Born August 13, 1979, in Atlanta. ... 5-9/175. ... Bats left, throws right. ... Full name: Donald Corey Patterson. ... Son of Don Patterson, defensive back with Detroit Lions (1979) and New York Giants (1980).
HIGH SCHOOL: Harrison (Kennesaw, Ga.).
TRANSACTIONS/CAREER NOTES: Selected by Chicago Cubs organization in first round (third pick overall) of free-agent draft (June 2, 1998). ... On disabled list (May 27-June 11, 1999).
2002 GAMES PLAYED BY POSITION (MLB): OF—147.

		BATTING														FIELDING	
Year Team (League)	Pos.	G	AB	R	H	2B	3B	HR	RBI	BB	SO	SB-CS	Avg.	OBP	SLG	E	Avg.
1999—Lansing (Midw.)	OF	112	475	94	152	35	*17	20	79	25	85	33-9	.320	.358	*.592	9	.965
2000—West Tenn (Sou.)	OF	118	444	73	116	26	5	22	82	45	115	27-15	.261	.338	.491	3	.990
—Chicago (N.L.)	OF	11	42	9	7	1	0	2	2	3	14	1-1	.167	.239	.333	1	.963
2001—Iowa (PCL)	OF	89	367	63	93	22	3	7	32	29	65	19-8	.253	.308	.387	6	.968
—Chicago (N.L.)	OF	59	131	26	29	3	0	4	14	6	33	4-0	.221	.266	.336	2	.976
2002—Chicago (N.L.)	OF	153	592	71	150	30	5	14	54	19	142	18-3	.253	.284	.392	3	.990
Major League totals (3 years)		223	765	106	186	34	5	20	70	28	189	23-4	.243	.278	.379	6	.986

PATTERSON, DANNY — P — TIGERS

PERSONAL: Born February 17, 1971, in San Gabriel, Calif. ... 6-0/185. ... Throws right, bats right. ... Full name: Daniel Shane Patterson.
HIGH SCHOOL: San Gabriel (Calif.).
JUNIOR COLLEGE: Cerritos College (Calif.).
TRANSACTIONS/CAREER NOTES: Selected by Texas Rangers organization in 47th round of free-agent draft (June 5, 1989). ... On Texas disabled list (May 22-June 14, 1997); included rehabilitation assignment to Tulsa (June 9-14). ... On Texas disabled list (March 22-April 17, 1998); included rehabilitation assignments to Tulsa (April 7-12) and Oklahoma (April 13-17). ... Traded by Rangers with OF Juan Gonzalez and C Gregg Zaun to Detroit Tigers for P Justin Thompson, P Francisco Cordero, OF Gabe Kapler, C Bill Haselman, 2B Frank Catalanotto and P Alan Webb (November 2, 1999). ... On disabled list (July 22-August 7, 2000). ... On Detroit disabled list (April 4-May 31 and June 9, 2002-remainder of season) included rehabilitation assignment to Toledo (May 22-31).
CAREER HITTING (MLB): 0-for-1 (.000), 0 R, 0 2B, 0 3B, 0 HR, 0 RBI.

Year League	W	L	Pct.	ERA	G	GS	CG	ShO	Sv.-Opp.	IP	H	R	ER	HR	BB-IBB	SO
1990—Butte (Pio.)	0	3	.000	6.35	13	3	0	0	1-...	28.1	36	23	20	3	14-1	18
1991—Gulf Coast Rangers (GCL)	5	3	.625	3.24	11	9	0	0	0-...	50.0	43	21	18	1	12-0	46
1992—Gastonia (S.Atl.)	4	6	.400	3.59	23	21	3	1	0-...	105.1	106	47	42	9	33-3	84
1993—Charlotte (FSL)	5	6	.455	2.51	47	0	0	0	7-...	68.0	55	22	19	2	28-4	41
1994—Charlotte (FSL)	1	0	1.000	4.61	7	0	0	0	0-...	13.2	13	7	7	1	5-0	9
—Tulsa (Texas)	1	4	.200	1.64	30	1	0	0	6-...	44.0	35	13	8	2	17-1	33
1995—Tulsa (Texas)	2	2	.500	6.19	26	0	0	0	5-...	36.1	45	27	25	2	13-2	24
—Oklahoma City (A.A.)	1	0	1.000	1.65	14	0	0	0	2-...	27.1	23	8	5	0	9-2	9
1996—Oklahoma City (A.A.)	6	2	.750	1.68	44	0	0	0	10-...	80.1	79	22	15	5	15-3	53
—Texas (A.L.)	0	0	...	0.00	7	0	0	0	0-0	8.2	10	4	0	0	3-1	5
1997—Texas (A.L.)	10	6	.625	3.42	54	0	0	0	1-8	71.0	70	29	27	3	23-4	69
—Tulsa (Texas)	0	0	...	4.50	2	2	0	0	0-...	2.0	5	4	1	0	0-0	0
1998—Tulsa (Texas)	0	0	...	4.50	2	1	0	0	0-...	4.0	3	2	2	1	0-0	4
—Oklahoma (PCL)	0	0	...	4.50	1	0	0	0	0-...	2.0	4	1	1	0	1-0	2
—Texas (A.L.)	2	5	.286	4.45	56	0	0	0	2-2	60.2	64	31	30	11	19-2	33
1999—Texas (A.L.)	2	0	1.000	5.67	53	0	0	0	0-1	60.1	77	38	38	5	19-3	43
—Oklahoma (PCL)	1	0	1.000	0.00	2	0	0	0	0-...	3.0	1	0	0	0	1-...	4
2000—Detroit (A.L.)■	5	1	.833	3.97	58	0	0	0	0-2	56.2	69	26	25	4	14-2	29
2001—Detroit (A.L.)	5	4	.556	3.06	60	0	0	0	1-5	64.2	64	24	22	4	12-5	27
2002—Detroit (A.L.)	0	2	.000	15.00	6	0	0	0	0-1	3.0	5	5	5	0	2-0	1
—Toledo (I.L.)	0	0	...	0.00	5	1	0	0	0-...	5.0	1	0	0	0	0-0	3
Major League totals (7 years)	24	18	.571	4.07	294	0	0	0	4-19	325.0	359	157	147	27	92-17	207

DIVISION SERIES RECORD

Year League	W	L	Pct.	ERA	G	GS	CG	ShO	Sv.-Opp.	IP	H	R	ER	HR	BB-IBB	SO
1996—Texas (A.L.)	0	0	...	0.00	1	0	0	0	0-0	.1	1	0	0	0	0-0	0
1999—Texas (A.L.)	0	0	...	0.00	1	0	0	0	0-0	1.0	1	0	0	0	0-0	0
Division series totals (2 years)	0	0	...	0.00	2	0	0	0	0-0	1.1	2	0	0	0	0-0	0

PATTERSON, JOHN — P — DIAMONDBACKS

PERSONAL: Born January 30, 1978, in Orange, Texas. ... 6-5/183. ... Throws right, bats right. ... Full name: John Hollis Patterson.
HIGH SCHOOL: West Orange-Stark (Orange, Texas).
TRANSACTIONS/CAREER NOTES: Signed as non-drafted free agent by Arizona Diamondbacks organization (November 7, 1996). ... On disabled list (April 6-24 and May 6-September 8, 2000). ... On El Paso disabled list (April 5-19 and April 25-May 13, 2001). ... On Tucson disabled list (April 4-May 5, 2002).
CAREER HITTING (MLB): 1-for-10 (.100), 1 R, 0 2B, 0 3B, 0 HR, 0 RBI.

Year League	W	L	Pct.	ERA	G	GS	CG	ShO	Sv.-Opp.	IP	H	R	ER	HR	BB-IBB	SO
1997—South Bend (Midw.)	1	9	.100	3.23	18	18	0	0	0-...	78.0	63	32	28	3	34-0	95
1998—High Desert (Calif.)	8	7	.533	*2.83	25	25	0	0	0-...	127.0	102	54	40	12	42-0	148
1999—El Paso (Texas)	8	6	.571	4.77	18	18	2	0	0-...	100.0	98	61	53	16	42-0	117
—Tucson (PCL)	1	5	.167	7.04	7	6	0	0	0-...	30.2	43	26	24	3	18-0	29
2000—Tucson (PCL)	0	2	.000	7.80	3	2	0	0	0-...	15.0	21	14	13	1	9-0	10
2001—Lancaster (Calif.)	0	0	...	5.79	2	2	0	0	0-...	9.1	9	6	6	3	3-0	9
—El Paso (Texas)	1	2	.333	4.26	5	5	0	0	0-...	25.1	30	15	12	2	9-0	19
—Tucson (PCL)	2	7	.222	5.85	13	12	0	0	0-...	67.2	82	50	44	9	31-3	40
2002—Tucson (PCL)	10	5	.667	4.23	19	18	0	0	0-...	112.2	117	59	53	14	45-1	104
—Arizona (N.L.)	2	0	1.000	3.23	7	5	0	0	0-0	30.2	27	11	11	7	7-0	31
Major League totals (1 year)	2	0	1.000	3.23	7	5	0	0	0-0	30.2	27	11	11	7	7-0	31

PAUL, JOSH — C — WHITE SOX

PERSONAL: Born May 19, 1975, in Evanston, Ill. ... 6-1/200. ... Bats right, throws right. ... Full name: Joshua William Paul.
HIGH SCHOOL: Buffalo Grove (Ill.).
COLLEGE: Vanderbilt.
TRANSACTIONS/CAREER NOTES: Selected by Chicago White Sox organization in second round of free-agent draft (June 4, 1996). ... On Birmingham disabled list (April 13-July 13, 1997; and July 9-27, 1999). ... On Charlotte disabled list (July 5-August 3, 2000). ... On Charlotte disabled list (July 25-August 9, 2001).

STATISTICAL NOTES: Led Carolina League catchers with 818 putouts, 118 assists and 939 total chances in 1998.
2002 GAMES PLAYED BY POSITION (MLB): C—32; OF—1.

			BATTING														FIELDING	
Year	Team (League)	Pos.	G	AB	R	H	2B	3B	HR	RBI	BB	SO	SB-CS	Avg.	OBP	SLG	E	Avg.
1996—	Hickory (S.Atl.)	C	59	226	41	74	16	0	8	37	21	53	13-4	.327	.386	.504	2	.991
1997—	Birmingham (Sou.)	C	34	115	18	34	5	0	1	16	12	25	6-2	.296	.367	.365	3	.988
—	GC White Sox (GCL)	C	5	14	3	6	0	1	0	0	1	3	1-0	.429	.467	.571	3	.900
1998—	Win.-Salem (Caro.)	C	123	444	66	113	20	7	11	63	38	91	20-8	.255	.319	.405	3	*.997
1999—	Birmingham (Sou.)	C-DH	93	319	47	89	19	3	4	42	29	68	6-6	.279	.345	.395	5	*.992
—	Chicago (A.L.)	C	6	18	2	4	1	0	0	1	0	4	0-0	.222	.222	.278	0	1.000
2000—	Chicago (A.L.)	C-OF	36	71	15	20	3	2	1	8	5	17	1-0	.282	.338	.423	4	.974
—	Charlotte (I.L.)	C-OF	51	168	28	40	5	1	4	19	13	38	6-2	.238	.299	.351	2	.994
2001—	Chicago (A.L.)	C	57	139	20	37	11	0	3	18	13	25	6-2	.266	.327	.410	6	.980
—	Charlotte (I.L.)	C	22	75	11	21	4	0	4	14	7	18	0-0	.280	.337	.493	0	1.000
2002—	Charlotte (I.L.)	C-1B-OF	65	231	18	63	15	2	0	17	17	45	10-4	.273	.323	.355	3	.993
—	Chicago (A.L.)	C-OF	33	104	11	25	4	0	0	11	9	22	2-0	.240	.302	.279	2	.991
Major League totals (4 years)			132	332	48	86	19	2	4	38	27	68	9-2	.259	.316	.364	12	.983

DIVISION SERIES RECORD

			BATTING														FIELDING	
Year	Team (League)	Pos.	G	AB	R	H	2B	3B	HR	RBI	BB	SO	SB-CS	Avg.	OBP	SLG	E	Avg.
2000—	Chicago (A.L.)	PR-C	1	0	0	0	0	0	0	0	0	0	0-0	...	...	...	0	1.000

PAVANO, CARL — P — MARLINS

PERSONAL: Born January 8, 1976, in New Britain, Conn. ... 6-5/230. ... Throws right, bats right. ... Full name: Carl Anthony Pavano.
HIGH SCHOOL: Southington (Conn.).
TRANSACTIONS/CAREER NOTES: Selected by Boston Red Sox organization in 13th round of free-agent draft (June 2, 1994). ... Traded by Red Sox with a player to be named later to Montreal Expos for P Pedro Martinez (November 18, 1997); Expos acquired P Tony Armas Jr. to complete deal (December 18, 1997). ... On Montreal disabled list (July 12-September 11, 1999); included rehabilitation assignments to Ottawa (July 29-30 and September 6-7). ... On disabled list (June 25, 2000-remainder of season). ... On Montreal disabled list (March 23-August 15, 2001); included rehabilitation assignments to Jupiter (July 14-29) and Ottawa (July 30-August 9). ... Traded by Expos with P Graeme Lloyd, IF Mike Mordecai and P Justin Wayne to Florida Marlins for OF Cliff Floyd, P Claudio Vargas, 2B/OF Wilton Guerrero, cash considerations and a player to be named later (July 11, 2002); Expos acquired P Don Levinski to complete deal (August 6, 2002).
HONORS: Named Eastern League Pitcher of the Year (1996).
CAREER HITTING (MLB): 22-for-159 (.138), 6 R, 3 2B, 1 3B, 0 HR, 7 RBI.

Year	League	W	L	Pct.	ERA	G	GS	CG	ShO	Sv.-Opp.	IP	H	R	ER	HR	BB-IBB	SO
1994—	Gulf Coast Red Sox (GCL)	4	3	.571	1.84	9	7	0	0	0-...	44.0	31	14	9	1	7-0	47
1995—	Michigan (Midw.)	6	6	.500	3.45	22	22	1	0	0-...	141.0	118	63	54	7	52-0	138
1996—	Trenton (East.)	16	5	.762	2.63	27	26	6	2	0-...	185.0	154	66	54	16	47-2	146
1997—	Pawtucket (I.L.)	11	6	.647	3.12	23	23	3	0	0-...	161.2	148	62	56	13	34-2	147
1998—	Jupiter (FSL)■	0	0	...	6.60	4	4	0	0	0-...	15.0	20	11	11	1	3-0	14
—	Ottawa (I.L.)	1	0	1.000	2.41	3	3	0	0	0-...	18.2	12	5	5	1	7-0	14
—	Montreal (N.L.)	6	9	.400	4.21	24	23	0	0	0-0	134.2	130	70	63	18	43-1	83
1999—	Montreal (N.L.)	6	8	.429	5.63	19	18	1	1	0-0	104.0	117	66	65	8	35-1	70
—	Ottawa (I.L.)	0	1	.000	9.00	2	2	0	0	0-...	5.0	7	5	5	1	0-0	3
2000—	Montreal (N.L.)	8	4	.667	3.06	15	15	0	0	0-0	97.0	89	40	33	8	34-1	64
2001—	Jupiter (FSL)	1	1	.500	2.19	3	3	0	0	0-...	12.1	10	7	3	1	2-0	11
—	Ottawa (I.L.)	2	1	.667	3.58	4	4	0	0	0-...	27.2	27	13	11	4	5-0	19
—	Montreal (N.L.)	1	6	.143	6.33	8	8	0	0	0-0	42.2	59	33	30	7	16-1	36
2002—	Montreal (N.L.)	3	8	.273	6.30	15	14	0	0	0-0	74.1	98	55	52	14	31-5	51
—	Ottawa (I.L.)	3	0	1.000	3.10	3	3	0	0	0-...	20.1	23	8	7	2	2-0	9
—	Florida (N.L.)■	3	2	.600	3.79	22	8	0	0	0-0	61.2	76	33	26	5	14-3	41
Major League totals (5 years)		27	37	.422	4.71	103	86	1	1	0-0	514.1	569	297	269	60	173-12	345

PAYTON, JAY — OF — ROCKIES

PERSONAL: Born November 22, 1972, in Zanesville, Ohio. ... 5-10/185. ... Bats right, throws right. ... Full name: Jason Lee Payton.
HIGH SCHOOL: Zanesville (Ohio).
COLLEGE: Georgia Tech.
TRANSACTIONS/CAREER NOTES: Selected by New York Mets organization in supplemental round ("sandwich pick" between first and second round, 29th pick overall) of free-agent draft (June 2, 1994); pick received as part of compensation for Baltimore Orioles signing Type A free-agent P Sid Fernandez. ... On Norfolk disabled list (April 29-July 3, 1996). ... On disabled list (April 3, 1997-entire season). ... On Norfolk disabled list (May 27-June 15 and June 24-July 20, 1998). ... On New York disabled list (March 21-June 8, 1999); included rehabilitation assignment to St. Lucie (May 30-June 8). ... On Norfolk disabled list (July 10-August 19, 1999). ... On New York disabled list (May 8-June 26, 2001); included rehabilitation assignment to St. Lucie (June 22-26). ... Traded by Mets with P Mark Corey and OF Robert Stratton to Colorado Rockies for P John Thomson and OF Mark Little (July 31, 2002).
STATISTICAL NOTES: Career major league grand slams: 1.
2002 GAMES PLAYED BY POSITION (MLB): OF—126.

			BATTING														FIELDING	
Year	Team (League)	Pos.	G	AB	R	H	2B	3B	HR	RBI	BB	SO	SB-CS	Avg.	OBP	SLG	E	Avg.
1994—	Pittsfield (NY-Penn)	OF	58	219	47	80	16	2	3	37	23	18	10-2	.365	.439	.498	5	.964
—	Binghamton (East.)	OF	8	25	3	7	1	0	0	1	2	3	1-1	.280	.357	.320	1	.917
1995—	Binghamton (East.)	OF	85	357	59	123	20	3	14	54	29	32	16-7	.345	.395	.535	3	.988
—	Norfolk (I.L.)	OF	50	196	33	47	11	4	4	30	11	22	11-3	.240	.284	.398	2	.982
1996—	Norfolk (I.L.)	DH-OF	55	153	30	47	6	3	6	26	11	26	10-1	.307	.363	.503	0	1.000
—	GC Mets (GCL)	DH	3	13	3	5	1	0	1	2	0	1	1-0	.385	.385	.692	...	...
—	St. Lucie (FSL)	DH	9	26	4	8	2	0	0	1	4	5	2-1	.308	.400	.385	...	...
—	Binghamton (East.)	DH	4	10	0	2	0	0	0	2	2	2	0-1	.200	.286	.200	...	...

									BATTING								FIELDING	
Year	Team (League)	Pos.	G	AB	R	H	2B	3B	HR	RBI	BB	SO	SB-CS	Avg.	OBP	SLG	E	Avg.
1997—	....								Did not play.									
1998—	Norfolk (I.L.)	OF-1B-DH	82	322	45	84	14	4	8	30	26	50	12-7	.261	.318	.404	7	.980
—	St. Lucie (FSL)	OF	3	7	0	1	0	0	0	0	3	1	0-0	.143	.400	.143	0	1.000
—	New York (N.L.)..........	OF	15	22	2	7	1	0	0	0	1	4	0-0	.318	.348	.364	0	1.000
1999—	St. Lucie (FSL)	OF	7	26	3	9	1	1	0	3	4	5	0-1	.346	.433	.462	1	.955
—	Norfolk (I.L.)	OF-DH	38	144	27	56	13	2	8	35	12	13	2-2	.389	.437	.674	1	.984
—	New York (N.L.)..........	OF	13	8	1	2	1	0	0	1	0	2	1-2	.250	.333	.375	0	1.000
2000—	New York (N.L.)..........	OF	149	488	63	142	23	1	17	62	30	60	5-11	.291	.331	.447	6	.981
2001—	New York (N.L.)..........	OF	104	361	44	92	16	1	8	34	18	52	4-3	.255	.298	.371	4	.984
—	St. Lucie (FSL)	OF	4	16	7	6	3	0	0	0	4	1	0-0	.375	.500	.563	0	1.000
2002—	New York (N.L.)..........	OF	87	275	33	78	6	3	8	31	21	34	4-1	.284	.336	.415	1	.994
—	Colorado (N.L.)■	OF	47	170	36	57	14	4	8	28	8	20	3-3	.335	.376	.606	0	1.000
Major League totals (5 years)			415	1324	179	378	61	9	41	156	78	172	17-20	.285	.329	.438	11	.987

DIVISION SERIES RECORD

									BATTING								FIELDING	
Year	Team (League)	Pos.	G	AB	R	H	2B	3B	HR	RBI	BB	SO	SB-CS	Avg.	OBP	SLG	E	Avg.
2000—	New York (N.L.)..........	OF	4	17	1	3	0	0	0	2	0	4	1-1	.176	.167	.176	0	1.000

CHAMPIONSHIP SERIES RECORD

									BATTING								FIELDING	
Year	Team (League)	Pos.	G	AB	R	H	2B	3B	HR	RBI	BB	SO	SB-CS	Avg.	OBP	SLG	E	Avg.
2000—	New York (N.L.)..........	OF	5	19	1	3	0	0	1	3	2	5	0-0	.158	.273	.316	0	1.000

WORLD SERIES RECORD

									BATTING								FIELDING	
Year	Team (League)	Pos.	G	AB	R	H	2B	3B	HR	RBI	BB	SO	SB-CS	Avg.	OBP	SLG	E	Avg.
2000—	New York (N.L.)..........	OF	5	21	3	7	0	0	1	3	0	5	0-0	.333	.333	.476	2	.895

PEARCE, JOSH — P — CARDINALS

PERSONAL: Born August 20, 1977, in Yakima, Wash. ... 6-3/215. ... Throws right, bats right. ... Full name: Joshua Ray Pearce.
HIGH SCHOOL: West Valley (Yakima, Wash.).
COLLEGE: Portland, then Arizona.
TRANSACTIONS/CAREER NOTES: Selected by New York Mets organization in 40th round of free-agent draft (June 4, 1996); did not sign. ... Selected by St. Louis Cardinals organization in supplemental round ("sandwich pick" between second and third round) of free-agent draft (June 2, 1999); pick received as compensation for Seattle Mariners signing Type C free agent C Tom Lampkin. ... On Memphis disabled list (May 11-August 30, 2002). ... On St. Louis disabled list (August 30, 2002-remainder of season).
CAREER HITTING (MLB): 1-for-4 (.250), 0 R, 0 2B, 0 3B, 0 HR, 1 RBI.

Year	League	W	L	Pct.	ERA	G	GS	CG	ShO	Sv.-Opp.	IP	H	R	ER	HR	BB-IBB	SO
1999—	New Jersey (NY-Penn).....	3	7	.300	4.98	14	14	1	1	0-...	77.2	78	45	43	8	20-0	78
2000—	Potomac (Caro.)...............	5	3	.625	3.45	10	10	1	0	0-...	62.2	70	25	24	5	10-0	42
—	Arkansas (Texas).............	5	6	.455	5.46	17	17	0	0	0-...	97.1	117	68	59	13	35-2	63
2001—	New Haven (East.)............	6	8	.429	2.34	18	18	0	0	0-...	185.0	111	55	48	11	34-1	96
—	Memphis (PCL)................	4	4	.500	2.58	10	10	0	0	0-...	115.1	72	43	33	11	12-1	36
2002—	Memphis (PCL)................	0	4	.000	7.65	4	4	0	0	0-...	20.0	28	18	17	8	3-0	17
—	St. Louis (N.L.)................	0	0	...	7.62	3	3	0	0	0-0	13.0	20	13	11	1	8-0	1
Major League totals (1 year).......		0	0	...	7.62	3	3	0	0	0-0	13.0	20	13	11	1	8-0	1

PEARSON, JASON — P

PERSONAL: Born December 29, 1975, in Freeport, Ill. ... 6-0/195. ... Throws left, bats left. ... Full name: Jason John Pearson.
HIGH SCHOOL: Freeport (Ill.).
COLLEGE: Illinois State.
TRANSACTIONS/CAREER NOTES: Signed as non-drafted free agent by Florida Marlins organization (June 16, 1998). ... Released by Marlins (April 5, 1999). ... Signed by Sioux Falls, Northern League (May 1999). ... Signed by Fargo-Moorhead, Northern League (May 2000). ... Signed by Cincinnati Reds organization (October 10, 2000). ... Selected by San Diego Padres from Reds organization in Rule 5 minor league draft (December 11, 2000). ... Claimed on waivers by San Francisco Giants (June 10, 2002). ... Granted free agency (October 15, 2002).
CAREER HITTING (MLB): 0-for-0 (.000), 0 R, 0 2B, 0 3B, 0 HR, 0 RBI.

Year	League	W	L	Pct.	ERA	G	GS	CG	ShO	Sv.-Opp.	IP	H	R	ER	HR	BB-IBB	SO
1998—	Gulf Coast Marlins (GCL).	4	0	1.000	1.57	11	3	0	0	2-...	34.1	28	8	6	0	5-0	36
—	Kane County (Midw.)........	0	0	...	3.38	2	0	0	0	0-...	2.2	3	3	1	0	1-0	1
1999—	Sioux Falls (Nor.)■	2	3	.400	3.00	27	2	0	...	0-...	63.0	57	29	21	6	28-2	48
2000—	Fargo-Moorhead (Nor.)■.	10	2	.833	3.00	18	16	1	...	0-...	108.0	90	45	36	6	49-1	82
2001—	Mobile (Sou.)..................	5	5	.500	4.17	54	5	0	0	1-...	86.1	88	40	40	5	30-3	67
2002—	Portland (PCL)■	3	0	1.000	1.50	23	0	0	0	0-...	30.0	25	5	5	3	9-0	18
—	San Diego (N.L.)	0	0	...	0.00	2	0	0	0	0-0	1.2	1	0	0	0	0-0	3
—	Fresno (PCL)■.................	0	0	...	3.75	34	0	0	0	0-...	36.0	35	20	15	5	16-1	28
Major League totals (1 year).......		0	0	...	0.00	2	0	0	0	0-0	1.2	1	0	0	0	0-0	3

PEARSON, TERRY — P — TIGERS

PERSONAL: Born November 10, 1971, in Tuscaloosa, Ala. ... 6-0/200. ... Throws right, bats right. ... Full name: Terry G. Pearson.
JUNIOR COLLEGE: Shelton State Junior College (Ala.).
COLLEGE: West Alabama.
TRANSACTIONS/CAREER NOTES: Signed by Zanesville of Frontier League (June 1995). ... Signed by Sioux Falls of Northern League (May 1997). ... Signed by Duluth-Superior of Northern League (July 2000). ... Signed as non-drafted free agent by Detroit Tigers organization (March 29, 2001).
CAREER HITTING (MLB): 0-for-0 (.000), 0 R, 0 2B, 0 3B, 0 HR, 0 RBI.

Year League	W	L	Pct.	ERA	G	GS	CG	ShO	Sv.-Opp.	IP	H	R	ER	HR	BB-IBB	SO
1995—Zanesville (Fron.)	6	2	.750	3.21	14	14	0	0	0-...	84.0	80	45	30	5	37-0	55
1996—Zanesville (Fron.)	4	1	.800	0.50	31	0	0	0	20-...	36.0	30	12	2	0	8-0	43
1997—Sioux Falls (Nor.)■	2	3	.400	4.14	41	0	0	0	1-...	63.0	85	54	29	5	30-3	46
1998—									Did not play.							
1999—									Did not play.							
2000—Sioux Falls (Nor.)	2	2	.500	4.50	19	0	0	0	6-...	22.0	27	17	11	1	7-2	14
—Duluth/Superior (Nor.)■	2	2	.500	6.75	18	0	0	0	3-...	20.0	28	18	15	0	4-0	18
2001—Erie (East.)	4	4	.500	2.93	59	0	0	0	23-...	61.1	65	26	20	1	16-2	62
2002—Toledo (I.L.)	3	8	.273	4.79	40	0	0	0	2-...	47.0	52	29	25	1	18-4	30
—Erie (East.)	0	0	...	3.68	15	0	0	0	4-...	14.2	25	7	6	1	2-0	11
—Detroit (A.L.)	0	0	...	10.50	4	0	0	0	0-0	6.0	8	7	7	2	2-1	4
Major League totals (1 year)	0	0	...	10.50	4	0	0	0	0-0	6.0	8	7	7	2	2-1	4

PEAVY, JAKE — P — PADRES

PERSONAL: Born May 31, 1981, in Mobile, Ala. ... 6-1/180. ... Throws right, bats right. ... Full name: Jacob Edward Peavy.
HIGH SCHOOL: St. Paul (Mobile, Ala.).
TRANSACTIONS/CAREER NOTES: Selected by San Diego Padres organization in 15th round of free-agent draft (June 2, 1999).
CAREER HITTING (MLB): 7-for-33 (.212), 4 R, 3 2B, 0 3B, 0 HR, 2 RBI.

Year League	W	L	Pct.	ERA	G	GS	CG	ShO	Sv.-Opp.	IP	H	R	ER	HR	BB-IBB	SO
1999—Arizona Padres (Ariz.)	7	1	.875	1.34	13	11	1	0	0-...	73.2	52	16	11	4	23-0	90
—Idaho Falls (Pio.)	2	0	1.000	0.00	2	2	0	0	0-...	11.0	5	0	0	0	1-0	13
2000—Fort Wayne (Midw.)	13	8	.619	2.90	26	25	0	0	0-...	133.2	107	61	43	6	53-0	164
2001—Lake Elsinore (Calif.)	7	5	.583	3.08	19	19	0	0	0-...	105.1	76	41	36	6	33-1	144
—Mobile (Sou.)	2	1	.667	2.57	5	5	0	0	0-...	28.0	19	8	8	3	12-1	44
2002—Mobile (Sou.)	4	5	.444	2.80	14	14	0	0	0-...	80.1	65	26	25	4	30-0	89
—San Diego (N.L.)	6	7	.462	4.52	17	17	0	0	0-0	97.2	106	54	49	11	33-4	90
Major League totals (1 year)	6	7	.462	4.52	17	17	0	0	0-0	97.2	106	54	49	11	33-4	90

PELAEZ, ALEX — 3B — PADRES

PERSONAL: Born April 6, 1976, in San Diego. ... 5-9/190. ... Bats right, throws right. ... Full name: Alejandro Pelaez.
HIGH SCHOOL: Chula Vista (Calif.).
COLLEGE: San Diego State.
TRANSACTIONS/CAREER NOTES: Selected by San Diego Padres organization in 42nd round of free-agent draft (June 2, 1998).
2002 GAMES PLAYED BY POSITION (MLB): 1B—1; 2B—1; 3B—1.

		BATTING														FIELDING	
Year Team (League)	Pos.	G	AB	R	H	2B	3B	HR	RBI	BB	SO	SB-CS	Avg.	OBP	SLG	E	Avg.
1998—Idaho Falls (Pio.)	3B	63	262	52	89	17	1	8	51	29	32	3-1	.340	.405	.504	6	.967
1999—Rancho Cuca. (Calif.)	3B-2B-1B	117	443	62	132	21	4	4	54	35	53	7-3	.298	.349	.391	9	.970
—Las Vegas (PCL)	3B-2B	5	13	1	4	0	0	0	0	0	2	0-0	.308	.308	.308	1	.875
2000—Rancho Cuca. (Calif.)	3B-2B-1B	62	235	29	66	20	0	2	28	23	27	2-2	.281	.340	.391	8	.949
—Las Vegas (PCL)	3B-1B-2B	34	108	13	27	3	0	1	15	4	20	0-0	.250	.281	.306	0	1.000
—Mobile (Sou.)	3B-2B-1B	28	90	8	24	3	0	2	11	10	15	0-0	.267	.337	.367	4	.958
2001—Mobile (Sou.)	3B-1B-P-2B	114	416	44	117	22	1	10	53	32	52	2-0	.281	.332	.411	8	.980
2002—Portland (PCL)	3B-2B-1B	112	411	47	127	31	1	11	64	20	40	0-1	.309	.339	.470	7	.982
—San Diego (N.L.)	1B-2B-3B	3	8	0	2	0	0	0	0	0	0	0-0	.250	.250	.250	0	1.000
Major League totals (1 year)		3	8	0	2	0	0	0	0	0	0	0-0	.250	.250	.250	0	1.000

RECORD AS PITCHER

Year League	W	L	Pct.	ERA	G	GS	CG	ShO	Sv.-Opp.	IP	H	R	ER	HR	BB-IBB	SO
2001—Mobile (Sou.)	1	1	.500	3.48	8	0	0	0	0-...	10.1	13	4	4	2	3-2	1

PELLOW, KIT — 1B

PERSONAL: Born August 28, 1973, in Kansas City, Mo. ... 6-1/200. ... Bats right, throws right. ... Full name: Kit Donovan Pellow.
HIGH SCHOOL: Olathe North (Kan.).
JUNIOR COLLEGE: Johnson County Community College (Kan.).
COLLEGE: Arkansas.
TRANSACTIONS/CAREER NOTES: Selected by Kansas City Royals organization in 22nd round of free-agent draft (June 4, 1996). ... Granted free agency (October 15, 2002).
2002 GAMES PLAYED BY POSITION (MLB): 3B—12; 1B—10; DH—5.

		BATTING														FIELDING	
Year Team (League)	Pos.	G	AB	R	H	2B	3B	HR	RBI	BB	SO	SB-CS	Avg.	OBP	SLG	E	Avg.
1996—Spokane (N'West)	1B-OF-3B-C	71	279	48	80	18	2	18	66	20	52	8-3	.287	.344	.559	14	.971
1997—Lansing (Midw.)	1B-3B	65	256	39	76	17	2	11	52	24	74	2-0	.297	.366	.508	33	.890
—Wichita (Texas)	3B	68	241	40	60	12	1	10	41	21	72	5-2	.249	.311	.432	24	.898
1998—Wichita (Texas)	3B	103	374	70	100	24	3	29	73	27	107	4-3	.267	.324	.580	26	.904
—Omaha (PCL)	3B	14	54	8	10	3	0	2	6	2	19	2-0	.185	.207	.352	3	.919
1999—Omaha (PCL)	3B-1B	131	475	88	136	28	4	35	99	20	117	6-5	.286	.335	.583	33	.906
2000—Omaha (PCL)	1B	117	421	61	105	17	3	22	75	38	89	6-4	.249	.331	.461	8	.992
2001—Omaha (PCL)	1B	129	484	81	141	15	0	20	81	37	101	4-3	.291	.353	.446	8	.993
2002—Omaha (PCL)	3B-1B	105	402	65	116	25	2	27	76	21	82	4-2	.289	.350	.562	19	.950
—Kansas City (A.L.)	3B-1B-DH	29	63	6	15	1	0	1	5	9	21	1-1	.238	.342	.302	5	.929
Major League totals (1 year)		29	63	6	15	1	0	1	5	9	21	1-1	.238	.342	.302	5	.929

PEMBER, DAVE — P — BREWERS

PERSONAL: Born May 24, 1978, in Cincinnati. ... 6-5/225. ... Throws right, bats right. ... Full name: David J. Pember.
COLLEGE: Western Carolina.
TRANSACTIONS/CAREER NOTES: Selected by Milwaukee Brewers organization in eighth round of free-agent draft (June 2, 1999).
CAREER HITTING (MLB): 0-for-1 (.000), 0 R, 0 2B, 0 3B, 0 HR, 0 RBI.

Year	League	W	L	Pct.	ERA	G	GS	CG	ShO	Sv.-Opp.	IP	H	R	ER	HR	BB-IBB	SO
2000—	Beloit (Midw.)	2	10	.167	4.68	17	16	0	0	0-...	98.0	118	56	51	9	25-2	70
2001—	Beloit (Midw.)	3	4	.429	3.27	8	8	0	0	0-...	44.0	49	20	16	3	10-0	39
	—High Desert (Calif.)	9	6	.600	4.82	20	20	0	0	0-...	121.1	135	73	65	12	35-1	96
2002—	Huntsville (Sou.)	10	6	.625	3.17	27	27	2	0	0-...	156.0	157	69	55	13	53-1	111
	—Milwaukee (N.L.)	0	1	.000	5.19	4	1	0	0	0-0	8.2	7	6	5	1	6-0	5
Major League totals (1 year)		0	1	.000	5.19	4	1	0	0	0-0	8.2	7	6	5	1	6-0	5

PENA, CARLOS — 1B — TIGERS

PERSONAL: Born May 17, 1978, in Santo Domingo, Dominican Republic. ... 6-2/210. ... Bats left, throws left.
HIGH SCHOOL: Haverhill (Mass.).
COLLEGE: Wright State, Northeastern.
TRANSACTIONS/CAREER NOTES: Selected by Texas Rangers organization in first round (10th pick overall) of free-agent draft (June 2, 1998). ... Traded by Rangers with P Mike Venafro to Oakland Athletics for 1B Jason Hart, P Marion Ramos, C Gerald Laird and OF Ryan Ludwick (January 14, 2002). ... Traded by A's to Detroit Tigers with P Franklyn German and a player to be named later as part of three-way deal in which New York Yankees acquired P Jeff Weaver from Tigers and A's acquired P Ted Lilly, OF John-Ford Griffin and P Jason Arnold from Yankees (July 5, 2002); Tigers acquired P Jeremy Bonderman to complete deal (August 22, 2002).
STATISTICAL NOTES: Led Florida State League first basemen with 121 double plays in 1999.
2002 GAMES PLAYED BY POSITION (MLB): 1B—113; DH—2.

			BATTING													FIELDING	
Year	Team (League)	Pos.	G	AB	R	H	2B	3B	HR	RBI	BB	SO	SB-CS	Avg.	OBP	SLG	E	Avg.
1998—	GC Rangers (GCL)	1B	2	5	1	2	0	0	0	0	3	1	1-1	.400	.625	.400	0	1.000
	—Savannah (S.Atl.)	1B-OF	30	117	22	38	14	0	6	20	8	26	3-2	.325	.385	.598	3	.986
	—Charlotte (FSL)	1B	7	22	1	6	1	0	0	3	2	8	0-1	.273	.360	.318	1	.977
1999—	Charlotte (FSL)	1B	136	501	85	128	31	8	18	103	74	135	2-5	.255	.365	.457	16	.986
2000—	Tulsa (Texas)	1B	138	529	117	158	36	2	28	105	101	108	12-0	.299	.414	.533	22	.982
2001—	Oklahoma (PCL)	1B	119	431	71	124	38	3	23	74	80	127	11-3	.288	.408	.550	11	.989
	—Texas (A.L.)	1B-DH	22	62	6	16	4	1	3	12	10	17	0-0	.258	.361	.500	2	.987
2002—	Oakland (A.L.)■	1B	40	124	12	27	4	0	7	16	15	38	0-0	.218	.305	.419	1	.997
	—Sacramento (PCL)	1B	44	175	30	42	10	1	10	33	24	49	3-0	.240	.340	.480	3	.992
	—Detroit (A.L.)■	1B-DH	75	273	31	69	13	4	12	36	26	73	2-2	.253	.321	.462	3	.996
Major League totals (2 years)			137	459	49	112	21	5	22	64	51	128	2-2	.244	.322	.455	6	.995

PENA, WILY — OF — REDS

PERSONAL: Born January 23, 1982, in Lagunda Salada, Dominican Republic. ... 6-3/215. ... Bats right, throws right. ... Full name: Wily Modesto Pena.
TRANSACTIONS/CAREER NOTES: Signed by New York Mets organization (1998); contract nullified by Baseball Commissioner's Office. ... Declared a free agent (March 7, 1999). ... Signed by New York Yankees organization (April 1, 1999). ... On New York disabled list (July 13, 2000-remainder of season). ... Traded by Yankees to Cincinnati Reds for 3B Drew Henson and OF Michael Coleman (March 21, 2001). ... On Chattanooga disabled list (April 17-May 11, 2002).
STATISTICAL NOTES: Led Midwest League outfielders with three double plays in 2001.
2002 GAMES PLAYED BY POSITION (MLB): OF—4.

			BATTING													FIELDING	
Year	Team (League)	Pos.	G	AB	R	H	2B	3B	HR	RBI	BB	SO	SB-CS	Avg.	OBP	SLG	E	Avg.
1999—	GC Yankees (GCL)	OF	45	166	21	41	10	1	7	26	12	54	3-2	.247	.323	.446	2	.947
2000—	Greensboro (S.Atl.)	OF	67	249	41	51	7	1	10	28	18	91	6-5	.205	.268	.361	4	.964
	—Staten Island (NY-P)	OF	20	73	7	22	1	2	0	10	2	23	2-0	.301	.354	.370	0	1.000
2001—	Dayton (Midw.)■	OF	*135	511	87	135	25	5	26	*113	33	*177	26-10	.264	.327	.485	9	.972
2002—	Chattanooga (Sou.)	OF	105	388	47	99	23	1	11	47	36	126	8-0	.255	.330	.405	4	.979
	—Cincinnati (N.L.)	OF	13	18	1	4	0	0	1	1	0	11	0-0	.222	.222	.389	0	1.000
Major League totals (1 year)			13	18	1	4	0	0	1	1	0	11	0-0	.222	.222	.389	0	1.000

PENNY, BRAD — P — MARLINS

PERSONAL: Born May 24, 1978, in Broken Arrow, Okla. ... 6-4/247. ... Throws right, bats right. ... Full name: Bradley Wayne Penny.
HIGH SCHOOL: Broken Arrow (Okla.).
TRANSACTIONS/CAREER NOTES: Selected by Arizona Diamondbacks organization in fifth round of free-agent draft (June 4, 1996). ... On El Paso disabled list (April 20-30, 1999). ... Traded by Diamondbacks with P Vladimir Nunez and a player to be named later to Florida Marlins for P Matt Mantei (July 9, 1999); Marlins acquired OF Abraham Nunez to complete deal (December 13, 1999). ... On Florida disabled list (July 20-September 2, 2000); included rehabilitation assignments to Brevard County (August 5-15) and Calgary (August 16-September 2). ... On Florida disabled list (May 19-July 2, 2002); included rehabilitation assignment to Jupiter (June 23-July 2).
HONORS: Named California League Most Valuable Player and Pitcher of the Year (1998).
MISCELLANEOUS: Flied out in only appearance as pinch hitter (2000).
CAREER HITTING (MLB): 23-for-155 (.148), 8 R, 3 2B, 1 3B, 0 HR, 4 RBI.

Year	League	W	L	Pct.	ERA	G	GS	CG	ShO	Sv.-Opp.	IP	H	R	ER	HR	BB-IBB	SO
1996—	Ariz. D-backs (Ariz.)	2	2	.500	2.36	11	8	0	0	0-...	49.2	36	18	13	1	14-0	52
1997—	South Bend (Midw.)	10	5	.667	2.73	25	25	0	0	0-...	118.2	91	44	36	4	43-2	116
1998—	High Desert (Calif.)	*14	5	.737	2.96	28	•28	1	0	0-...	164.0	138	65	54	15	35-0	*207
1999—	El Paso (Texas)	2	7	.222	4.80	17	17	0	0	0-...	90.0	109	56	48	9	25-0	100
	— Portland (East.)■	1	0	1.000	3.90	6	6	0	0	0-...	32.1	28	15	14	3	14-0	35
2000—	Florida (N.L.)	8	7	.533	4.81	23	22	0	0	0-0	119.2	120	70	64	13	60-4	80
	— Brevard County (FSL)	0	1	.000	1.13	2	2	0	0	0-...	8.0	5	2	1	0	4-0	11
	— Calgary (PCL)	2	0	1.000	1.80	3	3	0	0	0-...	15.0	8	8	3	1	10-0	16
2001—	Florida (N.L.)	10	10	.500	3.69	31	31	1	1	0-0	205.0	183	92	84	15	54-3	154
2002—	Florida (N.L.)	8	7	.533	4.66	24	24	1	1	0-0	129.1	148	76	67	18	50-7	93
	— Jupiter (FSL)	0	0	...	0.00	2	2	0	0	0-...	7.2	5	0	0	0	0-0	9
Major League totals (3 years)		26	24	.520	4.26	78	77	2	2	0-0	454.0	451	238	215	46	164-14	327

PERCIVAL, TROY — P — ANGELS

PERSONAL: Born August 9, 1969, in Fontana, Calif. ... 6-3/235. ... Throws right, bats right. ... Full name: Troy Eugene Percival. ... Name pronounced PER-sih-vol.

HIGH SCHOOL: Moreno Valley (Calif.).

COLLEGE: UC Riverside.

TRANSACTIONS/CAREER NOTES: Selected by California Angels organization in sixth round of free-agent draft (June 5, 1990). ... On Palm Springs disabled list (June 3-July 2, 1992). ... On disabled list (May 28, 1993-remainder of season). ... Angels franchise renamed Anaheim Angels for 1997 season. ... On disabled list (April 7-May 16, 1997); included rehabilitation assignment to Lake Elsinore (May 13-16). ... On Anaheim disabled list (August 5-26, 2000); included rehabilitation assignment to Lake Elsinore (August 22-26). ... On disabled list (April 3-18 and July 12-27, 2002).

MISCELLANEOUS: Played catcher (1990). ... Struck out in only appearance as pinch hitter (1996). ... Holds Anaheim Angels franchise all-time records for most games pitched (475) and most saves (250).

CAREER HITTING (MLB): 0-for-1 (.000), 0 R, 0 2B, 0 3B, 0 HR, 0 RBI.

Year	League	W	L	Pct.	ERA	G	GS	CG	ShO	Sv.-Opp.	IP	H	R	ER	HR	BB-IBB	SO
1991—	Boise (N'West)	2	0	1.000	1.41	28	0	0	0	*12-...	38.1	23	7	6	0	18-1	63
1992—	Palm Springs (Calif.)	1	1	.500	5.06	11	0	0	0	2-...	10.2	6	7	6	0	8-1	16
	— Midland (Texas)	3	0	1.000	2.37	20	0	0	0	5-...	19.0	18	5	5	1	11-1	21
1993—	Vancouver (PCL)	0	1	.000	6.27	18	0	0	0	4-...	18.2	24	14	13	0	13-1	19
1994—	Vancouver (PCL)	2	6	.250	4.13	49	0	0	0	15-...	61.0	63	31	28	4	29-5	73
1995—	California (A.L.)	3	2	.600	1.95	62	0	0	0	3-6	74.0	37	19	16	6	26-2	94
1996—	California (A.L.)	0	2	.000	2.31	62	0	0	0	36-39	74.0	38	20	19	8	31-4	100
1997—	Anaheim (A.L.)	5	5	.500	3.46	55	0	0	0	27-31	52.0	40	20	20	6	22-2	72
	— Lake Elsinore (Calif.)	0	0	...	0.00	2	1	0	0	0-...	2.0	1	0	0	0	0-0	3
1998—	Anaheim (A.L.)	2	7	.222	3.64	67	0	0	0	42-48	66.2	45	31	27	5	37-4	87
1999—	Anaheim (A.L.)	4	6	.400	3.79	60	0	0	0	31-39	57.0	38	24	24	9	22-0	58
2000—	Anaheim (A.L.)	5	5	.500	4.50	54	0	0	0	32-42	50.0	42	27	25	7	30-4	49
	— Lake Elsinore (Calif.)	0	0	...	4.50	2	2	0	0	0-...	2.0	1	1	1	0	1-0	1
2001—	Anaheim (A.L.)	4	2	.667	2.65	57	0	0	0	39-42	57.2	39	19	17	3	18-1	71
2002—	Anaheim (A.L.)	4	1	.800	1.92	58	0	0	0	40-44	56.1	38	12	12	5	25-1	68
Major League totals (8 years)		27	30	.474	2.95	475	0	0	0	250-291	487.2	317	172	160	49	211-18	599

DIVISION SERIES RECORD

Year	League	W	L	Pct.	ERA	G	GS	CG	ShO	Sv.-Opp.	IP	H	R	ER	HR	BB-IBB	SO
2002—	Anaheim (A.L.)	0	0	...	5.40	3	0	0	0	2-2	3.1	6	2	2	0	0-0	4

CHAMPIONSHIP SERIES RECORD

Year	League	W	L	Pct.	ERA	G	GS	CG	ShO	Sv.-Opp.	IP	H	R	ER	HR	BB-IBB	SO
2002—	Anaheim (A.L.)	0	0	...	0.00	3	0	0	0	2-2	3.1	0	0	0	0	0-0	3

WORLD SERIES RECORD

NOTES: Member of World Series championship team (2002).

Year	League	W	L	Pct.	ERA	G	GS	CG	ShO	Sv.-Opp.	IP	H	R	ER	HR	BB-IBB	SO
2002—	Anaheim (A.L.)	0	0	...	3.00	3	0	0	0	3-3	3.0	2	1	1	1	1-0	3

ALL-STAR GAME RECORD

	W	L	Pct.	ERA	GS	CG	ShO	Sv.-Opp.	IP	H	R	ER	HR	BB-IBB	SO
All-Star Game totals (3 years)	0	0	...	0.00	0	0	0	0-0	3.0	2	0	0	0	1-0	4

RECORD AS POSITION PLAYER

			BATTING														FIELDING	
Year	Team (League)	Pos.	G	AB	R	H	2B	3B	HR	RBI	BB	SO	SB-CS	Avg.	OBP	SLG	E	Avg.
1990—	Boise (N'West)	C	29	79	12	16	0	0	0	5	19	25	0-0	.203	.370	.203	5	.980

PEREZ, ANTONIO — SS — DEVIL RAYS

PERSONAL: Born January 26, 1980, in Bani, Dominican Republic. ... 5-11/175. ... Bats right, throws right. ... Full name: Antonio Miguel Perez.

TRANSACTIONS/CAREER NOTES: Signed as non-drafted free agent by Cincinnati Reds organization (March 21, 1998). ... Traded by Reds with OF Mike Cameron, P Brett Tomko and P Jake Meyer to Seattle Mariners for OF Ken Griffey Jr. (February 10, 2000). ... On disabled list (May 2-June 5, 2000). ... On disabled list (April 5-June 1 and June 6, 2001-remainder of season). ... On San Antonio disabled list (May 3-July 5, 2002). ... Traded by Mariners to Tampa Bay Devil Rays for OF Randy Winn (October 28, 2002).

STATISTICAL NOTES: Tied for Midwest League lead in caught stealing with 24 in 1999.

			BATTING														FIELDING	
Year	Team (League)	Pos.	G	AB	R	H	2B	3B	HR	RBI	BB	SO	SB-CS	Avg.	OBP	SLG	E	Avg.
1998—	Dom. Reds (DSL)		63	212	57	54	11	0	2	24	53	33	58-...	.255	...	.335	...	...
1999—	Rockford (Midw.)	SS-2B	119	385	69	111	20	3	7	41	43	80	35-24	.288	.376	.410	36	.929
2000—	Lancaster (Calif.)■	SS	98	395	90	109	36	6	17	63	58	99	28-16	.276	.376	*.527	27	.939
2001—	San Antonio (Texas)	SS	5	21	3	3	0	0	0	0	0	7	0-0	.143	.143	.143	6	.818
2002—	San Antonio (Texas)	2B-SS	72	240	30	62	8	2	2	24	11	64	15-9	.258	.312	.333	13	.955
	— Ariz. Mariners (Ariz.)	2B-SS	6	15	3	5	1	0	1	3	4	2	4-0	.333	.476	.600	0	1.000

PEREZ, EDDIE C

PERSONAL: Born May 4, 1968, in Cuidad Ojeda, Venezuela. ... 6-1/220. ... Bats right, throws right. ... Full name: Eduardo Rafael Perez.
HIGH SCHOOL: Doctor Raul Cuenca (Cuidad Ojeda, Venezuela).
TRANSACTIONS/CAREER NOTES: Signed as non-drafted free agent by Atlanta Braves organization (September 27, 1986). ... On disabled list (August 30-September 14, 1996; and May 5, 2000-remainder of season). ... On Atlanta disabled list (March 28-September 1, 2001); included rehabilitation assignment to Greenville (August 21-September 1). ... Granted free agency (November 14, 2001). ... Re-signed by Braves organization (December 17, 2001). ... Traded by Braves to Cleveland Indians for a player to be named later (March 21, 2002). ... Granted free agency (November 1, 2002).
STATISTICAL NOTES: Led South Atlantic League catchers with 13 errors in 1989. ... Tied for International League lead in errors by catcher with 11 in 1994. ... Led International League catchers with 539 putouts, 69 assists and 615 total chances in 1995. ... Tied for International League lead with seven double plays in 1995. ... Career major league grand slams: 1.
2002 GAMES PLAYED BY POSITION (MLB): C—42.

		BATTING														FIELDING	
Year Team (League)	Pos.	G	AB	R	H	2B	3B	HR	RBI	BB	SO	SB-CS	Avg.	OBP	SLG	E	Avg.
1987—GC Braves (GCL)	C	31	89	8	18	1	0	1	5	8	14	0-0	.202	.273	.247	4	.980
1988—Burlington (Midw.)	C-1B	64	186	14	43	8	0	4	19	10	33	1-0	.231	.269	.339	11	.963
1989—Sumter (S.Atl.)	C-1B	114	401	39	93	21	0	5	44	44	68	2-6	.232	.312	.322	†13	.985
1990—Sumter (S.Atl.)	C-1B	41	123	11	22	7	1	3	17	14	18	0-0	.179	.271	.325	3	.991
—Durham (Caro.)	C-1B	31	93	9	22	1	0	3	10	1	12	0-0	.237	.250	.344	3	.986
1991—Durham (Caro.)	C-1B	92	277	38	75	10	1	9	41	17	33	0-3	.271	.317	.412	8	.986
—Greenville (Sou.)	1B	1	4	0	1	0	0	0	0	0	1	0-0	.250	.250	.250	0	1.000
1992—Greenville (Sou.)	C-1B	91	275	28	63	16	0	6	41	24	41	3-3	.229	.292	.353	14	.980
1993—Greenville (Sou.)	1B-C	28	84	15	28	6	0	6	17	2	8	1-0	.333	.341	.619	3	.982
1994—Richmond (I.L.)	C-1B	113	388	37	101	16	2	9	49	18	47	1-1	.260	.294	.381	‡12	.985
1995—Richmond (I.L.)	C-DH-1B	92	324	31	86	19	0	5	40	12	58	1-2	.265	.294	.370	7	.989
—Atlanta (N.L.)	C-1B	7	13	1	4	1	0	1	4	0	2	0-0	.308	.308	.615	0	1.000
1996—Atlanta (N.L.)	C-1B	68	156	19	40	9	1	4	17	8	19	0-0	.256	.293	.404	3	.990
1997—Atlanta (N.L.)	C-1B	73	191	20	41	5	0	6	18	10	35	0-1	.215	.259	.335	5	.989
1998—Atlanta (N.L.)	C-1B-DH	61	149	18	50	12	0	6	32	15	28	1-1	.336	.404	.537	2	.994
1999—Atlanta (N.L.)	C-1B	104	309	30	77	17	0	7	30	17	40	0-1	.249	.299	.372	5	.993
2000—Atlanta (N.L.)	C	7	22	0	4	1	0	0	3	0	2	0-0	.182	.182	.227	1	.976
2001—Greenville (Sou.)	C-1B	10	38	7	13	2	0	4	5	0	9	0-0	.342	.359	.711	1	.984
—Atlanta (N.L.)	C	5	10	0	3	0	0	0	0	0	2	0-0	.300	.300	.300	0	1.000
2002—Cleveland (A.L.)■	C	42	117	6	25	9	0	0	4	5	25	0-0	.214	.252	.291	3	.988
American League totals (1 year)		42	117	6	25	9	0	0	4	5	25	0-0	.214	.252	.291	3	.988
National League totals (7 years)		325	850	88	219	45	1	24	104	50	128	1-3	.258	.305	.398	16	.991
Major League totals (8 years)		367	967	94	244	54	1	24	108	55	153	1-3	.252	.299	.385	19	.991

DIVISION SERIES RECORD

RECORDS: Shares career record for most grand slams—1 (October 3, 1998). ... Shares single-inning record for most runs batted in—4 (October 3, 1998, eighth inning).

		BATTING														FIELDING	
Year Team (League)	Pos.	G	AB	R	H	2B	3B	HR	RBI	BB	SO	SB-CS	Avg.	OBP	SLG	E	Avg.
1995—Atlanta (N.L.)								Did not play.									
1996—Atlanta (N.L.)	C	1	3	0	1	0	0	0	0	0	0	0-0	.333	.333	.333	0	1.000
1997—Atlanta (N.L.)	C	1	3	0	0	0	0	0	0	0	1	0-0	.000	.000	.000	0	1.000
1998—Atlanta (N.L.)	C	1	5	1	1	0	0	1	4	0	2	0-0	.200	.200	.800	0	1.000
1999—Atlanta (N.L.)	C	4	16	1	4	0	0	0	3	0	3	0-0	.250	.235	.250	0	1.000
2001—Atlanta (N.L.)								Did not play.									
Division series totals (4 years)		7	27	2	6	0	0	1	7	0	6	0-0	.222	.214	.333	0	1.000

CHAMPIONSHIP SERIES RECORD

NOTES: Named Most Valuable Player (1999).

		BATTING														FIELDING	
Year Team (League)	Pos.	G	AB	R	H	2B	3B	HR	RBI	BB	SO	SB-CS	Avg.	OBP	SLG	E	Avg.
1995—Atlanta (N.L.)								Did not play.									
1996—Atlanta (N.L.)	C-1B	4	1	0	0	0	0	0	0	1	0	0-0	.000	.500	.000	0	1.000
1997—Atlanta (N.L.)	C	2	3	0	0	0	0	0	0	0	0	0-0	.000	.000	.000	0	1.000
1998—Atlanta (N.L.)	C	3	4	0	3	0	0	0	0	0	0	0-0	.750	.750	.750	0	1.000
1999—Atlanta (N.L.)	C	6	20	2	10	2	0	2	5	1	3	0-0	.500	.524	.900	0	1.000
2001—Atlanta (N.L.)								Did not play.									
Championship series totals (4 years)		15	28	2	13	2	0	2	5	2	3	0-0	.464	.500	.750	0	1.000

WORLD SERIES RECORD

NOTES: Member of World Series championship team (1995).

		BATTING														FIELDING	
Year Team (League)	Pos.	G	AB	R	H	2B	3B	HR	RBI	BB	SO	SB-CS	Avg.	OBP	SLG	E	Avg.
1995—Atlanta (N.L.)								Did not play.									
1996—Atlanta (N.L.)	C	2	1	0	0	0	0	0	0	0	0	0-0	.000	.000	.000	0	1.000
1999—Atlanta (N.L.)	C	3	8	0	1	0	0	0	0	1	3	0-0	.125	.222	.125	0	1.000
World Series totals (2 years)		5	9	0	1	0	0	0	0	1	3	0-0	.111	.200	.111	0	1.000

PEREZ, EDUARDO 1B/OF CARDINALS

PERSONAL: Born September 11, 1969, in Cincinnati. ... 6-4/215. ... Bats right, throws right. ... Full name: Eduardo Antanacio Perez. ... Son of Tony Perez, special assistant to general manager, Florida Marlins; major league infielder with four teams (1964-86) and manager, Cincinnati Reds (1993); and brother of Victor Perez, minor league outfielder/first baseman (1990).
HIGH SCHOOL: Robinson (Santurce, Puerto Rico).
COLLEGE: Florida State.

TRANSACTIONS/CAREER NOTES: Selected by California Angels organization in first round (17th pick overall) of free-agent draft (June 3, 1991). ... On Palm Springs disabled list (May 9-19, 1992). ... On Vancouver disabled list (June 26-July 7, 1994). ... Traded by Angels to Cincinnati Reds for P Will Pennyfeather (April 5, 1996). ... Released by Reds (December 14, 1998). ... Signed by St. Louis Cardinals organization (February 16, 1999). ... Granted free agency (October 15, 1999). ... Re-signed by Cardinals organization (February 3, 2000). ... On St. Louis disabled list (June 25-July 13 and August 13-September 1, 2000); included rehabilitation assignment to Memphis (August 24-September 1). ... Contract sold by Cardinals to Hanshin Tigers of Japan Central League (December 20, 2000). ... Re-signed by Cardinals organization (February 8, 2002).
STATISTICAL NOTES: Career major league grand slams: 1.
2002 GAMES PLAYED BY POSITION (MLB): OF—35; 1B—10; 3B—6; DH—1.

			BATTING														FIELDING	
Year	Team (League)	Pos.	G	AB	R	H	2B	3B	HR	RBI	BB	SO	SB-CS	Avg.	OBP	SLG	E	Avg.
1991—	Boise (N'West)	OF-1B	46	160	35	46	13	0	1	22	19	39	12-3	.288	.375	.388	3	.969
1992—	Palm Springs (Calif.)	3B-SS-OF	54	204	37	64	8	4	3	35	23	33	14-3	.314	.386	.436	16	.882
—	Midland (Texas)	3B-OF-1B	62	235	27	54	8	1	3	23	22	49	19-7	.230	.295	.311	13	.920
1993—	Vancouver (PCL)	3B-1B-OF	96	363	66	111	23	6	12	70	28	83	21-7	.306	.360	.501	23	.922
—	California (A.L.)	3B-DH	52	180	16	45	6	2	4	30	9	39	5-4	.250	.292	.372	5	.962
1994—	California (A.L.)	1B	38	129	10	27	7	0	5	16	12	29	3-0	.209	.275	.380	1	.997
—	Vancouver (PCL)	3B-DH	61	219	37	65	14	3	7	38	34	53	9-4	.297	.394	.484	12	.926
—	Arizona Angels (Ariz.)	3B	1	3	0	0	0	0	0	0	1	1	0-0	.000	.250	.000	0	1.000
1995—	California (A.L.)	3B-DH	29	71	9	12	4	1	1	7	12	9	0-2	.169	.302	.296	7	.883
—	Vancouver (PCL)	3B-DH-1B	69	246	39	80	12	7	6	37	25	34	6-2	.325	.386	.504	6	.968
1996—	Indianapolis (A.A.)■	3B-1B-DH	122	451	84	132	29	5	21	84	51	69	11-0	.293	.371	.519	21	.939
—	Cincinnati (N.L.)	1B-3B	18	36	8	8	0	0	3	5	5	9	0-0	.222	.317	.472	0	1.000
1997—	Cincinnati (N.L.)	1-O-3-D	106	297	44	75	18	0	16	52	29	76	5-1	.253	.321	.475	2	.996
1998—	Cincinnati (N.L.)	1B-3B-OF	84	172	20	41	4	0	4	30	21	45	0-1	.238	.325	.331	5	.985
1999—	Memphis (PCL)■	1B-3B-DH	119	416	67	133	31	0	18	82	45	92	7-8	.320	.393	.524	9	.989
—	St. Louis (N.L.)	OF-1B	21	32	6	11	2	0	1	9	7	6	0-0	.344	.462	.500	1	.970
2000—	St. Louis (N.L.)	1B-OF-3B	35	91	9	27	4	0	3	10	5	19	1-0	.297	.350	.440	0	1.000
—	Memphis (PCL)	1B-3B-OF	77	277	57	80	12	3	19	66	43	48	10-4	.289	.383	.560	8	.980
2001—	Hanshin (Jap. Cen.)■		52	167	20	37	11	0	3	19	21	48	3-...	.222	...	.341	...	...
2002—	St. Louis (N.L.)■	OF-1B-3B-DH	96	154	22	31	9	0	10	26	17	36	0-0	.201	.290	.455	2	.982
American League totals (3 years)			119	380	35	84	17	3	10	53	33	77	8-6	.221	.288	.361	13	.975
National League totals (6 years)			360	782	109	193	37	0	37	132	84	191	6-2	.247	.325	.436	10	.992
Major League totals (9 years)			479	1162	144	277	54	3	47	185	117	268	14-8	.238	.313	.411	23	.987

DIVISION SERIES RECORD

			BATTING														FIELDING	
Year	Team (League)	Pos.	G	AB	R	H	2B	3B	HR	RBI	BB	SO	SB-CS	Avg.	OBP	SLG	E	Avg.
2002—	St. Louis (N.L.)	PH	1	1	0	0	0	0	0	0	0	0	0-0	.000	.000	.000	0	...

CHAMPIONSHIP SERIES RECORD

			BATTING														FIELDING	
Year	Team (League)	Pos.	G	AB	R	H	2B	3B	HR	RBI	BB	SO	SB-CS	Avg.	OBP	SLG	E	Avg.
2002—	St. Louis (N.L.)	OF	3	4	1	1	0	0	1	1	1	0	0-0	.250	.400	1.000	0	1.000

PEREZ, NEIFI — SS — ROYALS

PERSONAL: Born June 2, 1973, in Villa Mella, Dominican Republic. ... 6-0/175. ... Bats both, throws right. ... Full name: Neifi Neftali Perez Diaz.
TRANSACTIONS/CAREER NOTES: Signed as non-drafted free agent by Colorado Rockies organization (November 9, 1992). ... On Colorado disabled list (April 8-23, 2001). ... Traded by Rockies to Kansas City Royals for OF Jermaine Dye (July 25, 2001).
RECORDS: Holds N.L. single-season record for most at-bats with no intentional bases on balls—690 (1999).
HONORS: Won N.L. Gold Glove as shortstop (2000).
STATISTICAL NOTES: Led California League shortstops with 223 putouts, 650 total chances and 86 double plays in 1994. ... Tied for Eastern League lead in double plays by shortstop with 80 in 1995. ... Led Pacific Coast League shortstops with 244 putouts, 409 assists, 678 total chances and 91 double plays in 1996. ... Hit for the cycle (July 25, 1998). ... Had 15-game hitting streak (July 27-August 11, 1998). ... Led N.L. with 22 sacrifice hits in 1998. ... Led N.L. shortstops with 272 putouts, 516 assists, 808 total chances and 127 double plays in 1998. ... Led N.L. shortstops with 260 putouts, 481 assists, 755 total chances and 124 double plays in 1999. ... Led N.L. shortstops with 288 putouts, 523 assists, 829 total chances and 120 double plays in 2000. ... Had 17-game hitting streak (June 1-19, 2001). ... Career major league grand slams: 1.
MISCELLANEOUS: Holds Colorado Rockies all-time record for most triples (49).
2002 GAMES PLAYED BY POSITION (MLB): SS—139; 2B—5.

			BATTING														FIELDING	
Year	Team (League)	Pos.	G	AB	R	H	2B	3B	HR	RBI	BB	SO	SB-CS	Avg.	OBP	SLG	E	Avg.
1993—	Bend (N'West)	SS-2B	75	296	35	77	11	4	3	32	19	43	19-14	.260	.306	.355	25	.937
1994—	Central Valley (Calif.)	SS	•134	506	64	121	16	7	1	35	32	79	9-7	.239	.284	.304	*39	.940
1995—	Colo. Springs (PCL)	SS	11	36	4	10	4	0	0	2	0	5	1-1	.278	.278	.389	3	.936
—	New Haven (East.)	SS	116	427	59	108	28	3	5	43	24	52	5-2	.253	.295	.368	18	*.967
1996—	Colo. Springs (PCL)	SS	133	*570	77	180	28	12	7	72	21	48	16-13	.316	.337	.444	*25	.963
—	Colorado (N.L.)	SS-2B	17	45	4	7	2	0	0	3	0	8	2-2	.156	.156	.200	2	.961
1997—	Colo. Springs (PCL)	SS	68	303	68	110	24	3	8	46	17	27	8-2	.363	.393	.541	8	.975
—	Colorado (N.L.)	SS-2B-3B	83	313	46	91	13	10	5	31	21	43	4-3	.291	.333	.444	9	.981
1998—	Colorado (N.L.)	SS-C	•162	647	80	177	25	9	9	59	38	70	5-6	.274	.313	.382	20	.975
1999—	Colorado (N.L.)	SS	157	*690	108	193	27	•11	12	70	28	54	13-5	.280	.307	.403	14	.981
2000—	Colorado (N.L.)	SS	•162	651	92	187	39	11	10	71	30	63	3-6	.287	.314	.427	18	.978
2001—	Colorado (N.L.)	SS	87	382	65	114	19	8	7	47	16	49	6-2	.298	.326	.445	10	.976
—	Kansas City (A.L.)■	SS-2B	49	199	18	48	7	1	1	12	10	19	3-4	.241	.277	.302	5	.980
2002—	Kansas City (A.L.)	SS-2B	145	554	65	131	20	4	3	37	20	53	8-9	.236	.260	.303	20	.971
American League totals (2 years)			194	753	83	179	27	5	4	49	30	72	11-13	.238	.265	.303	25	.974
National League totals (6 years)			668	2728	395	769	125	49	43	281	133	287	33-24	.282	.313	.411	73	.978
Major League totals (7 years)			862	3481	478	948	152	54	47	330	163	359	44-37	.272	.303	.388	98	.977

PEREZ, ODALIS — P — DODGERS

PERSONAL: Born June 11, 1977, in Las Matas de Farfan, Dominican Republic. ... 6-0/150. ... Throws left, bats left. ... Full name: Odalis Amadol Perez.

HIGH SCHOOL: Damian Davis Ortiz (Las Matas de Farfan, Dominican Republic).

TRANSACTIONS/CAREER NOTES: Signed as non-drafted free agent by Atlanta Braves organization (July 2, 1994). ... On disabled list (July 23, 1999-remainder of season; and April 2, 2000-entire season). ... On Atlanta disabled list (July 22-September 1, 2001); included rehabilitation assignment to Richmond (August 9-September 1). ... Traded by Braves with OF Brian Jordan and P Andrew Brown to Los Angeles Dodgers for OF Gary Sheffield (January 15, 2002).

STATISTICAL NOTES: Tied for N.L. lead with three balks in 2001. ... Pitched 10-0 one-hit, complete-game victory against Chicago Cubs (April 26, 2002). ... Pitched 4-0 one-hit, complete-game victory against Colorado (June 25, 2002).

CAREER HITTING (MLB): 19-for-120 (.158), 7 R, 6 2B, 0 3B, 1 HR, 8 RBI.

Year League	W	L	Pct.	ERA	G	GS	CG	ShO	Sv.-Opp.	IP	H	R	ER	HR	BB-IBB	SO
1995—Gulf Coast Braves (GCL)	3	5	.375	2.22	12	12	1	1	0-...	65.0	48	22	16	0	18-0	62
1996—Eugene (N'West)	2	1	.667	3.80	10	6	0	0	0-...	23.2	26	16	10	2	11-0	38
1997—Macon (S.Atl.)	4	5	.444	1.65	36	0	0	0	5-...	87.1	67	31	16	4	27-1	100
1998—Greenville (Sou.)	6	5	.545	4.02	23	21	0	0	0-...	132.0	127	67	59	15	53-2	143
—Richmond (I.L.)	1	2	.333	2.96	13	0	0	0	3-...	24.1	26	10	8	4	7-1	22
—Atlanta (N.L.)	0	1	.000	4.22	10	0	0	0	0-1	10.2	10	5	5	1	4-0	5
1999—Atlanta (N.L.)	4	6	.400	6.00	18	17	0	0	0-0	93.0	100	65	62	12	53-2	82
2000—Atlanta (N.L.)									Did not play.							
2001—Atlanta (N.L.)	7	8	.467	4.91	24	16	0	0	0-0	95.1	108	55	52	7	39-0	71
—Richmond (I.L.)	1	0	1.000	2.74	5	5	0	0	0-...	23.0	23	7	7	1	2-0	22
2002—Los Angeles (N.L.)■	15	10	.600	3.00	32	32	4	2	0-0	222.1	182	76	74	21	38-5	155
Major League totals (4 years)	26	25	.510	4.12	84	65	4	2	0-1	421.1	400	201	193	41	134-7	313

DIVISION SERIES RECORD

Year League	W	L	Pct.	ERA	G	GS	CG	ShO	Sv.-Opp.	IP	H	R	ER	HR	BB-IBB	SO
1998—Atlanta (N.L.)	1	0	1.000	0.00	1	0	0	0	0-0	.2	0	0	0	0	0-0	1

CHAMPIONSHIP SERIES RECORD

Year League	W	L	Pct.	ERA	G	GS	CG	ShO	Sv.-Opp.	IP	H	R	ER	HR	BB-IBB	SO
1998—Atlanta (N.L.)	0	0	...	54.00	2	0	0	0	0-0	.1	5	2	2	0	2-1	0

ALL-STAR GAME RECORD

	W	L	Pct.	ERA	GS	CG	ShO	Sv.-Opp.	IP	H	R	ER	HR	BB-IBB	SO
All-Star Game totals (1 year)	0	0	...	0.00	0	0	0	0-0	1.0	2	1	0	0	0-0	2

PEREZ, OLIVER — P — PADRES

PERSONAL: Born August 15, 1981, in Culiacan, Mexico. ... 6-3/160. ... Throws left, bats left.

TRANSACTIONS/CAREER NOTES: Signed as non-drafted free agent by San Diego Padres organization (March 4, 1999). ... Loaned by Padres to Yucatan of Mexican League (June 2-22 and July 18, 2000-remainder of season). ... On San Diego disabled list (August 7-September 2, 2002).

CAREER HITTING (MLB): 4-for-30 (.133), 1 R, 0 2B, 0 3B, 0 HR, 0 RBI.

Year League	W	L	Pct.	ERA	G	GS	CG	ShO	Sv.-Opp.	IP	H	R	ER	HR	BB-IBB	SO
1999—Arizona Padres (Ariz.)	1	2	.333	5.08	15	2	0	0	3-...	28.1	28	20	16	1	16-0	37
2000—Yucatan (Mex.)■	3	2	.600	4.40	11	6	0	0	1-...	43.0	39	24	21	...	17-...	37
—Idaho Falls (Pio.)■	3	1	.750	4.07	5	5	0	0	0-...	24.1	24	14	11	1	9-0	27
2001—Fort Wayne (Midw.)	8	5	.615	3.46	19	19	0	0	0-...	101.1	84	46	39	9	43-0	98
—Lake Elsinore (Calif.)	2	4	.333	2.72	9	9	0	0	0-...	53.0	45	22	16	4	25-0	62
2002—Lake Elsinore (Calif.)	3	3	.500	1.85	9	8	0	0	0-...	48.2	36	13	10	0	24-0	66
—Mobile (Sou.)	1	0	1.000	1.17	4	4	0	0	0-...	23.0	11	3	3	1	16-0	34
—San Diego (N.L.)	4	5	.444	3.50	16	15	0	0	0-0	90.0	71	37	35	13	48-1	94
Major League totals (1 year)	4	5	.444	3.50	16	15	0	0	0-0	90.0	71	37	35	13	48-1	94

PEREZ, TIMO — OF — METS

PERSONAL: Born April 8, 1975, in Bani, Dominican Republic. ... 5-9/167. ... Bats left, throws left. ... Full name: Timoniel Perez.

TRANSACTIONS/CAREER NOTES: Played with Hiroshima Toyo Carp of Japan Central League (1996-99). ... Signed as non-drafted free agent by New York Mets organization (March 17, 2000). ... On New York disabled list (April 9-27, 2001); included rehabilitation assignment to Norfolk (April 20-27).

2002 GAMES PLAYED BY POSITION (MLB): OF—122.

		BATTING														FIELDING	
Year Team (League)	Pos.	G	AB	R	H	2B	3B	HR	RBI	BB	SO	SB-CS	Avg.	OBP	SLG	E	Avg.
1994—Hiroshima (DSL)		51	206	40	70	9	8	0	21	31	7	8-...	.340	...	.461	...	...
1995—						Japanese minor league statistics unavailable.											
1996—Hiroshima (Jap. Cen.)		31	54	8	15	1	0	1	7	2	7	3-...	.278	...	.352	...	...
1997—Hiroshima (Jp. West.)		19	69	9	21	3	1	2	12	10	3	9-...	.304	...	.464	...	...
—Hiroshima (Jap. Cen.)		86	139	17	34	4	2	3	15	10	16	4-...	.245	...	.367	...	...
1998—Hiroshima (Jp. West.)		2	7	0	2	0	0	0	0	0	0	0-...	.286	...	.286	...	...
—Hiroshima (Jap. Cen.)		98	230	22	68	8	1	5	35	20	21	2-...	.296	...	.404	...	...
1999—Hiroshima (Jp. West.)		60	160	19	58	13	4	1	24	34	13	6-...	.363	...	.513	...	...
—Hiroshima (Jap. Cen.)		12	23	2	4	0	0	0	2	3	3	0-...	.174	...	.174	...	...
2000—St. Lucie (FSL)■	OF	8	31	3	11	4	0	1	8	2	1	3-3	.355	.400	.581	0	1.000
—Norfolk (I.L.)	OF	72	291	45	104	17	5	6	37	16	25	13-7	.357	.392	.512	5	.976
—New York (N.L.)	OF	24	49	11	14	4	1	1	3	3	5	1-1	.286	.333	.469	1	.970
2001—New York (N.L.)	OF	85	239	26	59	9	1	5	22	12	25	1-6	.247	.287	.356	0	1.000
—Norfolk (I.L.)	OF	48	192	37	69	10	2	6	19	12	18	15-2	.359	.399	.526	5	.951
2002—Norfolk (I.L.)	OF	5	21	5	12	2	1	1	5	2	2	3-1	.571	.609	.905	0	1.000
—New York (N.L.)	OF	136	444	52	131	27	6	8	47	23	36	10-6	.295	.331	.437	6	.979
Major League totals (3 years)		245	732	89	204	40	8	14	72	38	66	12-13	.279	.317	.413	7	.984

P

DIVISION SERIES RECORD

Year	Team (League)	Pos.	G	AB	R	H	2B	3B	HR	RBI	BB	SO	SB-CS	Avg.	OBP	SLG	E	Avg.
				BATTING													FIELDING	
2000—	New York (N.L.)..........	PH-RF	4	17	2	5	1	0	0	3	0	2	1-0	.294	.294	.353	0	1.000

CHAMPIONSHIP SERIES RECORD

Year	Team (League)	Pos.	G	AB	R	H	2B	3B	HR	RBI	BB	SO	SB-CS	Avg.	OBP	SLG	E	Avg.
				BATTING													FIELDING	
2000—	New York (N.L.)..........	OF	5	23	8	7	2	0	0	0	1	3	2-1	.304	.333	.391	1	.947

WORLD SERIES RECORD

Year	Team (League)	Pos.	G	AB	R	H	2B	3B	HR	RBI	BB	SO	SB-CS	Avg.	OBP	SLG	E	Avg.
				BATTING													FIELDING	
2000—	New York (N.L.)..........	OF	5	16	1	2	0	0	0	0	1	4	0-0	.125	.176	.125	1	.900

PEREZ, TOMAS — IF — PHILLIES

PERSONAL: Born December 29, 1973, in Barquisimeto, Venezuela. ... 5-11/177. ... Bats both, throws right. ... Full name: Tomas Orlando Perez.

TRANSACTIONS/CAREER NOTES: Signed as non-drafted free agent by Montreal Expos organization (July 11, 1991). ... Selected by California Angels from Expos organization in Rule 5 major league draft (December 5, 1994). ... Contract sold by Angels to Toronto Blue Jays (December 5, 1994). ... On Toronto disabled list (June 25-July 25, 1997); included rehabilitation assignment to Syracuse (July 12-24). ... Traded by Blue Jays to Angels for IF Dave Hollins and cash (March 30, 1999). ... On Edmonton disabled list (April 21-June 10, 1999). ... Granted free agency (October 15, 1999). ... Signed by Philadelphia Phillies organization (December 15, 1999). ... On Philadelphia disabled list (March 26-April 16, 2002); included rehabilitation assignment to Reading (April 13-15).

STATISTICAL NOTES: Led Gulf Coast League with 121 putouts, 205 assists, 338 total chances and 39 double plays in 1993. ... Led Midwest League shortstops with 217 putouts and 65 double plays in 1994. ... Led International League with 14 sacrifice hits in 1997. ... Led International League shortstops with .977 fielding percentage in 1998. ... Switch-hit home runs in one game (July 24, 2001).

2002 GAMES PLAYED BY POSITION (MLB): 2B—50; 3B—14; SS—13; 1B—3.

Year	Team (League)	Pos.	G	AB	R	H	2B	3B	HR	RBI	BB	SO	SB-CS	Avg.	OBP	SLG	E	Avg.
				BATTING													FIELDING	
1992—	Dom. Expos (DSL).....	IF	44	151	35	46	7	0	1	19	27	20	12-...	.305	...	.371	12	.954
1993—	GC Expos (GCL).........	SS	52	189	27	46	3	1	2	21	23	25	8-3	.243	.322	.302	12	.964
1994—	Burlington (Midw.).....	SS-2B	119	465	76	122	22	1	8	47	48	78	8-10	.262	.329	.366	34	.944
1995—	Toronto (A.L.)■.........	SS-2B-3B	41	98	12	24	3	1	1	8	7	18	0-1	.245	.292	.327	5	.962
1996—	Syracuse (I.L.)...........	SS-2B	40	123	15	34	10	1	1	13	7	19	8-1	.276	.313	.398	7	.962
—	Toronto (A.L.)............	2B-3B-SS	91	295	24	74	13	4	1	19	25	29	1-2	.251	.311	.332	15	.964
1997—	Syracuse (I.L.)...........	SS	89	303	32	68	13	0	1	20	37	67	3-4	.224	.308	.277	12	.973
—	Toronto (A.L.)............	SS-2B	40	123	9	24	3	2	0	9	11	28	1-1	.195	.267	.252	3	.984
1998—	Syracuse (I.L.)...........	SS-2B	116	404	40	102	15	4	3	37	18	67	4-7	.252	.284	.332	15	†.977
—	Toronto (A.L.)............	SS-2B	6	9	1	1	0	0	0	0	1	3	0-0	.111	.200	.111	0	1.000
1999—	Edmonton (PCL)■.....	SS-2B	83	296	31	77	17	1	4	40	19	43	2-2	.260	.306	.365	11	.973
2000—	Reading (East.)■.......	PR	0	0	0	0	0	0	0	0	0	0	0-0	...	...	...	...	...
—	Philadelphia (N.L.)......	SS	45	140	17	31	7	1	1	13	11	30	1-1	.221	.278	.307	4	.976
—	Scranton/W.B. (I.L.)...	3B-SS-2B	77	279	44	82	16	2	10	56	16	48	4-1	.294	.334	.473	9	.962
2001—	Philadelphia (N.L.)......	2B-3B-SS-OF	62	135	11	41	7	1	3	19	7	22	0-1	.304	.347	.437	1	.993
2002—	Reading (East.)...........	2B-SS	2	9	2	4	0	0	0	1	0	1	0-0	.444	.444	.444	0	1.000
—	Philadelphia (N.L.)......	2-3-S-1-P	92	212	22	53	13	1	5	20	21	40	1-0	.250	.319	.392	4	.985
American League totals (4 years)			178	525	46	123	19	7	2	36	44	78	2-4	.234	.295	.309	23	.969
National League totals (3 years)			199	487	50	125	27	3	9	52	39	92	2-2	.257	.315	.380	9	.984
Major League totals (7 years)			377	1012	96	248	46	10	11	88	83	170	4-6	.245	.305	.343	32	.976

RECORD AS PITCHER

Year	League	W	L	Pct.	ERA	G	GS	CG	ShO	Sv.-Opp.	IP	H	R	ER	HR	BB-IBB	SO
2002—	Philadelphia (N.L.)...........	0	0	.000	0.00	1	0	0	0	0-0	.1	0	0	0	0	0-0	0

PEREZ, YORKIS — P

PERSONAL: Born September 30, 1967, in Bajos de Haina, Dominican Republic. ... 6-0/213. ... Throws left, bats both. ... Full name: Yorkis Miguel Perez.

TRANSACTIONS/CAREER NOTES: Signed as non-drafted free agent by Minnesota Twins organization (February 23, 1983). ... Traded by Twins with P Neal Heaton, P Al Cardwood and C Jeff Reed to Montreal Expos for P Jeff Reardon and C Tom Nieto (February 3, 1987). ... Granted free agency (October 15, 1990). ... Signed by Atlanta Braves organization (February 1, 1991). ... Traded by Braves with P Turk Wendell to Chicago Cubs for P Mike Bielecki and C Damon Berryhill (September 29, 1991). ... Released by Cubs (December 11, 1991). ... Signed by Yomiuri Giants of Japan Central League (1992). ... Released by Yomiuri (August 17, 1992). ... Signed as free agent by Seattle Mariners organization (August 19, 1992). ... Released by Mariners (January 11, 1993). ... Signed by Montreal Expos organization (February 15, 1993). ... Granted free agency (October 15, 1993). ... Signed by Florida Marlins organization (December 15, 1993). ... On Florida disabled list (June 10-30, 1994); included rehabilitation assignment to Portland (June 25-30). ... Traded by Marlins to Braves for P Martin Sanchez (December 13, 1996). ... Claimed on waivers by New York Mets (March 31, 1997). ... On New York disabled list (April 5-June 5, 1997); included rehabilitation assignment to Norfolk (May 15-June 5). ... Granted free agency (October 15, 1997). ... Signed by Philadelphia Phillies organization (January 23, 1998). ... On Scranton/Wilkes-Barre disabled list (April 9-16, 1998). ... On Philadelphia disabled list (May 25-June 17, 1998); included rehabilitation assignments to Reading (June 14) and Scranton/Wilkes-Barre (June 16). ... On disabled list (July 2, 1999-remainder of season). ... Granted free agency (October 8, 1999). ... Signed by Philadelphia Phillies organization (December 17, 1999). ... Traded by Phillies to Houston Astros for P Trever Miller (March 29, 2000). ... Released by Astros (July 24, 2000). ... Signed by Los Angeles Dodgers organization (December 23, 2000). ... Released by Dodgers (March 31, 2001). ... Signed by Mexico City Red Devils, Mexican League (April 2001). ... Signed by Arizona Diamondbacks organization (December 3, 2001). ... Released by Diamondbacks (March 27, 2002). ... Signed by Baltimore Orioles organization (March 27, 2002). ... On Baltimore disabled list (September 16, 2002-remainder of season). ... Released by Orioles (October 1, 2002).

CAREER HITTING (MLB): 0-for-11 (.000), 0 R, 0 2B, 0 3B, 0 HR, 0 RBI.

Year League	W	L	Pct.	ERA	G	GS	CG	ShO	Sv.-Opp.	IP	H	R	ER	HR	BB-IBB	SO
1983— Elizabethton (Appl.)	0	1	.000	20.25	3	1	0	0	0-...	4.0	5	9	9	1	9-0	6
1984— Elizabethton (Appl.)	0	0	...	0.00	1	0	0	0	0-...	1.1	1	0	0	0	1-0	1
1985— Santiago (DSL)	6	8	.429	3.17	21	16	7	2	1-...	122.0	104	58	43	...	63-...	69
1986— Kenosha (Midw.)	4	11	.267	5.15	31	18	3	0	0-...	131.0	120	81	75	9	88-1	144
1987— West Palm Beach (FSL)■	6	2	.750	2.34	15	15	3	0	0-...	100.0	78	36	26	4	46-0	111
— Jacksonville (Sou.)	2	7	.222	4.05	12	10	1	1	1-...	60.0	61	34	27	4	30-0	60
1988— Jacksonville (Sou.)	8	12	.400	5.82	27	25	2	1	0-...	130.0	142	96	84	11	94-0	105
1989— West Palm Beach (FSL)	7	6	.538	2.76	18	12	0	0	1-...	94.2	62	34	29	2	54-0	85
— Jacksonville (Sou.)	4	3	.571	3.60	20	0	0	0	0-...	35.0	25	16	14	0	34-1	50
1990— Jacksonville (Sou.)	2	2	.500	6.00	28	2	0	0	1-...	42.0	36	34	28	5	34-2	39
— Indianapolis (A.A.)	1	1	.500	2.31	9	0	0	0	0-...	11.2	8	5	3	1	6-0	8
1991— Richmond (I.L.)■	•12	3	•.800	3.79	36	10	0	0	1-...	107.0	99	47	45	7	53-1	102
— Chicago (N.L.)■	1	0	1.000	2.08	3	0	0	0	0-1	4.1	2	1	1	0	2-0	3
1992— Yomiuri Giants (Jap. Cn.)■	0	1	.000	7.11	3	0	0	0	0-...	6.1	8	6	5	0	3-...	6
1993— Harrisburg (East.)■	4	2	.667	3.45	34	0	0	0	3-...	44.1	49	26	17	3	20-1	58
— Ottawa (I.L.)	0	1	.000	3.60	20	0	0	0	5-...	20.0	14	12	8	0	7-0	17
1994— Florida (N.L.)■	3	0	1.000	3.54	44	0	0	0	0-2	40.2	33	18	16	4	14-3	41
— Portland (East.)	0	0	...	0.00	2	0	0	0	0-...	2.0	1	0	0	0	0-0	2
1995— Florida (N.L.)	2	6	.250	5.21	69	0	0	0	1-4	46.2	35	29	27	6	28-4	47
1996— Florida (N.L.)	3	4	.429	5.29	64	0	0	0	0-2	47.2	51	28	28	2	31-4	47
— Charlotte (I.L.)	3	0	1.000	4.22	9	0	0	0	0-...	10.2	6	5	5	1	3-0	13
1997— New York (N.L.)■	0	1	.000	8.31	9	0	0	0	0-1	8.2	15	8	8	2	4-0	7
— Norfolk (I.L.)	1	0	1.000	3.48	17	0	0	0	3-...	20.2	22	9	8	2	7-0	24
— Binghamton (East.)	2	1	.667	0.66	12	3	0	0	0-...	27.1	15	4	2	1	12-1	39
1998— Scranton/W.B. (I.L.)■	0	0	...	0.00	4	1	0	0	0-...	4.1	2	1	0	0	1-0	3
— Philadelphia (N.L.)	0	2	.000	3.81	57	0	0	0	0-0	52.0	40	23	22	3	25-0	42
— Reading (East.)	0	0	...	0.00	1	1	0	0	0-...	1.0	0	0	0	0	0-0	1
1999— Philadelphia (N.L.)	3	1	.750	3.94	35	0	0	0	0-1	32.0	29	15	14	4	15-1	26
2000— Houston (N.L.)■	2	1	.667	5.16	33	0	0	0	0-2	22.2	25	18	13	4	14-2	21
2001— MC Red Devils (Mex.)■	2	4	.333	3.51	57	0	0	0	0-...	51.1	52	22	20	4	15-0	56
2002— Rochester (I.L.)■	1	1	.500	3.79	28	0	0	0	0-...	40.1	42	20	17	4	20-1	44
— Baltimore (A.L.)	0	0	...	3.29	23	0	0	0	1-1	27.1	21	12	10	4	14-1	25
A.L. totals (1 year)	0	0	...	3.29	23	0	0	0	1-1	27.1	21	12	10	4	14-1	25
N.L. totals (8 years)	14	15	.483	4.56	314	0	0	0	1-13	254.2	230	140	129	25	133-14	234
Major League totals (9 years)	14	15	.483	4.44	337	0	0	0	2-14	282.0	251	152	139	29	147-15	259

PERISHO, MATT — P — DEVIL RAYS

PERSONAL: Born June 8, 1975, in Burlington, Iowa. ... 6-0/200. ... Throws left, bats left. ... Full name: Matthew Alan Perisho.

HIGH SCHOOL: McClintock (Tempe, Ariz.).

TRANSACTIONS/CAREER NOTES: Selected by California Angels organization in third round of free-agent draft (June 3, 1993). ... Angels franchise renamed Anaheim Angels for 1997 season. ... Traded by Angels to Texas Rangers for IF Mike Bell (October 31, 1997). ... On Oklahoma disabled list (June 29-July 25, 1998). ... Traded by Rangers to Detroit Tigers for P Kevin Mobley and P Brandon Villafuerte (December 15, 2000). ... On Detroit disabled list (May 5-25, 2001); included rehabilitation assignment to Toledo (May 16-25). ... Released by Tigers (October 1, 2002). ... Signed by Tampa Bay Devil Rays organization (November 6, 2002).

CAREER HITTING (MLB): 0-for-5 (.000), 0 R, 0 2B, 0 3B, 0 HR, 0 RBI.

Year League	W	L	Pct.	ERA	G	GS	CG	ShO	Sv.-Opp.	IP	H	R	ER	HR	BB-IBB	SO
1993— Arizona Angels (Ariz.)	7	3	.700	3.66	11	11	1	1	0-...	64.0	58	32	26	1	23-0	65
1994— Cedar Rapids (Midw.)	12	9	.571	4.33	27	27	0	0	0-...	147.2	165	90	71	11	88-0	107
1995— Lake Elsinore (Calif.)	8	9	.471	6.32	24	22	0	0	0-...	115.1	137	91	81	10	60-0	68
1996— Lake Elsinore (Calif.)	7	5	.583	4.20	21	18	1	1	0-...	128.2	131	72	60	9	58-0	97
— Midland (Texas)	3	2	.600	3.21	8	8	0	0	0-...	53.1	48	22	19	4	20-0	50
1997— Midland (Texas)	5	2	.714	2.96	10	10	3	•1	0-...	73.0	60	26	24	5	26-1	62
— Anaheim (A.L.)	0	2	.000	6.00	11	8	0	0	0-0	45.0	59	34	30	6	28-0	35
— Vancouver (PCL)	4	4	.500	5.33	9	9	1	0	0-...	52.1	68	42	31	3	29-1	47
1998— Tulsa (Texas)■	0	0	...	6.00	1	1	0	0	0-...	3.0	3	2	2	0	3-0	1
— Oklahoma (PCL)	8	5	.615	3.89	15	15	1	0	0-...	90.1	91	41	39	6	42-0	60
— Texas (A.L.)	0	2	.000	27.00	2	2	0	0	0-0	5.0	15	17	15	2	8-0	2
1999— Oklahoma (PCL)	*15	7	.682	4.61	27	27	2	0	0-...	156.1	160	86	80	14	*78-1	150
— Texas (A.L.)	0	0	...	2.61	4	1	0	0	0-0	10.1	8	3	3	0	2-1	17
2000— Texas (A.L.)■	2	7	.222	7.37	34	13	0	0	0-1	105.0	136	99	86	20	67-3	74
2001— Detroit (A.L.)■	2	3	.400	5.72	30	4	0	0	0-2	39.1	54	29	25	5	14-1	19
— Toledo (I.L.)	2	3	.400	1.71	25	2	0	0	9-...	42.0	42	10	8	3	11-0	28
2002— Toledo (I.L.)	4	4	.500	2.45	51	2	0	0	1-...	66.0	62	20	18	4	19-4	44
— Detroit (A.L.)	0	0	...	8.71	5	0	0	0	0-0	10.1	16	11	10	2	6-0	3
Major League totals (6 years)	4	14	.222	7.07	86	28	0	0	0-3	215.0	288	193	169	35	125-5	150

PERRY, CHAN — 1B

PERSONAL: Born September 13, 1972, in Live Oak, Fla. ... 6-2/200. ... Bats right, throws right. ... Full name: Chan Everett Perry. ... Brother of Herbert Perry, third baseman, Texas Rangers.

HIGH SCHOOL: Lafayette (Mayo, Fla.).

COLLEGE: Florida.

TRANSACTIONS/CAREER NOTES: Selected by Cleveland Indians organization in 44th round of free-agent draft (June 2, 1994). ... On Buffalo disabled list (June 26-July 21, 2000). ... Granted free agency (October 15, 2000). ... Signed by Atlanta Braves organization (November 9, 2000). ... On disabled list (August 7, 2001-remainder of season). ... Granted free agency (October 15, 2001). ... Signed by Kansas City Royals organization (January 24, 2002). ... On Wichita disabled list (June 8-19, 2002). ... Released by Royals (October 10, 2002).

STATISTICAL NOTES: Led Texas League first basemen with 98 double plays in 2002.

2002 GAMES PLAYED BY POSITION (MLB): 1B—5.

Year	Team (League)	Pos.	G	AB	R	H	2B	3B	HR	RBI	BB	SO	SB-CS	Avg.	OBP	SLG	E	Avg.
			BATTING														FIELDING	
1994—	Burlington (Appl.)	1B-OF	52	185	28	58	16	1	5	32	18	28	6-0	.314	.370	.492	5	.981
1995—	Columbus (S.Atl.)	1B-OF	113	411	64	117	30	4	9	50	53	49	7-2	.285	.366	.443	2	.997
1996—	Kinston (Caro.)	1B-OF-3B	96	358	44	104	27	1	10	62	36	33	2-3	.291	.356	.455	2	.993
1997—	Akron (East.)	1B-OF-3B	119	476	74	150	•34	2	20	96	28	61	3-3	.315	.355	.521	3	.994
1998—	Buffalo (I.L.)	1B-OF	13	49	8	11	4	0	0	3	6	10	1-0	.224	.333	.306	2	.974
	—Akron (East.)	OF-1B	54	203	36	57	17	2	5	27	23	43	3-2	.281	.352	.458	1	.987
1999—	Buffalo (I.L.)	1B-OF	79	273	44	77	17	0	10	59	19	34	5-1	.282	.328	.454	7	.985
	—Akron (East.)	1B-OF	37	154	24	43	14	0	7	30	11	27	1-0	.279	.329	.506	2	.983
2000—	Buffalo (I.L.)	OF-1B	92	362	48	107	18	1	10	65	21	55	1-2	.296	.336	.434	3	.990
	—Cleveland (A.L.)	OF-1B	13	14	1	1	0	0	0	0	0	5	0-0	.071	.071	.071	0	1.000
2001—	Richmond (I.L.)■	1B-OF-3B	98	350	38	96	15	3	8	39	19	60	1-6	.274	.316	.403	6	.990
2002—	Wichita (Texas)■	1B	105	399	59	126	20	2	14	73	29	44	6-5	.316	.359	.481	2	.998
	—Kansas City (A.L.)	1B	5	11	0	1	0	0	0	3	0	1	0-0	.091	.091	.091	0	1.000
Major League totals (2 years)			18	25	1	2	0	0	0	3	0	6	0-0	.080	.080	.080	0	1.000

PERRY, HERBERT 3B RANGERS

PERSONAL: Born September 15, 1969, in Mayo, Fla. ... 6-2/225. ... Bats right, throws right. ... Full name: Herbert Edward Perry Jr. ... Brother of Chan Perry, first baseman with Cleveland Indians (2000) and Kansas City Royals (2002).

HIGH SCHOOL: Lafayette (Mayo, Fla.).

COLLEGE: Florida.

TRANSACTIONS/CAREER NOTES: Selected by Cleveland Indians organization in second round of free-agent draft (June 3, 1991). ... On disabled list (June 18-July 13, 1991; and July 23, 1993-remainder of season). ... On Buffalo disabled list (June 7-27, 1996). ... On Cleveland disabled list (September 11, 1996-remainder of season; and March 26, 1997-entire season). ... Selected by Tampa Bay Devil Rays in third round (68th pick overall) of expansion draft (November 18, 1997). ... On Tampa Bay disabled list (March 25, 1998-entire season); included rehabilitation assignments to Durham (June 1-7), Gulf Coast Devil Rays (August 17-25) and St. Petersburg (August 27-28). ... On Tampa Bay disabled list (July 22-September 1, 1999); included rehabilitation assignment to Durham (August 25-31). ... Claimed on waivers by Chicago White Sox (April 21, 2000). ... On disabled list (June 8-22, 2001). ... Traded by White Sox to Texas Rangers for a player to be named later (November 27, 2001); White Sox acquired P Corey Lee to complete deal (December 17, 2001).

STATISTICAL NOTES: Led Eastern League in being hit by pitch with 15 in 1993.

2002 GAMES PLAYED BY POSITION (MLB): 3B—112; 1B—12; DH—6; OF—1.

Year	Team (League)	Pos.	G	AB	R	H	2B	3B	HR	RBI	BB	SO	SB-CS	Avg.	OBP	SLG	E	Avg.
			BATTING														FIELDING	
1991—	Watertown (NY-Penn)	DH	14	52	3	11	2	0	0	5	8	7	0-0	.212	.339	.250	...	...
1992—	Kinston (Caro.)	1B-OF-3B	121	449	74	125	16	1	19	77	46	89	12-0	.278	.358	.445	5	.985
1993—	Canton/Akron (East.)	1B-3B-DH-OF	89	327	52	88	21	1	9	55	37	47	7-4	.269	.364	.422	10	.979
1994—	Charlotte (I.L.)	1-3-DH-O	102	376	67	123	20	4	13	70	41	55	9-4	.327	.397	.505	6	.993
	—Cleveland (A.L.)	1B-3B	4	9	1	1	0	0	0	1	3	1	0-0	.111	.357	.111	1	.968
1995—	Buffalo (A.A.)	1B-DH	49	180	27	57	14	1	2	17	15	18	1-0	.317	.375	.439	3	.994
	—Cleveland (A.L.)	1B-DH-3B	52	162	23	51	13	1	3	23	13	28	1-3	.315	.376	.463	0	1.000
1996—	Buffalo (A.A.)	1B-3B-DH-OF	40	151	21	51	7	1	5	30	7	19	4-0	.338	.375	.497	4	.984
	—Cleveland (A.L.)	1B-3B	7	12	1	1	1	0	0	0	1	2	1-0	.083	.154	.167	0	1.000
1997—	Cleveland (A.L.)								Did not play.									
1998—	Durham (I.L.)■	1B-DH	5	17	1	5	4	0	0	1	0	2	0-0	.294	.333	.529	0	1.000
	—GC Devil Rays (GCL)	DH-3B	8	26	1	3	0	0	0	1	3	5	0-0	.115	.233	.115	1	.900
	—St. Petersburg (FSL)	3B	2	8	1	1	0	0	0	0	2	2	0-0	.125	.300	.125	1	.875
1999—	Durham (I.L.)	DH-1B-3B	27	103	21	32	8	0	5	20	6	21	0-0	.311	.360	.534	2	.971
	—Tampa Bay (A.L.)	3B-1B-OF-DH	66	209	29	53	10	1	6	32	16	42	0-0	.254	.331	.397	5	.975
2000—	Tampa Bay (A.L.)	3B-1B	7	28	2	6	1	0	0	1	2	7	0-0	.214	.267	.250	1	.944
	—Chicago (A.L.)■	3B-DH-1B	109	383	69	118	29	1	12	61	22	68	4-1	.308	.356	.483	9	.970
2001—	Chicago (A.L.)	3B-1B-DH	92	285	38	73	21	1	7	32	23	55	2-2	.256	.326	.411	10	.957
2002—	Texas (A.L.)■	3-1-D-O	132	450	64	124	24	1	22	77	34	66	4-2	.276	.333	.480	14	.960
Major League totals (7 years)			469	1538	227	427	99	5	50	227	114	269	12-8	.278	.339	.446	40	.975

DIVISION SERIES RECORD

Year	Team (League)	Pos.	G	AB	R	H	2B	3B	HR	RBI	BB	SO	SB-CS	Avg.	OBP	SLG	E	Avg.
			BATTING														FIELDING	
1995—	Cleveland (A.L.)	PH	1	1	0	0	0	0	0	0	0	0	0-0	.000	.000	.000	...	...
2000—	Chicago (A.L.)	3B	3	9	0	4	1	0	0	1	2	2	0-0	.444	.500	.556	0	1.000
Division series totals (2 years)			4	10	0	4	1	0	0	1	2	2	0-0	.400	.462	.500	0	1.000

CHAMPIONSHIP SERIES RECORD

Year	Team (League)	Pos.	G	AB	R	H	2B	3B	HR	RBI	BB	SO	SB-CS	Avg.	OBP	SLG	E	Avg.
			BATTING														FIELDING	
1995—	Cleveland (A.L.)	1B	3	8	0	0	0	0	0	0	1	3	0-1	.000	.111	.000	0	1.000

WORLD SERIES RECORD

Year	Team (League)	Pos.	G	AB	R	H	2B	3B	HR	RBI	BB	SO	SB-CS	Avg.	OBP	SLG	E	Avg.
			BATTING														FIELDING	
1995—	Cleveland (A.L.)	1B	3	5	0	0	0	0	0	0	0	2	0-0	.000	.000	.000	0	1.000

PERSON, ROBERT P

PERSONAL: Born October 6, 1969, in St. Louis. ... 6-0/193. ... Throws right, bats right. ... Full name: Robert Alan Person.

HIGH SCHOOL: University City (Mo.).

JUNIOR COLLEGE: Seminole (Okla.) Junior College.

TRANSACTIONS/CAREER NOTES: Selected by Cleveland Indians organization in 25th round of free-agent draft (June 5, 1989). ... Loaned by Indians organization to Bend, independent (June 12-25, 1991). ... Traded by Indians to Chicago White Sox for P Grady Hall (June 27, 1991).

... On disabled list (April 10-May 13, 1992). ... Selected by Florida Marlins in second round (47th pick overall) of expansion draft (November 17, 1992). ... Granted free agency (December 19, 1992). ... Re-signed by Marlins organization (January 8, 1993). ... Traded by Marlins to New York Mets for P Steve Long (March 30, 1994). ... Traded by Mets to Toronto Blue Jays for 1B John Olerud and cash (December 20, 1996). ... On Toronto disabled list (May 8-26 and September 9-28, 1997). ... On Syracuse disabled list (April 19-27, 1998). ... On Toronto disabled list (March 25-April 12, 1999); included rehabilitation assignment to Dunedin (April 9-10). ... Traded by Blue Jays to Philadelphia Phillies for P Paul Spoljaric (May 5, 1999). ... On Philadelphia disabled list (June 19-July 22, 2000); included rehabilitation assignments to Clearwater (July 12-16) and Reading (July 17-22). ... On suspended list (June 22-28, 2001). ... On Philadelphia disabled list (April 30-June 2 and July 23, 2002-remainder of season); included rehabilitation assignment to Scranton (May 21-June 2). ... Granted free agency (October 28, 2002).

MISCELLANEOUS: Appeared in two games as pinch runner with New York (1996).

CAREER HITTING (MLB): 25-for-213 (.117), 13 R, 5 2B, 0 3B, 4 HR, 16 RBI.

Year	League	W	L	Pct.	ERA	G	GS	CG	ShO	Sv.-Opp.	IP	H	R	ER	HR	BB-IBB	SO
1989—	Burlington (Appl.)	0	1	.000	3.18	10	5	0	0	1-...	34.0	23	13	12	1	17-0	19
1990—	Watertown (NY-Penn)	1	0	1.000	1.10	5	2	0	0	0-...	16.1	8	2	2	0	7-0	19
—	Kinston (Caro.)	1	0	1.000	2.70	4	3	0	0	0-...	16.2	17	6	5	0	9-0	7
—	Gulf Coast Indians (GCL)	0	2	.000	7.36	24	0	0	0	2-...	7.1	10	7	6	0	4-1	8
1991—	Kinston (Caro.)	3	5	.375	4.67	11	11	0	0	0-...	52.0	56	37	27	2	42-0	45
—	Bend (N'West)■	1	1	.500	3.60	2	2	0	0	0-...	10.0	6	6	4	0	5-0	6
—	South Bend (Midw.)■	4	3	.571	3.30	13	13	0	0	0-...	76.1	50	35	28	3	56-1	66
1992—	Sarasota (FSL)	5	7	.417	3.59	19	18	1	0	0-...	105.1	90	48	42	7	62-1	85
1993—	High Desert (Calif.)■	12	10	.545	4.69	28	26	4	0	0-...	169.0	184	*115	88	13	48-0	107
1994—	Binghamton (East.)■	9	6	.600	3.45	31	23	3	2	0-...	159.0	124	68	61	18	68-3	130
1995—	Binghamton (East.)	5	4	.556	3.11	26	7	1	0	7-...	66.2	46	27	23	4	25-0	65
—	Norfolk (I.L.)	2	1	.667	4.50	5	4	0	0	0-...	32.0	30	17	16	2	13-0	33
—	New York (N.L.)	1	0	1.000	0.75	3	1	0	0	0-0	12.0	5	1	1	1	2-0	10
1996—	New York (N.L.)	4	5	.444	4.52	27	13	0	0	0-0	89.2	86	50	45	16	35-3	76
—	Norfolk (I.L.)	5	0	1.000	3.35	8	8	0	0	0-...	43.0	33	16	16	7	21-0	32
1997—	Toronto (A.L.)■	5	10	.333	5.61	23	22	0	0	0-0	128.1	125	86	80	19	60-2	99
—	Syracuse (I.L.)	1	0	1.000	0.00	1	1	0	0	0-...	7.0	4	1	0	0	2-0	5
1998—	Toronto (A.L.)	3	1	.750	7.04	27	0	0	0	6-8	38.1	45	31	30	9	22-1	31
—	Syracuse (I.L.)	3	3	.500	2.29	20	6	1	0	6-...	59.0	38	17	15	9	29-2	55
1999—	Dunedin (FSL)	0	0	...	3.00	1	1	0	0	0-...	3.0	4	1	1	0	1-0	3
—	Toronto (A.L.)	0	2	.000	9.82	11	0	0	0	2-2	11.0	9	12	12	1	15-1	12
—	Philadelphia (N.L.)■	10	5	.667	4.27	31	22	0	0	0-0	137.0	130	72	65	23	70-1	127
2000—	Philadelphia (N.L.)	9	7	.563	3.63	28	28	1	1	0-0	173.1	144	73	70	13	95-1	164
—	Clearwater (FSL)	0	0	...	6.75	1	1	0	0	0-...	2.2	3	2	2	0	1-0	2
—	Reading (East.)	1	0	1.000	5.79	1	0	0	0	0-...	4.2	3	3	3	1	3-0	7
2001—	Philadelphia (N.L.)	15	7	.682	4.19	33	33	3	1	0-0	208.1	179	103	97	34	80-3	183
2002—	Philadelphia (N.L.)	4	5	.444	5.44	16	16	0	0	0-0	87.2	79	58	53	13	51-0	61
—	Scranton/W.B. (I.L.)	0	1	.000	4.32	2	2	0	0	0-...	8.1	8	4	4	2	1-0	7
A.L. totals (3 years)		8	13	.381	6.18	61	22	0	0	8-10	177.2	179	129	122	29	97-4	142
N.L. totals (6 years)		43	29	.597	4.21	138	113	4	2	0-0	708.0	623	357	331	100	333-8	621
Major League totals (8 years)		51	42	.548	4.60	199	135	4	2	8-10	885.2	802	486	453	129	430-12	763

RECORD AS POSITION PLAYER

			BATTING														FIELDING	
Year	Team (League)	Pos.	G	AB	R	H	2B	3B	HR	RBI	BB	SO	SB-CS	Avg.	OBP	SLG	E	Avg.
1990—	GC Indians (GCL)	OF	24	46	6	4	0	0	0	3	10	12	1-1	.087	.250	.087	0	1.000

PETRICK, BEN — OF/C — ROCKIES

PERSONAL: Born April 7, 1977, in Hillsboro, Ore. ... 6-0/200. ... Bats right, throws right. ... Full name: Benjamin Wayne Petrick.

HIGH SCHOOL: Glencoe (Hillsboro, Ore.).

TRANSACTIONS/CAREER NOTES: Selected by Colorado Rockies organization in second round of free-agent draft (June 3, 1995). ... On Carolina disabled list (April 26-May 6, 1999). ... On Colorado disabled list (August 2-September 1, 2001); included rehabilitation assignment to Colorado Springs (August 9-29).

STATISTICAL NOTES: Led Pacific Coast League catchers with 14 passed balls in 1999.

2002 GAMES PLAYED BY POSITION (MLB): OF—16; C—14.

			BATTING														FIELDING	
Year	Team (League)	Pos.	G	AB	R	H	2B	3B	HR	RBI	BB	SO	SB-CS	Avg.	OBP	SLG	E	Avg.
1996—	Asheville (S.Atl.)	C-DH	122	446	74	105	24	2	14	52	75	98	19-9	.235	.350	.392	12	.986
1997—	Salem (Caro.)	C-DH	121	412	68	102	23	3	15	56	62	100	30-11	.248	.347	.427	10	.988
1998—	New Haven (East.)	C-DH-OF	106	349	52	83	21	3	18	50	56	89	7-7	.238	.345	.470	5	.991
1999—	Carolina (Sou.)	C-DH	20	68	18	21	5	1	4	22	9	15	3-1	.309	.388	.588	1	.992
—	Colo. Springs (PCL)	C-DH-OF	84	282	56	88	16	5	19	64	44	58	9-6	.312	.403	.606	9	.980
—	Colorado (N.L.)	C	19	62	13	20	3	0	4	12	10	13	1-0	.323	.417	.565	2	.982
2000—	Colo. Springs (PCL)	C	63	248	38	78	22	3	9	47	32	40	7-2	.315	.390	.536	6	.986
—	Colorado (N.L.)	C	52	146	32	47	10	1	3	20	20	33	1-2	.322	.401	.466	4	.985
2001—	Colorado (N.L.)	C-1B	85	244	41	58	15	3	11	39	31	67	3-3	.238	.327	.459	8	.984
—	Colo. Springs (PCL)	OF-C-1B	18	64	11	16	2	0	1	9	13	21	1-0	.250	.367	.328	4	.957
2002—	Colorado (N.L.)	OF-C	38	95	10	20	3	1	5	11	9	33	0-1	.211	.283	.421	3	.974
—	Colo. Springs (PCL)	OF-C-1B	79	265	51	85	18	4	16	54	40	77	10-6	.321	.406	.600	5	.969
Major League totals (4 years)			194	547	96	145	31	5	23	82	70	146	5-6	.265	.350	.466	17	.983

PETTITTE, ANDY — P — YANKEES

PERSONAL: Born June 15, 1972, in Baton Rouge, La. ... 6-5/225. ... Throws left, bats left. ... Full name: Andrew Eugene Pettitte.

HIGH SCHOOL: Deer Park (Texas).

JUNIOR COLLEGE: San Jacinto (North) College (Texas).

TRANSACTIONS/CAREER NOTES: Selected by New York Yankees organization in 22nd round of free-agent draft (June 4, 1990); did not sign. ... Signed as non-drafted free agent by Yankees organization (May 25, 1991). ... On Albany temporarily inactive list (June 5-10, 1994). ...

On New York disabled list (March 26-April 17, 1999); included rehabilitation assignment to Tampa (April 12). ... On disabled list (April 13-26, 2000; and June 15-July 1, 2001). ... On New York disabled list (April 16-June 14, 2002); included rehabilitation assignments to Tampa (May 22-June 5) and Norwich (June 6-14).

HONORS: Named lefthanded pitcher on The Sporting News A.L. All-Star team (1996).

CAREER HITTING (MLB): 2-for-21 (.095), 0 R, 1 2B, 0 3B, 0 HR, 1 RBI.

Year League	W	L	Pct.	ERA	G	GS	CG	ShO	Sv.-Opp.	IP	H	R	ER	HR	BB-IBB	SO
1991—Gulf Coast Yankees (GCL)	4	1	.800	0.98	6	6	0	0	0-...	36.2	16	6	4	0	8-0	51
—Oneonta (NY-Penn)	2	2	.500	2.18	6	6	1	0	0-...	33.0	33	18	8	1	16-0	32
1992—Greensboro (S.Atl.)	10	4	.714	2.20	27	27	2	1	0-...	168.0	141	53	41	4	55-0	130
1993—Prince William (Caro.)	11	9	.550	3.04	26	26	2	1	0-...	159.2	146	68	54	7	47-0	129
—Albany (East.)	1	0	1.000	3.60	1	1	0	0	0-...	5.0	5	4	2	0	2-0	6
1994—Albany/Colonie (East.)	7	2	.778	2.71	11	11	0	0	0-...	73.0	60	32	22	5	18-1	50
—Columbus (I.L.)	7	2	.778	2.98	16	16	3	0	0-...	96.2	101	40	32	3	21-0	61
1995—New York (A.L.)	12	9	.571	4.17	31	26	3	0	0-0	175.0	183	86	81	15	63-3	114
—Columbus (I.L.)	0	0	...	0.00	2	2	0	0	0-...	11.2	7	0	0	0	0-0	8
1996—New York (A.L.)	*21	8	.724	3.87	35	34	2	0	0-0	221.0	229	105	95	23	72-2	162
1997—New York (A.L.)	18	7	.720	2.88	35	•35	4	1	0-0	240.1	233	86	77	7	65-0	166
1998—New York (A.L.)	16	11	.593	4.24	33	32	5	0	0-0	216.1	226	110	102	20	87-1	146
1999—Tampa (FSL)	1	0	1.000	0.00	1	1	0	0	0-...	5.0	4	0	0	0	2-0	8
—New York (A.L.)	14	11	.560	4.70	31	31	0	0	0-0	191.2	216	105	100	20	89-3	121
2000—New York (A.L.)	19	9	.679	4.35	32	32	3	1	0-0	204.2	219	111	99	17	80-4	125
2001—New York (A.L.)	15	10	.600	3.99	31	31	2	0	0-0	200.2	224	103	89	14	41-3	164
2002—New York (A.L.)	13	5	.722	3.27	22	22	3	1	0-0	134.2	144	58	49	6	32-2	97
—Tampa (FSL)	0	0	...	0.00	2	2	0	0	0-...	5.0	3	0	0	0	0-0	4
—Norwich (East.)	0	0	...	1.42	1	1	0	0	0-...	6.1	2	1	1	0	0-0	5
Major League totals (8 years)	128	70	.646	3.93	250	243	22	3	0-0	1584.1	1674	764	692	122	529-18	1095

DIVISION SERIES RECORD

RECORDS: Holds A.L. career records for most games started—10; hits allowed—68; runs allowed—31; earned runs allowed—31 and strikeouts—33. ... Shares A.L. career record for most wins—3; and losses—3. ... Shares career record for most innings pitched—60.

Year League	W	L	Pct.	ERA	G	GS	CG	ShO	Sv.-Opp.	IP	H	R	ER	HR	BB-IBB	SO
1995—New York (A.L.)	0	0	...	5.14	1	1	0	0	0-0	7.0	9	4	4	1	3-0	0
1996—New York (A.L.)	0	0	...	5.68	1	1	0	0	0-0	6.1	4	4	4	2	6-0	3
1997—New York (A.L.)	0	2	.000	8.49	2	2	0	0	0-0	11.2	15	11	11	1	1-0	5
1998—New York (A.L.)	1	0	1.000	1.29	1	1	0	0	0-0	7.0	3	1	1	0	0-0	8
1999—New York (A.L.)	1	0	1.000	1.23	1	1	0	0	0-0	7.1	7	1	1	1	0-0	5
2000—New York (A.L.)	1	0	1.000	3.97	2	2	0	0	0-0	11.1	15	5	5	0	3-0	7
2001—New York (A.L.)	0	1	.000	1.42	1	1	0	0	0-0	6.1	7	1	1	1	2-0	4
2002—New York (A.L.)	0	0	...	12.00	1	1	0	0	0-0	3.0	8	4	4	2	0-0	1
Division series totals (8 years)	3	3	.500	4.65	10	10	0	0	0-0	60.0	68	31	31	8	15-0	33

CHAMPIONSHIP SERIES RECORD

NOTES: Named Most Valuable Player (2001).

Year League	W	L	Pct.	ERA	G	GS	CG	ShO	Sv.-Opp.	IP	H	R	ER	HR	BB-IBB	SO
1996—New York (A.L.)	1	0	1.000	3.60	2	2	0	0	0-0	15.0	10	6	6	4	5-0	7
1998—New York (A.L.)	0	1	.000	11.57	1	1	0	0	0-0	4.2	8	6	6	4	3-0	1
1999—New York (A.L.)	1	0	1.000	2.45	1	1	0	0	0-0	7.1	8	2	2	0	1-0	5
2000—New York (A.L.)	1	0	1.000	2.70	1	1	0	0	0-0	6.2	9	2	2	0	1-0	2
2001—New York (A.L.)	2	0	1.000	2.51	2	2	0	0	0-0	14.1	11	4	4	0	2-0	8
Champ. series totals (5 years)	5	1	.833	3.75	7	7	0	0	0-0	48.0	46	20	20	8	12-0	23

WORLD SERIES RECORD

NOTES: Member of World Series championship team (1996, 1998, 1999 and 2000).

Year League	W	L	Pct.	ERA	G	GS	CG	ShO	Sv.-Opp.	IP	H	R	ER	HR	BB-IBB	SO
1996—New York (A.L.)	1	1	.500	5.91	2	2	0	0	0-0	10.2	11	7	7	1	4-0	5
1998—New York (A.L.)	1	0	1.000	0.00	1	1	0	0	0-0	7.1	5	0	0	0	3-0	4
1999—New York (A.L.)	0	0	...	12.27	1	1	0	0	0-0	3.2	10	5	5	0	1-0	1
2000—New York (A.L.)	0	0	...	1.98	2	2	0	0	0-0	13.2	16	5	3	0	4-1	9
2001—New York (A.L.)	0	2	.000	10.00	2	2	0	0	0-0	9.0	12	10	10	1	2-1	9
World Series totals (5 years)	2	3	.400	5.08	8	8	0	0	0-0	44.1	54	27	25	2	14-2	28

ALL-STAR GAME RECORD

	W	L	Pct.	ERA	GS	CG	ShO	Sv.-Opp.	IP	H	R	ER	HR	BB-IBB	SO
All-Star Game totals (1 year)	0	0	...	0.00	0	0	0	0-0	1.0	1	0	0	0	0-0	1

PETTYJOHN, ADAM P TIGERS

PERSONAL: Born June 11, 1977, in Phoenix, Ariz. ... 6-3/190. ... Throws left, bats right. ... Full name: Adam Christopher Pettyjohn.

HIGH SCHOOL: Exeter Union (Exeter, Calif.).

COLLEGE: Fresno State.

TRANSACTIONS/CAREER NOTES: Selected by Detroit Tigers organization in second round of free agent draft (June 2, 1998); choice received as part of compensation for Arizona Diamondbacks signing Type A free agent P Willie Blair. ... On Jacksonville disabled list (April 10-June 10, 2000). ... On disabled list (March 31, 2002-entire season).

CAREER HITTING (MLB): 0-for-2 (.000), 0 R, 0 2B, 0 3B, 0 HR, 0 RBI.

Year League	W	L	Pct.	ERA	G	GS	CG	ShO	Sv.-Opp.	IP	H	R	ER	HR	BB-IBB	SO
1998—Jamestown (NY-Penn)	2	2	.500	2.86	4	4	0	0	0-...	22.0	21	10	7	0	4-0	24
—West Michigan (Midw.)	4	2	.667	1.97	8	8	1	1	0-...	50.1	46	15	11	3	9-0	64
1999—Lakeland (FSL)	3	4	.429	3.77	9	9	2	0	0-...	59.2	62	35	25	2	11-0	51
—Jacksonville (Sou.)	9	5	.643	4.69	20	20	0	0	0-...	126.2	134	75	66	13	35-0	92
2000—Jacksonville (Sou.)	2	2	.500	3.40	8	8	0	0	0-...	50.1	43	20	19	4	12-0	45
—Toledo (I.L.)	0	4	.000	6.69	7	7	0	0	0-...	39.0	45	34	29	5	22-0	23
2001—Toledo (I.L.)	5	8	.385	3.44	17	17	0	0	0-...	107.1	107	51	41	9	26-0	78
—Detroit (A.L.)	1	6	.143	5.82	16	9	0	0	0-0	65.0	81	48	42	10	21-2	40
2002—Detroit (A.L.)									Did not play.							
Major League totals (1 year)	1	6	.143	5.82	16	9	0	0	0-0	65.0	81	48	42	10	21-2	40

PHELPS, JOSH — C — BLUE JAYS

PERSONAL: Born May 12, 1978, in Anchorage, Alaska. ... 6-3/220. ... Bats right, throws right. ... Full name: Joshua Lee Phelps.
HIGH SCHOOL: Lakeland (Rathdrum, Idaho).
TRANSACTIONS/CAREER NOTES: Selected by Toronto Blue Jays organization in 10th round of free-agent draft (June 4, 1996). ... On Tennessee disabled list (April 6-May 1, 2000).
HONORS: Named Southern League Most Valuable Player (2001).
STATISTICAL NOTES: Led South Atlantic League catchers with 19 errors in 1998. ... Led Southern League with 273 total bases in 2001.
2002 GAMES PLAYED BY POSITION (MLB): DH—71; 1B—2.

		BATTING														FIELDING	
Year Team (League)	Pos.	G	AB	R	H	2B	3B	HR	RBI	BB	SO	SB-CS	Avg.	OBP	SLG	E	Avg.
1996—Medicine Hat (Pio.)	C-OF	59	191	26	46	3	0	5	29	27	65	5-3	.241	.351	.335	9	.964
1997—Hagerstown (S.Atl.)	C	68	233	26	49	9	1	7	24	15	72	3-2	.210	.279	.348	21	.965
1998—Hagerstown (S.Atl.)	C-3B-OF	117	385	48	102	24	1	8	44	40	80	2-0	.265	.342	.395	†19	.975
1999—Dunedin (FSL)	DH-C	110	406	72	133	27	4	20	88	28	104	6-3	.328	.379	*.562	1	.994
2000—Tennessee (Sou.)	C	56	184	23	42	9	1	9	28	15	66	1-0	.228	.308	.435	5	.983
—Toronto (A.L.)	C	1	1	0	0	0	0	0	0	0	1	0-0	.000	.000	.000	0	1.000
—Dunedin (FSL)	C	30	113	26	36	7	0	12	34	12	34	0-0	.319	.386	.699	1	.992
2001—Tennessee (Sou.)	C	•136	486	95	142	*36	1	*31	97	80	127	3-3	.292	.406	.562	2	.996
—Toronto (A.L.)	C	8	12	3	0	0	0	0	1	2	5	1-0	.000	.143	.000	0	1.000
2002—Syracuse (I.L.)	C-1B	70	257	50	75	20	1	24	64	32	83	0-0	.292	.380	.658	4	.985
—Toronto (A.L.)	DH-1B	74	265	41	82	20	1	15	58	19	82	0-0	.309	.362	.562	0	1.000
Major League totals (3 years)		83	278	44	82	20	1	15	59	21	88	1-0	.295	.351	.536	0	1.000

PHELPS, TRAVIS — P — DEVIL RAYS

PERSONAL: Born July 25, 1977, in Rocky Comfort, Mo. ... 6-2/166. ... Throws right, bats right.
HIGH SCHOOL: Wheaton (Mo.).
JUNIOR COLLEGE: Crowder College (Mo.).
TRANSACTIONS/CAREER NOTES: Selected by Tampa Bay Devil Rays organization in 89th round of free-agent draft (June 4, 1996).
CAREER HITTING (MLB): 0-for-0 (.000), 0 R, 0 2B, 0 3B, 0 HR, 0 RBI.

Year League	W	L	Pct.	ERA	G	GS	CG	ShO	Sv.-Opp.	IP	H	R	ER	HR	BB-IBB	SO
1997—Princeton (Appl.)	4	3	.571	4.88	14	13	1	0	0-...	62.2	73	42	34	4	23-0	60
1998—Charleston, S.C. (S.Atl.)	5	8	.385	4.85	18	18	0	0	0-...	91.0	100	54	49	4	35-0	96
1999—St. Petersburg (FSL)	10	8	.556	4.24	24	23	1	1	0-...	133.2	148	70	63	6	39-0	101
2000—Orlando (Sou.)	7	8	.467	3.00	21	21	2	0	0-...	108.0	85	44	36	5	46-0	106
—Durham (I.L.)	3	1	.750	4.85	6	6	0	0	0-...	29.2	29	17	16	6	16-0	21
2001—Durham (I.L.)	2	0	1.000	0.00	9	0	0	0	0-...	15.2	11	0	0	0	1-0	12
—Tampa Bay (A.L.)	2	2	.500	3.48	49	0	0	0	5-6	62.0	53	30	24	6	24-1	54
2002—Tampa Bay (A.L.)	1	2	.333	4.78	26	0	0	0	0-0	37.2	30	20	20	7	27-0	36
—Durham (I.L.)	3	2	.600	4.35	27	0	0	0	8-...	31.0	29	15	15	2	14-1	34
Major League totals (2 years)	3	4	.429	3.97	75	0	0	0	5-6	99.2	83	50	44	13	51-1	90

PHILLIPS, BRANDON — SS — INDIANS

PERSONAL: Born June 28, 1981, in Raleigh, N.C. ... 5-11/185. ... Bats right, throws right. ... Full name: Brandon Emil Phillips.
HIGH SCHOOL: Redan (Stone Mountain, Ga.).
TRANSACTIONS/CAREER NOTES: Selected by Montreal Expos organization in second round of free-agent draft (June 2, 1999). ... Traded by Expos with 1B Lee Stevens, P Cliff Lee and OF Grady Sizemore to Cleveland Indians for P Bartolo Colon and future considerations (June 27, 2002); Expos acquired P Tim Drew to complete deal (June 28, 2002).
2002 GAMES PLAYED BY POSITION (MLB): 2B—11.

		BATTING														FIELDING	
Year Team (League)	Pos.	G	AB	R	H	2B	3B	HR	RBI	BB	SO	SB-CS	Avg.	OBP	SLG	E	Avg.
1999—GC Expos (GCL)	SS	47	169	23	49	11	3	1	21	15	35	12-3	.290	.358	.408	17	.915
2000—Cape Fear (S.Atl.)	SS-2B	126	484	74	117	17	8	11	72	38	97	23-8	.242	.306	.378	36	.940
2001—Jupiter (FSL)	SS	55	194	36	55	12	2	4	23	38	45	17-3	.284	.414	.428	18	.930
—Harrisburg (East.)	SS-2B-3B	67	265	35	79	19	0	7	36	12	42	13-6	.298	.337	.449	12	.958
2002—Harrisburg (East.)	SS	60	245	40	80	13	2	9	35	16	33	6-3	.327	.380	.506	14	.936
—Ottawa (I.L.)	SS	10	35	1	9	4	0	1	5	2	6	0-0	.257	.297	.457	0	1.000
—Buffalo (I.L.)■	SS-2B	55	223	30	63	14	0	8	27	14	39	8-2	.283	.321	.453	15	.952
—Cleveland (A.L.)	2B	11	31	5	8	3	1	0	4	3	6	0-0	.258	.343	.419	2	.957
Major League totals (1 year)		11	31	5	8	3	1	0	4	3	6	0-0	.258	.343	.419	2	.957

PHILLIPS, JASON — P — INDIANS

PERSONAL: Born March 22, 1974, in Williamsport, Pa. ... 6-6/225. ... Throws right, bats right. ... Full name: Jason Charles Phillips.
HIGH SCHOOL: Hughesville (Pa.).
TRANSACTIONS/CAREER NOTES: Selected by Pittsburgh Pirates organization in 14th round of free-agent draft (June 1, 1992). ... On Nashville disabled list (May 26, 1999-remainder of season). ... Granted free agency (October 15, 1999). ... Re-signed by Pirates organization (January 6, 1999). ... On Nashville disabled list (May 9-September 6, 2000). ... Granted free agency (October 18, 2000). ... Re-signed by Pirates organization (January 9, 2001). ... On Lynchburg disabled list (April 5-May 10, 2001). ... Released by Pirates (June 4, 2001). ... Signed by Cleveland Indians organization (June 7, 2001). ... On Buffalo disabled list (July 27-August 3, 2001). ... Granted free agency (October 15, 2001). ... Re-signed by Indians organization (October 26, 2001). ... On Cleveland disabled list (August 28, 2002-remainder of season).
CAREER HITTING (MLB): 0-for-0 (.000), 0 R, 0 2B, 0 3B, 0 HR, 0 RBI.

Year	League	W	L	Pct.	ERA	G	GS	CG	ShO	Sv.-Opp.	IP	H	R	ER	HR	BB-IBB	SO
1992—	Gulf Coast Pirates (GCL)..	1	2	.333	8.47	4	4	0	0	0-...	17.0	21	21	16	0	13-0	10
1993—	Welland (NY-Penn)..........	4	6	.400	3.53	14	14	0	0	0-...	71.1	60	44	28	2	36-0	66
1994—	Augusta (S.Atl.)...............	6	12	.333	6.73	23	23	1	0	0-...	108.1	118	97	81	4	88-1	108
1995—	Augusta (S.Atl.)...............	4	3	.571	3.60	30	6	0	0	0-...	80.0	76	46	32	2	53-1	65
1996—	Augusta (S.Atl.)...............	5	4	.556	2.41	14	14	1	1	0-...	89.2	79	35	24	3	29-1	75
	—Lynchburg (Caro.)...........	5	6	.455	4.52	13	13	1	1	0-...	73.2	82	47	37	3	35-0	63
1997—	Lynchburg (Caro.)...........	11	6	.647	3.76	23	23	2	1	0-...	138.2	129	66	58	10	35-0	140
	—Carolina (Sou.)................	1	2	.333	2.32	4	4	2	1	0-...	31.0	21	8	8	1	9-0	22
1998—	Carolina (Sou.)................	7	•13	.350	4.71	25	25	1	1	0-...	151.0	161	89	79	14	52-3	114
	—Nashville (PCL)...............	2	0	1.000	2.59	5	5	0	0	0-...	31.1	38	10	9	3	12-0	21
1999—	Pittsburgh (N.L.).............	0	0	...	11.57	6	0	0	0	0-0	7.0	11	9	9	2	6-1	7
	—Nashville (PCL)...............	0	0	...	15.00	1	1	0	0	0-...	3.0	6	6	5	0	5-1	5
2000—	Nashville (PCL)...............	2	4	.333	4.70	6	6	0	0	0-...	30.2	30	20	16	4	18-0	18
2001—	Altoona (East.)................	0	1	.000	10.00	6	1	0	0	0-...	9.0	18	11	10	0	4-0	4
	—Akron (East.)■................	2	1	.667	4.13	10	3	0	0	0-...	24.0	18	11	11	2	15-0	20
	—Buffalo (I.L.)....................	2	2	.500	3.34	8	6	1	0	0-...	35.0	27	15	13	3	8-0	25
2002—	Buffalo (I.L.)....................	7	4	.636	3.39	16	16	1	0	0-...	98.1	88	37	37	8	17-0	71
	—Cleveland (A.L.)...............	1	3	.250	4.97	8	6	0	0	0-0	41.2	41	24	23	7	20-0	23
A.L. totals (1 year)		1	3	.250	4.97	8	6	0	0	0-0	41.2	41	24	23	7	20-0	23
N.L. totals (1 year)		0	0	...	11.57	6	0	0	0	0-0	7.0	11	9	9	2	6-1	7
Major League totals (2 years)		1	3	.250	5.92	14	6	0	0	0-0	48.2	52	33	32	9	26-1	30

PHILLIPS, JASON — C — METS

PERSONAL: Born September 27, 1976, in La Mesa, Calif. ... 6-1/177. ... Bats right, throws right. ... Full name: Jason Lloyd Phillips.
HIGH SCHOOL: El Capitan (Lakeside, Calif.).
COLLEGE: San Diego State.
TRANSACTIONS/CAREER NOTES: Selected by New York Mets organization in 24th round of free-agent draft (June 3, 1997). ... On Norfolk disabled list (July 25-August 12, 2002).
STATISTICAL NOTES: Tied for International League lead with six double plays by catcher in 2002.
2002 GAMES PLAYED BY POSITION (MLB): C—7.

			BATTING															FIELDING	
Year	Team (League)	Pos.	G	AB	R	H	2B	3B	HR	RBI	BB	SO	SB-CS	Avg.	OBP	SLG	E	Avg.
1997—	Pittsfield (NY-Penn)....	C	48	155	15	32	9	0	2	17	13	24	4-0	.206	.282	.303	4	.990
1998—	Capital City (S.Atl.).....	C	69	251	36	68	15	1	5	37	23	35	5-2	.271	.343	.398	4	.994
	—St. Lucie (FSL)..........	C	8	28	4	13	2	0	0	2	2	1	0-0	.464	.500	.536	0	1.000
1999—	St. Lucie (FSL)..........	C	81	283	36	73	12	1	9	48	43	28	0-1	.258	.367	.403	4	.992
	—Binghamton (East.)....	C	39	141	13	32	5	0	7	23	13	20	0-0	.227	.304	.411	5	.984
2000—	St. Lucie (FSL)..........	C	80	297	53	82	21	0	6	41	23	19	1-1	.276	.343	.407	6	.989
	—Binghamton (East.)....	C	27	98	16	38	4	0	0	13	7	9	0-0	.388	.435	.429	3	.983
2001—	Binghamton (East.)....	C	93	317	42	93	21	0	11	55	31	25	0-1	.293	.362	.464	3	*.995
	—New York (N.L.)..........	C	6	7	2	1	1	0	0	0	0	1	0-0	.143	.143	.286	0	1.000
	—Norfolk (I.L.).............	C	19	66	8	20	2	0	2	14	7	8	0-0	.303	.365	.424	0	1.000
2002—	Norfolk (I.L.).............	C	88	323	35	91	22	1	13	65	24	29	1-0	.282	.327	.477	4	.993
	—New York (N.L.)..........	C	11	19	4	7	0	0	1	3	1	1	0-0	.368	.409	.526	0	1.000
Major League totals (2 years)			17	26	6	8	1	0	1	3	1	2	0-0	.308	.345	.462	0	1.000

PIATT, ADAM — OF/DH — ATHLETICS

PERSONAL: Born February 8, 1976, in Chicago. ... 6-2/205. ... Bats right, throws right. ... Full name: Adam David Piatt.
HIGH SCHOOL: Bishop Verot (Fort Myers, Fla.).
COLLEGE: Mississippi State.
TRANSACTIONS/CAREER NOTES: Selected by Oakland Athletics organization in eighth round of free-agent draft (June 3, 1997). ... On Oakland disabled list (June 6-September 1, 2001); included rehabilitation assignments to Sacramento (July 12-28 and August 17-27) and Modesto (August 27-September 1).
HONORS: Named Texas League Most Valuable Player (1999).
STATISTICAL NOTES: Led California League third basemen with 32 errors in 1998. ... Led Texas League with 335 total bases and 10 intentional bases on balls received in 1999.
2002 GAMES PLAYED BY POSITION (MLB): OF—50; 1B—1.

			BATTING															FIELDING	
Year	Team (League)	Pos.	G	AB	R	H	2B	3B	HR	RBI	BB	SO	SB-CS	Avg.	OBP	SLG	E	Avg.
1997—	S. Oregon (N'West)....	3B-1B	57	216	63	63	9	1	13	35	35	58	19-4	.292	.391	.523	21	.864
1998—	Modesto (Calif.).........	3B-2B	133	500	91	144	•40	3	20	*107	80	99	20-6	.288	.381	.500	†32	.892
1999—	Midland (Texas)..........	3B-SS-DH	129	476	*128	164	48	3	*39	*135	•93	101	7-3	*.345	*.451	*.704	31	.917
	—Vancouver (PCL)........	3B-SS	6	18	1	4	1	0	0	3	6	2	0-0	.222	.417	.278	2	.917
2000—	Sacramento (PCL)......	OF-3B-1B	65	254	36	72	15	0	8	42	26	57	3-2	.283	.355	.437	9	.959
	—Oakland (A.L.)...........	OF-DH-3B-1B	60	157	24	47	5	5	5	23	23	44	0-1	.299	.392	.490	2	.967
2001—	Oakland (A.L.)............	OF-DH	36	95	9	20	5	1	0	6	13	26	0-0	.211	.300	.284	2	.962
	—Sacramento (PCL)......	OF	35	109	14	28	9	0	1	15	11	27	2-0	.257	.339	.367	3	.933
	—Modesto (Calif.).........	OF	4	15	4	7	2	0	1	2	1	5	0-0	.467	.529	.800	0	1.000
2002—	Sacramento (PCL)......	OF-1B	62	234	46	69	15	0	8	44	35	30	4-3	.295	.385	.462	2	.981
	—Oakland (A.L.)...........	OF-1B	55	137	18	32	8	0	5	18	12	33	2-1	.234	.303	.401	0	1.000
Major League totals (3 years)			151	389	51	99	18	6	10	47	48	103	2-2	.254	.339	.409	4	.978

DIVISION SERIES RECORD

			BATTING															FIELDING	
Year	Team (League)	Pos.	G	AB	R	H	2B	3B	HR	RBI	BB	SO	SB-CS	Avg.	OBP	SLG	E	Avg.
2000—	Oakland (A.L.)...........	OF-PR-DH	3	6	2	1	0	0	0	0	0	1	0-0	.167	.167	.167	0	1.000
2002—	Oakland (A.L.)...........	OF	3	3	0	1	1	0	0	0	0	1	0-0	.333	.333	.667	0	...
Division series totals (2 years)			6	9	2	2	1	0	0	0	0	2	0-0	.222	.222	.333	0	1.000

PIAZZA, MIKE   C   METS

PERSONAL: Born September 4, 1968, in Norristown, Pa. ... 6-3/215. ... Bats right, throws right. ... Full name: Michael Joseph Piazza. ... Name pronounced pee-AH-za.

HIGH SCHOOL: Phoenixville (Pa.) Area.

JUNIOR COLLEGE: Miami-Dade (North) Community College.

TRANSACTIONS/CAREER NOTES: Selected by Los Angeles Dodgers organization in 62nd round of free-agent draft (June 1, 1988). ... On disabled list (May 11-June 4, 1995). ... Traded by Dodgers with 3B Todd Zeile to Florida Marlins for OF Gary Sheffield, 3B Bobby Bonilla, C Charles Johnson, OF Jim Eisenreich and P Manuel Barrios (May 15, 1998). ... Traded by Marlins to New York Mets for OF Preston Wilson, P Ed Yarnall and P Geoff Goetz (May 22, 1998). ... On disabled list (April 10-25, 1999).

RECORDS: Shares major league single-season record for most major league ballparks, one or more home runs—18 (2000). ... Shares major league record for most grand slams in two consecutive games—2 (April 9 and 10, 1998). ... Shares major league single-month record for most grand slams—3 (April 1998). ... Holds single-season record for highest batting average by a catcher (100 or more games)—.362 (1997). ... Holds N.L. career record for most home runs by catcher—336.

HONORS: Named N.L. Rookie Player of the Year by The Sporting News (1993). ... Named catcher on The Sporting News N.L. All-Star team (1993-2002). ... Named catcher on The Sporting News N.L. Silver Slugger team (1993-2000). ... Named N.L. Rookie of the Year by Baseball Writers' Association of America (1993). ... Named catcher on N.L. Silver Slugger team (2001 and 2002).

STATISTICAL NOTES: Led California League in grounding into double plays with 19 in 1991. ... Led N.L. catchers with 98 assists and tied for lead with 11 errors in 1993. ... Led N.L. catchers in total chances with 866 in 1995 and 1,055 in 1996. ... Led N.L. catchers in passed balls with 12 in 1995 and 12 in 1996. ... Led N.L. catchers with 805 putouts in 1995, 1,055 in 1996, 1045 in 1997 and 953 in 1999. ... Hit three home runs in one game (June 29, 1996). ... Led N.L. catchers in total chances with 1,135 in 1997. ... Led N.L. catchers with 83 assists in 1998. ... Had 24-game hitting streak (May 25-June 22, 1999). ... Led N.L. in grounding into double plays with 27 in 1999. ... Led N.L. catchers in total chances with 1,011 in 1999. ... Had 21-game hitting streak (June 7-July 3, 2000). ... Career major league grand slams: 14.

MISCELLANEOUS: Holds New York Mets all-time record for highest career batting average (.310).

2002 GAMES PLAYED BY POSITION (MLB): C—121; DH—6.

		BATTING														FIELDING	
Year Team (League)	Pos.	G	AB	R	H	2B	3B	HR	RBI	BB	SO	SB-CS	Avg.	OBP	SLG	E	Avg.
1989—Salem (N'West)	C	57	198	22	53	11	0	8	25	13	51	0-0	.268	.318	.444	6	.977
1990—Vero Beach (FSL)	C-1B	88	272	27	68	20	0	6	45	11	68	0-1	.250	.281	.390	16	.967
1991—Bakersfield (Calif.)	C-1B	117	448	71	124	27	2	29	80	47	83	0-3	.277	.344	*.540	15	.981
1992—San Antonio (Texas)	C	31	114	18	43	11	0	7	21	13	18	0-0	.377	.441	.658	4	.981
—Albuquerque (PCL)	C-1B	94	358	54	122	22	5	16	69	37	57	1-3	.341	.405	.564	9	.985
—Los Angeles (N.L.)	C	21	69	5	16	3	0	1	7	4	12	0-0	.232	.284	.319	1	.990
1993—Los Angeles (N.L.)	C-1B	149	547	81	174	24	2	35	112	46	86	3-4	.318	.370	.561	‡11	.989
1994—Los Angeles (N.L.)	C	107	405	64	129	18	0	24	92	33	65	1-3	.319	.370	.541	*10	.985
1995—Los Angeles (N.L.)	C	112	434	82	150	17	0	32	93	39	80	1-0	.346	.400	.606	9	.990
1996—Los Angeles (N.L.)	C	148	547	87	184	16	0	36	105	81	93	0-3	.336	.422	.563	9	.992
1997—Los Angeles (N.L.)	C-DH	152	556	104	201	32	1	40	124	69	77	5-1	.362	.431	.638	*16	.986
1998—Los Angeles (N.L.)	C	37	149	20	42	5	0	9	30	11	27	0-0	.282	.329	.497	2	.993
—Florida (N.L.)■	C	5	18	1	5	0	1	0	5	0	0	0-0	.278	.263	.389	1	.968
—New York (N.L.)■	C-DH	109	394	67	137	33	0	23	76	47	53	1-0	.348	.417	.607	8	.989
1999—New York (N.L.)	C-DH	141	534	100	162	25	0	40	124	51	70	2-2	.303	.361	.575	11	.989
2000—New York (N.L.)	C-DH	136	482	90	156	26	0	38	113	58	69	4-2	.324	.398	.614	3	*.997
2001—New York (N.L.)	C-DH	141	503	81	151	29	0	36	94	67	87	0-2	.300	.384	.573	9	.991
2002—New York (N.L.)	C-DH	135	478	69	134	23	2	33	98	57	82	0-3	.280	.359	.544	*12	.986
Major League totals (11 years)		1393	5116	851	1641	251	6	347	1073	563	801	17-20	.321	.388	.576	102	.990

DIVISION SERIES RECORD

		BATTING														FIELDING	
Year Team (League)	Pos.	G	AB	R	H	2B	3B	HR	RBI	BB	SO	SB-CS	Avg.	OBP	SLG	E	Avg.
1995—Los Angeles (N.L.)	C	3	14	1	3	1	0	1	1	0	2	0-0	.214	.214	.500	0	1.000
1996—Los Angeles (N.L.)	C	3	10	1	3	0	0	0	2	1	2	0-0	.300	.333	.300	0	1.000
1999—New York (N.L.)	C	2	9	0	2	0	0	0	0	0	4	0-0	.222	.222	.222	0	1.000
2000—New York (N.L.)	C	4	14	1	3	1	0	0	0	4	3	0-0	.214	.389	.286	0	1.000
Division series totals (4 years)		12	47	3	11	2	0	1	3	5	11	0-0	.234	.302	.340	0	1.000

CHAMPIONSHIP SERIES RECORD

		BATTING														FIELDING	
Year Team (League)	Pos.	G	AB	R	H	2B	3B	HR	RBI	BB	SO	SB-CS	Avg.	OBP	SLG	E	Avg.
1999—New York (N.L.)	C	6	24	1	4	0	0	1	4	1	6	0-0	.167	.192	.292	3	.940
2000—New York (N.L.)	C	5	17	7	7	3	0	2	4	5	0	0-0	.412	.545	.941	0	1.000
Championship series totals (2 years)		11	41	8	11	3	0	3	8	6	6	0-0	.268	.354	.561	3	.967

WORLD SERIES RECORD

		BATTING														FIELDING	
Year Team (League)	Pos.	G	AB	R	H	2B	3B	HR	RBI	BB	SO	SB-CS	Avg.	OBP	SLG	E	Avg.
2000—New York (N.L.)	DH-C	5	22	3	6	2	0	2	4	0	4	0-1	.273	.273	.636	0	1.000

ALL-STAR GAME RECORD

NOTES: Named Most Valuable Player (1996).

	AB	R	H	2B	3B	HR	RBI	BB	SO	SB-CS	Avg.	OBP	SLG	E	Avg.
All-Star Game totals (9 years)	21	2	6	1	0	2	5	1	3	0-0	.286	.318	.619	0	1.000

PICHARDO, HIPOLITO   P

P

PERSONAL: Born August 22, 1969, in Esperanza, Dominican Republic. ... 6-1/195. ... Throws right, bats right. ... Full name: Hipolito Antonio Pichardo. ... Name pronounced ee-POL-uh-toe puh-CHAR-doh.

HIGH SCHOOL: Liceo Enriguillo (Jicome Esperanza, Dominican Republic).

TRANSACTIONS/CAREER NOTES: Signed as non-drafted free agent by Kansas City Royals organization (December 16, 1987). ... On disabled list (August 14-September 1, 1993; and August 15-September 1, 1995). ... On Kansas City disabled list (July 5-August 25, 1997); included rehabilitation assignment to Omaha (July 25-August 25). ... Granted free agency (October 31, 1997). ... Re-signed by Royals (December 4, 1997). ... On Kansas City disabled list (May 6-23 and August 21, 1998-remainder of season); included rehabilitation assignment to Lansing (August 21). ... On disabled list (March 28, 1999-entire season). ... Granted free agency (November 11, 1999). ... Signed by Boston Red Sox organization (February 16, 2000). ... On Pawtucket disabled list (April 6-20, 2000). ... On Boston disabled list (March 21-May 14 and August 3-18, 2001); included rehabilitation assignments to Sarasota (April 18-May 6) and Pawtucket (May 7-14). ... Announced retirement (August 20, 2001). ... Signed by Houston Astros (February 22, 2002). ... On Houston disabled list (March 31-May 3, 2002); included rehabilitation assignment to New Orleans (April 22-May 3). ... Announced retirement (May 15, 2002). ... Granted free agency (October 15, 2002).

STATISTICAL NOTES: Pitched 8-0 one-hit, complete-game victory for Kansas City against Boston (July 21, 1992).

MISCELLANEOUS: Struck out in only appearance as pinch hitter (2000).

CAREER HITTING (MLB): 0-for-5 (.000), 0 R, 0 2B, 0 3B, 0 HR, 0 RBI.

Year League	W	L	Pct.	ERA	G	GS	CG	ShO	Sv.-Opp.	IP	H	R	ER	HR	BB-IBB	SO
1988— Gulf Coast Royals (GCL)	0	0	...	13.50	1	0	0	0	0-...	1.1	3	2	2	0	1-0	3
1989— Appleton (Midw.)	5	4	.556	2.97	12	12	2	0	0-...	75.2	58	29	25	4	18-0	50
1990— Baseball City (FSL)	1	6	.143	3.80	11	10	0	0	0-...	45.0	47	28	19	1	25-0	40
1991— Memphis (Sou.)	3	11	.214	4.27	34	11	0	0	0-...	99.0	116	56	47	4	38-5	75
1992— Memphis (Sou.)	0	0	...	0.64	2	2	0	0	0-...	14.0	13	2	1	0	1-0	10
— Kansas City (A.L.)	9	6	.600	3.95	31	24	1	1	0-0	143.2	148	71	63	9	49-1	59
1993— Kansas City (A.L.)	7	8	.467	4.04	30	25	2	0	0-0	165.0	183	85	74	10	53-2	70
1994— Kansas City (A.L.)	5	3	.625	4.92	45	0	0	0	3-5	67.2	82	42	37	4	24-5	36
1995— Kansas City (A.L.)	8	4	.667	4.36	44	0	0	0	1-2	64.0	66	34	31	4	30-7	43
1996— Kansas City (A.L.)	3	5	.375	5.43	57	0	0	0	3-5	68.0	74	41	41	5	26-5	43
1997— Kansas City (A.L.)	3	5	.375	4.22	47	0	0	0	11-13	49.0	51	24	23	7	24-8	34
— Omaha (A.A.)	0	0	...	5.79	5	1	0	0	1-...	4.2	5	3	3	1	3-0	3
1998— Kansas City (A.L.)	7	8	.467	5.13	27	18	0	0	1-1	112.1	126	73	64	11	43-2	55
— Lansing (Midw.)	0	0	...	0.00	1	0	0	0	0-...	1.0	0	0	0	0	0-0	0
1999— Kansas City (A.L.)									Did not play.							
2000— Sarasota (FSL)■	1	1	.500	1.38	7	2	0	0	0-...	13.0	9	3	2	1	0-0	12
— Pawtucket (I.L.)	0	0	...	0.00	3	0	0	0	0-...	4.2	2	0	0	0	0-0	4
— Boston (A.L.)	6	3	.667	3.46	38	1	0	0	1-2	65.0	63	29	25	1	26-2	37
2001— Sarasota (FSL)	0	0	...	4.50	3	3	0	0	0-...	6.0	8	3	3	1	2-0	8
— Pawtucket (I.L.)	0	0	...	5.40	3	3	0	0	0-...	5.0	3	3	3	0	4-0	2
— Boston (A.L.)	2	1	.667	4.93	30	0	0	0	0-3	34.2	42	23	19	3	10-3	17
2002— New Orleans (PCL)■	0	0	...	0.00	5	1	0	0	0-...	6.2	6	0	0	0	1-0	4
— Houston (N.L.)	0	1	.000	81.00	1	0	0	0	0-0	.1	3	3	3	0	2-1	0
A.L. totals (9 years)	50	43	.538	4.41	349	68	3	1	20-31	769.1	835	422	377	54	285-35	394
N.L. totals (1 year)	0	1	.000	81.00	1	0	0	0	0-0	.1	3	3	3	0	2-1	0
Major League totals (10 years)	50	44	.532	4.44	350	68	3	1	20-31	769.2	838	425	380	54	287-36	394

PICKFORD, KEVIN — P

PERSONAL: Born March 12, 1975, in Fresno, Calif. ... 6-4/200. ... Throws left, bats left. ... Full name: Kevin Patrick Pickford.

HIGH SCHOOL: Clovis West (Fresno, Calif.).

TRANSACTIONS/CAREER NOTES: Selected by Pittsburgh Pirates organization in second round of free-agent draft (June 3, 1993); pick received as part of compensation for Houston Astros signing of Type A free-agent P Doug Drabek. ... On disabled list (April 8, 1999-entire season). ... On Altoona disabled list (May 12-June 2, 2000). ... Granted free agency (October 18, 2000). ... On Lynchburg disabled list (April 5-16, 2001). ... Released by Pirates (April 16, 2001). ... Signed by Sonoma County, Western League (2001). ... Signed by San Diego Padres organization (February 1, 2002). ... Released by Padres (September 30, 2002).

CAREER HITTING (MLB): 0-for-5 (.000), 0 R, 0 2B, 0 3B, 0 HR, 0 RBI.

Year League	W	L	Pct.	ERA	G	GS	CG	ShO	Sv.-Opp.	IP	H	R	ER	HR	BB-IBB	SO
1993— Gulf Coast Pirates (GCL)	0	4	.000	3.41	9	7	0	0	0-...	34.1	24	19	13	1	20-0	28
1994— Augusta (S.Atl.)	0	1	.000	4.15	2	2	0	0	0-...	8.2	9	6	4	1	5-0	7
— Welland (NY-Penn)	5	8	.385	4.89	•15	15	1	1	0-...	84.2	86	52	46	7	36-0	52
1995— Augusta (S.Atl.)	7	3	.700	2.00	16	16	0	0	0-...	85.2	85	28	19	5	16-1	59
— Lynchburg (Caro.)	0	3	.000	4.94	4	4	0	0	0-...	27.1	31	15	15	5	0-0	15
1996— Lynchburg (Caro.)	11	11	.500	4.07	28	•28	•4	1	0-...	*172.1	*195	99	78	15	25-0	100
1997— Carolina (Sou.)	1	2	.333	7.36	21	1	0	0	1-...	29.1	48	29	24	3	15-3	24
— Lynchburg (Caro.)	3	4	.429	3.56	14	10	0	0	1-...	73.1	72	31	29	3	11-0	50
1998— Carolina (Sou.)	5	1	.833	3.90	13	8	1	0	0-...	57.2	48	26	25	7	15-1	43
— Nashville (PCL)	6	1	.857	3.49	13	12	0	0	0-...	80.0	84	33	31	7	20-2	59
1999— Nashville (PCL)									Did not play.							
2000— Altoona (East.)	0	5	.000	9.97	10	4	0	0	0-...	21.2	38	29	24	2	14-0	9
— Lynchburg (Caro.)	1	2	.333	6.16	10	6	0	0	0-...	30.2	42	30	21	3	14-0	13
2001— Sonoma County (West.)■	3	5	.375	8.29	9	9	0	0	0-...	38.0	51	45	35	2	23-...	19
2002— Portland (PCL)■	4	7	.364	5.94	20	12	1	0	1-...	69.2	79	50	46	5	31-1	40
— San Diego (N.L.)	0	2	.000	6.00	16	4	0	0	0-0	30.0	37	23	20	3	20-1	18
Major League totals (1 year)	0	2	.000	6.00	16	4	0	0	0-0	30.0	37	23	20	3	20-1	18

PIERRE, JUAN — OF — ROCKIES

PERSONAL: Born August 14, 1977, in Mobile, Ala. ... 6-0/180. ... Bats left, throws left. ... Full name: Juan D'Vaughn Pierre.

HIGH SCHOOL: Alexandria (La.).

COLLEGE: South Alabama.

TRANSACTIONS/CAREER NOTES: Selected by Colorado Rockies organization in 13th round of free-agent draft (June 2, 1998).

STATISTICAL NOTES: Tied for South Atlantic League lead in double plays by outfielder with four in 1999. ... Had 16-game hitting streak (August 8-23, 2000). ... Had 15-game hitting streak (September 6-22, 2000). ... Led N.L. in caught stealing with 17 in 2001.

2002 GAMES PLAYED BY POSITION (MLB): OF—149.

Year Team (League)	Pos.	G	AB	R	H	2B	3B	HR	RBI	BB	SO	SB-CS	Avg.	OBP	SLG	E	Avg.
		BATTING														FIELDING	
1998—Portland (N'West)	OF	64	264	55	93	9	2	0	30	19	11	*38-9	*.352	.399	.402	5	.955
1999—Asheville (S.Atl.)	OF	*140	*585	93	*187	28	5	1	55	38	37	66-19	.320	.366	.390	4	.981
2000—Carolina (Sou.)	OF	107	439	63	143	16	4	0	32	33	26	46-12	.326	.376	.380	2	.992
—Colo. Springs (PCL)	OF	4	17	3	8	0	1	0	1	0	0	1-1	.471	.471	.588	0	1.000
—Colorado (N.L.)	OF	51	200	26	62	2	0	0	20	13	15	7-6	.310	.353	.320	3	.975
2001—Colorado (N.L.)	OF	156	617	108	202	26	11	2	55	41	29	•46-17	.327	.378	.415	8	.979
2002—Colorado (N.L.)	OF	152	592	90	170	20	5	1	35	31	52	47-12	.287	.332	.343	2	.995
Major League totals (3 years)		359	1409	224	434	48	16	3	110	85	96	100-35	.308	.356	.371	13	.985

PIERZYNSKI, A.J. C TWINS

PERSONAL: Born December 30, 1976, in Bridgehampton, N.Y. ... 6-3/220. ... Bats left, throws right. ... Full name: Anthony John Pierzynski.
HIGH SCHOOL: Dr. Phillips (Orlando).
TRANSACTIONS/CAREER NOTES: Selected by Minnesota Twins organization in third round of free-agent draft (June 2, 1994). ... On Salt Lake disabled list (August 24, 1999-remainder of season).
STATISTICAL NOTES: Tied for Appalachian League lead in errors by catcher with 12 in 1995. ... Led Appalachian League catchers with 71 assists in 1995. ... Led Midwest League catchers with 22 passed balls and tied for lead with 20 errors by catcher in 1996. ... Had 16-game hitting streak (May 26-June 14, 2002).
2002 GAMES PLAYED BY POSITION (MLB): C—124.

Year Team (League)	Pos.	G	AB	R	H	2B	3B	HR	RBI	BB	SO	SB-CS	Avg.	OBP	SLG	E	Avg.
		BATTING														FIELDING	
1994—GC Twins (GCL)	C-DH	43	152	21	44	8	1	1	19	12	19	0-2	.289	.337	.375	8	.966
1995—Fort Wayne (Midw.)	C	22	84	10	26	5	1	2	14	2	10	0-0	.310	.322	.464	10	.939
—Elizabethton (Appl.)	C-1B	56	205	29	68	13	1	7	45	14	23	0-2	.332	.373	.507	‡12	.974
1996—Fort Wayne (Midw.)	C-DH-OF	114	431	48	118	30	3	7	70	22	53	0-4	.274	.308	.406	†21	.972
1997—Fort Myers (FSL)	C-DH-1B	118	412	49	115	23	1	9	64	16	59	2-1	.279	.313	.405	10	.987
1998—New Britain (East.)	C-DH	59	212	30	63	11	0	3	17	10	25	0-2	.297	.333	.392	2	.996
—Salt Lake (PCL)	C	59	208	29	53	7	2	7	30	9	24	3-1	.255	.284	.409	7	.983
—Minnesota (A.L.)	C	7	10	1	3	0	0	0	1	1	2	0-0	.300	.385	.300	0	1.000
1999—Salt Lake (PCL)	C-DH	67	228	29	59	10	0	1	25	16	29	0-0	.259	.307	.316	7	.984
—Minnesota (A.L.)	C	9	22	3	6	2	0	0	3	1	4	0-0	.273	.333	.364	0	1.000
2000—New Britain (East.)	C	62	228	36	68	17	2	4	34	8	22	0-0	.298	.341	.443	6	.982
—Salt Lake (PCL)	C	41	155	22	52	14	1	4	25	5	22	1-1	.335	.354	.516	3	.990
—Minnesota (A.L.)	C	33	88	12	27	5	1	2	11	5	14	1-0	.307	.354	.455	0	1.000
2001—Minnesota (A.L.)	C-DH	114	381	51	110	33	2	7	55	16	57	1-7	.289	.322	.441	10	.985
2002—Minnesota (A.L.)	C	130	440	54	132	31	6	6	49	13	61	1-2	.300	.334	.439	3	.996
Major League totals (5 years)		293	941	121	278	71	9	15	119	36	138	3-9	.295	.332	.438	13	.992

DIVISION SERIES RECORD

Year Team (League)	Pos.	G	AB	R	H	2B	3B	HR	RBI	BB	SO	SB-CS	Avg.	OBP	SLG	E	Avg.
		BATTING														FIELDING	
2002—Minnesota (A.L.)	C	5	16	4	7	0	1	1	4	2	2	0-0	.438	.500	.750	1	.969

CHAMPIONSHIP SERIES RECORD

Year Team (League)	Pos.	G	AB	R	H	2B	3B	HR	RBI	BB	SO	SB-CS	Avg.	OBP	SLG	E	Avg.
		BATTING														FIELDING	
2002—Minnesota (A.L.)	C	5	16	1	4	0	0	0	2	0	2	0-1	.250	.235	.250	2	.938

ALL-STAR GAME RECORD

	AB	R	H	2B	3B	HR	RBI	BB	SO	SB-CS	Avg.	OBP	SLG	E	Avg.
All-Star Game totals (1 year)	3	0	0	0	0	0	0	0	0	0-0	.000	.000	.000	0	1.000

PINEDA, LUIS P

PERSONAL: Born October 17, 1974, in San Cristobal, Dominican Republic. ... 6-1/178. ... Throws right, bats right. ... Full name: Luis A. Pineda.
TRANSACTIONS/CAREER NOTES: Signed as non-drafted free agent by Texas Rangers organization (June 14, 1995). ... Released by Rangers (May 22, 1997). ... Signed by Arizona Diamondbacks organization (June 25, 1998). ... Released by Diamondbacks (July 4, 1998). ... Signed by Detroit Tigers organization (July 30, 1998). ... Granted free agency (October 16, 1998). ... Re-signed by Tigers organization (December 29, 1998). ... On Lakeland disabled list (June 8-September 18, 2000). ... On Erie disabled list (June 14-July 13, 2001). ... Traded by Tigers with OF Juan Encarnacion to Cincinnati Reds for OF Dmitri Young (December 11, 2001). ... On Cincinnati disabled list (July 1, 2002-remainder of season). ... Granted free agency (October 15, 2002).
CAREER HITTING (MLB): 0-for-3 (.000), 0 R, 0 2B, 0 3B, 0 HR, 0 RBI.

Year League	W	L	Pct.	ERA	G	GS	CG	ShO	Sv.-Opp.	IP	H	R	ER	HR	BB-IBB	SO
1995—Dom. Rangers (DSL)	6	1	.857	3.00	12	5	0	0	0-...	39.0	36	17	13	...	31-...	19
1996—Gulf Coast Rangers (GCL)	6	3	.667	3.52	11	11	1	0	0-...	71.2	67	31	28	6	25-0	66
1997—									Did not play.							
1998—Dominican Tigers (DSL)■	2	0	1.000	0.89	12	0	0	0	5-...	20.1	7	3	2	...	14-...	43
1999—West Michigan (Midw.)	0	2	.000	7.45	24	3	0	0	7-...	19.1	30	18	16	2	26-2	55
—Lakeland (FSL)	0	1	.000	1.04	8	0	0	0	0-...	8.2	6	2	1	0	7-0	8
2000—Lakeland (FSL)	1	3	.250	3.38	18	0	0	0	4-...	26.2	23	13	10	3	19-0	42
2001—Erie (East.)	6	2	.750	3.05	16	12	2	1	0-...	85.2	68	33	29	8	28-0	92
—Toledo (I.L.)	1	0	1.000	0.00	2	0	0	0	0-...	8.0	3	0	0	0	0-0	6
—Detroit (A.L.)	0	1	.000	4.91	16	0	0	0	0-0	18.1	16	10	10	2	14-2	13
2002—Cincinnati (N.L.)■	1	3	.250	4.18	26	2	0	0	0-0	32.1	25	16	15	4	24-1	31
—Louisville (I.L.)	0	1	.000	4.26	3	3	0	0	0-...	12.2	9	6	6	1	4-0	12
A.L. totals (1 year)	0	1	.000	4.91	16	0	0	0	0-0	18.1	16	10	10	2	14-2	13
N.L. totals (1 year)	1	3	.250	4.18	26	2	0	0	0-0	32.1	25	16	15	4	24-1	31
Major League totals (2 years)	1	4	.200	4.44	42	2	0	0	0-0	50.2	41	26	25	6	38-3	44

PINEIRO, JOEL — P — MARINERS

PERSONAL: Born September 25, 1978, in Rio Pedres, Puerto Rico. ... 6-1/180. ... Throws right, bats right. ... Full name: Joel Alberto Pineiro.
HIGH SCHOOL: Colonial (Orlando).
JUNIOR COLLEGE: Edison Community College (Fla.).
TRANSACTIONS/CAREER NOTES: Selected by Seattle Mariners organization in 12th round of free-agent draft (June 3, 1997). ... On suspended list (October 3-6, 2001).
CAREER HITTING (MLB): 1-for-7 (.143), 0 R, 0 2B, 0 3B, 0 HR, 2 RBI.

Year	League	W	L	Pct.	ERA	G	GS	CG	ShO	Sv.-Opp.	IP	H	R	ER	HR	BB-IBB	SO
1997	Arizona Mariners (Ariz.)	1	0	1.000	0.00	1	0	0	0	0-...	3.0	1	0	0	0	0-0	4
—	Everett (N'West)	4	2	.667	5.33	18	6	0	0	2-...	49.0	54	33	29	2	18-1	59
1998	Wisconsin (Midw.)	8	4	.667	3.19	16	16	1	0	0-...	96.0	92	40	34	8	28-1	84
—	Lancaster (Calif.)	2	0	1.000	7.80	9	9	1	•1	0-...	45.0	58	40	39	6	22-0	48
—	Orlando (Sou.)	1	0	1.000	5.40	1	1	0	0	0-...	5.0	7	4	3	0	2-0	2
1999	New Haven (East.)	10	*15	.400	4.72	28	25	4	0	0-...	166.0	190	105	87	18	52-0	116
2000	New Haven (East.)	2	1	.667	4.13	9	9	0	0	0-...	52.1	42	25	24	6	12-0	43
—	Tacoma (PCL)	7	1	.875	2.80	10	9	2	2	0-...	61.0	53	20	19	3	22-1	41
—	Seattle (A.L.)	1	0	1.000	5.59	8	1	0	0	0-0	19.1	25	13	12	3	13-0	10
2001	Tacoma (PCL)	6	3	.667	3.62	18	10	0	0	0-...	77.0	68	31	31	8	33-0	64
—	Seattle (A.L.)	6	2	.750	2.03	17	11	0	0	0-0	75.1	50	24	17	2	21-0	56
2002	Seattle (A.L.)	14	7	.667	3.24	37	28	2	1	0-0	194.1	189	75	70	24	54-1	136
Major League totals (3 years)		21	9	.700	3.08	62	40	2	1	0-0	289.0	264	112	99	29	88-1	202

DIVISION SERIES RECORD

Year	League	W	L	Pct.	ERA	G	GS	CG	ShO	Sv.-Opp.	IP	H	R	ER	HR	BB-IBB	SO
2001	Seattle (A.L.)	Did not play.															

CHAMPIONSHIP SERIES RECORD

Year	League	W	L	Pct.	ERA	G	GS	CG	ShO	Sv.-Opp.	IP	H	R	ER	HR	BB-IBB	SO
2001	Seattle (A.L.)	0	0	...	4.50	1	0	0	0	0-0	2.0	4	1	1	0	2-0	5

PLESAC, DAN — P

PERSONAL: Born February 4, 1962, in Gary, Ind. ... 6-5/217. ... Throws left, bats left. ... Full name: Daniel Thomas Plesac. ... Name pronounced PLEE-sack.
HIGH SCHOOL: Crown Point (Ind.).
COLLEGE: North Carolina State.
TRANSACTIONS/CAREER NOTES: Selected by St. Louis Cardinals organization in second round of free-agent draft (June 3, 1980); did not sign. ... Selected by Milwaukee Brewers organization in first round (26th pick overall) of free-agent draft (June 6, 1983). ... Granted free agency (October 27, 1992). ... Signed by Chicago Cubs (December 8, 1992). ... Granted free agency (October 25, 1994). ... Signed by Pittsburgh Pirates (November 9, 1994). ... Traded by Pirates with OF Orlando Merced and IF Carlos Garcia to Toronto Blue Jays for P Jose Silva, P Jose Pett, IF Brandon Cromer and three players to be named later (November 14, 1996); Pirates acquired P Mike Halperin, IF Abraham Nunez and C/OF Craig Wilson to complete deal (December 11, 1996). ... Traded by Blue Jays to Arizona Diamondbacks for SS Tony Batista and P John Frascatore (June 12, 1999). ... Granted free agency (October 30, 2000). ... Signed by Blue Jays (December 8, 2000). ... Traded by Blue Jays to Philadelphia Phillies for P Cliff Politte (May 26, 2002). ... Granted free agency (October 29, 2002).
STATISTICAL NOTES: Led Appalachian League pitchers with three balks in 1983.
MISCELLANEOUS: Holds Milwaukee Brewers franchise all-time records for most games pitched (365), most saves (133) and lowest career earned-run average (3.21).
CAREER HITTING (MLB): 1-for-15 (.067), 0 R, 0 2B, 0 3B, 0 HR, 0 RBI.

Year	League	W	L	Pct.	ERA	G	GS	CG	ShO	Sv.-Opp.	IP	H	R	ER	HR	BB-IBB	SO
1983	Paintsville (Appl.)	*9	1	*.900	3.50	14	•14	2	0	0-...	82.1	76	44	32	6	57-0	*85
1984	Stockton (Calif.)	6	6	.500	3.32	16	16	2	0	0-...	108.1	106	51	40	7	50-0	101
—	El Paso (Texas)	2	2	.500	3.46	7	7	0	0	0-...	39.0	43	19	15	2	16-0	24
1985	El Paso (Texas)	12	5	.706	4.97	25	24	2	0	0-...	150.1	171	91	83	12	68-1	128
1986	Milwaukee (A.L.)	10	7	.588	2.97	51	0	0	0	14-18	91.0	81	34	30	5	29-1	75
1987	Milwaukee (A.L.)	5	6	.455	2.61	57	0	0	0	23-36	79.1	63	30	23	8	23-1	89
1988	Milwaukee (A.L.)	1	2	.333	2.41	50	0	0	0	30-35	52.1	46	14	14	2	12-2	52
1989	Milwaukee (A.L.)	3	4	.429	2.35	52	0	0	0	33-40	61.1	47	16	16	6	17-1	52
1990	Milwaukee (A.L.)	3	7	.300	4.43	66	0	0	0	24-34	69.0	67	36	34	5	31-6	65
1991	Milwaukee (A.L.)	2	7	.222	4.29	45	10	0	0	8-12	92.1	92	49	44	12	39-1	61
1992	Milwaukee (A.L.)	5	4	.556	2.96	44	4	0	0	1-3	79.0	64	28	26	5	35-5	54
1993	Chicago (N.L.)■	2	1	.667	4.74	57	0	0	0	0-2	62.2	74	37	33	10	21-6	47
1994	Chicago (N.L.)	2	3	.400	4.61	54	0	0	0	1-3	54.2	61	30	28	9	13-0	53
1995	Pittsburgh (N.L.)■	4	4	.500	3.58	58	0	0	0	3-5	60.1	53	26	24	3	27-7	57
1996	Pittsburgh (N.L.)	6	5	.545	4.09	73	0	0	0	11-17	70.1	67	35	32	4	24-6	76
1997	Toronto (A.L.)■	2	4	.333	3.58	73	0	0	0	1-5	50.1	47	22	20	8	19-4	61
1998	Toronto (A.L.)	4	3	.571	3.78	78	0	0	0	4-5	50.0	41	23	21	4	16-1	55
1999	Toronto (A.L.)	0	3	.000	8.34	30	0	0	0	0-2	22.2	28	21	21	4	9-1	26
—	Arizona (N.L.)■	2	1	.667	3.32	34	0	0	0	1-1	21.2	22	9	8	3	8-1	27
2000	Arizona (N.L.)	5	1	.833	3.15	62	0	0	0	0-4	40.0	34	21	14	4	26-2	45
2001	Toronto (A.L.)■	4	5	.444	3.57	62	0	0	0	1-2	45.1	34	18	18	4	24-5	68
2002	Toronto (A.L.)	1	2	.333	3.38	19	0	0	0	0-1	13.1	11	5	5	1	6-0	14
—	Philadelphia (N.L.)■	2	1	.667	4.70	41	0	0	0	1-3	23.0	16	12	12	5	12-3	27
A.L. totals (12 years)		40	54	.426	3.47	627	14	0	0	139-193	706.0	621	296	272	64	260-28	672
N.L. totals (7 years)		23	16	.590	4.09	379	0	0	0	17-35	332.2	327	170	151	38	131-25	332
Major League totals (17 years)		63	70	.474	3.67	1006	14	0	0	156-228	1038.2	948	466	423	102	391-53	1004

DIVISION SERIES RECORD

Year	League	W	L	Pct.	ERA	G	GS	CG	ShO	Sv.-Opp.	IP	H	R	ER	HR	BB-IBB	SO
1999	Arizona (N.L.)	0	0	...	54.00	1	0	0	0	0-0	.1	3	2	2	0	0-0	0

ALL-STAR GAME RECORD

	W	L	Pct.	ERA	GS	CG	ShO	Sv.-Opp.	IP	H	R	ER	HR	BB-IBB	SO
All-Star Game totals (3 years)	0	0	...	0.00	0	0	0	0-0	1.1	1	0	0	0	0-0	2

PODSEDNIK, SCOTT — OF — BREWERS

PERSONAL: Born March 18, 1976, in West, Texas. ... 6-0/170. ... Bats left, throws left. ... Full name: Scott Eric Podsednik.
HIGH SCHOOL: West (Texas).
TRANSACTIONS/CAREER NOTES: Selected by Texas Rangers organization in third round of free-agent draft (June 2, 1994). ... Traded by Rangers to Florida Marlins (October 8, 1995), completing deal in which Marlins traded P Bobby Witt to Texas Rangers for two players to be named (August 8, 1995); Rangers also sent P Wilson Heredia to Marlins (August 11, 1995). ... Selected by Rangers from Marlins organization in Rule 5 minor league draft (December 15, 1997). ... On Charlotte disabled list (April 6-May 22, 2000). ... Granted free agency (October 15, 2000). ... Signed by Seattle Mariners organization (November 1, 2000). ... On Tacoma disabled list (May 4-June 12 and August 14-26, 2001). ... Claimed on waivers by Milwaukee Brewers (October 13, 2002).
STATISTICAL NOTES: Led Gulf Coast League outfielders with 112 putouts and 118 total chances in 1994. ... Tied for Florida State League lead in double plays by outfielder with four in 1996. ... Led Pacific Coast League outfielders with 322 putouts and 329 total chances in 2002.
2002 GAMES PLAYED BY POSITION (MLB): OF—11; DH—2.

		BATTING														FIELDING	
Year Team (League)	Pos.	G	AB	R	H	2B	3B	HR	RBI	BB	SO	SB-CS	Avg.	OBP	SLG	E	Avg.
1994—GC Rangers (GCL)	OF	60	211	34	48	7	1	1	17	•41	34	18-5	.227	.357	.284	0	*1.000
1995—Hudson Valley (NY-P)	OF	65	252	42	67	3	0	0	20	35	31	20-6	.266	.355	.278	3	.978
1996—Brevard Co. (FSL)■	OF	108	383	39	100	9	2	0	30	45	65	20-10	.261	.343	.295	4	.984
1997—Kane County (Midw.)	OF	*135	*531	80	147	23	4	3	49	60	72	28-11	.277	.352	.352	5	.977
1998—Charlotte (FSL)■	OF	81	302	55	86	12	4	4	39	44	32	26-8	.285	.369	.391	2	.986
—Tulsa (Texas)	OF	17	75	9	18	4	1	0	4	6	11	5-2	.240	.296	.320	0	1.000
1999—GC Rangers (GCL)	OF	5	17	6	7	2	0	0	5	2	3	1-0	.412	.474	.529	0	1.000
—Tulsa (Texas)	OF	37	116	10	18	4	0	0	1	5	13	6-2	.155	.190	.190	1	.987
2000—Tulsa (Texas)	OF	49	169	20	42	7	2	2	13	30	33	19-4	.249	.361	.349	3	.968
2001—Tacoma (PCL)■	OF	66	269	46	78	15	4	3	30	13	46	12-5	.290	.327	.409	5	.967
—Seattle (A.L.)	OF	5	6	1	1	0	1	0	3	0	1	0-0	.167	.167	.500	0	1.000
2002—Tacoma (PCL)	OF	125	438	63	122	25	6	9	61	43	70	35-13	.279	.347	.425	5	.985
—Seattle (A.L.)	OF-DH	14	20	2	4	0	0	1	5	4	6	0-0	.200	.320	.350	1	.938
Major League totals (2 years)		19	26	3	5	0	1	1	8	4	7	0-0	.192	.290	.385	1	.947

POLANCO, PLACIDO — 3B — PHILLIES

PERSONAL: Born October 10, 1975, in Santo Domingo, Dominican Republic. ... 5-10/168. ... Bats right, throws right. ... Full name: Placido Enrique Polanco. ... Name pronounced Plah-SEE-doh Poh-LAHN-co.
HIGH SCHOOL: Santo Clara (Santo Domingo, Dominican Republic).
JUNIOR COLLEGE: Miami-Dade (Wolfson) Community College.
TRANSACTIONS/CAREER NOTES: Selected by St. Louis Cardinals in 19th round of free-agent draft (June 3, 1994). ... On Memphis suspended list (August 28-29, 1999). ... On disabled list (July 1-16, 2000). ... Traded by Cardinals with P Bud Smith and P Mike Timlin to Philadelphia Phillies for 3B Scott Rolen and P Doug Nickle (July 29, 2002).
STATISTICAL NOTES: Led Florida State League in grounding into double plays with 31 in 1996. ... Led Florida State League second basemen with 383 assists in 1996. ... Led Texas League second basemen with 425 assists and tied for lead with 110 double plays in 1997. ... Had 20-game hitting streak (July 21-August 11, 2001). ... Career major league grand slams: 1.
2002 GAMES PLAYED BY POSITION (MLB): 3B—131; SS—13; 2B—6.

		BATTING														FIELDING	
Year Team (League)	Pos.	G	AB	R	H	2B	3B	HR	RBI	BB	SO	SB-CS	Avg.	OBP	SLG	E	Avg.
1994—Ariz. Cardinals (Ariz.)	SS-2B	32	127	17	27	4	0	1	10	7	15	4-2	.213	.259	.268	10	.932
1995—Peoria (Midw.)	SS-2B	103	361	43	96	7	4	2	41	18	30	7-6	.266	.303	.324	21	.950
1996—St. Petersburg (FSL)	2B	*137	*540	65	*157	29	5	0	51	24	34	4-4	.291	.323	.363	4	*.993
1997—Arkansas (Texas)	2B	129	508	71	148	16	3	2	51	29	51	19-5	.291	.331	.346	14	*.979
1998—Memphis (PCL)	2B-SS	70	246	36	69	19	1	1	21	16	15	6-3	.280	.331	.378	5	.984
—St. Louis (N.L.)	SS-2B	45	114	10	29	3	2	1	11	5	9	2-0	.254	.292	.342	7	.961
1999—St. Louis (N.L.)	2B-3B-SS	88	220	24	61	9	3	1	19	15	24	1-3	.277	.321	.359	8	.972
—Memphis (PCL)	2B-SS-3B	29	120	18	33	4	1	0	10	3	11	2-0	.275	.296	.325	2	.984
2000—St. Louis (N.L.)	2B-3B-SS-1B	118	323	50	102	12	3	5	39	16	26	4-4	.316	.347	.418	3	.991
2001—St. Louis (N.L.)	3-S-2-D	144	564	87	173	26	4	3	38	25	43	12-3	.307	.342	.383	4	.992
2002—St. Louis (N.L.)	3B-SS-2B	94	342	47	97	19	1	5	27	12	27	3-1	.284	.316	.389	6	.978
—Philadelphia (N.L.)■	3B	53	206	28	61	13	1	4	22	14	14	2-2	.296	.353	.427	3	.983
Major League totals (5 years)		542	1769	246	523	82	14	19	156	87	143	24-13	.296	.333	.390	31	.982

DIVISION SERIES RECORD

		BATTING														FIELDING	
Year Team (League)	Pos.	G	AB	R	H	2B	3B	HR	RBI	BB	SO	SB-CS	Avg.	OBP	SLG	E	Avg.
2000—St. Louis (N.L.)	3B	3	10	1	3	0	0	0	3	1	0	1-0	.300	.364	.300	0	1.000
2001—St. Louis (N.L.)	3B	5	15	1	4	0	0	0	1	1	1	1-0	.267	.294	.267	1	.941
Division series totals (2 years)		8	25	2	7	0	0	0	4	2	1	2-0	.280	.321	.280	1	.957

CHAMPIONSHIP SERIES RECORD

		BATTING														FIELDING	
Year Team (League)	Pos.	G	AB	R	H	2B	3B	HR	RBI	BB	SO	SB-CS	Avg.	OBP	SLG	E	Avg.
2000—St. Louis (N.L.)	3B-PH	4	5	0	1	0	0	0	0	2	1	0-0	.200	.429	.200	0	1.000

POLITTE, CLIFF — P — BLUE JAYS

PERSONAL: Born February 27, 1974, in St. Louis. ... 5-11/185. ... Throws right, bats right. ... Full name: Cliff Anthony Politte. ... Son of Clifford Politte, pitcher in St. Louis Cardinals organization (1959-65). ... Name pronounced po-LEET.
HIGH SCHOOL: Vianney (Kirkwood, Mo.).
JUNIOR COLLEGE: Jefferson College (Mo.).

TRANSACTIONS/CAREER NOTES: Selected by St. Louis Cardinals organization in 54th round of free agent draft (June 1, 1995). ... Traded by Cardinals with OF Ron Gant and P Jeff Brantley to Philadelphia Phillies for P Ricky Bottalico and P Garrett Stephenson (November 19, 1998). ... On Scranton/Wilkes-Barre disabled list (April 30-May 9, 2000). ... On Philadelphia disabled list (March 31-July 6, 2001); included rehabilitation assignment to Clearwater (June 18-July 6). ... Traded by Phillies to Toronto Blue Jays for P Dan Plesac (May 26, 2002).
HONORS: Named Carolina League Pitcher of the Year (1997).
CAREER HITTING (MLB): 3-for-32 (.094), 2 R, 1 2B, 0 3B, 0 HR, 2 RBI.

Year League	W	L	Pct.	ERA	G	GS	CG	ShO	Sv.-Opp.	IP	H	R	ER	HR	BB-IBB	SO
1996— Peoria (Midw.)	14	6	.700	2.59	25	25	0	0	0-...	149.2	108	50	43	8	47-0	151
1997— Prince William (Caro.)	11	1	*.917	*2.24	19	19	0	0	0-...	120.1	89	37	30	11	31-0	118
— Arkansas (Texas)	4	1	.800	2.15	6	6	0	0	0-...	37.2	35	15	9	3	9-1	26
1998— St. Louis (N.L.)	2	3	.400	6.32	8	8	0	0	0-0	37.0	45	32	26	6	18-0	22
— Memphis (PCL)	1	4	.200	7.64	10	10	0	0	0-...	50.2	71	46	43	10	24-0	42
— Arkansas (Texas)	5	3	.625	2.96	10	10	1	•1	0-...	67.0	56	25	22	6	16-0	61
1999— Reading (East.)■	9	8	.529	3.63	37	13	1	0	5-...	109.0	112	45	44	12	33-3	97
— Philadelphia (N.L.)	1	0	1.000	7.13	13	0	0	0	0-0	17.2	19	14	14	2	15-0	15
2000— Scranton/W.B. (I.L.)	8	4	.667	3.12	21	20	1	0	0-...	112.2	94	45	39	8	41-2	106
— Philadelphia (N.L.)	4	3	.571	3.66	12	8	0	0	0-0	59.0	55	24	24	8	27-1	50
2001— Clearwater (FSL)	0	1	.000	2.45	7	7	0	0	0-...	11.0	8	4	3	0	3-0	15
— Philadelphia (N.L.)	2	3	.400	2.42	23	0	0	0	0-0	26.0	24	8	7	2	8-3	23
2002— Philadelphia (N.L.)	2	0	1.000	3.86	13	0	0	0	0-1	16.1	19	10	7	0	9-1	15
— Toronto (A.L.)■	1	3	.250	3.61	55	0	0	0	1-3	57.1	38	23	23	5	19-1	57
A.L. totals (1 year)	1	3	.250	3.61	55	0	0	0	1-3	57.1	38	23	23	5	19-1	57
N.L. totals (5 years)	11	9	.550	4.50	69	16	0	0	0-1	156.0	162	88	78	18	77-5	125
Major League totals (5 years)	12	12	.500	4.26	124	16	0	0	1-4	213.1	200	111	101	23	96-6	182

PONSON, SIDNEY P ORIOLES

PERSONAL: Born November 2, 1976, in Noord, Aruba. ... 6-1/225. ... Throws right, bats right. ... Full name: Sidney Alton Ponson.
COLLEGE: Maria (Aruba).
TRANSACTIONS/CAREER NOTES: Signed as non-drafted free agent by Baltimore Orioles organization (August 17, 1993). ... On Bowie disabled list (June 13-July 15, 1997). ... On Baltimore disabled list (April 16-May 9, 2001); included rehabilitation assignment to Bowie (May 4-9). ... On disabled list (August 7-September 1, 2002).
CAREER HITTING (MLB): 3-for-14 (.214), 2 R, 1 2B, 0 3B, 0 HR, 0 RBI.

Year League	W	L	Pct.	ERA	G	GS	CG	ShO	Sv.-Opp.	IP	H	R	ER	HR	BB-IBB	SO
1994— Gulf Coast Orioles (GCL)	4	3	.571	2.96	12	10	1	0	0-...	•73.0	68	30	24	5	17-0	53
1995— Bluefield (Appl.)	6	3	.667	4.17	13	13	0	0	0-...	77.2	79	44	36	7	16-0	56
1996— Frederick (Caro.)	7	6	.538	3.45	18	16	3	0	0-...	107.0	98	56	41	6	28-0	110
1997— Bowie (East.)	2	7	.222	5.42	13	13	1	1	0-...	74.2	77	51	45	11	32-2	56
— Gulf Coast Orioles (GCL)	1	0	1.000	0.00	1	0	0	0	0-...	2.0	0	0	0	0	0-0	1
1998— Rochester (I.L.)	1	0	1.000	0.00	1	1	0	0	0-...	5.0	4	0	0	0	1-0	3
— Baltimore (A.L.)	8	9	.471	5.27	31	20	0	0	1-2	135.0	157	82	79	19	42-2	85
1999— Baltimore (A.L.)	12	12	.500	4.71	32	32	6	0	0-0	210.0	227	118	110	35	80-2	112
2000— Baltimore (A.L.)	9	13	.409	4.82	32	32	6	1	0-0	222.0	223	125	119	30	83-0	152
2001— Baltimore (A.L.)	5	10	.333	4.94	23	23	3	1	0-0	138.1	161	83	76	21	37-0	84
— Bowie (East.)	0	0	...	0.00	1	1	0	0	0-...	4.0	3	0	0	0	1-0	2
2002— Baltimore (A.L.)	7	9	.438	4.09	28	28	3	0	0-0	176.0	172	84	80	26	63-1	120
Major League totals (5 years)	41	53	.436	4.74	146	135	18	2	1-2	881.1	940	492	464	131	305-5	553

PORZIO, MIKE P WHITE SOX

PERSONAL: Born August 20, 1972, in Waterbury, Conn. ... 6-3/190. ... Throws left, bats left. ... Full name: Lawrence Michael Porzio.
HIGH SCHOOL: Fairfield Prep (Fairfield, Conn.).
COLLEGE: Villanova.
TRANSACTIONS/CAREER NOTES: Signed as non-drafted free agent by Chicago Cubs organization (June 30, 1993). ... Released by Cubs organization (July 19, 1994). ... Signed by Boston Red Sox organization (February 20, 1995). ... Released by Red Sox organization (April 1, 1995). ... Signed by Moblie, Texas-Louisiana League (May 1995). ... Signed by Ogden, Pioneer League (July 26, 1995). ... Signed by Tennessee, Big South League (June 1996). ... Signed by Baltimore Orioles organization (March 2, 1997). ... Released by Orioles organization (March 25, 1997). ... Signed by Sioux City, Northern League (May 1997). ... Signed by Atlanta Braves organization (March 8, 1998). ... Traded by Braves with P David Cortes and a player to be named later to Colorado Rockies for 1B Greg Colbrunn (July 30, 1998); Rockies acquired P Anthony Briggs to complete deal (September 9, 1998). ... On Colorado Springs disabled list (June 6-25, 1999). ... Granted free agency (October 18, 2000). ... Signed by Chicago White Sox organization (January 13, 2001). ... Granted free agency (October 15, 2001). ... Re-signed by White Sox organization (January 22, 2002).
CAREER HITTING (MLB): 0-for-0 (.000), 0 R, 0 2B, 0 3B, 0 HR, 0 RBI.

Year League	W	L	Pct.	ERA	G	GS	CG	ShO	Sv.-Opp.	IP	H	R	ER	HR	BB-IBB	SO
1993— Gulf Coast Cubs (GCL)	1	3	.250	3.83	10	8	0	0	0-...	42.1	42	26	18	1	30-0	30
1994— Gulf Coast Cubs (GCL)	0	3	.000	5.93	7	0	0	0	1-...	13.2	19	10	9	0	6-0	5
1995— Mobile (Tex.-La.)■	0	3	.000	5.46	16	2	0	0	0-...	28.0	32	19	17	2	13-2	15
— Ogden (Pio.)■	4	3	.571	6.38	8	8	2	0	0-...	48.0	66	39	34	4	15-0	26
1996— Tennessee (BSL)■	7	4	.636	3.64	15	15	3	0	0-...	99.0	94	55	40	9	30-1	54
1997— Sioux City (Nor.)■	2	2	.500	4.28	27	5	1	1	0-...	61.0	75	32	29	6	27-1	63
1998— Danville (Caro.)■	3	2	.600	2.51	26	11	1	0	2-...	97.0	74	34	27	7	30-5	95
— Salem (Caro.)■	2	3	.400	2.76	7	7	0	0	0-...	42.1	40	20	13	6	12-0	46
1999— Colorado Springs (PCL)	5	1	.833	3.38	35	0	0	0	0-...	42.2	44	16	16	5	30-4	33
— Colorado (N.L.)	0	0	...	8.59	16	0	0	0	0-0	14.2	21	14	14	5	10-0	10
2000— Carolina (Sou.)	7	4	.636	3.41	20	18	1	1	0-...	121.1	111	53	46	11	31-0	90
— Colorado Springs (PCL)	0	3	.000	10.04	6	6	0	0	0-...	26.0	39	30	29	7	20-0	26
2001— Birmingham (Sou.)■	1	0	1.000	1.38	2	2	0	0	0-...	13.0	3	2	2	1	5-0	10
— Charlotte (I.L.)	6	6	.500	4.35	31	23	0	0	0-...	134.1	138	76	65	14	55-2	107
2002— Chicago (A.L.)	2	2	.500	4.81	32	0	0	0	0-0	43.0	40	25	23	10	23-2	33
— Charlotte (I.L.)	6	5	.545	4.52	14	13	0	0	0-...	75.2	83	43	38	9	29-0	59
A.L. totals (1 year)	2	2	.500	4.81	32	0	0	0	0-0	43.0	40	25	23	10	23-2	33
N.L. totals (1 year)	0	0	...	8.59	16	0	0	0	0-0	14.2	21	14	14	5	10-0	10
Major League totals (2 years)	2	2	.500	5.77	48	0	0	0	0-0	57.2	61	39	37	15	33-2	43

POSADA, JORGE — C — YANKEES

PERSONAL: Born August 17, 1971, in Santurce, Puerto Rico. ... 6-2/205. ... Bats both, throws right. ... Full name: Jorge Rafael Posada Jr. ... Name pronounced HOR-hay po-SOD-a.

HIGH SCHOOL: Colegio Alejandrino (Puerto Rico).

JUNIOR COLLEGE: Calhoon Community College (Ala.).

TRANSACTIONS/CAREER NOTES: Selected by New York Yankees organization in 24th round of free-agent draft (June 4, 1990). ... On disabled list (July 26-September 4, 1994). ... On Columbus disabled list (May 3-12, 1995). ... On suspended list (July 17-18, 2000; and September 26-October 2, 2001).

RECORDS: Shares major league single-season record for most unassisted double plays by catcher—2 (2000).

HONORS: Named catcher on The Sporting News A.L. All-Star team (2000-02). ... Named catcher on The Sporting News A.L. Silver Slugger team (2000). ... Named catcher on A.L. Silver Slugger team (2001 and 2002).

STATISTICAL NOTES: Led New York-Pennsylvania League second basemen with 42 double plays in 1991. ... Led Carolina League with 38 passed balls in 1993. ... Tied for Carolina League lead in intentional bases on balls received with four in 1993. ... Tied for International League lead in errors by catcher with 11 in 1994. ... Tied for International League lead in double plays by catcher with seven in 1995. ... Led International League with 14 passed balls in 1995. ... Switch-hit home runs in one game four times (August 23, 1998; July 10, 1999; April 23, 2000; June 28, 2002). ... Led A.L. with 23 grounded into double plays in 2002. ... Led A.L. catchers with 965 putouts and 1,073 total chances in 2002. ... Career major league grand slams: 5.

2002 GAMES PLAYED BY POSITION (MLB): C—138; DH—5.

			BATTING													FIELDING	
Year	Team (League)	Pos.	G	AB	R	H	2B	3B	HR	RBI	BB	SO	SB-CS	Avg.	OBP	SLG	E	Avg.
1991—	Oneonta (NY-Penn)	2B-C	71	217	34	51	5	5	4	33	51	51	6-4	.235	.388	.359	21	.947
1992—	Greensboro (S.Atl.)	C-3B	101	339	60	94	22	4	12	58	58	87	11-6	.277	.389	.472	11	.965
1993—	Prince William (Caro.)	C-3B	118	410	71	106	27	2	17	61	67	90	17-5	.259	.366	.459	15	.981
	—Albany (East.)	C	7	25	3	7	0	0	0	0	2	7	0-0	.280	.333	.280	2	.958
1994—	Columbus (I.L.)	C-OF	92	313	46	75	13	3	11	48	32	81	5-5	.240	.308	.406	‡11	.977
1995—	Columbus (I.L.)	C-DH	108	368	60	94	32	5	8	51	54	101	4-4	.255	.350	.435	4	*.993
	—New York (A.L.)	C	1	0	0	0	0	0	0	0	0	0	0-0	...	...	...	0	1.000
1996—	Columbus (I.L.)	C-DH-OF	106	354	76	96	22	6	11	62	*79	86	3-3	.271	.405	.460	10	.985
	—New York (A.L.)	C-DH	8	14	1	1	0	0	0	0	1	6	0-0	.071	.133	.071	0	1.000
1997—	New York (A.L.)	C	60	188	29	47	12	0	6	25	30	33	1-2	.250	.359	.410	3	.992
1998—	New York (A.L.)	C-DH-1B	111	358	56	96	23	0	17	63	47	92	0-1	.268	.350	.475	4	.994
1999—	New York (A.L.)	C-DH-1B	112	379	50	93	19	2	12	57	53	91	1-0	.245	.341	.401	5	.993
2000—	New York (A.L.)	C-1B-DH	151	505	92	145	35	1	28	86	107	151	2-2	.287	.417	.527	8	.992
2001—	New York (A.L.)	C-DH-1B	138	484	59	134	28	1	22	95	62	132	2-6	.277	.363	.475	11	.990
2002—	New York (A.L.)	C-DH	143	511	79	137	40	1	20	99	81	143	1-0	.268	.370	.468	12	.988
Major League totals (8 years)			724	2439	366	653	157	5	105	425	381	648	7-11	.268	.369	.465	43	.991

DIVISION SERIES RECORD

			BATTING													FIELDING	
Year	Team (League)	Pos.	G	AB	R	H	2B	3B	HR	RBI	BB	SO	SB-CS	Avg.	OBP	SLG	E	Avg.
1995—	New York (A.L.)	PR	1	0	1	0	0	0	0	0	0	0	0-0	...	...	...	...	...
1997—	New York (A.L.)	C-PH	2	2	0	0	0	0	0	0	0	1	0-0	.000	.000	.000	0	1.000
1998—	New York (A.L.)	C	1	2	1	0	0	0	0	0	1	2	0-0	.000	.333	.000	0	1.000
1999—	New York (A.L.)	C	1	4	0	1	1	0	0	0	0	0	0-0	.250	.250	.500	0	1.000
2000—	New York (A.L.)	C	5	17	2	4	2	0	0	1	3	5	0-0	.235	.350	.353	0	1.000
2001—	New York (A.L.)	C	5	18	3	8	1	0	1	2	2	2	1-0	.444	.500	.667	0	1.000
2002—	New York (A.L.)	C	4	17	2	4	0	0	1	3	0	3	0-0	.235	.222	.412	1	.955
Division series totals (7 years)			19	60	9	17	4	0	2	6	6	13	1-0	.283	.343	.450	1	.991

CHAMPIONSHIP SERIES RECORD

			BATTING													FIELDING	
Year	Team (League)	Pos.	G	AB	R	H	2B	3B	HR	RBI	BB	SO	SB-CS	Avg.	OBP	SLG	E	Avg.
1998—	New York (A.L.)	C-PH	5	11	1	2	0	0	1	2	4	2	0-1	.182	.400	.455	0	1.000
1999—	New York (A.L.)	C	3	10	1	1	0	0	1	2	1	2	0-0	.100	.182	.400	1	.955
2000—	New York (A.L.)	C	6	19	2	3	1	0	0	3	5	5	0-1	.158	.360	.211	0	1.000
2001—	New York (A.L.)	C	5	14	4	3	1	0	0	0	6	7	0-0	.214	.450	.286	0	1.000
Championship series totals (4 years)			19	54	8	9	2	0	2	7	16	16	0-2	.167	.366	.315	1	.993

WORLD SERIES RECORD

NOTES: Member of World Series championship team (1998, 1999 and 2000).

			BATTING													FIELDING	
Year	Team (League)	Pos.	G	AB	R	H	2B	3B	HR	RBI	BB	SO	SB-CS	Avg.	OBP	SLG	E	Avg.
1998—	New York (A.L.)	C-PH	3	9	2	3	0	0	1	2	2	2	0-0	.333	.455	.667	0	1.000
1999—	New York (A.L.)	C	2	8	0	2	1	0	0	1	0	3	0-0	.250	.250	.375	0	1.000
2000—	New York (A.L.)	C	5	18	2	4	1	0	0	1	5	4	0-0	.222	.391	.278	0	1.000
2001—	New York (A.L.)	C	7	23	2	4	1	0	1	1	3	8	0-0	.174	.269	.348	1	.986
World Series totals (4 years)			17	58	6	13	3	0	2	5	10	17	0-0	.224	.338	.379	1	.994

ALL-STAR GAME RECORD

	AB	R	H	2B	3B	HR	RBI	BB	SO	SB-CS	Avg.	OBP	SLG	E	Avg.
All-Star Game totals (3 years)	6	0	1	1	0	0	0	0	3	0-0	.167	.167	.333	0	1.000

POTE, LOU — P — ANGELS

P

PERSONAL: Born August 21, 1971, in Evergreen Park, Ill. ... 6-3/208. ... Throws right, bats right. ... Full name: Louis William Pote.

HIGH SCHOOL: De La Salle Institute (Chicago).

JUNIOR COLLEGE: Kishwaukee (Illinois).

TRANSACTIONS/CAREER NOTES: Selected by San Francisco Giants organization in 29th round of free-agent draft (June 4, 1990). ... On Shreveport disabled list (April 8-July 31, 1994). ... Traded by Giants to Montreal Expos for P Luis Aquino (July 24, 1995). ... Released by Expos

(March 28, 1997). ... Signed by St. Louis Cardinals organization (August 7, 1997). ... Granted free agency (October 17, 1997). ... Signed by Anaheim Angels organization (December 15, 1997).

CAREER HITTING (MLB): 0-for-0 (.000), 0 R, 0 2B, 0 3B, 0 HR, 0 RBI.

Year	League	W	L	Pct.	ERA	G	GS	CG	ShO	Sv.-Opp.	IP	H	R	ER	HR	BB-IBB	SO
1991—	Arizona Giants (Ariz.)	2	3	.400	2.55	8	8	0	0	0-...	42.1	38	23	12	0	19-0	41
—	Everett (N'West)	2	0	1.000	2.51	5	4	0	0	0-...	28.2	24	8	8	2	7-0	26
1992—	Shreveport (Texas)	4	2	.667	0.96	20	3	0	0	0-...	37.2	20	7	4	1	15-2	26
—	San Jose (Calif.)	0	1	.000	4.66	4	3	0	0	0-...	9.2	11	5	5	0	7-0	8
1993—	Shreveport (Texas)	8	7	.533	4.07	19	19	0	0	0-...	108.1	111	53	49	10	45-1	81
1994—	Arizona Giants (Ariz.)	1	0	1.000	0.00	4	4	0	0	0-...	19.2	9	0	0	0	6-0	30
—	Shreveport (Texas)	2	2	.500	2.83	5	5	0	0	0-...	28.2	31	11	9	2	7-0	15
1995—	Shreveport (Texas)	2	2	.500	5.33	28	0	0	0	3-...	50.2	63	41	30	8	26-1	30
—	Harrisburg (East.)■	0	1	.000	5.40	9	4	0	0	0-...	28.1	32	17	17	3	7-0	24
1996—	Harrisburg (East.)	1	7	.125	5.07	25	18	0	0	1-...	104.2	114	66	59	15	48-2	61
1997—	Arkansas (Texas)■	0	0	...	1.54	7	3	0	0	0-...	23.1	15	10	4	1	8-0	21
1998—	Midland (Texas)■	8	10	.444	5.31	32	19	*6	•1	0-...	154.1	194	110	91	18	54-1	117
1999—	Edmonton (PCL)	7	9	.438	4.50	24	23	3	0	0-...	150.0	171	80	75	19	41-0	118
—	Anaheim (A.L.)	1	1	.500	2.15	20	0	0	0	3-3	29.1	23	9	7	1	12-1	20
2000—	Anaheim (A.L.)	1	1	.500	3.40	32	1	0	0	1-1	50.1	52	23	19	4	17-1	44
—	Edmonton (PCL)	2	1	.667	3.52	24	0	0	0	12-...	30.2	27	14	12	2	14-0	28
2001—	Anaheim (A.L.)	2	0	1.000	4.15	44	1	0	0	2-3	86.2	88	41	40	11	32-5	66
2002—	Anaheim (A.L.)	0	2	.000	3.22	31	0	0	0	0-1	50.1	33	20	18	7	26-2	32
—	Salt Lake (PCL)	2	1	.667	6.00	7	7	0	0	0-...	39.0	42	29	26	3	10-0	43
Major League totals (4 years)		4	4	.500	3.49	127	2	0	0	6-8	216.2	196	93	84	23	87-9	162

POWELL, BRIAN — P

PERSONAL: Born October 10, 1973, in Bainbridge, Ga. ... 6-2/205. ... Throws right, bats right. ... Full name: William Brian Powell.

HIGH SCHOOL: Bainbridge (Ga.).

COLLEGE: Georgia.

TRANSACTIONS/CAREER NOTES: Selected by Detroit Tigers organization in second round of free-agent draft (June 1, 1995). ... Traded by Tigers with C Paul Bako, P Dean Crow, P Mark Persails and 3B Carlos Villalobos to Houston Astros for C Brad Ausmus and P C.J. Nitkowski (January 14, 1999). ... On disabled list (May 25, 1999-remainder of season). ... On New Orleans disabled list (April 6-22, 2000). ... Granted free agency (October 8, 2001). ... Signed by Tigers organization (December 19, 2001). ... Released by Tigers (October 2, 2002).

CAREER HITTING (MLB): 2-for-11 (.182), 2 R, 1 2B, 0 3B, 0 HR, 0 RBI.

Year	League	W	L	Pct.	ERA	G	GS	CG	ShO	Sv.-Opp.	IP	H	R	ER	HR	BB-IBB	SO
1995—	Jamestown (NY-Penn)	2	1	.667	3.08	5	5	0	0	0-...	26.1	19	12	9	1	8-0	15
—	Fayetteville (S.Atl.)	4	0	1.000	1.61	5	5	0	0	0-...	28.0	15	5	5	0	11-0	37
1996—	Lakeland (FSL)	8	13	.381	4.90	29	27	*5	0	0-...	•174.1	*195	106	*95	12	47-0	84
1997—	Lakeland (FSL)	13	9	.591	2.50	27	27	*8	•2	0-...	*183.1	153	70	51	9	35-2	122
1998—	Jacksonville (Sou.)	10	2	*.833	3.07	14	14	2	1	0-...	93.2	84	37	32	5	24-0	51
—	Toledo (I.L.)	0	0	...	0.00	1	1	0	0	0-...	7.0	5	0	0	0	0-0	7
—	Detroit (A.L.)	3	8	.273	6.35	18	16	0	0	0-0	83.2	101	67	59	17	36-2	46
1999—	New Orleans (PCL)■	4	4	.500	6.19	9	9	0	0	0-...	48.0	54	39	33	5	21-0	36
2000—	New Orleans (PCL)	9	4	.692	4.95	18	18	1	0	0-...	103.2	103	63	57	9	41-1	57
—	Houston (N.L.)	2	1	.667	5.74	9	5	0	0	0-0	31.1	34	21	20	8	13-0	14
2001—	New Orleans (PCL)	9	8	.529	3.17	24	23	3	•2	0-...	144.2	142	65	51	13	39-1	96
—	Houston (N.L.)	0	1	.000	18.00	1	1	0	0	0-0	3.0	5	6	6	1	3-0	3
2002—	Toledo (I.L.)■	10	3	.769	3.92	20	20	0	0	0-...	119.1	127	54	52	8	26-0	82
—	Detroit (A.L.)	1	5	.167	4.84	13	9	0	0	0-0	57.2	64	34	31	11	21-0	30
A.L. totals (2 years)		4	13	.235	5.73	31	25	0	0	0-0	141.1	165	101	90	28	57-2	76
N.L. totals (2 years)		2	2	.500	6.82	10	6	0	0	0-0	34.1	39	27	26	9	16-0	17
Major League totals (4 years)		6	15	.286	5.94	41	31	0	0	0-0	175.2	204	128	116	37	73-2	93

POWELL, JAY — P — RANGERS

PERSONAL: Born January 9, 1972, in Meridian, Miss. ... 6-4/225. ... Throws right, bats right. ... Full name: James Willard Powell Jr. ... Brother-in-law of Bud Brown, defensive back with Miami Dolphins (1984-88).

HIGH SCHOOL: West Lauderdale (Collinsville, Miss.).

COLLEGE: Mississippi State.

TRANSACTIONS/CAREER NOTES: Selected by San Diego Padres organization in 11th round of free-agent draft (June 4, 1990); did not sign. ... Selected by Baltimore Orioles organization in first round (19th pick overall) of free-agent draft (June 3, 1993). ... On disabled list (April 7-26, 1994). ... Traded by Orioles to Florida Marlins for IF Bret Barberie (December 6, 1994). ... On Florida disabled list (April 20-May 10, 1996); included rehabilitation assignment to Brevard County (May 8-10). ... Traded by Marlins with C Scott Makarewicz to Houston Astros for C Ramon Castro (July 6, 1998). ... On Houston disabled list (May 17-June 3, June 19-August 6 and August 18, 2000-remainder of season); included rehabilitation assignments to New Orleans (May 30-June 3) and Round Rock (August 3). ... Traded by Astros to Colorado Rockies for P Ron Villone (June 27, 2001). ... Granted free agency (November 5, 2001). ... Signed by Texas Rangers (December 13, 2001). ... On Texas disabled list (March 31-June 10, 2002); included rehabilitation assignment to Tulsa (May 21-24) and Oklahoma (May 25-June 10).

MISCELLANEOUS: Struck out in only appearance as pinch hitter with Florida (1996). ... Struck out in only appearance as pinch hitter (2000).

CAREER HITTING (MLB): 2-for-12 (.167), 0 R, 0 2B, 0 3B, 0 HR, 1 RBI.

Year	League	W	L	Pct.	ERA	G	GS	CG	ShO	Sv.-Opp.	IP	H	R	ER	HR	BB-IBB	SO
1993—	Albany (S.Atl.)	0	2	.000	4.55	6	6	0	0	0-...	27.2	29	19	14	0	13-0	29
1994—	Frederick (Caro.)	7	7	.500	4.96	26	20	0	0	1-...	123.1	132	79	68	13	54-0	87
1995—	Portland (East.)■	5	4	.556	1.87	50	0	0	0	*24-...	53.0	42	12	11	2	15-1	53
—	Florida (N.L.)	0	0	...	1.08	9	0	0	0	0-0	8.1	7	2	1	0	6-1	4
1996—	Florida (N.L.)	4	3	.571	4.54	67	0	0	0	2-5	71.1	71	41	36	5	36-1	52
—	Brevard County (FSL)	0	0	...	0.00	1	1	0	0	0-...	2.0	0	0	0	0	0-0	4
1997—	Florida (N.L.)	7	2	.778	3.28	74	0	0	0	2-4	79.2	71	35	29	3	30-3	65
1998—	Florida (N.L.)	4	4	.500	4.21	33	0	0	0	3-6	36.1	36	19	17	5	22-6	24
—	Houston (N.L.)■	3	3	.500	2.38	29	0	0	0	4-5	34.0	22	9	9	1	15-3	38

P

Year	League	W	L	Pct.	ERA	G	GS	CG	ShO	Sv.-Opp.	IP	H	R	ER	HR	BB-IBB	SO
1999—	Houston (N.L.)	5	4	.556	4.32	67	0	0	0	4-7	75.0	82	38	36	3	40-4	77
2000—	Houston (N.L.)	1	1	.500	5.67	29	0	0	0	0-0	27.0	29	18	17	1	19-1	16
	—New Orleans (PCL)	0	0	...	4.50	2	1	0	0	0-...	2.0	2	1	1	0	2-0	2
	—Round Rock (Texas)	0	0	...	0.00	1	1	0	0	0-...	2.0	0	0	0	0	1-0	1
2001—	Houston (N.L.)	2	2	.500	3.72	35	0	0	0	0-5	36.1	41	18	15	4	19-0	28
	—Colorado (N.L.)■	3	1	.750	2.79	39	0	0	0	7-8	38.2	34	18	12	5	12-3	26
2002—	Tulsa (Texas)■	0	0	...	0.00	2	0	0	0	0-...	2.0	0	0	0	0	1-0	0
	—Oklahoma (PCL)	2	0	1.000	12.38	8	0	0	0	0-...	8.0	14	11	11	2	3-1	8
	—Texas (A.L.)	3	2	.600	3.44	51	0	0	0	0-4	49.2	50	28	19	5	24-4	35
A.L. totals (1 year)		3	2	.600	3.44	51	0	0	0	0-4	49.2	50	28	19	5	24-4	35
N.L. totals (7 years)		29	20	.592	3.81	382	0	0	0	22-40	406.2	393	198	172	27	199-22	330
Major League totals (8 years)		32	22	.593	3.77	433	0	0	0	22-44	456.1	443	226	191	32	223-26	365

DIVISION SERIES RECORD

Year	League	W	L	Pct.	ERA	G	GS	CG	ShO	Sv.-Opp.	IP	H	R	ER	HR	BB-IBB	SO
1997—	Florida (N.L.)									Did not play.							
1998—	Houston (N.L.)	0	0	...	11.57	3	0	0	0	0-0	2.1	2	3	3	1	3-1	3
1999—	Houston (N.L.)	0	1	.000	6.00	3	0	0	0	0-0	3.0	3	2	2	0	1-1	3
Division series totals (2 years)		0	1	.000	8.44	6	0	0	0	0-0	5.1	5	5	5	1	4-2	6

CHAMPIONSHIP SERIES RECORD

Year	League	W	L	Pct.	ERA	G	GS	CG	ShO	Sv.-Opp.	IP	H	R	ER	HR	BB-IBB	SO
1997—	Florida (N.L.)	0	0	...	0.00	1	0	0	0	0-0	.2	0	0	0	0	0-0	1

WORLD SERIES RECORD

NOTES: Member of World Series championship team (1997).

Year	League	W	L	Pct.	ERA	G	GS	CG	ShO	Sv.-Opp.	IP	H	R	ER	HR	BB-IBB	SO
1997—	Florida (N.L.)	1	0	1.000	7.36	4	0	0	0	0-0	3.2	5	3	3	1	4-0	2

PRATT, ANDY — P — BRAVES

PERSONAL: Born August 27, 1979, in Mesa, Ariz. ... 5-11/160. ... Throws left, bats left. ... Full name: Andrew Elias Pratt.
HIGH SCHOOL: Chino Valley (Ariz.).
TRANSACTIONS/CAREER NOTES: Selected by Texas Rangers organization in ninth round of free-agent draft (June 2, 1998). ... Traded by Rangers to Atlanta Braves for P Ben Kozlowski (April 9, 2002).
CAREER HITTING (MLB): 0-for-0 (.000), 0 R, 0 2B, 0 3B, 0 HR, 0 RBI.

Year	League	W	L	Pct.	ERA	G	GS	CG	ShO	Sv.-Opp.	IP	H	R	ER	HR	BB-IBB	SO
1998—	Gulf Coast Rangers (GCL)	4	3	.571	3.86	12	8	0	0	0-...	56.0	49	25	24	4	14-0	49
1999—	Savannah (S.Atl.)	4	4	.500	2.89	13	13	1	1	0-...	71.2	66	30	23	4	16-0	100
2000—	Charlotte (FSL)	7	4	.636	2.72	16	16	2	1	0-...	92.2	68	37	28	8	26-0	95
	—Tulsa (Texas)	1	6	.143	7.22	11	11	0	0	0-...	52.1	66	48	42	7	33-0	42
2001—	Tulsa (Texas)	8	10	.444	4.61	27	26	3	1	0-...	168.0	175	99	86	18	57-0	132
2002—	Greenville (Sou.)■	4	9	.308	4.26	20	18	1	1	0-...	93.0	92	54	44	5	44-0	67
	—Richmond (I.L.)	4	2	.667	3.10	6	6	1	1	0-...	40.2	35	15	14	2	9-0	36
	—Atlanta (N.L.)	0	0	...	6.75	1	0	0	0	0-0	1.1	1	1	1	0	4-0	1
Major League totals (1 year)		0	0	...	6.75	1	0	0	0	0-0	1.1	1	1	1	0	4-0	1

PRATT, TODD — C

PERSONAL: Born February 9, 1967, in Bellevue, Neb. ... 6-3/230. ... Bats right, throws right. ... Full name: Todd Alan Pratt.
HIGH SCHOOL: Hilltop (Chula Vista, Calif.).
TRANSACTIONS/CAREER NOTES: Selected by Boston Red Sox organization in sixth round of free-agent draft (June 3, 1985). ... Selected by Cleveland Indians organization from Red Sox organization in Rule 5 minor league draft (December 7, 1987). ... Returned to Red Sox organization (March 28, 1988). ... Granted free agency (October 15, 1991). ... Signed by Baltimore Orioles organization (November 13, 1991). ... Selected by Philadelphia Phillies from Orioles organization in Rule 5 major league draft (December 9, 1991). ... On Philadelphia disabled list (April 28-May 27, 1993); included rehabilitation assignment to Scranton/Wilkes-Barre (May 23-27). ... Granted free agency (December 23, 1994). ... Signed by Chicago Cubs organization (April 8, 1995). ... Granted free agency (October 16, 1995). ... Signed by Seattle Mariners organization (January 25, 1996). ... Released by Mariners (March 27, 1996). ... Signed by New York Mets organization (December 23, 1996). ... On New York disabled list (May 7-June 23, 1998); included rehabilitation assignments to St. Lucie (June 14-18), Gulf Coast Mets (June 19-21) and Norfolk (June 22-23). ... Traded by Mets to Phillies for C Gary Bennett (July 23, 2001). ... Granted free agency (November 5, 2001). ... Re-signed by Phillies (December 15, 2001). ... Granted free agency (October 29, 2002).
STATISTICAL NOTES: Led South Atlantic League catchers with 660 putouts and nine double plays and tied for lead with 13 errors in 1986. ... Led Eastern League catchers with 11 errors in 1989. ... Career major league grand slams: 1.
2002 GAMES PLAYED BY POSITION (MLB): C—34; 1B—2.

			BATTING														FIELDING	
Year	Team (League)	Pos.	G	AB	R	H	2B	3B	HR	RBI	BB	SO	SB-CS	Avg.	OBP	SLG	E	Avg.
1985—	Elmira (NY-Penn)	C	39	119	7	16	1	1	0	5	10	27	0-1	.134	.206	.160	6	.979
1986—	Greensboro (S.Atl.)	C-1B	107	348	63	84	16	0	12	56	75	114	0-1	.241	.380	.391	‡15	.983
1987—	Winter Haven (FSL)	C-1B-OF	118	407	57	105	22	0	12	65	70	94	0-1	.258	.364	.400	15	.980
1988—	New Britain (East.)	C-1B	124	395	41	89	15	2	8	49	41	110	1-4	.225	.299	.334	15	.975
1989—	New Britain (East.)	C-1B	109	338	30	77	17	1	2	35	44	66	1-2	.228	.325	.302	†11	.977
1990—	New Britain (East.)	C-1B	70	195	15	45	14	1	2	22	18	56	0-1	.231	.293	.344	4	.978
1991—	Pawtucket (I.L.)	C-1B	68	219	68	64	16	0	11	41	23	42	0-3	.292	.367	.516	4	.985
1992—	Reading (East.)■	C	41	132	20	44	6	1	6	26	24	28	2-0	.333	.436	.530	3	.970
	—Scranton/W.B. (I.L.)	C-1B	41	125	20	40	9	1	7	28	30	14	1-0	.320	.446	.576	4	.977
	—Philadelphia (N.L.)	C	16	46	6	13	1	0	2	10	4	12	0-0	.283	.340	.435	2	.972
1993—	Philadelphia (N.L.)	C	33	87	8	25	6	0	5	13	5	19	0-0	.287	.330	.529	2	.989
	—Scranton/W.B. (I.L.)	C	3	9	1	2	1	0	0	1	3	1	0-0	.222	.417	.333	0	1.000
1994—	Philadelphia (N.L.)	C	28	102	10	20	6	1	2	9	12	29	0-1	.196	.281	.333	0	1.000
1995—	Chicago (N.L.)■	C	25	60	3	8	2	0	0	4	6	21	0-0	.133	.209	.167	3	.981
	—Iowa (A.A.)	C-1B-DH	23	58	3	19	1	0	0	5	4	17	0-0	.328	.371	.345	2	.978

Year Team (League)	Pos.	G	AB	R	H	2B	3B	HR	RBI	BB	SO	SB-CS	Avg.	OBP	SLG	E	Avg.
		BATTING														FIELDING	
1996—		Out of organized baseball.															
1997—Norfolk (I.L.)■	C-DH	59	206	42	62	8	3	9	34	26	48	1-2	.301	.383	.500	4	.988
—New York (N.L.)	C	39	106	12	30	6	0	2	19	13	32	0-1	.283	.372	.396	2	.990
1998—Norfolk (I.L.)	DH-C-OF-1B	35	118	16	42	6	0	7	30	15	19	2-0	.356	.442	.585	2	.984
—New York (N.L.)	C-1B	41	69	9	19	9	1	2	18	2	20	0-0	.275	.296	.522	2	.976
—St. Lucie (FSL)	C-1B-OF	5	20	2	9	1	0	1	3	1	5	1-0	.450	.522	.650	0	1.000
—GC Mets (GCL)	C-OF	2	4	1	1	0	0	0	0	4	1	0-0	.250	.625	.250	0	1.000
1999—New York (N.L.)	C-1B-OF	71	140	18	41	4	0	3	21	15	32	2-0	.293	.369	.386	1	.996
2000—New York (N.L.)	C-DH	80	160	33	44	6	0	8	25	22	31	0-0	.275	.378	.463	1	.997
2001—New York (N.L.)	C	45	80	6	13	5	0	2	4	15	36	1-0	.163	.306	.300	1	.994
—Philadelphia (N.L.)■	C-1B	35	93	12	19	3	0	2	7	19	25	0-0	.204	.345	.301	3	.986
2002—Philadelphia (N.L.)	C-1B	39	106	14	33	11	0	3	16	24	28	2-0	.311	.449	.500	0	1.000
Major League totals (10 years)		452	1049	131	265	59	2	31	146	137	285	5-2	.253	.347	.401	17	.992

DIVISION SERIES RECORD

Year Team (League)	Pos.	G	AB	R	H	2B	3B	HR	RBI	BB	SO	SB-CS	Avg.	OBP	SLG	E	Avg.
		BATTING														FIELDING	
1999—New York (N.L.)	PH-C	3	8	2	1	0	0	1	1	2	1	0-0	.125	.300	.500	0	1.000
2000—New York (N.L.)	PH-C	1	1	0	0	0	0	0	0	0	0	0-0	.000	.000	.000	0	1.000
Division series totals (2 years)		4	9	2	1	0	0	1	1	2	1	0-0	.111	.273	.444	0	1.000

CHAMPIONSHIP SERIES RECORD

Year Team (League)	Pos.	G	AB	R	H	2B	3B	HR	RBI	BB	SO	SB-CS	Avg.	OBP	SLG	E	Avg.
		BATTING														FIELDING	
1993—Philadelphia (N.L.)	C	1	1	0	0	0	0	0	0	0	1	0-0	.000	.000	.000	0	1.000
1999—New York (N.L.)	PH-C	4	2	0	1	0	0	0	3	1	1	0-0	.500	.500	.500	0	1.000
Championship series totals (2 years)		5	3	0	1	0	0	0	3	1	2	0-0	.333	.400	.333	0	1.000

WORLD SERIES RECORD

Year Team (League)	Pos.	G	AB	R	H	2B	3B	HR	RBI	BB	SO	SB-CS	Avg.	OBP	SLG	E	Avg.
		BATTING														FIELDING	
1993—Philadelphia (N.L.)		Did not play.															
2000—New York (N.L.)	C	1	2	1	0	0	0	0	0	1	2	0-0	.000	.600	.000	0	1.000

PRINCE, TOM C TWINS

PERSONAL: Born August 13, 1964, in Kankakee, Ill. ... 5-11/206. ... Bats right, throws right. ... Full name: Thomas Albert Prince.
HIGH SCHOOL: Bradley-Bourbonnais (Bradley, Ill.).
JUNIOR COLLEGE: Kankakee (Ill.) Community College.
TRANSACTIONS/CAREER NOTES: Selected by Atlanta Braves organization in eighth round of free-agent draft (January 11, 1983); did not sign. ... Selected by Braves organization in secondary phase of free-agent draft (June 6, 1983); did not sign. ... Selected by Pittsburgh Pirates organization in secondary phase of free-agent draft (January 17, 1984). ... On Pittsburgh disabled list (August 13-September 1, 1991); included rehabilitation assignment to Buffalo (August 28-September 1). ... Granted free agency (October 15, 1993). ... Signed by Los Angeles Dodgers organization (November 12, 1993). ... On Albuquerque disabled list (April 30-May 7, 1994). ... Released by Dodgers (December 5, 1994). ... Re-signed by Dodgers organization (January 5, 1995). ... On Los Angeles disabled list (June 4-July 10, 1995); included rehabilitation assignment to Albuquerque (June 26-July 10). ... Granted free agency (October 15, 1995). ... Re-signed by Dodgers organization (November 1, 1995). ... Granted free agency (October 22, 1998). ... Signed by Philadelphia Phillies (December 18, 1998). ... On Philadelphia disabled list (March 23-September 3, 1999); included rehabilitation assignments to Gulf Coast Phillies (July 21-28), Clearwater (July 29-August 9) and Scranton (August 10-29). ... Granted free agency (October 31, 2000). ... Signed by Minnesota Twins organization (December 19, 2000).
STATISTICAL NOTES: Led South Atlantic League catchers with 810 putouts, 101 assists, 930 total chances, 10 double plays and 27 passed balls in 1985. ... Led Carolina League catchers with 821 putouts, 954 total chances and 15 passed balls and tied for lead with 113 assists in 1986. ... Led Eastern League catchers with 622 putouts, 88 assists, 721 total chances and nine double plays in 1987. ... Led American Association catchers with 12 double plays in 1992. ... Led Pacific Coast League catchers with 75 assists, 677 total chances and nine double plays in 1994.
2002 GAMES PLAYED BY POSITION (MLB): C—50.

Year Team (League)	Pos.	G	AB	R	H	2B	3B	HR	RBI	BB	SO	SB-CS	Avg.	OBP	SLG	E	Avg.
		BATTING														FIELDING	
1984—Watertown (NY-Penn)	C-3B	23	69	6	14	3	0	2	13	9	13	0-0	.203	.304	.333	2	.989
—GC Pirates (GCL)	C-1B	18	48	4	11	0	0	1	6	8	10	1-0	.229	.351	.292	4	.958
1985—Macon (S.Atl.)	C	124	360	60	75	20	1	10	42	96	92	13-3	.208	.387	.353	*19	.980
1986—Prince William (Caro.)	C	121	395	59	100	34	1	10	47	50	74	4-5	.253	.346	.420	20	.979
1987—Harrisburg (East.)	C	113	365	41	112	23	2	6	54	51	46	6-3	.307	.401	.430	•11	.985
—Pittsburgh (N.L.)	C	4	9	1	2	1	0	1	2	0	2	0-0	.222	.222	.667	0	1.000
1988—Buffalo (A.A.)	C	86	304	35	79	16	0	14	42	23	53	3-6	.260	.325	.451	*12	.977
—Pittsburgh (N.L.)	C	29	74	3	13	2	0	0	6	4	15	0-0	.176	.218	.203	2	.983
1989—Buffalo (A.A.)	C	65	183	21	37	8	1	6	33	22	30	2-3	.202	.289	.355	5	.985
—Pittsburgh (N.L.)	C	21	52	1	7	4	0	0	5	6	12	1-1	.135	.220	.212	4	.960
1990—Pittsburgh (N.L.)	C	4	10	1	1	0	0	0	0	1	2	0-1	.100	.182	.100	0	1.000
—Buffalo (A.A.)	C-1B	94	284	38	64	13	0	7	37	39	46	4-7	.225	.326	.345	8	.985
1991—Pittsburgh (N.L.)	C-1B	26	34	4	9	3	0	1	2	7	3	0-0	.265	.405	.441	1	.984
—Buffalo (A.A.)	C	80	221	29	46	8	3	6	32	37	31	3-4	.208	.336	.353	5	.989
1992—Pittsburgh (N.L.)	C-3B	27	44	1	4	2	0	0	5	6	9	1-1	.091	.192	.136	2	.977
—Buffalo (A.A.)	C-OF	75	244	34	64	17	0	9	35	20	35	3-1	.262	.333	.443	8	.978
1993—Pittsburgh (N.L.)	C	66	179	14	35	14	0	2	24	13	38	1-1	.196	.272	.307	5	.984
1994—Albuquerque (PCL)■	C-DH	103	330	61	94	31	2	20	54	51	67	2-2	.285	.396	.573	9	.987
—Los Angeles (N.L.)	C	3	6	2	2	0	0	0	1	1	3	0-0	.333	.429	.333	0	1.000
1995—Albuquerque (PCL)	C-DH	61	192	30	61	15	0	7	36	27	41	0-0	.318	.407	.505	4	.989
—Los Angeles (N.L.)	C	18	40	3	8	2	1	1	4	4	10	0-0	.200	.273	.375	1	.988
1996—Albuquerque (PCL)	C-DH-3B-OF	32	95	24	39	5	1	7	22	15	14	0-2	.411	.500	.705	1	.991
—Los Angeles (N.L.)	C	40	64	6	19	6	0	1	11	6	15	0-0	.297	.365	.438	1	.994

P

Year	Team (League)	Pos.	G	AB	R	H	2B	3B	HR	RBI	BB	SO	SB-CS	Avg.	OBP	SLG	E	Avg.
			BATTING														FIELDING	
1997—	Los Angeles (N.L.)	C	47	100	17	22	5	0	3	14	5	15	0-0	.220	.275	.360	1	.996
1998—	Los Angeles (N.L.)	C	37	81	7	15	5	1	0	5	7	24	0-0	.185	.267	.272	0	1.000
1999—	GC Phillies (GCL)■	C-DH	7	21	3	5	3	0	0	3	4	0	0-0	.238	.385	.381	0	1.000
—	Clearwater (FSL)	C	9	33	5	12	0	0	2	9	3	3	1-0	.364	.432	.545	1	.981
—	Scranton/W.B. (I.L.)	C-DH	7	22	2	2	0	0	1	1	3	5	1-0	.091	.231	.227	0	1.000
—	Philadelphia (N.L.)	C	4	6	1	1	0	0	0	0	1	1	0-0	.167	.286	.167	0	1.000
2000—	Philadelphia (N.L.)	C	46	122	14	29	9	0	2	16	13	31	1-0	.238	.321	.361	1	.996
2001—	Minnesota (A.L.)■	C	64	196	19	43	4	1	7	23	12	39	3-1	.219	.284	.357	0	1.000
2002—	Minnesota (A.L.)	C	51	125	14	28	7	1	4	16	14	26	1-3	.224	.317	.392	1	.997
American League totals (2 years)			115	321	33	71	11	2	11	39	26	65	4-4	.221	.297	.371	1	.999
National League totals (14 years)			372	821	75	167	53	2	11	95	74	180	4-4	.203	.280	.313	18	.989
Major League totals (16 years)			487	1142	108	238	64	4	22	134	100	245	8-8	.208	.285	.329	19	.992

DIVISION SERIES RECORD

Year	Team (League)	Pos.	G	AB	R	H	2B	3B	HR	RBI	BB	SO	SB-CS	Avg.	OBP	SLG	E	Avg.
			BATTING														FIELDING	
2002—	Minnesota (A.L.)	C	1	2	0	0	0	0	0	0	0	2	0-0	.000	.000	.000	0	1.000

CHAMPIONSHIP SERIES RECORD

Year	Team (League)	Pos.	G	AB	R	H	2B	3B	HR	RBI	BB	SO	SB-CS	Avg.	OBP	SLG	E	Avg.
			BATTING														FIELDING	
2002—	Minnesota (A.L.)	C	1	1	0	0	0	0	0	0	0	0	0-0	.000	.000	.000	0	1.000

PRINZ, BRET — P — DIAMONDBACKS

PERSONAL: Born June 15, 1977, in Chicago Heights, Ill. ... 6-3/185. ... Throws right, bats right. ... Full name: Bret Randolph Prinz.
HIGH SCHOOL: Centennial (Peoria, Ariz.).
JUNIOR COLLEGE: Phoenix College.
TRANSACTIONS/CAREER NOTES: Selected by Arizona Diamondbacks organization in 18th round of 1998 free-agent draft (June 3, 1998).
CAREER HITTING (MLB): 0-for-0 (.000), 0 R, 0 2B, 0 3B, 0 HR, 0 RBI.

Year	League	W	L	Pct.	ERA	G	GS	CG	ShO	Sv.-Opp.	IP	H	R	ER	HR	BB-IBB	SO
1998—	Ariz. D-backs (Ariz.)	0	0	...	3.38	4	0	0	0	0-...	5.1	7	3	2	0	0-0	3
—	Lethbridge (Pio.)	4	2	.667	3.09	11	10	0	0	0-...	46.2	49	26	16	2	13-0	30
1999—	South Bend (Midw.)	6	10	.375	4.48	30	23	0	0	0-...	138.2	129	82	69	16	52-0	98
2000—	South Bend (Midw.)	1	0	1.000	0.00	6	0	0	0	1-...	7.1	2	2	0	0	1-0	10
—	El Paso (Texas)	9	1	.900	3.56	53	0	0	0	26-...	60.2	71	24	24	6	16-3	69
2001—	Tucson (PCL)	0	0	...	0.00	5	0	0	0	3-...	5.2	1	0	0	0	0-0	6
—	Arizona (N.L.)	4	1	.800	2.63	46	0	0	0	9-12	41.0	33	13	12	4	19-1	27
2002—	Arizona (N.L.)	0	2	.000	9.45	20	0	0	0	0-2	13.1	23	14	14	1	10-1	10
—	Tucson (PCL)	1	0	1.000	2.97	37	0	0	0	18-...	39.1	42	14	13	4	9-1	34
—	Lancaster (Calif.)	1	0	1.000	0.00	5	0	0	0	0-...	7.0	2	0	0	0	1-0	6
Major League totals (2 years)		4	3	.571	4.31	66	0	0	0	9-14	54.1	56	27	26	5	29-2	37

PRIOR, MARK — P — CUBS

PERSONAL: Born September 7, 1980, in San Diego. ... 6-5/225. ... Throws right, bats right. ... Full name: Mark William Prior.
COLLEGE: Vanderbilt, then Southern California.
TRANSACTIONS/CAREER NOTES: Selected by New York Yankees organization in first round (43rd pick overall) of free-agent draft (June 2, 1998); did not sign. ... Selected by Chicago Cubs organization in first round (second pick overall) of free-agent draft (June 5, 2001). ... On Chicago disabled list (September 2-17, 2002).
CAREER HITTING (MLB): 6-for-35 (.171), 3 R, 4 2B, 0 3B, 0 HR, 4 RBI.

Year	League	W	L	Pct.	ERA	G	GS	CG	ShO	Sv.-Opp.	IP	H	R	ER	HR	BB-IBB	SO
2002—	West Tenn (Sou.)	4	1	.800	2.60	6	6	0	0	0-...	34.2	26	16	10	0	10-0	55
—	Iowa (PCL)	1	1	.500	1.65	3	3	0	0	0-...	16.1	13	10	3	1	8-0	24
—	Chicago (N.L.)	6	6	.500	3.32	19	19	1	0	0-0	116.2	98	45	43	14	38-0	147
Major League totals (1 year)		6	6	.500	3.32	19	19	1	0	0-0	116.2	98	45	43	14	38-0	147

PROKOPEC, LUKE — P — DODGERS

PERSONAL: Born February 23, 1978, in Blackwood, South Australia. ... 5-11/175. ... Throws right, bats left. ... Full name: Kenneth Luke Prokopec.
HIGH SCHOOL: Renmark (South Australia).
TRANSACTIONS/CAREER NOTES: Signed as non-drafted free agent by Los Angeles Dodgers organization (August 28, 1994). ... On San Antonio disabled list (April 29-May 12 and July 8-21, 2000). ... On Los Angeles disabled list (August 9-25, 2001). ... Traded by Dodgers with P Chad Ricketts to Toronto Blue Jays for P Paul Quantrill and 2B/SS Cesar Izturis (December 13, 2001). ... On Toronto disabled list (June 14-July 21 and August 24, 2002-remainder of season); included rehabilitation assignment to Syracuse (July 17-21). ... Granted free agency (October 15, 2002). ... Signed by Dodgers organization (November 4, 2002).
MISCELLANEOUS: Appeared in one game as pinch runner (2000). ... Appeared in one game as pinch runner (2001).
CAREER HITTING (MLB): 7-for-41 (.171), 1 R, 1 2B, 0 3B, 0 HR, 0 RBI.

Year	League	W	L	Pct.	ERA	G	GS	CG	ShO	Sv.-Opp.	IP	H	R	ER	HR	BB-IBB	SO
1997—	Savannah (S.Atl.)	3	1	.750	4.07	13	6	0	0	0-...	42.0	37	21	19	8	12-0	45
1998—	San Bernardino (Calif.)	8	5	.615	2.69	20	20	0	0	0-...	110.1	99	43	33	11	33-1	148
—	San Antonio (Texas)	3	0	1.000	1.38	5	5	0	0	0-...	26.0	16	5	4	0	13-0	25
1999—	San Antonio (Texas)	8	12	.400	5.42	27	27	0	0	0-...	157.2	172	113	95	18	46-0	128
2000—	San Antonio (Texas)	7	3	.700	2.45	22	22	1	0	0-...	128.2	118	40	35	8	23-1	124
—	Los Angeles (N.L.)	1	1	.500	3.00	5	3	0	0	0-0	21.0	19	10	7	2	9-0	12

Year	League	W	L	Pct.	ERA	G	GS	CG	ShO	Sv.-Opp.	IP	H	R	ER	HR	BB-IBB	SO
2001—	Los Angeles (N.L.)	8	7	.533	4.88	29	22	0	0	0-0	138.1	146	80	75	27	40-1	91
—	Las Vegas (PCL)	1	0	1.000	3.00	1	1	0	0	0-...	6.0	3	2	2	1	2-0	8
2002—	Toronto (A.L.)■	2	9	.182	6.78	22	12	0	0	0-0	71.2	90	57	54	19	25-2	41
—	Syracuse (I.L.)	0	0	...	0.00	2	0	0	0	0-...	2.0	0	0	0	0	0-0	2
A.L. totals (1 year)		2	9	.182	6.78	22	12	0	0	0-0	71.2	90	57	54	19	25-2	41
N.L. totals (2 years)		9	8	.529	4.63	34	25	0	0	0-0	159.1	165	90	82	29	49-1	103
Major League totals (3 years)		11	17	.393	5.30	56	37	0	0	0-0	231.0	255	147	136	48	74-3	144

RECORD AS POSITION PLAYER

			BATTING														FIELDING	
Year	Team (League)	Pos.	G	AB	R	H	2B	3B	HR	RBI	BB	SO	SB-CS	Avg.	OBP	SLG	E	Avg.
1995—	Great Falls (Pio.)	OF	43	119	16	29	6	2	2	24	8	37	5-2	.244	.288	.378	0	1.000
1996—	Savannah (S.Atl.)	OF	82	245	34	53	12	1	4	29	27	78	0-5	.216	.300	.322	8	.889
1997—	Savannah (S.Atl.)	OF-P	61	164	11	38	7	3	2	20	12	49	3-1	.232	.291	.348	2	.978

PUFFER, BRANDON — P — ASTROS

PERSONAL: Born October 5, 1975, in Downey, Calif. ... 6-3/190. ... Throws right, bats right. ... Full name: Brandon Duane Puffer.
HIGH SCHOOL: Capistrano Valley (Mission Viejo, Calif.).
TRANSACTIONS/CAREER NOTES: Selected by Minnesota Twins organization in 27th round of free-agent draft (June 2, 1994). ... Released by Twins (May 6, 1996). ... Signed by California Angels organization (May 28, 1996). ... Released by Angels (December 15, 1997). ... Signed by Cincinnati Reds organization (January 14, 1998). ... Granted free agency (October 16, 1998). ... Re-signed by Reds organization (November 17, 1998). ... Granted free agency (October 15, 1999). ... Signed by Colorado Rockies organization (November 18, 1999). ... Released by Rockies (May 18, 2000). ... Signed by Somerset, Atlantic League (May 2000). ... Contract sold by Somerset to Houston Astros organization (July 17, 2000).
STATISTICAL NOTES: Led Midwest League pitchers with 55 games finished in 1999.
CAREER HITTING (MLB): 0-for-6 (.000), 0 R, 0 2B, 0 3B, 0 HR, 0 RBI.

Year	League	W	L	Pct.	ERA	G	GS	CG	ShO	Sv.-Opp.	IP	H	R	ER	HR	BB-IBB	SO
1994—	Gulf Coast Twins (GCL)	2	2	.500	3.06	18	0	0	0	2-...	35.1	33	18	12	1	19-0	40
1995—	Gulf Coast Twins (GCL)	0	3	.000	2.88	14	5	0	0	1-...	40.2	29	21	13	0	21-0	35
1996—	Arizona Angels (Ariz.)■	0	1	.000	3.60	1	1	0	0	0-...	5.0	7	2	2	0	1-0	3
—	Boise (N'West)	2	0	1.000	4.45	16	0	0	0	1-...	30.1	27	19	15	3	11-0	22
1997—	Boise (N'West)	0	0	...	2.35	6	0	0	0	1-...	15.1	10	5	4	0	2-0	15
—	Cedar Rapids (Midw.)	0	0	...	2.60	10	0	0	0	0-...	17.1	8	6	5	0	10-0	11
1998—	Charl., W.Va. (S.Atl.)■	2	7	.222	6.93	29	0	0	0	1-...	50.2	68	45	39	4	23-4	36
—	Chattanooga (Sou.)	0	0	...	3.12	7	0	0	0	0-...	8.2	2	3	3	2	3-0	6
1999—	Clinton (Midw.)	1	2	.333	1.99	59	0	0	0	*34-...	63.1	53	20	14	2	24-3	60
2000—	Asheville (S.Atl.)■	0	0	...	8.16	14	0	0	0	5-...	14.1	19	16	13	3	11-3	15
—	Somerset (Atl.)■	2	2	.500	3.52	15	0	0	0	1-...	23.0	25	12	9	...	9-...	21
—	Kissimmee (FSL)■	2	3	.400	1.27	18	0	0	0	9-...	21.1	18	6	3	0	11-4	26
2001—	Round Rock (Texas)	6	1	.857	2.07	56	0	0	0	8-...	82.2	52	19	19	4	35-2	91
2002—	New Orleans (PCL)	2	1	.667	1.80	11	0	0	0	0-...	15.0	8	3	3	1	4-0	13
—	Houston (N.L.)	3	3	.500	4.43	55	0	0	0	0-0	69.0	67	37	34	3	38-8	48
Major League totals (1 year)		3	3	.500	4.43	55	0	0	0	0-0	69.0	67	37	34	3	38-8	48

PUJOLS, ALBERT — 3B — CARDINALS

PERSONAL: Born January 16, 1980, in Santo Domingo, Dominican Republic. ... 6-3/210. ... Bats right, throws right. ... Full name: Jose Albert Pujols.
HIGH SCHOOL: Fort Osage (Independence, Mo.).
JUNIOR COLLEGE: Maple Woods.
TRANSACTIONS/CAREER NOTES: Selected by St. Louis Cardinals organization in 13th round of free-agent draft (June 2, 1999).
RECORDS: Holds N.L. single-season rookie record for most total bases—360 (2001); and most runs batted in—130 (2001).
HONORS: Named Midwest League Most Valuable Player (2000). ... Named third baseman on N.L. Silver Slugger team (2001). ... Named N.L. Rookie of the Year by The Sporting News (2001). ... Named N.L. Rookie of the Year by Baseball Writers' Association of America (2001).
STATISTICAL NOTES: Had 17-game hitting streak (July 31-August 16, 2001). ... Career major league grand slams: 3.
2002 GAMES PLAYED BY POSITION (MLB): OF—118; 3B—41; 1B—21; DH—2; SS—1.

			BATTING														FIELDING	
Year	Team (League)	Pos.	G	AB	R	H	2B	3B	HR	RBI	BB	SO	SB-CS	Avg.	OBP	SLG	E	Avg.
2000—	Peoria (Midw.)	3B	109	395	62	128	32	6	17	84	38	37	2-4	.324	.389	.565	19	.948
—	Potomac (Caro.)	3B	21	81	11	23	8	1	2	10	7	8	1-1	.284	.341	.481	3	.957
—	Memphis (PCL)	3B-OF	3	14	1	3	1	0	0	2	1	2	1-0	.214	.267	.286	0	1.000
2001—	St. Louis (N.L.)	O-3-1-D	161	590	112	194	47	4	37	130	69	93	1-3	.329	.403	.610	20	.967
2002—	St. Louis (N.L.)	O-3-1-D-S	157	590	118	185	40	2	34	127	72	69	2-4	.314	.394	.561	11	.975
Major League totals (2 years)			318	1180	230	379	87	6	71	257	141	162	3-7	.321	.399	.586	31	.970

DIVISION SERIES RECORD

			BATTING														FIELDING	
Year	Team (League)	Pos.	G	AB	R	H	2B	3B	HR	RBI	BB	SO	SB-CS	Avg.	OBP	SLG	E	Avg.
2001—	St. Louis (N.L.)	OF-1B	5	18	1	2	0	0	1	2	2	2	0-0	.111	.200	.278	1	.964
2002—	St. Louis (N.L.)	OF	3	10	3	3	0	1	0	3	3	1	0-0	.300	.462	.500	1	.833
Division series totals (2 years)			8	28	4	5	0	1	1	5	5	3	0-0	.179	.303	.357	2	.941

CHAMPIONSHIP SERIES RECORD

			BATTING														FIELDING	
Year	Team (League)	Pos.	G	AB	R	H	2B	3B	HR	RBI	BB	SO	SB-CS	Avg.	OBP	SLG	E	Avg.
2002—	St. Louis (N.L.)	OF-3B-1B	5	19	2	5	1	0	1	2	2	5	0-0	.263	.364	.474	0	1.000

ALL-STAR GAME RECORD

	AB	R	H	2B	3B	HR	RBI	BB	SO	SB-CS	Avg.	OBP	SLG	E	Avg.
All-Star Game totals (1 year)	0	0	0	0	0	0	0	1	0	0-0	...	1.000	...	0	1.000

P Q

PUNTO, NICK — SS — PHILLIES

PERSONAL: Born November 8, 1977, in San Diego. ... 5-9/170. ... Bats both, throws right. ... Full name: Nicholas Paul Punto.
HIGH SCHOOL: Trabuco Hills (Mission Vieh Vijo, Calif.).
JUNIOR COLLEGE: Saddleback.
TRANSACTIONS/CAREER NOTES: Selected by Minnesota Twins organization in 33rd round of free-agent draft (June 3, 1997); did not sign. ... Selected by Philadelphia Phillies organization in 21st round of free-agent draft (June 2, 1998). ... On Scranton/Wilkes-Barre disabled list (June 8-16, 2001). ... On Scranton/Wilkes-Barre disabled list (June 19-July 2, 2002).
STATISTICAL NOTES: Led New York-Pennsylvania League shortstops with 45 double plays in 1998. ... Led International League shortstops with 398 assists in 2001. ... Led International League shortstops with 101 double plays in 2002.
2002 GAMES PLAYED BY POSITION (MLB): SS—1; 2B—1.

		BATTING														FIELDING	
Year Team (League)	Pos.	G	AB	R	H	2B	3B	HR	RBI	BB	SO	SB-CS	Avg.	OBP	SLG	E	Avg.
1998—Batavia (NY-Penn)	SS-2B	72	279	51	69	9	4	1	20	42	48	19-7	.247	.347	.319	27	.924
1999—Clearwater (FSL)	SS	106	400	65	122	18	6	1	48	67	53	16-6	.305	.404	.388	24	.958
2000—Reading (East.)	SS	121	456	77	116	15	4	5	47	69	71	33-10	.254	.351	.338	20	.963
2001—Scranton/W.B. (I.L.)	SS	123	463	57	106	19	5	1	39	68	114	33-9	.229	.327	.298	21	.964
—Philadelphia (N.L.)	SS	4	5	0	2	0	0	0	0	0	0	0-0	.400	.400	.400	0	1.000
2002—Philadelphia (N.L.)	SS-2B	9	6	0	1	0	0	0	0	0	3	0-0	.167	.167	.167	1	.750
—Scranton/W.B. (I.L.)	SS	115	443	74	120	12	5	1	29	76	84	•42-8	.271	.378	.327	19	.967
Major League totals (2 years)		13	11	0	3	0	0	0	0	0	3	0-0	.273	.273	.273	1	.857

QUANTRILL, PAUL — P — DODGERS

PERSONAL: Born November 3, 1968, in London, Ont. ... 6-1/195. ... Throws right, bats left. ... Full name: Paul John Quantrill. ... Name pronounced KWON-trill.
HIGH SCHOOL: Okemos (Mich.).
COLLEGE: Wisconsin.
TRANSACTIONS/CAREER NOTES: Selected by Los Angeles Dodgers organization in 26th round of free-agent draft (June 2, 1986); did not sign. ... Selected by Boston Red Sox organization in sixth round of free-agent draft (June 5, 1989). ... Traded by Red Sox with OF Billy Hatcher to Philadelphia Phillies for OF Wes Chamberlain and P Mike Sullivan (May 31, 1994). ... Traded by Phillies to Toronto Blue Jays for 3B Howard Battle and P Ricardo Jordan (December 6, 1995). ... On Toronto disabled list (March 27-June 15, 1999); included rehabilitation assignments to Dunedin (June 4-10) and Syracuse (June 11-13). ... Traded by Blue Jays with 2B/SS Cesar Izturis to Los Angeles Dodgers for P Luke Prokopec and P Chad Ricketts (December 13, 2001).
STATISTICAL NOTES: Led A.L. with 14 intentional bases on balls issued in 1993.
CAREER HITTING (MLB): 7-for-64 (.109), 5 R, 0 2B, 0 3B, 0 HR, 0 RBI.

Year League	W	L	Pct.	ERA	G	GS	CG	ShO	Sv.-Opp.	IP	H	R	ER	HR	BB-IBB	SO
1989—Gulf Coast Red Sox (GCL)	0	0	...	0.00	2	0	0	0	2-...	5.0	2	0	0	0	0-0	5
—Elmira (NY-Penn)	5	4	.556	3.43	20	7	•5	0	2-...	76.0	90	37	29	5	12-2	57
1990—Winter Haven (FSL)	2	5	.286	4.14	7	7	1	0	0-...	45.2	46	24	21	3	6-0	14
—New Britain (East.)	7	11	.389	3.53	22	22	1	1	0-...	132.2	148	65	52	3	23-2	53
1991—New Britain (East.)	2	1	.667	2.06	5	5	1	0	0-...	35.0	32	14	8	2	8-0	18
—Pawtucket (I.L.)	10	7	.588	4.45	25	23	•6	2	0-...	155.2	169	81	77	14	30-1	75
1992—Pawtucket (I.L.)	6	8	.429	4.46	19	18	4	1	0-...	119.0	143	63	59	16	20-1	56
—Boston (A.L.)	2	3	.400	2.19	27	0	0	0	1-5	49.1	55	18	12	1	15-5	24
1993—Boston (A.L.)	6	12	.333	3.91	49	14	1	1	1-2	138.0	151	73	60	13	44-14	66
1994—Boston (A.L.)	1	1	.500	3.52	17	0	0	0	0-2	23.0	25	10	9	4	5-1	15
—Philadelphia (N.L.)■	2	2	.500	6.00	18	1	0	0	1-2	30.0	39	21	20	3	10-3	13
—Scranton/W.B. (I.L.)	3	3	.500	3.47	8	8	1	1	0-...	57.0	55	25	22	5	6-0	36
1995—Philadelphia (N.L.)	11	12	.478	4.67	33	29	0	0	0-0	179.1	212	102	93	20	44-3	103
1996—Toronto (A.L.)■	5	14	.263	5.43	38	20	0	0	0-2	134.1	172	90	81	27	51-3	86
1997—Toronto (A.L.)	6	7	.462	1.94	77	0	0	0	5-10	88.0	103	25	19	5	17-3	56
1998—Toronto (A.L.)	3	4	.429	2.59	82	0	0	0	7-14	80.0	88	26	23	5	22-6	59
1999—Dunedin (FSL)	0	1	.000	4.50	5	4	0	0	0-...	6.0	5	3	3	1	1-0	2
—Syracuse (I.L.)	0	0	...	0.00	2	0	0	0	0-...	2.0	1	0	0	0	0-0	1
—Toronto (A.L.)	3	2	.600	3.33	41	0	0	0	0-4	48.2	53	19	18	5	17-1	28
2000—Toronto (A.L.)	2	5	.286	4.52	68	0	0	0	1-3	83.2	100	45	42	7	25-1	47
2001—Toronto (A.L.)	11	2	.846	3.04	*80	0	0	0	2-9	83.0	86	29	28	6	12-7	58
2002—Los Angeles (N.L.)■	5	4	.556	2.70	*86	0	0	0	1-3	76.2	80	27	23	1	25-7	53
A.L. totals (9 years)	39	50	.438	3.61	479	34	1	1	17-51	728.0	833	335	292	73	208-41	439
N.L. totals (3 years)	18	18	.500	4.28	137	30	0	0	2-5	286.0	331	150	136	24	79-13	169
Major League totals (11 years)	57	68	.456	3.80	616	64	1	1	19-56	1014.0	1164	485	428	97	287-54	608

ALL-STAR GAME RECORD

	W	L	Pct.	ERA	GS	CG	ShO	Sv.-Opp.	IP	H	R	ER	HR	BB-IBB	SO
All-Star Game totals (1 year)	0	0	...	27.00	0	0	0	0-0	.1	2	1	1	0	0-0	0

QUEVEDO, RUBEN — P — BREWERS

PERSONAL: Born January 5, 1979, in Valencia, Venezuela. ... 6-1/245. ... Throws right, bats right. ... Full name: Ruben Eduardo Quevedo Yetez. ... Name pronounced keh-VAY-doh.
HIGH SCHOOL: Don Bosco (Valencia, Venezuela).
TRANSACTIONS/CAREER NOTES: Signed as non-drafted free agent by Atlanta Braves organization (September 6, 1995). ... Traded by Braves with P Micah Bowie and a player to be named later to Chicago Cubs for P Terry Mulholland and SS Jose Hernandez (July 31, 1999); Cubs acquired P Joey Nation to complete deal (August 24, 1999). ... Traded by Cubs with OF Peter Zoccolillo to Milwaukee Brewers for P David Weathers and P Roberto Miniel (July 30, 2001).
CAREER HITTING (MLB): 12-for-88 (.136), 4 R, 0 2B, 0 3B, 0 HR, 5 RBI.

Year	League	W	L	Pct.	ERA	G	GS	CG	ShO	Sv.-Opp.	IP	H	R	ER	HR	BB-IBB	SO
1996—	Gulf Coast Braves (GCL) ..	2	6	.250	2.29	10	10	0	0	0-...	55.0	50	19	14	1	9-0	49
1997—	Danville (Appl.)................	1	5	.167	3.56	13	11	0	0	0-...	68.1	46	37	27	6	27-0	78
1998—	Macon (S.Atl.)..................	11	3	.786	3.13	25	15	1	0	0-...	112.0	114	50	39	13	31-0	117
—	Danville (Caro.)...............	0	2	.000	3.58	6	6	0	0	0-...	32.2	28	22	13	2	13-1	35
1999—	Richmond (I.L.)...............	6	5	.545	5.37	21	21	0	0	0-...	105.2	112	65	63	26	34-0	98
—	Iowa (PCL)■.....................	3	1	.750	3.45	7	7	1	1	0-...	44.1	34	18	17	1	21-0	50
2000—	Iowa (PCL).......................	7	2	.778	4.22	13	13	0	0	0-...	74.2	68	37	35	7	31-0	77
—	Chicago (N.L.).................	3	10	.231	7.47	21	15	1	0	0-0	88.0	96	81	73	21	54-4	65
2001—	Iowa (PCL).......................	9	5	.643	2.99	22	22	1	1	0-...	141.2	124	54	47	13	48-3	150
—	Milwaukee (N.L.)■..........	4	5	.444	4.61	10	10	0	0	0-0	56.2	56	30	29	9	30-4	60
2002—	Milwaukee (N.L.)............	6	11	.353	5.76	26	25	1	1	0-0	139.0	159	100	89	28	68-3	93
—	Indianapolis (I.L.)...........	0	0	...	0.00	1	1	0	0	0-...	2.0	1	0	0	0	1-0	3
Major League totals (3 years).....		13	26	.333	6.06	57	50	2	1	0-0	283.2	311	211	191	58	152-11	218

Q
R

QUINLAN, ROBB — 1B — ANGELS

PERSONAL: Born March 17, 1977, in Maplewood, Minn. ... 6-1/195. ... Bats right, throws right. ... Full name: Robb William Quinlan.
COLLEGE: Minnesota.
TRANSACTIONS/CAREER NOTES: Selected by Anaheim Angels organization in 10th round of free-agent draft (June 2, 1999).
HONORS: Named Northwest League Most Valuable Player (1999). ... Named Pacific Coast League Most Valuable Player (2002).
STATISTICAL NOTES: Led Pacific Coast League with 15 sacrifice flies in 2002.

			BATTING														FIELDING	
Year	Team (League)	Pos.	G	AB	R	H	2B	3B	HR	RBI	BB	SO	SB-CS	Avg.	OBP	SLG	E	Avg.
1999—	Boise (N'West)..........	3B-2B-1B	73	295	51	95	20	1	9	77	35	52	5-3	.322	.400	.488	27	.892
2000—	Lake Elsinore (Calif.) ..	1B-OF	127	482	79	153	35	5	5	85	67	82	6-4	.317	.396	.442	16	.986
2001—	Arkansas (Texas)........	1B-OF	129	492	82	145	33	7	14	79	53	84	0-4	.295	.366	.476	8	.993
2002—	Salt Lake (PCL)..........	OF-1B	136	528	95	176	31	13	20	*112	41	93	8-2	.333	.376	.555	3	.988

QUINN, MARK — OF — ROYALS

PERSONAL: Born May 21, 1974, in La Miranda, Calif. ... 6-1/195. ... Bats right, throws right. ... Full name: Mark David Quinn.
HIGH SCHOOL: Clements (Sugar Land, Texas).
COLLEGE: Rice.
TRANSACTIONS/CAREER NOTES: Selected by Kansas City Royals organization in 11th round of free-agent draft (June 1, 1995). ... On Kansas City disabled list (June 9-July 6, 2001); included rehabilitation assignment to Omaha (June 25-July 6). ... On Kansas City disabled list (March 22-May 12 and June 8, 2002-remainder of season); included rehabilitation assignment to Omaha (April 11-May 10) and Wichita (May 11-12).
RECORDS: Shares major league record for most home runs, first game in major leagues—2 (September 14, 1999, second game).
HONORS: Named A.L. Rookie Player of the Year by The Sporting News (2000).
STATISTICAL NOTES: Career major league grand slams: 1.
2002 GAMES PLAYED BY POSITION (MLB): OF—15; DH—7.

			BATTING														FIELDING	
Year	Team (League)	Pos.	G	AB	R	H	2B	3B	HR	RBI	BB	SO	SB-CS	Avg.	OBP	SLG	E	Avg.
1995—	Spokane (N'West)......	3B	44	162	28	46	12	2	6	36	15	28	0-1	.284	.357	.494	8	.837
1996—	Lansing (Midw.).........	OF	113	437	63	132	23	3	9	71	43	54	14-8	.302	.367	.430	7	.958
1997—	Wilmington (Caro.).....	OF	87	299	51	92	22	3	16	71	42	47	3-2	.308	.400	.562	6	.932
—	Wichita (Texas)..........	OF	26	96	26	36	13	0	2	19	15	19	1-1	.375	.474	.573	1	.972
1998—	Wichita (Texas)..........	OF	100	372	82	130	26	6	16	84	43	54	4-1	*.349	.424	.581	8	.955
1999—	Omaha (PCL)..............	OF-DH	107	428	67	154	27	0	25	84	28	69	7-9	*.360	.409	.598	4	.983
—	Kansas City (A.L.)......	OF-DH	17	60	11	20	4	1	6	18	4	11	1-0	.333	.385	.733	1	.964
2000—	Kansas City (A.L.)......	OF-DH	135	500	76	147	33	2	20	78	35	91	5-2	.294	.342	.488	2	.988
—	Omaha (PCL)..............	OF	13	61	8	23	5	0	3	13	0	8	0-1	.377	.371	.607	0	1.000
2001—	Kansas City (A.L.)......	OF-DH	118	453	57	122	31	2	17	60	12	69	9-5	.269	.298	.459	5	.976
—	Omaha (PCL)..............	OF	11	43	4	8	1	0	2	3	0	9	0-0	.186	.186	.349	0	1.000
2002—	Omaha (PCL)..............	OF	12	39	4	7	2	1	0	2	4	7	0-0	.179	.289	.282	0	1.000
—	Wichita (Texas)..........	OF	2	8	0	2	1	0	0	1	0	1	0-0	.250	.250	.375	1	.000
—	Kansas City (A.L.)......	OF-DH	23	76	9	18	4	0	2	11	5	15	2-1	.237	.301	.368	0	1.000
Major League totals (4 years)			293	1089	153	307	72	5	45	167	56	186	17-8	.282	.324	.481	8	.981

RADKE, BRAD — P — TWINS

PERSONAL: Born October 27, 1972, in Eau Claire, Wis. ... 6-2/188. ... Throws right, bats right. ... Full name: Brad William Radke.
HIGH SCHOOL: Jesuit (Tampa).
TRANSACTIONS/CAREER NOTES: Selected by Minnesota Twins organization in eighth round of free-agent draft (June 3, 1991). ... On disabled list (August 4-21, 2001). ... On Minnesota disabled list (May 14-30 and May 31-August 3, 2002); included rehabilitation assignments to Gulf Coast Twins (July 19-24) and Fort Myers (July 25-30).
CAREER HITTING (MLB): 2-for-16 (.125), 0 R, 0 2B, 0 3B, 0 HR, 0 RBI.

Year	League	W	L	Pct.	ERA	G	GS	CG	ShO	Sv.-Opp.	IP	H	R	ER	HR	BB-IBB	SO
1991—	Gulf Coast Twins (GCL)....	3	4	.429	3.08	10	9	1	0	1-...	49.2	41	21	17	0	14-0	46
1992—	Kenosha (Midw.).............	10	10	.500	2.93	26	25	4	1	0-...	165.2	149	70	54	8	47-1	127
1993—	Fort Myers (FSL).............	3	5	.375	3.82	14	14	0	0	0-...	92.0	85	42	39	3	21-1	69
—	Nashville (Sou.)...............	2	6	.250	4.62	13	13	1	0	0-...	76.0	81	42	39	6	16-0	76
1994—	Nashville (Sou.)...............	12	9	.571	2.66	29	*28	5	1	0-...	186.1	167	66	55	9	34-0	123
1995—	Minnesota (A.L.).............	11	14	.440	5.32	29	28	2	1	0-0	181.0	195	112	107	*32	47-0	75
1996—	Minnesota (A.L.).............	11	16	.407	4.46	35	35	3	0	0-0	232.0	231	125	115	•40	57-2	148
1997—	Minnesota (A.L.).............	20	10	.667	3.87	35	•35	4	1	0-0	239.2	238	114	103	28	48-1	174
1998—	Minnesota (A.L.).............	12	14	.462	4.30	32	32	5	1	0-0	213.2	238	109	102	23	43-1	146

Year	League	W	L	Pct.	ERA	G	GS	CG	ShO	Sv.-Opp.	IP	H	R	ER	HR	BB-IBB	SO
1999—	Minnesota (A.L.)	12	14	.462	3.75	33	33	4	0	0-0	218.2	239	97	91	28	44-0	121
2000—	Minnesota (A.L.)	12	*16	.429	4.45	34	34	4	1	0-0	226.2	261	119	112	27	51-1	141
2001—	Minnesota (A.L.)	15	11	.577	3.94	33	33	6	2	0-0	226.0	235	105	99	24	26-0	137
2002—	Minnesota (A.L.)	9	5	.643	4.72	21	21	2	1	0-0	118.1	124	64	62	12	20-0	62
—	Gulf Coast Twins (GCL)	0	0	...	0.00	1	1	0	0	0-...	3.0	2	0	0	0	0-0	4
—	Fort Myers (FSL)	0	1	.000	3.12	2	2	0	0	0-...	8.2	11	6	3	1	0-0	6
Major League totals (8 years)		102	100	.505	4.30	252	251	30	7	0-0	1656.0	1761	845	791	214	336-5	1004

DIVISION SERIES RECORD

Year	League	W	L	Pct.	ERA	G	GS	CG	ShO	Sv.-Opp.	IP	H	R	ER	HR	BB-IBB	SO
2002—	Minnesota (A.L.)	2	0	1.000	1.54	2	2	0	0	0-0	11.2	14	6	2	1	1-0	7

CHAMPIONSHIP SERIES RECORD

Year	League	W	L	Pct.	ERA	G	GS	CG	ShO	Sv.-Opp.	IP	H	R	ER	HR	BB-IBB	SO
2002—	Minnesota (A.L.)	0	1	.000	2.70	1	1	0	0	0-0	6.2	5	2	2	0	1-0	4

ALL-STAR GAME RECORD

	W	L	Pct.	ERA	GS	CG	ShO	Sv.-Opp.	IP	H	R	ER	HR	BB-IBB	SO
All-Star Game totals (1 year)	0	0	...	9.00	0	0	0	0-0	1.0	2	1	1	0	1-0	1

RAINES, TIM — OF

PERSONAL: Born September 16, 1959, in Sanford, Fla. ... 5-9/202. ... Bats both, throws right. ... Full name: Timothy Raines. ... Father of Tim Raines Jr., outfielder, Baltimore Orioles; and brother of Ned Raines, minor league outfielder (1978-80).

HIGH SCHOOL: Seminole (Sanford, Fla.).

TRANSACTIONS/CAREER NOTES: Selected by Montreal Expos organization in fifth round of free-agent draft (June 7, 1977). ... On disabled list (May 23-June 5, 1978). ... Granted free agency (November 12, 1986). ... Re-signed by Expos (May 2, 1987). ... On disabled list (June 24-July 9, 1988 and June 25-July 10, 1990). ... Traded by Expos with P Jeff Carter and a player to be named later to Chicago White Sox for OF Ivan Calderon and P Barry Jones (December 23, 1990); White Sox acquired P Mario Brito to complete deal (February 15, 1991). ... On Chicago disabled list (April 10-May 22, 1993); included rehabilitation assignment to Nashville (May 19-22). ... Granted free agency (November 1, 1993). ... Re-signed by White Sox (December 22, 1993). ... Traded by White Sox to New York Yankees for a player to be named later (December 28, 1995); White Sox acquired 3B Blaise Kozeniewski to complete deal (February 6, 1996). ... On New York disabled list (March 21-April 16 and May 22-August 11, 1996); included rehabilitation assignments to Tampa (April 12-13 and July 25-August 2), Columbus (April 13-16 and June 23-24), Gulf Coast Yankees (June 22-23) and Norwich (August 2-10). ... On New York disabled list (March 27-April 11 and July 2-August 12, 1997); included rehabilitation assignment to Tampa (April 7-10, July 24-27, and August 5-7), Gulf Coast Yankees (July 24), Norwich (July 26-27) and Columbus (August 8-11). ... Granted free agency (October 29, 1997). ... Re-signed by Yankees (December 19, 1997). ... Granted free agency (October 26, 1998). ... Signed by Oakland Athletics (January 25, 1999). ... On disabled list (July 19, 1999-remainder of season). ... Granted free agency (November 5, 1999). ... Signed by Yankees organization (February 1, 2000). ... Announced retirement (March 23, 2000). ... Signed by Somerset, Atlantic League (July 8, 2000). ... Signed by Expos organization (December 21, 2000). ... On Montreal disabled list (May 4-August 22, 2001); included rehabilitation assignments to Jupiter (August 9-20) and Ottawa (August 21-22). ... Traded by Expos to Baltimore Orioles for a player to be named later (October 3, 2001). ... Granted free agency (November 6, 2001). ... Signed by Florida Marlins organization (February 18, 2002). ... Announced retirement (September 29, 2002). ... Granted free agency (October 28, 2002).

RECORDS: Holds major league single-season record for most intentional bases on balls received by switch hitter—26 (1987). ... Holds A.L. career records for most consecutive stolen bases without being caught stealing—40 (July 23, 1993 through August 4, 1995); and highest stolen-base percentage (300 or more attempts)—.857. ... Holds major league career record for highest stolen-base percentage (300 or more attempts)—.847. ... Shares A.L. single-game record for most consecutive times reached base safely—7 (April 20, 1994, 12 innings).

HONORS: Named Minor League Player of the Year by THE SPORTING NEWS (1980). ... Named N.L. Rookie Player of the Year by THE SPORTING NEWS (1981). ... Named outfielder on THE SPORTING NEWS N.L. All-Star team (1983 and 1986). ... Won THE SPORTING NEWS Gold Shoe Award (1984). ... Named outfielder on THE SPORTING NEWS N.L. Silver Slugger team (1986).

STATISTICAL NOTES: Led Southern League second basemen with 341 putouts, 413 assists and 777 total chances in 1979. ... Led N.L. outfielders with 21 assists in 1983. ... Hit for the cycle (August 16, 1987). ... Switch-hit home runs in one game (July 16, 1988 and August 31, 1993). ... Hit three home runs in one game (April 18, 1994). ... Career major league grand slams: 6.

MISCELLANEOUS: Holds Montreal Expos all-time records for most runs (947), triples (82) and stolen bases (635).

2002 GAMES PLAYED BY POSITION (MLB): OF—14; DH—1.

			BATTING														FIELDING	
Year	Team (League)	Pos.	G	AB	R	H	2B	3B	HR	RBI	BB	SO	SB-CS	Avg.	OBP	SLG	E	Avg.
1977—	GC Expos (GCL)	2B-3B-OF	49	161	28	45	6	2	0	21	27	16	29-2	.280	.381	.342	13	.921
1978—	W. Palm Beach (FSL)	2B-SS	100	359	67	103	10	0	0	23	64	44	57-21	.287	.400	.315	24	.953
1979—	Memphis (Sou.)	2B	•145	552	*104	160	25	10	5	50	90	51	59-12	.290	.390	.399	*23	.970
—	Montreal (N.L.)	PR	6	0	3	0	0	0	0	0	0	0	2-0	...	...	...	...	...
1980—	Denver (A.A.)	2B	108	429	105	152	23	•11	6	64	61	42	*77-13	*.354	.439	.501	16	.972
—	Montreal (N.L.)	2B-OF	15	20	5	1	0	0	0	0	6	3	5-0	.050	.269	.050	0	1.000
1981—	Montreal (N.L.)	OF-2B	88	313	61	95	13	7	5	37	45	31	*71-11	.304	.391	.438	4	.977
1982—	Montreal (N.L.)	OF-2B	156	647	90	179	32	8	4	43	75	83	*78-16	.277	.353	.369	8	.981
1983—	Montreal (N.L.)	OF-2B	156	615	*133	183	32	8	11	71	97	70	*90-14	.298	.393	.429	4	.988
1984—	Montreal (N.L.)	OF-2B	160	622	106	192	•38	9	8	60	87	69	*75-10	.309	.393	.437	6	.986
1985—	Montreal (N.L.)	OF	150	575	115	184	30	13	11	41	81	60	70-9	.320	.405	.475	2	.993
1986—	Montreal (N.L.)	OF	151	580	91	194	35	10	9	62	78	60	70-9	*.334	*.413	.476	6	.979
1987—	Montreal (N.L.)	OF	139	530	*123	175	34	8	18	68	90	52	50-5	.330	.429	.526	4	.987
1988—	Montreal (N.L.)	OF	109	429	66	116	19	7	12	48	53	44	33-7	.270	.350	.431	3	.988
1989—	Montreal (N.L.)	OF	145	517	76	148	29	6	9	60	93	48	41-9	.286	.395	.418	1	.996
1990—	Montreal (N.L.)	OF	130	457	65	131	11	5	9	62	70	43	49-16	.287	.379	.392	6	.976
1991—	Chicago (A.L.)■	OF-DH	155	609	102	163	20	6	5	50	83	68	51-15	.268	.359	.345	3	.990
1992—	Chicago (A.L.)	OF-DH	144	551	102	162	22	9	7	54	81	48	45-6	.294	.380	.405	2	.994
1993—	Chicago (A.L.)	OF	115	415	75	127	16	4	16	54	64	35	21-7	.306	.401	.480	0	*1.000
—	Nashville (A.A.)	OF	3	11	3	5	1	0	0	2	2	0	2-1	.455	.538	.545	0	1.000
1994—	Chicago (A.L.)	OF	101	384	80	102	15	5	10	52	61	43	13-0	.266	.365	.409	4	.981
1995—	Chicago (A.L.)	OF-DH	133	502	81	143	25	4	12	67	70	52	13-2	.285	.374	.422	4	.980
1996—	Tampa (FSL)■	OF-DH	9	36	9	13	2	0	2	11	8	3	0-0	.361	.477	.583	0	1.000
—	Columbus (I.L.)	DH-OF	4	12	3	3	1	0	0	0	1	3	1-0	.250	.308	.333	0	1.000
—	New York (A.L.)	OF-DH	59	201	45	57	10	0	9	33	34	29	10-1	.284	.383	.468	1	.988
—	GC Yankees (GCL)	DH	1	5	2	3	2	0	0	3	1	0	0-0	.600	.667	1.000	...	...
—	Norwich (East.)	OF-DH	8	27	8	5	1	0	1	1	9	2	2-0	.185	.405	.333	0	1.000

Year	Team (League)	Pos.	G	AB	R	H	2B	3B	HR	RBI	BB	SO	SB-CS	Avg.	OBP	SLG	E	Avg.
			BATTING														FIELDING	
1997—	Tampa (FSL)	OF-DH	11	35	8	12	0	0	2	5	11	1	1-0	.343	.500	.514	0	1.000
—	New York (A.L.)	OF-DH	74	271	56	87	20	2	4	38	41	34	8-5	.321	.403	.454	1	.988
—	GC Yankees (GCL)	OF	1	4	0	1	0	0	0	2	1	1	0-0	.250	.400	.250	0	1.000
—	Norwich (East.)	OF	2	7	0	2	1	0	0	2	0	2	0-0	.286	.286	.429	0	1.000
—	Columbus (I.L.)	OF	4	13	1	2	0	0	0	0	3	2	0-0	.154	.313	.154	0	1.000
1998—	New York (A.L.)	DH-OF	109	321	53	93	13	1	5	47	55	49	8-3	.290	.395	.383	1	.985
1999—	Oakland (A.L.)■	OF-DH	58	135	20	29	5	0	4	17	26	17	4-1	.215	.337	.341	0	1.000
2000—	Somerset (Atl.)■		7	26	5	9	3	0	0	2	5	2	0-...	.346	...	.462	...	...
2001—	Montreal (N.L.)■	OF	47	78	13	24	8	1	0	4	18	6	1-0	.308	.433	.436	0	1.000
—	Jupiter (FSL)	OF	8	23	7	8	1	1	1	5	5	4	1-0	.348	.448	.609	0	1.000
—	Ottawa (I.L.)	DH	2	7	1	1	1	0	0	0	1	1	0-0	.143	.250	.286	...	...
—	Baltimore (A.L.)■	OF-DH	4	11	1	3	0	0	1	5	0	3	0-0	.273	.250	.545	0	1.000
2002—	Florida (N.L.)■	OF-DH	98	89	9	17	3	0	1	7	22	19	0-0	.191	.351	.258	1	.917
American League totals (10 years)			952	3400	615	966	146	31	73	417	515	378	173-40	.284	.377	.410	16	.990
National League totals (14 years)			1550	5472	956	1639	284	82	97	563	815	588	635-106	.300	.390	.435	45	.985
Major League totals (23 years)			2502	8872	1571	2605	430	113	170	980	1330	966	808-146	.294	.385	.425	61	.987

DIVISION SERIES RECORD

Year	Team (League)	Pos.	G	AB	R	H	2B	3B	HR	RBI	BB	SO	SB-CS	Avg.	OBP	SLG	E	Avg.
			BATTING														FIELDING	
1996—	New York (A.L.)	OF	4	16	3	4	0	0	0	0	3	1	0-0	.250	.368	.250	0	1.000
1997—	New York (A.L.)	DH-OF	5	19	4	4	0	0	1	3	3	1	2-0	.211	.304	.368	0	1.000
1998—	New York (A.L.)	PH-DH	2	4	1	1	1	0	0	0	1	1	0-0	.250	.400	.500	...	...
Division series totals (3 years)			11	39	8	9	1	0	1	3	7	3	2-0	.231	.340	.333	0	1.000

CHAMPIONSHIP SERIES RECORD

RECORDS: Holds single-series record for most singles—10 (1993). ... Shares A.L. single-series record for most hits—12 (1993).

Year	Team (League)	Pos.	G	AB	R	H	2B	3B	HR	RBI	BB	SO	SB-CS	Avg.	OBP	SLG	E	Avg.
			BATTING														FIELDING	
1981—	Montreal (N.L.)	OF	5	21	1	5	2	0	0	1	0	3	0-1	.238	.238	.333	0	1.000
1993—	Chicago (A.L.)	OF	6	27	5	12	2	0	0	1	2	2	1-1	.444	.483	.519	0	1.000
1996—	New York (A.L.)	OF	5	15	2	4	1	0	0	0	1	1	0-0	.267	.313	.333	0	1.000
1998—	New York (A.L.)	DH-OF	3	10	0	1	0	0	0	1	2	5	0-0	.100	.250	.100	0	1.000
Championship series totals (4 years)			19	73	8	22	5	0	0	3	5	11	1-2	.301	.346	.370	0	1.000

WORLD SERIES RECORD

NOTES: Member of World Series championship team (1996 and 1998).

Year	Team (League)	Pos.	G	AB	R	H	2B	3B	HR	RBI	BB	SO	SB-CS	Avg.	OBP	SLG	E	Avg.
			BATTING														FIELDING	
1996—	New York (A.L.)	OF	4	14	2	3	0	0	0	0	2	1	0-1	.214	.313	.214	1	.833
1998—	New York (A.L.)								Did not play.									

ALL-STAR GAME RECORD

NOTES: Named Most Valuable Player (1987).

	AB	R	H	2B	3B	HR	RBI	BB	SO	SB-CS	Avg.	OBP	SLG	E	Avg.
All-Star Game totals (7 years)	10	1	3	0	1	0	2	2	4	3-0	.300	.417	.500	0	1.000

RAMIREZ, ARAMIS — 3B — PIRATES

PERSONAL: Born June 25, 1978, in Santo Domingo, Dominican Republic. ... 6-1/211. ... Bats right, throws right. ... Full name: Aramis Nin Ramirez.

TRANSACTIONS/CAREER NOTES: Signed as non-drafted free agent by Pittsburgh Pirates organization (November 7, 1994). ... On suspended list (July 24-29, 1998). ... On Pittsburgh disabled list (August 10-September 4, 1998); included rehabilitation assignment to Nashville (August 27). ... On Pittsburgh disabled list (August 29, 2000-remainder of season).

HONORS: Named Carolina League Most Valuable Player (1997).

STATISTICAL NOTES: Led Carolina League third basemen with 265 assists and 379 total chances in 1997. ... Hit three home runs in one game (April 8, 2001). ... Tied for N.L. lead with 11 sacrifice flies in 2002. ... Career major league grand slams: 3.

2002 GAMES PLAYED BY POSITION (MLB): 3B—131; DH—3.

Year	Team (League)	Pos.	G	AB	R	H	2B	3B	HR	RBI	BB	SO	SB-CS	Avg.	OBP	SLG	E	Avg.
			BATTING														FIELDING	
1995—	Dom. Pirates (DSL)	3B	64	214	41	63	13	0	11	54	42	26	2-...	.294	...	.509	19	.886
1996—	Erie (NY-Penn)	3B	61	223	37	68	14	4	9	42	31	41	0-0	.305	.403	.525	17	.896
—	Augusta (S.Atl.)	3B	6	20	3	4	1	0	1	2	1	7	0-2	.200	.304	.400	2	.833
1997—	Lynchburg (Caro.)	3B-DH	137	482	85	134	24	2	29	*114	80	103	5-3	.278	.390	.517	*39	.897
1998—	Nashville (PCL)	3B-DH-SS	47	168	19	46	10	0	5	18	24	28	0-2	.274	.374	.423	8	.932
—	Pittsburgh (N.L.)	3B	72	251	23	59	9	1	6	24	18	72	0-1	.235	.296	.351	9	.941
1999—	Nashville (PCL)	3B-DH	131	460	92	151	35	1	21	74	73	56	5-3	.328	.425	.546	*42	.884
—	Pittsburgh (N.L.)	3B	18	56	2	10	2	1	0	7	6	9	0-0	.179	.254	.250	3	.930
2000—	Pittsburgh (N.L.)	3B	73	254	19	65	15	2	6	35	10	36	0-0	.256	.293	.402	14	.917
—	Nashville (PCL)	3B	44	167	28	59	12	2	4	26	11	26	2-1	.353	.407	.521	9	.930
2001—	Pittsburgh (N.L.)	3B	158	603	83	181	40	0	34	112	40	100	5-4	.300	.350	.536	25	.945
2002—	Pittsburgh (N.L.)	3B-DH	142	522	51	122	26	0	18	71	29	95	2-0	.234	.279	.387	19	.946
Major League totals (5 years)			463	1686	178	437	92	4	64	249	103	312	7-5	.259	.308	.432	70	.940

RAMIREZ, JULIO — OF

PERSONAL: Born August 10, 1977, in San Juan de la Maguana, Dominican Republic. ... 5-11/170. ... Bats right, throws right. ... Full name: Julio Cesar Ramirez.

HIGH SCHOOL: Escuela Otilia Pelaez (Santo Domingo, Dominican Republic).

TRANSACTIONS/CAREER NOTES: Signed as non-drafted free agent by Florida Marlins organization (December 6, 1993). ... On Calgary disabled list (April 15-May 2 and July 18-August 14, 2000). ... Traded by Marlins to Chicago White Sox for OF Jeff Abbott (December 10, 2000). ... On Charlotte disabled list (August 13-20, 2001). ... Released by White Sox (March 13, 2002). ... Signed by Anaheim Angels organization (March 16, 2002). ... On Anaheim disabled list (June 16-September 1, 2002); included rehabilitation assignment to Salt Lake (August 15-September 1). ... Released by Angels (November 6, 2002).
STATISTICAL NOTES: Led Florida State League outfielders with 365 putouts and 390 total chances and tied for lead with 17 assists in 1998. ... Led Eastern League outfielders with 326 putouts and 351 total chances in 1999.
2002 GAMES PLAYED BY POSITION (MLB): OF—23; DH—1.

		BATTING														FIELDING	
Year Team (League)	**Pos.**	**G**	**AB**	**R**	**H**	**2B**	**3B**	**HR**	**RBI**	**BB**	**SO**	**SB-CS**	**Avg.**	**OBP**	**SLG**	**E**	**Avg.**
1994—Dom. Marlins (DSL)...	OF	67	274	54	75	18	0	7	32	28	41	29-...	.274	...	.416	10	.936
1995—GC Marlins (GCL).......	OF	48	204	35	58	9	4	2	13	13	42	17-6	.284	.330	.397	2	.983
1996—GC Marlins (GCL).......	OF	43	174	35	50	5	4	0	16	15	34	26-8	.287	.354	.362	2	.980
—Brevard County (FSL).	OF	17	61	11	15	0	1	0	2	4	18	2-3	.246	.288	.279	1	.933
1997—Kane County (Midw.)..	OF	99	376	70	96	18	7	14	53	37	122	41-6	.255	.329	.452	4	.979
1998—Brevard County (FSL).	OF	135	559	90	156	20	12	13	58	45	147	71-27	.279	.336	.428	8	.979
1999—Portland (East.)..........	OF	138	*568	87	148	30	10	13	64	39	150	*64-14	.261	.308	.417	•11	.969
—Florida (N.L.)..............	OF	15	21	3	3	1	0	0	2	1	6	0-1	.143	.182	.190	1	.950
2000—Calgary (PCL).............	OF	94	350	45	93	18	3	7	52	21	86	20-14	.266	.310	.394	*11	.954
2001—Chicago (A.L.)■.........	OF	22	37	2	3	0	0	0	1	2	15	2-0	.081	.128	.081	1	.978
—Charlotte (I.L.)............	OF	88	319	36	69	11	1	8	25	20	80	15-6	.216	.266	.332	8	.962
2002—Salt Lake (PCL)■.......	OF	39	139	17	38	3	5	2	10	4	31	8-3	.273	.299	.410	2	.976
—Anaheim (A.L.)...........	OF-DH	29	32	6	9	0	1	1	7	2	14	0-2	.281	.343	.438	0	1.000
American League totals (2 years)		51	69	8	12	0	1	1	8	4	29	2-2	.174	.230	.246	1	.986
National League totals (1 year)		15	21	3	3	1	0	0	2	1	6	0-1	.143	.182	.190	1	.950
Major League totals (3 years)		66	90	11	15	1	1	1	10	5	35	2-3	.167	.219	.233	2	.978

RAMIREZ, MANNY — OF — RED SOX

PERSONAL: Born May 30, 1972, in Santo Domingo, Dominican Republic. ... 6-0/213. ... Bats right, throws right. ... Full name: Manuel Aristides Ramirez.
HIGH SCHOOL: George Washington (New York).
TRANSACTIONS/CAREER NOTES: Selected by Cleveland Indians organization in first round (13th pick overall) of free-agent draft (June 3, 1991). ... On disabled list (July 10, 1992-remainder of season). ... On suspended list (June 8-11, 1999). ... On Cleveland disabled list (May 30-July 13, 2000); included rehabilitation assignments to Akron (June 16-23) and Buffalo (July 6-13). ... Granted free agency (October 27, 2000). ... Signed by Boston Red Sox (December 13, 2000). ... On Boston disabled list (May 14-June 25, 2002); included rehabilitation assignment to Pawtucket (June 13-25).
RECORDS: Shares major league record for most consecutive home runs—4 (September 15 [3], 16 [1], 1998); most home runs in two consecutive games—5 (September 15 [3], 16 [2], 1998); and most home runs in three consecutive games—6 (September 15 [3], 16 [2], 17 [1], 1998).
HONORS: Named Appalachian League Most Valuable Player (1991). ... Named outfielder on The Sporting News A.L. All-Star team (1995, 1999 and 2001). ... Named outfielder on The Sporting News A.L. Silver Slugger team (1995, 1999 and 2000). ... Named outfielder on A.L. Silver Slugger team (2001). ... Named designated hitter on The Sporting News A.L. All-Star team (2002). ... Named designated hitter on A.L. Silver Slugger team (2002).
STATISTICAL NOTES: Led Appalachian League with 146 total bases and tied for lead with five intentional bases on balls received in 1991. ... Led A.L. outfielders with 19 assists in 1996. ... Hit three home runs in one game (September 15, 1998 and August 25, 1999). ... Had 20-game hitting streak (August 15-September 5, 2000). ... Led A.L. with 25 intentional bases on balls received in 2001. ... Career major league grand slams: 15.
2002 GAMES PLAYED BY POSITION (MLB): OF—68; DH—51.

		BATTING														FIELDING	
Year Team (League)	**Pos.**	**G**	**AB**	**R**	**H**	**2B**	**3B**	**HR**	**RBI**	**BB**	**SO**	**SB-CS**	**Avg.**	**OBP**	**SLG**	**E**	**Avg.**
1991—Burlington (Appl.).......	OF	59	215	44	70	11	4	*19	*63	34	41	7-8	.326	.426	*.679	3	.966
1992—Kinston (Caro.)...........	OF	81	291	52	81	18	4	13	63	45	74	1-3	.278	.379	.502	6	.956
1993—Canton/Akron (East.)..	OF	89	344	67	117	32	0	17	79	45	68	2-2	*.340	.414	.581	5	.967
—Charlotte (I.L.)............	OF	40	145	38	46	12	0	14	36	27	35	1-1	.317	.424	.690	3	.961
—Cleveland (A.L.)..........	DH-OF	22	53	5	9	1	0	2	5	2	8	0-0	.170	.200	.302	0	1.000
1994—Cleveland (A.L.)..........	OF-DH	91	290	51	78	22	0	17	60	42	72	4-2	.269	.357	.521	1	.994
1995—Cleveland (A.L.)..........	OF-DH	137	484	85	149	26	1	31	107	75	112	6-6	.308	.402	.558	5	.978
1996—Cleveland (A.L.)..........	OF-DH	152	550	94	170	45	3	33	112	85	104	8-5	.309	.399	.582	9	.970
1997—Cleveland (A.L.)..........	OF-DH	150	561	99	184	40	0	26	88	79	115	2-3	.328	.415	.538	7	.975
1998—Cleveland (A.L.)..........	OF-DH	150	571	108	168	35	2	45	145	76	121	5-3	.294	.377	.599	7	.977
1999—Cleveland (A.L.)..........	OF-DH	147	522	131	174	34	3	44	*165	96	131	2-4	.333	.442	*.663	7	.975
2000—Cleveland (A.L.)..........	OF-DH	118	439	92	154	34	2	38	122	86	117	1-1	.351	.457	*.697	2	.986
—Akron (East.).............	DH	1	2	1	1	0	0	1	2	2	1	0-0	.500	.750	2.000	...	...
—Buffalo (I.L.)..............	DH	5	11	5	5	1	0	3	7	6	1	0-0	.455	.647	1.364	...	...
2001—Boston (A.L.)■...........	DH-OF	142	529	93	162	33	2	41	125	81	147	0-1	.306	.405	.609	0	1.000
2002—Boston (A.L.).............	OF-DH	120	436	84	152	31	0	33	107	73	85	0-0	*.349	*.450	.647	5	.959
—Pawtucket (I.L.).........	OF	11	30	2	3	1	0	1	2	8	9	0-0	.100	.308	.233	0	1.000
Major League totals (10 years)		1229	4435	842	1400	301	13	310	1036	695	1012	28-25	.316	.411	.599	43	.978

DIVISION SERIES RECORD

RECORDS: Shares career record for most extra-base hits—10. ... Shares single-game record for most home runs—2 (October 2, 1998).

		BATTING														FIELDING	
Year Team (League)	**Pos.**	**G**	**AB**	**R**	**H**	**2B**	**3B**	**HR**	**RBI**	**BB**	**SO**	**SB-CS**	**Avg.**	**OBP**	**SLG**	**E**	**Avg.**
1995—Cleveland (A.L.)..........	OF	3	12	1	0	0	0	0	0	1	2	0-0	.000	.143	.000	0	1.000
1996—Cleveland (A.L.)..........	OF	4	16	4	6	2	0	2	2	1	4	0-0	.375	.412	.875	0	1.000
1997—Cleveland (A.L.)..........	OF	5	21	2	3	1	0	0	3	0	3	0-0	.143	.143	.190	1	.750
1998—Cleveland (A.L.)..........	OF	4	14	2	5	2	0	2	3	1	4	0-0	.357	.471	.929	0	1.000
1999—Cleveland (A.L.)..........	OF	5	18	5	1	1	0	0	1	4	8	0-0	.056	.261	.111	0	1.000
Division series totals (5 years)		21	81	14	15	6	0	4	9	7	21	0-0	.185	.283	.407	1	.967

CHAMPIONSHIP SERIES RECORD

Year	Team (League)	Pos.	G	AB	R	H	2B	3B	HR	RBI	BB	SO	SB-CS	Avg.	OBP	SLG	E	Avg.
			BATTING														FIELDING	
1995—	Cleveland (A.L.)	OF	6	21	2	6	0	0	2	2	2	5	0-0	.286	.348	.571	0	1.000
1997—	Cleveland (A.L.)	OF	6	21	3	6	1	0	2	3	5	5	0-0	.286	.444	.619	1	.933
1998—	Cleveland (A.L.)	OF	6	21	2	7	1	0	2	4	4	9	0-0	.333	.423	.667	0	1.000
Championship series totals (3 years)			18	63	7	19	2	0	6	9	11	19	0-0	.302	.408	.619	1	.972

WORLD SERIES RECORD

Year	Team (League)	Pos.	G	AB	R	H	2B	3B	HR	RBI	BB	SO	SB-CS	Avg.	OBP	SLG	E	Avg.
			BATTING														FIELDING	
1995—	Cleveland (A.L.)	OF	6	18	2	4	0	0	1	2	4	5	1-0	.222	.364	.389	0	1.000
1997—	Cleveland (A.L.)	OF	7	26	3	4	0	0	2	6	6	5	0-0	.154	.294	.385	1	.944
World Series totals (2 years)			13	44	5	8	0	0	3	8	10	10	1-0	.182	.321	.386	1	.962

ALL-STAR GAME RECORD

	AB	R	H	2B	3B	HR	RBI	BB	SO	SB-CS	Avg.	OBP	SLG	E	Avg.
All-Star Game totals (5 years)	5	1	2	0	0	0	2	3	2	0-0	.400	.500	.400	0	1.000

RAMSAY, ROBERT — P — PADRES

PERSONAL: Born December 3, 1973, in Vancouver, Wash. ... 6-5/215. ... Throws left, bats left. ... Full name: Robert Arthur Ramsay.
HIGH SCHOOL: Mountain View (Vancouver, Wash.).
COLLEGE: Washington State.
TRANSACTIONS/CAREER NOTES: Selected by Boston Red Sox organization in seventh round of free-agent draft (June 2, 1996). ... Traded by Red Sox to Seattle Mariners for OF Butch Huskey (July 26, 1999). ... On Seattle disabled list (August 14-29, 2000); included rehabilitation assignment to Everett (August 26-29). ... On disabled list (September 10, 2001-remainder of season). ... Claimed on waivers by San Diego Padres (November 20, 2001). ... On disabled list (March 27, 2002-entire season).
STATISTICAL NOTES: Led Pacific Coast League with 10 sacrifice flies allowed in 2001.
CAREER HITTING (MLB): 0-for-0 (.000), 0 R, 0 2B, 0 3B, 0 HR, 0 RBI.

Year	League	W	L	Pct.	ERA	G	GS	CG	ShO	Sv.-Opp.	IP	H	R	ER	HR	BB-IBB	SO
1996—	Gulf Coast Red Sox (GCL)	0	1	.000	4.91	2	0	0	0	0-...	3.2	5	2	2	0	3-0	5
—	Sarasota (FSL)	2	2	.500	6.09	12	7	0	0	0-...	34.0	42	23	23	1	27-0	32
1997—	Sarasota (FSL)	9	9	.500	4.78	23	22	1	0	0-...	135.2	134	90	72	16	63-0	115
1998—	Trenton (East.)	12	6	.667	3.49	27	27	1	1	0-...	162.2	137	67	63	10	50-1	166
1999—	Pawtucket (I.L.)	6	6	.500	5.35	20	20	0	0	0-...	114.1	114	81	68	21	36-1	79
—	Tacoma (PCL)■	4	1	.800	1.08	5	5	0	0	0-...	33.1	20	6	4	2	14-1	37
—	Seattle (A.L.)	0	2	.000	6.38	6	3	0	0	0-0	18.1	23	13	13	3	9-1	11
2000—	Tacoma (PCL)	0	1	.000	4.50	3	3	0	0	0-...	16.0	16	8	8	1	6-0	6
—	Seattle (A.L.)	1	1	.500	3.40	37	1	0	0	0-0	50.1	43	22	19	3	40-3	32
—	Everett (N'West)	0	0	...	0.00	1	1	0	0	0-...	2.0	2	0	0	0	0-0	4
2001—	Tacoma (PCL)	10	11	.476	4.82	26	26	0	0	0-...	149.1	160	98	80	26	60-0	113
2002—	San Diego (N.L.)■	Did not play.															
Major League totals (2 years)		1	3	.250	4.19	43	4	0	0	0-0	68.2	66	35	32	6	49-4	43

CHAMPIONSHIP SERIES RECORD

Year	League	W	L	Pct.	ERA	G	GS	CG	ShO	Sv.-Opp.	IP	H	R	ER	HR	BB-IBB	SO
2000—	Seattle (A.L.)	0	0	...	0.00	2	0	0	0	0-0	1.2	2	0	0	0	0-0	1

RANDA, JOE — 3B — ROYALS

PERSONAL: Born December 18, 1969, in Milwaukee. ... 5-11/190. ... Bats right, throws right. ... Full name: Joseph Gregory Randa.
HIGH SCHOOL: Kettle-Moraine (Wales, Wis.).
JUNIOR COLLEGE: Indian River Community College (Fla.).
COLLEGE: Tennessee.
TRANSACTIONS/CAREER NOTES: Selected by California Angels organization in 30th round of free-agent draft (June 5, 1989); did not sign. ... Selected by Kansas City Royals organization in 11th round of free-agent draft (June 3, 1991). ... On Kansas City disabled list (May 5-27, 1996); included rehabilitation assignment to Omaha (May 23-27). ... Traded by Royals with P Jeff Granger, P Jeff Martin and P Jeff Wallace to Pittsburgh Pirates for SS Jay Bell and 1B Jeff King (December 13, 1996). ... On Pittsburgh disabled list (June 28-July 27, 1997); included rehabilitation assignment to Calgary (July 25-27). ... Selected by Arizona Diamondbacks in third round (57th pick overall) of expansion draft (November 18, 1997). ... Traded by Diamondbacks with P Matt Drews and 3B Gabe Alvarez to Detroit Tigers for 3B Travis Fryman (November 18, 1997). ... Traded by Tigers to New York Mets for P Willie Blair (December 4, 1998). ... Traded by Mets to Royals for OF Juan LeBron (December 10, 1998).
RECORDS: Holds A.L. single-season record for fewest putouts by third baseman for leader—111 (2001).
HONORS: Named Northwest League Most Valuable Player (1991).
STATISTICAL NOTES: Led Northwest League with 150 total bases in 1991. ... Led Northwest League third basemen with 57 putouts, 111 assists, 182 total chances and 12 double plays in 1991. ... Led Southern League with 10 sacrifice flies in 1993. ... Led Southern League third basemen with 97 putouts in 1993. ... Led American Association third basemen with 85 putouts, 324 assists, 433 total chances and 28 double plays in 1994. ... Had 18-game hitting streak (July 1-21, 1999). ... Led A.L. third baseman with 119 putouts, 314 assists, 455 total chances and 28 double plays in 1999. ... Led A.L. third basemen with 132 putouts in 2000. ... Led A.L. third basemen with 111 putouts in 2001. ... Career major league grand slams: 1.
2002 GAMES PLAYED BY POSITION (MLB): 3B—129; DH—19.

Year	Team (League)	Pos.	G	AB	R	H	2B	3B	HR	RBI	BB	SO	SB-CS	Avg.	OBP	SLG	E	Avg.
			BATTING														FIELDING	
1991—	Eugene (N'West)	3B	72	275	53	*93	20	2	11	59	46	29	6-1	.338	*.438	.545	14	*.923
1992—	Appleton (Midw.)	3B	72	266	55	80	13	0	5	43	34	37	6-2	.301	.385	.406	12	.941
—	Baseball City (FSL)	3B-SS	51	189	22	52	7	0	1	12	12	21	4-3	.275	.324	.328	6	.961
1993—	Memphis (Sou.)	3B	131	505	74	149	31	5	11	72	39	64	8-7	.295	.343	.442	25	.942
1994—	Omaha (A.A.)	3B	127	455	65	125	27	2	10	51	30	49	5-2	.275	.327	.409	*24	.945

Year	Team (League)	Pos.	G	AB	R	H	2B	3B	HR	RBI	BB	SO	SB-CS	Avg.	OBP	SLG	E	Avg.
			BATTING														FIELDING	
1995—	Kansas City (A.L.)	3B-2B-DH	34	70	6	12	2	0	1	5	6	17	0-1	.171	.237	.243	3	.952
—	Omaha (A.A.)	3B	64	233	33	64	10	2	8	33	22	33	2-2	.275	.341	.438	6	.958
1996—	Kansas City (A.L.)	3-2-1-DH	110	337	36	102	24	1	6	47	26	47	13-4	.303	.351	.433	10	.960
—	Omaha (A.A.)	3B	3	9	1	1	0	1	0	0	1	1	0-0	.111	.200	.333	0	1.000
1997—	Pittsburgh (N.L.)■	3B-2B	126	443	58	134	27	9	7	60	41	64	4-2	.302	.366	.451	21	.948
—	Calgary (PCL)	3B	3	11	4	4	1	0	1	4	3	4	0-0	.364	.500	.727	1	.900
1998—	Detroit (A.L.)■	3-2-DH-1	138	460	56	117	21	2	9	50	41	70	8-7	.254	.323	.367	7	.981
1999—	Kansas City (A.L.)■	3B	156	628	92	197	36	8	16	84	50	80	5-4	.314	.363	.473	22	.952
2000—	Kansas City (A.L.)	3B-DH	158	612	88	186	29	4	15	106	36	66	6-3	.304	.343	.438	19	.957
2001—	Kansas City (A.L.)	3B-DH-2B	151	581	59	147	34	2	13	83	42	80	3-2	.253	.307	.386	13	.966
2002—	Kansas City (A.L.)	3B-DH	151	549	63	155	36	5	11	80	46	69	2-1	.282	.341	.426	10	.972
American League totals (7 years)			898	3237	400	916	182	22	71	455	247	429	37-22	.283	.336	.419	84	.964
National League totals (1 year)			126	443	58	134	27	9	7	60	41	64	4-2	.302	.366	.451	21	.948
Major League totals (8 years)			1024	3680	458	1050	209	31	78	515	288	493	41-24	.285	.340	.423	105	.961

R

RANSOM, CODY — SS — GIANTS

PERSONAL: Born February 17, 1976, in Mesa, Ariz. ... 6-2/196. ... Bats right, throws right. ... Full name: Bryan Cody Ransom.
HIGH SCHOOL: Chandler (Ariz.).
JUNIOR COLLEGE: South Mountain (Ariz.).
COLLEGE: Grand Canyon.
TRANSACTIONS/CAREER NOTES: Selected by San Francisco Giants organization in ninth round of free-agent draft (June 2, 1998).
STATISTICAL NOTES: Tied for Northwest League lead in double plays by shortstop with 37 in 1998. ... Led Pacific Coast League with 12 sacrifice hits in 2002.
2002 GAMES PLAYED BY POSITION (MLB): SS—3.

Year	Team (League)	Pos.	G	AB	R	H	2B	3B	HR	RBI	BB	SO	SB-CS	Avg.	OBP	SLG	E	Avg.
			BATTING														FIELDING	
1998—	Salem-Kaizer (NW)	SS	71	236	52	55	12	7	6	27	43	56	19-6	.233	.351	.419	*24	.928
1999—	Bakersfield (Calif.)	SS	99	356	69	98	12	6	11	47	54	108	15-8	.275	.382	.435	30	.938
—	Shreveport (Texas)	SS	14	41	6	5	0	0	2	4	4	22	0-0	.122	.208	.268	3	.953
2000—	Shreveport (Texas)	SS	130	459	58	92	21	3	7	47	40	141	9-3	.200	.263	.305	25	.958
2001—	Fresno (PCL)	SS	134	469	77	113	21	6	23	78	44	137	17-2	.241	.303	.458	12	*.980
—	San Francisco (N.L.)	SS	9	7	1	0	0	0	0	0	0	5	0-0	.000	.000	.000	0	1.000
2002—	Fresno (PCL)	SS	135	449	53	93	18	4	13	46	47	151	6-4	.207	.283	.352	15	.973
—	San Francisco (N.L.)	SS	7	3	2	2	0	0	0	1	1	1	0-0	.667	.750	.667	0	1.000
Major League totals (2 years)			16	10	3	2	0	0	0	1	1	6	0-0	.200	.273	.200	0	1.000

RAUCH, JON — P — WHITE SOX

PERSONAL: Born September 27, 1978, in Louisville, Ky. ... 6-10/230. ... Throws right, bats right. ... Full name: Jon Erich Rauch.
HIGH SCHOOL: Oldham County (Buckner, Ky.).
COLLEGE: Morehead State (Ky.).
TRANSACTIONS/CAREER NOTES: Selected by Chicago White Sox organization in third round of free-agent draft (June 2, 1999). ... On disabled list (April 9-22 and May 14, 2001-remainder of season). ... On Charlotte disabled list (June 19-27, 2002).
HONORS: Named Minor League Player of the Year by The Sporting News (2000).
MISCELLANEOUS: Member of 2000 Olympic baseball team.
CAREER HITTING (MLB): 0-for-0 (.000), 0 R, 0 2B, 0 3B, 0 HR, 0 RBI.

Year	League	W	L	Pct.	ERA	G	GS	CG	ShO	Sv.-Opp.	IP	H	R	ER	HR	BB-IBB	SO
1999—	Bristol (Appl.)	4	4	.500	4.45	14	9	0	0	2-...	56.2	65	44	28	4	16-1	66
—	Winston-Salem (Caro.)	0	0	...	3.00	1	1	0	0	0-...	6.0	4	3	2	1	3-0	7
2000—	Winston-Salem (Caro.)	11	3	.786	2.86	18	18	1	0	0-...	110.0	102	49	35	10	33-0	124
—	Birmingham (Sou.)	5	1	.833	2.25	8	8	2	2	0-...	56.0	36	18	14	4	16-0	63
2001—	Charlotte (I.L.)	1	3	.250	5.79	6	6	0	0	0-...	28.0	28	20	18	8	7-0	27
2002—	Chicago (A.L.)	2	1	.667	6.59	8	6	0	0	0-0	28.2	28	26	21	7	14-2	19
—	Charlotte (I.L.)	7	8	.467	4.28	19	19	1	0	0-...	109.1	91	60	52	14	42-2	97
Major League totals (1 year)		2	1	.667	6.59	8	6	0	0	0-0	28.2	28	26	21	7	14-2	19

REAMES, BRITT — P — EXPOS

PERSONAL: Born August 19, 1973, in Seneca, S.C. ... 5-11/175. ... Throws right, bats right. ... Full name: William Britt Reames.
HIGH SCHOOL: Seneca (S.C.).
COLLEGE: The Citadel.
TRANSACTIONS/CAREER NOTES: Selected by St. Louis Cardinals organization in 17th round of free-agent draft (June 1, 1995). ... On disabled list (April 4, 1997-entire season; and April 10, 1998-entire season). ... On Potomac disabled list (April 23-June 10 and June 14-August 10, 1999). ... On Arkansas disabled list (April 19-29, 2000). ... On Memphis disabled list (July 7-14 and July 20-August 3, 2000). ... Traded by Cardinals with 3B Fernando Tatis to Montreal Expos for P Dustin Hermanson and P Steve Kline (December 14, 2000).
MISCELLANEOUS: Appeared in two games as pinch runner (2000).
CAREER HITTING (MLB): 5-for-38 (.132), 3 R, 0 2B, 0 3B, 1 HR, 3 RBI.

Year	League	W	L	Pct.	ERA	G	GS	CG	ShO	Sv.-Opp.	IP	H	R	ER	HR	BB-IBB	SO
1995—	New Jersey (NY-Penn)	2	1	.667	1.52	5	5	0	0	0-...	29.2	19	7	5	1	12-0	42
—	Savannah (S.Atl.)	3	5	.375	3.46	10	10	1	0	0-...	54.2	41	23	21	7	15-0	63
1996—	Peoria (Midw.)	15	7	.682	*1.90	25	25	2	•1	0-...	161.0	97	43	34	5	41-0	*167
1997—										Did not play.							
1998—										Did not play.							
1999—	Potomac (Caro.)	3	2	.600	3.19	10	8	0	0	0-...	36.2	34	21	13	2	21-0	22

Year League	W	L	Pct.	ERA	G	GS	CG	ShO	Sv.-Opp.	IP	H	R	ER	HR	BB-IBB	SO
2000—Arkansas (Texas)	2	3	.400	6.13	8	8	0	0	0-...	39.2	46	28	27	4	18-0	39
—Memphis (PCL)	6	2	.750	2.28	13	13	2	1	0-...	75.0	55	20	19	2	20-0	77
—St. Louis (N.L.)	2	1	.667	2.88	8	7	0	0	0-0	40.2	30	17	13	4	23-1	31
2001—Montreal (N.L.)■	4	8	.333	5.59	41	13	0	0	0-1	95.0	101	68	59	16	48-3	86
—Ottawa (I.L.)	4	3	.571	3.50	8	8	1	0	0-...	54.0	47	24	21	4	13-0	38
2002—Montreal (N.L.)	1	4	.200	5.03	42	6	0	0	0-1	68.0	70	42	38	8	38-6	76
—Ottawa (I.L.)	3	2	.600	2.79	7	7	0	0	0-...	42.0	31	16	13	3	14-0	26
Major League totals (3 years)	7	13	.350	4.86	91	26	0	0	0-2	203.2	201	127	110	28	109-10	193

DIVISION SERIES RECORD

Year League	W	L	Pct.	ERA	G	GS	CG	ShO	Sv.-Opp.	IP	H	R	ER	HR	BB-IBB	SO
2000—St. Louis (N.L.)	1	0	1.000	0.00	2	0	0	0	0-0	3.1	0	0	0	0	3-0	2

CHAMPIONSHIP SERIES RECORD

Year League	W	L	Pct.	ERA	G	GS	CG	ShO	Sv.-Opp.	IP	H	R	ER	HR	BB-IBB	SO
2000—St. Louis (N.L.)	0	0	...	1.42	2	0	0	0	0-0	6.1	5	1	1	1	4-1	6

REBOULET, JEFF IF

PERSONAL: Born April 30, 1964, in Dayton, Ohio. ... 6-0/175. ... Bats right, throws right. ... Full name: Jeffrey Allen Reboulet. ... Brother of Jim Reboulet, second baseman in St. Louis Cardinals and Pittsburgh Pirates organizations. ... Name pronounced REB-uh-lay.
HIGH SCHOOL: Alter (Kettering, Ohio).
JUNIOR COLLEGE: Triton Junior College (Ill.).
COLLEGE: Louisiana State.
TRANSACTIONS/CAREER NOTES: Selected by Houston Astros organization in 26th round of free-agent draft (June 3, 1985); did not sign. ... Selected by Minnesota Twins organization in 10th round of free-agent draft (June 2, 1986). ... Granted free agency (October 4, 1996). ... Signed by Baltimore Orioles organization (January 30, 1997). ... Traded by Orioles to Kansas City Royals for a player to be named later (December 12, 1999). ... Granted free agency (October 31, 2000). ... Signed by Los Angeles Dodgers organization (February 20, 2001). ... On Los Angeles disabled list (July 21-September 1, 2002); included rehabilitation assignment to Las Vegas (August 10-August 29). ... Granted free agency (October 29, 2002).
STATISTICAL NOTES: Led Southern League shortstops with 225 putouts and 602 total chances in 1988. ... Led Pacific Coast League with 17 sacrifice hits in 1991. ... Led Pacific Coast League shortstops with 202 putouts and 649 total chances in 1991.
2002 GAMES PLAYED BY POSITION (MLB): 2B—11; SS—5; 3B—3; DH—1.

		BATTING														FIELDING	
Year Team (League)	Pos.	G	AB	R	H	2B	3B	HR	RBI	BB	SO	SB-CS	Avg.	OBP	SLG	E	Avg.
1986—Visalia (Calif.)	SS	72	254	54	73	13	1	0	29	54	33	14-11	.287	.412	.346	20	.939
1987—Orlando (Sou.)	SS-2B-3B	129	422	52	108	15	1	1	35	58	56	9-5	.256	.347	.303	26	.958
1988—Orlando (Sou.)	SS	125	439	57	112	24	2	4	41	53	55	18-8	.255	.338	.346	30	.950
—Portland (PCL)	2B-SS	4	12	0	1	0	0	0	1	3	2	0-0	.083	.267	.083	1	.955
1989—Portland (PCL)	SS-2B-3B-OF	26	65	9	16	1	0	0	3	12	11	2-1	.246	.354	.262	7	.935
—Orlando (Sou.)	SS-2B-OF	81	291	43	63	5	1	0	26	49	33	11-6	.216	.328	.241	22	.942
1990—Orlando (Sou.)	2-3-S-0-1	97	287	43	66	12	2	2	28	57	37	10-5	.230	.357	.307	12	.968
1991—Portland (PCL)	SS	134	391	50	97	27	3	3	46	57	52	5-2	.248	.345	.355	*32	.951
1992—Portland (PCL)	SS	48	161	21	46	11	1	2	21	35	18	3-3	.286	.414	.404	7	.968
—Minnesota (A.L.)	S-3-2-O-DH	73	137	15	26	7	1	1	16	23	26	3-2	.190	.311	.277	5	.979
1993—Minnesota (A.L.)	S-3-2-O-DH	109	240	33	62	8	0	1	15	35	37	5-5	.258	.356	.304	6	.983
1994—Minnesota (A.L.)	S-2-1-3-O-DH	74	189	28	49	11	1	3	23	18	23	0-0	.259	.327	.376	7	.976
1995—Minnesota (A.L.)	S-3-1-2-C	87	216	39	63	11	0	4	23	27	34	1-2	.292	.373	.398	4	.988
1996—Minnesota (A.L.)	IF-OF-DH	107	234	20	52	9	0	0	23	25	34	4-2	.222	.298	.261	2	.992
1997—Baltimore (A.L.)■	2B-SS-3B-OF	99	228	26	54	9	0	4	27	23	44	3-0	.237	.307	.329	7	.975
1998—Baltimore (A.L.)	2B-SS-3B	79	126	20	31	6	0	1	8	19	34	0-1	.246	.351	.317	6	.966
1999—Baltimore (A.L.)	3B-2B-SS	99	154	25	25	4	0	0	4	33	29	1-0	.162	.317	.188	2	.991
2000—Kansas City (A.L.)■	2B-3B-SS-DH	66	182	29	44	7	0	0	14	23	32	3-1	.242	.325	.280	9	.965
2001—Los Angeles (N.L.)■	SS-2B-3B-OF	94	214	35	57	15	2	3	22	33	48	0-1	.266	.367	.397	10	.960
2002—Los Angeles (N.L.)	2B-SS-3B-DH	38	48	3	10	3	0	0	2	6	13	0-0	.208	.291	.271	4	.892
—Las Vegas (PCL)	2B-3B-SS	18	63	10	16	2	0	1	3	6	9	2-0	.254	.314	.333	2	.966
American League totals (9 years)		793	1706	235	406	72	2	14	153	226	293	20-13	.238	.330	.307	48	.980
National League totals (2 years)		132	262	38	67	18	2	3	24	39	61	0-1	.256	.353	.374	14	.951
Major League totals (11 years)		925	1968	273	473	90	4	17	177	265	354	20-14	.240	.333	.316	62	.977

DIVISION SERIES RECORD

		BATTING														FIELDING	
Year Team (League)	Pos.	G	AB	R	H	2B	3B	HR	RBI	BB	SO	SB-CS	Avg.	OBP	SLG	E	Avg.
1997—Baltimore (A.L.)	2B	2	5	1	1	0	0	1	1	0	2	0-0	.200	.200	.800	0	1.000

CHAMPIONSHIP SERIES RECORD

		BATTING														FIELDING	
Year Team (League)	Pos.	G	AB	R	H	2B	3B	HR	RBI	BB	SO	SB-CS	Avg.	OBP	SLG	E	Avg.
1997—Baltimore (A.L.)	SS-PR	1	2	1	0	0	0	0	0	0	1	0-0	.000	.000	.000	0	...

REDDING, TIM P ASTROS

PERSONAL: Born February 12, 1978, in Rochester, N.Y. ... 6-0/195. ... Throws right, bats right. ... Full name: Timothy J. Redding.
JUNIOR COLLEGE: Monroe (Rochester, N.Y.).
TRANSACTIONS/CAREER NOTES: Selected by Houston Astros organization in 20th round of free-agent draft (June 3, 1997). ... On New Orleans disabled list (August 20-28, 2002).
HONORS: Named Florida State League Most Valuable Pitcher (2000). ... Named Texas League Pitcher of the Year (2001).
CAREER HITTING (MLB): 5-for-34 (.147), 0 R, 0 2B, 0 3B, 0 HR, 3 RBI.

Year League	W	L	Pct.	ERA	G	GS	CG	ShO	Sv.-Opp.	IP	H	R	ER	HR	BB-IBB	SO
1998— Auburn (NY-Penn)...........	7	3	.700	4.52	16	15	0	0	1-...	73.2	49	44	37	2	*50-0	98
1999— Michigan (Midw.)............	8	6	.571	4.97	43	11	0	0	14-...	105.0	84	69	58	4	76-1	144
2000— Kissimmee (FSL).............	12	5	.706	2.68	24	24	0	0	0-...	154.2	125	62	46	5	57-1	*170
— Round Rock (Texas).........	2	0	1.000	3.46	5	5	0	0	0-...	26.0	14	12	10	4	22-0	22
2001— Round Rock (Texas).........	10	2	.833	2.18	14	14	1	1	0-...	90.2	64	26	22	5	25-0	113
— New Orleans (PCL)..........	4	1	.800	4.54	6	6	0	0	0-...	37.2	22	21	19	4	19-0	42
— Houston (N.L.)................	3	1	.750	5.50	13	9	0	0	0-0	55.2	62	38	34	11	24-0	55
2002— New Orleans (PCL)..........	3	3	.500	5.21	11	7	0	0	0-...	38.0	32	22	22	6	13-1	50
— Houston (N.L.)................	3	6	.333	5.40	18	14	0	0	0-0	73.1	78	49	44	10	35-3	63
Major League totals (2 years).....	6	7	.462	5.44	31	23	0	0	0-0	129.0	140	87	78	21	59-3	118

REDMAN, MARK — P — TIGERS

PERSONAL: Born January 5, 1974, in San Diego. ... 6-5/245. ... Throws left, bats left. ... Full name: Mark Allen Redman.

HIGH SCHOOL: Escondido (Calif.).

COLLEGE: The Master's College (Calif.), then Oklahoma.

TRANSACTIONS/CAREER NOTES: Selected by Detroit Tigers organization in 41st round of free-agent draft (June 1, 1992); did not sign. ... Selected by Minnesota Twins organization in first round (13th pick overall) of free-agent draft (June 1, 1995). ... On Salt Lake disabled list (August 1-8, 1998). ... On Minnesota disabled list (July 25-August 10, 1999). ... On Minnesota disabled list (May 21-July 28, 2001); included rehabilitation assignment to Edmonton (June 15-27). ... Traded by Twins to Tigers for P Todd Jones (July 28, 2001). ... On Detroit disabled list (July 28-August 22, 2001); included rehabilitation assignment to Toledo (August 6-22).

CAREER HITTING (MLB): 1-for-9 (.111), 1 R, 0 2B, 0 3B, 0 HR, 0 RBI.

Year League	W	L	Pct.	ERA	G	GS	CG	ShO	Sv.-Opp.	IP	H	R	ER	HR	BB-IBB	SO
1995— Fort Myers (FSL).............	2	1	.667	2.76	8	5	0	0	0-...	32.2	28	13	10	4	13-0	26
1996— Fort Myers (FSL).............	3	4	.429	1.85	13	13	0	0	0-...	82.2	63	24	17	1	34-0	75
— New Britain (East.)..........	7	7	.500	3.81	16	16	3	0	0-...	106.1	101	51	45	5	50-1	96
— Salt Lake (PCL)...............	0	0	...	9.00	1	1	0	0	0-...	4.0	7	4	4	1	2-0	4
1997— Salt Lake (PCL)...............	8	*15	.348	6.31	29	28	0	0	1-...	158.1	204	*123	111	19	80-3	125
1998— New Britain (East.)..........	4	2	.667	1.52	8	8	0	0	0-...	47.1	40	11	8	3	17-0	51
— Salt Lake (PCL)...............	6	7	.462	5.53	19	18	0	0	0-...	99.1	111	75	61	13	41-1	88
1999— Salt Lake (PCL)...............	9	9	.500	5.05	24	24	1	0	0-...	133.2	141	87	75	12	51-1	114
— Minnesota (A.L.).............	1	0	1.000	8.53	5	1	0	0	0-0	12.2	17	13	12	3	7-0	11
2000— Minnesota (A.L.).............	12	9	.571	4.76	32	24	0	0	0-0	151.1	168	81	80	22	45-0	117
2001— Minnesota (A.L.).............	2	4	.333	4.22	9	9	0	0	0-0	49.0	57	26	23	6	19-0	29
— Edmonton (PCL).............	0	0	...	13.50	1	1	0	0	0-...	1.1	3	2	2	0	1-0	0
— Toledo (I.L.)■..................	0	1	.000	5.27	3	3	0	0	0-...	13.2	14	10	8	3	1-0	12
— Detroit (A.L.)..................	0	2	.000	6.00	2	2	0	0	0-0	9.0	11	6	6	1	4-0	4
2002— Detroit (A.L.)..................	8	15	.348	4.21	30	30	3	0	0-0	203.0	211	107	95	15	51-2	109
Major League totals (4 years).....	23	30	.434	4.57	78	66	3	0	0-0	425.0	464	233	216	47	126-2	270

REDMOND, MIKE — C — MARLINS

PERSONAL: Born May 5, 1971, in Seattle. ... 5-11/208. ... Bats right, throws right. ... Full name: Michael Patrick Redmond.

HIGH SCHOOL: Gonzaga Prep (Spokane, Wash.).

COLLEGE: Gonzaga.

TRANSACTIONS/CAREER NOTES: Signed as a non-drafted free agent by Florida Marlins organization (August 18, 1992). ... On Florida disabled list (August 24-September 8, 1998).

STATISTICAL NOTES: Led Eastern League catchers with 95 assists in 1995. ... Led Eastern League catchers with 814 putouts and 906 total chances in 1996.

2002 GAMES PLAYED BY POSITION (MLB): C—80; 1B—2.

		BATTING														FIELDING	
Year Team (League)	Pos.	G	AB	R	H	2B	3B	HR	RBI	BB	SO	SB-CS	Avg.	OBP	SLG	E	Avg.
1993— Kane County (Midw.)..	C	43	100	10	20	2	0	0	10	6	17	2-0	.200	.273	.220	1	.996
1994— Kane County (Midw.)..	C	92	306	39	83	10	0	1	24	26	31	3-4	.271	.344	.314	6	.992
— Brevard County (FSL).	C	12	42	4	11	4	0	0	2	3	4	0-0	.262	.326	.357	0	1.000
1995— Portland (East.)..........	C-3B	105	333	37	85	11	1	3	39	22	27	2-2	.255	.305	.321	6	.992
1996— Portland (East.)..........	C	120	394	43	113	22	0	4	44	26	45	3-4	.287	.335	.373	4	.996
1997— Charlotte (I.L.)............	C	22	61	8	13	5	1	1	2	1	10	0-1	.213	.262	.377	2	.985
— GC Marlins (GCL).......	DH	16	55	7	19	3	0	0	5	9	5	2-0	.345	.463	.400	...	...
— Brevard County (FSL).	1B	5	17	2	0	0	0	0	0	2	2	0-0	.000	.105	.000	0	1.000
1998— Portland (East.)..........	C	8	28	7	9	4	0	1	7	2	2	0-0	.321	.406	.571	1	.983
— Charlotte (I.L.)............	C	18	58	4	14	2	0	2	7	0	3	0-0	.241	.246	.379	0	1.000
— Florida (N.L.)..............	C	37	118	10	39	9	0	2	12	5	16	0-0	.331	.368	.458	2	.992
1999— Florida (N.L.)..............	C	84	242	22	73	9	0	1	27	26	34	0-0	.302	.381	.351	4	.992
2000— Florida (N.L.)..............	C	87	210	17	53	8	1	0	15	13	19	0-0	.252	.316	.300	2	.996
2001— Florida (N.L.)..............	C	48	141	19	44	4	0	4	14	13	13	0-0	.312	.376	.426	2	.994
2002— Florida (N.L.)..............	C-1B	89	256	19	78	15	0	2	28	21	34	0-2	.305	.372	.387	4	.993
Major League totals (5 years)		345	967	87	287	45	1	9	96	78	116	0-2	.297	.362	.373	14	.993

REED, RICK — P — TWINS

PERSONAL: Born August 16, 1965, in Huntington, W.Va. ... 6-1/195. ... Throws right, bats right. ... Full name: Richard Allen Reed.

HIGH SCHOOL: Huntington (W.Va.).

COLLEGE: Marshall.

TRANSACTIONS/CAREER NOTES: Selected by Pittsburgh Pirates organization in 26th round of free-agent draft (June 2, 1986). ... On Buffalo disabled list (May 2-13, 1991). ... Granted free agency (April 3, 1992). ... Signed by Kansas City Royals organization (April 4, 1992). ... Granted free agency (August 5, 1993). ... Signed by Texas Rangers organization (August 11, 1993). ... Claimed on waivers by Cincinnati Reds (May

13, 1994). ... On Indianapolis disabled list (May 29-June 9, 1995). ... Granted free agency (October 16, 1995). ... Signed by New York Mets organization (November 7, 1995). ... On New York disabled list (April 12-May 3 and August 9-September 4, 1999); included rehabilitation assignments to Norfolk (August 27-31) and Binghamton (September 1-4). ... On disabled list (June 30-July 17, 2000). ... Granted free agency (November 8, 2000). ... Re-signed by Mets (December 6, 2000). ... Traded by Mets to Minnesota Twins for OF Matt Lawton (July 30, 2001).

HONORS: Named American Association Most Valuable Pitcher (1991).

MISCELLANEOUS: Appeared in one game as outfielder with no chances (1999).

CAREER HITTING (MLB): 51-for-297 (.172), 23 R, 9 2B, 0 3B, 2 HR, 24 RBI.

Year League	W	L	Pct.	ERA	G	GS	CG	ShO	Sv.-Opp.	IP	H	R	ER	HR	BB-IBB	SO
1986— Gulf Coast Pirates (GCL)..	0	2	.000	3.75	8	3	0	0	0-...	24.0	20	12	10	0	6-0	15
— Macon (S.Atl.)	0	0	...	2.84	1	1	0	0	0-...	6.1	5	3	2	0	2-0	1
1987— Macon (S.Atl.)	8	4	.667	2.50	46	0	0	0	7-...	93.2	80	38	26	6	29-3	92
1988— Salem (Caro.)	6	2	.750	2.74	15	8	4	1	0-...	72.1	56	28	22	6	17-1	73
— Harrisburg (East.)	1	0	1.000	1.13	2	2	0	0	0-...	16.0	11	2	2	0	2-0	17
— Buffalo (A.A.)	5	2	.714	1.64	10	9	3	2	0-...	77.0	62	15	14	0	12-2	50
— Pittsburgh (N.L.)	1	0	1.000	3.00	2	2	0	0	0-0	12.0	10	4	4	1	2-0	6
1989— Buffalo (A.A.)	9	8	.529	3.72	20	20	3	0	0-...	125.2	130	58	52	9	28-0	75
— Pittsburgh (N.L.)	1	4	.200	5.60	15	7	0	0	0-0	54.2	62	35	34	5	11-3	34
1990— Buffalo (A.A.)	7	4	.636	3.46	15	15	2	2	0-...	91.0	82	37	35	4	21-0	63
— Pittsburgh (N.L.)	2	3	.400	4.36	13	8	1	1	1-1	53.2	62	32	26	6	12-6	27
1991— Buffalo (A.A.)	*14	4	*.778	*2.15	25	25	•5	2	0-...	167.2	151	45	40	3	26-3	102
— Pittsburgh (N.L.)	0	0	...	10.38	1	1	0	0	0-0	4.1	8	6	5	1	1-0	2
1992— Omaha (A.A.)■	5	4	.556	4.35	11	10	3	0	1-...	62.0	67	33	30	8	12-0	35
— Kansas City (A.L.)	3	7	.300	3.68	19	18	1	1	0-0	100.1	105	47	41	10	20-3	49
1993— Omaha (A.A.)	11	4	.733	3.09	19	19	3	*2	0-...	128.1	116	48	44	19	14-1	58
— Kansas City (A.L.)	0	0	...	9.82	1	0	0	0	0-0	3.2	6	4	4	0	1-0	3
— Oklahoma City (A.A.)■	1	3	.250	4.19	5	5	1	0	0-...	34.1	43	20	16	2	2-0	21
— Texas (A.L.)	1	0	1.000	2.25	2	0	0	0	0-0	4.0	6	1	1	1	1-0	2
1994— Oklahoma City (A.A.)	1	1	.500	3.86	2	2	0	0	0-...	11.2	10	5	5	0	0-0	8
— Texas (A.L.)	1	1	.500	5.94	4	3	0	0	0-0	16.2	17	13	11	3	7-0	12
— Indianapolis (A.A.)■	9	5	.643	4.68	21	21	3	1	0-...	140.1	162	80	73	20	19-0	79
1995— Indianapolis (A.A.)	11	4	.733	3.33	22	21	3	1	0-...	135.0	127	60	50	16	26-2	92
— Cincinnati (N.L.)	0	0	...	5.82	4	3	0	0	0-0	17.0	18	12	11	5	3-0	10
1996— Norfolk (I.L.)■	8	10	.444	3.16	28	28	1	0	0-...	182.0	164	72	64	13	33-2	128
1997— New York (N.L.)	13	9	.591	2.89	33	31	2	0	0-0	208.1	186	76	67	19	31-4	113
1998— New York (N.L.)	16	11	.593	3.48	31	31	2	1	0-0	212.1	208	84	82	30	29-2	153
1999— New York (N.L.)	11	5	.688	4.58	26	26	1	1	0-0	149.1	163	77	76	23	47-2	104
— Norfolk (I.L.)	0	1	.000	27.00	1	1	0	0	0-...	3.0	10	9	9	1	2-0	2
— Binghamton (East.)	0	0	...	1.80	1	1	0	0	0-...	5.0	1	1	1	1	1-0	5
2000— New York (N.L.)	11	5	.688	4.11	30	30	0	0	0-0	184.0	192	90	84	28	34-3	121
2001— New York (N.L.)	8	6	.571	3.48	20	20	3	1	0-0	134.2	119	53	52	16	17-3	99
— Minnesota (A.L.)■	4	6	.400	5.19	12	12	0	0	0-0	67.2	92	45	39	12	14-0	43
2002— Minnesota (A.L.)	15	7	.682	3.78	33	32	2	1	0-0	188.0	192	89	79	32	26-0	121
A.L. totals (5 years)	24	21	.533	4.14	71	65	3	2	0-0	380.1	418	199	175	58	69-3	230
N.L. totals (10 years)	63	43	.594	3.85	175	159	9	4	1-1	1030.1	1028	469	441	134	187-23	669
Major League totals (14 years)	87	64	.576	3.93	246	224	12	6	1-1	1410.2	1446	668	616	192	256-26	899

DIVISION SERIES RECORD

Year League	W	L	Pct.	ERA	G	GS	CG	ShO	Sv.-Opp.	IP	H	R	ER	HR	BB-IBB	SO
1999— New York (N.L.)	1	0	1.000	3.00	1	1	0	0	0-0	6.0	4	2	2	1	3-0	2
2000— New York (N.L.)	0	0	...	3.00	1	1	0	0	0-0	6.0	7	2	2	0	2-1	6
2002— Minnesota (A.L.)	0	1	.000	7.20	1	1	0	0	0-0	5.0	6	4	4	4	2-0	8
Division series totals (3 years)	1	1	.500	4.24	3	3	0	0	0-0	17.0	17	8	8	5	7-1	16

CHAMPIONSHIP SERIES RECORD

Year League	W	L	Pct.	ERA	G	GS	CG	ShO	Sv.-Opp.	IP	H	R	ER	HR	BB-IBB	SO
1999— New York (N.L.)	0	0	...	2.57	1	1	0	0	0-0	7.0	3	2	2	2	0-0	5
2000— New York (N.L.)	0	1	.000	10.80	1	1	0	0	0-0	3.1	8	5	4	0	1-0	4
2002— Minnesota (A.L.)	0	1	.000	10.13	1	1	0	0	0-0	5.1	8	6	6	2	0-0	0
Champ. series totals (3 years)	0	2	.000	6.89	3	3	0	0	0-0	15.2	19	13	12	4	1-0	9

WORLD SERIES RECORD

Year League	W	L	Pct.	ERA	G	GS	CG	ShO	Sv.-Opp.	IP	H	R	ER	HR	BB-IBB	SO
2000— New York (N.L.)	0	0	...	3.00	1	1	0	0	0-0	6.0	6	2	2	0	1-0	8

ALL-STAR GAME RECORD

	W	L	Pct.	ERA	GS	CG	ShO	Sv.-Opp.	IP	H	R	ER	HR	BB-IBB	SO
All-Star Game totals (1 year)	1998—Selected, did not play.														

REED, STEVE P

PERSONAL: Born March 11, 1966, in Los Angeles. ... 6-2/212. ... Throws right, bats right. ... Full name: Steven Vincent Reed.

HIGH SCHOOL: Chatsworth (Calif.).

COLLEGE: Lewis-Clark State College (Idaho).

TRANSACTIONS/CAREER NOTES: Signed as non-drafted free agent by San Francisco Giants organization (June 24, 1988). ... On disabled list (July 17-August 13, 1990). ... Selected by Colorado Rockies in third round (60th pick overall) of expansion draft (November 17, 1992). ... Granted free agency (December 21, 1997). ... Signed by Giants (December 24, 1997). ... Traded by Giants with OF Jacob Cruz to Cleveland Indians for P Jose Mesa, IF Shawon Dunston and P Alvin Morman (July 23, 1998). ... Traded by Indians with P Steve Karsay to Atlanta Braves for P John Rocker and 3B Troy Cameron (June 22, 2001). ... Granted free agency (November 5, 2001). ... Signed by San Diego Padres organization (January 23, 2002). ... Traded by Padres with P Jason Middlebrook to New York Mets for P Bobby M. Jones, P Josh Reynolds and OF Jay Bay (July 31, 2002). ... Granted free agency (October 28, 2002).

MISCELLANEOUS: Holds Colorado Rockies all-time record for lowest earned-run average (3.68).

CAREER HITTING (MLB): 3-for-23 (.130), 0 R, 0 2B, 0 3B, 0 HR, 0 RBI.

Year League	W	L	Pct.	ERA	G	GS	CG	ShO	Sv.-Opp.	IP	H	R	ER	HR	BB-IBB	SO
1988—Pocatello (Pio.)	4	1	.800	2.54	31	0	0	0	*13-...	46.0	42	20	13	3	8-1	49
1989—Clinton (Midw.)	5	3	.625	1.05	60	0	0	0	26-...	94.2	54	16	11	1	38-10	104
—San Jose (Calif.)	0	0	...	0.00	2	0	0	0	0-...	2.0	0	0	0	0	1-0	3
1990—Shreveport (Texas)	3	1	.750	1.64	45	1	0	0	8-...	60.1	53	20	11	2	20-6	59
1991—Shreveport (Texas)	2	0	1.000	0.83	15	0	0	0	7-...	21.2	17	2	2	1	3-0	26
—Phoenix (PCL)	2	3	.400	4.31	41	0	0	0	6-...	56.1	62	33	27	5	12-0	46
1992—Shreveport (Texas)	1	0	1.000	0.62	27	0	0	0	23-...	29.0	18	3	2	1	0-0	33
—Phoenix (PCL)	0	1	.000	3.48	29	0	0	0	20-...	31.0	27	13	12	2	10-3	30
—San Francisco (N.L.)	1	0	1.000	2.30	18	0	0	0	0-0	15.2	13	5	4	2	3-0	11
1993—Colorado (N.L.)■	9	5	.643	4.48	64	0	0	0	3-6	84.1	80	47	42	13	30-5	51
—Colorado Springs (PCL)	0	0	...	0.00	11	0	0	0	7-...	12.1	8	1	0	0	3-1	10
1994—Colorado (N.L.)	3	2	.600	3.94	*61	0	0	0	3-10	64.0	79	33	28	9	26-3	51
1995—Colorado (N.L.)	5	2	.714	2.14	71	0	0	0	3-6	84.0	61	24	20	8	21-3	79
1996—Colorado (N.L.)	4	3	.571	3.96	70	0	0	0	0-6	75.0	66	38	33	11	19-0	51
1997—Colorado (N.L.)	4	6	.400	4.04	63	0	0	0	6-13	62.1	49	28	28	10	27-1	43
1998—San Francisco (N.L.)■	2	1	.667	1.48	50	0	0	0	1-5	54.2	30	10	9	4	19-5	50
—Cleveland (A.L.)■	2	2	.500	6.66	20	0	0	0	0-1	25.2	26	19	19	4	8-0	23
1999—Cleveland (A.L.)	3	2	.600	4.23	63	0	0	0	0-3	61.2	69	33	29	10	20-5	44
2000—Cleveland (A.L.)	2	0	1.000	4.34	57	0	0	0	0-1	56.0	58	30	27	7	21-4	39
2001—Cleveland (A.L.)	1	1	.500	3.62	31	0	0	0	0-1	27.1	22	11	11	3	10-2	21
—Atlanta (N.L.)■	2	2	.500	3.48	39	0	0	0	1-1	31.0	30	14	12	3	13-3	25
2002—San Diego (N.L.)■	2	4	.333	1.98	40	0	0	0	1-3	41.0	33	9	9	2	10-2	36
—New York (N.L.)■	0	1	.000	2.08	24	0	0	0	0-1	26.0	23	6	6	0	4-1	14
A.L. totals (4 years)	8	5	.615	4.54	171	0	0	0	0-6	170.2	175	93	86	24	59-11	127
N.L. totals (9 years)	32	26	.552	3.20	500	0	0	0	18-51	538.0	464	214	191	62	172-23	411
Major League totals (11 years)	40	31	.563	3.52	671	0	0	0	18-57	708.2	639	307	277	86	231-34	538

DIVISION SERIES RECORD

Year League	W	L	Pct.	ERA	G	GS	CG	ShO	Sv.-Opp.	IP	H	R	ER	HR	BB-IBB	SO
1995—Colorado (N.L.)	0	0	...	0.00	3	0	0	0	0-1	2.2	2	0	0	0	1-1	3
1998—Cleveland (A.L.)	1	0	1.000	40.50	2	0	0	0	0-0	.2	1	3	3	0	1-0	1
1999—Cleveland (A.L.)	0	0	...	30.86	2	0	0	0	0-0	2.1	9	8	8	1	1-0	1
2001—Atlanta (N.L.)	0	0	...	0.00	1	0	0	0	0-0	.1	0	0	0	0	0-0	0
Division series totals (4 years)	1	0	1.000	16.50	8	0	0	0	0-1	6.0	12	11	11	1	3-1	5

CHAMPIONSHIP SERIES RECORD

Year League	W	L	Pct.	ERA	G	GS	CG	ShO	Sv.-Opp.	IP	H	R	ER	HR	BB-IBB	SO
1998—Cleveland (A.L.)	0	0	...	0.00	3	0	0	0	0-0	1.2	0	0	0	0	1-0	0

REESE, POKEY — 2B — PIRATES

PERSONAL: Born June 10, 1973, in Columbia, S.C. ... 5-11/188. ... Bats right, throws right. ... Full name: Calvin Reese Jr.
HIGH SCHOOL: Lower Richland (Hopkins, S.C.).
TRANSACTIONS/CAREER NOTES: Selected by Cincinnati Reds organization in first round (20th pick overall) of free-agent draft (June 3, 1991). ... On disabled list (June 23-July 25, 1995; September 17, 1996-remainder of season; and July 31, 1998-remainder of season). ... Traded by Reds with P Dennys Reyes to Colorado Rockies for P Gabe White and P Luke Hudson (December 18, 2001). ... Traded by Rockies to Boston Red Sox for C Scott Hatteberg (December 19, 2001). ... Granted free agency (December 21, 2001). ... Signed by Pittsburgh Pirates organization (January 30, 2002). ... On disabled list (April 20-May 5, 2002).
RECORDS: Shares N.L. record for most errors by shortstop in opening game of season (nine-inning game) since 1900—4 (March 31, 1998).
HONORS: Won N.L. Gold Glove at second base (1999 and 2000).
STATISTICAL NOTES: Led Southern League shortstops with 221 putouts in 1994.
2002 GAMES PLAYED BY POSITION (MLB): 2B—117.

		BATTING													FIELDING	
Year Team (League)	Pos.	G	AB	R	H	2B	3B	HR	RBI	BB	SO	SB-CS	Avg.	OBP	SLG	E	Avg.
1991—Princeton (Appl.)	SS	62	231	30	55	8	3	3	27	23	44	10-8	.238	.305	.338	*31	.885
1992—Charl., W.Va. (S.Atl.)	SS	106	380	50	102	19	3	6	53	24	75	19-8	.268	.315	.382	34	.932
1993—Chattanooga (Sou.)	SS	102	345	35	73	17	4	3	37	23	77	8-5	.212	.258	.310	25	.951
1994—Chattanooga (Sou.)	SS	134	484	77	130	23	4	12	49	43	75	21-4	.269	.336	.407	38	.939
1995—Indianapolis (A.A.)	SS	89	343	51	82	21	1	10	46	36	81	8-5	.239	.316	.394	27	.935
1996—Indianapolis (A.A.)	SS-3B	79	280	26	65	16	0	1	23	21	46	5-2	.232	.294	.300	22	.944
1997—Cincinnati (N.L.)	SS-2B-3B	128	397	48	87	15	0	4	26	31	82	25-7	.219	.284	.287	15	.969
—Indianapolis (A.A.)	SS-2B	17	72	12	17	2	0	4	11	9	12	4-0	.236	.321	.431	3	.966
1998—Cincinnati (N.L.)	3B-SS-2B	59	133	20	34	2	2	1	16	14	28	3-2	.256	.322	.323	8	.941
1999—Cincinnati (N.L.)	2B-SS	149	585	85	167	37	5	10	52	35	81	38-7	.285	.330	.417	7	.991
2000—Cincinnati (N.L.)	2B	135	518	76	132	20	6	12	46	45	86	29-3	.255	.319	.386	14	.980
2001—Cincinnati (N.L.)	SS-2B	133	428	50	96	20	2	9	40	34	82	25-4	.224	.284	.343	15	.975
2002—Pittsburgh (N.L.)■	2B	119	421	46	111	25	0	4	50	41	81	12-1	.264	.330	.352	8	.988
Major League totals (6 years)		723	2482	325	627	119	15	40	230	200	440	132-24	.253	.312	.361	67	.980

REICHERT, DAN — P — DEVIL RAYS

PERSONAL: Born July 12, 1976, in Monterey, Calif. ... 6-3/175. ... Throws right, bats right. ... Full name: Daniel Robert Reichert.
HIGH SCHOOL: Turlock (Calif.).
COLLEGE: Pacific.
TRANSACTIONS/CAREER NOTES: Selected by Kansas City Royals organization in first round (seventh pick overall) of free-agent draft (June 3, 1997). ... On Kansas City disabled list (August 25, 1999-remainder of season). ... Claimed on waivers by Tampa Bay Devil Rays (September 20, 2002).
STATISTICAL NOTES: Led A.L. in wild pitches with 18 in 2000.
CAREER HITTING (MLB): 1-for-9 (.111), 0 R, 0 2B, 0 3B, 0 HR, 0 RBI.

Year	League	W	L	Pct.	ERA	G	GS	CG	ShO	Sv.-Opp.	IP	H	R	ER	HR	BB-IBB	SO
1997—	Spokane (N'West)	3	4	.429	2.84	9	9	0	0	0-...	38.0	40	25	12	2	16-0	39
1998—	Wichita (Texas)	1	4	.200	9.75	8	8	0	0	0-...	36.0	52	40	39	7	29-1	24
—	Lansing (Midw.)	1	1	.500	3.28	13	6	0	0	0-...	35.2	25	16	13	0	20-0	35
—	Wilmington (Caro.)	2	0	1.000	3.21	2	2	0	0	0-...	14.0	13	5	5	0	4-0	10
—	Omaha (PCL)	1	1	.500	4.67	3	3	0	0	0-...	17.1	14	10	9	2	2-0	11
1999—	Omaha (PCL)	9	2	.818	3.71	17	17	1	0	0-...	111.2	92	51	46	9	50-0	123
—	Kansas City (A.L.)	2	2	.500	9.08	8	8	0	0	0-0	36.2	48	38	37	2	32-1	20
2000—	Kansas City (A.L.)	8	10	.444	4.70	44	18	1	1	2-6	153.1	157	92	80	15	91-1	94
2001—	Kansas City (A.L.)	8	8	.500	5.63	27	19	0	0	0-0	123.0	131	83	77	14	67-2	77
—	Omaha (PCL)	1	5	.167	8.27	10	5	1	0	0-...	32.2	45	30	30	4	16-0	30
2002—	Kansas City (A.L.)	3	5	.375	5.32	30	6	0	0	0-0	66.0	77	48	39	10	25-2	36
—	Omaha (PCL)	0	0	...	5.40	5	0	0	0	0-...	5.0	6	3	3	0	4-1	3
—	Wichita (Texas)	0	1	.000	11.45	8	0	0	0	0-...	11.0	16	15	14	0	9-0	11
Major League totals (4 years)		21	25	.457	5.53	109	51	1	1	2-6	379.0	413	261	233	41	215-6	227

R

REITSMA, CHRIS — P — REDS

PERSONAL: Born December 31, 1977, in Minneapolis. ... 6-5/215. ... Throws right, bats right. ... Full name: Christopher Michael Reitsma.

HIGH SCHOOL: Calgary (Alta.) Christian.

TRANSACTIONS/CAREER NOTES: Selected by Boston Red Sox organization as "sandwich pick" between first and second round of free-agent draft (June 4, 1996); pick received as compensation for Toronto Blue Jays signing P Erik Hanson. ... On disabled list (June 5-September 8, 1997). ... On disabled list (April 8-May 3, 1999). ... Selected by Tampa Bay Devil Rays from Red Sox organization in Rule 5 major league draft (December 13, 1999). ... Returned to Red Sox (March 28, 2000). ... On Trenton disabled list (July 14-22, 2000). ... Traded by Red Sox with P John Curtice to Cincinnati Reds for OF Dante Bichette (August 31, 2000).

MISCELLANEOUS: Appeared in two games as pinch runner (2001).

CAREER HITTING (MLB): 8-for-78 (.103), 3 R, 1 2B, 0 3B, 0 HR, 3 RBI.

Year	League	W	L	Pct.	ERA	G	GS	CG	ShO	Sv.-Opp.	IP	H	R	ER	HR	BB-IBB	SO
1996—	Gulf Coast Red Sox (GCL)	3	1	.750	1.35	7	6	0	0	0-...	26.2	24	7	4	0	1-0	32
1997—	Michigan (Midw.)	4	1	.800	2.90	9	9	0	0	0-...	49.2	57	23	16	4	13-0	41
1998—	Sarasota (FSL)	0	0	...	2.84	8	8	0	0	0-...	12.2	12	6	4	0	5-0	9
1999—	Sarasota (FSL)	4	10	.286	5.61	19	19	0	0	0-...	96.1	116	71	60	11	31-1	79
2000—	Sarasota (FSL)	3	4	.429	3.66	11	11	0	0	0-...	64.0	57	29	26	3	17-0	47
—	Trenton (East.)	7	2	.778	2.58	14	14	1	0	0-...	90.2	78	28	26	7	21-1	58
2001—	Cincinnati (N.L.)■	7	15	.318	5.29	36	29	0	0	0-0	182.0	209	121	107	23	49-6	96
2002—	Cincinnati (N.L.)	6	12	.333	3.64	32	21	1	1	0-0	138.1	144	73	56	17	45-5	84
—	Louisville (I.L.)	2	0	1.000	3.86	3	3	1	0	0-...	21.0	17	10	9	2	8-1	13
Major League totals (2 years)		13	27	.325	4.58	68	50	1	1	0-0	320.1	353	194	163	40	94-11	180

REKAR, BRYAN — P

PERSONAL: Born June 3, 1972, in Oak Lawn, Ill. ... 6-3/220. ... Throws right, bats right. ... Full name: Bryan Robert Rekar. ... Cousin of Pete Bercich, linebacker with Minnesota Vikings (1994-2000); and nephew of Bob Bercich, defensive back with Dallas Cowboys (1960 and 1961).

HIGH SCHOOL: Providence Catholic (New Lenox, Ill.).

COLLEGE: Bradley.

TRANSACTIONS/CAREER NOTES: Selected by Colorado Rockies organization in second round of free-agent draft (June 3, 1993). ... Selected by Tampa Bay Devil Rays in second round (38th pick overall) of expansion draft (November 18, 1997). ... On Tampa Bay disabled list (March 19-July 6, 1998); included rehabilitation assignments to St. Petersburg (May 16-25 and June 25-July 4) and Durham (May 26-June 1 and July 4-6). ... On Tampa Bay disabled list (March 31-April 30, 2000); included rehabilitation assignment to Durham (April 9-30). ... On Tampa Bay disabled list (July 20-August 26, 2001); included rehabilitation assignment to Orlando (August 9-26). ... Released by Devil Rays (December 13, 2001). ... Signed by Kansas City Royals organization (December 23, 2001). ... Traded by Royals to Rockies for P Eduardo Villacis (May 17, 2002). ... Released by Rockies (September 30, 2002).

STATISTICAL NOTES: Tied for Pacific Coast League lead with 203 hits allowed in 2002.

MISCELLANEOUS: Holds Tampa Bay Devil Rays all-time record for most innings pitched (495 1/3).

CAREER HITTING (MLB): 8-for-55 (.145), 4 R, 2 2B, 0 3B, 0 HR, 1 RBI.

Year	League	W	L	Pct.	ERA	G	GS	CG	ShO	Sv.-Opp.	IP	H	R	ER	HR	BB-IBB	SO
1993—	Bend (N'West)	3	5	.375	4.08	13	13	1	0	0-...	75.0	81	36	34	8	18-2	59
1994—	Central Valley (Calif.)	6	6	.500	3.48	22	19	0	0	0-...	111.1	120	52	43	3	31-2	91
1995—	New Haven (East.)	6	3	.667	2.13	12	12	1	1	0-...	80.1	65	28	19	4	16-1	80
—	Colorado Springs (PCL)	4	2	.667	1.49	7	7	2	1	0-...	48.1	29	10	8	0	13-0	39
—	Colorado (N.L.)	4	6	.400	4.98	15	14	1	0	0-0	85.0	95	51	47	11	24-2	60
1996—	Colorado (N.L.)	2	4	.333	8.95	14	11	0	0	0-1	58.1	87	61	58	11	26-1	25
—	Colorado Springs (PCL)	8	8	.500	4.46	19	19	0	0	0-...	123.0	138	68	61	13	36-1	75
1997—	Colorado Springs (PCL)	10	9	.526	5.46	28	25	0	0	0-...	145.0	169	96	88	21	39-2	116
—	Colorado (N.L.)	1	0	1.000	5.79	2	2	0	0	0-0	9.1	11	7	6	3	6-0	4
1998—	St. Petersburg (FSL)■	0	0	...	0.69	4	4	0	0	0-...	13.0	6	2	1	0	2-0	15
—	Durham (I.L.)	0	1	.000	3.27	3	3	0	0	0-...	11.0	10	4	4	3	2-0	9
—	Tampa Bay (A.L.)	2	8	.200	4.98	16	15	1	0	0-0	86.2	95	56	48	16	21-0	55
1999—	Durham (I.L.)	4	1	.800	3.86	6	5	0	0	0-...	35.0	29	15	15	3	8-0	26
—	Tampa Bay (A.L.)	6	6	.500	5.80	27	12	0	0	0-0	94.2	121	68	61	14	41-2	55
2000—	Durham (I.L.)	3	0	1.000	2.05	4	4	0	0	0-...	22.0	16	5	5	1	4-0	18
—	Tampa Bay (A.L.)	7	10	.412	4.41	30	27	2	0	0-0	173.1	200	92	85	22	39-0	95
2001—	Tampa Bay (A.L.)	3	13	.188	5.89	25	25	0	0	0-0	140.2	167	104	92	21	45-2	87
—	Orlando (Sou.)	1	0	1.000	2.25	3	3	0	0	0-...	12.0	8	3	3	0	1-0	11
2002—	Omaha (PCL)■	0	0	...	4.50	5	4	0	0	0-...	24.0	30	16	12	4	5-0	20
—	Kansas City (A.L.)	0	2	.000	15.43	2	2	0	0	0-0	7.0	12	12	12	1	6-0	2
—	Colorado Springs (PCL)■	7	10	.412	5.93	20	20	0	0	0-...	123.0	§173	91	81	14	35-1	88
A.L. totals (5 years)		18	39	.316	5.34	100	81	3	0	0-0	502.1	595	332	298	74	152-4	294
N.L. totals (3 years)		7	10	.412	6.54	31	27	1	0	0-1	152.2	193	119	111	25	56-3	89
Major League totals (8 years)		25	49	.338	5.62	131	108	4	0	0-1	655.0	788	451	409	99	208-7	383

RELAFORD, DESI SS MARINERS

PERSONAL: Born September 16, 1973, in Valdosta, Ga. ... 5-9/174. ... Bats both, throws right. ... Full name: Desmond Lamont Relaford.
HIGH SCHOOL: Sandalwood (Jacksonville).
TRANSACTIONS/CAREER NOTES: Selected by Seattle Mariners organization in fourth round of free-agent draft (June 3, 1991). ... Traded by Mariners to Philadelphia Phillies for P Terry Mulholland (July 31, 1996). ... On Philadelphia disabled list (June 17-September 13, 1999); included rehabilitation assignment to Clearwater (September 4-13). ... Traded by Phillies to San Diego Padres for a player to be named later (August 4, 2000); Phillies acquired IF David Newhan to complete deal (August 7, 2000). ... Claimed on waivers by New York Mets (October 12, 2000). ... Traded by Mets with OF Tsuyoshi Shinjo to San Francisco Giants for P Shawn Estes (December 16, 2001). ... Traded by Giants with cash to Mariners for 3B David Bell (January 25, 2002).
STATISTICAL NOTES: Led Carolina League shortstops with 382 assists in 1992. ... Tied for Southern League lead in errors by shortstops with 35 in 1993. ... Led International League shortstops with 373 assists, 587 total chances and 81 double plays in 1997. ... Led N.L. shortstops with 31 errors in 2000.
2002 GAMES PLAYED BY POSITION (MLB): SS—40; 3B—38; OF—35; 2B—11; DH—4.

			BATTING														FIELDING	
Year	Team (League)	Pos.	G	AB	R	H	2B	3B	HR	RBI	BB	SO	SB-CS	Avg.	OBP	SLG	E	Avg.
1991—	Ariz. Mariners (Ariz.)	SS-2B	46	163	36	44	7	3	0	18	22	24	17-3	.270	.351	.350	24	.885
1992—	Peninsula (Caro.)	SS	130	445	53	96	18	1	3	34	39	88	27-7	.216	.277	.281	*52	.913
1993—	Jacksonville (Sou.)	SS-2B-3B	133	472	49	115	16	4	8	47	50	103	16-12	.244	.323	.345	‡38	.935
1994—	Jacksonville (Sou.)	SS	37	143	24	29	7	3	3	11	22	28	10-1	.203	.305	.357	4	.979
—	Riverside (Calif.)	SS	99	374	95	116	27	5	5	59	78	78	27-6	.310	.429	.449	36	.921
1995—	Port City (Sou.)	SS-2B-DH	90	352	51	101	11	2	7	27	41	58	25-9	.287	.365	.389	31	.930
—	Tacoma (PCL)	2B-SS	30	113	20	27	5	1	2	7	13	24	6-0	.239	.313	.354	6	.960
1996—	Tacoma (PCL)	2B-SS-DH	93	317	27	65	12	0	4	32	23	58	10-6	.205	.259	.281	20	.960
—	Philadelphia (N.L.)■	SS-2B	15	40	2	7	2	0	0	1	3	9	1-0	.175	.233	.225	2	.959
—	Scranton/W.B. (I.L.)	SS	21	85	12	20	4	1	1	11	8	19	7-1	.235	.305	.341	6	.938
1997—	Scranton/W.B. (I.L.)	SS	131	517	82	138	34	4	9	53	43	77	29-8	.267	.329	.400	34	.942
—	Philadelphia (N.L.)	SS	15	38	3	7	1	2	0	6	5	6	3-0	.184	.279	.316	1	.977
1998—	Philadelphia (N.L.)	SS	142	494	45	121	25	3	5	41	33	87	9-5	.245	.293	.338	24	.960
1999—	Philadelphia (N.L.)	SS	65	211	31	51	11	2	1	26	19	34	4-3	.242	.322	.327	14	.952
—	Clearwater (FSL)	SS	2	7	1	2	0	0	0	1	1	1	0-0	.286	.375	.286	1	.800
2000—	Philadelphia (N.L.)	SS	83	253	29	56	12	3	3	30	48	45	5-0	.221	.363	.328	24	.930
—	San Diego (N.L.)■	SS	45	157	26	32	2	0	2	16	27	26	8-0	.204	.330	.255	§7	.965
2001—	New York (N.L.)■	2B-SS-3B-P	120	301	43	91	27	0	8	36	27	65	13-5	.302	.364	.472	11	.963
2002—	Seattle (A.L.)■	S-3-O-2-D	112	329	55	88	13	2	6	43	33	51	10-3	.267	.339	.374	10	.965
American League totals (1 year)			112	329	55	88	13	2	6	43	33	51	10-3	.267	.339	.374	10	.965
National League totals (6 years)			485	1494	179	365	80	10	19	156	162	272	43-13	.244	.326	.349	83	.954
Major League totals (7 years)			597	1823	234	453	93	12	25	199	195	323	53-16	.248	.329	.354	93	.956

RECORD AS PITCHER

Year	League	W	L	Pct.	ERA	G	GS	CG	ShO	Sv.-Opp.	IP	H	R	ER	HR	BB-IBB	SO
2001—	New York (N.L.)	0	0	...	0.00	1	0	0	0	0-0	1.0	0	0	0	0	0-0	1

REMLINGER, MIKE P

PERSONAL: Born March 23, 1966, in Middletown, N.Y. ... 6-1/210. ... Throws left, bats left. ... Full name: Michael John Remlinger. ... Name pronounced REM-lynn-jer.
HIGH SCHOOL: Carver (Plymouth, Mass.).
COLLEGE: Dartmouth.
TRANSACTIONS/CAREER NOTES: Selected by San Francisco Giants organization in first round (16th pick overall) of free-agent draft (June 2, 1987). ... On disabled list (April 30, 1988-remainder of season). ... Traded by Giants with OF Kevin Mitchell to Seattle Mariners for P Bill Swift, P Mike Jackson and P Dave Burba (December 11, 1991). ... On Jacksonville disabled list (July 30, 1992-remainder of season). ... Granted free agency (October 15, 1993). ... Signed by New York Mets organization (November 22, 1993). ... Traded by Mets to Cincinnati Reds for OF Cobi Cradle (May 11, 1995). ... Granted free agency (October 6, 1995). ... Re-signed by Reds (October 22, 1995). ... Traded by Reds to Kansas City Royals as part of a three-team deal in which Reds sent SS Luis Ordaz to St. Louis Cardinals for OF Andre King. Royals then sent OF Miguel Mejia to Cardinals to complete deal (December 4, 1995). ... Claimed on waivers by Reds (April 4, 1996). ... Traded by Reds with 2B Bret Boone to Atlanta Braves for P Denny Neagle, OF Michael Tucker and P Rob Bell (November 10, 1998). ... On disabled list (April 3-18, 1999; and June 23-July 13, 2000; and August 8-24, 2002). ... Granted free agency (October 28, 2002).
RECORDS: Shares major league record for pitching shutout in first major league game (June 15, 1991).
STATISTICAL NOTES: Led American Association with 18 wild pitches in 1996. ... Led N.L. with 12 wild pitches in 1997.
MISCELLANEOUS: Appeared in two games as pinch runner (1997).
CAREER HITTING (MLB): 8-for-108 (.074), 5 R, 3 2B, 0 3B, 0 HR, 8 RBI.

Year	League	W	L	Pct.	ERA	G	GS	CG	ShO	Sv.-Opp.	IP	H	R	ER	HR	BB-IBB	SO
1987—	Everett (N'West)	0	0	...	3.60	2	1	0	0	0-...	5.0	1	2	2	0	5-0	11
—	Clinton (Midw.)	2	1	.667	3.30	6	5	0	0	0-...	30.0	21	12	11	2	14-0	43
—	Shreveport (Texas)	4	2	.667	2.36	6	6	0	0	0-...	34.1	14	11	9	2	22-0	51
1988—	Shreveport (Texas)	1	0	1.000	0.69	3	3	0	0	0-...	13.0	7	4	1	0	4-0	18
1989—	Shreveport (Texas)	4	6	.400	2.98	16	16	0	0	0-...	90.2	68	43	30	2	73-0	92
—	Phoenix (PCL)	1	6	.143	9.21	11	10	0	0	0-...	43.0	51	47	44	8	52-0	28
1990—	Shreveport (Texas)	9	11	.450	3.90	25	25	2	1	0-...	147.2	149	82	64	9	72-1	75
1991—	Phoenix (PCL)	5	5	.500	6.38	19	19	1	1	0-...	108.2	134	86	77	15	59-0	68
—	San Francisco (N.L.)	2	1	.667	4.37	8	6	1	1	0-0	35.0	36	17	17	5	20-1	19
1992—	Calgary (PCL)■	1	7	.125	6.65	21	11	0	0	0-...	70.1	97	65	52	7	48-1	24
—	Jacksonville (Sou.)	1	1	.500	3.46	5	5	0	0	0-...	26.0	25	15	10	1	11-0	21
1993—	Calgary (PCL)	4	3	.571	5.53	19	18	0	0	0-...	84.2	100	57	52	8	52-0	51
—	Jacksonville (Sou.)	1	3	.250	6.58	7	7	0	0	0-...	39.2	40	30	29	7	19-0	23
1994—	Norfolk (I.L.)■	2	4	.333	3.14	12	9	0	0	0-...	63.0	57	29	22	5	25-0	45
—	New York (N.L.)	1	5	.167	4.61	10	9	0	0	0-0	54.2	55	30	28	9	35-4	33
1995—	New York (N.L.)	0	1	.000	6.35	5	0	0	0	0-1	5.2	7	5	4	1	2-0	6
—	Cincinnati (N.L.)■	0	0	...	9.00	2	0	0	0	0-0	1.0	2	1	1	0	3-0	1
—	Indianapolis (A.A.)	5	3	.625	4.05	41	1	0	0	0-...	46.2	40	24	21	4	32-4	58

Year	League	W	L	Pct.	ERA	G	GS	CG	ShO	Sv.-Opp.	IP	H	R	ER	HR	BB-IBB	SO
1996—	Indianapolis (A.A.)	4	3	.571	2.52	28	13	0	0	0-...	89.1	64	29	25	4	44-0	97
—	Cincinnati (N.L.)	0	1	.000	5.60	19	4	0	0	0-0	27.1	24	17	17	4	19-2	19
1997—	Cincinnati (N.L.)	8	8	.500	4.14	69	12	2	0	2-2	124.0	100	61	57	11	60-6	145
1998—	Cincinnati (N.L.)	8	15	.348	4.82	35	28	1	1	0-0	164.1	164	96	88	23	87-1	144
1999—	Atlanta (N.L.)■	10	1	.909	2.37	73	0	0	0	1-3	83.2	66	24	22	9	35-5	81
2000—	Atlanta (N.L.)	5	3	.625	3.47	71	0	0	0	12-16	72.2	55	29	28	6	37-1	72
2001—	Atlanta (N.L.)	3	3	.500	2.76	74	0	0	0	1-5	75.0	67	25	23	9	23-4	93
2002—	Atlanta (N.L.)	7	3	.700	1.99	73	0	0	0	0-5	68.0	48	17	15	3	28-3	69
Major League totals (10 years)		44	41	.518	3.80	439	59	4	2	16-32	711.1	624	322	300	80	349-27	682

DIVISION SERIES RECORD

Year	League	W	L	Pct.	ERA	G	GS	CG	ShO	Sv.-Opp.	IP	H	R	ER	HR	BB-IBB	SO
1999—	Atlanta (N.L.)	0	0	...	9.82	2	0	0	0	0-1	3.2	4	4	4	1	3-2	4
2000—	Atlanta (N.L.)	0	0	...	2.70	3	0	0	0	0-0	3.1	6	1	1	1	0-0	3
2001—	Atlanta (N.L.)	0	0	...	0.00	1	0	0	0	0-0	.1	0	0	0	0	0-0	0
2002—	Atlanta (N.L.)	0	0	...	4.50	3	0	0	0	0-0	2.0	3	1	1	0	2-0	3
Division series totals (4 years)		0	0	...	5.79	9	0	0	0	0-1	9.1	13	6	6	2	5-2	10

CHAMPIONSHIP SERIES RECORD

Year	League	W	L	Pct.	ERA	G	GS	CG	ShO	Sv.-Opp.	IP	H	R	ER	HR	BB-IBB	SO
1999—	Atlanta (N.L.)	0	1	.000	3.18	5	0	0	0	0-0	5.2	3	2	2	0	3-0	4
2001—	Atlanta (N.L.)	0	0	...	0.00	3	0	0	0	0-0	2.1	3	0	0	0	2-0	2
Champ. series totals (2 years)		0	1	.000	2.25	8	0	0	0	0-0	8.0	6	2	2	0	5-0	6

WORLD SERIES RECORD

Year	League	W	L	Pct.	ERA	G	GS	CG	ShO	Sv.-Opp.	IP	H	R	ER	HR	BB-IBB	SO
1999—	Atlanta (N.L.)	0	1	.000	9.00	2	0	0	0	0-0	1.0	1	1	1	1	1-0	0

ALL-STAR GAME RECORD

	W	L	Pct.	ERA	GS	CG	ShO	Sv.-Opp.	IP	H	R	ER	HR	BB-IBB	SO
All-Star Game totals (1 year)	0	0	...	27.00	0	0	0	0-0	.2	1	2	2	0	1-0	0

RENTERIA, EDGAR — SS — CARDINALS

PERSONAL: Born August 7, 1975, in Barranquilla, Colombia. ... 6-1/180. ... Bats right, throws right. ... Full name: Edgar Enrique Renteria. ... Brother of Edinson Renteria, infielder in Houston Astros and Florida Marlins organizations (1985-94).

HIGH SCHOOL: Instituto Los Alpes (Barranquilla, Colombia).

TRANSACTIONS/CAREER NOTES: Signed as non-drafted free agent by Florida Marlins organization (February 14, 1992). ... On Florida disabled list (June 24-July 11, 1996); included rehabilitation assignment to Charlotte (July 3-11). ... On disabled list (August 25-September 9, 1998). ... Traded by Marlins to St. Louis Cardinals for P Braden Looper, P Armando Almanza and SS Pablo Ozuna (December 14, 1998).

HONORS: Named shortstop on The Sporting News N.L. All-Star team (2000 and 2002). ... Named shortstop on The Sporting News N.L. Silver Slugger team (2000). ... Named shortstop on N.L. Silver Slugger team (2002). ... Won N.L. Gold Glove at shortstop (2002).

STATISTICAL NOTES: Tied for Midwest League lead with 173 putouts by shortstop in 1993. ... Had 22-game hitting streak (July 25-August 16, 1996). ... Led N.L. with 19 sacrifice hits in 1997. ... Led N.L. shortstops with 242 putouts in 1997. ... Led N.L. in caught stealing with 22 in 1998. ... Career major league grand slams: 2.

2002 GAMES PLAYED BY POSITION (MLB): SS—149.

			BATTING														FIELDING	
Year	Team (League)	Pos.	G	AB	R	H	2B	3B	HR	RBI	BB	SO	SB-CS	Avg.	OBP	SLG	E	Avg.
1992—	GC Marlins (GCL)	SS	43	163	25	47	8	1	0	9	8	29	10-6	.288	.329	.350	*24	.897
1993—	Kane County (Midw.)	SS	116	384	40	78	8	0	1	35	35	94	7-8	.203	.268	.232	34	.934
1994—	Brevard County (FSL)	SS	128	439	46	111	15	1	0	36	35	56	6-11	.253	.307	.292	23	.959
1995—	Portland (East.)	SS	135	508	70	147	15	7	7	68	32	85	30-11	.289	.329	.388	33	.944
1996—	Charlotte (I.L.)	SS	35	132	17	37	8	0	2	16	9	17	10-4	.280	.326	.386	7	.959
—	Florida (N.L.)	SS	106	431	68	133	18	3	5	31	33	68	16-2	.309	.358	.399	11	.979
1997—	Florida (N.L.)	SS	154	617	90	171	21	3	4	52	45	108	32-15	.277	.327	.340	17	.975
1998—	Florida (N.L.)	SS	133	517	79	146	18	2	3	31	48	78	41-22	.282	.347	.342	20	.966
1999—	St. Louis (N.L.)■	SS	154	585	92	161	36	2	11	63	53	82	37-8	.275	.334	.400	26	.959
2000—	St. Louis (N.L.)	SS	150	562	94	156	32	1	16	76	63	77	21-13	.278	.346	.423	27	.958
2001—	St. Louis (N.L.)	SS-1B-DH	141	493	54	128	19	3	10	57	39	73	17-4	.260	.314	.371	24	.961
2002—	St. Louis (N.L.)	SS	152	544	77	166	36	2	11	83	49	57	22-7	.305	.364	.439	19	.970
Major League totals (7 years)			990	3749	554	1061	180	16	60	393	330	543	186-71	.283	.341	.388	144	.967

DIVISION SERIES RECORD

			BATTING														FIELDING	
Year	Team (League)	Pos.	G	AB	R	H	2B	3B	HR	RBI	BB	SO	SB-CS	Avg.	OBP	SLG	E	Avg.
1997—	Florida (N.L.)	SS	3	13	1	2	0	0	0	1	2	4	0-0	.154	.267	.154	2	.909
2000—	St. Louis (N.L.)	SS	3	10	5	2	0	0	0	0	4	1	2-0	.200	.429	.200	1	.909
2001—	St. Louis (N.L.)	SS	5	17	2	4	1	0	1	1	2	4	0-0	.235	.316	.471	1	.955
2002—	St. Louis (N.L.)	SS	3	12	3	3	0	0	0	0	1	1	2-0	.250	.308	.250	1	.909
Division series totals (4 years)			14	52	11	11	1	0	1	2	9	10	4-0	.212	.328	.288	5	.924

CHAMPIONSHIP SERIES RECORD

RECORDS: Shares N.L. single-game record for most stolen bases—3 (October 12, 2000).

			BATTING														FIELDING	
Year	Team (League)	Pos.	G	AB	R	H	2B	3B	HR	RBI	BB	SO	SB-CS	Avg.	OBP	SLG	E	Avg.
1997—	Florida (N.L.)	SS	6	22	4	5	1	0	0	0	3	6	1-0	.227	.346	.273	0	1.000
2000—	St. Louis (N.L.)	SS	5	20	4	6	1	0	0	4	0	2	3-0	.300	.286	.350	0	1.000
2002—	St. Louis (N.L.)	SS	5	19	0	3	0	0	0	1	0	2	0-0	.158	.190	.158	1	.900
Championship series totals (3 years)			16	61	8	14	2	0	0	5	3	10	4-0	.230	.279	.262	1	.982

WORLD SERIES RECORD

RECORDS: Holds record for most strikeouts in one inning—2 (October 23, 1997, sixth inning).
NOTES: Member of World Series championship team (1997).

							BATTING										FIELDING	
Year	Team (League)	Pos.	G	AB	R	H	2B	3B	HR	RBI	BB	SO	SB-CS	Avg.	OBP	SLG	E	Avg.
1997—	Florida (N.L.)	SS	7	31	3	9	2	0	0	3	3	5	0-0	.290	.353	.355	1	.974

ALL-STAR GAME RECORD

	AB	R	H	2B	3B	HR	RBI	BB	SO	SB-CS	Avg.	OBP	SLG	E	Avg.
All-Star Game totals (2 years)	3	1	0	0	0	0	0	0	0	0-0	.000	.000	.000	0	1.000

RESTOVICH, MICHAEL — OF — TWINS

PERSONAL: Born January 3, 1979, in Rochester, Minn. ... 6-4/233. ... Bats right, throws right. ... Full name: Michael Jerome Restovich.
HIGH SCHOOL: Mayo (Rochester, Minn.).
TRANSACTIONS/CAREER NOTES: Selected by Minnesota Twins organization in second round of free-agent draft (June 3, 1997).
HONORS: Named Appalachian League Player of the Year (1998).
STATISTICAL NOTES: Tied for Appalachian League lead in hit by pitch with nine in 1998. ... Tied for Eastern League lead with eight intentional bases on balls received in 2001.
2002 GAMES PLAYED BY POSITION (MLB): OF—5; DH—2.

							BATTING										FIELDING	
Year	Team (League)	Pos.	G	AB	R	H	2B	3B	HR	RBI	BB	SO	SB-CS	Avg.	OBP	SLG	E	Avg.
1998—	Elizabethton (Appl.)	OF	65	242	*68	86	20	1	13	*64	*54	58	5-2	.355	*.489	.607	9	.912
—	Fort Wayne (Midw.)	OF	11	45	9	20	5	2	0	6	4	12	0-0	.444	.490	.644	0	1.000
1999—	Quad City (Midw.)	OF-3B	131	493	91	154	30	6	19	107	74	100	7-9	.312	.412	.513	9	.958
2000—	Fort Myers (FSL)	OF	135	475	73	125	27	9	8	64	61	100	19-7	.263	.350	.408	6	.975
2001—	New Britain (East.)	OF-1B	140	501	69	135	33	4	23	84	54	125	15-7	.269	.345	.489	3	.989
2002—	Edmonton (PCL)	OF	138	518	95	148	32	7	29	98	53	151	11-7	.286	.353	.542	6	.976
—	Minnesota (A.L.)	OF-DH	8	13	3	4	0	0	1	1	1	4	1-0	.308	.357	.538	0	1.000
Major League totals (1 year)			8	13	3	4	0	0	1	1	1	4	1-0	.308	.357	.538	0	1.000

REYES, AL — P — PIRATES

PERSONAL: Born April 10, 1971, in San Cristobal, Dominican Republic. ... 6-1/206. ... Throws right, bats right. ... Full name: Rafael Alberto Reyes.
HIGH SCHOOL: Francisco del Rosario Sanche (Santo Domingo, Dominican Republic).
TRANSACTIONS/CAREER NOTES: Signed as non-drafted free agent by Montreal Expos organization (February 17, 1988). ... On disabled list (May 23, 1991-remainder of season). ... Selected by Milwaukee Brewers from Expos organization in Rule 5 major league draft (December 5, 1994). ... On disabled list (July 19, 1995-remainder of season). ... On New Orleans disabled list (April 4-August 2, 1996). ... On Milwaukee disabled list (July 25-September 8, 1998); included rehabilitation assignment to Louisville (September 1-8). ... Traded by Brewers to Baltimore Orioles (July 21, 1999), completing deal in which Orioles traded P Rocky Coppinger to Brewers for a player to be named later (July 16, 1999). ... Traded by Orioles to Los Angeles Dodgers for P Alan Mills and cash considerations (June 13, 2000). ... On Las Vegas disabled list (April 5-May 8, 2001). ... Granted free agency (October 17, 2001). ... Signed by Pittsburgh Pirates organization (January 25, 2002).
CAREER HITTING (MLB): 2-for-10 (.200), 2 R, 0 2B, 0 3B, 0 HR, 0 RBI.

Year	League	W	L	Pct.	ERA	G	GS	CG	ShO	Sv.-Opp.	IP	H	R	ER	HR	BB-IBB	SO
1989—	Dominican Expos (DSL)	3	4	.429	2.79	12	10	1	0	0-...	71.0	68	36	22	...	33-...	49
1990—	West Palm Beach (FSL)	5	4	.556	4.74	16	10	0	0	1-...	57.0	58	32	30	4	32-2	47
1991—	Rockford (Midw.)	0	1	.000	5.56	3	3	0	0	0-...	11.1	14	8	7	1	2-0	10
1992—	Albany (S.Atl.)	0	2	.000	3.95	27	0	0	0	4-...	27.1	24	14	12	0	13-0	29
1993—	Burlington (Midw.)	7	6	.538	2.68	53	0	0	0	11-...	74.0	52	33	22	7	26-3	80
1994—	Harrisburg (East.)	2	2	.500	3.25	60	0	0	0	*35-...	69.1	68	26	25	4	13-0	60
1995—	Milwaukee (A.L.)■	1	1	.500	2.43	27	0	0	0	1-1	33.1	19	9	9	3	18-2	29
1996—	Beloit (Midw.)	1	0	1.000	1.83	13	0	0	0	0-...	19.2	17	7	4	1	6-0	22
—	Milwaukee (A.L.)	1	0	1.000	7.94	5	0	0	0	0-0	5.2	8	5	5	1	2-0	2
1997—	Tucson (PCL)	2	4	.333	5.02	38	0	0	0	7-...	57.1	52	39	32	12	34-2	70
—	Milwaukee (A.L.)	1	2	.333	5.46	19	0	0	0	1-1	29.2	32	19	18	4	9-0	28
1998—	Milwaukee (N.L.)	5	1	.833	3.95	50	0	0	0	0-1	57.0	55	26	25	9	31-1	58
—	Louisville (I.L.)	0	1	.000	8.31	3	2	0	0	0-...	4.1	5	5	4	1	2-0	5
1999—	Louisville (I.L.)	0	2	.000	8.38	6	0	0	0	0-...	9.2	12	9	9	0	7-2	8
—	Milwaukee (N.L.)	2	0	1.000	4.25	26	0	0	0	0-1	36.0	27	17	17	5	25-1	39
—	Baltimore (A.L.)■	2	3	.400	4.85	27	0	0	0	0-3	29.2	23	16	16	4	16-2	28
2000—	Rochester (I.L.)	0	1	.000	7.71	9	0	0	0	2-...	11.2	13	11	10	2	9-1	17
—	Baltimore (A.L.)	1	0	1.000	6.92	13	0	0	0	0-1	13.0	13	10	10	2	11-1	10
—	Albuquerque (PCL)■	3	2	.600	3.72	30	0	0	0	8-...	38.2	33	20	16	5	21-0	39
—	Los Angeles (N.L.)	0	0	...	0.00	6	0	0	0	0-0	6.2	2	0	0	0	1-0	8
2001—	Las Vegas (PCL)	0	1	.000	3.38	19	0	0	0	0-...	29.1	24	11	11	3	10-1	37
—	Los Angeles (N.L.)	2	1	.667	3.86	19	0	0	0	1-2	25.2	28	13	11	3	13-1	23
2002—	Nashville (PCL)■	7	3	.700	2.70	43	0	0	0	1-...	66.2	40	21	20	5	22-2	90
—	Pittsburgh (N.L.)	0	0	...	2.65	15	0	0	0	0-1	17.0	9	5	5	1	7-0	21
A.L. totals (5 years)		6	6	.500	4.69	91	0	0	0	2-6	111.1	95	59	58	14	56-5	97
N.L. totals (5 years)		9	2	.818	3.67	116	0	0	0	1-5	142.1	121	61	58	18	77-3	149
Major League totals (8 years)		15	8	.652	4.12	207	0	0	0	3-11	253.2	216	120	116	32	133-8	246

REYES, DENNYS — P — RANGERS

PERSONAL: Born April 19, 1977, in Higuera de Zaragoza, Mexico. ... 6-3/246. ... Throws left, bats right.
HIGH SCHOOL: Ignacio Zaragoza (Higuera de Zaragoza, Mexico).

TRANSACTIONS/CAREER NOTES: Signed as non-drafted free agent by Los Angeles Dodgers organization (July 5, 1993). ... Loaned by Dodgers organization to Mexico City Red Devils, Mexican League (March 28-August 22, 1995). ... Traded by Dodgers with 1B/3B Paul Konerko to Cincinnati Reds for P Jeff Shaw (July 4, 1998). ... On Cincinnati disabled list (May 30-July 2, 2001). ... Traded by Reds with 2B Pokey Reese to Colorado Rockies for P Gabe White and P Luke Hudson (December 18, 2001). ... Traded by Rockies with OF Todd Hollandsworth to Texas Rangers for OF Gabe Kapler and 2B Jason Romano (July 31, 2002).
MISCELLANEOUS: Appeared in one game as pinch hitter (2001).
CAREER HITTING (MLB): 3-for-43 (.070), 2 R, 1 2B, 0 3B, 0 HR, 0 RBI.

Year League	W	L	Pct.	ERA	G	GS	CG	ShO	Sv.-Opp.	IP	H	R	ER	HR	BB-IBB	SO
1993— MC Red Devils (Mex.)	0	1	.000	5.06	7	1	0	0	0-...	5.1	4	4	3	1	9-0	5
1994— Vero Beach (FSL)■	2	4	.333	6.70	9	9	0	0	0-...	41.2	58	37	31	6	18-0	25
— Great Falls (Pio.)	7	1	.875	3.78	14	9	0	0	0-...	66.2	71	37	28	0	25-0	70
1995— MC Red Devils (Mex.)■	5	5	.500	6.60	17	15	1	0	0-...	58.2	76	49	43	4	41-0	44
— Vero Beach (FSL)■	1	0	1.000	1.80	3	2	0	0	0-...	10.0	8	2	2	0	6-0	9
1996— San Bernardino (Calif.)■	11	12	.478	4.17	29	•28	0	0	0-...	166.0	166	106	77	11	77-0	176
1997— San Antonio (Texas)	8	1	.889	3.02	12	12	1	0	0-...	80.1	79	33	27	6	28-1	66
— Albuquerque (PCL)	6	3	.667	5.65	10	10	1	0	0-...	57.1	70	40	36	4	33-0	45
— Los Angeles (N.L.)	2	3	.400	3.83	14	5	0	0	0-0	47.0	51	21	20	4	18-3	36
1998— Albuquerque (PCL)	1	4	.200	1.44	7	7	1	1	0-...	43.2	31	13	7	5	18-0	58
— Los Angeles (N.L.)	0	4	.000	4.71	11	3	0	0	0-0	28.2	27	17	15	1	20-4	33
— Indianapolis (I.L.)■	2	0	1.000	3.00	4	4	0	0	0-...	24.0	20	10	8	1	14-0	27
— Cincinnati (N.L.)	3	1	.750	4.42	8	7	0	0	0-0	38.2	35	19	19	2	27-1	44
1999— Cincinnati (N.L.)	2	2	.500	3.79	65	1	0	0	2-3	61.2	53	30	26	5	39-1	72
2000— Cincinnati (N.L.)	2	1	.667	4.53	62	0	0	0	0-1	43.2	43	31	22	5	29-0	36
2001— Cincinnati (N.L.)	2	6	.250	4.92	35	6	0	0	0-0	53.0	51	35	29	5	35-1	52
— Louisville (I.L.)	4	2	.667	3.67	7	6	0	0	0-...	34.1	34	15	14	3	16-0	34
2002— Colorado (N.L.)■	0	1	.000	4.24	43	0	0	0	0-0	40.1	43	19	19	1	24-3	30
— Texas (A.L.)■	4	3	.571	6.38	15	5	0	0	0-0	42.1	55	33	30	9	21-1	29
A.L. totals (1 year)	4	3	.571	6.38	15	5	0	0	0-0	42.1	55	33	30	9	21-1	29
N.L. totals (6 years)	11	18	.379	4.31	238	22	0	0	2-4	313.0	303	172	150	23	192-13	303
Major League totals (6 years)	15	21	.417	4.56	253	27	0	0	2-4	355.1	358	205	180	32	213-14	332

REYNOLDS, SHANE P

PERSONAL: Born March 26, 1968, in Bastrop, La. ... 6-3/215. ... Throws right, bats right. ... Full name: Richard Shane Reynolds.
HIGH SCHOOL: Ouachita Christian (Monroe, La.).
JUNIOR COLLEGE: Faulkner State Junior College (Ala.).
COLLEGE: Texas.
TRANSACTIONS/CAREER NOTES: Selected by Houston Astros organization in third round of free-agent draft (June 5, 1989). ... On Houston disabled list (June 10-July 14, 1997); included rehabilitation assignment to New Orleans (July 10-14). ... On disabled list (August 2, 2000-remainder of season). ... On Houston disabled list (March 31-April 18 and August 14-September 1, 2001); included rehabilitation assignments to Round Rock (April 3-5) and New Orleans (April 5-18). ... On disabled list (June 14, 2002-remainder of season). ... Granted free agency (October 28, 2002).
STATISTICAL NOTES: Led N.L. with 17 sacrifice hits in 1999.
MISCELLANEOUS: Appeared in one game as pinch runner (1995).
CAREER HITTING (MLB): 72-for-492 (.146), 34 R, 15 2B, 0 3B, 5 HR, 40 RBI.

Year League	W	L	Pct.	ERA	G	GS	CG	ShO	Sv.-Opp.	IP	H	R	ER	HR	BB-IBB	SO
1989— Auburn (NY-Penn)	3	2	.600	2.31	6	6	1	0	0-...	35.0	36	16	9	1	14-0	23
— Asheville (S.Atl.)	5	3	.625	3.68	8	8	2	1	0-...	51.1	53	25	21	2	21-0	33
1990— Columbus (Sou.)	9	10	.474	4.81	29	27	2	1	0-...	155.1	•181	104	83	14	70-1	92
1991— Jackson (Texas)	8	9	.471	4.47	27	•27	2	0	0-...	151.0	165	93	75	8	62-1	116
1992— Tucson (PCL)	9	8	.529	3.68	25	22	2	0	1-...	142.0	156	73	58	4	34-2	106
— Houston (N.L.)	1	3	.250	7.11	8	5	0	0	0-0	25.1	42	22	20	2	6-1	10
1993— Tucson (PCL)	10	6	.625	3.62	25	20	2	0	1-...	139.1	147	74	56	4	21-0	106
— Houston (N.L.)	0	0	...	0.82	5	1	0	0	0-0	11.0	11	4	1	0	6-1	10
1994— Houston (N.L.)	8	5	.615	3.05	33	14	1	1	0-0	124.0	128	46	42	10	21-3	110
1995— Houston (N.L.)	10	11	.476	3.47	30	30	3	2	0-0	189.1	196	87	73	15	37-6	175
1996— Houston (N.L.)	16	10	.615	3.65	35	35	4	1	0-0	239.0	227	103	97	20	44-3	204
1997— Houston (N.L.)	9	10	.474	4.23	30	30	2	0	0-0	181.0	189	92	85	19	47-5	152
— New Orleans (A.A.)	1	0	1.000	0.00	1	1	0	0	0-...	5.0	3	0	0	0	1-0	6
1998— Houston (N.L.)	19	8	.704	3.51	35	•35	3	1	0-0	233.1	257	99	91	25	53-2	209
1999— Houston (N.L.)	16	14	.533	3.85	35	•35	4	2	0-0	231.2	250	108	99	23	37-0	197
2000— Houston (N.L.)	7	8	.467	5.22	22	22	0	0	0-0	131.0	150	86	76	20	45-2	93
2001— Round Rock (Texas)	1	0	1.000	1.29	1	1	0	0	0-...	7.0	5	1	1	0	2-0	5
— New Orleans (PCL)	1	0	1.000	0.00	1	1	0	0	0-...	7.0	8	0	0	0	0-0	7
— Houston (N.L.)	14	11	.560	4.34	28	28	3	0	0-0	182.2	208	95	88	24	36-2	102
2002— Houston (N.L.)	3	6	.333	4.86	13	13	0	0	0-0	74.0	80	43	40	13	26-2	47
Major League totals (11 years)	103	86	.545	3.95	274	248	20	7	0-0	1622.1	1738	785	712	171	358-27	1309

DIVISION SERIES RECORD

Year League	W	L	Pct.	ERA	G	GS	CG	ShO	Sv.-Opp.	IP	H	R	ER	HR	BB-IBB	SO
1997— Houston (N.L.)	0	1	.000	3.00	1	1	0	0	0-0	6.0	5	2	2	1	1-0	5
1998— Houston (N.L.)	0	0	...	2.57	1	1	0	0	0-0	7.0	4	2	2	0	1-0	5
1999— Houston (N.L.)	1	1	.500	4.09	2	2	0	0	0-0	11.0	16	5	5	0	3-0	5
2001— Houston (N.L.)	0	1	.000	9.00	1	1	0	0	0-0	4.0	6	4	4	2	1-0	1
Division series totals (4 years)	1	3	.250	4.18	5	5	0	0	0-0	28.0	31	13	13	3	6-0	16

ALL-STAR GAME RECORD

	W	L	Pct.	ERA	GS	CG	ShO	Sv.-Opp.	IP	H	R	ER	HR	BB-IBB	SO
All-Star Game totals (1 year)	2000—Selected, did not play.														

REYNOSO, ARMANDO P

PERSONAL: Born May 1, 1966, in San Luis Potosi, Mexico. ... 6-0/210. ... Throws right, bats right. ... Full name: Martin Armando Gutierrez Reynoso. ... Name pronounced ray-NO-so.

HIGH SCHOOL: Escuela Secandaria Mita del Estado (Jalisco, Mexico).

TRANSACTIONS/CAREER NOTES: Signed as free agent by Saltillo of Mexican League (1988). ... Contract sold by Saltillo to Atlanta Braves organization (August 15, 1990). ... Selected by Colorado Rockies in third round (58th pick overall) of expansion draft (November 17, 1992). ... On disabled list (May 21, 1994-remainder of season). ... On Colorado disabled list (April 17-June 18, 1995); included rehabilitation assignments to Colorado Springs (May 9-20 and June 8-14). ... Traded by Rockies to New York Mets for P Jerry Dipoto (November 27, 1996). ... On New York disabled list (March 24-April 15 and July 17, 1997-remainder of season); included rehabilitation assignment to St. Lucie (April 5-15). ... On New York disabled list (March 24-July 24, 1998); included rehabilitation assignments to St. Lucie (June 18-July 3) and Norfolk (July 12-17). ... Granted free agency (October 26, 1998). ... Signed by Arizona Diamondbacks (December 2, 1998). ... Granted free agency (November 1, 2000). ... Re-signed by Diamondbacks (December 6, 2000). ... On Arizona disabled list (May 5-29 and June 10, 2001-remainder of season); included rehabilitation assignment to Tucson (May 24-29). ... On Arizona disabled list (March 22-September 5, 2002); included rehabilitation assignment to Tucson (July 12-August 10). ... Granted free agency (October 28, 2002).

STATISTICAL NOTES: Led International League with six balks in 1991 and five in 1992. ... Tied for International League lead with 10 hit batsmen in 1991.

MISCELLANEOUS: Appeared in one game as pinch runner with Colorado (1993).

CAREER HITTING (MLB): 50-for-337 (.148), 17 R, 6 2B, 0 3B, 3 HR, 13 RBI.

Year	League	W	L	Pct.	ERA	G	GS	CG	ShO	Sv.-Opp.	IP	H	R	ER	HR	BB-IBB	SO
1988	—Saltillo (Mex.)	11	11	.500	4.30	32	29	10	2	2-...	180.0	176	98	86	15	85-10	92
1989	—Saltillo (Mex.)	13	9	.591	3.48	27	25	7	2	0-...	160.1	155	78	62	10	64-7	107
1990	—Saltillo (Mex.)	*20	3	.870	2.60	27	•27	12	5	0-...	200.2	174	61	58	7	73-7	*170
	—Richmond (I.L.)■	3	1	.750	2.25	4	3	0	0	0-...	24.0	26	7	6	3	7-0	15
1991	—Richmond (I.L.)	10	6	.625	*2.61	22	19	3	•3	0-...	131.0	117	44	38	9	39-1	97
	—Atlanta (N.L.)	2	1	.667	6.17	6	5	0	0	0-0	23.1	26	18	16	4	10-1	10
1992	—Richmond (I.L.)	12	9	.571	2.66	28	27	4	1	0-...	169.1	156	65	50	12	52-6	108
	—Atlanta (N.L.)	1	0	1.000	4.70	3	1	0	0	1-1	7.2	11	4	4	2	2-1	2
1993	—Colorado Springs (PCL)■	2	1	.667	3.22	4	4	0	0	0-...	22.1	19	10	8	1	8-0	22
	—Colorado (N.L.)	12	11	.522	4.00	30	30	4	0	0-0	189.0	206	101	84	22	63-7	117
1994	—Colorado (N.L.)	3	4	.429	4.82	9	9	1	0	0-0	52.1	54	30	28	5	22-1	25
1995	—Colorado Springs (PCL)	2	1	.667	1.57	5	5	0	0	0-...	23.0	14	4	4	1	6-1	17
	—Colorado (N.L.)	7	7	.500	5.32	20	18	0	0	0-0	93.0	116	61	55	12	36-3	40
1996	—Colorado (N.L.)	8	9	.471	4.96	30	30	0	0	0-0	168.2	195	97	93	27	49-0	88
1997	—St. Lucie (FSL)■	1	1	.500	2.70	2	2	0	0	0-...	10.0	9	3	3	0	1-0	6
	—New York (N.L.)	6	3	.667	4.53	16	16	1	1	0-0	91.1	95	47	46	7	29-4	47
1998	—St. Lucie (FSL)	0	1	.000	3.75	4	4	0	0	0-...	12.0	14	6	5	2	1-0	6
	—Norfolk (I.L.)	0	2	.000	10.61	2	2	0	0	0-...	9.1	14	11	11	1	4-1	8
	—New York (N.L.)	7	3	.700	3.82	11	11	0	0	0-0	68.1	64	31	29	4	32-3	40
1999	—Arizona (N.L.)■	10	6	.625	4.37	31	27	0	0	0-0	167.0	178	90	81	20	67-7	79
2000	—Arizona (N.L.)	11	12	.478	5.27	31	30	2	0	0-0	170.2	179	102	100	22	52-5	89
2001	—Arizona (N.L.)	1	6	.143	5.98	9	9	0	0	0-0	46.2	58	32	31	13	13-2	15
	—Tucson (PCL)	0	0	...	0.00	1	1	0	0	0-...	3.2	3	0	0	0	2-0	5
2002	—Tucson (PCL)	1	2	.333	5.20	6	6	0	0	0-...	27.2	29	16	16	2	9-...	16
	—Arizona (N.L.)	0	0	...	10.80	2	0	0	0	0-0	1.2	3	2	2	0	1-0	2
Major League totals (12 years)		68	62	.523	4.74	198	186	8	1	1-1	1079.2	1185	615	569	138	376-34	554

DIVISION SERIES RECORD

Year	League	W	L	Pct.	ERA	G	GS	CG	ShO	Sv.-Opp.	IP	H	R	ER	HR	BB-IBB	SO
1995	—Colorado (N.L.)	0	0	...	0.00	1	0	0	0	0-0	1.0	2	0	0	0	0-0	0
1999	—Arizona (N.L.)									Did not play.							

RHODES, ARTHUR P MARINERS

PERSONAL: Born October 24, 1969, in Waco, Texas. ... 6-2/205. ... Throws left, bats left. ... Full name: Arthur Lee Rhodes Jr. ... Brother of Ricky Rhodes, pitcher in New York Yankees organization (1988-92).

HIGH SCHOOL: LaVega (Waco, Texas).

TRANSACTIONS/CAREER NOTES: Selected by Baltimore Orioles organization in second round of free-agent draft (June 1, 1988). ... On Hagerstown disabled list (May 13-June 5, 1991). ... On Baltimore disabled list (May 16-August 2, 1993); included rehabilitation assignment to Rochester (July 4-August 2). ... On Baltimore disabled list (May 2-20, 1994); included rehabilitation assignment to Frederick (May 16-20). ... On Baltimore disabled list (August 25, 1995-remainder of season). ... On disabled list (July 14-August 2 and August 6-September 27, 1996). ... On Baltimore disabled list (July 5-August 17, 1998); included rehabilitation assignment to Rochester (August 15-17). ... Granted free agency (November 1, 1999). ... Signed by Seattle Mariners (December 21, 1999).

HONORS: Named Eastern League Pitcher of the Year (1991).

MISCELLANEOUS: Appeared in one game as pinch runner (1997).

CAREER HITTING (MLB): 1-for-4 (.250), 0 R, 0 2B, 0 3B, 0 HR, 0 RBI.

Year	League	W	L	Pct.	ERA	G	GS	CG	ShO	Sv.-Opp.	IP	H	R	ER	HR	BB-IBB	SO
1988	—Bluefield (Appl.)	3	4	.429	3.31	11	7	0	0	0-...	35.1	29	17	13	1	15-0	44
1989	—Erie (NY-Penn)	2	0	1.000	1.16	5	5	1	0	0-...	31.0	13	7	4	1	10-0	45
	—Frederick (Caro.)	2	2	.500	5.18	7	6	0	0	0-...	24.1	19	16	14	2	19-0	28
1990	—Frederick (Caro.)	4	6	.400	2.12	13	13	3	0	0-...	80.2	62	25	19	6	21-0	103
	—Hagerstown (East.)	3	4	.429	3.73	12	12	0	0	0-...	72.1	62	32	30	3	39-0	60
1991	—Hagerstown (East.)	7	4	.636	2.70	19	19	2	2	0-...	106.2	73	37	32	2	47-1	115
	—Baltimore (A.L.)	0	3	.000	8.00	8	8	0	0	0-0	36.0	47	35	32	4	23-0	23
1992	—Rochester (I.L.)	6	6	.500	3.72	17	17	1	0	0-...	101.2	84	48	42	7	46-0	115
	—Baltimore (A.L.)	7	5	.583	3.63	15	15	2	1	0-0	94.1	87	39	38	6	38-2	77
1993	—Baltimore (A.L.)	5	6	.455	6.51	17	17	0	0	0-0	85.2	91	62	62	16	49-1	49
	—Rochester (I.L.)	1	1	.500	4.05	6	6	0	0	0-...	26.2	26	12	12	5	15-0	33
1994	—Baltimore (A.L.)	3	5	.375	5.81	10	10	3	2	0-0	52.2	51	34	34	8	30-1	47
	—Frederick (Caro.)	0	0	...	0.00	1	1	0	0	0-...	5.0	3	0	0	0	0-0	7
	—Rochester (I.L.)	7	5	.583	2.79	15	15	3	0	0-...	90.1	70	41	28	7	34-1	86

Year League	W	L	Pct.	ERA	G	GS	CG	ShO	Sv.-Opp.	IP	H	R	ER	HR	BB-IBB	SO
1995— Baltimore (A.L.)	2	5	.286	6.21	19	9	0	0	0-1	75.1	68	53	52	13	48-1	77
— Rochester (I.L.)	2	1	.667	2.70	4	4	1	0	0-...	30.0	27	12	9	2	8-0	33
1996— Baltimore (A.L.)	9	1	.900	4.08	28	2	0	0	1-1	53.0	48	28	24	6	23-3	62
1997— Baltimore (A.L.)	10	3	.769	3.02	53	0	0	0	1-2	95.1	75	32	32	9	26-5	102
1998— Baltimore (A.L.)	4	4	.500	3.51	45	0	0	0	4-8	77.0	65	30	30	8	34-2	83
— Rochester (I.L.)	0	0	...	4.50	1	1	0	0	0-...	2.0	3	1	1	0	1-0	1
1999— Baltimore (A.L.)	3	4	.429	5.43	43	0	0	0	3-5	53.0	43	37	32	9	45-6	59
2000— Seattle (A.L.)■	5	8	.385	4.28	72	0	0	0	0-7	69.1	51	34	33	6	29-3	77
2001— Seattle (A.L.)	8	0	1.000	1.72	71	0	0	0	3-7	68.0	46	14	13	5	12-0	83
2002— Seattle (A.L.)	10	4	.714	2.33	66	0	0	0	2-7	69.2	45	18	18	4	13-1	81
Major League totals (12 years)	66	48	.579	4.34	447	61	5	3	14-38	829.1	717	416	400	94	370-25	820

DIVISION SERIES RECORD

Year League	W	L	Pct.	ERA	G	GS	CG	ShO	Sv.-Opp.	IP	H	R	ER	HR	BB-IBB	SO
1996— Baltimore (A.L.)	0	0	...	9.00	2	0	0	0	0-0	1.0	1	1	1	0	1-0	1
1997— Baltimore (A.L.)	0	0	...	0.00	1	0	0	0	0-0	2.1	0	0	0	0	0-0	4
2000— Seattle (A.L.)	0	0	...	0.00	3	0	0	0	0-0	2.2	0	0	0	0	2-0	2
2001— Seattle (A.L.)	0	0	...	0.00	3	0	0	0	0-0	2.2	1	0	0	0	0-0	1
Division series totals (4 years)	0	0	...	1.04	9	0	0	0	0-0	8.2	2	1	1	0	3-0	8

CHAMPIONSHIP SERIES RECORD

Year League	W	L	Pct.	ERA	G	GS	CG	ShO	Sv.-Opp.	IP	H	R	ER	HR	BB-IBB	SO
1996— Baltimore (A.L.)	0	0	...	0.00	3	0	0	0	0-0	2.0	2	0	0	0	0-0	2
1997— Baltimore (A.L.)	0	0	...	0.00	2	0	0	0	0-0	2.1	2	0	0	0	3-1	2
2000— Seattle (A.L.)	0	1	.000	31.50	4	0	0	0	0-2	2.0	8	7	7	1	4-1	5
2001— Seattle (A.L.)	0	0	...	4.50	2	0	0	0	0-1	2.0	2	1	1	1	0-0	2
Champ. series totals (4 years)	0	1	.000	8.64	11	0	0	0	0-3	8.1	14	8	8	2	7-2	11

RICHARD, CHRIS — OF/1B — ORIOLES

PERSONAL: Born June 7, 1974, in San Diego. ... 6-2/190. ... Bats left, throws left. ... Full name: Christopher Robert Richard.
HIGH SCHOOL: University City (San Diego).
JUNIOR COLLEGE: San Diego City College, then San Diego Mesa College.
COLLEGE: Oklahoma State.
TRANSACTIONS/CAREER NOTES: Selected by St. Louis Cardinals organization in 19th round of free-agent draft (June 1, 1995). ... On Arkansas disabled list (April 2-June 16, 1998 and July 31-August 11, 1998). ... On Prince William disabled list (June 28-July 16, 1998). ... Traded by Cardinals with P Mark Nussbeck to Baltimore Orioles for P Mike Timlin and cash (July 29, 2000). ... On disabled list (June 20-July 5, 2001). ... On Baltimore disabled list (March 30-July 31, 2002); included rehabilitation assignments to Gulf Coast Orioles (July 2-4), Bowie (July 5-8), Aberdeen (July 9-10) and Rochester (July 15-31).
STATISTICAL NOTES: Led Texas League first baseman with 119 double plays in 1999. ... Hit home run in first major league at-bat (July 17, 2000).
2002 GAMES PLAYED BY POSITION (MLB): DH—36; 1B—9.

		BATTING														FIELDING	
Year Team (League)	Pos.	G	AB	R	H	2B	3B	HR	RBI	BB	SO	SB-CS	Avg.	OBP	SLG	E	Avg.
1995— New Jersey (NY-P)	1B	75	284	36	80	14	3	3	43	47	31	6-6	.282	.392	.384	11	.984
1996— St. Petersburg (FSL)	1B-OF	129	460	65	130	28	6	14	82	57	50	7-3	.283	.369	.461	7	.994
1997— Arkansas (Texas)	1B-OF	113	390	62	105	24	3	11	58	60	59	6-4	.269	.371	.431	10	.990
1998— Prince William (Caro.)	DH	8	30	5	8	2	0	0	1	1	5	1-0	.267	.290	.333	...	...
— Arkansas (Texas)	1B	28	89	7	18	5	1	2	17	9	10	0-1	.202	.280	.348	3	.986
1999— Arkansas (Texas)	1B-OF	133	442	78	130	26	3	29	94	43	75	7-7	.294	.363	.563	13	.989
— Memphis (PCL)	1B	4	17	3	7	2	0	1	4	1	2	0-0	.412	.444	.706	0	1.000
2000— Memphis (PCL)	OF-1B	95	375	64	104	24	0	16	75	50	70	9-3	.277	.366	.469	2	.993
— St. Louis (N.L.)	OF-1B	6	16	1	2	0	0	1	1	2	2	0-0	.125	.222	.313	0	1.000
— Baltimore (A.L.)■	1B-DH-OF	56	199	38	55	14	2	13	36	15	38	7-5	.276	.335	.563	5	.989
2001— Baltimore (A.L.)	OF-DH-1B	136	483	74	128	31	3	15	61	45	100	11-9	.265	.335	.435	0	1.000
2002— GC Orioles (GCL)	DH	1	1	1	1	0	0	0	0	1	0	0-0	1.000	1.000	1.000	...	...
— Bowie (East.)	DH	2	6	0	2	1	0	0	1	1	2	0-0	.333	.375	.500	...	...
— Aberdeen (NY-Penn)	DH	1	5	2	3	1	0	1	3	0	1	0-0	.600	.600	1.400	...	...
— Rochester (I.L.)	DH	14	53	10	17	6	0	6	18	6	14	0-0	.321	.397	.774	...	...
— Baltimore (A.L.)	DH-1B	50	155	15	36	11	0	4	21	12	30	0-3	.232	.292	.381	0	1.000
American League totals (3 years)		242	837	127	219	56	5	32	118	72	168	18-17	.262	.327	.455	5	.994
National League totals (1 year)		6	16	1	2	0	0	1	1	2	2	0-0	.125	.222	.313	0	1.000
Major League totals (3 years)		248	853	128	221	56	5	33	119	74	170	18-17	.259	.325	.453	5	.995

RIEDLING, JOHN — P — REDS

PERSONAL: Born August 29, 1975, in Fort Lauderdale, Fla. ... 5-11/190. ... Throws right, bats right. ... Full name: John Richard Riedling Jr.
HIGH SCHOOL: Ely (Pompano Beach, Fla.).
TRANSACTIONS/CAREER NOTES: Selected by Cincinnati Reds organization in 22nd round of free-agent draft (June 2, 1994). ... Released by Reds (December 14, 1998). ... Re-signed by Reds organization (January 5, 1999). ... On Cincinnati disabled list (May 27-August 12 and August 31, 2001-remainder of season); included rehabilitation assignment to Louisville (August 10-12). ... On Cincinnati disabled list (March 26-May 1 and August 20-September 4, 2002).
CAREER HITTING (MLB): 0-for-4 (.000), 0 R, 0 2B, 0 3B, 0 HR, 0 RBI.

Year League	W	L	Pct.	ERA	G	GS	CG	ShO	Sv.-Opp.	IP	H	R	ER	HR	BB-IBB	SO
1994—Billings (Pio.)	4	1	.800	5.48	15	15	0	0	0-...	44.1	62	36	27	0	28-0	27
1995—Billings (Pio.)	2	2	.500	7.04	13	7	0	0	1-...	38.1	51	38	30	4	21-2	28
1996—Charleston, W.Va. (S.Atl.)	6	10	.375	3.99	26	26	0	0	0-...	140.0	135	85	62	2	66-6	90
1997—Burlington (Midw.)	4	6	.400	5.26	35	16	0	0	0-...	102.2	101	70	60	8	47-0	104
1998—Chattanooga (Sou.)	3	10	.231	5.00	24	20	0	0	0-...	102.2	112	70	57	10	60-5	86
1999—Chattanooga (Sou.)	9	5	.643	3.43	40	0	0	0	5-...	42.0	41	23	16	2	20-3	38
—Indianapolis (I.L.)	1	0	1.000	1.54	24	0	0	0	1-...	35.0	19	9	6	1	18-2	26
2000—Louisville (I.L.)	6	3	.667	2.52	53	0	0	0	5-...	75.0	63	24	21	7	30-3	75
—Cincinnati (N.L.)	3	1	.750	2.35	13	0	0	0	1-2	15.1	11	7	4	1	8-0	18
2001—Cincinnati (N.L.)	1	1	.500	2.41	29	0	0	0	1-3	33.2	22	9	9	1	14-0	23
—Louisville (I.L.)	0	0	...	0.00	1	0	0	0	0-...	1.0	0	0	0	0	1-0	1
2002—Chattanooga (Sou.)	1	1	.500	11.05	6	0	0	0	0-...	7.1	13	11	9	0	5-2	5
—Louisville (I.L.)	1	0	1.000	4.66	7	0	0	0	0-...	9.2	10	6	5	0	4-0	10
—Cincinnati (N.L.)	2	4	.333	2.70	33	0	0	0	0-0	46.2	39	16	14	2	26-6	30
Major League totals (3 years)	6	6	.500	2.54	75	0	0	0	2-5	95.2	72	32	27	4	48-6	71

RIGDON, PAUL — P — BREWERS

PERSONAL: Born November 2, 1975, in Jacksonville, Fla. ... 6-5/242. ... Throws right, bats right. ... Full name: Paul David Rigdon.
HIGH SCHOOL: Trinity Christian Academy (Jacksonville, Fla.).
COLLEGE: Florida.
TRANSACTIONS/CAREER NOTES: Selected by Cleveland Indians organization in sixth-round of free-agent draft (June 4, 1996). ... On disabled list (June 17, 1997-entire season). ... Traded by Indians with 1B/OF Richie Sexson, P Kane Davis and a player to be named later to Milwaukee Brewers for P Bob Wickman, P Steve Woodard and P Jason Bere (July 28, 2000); Brewers acquired 2B Marcos Scutaro to complete deal (August 30). ... On Milwaukee disabled list (May 22-June 7, 2000). ... On disabled list (June 9-24 and July 2, 2001-remainder of season). ... On Milwaukee disabled list (March 28, 2002-entire season); included rehabilitation assignment to Indianapolis (April 26-May 6).

Year League	W	L	Pct.	ERA	G	GS	CG	ShO	Sv.-Opp.	IP	H	R	ER	HR	BB-IBB	SO
1996—Watertown (NY-Penn)	2	2	.500	4.08	22	0	0	0	6-...	39.2	41	24	18	4	10-0	46
1997—									Did not play.							
1998—Kinston (Caro.)	11	7	.611	4.03	24	24	0	0	0-...	127.1	126	65	57	9	35-1	97
1999—Akron (East.)	7	0	1.000	0.90	8	7	0	0	0-...	50.0	20	5	5	2	10-0	25
—Buffalo (I.L.)	7	4	.636	4.53	19	19	0	0	0-...	103.1	114	60	52	11	28-0	60
2000—Buffalo (I.L.)	6	1	.857	3.30	12	12	1	0	0-...	71.0	72	27	26	4	18-0	41
—Cleveland (A.L.)	1	1	.500	7.64	5	4	0	0	0-0	17.2	21	15	15	4	9-1	15
—Milwaukee (N.L.)■	4	4	.500	4.52	12	12	0	0	0-0	69.2	68	37	35	14	26-4	48
2001—Milwaukee (N.L.)	3	5	.375	5.79	15	15	0	0	0-0	79.1	86	52	51	13	46-6	49
2002—Indianapolis (I.L.)	0	1	.000	5.06	3	3	0	0	0-...	10.2	11	6	6	1	2-0	6
A.L. totals (1 year)	1	1	.500	7.64	5	4	0	0	0-0	17.2	21	15	15	4	9-1	15
N.L. totals (2 years)	7	9	.438	5.19	27	27	0	0	0-0	149.0	154	89	86	27	72-10	97
Major League totals (2 years)	8	10	.444	5.45	32	31	0	0	0-0	166.2	175	104	101	31	81-11	112

RIGGAN, JERROD — P — INDIANS

PERSONAL: Born May 16, 1974, in Brewster, Wash. ... 6-3/197. ... Throws right, bats right. ... Full name: Jerrod Ashley Riggan.
HIGH SCHOOL: Brewster (Wash.).
COLLEGE: San Diego State.
TRANSACTIONS/CAREER NOTES: Selected by California Angels organization in eighth round of free-agent draft (June 4, 1996). ... Angels franchise renamed Anaheim Angels for 1997 season. ... Released by Angels (April 17, 1998). ... Signed by New York Mets organization (July 9, 1998). ... Traded by Mets with OF Matt Lawton, OF Alex Escobar and two players to be named later to Cleveland Indians for 2B Roberto Alomar, P Mike Bacsik and OF Danny Peoples (December 11, 2001); Indians acquired P Billy Traber and 1B Earl Snyder to complete deal (December 13, 2001).
CAREER HITTING (MLB): 0-for-2 (.000), 0 R, 0 2B, 0 3B, 0 HR, 0 RBI.

Year League	W	L	Pct.	ERA	G	GS	CG	ShO	Sv.-Opp.	IP	H	R	ER	HR	BB-IBB	SO
1996—Boise (N'West)	3	5	.375	4.63	15	15	•1	0	0-...	89.1	90	62	46	10	38-5	80
1997—Cedar Rapids (Midw.)	9	8	.529	4.89	19	19	3	1	0-...	116.0	132	70	63	15	36-2	65
—Lake Elsinore (Calif.)	2	5	.286	6.07	8	8	0	0	0-...	43.0	60	36	29	1	16-0	31
1998—Capital City (S.Atl.)■	4	1	.800	3.70	14	0	0	0	1-...	41.1	38	21	17	5	14-1	40
1999—St. Lucie (FSL)	5	5	.500	3.33	44	0	0	0	12-...	73.0	69	33	27	4	24-5	66
2000—Binghamton (East.)	2	0	1.000	1.11	52	0	0	0	•28-...	65.0	43	9	8	2	18-0	79
—New York (N.L.)	0	0	...	0.00	1	0	0	0	0-0	2.0	3	2	0	0	0-0	1
2001—Norfolk (I.L.)	2	0	1.000	1.95	28	0	0	0	13-...	32.1	26	7	7	4	4-1	37
—New York (N.L.)	3	3	.500	3.40	35	0	0	0	0-1	47.2	42	19	18	5	24-7	41
2002—Cleveland (A.L.)■	2	1	.667	7.64	29	0	0	0	0-0	33.0	53	28	28	3	18-4	22
—Buffalo (I.L.)	4	1	.800	2.38	27	0	0	0	3-...	45.1	40	12	12	3	11-2	37
A.L. totals (1 year)	2	1	.667	7.64	29	0	0	0	0-0	33.0	53	28	28	3	18-4	22
N.L. totals (2 years)	3	3	.500	3.26	36	0	0	0	0-1	49.2	45	21	18	5	24-7	42
Major League totals (3 years)	5	4	.556	5.01	65	0	0	0	0-1	82.2	98	49	46	8	42-11	64

RIJO, JOSE — P

PERSONAL: Born May 13, 1965, in San Cristobal, Dominican Republic. ... 6-3/200. ... Throws right, bats right. ... Full name: Jose Antonio Abreau Rijo. ... Name pronounced REE-ho.
TRANSACTIONS/CAREER NOTES: Signed as non-drafted free agent by New York Yankees organization (August 1, 1980). ... Traded by Yankees with OF Stan Javier, P Jay Howell, P Eric Plunk and P Tim Birtsas to Oakland Athletics for OF Rickey Henderson, P Bert Bradley and cash (December 5, 1984). ... Traded by A's with P Tim Birtsas to Cincinnati Reds for OF Dave Parker (December 8, 1987). ... On disabled list (August 18-September 8, 1988; and July 17-September 1, 1989). ... On Cincinnati disabled list (June 29-July 21, 1990); included rehabilitation assignment to Nashville (July 16-20). ... On disabled list (June 21-July 25, 1991; April 18-May 3, 1992; June 2-17 and July 19, 1995-remainder of season; March 23, 1996-entire season; and February 17, 1997-entire season). ... Granted free agency (October 29, 1997). ...

Re-signed by Cincinnati Reds organization (January 8, 1998). ... On disabled list (April 9, 1998-entire season). ... Granted free agency (October 15, 1998). ... Signed by Reds organization (July 1, 2001). ... Granted free agency (November 5, 2001). ... Re-signed by Reds organization (January 7, 2002). ... On disabled list (June 2-July 13, 2002). ... Granted free agency (October 30, 2002).

HONORS: Named Florida State League Most Valuable Player (1983). ... Named righthanded pitcher on THE SPORTING NEWS N.L. All-Star team (1991).

STATISTICAL NOTES: Led Pacific Coast League with 11 balks in 1985. ... Struck out 16 batters in one game (April 19, 1986). ... Tied for N.L. lead with five balks in 1990. ... Pitched 6-0 one-hit, complete-game victory against Colorado (September 25, 1993).

MISCELLANEOUS: Struck out in only appearance as pinch hitter (1991).

CAREER HITTING (MLB): 85-for-445 (.191), 25 R, 13 2B, 0 3B, 2 HR, 29 RBI.

Year	League	W	L	Pct.	ERA	G	GS	CG	ShO	Sv.-Opp.	IP	H	R	ER	HR	BB-IBB	SO
1981—	Gulf Coast Yankees (GCL)	3	3	.500	4.50	11	1	0	0	1-...	22.0	37	16	11	2	7-0	22
1982—	Paintsville (Appl.)	8	4	.667	2.50	13	12	6	•3	0-...	79.1	76	33	22	6	22-0	66
1983—	Fort Lauderdale (FSL)	*15	5	.750	*1.68	21	21	*15	•4	0-...	160.1	129	38	30	6	43-3	152
—	Nashville (Sou.)	3	2	.600	2.68	5	5	3	0	0-...	40.1	31	12	12	1	22-0	32
1984—	New York (A.L.)	2	8	.200	4.76	24	5	0	0	2-3	62.1	74	40	33	5	33-1	47
—	Columbus (I.L.)	3	3	.500	4.41	11	11	0	0	0-...	65.1	67	35	32	7	40-0	47
1985—	Tacoma (PCL)■	7	10	.412	2.90	24	24	3	1	0-...	149.0	116	64	48	6	*108-3	*179
—	Oakland (A.L.)	6	4	.600	3.53	12	9	0	0	0-1	63.2	57	26	25	6	28-2	65
1986—	Oakland (A.L.)	9	11	.450	4.65	39	26	4	0	1-3	193.2	172	116	100	24	108-7	176
1987—	Oakland (A.L.)	2	7	.222	5.90	21	14	1	0	0-0	82.1	106	67	54	10	41-1	67
—	Tacoma (PCL)	2	4	.333	3.95	9	8	0	0	0-...	54.2	44	27	24	5	28-0	67
1988—	Cincinnati (N.L.)■	13	8	.619	2.39	49	19	0	0	0-2	162.0	120	47	43	7	63-7	160
1989—	Cincinnati (N.L.)	7	6	.538	2.84	19	19	1	1	0-0	111.0	101	39	35	6	48-3	86
1990—	Cincinnati (N.L.)	14	8	.636	2.70	29	29	7	1	0-0	197.0	151	65	59	10	78-1	152
—	Nashville (A.A.)	0	0	...	8.31	1	1	0	0	0-...	4.1	5	4	4	0	2-0	2
1991—	Cincinnati (N.L.)	15	6	•.714	2.51	30	30	3	1	0-0	204.1	165	69	57	8	55-4	172
1992—	Cincinnati (N.L.)	15	10	.600	2.56	33	33	2	0	0-0	211.0	185	67	60	15	44-1	171
1993—	Cincinnati (N.L.)	14	9	.609	2.48	36	•36	2	1	0-0	257.1	218	76	71	19	62-2	*227
1994—	Cincinnati (N.L.)	9	6	.600	3.08	26	*26	2	0	0-0	172.1	177	73	59	16	52-1	171
1995—	Cincinnati (N.L.)	5	4	.556	4.17	14	14	0	0	0-0	69.0	76	33	32	6	22-1	62
1996—	Cincinnati (N.L.)									Did not play.							
1997—	Cincinnati (N.L.)									Did not play.							
1998—	Indianapolis (I.L.)									Did not play.							
1999—										Did not play.							
2000—										Did not play.							
2001—	Dayton (Midw.)	0	0	...	3.00	1	1	0	0	0-...	3.0	3	1	1	0	0-0	1
—	Chattanooga (Sou.)	0	0	...	0.00	1	1	0	0	0-...	3.0	1	0	0	0	1-0	3
—	Louisville (I.L.)	0	0	...	5.14	6	4	0	0	0-...	14.0	16	9	8	2	5-0	7
—	Cincinnati (N.L.)	0	0	...	2.12	13	0	0	0	0-0	17.0	19	6	4	2	9-2	12
2002—	Cincinnati (N.L.)	5	4	.556	5.14	31	9	0	0	0-0	77.0	89	48	44	13	20-1	38
A.L. totals (4 years)		19	30	.388	4.75	96	54	5	0	3-7	402.0	409	249	212	45	210-11	355
N.L. totals (10 years)		97	61	.614	2.83	280	215	17	4	0-2	1478.0	1301	523	464	102	453-23	1251
Major League totals (14 years)		116	91	.560	3.24	376	269	22	4	3-9	1880.0	1710	772	676	147	663-34	1606

CHAMPIONSHIP SERIES RECORD

Year	League	W	L	Pct.	ERA	G	GS	CG	ShO	Sv.-Opp.	IP	H	R	ER	HR	BB-IBB	SO
1990—	Cincinnati (N.L.)	1	0	1.000	4.38	2	2	0	0	0-0	12.1	10	6	6	2	7-1	15

WORLD SERIES RECORD

NOTES: Named Most Valuable Player (1990). ... Member of World Series championship team (1990).

Year	League	W	L	Pct.	ERA	G	GS	CG	ShO	Sv.-Opp.	IP	H	R	ER	HR	BB-IBB	SO
1990—	Cincinnati (N.L.)	2	0	1.000	0.59	2	2	0	0	0-0	15.1	9	1	1	0	5-1	14

ALL-STAR GAME RECORD

	W	L	Pct.	ERA	GS	CG	ShO	Sv.-Opp.	IP	H	R	ER	HR	BB-IBB	SO
All-Star Game totals (1 year)					1994—Selected, did not play-injured.										

RINCON, JUAN — P — TWINS

PERSONAL: Born January 23, 1979, in Maracaibo, Venezuela. ... 5-11/190. ... Throws right, bats right. ... Full name: Juan Manuel Rincon.

HIGH SCHOOL: Instituto Cervantes (Maracaibo, Venezuela).

TRANSACTIONS/CAREER NOTES: Signed as non-drafted free agent by Minnesota Twins organization (November 15, 1996).

CAREER HITTING (MLB): 1-for-1 (1.000), 0 R, 0 2B, 0 3B, 0 HR, 0 RBI.

Year	League	W	L	Pct.	ERA	G	GS	CG	ShO	Sv.-Opp.	IP	H	R	ER	HR	BB-IBB	SO
1997—	Gulf Coast Twins (GCL)	3	3	.500	2.95	11	10	1	0	0-...	58.0	55	21	19	0	24-0	46
—	Elizabethton (Appl.)	0	1	.000	3.86	2	1	0	0	0-...	9.1	11	4	4	0	3-0	7
1998—	Fort Wayne (Midw.)	6	4	.600	3.83	37	13	0	0	6-...	96.1	84	51	41	6	54-1	74
1999—	Quad City (Midw.)	14	8	.636	2.92	28	•28	0	0	0-...	163.1	146	67	53	8	66-3	*153
2000—	Fort Myers (FSL)	5	3	.625	2.13	13	13	0	0	0-...	76.0	67	26	18	3	23-2	55
—	New Britain (East.)	3	9	.250	4.65	15	15	2	0	0-...	89.0	96	55	46	9	39-0	79
2001—	New Britain (East.)	14	6	.700	2.88	29	23	2	1	0-...	153.1	130	60	49	9	57-5	133
—	Minnesota (A.L.)	0	0	...	6.35	4	0	0	0	0-0	5.2	7	5	4	1	5-0	4
2002—	Edmonton (PCL)	7	4	.636	4.78	19	16	•3	0	0-...	101.2	111	56	54	12	35-0	75
—	Minnesota (A.L.)	0	2	.000	6.28	10	3	0	0	0-1	28.2	44	23	20	5	9-0	21
Major League totals (2 years)		0	2	.000	6.29	14	3	0	0	0-1	34.1	51	28	24	6	14-0	25

RINCON, RICKY — P — ATHLETICS

PERSONAL: Born April 13, 1970, in Veracruz, Mexico. ... 5-9/187. ... Throws left, bats left. ... Full name: Ricardo Rincon Espinoza.

TRANSACTIONS/CAREER NOTES: Signed as non-drafted free agent by Pittsburgh Pirates organization (March 30, 1997). ... On Pittsburgh disabled list (March 22-April 14, 1998); included rehabilitation assignments to Carolina (April 6) and Nashville (April 11-April 14). ... Traded by Pirates to Cleveland Indians for OF Brian Giles (November 18, 1998). ... On Cleveland disabled list (April 12-May 14, 1999); included rehabilitation assignment to Akron (May 11-14). ... On Cleveland disabled list (May 17-August 23, 2000); included rehabilitation assignment to Buffalo (August 20-23). ... Traded by Indians to Oakland Athletics for IF Marshall McDougall (July 30, 2002).

STATISTICAL NOTES: Pitched one inning, combining with Francisco Cordova (eight innings) in 3-0 no-hit victory against Houston (July 12, 1997).

CAREER HITTING (MLB): 0-for-4 (.000), 0 R, 0 2B, 0 3B, 0 HR, 0 RBI.

Year League	W	L	Pct.	ERA	G	GS	CG	ShO	Sv.-Opp.	IP	H	R	ER	HR	BB-IBB	SO
1990— Union Laguna (Mex.)	3	0	1.000	3.78	19	4	0	0	0-...	47.2	53	22	20	6	32-0	29
1991— Union Laguna (Mex.)	2	8	.200	6.54	32	9	0	0	1-...	74.1	99	60	54	12	48-3	66
1992— Union Laguna (Mex.)	6	5	.545	3.91	49	9	0	0	4-...	89.2	87	45	39	4	46-8	91
1993— Torreon (Mex.)■	7	3	.700	3.17	57	4	0	0	8-...	82.1	80	33	29	8	36-3	81
1994— MC Red Devils (Mex.)■	2	4	.333	3.21	20	9	0	0	1-...	53.1	57	23	19	4	20-0	38
1995— MC Red Devils (Mex.)	6	6	.500	5.16	27	11	0	0	3-...	75.0	86	45	43	7	41-0	41
1996— MC Red Devils (Mex.)	5	3	.625	2.97	50	0	0	0	10-...	78.2	58	28	26	2	27-2	60
1997— Pittsburgh (N.L.)■	4	8	.333	3.45	62	0	0	0	4-6	60.0	51	26	23	5	24-6	71
1998— Carolina (Sou.)	0	0	...	6.00	2	0	0	0	0-...	3.0	5	2	2	1	2-0	1
— Nashville (PCL)	0	0	...	0.00	1	0	0	0	0-...	1.0	0	0	0	0	0-0	1
— Pittsburgh (N.L.)	0	2	.000	2.91	60	0	0	0	14-17	65.0	50	31	21	6	29-2	64
1999— Cleveland (A.L.)■	2	3	.400	4.43	59	0	0	0	0-2	44.2	41	22	22	6	24-5	30
— Akron (East.)	0	0	...	5.40	2	2	0	0	0-...	1.2	2	1	1	1	0-0	2
2000— Cleveland (A.L.)	2	0	1.000	2.70	35	0	0	0	0-0	20.0	17	7	6	1	13-1	20
— Buffalo (I.L.)	0	0	...	0.00	2	0	0	0	0-...	2.0	1	1	0	0	0-0	2
2001— Cleveland (A.L.)	2	1	.667	2.83	67	0	0	0	2-4	54.0	44	18	17	3	21-5	50
2002— Cleveland (A.L.)	1	4	.200	4.79	46	0	0	0	0-3	35.2	36	21	19	3	8-1	30
— Oakland (A.L.)■	0	0	...	3.10	25	0	0	0	1-2	20.1	11	7	7	1	3-0	19
A.L. totals (4 years)	7	8	.467	3.66	232	0	0	0	3-11	174.2	149	75	71	14	69-12	149
N.L. totals (2 years)	4	10	.286	3.17	122	0	0	0	18-23	125.0	101	57	44	11	53-8	135
Major League totals (6 years)	11	18	.379	3.45	354	0	0	0	21-34	299.2	250	132	115	25	122-20	284

DIVISION SERIES RECORD

Year League	W	L	Pct.	ERA	G	GS	CG	ShO	Sv.-Opp.	IP	H	R	ER	HR	BB-IBB	SO
1999— Cleveland (A.L.)	0	0	...	40.50	1	0	0	0	0-0	.2	2	3	3	1	1-0	1
2001— Cleveland (A.L.)	0	0	...	9.00	3	0	0	0	0-0	2.0	2	2	2	0	0-0	3
2002— Oakland (A.L.)	0	0	...	0.00	2	0	0	0	0-0	3.0	2	0	0	0	0-0	2
Division series totals (3 years)	0	0	...	7.94	6	0	0	0	0-0	5.2	6	5	5	1	1-0	6

RIOS, ARMANDO — OF — PIRATES

PERSONAL: Born September 13, 1971, in Santurce, Puerto Rico. ... 5-9/185. ... Bats left, throws left.

HIGH SCHOOL: Villa Fontana (Carolina, Puerto Rico).

COLLEGE: UNC Charlotte, then Louisiana State.

TRANSACTIONS/CAREER NOTES: Signed as non-drafted free agent by San Francisco Giants organization (January 6, 1994). ... On disabled list (May 15-29, 1996). ... On San Francisco disabled list (June 22-September 2, 1999); included rehabilitation assignment to Fresno (July 23-30 and August 12-31). ... Traded by Giants with P Ryan Vogelsong to Pittsburgh Pirates for P Jason Schmidt and OF John Vander Wal (July 30, 2001). ... On Pittsburgh disabled list (August 2, 2001-remainder of season). ... On Pittsburgh disabled list (May 17-August 2, 2002); included rehabilitation assignments to Altoona (June 9-10) and Nashville (July 15-August 2).

STATISTICAL NOTES: Led Texas League outfielders with 15 assists in 1996 and 17 in 1997. ... Career major league grand slams: 2.

2002 GAMES PLAYED BY POSITION (MLB): OF—56.

		BATTING														FIELDING	
Year Team (League)	Pos.	G	AB	R	H	2B	3B	HR	RBI	BB	SO	SB-CS	Avg.	OBP	SLG	E	Avg.
1994— Clinton (Midw.)	OF	119	407	67	120	23	4	8	60	59	69	16-12	.295	.384	.430	12	.951
1995— San Jose (Calif.)	OF	128	488	76	143	34	3	8	75	74	75	51-10	.293	.382	.424	9	.963
1996— Shreveport (Texas)	OF	92	329	62	93	22	2	12	49	44	42	9-9	.283	.365	.471	7	.963
1997— Shreveport (Texas)	OF-DH	127	461	86	133	30	6	14	79	63	85	17-7	.289	.370	.471	6	.972
1998— Fresno (PCL)	OF-DH-1B	125	445	85	134	23	1	26	103	55	73	17-5	.301	.378	.533	7	.972
— San Francisco (N.L.)	OF	12	7	3	4	0	0	2	3	3	2	0-0	.571	.700	1.429	0	1.000
1999— Fresno (PCL)	OF-DH-1B	31	109	24	30	3	0	4	21	11	22	3-1	.275	.363	.413	0	1.000
— San Francisco (N.L.)	OF	72	150	32	49	9	0	7	29	24	35	7-4	.327	.420	.527	2	.978
2000— San Francisco (N.L.)	OF-1B	115	233	38	62	15	5	10	50	31	43	3-2	.266	.347	.502	6	.959
2001— San Francisco (N.L.)	OF	93	316	38	82	17	3	14	49	34	73	3-2	.259	.330	.465	6	.971
— Pittsburgh (N.L.)■	OF	2	3	0	1	0	0	0	1	2	1	0-0	.333	.500	.333	0	...
2002— Pittsburgh (N.L.)	OF	76	208	20	55	11	0	1	24	16	39	1-1	.264	.319	.332	0	1.000
— Altoona (East.)	OF	1	2	0	0	0	0	0	0	1	0	0-0	.000	.333	.000	0	1.000
— Nashville (PCL)	OF	15	52	6	13	2	0	0	6	5	10	1-2	.250	.322	.288	1	.923
Major League totals (5 years)		370	917	131	253	52	8	34	156	110	193	14-9	.276	.352	.461	14	.974

DIVISION SERIES RECORD

		BATTING														FIELDING	
Year Team (League)	Pos.	G	AB	R	H	2B	3B	HR	RBI	BB	SO	SB-CS	Avg.	OBP	SLG	E	Avg.
2000— San Francisco (N.L.)	PH	2	2	0	1	0	0	0	0	0	0	0-0	.500	.500	.500	...	...

RISKE, DAVE — P — INDIANS

PERSONAL: Born October 23, 1976, in Renton, Wash. ... 6-2/175. ... Throws right, bats right. ... Full name: David R. Riske.

HIGH SCHOOL: Lindbergh (Renton, Wash.).

JUNIOR COLLEGE: Green River (Wash.) Community College.

TRANSACTIONS/CAREER NOTES: Selected by Cleveland Indians organization in 56th round of free-agent draft (June 4, 1996). ... On Cleveland disabled list (March 25-April 28 and May 29-September 4 and September 14, 2000-remainder of season); included rehabilitation assignment to Akron (April 22-26 and August 28-September 4). ... On Cleveland disabled list (June 19-July 17, 2002); included rehabilitation assignment to Akron (July 4-17).

CAREER HITTING (MLB): 0-for-0 (.000), 0 R, 0 2B, 0 3B, 0 HR, 0 RBI.

Year	League	W	L	Pct.	ERA	G	GS	CG	ShO	Sv.-Opp.	IP	H	R	ER	HR	BB-IBB	SO
1997—	Kinston (Caro.)	4	4	.500	2.25	39	0	0	0	2-...	72.0	58	22	18	3	33-4	90
1998—	Kinston (Caro.)	1	1	.500	2.33	53	0	0	0	*33-...	54.0	48	15	14	4	15-0	67
—	Akron (East.)	0	0	...	0.00	2	0	0	0	1-...	3.0	1	0	0	0	1-0	5
1999—	Akron (East.)	0	0	...	1.90	23	0	0	0	12-...	23.2	5	6	5	1	13-0	33
—	Buffalo (I.L.)	3	0	1.000	0.65	23	0	0	0	6-...	27.2	14	3	2	0	7-0	22
—	Cleveland (A.L.)	1	1	.500	8.36	12	0	0	0	0-1	14.0	20	15	13	2	6-0	16
2000—	Akron (East.)	0	0	...	0.00	3	1	0	0	1-...	4.0	2	0	0	0	0-0	4
—	Buffalo (I.L.)	0	0	...	3.00	2	0	0	0	0-...	3.0	2	1	1	0	2-0	2
2001—	Buffalo (I.L.)	1	2	.333	2.36	38	0	0	0	15-...	53.1	45	16	14	2	17-0	72
—	Cleveland (A.L.)	2	0	1.000	1.98	26	0	0	0	1-1	27.1	20	7	6	3	18-3	29
2002—	Cleveland (A.L.)	2	2	.500	5.26	51	0	0	0	1-1	51.1	49	32	30	8	35-4	65
—	Akron (East.)	0	0	...	3.00	4	2	0	0	0-...	6.0	5	2	2	1	1-0	10
—	Buffalo (I.L.)	0	1	.000	3.72	9	0	0	0	3-...	9.2	6	4	4	2	4-0	17
Major League totals (3 years)		5	3	.625	4.76	89	0	0	0	2-3	92.2	89	54	49	13	59-7	110

DIVISION SERIES RECORD

Year	League	W	L	Pct.	ERA	G	GS	CG	ShO	Sv.-Opp.	IP	H	R	ER	HR	BB-IBB	SO
2001—	Cleveland (A.L.)	0	0	...	0.00	3	0	0	0	0-0	3.1	2	0	0	0	1-0	5

RITCHIE, TODD — P — WHITE SOX

PERSONAL: Born November 7, 1971, in Portsmouth, Va. ... 6-3/210. ... Throws right, bats right. ... Full name: Todd Everett Ritchie.
HIGH SCHOOL: Duncanville (Texas).
TRANSACTIONS/CAREER NOTES: Selected by Minnesota Twins organization in first round (12th pick overall) of free-agent draft (June 4, 1990). ... On disabled list (August 19, 1991-remainder of season; June 24-July 9, 1993; and April 28, 1994-remainder of season). ... Released by Twins (October 3, 1998). ... Signed by Pittsburgh Pirates organization (December 22, 1998). ... On Pittsburgh disabled list (August 21-September 6, 1999). ... On disabled list (July 24-August 11, 2000). ... Traded by Pirates with C Lee Evans to Chicago White Sox for P Kip Wells, P Sean Lowe and P Josh Fogg (December 13, 2001). ... On disabled list (August 4-September 10, 2002).
STATISTICAL NOTES: Pitched 1-0 one-hit, complete-game victory against Kansas City (July 13, 2001).
MISCELLANEOUS: Grounded out in only appearance as pinch hitter (1999).
CAREER HITTING (MLB): 31-for-178 (.174), 9 R, 5 2B, 0 3B, 0 HR, 6 RBI.

Year	League	W	L	Pct.	ERA	G	GS	CG	ShO	Sv.-Opp.	IP	H	R	ER	HR	BB-IBB	SO
1990—	Elizabethton (Appl.)	5	2	.714	1.94	11	11	1	0	0-...	65.0	45	22	14	5	24-0	49
1991—	Kenosha (Midw.)	7	6	.538	3.55	21	21	0	0	0-...	116.2	113	53	46	3	50-0	101
1992—	Visalia (Calif.)	11	9	.550	5.06	28	•28	3	1	0-...	172.2	193	113	97	13	65-2	129
1993—	Nashville (Sou.)	3	2	.600	3.66	12	10	0	0	0-...	46.2	46	21	19	2	15-0	41
1994—	Nashville (Sou.)	0	2	.000	4.24	4	4	0	0	0-...	17.0	24	10	8	1	7-0	9
1995—	New Britain (East.)	4	9	.308	5.73	24	21	0	0	0-...	113.0	135	78	72	12	54-0	60
1996—	New Britain (East.)	3	7	.300	5.44	29	10	0	0	4-...	82.2	101	55	50	6	30-1	53
—	Salt Lake (PCL)	0	4	.000	5.47	16	0	0	0	0-...	24.2	27	15	15	5	11-0	19
1997—	Minnesota (A.L.)	2	3	.400	4.58	42	0	0	0	0-2	74.2	87	41	38	11	28-0	44
1998—	Minnesota (A.L.)	0	0	...	5.63	15	0	0	0	0-0	24.0	30	17	15	1	9-0	21
—	Salt Lake (PCL)	1	3	.250	4.15	36	0	0	0	4-...	60.2	55	38	28	5	31-3	62
1999—	Nashville (PCL)■	0	0	...	1.80	1	1	0	0	0-...	5.0	6	1	1	0	1-0	2
—	Pittsburgh (N.L.)	15	9	.625	3.50	28	26	2	0	0-0	172.1	169	79	67	17	54-3	107
2000—	Pittsburgh (N.L.)	9	8	.529	4.81	31	31	1	1	0-0	187.0	208	111	100	26	51-1	124
2001—	Pittsburgh (N.L.)	11	15	.423	4.47	33	33	4	2	0-0	207.1	211	118	103	23	52-7	124
2002—	Chicago (A.L.)■	5	15	.250	6.06	26	23	0	0	0-0	133.2	176	104	90	18	52-2	77
A.L. totals (3 years)		7	18	.280	5.54	83	23	0	0	0-2	232.1	293	162	143	30	89-2	142
N.L. totals (3 years)		35	32	.522	4.29	92	90	7	3	0-0	566.2	588	308	270	66	157-11	355
Major League totals (6 years)		42	50	.457	4.65	175	113	7	3	0-2	799.0	881	470	413	96	246-13	497

RIVAS, LUIS — 2B — TWINS

PERSONAL: Born August 30, 1979, in La Guaria, Venezuela. ... 5-11/175. ... Bats right, throws right. ... Full name: Luis Wilfredo Rivas.
HIGH SCHOOL: Riceniado Le Guaria (La Guaria, Venezuela).
TRANSACTIONS/CAREER NOTES: Signed as non-drafted free agent by Minnesota Twins organization (October 9, 1995). ... On New Britain disabled list (July 7-21, 2000). ... On Minnesota disabled list (April 7-June 4, 2002); included rehabilitation assignment to Fort Myers (May 28-June 4).
RECORDS: Shares A.L. single-season record for fewest putouts by second baseman (150 or more games)—230 (2001). ... Shares major league single-season record for fewest double plays by second baseman (150 or more games)—65 (2001).
STATISTICAL NOTES: Led Gulf Coast League shortstops with 40 double plays in 1996. ... Led Midwest League shortstops with 394 assists, 621 total chances and 92 double plays in 1997. ... Led Florida State League shortstops with 415 assists and 78 double plays in 1998. ... Led Eastern League shortstops with 37 errors in 1999.
2002 GAMES PLAYED BY POSITION (MLB): 2B—93.

			BATTING														FIELDING	
Year	Team (League)	Pos.	G	AB	R	H	2B	3B	HR	RBI	BB	SO	SB-CS	Avg.	OBP	SLG	E	Avg.
1996—	GC Twins (GCL)	SS	53	201	29	52	12	1	1	13	18	37	•35-10	.259	.320	.343	21	.922
1997—	Fort Wayne (Midw.)	SS	121	419	61	100	20	6	1	30	33	90	28-18	.239	.301	.322	*58	.907
1998—	Fort Myers (FSL)	SS	126	463	58	130	21	5	4	51	14	75	34-8	.281	.302	.374	55	.913
1999—	New Britain (East.)	SS-2B	132	527	78	134	30	7	7	49	41	92	31-14	.254	.309	.378	†39	.934
2000—	New Britain (East.)	2B-SS	82	328	56	82	23	6	3	40	36	41	11-4	.250	.329	.384	11	.971
—	Salt Lake (PCL)	2B-SS	41	157	33	50	14	1	3	25	13	21	7-4	.318	.376	.478	2	.989
—	Minnesota (A.L.)	2B-SS	16	58	8	18	4	1	0	6	2	4	2-0	.310	.323	.414	1	.984
2001—	Minnesota (A.L.)	2B	153	563	70	150	21	6	7	47	40	99	31-11	.266	.319	.362	15	.974
2002—	Minnesota (A.L.)	2B	93	316	46	81	23	4	4	35	19	51	9-4	.256	.305	.392	5	.986
—	Fort Myers (FSL)	2B	6	22	1	2	0	1	0	3	2	2	1-0	.091	.167	.182	2	.900
Major League totals (3 years)			262	937	124	249	48	11	11	88	61	154	42-15	.266	.315	.376	21	.979

DIVISION SERIES RECORD

Year	Team (League)	Pos.	G	AB	R	H	2B	3B	HR	RBI	BB	SO	SB-CS	Avg.	OBP	SLG	E	Avg.
				BATTING													FIELDING	
2002—	Minnesota (A.L.)	2B	4	12	2	3	1	0	0	0	1	2	0-0	.250	.308	.333	0	1.000

CHAMPIONSHIP SERIES RECORD

Year	Team (League)	Pos.	G	AB	R	H	2B	3B	HR	RBI	BB	SO	SB-CS	Avg.	OBP	SLG	E	Avg.
				BATTING													FIELDING	
2002—	Minnesota (A.L.)	2B	5	12	1	3	0	0	0	0	1	3	0-0	.250	.308	.250	0	1.000

RIVERA, JUAN — OF — YANKEES

PERSONAL: Born July 3, 1978, in Guarenas, Venezuela. ... 6-2/170. ... Bats right, throws right. ... Full name: Juan Luis Rivera.

TRANSACTIONS/CAREER NOTES: Signed as non-drafted free agent by New York Yankees organization (April 12, 1996). ... On Columbus disabled list (April 16-27, 2002). ... On New York disabled list (June 9-August 19, 2002); included rehabilitation assignments to Gulf Coast Yankees (July 31-August 7) and Columbus (August 8-19).

STATISTICAL NOTES: Led Gulf Coast League with 117 total bases in 1998. ... Led Gulf Coast League outfielders with four double plays and tied for lead with eight assists in 1998. ... Tied for International League lead with 14 assists by outfielders in 2002.

2002 GAMES PLAYED BY POSITION (MLB): OF—28.

Year	Team (League)	Pos.	G	AB	R	H	2B	3B	HR	RBI	BB	SO	SB-CS	Avg.	OBP	SLG	E	Avg.
				BATTING													FIELDING	
1996—	Dom. Yankees (DSL)..	OF	10	18	0	3	0	0	0	2	0	1	0-...	.167	...	.167	0	1.000
1997—	Maracay 1 (VSL)		52	142	25	40	9	0	0	14	12	16	12-...	.282	...	.345	...	...
1998—	GC Yankees (GCL)......	OF	57	210	43	70	9	1	*12	*45	26	27	8-5	.333	.408	.557	2	.979
	—Oneonta (NY-Penn)	OF	6	18	2	5	0	0	1	3	1	4	1-1	.278	.316	.444	0	1.000
1999—	Tampa (FSL)...............	OF	109	426	50	112	20	2	14	77	26	67	5-3	.263	.308	.418	4	.979
	—GC Yankees (GCL)......	OF	5	18	7	6	0	0	1	4	4	1	0-0	.333	.455	.500	0	1.000
2000—	Norwich (East.)	OF	17	62	9	14	5	0	2	12	6	15	0-0	.226	.294	.403	1	.955
	—Tampa (FSL)...............	OF-1B	115	409	62	113	26	1	14	69	33	56	11-7	.276	.336	.447	5	.978
2001—	Norwich (East.)	OF	77	316	50	101	18	3	14	58	15	50	5-7	.320	.353	.528	6	.963
	—Columbus (I.L.)..........	OF	55	199	39	65	11	1	14	40	15	31	4-5	.327	.372	.603	4	.970
	—New York (A.L.)..........	OF	3	4	0	0	0	0	0	0	0	0	0-0	.000	.000	.000	0	1.000
2002—	Columbus (I.L.)..........	OF	65	265	40	86	21	1	8	47	13	39	5-1	.325	.355	.502	6	.955
	—New York (A.L.)..........	OF	28	83	9	22	5	0	1	6	6	10	1-1	.265	.311	.361	2	.966
	—GC Yankees (GCL)......	OF	4	13	1	4	2	0	0	4	2	3	0-0	.308	.438	.462	0	1.000
Major League totals (2 years)			31	87	9	22	5	0	1	6	6	10	1-1	.253	.298	.345	2	.966

DIVISION SERIES RECORD

Year	Team (League)	Pos.	G	AB	R	H	2B	3B	HR	RBI	BB	SO	SB-CS	Avg.	OBP	SLG	E	Avg.
				BATTING													FIELDING	
2002—	New York (A.L.)..........	OF	4	12	2	3	0	0	0	3	1	3	0-0	.250	.308	.250	0	1.000

RIVERA, LUIS — P — ORIOLES

PERSONAL: Born June 21, 1978, in Chihuahua, Mexico. ... 6-3/163. ... Throws right, bats right. ... Full name: Luis Gutierrez Rivera.

HIGH SCHOOL: Sistema Preparatoria Abierta (Telucha, Mexico).

TRANSACTIONS/CAREER NOTES: Signed as non-drafted free agent by Atlanta Braves organization (February 18, 1995). ... Loaned by Braves organization to Mexico City Tigres, Mexican League (May 4-October 18, 1995); did not play. ... On Myrtle Beach disabled list (April 18-May 14, 1999) ... On Richmond disabled list (May 5-June 29, 2000). ... Traded by Braves with OF Trenidad Hubbard and C Fernando Lunar to Baltimore Orioles for OF B.J. Surhoff and P Gabe Molina (July 31, 2000). ... On disabled list (March 30, 2001-entire season; and March 29, 2002-entire season).

STATISTICAL NOTES: Tied for International League lead with four balks in 2000.

CAREER HITTING (MLB): 0-for-0 (.000), 0 R, 0 2B, 0 3B, 0 HR, 0 RBI.

Year	League	W	L	Pct.	ERA	G	GS	CG	ShO	Sv.-Opp.	IP	H	R	ER	HR	BB-IBB	SO
1996—	Gulf Coast Braves (GCL) ..	1	1	.500	2.59	8	6	0	0	0-...	24.1	18	9	7	0	7-1	26
1997—	Danville (Appl.)................	3	1	.750	2.41	9	9	0	0	0-...	41.0	28	15	11	2	17-0	57
	—Macon (S.Atl.).................	2	0	1.000	1.29	4	4	0	0	0-...	21.0	13	4	3	1	7-0	27
1998—	Macon (S.Atl.).................	5	5	.500	3.98	20	20	0	0	0-...	92.2	78	53	41	8	41-0	118
1999—	Myrtle Beach (Caro.)	0	2	.000	3.11	25	13	0	0	0-...	66.2	45	25	23	3	23-0	81
2000—	Atlanta (N.L.)....................	1	0	1.000	1.35	5	0	0	0	0-0	6.2	4	1	1	0	5-1	5
	—Richmond (I.L.)................	0	2	.000	8.06	8	7	0	0	0-...	22.1	29	20	20	3	18-0	12
	—Gulf Coast Braves (GCL) ..	0	0	...	0.00	3	3	0	0	0-...	4.0	2	0	0	0	1-0	2
	—Rochester (I.L.)■............	0	1	.000	3.38	3	3	0	0	0-...	8.0	11	5	3	0	5-1	4
	—Baltimore (A.L.)................	0	0	...	0.00	1	0	0	0	0-0	.2	1	0	0	0	1-0	0
2001—	Baltimore (A.L.)..................									Did not play.							
2002—	Baltimore (A.L.)..................									Did not play.							
A.L. totals (1 year)		0	0	...	0.00	1	0	0	0	0-0	.2	1	0	0	0	1-0	0
N.L. totals (1 year)		1	0	1.000	1.35	5	0	0	0	0-0	6.2	4	1	1	0	5-1	5
Major League totals (1 year)		1	0	1.000	1.23	6	0	0	0	0-0	7.1	5	1	1	0	6-1	5

RIVERA, MARIANO — P — YANKEES

PERSONAL: Born November 29, 1969, in Panama City, Panama. ... 6-2/185. ... Throws right, bats right. ... Cousin of Ruben Rivera, outfielder with four major league teams (1995-2002).

TRANSACTIONS/CAREER NOTES: Signed as non-drafted free agent by New York Yankees organization (February 17, 1990). ... On disabled list (April 10-May 19, July 11-28 and August 12-September 8, 1992). ... On Albany/Colonie disabled list (April 9-June 28, 1993). ... On Greensboro disabled list (September 6, 1993-remainder of season). ... On Tampa disabled list (April 23-May 9, 1994). ... On Columbus disabled list (August 4-14, 1994). ... On disabled list (April 6-24, 1998). ... On New York disabled list (June 10-25, July 21-August 8 and August 18-September 21, 2002); included rehabilitation assignment to Gulf Coast Yankees (August 6-8).

HONORS: Named A.L. Fireman of the Year by The Sporting News (1997 and 1999). ... Named A.L. Reliever of the Year by The Sporting News (2001).

STATISTICAL NOTES: Pitched seven-inning, 3-0 no-hit victory against Gulf Coast Pirates (August 31, 1990). ... Pitched five-inning, 3-0 no-hit victory for Columbus against Rochester (June 26, 1995). ... Led A.L. with 52 save opportunities in 1997 and 57 in 2001.

MISCELLANEOUS: Holds New York Yankees all-time record for most saves (243).
CAREER HITTING (MLB): 0-for-0 (.000), 0 R, 0 2B, 0 3B, 0 HR, 0 RBI.

Year	League	W	L	Pct.	ERA	G	GS	CG	ShO	Sv.-Opp.	IP	H	R	ER	HR	BB-IBB	SO
1990—	Gulf Coast Yankees (GCL)	5	1	.833	*0.17	22	1	1	1	1-...	52.0	17	3	1	0	7-0	58
1991—	Greensboro (S.Atl.)	4	9	.308	2.75	29	15	1	0	0-...	114.2	103	48	35	2	36-0	123
1992—	Fort Lauderdale (FSL)	5	3	.625	2.28	10	10	3	1	0-...	59.1	40	17	15	5	5-0	42
1993—	Greensboro (S.Atl.)	1	0	1.000	2.06	10	10	0	0	0-...	39.1	31	12	9	0	15-0	32
	—Gulf Coast Yankees (GCL)	0	1	.000	2.25	2	2	0	0	0-...	4.0	2	1	1	0	1-0	6
1994—	Tampa (FSL)	3	0	1.000	2.21	7	7	0	0	0-...	36.2	34	12	9	2	12-0	27
	—Albany/Colonie (East.)	3	0	1.000	2.27	9	9	0	0	0-...	63.1	58	20	16	5	8-0	39
	—Columbus (I.L.)	4	2	.667	5.81	6	6	1	0	0-...	31.0	34	22	20	5	10-0	23
1995—	Columbus (I.L.)	2	2	.500	2.10	7	7	1	1	0-...	30.0	25	10	7	2	3-0	30
	—New York (A.L.)	5	3	.625	5.51	19	10	0	0	0-1	67.0	71	43	41	11	30-0	51
1996—	New York (A.L.)	8	3	.727	2.09	61	0	0	0	5-8	107.2	73	25	25	1	34-3	130
1997—	New York (A.L.)	6	4	.600	1.88	66	0	0	0	43-52	71.2	65	17	15	5	20-6	68
1998—	New York (A.L.)	3	0	1.000	1.91	54	0	0	0	36-41	61.1	48	13	13	3	17-1	36
1999—	New York (A.L.)	4	3	.571	1.83	66	0	0	0	*45-49	69.0	43	15	14	2	18-3	52
2000—	New York (A.L.)	7	4	.636	2.85	66	0	0	0	36-41	75.2	58	26	24	4	25-3	58
2001—	New York (A.L.)	4	6	.400	2.34	71	0	0	0	*50-57	80.2	61	24	21	5	12-2	83
2002—	New York (A.L.)	1	4	.200	2.74	45	0	0	0	28-32	46.0	35	16	14	3	11-2	41
	—Gulf Coast Yankees (GCL)	0	0	...	0.00	1	1	0	0	0-...	2.0	2	0	0	0	1-0	2
Major League totals (8 years)		38	27	.585	2.60	448	10	0	0	243-281	579.0	454	179	167	34	167-20	519

DIVISION SERIES RECORD

RECORDS: Holds A.L. career record for most saves—11. ... Shares A.L. career record for most games pitched—19.

Year	League	W	L	Pct.	ERA	G	GS	CG	ShO	Sv.-Opp.	IP	H	R	ER	HR	BB-IBB	SO
1995—	New York (A.L.)	1	0	1.000	0.00	3	0	0	0	0-0	5.1	3	0	0	0	1-1	8
1996—	New York (A.L.)	0	0	...	0.00	2	0	0	0	0-0	4.2	0	0	0	0	1-0	1
1997—	New York (A.L.)	0	0	...	4.50	2	0	0	0	1-2	2.0	2	1	1	1	0-0	1
1998—	New York (A.L.)	0	0	...	0.00	3	0	0	0	2-2	3.1	1	0	0	0	1-0	2
1999—	New York (A.L.)	0	0	...	0.00	2	0	0	0	2-2	3.0	1	0	0	0	0-0	3
2000—	New York (A.L.)	0	0	...	0.00	3	0	0	0	3-3	5.0	2	0	0	0	0-0	2
2001—	New York (A.L.)	0	0	...	0.00	3	0	0	0	2-2	5.0	4	1	0	0	0-0	4
2002—	New York (A.L.)	0	0	...	0.00	1	0	0	0	1-1	1.0	1	0	0	0	0-0	0
Division series totals (8 years)		1	0	1.000	0.31	19	0	0	0	11-12	29.1	14	2	1	1	3-1	21

CHAMPIONSHIP SERIES RECORD

Year	League	W	L	Pct.	ERA	G	GS	CG	ShO	Sv.-Opp.	IP	H	R	ER	HR	BB-IBB	SO
1996—	New York (A.L.)	1	0	1.000	0.00	2	0	0	0	0-0	4.0	6	0	0	0	1-0	5
1998—	New York (A.L.)	0	0	...	0.00	4	0	0	0	1-1	5.2	0	0	0	0	1-0	5
1999—	New York (A.L.)	1	0	1.000	0.00	3	0	0	0	2-2	4.2	5	0	0	0	0-0	3
2000—	New York (A.L.)	0	0	...	1.93	3	0	0	0	1-1	4.2	4	1	1	0	0-0	1
2001—	New York (A.L.)	1	0	1.000	1.93	4	0	0	0	2-2	4.2	2	1	1	0	1-0	3
Champ. series totals (5 years)		3	0	1.000	0.76	16	0	0	0	6-6	23.2	17	2	2	0	3-0	17

WORLD SERIES RECORD

RECORDS: Holds career record for most saves—8.
NOTES: Named Most Valuable Player (1999). ... Member of World Series championship team (1996, 1998, 1999 and 2000).

Year	League	W	L	Pct.	ERA	G	GS	CG	ShO	Sv.-Opp.	IP	H	R	ER	HR	BB-IBB	SO
1996—	New York (A.L.)	0	0	...	1.59	4	0	0	0	0-0	5.2	4	1	1	0	3-0	4
1998—	New York (A.L.)	0	0	...	0.00	3	0	0	0	3-3	4.1	5	0	0	0	0-0	4
1999—	New York (A.L.)	1	0	1.000	0.00	3	0	0	0	2-2	4.2	3	0	0	0	1-0	3
2000—	New York (A.L.)	0	0	...	3.00	4	0	0	0	2-2	6.0	4	2	2	1	1-0	7
2001—	New York (A.L.)	1	1	.500	1.42	4	0	0	0	1-2	6.1	6	2	1	0	1-1	7
World Series totals (5 years)		2	1	.667	1.33	18	0	0	0	8-9	27.0	22	5	4	1	6-1	25

ALL-STAR GAME RECORD

	W	L	Pct.	ERA	GS	CG	ShO	Sv.-Opp.	IP	H	R	ER	HR	BB-IBB	SO
All-Star Game totals (3 years)	0	0	...	0.00	0	0	0	1-1	3.0	3	1	0	0	0-0	1

RIVERA, MIKE — C — TIGERS

PERSONAL: Born September 8, 1976, in Rio Piedras, Puerto Rico. ... 6-0/210. ... Bats right, throws right. ... Full name: Michael R. Rivera.
HIGH SCHOOL: Dr. Augustin Stahl (Bayamon, Puerto Rico).
TRANSACTIONS/CAREER NOTES: Signed as non-drafted free agent by Detroit Tigers organization (January 20, 1997). ... On Toledo disabled list (July 24-August 2, 2002).
STATISTICAL NOTES: Tied for Gulf Coast League lead in intentional bases on balls received with two in 1997. ... Led Midwest League catchers with 889 putouts and 1,007 total chances in 1998. ... Led Florida State League catchers with 104 assists in 1999. ... Led Eastern League catchers with 793 putouts, 83 assists and 886 total chances in 2001.
2002 GAMES PLAYED BY POSITION (MLB): C—37; DH—1.

			BATTING														FIELDING	
Year	Team (League)	Pos.	G	AB	R	H	2B	3B	HR	RBI	BB	SO	SB-CS	Avg.	OBP	SLG	E	Avg.
1997—	GC Tigers (GCL)	C-1B	47	154	34	44	9	2	*10	36	18	25	0-0	.286	.367	.565	1	.996
1998—	West Mich. (Midw.)	C	108	403	40	111	34	3	9	67	15	68	0-2	.275	.301	.442	10	.990
1999—	Lakeland (FSL)	C	104	370	44	103	20	2	14	72	20	59	1-1	.278	.314	.457	8	.989
	—Jacksonville (Sou.)	C	7	23	3	4	1	0	2	6	2	5	0-0	.174	.240	.478	0	1.000
2000—	Lakeland (FSL)	C	64	243	30	71	19	4	11	53	16	45	2-0	.292	.336	.539	5	.988
	—Toledo (I.L.)	C	4	13	0	3	3	0	0	1	0	2	0-0	.231	.231	.462	1	.968
	—Jacksonville (Sou.)	C	39	150	10	29	8	1	2	9	7	30	0-0	.193	.228	.300	8	.969
2001—	Erie (East.)	C	112	415	76	120	19	1	*33	101	44	96	2-2	.289	.368	.578	10	.989
	—Detroit (A.L.)	C	4	12	2	4	2	0	0	1	0	2	0-0	.333	.333	.500	2	.929
2002—	Detroit (A.L.)	C-DH	39	132	11	30	8	1	1	11	4	35	0-0	.227	.254	.326	2	.990
	—Toledo (I.L.)	C	74	265	43	66	11	1	20	53	35	64	0-1	.249	.341	.525	3	.993
Major League totals (2 years)			43	144	13	34	10	1	1	12	4	37	0-0	.236	.260	.340	4	.983

RIVERA, RUBEN — OF

PERSONAL: Born November 14, 1973, in La Chorrera, Panama. ... 6-3/208. ... Bats right, throws right. ... Full name: Ruben Moreno Rivera. ... Cousin of Mariano Rivera, pitcher, New York Yankees.
TRANSACTIONS/CAREER NOTES: Signed as non-drafted free agent by New York Yankees organization (November 21, 1990). ... On New York disabled list (March 27-May 30, 1997). ... Traded by Yankees with P Rafael Medina and $3 million to San Diego Padres for the rights to P Hideki Irabu, 2B Homer Bush, OF Gordon Amerson and a player to be named later (April 22, 1997); Yankees acquired OF Vernon Maxwell to complete deal (June 9, 1997). ... On San Diego disabled list (May 30-August 13, 1997); included rehabilitation assignments to Rancho Cucamonga (May 30-July 22) and Las Vegas (July 23-August 4). ... On San Diego disabled list (April 12-May 5, 2000); included rehabilitation assignment to Las Vegas (May 3-5). ... Released by Padres (March 14, 2001). ... Signed by Cincinnati Reds (March 21, 2001). ... Claimed on waivers by San Francisco Giants (November 16, 2001). ... Granted free agency (December 21, 2001). ... Signed by Yankees (February 14, 2002). ... Released by Yankees (March 11, 2002). ... Signed by Texas Rangers organization (March 31, 2002). ... Released by Rangers (September 30, 2002).
HONORS: Named New York-Pennsylvania League Most Valuable Player (1993). ... Named South Atlantic League Most Valuable Player (1994).
STATISTICAL NOTES: Tied for New York-Pennsylvania League lead in double plays by outfielders with three in 1993. ... Career major league grand slams: 2.
2002 GAMES PLAYED BY POSITION (MLB): OF—67; DH—2.

		BATTING														FIELDING	
Year Team (League)	Pos.	G	AB	R	H	2B	3B	HR	RBI	BB	SO	SB-CS	Avg.	OBP	SLG	E	Avg.
1991—Dom. Yankees (DSL)..		51	170	27	34	3	2	2	16	23	37	14-...	.200	...	.276	...	...
1992—GC Yankees (GCL)......	OF	53	194	37	53	10	3	1	20	42	49	21-6	.273	.417	.371	4	.951
1993—Oneonta (NY-Penn)....	OF	55	199	45	55	7	6	13	47	32	66	12-5	.276	.385	.568	3	.976
1994—Greensboro (S.Atl.)....	OF	105	400	83	115	24	3	•28	81	47	125	36-5	.288	.372	*.573	5	.979
—Tampa (FSL)..............	OF	34	134	18	35	4	3	5	20	8	38	12-5	.261	.308	.448	2	.976
1995—Norwich (East.)..........	OF	71	256	49	75	16	8	9	39	37	77	16-8	.293	.402	.523	3	.984
—Columbus (I.L.)..........	OF	48	174	37	47	8	2	15	35	26	62	8-4	.270	.373	.598	3	.975
—New York (A.L.)..........	OF	5	1	0	0	0	0	0	0	0	1	0-0	.000	.000	.000	0	1.000
1996—Columbus (I.L.)..........	OF	101	362	59	85	20	4	10	46	40	96	15-10	.235	.324	.395	7	.972
—New York (A.L.)..........	OF	46	88	17	25	6	1	2	16	13	26	6-2	.284	.381	.443	0	1.000
1997—Rancho Cuca. (Calif.)■	DH	6	23	6	4	1	0	1	3	3	9	1-0	.174	.259	.348	...	...
—Las Vegas (PCL)........	DH-1B	12	48	6	12	5	1	1	6	1	20	1-0	.250	.280	.458	0	1.000
—San Diego (N.L.)........	OF	17	20	2	5	1	0	0	1	2	9	2-1	.250	.318	.300	0	1.000
1998—Las Vegas (PCL)........	OF	30	104	9	15	3	0	3	11	11	42	4-0	.144	.222	.260	0	1.000
—San Diego (N.L.)........	OF	95	172	31	36	7	2	6	29	28	52	5-1	.209	.325	.378	3	.973
1999—San Diego (N.L.)........	OF	147	411	65	80	16	1	23	48	55	143	18-7	.195	.295	.406	8	.976
2000—San Diego (N.L.)........	OF	135	423	62	88	18	6	17	57	44	137	8-4	.208	.296	.400	5	.984
—Las Vegas (PCL)........	OF	2	10	1	2	0	0	0	1	0	3	0-0	.200	.200	.200	0	1.000
2001—Cincinnati (N.L.)■......	OF	117	263	37	67	13	1	10	34	21	83	6-3	.255	.321	.426	3	.983
2002—Tulsa (Texas)■..........	OF	59	205	38	64	17	4	10	43	23	46	4-3	.312	.388	.580	2	.986
—Oklahoma (PCL)........	OF	27	98	19	27	2	4	7	23	13	23	2-0	.276	.366	.592	3	.955
—Texas (A.L.)...............	OF-DH	69	158	17	33	4	0	4	14	17	45	4-2	.209	.302	.310	3	.983
American League totals (3 years)		120	247	34	58	10	1	6	30	30	72	10-4	.235	.330	.356	3	.988
National League totals (5 years)		511	1289	197	276	55	10	56	169	150	424	39-16	.214	.305	.403	19	.980
Major League totals (8 years)		631	1536	231	334	65	11	62	199	180	496	49-20	.217	.309	.395	22	.982

DIVISION SERIES RECORD

		BATTING														FIELDING	
Year Team (League)	Pos.	G	AB	R	H	2B	3B	HR	RBI	BB	SO	SB-CS	Avg.	OBP	SLG	E	Avg.
1996—New York (A.L.)..........	OF-PH	2	1	0	0	0	0	0	0	0	1	0-0	.000	.000	.000	0	...
1998—San Diego (N.L.)........	OF	3	6	0	0	0	0	0	0	0	3	0-0	.000	.000	.000	0	1.000
Division series totals (2 years)		5	7	0	0	0	0	0	0	0	4	0-0	.000	.000	.000	0	1.000

CHAMPIONSHIP SERIES RECORD

		BATTING														FIELDING	
Year Team (League)	Pos.	G	AB	R	H	2B	3B	HR	RBI	BB	SO	SB-CS	Avg.	OBP	SLG	E	Avg.
1996— New York (A.L.).........								Did not play.									
1998—San Diego (N.L.)........	OF-PH	6	13	1	3	2	0	0	0	0	7	1-0	.231	.231	.385	0	1.000

WORLD SERIES RECORD

NOTES: Member of World Series championship team (1996); inactive due to injury.

		BATTING														FIELDING	
Year Team (League)	Pos.	G	AB	R	H	2B	3B	HR	RBI	BB	SO	SB-CS	Avg.	OBP	SLG	E	Avg.
1996— New York (A.L.).........								Did not play.									
1998—San Diego (N.L.)........	PH-OF-PR	3	5	1	4	2	0	0	1	0	0	0-0	.800	.800	1.200	0	1.000

ROA, JOE — P — PHILLIES

PERSONAL: Born October 11, 1971, in Southfield, Mich. ... 6-1/194. ... Throws right, bats right. ... Full name: Joe Rodger Roa. ... Name pronounced ROE-ah.
HIGH SCHOOL: Hazel Park (Mich.).
TRANSACTIONS/CAREER NOTES: Selected by Atlanta Braves organization in 18th round of free-agent draft (June 5, 1989). ... Traded by Braves to New York Mets organization (August 29, 1991), completing deal in which Mets traded P Alejandro Pena to Braves for P Tony Castillo and a player to be named (August 28, 1991). ... On Norfolk suspended list (July 31-August 2, 1994). ... Traded by Mets with OF Jeromy Burnitz to Cleveland Indians for P Dave Mlicki, P Paul Byrd, P Jerry DiPoto and a player to be named (November 18, 1994); Mets acquired 2B Jesus Azuaje to complete deal (December 6, 1994). ... Traded by Indians to San Francisco Giants for OF Trenidad Hubbard (December 16, 1996), completing deal in which Giants traded 3B Matt Williams and a player to be named later to Indians for IF Jeff Kent, IF Jose Vizcaino, P Julian Tavarez and a player to be named later (November 13, 1996). ... On Fresno disabled list (June 29-July 11, 1998). ... Granted free agency (October 15, 1998). ... Signed by Kansas City Royals organization (December 17, 1998). ... Released by Royals (March 29, 1999). ... Signed by Indians organization (March 28, 2000). ... On Buffalo disabled list (April 6-May 19, 2000). ... Granted free agency (October 18, 2000). ... Signed by Florida Marlins organization (December 28, 2000). ... Granted free agency (October 15, 2001). ... Re-signed by Marlins organization

(November 20, 2001). ... On Portland disabled list (April 15-May 2, 2001). ... Released by Marlins (March 19, 2002). ... Signed by Pittsburgh Pirates organization (March 22, 2002). ... Traded by Pirates to Philadelphia Phillies for future considerations (March 28, 2002).

HONORS: Named International League Most Valuable Pitcher (2002).

CAREER HITTING (MLB): 8-for-40 (.200), 1 R, 1 2B, 0 3B, 0 HR, 2 RBI.

Year League	W	L	Pct.	ERA	G	GS	CG	ShO	Sv.-Opp.	IP	H	R	ER	HR	BB-IBB	SO
1989—Gulf Coast Braves (GCL)	2	2	.500	2.89	13	4	0	0	0-...	37.1	40	18	12	2	10-1	21
1990—Pulaski (Appl.)	4	2	.667	2.97	14	11	3	1	0-...	75.2	55	29	25	3	26-0	49
1991—Macon (S.Atl.)	13	3	.813	2.17	30	18	4	2	1-...	141.0	106	46	34	6	33-4	96
1992—St. Lucie (FSL)■	9	7	.563	3.63	26	24	2	1	0-...	156.1	176	80	63	9	15-1	61
1993—Binghamton (East.)	12	7	.632	3.87	32	23	2	1	0-...	167.1	190	80	72	9	24-0	73
1994—Binghamton (East.)	2	1	.667	1.80	3	3	0	0	0-...	20.0	18	6	4	0	1-0	11
—Norfolk (I.L.)	8	8	.500	3.49	25	25	5	0	0-...	167.2	184	82	65	16	34-1	74
1995—Buffalo (A.A.)■	*17	3	.850	3.50	25	24	3	0	0-...	164.2	168	71	64	9	28-1	93
—Cleveland (A.L.)	0	1	.000	6.00	1	1	0	0	0-0	6.0	9	4	4	1	2-0	0
1996—Buffalo (A.A.)	11	8	.579	3.27	26	24	5	0	0-...	165.1	161	66	60	19	36-0	82
—Cleveland (A.L.)	0	0	...	10.80	1	0	0	0	0-0	1.2	4	2	2	0	3-0	0
1997—San Francisco (N.L.)■	2	5	.286	5.21	28	3	0	0	0-0	65.2	86	40	38	8	20-5	34
—Phoenix (PCL)	3	1	.750	4.75	6	5	0	0	0-...	36.0	43	21	19	4	11-0	16
1998—Fresno (PCL)	12	9	.571	5.17	27	27	2	1	0-...	162.0	192	102	93	26	32-0	97
1999—									Did not play.							
2000—Akron (East.)■	6	5	.545	3.41	19	14	1	0	0-...	103.0	91	48	39	7	38-0	59
2001—Portland (East.)■	0	2	.000	3.00	7	7	0	0	0-...	36.0	36	15	12	2	3-1	26
—Calgary (PCL)	6	6	.500	3.92	19	19	1	0	0-...	124.0	134	58	54	16	12-2	81
2002—Scranton/W.B. (I.L.)■	14	0	*1.000	1.86	17	17	1	0	0-...	111.0	83	24	23	4	16-2	74
—Philadelphia (N.L.)	4	4	.500	4.04	14	11	0	0	0-0	71.1	78	33	32	11	13-2	35
A.L. totals (2 years)	0	1	.000	7.04	2	1	0	0	0-0	7.2	13	6	6	1	5-0	0
N.L. totals (2 years)	6	9	.400	4.60	42	14	0	0	0-0	137.0	164	73	70	19	33-7	69
Major League totals (4 years)	6	10	.375	4.73	44	15	0	0	0-0	144.2	177	79	76	20	38-7	69

ROBERTS, BRIAN — SS — ORIOLES

PERSONAL: Born October 9, 1977, in Durham, N.C. ... 5-9/170. ... Bats both, throws right. ... Full name: Brian Michael Roberts.

HIGH SCHOOL: Chapel Hill (N.C.).

COLLEGE: North Carolina, then South Carolina.

TRANSACTIONS/CAREER NOTES: Selected by Baltimore Orioles organization in supplemental round ("sandwich pick" between first and second round, 50th pick overall) of free-agent draft (June 2, 1999); pick received as part of compensation for Texas Rangers signing Type A free agent 1B Rafael Palmeiro. ... On Frederick disabled list (April 19-July 13, 2000); included rehabilitation assignment to Gulf Coast Orioles (July 2-13).

STATISTICAL NOTES: Had 15-game hitting streak (June 22-July 12, 2001).

2002 GAMES PLAYED BY POSITION (MLB): 2B—25; DH—8.

		BATTING														FIELDING	
Year Team (League)	Pos.	G	AB	R	H	2B	3B	HR	RBI	BB	SO	SB-CS	Avg.	OBP	SLG	E	Avg.
1999—Delmarva (S.Atl.)	SS	47	167	22	40	12	1	0	21	27	42	17-5	.240	.347	.323	8	.964
2000—Frederick (Caro.)	SS	48	163	27	49	6	3	0	16	27	24	13-10	.301	.403	.374	8	.952
—GC Orioles (GCL)	SS	9	29	8	9	1	2	1	3	7	4	7-1	.310	.432	.586	2	.905
2001—Bowie (East.)	2B-SS	22	81	12	24	7	0	1	7	9	12	10-0	.296	.366	.420	3	.968
—Rochester (I.L.)	SS	44	161	16	43	4	1	1	12	28	22	23-3	.267	.376	.323	13	.927
—Baltimore (A.L.)	SS-2B-DH	75	273	42	69	12	3	2	17	13	36	12-3	.253	.284	.341	16	.941
2002—Rochester (I.L.)	2B	78	313	49	86	9	7	3	30	40	46	22-4	.275	.361	.377	7	.978
—Baltimore (A.L.)	2B-DH	38	128	18	29	6	0	1	11	15	21	9-2	.227	.308	.297	3	.977
Major League totals (2 years)		113	401	60	98	18	3	3	28	28	57	21-5	.244	.292	.327	19	.952

ROBERTS, DAVE — OF — DODGERS

PERSONAL: Born May 31, 1972, in Okinawa, Japan. ... 5-10/180. ... Bats left, throws left. ... Full name: David Ray Roberts.

HIGH SCHOOL: Rancho Buena Vista (Oceanside, Calif.).

COLLEGE: UCLA.

TRANSACTIONS/CAREER NOTES: Selected by Detroit Tigers organization in 28th round of free-agent draft (June 2, 1994). ... Loaned by Tigers to Visalia, Oakland Athletics organization (March 30-August 30, 1996). ... Traded by Tigers with P Tim Worrell to Cleveland Indians for OF Geronimo Berroa (June 24, 1998). ... On Akron disabled list (August 10-18, 1998). ... On Cleveland disabled list (March 31-June 24, 2001); included rehabilitation assignment to Akron (June 4-24). ... Traded by Indians to Los Angeles Dodgers for P Christian Bridenbaugh and P Nial Hughes (December 21, 2001).

STATISTICAL NOTES: Career major league grand slams: 2.

2002 GAMES PLAYED BY POSITION (MLB): OF—117.

		BATTING														FIELDING	
Year Team (League)	Pos.	G	AB	R	H	2B	3B	HR	RBI	BB	SO	SB-CS	Avg.	OBP	SLG	E	Avg.
1994—Jamestown (NY-P)	OF	54	178	33	52	7	2	0	12	29	27	12-8	.292	.392	.354	0	1.000
1995—Lakeland (FSL)	OF	92	357	67	108	10	5	3	30	39	43	30-8	.303	.371	.384	1	.985
1996—Visalia (Calif.)■	OF	126	482	*112	131	24	7	5	37	98	105	*65-21	.272	.391	.382	5	.977
—Jacksonville (Sou.)■	OF	3	9	0	2	0	0	0	0	1	0	0-1	.222	.300	.222	0	1.000
1997—Jacksonville (Sou.)	OF	105	415	76	123	24	2	4	41	45	62	23-5	.296	.366	.393	4	.954
1998—Jacksonville (Sou.)	OF	69	279	71	91	14	5	5	42	53	59	21-9	.326	.434	.466	0	1.000
—Akron (East.)■	OF	56	227	49	82	10	5	7	33	35	30	28-6	.361	.447	.542	1	.992
—Buffalo (I.L.)	OF	5	15	2	2	0	0	0	2	0	3	2-0	.133	.125	.133	0	1.000
1999—Buffalo (I.L.)	OF-DH	89	350	65	95	17	*10	0	38	43	52	39-3	.271	.351	.377	1	.996
—Cleveland (A.L.)	OF	41	143	26	34	4	0	2	12	9	16	11-3	.238	.281	.308	0	1.000
2000—Buffalo (I.L.)	OF	120	462	93	135	16	3	13	55	59	68	39-11	.292	.373	.424	1	*.997
—Cleveland (A.L.)	OF	19	10	1	2	0	0	0	0	2	2	1-1	.200	.333	.200	0	1.000

		BATTING														FIELDING	
Year Team (League)	Pos.	G	AB	R	H	2B	3B	HR	RBI	BB	SO	SB-CS	Avg.	OBP	SLG	E	Avg.
2001—Akron (East.)	OF	17	64	9	13	5	0	0	2	9	8	4-0	.203	.307	.281	1	.969
—Buffalo (I.L.)	OF	62	241	34	73	12	4	0	22	18	44	17-6	.303	.352	.386	3	.978
—Cleveland (A.L.)	OF-DH	15	12	3	4	1	0	0	2	1	2	0-1	.333	.385	.417	0	1.000
2002—Los Angeles (N.L.)■	OF	127	422	63	117	14	7	3	34	48	51	45-10	.277	.353	.365	0	•1.000
American League totals (3 years)		75	165	30	40	5	0	2	14	12	20	12-5	.242	.292	.309	0	1.000
National League totals (1 year)		127	422	63	117	14	7	3	34	48	51	45-10	.277	.353	.365	0	1.000
Major League totals (4 years)		202	587	93	157	19	7	5	48	60	71	57-15	.267	.336	.349	0	1.000

DIVISION SERIES RECORD

		BATTING														FIELDING	
Year Team (League)	Pos.	G	AB	R	H	2B	3B	HR	RBI	BB	SO	SB-CS	Avg.	OBP	SLG	E	Avg.
1999—Cleveland (A.L.)	PH-OF	2	3	0	0	0	0	0	0	0	2	0-0	.000	.000	.000	0	1.000

ROBERTS, GRANT — P — METS

PERSONAL: Born September 13, 1977, in El Cajon, Calif. ... 6-3/205. ... Throws right, bats right. ... Full name: Grant William Roberts.

HIGH SCHOOL: Grossmont (La Mesa, Calif.).

TRANSACTIONS/CAREER NOTES: Selected by New York Mets organization in 11th round of free-agent draft (June 1, 1995). ... On New York disabled list (June 9-30 and July 13-September 10, 2002); included rehabilitation assignment to Binghamton (June 28-30).

STATISTICAL NOTES: Tied for International League lead with 12 wild pitches in 2000.

CAREER HITTING (MLB): 1-for-4 (.250), 1 R, 0 2B, 0 3B, 0 HR, 0 RBI.

Year League	W	L	Pct.	ERA	G	GS	CG	ShO	Sv.-Opp.	IP	H	R	ER	HR	BB-IBB	SO
1995—Gulf Coast Mets (GCL)	2	1	.667	2.15	11	3	0	0	0-...	29.1	19	13	7	1	14-1	24
1996—Kingsport (Appl.)	*9	1	*.900	2.10	13	13	2	*2	0-...	68.2	43	18	16	3	37-1	*92
1997—Capital City (S.Atl.)	11	3	*.786	2.36	22	22	2	1	0-...	129.2	98	37	34	1	44-0	122
1998—St. Lucie (FSL)	4	5	.444	4.23	17	17	0	0	0-...	72.1	72	37	34	11	37-0	70
1999—Binghamton (East.)	7	6	.538	4.87	23	23	0	0	0-...	131.1	135	81	71	9	49-0	94
—Norfolk (I.L.)	2	1	.667	4.50	5	5	0	0	0-...	28.0	32	15	14	1	11-2	30
2000—Norfolk (I.L.)	7	8	.467	3.38	25	25	5	0	0-...	157.1	154	67	59	6	63-5	115
—New York (N.L.)	0	0	...	11.57	4	1	0	0	0-0	7.0	11	10	9	0	4-1	6
2001—Norfolk (I.L.)	3	5	.375	4.52	30	6	0	0	2-...	67.2	80	38	34	4	19-1	54
—New York (N.L.)	1	0	1.000	3.81	16	0	0	0	0-1	26.0	24	11	11	2	8-1	29
2002—New York (N.L.)	3	1	.750	2.20	34	0	0	0	0-0	45.0	43	12	11	3	16-7	31
—Binghamton (East.)	0	0	...	0.00	1	1	0	0	0-...	1.0	0	0	0	0	0-0	1
Major League totals (3 years)	4	1	.800	3.58	54	1	0	0	0-1	78.0	78	33	31	5	28-9	66

ROBERTS, WILLIS — P — ORIOLES

PERSONAL: Born June 19, 1975, in San Cristobal, Dominican Republic. ... 6-3/175. ... Throws right, bats right. ... Full name: Willis Augusto Roberts.

TRANSACTIONS/CAREER NOTES: Signed as non-drafted free agent by Detroit Tigers organization (February 18, 1992). ... On disabled list (July 14-August 1 and August 1-September 13, 1994). ... On Toledo disabled list (May 3-20, 1999). ... Released by Tigers (February 1, 2000). ... Signed by Cincinnati Reds organization (February 1, 2000). ... Granted free agency (October 18, 2000). ... Signed by Baltimore Orioles organization (November 16, 2000). ... On suspended list (September 13-18, 2002).

CAREER HITTING (MLB): 1-for-4 (.250), 0 R, 0 2B, 0 3B, 0 HR, 0 RBI.

Year League	W	L	Pct.	ERA	G	GS	CG	ShO	Sv.-Opp.	IP	H	R	ER	HR	BB-IBB	SO
1992—Dominican Tigers (DSL)	0	6	.000	8.23	12	7	1	0	0-...	35.0	43	49	32	...	46-...	17
1993—Bristol (Appl.)	2	3	.400	1.38	10	2	0	0	1-...	26.0	24	16	4	0	11-0	23
1994—Bristol (Appl.)	1	2	.333	3.92	4	4	0	0	0-...	20.2	9	9	9	1	8-0	17
1995—Fayetteville (S.Atl.)	6	3	.667	2.70	17	15	0	0	0-...	80.0	72	33	24	2	40-0	52
1996—Lakeland (FSL)	9	7	.563	2.89	23	22	2	0	0-...	149.1	133	60	48	5	69-0	105
1997—Jacksonville (Sou.)	6	*15	.286	6.28	26	26	2	0	0-...	149.0	181	*120	*104	18	64-0	86
1998—Jacksonville (Sou.)	3	1	.750	2.19	12	2	0	0	0-...	24.2	21	10	6	0	10-1	15
—Toledo (I.L.)	3	3	.500	4.61	39	0	0	0	2-...	54.2	63	33	28	4	28-2	40
1999—Toledo (I.L.)	5	8	.385	6.26	31	12	2	0	0-...	92.0	112	68	64	10	59-3	52
—Detroit (A.L.)	0	0	...	13.50	1	0	0	0	0-0	1.1	3	4	2	0	0-0	0
2000—Chattanooga (Sou.)■	4	0	1.000	3.06	5	5	0	0	0-...	32.1	33	12	11	0	13-1	28
—Louisville (I.L.)	7	8	.467	5.66	25	20	2	1	0-...	124.0	138	80	78	19	55-0	66
2001—Baltimore (A.L.)■	9	10	.474	4.91	46	18	1	0	6-10	132.0	142	75	72	15	55-1	95
2002—Baltimore (A.L.)	5	4	.556	3.36	66	0	0	0	1-3	75.0	79	34	28	5	32-3	51
Major League totals (3 years)	14	14	.500	4.41	113	18	1	0	7-13	208.1	224	113	102	20	87-4	146

ROBERTSON, JERIOME — P — ASTROS

PERSONAL: Born March 30, 1977, in San Jose, Calif. ... 6-1/190. ... Throws left, bats left. ... Full name: Jeriome Paul Robertson.

HIGH SCHOOL: Exeter (Calif.) Union.

TRANSACTIONS/CAREER NOTES: Selected by Houston Astros organization in 24th round of free-agent draft (June 1, 1995). ... On Round Rock disabled list (April 6-24, 2000).

HONORS: Named Pacific Coast League Pitcher of the Year (2002).

STATISTICAL NOTES: Tied for Florida State League lead in balks with six in 1998. ... Led Texas League with seven balks in 1999.

CAREER HITTING (MLB): 0-for-0 (.000), 0 R, 0 2B, 0 3B, 0 HR, 0 RBI.

Year League	W	L	Pct.	ERA	G	GS	CG	ShO	Sv.-Opp.	IP	H	R	ER	HR	BB-IBB	SO
1996—Gulf Coast Astros (GCL)	5	3	.625	1.72	13	•13	1	1	0-...	78.1	51	20	15	2	15-0	*98
—Kissimmee (FSL)	0	0	...	2.57	1	1	0	0	0-...	7.0	4	4	2	0	1-0	2
1997—Quad City (Midw.)	11	8	.579	4.07	26	25	2	1	1-...	146.0	151	86	66	12	56-1	135
1998—Kissimmee (FSL)	10	10	.500	3.70	28	•28	2	0	0-...	*175.0	185	83	72	13	53-3	131
1999—Jackson (Texas)	*15	7	.682	3.06	28	•28	1	0	0-...	*191.0	184	81	65	22	45-2	133

Year	League	W	L	Pct.	ERA	G	GS	CG	ShO	Sv.-Opp.	IP	H	R	ER	HR	BB-IBB	SO
2000—	Kissimmee (FSL)	2	1	.667	4.66	5	5	1	1	0-...	29.0	28	19	15	1	5-0	13
	— Round Rock (Texas)	2	2	.500	4.13	11	10	0	0	0-...	61.0	62	36	28	8	18-1	30
	— New Orleans (PCL)	1	7	.125	7.07	9	9	0	0	0-...	49.2	64	42	39	10	23-1	27
2001—	Round Rock (Texas)	5	1	.833	3.91	57	0	0	0	3-...	73.2	89	33	32	10	21-0	72
2002—	New Orleans (PCL)	12	8	.600	*2.55	27	27	2	1	0-...	*180.0	160	59	51	13	45-0	114
	— Houston (N.L.)	0	2	.000	6.52	11	1	0	0	0-0	9.2	13	8	7	4	5-3	6
Major League totals (1 year)		0	2	.000	6.52	11	1	0	0	0-0	9.2	13	8	7	4	5-3	6

ROBERTSON, NATE — P — MARLINS

PERSONAL: Born September 3, 1977, in Wichita, Kan. ... 6-2/215. ... Throws left, bats right. ... Full name: Nathan D. Robertson.
COLLEGE: Wichita State.
TRANSACTIONS/CAREER NOTES: Selected by Florida Marlins organization in fifth round of free-agent draft (June 2, 1999).

Year	League	W	L	Pct.	ERA	G	GS	CG	ShO	Sv.-Opp.	IP	H	R	ER	HR	BB-IBB	SO
1999—	Utica (NY-Penn)	2	0	1.000	2.77	5	5	0	0	0-...	26.0	22	9	8	0	8-0	26
	— Kane County (Midw.)	6	1	.857	2.29	8	8	1		0-...	51.0	42	14	13	1	12-0	33
2000—	Kane County (Midw.)	0	2	.000	5.09	6	6	0	0	0-...	17.2	24	13	10	0	6-0	15
2001—	Brevard County (FSL)	11	4	.733	2.88	19	19	2	0	0-...	106.1	95	44	34	3	43-1	67
2002—	Portland (East.)	10	9	.526	3.42	27	27	3	0	0-...	163.0	156	77	62	12	50-2	109
	— Florida (N.L.)	0	1	.000	11.88	6	1	0	0	0-0	8.1	15	11	11	3	4-3	1
Major League totals (1 year)		0	1	.000	11.88	6	1	0	0	0-0	8.1	15	11	11	3	4-3	1

ROBINSON, KERRY — OF — CARDINALS

PERSONAL: Born October 3, 1973, in St. Louis. ... 6-0/175. ... Bats left, throws left. ... Full name: Kerry Keith Robinson. ... Son of Rogers Robinson, outfielder in St. Louis Cardinals organization (1957-69).
HIGH SCHOOL: Hazelwood East (St. Louis).
COLLEGE: Southeast Missouri State.
TRANSACTIONS/CAREER NOTES: Selected by St. Louis Cardinals organization in 34th round of free-agent draft (June 1, 1995). ... Selected by Tampa Bay Devil Rays in second round (44th pick overall) of expansion draft (November 18, 1997). ... Claimed on waivers by Seattle Mariners (November 19, 1998). ... Traded by Mariners to Cincinnati Reds for P Todd Williams (July 22, 1999). ... Granted free agency (October 18, 2000). ... Signed by Cardinals organization (May 17, 2001).
STATISTICAL NOTES: Led Midwest League in caught stealing with 26 in 1996. ... Led Texas League in caught stealing with 23 in 1997.
2002 GAMES PLAYED BY POSITION (MLB): OF—76; DH—1.

			BATTING														FIELDING	
Year	Team (League)	Pos.	G	AB	R	H	2B	3B	HR	RBI	BB	SO	SB-CS	Avg.	OBP	SLG	E	Avg.
1995—	Johnson City (Appl.)	OF	60	250	44	74	12	8	1	26	16	30	14-10	.296	.336	.420	6	.938
1996—	Peoria (Midw.)	OF	123	440	98	158	17	4	2	47	51	51	•50-26	*.359	.422	.430	7	.962
1997—	Arkansas (Texas)	OF	135	*523	80	168	16	3	2	62	54	64	40-23	.321	.386	.375	7	.966
	— Louisville (A.A.)	OF	2	9	0	1	0	0	0	0	0	1	0-0	.111	.111	.111	0	1.000
1998—	Orlando (Sou.)■	OF	72	309	45	83	7	5	2	26	27	28	28-9	.269	.325	.343	0	1.000
	— Durham (I.L.)	OF	58	242	28	73	7	4	1	28	23	30	18-11	.302	.361	.376	2	.987
	— Tampa Bay (A.L.)	OF	2	3	0	0	0	0	0	0	0	1	0-0	.000	.000	.000	0	1.000
1999—	Tacoma (PCL)■	OF-DH	79	335	53	108	16	•9	0	34	14	44	30-7	.322	.348	.424	4	.974
	— Indianapolis (I.L.)■	OF	34	129	24	34	3	2	1	14	4	12	14-4	.264	.285	.341	2	.977
	— Cincinnati (N.L.)	OF	9	1	4	0	0	0	0	0	0	1	0-1	.000	.000	.000	0	...
2000—	Columbus (I.L.)■	OF	119	437	71	139	17	9	0	32	41	40	37-18	.318	.378	.398	3	.988
2001—	Memphis (PCL)	OF	10	40	4	13	1	0	0	3	4	10	4-1	.325	.386	.350	0	1.000
	— St. Louis (N.L.)	OF	114	186	34	53	6	1	1	15	12	20	11-2	.285	.330	.344	2	.981
2002—	St. Louis (N.L.)	OF-DH	124	181	27	47	7	4	1	15	11	29	7-4	.260	.301	.359	2	.977
American League totals (1 year)			2	3	0	0	0	0	0	0	0	1	0-0	.000	.000	.000	0	1.000
National League totals (3 years)			247	368	65	100	13	5	2	30	23	50	18-7	.272	.315	.351	4	.979
Major League totals (4 years)			249	371	65	100	13	5	2	30	23	51	18-7	.270	.313	.348	4	.980

DIVISION SERIES RECORD

			BATTING														FIELDING	
Year	Team (League)	Pos.	G	AB	R	H	2B	3B	HR	RBI	BB	SO	SB-CS	Avg.	OBP	SLG	E	Avg.
2001—	St. Louis (N.L.)	PH-OF	4	2	0	1	0	0	0	1	0	0	0-0	.500	.500	.500	0	...
2002—	St. Louis (N.L.)	PH	2	2	0	1	0	0	0	1	0	0	0-0	.500	.500	.500	0	...
Division series totals (2 years)			6	4	0	2	0	0	0	2	0	0	0-0	.500	.500	.500	0	...

CHAMPIONSHIP SERIES RECORD

			BATTING														FIELDING	
Year	Team (League)	Pos.	G	AB	R	H	2B	3B	HR	RBI	BB	SO	SB-CS	Avg.	OBP	SLG	E	Avg.
2002—	St. Louis (N.L.)	OF	3	2	1	0	0	0	0	0	1	1	0-1	.000	.333	.000	0	...

ROCKER, JOHN — P

PERSONAL: Born October 17, 1974, in Statesboro, Ga. ... 6-4/225. ... Throws left, bats right. ... Full name: John Loy Rocker.
HIGH SCHOOL: First Presbyterian Day School (Macon, Ga.).
COLLEGE: Mercer (Ga.).
TRANSACTIONS/CAREER NOTES: Selected by Atlanta Braves organization in 18th round of free-agent draft (June 3, 1993). ... On suspended list (April 3-18, 2000). ... Traded by Braves with 3B Troy Cameron to Cleveland Indians for P Steve Karsay and P Steve Reed (June 22, 2001). ... Traded by Indians to Texas Rangers for P David Elder (December 18, 2001). ... On Texas disabled list (July 4, 2002-remainder of season); included rehabilitation assignment to Tulsa (August 8-21). ... Released by Rangers (October 3, 2002).
STATISTICAL NOTES: Pitched 2-0 no-hit victory against Charleston, S.C. (June 9, 1996). ... Led Southern League in wild pitches with 17 in 1997.
CAREER HITTING (MLB): 0-for-0 (.000), 0 R, 0 2B, 0 3B, 0 HR, 0 RBI.

Year League	W	L	Pct.	ERA	G	GS	CG	ShO	Sv.-Opp.	IP	H	R	ER	HR	BB-IBB	SO
1994—Danville (Appl.)	1	5	.167	3.53	12	12	1	0	0-...	63.2	50	36	25	4	38-1	72
1995—Macon (S.Atl.)	4	4	.500	4.50	16	16	0	0	0-...	86.0	86	50	43	5	52-0	61
—Eugene (N'West)	1	5	.167	5.16	12	12	0	0	0-...	59.1	45	40	34	4	36-0	74
1996—Macon (S.Atl.)	5	3	.625	3.89	20	19	2	2	0-...	106.1	85	60	46	7	63-1	107
—Durham (Caro.)	4	3	.571	3.39	9	9	0	0	0-...	58.1	63	24	22	4	25-0	43
1997—Durham (Caro.)	1	1	.500	4.33	11	1	0	0	0-...	35.1	33	21	17	3	22-0	39
—Greenville (Sou.)	5	6	.455	4.86	22	18	0	0	0-...	113.0	119	69	61	12	61-0	96
1998—Richmond (I.L.)	1	1	.500	1.42	9	0	0	0	1-...	19.0	13	4	3	1	10-0	22
—Atlanta (N.L.)	1	3	.250	2.13	47	0	0	0	2-4	38.0	22	10	9	4	22-4	42
1999—Atlanta (N.L.)	4	5	.444	2.49	74	0	0	0	38-45	72.1	47	24	20	5	37-4	104
2000—Atlanta (N.L.)	1	2	.333	2.89	59	0	0	0	24-27	53.0	42	25	17	5	48-4	77
—Richmond (I.L.)	0	0	...	3.00	3	0	0	0	1-...	3.0	3	1	1	0	1-0	6
2001—Atlanta (N.L.)	2	2	.500	3.09	30	0	0	0	19-23	32.0	25	13	11	2	16-1	36
—Cleveland (A.L.)■	3	7	.300	5.45	38	0	0	0	4-7	34.2	33	23	21	2	25-3	43
2002—Texas (A.L.)■	2	3	.400	6.66	30	0	0	0	1-4	24.1	29	19	18	5	13-1	30
—Oklahoma (PCL)	1	0	1.000	0.00	6	0	0	0	0-...	8.2	4	0	0	0	2-0	14
—Tulsa (Texas)	0	1	.000	13.50	3	0	0	0	0-...	2.2	3	4	4	0	2-0	5
A.L. totals (2 years)	5	10	.333	5.95	68	0	0	0	5-11	59.0	62	42	39	7	38-4	73
N.L. totals (4 years)	8	12	.400	2.63	210	0	0	0	83-99	195.1	136	72	57	16	123-13	259
Major League totals (5 years)	13	22	.371	3.40	278	0	0	0	88-110	254.1	198	114	96	23	161-17	332

DIVISION SERIES RECORD

Year League	W	L	Pct.	ERA	G	GS	CG	ShO	Sv.-Opp.	IP	H	R	ER	HR	BB-IBB	SO
1998—Atlanta (N.L.)	0	0	...	0.00	2	0	0	0	0-0	1.1	1	0	0	0	0-0	2
1999—Atlanta (N.L.)	1	0	1.000	0.00	2	0	0	0	1-1	3.1	0	0	0	0	2-0	5
2000—Atlanta (N.L.)	0	0	...	0.00	1	0	0	0	0-0	.2	0	0	0	0	1-0	0
2001—Cleveland (A.L.)	0	0	...	0.00	1	0	0	0	0-0	1.0	1	0	0	0	0-0	1
Division series totals (4 years)	1	0	1.000	0.00	6	0	0	0	1-1	6.1	2	0	0	0	3-0	8

CHAMPIONSHIP SERIES RECORD

RECORDS: Shares single-series record for most games pitched—6 (1998 and 1999).

Year League	W	L	Pct.	ERA	G	GS	CG	ShO	Sv.-Opp.	IP	H	R	ER	HR	BB-IBB	SO
1998—Atlanta (N.L.)	1	0	1.000	0.00	6	0	0	0	0-0	4.2	3	0	0	0	1-0	5
1999—Atlanta (N.L.)	0	0	...	0.00	6	0	0	0	2-3	6.2	3	2	0	0	2-1	9
Champ. series totals (2 years)	1	0	1.000	0.00	12	0	0	0	2-3	11.1	6	2	0	0	3-1	14

WORLD SERIES RECORD

Year League	W	L	Pct.	ERA	G	GS	CG	ShO	Sv.-Opp.	IP	H	R	ER	HR	BB-IBB	SO
1999—Atlanta (N.L.)	0	0	...	0.00	2	0	0	0	0-0	3.0	2	0	0	0	2-1	4

RODNEY, FERNANDO — P — TIGERS

PERSONAL: Born March 18, 1977, in Samana, Dominican Republic. ... 5-11/170. ... Throws right, bats right.

TRANSACTIONS/CAREER NOTES: Signed as non-drafted free agent by Detroit Tigers organization (November 1, 1997). ... On disabled list (August 14, 2000-remainder of season). ... On Lakeland disabled list (May 22-June 30 and July 13-18, 2001).

CAREER HITTING (MLB): 0-for-0 (.000), 0 R, 0 2B, 0 3B, 0 HR, 0 RBI.

Year League	W	L	Pct.	ERA	G	GS	CG	ShO	Sv.-Opp.	IP	H	R	ER	HR	BB-IBB	SO
1998—Dominican Tigers (DSL)	1	3	.250	3.38	11	5	0	0	1-...	32.0	25	16	12	...	19-...	37
1999—Gulf Coast Tigers (GCL)	3	3	.500	2.40	22	0	0	0	9-...	30.0	20	8	8	1	21-0	39
—Lakeland (FSL)	1	0	1.000	1.42	4	0	0	0	2-...	6.1	7	1	1	0	1-0	5
2000—West Michigan (Midw.)	6	4	.600	2.94	22	10	0	0	0-...	82.2	74	34	27	2	35-0	56
2001—Lakeland (FSL)	4	2	.667	3.42	16	9	0	0	0-...	55.1	53	26	21	2	19-1	44
—Gulf Coast Tigers (GCL)	0	0	...	0.00	1	1	0	0	0-...	1.0	0	0	0	0	1-0	1
—Erie (East.)	0	0	...	4.26	4	0	0	0	1-...	6.1	7	3	3	1	3-0	8
2002—Erie (East.)	1	0	1.000	1.33	21	0	0	0	11-...	20.1	14	4	3	0	5-0	18
—Detroit (A.L.)	1	3	.250	6.00	20	0	0	0	0-4	18.0	25	15	12	2	10-2	10
—Toledo (I.L.)	1	1	.500	0.81	20	0	0	0	4-...	22.1	13	4	2	1	9-0	25
Major League totals (1 year)	1	3	.250	6.00	20	0	0	0	0-4	18.0	25	15	12	2	10-2	10

RODRIGUEZ, ALEX — SS — RANGERS

PERSONAL: Born July 27, 1975, in New York. ... 6-3/210. ... Bats right, throws right. ... Full name: Alexander Emmanuel Rodriguez.

HIGH SCHOOL: Westminster Christian (Miami).

TRANSACTIONS/CAREER NOTES: Selected by Seattle Mariners organization in first round (first pick overall) of free-agent draft (June 3, 1993). ... On Seattle disabled list (April 22-May 7, 1996); included rehabilitation assignment to Tacoma (May 5-7). ... On disabled list (June 12-27, 1997; April 7-May 14, 1999; and July 8-24, 2000). ... Granted free agency (October 30, 2000). ... Signed by Texas Rangers (December 11, 2000).

RECORDS: Hold major league single-season record for most home runs by shortstop—57 (2002). ... Shares major league career record for most home runs in two consecutive games—5 (August 17 [3] and 18 [2], 2002). ... Holds A.L. record for most home runs in consecutive years—109 (2001-02). ... Shares A.L. career record for most home runs in three straight game—6 (August 16 [1], 17 [3] and 18 [2], 2002).

HONORS: Named Major League Player of the Year by The Sporting News (1996 and 2002). ... Named shortstop on The Sporting News A.L. All-Star team (1996, 1998 and 2000-02). ... Named shortstop on The Sporting News A.L. Silver Slugger team (1996, 1998-99 and 2000). ... Named shortstop on A.L. Silver Slugger team (2001 and 2002). ... Won A.L Gold Glove at shortstop (2002).

STATISTICAL NOTES: Had 20-game hitting streak (August 16-September 4, 1996). ... Led A.L. with 379 total bases in 1996, 393 in 2001 and 389 in 2002. ... Hit for the cycle (June 5, 1997). ... Led A.L. shortstops with 731 total chances in 1998. ... Hit three home runs in one game (April 16, 2000; and August 17, 2002). ... Had 17-game hitting streak (May 5-23, 2000). ... Led A.L. shortstops with 123 double plays in 2000. ... Led A.L. shortstops with 259 putouts and 108 double plays in 2002. ... Career major league grand slams: 9.

2002 GAMES PLAYED BY POSITION (MLB): SS—162.

Year	Team (League)	Pos.	G	AB	R	H	2B	3B	HR	RBI	BB	SO	SB-CS	Avg.	OBP	SLG	E	Avg.
			BATTING														FIELDING	
1994—	Appleton (Midw.)	SS-DH	65	248	49	79	17	6	14	55	24	44	16-5	.319	.379	.605	19	.934
	— Jacksonville (Sou.)	SS	17	59	7	17	4	1	1	8	10	13	2-1	.288	.391	.441	3	.964
	— Seattle (A.L.)	SS	17	54	4	11	0	0	0	2	3	20	3-0	.204	.241	.204	6	.915
	— Calgary (PCL)	SS	32	119	22	37	7	4	6	21	8	25	2-4	.311	.359	.588	3	.980
1995—	Tacoma (PCL)	SS-DH	54	214	37	77	12	3	15	45	18	44	2-4	.360	.411	.654	10	.961
	— Seattle (A.L.)	SS-DH	48	142	15	33	6	2	5	19	6	42	4-2	.232	.264	.408	8	.953
1996—	Seattle (A.L.)	SS	146	601	*141	215	*54	1	36	123	59	104	15-4	*.358	.414	.631	15	.977
	— Tacoma (PCL)	SS	2	5	0	1	0	0	0	0	2	1	0-0	.200	.429	.200	1	.833
1997—	Seattle (A.L.)	SS-DH	141	587	100	176	40	3	23	84	41	99	29-6	.300	.350	.496	*24	.962
1998—	Seattle (A.L.)	SS-DH	161	*686	123	*213	35	5	42	124	45	121	46-13	.310	.360	.560	18	.975
1999—	Seattle (A.L.)	SS	129	502	110	143	25	0	42	111	56	109	21-7	.285	.357	.586	14	.977
2000—	Seattle (A.L.)	SS	148	554	134	175	34	2	41	132	100	121	15-4	.316	.420	.606	10	.986
2001—	Texas (A.L.)■	SS-DH	•162	632	*133	201	34	1	*52	135	75	131	18-3	.318	.399	.622	18	.976
2002—	Texas (A.L.)	SS	•162	624	125	187	27	2	*57	*142	87	122	9-4	.300	.392	.623	10	.987
Major League totals (9 years)			1114	4382	885	1354	255	16	298	872	472	869	160-43	.309	.380	.579	123	.976

DIVISION SERIES RECORD

Year	Team (League)	Pos.	G	AB	R	H	2B	3B	HR	RBI	BB	SO	SB-CS	Avg.	OBP	SLG	E	Avg.
			BATTING														FIELDING	
1995—	Seattle (A.L.)	SS-PR	1	1	1	0	0	0	0	0	0	0	0-0	.000	.000	.000	0	...
1997—	Seattle (A.L.)	SS	4	16	1	5	1	0	1	1	0	5	0-0	.313	.313	.563	0	1.000
2000—	Seattle (A.L.)	SS	3	13	0	4	0	0	0	2	0	2	0-1	.308	.308	.308	0	1.000
Division series totals (3 years)			8	30	2	9	1	0	1	3	0	7	0-1	.300	.300	.433	0	1.000

CHAMPIONSHIP SERIES RECORD

RECORDS: Shares A.L. single-game record for most long hits—3 (October 17, 2000).

Year	Team (League)	Pos.	G	AB	R	H	2B	3B	HR	RBI	BB	SO	SB-CS	Avg.	OBP	SLG	E	Avg.
			BATTING														FIELDING	
1995—	Seattle (A.L.)	PH	1	1	0	0	0	0	0	0	0	1	0-0	.000	.000	.000	...	...
2000—	Seattle (A.L.)	SS	6	22	4	9	2	0	2	5	3	8	1-0	.409	.480	.773	0	1.000
Championship series totals (2 years)			7	23	4	9	2	0	2	5	3	9	1-0	.391	.462	.739	0	1.000

ALL-STAR GAME RECORD

	AB	R	H	2B	3B	HR	RBI	BB	SO	SB-CS	Avg.	OBP	SLG	E	Avg.
All-Star Game totals (5 years)	11	2	3	0	0	1	1	0	7	0-0	.273	.273	.545	0	1.000

RODRIGUEZ, FELIX — P — GIANTS

PERSONAL: Born September 9, 1972, in Monte Cristi, Dominican Republic. ... 6-1/198. ... Throws right, bats right. ... Full name: Felix Antonio Rodriguez.

HIGH SCHOOL: Liceo Bijiador (Monte Cristi, Dominican Republic).

TRANSACTIONS/CAREER NOTES: Signed as non-drafted free agent by Los Angeles Dodgers organization (October 17, 1989). ... On disabled list (August 11, 1992-remainder of season). ... On Albuquerque disabled list (July 5-18, 1995). ... On disabled list (April 20-May 2 and May 12-27, 1996). ... Claimed on waivers by Cincinnati Reds (December 18, 1996). ... Traded by Reds to Arizona Diamondbacks for a player to be named later (November 11, 1997); Reds acquired P Scott Winchester to complete deal (November 18, 1997). ... On Arizona disabled list (June 21-July 30, 1998); included rehabilitation assignments to Arizona League Diamondbacks (July 20-27) and Tucson (July 28-30). ... Traded by Diamondbacks to San Francisco Giants for future considerations (December 8, 1998); Diamondbacks acquired P Troy Brohawn and OF Chris Van Rossum to complete deal (December 21, 1998).

STATISTICAL NOTES: Pitched 11-0 no-hit victory against Sarasota (August 28, 1993).

CAREER HITTING (MLB): 3-for-14 (.214), 4 R, 1 2B, 0 3B, 1 HR, 3 RBI.

Year	League	W	L	Pct.	ERA	G	GS	CG	ShO	Sv.-Opp.	IP	H	R	ER	HR	BB-IBB	SO
1993—	Vero Beach (FSL)	8	8	.500	3.75	32	20	2	1	0-...	132.0	109	71	55	15	71-1	80
1994—	San Antonio (Texas)	6	8	.429	4.03	26	26	0	0	0-...	136.1	106	70	61	8	*88-3	126
1995—	Albuquerque (PCL)	3	2	.600	4.24	14	11	0	0	0-...	51.0	52	29	24	5	26-0	46
	— Los Angeles (N.L.)	1	1	.500	2.53	11	0	0	0	0-1	10.2	11	3	3	2	5-0	5
1996—	Albuquerque (PCL)	3	9	.250	5.53	27	19	0	0	0-...	107.1	111	70	66	17	60-1	65
1997—	Indianapolis (A.A.)■	3	3	.500	1.01	23	0	0	0	1-...	26.2	22	10	3	0	16-1	26
	— Cincinnati (N.L.)	0	0	...	4.30	26	1	0	0	0-0	46.0	48	23	22	2	28-2	34
1998—	Arizona (N.L.)■	0	2	.000	6.14	43	0	0	0	5-8	44.0	44	31	30	5	29-1	36
	— Ariz. D-backs (Ariz.)	0	0	...	4.15	3	2	0	0	0-...	4.1	3	4	2	0	2-0	5
	— Tucson (PCL)	0	0	...	9.00	1	0	0	0	0-...	1.0	1	1	1	0	2-0	0
1999—	San Francisco (N.L.)■	2	3	.400	3.80	47	0	0	0	0-1	66.1	67	32	28	6	29-2	55
2000—	San Francisco (N.L.)	4	2	.667	2.64	76	0	0	0	3-8	81.2	65	29	24	5	42-2	95
2001—	San Francisco (N.L.)	9	1	.900	1.68	80	0	0	0	0-3	80.1	53	16	15	5	27-2	91
2002—	San Francisco (N.L.)	8	6	.571	4.17	71	0	0	0	0-6	69.0	53	33	32	5	29-1	58
Major League totals (7 years)		24	15	.615	3.48	354	1	0	0	8-27	398.0	341	167	154	30	189-10	374

DIVISION SERIES RECORD

Year	League	W	L	Pct.	ERA	G	GS	CG	ShO	Sv.-Opp.	IP	H	R	ER	HR	BB-IBB	SO
2000—	San Francisco (N.L.)	0	1	.000	6.23	3	0	0	0	0-0	4.1	6	3	3	1	1-0	6
2002—	San Francisco (N.L.)	0	0	...	0.00	3	0	0	0	0-0	3.0	1	0	0	0	2-0	2
Division series totals (2 years)		0	1	.000	3.68	6	0	0	0	0-0	7.1	7	3	3	1	3-0	8

CHAMPIONSHIP SERIES RECORD

Year	League	W	L	Pct.	ERA	G	GS	CG	ShO	Sv.-Opp.	IP	H	R	ER	HR	BB-IBB	SO
2002—	San Francisco (N.L.)	0	0	...	1.93	4	0	0	0	0-0	4.2	3	1	1	0	2-0	2

WORLD SERIES RECORD

Year	League	W	L	Pct.	ERA	G	GS	CG	ShO	Sv.-Opp.	IP	H	R	ER	HR	BB-IBB	SO
2002—	San Francisco (N.L.)	0	1	.000	4.76	6	0	0	0	0-0	5.2	4	3	3	2	1-0	3

RECORD AS POSITION PLAYER

Year	Team (League)	Pos.	G	AB	R	H	2B	3B	HR	RBI	BB	SO	SB-CS	Avg.	OBP	SLG	E	Avg.
			BATTING														FIELDING	
1990—	Dom. Dodgers (DSL)		63	241	23	55	10	0	2	33	15	52	4-0	.228	...	.295	...	...
1991—	GC Dodgers (GCL)	C	45	139	15	37	8	1	2	21	6	32	1-0	.266	.301	.381	5	.973
1992—	Great Falls (Pio.)	C-OF	32	110	20	32	8	0	2	20	1	16	2-0	.291	.301	.418	2	.992

RODRIGUEZ, FRANCISCO — P — ANGELS

PERSONAL: Born January 7, 1982, in Caracas, Venezuela. ... 6-0/175. ... Throws right, bats right. ... Full name: Francisco Jose Rodriguez.
TRANSACTIONS/CAREER NOTES: Signed as non-drafted free agent by Anaheim Angels organization (September 24, 1998).
CAREER HITTING (MLB): 0-for-0 (.000), 0 R, 0 2B, 0 3B, 0 HR, 0 RBI.

Year	League	W	L	Pct.	ERA	G	GS	CG	ShO	Sv.-Opp.	IP	H	R	ER	HR	BB-IBB	SO
1999	—Butte (Pio.)	1	1	.500	3.31	12	9	1	0	0-...	51.2	33	21	19	1	21-1	69
	—Boise (N'West)	1	0	1.000	5.40	1	1	0	0	0-...	5.0	3	4	3	0	1-0	6
2000	—Lake Elsinore (Calif.)	4	4	.500	2.81	13	12	0	0	0-...	64.0	43	29	20	2	32-0	79
2001	—Rancho Cuca. (Calif.)	5	7	.417	5.38	20	20	1	1	0-...	113.2	127	72	68	13	55-1	147
2002	—Arkansas (Texas)	3	3	.500	1.96	23	0	0	0	9-...	41.1	32	13	9	2	15-0	61
	—Salt Lake (PCL)	2	3	.400	2.57	27	0	0	0	6-...	42.0	30	13	12	1	13-0	59
	—Anaheim (A.L.)	0	0	...	0.00	5	0	0	0	0-0	5.2	3	0	0	0	2-1	13
Major League totals (1 year)		0	0	...	0.00	5	0	0	0	0-0	5.2	3	0	0	0	2-1	13

DIVISION SERIES RECORD

Year	League	W	L	Pct.	ERA	G	GS	CG	ShO	Sv.-Opp.	IP	H	R	ER	HR	BB-IBB	SO
2002	—Anaheim (A.L.)	2	0	1.000	3.18	3	0	0	0	0-1	5.2	2	2	2	1	2-0	8

CHAMPIONSHIP SERIES RECORD

Year	League	W	L	Pct.	ERA	G	GS	CG	ShO	Sv.-Opp.	IP	H	R	ER	HR	BB-IBB	SO
2002	—Anaheim (A.L.)	2	0	1.000	0.00	4	0	0	0	0-1	4.1	2	0	0	0	2-0	7

WORLD SERIES RECORD

NOTES: Member of World Series championship team (2002).

Year	League	W	L	Pct.	ERA	G	GS	CG	ShO	Sv.-Opp.	IP	H	R	ER	HR	BB-IBB	SO
2002	—Anaheim (A.L.)	1	1	.500	2.08	4	0	0	0	0-0	8.2	6	3	2	1	1-0	13

RODRIGUEZ, HENRY — OF

PERSONAL: Born November 8, 1967, in Santo Domingo, Dominican Republic. ... 6-2/225. ... Bats left, throws left. ... Full name: Henry Anderson Lorenzo Rodriguez Garcia.
HIGH SCHOOL: Liceo Republica de Paraguay. (Santo Domingo).
TRANSACTIONS/CAREER NOTES: Signed as non-drafted free agent by Los Angeles Dodgers organization (July 14, 1985). ... Traded by Dodgers with IF Jeff Treadway to Montreal Expos for OF Roberto Kelly and P Joey Eischen (May 23, 1995). ... On Montreal disabled list (June 2-September 1, 1995); included rehabilitation assignment to Ottawa (August 7-16). ... On suspended list (August 16-19, 1996). ... Traded by Expos to Chicago Cubs for P Miguel Batista (December 12, 1997). ... On disabled list (August 24-September 8, 1998). ... Granted free agency (October 23, 1998). ... Re-signed by Cubs (December 2, 1998). ... Traded by Cubs to Florida Marlins for 1B/OF Ross Gload and P Dave Noyce (July 31, 2000). ... Granted free agency (November 1, 2000). ... Signed by New York Yankees (February 15, 2001). ... On New York disabled list (March 31-May 23, 2001); included rehabilitation assignment to Columbus (May 1-20). ... Released by Yankees (June 19, 2001). ... Signed by Expos organization (March 28, 2002). ... Released by Expos (May 16, 2002).
HONORS: Named Texas League Most Valuable Player (1990).
STATISTICAL NOTES: Tied for Gulf Coast League lead with seven intentional bases on balls received in 1987. ... Tied for Northwest League lead with 38 assists by first basemen in 1988. ... Led Texas League with 14 sacrifice flies in 1990. ... Tied for Pacific Coast League lead with 10 sacrifice flies in 1992. ... Had 15-game hitting streak (July 31-August 14, 1999). ... Career major league grand slams: 5.
2002 GAMES PLAYED BY POSITION (MLB): OF—5.

			BATTING														FIELDING	
Year	Team (League)	Pos.	G	AB	R	H	2B	3B	HR	RBI	BB	SO	SB-CS	Avg.	OBP	SLG	E	Avg.
1987	—GC Dodgers (GCL)	1B-SS	49	148	23	49	7	3	0	15	16	15	3-1	*.331	.402	.419	6	.982
1988	—Dom. Dodgers (DSL)	N	19	21	9	8	2	0	0	10	10	6	4-...	.381	...	.476	...	...
	—Salem (N'West)	1B	72	291	47	84	14	4	2	39	21	42	14-2	.289	.339	.385	7	.989
1989	—Vero Beach (FSL)	1B-OF	126	433	53	123	*33	1	10	73	48	58	7-6	.284	.354	.434	12	.990
	—Bakersfield (Calif.)	1B	3	9	2	2	0	0	1	2	0	3	0-0	.222	.222	.556	0	1.000
1990	—San Antonio (Texas)	OF	129	495	82	144	22	9	*28	*109	61	66	5-4	.291	.362	.541	10	.958
1991	—Albuquerque (PCL)	OF-1B	121	446	61	121	22	5	10	67	25	62	4-5	.271	.308	.410	5	.980
1992	—Albuquerque (PCL)	1B-OF	94	365	59	111	21	5	14	72	31	57	1-5	.304	.351	.504	10	.981
	—Los Angeles (N.L.)	OF-1B	53	146	11	32	7	0	3	14	8	30	0-0	.219	.258	.329	3	.962
1993	—Albuquerque (PCL)	1B-OF	46	179	26	53	13	5	4	30	14	37	1-2	.296	.348	.492	5	.983
	—Los Angeles (N.L.)	OF-1B	76	176	20	39	10	0	8	23	11	39	1-0	.222	.266	.415	1	.993
1994	—Los Angeles (N.L.)	OF-1B	104	306	33	82	14	2	8	49	17	58	0-1	.268	.307	.405	2	.990
1995	—Los Angeles (N.L.)	OF-1B	21	80	6	21	4	1	1	10	5	17	0-1	.263	.306	.375	0	1.000
	—Montreal (N.L.)■	1B-OF	24	58	7	12	0	0	1	5	6	11	0-0	.207	.277	.259	1	.990
	—Ottawa (I.L.)	DH	4	15	0	3	1	0	0	2	1	4	0-0	.200	.250	.267	...	...
1996	—Montreal (N.L.)	OF-1B	145	532	81	147	42	1	36	103	37	*160	2-0	.276	.325	.562	11	.981
1997	—Montreal (N.L.)	OF-1B	132	476	55	116	28	3	26	83	42	149	3-3	.244	.306	.479	3	.987
1998	—Chicago (N.L.)■	OF-DH	128	415	56	104	21	1	31	85	54	113	1-3	.251	.334	.530	1	.996
1999	—Chicago (N.L.)	OF-DH	130	447	72	136	29	0	26	87	56	113	2-4	.304	.381	.544	6	.974
2000	—Chicago (N.L.)	OF	76	259	37	65	15	1	18	51	22	76	1-2	.251	.314	.525	2	.983
	—Florida (N.L.)■	OF	36	108	10	29	6	0	2	10	14	23	0-0	.269	.358	.380	0	1.000
2001	—Columbus (I.L.)■	OF	18	63	9	15	2	0	5	13	7	21	0-0	.238	.319	.508	0	1.000
	—New York (A.L.)	DH	5	8	0	0	0	0	0	0	0	6	0-0	.000	.000	.000	...	...
2002	—Montreal (N.L.)■	OF	20	20	1	1	0	0	0	3	4	8	0-0	.050	.200	.050	0	...
American League totals (1 year)			5	8	0	0	0	0	0	0	0	6	0-0	.000	.000	.000	0	...
National League totals (10 years)			945	3023	389	784	176	9	160	523	276	797	10-14	.259	.321	.482	30	.985
Major League totals (11 years)			950	3031	389	784	176	9	160	523	276	803	10-14	.259	.321	.481	30	.985

DIVISION SERIES RECORD

			BATTING														FIELDING	
Year	Team (League)	Pos.	G	AB	R	H	2B	3B	HR	RBI	BB	SO	SB-CS	Avg.	OBP	SLG	E	Avg.
1998	—Chicago (N.L.)	OF-PH	3	7	0	1	1	0	0	0	1	2	0-0	.143	.250	.286	0	1.000

ALL-STAR GAME RECORD

	AB	R	H	2B	3B	HR	RBI	BB	SO	SB-CS	Avg.	OBP	SLG	E	Avg.
All-Star Game totals (1 year)	1	0	1	0	0	0	1	0	0	0-0	1.000	1.000	1.000	0	...

RODRIGUEZ, IVAN — C

PERSONAL: Born November 30, 1971, in Vega Baja, Puerto Rico. ... 5-9/205. ... Bats right, throws right. ... Nickname: Pudge.
HIGH SCHOOL: Lina Padron Rivera (Vega Baja, Puerto Rico).
TRANSACTIONS/CAREER NOTES: Signed as non-drafted free agent by Texas Rangers organization (July 27, 1988). ... On disabled list (June 6-27, 1992; July 25, 2000-remainder of season; May 2-17 and August 31, 2001-remainder of season). ... On Texas disabled list (April 15-June 7, 2002); included rehabilitation assignment to Charlotte (June 2-7). ... On suspended list (September 28-29, 2002). ... Granted free agency (October 28, 2002).
RECORDS: Shares major league single-inning record for most doubles—2 (June 14, 2000, fourth inning). ... Holds A.L. single-season record for most home runs by catcher—35 (1999).
HONORS: Won A.L. Gold Glove at catcher (1992-2001). ... Named catcher on THE SPORTING NEWS A.L. All-Star team (1994-99). ... Named catcher on THE SPORTING NEWS A.L. Silver Slugger team (1994-99). ... Named A.L. Most Valuable Player by Baseball Writers' Association of America (1999).
STATISTICAL NOTES: Led South Atlantic League catchers with 96 assists and 34 double plays in 1989. ... Led Florida State League catchers with 727 putouts and 842 total chances in 1990. ... Led A.L. catchers with 67 assists in 1995 and 75 in 1997. ... Led A.L. catchers with 850 putouts, 81 assists, 941 total chances and 11 double plays in 1996. ... Hit three home runs in one game (September 11, 1997). ... Led A.L. catchers with 864 putouts, 72 assists and 942 total chances in 1998. ... Had 20-game hitting streak (May 8-June 1, 1999). ... Led A.L. in grounding into double plays with 31 in 1999. ... Led A.L. catchers with 10 double plays in 2000. ... Career major league grand slams: 5.
MISCELLANEOUS: Holds Texas Rangers franchise all-time records for most hits (1,723) and most doubles (344).
2002 GAMES PLAYED BY POSITION (MLB): C—100; DH—6.

			BATTING														FIELDING	
Year	Team (League)	Pos.	G	AB	R	H	2B	3B	HR	RBI	BB	SO	SB-CS	Avg.	OBP	SLG	E	Avg.
1989—	Gastonia (S.Atl.)	C	112	386	38	92	22	1	7	42	21	58	2-5	.238	.278	.355	11	.986
1990—	Charlotte (FSL)	C	109	408	48	117	17	7	2	55	12	50	1-0	.287	.316	.377	14	.983
1991—	Tulsa (Texas)	C	50	175	16	48	7	2	3	28	6	27	1-2	.274	.294	.389	3	.988
—	Texas (A.L.)	C	88	280	24	74	16	0	3	27	5	42	0-1	.264	.276	.354	10	.983
1992—	Texas (A.L.)	C-DH	123	420	39	109	16	1	8	37	24	73	0-0	.260	.300	.360	*15	.983
1993—	Texas (A.L.)	C-DH	137	473	56	129	28	4	10	66	29	70	8-7	.273	.315	.412	8	.991
1994—	Texas (A.L.)	C	99	363	56	108	19	1	16	57	31	42	6-3	.298	.360	.488	5	.992
1995—	Texas (A.L.)	C-DH	130	492	56	149	32	2	12	67	16	48	0-2	.303	.327	.449	8	.990
1996—	Texas (A.L.)	C-DH	153	639	116	192	47	3	19	86	38	55	5-0	.300	.342	.473	•10	.989
1997—	Texas (A.L.)	C-DH	150	597	98	187	34	4	20	77	38	89	7-3	.313	.360	.484	7	.992
1998—	Texas (A.L.)	C-DH	145	579	88	186	40	4	21	91	32	88	9-0	.321	.358	.513	6	.994
1999—	Texas (A.L.)	C-DH	144	600	116	199	29	1	35	113	24	64	25-12	.332	.356	.558	7	.993
2000—	Texas (A.L.)	C-DH	91	363	66	126	27	4	27	83	19	48	5-5	.347	.375	.667	2	*.996
2001—	Texas (A.L.)	C-DH	111	442	70	136	24	2	25	65	23	73	10-3	.308	.347	.541	7	.990
2002—	Texas (A.L.)	C-DH	108	408	67	128	32	2	19	60	25	71	5-4	.314	.353	.542	7	.990
—	Charlotte (FSL)	C	3	9	1	3	0	0	0	0	0	3	0-0	.333	.333	.333	0	1.000
Major League totals (12 years)			1479	5656	852	1723	344	28	215	829	304	763	80-40	.305	.342	.489	92	.990

DIVISION SERIES RECORD

			BATTING														FIELDING	
Year	Team (League)	Pos.	G	AB	R	H	2B	3B	HR	RBI	BB	SO	SB-CS	Avg.	OBP	SLG	E	Avg.
1996—	Texas (A.L.)	C	4	16	1	6	1	0	0	2	2	3	0-0	.375	.444	.438	0	1.000
1998—	Texas (A.L.)	C	3	10	0	1	0	0	0	1	0	5	0-0	.100	.100	.100	0	1.000
1999—	Texas (A.L.)	C	3	12	0	3	1	0	0	0	0	2	1-0	.250	.250	.333	0	1.000
Division series totals (3 years)			10	38	1	10	2	0	0	3	2	10	1-0	.263	.300	.316	0	1.000

ALL-STAR GAME RECORD

RECORDS: Shares single-game record for most at-bats (nine-inning game)—5 (July 12, 1994). ... Shares single-game records for most putouts by catcher—10; and most chances accepted by catcher—11 (1999).

	AB	R	H	2B	3B	HR	RBI	BB	SO	SB-CS	Avg.	OBP	SLG	E	Avg.
All-Star Game totals (10 years)	27	3	8	1	0	0	2	0	5	1-0	.296	.296	.333	0	1.000

RODRIGUEZ, JOSE — P

PERSONAL: Born December 18, 1974, in Santurce, Puerto Rico. ... 6-1/215. ... Throws left, bats left. ... Full name: Jose Ilich Rodriguez.
COLLEGE: Florida International.
TRANSACTIONS/CAREER NOTES: Selected by St. Louis Cardinals organization in 24th round of free-agent draft (June 4, 1997). ... Released by Cardinals (June 9, 2002). ... Signed by Minnesota Twins organization (June 19, 2002). ... On Minnesota disabled list (July 14, 2002-remainder of season). ... Released by Twins (October 21, 2002).
CAREER HITTING (MLB): 0-for-1 (.000), 0 R, 0 2B, 0 3B, 0 HR, 0 RBI.

Year	League	W	L	Pct.	ERA	G	GS	CG	ShO	Sv.-Opp.	IP	H	R	ER	HR	BB-IBB	SO
1997—	Johnson City (Appl.)	0	0	...	4.05	4	0	0	0	0-...	6.2	4	3	3	1	3-1	8
1998—	Peoria (Midw.)	2	4	.333	4.58	40	40	0	0	0-...	39.1	47	32	20	0	19-1	30
1999—	Arkansas (Texas)	1	2	.333	3.25	30	0	0	0	0-...	36.0	38	16	13	6	25-0	30
—	Peoria (Midw.)	2	3	.400	3.31	15	0	0	0	0-...	16.1	14	7	6	1	8-0	15
2000—	Arkansas (Texas)	1	0	1.000	2.45	10	0	0	0	1-...	11.0	7	3	3	0	4-2	8
—	Memphis (PCL)	4	2	.667	3.80	40	0	0	0	3-...	47.1	48	21	20	4	19-1	37
—	St. Louis (N.L.)	0	0	...	0.00	6	0	0	0	0-0	4.0	2	2	0	0	3-0	2
2001—	Memphis (PCL)	2	1	.667	3.56	54	0	0	0	1-...	60.2	52	25	24	7	31-0	54
2002—	Memphis (PCL)	2	1	.667	3.44	22	0	0	0	2-...	18.1	26	13	7	2	7-0	14
—	St. Louis (N.L.)	0	0	...	54.00	2	0	0	0	0-0	.1	4	2	2	0	2-0	0
—	Edmonton (PCL)■	0	0	...	0.00	4	0	0	0	1-...	5.2	4	0	0	0	1-0	6
—	Minnesota (A.L.)	0	1	.000	14.73	4	0	0	0	0-0	3.2	8	6	6	0	4-1	1
A.L. totals (1 year)		0	1	.000	14.73	4	0	0	0	0-0	3.2	8	6	6	0	4-1	1
N.L. totals (2 years)		0	0	...	4.15	8	0	0	0	0-0	4.1	6	4	2	0	5-0	2
Major League totals (2 years)		0	1	.000	9.00	12	0	0	0	0-0	8.0	14	10	8	0	9-1	3

RODRIGUEZ, NERIO — P

PERSONAL: Born March 4, 1971, in Bani, Dominican Republic. ... 6-1/205. ... Throws right, bats right.

TRANSACTIONS/CAREER NOTES: Signed as non-drafted free agent by Chicago White Sox organization (February 2, 1990). ... Selected by Baltimore Orioles organization from White Sox organization in Rule 5 minor league draft (December 5, 1994). ... On Frederick disabled list (April 5-August 11, 1996). ... On Baltimore disabled list (May 26-June 30, 1998); included rehabilitation assignment to Bowie (June 24-30). ... Traded by Orioles with OF Shannon Carter to Toronto Blue Jays for P Juan Guzman (July 31, 1998). ... Claimed on waivers by New York Mets (March 28, 2000). ... Claimed on waivers by Boston Red Sox (March 30, 2000). ... Granted free agency (October 18, 2000). ... Signed by Mets organization (November 17, 2000). ... On Norfolk disabled list (April 12-19, 2001). ... Granted free agency (October 15, 2001). ... Signed by Cleveland Indians organization (June 7, 2002). ... Contract purchased by St. Louis Cardinals organization from Indians (July 11, 2002). ... Released by Cardinals (October 11, 2002).

STATISTICAL NOTES: Led Gulf Coast League catchers with 312 total chances and four double plays in 1992.

CAREER HITTING (MLB): 0-for-1 (.000), 0 R, 0 2B, 0 3B, 0 HR, 0 RBI.

Year League	W	L	Pct.	ERA	G	GS	CG	ShO	Sv.-Opp.	IP	H	R	ER	HR	BB-IBB	SO
1995— High Desert (Calif.)	0	0	...	1.80	7	0	0	0	0-...	10.0	8	2	2	0	7-0	10
1996— Frederick (Caro.)	8	7	.533	2.26	24	17	1	0	2-...	111.1	83	42	28	10	40-0	114
— Rochester (I.L.)	1	0	1.000	1.80	2	2	0	0	0-...	15.0	10	3	3	0	2-0	6
— Baltimore (A.L.)	0	1	.000	4.32	8	1	0	0	0-0	16.2	18	11	8	2	7-0	12
1997— Rochester (I.L.)	11	10	.524	3.90	27	27	1	1	0-...	168.1	124	82	73	23	62-0	*160
— Baltimore (A.L.)	2	1	.667	4.91	6	2	0	0	0-1	22.0	21	15	12	2	8-0	11
1998— Rochester (I.L.)	1	4	.200	5.47	5	5	0	0	0-...	24.2	24	16	15	6	10-0	19
— Baltimore (A.L.)	1	3	.250	8.05	6	4	0	0	0-0	19.0	25	17	17	0	9-0	8
— Bowie (East.)	0	1	.000	4.50	2	2	0	0	0-...	4.0	6	2	2	0	0-0	7
— Toronto (A.L.)■	1	0	1.000	9.72	7	0	0	0	0-0	8.1	10	9	9	1	8-0	3
1999— Syracuse (I.L.)	10	8	.556	4.54	27	27	1	1	0-...	162.2	161	84	82	17	53-0	137
— Toronto (A.L.)	0	1	.000	13.50	2	0	0	0	0-0	2.0	2	3	3	2	2-0	2
2000— Pawtucket (I.L.)■	0	1	.000	9.49	12	1	0	0	0-...	24.2	38	28	26	9	9-0	23
— Trenton (East.)	7	7	.500	4.77	19	19	1	0	0-...	109.1	115	64	58	9	34-0	93
2001— Norfolk (I.L.)■	0	0	...	...	1	0	0	0	0-...	.0	2	2	2	0	0-0	0
— Buffalo (I.L.)■	2	3	.400	5.35	11	5	0	0	1-...	38.2	41	24	23	5	15-1	21
— Akron (East.)	6	2	.750	3.91	11	11	2	1	0-...	71.1	64	34	31	10	17-0	49
2002— Buffalo (I.L.)	4	2	.667	1.82	13	10	1	0	0-...	74.1	55	20	15	6	12-0	44
— Cleveland (A.L.)	0	0	...	0.00	1	0	0	0	0-0	.1	0	0	0	0	0-0	0
— Memphis (PCL)■	3	1	.750	2.79	8	8	0	0	0-...	51.2	42	22	16	7	10-0	43
— St. Louis (N.L.)	0	0	...	4.15	2	0	0	0	0-0	4.1	4	3	2	1	1-0	2
A.L. totals (5 years)	4	6	.400	6.45	30	7	0	0	0-1	68.1	76	55	49	7	34-0	36
N.L. totals (1 year)	0	0	...	4.15	2	0	0	0	0-0	4.1	4	3	2	1	1-0	2
Major League totals (5 years)	4	6	.400	6.32	32	7	0	0	0-1	72.2	80	58	51	8	35-0	38

RECORD AS POSITION PLAYER

		BATTING														FIELDING	
Year Team (League)	Pos.	G	AB	R	H	2B	3B	HR	RBI	BB	SO	SB-CS	Avg.	OBP	SLG	E	Avg.
1990— Dom. Orioles/WS (DSL)		46	141	24	33	6	0	5	21	12	35	1-...	.234	...	.383	...	...
1991— Dom. Orioles/WS (DSL)		14	54	11	20	4	0	1	10	5	13	3-...	.370	...	.500	...	...
— GC White Sox (GCL)	C	26	89	4	20	1	0	0	8	2	24	3-2	.225	.242	.236	5	.972
1992— GC White Sox (GCL)	C	41	122	18	33	8	1	2	13	10	31	1-5	.270	.324	.402	*12	.962
1993— Hickory (S.Atl.)	C	82	262	31	54	9	2	4	32	27	70	4-0	.206	.286	.302	13	.976
1994— South Bend (Midw.)	C	18	59	4	13	4	0	0	8	2	14	0-2	.220	.258	.288	0	1.000
— Prince William (Caro.)	C	6	19	2	4	1	1	0	1	1	9	0-1	.211	.250	.368	0	1.000
1995— High Desert (Calif.)■	C-P	58	144	20	34	7	0	4	12	18	50	5-3	.236	.323	.368	8	.978
— Bowie (East.)	C	3	4	0	0	0	0	0	0	2	2	0-0	.000	.333	.000	0	1.000

RODRIGUEZ, RICARDO — P — INDIANS

PERSONAL: Born May 21, 1978, in Manga, Dominican Republic. ... 6-3/165. ... Throws right, bats right. ... Full name: Ricardo Antonio Rodriguez.

TRANSACTIONS/CAREER NOTES: Signed as non-drafted free agent by Los Angeles Dodgers organization (September 2, 1996). ... On Jacksonville disabled list (April 4-May 17, 2002). ... Traded by Dodgers with P Terry Mulholland and P Francisco Cruceta to Cleveland Indians for P Paul Shuey (July 28, 2002).

HONORS: Named Florida State League Most Valuable Pitcher (2001).

STATISTICAL NOTES: Led Florida State League with 18 wild pitches in 2001.

CAREER HITTING (MLB): 0-for-0 (.000), 0 R, 0 2B, 0 3B, 0 HR, 0 RBI.

Year League	W	L	Pct.	ERA	G	GS	CG	ShO	Sv.-Opp.	IP	H	R	ER	HR	BB-IBB	SO
1997— Dom. Dodgers (DSL)	1	2	.333	6.40	12	10	0	0	0-...	32.1	42	39	23	6	26-...	20
1998— Dom. Dodgers (DSL)	1	1	.500	3.55	13	9	1	1	0-...	33.0	28	19	13	1	34-...	36
1999— Dom. Dodgers (DSL)	3	2	.600	3.43	9	9	0	0	0-...	42.0	34	22	16	2	18-...	51
2000— Great Falls (Pio.)	*10	3	.769	1.88	15	15	*2	0	0-...	*95.2	66	32	20	2	23-0	*129
2001— Vero Beach (FSL)	*14	6	.700	3.21	26	26	2	0	0-...	154.1	133	67	55	13	60-0	*154
2002— Jacksonville (Sou.)	5	4	.556	1.99	11	11	2	0	0-...	68.0	56	21	15	4	13-0	44
— Las Vegas (PCL)	1	0	1.000	3.86	2	2	0	0	0-...	11.2	13	5	5	1	5-0	7
— Buffalo (I.L.)■	3	1	.750	3.60	4	4	0	0	0-...	25.0	26	10	10	1	7-0	14
— Cleveland (A.L.)	2	2	.500	5.66	7	7	0	0	0-0	41.1	40	27	26	5	18-3	24
Major League totals (1 year)	2	2	.500	5.66	7	7	0	0	0-0	41.1	40	27	26	5	18-3	24

RODRIGUEZ, RICH — P

PERSONAL: Born March 1, 1963, in Downey, Calif. ... 6-0/205. ... Throws left, bats left. ... Full name: Richard Anthony Rodriguez.

HIGH SCHOOL: Mountain View (El Monte, Calif.).

COLLEGE: Tennessee.

TRANSACTIONS/CAREER NOTES: Selected by Kansas City Royals organization in 17th round of free-agent draft (June 8, 1981); did not sign. ... Selected by New York Mets organization in ninth round of free-agent draft (June 4, 1984). ... Traded by Mets to San Diego Padres for 1B

Brad Pounders and 1B Bill Stevenson (January 13, 1989). ... Traded by Padres with 3B Gary Sheffield to Florida Marlins for P Trevor Hoffman, P Jose Martinez and P Andres Berumen (June 24, 1993). ... Released by Marlins (March 29, 1994). ... Signed by St. Louis Cardinals (April 1, 1994). ... On disabled list (April 27, 1995-remainder of season). ... Released by Cardinals (November 20, 1995). ... Signed by Cincinnati Reds organization (January 2, 1996). ... Released by Reds (March 24, 1996). ... Signed by Kansas City Royals organization (April 9, 1996). ... On disabled list (May 18-29, 1996). ... Granted free agency (October 15, 1996). ... Signed by San Francisco Giants organization (November 25, 1996). ... Granted free agency (October 30, 1997). ... Re-signed by Giants (December 7, 1997). ... Granted free agency (October 28, 1999). ... Signed by Mets (February 8, 2000). ... Released by Mets (March 29, 2001). ... Signed by Cleveland Indians organization (April 8, 2001). ... Granted free agency (November 6, 2001). ... Signed by Atlanta Braves organization (February 1, 2002). ... Traded by Braves to Texas Rangers for a player to be named (March 25, 2002). ... On Texas disabled list (April 6-July 11, 2002); included rehabilitation assignments to Tulsa (June 27-July 4) and Oklahoma (July 5-11). ... Granted free agency (October 30, 2002).

MISCELLANEOUS: Appeared in one game as pinch runner (1991). ... Had sacrifice hit in only appearance as pinch hitter (1992).

CAREER HITTING (MLB): 3-for-28 (.107), 3 R, 0 2B, 0 3B, 0 HR, 1 RBI.

Year League	W	L	Pct.	ERA	G	GS	CG	ShO	Sv.-Opp.	IP	H	R	ER	HR	BB-IBB	SO
1984— Little Falls (NY-Penn)	2	1	.667	2.80	25	1	0	0	0-...	35.1	28	21	11	0	36-7	27
1985— Columbia (S.Atl.)	6	3	.667	4.03	49	3	0	0	6-...	80.1	89	41	36	4	36-2	71
1986— Lynchburg (Caro.)	2	1	.667	3.57	36	0	0	0	3-...	45.1	37	20	18	2	19-0	38
— Jackson (Texas)	3	4	.429	9.00	13	5	1	0	0-...	33.0	51	35	33	5	15-2	15
1987— Lynchburg (Caro.)	3	1	.750	2.78	*69	0	0	0	5-...	68.0	69	23	21	3	26-6	59
1988— Jackson (Texas)	2	7	.222	2.87	47	1	0	0	6-...	78.1	66	35	25	3	42-6	68
1989— Wichita (Texas)■	8	3	.727	3.63	54	0	0	0	8-...	74.1	74	30	30	3	37-11	40
1990— Las Vegas (PCL)	3	4	.429	3.51	27	2	0	0	8-...	59.0	50	24	23	5	22-1	46
— San Diego (N.L.)	1	1	.500	2.83	32	0	0	0	1-1	47.2	52	17	15	2	16-4	22
1991— San Diego (N.L.)	3	1	.750	3.26	64	1	0	0	0-2	80.0	66	31	29	8	44-8	40
1992— San Diego (N.L.)	6	3	.667	2.37	61	1	0	0	0-1	91.0	77	28	24	4	29-4	64
1993— San Diego (N.L.)	2	3	.400	3.30	34	0	0	0	2-5	30.0	34	15	11	2	9-3	22
— Florida (N.L.)■	0	1	.000	4.11	36	0	0	0	1-2	46.0	39	23	21	8	24-5	21
1994— St. Louis (N.L.)■	3	5	.375	4.03	56	0	0	0	0-3	60.1	62	30	27	6	26-4	43
1995— St. Louis (N.L.)	0	0	...	0.00	1	0	0	0	0-0	1.2	0	0	0	0	0-0	0
1996— Omaha (A.A.)■	2	3	.400	3.99	47	0	0	0	3-...	70.0	75	40	31	11	20-1	68
1997— San Francisco (N.L.)■	4	3	.571	3.17	71	0	0	0	1-5	65.1	65	24	23	7	21-4	32
1998— San Francisco (N.L.)	4	0	1.000	3.70	68	0	0	0	2-6	65.2	69	28	27	7	20-5	44
1999— San Francisco (N.L.)	3	0	1.000	5.24	62	0	0	0	0-2	56.2	60	33	33	8	28-5	44
2000— New York (N.L.)■	0	1	.000	7.78	32	0	0	0	0-0	37.0	59	40	32	7	15-0	18
— Norfolk (I.L.)	0	1	.000	3.05	14	3	0	0	1-...	20.2	17	7	7	2	6-3	16
2001— Akron (East.)■	0	0	...	0.00	4	0	0	0	1-...	5.0	2	0	0	0	0-0	4
— Cleveland (A.L.)	2	2	.500	4.15	53	0	0	0	0-2	39.0	41	24	18	2	17-3	31
2002— Texas (A.L.)■	3	2	.600	5.40	36	0	0	0	1-3	16.2	14	10	10	1	11-1	12
— Tulsa (Texas)	0	0	...	6.75	3	0	0	0	0-...	2.2	4	2	2	0	2-0	3
— Oklahoma (PCL)	0	0	...	13.50	3	0	0	0	0-...	2.2	6	4	4	0	0-0	1
A.L. totals (2 years)	5	4	.556	4.53	89	0	0	0	1-5	55.2	55	34	28	3	28-4	43
N.L. totals (10 years)	26	18	.591	3.75	517	2	0	0	7-27	581.1	583	269	242	59	232-42	350
Major League totals (12 years)	31	22	.585	3.81	606	2	0	0	8-32	637.0	638	303	270	62	260-46	393

DIVISION SERIES RECORD

Year League	W	L	Pct.	ERA	G	GS	CG	ShO	Sv.-Opp.	IP	H	R	ER	HR	BB-IBB	SO
1997— San Francisco (N.L.)	0	0	...	0.00	2	0	0	0	0-0	1.0	1	0	0	0	0-0	0

ROGERS, EDDIE — SS — ORIOLES

PERSONAL: Born August 29, 1978, in San Pedro de Macoris, Dominican Republic. ... 6-1/172. ... Bats right, throws right. ... Full name: Edward Antonio Rogers. ... Brother of Omar Rogers, second baseman, Baltimore Orioles organization.

TRANSACTIONS/CAREER NOTES: Signed as non-drafted free agent by Baltimore Orioles organization (November 1, 1997). ... On Delmarva disabled list (April 6-22, 2000). ... On Bowie disabled list (August 8, 2000-remainder of season). ... On Bowie disabled list (June 4-24, 2002).

2002 GAMES PLAYED BY POSITION (MLB): SS—4.

		BATTING														FIELDING	
Year Team (League)	Pos.	G	AB	R	H	2B	3B	HR	RBI	BB	SO	SB-CS	Avg.	OBP	SLG	E	Avg.
1998— Dom. Orioles (DSL)		58	194	33	56	9	2	2	27	26	29	8-...	.289	...	.387	...	...
1999— GC Orioles (GCL)	SS-3B-2B	53	177	34	51	5	1	1	19	23	22	20-3	.288	.379	.345	10	.947
2000— Delmarva (S.Atl.)	SS-2B	80	332	46	91	14	5	5	42	22	63	27-6	.274	.317	.392	19	.947
— Bowie (East.)	SS	13	49	4	14	3	0	1	8	3	15	1-1	.286	.321	.408	0	1.000
2001— Bowie (East.)	SS	53	191	11	38	10	1	0	13	6	40	10-2	.199	.231	.262	10	.960
— Frederick (Caro.)	SS	73	292	39	76	20	3	8	41	14	47	18-6	.260	.310	.432	14	.956
2002— Bowie (East.)	SS	112	422	59	110	26	2	11	57	16	70	14-4	.261	.300	.410	20	.958
— Baltimore (A.L.)	SS	5	3	0	0	0	0	0	0	0	0	0-0	.000	.000	.000	0	1.000
Major League totals (1 year)		5	3	0	0	0	0	0	0	0	0	0-0	.000	.000	.000	0	1.000

ROGERS, KENNY — P

PERSONAL: Born November 10, 1964, in Savannah, Ga. ... 6-1/217. ... Throws left, bats left. ... Full name: Kenneth Scott Rogers.

HIGH SCHOOL: Plant City (Fla.).

TRANSACTIONS/CAREER NOTES: Selected by Texas Rangers organization in 39th round of free-agent draft (June 7, 1982). ... On Tulsa disabled list (April 12-30, 1986). ... Granted free agency (October 31, 1995). ... Signed by New York Yankees (December 30, 1995). ... Traded by Yankees with IF Mariano Duncan and P Kevin Henthorne to San Diego Padres for OF Greg Vaughn, P Kerry Taylor and P Chris Clark (July 4, 1997); trade later voided because Vaughn failed physical (July 6). ... Traded by Yankees with cash to Oakland Athletics for a player to be named later (November 7, 1997); Yankees acquired 3B Scott Brosius to complete deal (November 18, 1997). ... Traded by A's to New York Mets for OF Terrance Long and P Leo Vasquez (July 23, 1999). ... Granted free agency (October 29, 1999). ... Signed by Rangers (December 29, 1999). ... On disabled list (July 24, 2001-remainder of season). ... Granted free agency (October 29, 2002).

HONORS: Won A.L. Gold Glove as pitcher (2000 and 2002).

STATISTICAL NOTES: Tied for A.L. lead with five balks in 1993. ... Pitched 4-0 perfect game against California (July 28, 1994).

MISCELLANEOUS: Holds Texas Rangers franchise all-time record for most games pitched (463).

CAREER HITTING (MLB): 7-for-44 (.159), 3 R, 0 2B, 0 3B, 0 HR, 3 RBI.

Year League	W	L	Pct.	ERA	G	GS	CG	ShO	Sv.-Opp.	IP	H	R	ER	HR	BB-IBB	SO
1982— Gulf Coast Rangers (GCL)	0	0	...	0.00	2	0	0	0	0-...	3.0	0	0	0	0	0-0	4
1983— Gulf Coast Rangers (GCL)	4	1	.800	2.36	15	6	0	0	1-...	53.1	40	21	14	0	20-0	36
1984— Burlington (Midw.)	4	7	.364	3.98	39	4	1	0	3-...	92.2	87	52	41	9	33-3	93
1985— Daytona Beach (FSL)	0	1	.000	7.20	6	0	0	0	0-...	10.0	12	9	8	0	11-1	9
— Burlington (Midw.)	2	5	.286	2.84	33	4	2	1	4-...	95.0	67	34	30	3	62-9	96
1986— Tulsa (Texas)	0	3	.000	9.91	10	4	0	0	0-...	26.1	39	30	29	4	18-1	23
— Salem (Caro.)	2	7	.222	6.27	12	12	0	0	0-...	66.0	75	54	46	9	26-0	46
1987— Charlotte (FSL)	0	3	.000	4.76	5	3	0	0	0-...	17.0	17	13	9	1	8-0	14
— Tulsa (Texas)	1	5	.167	5.35	28	6	0	0	2-...	69.0	80	51	41	5	35-3	59
1988— Charlotte (FSL)	2	0	1.000	1.27	8	6	0	0	1-...	35.1	22	8	5	1	11-0	26
— Tulsa (Texas)	4	6	.400	4.00	13	13	2	0	0-...	83.1	73	43	37	6	34-0	76
1989— Texas (A.L.)	3	4	.429	2.93	73	0	0	0	2-5	73.2	60	28	24	2	42-9	63
1990— Texas (A.L.)	10	6	.625	3.13	69	3	0	0	15-23	97.2	93	40	34	6	42-5	74
1991— Texas (A.L.)	10	10	.500	5.42	63	9	0	0	5-6	109.2	121	80	66	14	61-7	73
1992— Texas (A.L.)	3	6	.333	3.09	*81	0	0	0	6-10	78.2	80	32	27	7	26-8	70
1993— Texas (A.L.)	16	10	.615	4.10	35	33	5	0	0-0	208.1	210	108	95	18	71-2	140
1994— Texas (A.L.)	11	8	.579	4.46	24	24	6	2	0-0	167.1	169	93	83	24	52-1	120
1995— Texas (A.L.)	17	7	.708	3.38	31	31	3	1	0-0	208.0	192	87	78	26	76-1	140
1996— New York (A.L.)■	12	8	.600	4.68	30	30	2	1	0-0	179.0	179	97	93	16	83-2	92
1997— New York (A.L.)	6	7	.462	5.65	31	22	1	0	0-0	145.0	161	100	91	18	62-1	78
1998— Oakland (A.L.)■	16	8	.667	3.17	34	34	7	1	0-0	238.2	215	96	84	19	67-0	138
1999— Oakland (A.L.)	5	3	.625	4.30	19	19	3	0	0-0	119.1	135	66	57	8	41-0	68
— New York (N.L.)■	5	1	.833	4.03	12	12	2	1	0-0	76.0	71	35	34	8	28-1	58
2000— Texas (A.L.)■	13	13	.500	4.55	34	34	2	0	0-0	227.1	257	126	115	20	78-2	127
2001— Texas (A.L.)	5	7	.417	6.19	20	20	0	0	0-0	120.2	150	88	83	18	49-2	74
2002— Texas (A.L.)	13	8	.619	3.84	33	33	2	1	0-0	210.2	212	101	90	21	70-1	107
A.L. totals (14 years)	140	105	.571	4.20	577	292	31	6	28-44	2184.0	2234	1142	1020	217	820-41	1364
N.L. totals (1 year)	5	1	.833	4.03	12	12	2	1	0-0	76.0	71	35	34	8	28-1	58
Major League totals (14 years)	145	106	.578	4.20	589	304	33	7	28-44	2260.0	2305	1177	1054	225	848-42	1422

DIVISION SERIES RECORD

Year League	W	L	Pct.	ERA	G	GS	CG	ShO	Sv.-Opp.	IP	H	R	ER	HR	BB-IBB	SO
1996— New York (A.L.)	0	0	...	9.00	2	1	0	0	0-0	2.0	5	2	2	0	2-0	1
1999— New York (N.L.)	0	1	.000	8.31	1	1	0	0	0-0	4.1	5	4	4	0	2-0	6
Division series totals (2 years)	0	1	.000	8.53	3	2	0	0	0-0	6.1	10	6	6	0	4-0	7

CHAMPIONSHIP SERIES RECORD

Year League	W	L	Pct.	ERA	G	GS	CG	ShO	Sv.-Opp.	IP	H	R	ER	HR	BB-IBB	SO
1996— New York (A.L.)	0	0	...	12.00	1	1	0	0	0-0	3.0	5	4	4	1	2-0	3
1999— New York (N.L.)	0	2	.000	5.87	3	1	0	0	0-0	7.2	11	5	5	2	7-2	2
Champ. series totals (2 years)	0	2	.000	7.59	4	2	0	0	0-0	10.2	16	9	9	3	9-2	5

WORLD SERIES RECORD

NOTES: Member of World Series championship team (1996).

Year League	W	L	Pct.	ERA	G	GS	CG	ShO	Sv.-Opp.	IP	H	R	ER	HR	BB-IBB	SO
1996— New York (A.L.)	0	0	...	22.50	1	1	0	0	0-0	2.0	5	5	5	1	2-0	0

ALL-STAR GAME RECORD

	W	L	Pct.	ERA	GS	CG	ShO	Sv.-Opp.	IP	H	R	ER	HR	BB-IBB	SO
All-Star Game totals (1 year)	0	0	...	9.00	0	0	0	0-1	1.0	1	1	1	1	0-0	2

ROLEN, SCOTT 3B CARDINALS

PERSONAL: Born April 4, 1975, in Jasper, Ind. ... 6-4/226. ... Bats right, throws right. ... Full name: Scott Bruce Rolen.

HIGH SCHOOL: Jasper (Ind.).

TRANSACTIONS/CAREER NOTES: Selected by Philadelphia Phillies organization in second round of free-agent draft (June 3, 1993). ... On disabled list (May 24-June 8, 2000). ... Traded by Phillies with P Doug Nickle to St. Louis Cardinals for IF/OF Placido Polanco, P Bud Smith and P Mike Timlin (July 29, 2002).

RECORDS: Shares major league single-game record for most strikeouts (nine-inning game)—5 (August 23, 1999).

HONORS: Named N.L. Rookie Player of the Year by The Sporting News (1997). ... Named N.L. Rookie of the Year by Baseball Writers' Association of America (1997). ... Won N.L. Gold Glove at third base (1998 and 2000-02). ... Named third baseman on The Sporting News N.L. All-Star team (2002). ... Named third baseman on N.L. Silver Slugger team (2002).

STATISTICAL NOTES: Led South Atlantic League third basemen with 323 assists, 457 total chances and 36 double plays and tied for lead with 96 putouts in 1994. ... Led N.L. third basemen with 459 total chances in 1997 and 468 in 1998. ... Led N.L. third basemen with 144 putouts in 1997 and 135 in 1998. ... Led N.L. third basemen with 335 assists and 484 total chances in 2002. ... Career major league grand slams: 2.

2002 GAMES PLAYED BY POSITION (MLB): 3B—155.

		BATTING														FIELDING	
Year Team (League)	Pos.	G	AB	R	H	2B	3B	HR	RBI	BB	SO	SB-CS	Avg.	OBP	SLG	E	Avg.
1993— Martinsville (Appl.)	3B	25	80	8	25	5	0	0	12	10	15	3-4	.313	.429	.375	10	.889
1994— Spartanburg (S.Atl.)	3B	138	513	83	151	34	5	14	72	55	90	6-8	.294	.363	.462	38	.917
1995— Clearwater (FSL)	3B	66	238	45	69	13	2	10	39	37	46	4-0	.290	.392	.487	20	.899
— Reading (East.)	3B	20	76	16	22	3	0	3	15	7	14	1-0	.289	.353	.447	4	.934
1996— Reading (East.)	3B	61	230	44	83	22	2	9	42	34	32	8-3	.361	.445	.591	9	.949
— Scranton/W.B. (I.L.)	3B	45	168	23	46	17	0	2	19	28	28	4-5	.274	.376	.411	6	.952
— Philadelphia (N.L.)	3B	37	130	10	33	7	0	4	18	13	27	0-2	.254	.322	.400	4	.954
1997— Philadelphia (N.L.)	3B	156	561	93	159	35	3	21	92	76	138	16-6	.283	.377	.469	24	.948
1998— Philadelphia (N.L.)	3B	160	601	120	174	45	4	31	110	93	141	14-7	.290	.391	.532	14	.970
1999— Philadelphia (N.L.)	3B	112	421	74	113	28	1	26	77	67	114	12-2	.268	.368	.525	14	.960
2000— Philadelphia (N.L.)	3B	128	483	88	144	32	6	26	89	51	99	8-1	.298	.370	.551	10	.971
2001— Philadelphia (N.L.)	3B	151	554	96	160	39	1	25	107	74	127	16-5	.289	.378	.498	12	.973
2002— Philadelphia (N.L.)	3B	100	375	52	97	21	4	17	66	52	68	5-2	.259	.358	.472	8	.973
— St. Louis (N.L.)■	3B	55	205	37	57	8	4	14	44	20	34	3-2	.278	.354	.561	8	.958
Major League totals (7 years)		899	3330	570	937	215	23	164	603	446	748	74-27	.281	.372	.508	94	.964

DIVISION SERIES RECORD

			BATTING														FIELDING	
Year	Team (League)	Pos.	G	AB	R	H	2B	3B	HR	RBI	BB	SO	SB-CS	Avg.	OBP	SLG	E	Avg.
2002—	St. Louis (N.L.)..........	3B	2	7	1	3	0	0	1	2	0	2	0-0	.429	.500	.857	0	1.000

ALL-STAR GAME RECORD

	AB	R	H	2B	3B	HR	RBI	BB	SO	SB-CS	Avg.	OBP	SLG	E	Avg.
All-Star Game totals (1 year)	3	0	0	0	0	0	0	0	1	0-0	.000	.000	.000	0	...

ROLLINS, JIMMY — SS — PHILLIES

PERSONAL: Born November 27, 1978, in Oakland. ... 5-8/165. ... Bats both, throws right. ... Full name: James Calvin Rollins. ... Cousin of Tony Tarasco, outfielder with six major league teams (1988-99).
HIGH SCHOOL: Encinal (Alameda, Calif.).
TRANSACTIONS/CAREER NOTES: Selected by Philadelphia Phillies organization in second round of free-agent draft (June 4, 1996).
STATISTICAL NOTES: Led South Atlantic League shortstops wth 201 putouts, 421 assists and 648 total chances in 1997. ... Led International League shortstops with 411 assists in 2000.
2002 GAMES PLAYED BY POSITION (MLB): SS—152; 2B—1.

			BATTING														FIELDING	
Year	Team (League)	Pos.	G	AB	R	H	2B	3B	HR	RBI	BB	SO	SB-CS	Avg.	OBP	SLG	E	Avg.
1996—	Martinsville (Appl.).....	SS	49	172	22	41	3	1	1	16	28	20	11-5	.238	.351	.285	20	.906
1997—	Piedmont (S.Atl.)........	SS	139	560	94	151	22	8	6	59	52	80	46-6	.270	.330	.370	26	*.960
1998—	Clearwater (FSL)	SS	119	495	72	121	18	9	6	35	41	62	23-9	.244	.306	.354	29	*.952
1999—	Reading (East.)...........	SS	133	532	81	145	21	8	11	56	51	47	24-12	.273	.336	.404	22	.965
—	Scranton/W.B. (I.L.) ...	SS	4	13	0	1	1	0	0	0	1	1	1-0	.077	.143	.154	1	.960
2000—	Scranton/W.B. (I.L.) ...	SS	133	470	67	129	28	•11	12	69	49	55	24-7	.274	.341	.457	26	.958
—	Philadelphia (N.L.)......	SS	14	53	5	17	1	1	0	5	2	7	3-0	.321	.345	.377	1	.978
2001—	Philadelphia (N.L.)......	SS	158	656	97	180	29	*12	14	54	48	108	•46-8	.274	.323	.419	14	.979
2002—	Philadelphia (N.L.)......	SS-2B	154	*637	82	156	33	*10	11	60	54	103	31-13	.245	.306	.380	14	.980
Major League totals (3 years)			326	1346	184	353	63	23	25	119	104	218	80-21	.262	.316	.399	29	.979

ALL-STAR GAME RECORD

	AB	R	H	2B	3B	HR	RBI	BB	SO	SB-CS	Avg.	OBP	SLG	E	Avg.
All-Star Game totals (2 years)	2	2	2	0	0	0	0	1	0	1-0	1.000	1.000	1.000	0	1.000

ROLLS, DAMIAN — 3B — DEVIL RAYS

PERSONAL: Born September 15, 1977, in Manhattan, Kan. ... 6-2/215. ... Bats right, throws right. ... Full name: Damian Michael Rolls.
HIGH SCHOOL: F.L. Schlagle (Kansas City, Kan.).
TRANSACTIONS/CAREER NOTES: Selected by Los Angeles Dodgers organization in first round (23rd pick overall) of free-agent draft (June 4, 1996). ... Selected by Kansas City Royals from Dodgers organization in Rule 5 major league draft (December 13, 1999). ... Traded by Royals to Tampa Bay Devil Rays for a player to be named later and cash (December 13, 1999). ... On Tampa Bay disabled list (March 25-September 1, 2000); included rehabilitation assignments to St. Petersburg (August 12-18) and Orlando (August 19-September 1). ... On Durham disabled list (May 30-August 13, 2002).
STATISTICAL NOTES: Led Northwest League third basemen with 58 putouts, 134 assists and 215 total chances in 1996. ... Led South Atlantic League third basemen with 111 putouts, 246 assists and 388 total chances in 1997.
2002 GAMES PLAYED BY POSITION (MLB): OF—21.

			BATTING														FIELDING	
Year	Team (League)	Pos.	G	AB	R	H	2B	3B	HR	RBI	BB	SO	SB-CS	Avg.	OBP	SLG	E	Avg.
1996—	Yakima (N'West)	3B	66	257	31	68	11	1	4	27	7	46	8-3	.265	.291	.362	•23	.893
1997—	Savannah (S.Atl.)	3B	130	475	57	100	17	5	5	47	38	83	11-3	.211	.274	.299	31	.920
1998—	Vero Beach (FSL)	3B	73	266	28	65	9	0	0	30	23	43	13-3	.244	.307	.278	13	.951
—	San Antonio (Texas)...	3B	50	160	18	35	6	0	1	9	6	28	2-0	.219	.246	.275	9	.947
1999—	Vero Beach (FSL)	3B-2B	127	474	68	141	26	2	9	54	36	66	24-13	.297	.361	.418	25	.924
2000—	St. Pete. (FSL)■.........	3B	5	16	2	3	2	0	0	0	2	3	1-0	.188	.316	.313	0	1.000
—	Orlando (Sou.)	3B	14	51	6	13	5	0	0	3	7	6	1-1	.255	.350	.353	3	.906
—	Tampa Bay (A.L.)........	DH-3B	4	3	0	1	0	0	0	0	0	1	0-0	.333	.333	.333	0	...
2001—	Tampa Bay (A.L.)........	2B-OF-DH-3B	81	237	33	62	11	1	2	12	10	47	12-4	.262	.291	.342	6	.974
2002—	Orlando (Sou.)	OF	2	7	1	3	0	1	0	0	1	0	0-1	.429	.500	.714	0	1.000
—	Durham (I.L.)	OF-3B	67	244	41	65	6	4	6	35	21	43	15-0	.266	.332	.398	6	.962
—	Tampa Bay (A.L.)........	OF	21	89	15	26	6	1	0	6	3	16	2-5	.292	.330	.382	3	.947
Major League totals (3 years)			106	329	48	89	17	2	2	18	13	64	14-9	.271	.302	.353	9	.969

ROMANO, JASON — 2B — ROCKIES

PERSONAL: Born June 24, 1979, in Tampa, Fla. ... 6-0/185. ... Bats right, throws right. ... Full name: Jason Anthony Romano. ... Brother of Jimmie Romano, catcher, Texas Rangers organization.
HIGH SCHOOL: Hillsborough (Tampa, Fla.).
TRANSACTIONS/CAREER NOTES: Selected by Texas Rangers organization in supplemental round ("sandwich pick" between first and second round, 39th pick overall) of free-agent draft (June 3, 1997); pick received as part of compensation of New York Yankees signed Type-A free agent P Mike Stanton. ... On Oklahoma disabled list (June 17-August 9, 2001). ... Traded by Rangers with OF Gabe Kapler to Colorado Rockies for OF Todd Hollandsworth and P Dennys Reyes (July 31, 2002).
STATISTICAL NOTES: Led South Atlantic League second basemen with 305 putouts in 1998. ... Led Texas League with 16 sacrifice hits in 2000.
2002 GAMES PLAYED BY POSITION (MLB): OF—21; 2B—20; SS—5; DH—4; 3B—2.

								BATTING								FIELDING	
Year Team (League)	Pos.	G	AB	R	H	2B	3B	HR	RBI	BB	SO	SB-CS	Avg.	OBP	SLG	E	Avg.
1997—GC Rangers (GCL)......	3B	34	109	27	28	5	3	2	11	13	19	13-4	.257	.349	.413	15	.810
1998—Savannah (S.Atl.).......	2B	134	524	72	142	19	4	7	52	46	94	40-17	.271	.336	.363	•32	.952
—Charlotte (FSL)...........	2B	7	24	3	5	1	0	0	1	2	2	1-2	.208	.259	.250	1	.978
1999—Charlotte (FSL)...........	2B	120	459	84	143	27	*14	13	71	39	72	34-15	.312	.376	.516	23	.957
2000—Tulsa (Texas).............	2B	131	535	87	145	35	2	8	70	56	84	25-10	.271	.343	.389	24	.963
2001—Tulsa (Texas).............	2B	46	186	19	45	9	1	1	19	16	31	8-3	.242	.304	.317	8	.962
—Oklahoma (PCL).........	2B-OF	41	149	32	47	6	1	4	13	20	28	3-4	.315	.394	.450	2	.981
—GC Rangers (GCL)......	2B-OF	5	21	2	3	0	0	0	0	1	8	1-0	.143	.182	.143	5	.808
—Charlotte (FSL)...........	OF	3	10	3	4	2	0	0	1	4	1	1-0	.400	.571	.600	0	1.000
2002—Oklahoma (PCL).........	OF-2B-SS-3B	48	196	28	53	8	1	4	28	19	41	10-3	.270	.329	.383	5	.972
—Texas (A.L.)................	OF-2B-DH-3B	29	54	8	11	4	0	0	4	4	13	2-0	.204	.254	.278	1	.981
—Colo. Springs (PCL)■	OF-2B-SS-3B	31	129	20	40	7	2	0	9	6	27	8-3	.310	.338	.395	3	.973
—Colorado (N.L.)..........	2B-SS-OF-3B	18	37	9	12	0	1	0	1	3	11	4-1	.324	.375	.378	4	.907
American League totals (1 year)		29	54	8	11	4	0	0	4	4	13	2-0	.204	.254	.278	1	.981
National League totals (1 year)		18	37	9	12	0	1	0	1	3	11	4-1	.324	.375	.378	4	.907
Major League totals (1 year)		47	91	17	23	4	1	0	5	7	24	6-1	.253	.303	.319	5	.947

ROMERO, J.C. — P — TWINS

PERSONAL: Born June 4, 1976, in Rio Piedras, Puerto Rico. ... 5-11/195. ... Throws left, bats both. ... Full name: Juan C. Romero.
HIGH SCHOOL: Berwing (San Juan, Puerto Rico).
COLLEGE: Mobile.
TRANSACTIONS/CAREER NOTES: Selected by Minnesota Twins organization in 21st round of free-agent draft (June 3, 1997). ... On Minnesota disabled list (March 25-May 10, 2000); included rehabilitation assignment to Fort Myers (May 3-10).
CAREER HITTING (MLB): 1-for-2 (.500), 1 R, 1 2B, 0 3B, 0 HR, 0 RBI.

Year League	W	L	Pct.	ERA	G	GS	CG	ShO	Sv.-Opp.	IP	H	R	ER	HR	BB-IBB	SO
1997—Elizabethton (Appl.)..........	3	2	.600	4.88	18	0	0	0	3-...	24.0	27	16	13	4	7-0	29
—Fort Myers (FSL).............	1	1	.500	4.38	7	1	0	0	0-...	12.1	11	6	6	1	4-0	9
1998—New Britain (East.)...........	6	3	.667	2.19	51	1	0	0	2-...	78.0	48	28	19	3	43-3	79
1999—New Britain (East.)...........	4	4	.500	3.40	36	1	0	0	7-...	53.0	51	25	20	6	34-0	53
—Salt Lake (PCL)................	4	1	.800	3.20	15	0	0	0	1-...	19.2	18	11	7	1	14-0	20
—Minnesota (A.L.).............	0	0	...	3.72	5	0	0	0	0-0	9.2	13	4	4	0	0-0	4
2000—Fort Myers (FSL).............	0	0	...	1.93	2	0	0	0	0-...	4.2	4	1	1	0	1-0	3
—Salt Lake (PCL)................	4	2	.667	3.44	17	11	1	0	4-...	65.1	60	40	25	6	25-0	38
—Minnesota (A.L.).............	2	7	.222	7.02	12	11	0	0	0-0	57.2	72	51	45	8	30-0	50
2001—Minnesota (A.L.).............	1	4	.200	6.23	14	11	0	0	0-0	65.0	71	48	45	10	24-1	39
—Edmonton (PCL)...............	3	3	.500	3.68	12	10	0	0	0-...	63.2	67	33	26	4	24-0	55
2002—Minnesota (A.L.).............	9	2	.818	1.89	81	0	0	0	1-5	81.0	62	17	17	3	36-4	76
Major League totals (4 years).....	12	13	.480	4.68	112	22	0	0	1-5	213.1	218	120	111	21	90-5	169

DIVISION SERIES RECORD

Year League	W	L	Pct.	ERA	G	GS	CG	ShO	Sv.-Opp.	IP	H	R	ER	HR	BB-IBB	SO
2002—Minnesota (A.L.).............	0	0	...	0.00	3	0	0	0	0-0	3.1	3	0	0	0	1-0	2

CHAMPIONSHIP SERIES RECORD

Year League	W	L	Pct.	ERA	G	GS	CG	ShO	Sv.-Opp.	IP	H	R	ER	HR	BB-IBB	SO
2002—Minnesota (A.L.).............	0	1	.000	22.50	4	0	0	0	0-0	2.0	4	5	5	1	2-0	3

ROSS, DAVE — C — DODGERS

PERSONAL: Born March 19, 1977, in Bainbridge, Ga. ... 6-2/205. ... Bats right, throws right. ... Full name: David Wade Ross.
COLLEGE: Florida.
TRANSACTIONS/CAREER NOTES: Selected by Los Angeles Dodgers organization in seventh round of free-agent draft (June 2, 1998).
2002 GAMES PLAYED BY POSITION (MLB): C—6.

								BATTING								FIELDING	
Year Team (League)	Pos.	G	AB	R	H	2B	3B	HR	RBI	BB	SO	SB-CS	Avg.	OBP	SLG	E	Avg.
1998—Yakima (N'West)........	C	59	191	31	59	14	1	6	25	34	49	2-2	.309	.412	.487	10	.979
1999—Vero Beach (FSL).......	C-1B-OF	114	375	47	85	19	1	7	39	46	111	5-9	.227	.318	.339	16	.979
2000—San Bern. (Calif.)........	C	51	191	27	49	11	1	7	21	17	43	3-2	.257	.319	.435	3	.992
—San Antonio (Texas)...	C	24	67	11	14	2	1	3	12	9	17	1-0	.209	.308	.403	1	.994
2001—Jacksonville (Sou.).....	C	74	246	35	65	13	1	11	45	34	72	1-1	.264	.372	.459	9	.985
2002—Las Vegas (PCL)........	C	92	293	48	87	16	2	15	68	35	86	1-1	.297	.384	.519	7	.989
—Los Angeles (N.L.).....	C	8	10	2	2	1	0	1	2	2	4	0-0	.200	.385	.600	0	1.000
Major League totals (1 year)		8	10	2	2	1	0	1	2	2	4	0-0	.200	.385	.600	0	1.000

ROWAND, AARON — OF — WHITE SOX

PERSONAL: Born August 29, 1977, in Portland, Ore. ... 6-1/200. ... Bats right, throws right. ... Full name: Aaron Ryan Rowand.
HIGH SCHOOL: Glendora (Calif.).
COLLEGE: Cal State-Fullerton.
TRANSACTIONS/CAREER NOTES: Selected by New York Mets organization in 40th round of free-agent draft (June 1, 1995); did not sign. ... Selected by Chicago White Sox organization in supplemental round ("sandwich pick" between first and second round, 35th pick overall) of free-agent draft (June 2, 1998); pick received as part of compensation for Tampa Bay Devil Rays signing Type A free agent OF Dave Martinez.
STATISTICAL NOTES: Led Carolina League with 258 total bases in 1999.
2002 GAMES PLAYED BY POSITION (MLB): OF—120.

Year Team (League)	Pos.	G	AB	R	H	2B	3B	HR	RBI	BB	SO	SB-CS	Avg.	OBP	SLG	E	Avg.
		BATTING														FIELDING	
1998—Hickory (S.Atl.)	OF	61	222	42	76	13	3	5	32	21	36	7-3	.342	.410	.495	3	.966
1999—Win.-Salem (Caro.)	OF	133	512	•96	143	37	3	24	88	33	94	15-9	.279	.336	.504	5	.973
2000—Birmingham (Sou.)	OF	139	532	80	137	26	5	20	98	38	117	22-7	.258	.321	.438	8	.975
2001—Charlotte (I.L.)	OF	82	329	54	97	28	0	16	48	21	47	8-2	.295	.353	.526	6	.966
—Chicago (A.L.)	OF	63	123	21	36	5	0	4	20	15	28	5-1	.293	.385	.431	1	.991
2002—Chicago (A.L.)	OF	126	302	41	78	16	2	7	29	12	54	0-1	.258	.298	.394	4	.983
Major League totals (2 years)		189	425	62	114	21	2	11	49	27	82	5-2	.268	.325	.405	5	.985

RUAN, WILKIN — OF — DODGERS

PERSONAL: Born September 18, 1978, in Ramon Santana, Dominican Republic. ... 6-0/170. ... Bats right, throws right. ... Full name: Wilkin Chal Ruan.

TRANSACTIONS/CAREER NOTES: Signed as non-drafted free agent by Montreal Expos organization (November 15, 1996). ... On Harrisburg disabled list (July 12-August 11, 2001). ... Traded by Expos with P Guillermo Mota to Los Angeles Dodgers for P Matt Herges and IF Jorge Nunez (March 24, 2002). ... On Jacksonville disabled list (July 19-August 10, 2002).

STATISTICAL NOTES: Led South Atlantic League outfielders with 285 total chances and tied for the lead in double plays with four in 1999.

2002 GAMES PLAYED BY POSITION (MLB): OF—5.

Year Team (League)	Pos.	G	AB	R	H	2B	3B	HR	RBI	BB	SO	SB-CS	Avg.	OBP	SLG	E	Avg.
		BATTING														FIELDING	
1997—Dom. Expos (DSL)	OF	69	293	53	102	16	5	4	46	31	34	33-...	.348	...	.478	...	...
1998—Jupiter (FSL)	OF	5	18	2	3	0	0	0	0	1	3	2-0	.167	.211	.167	0	1.000
—GC Expos (GCL)	OF	54	201	22	48	9	3	1	19	5	43	13-13	.239	.262	.328	1	*.991
1999—Cape Fear (S.Atl.)	OF	112	397	43	89	16	4	1	47	18	79	29-17	.224	.268	.292	4	.986
2000—Cape Fear (S.Atl.)	OF	134	574	95	165	29	10	0	51	24	75	64-10	.287	.323	.373	3	.990
2001—Jupiter (FSL)	OF	72	293	41	83	8	2	2	26	10	35	25-14	.283	.313	.345	7	.964
—Harrisburg (East.)	OF	30	117	14	29	7	0	0	6	3	18	6-0	.248	.279	.308	2	.976
2002—Jacksonville (Sou.)■	OF	78	324	44	82	16	6	3	34	17	33	23-3	.253	.306	.367	4	.979
—Las Vegas (PCL)	OF	40	153	18	50	7	3	0	29	2	17	12-0	.327	.335	.412	0	1.000
—Los Angeles (N.L.)	OF	12	11	2	3	1	0	0	3	0	2	0-0	.273	.273	.364	0	1.000
Major League totals (1 year)		12	11	2	3	1	0	0	3	0	2	0-0	.273	.273	.364	0	1.000

RUETER, KIRK — P — GIANTS

PERSONAL: Born December 1, 1970, in Centralia, Ill. ... 6-3/212. ... Throws left, bats left. ... Full name: Kirk Wesley Rueter. ... Name pronounced REE-ter.

HIGH SCHOOL: Nashville (Ill.) Community.

COLLEGE: Murray State.

TRANSACTIONS/CAREER NOTES: Selected by Montreal Expos organization in 18th round of free-agent draft (June 3, 1991). ... On Montreal disabled list (May 10-26, 1996); included rehabilitation assignment to Ottawa (May 20-24). ... Traded by Expos with P Tim Scott to San Francisco Giants for P Mark Leiter (July 30, 1996).

HONORS: Named N.L. Rookie Pitcher of the Year by The Sporting News (1993).

STATISTICAL NOTES: Pitched 1-0 one-hit, complete-game victory for Montreal against San Francisco (August 27, 1995).

MISCELLANEOUS: Caught stealing in only appearance as pinch runner (1998). ... Scored one run in two appearances as pinch runner (2000). ... Appeared in one game as pinch runner (2001). ... Appeared in one game as pinch hitter (2001).

CAREER HITTING (MLB): 75-for-478 (.157), 34 R, 6 2B, 0 3B, 0 HR, 34 RBI.

Year League	W	L	Pct.	ERA	G	GS	CG	ShO	Sv.-Opp.	IP	H	R	ER	HR	BB-IBB	SO
1991—Gulf Coast Expos (GCL)	1	1	.500	0.95	5	4	0	0	0-...	19.0	16	5	2	0	4-0	19
—Sumter (S.Atl.)	3	1	.750	1.33	8	5	0	0	0-...	40.2	32	8	6	3	10-0	27
1992—Rockford (Midw.)	11	9	.550	2.58	26	26	6	•2	0-...	174.1	150	68	50	5	36-2	153
1993—Harrisburg (East.)	5	0	1.000	1.36	9	8	1	1	0-...	59.2	47	10	9	4	7-0	36
—Ottawa (I.L.)	4	2	.667	2.70	7	7	1	0	0-...	43.1	46	20	13	7	3-0	27
—Montreal (N.L.)	8	0	1.000	2.73	14	14	1	0	0-0	85.2	85	33	26	5	18-1	31
1994—Montreal (N.L.)	7	3	.700	5.17	20	20	0	0	0-0	92.1	106	60	53	11	23-1	50
—Ottawa (I.L.)	0	0	...	4.50	1	1	0	0	0-...	2.0	1	1	1	1	0-0	1
1995—Montreal (N.L.)	5	3	.625	3.23	9	9	1	1	0-0	47.1	38	17	17	3	9-0	28
—Ottawa (I.L.)	9	7	.563	3.06	20	20	3	1	0-...	120.2	120	50	41	7	25-0	67
1996—Ottawa (I.L.)	1	2	.333	4.20	3	3	1	0	0-...	15.0	21	7	7	3	3-0	3
—Montreal (N.L.)	5	6	.455	4.58	16	16	0	0	0-0	78.2	91	44	40	12	22-0	30
—San Francisco (N.L.)■	1	2	.333	1.93	4	3	0	0	0-0	23.1	18	6	5	0	5-0	16
—Phoenix (PCL)	1	2	.333	3.51	5	5	0	0	0-...	25.2	25	12	10	2	12-0	15
1997—San Francisco (N.L.)	13	6	.684	3.45	32	32	0	0	0-0	190.2	194	83	73	17	51-8	115
1998—San Francisco (N.L.)	16	9	.640	4.36	33	33	1	0	0-0	187.2	193	100	91	27	57-3	102
1999—San Francisco (N.L.)	15	10	.600	5.41	33	33	1	0	0-0	184.2	219	118	111	28	55-2	94
2000—San Francisco (N.L.)	11	9	.550	3.96	32	31	0	0	0-0	184.0	205	92	81	23	62-5	71
2001—San Francisco (N.L.)	14	12	.538	4.42	34	34	0	0	0-0	195.1	213	105	96	25	66-4	83
2002—San Francisco (N.L.)	14	8	.636	3.23	33	33	0	0	0-0	203.2	204	83	73	22	54-7	76
Major League totals (10 years)	109	68	.616	4.07	260	258	4	1	0-0	1473.1	1566	741	666	173	422-31	696

DIVISION SERIES RECORD

Year League	W	L	Pct.	ERA	G	GS	CG	ShO	Sv.-Opp.	IP	H	R	ER	HR	BB-IBB	SO
1997—San Francisco (N.L.)	0	0	...	1.29	1	1	0	0	0-0	7.0	4	1	1	1	3-0	5
2000—San Francisco (N.L.)	0	0	...	0.00	1	0	0	0	0-0	4.1	3	0	0	0	1-0	1
2002—San Francisco (N.L.)	0	1	.000	18.00	1	1	0	0	0-0	3.0	7	7	6	2	2-0	1
Division series totals (3 years)	0	1	.000	4.40	3	2	0	0	0-0	14.1	14	8	7	3	6-0	7

CHAMPIONSHIP SERIES RECORD

Year League	W	L	Pct.	ERA	G	GS	CG	ShO	Sv.-Opp.	IP	H	R	ER	HR	BB-IBB	SO
2002—San Francisco (N.L.)	1	0	1.000	4.09	2	2	0	0	0-0	11.0	15	5	5	2	2-0	3

WORLD SERIES RECORD

Year League	W	L	Pct.	ERA	G	GS	CG	ShO	Sv.-Opp.	IP	H	R	ER	HR	BB-IBB	SO
2002—San Francisco (N.L.)	0	0	...	2.70	2	1	0	0	0-0	10.0	10	3	3	1	1-0	5

RUPE, RYAN — P — DEVIL RAYS

PERSONAL: Born March 31, 1975, in Houston. ... 6-5/248. ... Throws right, bats right. ... Full name: Ryan Kittman Rupe.
HIGH SCHOOL: Northbrook (Houston).
COLLEGE: Texas A&M.
TRANSACTIONS/CAREER NOTES: Selected by New York Mets organization in 19th round of free-agent draft (June 3, 1993); did not sign. ... Selected by Kansas City Royals organization in 36th round of free-agent draft (June 4, 1996); did not sign. ... Selected by Tampa Bay Devil Rays organization in sixth round of free-agent draft (June 2, 1998). ... On Durham disabled list (May 9-June 16, 2000). ... On Tampa Bay disabled list (September 11, 2000-remainder of season). ... On disabled list (June 20-July 11 and July 16, 2002-remainder of season).
CAREER HITTING (MLB): 1-for-9 (.111), 1 R, 1 2B, 0 3B, 0 HR, 0 RBI.

Year	League	W	L	Pct.	ERA	G	GS	CG	ShO	Sv.-Opp.	IP	H	R	ER	HR	BB-IBB	SO
1998	Hudson Valley (NY-Penn)	1	0	1.000	0.68	3	3	0	0	0-...	13.1	8	1	1	0	2-0	18
	Charleston, S.C. (S.Atl.)	6	1	.857	2.40	10	10	0	0	0-...	56.1	33	18	15	3	9-0	62
1999	Orlando (Sou.)	2	2	.500	2.73	5	5	0	0	0-...	26.1	18	13	8	1	6-0	22
	Tampa Bay (A.L.)	8	9	.471	4.55	24	24	0	0	0-0	142.1	136	81	72	17	57-2	97
2000	Tampa Bay (A.L.)	5	6	.455	6.92	18	18	0	0	0-0	91.0	121	75	70	19	31-3	61
	Durham (I.L.)	0	1	.000	6.52	5	5	0	0	0-...	19.1	24	16	14	3	7-0	18
2001	Tampa Bay (A.L.)	5	12	.294	6.59	28	26	0	0	0-1	143.1	161	111	105	30	48-0	123
	Durham (I.L.)	0	1	.000	0.82	2	2	0	0	0-...	11.0	3	1	1	0	1-0	17
2002	Tampa Bay (A.L.)	5	10	.333	5.60	15	15	2	0	0-0	90.0	83	60	56	11	25-0	67
Major League totals (4 years)		23	37	.383	5.84	85	83	2	0	0-1	466.2	501	327	303	77	161-5	348

RUSCH, GLENDON — P — BREWERS

PERSONAL: Born November 7, 1974, in Seattle. ... 6-1/200. ... Throws left, bats left. ... Full name: Glendon James Rusch.
HIGH SCHOOL: Shorecrest (Seattle).
TRANSACTIONS/CAREER NOTES: Selected by Kansas City Royals organization in 17th round of free-agent draft (June 3, 1993). ... On Kansas City disabled list (June 16-July 1, 1997); included rehabilitation assignment to Omaha (June 26-July 1). ... On Kansas City disabled list (August 9-September 4, 1998); included rehabilitation assignment to Omaha (August 24-September 4). ... On Omaha disabled list (May 31-July 1, 1999). ... Traded by Royals to New York Mets for P Dan Murray (September 14, 1999). ... Traded by Mets to Milwaukee Brewers as part of three-way deal in which Brewers traded P Jeff D'Amico, OF Jeromy Burnitz, IF Lou Collier, OF/1B Mark Sweeney and cash to Mets, Colorado Rockies traded OF Alex Ochoa to Brewers, Mets traded 1B/3B Todd Zeile, OF Benny Agbayani, IF/OF Lenny Harris and cash to Rockies and Rockies traded 1B/OF Ross Gload and P Craig House to Mets (January 21, 2002).
STATISTICAL NOTES: Pitched 9-0 no-hit victory against Kane County (August 7, 1994).
CAREER HITTING (MLB): 25-for-176 (.142), 8 R, 0 2B, 0 3B, 1 HR, 14 RBI.

Year	League	W	L	Pct.	ERA	G	GS	CG	ShO	Sv.-Opp.	IP	H	R	ER	HR	BB-IBB	SO
1993	Gulf Coast Royals (GCL)	4	2	.667	1.60	11	10	0	0	0-...	62.0	43	14	11	0	11-0	48
	Rockford (Midw.)	0	1	.000	3.38	2	2	0	0	0-...	8.0	10	6	3	0	7-0	8
1994	Rockford (Midw.)	8	5	.615	4.66	28	17	1	1	1-...	114.0	111	61	59	5	34-2	122
1995	Wilmington (Caro.)	*14	6	.700	*1.74	26	26	1	1	0-...	165.2	110	41	32	5	34-3	147
1996	Omaha (A.A.)	11	9	.550	3.98	28	28	1	0	0-...	169.2	177	88	75	15	40-3	117
1997	Kansas City (A.L.)	6	9	.400	5.50	30	27	1	0	0-0	170.1	206	111	104	28	52-0	116
	Omaha (A.A.)	0	1	.000	4.50	1	1	0	0	0-...	6.0	7	3	3	3	1-0	2
1998	Kansas City (A.L.)	6	15	.286	5.88	29	24	1	1	1-1	154.2	191	104	101	22	50-0	94
	Omaha (PCL)	1	1	.500	7.98	3	3	0	0	0-...	14.2	20	18	13	4	6-0	14
1999	Omaha (PCL)	4	7	.364	4.42	20	20	1	0	0-...	114.0	143	68	56	10	33-0	102
	Gulf Coast Royals (GCL)	0	0	...	1.50	2	2	0	0	0-...	6.0	3	1	1	0	3-0	9
	Kansas City (A.L.)	0	1	.000	15.75	3	0	0	0	0-0	4.0	7	7	7	1	3-0	4
	New York (N.L.)■	0	0	...	0.00	1	0	0	0	0-0	1.0	1	0	0	0	0-0	0
2000	New York (N.L.)	11	11	.500	4.01	31	30	2	0	0-0	190.2	196	91	85	18	44-2	157
2001	New York (N.L.)	8	12	.400	4.63	33	33	1	0	0-0	179.0	216	101	92	23	43-2	156
2002	Milwaukee (N.L.)■	10	•16	.385	4.70	34	34	4	1	0-0	210.2	227	118	110	30	76-1	140
A.L. totals (3 years)		12	25	.324	5.80	62	51	2	1	1-1	329.0	404	222	212	51	105-0	214
N.L. totals (4 years)		29	39	.426	4.44	99	97	7	1	0-0	581.1	640	310	287	71	163-5	453
Major League totals (6 years)		41	64	.390	4.93	161	148	9	2	1-1	910.1	1044	532	499	122	268-5	667

DIVISION SERIES RECORD

Year	League	W	L	Pct.	ERA	G	GS	CG	ShO	Sv.-Opp.	IP	H	R	ER	HR	BB-IBB	SO
2000	New York (N.L.)	0	0	...	0.00	1	0	0	0	0-0	.2	0	0	0	0	0-0	2

CHAMPIONSHIP SERIES RECORD

Year	League	W	L	Pct.	ERA	G	GS	CG	ShO	Sv.-Opp.	IP	H	R	ER	HR	BB-IBB	SO
2000	New York (N.L.)	1	0	1.000	0.00	2	0	0	0	0-0	3.2	3	0	0	0	0-0	3

WORLD SERIES RECORD

Year	League	W	L	Pct.	ERA	G	GS	CG	ShO	Sv.-Opp.	IP	H	R	ER	HR	BB-IBB	SO
2000	New York (N.L.)	0	0	...	2.25	3	0	0	0	0-0	4.0	6	1	1	0	2-1	2

RUSHFORD, JIM — OF — BREWERS

PERSONAL: Born March 24, 1974, in Chicago. ... 6-1/190. ... Bats left, throws left. ... Full name: James Thomas Rushford.
COLLEGE: San Diego State.
TRANSACTIONS/CAREER NOTES: Signed by Dubois County of Heartland League (June 1996). ... Signed by Schaumburg of Northern League (May 1999). ... Signed by Duluth-Superior of Northern League (May 2000). ... Signed as non-drafted free agent by Milwaukee Brewers organization (November 22, 2000).
2002 GAMES PLAYED BY POSITION (MLB): OF—22.

Year Team (League)	Pos.	G	AB	R	H	2B	3B	HR	RBI	BB	SO	SB-CS	Avg.	OBP	SLG	E	Avg.
		BATTING														FIELDING	
1996— Dubois County (HBL)		40	44	9	15	2	0	2	6	6	10	6-0	.341	.444	.523	...	...
1997—								Did not play.									
1998—								Did not play.									
1999— Schaumburg (Nor.)■		47	166	26	48	12	2	2	28	23	27	7-...	.289	...	.422	...	...
2000— Dul./Superior (Nor.)■		75	289	53	95	16	3	12	53	25	32	13-...	.329	...	.529	...	...
2001— High Desert (Calif.)■	OF-1B	65	259	68	94	22	2	14	61	38	35	3-3	.363	.449	.625	6	.983
— Huntsville (Sou.)	OF	57	187	35	64	16	1	7	30	23	22	3-2	.342	.422	.551	1	.989
2002— Indianapolis (I.L.)	OF	117	405	54	128	33	3	7	68	45	41	0-2	.316	.391	.464	2	.988
— Milwaukee (N.L.)	OF	23	77	8	11	2	0	1	6	6	9	0-0	.143	.214	.208	2	.956
Major League totals (1 year)		23	77	8	11	2	0	1	6	6	9	0-0	.143	.214	.208	2	.956

RYAN, B.J. — P — ORIOLES

PERSONAL: Born December 28, 1975, in Bossier City, La. ... 6-6/230. ... Throws left, bats left. ... Full name: Robert Victor Ryan Jr.
HIGH SCHOOL: Airline (Bossier City, La.).
COLLEGE: Southwestern Louisiana.
TRANSACTIONS/CAREER NOTES: Selected by Cincinnati Reds organization in 17th round of free-agent draft (June 2, 1998). ... Traded by Reds with P Jacobo Sequea to Baltimore Orioles for P Juan Guzman (July 31, 1999).
CAREER HITTING (MLB): 0-for-2 (.000), 0 R, 0 2B, 0 3B, 0 HR, 0 RBI.

Year League	W	L	Pct.	ERA	G	GS	CG	ShO	Sv.-Opp.	IP	H	R	ER	HR	BB-IBB	SO
1998— Billings (Pio.)	2	1	.667	1.93	14	0	0	0	4-...	18.2	15	4	4	0	5-0	25
— Charleston, W.Va. (S.Atl.)	0	0	...	2.08	3	0	0	0	2-...	4.1	1	1	1	0	1-0	5
— Chattanooga (Sou.)	1	0	1.000	2.20	16	0	0	0	4-...	16.1	13	4	4	0	6-0	21
1999— Chattanooga (Sou.)	2	1	.667	2.59	35	0	0	0	6-...	41.2	33	13	12	1	17-0	46
— Indianapolis (I.L.)	1	0	1.000	4.00	11	0	0	0	0-...	9.0	9	4	4	0	3-1	12
— Cincinnati (N.L.)	0	0	...	4.50	1	0	0	0	0-0	2.0	4	1	1	0	1-0	1
— Rochester (I.L.)■	0	0	...	2.51	11	0	0	0	1-...	14.1	8	4	4	2	4-1	20
— Baltimore (A.L.)	1	0	1.000	2.95	13	0	0	0	0-0	18.1	9	6	6	0	12-1	28
2000— Baltimore (A.L.)	2	3	.400	5.91	42	0	0	0	0-3	42.2	36	29	28	7	31-1	41
— Rochester (I.L.)	0	1	.000	4.74	14	4	0	0	0-...	24.2	23	13	13	4	9-0	28
2001— Baltimore (A.L.)	2	4	.333	4.25	61	0	0	0	2-4	53.0	47	31	25	6	30-4	54
2002— Baltimore (A.L.)	2	1	.667	4.68	67	0	0	0	1-2	57.2	51	31	30	7	33-4	56
A.L. totals (4 years)	7	8	.467	4.67	183	0	0	0	3-9	171.2	143	97	89	20	106-10	179
N.L. totals (1 year)	0	0	...	4.50	1	0	0	0	0-0	2.0	4	1	1	0	1-0	1
Major League totals (4 years)	7	8	.467	4.66	184	0	0	0	3-9	173.2	147	98	90	20	107-10	180

RYAN, MICHAEL — OF — TWINS

PERSONAL: Born July 6, 1977, in Indiana, Pa. ... 6-0/185. ... Bats left, throws right. ... Full name: Michael Sean Ryan.
HIGH SCHOOL: Indiana (Pa.).
TRANSACTIONS/CAREER NOTES: Selected by Minnesota Twins organization in fifth round of free-agent draft (June 4, 1996).
2002 GAMES PLAYED BY POSITION (MLB): OF—5; DH—1.

Year Team (League)	Pos.	G	AB	R	H	2B	3B	HR	RBI	BB	SO	SB-CS	Avg.	OBP	SLG	E	Avg.
		BATTING														FIELDING	
1996— GC Twins (GCL)	3B	43	157	12	31	8	2	0	13	13	20	3-0	.197	.260	.274	10	.910
1997— Elizabethton (Appl.)	3B	62	220	44	66	10	0	3	29	38	39	2-2	.300	.404	.386	28	.825
1998— Fort Wayne (Midw.)	3B-1B	113	412	68	131	24	6	9	72	44	92	7-3	.318	.382	.471	33	.906
1999— Fort Myers (FSL)	2B	131	507	85	139	26	5	8	71	63	60	3-4	.274	.356	.393	35	.949
2000— New Britain (East.)	OF-2B	122	481	64	133	23	8	11	69	34	79	4-3	.277	.323	.426	9	.965
— Salt Lake (PCL)	OF	3	9	1	2	0	0	0	2	3	2	0-0	.222	.417	.222	0	1.000
2001— Edmonton (PCL)	OF-2B	135	527	89	152	36	7	18	73	52	121	1-6	.288	.353	.486	11	.966
2002— Edmonton (PCL)	OF	131	540	92	141	36	6	31	101	55	124	4-5	.261	.330	.522	3	.987
— Minnesota (A.L.)	OF-DH	7	11	3	1	0	0	0	0	0	2	0-0	.091	.091	.091	0	1.000
Major League totals (1 year)		7	11	3	1	0	0	0	0	0	2	0-0	.091	.091	.091	0	1.000

SAARLOOS, KIRK — P — ASTROS

PERSONAL: Born May 23, 1979, in Long Beach, Calif. ... 6-0/185. ... Throws right, bats right. ... Full name: Kirk Craig Saarloos.
COLLEGE: Cal State Fullerton.
TRANSACTIONS/CAREER NOTES: Selected by Houston Astros organization in third round of free-agent draft (June 1, 2001).
HONORS: Named Texas League Pitcher of the Year (2002).
CAREER HITTING (MLB): 2-for-30 (.067), 0 R, 1 2B, 0 3B, 0 HR, 2 RBI.

Year League	W	L	Pct.	ERA	G	GS	CG	ShO	Sv.-Opp.	IP	H	R	ER	HR	BB-IBB	SO
2001— Lexington (S.Atl.)	1	1	.500	1.17	22	0	0	0	11-...	30.2	18	5	4	1	7-0	40
2002— Round Rock (Texas)	10	1	*.909	1.40	13	13	1	1	0-...	83.1	48	17	13	1	21-0	82
— New Orleans (PCL)	2	0	1.000	2.25	4	2	0	0	0-...	16.0	12	4	4	1	2-0	19
— Houston (N.L.)	6	7	.462	6.01	17	17	1	1	0-0	85.1	100	59	57	12	27-5	54
Major League totals (1 year)	6	7	.462	6.01	17	17	1	1	0-0	85.1	100	59	57	12	27-5	54

SABATHIA, C.C. — P — INDIANS

PERSONAL: Born July 21, 1980, in Vallejo, Calif. ... 6-7/270. ... Throws left, bats left. ... Full name: Carsten Charles Sabathia.
HIGH SCHOOL: Vallejo (Calif.).
TRANSACTIONS/CAREER NOTES: Selected by Cleveland Indians organization in first round (20th pick overall) of free-agent draft (June 2, 1998).
HONORS: Named A.L. Rookie Pitcher of the Year by The Sporting News (2001).
STATISTICAL NOTES: Tied for A.L. lead with three balks in 2002.
CAREER HITTING (MLB): 1-for-9 (.111), 0 R, 0 2B, 0 3B, 0 HR, 0 RBI.

Year	League	W	L	Pct.	ERA	G	GS	CG	ShO	Sv.-Opp.	IP	H	R	ER	HR	BB-IBB	SO
1998—	Burlington (Appl.)	1	0	1.000	4.50	5	5	0	0	0-...	18.0	20	14	9	1	8-0	35
1999—	Mahoning Valley (NY-P)	0	0	...	1.83	6	6	0	0	0-...	19.2	9	5	4	0	12-0	57
	—Columbus (S.Atl.)	2	0	1.000	1.08	3	3	0	0	0-...	16.2	8	2	2	1	5-0	20
	—Kinston (Caro.)	3	3	.500	5.34	7	7	0	0	0-...	32.0	30	22	19	3	19-0	29
2000—	Kinston (Caro.)	3	2	.600	3.54	10	10	2	2	0-...	56.0	48	23	22	4	24-0	69
	—Akron (East.)	3	7	.300	3.59	17	17	0	0	0-...	90.1	75	41	36	6	48-0	90
2001—	Cleveland (A.L.)	17	5	.773	4.39	33	33	0	0	0-0	180.1	149	93	88	19	95-1	171
2002—	Cleveland (A.L.)	13	11	.542	4.37	33	33	2	0	0-0	210.0	198	109	102	17	88-2	149
Major League totals (2 years)		30	16	.652	4.38	66	66	2	0	0-0	390.1	347	202	190	36	183-3	320

DIVISION SERIES RECORD

Year	League	W	L	Pct.	ERA	G	GS	CG	ShO	Sv.-Opp.	IP	H	R	ER	HR	BB-IBB	SO
2001—	Cleveland (A.L.)	1	0	1.000	3.00	1	1	0	0	0-0	6.0	6	2	2	0	5-1	5

SABEL, ERIK — P

PERSONAL: Born October 14, 1974, in West Lafayette, Ind. ... 6-3/195. ... Throws right, bats right. ... Full name: Erik Douglas Sabel.
HIGH SCHOOL: Harrison (West Lafayette, Ind.).
COLLEGE: Tennessee Tech.
TRANSACTIONS/CAREER NOTES: Selected by Arizona Diamondbacks organization in 42nd round of free-agent draft (June 4, 1996). ... Loaned by Diamondbacks to Tulsa, Texas Rangers organization (June 3-September 14, 1998). ... On Tucson disabled list (May 26-June 15, 1999; and August 7-September 8, 2000). ... Claimed on waivers by Detroit Tigers (July 24, 2002). ... Released by Tigers (October 14, 2002).
CAREER HITTING (MLB): 0-for-2 (.000), 0 R, 0 2B, 0 3B, 0 HR, 0 RBI.

Year	League	W	L	Pct.	ERA	G	GS	CG	ShO	Sv.-Opp.	IP	H	R	ER	HR	BB-IBB	SO
1996—	Lethbridge (Pio.)	1	4	.200	2.79	20	3	0	0	1-...	42.0	43	23	13	3	7-0	41
1997—	High Desert (Calif.)	11	11	.500	5.32	31	22	0	0	1-...	143.2	174	101	85	21	40-0	86
1998—	High Desert (Calif.)	0	1	.000	3.18	14	0	0	0	4-...	22.2	25	8	8	2	4-3	18
	—Tucson (PCL)	1	0	1.000	8.71	7	0	0	0	0-...	10.1	17	10	10	0	5-1	7
	—Tulsa (Texas)■	7	0	1.000	3.20	24	2	0	0	2-...	56.1	46	24	20	6	13-1	33
1999—	El Paso (Texas)■	0	1	.000	6.30	8	1	0	0	1-...	10.0	16	9	7	1	4-0	7
	—Tucson (PCL)	5	2	.714	3.34	22	9	0	0	2-...	72.2	79	36	27	4	24-4	38
	—Arizona (N.L.)	0	0	...	6.52	7	0	0	0	0-0	9.2	12	7	7	1	6-2	6
2000—	Tucson (PCL)	4	11	.267	7.23	29	15	0	0	1-...	98.1	149	90	79	16	31-4	61
2001—	Tucson (PCL)	2	2	.500	2.95	18	2	0	0	2-...	39.2	35	14	13	3	7-1	32
	—Arizona (N.L.)	3	2	.600	4.38	42	0	0	0	0-0	51.1	57	26	25	8	12-3	25
2002—	Tucson (PCL)	4	5	.444	4.32	25	7	0	0	1-...	66.2	67	37	32	7	19-1	46
	—Detroit (A.L.)■	0	0	...	...	1	0	0	0	0-0	.0	2	2	2	1	0-0	0
	—Toledo (I.L.)	1	0	1.000	6.55	14	0	0	0	0-...	11.0	15	8	8	0	4-0	7
A.L. totals (1 year)		0	0	...	...	1	0	0	0	0-0	.0	2	2	2	1	0-0	0
N.L. totals (2 years)		3	2	.600	4.72	49	0	0	0	0-0	61.0	69	33	32	9	18-5	31
Major League totals (3 years)		3	2	.600	5.02	50	0	0	0	0-0	61.0	71	35	34	10	18-5	31

SADLER, CARL — P — INDIANS

PERSONAL: Born October 11, 1976, in Gainesville, Fla. ... 6-2/180. ... Throws left, bats left. ... Full name: William Carl Sadler.
HIGH SCHOOL: Taylor County (Perry, Fla.).
TRANSACTIONS/CAREER NOTES: Selected by Montreal Expos organization in 34th round of free-agent draft (June 4, 1996). ... Released by Expos (April 1, 1998). ... Signed by Cleveland Indians organization (April 3, 1998). ... On disabled list (June 16, 1998-entire season).
CAREER HITTING (MLB): 0-for-0 (.000), 0 R, 0 2B, 0 3B, 0 HR, 0 RBI.

Year	League	W	L	Pct.	ERA	G	GS	CG	ShO	Sv.-Opp.	IP	H	R	ER	HR	BB-IBB	SO
1996—	Gulf Coast Expos (GCL)	2	2	.500	3.89	17	3	0	0	1-...	37.0	41	24	16	2	12-0	24
1997—	Gulf Coast Expos (GCL)	0	2	.000	4.35	9	3	0	0	0-...	20.2	26	11	10	0	5-0	14
	—Vermont (NY-Penn)	2	2	.500	4.21	7	6	0	0	0-...	36.1	33	20	17	2	23-0	27
1998—										Did not play.							
1999—	Burlington (Appl.)■	1	0	1.000	3.13	5	5	0	0	0-...	23.0	18	10	8	0	10-0	22
	—Mahoning Valley (NY-P)	0	1	.000	31.50	1	1	0	0	0-...	2.0	8	7	7	0	3-0	3
2000—	Mahoning Valley (NY-P)	0	0	...	3.00	5	0	0	0	0-...	6.0	5	2	2	0	3-0	3
	—Columbus (S.Atl.)	1	3	.250	6.61	10	0	0	0	0-...	16.1	20	13	12	0	7-0	21
2001—	Kinston (Caro.)	6	0	1.000	1.88	27	2	0	0	2-...	62.1	51	19	13	2	18-1	78
	—Akron (East.)	2	3	.400	6.50	11	0	0	0	0-...	18.0	23	16	13	1	9-0	14
2002—	Akron (East.)	4	1	.800	2.33	21	0	0	0	2-...	46.1	39	12	12	0	12-1	37
	—Buffalo (I.L.)	1	1	.500	1.93	12	0	0	0	1-...	18.2	19	7	4	1	8-1	13
	—Cleveland (A.L.)	1	2	.333	4.43	24	0	0	0	0-1	20.1	15	10	10	2	11-0	23
Major League totals (1 year)		1	2	.333	4.43	24	0	0	0	0-1	20.1	15	10	10	2	11-0	23

SADLER, DONNIE — IF — RANGERS

PERSONAL: Born June 17, 1975, in Gohlson, Texas. ... 5-6/175. ... Bats right, throws right. ... Full name: Donnie Lamont Sadler.
HIGH SCHOOL: Valley Mills (Texas).
TRANSACTIONS/CAREER NOTES: Selected by Boston Red Sox organization in 11th round of free-agent draft (June 2, 1994). ... On Pawtucket disabled list (May 4-June 4 and June 23-30, 1998; and June 25-July 18, 1999). ... Traded by Red Sox with OF Michael Coleman to Cincinnati Reds for IF Chris Stynes (November 16, 2000). ... Traded by Reds to Kansas City Royals for P Cary Ammons (June 20, 2001). ... Granted free agency (December 21, 2001). ... Re-signed by Royals (January 7, 2002). ... On Kansas City disabled list (June 14-July 8, 2002); included rehabilitation assignment to Omaha (July 3-8). ... Claimed on waivers by Texas Rangers (July 8, 2002). ... Released by Rangers (September 30, 2002). ... Re-signed by Rangers organization (November 13, 2002).
STATISTICAL NOTES: Tied for International League lead in errors by second baseman with 12 in 1997. ... Tied for International League lead in caught stealing with 14 in 1997.
2002 GAMES PLAYED BY POSITION (MLB): OF—33; SS—16; 3B—15; 2B—6; DH—4.

Year	Team (League)	Pos.	G	AB	R	H	2B	3B	HR	RBI	BB	SO	SB-CS	Avg.	OBP	SLG	E	Avg.
			BATTING														FIELDING	
1994—	GC Red Sox (GCL)	SS-3B-2B	53	206	52	56	8	6	1	16	23	27	32-8	.272	.349	.383	18	.928
1995—	Michigan (Midw.)	SS	118	438	*103	124	25	8	9	55	79	85	41-13	.283	.397	.438	28	.944
1996—	Trenton (East.)	SS-OF	115	454	68	121	20	8	6	46	38	75	34-8	.267	.329	.385	27	.940
1997—	Pawtucket (I.L.)	2B-SS-OF	125	481	74	102	18	2	11	36	57	121	20-14	.212	.295	.326	‡15	.976
1998—	Boston (A.L.)	2B-DH-SS	58	124	21	28	4	4	3	15	6	28	4-0	.226	.276	.395	5	.973
—	Pawtucket (I.L.)	2B-SS	36	131	25	29	5	1	2	10	26	23	11-1	.221	.348	.321	4	.978
1999—	Boston (A.L.)	S-2-3-O-DH	49	107	18	30	5	1	0	4	5	20	2-1	.280	.313	.346	9	.916
—	Pawtucket (I.L.)	SS-DH	43	172	23	50	12	4	1	17	16	36	4-2	.291	.361	.424	10	.944
—	GC Red Sox (GCL)	SS	4	13	2	5	2	0	0	1	2	1	0-0	.385	.467	.538	1	.950
2000—	Pawtucket (I.L.)	OF-SS-2B	91	313	45	63	6	5	5	23	45	60	10-1	.201	.306	.300	7	.979
—	Boston (A.L.)	S-O-2-3-DH	49	99	14	22	5	0	1	10	5	18	3-1	.222	.262	.303	3	.976
2001—	Cincinnati (N.L.)■	2B-SS-OF-DH	39	84	9	17	3	0	1	3	9	20	3-3	.202	.280	.274	3	.965
—	Kansas City (A.L.)■	O-3-2-S-DH	54	101	19	13	3	0	0	2	9	17	4-1	.129	.212	.158	2	.987
2002—	Kansas City (A.L.)	O-3-S-2-D	35	68	10	13	1	1	0	5	4	12	3-1	.191	.233	.235	3	.943
—	Omaha (PCL)	3B-SS-2B	5	21	6	7	0	0	0	0	2	3	0-2	.333	.417	.333	0	1.000
—	Texas (A.L.)■	O-S-3-2-D	38	30	6	3	1	0	0	2	3	7	2-2	.100	.229	.133	0	1.000
—	Oklahoma (PCL)	OF-2B	12	43	7	10	3	1	0	4	6	7	2-1	.233	.340	.349	1	.978
American League totals (5 years)			283	529	88	109	19	6	4	38	32	102	18-6	.206	.260	.287	22	.967
National League totals (1 year)			39	84	9	17	3	0	1	3	9	20	3-3	.202	.280	.274	3	.965
Major League totals (5 years)			322	613	97	126	22	6	5	41	41	122	21-9	.206	.262	.285	25	.967

DIVISION SERIES RECORD

Year	Team (League)	Pos.	G	AB	R	H	2B	3B	HR	RBI	BB	SO	SB-CS	Avg.	OBP	SLG	E	Avg.
			BATTING														FIELDING	
1998—	Boston (A.L.)	2B-PR	3	0	0	0	0	0	0	0	0	0	0-0	...	...	...	0	1.000
1999—	Boston (A.L.)	PH-3B-PR-DH	2	2	1	1	1	0	0	0	0	1	0-0	.500	.500	1.000	0	1.000
Division series totals (2 years)			5	2	1	1	1	0	0	0	0	1	0-0	.500	.500	1.000	0	1.000

CHAMPIONSHIP SERIES RECORD

Year	Team (League)	Pos.	G	AB	R	H	2B	3B	HR	RBI	BB	SO	SB-CS	Avg.	OBP	SLG	E	Avg.
			BATTING														FIELDING	
1999—	Boston (A.L.)	PR-OF-DH	2	0	0	0	0	0	0	0	0	0	0-0	...	...	...	0	...

SAENZ, OLMEDO 3B/1B

PERSONAL: Born October 8, 1970, in Chitre Herrera, Panama. ... 5-11/221. ... Bats right, throws right. ... Full name: Olmedo Sanchez Saenz. ... Name pronounced SIGNS.

TRANSACTIONS/CAREER NOTES: Signed as non-drafted free agent by Chicago White Sox organization (May 11, 1990). ... Granted free agency (October 15, 1997). ... Re-signed by White Sox organization (January 25, 1998). ... Granted free agency (October 15, 1998). ... Signed by Oakland Athletics (November 13, 1998). ... On Oakland disabled list (July 26-August 16, 1999); included rehabilitation assignment to Vancouver (August 13-16). ... On Oakland disabled list (August 1-September 19, 2000); included rehabilitation assignment to Sacramento (August 29-30). ... Granted free agency (November 1, 2002).

STATISTICAL NOTES: Led American Association third basemen with 82 putouts, 289 assists and 395 total chances in 1995. ... Tied for American Association lead in being hit by pitch with 13 in 1996. ... Led American Association third basemen with 97 putouts, 363 total chances and 24 double plays in 1996. ... Led Pacific Coast League in being hit by pitch with 22 in 1998.

2002 GAMES PLAYED BY POSITION (MLB): 1B—34; 3B—15; DH—7.

Year	Team (League)	Pos.	G	AB	R	H	2B	3B	HR	RBI	BB	SO	SB-CS	Avg.	OBP	SLG	E	Avg.
			BATTING														FIELDING	
1991—	South Bend (Midw.)	3B	56	192	23	47	10	1	2	22	21	48	5-3	.245	.332	.339	12	.890
—	Sarasota (FSL)	3B	5	19	1	2	0	1	0	2	2	0	0-1	.105	.190	.211	3	.842
1992—	South Bend (Midw.)	3B-1B	132	493	66	121	26	4	7	59	36	52	16-13	.245	.309	.357	48	.895
1993—	Sarasota (FSL)	3B	33	121	13	31	9	4	0	27	9	18	3-1	.256	.316	.397	5	.933
—	South Bend (Midw.)	3B	13	50	3	18	4	1	0	7	7	7	1-1	.360	.439	.480	4	.913
—	Birmingham (Sou.)	3B	49	173	30	60	17	2	6	29	20	21	2-1	.347	.427	.572	14	.899
1994—	Nashville (A.A.)	3B-DH	107	383	48	100	27	2	12	59	30	57	3-2	.261	.326	.436	22	.917
—	Chicago (A.L.)	3B	5	14	2	2	0	1	0	0	0	5	0-0	.143	.143	.286	0	1.000
1995—	Nashville (A.A.)	3B	111	415	60	126	26	1	13	74	45	60	0-2	.304	.385	.465	*24	*.939
1996—	Nashville (A.A.)	3B-DH	134	476	86	124	29	1	18	63	53	80	4-2	.261	.350	.439	22	.939
1997—	GC White Sox (GCL)	DH	2	1	0	1	1	0	0	0	0	0	0-0	1.000	1.000	2.000	...	...
1998—	Calgary (PCL)	3B-DH	124	466	89	146	29	0	29	102	45	49	3-3	.313	.394	.562	21	.937
1999—	Oakland (A.L.)■	3B-1B-DH	97	255	41	70	18	0	11	41	22	47	1-1	.275	.363	.475	8	.971
—	Vancouver (PCL)	3B	2	5	1	3	1	0	0	2	0	0	0-0	.600	.571	.800	0	1.000
2000—	Oakland (A.L.)	DH-3B-1B	76	214	40	67	12	2	9	33	25	40	1-0	.313	.401	.514	4	.977
—	Sacramento (PCL)	DH	1	4	1	2	0	0	0	1	0	0	0-0	.500	.500	.500	...	...
2001—	Oakland (A.L.)	DH-1B-3B	106	305	33	67	21	1	9	32	19	64	0-1	.220	.291	.384	5	.979
2002—	Oakland (A.L.)	1B-3B-DH	68	156	15	43	10	1	6	18	13	31	1-1	.276	.354	.468	5	.980
Major League totals (5 years)			352	944	131	249	61	5	35	124	79	187	3-3	.264	.345	.450	22	.977

DIVISION SERIES RECORD

RECORDS: Holds A.L. career record for most games by pinch-hitter—4.

Year	Team (League)	Pos.	G	AB	R	H	2B	3B	HR	RBI	BB	SO	SB-CS	Avg.	OBP	SLG	E	Avg.
			BATTING														FIELDING	
2000—	Oakland (A.L.)	PH-DH	4	13	1	3	0	0	1	4	0	2	0-0	.231	.267	.462	...	...
2001—	Oakland (A.L.)	PH-DH	3	4	0	0	0	0	0	0	0	1	0-0	.000	.000	.000	...	...
2002—	Oakland (A.L.)	1B	1	0	0	0	0	0	0	0	1	0	0-0	...	1.000	...	0	1.000
Division series totals (3 years)			8	17	1	3	0	0	1	4	1	3	0-0	.176	.250	.353	0	1.000

SALAZAR, OSCAR — IF

PERSONAL: Born June 27, 1978, in Maracay, Venezuela. ... 5-11/178. ... Bats right, throws right. ... Full name: Oscar Enrique Salazar.
TRANSACTIONS/CAREER NOTES: Signed as non-drafted free agent by Oakland Athletics organization (July 2, 1994). ... Claimed on waivers by Detroit Tigers (January 24, 2002). ... Claimed on waivers by New York Mets (July 31, 2002). ... Granted free agency (October 15, 2002).
2002 GAMES PLAYED BY POSITION (MLB): 2B—6; 3B—1; SS—1.

			BATTING														FIELDING	
Year	**Team (League)**	**Pos.**	**G**	**AB**	**R**	**H**	**2B**	**3B**	**HR**	**RBI**	**BB**	**SO**	**SB-CS**	**Avg.**	**OBP**	**SLG**	**E**	**Avg.**
1995—	Dom. Athletics (DSL)	SS	53	166	29	45	10	1	0	23	22	23	5-...	.271	...	.343	32	.888
1996—	Dom. Athletics (DSL)	2B	69	219	49	56	9	4	3	29	47	37	9-138	.256	...	.374	11	.966
1997—	Dom. Athletics (DSL)		66	268	65	80	20	4	12	48	34	39	3-...	.299	...	.537	...	...
1998—	Ariz. Athletics (Ariz.)	3B-SS-2B	26	102	29	33	7	5	2	18	12	15	4-1	.324	.400	.549	9	.908
—	S. Oregon (N'West)	3B-2B-SS	28	101	19	32	4	1	5	28	16	22	5-2	.317	.400	.525	13	.883
1999—	Modesto (Calif.)	2B-3B-SS-1B	130	525	100	155	26	18	18	105	39	106	14-6	.295	.340	.516	22	.928
2000—	Midland (Texas)	SS-OF-3B	111	427	70	128	27	1	13	57	39	71	4-4	.300	.359	.459	34	.933
—	Sacramento (PCL)	SS	4	13	0	2	1	0	0	1	1	1	1-0	.154	.214	.231	0	1.000
2001—	Midland (Texas)	SS-3B-2B-OF	130	521	75	139	31	4	18	95	49	100	10-3	.267	.329	.445	37	.937
—	Sacramento (PCL)	2B-3B	5	16	0	1	0	0	0	1	1	5	0-0	.063	.118	.063	0	1.000
2002—	Toledo (I.L.)■	SS-2B	8	19	0	6	0	0	0	1	3	1	0-1	.316	.409	.316	1	.964
—	Erie (East.)	2B-SS-OF-1B	53	191	16	41	18	1	6	26	14	36	2-1	.215	.279	.414	3	.983
—	Detroit (A.L.)	2B-3B-SS	8	21	2	4	1	0	1	3	1	2	0-0	.190	.227	.381	1	.952
—	Binghamton (East.)■	2B-3B	28	75	6	13	2	0	1	5	5	19	0-1	.173	.232	.240	3	.961
Major League totals (1 year)			8	21	2	4	1	0	1	3	1	2	0-0	.190	.227	.381	1	.952

SALMON, TIM — OF — ANGELS

PERSONAL: Born August 24, 1968, in Long Beach, Calif. ... 6-3/225. ... Bats right, throws right. ... Full name: Timothy James Salmon. ... Brother of Mike Salmon, safety with San Francisco 49ers (1997). ... Name pronounced SA-mon.
HIGH SCHOOL: Greenway (Phoenix).
COLLEGE: Grand Canyon (Ariz.).
TRANSACTIONS/CAREER NOTES: Selected by Atlanta Braves organization in 18th round of free-agent draft (June 2, 1986); did not sign. ... Selected by California Angels organization in third round of free-agent draft (June 5, 1989). ... On disabled list (May 12-23 and May 27-August 7, 1990; and July 18-August 3, 1994). ... Angels franchise renamed Anaheim Angels for 1997 season. ... On disabled list (April 23-May 9, 1998). ... On Anaheim disabled list (May 4-July 17, 1999); included rehabilitation assignment to Lake Elsinore (July 16-17). ... On Anaheim disabled list (July 1-19, 2001); included rehabilitation assignment to Rancho Cucamonga (July 17-19). ... On disabled list (August 14-September 1, 2002).
RECORDS: Shares major league record for fewest double plays by outfielder (150 or more games)—0 (1996). ... Shares major league single-inning record for most doubles—2 (September 23, 2000, second inning). ... Shares A.L. record for most hits in three consecutive games—13 (May 10 [4], 11 [4] and 13 [5], 1994).
HONORS: Named Minor League Player of the Year by The Sporting News (1992). ... Named Pacific Coast League Most Valuable Player (1992). ... Named A.L. Rookie Player of the Year by The Sporting News (1993). ... Named A.L. Rookie of the Year by Baseball Writers' Association of America (1993). ... Named outfielder on The Sporting News A.L. All-Star team (1995 and 1997). ... Named outfielder on The Sporting News Silver Slugger team (1995). ... Named A.L. Comeback Player of the Year by The Sporting News (2002).
STATISTICAL NOTES: Led Pacific Coast League with 275 total bases, .672 slugging percentage and .469 on-base percentage in 1992. ... Led A.L. outfielders with four double plays in 1994. ... Tied for A.L. lead in double plays by outfielder with five in 1997. ... Had 17-game hitting streak (July 23-August 9, 2000). ... Career major league grand slams: 6.
MISCELLANEOUS: Holds Anaheim Angels franchise all-time records for home runs (269) and most runs batted in (894).
2002 GAMES PLAYED BY POSITION (MLB): OF—111; DH—25.

			BATTING														FIELDING	
Year	**Team (League)**	**Pos.**	**G**	**AB**	**R**	**H**	**2B**	**3B**	**HR**	**RBI**	**BB**	**SO**	**SB-CS**	**Avg.**	**OBP**	**SLG**	**E**	**Avg.**
1989—	Bend (N'West)	OF	55	196	37	48	6	5	6	31	33	60	2-4	.245	.367	.418	4	.958
1990—	Palm Springs (Calif.)	OF	36	118	19	34	6	0	2	21	21	44	11-1	.288	.413	.390	1	.985
—	Midland (Texas)	OF	27	97	17	26	3	1	3	16	18	38	1-0	.268	.385	.412	3	.950
1991—	Midland (Texas)	OF	131	465	100	114	26	4	23	94	*89	*166	12-6	.245	.372	.467	10	.966
1992—	Edmonton (PCL)	OF	118	409	•101	142	38	4	*29	*105	91	103	9-7	.347	*.469	.672	3	.988
—	California (A.L.)	OF	23	79	8	14	1	0	2	6	11	23	1-1	.177	.283	.266	2	.953
1993—	California (A.L.)	OF-DH	142	515	93	146	35	1	31	95	82	135	5-6	.283	.382	.536	7	.980
1994—	California (A.L.)	OF	100	373	67	107	18	2	23	70	54	102	1-3	.287	.382	.531	8	.966
1995—	California (A.L.)	OF-DH	143	537	111	177	34	3	34	105	91	111	5-5	.330	.429	.594	4	.988
1996—	California (A.L.)	OF-DH	156	581	90	166	27	4	30	98	93	125	4-2	.286	.386	.501	8	.975
1997—	Anaheim (A.L.)	OF-DH	157	582	95	172	28	1	33	129	95	142	9-12	.296	.394	.517	11	.971
1998—	Anaheim (A.L.)	DH-OF	136	463	84	139	28	1	26	88	90	100	0-1	.300	.410	.533	2	.959
1999—	Anaheim (A.L.)	OF-DH	98	353	60	94	24	2	17	69	63	82	4-1	.266	.372	.490	4	.981
—	Lake Elsinore (Calif.)	DH	1	5	0	3	2	0	0	2	0	1	0-0	.600	.600	1.000	...	...
2000—	Anaheim (A.L.)	OF-DH	158	568	108	165	36	2	34	97	104	139	0-2	.290	.404	.540	6	.979
2001—	Anaheim (A.L.)	OF-DH	137	475	63	108	21	1	17	49	96	121	9-3	.227	.365	.383	3	.989
—	Rancho Cuca. (Calif.)	OF	2	7	1	1	1	0	0	0	1	4	0-0	.143	.250	.286	1	.667
2002—	Anaheim (A.L.)	OF-DH	138	483	84	138	37	1	22	88	71	102	6-3	.286	.380	.503	3	.986
Major League totals (11 years)			1388	5009	863	1426	289	18	269	894	850	1182	44-39	.285	.390	.511	58	.978

DIVISION SERIES RECORD

			BATTING														FIELDING	
Year	**Team (League)**	**Pos.**	**G**	**AB**	**R**	**H**	**2B**	**3B**	**HR**	**RBI**	**BB**	**SO**	**SB-CS**	**Avg.**	**OBP**	**SLG**	**E**	**Avg.**
2002—	Anaheim (A.L.)	OF	4	19	3	5	1	0	2	7	1	5	0-0	.263	.300	.632	0	1.000

CHAMPIONSHIP SERIES RECORD

			BATTING														FIELDING	
Year	**Team (League)**	**Pos.**	**G**	**AB**	**R**	**H**	**2B**	**3B**	**HR**	**RBI**	**BB**	**SO**	**SB-CS**	**Avg.**	**OBP**	**SLG**	**E**	**Avg.**
2002—	Anaheim (A.L.)	OF	5	14	0	3	0	0	0	0	3	1	0-0	.214	.353	.214	0	1.000

WORLD SERIES RECORD

NOTES: Member of World Series championship team (2002).

			BATTING														FIELDING	
Year	**Team (League)**	**Pos.**	**G**	**AB**	**R**	**H**	**2B**	**3B**	**HR**	**RBI**	**BB**	**SO**	**SB-CS**	**Avg.**	**OBP**	**SLG**	**E**	**Avg.**
2002—	Anaheim (A.L.)	OF	7	26	7	9	1	0	2	5	4	7	1-0	.346	.452	.615	1	.917

SANCHEZ, ALEX — OF — BREWERS

PERSONAL: Born August 26, 1976, in Havana, Cuba. ... 5-10/159. ... Bats left, throws left. ... Full name: Alexis Sanchez.
JUNIOR COLLEGE: Miami-Dade (Wolfson) Community College.
TRANSACTIONS/CAREER NOTES: Selected by Tampa Bay Devil Rays organization in fifth round of free-agent draft (June 4, 1996). ... Claimed on waivers by Milwaukee Brewers (April 6, 2001). ... On Milwaukee disabled list (July 16-31, 2001). ... On disabled list (September 2, 2002-remainder of season).
STATISTICAL NOTES: Led Gulf Coast League with 12 caught stealing in 1996. ... Led South Atlantic League outfielders with 296 total chances in 1997. ... Led South Atlantic League in caught stealing with 40 in 1997. ... Led Florida State League in caught stealing with 33 and sacrifice flies with 12 in 1998. ... Led Southern League in caught stealing with 27 and sacrifice hits with 10 in 1999. ... Led International League in caught stealing with 20 in 2000.
2002 GAMES PLAYED BY POSITION (MLB): OF—100.

		BATTING														FIELDING	
Year Team (League)	Pos.	G	AB	R	H	2B	3B	HR	RBI	BB	SO	SB-CS	Avg.	OBP	SLG	E	Avg.
1996—GC Devil Rays (GCL)	OF	56	227	36	64	7	6	1	22	10	35	20-12	.282	.328	.379	3	.968
1997—Charl., S.C. (S.Atl.)	OF	131	537	73	155	15	6	0	34	37	72	92-40	.289	.336	.339	11	.963
1998—St. Petersburg (FSL)	OF	128	545	77	*180	17	9	1	50	31	70	66-33	.330	.360	.400	•12	.965
1999—Orlando (Sou.)	OF	121	500	68	127	12	4	2	29	26	88	48-26	.254	.290	.306	*14	.958
—Durham (I.L.)	OF	3	10	2	2	1	0	0	0	1	0	0-0	.200	.273	.300	0	1.000
2000—Durham (I.L.)	OF	107	446	76	130	18	3	2	33	30	66	*52-20	.291	.342	.359	6	.977
—Orlando (Sou.)	OF	20	86	12	25	2	1	0	4	1	13	2-6	.291	.307	.337	1	.972
2001—Indianapolis (I.L.)■	OF	83	335	52	105	14	5	1	26	22	44	27-8	.313	.359	.394	6	.968
—Milwaukee (N.L.)	OF	30	68	7	14	3	2	0	4	5	13	6-2	.206	.260	.309	1	.963
2002—Milwaukee (N.L.)	OF	112	394	55	114	10	7	1	33	31	62	37-14	.289	.343	.358	5	.982
Major League totals (2 years)		142	462	62	128	13	9	1	37	36	75	43-16	.277	.331	.351	6	.980

SANCHEZ, DUANER — P — PIRATES

PERSONAL: Born October 14, 1979, in Cotui, Dominican Republic. ... 6-0/190. ... Throws right, bats right.
HIGH SCHOOL: Francisco H. Carvajal (Cotui, Dominican Repblic).
TRANSACTIONS/CAREER NOTES: Signed as non-drafted free agent by Arizona Diamondbacks organization (October 16, 1996). ... On El Paso disabled list (June 12-July 16, 2001). ... Traded by Diamondbacks to Pittsbugh Pirates for P Mike Fetters (July 6, 2002).
CAREER HITTING (MLB): 0-for-0 (.000), 0 R, 0 2B, 0 3B, 0 HR, 0 RBI.

Year League	W	L	Pct.	ERA	G	GS	CG	ShO	Sv.-Opp.	IP	H	R	ER	HR	BB-IBB	SO
1997—Dom. D-backs (DSL)	4	4	.500	5.13	21	6	0	0	1-...	59.2	57	50	34	...	48-...	44
1998—Dom. D-backs (DSL)	2	3	.400	1.79	14	8	1	0	1-...	50.1	36	19	10	...	24-...	44
1999—High Desert (Calif.)	0	0	...	7.53	3	3	0	0	0-...	14.1	15	13	12	2	9-0	9
—Missoula (Pio.)	5	3	.625	3.13	13	11	0	0	0-...	63.1	54	34	22	3	23-0	51
2000—South Bend (Midw.)	8	9	.471	3.65	28	28	4	0	0-...	165.1	152	80	67	6	54-1	121
2001—El Paso (Texas)	3	7	.300	6.78	13	13	0	0	0-...	70.1	92	56	53	5	25-1	41
—Lancaster (Calif.)	2	4	.333	4.58	10	10	1	0	0-...	59.0	65	44	30	7	18-0	49
2002—El Paso (Texas)	4	3	.571	3.03	31	0	0	0	13-...	35.2	31	16	12	1	13-1	37
—Arizona (N.L.)	0	0	...	4.91	6	0	0	0	0-1	3.2	3	2	2	1	5-0	4
—Tucson (PCL)	1	1	.500	6.75	4	0	0	0	1-...	5.1	6	4	4	1	1-0	9
—Nashville (PCL)■	0	3	.000	4.76	20	0	0	0	6-...	22.2	23	12	12	2	11-2	20
—Pittsburgh (N.L.)	0	0	...	15.43	3	0	0	0	0-0	2.1	3	4	4	1	2-0	2
Major League totals (1 year)	0	0	...	9.00	9	0	0	0	0-1	6.0	6	6	6	2	7-0	6

SANCHEZ, FREDDY — 2B — RED SOX

PERSONAL: Born December 21, 1977, in Hollywood, Calif. ... 5-11/185. ... Bats right, throws right. ... Full name: Frederick P. Sanchez.
COLLEGE: Oklahoma City.
TRANSACTIONS/CAREER NOTES: Selected by Boston Red Sox oragnization in 11th round of free-agent draft (June 5, 2000).
2002 GAMES PLAYED BY POSITION (MLB): 2B—5; SS—5; DH—1.

		BATTING														FIELDING	
Year Team (League)	Pos.	G	AB	R	H	2B	3B	HR	RBI	BB	SO	SB-CS	Avg.	OBP	SLG	E	Avg.
2000—Lowell (NY-Penn)	SS	34	132	24	38	13	2	1	14	9	16	2-4	.288	.347	.439	4	.974
—Augusta (S.Atl.)	SS	30	109	17	33	7	0	0	15	11	19	4-0	.303	.372	.367	3	.976
2001—Sarasota (FSL)	SS	69	280	40	95	19	4	1	24	22	30	5-3	.339	.388	.446	17	.944
—Trenton (East.)	SS	44	178	25	58	20	0	2	19	9	21	3-1	.326	.363	.472	9	.948
2002—Trenton (East.)	SS-2B	80	311	60	102	23	1	3	38	37	45	19-3	.328	.403	.437	16	.955
—Pawtucket (I.L.)	SS-2B	45	183	25	55	10	1	4	28	12	21	5-3	.301	.350	.432	13	.942
—Boston (A.L.)	2B-SS-DH	12	16	3	3	0	0	0	2	2	3	0-0	.188	.278	.188	0	1.000
Major League totals (1 year)		12	16	3	3	0	0	0	2	2	3	0-0	.188	.278	.188	0	1.000

SANCHEZ, JESUS — P

PERSONAL: Born October 11, 1974, in Nizao Bani, Dominican Republic. ... 5-11/175. ... Throws left, bats left. ... Full name: Jesus Paulino Sanchez.
TRANSACTIONS/CAREER NOTES: Signed as non-drafted free agent by New York Mets organization (June 7, 1992). ... On disabled list (April 4-May 28, 1996). ... Traded by Mets with P A.J. Burnett and OF Robert Stratton to Florida Marlins for P Al Leiter and 2B Ralph Milliard (February 6, 1998). ... Traded by Marlins to Chicago Cubs for P Nate Teut (December 11, 2001). ... Released by Cubs (October 1, 2002).
STATISTICAL NOTES: Led Dominican Summer League in home runs allowed with 14 in 1992.
MISCELLANEOUS: Appeared in two games as pinch runner (1998). ... Appeared in one game as pinch runner (1999). ... Scored two runs in 13 appearances as pinch runner (2000). ... Appeared in one game as pinch runner (2001).
CAREER HITTING (MLB): 25-for-138 (.181), 10 R, 0 2B, 1 3B, 0 HR, 6 RBI.

Year	League	W	L	Pct.	ERA	G	GS	CG	ShO	Sv.-Opp.	IP	H	R	ER	HR	BB-IBB	SO
1992—	Dominican Mets (DSL)	5	5	.500	4.19	15	15	1	0	0-...	81.2	86	52	38	...	38-...	72
1993—	Dominican Mets (DSL)	7	3	.700	2.40	16	13	2	•2	0-...	82.1	63	30	22	...	36-...	94
1994—	Kingsport (Appl.)	7	4	.636	1.96	13	12	•3	0	0-...	87.1	61	27	19	2	27-0	71
1995—	Capital City (S.Atl.)	9	7	.563	3.13	27	27	4	0	0-...	169.2	154	76	59	9	58-0	•177
1996—	St. Lucie (FSL)	9	3	.750	1.96	16	16	2	1	0-...	92.0	53	22	20	6	24-0	81
1997—	Binghamton (East.)	*13	10	.565	4.30	26	26	3	0	0-...	165.1	146	87	79	25	61-2	*176
1998—	Florida (N.L.)■	7	9	.438	4.47	35	29	0	0	0-1	173.0	178	98	86	18	91-2	137
1999—	Florida (N.L.)	5	7	.417	6.01	59	10	0	0	0-2	76.1	84	53	51	16	60-11	62
—	Calgary (PCL)	0	0	...	5.79	4	1	0	0	1-...	9.1	8	6	6	0	5-0	14
2000—	Florida (N.L.)	9	12	.429	5.34	32	32	2	2	0-0	182.0	197	118	108	32	76-4	123
2001—	Calgary (PCL)	6	1	.857	3.21	16	11	0	0	0-...	75.2	61	32	27	4	33-0	58
—	Florida (N.L.)	2	4	.333	4.74	16	9	0	0	0-0	62.2	61	33	33	7	31-2	46
2002—	Chicago (N.L.)■	0	0	...	12.96	8	0	0	0	0-0	8.1	15	12	12	4	10-1	6
—	Iowa (PCL)	8	9	.471	5.90	26	24	0	0	0-...	125.0	144	90	82	27	65-3	94
Major League totals (5 years)		23	32	.418	5.20	150	80	2	2	0-3	502.1	535	314	290	77	268-20	374

SANCHEZ, REY — 2B — RED SOX

PERSONAL: Born October 5, 1967, in Rio Piedras, Puerto Rico. ... 5-9/175. ... Bats right, throws right. ... Full name: Rey Francisco Guadalupe Sanchez.

HIGH SCHOOL: Live Oak (Morgan Hill, Calif.).

TRANSACTIONS/CAREER NOTES: Selected by Texas Rangers organization in 13th round of free-agent draft (June 2, 1986). ... Traded by Rangers to Chicago Cubs for IF Bryan House (January 3, 1990). ... On disabled list (April 6, 1990-entire season). ... On Chicago disabled list (May 6-21, 1992); included rehabilitation assignment to Iowa (May 13-21). ... On disabled list (July 24-August 9, 1995). ... On Chicago disabled list (June 5-July 20 and August 11-September 1, 1996); included rehabilitation assignment to Iowa (July 16-20). ... Traded by Cubs to New York Yankees for P Frisco Parotte (August 16, 1997). ... Granted free agency (November 3, 1997). ... Signed by San Francisco Giants (January 22, 1998). ... Granted free agency (November 5, 1998). ... Signed by Kansas City Royals (December 11, 1998). ... Granted free agency (October 29, 1999). ... Re-signed by Royals (December 7, 1999). ... Traded by Royals to Atlanta Braves for P Brad Voyles and IF Alejandro Machado (July 31, 2001). ... Granted free agency (November 5, 2001). ... Signed by Boston Red Sox organization (February 27, 2002). ... On disabled list (June 13-July 11, 2002). ... On suspended list (September 15-16, 2002).

STATISTICAL NOTES: Led Gulf Coast League shortstops with .932 fielding percentage in 1986. ... Led Florida State League shortstops with 415 in 1988. ... Led American Association shortstops with 237 putouts, 418 assists, 684 total chances and 104 double plays in 1989. ... Led American Association shortstops with 375 assists, 596 total chances and 81 double plays in 1991. ... Had 21-game hitting streak (May 11-June 3, 2001).

2002 GAMES PLAYED BY POSITION (MLB): 2B—100; SS—10.

			BATTING														FIELDING	
Year	Team (League)	Pos.	G	AB	R	H	2B	3B	HR	RBI	BB	SO	SB-CS	Avg.	OBP	SLG	E	Avg.
1986—	GC Rangers (GCL)	SS-2B	52	169	27	49	3	1	0	23	41	18	10-10	.290	.435	.320	15	†.938
1987—	Gastonia (S.Atl.)	SS	50	160	19	35	1	2	1	10	22	17	6-3	.219	.321	.269	18	.933
—	Butte (Pio.)	SS	49	189	36	69	10	6	0	25	21	12	22-6	.365	.430	.481	12	.953
1988—	Charlotte (FSL)	SS	128	418	60	128	6	5	0	38	35	24	29-11	.306	.364	.344	35	.948
1989—	Oklahoma City (A.A.)	SS	134	464	38	104	10	4	1	39	21	50	4-4	.224	.259	.269	29	*.958
1990—	Iowa (A.A.)■								Did not play.									
1991—	Iowa (A.A.)	SS	126	417	60	121	16	5	2	46	37	27	13-7	.290	.356	.367	17	*.971
—	Chicago (N.L.)	SS-2B	13	23	1	6	0	0	0	2	4	3	0-0	.261	.370	.261	0	1.000
1992—	Iowa (A.A.)	SS-2B	20	76	12	26	3	0	0	3	4	1	6-3	.342	.375	.382	5	.956
—	Chicago (N.L.)	SS-2B	74	255	24	64	14	3	1	19	10	17	2-1	.251	.285	.341	9	.975
1993—	Chicago (N.L.)	SS	105	344	35	97	11	2	0	28	15	22	1-1	.282	.316	.326	15	.969
1994—	Chicago (N.L.)	2B-SS-3B	96	291	26	83	13	1	0	24	20	29	2-5	.285	.345	.337	9	.979
1995—	Chicago (N.L.)	2B-SS	114	428	57	119	22	2	3	27	14	48	6-4	.278	.301	.360	7	.987
1996—	Chicago (N.L.)	SS	95	289	28	61	9	0	1	12	22	42	7-1	.211	.272	.253	11	.977
—	Iowa (A.A.)	SS	3	12	2	2	0	0	0	1	1	2	2-0	.167	.231	.167	1	.933
1997—	Chicago (N.L.)	SS-2B-3B	97	205	14	51	9	0	1	12	11	26	4-2	.249	.287	.307	6	.977
—	New York (A.L.)■	2B-SS	38	138	21	43	12	0	1	15	5	21	0-4	.312	.338	.420	4	.978
1998—	San Fran. (N.L.)■	SS-2B	109	316	44	90	14	2	2	30	16	47	0-0	.285	.325	.361	8	.981
1999—	Kansas City (A.L.)■	SS	134	479	66	141	18	6	2	56	22	48	11-5	.294	.329	.370	13	.982
2000—	Kansas City (A.L.)	SS	143	509	68	139	18	2	1	38	28	55	7-3	.273	.314	.322	4	.994
2001—	Kansas City (A.L.)	SS	100	390	46	118	14	5	0	28	11	34	9-1	.303	.322	.364	3	.994
—	Atlanta (N.L.)■	SS	49	154	10	35	4	1	0	9	4	15	2-0	.227	.245	.266	3	.986
2002—	Boston (A.L.)■	2B-SS	107	357	46	102	12	3	1	38	17	31	2-2	.286	.318	.345	5	.989
American League totals (5 years)			522	1873	247	543	74	16	5	175	83	189	29-15	.290	.322	.355	29	.988
National League totals (9 years)			752	2305	239	606	96	11	8	163	116	249	24-14	.263	.303	.325	68	.979
Major League totals (12 years)			1274	4178	486	1149	170	27	13	338	199	438	53-29	.275	.311	.338	97	.983

DIVISION SERIES RECORD

			BATTING														FIELDING	
Year	Team (League)	Pos.	G	AB	R	H	2B	3B	HR	RBI	BB	SO	SB-CS	Avg.	OBP	SLG	E	Avg.
1997—	New York (A.L.)	2B	5	15	1	3	1	0	0	1	1	2	0-0	.200	.250	.267	0	1.000
2001—	Atlanta (N.L.)	SS	3	9	1	2	1	0	0	0	0	2	0-0	.222	.222	.333	1	.944
Division series totals (2 years)			8	24	2	5	2	0	0	1	1	4	0-0	.208	.240	.292	1	.979

CHAMPIONSHIP SERIES RECORD

			BATTING														FIELDING	
Year	Team (League)	Pos.	G	AB	R	H	2B	3B	HR	RBI	BB	SO	SB-CS	Avg.	OBP	SLG	E	Avg.
2001—	Atlanta (N.L.)	SS	5	17	1	5	1	0	0	1	0	4	0-0	.294	.294	.353	2	.900

SANDBERG, JARED — 3B — DEVIL RAYS

PERSONAL: Born March 2, 1978, in Olympia, Wash. ... 6-3/226. ... Bats right, throws right. ... Full name: Jared Lawrence Sandberg. ... Nephew of Ryne Sandberg, second baseman with Philadelphia Phillies (1981) and Chicago Cubs (1982-94 and 1996-97).

HIGH SCHOOL: Capital (Olympia, Wash.).

TRANSACTIONS/CAREER NOTES: Selected by Tampa Bay Devil Rays organization in 16th round of free-agent draft (June 4, 1996). ... On Orlando disabled list (April 13-25 and May 9-June 30, 2000).

RECORDS: Shares major league single-game record for most home runs in one inning—2 (June 11, 2002, fifth inning).

HONORS: Named Appalachian League Player of the Year (1997).

STATISTICAL NOTES: Led Appalachian League with 157 total bases and five intentional bases on balls received in 1997. ... Led New York-Pennsylvania League with 133 total bases in 1998. ... Led New York-Pennsylvania League third basemen with 55 putouts, 234 total chances and 15 double plays and tied for lead with 159 assists in 1998. ... Led Florida State League third basemen with 102 putouts, 284 assists and 423 total chances in 1999. ... Tied for Florida State League lead with 25 double plays by third basemen in 1999. ... Career major league grand slams: 1.

2002 GAMES PLAYED BY POSITION (MLB): 3B—97; 1B—3; DH—2.

			BATTING														FIELDING	
Year	Team (League)	Pos.	G	AB	R	H	2B	3B	HR	RBI	BB	SO	SB-CS	Avg.	OBP	SLG	E	Avg.
1996	GC Devil Rays (GCL)	2B	22	77	6	13	2	1	0	7	9	26	1-0	.169	.256	.221	3	.969
1997	St. Petersburg (FSL)	2B	2	3	1	1	0	0	0	2	2	2	0-0	.333	.600	.333	0	1.000
	Princeton (Appl.)	2B-3B	•67	*268	61	81	15	5	17	*68	42	*94	12-3	.302	.401	.586	13	.949
1998	Charl., S.C. (S.Atl.)	3B	56	191	31	35	11	0	3	15	27	76	4-0	.183	.293	.288	22	.862
	Hudson Valley (NY-P)	3B	73	271	49	78	15	2	•12	54	42	76	13-3	.288	.388	.491	20	.915
1999	St. Petersburg (FSL)	3B	136	504	73	139	24	1	22	96	51	133	8-2	.276	.350	.458	*37	.913
2000	Orlando (Sou.)	3B	67	244	30	63	15	1	5	35	33	55	5-3	.258	.348	.389	10	.946
	Durham (I.L.)	3B	3	15	2	6	3	0	2	7	0	6	0-0	.400	.400	1.000	1	.933
2001	Orlando (Sou.)	3B-1B	8	28	4	8	2	0	1	4	6	10	0-0	.286	.412	.464	0	1.000
	Durham (I.L.)	3B	93	322	39	77	16	0	16	50	38	81	0-1	.239	.331	.438	13	.948
	Tampa Bay (A.L.)	3B-1B	39	136	13	28	7	0	1	15	10	45	1-0	.206	.265	.279	6	.944
2002	Durham (I.L.)	3B-1B	30	114	20	32	9	0	4	21	14	42	1-0	.281	.369	.465	5	.933
	Tampa Bay (A.L.)	3B-1B-DH	102	358	55	82	21	1	18	54	39	139	3-2	.229	.305	.444	15	.949
Major League totals (2 years)			141	494	68	110	28	1	19	69	49	184	4-2	.223	.294	.399	21	.948

SANDERS, REGGIE — OF

PERSONAL: Born December 1, 1967, in Florence, S.C. ... 6-1/205. ... Bats right, throws right. ... Full name: Reginald Laverne Sanders.

HIGH SCHOOL: Wilson (Florence, S.C.).

COLLEGE: Spartanburg (S.C.) Methodist.

TRANSACTIONS/CAREER NOTES: Selected by Cincinnati Reds organization in seventh round of free-agent draft (June 2, 1987). ... On disabled list (July 11-September 15, 1988; and July 15-September 5, 1989). ... On Chattanooga disabled list (June 30-July 26, 1991). ... On Cincinnati disabled list (August 24-September 20, 1991; and May 13-29 and July 17-August 2, 1992). ... On suspended list (June 3-9, 1994). ... On Cincinnati disabled list (April 20-May 22, May 31-June 15 and September 17, 1996-remainder of season); included rehabilitation assignment to Indianapolis (May 17-22). ... On Cincinnati disabled list (April 19-May 6 and May 24-July 23, 1997); included rehabilitation assignments to Chattanooga (May 3-5) and Indianapolis (July 15-22). ... Traded by Reds with SS Damian Jackson and P Josh Harris to San Diego Padres for OF Greg Vaughn and OF/1B Mark Sweeney (February 2, 1999). ... On disabled list (June 3-18, 1999). ... Traded by Padres with 2B Quilvio Veras and 1B Wally Joyner to Atlanta Braves for OF/1B Ryan Klesko, 2B Bret Boone and P Jason Shiell (December 22, 1999). ... On disabled list (April 30-May 23 and July 28-August 15, 2000). ... Granted free agency (October 31, 2000). ... Signed by Arizona Diamondbacks (January 5, 2001). ... On Arizona disabled list (March 23-April 8, 2001); included rehabilitation assignment to Tuscon (April 5-8). ... Granted free agency (November 6, 2001). ... Signed by San Francisco Giants (January 8, 2002). ... Granted free agency (October 31, 2002).

HONORS: Named Midwest League Most Valuable Player (1990). ... Named outfielder on The Sporting News N.L. All-Star team (1995).

STATISTICAL NOTES: Hit three home runs in one game (August 15, 1995). ... Career major league grand slams: 2.

2002 GAMES PLAYED BY POSITION (MLB): OF—137.

			BATTING														FIELDING	
Year	Team (League)	Pos.	G	AB	R	H	2B	3B	HR	RBI	BB	SO	SB-CS	Avg.	OBP	SLG	E	Avg.
1988	Billings (Pio.)	SS	17	64	11	15	1	1	0	3	6	4	10-2	.234	.296	.281	3	.944
1989	Greensboro (S.Atl.)	SS	81	315	53	91	18	5	9	53	29	63	21-7	.289	.353	.463	42	.875
1990	Cedar Rapids (Midw.)	OF	127	466	89	133	21	4	17	63	59	97	40-15	.285	.370	.457	10	.962
1991	Chattanooga (Sou.)	OF	86	302	50	95	15	•8	8	49	41	67	15-2	.315	.394	.497	3	.982
	Cincinnati (N.L.)	OF	9	40	6	8	0	0	1	3	0	9	1-1	.200	.200	.275	0	1.000
1992	Cincinnati (N.L.)	OF	116	385	62	104	26	6	12	36	48	98	16-7	.270	.356	.462	6	.978
1993	Cincinnati (N.L.)	OF	138	496	90	136	16	4	20	83	51	118	27-10	.274	.343	.444	8	.975
1994	Cincinnati (N.L.)	OF	107	400	66	105	20	8	17	62	41	*114	21-9	.263	.332	.480	6	.975
1995	Cincinnati (N.L.)	OF	133	484	91	148	36	6	28	99	69	122	36-12	.306	.397	.579	5	.982
1996	Cincinnati (N.L.)	OF	81	287	49	72	17	1	14	33	44	86	24-8	.251	.353	.463	2	.988
	Indianapolis (A.A.)	OF-DH	4	12	3	5	2	0	0	1	1	4	0-1	.417	.500	.583	0	1.000
1997	Cincinnati (N.L.)	OF	86	312	52	79	19	2	19	56	42	93	13-7	.253	.347	.510	5	.974
	Chattanooga (Sou.)	OF	3	11	3	6	1	1	1	3	1	2	0-0	.545	.615	1.091	0	1.000
	Indianapolis (A.A.)	OF	5	19	1	4	0	0	0	1	1	6	0-0	.211	.250	.211	2	.750
1998	Cincinnati (N.L.)	OF	135	481	83	129	18	6	14	59	51	137	20-9	.268	.346	.418	6	.978
1999	San Diego (N.L.)■	OF-DH	133	478	92	136	24	7	26	72	65	108	36-13	.285	.376	.527	6	.975
2000	Atlanta (N.L.)■	OF	103	340	43	79	23	1	11	37	32	78	21-4	.232	.302	.403	6	.964
2001	Tucson (PCL)■	OF	2	6	0	2	1	0	0	1	2	0	1-0	.333	.500	.500	0	1.000
	Arizona (N.L.)	OF	126	441	84	116	21	3	33	90	46	126	14-10	.263	.337	.549	1	.996
2002	San Fran. (N.L.)■	OF	140	505	75	126	23	6	23	85	47	121	18-6	.250	.324	.455	5	.984
Major League totals (12 years)			1307	4649	793	1238	243	50	218	715	536	1210	247-96	.266	.347	.481	56	.980

DIVISION SERIES RECORD

RECORDS: Holds N.L. career record for most strikeouts—22.

Year Team (League)	Pos.	BATTING G	AB	R	H	2B	3B	HR	RBI	BB	SO	SB-CS	Avg.	OBP	SLG	FIELDING E	Avg.
1995— Cincinnati (N.L.)	OF	3	13	3	2	1	0	1	2	1	9	2-0	.154	.214	.462	1	.875
2000— Atlanta (N.L.)	OF	3	9	0	0	0	0	0	0	2	5	0-0	.000	.182	.000	0	1.000
2001— Arizona (N.L.)	OF	5	14	2	5	1	0	1	1	3	3	1-0	.357	.471	.643	0	1.000
2002— San Francisco (N.L.)	OF	5	18	1	4	1	0	0	1	3	5	0-0	.222	.333	.278	0	1.000
Division series totals (4 years)		16	54	6	11	3	0	2	4	9	22	3-0	.204	.317	.370	1	.971

CHAMPIONSHIP SERIES RECORD

Year Team (League)	Pos.	BATTING G	AB	R	H	2B	3B	HR	RBI	BB	SO	SB-CS	Avg.	OBP	SLG	FIELDING E	Avg.
1995— Cincinnati (N.L.)	OF	4	16	0	2	0	0	0	0	2	10	0-1	.125	.222	.125	1	.875
2001— Arizona (N.L.)	OF	5	17	2	2	0	0	0	1	5	5	1-0	.118	.318	.118	0	1.000
2002— San Francisco (N.L.)	OF	4	16	0	1	0	0	0	0	0	4	0-0	.063	.063	.063	0	1.000
Championship series totals (3 years)		13	49	2	5	0	0	0	1	7	19	1-1	.102	.214	.102	1	.973

WORLD SERIES RECORD

RECORDS: Shares single-inning record for most at-bats—2 (November 3, 2001, third inning).
NOTES: Member of World Series championship team (2001).

Year Team (League)	Pos.	BATTING G	AB	R	H	2B	3B	HR	RBI	BB	SO	SB-CS	Avg.	OBP	SLG	FIELDING E	Avg.
2001— Arizona (N.L.)	OF	6	23	6	7	1	0	0	1	1	7	1-0	.304	.360	.348	0	1.000
2002— San Francisco (N.L.)	OF	7	21	3	5	0	0	2	6	2	9	1-0	.238	.280	.524	0	1.000
World Series totals (2 years)		13	44	9	12	1	0	2	7	3	16	2-0	.273	.320	.432	0	1.000

ALL-STAR GAME RECORD

	AB	R	H	2B	3B	HR	RBI	BB	SO	SB-CS	Avg.	OBP	SLG	E	Avg.
All-Star Game totals (1 year)	1	0	0	0	0	0	0	0	1	0-0	.000	.000	.000	0	...

SANTANA, JOHAN — P — TWINS

PERSONAL: Born March 13, 1979, in Tovar, Venezuela. ... 6-0/195. ... Throws left, bats left. ... Full name: Johan Alexander Santana.
HIGH SCHOOL: Liceo Nucete Sardi (Venezuela).
TRANSACTIONS/CAREER NOTES: Signed as non-drafted free agent by Houston Astros organization (July 2, 1995). ... Selected by Florida Marlins from Astros organization in Rule 5 major league draft (December 13, 1999). ... Traded by Marlins with cash to Minnesota Twins for P Jared Camp (December 13, 1999). ... On disabled list (July 7-September 21, 2001).
STATISTICAL NOTES: Led New York-Pennsylvania League with 10 hit batsmen in 1998. ... Led A.L. with 15 wild pitches in 2002.
CAREER HITTING (MLB): 1-for-5 (.200), 0 R, 0 2B, 0 3B, 0 HR, 0 RBI.

Year League	W	L	Pct.	ERA	G	GS	CG	ShO	Sv.-Opp.	IP	H	R	ER	HR	BB-IBB	SO
1996— Dominican Astros (DSL)	4	3	.571	2.70	23	1	0	0	3-...	40.0	26	16	12	...	22-...	51
1997— Gulf Coast Astros (GCL)	0	4	.000	7.93	9	5	1	0	0-...	36.1	49	36	32	2	18-0	25
— Auburn (NY-Penn)	0	0	...	2.25	1	1	0	0	0-...	4.0	1	1	1	0	6-0	5
1998— Quad City (Midw.)	0	1	.000	9.45	2	1	0	0	0-...	6.2	14	7	7	1	3-0	6
— Auburn (NY-Penn)	7	5	.583	4.36	15	15	1	•1	0-...	86.2	81	52	42	9	21-0	88
1999— Michigan (Midw.)	8	8	.500	4.66	27	26	1	0	0-...	160.1	162	94	83	14	55-0	150
2000— Minnesota (A.L.)■	2	3	.400	6.49	30	5	0	0	0-0	86.0	102	64	62	11	54-0	64
2001— Minnesota (A.L.)	1	0	1.000	4.74	15	4	0	0	0-0	43.2	50	25	23	6	16-0	28
2002— Edmonton (PCL)	5	2	.714	3.14	11	9	0	0	0-...	48.2	37	24	17	7	27-0	75
— Minnesota (A.L.)	8	6	.571	2.99	27	14	0	0	1-1	108.1	84	41	36	7	49-0	137
Major League totals (3 years)	11	9	.550	4.58	72	23	0	0	1-1	238.0	236	130	121	24	119-0	229

DIVISION SERIES RECORD

Year League	W	L	Pct.	ERA	G	GS	CG	ShO	Sv.-Opp.	IP	H	R	ER	HR	BB-IBB	SO
2002— Minnesota (A.L.)	0	0	...	6.00	2	0	0	0	0-0	3.0	3	2	2	0	2-0	2

CHAMPIONSHIP SERIES RECORD

Year League	W	L	Pct.	ERA	G	GS	CG	ShO	Sv.-Opp.	IP	H	R	ER	HR	BB-IBB	SO
2002— Minnesota (A.L.)	0	1	.000	10.80	4	0	0	0	0-0	3.1	4	4	4	1	0-0	4

SANTANA, JULIO — P — TIGERS

PERSONAL: Born January 20, 1974, in San Pedro de Macoris, Dominican Republic ... 6-0/225. ... Throws right, bats right. ... Full name: Julio Franklin Santana. ... Nephew of Rico Carty, outfielder with seven major league teams (1963-79).
HIGH SCHOOL: Divina Providence (Dominican Republic).
TRANSACTIONS/CAREER NOTES: Signed as non-drafted free agent by Texas Rangers organization (February 18, 1990). ... On Texas disabled list (July 15-August 10, 1997). ... Claimed on waivers by Tampa Bay Devil Rays (April 27, 1998). ... On Tampa Bay disabled list (May 3-24, 1999). ... Traded by Devil Rays to Boston Red Sox for a player to be named later and cash (July 21, 1999); Devil Rays acquired P Will Silverthorn to complete deal (July 30, 1999). ... On Boston disabled list (July 22, 1999-remainder of season). ... Granted free agency (December 21, 1999). ... Re-signed by Red Sox organization (February 2, 2000). ... Released by Red Sox (June 15, 2000). ... Signed by Montreal Expos (June 18, 2000). ... Granted free agency (October 10, 2000). ... Signed by San Francisco Giants organization (November 11, 2000). ... Selected by New York Mets from Giants organization in Rule 5 major league draft (December 11, 2000). ... Returned to Giants organization (March 30, 2001). ... Granted free agency (October 15, 2001). ... Signed by Detroit Tigers organization (November 16, 2001). ... On Detroit disabled list (August 11, 2002-remainder of season).
CAREER HITTING (MLB): 2-for-14 (.143), 0 R, 0 2B, 0 3B, 0 HR, 1 RBI.

Year League	W	L	Pct.	ERA	G	GS	CG	ShO	Sv.-Opp.	IP	H	R	ER	HR	BB-IBB	SO
1992— San Pedro (DSL)	0	1	.000	3.24	4	1	0	0	0-...	8.1	8	5	3	...	7-...	5
1993— Gulf Coast Rangers (GCL)	4	1	.800	1.38	*26	0	0	0	7-...	39.0	31	9	6	0	7-0	50
1994— Charleston, S.C. (S.Atl.)	6	7	.462	2.46	16	16	0	0	0-...	91.1	65	38	25	3	44-0	103
— Tulsa (Texas)	7	2	.778	2.90	11	11	2	0	0-...	71.1	50	26	23	1	41-0	45
1995— Oklahoma City (A.A.)	0	2	.000	39.00	2	2	0	0	0-...	3.0	9	14	13	3	7-0	6
— Charlotte (FSL)	0	3	.000	3.73	5	5	1	0	0-...	31.1	32	16	13	1	16-0	27
— Tulsa (Texas)	6	4	.600	3.23	15	15	3	0	0-...	103.0	91	40	37	8	52-2	71
1996— Oklahoma City (A.A.)	11	12	.478	4.02	29	*29	4	1	0-...	*185.2	171	102	83	12	66-1	113
1997— Texas (A.L.)	4	6	.400	6.75	30	14	0	0	0-1	104.0	141	86	78	16	49-2	64
— Oklahoma City (A.A.)	0	0	...	15.00	1	1	0	0	0-...	3.0	9	6	5	0	2-0	1
1998— Texas (A.L.)	0	0	...	8.44	3	0	0	0	0-0	5.1	7	5	5	0	4-1	1
— Tampa Bay (A.L.)■	5	6	.455	4.23	32	19	1	0	0-0	140.1	144	72	66	18	58-2	60
1999— Tampa Bay (A.L.)	1	4	.200	7.32	22	5	0	0	0-0	55.1	66	49	45	10	32-0	34
2000— Pawtucket (I.L.)■	5	3	.625	4.71	12	12	0	0	0-...	65.0	61	34	34	7	23-0	55
— Montreal (N.L.)■	1	5	.167	5.67	36	4	0	0	0-2	66.2	69	45	42	11	33-2	58
2001— Fresno (PCL)■	8	8	.500	5.83	25	25	0	0	0-...	132.2	160	94	86	28	50-0	125
2002— Toledo (I.L.)■	0	1	.000	2.13	7	0	0	0	1-...	12.2	12	5	3	1	3-0	12
— Detroit (A.L.)	3	5	.375	2.84	38	0	0	0	0-1	57.0	49	19	18	8	28-2	38
A.L. totals (4 years)	13	21	.382	5.27	125	38	1	0	0-2	362.0	407	231	212	52	171-7	197
N.L. totals (1 year)	1	5	.167	5.67	36	4	0	0	0-2	66.2	69	45	42	11	33-2	58
Major League totals (5 years)	14	26	.350	5.33	161	42	1	0	0-4	428.2	476	276	254	63	204-9	255

RECORD AS POSITION PLAYER

		BATTING														FIELDING	
Year Team (League)	Pos.	G	AB	R	H	2B	3B	HR	RBI	BB	SO	SB-CS	Avg.	OBP	SLG	E	Avg.
1990— San Pedro (DSL)		11	34	4	7	0	0	1	3	5	7	0-0	.206	...	.294	...	...
1991— San Pedro (DSL)		55	161	27	42	7	0	2	12	27	37	5-2	.261	...	.342	...	...
1992— San Pedro (DSL)	OF-IF	17	48	7	11	2	0	2	2	11	8	0-2	.229	...	.396	4	.929

SANTIAGO, BENITO — C — GIANTS

PERSONAL: Born March 9, 1965, in Ponce, Puerto Rico. ... 6-1/200. ... Bats right, throws right. ... Full name: Benito Rivera Santiago.

HIGH SCHOOL: John F. Kennedy (Ponce, Puerto Rico).

TRANSACTIONS/CAREER NOTES: Signed as non-drafted free agent by San Diego Padres organization (September 1, 1982). ... On disabled list (June 21-July 2, 1985). ... On San Diego disabled list (June 15-August 10, 1990); included rehabilitation assignment to Las Vegas (August 2-9). ... On San Diego disabled list (May 31-July 11, 1992); included rehabilitation assignment to Las Vegas (July 7-11). ... Granted free agency (October 26, 1992). ... Signed by Florida Marlins (December 16, 1992). ... On suspended list (May 5-9, 1994). ... Granted free agency (October 20, 1994). ... Signed by Cincinnati Reds (April 17, 1995). ... On disabled list (May 8-July 4, 1995). ... Granted free agency (October 31, 1995). ... Signed by Philadelphia Phillies (January 30, 1996). ... Granted free agency (November 18, 1996). ... Signed by Toronto Blue Jays (December 9, 1996). ... On disabled list (April 14-29, 1997). ... On Toronto disabled list (March 18-September 3, 1998); included rehabilitation assignments to Dunedin (August 15-26) and Syracuse (August 28-September 3). ... Granted free agency (October 23, 1998). ... Signed by Chicago Cubs (December 10, 1998). ... Granted free agency (October 29, 1999). ... Signed by Reds organization (February 24, 2000). ... Granted free agency (November 3, 2000). ... Signed by San Francisco Giants organization (March 17, 2001). ... Granted free agency (November 7, 2001). ... Re-signed by Giants (December 7, 2001). ... On suspended list (September 20-22, 2002).

RECORDS: Holds major league rookie-season record for most consecutive games batted safely—34 (August 25-October 2, 1987). ... Shares major league single-season record for fewest passed balls (100 or more games)—0 (1992). ... Shares major league record for most consecutive home runs—4 (September 14 [1] and 15 [3], 1996).

HONORS: Named N.L. Rookie Player of the Year by The Sporting News (1987). ... Named catcher on The Sporting News N.L. All-Star team (1987, 1989 and 1991). ... Named catcher on The Sporting News N.L. Silver Slugger team (1987-88 and 1990-91). ... Named N.L. Rookie of the Year by Baseball Writers' Association of America (1987). ... Won N.L. Gold Glove at catcher (1988-90).

STATISTICAL NOTES: Led Florida State League catchers with 69 assists, 26 passed balls and 12 double plays in 1983. ... Led Texas League catchers with 78 assists and 16 passed balls in 1985. ... Led Pacific Coast League catchers with 563 putouts and 655 total chances in 1986. ... Had 34-game hitting streak (August 25-October 2, 1987). ... Led N.L. with 22 passed balls in 1987, 14 in 1989 and 23 in 1993. ... Led N.L. catchers with 75 assists in 1988 and 66 in 1994. ... Led N.L. in grounding into double plays with 21 in 1991. ... Tied for N.L. lead in double plays by catcher with 11 in 1988 and 14 in 1991. ... Led N.L. catchers with 100 assists and 14 errors in 1991. ... Tied for N.L. lead in errors by catcher with 11 in 1993. ... Led N.L. catchers with .996 fielding percentage in 1995. ... Hit three home runs in one game (September 15, 1996). ... Career major league grand slams: 8.

2002 GAMES PLAYED BY POSITION (MLB): C—125.

		BATTING														FIELDING	
Year Team (League)	Pos.	G	AB	R	H	2B	3B	HR	RBI	BB	SO	SB-CS	Avg.	OBP	SLG	E	Avg.
1983— Miami (FSL)	C	122	429	34	106	25	3	5	56	11	79	3-7	.247	.276	.354	*21	.963
1984— Reno (Calif.)	C	114	416	64	116	20	6	16	83	36	75	5-2	.279	.338	.471	25	.969
1985— Beaumont (Texas)	C-1B-3B	101	372	55	111	16	6	5	52	16	59	12-2	.298	.328	.414	15	.976
1986— Las Vegas (PCL)	C	117	437	55	125	26	3	17	71	17	81	19-7	.286	.312	.476	*21	.968
— San Diego (N.L.)	C	17	62	10	18	2	0	3	6	2	12	0-1	.290	.308	.468	5	.946
1987— San Diego (N.L.)	C	146	546	64	164	33	2	18	79	16	112	21-12	.300	.324	.467	*22	.976
1988— San Diego (N.L.)	C	139	492	49	122	22	2	10	46	24	82	15-7	.248	.282	.362	*12	.985
1989— San Diego (N.L.)	C	129	462	50	109	16	3	16	62	26	89	11-6	.236	.277	.387	*20	.975
1990— San Diego (N.L.)	C	100	344	42	93	8	5	11	53	27	55	5-5	.270	.323	.419	12	.980
— Las Vegas (PCL)	C	6	20	5	6	2	0	1	8	3	1	0-0	.300	.375	.550	0	1.000
1991— San Diego (N.L.)	C-OF	152	580	60	155	22	3	17	87	23	114	8-10	.267	.296	.403	†14	.985
1992— San Diego (N.L.)	C	106	386	37	97	21	0	10	42	21	52	2-5	.251	.287	.383	*12	.982
— Las Vegas (PCL)	C	4	13	3	4	0	0	1	2	1	1	0-0	.308	.357	.538	0	1.000
1993— Florida (N.L.)■	C-OF	139	469	49	108	19	6	13	50	37	88	10-7	.230	.291	.380	•11	.987
1994— Florida (N.L.)	C	101	337	35	92	14	2	11	41	25	57	1-2	.273	.322	.424	5	.991
1995— Cincinnati (N.L.)■	C-1B	81	266	40	76	20	0	11	44	24	48	2-2	.286	.351	.485	2	†.996
1996— Philadelphia (N.L.)■	C-1B	136	481	71	127	21	2	30	85	49	104	2-0	.264	.332	.503	11	.988
1997— Toronto (A.L.)■	C-DH	97	341	31	83	10	0	13	42	17	80	1-0	.243	.279	.387	2	.997
1998— Dunedin (FSL)	DH-C	11	37	4	6	1	0	1	5	3	9	3-0	.162	.225	.270	0	1.000
— Syracuse (I.L.)	C-DH	5	22	0	5	2	0	0	2	1	3	0-0	.227	.261	.318	0	1.000
— Toronto (A.L.)	C	15	29	3	9	5	0	0	4	1	6	0-0	.310	.333	.483	0	1.000

Year	Team (League)	Pos.	BATTING G	AB	R	H	2B	3B	HR	RBI	BB	SO	SB-CS	Avg.	OBP	SLG	FIELDING E	Avg.
1999—	Chicago (N.L.)■	C-1B	109	350	28	87	18	3	7	36	32	71	1-1	.249	.313	.377	6	.990
2000—	Cincinnati (N.L.)■	C	89	252	22	66	11	1	8	45	19	45	2-2	.262	.310	.409	3	.994
2001—	San Fran. (N.L.)■	C-1B	133	477	39	125	25	4	6	45	23	78	5-4	.262	.295	.369	5	.994
2002—	San Francisco (N.L.)	C	126	478	56	133	24	5	16	74	27	73	4-2	.278	.315	.450	4	.995
American League totals (2 years)			112	370	34	92	15	0	13	46	18	86	1-0	.249	.284	.395	2	.997
National League totals (15 years)			1703	5982	652	1572	276	38	187	795	375	1080	89-66	.263	.307	.415	144	.986
Major League totals (17 years)			1815	6352	686	1664	291	38	200	841	393	1166	90-66	.262	.305	.414	146	.987

DIVISION SERIES RECORD

NOTES: Hit home run in first at-bat (October 3, 1995).

Year	Team (League)	Pos.	BATTING G	AB	R	H	2B	3B	HR	RBI	BB	SO	SB-CS	Avg.	OBP	SLG	FIELDING E	Avg.
1995—	Cincinnati (N.L.)	C	3	9	2	3	0	0	1	3	3	3	0-0	.333	.462	.667	0	1.000
2002—	San Francisco (N.L.)	C	5	21	1	5	2	0	0	5	1	5	0-0	.238	.273	.333	1	.971
Division series totals (2 years)			8	30	3	8	2	0	1	8	4	8	0-0	.267	.343	.433	1	.982

CHAMPIONSHIP SERIES RECORD

NOTES: Named Most Valuable Player (2002).

Year	Team (League)	Pos.	BATTING G	AB	R	H	2B	3B	HR	RBI	BB	SO	SB-CS	Avg.	OBP	SLG	FIELDING E	Avg.
1995—	Cincinnati (N.L.)	C	4	13	0	3	0	0	0	0	2	3	0-0	.231	.333	.231	0	1.000
2002—	San Francisco (N.L.)	C	5	20	2	6	0	0	2	6	2	4	0-0	.300	.364	.600	0	1.000
Championship series totals (2 years)			9	33	2	9	0	0	2	6	4	7	0-0	.273	.351	.455	0	1.000

WORLD SERIES RECORD

Year	Team (League)	Pos.	BATTING G	AB	R	H	2B	3B	HR	RBI	BB	SO	SB-CS	Avg.	OBP	SLG	FIELDING E	Avg.
2002—	San Francisco (N.L.)	PH	7	26	2	6	0	0	0	5	3	4	0-0	.231	.300	.231	1	.976

ALL-STAR GAME RECORD

	AB	R	H	2B	3B	HR	RBI	BB	SO	SB-CS	Avg.	OBP	SLG	E	Avg.
All-Star Game totals (4 years)	7	0	1	0	0	0	0	0	4	0-0	.143	.143	.143	1	.875

SANTIAGO, JOSE — P — INDIANS

PERSONAL: Born November 5, 1974, in Fajardo, Puerto Rico. ... 6-3/215. ... Throws right, bats right. ... Full name: Jose Rafael Santiago.

HIGH SCHOOL: Carlos Escobar Lopez (Loiza, Puerto Rico).

TRANSACTIONS/CAREER NOTES: Selected by Kansas City Royals organization in 70th round of free agent draft (June 3, 1994). ... On Kansas City disabled list (June 26-July 9, 1997). ... On Kansas City disabled list (June 20-September 13, 1999); included rehabilitation assignments to Gulf Coast Royals (July 3-9), Wichita (July 10-11 and August 30-September 5) and Omaha (July 18-19 and September 6-12). ... Traded by Royals to Philadelphia Phillies for P Paul Byrd (June 5, 2001). ... Released by Phillies (October 11, 2002). ... Signed by Cleveland Indians organization (November 2, 2002).

CAREER HITTING (MLB): 0-for-5 (.000), 0 R, 0 2B, 0 3B, 0 HR, 0 RBI.

Year	League	W	L	Pct.	ERA	G	GS	CG	ShO	Sv.-Opp.	IP	H	R	ER	HR	BB-IBB	SO
1994—	Gulf Coast Royals (GCL)	1	0	1.000	2.37	10	1	0	0	2-...	19.0	17	7	5	1	7-0	10
1995—	Spokane (N'West)	2	4	.333	3.14	22	0	0	0	1-...	48.2	60	26	17	1	20-4	32
1996—	Lansing (Midw.)	7	6	.538	3.74	54	0	0	0	19-...	77.0	78	34	32	4	21-3	55
1997—	Wilmington (Caro.)	1	1	.500	4.91	4	0	0	0	2-...	3.2	3	3	2	0	1-0	1
—	Lansing (Midw.)	1	0	1.000	2.08	9	0	0	0	1-...	13.0	10	6	3	0	6-1	8
—	Kansas City (A.L.)	0	0	...	1.93	4	0	0	0	0-0	4.2	7	2	1	0	2-1	1
—	Wichita (Texas)	2	1	.667	4.00	22	0	0	0	3-...	27.0	32	13	12	1	8-1	12
1998—	Wichita (Texas)	3	4	.429	3.61	52	0	0	0	22-...	72.1	79	36	29	9	27-7	31
—	Kansas City (A.L.)	0	0	...	9.00	2	0	0	0	0-0	2.0	4	2	2	0	0-0	2
—	Omaha (PCL)	0	0	...	7.04	4	0	0	0	1-...	7.2	10	9	6	0	5-2	4
1999—	Kansas City (A.L.)	3	4	.429	3.42	34	0	0	0	2-3	47.1	46	23	18	7	14-2	15
—	Gulf Coast Royals (GCL)	0	0	...	1.80	3	3	0	0	0-...	5.0	1	1	1	0	0-0	4
—	Wichita (Texas)	0	1	.000	2.00	4	2	0	0	0-...	9.0	8	2	2	0	0-0	0
—	Omaha (PCL)	0	0	...	0.00	1	0	0	0	0-...	1.2	3	0	0	0	0-0	0
2000—	Kansas City (A.L.)	8	6	.571	3.91	45	0	0	0	2-8	69.0	70	33	30	7	26-3	44
—	Omaha (PCL)	0	1	.000	3.18	11	0	0	0	4-...	17.0	19	7	6	2	3-1	14
2001—	Kansas City (A.L.)	2	2	.500	6.75	20	0	0	0	0-1	29.1	40	22	22	2	9-1	15
—	Philadelphia (N.L.)■	2	4	.333	3.61	53	0	0	0	0-1	62.1	66	25	25	3	13-1	28
2002—	Philadelphia (N.L.)	1	3	.250	6.70	42	0	0	0	0-1	47.0	56	35	35	7	15-1	30
—	Scranton/W.B. (I.L.)	3	2	.600	1.29	22	0	0	0	7-...	28.0	28	6	4	0	7-1	21
A.L. totals (5 years)		13	12	.520	4.31	105	0	0	0	4-12	152.1	167	82	73	16	51-7	77
N.L. totals (2 years)		3	7	.300	4.94	95	0	0	0	0-2	109.1	122	60	60	10	28-2	58
Major League totals (6 years)		16	19	.457	4.57	200	0	0	0	4-14	261.2	289	142	133	26	79-9	135

SANTIAGO, RAMON — SS — TIGERS

PERSONAL: Born August 31, 1979, in Las Matas de Farfan, Dominican Republic. ... 5-11/150. ... Bats both, throws right. ... Full name: Ramon D. Santiago.

TRANSACTIONS/CAREER NOTES: Signed as non-drafted free agent by Detroit Tigers organization (July 29, 1998). ... On Detroit disabled list (July 24-September 1, 2002).

2002 GAMES PLAYED BY POSITION (MLB): SS—63; DH—1.

Year	Team (League)	Pos.	G	AB	R	H	2B	3B	HR	RBI	BB	SO	SB-CS	Avg.	OBP	SLG	E	Avg.
			BATTING														FIELDING	
1999—	GC Tigers (GCL)	SS	35	134	25	43	9	2	0	11	9	17	20-7	.321	.361	.418	4	.974
—	Oneonta (NY-Penn)	SS	12	50	9	17	1	2	1	8	2	12	5-0	.340	.377	.500	1	.979
2000—	West Mich. (Midw.)	SS	98	379	69	103	15	1	1	42	34	60	39-12	.272	.346	.325	8	.976
2001—	Lakeland (FSL)	DH	120	429	64	115	15	3	2	46	54	60	34-8	.268	.361	.331	...	...
2002—	Erie (East.)	SS	22	75	9	21	0	2	1	7	3	12	6-0	.280	.329	.373	3	.966
—	Toledo (I.L.)	SS	9	28	8	12	1	0	2	6	3	4	0-2	.429	.515	.679	2	.956
—	Detroit (A.L.)	SS-DH	65	222	33	54	5	5	4	20	13	48	8-5	.243	.306	.365	7	.977
Major League totals (1 year)			65	222	33	54	5	5	4	20	13	48	8-5	.243	.306	.365	7	.977

SANTOS, VICTOR — P — RANGERS

PERSONAL: Born October 2, 1976, in San Pedro de Macoris, Dominican Republic ... 6-3/195. ... Throws right, bats right. ... Full name: Victor Irving Santos.

HIGH SCHOOL: Passaic (N.J.).

TRANSACTIONS/CAREER NOTES: Signed as non-drafted free agent by Detroit Tigers organization (June 11, 1995). ... On Toledo disabled list (April 6-July 1, July 7-14 and July 19-September 18, 2000). ... Traded by Tigers with IF Ronnie Merrill to Colorado Rockies for P Jose Paniagua (March 25, 2002). ... On Colorado Springs disabled list (April 14-24, 2002). ... Released by Rockies (October 9, 2002). ... Signed by Texas Rangers organization (November 13, 2002).

CAREER HITTING (MLB): 1-for-2 (.500), 0 R, 0 2B, 0 3B, 0 HR, 0 RBI.

Year	League	W	L	Pct.	ERA	G	GS	CG	ShO	Sv.-Opp.	IP	H	R	ER	HR	BB-IBB	SO
1995—	Dominican Tigers (DSL)	7	5	.583	3.72	15	12	3	2	0-...	77.1	88	46	32	...	18-...	75
1996—	Lakeland (FSL)	2	2	.500	2.22	5	4	0	0	0-...	28.1	19	11	7	2	9-0	25
—	Gulf Coast Tigers (GCL)	3	2	.600	1.98	9	9	0	0	0-...	50.0	44	12	11	1	13-0	39
1997—	Lakeland (FSL)	10	5	.667	3.23	26	26	4	•2	0-...	145.0	136	74	52	10	59-1	108
1998—	Lakeland (FSL)	5	2	.714	2.51	16	15	0	0	1-...	100.1	88	38	28	9	24-1	74
—	Toledo (I.L.)	1	2	.333	11.05	5	3	0	0	0-...	14.2	24	22	18	5	10-0	12
—	Jacksonville (Sou.)	4	2	.667	4.17	6	6	0	0	0-...	36.2	40	20	17	2	15-1	37
1999—	Jacksonville (Sou.)	12	6	.667	3.49	28	•28	2	1	0-...	173.0	150	86	67	16	58-2	*146
2000—	Gulf Coast Tigers (GCL)	0	0	...	0.00	1	1	0	0	0-...	3.0	2	1	0	0	2-0	5
—	Lakeland (FSL)	1	0	1.000	0.00	1	1	0	0	0-...	5.0	5	0	0	0	1-0	4
—	Toledo (I.L.)	0	1	.000	11.37	2	2	0	0	0-...	6.1	7	8	8	4	6-0	2
2001—	Detroit (A.L.)	2	2	.500	3.30	33	7	0	0	0-0	76.1	62	33	28	9	49-4	52
—	Toledo (I.L.)	2	1	.667	6.37	6	6	0	0	0-...	35.1	50	27	25	6	12-0	22
2002—	Colorado Springs (PCL)■	4	9	.308	5.72	21	21	1	1	0-...	118.0	147	81	75	17	43-0	134
—	Colorado (N.L.)	0	4	.000	10.38	24	2	0	0	0-0	26.0	41	30	30	3	22-3	25
A.L. totals (1 year)		2	2	.500	3.30	33	7	0	0	0-0	76.1	62	33	28	9	49-4	52
N.L. totals (1 year)		0	4	.000	10.38	24	2	0	0	0-0	26.0	41	30	30	3	22-3	25
Major League totals (2 years)		2	6	.250	5.10	57	9	0	0	0-0	102.1	103	63	58	12	71-7	77

SARDINHA, DANE — C — REDS

PERSONAL: Born April 8, 1979, in Kahuku, Hawaii. ... 5-11/205. ... Bats right, throws right.

COLLEGE: Pepperdine.

TRANSACTIONS/CAREER NOTES: Selected by Cincinnati Reds organization in second round of free-agent draft (June 5, 2000).

STATISTICAL NOTES: Led California League catchers with 89 assists in 2001.

Year	Team (League)	Pos.	G	AB	R	H	2B	3B	HR	RBI	BB	SO	SB-CS	Avg.	OBP	SLG	E	Avg.
			BATTING														FIELDING	
2001—	Mudville (Calif.)	C	109	422	45	99	24	2	9	55	12	97	0-1	.235	.259	.365	10	.991
2002—	Chattanooga (Sou.)	C	106	394	34	81	20	0	4	40	14	114	0-2	.206	.234	.287	9	.990

SASAKI, KAZUHIRO — P — MARINERS

PERSONAL: Born February 22, 1968, in Sendai City, Japan. ... 6-4/220. ... Throws right, bats right.

COLLEGE: Tohoku Fukushi University (Sendai City, Japan).

TRANSACTIONS/CAREER NOTES: Signed as non-drafted free agent by Seattle Mariners (December 18, 1999).

RECORDS: Holds major league rookie-season record for most saves—37 (2000).

HONORS: Named A.L. Rookie Pitcher of the Year by The Sporting News (2000). ... Named A.L. Rookie of the Year by Baseball Writers' Association of America (2000).

MISCELLANEOUS: Holds Seattle Mariners all-time record for most saves (119).

CAREER HITTING (MLB): 0-for-0 (.000), 0 R, 0 2B, 0 3B, 0 HR, 0 RBI.

Year	League	W	L	Pct.	ERA	G	GS	CG	ShO	Sv.-Opp.	IP	H	R	ER	HR	BB-IBB	SO
1990—	Yokohama (Jap. Cen.)	2	4	.333	5.85	16	...	...	...	2-...	47.2	49	31	31	10	30-...	44
1991—	Yokohama (Jap. Cen.)	6	9	.400	2.00	58	...	...	...	17-...	117.0	72	33	26	7	55-...	137
1992—	Yokohama (Jap. Cen.)	12	6	.667	2.46	53	...	...	...	21-...	87.2	47	32	24	6	40-...	135
1993—	Yokohama (Jap. Cen.)	3	6	.333	3.27	38	...	...	...	20-...	55.0	35	24	20	6	23-...	84
1994—	Yokohama (Jap. Cen.)	3	1	.750	2.15	31	...	...	...	10-...	46.0	27	11	11	5	15-...	59
1995—	Yokohama (Jap. Cen.)	7	2	.778	1.75	47	...	...	...	32-...	56.2	30	12	11	5	17-...	78
1996—	Yokohama (Jap. Cen.)	4	3	.571	2.90	39	...	...	...	25-...	49.2	37	17	16	6	17-...	80
1997—	Yokohama (Jap. Cen.)	3	0	1.000	0.90	49	...	...	...	38-...	60.0	25	6	6	6	18-...	99
1998—	Yokohama (Jap. Cen.)	1	1	.500	0.64	51	...	...	...	45-...	56.0	32	7	4	1	14-...	78
1999—	Yokohama (Jap. Cen.)	1	1	.500	1.93	23	...	...	...	19-...	23.1	19	5	5	1	16-...	34
2000—	Seattle (A.L.)■	2	5	.286	3.16	63	0	0	0	37-40	62.2	42	25	22	10	31-5	78
2001—	Seattle (A.L.)	0	4	.000	3.24	69	0	0	0	45-52	66.2	48	24	24	6	11-2	62
2002—	Seattle (A.L.)	4	5	.444	2.52	61	0	0	0	37-45	60.2	44	24	17	6	20-4	73
Major League totals (3 years)		6	14	.300	2.98	193	0	0	0	119-137	190.0	134	73	63	22	62-11	213

DIVISION SERIES RECORD

Year	League	W	L	Pct.	ERA	G	GS	CG	ShO	Sv.-Opp.	IP	H	R	ER	HR	BB-IBB	SO
2000—	Seattle (A.L.)	0	0	...	0.00	2	0	0	0	2-2	2.0	1	0	0	0	0-0	5
2001—	Seattle (A.L.)	0	0	...	0.00	3	0	0	0	1-1	3.0	1	0	0	0	0-0	5
Division series totals (2 years)		0	0	...	0.00	5	0	0	0	3-3	5.0	2	0	0	0	0-0	10

CHAMPIONSHIP SERIES RECORD

Year	League	W	L	Pct.	ERA	G	GS	CG	ShO	Sv.-Opp.	IP	H	R	ER	HR	BB-IBB	SO
2000—	Seattle (A.L.)	0	0	...	0.00	2	0	0	0	1-1	2.2	3	0	0	0	1-0	3
2001—	Seattle (A.L.)	0	1	.000	54.00	1	0	0	0	0-0	.1	2	2	2	1	0-0	0
Champ. series totals (2 years)		0	1	.000	6.00	3	0	0	0	1-1	3.0	5	2	2	1	1-0	3

ALL-STAR GAME RECORD

	W	L	Pct.	ERA	GS	CG	ShO	Sv.-Opp.	IP	H	R	ER	HR	BB-IBB	SO
All-Star Game totals (2 years)	0	0	...	9.00	0	0	0	1-0	2.0	3	2	2	0	1-0	3

SAUERBECK, SCOTT — P — PIRATES

PERSONAL: Born November 9, 1971, in Cincinnati. ... 6-3/197. ... Throws left, bats right. ... Full name: Scott William Sauerbeck.
HIGH SCHOOL: Northwest (Cincinnati).
COLLEGE: Miami of Ohio.
TRANSACTIONS/CAREER NOTES: Selected by New York Mets organization in 23rd round of free-agent draft (June 2, 1994). ... Selected by Pittsburgh Pirates from Mets organization in Rule 5 major league draft (December 14, 1998). ... On Pittsburgh disabled list (June 14-July 3, 2000); included rehabilitation assignment to Nashville (June 29-July 3).
CAREER HITTING (MLB): 0-for-6 (.000), 0 R, 0 2B, 0 3B, 0 HR, 0 RBI.

Year	League	W	L	Pct.	ERA	G	GS	CG	ShO	Sv.-Opp.	IP	H	R	ER	HR	BB-IBB	SO
1994—	Pittsfield (NY-Penn)	3	1	.750	2.05	21	0	0	0	1-...	48.1	39	16	11	0	19-2	39
1995—	St. Lucie (FSL)	0	1	.000	2.03	20	1	0	0	0-...	26.2	26	10	6	0	14-1	25
—	Capital City (S.Atl.)	5	4	.556	3.27	19	0	0	0	2-...	33.0	28	14	12	2	14-1	33
1996—	St. Lucie (FSL)	6	6	.500	2.27	17	16	2	•2	0-...	99.1	101	37	25	1	27-0	62
—	Binghamton (East.)	3	3	.500	3.47	8	8	2	0	0-...	46.2	48	24	18	4	12-0	30
1997—	Binghamton (East.)	8	9	.471	4.93	27	20	2	0	0-...	131.1	144	89	72	15	50-0	88
—	Norfolk (I.L.)	1	0	1.000	3.60	1	1	0	0	0-...	5.0	3	2	2	0	4-0	4
1998—	Norfolk (I.L.)	7	13	.350	3.93	27	27	2	0	0-...	160.1	178	82	70	8	69-1	119
1999—	Pittsburgh (N.L.)■	4	1	.800	2.00	65	0	0	0	2-5	67.2	53	19	15	6	38-5	55
2000—	Pittsburgh (N.L.)	5	4	.556	4.04	75	0	0	0	1-4	75.2	76	36	34	4	61-8	83
—	Nashville (PCL)	0	0	...	0.00	2	0	0	0	0-...	2.0	1	0	0	0	0-0	0
2001—	Pittsburgh (N.L.)	2	2	.500	5.60	70	0	0	0	2-4	62.2	61	41	39	4	40-6	79
2002—	Pittsburgh (N.L.)	5	4	.556	2.30	78	0	0	0	0-0	62.2	50	18	16	4	27-4	70
Major League totals (4 years)		16	11	.593	3.48	288	0	0	0	5-13	268.2	240	114	104	18	166-23	287

SCHILLING, CURT — P — DIAMONDBACKS

PERSONAL: Born November 14, 1966, in Anchorage, Alaska. ... 6-4/231. ... Throws right, bats right. ... Full name: Curtis Montague Schilling.
HIGH SCHOOL: Shadow Mountain (Phoenix).
JUNIOR COLLEGE: Yavapai College (Ariz.).
TRANSACTIONS/CAREER NOTES: Selected by Boston Red Sox organization in second round of free-agent draft (January 14, 1986). ... Traded by Red Sox with OF Brady Anderson to Baltimore Orioles for P Mike Boddicker (July 29, 1988). ... Traded by Orioles with P Pete Harnisch and OF Steve Finley to Houston Astros for 1B Glenn Davis (January 10, 1991). ... Traded by Astros to Philadelphia Phillies for P Jason Grimsley (April 2, 1992). ... On Philadelphia disabled list (May 17-July 25, 1994); included rehabilitation assignments to Scranton/Wilkes-Barre (July 10-15) and Reading (July 15-20). ... On disabled list (July 19, 1995-remainder of season). ... On Philadelphia disabled list (March 23-May 14, 1996); included rehabilitation assignments to Clearwater (April 23-May 3) and Scranton/Wilkes-Barre (May 3-14). ... On disabled list (August 8-September 3, 1999). ... On Philadelphia disabled list (March 25-April 30, 2000); included rehabilitation assignments to Clearwater (April 6-29) and Scranton/Wilkes-Barre (April 30). ... Traded by Phillies to Arizona Diamondbacks for OF Travis Lee, P Omar Daal, P Vicente Padilla and P Nelson Figueroa (July 26, 2000).
RECORDS: Holds N.L. single-season record for most strikeouts by righthander—319 (1997) and fewest complete games for leader—6 (2001).
HONORS: Named N.L. Pitcher of the Year by The Sporting News (2001 and 2002). ... Named righthanded pitcher on The Sporting News N.L. All-Star team (2001 and 2002). ... Named Sportsman of the Year by The Sporting News (2001).
STATISTICAL NOTES: Tied for International League lead with six balks in 1989. ... Pitched 2-1 one-hit, complete-game victory against New York (September 9, 1992). ... Struck out 15 batters in one game (July 21, 1997; and April 5, 1998). ... Struck out 16 batters in one game (September 1, 1997). ... Pitched 2-0 one-hit, complete-game victory against Milwaukee (April 7, 2002). ... Struck out 17 batters in one game (April 7, 2002).
MISCELLANEOUS: Struck out once in two appearances as pinch hitter with Philadelphia (1996).
CAREER HITTING (MLB): 111-for-710 (.156), 35 R, 13 2B, 1 3B, 0 HR, 29 RBI.

Year	League	W	L	Pct.	ERA	G	GS	CG	ShO	Sv.-Opp.	IP	H	R	ER	HR	BB-IBB	SO
1986—	Elmira (NY-Penn)	7	3	.700	2.59	16	15	2	1	0-...	93.2	92	34	27	3	30-1	75
1987—	Greensboro (S.Atl.)	8	*15	.348	3.82	29	28	7	3	0-...	184.0	179	96	78	10	65-8	*189
1988—	New Britain (East.)	8	5	.615	2.97	21	17	4	1	0-...	106.0	91	44	35	3	40-0	62
—	Charlotte (Sou.)■	5	2	.714	3.18	7	7	2	1	0-...	45.1	36	19	16	3	23-0	32
—	Baltimore (A.L.)	0	3	.000	9.82	4	4	0	0	0-0	14.2	22	19	16	3	10-1	4
1989—	Rochester (I.L.)	•13	11	.542	3.21	27	•27	•9	•3	0-...	*185.1	176	76	66	11	59-0	109
—	Baltimore (A.L.)	0	1	.000	6.23	5	1	0	0	0-0	8.2	10	6	6	2	3-0	6
1990—	Rochester (I.L.)	4	4	.500	3.92	15	14	1	0	0-...	87.1	95	46	38	10	25-1	83
—	Baltimore (A.L.)	1	2	.333	2.54	35	0	0	0	3-9	46.0	38	13	13	1	19-0	32
1991—	Houston (N.L.)■	3	5	.375	3.81	56	0	0	0	8-11	75.2	79	35	32	2	39-7	71
—	Tucson (PCL)	0	1	.000	3.42	13	0	0	0	3-...	23.2	16	9	9	0	12-1	21
1992—	Philadelphia (N.L.)■	14	11	.560	2.35	42	26	10	4	2-3	226.1	165	67	59	11	59-4	147
1993—	Philadelphia (N.L.)	16	7	.696	4.02	34	34	7	2	0-0	235.1	234	114	105	23	57-6	186
1994—	Philadelphia (N.L.)	2	8	.200	4.48	13	13	1	0	0-0	82.1	87	42	41	10	28-3	58
—	Scranton/W.B. (I.L.)	0	0	...	1.80	2	2	0	0	0-...	10.0	6	2	2	0	5-0	6
—	Reading (East.)	0	0	...	0.00	1	1	0	0	0-...	4.0	6	0	0	0	1-0	4

Year	League	W	L	Pct.	ERA	G	GS	CG	ShO	Sv.-Opp.	IP	H	R	ER	HR	BB-IBB	SO
1995—	Philadelphia (N.L.)	7	5	.583	3.57	17	17	1	0	0-0	116.0	96	52	46	12	26-2	114
1996—	Clearwater (FSL)	2	0	1.000	1.29	2	2	0	0	0-...	14.0	9	2	2	0	1-0	17
—	Scranton/W.B. (I.L.)	1	0	1.000	1.38	2	2	0	0	0-...	13.0	9	2	2	0	5-0	10
—	Philadelphia (N.L.)	9	10	.474	3.19	26	26	*8	2	0-0	183.1	149	69	65	16	50-5	182
1997—	Philadelphia (N.L.)	17	11	.607	2.97	35	•35	7	2	0-0	254.1	208	96	84	25	58-3	*319
1998—	Philadelphia (N.L.)	15	14	.517	3.25	35	•35	*15	2	0-0	*268.2	236	101	97	23	61-3	*300
1999—	Philadelphia (N.L.)	15	6	.714	3.54	24	24	8	1	0-0	180.1	159	74	71	25	44-0	152
2000—	Clearwater (FSL)	1	0	1.000	1.31	4	4	0	0	0-...	20.2	10	3	3	0	2-0	23
—	Scranton/W.B. (I.L.)	0	0	...	3.60	1	1	0	0	0-...	5.0	9	2	2	0	1-0	7
—	Philadelphia (N.L.)	6	6	.500	3.91	16	16	4	1	0-0	112.2	110	49	49	17	32-4	96
—	Arizona (N.L.)■	5	6	.455	3.69	13	13	§4	1	0-0	97.2	94	41	40	10	13-0	72
2001—	Arizona (N.L.)	•22	6	.786	2.98	35	•35	*6	1	0-0	*256.2	237	86	85	•37	39-0	293
2002—	Arizona (N.L.)	23	7	.767	3.23	36	35	5	1	0-0	259.1	218	95	93	29	33-1	316
A.L. totals (3 years)		1	6	.143	4.54	44	5	0	0	3-9	69.1	70	38	35	6	32-1	42
N.L. totals (12 years)		154	102	.602	3.32	382	309	76	17	10-14	2348.2	2072	921	867	240	539-38	2306
Major League totals (15 years)		155	108	.589	3.36	426	314	76	17	13-23	2418.0	2142	959	902	246	571-39	2348

DIVISION SERIES RECORD

RECORDS: Holds N.L. career record for most complete games—2. ... Shares career record for most shutouts—1.

Year	League	W	L	Pct.	ERA	G	GS	CG	ShO	Sv.-Opp.	IP	H	R	ER	HR	BB-IBB	SO
2001—	Arizona (N.L.)	2	0	1.000	0.50	2	2	2	1	0-0	18.0	9	1	1	1	2-0	18
2002—	Arizona (N.L.)	0	0	...	1.29	1	1	0	0	0-0	7.0	7	1	1	1	1-0	7
Division series totals (2 years)		2	0	1.000	0.72	3	3	2	1	0-0	25.0	16	2	2	2	3-0	25

CHAMPIONSHIP SERIES RECORD

RECORDS: Holds single-game records for most consecutive strikeouts—5; and most consecutive strikeouts from start of the game—5 (October 6, 1993).

NOTES: Named N.L. Championship Series Most Valuable Player (1993).

Year	League	W	L	Pct.	ERA	G	GS	CG	ShO	Sv.-Opp.	IP	H	R	ER	HR	BB-IBB	SO
1993—	Philadelphia (N.L.)	0	0	...	1.69	2	2	0	0	0-0	16.0	11	4	3	0	5-0	19
2001—	Arizona (N.L.)	1	0	1.000	1.00	1	1	1	0	0-0	9.0	4	1	1	0	2-0	12
Champ. series totals (2 years)		1	0	1.000	1.44	3	3	1	0	0-0	25.0	15	5	4	0	7-0	31

WORLD SERIES RECORD

NOTES: Named co-Most Valuable Player (2001). ... Member of World Series championship team (2001).

Year	League	W	L	Pct.	ERA	G	GS	CG	ShO	Sv.-Opp.	IP	H	R	ER	HR	BB-IBB	SO
1993—	Philadelphia (N.L.)	1	1	.500	3.52	2	2	1	1	0-0	15.1	13	7	6	2	5-0	9
2001—	Arizona (N.L.)	1	0	1.000	1.69	3	3	0	0	0-0	21.1	12	4	4	2	2-0	26
World Series totals (2 years)		2	1	.667	2.45	5	5	1	1	0-0	36.2	25	11	10	4	7-0	35

ALL-STAR GAME RECORD

	W	L	Pct.	ERA	GS	CG	ShO	Sv.-Opp.	IP	H	R	ER	HR	BB-IBB	SO
All-Star Game totals (3 years)	0	1	.000	3.00	2	0	0	0-0	6.0	6	2	2	0	1-0	9

SCHMIDT, JASON — P — GIANTS

PERSONAL: Born January 29, 1973, in Lewiston, Idaho. ... 6-5/205. ... Throws right, bats right. ... Full name: Jason David Schmidt.

HIGH SCHOOL: Kelso (Wash.).

TRANSACTIONS/CAREER NOTES: Selected by Atlanta Braves organization in eighth round of free-agent draft (June 3, 1991). ... On Atlanta disabled list (July 15-August 30, 1996); included rehabilitation assignment to Greenville (August 11-30). ... Traded by Braves to Pittsburgh Pirates (August 30, 1996), completing deal in which Pirates traded P Denny Neagle to Braves for a player to be named later (August 28, 1996). ... On Pittsburgh disabled list (April 15-May 1 and June 10, 2000-remainder of season); included rehabilitation assignment to Gulf Coast Pirates (July 29-August 23). ... On Pittsburgh disabled list (March 31-May 10, 2001); included rehabilitation assignments to Altoona (April 13-May 5) and Nashville (May 5-7). ... Traded by Pirates with OF John Vander Wal to San Francisco Giants for OF Armando Rios and P Ryan Vogelsong (July 30, 2001). ... Granted free agency (November 5, 2001). ... Re-signed by Giants (December 18, 2001). ... On San Francisco disabled list (March 21-April 24, 2002); included rehabilitation assignment to Fresno (April 13-24).

RECORDS: Shares N.L. single-inning record for most consecutive home runs allowed—3 (August 22, 1999, first inning).

STATISTICAL NOTES: Led N.L. with 15 wild pitches in 1998. ... Tied for N.L. lead with four balks in 1999.

MISCELLANEOUS: Received base on balls in only appearance as pinch hitter with Atlanta (1995).

CAREER HITTING (MLB): 34-for-338 (.101), 15 R, 6 2B, 0 3B, 2 HR, 14 RBI.

Year	League	W	L	Pct.	ERA	G	GS	CG	ShO	Sv.-Opp.	IP	H	R	ER	HR	BB-IBB	SO
1991—	Gulf Coast Braves (GCL)	3	4	.429	2.38	11	11	0	0	0-...	45.1	32	21	12	0	23-0	44
1992—	Pulaski (Appl.)	3	4	.429	4.01	11	11	0	0	0-...	58.1	38	36	26	4	31-0	56
—	Macon (S.Atl.)	0	3	.000	4.01	7	7	0	0	0-...	24.2	31	18	11	2	19-0	33
1993—	Durham (Caro.)	7	11	.389	4.94	22	22	0	0	0-...	116.2	128	69	64	12	47-3	110
1994—	Greenville (Sou.)	8	7	.533	3.65	24	24	1	0	0-...	140.2	135	64	57	9	54-1	131
1995—	Atlanta (N.L.)	2	2	.500	5.76	9	2	0	0	0-1	25.0	27	17	16	2	18-3	19
—	Richmond (I.L.)	8	6	.571	*2.25	19	19	0	0	0-...	116.0	97	40	29	2	48-3	95
1996—	Atlanta (N.L.)	3	4	.429	6.75	13	11	0	0	0-0	58.2	69	48	44	8	32-0	48
—	Richmond (I.L.)	3	0	1.000	2.56	7	7	0	0	0-...	45.2	36	17	13	2	19-1	41
—	Greenville (Sou.)	0	0	...	9.00	1	1	0	0	0-...	2.0	4	2	2	0	0-0	2
—	Pittsburgh (N.L.)■	2	2	.500	4.06	6	6	1	0	0-0	37.2	39	19	17	2	21-0	26
1997—	Pittsburgh (N.L.)	10	9	.526	4.60	32	32	2	0	0-0	187.2	193	106	96	16	76-2	136
1998—	Pittsburgh (N.L.)	11	14	.440	4.07	33	33	0	0	0-0	214.1	228	106	97	24	71-3	158
1999—	Pittsburgh (N.L.)	13	11	.542	4.19	33	33	2	0	0-0	212.2	219	110	99	24	85-4	148
2000—	Pittsburgh (N.L.)	2	5	.286	5.40	11	11	0	0	0-0	63.1	71	43	38	6	41-2	51
—	Gulf Coast Pirates (GCL)	0	0	...	2.25	1	1	0	0	0-...	4.0	4	2	1	0	1-0	1
2001—	Altoona (East.)	0	1	.000	0.96	3	3	0	0	0-...	9.1	7	1	1	0	1-0	17
—	Nashville (PCL)	1	0	1.000	0.00	1	1	0	0	0-...	7.0	4	0	0	0	0-0	6
—	Pittsburgh (N.L.)	6	6	.500	4.61	14	14	1	0	0-0	84.0	81	46	43	11	28-2	77
—	San Francisco (N.L.)■	7	1	.875	3.39	11	11	0	0	0-0	66.1	57	29	25	2	33-1	65
2002—	Fresno (PCL)	2	0	1.000	3.00	2	2	0	0	0-...	12.0	11	4	4	0	2-0	12
—	San Francisco (N.L.)	13	8	.619	3.45	29	29	2	2	0-0	185.1	148	78	71	15	73-1	196
Major League totals (8 years)		69	62	.527	4.33	191	182	8	2	0-1	1135.0	1132	602	546	110	478-18	924

DIVISION SERIES RECORD

Year	League	W	L	Pct.	ERA	G	GS	CG	ShO	Sv.-Opp.	IP	H	R	ER	HR	BB-IBB	SO
2002—	San Francisco (N.L.)	0	1	.000	6.75	1	1	0	0	0-0	5.1	3	4	4	0	4-1	5

CHAMPIONSHIP SERIES RECORD

Year	League	W	L	Pct.	ERA	G	GS	CG	ShO	Sv.-Opp.	IP	H	R	ER	HR	BB-IBB	SO
2002—	San Francisco (N.L.)	1	0	1.000	1.17	1	1	0	0	0-0	7.2	4	1	1	1	1-0	8

WORLD SERIES RECORD

Year	League	W	L	Pct.	ERA	G	GS	CG	ShO	Sv.-Opp.	IP	H	R	ER	HR	BB-IBB	SO
2002—	San Francisco (N.L.)	1	0	1.000	5.23	2	2	0	0	0-0	10.1	16	6	6	2	4-0	14

SCHNEIDER, BRIAN — C — EXPOS

PERSONAL: Born November 26, 1976, in Jacksonville. ... 6-1/200. ... Bats left, throws right. ... Full name: Brian Duncan Schneider.
HIGH SCHOOL: Northampton (Pa.).
TRANSACTIONS/CAREER NOTES: Selected by Montreal Expos organization in fifth round of free-agent draft (June 1, 1995).
STATISTICAL NOTES: Led Eastern League catchers with 91 assists and .992 fielding percentage and tied for league lead with seven double plays by catcher in 1999. ... Tied for International League lead with nine sacrifice flies in 2000. ... Led International League catchers with 629 putouts, 79 assists and 712 total chances in 2001.
2002 GAMES PLAYED BY POSITION (MLB): C—65; OF—2.

			BATTING													FIELDING	
Year	Team (League)	Pos.	G	AB	R	H	2B	3B	HR	RBI	BB	SO	SB-CS	Avg.	OBP	SLG	E	Avg.
1995—	GC Expos (GCL)	C	30	97	7	22	3	0	0	4	14	23	2-4	.227	.330	.258	3	.982
1996—	GC Expos (GCL)	C	52	144	26	44	5	2	0	23	24	15	2-3	.306	.415	.368	3	.988
—	Delmarva (S.Atl.)	C	5	9	0	3	0	0	0	1	1	1	0-0	.333	.455	.333	0	1.000
1997—	Cape Fear (S.Atl.)	C	113	381	46	96	20	1	4	49	53	45	3-6	.252	.345	.341	10	.988
1998—	Cape Fear (S.Atl.)	C	38	134	33	40	7	2	7	30	16	9	6-3	.299	.381	.537	6	.980
—	Jupiter (FSL)	C	82	302	32	82	12	1	3	30	22	38	4-4	.272	.321	.348	11	.981
1999—	Harrisburg (East.)	C-DH-1B	121	421	48	111	19	1	17	66	32	56	2-2	.264	.318	.435	6	†.992
2000—	Ottawa (I.L.)	C-1B	67	238	22	59	22	3	4	31	16	42	1-0	.248	.285	.416	8	.982
—	Montreal (N.L.)	C	45	115	6	27	6	0	0	11	7	24	0-1	.235	.276	.287	6	.974
2001—	Ottawa (I.L.)	C	97	338	33	93	27	1	6	43	27	55	2-0	.275	.336	.414	4	.994
—	Montreal (N.L.)	C	27	41	4	13	3	0	1	6	6	3	0-0	.317	.396	.463	0	1.000
2002—	Montreal (N.L.)	C-OF	73	207	21	57	19	2	5	29	21	41	1-2	.275	.339	.459	3	.993
Major League totals (3 years)			145	363	31	97	28	2	6	46	34	68	1-3	.267	.327	.405	9	.988

SCHOENEWEIS, SCOTT — P — ANGELS

PERSONAL: Born October 2, 1973, in Long Branch, N.J. ... 6-0/185. ... Throws left, bats left. ... Full name: Scott David Schoeneweis.
HIGH SCHOOL: Lenape (Medford, N.J.).
COLLEGE: Duke.
TRANSACTIONS/CAREER NOTES: Selected by California Angels organization in third round of free-agent draft (June 4, 1996). ... Angels franchise renamed Anaheim Angels for 1997 season. ... On Anaheim disabled list (June 17-July 26, 2000); included rehabilitation assignments to Lake Elsinore (July 14-17) and Edmonton (July 18-24).
CAREER HITTING (MLB): 1-for-5 (.200), 0 R, 0 2B, 0 3B, 0 HR, 1 RBI.

Year	League	W	L	Pct.	ERA	G	GS	CG	ShO	Sv.-Opp.	IP	H	R	ER	HR	BB-IBB	SO
1996—	Lake Elsinore (Calif.)	8	3	.727	3.94	14	12	0	0	0-...	93.2	86	47	41	6	27-0	83
1997—	Midland (Texas)	7	5	.583	5.96	20	20	3	0	0-...	113.1	145	84	75	7	39-0	84
1998—	Vancouver (PCL)	11	8	.579	4.50	27	27	2	0	0-...	180.0	188	102	90	18	59-0	133
1999—	Anaheim (A.L.)	1	1	.500	5.49	31	0	0	0	0-0	39.1	47	27	24	4	14-1	22
—	Edmonton (PCL)	2	4	.333	7.64	9	7	0	0	0-...	35.1	58	35	30	6	12-0	29
2000—	Anaheim (A.L.)	7	10	.412	5.45	27	27	1	1	0-0	170.0	183	112	103	21	67-2	78
—	Lake Elsinore (Calif.)	0	0	...	1.93	1	1	0	0	0-...	4.2	3	1	1	0	3-0	3
—	Edmonton (PCL)	0	0	...	0.00	1	1	0	0	0-...	7.0	2	1	0	0	1-0	6
2001—	Anaheim (A.L.)	10	11	.476	5.08	32	32	1	0	0-0	205.1	227	122	116	21	77-2	104
2002—	Anaheim (A.L.)	9	8	.529	4.88	54	15	0	0	1-4	118.0	119	68	64	17	49-4	65
Major League totals (4 years)		27	30	.474	5.19	144	74	2	1	1-4	532.2	576	329	307	63	207-9	269

DIVISION SERIES RECORD

Year	League	W	L	Pct.	ERA	G	GS	CG	ShO	Sv.-Opp.	IP	H	R	ER	HR	BB-IBB	SO
2002—	Anaheim (A.L.)	0	0	...	27.00	3	0	0	0	0-1	.1	2	1	1	0	0-0	0

CHAMPIONSHIP SERIES RECORD

Year	League	W	L	Pct.	ERA	G	GS	CG	ShO	Sv.-Opp.	IP	H	R	ER	HR	BB-IBB	SO
2002—	Anaheim (A.L.)	0	0	...	0.00	1	0	0	0	0-0	.2	0	0	0	0	0-0	0

WORLD SERIES RECORD

NOTES: Member of World Series championship team (2002).

Year	League	W	L	Pct.	ERA	G	GS	CG	ShO	Sv.-Opp.	IP	H	R	ER	HR	BB-IBB	SO
2002—	Anaheim (A.L.)	0	0	...	0.00	2	0	0	0	0-0	2.0	1	0	0	0	1-0	2

SCUTARO, MARCOS — IF — METS

PERSONAL: Born October 30, 1975, in Yaracuy, Venezuela. ... 5-10/170. ... Bats right, throws right.
TRANSACTIONS/CAREER NOTES: Signed as non-drafted free agent by Cleveland Indians organization (July 26, 1994). ... Traded by Indians to Milwaukee Brewers (August 30, 2000); completed trade in which Indians traded OF Richie Sexson, P Paul Rigdon, P Kane Davis and a player to be named to Brewers for P Bob Wickman, P Jason Bere and P Steve Woodard (July 28, 2000). ... Claimed on waivers by New York Mets (April 5, 2002).

STATISTICAL NOTES: Led Eastern League second basemen in fielding percentage with .977 in 1998. ... Led International League second basemen with 250 putouts and 551 total chances in 2000. ... Led International League second basemen with .973 fielding percentage in 2001.
2002 GAMES PLAYED BY POSITION (MLB): 2B—12; SS—6; 3B—3; OF—1.

			BATTING														FIELDING	
Year	Team (League)	Pos.	G	AB	R	H	2B	3B	HR	RBI	BB	SO	SB-CS	Avg.	OBP	SLG	E	Avg.
1995—	Dom. Indians (DSL)	3B	66	262	71	103	18	6	0	38	20	11	32-...	.393	...	.508	17	.931
1996—	Columbus (S.Atl.)	2B-SS-3B	85	315	66	79	12	3	10	45	38	86	6-3	.251	.334	.403	17	.959
1997—	Kinston (Caro.)	2B-3B	97	378	58	103	17	6	10	59	35	72	23-7	.272	.346	.429	11	.972
	—Buffalo (A.A.)	2B-3B-SS	21	57	8	15	3	0	1	6	6	8	0-1	.263	.328	.368	3	.959
1998—	Akron (East.)	2B-SS	124	462	68	146	27	6	11	62	47	71	33-16	.316	.387	.472	15	†.976
	—Buffalo (I.L.)	2B-3B	8	26	3	6	3	0	0	4	0	2	0-0	.231	.231	.346	2	.939
1999—	Buffalo (I.L.)	2B-SS	129	462	76	126	24	2	8	51	61	69	21-6	.273	.362	.385	16	.974
2000—	Buffalo (I.L.)	2B-SS	124	425	67	117	20	5	5	54	61	53	9-6	.275	.373	.381	15	.976
	—Indianapolis (I.L.)■	2B-SS	4	13	5	7	1	1	1	3	1	2	1-0	.538	.571	1.000	0	1.000
2001—	Indianapolis (I.L.)	2B-3B-SS	132	495	87	146	29	3	11	50	62	83	11-11	.295	.382	.432	19	†.968
2002—	Norfolk (I.L.)■	2B-SS-OF-3B	97	354	48	113	22	6	7	28	30	61	7-8	.319	.375	.475	10	.974
	—New York (N.L.)	2B-SS-3B-OF	27	36	2	8	0	1	1	6	0	11	0-1	.222	.216	.361	1	.968
Major League totals (1 year)			27	36	2	8	0	1	1	6	0	11	0-1	.222	.216	.361	1	.968

SEANEZ, RUDY — P

PERSONAL: Born October 20, 1968, in Brawley, Calif. ... 5-11/205. ... Throws right, bats right. ... Full name: Rudy Caballero Seanez. ... Name pronounced see-AHN-yez.
HIGH SCHOOL: Brawley (Calif.) Union.
TRANSACTIONS/CAREER NOTES: Selected by Cleveland Indians organization in fourth round of free-agent draft (June 10, 1986). ... On disabled list (May 4-July 11 and August 9-29, 1987). ... On Cleveland disabled list (April 1-16 and July 30-September 2, 1991); included rehabilitation assignment to Colorado Springs (August 14-September 2). ... Traded by Indians to Los Angeles Dodgers for P Dennis Cook and P Mike Christopher (December 10, 1991). ... On disabled list (March 29, 1992-entire season). ... Traded by Dodgers to Colorado Rockies for 2B Jody Reed (November 17, 1992). ... On Colorado disabled list (April 4-July 16, 1993); included rehabilitation assignments to Central Valley (June 16-July 4) and Colorado Springs (July 4-15). ... Granted free agency (July 16, 1993). ... Signed by San Diego Padres organization (July 22, 1993). ... Released by Padres (November 18, 1993). ... Signed by Dodgers organization (January 12, 1994). ... On Los Angeles disabled list (May 28-June 16, 1995); included rehabilitation assignment to San Bernardino (June 9-16). ... Granted free agency (October 15, 1996). ... Signed by New York Mets organization (January 15, 1997). ... Traded by Mets to Kansas City Royals for future considerations (May 30, 1997). ... Granted free agency (October 15, 1997). ... Signed by Atlanta Braves organization (December 9, 1997). ... On disabled list (August 21, 1999-remainder of season). ... Granted free agency (November 2, 1999). ... Re-signed by Braves (December 12, 1999). ... On Atlanta disabled list (March 23-April 27, 2000 and June 14-remainder of season); included rehabilitation assignment to Greenville (April 22-27). ... Granted free agency (October 30, 2000). ... Signed by Padres organization (February 14, 2001). ... On Portland disabled list (April 5-May 6, 2001). ... On San Diego disabled list (June 6-21, 2001). ... Traded by Padres to Braves for a player to be named later (August 31, 2001); Padres acquired P Winston Abreu to complete deal (September 6, 2001). ... Granted free agency (November 5, 2001). ... Signed by Texas Rangers (January 28, 2002). ... On Texas disabled list (May 30-September 2, 2002); included rehabilitation assignments to Oklahoma (June 24-26 and August 24-September 2). ... Granted free agency (October 28, 2002).
STATISTICAL NOTES: Pitched 4-0 no-hit victory against Pulaski (August 2, 1986).
CAREER HITTING (MLB): 0-for-4 (.000), 1 R, 0 2B, 0 3B, 0 HR, 0 RBI.

Year	League	W	L	Pct.	ERA	G	GS	CG	ShO	Sv.-Opp.	IP	H	R	ER	HR	BB-IBB	SO
1986—	Burlington (Appl.)	5	2	.714	3.20	13	12	1	1	0-...	76.0	59	37	27	5	32-0	56
1987—	Waterloo (Midw.)	0	4	.000	6.75	10	10	0	0	0-...	34.2	35	29	26	6	23-0	23
1988—	Waterloo (Midw.)	6	6	.500	4.69	22	22	1	1	0-...	113.1	98	69	59	10	68-0	93
1989—	Kinston (Caro.)	8	10	.444	4.14	25	25	1	0	0-...	113.0	94	66	52	0	*111-1	149
	—Colorado Springs (PCL)	0	0	...	0.00	1	0	0	0	0-...	1.0	1	0	0	0	0-0	0
	—Cleveland (A.L.)	0	0	...	3.60	5	0	0	0	0-0	5.0	1	2	2	0	4-1	7
1990—	Canton/Akron (East.)	1	0	1.000	2.16	15	0	0	0	5-...	16.2	9	4	4	0	12-0	27
	—Cleveland (A.L.)	2	1	.667	5.60	24	0	0	0	0-0	27.1	22	17	17	2	25-1	24
	—Colorado Springs (PCL)	1	4	.200	6.75	12	0	0	0	1-...	12.0	15	10	9	2	10-0	7
1991—	Colorado Springs (PCL)	0	0	...	7.27	16	0	0	0	0-...	17.1	17	14	14	2	22-0	19
	—Canton/Akron (East.)	4	2	.667	2.58	25	0	0	0	7-...	38.1	17	12	11	2	30-1	73
	—Cleveland (A.L.)	0	0	...	16.20	5	0	0	0	0-1	5.0	10	12	9	2	7-0	7
1992—	Los Angeles (N.L.)■									Did not play.							
1993—	Central Valley (Calif.)■	0	2	.000	9.72	5	1	0	0	0-...	8.1	9	9	9	0	11-0	7
	—Colorado Springs (PCL)	0	0	...	9.00	3	0	0	0	0-...	3.0	3	3	3	1	1-0	5
	—Las Vegas (PCL)■	0	1	.000	6.41	14	0	0	0	0-...	19.2	24	15	14	2	11-0	14
	—San Diego (N.L.)	0	0	...	13.50	3	0	0	0	0-0	3.1	8	6	5	1	2-0	1
1994—	Albuquerque (PCL)■	2	1	.667	5.32	20	0	0	0	9-...	22.0	28	14	13	3	13-1	26
	—Los Angeles (N.L.)	1	1	.500	2.66	17	0	0	0	0-1	23.2	24	7	7	2	9-1	18
1995—	Los Angeles (N.L.)	1	3	.250	6.75	37	0	0	0	3-4	34.2	39	27	26	5	18-3	29
	—San Bernardino (Calif.)	2	0	1.000	0.00	4	0	0	0	1-...	6.0	2	0	0	0	3-0	5
1996—	Albuquerque (PCL)	0	2	.000	6.52	21	0	0	0	6-...	19.1	27	18	14	0	11-1	20
1997—	Norfolk (I.L.)■	1	0	1.000	4.05	9	0	0	0	0-...	13.1	12	8	6	1	11-0	17
	—Omaha (A.A.)■	2	5	.286	6.51	28	3	0	0	0-...	47.0	53	42	34	13	25-0	46
1998—	Richmond (I.L.)■	2	0	1.000	1.29	16	0	0	0	7-...	21.0	13	9	3	1	7-1	33
	—Atlanta (N.L.)	4	1	.800	2.75	34	0	0	0	2-4	36.0	25	13	11	2	16-0	50
1999—	Atlanta (N.L.)	6	1	.857	3.35	56	0	0	0	3-8	53.2	47	21	20	3	21-1	41
2000—	Greenville (Sou.)	0	0	...	0.00	2	1	0	0	0-...	2.0	2	0	0	0	0-0	3
	—Atlanta (N.L.)	2	4	.333	4.29	23	0	0	0	2-3	21.0	15	11	10	3	9-1	20
2001—	Lake Elsinore (Calif.)■	2	0	1.000	2.08	7	0	0	0	0-...	8.2	7	3	2	1	2-0	8
	—San Diego (N.L.)	0	2	.000	2.63	26	0	0	0	1-3	24.0	15	8	7	3	15-0	24
	—Atlanta (N.L.)■	0	0	...	3.00	12	0	0	0	0-0	12.0	8	4	4	1	4-0	17
2002—	Texas (A.L.)■	1	3	.250	5.73	33	0	0	0	0-4	33.0	28	25	21	5	24-1	40
	—Oklahoma (PCL)	0	0	...	4.50	4	0	0	0	0-...	4.0	4	2	2	0	0-0	3
A.L. totals (4 years)		3	4	.429	6.27	67	0	0	0	0-5	70.1	61	56	49	9	60-3	78
N.L. totals (7 years)		14	12	.538	3.89	208	0	0	0	11-23	208.1	181	97	90	20	94-6	200
Major League totals (11 years)		17	16	.515	4.49	275	0	0	0	11-28	278.2	242	153	139	29	154-9	278

DIVISION SERIES RECORD

Year League	W	L	Pct.	ERA	G	GS	CG	ShO	Sv.-Opp.	IP	H	R	ER	HR	BB-IBB	SO
1998— Atlanta (N.L.)	0	0	...	0.00	1	0	0	0	0-0	1.0	0	0	0	0	0-0	0
2001— Atlanta (N.L.)	1	0	1.000	0.00	1	0	0	0	0-0	1.0	0	0	0	0	1-0	0
Division series totals (2 years)	1	0	1.000	0.00	2	0	0	0	0-0	2.0	0	0	0	0	1-0	0

CHAMPIONSHIP SERIES RECORD

Year League	W	L	Pct.	ERA	G	GS	CG	ShO	Sv.-Opp.	IP	H	R	ER	HR	BB-IBB	SO
1998— Atlanta (N.L.)	0	0	...	6.00	4	0	0	0	0-0	3.0	2	2	2	0	1-0	4
2001— Atlanta (N.L.)	0	0	...	0.00	2	0	0	0	0-0	2.0	1	0	0	0	3-2	3
Champ. series totals (2 years)	0	0	...	3.60	6	0	0	0	0-0	5.0	3	2	2	0	4-2	7

SEARS, TODD — 1B — TWINS

PERSONAL: Born October 23, 1975, in Des Moines, Iowa. ... 6-5/215. ... Bats left, throws right. ... Full name: Todd A. Sears.
HIGH SCHOOL: Ankeny (Iowa).
COLLEGE: Nebraska.
TRANSACTIONS/CAREER NOTES: Selected by California Angels organization in 19th round of free-agent draft (June 2, 1994); did not sign. ... Selected by Colorado Rockies organization in third round of free-agent draft (June 3, 1997). ... Traded by Rockies with cash to Minnesota Twins for 2B Todd Walker and OF Butch Huskey (July 16, 2000).
STATISTICAL NOTES: Led Pacific Coast League first basemen with .993 fielding percentage in 2001.
2002 GAMES PLAYED BY POSITION (MLB): 1B—6.

		BATTING														FIELDING	
Year Team (League)	Pos.	G	AB	R	H	2B	3B	HR	RBI	BB	SO	SB-CS	Avg.	OBP	SLG	E	Avg.
1997— Portland (N'West)	1B	55	200	37	54	13	1	2	29	41	49	2-0	.270	.393	.375	6	.989
1998— Asheville (S.Atl.)	3B	130	459	71	133	26	2	11	82	72	89	10-4	.290	.387	.427	•31	.888
1999— Salem (Caro.)	1B-3B	109	385	58	108	21	0	14	59	58	99	11-2	.281	.379	.444	26	.950
2000— Carolina (Sou.)	1B	86	299	54	90	21	0	12	72	72	76	12-3	.301	.434	.492	12	.982
— New Britain (East.)■	1B	40	140	15	44	8	1	3	15	18	40	1-0	.314	.396	.450	2	.993
— Salt Lake (PCL)	1B	3	11	2	4	1	0	1	4	1	2	0-0	.364	.417	.727	0	1.000
2001— Edmonton (PCL)	1B-3B	118	408	61	127	25	2	13	50	41	71	2-1	.311	.376	.478	6	†.993
2002— Edmonton (PCL)	1B	129	484	88	150	36	4	20	100	59	142	2-1	.310	.388	.525	3	.997
— Minnesota (A.L.)	1B	7	12	2	4	2	0	0	0	0	1	0-0	.333	.333	.500	0	1.000
Major League totals (1 year)		7	12	2	4	2	0	0	0	0	1	0-0	.333	.333	.500	0	1.000

SEAY, BOBBY — P — DEVIL RAYS

PERSONAL: Born June 20, 1978, in Sarasota, Fla. ... 6-2/221. ... Throws left, bats left. ... Full name: Robery Michael Seay.
HIGH SCHOOL: Sarasota (Fla.).
TRANSACTIONS/CAREER NOTES: Selected by Chicago White Sox organization in first round (12th pick overall) of free-agent draft (June 4, 1996). ... Rights relinquished by White Sox (August 15, 1996). ... Signed by Tampa Bay Devil Rays organization (November 8, 1996). ... On disabled list (June 9, 1997-remainder of season). ... On Orlando disabled list (May 8-June 30, 2001). ... On Tampa Bay disabled list (March 22-June 3, 2002); included rehabilitation assignment to Orlando (May 7-June 3). ... On Orlando disabled list (June 9-July 7, 2002).
MISCELLANEOUS: Member of 2000 U.S. Olympic baseball team.
CAREER HITTING (MLB): 0-for-0 (.000), 0 R, 0 2B, 0 3B, 0 HR, 0 RBI.

Year League	W	L	Pct.	ERA	G	GS	CG	ShO	Sv.-Opp.	IP	H	R	ER	HR	BB-IBB	SO
1997— Charleston, S.C. (S.Atl.)	3	4	.429	4.55	13	13	0	0	0-...	61.1	56	35	31	2	37-0	64
1998— Charleston, S.C. (S.Atl.)	1	7	.125	4.30	15	15	0	0	0-...	69.0	59	40	33	10	29-0	74
1999— St. Petersburg (FSL)	2	6	.250	3.00	12	11	0	0	0-...	57.0	56	25	19	0	23-0	45
— Orlando (Sou.)	1	2	.333	7.94	6	6	0	0	0-...	17.0	22	15	15	2	15-0	16
2000— Orlando (Sou.)	8	7	.533	3.88	24	24	0	0	0-...	132.1	132	64	57	13	53-1	106
2001— Orlando (Sou.)	2	5	.286	5.98	15	13	0	0	0-...	64.2	81	48	43	9	26-0	49
— Tampa Bay (A.L.)	1	1	.500	6.23	12	0	0	0	0-0	13.0	13	11	9	3	5-1	12
2002— Orlando (Sou.)	2	0	1.000	3.28	15	3	0	0	0-...	35.2	31	16	13	2	15-0	24
— Durham (I.L.)	0	0	...	6.00	10	0	0	0	0-...	15.0	15	10	10	1	2-0	14
Major League totals (1 year)	1	1	.500	6.23	12	0	0	0	0-0	13.0	13	11	9	3	5-1	12

SEDLACEK, SHAWN — P — ROYALS

PERSONAL: Born June 29, 1977, in Cedar Rapids, Iowa. ... 6-4/200. ... Throws right, bats right. ... Full name: Shawn Patrick Sedlacek.
HIGH SCHOOL: Kennedy (Cedar Rapids, Iowa).
JUNIOR COLLEGE: Indian Hills Community College (Iowa).
COLLEGE: Iowa State.
TRANSACTIONS/CAREER NOTES: Selected by Kansas City Royals organization in 14th round of free-agent draft (June 2, 1998).
CAREER HITTING (MLB): 0-for-6 (.000), 0 R, 0 2B, 0 3B, 0 HR, 0 RBI.

Year League	W	L	Pct.	ERA	G	GS	CG	ShO	Sv.-Opp.	IP	H	R	ER	HR	BB-IBB	SO
1998— Spokane (N'West)	9	2	.818	3.45	16	13	0	0	0-...	86.0	89	43	33	2	18-0	62
1999— Wilmington (Caro.)	4	6	.400	5.28	17	17	1	0	0-...	92.0	111	61	54	7	26-0	69
2000— Wichita (Texas)	15	6	.714	3.66	35	16	1	0	3-...	140.1	153	69	57	10	43-4	81
2001— Wichita (Texas)	6	7	.462	3.63	14	14	1	1	0-...	86.2	85	37	35	7	14-1	66
— Omaha (PCL)	5	4	.556	5.00	14	13	0	0	0-...	81.0	98	49	45	13	22-2	44
2002— Wichita (Texas)	2	1	.667	1.47	3	3	0	0	0-...	18.1	14	6	3	0	4-0	16
— Kansas City (A.L.)	3	5	.375	6.72	16	14	0	0	0-0	84.1	99	64	63	16	36-2	52
— Omaha (PCL)	6	5	.545	3.70	11	11	2	1	0-...	80.1	67	37	33	6	15-0	66
Major League totals (1 year)	3	5	.375	6.72	16	14	0	0	0-0	84.1	99	64	63	16	36-2	52

SEGUI, DAVID — 1B/DH — ORIOLES

PERSONAL: Born July 19, 1966, in Kansas City, Kan. ... 6-1/202. ... Bats both, throws left. ... Full name: David Vincent Segui. ... Son of Diego Segui, pitcher with five major league teams (1962-75 and 1977); and brother of Dan Segui, minor league infielder (1987-90). ... Name pronounced seh-GHEE.

HIGH SCHOOL: Bishop Ward (Kansas City, Kan.).

JUNIOR COLLEGE: Kansas City Kansas Community College.

COLLEGE: Louisiana Tech.

TRANSACTIONS/CAREER NOTES: Selected by Baltimore Orioles organization in 18th round of free-agent draft (June 2, 1987). ... On Rochester disabled list (April 19-26, 1991). ... On suspended list (August 16-19, 1993). ... Traded by Orioles to New York Mets for SS Kevin Baez and P Tom Wegmann (March 27, 1994). ... On disabled list (June 20-July 5, 1994). ... Traded by Mets to Montreal Expos for P Reid Cornelius (June 8, 1995). ... On disabled list (July 4-August 16, 1996). ... On disabled list (June 4-21, 1997). ... On suspended list (July 26, 1997). ... Granted free agency (October 28, 1997). ... Signed by Seattle Mariners (December 12, 1997). ... Traded by Mariners to Toronto Blue Jays for P Tom Davey and P Steve Sinclair (July 28, 1999). ... On suspended list (July 30-31, 1999). ... On Toronto disabled list (August 8-September 2, 1999). ... Granted free agency (October 29, 1999). ... Re-signed by Blue Jays (January 18, 2000). ... Traded by Blue Jays with cash to Texas Rangers as part of three-way deal in which Rangers sent 1B Lee Stevens to Montreal Expos and Expos sent 1B Brad Fullmer to Blue Jays (March 16, 2000). ... Traded by Rangers to Cleveland Indians for OF Ricky Ledee (July 28, 2000). ... Granted free agency (October 30, 2000). ... Signed by Orioles (December 21, 2000). ... On disabled list (April 28-May 15 and July 16-August 4, 2001; and May 18, 2002-remainder of season).

STATISTICAL NOTES: Led N.L. first basemen with .996 fielding percentage in 1994. ... Switch-hit home runs in one game (April 1, 1998). ... Led A.L. first basemen with .999 fielding percentage in 1998. ... Had 15-game hitting streak (May 10-29, 1999). ... Career major league grand slams: 6.

2002 GAMES PLAYED BY POSITION (MLB): DH—19; 1B—7.

		BATTING														FIELDING	
Year Team (League)	Pos.	G	AB	R	H	2B	3B	HR	RBI	BB	SO	SB-CS	Avg.	OBP	SLG	E	Avg.
1988—Hagerstown (Caro.)	1B-OF	60	190	35	51	12	4	3	31	22	23	0-0	.268	.347	.421	9	.976
1989—Frederick (Caro.)	1B	83	284	43	90	19	0	10	50	41	32	2-1	.317	.407	.489	4	.995
—Hagerstown (East.)	1B	44	173	22	56	14	1	1	27	16	16	0-0	.324	.383	.434	1	.998
1990—Rochester (I.L.)	1B-OF	86	307	55	103	28	0	2	51	45	28	5-4	.336	.415	.446	3	.996
—Baltimore (A.L.)	1B-DH	40	123	14	30	7	0	2	15	11	15	0-0	.244	.311	.350	3	.990
1991—Rochester (I.L.)	1B-OF	28	96	9	26	2	0	1	10	15	6	1-1	.271	.365	.323	0	1.000
—Baltimore (A.L.)	OF-1B-DH	86	212	15	59	7	0	2	22	12	19	1-1	.278	.316	.340	3	.990
1992—Baltimore (A.L.)	1B-OF	115	189	21	44	9	0	1	17	20	23	1-0	.233	.306	.296	1	.998
1993—Baltimore (A.L.)	1B-DH	146	450	54	123	27	0	10	60	58	53	2-1	.273	.351	.400	5	.996
1994—New York (N.L.)■	1B-OF	92	336	46	81	17	1	10	43	33	43	0-0	.241	.308	.387	5	†.993
1995—New York (N.L.)	OF-1B	33	73	9	24	3	1	2	11	12	9	1-3	.329	.420	.479	0	1.000
—Montreal (N.L.)■	1B-OF	97	383	59	117	22	3	10	57	28	38	1-4	.305	.355	.457	3	.997
1996—Montreal (N.L.)	1B	115	416	69	119	30	1	11	58	60	54	4-4	.286	.375	.442	7	.993
1997—Montreal (N.L.)	1B	125	459	75	141	22	3	21	68	57	66	1-0	.307	.380	.505	6	.995
1998—Seattle (A.L.)■	1B-OF	143	522	79	159	36	1	19	84	49	80	3-1	.305	.359	.487	1	†.999
1999—Seattle (A.L.)	1B	90	345	43	101	22	3	9	39	32	43	1-2	.293	.352	.452	3	.996
—Toronto (A.L.)■	DH-1B	31	95	14	30	5	0	5	13	8	17	0-0	.316	.365	.526	1	.955
2000—Texas (A.L.)■	DH-1B	93	351	52	118	29	1	11	57	34	51	0-1	.336	.391	.519	0	1.000
—Cleveland (A.L.)■	1B-DH-OF	57	223	41	74	13	0	8	46	19	33	0-0	.332	.384	.498	0	1.000
2001—Baltimore (A.L.)■	1B-DH	82	292	48	88	18	1	10	46	49	61	1-1	.301	.406	.473	9	.983
2002—Baltimore (A.L.)	DH-1B	26	95	10	25	4	0	2	16	11	22	0-0	.263	.336	.368	0	1.000
American League totals (9 years)		909	2897	391	851	177	6	79	415	303	417	9-7	.294	.359	.441	26	.995
National League totals (4 years)		462	1667	258	482	94	9	54	237	190	210	7-11	.289	.361	.454	21	.995
Major League totals (13 years)		1371	4564	649	1333	271	15	133	652	493	627	16-18	.292	.359	.445	47	.995

SELBY, BILL — OF/IF — INDIANS

PERSONAL: Born June 11, 1970, in Monroeville, Ala. ... 5-10/195. ... Bats left, throws right. ... Full name: William Frank Selby.

HIGH SCHOOL: Horn Lake (Mich.).

JUNIOR COLLEGE: Northwest Mississippi Community College.

COLLEGE: Southern Mississippi.

TRANSACTIONS/CAREER NOTES: Selected by Boston Red Sox organization in 13th round of free-agent draft (June 1, 1992). ... Contract sold by Red Sox to Yokohama BayStars, Japan Central League (October 22, 1996). ... Signed by Cleveland Indians organization (February 1, 1998). ... Granted free agency (October 16, 1998). ... Re-signed by Indians organization (February 3, 1999). ... Granted free agency (October 15, 1999). ... Re-signed by Indians organization (December 23, 1999). ... Released by Indians (October 20, 2000). ... Signed by Cincinnati Reds organization (May 29, 2001). ... On Louisville disabled list (August 28, 2001-remainder of season). ... Granted free agency (October 15, 2001). ... Signed by Cleveland Indians organization (December 18, 2001).

STATISTICAL NOTES: Led New York-Pennsylvania League with six intentional bases on balls received in 1992. ... Career major league grand slams: 1.

2002 GAMES PLAYED BY POSITION (MLB): 3B—33; OF—18; 2B—6.

		BATTING														FIELDING	
Year Team (League)	Pos.	G	AB	R	H	2B	3B	HR	RBI	BB	SO	SB-CS	Avg.	OBP	SLG	E	Avg.
1992—Elmira (NY-Penn)	3B-2B	73	275	38	72	16	1	10	41	31	53	4-4	.262	.339	.436	16	.930
1993—Lynchburg (Caro.)	3B-1B	113	394	57	99	22	1	7	38	24	66	1-2	.251	.294	.365	8	.954
1994—Lynchburg (Caro.)	3B-2B-1B	97	352	58	109	20	2	19	69	28	62	3-1	.310	.367	.540	23	.924
—New Britain (East.)	3B	35	107	15	28	5	0	1	18	15	16	0-1	.262	.336	.336	6	.930
1995—Trenton (East.)	3B-2B-DH	117	451	64	129	29	2	13	68	46	52	4-6	.286	.350	.446	29	.918
1996—Pawtucket (I.L.)	2B-3B-OF	71	260	39	66	14	5	11	47	22	39	0-3	.254	.313	.473	16	.936
—Boston (A.L.)	2B-3B-OF	40	95	12	26	4	0	3	6	9	11	1-1	.274	.337	.411	4	.948
1997—Yokohama (Jap. Cen.)		90	171	19	39	4	1	5	17	21	37	3-...	.228	...	.351	...	...
1998—Buffalo (I.L.)■	3B-OF-2B	97	334	45	85	23	0	14	52	38	50	3-0	.254	.328	.449	4	.967
—Akron (East.)	OF-3B-2B	20	77	15	30	7	1	3	10	3	11	0-0	.390	.415	.623	1	.977
1999—Buffalo (I.L.)	3B-OF-2B	122	447	75	132	32	5	20	85	57	63	4-3	.295	.372	.523	5	.967
2000—Buffalo (I.L.)	3B-OF-2B	100	384	69	106	21	6	21	86	48	61	1-1	.276	.355	.526	15	.949
—Cleveland (A.L.)	OF-DH-2B-3B	30	46	8	11	1	0	0	4	1	9	0-0	.239	.271	.261	0	1.000

Year	Team (League)	Pos.	G	AB	R	H	2B	3B	HR	RBI	BB	SO	SB-CS	Avg.	OBP	SLG	E	Avg.
			BATTING														FIELDING	
2001	—Louisville (I.L.)■	2B-1B-3B-OF	88	330	47	85	19	1	14	56	25	47	1-0	.258	.310	.448	10	.975
	—Cincinnati (N.L.)	2B-3B-1B	36	92	7	21	7	1	2	12	5	13	0-0	.228	.273	.391	2	.981
2002	—Buffalo (I.L.)■	OF-2B-3B	51	184	28	55	14	2	5	22	20	33	4-1	.299	.364	.478	5	.962
	—Cleveland (A.L.)	3B-OF-2B	65	159	15	34	7	2	6	21	15	27	0-1	.214	.278	.396	5	.952
American League totals (3 years)			135	300	35	71	12	2	9	31	25	47	1-2	.237	.296	.380	9	.956
National League totals (1 year)			36	92	7	21	7	1	2	12	5	13	0-0	.228	.273	.391	2	.981
Major League totals (4 years)			171	392	42	92	19	3	11	43	30	60	1-2	.235	.290	.383	11	.964

SELE, AARON — P — ANGELS

PERSONAL: Born June 25, 1970, in Golden Valley, Minn. ... 6-5/220. ... Throws right, bats right. ... Full name: Aaron Helmer Sele. ... Name pronounced SEE-lee.

HIGH SCHOOL: North Kitsap (Poulsbo, Wash.).

COLLEGE: Washington State.

TRANSACTIONS/CAREER NOTES: Selected by Minnesota Twins organization in 37th round of free-agent draft (June 1, 1988); did not sign. ... Selected by Boston Red Sox organization in first round (23rd pick overall) of free-agent draft (June 3, 1991). ... On Boston disabled list (May 24, 1995-remainder of season); included rehabilitation assignments to Trenton (June 19-22), Sarasota (July 10-21 and August 7-16) and Pawtucket (August 16-23). ... On Boston disabled list (August 14-September 1, 1996); included rehabilitation assignment to Pawtucket (August 26-27). ... Traded by Red Sox with P Mark Brandenburg and C Bill Haselman to Texas Rangers for C Jim Leyritz and OF Damon Buford (November 6, 1997). ... Granted free agency (November 5, 1999). ... Signed by Seattle Mariners (January 10, 2000). ... Granted free agency (November 5, 2001). ... Signed by Anaheim Angels (January 4, 2002). ... On disabled list (August 21-September 29, 2002).

HONORS: Named A.L. Rookie Pitcher of the Year by The Sporting News (1993). ... Named International League Most Valuable Pitcher (1993).

STATISTICAL NOTES: Led Carolina League with 14 hit batsmen in 1992. ... Tied for A.L. lead with nine hit batsmen in 1994.

CAREER HITTING (MLB): 3-for-21 (.143), 2 R, 1 2B, 0 3B, 0 HR, 1 RBI.

Year	League	W	L	Pct.	ERA	G	GS	CG	ShO	Sv.-Opp.	IP	H	R	ER	HR	BB-IBB	SO
1991	—Winter Haven (FSL)	3	6	.333	4.96	13	11	4	0	1-...	69.0	65	42	38	2	32-2	51
1992	—Lynchburg (Caro.)	13	5	.722	2.91	20	19	2	1	0-...	127.0	104	51	41	5	46-0	112
	—New Britain (East.)	2	1	.667	6.27	7	6	1	0	0-...	33.0	43	29	23	2	15-0	29
1993	—Pawtucket (I.L.)	8	2	.800	2.19	14	14	2	1	0-...	94.1	74	30	23	8	23-0	87
	—Boston (A.L.)	7	2	.778	2.74	18	18	0	0	0-0	111.2	100	42	34	5	48-2	93
1994	—Boston (A.L.)	8	7	.533	3.83	22	22	2	0	0-0	143.1	140	68	61	13	60-2	105
1995	—Boston (A.L.)	3	1	.750	3.06	6	6	0	0	0-0	32.1	32	14	11	3	14-0	21
	—Trenton (East.)	0	1	.000	3.38	2	2	0	0	0-...	8.0	8	3	3	0	2-0	9
	—Sarasota (FSL)	0	0	...	0.00	2	2	0	0	0-...	7.0	6	0	0	0	1-0	8
	—Pawtucket (I.L.)	0	0	...	9.00	2	2	0	0	0-...	5.0	9	5	5	3	2-0	1
1996	—Boston (A.L.)	7	11	.389	5.32	29	29	1	0	0-0	157.1	192	110	93	14	67-2	137
	—Pawtucket (I.L.)	0	0	...	6.00	1	1	0	0	0-...	3.0	3	2	2	0	1-0	4
1997	—Boston (A.L.)	13	12	.520	5.38	33	33	1	0	0-0	177.1	196	115	106	25	80-4	122
1998	—Texas (A.L.)■	19	11	.633	4.23	33	33	3	2	0-0	212.2	239	116	100	14	84-6	167
1999	—Texas (A.L.)	18	9	.667	4.79	33	33	2	2	0-0	205.0	244	115	109	21	70-3	186
2000	—Seattle (A.L.)■	17	10	.630	4.51	34	34	2	2	0-0	211.2	221	110	106	17	74-7	137
2001	—Seattle (A.L.)	15	5	.750	3.60	34	33	2	1	0-0	215.0	216	93	86	25	51-2	114
2002	—Anaheim (A.L.)■	8	9	.471	4.89	26	26	1	1	0-0	160.0	190	92	87	21	49-2	82
Major League totals (10 years)		115	77	.599	4.39	268	267	14	8	0-0	1626.1	1770	875	793	158	597-30	1164

DIVISION SERIES RECORD

RECORDS: Shares A.L. career record for most losses—3.

Year	League	W	L	Pct.	ERA	G	GS	CG	ShO	Sv.-Opp.	IP	H	R	ER	HR	BB-IBB	SO
1998	—Texas (A.L.)	0	1	.000	6.00	1	1	0	0	0-0	6.0	8	4	4	2	1-0	4
1999	—Texas (A.L.)	0	1	.000	5.40	1	1	0	0	0-0	5.0	6	4	3	0	5-2	3
2000	—Seattle (A.L.)	0	0	...	1.23	1	1	0	0	0-0	7.1	3	1	1	0	3-0	1
2001	—Seattle (A.L.)	0	1	.000	9.00	1	1	0	0	0-0	2.0	5	4	2	0	0-0	0
Division series totals (4 years)		0	3	.000	4.43	4	4	0	0	0-0	20.1	22	13	10	2	9-2	8

CHAMPIONSHIP SERIES RECORD

Year	League	W	L	Pct.	ERA	G	GS	CG	ShO	Sv.-Opp.	IP	H	R	ER	HR	BB-IBB	SO
2000	—Seattle (A.L.)	0	1	.000	6.00	1	1	0	0	0-0	6.0	9	4	4	2	0-0	4
2001	—Seattle (A.L.)	0	2	.000	3.60	2	2	0	0	0-0	10.0	11	8	4	3	4-0	5
Champ. series totals (2 years)		0	3	.000	4.50	3	3	0	0	0-0	16.0	20	12	8	5	4-0	9

ALL-STAR GAME RECORD

	W	L	Pct.	ERA	GS	CG	ShO	Sv.-Opp.	IP	H	R	ER	HR	BB-IBB	SO
All-Star Game totals (1 year)	0	0	...	0.00	0	0	0	0-0	1.0	1	0	0	0	0-0	0

SEO, JAE — P — METS

PERSONAL: Born May 24, 1977, in Kwanju, South Korea. ... 6-1/215. ... Throws right, bats right. ... Full name: Jae Weong Seo.

HIGH SCHOOL: First (Kwanju, South Korea).

COLLEGE: Inha University (South Korea).

TRANSACTIONS/CAREER NOTES: Signed as non-drafted free agent by New York Mets organization (December 17, 1997). ... On Binghamton disabled list (May 4, 1999-remainder of season). ... On disabled list (April 6, 2000-entire season).

CAREER HITTING (MLB): 0-for-0 (.000), 0 R, 0 2B, 0 3B, 0 HR, 0 RBI.

Year	League	W	L	Pct.	ERA	G	GS	CG	ShO	Sv.-Opp.	IP	H	R	ER	HR	BB-IBB	SO
1998	—St. Lucie (FSL)	3	1	.750	2.27	8	7	0	0	0-...	35.2	26	13	9	2	10-0	37
	—Gulf Coast Mets (GCL)	0	0	...	0.00	2	0	0	0	0-...	5.0	4	0	0	0	0-0	0
1999	—St. Lucie (FSL)	2	0	1.000	1.84	3	3	0	0	0-...	14.2	8	3	3	0	2-0	14
2000	—St. Lucie (FSL)	Did not play.															
2001	—St. Lucie (FSL)	2	3	.400	3.55	6	5	0	0	0-...	25.1	21	11	10	2	6-0	19
	—Binghamton (East.)	5	1	.833	1.94	12	10	0	0	0-...	60.1	44	14	13	3	11-1	47
	—Norfolk (I.L.)	2	2	.500	3.42	9	9	0	0	0-...	47.1	53	18	18	4	6-1	25
2002	—Binghamton (East.)	0	0	...	5.40	1	0	0	0	0-...	5.0	5	3	3	1	1-0	6
	—Norfolk (I.L.)	6	9	.400	3.99	26	24	1	0	0-...	128.2	145	66	57	14	22-1	87
	—New York (N.L.)	0	0	...	0.00	1	0	0	0	0-0	1.0	0	0	0	0	0-0	1
Major League totals (1 year)		0	0	...	0.00	1	0	0	0	0-0	1.0	0	0	0	0	0-0	1

SEXSON, RICHIE — 1B — BREWERS

PERSONAL: Born December 29, 1974, in Portland. ... 6-8/227. ... Bats right, throws right. ... Full name: Richmond Lockwood Sexson.
HIGH SCHOOL: Prairie (Brush Prairie, Wash.).
TRANSACTIONS/CAREER NOTES: Selected by Cleveland Indians organization in 24th round of free-agent draft (June 2, 1993). ... Traded by Indians with P Paul Rigdon, P Kane Davis and a player to be named later to Milwaukee Brewers for P Bob Wickman, P Steve Woodard and P Jason Bere (July 28, 2000); Brewers acquired 2B Marcos Scutaro to complete deal (August 30).
RECORDS: Shares major league record for most home runs in month of October—5 (2001). ... Shares major league single-game record for most strikeouts (nine-inning game)—5 (May 29, 2001). ... Shares major league single-game record for most unassisted double plays by first baseman—2 (October 7, 2001).
STATISTICAL NOTES: Led Carolina League with 251 total bases in 1995. ... Led Carolina League first basemen with 1,135 putouts, 79 assists, 1,226 total chances and 109 double plays in 1995. ... Led American Association first basemen with 922 putouts, 77 assists, 1,003 total chances and 105 double plays in 1997. ... Hit three home runs in one game (September 25, 2001). ... Career major league grand slams: 6.
2002 GAMES PLAYED BY POSITION (MLB): 1B—154; DH—1.

			BATTING														FIELDING	
Year	Team (League)	Pos.	G	AB	R	H	2B	3B	HR	RBI	BB	SO	SB-CS	Avg.	OBP	SLG	E	Avg.
1993—	Burlington (Appl.)	1B	40	97	11	18	3	0	1	5	18	21	1-1	.186	.316	.247	4	.988
1994—	Columbus (S.Atl.)	1B	130	488	88	133	25	2	14	77	37	87	7-3	.273	.338	.418	10	.990
1995—	Kinston (Caro.)	1B	131	494	80	*151	*34	0	22	*85	43	115	4-6	.306	.368	.508	12	.990
1996—	Canton/Akron (East.)	1B	133	518	85	143	33	3	16	76	39	118	2-1	.276	.331	.444	11	.989
1997—	Buffalo (A.A.)	1B-DH	115	434	57	113	20	2	*31	88	27	87	5-1	.260	.307	.530	4	*.996
	—Cleveland (A.L.)	1B-DH	5	11	1	3	0	0	0	0	0	2	0-0	.273	.273	.273	0	1.000
1998—	Buffalo (I.L.)	OF-1B-DH	89	344	58	102	20	1	21	74	50	68	1-2	.297	.386	.544	3	.990
	—Cleveland (A.L.)	1B-OF-DH	49	174	28	54	14	1	11	35	6	42	1-1	.310	.344	.592	6	.984
1999—	Cleveland (A.L.)	1B-OF-DH	134	479	72	122	17	7	31	116	34	117	3-3	.255	.305	.514	7	.989
2000—	Cleveland (A.L.)	OF-1B-DH	91	324	45	83	16	1	16	44	25	96	1-0	.256	.315	.460	1	.997
	—Milwaukee (N.L.)■	1B	57	213	44	63	14	0	14	47	34	63	1-0	.296	.398	.559	5	.991
2001—	Milwaukee (N.L.)	1B	158	598	94	162	24	3	45	125	60	178	2-4	.271	.342	.547	8	.995
2002—	Milwaukee (N.L.)	1B-DH	157	570	86	159	37	2	29	102	70	136	0-0	.279	.363	.504	7	.995
American League totals (4 years)			279	988	146	262	47	9	58	195	65	257	5-4	.265	.314	.507	14	.989
National League totals (3 years)			372	1381	224	384	75	5	88	274	164	377	3-4	.278	.360	.531	20	.994
Major League totals (6 years)			651	2369	370	646	122	14	146	469	229	634	8-8	.273	.341	.521	34	.993

DIVISION SERIES RECORD

			BATTING														FIELDING	
Year	Team (League)	Pos.	G	AB	R	H	2B	3B	HR	RBI	BB	SO	SB-CS	Avg.	OBP	SLG	E	Avg.
1998—	Cleveland (A.L.)	1B	3	2	0	0	0	0	0	0	2	1	0-0	.000	.500	.000	0	1.000
1999—	Cleveland (A.L.)	PH-1B-OF	3	6	1	1	0	0	0	1	1	3	0-0	.167	.286	.167	0	1.000
Division series totals (2 years)			6	8	1	1	0	0	0	1	3	4	0-0	.125	.364	.125	0	1.000

CHAMPIONSHIP SERIES RECORD

			BATTING														FIELDING	
Year	Team (League)	Pos.	G	AB	R	H	2B	3B	HR	RBI	BB	SO	SB-CS	Avg.	OBP	SLG	E	Avg.
1998—	Cleveland (A.L.)	1B	3	6	0	0	0	0	0	0	0	3	0-0	.000	.000	.000	0	1.000

ALL-STAR GAME RECORD

	AB	R	H	2B	3B	HR	RBI	BB	SO	SB-CS	Avg.	OBP	SLG	E	Avg.
All-Star Game totals (1 year)	1	0	0	0	0	0	0	0	0	0-0	.000	.000	.000	0	1.000

SHEETS, ANDY — 2B/SS — DEVIL RAYS

PERSONAL: Born November 19, 1971, in Baton Rouge, La. ... 6-2/192. ... Bats right, throws right. ... Full name: Andrew Mark Sheets.
HIGH SCHOOL: St. Amant (La.).
COLLEGE: Tulane, then Louisiana State.
TRANSACTIONS/CAREER NOTES: Selected by Seattle Mariners organization in fourth round of free-agent draft (June 1, 1992). ... Selected by Tampa Bay Devil Rays in first round (24th pick overall) of expansion draft (November 18, 1997). ... Traded by Devil Rays with P Brian Boehringer to San Diego Padres for C John Flaherty (November 18, 1997). ... Traded by Padres with OF Gus Kennedy to Anaheim Angels for C Phil Nevin and P Keith Volkman (March 29, 1999). ... Granted free agency (December 21, 1999). ... Signed by Red Sox organization (January 23, 2000). ... Granted free agency (October 13, 2000). ... Signed by Devil Rays organization (November 15, 2000). ... Granted free agency (October 9, 2001). ... Re-signed by Devil Rays organization (January 28, 2002).
STATISTICAL NOTES: Led Pacific Coast League shortstops with .973 fielding percentage in 1997. ... Career major league grand slams: 1.
2002 GAMES PLAYED BY POSITION (MLB): 2B—26; SS—11; 3B—4.

			BATTING														FIELDING	
Year	Team (League)	Pos.	G	AB	R	H	2B	3B	HR	RBI	BB	SO	SB-CS	Avg.	OBP	SLG	E	Avg.
1993—	Riverside (Calif.)	SS	52	176	23	34	9	1	1	12	17	51	2-2	.193	.259	.273	17	.934
	—Appleton (Midw.)	SS-2B-OF	69	259	32	68	10	4	1	25	20	59	7-7	.263	.320	.344	11	.964
1994—	Riverside (Calif.)	SS	31	100	17	27	5	1	2	10	16	22	6-1	.270	.371	.400	14	.905
	—Jacksonville (Sou.)	SS	70	232	26	51	12	0	0	17	20	54	3-5	.220	.286	.272	17	.948
	—Calgary (PCL)	SS	26	93	22	32	8	1	2	16	11	20	1-1	.344	.415	.516	2	.982
1995—	Tacoma (PCL)	SS	132	437	57	128	29	9	2	47	32	83	8-3	.293	.338	.414	27	.952
1996—	Tacoma (PCL)	SS-2B-3B	62	232	44	83	16	5	5	33	25	56	6-4	.358	.415	.534	14	.951
	—Seattle (A.L.)	3B-2B-SS	47	110	18	21	8	0	0	9	10	41	2-0	.191	.262	.264	5	.959
1997—	Tacoma (PCL)	SS-2B-3B	113	401	57	104	23	0	14	53	46	97	7-2	.259	.337	.421	13	†.974
	—Seattle (A.L.)	3B-SS-2B	32	89	18	22	3	0	4	9	7	34	2-0	.247	.299	.416	8	.905
1998—	San Diego (N.L.)■	SS-3B-2B-1B	88	194	31	47	5	3	7	29	21	62	7-2	.242	.318	.407	9	.964
1999—	Anaheim (A.L.)■	SS-2B-3B	87	244	22	48	10	0	3	29	14	59	1-2	.197	.236	.275	12	.961
	—Edmonton (PCL)	SS-2B	12	45	6	13	1	1	0	4	2	11	0-1	.289	.319	.356	1	.979
2000—	Pawtucket (I.L.)■	SS-3B-2B-1B	83	281	38	64	9	3	8	36	38	48	4-2	.228	.321	.367	9	.969
	—Boston (A.L.)	SS-DH-1B	12	21	1	2	0	0	0	1	0	3	0-0	.095	.095	.095	0	1.000

Year	Team (League)	Pos.	G	AB	R	H	2B	3B	HR	RBI	BB	SO	SB-CS	Avg.	OBP	SLG	E	Avg.
			BATTING														FIELDING	
2001	—Durham (I.L.)■	S-3-0-1-2	66	225	28	63	14	2	4	22	25	45	8-3	.280	.356	.413	11	.960
	—Tampa Bay (A.L.)	SS	49	153	10	30	8	0	1	14	12	35	2-0	.196	.251	.268	2	.990
2002	—Durham (I.L.)	3B-2B-1B-SS	98	374	55	110	25	6	14	69	28	72	7-2	.294	.345	.505	10	.978
	—Tampa Bay (A.L.)	2B-SS-3B	41	149	18	37	4	0	4	22	12	41	2-3	.248	.301	.356	1	.995
American League totals (6 years)			268	766	87	160	33	0	12	84	55	213	9-5	.209	.259	.299	28	.970
National League totals (1 year)			88	194	31	47	5	3	7	29	21	62	7-2	.242	.318	.407	9	.964
Major League totals (7 years)			356	960	118	207	38	3	19	113	76	275	16-7	.216	.271	.321	37	.969

DIVISION SERIES RECORD

Year	Team (League)	Pos.	G	AB	R	H	2B	3B	HR	RBI	BB	SO	SB-CS	Avg.	OBP	SLG	E	Avg.
			BATTING														FIELDING	
1997	—Seattle (A.L.)	3B	2	3	0	1	0	0	0	0	0	2	0-0	.333	.333	.333	0	...
1998	—San Diego (N.L.)	PR-2B	2	0	0	0	0	0	0	0	0	0	0-0	...	...	...	0	...
Division series totals (2 years)			4	3	0	1	0	0	0	0	0	2	0-0	.333	.333	.333	0	...

CHAMPIONSHIP SERIES RECORD

Year	Team (League)	Pos.	G	AB	R	H	2B	3B	HR	RBI	BB	SO	SB-CS	Avg.	OBP	SLG	E	Avg.
			BATTING														FIELDING	
1998	—San Diego (N.L.)	SS-PH	3	3	0	0	0	0	0	0	0	1	0-0	.000	.000	.000	0	1.000

WORLD SERIES RECORD

Year	Team (League)	Pos.	G	AB	R	H	2B	3B	HR	RBI	BB	SO	SB-CS	Avg.	OBP	SLG	E	Avg.
			BATTING														FIELDING	
1998	—San Diego (N.L.)	SS	2	2	0	0	0	0	0	0	0	1	0-0	.000	.000	.000	0	1.000

SHEETS, BEN — P — BREWERS

PERSONAL: Born July 18, 1978, in Baton Rouge, La. ... 6-1/203. ... Throws right, bats right. ... Full name: Ben M. Sheets.
HIGH SCHOOL: St. Amant (La.).
COLLEGE: Northeast Louisiana.
TRANSACTIONS/CAREER NOTES: Selected by Milwaukee Brewers organization in first round (10th pick overall) of free-agent draft (June 2, 1999). ... On Milwaukee disabled list (August 6-September 21, 2001).
MISCELLANEOUS: Member of 2000 U.S. Olympic baseball team.
CAREER HITTING (MLB): 9-for-110 (.082), 6 R, 1 2B, 0 3B, 0 HR, 4 RBI.

Year	League	W	L	Pct.	ERA	G	GS	CG	ShO	Sv.-Opp.	IP	H	R	ER	HR	BB-IBB	SO
1999	—Ogden (Pio.)	0	1	.000	5.63	2	2	0	0	0-...	8.0	8	5	5	2	2-0	12
	—Stockton (Calif.)	1	0	1.000	3.58	5	5	0	0	0-...	27.2	23	11	11	1	14-0	28
2000	—Huntsville (Sou.)	5	3	.625	1.88	13	13	0	0	0-...	72.0	55	17	15	4	25-0	60
	—Indianapolis (I.L.)	3	5	.375	2.87	14	13	1	0	0-...	81.2	77	31	26	4	31-0	59
2001	—Milwaukee (N.L.)	11	10	.524	4.76	25	25	1	1	0-0	151.1	166	89	80	23	48-6	94
	—Indianapolis (I.L.)	1	1	.500	3.38	2	2	0	0	0-...	10.2	14	5	4	0	3-0	6
2002	—Milwaukee (N.L.)	11	•16	.407	4.15	34	34	1	0	0-0	216.2	237	105	100	21	70-10	170
Major League totals (2 years)		22	26	.458	4.40	59	59	2	1	0-0	368.0	403	194	180	44	118-16	264

ALL-STAR GAME RECORD

	W	L	Pct.	ERA	GS	CG	ShO	Sv.-Opp.	IP	H	R	ER	HR	BB-IBB	SO
All-Star Game totals (1 year)	0	0	...	0.00	0	0	0	0-0	.1	0	0	0	0	0-0	0

SHEFFIELD, GARY — OF — BRAVES

PERSONAL: Born November 18, 1968, in Tampa. ... 6-0/205. ... Bats right, throws right. ... Full name: Gary Antonian Sheffield. ... Nephew of Dwight Gooden, pitcher with five major league teams (1984-2000).
HIGH SCHOOL: Hillsborough (Tampa).
TRANSACTIONS/CAREER NOTES: Selected by Milwaukee Brewers organization in first round (sixth pick overall) of free-agent draft (June 2, 1986). ... On Milwaukee disabled list (July 14-September 9, 1989). ... On suspended list (August 31-September 3, 1990). ... On disabled list (June 15-July 3 and July 25, 1991-remainder of season). ... Traded by Brewers with P Geoff Kellogg to San Diego Padres for P Ricky Bones, SS Jose Valentin and OF Matt Mieske (March 27, 1992). ... Traded by Padres with P Rich Rodriguez to Florida Marlins for P Trevor Hoffman, P Jose Martinez and P Andres Berumen (June 24, 1993). ... On Florida suspended list (July 9-12, 1993). ... On Florida disabled list (May 10-25 and May 28-June 12, 1994); included rehabilitation assignment to Portland (June 10-12). ... On disabled list (June 11-September 1, 1995; and May 14-29, 1997). ... Traded by Marlins with 3B Bobby Bonilla, C Charles Johnson, OF Jim Eisenreich and P Manuel Barrios to Los Angeles Dodgers for C Mike Piazza and 3B Todd Zeile (May 15, 1998). ... On suspended list (August 4-6, 1998). ... On suspended list (August 23-27, 2000). ... On disabled list (May 24-June 8, 2001). ... Traded by Dodgers to Atlanta Braves for OF Brian Jordan, P Odalis Perez and P Andrew Brown (January 15, 2002).
RECORDS: Shares major league record for fewest double plays by outfielder (150 or more games)—0 (1996). ... Shares major league single-inning record for most home runs—2 (July 13, 1997, fourth inning).
HONORS: Named Minor League co-Player of the Year by The Sporting News (1988). ... Named Major League Player of the Year by The Sporting News (1992). ... Named N.L. Comeback Player of the Year by The Sporting News (1992). ... Named third baseman on The Sporting News N.L. All-Star team (1992). ... Named third baseman on The Sporting News N.L. Silver Slugger team (1992). ... Named outfielder on The Sporting News N.L. All-Star team (1996). ... Named outfielder on The Sporting News N.L. Silver Slugger team (1996).
STATISTICAL NOTES: Led Pioneer League shortstops with 34 double plays in 1986. ... Led California League shortstops with 77 double plays in 1987. ... Led N.L. with 323 total bases in 1992. ... Career major league grand slams: 8.
MISCELLANEOUS: Holds Florida Marlins all-time record for most home runs (122).
2002 GAMES PLAYED BY POSITION (MLB): OF—127; DH—4.

			BATTING														FIELDING	
Year	Team (League)	Pos.	G	AB	R	H	2B	3B	HR	RBI	BB	SO	SB-CS	Avg.	OBP	SLG	E	Avg.
1986—	Helena (Pio.)	SS	57	222	53	81	12	2	15	*71	20	14	14-4	.365	.413	.640	24	.911
1987—	Stockton (Calif.)	SS	129	469	84	130	23	3	17	*103	81	49	25-15	.277	.388	.448	39	.937
1988—	El Paso (Texas)	SS-3B-OF	77	296	70	93	19	3	19	65	35	41	5-4	.314	.386	.591	23	.936
—	Denver (A.A.)	3B-SS	57	212	42	73	9	5	9	54	21	22	8-4	.344	.407	.561	8	.950
—	Milwaukee (A.L.)	SS	24	80	12	19	1	0	4	12	7	7	3-1	.238	.295	.400	3	.967
1989—	Milwaukee (A.L.)	SS-3B-DH	95	368	34	91	18	0	5	32	27	33	10-6	.247	.303	.337	16	.955
—	Denver (A.A.)	SS	7	29	3	4	1	1	0	0	2	0	0-0	.138	.194	.241	0	1.000
1990—	Milwaukee (A.L.)	3B	125	487	67	143	30	1	10	67	44	41	25-10	.294	.350	.421	25	.934
1991—	Milwaukee (A.L.)	3B-DH	50	175	25	34	12	2	2	22	19	15	5-5	.194	.277	.320	8	.922
1992—	San Diego (N.L.)■	3B	146	557	87	184	34	3	33	100	48	40	5-6	*.330	.385	.580	16	.961
1993—	San Diego (N.L.)	3B	68	258	34	76	12	2	10	36	18	30	5-1	.295	.344	.473	15	.905
—	Florida (N.L.)■	3B	72	236	33	69	8	3	10	37	29	34	12-4	.292	.378	.479	19	.894
1994—	Florida (N.L.)	OF	87	322	61	89	16	1	27	78	51	50	12-6	.276	.380	.584	5	.970
—	Portland (East.)	OF	2	7	1	2	1	0	0	0	1	3	0-0	.286	.375	.429	0	1.000
1995—	Florida (N.L.)	OF	63	213	46	69	8	0	16	46	55	45	19-4	.324	.467	.587	7	.942
1996—	Florida (N.L.)	OF	161	519	118	163	33	1	42	120	142	66	16-9	.314	*.465	.624	6	.976
1997—	Florida (N.L.)	OF-DH	135	444	86	111	22	1	21	71	121	79	11-7	.250	.424	.446	5	.980
1998—	Florida (N.L.)	OF	40	136	21	37	11	1	6	28	26	16	4-2	.272	.392	.500	1	.986
—	Los Angeles (N.L.)■	OF	90	301	52	95	16	1	16	57	69	30	18-5	.316	.444	.535	1	.994
1999—	Los Angeles (N.L.)	OF-DH	152	549	103	165	20	0	34	101	101	64	11-5	.301	.407	.523	7	.972
2000—	Los Angeles (N.L.)	OF-DH	141	501	105	163	24	3	43	109	101	71	4-6	.325	.438	.643	•10	.954
2001—	Los Angeles (N.L.)	OF-DH	143	515	98	160	28	2	36	100	94	67	10-4	.311	.417	.583	6	.972
2002—	Atlanta (N.L.)■	OF-DH	135	492	82	151	26	0	25	84	72	53	12-2	.307	.404	.512	4	.984
American League totals (4 years)			294	1110	138	287	61	3	21	133	97	96	43-22	.259	.319	.376	52	.944
National League totals (11 years)			1433	5043	926	1532	258	18	319	967	927	645	139-61	.304	.416	.552	102	.962
Major League totals (15 years)			1727	6153	1064	1819	319	21	340	1100	1024	741	182-83	.296	.399	.520	154	.957

DIVISION SERIES RECORD

			BATTING														FIELDING	
Year	Team (League)	Pos.	G	AB	R	H	2B	3B	HR	RBI	BB	SO	SB-CS	Avg.	OBP	SLG	E	Avg.
1997—	Florida (N.L.)	OF	3	9	3	5	1	0	1	1	5	0	1-0	.556	.714	1.000	0	1.000
2002—	Atlanta (N.L.)	OF	5	16	3	1	0	0	1	1	7	3	0-0	.063	.348	.250	0	1.000
Division series totals (2 years)			8	25	6	6	1	0	2	2	12	3	1-0	.240	.486	.520	0	1.000

CHAMPIONSHIP SERIES RECORD

			BATTING														FIELDING	
Year	Team (League)	Pos.	G	AB	R	H	2B	3B	HR	RBI	BB	SO	SB-CS	Avg.	OBP	SLG	E	Avg.
1997—	Florida (N.L.)	OF	6	17	6	4	0	0	1	1	7	3	0-0	.235	.458	.412	0	1.000

WORLD SERIES RECORD

NOTES: Member of World Series championship team (1997).

			BATTING														FIELDING	
Year	Team (League)	Pos.	G	AB	R	H	2B	3B	HR	RBI	BB	SO	SB-CS	Avg.	OBP	SLG	E	Avg.
1997—	Florida (N.L.)	OF	7	24	4	7	1	0	1	5	8	5	0-0	.292	.485	.458	1	.941

ALL-STAR GAME RECORD

	AB	R	H	2B	3B	HR	RBI	BB	SO	SB-CS	Avg.	OBP	SLG	E	Avg.
All-Star Game totals (6 years)	9	2	2	0	0	1	2	1	0	0-0	.222	.300	.556	0	1.000

SHIBILO, ANDY — P — RED SOX

PERSONAL: Born September 16, 1976, in Massapequa Park, N.Y. ... 6-7/220. ... Throws right, bats right. ... Full name: Andrew Joseph Shibilo.
HIGH SCHOOL: Massapequa (N.Y.).
COLLEGE: Pepperdine.
TRANSACTIONS/CAREER NOTES: Selected by St. Louis Cardinals organization in 23rd round of free-agent draft (June 2, 1998). ... Released by Cardinals (March 2000). ... Signed by Lehigh Valley, Atlantic League (2000). ... Signed by San Diego Padres organization (March 2001). ... Traded by Padres with P Alan Embree to Boston Red Sox for P Brad Baker and P Dan Giese (June 26, 2002).

Year	League	W	L	Pct.	ERA	G	GS	CG	ShO	Sv.-Opp.	IP	H	R	ER	HR	BB-IBB	SO
1998—	New Jersey (NY-Penn)	4	4	.500	3.45	9	9	0	0	0-...	47.0	51	21	18	2	8-0	54
—	Peoria (Midw.)	1	3	.250	8.51	7	7	0	0	0-...	30.2	42	30	29	2	11-0	22
1999—	Peoria (Midw.)	4	*13	.235	5.11	27	24	2	0	0-...	135.2	157	*105	77	10	41-0	96
2000—	Lehigh Valley (Atl.)■	11	*13	.458	4.02	27	26	*11	...	0-...	179.0	173	99	80	...	61-...	128
2001—	Lake Elsinore (Calif.)■	10	2	.833	1.96	*60	0	0	0	15-...	82.2	66	24	18	4	27-1	105
2002—	Mobile (Sou.)	4	3	.571	4.89	29	0	0	0	0-...	42.1	49	26	23	2	16-2	42
—	Trenton (East.)■	1	0	1.000	3.19	21	0	0	0	6-...	31.0	27	11	11	1	7-0	34
—	Pawtucket (I.L.)	0	1	.000	5.19	6	0	0	0	0-...	8.2	9	7	5	0	2-0	9

SHIELDS, SCOT — P — ANGELS

PERSONAL: Born July 22, 1975, in Fort Lauderdale, Fla. ... 6-1/175. ... Throws right, bats right. ... Full name: Robert Scot Shields.
HIGH SCHOOL: Fort Lauderdale (Fla.).
COLLEGE: Lincoln Memorial University (Tenn.).
TRANSACTIONS/CAREER NOTES: Selected by Anaheim Angels organization in 38th round of free-agent draft (June 3, 1997).
STATISTICAL NOTES: Led Pacific Coast League with 14 hit batsmen in 2000.
CAREER HITTING (MLB): 0-for-0 (.000), 0 R, 0 2B, 0 3B, 0 HR, 0 RBI.

Year League	W	L	Pct.	ERA	G	GS	CG	ShO	Sv.-Opp.	IP	H	R	ER	HR	BB-IBB	SO
1997—Boise (N'West)	7	2	.778	2.94	30	0	0	0	2-...	52.0	45	20	17	1	24-4	61
1998—Cedar Rapids (Midw.)	6	5	.545	3.65	58	0	0	0	7-...	74.0	62	33	30	5	29-0	81
1999—Lake Elsinore (Calif.)	10	3	.769	2.52	24	9	2	1	1-...	107.1	91	37	30	1	39-4	113
—Erie (East.)	4	4	.500	2.89	10	10	1	1	0-...	74.2	57	26	24	10	26-0	81
2000—Edmonton (PCL)	7	•13	.350	5.41	27	27	4	1	0-...	163.0	158	114	98	16	82-0	*156
2001—Salt Lake (PCL)	6	11	.353	4.97	21	21	4	0	0-...	137.2	141	84	76	24	31-0	104
—Anaheim (A.L.)	0	0	...	0.00	8	0	0	0	0-0	11.0	8	1	0	0	7-0	7
2002—Salt Lake (PCL)	2	2	.500	3.06	28	1	0	0	1-...	47.0	39	18	16	5	6-0	50
—Anaheim (A.L.)	5	3	.625	2.20	29	1	0	0	0-0	49.0	31	13	12	4	21-1	30
Major League totals (2 years)	5	3	.625	1.80	37	1	0	0	0-0	60.0	39	14	12	4	28-1	37

WORLD SERIES RECORD

NOTES: Member of World Series championship team (2002).

Year League	W	L	Pct.	ERA	G	GS	CG	ShO	Sv.-Opp.	IP	H	R	ER	HR	BB-IBB	SO
2002—Anaheim (A.L.)	0	0	...	5.40	1	0	0	0	0-0	1.2	5	5	1	2	0-0	1

SHIELL, JASON — P — RED SOX

PERSONAL: Born October 19, 1976, in Savannah, Ga. ... 6-0/180. ... Throws right, bats right. ... Full name: Jason Alexander Shiell.

HIGH SCHOOL: Windsor-Forest (Savannah, Ga.).

TRANSACTIONS/CAREER NOTES: Selected by Atlanta Braves organization in 48th round of free-agent draft (June 1, 1995). ... On Myrtle Beach disabled list (September 3-20, 1999). ... Traded by Braves with OF/1B Ryan Klesko and 2B Bret Boone to San Diego Padres for 2B Quilvio Veras, 1B Wally Joyner and OF Reggie Sanders (December 22, 1999). ... On Rancho Cucamonga disabled list (July 8-September 13, 2000). ... Claimed on waivers by Boston Red Sox (October 2, 2002).

STATISTICAL NOTES: Tied for Southern League lead with eight sacrifice flies allowed in 2001.

CAREER HITTING (MLB): 0-for-0 (.000), 0 R, 0 2B, 0 3B, 0 HR, 0 RBI.

Year League	W	L	Pct.	ERA	G	GS	CG	ShO	Sv.-Opp.	IP	H	R	ER	HR	BB-IBB	SO
1995—Gulf Coast Braves (GCL)	1	3	.250	4.43	12	0	0	0	2-...	22.1	23	16	11	0	10-1	13
1996—Danville (Appl.)	3	1	.750	1.97	12	12	0	0	0-...	59.1	44	14	13	1	19-0	57
1997—Macon (S.Atl.)	10	5	.667	2.86	27	24	0	0	0-...	129.0	113	53	41	12	32-0	101
1998—Macon (S.Atl.)	0	1	.000	4.50	4	3	0	0	0-...	8.0	7	4	4	2	1-0	8
1999—Myrtle Beach (Caro.)	6	7	.462	3.77	26	17	0	0	0-...	114.2	118	51	48	5	36-0	90
2000—Rancho Cuca. (Calif.)■	7	5	.583	5.33	16	14	0	0	0-...	81.0	73	54	48	9	41-0	80
2001—Mobile (Sou.)	2	3	.400	4.44	45	2	0	0	0-...	81.0	91	46	40	5	32-2	60
2002—Portland (PCL)	4	3	.571	2.78	56	0	0	0	6-...	74.1	62	26	23	6	29-0	74
—San Diego (N.L.)	0	0	...	27.00	3	0	0	0	0-0	1.1	7	4	4	0	3-0	1
Major League totals (1 year)	0	0	...	27.00	3	0	0	0	0-0	1.1	7	4	4	0	3-0	1

SHINJO, TSUYOSHI — OF — GIANTS

PERSONAL: Born January 28, 1972, in Fukuoka, Japan. ... 6-1/185. ... Bats right, throws right.

HIGH SCHOOL: Nishinihon Tandai Fuzoku (Fukuoka, Japan).

TRANSACTIONS/CAREER NOTES: Signed by Hanshin Tigers of Japan Central League (1991). ... Signed as non-drafted free agent by New York Mets (December 11, 2000). ... On New York disabled list (June 18-July 16, 2001); included rehabilitation assignment to Brooklyn (July 14-16). ... Traded by Mets with SS Desi Relaford to San Francisco Giants for P Shawn Estes (December 16, 2001). ... On San Francisco disabled list (July 26-August 13, 2002); included rehabilitation assignment to Fresno (August 9-13).

STATISTICAL NOTES: Career major league grand slams: 2.

2002 GAMES PLAYED BY POSITION (MLB): OF—117.

		BATTING														FIELDING	
Year Team (League)	Pos.	G	AB	R	H	2B	3B	HR	RBI	BB	SO	SB-CS	Avg.	OBP	SLG	E	Avg.
1991—Hanshin Tigers (Jap. Cen.)		13	17	...	2	...	...	0	1	...	...	0-...	.118	...	.118	...	...
1992—Hanshin Tigers (Jap. Cen.)		95	353	...	98	...	...	11	46	...	...	5-...	.278	...	.371	...	...
1993—Hanshin Tigers (Jap. Cen.)		102	408	50	105	13	1	23	62	...	...	13-...	.257	...	.463	...	...
1994—Hanshin Tigers (Jap. Cen.)		122	466	...	117	...	...	17	68	...	...	7-...	.251	...	.361	...	...
1995—Hanshin Tigers (Jap. Cen.)		87	311	...	70	...	...	7	37	...	...	6-...	.225	...	.293	...	...
1996—Hanshin Tigers (Jap. Cen.)		113	408	97	97	...	...	19	66	...	...	2-...	.238	...	.377	...	...
1997—Hanshin Tigers (Jap. Cen.)		136	482	...	112	...	...	20	68	...	...	8-...	.232	...	.357	...	...
1998—Hanshin Tigers (Jap. Cen.)		132	414	...	92	...	...	6	27	...	...	1-...	.222	...	.266	...	...
1999—Hanshin Tigers (Jap. Cen.)		123	471	53	120	21	7	14	58	...	...	8-...	.255	...	.418	...	...
2000—Hanshin Tigers (Jap. Cen.)		131	511	71	142	23	1	28	85	32	93	15-...	.278	...	.491	...	...
2001—New York (N.L.)■	OF	123	400	46	107	23	1	10	56	25	70	4-5	.268	.320	.405	3	.989
—Brooklyn (NY-Penn)	OF	2	7	0	2	0	0	0	1	1	2	0-0	.286	.375	.286	0	1.000
2002—San Fran. (N.L.)■	OF	118	362	42	86	15	3	9	37	24	46	5-0	.238	.294	.370	6	.980
—Fresno (PCL)	OF	2	7	0	0	0	0	0	0	1	1	0-0	.000	.125	.000	0	1.000
Major League totals (2 years)		241	762	88	193	38	4	19	93	49	116	9-5	.253	.308	.388	9	.984

CHAMPIONSHIP SERIES RECORD

		BATTING														FIELDING	
Year Team (League)	Pos.	G	AB	R	H	2B	3B	HR	RBI	BB	SO	SB-CS	Avg.	OBP	SLG	E	Avg.
2002—San Francisco (N.L.)	OF	1	1	0	0	0	0	0	0	0	0	0-0	.000	.000	.000	0	1.000

WORLD SERIES RECORD

		BATTING														FIELDING	
Year Team (League)	Pos.	G	AB	R	H	2B	3B	HR	RBI	BB	SO	SB-CS	Avg.	OBP	SLG	E	Avg.
2002—San Francisco (N.L.)	DH-OF	3	6	1	1	0	0	0	0	0	3	0-0	.167	.167	.167	0	1.000

SHOUSE, BRIAN — P — RANGERS

PERSONAL: Born September 26, 1968, in Effingham, Ill. ... 5-11/180. ... Throws left, bats left. ... Full name: Brian Douglas Shouse.
HIGH SCHOOL: Effingham (Ill.).
COLLEGE: Bradley.
TRANSACTIONS/CAREER NOTES: Selected by Pittsburgh Pirates organization in 13th round of free-agent draft (June 4, 1990). ... Released by Pirates (May 16, 1996). ... Signed by Baltimore Orioles organization (May 22, 1996). ... Granted free agency (October 15, 1997). ... Signed by Boston Red Sox organization (October 28, 1997). ... Contract sold by Red Sox to Kintetsu Buffaloes of Japan Pacific League (June 25, 1998). ... Signed by Arizona Diamondbacks organization (November 19, 1998). ... On Tucson disabled list (April 24-May 28 and August 11-September 7, 1999). ... On Arizona disabled list (September 18, 1999-remainder of season). ... Granted free agency (October 15, 1999). ... Signed by New York Mets organization (December 2, 1999). ... Released by Mets (April 14, 2000). ... Signed by Baltimore Orioles organization (May 13, 2000). ... Granted free agency (October 18, 2000). ... Signed by Houston Astros organization (December 22, 2000). ... Granted free agency (October 15, 2001). ... Signed by Kansas City Royals organization (December 7, 2001). ... On Kansas City disabled list (April 28-May 13, 2002). ... Released by Royals (June 27, 2002). ... Signed by Astros organization (July 22, 2002). ... Granted free agency (October 15, 2002). ... Signed by Texas Rangers organization (November 13, 2002).
CAREER HITTING (MLB): 0-for-0 (.000), 0 R, 0 2B, 0 3B, 0 HR, 0 RBI.

Year League	W	L	Pct.	ERA	G	GS	CG	ShO	Sv.-Opp.	IP	H	R	ER	HR	BB-IBB	SO
1990—Welland (NY-Penn)	4	3	.571	5.22	17	1	0	0	2-...	39.2	50	27	23	2	7-0	39
1991—Augusta (S.Atl.)	2	3	.400	3.19	26	0	0	0	8-...	31.0	22	13	11	1	9-1	32
—Salem (Caro.)	2	1	.667	2.94	17	0	0	0	3-...	33.2	35	12	11	2	15-2	25
1992—Carolina (Sou.)	5	6	.455	2.44	59	0	0	0	4-...	77.1	71	31	21	3	28-4	79
1993—Buffalo (A.A.)	1	0	1.000	3.83	48	0	0	0	2-...	51.2	54	24	22	7	17-2	25
—Pittsburgh (N.L.)	0	0	...	9.00	6	0	0	0	0-0	4.0	7	4	4	1	2-0	3
1994—Buffalo (A.A.)	3	4	.429	3.63	43	0	0	0	0-...	52.0	44	22	21	6	15-4	31
1995—Carolina (Sou.)	7	6	.538	4.47	21	20	0	0	0-...	114.2	126	64	57	14	19-2	76
—Calgary (PCL)	4	4	.500	6.18	8	8	1	0	0-...	39.1	62	35	27	2	7-0	17
1996—Calgary (PCL)	1	0	1.000	10.66	12	1	0	0	0-...	12.2	22	15	15	4	4-1	12
—Rochester (I.L.)■	1	2	.333	4.50	32	0	0	0	2-...	50.0	53	27	25	6	16-1	45
1997—Rochester (I.L.)	6	2	.750	2.27	54	0	0	0	9-...	71.1	48	21	18	6	21-4	81
1998—Pawtucket (I.L.)■	2	0	1.000	2.90	22	1	0	0	6-...	31.0	21	11	10	7	7-0	25
—Boston (A.L.)	0	1	.000	5.63	7	0	0	0	0-0	8.0	9	5	5	2	4-0	5
—Kintetsu (Jap. Pac.)■	0	2	.000	6.58	13	3	0	0	0-...	26.0	40	20	19	...	13-...	20
—Kintetsu (Jp. West.)	1	0	1.000	1.38	5	2	0	0	0-...	13.0	9	2	2	...	7-...	9
1999—Tucson (PCL)■	3	4	.429	6.25	30	0	0	0	0-...	44.2	63	35	31	4	18-3	32
2000—Norfolk (I.L.)■	0	1	.000	15.00	4	0	0	0	0-...	3.0	6	5	5	2	2-0	1
—Rochester (I.L.)■	4	4	.500	2.79	43	0	0	0	2-...	58.0	63	20	18	4	14-1	52
2001—New Orleans (PCL)■	2	2	.500	2.89	56	1	0	0	1-...	53.0	51	21	17	4	15-0	56
2002—Kansas City (A.L.)■	0	0	...	6.14	23	0	0	0	0-0	14.2	15	10	10	3	9-1	11
—Omaha (PCL)	0	0	...	11.57	5	0	0	0	0-...	2.1	7	3	3	0	1-0	2
—New Orleans (PCL)■	1	0	1.000	3.43	19	0	0	0	0-...	21.0	17	10	8	2	3-0	20
A.L. totals (2 years)	0	1	.000	5.96	30	0	0	0	0-0	22.2	24	15	15	5	13-1	16
N.L. totals (1 year)	0	0	...	9.00	6	0	0	0	0-0	4.0	7	4	4	1	2-0	3
Major League totals (3 years)	0	1	.000	6.41	36	0	0	0	0-0	26.2	31	19	19	6	15-1	19

SHUEY, PAUL — P — DODGERS

PERSONAL: Born September 16, 1970, in Lima, Ohio. ... 6-3/215. ... Throws right, bats right. ... Full name: Paul Kenneth Shuey. ... Name pronounced SHOO-ee.
HIGH SCHOOL: Millbrook (Raleigh, N.C.).
COLLEGE: North Carolina.
TRANSACTIONS/CAREER NOTES: Selected by Cleveland Indians organization in first round (second pick overall) of free-agent draft (June 1, 1992). ... On Cleveland disabled list (June 27-July 21, 1994); included rehabilitation assignment to Charlotte (July 5-21). ... On Cleveland disabled list (May 4-22, 1995). ... On Buffalo disabled list (June 2-July 10, 1995). ... On Cleveland disabled list (April 25-May 18, June 19-July 4 and July 11-August 1, 1997); included rehabilitation assignments to Buffalo (May 5-10) and Akron (May 1-18). ... On Cleveland disabled list (April 11-June 15, 1998); included rehabilitation assignments to Akron (April 24) and Buffalo (May 23-June 14). ... On Cleveland disabled list (April 26-May 11, 1999); included rehabilitation assignment to Buffalo (May 9-11). ... On Cleveland disabled list (May 21-June 27, 2000); included rehabilitation assignment to Akron (June 24-27). ... On Cleveland disabled list (June 13-29 and July 22-September 18, 2001); included rehabilitation assignment to Akron (June 27). ... On Cleveland disabled list (June 10-25, 2002); included rehabilitation assignment to Akron (June 22-25). ... Traded by Indians to Los Angeles Dodgers for P Terry Mulholland, P Ricardo Rodriguez and P Francisco Cruceta (July 28, 2002).
RECORDS: Shares major single-inning league record for most strikeouts—4 (May 14, 1994, ninth inning).
CAREER HITTING (MLB): 1-for-5 (.200), 0 R, 0 2B, 0 3B, 0 HR, 0 RBI.

Year League	W	L	Pct.	ERA	G	GS	CG	ShO	Sv.-Opp.	IP	H	R	ER	HR	BB-IBB	SO
1992—Columbus (S.Atl.)	5	5	.500	3.35	14	14	0	0	0-...	78.0	62	35	29	2	47-2	73
1993—Canton/Akron (East.)	4	8	.333	7.30	27	7	0	0	0-...	61.2	76	50	50	13	36-3	41
—Kinston (Caro.)	1	0	1.000	4.84	15	0	0	0	0-...	22.1	29	12	12	1	8-0	27
1994—Kinston (Caro.)	1	0	1.000	3.75	13	0	0	0	8-...	12.0	10	5	5	1	3-0	16
—Cleveland (A.L.)	0	1	.000	8.49	14	0	0	0	5-5	11.2	14	11	11	1	12-1	16
—Charlotte (I.L.)	2	1	.667	1.93	20	0	0	0	10-...	23.1	15	9	5	1	10-0	25
1995—Cleveland (A.L.)	0	2	.000	4.26	7	0	0	0	0-0	6.1	5	4	3	0	5-0	5
—Buffalo (A.A.)	1	2	.333	2.63	25	0	0	0	11-...	27.1	21	9	8	2	7-0	27
1996—Buffalo (A.A.)	3	2	.600	0.81	19	0	0	0	4-...	33.1	14	4	3	1	9-2	57
—Cleveland (A.L.)	5	2	.714	2.85	42	0	0	0	4-7	53.2	45	19	17	6	26-3	44
1997—Cleveland (A.L.)	4	2	.667	6.20	40	0	0	0	2-3	45.0	52	31	31	5	28-3	46
—Buffalo (A.A.)	0	0	...	3.60	2	0	0	0	0-...	5.0	4	2	2	0	4-0	6
—Akron (East.)	0	0	...	3.38	3	0	0	0	0-...	8.0	10	3	3	1	0-0	9
1998—Cleveland (A.L.)	5	4	.556	3.00	43	0	0	0	2-5	51.0	44	19	17	6	25-5	58
—Akron (East.)	0	0	...	54.00	1	0	0	0	0-...	.1	3	2	2	0	1-0	0
—Buffalo (I.L.)	0	0	...	2.51	11	0	0	0	2-...	14.1	11	4	4	0	6-0	22
1999—Cleveland (A.L.)	8	5	.615	3.53	72	0	0	0	6-12	81.2	68	37	32	8	40-7	103
—Buffalo (I.L.)	0	0	...	0.00	1	0	0	0	0-...	1.0	0	0	0	0	1-0	1

Year	League	W	L	Pct.	ERA	G	GS	CG	ShO	Sv.-Opp.	IP	H	R	ER	HR	BB-IBB	SO
2000—	Cleveland (A.L.)	4	2	.667	3.39	57	0	0	0	0-5	63.2	51	25	24	4	30-3	69
	—Akron (East.)	0	0	...	4.50	2	1	0	0	0-...	2.0	1	1	1	0	1-0	1
2001—	Cleveland (A.L.)	5	3	.625	2.82	47	0	0	0	2-5	54.1	53	25	17	1	26-5	70
	—Akron (East.)	0	0	...	0.00	1	1	0	0	0-...	1.0	0	0	0	0	1-0	2
2002—	Cleveland (A.L.)	3	0	1.000	2.41	39	0	0	0	0-2	37.1	31	11	10	1	10-1	39
	—Akron (East.)	0	0	...	4.50	2	2	0	0	0-...	2.0	2	1	1	0	0-0	3
	—Los Angeles (N.L.)■	5	2	.714	4.40	28	0	0	0	1-3	30.2	25	18	15	2	21-1	24
A.L. totals (9 years)		34	21	.618	3.60	361	0	0	0	21-44	404.2	363	182	162	32	202-28	450
N.L. totals (1 year)		5	2	.714	4.40	28	0	0	0	1-3	30.2	25	18	15	2	21-1	24
Major League totals (9 years)		39	23	.629	3.66	389	0	0	0	22-47	435.1	388	200	177	34	223-29	474

DIVISION SERIES RECORD

Year	League	W	L	Pct.	ERA	G	GS	CG	ShO	Sv.-Opp.	IP	H	R	ER	HR	BB-IBB	SO
1996—	Cleveland (A.L.)	0	0	...	9.00	3	0	0	0	0-0	2.0	5	2	2	2	2-0	2
1998—	Cleveland (A.L.)	0	0	...	0.00	3	0	0	0	0-0	3.0	3	0	0	0	1-0	4
1999—	Cleveland (A.L.)	1	1	.500	11.25	3	0	0	0	0-0	4.0	4	5	5	1	4-1	5
2001—	Cleveland (A.L.)	0	0	...	6.75	2	0	0	0	0-0	1.1	3	1	1	1	0-0	2
Division series totals (4 years)		1	1	.500	6.97	11	0	0	0	0-0	10.1	15	8	8	4	7-1	13

CHAMPIONSHIP SERIES RECORD

Year	League	W	L	Pct.	ERA	G	GS	CG	ShO	Sv.-Opp.	IP	H	R	ER	HR	BB-IBB	SO
1998—	Cleveland (A.L.)	0	0	...	0.00	5	0	0	0	0-0	6.1	4	0	0	0	7-2	7

SHUMPERT, TERRY — IF/OF

PERSONAL: Born August 16, 1966, in Paducah, Ky. ... 6-0/198. ... Bats right, throws right. ... Full name: Terrance Darnell Shumpert.
HIGH SCHOOL: Paducah (Ky.) Tilghman.
COLLEGE: Kentucky.
TRANSACTIONS/CAREER NOTES: Selected by Kansas City Royals organization in second round of free-agent draft (June 2, 1987). ... On disabled list (July 19-August 13, 1989). ... On Kansas City disabled list (June 3-September 10, 1990); included rehabilitation assignment to Omaha (August 7-25). ... On Kansas City disabled list (August 7-September 7, 1992). ... Traded by Royals to Boston Red Sox for a player to be named later (December 13, 1994). ... Granted free agency (October 6, 1995). ... Signed by Chicago Cubs organization (March 12, 1996). ... On Chicago disabled list (August 19-September 3, 1996). ... Granted free agency (October 15, 1996). ... Signed by San Diego Padres (November 4, 1996). ... On San Diego disabled list (May 27-August 5, 1997). ... Released by Padres (August 5, 1997). ... Signed by Colorado Rockies organization (August 13, 1997). ... Granted free agency (October 15, 1998). ... Re-signed by Rockies organization (December 18, 1998). ... On Colorado Springs disabled list (May 13-23, 1999). ... Granted free agency (October 29, 1999). ... Re-signed by Rockies (January 1, 1999). ... Granted free agency (October 28, 2002).
STATISTICAL NOTES: Led American Association with 21 sacrifice hits in 1993. ... Career major league grand slams: 1.
2002 GAMES PLAYED BY POSITION (MLB): 2B—60; OF—8; SS—3; 3B—1.

			BATTING														FIELDING	
Year	Team (League)	Pos.	G	AB	R	H	2B	3B	HR	RBI	BB	SO	SB-CS	Avg.	OBP	SLG	E	Avg.
1987—	Eugene (N'West)	2B	48	186	38	54	16	1	4	22	27	41	16-4	.290	.385	.452	11	.945
1988—	Appleton (Midw.)	2B-OF	114	422	64	102	*37	2	7	38	56	90	36-3	.242	.331	.389	20	.962
1989—	Omaha (A.A.)	2B	113	355	54	88	29	2	4	22	25	63	23-7	.248	.315	.375	*22	.959
1990—	Omaha (A.A.)	2B	39	153	24	39	6	4	2	12	14	28	18-0	.255	.327	.386	7	.960
	—Kansas City (A.L.)	2B-DH	32	91	7	25	6	1	0	8	2	17	3-3	.275	.292	.363	3	.977
1991—	Kansas City (A.L.)	2B	144	369	45	80	16	4	5	34	30	75	17-11	.217	.283	.322	16	.975
1992—	Kansas City (A.L.)	2B-DH-SS	36	94	6	14	5	1	1	11	3	17	2-2	.149	.175	.255	4	.969
	—Omaha (A.A.)	2B-SS	56	210	23	42	12	0	1	14	13	33	3-5	.200	.259	.271	9	.967
1993—	Omaha (A.A.)	2B	111	413	70	124	29	1	14	59	41	62	*36-8	.300	.367	.477	14	.972
	—Kansas City (A.L.)	2B	8	10	0	1	0	0	0	0	2	2	1-0	.100	.250	.100	0	1.000
1994—	Kansas City (A.L.)	2B-3B-DH-SS	64	183	28	44	6	2	8	24	13	39	18-3	.240	.289	.426	8	.961
1995—	Boston (A.L.)■	2B-3B-SS-DH	21	47	6	11	3	0	0	3	4	13	3-1	.234	.294	.298	2	.966
	—Pawtucket (I.L.)	3B-2B-DH-OF	37	133	17	36	7	0	2	11	14	27	10-4	.271	.345	.368	11	.899
1996—	Iowa (A.A.)■	2-3-DH-1-S	72	246	45	68	13	4	5	32	24	44	13-3	.276	.342	.423	7	.976
	—Chicago (N.L.)	3B-2B-SS	27	31	5	7	1	0	2	6	2	11	0-1	.226	.286	.452	1	.952
1997—	Las Vegas (PCL)■	3B-2B-SS-DH	32	109	18	31	8	1	1	16	9	20	3-0	.284	.350	.404	4	.960
	—San Diego (N.L.)	2B-OF-3B	13	33	4	9	3	0	1	6	3	4	0-0	.273	.324	.455	2	.952
	—New Haven (East.)■	2B	5	17	2	4	0	0	1	1	0	2	0-0	.235	.235	.412	0	1.000
	—Colo. Springs (PCL)	SS-2B-3B-OF	10	37	8	11	3	0	1	2	2	7	0-0	.297	.333	.459	5	.848
1998—	Colo. Springs (PCL)	2-O-3-D-S	97	376	66	115	29	8	12	50	35	59	11-11	.306	.370	.521	4	.986
	—Colorado (N.L.)	2B	23	26	3	6	1	0	1	2	2	8	0-0	.231	.286	.385	0	1.000
1999—	Colo. Springs (PCL)	3B-2B-SS-OF	29	79	15	30	8	1	6	17	4	9	3-1	.380	.410	.734	5	.922
	—Colorado (N.L.)	2B-OF-3B-SS	92	262	58	91	26	3	10	37	31	41	14-0	.347	.413	.584	5	.983
2000—	Colorado (N.L.)	OF-IF-DH	115	263	52	68	11	7	9	40	28	40	8-4	.259	.340	.456	4	.977
2001—	Colorado (N.L.)	2B-OF-3B-SS	114	242	37	70	14	5	4	24	15	44	14-3	.289	.337	.438	8	.959
2002—	Colorado (N.L.)	2B-OF-SS-3B	106	234	30	55	12	1	6	21	21	41	4-1	.235	.304	.372	6	.975
American League totals (6 years)			305	794	92	175	36	8	14	80	54	163	44-20	.220	.273	.339	33	.972
National League totals (7 years)			490	1091	189	306	68	16	33	136	102	189	40-9	.280	.346	.463	26	.974
Major League totals (13 years)			795	1885	281	481	104	24	47	216	156	352	84-29	.255	.316	.411	59	.973

SIERRA, RUBEN — OF

PERSONAL: Born October 6, 1965, in Rio Piedras, Puerto Rico. ... 6-1/215. ... Bats both, throws right. ... Full name: Ruben Angel Garcia Sierra.
HIGH SCHOOL: Dr. Secario Rosario (Rio Piedras, Puerto Rico).
TRANSACTIONS/CAREER NOTES: Signed as non-drafted free agent by Texas Rangers organization (November 21, 1982). ... Traded by Rangers with P Jeff Russell, P Bobby Witt and cash to Oakland Athletics for OF Jose Canseco (August 31, 1992). ... Granted free agency (October 26, 1992). ... Re-signed by A's (December 21, 1992). ... On Oakland disabled list (July 7-22, 1995). ... Traded by A's with P Jason Beverlin to New York Yankees for OF/DH Danny Tartabull (July 28, 1995). ... Traded by Yankees with P Matt Drews to Detroit Tigers for 1B/DH Cecil Fielder (July 31, 1996). ... Traded by Tigers to Cincinnati Reds for OF Decomba Conner and P Ben Bailey (October 28, 1996). ... Released by Reds (May 9, 1997). ... Signed by Toronto Blue Jays organization (May 11, 1997). ... Released by Blue Jays (June 16, 1997). ... Signed by Chicago White Sox

organization (January 9, 1998). ... Released by White Sox (May 29, 1998). ... Signed by New York Mets organization (June 20, 1998). ... Granted free agency (October 16, 1998). ... Signed by Atlantic City, Atlantic League (May 1, 1999). ... Signed by Cleveland Indians organization (December 23, 1999). ... Released by Indians (March 20, 2000). ... Signed by Rangers organization (May 1, 2000). ... Granted free agency (October 30, 2000). ... Re-signed by Rangers organization (December 13, 2000). ... On Texas disabled list (July 27-August 11, 2001). ... Granted free agency (November 5, 2001). ... Signed by Seattle Mariners (January 3, 2002). ... Granted free agency (October 31, 2002).

HONORS: Named A.L. Player of the Year by THE SPORTING NEWS (1989). ... Named outfielder on THE SPORTING NEWS A.L. All-Star team (1989). ... Named outfielder on THE SPORTING NEWS A.L. Silver Slugger team (1989). ... Named A.L. Comeback Player of the Year by THE SPORTING NEWS (2001).

STATISTICAL NOTES: Switch-hit home runs in one game six times (September 13, 1986; August 27, 1988; June 8, 1989; June 7, 1994; June 22, 1996; and June 13, 2001). ... Led A.L. with 12 sacrifice flies in 1987. ... Led A.L. outfielders with six double plays and tied for lead with 17 assists in 1987. ... Led A.L. with 344 total bases in 1989. ... Led Pacific Coast League in grounding into double plays with 24 in 2000. ... Career major league grand slams: 6.

MISCELLANEOUS: Holds Texas Rangers franchise all-time record for most triples (44). ... Batted righthanded only (1983).

2002 GAMES PLAYED BY POSITION (MLB): OF—60; DH—52.

			BATTING														FIELDING	
Year	**Team (League)**	**Pos.**	**G**	**AB**	**R**	**H**	**2B**	**3B**	**HR**	**RBI**	**BB**	**SO**	**SB-CS**	**Avg.**	**OBP**	**SLG**	**E**	**Avg.**
1983—	GC Rangers (GCL)	OF	48	182	26	44	7	3	1	26	16	38	3-4	.242	.300	.330	4	.948
1984—	Burlington (Midw.)	OF	•138	482	55	127	33	5	6	75	49	97	13-9	.263	.331	.390	*20	.928
1985—	Tulsa (Texas)	OF	*137	*545	63	138	34	*8	13	74	35	111	22-7	.253	.297	.417	*15	.943
1986—	Oklahoma City (A.A.)	OF	46	189	31	56	11	2	9	41	15	27	8-2	.296	.341	.519	2	.983
—	Texas (A.L.)	OF-DH	113	382	50	101	13	10	16	55	22	65	7-8	.264	.302	.476	6	.972
1987—	Texas (A.L.)	OF	158	*643	97	169	35	4	30	109	39	114	16-11	.263	.302	.470	11	.963
1988—	Texas (A.L.)	OF-DH	156	615	77	156	32	2	23	91	44	91	18-4	.254	.301	.424	7	.979
1989—	Texas (A.L.)	OF	•162	634	101	194	35	*14	29	*119	43	82	8-2	.306	.347	*.543	9	.973
1990—	Texas (A.L.)	OF-DH	159	608	70	170	37	2	16	96	49	86	9-0	.280	.330	.426	10	.967
1991—	Texas (A.L.)	OF	161	661	110	203	44	5	25	116	56	91	16-4	.307	.357	.502	7	.979
1992—	Texas (A.L.)	OF-DH	124	500	66	139	30	6	14	70	31	59	12-4	.278	.315	.446	7	.970
—	Oakland (A.L.)■	OF-DH	27	101	17	28	4	1	3	17	14	9	2-0	.277	.359	.426	0	1.000
1993—	Oakland (A.L.)	OF-DH	158	630	77	147	23	5	22	101	52	97	25-5	.233	.288	.390	7	.977
1994—	Oakland (A.L.)	OF-DH	110	426	71	114	21	1	23	92	23	64	8-5	.268	.298	.484	*9	.948
1995—	Oakland (A.L.)	OF-DH	70	264	40	70	17	0	12	42	24	42	4-4	.265	.323	.466	4	.957
—	New York (A.L.)■	DH-OF	56	215	33	56	15	0	7	44	22	34	1-0	.260	.322	.428	1	.950
1996—	Campeche (Mex.)■	DH	1	1	1	0	0	0	0	0	0	0	0-0	.000	.000	.000	...	...
—	New York (A.L.)■	DH-OF	96	360	39	93	17	1	11	52	40	58	1-3	.258	.327	.403	1	.984
—	Detroit (A.L.)■	OF-DH	46	158	22	35	9	1	1	20	20	25	3-1	.222	.306	.310	5	.914
1997—	Cincinnati (N.L.)■	OF	25	90	6	22	5	1	2	7	6	21	0-0	.244	.292	.389	0	1.000
—	Syracuse (I.L.)■	OF	8	32	5	7	2	0	1	5	2	6	0-0	.219	.265	.375	1	.923
—	Toronto (A.L.)	OF-DH	14	48	4	10	0	2	1	5	3	13	0-0	.208	.250	.354	1	.929
1998—	Chicago (A.L.)■	OF-DH	27	74	7	16	4	1	4	11	3	11	2-0	.216	.247	.459	0	1.000
—	Norfolk (I.L.)■	OF-DH	28	108	16	28	5	0	3	19	13	18	3-0	.259	.331	.389	0	1.000
1999—	Atlantic City (Atl.)■	DH-OF	112	422	76	124	22	2	28	82	59	63	3-2	.294	...	.555	3	.960
2000—	Cancun (Mex.)■	OF	16	62	8	22	2	1	3	12	10	10	0-1	.355	.438	.565	0	1.000
—	Oklahoma (PCL)■	OF	112	439	70	143	26	3	18	82	55	63	5-2	.326	.398	.522	6	.962
—	Texas (A.L.)	DH	20	60	5	14	0	0	1	7	4	9	1-0	.233	.281	.283	...	...
2001—	Oklahoma (PCL)	OF	24	94	14	25	2	1	3	12	10	14	2-0	.266	.337	.404	0	1.000
—	Texas (A.L.)	DH-OF	94	344	55	100	22	1	23	67	19	52	2-0	.291	.322	.561	4	.937
2002—	Seattle (A.L.)	OF-DH	122	419	47	113	23	0	13	60	31	66	4-0	.270	.319	.418	2	.979
American League totals (16 years)			1873	7142	988	1928	381	56	274	1174	539	1068	139-51	.270	.317	.454	91	.970
National League totals (1 year)			25	90	6	22	5	1	2	7	6	21	0-0	.244	.292	.389	0	1.000
Major League totals (16 years)			1898	7232	994	1950	386	57	276	1181	545	1089	139-51	.270	.317	.453	91	.970

DIVISION SERIES RECORD

RECORDS: Shares single-game record for most at-bats—7 (October 4, 1995).

			BATTING														FIELDING	
Year	**Team (League)**	**Pos.**	**G**	**AB**	**R**	**H**	**2B**	**3B**	**HR**	**RBI**	**BB**	**SO**	**SB-CS**	**Avg.**	**OBP**	**SLG**	**E**	**Avg.**
1995—	New York (A.L.)	DH	5	23	2	4	2	0	2	5	2	7	0-0	.174	.231	.522	...	...

CHAMPIONSHIP SERIES RECORD

			BATTING														FIELDING	
Year	**Team (League)**	**Pos.**	**G**	**AB**	**R**	**H**	**2B**	**3B**	**HR**	**RBI**	**BB**	**SO**	**SB-CS**	**Avg.**	**OBP**	**SLG**	**E**	**Avg.**
1992—	Oakland (A.L.)	OF	6	24	4	8	2	1	1	7	2	1	1-2	.333	.357	.625	0	1.000

ALL-STAR GAME RECORD

	AB	**R**	**H**	**2B**	**3B**	**HR**	**RBI**	**BB**	**SO**	**SB-CS**	**Avg.**	**OBP**	**SLG**	**E**	**Avg.**
All-Star Game totals (4 years)	9	3	4	0	0	1	3	0	2	0-0	.444	.444	.778	0	1.000

SILVA, CARLOS — P — PHILLIES

PERSONAL: Born April 23, 1979, in Bolivar, Venezuela. ... 6-4/225. ... Throws right, bats right.

HIGH SCHOOL: U.E. General Ezequiel Zamora Bolivar.

TRANSACTIONS/CAREER NOTES: Signed as non-drafted free agent by Philadelphia Phillies organization (March 22, 1996). ... On Philadelphia disabled list (May 27-June 14, 2002); included rehabilitation assignment to Reading (June 11-14).

CAREER HITTING (MLB): 0-for-2 (.000), 0 R, 0 2B, 0 3B, 0 HR, 0 RBI.

Year	**League**	**W**	**L**	**Pct.**	**ERA**	**G**	**GS**	**CG**	**ShO**	**Sv.-Opp.**	**IP**	**H**	**R**	**ER**	**HR**	**BB-IBB**	**SO**
1996—	Martinsville (Appl.)	0	0	...	4.00	7	1	0	0	0-...	18.0	20	11	8	1	5-0	16
1997—	Martinsville (Appl.)	2	2	.500	5.15	11	11	0	0	0-...	57.2	66	46	33	9	14-0	31
1998—	Martinsville (Appl.)	1	4	.200	5.05	7	7	1	0	0-...	41.0	48	24	23	2	4-0	21
—	Batavia (NY-Penn)	2	3	.400	6.35	9	7	0	0	0-...	45.1	61	37	32	4	9-0	27
1999—	Piedmont (S.Atl.)	11	8	.579	3.12	26	26	3	1	0-...	164.1	176	79	57	6	41-2	99
2000—	Clearwater (FSL)	8	*13	.381	3.57	26	24	*4	0	0-...	176.1	*229	99	70	7	26-1	82
2001—	Reading (East.)	15	8	.652	3.90	28	28	4	1	0-...	180.0	*197	85	78	20	27-0	100
2002—	Philadelphia (N.L.)	5	0	1.000	3.21	68	0	0	0	1-5	84.0	88	34	30	4	22-6	41
—	Reading (East.)	0	0	...	0.00	2	0	0	0	1-...	3.0	0	0	0	0	0-0	1
Major League totals (1 year)		5	0	1.000	3.21	68	0	0	0	1-5	84.0	88	34	30	4	22-6	41

SILVA, JOSE — P

PERSONAL: Born December 19, 1973, in Tijuana, Mexico. ... 6-6/235. ... Throws right, bats right. ... Full name: Jose Leonel Silva.
HIGH SCHOOL: Hilltop (Chula Vista, Calif.).
TRANSACTIONS/CAREER NOTES: Selected by Toronto Blue Jays organization in sixth round of free-agent draft (June 3, 1991). ... On disabled list (April 6-August 17, 1995). ... On Knoxville disabled list (April 4-June 5, 1996). ... Traded by Blue Jays with IF Jose Pett, IF Brandon Cromer and three players to be named later to Pittsburgh Pirates for OF Orlando Merced, IF Carlos Garcia and P Dan Plesac (November 14, 1996); Pirates acquired P Mike Halperin, IF Abraham Nunez and C/OF Craig Wilson to complete deal (December 11, 1996). ... On Calgary disabled list (April 29-June 2, 1997). ... On Pittsburgh disabled list (June 17-September 10, 1998); included rehabilitation assignment to Nashville (August 25-September 6). ... On Pittsburgh disabled list (March 26-April 23, 1999); included rehabilitation assignment to Nashville (April 14-23). ... On Pittsburgh disabled list (June 5, 2001-remainder of season); included rehabilitation assignments to Altoona (August 27-September 2) and Williamsport (September 2-13). ... Traded Pirates to Cincinnati Reds for P Ben Shaffar (December 20, 2001). ... On Cincinnati disabled list (March 21-June 6 and June 27-September 1, 2002); included rehabilitation assignments to Louisville (May 13-June 6, July 19-August 8 and August 22-September 1). ... Released by Reds (October 2, 2002).
CAREER HITTING (MLB): 10-for-90 (.111), 1 R, 1 2B, 0 3B, 0 HR, 5 RBI.

Year League	W	L	Pct.	ERA	G	GS	CG	ShO	Sv.-Opp.	IP	H	R	ER	HR	BB-IBB	SO
1992— GC Blue Jays (GCL)	6	4	.600	2.28	12	•12	0	0	0-...	59.1	42	23	15	1	18-0	78
1993— Hagerstown (S.Atl.)	12	5	.706	2.52	24	24	0	0	0-...	142.2	103	50	40	6	62-0	161
1994— Dunedin (FSL)	0	2	.000	3.77	8	7	0	0	0-...	43.0	41	32	18	4	24-0	41
— Knoxville (Sou.)	4	8	.333	4.14	16	16	1	1	0-...	91.1	89	47	42	9	31-0	71
1995— Knoxville (Sou.)	0	0	...	9.00	3	0	0	0	0-...	2.0	3	2	2	0	6-0	2
1996— Knoxville (Sou.)	2	3	.400	4.91	22	6	0	0	0-...	44.0	45	27	24	3	22-2	26
— Toronto (A.L.)	0	0	...	13.50	2	0	0	0	0-0	2.0	5	3	3	1	0-0	0
1997— Calgary (PCL)■	5	1	.833	3.41	17	11	0	0	0-...	66.0	74	27	25	3	22-0	54
— Pittsburgh (N.L.)	2	1	.667	5.94	11	4	0	0	0-0	36.1	52	26	24	4	16-3	30
1998— Pittsburgh (N.L.)	6	7	.462	4.40	18	18	1	0	0-0	100.1	104	55	49	7	30-2	64
— Nashville (PCL)	0	0	...	4.82	3	3	0	0	0-...	9.1	10	5	5	2	4-0	6
1999— Nashville (PCL)	2	0	1.000	1.50	2	2	0	0	0-...	12.0	14	4	2	0	4-0	10
— Pittsburgh (N.L.)	2	8	.200	5.73	34	12	0	0	4-5	97.1	108	70	62	10	39-0	77
2000— Pittsburgh (N.L.)	11	9	.550	5.56	51	19	1	0	0-2	136.0	178	96	84	16	50-7	98
2001— Pittsburgh (N.L.)	3	3	.500	6.75	26	0	0	0	0-2	32.0	35	24	24	6	9-1	23
— Altoona (East.)	0	0	...	0.00	2	0	0	0	0-...	1.1	2	0	0	0	1-0	2
— Williamsport (NY-Penn)	0	0	...	0.00	2	2	0	0	0-...	2.0	2	0	0	0	0-0	2
2002— Louisville (I.L.)■	1	2	.333	2.27	20	3	0	0	1-...	35.2	41	15	9	1	4-0	28
— Cincinnati (N.L.)	1	0	1.000	4.24	12	0	0	0	0-0	23.1	25	11	11	3	10-3	6
A.L. totals (1 year)	0	0	...	13.50	2	0	0	0	0-0	2.0	5	3	3	1	0-0	0
N.L. totals (6 years)	25	28	.472	5.37	152	53	2	0	4-9	425.1	502	282	254	46	154-16	298
Major League totals (7 years)	25	28	.472	5.41	154	53	2	0	4-9	427.1	507	285	257	47	154-16	298

SIMON, RANDALL — 1B — TIGERS

PERSONAL: Born May 26, 1975, in Willemstad, Curacao. ... 6-0/230. ... Bats left, throws left. ... Full name: Randall Carlito Simon.
HIGH SCHOOL: Juan Pablo Duarte Tech (Willemstad, Curacao).
TRANSACTIONS/CAREER NOTES: Signed as non-drafted free agent by Atlanta Braves organization (July 17, 1992). ... Released by Braves (March 31, 2000). ... Signed by Florida Marlins organization (April 5, 2000). ... Released by Marlins (May 8, 2000). ... Signed by New York Yankees organization (May 14, 2000). ... On Columbus disabled list (July 6-13, 2000). ... Granted free agency (October 18, 2000). ... Signed by Detroit Tigers organization (January 18, 2001).
STATISTICAL NOTES: Led Carolina League with 14 intentional bases on balls received in 1995. ... Led International League first basemen with 1,063 putouts and 1,149 total chances in 1997. ... Tied for International League lead in grounding into double plays with 18 in 1997. ... Led International League in grounding into double plays with 22 in 1998. ... Career major league grand slams: 2.
2002 GAMES PLAYED BY POSITION (MLB): DH—65; 1B—59.

		BATTING														FIELDING	
Year Team (League)	Pos.	G	AB	R	H	2B	3B	HR	RBI	BB	SO	SB-CS	Avg.	OBP	SLG	E	Avg.
1992— Dom. Braves (DSL)	C	11	43	7	12	4	2	0	7	5	6	1-...	.279	...	.465	4	.979
1993— Danville (Appl.)	1B	61	232	28	59	17	1	3	31	10	34	1-1	.254	.289	.375	10	.980
1994— Macon (S.Atl.)	1B	106	358	48	105	23	1	10	54	6	56	7-6	.293	.305	.447	9	.986
1995— Durham (Caro.)	1B	122	420	56	111	18	1	18	79	36	63	6-5	.264	.326	.440	10	.989
1996— Greenville (Sou.)	1B-OF	134	498	74	139	26	2	18	77	37	61	4-9	.279	.331	.448	16	.980
1997— Richmond (I.L.)	1B-DH	133	519	62	160	*45	1	14	*102	17	76	1-6	.308	.335	.480	•14	.988
— Atlanta (N.L.)	1B	13	14	2	6	1	0	0	1	1	2	0-0	.429	.467	.500	0	1.000
1998— Richmond (I.L.)	1B-DH	126	484	52	124	20	1	13	70	24	62	4-4	.256	.292	.382	*11	.989
— Atlanta (N.L.)	1B	7	16	2	3	0	0	0	4	0	1	0-0	.188	.176	.188	0	1.000
1999— Atlanta (N.L.)	1B	90	218	26	69	16	0	5	25	17	25	2-2	.317	.367	.459	3	.994
— Richmond (I.L.)	1B-DH	15	59	7	16	4	0	1	8	3	10	0-1	.271	.302	.390	0	1.000
2000— Calgary (PCL)■	1B	22	68	5	20	3	0	1	11	0	3	0-0	.294	.290	.382	4	.966
— Columbus (I.L.)■	1B-OF	94	364	52	97	20	4	17	74	35	42	6-5	.266	.325	.484	9	.987
2001— Toledo (I.L.)■	1B	59	222	27	75	13	0	10	31	21	21	0-3	.338	.400	.532	7	.986
— Detroit (A.L.)	1B-DH	81	256	28	78	14	2	6	37	15	28	0-1	.305	.341	.445	3	.992
2002— Detroit (A.L.)	DH-1B	130	482	51	145	17	1	19	82	13	30	0-1	.301	.320	.459	7	.988
American League totals (2 years)		211	738	79	223	31	3	25	119	28	58	0-2	.302	.327	.454	10	.990
National League totals (3 years)		110	248	30	78	17	0	5	30	18	28	2-2	.315	.361	.444	3	.995
Major League totals (5 years)		321	986	109	301	48	3	30	149	46	86	2-4	.305	.336	.451	13	.991

DIVISION SERIES RECORD

		BATTING														FIELDING	
Year Team (League)	Pos.	G	AB	R	H	2B	3B	HR	RBI	BB	SO	SB-CS	Avg.	OBP	SLG	E	Avg.
1999— Atlanta (N.L.)								Did not play.									

CHAMPIONSHIP SERIES RECORD

		BATTING														FIELDING	
Year Team (League)	Pos.	G	AB	R	H	2B	3B	HR	RBI	BB	SO	SB-CS	Avg.	OBP	SLG	E	Avg.
1999— Atlanta (N.L.)								Did not play.									

WORLD SERIES RECORD

		BATTING														FIELDING	
Year Team (League)	Pos.	G	AB	R	H	2B	3B	HR	RBI	BB	SO	SB-CS	Avg.	OBP	SLG	E	Avg.
1999— Atlanta (N.L.)								Did not play.									

SIMONTACCHI, JASON — P — CARDINALS

PERSONAL: Born November 13, 1973, in Mountain View, Calif. ... 6-2/185. ... Throws right, bats right. ... Full name: Jason William Simontacchi.

COLLEGE: Albertson College (Idaho).

TRANSACTIONS/CAREER NOTES: Selected by Kansas City Royals organization in 21st round of free-agent draft (June 4, 1996). ... Released by Royals (July 30, 1997). ... Signed by Springfield of the Frontier League (June 1998). ... Signed by Pittsburgh Pirates organization (January 6, 1999). ... Released by Pirates (September 29, 1999). ... Signed by Minnesota Twins organization (September 27, 2000). ... Granted free agency (October 15, 2001). ... Signed by St. Louis Cardinals organization (December 21, 2001).

CAREER HITTING (MLB): 12-for-50 (.240), 5 R, 0 2B, 0 3B, 0 HR, 2 RBI.

Year	League	W	L	Pct.	ERA	G	GS	CG	ShO	Sv.-Opp.	IP	H	R	ER	HR	BB-IBB	SO
1996—	Spokane (N'West)	2	5	.286	5.17	14	6	0	0	2-...	47.0	59	37	27	8	15-0	43
1997—	Lansing (Midw.)	3	7	.300	6.97	29	1	0	0	2-...	60.2	93	56	47	7	15-1	38
1998—	Springfield (Fron.)■	10	2	.833	2.95	16	16	3	...	0-...	110.0	103	43	36	14	21-3	92
1999—	Hickory (S.Atl.)■	4	6	.400	4.02	23	7	0	0	1-...	69.1	71	34	31	8	19-1	66
2000—										Did not play.							
2001—	Edmonton (PCL)■	7	13	.350	5.34	32	18	2	0	0-...	143.1	192	97	85	21	23-1	83
2002—	Memphis (PCL)■	5	1	.833	2.34	6	6	0	0	0-...	42.1	44	12	11	2	5-1	28
—	St. Louis (N.L.)	11	5	.688	4.02	24	24	0	0	0-0	143.1	134	68	64	18	54-4	72
Major League totals (1 year)		11	5	.688	4.02	24	24	0	0	0-0	143.1	134	68	64	18	54-4	72

SINGLETON, CHRIS — OF — ORIOLES

PERSONAL: Born August 15, 1972, in Mesa, Ariz. ... 6-2/210. ... Bats left, throws left. ... Full name: Christopher Verdell Singleton.

HIGH SCHOOL: Pinole (Calif.) Valley.

COLLEGE: Nevada.

TRANSACTIONS/CAREER NOTES: Selected by San Francisco Giants organization in second round of free-agent draft (June 3, 1993). ... Traded by Giants with P Alberto Castillo to New York Yankees for 3B Charlie Hayes and cash (November 11, 1997). ... Traded by Yankees to Chicago White Sox for a player to be named later (December 8, 1998); Yankees acquired P Rich Pratt to complete deal (January 10, 1999). ... Traded by White Sox to Baltimore Orioles for 2B/OF Willie Harris (January 29, 2002).

STATISTICAL NOTES: Led Texas League with nine sacrifice flies in 1997. ... Led Texas League outfielders with 253 putouts and 271 total chances and tied for league lead with four double plays in 1997. ... Tied for Texas League lead with four intentional bases on balls received in 1997. ... Hit for the cycle (July 6, 1999). ... Had 15-game hitting streak (May 6-26, 2002).

2002 GAMES PLAYED BY POSITION (MLB): OF—126; DH—1.

			BATTING														FIELDING	
Year	Team (League)	Pos.	G	AB	R	H	2B	3B	HR	RBI	BB	SO	SB-CS	Avg.	OBP	SLG	E	Avg.
1993—	Everett (N'West)	OF	58	219	39	58	14	4	3	18	18	46	14-3	.265	.322	.406	3	.974
1994—	San Jose (Calif.)	OF	113	425	51	106	17	5	2	49	27	62	19-6	.249	.297	.327	13	.952
1995—	San Jose (Calif.)	OF	94	405	55	112	13	5	2	31	17	49	33-13	.277	.313	.348	7	.955
1996—	Shreveport (Texas)	OF	129	500	68	149	31	9	5	72	24	58	27-12	.298	.333	.426	4	.986
—	Phoenix (PCL)	OF	9	32	3	4	0	0	0	0	1	2	0-0	.125	.152	.125	0	1.000
1997—	Shreveport (Texas)	OF	126	464	85	147	26	10	9	61	22	50	27-11	.317	.343	.474	7	.974
1998—	Columbus (I.L.)■	OF	121	413	55	105	17	10	6	45	27	78	9-3	.254	.304	.387	7	.974
1999—	Chicago (A.L.)■	OF-DH	133	496	72	149	31	6	17	72	22	45	20-5	.300	.328	.490	4	.990
2000—	Chicago (A.L.)	OF-DH	147	511	83	130	22	5	11	62	35	85	22-7	.254	.301	.382	3	.992
2001—	Chicago (A.L.)	OF-DH	140	392	57	117	21	5	7	45	20	61	12-11	.298	.331	.431	3	.991
2002—	Baltimore (A.L.)■	OF-DH	136	466	67	122	30	6	9	50	21	83	20-2	.262	.296	.410	4	.986
Major League totals (4 years)			556	1865	279	518	104	22	44	229	98	274	74-25	.278	.313	.428	14	.990

DIVISION SERIES RECORD

			BATTING														FIELDING	
Year	Team (League)	Pos.	G	AB	R	H	2B	3B	HR	RBI	BB	SO	SB-CS	Avg.	OBP	SLG	E	Avg.
2000—	Chicago (A.L.)	OF	3	9	1	1	0	1	0	1	0	2	0-0	.111	.111	.333	0	1.000

SIROTKA, MIKE — P — CUBS

PERSONAL: Born May 13, 1971, in Chicago. ... 6-1/200. ... Throws left, bats left. ... Full name: Michael Robert Sirotka.

HIGH SCHOOL: Westfield (Houston).

COLLEGE: Louisiana State.

TRANSACTIONS/CAREER NOTES: Selected by Chicago White Sox organization in 15th round of free-agent draft (June 3, 1993). ... On Hickory disabled list (July 1-28, 1993). ... On South Bend temporarily inactive list (August 27-October 4, 1993). ... Traded by White Sox with P Kevin Beirne, OF Brian Simmons and P Mike Williams to Toronto Blue Jays P David Wells and P Matt DeWitt (January 14, 2001). ... On disabled list (March 23, 2001-entire season). ... On disabled list (March 31, 2002-entire season). ... Released by Blue Jays (October 9, 2002). ... Signed by Chicago Cubs organization (October 30, 2002).

RECORDS: Shares major league single-inning record for most errors by pitcher—3 (April 9, 1999, fifth inning).

CAREER HITTING (MLB): 2-for-17 (.118), 1 R, 0 2B, 0 3B, 0 HR, 0 RBI.

Year	League	W	L	Pct.	ERA	G	GS	CG	ShO	Sv.-Opp.	IP	H	R	ER	HR	BB-IBB	SO
1993—	GC White Sox (GCL)	0	0	...	0.00	3	0	0	0	0-...	5.0	4	1	0	0	2-0	8
—	South Bend (Midw.)	0	1	.000	6.10	7	1	0	0	0-...	10.1	12	8	7	3	6-0	12
1994—	South Bend (Midw.)	12	9	.571	3.07	27	27	8	2	0-...	196.2	183	99	67	11	58-1	173
1995—	Birmingham (Sou.)	7	6	.538	3.20	16	16	1	0	0-...	101.1	95	42	36	11	22-0	79
—	Chicago (A.L.)	1	2	.333	4.19	6	6	0	0	0-0	34.1	39	16	16	2	17-0	19
—	Nashville (A.A.)	1	5	.167	2.83	8	8	0	0	0-...	54.0	51	21	17	4	13-1	34
1996—	Nashville (A.A.)	7	5	.583	3.60	15	15	1	1	0-...	90.0	90	44	36	10	24-0	58
—	Chicago (A.L.)	1	2	.333	7.18	15	4	0	0	0-0	26.1	34	27	21	3	12-0	11
1997—	Nashville (A.A.)	7	5	.583	3.28	19	19	1	0	0-...	112.1	115	49	41	13	22-0	92
—	Chicago (A.L.)	3	0	1.000	2.25	7	4	0	0	0-0	32.0	36	9	8	4	5-1	24
1998—	Chicago (A.L.)	14	15	.483	5.06	33	33	5	0	0-0	211.2	255	137	119	30	47-0	128

Year League	W	L	Pct.	ERA	G	GS	CG	ShO	Sv.-Opp.	IP	H	R	ER	HR	BB-IBB	SO
1999—Chicago (A.L.)	11	13	.458	4.00	32	32	3	1	0-0	209.0	236	108	93	24	57-2	125
2000—Chicago (A.L.)	15	10	.600	3.79	32	32	1	0	0-0	197.0	203	101	83	23	69-1	128
2001—Toronto (A.L.)■	Did not play.															
2002—Toronto (A.L.)	Did not play.															
Major League totals (6 years)	45	42	.517	4.31	125	111	9	1	0-0	710.1	803	398	340	86	207-4	435

DIVISION SERIES RECORD

Year League	W	L	Pct.	ERA	G	GS	CG	ShO	Sv.-Opp.	IP	H	R	ER	HR	BB-IBB	SO
2000—Chicago (A.L.)	0	1	.000	4.76	1	1	0	0	0-0	5.2	7	4	3	1	2-0	0

SMALL, AARON P

PERSONAL: Born November 23, 1971, in Oxnard, Calif. ... 6-5/237. ... Throws right, bats right. ... Full name: Aaron James Small.

HIGH SCHOOL: South Hills (Covina, Calif.).

TRANSACTIONS/CAREER NOTES: Selected by Toronto Blue Jays organization in 22nd round of free-agent draft (June 5, 1989). ... Traded by Blue Jays to Florida Marlins for a player to be named later (April 26, 1995); Blue Jays acquired P Ernie Delgado to complete deal (September 19, 1995). ... On Charlotte disabled list (May 3-June 14, 1995). ... Claimed on waivers by Seattle Mariners (January 23, 1996). ... Claimed on waivers by Oakland Athletics (January 29, 1996). ... Claimed on waivers by Arizona Diamondbacks (June 26, 1998). ... Released by Diamondbacks (March 30, 1999). ... Signed by Milwaukee Brewers organization (April 12, 1999). ... On Louisville disabled list (April 12-20, 1999). ... Released by Brewers (May 23, 1999). ... Signed by Tampa Bay Devil Rays organization (May 27, 1999). ... On Durham disabled list (September 2, 1999-remainder of season). ... Granted free agency (October 15, 1999). ... Signed by Colorado Rockies organization (January 5, 2000). ... Granted free agency (October 18, 2000). ... Signed by Anaheim Angels organization (December 21, 2000). ... On Salt Lake disabled list (April 5-20, 2001). ... Released by Angels (May 4, 2001). ... Signed by Atlanta Braves organization (May 10, 2001). ... Granted free agency (October 15, 2001). ... Re-signed by Braves organization (April 6, 2002). ... On Richmond disabled list (May 8-July 9 and July 22, 2002-remainder of season). ... Released by Braves (September 30, 2002).

STATISTICAL NOTES: Pitched 6-0 no-hit victory for Edmonton against Vancouver (August 8, 1996).

CAREER HITTING (MLB): 0-for-1 (.000), 0 R, 0 2B, 0 3B, 0 HR, 0 RBI.

Year League	W	L	Pct.	ERA	G	GS	CG	ShO	Sv.-Opp.	IP	H	R	ER	HR	BB-IBB	SO
1989—Medicine Hat (Pio.)	1	7	.125	5.86	15	14	0	0	0-...	70.2	80	55	46	2	31-1	40
1990—Myrtle Beach (S.Atl.)	9	9	.500	2.80	27	27	1	0	0-...	147.2	150	72	46	6	56-2	96
1991—Dunedin (FSL)	8	7	.533	2.73	24	23	1	0	0-...	148.1	129	51	45	5	42-1	92
1992—Knoxville (Sou.)	5	12	.294	5.27	27	24	2	1	0-...	135.0	152	94	79	13	61-0	79
1993—Knoxville (Sou.)	4	4	.500	3.39	48	9	0	0	16-...	93.0	99	44	35	5	40-4	44
1994—Knoxville (Sou.)	5	5	.500	2.99	29	11	1	1	5-...	96.1	92	37	32	4	38-0	75
—Syracuse (I.L.)	3	2	.600	2.22	13	0	0	0	0-...	24.1	19	8	6	2	9-2	15
—Toronto (A.L.)	0	0	...	9.00	1	0	0	0	0-0	2.0	5	2	2	1	2-0	0
1995—Syracuse (I.L.)	0	0	...	5.40	1	0	0	0	0-...	1.2	3	1	1	1	1-0	2
—Charlotte (I.L.)■	2	1	.667	2.88	33	0	0	0	10-...	40.2	36	15	13	2	10-1	31
—Florida (N.L.)	1	0	1.000	1.42	7	0	0	0	0-0	6.1	7	2	1	1	6-0	5
1996—Oakland (A.L.)■	1	3	.250	8.16	12	3	0	0	0-0	28.2	37	28	26	3	22-1	17
—Edmonton (PCL)	8	6	.571	4.29	25	19	1	1	1-...	119.2	111	65	57	9	28-0	83
1997—Edmonton (PCL)	1	0	1.000	0.00	1	1	0	0	0-...	5.0	1	0	0	0	0-0	4
—Oakland (A.L.)	9	5	.643	4.28	71	0	0	0	4-6	96.2	109	50	46	6	40-6	57
1998—Oakland (A.L.)	1	1	.500	7.25	24	0	0	0	0-0	36.0	51	34	29	3	14-3	19
—Arizona (N.L.)■	3	1	.750	3.69	23	0	0	0	0-2	31.2	32	14	13	5	8-1	14
1999—Louisville (I.L.)■	1	1	.500	9.43	11	0	0	0	0-...	21.0	38	23	22	3	15-1	11
—Durham (I.L.)■	4	6	.400	6.34	21	18	0	0	0-...	99.1	118	81	70	16	32-2	52
2000—Colorado Springs (PCL)■	11	6	.647	5.61	36	18	0	0	0-...	131.2	152	87	82	14	43-0	85
2001—Salt Lake (PCL)■	0	1	.000	1.69	3	0	0	0	0-...	5.1	8	1	1	1	1-0	5
—Richmond (I.L.)■	10	7	.588	3.83	41	11	0	0	0-...	96.1	97	50	41	14	31-5	61
2002—Richmond (I.L.)	0	3	.000	6.39	14	4	0	0	0-...	31.0	48	27	22	2	14-1	19
—Atlanta (N.L.)	0	0	...	27.00	1	0	0	0	0-0	.1	2	1	1	0	2-0	1
—Gulf Coast Braves (GCL)	0	0	...	6.00	5	5	0	0	0-...	6.0	9	4	4	0	0-0	3
A.L. totals (4 years)	11	9	.550	5.68	108	3	0	0	4-6	163.1	202	114	103	13	78-10	93
N.L. totals (3 years)	4	1	.800	3.52	31	0	0	0	0-2	38.1	41	17	15	6	16-1	20
Major League totals (6 years)	15	10	.600	5.27	139	3	0	0	4-8	201.2	243	131	118	19	94-11	113

SMITH, BOBBY IF BREWERS

PERSONAL: Born May 10, 1974, in Oakland. ... 6-3/199. ... Bats right, throws right. ... Full name: Robert Eugene Smith.

HIGH SCHOOL: Fremont (Oakland).

TRANSACTIONS/CAREER NOTES: Selected by Atlanta Braves organization in 11th round of free-agent draft (June 1, 1992). ... Selected by Tampa Bay Devil Rays in first round (12th pick overall) of expansion draft (November 18, 1997). ... On disabled list (May 13-28, 1998). ... On Tampa Bay disabled list (July 6-August 19, 2000); included rehabilitation assignment to Durham (August 14-19). ... On suspended list (September 8-9, 2000). ... On Durham disabled list (April 30-May 14, 2001). ... Released by Devil Rays (May 8, 2002). ... Signed by Milwaukee Brewers organization (May 28, 2002). ... On Indianapolis disabled list (August 26-September 3, 2002).

STATISTICAL NOTES: Tied for Carolina League lead in grounding into double plays with 19 in 1994. ... Led Carolina League third basemen with 104 putouts, 388 total chances and 27 double plays in 1994. ... Led Southern League third basemen with 120 putouts in 1995.

2002 GAMES PLAYED BY POSITION (MLB): 3B—10; 1B—6; OF—2; DH—1.

					BATTING										FIELDING	
Year Team (League)	Pos.	G	AB	R	H	2B	3B	HR	RBI	BB	SO	SB-CS	Avg.	OBP	SLG	E	Avg.
1992—GC Braves (GCL)	3B	57	217	31	51	9	1	3	28	17	55	5-6	.235	.297	.327	15	.910
1993—Macon (S.Atl.)	3B	108	384	53	94	16	7	4	38	23	81	12-8	.245	.296	.354	30	.885
1994—Durham (Caro.)	3B	127	478	49	127	27	2	12	71	41	112	18-7	.266	.329	.406	31	*.920
1995—Greenville (Sou.)	3B	127	444	75	116	27	3	14	58	40	109	12-6	.261	.331	.430	26	.937
1996—Richmond (I.L.)	3B-SS-DH	124	445	49	114	27	0	8	58	32	114	15-9	.256	.310	.371	24	.935
1997—Richmond (I.L.)	SS-DH	100	357	47	88	10	2	12	47	44	109	6-5	.246	.340	.387	23	.952
1998—Tampa Bay (A.L.)■	3-DH-S-2	117	370	44	102	15	3	11	55	34	110	5-3	.276	.343	.422	13	.957
1999—Tampa Bay (A.L.)	3B-2B	68	199	18	36	4	1	3	19	16	64	4-4	.181	.244	.256	11	.942
—Durham (I.L.)	3B-SS	57	225	52	75	15	3	14	47	27	61	13-3	.333	.409	.613	10	.945

Year	Team (League)	Pos.	G	AB	R	H	2B	3B	HR	RBI	BB	SO	SB-CS	Avg.	OBP	SLG	E	Avg.
			BATTING														FIELDING	
2000—	Durham (I.L.)	2B-SS-3B	66	261	48	76	20	2	17	58	23	61	15-2	.291	.351	.579	9	.971
	—Tampa Bay (A.L.)	2B-3B	49	175	21	41	8	0	6	26	14	59	2-2	.234	.293	.383	8	.967
2001—	Tampa Bay (A.L.)	2B	6	19	1	2	0	0	0	1	3	10	0-0	.105	.227	.105	1	.958
	—Durham (I.L.)	0-2-S-3-1	107	396	67	119	25	2	22	70	46	91	10-2	.301	.380	.540	7	.977
2002—	Tampa Bay (A.L.)	3B-1B-OF-DH	18	63	4	11	2	0	1	6	3	25	0-0	.175	.212	.254	4	.954
	—Indianapolis (I.L.)■	3B-1B-2B-OF	80	293	26	70	21	0	7	31	25	57	11-2	.239	.307	.382	13	.958
Major League totals (5 years)			258	826	88	192	29	4	21	107	70	268	11-9	.232	.297	.354	37	.956

SMITH, BUD — P — PHILLIES

PERSONAL: Born October 23, 1979, in Torrance, Calif. ... 6-0/170. ... Throws left, bats left. ... Full name: Robert Allan Smith.
HIGH SCHOOL: St. John Bosco (Bellflower, Calif.).
JUNIOR COLLEGE: Los Angeles Harbor.
TRANSACTIONS/CAREER NOTES: Selected by St. Louis Cardinals organization in fourth round of free-agent draft (June 2, 1998). ... On St. Louis disabled list (April 22-May 7, 2002). ... Traded by Cardinals with IF/OF Placido Polanco and P Mike Timlin to Philadelphia Phillies for 3B Scott Rolen and P Doug Nickle (July 29, 2002). ... On Scranton/Wilkes-Barre disabled list (August 15, 2002-remainder of season).
HONORS: Named Texas League Pitcher of the Year (2000).
STATISTICAL NOTES: Pitched 5-0 no-hit victory for Arkansas against Midland (May 6, 2000, second game). ... Pitched 1-0 no-hit victory for Arkansas against San Antonio (June 11, 2000, second game). ... Pitched 3-0 no-hit victory against San Diego (September 3, 2001).
CAREER HITTING (MLB): 7-for-39 (.179), 0 R, 1 2B, 0 3B, 0 HR, 2 RBI.

Year	League	W	L	Pct.	ERA	G	GS	CG	ShO	Sv.-Opp.	IP	H	R	ER	HR	BB-IBB	SO
1998—	Johnson City (Appl.)	3	3	.500	5.18	14	•14	0	0	0-...	64.1	85	47	37	9	34-1	65
1999—	Peoria (Midw.)	4	1	.800	2.83	9	9	0	0	0-...	54.0	53	20	17	4	16-0	59
	—Potomac (Caro.)	4	9	.308	2.96	18	18	0	0	0-...	103.1	91	47	34	2	32-0	93
2000—	Arkansas (Texas)	12	1	.923	2.32	18	18	•3	*3	0-...	108.2	93	32	28	5	27-1	102
	—Memphis (PCL)	5	1	.833	2.15	9	8	0	0	0-...	54.1	40	24	13	4	15-0	34
2001—	Memphis (PCL)	8	5	.615	2.75	17	17	0	0	0-...	108.0	114	38	33	6	28-2	78
	—St. Louis (N.L.)	6	3	.667	3.83	16	14	1	1	0-0	84.2	79	40	36	12	24-5	59
2002—	Memphis (PCL)	3	0	1.000	2.13	6	6	0	0	0-...	38.0	33	10	9	1	13-0	34
	—St. Louis (N.L.)	1	5	.167	6.94	11	10	0	0	0-0	48.0	67	39	37	4	22-2	22
	—Scranton/W.B. (I.L.)■	0	1	.000	4.15	3	3	0	0	0-...	17.1	21	8	8	0	6-0	11
Major League totals (2 years)		7	8	.467	4.95	27	24	1	1	0-0	132.2	146	79	73	16	46-7	81

DIVISION SERIES RECORD

Year	League	W	L	Pct.	ERA	G	GS	CG	ShO	Sv.-Opp.	IP	H	R	ER	HR	BB-IBB	SO
2001—	St. Louis (N.L.)	1	0	1.000	1.80	1	1	0	0	0-0	5.0	4	1	1	0	4-0	2

SMITH, DAN — P — EXPOS

PERSONAL: Born September 15, 1975, in Flemington, N.J. ... 6-3/210. ... Throws right, bats right. ... Full name: Daniel Charles Smith Jr.
HIGH SCHOOL: Girard (Kan.).
TRANSACTIONS/CAREER NOTES: Selected by Texas Rangers organization in seventh round of free-agent draft (June 3, 1993). ... On Charlotte disabled list (June 12-July 7, 1995). ... Claimed on waivers by Montreal Expos (December 14, 1998). ... Granted free agency (December 21, 1999). ... Signed by Boston Red Sox organization (June 2, 2000). ... Granted free agency (October 18, 2000). ... Signed by Cleveland Indians organization (November 15, 2000). ... On disabled list (April 16-May 19, 2001). ... Granted free agency (October 15, 2001). ... Signed by Expos organization (January 11, 2002).
STATISTICAL NOTES: Led South Atlantic League with 19 hit batsmen in 1994.
CAREER HITTING (MLB): 2-for-27 (.074), 3 R, 0 2B, 0 3B, 0 HR, 1 RBI.

Year	League	W	L	Pct.	ERA	G	GS	CG	ShO	Sv.-Opp.	IP	H	R	ER	HR	BB-IBB	SO
1993—	Gulf Coast Rangers (GCL)	3	2	.600	2.87	12	10	1	0	0-...	53.1	50	19	17	1	8-0	27
1994—	Charleston, S.C. (S.Atl.)	7	10	.412	4.92	27	27	4	0	0-...	157.1	171	*111	86	12	55-0	86
1995—	Gulf Coast Rangers (GCL)	0	3	.000	4.26	4	3	0	0	0-...	19.0	19	9	9	0	5-0	12
	—Charlotte (FSL)	5	1	.833	2.95	9	9	1	1	0-...	58.0	53	23	19	4	16-0	34
1996—	Charlotte (FSL)	3	7	.300	5.07	18	18	1	0	0-...	87.0	100	61	49	6	38-0	55
1997—	Charlotte (FSL)	8	10	.444	4.43	26	25	2	0	0-...	160.2	169	93	79	17	66-1	113
1998—	Tulsa (Texas)	13	9	.591	5.81	26	25	1	0	0-...	153.1	162	101	99	27	58-1	105
	—Oklahoma (PCL)	0	0	...	6.00	1	1	0	0	0-...	6.0	6	4	4	2	1-0	3
1999—	Ottawa (I.L.)■	5	4	.556	3.68	11	11	0	0	0-...	71.0	61	31	29	7	27-0	59
	—Montreal (N.L.)	4	9	.308	6.02	20	17	0	0	0-1	89.2	104	64	60	12	39-0	72
2000—	Pawtucket (I.L.)■	7	10	.412	4.84	24	21	2	1	0-...	124.2	134	72	67	15	41-1	70
	—Boston (A.L.)	0	0	...	8.10	2	0	0	0	0-0	3.1	2	3	3	0	3-0	1
2001—	Buffalo (I.L.)■	6	4	.600	4.50	21	16	1	0	0-...	106.0	110	58	53	17	44-0	68
2002—	Ottawa (I.L.)■	5	4	.556	3.24	14	14	1	0	0-...	83.1	71	30	30	10	18-1	61
	—Montreal (N.L.)	1	1	.500	3.47	33	0	0	0	2-2	46.2	34	18	18	6	21-0	34
A.L. totals (1 year)		0	0	...	8.10	2	0	0	0	0-0	3.1	2	3	3	0	3-0	1
N.L. totals (2 years)		5	10	.333	5.15	53	17	0	0	2-3	136.1	138	82	78	18	60-0	106
Major League totals (3 years)		5	10	.333	5.22	55	17	0	0	2-3	139.2	140	85	81	18	63-0	107

SMITH, JASON — SS — DEVIL RAYS

PERSONAL: Born July 24, 1977, in Meridian, Miss. ... 6-3/199. ... Bats left, throws right. ... Full name: Jason William Smith.
HIGH SCHOOL: Demopolis (Ala.).
JUNIOR COLLEGE: Meridian (Miss.) Community College.
TRANSACTIONS/CAREER NOTES: Selected by Chicago Cubs organization in 23rd round free-agent draft (June 4, 1996). ... On Iowa disabled list (July 9-August 2, 2001). ... Traded by Cubs to Tampa Bay Devil Rays (August 5, 2001), completing deal in which Devil Rays traded 1B Fred McGriff to Cubs for P Manny Aybar and a player to be named later (July 27, 2001).
2002 GAMES PLAYED BY POSITION (MLB): 3B—12; SS—9; 2B—1; DH—1.

Year Team (League)	Pos.	G	AB	R	H	2B	3B	HR	RBI	BB	SO	SB-CS	Avg.	OBP	SLG	E	Avg.
		BATTING														FIELDING	
1997—Williamsport (NY-P)...	SS	51	205	25	59	5	2	0	11	10	44	9-2	.288	.321	.332	19	.930
—Rockford (Midw.).......	SS	9	33	4	6	0	1	0	3	2	11	1-0	.182	.229	.242	5	.884
1998—Rockford (Midw.).......	SS	126	464	67	111	15	9	7	60	31	122	23-6	.239	.286	.356	38	.939
1999—Daytona (FSL)...........	SS	39	142	22	37	5	2	5	26	12	29	9-3	.261	.329	.430	7	.953
2000—West Tenn (Sou.).......	SS	119	481	55	114	22	7	12	61	22	130	16-10	.237	.273	.387	37	.927
2001—Iowa (PCL)................	SS	70	240	31	56	8	6	4	15	12	71	6-3	.233	.271	.367	19	.942
—Chicago (N.L.)...........	SS	2	1	0	0	0	0	0	0	0	1	0-0	.000	.000	.000	0	1.000
—Durham (I.L.)■.........	SS	8	31	2	6	1	0	0	3	0	11	0-0	.194	.194	.226	3	.917
2002—Tampa Bay (A.L.)........	3B-SS-2B-DH	26	65	9	13	1	2	1	6	2	24	3-0	.200	.224	.323	6	.905
—Durham (I.L.)............	SS-3B	54	206	29	57	11	2	4	28	10	44	5-1	.277	.312	.408	16	.936
American League totals (1 year)		26	65	9	13	1	2	1	6	2	24	3-0	.200	.224	.323	6	.905
National League totals (1 year)		2	1	0	0	0	0	0	0	0	1	0-0	.000	.000	.000	0	1.000
Major League totals (2 years)		28	66	9	13	1	2	1	6	2	25	3-0	.197	.221	.318	6	.908

SMITH, MIKE P BLUE JAYS

PERSONAL: Born September 19, 1977, in Norwood, Mass. ... 5-11/195. ... Throws right, bats right. ... Full name: Michael Anthony Smith.
COLLEGE: Richmond.
TRANSACTIONS/CAREER NOTES: Selected by Toronto Blue Jays organization in fifth round of free-agent draft (June 15, 2000).
CAREER HITTING (MLB): 0-for-0 (.000), 0 R, 0 2B, 0 3B, 0 HR, 0 RBI.

Year League	W	L	Pct.	ERA	G	GS	CG	ShO	Sv.-Opp.	IP	H	R	ER	HR	BB-IBB	SO
2000—Queens (NY-Penn)............	2	2	.500	2.29	14	12	0	0	0-...	51.0	41	18	13	1	17-0	55
2001—Charleston, W.Va. (S.Atl.).	5	5	.500	2.10	14	14	2	1	0-...	94.1	78	32	22	2	21-0	85
—Tennessee (Sou.)............	6	2	.750	2.42	14	14	1	0	0-...	93.0	80	32	25	7	26-2	77
2002—Syracuse (I.L.)..................	8	4	.667	3.48	20	20	1	1	0-...	121.2	106	51	47	10	43-0	76
—Toronto (A.L.)..................	0	3	.000	6.62	14	6	0	0	0-0	35.1	43	28	26	3	20-0	16
Major League totals (1 year)......	0	3	.000	6.62	14	6	0	0	0-0	35.1	43	28	26	3	20-0	16

SMITH, ROY P ATHLETICS

PERSONAL: Born May 18, 1976, in St. Petersburg, Fla. ... 6-6/235. ... Throws right, bats right. ... Full name: Walter Roy Smith.
HIGH SCHOOL: Dixie Hollins (St. Petersburg, Fla.).
JUNIOR COLLEGE: St. Petersburg.
TRANSACTIONS/CAREER NOTES: Selected by Seattle Mariners organization in 13th round of free-agent draft (June 2, 1994). ... Released by Mariners (March 24, 1998). ... Signed by St. Paul, Northern League (May, 1998). ... Signed by Cleveland Indians organization (January 17, 2000). ... Granted free agency (October 15, 2000). ... Re-signed by Indians organization (December 20, 2000). ... Traded by Indians to Oakland Athletics for cash considerations (November 13, 2002).
CAREER HITTING (MLB): 0-for-0 (.000), 0 R, 0 2B, 0 3B, 0 HR, 0 RBI.

Year League	W	L	Pct.	ERA	G	GS	CG	ShO	Sv.-Opp.	IP	H	R	ER	HR	BB-IBB	SO
1994—Arizona Mariners (Ariz.)...	3	1	.750	1.60	11	5	0	0	0-...	45.0	30	9	8	2	4-0	35
1995—Wisconsin (Midw.)...........	7	14	.333	5.38	27	•27	1	0	0-...	149.0	*179	*100	*89	9	54-2	109
1996—Wisconsin (Midw.)...........	6	13	.316	5.12	27	27	0	0	0-...	146.0	164	113	83	9	73-3	99
1997—Wisconsin (Midw.)...........	3	4	.429	5.59	18	11	0	0	0-...	66.0	81	50	41	3	31-0	38
—Memphis (Sou.)...............	0	0	...	10.38	4	0	0	0	0-...	4.1	6	5	5	0	1-0	6
1998—St. Paul (Nor.)■...............	6	7	.462	5.03	18	18	1	•1	0-...	105.2	119	75	59	10	36-0	74
1999—St. Paul (Nor.).................	4	2	.667	3.21	8	7	1	1	0-...	42.0	38	18	15	3	23-0	43
2000—Kinston (Caro.)■.............	2	2	.500	2.80	21	0	0	0	2-...	45.0	35	15	14	0	21-1	45
—Akron (East.)..................	5	1	.833	1.96	28	0	0	0	6-...	55.0	36	14	12	0	22-2	50
2001—Buffalo (I.L.).....................	0	5	.000	2.19	48	0	0	0	18-...	74.0	59	25	18	2	29-4	86
—Cleveland (A.L.)...............	0	0	...	6.06	9	0	0	0	0-0	16.1	16	14	11	3	13-1	17
2002—Buffalo (I.L.).....................	5	4	.556	3.84	36	3	0	0	1-...	70.1	65	37	30	2	29-0	65
—Cleveland (A.L.)...............	0	0	...	3.00	4	1	0	0	0-0	6.0	9	4	2	1	5-0	2
Major League totals (2 years).....	0	0	...	5.24	13	1	0	0	0-0	22.1	25	18	13	4	18-1	19

SMITH, TRAVIS P

PERSONAL: Born November 7, 1972, in Springfield, Ore. ... 5-10/165. ... Throws right, bats right. ... Full name: Travis William Smith.
HIGH SCHOOL: Bend (Ore.).
COLLEGE: Texas Tech.
TRANSACTIONS/CAREER NOTES: Selected by Milwaukee Brewers organization in 19th round of free-agent draft (June 1, 1995). ... On Louisville disabled list (April 9-18, 1998). ... On Milwaukee disabled list (June 23, 1998-remainder of season). ... Released by Brewers (October 5, 1998). ... Resigned by Brewers organization (March 30, 1999). ... On Louisville disabled list (April 8-July 6, 1999). ... Released by Brewers (October 14, 1999). ... Re-signed by Brewers (December 7, 1999). ... Granted free agency (October 18, 2000). ... Signed by Houston Astros organization (November 1, 2000). ... Granted free agency (October 15, 2001). ... Signed by St. Louis Cardinals organization (November 21, 2001). ... Granted free agency (October 15, 2002).
CAREER HITTING (MLB): 3-for-19 (.158), 0 R, 0 2B, 0 3B, 0 HR, 2 RBI.

Year League	W	L	Pct.	ERA	G	GS	CG	ShO	Sv.-Opp.	IP	H	R	ER	HR	BB-IBB	SO
1995—Helena (Pio.)....................	4	2	.667	2.41	20	7	0	0	5-...	56.0	41	16	15	4	19-0	63
1996—Stockton (Calif.)...............	6	1	.857	1.84	14	6	0	0	1-...	58.2	56	17	12	4	21-0	48
—El Paso (Texas)................	7	4	.636	4.18	17	17	3	1	0-...	107.2	119	56	50	6	39-0	68
1997—El Paso (Texas)................	*16	3	*.842	4.15	28	28	5	•1	0-...	184.1	210	106	85	12	58-2	107
1998—Louisville (I.L.)................	4	6	.400	5.32	12	11	0	0	0-...	67.2	77	44	40	9	25-1	36
—Milwaukee (N.L.)...............	0	0	...	0.00	1	0	0	0	0-0	2.0	1	0	0	0	0-0	1
1999—Ogden (Pio.).....................	0	0	...	0.00	1	1	0	0	0-...	1.0	0	1	0	0	0-0	3
—Stockton (Calif.)...............	0	2	.000	6.14	3	3	0	0	0-...	7.1	9	6	5	1	3-0	8
—Huntsville (Sou.)..............	3	2	.600	5.87	7	7	0	0	0-...	38.1	40	27	25	3	18-0	23
2000—Huntsville (Sou.).............	12	7	.632	3.73	27	24	1	1	0-...	154.1	141	77	64	13	37-0	113
—Indianapolis (I.L.)............	1	1	.500	12.66	3	3	0	0	0-...	10.2	19	18	15	6	9-1	5

Year	League	W	L	Pct.	ERA	G	GS	CG	ShO	Sv.-Opp.	IP	H	R	ER	HR	BB-IBB	SO
2001—	Round Rock (Texas)■	*15	8	.652	3.09	29	22	1	0	1-...	160.1	154	66	55	7	26-0	85
—	New Orleans (PCL)	0	0	...	0.00	1	0	0	0	0-...	2.0	3	0	0	0	1-0	0
2002—	Memphis (PCL)■	4	7	.364	2.31	16	13	1	0	0-...	85.2	76	24	22	7	14-1	62
—	St. Louis (N.L.)	4	2	.667	7.17	12	10	0	0	0-0	54.0	69	44	43	10	20-0	32
Major League totals (2 years)		4	2	.667	6.91	13	10	0	0	0-0	56.0	70	44	43	10	20-0	33

SMOLTZ, JOHN — P — BRAVES

PERSONAL: Born May 15, 1967, in Warren, Mich. ... 6-3/220. ... Throws right, bats right. ... Full name: John Andrew Smoltz.

HIGH SCHOOL: Waverly (Lansing, Mich.).

TRANSACTIONS/CAREER NOTES: Selected by Detroit Tigers organization in 22nd round of free-agent draft (June 3, 1985). ... Traded by Tigers to Atlanta Braves for P Doyle Alexander (August 12, 1987). ... On suspended list (June 20-29, 1994). ... Granted free agency (October 31, 1996). ... Re-signed by Braves (November 20, 1996). ... On Atlanta disabled list (March 29-April 15, and May 24-June 20, 1998); included rehabilitation assignments to Greenville (April 2-10 and June 10-14) and Macon (April 10-14 and June 14-16). ... On Atlanta disabled list (May 17-June 1 and July 5-24, 1999); included rehabilitation assignment to Greenville (July 15-18). ... On disabled list (April 2, 2000-entire season). ... On Atlanta disabled list (March 23-May 17 and June 10-July 22, 2001); included rehabilitation assignments to Macon (May 9-17) and Greenville (May 5-8 and July 17-22). ... Granted free agency (November 5, 2001). ... Re-signed by Braves (December 4, 2001).

RECORDS: Shares major league record for most home runs allowed in one inning—4 (June 19, 1994, first inning). ... Holds N.L. single-season record for most saves—55 (2002).

HONORS: Named N.L. Pitcher of the Year by The Sporting News (1996). ... Named righthanded pitcher on The Sporting News N.L. All-Star team (1996). ... Named N.L. Cy Young Award winner by Baseball Writers' Association of America (1996). ... Named pitcher on The Sporting News N.L. Silver Slugger team (1997). ... Named N.L. Relief Pitcher of the Year by The Sporting News (2002).

STATISTICAL NOTES: Tied for Florida State League lead with six balks in 1986. ... Led N.L. with 14 wild pitches in 1990, 20 in 1991 and 17 in 1992. ... Struck out 15 batters in one game (May 24, 1992). ... Pitched 3-0 one-hit, complete-game victory against Cincinnati (May 28, 1995). ... Led N.L. with 59 save opportunities in 2002.

MISCELLANEOUS: Appeared in three games as pinch runner and struck out in only appearance in pinch hitter (1989). ... Appeared in four games as pinch runner (1990). ... Appeared in two games as pinch runner (1991). ... Struck out in only appearance as pinch hitter (1992). ... Appeared in one game as pinch runner (1997).

CAREER HITTING (MLB): 127-for-736 (.173), 69 R, 20 2B, 1 3B, 5 HR, 51 RBI.

Year	League	W	L	Pct.	ERA	G	GS	CG	ShO	Sv.-Opp.	IP	H	R	ER	HR	BB-IBB	SO
1986—	Lakeland (FSL)	7	8	.467	3.56	17	14	2	1	0-...	96.0	86	44	38	7	31-0	47
1987—	Glens Falls (East.)	4	10	.286	5.68	21	21	0	0	0-...	130.0	131	89	82	17	81-2	86
—	Richmond (I.L.)■	0	1	.000	6.19	3	3	0	0	0-...	16.0	17	11	11	2	11-0	5
1988—	Richmond (I.L.)	10	5	.667	2.79	20	20	3	0	0-...	135.1	118	49	42	5	37-1	115
—	Atlanta (N.L.)	2	7	.222	5.48	12	12	0	0	0-0	64.0	74	40	39	10	33-4	37
1989—	Atlanta (N.L.)	12	11	.522	2.94	29	29	5	0	0-0	208.0	160	79	68	15	72-2	168
1990—	Atlanta (N.L.)	14	11	.560	3.85	34	34	6	2	0-0	231.1	206	109	99	20	*90-3	170
1991—	Atlanta (N.L.)	14	13	.519	3.80	36	36	5	0	0-0	229.2	206	101	97	16	77-1	148
1992—	Atlanta (N.L.)	15	12	.556	2.85	35	•35	9	3	0-0	246.2	206	90	78	17	80-5	*215
1993—	Atlanta (N.L.)	15	11	.577	3.62	35	35	3	1	0-0	243.2	208	104	98	23	100-12	208
1994—	Atlanta (N.L.)	6	10	.375	4.14	21	21	1	0	0-0	134.2	120	69	62	15	48-4	113
1995—	Atlanta (N.L.)	12	7	.632	3.18	29	29	2	1	0-0	192.2	166	76	68	15	72-8	193
1996—	Atlanta (N.L.)	*24	8	*.750	2.94	35	35	6	2	0-0	*253.2	199	93	83	19	55-3	*276
1997—	Atlanta (N.L.)	15	12	.556	3.02	35	•35	7	2	0-0	*256.0	*234	97	86	21	63-9	241
1998—	Greenville (Sou.)	0	1	.000	2.57	3	3	0	0	0-...	14.0	11	4	4	2	3-0	16
—	Macon (S.Atl.)	0	0	...	3.60	2	2	0	0	0-...	10.0	7	4	4	1	1-0	14
—	Atlanta (N.L.)	17	3	*.850	2.90	26	26	2	2	0-0	167.2	145	58	54	10	44-2	173
1999—	Atlanta (N.L.)	11	8	.579	3.19	29	29	1	1	0-0	186.1	168	70	66	14	40-2	156
—	Greenville (Sou.)	0	0	...	4.50	2	1	0	0	0-...	4.0	5	2	2	0	1-0	7
2000—	Atlanta (N.L.)									Did not play.							
2001—	Greenville (Sou.)	0	0	...	0.00	3	1	0	0	0-...	6.0	3	0	0	0	0-0	6
—	Macon (S.Atl.)	0	0	...	1.80	1	1	0	0	0-...	5.0	4	1	1	0	0-0	5
—	Atlanta (N.L.)	3	3	.500	3.36	36	5	0	0	10-11	59.0	53	24	22	7	10-2	57
2002—	Atlanta (N.L.)	3	2	.600	3.25	75	0	0	0	*55-59	80.1	59	30	29	4	24-1	85
Major League totals (14 years)		163	118	.580	3.34	467	361	47	14	65-70	2553.2	2204	1040	949	206	808-58	2240

DIVISION SERIES RECORD

RECORDS: Holds N.L. career record for most strikeouts—43. ... Shares N.L. career record for most games pitched—10.

Year	League	W	L	Pct.	ERA	G	GS	CG	ShO	Sv.-Opp.	IP	H	R	ER	HR	BB-IBB	SO
1995—	Atlanta (N.L.)	0	0	...	7.94	1	1	0	0	0-0	5.2	5	5	5	2	1-0	6
1996—	Atlanta (N.L.)	1	0	1.000	1.00	1	1	0	0	0-0	9.0	4	1	1	0	2-0	7
1997—	Atlanta (N.L.)	1	0	1.000	1.00	1	1	1	0	0-0	9.0	3	1	1	1	1-0	11
1998—	Atlanta (N.L.)	1	0	1.000	1.17	1	1	0	0	0-0	7.2	5	1	1	1	0-0	6
1999—	Atlanta (N.L.)	1	0	1.000	5.14	1	1	0	0	0-0	7.0	6	4	4	2	3-0	3
2001—	Atlanta (N.L.)	0	0	...	2.25	3	0	0	0	2-2	4.0	3	1	1	1	0-0	3
2002—	Atlanta (N.L.)	0	0	...	2.70	2	0	0	0	0-0	3.1	2	1	1	1	2-0	7
Division series totals (7 years)		4	0	1.000	2.76	10	5	1	0	2-2	45.2	28	14	14	8	9-0	43

CHAMPIONSHIP SERIES RECORD

RECORDS: Holds career records for most innings pitched—95 1/3; and most strikeouts—89. ... Shares N.L. career records for most wins—6; and home runs allowed—8.

NOTES: Named Most Valuable Player (1992).

Year	League	W	L	Pct.	ERA	G	GS	CG	ShO	Sv.-Opp.	IP	H	R	ER	HR	BB-IBB	SO
1991—	Atlanta (N.L.)	2	0	1.000	1.76	2	2	1	1	0-0	15.1	14	3	3	2	3-0	15
1992—	Atlanta (N.L.)	2	0	1.000	2.66	3	3	0	0	0-0	20.1	14	7	6	1	10-2	19
1993—	Atlanta (N.L.)	0	1	.000	0.00	1	1	0	0	0-0	6.1	8	2	0	0	5-0	10
1995—	Atlanta (N.L.)	0	0	...	2.57	1	1	0	0	0-0	7.0	7	2	2	0	2-0	2
1996—	Atlanta (N.L.)	2	0	1.000	1.20	2	2	0	0	0-0	15.0	12	2	2	0	3-0	12
1997—	Atlanta (N.L.)	0	1	.000	7.50	1	1	0	0	0-0	6.0	5	5	5	1	5-2	9
1998—	Atlanta (N.L.)	0	0	...	3.95	2	2	0	0	0-0	13.2	13	6	6	2	6-0	13
1999—	Atlanta (N.L.)	0	0	...	6.23	3	1	0	0	1-1	8.2	8	6	6	2	0-0	8
2001—	Atlanta (N.L.)	0	0	...	0.00	2	0	0	0	0-0	3.0	0	0	0	0	0-0	1
Champ. series totals (9 years)		6	2	.750	2.83	17	13	1	1	1-1	95.1	81	33	30	8	34-4	89

WORLD SERIES RECORD

NOTES: Appeared in one game as pinch runner (1992). ... Member of World Series championship team (1995).

Year League	W	L	Pct.	ERA	G	GS	CG	ShO	Sv.-Opp.	IP	H	R	ER	HR	BB-IBB	SO
1991—Atlanta (N.L.)	0	0	...	1.26	2	2	0	0	0-0	14.1	13	2	2	1	1-0	11
1992—Atlanta (N.L.)	1	0	1.000	2.70	2	2	0	0	0-0	13.1	13	5	4	0	7-0	12
1995—Atlanta (N.L.)	0	0	...	15.43	1	1	0	0	0-0	2.1	6	4	4	0	2-0	4
1996—Atlanta (N.L.)	1	1	.500	0.64	2	2	0	0	0-0	14.0	6	2	1	0	8-0	14
1999—Atlanta (N.L.)	0	1	.000	3.86	1	1	0	0	0-0	7.0	6	3	3	0	3-1	11
World Series totals (5 years)	2	2	.500	2.47	8	8	0	0	0-0	51.0	44	16	14	1	21-1	52

ALL-STAR GAME RECORD

RECORDS: Shares single-game record for most wild pitches—2 (July 13, 1993). ... Shares single-inning record for most wild pitches—2 (July 13, 1993, sixth inning).

	W	L	Pct.	ERA	GS	CG	ShO	Sv.-Opp.	IP	H	R	ER	HR	BB-IBB	SO
All-Star Game totals (5 years)	1	1	.500	1.93	1	0	0	0-0	4.2	5	1	1	0	1-0	2

SMYTH, STEVE — P — CUBS

S

PERSONAL: Born June 3, 1978, in Brawley, Calif. ... 6-1/195. ... Throws left, bats left. ... Full name: Steven Delton Smyth.
HIGH SCHOOL: Temecula Valley (Temecula, Calif.).
JUNIOR COLLEGE: Cypress.
COLLEGE: Southern California.
TRANSACTIONS/CAREER NOTES: Selected by Chicago Cubs organization in fourth round of free-agent draft (June 2, 1999). ... On disabled list (July 16, 2001-remainder of season). ... On West Tenn disabled list (April 4-May 11, 2002).
CAREER HITTING (MLB): 2-for-9 (.222), 1 R, 0 2B, 0 3B, 0 HR, 1 RBI.

Year League	W	L	Pct.	ERA	G	GS	CG	ShO	Sv.-Opp.	IP	H	R	ER	HR	BB-IBB	SO
1999—Eugene (N'West)	1	1	.500	4.38	5	5	0	0	0-...	24.2	29	17	12	2	7-0	14
—Lansing (Midw.)	5	3	.625	6.93	10	10	0	0	0-...	50.2	68	40	39	5	30-0	46
2000—Daytona (FSL)	8	8	.500	3.25	24	23	1	0	0-...	138.1	134	62	50	9	57-0	100
2001—West Tenn (Sou.)	9	3	.750	2.54	18	18	3	1	0-...	120.1	110	38	34	9	40-1	93
2002—West Tenn (Sou.)	4	4	.500	3.58	11	11	0	0	0-...	73.0	62	34	29	7	18-0	74
—Iowa (PCL)	3	2	.600	5.81	6	6	0	0	0-...	31.0	35	21	20	4	10-0	25
—Chicago (N.L.)	1	3	.250	9.35	8	7	0	0	0-0	26.0	34	28	27	9	10-0	16
Major League totals (1 year)	1	3	.250	9.35	8	7	0	0	0-0	26.0	34	28	27	9	10-0	16

SNEAD, ESIX — OF — METS

PERSONAL: Born June 7, 1976, in Fort Myers, Fla. ... 5-10/175. ... Bats both, throws right.
HIGH SCHOOL: Williston (Fla.).
COLLEGE: Central Florida.
TRANSACTIONS/CAREER NOTES: Selected by St. Louis Cardinals organization in 18th round of free-agent draft (June 2, 1998). ... On disabled list (August 20-September 5, 2001). ... Claimed on waivers by New York Mets (November 20, 2001).
STATISTICAL NOTES: Led Carolina League in caught stealing with 35 in 2000. ... Led Eastern League in caught stealing with 23 in 2001. ... Led Eastern League outfielders with 347 putouts and 363 total chances in 2001. ... Tied for Eastern League lead with 18 caught stealing in 2002.
2002 GAMES PLAYED BY POSITION (MLB): OF—6.

		BATTING														FIELDING	
Year Team (League)	Pos.	G	AB	R	H	2B	3B	HR	RBI	BB	SO	SB-CS	Avg.	OBP	SLG	E	Avg.
1998—New Jersey (NY-P)	OF	58	193	38	45	4	4	1	16	33	54	*42-11	.233	.365	.311	3	.976
1999—Potomac (Caro.)	OF	67	249	37	45	8	5	0	14	32	57	45-12	.181	.281	.253	2	.989
—Peoria (Midw.)	OF	59	181	35	35	7	1	2	18	35	42	29-9	.193	.329	.276	4	.975
2000—Potomac (Caro.)	OF	132	493	82	116	14	3	1	34	72	98	109-35	.235	.340	.282	7	.979
2001—New Haven (East.)	OF	133	520	71	121	21	6	1	33	44	115	64-23	.233	.307	.302	6	.983
2002—Binghamton (East.)■	OF	125	401	62	101	9	6	3	42	45	72	*66-18	.252	.335	.327	4	.985
—New York (N.L.)	OF	17	13	3	4	0	0	1	3	1	4	4-3	.308	.357	.538	0	1.000
Major League totals (1 year)		17	13	3	4	0	0	1	3	1	4	4-3	.308	.357	.538	0	1.000

SNELLING, CHRIS — OF — MARINERS

PERSONAL: Born December 3, 1981, in North Miami. ... 5-10/165. ... Bats left, throws left. ... Full name: Christopher Doyle Snelling.
HIGH SCHOOL: Corpus Christi College Tuggerah (Australia).
TRANSACTIONS/CAREER NOTES: Signed as non-drafted free agent by Seattle Mariners organization (March 2, 1999). ... On San Antonio disabled list (April 4-May 1, 2002). ... On Seattle disabled list (June 5, 2002-remainder of season).
2002 GAMES PLAYED BY POSITION (MLB): OF—8.

		BATTING														FIELDING	
Year Team (League)	Pos.	G	AB	R	H	2B	3B	HR	RBI	BB	SO	SB-CS	Avg.	OBP	SLG	E	Avg.
1999—Everett (N'West)	OF	69	265	46	81	15	3	10	50	33	24	8-9	.306	.388	.498	1	.993
2000—Wisconsin (Midw.)	OF	72	259	44	79	9	5	9	56	34	34	7-4	.305	.386	.483	2	.983
2001—San Bern. (Calif.)	OF	114	450	90	151	29	10	7	73	45	63	12-5	.336	.418	.491	4	.978
2002—San Antonio (Texas)	OF	23	89	10	29	9	2	1	12	12	11	5-1	.326	.429	.506	0	1.000
—Seattle (A.L.)	OF	8	27	2	4	0	0	1	3	2	4	0-0	.148	.207	.259	0	1.000
Major League totals (1 year)		8	27	2	4	0	0	1	3	2	4	0-0	.148	.207	.259	0	1.000

SNOW, J.T. — 1B — GIANTS

PERSONAL: Born February 26, 1968, in Long Beach, Calif. ... 6-2/209. ... Bats left, throws left. ... Full name: Jack Thomas Snow Jr. ... Son of Jack Snow, wide receiver with Los Angeles Rams (1965-75).
HIGH SCHOOL: Los Alamitos (Calif.).
COLLEGE: Arizona.
TRANSACTIONS/CAREER NOTES: Selected by New York Yankees organization in fifth round of free-agent draft (June 5, 1989). ... Traded by Yankees with P Jerry Nielsen and P Russ Springer to California Angels for P Jim Abbott (December 6, 1992). ... Traded by Angels to San Francisco Giants for P Allen Watson and P Fausto Macey (November 27, 1996). ... On San Francisco disabled list (May 27-June 14, June 24-July 15 and July 27-August 7, 2001); included rehabilitation assignments to Fresno (June 12-14 and July 12-15).
RECORDS: Shares major league career record for highest fielding percentage for first baseman—.996.
HONORS: Named International League Most Valuable Player (1992). ... Won A.L. Gold Glove at first base (1995-96). ... Won N.L. Gold Glove at first base (1997-2000).
STATISTICAL NOTES: Led New York-Pennsylvania League first basemen with 590 putouts and 649 total chances in 1989. ... Led Carolina League in grounding into double plays with 20 in 1990. ... Led Carolina League first basemen with 1,208 putouts, 78 assists, 1,298 total chances and 120 double plays in 1990. ... Tied for Eastern League lead with 10 sacrifice flies in 1991. ... Led Eastern League first basemen with 1,108 putouts and 1,200 total chances in 1991. ... Led International League with 11 intentional bases on balls received in 1992. ... Led International League first basemen with .995 fielding percentage, 1,097 putouts, 93 assists, 1,196 total chances and 107 double plays in 1992. ... Switch-hit home runs in one game (June 9, 1996). ... Led N.L. in sacrifice flies with 14 in 2000. ... Career major league grand slams: 7.
MISCELLANEOUS: Batted as switch-hitter (1989-98).
2002 GAMES PLAYED BY POSITION (MLB): 1B—135.

			BATTING														FIELDING	
Year	Team (League)	Pos.	G	AB	R	H	2B	3B	HR	RBI	BB	SO	SB-CS	Avg.	OBP	SLG	E	Avg.
1989—	Oneonta (NY-Penn)	1B	73	274	41	80	18	2	8	51	29	35	4-1	.292	.359	.460	6	*.991
1990—	Prince William (Caro.)	1B	*138	520	57	133	25	1	8	72	46	65	2-0	.256	.318	.354	12	.991
1991—	Albany/Colonie (East.)	1B	132	477	78	133	33	3	13	76	67	78	5-1	.279	.364	.442	8	*.993
1992—	Columbus (I.L.)	1B-OF	135	492	81	154	26	4	15	78	70	65	3-3	•.313	.395	.474	8	†.993
—	New York (A.L.)	1B-DH	7	14	1	2	1	0	0	2	5	5	0-0	.143	.368	.214	0	1.000
1993—	California (A.L.)■	1B	129	419	60	101	18	2	16	57	55	88	3-0	.241	.328	.408	6	.995
—	Vancouver (PCL)	1B	23	94	19	32	9	1	5	24	10	13	0-0	.340	.410	.617	2	.991
1994—	Vancouver (PCL)	1B-DH	53	189	35	56	13	2	8	43	22	32	1-2	.296	.364	.513	1	.998
—	California (A.L.)	1B	61	223	22	49	4	0	8	30	19	48	0-1	.220	.289	.345	2	.996
1995—	California (A.L.)	1B	143	544	80	157	22	1	24	102	52	91	2-1	.289	.353	.465	4	.997
1996—	California (A.L.)	1B	155	575	69	148	20	1	17	67	56	96	1-6	.257	.327	.384	10	.993
1997—	San Fran. (N.L.)■	1B	157	531	81	149	36	1	28	104	96	124	6-4	.281	.387	.510	7	.995
1998—	San Francisco (N.L.)	1B	138	435	65	108	29	1	15	79	58	84	1-2	.248	.332	.423	1	*.999
1999—	San Francisco (N.L.)	1B	161	570	93	156	25	2	24	98	86	121	0-4	.274	.370	.451	6	.996
2000—	San Francisco (N.L.)	1B	155	536	82	152	33	2	19	96	66	129	1-3	.284	.365	.459	6	.995
2001—	San Francisco (N.L.)	1B	101	285	43	70	12	1	8	34	55	81	0-0	.246	.371	.379	1	.999
—	Fresno (PCL)	1B	4	12	1	0	0	0	0	0	2	7	0-0	.000	.143	.000	0	1.000
2002—	San Francisco (N.L.)	1B	143	422	47	104	26	2	6	53	59	90	0-0	.246	.344	.360	7	.993
American League totals (5 years)			495	1775	232	457	65	4	65	258	187	328	6-8	.257	.331	.408	22	.995
National League totals (6 years)			855	2779	411	739	161	9	100	464	420	629	8-13	.266	.363	.438	28	.996
Major League totals (11 years)			1350	4554	643	1196	226	13	165	722	607	957	14-21	.263	.351	.427	50	.996

DIVISION SERIES RECORD

			BATTING														FIELDING	
Year	Team (League)	Pos.	G	AB	R	H	2B	3B	HR	RBI	BB	SO	SB-CS	Avg.	OBP	SLG	E	Avg.
1997—	San Francisco (N.L.)	1B	3	6	0	1	0	0	0	0	1	1	0-0	.167	.286	.167	0	1.000
2000—	San Francisco (N.L.)	1B-PH	4	10	1	4	0	0	1	3	4	1	0-0	.400	.571	.700	0	1.000
2002—	San Francisco (N.L.)	1B	5	19	3	6	2	0	1	3	1	5	0-0	.316	.350	.579	0	1.000
Division series totals (3 years)			12	35	4	11	2	0	2	6	6	7	0-0	.314	.415	.543	0	1.000

CHAMPIONSHIP SERIES RECORD

			BATTING														FIELDING	
Year	Team (League)	Pos.	G	AB	R	H	2B	3B	HR	RBI	BB	SO	SB-CS	Avg.	OBP	SLG	E	Avg.
2002—	San Francisco (N.L.)	1B	5	20	1	5	1	1	0	2	1	4	0-0	.250	.286	.400	0	1.000

WORLD SERIES RECORD

			BATTING														FIELDING	
Year	Team (League)	Pos.	G	AB	R	H	2B	3B	HR	RBI	BB	SO	SB-CS	Avg.	OBP	SLG	E	Avg.
2002—	San Francisco (N.L.)	1B	7	27	6	11	1	0	1	4	2	1	0-0	.407	.448	.556	0	1.000

SNYDER, EARL — 1B — INDIANS

PERSONAL: Born May 6, 1976, in New Britain, Conn. ... 6-0/207. ... Bats right, throws right. ... Full name: Earl Clifford Snyder.
COLLEGE: Hartford.
TRANSACTIONS/CAREER NOTES: Selected by New York Mets organization in 36th round of free-agent draft (June 2, 1998). ... Traded by Mets with P Billy Traber to Cleveland Indians (December 13, 2001), completing deal in which Mets traded OF Matt Lawton, OF Alex Escobar, P Jerrod Riggan and two players to be named later to Indians for 2B Roberto Alomar, P Mike Bacsik and OF Danny Peoples (December 11, 2001).
2002 GAMES PLAYED BY POSITION (MLB): 1B—12; 3B—2; DH—1.

			BATTING														FIELDING	
Year	Team (League)	Pos.	G	AB	R	H	2B	3B	HR	RBI	BB	SO	SB-CS	Avg.	OBP	SLG	E	Avg.
1998—	Pittsfield (NY-Penn)	1B-OF	71	262	39	66	8	1	11	40	23	60	0-1	.252	.316	.416	5	.989
1999—	Capital City (S.Atl.)	1B-3B	136	486	73	130	25	4	28	97	55	117	2-1	.267	.339	.508	13	.989
2000—	St. Lucie (FSL)	1B	134	514	84	145	36	0	25	93	57	127	4-4	.282	.358	.498	15	.988
2001—	Binghamton (East.)	1B-3B-OF	114	405	69	114	35	2	20	75	58	111	4-2	.281	.374	.526	9	.989
—	Norfolk (I.L.)	1B	6	19	5	9	3	0	0	3	3	1	0-1	.474	.565	.632	1	.981
2002—	Buffalo (I.L.)■	3B-1B-OF	110	400	69	105	29	1	19	66	43	96	0-2	.263	.341	.483	19	.965
—	Cleveland (A.L.)	1B-3B-DH	18	55	5	11	2	0	1	4	6	21	0-0	.200	.279	.291	2	.982
Major League totals (1 year)			18	55	5	11	2	0	1	4	6	21	0-0	.200	.279	.291	2	.982

SORIANO, ALFONSO 2B YANKEES

PERSONAL: Born January 7, 1978, in San Pedro de Macoris, Dominican Republi ... 6-1/180. ... Bats right, throws right.
HIGH SCHOOL: Eugenio Maria de Osto (Dominican Republic).
TRANSACTIONS/CAREER NOTES: Signed by Hiroshima Toyo Carp of Japan Central League (November 1994). ... Played in Toyo Carp organization (1995-97). ... Retired from Japan Central League and declared free agent by Major League Baseball (1998). ... Signed by New York Yankees (September 29, 1998). ... On Norwich disabled list (July 15-August 15, 1999).
RECORDS: Holds A.L. single-season records for most at-bats by righthander—696 (2002); and most home runs by second baseman—39 (2002).
HONORS: Named second baseman on The Sporting News A.L. All-Star team (2002). ... Named second baseman on A.L. Silver Slugger team (2002).
STATISTICAL NOTES: Led A.L. second basemen with 300 putouts in 2002.
2002 GAMES PLAYED BY POSITION (MLB): 2B—155; DH—1.

			BATTING														FIELDING	
Year	Team (League)	Pos.	G	AB	R	H	2B	3B	HR	RBI	BB	SO	SB-CS	Avg.	OBP	SLG	E	Avg.
1995—	....		Japan minor league statistics unavailable.															
	—Hiroshima (DSL)		63	227	52	83	12	3	4	55	30	19	8-...	.366	...	.498	...	...
1996—	....		Japan minor league statistics unavailable.															
	—Hiroshima (Jp. W)■...		57	131	11	28	...	...	0	13	...	...	...-...	.214	...	.214	...	...
1997—	Hiroshima (Jp. West.)		68	242	28	61	13	2	8	34	13	35	14-...	.252	...	.421	...	...
	—Hiroshima (Jap. Cen.)	OF	9	17	2	2	0	0	0	0	2	4	0-...	.118	...	.118	...	...
1998—	....		Out of organized baseball.															
1999—	Norwich (East.)■	SS-DH	89	361	57	110	20	3	15	68	32	67	24-16	.305	.363	.501	27	.937
	—GC Yankees (GCL)......	SS-DH	5	19	7	5	2	0	1	5	1	3	0-0	.263	.318	.526	1	.929
	—Columbus (I.L.).......	SS-3B-2B	20	82	8	15	5	1	2	11	5	18	1-1	.183	.225	.341	3	.955
	—New York (A.L.)..........	DH-SS	9	8	2	1	0	0	1	1	0	3	0-1	.125	.125	.500	1	.500
2000—	Columbus (I.L.)..........	SS-2B	111	459	90	133	32	6	12	66	25	85	14-7	.290	.327	.464	21	.952
	—New York (A.L.)..........	3B-SS-DH-2B	22	50	5	9	3	0	2	3	1	15	2-0	.180	.196	.360	7	.837
2001—	New York (A.L.)..........	2B-DH	158	574	77	154	34	3	18	73	29	125	43-14	.268	.304	.432	19	.973
2002—	New York (A.L.)..........	2B-DH	156	*696	*128	*209	51	2	39	102	23	157	*41-13	.300	.332	.547	*23	.968
Major League totals (4 years)			345	1328	212	373	88	5	60	179	53	300	86-28	.281	.314	.490	50	.966

DIVISION SERIES RECORD

			BATTING														FIELDING	
Year	Team (League)	Pos.	G	AB	R	H	2B	3B	HR	RBI	BB	SO	SB-CS	Avg.	OBP	SLG	E	Avg.
2001—	New York (A.L.)..........	2B	5	18	2	4	0	0	0	3	1	5	2-1	.222	.263	.222	0	1.000
2002—	New York (A.L.)..........	2B	4	17	2	2	1	0	1	2	1	4	1-0	.118	.211	.353	1	.958
Division series totals (2 years)			9	35	4	6	1	0	1	5	2	9	3-1	.171	.237	.286	1	.975

CHAMPIONSHIP SERIES RECORD

			BATTING														FIELDING	
Year	Team (League)	Pos.	G	AB	R	H	2B	3B	HR	RBI	BB	SO	SB-CS	Avg.	OBP	SLG	E	Avg.
2001—	New York (A.L.)..........	2B	5	15	5	6	0	0	1	2	3	3	2-0	.400	.526	.600	1	.955

WORLD SERIES RECORD

			BATTING														FIELDING	
Year	Team (League)	Pos.	G	AB	R	H	2B	3B	HR	RBI	BB	SO	SB-CS	Avg.	OBP	SLG	E	Avg.
2001—	New York (A.L.)..........	2B	7	25	1	6	0	0	1	2	0	7	0-1	.240	.240	.360	3	.927

ALL-STAR GAME RECORD

	AB	R	H	2B	3B	HR	RBI	BB	SO	SB-CS	Avg.	OBP	SLG	E	Avg.
All-Star Game totals (1 year)	2	1	1	0	0	1	1	0	1	0-0	.500	.500	2.000	0	1.000

SORIANO, RAFAEL P MARINERS

PERSONAL: Born December 19, 1979, in San Jose, Dominican Republic. ... 6-1/175. ... Throws right, bats right.
TRANSACTIONS/CAREER NOTES: Signed as non-drafted free agent by Seattle Mariners organization (August 30, 1996). ... On Wisconsin disabled list (April 6-May 5, 2000). ... On San Bernardino disabled list (April 26-May 6, 2001). ... On San Antonio disabled list (July 4-12 and August 31, 2001-remainder of season). ... On disabled list (July 3-August 2, 2002).
CAREER HITTING (MLB): 0-for-4 (.000), 0 R, 0 2B, 0 3B, 0 HR, 0 RBI.

Year	League	W	L	Pct.	ERA	G	GS	CG	ShO	Sv.-Opp.	IP	H	R	ER	HR	BB-IBB	SO
1999—	Everett (N'West)..............	5	4	.556	3.11	14	14	0	0	0-...	75.1	56	34	26	8	49-0	83
2000—	Wisconsin (Midw.)...........	8	4	.667	2.87	21	21	1	0	0-...	122.1	97	41	39	3	50-0	90
2001—	San Bernardino (Calif.).....	6	3	.667	2.53	15	15	*2	1	0-...	89.0	49	28	25	4	39-0	98
	—San Antonio (Texas).........	2	2	.500	3.35	8	8	0	0	0-...	48.1	34	18	18	5	14-0	53
2002—	San Antonio (Texas).........	2	3	.400	2.31	10	8	0	0	0-...	46.2	32	13	12	6	15-0	52
	—Seattle (A.L.)....................	0	3	.000	4.56	10	8	0	0	1-1	47.1	45	25	24	8	16-1	32
Major League totals (1 year).......		0	3	.000	4.56	10	8	0	0	1-1	47.1	45	25	24	8	16-1	32

RECORD AS POSITION PLAYER

			BATTING														FIELDING	
Year	Team (League)	Pos.	G	AB	R	H	2B	3B	HR	RBI	BB	SO	SB-CS	Avg.	OBP	SLG	E	Avg.
1997—	Ariz. Mariners (Ariz.)..	1B-OF	38	119	19	32	3	2	0	12	14	31	7-4	.269	.351	.328	6	.970
1998—	Ariz. Mariners (Ariz.)..	1B-OF	32	108	17	18	4	0	0	6	11	34	5-3	.167	.250	.204	5	.975

SOSA, JORGE P DEVIL RAYS

PERSONAL: Born April 28, 1977, in Santo Domingo, Dominican Republic. ... 6-2/177. ... Throws right, bats both. ... Full name: Jorge Bolivar Sosa.
TRANSACTIONS/CAREER NOTES: Signed as non-drafted free agent by Colorado Rockies organization (June 23, 1995). ... Selected by Seattle Mariners from Rockies organization in Rule 5 minor league draft (December 11, 2000). ... Selected by Milwaukee Brewers from Mariners organization in Rule 5 major league draft (December 13, 2001). ... Claimed on waivers by Tampa Bay Devils Rays (March 18, 2002). ... On Tampa Bay disabled list (May 26-June 25, 2002); included rehabilitation assignment to Orlando (June 14-25).
CAREER HITTING (MLB): 0-for-0 (.000), 0 R, 0 2B, 0 3B, 0 HR, 0 RBI.

Year	League	W	L	Pct.	ERA	G	GS	CG	ShO	Sv.-Opp.	IP	H	R	ER	HR	BB-IBB	SO
2001—	Everett (N'West)■	3	1	.750	1.69	21	7	0	0	7-...	58.2	45	22	11	2	19-0	57
—	Wisconsin (Midw.)	0	0	...	9.00	2	0	0	0	0-...	2.0	3	2	2	1	0-0	4
2002—	Tampa Bay (A.L.)■	2	7	.222	5.53	31	14	0	0	0-0	99.1	88	63	61	16	54-0	48
—	Orlando (Sou.)	0	0	...	0.00	2	2	0	0	0-...	7.0	4	2	0	1	1-0	3
Major League totals (1 year)		2	7	.222	5.53	31	14	0	0	0-0	99.1	88	63	61	16	54-0	48

RECORD AS POSITION PLAYER

			BATTING														FIELDING	
Year	Team (League)	Pos.	G	AB	R	H	2B	3B	HR	RBI	BB	SO	SB-CS	Avg.	OBP	SLG	E	Avg.
1995—	Dom. Rockies (DSL)	SS	32	91	10	23	3	0	0	1	8	26	1-...	.253	...	.286	15	.797
1996—	Dom. Rockies (DSL)		51	162	29	39	13	2	3	25	25	54	2-...	.241	...	.401	...	...
1997—	Ariz. Rockies (Ariz.)	OF	29	93	13	13	1	2	0	6	13	36	6-0	.140	.273	.194	4	.892
1998—	Ariz. Rockies (Ariz.)	OF	45	152	23	36	6	1	2	11	12	57	4-3	.237	.299	.329	5	.928
1999—	Portland (N'West)	OF	35	113	15	23	3	0	2	8	13	57	2-3	.204	.291	.283	3	.940
2000—	Portland (N'West)	OF	62	200	24	46	7	5	4	26	37	102	4-6	.230	.357	.375	7	.903

SOSA, SAMMY — OF — CUBS

PERSONAL: Born November 12, 1968, in San Pedro de Macoris, Dominican Repubic. ... 6-0/220. ... Bats right, throws right. ... Full name: Samuel Sosa Peralta.

TRANSACTIONS/CAREER NOTES: Signed as non-drafted free agent by Texas Rangers organization (July 30, 1985). ... Traded by Rangers with SS Scott Fletcher and P Wilson Alvarez to Chicago White Sox for OF Harold Baines and IF Fred Manrique (July 29, 1989). ... Traded by White Sox with P Ken Patterson to Chicago Cubs for OF George Bell (March 30, 1992). ... On Chicago disabled list (June 13-July 27, and August 7-September 16, 1992); included rehabilitation assignment to Iowa (July 21-27). ... On disabled list (August 21, 1996-remainder of season).

RECORDS: Holds major league single-season record for most intentional bases on balls by righthander—37 (2001). ... Holds N.L. single-season record for most at-bats without a triple—643 (1998). ... Holds major league single-month record for most home runs—20 (June 1998). ... Shares major league career record for most times hitting three or more home runs in a game—6; and for most times hitting three or more consecutive home runs in a game—4. ... Shares major league single-season record for most major league ballparks, one or more home runs—18 (1998); and most times hitting three or more home runs in a game—2 (2001). ... Shares major league record for most grand slams in two consecutive games—2 (July 27 and 28, 1998); and most consecutive seasons with 50 or more home runs—4 (1998-2001). ... Shares major league single-season record for most times hitting two or more home runs in a game—11 (1998). ... Shares major league single-inning record for most home runs—2 (May 16, 1996, seventh inning). ... Shares N.L. single-month record for most home runs—17 (August 2001). ... Shares N.L. career record most consecutive years with 40 or more home runs—5 (1998-2002). ... Shares major league record for most home runs in month of October—5 (2001). ... Holds N.L. record for most runs batted in, two consecutive games—14 (August 10 [9] and 11 [5], 2002).

HONORS: Named outfielder on The Sporting News N.L. All-Star team (1995 and 1998-2002). ... Named outfielder on The Sporting News N.L. Silver Slugger team (1995, 1998, 1999 and 2000). ... Named co-Sportsman of the Year by The Sporting News (1998). ... Named Major League Player of the Year by The Sporting News (1998). ... Named N.L. Most Valuable Player by Baseball Writers' Association of America (1998). ... Named outfielder on N.L. Silver Slugger team (2001 and 2002).

STATISTICAL NOTES: Led Gulf Coast League with 96 total bases in 1986. ... Tied for South Atlantic League lead in double plays by outfielder with four in 1987. ... Collected six hits in one game (July 2, 1993). ... Tied for N.L. lead in double plays by outfielder with four in 1995. ... Hit three home runs in one game (June 5, 1996; June 15, 1998; August 9, August 22 and September 23, 2001; and August 10, 2002). ... Led N.L. with 416 total bases in 1998. ... Had 18-game hitting streak (May 26-June 15, 1999). ... Led N.L. with 397 total bases in 1999. ... Had 15-game hitting streak (July 4-22, 2000). ... Led N.L. with 425 total bases and with 37 intentional bases on balls received in 2001. ... Career major league grand slams: 7.

2002 GAMES PLAYED BY POSITION (MLB): OF—150.

			BATTING														FIELDING	
Year	Team (League)	Pos.	G	AB	R	H	2B	3B	HR	RBI	BB	SO	SB-CS	Avg.	OBP	SLG	E	Avg.
1986—	GC Rangers (GCL)	OF	61	229	38	63	*19	1	4	28	22	51	11-3	.275	.336	.419	•6	.944
1987—	Gastonia (S.Atl.)	OF	129	519	73	145	27	4	11	59	21	123	22-8	.279	.312	.410	17	.920
1988—	Charlotte (FSL)	OF	131	507	70	116	13	*12	9	51	35	106	42-24	.229	.282	.355	7	.971
1989—	Tulsa (Texas)	OF	66	273	45	81	15	4	7	31	15	52	16-11	.297	.338	.458	4	.967
—	Texas (A.L.)	OF-DH	25	84	8	20	3	0	1	3	0	20	0-2	.238	.238	.310	2	.944
—	Oklahoma City (A.A.)	OF	10	39	2	4	2	0	0	3	2	8	4-2	.103	.146	.154	2	.917
—	Vancouver (PCL)	OF	13	49	7	18	3	0	1	5	0	20	0-1	.367	.367	.490	0	1.000
—	Chicago (A.L.)■	OF	33	99	19	27	5	0	3	10	11	27	7-3	.273	.351	.414	2	.969
1990—	Chicago (A.L.)	OF	153	532	72	124	26	10	15	70	33	150	32-16	.233	.282	.404	*13	.962
1991—	Chicago (A.L.)	OF-DH	116	316	39	64	10	1	10	33	14	98	13-6	.203	.240	.335	6	.973
—	Vancouver (PCL)	OF	32	116	19	31	7	2	3	19	17	32	9-2	.267	.358	.440	3	.970
1992—	Chicago (N.L.)■	OF	67	262	41	68	7	2	8	25	19	63	15-7	.260	.317	.393	6	.961
—	Iowa (A.A.)	OF	5	19	3	6	2	0	0	1	1	2	5-0	.316	.350	.421	0	1.000
1993—	Chicago (N.L.)	OF	159	598	92	156	25	5	33	93	38	135	36-11	.261	.309	.485	9	.976
1994—	Chicago (N.L.)	OF	105	426	59	128	17	6	25	70	25	92	22-13	.300	.339	.545	7	.973
1995—	Chicago (N.L.)	OF	•144	564	89	151	17	3	36	119	58	134	34-7	.268	.340	.500	*13	.962
1996—	Chicago (N.L.)	OF	124	498	84	136	21	2	40	100	34	134	18-5	.273	.323	.564	10	.964
1997—	Chicago (N.L.)	OF	•162	642	90	161	31	4	36	119	45	*174	22-12	.251	.300	.480	8	.977
1998—	Chicago (N.L.)	OF	159	643	*134	198	20	0	66	*158	73	*171	18-9	.308	.377	.647	9	.975
1999—	Chicago (N.L.)	OF	•162	625	114	180	24	2	63	141	78	*171	7-8	.288	.367	.635	9	.978
2000—	Chicago (N.L.)	OF	156	604	106	193	38	1	*50	138	91	168	7-4	.320	.406	.634	•10	.970
2001—	Chicago (N.L.)	OF	160	577	*146	189	34	5	64	*160	116	153	0-2	.328	.437	.737	6	.982
2002—	Chicago (N.L.)	OF	150	556	*122	160	19	2	*49	108	103	144	2-0	.288	.399	.594	6	.980
American League totals (3 years)			327	1031	138	235	44	11	29	116	58	295	52-27	.228	.273	.376	23	.966
National League totals (11 years)			1548	5995	1077	1720	253	32	470	1231	680	1539	181-78	.287	.360	.575	93	.973
Major League totals (14 years)			1875	7026	1215	1955	297	43	499	1347	738	1834	233-105	.278	.348	.546	116	.972

DIVISION SERIES RECORD

			BATTING														FIELDING	
Year	Team (League)	Pos.	G	AB	R	H	2B	3B	HR	RBI	BB	SO	SB-CS	Avg.	OBP	SLG	E	Avg.
1998—	Chicago (N.L.)	OF	3	11	0	2	1	0	0	0	1	4	0-2	.182	.250	.273	0	1.000

ALL-STAR GAME RECORD

NOTES: Named to All-Star team for 1998 game; replaced by Bret Boone due to injury.

	AB	R	H	2B	3B	HR	RBI	BB	SO	SB-CS	Avg.	OBP	SLG	E	Avg.
All-Star Game totals (5 years)	11	0	1	0	0	0	0	0	4	0-0	.091	.091	.091	0	1.000

S

SPARKS, STEVE — P — TIGERS

PERSONAL: Born July 2, 1965, in Tulsa, Okla. ... 6-0/195. ... Throws right, bats right. ... Full name: Steven William Sparks.
HIGH SCHOOL: Holland Hall (Tulsa, Okla.).
COLLEGE: Sam Houston State.
TRANSACTIONS/CAREER NOTES: Selected by Milwaukee Brewers organization in fifth round of free-agent draft (June 2, 1987). ... On disabled list (March 24, 1997-entire season). ... Granted free agency (October 15, 1997). ... Signed by Anaheim Angels (February 23, 1998). ... On Cedar Rapids disabled list (April 9-19, 1998). ... Granted free agency (October 15, 1999). ... Signed by Philadelphia Phillies organization (February 1, 2000). ... Released by Phillies (February 28, 2000). ... Signed by Detroit Tigers organization (March 2, 2000).
RECORDS: Shares major league single-inning record for most hit batsmen—3 (May 22, 1999, third inning). ... Shares A.L. single-game record for most hit batsmen (nine innings)—4 (May 22, 1999).
MISCELLANEOUS: Appeared in one game as pinch runner (1999). ... Appeared in one game as pinch runner (2001).
CAREER HITTING (MLB): 1-for-10 (.100), 1 R, 1 2B, 0 3B, 0 HR, 2 RBI.

Year League	W	L	Pct.	ERA	G	GS	CG	ShO	Sv.-Opp.	IP	H	R	ER	HR	BB-IBB	SO
1987—Helena (Pio.)	6	3	.667	4.68	10	9	2	0	0-...	57.2	68	44	30	8	20-1	47
1988—Beloit (Midw.)	9	13	.409	3.79	25	24	5	1	0-...	164.0	162	80	69	8	51-2	96
1989—Stockton (Calif.)	•13	5	.722	2.41	23	22	3	2	0-...	164.0	125	55	44	6	53-0	126
1990—Stockton (Calif.)	10	7	.588	3.69	19	19	5	1	0-...	129.1	136	63	53	4	31-0	77
—El Paso (Texas)	1	2	.333	6.53	7	6	1	0	0-...	30.1	43	24	22	4	15-0	17
1991—Stockton (Calif.)	9	10	.474	3.06	24	24	•8	2	0-...	179.2	160	70	61	4	98-2	139
—El Paso (Texas)	1	2	.333	9.53	4	4	0	0	0-...	17.0	30	22	18	1	9-0	10
1992—El Paso (Texas)	9	8	.529	5.37	28	22	3	0	1-...	140.2	159	99	84	11	50-1	79
1993—New Orleans (A.A.)	9	13	.409	3.84	29	•28	*7	1	0-...	*180.1	174	89	77	17	*80-1	104
1994—New Orleans (A.A.)	10	12	.455	4.46	28	27	5	1	0-...	*183.2	183	101	91	23	68-0	105
1995—Milwaukee (A.L.)	9	11	.450	4.63	33	27	3	0	0-0	202.0	210	111	104	17	86-1	96
1996—Milwaukee (A.L.)	4	7	.364	6.60	20	13	1	0	0-0	88.2	103	66	65	19	52-0	21
—New Orleans (A.A.)	2	6	.250	4.99	11	10	3	2	0-...	57.2	64	43	32	8	35-0	27
1997—Milwaukee (A.L.)									Did not play.							
1998—Midland (Texas)■	0	4	.000	7.08	7	7	0	0	0-...	40.2	49	38	32	3	15-0	34
—Vancouver (PCL)	0	4	.000	2.89	4	4	2	0	0-...	28.0	23	11	9	2	6-0	19
—Anaheim (A.L.)	9	4	.692	4.34	22	20	0	0	0-0	128.2	130	66	62	14	58-0	90
1999—Anaheim (A.L.)	5	11	.313	5.42	28	26	0	0	0-0	147.2	165	101	89	21	82-0	73
2000—Toledo (I.L.)■	5	7	.417	3.77	16	14	1	0	0-...	90.2	86	53	38	8	41-0	44
—Detroit (A.L.)	7	5	.583	4.07	20	15	1	1	1-1	104.0	108	55	47	7	29-0	53
2001—Detroit (A.L.)	14	9	.609	3.65	35	33	*8	1	0-0	232.0	244	110	94	22	64-1	116
2002—Detroit (A.L.)	8	16	.333	5.52	32	30	3	0	0-0	189.0	238	134	116	23	67-3	98
Major League totals (7 years)	56	63	.471	4.76	190	164	16	2	1-1	1092.0	1198	643	577	123	438-5	547

SPEIER, JUSTIN — P — ROCKIES

PERSONAL: Born November 6, 1973, in Walnut Creek, Calif. ... 6-4/205. ... Throws right, bats right. ... Full name: Justin James Speier. ... Son of Chris Speier, infielder with five major league teams (1971-89).
HIGH SCHOOL: Brophy College Prep (Phoenix).
COLLEGE: San Francisco, then Nicholls State.
TRANSACTIONS/CAREER NOTES: Selected by Chicago Cubs organization in 55th round of free-agent draft (June 1, 1995). ... Traded by Cubs with 3B Kevin Orie and P Todd Noel to Florida Marlins for P Felix Heredia and P Steve Hoff (July 31, 1998). ... Traded by Marlins to Atlanta Braves for a player to be named (April 1, 1999); Marlins acquired P Matthew Targac to complete deal (June 11, 1999). ... Claimed on waivers by Cleveland Indians (November 23, 1999). ... Traded by Indians to New York Mets for OF Brian Jenkins (May 19, 2001). ... Claimed on waivers by Colorado Rockies (May 29, 2001). ... On Colorado disabled list (March 31-May 6, 2002); included rehabilitation assignment to Colorado Springs (April 8-May 6)
CAREER HITTING (MLB): 3-for-15 (.200), 0 R, 0 2B, 0 3B, 0 HR, 0 RBI.

Year League	W	L	Pct.	ERA	G	GS	CG	ShO	Sv.-Opp.	IP	H	R	ER	HR	BB-IBB	SO
1995—Williamsport (NY-Penn)	2	1	.667	1.49	30	0	0	0	12-...	36.1	27	6	6	1	4-0	39
1996—Daytona (FSL)	2	4	.333	3.76	33	0	0	0	13-...	38.1	32	19	16	3	19-3	34
—Orlando (Sou.)	4	1	.800	2.05	24	0	0	0	6-...	26.1	23	7	6	2	5-1	14
1997—Orlando (Sou.)	6	5	.545	4.48	50	0	0	0	6-...	78.1	77	46	39	8	23-0	63
—Iowa (A.A.)	2	0	1.000	0.00	8	0	0	0	1-...	12.1	5	0	0	0	1-0	9
1998—Iowa (PCL)	3	3	.500	5.05	45	0	0	0	12-...	51.2	52	31	29	10	19-1	49
—Chicago (N.L.)	0	0	...	13.50	1	0	0	0	0-0	1.1	2	2	2	0	1-0	2
—Florida (N.L.)■	0	3	.000	8.38	18	0	0	0	0-1	19.1	25	18	18	7	12-1	15
1999—Richmond (I.L.)■	2	4	.333	5.62	27	0	0	0	3-...	41.2	51	28	26	4	22-4	39
—Atlanta (N.L.)	0	0	...	5.65	19	0	0	0	0-0	28.2	28	18	18	8	13-1	22
2000—Buffalo (I.L.)■	0	0	...	4.15	13	0	0	0	9-...	13.0	13	6	6	0	3-0	12
—Cleveland (A.L.)	5	2	.714	3.29	47	0	0	0	0-1	68.1	57	27	25	9	28-3	69
2001—Cleveland (A.L.)	2	0	1.000	6.97	12	0	0	0	0-0	20.2	24	16	16	5	8-0	15
—Colorado (N.L.)■	4	3	.571	3.70	42	0	0	0	0-1	56.0	47	24	23	8	12-3	47
—Colorado Springs (PCL)	1	0	1.000	1.46	11	0	0	0	2-...	12.1	10	2	2	0	7-0	16
2002—Colorado Springs (PCL)	2	0	1.000	3.86	12	0	0	0	2-...	14.0	20	7	6	2	3-1	14
—Colorado (N.L.)	5	1	.833	4.33	63	0	0	0	1-4	62.1	51	31	30	9	19-4	47
A.L. totals (2 years)	7	2	.778	4.15	59	0	0	0	0-1	89.0	81	43	41	14	36-3	84
N.L. totals (4 years)	9	7	.563	4.88	143	0	0	0	1-6	167.2	153	93	91	32	57-9	133
Major League totals (5 years)	16	9	.640	4.63	202	0	0	0	1-7	256.2	234	136	132	46	93-12	217

SPENCER, SHANE — OF — YANKEES

PERSONAL: Born February 20, 1972, in Key West, Fla. ... 5-11/225. ... Bats right, throws right. ... Full name: Michael Shane Spencer.
HIGH SCHOOL: Granite Hills (El Cajon, Calif.).
TRANSACTIONS/CAREER NOTES: Selected by New York Yankees organization in 28th round of free-agent draft (June 4, 1990). ... On disabled list (April 10-May 9, 1994). ... On New York disabled list (July 3-27, 1999); included rehabilitation assignment to Columbus (July 21-27). ...

On disabled list (July 12, 2000-remainder of season). ... On New York disabled list (March 31-April 29, 2001); included rehabilitation assignment to Columbus (April 14-29).
RECORDS: Shares major league single-month record for most grand slams—3 (September 1998).
HONORS: Named Florida State League Most Valuable Player (1995).
STATISTICAL NOTES: Led Florida State League with 235 total bases in 1995. ... Career major league grand slams: 4.
2002 GAMES PLAYED BY POSITION (MLB): OF—91; DH—1.

		BATTING														FIELDING	
Year Team (League)	Pos.	G	AB	R	H	2B	3B	HR	RBI	BB	SO	SB-CS	Avg.	OBP	SLG	E	Avg.
1990—GC Yankees (GCL)......	OF	42	147	20	27	4	0	0	7	20	23	11-2	.184	.284	.211	3	.965
1991—GC Yankees (GCL)......	OF	44	160	25	49	7	0	0	30	14	19	9-2	.306	.361	.350	3	.959
—Oneonta (NY-Penn)....	OF	18	53	10	13	2	1	0	3	10	9	2-2	.245	.375	.321	1	.917
1992—Greensboro (S.Atl.)....	OF-P	83	258	43	74	10	2	3	27	33	37	8-2	.287	.372	.376	0	1.000
1993—Greensboro (S.Atl.)....	OF-P	122	431	89	116	35	2	12	80	52	62	14-2	.269	.346	.443	5	.967
1994—Tampa (FSL)..............	OF	90	334	44	97	22	3	8	53	30	53	5-3	.290	.350	.446	4	.962
1995—Tampa (FSL)..............	OF	•134	500	87	*150	31	3	16	*88	61	60	14-8	.300	.382	.470	6	.966
1996—Norwich (East.)..........	OF-1B-3B	126	450	70	114	19	0	29	89	68	99	4-2	.253	.353	.489	3	.988
—Columbus (I.L.)..........	OF	9	31	7	11	4	0	3	6	5	5	0-1	.355	.459	.774	1	.963
1997—Columbus (I.L.)..........	OF-DH-3B	125	452	78	109	34	4	30	86	71	105	0-2	.241	.346	.533	4	.980
1998—New York (A.L.)..........	OF-DH-1B	27	67	18	25	6	0	10	27	5	12	0-1	.373	.411	.910	0	1.000
—Columbus (I.L.)..........	OF-DH-1B	87	342	66	110	29	1	18	67	41	59	1-3	.322	.397	.570	5	.979
1999—New York (A.L.)..........	OF-DH	71	205	25	48	8	0	8	20	18	51	0-4	.234	.301	.390	0	1.000
—Columbus (I.L.)..........	OF-DH	14	50	17	18	2	0	2	10	9	8	0-0	.360	.458	.520	1	.958
2000—New York (A.L.)..........	OF-DH	73	248	33	70	11	3	9	40	19	45	1-2	.282	.330	.460	1	.989
2001—Columbus (I.L.)..........	OF	49	173	17	40	10	1	3	14	23	21	4-1	.231	.323	.353	1	.985
—New York (A.L.)..........	OF-DH	80	283	40	73	14	2	10	46	21	58	4-1	.258	.315	.428	1	.993
2002—New York (A.L.)..........	OF-DH	94	288	32	71	15	2	6	34	31	62	0-3	.247	.324	.375	4	.975
Major League totals (5 years)		345	1091	148	287	54	7	43	167	94	228	5-11	.263	.324	.444	6	.989

DIVISION SERIES RECORD

		BATTING														FIELDING	
Year Team (League)	Pos.	G	AB	R	H	2B	3B	HR	RBI	BB	SO	SB-CS	Avg.	OBP	SLG	E	Avg.
1998—New York (A.L.)..........	OF	2	6	3	3	0	0	2	4	0	1	0-0	.500	.500	1.500	0	1.000
1999—New York (A.L.).........								Did not play.									
2001—New York (A.L.)..........	OF-PH	3	8	1	2	1	0	0	0	1	4	0-0	.250	.333	.375	0	1.000
2002—New York (A.L.)..........	OF	1	0	0	0	0	0	0	0	0	0	0-0	...	...	...	0	...
Division series totals (3 years)		6	14	4	5	1	0	2	4	1	5	0-0	.357	.400	.857	0	1.000

CHAMPIONSHIP SERIES RECORD

		BATTING														FIELDING	
Year Team (League)	Pos.	G	AB	R	H	2B	3B	HR	RBI	BB	SO	SB-CS	Avg.	OBP	SLG	E	Avg.
1998—New York (A.L.)..........	OF	3	10	1	1	0	0	0	0	1	3	0-0	.100	.182	.100	0	1.000
1999—New York (A.L.)..........	OF	3	9	1	1	0	0	0	0	1	6	0-0	.111	.200	.111	0	1.000
2001—New York (A.L.)..........	PH-OF-PR	5	7	1	2	1	0	0	0	1	1	1-0	.286	.375	.429	0	1.000
Championship series totals (3 years)		11	26	3	4	1	0	0	0	3	10	1-0	.154	.241	.192	0	1.000

WORLD SERIES RECORD

NOTES: Member of World Series championship team (1998 and 1999).

		BATTING														FIELDING	
Year Team (League)	Pos.	G	AB	R	H	2B	3B	HR	RBI	BB	SO	SB-CS	Avg.	OBP	SLG	E	Avg.
1998—New York (A.L.)..........	OF	1	3	1	1	1	0	0	0	0	2	0-0	.333	.333	.667	0	1.000
1999—New York (A.L.).........								Did not play.									
2001—New York (A.L.)..........	PH-OF	7	20	1	4	0	0	1	2	2	6	0-0	.200	.273	.350	0	1.000
World Series totals (2 years)		8	23	2	5	1	0	1	2	2	8	0-0	.217	.280	.391	0	1.000

RECORD AS PITCHER

Year League	W	L	Pct.	ERA	G	GS	CG	ShO	Sv.-Opp.	IP	H	R	ER	HR	BB-IBB	SO
1992—Greensboro (S.Atl.)..........	0	0	...	0.00	1	0	0	0	0-...	1.0	2	0	0	0	1-0	1
1993—Greensboro (S.Atl.)..........	0	0	...	4.50	2	0	0	0	0-...	4.0	5	2	2	0	2-0	5

SPIEZIO, SCOTT 1B/DH ANGELS

PERSONAL: Born September 21, 1972, in Joliet, Ill. ... 6-2/225. ... Bats both, throws right. ... Full name: Scott Edward Spiezio. ... Son of Ed Spiezio, third baseman with St. Louis Cardinals (1964-68), San Diego Padres (1969-72) and Chicago White Sox (1972).
HIGH SCHOOL: Morris (Ill.).
COLLEGE: Illinois.
TRANSACTIONS/CAREER NOTES: Selected by Oakland Athletics organization in sixth round of free-agent draft (June 3, 1993). ... On Oakland disabled list (June 8-25, 1997); included rehabilitation assignment to Southern Oregon (June 23-25). ... On Oakland disabled list (June 15-July 31, 1998); included rehabilitation assignment to Edmonton (July 26-31). ... Granted free agency (December 21, 1999). ... Signed by Anaheim Angels (January 11, 2000).
RECORDS: Shares A.L. single-season record for highest fielding percentage for first baseman (100 or more games)—.999.
STATISTICAL NOTES: Led California League third basemen with .948 fielding percentage in 1994. ... Led Southern League with 14 sacrifice flies in 1995. ... Led Southern League third basemen with 291 assists, 29 errors, 424 total chances and 34 double plays in 1995. ... Led Pacific Coast League third basemen with 91 putouts, 302 assists, 405 total chances and .970 fielding percentage in 1996. ... Led A.L. second basemen with .990 fielding percentage in 1997. ... Had 18-game hitting streak (May 21-June 9, 1998). ... Career major league grand slams: 3.
2002 GAMES PLAYED BY POSITION (MLB): 1B—143; 3B—20; OF—10; 2B—1.

								BATTING									FIELDING	
Year	Team (League)	Pos.	G	AB	R	H	2B	3B	HR	RBI	BB	SO	SB-CS	Avg.	OBP	SLG	E	Avg.
1993—	S. Oregon (N'West)	3B-1B	31	125	32	41	10	2	3	19	16	18	0-1	.328	.404	.512	9	.928
—	Modesto (Calif.)	3B-1B	32	110	12	28	9	1	1	13	23	19	1-5	.255	.388	.382	5	.949
1994—	Modesto (Calif.)	3B-1B-SS	127	453	84	127	32	5	14	68	88	72	5-0	.280	.399	.466	18	†.951
1995—	Huntsville (Sou.)	3B-1B-2B	141	528	78	149	33	8	13	86	67	78	10-3	.282	.359	.449	†29	.935
1996—	Edmonton (PCL)	3B-1B-DH	*140	523	87	137	30	4	20	91	56	66	6-5	.262	.335	.449	15	†.970
—	Oakland (A.L.)	3B-DH	9	29	6	9	2	0	2	8	4	4	0-1	.310	.394	.586	2	.846
1997—	Oakland (A.L.)	2B-3B	147	538	58	131	28	4	14	65	44	75	9-3	.243	.300	.388	7	†.990
—	S. Oregon (N'West)	DH-2B	2	9	1	5	0	0	0	2	2	1	0-0	.556	.583	.556	1	.875
1998—	Oakland (A.L.)	2B-DH	114	406	54	105	19	1	9	50	44	56	1-3	.259	.333	.377	13	.975
—	Edmonton (PCL)	2B-DH	5	13	3	3	1	0	1	4	3	2	0-0	.231	.375	.538	1	.889
1999—	Oakland (A.L.)	2B-3B-1B-DH	89	247	31	60	24	0	8	33	29	36	0-0	.243	.324	.437	7	.976
—	Vancouver (PCL)	2B-DH-3B	28	105	27	41	7	1	6	27	15	16	0-0	.390	.475	.648	4	.969
2000—	Anaheim (A.L.)■	DH-1-3-0-2	123	297	47	72	11	2	17	49	40	56	1-2	.242	.334	.465	3	.984
2001—	Anaheim (A.L.)	1-D-0-3	139	457	57	124	29	4	13	54	34	65	5-2	.271	.326	.438	2	.998
2002—	Anaheim (A.L.)	1-3-0-2	153	491	80	140	34	2	12	82	67	52	6-7	.285	.371	.436	5	*.996
Major League totals (7 years)			774	2465	333	641	147	13	75	341	262	344	22-18	.260	.332	.422	39	.990

DIVISION SERIES RECORD

								BATTING									FIELDING	
Year	Team (League)	Pos.	G	AB	R	H	2B	3B	HR	RBI	BB	SO	SB-CS	Avg.	OBP	SLG	E	Avg.
2002—	Anaheim (A.L.)	1B	4	15	2	6	1	0	1	6	2	1	0-0	.400	.471	.667	0	1.000

CHAMPIONSHIP SERIES RECORD

RECORDS: Shares single-inning record for most hits—2 (October 13, 2002, seventh inning). ... Shares A.L. single-inning record for most runs—2 (October 13, 2002, seventh inning).

								BATTING									FIELDING	
Year	Team (League)	Pos.	G	AB	R	H	2B	3B	HR	RBI	BB	SO	SB-CS	Avg.	OBP	SLG	E	Avg.
2002—	Anaheim (A.L.)	1B	5	17	5	6	2	0	1	5	2	1	1-0	.353	.421	.647	0	1.000

WORLD SERIES RECORD

NOTES: Member of World Series championship team (2002).

								BATTING									FIELDING	
Year	Team (League)	Pos.	G	AB	R	H	2B	3B	HR	RBI	BB	SO	SB-CS	Avg.	OBP	SLG	E	Avg.
2002—	Anaheim (A.L.)	1B	7	23	3	6	1	1	1	8	6	1	1-0	.261	.400	.522	0	1.000

SPIVEY, JUNIOR — 2B — DIAMONDBACKS

PERSONAL: Born January 28, 1975, in Oklahoma City. ... 6-0/185. ... Bats right, throws right. ... Full name: Ernest Lee Spivey Jr.
HIGH SCHOOL: Douglass (Oklahoma City).
JUNIOR COLLEGE: Cowley County Community College (Kan.).
TRANSACTIONS/CAREER NOTES: Selected by Arizona Diamondbacks organization in 36th round of free-agent draft (June 4, 1996). ... Loaned by Diamondbacks to Tulsa, Texas Rangers organization (July 18-August 29, 1998). ... On El Paso disabled list (April 8-May 15 and July 4-August 19, 1999). ... On Arizona disabled list (August 19, 1999-remainder of season). ... On Tucson disabled list (May 8-June 14, 2000). ... On El Paso disabled list (June 25-August 17, 2000). ... On Arizona disabled list (August 31, 2000-remainder of season). ... On disabled list (June 14-26, 2002).
STATISTICAL NOTES: Led California League second basemen with 394 assists and 653 total chances in 1997. ... Tied for California League lead with 20 errors by second baseman in 1998. ... Had 18-game hitting streak (May 31-July 4, 2002).
2002 GAMES PLAYED BY POSITION (MLB): 2B—143.

								BATTING									FIELDING	
Year	Team (League)	Pos.	G	AB	R	H	2B	3B	HR	RBI	BB	SO	SB-CS	Avg.	OBP	SLG	E	Avg.
1996—	Ariz. D-backs (Ariz.)	2B-SS-3B	20	69	13	23	0	0	0	3	12	16	11-2	.333	.453	.333	3	.970
—	Lethbridge (Pio.)	2B-SS	31	107	30	36	3	4	2	25	23	24	8-3	.336	.459	.495	10	.930
1997—	High Desert (Calif.)	2B	136	491	88	134	24	6	6	53	69	115	14-9	.273	.373	.383	*33	.949
1998—	High Desert (Calif.)	2B-3B-SS	79	285	64	80	14	5	5	35	64	61	34-12	.281	.416	.418	‡20	.949
—	Tulsa (Texas)■	2B	34	119	26	37	10	1	3	16	28	25	8-4	.311	.450	.487	3	.980
1999—	El Paso (Texas)■	2B-SS	44	164	40	48	10	4	3	19	36	27	14-10	.293	.424	.457	9	.963
2000—	Tucson (PCL)	2B-SS-3B	28	117	21	33	8	4	3	16	11	17	3-1	.282	.341	.496	6	.958
—	El Paso (Texas)	2B	6	19	5	8	5	0	1	2	0	5	0-0	.421	.421	.842	0	1.000
2001—	Tucson (PCL)	2B-SS	54	194	25	45	6	0	6	27	27	32	9-6	.232	.326	.356	3	.990
—	Arizona (N.L.)	2B-SS	72	163	33	42	6	3	5	21	23	47	3-0	.258	.354	.423	3	.985
2002—	Arizona (N.L.)	2B	143	538	103	162	34	6	16	78	65	100	11-6	.301	.389	.476	15	.977
Major League totals (2 years)			215	701	136	204	40	9	21	99	88	147	14-6	.291	.381	.464	18	.979

DIVISION SERIES RECORD

								BATTING									FIELDING	
Year	Team (League)	Pos.	G	AB	R	H	2B	3B	HR	RBI	BB	SO	SB-CS	Avg.	OBP	SLG	E	Avg.
2002—	Arizona (N.L.)	2B	3	13	0	2	0	0	0	0	1	3	0-0	.154	.214	.154	0	1.000

ALL-STAR GAME RECORD

	AB	R	H	2B	3B	HR	RBI	BB	SO	SB-CS	Avg.	OBP	SLG	E	Avg.
All-Star Game totals (1 year)	2	0	0	0	0	0	0	0	1	0-0	.000	.000	.000	0	1.000

SPOONEYBARGER, TIM — P — BRAVES

PERSONAL: Born October 21, 1979, in San Diego, Calif. ... 6-3/190. ... Throws right, bats right. ... Full name: Timothy F. Spooneybarger.
HIGH SCHOOL: Pine Forest (Pensacola, Fla.).
JUNIOR COLLEGE: Okaloosa-Walton.

TRANSACTIONS/CAREER NOTES: Selected by Atlanta Braves organization in 29th round of free-agent draft (June 2, 1998). ... On disabled list (May 21-July 22, 2000).

CAREER HITTING (MLB): 0-for-1 (.000), 0 R, 0 2B, 0 3B, 0 HR, 0 RBI.

Year	League	W	L	Pct.	ERA	G	GS	CG	ShO	Sv.-Opp.	IP	H	R	ER	HR	BB-IBB	SO
1999—	Danville (Appl.)	3	0	1.000	2.22	12	0	0	0	0-...	24.1	15	11	6	0	14-0	36
—	Macon (S.Atl.)	0	1	.000	3.60	7	0	0	0	0-...	10.0	7	4	4	1	10-1	17
2000—	Myrtle Beach (Caro.)	3	0	1.000	0.91	19	6	0	0	0-...	49.2	18	7	5	0	19-0	57
2001—	Greenville (Sou.)	1	1	.500	5.14	15	0	0	0	0-...	21.0	20	12	12	1	4-0	24
—	Richmond (I.L.)	3	0	1.000	0.71	42	0	0	0	5-...	50.2	33	5	4	1	21-1	58
—	Atlanta (N.L.)	0	1	.000	2.25	4	0	0	0	0-0	4.0	5	1	1	0	2-1	3
2002—	Atlanta (N.L.)	1	0	1.000	2.63	51	0	0	0	1-1	51.1	38	16	15	4	26-5	33
—	Richmond (I.L.)	1	0	1.000	0.90	18	0	0	0	11-...	20.0	13	2	2	1	8-0	21
Major League totals (2 years)		1	1	.500	2.60	55	0	0	0	1-1	55.1	43	17	16	4	28-6	36

SPRINGER, DENNIS — P

PERSONAL: Born February 12, 1965, in Fresno, Calif. ... 5-10/185. ... Throws right, bats right. ... Full name: Dennis LeRoy Springer.

HIGH SCHOOL: Washington (Fresno, Calif.).

JUNIOR COLLEGE: Kings River Community College (Calif.).

COLLEGE: Fresno State.

TRANSACTIONS/CAREER NOTES: Selected by Los Angeles Dodgers organization in 21st round of free-agent draft (June 2, 1987). ... On San Antonio disabled list (April 19-27, 1992). ... On disabled list (August 24-September 6, 1993). ... Granted free agency (October 15, 1993). ... Signed by Philadelphia Phillies organization (May 19, 1994). ... Granted free agency (December 21, 1995). ... Signed by California Angels organization (January 5, 1996). ... Angels franchise renamed Anaheim Angels for 1997 season. ... Selected by Tampa Bay Devil Rays in first round (26th pick overall) of expansion draft (November 18, 1997). ... Released by Devil Rays (November 3, 1998). ... Signed by Florida Marlins organization (January 29, 1999). ... Granted free agency (October 6, 1999). ... Signed by New York Mets organization (February 4, 2000). ... Granted free agency (October 18, 2000). ... Signed by Los Angeles Dodgers organization (May 11, 2001). ... Granted free agency (October 15, 2001). ... Re-signed by Dodgers organization (January 4, 2002). ... On Las Vegas disabled list (July 18-25, 2002). ... Released by Dodgers (October 1, 2002).

CAREER HITTING (MLB): 7-for-72 (.097), 2 R, 1 2B, 0 3B, 0 HR, 2 RBI.

Year	League	W	L	Pct.	ERA	G	GS	CG	ShO	Sv.-Opp.	IP	H	R	ER	HR	BB-IBB	SO
1987—	Great Falls (Pio.)	4	3	.571	2.88	23	5	1	0	6-...	65.2	70	38	21	3	16-2	54
1988—	Bakersfield (Calif.)	13	7	.650	3.27	32	20	6	•4	2-...	154.0	135	75	56	13	62-4	108
—	Vero Beach (FSL)	0	0	...	4.76	1	1	0	0	0-...	5.2	6	3	3	0	2-0	4
1989—	San Antonio (Texas)	6	8	.429	3.15	19	19	4	1	0-...	140.0	128	58	49	13	46-2	89
—	Albuquerque (PCL)	4	1	.800	4.83	8	7	0	0	0-...	41.0	58	28	22	5	14-0	18
1990—	Albuquerque (PCL)	0	0	...	5.68	2	2	0	0	0-...	6.1	10	4	4	1	7-0	2
—	San Antonio (Texas)	8	6	.571	3.31	24	24	3	0	0-...	*163.1	147	76	60	8	73-0	77
1991—	San Antonio (Texas)	10	10	.500	4.43	30	24	2	0	0-...	164.2	153	96	81	18	91-2	*138
1992—	San Antonio (Texas)	6	7	.462	4.35	18	18	4	0	0-...	122.0	114	61	59	6	49-3	73
—	Albuquerque (PCL)	2	7	.222	5.66	11	11	1	0	0-...	62.0	70	45	39	7	22-0	36
1993—	Albuquerque (PCL)	3	8	.273	5.99	35	18	0	0	0-...	130.2	173	104	87	18	39-1	69
1994—	Reading (East.)■	5	8	.385	3.40	24	19	2	0	2-...	135.0	125	74	51	11	44-1	118
1995—	Scranton/W.B. (I.L.)	10	11	.476	4.68	30	23	•4	0	0-...	171.0	163	*101	89	19	47-1	115
—	Philadelphia (N.L.)	0	3	.000	4.84	4	4	0	0	0-0	22.1	21	15	12	3	9-1	15
1996—	California (A.L.)■	5	6	.455	5.51	20	15	2	1	0-0	94.2	91	65	58	24	43-0	64
—	Vancouver (PCL)	10	3	.769	2.72	16	12	6	0	0-...	109.1	89	35	33	9	36-1	78
1997—	Anaheim (A.L.)	9	9	.500	5.18	32	28	3	1	0-0	194.2	199	118	112	32	73-0	75
—	Vancouver (PCL)	1	1	.500	3.00	2	2	2	0	0-...	15.0	12	6	5	1	6-0	7
1998—	Tampa Bay (A.L.)■	3	11	.214	5.45	29	17	1	0	0-0	115.2	120	77	70	21	60-1	46
—	Durham (I.L.)	2	3	.400	2.87	5	5	0	0	0-...	37.2	34	13	12	1	15-0	23
1999—	Florida (N.L.)■	6	16	.273	4.86	38	29	3	2	1-1	196.1	231	121	106	23	64-3	83
2000—	Norfolk (I.L.)■	5	5	.500	4.38	25	17	1	1	0-...	117.0	120	65	57	15	35-1	35
—	New York (N.L.)	0	1	.000	8.74	2	2	0	0	0-0	11.1	20	11	11	2	5-0	5
2001—	Las Vegas (PCL)■	7	7	.500	5.27	19	18	2	1	0-...	114.1	142	74	67	16	28-1	51
—	Los Angeles (N.L.)	1	1	.500	3.32	4	3	0	0	0-0	19.0	19	7	7	3	2-0	7
2002—	Las Vegas (PCL)	7	8	.467	5.85	26	22	1	1	1-...	143.0	•203	100	93	21	37-0	38
—	Los Angeles (N.L.)	0	1	.000	6.75	1	0	0	0	0-0	1.1	1	1	1	0	2-0	1
A.L. totals (3 years)		17	26	.395	5.33	81	60	6	2	0-0	405.0	410	260	240	77	176-1	185
N.L. totals (5 years)		7	22	.241	4.93	49	38	3	2	1-1	250.1	292	155	137	31	82-4	111
Major League totals (8 years)		24	48	.333	5.18	130	98	9	4	1-1	655.1	702	415	377	108	258-5	296

STAIRS, MATT — OF

PERSONAL: Born February 27, 1968, in Saint John, N.B. ... 5-9/215. ... Bats left, throws right. ... Full name: Matthew Wade Stairs.

HIGH SCHOOL: Fredericton (N.B.).

TRANSACTIONS/CAREER NOTES: Signed as non-drafted free agent by Montreal Expos organization (January 17, 1989). ... On disabled list (May 16-23, 1991). ... On Ottawa disabled list (May 7-18, 1993). ... Contract sold by Expos to Chunichi Dragons of Japan Central League (June 8, 1993). ... Signed by Expos organization (December 15, 1993). ... Traded by Expos with P Pete Young to Boston Red Sox for cash (February 18, 1994). ... Granted free agency (October 14, 1995). ... Signed by Oakland Athletics organization (December 1, 1995). ... Traded by A's to Chicago Cubs for P Eric Ireland (November 20, 2000). ... Granted free agency (November 5, 2001). ... Signed by Milwaukee Brewers (January 25, 2002). ... On disabled list (May 16-June 3, 2002). ... Granted free agency (October 28, 2002).

RECORDS: Shares A.L. single-inning record for most runs batted in—6 (July 5, 1996, first inning).

HONORS: Named Eastern League Most Valuable Player (1991).

STATISTICAL NOTES: Led Eastern League with 257 total bases and tied for lead with eight intentional bases on balls received in 1991. ... Career major league grand slams: 7.

MISCELLANEOUS: Member of 1988 Canadian Olympic baseball team.

2002 GAMES PLAYED BY POSITION (MLB): OF—84.

Year	Team (League)	Pos.	G	AB	R	H	2B	3B	HR	RBI	BB	SO	SB-CS	Avg.	OBP	SLG	E	Avg.
			BATTING														FIELDING	
1989—	W. Palm Beach (FSL)	3B-SS-2B	36	111	12	21	3	1	1	9	9	18	0-0	.189	.248	.261	4	.956
—	Jamestown (NY-P)	2B-3B	14	43	8	11	1	0	1	5	3	5	1-2	.256	.304	.349	6	.893
—	Rockford (Midw.)	3B	44	141	20	40	9	2	2	14	15	29	5-4	.284	.358	.418	7	.929
1990—	W. Palm Beach (FSL)	3B-2B	55	183	30	62	9	3	3	30	41	19	15-2	.339	.468	.470	17	.899
—	Jacksonville (Sou.)	3B-OF-2B-SS	79	280	26	71	17	0	3	34	22	43	5-3	.254	.310	.346	22	.893
1991—	Harrisburg (East.)	2B-3B-OF	129	505	87	*168	30	•10	13	78	66	47	23-11	*.333	.411	*.509	22	.958
1992—	Indianapolis (A.A.)	OF	110	401	57	107	23	4	11	56	49	61	11-11	.267	.351	.426	3	.985
—	Montreal (N.L.)	OF	13	30	2	5	2	0	0	5	7	7	0-0	.167	.316	.233	1	.933
1993—	Ottawa (I.L.)	OF	34	125	18	35	4	2	3	20	11	15	4-1	.280	.348	.416	0	1.000
—	Montreal (N.L.)	OF	6	8	1	3	1	0	0	2	0	1	0-0	.375	.375	.500	0	1.000
—	Chunichi (Jp.Cn.)■		60	132	10	33	6	0	6	23	7	34	1-...	.250	...	.432	...	...
1994—	New Britain (East.)■	OF-DH-1B	93	317	44	98	25	2	9	61	53	38	10-7	.309	.407	.486	3	.975
1995—	Pawtucket (I.L.)	OF-DH	75	271	40	77	17	0	13	56	29	41	3-3	.284	.352	.491	0	1.000
—	Boston (A.L.)	OF-DH	39	88	8	23	7	1	1	17	4	14	0-1	.261	.298	.398	2	.913
1996—	Oakland (A.L.)■	OF-DH-1B	61	137	21	38	5	1	10	23	19	23	1-1	.277	.367	.547	1	.987
—	Edmonton (PCL)	DH-OF-1B	51	180	35	62	16	1	8	41	21	34	0-0	.344	.401	.578	3	.944
1997—	Oakland (A.L.)	OF-DH-1B	133	352	62	105	19	0	27	73	50	60	3-2	.298	.386	.582	4	.974
1998—	Oakland (A.L.)	DH-OF-1B	149	523	88	154	33	1	26	106	59	93	8-3	.294	.370	.511	0	1.000
1999—	Oakland (A.L.)	OF-DH-1B	146	531	94	137	26	3	38	102	89	124	2-7	.258	.366	.533	5	.981
2000—	Oakland (A.L.)	OF-DH-1B	143	476	74	108	26	0	21	81	78	122	5-2	.227	.333	.414	4	.980
2001—	Chicago (N.L.)■	1-O-D-2	128	340	48	85	21	0	17	61	52	76	2-3	.250	.358	.462	4	.993
2002—	Milwaukee (N.L.)■	OF	107	270	41	66	15	0	16	41	36	50	2-0	.244	.349	.478	1	.993
American League totals (6 years)			671	2107	347	565	116	6	123	402	299	436	19-16	.268	.360	.504	16	.980
National League totals (4 years)			254	648	92	159	39	0	33	109	95	134	4-3	.245	.353	.458	6	.992
Major League totals (10 years)			925	2755	439	724	155	6	156	511	394	570	23-19	.263	.358	.493	22	.986

S

DIVISION SERIES RECORD

Year	Team (League)	Pos.	G	AB	R	H	2B	3B	HR	RBI	BB	SO	SB-CS	Avg.	OBP	SLG	E	Avg.
			BATTING														FIELDING	
1995—	Boston (A.L.)	PH	1	1	0	0	0	0	0	0	0	1	0-0	.000	.000	.000	...	...
2000—	Oakland (A.L.)	OF-PH	3	9	0	1	1	0	0	0	0	1	0-0	.111	.111	.222	0	1.000
Division series totals (2 years)			4	10	0	1	1	0	0	0	0	2	0-0	.100	.100	.200	0	1.000

STANDRIDGE, JASON — P — DEVIL RAYS

PERSONAL: Born November 9, 1978, in Birmingham, Ala. ... 6-4/230. ... Throws right, bats right. ... Full name: Jason Wayne Standridge.

HIGH SCHOOL: Hewitt-Trussville (Ala.).

TRANSACTIONS/CAREER NOTES: Selected by Tampa Bay Devil Rays organization in first round (31st pick overall) of free-agent draft (June 3, 1997).

HONORS: Named South Atlantic League Most Valuable Pitcher (1999).

CAREER HITTING (MLB): 0-for-0 (.000), 0 R, 0 2B, 0 3B, 0 HR, 0 RBI.

Year	League	W	L	Pct.	ERA	G	GS	CG	ShO	Sv.-Opp.	IP	H	R	ER	HR	BB-IBB	SO
1997—	GC Devil Rays (GCL)	0	6	.000	3.59	13	13	0	0	0-...	57.2	56	30	23	3	13-1	55
1998—	Princeton (Appl.)	4	4	.500	7.00	12	12	0	0	0-...	63.0	82	61	49	4	28-0	47
1999—	Charleston, S.C. (S.Atl.)	9	1	.900	2.02	18	18	3	3	0-...	116.0	80	35	26	5	31-1	84
—	St. Petersburg (FSL)	4	4	.500	3.91	8	8	0	0	0-...	48.1	49	21	21	0	20-0	26
2000—	St. Petersburg (FSL)	2	4	.333	3.38	10	10	1	0	0-...	56.0	45	28	21	4	31-0	41
—	Orlando (Sou.)	6	8	.429	3.62	17	17	2	0	0-...	97.0	85	46	39	4	43-0	55
2001—	Durham (I.L.)	5	10	.333	5.28	20	20	0	0	0-...	102.1	130	73	60	13	50-0	48
—	Tampa Bay (A.L.)	0	0	...	4.66	9	1	0	0	0-0	19.1	19	10	10	5	14-1	9
—	Orlando (Sou.)	0	2	.000	5.59	2	2	0	0	0-...	9.2	12	6	6	0	4-0	7
2002—	Durham (I.L.)	10	9	.526	3.12	29	•29	0	0	0-...	173.0	168	71	60	12	64-1	111
—	Tampa Bay (A.L.)	0	0	...	9.00	1	0	0	0	0-0	3.0	7	3	3	1	4-0	1
Major League totals (2 years)		0	0	...	5.24	10	1	0	0	0-0	22.1	26	13	13	6	18-1	10

STANTON, MIKE — P

PERSONAL: Born June 2, 1967, in Houston. ... 6-1/215. ... Throws left, bats left. ... Full name: William Michael Stanton.

HIGH SCHOOL: Midland (Texas).

JUNIOR COLLEGE: Alvin (Texas) Community College.

TRANSACTIONS/CAREER NOTES: Selected by Atlanta Braves organization in 13th round of free-agent draft (June 2, 1987). ... On Atlanta disabled list (April 27, 1990-remainder of season); included rehabilitation assignments to Greenville (May 31-June 5 and August 21-29). ... Granted free agency (December 23, 1994). ... Re-signed by Braves (April 12, 1995). ... Traded by Braves with a player to be named later to Boston Red Sox for two players to be named later (July 31, 1995); Red Sox acquired P Matt Murray and Braves acquired OF Marc Lewis and P Mike Jacobs to complete deal (August 31, 1995). ... Traded by Red Sox to Texas Rangers for P Mark Brandenburg and P Kerry Lacy (July 31, 1996). ... Granted free agency (October 27, 1996). ... Signed by New York Yankees (December 11, 1996). ... On suspended list (July 3-10, 1998). ... Granted free agency (November 5, 1999). ... Re-signed by Yankees (November 29, 1999). ... Granted free agency (October 30, 2002).

STATISTICAL NOTES: Led A.L. with nine intentional bases on balls issued in 2001.

CAREER HITTING (MLB): 7-for-16 (.438), 2 R, 1 2B, 0 3B, 0 HR, 2 RBI.

Year	League	W	L	Pct.	ERA	G	GS	CG	ShO	Sv.-Opp.	IP	H	R	ER	HR	BB-IBB	SO
1987—	Pulaski (Appl.)	4	8	.333	3.24	15	13	3	2	0-...	83.1	64	37	30	7	42-0	82
1988—	Burlington (Midw.)	11	5	.688	3.62	30	23	1	1	0-...	154.0	154	86	62	7	69-2	160
—	Durham (Caro.)	1	0	1.000	1.46	2	2	1	1	0-...	12.1	14	3	2	0	5-0	14
1989—	Greenville (Sou.)	4	1	.800	1.58	47	0	0	0	19-...	51.1	32	10	9	1	31-3	58
—	Richmond (I.L.)	2	0	1.000	0.00	13	0	0	0	8-...	20.0	6	0	0	0	13-2	20
—	Atlanta (N.L.)	0	1	.000	1.50	20	0	0	0	7-8	24.0	17	4	4	0	8-1	27
1990—	Atlanta (N.L.)	0	3	.000	18.00	7	0	0	0	2-3	7.0	16	16	14	1	4-2	7
—	Greenville (Sou.)	0	1	.000	1.59	4	4	0	0	0-...	5.2	7	1	1	1	3-0	4

Year League	W	L	Pct.	ERA	G	GS	CG	ShO	Sv.-Opp.	IP	H	R	ER	HR	BB-IBB	SO
1991— Atlanta (N.L.)	5	5	.500	2.88	74	0	0	0	7-10	78.0	62	27	25	6	21-6	54
1992— Atlanta (N.L.)	5	4	.556	4.10	65	0	0	0	8-11	63.2	59	32	29	6	20-2	44
1993— Atlanta (N.L.)	4	6	.400	4.67	63	0	0	0	27-33	52.0	51	35	27	4	29-7	43
1994— Atlanta (N.L.)	3	1	.750	3.55	49	0	0	0	3-4	45.2	41	18	18	2	26-3	35
1995— Atlanta (N.L.)	1	1	.500	5.59	26	0	0	0	1-2	19.1	31	14	12	3	6-2	13
— Boston (A.L.)■	1	0	1.000	3.00	22	0	0	0	0-1	21.0	17	9	7	3	8-0	10
1996— Boston (A.L.)	4	3	.571	3.83	59	0	0	0	1-5	56.1	58	24	24	9	23-4	46
— Texas (A.L.)■	0	1	.000	3.22	22	0	0	0	0-1	22.1	20	8	8	2	4-1	14
1997— New York (A.L.)■	6	1	.857	2.57	64	0	0	0	3-5	66.2	50	19	19	3	34-2	70
1998— New York (A.L.)	4	1	.800	5.47	67	0	0	0	6-10	79.0	71	51	48	13	26-1	69
1999— New York (A.L.)	2	2	.500	4.33	73	1	0	0	0-5	62.1	71	30	30	5	18-4	59
2000— New York (A.L.)	2	3	.400	4.10	69	0	0	0	0-4	68.0	68	32	31	5	24-2	75
2001— New York (A.L.)	9	4	.692	2.58	76	0	0	0	0-1	80.1	80	25	23	4	29-9	78
2002— New York (A.L.)	7	1	.875	3.00	79	0	0	0	6-9	78.0	73	29	26	4	28-3	44
A.L. totals (8 years)	35	16	.686	3.64	531	1	0	0	16-41	534.0	508	227	216	48	194-26	465
N.L. totals (7 years)	18	21	.462	4.01	304	0	0	0	55-71	289.2	277	146	129	22	114-23	223
Major League totals (14 years)	53	37	.589	3.77	835	1	0	0	71-112	823.2	785	373	345	70	308-49	688

DIVISION SERIES RECORD

Year League	W	L	Pct.	ERA	G	GS	CG	ShO	Sv.-Opp.	IP	H	R	ER	HR	BB-IBB	SO
1995— Boston (A.L.)	0	0	...	0.00	1	0	0	0	0-0	2.1	1	0	0	0	0-0	4
1996— Texas (A.L.)	0	1	.000	2.70	3	0	0	0	0-0	3.1	2	2	1	1	3-0	3
1997— New York (A.L.)	0	0	...	0.00	3	0	0	0	0-0	1.0	1	0	0	0	1-0	3
1998— New York (A.L.)	Did not play.															
1999— New York (A.L.)	Did not play.															
2000— New York (A.L.)	1	0	1.000	2.08	3	0	0	0	0-0	4.1	5	1	1	0	1-0	3
2001— New York (A.L.)	1	0	1.000	0.00	3	0	0	0	0-0	4.2	3	0	0	0	0-0	1
2002— New York (A.L.)	0	1	.000	10.13	3	0	0	0	0-1	2.2	6	3	3	0	1-1	1
Division series totals (6 years)	2	2	.500	2.45	16	0	0	0	0-1	18.1	18	6	5	1	6-1	15

CHAMPIONSHIP SERIES RECORD

Year League	W	L	Pct.	ERA	G	GS	CG	ShO	Sv.-Opp.	IP	H	R	ER	HR	BB-IBB	SO
1991— Atlanta (N.L.)	0	0	...	2.45	3	0	0	0	0-0	3.2	4	1	1	0	3-1	3
1992— Atlanta (N.L.)	0	0	...	0.00	5	0	0	0	0-0	4.1	2	1	0	0	2-1	5
1993— Atlanta (N.L.)	0	0	...	0.00	1	0	0	0	0-0	1.0	1	0	0	0	1-0	0
1998— New York (A.L.)	0	0	...	0.00	3	0	0	0	0-0	3.2	2	0	0	0	1-1	4
1999— New York (A.L.)	0	0	...	0.00	3	0	0	0	0-0	.1	1	0	0	0	1-0	0
2000— New York (A.L.)	Did not play.															
2001— New York (A.L.)	0	0	...	27.00	2	0	0	0	0-0	1.0	1	3	3	0	2-1	0
Champ. series totals (6 years)	0	0	...	2.57	17	0	0	0	0-0	14.0	11	5	4	0	10-4	12

WORLD SERIES RECORD

RECORDS: Holds record for most games as relief pitcher—20.

NOTES: Member of World Series championship team (1998, 1999 and 2000).

Year League	W	L	Pct.	ERA	G	GS	CG	ShO	Sv.-Opp.	IP	H	R	ER	HR	BB-IBB	SO
1991— Atlanta (N.L.)	1	0	1.000	0.00	5	0	0	0	0-0	7.1	5	0	0	0	2-2	7
1992— Atlanta (N.L.)	0	0	...	0.00	4	0	0	0	1-1	5.0	3	0	0	0	2-2	1
1998— New York (A.L.)	0	0	...	27.00	1	0	0	0	0-0	.2	3	2	2	0	0-0	1
1999— New York (A.L.)	0	0	...	0.00	1	0	0	0	0-0	.1	0	0	0	0	0-0	1
2000— New York (A.L.)	2	0	1.000	0.00	4	0	0	0	0-0	4.1	0	0	0	0	0-0	7
2001— New York (A.L.)	0	0	...	3.18	5	0	0	0	0-0	5.2	3	2	2	0	1-0	3
World Series totals (6 years)	3	0	1.000	1.54	20	0	0	0	1-1	23.1	14	4	4	0	5-4	20

ALL-STAR GAME RECORD

	W	L	Pct.	ERA	GS	CG	ShO	Sv.-Opp.	IP	H	R	ER	HR	BB-IBB	SO
All-Star Game totals (1 year)	0	0	...	0.00	0	0	0	0-0	.2	0	0	0	0	0-0	0

STARK, DENNIS — P — ROCKIES

PERSONAL: Born October 27, 1974, in Hicksville, Ohio. ... 6-2/210. ... Throws right, bats right.

HIGH SCHOOL: Edgerton (Ohio).

COLLEGE: Toledo.

TRANSACTIONS/CAREER NOTES: Selected by Seattle Mariners organization in fourth round of free-agent draft (June 4, 1996). ... On Lancaster disabled list (April 26, 1998-remainder of season); included rehabilitation assignment to Arizona League Mariners (July 30-August 11). ... On New Haven disabled list (May 20-August 30, 2000). ... On Seattle disabled list (August 31, 2000-remainder of season). ... Traded by Mariners with P Jose Paniagua and P Brian Fuentes to Colorado Rockies for 3B Jeff Cirillo (December 15, 2001).

HONORS: Named Pacific Coast League Pitcher of the Year (2001).

CAREER HITTING (MLB): 7-for-41 (.171), 4 R, 3 2B, 0 3B, 1 HR, 4 RBI.

Year League	W	L	Pct.	ERA	G	GS	CG	ShO	Sv.-Opp.	IP	H	R	ER	HR	BB-IBB	SO
1996— Everett (N'West)	1	3	.250	4.45	12	4	0	0	0-...	30.1	25	19	15	2	17-0	49
1997— Wisconsin (Midw.)	6	3	.667	1.97	16	15	1	0	0-...	91.1	52	27	20	3	33-0	105
— Lancaster (Calif.)	1	1	.500	3.24	3	3	0	0	0-...	16.2	13	7	6	1	10-0	17
1998— Lancaster (Calif.)	1	2	.333	4.29	5	5	0	0	0-...	21.0	18	12	10	1	17-0	21
— Arizona Mariners (Ariz.)	0	0	...	2.16	3	1	0	0	0-...	8.1	9	2	2	0	2-0	13
1999— New Haven (East.)	9	11	.450	4.40	26	26	2	1	0-...	147.1	151	82	72	14	62-0	103
— Seattle (A.L.)	0	0	...	9.95	5	0	0	0	0-0	6.1	10	8	7	0	4-0	4
2000— New Haven (East.)	4	3	.571	2.19	8	8	1	0	0-...	49.1	31	13	12	1	17-0	42
2001— Tacoma (PCL)	*14	2	*.875	2.37	24	24	0	0	0-...	151.2	124	52	40	12	41-0	130
— Seattle (A.L.)	1	1	.500	9.20	4	3	0	0	0-0	14.2	21	15	15	5	4-0	12
— San Antonio (Texas)	1	0	1.000	0.00	1	1	0	0	0-...	6.0	2	0	0	0	3-0	7
2002— Colorado Springs (PCL)■	1	2	.333	3.82	7	7	0	0	0-...	37.2	35	20	16	4	14-0	38
— Colorado (N.L.)	11	4	.733	4.00	32	20	0	0	0-1	128.1	108	69	57	25	64-4	64
A.L. totals (2 years)	1	1	.500	9.43	9	3	0	0	0-0	21.0	31	23	22	5	8-0	16
N.L. totals (1 year)	11	4	.733	4.00	32	20	0	0	0-1	128.1	108	69	57	25	64-4	64
Major League totals (3 years)	12	5	.706	4.76	41	23	0	0	0-1	149.1	139	92	79	30	72-4	80

STECHSCHULTE, GENE — P — CARDINALS

PERSONAL: Born August 12, 1973, in Lima, Ohio. ... 6-5/210. ... Throws right, bats right. ... Full name: Eugene Urban Stechschulte.
HIGH SCHOOL: Kalida (Ohio).
COLLEGE: Ashland (Ohio).
TRANSACTIONS/CAREER NOTES: Signed as non-drafted free agent by St. Louis Cardinals organization (June 13, 1996). ... On Arkansas disabled list (July 31-September 1, 1999). ... On Memphis disabled list (August 4, 2002-remainder of season).
STATISTICAL NOTES: Hit home run in first major league at-bat (April 17, 2001).
MISCELLANEOUS: Appeared in two games as pinch hitter (2001).
CAREER HITTING (MLB): 2-for-5 (.400), 1 R, 0 2B, 0 3B, 1 HR, 3 RBI.

Year	League	W	L	Pct.	ERA	G	GS	CG	ShO	Sv.-Opp.	IP	H	R	ER	HR	BB-IBB	SO
1996—	New Jersey (NY-Penn)	1	2	.333	3.27	20	1	0	0	0-...	33.0	41	17	12	0	16-2	27
1997—	New Jersey (NY-Penn)	1	1	.500	3.22	30	0	0	0	1-...	36.1	45	16	13	2	16-0	28
1998—	Peoria (Midw.)	4	8	.333	2.59	57	0	0	0	*33-...	66.0	58	26	19	1	21-2	70
1999—	Arkansas (Texas)	2	6	.250	3.40	39	0	0	0	19-...	42.1	41	26	16	4	20-1	41
	—Memphis (PCL)	0	0	...	7.71	2	0	0	0	0-...	2.1	2	2	2	0	5-0	2
2000—	Memphis (PCL)	4	1	.800	2.45	41	0	0	0	26-...	47.2	38	13	13	4	18-4	37
	—St. Louis (N.L.)	1	0	1.000	6.31	20	0	0	0	0-1	25.2	24	22	18	6	17-1	12
	—Arkansas (Texas)	0	0	...	0.00	2	0	0	0	0-...	2.0	0	0	0	0	0-0	3
2001—	St. Louis (N.L.)	1	5	.167	3.86	67	0	0	0	6-8	70.0	71	35	30	10	30-2	51
2002—	St. Louis (N.L.)	6	2	.750	4.78	29	0	0	0	0-2	32.0	27	19	17	4	17-1	21
	—Memphis (PCL)	1	0	1.000	1.80	10	0	0	0	5-...	10.0	8	2	2	0	2-0	7
Major League totals (3 years)		8	7	.533	4.58	116	0	0	0	6-11	127.2	122	76	65	20	64-4	84

DIVISION SERIES RECORD

Year	League	W	L	Pct.	ERA	G	GS	CG	ShO	Sv.-Opp.	IP	H	R	ER	HR	BB-IBB	SO
2001—	St. Louis (N.L.)	0	0	...	0.00	2	0	0	0	0-0	.1	3	0	0	0	0-0	0

STEIN, BLAKE — P

PERSONAL: Born August 3, 1973, in McComb, Miss. ... 6-7/240. ... Throws right, bats right. ... Full name: William Blake Stein.
HIGH SCHOOL: Covington (La.).
COLLEGE: Spring Hill College (Ala.).
TRANSACTIONS/CAREER NOTES: Selected by St. Louis Cardinals organization in sixth round of free-agent draft (June 2, 1994). ... Traded by Cardinals with P T.J. Mathews and P Eric Ludwick to Oakland Athletics for 1B Mark McGwire (July 31, 1997). ... Traded by A's with P Jeff D'Amico and P Brad Rigby to Kansas City Royals for P Kevin Appier (July 31, 1999). ... On Kansas City disabled list (March 24-July 5, 2000); included rehabilitation assignments to Wilmington (June 7-18), Wichita (June 21-22) and Omaha (June 23-July 5). ... On Kansas City disabled list (May 27-July 27, 2002); included rehabilitation assignment to Wichita (July 11-27). ... Released by Royals (September 9, 2002).
RECORDS: Shares major league single-inning record for most strikeouts—4 (July 27, 1998, fourth inning).
CAREER HITTING (MLB): 0-for-9 (.000), 0 R, 0 2B, 0 3B, 0 HR, 0 RBI.

Year	League	W	L	Pct.	ERA	G	GS	CG	ShO	Sv.-Opp.	IP	H	R	ER	HR	BB-IBB	SO
1994—	Johnson City (Appl.)	4	1	.800	2.87	13	13	1	0	0-...	59.2	44	21	19	4	24-0	69
1995—	Peoria (Midw.)	10	6	.625	3.80	27	•27	1	0	0-...	139.2	122	69	59	12	61-0	133
1996—	St. Petersburg (FSL)	•16	5	.762	*2.15	28	27	2	1	1-...	172.0	122	48	41	4	54-0	*159
1997—	Arkansas (Texas)	8	7	.533	4.24	22	22	1	0	0-...	133.2	128	67	63	17	49-2	114
	—Huntsville (Sou.)■	3	2	.600	5.71	7	7	0	0	0-...	34.2	36	24	22	3	20-1	25
1998—	Edmonton (PCL)	3	1	.750	3.47	5	4	0	0	0-...	23.1	22	13	9	1	11-0	31
	—Oakland (A.L.)	5	9	.357	6.37	24	20	1	1	0-0	117.1	117	92	83	22	71-3	89
1999—	Vancouver (PCL)	4	2	.667	4.10	19	19	0	0	0-...	109.2	94	54	50	9	43-0	111
	—Oakland (A.L.)	0	0	...	16.88	1	1	0	0	0-0	2.2	6	5	5	1	6-0	4
	—Kansas City (A.L.)■	1	2	.333	4.09	12	11	0	0	0-0	70.1	59	33	32	10	41-1	43
2000—	Wilmington (Caro.)	0	0	...	6.75	2	2	0	0	0-...	5.1	6	4	4	1	2-0	12
	—Wichita (Texas)	1	0	1.000	6.23	2	2	0	0	0-...	8.2	10	6	6	2	1-0	12
	—Omaha (PCL)	2	0	1.000	0.73	2	2	0	0	0-...	12.1	9	1	1	1	2-0	14
	—Kansas City (A.L.)	8	5	.615	4.68	17	17	1	0	0-0	107.2	98	57	56	19	57-1	78
2001—	Kansas City (A.L.)	7	8	.467	4.74	36	15	0	0	1-2	131.0	112	73	69	20	79-2	113
2002—	Kansas City (A.L.)	0	4	.000	7.91	27	2	0	0	1-2	46.2	59	41	41	6	27-1	42
	—Wichita (Texas)	0	1	.000	3.48	6	3	0	0	0-...	10.1	11	4	4	1	7-0	7
Major League totals (5 years)		21	28	.429	5.41	117	66	2	1	2-4	475.2	451	301	286	78	281-8	369

STENSON, DERNELL — OF — RED SOX

PERSONAL: Born June 17, 1978, in La Grange, Ga. ... 6-1/230. ... Bats left, throws left. ... Full name: Dernell Renauld Stenson.
HIGH SCHOOL: La Grange (Ga.).
TRANSACTIONS/CAREER NOTES: Selected by Boston Red Sox organization in third round of free-agent draft (June 2, 1996). ... On Pawtucket disabled list (June 24-July 15, 1999). ... On disabled list (April 17-May 10 and June 1-18, 2000; and May 8-17, 2001).
STATISTICAL NOTES: Led Eastern League outfielders with 15 assists in 1998.

			BATTING														FIELDING	
Year	Team (League)	Pos.	G	AB	R	H	2B	3B	HR	RBI	BB	SO	SB-CS	Avg.	OBP	SLG	E	Avg.
1996—	GC Red Sox (GCL)	OF	32	97	16	21	3	1	2	15	16	26	4-3	.216	.358	.330	0	1.000
1997—	Michigan (Midw.)	OF	131	471	79	137	35	2	15	80	72	105	6-4	.291	.400	.469	14	.918
1998—	Trenton (East.)	OF	138	505	90	130	21	1	24	71	84	135	5-3	.257	.376	.446	6	.975
1999—	Pawtucket (I.L.)	1B-DH	121	440	64	119	28	2	18	82	55	119	2-1	.270	.356	.466	*34	.966
	—GC Red Sox (GCL)	DH-1B	6	23	2	5	0	0	2	7	3	5	0-0	.217	.308	.478	1	.947
2000—	Pawtucket (I.L.)	1B-OF	98	380	59	102	14	0	23	71	45	99	0-0	.268	.349	.487	12	.980
2001—	Pawtucket (I.L.)	OF	122	464	53	110	18	1	16	69	43	116	0-0	.237	.302	.384	8	.964
2002—	Pawtucket (I.L.)	OF	107	368	44	92	20	1	9	36	37	96	4-3	.250	.321	.383	9	.957

STEPHENS, JOHN — P — ORIOLES

PERSONAL: Born November 15, 1979, in Sydney, Australia. ... 6-1/204. ... Throws right, bats right. ... Full name: John M. Stephens.
HIGH SCHOOL: Parramatta Marist (Westmead, Australia).
TRANSACTIONS/CAREER NOTES: Signed as non-drafted free agent by Baltimore Orioles organization (July 3, 1996). ... On disabled list (May 11, 1998-remainder of season).
HONORS: Named Eastern League Pitcher of the Year (2001).
CAREER HITTING (MLB): 0-for-0 (.000), 0 R, 0 2B, 0 3B, 0 HR, 0 RBI.

Year League	W	L	Pct.	ERA	G	GS	CG	ShO	Sv.-Opp.	IP	H	R	ER	HR	BB-IBB	SO
1997—Gulf Coast Orioles (GCL)..	3	0	1.000	0.82	9	3	0	0	1-...	33.0	15	3	3	1	9-0	43
—Bluefield (Appl.)	2	0	1.000	2.25	4	4	0	0	0-...	24.0	17	6	6	4	5-0	34
1998—Delmarva (S.Atl.)	1	2	.333	2.60	6	6	1	1	0-...	34.2	25	11	10	3	13-0	40
1999—Delmarva (S.Atl.)	10	8	.556	3.22	28	27	•4	2	0-...	170.1	148	75	61	10	36-0	*217
2000—Frederick (Caro.)	7	6	.538	3.05	20	20	0	0	0-...	118.0	119	45	40	5	22-1	121
2001—Bowie (East.)	11	4	.733	1.84	18	17	3	•3	0-...	132.0	95	32	27	10	21-1	130
—Rochester (I.L.)	2	5	.286	4.03	9	9	0	0	0-...	58.0	52	31	26	5	19-1	61
2002—Rochester (I.L.)	11	5	.688	3.03	21	21	1	0	0-...	142.2	126	51	48	10	23-0	118
—Baltimore (A.L.)	2	5	.286	6.09	12	11	0	0	0-0	65.0	68	44	44	13	22-2	56
Major League totals (1 year)	2	5	.286	6.09	12	11	0	0	0-0	65.0	68	44	44	13	22-2	56

STEPHENSON, GARRETT — P — CARDINALS

PERSONAL: Born January 2, 1972, in Takoma Park, Md. ... 6-5/208. ... Throws right, bats right. ... Full name: Garrett Charles Stephenson.
HIGH SCHOOL: Boonsboro (Md.).
JUNIOR COLLEGE: Ricks College (Idaho).
COLLEGE: Idaho State.
TRANSACTIONS/CAREER NOTES: Selected by Baltimore Orioles organization in 18th round of free-agent draft (June 1, 1992). ... Traded by Orioles with P Calvin Maduro to Philadelphia Phillies (September 4, 1996), completing deal in which Phillies traded 3B Todd Zeile and OF Pete Incaviglia to Orioles for two players to be named later (August 29, 1996). ... On Philadelphia disabled list (June 5-22 and August 18-September 2, 1997). ... On Scranton/Wilkes-Barre disabled list (July 8-August 3, 1998). ... Traded by Phillies with P Ricky Bottalico to St. Louis Cardinals for OF Ron Gant, P Jeff Brantley and P Cliff Politte (November 19, 1998). ... On Memphis disabled list (April 8-June 13, 1999). ... On St. Louis disabled list (March 28, 2001-entire season); included rehabilitation assignment to Memphis (April 5-9). ... On St. Louis disabled list (April 15-May 14 and May 30-August 28, 2002); included rehabilitation assignments to Peoria (May 8-14 and July 31-August 4) and Memphis (August 5-28).
STATISTICAL NOTES: Led Eastern League with 18 hit batsmen in 1995.
CAREER HITTING (MLB): 9-for-136 (.066), 1 R, 2 2B, 0 3B, 0 HR, 5 RBI.

Year League	W	L	Pct.	ERA	G	GS	CG	ShO	Sv.-Opp.	IP	H	R	ER	HR	BB-IBB	SO
1992—Bluefield (Appl.)	3	1	.750	4.73	12	3	0	0	0-...	32.1	35	22	17	4	7-0	30
1993—Albany (S.Atl.)	16	7	.696	2.84	30	24	3	•2	1-...	171.1	142	65	54	6	44-0	147
1994—Frederick (Caro.)	7	5	.583	4.02	18	17	1	0	0-...	107.1	91	62	48	13	36-2	133
—Bowie (East.)	3	2	.600	5.15	7	7	1	1	0-...	36.2	47	22	21	2	11-1	32
1995—Bowie (East.)	7	10	.412	3.64	29	*29	1	0	0-...	175.1	154	87	71	*23	47-0	139
1996—Rochester (I.L.)	7	6	.538	4.81	23	21	3	1	0-...	121.2	123	66	65	13	44-0	86
—Baltimore (A.L.)	0	1	.000	12.79	3	0	0	0	0-0	6.1	13	9	9	1	3-1	3
1997—Scranton/W.B. (I.L.)■	3	1	.750	5.90	7	3	0	0	0-...	29.0	27	19	19	6	12-0	27
—Philadelphia (N.L.)	8	6	.571	3.15	20	18	2	0	0-0	117.0	104	45	41	11	38-0	81
1998—Philadelphia (N.L.)	0	2	.000	9.00	6	6	0	0	0-0	23.0	31	24	23	3	19-0	17
—Scranton/W.B. (I.L.)	1	8	.111	5.25	13	11	2	0	0-...	73.2	81	49	43	15	16-0	48
1999—Memphis (PCL)■	1	1	.500	3.16	4	4	0	0	0-...	25.2	22	9	9	2	7-0	19
—Arkansas (Texas)	0	0	...	3.38	1	1	0	0	0-...	5.1	8	3	2	1	1-0	2
—St. Louis (N.L.)	6	3	.667	4.22	18	12	0	0	0-0	85.1	90	43	40	11	29-1	59
2000—St. Louis (N.L.)	16	9	.640	4.49	32	31	3	2	0-0	200.1	209	105	100	31	63-0	123
2001—Memphis (PCL)	0	0	...	0.00	1	1	0	0	0-...	2.0	2	0	0	0	0-0	2
2002—St. Louis (N.L.)	2	5	.286	5.40	12	10	0	0	0-0	45.0	48	27	27	4	25-0	34
—Peoria (Midw.)	0	0	...	0.00	2	2	0	0	0-...	8.2	0	0	0	0	0-0	11
—Memphis (PCL)	0	1	.000	3.55	3	3	0	0	0-...	12.2	12	5	5	0	2-0	12
A.L. totals (1 year)	0	1	.000	12.79	3	0	0	0	0-0	6.1	13	9	9	1	3-1	3
N.L. totals (5 years)	32	25	.561	4.42	88	77	5	2	0-0	470.2	482	244	231	60	174-1	314
Major League totals (6 years)	32	26	.552	4.53	91	77	5	2	0-0	477.0	495	253	240	61	177-2	317

DIVISION SERIES RECORD

Year League	W	L	Pct.	ERA	G	GS	CG	ShO	Sv.-Opp.	IP	H	R	ER	HR	BB-IBB	SO
2000—St. Louis (N.L.)	0	0	...	2.45	1	1	0	0	0-0	3.2	3	1	1	0	2-0	2

STEVENS, LEE — 1B

PERSONAL: Born October 3, 1967, in Kansas City, Mo. ... 6-4/235. ... Bats left, throws left. ... Full name: DeWain Lee Stevens.
HIGH SCHOOL: Lawrence (Kan.).
TRANSACTIONS/CAREER NOTES: Selected by California Angels organization in first round (22nd pick overall) of free-agent draft (June 2, 1986). ... Traded by Angels to Montreal Expos for P Jeff Tuss (January 15, 1993); Tuss announced his retirement and Angels acquired P Keith Morrison to complete deal (January 21, 1993). ... Released by Expos (March 30, 1993). ... Signed by Toronto Blue Jays organization (April 8, 1993). ... Granted free agency (October 15, 1993). ... Signed by Angels organization (October 25, 1993). ... Contract sold by Angels to Kintetsu Buffaloes of Japan Pacific League (November 16, 1993). ... Signed by Texas Rangers organization (April 3, 1996). ... On Texas disabled list (August 4-September 1, 1996); included rehabilitation assignment to Oklahoma City (August 13-September 1, 1996). ... On Texas disabled list (August 8-September 1, 1998); included rehabilitation assignment to Oklahoma (August 25-September 1). ... Traded by Rangers to Expos as part of three-way deal in which Expos sent 1B Brad Fullmer to Toronto Blue Jays and Blue Jays sent 1B/DH David Segui and cash to Rangers (March 16, 2000). ... Traded by Expos with SS Brandon Phillips, P Cliff Lee and OF Grady Sizemore to Cleveland Indians for P Bartolo Colon and future considerations (June 27, 2002); Expos acquired P Tim Drew to complete deal (June 28, 2002). ... Granted free agency (October 28, 2002).

HONORS: Named American Association Most Valuable Player (1996).

STATISTICAL NOTES: Led California League first basemen with .986 fielding percentage, 1,028 putouts and 66 assists in 1987. ... Led Texas League outfielders with 12 errors in 1988. ... Tied for Pacific Coast League lead with 11 intentional bases on balls received in 1990. ... Led American Association with 277 total bases in 1996. ... Tied for American Association lead with eight intentional bases on balls received in 1996. ... Hit three home runs in one game (April 13, 1998). ... Career major league grand slams: 2.

2002 GAMES PLAYED BY POSITION (MLB): 1B—83; OF—16; DH—3.

					BATTING											FIELDING	
Year	Team (League)	Pos.	G	AB	R	H	2B	3B	HR	RBI	BB	SO	SB-CS	Avg.	OBP	SLG	E	Avg.
1986—	Salem (N'West)	OF-1B	72	267	45	75	18	2	6	47	45	49	13-6	.281	.387	.431	5	.980
1987—	Palm Springs (Calif.)	1B-OF	140	532	82	130	29	2	19	97	61	117	1-9	.244	.324	.414	18	†.984
1988—	Midland (Texas)	OF-1B	116	414	79	123	26	2	23	76	58	108	0-5	.297	.388	.536	†14	.943
1989—	Edmonton (PCL)	1B-OF	127	446	72	110	29	9	14	74	61	115	5-3	.247	.341	.446	7	.990
1990—	Edmonton (PCL)	OF-1B	90	338	57	99	31	2	16	66	55	83	1-2	.293	.390	.538	6	.980
—	California (A.L.)	1B	67	248	28	53	10	0	7	32	22	75	1-1	.214	.275	.339	4	.994
1991—	Edmonton (PCL)	OF-1B	123	481	75	151	29	3	19	96	37	79	3-1	.314	.363	.505	7	.987
—	California (A.L.)	OF-1B	18	58	8	17	7	0	0	9	6	12	1-2	.293	.354	.414	1	.991
1992—	California (A.L.)	1B-DH	106	312	25	69	19	0	7	37	29	64	1-4	.221	.288	.349	4	.995
1993—	Syracuse (I.L.)■	OF-1B	116	401	61	106	30	1	14	66	39	85	2-4	.264	.328	.449	3	.986
1994—	Kintetsu (Jap. Pac.)■	OF	93	302	44	87	21	0	20	66	28	100	3-...	.288	...	.556	...	...
1995—	Kintetsu (Jap. Pac.)	OF	129	476	54	117	29	1	23	70	46	129	0-...	.246	...	.456	...	...
1996—	Okla. City (A.A.)■	DH-1B-OF	117	431	84	140	*37	2	*32	94	58	90	3-0	.325	*.404	*.643	3	.992
—	Texas (A.L.)	1B-OF	27	78	6	18	2	3	3	12	6	22	0-0	.231	.291	.449	1	.994
1997—	Texas (A.L.)	1B-DH-OF	137	426	58	128	24	2	21	74	23	83	1-3	.300	.336	.514	3	.994
1998—	Texas (A.L.)	DH-1B-OF	120	344	52	91	17	4	20	59	31	93	0-2	.265	.324	.512	1	.996
—	Oklahoma (PCL)	DH-1B	3	12	2	4	0	0	1	1	0	2	0-0	.333	.333	.583	0	1.000
1999—	Texas (A.L.)	1B-DH	146	517	76	146	31	1	24	81	52	132	2-3	.282	.344	.485	8	.994
2000—	Montreal (N.L.)■	1B	123	449	60	119	27	2	22	75	48	105	0-0	.265	.337	.481	11	.991
2001—	Montreal (N.L.)	1B	152	542	77	133	35	1	25	95	74	157	2-1	.245	.338	.452	19	.986
2002—	Montreal (N.L.)	1B	63	205	28	39	6	1	10	31	39	57	1-0	.190	.318	.376	4	.993
—	Cleveland (A.L.)■	1B-OF-DH	53	153	22	34	7	1	5	26	15	32	0-0	.222	.285	.379	3	.988
American League totals (8 years)			674	2136	275	556	117	11	87	330	184	513	6-15	.260	.317	.448	25	.994
National League totals (3 years)			338	1196	165	291	68	4	57	201	161	319	3-1	.243	.334	.450	34	.989
Major League totals (10 years)			1012	3332	440	847	185	15	144	531	345	832	9-16	.254	.323	.448	59	.992

DIVISION SERIES RECORD

					BATTING											FIELDING	
Year	Team (League)	Pos.	G	AB	R	H	2B	3B	HR	RBI	BB	SO	SB-CS	Avg.	OBP	SLG	E	Avg.
1998—	Texas (A.L.)	DH	1	3	0	0	0	0	0	0	0	1	0-0	.000	.000	.000	...	...
1999—	Texas (A.L.)	1B	3	9	0	1	1	0	0	0	1	2	0-0	.111	.200	.222	0	1.000
Division series totals (2 years)			4	12	0	1	1	0	0	0	1	3	0-0	.083	.154	.167	0	1.000

STEWART, SCOTT — P — EXPOS

PERSONAL: Born August 14, 1975, in Stoughton, Mass. ... 6-2/225. ... Throws left, bats right. ... Full name: Scott Edward Stewart.

HIGH SCHOOL: East Gaston (Mount Holly, N.C.).

TRANSACTIONS/CAREER NOTES: Selected by Texas Rangers organization in 20th round of free-agent draft (June 2, 1994). ... Released by Rangers (May 30, 1995). ... Signed by Minnesota Twins organization (June 13, 1995). ... Released by Twins (July 13, 1995). ... Signed by St. Paul, Northern League (June 1996). ... Sold by St. Paul to New York Mets organization (February 25, 1997). ... Granted free agency (October 15, 2000). ... Signed by Montreal Expos organization (November 17, 2000). ... On Montreal disabled list (May 11-June 2, 2001); included rehabilitation assignment to Ottawa (May 19-June 2).

STATISTICAL NOTES: Led Gulf Coast League with nine balks in 1994. ... Tied for Florida State League lead in balks with seven in 1997. ... Led Eastern League with four balks in 1998.

CAREER HITTING (MLB): 0-for-2 (.000), 0 R, 0 2B, 0 3B, 0 HR, 0 RBI.

Year	League	W	L	Pct.	ERA	G	GS	CG	ShO	Sv.-Opp.	IP	H	R	ER	HR	BB-IBB	SO
1994—	Gulf Coast Rangers (GCL)	4	1	.800	2.82	14	8	0	0	1-...	54.1	47	22	17	1	12-0	62
1995—	Charleston, S.C. (S.Atl.)	1	7	.125	3.69	11	11	1	0	0-...	75.2	76	38	31	6	14-1	47
—	Gulf Coast Twins (GCL)■	0	0	...	6.35	3	1	0	0	0-...	5.2	7	4	4	0	4-0	9
1996—	St. Paul (Nor.)■	6	8	.429	5.84	19	18	0	0	0-...	86.1	121	70	56	13	42-2	54
1997—	St. Lucie (FSL)■	5	10	.333	4.01	22	18	4	0	0-...	123.1	114	62	55	8	18-1	64
1998—	Binghamton (East.)	8	5	.615	3.70	24	13	0	0	2-...	90.0	91	44	37	12	29-2	65
—	Norfolk (I.L.)	0	6	.000	6.66	9	9	0	0	0-...	51.1	60	43	38	12	22-0	32
1999—	Norfolk (I.L.)	6	4	.600	4.42	35	14	0	0	0-...	99.2	109	55	49	9	36-1	85
—	Binghamton (East.)	1	0	1.000	0.00	1	1	0	0	0-...	5.0	3	0	0	0	0-0	5
2000—	Norfolk (I.L.)	3	5	.375	3.50	53	1	0	0	5-...	72.0	80	32	28	3	18-2	57
2001—	Montreal (N.L.)■	3	1	.750	3.78	62	0	0	0	3-4	47.2	43	20	20	5	13-0	39
—	Ottawa (I.L.)	0	0	...	1.80	4	0	0	0	0-...	5.0	5	1	1	0	1-0	4
2002—	Montreal (N.L.)	4	2	.667	3.09	67	0	0	0	17-19	64.0	49	29	22	4	22-5	67
Major League totals (2 years)		7	3	.700	3.39	129	0	0	0	20-23	111.2	92	49	42	9	35-5	106

STEWART, SHANNON — OF — BLUE JAYS

PERSONAL: Born February 25, 1974, in Cincinnati. ... 6-1/210. ... Bats right, throws right. ... Full name: Shannon Harold Stewart.

HIGH SCHOOL: Southridge Senior (Miami).

TRANSACTIONS/CAREER NOTES: Selected by Toronto Blue Jays organization in first round (19th pick overall) of free-agent draft (June 1, 1992); pick received as part of compensation for Los Angeles Dodgers signing Type A free-agent P Tom Candiotti. ... On disabled list (June 13, 1994-remainder of season). ... On Syracuse disabled list (May 13-31, 1996). ... On Toronto disabled list (May 1-14, 2000); included rehabilitation assignment to Dunedin (May 12-14). ... On disabled list (May 1-16, 2002).

RECORDS: Shares major league single-game record for most doubles—4 (July 18, 2000).

STATISTICAL NOTES: Led International League outfielders with 274 putouts and 286 total chances in 1996. ... Had 16-game hitting streak (June 15-30, 1999). ... Had 26-game hitting streak (August 1-29, 1999). ... Tied for A.L. lead in caught stealing with 14 in 1999. ... Had 16-game hitting streak (May 9-26, 2001).

2002 GAMES PLAYED BY POSITION (MLB): OF—99; DH—38.

			BATTING														FIELDING	
Year	**Team (League)**	**Pos.**	**G**	**AB**	**R**	**H**	**2B**	**3B**	**HR**	**RBI**	**BB**	**SO**	**SB-CS**	**Avg.**	**OBP**	**SLG**	**E**	**Avg.**
1992—	GC Blue Jays (GCL)....	OF	50	172	44	40	1	0	1	11	24	27	*32-5	.233	.333	.256	1	.988
1993—	St. Catharines (NY-P).	OF	75	*301	•53	84	15	2	3	29	33	43	25-10	.279	.351	.372	0	1.000
1994—	Hagerstown (S.Atl.)....	OF	56	225	39	73	10	5	4	25	23	39	15-11	.324	.386	.467	1	.990
1995—	Knoxville (Sou.)..........	OF-DH	138	498	89	143	24	6	5	55	*89	61	42-16	.287	.398	.390	6	.980
—	Toronto (A.L.)............	OF	12	38	2	8	0	0	0	1	5	5	2-0	.211	.318	.211	1	.955
1996—	Syracuse (I.L.)...........	OF	112	420	77	125	26	8	6	42	54	61	*35-8	.298	.377	.440	5	.983
—	Toronto (A.L.)............	OF	7	17	2	3	1	0	0	2	1	4	1-0	.176	.222	.235	1	.800
1997—	Toronto (A.L.)............	OF-DH	44	168	25	48	13	7	0	22	19	24	10-3	.286	.368	.446	2	.980
—	Syracuse (I.L.)...........	OF	58	208	41	72	13	1	5	24	36	26	9-6	.346	.452	.490	2	.983
1998—	Toronto (A.L.)............	OF	144	516	90	144	29	3	12	55	67	77	51-18	.279	.377	.417	6	.980
1999—	Toronto (A.L.)............	OF-DH	145	608	102	185	28	2	11	67	59	83	37-14	.304	.371	.411	5	.981
2000—	Toronto (A.L.)............	OF	136	583	107	186	43	5	21	69	37	79	20-5	.319	.363	.518	2	.993
—	Dunedin (FSL)............	OF	1	3	2	3	1	0	0	1	2	0	0-1	1.000	1.000	1.333	0	...
2001—	Toronto (A.L.)............	OF-DH	155	640	103	202	44	7	12	60	46	72	27-10	.316	.371	.463	5	.981
2002—	Toronto (A.L.)............	OF-DH	141	577	103	175	38	6	10	45	54	60	14-2	.303	.371	.442	2	.990
Major League totals (8 years)			784	3147	534	951	196	30	66	321	288	404	162-52	.302	.369	.446	24	.984

STINNETT, KELLY — C — REDS

PERSONAL: Born February 4, 1970, in Lawton, Okla. ... 5-11/225. ... Bats right, throws right. ... Full name: Kelly Lee Stinnett. ... Name pronounced stih-NET.

HIGH SCHOOL: Lawton (Okla.).

JUNIOR COLLEGE: Seminole (Okla.) Junior College.

TRANSACTIONS/CAREER NOTES: Selected by Cleveland Indians organization in 11th round of free-agent draft (June 5, 1989). ... Selected by New York Mets from Indians organization in Rule 5 major league draft (December 13, 1993). ... Traded by Mets to Milwaukee Brewers for P Cory Lidle (January 17, 1996). ... On Milwaukee disabled list (July 27-September 2, 1997). ... Selected by Arizona Diamondbacks in third round (65th pick overall) of expansion draft (November 18, 1997). ... Granted free agency (December 21, 2000). ... Signed by Cincinnati Reds (January 9, 2001). ... On disabled list (September 4, 2001-remainder of season). ... On Cincinnati disabled list (April 6-July 15, 2002); included rehabilitation assignments to Louisville (May 24-June 11 and June 26-July 15).

STATISTICAL NOTES: Led New York-Pennsylvania League catchers with 18 errors in 1990. ... Led South Atlantic League catchers with 27 errors in 1991. ... Tied for American Association lead in being hit by pitch with 13 in 1996. ... Led American Association catchers with 10 errors and tied for lead with nine double plays in 1996. ... Career major league grand slams: 1.

2002 GAMES PLAYED BY POSITION (MLB): C—30.

			BATTING														FIELDING	
Year	**Team (League)**	**Pos.**	**G**	**AB**	**R**	**H**	**2B**	**3B**	**HR**	**RBI**	**BB**	**SO**	**SB-CS**	**Avg.**	**OBP**	**SLG**	**E**	**Avg.**
1990—	Watertown (NY-Penn)	C-1B	60	192	29	46	10	2	2	21	40	43	3-7	.240	.378	.344	†18	.957
1991—	Columbus (S.Atl.).......	C-1B	102	384	49	101	15	1	14	74	26	70	4-1	.263	.321	.417	†28	.966
1992—	Canton/Akron (East.)..	C	91	296	37	84	10	0	6	32	16	43	7-6	.284	.326	.378	*13	.979
1993—	Charlotte (I.L.)...........	C	98	288	42	79	10	3	6	33	17	52	0-0	.274	.318	.392	8	.985
1994—	New York (N.L.)■	C	47	150	20	38	6	2	2	14	11	28	2-0	.253	.323	.360	5	.979
1995—	New York (N.L.)........	C	77	196	23	43	8	1	4	18	29	65	2-0	.219	.338	.332	7	.983
1996—	Milwaukee (A.L.)■.....	C-DH	14	26	1	2	0	0	0	0	2	11	0-0	.077	.172	.077	2	.960
—	New Orleans (A.A.).....	C-DH-3B	95	334	63	96	21	1	27	70	31	83	3-3	.287	.366	.599	†11	.980
1997—	Tucson (PCL)	C-DH-1B	64	209	50	67	15	3	10	43	42	46	1-1	.321	.444	.565	2	.993
—	Milwaukee (A.L.)	C-DH	30	36	2	9	4	0	0	3	3	9	0-0	.250	.308	.361	1	.989
1998—	Arizona (N.L.)■..........	C-DH	92	274	35	71	14	1	11	34	35	74	0-1	.259	.353	.438	8	.984
1999—	Arizona (N.L.)............	C	88	284	36	66	13	0	14	38	24	83	2-1	.232	.302	.426	6	.990
2000—	Arizona (N.L.)............	C	76	240	22	52	7	0	8	33	19	56	0-1	.217	.291	.346	6	.990
2001—	Cincinnati (N.L.)■......	C-DH	63	187	27	48	11	0	9	25	17	61	2-2	.257	.333	.460	12	.966
2002—	Cincinnati (N.L.)........	C	34	93	10	21	5	0	3	13	15	25	2-0	.226	.333	.376	2	.990
—	Louisville (I.L.)	C	30	86	6	17	6	0	0	5	3	24	0-0	.198	.225	.267	2	.988
American League totals (2 years)			44	62	3	11	4	0	0	3	5	20	0-0	.177	.250	.242	3	.978
National League totals (7 years)			477	1424	173	339	64	4	51	175	150	392	10-5	.238	.324	.396	46	.984
Major League totals (9 years)			521	1486	176	350	68	4	51	178	155	412	10-5	.236	.321	.390	49	.984

DIVISION SERIES RECORD

			BATTING														FIELDING	
Year	**Team (League)**	**Pos.**	**G**	**AB**	**R**	**H**	**2B**	**3B**	**HR**	**RBI**	**BB**	**SO**	**SB-CS**	**Avg.**	**OBP**	**SLG**	**E**	**Avg.**
1999—	Arizona (N.L.)............	C	4	14	1	2	1	0	0	0	1	4	0-0	.143	.200	.214	0	1.000

STONE, RICKY — P — ASTROS

PERSONAL: Born February 28, 1975, in Hamilton, Ohio. ... 6-1/190. ... Throws right, bats right. ... Full name: Ricky L. Stone.

HIGH SCHOOL: Hamilton (Ohio).

TRANSACTIONS/CAREER NOTES: Selected by Los Angeles Dodgers organization in fourth round of free-agent draft (June 2, 1994). ... Granted free agency (October 18, 2000). ... Signed by Houston Astros organization (January 8, 2001).

RECORDS: Shares N.L. rookie-season record for most games pitched—78 (2002).

CAREER HITTING (MLB): 0-for-4 (.000), 0 R, 0 2B, 0 3B, 0 HR, 0 RBI.

Year League	W	L	Pct.	ERA	G	GS	CG	ShO	Sv.-Opp.	IP	H	R	ER	HR	BB-IBB	SO
1994—Great Falls (Pio.)	2	2	.500	4.44	13	7	0	0	2-...	50.2	55	40	25	5	24-0	48
1995—San Bernardino (Calif.)	3	5	.375	6.52	12	12	0	0	0-...	58.0	79	50	42	7	25-0	31
—Yakima (N'West)	4	4	.500	5.25	16	6	0	0	2-...	48.0	54	31	28	5	20-0	28
1996—Savannah (S.Atl.)	2	1	.667	3.98	5	5	0	0	0-...	31.2	34	15	14	2	9-0	31
—Vero Beach (FSL)	8	6	.571	3.83	21	21	1	0	0-...	112.2	115	58	48	9	46-0	74
1997—San Antonio (Texas)	0	3	.000	5.47	25	5	0	0	3-...	52.2	63	33	32	4	30-0	46
—San Bernardino (Calif.)	3	3	.500	3.35	8	8	0	0	0-...	53.2	40	22	20	4	10-0	40
1998—San Antonio (Texas)	7	2	.778	3.84	13	13	1	1	0-...	82.0	76	40	35	7	26-0	69
—Albuquerque (PCL)	5	5	.500	5.38	18	16	0	0	0-...	105.1	120	69	63	13	41-0	85
1999—Albuquerque (PCL)	6	10	.375	5.50	27	27	2	0	0-...	167.0	205	*123	•102	23	71-4	132
2000—Albuquerque (PCL)	9	5	.643	4.94	48	7	0	0	5-...	120.1	146	79	66	9	42-3	75
2001—New Orleans (PCL)	6	3	.667	3.59	51	8	0	0	2-...	95.1	98	42	38	8	27-4	78
—Houston (N.L.)■	0	0	...	2.35	6	0	0	0	0-0	7.2	8	3	2	1	2-1	4
2002—Houston (N.L.)	3	3	.500	3.61	78	0	0	0	1-2	77.1	78	36	31	9	34-3	63
Major League totals (2 years)	3	3	.500	3.49	84	0	0	0	1-2	85.0	86	39	33	10	36-4	67

STOTTLEMYRE, TODD P

PERSONAL: Born May 20, 1965, in Yakima, Wash. ... 6-2/210. ... Throws right, bats left. ... Full name: Todd Vernon Stottlemyre. ... Son of Mel Stottlemyre Sr., pitching coach, New York Yankees; pitcher with New York Yankees (1964-74) and pitching coach for New York Mets (1984-93); and brother of Mel Stottlemyre Jr., pitcher with Kansas City Royals (1990).

HIGH SCHOOL: A.C. Davis (Yakima, Wash.).

JUNIOR COLLEGE: Yakima (Wash.) Valley College.

COLLEGE: UNLV.

TRANSACTIONS/CAREER NOTES: Selected by New York Yankees organization in fifth round of free-agent draft (June 6, 1983); did not sign. ... Selected by St. Louis Cardinals organization in secondary phase of free-agent draft (January 9, 1985); did not sign. ... Selected by Toronto Blue Jays organization in secondary phase of free-agent draft (June 3, 1985). ... On disabled list (June 20-July 13, 1992). ... On suspended list (September 23-28, 1992). ... On disabled list (May 23-June 13, 1993). ... Granted free agency (October 18, 1994). ... Signed by Oakland Athletics (April 11, 1995). ... Traded by A's to St. Louis Cardinals for P Bret Wagner, P Jay Witasick and P Carl Dale (January 9, 1996). ... Traded by Cardinals with SS Royce Clayton to Texas Rangers for P Darren Oliver, 3B Fernando Tatis and a player to be named later (July 31, 1998); Cardinals acquired OF Mark Little to complete deal (August 9, 1998). ... Granted free agency (October 22, 1998). ... Signed by Arizona Diamondbacks (December 2, 1998). ... On Arizona disabled list (May 18-August 19, 1999); included rehabilitation assignment to Arizona League Diamondbacks (August 3-15). ... On Arizona disabled list (May 30-June 15 and June 26-September 1, 2000); included rehabilitation assignment to Arizona League Diamondbacks (August 23-September 1). ... On disabled list (March 23, 2001-entire season). ... On Arizona disabled list (March 22-April 9, May 2-June 25 and June 27, 2002-remainder of season); included rehabilitation assignments to Tucson (June 15-25 and August 13-September 3). ... Announced retirement (October 30, 2002).

STATISTICAL NOTES: Pitched 9-0 one-hit, complete-game victory against Chicago (August 26, 1992). ... Struck out 15 batters in one game (June 16, 1995).

MISCELLANEOUS: Struck out in only appearance as pinch hitter (1997).

CAREER HITTING (MLB): 50-for-242 (.207), 23 R, 7 2B, 1 3B, 1 HR, 11 RBI.

Year League	W	L	Pct.	ERA	G	GS	CG	ShO	Sv.-Opp.	IP	H	R	ER	HR	BB-IBB	SO
1986—Ventura County (Calif.)	9	4	.692	2.43	17	17	2	0	0-...	103.2	76	39	28	4	36-0	104
—Knoxville (Sou.)	8	7	.533	4.18	18	18	1	0	0-...	99.0	93	56	46	5	49-1	81
1987—Syracuse (I.L.)	11	•13	.458	4.44	34	*34	1	0	0-...	186.2	189	•103	*92	14	*87-3	143
1988—Toronto (A.L.)	4	8	.333	5.69	28	16	0	0	0-1	98.0	109	70	62	15	46-5	67
—Syracuse (I.L.)	5	0	1.000	2.05	7	7	1	0	0-...	48.1	36	12	11	1	8-0	51
1989—Toronto (A.L.)	7	7	.500	3.88	27	18	0	0	0-0	127.2	137	56	55	11	44-4	63
—Syracuse (I.L.)	3	2	.600	3.23	10	9	2	0	0-...	55.2	46	23	20	4	15-0	45
1990—Toronto (A.L.)	13	17	.433	4.34	33	33	4	0	0-0	203.0	214	101	98	18	69-4	115
1991—Toronto (A.L.)	15	8	.652	3.78	34	34	1	0	0-0	219.0	194	97	92	21	75-3	116
1992—Toronto (A.L.)	12	11	.522	4.50	28	27	6	2	0-0	174.0	175	99	87	20	63-4	98
1993—Toronto (A.L.)	11	12	.478	4.84	30	28	1	1	0-0	176.2	204	107	95	11	69-5	98
1994—Toronto (A.L.)	7	7	.500	4.22	26	19	3	1	1-3	140.2	149	67	66	19	48-2	105
1995—Oakland (A.L.)■	14	7	.667	4.55	31	31	2	0	0-0	209.2	228	117	106	26	80-7	205
1996—St. Louis (N.L.)■	14	11	.560	3.87	34	33	5	2	0-0	223.1	191	100	96	30	93-8	194
1997—St. Louis (N.L.)	12	9	.571	3.88	28	28	0	0	0-0	181.0	155	86	78	16	65-3	160
1998—St. Louis (N.L.)	9	9	.500	3.51	23	23	3	0	0-0	161.1	146	74	63	20	51-0	147
—Texas (A.L.)■	5	4	.556	4.33	10	10	0	0	0-0	60.1	68	33	29	5	30-1	57
1999—Arizona (N.L.)■	6	3	.667	4.09	17	17	0	0	0-0	101.1	106	51	46	12	40-1	74
—Ariz. D-backs (Ariz.)	2	0	1.000	0.53	3	3	1	0	0-...	17.0	11	1	1	0	1-0	25
2000—Arizona (N.L.)	9	6	.600	4.91	18	18	0	0	0-0	95.1	98	55	52	18	36-2	76
—Ariz. D-backs (Ariz.)	1	1	.500	3.60	2	2	0	0	0-...	10.0	10	4	4	0	1-0	10
2001—Arizona (N.L.)									Did not play.							
2002—Tucson (PCL)	1	1	.500	3.45	11	0	0	0	1-...	15.2	13	6	6	0	4-1	12
—Arizona (N.L.)	0	2	.000	7.52	5	4	0	0	0-0	20.1	26	17	17	4	7-0	12
A.L. totals (9 years)	88	81	.521	4.41	247	216	17	4	1-4	1409.0	1478	747	690	146	524-35	924
N.L. totals (6 years)	50	40	.556	4.05	125	123	8	2	0-0	782.2	722	383	352	100	292-14	663
Major League totals (14 years)	138	121	.533	4.28	372	339	25	6	1-4	2191.2	2200	1130	1042	246	816-49	1587

DIVISION SERIES RECORD

Year League	W	L	Pct.	ERA	G	GS	CG	ShO	Sv.-Opp.	IP	H	R	ER	HR	BB-IBB	SO
1996—St. Louis (N.L.)	1	0	1.000	1.35	1	1	0	0	0-0	6.2	5	1	1	1	2-0	7
1998—Texas (A.L.)	0	1	.000	2.25	1	1	1	0	0-0	8.0	6	2	2	0	4-0	8
1999—Arizona (N.L.)	1	0	1.000	1.35	1	1	0	0	0-0	6.2	4	1	1	0	5-0	6
Division series totals (3 years)	2	1	.667	1.69	3	3	1	0	0-0	21.1	15	4	4	1	11-0	21

CHAMPIONSHIP SERIES RECORD

RECORDS: Shares single-series record for most earned runs allowed—11 (1996). ... Shares single-game record for most earned runs allowed—7 (October 14, 1996). ... Shares record for most hits allowed in one inning—6 (October 14, 1996, first inning).

Year	League	W	L	Pct.	ERA	G	GS	CG	ShO	Sv.-Opp.	IP	H	R	ER	HR	BB-IBB	SO
1989—	Toronto (A.L.)	0	1	.000	7.20	1	1	0	0	0-0	5.0	7	4	4	1	2-0	3
1991—	Toronto (A.L.)	0	1	.000	9.82	1	1	0	0	0-0	3.2	7	4	4	1	1-0	3
1992—	Toronto (A.L.)	0	0	...	2.45	1	0	0	0	0-0	3.2	3	1	1	0	0-0	1
1993—	Toronto (A.L.)	0	1	.000	7.50	1	1	0	0	0-0	6.0	6	5	5	2	4-0	4
1996—	St. Louis (N.L.)	1	1	.500	12.38	3	2	0	0	0-0	8.0	15	11	11	1	3-0	11
Champ. series totals (5 years)		1	4	.200	8.54	7	5	0	0	0-0	26.1	38	25	25	5	10-0	22

WORLD SERIES RECORD

RECORDS: Shares records for most bases on balls allowed in one inning—4 (October 20, 1993, first inning); and most consecutive bases on balls allowed in one inning—3 (October 20, 1993, first inning).

NOTES: Member of World Series championship team (1992, 1993 and 2001).

Year	League	W	L	Pct.	ERA	G	GS	CG	ShO	Sv.-Opp.	IP	H	R	ER	HR	BB-IBB	SO
1992—	Toronto (A.L.)	0	0	...	0.00	4	0	0	0	0-0	3.2	4	0	0	0	0-0	4
1993—	Toronto (A.L.)	0	0	...	27.00	1	1	0	0	0-0	2.0	3	6	6	1	4-0	1
World Series totals (2 years)		0	0	...	9.53	5	1	0	0	0-0	5.2	7	6	6	1	4-0	5

STRANGE, PAT P METS

PERSONAL: Born August 23, 1980, in Springfield, Mass. ... 6-5/243. ... Throws right, bats right. ... Full name: Patrick Martin Strange.

HIGH SCHOOL: Springfield Central (Springfield, Mass.).

TRANSACTIONS/CAREER NOTES: Selected by New York Mets organization in second round of free-agent draft (June 2, 1998).

CAREER HITTING (MLB): 0-for-0 (.000), 0 R, 0 2B, 0 3B, 0 HR, 0 RBI.

Year	League	W	L	Pct.	ERA	G	GS	CG	ShO	Sv.-Opp.	IP	H	R	ER	HR	BB-IBB	SO
1998—	Gulf Coast Mets (GCL)	1	1	.500	1.42	4	4	0	0	0-...	19.0	18	3	3	0	7-0	19
1999—	Capital City (S.Atl.)	12	5	.706	2.63	28	21	2	0	1-...	154.0	138	57	45	4	29-1	113
2000—	St. Lucie (FSL)	10	1	.909	3.58	19	13	2	0	0-...	88.0	78	48	35	4	32-0	77
—	Binghamton (East.)	4	3	.571	4.55	10	10	0	0	0-...	55.1	62	30	28	2	30-0	36
2001—	Binghamton (East.)	11	6	.647	4.87	26	24	1	0	0-...	153.1	171	94	83	18	52-1	106
—	Norfolk (I.L.)	1	0	1.000	0.00	1	1	0	0	0-...	6.0	4	0	0	0	1-0	6
2002—	Norfolk (I.L.)	10	10	.500	3.82	29	25	2	0	0-...	165.0	165	77	70	12	59-2	109
—	New York (N.L.)	0	0	...	1.13	5	0	0	0	0-0	8.0	6	1	1	0	1-1	4
Major League totals (1 year)		0	0	...	1.13	5	0	0	0	0-0	8.0	6	1	1	0	1-1	4

STRICKLAND, SCOTT P METS

PERSONAL: Born April 26, 1976, in Houston. ... 5-11/180. ... Throws right, bats right. ... Full name: Scott Michael Strickland.

HIGH SCHOOL: Klein Oak (Spring, Texas).

COLLEGE: New Mexico.

TRANSACTIONS/CAREER NOTES: Selected by Montreal Expos organization in 10th round of free-agent draft (June 3, 1997). ... On Montreal disabled list (May 3-July 3, 2000); included rehabilitation assignment to Ottawa (June 25-July 1). ... Traded by Expos with OF Matt Watson and P Philip Seibel to New York Mets for P Bruce Chen, P Dicky Gonzalez and SS/2B Luis Figueroa (April 5, 2002).

CAREER HITTING (MLB): 0-for-5 (.000), 0 R, 0 2B, 0 3B, 0 HR, 0 RBI.

Year	League	W	L	Pct.	ERA	G	GS	CG	ShO	Sv.-Opp.	IP	H	R	ER	HR	BB-IBB	SO
1997—	Vermont (NY-Penn)	5	2	.714	3.82	15	9	1	0	0-...	61.1	56	27	26	5	20-0	69
—	Cape Fear (S.Atl.)	0	1	.000	6.35	3	1	0	0	1-...	5.2	8	7	4	0	1-0	8
1998—	Cape Fear (S.Atl.)	0	3	.000	4.46	15	2	0	0	4-...	36.1	36	19	18	3	12-0	53
—	Jupiter (FSL)	4	3	.571	3.39	22	11	0	0	2-...	69.0	64	28	26	5	20-0	51
1999—	Jupiter (FSL)	1	1	.500	3.51	12	1	0	0	2-...	25.2	21	11	10	1	4-1	33
—	Harrisburg (East.)	1	1	.500	2.48	14	1	0	0	3-...	29.0	25	8	8	1	10-0	36
—	Ottawa (I.L.)	3	0	1.000	1.63	19	0	0	0	5-...	27.2	23	5	5	0	11-2	34
—	Montreal (N.L.)	0	1	.000	4.50	17	0	0	0	0-0	18.0	15	10	9	3	11-0	23
2000—	Montreal (N.L.)	4	3	.571	3.00	49	0	0	0	9-13	48.0	38	18	16	3	16-2	48
—	Ottawa (I.L.)	0	0	...	0.00	3	0	0	0	0-...	4.0	1	0	0	0	0-0	4
2001—	Montreal (N.L.)	2	6	.250	3.21	77	0	0	0	9-12	81.1	67	36	29	9	41-5	85
2002—	Montreal (N.L.)	0	0	...	0.00	1	0	0	0	0-0	1.0	0	0	0	0	0-0	2
—	New York (N.L.)■	6	9	.400	3.59	68	0	0	0	2-6	67.2	61	29	27	7	33-9	67
Major League totals (4 years)		12	19	.387	3.38	212	0	0	0	20-31	216.0	181	93	81	22	101-16	225

STRONG, JAMAL OF MARINERS

PERSONAL: Born August 5, 1978, in Pasadena, Calif. ... 5-10/180. ... Bats right, throws right. ... Full name: Jamal N. Strong.

COLLEGE: Nebraska.

TRANSACTIONS/CAREER NOTES: Selected by Seattle Mariners organization in sixth round of free-agent draft (June 5, 2000). ... On San Antonio disabled list (May 17-24, 2002).

HONORS: Shared Northwest League Most Valuable Player (2000).

STATISTICAL NOTES: Led Northwest League outfielders with 159 putouts in 2000. ... Led Texas League outfielders with 280 putouts, 299 total chances and five double plays in 2002.

				BATTING												FIELDING	
Year	Team (League)	Pos.	G	AB	R	H	2B	3B	HR	RBI	BB	SO	SB-CS	Avg.	OBP	SLG	E	Avg.
2000—	Everett (N'West)	OF	•75	296	63	93	7	3	1	28	52	29	*60-14	.314	.422	.368	2	.988
2001—	Wisconsin (Midw.)	OF	51	184	41	65	12	1	0	19	40	27	35-4	.353	.478	.429	1	.988
—	San Bern. (Calif.)	OF	81	331	74	103	11	2	0	32	51	60	47-8	.311	.411	.356	4	.977
2002—	San Antonio (Texas)	OF	127	503	63	140	16	5	1	31	62	87	*46-16	.278	.366	.336	6	.980

STULL, EVERETT — P

PERSONAL: Born August 24, 1971, in Fort Riley, Ga. ... 6-3/200. ... Throws right, bats right. ... Full name: Everett James Stull.

HIGH SCHOOL: Redan (Stone Mountain, Ga.).

COLLEGE: Tennessee State.

TRANSACTIONS/CAREER NOTES: Selected by Montreal Expos organization in third round of free-agent draft (June 1, 1992). ... Traded by Expos to Baltimore Orioles (October 31, 1997), completing deal in which Orioles traded P Mike Johnson to Expos for a player to be named later (July 31, 1997). ... On Baltimore disabled list (March 19-July 27, 1998); included rehabilitation assignment to Rochester (June 13-July 27). ... Granted free agency (October 15, 1998). ... Signed by Atlanta Braves organization (January 20, 1999). ... Granated free agency (March 20, 2000). ... Signed by Milwaukee Brewers organization (March 30, 2000). ... On Milwaukee disabled list (March 27-August 12, 2001); included rehabilitation assignments to Arizona League Brewers (July 15-24), High Desert (July 25-31) and Huntsville (August 1-12). ... Granted free agency (October 8, 2001). ... Signed by Milwaukee Brewers organization (December 20, 2001). ... Released by Brewers (September 30, 2002).

STATISTICAL NOTES: Led New York-Pennsylvania League with 18 wild pitches in 1992. ... Led International League with 25 home runs allowed in 1997.

CAREER HITTING (MLB): 1-for-12 (.083), 0 R, 0 2B, 0 3B, 0 HR, 0 RBI.

Year League	W	L	Pct.	ERA	G	GS	CG	ShO	Sv.-Opp.	IP	H	R	ER	HR	BB-IBB	SO
1992—Jamestown (NY-Penn)	3	5	.375	5.40	14	14	0	0	0-...	63.1	52	49	38	2	*61-0	64
1993—Burlington (Midw.)	4	9	.308	3.83	15	15	0	0	0-...	82.1	68	44	35	8	59-0	85
1994—West Palm Beach (FSL)	10	10	.500	3.31	27	26	3	1	0-...	147.0	116	60	54	3	78-0	165
1995—Harrisburg (East.)	3	•12	.200	5.54	24	24	0	0	0-...	126.2	114	88	78	12	79-2	132
1996—Harrisburg (East.)	6	3	.667	3.15	14	14	0	0	0-...	80.0	64	31	28	8	52-1	81
—Ottawa (I.L.)	2	6	.250	6.33	13	13	1	0	0-...	69.2	87	57	49	7	39-1	69
1997—Ottawa (I.L.)	8	10	.444	5.82	27	27	1	0	0-...	159.1	166	110	*103	25	86-0	130
—Montreal (N.L.)	0	1	.000	16.20	3	0	0	0	0-0	3.1	7	7	6	1	4-0	2
1998—Rochester (I.L.)■	1	4	.200	8.86	21	7	0	0	0-...	42.2	49	44	42	9	45-0	39
1999—Richmond (I.L.)■	8	8	.500	4.47	30	22	0	0	0-...	139.0	124	75	69	17	73-0	126
—Atlanta (N.L.)	0	0	...	13.50	1	0	0	0	0-0	.2	2	3	1	0	2-0	0
2000—Milwaukee (N.L.)■	2	3	.400	5.82	20	4	0	0	0-0	43.1	41	30	28	7	30-3	33
—Indianapolis (I.L.)	7	5	.583	2.95	16	16	1	1	0-...	103.2	95	41	34	3	43-0	74
2001—Arizona Brewers (Ariz.)	0	0	...	0.00	2	1	0	0	0-...	4.1	2	0	0	0	0-0	4
—High Desert (Calif.)	0	1	.000	16.88	1	1	0	0	0-...	2.2	6	5	5	1	1-0	1
—Huntsville (Sou.)	1	1	.500	3.86	6	4	0	0	1-...	25.2	21	11	11	3	5-0	23
2002—Indianapolis (I.L.)	11	11	.500	3.87	24	24	0	0	0-...	151.0	149	72	65	13	49-2	119
—Milwaukee (N.L.)	0	1	.000	6.30	2	2	0	0	0-0	10.0	15	7	7	0	9-2	7
Major League totals (4 years)	2	5	.286	6.59	26	6	0	0	0-0	57.1	65	47	42	8	45-5	42

STURTZE, TANYON — P — DEVIL RAYS

PERSONAL: Born October 12, 1970, in Worcester, Mass. ... 6-5/221. ... Throws right, bats right. ... Full name: Tanyon James Sturtze. ... Name pronounced STURTS.

HIGH SCHOOL: St. Peter-Marian (Worcester, Mass.).

JUNIOR COLLEGE: Quinsigamond Community College (Mass.).

TRANSACTIONS/CAREER NOTES: Selected by Oakland Athletics organization in 23rd round of free-agent draft (June 4, 1990). ... On Huntsville disabled list (April 7-16, 1994). ... Selected by Chicago Cubs from A's organization in Rule 5 major league draft (December 5, 1994). ... Granted free agency (October 15, 1996). ... Signed by Texas Rangers (November 20, 1996). ... Released by Rangers (March 6, 1998). ... Re-signed by Rangers organization (March 11, 1998). ... Granted free agency (October 15, 1998). ... Signed by Florida Marlins organization (November 23, 1998). ... Signed by Chicago White Sox organization (November 23, 1998). ... On suspended list (May 1-3, 2000). ... Traded by White Sox to Tampa Bay Devil Rays for 2B/SS Tony Graffanino (May 31, 2000). ... On Tampa Bay disabled list (August 27, 2000-remainder of season).

STATISTICAL NOTES: Pitched 5-0 no-hit victory against Chattanooga (June 13, 1993).

CAREER HITTING (MLB): 1-for-13 (.077), 0 R, 0 2B, 0 3B, 0 HR, 0 RBI.

Year League	W	L	Pct.	ERA	G	GS	CG	ShO	Sv.-Opp.	IP	H	R	ER	HR	BB-IBB	SO
1990—Arizona Athletics (Ariz.)	2	5	.286	5.44	12	10	0	0	0-...	48.0	55	41	29	3	27-0	30
1991—Madison (Midw.)	10	5	.667	3.09	27	27	0	0	0-...	163.0	136	77	56	5	58-5	88
1992—Modesto (Calif.)	7	11	.389	3.75	25	25	1	0	0-...	151.0	143	72	63	6	78-1	126
1993—Huntsville (Sou.)	5	12	.294	4.78	28	•28	1	1	0-...	165.2	169	102	*88	16	85-2	112
1994—Huntsville (Sou.)	6	3	.667	3.22	17	17	1	0	0-...	103.1	100	40	37	5	39-1	63
—Tacoma (PCL)	4	5	.444	4.04	11	9	0	0	0-...	64.2	73	36	29	5	34-2	28
1995—Chicago (N.L.)■	0	0	...	9.00	2	0	0	0	0-0	2.0	2	2	2	1	1-0	0
—Iowa (A.A.)	4	7	.364	6.80	23	17	1	1	0-...	86.0	108	66	65	18	42-1	48
1996—Iowa (A.A.)	6	4	.600	4.85	51	1	0	0	4-...	72.1	80	42	39	7	33-2	51
—Chicago (N.L.)	1	0	1.000	9.00	6	0	0	0	0-0	11.0	16	11	11	3	5-0	7
1997—Oklahoma City (A.A.)■	8	6	.571	5.10	25	19	1	0	0-...	114.2	133	76	65	10	47-1	79
—Texas (A.L.)	1	1	.500	8.27	9	5	0	0	0-0	32.2	45	30	30	6	18-0	18
1998—Gulf Coast Rangers (GCL)	0	1	.000	7.71	3	3	0	0	0-...	7.0	12	7	6	1	4-0	10
—Charlotte (FSL)	0	1	.000	6.00	1	0	0	0	0-...	3.0	2	3	2	0	1-0	3
—Tulsa (Texas)	1	0	1.000	5.40	1	0	0	0	0-...	1.2	2	1	1	1	2-0	3
—Oklahoma (PCL)	3	1	.750	3.34	13	3	0	0	0-...	35.0	33	13	13	3	18-0	31
1999—Charlotte (I.L.)■	9	4	.692	4.05	33	14	2	1	3-...	104.1	83	53	47	7	41-1	107
—Chicago (A.L.)	0	0	...	0.00	1	1	0	0	0-0	6.0	4	0	0	0	2-0	2
2000—Chicago (A.L.)	1	2	.333	12.06	10	1	0	0	0-0	15.2	25	23	21	4	15-0	6
—Tampa Bay (A.L.)■	4	0	1.000	2.56	19	5	0	0	0-0	52.2	47	16	15	4	14-1	38
2001—Tampa Bay (A.L.)	11	12	.478	4.42	39	27	0	0	1-3	195.1	200	98	96	23	79-0	110
2002—Tampa Bay (A.L.)	4	*18	.182	5.18	33	33	4	0	0-0	224.0	*271	*141	*129	33	*89-2	137
A.L. totals (5 years)	21	33	.389	4.98	111	72	4	0	1-3	526.1	592	308	291	70	217-3	311
N.L. totals (2 years)	1	0	1.000	9.00	8	0	0	0	0-0	13.0	18	13	13	4	6-0	7
Major League totals (7 years)	22	33	.400	5.07	119	72	4	0	1-3	539.1	610	321	304	74	223-3	318

STYNES, CHRIS — 3B/2B — CUBS

PERSONAL: Born January 19, 1973, in Queens, N.Y. ... 5-10/205. ... Bats right, throws right. ... Full name: Christopher Desmond Stynes.
HIGH SCHOOL: Boca Raton (Fla.).
TRANSACTIONS/CAREER NOTES: Selected by Toronto Blue Jays in third round of free-agent draft (June 3, 1991). ... Traded by Blue Jays with P David Sinnes and IF Tony Medrano to Kansas City Royals for P David Cone (April 6, 1995). ... Traded by Royals with OF Jon Nunnally to Cincinnati Reds for P Hector Carrasco and P Scott Service (July 15, 1997). ... Traded by Reds to Boston Red Sox for OF Michael Coleman and IF Donnie Sadler (November 16, 2000). ... On Boston disabled list (April 6-24 and May 10-June 7, 2001); included rehabilitation assignment to Pawtucket (June 3-7). ... Granted free agency (December 21, 2001). ... Signed by Chicago Cubs (January 2, 2002).
STATISTICAL NOTES: Led Gulf Coast League third basemen with 138 assists in 1991. ... Tied for Florida State League lead in double plays by third basemen with 22 in 1993. ... Led Southern League with 237 total bases in 1994. ... Tied for Southern League lead with 366 assists by second basemen in 1994.
2002 GAMES PLAYED BY POSITION (MLB): 3B—40; 2B—20.

								BATTING								FIELDING	
Year Team (League)	Pos.	G	AB	R	H	2B	3B	HR	RBI	BB	SO	SB-CS	Avg.	OBP	SLG	E	Avg.
1991—GC Blue Jays (GCL)....	3B	57	219	29	67	15	1	4	39	9	39	10-3	.306	.336	.438	8	*.957
1992—Myrtle Beach (S.Atl.)..	3B	127	489	67	139	36	0	7	46	16	43	28-14	.284	.315	.401	26	.919
1993—Dunedin (FSL)...........	3B	123	496	72	151	28	5	7	48	25	40	19-9	.304	.339	.423	21	*.938
1994—Knoxville (Sou.)..........	2B	136	*545	79	*173	32	4	8	79	23	36	28-12	.317	.351	.435	20	.968
1995—Omaha (A.A.)■	2B-3B	83	306	51	84	12	5	9	42	27	24	4-5	.275	.338	.435	13	.964
—Kansas City (A.L.)	2B-DH	22	35	7	6	1	0	0	2	4	3	0-0	.171	.256	.200	1	.982
1996—Omaha (A.A.).............	OF-3B-2B-DH	72	284	50	101	22	2	10	40	18	17	7-3	.356	.398	.553	9	.951
—Kansas City (A.L.)	OF-2B-DH-3B	36	92	8	27	6	0	0	6	2	5	5-2	.293	.309	.359	3	.939
1997—Omaha (A.A.).............	2B-OF-DH-3B	82	332	53	88	18	1	8	44	19	25	3-1	.265	.303	.398	10	.948
—Indianapolis (A.A.)■ ..	2B	21	86	14	31	8	0	1	17	2	5	4-1	.360	.374	.488	2	.982
—Cincinnati (N.L.)	OF-2B-3B	49	198	31	69	7	1	6	28	11	13	11-2	.348	.394	.485	2	.984
1998—Cincinnati (N.L.)	0-3-2-S	123	347	52	88	10	1	6	27	32	36	15-1	.254	.323	.340	2	.990
1999—Cincinnati (N.L.)	2B-3B-OF	73	113	18	27	1	0	2	14	12	13	5-2	.239	.310	.301	6	.953
2000—Cincinnati (N.L.)	3B-2B-OF	119	380	71	127	24	1	12	40	32	54	5-2	.334	.386	.497	7	.970
2001—Boston (A.L.)■...........	3B-2B-OF	96	361	52	101	19	2	8	33	20	56	4-5	.280	.322	.410	6	.980
—Pawtucket (I.L.)..........	2B-3B	4	15	1	5	1	0	0	1	1	2	0-0	.333	.412	.400	0	1.000
2002—Chicago (N.L.)■.........	3B-2B	98	195	25	47	9	1	5	26	21	29	1-1	.241	.314	.374	5	.957
American League totals (3 years)		154	488	67	134	26	2	8	41	26	64	9-7	.275	.315	.385	10	.975
National League totals (5 years)		462	1233	197	358	51	4	31	135	108	145	37-8	.290	.351	.414	22	.973
Major League totals (8 years)		616	1721	264	492	77	6	39	176	134	209	46-15	.286	.341	.406	32	.973

SULLIVAN, SCOTT — P — REDS

PERSONAL: Born March 13, 1971, in Carrollton, Ala. ... 6-3/210. ... Throws right, bats right. ... Full name: William Scott Sullivan.
HIGH SCHOOL: Pickens Academy (Carrollton, Ala.).
COLLEGE: Auburn.
TRANSACTIONS/CAREER NOTES: Selected by Cincinnati Reds organization in second round of free-agent draft (June 3, 1993). ... On Indianapolis disabled list (August 21, 1995-remainder of season). ... On disabled list (August 10-25, 2002).
MISCELLANEOUS: Appeared in one game as pinch runner (2000).
CAREER HITTING (MLB): 4-for-48 (.083), 1 R, 0 2B, 0 3B, 0 HR, 1 RBI.

Year League	W	L	Pct.	ERA	G	GS	CG	ShO	Sv.-Opp.	IP	H	R	ER	HR	BB-IBB	SO
1993—Billings (Pio.)	5	0	1.000	1.67	18	7	2	2	3-...	54.0	33	13	10	1	25-0	79
1994—Chattanooga (Sou.)..........	11	7	.611	3.41	34	13	2	0	7-...	121.1	101	60	46	8	40-1	111
1995—Indianapolis (A.A.)...........	4	3	.571	3.53	44	0	0	0	1-...	58.2	51	31	23	2	24-4	54
—Cincinnati (N.L.)	0	0	...	4.91	3	0	0	0	0-0	3.2	4	2	2	0	2-0	2
1996—Indianapolis (A.A.)...........	5	2	.714	2.73	53	3	0	0	1-...	108.2	95	38	33	10	37-3	77
—Cincinnati (N.L.)	0	0	...	2.25	7	0	0	0	0-0	8.0	7	2	2	0	5-0	3
1997—Cincinnati (N.L.)	5	3	.625	3.24	59	0	0	0	1-2	97.1	79	36	35	12	30-8	96
—Indianapolis (A.A.)...........	3	1	.750	1.30	19	0	0	0	2-...	27.2	16	4	4	0	4-1	23
1998—Cincinnati (N.L.)	5	5	.500	5.21	67	0	0	0	1-4	102.0	98	62	59	14	36-4	86
1999—Cincinnati (N.L.)	5	4	.556	3.01	79	0	0	0	3-5	113.2	88	41	38	10	47-4	78
2000—Cincinnati (N.L.)	3	6	.333	3.47	79	0	0	0	3-6	106.1	87	44	41	14	38-8	96
2001—Cincinnati (N.L.)	7	1	.875	3.31	79	0	0	0	0-3	103.1	94	44	38	10	36-8	82
2002—Cincinnati (N.L.)	6	5	.545	6.06	71	0	0	0	1-3	78.2	93	60	53	15	31-11	78
Major League totals (8 years).....	31	24	.564	3.93	444	0	0	0	9-23	613.0	550	291	268	75	225-43	521

SUPPAN, JEFF — P — ROYALS

PERSONAL: Born January 2, 1975, in Oklahoma City. ... 6-2/210. ... Throws right, bats right. ... Full name: Jeffrey Scot Suppan.
HIGH SCHOOL: Crespi (Encino, Calif.).
TRANSACTIONS/CAREER NOTES: Selected by Boston Red Sox organization in second round of free-agent draft (June 3, 1993). ... On Trenton disabled list (April 9-29, 1995). ... On Boston disabled list (August 25, 1996-remainder of season). ... Selected by Arizona Diamondbacks in first round (third pick overall) of expansion draft (November 18, 1997). ... Contract purchased by Kansas City Royals from Diamondbacks (September 3, 1998).
CAREER HITTING (MLB): 9-for-38 (.237), 1 R, 0 2B, 0 3B, 0 HR, 2 RBI.

Year League	W	L	Pct.	ERA	G	GS	CG	ShO	Sv.-Opp.	IP	H	R	ER	HR	BB-IBB	SO
1993—Gulf Coast Red Sox (GCL)	4	3	.571	2.18	10	9	2	1	0-...	57.2	52	20	14	0	16-0	64
1994—Sarasota (FSL)	•13	7	.650	3.26	27	27	4	2	0-...	174.0	153	74	63	10	50-0	*173
1995—Trenton (East.)	6	2	.750	2.36	15	15	1	1	0-...	99.0	86	35	26	5	26-1	88
—Boston (A.L.)...................	1	2	.333	5.96	8	3	0	0	0-0	22.2	29	15	15	4	5-1	19
—Pawtucket (I.L.)................	2	3	.400	5.32	7	7	0	0	0-...	45.2	50	29	27	9	9-0	32
1996—Boston (A.L.).....................	1	1	.500	7.54	8	4	0	0	0-0	22.2	29	19	19	3	13-0	13
—Pawtucket (I.L.)................	10	6	.625	3.22	22	22	7	1	0-...	145.1	130	66	52	16	25-1	142

Year	League	W	L	Pct.	ERA	G	GS	CG	ShO	Sv.-Opp.	IP	H	R	ER	HR	BB-IBB	SO
1997—	Pawtucket (I.L.)	5	1	.833	3.71	9	9	2	1	0-...	60.2	51	26	25	7	15-0	40
—	Boston (A.L.)	7	3	.700	5.69	23	22	0	0	0-0	112.1	140	75	71	12	36-1	67
1998—	Arizona (N.L.)■	1	7	.125	6.68	13	13	1	0	0-0	66.0	82	55	49	12	21-1	39
—	Tucson (PCL)	4	3	.571	3.63	13	12	0	0	0-...	67.0	75	29	27	4	17-1	62
—	Kansas City (A.L.)■	0	0	...	0.71	4	1	0	0	0-0	12.2	9	1	1	1	1-0	12
1999—	Kansas City (A.L.)	10	12	.455	4.53	32	32	4	1	0-0	208.2	222	113	105	28	62-4	103
2000—	Kansas City (A.L.)	10	9	.526	4.94	35	33	3	1	0-0	217.0	240	121	119	*36	84-3	128
2001—	Kansas City (A.L.)	10	14	.417	4.37	34	34	1	0	0-0	218.1	227	120	106	26	74-3	120
2002—	Kansas City (A.L.)	9	16	.360	5.32	33	33	3	1	0-0	208.0	229	134	123	32	68-3	109
A.L. totals (8 years)		48	57	.457	4.92	177	162	11	3	0-0	1022.1	1125	598	559	142	343-15	571
N.L. totals (1 year)		1	7	.125	6.68	13	13	1	0	0-0	66.0	82	55	49	12	21-1	39
Major League totals (8 years)		49	64	.434	5.03	190	175	12	3	0-0	1088.1	1207	653	608	154	364-16	610

SURHOFF, B.J. 1B/OF

PERSONAL: Born August 4, 1964, in Bronx, N.Y. ... 6-1/200. ... Bats left, throws right. ... Full name: William James Surhoff. ... Son of Dick Surhoff, forward with New York Knicks and Milwaukee Hawks of National Basketball Association (1952-53 and 1953-54); and brother of Rich Surhoff, pitcher with Philadelphia Phillies and Texas Rangers (1985).

HIGH SCHOOL: Rye (N.Y.).

COLLEGE: North Carolina.

TRANSACTIONS/CAREER NOTES: Selected by New York Yankees organization in fifth round of free-agent draft (June 7, 1982); did not sign. ... Selected by Milwaukee Brewers organization in first round (first pick overall) of free-agent draft (June 3, 1985). ... On suspended list (August 23-25, 1990). ... On Milwaukee disabled list (March 25-April 16, April 20-May 23 and July 7, 1994-remainder of season); included rehabilitation assignments to El Paso (April 12-16) and New Orleans (May 17-23). ... Granted free agency (October 20, 1994). ... Re-signed by Brewers organization (April 7, 1995). ... Granted free agency (November 6, 1995). ... Signed by Baltimore Orioles (December 20, 1995). ... On disabled list (May 18-June 2, 1996). ... Granted free agency (October 26, 1998). ... Re-signed by Orioles (December 7, 1998). ... Traded by Orioles with P Gabe Molina to Atlanta Braves for OF Trenidad Hubbard, C Fernando Lunar and P Luis Rivera (July 31, 2000). ... On disabled list (April 28, 2002-remainder of season). ... Granted free agency (October 28, 2002).

RECORDS: Shares major league single-inning record for most doubles—2 (September 14, 1999, fifth inning).

HONORS: Named College Player of the Year by The Sporting News (1985). ... Named catcher on The Sporting News college All-America team (1985).

STATISTICAL NOTES: Tied for Pacific Coast League lead in double plays by catcher with 10 in 1986. ... Led A.L. catchers with 68 assists in 1991. ... Had 15-game hitting streak (May 9-25, 1999). ... Had 21-game hitting streak (May 29-June 20, 1999). ... Led A.L. outfielders with 1.000 fielding percentage in 1999. ... Had 21-game hitting streak (June 5-28, 2000). ... Career major league grand slams: 5.

MISCELLANEOUS: Member of 1984 U.S. Olympic baseball team.

2002 GAMES PLAYED BY POSITION (MLB): 1B—11; OF—9.

			BATTING														FIELDING	
Year	Team (League)	Pos.	G	AB	R	H	2B	3B	HR	RBI	BB	SO	SB-CS	Avg.	OBP	SLG	E	Avg.
1985—	Beloit (Midw.)	C	76	289	39	96	13	4	7	58	22	35	10-9	.332	.373	.478	3	.994
1986—	Vancouver (PCL)	C	116	458	71	141	19	3	5	59	29	30	21-8	.308	.356	.395	7	*.989
1987—	Milwaukee (A.L.)	C-3-DH-1	115	395	50	118	22	3	7	68	36	30	11-10	.299	.350	.423	11	.985
1988—	Milwaukee (A.L.)	C-3-1-S-O	139	493	47	121	21	0	5	38	31	49	21-6	.245	.292	.318	8	.988
1989—	Milwaukee (A.L.)	C-DH-3B	126	436	42	108	17	4	5	55	25	29	14-12	.248	.287	.339	10	.983
1990—	Milwaukee (A.L.)	C-3B	135	474	55	131	21	4	6	59	41	37	18-7	.276	.331	.376	12	.983
1991—	Milwaukee (A.L.)	C-DH-3-O-2	143	505	57	146	19	4	5	68	26	33	5-8	.289	.319	.372	4	.995
1992—	Milwaukee (A.L.)	C-1-DH-O-3	139	480	63	121	19	1	4	62	46	41	14-8	.252	.314	.321	6	.992
1993—	Milwaukee (A.L.)	3-O-1-C-DH	148	552	66	151	38	3	7	79	36	47	12-9	.274	.318	.391	18	.956
1994—	El Paso (Texas)	OF	3	12	2	3	1	0	0	0	0	2	0-0	.250	.250	.333	0	1.000
—	Milwaukee (A.L.)	3-C-1-O-DH	40	134	20	35	11	2	5	22	16	14	0-1	.261	.336	.485	4	.974
—	New Orleans (A.A.)	3B-OF-C-1B	5	19	3	6	2	0	0	1	1	2	0-0	.316	.350	.421	0	1.000
1995—	Milwaukee (A.L.)	O-1-C-DH	117	415	72	133	26	3	13	73	37	43	7-3	.320	.378	.492	5	.991
1996—	Baltimore (A.L.)■	3-O-DH-1	143	537	74	157	27	6	21	82	47	79	0-1	.292	.352	.482	15	.955
1997—	Baltimore (A.L.)	O-DH-1-3	147	528	80	150	30	4	18	88	49	60	1-1	.284	.345	.458	2	.993
1998—	Baltimore (A.L.)	OF-1B	162	573	79	160	34	1	22	92	49	81	9-7	.279	.332	.457	3	.989
1999—	Baltimore (A.L.)	OF-DH-3B	*162	*673	104	207	38	1	28	107	43	78	5-1	.308	.347	.492	0	†1.000
2000—	Baltimore (A.L.)	OF-DH	103	411	56	120	27	0	13	57	29	46	7-2	.292	.341	.453	3	.987
—	Atlanta (N.L.)■	OF	44	128	13	37	9	2	1	11	12	12	3-0	.289	.352	.414	0	1.000
2001—	Atlanta (N.L.)	OF-DH	141	484	68	131	33	1	10	58	38	48	9-3	.271	.321	.405	3	.986
2002—	Atlanta (N.L.)	1B-OF	25	75	5	22	5	0	0	9	9	5	1-3	.293	.369	.360	0	1.000
American League totals (14 years)			1819	6606	865	1858	350	36	159	950	511	667	124-76	.281	.331	.417	101	.985
National League totals (3 years)			210	687	86	190	47	3	11	78	59	65	13-6	.277	.332	.402	3	.992
Major League totals (16 years)			2029	7293	951	2048	397	39	170	1028	570	732	137-82	.281	.331	.416	104	.985

DIVISION SERIES RECORD

RECORDS: Shares single-game record for most home runs—2 (October 1, 1996).

			BATTING														FIELDING	
Year	Team (League)	Pos.	G	AB	R	H	2B	3B	HR	RBI	BB	SO	SB-CS	Avg.	OBP	SLG	E	Avg.
1996—	Baltimore (A.L.)	OF-PH	4	13	3	5	0	0	3	5	0	1	0-0	.385	.385	1.077	0	1.000
1997—	Baltimore (A.L.)	OF-PH	3	11	0	3	1	0	0	2	0	2	0-0	.273	.273	.364	0	1.000
2000—	Atlanta (N.L.)	PH	2	2	0	1	0	0	0	0	0	0	0-0	.500	.500	.500	...	...
2001—	Atlanta (N.L.)	OF	3	11	1	3	1	0	0	0	0	0	1-0	.273	.333	.364	0	1.000
Division series totals (4 years)			12	37	4	12	2	0	3	7	0	3	1-0	.324	.342	.622	0	1.000

CHAMPIONSHIP SERIES RECORD

			BATTING														FIELDING	
Year	Team (League)	Pos.	G	AB	R	H	2B	3B	HR	RBI	BB	SO	SB-CS	Avg.	OBP	SLG	E	Avg.
1996—	Baltimore (A.L.)	OF-PH	5	15	0	4	0	0	0	2	1	2	0-0	.267	.294	.267	0	1.000
1997—	Baltimore (A.L.)	OF-1B	6	25	1	5	2	0	0	1	2	2	0-0	.200	.259	.280	0	1.000
2001—	Atlanta (N.L.)	OF-PH	4	13	1	3	0	0	1	2	0	1	0-1	.231	.231	.462	0	1.000
Championship series totals (3 years)			15	53	2	12	2	0	1	5	3	5	0-1	.226	.263	.321	0	1.000

ALL-STAR GAME RECORD

	AB	R	H	2B	3B	HR	RBI	BB	SO	SB-CS	Avg.	OBP	SLG	E	Avg.
All-Star Game totals (1 year)	2	0	0	0	0	0	0	0	0	0-0	.000	.000	.000	0	...

SUTTON, LARRY 1B/OF

PERSONAL: Born May 14, 1970, in West Covina, Calif. ... 6-0/185. ... Bats left, throws left. ... Full name: Larry James Sutton.
HIGH SCHOOL: Mater Dei (Santa Ana, Calif.).
COLLEGE: Illinois.
TRANSACTIONS/CAREER NOTES: Selected by Kansas City organization in 21st round of free-agent draft (June 1, 1992). ... On Kansas City disabled list (June 6-July 27, 1999); included rehabilitation assignments to Gulf Coast Royals (July 5-15) and Omaha (July 16-25). ... Granted free agency (October 18, 1999). ... Signed by St. Louis Cardinals organization (December 8, 1999). ... Traded by Cardinals to Minnesota Twins for SS Hanley Frias (July 2, 2001). ... Granted free agency (October 15, 2001). ... Signed by Oakland Athletics organization (January 24, 2002). ... On Sacramento disabled list (June 17-24, 2002). ... Released by A's (October 7, 2002).
HONORS: Named Northwest League Most Valuable Player (1992). ... Named Carolina League Most Valuable Player (1994).
STATISTICAL NOTES: Led Northwest League with 142 total bases in 1992. ... Led Midwest League first basemen with 92 double plays in 1993. ... Led Carolina League with 10 intentional bases on balls received and nine sacrifice flies in 1994. ... Led Texas League first basemen with .989 fielding percentage in 1996. ... Career major league grand slams: 1.
2002 GAMES PLAYED BY POSITION (MLB): 1B—6; OF—3.

			BATTING														FIELDING	
Year	Team (League)	Pos.	G	AB	R	H	2B	3B	HR	RBI	BB	SO	SB-CS	Avg.	OBP	SLG	E	Avg.
1992	—Eugene (N'West)	1B	70	238	45	74	17	3	*15	*58	48	33	3-6	.311	.433	.597	14	.975
	—Appleton (Midw.)	DH	1	2	1	0	0	0	0	0	2	1	0-1	.000	.500	.000	...	...
1993	—Rockford (Midw.)	1B	113	361	67	97	24	1	7	50	*95	65	3-5	.269	.424	.399	11	.989
1994	—Wilmington (Caro.)	1B	129	480	91	147	33	1	26	94	*81	71	2-1	.306	.406	*.542	12	*.990
1995	—Wichita (Texas)	1B	53	197	31	53	11	1	5	32	26	33	1-1	.269	.357	.411	7	.986
1996	—Wichita (Texas)	1B-OF-DH	125	463	84	137	22	2	22	84	77	66	4-1	.296	.401	.495	13	*.989
1997	—Omaha (A.A.)	1B-DH	106	380	61	114	27	1	19	72	61	57	0-0	.300	.395	.526	5	.994
	—Kansas City (A.L.)	1B-DH-OF	27	69	9	20	2	0	2	8	5	12	0-0	.290	.338	.406	0	1.000
1998	—Kansas City (A.L.)	OF-1B-DH	111	310	29	76	14	2	5	42	29	46	3-3	.245	.311	.352	2	.989
1999	—Kansas City (A.L.)	1B-DH-OF	43	102	14	23	6	0	2	15	13	17	1-0	.225	.308	.343	3	.987
	—GC Royals (GCL)	1B-DH-OF	9	31	7	8	2	0	1	6	7	6	0-0	.258	.410	.419	1	.977
	—Omaha (PCL)	1B-OF	39	148	28	41	8	1	3	12	27	24	4-1	.277	.390	.405	4	.985
2000	—Memphis (PCL)■	1B	95	347	61	89	21	2	12	70	67	56	4-1	.256	.377	.432	8	.991
	—St. Louis (N.L.)	1B-OF	23	25	5	8	0	0	1	6	5	7	0-0	.320	.406	.440	0	1.000
2001	—St. Louis (N.L.)	1B-OF	33	42	3	5	1	0	1	3	1	10	0-0	.119	.140	.214	0	1.000
	—Memphis (PCL)	1B	29	99	12	26	5	0	2	13	21	16	1-1	.263	.392	.374	1	.995
	—Edmonton (PCL)■	OF-1B	45	147	23	37	7	3	3	24	23	32	0-1	.252	.351	.401	2	.984
2002	—Sacramento (PCL)■	1B-OF	116	431	83	126	40	2	12	81	93	108	2-0	.292	.417	.478	11	.978
	—Oakland (A.L.)	1B-OF	7	19	3	2	0	0	1	3	1	8	0-0	.105	.150	.263	0	1.000
American League totals (4 years)			188	500	55	121	22	2	10	68	48	83	4-3	.242	.308	.354	5	.991
National League totals (2 years)			56	67	8	13	1	0	2	9	6	17	0-0	.194	.253	.299	0	1.000
Major League totals (6 years)			244	567	63	134	23	2	12	77	54	100	4-3	.236	.302	.347	5	.992

SUZUKI, ICHIRO OF MARINERS

PERSONAL: Born October 22, 1973, in Kasugai, Japan. ... 5-9/160. ... Bats left, throws right.
HIGH SCHOOL: Aikoudai Meiden (Kasugai, Japan).
TRANSACTIONS/CAREER NOTES: Signed as non-drafted free agent by Seattle Mariners organization (November 18, 2000).
RECORDS: Holds major league rookie-season record for most hits—242 (2001). ... Holds A.L. rookie-season record for highest batting average (100 or more games)—.350; most at-bats—692; and most singles—192 (2001). ... Holds A.L. single-season record for most at-bats by lefthander—692; and most singles—192 (2001). ... Shares major league single-season record for most games with at least one hit—135 (2001). ... Shares major league single-season record for fewest double plays by outfielder (150 or more games)—0 (2002).
HONORS: Named outfielder on A.L. Silver Slugger team (2001). ... Named A.L. Rookie of the Year by The Sporting News (2001). ... Named outfielder on The Sporting News A.L. All-Star team (2001). ... Named A.L. Rookie of the Year by Baseball Writers' Association of America (2001). ... Named A.L. Most Valuable Player by Baseball Writers' Association of America (2001). ... Won A.L. Gold Glove as outfielder (2001-02).
STATISTICAL NOTES: Had 15-game hitting streak (April 4-20, 2001). ... Had 23-game hitting streak (April 22-May 18, 2001). ... Had 21-game hitting streak (August 3-24, 2001). ... Had 15-game hitting streak (May 22-June 6, 2002). ... Led A.L. with 15 caught stealing in 2002.
2002 GAMES PLAYED BY POSITION (MLB): OF—152; DH—4.

			BATTING														FIELDING	
Year	Team (League)	Pos.	G	AB	R	H	2B	3B	HR	RBI	BB	SO	SB-CS	Avg.	OBP	SLG	E	Avg.
1992	—Orix (Jap. Pac.)		40	95	9	24	5	0	0	5	3	11	3-2	.253	...	.305	...	...
1993	—Orix (Jap. Pac.)		43	64	4	12	2	0	1	3	2	7	0-2	.188	...	.266	...	...
1994	—Orix (Jap. Pac.)		130	546	111	210	41	5	13	54	51	53	29-7	.385	...	.549	...	...
1995	—Orix (Jap. Pac.)		130	524	104	179	23	4	25	80	68	52	49-9	.342	...	.544	...	...
1996	—Orix (Jap. Pac.)		130	542	104	193	24	4	16	84	56	52	35-3	.356	...	.504	...	...
1997	—Orix (Jap. Pac.)		135	536	94	185	31	4	17	91	62	36	39-4	.345	...	.513	...	...
1998	—Orix (Jap. Pac.)		135	506	79	181	36	3	13	71	43	35	11-4	.358	...	.518	...	...
1999	—Orix (Jap. Pac.)		103	411	80	141	27	2	21	68	45	46	12-1	.343	...	.572	...	...
2000	—Orix (Jap. Pac.)		105	395	73	153	22	1	12	74	54	36	21-...	.387	...	.539	...	...
2001	—Seattle (A.L.)■	OF-DH	157	*692	127	*242	34	8	8	69	30	53	*56-14	*.350	.381	.457	1	.997
2002	—Seattle (A.L.)	OF-DH	157	647	111	208	27	8	8	51	68	62	31-15	.321	.388	.425	3	.991
Major League totals (2 years)			314	1339	238	450	61	16	16	120	98	115	87-29	.336	.385	.441	4	.994

DIVISION SERIES RECORD

RECORDS: Shares single-series record for most hits—12 (2001).

			BATTING														FIELDING	
Year	Team (League)	Pos.	G	AB	R	H	2B	3B	HR	RBI	BB	SO	SB-CS	Avg.	OBP	SLG	E	Avg.
2001	—Seattle (A.L.)	OF	5	20	4	12	1	0	0	2	1	0	1-2	.600	.619	.650	1	.900

CHAMPIONSHIP SERIES RECORD

			BATTING														FIELDING	
Year	Team (League)	Pos.	G	AB	R	H	2B	3B	HR	RBI	BB	SO	SB-CS	Avg.	OBP	SLG	E	Avg.
2001	—Seattle (A.L.)	OF	5	18	3	4	1	0	0	1	4	4	2-0	.222	.364	.278	0	1.000

ALL-STAR GAME RECORD

	AB	R	H	2B	3B	HR	RBI	BB	SO	SB-CS	Avg.	OBP	SLG	E	Avg.
All-Star Game totals (2 years)	5	0	1	0	0	0	0	0	0	1-0	.200	.200	.200	0	...

SUZUKI, MAC — P

PERSONAL: Born May 31, 1975, in Kobe, Japan. ... 6-3/205. ... Throws right, bats right. ... Full name: Makoto Suzuki.
HIGH SCHOOL: Takigawa Daini (Kobe, Japan).
TRANSACTIONS/CAREER NOTES: Played with Salinas, independent (August 30, 1992). ... Signed by San Bernardino, independent (April 9, 1993). ... Contract purchased by Seattle Mariners organization from San Bernardino (September 5, 1993). ... On disabled list (April 19-June 15 and July 10, 1994-remainder of season). ... On Riverside temporarily inactive list (April 22-August 3, 1995). ... On Riverside disabled list (August 3-18, 1995). ... On Port City disabled list (May 8-17, 1996). ... Traded by Mariners with a player to be named later to New York Mets for P Allen Watson and cash (June 18, 1999); Mets acquired P Justin Dunning to complete deal (September 14, 1999). ... Claimed on waivers by Kansas City Royals (June 22, 1999). ... Traded by Royals with C Sal Fasano to Colorado Rockies for C Brent Mayne (June 24, 2001). ... Claimed on waivers by Milwaukee Brewers (July 12, 2001). ... Released by Brewers (October 12, 2001). ... Signed by Royals organization (November 28, 2001). ... Released by Royals (September 30, 2002).
CAREER HITTING (MLB): 2-for-25 (.080), 1 R, 0 2B, 0 3B, 0 HR, 0 RBI.

Year League	W	L	Pct.	ERA	G	GS	CG	ShO	Sv.-Opp.	IP	H	R	ER	HR	BB-IBB	SO
1992—Salinas (Calif.)	0	0	...	0.00	1	0	0	0	0-...	1.0	0	0	0	0	0-0	1
1993—San Bernardino (Calif.)■	4	4	.500	3.68	48	1	0	0	12-...	80.2	59	37	33	5	56-4	87
1994—Jacksonville (Sou.)■	1	0	1.000	2.84	8	0	0	0	1-...	12.2	15	4	4	1	6-0	10
1995—Arizona Mariners (Ariz.)	1	0	1.000	6.75	4	3	0	0	0-...	4.0	5	4	3	1	0-0	3
—Riverside (Calif.)	0	1	.000	4.70	6	0	0	0	0-...	7.2	10	4	4	0	6-0	6
1996—Port City (Sou.)	3	6	.333	4.72	16	16	0	0	0-...	74.1	69	41	39	10	32-0	66
—Seattle (A.L.)	0	0	...	20.25	1	0	0	0	0-0	1.1	2	3	3	0	2-1	1
—Tacoma (PCL)	0	3	.000	7.25	13	2	0	0	0-...	22.1	31	19	18	3	12-2	14
1997—Tacoma (PCL)	4	9	.308	5.94	32	10	0	0	0-...	83.1	79	60	55	13	64-1	63
1998—Tacoma (PCL)	9	10	.474	4.37	28	21	2	1	0-...	131.2	130	70	64	19	70-0	117
—Seattle (A.L.)	1	2	.333	7.18	6	5	0	0	0-0	26.1	34	23	21	3	15-0	19
1999—Seattle (A.L.)	0	2	.000	9.43	16	4	0	0	0-0	42.0	47	47	44	7	34-2	32
—Kansas City (A.L.)■	2	3	.400	5.16	22	9	0	0	0-0	68.0	77	45	39	9	30-1	36
2000—Kansas City (A.L.)	8	10	.444	4.34	32	29	1	1	0-0	188.2	195	100	91	26	94-6	135
2001—Kansas City (A.L.)	2	5	.286	5.30	15	9	0	0	0-0	56.0	61	38	33	12	25-1	37
—Colorado (N.L.)■	0	2	.000	15.63	3	1	0	0	0-0	6.1	9	12	11	3	11-0	5
—Milwaukee (N.L.)■	3	5	.375	5.30	15	9	0	0	0-0	56.0	52	37	33	5	37-3	47
2002—Wichita (Texas)	0	0	...	0.00	1	1	0	0	0-...	5.0	0	0	0	0	2-0	3
—Omaha (PCL)	0	4	.000	4.53	29	1	0	0	0-...	53.2	63	30	27	6	21-2	46
—Kansas City (A.L.)	0	2	.000	9.00	7	1	0	0	0-0	21.0	24	21	21	2	17-2	15
A.L. totals (6 years)	13	24	.351	5.62	99	57	1	1	0-0	403.1	440	277	252	59	217-13	275
N.L. totals (1 year)	3	7	.300	6.35	18	10	0	0	0-0	62.1	61	49	44	8	48-3	52
Major League totals (6 years)	16	31	.340	5.72	117	67	1	1	0-0	465.2	501	326	296	67	265-16	327

SWANN, PEDRO — OF

PERSONAL: Born October 27, 1970, in Wilmington, Del. ... 6-0/200. ... Bats left, throws right. ... Full name: Pedro Maurice Swann.
HIGH SCHOOL: St. Mark's (Wilmington, Del.).
COLLEGE: Delaware State.
TRANSACTIONS/CAREER NOTES: Selected by Atlanta Braves organization in 26th round of free-agent draft (June 3, 1991). ... Granted free agency (October 17, 1997). ... Signed by Detroit Tigers organization (December 8, 1997). ... Granted free agency (October 16, 1998). ... Re-signed by Tigers organization (December 17, 1998). ... Granted free agency (October 15, 1999). ... Signed by Braves organization (December 18, 1999). ... On Richmond disabled list (July 9-24, 2000). ... Granted free agency (October 18, 2000). ... Re-signed by Braves organization (January 22, 2001). ... Granted free agency (October 15, 2001). ... Signed by Toronto Blue Jays organization (February 15, 2002). ... Granted free agency (October 15, 2002).
STATISTICAL NOTES: Led Appalachian League outfielders with 10 assists in 1992. ... Led International League with 10 sacrifice flies in 2001.
2002 GAMES PLAYED BY POSITION (MLB): DH—3; OF—1.

		BATTING														FIELDING	
Year Team (League)	Pos.	G	AB	R	H	2B	3B	HR	RBI	BB	SO	SB-CS	Avg.	OBP	SLG	E	Avg.
1991—Idaho Falls (Pio.)	OF	55	174	35	48	6	1	3	28	33	45	8-5	.276	.393	.374	5	.935
1992—Pulaski (Appl.)	OF	59	203	36	61	*18	1	5	34	32	33	13-6	.300	.412	.473	8	.912
1993—Durham (Caro.)	OF-1B	61	182	27	63	8	2	6	27	19	38	6-12	.346	.411	.511	2	.958
—Greenville (Sou.)	OF	44	157	19	48	9	2	3	21	9	23	2-2	.306	.347	.446	3	.932
1994—Greenville (Sou.)	OF	126	428	55	121	25	2	10	49	46	85	16-9	.283	.356	.421	6	.943
1995—Richmond (I.L.)	OF	15	38	2	8	1	0	0	3	1	2	0-2	.211	.250	.237	0	1.000
—Greenville (Sou.)	OF-1B	102	339	57	110	24	2	11	64	45	63	14-11	.324	.405	.504	6	.961
1996—Greenville (Sou.)	OF	35	129	15	40	5	0	3	20	18	23	4-4	.310	.404	.419	3	.949
—Richmond (I.L.)	OF	93	296	42	74	11	4	4	35	22	56	7-7	.250	.308	.355	3	.983
1997—Greenville (Sou.)	OF	124	465	78	133	29	2	24	83	49	75	5-5	.286	.358	.512	7	.957
1998—Toledo (I.L.)■	OF	120	419	56	122	28	2	15	66	41	74	6-3	.291	.355	.475	2	.985
1999—Toledo (I.L.)	OF	103	332	51	86	14	2	10	37	36	67	3-1	.259	.338	.404	1	.993
2000—Richmond (I.L.)■	OF-1B	125	442	70	135	22	2	9	57	54	68	6-5	.305	.386	.425	3	.987
—Atlanta (N.L.)	OF	4	2	0	0	0	0	0	0	0	2	0-0	.000	.000	.000	0	...
2001—Richmond (I.L.)	OF	139	488	68	142	33	5	8	72	52	95	12-6	.291	.362	.428	4	.985
2002—Syracuse (I.L.)■	OF	97	368	52	102	17	4	14	62	37	77	1-3	.277	.353	.459	1	.994
—Toronto (A.L.)	DH-OF	13	12	3	1	0	0	0	1	1	6	0-0	.083	.154	.083	0	...
American League totals (1 year)		13	12	3	1	0	0	0	1	1	6	0-0	.083	.154	.083	0	...
National League totals (1 year)		4	2	0	0	0	0	0	0	0	2	0-0	.000	.000	.000	0	...
Major League totals (2 years)		17	14	3	1	0	0	0	1	1	8	0-0	.071	.133	.071	0	...

SWEENEY, MARK — OF/1B

PERSONAL: Born October 26, 1969, in Framingham, Mass. ... 6-1/215. ... Bats left, throws left. ... Full name: Mark Patrick Sweeney.
HIGH SCHOOL: Holliston (Mass.).
COLLEGE: Maine.

TRANSACTIONS/CAREER NOTES: Selected by Los Angeles Dodgers organization in 39th round of free-agent draft (June 4, 1990); did not sign. ... Selected by California Angels organization in ninth round of free-agent draft (June 3, 1991). ... Traded by Angels with a player to be named later to St. Louis Cardinals for P John Habyan (July 8, 1995); Cardinals acquired IF Rod Correia to complete deal (January 31, 1996). ... Traded by Cardinals with P Danny Jackson and P Rich Batchelor to San Diego Padres for P Fernando Valenzuela, 3B Scott Livingstone and OF Phil Plantier (June 13, 1997). ... Traded by Padres with OF Greg Vaughn to Cincinnati Reds for OF Reggie Sanders, SS Damian Jackson and P Josh Harris (February 2, 1999). ... Traded by Reds with a player to be named later to Milwaukee Brewers for OF Alex Ochoa (January 14, 2000); Brewers acquired P Gene Altman to complete deal (May 15, 2000). ... On Milwaukee disabled list (March 31-May 7 and July 18-August 14, 2000); included rehabilitation assignments to Indianapolis (July 21-26 and August 3-14). ... Granted free agency (October 5, 2000). ... Re-signed by Brewers organization (January 3, 2001). ... Traded by Brewers to New York Mets as part of three-way deal in which Mets traded P Glendon Rusch to Brewers, Colorado Rockies traded 1B/OF Ross Gload and P Craig House to Mets, Brewers traded P Jeff D'Amico, OF Jeromy Burnitz, IF Lou Collier and cash to Mets, Mets traded 1B/3B Todd Zeile, OF Benny Agbayani, IF/OF Lenny Harris and cash to Rockies and Rockies traded OF Alex Ochoa to Brewers (January 21, 2002). ... Released by Mets (March 13, 2002). ... Signed by Padres organization (March 16, 2001). ... On San Diego disabled list (June 6-26, 2002). ... Released by Padres (July 15, 2002).
2002 GAMES PLAYED BY POSITION (MLB): 1B—11; OF—5; DH—1.

			BATTING														FIELDING	
Year	Team (League)	Pos.	G	AB	R	H	2B	3B	HR	RBI	BB	SO	SB-CS	Avg.	OBP	SLG	E	Avg.
1991—	Boise (N'West)	OF	70	234	45	66	10	3	4	34	*51	42	9-5	.282	.416	.402	4	.954
1992—	Quad City (Midw.)	OF	120	424	65	115	20	5	14	76	47	85	15-11	.271	.346	.441	4	.981
1993—	Palm Springs (Calif.)	OF-1B-DH	66	245	41	87	18	3	3	47	42	29	9-6	.355	.449	.490	7	.955
—	Midland (Texas)	OF	51	188	41	67	13	2	9	32	27	22	1-1	.356	.444	.590	1	.989
1994—	Vancouver (PCL)	DH-1B-OF	103	344	59	98	12	3	8	49	59	50	3-3	.285	.394	.407	2	.994
—	Midland (Texas)	OF-1B-DH	14	50	13	15	3	0	3	18	10	10	1-1	.300	.403	.540	2	.973
1995—	Vancouver (PCL)	OF-DH-1B	69	226	48	78	14	2	7	59	43	33	3-1	.345	.452	.518	2	.981
—	Louisville (A.A.)■	1B	22	76	15	28	8	0	2	22	14	8	2-0	.368	.468	.553	2	.990
—	St. Louis (N.L.)	1B-OF	37	77	5	21	2	0	2	13	10	15	1-1	.273	.348	.377	2	.988
1996—	St. Louis (N.L.)	OF-1B	98	170	32	45	9	0	3	22	33	29	3-0	.265	.387	.371	3	.977
1997—	St. Louis (N.L.)	OF-1B	44	61	5	13	3	0	0	4	9	14	0-1	.213	.319	.262	0	1.000
—	San Diego (N.L.)■	OF-1B	71	103	11	33	4	0	2	19	11	18	2-2	.320	.383	.417	2	.957
1998—	San Diego (N.L.)	OF-1B-DH	122	192	17	45	8	3	2	15	26	37	1-2	.234	.324	.339	1	.994
1999—	Cincinnati (N.L.)■	1B-OF	37	31	6	11	3	0	2	7	4	9	0-0	.355	.429	.645	0	1.000
—	Indianapolis (I.L.)	OF-DH-1B	86	311	66	100	17	1	12	51	59	40	3-2	.322	.432	.498	5	.982
2000—	Milwaukee (N.L.)■	DH-OF-1B	71	73	9	16	6	0	1	6	12	18	0-0	.219	.337	.342	0	1.000
—	Indianapolis (I.L.)	1B-OF	18	55	13	28	8	0	2	14	10	8	0-0	.509	.585	.764	0	1.000
2001—	Indianapolis (I.L.)	OF-1B	109	404	65	116	34	1	6	69	56	71	3-1	.287	.373	.421	1	.994
—	Milwaukee (N.L.)	OF-1B	48	89	9	23	3	1	3	11	12	23	2-1	.258	.347	.416	1	.971
2002—	San Diego (N.L.)■	1B-OF-DH	48	65	3	11	3	0	1	4	4	19	0-0	.169	.217	.262	2	.956
—	Portland (PCL)	1B	1	1	0	1	0	0	0	0	0	0	0-0	1.000	1.000	1.000	0	...
Major League totals (8 years)			576	861	97	218	41	4	16	101	121	182	9-7	.253	.345	.366	11	.983

DIVISION SERIES RECORD

			BATTING														FIELDING	
Year	Team (League)	Pos.	G	AB	R	H	2B	3B	HR	RBI	BB	SO	SB-CS	Avg.	OBP	SLG	E	Avg.
1996—	St. Louis (N.L.)	PH	1	1	0	1	0	0	0	0	0	0	0-0	1.000	1.000	1.000	...	...
1998—	San Diego (N.L.)	PH	2	1	0	0	0	0	0	0	1	0	0-1	.000	.500	.000	...	...
Division series totals (2 years)			3	2	0	1	0	0	0	0	1	0	0-1	.500	.667	.500	0	...

CHAMPIONSHIP SERIES RECORD

			BATTING														FIELDING	
Year	Team (League)	Pos.	G	AB	R	H	2B	3B	HR	RBI	BB	SO	SB-CS	Avg.	OBP	SLG	E	Avg.
1996—	St. Louis (N.L.)	PH-OF	5	4	1	0	0	0	0	0	0	2	0-0	.000	.000	.000	0	1.000
1998—	San Diego (N.L.)	PH	3	2	1	0	0	0	0	0	1	1	0-0	.000	.333	.000	...	...
Championship series totals (2 years)			8	6	2	0	0	0	0	0	1	3	0-0	.000	.143	.000	0	1.000

WORLD SERIES RECORD

			BATTING														FIELDING	
Year	Team (League)	Pos.	G	AB	R	H	2B	3B	HR	RBI	BB	SO	SB-CS	Avg.	OBP	SLG	E	Avg.
1998—	San Diego (N.L.)	PH	3	3	0	2	0	0	0	1	0	0	0-0	.667	.667	.667	...	...

SWEENEY, MIKE 1B ROYALS

PERSONAL: Born July 22, 1973, in Orange, Calif. ... 6-3/225. ... Bats right, throws right. ... Full name: Michael John Sweeney.
HIGH SCHOOL: Ontario (Calif.).
TRANSACTIONS/CAREER NOTES: Selected by Kansas City Royals organization in 10th round of free-agent draft (June 3, 1991). ... On disabled list (May 24-July 5, 1994). ... On suspended list (August 17-27, 2001). ... On Kansas City disabled list (July 14-August 13, 2002); included rehabilitation assignment to Omaha (August 9-13).
RECORDS: Shares A.L. single-season record for most consecutive games with one or more runs batted in—13 (June 23-July 4, 1999).
STATISTICAL NOTES: Tied for A.L. lead in double plays by catcher with 13 in 1997. ... Had 16-game hitting streak (June 22-July 7, 1999). ... Had 25-game hitting streak (July 18-August 13, 1999). ... Had 16-game hitting streak (August 13-30, 2000). ... Tied for A.L. lead in being hit by pitch with 15 in 2000. ... Led A.L. first basemen with 105 assists in 2002. ... Career major league grand slams: 1.
MISCELLANEOUS: Holds Kansas City Royals all-time record for highest career batting average (.309).
2002 GAMES PLAYED BY POSITION (MLB): 1B—102; DH—24.

			BATTING														FIELDING	
Year	Team (League)	Pos.	G	AB	R	H	2B	3B	HR	RBI	BB	SO	SB-CS	Avg.	OBP	SLG	E	Avg.
1991—	GC Royals (GCL)	C-1B	38	102	8	22	3	0	1	11	11	9	1-0	.216	.287	.275	4	.972
1992—	Eugene (N'West)	C	59	199	17	44	12	1	4	28	13	54	3-3	.221	.280	.352	14	.967
1993—	Eugene (N'West)	C	53	175	32	42	10	2	6	29	30	41	1-0	.240	.359	.423	7	.983
1994—	Rockford (Midw.)	C	86	276	47	83	20	3	10	52	55	43	0-1	.301	.427	.504	6	.988
1995—	Wilmington (Caro.)	C-DH-3B	99	332	61	103	23	1	18	53	60	39	6-1	*.310	.424	*.548	7	.989
—	Kansas City (A.L.)	C	4	4	1	1	0	0	0	0	0	0	0-0	.250	.250	.250	1	.875
1996—	Wichita (Texas)	DH-C	66	235	45	75	18	1	14	51	32	29	3-2	.319	.399	.583	1	.995
—	Omaha (A.A.)	C-DH	25	101	14	26	9	0	3	16	6	13	0-0	.257	.318	.436	0	1.000
—	Kansas City (A.L.)	C-DH	50	165	23	46	10	0	4	24	18	21	1-2	.279	.358	.412	1	.994

Year	Team (League)	Pos.	G	AB	R	H	2B	3B	HR	RBI	BB	SO	SB-CS	Avg.	OBP	SLG	E	Avg.
								BATTING									FIELDING	
1997—	Kansas City (A.L.)	C-DH	84	240	30	58	8	0	7	31	17	33	3-2	.242	.306	.363	3	.993
—	Omaha (A.A.)	C-DH	40	144	22	34	8	1	10	29	18	20	0-2	.236	.323	.514	1	.996
1998—	Kansas City (A.L.)	C	92	282	32	73	18	0	8	35	24	38	2-3	.259	.320	.408	•9	.984
1999—	Kansas City (A.L.)	1B-DH-C	150	575	101	185	44	2	22	102	54	48	6-1	.322	.387	.520	12	.981
2000—	Kansas City (A.L.)	1B-DH	159	618	105	206	30	0	29	144	71	67	8-3	.333	.407	.523	9	.991
2001—	Kansas City (A.L.)	1B-DH	147	559	97	170	46	0	29	99	64	64	10-3	.304	.374	.542	12	.989
2002—	Kansas City (A.L.)	1B-DH	126	471	81	160	31	1	24	86	61	46	9-7	.340	.417	.563	9	.991
—	Omaha (PCL)	1B	3	12	2	3	1	0	1	4	1	2	0-0	.250	.286	.583	0	1.000
Major League totals (8 years)			812	2914	470	899	187	3	123	521	309	317	39-21	.309	.379	.501	56	.989

ALL-STAR GAME RECORD

	AB	R	H	2B	3B	HR	RBI	BB	SO	SB-CS	Avg.	OBP	SLG	E	Avg.
All-Star Game totals (3 years)	3	0	0	0	0	0	0	0	0	0-0	.000	.000	.000	0	1.000

SWINDELL, GREG P DIAMONDBACKS

PERSONAL: Born January 2, 1965, in Fort Worth, Texas. ... 6-3/239. ... Throws left, bats right. ... Full name: Forest Gregory Swindell.

HIGH SCHOOL: Sharpstown (Houston).

COLLEGE: Texas.

TRANSACTIONS/CAREER NOTES: Selected by Cleveland Indians organization in first round (second pick overall) of free-agent draft (June 2, 1986). ... On disabled list (June 30, 1987-remainder of season; and July 26-August 30, 1989). ... Traded by Indians to Cincinnati Reds for P Jack Armstrong, P Scott Scudder and P Joe Turek (November 15, 1991). ... On disabled list (August 23-September 7, 1992). ... Granted free agency (October 26, 1992). ... Signed by Houston Astros (December 4, 1992). ... On disabled list (July 6-26, 1993). ... On Houston disabled list (April 20-May 22, 1996). ... Released by Astros (June 3, 1996). ... Signed by Indians (June 15, 1996). ... On Cleveland disabled list (July 4-21, 1996). ... Granted free agency (October 3, 1996). ... Signed by Minnesota Twins organization (December 18, 1996). ... Traded by Twins with 1B Orlando Merced to Boston Red Sox for P Matt Kinney, P Joe Thomas and P John Barnes (July 31, 1998). ... Granted free agency (October 27, 1998). ... Signed by Arizona Diamondbacks (November 13, 1998). ... On disabled list (June 13-28, 1999). ... On Arizona disabled list (March 23-May 5 and August 18-September 6, 2002); included rehabilitation assignment to Tucson (May 3-4).

HONORS: Named lefthanded pitcher on The Sporting News college All-America team (1985-86).

STATISTICAL NOTES: Struck out 15 batters in one game (May 10, 1987).

MISCELLANEOUS: Holds Arizona Diamondbacks all-time records for most games pitched (191). ... Struck out in only appearance as pinch hitter (1995).

CAREER HITTING (MLB): 46-for-245 (.188), 10 R, 10 2B, 0 3B, 0 HR, 13 RBI.

Year	League	W	L	Pct.	ERA	G	GS	CG	ShO	Sv.-Opp.	IP	H	R	ER	HR	BB-IBB	SO
1986—	Waterloo (Midw.)	2	1	.667	1.00	3	3	0	0	0-...	18.0	12	2	2	1	3-0	25
—	Cleveland (A.L.)	5	2	.714	4.23	9	9	1	0	0-0	61.2	57	35	29	9	15-0	46
1987—	Cleveland (A.L.)	3	8	.273	5.10	16	15	4	1	0-0	102.1	112	62	58	18	37-1	97
1988—	Cleveland (A.L.)	18	14	.563	3.20	33	33	12	4	0-0	242.0	234	97	86	18	45-3	180
1989—	Cleveland (A.L.)	13	6	.684	3.37	28	28	5	2	0-0	184.1	170	71	69	16	51-1	129
1990—	Cleveland (A.L.)	12	9	.571	4.40	34	34	3	0	0-0	214.2	245	110	105	27	47-2	135
1991—	Cleveland (A.L.)	9	16	.360	3.48	33	33	7	0	0-0	238.0	241	112	92	21	31-1	169
1992—	Cincinnati (N.L.)■	12	8	.600	2.70	31	30	5	3	0-0	213.2	210	72	64	14	41-4	138
1993—	Houston (N.L.)■	12	13	.480	4.16	31	30	1	1	0-0	190.1	215	98	88	24	40-3	124
1994—	Houston (N.L.)	8	9	.471	4.37	24	24	1	0	0-0	148.1	175	80	72	20	26-2	74
1995—	Houston (N.L.)	10	9	.526	4.47	33	26	1	1	0-2	153.0	180	86	76	21	39-2	96
1996—	Houston (N.L.)	0	3	.000	7.83	8	4	0	0	0-2	23.0	35	25	20	5	11-0	15
—	Cleveland (A.L.)■	1	1	.500	6.59	13	2	0	0	0-0	28.2	31	21	21	8	8-0	21
1997—	Minnesota (A.L.)■	7	4	.636	3.58	65	1	0	0	1-7	115.2	102	46	46	12	25-3	75
1998—	Minnesota (A.L.)	3	3	.500	3.66	52	0	0	0	2-4	66.1	67	27	27	10	18-2	45
—	Boston (A.L.)■	2	3	.400	3.38	29	0	0	0	0-1	24.0	25	13	9	3	13-1	18
1999—	Arizona (N.L.)■	4	0	1.000	2.51	63	0	0	0	1-2	64.2	54	19	18	8	21-1	51
2000—	Arizona (N.L.)	2	6	.250	3.20	64	0	0	0	1-1	76.0	71	29	27	7	20-5	64
2001—	Arizona (N.L.)	2	6	.250	4.53	64	0	0	0	2-5	53.2	51	27	27	12	8-2	42
2002—	Tucson (PCL)	0	0	...	0.00	1	1	0	0	0-...	1.0	0	0	0	0	0-0	0
—	Arizona (N.L.)	0	2	.000	6.27	34	0	0	0	0-1	33.0	38	23	23	9	5-1	23
A.L. totals (9 years)		73	66	.525	3.82	312	155	32	7	3-12	1277.2	1284	594	542	142	290-14	915
N.L. totals (9 years)		50	56	.472	3.91	352	114	8	5	4-13	955.2	1029	459	415	120	211-20	627
Major League totals (17 years)		123	122	.502	3.86	664	269	40	12	7-25	2233.1	2313	1053	957	262	501-34	1542

DIVISION SERIES RECORD

Year	League	W	L	Pct.	ERA	G	GS	CG	ShO	Sv.-Opp.	IP	H	R	ER	HR	BB-IBB	SO
1998—	Boston (A.L.)	0	0	...	0.00	1	0	0	0	0-0	1.1	0	0	0	0	1-0	1
1999—	Arizona (N.L.)	0	0	...	0.00	3	0	0	0	0-1	3.1	1	0	0	0	3-1	1
2001—	Arizona (N.L.)	0	0	...	0.00	2	0	0	0	0-0	1.2	1	0	0	0	0-0	2
2002—	Arizona (N.L.)	0	0	...	27.00	2	0	0	0	0-0	.1	2	4	1	0	1-0	0
Division series totals (4 years)		0	0	...	1.35	8	0	0	0	0-1	6.2	4	4	1	0	5-1	4

CHAMPIONSHIP SERIES RECORD

Year	League	W	L	Pct.	ERA	G	GS	CG	ShO	Sv.-Opp.	IP	H	R	ER	HR	BB-IBB	SO
2001—	Arizona (N.L.)	0	0	...	27.00	2	0	0	0	0-0	.1	1	1	1	1	0-0	0

WORLD SERIES RECORD

NOTES: Member of World Series championship team (2001).

Year	League	W	L	Pct.	ERA	G	GS	CG	ShO	Sv.-Opp.	IP	H	R	ER	HR	BB-IBB	SO
2001—	Arizona (N.L.)	0	0	...	0.00	3	0	0	0	0-0	2.2	1	0	0	0	1-0	2

ALL-STAR GAME RECORD

	W	L	Pct.	ERA	GS	CG	ShO	Sv.-Opp.	IP	H	R	ER	HR	BB-IBB	SO
All-Star Game totals (1 year)	0	0	...	0.00	0	0	0	0-0	1.2	2	0	0	0	0-0	3

SYLVESTER, BILLY — P — BRAVES

PERSONAL: Born October 1, 1976, in Darlington, S.C. ... 6-5/220. ... Throws right, bats right. ... Full name: William Eugene Sylvester.
JUNIOR COLLEGE: Spartanburg (S.C.) Methodist.
TRANSACTIONS/CAREER NOTES: Signed as non-drafted free agent by Atlanta Braves organization (June 18, 1997). ... On disabled list (July 17-September 11, 2000).

Year	League	W	L	Pct.	ERA	G	GS	CG	ShO	Sv.-Opp.	IP	H	R	ER	HR	BB-IBB	SO
1997—	Gulf Coast Braves (GCL) ..	3	4	.429	3.91	12	9	0	0	0-...	53.0	45	25	23	2	28-0	58
1998—	Eugene (N'West)	0	*11	.000	6.51	16	•16	0	0	0-...	55.1	73	61	40	7	24-0	42
1999—	Macon (S.Atl.)	5	4	.556	3.12	44	1	0	0	2-...	83.2	78	37	29	3	37-2	75
2000—	Myrtle Beach (Caro.)	3	0	1.000	0.79	32	0	0	0	16-...	45.2	16	8	4	2	15-1	48
2001—	Greenville (Sou.)	1	0	1.000	2.37	26	0	0	0	12-...	30.1	18	8	8	3	24-0	41
—	Richmond (I.L.)	0	4	.000	5.11	36	0	0	0	11-...	37.0	28	21	21	2	27-2	41
2002—	Richmond (I.L.)	0	0	...	3.86	7	0	0	0	1-...	9.1	10	4	4	1	5-0	5
—	Greenville (Sou.)	2	3	.400	3.47	51	0	0	0	25-...	49.1	31	20	19	6	32-1	48

TAGUCHI, SO — OF — CARDINALS

PERSONAL: Born July 2, 1969, in Hyogo Prefecture, Japan. ... 5-10/163. ... Bats right, throws right.
TRANSACTIONS/CAREER NOTES: Played with Orix Blue Wave of Japan Pacific League (1992-2001). ... Signed as non-drafted free agent by St. Louis Cardinals (January 9, 2002).
2002 GAMES PLAYED BY POSITION (MLB): OF—14.

			BATTING														FIELDING	
Year	Team (League)	Pos.	G	AB	R	H	2B	3B	HR	RBI	BB	SO	SB-CS	Avg.	OBP	SLG	E	Avg.
1992—	Orix (Jap. Pac.)	OF	47	123	...	33	...	...	1	7	...	...	5-...	.268	...	.293	...	...
1993—	Orix (Jap. Pac.)	OF	31	83	...	23	...	...	0	5	...	...	3-...	.277	...	.277	...	...
1994—	Orix (Jap. Pac.)	OF	108	329	...	101	...	...	6	43	...	...	10-...	.307	...	.362	...	...
1995—	Orix (Jap. Pac.)	OF	130	495	...	122	...	...	9	61	...	...	14-...	.246	...	.301	...	...
1996—	Orix (Jap. Pac.)	OF	128	509	...	142	...	...	7	44	...	...	10-...	.279	...	.320	...	...
1997—	Orix (Jap. Pac.)	OF	135	572	...	168	...	...	10	56	...	...	7-...	.294	...	.346	...	...
1998—	Orix (Jap. Pac.)	OF	132	497	...	135	...	...	9	41	...	...	8-...	.272	...	.326	...	...
1999—	Orix (Jap. Pac.)	OF	133	524	...	141	...	...	9	56	...	...	11-...	.269	...	.321	...	...
2000—	Orix (Jap. Pac.)	OF	129	509	...	142	...	...	8	49	...	...	9-...	.279	...	.326	...	...
2001—	Orix (Jap. Pac.)	OF	134	453	70	127	21	6	8	42	43	88	6-...	.280	...	.333	...	...
2002—	Memphis (PCL)■	OF	91	304	37	75	17	0	5	36	13	44	6-3	.247	.286	.352	2	.990
—	St. Louis (N.L.)	OF	19	15	4	6	0	0	0	2	2	1	1-0	.400	.471	.400	1	.929
—	New Haven (East.)	OF	26	107	21	33	10	0	1	15	9	15	3-1	.308	.375	.430	2	.970
Major League totals (1 year)			19	15	4	6	0	0	0	2	2	1	1-0	.400	.471	.400	1	.929

TALLET, BRIAN — P — INDIANS

PERSONAL: Born September 21, 1977, in Midwest City, Okla. ... 6-7/208. ... Throws left, bats left. ... Full name: Brian Curtis Tallet.
COLLEGE: Louisiana State.
TRANSACTIONS/CAREER NOTES: Selected by Cleveland Indians organization in second round of free-agent draft (June 5, 2000).
CAREER HITTING (MLB): 0-for-0 (.000), 0 R, 0 2B, 0 3B, 0 HR, 0 RBI.

Year	League	W	L	Pct.	ERA	G	GS	CG	ShO	Sv.-Opp.	IP	H	R	ER	HR	BB-IBB	SO
2000—	Mahoning Valley (NY-P) ...	0	0	...	1.15	6	6	0	0	0-...	15.2	10	2	2	0	3-0	20
2001—	Kinston (Caro.)	9	7	.563	3.04	27	27	2	0	0-...	160.0	134	62	54	12	38-0	164
2002—	Akron (East.)	10	1	.909	3.08	18	16	1	0	0-...	102.1	93	41	35	9	32-0	73
—	Buffalo (I.L.)	2	3	.400	3.07	8	7	0	0	0-...	44.0	47	17	15	1	16-0	25
—	Cleveland (A.L.)	1	0	1.000	1.50	2	2	0	0	0-0	12.0	9	3	2	0	4-0	5
Major League totals (1 year)		1	0	1.000	1.50	2	2	0	0	0-0	12.0	9	3	2	0	4-0	5

TAM, JEFF — P — BLUE JAYS

PERSONAL: Born August 19, 1970, in Fullerton, Calif. ... 6-1/219. ... Throws right, bats right. ... Full name: Jeffery Eugene Tam.
HIGH SCHOOL: Eau Gaille (Melbourne, Fla.).
COLLEGE: Florida State.
TRANSACTIONS/CAREER NOTES: Signed as a non-drafted free agent by New York Mets organization (June 27, 1993). ... On New York disabled list (March 21-May 16, 1999); included rehabilitation assignment to St. Lucie (May 2-16). ... Claimed on waivers by Cleveland Indians (June 18, 1999). ... On Buffalo disabled list (July 23-August 1, 1999). ... Claimed on waivers by Mets (August 11, 1999). ... Granted free agency (October 15, 1999). ... Signed by Oakland Athletics organization (November 23, 1999). ... Released by A's (October 15, 2002). ... Signed by Toronto Blue Jays organization (November 1, 2002).
CAREER HITTING (MLB): 0-for-1 (.000), 0 R, 0 2B, 0 3B, 0 HR, 0 RBI.

Year	League	W	L	Pct.	ERA	G	GS	CG	ShO	Sv.-Opp.	IP	H	R	ER	HR	BB-IBB	SO
1993—	Pittsfield (NY-Penn)	3	3	.500	3.35	21	1	0	0	0-...	40.1	50	21	15	0	7-0	31
1994—	Capital City (S.Atl.)	1	1	.500	1.29	26	0	0	0	18-...	28.0	23	14	4	0	6-0	22
—	St. Lucie (FSL)	0	0	...	0.00	24	0	0	0	16-...	26.2	13	0	0	0	6-1	15
—	Binghamton (East.)	0	0	...	8.10	4	0	0	0	0-...	6.2	9	6	6	0	5-0	7
1995—	Binghamton (East.)	0	2	.000	4.50	14	0	0	0	3-...	18.0	20	11	9	1	4-2	9
—	Gulf Coast Mets (GCL)	0	0	...	3.00	2	1	0	0	0-...	3.0	2	1	1	0	1-0	2
1996—	Binghamton (East.)	6	2	.750	2.44	49	0	0	0	2-...	62.2	51	19	17	6	16-3	48
1997—	Norfolk (I.L.)	7	5	.583	4.67	40	11	0	0	6-...	111.2	137	72	58	9	14-4	67
1998—	Norfolk (I.L.)	3	3	.500	1.83	45	0	0	0	11-...	64.0	42	14	13	3	6-0	54
—	New York (N.L.)	1	1	.500	6.28	15	0	0	0	0-1	14.1	13	10	10	2	4-1	8

Year League	W	L	Pct.	ERA	G	GS	CG	ShO	Sv.-Opp.	IP	H	R	ER	HR	BB-IBB	SO
1999— St. Lucie (FSL)	0	0	...	3.38	2	0	0	0	0-...	2.2	4	1	1	0	0-0	3
— Norfolk (I.L.)	0	1	.000	3.10	16	0	0	0	3-...	20.1	24	7	7	1	3-1	10
— Buffalo (I.L.)■	2	2	.500	2.08	16	0	0	0	0-...	26.0	23	9	6	2	8-1	13
— Cleveland (A.L.)	0	0	...	81.00	1	0	0	0	0-0	.1	2	3	3	0	1-1	0
— New York (N.L.)■	0	0	...	3.18	9	0	0	0	0-0	11.1	6	4	4	3	3-0	8
2000— Oakland (A.L.)■	3	3	.500	2.63	72	0	0	0	3-6	85.2	86	30	25	3	23-8	46
2001— Oakland (A.L.)	2	4	.333	3.01	70	0	0	0	3-6	74.2	68	27	25	3	29-9	44
2002— Oakland (A.L.)	1	2	.333	5.13	40	0	0	0	0-4	40.1	56	26	23	2	13-5	14
— Sacramento (PCL)	1	3	.250	5.59	20	0	0	0	2-...	29.0	31	20	18	2	5-0	26
A.L. totals (4 years)	6	9	.400	3.40	183	0	0	0	6-16	201.0	212	86	76	8	66-23	104
N.L. totals (2 years)	1	1	.500	4.91	24	0	0	0	0-1	25.2	19	14	14	5	7-1	16
Major League totals (5 years)	7	10	.412	3.57	207	0	0	0	6-17	226.2	231	100	90	13	73-24	120

DIVISION SERIES RECORD

Year League	W	L	Pct.	ERA	G	GS	CG	ShO	Sv.-Opp.	IP	H	R	ER	HR	BB-IBB	SO
2000— Oakland (A.L.)	0	0	...	0.00	3	0	0	0	0-0	2.0	3	1	0	0	1-1	1
2001— Oakland (A.L.)	0	0	...	18.00	1	0	0	0	0-0	1.0	3	2	2	0	0-0	0
Division series totals (2 years)	0	0	...	6.00	4	0	0	0	0-0	3.0	6	3	2	0	1-1	1

TANKERSLEY, DENNIS P PADRES

PERSONAL: Born February 24, 1979, in Troy, Mo. ... 6-2/185. ... Throws right, bats right. ... Full name: Dennis Lee Tankersley Jr.
HIGH SCHOOL: St. Charles (Mo.).
JUNIOR COLLEGE: Meramec (Mo.).
TRANSACTIONS/CAREER NOTES: Selected by Boston Red Sox organization in 38th round of free-agent draft (June 2, 1998). ... Traded by Red Sox with IF Cesar Saba to San Diego Padres for 3B Ed Sprague (June 30, 2000).
CAREER HITTING (MLB): 4-for-13 (.308), 2 R, 1 2B, 0 3B, 1 HR, 1 RBI.

Year League	W	L	Pct.	ERA	G	GS	CG	ShO	Sv.-Opp.	IP	H	R	ER	HR	BB-IBB	SO
1999— Gulf Coast Red Sox (GCL)	1	0	1.000	0.76	11	6	0	0	1-...	35.2	14	7	3	2	9-1	57
2000— Augusta (S.Atl.)	5	3	.625	4.06	15	15	1	1	0-...	75.1	73	41	34	4	32-0	74
— Fort Wayne (Midw.)■	5	2	.714	2.85	12	12	0	0	0-...	66.1	48	25	21	5	25-0	87
2001— Lake Elsinore (Calif.)	5	1	.833	0.52	9	8	0	0	0-...	52.1	29	5	3	1	12-0	68
— Mobile (Sou.)	4	1	.800	2.07	13	13	0	0	0-...	69.2	44	23	16	6	24-1	89
— Portland (PCL)	1	2	.333	6.91	3	3	0	0	0-...	14.1	16	13	11	2	8-0	16
2002— Mobile (Sou.)	3	3	.500	3.02	10	10	0	0	0-...	50.2	47	20	17	1	21-0	56
— San Diego (N.L.)	1	4	.200	8.06	17	9	0	0	0-0	51.1	59	46	46	10	40-3	39
— Portland (PCL)	3	4	.429	3.88	9	9	0	0	0-...	51.0	43	29	22	6	30-0	51
Major League totals (1 year)	1	4	.200	8.06	17	9	0	0	0-0	51.1	59	46	46	10	40-3	39

TARASCO, TONY OF METS

PERSONAL: Born December 9, 1970, in New York. ... 6-0/205. ... Bats left, throws right. ... Full name: Anthony Giacinto Tarasco.
HIGH SCHOOL: Santa Monica (Calif.).
TRANSACTIONS/CAREER NOTES: Selected by Atlanta Braves organization in 15th round of free-agent draft (June 1, 1988). ... On disabled list (August 4-September 12, 1991). ... Traded by Braves with OF Roberto Kelly and P Esteban Yan to Montreal Expos for OF Marquis Grissom (April 6, 1995). ... Traded by Expos to Baltimore Orioles for OF Sherman Obando (March 13, 1996). ... On Rochester disabled list (June 16-August 25, 1996). ... On Baltimore disabled list (August 25-September 13, 1996); included rehabilitation assignments to Frederick (August 25-September 8) and Rochester (September 9-13). ... Claimed on waivers by Cincinnati Reds (March 24, 1998). ... On Indianapolis disabled list (April 26-May 29, 1998). ... Released by Reds (November 10, 1998). ... Signed by Kansas City Royals organization (January 25, 1999). ... Released by Royals (March 18, 1999). ... Signed by New York Yankees organization (March 26, 1999). ... Granted free agency (October 4, 1999). ... Signed by Hanshin Tigers of Japan Central League (2000). ... Signed by New York Mets organization (March 6, 2001). ... Granted free agency (October 15, 2001). ... Re-signed by Mets organization (January 21, 2002).
STATISTICAL NOTES: Tied for International League lead with eight intentional bases on balls received in 2001. ... Tied for International League lead with 13 assists by outfielder in 2001. ... Career major league grand slams: 1.
2002 GAMES PLAYED BY POSITION (MLB): OF—29; 1B—7; DH—2.

		BATTING														FIELDING	
Year Team (League)	Pos.	G	AB	R	H	2B	3B	HR	RBI	BB	SO	SB-CS	Avg.	OBP	SLG	E	Avg.
1988— Idaho Falls (Pio.)	OF	7	10	1	0	0	0	0	1	5	2	1-0	.000	.333	.000	1	.667
— GC Braves (GCL)	OF	21	64	10	15	6	1	0	4	7	7	3-2	.234	.319	.359	1	.963
1989— Pulaski (Appl.)	OF	49	156	22	53	8	2	2	22	21	20	7-2	.340	.413	.455	3	.942
1990— Sumter (S.Atl.)	OF	107	355	42	94	13	3	3	37	37	57	9-5	.265	.333	.344	9	.954
1991— Durham (Caro.)	OF	78	248	31	62	8	2	12	38	21	64	11-9	.250	.308	.444	3	.977
1992— Greenville (Sou.)	OF-2B	133	489	73	140	22	2	15	54	27	84	33-19	.286	.321	.431	5	.978
1993— Richmond (I.L.)	OF	93	370	73	122	15	7	15	53	36	54	19-11	.330	.388	.530	2	.987
— Atlanta (N.L.)	OF	24	35	6	8	2	0	0	2	0	5	0-1	.229	.243	.286	0	1.000
1994— Atlanta (N.L.)	OF	87	132	16	36	6	0	5	19	9	17	5-0	.273	.313	.432	0	1.000
1995— Montreal (N.L.)■	OF	126	438	64	109	18	4	14	40	51	78	24-3	.249	.329	.404	5	.979
1996— Baltimore (A.L.)■	OF-DH	31	84	14	20	3	0	1	9	7	15	5-3	.238	.297	.310	0	1.000
— Rochester (I.L.)	DH-OF	29	103	18	27	6	0	2	9	17	20	4-4	.262	.364	.379	0	1.000
— GC Orioles (GCL)	DH	3	8	2	3	1	0	0	3	2	1	0-0	.375	.455	.500	0	...
— Frederick (Caro.)	DH	9	35	6	8	3	0	1	5	4	4	0-1	.229	.325	.400	0	...
1997— Baltimore (A.L.)	OF-DH	100	166	26	34	8	1	7	26	25	33	2-2	.205	.313	.392	1	.991
— Rochester (I.L.)	OF	10	35	4	7	0	0	2	6	7	7	0-0	.200	.326	.371	0	1.000
1998— Indianapolis (I.L.)■	OF-DH	90	319	53	100	19	1	16	45	43	46	3-2	.313	.395	.530	0	1.000
— Cincinnati (N.L.)	OF	15	24	5	5	2	0	1	4	3	5	0-0	.208	.296	.417	0	1.000
1999— Columbus (I.L.)■	OF-DH	95	346	72	102	23	0	19	61	49	39	9-5	.295	.383	.526	2	.990
— New York (A.L.)	OF-DH	14	31	5	5	2	0	0	3	3	5	1-0	.161	.229	.226	0	1.000
2000— Hanshin (Jap. Cen.)■		102	380	40	91	13	1	99	57	38	88	1-...	.239	...	1.061	...	...
— Hanshin (Jp. West.)		6	17	1	2	2	0	0	2	2	3	0-...	.118	...	.235	...	...

Year	Team (League)	Pos.	G	AB	R	H	2B	3B	HR	RBI	BB	SO	SB-CS	Avg.	OBP	SLG	E	Avg.
			BATTING														FIELDING	
2001	—St. Lucie (FSL)■	OF	3	13	1	3	2	0	0	2	0	4	0-0	.231	.231	.385	0	1.000
	—Norfolk (I.L.)	OF	105	366	53	107	31	4	7	57	48	43	14-8	.292	.371	.456	2	.991
2002	—Norfolk (I.L.)	OF-1B	42	153	21	43	7	1	1	18	9	15	5-3	.281	.323	.359	0	1.000
	—New York (N.L.)	OF-1B-DH	60	96	15	24	5	0	6	15	8	13	2-1	.250	.305	.490	1	.982
American League totals (3 years)			145	281	45	59	13	1	8	38	35	53	8-5	.210	.299	.349	1	.994
National League totals (5 years)			312	725	106	182	33	4	26	80	71	118	31-5	.251	.318	.415	6	.983
Major League totals (8 years)			457	1006	151	241	46	5	34	118	106	171	39-10	.240	.313	.397	7	.987

DIVISION SERIES RECORD

Year	Team (League)	Pos.	G	AB	R	H	2B	3B	HR	RBI	BB	SO	SB-CS	Avg.	OBP	SLG	E	Avg.
			BATTING														FIELDING	
1996	— Baltimore (A.L.)		Did not play.															

CHAMPIONSHIP SERIES RECORD

Year	Team (League)	Pos.	G	AB	R	H	2B	3B	HR	RBI	BB	SO	SB-CS	Avg.	OBP	SLG	E	Avg.
			BATTING														FIELDING	
1993	—Atlanta (N.L.)	OF-PR	2	1	0	0	0	0	0	0	0	1	0-0	.000	.000	.000	0	...
1996	—Baltimore (A.L.)	OF	2	1	0	0	0	0	0	0	0	1	0-0	.000	.000	.000	0	1.000
Championship series totals (2 years)			4	2	0	0	0	0	0	0	0	2	0-0	.000	.000	.000	0	1.000

TATIS, FERNANDO — 3B — EXPOS

PERSONAL: Born January 1, 1975, in San Pedro de Macoris, Dominican Republic ... 5-10/180. ... Bats right, throws right. ... Full name: Fernando Tatis Jr. ... Name pronounced ta-TEES.

TRANSACTIONS/CAREER NOTES: Signed as non-drafted free agent by Texas Rangers organization (August 25, 1992). ... Traded by Rangers with P Darren Oliver and a player to be named later to St. Louis Cardinals for P Todd Stottlemyre and SS Royce Clayton (July 31, 1998); Cardinals acquired OF Mark Little to complete deal (August 9, 1998). ... On St. Louis disabled list (April 30-June 30, 2000); included rehabilitation assignment to Memphis (June 26-30). ... Traded by Cardinals with P Britt Reames to Montreal Expos for P Dustin Hermanson and P Steve Kline (December 14, 2000). ... On disabled list (May 11-26 and June 3, 2001-remainder of season). ... On suspended list (July 8-9, 2001). ... On Montreal disabled list (March 22-April 28, 2002); included rehabilitation assignment to Brevard County (April 22-29). ... On suspended list (August 31-September 3, 2002).

RECORDS: Holds major league single-inning records for most grand slams—2; and most runs batted in—8 (April 23, 1999, third inning). ... Shares major league single-game record for most grand slams—2 (April 23, 1999). ... Shares major league single-inning record for most home runs—2 (April 23, 1999, third inning).

STATISTICAL NOTES: Led Gulf Coast League with four intentional bases on balls received in 1994. ... Led Gulf Coast League third basemen with 165 assists, 227 total chances and .925 fielding percentage in 1994. ... Tied for Texas League lead with four intentional bases on balls received in 1997. ... Career major league grand slams: 6.

2002 GAMES PLAYED BY POSITION (MLB): 3B—99; DH—4.

Year	Team (League)	Pos.	G	AB	R	H	2B	3B	HR	RBI	BB	SO	SB-CS	Avg.	OBP	SLG	E	Avg.
			BATTING														FIELDING	
1993	—Dom. Rangers (DSL)	IF	59	198	22	54	5	1	4	34	27	12	7-...	.273	...	.369	11	.940
1994	—GC Rangers (GCL)	3B-2B	•60	212	34	70	10	2	6	32	25	33	21-4	.330	.405	.481	17	†.927
1995	—Charl., S.C. (SAL)	3B	131	499	74	•151	*43	4	15	84	45	94	22-19	.303	.366	.495	37	.900
1996	—Charlotte (FSL)	3B	85	325	46	93	25	0	12	53	30	48	9-3	.286	.353	.474	24	.893
	—Oklahoma City (A.A.)	3B	2	4	0	2	1	0	0	0	0	1	0-0	.500	.500	.750	0	1.000
1997	—Tulsa (Texas)	3B-DH	102	382	73	120	26	1	24	61	46	72	17-8	.314	.390	.576	21	.921
	—Texas (A.L.)	3B	60	223	29	57	9	0	8	29	14	42	3-0	.256	.297	.404	7	.951
1998	—Texas (A.L.)	3B	95	330	41	89	17	2	3	32	12	66	6-2	.270	.303	.361	15	.945
	—St. Louis (N.L.)■	3B-SS	55	202	28	58	16	2	8	26	24	57	7-3	.287	.367	.505	12	.930
1999	—St. Louis (N.L.)	3B	149	537	104	160	31	2	34	107	82	128	21-9	.298	.404	.553	16	.958
2000	—St. Louis (N.L.)	3B-DH-1B	96	324	59	82	21	1	18	64	57	94	2-3	.253	.379	.491	8	.955
	—Memphis (PCL)	3B	3	9	0	0	0	0	0	0	1	3	0-0	.000	.100	.000	0	1.000
2001	—Montreal (N.L.)■	3B	41	145	20	37	9	0	2	11	16	43	0-0	.255	.339	.359	9	.889
2002	—Brevard County (FSL)	3B	6	17	2	4	1	0	0	2	3	4	0-0	.235	.391	.294	1	.929
	—Montreal (N.L.)	3B-DH	114	381	43	87	18	1	15	55	35	90	2-2	.228	.303	.399	13	.948
American League totals (2 years)			155	553	70	146	26	2	11	61	26	108	9-2	.264	.301	.378	22	.947
National League totals (5 years)			455	1589	254	424	95	6	77	263	214	412	32-17	.267	.365	.480	58	.946
Major League totals (6 years)			610	2142	324	570	121	8	88	324	240	520	41-19	.266	.350	.453	80	.946

DIVISION SERIES RECORD

Year	Team (League)	Pos.	G	AB	R	H	2B	3B	HR	RBI	BB	SO	SB-CS	Avg.	OBP	SLG	E	Avg.
			BATTING														FIELDING	
2000	— St. Louis (N.L.)		Did not play.															

CHAMPIONSHIP SERIES RECORD

Year	Team (League)	Pos.	G	AB	R	H	2B	3B	HR	RBI	BB	SO	SB-CS	Avg.	OBP	SLG	E	Avg.
			BATTING														FIELDING	
2000	—St. Louis (N.L.)	PH-3B	5	13	1	3	2	0	0	2	1	5	0-0	.231	.267	.385	2	.800

TAUBENSEE, EDDIE — C — INDIANS

PERSONAL: Born October 31, 1968, in Beeville, Texas. ... 6-3/230. ... Bats left, throws right. ... Full name: Edward Kenneth Taubensee. ... Name pronounced TAW-ben-see.

HIGH SCHOOL: Lake Howell (Casselberry, Fla.).

TRANSACTIONS/CAREER NOTES: Selected by Cincinnati Reds organization in sixth round of free-agent draft (June 2, 1986). ... Selected by Oakland Athletics from Reds organization in Rule 5 major league draft (December 3, 1990). ... Claimed on waivers by Cleveland Indians (April 4, 1991). ... Traded by Indians with P Willie Blair to Houston Astros for OF Kenny Lofton and IF Dave Rohde (December 10, 1991). ... Traded by Astros to Reds for P Ross Powell and P Marty Lister (April 19, 1994). ... On disabled list (August 1, 2000-remainder of season). ... Traded

T

by Reds to Indians for P Jim Brower and P Robert Pugmire (November 16, 2000). ... On Cleveland disabled list (June 17-July 27, 2001); included rehabilitation assignments to Buffalo (July 16-24) and Akron (July 25-26). ... On disabled list (March 30, 2002-entire season).
STATISTICAL NOTES: Led Pioneer League with 19 passed balls in 1987. ... Tied for South Atlantic League lead in double plays by catcher with seven in 1988. ... Had 16-game hitting streak (May 22-June 13, 1999). ... Career major league grand slams: 1.

		BATTING														FIELDING	
Year Team (League)	**Pos.**	**G**	**AB**	**R**	**H**	**2B**	**3B**	**HR**	**RBI**	**BB**	**SO**	**SB-CS**	**Avg.**	**OBP**	**SLG**	**E**	**Avg.**
1986— GC Reds (GCL)	C-1B	35	107	8	21	3	0	1	11	11	33	0-1	.196	.271	.252	8	.967
1987— Billings (Pio.)	C	55	162	24	43	7	0	5	28	25	47	2-2	.265	.363	.401	6	.984
1988— Greensboro (S.Atl.)	C	103	330	36	85	16	1	10	41	44	93	8-4	.258	.354	.403	15	.979
— Chattanooga (Sou.)	C	5	12	2	2	0	0	1	1	3	4	0-0	.167	.333	.417	1	.957
1989— Cedar Rapids (Midw.)	C	59	196	25	39	5	0	8	22	25	55	4-1	.199	.296	.347	1	.998
— Chattanooga (Sou.)	C	45	127	11	24	2	0	3	13	11	28	0-0	.189	.248	.276	6	.976
1990— Cedar Rapids (Midw.)	C	122	417	57	108	21	1	16	62	51	98	11-4	.259	.342	.429	16	.982
1991— Colo. Springs (PCL)■	C	91	287	53	89	23	3	13	39	31	61	0-0	.310	.377	.547	12	.975
— Cleveland (A.L.)	C	26	66	5	16	2	1	0	8	5	16	0-0	.242	.288	.303	2	.979
1992— Houston (N.L.)■	C	104	297	23	66	15	0	5	28	31	78	2-1	.222	.299	.323	5	.992
— Tucson (PCL)	C	20	74	13	25	8	1	1	10	8	17	0-1	.338	.402	.514	4	.972
1993— Houston (N.L.)	C	94	288	26	72	11	1	9	42	21	44	1-0	.250	.299	.389	5	.992
1994— Houston (N.L.)	C	5	10	0	1	0	0	0	0	0	3	0-0	.100	.100	.100	0	1.000
— Cincinnati (N.L.)■	C	61	177	29	52	8	2	8	21	15	28	2-0	.294	.345	.497	4	.990
1995— Cincinnati (N.L.)	C-1B	80	218	32	62	14	2	9	44	22	52	2-2	.284	.354	.491	6	.984
1996— Cincinnati (N.L.)	C	108	327	46	95	20	0	12	48	26	64	3-4	.291	.338	.462	11	.981
1997— Cincinnati (N.L.)	C-OF-1B-DH	108	254	26	68	18	0	10	34	22	66	0-1	.268	.323	.457	5	.989
1998— Cincinnati (N.L.)	C	130	431	61	120	27	0	11	72	52	93	1-0	.278	.352	.418	10	.988
1999— Cincinnati (N.L.)	C	126	424	58	132	22	2	21	87	30	67	0-2	.311	.354	.521	9	.989
2000— Cincinnati (N.L.)	C	81	266	29	71	12	0	6	24	21	44	0-0	.267	.324	.380	5	.989
2001— Cleveland (A.L.)■	C-DH	52	116	16	29	2	1	3	11	10	19	0-0	.250	.315	.362	3	.986
— Buffalo (I.L.)	C	7	26	5	7	1	0	2	7	2	6	0-0	.269	.321	.538	1	.960
— Akron (East.)	C	2	7	1	1	0	0	0	1	1	1	0-0	.143	.250	.143	0	1.000
2002— Cleveland (A.L.)		Did not play.															
American League totals (2 years)		78	182	21	45	4	2	3	19	15	35	0-0	.247	.288	.341	5	.984
National League totals (9 years)		897	2692	330	739	147	7	91	400	240	539	11-10	.275	.333	.436	60	.988
Major League totals (11 years)		975	2874	351	784	151	9	94	419	255	574	11-10	.273	.331	.430	65	.988

CHAMPIONSHIP SERIES RECORD

		BATTING														FIELDING	
Year Team (League)	**Pos.**	**G**	**AB**	**R**	**H**	**2B**	**3B**	**HR**	**RBI**	**BB**	**SO**	**SB-CS**	**Avg.**	**OBP**	**SLG**	**E**	**Avg.**
1995— Cincinnati (N.L.)	PH-C	2	2	0	1	0	0	0	0	0	0	0-0	.500	.500	.500	0	...

TAVAREZ, JULIAN — P

PERSONAL: Born May 22, 1973, in Santiago, Dominican Republic. ... 6-2/195. ... Throws right, bats left.
HIGH SCHOOL: Santiago (Dominican Republic) Public School.
TRANSACTIONS/CAREER NOTES: Signed as non-drafted free agent by Cleveland Indians organization (March 16, 1990). ... On Cleveland suspended list (June 18-21, 1996). ... Traded by Indians with IF Jeff Kent, IF Jose Vizcaino and a player to be named later to San Francisco Giants for 3B Matt Williams and a player to be named later (November 13, 1996); Indians traded P Joe Roa to Giants for OF Trenidad Hubbard to complete deal (December 16, 1996). ... On San Francisco disabled list (July 13-August 7, 1998); included rehabilitation assignment to Fresno (August 5-7). ... On suspended list (September 14-16, 1998). ... On San Francisco disabled list (May 1-June 1, 1999); included rehabilitation assignment to Fresno (May 25-June 1). ... Claimed on waivers by Colorado Rockies (November 21, 1999). ... Granted free agency (October 31, 2000). ... Signed by Chicago Cubs (November 16, 2000). ... On suspended list (April 29-May 5, 2001). ... Traded by Cubs with P Jose Cueto, P Dontrelle Willis and C Ryan Jorgensen to Florida Marlins for P Antonio Alfonseca and P Matt Clement (March 27, 2002). ... On disabled list (April 17-May 12, 2002). ... Granted free agency (October 28, 2002).
HONORS: Named A.L. Rookie Pitcher of the Year by THE SPORTING NEWS (1995).
STATISTICAL NOTES: Led Appalachian League with 10 hit batsmen in 1992.
CAREER HITTING (MLB): 15-for-131 (.115), 8 R, 0 2B, 0 3B, 0 HR, 9 RBI.

Year League	**W**	**L**	**Pct.**	**ERA**	**G**	**GS**	**CG**	**ShO**	**Sv.-Opp.**	**IP**	**H**	**R**	**ER**	**HR**	**BB-IBB**	**SO**
1990— Dominican Indians (DSL)	5	5	.500	3.29	14	12	3	0	0-...	82.0	85	53	30	...	48-...	33
1991— Dominican Indians (DSL)	8	2	.800	2.67	19	18	1	0	0-...	121.1	95	41	36	...	28-...	75
1992— Burlington (Appl.)	6	3	.667	2.68	14	*14	2	•2	0-...	87.1	86	41	26	3	12-0	69
1993— Kinston (Caro.)	11	5	.688	2.42	18	18	2	0	0-...	119.0	102	48	32	6	28-0	107
— Canton/Akron (East.)	2	1	.667	0.95	3	2	1	1	0-...	19.0	14	2	2	0	1-0	11
— Cleveland (A.L.)	2	2	.500	6.57	8	7	0	0	0-0	37.0	53	29	27	7	13-2	19
1994— Charlotte (I.L.)	•15	6	.714	3.48	26	26	2	2	0-...	176.0	167	79	68	15	43-0	102
— Cleveland (A.L.)	0	1	.000	21.60	1	1	0	0	0-0	1.2	6	8	4	1	1-1	0
1995— Cleveland (A.L.)	10	2	.833	2.44	57	0	0	0	0-4	85.0	76	36	23	7	21-0	68
1996— Cleveland (A.L.)	4	7	.364	5.36	51	4	0	0	0-0	80.2	101	49	48	9	22-5	46
— Buffalo (A.A.)	1	0	1.000	1.29	2	2	0	0	0-...	14.0	10	2	2	0	3-0	10
1997— San Francisco (N.L.)■	6	4	.600	3.87	*89	0	0	0	0-3	88.1	91	43	38	6	34-5	38
1998— San Francisco (N.L.)	5	3	.625	3.80	60	0	0	0	1-6	85.1	96	41	36	5	36-11	52
— Fresno (PCL)	0	0	...	19.29	1	0	0	0	0-...	2.1	6	5	5	0	0-0	1
1999— San Francisco (N.L.)	2	0	1.000	5.93	47	0	0	0	0-2	54.2	65	38	36	7	25-3	33
— Fresno (PCL)	0	0	...	2.25	4	1	0	0	0-...	8.0	3	2	2	1	3-0	9
— San Jose (Calif.)	0	0	...	0.00	1	1	0	0	0-...	4.0	1	0	0	0	1-0	3
2000— Colorado (N.L.)■	11	5	.688	4.43	51	12	1	0	1-1	120.0	124	68	59	11	53-9	62
2001— Chicago (N.L.)■	10	9	.526	4.52	34	28	0	0	0-0	161.1	172	98	81	13	69-4	107
2002— Florida (N.L.)■	10	12	.455	5.39	29	27	0	0	0-1	153.2	188	100	92	9	74-7	67
A.L. totals (4 years)	16	12	.571	4.49	117	12	0	0	0-4	204.1	236	122	102	24	57-8	133
N.L. totals (6 years)	44	33	.571	4.64	310	67	1	0	2-13	663.1	736	388	342	51	291-39	359
Major League totals (10 years)	60	45	.571	4.61	427	79	1	0	2-17	867.2	972	510	444	75	348-47	492

DIVISION SERIES RECORD

Year	League	W	L	Pct.	ERA	G	GS	CG	ShO	Sv.-Opp.	IP	H	R	ER	HR	BB-IBB	SO
1995—	Cleveland (A.L.)	0	0	...	6.75	3	0	0	0	0-1	2.2	5	2	2	1	0-0	3
1996—	Cleveland (A.L.)	0	0	...	0.00	2	0	0	0	0-0	1.1	1	0	0	0	2-0	1
1997—	San Francisco (N.L.)	0	1	.000	4.50	3	0	0	0	0-0	4.0	4	2	2	1	2-1	0
Division series totals (3 years)		0	1	.000	4.50	8	0	0	0	0-1	8.0	10	4	4	2	4-1	4

CHAMPIONSHIP SERIES RECORD

Year	League	W	L	Pct.	ERA	G	GS	CG	ShO	Sv.-Opp.	IP	H	R	ER	HR	BB-IBB	SO
1995—	Cleveland (A.L.)	0	1	.000	2.70	4	0	0	0	0-0	3.1	3	1	1	0	1-1	2

WORLD SERIES RECORD

Year	League	W	L	Pct.	ERA	G	GS	CG	ShO	Sv.-Opp.	IP	H	R	ER	HR	BB-IBB	SO
1995—	Cleveland (A.L.)	0	0	...	0.00	5	0	0	0	0-0	4.1	3	0	0	0	2-0	1

TAYLOR, AARON — P — MARINERS

PERSONAL: Born August 20, 1977, in Valdosta, Ga. ... 6-7/230. ... Throws right, bats right. ... Full name: Aaron Wade Taylor.
HIGH SCHOOL: Lowndes (Valdosta, Ga.).
TRANSACTIONS/CAREER NOTES: Selected by Atlanta Braves organization in 11th round of free-agent draft (June 4, 1996). ... Selected by Seattle Mariners organization from Braves organization in Rule 5 minor league draft (December 13, 1999).
STATISTICAL NOTES: Led Gulf Coast League in wild pitches with 14 in 1996.
CAREER HITTING (MLB): 0-for-0 (.000), 0 R, 0 2B, 0 3B, 0 HR, 0 RBI.

Year	League	W	L	Pct.	ERA	G	GS	CG	ShO	Sv.-Opp.	IP	H	R	ER	HR	BB-IBB	SO
1996—	Gulf Coast Braves (GCL)	0	*9	.000	7.74	13	9	0	0	0-...	52.1	68	*54	45	0	28-0	33
1997—	Danville (Appl.)	1	•8	.111	5.53	15	7	0	0	0-...	55.1	65	49	34	4	31-0	38
1998—	Danville (Appl.)	3	6	.333	6.25	14	•14	1	0	0-...	72.0	87	60	*50	9	36-0	55
1999—	Macon (S.Atl.)	6	7	.462	4.88	27	8	0	0	1-...	79.1	86	56	43	9	27-2	78
2000—	Everett (N'West)■	1	4	.200	7.43	15	14	0	0	0-...	63.0	76	54	52	5	37-0	57
2001—	Wisconsin (Midw.)	3	1	.750	2.45	28	0	0	0	9-...	29.1	19	9	8	1	11-2	50
2002—	San Antonio (Texas)	4	3	.571	2.34	61	0	0	0	24-...	77.0	51	28	20	5	34-0	93
—	Seattle (A.L.)	0	0	...	9.00	5	0	0	0	0-1	5.0	8	5	5	2	0-0	6
Major League totals (1 year)		0	0	...	9.00	5	0	0	0	0-1	5.0	8	5	5	2	0-0	6

TAYLOR, REGGIE — OF — REDS

PERSONAL: Born January 12, 1977, in Newberry, S.C. ... 6-1/178. ... Bats left, throws right. ... Full name: Reginald Tremain Taylor.
HIGH SCHOOL: Newberry (S.C.).
TRANSACTIONS/CAREER NOTES: Selected by Philadelphia Phillies organization in first round (14th pick overall) of free-agent draft (June 1, 1995). ... On disabled list (July 23, 1998-remainder of season). ... On Scranton/Wilkes-Barre disabled list (April 6-May 26, 2000; and April 6-May 1, 2001). ... Traded by Phillies to Cincinnati Reds for a player to be named (March 28, 2002); Phillies acquired P Hector Mercado to complete deal (March 30, 2002).
STATISTICAL NOTES: Led Appalachian League outfielders with three double plays in 1995. ... Led Florida State League outfielders with 19 assists and 354 total chances in 1997. ... Led Eastern League in caught stealing with 20 in 1999. ... Led International League in caught stealing with 15 in 2001. ... Career major league grand slams: 1.
2002 GAMES PLAYED BY POSITION (MLB): OF—103.

			BATTING															FIELDING	
Year	Team (League)	Pos.	G	AB	R	H	2B	3B	HR	RBI	BB	SO	SB-CS	Avg.	OBP	SLG		E	Avg.
1995—	Martinsville (Appl.)	OF	64	239	36	53	4	6	2	32	23	58	18-7	.222	.301	.314		8	.940
1996—	Piedmont (S.Atl.)	OF	128	499	68	131	20	6	0	31	29	136	36-17	.263	.305	.327		•12	.961
1997—	Clearwater (FSL)	OF	134	545	73	133	18	6	12	47	30	130	40-23	.244	.285	.365		11	.969
1998—	Reading (East.)	OF	79	337	49	92	14	6	5	22	12	73	22-10	.273	.300	.395		10	.944
1999—	Reading (East.)	OF	127	526	75	140	17	10	15	61	18	79	38-20	.266	.293	.422		9	.971
2000—	Scranton/W.B. (I.L.)	OF	98	422	60	116	10	8	15	43	21	87	23-13	.275	.310	.443		5	.980
—	Philadelphia (N.L.)	OF	9	11	1	1	0	0	0	0	0	8	1-0	.091	.091	.091		1	.750
2001—	Scranton/W.B. (I.L.)	OF	111	464	56	122	20	9	7	50	24	94	31-15	.263	.301	.390		5	.980
—	Philadelphia (N.L.)	OF	5	7	1	0	0	0	0	0	1	1	0-0	.000	.125	.000		0	1.000
2002—	Cincinnati (N.L.)■	OF	135	287	41	73	15	4	9	38	14	79	11-8	.254	.291	.429		5	.973
Major League totals (3 years)			149	305	43	74	15	4	9	38	15	88	12-8	.243	.280	.407		6	.969

TEIXEIRA, MARK — 3B — RANGERS

PERSONAL: Born April 11, 1980, in Annapolis, Md. ... 6-3/225. ... Bats both, throws right. ... Full name: Mark Charles Teixeira.
HIGH SCHOOL: Mount St. Joseph (Baltimore).
COLLEGE: Georgia Tech.
TRANSACTIONS/CAREER NOTES: Selected by Boston Red Sox organization in ninth round of free-agent draft (June 2, 1998); did not sign. ... Selected by Texas Rangers organization in first round (fifth pick overall) of free-agent draft (June 5, 2001).

			BATTING															FIELDING	
Year	Team (League)	Pos.	G	AB	R	H	2B	3B	HR	RBI	BB	SO	SB-CS	Avg.	OBP	SLG		E	Avg.
2001—									Did not play.										
2002—	Charlotte (FSL)	3B	38	150	32	48	10	2	9	41	21	24	2-0	.320	.411	.593		9	.902
—	Tulsa (Texas)	3B	48	171	31	54	11	3	10	28	25	36	3-2	.316	.415	.591		12	.925

TEJADA, MIGUEL — SS — ATHLETICS

PERSONAL: Born May 25, 1976, in Bani, Dominican Republic. ... 5-9/200. ... Bats right, throws right. ... Full name: Miguel Odalis Tejada.
TRANSACTIONS/CAREER NOTES: Signed as non-drafted free agent by Oakland Athletics organization (July 17, 1993). ... On suspended list (July 4-7, 1996). ... On disabled list (July 20-August 10, 1996). ... On Oakland disabled list (March 22-May 20, 1998); included rehabilitation assignments to Edmonton (May 11-12) and Huntsville (May 12-20).

T

RECORDS: Holds major league single-season record for most at-bats without a triple—662 (2002).
HONORS: Named A.L. Most Valuable Player by Baseball Writers' Association of America (2002).
STATISTICAL NOTES: Led Northwest League shortstops with 129 putouts, 214 assists and 369 total chances in 1995. ... Led California League shortstops with 44 errors in 1996. ... Led Southern League shortstops with 229 putouts, 423 assists, 688 total chances and 97 double plays in 1997. ... Hit three home runs in one game (June 11, 1999 and June 30, 2001). ... Led A.L. shortstops with 292 putouts in 1999. ... Led A.L. shortstops with 501 assists and 755 total chances in 2000. ... Hit for the cycle (September 29, 2001). ... Had 15-game hitting streak (April 17-May 3, 2002). ... Had 24-game hitting streak (July 11-August 4, 2002). ... Led A.L. shortstops with 504 assists and 753 total chances in 2002. ... Career major league grand slams: 5.
2002 GAMES PLAYED BY POSITION (MLB): SS—162.

		BATTING														FIELDING	
Year Team (League)	Pos.	G	AB	R	H	2B	3B	HR	RBI	BB	SO	SB-CS	Avg.	OBP	SLG	E	Avg.
1994— Dom. Athletics (DSL)	2B	74	218	51	64	9	1	18	62	37	36	13-...	.294	...	.592	16	.927
1995— S. Oregon (N'West)	SS	74	269	45	66	15	5	8	44	41	54	19-2	.245	.346	.428	26	.930
1996— Modesto (Calif.)	SS-DH-3B	114	458	97	128	12	5	20	72	51	93	27-16	.279	.352	.459	†45	.925
1997— Huntsville (Sou.)	SS	128	502	85	138	20	3	22	97	50	99	15-11	.275	.344	.458	*36	.948
— Oakland (A.L.)	SS	26	99	10	20	3	2	2	10	2	22	2-0	.202	.240	.333	4	.969
1998— Edmonton (PCL)	SS	1	3	0	0	0	0	0	0	1	1	0-0	.000	.250	.000	0	1.000
— Huntsville (Sou.)	SS-DH	15	52	9	17	6	0	2	7	4	8	1-0	.327	.362	.558	5	.922
— Oakland (A.L.)	SS	105	365	53	85	20	1	11	45	28	86	5-6	.233	.298	.384	26	.951
1999— Oakland (A.L.)	SS	159	593	93	149	33	4	21	84	57	94	8-7	.251	.325	.427	21	.973
2000— Oakland (A.L.)	SS	160	607	105	167	32	1	30	115	66	102	6-0	.275	.349	.479	21	.972
2001— Oakland (A.L.)	SS	•162	622	107	166	31	3	31	113	43	89	11-5	.267	.326	.476	20	.973
2002— Oakland (A.L.)	SS	•162	662	108	204	30	0	34	131	38	84	7-2	.308	.354	.508	19	.975
Major League totals (6 years)		774	2948	476	791	149	11	129	498	234	477	39-20	.268	.330	.458	111	.970

DIVISION SERIES RECORD

		BATTING														FIELDING	
Year Team (League)	Pos.	G	AB	R	H	2B	3B	HR	RBI	BB	SO	SB-CS	Avg.	OBP	SLG	E	Avg.
2000— Oakland (A.L.)	SS	5	20	5	7	2	0	0	1	2	2	1-0	.350	.409	.450	0	1.000
2001— Oakland (A.L.)	SS	5	21	1	6	3	0	0	1	0	3	0-0	.286	.304	.429	1	.958
2002— Oakland (A.L.)	SS	5	21	3	3	1	0	1	4	1	7	0-0	.143	.174	.333	1	.947
Division series totals (3 years)		15	62	9	16	6	0	1	6	3	12	1-0	.258	.294	.403	2	.969

ALL-STAR GAME RECORD

	AB	R	H	2B	3B	HR	RBI	BB	SO	SB-CS	Avg.	OBP	SLG	E	Avg.
All-Star Game totals (1 year)	2	1	1	0	0	0	0	0	0	0-0	.500	.500	.500	0	1.000

TEJERA, MICHAEL — P — MARLINS

PERSONAL: Born October 18, 1976, in Havana, Cuba. ... 5-9/175. ... Throws left, bats left.
HIGH SCHOOL: Southwest (Miami).
TRANSACTIONS/CAREER NOTES: Selected by Florida Marlins organization in sixth round of free-agent draft (June 1, 1995). ... On disabled list (April 2, 2000-entire season).
HONORS: Named Eastern League Pitcher of the Year (1999).
CAREER HITTING (MLB): 7-for-37 (.189), 5 R, 0 2B, 0 3B, 1 HR, 5 RBI.

Year League	W	L	Pct.	ERA	G	GS	CG	ShO	Sv.-Opp.	IP	H	R	ER	HR	BB-IBB	SO
1995— Gulf Coast Marlins (GCL)	3	1	.750	2.65	11	3	0	0	2-...	34.0	28	13	10	2	16-1	28
1996— Gulf Coast Marlins (GCL)	1	0	1.000	3.60	2	0	0	0	0-...	5.0	6	2	2	0	0-0	2
1997— Utica (NY-Penn)	3	3	.500	3.76	12	12	0	0	0-...	69.1	65	36	29	8	11-0	67
1998— Kane County (Midw.)	6	1	.857	2.77	10	10	0	0	0-...	55.1	44	20	17	3	13-0	47
— Portland (East.)	9	5	.643	4.11	18	18	2	2	0-...	107.1	113	55	49	15	36-2	97
1999— Portland (East.)	13	4	.765	2.62	25	25	0	0	0-...	154.2	137	55	45	13	45-1	152
— Calgary (PCL)	0	2	.000	12.00	2	2	0	0	0-...	9.0	19	14	12	2	4-0	5
— Florida (N.L.)	0	0	...	11.37	3	1	0	0	0-0	6.1	10	8	8	1	5-0	7
2000— Florida (N.L.)									Did not play.							
2001— Portland (East.)	9	8	.529	3.57	25	25	0	0	0-...	141.0	143	61	56	17	41-0	131
2002— Florida (N.L.)	8	8	.500	4.45	47	18	0	0	1-3	139.2	144	71	69	17	60-3	95
Major League totals (2 years)	8	8	.500	4.75	50	19	0	0	1-3	146.0	154	79	77	18	65-3	102

TELFORD, ANTHONY — P

PERSONAL: Born March 6, 1966, in San Jose, Calif. ... 6-0/195. ... Throws right, bats right. ... Full name: Anthony Charles Telford.
HIGH SCHOOL: Silver Creek (Calif.).
COLLEGE: San Jose State.
TRANSACTIONS/CAREER NOTES: Selected by Baltimore Orioles organization in third round of free-agent draft (June 2, 1987). ... On disabled list (April 20, 1988-remainder of season). ... On Frederick disabled list (April 7-18, 1989). ... On Erie disabled list (June 16-30, 1989). ... Granted free agency (October 15, 1993). ... Signed by Atlanta Braves organization (November 23, 1993). ... Granted free agency (October 15, 1994). ... Signed by Oakland Athletics organization (January 20, 1995). ... Released by A's (May 16, 1995). ... Signed by Cleveland Indians organization (June 15, 1995). ... Granted free agency (October 16, 1995). ... Signed by Montreal Expos organization (February 22, 1996). ... Granted free agency (October 15, 1996). ... Re-signed by Expos organization (December 18, 1996). ... On disabled list (May 19-June 3, 2000). ... On Montreal disabled list (March 23-April 25, 2001); included rehabilitation assignments to Jupiter (April 8-9 and April 24-25). ... Granted free agency (October 15, 2001). ... Signed by Texas Rangers organization (November 20, 2001). ... Released by Rangers (September 30, 2002).
CAREER HITTING (MLB): 4-for-23 (.174), 0 R, 1 2B, 0 3B, 0 HR, 3 RBI.

Year League	W	L	Pct.	ERA	G	GS	CG	ShO	Sv.-Opp.	IP	H	R	ER	HR	BB-IBB	SO
1987— Newark (NY-Penn)	1	0	1.000	1.02	6	2	0	0	0-...	17.2	16	2	2	0	3-0	27
— Hagerstown (Caro.)	1	0	1.000	1.59	2	2	0	0	0-...	11.1	9	2	2	0	5-0	10
— Rochester (I.L.)	0	0	...	0.00	1	0	0	0	0-...	2.0	0	0	0	0	3-0	3
1988— Hagerstown (Caro.)	1	0	1.000	0.00	1	1	0	0	0-...	7.0	3	0	0	0	0-0	10
1989— Frederick (Caro.)	2	1	.667	4.21	9	5	0	0	1-...	25.2	25	15	12	1	12-0	19

Year	League	W	L	Pct.	ERA	G	GS	CG	ShO	Sv.-Opp.	IP	H	R	ER	HR	BB-IBB	SO
1990—	Frederick (Caro.)	4	2	.667	1.68	8	8	1	0	0-...	53.2	35	15	10	1	11-1	49
—	Hagerstown (East.)	10	2	.833	1.97	14	13	3	1	0-...	96.0	80	26	21	3	25-1	73
—	Baltimore (A.L.)	3	3	.500	4.95	8	8	0	0	0-0	36.1	43	22	20	4	19-0	20
1991—	Rochester (I.L.)	•12	9	.571	3.95	27	25	3	0	0-...	157.1	166	82	69	18	48-2	115
—	Baltimore (A.L.)	0	0	...	4.05	9	1	0	0	0-0	26.2	27	12	12	3	6-1	24
1992—	Rochester (I.L.)	12	7	.632	4.18	27	26	3	0	0-...	*181.0	*183	89	84	15	64-0	129
1993—	Rochester (I.L.)	7	7	.500	4.27	38	6	0	0	2-...	90.2	98	51	43	10	33-3	66
—	Baltimore (A.L.)	0	0	...	9.82	3	0	0	0	0-0	7.1	11	8	8	3	1-0	6
1994—	Richmond (I.L.)■	10	6	.625	4.23	38	20	3	1	0-...	142.2	148	82	67	17	41-2	111
1995—	Edmonton (PCL)■	3	2	.600	7.18	8	6	0	0	0-...	36.1	47	32	29	5	16-0	17
—	Canton/Akron (East.)■	2	0	1.000	0.82	2	2	0	0	0-...	11.0	6	2	1	0	4-1	4
—	Buffalo (A.A.)	4	1	.800	3.46	16	2	0	0	0-...	39.0	35	15	15	1	10-3	24
1996—	Ottawa (I.L.)■	7	2	.778	4.11	30	15	1	1	0-...	118.1	128	62	54	12	34-1	69
1997—	Montreal (N.L.)	4	6	.400	3.24	65	0	0	0	1-5	89.0	77	34	32	11	33-4	61
1998—	Montreal (N.L.)	3	6	.333	3.86	77	0	0	0	1-5	91.0	85	45	39	9	36-1	59
1999—	Montreal (N.L.)	5	4	.556	3.94	79	0	0	0	2-9	96.0	112	52	42	3	38-3	69
2000—	Montreal (N.L.)	5	4	.556	3.79	64	0	0	0	3-5	78.1	76	38	33	10	23-1	68
2001—	Jupiter (FSL)	0	1	.000	7.20	4	2	0	0	0-...	5.0	9	5	4	0	1-0	5
—	Montreal (N.L.)	0	1	.000	10.29	8	0	0	0	0-0	7.0	14	12	8	2	5-1	5
—	Ottawa (I.L.)	3	5	.375	4.50	28	8	0	0	1-...	76.0	79	42	38	7	17-0	62
2002—	Oklahoma (PCL)■	8	2	.800	3.40	35	0	0	0	5-...	50.1	47	19	19	3	21-2	35
—	Texas (A.L.)	2	1	.667	6.46	20	0	0	0	1-2	23.2	30	18	17	3	15-2	19
A.L. totals (4 years)		5	4	.556	5.46	40	9	0	0	1-2	94.0	111	60	57	13	41-3	69
N.L. totals (5 years)		17	21	.447	3.84	293	0	0	0	7-24	361.1	364	181	154	35	135-10	262
Major League totals (9 years)		22	25	.468	4.17	333	9	0	0	8-26	455.1	475	241	211	48	176-13	331

TESSMER, JAY — P

PERSONAL: Born December 26, 1971, in Meadville, Pa. ... 6-3/188. ... Throws right, bats right. ... Full name: Jay Weldon Tessmer.
HIGH SCHOOL: Cochranton (Pa.).
COLLEGE: Miami (Fla.).
TRANSACTIONS/CAREER NOTES: Selected by New York Yankees organization in 19th round of free-agent draft (June 1, 1995). ... Traded by Yankees with SS Seth Taylor to Colorado Rockies for P David Lee (January 3, 2001). ... Traded by Rockies to Milwaukee Brewers for a player to be named later (May 12, 2001). ... Granted free agency (October 15, 2001). ... Signed by Yankees organization (January 18, 2002). ... Granted free agency (October 15, 2002).
HONORS: Name Florida State League Most Valuable Player (1996).
CAREER HITTING (MLB): 0-for-0 (.000), 0 R, 0 2B, 0 3B, 0 HR, 0 RBI.

Year	League	W	L	Pct.	ERA	G	GS	CG	ShO	Sv.-Opp.	IP	H	R	ER	HR	BB-IBB	SO
1995—	Oneonta (NY-Penn)	2	0	1.000	0.95	34	0	0	0	20-...	38.0	27	8	4	0	12-2	52
1996—	Tampa (FSL)	12	4	.750	1.48	*68	0	0	0	*35-...	97.1	68	18	16	2	19-3	104
1997—	Norwich (East.)	3	6	.333	5.31	55	0	0	0	17-...	62.2	78	41	37	7	24-2	51
1998—	Norwich (East.)	3	4	.429	1.09	45	0	0	0	29-...	49.2	50	8	6	0	13-5	57
—	Columbus (I.L.)	1	1	.500	0.49	12	0	0	0	5-...	18.1	8	2	1	1	1-0	14
—	New York (A.L.)	1	0	1.000	3.12	7	0	0	0	0-0	8.2	4	3	3	1	4-0	6
1999—	Columbus (I.L.)	3	3	.500	3.34	51	0	0	0	*28-...	56.2	52	22	21	4	12-1	42
—	New York (A.L.)	0	0	...	14.85	6	0	0	0	0-0	6.2	16	11	11	1	4-2	3
2000—	Columbus (I.L.)	4	8	.333	3.80	*60	0	0	0	34-...	66.1	73	36	28	5	19-7	40
—	New York (A.L.)	0	0	...	6.75	7	0	0	0	0-0	6.2	9	6	5	3	1-1	5
2001—	Colorado Springs (PCL)■	1	0	1.000	6.59	10	0	0	0	0-...	13.2	23	14	10	4	6-2	10
—	Indianapolis (I.L.)■	7	5	.583	2.79	35	0	0	0	4-...	58.0	56	23	18	3	9-2	39
2002—	New York (A.L.)■	0	0	...	6.75	2	0	0	0	0-0	1.1	0	1	1	0	2-0	0
—	Columbus (I.L.)	5	4	.556	4.37	63	0	0	0	4-...	78.1	109	42	38	6	14-4	54
Major League totals (4 years)		1	0	1.000	7.71	22	0	0	0	0-0	23.1	29	21	20	5	11-3	14

TEUT, NATHAN — P — MARLINS

PERSONAL: Born March 11, 1976, in Newton, Iowa. ... 6-6/225. ... Throws left, bats right. ... Full name: Nathan Mark Teut. ... Name pronounced TOIT.
HIGH SCHOOL: Paton-Churdan (Churdan, Iowa).
COLLEGE: Iowa State.
TRANSACTIONS/CAREER NOTES: Selected by Chicago Cubs organization in fourth round of free-agent draft (June 3, 1997). ... Traded by Cubs to Florida Marlins for P Jesus Sanchez (December 11, 2001).
CAREER HITTING (MLB): 0-for-2 (.000), 0 R, 0 2B, 0 3B, 0 HR, 0 RBI.

Year	League	W	L	Pct.	ERA	G	GS	CG	ShO	Sv.-Opp.	IP	H	R	ER	HR	BB-IBB	SO
1997—	Williamsport (NY-Penn)	3	4	.429	2.57	9	9	0	0	0-...	49.0	55	23	14	0	6-1	37
—	Rockford (Midw.)	0	1	.000	10.13	2	2	0	0	0-...	10.2	18	12	12	1	2-0	6
1998—	Rockford (Midw.)	8	5	.615	3.31	16	16	1	0	0-...	103.1	99	49	38	9	23-0	67
—	Daytona (FSL)	5	3	.625	5.48	11	11	1	0	0-...	65.2	88	48	40	7	19-0	54
1999—	Daytona (FSL)	5	12	.294	6.38	26	26	1	0	0-...	132.2	180	*113	•94	16	41-0	91
2000—	West Tenn (Sou.)	11	6	.647	3.06	27	21	1	1	0-...	138.1	133	53	47	13	44-0	106
2001—	Iowa (PCL)	13	8	.619	5.12	29	•29	0	0	0-...	167.0	184	109	95	28	69-3	125
2002—	Calgary (PCL)■	5	6	.455	5.28	27	19	0	0	0-...	116.0	132	81	68	19	52-2	82
—	Florida (N.L.)	0	1	.000	9.82	2	1	0	0	0-0	7.1	13	8	8	0	3-1	4
Major League totals (1 year)		0	1	.000	9.82	2	1	0	0	0-0	7.1	13	8	8	0	3-1	4

THAMES, MARCUS — OF — YANKEES

PERSONAL: Born March 6, 1977, in Louisville, Miss. ... 6-2/205. ... Bats right, throws right. ... Full name: Marcus Markey Thames.
JUNIOR COLLEGE: East Central (Miss.).
TRANSACTIONS/CAREER NOTES: Selected by New York Yankees organization in 30th round of free-agent draft (June 4, 1996). ... On Columbus disabled list (May 2-18, 2002).

T

STATISTICAL NOTES: Led Gulf Coast League with 113 total bases in 1997. ... Led Eastern League with 311 total bases in 2001. ... Tied for Eastern League lead with eight intentional bases on balls received in 2001. ... Hit home run in first major league at-bat (June 10, 2002).
2002 GAMES PLAYED BY POSITION (MLB): OF—7.

		BATTING														FIELDING	
Year Team (League)	Pos.	G	AB	R	H	2B	3B	HR	RBI	BB	SO	SB-CS	Avg.	OBP	SLG	E	Avg.
1997—GC Yankees (GCL)	OF	57	195	*51	67	*17	4	7	36	16	26	6-4	.344	.394	*.579	2	.978
—Greensboro (S.Atl.)	OF	4	16	2	5	1	0	0	2	0	3	1-0	.313	.313	.375	0	1.000
1998—Tampa (FSL)	OF	122	457	62	130	18	3	11	59	24	78	13-6	.284	.328	.409	9	.970
1999—Norwich (East.)	OF	51	182	25	41	6	2	4	26	22	40	0-1	.225	.316	.346	7	.929
—Tampa (FSL)	OF	69	266	47	65	12	4	11	38	33	58	3-0	.244	.332	.444	3	.974
2000—Norwich (East.)	OF	131	474	72	114	30	2	15	79	50	89	1-5	.241	.313	.407	•9	.959
2001—Norwich (East.)	OF	139	520	*114	167	*43	4	31	97	73	101	10-4	.321	*.410	*.598	8	.973
2002—Columbus (I.L.)	OF	107	386	51	80	21	3	13	45	43	71	5-4	.207	.297	.378	5	.983
—New York (A.L.)	OF	7	13	2	3	1	0	1	2	0	4	0-0	.231	.231	.538	0	1.000
Major League totals (1 year)		7	13	2	3	1	0	1	2	0	4	0-0	.231	.231	.538	0	1.000

THOMAS, FRANK DH/1B

PERSONAL: Born May 27, 1968, in Columbus, Ga. ... 6-5/275. ... Bats right, throws right. ... Full name: Frank Edward Thomas.
HIGH SCHOOL: Columbus (Ga.).
COLLEGE: Auburn.
TRANSACTIONS/CAREER NOTES: Selected by Chicago White Sox organization in first round (seventh pick overall) of free-agent draft (June 5, 1989). ... On disabled list (July 11-30, 1996; June 7-22, 1997; and May 10, 2001-remainder of season). ... Granted free agency (October 31, 2002).
RECORDS: Shares major league single-inning record for most doubles—2 (September 3, 2000, first inning). ... Shares A.L. single-season record for most intentional bases on balls received by righthanded batter—29 (1995).
HONORS: Named first baseman on The Sporting News college All-America team (1989). ... Named designated hitter on The Sporting News A.L. All-Star team (1991). ... Named designated hitter on The Sporting News A.L. Silver Slugger team (1991 and 2000). ... Named Major League Player of the Year by The Sporting News (1993). ... Named first baseman on The Sporting News A.L. All-Star team (1993-94). ... Named first baseman on The Sporting News A.L. Silver Slugger team (1993-94). ... Named A.L. Most Valuable Player by Baseball Writers' Association of America (1993-94). ... Named A.L. Comeback Player of the Year by The Sporting News (2000).
STATISTICAL NOTES: Led A.L. first basemen with 1,428 putouts and 1,533 total chances in 1992. ... Led A.L. with 12 sacrifice flies in 1995. ... Led A.L. with 29 intentional bases on balls received in 1995 and 26 in 1996. ... Hit three home runs in one game (September 15, 1996) ... Had 21-game hitting streak (May 24-June 15, 1999). ... Career major league grand slams: 7.
MISCELLANEOUS: Holds Chicago White Sox all-time records for most home runs (376) and most runs batted in (1,285).
2002 GAMES PLAYED BY POSITION (MLB): DH—140; 1B—4.

		BATTING														FIELDING	
Year Team (League)	Pos.	G	AB	R	H	2B	3B	HR	RBI	BB	SO	SB-CS	Avg.	OBP	SLG	E	Avg.
1989—GC White Sox (GCL)	1B	17	52	8	19	5	0	1	11	10	24	4-0	.365	.462	.519	2	.986
—Sarasota (FSL)	1B	55	188	27	52	9	1	4	30	31	33	0-1	.277	.386	.399	7	.985
1990—Birmingham (Sou.)	1B	109	353	85	114	27	5	18	71	*112	74	7-5	.323	*.487	*.581	14	.987
—Chicago (A.L.)	1B-DH	60	191	39	63	11	3	7	31	44	54	0-1	.330	.454	.529	5	.989
1991—Chicago (A.L.)	DH-1B	158	559	104	178	31	2	32	109	*138	112	1-2	.318	*.453	.553	2	.996
1992—Chicago (A.L.)	1B-DH	160	573	108	185	•46	2	24	115	•122	88	6-3	.323	*.439	.536	13	.992
1993—Chicago (A.L.)	1B-DH	153	549	106	174	36	0	41	128	112	54	4-2	.317	.426	.607	15	.989
1994—Chicago (A.L.)	1B-DH	113	399	*106	141	34	1	38	101	*109	61	2-3	.353	*.487	*.729	7	.991
1995—Chicago (A.L.)	1B-DH	•145	493	102	152	27	0	40	111	*136	74	3-2	.308	.454	.606	7	.991
1996—Chicago (A.L.)	1B	141	527	110	184	26	0	40	134	109	70	1-1	.349	.459	.626	9	.992
1997—Chicago (A.L.)	1B-DH	146	530	110	184	35	0	35	125	109	69	1-1	*.347	*.456	.611	11	.986
1998—Chicago (A.L.)	DH-1B	160	585	109	155	35	2	29	109	110	93	7-0	.265	.381	.480	2	.984
1999—Chicago (A.L.)	DH-1B	135	486	74	148	36	0	15	77	87	66	3-3	.305	.414	.471	4	.990
2000—Chicago (A.L.)	DH-1B	159	582	115	191	44	0	43	143	112	94	1-3	.328	.436	.625	1	.996
2001—Chicago (A.L.)	DH-1B	20	68	8	15	3	0	4	10	10	12	0-0	.221	.316	.441	1	.955
2002—Chicago (A.L.)	DH-1B	148	523	77	132	29	1	28	92	88	115	3-0	.252	.361	.472	2	.955
Major League totals (13 years)		1698	6065	1168	1902	393	11	376	1285	1286	962	32-21	.314	.432	.568	79	.990

DIVISION SERIES RECORD

		BATTING														FIELDING	
Year Team (League)	Pos.	G	AB	R	H	2B	3B	HR	RBI	BB	SO	SB-CS	Avg.	OBP	SLG	E	Avg.
2000—Chicago (A.L.)	DH-1B	3	9	0	0	0	0	0	0	4	0	0-0	.000	.308	.000	0	1.000

CHAMPIONSHIP SERIES RECORD

RECORDS: Shares single-series record for most bases on balls received—10 (1993). ... Shares single-game record for most bases on balls received—4 (October 5, 1993).

		BATTING														FIELDING	
Year Team (League)	Pos.	G	AB	R	H	2B	3B	HR	RBI	BB	SO	SB-CS	Avg.	OBP	SLG	E	Avg.
1993—Chicago (A.L.)	1B-DH	6	17	2	6	0	0	1	3	10	5	0-0	.353	.593	.529	0	1.000

ALL-STAR GAME RECORD

	AB	R	H	2B	3B	HR	RBI	BB	SO	SB-CS	Avg.	OBP	SLG	E	Avg.
All-Star Game totals (3 years)	5	2	4	0	0	1	3	1	0	0-0	.800	.833	1.400	0	1.000

THOME, JIM 1B

PERSONAL: Born August 27, 1970, in Peoria, Ill. ... 6-4/220. ... Bats left, throws right. ... Full name: James Howard Thome. ... Name pronounced TOE-me.
HIGH SCHOOL: Limestone (Bartonville, Ill.).
JUNIOR COLLEGE: Illinois Central College.
TRANSACTIONS/CAREER NOTES: Selected by Cleveland Indians organization in 13th round of free-agent draft (June 5, 1989). ... On Cleveland disabled list (March 28-May 18, 1992); included rehabilitation assignment to Canton/Akron (May 9-18). ... On Cleveland disabled list (May 20-

June 15, 1992); included rehabilitation assignment to Canton/Akron (June 1-15). ... On disabled list (August 8-September 16, 1998). ... Granted free agency (October 28, 2002).

RECORDS: Shares major league single-game record for most strikeouts (nine-inning game)—5 (April 9, 2000).

HONORS: Named International League Most Valuable Player (1993). ... Named third baseman on The Sporting News A.L. All-Star team (1995 and 1996). ... Named third baseman on The Sporting News A.L. Silver Slugger team (1996). ... Named first baseman on The Sporting News A.L. All-Star team (2001).

STATISTICAL NOTES: Hit three home runs in one game (July 22, 1994; and July 6, 2001). ... Had 16-game hitting streak (May 25-June 10, 1998). ... Career major league grand slams: 7.

MISCELLANEOUS: Holds Cleveland Indians all-time record for most home runs (334).

2002 GAMES PLAYED BY POSITION (MLB): 1B—128; DH—18.

		BATTING														FIELDING	
Year Team (League)	**Pos.**	**G**	**AB**	**R**	**H**	**2B**	**3B**	**HR**	**RBI**	**BB**	**SO**	**SB-CS**	**Avg.**	**OBP**	**SLG**	**E**	**Avg.**
1989—GC Indians (GCL)	SS-3B	55	186	22	44	5	3	0	22	21	33	6-4	.237	.314	.296	21	.909
1990—Burlington (Appl.)	3B	34	118	31	44	7	1	12	34	27	18	6-3	.373	.503	.754	11	.907
—Kinston (Caro.)	3B	33	117	19	36	4	1	4	16	24	26	4-1	.308	.427	.462	8	.905
1991—Canton/Akron (East.)	3B	84	294	47	99	20	2	5	45	44	58	8-2	.337	.426	.469	17	.924
—Colo. Springs (PCL)	3B	41	151	20	43	7	3	2	28	12	29	0-0	.285	.331	.411	6	.949
—Cleveland (A.L.)	3B	27	98	7	25	4	2	1	9	5	16	1-1	.255	.298	.367	8	.900
1992—Colo. Springs (PCL)	3B	12	48	11	15	4	1	2	14	6	16	0-0	.313	.400	.563	8	.784
—Cleveland (A.L.)	3B	40	117	8	24	3	1	2	12	10	34	2-0	.205	.275	.299	11	.882
—Canton/Akron (East.)	3B	30	107	16	36	9	2	1	14	24	30	0-2	.336	.462	.486	4	.920
1993—Charlotte (I.L.)	3B-DH	115	410	85	136	21	4	25	*102	76	94	1-3	*.332	*.441	.585	15	.951
—Cleveland (A.L.)	3B	47	154	28	41	11	0	7	22	29	36	2-1	.266	.385	.474	6	.950
1994—Cleveland (A.L.)	3B	98	321	58	86	20	1	20	52	46	84	3-3	.268	.359	.523	15	.940
1995—Cleveland (A.L.)	3B-DH	137	452	92	142	29	3	25	73	97	113	4-3	.314	.438	.558	16	.948
1996—Cleveland (A.L.)	3B-DH	151	505	122	157	28	5	38	116	123	141	2-2	.311	.450	.612	17	.953
1997—Cleveland (A.L.)	1B	147	496	104	142	25	0	40	102	*120	146	1-1	.286	.423	.579	10	.993
1998—Cleveland (A.L.)	1B-DH	123	440	89	129	34	2	30	85	89	141	1-0	.293	.413	.584	10	.991
1999—Cleveland (A.L.)	1B-DH	146	494	101	137	27	2	33	108	*127	*171	0-0	.277	.426	.540	6	.994
2000—Cleveland (A.L.)	1B-DH	158	557	106	150	33	1	37	106	118	171	1-0	.269	.398	.531	5	.995
2001—Cleveland (A.L.)	1B-DH	156	526	101	153	26	1	49	124	111	*185	0-1	.291	.416	.624	10	.992
2002—Cleveland (A.L.)	1B-DH	147	480	101	146	19	2	52	118	*122	139	1-2	.304	.445	*.677	10	.991
Major League totals (12 years)		1377	4640	917	1332	259	20	334	927	997	1377	18-14	.287	.414	.567	124	.985

DIVISION SERIES RECORD

RECORDS: Holds major league career record for most strikeouts—34. ... Shares A.L. career record for most home runs—8. ... Shares single-game records for most home runs—2 (October 11, 1999); and most grand slams—1 (October 7, 1999). ... Shares single-inning record for most runs batted in—4 (October 7, 1999, fourth inning). ... Shares single-game record for most at-bats (nine-inning game)—6 (October 13, 2001).

		BATTING														FIELDING	
Year Team (League)	**Pos.**	**G**	**AB**	**R**	**H**	**2B**	**3B**	**HR**	**RBI**	**BB**	**SO**	**SB-CS**	**Avg.**	**OBP**	**SLG**	**E**	**Avg.**
1995—Cleveland (A.L.)	3B	3	13	1	2	0	0	1	3	1	6	0-0	.154	.214	.385	0	1.000
1996—Cleveland (A.L.)	3B	4	10	1	3	0	0	0	0	1	5	0-0	.300	.417	.300	0	1.000
1997—Cleveland (A.L.)	1B	4	15	1	3	0	0	0	1	0	5	0-0	.200	.200	.200	0	1.000
1998—Cleveland (A.L.)	1B-DH	4	15	2	2	0	0	2	2	2	5	0-0	.133	.235	.533	0	1.000
1999—Cleveland (A.L.)	1B	5	17	7	6	0	0	4	10	4	5	0-0	.353	.476	1.059	0	1.000
2001—Cleveland (A.L.)	1B	5	19	2	3	0	0	1	1	2	8	0-0	.158	.238	.316	0	1.000
Division series totals (6 years)		25	89	14	19	0	0	8	17	10	34	0-0	.213	.300	.483	0	1.000

CHAMPIONSHIP SERIES RECORD

RECORDS: Shares single-game record for most grand slams—1 (October 13, 1998). ... Shares single-inning record for most runs batted in—4 (October 13, 1998, fifth inning). ... Shares A.L. single series record for most home runs—4 (1998).

		BATTING														FIELDING	
Year Team (League)	**Pos.**	**G**	**AB**	**R**	**H**	**2B**	**3B**	**HR**	**RBI**	**BB**	**SO**	**SB-CS**	**Avg.**	**OBP**	**SLG**	**E**	**Avg.**
1995—Cleveland (A.L.)	3B	5	15	2	4	0	0	2	5	2	3	0-0	.267	.353	.667	1	.857
1997—Cleveland (A.L.)	1B-PH	6	14	3	1	0	0	0	0	5	4	0-0	.071	.316	.071	0	1.000
1998—Cleveland (A.L.)	DH-1B	6	23	4	7	0	0	4	8	1	8	0-0	.304	.360	.826	0	1.000
Championship series totals (3 years)		17	52	9	12	0	0	6	13	8	15	0-0	.231	.344	.577	1	.989

WORLD SERIES RECORD

		BATTING														FIELDING	
Year Team (League)	**Pos.**	**G**	**AB**	**R**	**H**	**2B**	**3B**	**HR**	**RBI**	**BB**	**SO**	**SB-CS**	**Avg.**	**OBP**	**SLG**	**E**	**Avg.**
1995—Cleveland (A.L.)	3B-PH	6	19	1	4	1	0	1	2	2	5	0-0	.211	.286	.421	1	.889
1997—Cleveland (A.L.)	1B	7	28	8	8	0	1	2	4	5	7	0-0	.286	.394	.571	1	.984
World Series totals (2 years)		13	47	9	12	1	1	3	6	7	12	0-0	.255	.352	.511	2	.972

ALL-STAR GAME RECORD

	AB	**R**	**H**	**2B**	**3B**	**HR**	**RBI**	**BB**	**SO**	**SB-CS**	**Avg.**	**OBP**	**SLG**	**E**	**Avg.**
All-Star Game totals (3 years)	5	2	1	0	0	0	1	3	1	0-0	.200	.500	.200	0	1.000

THOMPSON, RYAN OF BREWERS

PERSONAL: Born November 4, 1967, in Chestertown, Md. ... 6-3/215. ... Bats right, throws right. ... Full name: Ryan Orlando Thompson.

HIGH SCHOOL: Kent County (Rock Hall, Md.).

TRANSACTIONS/CAREER NOTES: Selected by Toronto Blue Jays organization in 13th round of free-agent draft (June 2, 1987). ... On disabled list (May 29-June 7, 1991). ... On Syracuse disabled list (May 4-11 and July 20-27, 1992). ... Traded by Blue Jays to New York Mets (September 1, 1992), completing deal in which Mets traded P David Cone to Blue Jays for IF Jeff Kent and a player to be named later (August 27, 1992). ... On New York disabled list (April 18-May 30 and July 18-August 18, 1995); included rehabilitation assignments to Norfolk (May 13-30) and Binghamton (August 16-18). ... Traded by Mets with P Reid Cornelius to Cleveland Indians for P Mark Clark (March 30, 1996). ... Granted free agency (December 20, 1996). ... Signed by Kansas City Royals organization (January 16, 1997). ... Released by Royals (March 26, 1997). ... Signed by Indians organization (April 21, 1997). ... Traded by Indians to Toronto Blue Jays for IF Jeff Manto (June 6, 1997). ...

Granted free agency (October 15, 1997). ... Signed to play for Fukuoka Dalei Hawks of Japan Pacific League (1998). ... Signed by Houston Astros organization (January 21, 1999). ... On New Orleans disabled list (August 5-13, 1999). ... Granted free agency (October 20, 1999). ... Signed by New York Yankees organization (December 15, 1999). ... Released by Yankees (April 2, 2000). ... Re-signed by Yankees organization (May 1, 2000). ... Released by Yankees (November 15, 2000). ... Signed by Blue Jays organization (December 13, 2000). ... Released by Blue Jays (April 2, 2001). ... Signed by Florida Marlins organization (April 6, 2001). ... Released by Marlins (August 1, 2001). ... Signed by Montreal Expos organization (August 3, 2001). ... Granted free agency (October 15, 2001). ... Signed by Milwaukee Brewers organization (December 20, 2001).

STATISTICAL NOTES: Tied for New York-Pennsylvania League lead with 11 assists by outfielder in 1989. ... Led American Association outfielders with 317 putouts and 334 total chances in 1996. ... Career major league grand slams: 1.

2002 GAMES PLAYED BY POSITION (MLB): OF—51.

		BATTING														FIELDING	
Year Team (League)	**Pos.**	**G**	**AB**	**R**	**H**	**2B**	**3B**	**HR**	**RBI**	**BB**	**SO**	**SB-CS**	**Avg.**	**OBP**	**SLG**	**E**	**Avg.**
1987—Medicine Hat (Pio.)	OF	40	110	13	27	3	1	1	9	6	34	1-2	.245	.284	.318	4	.935
1988—St. Catharines (NY-P)	OF	23	57	13	10	4	0	0	2	24	21	2-2	.175	.447	.246	4	.882
—Dunedin (FSL)	OF	17	29	2	4	0	0	1	2	2	12	0-0	.138	.219	.241	0	1.000
1989—St. Catharines (NY-P)	OF	74	278	39	76	14	1	6	36	16	60	9-6	.273	.319	.396	5	.961
1990—Dunedin (FSL)	OF	117	438	56	101	15	5	6	37	20	100	18-5	.231	.265	.329	7	.972
1991—Knoxville (Sou.)	OF	114	403	48	97	14	3	8	40	26	88	17-10	.241	.291	.350	4	.983
1992—Syracuse (I.L.)	OF	112	429	74	121	20	7	14	46	43	114	10-4	.282	.351	.459	4	.986
—New York (N.L.)■	OF	30	108	15	24	7	1	3	10	8	24	2-2	.222	.274	.389	1	.988
1993—New York (N.L.)	OF	80	288	34	72	19	2	11	26	19	81	2-7	.250	.302	.444	3	.987
—Norfolk (I.L.)	OF	60	224	39	58	11	2	12	34	24	81	6-3	.259	.341	.487	4	.973
1994—New York (N.L.)	OF	98	334	39	75	14	1	18	59	28	94	1-1	.225	.301	.434	3	.989
1995—Norfolk (I.L.)	OF-DH	15	53	7	18	3	0	2	11	4	15	4-1	.340	.361	.509	0	1.000
—New York (N.L.)	OF	75	267	39	67	13	0	7	31	19	77	3-1	.251	.306	.378	3	.985
—Binghamton (East.)	OF	2	8	2	4	0	0	1	4	1	2	0-0	.500	.556	.875	0	1.000
1996—Buffalo (A.A.)■	OF-DH	•138	*540	79	140	26	4	21	83	21	119	12-5	.259	.294	.439	*9	.973
—Cleveland (A.L.)	OF	8	22	2	7	0	0	1	5	1	6	0-0	.318	.348	.455	0	1.000
1997—Buffalo (A.A.)	OF-DH	24	66	10	16	0	0	1	6	5	16	2-0	.242	.296	.288	1	.955
—Syracuse (I.L.)■	OF-DH	83	330	37	95	23	1	16	58	21	59	4-3	.288	.333	.509	1	.992
1998—Fukuoka (Jp. West.)■		8	23	3	6	1	0	1	6	1	5	0-...	.261	...	.435	...	...
—Fukuoka (Jap. Pac.)		26	107	10	29	7	0	2	16	12	32	1-...	.271	...	.393	...	...
1999—New Orleans (PCL)■	OF-DH	112	404	60	125	23	2	16	58	37	78	4-8	.309	.369	.495	8	.965
—Houston (N.L.)	OF	12	20	2	4	1	0	1	5	2	7	0-0	.200	.273	.400	1	.800
2000—Columbus (I.L.)■	OF	86	326	45	93	23	3	23	75	27	72	10-3	.285	.342	.586	2	.988
—New York (A.L.)	OF	33	50	12	13	3	0	3	14	5	12	0-1	.260	.339	.500	0	1.000
2001—Calgary (PCL)■	OF	78	300	53	93	26	0	19	69	14	65	4-3	.310	.342	.587	9	.948
—Florida (N.L.)	OF	18	31	6	9	5	0	0	2	1	8	0-0	.290	.313	.452	1	.923
—Ottawa (I.L.)■	OF-1B	21	85	6	14	4	0	2	9	3	22	0-2	.165	.202	.282	1	.983
2002—Indianapolis (I.L.)■	OF	70	273	36	80	12	3	12	40	11	46	0-4	.293	.324	.491	2	.984
—Milwaukee (N.L.)	OF	62	137	16	34	9	2	8	24	7	38	1-0	.248	.295	.518	1	.985
American League totals (2 years)		41	72	14	20	3	0	4	19	6	18	0-1	.278	.342	.486	0	1.000
National League totals (7 years)		375	1185	151	285	68	6	48	157	84	329	9-11	.241	.299	.430	13	.985
Major League totals (9 years)		416	1257	165	305	71	6	52	176	90	347	9-12	.243	.301	.433	13	.986

THOMSON, JOHN P METS

PERSONAL: Born October 1, 1973, in Vicksburg, Miss. ... 6-3/190. ... Throws right, bats right. ... Full name: John Carl Thomson.

HIGH SCHOOL: Sulphur (La.).

JUNIOR COLLEGE: Blinn College (Texas).

COLLEGE: McNeese State.

TRANSACTIONS/CAREER NOTES: Selected by Colorado Rockies organization in seventh round of free-agent draft (June 3, 1993). ... On Colorado disabled list (June 16-July 26, 1998); included rehabilitation assignment to Asheville (July 16-22). ... On Colorado Springs disabled list (May 19-July 19, 1999); included rehabilitation assignment to Salem (July 17-19). ... On Colorado disabled list (March 23, 2000-remainder of season); included rehabilitation assignments to Arizona League Rockies (August 16-September 1) and Portland (September 2-4). ... On Colorado disabled list (March 23-May 12 and May 26-August 2, 2001); included rehabilitation assignments to Colorado Springs (April 1-6, April 17-May 12 and June 24-July 23). ... Traded by Rockies with OF Mark Little to New York Mets for OF Jay Payton, P Mark Corey and OF Robert Stratton (July 31, 2002).

STATISTICAL NOTES: Tied for Arizona League lead with 14 wild pitches in 1993.

MISCELLANEOUS: Shares Colorado Rockies all-time record for most shutouts (2).

CAREER HITTING (MLB): 37-for-196 (.189), 14 R, 1 2B, 1 3B, 0 HR, 12 RBI.

Year League	**W**	**L**	**Pct.**	**ERA**	**G**	**GS**	**CG**	**ShO**	**Sv.-Opp.**	**IP**	**H**	**R**	**ER**	**HR**	**BB-IBB**	**SO**
1993—Arizona Rockies (Ariz.)	3	5	.375	4.62	11	11	0	0	0-...	50.2	43	40	26	0	31-0	36
1994—Asheville (S.Atl.)	6	6	.500	2.85	19	15	1	1	0-...	88.1	70	34	28	3	33-1	79
—Central Valley (Calif.)	3	1	.750	3.28	9	8	0	0	0-...	49.1	43	20	18	0	18-1	41
1995—New Haven (East.)	7	8	.467	4.18	26	24	0	0	0-...	131.1	132	69	61	8	56-0	82
1996—New Haven (East.)	9	4	.692	2.86	16	16	1	0	0-...	97.2	82	35	31	8	27-1	86
—Colorado Springs (PCL)	4	7	.364	5.04	11	11	0	0	0-...	69.2	76	45	39	6	26-2	62
1997—Colorado Springs (PCL)	4	2	.667	3.43	7	7	0	0	0-...	42.0	36	18	16	4	14-1	49
—Colorado (N.L.)	7	9	.438	4.71	27	27	2	1	0-0	166.1	193	94	87	15	51-0	106
1998—Colorado (N.L.)	8	11	.421	4.81	26	26	2	0	0-0	161.0	174	86	86	21	49-0	106
—Asheville (S.Atl.)	1	0	1.000	0.00	2	2	0	0	0-...	9.0	5	1	0	0	1-0	12
1999—Colorado (N.L.)	1	10	.091	8.04	14	13	1	0	0-0	62.2	85	62	56	11	36-1	34
—Colorado Springs (PCL)	0	2	.000	9.45	5	5	1	0	0-...	20.0	36	25	21	3	8-0	19
—Salem (Caro.)	0	1	.000	9.00	1	1	0	0	0-...	2.0	4	2	2	0	0-0	2
2000—Arizona Rockies (Ariz.)	0	1	.000	13.50	3	3	0	0	0-...	5.1	8	8	8	0	4-0	7
—Portland (N'West)	0	0	...	2.25	1	1	0	0	0-...	4.0	4	1	1	0	1-0	3
2001—Colorado Springs (PCL)	5	3	.625	3.31	12	12	0	0	0-...	68.0	74	29	25	6	13-0	52
—Colorado (N.L.)	4	5	.444	4.04	14	14	1	1	0-0	93.2	84	46	42	15	25-3	68
2002—Colorado (N.L.)	7	8	.467	4.88	21	21	0	0	0-0	127.1	136	77	69	21	27-6	76
—New York (N.L.)■	2	6	.250	4.31	9	9	0	0	0-0	54.1	65	39	26	7	17-3	31
Major League totals (5 years)	29	49	.372	4.95	111	110	6	2	0-0	665.1	737	404	366	90	205-13	421

THURMAN, COREY — P — BLUE JAYS

PERSONAL: Born November 5, 1978, in Augusta, Ga. ... 6-1/215. ... Throws right, bats right. ... Full name: Corey Lamar Thurman.
HIGH SCHOOL: Texas (Texarkana, Texas).
TRANSACTIONS/CAREER NOTES: Selected by Kansas City Royals organization in fourth round of free-agent draft (June 4, 1996). ... Selected by Toronto Blue Jays from Royals organization in Rule 5 major league draft (December 13, 2001).
CAREER HITTING (MLB): 0-for-1 (.000), 0 R, 0 2B, 0 3B, 0 HR, 0 RBI.

Year League	W	L	Pct.	ERA	G	GS	CG	ShO	Sv.-Opp.	IP	H	R	ER	HR	BB-IBB	SO
1996—Gulf Coast Royals (GCL)	1	6	.143	6.08	11	11	0	0	0-...	47.1	53	32	32	2	28-0	52
1997—Gulf Coast Royals (GCL)	2	1	.667	2.38	8	8	1	0	0-...	34.0	28	12	9	1	22-0	42
—Spokane (N'West)	1	2	.333	5.16	5	5	0	0	0-...	22.2	23	19	13	2	13-0	24
1998—Lansing (Midw.)	5	6	.455	3.61	14	11	0	0	0-...	62.1	47	31	25	6	30-0	61
—Spokane (N'West)	3	3	.500	4.05	12	12	0	0	0-...	60.0	72	35	27	3	31-0	49
1999—Wilmington (Caro.)	8	11	.421	4.88	27	27	0	0	0-...	149.1	160	89	81	11	64-0	131
2000—Wilmington (Caro.)	10	5	.667	2.26	19	19	1	0	0-...	115.2	97	33	29	6	46-0	96
—Wichita (Texas)	4	5	.444	4.83	9	9	0	0	0-...	50.1	46	34	27	10	24-0	47
2001—Wichita (Texas)	13	5	.722	3.37	25	25	0	0	0-...	155.0	117	66	58	16	65-1	148
—Omaha (PCL)	0	0	...	5.40	1	1	0	0	0-...	5.0	6	4	3	0	2-0	4
2002—Toronto (A.L.)■	2	3	.400	4.37	43	1	0	0	0-2	68.0	65	34	33	11	45-2	56
Major League totals (1 year)	2	3	.400	4.37	43	1	0	0	0-2	68.0	65	34	33	11	45-2	56

THURMAN, MIKE — P

PERSONAL: Born July 22, 1973, in Corvallis, Ore. ... 6-5/210. ... Throws right, bats right. ... Full name: Michael Richard Thurman.
HIGH SCHOOL: Philomath (Ore.).
COLLEGE: Oregon State.
TRANSACTIONS/CAREER NOTES: Selected by Montreal Expos organization in supplemental round ("sandwich pick" between first and second round, 31st pick overall) of free-agent draft (June 2, 1994); pick received as compensation for Cleveland Indians signing Type A free-agent P Dennis Martinez. ... On Harrisburg disabled list (June 17-July 5, 1997). ... On Montreal disabled list (March 23-May 12 and May 25-July 21, 2000); included rehabilitation assignments to Jupiter (April 21-May 7) and Ottawa (May 8-9, June 29-July 10 and July 17-19) and Harrisburg (July 11-16). ... On Montreal disabled list (May 24-June 26, 2001); included rehabilitation assignment to Jupiter (June 21-26). ... Granted free agency (December 21, 2001). ... Signed by New York Yankees organization (January 29, 2002). ... Released by Yankees (October 10, 2002).
CAREER HITTING (MLB): 4-for-131 (.031), 6 R, 0 2B, 0 3B, 0 HR, 0 RBI.

Year League	W	L	Pct.	ERA	G	GS	CG	ShO	Sv.-Opp.	IP	H	R	ER	HR	BB-IBB	SO
1994—Vermont (NY-Penn)	0	1	.000	5.40	2	2	0	0	0-...	6.2	6	4	4	1	2-0	3
1995—Albany (S.Atl.)	3	8	.273	5.47	22	22	2	0	0-...	110.1	133	79	67	4	32-0	77
1996—West Palm Beach (FSL)	6	8	.429	3.33	19	19	0	0	0-...	113.2	122	53	42	3	23-0	68
—Harrisburg (East.)	3	1	.750	5.11	4	4	1	0	0-...	24.2	25	14	14	6	5-0	14
1997—Harrisburg (East.)	9	6	.600	3.81	20	20	1	0	0-...	115.2	102	54	49	16	30-0	85
—Ottawa (I.L.)	1	3	.250	5.49	4	4	0	0	0-...	19.2	17	13	12	1	9-0	15
—Montreal (N.L.)	1	0	1.000	5.40	5	2	0	0	0-0	11.2	8	9	7	3	4-0	8
1998—Ottawa (I.L.)	7	7	.500	3.41	19	19	0	0	0-...	105.2	107	50	40	13	49-0	76
—Montreal (N.L.)	4	5	.444	4.70	14	13	0	0	0-0	67.0	60	38	35	7	26-2	32
1999—Montreal (N.L.)	7	11	.389	4.05	29	27	0	0	0-0	146.2	140	84	66	17	52-4	85
2000—Jupiter (FSL)	1	1	.500	2.08	3	3	0	0	0-...	13.0	14	3	3	1	0-0	6
—Ottawa (I.L.)	0	3	.000	7.71	4	4	0	0	0-...	16.1	23	14	14	1	9-0	8
—Montreal (N.L.)	4	9	.308	6.42	17	17	0	0	0-0	88.1	112	69	63	9	46-4	52
—Harrisburg (East.)	0	0	...	4.15	1	0	0	0	0-...	4.1	4	2	2	0	3-0	1
2001—Montreal (N.L.)	9	11	.450	5.33	28	26	0	0	0-0	147.0	172	90	87	21	50-7	96
—Jupiter (FSL)	1	0	1.000	0.00	1	1	1	1	0-...	5.0	2	0	0	0	0-0	3
2002—Columbus (I.L.)■	7	3	.700	3.52	12	12	0	0	0-...	76.2	83	34	30	8	14-0	51
—New York (A.L.)	1	0	1.000	5.18	12	2	0	0	0-1	33.0	45	21	19	2	12-1	23
A.L. totals (1 year)	1	0	1.000	5.18	12	2	0	0	0-1	33.0	45	21	19	2	12-1	23
N.L. totals (5 years)	25	36	.410	5.04	93	85	0	0	0-0	460.2	492	290	258	57	178-17	273
Major League totals (6 years)	26	36	.419	5.05	105	87	0	0	0-1	493.2	537	311	277	59	190-18	296

THURSTON, JOE — 2B — DODGERS

PERSONAL: Born September 29, 1979, in Fairfield, Calif. ... 5-11/175. ... Bats left, throws right. ... Full name: Joseph William Thurston.
HIGH SCHOOL: Vallejo (Calif.).
JUNIOR COLLEGE: Sacramento City College (Calif.).
TRANSACTIONS/CAREER NOTES: Selected by Los Angeles Dodgers organization in fourth round of free-agent draft (June 2, 1999).
STATISTICAL NOTES: Led Northwest League in caught stealing with 18 in 1999. ... Led Northwest League shortstops with 246 assists, 29 errors and 43 double plays in 1999. ... Led California League in caught stealing with 25 in 2000. ... Led California League shortstops with 374 assists in 2000. ... Led Pacific Coast League with 297 total bases in 2002. ... Led Pacific Coast League second basemen with 285 putouts and 682 total chances in 2002.
2002 GAMES PLAYED BY POSITION (MLB): 2B—4.

		BATTING														FIELDING	
Year Team (League)	Pos.	G	AB	R	H	2B	3B	HR	RBI	BB	SO	SB-CS	Avg.	OBP	SLG	E	Avg.
1999—Yakima (N'West)	SS-1B	71	277	48	79	10	3	0	32	27	34	27-17	.285	.387	.343	†29	.899
—San Bern. (Calif.)	SS	2	3	0	0	0	0	0	0	0	1	0-0	.000	.250	.000	0	1.000
2000—San Bern. (Calif.)	SS-2B	•138	551	97	*167	31	8	4	70	56	61	43-25	.303	.380	.410	34	.953
2001—Jacksonville (Sou.)	2B-SS	134	544	80	145	25	7	7	46	48	65	20-18	.267	.338	.377	17	.973
2002—Las Vegas (PCL)	2B-SS	136	*587	*106	*196	39	13	12	55	25	60	22-9	.334	.372	.506	21	.973
—Los Angeles (N.L.)	2B	8	13	1	6	1	0	0	1	0	1	0-0	.462	.429	.538	0	1.000
Major League totals (1 year)		8	13	1	6	1	0	0	1	0	1	0-0	.462	.429	.538	0	1.000

TIMLIN, MIKE P

PERSONAL: Born March 10, 1966, in Midland, Texas. ... 6-4/210. ... Throws right, bats right. ... Full name: Michael August Timlin.

HIGH SCHOOL: Midland (Texas).

COLLEGE: Southwestern University (Texas).

TRANSACTIONS/CAREER NOTES: Selected by Toronto Blue Jays organization in fifth round of free-agent draft (June 2, 1987). ... On disabled list (April 4-May 2, 1989 and August 2-17, 1991). ... On Toronto disabled list (March 27-June 12, 1992); included rehabilitation assignments to Dunedin (April 11-15 and May 24-June 5) and Syracuse (June 5-12). ... On disabled list (May 25-June 9, 1994). ... On Toronto disabled list (June 22-August 18, 1995); included rehabilitation assignment to Syracuse (July 31-August 18). ... Traded by Blue Jays with P Paul Spoljaric to Seattle Mariners for OF Jose Cruz Jr. (July 31, 1997). ... Granted free agency (October 22, 1998). ... Signed by Baltimore Orioles (November 16, 1998). ... On Baltimore disabled list (April 2-17, 2000). ... Traded by Orioles with cash to St. Louis Cardinals for 1B Chris Richard and P Mark Nussbeck (July 29, 2000). ... On disabled list (July 26-August 17, 2001). ... Traded by Cardinals with IF/OF Placido Polanco and P Bud Smith to Philadelphia Phillies for 3B Scott Rolen and P Doug Nickle (July 29, 2002). ... Granted free agency (October 28, 2002).

STATISTICAL NOTES: Led South Atlantic League with 19 hit batsmen in 1988.

CAREER HITTING (MLB): 0-for-7 (.000), 0 R, 0 2B, 0 3B, 0 HR, 0 RBI.

Year League	W	L	Pct.	ERA	G	GS	CG	ShO	Sv.-Opp.	IP	H	R	ER	HR	BB-IBB	SO
1987— Medicine Hat (Pio.)	4	8	.333	5.14	13	12	2	0	0-...	75.1	79	50	43	4	26-0	66
1988— Myrtle Beach (S.Atl.)	10	6	.625	2.86	35	22	0	0	0-...	151.0	119	68	48	4	77-2	106
1989— Dunedin (FSL)	5	8	.385	3.25	33	7	1	0	7-...	88.2	90	44	32	2	36-2	64
1990— Dunedin (FSL)	7	2	.778	1.43	42	0	0	0	22-...	50.1	36	11	8	0	16-2	46
— Knoxville (Sou.)	1	2	.333	1.73	17	0	0	0	8-...	26.0	20	6	5	0	7-1	21
1991— Toronto (A.L.)	11	6	.647	3.16	63	3	0	0	3-8	108.1	94	43	38	6	50-11	85
1992— Dunedin (FSL)	0	0	...	0.90	6	1	0	0	1-...	10.0	9	2	1	0	2-0	7
— Syracuse (I.L.)	0	1	.000	8.74	7	1	0	0	3-...	11.1	15	11	11	3	5-1	7
— Toronto (A.L.)	0	2	.000	4.12	26	0	0	0	1-1	43.2	45	23	20	0	20-5	35
1993— Toronto (A.L.)	4	2	.667	4.69	54	0	0	0	1-4	55.2	63	32	29	7	27-3	49
— Dunedin (FSL)	0	0	...	1.00	4	0	0	0	1-...	9.0	4	1	1	0	0-0	8
1994— Toronto (A.L.)	0	1	.000	5.18	34	0	0	0	2-4	40.0	41	25	23	5	20-0	38
1995— Toronto (A.L.)	4	3	.571	2.14	31	0	0	0	5-9	42.0	38	13	10	1	17-5	36
— Syracuse (I.L.)	1	1	.500	1.04	8	0	0	0	0-...	17.1	13	6	2	2	4-0	13
1996— Toronto (A.L.)	1	6	.143	3.65	59	0	0	0	31-38	56.2	47	25	23	4	18-4	52
1997— Toronto (A.L.)	3	2	.600	2.87	38	0	0	0	9-13	47.0	41	17	15	6	15-4	36
— Seattle (A.L.)■	3	2	.600	3.86	26	0	0	0	1-5	25.2	28	13	11	2	5-1	9
1998— Seattle (A.L.)	3	3	.500	2.95	70	0	0	0	19-24	79.1	78	26	26	5	16-2	60
1999— Baltimore (A.L.)■	3	9	.250	3.57	62	0	0	0	27-36	63.0	51	30	25	9	23-3	50
2000— Baltimore (A.L.)	2	3	.400	4.89	37	0	0	0	11-15	35.0	37	22	19	6	15-3	26
— St. Louis (N.L.)■	3	1	.750	3.34	25	0	0	0	1-3	29.2	30	11	11	2	20-3	26
2001— St. Louis (N.L.)	4	5	.444	4.09	67	0	0	0	3-7	72.2	78	35	33	6	19-4	47
2002— St. Louis (N.L.)	1	3	.250	2.51	42	1	0	0	0-2	61.0	48	19	17	9	7-2	35
— Philadelphia (N.L.)■	3	3	.500	3.79	30	0	0	0	0-2	35.2	27	16	15	6	7-0	15
A.L. totals (10 years)	34	39	.466	3.61	500	3	0	0	110-157	596.1	563	269	239	51	226-41	476
N.L. totals (3 years)	11	12	.478	3.44	164	1	0	0	4-14	199.0	183	81	76	23	53-9	123
Major League totals (12 years)	45	51	.469	3.56	664	4	0	0	114-171	795.1	746	350	315	74	279-50	599

DIVISION SERIES RECORD

Year League	W	L	Pct.	ERA	G	GS	CG	ShO	Sv.-Opp.	IP	H	R	ER	HR	BB-IBB	SO
1997— Seattle (A.L.)	0	0	...	54.00	1	0	0	0	0-0	.2	3	4	4	1	1-1	1
2000— St. Louis (N.L.)	0	0	...	10.80	2	0	0	0	0-0	1.2	5	2	2	1	1-0	2
2001— St. Louis (N.L.)	0	0	...	0.00	1	0	0	0	0-0	1.1	1	0	0	0	0-0	0
Division series totals (3 years)	0	0	...	14.73	4	0	0	0	0-0	3.2	9	6	6	2	2-1	3

CHAMPIONSHIP SERIES RECORD

Year League	W	L	Pct.	ERA	G	GS	CG	ShO	Sv.-Opp.	IP	H	R	ER	HR	BB-IBB	SO
1991— Toronto (A.L.)	0	1	.000	3.18	4	0	0	0	0-1	5.2	5	4	2	1	2-1	5
1992— Toronto (A.L.)	0	0	...	6.75	2	0	0	0	0-0	1.1	4	1	1	0	0-0	1
1993— Toronto (A.L.)	0	0	...	3.86	1	0	0	0	0-0	2.1	3	1	1	0	0-0	2
2000— St. Louis (N.L.)	0	1	.000	0.00	3	0	0	0	0-0	3.1	1	3	0	0	2-0	0
Champ. series totals (4 years)	0	2	.000	2.84	10	0	0	0	0-1	12.2	13	9	4	1	4-1	8

WORLD SERIES RECORD

NOTES: Member of World Series championship team (1992 and 1993).

Year League	W	L	Pct.	ERA	G	GS	CG	ShO	Sv.-Opp.	IP	H	R	ER	HR	BB-IBB	SO
1992— Toronto (A.L.)	0	0	...	0.00	2	0	0	0	1-1	1.1	0	0	0	0	0-0	0
1993— Toronto (A.L.)	0	0	...	0.00	2	0	0	0	0-0	2.1	2	0	0	0	0-0	4
World Series totals (2 years)	0	0	...	0.00	4	0	0	0	1-1	3.2	2	0	0	0	0-0	4

TOLLBERG, BRIAN P PADRES

PERSONAL: Born September 16, 1972, in Tampa. ... 6-3/195. ... Throws right, bats right. ... Full name: Brian Patrick Tollberg.

HIGH SCHOOL: Manatee (Bradenton, Fla.).

COLLEGE: North Florida.

TRANSACTIONS/CAREER NOTES: Signed by Chillicothe, Frontier League (1994). ... Signed as non-drafted free agent by Milwaukee Brewers organization (January 31, 1995). ... Traded by Brewers to San Diego Padres for 3B Antonio Fernandez (March 13, 1997). ... On Las Vegas disabled list (May 6, 1999-remainder of season). ... On San Diego disabled list (May 7-July 16, 2001); included rehabilitation assignments to Lake Elsinore (July 2-6 and July 11-16) and Portland (June 27-July 1 and July 7-10). ... On disabled list (May 30, 2002-remainder of season).

CAREER HITTING (MLB): 14-for-91 (.154), 5 R, 1 2B, 0 3B, 0 HR, 2 RBI.

Year League	W	L	Pct.	ERA	G	GS	CG	ShO	Sv.-Opp.	IP	H	R	ER	HR	BB-IBB	SO
1994— Chillicothe (Fron.)	7	4	.636	2.85	13	13	4	0	0-...	94.2	90	34	30	5	27-2	69
1995— Beloit (Midw.)■	13	4	.765	3.41	22	22	1	1	0-...	132.0	119	59	50	10	27-0	110
1996— El Paso (Texas)	7	5	.583	4.90	26	26	0	0	0-...	154.1	183	90	84	15	23-0	109
1997— Mobile (Sou.)■	6	3	.667	3.72	31	13	1	0	0-...	123.1	123	60	51	15	24-2	108

Year	League	W	L	Pct.	ERA	G	GS	CG	ShO	Sv.-Opp.	IP	H	R	ER	HR	BB-IBB	SO
1998—	Mobile (Sou.)	3	2	.600	2.41	6	6	1	0	0-...	41.0	31	11	11	3	4-0	45
—	Las Vegas (PCL)	6	6	.500	6.38	33	15	1	0	3-...	110.0	138	85	78	21	27-2	109
1999—	Las Vegas (PCL)	1	2	.333	4.85	5	5	0	0	0-...	29.2	34	17	16	3	6-0	23
—	Arizona Padres (Ariz.)	0	0	...	4.50	2	2	0	0	0-...	4.0	4	2	2	0	0-0	6
2000—	Las Vegas (PCL)	6	0	1.000	2.83	13	13	0	0	0-...	76.1	72	28	24	5	11-0	60
—	San Diego (N.L.)	4	5	.444	3.58	19	19	1	0	0-0	118.0	126	58	47	13	35-4	76
2001—	San Diego (N.L.)	10	4	.714	4.30	19	19	0	0	0-0	117.1	133	58	56	15	25-3	71
—	Portland (PCL)	1	0	1.000	4.50	4	4	0	0	0-...	20.0	24	11	10	3	4-0	10
—	Lake Elsinore (Calif.)	0	2	.000	6.30	2	2	0	0	0-...	10.0	18	11	7	1	1-0	9
2002—	San Diego (N.L.)	1	5	.167	6.13	12	11	0	0	0-0	61.2	88	47	42	11	19-2	33
Major League totals (3 years)		15	14	.517	4.39	50	49	1	0	0-0	297.0	347	163	145	39	79-9	180

TOMKO, BRETT — P — PADRES

PERSONAL: Born April 7, 1973, in San Diego. ... 6-4/215. ... Throws right, bats right. ... Full name: Brett Daniel Tomko.
HIGH SCHOOL: El Dorado (Placentia, Calif.).
JUNIOR COLLEGE: Mount San Antonio College (Calif.).
COLLEGE: Florida Southern.
TRANSACTIONS/CAREER NOTES: Selected by Los Angeles Dodgers organization in 20th round of free-agent draft (June 2, 1994); did not sign. ... Selected by Cincinnati Reds organization in second round of free-agent draft (June 1, 1995). ... Traded by Reds with OF Mike Cameron, IF Antonio Perez and P Jake Meyer to Seattle Mariners for OF Ken Griffey Jr. (February 10, 2000). ... On disabled list (June 7-24, 2000). ... Traded by Mariners with C Tom Lampkin and SS Ramon Vazquez to San Diego Padres for C Ben Davis, P Wascar Serrano and SS Alex Arias (December 11, 2001).
RECORDS: Shares N.L. single-inning record for most consecutive home runs allowed—3 (April 28, 1999, first inning).
MISCELLANEOUS: Appeared in two games as pinch runner (1997). ... Appeared in one game as pinch runner and struck out in only appearance as pinch hitter (1998).
CAREER HITTING (MLB): 34-for-214 (.159), 11 R, 6 2B, 0 3B, 0 HR, 14 RBI.

Year	League	W	L	Pct.	ERA	G	GS	CG	ShO	Sv.-Opp.	IP	H	R	ER	HR	BB-IBB	SO
1995—	Charleston, W.Va. (S.Atl.)	4	2	.667	1.84	9	7	0	0	0-...	49.0	41	12	10	1	9-1	46
1996—	Chattanooga (Sou.)	11	7	.611	3.88	27	27	0	0	0-...	157.2	131	73	68	20	54-4	164
1997—	Indianapolis (A.A.)	6	3	.667	2.95	10	10	0	0	0-...	61.0	53	21	20	7	9-0	60
—	Cincinnati (N.L.)	11	7	.611	3.43	22	19	0	0	0-0	126.0	106	50	48	14	47-4	95
1998—	Cincinnati (N.L.)	13	12	.520	4.44	34	34	1	0	0-0	210.2	198	111	104	22	64-3	162
1999—	Cincinnati (N.L.)	5	7	.417	4.92	33	26	1	0	0-0	172.0	175	103	94	31	60-10	132
—	Indianapolis (I.L.)	2	0	1.000	4.97	2	2	0	0	0-...	12.2	15	7	7	1	1-0	9
2000—	Tacoma (PCL)■	1	0	1.000	2.84	2	2	0	0	0-...	12.2	13	4	4	1	5-1	8
—	Seattle (A.L.)	7	5	.583	4.68	32	8	0	0	1-2	92.1	92	53	48	12	40-4	59
2001—	Seattle (A.L.)	3	1	.750	5.19	11	4	0	0	0-1	34.2	42	24	20	9	15-2	22
—	Tacoma (PCL)	10	6	.625	4.04	19	18	3	•2	0-...	127.0	124	64	57	12	25-1	117
2002—	San Diego (N.L.)■	10	10	.500	4.49	32	32	3	0	0-0	204.1	212	107	102	31	60-9	126
A.L. totals (2 years)		10	6	.625	4.82	43	12	0	0	1-3	127.0	134	77	68	21	55-6	81
N.L. totals (4 years)		39	36	.520	4.39	121	111	5	0	0-0	713.0	691	371	348	98	231-26	515
Major League totals (6 years)		49	42	.538	4.46	164	123	5	0	1-3	840.0	825	448	416	119	286-32	596

DIVISION SERIES RECORD

Year	League	W	L	Pct.	ERA	G	GS	CG	ShO	Sv.-Opp.	IP	H	R	ER	HR	BB-IBB	SO
2000—	Seattle (A.L.)	0	0	...	0.00	1	0	0	0	0-0	2.2	1	0	0	0	1-0	0

CHAMPIONSHIP SERIES RECORD

Year	League	W	L	Pct.	ERA	G	GS	CG	ShO	Sv.-Opp.	IP	H	R	ER	HR	BB-IBB	SO
2000—	Seattle (A.L.)	0	0	...	7.20	2	0	0	0	0-0	5.0	3	4	4	0	4-1	4

TORCATO, TONY — OF — GIANTS

PERSONAL: Born October 25, 1979, in Woodland, Calif. ... 6-1/195. ... Bats left, throws right. ... Full name: Anthony Dale Torcato.
HIGH SCHOOL: Woodland (Calif.).
TRANSACTIONS/CAREER NOTES: Selected by San Francisco Giants organization in first round (19th pick overall) of free-agent draft (June 2, 1998); pick received from Houston Astros as part of compensation for signing Type B free agent P Doug Henry.
STATISTICAL NOTES: Led California League with eight intentional bases on balls received in 2000. ... Led California League third basemen with 24 double plays in 2000.
2002 GAMES PLAYED BY POSITION (MLB): OF—3.

			BATTING													FIELDING	
Year	Team (League)	Pos.	G	AB	R	H	2B	3B	HR	RBI	BB	SO	SB-CS	Avg.	OBP	SLG	E	Avg.
1998—	Salem-Kaizer (NW)	3B	59	220	31	64	15	2	3	43	14	38	4-2	.291	.333	.418	17	.886
1999—	Bakersfield (Calif.)	3B	110	422	50	123	25	0	4	58	30	67	2-1	.291	.338	.379	28	.886
2000—	San Jose (Calif.)	3B	119	490	77	159	37	2	7	88	41	62	19-4	.324	.379	.451	40	.882
—	Shreveport (Texas)	3B	2	8	1	4	0	0	0	2	0	1	0-0	.500	.500	.500	0	1.000
2001—	San Jose (Calif.)	OF	67	258	38	88	21	2	2	47	17	40	9-3	.341	.381	.461	1	.952
—	Shreveport (Texas)	OF	36	147	13	43	9	1	1	23	9	15	0-1	.293	.344	.388	2	.975
—	Fresno (PCL)	OF	35	150	20	48	8	1	2	8	2	20	0-1	.320	.329	.427	1	.985
2002—	Fresno (PCL)	OF	130	490	64	142	23	3	13	64	29	65	4-6	.290	.330	.429	8	.964
—	San Francisco (N.L.)	OF	5	11	0	3	1	0	0	0	0	2	0-0	.273	.273	.364	0	1.000
Major League totals (1 year)			5	11	0	3	1	0	0	0	0	2	0-0	.273	.273	.364	0	1.000

TORREALBA, STEVE — C

PERSONAL: Born February 24, 1978, in Barquisimeto, Venezuela. ... 6-0/175. ... Bats right, throws right. ... Full name: Steve Alexander Torrealba.
HIGH SCHOOL: Mario Bricamo Iragorri (Barquisimeto, Venezuela).

T

TRANSACTIONS/CAREER NOTES: Signed as non-drafted free agent by Atlanta Braves organization (March 1, 1995). ... On Greenville disabled list (April 13-May 10, 2001). ... Granted free agency (October 15, 2002).
STATISTICAL NOTES: Led Appalachian League catchers with 398 putouts and 457 total chances in 1997. ... Led Carolina League catchers with 723 putouts and 815 total chances in 2000.
2002 GAMES PLAYED BY POSITION (MLB): C—12.

			BATTING													FIELDING	
Year	Team (League)	Pos.	G	AB	R	H	2B	3B	HR	RBI	BB	SO	SB-CS	Avg.	OBP	SLG	E	Avg.
1995—	GC Braves (GCL)	C	30	92	3	19	4	0	0	10	11	20	0-0	.207	.302	.250	4	.982
1996—	GC Braves (GCL)	C-1B-OF	52	146	9	25	2	0	0	7	16	19	1-2	.171	.262	.185	4	.987
—	Danville (Appl.)	C	2	5	1	1	0	0	0	0	0	2	0-1	.200	.200	.200	1	.917
1997—	Danville (Appl.)	C	44	150	17	34	9	0	2	18	15	27	0-1	.227	.302	.327	*18	.961
1998—	Macon (S.Atl.)	C-3B	67	209	28	57	10	0	10	37	20	31	3-0	.273	.336	.464	7	.988
1999—	Myrtle Beach (Caro.)	C	52	175	23	37	9	0	6	23	13	47	1-0	.211	.274	.366	10	.978
2000—	Myrtle Beach (Caro.)	C	99	334	43	90	16	0	7	35	31	79	5-1	.269	.328	.380	10	.988
2001—	Greenville (Sou.)	C	90	295	37	80	21	0	8	34	33	54	0-0	.271	.347	.424	*14	.979
—	Atlanta (N.L.)	C	2	2	0	1	0	0	0	0	0	0	0-0	.500	.500	.500	0	1.000
2002—	Richmond (I.L.)	C	61	191	19	45	11	0	3	18	19	31	0-0	.236	.313	.340	9	.979
—	Atlanta (N.L.)	C	13	17	1	1	0	0	0	1	3	4	0-0	.059	.200	.059	0	1.000
Major League totals (2 years)			15	19	1	2	0	0	0	1	3	4	0-0	.105	.227	.105	0	1.000

DIVISION SERIES RECORD

			BATTING													FIELDING	
Year	Team (League)	Pos.	G	AB	R	H	2B	3B	HR	RBI	BB	SO	SB-CS	Avg.	OBP	SLG	E	Avg.
2001—	Atlanta (N.L.)	C	1	1	0	1	1	0	0	0	0	0	0-0	1.000	1.000	2.000	0	1.000

CHAMPIONSHIP SERIES RECORD

			BATTING													FIELDING	
Year	Team (League)	Pos.	G	AB	R	H	2B	3B	HR	RBI	BB	SO	SB-CS	Avg.	OBP	SLG	E	Avg.
2001—	Atlanta (N.L.)								Did not play.									

TORREALBA, YORVIT — C — GIANTS

PERSONAL: Born July 19, 1978, in Caracas, Venezuela. ... 5-11/180. ... Bats right, throws right. ... Full name: Yorvit Adolfo Torrealba.
HIGH SCHOOL: Vincente Emilio Sojo (Venezuela).
COLLEGE: Alberto Sequin Vera (Venezuela).
TRANSACTIONS/CAREER NOTES: Signed as non-drafted free agent by San Francisco Giants organization (September 14, 1994).
STATISTICAL NOTES: Led California League catchers with 119 assists and 10 double plays in 1997. ... Led Pacific Coast League catchers with 779 putouts, 62 assists and 850 total chances in 2001.
2002 GAMES PLAYED BY POSITION (MLB): C—53.

			BATTING													FIELDING	
Year	Team (League)	Pos.	G	AB	R	H	2B	3B	HR	RBI	BB	SO	SB-CS	Avg.	OBP	SLG	E	Avg.
1995—	Bellingham (N'West)	C	26	71	2	11	3	0	0	8	2	14	0-1	.155	.187	.197	5	.973
1996—	San Jose (Calif.)	C	2	5	0	0	0	0	0	0	1	1	0-0	.000	.167	.000	0	1.000
—	Burlington (Midw.)	C	1	4	0	0	0	0	0	0	0	1	0-0	.000	.000	.000	0	1.000
—	Bellingham (N'West)	C	48	150	23	40	4	0	1	10	9	27	4-1	.267	.304	.313	2	.994
1997—	Bakersfield (Calif.)	C	119	446	52	122	15	3	4	40	31	58	4-2	.274	.326	.348	6	.993
1998—	Shreveport (Texas)	C	59	196	18	46	7	0	0	13	18	30	0-5	.235	.311	.270	2	.996
—	San Jose (Calif.)	C	21	70	10	20	2	0	0	10	1	6	2-2	.286	.292	.314	2	.989
—	Fresno (PCL)	C	4	11	1	2	1	0	0	1	1	4	0-0	.182	.250	.273	0	1.000
1999—	Shreveport (Texas)	C-DH	65	217	25	53	10	1	4	19	9	34	0-2	.244	.278	.355	2	.994
—	Fresno (PCL)	C	17	63	9	16	2	0	2	10	4	11	0-1	.254	.319	.381	2	.988
—	San Jose (Calif.)	C	19	73	10	23	3	0	2	14	6	15	0-0	.315	.370	.438	5	.975
2000—	Shreveport (Texas)	C	108	398	50	114	21	1	4	32	34	55	2-3	.286	.350	.374	8	.990
2001—	Fresno (PCL)	C	115	394	56	108	23	3	8	36	19	65	2-3	.274	.313	.409	9	.989
—	San Francisco (N.L.)	C	3	4	0	2	0	1	0	2	0	0	0-0	.500	.500	1.000	0	1.000
2002—	San Francisco (N.L.)	C	53	136	17	38	10	0	2	14	14	20	0-0	.279	.355	.397	2	.993
Major League totals (2 years)			56	140	17	40	10	1	2	16	14	20	0-0	.286	.359	.414	2	.993

TORRES, ANDRES — OF — TIGERS

PERSONAL: Born January 26, 1978, in Aguada, Puerto Rico. ... 5-10/175. ... Bats both, throws right.
JUNIOR COLLEGE: Miami-Dade North.
TRANSACTIONS/CAREER NOTES: Selected by Florida Marlins organization in 23rd round of free-agent draft (June 3, 1997); did not sign. ... Selected by Detroit Tigers organization in fourth round of free-agent draft (June 2, 1998). ... On disabled list (July 2, 2001-remainder of season).
STATISTICAL NOTES: Led Florida State League outfielders with 18 assists in 2000.
2002 GAMES PLAYED BY POSITION (MLB): OF—19.

			BATTING													FIELDING	
Year	Team (League)	Pos.	G	AB	R	H	2B	3B	HR	RBI	BB	SO	SB-CS	Avg.	OBP	SLG	E	Avg.
1998—	Jamestown (NY-P)	OF	48	192	28	45	2	6	1	21	25	50	13-2	.234	.323	.323	5	.944
1999—	West Mich. (Midw.)	OF	117	407	72	96	20	5	2	34	92	116	39-18	.236	.385	.324	7	.972
2000—	Lakeland (FSL)	OF	108	398	82	118	11	11	3	33	63	82	65-16	.296	.399	.402	6	.979
—	Jacksonville (Sou.)	OF	14	54	3	8	0	0	0	0	5	14	2-0	.148	.220	.148	1	.971
2001—	Erie (East.)	OF	64	252	54	74	16	3	1	23	36	50	19-11	.294	.391	.393	1	.993
2002—	Toledo (I.L.)	OF	115	462	80	123	17	8	4	42	53	116	•42-12	.266	.345	.364	10	.967
—	Detroit (A.L.)	OF	19	70	7	14	1	1	0	3	6	16	2-2	.200	.266	.243	1	.981
Major League totals (1 year)			19	70	7	14	1	1	0	3	6	16	2-2	.200	.266	.243	1	.981

TORRES, SALOMON — P — PIRATES

PERSONAL: Born March 11, 1972, in San Pedro de Macoris, Dominican Republic. ... 5-11/165. ... Throws right, bats right. ... Full name: Salomon Ramirez Torres.

HIGH SCHOOL: Centro Academico Rogus (San Pedro de Macoris, Dominican Republic).

TRANSACTIONS/CAREER NOTES: Signed as non-drafted free agent by San Francisco Giants organization (September 15, 1989). ... Traded by Giants to Seattle Mariners for P Shawn Estes and IF Wilson Delgado (May 21, 1995). ... Claimed on waivers by Montreal Expos (April 18, 1997). ... On voluntarily retired list (August 1, 1997-January 29, 2001). ... Released by Expos (January 29, 2001). ... Signed by Samsung, Korean League (2001). ... Signed by Pittsburgh Pirates organization (January 8, 2002). ... On Nashville disabled list (July 2-15, 2002).

HONORS: Named Midwest League Most Valuable Player (1991).

CAREER HITTING (MLB): 9-for-59 (.153), 2 R, 0 2B, 0 3B, 0 HR, 0 RBI.

Year League	W	L	Pct.	ERA	G	GS	CG	ShO	Sv.-Opp.	IP	H	R	ER	HR	BB-IBB	SO
1990—San Pedro (DSL)	11	1	.917	0.50	13	13	6	0	0-...	90.0	44	15	5	...	30-...	101
1991—Clinton (Midw.)	•16	5	.762	*1.41	28	28	*8	3	0-...	*210.1	148	48	33	4	47-2	*214
1992—Shreveport (Texas)	6	10	.375	4.21	25	25	4	2	0-...	162.1	167	93	76	10	34-2	151
1993—Shreveport (Texas)	7	4	.636	2.70	12	12	2	1	0-...	83.1	67	27	25	6	12-0	67
—Phoenix (PCL)	7	4	.636	3.50	14	14	•4	1	0-...	105.1	105	43	41	5	27-0	99
—San Francisco (N.L.)	3	5	.375	4.03	8	8	0	0	0-0	44.2	37	21	20	5	27-3	23
1994—San Francisco (N.L.)	2	8	.200	5.44	16	14	1	0	0-0	84.1	95	55	51	10	34-2	42
—Phoenix (PCL)	5	6	.455	4.22	13	13	0	0	0-...	79.0	85	49	37	7	31-0	64
1995—San Francisco (N.L.)	0	1	.000	9.00	4	1	0	0	0-0	8.0	13	8	8	4	7-0	2
—Phoenix (PCL)	0	0	...	0.00	1	0	0	0	0-...	2.0	2	0	0	0	0-0	5
—Tacoma (PCL)■	1	1	.500	3.21	5	4	0	0	0-...	28.0	20	10	10	2	13-1	19
—Seattle (A.L.)	3	8	.273	6.00	16	13	1	0	0-0	72.0	87	53	48	12	42-3	45
1996—Tacoma (PCL)	7	10	.412	5.29	22	21	3	1	0-...	134.1	150	87	79	16	52-1	121
—Seattle (A.L.)	3	3	.500	4.59	10	7	1	1	0-0	49.0	44	27	25	5	23-2	36
1997—Seattle (A.L.)	0	0	...	27.00	2	0	0	0	0-0	3.1	7	10	10	0	3-0	0
—Montreal (N.L.)■	0	0	...	7.25	12	0	0	0	0-0	22.1	25	19	18	2	12-0	11
—Ottawa (I.L.)	0	0	...	5.40	2	1	0	0	0-...	5.0	7	5	3	0	2-0	2
1998—									Did not play.							
1999—									Did not play.							
2000—									Did not play.							
2001—Samsung (Korean)■	0	2	.000	32.40	2	...	...	...	0-...	5.0	...	...	...	...	10-...	5
2002—Nashville (PCL)	8	5	.615	3.83	26	24	2	1	0-...	162.1	169	78	69	12	39-2	136
—Pittsburgh (N.L.)	2	1	.667	2.70	5	5	0	0	0-0	30.0	28	10	9	2	13-1	12
A.L. totals (3 years)	6	11	.353	6.01	28	20	2	1	0-0	124.1	138	90	83	17	68-5	81
N.L. totals (5 years)	7	15	.318	5.04	45	28	1	0	0-0	189.1	198	113	106	23	93-6	90
Major League totals (6 years)	13	26	.333	5.42	73	48	3	1	0-0	313.2	336	203	189	40	161-11	171

TOWERS, JOSH — P — BLUE JAYS

PERSONAL: Born February 26, 1977, in Port Hueneme, Calif. ... 6-1/165. ... Throws right, bats right. ... Full name: Joshua Eric Towers. ... Nephew of Roger Frash, infielder/outfielder with New York Mets organization (1980-82).

HIGH SCHOOL: Hueneme (Oxnard, Calif.).

JUNIOR COLLEGE: Oxnard (Calif.) College.

TRANSACTIONS/CAREER NOTES: Selected by Baltimore Orioles organization in 15th round of free-agent draft (June 4, 1996). ... On Rochester disabled list (May 30-June 13 and August 5-24, 2000). ... On disabled list (October 1, 2001-remainder of season). ... On Rochester disabled list (June 12-July 5 and August 18-30, 2002). ... Granted free agency (October 15, 2002). ... Signed by Toronto Blue Jays organization (November 8, 2002).

STATISTICAL NOTES: Tied Carolina League lead in sacrifice hits allowed with 12 in 1996.

CAREER HITTING (MLB): 0-for-2 (.000), 0 R, 0 2B, 0 3B, 0 HR, 0 RBI.

Year League	W	L	Pct.	ERA	G	GS	CG	ShO	Sv.-Opp.	IP	H	R	ER	HR	BB-IBB	SO
1996—Bluefield (Appl.)	4	1	.800	5.24	14	9	0	0	0-...	55.0	63	35	32	9	5-0	61
1997—Delmarva (S.Atl.)	0	0	...	3.44	9	1	0	0	1-...	18.1	18	8	7	1	2-0	16
—Frederick (Caro.)	6	2	.750	4.86	25	3	0	0	1-...	53.2	74	36	29	4	18-0	64
1998—Frederick (Caro.)	8	7	.533	3.34	25	20	3	0	1-...	145.1	137	58	54	11	9-0	122
—Bowie (East.)	2	1	.667	3.50	5	2	0	0	0-...	18.0	20	9	7	1	4-0	7
1999—Bowie (East.)	12	7	.632	3.76	29	•28	5	•2	0-...	*189.0	*204	86	79	*26	26-1	106
2000—Rochester (I.L.)	8	6	.571	3.47	24	24	5	1	0-...	148.0	157	63	57	17	21-0	102
2001—Rochester (I.L.)	3	1	.750	3.51	6	6	1	1	0-...	41.0	40	18	16	2	8-2	27
—Baltimore (A.L.)	8	10	.444	4.49	24	20	1	1	0-0	140.1	165	74	70	21	16-0	58
2002—Baltimore (A.L.)	0	3	.000	7.90	5	3	0	0	0-0	27.1	42	24	24	11	5-0	13
—Rochester (I.L.)	0	9	.000	7.57	15	13	1	0	0-...	69.0	109	65	58	16	14-0	43
Major League totals (2 years)	8	13	.381	5.05	29	23	1	1	0-0	167.2	207	98	94	32	21-0	71

TRACHSEL, STEVE — P

PERSONAL: Born October 31, 1970, in Oxnard, Calif. ... 6-4/205. ... Throws right, bats right. ... Full name: Stephen Christopher Trachsel. ... Name pronounced TRACK-sul.

HIGH SCHOOL: Troy (Fullerton, Calif.).

JUNIOR COLLEGE: Fullerton (Calif.) College.

COLLEGE: Long Beach State.

TRANSACTIONS/CAREER NOTES: Selected by Chicago Cubs organization in eighth round of free-agent draft (June 3, 1991). ... On Chicago disabled list (July 20-August 4, 1994). ... Granted free agency (October 28, 1999). ... Signed by Tampa Bay Devil Rays (January 28, 2000). ... Traded by Devil Rays with P Mark Guthrie to Toronto Blue Jays for 2B Brent Abernathy and a player to be named later (July 31, 2000). ... Granted free agency (October 31, 2000). ... Signed by New York Mets (December 11, 2000). ... On New York disabled list (July 1-22, 2002); included rehabilitation assignment to Binghamton (July 16-18). ... Granted free agency (October 28, 2002).

RECORDS: Shares major league record for most home runs allowed in one inning—4 (May 17, 2001, third inning).

HONORS: Named N.L. Rookie Pitcher of the Year by The Sporting News (1994).

STATISTICAL NOTES: Pitched 4-2 no-hit victory for Winston-Salem against Peninsula (July 12, 1991, second game). ... Pitched 6-0 one-hit, complete-game victory against Houston (May 13, 1996).
CAREER HITTING (MLB): 75-for-457 (.164), 36 R, 13 2B, 1 3B, 2 HR, 29 RBI.

Year	League	W	L	Pct.	ERA	G	GS	CG	ShO	Sv.-Opp.	IP	H	R	ER	HR	BB-IBB	SO
1991—	Geneva (NY-Penn)	1	0	1.000	1.26	2	2	0	0	0-...	14.1	10	2	2	0	6-0	7
—	Winston-Salem (Caro.)	4	4	.500	3.67	12	12	1	0	0-...	73.2	70	38	30	3	19-0	69
1992—	Charlotte (Sou.)	•13	8	.619	3.06	29	•29	5	2	0-...	*191.0	180	76	65	19	35-3	135
1993—	Iowa (A.A.)	13	6	.684	3.96	27	26	1	1	0-...	170.2	170	78	75	20	45-0	135
—	Chicago (N.L.)	0	2	.000	4.58	3	3	0	0	0-0	19.2	16	10	10	4	3-0	14
1994—	Chicago (N.L.)	9	7	.563	3.21	22	22	1	0	0-0	146.0	133	57	52	19	54-4	108
—	Iowa (A.A.)	0	2	.000	10.00	2	2	0	0	0-...	9.0	11	10	10	1	7-0	8
1995—	Chicago (N.L.)	7	13	.350	5.15	30	29	2	0	0-0	160.2	174	104	92	25	76-8	117
1996—	Orlando (Sou.)	0	1	.000	2.77	2	2	0	0	0-...	13.0	11	6	4	0	0-0	12
—	Chicago (N.L.)	13	9	.591	3.03	31	31	3	2	0-0	205.0	181	82	69	30	62-3	132
1997—	Chicago (N.L.)	8	12	.400	4.51	34	34	0	0	0-0	201.1	225	110	101	*32	69-6	160
1998—	Chicago (N.L.)	15	8	.652	4.46	33	33	1	0	0-0	208.0	204	107	103	27	84-5	149
1999—	Chicago (N.L.)	8	*18	.308	5.56	34	34	4	0	0-0	205.2	226	133	127	32	64-4	149
2000—	Tampa Bay (A.L.)■	6	10	.375	4.58	23	23	3	1	0-0	137.2	160	76	70	16	49-1	78
—	Toronto (A.L.)■	2	5	.286	5.29	11	11	0	0	0-0	63.0	72	40	37	10	25-1	32
2001—	New York (N.L.)■	11	13	.458	4.46	28	28	1	1	0-0	173.2	168	90	86	28	47-7	144
—	Norfolk (I.L.)	2	0	1.000	2.79	3	3	1	1	0-...	19.1	13	6	6	0	6-0	12
2002—	New York (N.L.)	11	11	.500	3.37	30	30	1	1	0-0	173.2	170	80	65	16	69-4	105
—	Binghamton (East.)	1	0	1.000	0.00	1	1	0	0	0-...	5.2	3	1	0	0	4-0	5
A.L. totals (1 year)		8	15	.348	4.80	34	34	3	1	0-0	200.2	232	116	107	26	74-2	110
N.L. totals (9 years)		82	93	.469	4.25	245	244	13	4	0-0	1493.2	1497	773	705	213	528-41	1078
Major League totals (10 years)		90	108	.455	4.31	279	278	16	5	0-0	1694.1	1729	889	812	239	602-43	1188

ALL-STAR GAME RECORD

	W	L	Pct.	ERA	GS	CG	ShO	Sv.-Opp.	IP	H	R	ER	HR	BB-IBB	SO
All-Star Game totals (1 year)	0	0	...	0.00	0	0	0	0-0	1.0	0	0	0	0	0-0	3

TRACY, CHAD — 3B — DIAMONDBACKS

PERSONAL: Born May 22, 1980, in Charlotte. ... 6-2/190. ... Bats left, throws right. ... Full name: Chad A. Tracy.
COLLEGE: East Carolina.
TRANSACTIONS/CAREER NOTES: Selected by Arizona Diamondbacks organization in seventh round of free-agent draft (June 5, 2001).
HONORS: Named Texas League Player of the Year (2002).
STATISTICAL NOTES: Led Texas League third basemen with 25 errors in 2002.

			BATTING														FIELDING	
Year	Team (League)	Pos.	G	AB	R	H	2B	3B	HR	RBI	BB	SO	SB-CS	Avg.	OBP	SLG	E	Avg.
2001—	Yakima (N'West)	3B	10	36	2	10	1	0	0	5	3	5	1-0	.278	.350	.306	0	1.000
—	South Bend (Midw.)	3B	54	215	43	73	11	0	4	36	19	19	3-0	.340	.393	.447	17	.895
2002—	El Paso (Texas)	3B-1B	129	514	80	*177	*39	5	8	74	38	51	2-3	*.344	.389	.486	†26	.931

TRAMMELL, BUBBA — OF — PADRES

PERSONAL: Born November 6, 1971, in Knoxville, Tenn. ... 6-2/220. ... Bats right, throws right. ... Full name: Thomas Bubba Trammell.
HIGH SCHOOL: Knoxville (Tenn.) Central.
JUNIOR COLLEGE: Cleveland (Tenn.) State Community College.
COLLEGE: Tennessee.
TRANSACTIONS/CAREER NOTES: Selected by Detroit Tigers organization in 11th round of free-agent draft (June 2, 1994). ... Selected by Tampa Bay Devil Rays in first round (22nd pick overall) of expansion draft (November 18, 1997). ... On Durham disabled list (May 17-25, 1999). ... Traded by Devil Rays with P Rick White to New York Mets for OF Jason Tyner and P Paul Wilson (July 28, 2000). ... Traded by Mets to San Diego Padres for P Donne Wall (December 11, 2000).
STATISTICAL NOTES: Career major league grand slams: 2.
2002 GAMES PLAYED BY POSITION (MLB): OF—122; DH—2.

			BATTING														FIELDING	
Year	Team (League)	Pos.	G	AB	R	H	2B	3B	HR	RBI	BB	SO	SB-CS	Avg.	OBP	SLG	E	Avg.
1994—	Jamestown (NY-P)	OF	65	235	37	70	18	6	5	41	23	32	9-7	.298	.365	.489	5	.941
1995—	Lakeland (FSL)	OF	122	454	61	129	32	6	16	72	48	80	13-3	.284	.355	.487	5	.973
1996—	Jacksonville (Sou.)	OF	83	311	63	102	23	2	27	75	32	61	3-2	.328	.403	.675	5	.955
—	Toledo (I.L.)	OF	51	180	32	53	14	1	6	24	22	44	5-1	.294	.369	.483	1	.987
1997—	Detroit (A.L.)	OF-DH	44	123	14	28	5	0	4	13	15	35	3-1	.228	.307	.366	0	1.000
—	Toledo (I.L.)	OF-DH	90	319	56	80	15	1	28	75	38	91	2-2	.251	.336	.567	3	.972
1998—	Tampa Bay (A.L.)■	OF-DH	59	199	28	57	18	1	12	35	16	45	0-2	.286	.338	.568	0	1.000
—	Durham (I.L.)	OF	57	217	46	63	12	0	16	48	38	42	6-1	.290	.395	.567	2	.983
1999—	Durham (I.L.)	OF-DH-3B	47	186	25	50	12	0	7	31	15	36	0-0	.269	.317	.446	3	.961
—	Tampa Bay (A.L.)	OF-DH	82	283	49	82	19	0	14	39	43	37	0-2	.290	.384	.505	1	.993
2000—	Tampa Bay (A.L.)	OF-DH	66	189	19	52	11	2	7	33	21	30	3-0	.275	.352	.466	0	1.000
—	New York (N.L.)■	OF	36	56	9	13	2	0	3	12	8	19	1-0	.232	.323	.429	1	.963
2001—	San Diego (N.L.)■	OF-DH	142	490	66	128	20	3	25	92	48	78	2-2	.261	.330	.467	4	.985
2002—	San Diego (N.L.)	OF-DH	133	403	54	98	16	1	17	56	53	71	1-3	.243	.333	.414	5	.973
American League totals (4 years)			251	794	110	219	53	3	37	120	95	147	6-5	.276	.353	.490	1	.997
National League totals (3 years)			311	949	129	239	38	4	45	160	109	168	4-5	.252	.331	.443	10	.979
Major League totals (6 years)			562	1743	239	458	91	7	82	280	204	315	10-10	.263	.341	.464	11	.986

DIVISION SERIES RECORD

			BATTING														FIELDING	
Year	Team (League)	Pos.	G	AB	R	H	2B	3B	HR	RBI	BB	SO	SB-CS	Avg.	OBP	SLG	E	Avg.
2000—	New York (N.L.)								Did not play.									

CHAMPIONSHIP SERIES RECORD

Year	Team (League)	Pos.	G	AB	R	H	2B	3B	HR	RBI	BB	SO	SB-CS	Avg.	OBP	SLG	E	Avg.
				BATTING													FIELDING	
2000—	New York (N.L.)	PH	3	3	0	0	0	0	0	0	0	2	0-0	.000	.000	.000	...	...

WORLD SERIES RECORD

Year	Team (League)	Pos.	G	AB	R	H	2B	3B	HR	RBI	BB	SO	SB-CS	Avg.	OBP	SLG	E	Avg.
				BATTING													FIELDING	
2000—	New York (N.L.)	PH-OF	4	5	1	2	0	0	0	3	1	1	0-0	.400	.429	.400	1	.750

TROMBLEY, MIKE P

PERSONAL: Born April 14, 1967, in Springfield, Mass. ... 6-2/204. ... Throws right, bats right. ... Full name: Michael Scott Trombley.
HIGH SCHOOL: Minnechaug Regional (Wilbraham, Mass.).
COLLEGE: Duke.
TRANSACTIONS/CAREER NOTES: Selected by Minnesota Twins organization in 14th round of free-agent draft (June 5, 1989). ... Granted free agency (October 29, 1999). ... Signed by Baltimore Orioles (November 18, 1999). ... Traded by Orioles to Los Angeles Dodgers for P Kris Foster and C Geronimo Gil (July 31, 2001). ... Released by Dodgers (April 8, 2002). ... Signed by Twins organization (April 15, 2002). ... Released by Twins (June 3, 2002).
STATISTICAL NOTES: Pitched 3-0 no-hit victory against Knoxville (August 8, 1991).
CAREER HITTING (MLB): 0-for-2 (.000), 0 R, 0 2B, 0 3B, 0 HR, 0 RBI.

Year	League	W	L	Pct.	ERA	G	GS	CG	ShO	Sv.-Opp.	IP	H	R	ER	HR	BB-IBB	SO
1989—	Kenosha (Midw.)	5	1	.833	3.12	12	3	0	0	2-...	49.0	45	23	17	1	13-0	41
—	Visalia (Calif.)	2	2	.500	2.14	6	6	2	1	0-...	42.0	31	12	10	2	11-0	36
1990—	Visalia (Calif.)	14	6	.700	3.43	27	25	3	1	0-...	176.0	163	79	67	12	50-0	164
1991—	Orlando (Sou.)	12	7	.632	2.54	27	27	7	2	0-...	*191.0	153	65	54	12	57-3	*175
1992—	Portland (PCL)	10	8	.556	3.65	25	25	2	0	0-...	165.0	149	70	67	*18	58-1	*138
—	Minnesota (A.L.)	3	2	.600	3.30	10	7	0	0	0-0	46.1	43	20	17	5	17-0	38
1993—	Minnesota (A.L.)	6	6	.500	4.88	44	10	0	0	2-5	114.1	131	72	62	15	41-4	85
1994—	Minnesota (A.L.)	2	0	1.000	6.33	24	0	0	0	0-1	48.1	56	36	34	10	18-2	32
—	Salt Lake (PCL)	4	4	.500	5.04	11	10	0	0	0-...	60.2	75	37	34	7	20-1	63
1995—	Salt Lake (PCL)	5	3	.625	3.62	12	12	0	0	0-...	69.2	71	32	28	3	26-1	59
—	Minnesota (A.L.)	4	8	.333	5.62	20	18	0	0	0-0	97.2	107	68	61	18	42-1	68
1996—	Salt Lake (PCL)	2	2	.500	2.45	24	0	0	0	10-...	36.2	24	12	10	3	10-0	38
—	Minnesota (A.L.)	5	1	.833	3.01	43	0	0	0	6-9	68.2	61	24	23	2	25-8	57
1997—	Minnesota (A.L.)	2	3	.400	4.37	67	0	0	0	1-1	82.1	77	43	40	7	31-4	74
1998—	Minnesota (A.L.)	6	5	.545	3.63	77	1	0	0	1-4	96.2	90	41	39	16	41-3	89
1999—	Minnesota (A.L.)	2	8	.200	4.33	75	0	0	0	24-30	87.1	93	42	42	15	28-2	82
2000—	Baltimore (A.L.)■	4	5	.444	4.13	75	0	0	0	4-11	72.0	67	34	33	15	38-8	72
2001—	Baltimore (A.L.)	3	4	.429	3.46	50	0	0	0	6-9	54.2	38	23	21	4	27-2	45
—	Los Angeles (N.L.)■	0	4	.000	6.56	19	0	0	0	0-0	23.1	27	17	17	5	10-3	27
2002—	Fort Myers (FSL)	0	0	...	0.00	1	0	0	0	0-...	2.0	2	1	0	0	0-0	3
—	Edmonton (PCL)	0	1	.000	5.19	9	0	0	0	0-...	8.2	11	6	5	1	2-0	13
—	Minnesota (A.L.)	0	1	.000	15.75	5	0	0	0	0-1	4.0	10	7	7	2	1-0	3
A.L. totals (11 years)		37	43	.463	4.42	490	36	0	0	44-71	772.1	773	410	379	109	309-34	645
N.L. totals (1 year)		0	4	.000	6.56	19	0	0	0	0-0	23.1	27	17	17	5	10-3	27
Major League totals (11 years)		37	47	.440	4.48	509	36	0	0	44-71	795.2	800	427	396	114	319-37	672

TRUBY, CHRIS 3B

PERSONAL: Born December 9, 1973, in Palm Springs, Calif. ... 6-2/215. ... Bats right, throws right. ... Full name: Christopher John Truby.
HIGH SCHOOL: Damien (Hawaii).
TRANSACTIONS/CAREER NOTES: Signed as non-drafted free agent by Houston Astros organization (August 25, 1992). ... On disabled list (April 26-May 11, 1999). ... Traded by Astros to Montreal Expos for 3B/OF Geoff Blum (March 12, 2002). ... Traded by Expos to Detroit Tigers for 2B Jose Macias (May 16, 2002). ... On Detroit disabled list (July 4-29, 2002); included rehabilitation assignment to Toledo (July 26-29). ... Granted free agency (October 15, 2002).
STATISTICAL NOTES: Tied for Gulf Coast League lead with 21 errors by third basemen in 1993. ... Led New York-Pennsylvania League with 141 total bases and eight sacrifice flies in 1994. ... Led Midwest League third basemen with 279 assists and 26 double plays in 1995. ... Led Texas League with 12 sacrifice flies in 1999. ... Led Texas League third baseman with 93 putouts, 35 double plays and a .950 fielding percentage in 1999. ... Career major league grand slams: 1.
2002 GAMES PLAYED BY POSITION (MLB): 3B—120; 1B—2; OF—1.

Year	Team (League)	Pos.	G	AB	R	H	2B	3B	HR	RBI	BB	SO	SB-CS	Avg.	OBP	SLG	E	Avg.
				BATTING													FIELDING	
1993—	GC Astros (GCL)	3B-SS	57	215	30	49	10	2	1	24	22	30	16-1	.228	.301	.307	‡26	.885
—	Osceola (FSL)	3B	3	13	0	0	0	0	0	0	0	2	0-0	.000	.000	.000	2	.857
1994—	Quad City (Midw.)	3B-1B	36	111	12	24	4	1	2	19	3	29	1-1	.216	.246	.324	6	.933
—	Auburn (NY-Penn)	3B	73	282	*56	*91	17	6	7	*61	23	48	20-4	.323	.370	.500	•27	.882
1995—	Quad City (Midw.)	3B-OF	118	400	68	93	23	4	9	64	41	66	27-8	.233	.306	.378	38	.903
1996—	Quad City (Midw.)	1B-3B	109	362	45	91	15	3	8	37	28	74	6-10	.251	.305	.376	17	.975
1997—	Quad City (Midw.)	3B	68	268	34	75	14	1	7	46	22	32	13-4	.280	.334	.418	15	.926
—	Kissimmee (FSL)	3B-1B-SS-2B	57	199	23	49	11	0	2	29	8	40	8-3	.246	.278	.332	16	.916
1998—	Kissimmee (FSL)	3B	52	212	36	66	16	1	14	48	19	30	6-1	.311	.373	.594	9	.951
—	Jackson (Texas)	3B-1B	80	308	46	89	20	5	16	63	20	50	8-3	.289	.335	.542	15	.944
—	New Orleans (PCL)	3B	5	17	6	7	1	1	1	1	1	3	1-0	.412	.444	.765	1	.917
1999—	Jackson (Texas)	3B-SS	124	465	78	131	21	3	28	87	36	88	20-8	.282	.329	.520	20	†.949
2000—	Houston (N.L.)	3B	78	258	28	67	15	4	11	59	10	56	2-1	.260	.295	.477	14	.926
—	New Orleans (PCL)	3B	64	268	31	76	11	3	2	30	17	32	6-2	.284	.318	.369	12	.943
2001—	Houston (N.L.)	3B-1B	48	136	11	28	6	1	8	23	13	38	1-2	.206	.276	.441	6	.924
—	New Orleans (PCL)	3B-1B	81	321	53	100	25	6	12	71	24	66	10-5	.312	.365	.539	11	.973

T

Year	Team (League)	Pos.	G	AB	R	H	2B	3B	HR	RBI	BB	SO	SB-CS	Avg.	OBP	SLG	E	Avg.
			BATTING														FIELDING	
2002	—Montreal (N.L.)■	3B-1B-OF	35	105	12	27	5	2	2	7	5	27	1-1	.257	.297	.400	5	.934
	—Detroit (A.L.)■	3B	89	277	23	55	13	2	2	15	5	71	1-1	.199	.215	.282	11	.958
	—Toledo (I.L.)	3B	3	12	2	4	0	2	1	1	2	1	0-0	.333	.429	.917	2	.818
American League totals (1 year)			89	277	23	55	13	2	2	15	5	71	1-1	.199	.215	.282	11	.958
National League totals (3 years)			161	499	51	122	26	7	21	89	28	121	4-4	.244	.290	.451	25	.928
Major League totals (3 years)			250	776	74	177	39	9	23	104	33	192	5-5	.228	.264	.390	36	.941

DIVISION SERIES RECORD

Year	Team (League)	Pos.	G	AB	R	H	2B	3B	HR	RBI	BB	SO	SB-CS	Avg.	OBP	SLG	E	Avg.
			BATTING														FIELDING	
2001	—Houston (N.L.)	PH	1	1	0	0	0	0	0	0	0	1	0-0	.000	.000	.000	...	...

TRUJILLO, J.J. — P — PADRES

PERSONAL: Born October 9, 1975, in Corpus Christi, Texas. ... 6-0/180. ... Throws right, bats right. ... Full name: John Trujillo.
HIGH SCHOOL: W.B. Ray (Texas).
JUNIOR COLLEGE: Schrainer College (Texas), then Laredo Junior College (Texas).
COLLEGE: Dallas Baptist.
TRANSACTIONS/CAREER NOTES: Signed by Johnstown, Frontier League (June 1999). ... Signed as non-drafted free agent by San Diego Padres organization (October 12, 1999). ... On Portland disabled list (July 1-August 1, 2002).
CAREER HITTING (MLB): 0-for-0 (.000), 0 R, 0 2B, 0 3B, 0 HR, 0 RBI.

Year	League	W	L	Pct.	ERA	G	GS	CG	ShO	Sv.-Opp.	IP	H	R	ER	HR	BB-IBB	SO
1999	—Johnstown (Fron.)	1	3	.250	1.57	39	0	0	0	14-...	46.0	33	11	8	...	21-...	60
2000	—Fort Wayne (Midw.)	3	4	.429	1.33	63	0	0	0	42-...	74.2	39	16	11	3	25-1	85
2001	—Lake Elsinore (Calif.)	4	1	.800	1.86	23	0	0	0	13-...	29.0	20	7	6	1	13-2	31
	—Mobile (Sou.)	3	3	.500	2.65	43	0	0	0	6-...	51.0	44	20	15	1	20-2	44
2002	—Mobile (Sou.)	3	0	1.000	0.66	31	0	0	0	20-...	41.0	25	3	3	1	12-0	49
	—Portland (PCL)	2	0	1.000	4.33	18	1	0	0	0-...	27.0	30	14	13	2	8-0	28
	—San Diego (N.L.)	0	1	.000	10.13	4	0	0	0	0-0	2.2	4	3	3	1	6-0	3
Major League totals (1 year)		0	1	.000	10.13	4	0	0	0	0-0	2.2	4	3	3	1	6-0	3

TUCKER, MICHAEL — OF — ROYALS

PERSONAL: Born June 25, 1971, in South Boston, Va. ... 6-2/195. ... Bats left, throws right. ... Full name: Michael Anthony Tucker.
HIGH SCHOOL: Bluestone (Skipwith, Va.).
COLLEGE: Longwood (Va.).
TRANSACTIONS/CAREER NOTES: Selected by Kansas City Royals organization in first round (10th pick overall) of free-agent draft (June 1, 1992). ... On Kansas City disabled list (June 4-21 and August 28, 1996-remainder of season); included rehabilitation assignment to Wichita (June 15-21). ... Traded by Royals with IF Keith Lockhart to Atlanta Braves for OF Jermaine Dye and P Jamie Walker (March 27, 1997). ... Traded by Braves with P Denny Neagle and P Rob Bell to Cincinnati Reds for 2B Bret Boone and P Mike Remlinger (November 10, 1998). ... Traded by Reds to Chicago Cubs for P Chris Booker and P Ben Shaffar (July 20, 2001). ... Traded by Cubs to Royals for a player to be named later (December 19, 2001); Cubs acquired P Shawn Sonnier to complete deal (March 15, 2002).
STATISTICAL NOTES: Tied for Carolina League lead with four intentional bases on balls received in 1994.
2002 GAMES PLAYED BY POSITION (MLB): OF—108; DH—23; 1B—5; 2B—2.

Year	Team (League)	Pos.	G	AB	R	H	2B	3B	HR	RBI	BB	SO	SB-CS	Avg.	OBP	SLG	E	Avg.
			BATTING														FIELDING	
1993	—Wilmington (Caro.)	2B	61	239	42	73	14	2	6	44	34	49	12-2	.305	.391	.456	10	.965
	—Memphis (Sou.)	2B	72	244	38	68	7	4	9	35	42	51	12-5	.279	.392	.451	13	.962
1994	—Omaha (A.A.)	OF	132	485	75	134	16	7	21	77	69	111	11-3	.276	.366	.468	•7	.967
1995	—Kansas City (A.L.)	OF-DH	62	177	23	46	10	0	4	17	18	51	2-3	.260	.332	.384	1	.986
	—Omaha (A.A.)	OF	71	275	37	84	18	4	4	28	24	39	11-4	.305	.367	.444	2	.986
1996	—Kansas City (A.L.)	OF-1B-DH	108	339	55	88	18	4	12	53	40	69	10-4	.260	.346	.442	2	.992
	—Wichita (Texas)	OF-1B	6	20	4	9	1	3	0	7	5	4	0-2	.450	.538	.800	0	1.000
1997	—Atlanta (N.L.)■	OF	138	499	80	141	25	7	14	56	44	116	12-7	.283	.347	.445	5	.980
1998	—Atlanta (N.L.)	OF	130	414	54	101	27	3	13	46	49	112	8-3	.244	.327	.418	1	.995
1999	—Cincinnati (N.L.)■	OF	133	296	55	75	8	5	11	44	37	81	11-4	.253	.338	.426	2	.990
2000	—Cincinnati (N.L.)	OF-2B	148	270	55	72	13	4	15	36	44	64	13-6	.267	.381	.511	5	.969
2001	—Cincinnati (N.L.)	OF	86	231	31	56	10	1	7	30	23	55	12-5	.242	.308	.385	3	.978
	—Chicago (N.L.)■	OF-1B	63	205	31	54	9	7	5	31	23	47	4-3	.263	.339	.449	3	.978
2002	—Kansas City (A.L.)■	O-D-1-2	144	475	65	118	27	6	12	56	56	105	23-9	.248	.330	.406	4	.985
American League totals (3 years)			314	991	143	252	55	10	28	126	114	225	35-16	.254	.336	.415	7	.988
National League totals (5 years)			698	1915	306	499	92	27	65	243	220	475	60-28	.261	.341	.439	19	.982
Major League totals (8 years)			1012	2906	449	751	147	37	93	369	334	700	95-44	.258	.339	.430	26	.984

DIVISION SERIES RECORD

Year	Team (League)	Pos.	G	AB	R	H	2B	3B	HR	RBI	BB	SO	SB-CS	Avg.	OBP	SLG	E	Avg.
			BATTING														FIELDING	
1997	—Atlanta (N.L.)	OF	2	6	0	1	0	0	0	1	0	1	0-0	.167	.167	.167	0	1.000
1998	—Atlanta (N.L.)	OF	3	8	1	2	0	0	1	2	2	0	1-0	.250	.400	.625	0	1.000
Division series totals (2 years)			5	14	1	3	0	0	1	3	2	1	1-0	.214	.313	.429	0	1.000

CHAMPIONSHIP SERIES RECORD

Year	Team (League)	Pos.	G	AB	R	H	2B	3B	HR	RBI	BB	SO	SB-CS	Avg.	OBP	SLG	E	Avg.
			BATTING														FIELDING	
1997	—Atlanta (N.L.)	OF-PH	5	10	1	1	0	0	1	1	3	4	0-0	.100	.308	.400	0	1.000
1998	—Atlanta (N.L.)	OF-PH	6	13	1	5	1	0	1	5	2	5	0-0	.385	.467	.692	0	1.000
Championship series totals (2 years)			11	23	2	6	1	0	2	6	5	9	0-0	.261	.393	.565	0	1.000

TUCKER, T.J. P EXPOS

PERSONAL: Born August 20, 1978, in Clearwater, Fla. ... 6-3/245. ... Throws right, bats right. ... Full name: Thomas John Tucker.
HIGH SCHOOL: River Ridge (New Port Richey, Fla.).
TRANSACTIONS/CAREER NOTES: Selected by Montreal Expos organization in supplemental round ("sandwich pick" between first and second round, 47th pick overall) of free-agent draft (June 3, 1997); pick received as compensation for Chicago Cubs signing P Mel Rojas. ... On Harrisburg disabled list (April 6-23, 2000). ... On Montreal disabled list (June 10, 2000-remainder of season). ... On Harrisburg disabled list (May 25-June 6, 2001). ... On disabled list (August 18-September 6, 2002).
CAREER HITTING (MLB): 4-for-5 (.800), 2 R, 0 2B, 0 3B, 0 HR, 0 RBI.

Year League	W	L	Pct.	ERA	G	GS	CG	ShO	Sv.-Opp.	IP	H	R	ER	HR	BB-IBB	SO
1997— Gulf Coast Expos (GCL) ...	1	0	1.000	1.93	3	2	0	0	0-...	4.2	5	1	1	0	1-0	11
1998— Gulf Coast Expos (GCL) ...	1	0	1.000	0.75	7	7	0	0	0-...	36.0	23	5	3	1	5-0	40
— Vermont (NY-Penn)	3	1	.750	2.18	6	6	0	0	0-...	33.0	24	9	8	0	15-0	34
— Jupiter (FSL)	1	1	.500	1.00	2	1	0	0	0-...	9.0	5	1	1	0	0-0	10
1999— Jupiter (FSL)	5	1	.833	1.23	7	7	0	0	0-...	44.0	24	7	6	2	16-0	35
— Harrisburg (East.)	8	5	.615	4.10	19	19	1	1	0-...	116.1	110	55	53	12	38-0	85
2000— Harrisburg (East.)	2	1	.667	3.60	8	8	0	0	0-...	45.0	33	19	18	7	17-0	24
— Montreal (N.L.)	0	1	.000	11.57	2	2	0	0	0-0	7.0	11	9	9	5	3-0	2
2001— Harrisburg (East.)	5	5	.500	3.73	13	13	0	0	0-...	82.0	77	38	34	10	37-0	57
— Ottawa (I.L.)	3	5	.375	3.11	14	14	1	0	0-...	84.0	68	42	29	11	33-0	63
2002— Montreal (N.L.)	6	3	.667	4.11	57	0	0	0	4-7	61.1	69	32	28	5	31-9	42
Major League totals (2 years)	6	4	.600	4.87	59	2	0	0	4-7	68.1	80	41	37	10	34-9	44

TYNER, JASON OF DEVIL RAYS

PERSONAL: Born April 23, 1977, in Beaumont, Texas. ... 6-1/168. ... Bats left, throws left. ... Full name: Jason Renyt Tyner.
HIGH SCHOOL: Westbrook (Beaumont, Texas).
COLLEGE: Texas A&M.
TRANSACTIONS/CAREER NOTES: Selected by New York Mets organization in first round (21st pick overall) of free-agent draft (June 2, 1998). ... Traded by Mets with P Paul Wilson to Tampa Bay Devil Rays for P Rick White and OF Bubba Trammell (July 28, 2000).
2002 GAMES PLAYED BY POSITION (MLB): OF—42; DH—1.

		BATTING														FIELDING	
Year Team (League)	Pos.	G	AB	R	H	2B	3B	HR	RBI	BB	SO	SB-CS	Avg.	OBP	SLG	E	Avg.
1998— St. Lucie (FSL)	OF	50	201	30	61	2	3	0	16	17	20	15-11	.303	.361	.343	2	.976
1999— Binghamton (East.)	OF	129	518	91	162	19	5	0	33	62	46	49-15	.313	.387	.369	2	.993
— Norfolk (I.L.)	OF	3	8	0	0	0	0	0	0	0	5	0-0	.000	.000	.000	0	1.000
2000— Norfolk (I.L.)	OF	84	327	54	105	5	2	0	28	30	32	33-14	.321	.380	.349	1	.995
— New York (N.L.)	OF	13	41	3	8	2	0	0	5	1	4	1-1	.195	.222	.244	2	.920
— Tampa Bay (A.L.)■	OF-DH	37	83	6	20	2	0	0	8	4	12	6-1	.241	.281	.265	0	1.000
2001— Durham (I.L.)	OF	39	157	25	49	2	1	0	12	15	10	11-5	.312	.371	.338	0	1.000
— Tampa Bay (A.L.)	OF	105	396	51	111	8	5	0	21	15	42	31-6	.280	.311	.326	5	.978
2002— Tampa Bay (A.L.)	OF-DH	44	168	17	36	2	1	0	9	7	19	7-1	.214	.249	.238	1	.990
— Durham (I.L.)	OF	88	351	59	102	12	4	0	27	34	27	20-7	.291	.362	.348	1	.994
American League totals (3 years)		186	647	74	167	12	6	0	38	26	73	44-8	.258	.291	.295	6	.985
National League totals (1 year)		13	41	3	8	2	0	0	5	1	4	1-1	.195	.222	.244	2	.920
Major League totals (3 years)		199	688	77	175	14	6	0	43	27	77	45-9	.254	.287	.292	8	.981

UGUETO, LUIS SS MARINERS

PERSONAL: Born February 15, 1979, in Caracas, Venezuela. ... 5-11/170. ... Bats both, throws right. ... Full name: Luis Enrique Ugueto.
HIGH SCHOOL: Liceo Juan Pablo II (Macaracuay, Venezuela).
TRANSACTIONS/CAREER NOTES: Signed as non-drafted free agent by Florida Marlins organization (April 28, 1996). ... Selected by Pittsburgh Pirates from Marlins organization in Rule 5 major league draft (December 13, 2001). ... Traded by Pirates to Seattle Mariners for cash considerations (December 13, 2001). ... On Seattle disabled list (August 8-September 1, 2002); included rehabilitation assignment to Tacoma (August 19-September 1).
2002 GAMES PLAYED BY POSITION (MLB): DH—16; 2B—11; SS—8; 3B—1.

		BATTING														FIELDING	
Year Team (League)	Pos.	G	AB	R	H	2B	3B	HR	RBI	BB	SO	SB-CS	Avg.	OBP	SLG	E	Avg.
1996— Dom. Marlins (DSL) ...	SS	70	240	37	61	4	2	0	12	41	33	14-...	.254	...	.288	34	.912
1997— Ven. Marlins (VSL)		50	111	17	20	3	2	0	17	18	16	7-...	.180	...	.243	...	...
1998— Brevard County (FSL).	SS	3	11	0	2	0	0	0	0	0	5	0-0	.182	.182	.182	2	.857
— GC Marlins (GCL)	SS	50	166	20	38	8	2	0	15	8	37	7-1	.229	.270	.301	15	.925
1999— Brevard County (FSL).	SS	12	30	1	4	0	0	0	3	7	5	1-0	.133	.297	.133	2	.958
— GC Marlins (GCL)	DH	1	3	0	0	0	0	0	2	1	0	0-0	.000	.200	.000	...	...
— Utica (NY-Penn)	SS	56	217	33	60	11	2	1	26	18	46	9-4	.276	.335	.359	17	.940
2000— Kane County (Midw.)..	SS	114	393	43	92	13	2	1	32	28	83	12-14	.234	.291	.285	33	.941
2001— Brevard County (FSL).	SS-2B	121	392	53	103	12	5	3	43	38	96	22-7	.263	.330	.342	30	.950
2002— Seattle (A.L.)■	DH-2B-SS-3B	62	23	19	5	0	0	1	1	2	8	8-4	.217	.280	.348	3	.923
— Tacoma (PCL)	SS	12	51	5	13	1	0	0	5	3	13	2-1	.255	.291	.275	0	1.000
Major League totals (1 year)		62	23	19	5	0	0	1	1	2	8	8-4	.217	.280	.348	3	.923

URBINA, UGUETH P

PERSONAL: Born February 15, 1974, in Caracas, Venezuela. ... 6-0/205. ... Throws right, bats right. ... Full name: Ugueth Urtain Urbina. ... Name pronounced OOO-get.
HIGH SCHOOL: Liceo Peres Bonalde de Miranda (Miranda, Venezuala).

TRANSACTIONS/CAREER NOTES: Signed as non-drafted free agent by Montreal Expos organization (July 2, 1990). ... On disabled list (April 8-17, 1994). ... On temporarily inactive list (May 9-June 6, 1994). ... On Ottawa disabled list (August 10-September 14, 1995). ... On disabled list (May 9, 2000-remainder of season). ... Traded by Expos to Boston Red Sox for P Tomo Ohka and P Rich Rundles (July 31, 2001). ... Granted free agency (October 28, 2002).

HONORS: Named N.L. Fireman of the Year by THE SPORTING NEWS (1999).

STATISTICAL NOTES: Led N.L. with 50 save opportunities in 1999.

CAREER HITTING (MLB): 5-for-53 (.094), 3 R, 0 2B, 0 3B, 0 HR, 1 RBI.

Year League	W	L	Pct.	ERA	G	GS	CG	ShO	Sv.-Opp.	IP	H	R	ER	HR	BB-IBB	SO
1991—Gulf Coast Expos (GCL)	3	3	.500	2.29	10	10	3	1	0-...	63.0	58	24	16	2	10-0	51
1992—Albany (S.Atl.)	7	•13	.350	3.22	24	24	5	2	0-...	142.1	111	68	51	14	54-0	100
1993—Burlington (Midw.)	2	3	.400	4.50	10	8	0	0	0-...	46.0	41	31	23	7	22-1	30
—Harrisburg (East.)	4	5	.444	3.99	11	11	3	1	0-...	70.0	66	32	31	5	32-1	45
1994—Harrisburg (East.)	9	3	.750	3.28	21	21	0	0	0-...	120.2	95	49	44	11	43-0	86
1995—West Palm Beach (FSL)	1	0	1.000	0.00	2	2	0	0	0-...	9.0	4	0	0	0	1-0	11
—Ottawa (I.L.)	6	2	.750	3.04	13	11	2	1	0-...	68.0	46	26	23	1	26-0	55
—Montreal (N.L.)	2	2	.500	6.17	7	4	0	0	0-0	23.1	26	17	16	6	14-1	15
1996—West Palm Beach (FSL)	1	1	.500	1.29	3	3	0	0	0-...	14.0	13	3	2	0	3-0	21
—Ottawa (I.L.)	2	0	1.000	2.66	5	5	0	0	0-...	23.2	17	9	7	2	6-0	28
—Montreal (N.L.)	10	5	.667	3.71	33	17	0	0	0-1	114.0	102	54	47	18	44-4	108
1997—Montreal (N.L.)	5	8	.385	3.78	63	0	0	0	27-32	64.1	52	29	27	9	29-2	84
1998—Montreal (N.L.)	6	3	.667	1.30	64	0	0	0	34-38	69.1	37	11	10	2	33-2	94
1999—Montreal (N.L.)	6	6	.500	3.69	71	0	0	0	*41-50	75.2	59	35	31	6	36-6	100
2000—Montreal (N.L.)	0	1	.000	4.05	13	0	0	0	8-10	13.1	11	6	6	1	5-0	22
2001—Montreal (N.L.)	2	1	.667	4.24	45	0	0	0	15-18	46.2	42	24	22	8	21-1	57
—Boston (A.L.)■	0	1	.000	2.25	19	0	0	0	9-10	20.0	16	5	5	1	3-0	32
2002—Boston (A.L.)	1	6	.143	3.00	61	0	0	0	40-46	60.0	44	21	20	8	20-5	71
A.L. totals (2 years)	1	7	.125	2.81	80	0	0	0	49-56	80.0	60	26	25	9	23-5	103
N.L. totals (7 years)	31	26	.544	3.52	296	21	0	0	125-149	406.2	329	176	159	50	182-16	480
Major League totals (8 years)	32	33	.492	3.40	376	21	0	0	174-205	486.2	389	202	184	59	205-21	583

ALL-STAR GAME RECORD

	W	L	Pct.	ERA	GS	CG	ShO	Sv.-Opp.	IP	H	R	ER	HR	BB-IBB	SO
All-Star Game totals (2 years)	0	1	.000	13.50	0	0	0	0-2	2.0	3	3	3	0	1-0	3

URIBE, JUAN — SS — ROCKIES

PERSONAL: Born July 22, 1979, in Bani, Dominican Republic. ... 5-11/173. ... Bats right, throws right. ... Full name: Juan C. Uribe.

HIGH SCHOOL: Abel Uribe (Dominican Republic).

TRANSACTIONS/CAREER NOTES: Signed as non-drafted free agent by Colorado Rockies organization (January 15, 1997).

STATISTICAL NOTES: Led South Atlantic League shortstops with 390 assists, 615 total chances and 72 double plays in 1999. ... Had 17-game hitting streak (April 16-May 5, 2002). ... Led N.L. shortstops with 261 putouts, 505 assists, 793 total chances and 118 double plays in 2002.

2002 GAMES PLAYED BY POSITION (MLB): SS—155.

		BATTING														FIELDING	
Year Team (League)	Pos.	G	AB	R	H	2B	3B	HR	RBI	BB	SO	SB-CS	Avg.	OBP	SLG	E	Avg.
1997—DSL Rockies (DSL)		65	234	32	63	12	0	0	29	31	22	7-...	.269	...	.321	...	...
1998—Ariz. Rockies (Ariz.)	SS	40	148	25	41	5	3	0	17	12	25	8-1	.277	.339	.351	14	.927
1999—Asheville (S.Atl.)	SS	125	430	57	115	28	3	9	46	20	79	11-7	.267	.307	.409	38	.938
2000—Salem (Caro.)	SS	134	485	64	124	22	7	13	65	38	100	22-5	.256	.314	.410	26	.961
2001—Carolina (Sou.)	SS	3	13	1	3	1	0	0	1	0	4	1-0	.231	.231	.308	2	.833
—Colorado (N.L.)	SS	72	273	32	82	15	11	8	53	8	55	3-0	.300	.325	.524	5	.983
—Colo. Springs (PCL)	SS	74	281	40	87	27	7	7	48	12	43	11-8	.310	.340	.530	16	.960
2002—Colorado (N.L.)	SS	155	566	69	136	25	7	6	49	34	120	9-2	.240	.286	.341	27	.966
Major League totals (2 years)		227	839	101	218	40	18	14	102	42	175	12-2	.260	.299	.400	32	.971

UTLEY, CHASE — 3B — PHILLIES

PERSONAL: Born December 17, 1978, in Pasadena, Calif. ... 6-1/185. ... Bats left, throws right. ... Full name: Chase Cameron Utley.

COLLEGE: UCLA.

TRANSACTIONS/CAREER NOTES: Selected by Philadelphia Phillies organization in first round (15th pick overall) of free-agent draft (June 5, 2000).

STATISTICAL NOTES: Led International League third basemen with 88 putouts, 224 assists and 340 total chances in 2002.

		BATTING														FIELDING	
Year Team (League)	Pos.	G	AB	R	H	2B	3B	HR	RBI	BB	SO	SB-CS	Avg.	OBP	SLG	E	Avg.
2000—Batavia (NY-Penn)	2B	40	153	21	47	13	1	2	22	18	23	5-3	.307	.383	.444	3	.983
2001—Clearwater (FSL)	2B	122	467	65	120	25	2	16	59	37	88	19-8	.257	.324	.422	17	.970
2002—Scranton/W.B. (I.L.)	3B	123	464	73	122	*39	1	17	70	46	89	8-3	.263	.352	.461	28	.918

VALDES, ISMAEL — P

PERSONAL: Born August 21, 1973, in Victoria, Mexico. ... 6-4/225. ... Throws right, bats right.

HIGH SCHOOL: Mexico (Ciudad Victoria).

TRANSACTIONS/CAREER NOTES: Signed as non-drafted free agent by Los Angeles Dodgers (June 14, 1991). ... Loaned by Dodgers organization to Mexico City Tigers of Mexican League (April 21-June 26, 1992; and March 17-August 19, 1993). ... On disabled list (July 6-28, 1997). ... On Los Angeles disabled list (July 26-September 1, 1998); included rehabilitation assignments to Vero Beach (August 22) and San Bernardino (August 27). ... Traded by Dodgers with 2B Eric Young to Chicago Cubs for P Terry Adams, P Chad Ricketts and a player to be named later (December 12, 1999); Dodgers acquired P Brian Stephenson to complete deal (December 16, 1999). ... On Chicago disabled list (March 20-May 4, 2000); included rehabilitation assignment to Daytona (April 29-May 1). ... Traded by Cubs to Dodgers for P Jamie Arnold, OF Jorge Piedra and cash (July 26, 2000). ... On suspended list (September 12-18, 2000). ... Granted free agency (October 30, 2000). ...

Signed by Anaheim Angels (January 4, 2001). ... On disabled list (March 29-April 14 and June 15-July 4, 2001). ... Granted free agency (November 5, 2001). ... Signed by Texas Rangers (January 28, 2002). ... Traded by Rangers to Seattle Mariners for 2B Jermaine Clark and P Derrick Van Dusen (August 18, 2002). ... Granted free agency (October 29, 2002).

STATISTICAL NOTES: Led N.L. with five balks in 1996. ... Pitched 2-0 one-hit, complete-game victory against Pittsburgh (June 27, 1998).

MISCELLANEOUS: Had sacrifice hit in only appearance as pinch hitter (2000).

CAREER HITTING (MLB): 40-for-330 (.121), 14 R, 5 2B, 0 3B, 1 HR, 12 RBI.

Year League	W	L	Pct.	ERA	G	GS	CG	ShO	Sv.-Opp.	IP	H	R	ER	HR	BB-IBB	SO
1991—Gulf Coast Dodgers (GCL)	2	2	.500	2.32	10	10	0	0	0-...	50.1	44	15	13	0	13-0	44
1992—MC Tigres (Mex.)■	0	0	...	19.64	5	0	0	0	0-...	3.2	15	9	8	1	1-0	2
—La Vega (DSL)■	3	0	1.000	1.42	6	0	0	0	0-...	38.0	27	9	6	...	17-...	34
1993—MC Tigres (Mex.)■	16	7	.696	3.94	26	25	11	1	0-...	173.2	192	87	76	16	55-3	113
—San Antonio (Texas)■	1	0	1.000	1.38	3	2	0	0	0-...	13.0	12	2	2	0	0-0	11
1994—San Antonio (Texas)	2	3	.400	3.38	8	8	0	0	0-...	53.1	54	22	20	4	9-1	55
—Albuquerque (PCL)	4	1	.800	3.40	8	8	0	0	0-...	45.0	44	21	17	1	13-0	39
—Los Angeles (N.L.)	3	1	.750	3.18	21	1	0	0	0-0	28.1	21	10	10	2	10-2	28
1995—Los Angeles (N.L.)	13	11	.542	3.05	33	27	6	2	1-1	197.2	168	76	67	17	51-5	150
1996—Los Angeles (N.L.)	15	7	.682	3.32	33	33	0	0	0-0	225.0	219	94	83	20	54-10	173
1997—Los Angeles (N.L.)	10	11	.476	2.65	30	30	0	0	0-0	196.2	171	68	58	16	47-1	140
1998—Los Angeles (N.L.)	11	10	.524	3.98	27	27	2	2	0-0	174.0	171	82	77	17	66-4	122
—Vero Beach (FSL)	0	0	...	0.00	1	1	0	0	0-...	3.0	2	0	0	0	1-0	3
—San Bernardino (Calif.)	1	0	1.000	2.84	1	1	0	0	0-...	6.1	7	2	2	0	1-0	4
1999—Los Angeles (N.L.)	9	14	.391	3.98	32	32	2	1	0-0	203.1	213	97	90	32	58-2	143
2000—Daytona (FSL)■	1	0	1.000	1.80	1	1	0	0	0-...	5.0	3	2	1	0	3-0	5
—Chicago (N.L.)	2	4	.333	5.37	12	12	0	0	0-0	67.0	71	40	40	17	27-2	45
—Los Angeles (N.L.)■	0	3	.000	6.07	9	8	0	0	0-0	40.0	53	29	27	5	13-0	29
2001—Anaheim (A.L.)■	9	13	.409	4.45	27	27	1	0	0-0	163.2	177	82	81	20	50-3	100
2002—Texas (A.L.)■	6	9	.400	3.93	23	23	0	0	0-0	146.2	135	65	64	19	36-1	75
—Seattle (A.L.)■	2	3	.400	4.93	8	8	1	0	0-0	49.1	59	29	27	7	11-0	27
A.L. totals (2 years)	17	25	.405	4.30	58	58	2	0	0-0	359.2	371	176	172	46	97-4	202
N.L. totals (7 years)	63	61	.508	3.59	197	170	10	5	1-1	1132.0	1087	496	452	126	326-26	830
Major League totals (9 years)	80	86	.482	3.76	255	228	12	5	1-1	1491.2	1458	672	624	172	423-30	1032

DIVISION SERIES RECORD

Year League	W	L	Pct.	ERA	G	GS	CG	ShO	Sv.-Opp.	IP	H	R	ER	HR	BB-IBB	SO
1995—Los Angeles (N.L.)	0	0	...	0.00	1	1	0	0	0-0	7.0	3	2	0	1	1-0	6
1996—Los Angeles (N.L.)	0	1	.000	4.26	1	1	0	0	0-0	6.1	5	3	3	3	0-0	5
Division series totals (2 years)	0	1	.000	2.03	2	2	0	0	0-0	13.1	8	5	3	4	1-0	11

VALENT, ERIC — OF — PHILLIES

PERSONAL: Born April 4, 1977, in La Mirada, Calif. ... 6-0/191. ... Bats left, throws left. ... Full name: Eric Christian Valent.

HIGH SCHOOL: Canyon (Anaheim, Calif.).

COLLEGE: UCLA.

TRANSACTIONS/CAREER NOTES: Selected by Detroit Tigers organization in 26th round of free-agent draft (June 1, 1995); did not sign. ... Selected by Philadelphia Phillies organization in supplemental round ('sandwich pick" between first and second round, 42nd pick overall) of free-agent draft (June 2, 1998); pick received for failure to sign 1997 first-round pick J.D. Drew.

STATISTICAL NOTES: Tied for International League lead with 14 assists by outfielders in 2002.

2002 GAMES PLAYED BY POSITION (MLB): OF—2; 1B—1.

		BATTING														FIELDING	
Year Team (League)	Pos.	G	AB	R	H	2B	3B	HR	RBI	BB	SO	SB-CS	Avg.	OBP	SLG	E	Avg.
1998—Piedmont (S.Atl.)	OF	22	89	24	38	12	0	8	28	14	19	0-0	.427	.500	.831	2	.952
—Clearwater (FSL)	OF	34	125	24	33	8	1	5	25	16	29	1-2	.264	.359	.464	0	1.000
1999—Clearwater (FSL)	OF	134	520	91	150	31	9	20	*106	58	110	5-3	.288	.359	.498	9	.969
2000—Reading (East.)	OF	128	469	81	121	22	5	22	90	70	89	2-3	.258	.356	.467	4	.984
2001—Scranton/W.B. (I.L.)	OF-1B	117	448	65	122	30	2	21	78	49	105	0-1	.272	.352	.489	3	.992
—Philadelphia (N.L.)	OF-DH	22	41	3	4	2	0	0	1	4	11	0-0	.098	.196	.146	0	1.000
2002—Scranton/W.B. (I.L.)	OF-1B	140	546	69	137	34	2	9	84	49	94	0-2	.251	.311	.370	10	.980
—Philadelphia (N.L.)	OF-1B	7	10	1	2	0	0	0	0	0	3	0-0	.200	.200	.200	1	.750
Major League totals (2 years)		29	51	4	6	2	0	0	1	4	14	0-0	.118	.196	.157	1	.962

VALENTIN, JAVIER — C — TWINS

PERSONAL: Born September 19, 1975, in Manati, Puerto Rico. ... 5-10/192. ... Bats both, throws right. ... Full name: Jose Javier Valentin. ... Brother of Jose Valentin, shortstop, Chicago White Sox. ... Name pronounced VAL-un-TEEN.

HIGH SCHOOL: Fernando Callejo (Manati, Puerto Rico).

TRANSACTIONS/CAREER NOTES: Selected by Minnesota Twins organization in third round of free-agent draft (June 3, 1993). ... On disabled list (May 25-July 5 and September 4-20, 2000).

STATISTICAL NOTES: Led Appalachian League catchers with 48 assists and 348 total chances in 1993. ... Led Midwest League catchers with 730 putouts, 108 assists, 861 total chances, 23 errors and 11 double plays in 1995.

2002 GAMES PLAYED BY POSITION (MLB): C—4.

		BATTING														FIELDING	
Year Team (League)	Pos.	G	AB	R	H	2B	3B	HR	RBI	BB	SO	SB-CS	Avg.	OBP	SLG	E	Avg.
1993—GC Twins (GCL)	C-DH-3B	32	103	18	27	6	1	1	19	14	19	0-2	.262	.344	.369	5	.966
—Elizabethton (Appl.)	C	9	24	3	5	1	0	0	3	4	2	0-0	.208	.345	.250	2	.977
1994—Elizabethton (Appl.)	C-3B	54	210	23	44	5	0	9	27	15	44	0-1	.210	.263	.362	12	.966
1995—Fort Wayne (Midw.)	C-3B	112	383	59	124	26	5	19	65	47	75	0-5	.324	.400	.567	†23	.974
1996—Fort Myers (FSL)	C-DH-3B	87	338	34	89	26	1	7	54	32	65	1-0	.263	.330	.408	4	.991
—New Britain (East.)	C-3B-DH	48	165	22	39	8	0	3	14	16	35	0-3	.236	.308	.339	5	.978

Year	Team (League)	Pos.	BATTING														FIELDING	
			G	AB	R	H	2B	3B	HR	RBI	BB	SO	SB-CS	Avg.	OBP	SLG	E	Avg.
1997—	New Britain (East.).....	C-DH-3B	102	370	41	90	17	0	8	50	30	61	2-3	.243	.297	.354	6	.990
—	Minnesota (A.L.).........	C	4	7	1	2	0	0	0	0	0	3	0-0	.286	.286	.286	0	1.000
1998—	Minnesota (A.L.).........	C-DH	55	162	11	32	7	1	3	18	11	30	0-0	.198	.247	.309	5	.983
1999—	Minnesota (A.L.).........	C	78	218	22	54	12	1	5	28	22	39	0-0	.248	.313	.381	1	.998
2000—	Salt Lake (PCL)..........	C	39	140	25	50	16	2	7	35	9	27	1-0	.357	.397	.650	1	.994
2001—	Edmonton (PCL).........	C-3B-1B	121	431	53	121	29	2	17	71	47	108	0-1	.281	.352	.476	14	.977
2002—	Edmonton (PCL).........	C-3B-1B	127	455	69	130	33	1	21	80	41	96	0-1	.286	.346	.501	9	.984
—	Minnesota (A.L.).........	C	4	4	0	2	0	0	0	0	0	0	0-0	.500	.500	.500	0	1.000
Major League totals (4 years)			141	391	34	90	19	2	8	46	33	72	0-0	.230	.288	.350	6	.992

VALENTIN, JOHN — 3B

PERSONAL: Born February 18, 1967, in Mineola, N.Y. ... 6-0/185. ... Bats right, throws right. ... Full name: John William Valentin.

HIGH SCHOOL: St. Anthony (Jersey City, N.J.).

COLLEGE: Seton Hall.

TRANSACTIONS/CAREER NOTES: Selected by Boston Red Sox organization in fifth round of free-agent draft (June 1, 1988). ... On Boston disabled list (April 1-20, 1993); included rehabilitation assignment to Pawtucket (April 16-20). ... On Boston disabled list (May 4-June 6, 1994); included rehabilitation assignment to Pawtucket (May 31-June 6). ... On disabled list (August 3-18, 1996; and June 26-July 11 and August 31-September 23, 1999; April 16-May 19 and May 31, 2000-remainder of season). ... On disabled list (April 6-May 19 and May 31, 2000-remainder of season). ... On Boston disabled list (March 21-May 9 and June 7, 2001-remainder of season); included rehabilitation assignments to Pawtucket (April 24-28, May 4-9 and June 26-28) and Trenton (April 29-May 3). ... Granted free agency (November 5, 2001). ... Signed by New York Mets organization (January 30, 2002). ... On disabled list (May 15-31, 2002). ... Granted free agency (October 28, 2002).

HONORS: Named shortstop on The Sporting News A.L. Silver Slugger team (1995).

STATISTICAL NOTES: Led New York-Pennsylvania League shortstops with .949 fielding percentage in 1988. ... Led International League shortstops with 358 assists in 1992. ... Hit three home runs in one game (June 2, 1995). ... Led A.L. shortstops with 414 assists and 659 total chances in 1995. ... Hit for the cycle (June 6, 1996). ... Led A.L. third basemen with 121 putouts in 1998. ... Career major league grand slams: 3.

MISCELLANEOUS: Turned unassisted triple play while playing shortstop (July 8, 1994, sixth inning); 10th player ever to accomplish feat.

2002 GAMES PLAYED BY POSITION (MLB): SS—24; 1B—22; 3B—18; 2B—3; DH—2.

Year	Team (League)	Pos.	BATTING														FIELDING	
			G	AB	R	H	2B	3B	HR	RBI	BB	SO	SB-CS	Avg.	OBP	SLG	E	Avg.
1988—	Elmira (NY-Penn).......	SS-3B	60	207	18	45	5	1	2	16	36	35	5-4	.217	.331	.280	14	†.951
1989—	Winter Haven (FSL)....	SS-3B	55	215	27	58	13	1	3	18	13	29	4-4	.270	.310	.381	12	.958
—	Lynchburg (Caro.)......	SS	75	264	47	65	7	2	8	34	41	40	5-2	.246	.350	.379	16	.953
1990—	New Britain (East.).....	SS	94	312	20	68	18	1	2	31	25	46	1-2	.218	.274	.301	21	.951
1991—	New Britain (East.).....	SS	23	81	8	16	3	0	0	5	9	14	1-1	.198	.278	.235	3	.975
—	Pawtucket (I.L.)..........	SS	100	329	52	87	22	4	9	49	60	42	0-1	.264	.374	.438	25	.951
1992—	Pawtucket (I.L.)..........	SS	97	331	47	86	18	1	9	29	48	50	1-2	.260	.358	.402	20	.962
—	Boston (A.L.)..............	SS	58	185	21	51	13	0	5	25	20	17	1-0	.276	.351	.427	10	.963
1993—	Pawtucket (I.L.)..........	SS	2	9	3	3	0	0	1	1	0	1	0-0	.333	.333	.667	0	1.000
—	Boston (A.L.)..............	SS	144	468	50	130	40	3	11	66	49	77	3-4	.278	.346	.447	20	.971
1994—	Boston (A.L.)..............	SS-DH	84	301	53	95	26	2	9	49	42	38	3-1	.316	.400	.505	8	.979
—	Pawtucket (I.L.)..........	SS	5	18	2	6	0	0	1	2	3	4	0-0	.333	.409	.500	3	.885
1995—	Boston (A.L.)..............	SS	135	520	108	155	37	2	27	102	81	67	20-5	.298	.399	.533	•18	.973
1996—	Boston (A.L.)..............	SS-3B-DH	131	527	84	156	29	3	13	59	63	59	9-10	.296	.374	.436	17	.970
1997—	Boston (A.L.)..............	2B-3B	143	575	95	176	*47	5	18	77	58	66	7-4	.306	.372	.499	22	.966
1998—	Boston (A.L.)..............	3B-2B	153	588	113	145	44	1	23	73	77	82	4-5	.247	.340	.442	15	.965
1999—	Boston (A.L.)..............	3B-DH	113	450	58	114	27	1	12	70	40	68	0-1	.253	.315	.398	14	.954
2000—	Boston (A.L.)..............	3B	10	35	6	9	1	0	2	2	2	5	0-1	.257	.297	.457	0	1.000
2001—	Pawtucket (I.L.)..........	3B	10	36	7	9	1	0	2	4	8	4	0-0	.250	.386	.444	3	.850
—	Trenton (East.)...........	SS	3	13	1	2	1	0	0	0	1	3	0-0	.154	.214	.231	1	.917
—	Boston (A.L.)..............	SS-3B	20	60	8	12	2	0	1	5	9	8	0-0	.200	.314	.283	2	.971
2002—	New York (N.L.)■......	S-1-3-2-D	114	208	18	50	15	0	3	30	22	37	0-0	.240	.339	.356	10	.957
American League totals (10 years)			991	3709	596	1043	266	17	121	528	441	487	47-31	.281	.361	.460	126	.969
National League totals (1 year)			114	208	18	50	15	0	3	30	22	37	0-0	.240	.339	.356	10	.957
Major League totals (11 years)			1105	3917	614	1093	281	17	124	558	463	524	47-31	.279	.360	.454	136	.968

DIVISION SERIES RECORD

RECORDS: Shares single-game records for most home runs—2; and most runs batted in—7 (October 10, 1999).

Year	Team (League)	Pos.	BATTING														FIELDING	
			G	AB	R	H	2B	3B	HR	RBI	BB	SO	SB-CS	Avg.	OBP	SLG	E	Avg.
1995—	Boston (A.L.)..............	SS	3	12	1	3	1	0	1	2	3	1	0-1	.250	.400	.583	1	.909
1998—	Boston (A.L.)..............	3B	4	15	5	7	1	0	0	0	3	1	0-0	.467	.556	.533	0	1.000
1999—	Boston (A.L.)..............	3B	5	22	6	7	2	0	3	12	0	4	0-0	.318	.304	.818	2	.889
Division series totals (3 years)			12	49	12	17	4	0	4	14	6	6	0-1	.347	.411	.673	3	.932

CHAMPIONSHIP SERIES RECORD

RECORDS: Shares single-game record for most at-bats (nine-inning game)—6 (October 16, 1999). ... Shares A.L. single-game record for most runs batted in—5 (October 16, 1999).

Year	Team (League)	Pos.	BATTING														FIELDING	
			G	AB	R	H	2B	3B	HR	RBI	BB	SO	SB-CS	Avg.	OBP	SLG	E	Avg.
1999—	Boston (A.L.)..............	3B	5	23	3	8	2	0	1	5	2	4	0-0	.348	.400	.565	0	1.000

VALENTIN, JOSE — 3B/SS — WHITE SOX

PERSONAL: Born October 12, 1969, in Manati, Puerto Rico. ... 5-10/185. ... Bats both, throws right. ... Full name: Jose Antonio Valentin. ... Brother of Javier Valentin, catcher, Minnesota Twins organization.

HIGH SCHOOL: Fernando Callejo (Manati, Puerto Rico).

TRANSACTIONS/CAREER NOTES: Signed as non-drafted free agent by San Diego Padres organization (October 12, 1986). ... On disabled list (April 16-May 1 and May 18-July 11, 1990). ... Traded by Padres with P Ricky Bones and OF Matt Mieske to Milwaukee Brewers for 3B Gary Sheffield and P Geoff Kellogg (March 27, 1992). ... On Milwaukee disabled list (April 14-May 5, 1997); included rehabilitation assignment to Beloit (May 3-5). ... On Milwaukee disabled list (April 13-June 16, 1999); included rehabilitation assignment to Louisville (June 9-16). ... Traded by Brewers with P Cal Eldred to Chicago White Sox for P Jaime Navarro and P John Snyder (January 12, 2000). ... Granted free agency (October 30, 2000). ... Re-signed by White Sox (November 22, 2000). ... On disabled list (June 8-24, 2001).

STATISTICAL NOTES: Led Texas League shortstops with 442 putouts and 658 total chances in 1991. ... Led American Association shortstops with 187 putouts, 414 assists, 639 total chances and 70 double plays in 1992. ... Led American Association shortstops with 211 putouts and 80 double plays in 1993. ... Led A.L. shortstops with 20 errors in 1994. ... Hit three home runs in one game (April 3, 1998). ... Hit for the cycle (April 27, 2000). ... Switch-hit home runs in one game twice (September 30, 2000; and August 13, 2002). ... Led A.L. shortstops with 36 errors in 2000. ... Career major league grand slams: 6.

2002 GAMES PLAYED BY POSITION (MLB): 3B—83; SS—50; DH—1.

			BATTING														FIELDING	
Year	Team (League)	Pos.	G	AB	R	H	2B	3B	HR	RBI	BB	SO	SB-CS	Avg.	OBP	SLG	E	Avg.
1987—	Spokane (N'West)	SS	70	244	52	61	8	2	2	24	35	38	8-5	.250	.346	.324	26	.914
1988—	Charl., S.C. (S.Atl.)	SS	133	444	56	103	20	1	6	44	45	83	11-4	.232	.304	.322	60	.911
1989—	Riverside (Calif.)	SS	114	381	40	74	10	5	10	41	37	93	8-7	.194	.273	.325	*46	.924
—	Wichita (Texas)	SS-3B	18	49	8	12	1	0	2	5	5	12	1-0	.245	.315	.388	8	.899
1990—	Wichita (Texas)	SS	11	36	4	10	2	0	0	2	5	7	2-1	.278	.366	.333	2	.959
1991—	Wichita (Texas)	SS	129	447	73	112	22	5	17	68	55	115	8-6	.251	.335	.436	40	.939
1992—	Denver (A.A.)■	SS	*139	492	78	118	19	11	3	45	53	99	9-4	.240	.317	.341	*38	.941
—	Milwaukee (A.L.)	SS-2B	4	3	1	0	0	0	0	1	0	0	0-0	.000	.000	.000	1	.667
1993—	New Orleans (A.A.)	SS-1B	122	389	56	96	22	5	9	53	47	87	9-10	.247	.337	.398	29	.951
—	Milwaukee (A.L.)	SS	19	53	10	13	1	2	1	7	7	16	1-0	.245	.344	.396	6	.922
1994—	Milwaukee (A.L.)	SS-2B-DH-3B	97	285	47	68	19	0	11	46	38	75	12-3	.239	.330	.421	†20	.961
1995—	Milwaukee (A.L.)	SS-DH-3B	112	338	62	74	23	3	11	49	37	83	16-8	.219	.293	.402	15	.971
1996—	Milwaukee (A.L.)	SS	154	552	90	143	33	7	24	95	66	145	17-4	.259	.336	.475	*37	.950
1997—	Milwaukee (A.L.)	SS-DH	136	494	58	125	23	1	17	58	39	109	19-8	.253	.310	.407	20	.967
—	Beloit (Midw.)	SS	2	6	3	3	1	0	0	1	2	1	0-0	.500	.625	.667	0	1.000
1998—	Milwaukee (N.L.)	SS-DH	151	428	65	96	24	0	16	49	63	105	10-7	.224	.323	.393	21	.963
1999—	Milwaukee (N.L.)	SS	89	256	45	58	9	5	10	38	48	52	3-2	.227	.347	.418	22	.937
—	Louisville (I.L.)	SS	6	20	6	5	0	0	3	3	4	3	0-1	.250	.375	.700	0	1.000
2000—	Chicago (A.L.)■	SS-OF	144	568	107	155	37	6	25	92	59	106	19-2	.273	.343	.491	†36	.950
2001—	Chicago (A.L.)	3B-SS-OF	124	438	74	113	22	2	28	68	50	114	9-6	.258	.336	.509	22	.947
2002—	Chicago (A.L.)	3B-SS-DH	135	474	70	118	26	4	25	75	43	99	3-3	.249	.311	.479	19	.957
American League totals (9 years)			925	3205	519	809	184	25	142	491	339	747	96-34	.252	.324	.458	176	.956
National League totals (2 years)			240	684	110	154	33	5	26	87	111	157	13-9	.225	.333	.402	43	.953
Major League totals (11 years)			1165	3889	629	963	217	30	168	578	450	904	109-43	.248	.326	.448	219	.956

DIVISION SERIES RECORD

			BATTING														FIELDING	
Year	Team (League)	Pos.	G	AB	R	H	2B	3B	HR	RBI	BB	SO	SB-CS	Avg.	OBP	SLG	E	Avg.
2000—	Chicago (A.L.)	SS	3	10	2	3	2	0	0	1	2	2	3-0	.300	.417	.500	1	.964

VAN HEKKEN, ANDY — P — TIGERS

PERSONAL: Born July 31, 1979, in Holland, Mich. ... 6-3/175. ... Throws left, bats right. ... Full name: Andrew William Van Hekken.

HIGH SCHOOL: Holland (Mich.).

TRANSACTIONS/CAREER NOTES: Selected by Seattle Mariners organization in third round of free-agent draft (June 2, 1998). ... Traded by Mariners to Detroit Tigers (June 26, 1999); part of trade in which Tigers traded OF Brian Hunter to Mariners for two players to be named later (April 21, 1999); Mariners traded OF Jerry Amador to Tigers to complete deal (August 26, 1999).

STATISTICAL NOTES: Pitched shutout in first major league game (September 3, 2002).

CAREER HITTING (MLB): 0-for-0 (.000), 0 R, 0 2B, 0 3B, 0 HR, 0 RBI.

Year	League	W	L	Pct.	ERA	G	GS	CG	ShO	Sv.-Opp.	IP	H	R	ER	HR	BB-IBB	SO
1998—	Arizona Mariners (Ariz.)	6	3	.667	4.43	11	8	0	0	0-...	40.2	34	23	20	1	18-0	55
1999—	Oneonta (NY-Penn)■	4	2	.667	2.15	11	10	0	0	0-...	50.1	44	17	12	3	16-0	50
2000—	West Michigan (Midw.)	•16	6	.727	2.45	26	25	3	1	1-...	158.0	139	48	43	3	37-0	126
2001—	Lakeland (FSL)	10	4	.714	3.17	19	19	2	0	0-...	110.2	105	43	39	8	33-0	82
—	Erie (East.)	5	0	1.000	4.69	8	8	0	0	0-...	48.0	63	29	25	5	8-0	29
2002—	Erie (East.)	4	7	.364	3.83	21	21	1	0	0-...	134.0	138	69	57	10	34-0	97
—	Toledo (I.L.)	5	0	1.000	1.82	7	7	1	1	0-...	49.1	41	14	10	4	11-0	19
—	Detroit (A.L.)	1	3	.250	3.00	5	5	1	1	0-0	30.0	38	13	10	2	6-0	5
Major League totals (1 year)		1	3	.250	3.00	5	5	1	1	0-0	30.0	38	13	10	2	6-0	5

VAN POPPEL, TODD — P — RANGERS

PERSONAL: Born December 9, 1971, in Hinsdale, Ill. ... 6-5/240. ... Throws right, bats right. ... Full name: Todd Matthew Van Poppel.

HIGH SCHOOL: St. Martin (Arlington, Texas).

TRANSACTIONS/CAREER NOTES: Selected by Oakland Athletics organization in first round (14th pick overall) of free-agent draft (June 4, 1990); pick received as part of compensation for Milwaukee Brewers signing Type A free-agent DH Dave Parker. ... On disabled list (May 28-September 11, 1992). ... Claimed on waivers by Detroit Tigers (August 6, 1996). ... Claimed on waivers by California Angels (November 12, 1996). ... Released by Angels (March 26, 1997). ... Signed by Kansas City Royals organization (April 17, 1997). ... Released by Royals (June 6, 1997). ... Signed by Texas Rangers organization (June 20, 1997). ... Traded by Rangers with 2B Warren Morris to Pittsburgh Pirates for P

Esteban Loaiza (July 17, 1998). ... Granted free agency (October 15, 1998). ... Re-signed by Pirates (January 18, 1999). ... Granted free agency (October 15, 1999). ... Signed by Chicago Cubs organization (November 22, 1999). ... Granted free agency (November 5, 2001). ... Signed by Texas Rangers (November 26, 2001).

CAREER HITTING (MLB): 5-for-31 (.161), 4 R, 1 2B, 0 3B, 0 HR, 1 RBI.

Year League	W	L	Pct.	ERA	G	GS	CG	ShO	Sv.-Opp.	IP	H	R	ER	HR	BB-IBB	SO
1990— S. Oregon (N'West)	1	1	.500	1.13	5	5	0	0	0-...	24.0	10	5	3	1	9-0	32
— Madison (Midw.)	2	1	.667	3.95	3	3	0	0	0-...	13.2	8	11	6	0	10-0	17
1991— Huntsville (Sou.)	6	*13	.316	3.47	24	24	1	1	0-...	132.1	118	69	51	2	90-0	115
— Oakland (A.L.)	0	0	...	9.64	1	1	0	0	0-0	4.2	7	5	5	1	2-0	6
1992— Tacoma (PCL)	4	2	.667	3.97	9	9	0	0	0-...	45.1	44	22	20	1	35-0	29
1993— Tacoma (PCL)	4	8	.333	5.83	16	16	0	0	0-...	78.2	67	53	51	5	54-0	71
— Oakland (A.L.)	6	6	.500	5.04	16	16	0	0	0-0	84.0	76	50	47	10	62-0	47
1994— Oakland (A.L.)	7	10	.412	6.09	23	23	0	0	0-0	116.2	108	80	79	20	•89-2	83
1995— Oakland (A.L.)	4	8	.333	4.88	36	14	1	0	0-0	138.1	125	77	75	16	56-1	122
1996— Oakland (A.L.)	1	5	.167	7.71	28	6	0	0	1-2	63.0	86	56	54	13	33-3	37
— Detroit (A.L.)■	2	4	.333	11.39	9	9	1	1	0-0	36.1	53	51	46	11	29-0	16
1997— Omaha (A.A.)■	1	5	.167	8.03	11	6	0	0	0-...	37.0	50	36	33	10	24-0	27
— Charlotte (FSL)■	0	4	.000	4.04	6	6	2	0	0-...	35.2	36	19	16	3	10-0	33
— Tulsa (Texas)	3	3	.500	5.06	7	7	0	0	0-...	42.2	53	27	24	2	15-0	26
1998— Tulsa (Texas)■	0	0	...	4.50	1	1	0	0	0-...	4.0	2	2	2	1	4-0	2
— Oklahoma (PCL)	5	5	.500	3.72	15	13	2	0	0-...	87.0	88	44	36	11	25-0	69
— Texas (A.L.)	1	2	.333	8.84	4	4	0	0	0-0	19.1	26	20	19	5	10-0	10
— Pittsburgh (N.L.)■	1	2	.333	5.36	18	7	0	0	0-0	47.0	53	32	28	4	18-3	32
1999— Nashville (PCL)	10	6	.625	4.95	27	27	2	0	0-...	163.2	173	95	90	23	62-1	*157
2000— Iowa (PCL)■	3	4	.429	3.10	10	6	0	0	0-...	40.2	37	18	14	2	10-0	52
— Chicago (N.L.)	4	5	.444	3.75	51	2	0	0	2-5	86.1	80	38	36	10	48-2	77
2001— Chicago (N.L.)	4	1	.800	2.52	59	0	0	0	0-0	75.0	63	22	21	9	38-4	90
2002— Texas (A.L.)■	3	2	.600	5.45	50	0	0	0	1-2	72.2	80	44	44	14	29-1	85
A.L. totals (7 years)	24	37	.393	6.21	167	73	2	1	2-4	535.0	561	383	369	90	310-7	406
N.L. totals (3 years)	9	8	.529	3.67	128	9	0	0	2-5	208.1	196	92	85	23	104-9	199
Major League totals (9 years)	33	45	.423	5.50	295	82	2	1	4-9	743.1	757	475	454	113	414-16	605

VANCE, CORY — P — ROCKIES

PERSONAL: Born June 20, 1979, in Dayton, Ohio. ... 6-1/195. ... Throws left, bats left.

HIGH SCHOOL: Butler (Vandalia, Ohio).

COLLEGE: Georgia Tech.

TRANSACTIONS/CAREER NOTES: Selected by Colorado Rockies organization in fourth round of free-agent draft (June 5, 2000).

CAREER HITTING (MLB): 0-for-1 (.000), 0 R, 0 2B, 0 3B, 0 HR, 0 RBI.

Year League	W	L	Pct.	ERA	G	GS	CG	ShO	Sv.-Opp.	IP	H	R	ER	HR	BB-IBB	SO
2000— Portland (N'West)	0	2	.000	1.11	7	3	0	0	0-...	24.1	11	5	3	1	8-0	26
2001— Salem (Caro.)	10	8	.556	3.10	26	26	1	0	0-...	154.0	129	65	53	9	65-0	142
2002— Carolina (Sou.)	10	8	.556	3.77	25	25	1	0	0-...	150.1	142	73	63	8	76-1	114
— Colorado (N.L.)	0	0	...	6.75	2	1	0	0	0-0	4.0	4	3	3	2	4-0	1
Major League totals (1 year)	0	0	...	6.75	2	1	0	0	0-0	4.0	4	3	3	2	4-0	1

VANDER WAL, JOHN — OF/1B

PERSONAL: Born April 29, 1966, in Grand Rapids, Mich. ... 6-1/197. ... Bats left, throws left. ... Full name: John Henry Vander Wal.

HIGH SCHOOL: Hudsonville (Mich.).

COLLEGE: Western Michigan.

TRANSACTIONS/CAREER NOTES: Selected by Houston Astros organization in eighth round of free-agent draft (June 4, 1984); did not sign. ... Selected by Montreal Expos organization in third round of free-agent draft (June 2, 1987). ... Contract purchased by Rockies with OF Ronnie Hall from Expos (March 31, 1994). ... Traded by Rockies to San Diego Padres for a player to be named later (August 31, 1998). ... Granted free agency (October 26, 1998). ... Re-signed by Padres (November 13, 1998). ... Traded by Padres with P Geraldo Padua and P James Sak to Pittsburgh Pirates for OF Al Martin and cash (February 23, 2000). ... Traded by Pirates with P Jason Schmidt to San Francisco Giants for OF Armando Rios and P Ryan Vogelsong (July 30, 2001). ... Traded by Giants to New York Yankees for P Jay Witasick (December 13, 2001). ... Granted free agency (October 28, 2002).

RECORDS: Holds major league single-season record for most hits by pinch hitter—28 (1995).

STATISTICAL NOTES: Had 16-game hitting streak (August 29-September 16, 2000). ... Career major league grand slams: 2.

2002 GAMES PLAYED BY POSITION (MLB): OF—57; DH—16; 1B—6.

		BATTING														FIELDING	
Year Team (League)	Pos.	G	AB	R	H	2B	3B	HR	RBI	BB	SO	SB-CS	Avg.	OBP	SLG	E	Avg.
1987— Jamestown (NY-P)	OF	18	69	24	33	12	3	3	15	3	14	3-2	.478	.493	.870	0	1.000
— W. Palm Beach (FSL)	OF	50	189	29	54	11	2	2	22	30	25	8-3	.286	.378	.397	3	.972
1988— W. Palm Beach (FSL)	OF	62	231	50	64	15	2	10	33	32	40	11-4	.277	.368	.489	1	.991
— Jacksonville (Sou.)	OF	58	208	22	54	14	0	3	14	17	49	3-4	.260	.317	.370	0	1.000
1989— Jacksonville (Sou.)	OF	71	217	30	55	9	2	6	24	22	51	2-3	.253	.322	.396	1	.987
1990— Jacksonville (Sou.)	OF	77	277	45	84	25	3	8	40	39	46	6-3	.303	.393	.502	1	.991
— Indianapolis (A.A.)	OF	51	135	16	40	6	0	2	14	13	28	0-1	.296	.358	.385	2	.963
1991— Indianapolis (A.A.)	OF	133	478	84	140	36	8	15	71	79	118	8-1	.293	.393	.496	1	*.995
— Montreal (N.L.)	OF	21	61	4	13	4	1	1	8	1	18	0-0	.213	.222	.361	0	1.000
1992— Montreal (N.L.)	OF-1B	105	213	21	51	8	2	4	20	24	36	3-0	.239	.316	.352	2	.985
1993— Montreal (N.L.)	1B-OF	106	215	34	50	7	4	5	30	27	30	6-3	.233	.320	.372	4	.986
1994— Colorado (N.L.)■	1B-OF	91	110	12	27	3	1	5	15	16	31	2-1	.245	.339	.427	0	1.000
1995— Colorado (N.L.)	1B-OF	105	101	15	35	8	1	5	21	16	23	1-1	.347	.432	.594	2	.965
1996— Colorado (N.L.)	OF-1B	104	151	20	38	6	2	5	31	19	38	2-2	.252	.335	.417	1	.987
1997— Colorado (N.L.)	OF-1B-DH	76	92	7	16	2	0	1	11	10	33	1-1	.174	.255	.228	1	.974
— Colo. Springs (PCL)	1B-OF-DH	25	103	29	42	12	1	3	19	11	28	1-1	.408	.465	.631	4	.977

Year Team (League)	Pos.	G	AB	R	H	2B	3B	HR	RBI	BB	SO	SB-CS	Avg.	OBP	SLG	E	Avg.
		BATTING														FIELDING	
1998—Colorado (N.L.)	OF-DH-1B	89	104	18	30	10	1	5	20	16	29	0-0	.288	.380	.548	0	1.000
—San Diego (N.L.)■	OF-1B	20	25	3	6	3	0	0	0	6	5	0-0	.240	.387	.360	0	1.000
1999—San Diego (N.L.)	OF-1B-DH	132	246	26	67	18	0	6	41	37	59	2-1	.272	.368	.419	1	.996
2000—Pittsburgh (N.L.)■	OF-1B-DH	134	384	74	115	29	0	24	94	72	92	11-2	.299	.410	.563	6	.985
2001—Pittsburgh (N.L.)	OF-1B-DH	97	313	39	87	22	3	11	50	42	84	7-4	.278	.361	.473	4	.982
—San Fran. (N.L.)■	OF-1B	49	139	19	35	6	1	3	20	26	38	1-2	.252	.370	.374	0	1.000
2002—New York (A.L.)■	OF-DH-1B	84	219	30	57	17	1	6	20	23	58	1-1	.260	.327	.429	2	.983
American League totals (1 year)		84	219	30	57	17	1	6	20	23	58	1-1	.260	.327	.429	2	.983
National League totals (11 years)		1129	2154	292	570	126	16	75	361	312	516	36-17	.265	.357	.442	21	.988
Major League totals (12 years)		1213	2373	322	627	143	17	81	381	335	574	37-18	.264	.354	.441	23	.988

DIVISION SERIES RECORD

RECORDS: Holds N.L. career record for most games by pinch-hitter—7. ... Shares career record for most triples—1.

Year Team (League)	Pos.	G	AB	R	H	2B	3B	HR	RBI	BB	SO	SB-CS	Avg.	OBP	SLG	E	Avg.
		BATTING														FIELDING	
1995—Colorado (N.L.)	PH	4	4	0	0	0	0	0	0	0	2	0-0	.000	.000	.000	...	...
1998—San Diego (N.L.)	PH	3	3	1	1	0	1	0	2	0	1	0-0	.333	.333	1.000	...	...
2002—New York (A.L.)	OF	2	2	0	0	0	0	0	0	0	1	0-0	.000	.000	.000	0	...
Division series totals (3 years)		9	9	1	1	0	1	0	2	0	4	0-0	.111	.111	.333	0	...

CHAMPIONSHIP SERIES RECORD

Year Team (League)	Pos.	G	AB	R	H	2B	3B	HR	RBI	BB	SO	SB-CS	Avg.	OBP	SLG	E	Avg.
		BATTING														FIELDING	
1998—San Diego (N.L.)	OF-PH	3	7	1	3	0	0	1	2	0	2	0-0	.429	.429	.857	0	1.000

WORLD SERIES RECORD

Year Team (League)	Pos.	G	AB	R	H	2B	3B	HR	RBI	BB	SO	SB-CS	Avg.	OBP	SLG	E	Avg.
		BATTING														FIELDING	
1998—San Diego (N.L.)	OF-PH	4	5	0	2	1	0	0	0	0	2	0-0	.400	.400	.600	0	1.000

VARITEK, JASON — C — RED SOX

PERSONAL: Born April 11, 1972, in Rochester, Minn. ... 6-2/237. ... Bats both, throws right. ... Full name: Jason A. Varitek.
HIGH SCHOOL: Lake Brantley (Longwood, Fla.).
COLLEGE: Georgia Tech.
TRANSACTIONS/CAREER NOTES: Selected by Minnesota Twins organization first round (21st pick overall) of free-agent draft (June 3, 1993); did not sign. ... Selected by Seattle Mariners organization in first round (14th pick overall) of free-agent draft (June 2, 1994). ... Traded by Mariners with P Derek Lowe to Boston Red Sox for P Heathcliff Slocumb (July 31, 1997). ... On disabled list (June 8, 2001-remainder of season). ... On suspended list (September 16-20, 2002).
STATISTICAL NOTES: Led Southern league catchers with .993 fielding percentage and 21 passed balls and tied for lead in double plays by catcher with 10 in 1996. ... Led A.L. catchers with 972 putouts, 1,049 total chances and 25 passed balls in 1999. ... Led A.L. catchers with 14 passed balls in 2000. ... Hit three home runs in one game (May 20, 2001). ... Had 16-game hitting streak (July 14-30, 2002).
2002 GAMES PLAYED BY POSITION (MLB): C—127; DH—1.

Year Team (League)	Pos.	G	AB	R	H	2B	3B	HR	RBI	BB	SO	SB-CS	Avg.	OBP	SLG	E	Avg.
		BATTING														FIELDING	
1995—Port City (Sou.)	C	104	352	42	79	14	3	10	44	61	126	0-1	.224	.340	.366	8	.988
1996—Port City (Sou.)	C-DH-3B-OF	134	503	63	132	34	1	12	67	66	93	7-6	.262	.350	.406	5	*.993
1997—Tacoma (PCL)	C-DH	87	307	54	78	13	0	15	48	34	71	0-1	.254	.329	.443	3	*.995
—Pawtucket (I.L.)■	C	20	66	6	13	5	0	1	5	8	12	0-0	.197	.284	.318	1	.993
—Boston (A.L.)	C	1	1	0	1	0	0	0	0	0	0	0-0	1.000	1.000	1.000	0	1.000
1998—Boston (A.L.)	C-DH	86	221	31	56	13	0	7	33	17	45	2-2	.253	.309	.407	5	.988
1999—Boston (A.L.)	C-DH	144	483	70	130	39	2	20	76	46	85	1-2	.269	.330	.482	*11	.990
2000—Boston (A.L.)	C-DH	139	448	55	111	31	1	10	65	60	84	1-1	.248	.342	.388	7	.992
2001—Boston (A.L.)	C	51	174	19	51	11	1	7	25	21	35	0-0	.293	.371	.489	2	.996
2002—Boston (A.L.)	C-DH	132	467	58	124	27	1	10	61	41	95	4-3	.266	.332	.392	4	.996
Major League totals (6 years)		553	1794	233	473	121	5	54	260	185	344	8-8	.264	.335	.427	29	.992

DIVISION SERIES RECORD

RECORDS: Holds single-game record for most runs scored—5 (October 10, 1999). ... Shares career and single-series record for most consecutive hits—5 (October 9-10, 1999).

Year Team (League)	Pos.	G	AB	R	H	2B	3B	HR	RBI	BB	SO	SB-CS	Avg.	OBP	SLG	E	Avg.
		BATTING														FIELDING	
1998—Boston (A.L.)	C	1	4	0	1	0	0	0	1	0	1	0-0	.250	.250	.250	0	1.000
1999—Boston (A.L.)	C	5	21	7	5	3	0	1	3	0	4	0-0	.238	.273	.524	0	1.000
Division series totals (2 years)		6	25	7	6	3	0	1	4	0	5	0-0	.240	.269	.480	0	1.000

CHAMPIONSHIP SERIES RECORD

Year Team (League)	Pos.	G	AB	R	H	2B	3B	HR	RBI	BB	SO	SB-CS	Avg.	OBP	SLG	E	Avg.
		BATTING														FIELDING	
1999—Boston (A.L.)	C	5	20	1	4	1	1	1	1	1	4	0-0	.200	.238	.500	1	.978

VAUGHN, GREG — OF/DH — DEVIL RAYS

PERSONAL: Born July 3, 1965, in Sacramento. ... 6-0/206. ... Bats right, throws right. ... Full name: Gregory Lamont Vaughn. ... Cousin of Mo Vaughn, first baseman, New York Mets; and cousin of Jerry Royster, infielder with five major league teams (1973-88).
HIGH SCHOOL: John F. Kennedy (Sacramento).
JUNIOR COLLEGE: Sacramento City College.
COLLEGE: Miami (Fla.).

TRANSACTIONS/CAREER NOTES: Selected by St. Louis Cardinals organization in fifth round of free-agent draft (January 17, 1984); did not sign. ... Selected by Milwaukee Brewers organization in secondary phase of free-agent draft (June 4, 1984); did not sign. ... Selected by Pittsburgh Pirates organization in secondary phase of free-agent draft (January 9, 1985); did not sign. ... Selected by California Angels organization in secondary phase of free-agent draft (June 3, 1985); did not sign. ... Selected by Brewers organization in secondary phase of free-agent draft (June 2, 1986). ... On disabled list (May 26-June 10, 1990). ... On Milwaukee disabled list (April 8-27, 1994); included rehabilitation assignment to Beloit (April 25-27). ... Traded by Brewers with a player to be named later to San Diego Padres for P Bryce Florie, P Ron Villone and OF Marc Newfield (July 31, 1996); Padres acquired OF Gerald Parent to complete deal (September 16, 1996). ... Granted free agency (October 28, 1996). ... Re-signed by Padres (December 19, 1996). ... Traded by Padres with P Kerry Taylor and P Chris Clark to New York Yankees for P Kenny Rogers, IF Mariano Duncan and P Kevin Henthorne (July 4, 1997); trade later voided because Vaughn failed physical (July 6, 1997). ... Traded by Padres with OF/1B Mark Sweeney to Cincinnati Reds for OF Reggie Sanders, SS Damian Jackson and P Josh Harris (February 2, 1999). ... Granted free agency (October 28, 1999). ... Signed by Tampa Bay Devil Rays (December 13, 1999). ... On disabled list (June 18-July 7, 2000; and June 23-September 1, 2002).
HONORS: Named Midwest League co-Most Valuable Player (1987). ... Named American Association Most Valuable Player (1989). ... Named N.L. Comeback Player of the Year by The Sporting News (1998). ... Named outfielder on The Sporting News N.L. All-Star team (1998). ... Named outfielder on The Sporting News N.L. Silver Slugger team (1998).
STATISTICAL NOTES: Led Midwest League with 292 total bases in 1987. ... Led Texas League with 279 total bases in 1988. ... Hit three home runs in one game (September 7, 1999). ... Career major league grand slams: 6.
2002 GAMES PLAYED BY POSITION (MLB): DH—38; OF—31.

		BATTING														FIELDING	
Year Team (League)	**Pos.**	**G**	**AB**	**R**	**H**	**2B**	**3B**	**HR**	**RBI**	**BB**	**SO**	**SB-CS**	**Avg.**	**OBP**	**SLG**	**E**	**Avg.**
1986—Helena (Pio.)	OF	66	258	64	75	13	2	16	54	30	69	23-5	.291	.363	.543	3	.972
1987—Beloit (Midw.)	OF	139	492	*120	150	31	6	*33	105	102	115	36-9	.305	.425	.593	10	.963
1988—El Paso (Texas)	OF	131	505	*104	152	*39	2	*28	*105	63	120	22-5	.301	.379	.552	7	.970
1989—Denver (A.A.)	OF	110	387	74	107	17	5	*26	*92	62	94	20-3	.276	.376	*.548	3	.980
—Milwaukee (A.L.)	OF-DH	38	113	18	30	3	0	5	23	13	23	4-1	.265	.336	.425	2	.943
1990—Milwaukee (A.L.)	OF-DH	120	382	51	84	26	2	17	61	33	91	7-4	.220	.280	.432	7	.967
1991—Milwaukee (A.L.)	OF-DH	145	542	81	132	24	5	27	98	62	125	2-2	.244	.319	.456	2	.994
1992—Milwaukee (A.L.)	OF-DH	141	501	77	114	18	2	23	78	60	123	15-15	.228	.313	.409	3	.990
1993—Milwaukee (A.L.)	OF-DH	154	569	97	152	28	2	30	97	89	118	10-7	.267	.369	.482	3	.986
1994—Milwaukee (A.L.)	OF-DH	95	370	59	94	24	1	19	55	51	93	9-5	.254	.345	.478	3	.982
—Beloit (Midw.)	DH	2	6	1	1	0	0	0	0	4	1	0-0	.167	.500	.167	...	...
1995—Milwaukee (A.L.)	DH	108	392	67	88	19	1	17	59	55	89	10-4	.224	.317	.408	...	...
1996—Milwaukee (A.L.)	OF-DH	102	375	78	105	16	0	31	95	58	99	5-2	.280	.378	.571	4	.980
—San Diego (N.L.)■	OF	43	141	20	29	3	1	10	22	24	31	4-1	.206	.329	.454	2	.974
1997—San Diego (N.L.)	OF-DH	120	361	60	78	10	0	18	57	56	110	7-4	.216	.322	.393	1	.994
1998—San Diego (N.L.)	OF-DH	158	573	112	156	28	4	50	119	79	121	11-4	.272	.363	.597	2	.993
1999—Cincinnati (N.L.)■	OF-DH	153	550	104	135	20	2	45	118	85	137	15-2	.245	.347	.535	4	.986
2000—Tampa Bay (A.L.)■	OF-DH	127	461	83	117	27	1	28	74	80	128	8-1	.254	.365	.499	1	.993
2001—Tampa Bay (A.L.)	DH-OF	136	485	74	113	25	0	24	82	71	130	11-5	.233	.333	.433	3	.978
2002—Tampa Bay (A.L.)	DH-OF	69	251	28	41	10	2	8	29	41	82	3-2	.163	.286	.315	1	.987
American League totals (11 years)		1235	4441	713	1070	220	16	229	751	613	1101	84-48	.241	.334	.452	29	.984
National League totals (4 years)		474	1625	296	398	61	7	123	316	244	399	37-11	.245	.345	.518	9	.989
Major League totals (14 years)		1709	6066	1009	1468	281	23	352	1067	857	1500	121-59	.242	.337	.470	38	.985

DIVISION SERIES RECORD

		BATTING														FIELDING	
Year Team (League)	**Pos.**	**G**	**AB**	**R**	**H**	**2B**	**3B**	**HR**	**RBI**	**BB**	**SO**	**SB-CS**	**Avg.**	**OBP**	**SLG**	**E**	**Avg.**
1996—San Diego (N.L.)	PH	3	3	0	0	0	0	0	0	0	1	0-0	.000	.000	.000	...	...
1998—San Diego (N.L.)	OF	4	15	2	5	1	0	1	1	0	4	0-1	.333	.333	.600	0	1.000
Division series totals (2 years)		7	18	2	5	1	0	1	1	0	5	0-1	.278	.278	.500	0	1.000

CHAMPIONSHIP SERIES RECORD

		BATTING														FIELDING	
Year Team (League)	**Pos.**	**G**	**AB**	**R**	**H**	**2B**	**3B**	**HR**	**RBI**	**BB**	**SO**	**SB-CS**	**Avg.**	**OBP**	**SLG**	**E**	**Avg.**
1998—San Diego (N.L.)	OF-PH	3	8	1	2	0	0	0	0	1	1	0-0	.250	.333	.250	0	1.000

WORLD SERIES RECORD

		BATTING														FIELDING	
Year Team (League)	**Pos.**	**G**	**AB**	**R**	**H**	**2B**	**3B**	**HR**	**RBI**	**BB**	**SO**	**SB-CS**	**Avg.**	**OBP**	**SLG**	**E**	**Avg.**
1998—San Diego (N.L.)	OF-DH	4	15	3	2	0	0	2	4	1	2	0-0	.133	.176	.533	1	.800

ALL-STAR GAME RECORD

	AB	**R**	**H**	**2B**	**3B**	**HR**	**RBI**	**BB**	**SO**	**SB-CS**	**Avg.**	**OBP**	**SLG**	**E**	**Avg.**
All-Star Game totals (2 years)	2	1	2	0	0	0	2	0	0	0-0	1.000	1.000	1.000	0	...

VAUGHN, MO — 1B — METS

PERSONAL: Born December 15, 1967, in Norwalk, Conn. ... 6-1/275. ... Bats left, throws right. ... Full name: Maurice Samuel Vaughn. ... Cousin of Greg Vaughn, outfielder/designated hitter, Tampa Bay Devil Rays.
HIGH SCHOOL: Trinity Pawling Prep (Pawling, N.Y.).
COLLEGE: Seton Hall.
TRANSACTIONS/CAREER NOTES: Selected by Boston Red Sox organization in first round (23rd pick overall) of free-agent draft (June 9, 1989). ... On disabled list (June 17-July 10, 1997). ... Granted free agency (October 23, 1998). ... Signed by Anaheim Angels (December 11, 1998). ... On disabled list (April 7-22, 1999; and March 23, 2001-entire season). ... Traded by Angels to New York Mets for P Kevin Appier (December 27, 2001). ... On disabled list (April 6-21, 2002).
RECORDS: Holds major league single-season record for most strikeouts by lefthander—181 (2000). ... Shares major league record for most seasons leading league in errors—7. ... Holds A.L. record for most seasons leading league in errors by first baseman—6.
HONORS: Named first baseman on The Sporting News A.L. All-Star team (1995). ... Named first baseman on The Sporting News A.L. Silver Slugger team (1995). ... Named A.L. Most Valuable Player by Baseball Writers' Association of America (1995).
STATISTICAL NOTES: Led A.L. with 20 intentional bases on balls received in 1994. ... Led A.L. first basemen with 103 double plays in 1994. ... Led A.L. first basemen with 1,262 putouts, 1,368 total chances and 128 double plays in 1995. ... Hit three home runs in one game

(September 24, 1996; and May 30, 1997). ... Had 16-game hitting streak (September 13-27, 1998). ... Led A.L. first basemen with 14 errors in 2000. ... Career major league grand slams: 10.
2002 GAMES PLAYED BY POSITION (MLB): 1B—134.

		BATTING														FIELDING	
Year Team (League)	**Pos.**	**G**	**AB**	**R**	**H**	**2B**	**3B**	**HR**	**RBI**	**BB**	**SO**	**SB-CS**	**Avg.**	**OBP**	**SLG**	**E**	**Avg.**
1989—New Britain (East.)	1B	73	245	28	68	15	0	8	38	25	47	1-3	.278	.350	.437	•10	.983
1990—Pawtucket (I.L.)	1B	108	386	62	114	26	1	22	72	44	87	3-2	.295	.374	.539	11	.988
1991—Pawtucket (I.L.)	1B	69	234	35	64	10	0	14	50	60	44	2-1	.274	.422	.496	3	.993
—Boston (A.L.)	1B-DH	74	219	21	57	12	0	4	32	26	43	2-1	.260	.339	.370	6	.985
1992—Boston (A.L.)	1B-DH	113	355	42	83	16	2	13	57	47	67	3-3	.234	.326	.400	*15	.982
—Pawtucket (I.L.)	1B	39	149	15	42	6	0	6	28	18	35	1-0	.282	.357	.443	8	.980
1993—Boston (A.L.)	1B-DH	152	539	86	160	34	1	29	101	79	130	4-3	.297	.390	.525	*16	.987
1994—Boston (A.L.)	1B-DH	111	394	65	122	25	1	26	82	57	112	4-4	.310	.408	.576	•10	.989
1995—Boston (A.L.)	1B-DH	140	550	98	165	28	3	39	•126	68	*150	11-4	.300	.388	.575	11	.992
1996—Boston (A.L.)	1B-DH	161	635	118	207	29	1	44	143	95	154	2-0	.326	.420	.583	*15	.988
1997—Boston (A.L.)	1B-DH	141	527	91	166	24	0	35	96	86	154	2-2	.315	.420	.560	*14	.988
1998—Boston (A.L.)	1B-DH	154	609	107	205	31	2	40	115	61	144	0-0	.337	.402	.591	12	.991
1999—Anaheim (A.L.)■	1B-DH	139	524	63	147	20	0	33	108	54	127	0-0	.281	.358	.508	3	.995
2000—Anaheim (A.L.)	1B-DH-OF	161	614	93	167	31	0	36	117	79	*181	2-0	.272	.365	.498	†14	.990
2001—Anaheim (A.L.)								Did not play.									
2002—New York (N.L.)■	1B	139	487	67	126	18	0	26	72	59	145	0-1	.259	.349	.456	18	.984
American League totals (10 years)		1346	4966	784	1479	250	10	299	977	652	1262	30-17	.298	.387	.533	116	.989
National League totals (1 year)		139	487	67	126	18	0	26	72	59	145	0-1	.259	.349	.456	18	.984
Major League totals (11 years)		1485	5453	851	1605	268	10	325	1049	711	1407	30-18	.294	.384	.526	134	.988

DIVISION SERIES RECORD

RECORDS: Shares single-game records for most home runs—2 (September 29, 1998); and most runs batted in—7 (September 29, 1998).
NOTES: Shares postseason single-game record for most runs batted in—7 (September 29, 1998).

		BATTING														FIELDING	
Year Team (League)	**Pos.**	**G**	**AB**	**R**	**H**	**2B**	**3B**	**HR**	**RBI**	**BB**	**SO**	**SB-CS**	**Avg.**	**OBP**	**SLG**	**E**	**Avg.**
1995—Boston (A.L.)	1B	3	14	0	0	0	0	0	0	1	7	0-0	.000	.067	.000	0	1.000
1998—Boston (A.L.)	1B	4	17	3	7	2	0	2	7	1	5	0-0	.412	.444	.882	0	1.000
Division series totals (2 years)		7	31	3	7	2	0	2	7	2	12	0-0	.226	.273	.484	0	1.000

ALL-STAR GAME RECORD

NOTES: Named to A.L. All-Star team for 1998 game; replaced by Rafael Palmeiro due to injury.

	AB	**R**	**H**	**2B**	**3B**	**HR**	**RBI**	**BB**	**SO**	**SB-CS**	**Avg.**	**OBP**	**SLG**	**E**	**Avg.**
All-Star Game totals (1 year)	2	0	0	0	0	0	0	0	2	0-0	.000	.000	.000	0	1.000

VAZQUEZ, JAVIER P EXPOS

PERSONAL: Born July 25, 1976, in Ponce, Puerto Rico. ... 6-2/195. ... Throws right, bats right. ... Full name: Javier Carlos Vazquez.
HIGH SCHOOL: Colegio de Ponce (Ponce, Puerto Rico).
TRANSACTIONS/CAREER NOTES: Selected by Montreal Expos organization in fifth round of free-agent draft (June 2, 1994). ... On suspended list (July 23-27, 1998).
STATISTICAL NOTES: Pitched 3-0 one-hit, complete-game victory against Los Angeles (September 14, 1999).
CAREER HITTING (MLB): 65-for-294 (.221), 23 R, 8 2B, 1 3B, 0 HR, 16 RBI.

Year League	**W**	**L**	**Pct.**	**ERA**	**G**	**GS**	**CG**	**ShO**	**Sv.-Opp.**	**IP**	**H**	**R**	**ER**	**HR**	**BB-IBB**	**SO**
1994—Gulf Coast Expos (GCL)	5	2	.714	2.53	15	11	1	1	0-...	67.2	37	25	19	0	15-0	56
1995—Albany (S.Atl.)	6	6	.500	5.08	21	21	1	0	0-...	102.2	109	67	58	8	47-0	87
1996—Delmarva (S.Atl.)	14	3	*.824	2.68	27	27	1	0	0-...	164.1	138	64	49	12	57-0	173
1997—West Palm Beach (FSL)	6	3	.667	2.16	19	19	1	0	0-...	112.2	98	40	27	8	28-0	100
—Harrisburg (East.)	4	0	1.000	1.07	6	6	1	0	0-...	42.0	15	5	5	2	12-0	47
1998—Montreal (N.L.)	5	15	.250	6.06	33	32	0	0	0-0	172.1	196	121	116	31	68-2	139
1999—Montreal (N.L.)	9	8	.529	5.00	26	26	3	1	0-0	154.2	154	98	86	20	52-4	113
—Ottawa (I.L.)	4	2	.667	4.85	7	7	0	0	0-...	42.2	45	24	23	7	16-0	46
2000—Montreal (N.L.)	11	9	.550	4.05	33	33	2	1	0-0	217.2	247	104	98	24	61-10	196
2001—Montreal (N.L.)	16	11	.593	3.42	32	32	5	•3	0-0	223.2	197	92	85	24	44-4	208
2002—Montreal (N.L.)	10	13	.435	3.91	34	34	2	0	0-0	230.1	*243	111	100	28	49-6	179
Major League totals (5 years)	51	56	.477	4.37	158	157	12	5	0-0	998.2	1037	526	485	127	274-26	835

VAZQUEZ, RAMON SS PADRES

PERSONAL: Born August 21, 1976, in Aibonito, Puerto Rico. ... 5-11/170. ... Bats left, throws right. ... Full name: Ramon Luis Vazquez.
JUNIOR COLLEGE: Indian Hills.
TRANSACTIONS/CAREER NOTES: Selected by Seattle Mariners organization in 27th round of free-agent draft (June 1, 1995). ... On disabled list (June 29-July 11, 2000). ... On Tacoma disabled list (June 20-29, 2001). ... Traded by Mariners with P Brett Tomko and C Tom Lampkin to San Diego Padres for C Ben Davis, P Wascar Serrano and SS Alex Arias (December 11, 2001).
STATISTICAL NOTES: Led Eastern League shortstops with 350 assists and 75 double plays in 2000. ... Career major league grand slams: 1.
2002 GAMES PLAYED BY POSITION (MLB): 2B—81; SS—41; 3B—20.

		BATTING														FIELDING	
Year Team (League)	**Pos.**	**G**	**AB**	**R**	**H**	**2B**	**3B**	**HR**	**RBI**	**BB**	**SO**	**SB-CS**	**Avg.**	**OBP**	**SLG**	**E**	**Avg.**
1995—Ariz. Mariners (Ariz.)	SS-3B-2B	39	141	20	29	3	1	0	11	19	27	4-3	.206	.309	.241	11	.941
1996—Everett (N'West)	SS	33	126	25	35	5	2	1	18	26	26	7-2	.278	.392	.373	20	.873
—Tacoma (PCL)	2B-SS	18	49	7	11	2	1	0	4	4	12	0-0	.224	.296	.306	1	.985
—Wisconsin (Midw.)	3B	3	10	1	3	1	0	0	1	2	2	0-0	.300	.417	.400	2	.818
1997—Wisconsin (Midw.)	SS	131	479	79	129	25	5	8	49	78	93	16-10	.269	.373	.392	35	.935
1998—Lancaster (Calif.)	SS	121	468	77	129	26	4	2	72	81	66	15-11	.276	.384	.361	31	.944
1999—New Haven (East.)	SS-3B-2B	127	438	58	113	27	3	5	45	62	77	8-1	.258	.354	.368	31	.942

Year	Team (League)	Pos.	G	AB	R	H	2B	3B	HR	RBI	BB	SO	SB-CS	Avg.	OBP	SLG	E	Avg.
			BATTING														FIELDING	
2000—	New Haven (East.)	SS	124	405	58	116	25	4	8	59	52	76	1-6	.286	.367	.427	22	.961
2001—	Tacoma (PCL)	SS	127	466	85	140	28	1	10	79	76	84	9-7	.300	.397	.429	12	.979
—	Seattle (A.L.)	SS-2B-3B-DH	17	35	5	8	0	0	0	4	0	3	0-0	.229	.222	.229	1	.969
2002—	San Diego (N.L.)■	2B-SS-3B	128	423	50	116	21	5	2	32	45	79	7-2	.274	.344	.362	7	.986
American League totals (1 year)			17	35	5	8	0	0	0	4	0	3	0-0	.229	.222	.229	1	.969
National League totals (1 year)			128	423	50	116	21	5	2	32	45	79	7-2	.274	.344	.362	7	.986
Major League totals (2 years)			145	458	55	124	21	5	2	36	45	82	7-2	.271	.335	.352	8	.985

DIVISION SERIES RECORD

Year	Team (League)	Pos.	G	AB	R	H	2B	3B	HR	RBI	BB	SO	SB-CS	Avg.	OBP	SLG	E	Avg.
			BATTING														FIELDING	
2001—	Seattle (A.L.)								Did not play.									

CHAMPIONSHIP SERIES RECORD

Year	Team (League)	Pos.	G	AB	R	H	2B	3B	HR	RBI	BB	SO	SB-CS	Avg.	OBP	SLG	E	Avg.
			BATTING														FIELDING	
2001—	Seattle (A.L.)								Did not play.									

VELARDE, RANDY 2B

PERSONAL: Born November 24, 1962, in Midland, Texas. ... 6-0/200. ... Bats right, throws right. ... Full name: Randy Lee Velarde. ... Name pronounced vel-ARE-dee.

HIGH SCHOOL: Robert E. Lee (Midland, Texas).

COLLEGE: Lubbock (Texas) Christian College.

TRANSACTIONS/CAREER NOTES: Selected by Chicago White Sox organization in 19th round of free-agent draft (June 3, 1985). ... Traded by White Sox with P Pete Filson to New York Yankees for P Scott Nielsen and IF Mike Soper (January 5, 1987). ... On New York disabled list (August 9-29, 1989). ... On New York disabled list (June 6-July 30, 1993); included rehabilitation assignment to Albany/Colonie (July 24-30). ... Granted free agency (December 23, 1994). ... Re-signed by Yankees organization (April 12, 1995). ... Granted free agency (November 2, 1995). ... Signed by California Angels (November 21, 1995). ... Angels franchise renamed Anaheim Angels for 1997 season. ... On disabled list (March 23-September 1 and September 2, 1997-remainder of season). ... On Anaheim disabled list (March 19-May 13 and May 16-August 3, 1998); included rehabilitation assignments to Lake Elsinore (May 7-13) and Vancouver (July 29-August 3). ... Granted free agency (October 23, 1998). ... Re-signed by Angels (December 7, 1998). ... Traded by Angels with P Omar Olivares to Oakland Athletics for P Elvin Nina, OF Jeff DaVanon and OF Nathan Hayes (July 29, 1999). ... On Oakland disabled list (April 2-May 8, 2000); included rehabilitation assignments to Midland (April 28-May 2) and Sacramento (May 3-8). ... Traded by A's to Texas Rangers for P Ryan Cullen and P Aaron Harang (November 17, 2000). ... On Texas disabled list (May 25-July 12, 2001); included rehabilitation assignment to Tulsa (July 4-12). ... Traded by Rangers to Yankees for two players to be named later (August 31, 2001); Rangers acquired P Randy Flores and P Rosman Garcia to complete deal (October 12, 2001). ... Granted free agency (November 5, 2001). ... Signed by A's (January 17, 2002). ... On Oakland disabled list (April 5-May 4, 2002); included rehabilitation assignment to Sacramento (April 29-May 4). ... Granted free agency (October 30, 2002).

STATISTICAL NOTES: Led Midwest League shortstops with 52 errors in 1986. ... Had 21-game hitting streak (June 9-July 4, 1996). ... Led A.L. second baseman with 493 assists and 805 total chances in 1999. ... Career major league grand slams: 1.

2002 GAMES PLAYED BY POSITION (MLB): 2B—38; DH—5; 1B—5; 3B—1.

Year	Team (League)	Pos.	G	AB	R	H	2B	3B	HR	RBI	BB	SO	SB-CS	Avg.	OBP	SLG	E	Avg.
			BATTING														FIELDING	
1985—	Niagara Falls (NY-P)	OF-SS-2B-3B	67	218	28	48	7	3	1	16	35	72	8-3	.220	.331	.294	15	.941
1986—	Appleton (Midw.)	SS-3B-OF	124	417	55	105	31	4	11	50	58	96	13-6	.252	.350	.424	†54	.903
—	Buffalo (A.A.)	SS	9	20	2	4	1	0	0	2	2	4	1-0	.200	.304	.250	3	.925
1987—	Alb./Colonie (East.)■	SS-OF	71	263	40	83	20	2	7	32	25	47	8-6	.316	.380	.487	17	.957
—	Columbus (I.L.)	SS	49	185	21	59	10	6	5	33	15	36	8-2	.319	.380	.519	16	.943
—	New York (A.L.)	SS	8	22	1	4	0	0	0	1	0	6	0-0	.182	.182	.182	2	.933
1988—	Columbus (I.L.)	SS-2B-3B	78	293	39	79	23	4	5	37	25	71	7-5	.270	.327	.427	25	.940
—	New York (A.L.)	2B-SS-3B	48	115	18	20	6	0	5	12	8	24	1-1	.174	.240	.357	8	.955
1989—	Columbus (I.L.)	SS-3B	103	387	59	103	26	3	11	53	38	105	3-5	.266	.340	.434	22	.953
—	New York (A.L.)	3B-SS	33	100	12	34	4	2	2	11	7	14	0-3	.340	.389	.480	4	.956
1990—	New York (A.L.)	3-S-O-2-DH	95	229	21	48	6	2	5	19	20	53	0-3	.210	.275	.319	12	.950
1991—	New York (A.L.)	3B-SS-OF	80	184	19	45	11	1	1	15	18	43	3-1	.245	.322	.332	15	.934
1992—	New York (A.L.)	S-3-O-2	121	412	57	112	24	1	7	46	38	78	7-2	.272	.333	.386	15	.967
1993—	New York (A.L.)	OF-SS-3B-DH	85	226	28	68	13	2	7	24	18	39	2-2	.301	.360	.469	9	.956
—	Alb./Colonie (East.)	SS-OF-DH	5	17	2	4	0	0	1	2	2	2	0-0	.235	.316	.412	2	.900
1994—	New York (A.L.)	SS-3B-OF-2B	77	280	47	78	16	1	9	34	22	61	4-2	.279	.338	.439	19	.936
1995—	New York (A.L.)	2-S-O-3	111	367	60	102	19	1	7	46	55	64	5-1	.278	.375	.392	10	.977
1996—	California (A.L.)■	2B-3B-SS	136	530	82	151	27	3	14	54	70	118	7-7	.285	.372	.426	16	.972
1997—	Anaheim (A.L.)	PR	1	0	0	0	0	0	0	0	0	0	0-0	...	...	...	...	...
1998—	Lake Elsinore (Calif.)	2B	5	20	6	11	2	1	1	7	2	0	1-1	.550	.609	.900	1	.966
—	Anaheim (A.L.)	2B	51	188	29	49	13	1	4	26	34	42	7-2	.261	.375	.404	4	.982
—	Vancouver (PCL)	2B-DH	4	16	0	4	2	0	0	2	1	4	1-1	.250	.333	.375	0	1.000
1999—	Anaheim (A.L.)	2B	95	376	57	115	15	4	9	48	43	56	13-4	.306	.383	.439	7	.986
—	Oakland (A.L.)■	2B	61	255	48	85	10	3	7	28	27	42	11-4	.333	.401	.478	7	.977
2000—	Midland (Texas)	2B	5	16	4	2	0	0	1	1	4	4	0-0	.125	.300	.313	1	.941
—	Sacramento (PCL)	2B	3	11	3	5	0	0	0	2	4	2	2-0	.455	.625	.455	0	1.000
—	Oakland (A.L.)	2B	122	485	82	135	23	0	12	41	54	95	9-3	.278	.354	.400	12	.982
2001—	Texas (A.L.)■	2-1-3-DH-O	78	296	46	88	16	2	9	31	29	73	4-2	.297	.369	.456	4	.988
—	Tulsa (Texas)	2B-3B	6	21	5	8	2	0	0	5	1	5	0-0	.381	.375	.476	0	1.000
—	New York (A.L.)■	3B-DH-OF-1B	15	46	4	7	3	0	0	1	5	13	2-0	.152	.278	.217	1	.973
2002—	Oakland (A.L.)■	2B-DH-1B-3B	56	133	22	30	8	0	2	8	15	32	3-0	.226	.325	.331	4	.979
—	Sacramento (PCL)	2B	4	17	3	8	3	0	1	4	1	3	1-0	.471	.526	.824	0	...
Major League totals (16 years)			1273	4244	633	1171	214	23	100	445	463	853	78-37	.276	.352	.408	149	.970

DIVISION SERIES RECORD

Year	Team (League)	Pos.	G	AB	R	H	2B	3B	HR	RBI	BB	SO	SB-CS	Avg.	OBP	SLG	E	Avg.
			BATTING														FIELDING	
1995—	New York (A.L.)	2B-3B-OF	5	17	3	3	0	0	0	1	6	4	0-1	.176	.417	.176	1	.963
2000—	Oakland (A.L.)	2B	5	20	2	5	1	0	0	3	2	3	1-0	.250	.318	.300	2	.920
2001—	New York (A.L.)	DH	2	5	0	1	0	0	0	0	0	1	0-0	.200	.200	.200	...	...
2002—	Oakland (A.L.)	1B-2B	4	5	1	3	1	0	0	1	0	1	0-0	.600	.600	.800	0	1.000
Division series totals (4 years)			16	47	6	12	2	0	0	5	8	9	1-1	.255	.375	.298	3	.949

CHAMPIONSHIP SERIES RECORD

Year	Team (League)	Pos.	G	AB	R	H	2B	3B	HR	RBI	BB	SO	SB-CS	Avg.	OBP	SLG	E	Avg.
			BATTING														FIELDING	
2001—	New York (A.L.)	PH-3B	1	1	0	0	0	0	0	0	0	0	0-0	.000	.000	.000	0	1.000

WORLD SERIES RECORD

Year	Team (League)	Pos.	G	AB	R	H	2B	3B	HR	RBI	BB	SO	SB-CS	Avg.	OBP	SLG	E	Avg.
			BATTING														FIELDING	
2001—	New York (A.L.)	1B	1	3	0	0	0	0	0	0	1	1	0-0	.000	.250	.000	0	1.000

VENAFRO, MIKE — P — ATHLETICS

PERSONAL: Born August 2, 1973, in Takoma Park, Md. ... 5-10/180. ... Throws left, bats left. ... Full name: Michael Robert Venafro.
HIGH SCHOOL: Paul VI (Fairfax, Va.).
COLLEGE: James Madison.
TRANSACTIONS/CAREER NOTES: Selected by Texas Rangers organization in 29th round of free-agent draft (June 1, 1995). ... Traded by Rangers with 1B Carlos Pena to Oakland Athletics for 1B Jason Hart, P Marion Ramos, C Gerald Laird and OF Ryan Ludwick (January 14, 2002). ... On Sacramento disabled list (August 17-31, 2002).
CAREER HITTING (MLB): 0-for-0 (.000), 0 R, 0 2B, 0 3B, 0 HR, 0 RBI.

Year	League	W	L	Pct.	ERA	G	GS	CG	ShO	Sv.-Opp.	IP	H	R	ER	HR	BB-IBB	SO
1995—	Hudson Valley (NY-Penn)	9	1	.900	2.13	32	0	0	0	2-...	50.2	37	13	12	0	21-2	32
1996—	Charleston, S.C. (S.Atl.)	1	3	.250	3.51	50	0	0	0	19-...	59.0	57	27	23	0	21-3	62
1997—	Charlotte (FSL)	4	2	.667	3.43	35	0	0	0	10-...	44.2	51	17	17	2	21-1	35
—	Tulsa (Texas)	0	1	.000	3.45	11	0	0	0	1-...	15.2	13	12	6	1	12-0	13
1998—	Tulsa (Texas)	3	4	.429	3.10	46	0	0	0	14-...	52.1	42	21	18	5	26-0	45
—	Oklahoma City (PCL)	0	0	...	6.35	13	0	0	0	0-...	17.0	19	12	12	3	10-0	15
1999—	Oklahoma (PCL)	0	0	...	5.40	6	0	0	0	1-...	11.2	16	7	7	2	0-0	7
—	Texas (A.L.)	3	2	.600	3.29	65	0	0	0	0-1	68.1	63	29	25	4	22-0	37
2000—	Texas (A.L.)	3	1	.750	3.83	77	0	0	0	1-2	56.1	64	27	24	2	21-4	32
2001—	Texas (A.L.)	5	5	.500	4.80	70	0	0	0	4-8	60.0	54	35	32	2	28-4	29
2002—	Oakland (A.L.)■	2	2	.500	4.62	47	0	0	0	0-0	37.0	45	22	19	5	14-2	16
—	Sacramento (PCL)	0	1	.000	6.97	8	0	0	0	0-...	10.1	12	8	8	2	1-0	14
Major League totals (4 years)		13	10	.565	4.06	259	0	0	0	5-11	221.2	226	113	100	13	85-10	114

DIVISION SERIES RECORD

Year	League	W	L	Pct.	ERA	G	GS	CG	ShO	Sv.-Opp.	IP	H	R	ER	HR	BB-IBB	SO
1999—	Texas (A.L.)	0	0	...	0.00	2	0	0	0	0-0	1.0	2	2	0	1	1-0	0

VENTURA, ROBIN — 3B

PERSONAL: Born July 14, 1967, in Santa Maria, Calif. ... 6-1/198. ... Bats left, throws right. ... Full name: Robin Mark Ventura.
HIGH SCHOOL: Righetti (Santa Maria, Calif.).
COLLEGE: Oklahoma State.
TRANSACTIONS/CAREER NOTES: Selected by Chicago White Sox organization in first round (10th pick overall) of free-agent draft (June 1, 1988). ... On suspended list (August 23-25, 1993). ... On disabled list (March 31-July 24, 1997); included rehabilitation assignments to Nashville (July 13-17) and Birmingham (July 18-22). ... Granted free agency (October 23, 1998). ... Signed by New York Mets (December 1, 1998). ... On disabled list (July 14-29, 2000). ... Traded by Mets to New York Yankees for OF David Justice (December 7, 2001). ... Granted free agency (October 29, 2002).
RECORDS: Holds A.L. single-season record for fewest chances accepted by third baseman for leader—372 (1996). ... Shares N.L. single-season record for highest fielding average by third baseman (150 or more games)—.980 (1999). ... Shares major league single-game record for most grand slams—2 (September 4, 1995).
HONORS: Named College Player of the Year by The Sporting News (1987-88). ... Named third baseman on The Sporting News college All-America team (1987-88). ... Named Golden Spikes Award winner by USA Baseball (1988). ... Won A.L. Gold Glove at third base (1991-93, 1996 and 1998). ... Won N.L. Gold Glove at third base (1999).
STATISTICAL NOTES: Led Southern League with 12 intentional bases on balls received in 1989. ... Led Southern League third basemen with .930 fielding percentage and tied for lead with 21 double plays in 1989. ... Led A.L. third basemen with 18 errors in 1991. ... Led A.L. third basemen in putouts with 134 in 1991, 141 in 1992 and 133 in 1996. ... Led A.L. third basemen in total chances with 536 in 1992, 404 in 1993 and 382 in 1996. ... Led A.L. third basemen with 372 assists and tied for lead in double plays with 29 in 1992. ... Led A.L. third basemen in double plays with 22 in 1994 and 34 in 1996 and tied for lead with 29 in 1992. ... Led A.L. with 15 intentional bases on balls received in 1998. ... Led A.L. third basemen with 330 assists, 447 total chances and 38 double plays in 1998. ... Led N.L. third basemen with 320 assists, 452 total chances and .980 fielding percentage in 1999. ... Career major league grand slams: 16.
MISCELLANEOUS: Member of 1988 U.S. Olympic baseball team.
2002 GAMES PLAYED BY POSITION (MLB): 3B—137; 1B—5.

Year	Team (League)	Pos.	G	AB	R	H	2B	3B	HR	RBI	BB	SO	SB-CS	Avg.	OBP	SLG	E	Avg.
			BATTING														FIELDING	
1989—	Birmingham (Sou.)	3B-1B-2B	129	454	75	126	25	2	3	67	93	51	9-7	.278	.403	.361	27	†.930
—	Chicago (A.L.)	3B	16	45	5	8	3	0	0	7	8	6	0-0	.178	.298	.244	2	.962
1990—	Chicago (A.L.)	3B-1B	150	493	48	123	17	1	5	54	55	53	1-4	.249	.324	.318	25	.939
1991—	Chicago (A.L.)	3B-1B	157	606	92	172	25	1	23	100	80	67	2-4	.284	.367	.442	†18	.966
1992—	Chicago (A.L.)	3B-1B	157	592	85	167	38	1	16	93	93	71	2-4	.282	.375	.431	23	.957

Year Team (League)	Pos.	G	AB	R	H	2B	3B	HR	RBI	BB	SO	SB-CS	Avg.	OBP	SLG	E	Avg.
		BATTING														FIELDING	
1993—Chicago (A.L.)	3B-1B	157	554	85	145	27	1	22	94	105	82	1-6	.262	.379	.433	14	.966
1994—Chicago (A.L.)	3B-1B-SS	109	401	57	113	15	1	18	78	61	69	3-1	.282	.373	.459	20	.931
1995—Chicago (A.L.)	3B-1B-DH	135	492	79	145	22	0	26	93	75	98	4-3	.295	.384	.498	19	.956
1996—Chicago (A.L.)	3B-1B	158	586	96	168	31	2	34	105	78	81	1-3	.287	.368	.520	11	.975
1997—Nashville (A.A.)	3B-DH	5	15	3	6	1	0	2	5	2	1	0-1	.400	.471	.867	0	1.000
—Birmingham (Sou.)	3B	4	17	3	5	1	0	1	2	1	1	0-0	.294	.333	.529	2	.714
—Chicago (A.L.)	3B	54	183	27	48	10	1	6	26	34	21	0-0	.262	.373	.426	7	.956
1998—Chicago (A.L.)	3B	161	590	84	155	31	4	21	91	79	111	1-1	.263	.349	.436	15	.966
1999—New York (N.L.)■	3B-1B	161	588	88	177	38	0	32	120	74	109	1-1	.301	.379	.529	9	†.980
2000—New York (N.L.)	3B-1B	141	469	61	109	23	1	24	84	75	91	3-5	.232	.338	.439	17	.955
2001—New York (N.L.)	3B	142	456	70	108	20	0	21	61	88	101	2-5	.237	.359	.419	16	.957
2002—New York (A.L.)■	3B-1B	141	465	68	115	17	0	27	93	90	101	3-1	.247	.368	.458	*23	.944
American League totals (11 years)		1395	5007	726	1359	236	12	198	834	758	760	18-27	.271	.365	.442	177	.957
National League totals (3 years)		444	1513	219	394	81	1	77	265	237	301	6-11	.260	.360	.468	42	.965
Major League totals (14 years)		1839	6520	945	1753	317	13	275	1099	995	1061	24-38	.269	.364	.448	219	.959

DIVISION SERIES RECORD

Year Team (League)	Pos.	G	AB	R	H	2B	3B	HR	RBI	BB	SO	SB-CS	Avg.	OBP	SLG	E	Avg.
		BATTING														FIELDING	
1999—New York (N.L.)	3B	4	14	1	3	2	0	0	1	4	2	0-0	.214	.389	.357	0	1.000
2000—New York (N.L.)	3B-1B	4	14	1	2	0	0	1	2	4	1	0-0	.143	.368	.357	0	1.000
2002—New York (A.L.)	3B	4	14	1	4	2	0	0	4	1	2	0-0	.286	.313	.429	0	1.000
Division series totals (3 years)		12	42	3	9	4	0	1	7	9	5	0-0	.214	.358	.381	0	1.000

CHAMPIONSHIP SERIES RECORD

Year Team (League)	Pos.	G	AB	R	H	2B	3B	HR	RBI	BB	SO	SB-CS	Avg.	OBP	SLG	E	Avg.
		BATTING														FIELDING	
1993—Chicago (A.L.)	3B-1B	6	20	2	4	0	0	1	5	6	6	0-0	.200	.370	.350	1	.938
1999—New York (N.L.)	3B	6	25	2	3	1	0	0	1	2	5	0-0	.120	.185	.160	0	1.000
2000—New York (N.L.)	3B	5	14	4	3	1	0	0	5	6	0	0-0	.214	.409	.286	1	.938
Championship series totals (3 years)		17	59	8	10	2	0	1	11	14	11	0-0	.169	.316	.254	2	.962

WORLD SERIES RECORD

Year Team (League)	Pos.	G	AB	R	H	2B	3B	HR	RBI	BB	SO	SB-CS	Avg.	OBP	SLG	E	Avg.
		BATTING														FIELDING	
2000—New York (N.L.)	3B	5	20	1	3	1	0	1	1	1	5	0-0	.150	.190	.350	0	1.000

ALL-STAR GAME RECORD

	AB	R	H	2B	3B	HR	RBI	BB	SO	SB-CS	Avg.	OBP	SLG	E	Avg.
All-Star Game totals (2 years)	3	1	2	1	0	0	1	0	1	0-0	.667	.667	1.000	0	1.000

VERES, DAVE P

PERSONAL: Born October 19, 1966, in Montgomery, Ala. ... 6-2/220. ... Throws right, bats right. ... Full name: David Scott Veres. ... Name pronounced VEERZ.

HIGH SCHOOL: Gresham (Ore.).

JUNIOR COLLEGE: Mount Hood Community College (Ore.).

TRANSACTIONS/CAREER NOTES: Selected by Oakland Athletics organization in fourth round of free-agent draft (January 14, 1986). ... Traded by A's to Los Angeles Dodgers for P Kevin Campbell (January 15, 1991). ... Loaned by Dodgers organization to Mexico City Tigers, Mexican League (April 3-May 15, 1992). ... Released by Dodgers (May 15, 1992). ... Signed by Houston Astros organization (May 28, 1992). ... Traded by Astros with C Raul Chavez to Montreal Expos for 3B Sean Berry (December 20, 1995). ... On disabled list (August 21-September 17, 1997). ... Traded by Expos with a player to be named later to Colorado Rockies for OF Terry Jones and a player to be named later (December 10, 1997). ... Traded by Rockies with P Darryl Kile and P Luther Hackman to St. Louis Cardinals for P Jose Jimenez, P Manny Aybar, P Rick Croushore and SS Brent Butler (November 16, 1999). ... Granted free agency (October 30, 2002).

STATISTICAL NOTES: Tied for California League lead with 29 wild pitches in 1987. ... Led Southern League with 16 wild pitches in 1989.

MISCELLANEOUS: Made an out in only appearance as pinch hitter (1998).

CAREER HITTING (MLB): 7-for-27 (.259), 1 R, 1 2B, 0 3B, 0 HR, 1 RBI.

Year League	W	L	Pct.	ERA	G	GS	CG	ShO	Sv.-Opp.	IP	H	R	ER	HR	BB-IBB	SO
1986—Medford (N'West)	5	2	.714	3.26	15	•15	0	0	0-...	77.1	58	38	28	5	57-0	60
1987—Modesto (Calif.)	8	9	.471	4.79	26	26	2	0	0-...	148.1	124	90	79	9	108-3	124
1988—Modesto (Calif.)	4	11	.267	3.31	19	19	3	0	0-...	125.0	100	61	46	7	78-1	91
—Huntsville (Sou.)	3	4	.429	4.15	8	8	0	0	0-...	39.0	50	20	18	1	15-2	17
1989—Huntsville (Sou.)	8	11	.421	4.86	29	28	2	1	0-...	159.1	160	93	86	15	83-1	105
1990—Tacoma (PCL)	11	8	.579	4.69	32	23	2	0	1-...	151.2	136	90	79	13	88-1	88
1991—Albuquerque (PCL)■	7	6	.538	4.47	57	3	0	0	5-...	100.2	89	52	50	8	52-5	81
1992—MC Tigres (Mex.)■	1	5	.167	8.10	14	1	0	0	1-...	23.1	29	21	21	5	12-2	12
—Tucson (PCL)■	2	3	.400	5.30	29	1	0	0	0-...	52.2	60	36	31	1	17-1	46
1993—Tucson (PCL)	6	10	.375	4.90	43	15	1	0	5-...	130.1	156	88	71	7	32-1	122
1994—Tucson (PCL)	1	1	.500	1.88	16	0	0	0	1-...	24.0	17	8	5	0	10-2	19
—Houston (N.L.)	3	3	.500	2.41	32	0	0	0	1-1	41.0	39	13	11	4	7-3	28
1995—Houston (N.L.)	5	1	.833	2.26	72	0	0	0	1-3	103.1	89	29	26	5	30-6	94
1996—Montreal (N.L.)■	6	3	.667	4.17	68	0	0	0	4-6	77.2	85	39	36	10	32-2	81
1997—Montreal (N.L.)	2	3	.400	3.48	53	0	0	0	1-4	62.0	68	28	24	5	27-3	47
1998—Colorado (N.L.)■	3	1	.750	2.83	63	0	0	0	8-13	76.1	67	26	24	6	27-2	74
1999—Colorado (N.L.)	4	8	.333	5.14	73	0	0	0	31-39	77.0	88	46	44	14	37-7	71
2000—St. Louis (N.L.)■	3	5	.375	2.85	71	0	0	0	29-36	75.2	65	26	24	6	25-2	67
2001—St. Louis (N.L.)	3	2	.600	3.70	71	0	0	0	15-19	65.2	57	29	27	12	28-1	61
2002—St. Louis (N.L.)	5	8	.385	3.48	71	0	0	0	4-8	82.2	67	34	32	12	39-4	68
Major League totals (9 years)	34	34	.500	3.38	574	0	0	0	94-129	661.1	625	270	248	74	252-30	591

DIVISION SERIES RECORD

Year League	W	L	Pct.	ERA	G	GS	CG	ShO	Sv.-Opp.	IP	H	R	ER	HR	BB-IBB	SO
2000—St. Louis (N.L.)	0	0	...	0.00	2	0	0	0	1-1	2.0	1	1	0	0	0-0	4
2001—St. Louis (N.L.)	0	0	...	0.00	2	0	0	0	0-0	1.0	1	0	0	0	1-1	1
Division series totals (2 years)	0	0	...	0.00	4	0	0	0	1-1	3.0	2	1	0	0	1-1	5

CHAMPIONSHIP SERIES RECORD

Year League	W	L	Pct.	ERA	G	GS	CG	ShO	Sv.-Opp.	IP	H	R	ER	HR	BB-IBB	SO
2000—St. Louis (N.L.)	0	0	...	0.00	3	0	0	0	0-0	2.1	2	0	0	0	0-0	3
2002—St. Louis (N.L.)	0	0	...	0.00	2	0	0	0	0-0	3.2	2	0	0	0	1-1	5
Champ. series totals (2 years)	0	0	...	0.00	5	0	0	0	0-0	6.0	4	0	0	0	1-1	8

VIDRO, JOSE — 2B — EXPOS

PERSONAL: Born August 27, 1974, in Mayaguez, Puerto Rico. ... 5-11/195. ... Bats both, throws right. ... Full name: Jose Angel Cetty Vidro.
HIGH SCHOOL: Blanco Morales (Sabana Grande, Puerto Rico).
TRANSACTIONS/CAREER NOTES: Selected by Montreal Expos organization in sixth round of free agent draft (June 1, 1992). ... On disabled list (June 1-15 and July 26, 1993-remainder of season). ... On disabled list (May 20-June 12, 2001).
RECORDS: Shares major league single-season record for fewest putouts by second baseman (150 or more games)—260 (2000).
STATISTICAL NOTES: Led N.L. second basemen with 442 assists in 2000 and 448 in 2002. ... Switch-hit home runs in one game (July 3, 2000). ... Had 21-game hitting streak (May 4-27, 2002). ... Led N.L. second basemen with 773 total chances in 2002. ... Career major league grand slams: 2.
2002 GAMES PLAYED BY POSITION (MLB): 2B—152.

		BATTING														FIELDING	
Year Team (League)	Pos.	G	AB	R	H	2B	3B	HR	RBI	BB	SO	SB-CS	Avg.	OBP	SLG	E	Avg.
1992—GC Expos (GCL)	2B	54	200	29	66	6	2	4	31	16	31	10-1	.330	.376	.440	4	*.982
1993—Burlington (Midw.)	2B	76	287	39	69	19	0	2	34	28	54	3-2	.240	.317	.328	7	.974
1994—W. Palm Beach (FSL)	2B	125	465	57	124	30	2	4	49	51	56	8-2	.267	.344	.366	20	.964
1995—W. Palm Beach (FSL)	IF	44	163	20	53	15	2	3	24	8	21	0-1	.325	.360	.497	4	.981
—Harrisburg (East.)	IF	64	246	33	64	16	2	4	38	20	37	7-7	.260	.315	.390	9	.966
1996—Harrisburg (East.)	IF	126	452	57	117	25	3	18	82	29	71	3-1	.259	.300	.447	15	.964
1997—Ottawa (I.L.)	3B-2B-DH	73	279	40	90	17	0	13	47	22	40	2-0	.323	.370	.523	8	.967
—Montreal (N.L.)	3B-DH-2B	67	169	19	42	12	1	2	17	11	20	1-0	.249	.297	.367	4	.955
1998—Montreal (N.L.)	2B-3B	83	205	24	45	12	0	0	18	27	33	2-2	.220	.318	.278	6	.972
—Ottawa (I.L.)	2B-3B-DH	63	235	35	68	14	2	2	32	24	25	5-2	.289	.361	.391	6	.973
1999—Montreal (N.L.)	2-1-0-3	140	494	67	150	45	2	12	59	29	51	0-4	.304	.346	.476	11	.981
2000—Montreal (N.L.)	2B	153	606	101	200	51	2	24	97	49	69	5-4	.330	.379	.540	10	.986
2001—Montreal (N.L.)	2B-DH	124	486	82	155	34	1	15	59	31	49	4-1	.319	.371	.486	9	.983
2002—Montreal (N.L.)	2B	152	604	103	190	43	3	19	96	60	70	2-1	.315	.378	.490	11	.986
Major League totals (6 years)		719	2564	396	782	197	9	72	346	207	292	14-12	.305	.360	.473	51	.982

ALL-STAR GAME RECORD

	AB	R	H	2B	3B	HR	RBI	BB	SO	SB-CS	Avg.	OBP	SLG	E	Avg.
All-Star Game totals (2 years)	3	0	0	0	0	0	0	0	0	0-0	.000	.000	.000	1	.667

VILLAFUERTE, BRANDON — P — PADRES

PERSONAL: Born December 17, 1975, in Hilo, Hawaii. ... 5-11/165. ... Throws right, bats right. ... Full name: Brandon Paul Villafuerte.
HIGH SCHOOL: Live Oak (Morgan Hill, Calif.).
JUNIOR COLLEGE: West Valley College (Calif.).
TRANSACTIONS/CAREER NOTES: Selected by New York Mets organization 66th round of free-agent draft (June 2, 1994). ... Traded by Mets with a player to be named later to Florida Marlins for OF Robert Stratton (March 20,1998); Marlins acquired 2B Cesar Crespo to complete deal (September 14, 1998). ... Traded by Marlins to Detroit Tigers for P Mike Drumright (July 31, 1999). ... Traded by Tigers with P Kevin Mobley to Texas Rangers for P Matt Perisho (December 15, 2000). ... Granted free agency (October 11, 2001). ... Signed by San Diego Padres organization (December 6, 2001).
STATISTICAL NOTES: Tied for International League lead with 12 wild pitches in 2000.
CAREER HITTING (MLB): 0-for-0 (.000), 0 R, 0 2B, 0 3B, 0 HR, 0 RBI.

Year League	W	L	Pct.	ERA	G	GS	CG	ShO	Sv.-Opp.	IP	H	R	ER	HR	BB-IBB	SO
1995—Kingsport (Appl.)	5	1	.833	5.63	20	0	0	0	0-...	32.0	28	21	20	0	26-0	42
1996—Pittsfield (NY-Penn)	8	3	.727	3.02	18	7	1	0	1-...	62.2	53	21	21	5	27-0	59
1997—Capital City (S.Atl.)	3	1	.750	2.38	47	3	0	0	7-...	75.2	58	23	20	6	33-0	88
1998—Brevard County (FSL)■	1	0	1.000	0.93	3	0	0	0	0-...	9.2	7	3	1	0	1-0	6
—Portland (East.)	0	2	.000	4.97	30	0	0	0	1-...	54.1	68	35	30	3	33-2	52
—Charlotte (I.L.)	1	0	1.000	6.35	10	0	0	0	0-...	11.1	15	8	8	2	8-0	9
1999—Portland (East.)	6	8	.429	3.50	22	12	0	0	0-...	100.1	97	45	39	11	40-3	85
—Jacksonville (Sou.)■	0	2	.000	1.88	15	0	0	0	5-...	24.0	17	6	5	0	12-0	20
2000—Toledo (I.L.)	4	9	.308	6.67	46	6	0	0	4-...	87.2	112	70	65	7	49-1	85
—Detroit (A.L.)	0	0	...	10.38	3	0	0	0	0-0	4.1	4	5	5	0	4-0	1
2001—Oklahoma (PCL)■	5	5	.500	2.83	38	0	0	0	10-...	63.2	63	21	20	4	26-1	65
—Texas (A.L.)	0	0	...	14.29	6	0	0	0	0-0	5.2	12	9	9	3	4-0	4
2002—Portland (PCL)■	8	4	.667	2.02	47	0	0	0	1-...	58.0	43	17	13	2	22-1	54
—San Diego (N.L.)	1	2	.333	1.41	31	0	0	0	1-1	32.0	29	5	5	2	12-2	25
A.L. totals (2 years)	0	0	...	12.60	9	0	0	0	0-0	10.0	16	14	14	3	8-0	5
N.L. totals (1 year)	1	2	.333	1.41	31	0	0	0	1-1	32.0	29	5	5	2	12-2	25
Major League totals (3 years)	1	2	.333	4.07	40	0	0	0	1-1	42.0	45	19	19	5	20-2	30

VILLONE, RON — P

PERSONAL: Born January 16, 1970, in Englewood, N.J. ... 6-4/235. ... Throws left, bats left. ... Full name: Ronald Thomas Villone Jr.

HIGH SCHOOL: South Bergenfield (Bergenfield, N.J.).

COLLEGE: Massachusetts.

TRANSACTIONS/CAREER NOTES: Selected by Seattle Mariners in first round (14th pick overall) of free-agent draft (June 1, 1992). ... On disabled list (April 19-26, 1994). ... Traded by Mariners with OF Marc Newfield to San Diego Padres for P Andy Benes and a player to be named later (July 31, 1995); Mariners acquired P Greg Keagle to complete deal (September 16, 1995). ... Traded by Padres with P Bryce Florie and OF Marc Newfield to Milwaukee Brewers for OF Greg Vaughn and a player to be named later (July 31, 1996); Padres acquired OF Gerald Parent to complete deal (September 16, 1996). ... Traded by Brewers with P Ben McDonald and P Mike Fetters to Cleveland Indians for OF Marquis Grissom and P Jeff Juden (December 8, 1997). ... On Cleveland disabled list (August 15-September 1, 1998); included rehabilitation assignment to Buffalo (August 22-September 1). ... Released by Indians (April 2, 1999). ... Signed by Cincinnati Reds organization (April 5, 1999). ... Traded by Reds to Colorado Rockies for two players to be named later (November 8, 2000); Reds acquired P Jeff Taglienti and P Justin Carter to complete deal (December 20, 2000). ... Traded by Rockies to Houston Astros for P Jay Powell (June 27, 2001). ... Granted free agency (November 5, 2001). ... Signed by Pittsburgh Pirates organization (February 12, 2002). ... On disabled list (August 15-September 1, 2002). ... Granted free agency (October 29, 2002).

STATISTICAL NOTES: Struck out 16 batters in one game (September 29, 2000).

MISCELLANEOUS: Member of 1992 U.S. Olympic baseball team.

CAREER HITTING (MLB): 15-for-126 (.119), 5 R, 2 2B, 1 3B, 0 HR, 5 RBI.

Year	League	W	L	Pct.	ERA	G	GS	CG	ShO	Sv.-Opp.	IP	H	R	ER	HR	BB-IBB	SO
1993	Riverside (Calif.)	7	4	.636	4.21	16	16	0	0	0-...	83.1	74	47	39	5	62-0	82
—	Jacksonville (Sou.)	3	4	.429	4.38	11	11	0	0	0-...	63.2	49	34	31	6	41-3	66
1994	Jacksonville (Sou.)	6	7	.462	3.86	41	5	0	0	8-...	79.1	56	37	34	7	68-3	94
1995	Seattle (A.L.)	0	2	.000	7.91	19	0	0	0	0-3	19.1	20	19	17	6	23-0	26
—	Tacoma (PCL)	1	0	1.000	0.61	22	0	0	0	13-...	29.2	9	6	2	1	19-0	43
—	San Diego (N.L.)■	2	1	.667	4.21	19	0	0	0	1-2	25.2	24	12	12	5	11-0	37
1996	Las Vegas (PCL)	2	1	.667	1.64	23	0	0	0	3-...	22.0	13	5	4	0	9-0	29
—	San Diego (N.L.)	1	1	.500	2.95	21	0	0	0	0-1	18.1	17	6	6	2	7-0	19
—	Milwaukee (A.L.)■	0	0	...	3.28	23	0	0	0	2-2	24.2	14	9	9	4	18-0	19
1997	Milwaukee (A.L.)	1	0	1.000	3.42	50	0	0	0	0-2	52.2	54	23	20	4	36-2	40
1998	Buffalo (I.L.)■	2	2	.500	2.01	23	0	0	0	7-...	22.1	20	11	5	2	11-1	28
—	Cleveland (A.L.)	0	0	...	6.00	25	0	0	0	0-0	27.0	30	18	18	3	22-0	15
1999	Indianapolis (I.L.)■	2	0	1.000	1.42	18	0	0	0	1-...	19.0	9	3	3	1	13-1	23
—	Cincinnati (N.L.)	9	7	.563	4.23	29	22	0	0	2-2	142.2	114	70	67	8	73-2	97
2000	Cincinnati (N.L.)	10	10	.500	5.43	35	23	2	0	0-0	141.0	154	95	85	22	78-3	77
2001	Colorado (N.L.)■	1	3	.250	6.36	22	6	0	0	0-0	46.2	56	35	33	6	29-4	48
—	Houston (N.L.)■	5	7	.417	5.56	31	6	0	0	0-0	68.0	77	46	42	12	24-1	65
2002	Pittsburgh (N.L.)■	4	6	.400	5.81	45	7	0	0	0-1	93.0	95	63	60	8	34-3	55
A.L. totals (4 years)		1	2	.333	4.66	117	0	0	0	2-7	123.2	118	69	64	17	99-2	100
N.L. totals (6 years)		32	35	.478	5.13	202	64	2	0	3-6	535.1	537	327	305	63	256-13	398
Major League totals (8 years)		33	37	.471	5.04	319	64	2	0	5-13	659.0	655	396	369	80	355-15	498

DIVISION SERIES RECORD

Year	League	W	L	Pct.	ERA	G	GS	CG	ShO	Sv.-Opp.	IP	H	R	ER	HR	BB-IBB	SO
2001	Houston (N.L.)	0	0	...	0.00	1	0	0	0	0-0	.2	0	0	0	0	0-0	0

VINA, FERNANDO — 2B — CARDINALS

PERSONAL: Born April 16, 1969, in Sacramento. ... 5-9/174. ... Bats left, throws right. ... Name pronounced VEEN-ya.

HIGH SCHOOL: Valley (Sacramento).

JUNIOR COLLEGE: Cosumnes River College (Calif.), then Sacramento City College.

COLLEGE: Arizona State.

TRANSACTIONS/CAREER NOTES: Selected by New York Yankees organization in 51st round of free-agent draft (June 1, 1988); did not sign. ... Selected by New York Mets organization in ninth round of free-agent draft (June 4, 1990). ... Selected by Seattle Mariners from Mets organization in Rule 5 major league draft (December 7, 1992). ... Returned to Mets organization (June 15, 1993). ... On New York disabled list (May 22-June 6, 1994). ... On Norfolk disabled list (August 30-September 6, 1994). ... Traded by Mets to Milwaukee Brewers (December 22, 1994), completing deal in which Brewers traded P Doug Henry for two players to be named later (November 30, 1994); Brewers acquired C Javier Gonzalez as partial completion of deal (December 6, 1994). ... On Milwaukee disabled list (April 20-July 17, 1997); included rehabilitation assignments to Stockton (July 9-11) and Tucson (July 12-17). ... On suspended list (May 11-13 and May 25-27, 1999). ... On Milwaukee disabled list (May 10-25 and June 4, 1999-remainder of season); included rehabilitation assignment to Beloit (August 6-8). ... Traded by Brewers to St. Louis Cardinals for P Juan Acevedo and two players to be named later (December 20, 1999); Brewers acquired P Matt Parker and C Eliezer Alfonzo to complete deal (June 13, 2000). ... On disabled list (June 20-July 4, 2000).

HONORS: Won N.L. Gold Glove at second base (2001-02).

STATISTICAL NOTES: Tied for South Atlantic League lead in caught stealing with 22 in 1991. ... Led South Atlantic League second basemen with 385 assists, 600 total chances and 61 double plays in 1991. ... Led Florida State League second basemen with 360 assists and 85 double plays in 1992. ... Led N.L. in being hit by pitch with 12 in 1994. ... Led A.L. second basemen with 333 putouts and 116 double plays in 1996. ... Led N.L. second basemen with 404 putouts, 468 assists, 884 total chances and 135 double plays in 1998. ... Had 17-game hitting streak (August 8-25, 2000). ... Led N.L. in being hit by pitch with 28 in 2000. ... Career major league grand slams: 2.

2002 GAMES PLAYED BY POSITION (MLB): 2B—150.

				BATTING													FIELDING	
Year	Team (League)	Pos.	G	AB	R	H	2B	3B	HR	RBI	BB	SO	SB-CS	Avg.	OBP	SLG	E	Avg.
1991	Columbia (S.Atl.)	2B	129	498	77	135	23	6	6	50	46	27	42-•22	.271	.344	.378	21	*.965
1992	St. Lucie (FSL)	2B	111	421	61	124	15	5	1	42	32	26	36-17	.295	.347	.361	17	.971
—	Tidewater (I.L.)	2B	11	30	3	6	0	0	0	2	0	2	0-0	.200	.194	.200	1	.978
1993	Seattle (A.L.)■	2B-SS-DH	24	45	5	10	2	0	0	2	4	3	6-0	.222	.327	.267	0	1.000
—	Norfolk (I.L.)■	SS-2B-DH-OF	73	287	24	66	6	4	4	27	7	17	16-11	.230	.258	.321	14	.964
1994	New York (N.L.)	2B-3B-SS-OF	79	124	20	31	6	0	0	6	12	11	3-1	.250	.372	.298	4	.963
—	Norfolk (I.L.)	SS-2B	6	17	2	3	0	0	0	1	1	1	1-1	.176	.250	.176	1	.952
1995	Milwaukee (A.L.)■	2B-SS-3B	113	288	46	74	7	7	3	29	22	28	6-3	.257	.327	.361	8	.982
1996	Milwaukee (A.L.)	2B	140	554	94	157	19	10	7	46	38	35	16-7	.283	.342	.392	*16	.979

Year	Team (League)	Pos.	G	AB	R	H	2B	3B	HR	RBI	BB	SO	SB-CS	Avg.	OBP	SLG	E	Avg.
			BATTING														FIELDING	
1997—	Milwaukee (A.L.)	2B-DH	79	324	37	89	12	2	4	28	12	23	8-7	.275	.312	.361	7	.982
—	Stockton (Calif.)	2B	3	9	2	4	0	1	0	3	0	0	0-2	.444	.444	.667	0	1.000
—	Tucson (PCL)	2B	6	19	3	9	3	0	1	5	3	1	0-1	.474	.583	.789	2	.923
1998—	Milwaukee (N.L.)	2B	159	637	101	198	39	7	7	45	54	46	22-16	.311	.386	.427	12	.986
1999—	Milwaukee (N.L.)	2B	37	154	17	41	7	0	1	16	14	6	5-2	.266	.339	.331	1	.995
—	Beloit (Midw.)	DH-2B	2	10	1	2	1	0	0	0	0	2	0-1	.200	.200	.300	2	.500
2000—	St. Louis (N.L.)■	2B	123	487	81	146	24	6	4	31	36	36	10-8	.300	.380	.398	7	*.988
2001—	St. Louis (N.L.)	2B	154	631	95	191	30	8	9	56	32	35	17-7	.303	.357	.418	9	.987
2002—	St. Louis (N.L.)	2B	150	622	75	168	29	5	1	54	44	36	17-11	.270	.333	.338	13	.981
American League totals (4 years)			356	1211	182	330	40	19	14	105	76	89	36-17	.273	.330	.372	31	.981
National League totals (6 years)			702	2655	389	775	135	26	22	208	192	170	74-45	.292	.362	.387	46	.986
Major League totals (10 years)			1058	3866	571	1105	175	45	36	313	268	259	110-62	.286	.352	.382	77	.984

DIVISION SERIES RECORD

Year	Team (League)	Pos.	G	AB	R	H	2B	3B	HR	RBI	BB	SO	SB-CS	Avg.	OBP	SLG	E	Avg.
			BATTING														FIELDING	
2000—	St. Louis (N.L.)	2B	3	13	3	4	0	0	1	3	1	1	0-1	.308	.400	.538	0	1.000
2001—	St. Louis (N.L.)	2B	5	19	2	6	0	0	1	2	0	1	1-0	.316	.350	.474	0	1.000
2002—	St. Louis (N.L.)	2B	3	15	3	9	0	0	0	1	1	0	0-1	.600	.625	.600	0	1.000
Division series totals (3 years)			11	47	8	19	0	0	2	6	2	2	1-2	.404	.451	.532	0	1.000

CHAMPIONSHIP SERIES RECORD

Year	Team (League)	Pos.	G	AB	R	H	2B	3B	HR	RBI	BB	SO	SB-CS	Avg.	OBP	SLG	E	Avg.
			BATTING														FIELDING	
2000—	St. Louis (N.L.)	2B	5	23	3	6	1	0	0	1	1	4	0-0	.261	.292	.304	1	.960
2002—	St. Louis (N.L.)	2B	5	23	2	6	2	0	0	2	0	0	0-0	.261	.250	.348	0	1.000
Championship series totals (2 years)			10	46	5	12	3	0	0	3	1	4	0-0	.261	.271	.326	1	.977

ALL-STAR GAME RECORD

	AB	R	H	2B	3B	HR	RBI	BB	SO	SB-CS	Avg.	OBP	SLG	E	Avg.
All-Star Game totals (1 year)	1	0	1	0	0	0	0	1	0	0-0	1.000	1.000	1.000	1	.667

VIZCAINO, JOSE — IF — ASTROS

PERSONAL: Born March 26, 1968, in San Cristobal, Dominican Republic. ... 6-1/185. ... Bats both, throws right. ... Full name: Jose Luis Pimental Vizcaino. ... Name pronounced VIS-ky-EE-no.

HIGH SCHOOL: Americo Tolentino (Palenque de San Cristobal, Dominican Republic).

TRANSACTIONS/CAREER NOTES: Signed as non-drafted free agent by Los Angeles Dodgers organization (February 18, 1986). ... Traded by Dodgers to Chicago Cubs for IF Greg Smith (December 14, 1990). ... On disabled list (April 20-May 6 and August 26-September 16, 1992). ... Traded by Cubs to New York Mets for P Anthony Young and P Ottis Smith (March 30, 1994). ... Traded by Mets with IF Jeff Kent to Cleveland Indians for 2B Carlos Baerga and IF Alvaro Espinoza (July 29, 1996). ... Traded by Indians with IF Jeff Kent, P Julian Tavarez and a player to be named later to San Francisco Giants for 3B Matt Williams and a player to be named later (November 13, 1996); Indians traded P Joe Roa to Giants for OF Trenidad Hubbard to complete deal (December 16, 1996). ... Granted free agency (October 29, 1997). ... Signed by Dodgers (December 8, 1997). ... On disabled list (June 22-September 9, 1998; and May 19-June 4, 1999). ... Traded by Dodgers to New York Yankees for IF/DH Jim Leyritz (June 20, 2000). ... Granted free agency (November 1, 2000). ... Signed by Houston Astros (November 20, 2000). ... Granted free agency (November 5, 2001). ... Re-signed by Astros (December 3, 2001).

STATISTICAL NOTES: Led Gulf Coast League shortstops with 23 double plays in 1987. ... Led Pacific Coast League shortstops with 191 putouts, 390 assists, 611 total chances and 82 double plays in 1989. ... Led N.L. shortstops in fielding percentage with .984 and tied for lead in assists by shortstop with 411 in 1995.

2002 GAMES PLAYED BY POSITION (MLB): SS—58; 3B—30; 2B—25; 1B—5.

Year	Team (League)	Pos.	G	AB	R	H	2B	3B	HR	RBI	BB	SO	SB-CS	Avg.	OBP	SLG	E	Avg.
			BATTING														FIELDING	
1987—	GC Dodgers (GCL)	SS-1B	49	150	26	38	5	1	0	12	22	24	8-5	.253	.347	.300	13	.933
1988—	Bakersfield (Calif.)	SS	122	433	77	126	11	4	0	38	50	54	13-14	.291	.372	.335	30	.946
1989—	Albuquerque (PCL)	SS	129	434	60	123	10	4	1	44	33	41	16-14	.283	.333	.332	*30	.951
—	Los Angeles (N.L.)	SS	7	10	2	2	0	0	0	0	0	1	0-0	.200	.200	.200	2	.882
1990—	Albuquerque (PCL)	2B-SS	81	276	46	77	10	2	2	38	30	33	13-6	.279	.346	.351	14	.964
—	Los Angeles (N.L.)	SS-2B	37	51	3	14	1	1	0	2	4	8	1-1	.275	.327	.333	2	.962
1991—	Chicago (N.L.)■	3B-SS-2B	93	145	7	38	5	0	0	10	5	18	2-1	.262	.283	.297	7	.960
1992—	Chicago (N.L.)	SS-3B-2B	86	285	25	64	10	4	1	17	14	35	3-0	.225	.260	.298	9	.970
1993—	Chicago (N.L.)	SS-3B-2B	151	551	74	158	19	4	4	54	46	71	12-9	.287	.340	.358	17	.974
1994—	New York (N.L.)■	SS	103	410	47	105	13	3	3	33	33	62	1-11	.256	.310	.324	13	.970
1995—	New York (N.L.)	SS-2B	135	509	66	146	21	5	3	56	35	76	8-3	.287	.332	.365	10	†.984
1996—	New York (N.L.)	2B	96	363	47	110	12	6	1	32	28	58	9-5	.303	.356	.377	6	.986
—	Cleveland (A.L.)■	2B-SS-DH	48	179	23	51	5	2	0	13	7	24	6-2	.285	.310	.335	4	.982
1997—	San Fran. (N.L.)■	SS-2B	151	568	77	151	19	7	5	50	48	87	8-8	.266	.323	.350	16	.976
1998—	Los Angeles (N.L.)■	SS	67	237	30	62	9	0	3	29	17	35	7-3	.262	.311	.338	4	.985
1999—	Los Angeles (N.L.)	SS-2B-3B-OF	94	266	27	67	9	0	1	29	20	23	2-1	.252	.304	.297	7	.976
2000—	Los Angeles (N.L.)	S-3-2-DH-1	40	93	9	19	2	1	0	4	10	15	1-0	.204	.288	.247	2	.978
—	New York (A.L.)■	2B-3B-DH-SS	73	174	23	48	8	1	0	10	12	28	5-7	.276	.319	.333	2	.991
2001—	Houston (N.L.)■	SS-2B-3B	107	256	38	71	8	3	1	14	15	33	3-2	.277	.322	.344	14	.939
2002—	Houston (N.L.)	S-3-2-1	125	406	53	123	19	2	5	37	24	40	3-5	.303	.342	.397	4	.989
American League totals (2 years)			121	353	46	99	13	3	0	23	19	52	11-9	.280	.315	.334	6	.986
National League totals (14 years)			1292	4150	505	1130	147	36	27	367	299	562	60-49	.272	.321	.345	113	.975
Major League totals (14 years)			1413	4503	551	1229	160	39	27	390	318	614	71-58	.273	.321	.344	119	.976

DIVISION SERIES RECORD

Year	Team (League)	Pos.	G	AB	R	H	2B	3B	HR	RBI	BB	SO	SB-CS	Avg.	OBP	SLG	E	Avg.
			BATTING														FIELDING	
1996—	Cleveland (A.L.)	2B	3	12	1	4	2	0	0	1	1	1	0-0	.333	.385	.500	1	.875
1997—	San Francisco (N.L.)	SS	3	11	1	2	1	0	0	0	0	5	0-0	.182	.182	.273	0	1.000
2000—	New York (A.L.)	PR-2B	1	0	1	0	0	0	0	0	0	0	0-0	...	...	...	0	1.000
2001—	Houston (N.L.)	PH-SS	3	6	0	1	0	0	0	0	0	1	0-0	.167	.167	.167	0	1.000
Division series totals (4 years)			10	29	3	7	3	0	0	1	1	7	0-0	.241	.267	.345	1	.964

CHAMPIONSHIP SERIES RECORD

Year	Team (League)	Pos.	G	AB	R	H	2B	3B	HR	RBI	BB	SO	SB-CS	Avg.	OBP	SLG	E	Avg.
			BATTING														FIELDING	
2000—	New York (A.L.)	PR-2B	4	2	3	2	1	0	0	2	0	0	2-0	1.000	.667	1.500	0	1.000

WORLD SERIES RECORD

NOTES: Member of World Series championship team (2000).

Year	Team (League)	Pos.	G	AB	R	H	2B	3B	HR	RBI	BB	SO	SB-CS	Avg.	OBP	SLG	E	Avg.
			BATTING														FIELDING	
2000—	New York (A.L.)	2B	4	17	0	4	0	0	0	1	0	5	0-1	.235	.235	.235	0	1.000

VIZCAINO, LUIS — P — BREWERS

PERSONAL: Born August 6, 1974, in Bani, Dominican Republic. ... 5-11/174. ... Throws right, bats right. ... Full name: Luis Viczaino Vizcaino.
TRANSACTIONS/CAREER NOTES: Signed as non-drafted free agent by Oakland Athletics organization (December 9, 1994). ... Traded by A's to Texas Rangers for P Justin Duchscherer (March 18, 2002). ... Traded by Rangers to Milwaukee Brewers for P Jesus Pena (March 24, 2002).
STATISTICAL NOTES: Tied for Arizona League lead with three balks in 1996.
CAREER HITTING (MLB): 0-for-2 (.000), 0 R, 0 2B, 0 3B, 0 HR, 0 RBI.

Year	League	W	L	Pct.	ERA	G	GS	CG	ShO	Sv.-Opp.	IP	H	R	ER	HR	BB-IBB	SO
1995—	Dom. Athletics (DSL)	10	2	.833	2.27	16	15	5	1	0-...	*115.0	93	41	29	...	29-...	89
1996—	Arizona Athletics (Ariz.)	6	3	.667	4.07	15	10	0	0	1-...	59.2	58	36	27	1	24-1	52
1997—	Modesto (Calif.)	0	3	.000	13.19	7	0	0	0	0-...	14.1	24	24	21	4	13-4	15
	—S. Oregon (N'West)	1	6	.143	7.93	22	5	0	0	0-...	47.2	62	51	42	5	27-0	42
1998—	Modesto (Calif.)	6	3	.667	2.74	23	16	0	0	0-...	102.0	72	39	31	5	43-1	108
	—Huntsville (Sou.)	3	2	.600	4.66	7	7	0	0	0-...	38.2	43	27	20	8	22-0	26
1999—	Midland (Texas)	8	7	.533	5.85	25	19	0	0	0-...	104.2	120	74	68	18	48-2	88
	—Oakland (A.L.)	0	0	...	5.40	1	0	0	0	0-0	3.1	3	2	2	1	3-0	2
	—Vancouver (PCL)	0	1	.000	1.38	7	0	0	0	0-...	13.0	13	4	2	0	6-0	7
2000—	Oakland (A.L.)	0	1	.000	7.45	12	0	0	0	0-0	19.1	25	17	16	2	11-0	18
	—Sacramento (PCL)	6	2	.750	5.03	33	2	0	0	5-...	48.1	48	27	27	4	21-0	41
2001—	Sacramento (PCL)	2	2	.500	2.14	27	0	0	0	7-...	42.0	35	10	10	5	10-4	56
	—Oakland (A.L.)	2	1	.667	4.66	36	0	0	0	1-1	36.2	38	19	19	8	12-1	31
2002—	Milwaukee (N.L.)■	5	3	.625	2.99	76	0	0	0	5-6	81.1	55	27	27	6	30-4	79
A.L. totals (3 years)		2	2	.500	5.61	49	0	0	0	1-1	59.1	66	38	37	11	26-1	51
N.L. totals (1 year)		5	3	.625	2.99	76	0	0	0	5-6	81.1	55	27	27	6	30-4	79
Major League totals (4 years)		7	5	.583	4.09	125	0	0	0	6-7	140.2	121	65	64	17	56-5	130

VIZQUEL, OMAR — SS — INDIANS

PERSONAL: Born April 24, 1967, in Caracas, Venezuela. ... 5-9/175. ... Bats both, throws right. ... Full name: Omar Enrique Vizquel. ... Name pronounced vis-KEL.
HIGH SCHOOL: Francisco Espejo (Caracas, Venezuela).
TRANSACTIONS/CAREER NOTES: Signed as non-drafted free agent by Seattle Mariners organization (April 1, 1984). ... On Seattle disabled list (April 7-May 13, 1990); included rehabilitation assignments to Calgary (May 3-7) and San Bernardino (May 8-12). ... On Seattle disabled list (April 13-May 11, 1992); included rehabilitation assignment to Calgary (May 5-11). ... Traded by Mariners to Cleveland Indians for SS Felix Fermin, 1B Reggie Jefferson and cash (December 20, 1993). ... On Cleveland disabled list (April 23-June 13, 1994); included rehabilitation assignment to Charlotte (June 6-13). ... On suspended list (September 17-18, 1998).
RECORDS: Shares major league career record for highest fielding percentage by shortstop (1,000 or more games)—.984; fewest errors by shortstop (150 or more games)—3 (2000); and most consecutive errorless games by shortstop—95 (September 26, 1999 through July 21, 2000).
HONORS: Won A.L. Gold Glove at shortstop (1993-2001).
STATISTICAL NOTES: Led Midwest League shortstops with .969 fielding percentage in 1986. ... Tied for A.L. lead in double plays by shortstop with 108 in 1993. ... Led A.L. with 16 sacrifice hits in 1997 and with 17 in 1999. ... Led A.L. shortstops with 273 putouts in 1998. ... Had 18-game hitting streak (July 14-August 1, 2002). ... Career major league grand slams: 4.
MISCELLANEOUS: Batted righthanded only (1984-88).
2002 GAMES PLAYED BY POSITION (MLB): SS—150.

Year	Team (League)	Pos.	G	AB	R	H	2B	3B	HR	RBI	BB	SO	SB-CS	Avg.	OBP	SLG	E	Avg.
			BATTING														FIELDING	
1984—	Butte (Pio.)	SS-2B	15	45	7	14	2	0	0	4	3	8	2-0	.311	.347	.356	5	.894
1985—	Bellingham (N'West)	SS-2B	50	187	24	42	9	0	5	17	12	27	4-3	.225	.270	.353	19	.932
1986—	Wausau (Midw.)	SS-2B	105	352	60	75	13	2	4	28	64	56	19-6	.213	.333	.295	16	†.968
1987—	Salinas (Calif.)	SS-2B	114	407	61	107	12	8	0	38	57	55	25-19	.263	.350	.332	25	.938
1988—	Vermont (East.)	SS	103	374	54	95	18	2	2	35	42	44	30-11	.254	.328	.329	19	*.959
	—Calgary (PCL)	SS	33	107	10	24	2	3	1	12	5	14	2-4	.224	.259	.327	6	.957
1989—	Seattle (A.L.)	SS	143	387	45	85	7	3	1	20	28	40	1-4	.220	.273	.261	18	.971
	—Calgary (PCL)	SS	7	28	3	6	2	0	0	3	3	4	0-2	.214	.313	.286	0	1.000
1990—	Calgary (PCL)	SS	48	150	18	35	6	2	0	8	13	10	4-3	.233	.299	.300	6	.972
	—San Bern. (Calif.)	SS	6	28	5	7	0	0	0	3	3	1	1-2	.250	.323	.250	3	.914
	—Seattle (A.L.)	SS	81	255	19	63	3	2	2	18	18	22	4-1	.247	.295	.298	7	.980
1991—	Seattle (A.L.)	SS-2B	142	426	42	98	16	4	1	41	45	37	7-2	.230	.302	.293	13	.980

Year	Team (League)	Pos.	G	AB	R	H	2B	3B	HR	RBI	BB	SO	SB-CS	Avg.	OBP	SLG	E	Avg.
			BATTING														FIELDING	
1992—	Seattle (A.L.)	SS	136	483	49	142	20	4	0	21	32	38	15-13	.294	.340	.352	7	*.989
—	Calgary (PCL)	SS	6	22	0	6	1	0	0	2	1	3	0-1	.273	.333	.318	1	.972
1993—	Seattle (A.L.)	SS-DH	158	560	68	143	14	2	2	31	50	71	12-14	.255	.319	.298	15	.980
1994—	Cleveland (A.L.)■	SS	69	286	39	78	10	1	1	33	23	23	13-4	.273	.325	.325	6	.981
—	Charlotte (I.L.)	SS	7	26	3	7	1	0	0	1	2	1	1-0	.269	.321	.308	1	.967
1995—	Cleveland (A.L.)	SS	136	542	87	144	28	0	6	56	59	59	29-11	.266	.333	.351	9	.986
1996—	Cleveland (A.L.)	SS	151	542	98	161	36	1	9	64	56	42	35-9	.297	.362	.417	20	.971
1997—	Cleveland (A.L.)	SS	153	565	89	158	23	6	5	49	57	58	43-12	.280	.347	.368	10	.985
1998—	Cleveland (A.L.)	SS	151	576	86	166	30	6	2	50	62	64	37-12	.288	.358	.372	5	*.993
1999—	Cleveland (A.L.)	SS-OF	144	574	112	191	36	4	5	66	65	50	42-9	.333	.397	.436	15	.976
2000—	Cleveland (A.L.)	SS	156	613	101	176	27	3	7	66	87	72	22-10	.287	.377	.375	3	*.995
2001—	Cleveland (A.L.)	SS	155	611	84	156	26	8	2	50	61	72	13-9	.255	.323	.334	7	.989
2002—	Cleveland (A.L.)	SS	151	582	85	160	31	5	14	72	56	64	18-10	.275	.341	.418	7	.990
Major League totals (14 years)			1926	7002	1004	1921	307	49	57	637	699	712	291-120	.274	.340	.357	142	.984

DIVISION SERIES RECORD

RECORDS: Holds A.L. career record for triples—2. ... Shares A.L. career records for most stolen bases—10; and hits—32. ... Shares single-game record for most at-bats (nine-inning game)—6 (October 13, 2001).

Year	Team (League)	Pos.	G	AB	R	H	2B	3B	HR	RBI	BB	SO	SB-CS	Avg.	OBP	SLG	E	Avg.
			BATTING														FIELDING	
1995—	Cleveland (A.L.)	SS	3	12	2	2	1	0	0	4	2	2	1-0	.167	.286	.250	0	1.000
1996—	Cleveland (A.L.)	SS	4	14	4	6	1	0	0	2	3	4	4-2	.429	.500	.500	0	1.000
1997—	Cleveland (A.L.)	SS	5	18	3	9	0	0	0	1	2	1	4-0	.500	.550	.500	0	1.000
1998—	Cleveland (A.L.)	SS	4	15	1	1	0	0	0	0	1	0	0-0	.067	.125	.067	0	1.000
1999—	Cleveland (A.L.)	SS	5	21	3	5	1	1	0	3	2	3	0-0	.238	.304	.381	0	1.000
2001—	Cleveland (A.L.)	SS	5	22	2	9	1	1	0	6	1	1	1-0	.409	.435	.545	1	.964
Division series totals (6 years)			26	102	15	32	4	2	0	16	11	11	10-2	.314	.377	.392	1	.992

CHAMPIONSHIP SERIES RECORD

Year	Team (League)	Pos.	G	AB	R	H	2B	3B	HR	RBI	BB	SO	SB-CS	Avg.	OBP	SLG	E	Avg.
			BATTING														FIELDING	
1995—	Cleveland (A.L.)	SS	6	23	2	2	1	0	0	2	5	2	3-0	.087	.241	.130	0	1.000
1997—	Cleveland (A.L.)	SS	6	25	1	1	0	0	0	0	2	10	0-0	.040	.143	.040	0	1.000
1998—	Cleveland (A.L.)	SS	6	25	2	11	0	1	0	0	1	3	4-1	.440	.481	.520	1	.974
Championship series totals (3 years)			18	73	5	14	1	1	0	2	8	15	7-1	.192	.286	.233	1	.990

WORLD SERIES RECORD

RECORDS: Shares single-inning record for most stolen bases—2 (October 26, 1997).

Year	Team (League)	Pos.	G	AB	R	H	2B	3B	HR	RBI	BB	SO	SB-CS	Avg.	OBP	SLG	E	Avg.
			BATTING														FIELDING	
1995—	Cleveland (A.L.)	SS	6	23	3	4	0	1	0	1	3	5	1-0	.174	.269	.261	0	1.000
1997—	Cleveland (A.L.)	SS	7	30	5	7	2	0	0	1	3	5	5-0	.233	.303	.300	0	1.000
World Series totals (2 years)			13	53	8	11	2	1	0	2	6	10	6-0	.208	.288	.283	0	1.000

ALL-STAR GAME RECORD

	AB	R	H	2B	3B	HR	RBI	BB	SO	SB-CS	Avg.	OBP	SLG	E	Avg.
All-Star Game totals (3 years)	5	0	2	0	1	0	1	1	0	0-0	.400	.500	.800	0	1.000

VOSBERG, ED — P

PERSONAL: Born September 28, 1961, in Tucson, Ariz. ... 6-1/210. ... Throws left, bats left. ... Full name: Edward John Vosberg. ... Nephew of Don Vosberg, defensive end with New York Giants (1941).

HIGH SCHOOL: Salpointe (Tucson, Ariz.).

COLLEGE: Arizona.

TRANSACTIONS/CAREER NOTES: Selected by St. Louis Cardinals organization in third round of free-agent draft (June 5, 1979); did not sign. ... Selected by Toronto Blue Jays organization in 11th round of free-agent draft (June 7, 1982); did not sign. ... Selected by San Diego Padres organization in third round of free-agent draft (June 6, 1983). ... Traded by Padres to Houston Astros for C Dan Walters (December 13, 1988). ... Traded by Astros to Los Angeles Dodgers (August 1, 1989), completing deal in which Dodgers traded OF Javier Ortiz to Astros for a player to be named later (July 22, 1989). ... Granted free agency (October 15, 1989). ... Signed by San Francisco Giants organization (March 13, 1990). ... Granted free agency (October 15, 1990). ... Signed by California Angels organization (December 4, 1990). ... Released by Angels (May 11, 1991). ... Signed by Seattle Mariners organization (May 20, 1991). ... Released by Mariners (July 10, 1991). ... Pitched in Italy (1992). ... Signed by Chicago Cubs organization (March 17, 1993). ... Granted free agency (October 15, 1993). ... Signed by Oakland Athletics organization (December 3, 1993). ... Granted free agency (October 15, 1994). ... Re-signed by A's organization (November 11, 1994). ... Selected by Los Angeles Dodgers from A's organization in Rule 5 major league draft (December 5, 1994). ... Granted free agency (April 24, 1995). ... Signed by Texas Rangers organization (April 26, 1995). ... Traded by Rangers to Florida Marlins for P Rick Helling (August 12, 1997). ... Traded by Marlins to Padres for P Chris Clark (November 20, 1997). ... On disabled list (March 25, 1998-entire season). ... On San Diego disabled list (March 30-April 24, 1999); included rehabilitation assignment to Las Vegas (April 8-24). ... Released by Padres (June 5, 1999). ... Signed by Arizona Diamondbacks organization (June 10, 1999). ... Granted free agency (October 15, 1999). ... Signed by Colorado Rockies organization (November 17, 1999). ... Traded by Rockies to Philadelphia Phillies for a player to be named later (June 28, 2000); Rockies acquired P Sean Fesh to complete deal (July 25, 2000). ... Granted free agency (October 12, 2000). ... Re-signed by Phillies organization (December 20, 2000). ... Granted free agency (October 8, 2001). ... Signed by Montreal Expos organization (February 19, 2002). ... Released by Expos (April 18, 2002).

STATISTICAL NOTES: Led Pacific Coast League with 11 balks in 1987.

CAREER HITTING (MLB): 0-for-2 (.000), 0 R, 0 2B, 0 3B, 0 HR, 0 RBI.

Year League	W	L	Pct.	ERA	G	GS	CG	ShO	Sv.-Opp.	IP	H	R	ER	HR	BB-IBB	SO
1983— Reno (Calif.)	6	6	.500	3.87	15	15	3	0	0-...	97.2	111	61	42	3	39-0	70
— Beaumont (Texas)	1	0	1.000	0.00	1	1	1	1	0-...	7.0	2	0	0	0	2-0	1
1984— Beaumont (Texas)	13	•11	.542	3.43	27	•27	5	2	0-...	183.2	196	87	70	12	74-5	100
1985— Beaumont (Texas)	9	11	.450	3.91	27	•27	2	1	0-...	175.0	178	92	76	6	69-3	124
1986— Las Vegas (PCL)	7	8	.467	4.72	25	24	2	1	0-...	129.2	136	80	68	13	64-2	93
— San Diego (N.L.)	0	1	.000	6.59	5	3	0	0	0-0	13.2	17	11	10	1	9-1	8
1987— Las Vegas (PCL)	9	8	.529	3.92	34	24	3	0	0-...	167.2	154	88	73	11	97-3	98
1988— Las Vegas (PCL)	11	7	.611	4.15	45	11	1	0	2-...	128.0	137	67	59	12	56-0	75
1989— Tucson (PCL)■	4	7	.364	6.78	23	14	0	0	1-...	87.2	122	70	66	9	49-5	68
— Albuquerque (PCL)■	2	1	.667	2.70	12	0	0	0	0-...	20.0	17	8	6	2	5-2	18
1990— Phoenix (PCL)■	1	3	.250	2.65	24	0	0	0	3-...	34.0	36	14	10	2	16-3	28
— San Francisco (N.L.)	1	1	.500	5.55	18	0	0	0	0-0	24.1	21	16	15	3	12-2	12
1991— Edmonton (PCL)■	0	1	.000	6.28	12	0	0	0	0-...	14.1	19	10	10	3	5-0	14
— Calgary (PCL)■	0	2	.000	7.23	16	0	0	0	2-...	23.2	38	26	19	1	12-0	15
1992—	Italian statistics unavailable.															
1993— Iowa (A.A.)■	5	1	.833	3.57	52	0	0	0	3-...	63.0	67	32	25	7	22-5	64
1994— Tacoma (PCL)■	4	2	.667	3.35	26	1	0	0	3-...	53.2	39	21	20	4	19-0	54
— Oakland (A.L.)	0	2	.000	3.95	16	0	0	0	0-1	13.2	16	7	6	2	5-0	12
1995— Oklahoma City (A.A.)■	1	0	1.000	0.00	1	0	0	0	0-...	1.2	1	0	0	0	1-0	2
— Texas (A.L.)	5	5	.500	3.00	44	0	0	0	4-8	36.0	32	15	12	3	16-1	36
1996— Texas (A.L.)	1	1	.500	3.27	52	0	0	0	8-9	44.0	51	17	16	4	21-4	32
1997— Texas (A.L.)	1	2	.333	4.61	42	0	0	0	0-1	41.0	44	23	21	3	15-6	29
— Florida (N.L.)■	1	1	.500	3.75	17	0	0	0	1-2	12.0	15	7	5	0	6-0	8
1998— San Diego (N.L.)■	Did not play.															
1999— Las Vegas (PCL)	0	0	...	1.08	8	0	0	0	1-...	8.1	3	1	1	1	4-0	12
— San Diego (N.L.)	0	0	...	9.72	15	0	0	0	0-2	8.1	16	11	9	1	3-0	6
— Tucson (PCL)■	1	0	1.000	0.78	26	0	0	0	7-...	34.2	26	5	3	0	8-1	30
— Arizona (N.L.)	0	1	.000	3.38	4	0	0	0	0-0	2.2	6	1	1	0	0-0	2
2000— Colorado Springs (PCL)■	1	2	.333	6.86	29	3	0	0	2-...	42.0	59	41	32	4	20-0	37
— Scranton/W.B. (I.L.)■	0	0	...	0.00	1	0	0	0	0-...	2.0	0	0	0	0	0-0	2
— Philadelphia (N.L.)	1	1	.500	4.13	31	0	0	0	0-0	24.0	21	11	11	4	18-0	23
2001— Scranton/W.B. (I.L.)	1	0	1.000	3.00	27	0	0	0	5-...	27.0	24	9	9	1	13-3	22
— Philadelphia (N.L.)	0	0	...	2.84	18	0	0	0	0-0	12.2	8	4	4	0	3-0	11
2002— Montreal (N.L.)■	0	0	...	18.00	4	0	0	0	0-0	1.0	3	3	2	1	1-0	0
— MC Red Devils (Mex.)■	3	4	.429	5.31	12	10	0	0	0-...	57.2	73	38	34	4	15-0	50
A.L. totals (4 years)	7	10	.412	3.68	154	0	0	0	12-19	134.2	143	62	55	12	57-11	109
N.L. totals (7 years)	3	5	.375	5.20	112	3	0	0	1-4	98.2	107	64	57	10	52-3	70
Major League totals (10 years)	10	15	.400	4.32	266	3	0	0	13-23	233.1	250	126	112	22	109-14	179

DIVISION SERIES RECORD

Year League	W	L	Pct.	ERA	G	GS	CG	ShO	Sv.-Opp.	IP	H	R	ER	HR	BB-IBB	SO
1996— Texas (A.L.)	0	0	...	...	1	0	0	0	0-0	.0	1	0	0	0	0-0	0

CHAMPIONSHIP SERIES RECORD

Year League	W	L	Pct.	ERA	G	GS	CG	ShO	Sv.-Opp.	IP	H	R	ER	HR	BB-IBB	SO
1997— Florida (N.L.)	0	0	...	0.00	2	0	0	0	0-0	2.2	2	0	0	0	1-0	3

WORLD SERIES RECORD

NOTES: Member of World Series championship team (1997).

Year League	W	L	Pct.	ERA	G	GS	CG	ShO	Sv.-Opp.	IP	H	R	ER	HR	BB-IBB	SO
1997— Florida (N.L.)	0	0	...	6.00	2	0	0	0	0-0	3.0	3	2	2	0	3-1	2

VOYLES, BRAD — P — ROYALS

PERSONAL: Born December 30, 1976, in Green Bay, Wis. ... 6-0/195. ... Throws right, bats right. ... Full name: Bradley Roy Voyles.
HIGH SCHOOL: Luxemburg-Casco (Luxemburg, Wis.).
JUNIOR COLLEGE: Kishwaukee (Ill.).
COLLEGE: Lincoln Memorial.
TRANSACTIONS/CAREER NOTES: Selected by Atlanta Braves organization in 45th round of free-agent draft (June 2, 1998). ... On Atlanta disabled list (March 28-June 8, 2001); included rehabilitation assignment to Myrtle Beach (June 3-8). ... Traded by Braves with IF Alejandro Machado to Kansas City Royals for SS Rey Sanchez (July 31, 2001).
CAREER HITTING (MLB): 0-for-0 (.000), 0 R, 0 2B, 0 3B, 0 HR, 0 RBI.

Year League	W	L	Pct.	ERA	G	GS	CG	ShO	Sv.-Opp.	IP	H	R	ER	HR	BB-IBB	SO
1998— Eugene (N'West)	0	0	...	3.09	7	0	0	0	0-...	11.2	9	5	4	0	10-1	22
1999— Macon (S.Atl.)	3	3	.500	2.98	38	0	0	0	14-...	51.1	27	21	17	0	39-2	65
— Myrtle Beach (Caro.)	1	1	.500	2.25	5	0	0	0	0-...	12.0	7	3	3	1	9-1	13
2000— Myrtle Beach (Caro.)	5	2	.714	1.11	39	0	0	0	19-...	56.2	21	8	7	1	25-2	70
2001— Myrtle Beach (Caro.)	0	0	...	0.00	2	0	0	0	1-...	1.2	0	0	0	0	1-0	3
— Greenville (Sou.)	0	0	...	1.08	15	0	0	0	6-...	16.2	11	3	2	0	10-1	25
— Wichita (Texas)■	1	0	1.000	0.00	11	0	0	0	4-...	15.1	8	0	0	0	10-1	19
— Kansas City (A.L.)	0	0	...	3.86	7	0	0	0	0-0	9.1	5	4	4	1	8-0	6
2002— Omaha (PCL)	3	4	.429	4.18	26	0	0	0	5-...	32.1	29	15	15	2	22-1	34
— Kansas City (A.L.)	0	2	.000	6.51	22	0	0	0	1-2	27.2	31	21	20	5	18-1	26
Major League totals (2 years)	0	2	.000	5.84	29	0	0	0	1-2	37.0	36	25	24	6	26-1	32

WAGNER, BILLY — P — ASTROS

PERSONAL: Born July 25, 1971, in Tannersville, Va. ... 5-11/195. ... Throws left, bats left. ... Full name: William Edward Wagner.
HIGH SCHOOL: Tazewell (Va.).
COLLEGE: Ferrum (Va.).
TRANSACTIONS/CAREER NOTES: Selected by Houston Astros organization in first round (12th pick overall) of free-agent draft (June 3, 1993). ... On Houston disabled list (August 23-September 7, 1996). ... On Houston disabled list (July 16-August 7, 1998); included rehabilitation

assignment to Jackson (August 1-7). ... On disabled list (June 21, 2000-remainder of season). ... On Houston disabled list (June 5-June 19, 2001); included rehabilitation assignment to Round Rock (June 16-17).

CAREER HITTING (MLB): 1-for-13 (.077), 0 R, 0 2B, 0 3B, 0 HR, 0 RBI.

Year League	W	L	Pct.	ERA	G	GS	CG	ShO	Sv.-Opp.	IP	H	R	ER	HR	BB-IBB	SO
1993—Auburn (NY-Penn)	1	3	.250	4.08	7	7	0	0	0-...	28.2	25	19	13	2	25-0	31
1994—Quad City (Midw.)	8	9	.471	3.29	26	26	2	0	0-...	153.0	99	71	56	9	*91-0	*204
1995—Jackson (Texas)	2	2	.500	2.57	12	12	0	0	0-...	70.0	49	25	20	7	36-1	77
—Tucson (PCL)	5	3	.625	3.18	13	13	0	0	0-...	76.1	70	28	27	3	32-0	80
—Houston (N.L.)	0	0	...	0.00	1	0	0	0	0-0	.1	0	0	0	0	0-0	0
1996—Tucson (PCL)	6	2	.750	3.28	12	12	1	1	0-...	74.0	62	32	27	2	33-0	86
—Houston (N.L.)	2	2	.500	2.44	37	0	0	0	9-13	51.2	28	16	14	6	30-2	67
1997—Houston (N.L.)	7	8	.467	2.85	62	0	0	0	23-29	66.1	49	23	21	5	30-1	106
1998—Houston (N.L.)	4	3	.571	2.70	58	0	0	0	30-35	60.0	46	19	18	6	25-1	97
—Jackson (Texas)	0	0	...	0.00	3	1	0	0	0-...	3.0	1	0	0	0	0-0	7
1999—Houston (N.L.)	4	1	.800	1.57	66	0	0	0	39-42	74.2	35	14	13	5	23-1	124
2000—Houston (N.L.)	2	4	.333	6.18	28	0	0	0	6-15	27.2	28	19	19	6	18-0	28
2001—Houston (N.L.)	2	5	.286	2.73	64	0	0	0	39-41	62.2	44	19	19	5	20-0	79
—Round Rock (Texas)	0	0	...	0.00	1	1	0	0	0-...	1.0	0	0	0	0	0-0	2
2002—Houston (N.L.)	4	2	.667	2.52	70	0	0	0	35-41	75.0	51	21	21	7	22-5	88
Major League totals (8 years)	25	25	.500	2.69	386	0	0	0	181-216	418.1	281	131	125	40	168-10	589

DIVISION SERIES RECORD

Year League	W	L	Pct.	ERA	G	GS	CG	ShO	Sv.-Opp.	IP	H	R	ER	HR	BB-IBB	SO
1997—Houston (N.L.)	0	0	...	18.00	1	0	0	0	0-0	1.0	3	2	2	0	0-0	2
1998—Houston (N.L.)	1	0	1.000	18.00	1	0	0	0	0-1	1.0	4	2	2	1	0-0	1
1999—Houston (N.L.)	0	0	...	0.00	1	0	0	0	0-0	1.0	0	0	0	0	0-0	1
2001—Houston (N.L.)	0	0	...	5.40	2	0	0	0	0-0	1.2	1	1	1	1	0-0	3
Division series totals (4 years)	1	0	1.000	9.64	5	0	0	0	0-1	4.2	8	5	5	2	0-0	7

ALL-STAR GAME RECORD

	W	L	Pct.	ERA	GS	CG	ShO	Sv.-Opp.	IP	H	R	ER	HR	BB-IBB	SO
All-Star Game totals (2 years)	0	0	...	0.00	0	0	0	0-0	1.0	0	0	0	0	0-0	2

WAKEFIELD, TIM — P — RED SOX

PERSONAL: Born August 2, 1966, in Melbourne, Fla. ... 6-2/214. ... Throws right, bats right. ... Full name: Timothy Stephen Wakefield.

HIGH SCHOOL: Eau Gallie (Melbourne, Fla.).

COLLEGE: Florida Tech.

TRANSACTIONS/CAREER NOTES: Selected by Pittsburgh Pirates organization in eighth round of free-agent draft (June 1, 1988). ... Released by Pirates (April 20, 1995). ... Signed by Boston Red Sox organization (April 26, 1995). ... On disabled list (April 15-May 6, 1997). ... Granted free agency (November 1, 2000). ... Re-signed by Red Sox (December 7, 2000).

RECORDS: Shares major league single-inning record for most strikeouts—4 (August 10, 1999, ninth inning).

HONORS: Named N.L. Rookie Pitcher of the Year by The Sporting News (1992). ... Named A.L. Comeback Player of the Year by The Sporting News (1995).

STATISTICAL NOTES: Led American Association with 23 hit batsmen in 1994. ... Led A.L. with 16 hit batsmen in 1997 and 18 in 2001.

MISCELLANEOUS: Appeared in one game as pinch runner with Pittsburgh (1992). ... Had a sacrifice hit in only appearance as pinch hitter (1998). ... Had a sacrifice hit in only appearance as pinch hitter (2000).

CAREER HITTING (MLB): 10-for-82 (.122), 3 R, 2 2B, 0 3B, 1 HR, 3 RBI.

Year League	W	L	Pct.	ERA	G	GS	CG	ShO	Sv.-Opp.	IP	H	R	ER	HR	BB-IBB	SO
1989—Welland (NY-Penn)	1	1	.500	3.40	18	1	0	0	2-...	39.2	30	17	15	1	21-0	42
1990—Salem (Caro.)	10	•14	.417	4.73	28	•28	2	0	0-...	*190.1	*187	109	*100	*24	*85-2	127
1991—Carolina (Sou.)	15	8	.652	2.90	26	25	•8	1	0-...	183.0	155	68	59	13	51-6	120
—Buffalo (A.A.)	0	1	.000	11.57	1	1	0	0	0-...	4.2	8	6	6	3	1-0	4
1992—Buffalo (A.A.)	10	3	.769	3.06	20	20	*6	1	0-...	135.1	122	52	46	10	51-1	71
—Pittsburgh (N.L.)	8	1	.889	2.15	13	13	4	1	0-0	92.0	76	26	22	3	35-1	51
1993—Pittsburgh (N.L.)	6	11	.353	5.61	24	20	3	2	0-0	128.1	145	83	80	14	75-2	59
—Carolina (Sou.)	3	5	.375	6.99	9	9	1	0	0-...	56.2	68	48	44	5	22-0	36
1994—Buffalo (A.A.)	5	*15	.250	5.84	30	•29	4	1	0-...	175.2	*197	*127	*114	*27	*98-0	83
1995—Pawtucket (I.L.)■	2	1	.667	2.52	4	4	0	0	0-...	25.0	23	10	7	1	9-0	14
—Boston (A.L.)	16	8	.667	2.95	27	27	6	1	0-0	195.1	163	76	64	22	68-0	119
1996—Boston (A.L.)	14	13	.519	5.14	32	32	6	0	0-0	211.2	238	*151	121	38	90-0	140
1997—Boston (A.L.)	12	•15	.444	4.25	35	29	4	2	0-0	201.1	193	109	95	24	87-5	151
1998—Boston (A.L.)	17	8	.680	4.58	36	33	2	0	0-0	216.0	211	123	110	30	79-1	146
1999—Boston (A.L.)	6	11	.353	5.08	49	17	0	0	15-18	140.0	146	93	79	19	72-2	104
2000—Boston (A.L.)	6	10	.375	5.48	51	17	0	0	0-1	159.1	170	107	97	31	65-3	102
2001—Boston (A.L.)	9	12	.429	3.90	45	17	0	0	3-5	168.2	156	84	73	13	73-5	148
2002—Boston (A.L.)	11	5	.688	2.81	45	15	0	0	3-5	163.1	121	57	51	15	51-2	134
A.L. totals (8 years)	91	82	.526	4.27	320	187	18	3	21-29	1455.2	1398	800	690	192	585-18	1044
N.L. totals (2 years)	14	12	.538	4.17	37	33	7	3	0-0	220.1	221	109	102	17	110-3	110
Major League totals (10 years)	105	94	.528	4.25	357	220	25	6	21-29	1676.0	1619	909	792	209	695-21	1154

DIVISION SERIES RECORD

Year League	W	L	Pct.	ERA	G	GS	CG	ShO	Sv.-Opp.	IP	H	R	ER	HR	BB-IBB	SO
1995—Boston (A.L.)	0	1	.000	11.81	1	1	0	0	0-0	5.1	5	7	7	1	5-0	4
1998—Boston (A.L.)	0	1	.000	33.75	1	1	0	0	0-0	1.1	3	5	5	0	2-0	1
1999—Boston (A.L.)	0	0	...	13.50	2	0	0	0	0-0	2.0	3	3	3	0	4-0	4
Division series totals (3 years)	0	2	.000	15.58	4	2	0	0	0-0	8.2	11	15	15	1	11-0	9

CHAMPIONSHIP SERIES RECORD

RECORDS: Shares single-series record for most complete games—2 (1992). ... Shares N.L. career record for most complete games—2.

Year League	W	L	Pct.	ERA	G	GS	CG	ShO	Sv.-Opp.	IP	H	R	ER	HR	BB-IBB	SO
1992—Pittsburgh (N.L.)	2	0	1.000	3.00	2	2	2	0	0-0	18.0	14	6	6	4	5-0	7
1999—Boston (A.L.)									Did not play.							

RECORD AS POSITION PLAYER

Year	Team (League)	Pos.	G	AB	R	H	2B	3B	HR	RBI	BB	SO	SB-CS	Avg.	OBP	SLG	E	Avg.
			BATTING														FIELDING	
1988—	Watertown (NY-Penn)	1B	54	159	24	30	6	2	3	20	25	57	3-3	.189	.328	.308	8	.980
1989—	Augusta (S.Atl.)..........	3B-1B	11	34	5	8	2	1	0	5	1	14	1-1	.235	.257	.353	3	.917
—	Welland (NY-Penn).....	3B-2B-1B	36	63	7	13	4	0	1	3	3	21	1-1	.206	.254	.317	8	.877

WALBECK, MATT — C

PERSONAL: Born October 2, 1969, in Sacramento. ... 5-11/188. ... Bats both, throws right. ... Full name: Matthew Lovick Walbeck.
HIGH SCHOOL: Sacramento High.
TRANSACTIONS/CAREER NOTES: Selected by Chicago Cubs organization in eighth round of free-agent draft (June 2, 1987). ... On Winston-Salem disabled list (April 12-July 11, 1990). ... On Charleston, W.Va. disabled list (September 5, 1992-remainder of season). ... Traded by Cubs with P Dave Stevens to Minnesota Twins for P Willie Banks (November 24, 1993). ... On Minnesota disabled list (March 31-June 17, 1996); included rehabilitation assignments to Fort Myers (May 31-June 11) and New Britain (June 12-17). ... Traded by Twins to Detroit Tigers for P Brent Stentz (December 11, 1996). ... On Detroit disabled list (April 19-July 9, 1997); included rehabilitation assignments to Lakeland (June 12-15) and Toledo (June 16-July 9). ... Traded by Tigers with 3B Phil Nevin to Anaheim Angels for P Nick Skuse (November 20, 1997). ... On disabled list (August 17-September 1, 2000). ... Granted free agency (November 1, 2000). ... Signed by Cincinnati Reds organization (February 9, 2001). ... Contract purchased Philadelphia Phillies organization from Reds (July 11, 2001). ... Granted free agency (October 8, 2001). ... Signed by San Diego Padres organization (January 2, 2002). ... Traded by Padres with IF Damian Jackson to Detroit Tigers for C Javier Cardona and OF Rich Gomez (March 24, 2002). ... Granted free agency (October 30, 2002).
STATISTICAL NOTES: Tied for Carolina League lead with 10 sacrifice flies in 1991. ... Led American Association catchers with 64 assists and 561 total chances and tied for lead with nine double plays in 1993. ... Led International League catchers with 1.000 fielding percentage in 2001. ... Career major league grand slams: 2.
MISCELLANEOUS: Batted righthanded only (1987-89).
2002 GAMES PLAYED BY POSITION (MLB): C—27.

Year	Team (League)	Pos.	G	AB	R	H	2B	3B	HR	RBI	BB	SO	SB-CS	Avg.	OBP	SLG	E	Avg.
			BATTING														FIELDING	
1987—	Wytheville (Appl.).......	C	51	169	24	53	9	3	1	28	22	39	0-1	.314	.387	.420	1	*.997
1988—	Charl., W.Va. (S.Atl.)..	C	104	312	28	68	9	0	2	24	30	44	7-5	.218	.292	.266	14	.978
1989—	Peoria (Midw.)............	C	94	341	38	86	19	0	4	47	20	47	5-2	.252	.297	.343	11	.984
1990—	Peoria (Midw.)............	C	25	66	2	15	1	0	0	5	5	7	1-0	.227	.301	.242	2	.987
1991—	Win.-Salem (Caro.)	C	91	260	25	70	11	0	3	41	20	23	3-2	.269	.315	.346	12	.978
1992—	Charlotte (Sou.)..........	C-1B	105	385	48	116	22	1	7	42	33	56	0-7	.301	.358	.418	10	.984
1993—	Chicago (N.L.)............	C	11	30	2	6	2	0	1	6	1	6	0-0	.200	.226	.367	0	1.000
—	Iowa (A.A.)................	C	87	331	31	93	18	2	6	43	18	47	1-2	.281	.320	.402	1	*.998
1994—	Minnesota (A.L.)■.....	C-DH	97	338	31	69	12	0	5	35	17	37	1-1	.204	.246	.284	4	.993
1995—	Minnesota (A.L.).......	C	115	393	40	101	18	1	1	44	25	71	3-1	.257	.302	.316	6	.991
1996—	Fort Myers (FSL)........	C-DH	9	33	4	9	1	1	0	9	4	2	0-1	.273	.350	.364	0	1.000
—	New Britain (East.).....	DH-C	7	24	1	5	0	0	0	0	1	1	0-0	.208	.240	.208	0	1.000
—	Minnesota (A.L.)........	C	63	215	25	48	10	0	2	24	9	34	3-1	.223	.252	.298	2	.994
1997—	Detroit (A.L.)■...........	C	47	137	18	38	3	0	3	10	12	19	3-3	.277	.331	.365	3	.988
—	Lakeland (FSL)..........	C-DH	4	10	4	5	1	0	0	3	4	1	0-1	.500	.643	.600	1	.933
—	Toledo (I.L.)...............	C-DH	17	59	6	18	2	1	1	8	4	15	0-0	.305	.338	.424	3	.955
1998—	Anaheim (A.L.)■........	C-DH	108	338	41	87	15	2	6	46	30	68	1-1	.257	.317	.367	7	.990
1999—	Anaheim (A.L.)..........	C-DH	107	288	26	69	8	1	3	22	26	46	2-3	.240	.308	.306	5	.989
2000—	Anaheim (A.L.)..........	C-1B-DH	47	146	17	29	5	0	6	12	7	22	0-1	.199	.240	.356	2	.991
2001—	Louisville (I.L.)■........	C	67	197	20	45	7	0	3	25	23	26	1-0	.228	.309	.310	0	1.000
—	Scranton/W.B. (I.L.)■	C-1B	40	141	18	42	11	0	2	21	11	20	0-2	.298	.355	.418	0	§1.000
—	Philadelphia (N.L.)......	PH	1	1	0	1	0	0	0	0	0	0	0-0	1.000	1.000	1.000	...	...
2002—	Toledo (I.L.)■............	C-1B	21	75	4	16	3	0	1	6	4	10	0-0	.213	.250	.293	3	.980
—	Detroit (A.L.).............	C	27	85	4	20	2	0	0	3	3	14	0-0	.235	.258	.259	1	.993
American League totals (8 years)			611	1940	202	461	73	4	26	196	129	311	13-11	.238	.286	.320	30	.991
National League totals (2 years)			12	31	2	7	2	0	1	6	1	6	0-0	.226	.250	.387	0	1.000
Major League totals (10 years)			623	1971	204	468	75	4	27	202	130	317	13-11	.237	.286	.321	30	.991

WALKER, JAMIE — P — TIGERS

PERSONAL: Born July 1, 1971, in McMinnville, Tenn. ... 6-2/190. ... Throws left, bats left. ... Full name: Jamie Ross Walker.
HIGH SCHOOL: Warren County (McMinnville, Tenn.).
COLLEGE: Austin Peay.
TRANSACTIONS/CAREER NOTES: Selected by Houston Astros organization in 10th round of free-agent draft (June 1, 1992). ... Selected by Atlanta Braves organization from Astros organization in Rule 5 major league draft (December 9, 1996). ... Traded by Braves with OF Jermaine Dye to Kansas City Royals for OF Michael Tucker and IF Keith Lockhart (March 27, 1997). ... On Kansas City disabled list (June 5-24, 1997); included rehabilitation assignment to Wichita (June 11-24). ... On Kansas City disabled list (June 1, 1998-remainder of season). ... Granted free agency (December 21, 1998). ... Re-signed by Royals organization (December 21, 1998). ... On Omaha disabled list (April 8-May 17 and May 25-August 27, 1999). ... Released by Royals (July 27, 2000). ... Signed by Cleveland Indians organization (February 9, 2001). ... Granted free agency (October 15, 2001). ... Signed by Detroit Tigers organization (December 19, 2001).
CAREER HITTING (MLB): 0-for-0 (.000), 0 R, 0 2B, 0 3B, 0 HR, 0 RBI.

Year	League	W	L	Pct.	ERA	G	GS	CG	ShO	Sv.-Opp.	IP	H	R	ER	HR	BB-IBB	SO
1992—	Auburn (NY-Penn)............	4	6	.400	3.13	15	14	0	0	0-...	83.1	75	35	29	4	21-0	67
1993—	Quad City (Midw.)............	3	11	.214	5.13	25	24	1	1	0-...	131.2	140	92	75	12	48-1	121
1994—	Quad City (Midw.)............	8	10	.444	4.18	32	18	0	0	1-...	125.0	133	80	58	10	42-2	104
1995—	Jackson (Texas)...............	4	2	.667	4.50	50	0	0	0	2-...	58.0	59	29	29	6	24-5	38
1996—	Jackson (Texas)...............	5	1	.833	2.50	45	7	0	0	2-...	101.0	94	34	28	7	35-2	79
1997—	Kansas City (A.L.)■.........	3	3	.500	5.44	50	0	0	0	0-1	43.0	46	28	26	6	20-3	24
—	Wichita (Texas)................	0	1	.000	9.45	5	0	0	0	0-...	6.2	6	8	7	1	5-0	6
1998—	Omaha (PCL).....................	5	1	.833	2.70	7	7	0	0	0-...	46.2	57	15	14	3	11-1	21
—	Kansas City (A.L.)............	0	1	.000	9.87	6	2	0	0	0-0	17.1	30	20	19	5	3-0	15

Year	League	W	L	Pct.	ERA	G	GS	CG	ShO	Sv.-Opp.	IP	H	R	ER	HR	BB-IBB	SO
1999—	Omaha (PCL)	0	1	.000	4.67	4	4	0	0	0-...	17.1	22	12	9	1	4-0	11
—	Gulf Coast Royals (GCL)	1	0	1.000	3.38	2	2	0	0	0-...	8.0	10	3	3	1	0-0	9
2000—	Omaha (PCL)	3	10	.231	5.22	24	15	0	0	0-...	101.2	138	65	59	25	25-1	52
2001—	Buffalo (I.L.)■	7	2	.778	3.87	38	8	0	0	2-...	93.0	104	44	40	12	27-1	51
2002—	Toledo (I.L.)■	0	1	.000	1.98	10	0	0	0	1-...	13.2	7	3	3	2	3-0	9
—	Detroit (A.L.)	1	1	.500	3.71	57	0	0	0	1-4	43.2	32	19	18	9	9-1	40
Major League totals (3 years)		4	5	.444	5.45	113	2	0	0	1-5	104.0	108	67	63	20	32-4	79

WALKER, KEVIN P PADRES

PERSONAL: Born September 20, 1976, in Irvin, Texas. ... 6-4/190. ... Throws left, bats left. ... Full name: Kevin Michael Walker.

HIGH SCHOOL: Grand Prairie (Texas).

TRANSACTIONS/CAREER NOTES: Selected by San Diego Padres organization in sixth round of free-agent draft (June 1, 1995). ... On Mobile disabled list (April 8-24, 1999). ... On Rancho Cucamonga disabled list (June 19-July 30, 1999). ... On disabled list (April 20-May 8 and May 23, 2001-remainder of season). ... On San Diego disabled list (March 27-August 8 and August 12-September 1, 2002); included rehabilitation assignments to Lake Elsinore (July 18-August 2) and Portland (August 3-8).

CAREER HITTING (MLB): 1-for-4 (.250), 0 R, 0 2B, 0 3B, 0 HR, 0 RBI.

Year	League	W	L	Pct.	ERA	G	GS	CG	ShO	Sv.-Opp.	IP	H	R	ER	HR	BB-IBB	SO
1995—	Arizona Padres (Ariz.)	5	5	.500	3.01	13	12	0	0	0-...	71.2	74	34	24	1	12-0	69
1996—	Idaho Falls (Pio.)	1	0	1.000	3.00	1	1	0	0	0-...	6.0	4	3	2	1	2-0	4
—	Clinton (Midw.)	4	6	.400	4.74	13	13	0	0	0-...	76.0	80	46	40	9	33-0	43
1997—	Clinton (Midw.)	6	10	.375	4.88	19	19	3	1	0-...	110.2	133	80	60	9	37-0	80
1998—	Clinton (Midw.)	2	0	1.000	1.23	2	2	0	0	0-...	14.2	11	2	2	0	7-0	10
—	Rancho Cuca. (Calif.)	11	7	.611	4.15	22	22	0	0	0-...	121.1	122	62	56	10	48-0	94
1999—	Rancho Cuca. (Calif.)	1	1	.500	3.46	27	1	0	0	4-...	39.0	35	19	15	2	19-3	35
2000—	Mobile (Sou.)	0	1	.000	2.25	4	0	0	0	0-...	4.0	1	1	1	1	1-0	6
—	San Diego (N.L.)	7	1	.875	4.18	70	0	0	0	0-0	66.2	49	35	31	5	38-6	56
2001—	San Diego (N.L.)	0	0	...	3.00	16	0	0	0	0-1	12.0	5	4	4	0	8-2	17
2002—	Lake Elsinore (Calif.)	0	0	...	0.00	5	1	0	0	0-...	7.0	3	0	0	0	0-0	10
—	Portland (PCL)	0	0	...	3.00	3	0	0	0	0-...	3.0	1	1	1	1	0-0	4
—	San Diego (N.L.)	0	1	.000	5.63	11	0	0	0	0-1	8.0	12	6	5	2	5-1	11
Major League totals (3 years)		7	2	.778	4.15	97	0	0	0	0-2	86.2	66	45	40	7	51-9	84

WALKER, LARRY OF ROCKIES

PERSONAL: Born December 1, 1966, in Maple Ridge, B.C. ... 6-3/233. ... Bats left, throws right. ... Full name: Larry Kenneth Robert Walker.

HIGH SCHOOL: Maple Ridge (B.C.) Senior Secondary School.

TRANSACTIONS/CAREER NOTES: Signed as non-drafted free agent by Montreal Expos organization (November 14, 1984). ... On disabled list (April 4, 1988-entire season; June 28-July 13, 1991; and May 26-June 10, 1993). ... On suspended list (June 24-28, 1994). ... Granted free agency (October 24, 1994). ... Signed by Colorado Rockies (April 8, 1995). ... On Colorado disabled list (June 10-August 15, 1996); included rehabilitation assignments to Salem (August 6-9) and Colorado Springs (August 9-15). ... On disabled list (June 18-July 3, 1998; March 29-April 14, 1999; May 11-June 9 and August 20, 2000-remainder of season).

RECORDS: Shares major league record for most extra-base hits in two consecutive games (May 21-22, 1996; 2 doubles, 3 triples and 1 home run). ... Shares major league single-season record for fewest assists by outfielder who led league in assists—14 (2002). ... Holds N.L. single-season record for most consecutive long hits—6 (May 21-22, 1996; 2 doubles, 3 triples and 1 home run).

HONORS: Named outfielder on The Sporting News N.L. All-Star team (1992, 1997 and 1999). ... Won N.L. Gold Glove as outfielder (1992-93, 1997-99 and 2001-02). ... Named outfielder on The Sporting News N.L. Silver Slugger team (1992, 1997 and 1999). ... Named N.L. Most Valuable Player by Baseball Writers' Association of America (1997).

STATISTICAL NOTES: Led American Association outfielders with 18 assists in 1989. ... Hit three home runs in one game (April 5, 1997; and April 28, 1999). ... Led N.L. with 409 total bases in 1997. ... Led N.L. outfielders in double plays with four in 1997 and tied for lead with four in 2000. ... Had 20-game hitting streak (May 4-25, 1998). ... Had 21-game hitting streak (April 25-May 21, 1999). ... Had 18-game hitting streak (June 14-July 3, 1999). ... Had 17-game hitting streak (July 15-August 3, 2002). ... Tied for N.L. lead with 14 assists by outfielder in 2002. ... Career major league grand slams: 4.

MISCELLANEOUS: Holds Colorado Rockies all-time record for most runs (784), most home runs (236) and highest career batting average (.341).

2002 GAMES PLAYED BY POSITION (MLB): OF—123; DH—7.

			BATTING														FIELDING	
Year	Team (League)	Pos.	G	AB	R	H	2B	3B	HR	RBI	BB	SO	SB-CS	Avg.	OBP	SLG	E	Avg.
1985—	Utica (NY-Penn)	1B-3B	62	215	24	48	8	2	2	26	18	57	12-6	.223	.297	.307	8	.981
1986—	Burlington (Midw.)	OF-3B	95	332	67	96	12	6	29	74	46	112	16-8	.289	.387	.623	10	.940
—	W. Palm Beach (FSL)	OF	38	113	20	32	7	5	4	16	26	32	2-2	.283	.423	.540	0	1.000
1987—	Jacksonville (Sou.)	OF	128	474	91	136	25	7	26	83	67	120	24-3	.287	.383	.534	9	.968
1988—	Montreal (N.L.)	Did not play.																
1989—	Indianapolis (A.A.)	OF	114	385	68	104	18	2	12	59	50	87	36-6	.270	.361	.421	*11	.959
—	Montreal (N.L.)	OF	20	47	4	8	0	0	0	4	5	13	1-1	.170	.264	.170	0	1.000
1990—	Montreal (N.L.)	OF	133	419	59	101	18	3	19	51	49	112	21-7	.241	.326	.434	4	.985
1991—	Montreal (N.L.)	OF-1B	137	487	59	141	30	2	16	64	42	102	14-9	.290	.349	.458	6	.990
1992—	Montreal (N.L.)	OF	143	528	85	159	31	4	23	93	41	97	18-6	.301	.353	.506	2	.993
1993—	Montreal (N.L.)	OF-1B	138	490	85	130	24	5	22	86	80	76	29-7	.265	.371	.469	6	.982
1994—	Montreal (N.L.)	OF-1B	103	395	76	127	*44	2	19	86	47	74	15-5	.322	.394	.587	9	.980
1995—	Colorado (N.L.)■	OF	131	494	96	151	31	5	36	101	49	72	16-3	.306	.381	.607	3	.988
1996—	Colorado (N.L.)	OF	83	272	58	75	18	4	18	58	20	58	18-2	.276	.342	.570	1	.994
—	Salem (Caro.)	DH	2	8	3	4	3	0	1	1	0	1	0-0	.500	.500	1.250	...	...
—	Colo. Springs (PCL)	OF	3	11	2	4	0	0	2	8	1	4	0-0	.364	.385	.909	0	1.000
1997—	Colorado (N.L.)	OF-1B-DH	153	568	143	208	46	4	*49	130	78	90	33-8	.366	*.452	*.720	2	.993
1998—	Colorado (N.L.)	O-DH-2-3	130	454	113	165	46	3	23	67	64	61	14-4	*.363	.445	.630	4	.984
1999—	Colorado (N.L.)	OF-DH	127	438	108	166	26	4	37	115	57	52	11-4	*.379	*.458	*.710	4	.982
2000—	Colorado (N.L.)	OF-DH	87	314	64	97	21	7	9	51	46	40	5-5	.309	.409	.506	1	.994
2001—	Colorado (N.L.)	OF-DH	142	497	107	174	35	3	38	123	82	103	14-5	*.350	.449	.662	4	.984
2002—	Colorado (N.L.)	OF-DH	136	477	95	161	40	4	26	104	65	73	6-5	.338	.421	.602	4	.984
Major League totals (14 years)			1663	5880	1152	1863	410	50	335	1133	725	1023	215-71	.317	.398	.574	50	.987

DIVISION SERIES RECORD

Year	Team (League)	Pos.	G	AB	R	H	2B	3B	HR	RBI	BB	SO	SB-CS	Avg.	OBP	SLG	E	Avg.
			BATTING														FIELDING	
1995—	Colorado (N.L.)	OF	4	14	3	3	0	0	1	3	3	4	1-0	.214	.389	.429	0	1.000

ALL-STAR GAME RECORD

	AB	R	H	2B	3B	HR	RBI	BB	SO	SB-CS	Avg.	OBP	SLG	E	Avg.
All-Star Game totals (5 years)	7	1	1	0	0	0	0	2	1	0-0	.143	.333	.143	0	1.000

WALKER, PETE P BLUE JAYS

PERSONAL: Born April 8, 1969, in Beverly, Mass. ... 6-2/195. ... Throws right, bats right. ... Full name: Peter Brian Walker.

HIGH SCHOOL: East Lyme (Conn.).

COLLEGE: Connecticut.

TRANSACTIONS/CAREER NOTES: Selected by New York Mets organization in seventh round of free-agent draft (June 4, 1990). ... On disabled list (June 6-18, 1992; and April 25-May 9, 1993). ... On Norfolk disabled list (April 7-May 16, 1994). ... On Norfolk suspended list (August 5-6, 1994). ... Traded by Mets with P Luis Arroyo to San Diego Padres for 1B Roberto Petagine and P Scott Adair (March 17, 1996). ... On Las Vegas disabled list (May 4-July 11, 1996). ... Granted free agency (October 15, 1996). ... Signed by Boston Red Sox organization (June 30, 1997). ... Granted free agency (October 17, 1997). ... Re-signed by Red Sox organization (January 14, 1998). ... On Pawtucket disabled list (June 11-22 and June 26-September 8, 1998). ... Granted free agency (October 16, 1998). ... Signed by Colorado Rockies organization (February 8, 1999). ... On Colorado Springs disabled list (July 16-August 6, 1999). ... Granted free agency (October 15, 1999). ... Re-signed by Rockies organization (November 17, 1999). ... Released by Rockies (November 13, 2000). ... Signed by Mets organization (December 26, 2000). ... Granted free agency (October 15, 2001). ... Re-signed by Mets organization (December 10, 2001). ... Claimed on waivers by Toronto Blue Jays (May 3, 2002).

CAREER HITTING (MLB): 0-for-1 (.000), 0 R, 0 2B, 0 3B, 0 HR, 0 RBI.

Year	League	W	L	Pct.	ERA	G	GS	CG	ShO	Sv.-Opp.	IP	H	R	ER	HR	BB-IBB	SO
1990—	Pittsfield (NY-Penn)	5	7	.417	4.16	16	13	1	0	0-...	80.0	74	43	37	2	46-0	73
1991—	St. Lucie (FSL)	10	12	.455	3.21	26	25	1	0	0-...	151.1	145	77	54	9	52-2	95
1992—	Binghamton (East.)	7	12	.368	4.12	24	23	4	0	0-...	139.2	159	77	64	9	46-0	72
1993—	Binghamton (East.)	4	9	.308	3.44	45	10	0	0	19-...	99.1	89	45	38	6	46-1	89
1994—	St. Lucie (FSL)	0	0	...	2.25	3	0	0	0	0-...	4.0	3	2	1	1	1-0	5
—	Norfolk (I.L.)	2	4	.333	3.97	37	0	0	0	3-...	47.2	48	22	21	3	24-2	42
1995—	Norfolk (I.L.)	5	2	.714	3.91	34	1	0	0	8-...	48.1	51	24	21	4	16-1	39
—	New York (N.L.)	1	0	1.000	4.58	13	0	0	0	0-0	17.2	24	9	9	3	5-0	5
1996—	Las Vegas (PCL)■	5	1	.833	6.83	26	0	0	0	0-...	27.2	37	22	21	7	14-2	23
—	Arizona Padres (Ariz.)	0	1	.000	2.25	2	2	0	0	0-...	4.0	4	1	1	0	0-0	5
—	San Diego (N.L.)	0	0	...	0.00	1	0	0	0	0-0	.2	0	0	0	0	3-0	1
1997—	GC Red Sox (GCL)■	0	0	...	0.96	4	3	0	0	0-...	9.1	5	1	1	0	1-0	14
—	Trenton (East.)	0	0	...	4.05	8	0	0	0	3-...	13.1	14	6	6	1	7-0	13
—	Pawtucket (I.L.)	0	0	...	5.40	7	0	0	0	0-...	11.2	14	8	7	2	7-1	8
1998—	Pawtucket (I.L.)	1	4	.200	5.94	22	0	0	0	0-...	33.1	34	26	22	8	17-1	19
1999—	Colorado Springs (PCL)■	8	4	.667	4.48	48	0	0	0	5-...	62.1	64	37	31	9	28-3	57
2000—	Colorado Springs (PCL)	7	3	.700	3.07	58	0	0	0	5-...	73.1	64	29	25	3	30-1	61
—	Colorado (N.L.)	0	0	...	17.36	3	0	0	0	0-0	4.2	10	9	9	1	4-0	2
2001—	Norfolk (I.L.)■	13	4	.765	2.99	26	26	0	0	0-...	168.1	145	64	56	12	46-5	106
—	New York (N.L.)	0	0	...	2.70	2	0	0	0	0-0	6.2	6	2	2	0	0-0	4
2002—	Norfolk (I.L.)	0	0	...	3.00	2	2	0	0	0-...	9.0	9	3	3	1	1-0	6
—	New York (N.L.)	0	0	...	9.00	1	0	0	0	0-0	1.0	2	1	1	0	0-0	0
—	Toronto (A.L.)■	10	5	.667	4.33	37	20	0	0	1-1	139.1	143	72	67	18	51-5	80
A.L. totals (1 year)		10	5	.667	4.33	37	20	0	0	1-1	139.1	143	72	67	18	51-5	80
N.L. totals (5 years)		1	0	1.000	6.16	20	0	0	0	0-0	30.2	42	21	21	4	12-0	12
Major League totals (5 years)		11	5	.688	4.66	57	20	0	0	1-1	170.0	185	93	88	22	63-5	92

WALKER, TODD 2B REDS

PERSONAL: Born May 25, 1973, in Bakersfield, Calif. ... 6-0/190. ... Bats left, throws right. ... Full name: Todd Arthur Walker.

HIGH SCHOOL: Airline (Bossier City, La.).

COLLEGE: Louisiana State.

TRANSACTIONS/CAREER NOTES: Selected by Texas Rangers organization in 51st round of free-agent draft (June 3, 1991); did not sign. ... Selected by Minnesota Twins organization in first round (eighth pick overall) of free-agent draft (June 2, 1994). ... Traded by Twins with OF/1B Butch Huskey to Colorado Rockies for 2B Todd Sears and cash considerations (July 16, 2000). ... Traded by Rockies with OF Robin Jennings to Cincinnati Reds for OF Alex Ochoa (July 19, 2001).

HONORS: Named Most Outstanding Player of College World Series (1993).

STATISTICAL NOTES: Led Pacific Coast League with 330 total bases and tied for lead in intentional bases on balls received with 11 in 1996. ... Led N.L. second basemen with 315 putouts in 2002. ... Career major league grand slams: 2.

2002 GAMES PLAYED BY POSITION (MLB): 2B—154.

Year	Team (League)	Pos.	G	AB	R	H	2B	3B	HR	RBI	BB	SO	SB-CS	Avg.	OBP	SLG	E	Avg.
			BATTING														FIELDING	
1994—	Fort Myers (FSL)	2B	46	171	29	52	5	2	10	34	32	15	6-3	.304	.406	.532	9	.959
1995—	New Britain (East.)	2B-3B	137	513	83	149	27	3	21	85	63	101	23-9	.290	.365	.478	27	.955
1996—	Salt Lake (PCL)	3B-2B-DH	135	551	94	*187	*41	9	*28	*111	57	91	13-8	.339	.400	*.599	19	.955
—	Minnesota (A.L.)	3B-2B-DH	25	82	8	21	6	0	0	6	4	13	2-0	.256	.281	.329	2	.965
1997—	Minnesota (A.L.)	3B-2B-DH	52	156	15	37	7	1	3	16	11	30	7-0	.237	.288	.353	4	.968
—	Salt Lake (PCL)	3B-DH	83	322	69	111	20	1	11	53	46	49	5-5	.345	.420	.516	*24	.901
1998—	Minnesota (A.L.)	2B-DH	143	528	85	167	41	3	12	62	47	65	19-7	.316	.372	.473	13	.978
1999—	Minnesota (A.L.)	2B-DH	143	531	62	148	37	4	6	46	52	83	18-10	.279	.343	.397	7	.984
2000—	Minnesota (A.L.)	2B-DH	23	77	14	18	1	0	2	8	7	10	3-0	.234	.287	.325	4	.946
—	Salt Lake (PCL)	2B	63	249	51	81	14	1	2	37	32	32	8-3	.325	.398	.414	11	.964
—	Colorado (N.L.)■	2B	57	171	28	54	10	4	7	36	20	19	4-1	.316	.385	.544	5	.975

Year	Team (League)	Pos.	G	AB	R	H	2B	3B	HR	RBI	BB	SO	SB-CS	Avg.	OBP	SLG	E	Avg.
			BATTING														FIELDING	
2001—	Colorado (N.L.)	2B	85	290	52	86	18	2	12	43	25	40	1-3	.297	.349	.497	7	.981
—	Cincinnati (N.L.)■	2B-SS	66	261	41	77	17	0	5	32	26	42	0-5	.295	.361	.418	4	.987
2002—	Cincinnati (N.L.)	2B	155	612	79	183	42	3	11	64	50	81	8-5	.299	.353	.431	8	*.989
American League totals (5 years)			386	1374	184	391	92	8	23	138	121	201	49-17	.285	.341	.413	30	.977
National League totals (3 years)			363	1334	200	400	87	9	35	175	121	182	13-14	.300	.358	.457	24	.985
Major League totals (7 years)			749	2708	384	791	179	17	58	313	242	383	62-31	.292	.349	.435	54	.982

WALKER, TYLER — P — METS

PERSONAL: Born May 15, 1976, in San Francisco. ... 6-3/255. ... Throws right, bats right. ... Full name: Tyler Lanier Walker.
HIGH SCHOOL: University (San Francisco).
COLLEGE: California.
TRANSACTIONS/CAREER NOTES: Selected by New York Mets organization in second round of free-agent draft (June 3, 1997). ... On Norfolk disabled list (August 11-20 and August 21-28, 2000).
CAREER HITTING (MLB): 0-for-2 (.000), 0 R, 0 2B, 0 3B, 0 HR, 0 RBI.

Year	League	W	L	Pct.	ERA	G	GS	CG	ShO	Sv.-Opp.	IP	H	R	ER	HR	BB-IBB	SO
1997—	Gulf Coast Mets (GCL)	0	0	...	1.00	5	0	0	0	3-...	9.0	8	1	1	0	2-1	9
—	Pittsfield (NY-Penn)	0	0	...	13.50	1	0	0	0	0-...	.2	2	2	1	1	1-0	1
1998—	Capital City (S.Atl.)	5	5	.500	4.12	34	13	0	0	1-...	115.2	122	63	53	9	38-0	110
1999—	St. Lucie (FSL)	6	5	.545	2.94	13	13	2	0	0-...	79.2	64	31	26	6	29-2	64
—	Binghamton (East.)	6	4	.600	6.22	13	13	0	0	0-...	68.0	78	49	47	11	32-0	59
2000—	Binghamton (East.)	7	6	.538	2.75	22	22	0	0	0-...	121.0	82	43	37	3	55-1	111
—	Norfolk (I.L.)	1	3	.250	2.39	5	5	0	0	0-...	26.1	29	7	7	0	9-0	17
2001—	St. Lucie (FSL)	0	2	.000	8.04	4	4	0	0	0-...	15.2	19	14	14	0	3-0	11
—	Binghamton (East.)	1	0	1.000	0.40	4	3	0	0	0-...	22.1	9	2	1	1	13-1	13
—	Norfolk (I.L.)	3	2	.600	4.02	8	8	0	0	0-...	40.1	34	19	18	7	8-0	35
2002—	Norfolk (I.L.)	10	5	.667	3.99	28	25	1	1	1-...	142.0	152	65	63	13	38-3	109
—	New York (N.L.)	1	0	1.000	5.91	5	1	0	0	0-0	10.2	11	7	7	3	5-1	7
Major League totals (1 year)		1	0	1.000	5.91	5	1	0	0	0-0	10.2	11	7	7	3	5-1	7

WALL, DONNE — P — ROCKIES

PERSONAL: Born July 11, 1967, in Potosi, Mo. ... 6-1/205. ... Throws right, bats right. ... Full name: Donnell Lee Wall. ... Name pronounced DON-ee.
HIGH SCHOOL: Festus (Mo.).
JUNIOR COLLEGE: Jefferson College (Mo.), then St. Louis Community College at Meramec.
COLLEGE: Southwestern Louisiana.
TRANSACTIONS/CAREER NOTES: Selected by Houston Astros organization in 18th round of free-agent draft (June 5, 1989). ... On disabled list (May 27-June 16, 1994). ... Claimed on waivers by Cincinnati Reds (October 7, 1997). ... Traded by Reds with C Paul Bako to Detroit Tigers for OF Melvin Nieves (November 11, 1997). ... Traded by Tigers with P Dan Miceli and 3B Ryan Balfe to San Diego Padres for P Tim Worrell and OF Trey Beamon (November 19, 1997). ... On San Diego disabled list (June 1-July 1, 2000); included rehabilitation assignment to Las Vegas (June 28-July 1). ... Traded by Padres to New York Mets for OF Bubba Trammell (December 11, 2000). ... On New York disabled list (May 27-July 4, 2001); included rehabilitation assignment to Binghamton (June 25-July 4). ... Granted free agency (October 15, 2001). ... Signed by Anaheim Angels organization (January 31, 2002). ... On Anaheim disabled list (April 29-May 20, 2002); included rehabilitation assignment to Salt Lake (May 17-20). ... Released by Angels (June 2, 2002). ... Signed by Colorado Rockies organization (June 21, 2002).
HONORS: Named Pacific Coast League Most Valuable Player (1995).
MISCELLANEOUS: Appeared in one game pinch runner (2001).
CAREER HITTING (MLB): 12-for-68 (.176), 6 R, 1 2B, 0 3B, 0 HR, 1 RBI.

Year	League	W	L	Pct.	ERA	G	GS	CG	ShO	Sv.-Opp.	IP	H	R	ER	HR	BB-IBB	SO
1989—	Auburn (NY-Penn)	7	0	*1.000	1.79	12	8	3	1	1-...	65.1	45	17	13	2	12-0	69
1990—	Asheville (S.Atl.)	6	8	.429	5.18	28	22	1	0	1-...	132.0	149	87	76	*18	47-1	111
1991—	Burlington (Midw.)	7	5	.583	2.03	16	16	3	1	0-...	106.2	73	30	24	4	21-1	102
—	Osceola (FSL)	6	3	.667	2.09	12	12	4	2	0-...	77.1	55	22	18	3	11-1	62
1992—	Osceola (FSL)	3	1	.750	2.63	7	7	0	0	0-...	41.0	37	13	12	1	8-0	30
—	Jackson (Texas)	9	6	.600	3.54	18	18	2	0	0-...	114.1	114	51	45	6	26-2	99
1993—	Tucson (PCL)	6	4	.600	3.83	25	22	0	0	0-...	131.2	147	73	56	11	25-3	89
1994—	Tucson (PCL)	11	8	.579	4.43	26	24	2	2	0-...	148.1	171	87	73	9	35-2	84
1995—	Tucson (PCL)	*17	6	.739	*3.30	28	•28	0	0	0-...	*177.1	190	72	65	5	32-1	*119
—	Houston (N.L.)	3	1	.750	5.55	6	5	0	0	0-0	24.1	33	19	15	5	5-0	16
1996—	Tucson (PCL)	3	3	.500	4.13	8	8	0	0	0-...	52.1	67	30	24	2	6-0	36
—	Houston (N.L.)	9	8	.529	4.56	26	23	2	1	0-0	150.0	170	84	76	17	34-3	99
1997—	New Orleans (A.A.)	8	7	.533	3.85	17	17	1	0	0-...	110.0	109	49	47	13	24-0	84
—	Houston (N.L.)	2	5	.286	6.26	8	8	0	0	0-0	41.2	53	31	29	8	16-0	25
1998—	Las Vegas (PCL)■	2	0	1.000	4.80	3	3	0	0	0-...	15.0	11	8	8	2	8-0	12
—	San Diego (N.L.)	5	4	.556	2.43	46	1	0	0	1-4	70.1	50	20	19	6	32-2	56
1999—	San Diego (N.L.)	7	4	.636	3.07	55	0	0	0	0-6	70.1	58	31	24	11	23-3	53
2000—	San Diego (N.L.)	5	2	.714	3.35	44	0	0	0	1-5	53.2	36	20	20	4	21-1	29
—	Las Vegas (PCL)	0	0	...	0.00	2	0	0	0	0-...	2.0	3	0	0	0	2-0	1
2001—	New York (N.L.)■	0	4	.000	4.85	32	0	0	0	0-0	42.2	51	24	23	8	17-6	31
—	Binghamton (East.)	0	0	...	0.00	4	4	0	0	0-...	5.0	1	0	0	0	1-0	5
—	Norfolk (I.L.)	0	0	...	10.38	4	0	0	0	1-...	4.1	8	6	5	1	5-0	1
2002—	Salt Lake (PCL)	0	1	.000	5.40	1	1	0	0	0-...	1.2	1	1	1	1	0-0	2
—	Anaheim (A.L.)	0	0	...	6.43	17	0	0	0	0-0	21.0	17	15	15	3	7-1	13
—	Colorado Springs (PCL)	1	2	.333	5.19	14	0	0	0	0-...	17.1	16	10	10	1	4-0	11
A.L. totals (1 year)		0	0	...	6.43	17	0	0	0	0-0	21.0	17	15	15	3	7-1	13
N.L. totals (7 years)		31	28	.525	4.09	217	37	2	1	2-15	453.0	451	229	206	59	148-15	309
Major League totals (8 years)		31	28	.525	4.20	234	37	2	1	2-15	474.0	468	244	221	62	155-16	322

DIVISION SERIES RECORD

Year League	W	L	Pct.	ERA	G	GS	CG	ShO	Sv.-Opp.	IP	H	R	ER	HR	BB-IBB	SO
1998—San Diego (N.L.)	0	0	...	9.00	1	0	0	0	0-0	1.0	2	1	1	1	0-0	2

CHAMPIONSHIP SERIES RECORD

Year League	W	L	Pct.	ERA	G	GS	CG	ShO	Sv.-Opp.	IP	H	R	ER	HR	BB-IBB	SO
1998—San Diego (N.L.)	0	0	...	3.00	3	0	0	0	1-1	3.0	3	2	1	0	4-1	4

WORLD SERIES RECORD

Year League	W	L	Pct.	ERA	G	GS	CG	ShO	Sv.-Opp.	IP	H	R	ER	HR	BB-IBB	SO
1998—San Diego (N.L.)	0	1	.000	6.75	2	0	0	0	0-1	2.2	3	2	2	1	3-0	1

WARD, DARYLE — OF/1B — ASTROS

PERSONAL: Born June 27, 1975, in Lynwood, Calif. ... 6-2/240. ... Bats left, throws left. ... Full name: Daryle Lamar Ward. ... Son of Gary Ward, outfielder with four major league teams (1979-90); and hitting coach, Charlotte Knights of International League.

HIGH SCHOOL: Brethren Christian (Riverside, Calif.).

JUNIOR COLLEGE: Rancho Santiago College (Calif.).

TRANSACTIONS/CAREER NOTES: Selected by Detroit Tigers organization in 15th round of free-agent draft (June 2, 1994). ... Traded by Tigers with C Brad Ausmus, P Jose Lima, P C.J. Nitkowski and P Trever Miller to Houston Astros for OF Brian Hunter, IF Orlando Miller, P Doug Brocail, P Todd Jones and cash (December 10, 1996).

STATISTICAL NOTES: Tied for Texas League lead with four intentional bases on balls in 1997. ... Had 15-game hitting streak (April 13-30, 2002). ... Career major league grand slams: 2.

2002 GAMES PLAYED BY POSITION (MLB): OF—122; DH—1.

		BATTING														FIELDING	
Year Team (League)	Pos.	G	AB	R	H	2B	3B	HR	RBI	BB	SO	SB-CS	Avg.	OBP	SLG	E	Avg.
1994—Bristol (Appl.)	1B	48	161	17	43	6	0	5	30	19	33	5-1	.267	.343	.398	11	.968
1995—Fayetteville (S.Atl.)	1B	137	524	75	149	32	0	14	106	46	111	1-2	.284	.344	.426	14	.987
1996—Lakeland (FSL)	1B-DH	128	464	65	135	29	4	10	68	57	77	1-1	.291	.373	.435	8	.993
—Toledo (I.L.)	1B	6	23	1	4	0	0	0	1	0	3	0-0	.174	.174	.174	1	.979
1997—Jackson (Texas)■	1B-DH	114	422	72	139	25	0	19	90	46	68	4-2	.329	.398	.524	12	.988
—New Orleans (A.A.)	1B-DH	14	48	4	18	1	0	2	8	7	7	0-0	.375	.455	.521	2	.976
1998—New Orleans (PCL)	OF-1B-DH	116	463	78	141	31	1	23	96	41	78	2-0	.305	.361	.525	13	.976
—Houston (N.L.)	PH	4	3	1	1	0	0	0	0	1	2	0-0	.333	.500	.333	...	...
1999—New Orleans (PCL)	1B-OF	61	241	56	85	15	1	28	65	23	43	1-1	.353	.416	.772	5	.991
—Houston (N.L.)	OF-1B-DH	64	150	11	41	6	0	8	30	9	31	0-0	.273	.311	.473	2	.973
2000—Houston (N.L.)	OF-1B-DH	119	264	36	68	10	2	20	47	15	61	0-0	.258	.295	.538	1	.992
2001—Houston (N.L.)	OF-1B-DH	95	213	21	56	15	0	9	39	19	48	0-0	.263	.323	.460	1	.988
2002—Houston (N.L.)	OF-DH	136	453	41	125	31	0	12	72	33	82	1-3	.276	.324	.424	3	.981
Major League totals (5 years)		418	1083	110	291	62	2	49	188	77	224	1-3	.269	.316	.465	7	.984

DIVISION SERIES RECORD

		BATTING														FIELDING	
Year Team (League)	Pos.	G	AB	R	H	2B	3B	HR	RBI	BB	SO	SB-CS	Avg.	OBP	SLG	E	Avg.
1999—Houston (N.L.)	OF-PH	3	7	1	1	0	0	1	1	0	2	0-0	.143	.143	.571	1	.750
2001—Houston (N.L.)	PH	2	2	1	1	0	0	1	2	0	0	0-0	.500	.500	2.000	...	...
Division series totals (2 years)		5	9	2	2	0	0	2	3	0	2	0-0	.222	.222	.889	1	.750

WASHBURN, JARROD — P — ANGELS

PERSONAL: Born August 13, 1974, in La Crosse, Wis. ... 6-1/187. ... Throws left, bats left. ... Full name: Jarrod Michael Washburn.

HIGH SCHOOL: Webster (Wis.).

COLLEGE: Wisconsin-Oshkosh.

TRANSACTIONS/CAREER NOTES: Selected by California Angels organizaiton in second round of free-agent draft (June 1, 1995). ... Angels franchise renamed Anaheim Angels for 1997 season. ... On Edmonton disabled list (April 26-June 17, 1999). ... On Anaheim disabled list (March 25-April 9, July 22-August 7 and August 8, 2000-remainder of season); included rehabilitation assignment to Lake Elsinore (April 7). ... On Anaheim disabled list (March 23-April 16, 2001); included rehabilitation assignment to Salt Lake (April 8-16).

STATISTICAL NOTES: Led Texas League with 23 home runs allowed in 1997.

CAREER HITTING (MLB): 5-for-14 (.357), 1 R, 0 2B, 0 3B, 0 HR, 2 RBI.

Year League	W	L	Pct.	ERA	G	GS	CG	ShO	Sv.-Opp.	IP	H	R	ER	HR	BB-IBB	SO
1995—Boise (N'West)	3	2	.600	3.33	8	8	0	0	0-...	46.0	35	17	17	1	14-0	54
—Cedar Rapids (Midw.)	0	1	.000	3.44	3	3	0	0	0-...	18.1	17	7	7	1	7-0	20
1996—Lake Elsinore (Calif.)	6	3	.667	3.30	14	14	3	0	0-...	92.2	79	38	34	5	33-0	93
—Midland (Texas)	5	6	.455	4.40	13	13	1	0	0-...	88.0	77	44	43	11	25-0	58
—Vancouver (PCL)	0	2	.000	10.80	2	2	0	0	0-...	8.1	12	16	10	1	12-0	5
1997—Midland (Texas)	15	•12	.556	4.80	29	*29	5	•1	0-...	*189.1	*211	*115	*101	23	65-0	*146
—Vancouver (PCL)	0	0	...	3.60	1	1	0	0	0-...	5.0	4	2	2	0	2-0	6
1998—Vancouver (PCL)	4	5	.444	4.32	14	14	2	0	0-...	91.2	91	44	44	7	43-0	66
—Anaheim (A.L.)	6	3	.667	4.62	15	11	0	0	0-0	74.0	70	40	38	11	27-1	48
—Midland (Texas)	0	1	.000	6.23	1	1	0	0	0-...	8.2	13	8	6	2	2-0	8
1999—Edmonton (PCL)	1	5	.167	4.73	11	11	1	0	0-...	59.0	50	31	31	6	17-0	55
—Anaheim (A.L.)	4	5	.444	5.25	16	10	0	0	0-0	61.2	61	36	36	6	26-0	39
2000—Lake Elsinore (Calif.)	0	0	...	6.00	1	1	0	0	0-...	3.0	3	2	2	0	2-0	7
—Edmonton (PCL)	3	0	1.000	3.52	5	5	0	0	0-...	30.2	35	13	12	2	13-0	20
—Anaheim (A.L.)	7	2	.778	3.74	14	14	0	0	0-0	84.1	64	38	35	16	37-0	49
2001—Salt Lake (PCL)	0	1	.000	5.87	1	1	0	0	0-...	7.2	9	5	5	1	1-0	5
—Anaheim (A.L.)	11	10	.524	3.77	30	30	1	0	0-0	193.1	196	89	81	25	54-4	126
2002—Anaheim (A.L.)	18	6	.750	3.15	32	32	1	0	0-0	206.0	183	75	72	19	59-1	139
Major League totals (5 years)	46	26	.639	3.81	107	97	2	0	0-0	619.1	574	278	262	77	203-6	401

DIVISION SERIES RECORD

Year	League	W	L	Pct.	ERA	G	GS	CG	ShO	Sv.-Opp.	IP	H	R	ER	HR	BB-IBB	SO
2002—	Anaheim (A.L.)	1	0	1.000	3.75	2	2	0	0	0-0	12.0	12	6	5	3	3-0	4

CHAMPIONSHIP SERIES RECORD

Year	League	W	L	Pct.	ERA	G	GS	CG	ShO	Sv.-Opp.	IP	H	R	ER	HR	BB-IBB	SO
2002—	Anaheim (A.L.)	0	0	...	1.29	1	1	0	0	0-0	7.0	6	1	1	0	0-0	7

WORLD SERIES RECORD

RECORDS: Shares single-inning record for most consecutive bases on balls allowed—3 (October 24, 2002, first inning).

NOTES: Member of World Series championship team (2002).

Year	League	W	L	Pct.	ERA	G	GS	CG	ShO	Sv.-Opp.	IP	H	R	ER	HR	BB-IBB	SO
2002—	Anaheim (A.L.)	0	2	.000	9.31	2	2	0	0	0-0	9.2	12	10	10	3	7-2	6

WATHAN, DUSTY — C

PERSONAL: Born August 22, 1973, in Jacksonville, Fla. ... 6-4/215. ... Bats right, throws right. ... Full name: Dustin James Wathan.

JUNIOR COLLEGE: Cerritos Junior College (Calif.).

TRANSACTIONS/CAREER NOTES: Signed as non-drafted free agent by Seattle Mariners organization (June 20, 1994). ... Granted free agency (October 15, 2000). ... Signed by Florida Marlins organization (January 15, 2001). ... Granted free agency (October 15, 2001). ... Signed by San Diego Padres organization (December 18, 2001). ... Traded by Padres to Milwaukee Brewers for 1B Kevin Barker (March 20, 2002). ... On Huntsville disabled list (April 26-May 11, 2002). ... Released by Brewers (May 11, 2002). ... Signed by Kansas City Royals organization (May 16, 2002). ... Granted free agency (October 15, 2002).

2002 GAMES PLAYED BY POSITION (MLB): C—3.

			BATTING														FIELDING	
Year	Team (League)	Pos.	G	AB	R	H	2B	3B	HR	RBI	BB	SO	SB-CS	Avg.	OBP	SLG	E	Avg.
1994—	Ariz. Mariners (Ariz.)	C-1B	35	86	14	18	2	0	1	7	11	13	0-0	.209	.320	.267	7	.970
1995—	Wisconsin (Midw.)	C	5	11	1	1	0	0	1	3	0	3	0-0	.091	.167	.364	0	1.000
—	Everett (N'West)	C-1B	53	181	32	49	9	1	6	25	17	26	2-1	.271	.356	.431	8	.982
1996—	Lancaster (Calif.)	C-1B	74	246	41	64	10	1	8	40	26	65	1-1	.260	.344	.407	8	.985
1997—	Lancaster (Calif.)	C	56	202	27	60	17	0	4	35	21	51	0-1	.297	.381	.441	7	.984
—	Memphis (Sou.)	C	49	149	20	40	4	1	4	19	19	28	1-1	.268	.368	.389	4	.987
1998—	Tacoma (PCL)	C	19	51	6	15	1	1	0	8	6	10	0-0	.294	.390	.353	1	.993
—	Orlando (Sou.)	C-1B	69	234	32	60	10	0	2	21	28	39	3-1	.256	.369	.325	1	.998
1999—	New Haven (East.)	C-1B-OF	96	333	37	93	16	2	4	37	24	60	4-1	.279	.349	.375	8	.989
2000—	Tacoma (PCL)	C-1B-3B	64	203	25	66	12	0	3	29	15	28	0-2	.325	.403	.429	2	.996
2001—	Portland (East.)	C-1B-3B	55	134	24	36	10	0	2	21	13	28	0-1	.269	.402	.388	3	.991
2002—	Huntsville (Sou.)■	C	9	25	2	4	2	0	0	2	2	4	0-0	.160	.276	.240	1	.983
—	Omaha (PCL)■	C	49	160	22	46	9	1	1	26	16	36	1-1	.288	.385	.375	4	.988
—	Kansas City (A.L.)	C	3	5	1	3	1	0	0	1	0	1	0-0	.600	.667	.800	0	1.000
Major League totals (1 year)			3	5	1	3	1	0	0	1	0	1	0-0	.600	.667	.800	0	1.000

WATSON, MARK — P — ROCKIES

PERSONAL: Born January 23, 1974, in Atlanta. ... 6-4/215. ... Throws left, bats right. ... Full name: Mark Bradford Watson.

HIGH SCHOOL: Marist (Atlanta).

COLLEGE: Clemson, then Georgia.

TRANSACTIONS/CAREER NOTES: Signed as non-drafted free agent by Milwaukee Brewers organization (June 16, 1996). ... Traded by Brewers to Cleveland Indians for P Ben McDonald (March 11, 1998); traded arranged as compensation for McDonald, who was injured and had been acquired by Indians (December 8, 1997). ... Claimed on waivers by Seattle Mariners (June 23, 2000). ... On Tacoma disabled list (August 27-September 21, 2000). ... Released by Mariners (May 4, 2001). ... Signed by Indians organization (May 24, 2001). ... Granted free agency (October 15, 2001). ... Signed by Chicago Cubs organization (December 14, 2001). ... Claimed on waivers by Colorado Rockies (July 26, 2002). ... On Colorado Springs disabled list (August 23-September 1, 2002).

CAREER HITTING (MLB): 0-for-0 (.000), 0 R, 0 2B, 0 3B, 0 HR, 0 RBI.

Year	League	W	L	Pct.	ERA	G	GS	CG	ShO	Sv.-Opp.	IP	H	R	ER	HR	BB-IBB	SO
1996—	Helena (Pio.)	5	2	.714	4.77	13	13	0	0	0-...	60.1	59	43	32	2	28-0	68
1997—	Beloit (Midw.)	0	3	.000	6.68	8	7	0	0	0-...	32.1	40	33	24	3	20-0	33
—	Ogden (Pio.)	4	3	.571	4.15	10	10	1	0	0-...	47.2	44	26	22	4	19-0	49
1998—	Columbus (S.Atl.)■	3	4	.429	4.05	31	12	1	0	0-...	97.2	95	53	44	10	32-0	77
—	Kinston (Caro.)	0	1	.000	0.00	1	1	0	0	0-...	6.1	3	4	0	0	2-0	8
1999—	Kinston (Caro.)	6	0	1.000	1.04	11	4	0	0	0-...	43.1	28	7	5	1	10-0	40
—	Akron (East.)	9	8	.529	4.34	19	17	0	0	0-...	110.0	143	64	53	9	38-0	57
2000—	Buffalo (I.L.)	1	2	.333	4.43	16	0	0	0	1-...	20.1	18	11	10	1	12-6	16
—	Cleveland (A.L.)	0	1	.000	8.53	6	0	0	0	0-0	6.1	12	7	6	0	2-0	4
—	Tacoma (PCL)■	2	1	.667	3.96	16	0	0	0	0-...	25.0	30	16	11	3	6-0	17
2001—	Tacoma (PCL)	0	1	.000	2.25	3	0	0	0	1-...	4.0	4	2	1	1	2-0	1
—	Akron (East.)■	3	1	.750	4.12	30	0	0	0	4-...	39.1	34	19	18	2	13-0	34
—	Buffalo (I.L.)	0	1	.000	13.50	3	0	0	0	0-...	4.0	9	7	6	1	3-1	3
2002—	Seattle (A.L.)	1	0	1.000	18.00	3	0	0	0	0-0	4.0	8	8	8	1	4-0	1
—	Iowa (PCL)	4	0	1.000	4.30	28	0	0	0	1-...	37.2	35	22	18	3	19-3	25
—	Tacoma (PCL)	2	0	1.000	0.73	6	0	0	0	2-...	12.1	10	2	1	0	3-0	8
—	Colorado Springs (PCL)	0	0	...	16.03	10	0	0	0	0-...	10.2	22	19	19	3	11-1	10
Major League totals (2 years)		1	1	.500	12.19	9	0	0	0	0-0	10.1	20	15	14	1	6-0	5

W

WAYNE, JUSTIN — P — MARLINS

PERSONAL: Born April 16, 1979, in Honolulu, Hawaii. ... 6-3/200. ... Throws right, bats right. ... Full name: Justin Morgan Wayne.

COLLEGE: Stanford.

TRANSACTIONS/CAREER NOTES: Selected by Montreal Expos organization in first round (fifth pick overall) of free-agent draft (June 5, 2000). ... Traded by Expos with P Carl Pavano, P Graeme Lloyd, and IF Mike Mordecai to Florida Marlins for P Claudio Vargas, OF/2B Wilton Guerrero, OF Cliff Floyd, cash considerations and a player to be named later (July 11, 2002); Expos acquired P Don Levinski to complete deal (August 5, 2002).

STATISTICAL NOTES: Led Eastern League with 13 sacrifice flies allowed in 2002.
CAREER HITTING (MLB): 0-for-7 (.000), 0 R, 0 2B, 0 3B, 0 HR, 0 RBI.

Year League	W	L	Pct.	ERA	G	GS	CG	ShO	Sv.-Opp.	IP	H	R	ER	HR	BB-IBB	SO
2000—Jupiter (FSL)	0	3	.000	5.81	5	5	0	0	0-...	26.1	26	22	17	2	11-0	24
2001—Jupiter (FSL)	2	3	.400	3.02	8	7	0	0	0-...	41.2	31	16	14	0	9-0	35
—Harrisburg (East.)	9	2	.818	2.62	14	14	2	0	0-...	92.2	87	28	27	4	34-0	70
2002—Harrisburg (East.)	5	2	.714	2.37	17	17	0	0	0-...	98.2	74	41	26	7	32-0	47
—Florida (N.L.)■	2	3	.400	5.32	5	5	0	0	0-0	23.2	22	16	14	3	13-0	16
—Portland (East.)	3	3	.500	4.85	7	7	1	1	0-...	42.2	43	26	23	3	13-0	30
—Calgary (PCL)	0	1	.000	6.35	2	2	0	0	0-...	11.1	8	8	8	3	6-0	10
Major League totals (1 year)	2	3	.400	5.32	5	5	0	0	0-0	23.2	22	16	14	3	13-0	16

WEATHERS, DAVE P METS

PERSONAL: Born September 25, 1969, in Lawrenceburg, Tenn. ... 6-3/230. ... Throws right, bats right. ... Full name: John David Weathers.
HIGH SCHOOL: Loretto (Tenn.).
JUNIOR COLLEGE: Motlow State Community College (Tenn.).
TRANSACTIONS/CAREER NOTES: Selected by Toronto Blue Jays organization in third round of free-agent draft (June 1, 1988). ... On Syracuse disabled list (May 11-July 31, 1992). ... Selected by Florida Marlins in second round (29th pick overall) of expansion draft (November 17, 1992). ... On Florida disabled list (June 26-July 13, 1995); included rehabilitation assignments to Brevard County (July 4-10) and Charlotte (July 11-13). ... Traded by Marlins to New York Yankees for P Mark Hutton (July 31, 1996). ... Traded by Yankees to Cleveland Indians for OF Chad Curtis (June 9, 1997). ... Claimed on waivers by Cincinnati Reds (December 20, 1997). ... Claimed on waivers by Milwaukee Brewers (June 24, 1998). ... Granted free agency (October 29, 1999). ... Re-signed by Brewers (December 2, 1999). ... On disabled list (August 2-22, 2000). ... Traded by Brewers with P Roberto Miniel to Chicago Cubs for P Ruben Quevedo and OF Peter Zoccolillo (July 30, 2001). ... Granted free agency (November 5, 2001). ... Signed by New York Mets (December 13, 2001). ... On suspended list (September 20-22, 2002).
MISCELLANEOUS: Appeared in two games as pinch runner (1994). ... Appeared in one game as pinch runner with Florida (1996). ... Struck out in only appearance as pinch hitter (1999).
CAREER HITTING (MLB): 14-for-132 (.106), 7 R, 0 2B, 0 3B, 2 HR, 4 RBI.

Year League	W	L	Pct.	ERA	G	GS	CG	ShO	Sv.-Opp.	IP	H	R	ER	HR	BB-IBB	SO
1988—St. Catharines (NY-Penn)	4	4	.500	3.02	15	12	0	0	0-...	62.2	58	30	21	3	26-0	36
1989—Myrtle Beach (S.Atl.)	11	•13	.458	3.86	31	*31	2	0	0-...	172.2	163	99	74	3	86-2	111
1990—Dunedin (FSL)	10	7	.588	3.70	27	•27	2	0	0-...	158.0	158	82	65	2	59-0	96
1991—Knoxville (Sou.)	10	7	.588	2.45	24	22	5	2	0-...	139.1	121	51	38	3	49-1	114
—Toronto (A.L.)	1	0	1.000	4.91	15	0	0	0	0-0	14.2	15	9	8	1	17-3	13
1992—Syracuse (I.L.)	1	4	.200	4.66	12	10	0	0	0-...	48.1	48	29	25	3	21-2	30
—Toronto (A.L.)	0	0	...	8.10	2	0	0	0	0-0	3.1	5	3	3	1	2-0	3
1993—Edmonton (PCL)■	11	4	•.733	3.83	22	22	3	1	0-...	141.0	150	77	60	12	47-2	117
—Florida (N.L.)	2	3	.400	5.12	14	6	0	0	0-0	45.2	57	26	26	3	13-1	34
1994—Florida (N.L.)	8	12	.400	5.27	24	24	0	0	0-0	135.0	166	87	79	13	59-9	72
1995—Florida (N.L.)	4	5	.444	5.98	28	15	0	0	0-0	90.1	104	68	60	8	52-3	60
—Brevard County (FSL)	0	0	...	0.00	1	1	0	0	0-...	4.0	4	0	0	0	1-0	3
—Charlotte (I.L.)	0	1	.000	9.00	1	1	0	0	0-...	5.0	10	5	5	0	5-0	0
1996—Florida (N.L.)	2	2	.500	4.54	31	8	0	0	0-0	71.1	85	41	36	7	28-4	40
—Charlotte (I.L.)	0	0	...	7.71	1	1	0	0	0-...	2.1	5	2	2	0	3-0	0
—New York (A.L.)■	0	2	.000	9.35	11	4	0	0	0-0	17.1	23	19	18	1	14-1	13
—Columbus (I.L.)	0	2	.000	5.40	3	3	0	0	0-...	16.2	20	13	10	1	5-0	7
1997—New York (A.L.)	0	1	.000	10.00	10	0	0	0	0-1	9.0	15	10	10	1	7-0	4
—Columbus (I.L.)	2	2	.500	3.19	5	5	1	0	0-...	36.2	35	18	13	3	7-0	35
—Buffalo (A.A.)■	4	3	.571	3.15	11	11	2	1	0-...	68.2	71	37	24	7	17-0	51
—Cleveland (A.L.)	1	2	.333	7.56	9	1	0	0	0-0	16.2	23	14	14	2	8-0	14
1998—Cincinnati (N.L.)■	2	4	.333	6.21	16	9	0	0	0-0	62.1	86	47	43	3	27-2	51
—Milwaukee (N.L.)■	4	1	.800	3.21	28	0	0	0	0-1	47.2	44	22	17	3	14-1	43
1999—Milwaukee (N.L.)	7	4	.636	4.65	63	0	0	0	2-6	93.0	102	49	48	14	38-3	74
2000—Milwaukee (N.L.)	3	5	.375	3.07	69	0	0	0	1-7	76.1	73	29	26	7	32-8	50
2001—Milwaukee (N.L.)	3	4	.429	2.03	52	0	0	0	4-7	57.2	37	14	13	3	25-7	46
—Chicago (N.L.)■	1	1	.500	3.18	28	0	0	0	0-3	28.1	28	10	10	3	9-1	20
2002—New York (N.L.)	6	3	.667	2.91	71	0	0	0	0-5	77.1	69	30	25	6	36-7	61
A.L. totals (4 years)	2	5	.286	7.82	47	5	0	0	0-1	61.0	81	55	53	6	48-4	47
N.L. totals (9 years)	42	44	.488	4.39	424	62	0	0	7-29	785.0	851	423	383	70	333-46	551
Major League totals (12 years)	44	49	.473	4.64	471	67	0	0	7-30	846.0	932	478	436	76	381-50	598

DIVISION SERIES RECORD

Year League	W	L	Pct.	ERA	G	GS	CG	ShO	Sv.-Opp.	IP	H	R	ER	HR	BB-IBB	SO
1996—New York (A.L.)	1	0	1.000	0.00	2	0	0	0	0-0	5.0	1	0	0	0	0-0	5

CHAMPIONSHIP SERIES RECORD

Year League	W	L	Pct.	ERA	G	GS	CG	ShO	Sv.-Opp.	IP	H	R	ER	HR	BB-IBB	SO
1996—New York (A.L.)	1	0	1.000	0.00	2	0	0	0	0-0	3.0	3	0	0	0	0-0	0

WORLD SERIES RECORD

NOTES: Member of World Series championship team (1996).

Year League	W	L	Pct.	ERA	G	GS	CG	ShO	Sv.-Opp.	IP	H	R	ER	HR	BB-IBB	SO
1996—New York (A.L.)	0	0	...	3.00	3	0	0	0	0-0	3.0	2	1	1	0	3-1	3

WEAVER, JEFF P YANKEES

PERSONAL: Born August 22, 1976, in Northridge, Calif. ... 6-5/200. ... Throws right, bats right. ... Full name: Jeffery Charles Weaver. ... Cousin of Jed Weaver, tight end, Miami Dolphins.
HIGH SCHOOL: Simi Valley (Calif.).
COLLEGE: Fresno State.
TRANSACTIONS/CAREER NOTES: Selected by Chicago White Sox organziation in second-round of free-agent draft (June 3, 1997); did not sign. ... Selected by Detroit Tigers organization in first round (14th pick overall) of free-agent draft (June 2, 1998). ... Traded by Tigers to New

York Yankees as part of three-way deal in which Oakland Athletics acquired P Ted Lilly, OF John-Ford Griffin and P Jason Arnold from Yankees and Tigers acquired 1B Carlos Pena, P Franklyn German and a player to be named later from A's (July 5, 2002); Tigers acquired P Jeremy Bonderman to complete deal (August 22, 2002).

STATISTICAL NOTES: Led A.L. pitchers with 17 hit batsmen in 1999 and 15 in 2000. ... Pitched 2-0 one-hit, complete-game victory against Cleveland (May 22, 2002). ... Led A.L. with three shutouts in 2002.

MISCELLANEOUS: Member of 1996 U.S. Olympic baseball team. ... Appeared in one game as pinch runner (1999).

CAREER HITTING (MLB): 4-for-19 (.211), 2 R, 1 2B, 0 3B, 0 HR, 1 RBI.

Year League	W	L	Pct.	ERA	G	GS	CG	ShO	Sv.-Opp.	IP	H	R	ER	HR	BB-IBB	SO
1998— Jamestown (NY-Penn)	1	0	1.000	1.50	3	3	0	0	0-...	12.0	6	4	2	0	1-0	12
— West Michigan (Midw.)	1	0	1.000	1.38	2	2	0	0	0-...	13.0	8	3	2	1	0-0	21
1999— Jacksonville (Sou.)	0	0	...	3.00	1	1	0	0	0-...	6.0	5	2	2	0	0-0	6
— Detroit (A.L.)	9	12	.429	5.55	30	29	0	0	0-0	163.2	176	104	101	27	56-2	114
2000— Toledo (I.L.)	0	1	.000	3.38	1	1	0	0	0-...	5.1	5	2	2	1	1-0	10
— Detroit (A.L.)	11	15	.423	4.32	31	30	2	0	0-0	200.0	205	102	96	26	52-2	136
2001— Detroit (A.L.)	13	16	.448	4.08	33	33	5	0	0-0	229.1	235	116	104	19	68-4	152
2002— Detroit (A.L.)	6	8	.429	3.18	17	17	3	3	0-0	121.2	112	50	43	4	33-1	75
— New York (A.L.)■	5	3	.625	4.04	15	8	0	§0	2-2	78.0	81	38	35	12	15-3	57
Major League totals (4 years)	44	54	.449	4.30	126	117	10	3	2-2	792.2	809	410	379	88	224-12	534

DIVISION SERIES RECORD

Year League	W	L	Pct.	ERA	G	GS	CG	ShO	Sv.-Opp.	IP	H	R	ER	HR	BB-IBB	SO
2002— New York (A.L.)	0	0	...	6.75	2	0	0	0	0-0	2.2	4	2	2	0	3-1	1

WEBER, BEN — P — ANGELS

PERSONAL: Born November 17, 1969, in Port Arthur, Texas. ... 6-4/210. ... Throws right, bats right. ... Full name: Benjamin Edward Weber.

HIGH SCHOOL: Port Neches-Groves (Port Neches, Texas).

COLLEGE: Houston.

TRANSACTIONS/CAREER NOTES: Selected by Toronto Blue Jays organization in 20th round of free-agent draft (June 3, 1991). ... Released by Blue Jays (March 24, 1996). ... Signed by Salinas, Western League (May 1996). ... Signed by Taipei, Taiwan League (1997). ... Signed by San Francisco Giants organization (October 30, 1998). ... Claimed on waivers by Anaheim Angels (August 30, 2000).

CAREER HITTING (MLB): 0-for-0 (.000), 0 R, 0 2B, 0 3B, 0 HR, 0 RBI.

Year League	W	L	Pct.	ERA	G	GS	CG	ShO	Sv.-Opp.	IP	H	R	ER	HR	BB-IBB	SO
1991— St. Catharines (NY-Penn)	6	3	.667	3.24	16	14	1	0	0-...	97.1	•105	43	35	3	24-2	60
1992— Myrtle Beach (S.Atl.)	4	7	.364	1.64	41	1	0	0	6-...	98.2	83	27	18	1	29-3	65
1993— Dunedin (FSL)	8	3	.727	2.92	55	0	0	0	12-...	83.1	87	36	27	4	25-5	45
1994— Dunedin (FSL)	3	2	.600	2.73	18	0	0	0	3-...	26.1	25	8	8	1	5-3	19
— Knoxville (Sou.)	4	3	.571	3.76	25	10	0	0	0-...	95.2	103	49	40	8	16-0	55
1995— Syracuse (I.L.)	4	5	.444	5.40	25	15	0	0	1-...	91.2	111	62	55	10	27-1	38
— Knoxville (Sou.)	4	1	.800	3.91	12	1	0	0	0-...	25.1	26	12	11	3	6-0	16
1996— Salinas (West.)■	•12	6	.667	3.47	22	22	2	...	0-...	148.0	138	68	57	11	42-1	102
1997— Taipei (Taiwan)■	7	3	.700	5.18	40	...	...	...	5-...	99.0	85	...	...	...	33-...	78
1998— Taipei (Taiwan)	12	7	.632	3.56	56	...	...	...	7-...	144.0	150	...	...	...	52-...	122
1999— Fresno (PCL)■	2	4	.333	3.34	51	0	0	0	8-...	86.1	78	34	32	6	28-2	67
2000— San Francisco (N.L.)	0	1	.000	14.63	9	0	0	0	0-2	8.0	16	13	13	0	4-0	6
— Fresno (PCL)	4	8	.333	2.42	38	3	0	0	7-...	78.0	72	31	21	7	20-0	66
— Erie (East.)■	0	1	.000	16.20	2	0	0	0	0-...	1.2	3	5	3	1	2-0	2
— Anaheim (A.L.)	1	0	1.000	1.84	10	0	0	0	0-0	14.2	12	6	3	0	2-1	8
2001— Anaheim (A.L.)	6	2	.750	3.42	56	0	0	0	0-1	68.1	66	28	26	4	31-8	40
2002— Anaheim (A.L.)	7	2	.778	2.54	63	0	0	0	7-11	78.0	70	25	22	4	22-3	43
A.L. totals (3 years)	14	4	.778	2.85	129	0	0	0	7-12	161.0	148	59	51	8	55-12	91
N.L. totals (1 year)	0	1	.000	14.63	9	0	0	0	0-2	8.0	16	13	13	0	4-0	6
Major League totals (3 years)	14	5	.737	3.41	138	0	0	0	7-14	169.0	164	72	64	8	59-12	97

DIVISION SERIES RECORD

Year League	W	L	Pct.	ERA	G	GS	CG	ShO	Sv.-Opp.	IP	H	R	ER	HR	BB-IBB	SO
2002— Anaheim (A.L.)	0	1	.000	18.00	2	0	0	0	0-0	1.0	2	2	2	0	2-0	0

CHAMPIONSHIP SERIES RECORD

Year League	W	L	Pct.	ERA	G	GS	CG	ShO	Sv.-Opp.	IP	H	R	ER	HR	BB-IBB	SO
2002— Anaheim (A.L.)	0	0	...	3.38	3	0	0	0	0-0	2.2	3	1	1	0	0-0	3

WORLD SERIES RECORD

NOTES: Member of World Series championship team (2002).

Year League	W	L	Pct.	ERA	G	GS	CG	ShO	Sv.-Opp.	IP	H	R	ER	HR	BB-IBB	SO
2002— Anaheim (A.L.)	0	0	...	13.50	4	0	0	0	0-0	4.2	10	7	7	1	2-1	5

WELLS, BOB — P

PERSONAL: Born November 1, 1966, in Yakima, Wash. ... 6-0/200. ... Throws right, bats right. ... Full name: Robert Lee Wells.

HIGH SCHOOL: Eisenhower (Yakima, Wash.).

JUNIOR COLLEGE: Spokane Falls Community College (Wash.).

TRANSACTIONS/CAREER NOTES: Signed as non-drafted free agent by Philadelphia Phillies organization (August 18, 1988). ... On Reading disabled list (July 21, 1991-remainder of season). ... On Scranton/Wilkes-Barre disabled list (April 9-28, 1992). ... On Reading disabled list (June 9, 1992-remainder of season; and April 8-June 13, 1993). ... Claimed on waivers by Seattle Mariners (June 30, 1994). ... On Seattle disabled list (April 16-May 19, 1998); included rehabilitation assignment to Wisconsin (May 12-19). ... Released by Mariners (November 19, 1998). ... Signed by Minnesota Twins organization (January 27, 1999). ... On Minnesota disabled list (June 12-July 23, 2002); included rehabilitation assignment to Edmonton (July 15-22). ... Granted free agency (November 5, 2002).

CAREER HITTING (MLB): 0-for-0 (.000), 1 R, 0 2B, 0 3B, 0 HR, 0 RBI.

Year	League	W	L	Pct.	ERA	G	GS	CG	ShO	Sv.-Opp.	IP	H	R	ER	HR	BB-IBB	SO
1989—	Martinsville (Appl.)	0	0	...	4.50	4	0	0	0	0-...	6.0	8	5	3	1	2-0	3
1990—	Spartanburg (S.Atl.)	5	8	.385	2.87	20	19	2	0	0-...	113.0	94	47	36	6	40-0	73
	—Clearwater (FSL)	0	2	.000	4.91	6	1	0	0	1-...	14.2	17	9	8	0	6-1	11
1991—	Clearwater (FSL)	7	2	.778	3.11	24	9	1	0	0-...	75.1	63	27	26	5	19-4	66
	—Reading (East.)	1	0	1.000	3.60	1	1	0	0	0-...	5.0	4	2	2	1	1-0	3
1992—	Clearwater (FSL)	1	0	1.000	3.86	9	0	0	0	5-...	9.1	10	4	4	0	3-2	9
	—Reading (East.)	0	1	.000	1.17	3	3	0	0	0-...	15.1	12	2	2	0	5-0	11
1993—	Clearwater (FSL)	1	0	1.000	0.98	12	1	0	0	2-...	27.2	23	5	3	0	6-1	24
	—Scranton/W.B. (I.L.)	1	1	.500	2.79	11	0	0	0	0-...	19.1	19	7	6	1	5-0	8
1994—	Reading (East.)	1	3	.250	2.79	14	0	0	0	4-...	19.1	18	6	6	3	3-1	19
	—Philadelphia (N.L.)	1	0	1.000	1.80	6	0	0	0	0-0	5.0	4	1	1	0	3-0	3
	—Scranton/W.B. (I.L.)	0	2	.000	2.45	11	0	0	0	0-...	14.2	18	6	4	1	6-1	13
	—Calgary (PCL)■	3	2	.600	6.54	6	6	0	0	0-...	31.2	43	27	23	9	9-0	17
	—Seattle (A.L.)	1	0	1.000	2.25	1	0	0	0	0-0	4.0	4	1	1	0	1-0	3
1995—	Seattle (A.L.)	4	3	.571	5.75	30	4	0	0	0-1	76.2	88	51	49	11	39-3	38
1996—	Seattle (A.L.)	12	7	.632	5.30	36	16	1	1	0-0	130.2	141	78	77	25	46-5	94
1997—	Seattle (A.L.)	2	0	1.000	5.75	46	1	0	0	2-4	67.1	88	49	43	11	18-1	51
1998—	Seattle (A.L.)	2	2	.500	6.10	30	0	0	0	0-1	51.2	54	38	35	12	16-1	29
	—Wisconsin (Midw.)	0	1	.000	3.00	1	1	0	0	0-...	3.0	4	2	1	1	0-0	2
1999—	Minnesota (A.L.)■	8	3	.727	3.81	•76	0	0	0	1-5	87.1	79	41	37	8	28-4	44
2000—	Minnesota (A.L.)	0	7	.000	3.65	76	0	0	0	10-20	86.1	80	39	35	14	15-2	76
2001—	Minnesota (A.L.)	8	5	.615	5.11	65	0	0	0	2-4	68.2	72	39	39	12	18-2	49
2002—	Minnesota (A.L.)	2	1	.667	5.90	48	0	0	0	0-0	58.0	78	41	38	8	16-1	30
A.L. totals (9 years)		39	28	.582	5.05	408	21	1	1	15-35	630.2	684	377	354	101	197-19	414
N.L. totals (1 year)		1	0	1.000	1.80	6	0	0	0	0-0	5.0	4	1	1	0	3-0	3
Major League totals (9 years)		40	28	.588	5.03	414	21	1	1	15-35	635.2	688	378	355	101	200-19	417

DIVISION SERIES RECORD

Year	League	W	L	Pct.	ERA	G	GS	CG	ShO	Sv.-Opp.	IP	H	R	ER	HR	BB-IBB	SO
1995—	Seattle (A.L.)	0	0	...	9.00	1	0	0	0	0-0	1.0	2	1	1	0	1-0	0
1997—	Seattle (A.L.)	0	0	...	0.00	1	0	0	0	0-0	1.1	1	0	0	0	0-0	1
Division series totals (2 years)		0	0	...	3.86	2	0	0	0	0-0	2.1	3	1	1	0	1-0	1

CHAMPIONSHIP SERIES RECORD

Year	League	W	L	Pct.	ERA	G	GS	CG	ShO	Sv.-Opp.	IP	H	R	ER	HR	BB-IBB	SO
1995—	Seattle (A.L.)	0	0	...	3.00	1	0	0	0	0-0	3.0	2	1	1	0	2-0	2
2002—	Minnesota (A.L.)	0	0	...	9.00	2	0	0	0	0-0	1.0	2	1	1	0	0-0	2
Champ. series totals (2 years)		0	0	...	4.50	3	0	0	0	0-0	4.0	4	2	2	0	2-0	4

WELLS, DAVID — P — YANKEES

PERSONAL: Born May 20, 1963, in Torrance, Calif. ... 6-4/240. ... Throws left, bats left. ... Full name: David Lee Wells.

HIGH SCHOOL: Point Loma (San Diego).

TRANSACTIONS/CAREER NOTES: Selected by Toronto Blue Jays organization in second round of free-agent draft (June 7, 1982). ... On Knoxville disabled list (June 28, 1984-remainder of season). ... On disabled list (April 10, 1985-entire season). ... On Knoxville disabled list (July 7-August 20, 1986). ... Released by Blue Jays (March 30, 1993). ... Signed by Detroit Tigers (April 3, 1993). ... On disabled list (August 1-20, 1993). ... Granted free agency (October 28, 1993). ... Re-signed by Tigers (December 13, 1993). ... On Detroit disabled list (April 19-June 6, 1994); included rehabilitation assignment to Lakeland (May 27-June 6). ... Traded by Tigers to Cincinnati Reds for P C.J. Nitkowski, P David Tuttle and a player to be named later (July 31, 1995); Tigers acquired IF Mark Lewis to complete deal (November 16, 1995). ... Traded by Reds to Baltimore Orioles for OF Curtis Goodwin and OF Trovin Valdez (December 26, 1995). ... Granted free agency (October 29, 1996). ... Signed by New York Yankees (December 24, 1996). ... Traded by Yankees with P Graeme Lloyd and 2B Homer Bush to Blue Jays for P Roger Clemens (February 18, 1999). ... Traded by Blue Jays with P Matt DeWitt to Chicago White Sox for P Mike Sirotka, P Kevin Beirne, OF Brian Simmons and P Mike Williams (January 14, 2001). ... On disabled list (July 2, 2001-remainder of season). ... Granted free agency (November 5, 2001). ... Signed by Yankees (January 17, 2002).

RECORDS: Holds major league single-season records for fewest innings pitched by leader—231 2/3 (1999). ... Shares major league single-season record for fewest complete games for leader—7 (1999). ... Holds A.L. single-season record for most consecutive batsmen retired—38 (May 12 [last 10], 17 [all 27] and 23 [first], 1998).

HONORS: Named lefthanded pitcher on The Sporting News A.L. All-Star team (1998 and 2000).

STATISTICAL NOTES: Struck out 16 batters in one game (July 30, 1997). ... Pitched 4-0 perfect game against Minnesota (May 17, 1998).

CAREER HITTING (MLB): 6-for-50 (.120), 2 R, 0 2B, 0 3B, 0 HR, 0 RBI.

Year	League	W	L	Pct.	ERA	G	GS	CG	ShO	Sv.-Opp.	IP	H	R	ER	HR	BB-IBB	SO
1982—	Medicine Hat (Pio.)	4	3	.571	5.18	12	12	1	0	0-...	64.1	71	42	37	5	32-1	53
1983—	Kinston (Caro.)	6	5	.545	3.73	25	25	5	0	0-...	157.0	141	81	65	13	71-2	115
1984—	Kinston (Caro.)	1	6	.143	4.71	7	7	0	0	0-...	42.0	51	29	22	1	19-1	44
	—Knoxville (Sou.)	3	2	.600	2.59	8	8	3	1	0-...	59.0	58	22	17	3	17-0	34
1985—	Syracuse (I.L.)									Did not play.							
1986—	Florence (S.Atl.)	0	0	...	3.55	4	1	0	0	0-...	12.2	7	6	5	1	9-0	14
	—Ventura (Calif.)	2	1	.667	1.89	5	2	0	0	0-...	19.0	13	5	4	0	4-0	26
	—Knoxville (Sou.)	1	3	.250	4.05	10	7	1	0	0-...	40.0	42	24	18	1	18-0	32
	—Syracuse (I.L.)	0	1	.000	9.82	3	0	0	0	0-...	3.2	6	4	4	0	1-0	2
1987—	Syracuse (I.L.)	4	6	.400	3.87	43	12	0	0	6-...	109.1	102	49	47	9	32-0	106
	—Toronto (A.L.)	4	3	.571	3.99	18	2	0	0	1-2	29.1	37	14	13	0	12-0	32
1988—	Toronto (A.L.)	3	5	.375	4.62	41	0	0	0	4-6	64.1	65	36	33	12	31-9	56
	—Syracuse (I.L.)	0	0	...	0.00	6	0	0	0	3-...	5.2	7	1	0	0	2-1	8
1989—	Toronto (A.L.)	7	4	.636	2.40	54	0	0	0	2-9	86.1	66	25	23	5	28-7	78
1990—	Toronto (A.L.)	11	6	.647	3.14	43	25	0	0	3-3	189.0	165	72	66	14	45-3	115
1991—	Toronto (A.L.)	15	10	.600	3.72	40	28	2	0	1-2	198.1	188	88	82	24	49-1	106
1992—	Toronto (A.L.)	7	9	.438	5.40	41	14	0	0	2-4	120.0	138	84	72	16	36-6	62
1993—	Detroit (A.L.)■	11	9	.550	4.19	32	30	0	0	0-0	187.0	183	93	87	26	42-6	139
1994—	Detroit (A.L.)	5	7	.417	3.96	16	16	5	1	0-0	111.1	113	54	49	13	24-6	71
	—Lakeland (FSL)	0	0	...	0.00	2	2	0	0	0-...	6.0	5	1	0	0	0-0	3

Year League	W	L	Pct.	ERA	G	GS	CG	ShO	Sv.-Opp.	IP	H	R	ER	HR	BB-IBB	SO
1995—Detroit (A.L.)	10	3	.769	3.04	18	18	3	0	0-0	130.1	120	54	44	17	37-5	83
—Cincinnati (N.L.)■	6	5	.545	3.59	11	11	3	0	0-0	72.2	74	34	29	6	16-4	50
1996—Baltimore (A.L.)■	11	14	.440	5.14	34	34	3	0	0-0	224.1	247	132	128	32	51-7	130
1997—New York (A.L.)■	16	10	.615	4.21	32	32	5	2	0-0	218.0	239	109	102	24	45-0	156
1998—New York (A.L.)	18	4	*.818	3.49	30	30	8	*5	0-0	214.1	195	86	83	29	29-0	163
1999—Toronto (A.L.)■	17	10	.630	4.82	34	34	*7	1	0-0	*231.2	*246	132	124	32	62-2	169
2000—Toronto (A.L.)	•20	8	.714	4.11	35	•35	*9	1	0-0	229.2	*266	115	105	23	31-0	166
2001—Chicago (A.L.)■	5	7	.417	4.47	16	16	1	0	0-0	100.2	120	55	50	12	21-1	59
2002—New York (A.L.)■	19	7	.731	3.75	31	31	2	1	0-0	206.1	210	100	86	21	45-2	137
A.L. totals (16 years)	179	116	.607	4.06	515	345	45	11	13-26	2541.0	2598	1249	1147	300	588-55	1722
N.L. totals (1 year)	6	5	.545	3.59	11	11	3	0	0-0	72.2	74	34	29	6	16-4	50
Major League totals (16 years)	185	121	.605	4.05	526	356	48	11	13-26	2613.2	2672	1283	1176	306	604-59	1772

DIVISION SERIES RECORD

RECORDS: Shares A.L. career record for most wins—3.

Year League	W	L	Pct.	ERA	G	GS	CG	ShO	Sv.-Opp.	IP	H	R	ER	HR	BB-IBB	SO
1995—Cincinnati (N.L.)	1	0	1.000	0.00	1	1	0	0	0-0	6.1	6	1	0	0	1-0	8
1996—Baltimore (A.L.)	1	0	1.000	4.61	2	2	0	0	0-0	13.2	15	7	7	1	4-1	6
1997—New York (A.L.)	1	0	1.000	1.00	1	1	1	0	0-0	9.0	5	1	1	0	0-0	1
1998—New York (A.L.)	1	0	1.000	0.00	1	1	0	0	0-0	8.0	5	0	0	0	1-0	9
2002—New York (A.L.)	0	1	.000	15.43	1	1	0	0	0-0	4.2	10	8	8	1	0-0	0
Division series totals (5 years)	4	1	.800	3.46	6	6	1	0	0-0	41.2	41	17	16	2	6-1	24

CHAMPIONSHIP SERIES RECORD

NOTES: Named A.L. Championship Series Most Valuable Player (1998).

Year League	W	L	Pct.	ERA	G	GS	CG	ShO	Sv.-Opp.	IP	H	R	ER	HR	BB-IBB	SO
1989—Toronto (A.L.)	0	0	...	0.00	1	0	0	0	0-0	1.0	0	1	0	0	2-0	1
1991—Toronto (A.L.)	0	0	...	2.35	4	0	0	0	0-0	7.2	6	2	2	0	2-1	9
1992—Toronto (A.L.)									Did not play.							
1995—Cincinnati (N.L.)	0	1	.000	4.50	1	1	0	0	0-0	6.0	8	3	3	1	2-0	3
1996—Baltimore (A.L.)	1	0	1.000	4.05	1	1	0	0	0-0	6.2	8	3	3	0	3-0	6
1998—New York (A.L.)	2	0	1.000	2.87	2	2	0	0	0-0	15.2	12	5	5	3	2-0	18
Champ. series totals (5 years)	3	1	.750	3.16	9	4	0	0	0-0	37.0	34	14	13	4	11-1	37

WORLD SERIES RECORD

NOTES: Member of World Series championship team (1992 and 1998).

Year League	W	L	Pct.	ERA	G	GS	CG	ShO	Sv.-Opp.	IP	H	R	ER	HR	BB-IBB	SO
1992—Toronto (A.L.)	0	0	...	0.00	4	0	0	0	0-0	4.1	1	0	0	0	2-0	3
1998—New York (A.L.)	1	0	1.000	6.43	1	1	0	0	0-0	7.0	7	5	5	3	2-0	4
World Series totals (2 years)	1	0	1.000	3.97	5	1	0	0	0-0	11.1	8	5	5	3	4-0	7

ALL-STAR GAME RECORD

	W	L	Pct.	ERA	GS	CG	ShO	Sv.-Opp.	IP	H	R	ER	HR	BB-IBB	SO
All-Star Game totals (3 years)	0	0	...	0.00	2	0	0	0-0	4.1	2	0	0	0	1-0	4

WELLS, KIP — P — PIRATES

PERSONAL: Born April 21, 1977, in Houston. ... 6-3/205. ... Throws right, bats right. ... Full name: Robert Kip Wells.

HIGH SCHOOL: Elkins (Fort Bend, Texas).

COLLEGE: Baylor.

TRANSACTIONS/CAREER NOTES: Selected by Milwaukee Brewers organization in 58th round of free-agent draft (June 1, 1995); did not sign. ... Selected by Chicago White Sox organization in first round (16th pick overall) of free-agent draft (June 2, 1998). ... Traded by White Sox with P Sean Lowe and P Josh Fogg to Pittsburgh Pirates for P Todd Ritchie and C Lee Evans (December 13, 2001).

STATISTICAL NOTES: Tied for A.L. lead with 14 wild pitches in 2001.

CAREER HITTING (MLB): 13-for-71 (.183), 5 R, 2 2B, 0 3B, 1 HR, 5 RBI.

Year League	W	L	Pct.	ERA	G	GS	CG	ShO	Sv.-Opp.	IP	H	R	ER	HR	BB-IBB	SO
1999—Winston-Salem (Caro.)	5	6	.455	3.57	14	14	0	0	0-...	85.2	78	39	34	4	34-1	95
—Birmingham (Sou.)	8	2	.800	2.94	11	11	0	0	0-...	70.1	49	24	23	5	31-0	44
—Chicago (A.L.)	4	1	.800	4.04	7	7	0	0	0-0	35.2	33	17	16	2	15-0	29
2000—Chicago (A.L.)	6	9	.400	6.02	20	20	0	0	0-0	98.2	126	76	66	15	58-4	71
—Charlotte (I.L.)	5	3	.625	5.37	12	12	2	1	0-...	62.0	67	38	37	10	27-1	38
2001—Charlotte (I.L.)	2	1	.667	3.55	4	4	0	0	0-...	25.1	26	11	10	2	8-0	24
—Chicago (A.L.)	10	11	.476	4.79	40	20	0	0	0-2	133.1	145	80	71	14	61-5	99
2002—Pittsburgh (N.L.)■	12	14	.462	3.58	33	33	1	1	0-0	198.1	197	92	79	21	71-11	134
A.L. totals (3 years)	20	21	.488	5.14	67	47	0	0	0-2	267.2	304	173	153	31	134-9	199
N.L. totals (1 year)	12	14	.462	3.58	33	33	1	1	0-0	198.1	197	92	79	21	71-11	134
Major League totals (4 years)	32	35	.478	4.48	100	80	1	1	0-2	466.0	501	265	232	52	205-20	333

WELLS, VERNON — OF — BLUE JAYS

PERSONAL: Born December 8, 1978, in Shreveport, La. ... 6-1/225. ... Bats right, throws right. ... Full name: Vernon Wells III.

HIGH SCHOOL: Bowie (Arlington, Texas).

TRANSACTIONS/CAREER NOTES: Selected by Toronto Blue Jays organization in first round (fifth pick overall) of free-agent draft (June 3, 1997). ... On Syracuse disabled list (April 14-24, 2001).

HONORS: Named Florida State League Most Valuable Player (1999).

2002 GAMES PLAYED BY POSITION (MLB): OF—159.

Year	Team (League)	Pos.	G	AB	R	H	2B	3B	HR	RBI	BB	SO	SB-CS	Avg.	OBP	SLG	E	Avg.
			BATTING														FIELDING	
1997—	St. Catharines (NY-P)	OF	66	264	52	81	20	1	10	31	30	44	8-6	.307	.377	.504	7	.953
1998—	Hagerstown (S.Atl.)	OF	134	509	86	145	35	2	11	65	49	84	13-8	.285	.348	.426	5	.980
1999—	Dunedin (FSL)	OF-DH	70	265	43	91	16	2	11	43	26	34	13-2	.343	.403	.543	1	.993
—	Knoxville (Sou.)	OF	26	106	18	36	6	2	3	17	12	15	6-2	.340	.400	.519	0	1.000
—	Syracuse (I.L.)	OF	33	129	20	40	8	1	4	21	10	22	5-1	.310	.357	.481	2	.976
—	Toronto (A.L.)	OF	24	88	8	23	5	0	1	8	4	18	1-1	.261	.293	.352	0	1.000
2000—	Syracuse (I.L.)	OF	127	493	76	120	31	7	16	66	48	88	23-4	.243	.313	.432	3	.990
—	Toronto (A.L.)	OF	3	2	0	0	0	0	0	0	0	0	0-0	.000	.000	.000	0	1.000
2001—	Syracuse (I.L.)	OF	107	413	57	116	27	4	12	52	29	68	15-11	.281	.333	.453	5	.978
—	Toronto (A.L.)	OF	30	96	14	30	8	0	1	6	5	15	5-0	.313	.350	.427	2	.969
2002—	Toronto (A.L.)	OF	159	608	87	167	34	4	23	100	27	85	9-4	.275	.305	.457	3	.992
Major League totals (4 years)			216	794	109	220	47	4	25	114	36	118	15-5	.277	.308	.441	5	.990

WENDELL, TURK — P — PHILLIES

PERSONAL: Born May 19, 1967, in Pittsfield, Mass. ... 6-2/205. ... Throws right, bats left. ... Full name: Steven John Wendell.

HIGH SCHOOL: Wahconah Regional (Dalton, Mass.).

COLLEGE: Quinnipiac College (Conn.).

TRANSACTIONS/CAREER NOTES: Selected by Atlanta Braves organization in fifth round of free-agent draft (June 1, 1988). ... Traded by Braves with P Yorkis Perez to Chicago Cubs for P Mike Bielecki and C Damon Berryhill (September 29, 1991). ... On disabled list (May 4, 1992-remainder of season). ... On Chicago disabled list (April 16-May 27, 1995); included rehabilitation assignments to Daytona (May 5-15) and Orlando (May 15-27). ... Traded by Cubs with OF Brian McRae and P Mel Rojas to New York Mets for OF Lance Johnson and two players to be named later (August 8, 1997); Cubs acquired P Mark Clark (August 11, 1997) and IF Manny Alexander (August 14, 1997) to complete deal. ... Granted free agency (November 3, 2000). ... Re-signed by Mets (December 1, 2000). ... Traded by Mets with P Dennis Cook to Philadelphia Phillies for P Bruce Chen and P Adam Walker (July 27, 2001). ... On disabled list (March 30, 2002-entire season).

CAREER HITTING (MLB): 3-for-39 (.077), 1 R, 0 2B, 0 3B, 0 HR, 0 RBI.

Year	League	W	L	Pct.	ERA	G	GS	CG	ShO	Sv.-Opp.	IP	H	R	ER	HR	BB-IBB	SO
1988—	Pulaski (Appl.)	3	•8	.273	3.83	14	14	*6	1	0-...	*101.0	85	50	43	3	30-0	87
1989—	Burlington (Midw.)	9	11	.450	2.21	22	22	•9	*5	0-...	159.0	127	63	39	7	41-1	153
—	Greenville (Sou.)	0	0	...	9.82	1	1	0	0	0-...	3.2	7	5	4	3	1-0	3
—	Durham (Caro.)	2	0	1.000	1.13	3	3	1	0	0-...	24.0	13	4	3	0	6-0	27
1990—	Greenville (Sou.)	4	9	.308	5.74	36	13	1	1	2-...	91.0	105	70	58	5	48-2	85
—	Durham (Caro.)	1	3	.250	1.86	6	5	1	0	0-...	38.2	24	10	8	3	15-1	26
1991—	Greenville (Sou.)	11	3	*.786	2.56	25	20	1	1	0-...	147.2	130	47	42	4	51-5	122
—	Richmond (I.L.)	0	2	.000	3.43	3	3	1	0	0-...	21.0	20	9	8	3	16-0	18
1992—	Iowa (A.A.)■	2	0	1.000	1.44	4	4	0	0	0-...	25.0	17	7	4	3	15-0	12
1993—	Iowa (A.A.)	10	8	.556	4.60	25	25	3	0	0-...	148.2	148	88	76	9	47-0	110
—	Chicago (N.L.)	1	2	.333	4.37	7	4	0	0	0-0	22.2	24	13	11	0	8-1	15
1994—	Iowa (A.A.)	11	6	.647	2.95	23	23	6	•3	0-...	168.0	141	58	55	12	28-1	118
—	Chicago (N.L.)	0	1	.000	11.93	6	2	0	0	0-0	14.1	22	20	19	3	10-1	9
1995—	Daytona (FSL)	0	0	...	1.17	4	2	0	0	0-...	7.2	5	2	1	0	1-0	8
—	Orlando (Sou.)	1	0	1.000	3.86	5	0	0	0	1-...	7.0	6	3	3	0	4-0	7
—	Chicago (N.L.)	3	1	.750	4.92	43	0	0	0	0-0	60.1	71	35	33	11	24-4	50
1996—	Chicago (N.L.)	4	5	.444	2.84	70	0	0	0	18-21	79.1	58	26	25	8	44-4	75
1997—	Chicago (N.L.)	3	5	.375	4.20	52	0	0	0	4-5	60.0	53	32	28	4	39-5	54
—	New York (N.L.)■	0	0	...	4.96	13	0	0	0	1-2	16.1	15	10	9	3	14-1	10
1998—	New York (N.L.)	5	1	.833	2.93	66	0	0	0	4-8	76.2	62	25	25	4	33-9	58
1999—	New York (N.L.)	5	4	.556	3.05	80	0	0	0	3-6	85.2	80	31	29	9	37-8	77
2000—	New York (N.L.)	8	6	.571	3.59	77	0	0	0	1-5	82.2	60	36	33	9	41-7	73
2001—	New York (N.L.)	4	3	.571	3.51	49	0	0	0	1-3	51.1	42	23	20	8	22-6	41
—	Philadelphia (N.L.)■	0	2	.000	7.47	21	0	0	0	0-0	15.2	21	13	13	4	12-3	15
2002—	Philadelphia (N.L.)									Did not play.							
Major League totals (9 years)		33	30	.524	3.90	484	6	0	0	32-50	565.0	508	264	245	63	284-49	477

DIVISION SERIES RECORD

Year	League	W	L	Pct.	ERA	G	GS	CG	ShO	Sv.-Opp.	IP	H	R	ER	HR	BB-IBB	SO
1999—	New York (N.L.)	1	0	1.000	0.00	2	0	0	0	0-0	2.0	0	0	0	0	2-0	0
2000—	New York (N.L.)	0	0	...	0.00	2	0	0	0	0-0	2.0	0	0	0	0	1-0	5
Division series totals (2 years)		1	0	1.000	0.00	4	0	0	0	0-0	4.0	0	0	0	0	3-0	5

CHAMPIONSHIP SERIES RECORD

Year	League	W	L	Pct.	ERA	G	GS	CG	ShO	Sv.-Opp.	IP	H	R	ER	HR	BB-IBB	SO
1999—	New York (N.L.)	1	0	1.000	4.76	5	0	0	0	0-0	5.2	2	3	3	0	4-2	5
2000—	New York (N.L.)	1	0	1.000	0.00	2	0	0	0	0-1	1.1	1	0	0	0	1-1	2
Champ. series totals (2 years)		2	0	1.000	3.86	7	0	0	0	0-1	7.0	3	3	3	0	5-3	7

WORLD SERIES RECORD

Year	League	W	L	Pct.	ERA	G	GS	CG	ShO	Sv.-Opp.	IP	H	R	ER	HR	BB-IBB	SO
2000—	New York (N.L.)	0	1	.000	5.40	2	0	0	0	0-0	1.2	3	1	1	0	2-1	2

WERTH, JAYSON — OF/C — BLUE JAYS

PERSONAL: Born May 20, 1979, in Springfield, Ill. ... 6-5/190. ... Bats right, throws right. ... Full name: Jayson Richard Werth. ... Grandson of Dick Schofield, infielder/outfielder with six major league teams (1953-71); nephew of Dick Schofield, infielder with four major league teams (1983-96); stepson of Dennis Werth, outfielder/first baseman with New York Yankees (1979) and Kansas City Royals (1980-82).

HIGH SCHOOL: Chatham Glenwood (Chatham, Ill.).

TRANSACTIONS/CAREER NOTES: Selected by Baltimore Orioles organization in first round (22nd pick overall) of free-agent draft (June 3, 1997). ... Traded by Orioles to Toronto Blue Jays for P John Bale (December 11, 2000). ... On Tennessee disabled list (April 5-14, 2001).

STATISTICAL NOTES: Tied for Gulf Coast League lead in double plays by catcher with four in 1997. ... Led South Atlantic League catchers with 131 assists in 1998.

2002 GAMES PLAYED BY POSITION (MLB): OF—15.

Year	Team (League)	Pos.	G	AB	R	H	2B	3B	HR	RBI	BB	SO	SB-CS	Avg.	OBP	SLG	E	Avg.
			BATTING														FIELDING	
1997—	GC Orioles (GCL)	C-1B	32	88	16	26	6	0	1	8	22	22	7-1	.295	.432	.398	9	.958
1998—	Delmarva (S.Atl.)	C	120	408	71	108	20	3	8	53	50	92	21-6	.265	.364	.387	9	.991
—	Bowie (East.)	C	5	19	2	3	2	0	0	1	2	6	1-0	.158	.238	.263	0	1.000
1999—	Frederick (Caro.)	C	66	236	41	72	10	1	3	30	37	37	16-3	.305	.403	.394	10	.981
—	Bowie (East.)	C-OF	35	121	18	33	5	1	1	11	17	26	7-1	.273	.364	.355	1	.996
2000—	Bowie (East.)	C-OF	85	276	47	63	16	2	5	26	54	50	9-3	.228	.361	.355	7	.988
—	Frederick (Caro.)	C	24	83	16	23	3	0	2	18	10	15	5-1	.277	.347	.386	2	.985
2001—	Dunedin (FSL)■	C	21	70	9	14	3	0	2	14	17	19	1-1	.200	.356	.329	0	1.000
—	Tennessee (Sou.)	C-1B	104	369	51	105	23	1	18	69	63	93	12-3	.285	.387	.499	7	.988
2002—	Toronto (A.L.)	OF	15	46	4	12	2	1	0	6	6	11	1-0	.261	.340	.348	0	1.000
—	Syracuse (I.L.)	OF-C	127	443	65	114	25	2	18	82	67	125	24-7	.257	.354	.445	5	.985
Major League totals (1 year)			15	46	4	12	2	1	0	6	6	11	1-0	.261	.340	.348	0	1.000

WESSON, BARRY — OF — ANGELS

PERSONAL: Born April 6, 1977, in Tupelo, Miss. ... 6-2/212. ... Bats right, throws right. ... Full name: Barry Jarvis Wesson.
HIGH SCHOOL: Brandon (Miss.).
TRANSACTIONS/CAREER NOTES: Selected by Houston Astros organization in 14th round of free-agent draft (June 1, 1995). ... Granted free agency (October 15, 2001). ... Re-signed by Astros organization (December 4, 2001). ... Claimed on waivers by Anaheim Angels (September 3, 2002).
2002 GAMES PLAYED BY POSITION (MLB): OF—15.

Year	Team (League)	Pos.	G	AB	R	H	2B	3B	HR	RBI	BB	SO	SB-CS	Avg.	OBP	SLG	E	Avg.
			BATTING														FIELDING	
1995—	GC Astros (GCL)	OF	45	138	14	26	2	2	2	18	19	40	4-0	.188	.289	.275	0	1.000
—	Jackson (Texas)	OF	4	3	2	2	0	1	0	1	0	0	0-0	.667	.667	1.333	0	1.000
1996—	Auburn (NY-Penn)	OF	55	176	11	28	7	0	0	12	12	46	5-3	.159	.214	.199	5	.943
1997—	Auburn (NY-Penn)	OF	58	208	24	54	7	3	3	26	10	45	8-4	.260	.295	.365	5	.956
1998—	Quad City (Midw.)	OF	138	493	71	124	21	2	7	43	32	90	22-12	.252	.304	.345	4	.986
1999—	Kissimmee (FSL)	OF	115	352	32	76	15	1	4	34	26	84	8-7	.216	.276	.298	2	.992
2000—	Round Rock (Texas)	OF-1B	39	110	12	26	1	2	2	15	10	32	6-2	.236	.295	.336	0	1.000
—	Kissimmee (FSL)	OF	81	308	50	84	21	3	5	35	33	66	24-5	.273	.346	.409	2	.988
2001—	Round Rock (Texas)	OF	133	472	67	119	23	7	16	54	41	135	20-10	.252	.317	.432	3	.990
2002—	Houston (N.L.)	OF	15	20	1	4	0	1	0	1	1	5	0-0	.200	.238	.300	0	1.000
—	New Orleans (PCL)	OF	111	413	43	121	25	5	11	61	16	100	4-7	.293	.325	.458	1	.996
Major League totals (1 year)			15	20	1	4	0	1	0	1	1	5	0-0	.200	.238	.300	0	1.000

WESTBROOK, JAKE — P — INDIANS

PERSONAL: Born September 29, 1977, in Athens, Ga. ... 6-3/185. ... Throws right, bats right. ... Full name: Jacob Cauthen Westbrook.
HIGH SCHOOL: Madison County (Danielsville, Ga.).
TRANSACTIONS/CAREER NOTES: Selected by Colorado Rockies organization in first round (21st pick overall) of free-agent draft (June 4, 1996). ... Traded by Rockies with P John Nicholson and OF Mark Hamlin to Montreal Expos for 2B Mike Lansing (December 16, 1997). ... Traded by Expos with two players to be named later to New York Yankees for P Hideki Irabu (December 22, 1999); Yankees acquired P Ted Lilly (March 17, 2000) and P Christian Parker (March 22, 2000) to complete deal. ... On Columbus disabled list (July 5-23, 2000). ... Traded by Yankees with P Zach Day to Cleveland Indians (July 25, 2000), completing deal in which Indians traded OF Dave Justice to Yankees for OF Ricky Ledee and two players to be named later (June 29, 2000). ... On Buffalo disabled list (July 25-September 1, 2000). ... On Cleveland disabled list (September 1, 2000-remainder of season). ... On Cleveland disabled list (March 30-July 11 and August 26, 2002-remainder of season); included rehabilitation assignments to Akron (June 16-July 6) and Buffalo (July 7-11).
CAREER HITTING (MLB): 0-for-1 (.000), 0 R, 0 2B, 0 3B, 0 HR, 0 RBI.

Year	League	W	L	Pct.	ERA	G	GS	CG	ShO	Sv.-Opp.	IP	H	R	ER	HR	BB-IBB	SO
1996—	Arizona Rockies (Ariz.)	4	2	.667	2.87	11	11	0	0	0-...	62.2	66	33	20	0	14-0	57
—	Portland (N'West)	1	1	.500	2.55	4	4	0	0	0-...	24.2	22	8	7	1	5-0	19
1997—	Asheville (S.Atl.)	*14	11	.560	4.82	28	27	3	2	0-...	170.0	176	93	91	16	55-0	92
1998—	Jupiter (FSL)■	11	6	.647	3.26	27	27	2	0	0-...	171.0	169	70	62	11	60-0	79
1999—	Harrisburg (East.)	11	5	.688	3.92	27	27	2	•2	0-...	174.2	180	88	76	14	63-1	90
2000—	Columbus (I.L.)■	5	7	.417	4.65	16	15	2	0	0-...	89.0	94	53	46	3	38-0	61
—	New York (A.L.)	0	2	.000	13.50	3	2	0	0	0-0	6.2	15	10	10	1	4-1	1
2001—	Buffalo (I.L.)■	8	1	.889	3.20	12	12	0	0	0-...	64.2	60	27	23	2	23-0	45
—	Cleveland (A.L.)	4	4	.500	5.85	23	6	0	0	0-0	64.2	79	43	42	6	22-4	48
2002—	Cleveland (A.L.)	1	3	.250	5.83	11	4	0	0	0-2	41.2	50	30	27	6	12-1	20
—	Akron (East.)	0	1	.000	4.80	3	3	0	0	0-...	15.0	13	8	8	0	1-0	8
—	Buffalo (I.L.)	1	0	1.000	6.00	1	1	0	0	0-...	6.0	8	4	4	1	0-0	2
Major League totals (3 years)		5	9	.357	6.29	37	12	0	0	0-2	113.0	144	83	79	13	38-6	69

WHITE, GABE — P — REDS

PERSONAL: Born November 20, 1971, in Sebring, Fla. ... 6-2/204. ... Throws left, bats left. ... Full name: Gabriel Allen White.
HIGH SCHOOL: Sebring (Fla.).
TRANSACTIONS/CAREER NOTES: Selected by Montreal Expos organization in supplemental round ("sandwich pick" between first and second round, 28th pick overall) of free-agent draft (June 4, 1990); pick received as part of compensation for California Angels signing Type A free-agent P Mark Langston. ... On Harrisburg disabled list (July 2-27, 1993). ... On Ottawa disabled list (April 7-May 6, 1994). ... Traded by Expos to Cincinnati Reds for 2B Jhonny Carvajal (December 15, 1995). ... On disabled list (September 17, 1996-remainder of season). ... Traded by Reds to Colorado Rockies for P Manny Aybar (April 7, 2000). ... Traded by Rockies with P Luke Hudson to Reds for 2B Pokey Reese and P Dennys Reyes (December 18, 2001). ... On disabled list (July 12-31 and August 29, 2002-remainder of season).
RECORDS: Shares N.L. record for most consecutive home runs allowed in one inning—3 (July 7, 1995, second inning).
CAREER HITTING (MLB): 4-for-36 (.111), 1 R, 0 2B, 0 3B, 1 HR, 3 RBI.

Year	League	W	L	Pct.	ERA	G	GS	CG	ShO	Sv.-Opp.	IP	H	R	ER	HR	BB-IBB	SO
1990—	Gulf Coast Expos (GCL)	4	2	.667	3.14	11	11	1	0	0-...	57.1	50	21	20	3	12-0	41
1991—	Sumter (S.Atl.)	6	9	.400	3.26	24	24	5	0	0-...	149.0	127	73	54	7	53-0	140
1992—	Rockford (Midw.)	14	8	.636	2.84	27	27	7	0	0-...	187.0	148	73	59	10	61-0	*176
1993—	Harrisburg (East.)	7	2	.778	2.16	16	16	2	1	0-...	100.0	80	30	24	4	28-0	80
—	Ottawa (I.L.)	2	1	.667	3.12	6	6	1	1	0-...	40.1	38	15	14	3	6-0	28
1994—	West Palm Beach (FSL)	1	0	1.000	1.50	1	1	0	0	0-...	6.0	2	2	1	0	1-0	4
—	Ottawa (I.L.)	8	3	.727	5.05	14	14	0	0	0-...	73.0	77	49	41	11	28-2	63
—	Montreal (N.L.)	1	1	.500	6.08	7	5	0	0	1-1	23.2	24	16	16	4	11-0	17
1995—	Ottawa (I.L.)	2	3	.400	3.90	12	12	0	0	0-...	62.1	58	31	27	10	17-0	37
—	Montreal (N.L.)	1	2	.333	7.01	19	1	0	0	0-0	25.2	26	21	20	7	9-0	25
1996—	Indianapolis (A.A.)■	6	3	.667	2.77	11	11	0	0	0-...	68.1	69	25	21	6	9-3	51
1997—	Indianapolis (A.A.)	7	4	.636	2.82	20	19	0	0	0-...	118.0	119	46	37	10	18-0	62
—	Cincinnati (N.L.)	2	2	.500	4.39	12	6	0	0	1-1	41.0	39	20	20	6	8-1	25
1998—	Cincinnati (N.L.)	5	5	.500	4.01	69	3	0	0	9-13	98.2	86	46	44	17	27-6	83
1999—	Cincinnati (N.L.)	1	2	.333	4.43	50	0	0	0	0-1	61.0	68	31	30	13	14-1	61
2000—	Cincinnati (N.L.)	0	0	...	18.00	1	0	0	0	0-0	1.0	2	2	2	1	1-0	2
—	Colorado (N.L.)■	11	2	.846	2.17	67	0	0	0	5-9	83.0	62	21	20	5	14-2	82
2001—	Colorado (N.L.)	1	7	.125	6.25	69	0	0	0	0-2	67.2	70	47	47	18	26-5	47
2002—	Cincinnati (N.L.)■	6	1	.857	2.98	62	0	0	0	0-1	54.1	49	19	18	3	10-2	41
Major League totals (8 years)		28	22	.560	4.28	356	15	0	0	16-28	456.0	426	223	217	74	120-17	383

WHITE, RICK P

PERSONAL: Born December 23, 1968, in Springfield, Ohio. ... 6-4/230. ... Throws right, bats right. ... Full name: Richard Allen White.

HIGH SCHOOL: Kenton Ridge (Springfield, Ohio).

JUNIOR COLLEGE: Paducah (Ky.) Community College.

TRANSACTIONS/CAREER NOTES: Selected by Pittsburgh Pirates organization in 15th round of free-agent draft (June 4, 1990). ... On Carolina disabled list (May 15-July 6, 1993). ... On Buffalo disabled list (August 28-September 4, 1993). ... On Pittsburgh disabled list (April 14-May 17, 1995); included rehabilitation assignment to Gulf Coast Pirates (April 26-May 17). ... Granted free agency (December 21, 1995). ... Re-signed by Pirates organization (December 21, 1995). ... On Calgary disabled list (April 4-August 7, 1996). ... On Carolina disabled list (August 7-23, 1996). ... Granted free agency (October 15, 1996). ... Signed by Tampa Bay Devil Rays organization (February 4, 1997). ... Loaned by Devil Rays to Orlando, Chicago Cubs organization (April 3-September 11, 1997). ... Traded by Devil Rays with OF Bubba Trammell to New York Mets for OF Jason Tyner and P Paul Wilson (July 28, 2000). ... On disabled list (March 31-April 21, 2001 and May 1-17, 2001). ... Granted free agency (December 21, 2001). ... Signed by Colorado Rockies (January 10, 2002). ... On disabled list (May 27-June 18, 2002); included rehabilitation assignment to Colorado Springs (June 14-18). ... Released by Rockies (August 12, 2002). ... Signed by St. Louis Cardinals organization (August 17, 2002). ... Granted free agency (October 29, 2002).

MISCELLANEOUS: Struck out and grounded out in two appearances as pinch hitter with New York (2000).

CAREER HITTING (MLB): 4-for-40 (.100), 1 R, 1 2B, 0 3B, 0 HR, 1 RBI.

Year	League	W	L	Pct.	ERA	G	GS	CG	ShO	Sv.-Opp.	IP	H	R	ER	HR	BB-IBB	SO
1990—	Gulf Coast Pirates (GCL)	3	1	.750	0.76	7	6	0	0	0-...	35.2	26	11	3	0	4-0	27
—	Welland (NY-Penn)	1	4	.200	3.26	9	5	1	0	0-...	38.2	39	19	14	2	14-2	43
1991—	Augusta (S.Atl.)	4	4	.500	3.00	34	0	0	0	6-...	63.0	68	26	21	2	18-2	52
—	Salem (Caro.)	2	3	.400	4.66	13	5	1	0	1-...	46.1	41	27	24	2	9-3	36
1992—	Salem (Caro.)	7	9	.438	3.80	18	18	•5	0	0-...	120.2	116	58	51	15	24-1	70
—	Carolina (Sou.)	1	7	.125	4.21	10	10	1	0	0-...	57.2	59	32	27	8	18-1	45
1993—	Carolina (Sou.)	4	3	.571	3.50	12	12	1	0	0-...	69.1	59	29	27	5	12-0	52
—	Buffalo (A.A.)	0	3	.000	3.54	7	3	0	0	0-...	28.0	25	13	11	1	8-0	16
1994—	Pittsburgh (N.L.)	4	5	.444	3.82	43	5	0	0	6-9	75.1	79	35	32	9	17-3	38
1995—	Pittsburgh (N.L.)	2	3	.400	4.75	15	9	0	0	0-0	55.0	66	33	29	3	18-0	29
—	Calgary (PCL)	6	4	.600	4.20	14	11	1	0	0-...	79.1	97	40	37	13	10-0	56
1996—	Gulf Coast Pirates (GCL)	0	0	...	2.25	3	3	0	0	0-...	12.0	8	4	3	0	3-0	8
—	Carolina (Sou.)	0	1	.000	11.37	2	1	0	0	0-...	6.1	9	8	8	2	1-0	7
1997—	Orlando (Sou.)■	5	7	.417	4.71	39	8	0	0	12-...	86.0	93	55	45	7	22-2	65
1998—	Durham (I.L.)■	4	2	.667	4.22	9	9	1	0	0-...	53.1	63	29	25	3	11-0	31
—	Tampa Bay (A.L.)	2	6	.250	3.80	38	3	0	0	0-0	68.2	66	32	29	8	23-2	39
1999—	Tampa Bay (A.L.)	5	3	.625	4.08	63	1	0	0	0-2	108.0	132	56	49	8	38-5	81
2000—	Tampa Bay (A.L.)	3	6	.333	3.41	44	0	0	0	2-5	71.1	57	30	27	7	26-3	47
—	New York (N.L.)■	2	3	.400	3.81	22	0	0	0	1-2	28.1	26	14	12	2	12-2	20
2001—	New York (N.L.)	4	5	.444	3.88	55	0	0	0	2-4	69.2	71	38	30	7	17-4	51
2002—	Colorado (N.L.)■	2	6	.250	6.20	41	0	0	0	0-1	40.2	49	30	28	4	18-4	27
—	St. Louis (N.L.)■	3	1	.750	0.82	20	0	0	0	0-0	22.0	13	3	2	0	3-1	14
A.L. totals (3 years)		10	15	.400	3.81	145	4	0	0	2-7	248.0	255	118	105	23	87-10	167
N.L. totals (5 years)		17	23	.425	4.11	196	14	0	0	9-16	291.0	304	153	133	25	85-14	179
Major League totals (7 years)		27	38	.415	3.97	341	18	0	0	11-23	539.0	559	271	238	48	172-24	346

DIVISION SERIES RECORD

Year	League	W	L	Pct.	ERA	G	GS	CG	ShO	Sv.-Opp.	IP	H	R	ER	HR	BB-IBB	SO
2000—	New York (N.L.)	1	0	1.000	0.00	2	0	0	0	0-0	2.2	6	0	0	0	2-0	4
2002—	St. Louis (N.L.)	0	0	...	0.00	2	0	0	0	0-1	2.0	1	1	0	0	1-0	1
Division series totals (2 years)		1	0	1.000	0.00	4	0	0	0	0-1	4.2	7	1	0	0	3-0	5

CHAMPIONSHIP SERIES RECORD

Year	League	W	L	Pct.	ERA	G	GS	CG	ShO	Sv.-Opp.	IP	H	R	ER	HR	BB-IBB	SO
2000—	New York (N.L.)	0	0	...	9.00	1	0	0	0	0-0	3.0	5	3	3	0	1-0	1
2002—	St. Louis (N.L.)	0	1	.000	4.50	3	0	0	0	0-1	4.0	2	2	2	1	2-1	5
Champ. series totals (2 years)		0	1	.000	6.43	4	0	0	0	0-1	7.0	7	5	5	1	3-1	6

WORLD SERIES RECORD

Year	League	W	L	Pct.	ERA	G	GS	CG	ShO	Sv.-Opp.	IP	H	R	ER	HR	BB-IBB	SO
2000—	New York (N.L.)	0	0	...	6.75	1	0	0	0	0-0	1.1	1	1	1	0	1-1	1

WHITE, RONDELL — OF — YANKEES

PERSONAL: Born February 23, 1972, in Milledgeville, Ga. ... 6-1/225. ... Bats right, throws right. ... Full name: Rondell Bernard White.
HIGH SCHOOL: Jones County (Gray, Ga.).
TRANSACTIONS/CAREER NOTES: Selected by Montreal Expos organization in first round (24th pick overall) of free-agent draft (June 4, 1990); pick received as part of compensation for California Angels signing Type A free-agent P Mark Langston. ... On Montreal disabled list (April 28-July 16, 1996); included rehabilitation assignments to West Palm Beach (July 5-10), Gulf Coast Expos (July 5-10) and Harrisburg (July 10-16). ... On disabled list (July 21, 1998-remainder of season; June 14-29 and July 2-17, 1999). ... On Montreal disabled list (July 8-August 31, 2000). ... Traded by Expos to Chicago Cubs for P Scott Downs (July 31, 2000). ... On Chicago disabled list (August 1-6 and August 27, 2000-remainder of season). ... On Chicago disabled list (June 26-July 12 and July 14-September 1, 2001); included rehabilitation assignment to West Tenn (August 15-September 1). ... Granted free agency (November 5, 2001). ... Signed by New York Yankees (December 21, 2001).
STATISTICAL NOTES: Led Gulf Coast League with 96 total bases in 1990. ... Hit for the cycle (June 11, 1995, 13 innings). ... Collected six hits in one game (June 11, 1995). ... Led N.L. outfielders with 376 putouts and 385 total chances in 1997. ... Had 17-game hitting streak (May 23-June 13, 2001). ... Career major league grand slams: 2.
2002 GAMES PLAYED BY POSITION (MLB): OF—113; DH—11.

			BATTING														FIELDING	
Year	Team (League)	Pos.	G	AB	R	H	2B	3B	HR	RBI	BB	SO	SB-CS	Avg.	OBP	SLG	E	Avg.
1990—	GC Expos (GCL)	OF	57	221	33	66	7	4	5	34	17	33	10-7	.299	.362	.434	2	.973
1991—	Sumter (S.Atl.)	OF	123	465	80	122	23	6	13	68	57	109	50-17	.262	.351	.422	3	*.987
1992—	W. Palm Beach (FSL)	OF	111	450	80	142	10	*12	4	41	46	78	42-16	.316	.384	.418	3	.984
	— Harrisburg (East.)	OF	21	89	22	27	7	1	2	7	6	14	6-1	.303	.374	.472	2	.938
1993—	Harrisburg (East.)	OF	90	372	72	122	16	10	12	52	22	72	21-6	.328	.371	.522	1	.995
	— Ottawa (I.L.)	OF-DH	37	150	28	57	8	2	7	32	12	20	10-1	.380	.436	.600	1	.988
	— Montreal (N.L.)	OF	23	73	9	19	3	1	2	15	7	16	1-2	.260	.321	.411	0	1.000
1994—	Montreal (N.L.)	OF	40	97	16	27	10	1	2	13	9	18	1-1	.278	.358	.464	2	.946
	— Ottawa (I.L.)	OF	42	169	23	46	7	0	7	18	15	17	9-2	.272	.344	.438	2	.979
1995—	Montreal (N.L.)	OF	130	474	87	140	33	4	13	57	41	87	25-5	.295	.356	.464	4	.986
1996—	Montreal (N.L.)	OF	88	334	35	98	19	4	6	41	22	53	14-6	.293	.340	.428	2	.990
	— W. Palm Beach (FSL)	DH-OF	3	10	0	2	1	0	0	2	0	4	0-1	.200	.200	.300	0	1.000
	— GC Expos (GCL)	OF	3	12	3	3	0	0	2	4	0	1	1-0	.250	.250	.750	0	1.000
	— Harrisburg (East.)	OF	5	20	5	7	1	0	3	6	1	1	1-1	.350	.381	.850	0	1.000
1997—	Montreal (N.L.)	OF	151	592	84	160	29	5	28	82	31	111	16-8	.270	.316	.478	3	*.992
1998—	Montreal (N.L.)	OF-DH	97	357	54	107	21	2	17	58	30	57	16-7	.300	.363	.513	1	.996
1999—	Montreal (N.L.)	OF	138	539	83	168	26	6	22	64	32	85	10-6	.312	.359	.505	11	.964
2000—	Montreal (N.L.)	OF	75	290	52	89	24	0	11	54	28	67	5-1	.307	.370	.503	1	.994
	— Chicago (N.L.)■	OF	19	67	7	22	2	0	2	7	5	12	0-2	.328	.392	.448	0	1.000
2001—	Chicago (N.L.)	OF	95	323	43	99	19	1	17	50	26	56	1-0	.307	.371	.529	3	.979
	— West Tenn (Sou.)	OF	9	28	2	4	1	0	2	4	1	7	0-0	.143	.226	.393	0	1.000
2002—	New York (A.L.)	OF-DH	126	455	59	109	21	0	14	62	25	86	1-2	.240	.288	.378	0	*1.000
American League totals (1 year)			126	455	59	109	21	0	14	62	25	86	1-2	.240	.288	.378	0	1.000
National League totals (9 years)			856	3146	470	929	186	24	120	441	231	562	89-38	.295	.351	.484	27	.985
Major League totals (10 years)			982	3601	529	1038	207	24	134	503	256	648	90-40	.288	.343	.471	27	.987

DIVISION SERIES RECORD

			BATTING														FIELDING	
Year	Team (League)	Pos.	G	AB	R	H	2B	3B	HR	RBI	BB	SO	SB-CS	Avg.	OBP	SLG	E	Avg.
2002—	New York (A.L.)	DH	1	3	1	1	0	0	1	1	0	0	0-0	.333	.333	1.333	0	...

WICKMAN, BOB — P — INDIANS

PERSONAL: Born February 6, 1969, in Green Bay, Wis. ... 6-1/240. ... Throws right, bats right. ... Full name: Robert Joe Wickman.
HIGH SCHOOL: Oconto Falls (Wis.).
COLLEGE: Wisconsin-Whitewater.
TRANSACTIONS/CAREER NOTES: Selected by Chicago White Sox organization in second round of free-agent draft (June 4, 1990). ... Traded by White Sox with P Melido Perez and P Domingo Jean to New York Yankees for 2B Steve Sax and cash (January 10, 1992). ... Traded by Yankees with OF Gerald Williams to Milwaukee Brewers for P Graeme Lloyd and OF Pat Listach (August 23, 1996). ... Traded by Brewers with P Steve Woodard and P Jason Bere to Cleveland Indians for 1B/OF Richie Sexson, P Paul Rigdon, P Kane Davis and a player to be named later (July 28, 2000); Brewers acquired 2B Marcos Scutaro to complete deal (August 30). ... On disabled list (July 22-August 10 and August 11, 2002-remainder of season).
CAREER HITTING (MLB): 0-for-2 (.000), 0 R, 0 2B, 0 3B, 0 HR, 0 RBI.

Year	League	W	L	Pct.	ERA	G	GS	CG	ShO	Sv.-Opp.	IP	H	R	ER	HR	BB-IBB	SO
1990—	GC White Sox (GCL)	2	0	1.000	2.45	2	2	0	0	0-...	11.0	7	4	3	0	1-0	15
	— Sarasota (FSL)	0	1	.000	1.98	2	2	0	0	0-...	13.2	17	7	3	0	4-0	8
	— South Bend (Midw.)	7	2	.778	1.38	9	9	3	0	0-...	65.1	50	16	10	1	16-0	50
1991—	Sarasota (FSL)	5	1	.833	2.05	7	7	1	1	0-...	44.0	43	16	10	2	11-0	32
	— Birmingham (Sou.)	6	10	.375	3.56	20	20	4	1	0-...	131.1	127	68	52	5	50-0	81
1992—	Columbus (I.L.)■	12	5	.706	2.92	23	23	2	1	0-...	157.0	131	61	51	12	55-0	108
	— New York (A.L.)	6	1	.857	4.11	8	8	0	0	0-0	50.1	51	25	23	2	20-0	21
1993—	New York (A.L.)	14	4	.778	4.63	41	19	1	1	4-8	140.0	156	82	72	13	69-7	70
1994—	New York (A.L.)	5	4	.556	3.09	*53	0	0	0	6-10	70.0	54	26	24	3	27-3	56
1995—	New York (A.L.)	2	4	.333	4.05	63	1	0	0	1-10	80.0	77	38	36	6	33-3	51
1996—	New York (A.L.)	4	1	.800	4.67	58	0	0	0	0-3	79.0	94	41	41	7	34-1	61
	— Milwaukee (A.L.)■	3	0	1.000	3.24	12	0	0	0	0-1	16.2	12	9	6	3	10-2	14
1997—	Milwaukee (A.L.)	7	6	.538	2.73	74	0	0	0	1-5	95.2	89	32	29	8	41-7	78
1998—	Milwaukee (N.L.)	6	9	.400	3.72	72	0	0	0	25-32	82.1	79	38	34	5	39-2	71
1999—	Milwaukee (N.L.)	3	8	.273	3.39	71	0	0	0	37-45	74.1	75	31	28	6	38-6	60
2000—	Milwaukee (N.L.)	2	2	.500	2.93	43	0	0	0	16-20	46.0	37	18	15	1	20-2	44
	— Cleveland (A.L.)■	1	3	.250	3.38	26	0	0	0	14-17	26.2	27	12	10	0	12-3	11
2001—	Cleveland (A.L.)	5	0	1.000	2.39	70	0	0	0	32-35	67.2	61	18	18	4	14-2	66
2002—	Cleveland (A.L.)	1	3	.250	4.46	36	0	0	0	20-22	34.1	42	22	17	3	10-0	36
A.L. totals (9 years)		48	26	.649	3.76	441	28	1	1	78-111	660.1	663	305	276	49	270-28	464
N.L. totals (3 years)		11	19	.367	3.42	186	0	0	0	78-97	202.2	191	87	77	12	97-10	175
Major League totals (11 years)		59	45	.567	3.68	627	28	1	1	156-208	863.0	854	392	353	61	367-38	639

DIVISION SERIES RECORD

Year	League	W	L	Pct.	ERA	G	GS	CG	ShO	Sv.-Opp.	IP	H	R	ER	HR	BB-IBB	SO
1995—	New York (A.L.)	0	0	...	0.00	3	0	0	0	0-0	3.0	5	0	0	0	0-0	3
2001—	Cleveland (A.L.)	0	0	...	0.00	1	0	0	0	0-0	1.0	0	0	0	0	0-0	2
Division series totals (2 years)		0	0	...	0.00	4	0	0	0	0-0	4.0	5	0	0	0	0-0	5

ALL-STAR GAME RECORD

	W	L	Pct.	ERA	GS	CG	ShO	Sv.-Opp.	IP	H	R	ER	HR	BB-IBB	SO
All-Star Game totals (1 year)	0	0	...	0.00	0	0	0	0-0	1.0	0	0	0	0	0-0	1

WIDGER, CHRIS — C

PERSONAL: Born May 21, 1971, in Wilmington, Del. ... 6-2/215. ... Bats right, throws right. ... Full name: Christopher Jon Widger. ... Nephew of Mike Widger, linebacker with Montreal Alouettes and Ottawa Rough Riders of Canadian Football League (1970-78).

HIGH SCHOOL: Pennsville (N.J.).

COLLEGE: George Mason.

TRANSACTIONS/CAREER NOTES: Selected by Seattle Mariners organization in third round of free-agent draft (June 1, 1992). ... On disabled list (June 6-16, 1993). ... Traded by Mariners with P Trey Moore and P Matt Wagner to Montreal Expos for P Jeff Fassero and P Alex Pacheco (October 29, 1996). ... On Montreal disabled list (May 25-June 9, 2000). ... Traded by Expos to Mariners for two players to be named later (August 8, 2000); Expos acquired OF Terrmel Sledge (September 28) and Sean Spencer (August 10) to complete deal. ... On Seattle disabled list (March 31, 2001-entire season); included rehabilitation assignment to Everett (June 24-July 6). ... Granted free agency (November 6, 2001). ... Signed by New York Yankees organization (February 1, 2002). ... Granted free agency (November 8, 2002).

STATISTICAL NOTES: Led N.L. catchers with 14 passed balls and tied for lead with 12 double plays in 1998. ... Career major league grand slams: 1.

2002 GAMES PLAYED BY POSITION (MLB): C—21.

			BATTING														FIELDING	
Year	Team (League)	Pos.	G	AB	R	H	2B	3B	HR	RBI	BB	SO	SB-CS	Avg.	OBP	SLG	E	Avg.
1992—	Bellingham (N'West)	C	51	166	28	43	7	2	5	30	22	36	8-1	.259	.340	.416	4	*.987
1993—	Riverside (Calif.)	C-OF	97	360	44	95	28	2	9	58	19	64	5-4	.264	.303	.428	14	.974
1994—	Jacksonville (Sou.)	C-OF-1B	116	388	58	101	15	3	16	59	39	69	8-7	.260	.334	.438	13	.980
1995—	Tacoma (PCL)	C-DH-OF	50	174	29	48	11	1	9	21	9	29	0-0	.276	.311	.506	4	.981
—	Seattle (A.L.)	C-OF-DH	23	45	2	9	0	0	1	2	3	11	0-0	.200	.245	.267	0	1.000
1996—	Tacoma (PCL)	C-DH	97	352	42	107	20	2	13	48	27	62	7-1	.304	.355	.483	8	.988
—	Seattle (A.L.)	C	8	11	1	2	0	0	0	0	0	5	0-0	.182	.250	.182	2	.905
1997—	Montreal (N.L.)■	C	91	278	30	65	20	3	7	37	22	59	2-0	.234	.290	.403	11	.981
1998—	Montreal (N.L.)	C	125	417	36	97	18	1	15	53	29	85	6-1	.233	.281	.388	*14	.983
1999—	Montreal (N.L.)	C	124	383	42	101	24	1	14	56	28	86	1-4	.264	.325	.441	6	.992
2000—	Montreal (N.L.)	C	86	281	31	67	17	2	12	34	29	61	1-2	.238	.311	.441	8	.985
—	Seattle (A.L.)■	C-DH-1B-OF	10	11	1	1	0	0	1	1	1	2	0-0	.091	.167	.364	0	1.000
2001—	Everett (N'West)	1B	5	13	2	1	0	0	0	0	6	1	0-0	.077	.368	.077	0	1.000
2002—	Columbus (I.L.)■	C-OF	61	217	26	53	14	1	10	39	17	31	0-3	.244	.300	.456	4	.990
—	New York (A.L.)	C	21	64	4	19	5	0	0	5	2	9	0-0	.297	.338	.375	2	.983
American League totals (4 years)			62	131	8	31	5	0	2	8	6	27	0-0	.237	.284	.321	4	.982
National League totals (4 years)			426	1359	139	330	79	7	48	180	108	291	10-7	.243	.302	.417	39	.985
Major League totals (7 years)			488	1490	147	361	84	7	50	188	114	318	10-7	.242	.300	.409	43	.985

DIVISION SERIES RECORD

			BATTING														FIELDING	
Year	Team (League)	Pos.	G	AB	R	H	2B	3B	HR	RBI	BB	SO	SB-CS	Avg.	OBP	SLG	E	Avg.
1995—	Seattle (A.L.)	C	2	3	0	0	0	0	0	0	0	3	0-0	.000	.000	.000	0	1.000
2000—	Seattle (A.L.)								Did not play.									

CHAMPIONSHIP SERIES RECORD

			BATTING														FIELDING	
Year	Team (League)	Pos.	G	AB	R	H	2B	3B	HR	RBI	BB	SO	SB-CS	Avg.	OBP	SLG	E	Avg.
1995—	Seattle (A.L.)	C	3	1	0	0	0	0	0	0	0	1	0-0	.000	.000	.000	0	1.000
2000—	Seattle (A.L.)								Did not play.									

WIGGINS, SCOTT — P — BLUE JAYS

PERSONAL: Born March 24, 1976, in Fort Thomas, Ky. ... 6-3/205. ... Throws left, bats left. ... Full name: Scott Joseph Wiggins.

COLLEGE: Northern Kentucky.

TRANSACTIONS/CAREER NOTES: Selected by New York Yankees organization in seventh round of free-agent draft (June 3, 1997).

CAREER HITTING (MLB): 0-for-0 (.000), 0 R, 0 2B, 0 3B, 0 HR, 0 RBI.

Year	League	W	L	Pct.	ERA	G	GS	CG	ShO	Sv.-Opp.	IP	H	R	ER	HR	BB-IBB	SO
1997—	Oneonta (NY-Penn)	6	2	.750	2.56	13	13	1	1	0-...	63.1	58	25	18	1	22-0	44
1998—	Greensboro (S.Atl.)	2	2	.500	2.98	14	4	0	0	1-...	42.1	37	17	14	4	11-0	56
—	Tampa (FSL)	1	1	.500	1.87	11	5	0	0	0-...	33.2	19	12	7	1	17-1	36
—	Gulf Coast Yankees (GCL)	0	0	...	0.00	1	1	0	0	0-...	1.2	2	1	0	0	0-0	2
1999—	Greensboro (S.Atl.)	7	1	.875	3.95	17	17	0	0	0-...	93.1	84	45	41	15	32-0	110
2000—	Tampa (FSL)	2	8	.200	4.11	28	15	1	1	0-...	100.2	106	61	46	4	46-0	68
2001—	Tampa (FSL)	4	3	.571	3.03	36	5	0	0	1-...	68.1	72	29	23	5	23-1	77
—	Norwich (East.)	0	0	...	0.00	4	0	0	0	0-...	4.0	0	0	0	0	1-0	5
2002—	Norwich (East.)	2	1	.667	2.28	24	0	0	0	0-...	27.2	19	8	7	1	9-1	26
—	Tennessee (Sou.)■	0	1	.000	0.93	16	0	0	0	1-...	19.1	18	3	2	0	5-1	19
—	Syracuse (I.L.)	2	0	1.000	2.57	12	0	0	0	0-...	14.0	11	6	4	0	7-0	14
—	Toronto (A.L.)	0	0	...	3.38	3	0	0	0	0-0	2.2	5	1	1	1	1-0	3
Major League totals (1 year)		0	0	...	3.38	3	0	0	0	0-0	2.2	5	1	1	1	1-0	3

WIGGINTON, TY — 3B — METS

PERSONAL: Born October 11, 1977, in San Diego. ... 6-0/200. ... Bats right, throws right. ... Full name: Ty Allen Wigginton.
COLLEGE: UNC Asheville.
TRANSACTIONS/CAREER NOTES: Selected by New York Mets organization in 17th round of free-agent draft (June 2, 1998).
2002 GAMES PLAYED BY POSITION (MLB): 3B—14; 1B—13; 2B—12; OF—2.

			BATTING														FIELDING	
Year	**Team (League)**	**Pos.**	**G**	**AB**	**R**	**H**	**2B**	**3B**	**HR**	**RBI**	**BB**	**SO**	**SB-CS**	**Avg.**	**OBP**	**SLG**	**E**	**Avg.**
1998—	Pittsfield (NY-Penn)	2B-3B-OF	70	272	39	65	14	4	8	29	16	72	11-2	.239	.284	.408	14	.949
1999—	St. Lucie (FSL)	2B	123	456	69	133	23	5	21	73	56	82	9-12	.292	.373	.502	16	.974
2000—	Binghamton (East.)	2B-3B	122	453	64	129	27	3	20	77	24	107	5-5	.285	.319	.490	23	.943
2001—	Norfolk (I.L.)	3-2-1-C-O	78	260	29	65	12	0	7	24	27	66	3-3	.250	.323	.377	17	.924
—	St. Lucie (FSL)	2B	3	9	1	3	1	0	0	1	4	2	0-0	.333	.571	.444	0	1.000
—	Binghamton (East.)	2B-3B	8	28	5	8	3	0	0	0	5	5	1-0	.286	.394	.393	3	.870
2002—	Norfolk (I.L.)	3B-2B-OF-1B	104	383	49	115	26	3	6	48	43	50	5-3	.300	.366	.431	11	.967
—	New York (N.L.)	3B-1B-2B-OF	46	116	18	35	8	0	6	18	8	19	2-1	.302	.354	.526	5	.966
Major League totals (1 year)			46	116	18	35	8	0	6	18	8	19	2-1	.302	.354	.526	5	.966

WILKERSON, BRAD — OF — EXPOS

PERSONAL: Born June 1, 1977, in Daviess County, Ky. ... 6-0/200. ... Bats left, throws left. ... Full name: Stephen Bradley Wilkerson.
HIGH SCHOOL: Apollo (Owensboro, Ky.).
COLLEGE: Florida.
TRANSACTIONS/CAREER NOTES: Selected by Montreal Expos organization in supplemental round ("sandwich pick" between first and second round, 33rd pick overall) of free-agent draft (June 2, 1998); pick received as part of compensation for Toronto Blue Jays signing Type A free agent C Darrin Fletcher. ... On Ottawa disabled list (April 5-May 5, 2001).
HONORS: Named N.L. Rookie of the Year by The Sporting News (2002).
2002 GAMES PLAYED BY POSITION (MLB): OF—129; 1B—23.

			BATTING														FIELDING	
Year	**Team (League)**	**Pos.**	**G**	**AB**	**R**	**H**	**2B**	**3B**	**HR**	**RBI**	**BB**	**SO**	**SB-CS**	**Avg.**	**OBP**	**SLG**	**E**	**Avg.**
1999—	Harrisburg (East.)	OF-1B	138	422	66	99	21	3	8	49	88	100	3-5	.235	.372	.355	7	.972
2000—	Harrisburg (East.)	OF-1B	66	229	53	77	36	2	6	44	42	38	8-4	.336	.442	.590	3	.983
—	Ottawa (I.L.)	OF	63	212	40	53	11	1	12	35	45	60	5-4	.250	.387	.481	6	.956
2001—	Jupiter (FSL)	DH	6	26	3	6	3	0	0	1	3	10	0-0	.231	.310	.346	...	...
—	Ottawa (I.L.)	OF	69	233	43	63	10	0	12	48	60	68	12-5	.270	.423	.468	3	.973
—	Montreal (N.L.)	OF	47	117	11	24	7	2	1	5	17	41	2-1	.205	.304	.325	2	.970
2002—	Montreal (N.L.)	OF-1B	153	507	92	135	27	8	20	59	81	161	7-8	.266	.370	.469	7	.984
Major League totals (2 years)			200	624	103	159	34	10	21	64	98	202	9-9	.255	.358	.442	9	.982

WILLIAMS, BERNIE — OF — YANKEES

PERSONAL: Born September 13, 1968, in San Juan, Puerto Rico. ... 6-2/205. ... Bats both, throws right. ... Full name: Bernabe Figueroa Williams.
HIGH SCHOOL: Escuela Libre de Musica (San Juan, Puerto Rico).
COLLEGE: Puerto Rico.
TRANSACTIONS/CAREER NOTES: Signed as non-drafted free agent by New York Yankees organization (September 13, 1985). ... On disabled list (July 15, 1988-remainder of seasonl; and May 13-June 7, 1993). ... On disabled list (May 11-May 26, 1996; June 16-July 2 and July 15-August 1, 1997). ... On New York disabled list (June 11-July 18, 1998); included rehabilitation assignments to Tampa (July 6-7) and Norwich (July 14-16). ... Granted free agency (October 26, 1998). ... Re-signed by Yankees (November 25, 1998).
RECORDS: Shares major league single-game record for most strikeouts (nine-inning game)—5 (August 21, 1991). ... Shares major league single-inning record for most doubles—2 (June 22, 1994, seventh inning). ... Shares modern major league record for most long hits in one inning—2 (June 22, 1994, seventh inning).
HONORS: Won A.L. Gold Glove as outfielder (1997-2000). ... Named outfielder on The Sporting News A.L. All-Star team (2000 and 2002). ... Named outfielder on A.L. Silver Slugger team (2002).
STATISTICAL NOTES: Led Gulf Coast League outfielders with 117 putouts and 123 total chances in 1986. ... Tied for Gulf Coast League lead in caught stealing with 12 in 1986. ... Led Eastern League in caught stealing with 18 in 1990. ... Led Eastern League outfielders with 288 putouts and 307 total chances and tied for lead with four double plays in 1990. ... Had 21-game hitting streak (August 1-23, 1993). ... Switch-hit home runs in one game eight times (June 6, 1994; September 12, 1996; September 4, 1998; May 4, 1999; April 23 and May 17, 2000; June 30, 2001; May 17, 2002). ... Led A.L. outfielders with 432 putouts and 441 total chances in 1995. ... Had 16-game hitting streak (July 31-August 14, 1998). ... Had 17-game hitting streak (June 8-July 6, 1999). ... Tied for A.L. lead with 17 intentional bases on balls received in 1999. ... Had 17-game hitting streak (June 19-July 7, 2000). ... Had 16-game hitting streak (August 16-September 1, 2001). ... Had 19-game hitting streak (August 7-28, 2002). ... Career major league grand slams: 9.
MISCELLANEOUS: Batted righthanded only (1986-88).
2002 GAMES PLAYED BY POSITION (MLB): OF—147; DH—7.

			BATTING														FIELDING	
Year	**Team (League)**	**Pos.**	**G**	**AB**	**R**	**H**	**2B**	**3B**	**HR**	**RBI**	**BB**	**SO**	**SB-CS**	**Avg.**	**OBP**	**SLG**	**E**	**Avg.**
1986—	GC Yankees (GCL)	OF	61	230	*45	62	5	3	2	25	39	40	33-•12	.270	.374	.343	3	.976
1987—	Fort Lauderdale (FSL)	OF	25	71	11	11	3	0	0	4	18	22	9-1	.155	.348	.197	0	1.000
—	Oneonta (NY-Penn)	OF	25	93	13	32	4	0	0	15	10	14	9-3	.344	.410	.387	2	.952
1988—	Prince William (Caro.)	OF	92	337	72	113	16	7	7	45	65	65	29-11	*.335	.447	.487	5	.975
1989—	Columbus (I.L.)	OF	50	162	21	35	8	1	2	16	25	38	11-5	.216	.325	.315	1	.991
—	Albany/Colonie (East.)	OF	91	314	63	79	11	8	11	42	60	72	26-13	.252	.381	.443	5	.974
1990—	Albany/Colonie (East.)	OF	134	466	*91	131	28	5	8	54	*98	97	*39-18	.281	.409	.414	4	.987
1991—	Columbus (I.L.)	OF	78	306	52	90	14	6	8	37	38	43	9-8	.294	.372	.458	1	.994
—	New York (A.L.)	OF	85	320	43	76	19	4	3	34	48	57	10-5	.238	.336	.350	5	.979

Year Team (League)	Pos.	G	AB	R	H	2B	3B	HR	RBI	BB	SO	SB-CS	Avg.	OBP	SLG	E	Avg.
		BATTING														FIELDING	
1992—New York (A.L.)..........	OF	62	261	39	73	14	2	5	26	29	36	7-6	.280	.354	.406	1	.995
—Columbus (I.L.)..........	OF	95	363	68	111	23	•9	8	50	52	61	20-8	.306	.389	.485	2	.990
1993—New York (A.L.)..........	OF	139	567	67	152	31	4	12	68	53	106	9-9	.268	.333	.400	4	.989
1994—New York (A.L.)..........	OF	108	408	80	118	29	1	12	57	61	54	16-9	.289	.384	.453	3	.990
1995—New York (A.L.)..........	OF	144	563	93	173	29	9	18	82	75	98	8-6	.307	.392	.487	•8	.982
1996—New York (A.L.)..........	OF-DH	143	551	108	168	26	7	29	102	82	72	17-4	.305	.391	.535	5	.986
1997—New York (A.L.)..........	OF	129	509	107	167	35	6	21	100	73	80	15-8	.328	.408	.544	2	.993
1998—New York (A.L.)..........	OF-DH	128	499	101	169	30	5	26	97	74	81	15-9	*.339	.422	.575	3	.990
—Tampa (FSL)...............	OF	1	2	0	1	1	0	0	0	1	0	0-0	.500	.667	1.000	0	1.000
—Norwich (East.)..........	OF	3	11	6	6	2	0	2	5	2	1	0-0	.545	.571	1.273	0	1.000
1999—New York (A.L.)..........	OF-DH	158	591	116	202	28	6	25	115	100	95	9-10	.342	.435	.536	5	.987
2000—New York (A.L.)..........	OF-DH	141	537	108	165	37	6	30	121	71	84	13-5	.307	.391	.566	0	*1.000
2001—New York (A.L.)..........	OF-DH	146	540	102	166	38	0	26	94	78	67	11-5	.307	.395	.522	2	.994
2002—New York (A.L.)..........	OF-DH	154	612	102	204	37	2	19	102	83	97	8-4	.333	.415	.493	5	.986
Major League totals (12 years)		1537	5958	1066	1833	353	52	226	998	827	927	138-80	.308	.392	.498	43	.989

DIVISION SERIES RECORD

RECORDS: Holds A.L. career records for most games—34; at-bats—128; runs—29; doubles—11; runs batted in—26; total bases—68; bases on balls—22; and extra-base hits—18. ... Shares single-game record for most home runs—2 (October 6, 1995 and October 5, 1996).

Year Team (League)	Pos.	G	AB	R	H	2B	3B	HR	RBI	BB	SO	SB-CS	Avg.	OBP	SLG	E	Avg.
		BATTING														FIELDING	
1995—New York (A.L.)..........	OF	5	21	8	9	2	0	2	5	7	3	1-0	.429	.571	.810	0	1.000
1996—New York (A.L.)..........	OF	4	15	5	7	0	0	3	5	2	1	1-1	.467	.500	1.067	0	1.000
1997—New York (A.L.)..........	OF	5	17	3	2	1	0	0	1	4	3	0-0	.118	.318	.176	0	1.000
1998—New York (A.L.)..........	OF	3	11	0	0	0	0	0	0	1	4	0-0	.000	.083	.000	0	1.000
1999—New York (A.L.)..........	OF	3	11	2	4	1	0	1	6	1	2	0-0	.364	.462	.727	0	1.000
2000—New York (A.L.)..........	OF	5	20	3	5	3	0	0	1	1	4	0-1	.250	.273	.400	0	1.000
2001—New York (A.L.)..........	OF	5	18	4	4	3	0	0	5	3	3	0-1	.222	.333	.389	0	1.000
2002—New York (A.L.)..........	OF	4	15	4	5	1	0	1	3	3	2	0-0	.333	.444	.600	0	1.000
Division series totals (8 years)		34	128	29	36	11	0	7	26	22	22	2-3	.281	.390	.531	0	1.000

CHAMPIONSHIP SERIES RECORD

RECORDS: Holds A.L. career record for runs batted in—21; and bases on balls received—21. ... Shares A.L. career record for most runs—22.

NOTES: Named Most Valuable Player (1996).

Year Team (League)	Pos.	G	AB	R	H	2B	3B	HR	RBI	BB	SO	SB-CS	Avg.	OBP	SLG	E	Avg.
		BATTING														FIELDING	
1996—New York (A.L.)..........	OF	5	19	6	9	3	0	2	6	5	4	1-0	.474	.583	.947	0	1.000
1998—New York (A.L.)..........	OF	6	21	4	8	1	0	0	5	7	4	1-1	.381	.536	.429	0	1.000
1999—New York (A.L.)..........	OF	5	20	3	5	1	0	1	2	2	5	1-0	.250	.318	.450	0	1.000
2000—New York (A.L.)..........	CF	6	23	5	10	1	0	1	3	2	3	1-0	.435	.481	.609	0	1.000
2001—New York (A.L.)..........	OF	5	17	4	4	0	0	3	5	5	4	0-1	.235	.409	.765	1	.900
Championship series totals (5 years)		27	100	22	36	6	0	7	21	21	20	4-2	.360	.472	.630	1	.986

WORLD SERIES RECORD

NOTES: Member of World Series championship team (1996, 1998, 1999 and 2000).

Year Team (League)	Pos.	G	AB	R	H	2B	3B	HR	RBI	BB	SO	SB-CS	Avg.	OBP	SLG	E	Avg.
		BATTING														FIELDING	
1996—New York (A.L.)..........	OF	6	24	3	4	0	0	1	4	3	6	1-0	.167	.259	.292	0	1.000
1998—New York (A.L.)..........	OF	4	16	2	1	0	0	1	3	2	5	0-0	.063	.167	.250	0	1.000
1999—New York (A.L.)..........	OF	4	13	2	3	0	0	0	0	4	2	1-0	.231	.412	.231	0	1.000
2000—New York (A.L.)..........	OF	5	18	2	2	0	0	1	1	5	5	0-0	.111	.304	.278	0	1.000
2001—New York (A.L.)..........	OF	7	24	2	5	1	0	0	1	4	6	0-0	.208	.321	.250	0	1.000
World Series totals (5 years)		26	95	11	15	1	0	3	9	18	24	2-0	.158	.292	.263	0	1.000

ALL-STAR GAME RECORD

NOTES: Named to All-Star team for 1998 game; replaced by Manny Ramirez due to injury.

	AB	R	H	2B	3B	HR	RBI	BB	SO	SB-CS	Avg.	OBP	SLG	E	Avg.
All-Star Game totals (4 years)	5	1	0	0	0	0	0	1	1	1-0	.000	.167	.000	0	1.000

WILLIAMS, DAVID — P — PIRATES

PERSONAL: Born March 12, 1979, in Anchorage, Alaska. ... 6-2/213. ... Throws left, bats left. ... Full name: David Aaron Williams.

JUNIOR COLLEGE: Delaware Tech (Georgetown, Del.).

TRANSACTIONS/CAREER NOTES: Selected by Pittsburgh Pirates organization in 17th round of free-agent draft (June 2, 1998). ... On disabled list (May 28, 2002-remainder of season).

CAREER HITTING (MLB): 6-for-50 (.120), 2 R, 2 2B, 0 3B, 1 HR, 5 RBI.

Year League	W	L	Pct.	ERA	G	GS	CG	ShO	Sv.-Opp.	IP	H	R	ER	HR	BB-IBB	SO
1998—Erie (NY-Penn)................	2	2	.500	3.23	22	2	0	0	0-...	47.1	45	21	17	6	14-0	38
1999—Williamsport (NY-Penn) ...	4	2	.667	2.56	7	7	1	1	0-...	45.2	33	17	13	2	11-0	47
—Hickory (S.Atl.)................	3	1	.750	3.20	9	9	1	1	0-...	59.0	42	22	21	5	11-0	46
2000—Hickory (S.Atl.)................	11	9	.550	2.96	24	24	1	1	0-...	170.0	145	66	56	14	39-2	193
—Lynchburg (Caro.)...........	1	0	1.000	6.55	2	2	0	0	0-...	11.0	18	8	8	2	3-0	8
2001—Altoona (East.)................	5	2	.714	2.61	9	8	1	0	0-...	58.2	45	17	17	8	12-0	39
—Nashville (PCL)...............	1	1	.500	3.38	2	2	0	0	0-...	10.2	9	5	4	3	5-0	6
—Pittsburgh (N.L.).............	3	7	.300	3.71	22	18	0	0	0-0	114.0	100	53	47	15	45-4	57
2002—Pittsburgh (N.L.).............	2	5	.286	4.98	9	9	0	0	0-0	43.1	38	26	24	9	24-2	33
Major League totals (2 years).....	5	12	.294	4.06	31	27	0	0	0-0	157.1	138	79	71	24	69-6	90

WILLIAMS, GERALD OF

PERSONAL: Born August 10, 1966, in New Orleans. ... 6-2/187. ... Bats right, throws right. ... Full name: Gerald Floyd Williams.
HIGH SCHOOL: East St. John (Reserve, La.).
COLLEGE: Grambling State.
TRANSACTIONS/CAREER NOTES: Selected by New York Yankees organization in 14th round of free-agent draft (June 2, 1987). ... Traded by Yankees with P Bob Wickman to Milwaukee Brewers for P Graeme Lloyd and OF Pat Listach (August 23, 1996). ... Traded by Brewers to Atlanta Braves for P Chad Fox (December 11, 1997). ... Granted free agency (November 3, 1999). ... Signed by Tampa Bay Devil Rays (December 19, 1999). ... On suspended list (September 22-25, 2000). ... Released by Devil Rays (June 24, 2001). ... Signed by New York Yankees (June 28, 2001). ... Released by Yankees (June 5, 2002). ... Signed by St. Louis Cardinals organization (June 12, 2002). ... Contract purchased by Cincinnati Reds organization from Cardinals (July 12, 2002). ... Granted free agency (October 15, 2002).
STATISTICAL NOTES: Led Carolina League outfielders with 292 putouts and 307 total chances in 1989. ... Led International League outfielders with 332 putouts, 14 assists and 354 total chances in 1992. ... Tied for International League lead in double plays by outfielder with five in 1992. ... Collected six hits in one game (May 1, 1996). ... Had 15-game hitting streak (July 23-August 13, 1999). ... Career major league grand slams: 3.
2002 GAMES PLAYED BY POSITION (MLB): OF—30; DH—1.

			BATTING														FIELDING	
Year	Team (League)	Pos.	G	AB	R	H	2B	3B	HR	RBI	BB	SO	SB-CS	Avg.	OBP	SLG	E	Avg.
1987—	Oneonta (NY-Penn)	OF	29	115	26	42	6	2	2	29	16	18	6-2	.365	.447	.504	3	.959
1988—	Prince William (Caro.)	OF	54	159	20	29	3	0	2	18	15	47	6-1	.182	.251	.239	3	.961
—	Fort Lauderdale (FSL)	OF	63	212	21	40	7	2	2	17	16	56	4-3	.189	.255	.269	6	.965
1989—	Prince William (Caro.)	OF	134	454	63	104	19	6	13	69	51	120	15-10	.229	.316	.383	8	.974
1990—	Fort Lauderdale (FSL)	OF	50	204	25	59	4	5	7	43	16	52	19-5	.289	.344	.461	3	.975
—	Albany/Colonie (East.)	OF	96	324	54	81	17	2	13	58	35	74	18-8	.250	.324	.435	7	.969
1991—	Albany/Colonie (East.)	OF	45	175	28	50	15	0	5	32	18	26	18-3	.286	.347	.457	3	.974
—	Columbus (I.L.)	OF	61	198	20	51	8	3	2	27	16	39	9-12	.258	.309	.359	3	.977
1992—	Columbus (I.L.)	OF	*142	547	92	*156	31	6	16	86	38	98	36-14	.285	.334	.452	8	.977
—	New York (A.L.)	OF	15	27	7	8	2	0	3	6	0	3	2-0	.296	.296	.704	2	.913
1993—	Columbus (I.L.)	OF	87	336	53	95	19	6	8	38	20	66	29-12	.283	.321	.446	3	.985
—	New York (A.L.)	OF-DH	42	67	11	10	2	3	0	6	1	14	2-0	.149	.183	.269	2	.956
1994—	New York (A.L.)	OF-DH	57	86	19	25	8	0	4	13	4	17	1-3	.291	.319	.523	2	.957
1995—	New York (A.L.)	OF-DH	100	182	33	45	18	2	6	28	22	34	4-2	.247	.327	.467	1	.993
1996—	New York (A.L.)	OF-DH	99	233	37	63	15	4	5	30	15	39	7-8	.270	.319	.433	3	.978
—	Milwaukee (A.L.)■	OF	26	92	6	19	4	0	0	4	4	18	3-1	.207	.247	.250	1	.987
1997—	Milwaukee (A.L.)	OF-DH	155	566	73	143	32	2	10	41	19	90	23-9	.253	.282	.369	3	.992
1998—	Atlanta (N.L.)■	OF	129	266	46	81	19	2	10	44	17	48	11-5	.305	.352	.504	5	.970
1999—	Atlanta (N.L.)	OF	143	422	76	116	24	1	17	68	33	67	19-11	.275	.335	.457	3	.985
2000—	Tampa Bay (A.L.)■	OF-DH	146	632	87	173	30	2	21	89	34	103	12-12	.274	.312	.427	6	.983
2001—	Tampa Bay (A.L.)	OF	62	232	30	48	17	0	4	17	13	42	10-4	.207	.261	.332	2	.989
—	New York (A.L.)■	OF-DH	38	47	12	8	1	0	0	2	5	13	3-1	.170	.264	.191	1	.967
2002—	New York (A.L.)	OF-DH	33	17	6	0	0	0	0	0	2	4	2-0	.000	.105	.000	0	1.000
—	Memphis (PCL)■	OF	21	73	11	11	3	0	1	3	3	8	2-0	.151	.195	.233	0	1.000
—	Louisville (I.L.)■	OF	48	205	29	54	10	3	2	12	11	36	6-4	.263	.307	.371	1	.992
American League totals (9 years)			773	2181	321	542	129	13	53	236	119	377	69-40	.249	.292	.392	23	.984
National League totals (2 years)			272	688	122	197	43	3	27	112	50	115	30-16	.286	.341	.475	8	.978
Major League totals (11 years)			1045	2869	443	739	172	16	80	348	169	492	99-56	.258	.304	.412	31	.983

DIVISION SERIES RECORD

			BATTING														FIELDING	
Year	Team (League)	Pos.	G	AB	R	H	2B	3B	HR	RBI	BB	SO	SB-CS	Avg.	OBP	SLG	E	Avg.
1995—	New York (A.L.)	OF-PR	5	5	1	0	0	0	0	0	2	3	0-0	.000	.286	.000	0	1.000
1998—	Atlanta (N.L.)	OF	2	2	1	1	0	0	0	1	0	1	0-0	.500	.500	.500	0	1.000
1999—	Atlanta (N.L.)	OF	4	18	2	7	1	0	0	3	0	3	1-0	.389	.389	.444	0	1.000
Division series totals (3 years)			11	25	4	8	1	0	0	4	2	7	1-0	.320	.370	.360	0	1.000

CHAMPIONSHIP SERIES RECORD

RECORDS: Shares single-game record for most strikeouts—4 (October 10, 1998).

			BATTING														FIELDING	
Year	Team (League)	Pos.	G	AB	R	H	2B	3B	HR	RBI	BB	SO	SB-CS	Avg.	OBP	SLG	E	Avg.
1998—	Atlanta (N.L.)	PH-OF	5	13	0	2	0	0	0	0	1	6	1-0	.154	.214	.154	0	1.000
1999—	Atlanta (N.L.)	OF	6	28	4	5	2	0	0	1	2	2	3-1	.179	.258	.250	1	.923
Championship series totals (2 years)			11	41	4	7	2	0	0	1	3	8	4-1	.171	.244	.220	1	.938

WORLD SERIES RECORD

			BATTING														FIELDING	
Year	Team (League)	Pos.	G	AB	R	H	2B	3B	HR	RBI	BB	SO	SB-CS	Avg.	OBP	SLG	E	Avg.
1999—	Atlanta (N.L.)	OF	4	17	2	3	0	1	0	0	0	4	0-0	.176	.176	.294	0	1.000

W

WILLIAMS, JEFF P DODGERS

PERSONAL: Born June 6, 1972, in Canberra, Australia. ... 6-0/185. ... Throws left, bats right. ... Full name: Jeffrey F. Williams.
COLLEGE: Hawker (Canberra, Australia), then Southeastern Louisiana.
TRANSACTIONS/CAREER NOTES: Signed as non-drafted free agent by Los Angeles Dodgers organization (July 3, 1996). ... On Los Angeles disabled list (April 20-June 27, 2000). ... On Las Vegas disabled list (April 25-May 6, 2001).
CAREER HITTING (MLB): 2-for-11 (.182), 2 R, 0 2B, 0 3B, 0 HR, 0 RBI.

Year	League	W	L	Pct.	ERA	G	GS	CG	ShO	Sv.-Opp.	IP	H	R	ER	HR	BB-IBB	SO
1997—	San Bernardino (Calif.).....	10	4	.714	3.10	18	18	0	0	0-...	116.0	101	52	40	8	34-0	72
	—San Antonio (Texas).........	2	1	.667	5.81	5	5	0	0	0-...	26.1	30	17	17	2	7-0	14
1998—	San Antonio (Texas).........	3	0	1.000	2.59	7	7	0	0	0-...	41.2	43	19	12	3	13-1	35
	—Albuquerque (PCL)...........	8	8	.500	4.98	21	21	0	0	0-...	121.0	160	87	67	14	49-0	93
1999—	Albuquerque (PCL)...........	9	7	.563	5.01	42	14	1	1	4-...	125.2	151	77	70	14	47-2	86
	—Los Angeles (N.L.)	2	0	1.000	4.08	5	3	0	0	0-0	17.2	12	10	8	2	9-0	7
2000—	Albuquerque (PCL)...........	4	3	.571	4.26	12	12	0	0	0-...	63.1	64	33	30	6	28-0	38
	—Los Angeles (N.L.)	0	0	...	15.88	7	0	0	0	0-1	5.2	12	11	10	1	8-0	3
2001—	Las Vegas (PCL)	7	5	.583	3.97	16	16	1	1	0-...	90.2	102	49	40	12	24-0	61
	—Los Angeles (N.L.)	2	1	.667	6.29	15	1	0	0	0-0	24.1	26	18	17	5	17-1	9
2002—	Las Vegas (PCL)	6	4	.600	2.60	56	0	0	0	*28-...	79.2	80	25	23	3	22-0	75
	—Los Angeles (N.L.)	0	0	...	11.70	10	0	0	0	0-0	10.0	15	13	13	2	7-0	11
Major League totals (4 years).....		4	1	.800	7.49	37	4	0	0	0-1	57.2	65	52	48	10	41-1	30

WILLIAMS, MATT — 3B — DIAMONDBACKS

PERSONAL: Born November 28, 1965, in Bishop, Calif. ... 6-2/219. ... Bats right, throws right. ... Full name: Matthew Derrick Williams. ... Grandson of Bartholomew (Bart) Griffith, outfielder/first baseman with Brooklyn Dodgers and Washington Senators (1922-24).

HIGH SCHOOL: Carson (Nev.).

COLLEGE: UNLV.

TRANSACTIONS/CAREER NOTES: Selected by New York Mets organization in 27th round of free-agent draft (June 6, 1983); did not sign. ... Selected by San Francisco Giants organization in first round (third pick overall) of free-agent draft (June 2, 1986). ... On disabled list (June 28-July 14, 1993). ... On San Francisco disabled list (June 4-August 19, 1995); included rehabilitation assignments to San Jose (July 24-25 and August 13-19). ... On disabled list (August 5, 1996-remainder of season). ... Traded by Giants with a player to be named later to Cleveland Indians for IF Jeff Kent, IF Jose Vizcaino, P Julian Tavarez and a player to be named later (November 13, 1996); Giants traded OF Trenidad Hubbard to Indians for P Joe Roa to complete deal (December 16, 1996). ... Traded by Indians to Arizona Diamondbacks for 3B Travis Fryman, P Tom Martin and cash (December 1, 1997). ... On Arizona disabled list (July 18-August 3, 1998); included rehabilitation assignment to Tucson (July 31-August 3). ... On Arizona disabled list (March 29-May 23 and June 25-July 13, 2000); included rehabilitation assignments to El Paso (May 16-23) and High Desert (July 8-10). ... On Arizona disabled list (May 18-July 12, 2001); included rehabilitation assignment to Tucson (July 4-12). ... On Arizona disabled list (March 22-July 11, 2002); included rehabilitation assignments to Tucson (June 26-July 4) and Lancaster (July 4-11).

RECORDS: Shares major league record for most home runs in two consecutive games—5 (April 25 [3] and 26 [2], 1997).

HONORS: Named shortstop on The Sporting News college All-America team (1986). ... Named third baseman on The Sporting News N.L. All-Star team (1990 and 1993-94). ... Named third baseman on The Sporting News N.L. Silver Slugger team (1990 and 1993-94). ... Won N.L. Gold Glove at third base (1991 and 1993-94). ... Named third baseman on The Sporting News A.L. All-Star team (1997). ... Won A.L. Gold Glove at third base (1997). ... Named third baseman on The Sporting News A.L. Silver Slugger team (1997).

STATISTICAL NOTES: Led N.L. third basemen with 33 double plays in 1990 and 1992 and 34 in 1993. ... Led N.L. third basemen with 140 putouts and tied for league lead with 465 total chances in 1990. ... Led N.L. third basemen with 131 putouts in 1991. ... Led N.L. third basemen with 235 assists and 326 total chances in 1994. ... Hit three home runs in one game (April 25, 1997). ... Had 24-game hitting streak (August 13-September 8, 1997). ... Had 19-game hitting streak (May 26-June 18, 1999). ... Career major league grand slams: 11.

2002 GAMES PLAYED BY POSITION (MLB): 3B—56.

			BATTING														FIELDING	
Year	Team (League)	Pos.	G	AB	R	H	2B	3B	HR	RBI	BB	SO	SB-CS	Avg.	OBP	SLG	E	Avg.
1986—	Everett (N'West).........	SS	4	17	3	4	0	1	1	10	1	4	0-0	.235	.263	.529	2	.882
	—Clinton (Midw.)	SS	68	250	32	60	14	3	7	29	23	62	3-3	.240	.308	.404	10	.960
1987—	Phoenix (PCL)...........	3B-2B-SS	56	211	36	61	15	2	6	37	19	53	6-2	.289	.345	.464	14	.931
	—San Francisco (N.L.) ..	SS-3B	84	245	28	46	9	2	8	21	16	68	4-3	.188	.240	.339	9	.975
1988—	Phoenix (PCL)...........	3B-SS-2B-OF	82	306	45	83	19	1	12	51	13	56	6-5	.271	.299	.458	13	.946
	—San Francisco (N.L.) ..	3B-SS	52	156	17	32	6	1	8	19	8	41	0-1	.205	.251	.410	7	.957
1989—	San Francisco (N.L.) ..	3B-SS	84	292	31	59	18	1	18	50	14	72	1-2	.202	.242	.455	10	.963
	—Phoenix (PCL)...........	3B-SS-OF	76	284	61	91	20	2	26	61	32	51	9-3	.320	.394	.680	11	.958
1990—	San Francisco (N.L.) ..	3B	159	617	87	171	27	2	33	*122	33	138	7-4	.277	.319	.488	19	.959
1991—	San Francisco (N.L.) ..	3B-SS	157	589	72	158	24	5	34	98	33	128	5-5	.268	.310	.499	16	.964
1992—	San Francisco (N.L.) ..	3B	146	529	58	120	13	5	20	66	39	109	7-7	.227	.286	.384	*23	.945
1993—	San Francisco (N.L.) ..	3B	145	579	105	170	33	4	38	110	27	80	1-3	.294	.325	.561	12	.970
1994—	San Francisco (N.L.) ..	3B	112	445	74	119	16	3	*43	96	33	87	1-0	.267	.319	.607	12	.963
1995—	San Francisco (N.L.) ..	3B	76	283	53	95	17	1	23	65	30	58	2-0	.336	.399	.647	10	.958
	—San Jose (Calif.).........	3B	4	11	2	2	0	0	1	2	0	3	0-0	.182	.250	.455	0	1.000
1996—	San Francisco (N.L.) ..	3B-1B-SS	105	404	69	122	16	1	22	85	39	91	1-2	.302	.367	.510	14	.962
1997—	Cleveland (A.L.)■.......	3B	151	596	86	157	32	3	32	105	34	108	12-4	.263	.307	.488	12	.970
1998—	Arizona (N.L.)■..........	3B	135	510	72	136	26	1	20	71	43	102	5-1	.267	.327	.439	11	.972
	—Tucson (PCL)	3B	2	5	0	1	0	0	0	0	0	0	0-0	.200	.200	.200	0	1.000
1999—	Arizona (N.L.)............	3B	154	627	98	190	37	2	35	142	41	93	2-0	.303	.344	.536	10	.977
2000—	El Paso (Texas)..........	3B	5	13	3	6	2	0	0	1	2	1	0-0	.462	.533	.615	0	1.000
	—Arizona (N.L.)............	3B-DH	96	371	43	102	18	2	12	47	20	51	1-2	.275	.315	.431	9	.964
	—High Desert (Calif.).....	3B	2	8	1	3	0	0	1	1	0	1	0-0	.375	.375	.750	0	1.000
2001—	Arizona (N.L.)............	3B-SS	106	408	58	112	30	0	16	65	22	70	1-0	.275	.314	.466	9	.964
	—Tucson (PCL)	3B	5	17	4	6	2	0	2	5	2	2	1-0	.353	.421	.824	1	.833
2002—	Arizona (N.L.)............	3B	60	215	29	56	7	2	12	40	21	41	3-1	.260	.324	.479	4	.969
	—Tucson (PCL)	3B	5	15	1	3	0	0	1	3	0	0	0-0	.200	.200	.400	1	.875
	—Lancaster (Calif.)........	3B	4	12	2	4	1	0	1	5	2	1	0-0	.333	.429	.667	1	.889
American League totals (1 year)			151	596	86	157	32	3	32	105	34	108	12-4	.263	.307	.488	12	.970
National League totals (15 years)			1671	6270	894	1688	297	32	342	1097	419	1229	41-31	.269	.317	.490	175	.964
Major League totals (16 years)			1822	6866	980	1845	329	35	374	1202	453	1337	53-35	.269	.316	.490	187	.965

DIVISION SERIES RECORD

			BATTING														FIELDING	
Year	Team (League)	Pos.	G	AB	R	H	2B	3B	HR	RBI	BB	SO	SB-CS	Avg.	OBP	SLG	E	Avg.
1997—	Cleveland (A.L.)..........	3B	5	17	4	4	1	0	1	3	3	3	0-0	.235	.381	.471	0	1.000
1999—	Arizona (N.L.)............	3B	4	16	3	6	1	0	0	0	0	1	0-0	.375	.375	.438	0	1.000
2001—	Arizona (N.L.)............	3B	5	16	0	1	1	0	0	0	4	4	0-0	.063	.250	.125	1	.944
2002—	Arizona (N.L.)............	3B	3	12	0	1	0	0	0	0	0	3	0-0	.083	.083	.083	0	1.000
Division series totals (4 years)			17	61	7	12	3	0	1	3	7	11	0-0	.197	.290	.295	1	.979

CHAMPIONSHIP SERIES RECORD

RECORDS: Holds N.L. single-series record for most runs batted in—9 (1989).

			BATTING														FIELDING	
Year	**Team (League)**	**Pos.**	**G**	**AB**	**R**	**H**	**2B**	**3B**	**HR**	**RBI**	**BB**	**SO**	**SB-CS**	**Avg.**	**OBP**	**SLG**	**E**	**Avg.**
1987—	San Francisco (N.L.) ..								Did not play.									
1989—	San Francisco (N.L.) ..	3B-SS	5	20	2	6	1	0	2	9	0	2	0-0	.300	.333	.650	0	1.000
1997—	Cleveland (A.L.).........	3B	6	23	1	5	1	0	0	2	3	7	1-0	.217	.308	.261	2	.923
2001—	Arizona (N.L.)............	3B	5	18	1	5	1	0	0	2	2	3	0-0	.278	.350	.333	3	.824
Championship series totals (3 years)			16	61	4	16	3	0	2	13	5	12	1-0	.262	.328	.410	5	.917

WORLD SERIES RECORD

RECORDS: Shares single-inning record for most at-bats—2 (November 3, 2001, third inning). ... Shares single-inning record for most hits—2 (November 3, 2001, third inning). ... Holds single-inning record for most doubles—2 (November 3, 2001, third inning).
NOTES: Member of World Series championship team (2001).

			BATTING														FIELDING	
Year	**Team (League)**	**Pos.**	**G**	**AB**	**R**	**H**	**2B**	**3B**	**HR**	**RBI**	**BB**	**SO**	**SB-CS**	**Avg.**	**OBP**	**SLG**	**E**	**Avg.**
1989—	San Francisco (N.L.) ..	SS-3B	4	16	1	2	0	0	1	1	0	6	0-0	.125	.125	.313	0	1.000
1997—	Cleveland (A.L.).........	3B	7	26	8	10	1	0	1	3	7	6	0-0	.385	.515	.538	0	1.000
2001—	Arizona (N.L.)............	3B	7	26	3	7	2	0	1	7	0	6	0-0	.269	.250	.462	0	1.000
World Series totals (3 years)			18	68	12	19	3	0	3	11	7	18	0-0	.279	.338	.456	0	1.000

ALL-STAR GAME RECORD

NOTES: Named to N.L. All-Star team for 1996 game; replaced by Ken Caminiti due to injury.

	AB	**R**	**H**	**2B**	**3B**	**HR**	**RBI**	**BB**	**SO**	**SB-CS**	**Avg.**	**OBP**	**SLG**	**E**	**Avg.**
All-Star Game totals (3 years)	7	0	1	0	0	0	0	0	4	0-1	.143	.143	.143	2	.500

WILLIAMS, MIKE   P   PIRATES

PERSONAL: Born July 29, 1968, in Radford, Va. ... 6-2/200. ... Throws right, bats right. ... Full name: Michael Darren Williams.
HIGH SCHOOL: Giles (Pearisburg, Va.).
COLLEGE: Virginia Tech.
TRANSACTIONS/CAREER NOTES: Selected by Philadelphia Phillies organization in 14th round of free-agent draft (June 4, 1990). ... On suspended list (September 26, 1996-remainder of season). ... Granted free agency (December 20, 1996). ... Signed by Boston Red Sox organization (February 15, 1997). ... Released by Red Sox (March 14, 1997). ... Signed by Kansas City Royals organization (April 30, 1997). ... On suspended list (May 16-18, 1997). ... Granted free agency (October 15, 1997). ... Signed by Pittsburgh Pirates organization (December 18, 1997). ... On disabled list (June 24-July 9, 1999). ... Traded by Pirates to Houston Astros for P Tony McKnight (July 31, 2001). ... Granted free agency (November 5, 2001). ... Signed by Pirates (January 7, 2002).
STATISTICAL NOTES: Led N.L. with 16 wild pitches in 1996.
MISCELLANEOUS: Appeared in one game as pinch runner (1996).
CAREER HITTING (MLB): 17-for-108 (.157), 7 R, 2 2B, 0 3B, 0 HR, 7 RBI.

Year	**League**	**W**	**L**	**Pct.**	**ERA**	**G**	**GS**	**CG**	**ShO**	**Sv.-Opp.**	**IP**	**H**	**R**	**ER**	**HR**	**BB-IBB**	**SO**
1990—	Batavia (NY-Penn)............	2	3	.400	2.30	27	0	0	0	11-...	47.0	39	17	12	0	13-4	42
1991—	Clearwater (FSL).............	7	3	.700	1.74	14	14	2	1	0-...	93.1	65	23	18	5	14-0	76
	—Reading (East.)................	7	5	.583	3.69	16	15	2	1	0-...	102.1	93	44	42	1	36-0	51
1992—	Reading (East.)..................	1	2	.333	5.17	3	3	0	0	0-...	15.2	17	10	9	1	7-0	12
	—Scranton/W.B. (I.L.).........	9	1	*.900	2.43	16	16	3	1	0-...	92.2	84	26	25	4	30-2	59
	—Philadelphia (N.L.)...........	1	1	.500	5.34	5	5	1	0	0-0	28.2	29	20	17	3	7-0	5
1993—	Scranton/W.B. (I.L.).........	9	2	*.818	2.87	14	13	1	1	0-...	97.1	93	34	31	7	16-0	53
	—Philadelphia (N.L.)...........	1	3	.250	5.29	17	4	0	0	0-0	51.0	50	32	30	5	22-2	33
1994—	Philadelphia (N.L.)...........	2	4	.333	5.01	12	8	0	0	0-0	50.1	61	31	28	7	20-3	29
	—Scranton/W.B. (I.L.).........	2	7	.222	5.79	14	14	1	0	0-...	84.0	91	55	54	14	36-0	53
1995—	Philadelphia (N.L.)...........	3	3	.500	3.29	33	8	0	0	0-0	87.2	78	37	32	10	29-2	57
	—Scranton/W.B. (I.L.).........	0	1	.000	4.66	3	3	1	0	0-...	9.2	8	5	5	0	2-0	8
1996—	Philadelphia (N.L.)...........	6	14	.300	5.44	32	29	0	0	0-0	167.0	188	107	101	25	67-6	103
1997—	Omaha (A.A.)■	3	6	.333	4.22	20	11	1	0	5-...	79.0	71	41	37	10	38-0	68
	—Kansas City (A.L.)...........	0	2	.000	6.43	10	0	0	0	1-1	14.0	20	11	10	1	8-1	10
1998—	Pittsburgh (N.L.)■	4	2	.667	1.94	37	1	0	0	0-1	51.0	39	12	11	1	16-4	59
	—Nashville (PCL)...............	0	2	.000	5.59	16	4	0	0	1-...	37.0	36	25	23	11	14-2	34
1999—	Pittsburgh (N.L.).............	3	4	.429	5.09	58	0	0	0	23-28	58.1	63	36	33	9	37-7	76
2000—	Pittsburgh (N.L.).............	3	4	.429	3.50	72	0	0	0	24-29	72.0	56	34	28	8	40-3	71
2001—	Pittsburgh (N.L.).............	2	4	.333	3.67	40	0	0	0	22-24	41.2	39	18	17	6	21-2	43
	—Houston (N.L.)■	4	0	1.000	4.03	25	0	0	0	0-1	22.1	21	10	10	3	14-1	16
2002—	Pittsburgh (N.L.)■	2	6	.250	2.93	59	0	0	0	46-50	61.1	54	24	20	6	21-3	43
A.L. totals (1 year).......................		0	2	.000	6.43	10	0	0	0	1-1	14.0	20	11	10	1	8-1	10
N.L. totals (10 years)....................		31	45	.408	4.26	390	55	1	0	115-133	691.1	678	361	327	83	294-33	535
Major League totals (11 years)...		31	47	.397	4.30	400	55	1	0	116-134	705.1	698	372	337	84	302-34	545

DIVISION SERIES RECORD

Year	**League**	**W**	**L**	**Pct.**	**ERA**	**G**	**GS**	**CG**	**ShO**	**Sv.-Opp.**	**IP**	**H**	**R**	**ER**	**HR**	**BB-IBB**	**SO**
2001—	Houston (N.L.).................	0	0	...	9.00	1	0	0	0	0-0	1.0	3	1	1	1	0-0	1

ALL-STAR GAME RECORD

	W	**L**	**Pct.**	**ERA**	**GS**	**CG**	**ShO**	**Sv.-Opp.**	**IP**	**H**	**R**	**ER**	**HR**	**BB-IBB**	**SO**
All-Star Game totals (1 year)........	0	0	...	0.00	0	0	0	0-0	1.0	0	0	0	0	0-0	2

WILLIAMS, WOODY   P

PERSONAL: Born August 19, 1966, in Houston. ... 6-0/195. ... Throws right, bats right. ... Full name: Gregory Scott Williams.
HIGH SCHOOL: Cypress-Fairbanks (Houston).
COLLEGE: Houston.
TRANSACTIONS/CAREER NOTES: Selected by Toronto Blue Jays organization in 28th round of free-agent draft (June 1, 1988). ... On disabled list (April 9-May 17, 1992). ... On Toronto disabled list (July 17, 1995-remainder of season); included rehabilitation assignment to Syracuse

(August 15-25). ... On Toronto disabled list (March 22-May 31 and June 11-July 26, 1996); included rehabilitation assignments to Dunedin (May 2-10), Syracuse (May 10-28 and July 13-20) and St. Catharines (July 20-26). ... Traded by Blue Jays with P Carlos Almanzar and OF Peter Tucci to San Diego Padres for P Joey Hamilton (December 13, 1998). ... On San Diego disabled list (May 2-July 2, 2000); included rehabilitation assignment to Rancho Cucamonga (June 22-27) and Las Vegas (June 28). ... Traded by Padres to St. Louis Cardinals for OF Ray Lankford and cash (August 2, 2001). ... On St. Louis disabled list (April 6-May 15 and July 7-August 29, 2002); included rehabilitation assignment to Memphis (August 24-26). ... Granted free agency (October 30, 2002).

MISCELLANEOUS: Appeared in one game as pinch runner (1999). ... Scored three runs in four appearances as pinch runner (2000). ... Struck out twice in two appearances as pinch hitter (2000). ... Appeared in two games as pinch runner (2001). ... Appeared in one game as pinch hitter (2001).

CAREER HITTING (MLB): 53-for-250 (.212), 28 R, 16 2B, 0 3B, 2 HR, 25 RBI.

Year League	W	L	Pct.	ERA	G	GS	CG	ShO	Sv.-Opp.	IP	H	R	ER	HR	BB-IBB	SO
1988—St. Catharines (NY-Penn)	8	2	.800	1.54	12	12	2	0	0-...	76.0	48	22	13	1	21-0	58
—Knoxville (Sou.)	2	2	.500	3.81	6	4	0	0	0-...	28.1	27	13	12	1	12-0	25
1989—Dunedin (FSL)	3	5	.375	2.32	20	9	0	0	3-...	81.1	63	26	21	3	27-1	60
—Knoxville (Sou.)	3	5	.375	3.55	14	12	2	•2	1-...	71.0	61	32	28	6	33-2	51
1990—Knoxville (Sou.)	7	9	.438	3.14	42	12	0	0	5-...	126.0	111	55	44	7	39-3	74
—Syracuse (I.L.)	0	1	.000	10.00	3	0	0	0	0-...	9.0	15	10	10	1	4-0	8
1991—Knoxville (Sou.)	3	2	.600	3.59	18	1	0	0	3-...	42.2	42	18	17	1	14-0	37
—Syracuse (I.L.)	3	4	.429	4.12	31	0	0	0	6-...	54.2	52	27	25	2	27-3	37
1992—Syracuse (I.L.)	6	8	.429	3.13	25	16	1	0	1-...	120.2	115	46	42	4	41-0	81
1993—Syracuse (I.L.)	1	1	.500	2.20	12	0	0	0	3-...	16.1	15	5	4	2	5-3	16
—Toronto (A.L.)	3	1	.750	4.38	30	0	0	0	0-2	37.0	40	18	18	2	22-3	24
—Dunedin (FSL)	0	0	...	0.00	2	0	0	0	0-...	4.0	0	0	0	0	2-0	2
1994—Toronto (A.L.)	1	3	.250	3.64	38	0	0	0	0-0	59.1	44	24	24	5	33-1	56
—Syracuse (I.L.)	0	0	...	0.00	1	0	0	0	1-...	1.2	0	0	0	0	0-0	1
1995—Toronto (A.L.)	1	2	.333	3.69	23	3	0	0	0-1	53.2	44	23	22	6	28-1	41
—Syracuse (I.L.)	0	0	...	3.52	5	1	0	0	1-...	7.2	5	3	3	0	5-0	13
1996—Dunedin (FSL)	0	2	.000	8.22	2	2	0	0	0-...	7.2	9	7	7	1	2-0	11
—Syracuse (I.L.)	3	1	.750	1.41	7	7	1	1	0-...	32.0	22	5	5	3	7-0	33
—Toronto (A.L.)	4	5	.444	4.73	12	10	1	0	0-0	59.0	64	33	31	8	21-1	43
—St. Catharines (NY-Penn)	0	0	...	3.68	2	2	0	0	0-...	7.1	7	3	3	0	4-0	12
1997—Toronto (A.L.)	9	14	.391	4.35	31	31	0	0	0-0	194.2	201	98	94	31	66-3	124
1998—Toronto (A.L.)	10	9	.526	4.46	32	32	1	1	0-0	209.2	196	112	104	36	81-3	151
1999—San Diego (N.L.)■	12	12	.500	4.41	33	33	0	0	0-0	208.1	213	106	102	33	73-5	137
2000—San Diego (N.L.)	10	8	.556	3.75	23	23	4	0	0-0	168.0	152	74	70	23	54-2	111
—Rancho Cuca. (Calif.)	0	0	...	0.00	1	1	0	0	0-...	5.0	3	0	0	0	0-0	10
—Las Vegas (PCL)	0	0	...	1.50	1	1	0	0	0-...	6.0	7	2	1	1	0-0	5
2001—San Diego (N.L.)	8	8	.500	4.97	23	23	0	0	0-0	145.0	170	88	80	28	37-4	102
—St. Louis (N.L.)■	7	1	.875	2.28	11	11	3	1	0-0	75.0	54	22	19	7	19-1	52
2002—St. Louis (N.L.)	9	4	.692	2.53	17	17	1	0	0-0	103.1	84	30	29	10	25-2	76
—Memphis (PCL)	1	0	1.000	1.80	1	1	0	0	0-...	5.0	1	1	1	0	1-0	7
A.L. totals (6 years)	28	34	.452	4.30	166	76	2	1	0-3	613.1	589	308	293	88	251-12	439
N.L. totals (4 years)	46	33	.582	3.86	107	107	8	1	0-0	699.2	673	320	300	101	208-14	478
Major League totals (10 years)	74	67	.525	4.06	273	183	10	2	0-3	1313.0	1262	628	593	189	459-26	917

DIVISION SERIES RECORD

Year League	W	L	Pct.	ERA	G	GS	CG	ShO	Sv.-Opp.	IP	H	R	ER	HR	BB-IBB	SO
2001—St. Louis (N.L.)	1	0	1.000	1.29	1	1	0	0	0-0	7.0	4	1	1	0	1-0	9

CHAMPIONSHIP SERIES RECORD

Year League	W	L	Pct.	ERA	G	GS	CG	ShO	Sv.-Opp.	IP	H	R	ER	HR	BB-IBB	SO
2002—St. Louis (N.L.)	0	1	.000	4.50	1	1	0	0	0-0	6.0	6	3	3	2	1-0	7

WILLIAMSON, SCOTT P REDS

PERSONAL: Born February 17, 1976, in Fort Polk, La. ... 6-0/185. ... Throws right, bats right. ... Full name: Scott Ryan Williamson.

HIGH SCHOOL: Friendswood (Texas).

COLLEGE: Tulane, then Oklahoma State.

TRANSACTIONS/CAREER NOTES: Selected by Cincinnati Reds organization in ninth round of free-agent draft (June 3, 1997). ... On disabled list (August 24-September 8, 2000; and April 4, 2001-remainder of season).

RECORDS: Shares N.L. single-game record for most consecutive strikeouts by relief pitcher—6 (May 27, 1999).

HONORS: Named N.L. Rookie Pitcher of the Year by The Sporting News (1999). ... Named N.L. Rookie of the Year by Baseball Writers' Association of America (1999).

STATISTICAL NOTES: Tied for Pioneer League lead with 12 wild pitches in 1997.

CAREER HITTING (MLB): 1-for-23 (.043), 1 R, 0 2B, 0 3B, 0 HR, 0 RBI.

Year League	W	L	Pct.	ERA	G	GS	CG	ShO	Sv.-Opp.	IP	H	R	ER	HR	BB-IBB	SO
1997—Billings (Pio.)	•8	2	.800	1.78	13	13	2	•1	0-...	86.0	66	25	17	5	23-0	*101
1998—Chattanooga (Sou.)	4	5	.444	3.78	18	18	0	0	0-...	100.0	85	49	42	4	46-4	105
—Indianapolis (I.L.)	0	0	...	3.48	5	5	0	0	0-...	20.2	20	9	8	2	9-0	17
1999—Cincinnati (N.L.)	12	7	.632	2.41	62	0	0	0	19-26	93.1	54	29	25	8	43-6	107
2000—Cincinnati (N.L.)	5	8	.385	3.29	48	10	0	0	6-8	112.0	92	45	41	7	75-7	136
2001—Cincinnati (N.L.)	0	0	...	0.00	2	0	0	0	0-0	.2	1	0	0	0	2-0	0
2002—Cincinnati (N.L.)	3	4	.429	2.92	63	0	0	0	8-12	74.0	46	27	24	5	36-5	84
Major League totals (4 years)	20	19	.513	2.89	175	10	0	0	33-46	280.0	193	101	90	20	156-18	327

ALL-STAR GAME RECORD

	W	L	Pct.	ERA	GS	CG	ShO	Sv.-Opp.	IP	H	R	ER	HR	BB-IBB	SO
All-Star Game totals (1 year)	1999—Selected, did not play.														

WILSON, CRAIG OF/1B PIRATES

PERSONAL: Born November 30, 1976, in Fountain Valley, Calif. ... 6-2/225. ... Bats right, throws right. ... Full name: Craig Alan Wilson.

HIGH SCHOOL: Marina (Huntington Beach, Calif.).

TRANSACTIONS/CAREER NOTES: Selected by Toronto Blue Jays organization in second round of free-agent draft (June 1, 1995). ... Traded by Blue jays to Pittsburgh Pirates (December 11, 1996), completing deal in which Pirates traded 2B Carlos Garcia, 1B Orlando Merced and P Dan Plesac to Blue Jays for P Mike Halperin, SS Abraham Nunez, P Jose Pett, P Jose Silva, SS Brandon Cromer and a player to be named later (November 14, 1996).

RECORDS: Shares major league single-season record for most home runs by pinch-hitter—7 (2001).

STATISTICAL NOTES: Led Carolina League catchers with 21 double plays in 1997. ... Led N.L. with 21 being hit by pitch in 2002.

2002 GAMES PLAYED BY POSITION (MLB): OF—75; 1B—42; C—5; DH—3.

			BATTING														FIELDING	
Year	Team (League)	Pos.	G	AB	R	H	2B	3B	HR	RBI	BB	SO	SB-CS	Avg.	OBP	SLG	E	Avg.
1995—	Medicine Hat (Pio.)	C	49	184	33	52	14	1	7	35	24	44	8-2	.283	.367	.484	5	.982
1996—	Hagerstown (S.Atl.)	C-OF	131	495	66	129	27	5	11	70	32	120	17-11	.261	.316	.402	9	.986
1997—	Lynchburg (Caro.)■	C	117	401	54	106	26	1	19	69	39	98	6-5	.264	.350	.476	12	.985
1998—	Lynchburg (Caro.)	C-1B	61	219	26	59	12	2	12	45	22	53	2-1	.269	.348	.507	6	.986
—	Carolina (Sou.)	C	45	148	20	49	11	0	5	21	14	32	4-1	.331	.399	.507	1	.995
1999—	Altoona (East.)	C-OF-1B	111	362	57	97	21	3	20	69	40	104	1-3	.268	.367	.508	9	.978
2000—	Nashville (PCL)	C-1B	124	396	83	112	24	1	33	86	44	121	1-2	.283	.383	.598	13	.982
2001—	Nashville (PCL)	1B-C	11	45	4	13	2	1	1	3	2	14	0-0	.289	.333	.444	2	.976
—	Pittsburgh (N.L.)	1B-OF-C-DH	88	158	27	49	3	1	13	32	15	53	3-1	.310	.390	.589	3	.987
2002—	Pittsburgh (N.L.)	OF-1B-C-DH	131	368	48	97	16	1	16	57	32	116	2-3	.264	.355	.443	5	.988
Major League totals (2 years)			219	526	75	146	19	2	29	89	47	169	5-4	.278	.365	.487	8	.988

WILSON, DAN C MARINERS

PERSONAL: Born March 25, 1969, in Arlington Heights, Ill. ... 6-3/214. ... Bats right, throws right. ... Full name: Daniel Allen Wilson.

HIGH SCHOOL: Barrington (Ill.).

COLLEGE: Minnesota.

TRANSACTIONS/CAREER NOTES: Selected by New York Mets organization in 26th round of free-agent draft (June 2, 1987); did not sign. ... Selected by Cincinnati Reds organization in first round (seventh pick overall) of free-agent draft (June 4, 1990). ... Traded by Reds with P Bobby Ayala to Seattle Mariners for P Erik Hanson and 2B Bret Boone (November 2, 1993). ... On disabled list (July 21-September 1, 1998). ... On Seattle disabled list (June 15-July 14, 2000); included rehabilitation assignments to Everett (July 12-13) and Tacoma (July 14).

RECORDS: Holds A.L. single-season record for most putouts by catcher—1,051 (1997). ... Shares major league single-game record for most putouts by catcher (nine-inning game)—20 (August 8, 1997); most putouts by catcher (extra-inning game)—21 (March 31, 1996, 12 innings); and most chances accepted by catcher (nine-inning game) since 1900—20 (August 8, 1997). ... Shares A.L. single-game record for most putouts by catcher (extra-inning game)—21 (March 31, 1996, 12 innings).

STATISTICAL NOTES: Led American Association catchers with 733 putouts, 69 assists and 810 total chances in 1992. ... Led A.L. catchers with 952 total chances in 1995 and 1,129 in 1997. ... Hit three home runs in one game (April 11, 1996). ... Led A.L. catchers with 1,051 putouts and tied for lead with 13 double plays in 1997. ... Career major league grand slams: 2.

2002 GAMES PLAYED BY POSITION (MLB): C—113; 1B—4.

			BATTING														FIELDING	
Year	Team (League)	Pos.	G	AB	R	H	2B	3B	HR	RBI	BB	SO	SB-CS	Avg.	OBP	SLG	E	Avg.
1990—	Charl., W.Va. (S.Atl.)	C	32	113	16	28	9	1	2	17	13	17	0-0	.248	.323	.398	1	.995
1991—	Charl., W.Va. (S.Atl.)	C	52	197	25	62	11	1	3	29	25	21	1-1	.315	.396	.426	3	.992
—	Chattanooga (Sou.)	C	81	292	32	75	19	2	2	38	21	39	2-2	.257	.303	.356	4	.993
1992—	Nashville (A.A.)	C	106	366	27	92	16	1	4	34	31	58	1-4	.251	.310	.333	*8	.990
—	Cincinnati (N.L.)	C	12	25	2	9	1	0	0	3	3	8	0-0	.360	.429	.400	0	1.000
1993—	Cincinnati (N.L.)	C	36	76	6	17	3	0	0	8	9	16	0-0	.224	.302	.263	1	.994
—	Indianapolis (A.A.)	C	51	191	18	50	11	1	1	17	19	31	1-0	.262	.330	.346	2	.994
1994—	Seattle (A.L.)■	C	91	282	24	61	14	2	3	27	10	57	1-2	.216	.244	.312	*9	.986
1995—	Seattle (A.L.)	C	119	399	40	111	22	3	9	51	33	63	2-1	.278	.336	.416	5	.995
1996—	Seattle (A.L.)	C	138	491	51	140	24	0	18	83	32	88	1-2	.285	.330	.444	4	.996
1997—	Seattle (A.L.)	C	146	508	66	137	31	1	15	74	39	72	7-2	.270	.326	.423	6	.995
1998—	Seattle (A.L.)	C	96	325	39	82	17	1	9	44	24	56	2-1	.252	.308	.394	4	.994
1999—	Seattle (A.L.)	C-1B	123	414	46	110	23	2	7	38	29	83	5-0	.266	.315	.382	4	.995
2000—	Seattle (A.L.)	C-1B-3B	90	268	31	63	12	0	5	27	22	51	1-2	.235	.291	.336	5	.990
—	Everett (N'West)	C	1	2	2	1	0	0	1	1	1	0	0-0	.500	.667	2.000	0	1.000
—	Tacoma (PCL)	DH	1	4	0	1	1	0	0	0	0	1	0-0	.250	.250	.500	...	...
2001—	Seattle (A.L.)	C-1B	123	377	44	100	20	1	10	42	20	69	3-2	.265	.305	.403	1	.999
2002—	Seattle (A.L.)	C-1B	115	359	35	106	16	1	6	44	18	81	1-0	.295	.326	.396	2	.997
American League totals (9 years)			1041	3423	376	910	179	11	82	430	227	620	23-12	.266	.313	.396	40	.994
National League totals (2 years)			48	101	8	26	4	0	0	11	12	24	0-0	.257	.333	.297	1	.995
Major League totals (11 years)			1089	3524	384	936	183	11	82	441	239	644	23-12	.266	.314	.394	41	.994

DIVISION SERIES RECORD

			BATTING														FIELDING	
Year	Team (League)	Pos.	G	AB	R	H	2B	3B	HR	RBI	BB	SO	SB-CS	Avg.	OBP	SLG	E	Avg.
1995—	Seattle (A.L.)	C	5	17	0	2	0	0	0	1	2	6	0-0	.118	.211	.118	0	1.000
1997—	Seattle (A.L.)	C	4	13	0	0	0	0	0	0	0	9	0-0	.000	.000	.000	0	1.000
2000—	Seattle (A.L.)	C	2	3	0	0	0	0	0	1	1	2	0-0	.000	.200	.000	1	.833
2001—	Seattle (A.L.)	C	5	15	0	3	1	0	0	0	0	5	0-0	.200	.200	.267	0	1.000
Division series totals (4 years)			16	48	0	5	1	0	0	2	3	22	0-0	.104	.154	.125	1	.991

CHAMPIONSHIP SERIES RECORD

			BATTING														FIELDING	
Year	Team (League)	Pos.	G	AB	R	H	2B	3B	HR	RBI	BB	SO	SB-CS	Avg.	OBP	SLG	E	Avg.
1995—	Seattle (A.L.)	C	6	16	0	0	0	0	0	0	0	4	0-0	.000	.000	.000	1	.974
2000—	Seattle (A.L.)	C	4	11	0	1	0	0	0	0	1	5	0-0	.091	.167	.091	1	.960
2001—	Seattle (A.L.)	C-PH	4	13	2	2	0	0	0	0	0	1	0-0	.154	.154	.154	0	1.000
Championship series totals (3 years)			14	40	2	3	0	0	0	0	1	10	0-0	.075	.098	.075	2	.977

ALL-STAR GAME RECORD

	AB	R	H	2B	3B	HR	RBI	BB	SO	SB-CS	Avg.	OBP	SLG	E	Avg.
All-Star Game totals (1 year)	1	0	0	0	0	0	0	0	0	0-0	.000	.000	.000	0	...

WILSON, ENRIQUE — IF — YANKEES

PERSONAL: Born July 27, 1973, in Santo Domingo, Dominican Republic. ... 5-11/195. ... Bats both, throws right. ... Full name: Enrique Martes Wilson.

HIGH SCHOOL: Liceo Ramon Amelio Jiminez (Santo Domingo, Dominican Republic).

TRANSACTIONS/CAREER NOTES: Signed as non-drafted free agent by Minnesota Twins organization (April 15, 1992). ... Traded by Twins to Cleveland Indians (February 21, 1994), completing deal in which Twins acquired P Shawn Bryant for a player to be named later (February 21, 1994). ... On Cleveland disabled list (April 4-June 15, 1998); included rehabilitation assignment to Buffalo (June 2-15). ... On Cleveland disabled list (July 14-July 28, 2000). ... Traded by Indians with OF Alex Ramirez to Pittsburgh Pirates for 1B/OF Wil Cordero (July 28, 2000). ... On Pittsburgh disabled list (July 29-August 1, 2000); included rehabilitation assignment to Nashville (July 31-August 1). ... Traded by Pirates to New York Yankees for P Damaso Marte (June 13, 2001).

STATISTICAL NOTES: Led South Atlantic League shortstops with 185 putouts, 407 assists, 625 total chances and 66 double plays in 1994. ... Led Carolina League with 10 sacrifice flies in 1995. ... Led Eastern League shortstops with 74 double plays in 1996. ... Career major league grand slams: 2.

2002 GAMES PLAYED BY POSITION (MLB): 3B—26; SS—14; 2B—7; DH—2; OF—1.

								BATTING								FIELDING	
Year Team (League)	Pos.	G	AB	R	H	2B	3B	HR	RBI	BB	SO	SB-CS	Avg.	OBP	SLG	E	Avg.
1992—GC Twins (GCL)	SS	13	44	12	15	1	0	0	8	4	4	3-0	.341	.434	.364	4	.897
1993—Elizabethton (Appl.)	SS-3B	58	197	42	57	8	4	13	50	14	18	5-4	.289	.352	.569	19	.909
1994—Columbus (S.Atl.)■	SS	133	512	82	143	28	12	10	72	44	34	21-13	.279	.341	.439	33	.947
1995—Kinston (Caro.)	SS-2B	117	464	55	124	24	•7	6	52	25	38	18-19	.267	.301	.388	21	.964
1996—Canton/Akron (East.)	SS-2B	117	484	70	147	17	5	5	50	31	46	23-16	.304	.346	.390	28	.949
—Buffalo (A.A.)	3B-SS	3	8	1	4	1	0	0	0	1	1	0-2	.500	.556	.625	1	.750
1997—Buffalo (A.A.)	SS-2B-3B	118	451	78	138	20	3	11	39	42	41	9-8	.306	.369	.437	20	.965
—Cleveland (A.L.)	SS-2B	5	15	2	5	0	0	0	1	0	2	0-0	.333	.333	.333	1	.952
1998—Cleveland (A.L.)	2B-SS-3B	32	90	13	29	6	0	2	12	4	8	2-4	.322	.354	.456	2	.983
—Buffalo (I.L.)	2B-SS	56	221	40	62	13	0	4	23	19	21	8-3	.281	.335	.394	6	.976
1999—Cleveland (A.L.)	3-S-2-DH	113	332	41	87	22	1	2	24	25	41	5-4	.262	.310	.352	8	.968
2000—Cleveland (A.L.)	3B-DH-2B-SS	40	117	16	38	9	0	2	12	7	11	2-1	.325	.360	.453	1	.985
—Nashville (PCL)■	2B-SS	2	7	0	2	0	0	0	1	0	0	0-0	.286	.286	.286	1	.889
—Pittsburgh (N.L.)	3B-2B-SS	40	122	11	32	6	1	3	15	11	13	0-1	.262	.321	.402	6	.942
2001—Pittsburgh (N.L.)	SS-2B-3B	46	129	7	24	3	0	1	8	3	23	0-3	.186	.203	.233	4	.974
—New York (A.L.)■	SS-3B-2B-DH	48	99	10	24	5	1	1	12	6	14	0-2	.242	.283	.343	2	.981
2002—New York (A.L.)	3-S-2-D-O	60	105	17	19	2	2	2	11	8	22	1-1	.181	.239	.295	5	.955
American League totals (6 years)		298	758	99	202	44	4	9	72	50	98	10-12	.266	.310	.371	19	.972
National League totals (2 years)		86	251	18	56	9	1	4	23	14	36	0-4	.223	.262	.315	10	.961
Major League totals (6 years)		384	1009	117	258	53	5	13	95	64	134	10-16	.256	.298	.357	29	.969

DIVISION SERIES RECORD

								BATTING								FIELDING	
Year Team (League)	Pos.	G	AB	R	H	2B	3B	HR	RBI	BB	SO	SB-CS	Avg.	OBP	SLG	E	Avg.
1998—Cleveland (A.L.)	2B	1	2	0	0	0	0	0	0	0	0	0-0	.000	.000	.000	0	1.000
1999—Cleveland (A.L.)	2B-PH	3	2	0	0	0	0	0	0	0	0	0-0	.000	.000	.000	0	1.000
2002—New York (A.L.)	PH	1	0	0	0	0	0	0	0	0	0	0-0	...	...	...	0	...
Division series totals (3 years)		5	4	0	0	0	0	0	0	0	0	0-0	.000	.000	.000	0	1.000

CHAMPIONSHIP SERIES RECORD

								BATTING								FIELDING	
Year Team (League)	Pos.	G	AB	R	H	2B	3B	HR	RBI	BB	SO	SB-CS	Avg.	OBP	SLG	E	Avg.
1998—Cleveland (A.L.)	PR-2B	5	14	2	3	0	0	0	1	1	3	0-0	.214	.267	.214	1	.960
2001—New York (A.L.)	SS	1	1	0	1	0	0	0	0	0	0	0-0	1.000	1.000	1.000	0	...
Championship series totals (2 years)		6	15	2	4	0	0	0	1	1	3	0-0	.267	.313	.267	1	.960

WORLD SERIES RECORD

								BATTING								FIELDING	
Year Team (League)	Pos.	G	AB	R	H	2B	3B	HR	RBI	BB	SO	SB-CS	Avg.	OBP	SLG	E	Avg.
2001—New York (A.L.)	PH-SS	2	3	0	0	0	0	0	0	0	0	0-0	.000	.000	.000	0	1.000

WILSON, JACK — SS — PIRATES

W

PERSONAL: Born December 29, 1977, in Westlake, Calif. ... 6-0/195. ... Bats right, throws right. ... Full name: Jack Eugene Wilson.

HIGH SCHOOL: Thousand Oaks (Calif.).

JUNIOR COLLEGE: Oxnard.

TRANSACTIONS/CAREER NOTES: Selected by St. Louis Cardinals organization in ninth round of free-agent draft (June 2, 1998). ... Traded by Cardinals to Pittsburgh Pirates for P Jason Christiansen (July 30, 2000).

STATISTICAL NOTES: Tied for N.L. lead with 17 sacrifice hits in 2001. ... Led N.L. with 17 sacrifice hits in 2002.

2002 GAMES PLAYED BY POSITION (MLB): SS—143.

								BATTING								FIELDING	
Year Team (League)	Pos.	G	AB	R	H	2B	3B	HR	RBI	BB	SO	SB-CS	Avg.	OBP	SLG	E	Avg.
1998—Johnson City (Appl.)	SS	61	241	50	90	18	4	4	29	18	30	22-6	*.373	.424	.531	16	.940
1999—Peoria (Midw.)	SS	64	251	47	86	22	4	3	28	15	23	11-5	.343	.384	.498	16	.943
—Potomac (Caro.)	SS	64	257	44	76	10	1	2	18	19	31	7-4	.296	.345	.366	18	.941
2000—Potomac (Caro.)	SS	13	47	7	13	0	1	2	7	5	10	2-3	.277	.340	.447	2	.967
—Arkansas (Texas)	SS	88	343	65	101	20	8	6	34	36	59	2-3	.294	.368	.452	12	.971
—Altoona (East.)■	SS	33	139	17	35	7	2	1	16	14	17	1-3	.252	.325	.353	5	.966
2001—Pittsburgh (N.L.)	SS	108	390	44	87	17	1	3	25	16	70	1-3	.223	.255	.295	16	.968
—Nashville (PCL)	SS	27	103	20	38	6	1	1	6	9	13	2-2	.369	.430	.476	3	.974
2002—Pittsburgh (N.L.)	SS	147	527	77	133	22	4	4	47	37	74	5-2	.252	.306	.332	15	.977
Major League totals (2 years)		255	917	121	220	39	5	7	72	53	144	6-5	.240	.285	.316	31	.973

WILSON, KRIS — P — ROYALS

PERSONAL: Born August 6, 1976, in Washington, D.C. ... 6-4/225. ... Throws right, bats right. ... Full name: Kristopher Kyle Wilson.
HIGH SCHOOL: Tarpon Springs (Fla.).
COLLEGE: Georgia Tech.
TRANSACTIONS/CAREER NOTES: Selected by Kansas City Royals organization in ninth round of free-agent draft (June 3, 1997). ... On Kansas City disabled list (March 22-May 26, 2002); included rehabilitation assignment to Omaha (May 25-26).
CAREER HITTING (MLB): 1-for-3 (.333), 1 R, 0 2B, 0 3B, 0 HR, 0 RBI.

Year	League	W	L	Pct.	ERA	G	GS	CG	ShO	Sv.-Opp.	IP	H	R	ER	HR	BB-IBB	SO
1997	—Spokane (N'West)	5	3	.625	4.52	15	15	0	0	0-...	73.2	101	50	37	6	21-1	72
1998	—Wilmington (Caro.)	0	3	.000	3.75	10	2	0	0	1-...	24.0	19	10	10	0	6-1	20
	—Lansing (Midw.)	10	5	.667	3.53	18	18	1	0	0-...	117.1	119	50	46	7	15-0	74
1999	—Wilmington (Caro.)	8	1	.889	1.13	14	4	0	0	0-...	48.0	25	7	6	0	11-0	45
	—Omaha (PCL)	0	1	.000	8.44	1	1	0	0	0-...	5.1	8	5	5	3	0-0	3
	—Wichita (Texas)	5	7	.417	5.45	23	10	0	0	0-...	74.1	91	51	45	11	14-0	45
2000	—Wichita (Texas)	7	3	.700	3.51	21	15	1	0	0-...	102.2	99	52	40	12	21-0	69
	—Kansas City (A.L.)	0	1	.000	4.19	20	0	0	0	0-1	34.1	38	16	16	3	11-3	17
2001	—Kansas City (A.L.)	6	5	.545	5.19	29	15	0	0	1-1	109.1	132	78	63	26	32-0	67
	—Omaha (PCL)	2	2	.500	2.79	6	5	0	0	0-...	29.0	31	9	9	2	6-0	18
2002	—Omaha (PCL)	2	0	1.000	3.08	8	3	0	0	1-...	26.1	38	9	9	0	1-0	17
	—Wichita (Texas)	3	3	.500	1.88	13	7	1	0	0-...	48.0	47	17	10	4	4-1	33
	—Kansas City (A.L.)	2	0	1.000	8.20	12	0	0	0	0-2	18.2	29	18	17	7	5-0	10
Major League totals (3 years)		8	6	.571	5.32	61	15	0	0	1-4	162.1	199	112	96	36	48-3	94

WILSON, PAUL — P — DEVIL RAYS

PERSONAL: Born March 28, 1973, in Orlando. ... 6-5/214. ... Throws right, bats right. ... Full name: Paul Anthony Wilson.
HIGH SCHOOL: William R. Boone (Orlando).
COLLEGE: Florida State.
TRANSACTIONS/CAREER NOTES: Selected by New York Mets organization in first round (first pick overall) of free-agent draft (June 2, 1994). ... On New York disabled list (June 5-July 15, 1996); included rehabilitation assignments to St. Lucie (June 28-July 10) and Binghamton (July 10-15). ... On New York disabled list (March 27, 1997-entire season); included rehabilitation assignments to Gulf Coast Mets (August 2-23) and St. Lucie (August 28-September 8). ... On New York disabled list (March 13-August 4, 1998); included rehabilitation assignment to St. Lucie (July 9-August 1). ... On disabled list (April 8, 1999-entire season). ... Traded by Mets with OF Jason Tyner to Tampa Bay Devil Rays for OF Bubba Trammell and P Rick White (July 28, 2000).
STATISTICAL NOTES: Named Eastern League Pitcher of the Year (1995).
CAREER HITTING (MLB): 4-for-55 (.073), 3 R, 0 2B, 0 3B, 1 HR, 4 RBI.

Year	League	W	L	Pct.	ERA	G	GS	CG	ShO	Sv.-Opp.	IP	H	R	ER	HR	BB-IBB	SO
1994	—Gulf Coast Mets (GCL)	0	2	.000	3.00	3	3	0	0	0-...	12.0	8	4	4	0	4-0	13
	—St. Lucie (FSL)	0	5	.000	5.06	8	8	0	0	0-...	37.1	32	23	21	3	17-1	37
1995	—Binghamton (East.)	6	3	.667	*2.17	16	16	4	1	0-...	120.1	89	34	29	5	24-2	127
	—Norfolk (I.L.)	5	3	.625	2.85	10	10	•4	2	0-...	66.1	59	25	21	3	20-0	67
1996	—New York (N.L.)	5	12	.294	5.38	26	26	1	0	0-0	149.0	157	102	89	15	71-11	109
	—St. Lucie (FSL)	0	1	.000	3.38	2	2	0	0	0-...	8.0	6	5	3	0	4-0	5
	—Binghamton (East.)	0	1	.000	7.20	1	1	0	0	0-...	5.0	6	4	4	0	5-0	5
1997	—Gulf Coast Mets (GCL)	1	0	1.000	1.45	4	3	0	0	1-...	18.2	14	7	3	0	4-0	18
	—St. Lucie (FSL)	0	0	...	2.57	1	1	0	0	0-...	7.0	6	2	2	1	0-0	6
1998	—St. Lucie (FSL)	0	1	.000	6.38	5	5	0	0	0-...	18.1	23	13	13	2	4-0	16
	—Norfolk (I.L.)	4	1	.800	4.42	7	7	0	0	0-...	38.2	42	19	19	2	9-0	30
1999	—Norfolk (I.L.)									Did not play.							
2000	—St. Lucie (FSL)	2	0	1.000	1.40	5	5	0	0	0-...	25.2	22	9	4	0	4-0	19
	—Norfolk (I.L.)	5	5	.500	4.23	15	13	0	0	0-...	83.0	85	40	39	7	25-1	56
	—Tampa Bay (A.L.)■	1	4	.200	3.35	11	7	0	0	0-0	51.0	38	20	19	1	16-2	40
2001	—Tampa Bay (A.L.)	8	9	.471	4.88	37	24	0	0	0-1	151.1	165	94	82	21	52-2	119
2002	—Tampa Bay (A.L.)	6	12	.333	4.83	30	30	1	0	0-0	193.2	219	113	104	29	67-2	111
A.L. totals (3 years)		15	25	.375	4.66	78	61	1	0	0-1	396.0	422	227	205	51	135-6	270
N.L. totals (1 year)		5	12	.294	5.38	26	26	1	0	0-0	149.0	157	102	89	15	71-11	109
Major League totals (4 years)		20	37	.351	4.86	104	87	2	0	0-1	545.0	579	329	294	66	206-17	379

WILSON, PRESTON — OF — MARLINS

PERSONAL: Born July 19, 1974, in Bamberg, S.C. ... 6-2/213. ... Bats right, throws right. ... Full name: Preston James Richard Wilson. ... Stepson of Mookie Wilson, first base/outfield coach, New York Mets; and outfielder with Mets (1980-89) and Toronto Blue Jays (1989-91).
HIGH SCHOOL: Bamberg Erhardt (Bamberg, S.C.).
TRANSACTIONS/CAREER NOTES: Selected by New York Mets organization in first round (ninth pick overall) of free-agent draft (June 1, 1992). ... On disabled list (April 4-29, May 21-July 13 and July 29-September 8, 1996). ... On Norfolk disabled list (April 20-May 2, 1998). ... Traded by Mets with P Ed Yarnall and P Geoff Goetz to Florida Marlins for C Mike Piazza (May 22, 1998). ... On Florida disabled list (July 2-August 10, 2001); included rehabilitation assignment to Calgary (August 7-10).
HONORS: Named N.L. Rookie Player of the Year by The Sporting News (1999).
STATISTICAL NOTES: Led Appalachian League third basemen with 45 putouts, 127 assists and 197 total chances in 1993. ... Career major league grand slams: 3.
2002 GAMES PLAYED BY POSITION (MLB): OF—138.

			BATTING														FIELDING	
Year	Team (League)	Pos.	G	AB	R	H	2B	3B	HR	RBI	BB	SO	SB-CS	Avg.	OBP	SLG	E	Avg.
1993	—Kingsport (Appl.)	3B	66	259	44	60	10	0	*16	48	24	75	6-2	.232	.303	.456	*25	.873
	—Pittsfield (NY-Penn)	3B	8	29	6	16	5	1	1	12	2	7	1-0	.552	.576	.897	6	.700
1994	—Capital City (S.Atl.)	3B	131	474	55	108	17	4	14	58	20	135	10-10	.228	.262	.369	47	.884
1995	—Capital City (S.Atl.)	OF	111	442	70	119	26	5	20	61	19	114	20-6	.269	.311	.486	8	.961

Year	Team (League)	Pos.	G	AB	R	H	2B	3B	HR	RBI	BB	SO	SB-CS	Avg.	OBP	SLG	E	Avg.
			BATTING														FIELDING	
1996—	St. Lucie (FSL)	OF	23	85	6	15	3	0	1	7	8	21	1-1	.176	.263	.247	2	.956
1997—	St. Lucie (FSL)	OF-DH	63	245	32	60	12	1	11	48	8	66	3-4	.245	.267	.437	3	.973
	— Binghamton (East.)	OF-DH-3B	70	259	37	74	12	1	19	47	21	71	7-1	.286	.340	.560	6	.952
1998—	Norfolk (I.L.)	OF	18	73	9	18	5	1	1	9	2	22	1-1	.247	.273	.384	2	.958
	— New York (N.L.)	OF	8	20	3	6	2	0	0	2	2	8	1-1	.300	.364	.400	1	.909
	— Charlotte (I.L.)■	OF-DH	94	356	71	99	25	3	25	77	34	121	14-6	.278	.341	.576	4	.979
	— Florida (N.L.)	OF	14	31	4	2	0	0	1	1	4	13	0-0	.065	.194	.161	0	1.000
1999—	Florida (N.L.)	OF	149	482	67	135	21	4	26	71	46	156	11-4	.280	.350	.502	9	.973
2000—	Florida (N.L.)	OF	161	605	94	160	35	3	31	121	55	*187	36-14	.264	.331	.486	5	.988
2001—	Florida (N.L.)	OF	123	468	70	128	30	2	23	71	36	107	20-8	.274	.331	.494	2	.993
	— Calgary (PCL)	OF	4	10	3	5	2	0	0	1	5	1	2-0	.500	.667	.700	0	1.000
2002—	Florida (N.L.)	OF	141	510	80	124	22	2	23	65	58	140	20-11	.243	.329	.429	6	.981
Major League totals (5 years)			596	2116	318	555	110	11	104	331	201	611	88-38	.262	.333	.472	23	.983

WILSON, TOM — C — BLUE JAYS

PERSONAL: Born December 19, 1970, in Fullerton, Calif. ... 6-3/220. ... Bats right, throws right. ... Full name: Thomas Leroy Wilson.
HIGH SCHOOL: Troy (Fullerton, Calif.).
JUNIOR COLLEGE: Fullerton.
TRANSACTIONS/CAREER NOTES: Selected by New York Yankees organization in 23rd round of free-agent draft (June 4, 1990). ... Traded by Yankees to Cleveland Indians for C Ryan Martindale and OF Marc Marini (April 6, 1996). ... Released by Indians (October 15, 1996). ... Signed by Yankees organization (February 1, 1997). ... Granted free agency (October 17, 1997). ... Signed by Arizona Diamondbacks organization (December 15, 1997). ... Granted free agency (October 16, 1998). ... Signed by Tampa Bay Devil Rays organization (November 23, 1998). ... Granted free agency (October 15, 1999). ... Signed by Yankees organization (November 9, 1999). ... Granted free agency (October 15, 2000). ... Signed by Oakland Athletics organization (November 7, 2000). ... Traded by A's to Toronto Blue Jays for C Mike Kremblas (January 2, 2002).
STATISTICAL NOTES: Led New York-Pennsylvania League catchers with 25 passes balls in 1991. ... Led South Atlantic League catchers with 23 passed balls in 1992. ... Led South Atlantic League catchers with 850 putouts in 1993. ... Led Eastern League catchers with 744 putouts and 822 total chances in 1994. ... Led Eastern League catchers with 694 putouts and 781 total chances in 1997. ... Tied for Pacific Coast League lead in errors by catcher with 12 in 1998.
2002 GAMES PLAYED BY POSITION (MLB): C—65; DH—12; 1B—11.

Year	Team (League)	Pos.	G	AB	R	H	2B	3B	HR	RBI	BB	SO	SB-CS	Avg.	OBP	SLG	E	Avg.
			BATTING														FIELDING	
1991—	Oneonta (NY-Penn)	C-OF	70	243	38	59	12	2	4	42	34	72	4-4	.243	.337	.358	17	.950
1992—	Greensboro (S.Atl.)	C-OF	117	395	50	83	22	0	6	48	68	128	2-1	.210	.325	.311	10	.984
1993—	Greensboro (S.Atl.)	C	120	394	55	98	20	1	10	63	•91	112	2-5	.249	.388	.381	13	.986
1994—	Albany (East.)	C-3B	123	408	54	100	20	1	7	42	58	100	4-6	.245	.345	.350	8	.990
1995—	Columbus (I.L.)	C	22	62	11	16	3	1	0	9	9	10	0-0	.258	.352	.339	5	.962
	— Norwich (East.)	C-3B	28	84	6	12	4	0	0	4	17	22	0-0	.143	.287	.190	6	.964
	— Tampa (FSL)	C	17	48	3	8	0	0	0	2	11	13	1-0	.167	.317	.167	0	1.000
1996—	Columbus (I.L.)	DH	1	1	0	0	0	0	0	0	1	0	0-0	.000	.500	.000	...	...
	— Buffalo (A.A.)■	C-SS	72	208	28	56	14	2	9	30	35	66	0-1	.269	.390	.486	5	.988
1997—	Norwich (East.)■	C-1B-3B	124	419	88	124	21	4	21	80	86	126	1-4	.296	.416	.516	8	.990
	— Columbus (I.L.)	C	1	3	0	0	0	0	0	0	1	0	0-0	.000	.250	.000	0	1.000
1998—	Tucson (PCL)■	C-1B-OF-3B	111	370	59	112	17	3	12	54	41	81	3-1	.303	.380	.462	‡16	.978
1999—	Durham (I.L.)■	C-OF-1B	67	215	41	60	19	0	16	44	49	59	0-2	.279	.411	.591	6	.987
	— Orlando (Sou.)	C	30	104	12	30	2	0	7	23	18	34	0-0	.288	.405	.510	4	.971
2000—	Columbus (I.L.)■	C-OF-3B	104	330	63	91	20	0	20	71	73	114	2-2	.276	.410	.518	8	.987
2001—	Sacramento (PCL)■	C-3B-OF-1B	77	259	43	73	15	1	8	48	49	62	0-1	.282	.394	.440	5	.988
	— Oakland (A.L.)	C	9	21	4	4	0	0	2	4	1	5	0-0	.190	.250	.476	1	.974
2002—	Toronto (A.L.)■	C-DH-1B	96	265	33	68	10	0	8	37	28	79	0-0	.257	.334	.385	4	.991
Major League totals (2 years)			105	286	37	72	10	0	10	41	29	84	0-0	.252	.328	.392	5	.989

WILSON, VANCE — C — METS

PERSONAL: Born March 17, 1973, in Mesa, Ariz. ... 5-11/190. ... Bats right, throws right. ... Full name: Vance Allen Wilson.
HIGH SCHOOL: Red Mountain (Mesa, Ariz.).
JUNIOR COLLEGE: Mesa (Ariz.) Community College.
TRANSACTIONS/CAREER NOTES: Selected by New York Mets organization in 44th round of free-agent draft (June 3, 1993). ... On Norfolk disabled list (May 2-July 18, 1998). ... On New York disabled list (September 8, 1998-remainder of season). ... On Norfolk disabled list (May 13-August 28, 1999). ... On New York disabled list (August 28, 1999-remainder of season).
STATISTICAL NOTES: Led International League with 706 total chances, 10 double plays and 14 passed balls in 2000.
2002 GAMES PLAYED BY POSITION (MLB): C—66; 1B—1.

Year	Team (League)	Pos.	G	AB	R	H	2B	3B	HR	RBI	BB	SO	SB-CS	Avg.	OBP	SLG	E	Avg.
			BATTING														FIELDING	
1994—	Pittsfield (NY-Penn)	C	44	166	22	51	12	0	2	20	5	27	4-1	.307	.343	.416	5	.977
1995—	Capital City (S.Atl.)	C	91	324	34	81	11	0	6	32	19	45	4-3	.250	.306	.340	*14	.981
1996—	St. Lucie (FSL)	C	93	311	29	76	14	2	6	44	31	41	2-4	.244	.321	.360	8	.987
1997—	Binghamton (East.)	C	92	322	46	89	17	0	15	40	20	46	2-5	.276	.328	.469	11	.984
1998—	Norfolk (I.L.)	C	46	154	18	40	3	0	4	16	9	29	0-3	.260	.305	.357	4	.990
	— GC Mets (GCL)	C	10	28	5	10	5	0	2	9	0	0	0-1	.357	.367	.750	2	.957
	— St. Lucie (FSL)	C	4	16	0	1	0	0	0	0	0	5	0-0	.063	.063	.063	0	1.000
1999—	Norfolk (I.L.)	C	15	53	10	14	3	0	3	5	4	8	1-0	.264	.328	.491	1	.991
	— New York (N.L.)	C	1	0	0	0	0	0	0	0	0	0	0-0	...	...	...	0	...
2000—	Norfolk (I.L.)	C	111	400	47	104	23	1	16	62	24	65	11-6	.260	.319	.443	3	.996
	— New York (N.L.)	C	4	4	0	0	0	0	0	0	0	2	0-0	.000	.000	.000	0	1.000
2001—	Norfolk (I.L.)	C	65	228	24	56	14	0	6	31	12	34	0-1	.246	.306	.386	8	.984
	— New York (N.L.)	C	32	57	3	17	3	0	0	6	2	16	0-1	.298	.339	.351	1	.993
2002—	New York (N.L.)	C-1B	74	163	19	40	7	0	5	26	5	32	0-1	.245	.301	.380	6	.983
Major League totals (4 years)			111	224	22	57	10	0	5	32	7	50	0-2	.254	.306	.366	7	.986

WINN, RANDY — OF — MARINERS

PERSONAL: Born June 9, 1974, in Los Angeles. ... 6-2/197. ... Bats both, throws right. ... Full name: Dwight Randolph Winn.
HIGH SCHOOL: San Ramon Valley (Danville, Calif.).
COLLEGE: Santa Clara.
TRANSACTIONS/CAREER NOTES: Selected by Florida Marlins organization in third round of free-agent draft (June 1, 1995). ... On disabled list (August 22-September 11, 1995). ... Selected by Tampa Bay Devil Rays in third round (58th pick overall) of expansion draft (November 18, 1997). ... Traded by Devil Rays to Seattle Mariners for SS Antonio Perez (October 28, 2002).
STATISTICAL NOTES: Led Eastern League in caught stealing with 20 in 1997. ... Career major league grand slams: 2.
MISCELLANEOUS: Holds Tampa Bay Devil Rays all-time record for most triples (28).
2002 GAMES PLAYED BY POSITION (MLB): OF—146; DH—4.

		BATTING														FIELDING	
Year Team (League)	Pos.	G	AB	R	H	2B	3B	HR	RBI	BB	SO	SB-CS	Avg.	OBP	SLG	E	Avg.
1995— Elmira (NY-Penn)	OF	51	213	38	67	7	4	0	22	15	31	19-7	.315	.365	.385	5	.954
1996— Kane County (Midw.)..	OF	130	514	90	139	16	3	0	35	47	115	30-18	.270	.340	.313	8	.970
1997— Brevard County (FSL).	OF	36	143	26	45	8	2	0	15	16	28	16-8	.315	.400	.399	0	1.000
— Portland (East.)..........	OF	96	384	66	112	15	6	8	36	42	92	35-20	.292	.371	.424	4	.979
1998— Durham (I.L.)■..........	OF	29	123	25	35	5	2	1	16	15	24	10-4	.285	.362	.382	2	.966
— Tampa Bay (A.L.)........	OF-DH	109	338	51	94	9	9	1	17	29	69	26-12	.278	.337	.367	4	.980
1999— Tampa Bay (A.L.)........	OF	79	303	44	81	16	4	2	24	17	63	9-9	.267	.307	.366	1	.995
— Durham (I.L.)	OF	46	207	38	73	20	3	3	30	16	27	9-6	.353	.402	.522	4	.966
2000— Durham (I.L.)	OF	79	303	67	100	24	5	7	40	48	53	18-5	.330	.425	.512	7	.960
— Tampa Bay (A.L.)........	OF-DH	51	159	28	40	5	0	1	16	26	25	6-7	.252	.362	.302	1	.990
2001— Tampa Bay (A.L.)........	OF-DH	128	429	54	117	25	6	6	50	38	81	12-10	.273	.339	.401	5	.981
2002— Tampa Bay (A.L.)........	OF-DH	152	607	87	181	39	9	14	75	55	109	27-8	.298	.360	.461	3	.993
Major League totals (5 years)		519	1836	264	513	94	28	24	182	165	347	80-46	.279	.342	.400	14	.988

ALL-STAR GAME RECORD

	AB	R	H	2B	3B	HR	RBI	BB	SO	SB-CS	Avg.	OBP	SLG	E	Avg.
All-Star Game totals (1 year)	2	1	1	1	0	0	0	1	1	1-0	.500	.667	1.000	0	1.000

WISE, DeWAYNE — OF — BLUE JAYS

PERSONAL: Born February 24, 1978, in Columbia, S.C. ... 6-1/180. ... Bats left, throws left. ... Full name: Larry DeWayne Wise.
HIGH SCHOOL: Chapin (S.C.).
TRANSACTIONS/CAREER NOTES: Selected by Cincinnati Reds organization in fifth round of free-agent draft (June 3, 1997). ... Selected by Toronto Blue Jays from Reds organization in Rule 5 major league draft (December 13, 1999). ... On Toronto disabled list (June 6-September 1, 2000); included rehabilitation assignment to Tennessee (August 11-30). ... On Tennessee disabled list (April 24-May 7, 2001).
STATISTICAL NOTES: Led Pioneer League outfielders with 118 putouts and 140 total chances in 1997. ... Led Midwest League with nine sacrifice flies in 1998. ... Led Midwest League with 14 sacrifice flies in 1999. ... Tied outfielders for Southern League lead with five double plays in 2001.
2002 GAMES PLAYED BY POSITION (MLB): OF—33; DH—3.

		BATTING														FIELDING	
Year Team (League)	Pos.	G	AB	R	H	2B	3B	HR	RBI	BB	SO	SB-CS	Avg.	OBP	SLG	E	Avg.
1997— Billings (Pio.)	OF	62	268	53	84	13	*9	7	41	9	47	18-8	.313	.337	.507	*13	.907
1998— Burlington (Midw.).....	OF	127	496	61	111	15	9	2	44	41	111	27-17	.224	.280	.302	7	.972
1999— Rockford (Midw.).......	OF	131	502	70	127	20	13	11	81	42	81	35-13	.253	.312	.410	8	.975
2000— Toronto (A.L.)■..........	OF-DH	28	22	3	3	0	0	0	0	1	5	1-0	.136	.208	.136	0	1.000
— Tennessee (Sou.)	OF	15	56	10	14	5	2	2	8	7	13	3-2	.250	.333	.518	4	.882
2001— Tennessee (Sou.)	OF	87	351	44	84	13	6	8	44	21	58	13-5	.239	.283	.379	5	.976
— Syracuse (I.L.)............	OF	3	13	1	3	0	0	0	0	0	8	0-1	.231	.231	.231	0	1.000
— Dunedin (FSL)............	OF	25	103	9	23	3	1	2	16	5	13	5-0	.223	.252	.330	0	1.000
2002— Toronto (A.L.)............	OF-DH	42	112	14	20	4	1	3	13	4	15	5-0	.179	.207	.313	0	1.000
— Tennessee (Sou.)	OF	86	340	59	101	21	4	10	49	29	49	15-8	.297	.350	.471	4	.981
Major League totals (2 years)		70	134	17	23	4	1	3	13	5	20	6-0	.172	.207	.284	0	1.000

WISE, MATT — P — ANGELS

PERSONAL: Born November 18, 1975, in Montclair, Calif. ... 6-4/195. ... Throws right, bats right. ... Full name: Matthew John Wise.
HIGH SCHOOL: Bonita (Calif.).
COLLEGE: Pepperdine, then Cal State-Fullerton.
TRANSACTIONS/CAREER NOTES: Selected by Anaheim Angels organization in sixth round of free-agent draft (June 3, 1997). ... On disabled list (July 9, 1999-remainder of season). ... On Salt Lake disabled list (August 14-September 3, 2002).
CAREER HITTING (MLB): 0-for-0 (.000), 0 R, 0 2B, 0 3B, 0 HR, 0 RBI.

Year League	W	L	Pct.	ERA	G	GS	CG	ShO	Sv.-Opp.	IP	H	R	ER	HR	BB-IBB	SO
1997— Boise (N'West)................	•9	1	*.900	3.25	15	15	0	0	0-...	83.0	82	37	30	5	34-0	86
1998— Midland (Texas)...............	9	10	.474	5.42	27	27	3	•1	0-...	167.2	195	111	101	23	48-0	131
1999— Erie (East.)	8	5	.615	3.77	16	16	3	0	0-...	98.0	102	48	41	10	24-0	72
2000— Edmonton (PCL)	9	6	.600	3.69	19	19	2	1	0-...	124.1	122	54	51	10	26-0	82
— Anaheim (A.L.).................	3	3	.500	5.54	8	6	0	0	0-0	37.1	40	23	23	7	13-1	20
2001— Anaheim (A.L.).................	1	4	.200	4.38	11	9	0	0	0-0	49.1	47	27	24	11	18-1	50
— Salt Lake (PCL)................	9	9	.500	5.04	21	21	0	0	0-...	123.1	134	79	69	19	17-0	111
2002— Salt Lake (PCL)	3	4	.429	5.42	16	16	0	0	0-...	78.0	102	51	47	12	15-0	76
— Anaheim (A.L.).................	0	0	...	3.24	7	0	0	0	0-0	8.1	7	3	3	0	1-0	6
Major League totals (3 years).....	4	7	.364	4.74	26	15	0	0	0-0	95.0	94	53	50	18	32-2	76

WITASICK, JAY P GIANTS

PERSONAL: Born August 28, 1972, in Baltimore. ... 6-4/235. ... Throws right, bats right. ... Full name: Gerald Alphonse Witasick Jr..
HIGH SCHOOL: C. Milton Wright (Bel Air, Md.).
JUNIOR COLLEGE: Brevard Community College (Fla.).
COLLEGE: Maryland-Baltimore County.
TRANSACTIONS/CAREER NOTES: Selected by St. Louis Cardinals organization in second round of free-agent draft (June 3, 1993). ... On disabled list (July 17, 1995-remainder of season). ... Traded by Cardinals with OF Allen Battle, P Bret Wagner and P Carl Dale to Oakland Athletics for P Todd Stottlemyre (January 9, 1996). ... On Oakland disabled list (March 31-June 14, 1997); included rehabilitation assignment to Modesto (June 11-14). ... Traded by A's to Kansas City Royals for a player to be named later and cash (March 30, 1999); A's acquired P Scott Chiasson to complete deal (June 10, 1999). ... Traded by Royals to San Diego Padres for P Brian Meadows (July 31, 2000). ... Traded by Padres to New York Yankees for IF D'Angelo Jimenez (June 23, 2001). ... Traded by Yankees to San Francisco Giants for OF John Vander Wal (December 13, 2001). ... On San Francisco disabled list (July 27-August 15, 2002); included rehabilitation assignment to Fresno (August 10-15).
CAREER HITTING (MLB): 3-for-37 (.081), 0 R, 0 2B, 0 3B, 0 HR, 3 RBI.

Year	League	W	L	Pct.	ERA	G	GS	CG	ShO	Sv.-Opp.	IP	H	R	ER	HR	BB-IBB	SO
1993	Johnson City (Appl.)	4	3	.571	4.12	12	12	0	0	0-...	67.2	65	42	31	8	19-0	74
	Savannah (S.Atl.)	1	0	1.000	4.50	1	1	0	0	0-...	6.0	7	3	3	0	2-0	8
1994	Madison (Midw.)	10	4	.714	2.32	18	18	2	0	0-...	112.1	74	36	29	5	42-0	141
1995	St. Petersburg (FSL)	7	7	.500	2.74	18	18	1	1	0-...	105.0	80	39	32	4	36-1	109
	Arkansas (Texas)	2	4	.333	6.88	7	7	0	0	0-...	34.0	46	29	26	4	16-1	26
1996	Huntsville (Sou.)■	0	3	.000	2.30	25	6	0	0	4-...	66.2	47	21	17	3	26-2	63
	Oakland (A.L.)	1	1	.500	6.23	12	0	0	0	0-1	13.0	12	9	9	5	5-0	12
	Edmonton (PCL)	0	0	...	4.15	6	0	0	0	2-...	8.2	9	4	4	1	6-0	9
1997	Modesto (Calif.)	0	1	.000	4.15	9	2	0	0	1-...	17.1	16	9	8	1	5-0	29
	Edmonton (PCL)	3	2	.600	4.28	13	1	0	0	0-...	27.1	25	13	13	3	15-3	17
	Oakland (A.L.)	0	0	...	5.73	8	0	0	0	0-0	11.0	14	7	7	2	6-0	8
1998	Edmonton (PCL)	11	7	.611	3.87	27	26	2	1	0-...	149.0	126	74	64	19	49-0	155
	Oakland (A.L.)	1	3	.250	6.33	7	3	0	0	0-0	27.0	36	24	19	9	15-1	29
1999	Kansas City (A.L.)■	9	12	.429	5.57	32	28	1	1	0-0	158.1	191	108	98	23	83-1	102
2000	Kansas City (A.L.)	3	8	.273	5.94	22	14	2	0	0-0	89.1	109	65	59	15	38-0	67
	San Diego (N.L.)■	3	2	.600	5.64	11	11	0	0	0-0	60.2	69	42	38	9	35-5	54
2001	San Diego (N.L.)	5	2	.714	1.86	31	0	0	0	1-3	38.2	31	14	8	3	15-3	53
	New York (A.L.)■	3	0	1.000	4.69	32	0	0	0	0-1	40.1	47	27	21	5	18-1	53
2002	San Francisco (N.L.)■	1	0	1.000	2.37	44	0	0	0	0-0	68.1	58	19	18	3	21-3	54
	Fresno (PCL)	0	0	...	4.50	2	2	0	0	0-...	2.0	1	1	1	0	1-0	2
A.L. totals (6 years)		17	24	.415	5.65	113	45	3	1	0-2	339.0	409	240	213	59	165-3	271
N.L. totals (3 years)		9	4	.692	3.44	86	11	0	0	1-3	167.2	158	75	64	15	71-11	161
Major League totals (7 years)		26	28	.481	4.92	199	56	3	1	1-5	506.2	567	315	277	74	236-14	432

DIVISION SERIES RECORD

Year	League	W	L	Pct.	ERA	G	GS	CG	ShO	Sv.-Opp.	IP	H	R	ER	HR	BB-IBB	SO
2001	New York (A.L.)	0	0	...	13.50	1	0	0	0	0-0	.2	1	1	1	0	1-0	0
2002	San Francisco (N.L.)	0	0	...	0.00	2	0	0	0	0-0	2.1	0	0	0	0	0-0	1
Division series totals (2 years)		0	0	...	3.00	3	0	0	0	0-0	3.0	1	1	1	0	1-0	1

CHAMPIONSHIP SERIES RECORD

Year	League	W	L	Pct.	ERA	G	GS	CG	ShO	Sv.-Opp.	IP	H	R	ER	HR	BB-IBB	SO
2001	New York (A.L.)	0	0	...	9.00	1	0	0	0	0-0	3.0	6	3	3	1	0-0	2
2002	San Francisco (N.L.)	0	1	.000	9.00	1	0	0	0	0-0	1.0	1	1	1	1	0-0	0
Champ. series totals (2 years)		0	1	.000	9.00	2	0	0	0	0-0	4.0	7	4	4	2	0-0	2

WORLD SERIES RECORD

RECORDS: Holds single-game record for most earned runs allowed—8 (November 3, 2001). ... Holds record for most hits allowed in one inning—8 (November 3, 2001, third inning). ... Shares record for most earned runs allowed in one inning—6 (November 3, 2001, third inning).

Year	League	W	L	Pct.	ERA	G	GS	CG	ShO	Sv.-Opp.	IP	H	R	ER	HR	BB-IBB	SO
2001	New York (A.L.)	0	0	...	54.00	1	0	0	0	0-0	1.1	10	9	8	0	0-0	4
2002	San Francisco (N.L.)	0	0	...	54.00	2	0	0	0	0-0	.1	3	2	2	0	2-0	1
World Series totals (2 years)		0	0	...	54.00	3	0	0	0	0-0	1.2	13	11	10	0	2-0	5

WOHLERS, MARK P INDIANS

W

PERSONAL: Born January 23, 1970, in Holyoke, Mass. ... 6-4/207. ... Throws right, bats right. ... Full name: Mark Edward Wohlers.
HIGH SCHOOL: Holyoke (Mass.).
TRANSACTIONS/CAREER NOTES: Selected by Atlanta Braves organization in eighth round of free-agent draft (June 1, 1988). ... On Atlanta disabled list (May 3-24 and August 21, 1998-remainder of season); included rehabilitation assignments to Greenville (May 23) and Richmond (August 25-September 8). ... Traded by Braves with cash to Cincinnati Reds for P John Hudek (April 16, 1999). ... On Cincinnati disabled list (April 17, 1999-remainder of season); included rehabilitation assignments to Indianapolis (May 2-3), Rockford (June 17-21) and Chattanooga (June 22-July 1). ... Granted free agency (November 5, 1999). ... Re-signed by Reds organization (January 28, 2000). ... On Louisville disabled list (April 6-May 29, 2000). ... Granted free agency (October 31, 2000). ... Re-signed by Reds (December 15, 2000). ... Traded by Reds to New York Yankees for P Ricardo Aromboles (June 30, 2001). ... Granted free agency (November 5, 2001). ... Signed by Cleveland Indians (January 10, 2002).
RECORDS: Shares major league single-inning record for most strikeouts—4 (June 7, 1995, ninth inning).
HONORS: Named Southern League Outstanding Pitcher (1991).
STATISTICAL NOTES: Pitched two innings, combining with starter Kent Mercker (six innings) and Alejandro Pena (one inning) in 1-0 no-hit victory for Atlanta against San Diego (September 11, 1991). ... Led International League with 17 wild pitches in 1998.
CAREER HITTING (MLB): 1-for-12 (.083), 1 R, 0 2B, 0 3B, 0 HR, 0 RBI.

Year League	W	L	Pct.	ERA	G	GS	CG	ShO	Sv.-Opp.	IP	H	R	ER	HR	BB-IBB	SO
1988— Pulaski (Appl.)	5	3	.625	3.32	13	9	1	0	0-...	59.2	47	37	22	0	50-0	49
1989— Sumter (S.Atl.)	2	7	.222	6.49	14	14	0	0	0-...	68.0	74	55	49	3	59-0	51
— Pulaski (Appl.)	1	1	.500	5.48	14	8	0	0	0-...	46.0	48	36	28	5	28-0	50
1990— Sumter (S.Atl.)	5	4	.556	1.88	37	2	0	0	5-...	52.2	27	13	11	1	20-0	85
— Greenville (Sou.)	0	1	.000	4.02	14	0	0	0	6-...	15.2	14	7	7	0	14-0	20
1991— Greenville (Sou.)	0	0	...	0.57	28	0	0	0	21-...	31.1	9	4	2	0	13-0	44
— Richmond (I.L.)	1	0	1.000	1.03	23	0	0	0	11-...	26.1	23	4	3	1	12-1	22
— Atlanta (N.L.)	3	1	.750	3.20	17	0	0	0	2-4	19.2	17	7	7	1	13-3	13
1992— Richmond (I.L.)	0	2	.000	3.93	27	2	0	0	9-...	34.1	32	16	15	5	17-3	33
— Atlanta (N.L.)	1	2	.333	2.55	32	0	0	0	4-6	35.1	28	11	10	0	14-4	17
1993— Richmond (I.L.)	1	3	.250	1.84	25	0	0	0	4-...	29.1	21	7	6	0	11-0	39
— Atlanta (N.L.)	6	2	.750	4.50	46	0	0	0	0-0	48.0	37	25	24	2	22-3	45
1994— Atlanta (N.L.)	7	2	.778	4.59	51	0	0	0	1-2	51.0	51	35	26	1	33-9	58
1995— Atlanta (N.L.)	7	3	.700	2.09	65	0	0	0	25-29	64.2	51	16	15	2	24-3	90
1996— Atlanta (N.L.)	2	4	.333	3.03	77	0	0	0	39-44	77.1	71	30	26	8	21-3	100
1997— Atlanta (N.L.)	5	7	.417	3.50	71	0	0	0	33-40	69.1	57	29	27	4	38-0	92
1998— Atlanta (N.L.)	0	1	.000	10.18	27	0	0	0	8-8	20.1	18	23	23	2	33-0	22
— Greenville (Sou.)	0	0	...	0.00	1	1	0	0	0-...	1.0	1	1	0	0	1-0	1
— Richmond (I.L.)	0	3	.000	20.43	16	0	0	0	0-...	12.1	21	28	28	5	36-0	16
1999— Atlanta (N.L.)	0	0	...	27.00	2	0	0	0	0-0	.2	1	2	2	0	6-0	0
— Indianapolis (I.L.)■	0	0	...	108.00	1	0	0	0	0-...	.1	1	4	4	0	5-0	1
— Rockford (Midw.)	0	0	...	4.50	2	0	0	0	0-...	2.0	1	1	1	0	2-0	4
— Chattanooga (Sou.)	0	0	...	16.20	2	0	0	0	0-...	1.2	1	3	3	1	3-0	3
2000— Dayton (Midw.)	0	0	...	3.00	3	3	0	0	0-...	3.0	1	1	1	1	1-0	7
— Louisville (I.L.)	1	2	.333	6.10	17	2	0	0	0-...	20.2	30	21	14	4	9-0	16
— Cincinnati (N.L.)	1	2	.333	4.50	20	0	0	0	0-0	28.0	19	14	14	3	17-0	20
2001— Cincinnati (N.L.)	3	1	.750	3.94	30	0	0	0	0-1	32.0	36	20	14	5	7-2	21
— New York (A.L.)■	1	0	1.000	4.54	31	0	0	0	0-0	35.2	33	20	18	3	18-0	33
2002— Cleveland (A.L.)■	3	4	.429	4.79	64	0	0	0	7-11	71.1	71	41	38	6	26-3	46
A.L. totals (2 years)	4	4	.500	4.71	95	0	0	0	7-11	107.0	104	61	56	9	44-3	79
N.L. totals (11 years)	35	25	.583	3.79	438	0	0	0	112-134	446.1	386	212	188	28	228-27	478
Major League totals (12 years)	39	29	.574	3.97	533	0	0	0	119-145	553.1	490	273	244	37	272-30	557

DIVISION SERIES RECORD

RECORDS: Holds N.L. career record for most saves—5.

Year League	W	L	Pct.	ERA	G	GS	CG	ShO	Sv.-Opp.	IP	H	R	ER	HR	BB-IBB	SO
1995— Atlanta (N.L.)	0	1	.000	6.75	3	0	0	0	2-2	2.2	6	2	2	0	2-1	4
1996— Atlanta (N.L.)	0	0	...	0.00	3	0	0	0	3-3	3.1	1	0	0	0	0-0	4
1997— Atlanta (N.L.)	0	0	...	0.00	1	0	0	0	0-0	1.0	1	0	0	0	0-0	1
2001— New York (A.L.)	Did not play.															
Division series totals (3 years)	0	1	.000	2.57	7	0	0	0	5-5	7.0	8	2	2	0	2-1	9

CHAMPIONSHIP SERIES RECORD

RECORDS: Holds N.L. career records for most games pitched—18; and most games as relief pitcher—18.

Year League	W	L	Pct.	ERA	G	GS	CG	ShO	Sv.-Opp.	IP	H	R	ER	HR	BB-IBB	SO
1991— Atlanta (N.L.)	0	0	...	0.00	3	0	0	0	0-0	1.2	3	0	0	0	1-0	1
1992— Atlanta (N.L.)	0	0	...	0.00	3	0	0	0	0-0	3.0	2	0	0	0	1-0	2
1993— Atlanta (N.L.)	0	1	.000	3.38	4	0	0	0	0-0	5.1	2	2	2	2	3-1	10
1995— Atlanta (N.L.)	1	0	1.000	1.80	4	0	0	0	0-0	5.0	2	1	1	0	0-0	8
1996— Atlanta (N.L.)	0	0	...	0.00	3	0	0	0	2-2	3.0	0	0	0	0	0-0	4
1997— Atlanta (N.L.)	0	0	...	0.00	1	0	0	0	0-0	1.0	0	0	0	0	1-0	1
2001— New York (A.L.)	0	0	...	13.50	1	0	0	0	0-0	.2	3	3	1	1	1-0	1
Champ. series totals (7 years)	1	1	.500	1.83	19	0	0	0	2-2	19.2	12	6	4	3	7-1	27

WORLD SERIES RECORD

NOTES: Member of World Series championship team (1995).

Year League	W	L	Pct.	ERA	G	GS	CG	ShO	Sv.-Opp.	IP	H	R	ER	HR	BB-IBB	SO
1991— Atlanta (N.L.)	0	0	...	0.00	3	0	0	0	0-0	1.2	2	0	0	0	2-0	1
1992— Atlanta (N.L.)	0	0	...	0.00	2	0	0	0	0-0	.2	0	0	0	0	1-1	0
1995— Atlanta (N.L.)	0	0	...	1.80	4	0	0	0	2-3	5.0	4	1	1	1	3-2	3
1996— Atlanta (N.L.)	0	0	...	6.23	4	0	0	0	0-1	4.1	7	3	3	1	2-1	4
2001— New York (A.L.)	Did not play.															
World Series totals (4 years)	0	0	...	3.09	13	0	0	0	2-4	11.2	13	4	4	2	8-4	8

ALL-STAR GAME RECORD

	W	L	Pct.	ERA	GS	CG	ShO	Sv.-Opp.	IP	H	R	ER	HR	BB-IBB	SO
All-Star Game totals (1 year)	0	0	...	0.00	0	0	0	0-0	.2	1	0	0	0	0-0	0

WOLF, RANDY P PHILLIES

PERSONAL: Born August 22, 1976, in Canoga Park, Calif. ... 6-0/194. ... Throws left, bats left. ... Full name: Randall C. Wolf.

HIGH SCHOOL: El Camino Real (Woodland Hills, Calif.).

COLLEGE: Pepperdine.

TRANSACTIONS/CAREER NOTES: Selected by Los Angeles Dodgers organization in 25th round of free-agent draft (June 2, 1994); did not sign. ... Selected by Philadelphia Phillies organization in second round of free-agent draft (June 3, 1997). ... On Philadelphia disabled list (August 2-September 1, 2001); included rehabilitation assignments to Scranton/Wilkes-Barre (August 17-28) and Reading (August 29-September 1). ... On Philadelphia disabled list (March 25-April 12, 2002); included rehabilitation assignment to Clearwater (April 6-12).

STATISTICAL NOTES: Pitched 8-0 one-hit, complete-game victory against Cincinnati (September 26, 2001).

CAREER HITTING (MLB): 34-for-191 (.178), 15 R, 7 2B, 0 3B, 1 HR, 10 RBI.

Year	League	W	L	Pct.	ERA	G	GS	CG	ShO	Sv.-Opp.	IP	H	R	ER	HR	BB-IBB	SO
1997—	Batavia (NY-Penn)............	4	0	1.000	1.58	7	7	0	0	0-...	40.0	29	8	7	1	8-0	53
1998—	Reading (East.).................	2	0	1.000	1.44	4	4	0	0	0-...	25.0	15	4	4	0	4-0	33
	—Scranton/W.B. (I.L.).........	9	7	.563	4.62	24	23	1	0	0-...	148.0	167	88	76	16	48-4	118
1999—	Scranton/W.B. (I.L.).........	4	5	.444	3.61	12	12	0	0	0-...	77.1	73	36	31	8	29-1	72
	—Philadelphia (N.L.)...........	6	9	.400	5.55	22	21	0	0	0-0	121.2	126	78	75	20	67-0	116
2000—	Philadelphia (N.L.)...........	11	9	.550	4.36	32	32	1	0	0-0	206.1	210	107	100	25	83-2	160
2001—	Philadelphia (N.L.)...........	10	11	.476	3.70	28	25	4	2	0-0	163.0	150	74	67	15	51-4	152
	—Scranton/W.B. (I.L.).........	0	1	.000	5.00	2	2	0	0	0-...	9.0	10	6	5	2	5-0	7
	—Reading (East.).................	0	0	...	4.50	1	1	0	0	0-...	6.0	5	3	3	0	2-0	7
2002—	Clearwater (FSL).............	0	0	...	0.00	1	1	0	0	0-...	5.0	1	0	0	0	1-0	8
	—Philadelphia (N.L.)...........	11	9	.550	3.20	31	31	3	2	0-0	210.2	172	77	75	23	63-5	172
Major League totals (4 years).....		38	38	.500	4.07	113	109	8	4	0-0	701.2	658	336	317	83	264-11	600

WOMACK, TONY — SS — DIAMONDBACKS

PERSONAL: Born September 25, 1969, in Danville, Va. ... 5-9/170. ... Bats left, throws right. ... Full name: Anthony Darrell Womack.

HIGH SCHOOL: Gretna (Va.).

COLLEGE: Guilford (N.C.); then UNC Greensboro (did not play).

TRANSACTIONS/CAREER NOTES: Selected by Pittsburgh Pirates organization in seventh round of free-agent draft (June 3, 1991). ... On disabled list (April 17-26 and August 28, 1992-remainder of season). ... Traded by Pirates to Arizona Diamondbacks for OF Paul Weichard and a player to be named later (February 26, 1999); Pirates acquired P Jason Boyd to complete deal (August 25, 1999). ... On Arizona disabled list (March 26-April 12, 1999); included rehabilitation assignment to Tucson (April 8-12). ... On Arizona disabled list (July 23-August 6, 2001); included rehabilitation assignment to Tucson (August 2-6).

STATISTICAL NOTES: Tied for American Association lead with 12 sacrifice hits in 1994. ... Led Pacific Coast League with 14 sacrifice hits in 1996. ... Led N.L. second basemen with 20 errors in 1997. ... Had 16-game hitting streak (July 3-22, 1998). ... Had 24-game hitting streak (May 2-29, 2000). ... Career major league grand slams: 2.

MISCELLANEOUS: Holds Arizona Diamondbacks all-time records for most triples (34) and most stolen bases (174).

2002 GAMES PLAYED BY POSITION (MLB): SS—149; OF—1.

			BATTING														FIELDING	
Year	Team (League)	Pos.	G	AB	R	H	2B	3B	HR	RBI	BB	SO	SB-CS	Avg.	OBP	SLG	E	Avg.
1991—	Welland (NY-Penn).....	SS-2B	45	166	30	46	3	0	1	8	17	39	26-5	.277	.344	.313	16	.921
1992—	Augusta (S.Atl.)..........	SS-2B	102	380	62	93	8	3	0	18	41	59	50-25	.245	.325	.282	40	.923
1993—	Salem (Caro.)............	SS	72	304	41	91	11	3	2	18	13	34	28-14	.299	.331	.375	28	.927
	—Carolina (Sou.)..........	SS	60	247	41	75	7	2	0	23	17	34	21-6	.304	.346	.348	11	.961
	—Pittsburgh (N.L.)........	SS	15	24	5	2	0	0	0	0	3	3	2-0	.083	.185	.083	1	.971
1994—	Buffalo (A.A.).............	SS-2B	106	421	40	93	9	2	0	18	19	76	41-10	.221	.253	.252	22	.957
	—Pittsburgh (N.L.)........	2B-SS	5	12	4	4	0	0	0	1	2	3	0-0	.333	.429	.333	2	.818
1995—	Calgary (PCL)............	2B-SS	30	107	12	30	3	1	0	6	12	11	7-5	.280	.353	.327	5	.963
	—Carolina (Sou.)..........	SS-2B	82	332	52	85	9	4	1	19	19	36	27-10	.256	.300	.316	18	.953
1996—	Calgary (PCL)............	S-2-O-DH	131	506	75	151	19	11	1	47	31	79	37-12	.298	.339	.385	24	.961
	—Pittsburgh (N.L.)........	OF-2B	17	30	11	10	3	1	0	7	6	1	2-0	.333	.459	.500	2	.905
1997—	Pittsburgh (N.L.)........	2B-SS	155	641	85	178	26	9	6	50	43	109	*60-7	.278	.326	.374	†20	.975
1998—	Pittsburgh (N.L.)........	2B-OF-SS	159	655	85	185	26	7	3	45	38	94	*58-8	.282	.319	.357	17	.978
1999—	Tucson (PCL)■..........	OF	4	16	1	4	1	0	1	3	2	3	0-1	.250	.333	.500	0	1.000
	—Arizona (N.L.)............	OF-2B-SS	144	614	111	170	25	10	4	41	52	68	*72-13	.277	.332	.370	5	.987
2000—	Arizona (N.L.)............	SS-OF	146	617	95	167	21	*14	7	57	30	74	45-11	.271	.307	.384	18	.970
2001—	Arizona (N.L.)............	SS-OF	125	481	66	128	19	5	3	30	23	54	28-7	.266	.307	.345	22	.955
	—Tucson (PCL)............	SS	4	13	1	5	0	1	0	2	0	1	0-1	.385	.385	.538	2	.846
2002—	Arizona (N.L.)............	SS-OF	153	590	90	160	23	5	5	57	46	80	29-12	.271	.325	.353	20	.964
Major League totals (9 years)			919	3664	552	1004	143	51	28	288	243	486	296-58	.274	.321	.364	107	.971

DIVISION SERIES RECORD

			BATTING														FIELDING	
Year	Team (League)	Pos.	G	AB	R	H	2B	3B	HR	RBI	BB	SO	SB-CS	Avg.	OBP	SLG	E	Avg.
1999—	Arizona (N.L.)............	OF-SS	4	18	2	2	0	1	0	0	0	6	0-0	.111	.111	.222	2	.833
2001—	Arizona (N.L.)............	SS	5	17	1	5	1	0	0	1	3	2	0-1	.294	.400	.353	2	.905
2002—	Arizona (N.L.)............	SS	3	13	1	2	0	0	0	0	1	1	0-0	.154	.214	.154	1	.941
Division series totals (3 years)			12	48	4	9	1	1	0	1	4	9	0-1	.188	.250	.250	5	.900

CHAMPIONSHIP SERIES RECORD

RECORDS: Shares N.L. single-game record for most at-bats—6 (October 20, 2001).

			BATTING														FIELDING	
Year	Team (League)	Pos.	G	AB	R	H	2B	3B	HR	RBI	BB	SO	SB-CS	Avg.	OBP	SLG	E	Avg.
2001—	Arizona (N.L.)............	SS	4	20	4	4	1	0	0	0	0	2	0-1	.200	.200	.250	0	1.000

WORLD SERIES RECORD

RECORDS: Shares single-game record for most at-bats—6 (November 3, 2001).

NOTES: Member of World Series championship team (2001).

			BATTING														FIELDING	
Year	Team (League)	Pos.	G	AB	R	H	2B	3B	HR	RBI	BB	SO	SB-CS	Avg.	OBP	SLG	E	Avg.
2001—	Arizona (N.L.)............	SS	7	32	3	8	3	0	0	3	1	7	1-1	.250	.294	.344	1	.968

ALL-STAR GAME RECORD

	AB	R	H	2B	3B	HR	RBI	BB	SO	SB-CS	Avg.	OBP	SLG	E	Avg.
All-Star Game totals (1 year)	1	0	0	0	0	0	0	0	0	0-0	.000	.000	.000	0	1.000

WOOD, KERRY — P — CUBS

PERSONAL: Born June 16, 1977, in Irving, Texas. ... 6-5/230. ... Throws right, bats right. ... Full name: Kerry Lee Wood.

HIGH SCHOOL: Grand Prairie (Texas).

TRANSACTIONS/CAREER NOTES: Selected by Chicago Cubs organization in first round (fourth pick overall) of free-agent draft (June 1, 1995). ... On disabled list (May 24-June 19, 1996). ... On disabled list (March 31, 1999-entire season). ... On Chicago disabled list (March 25-May 2 and July 30-August 22, 2000); included rehabilitation assignments to Daytona (April 13-23) and Iowa (April 23-April 28). ... On suspended list (September 8-11, 2000). ... On disabled list (August 4-September 7, 2001).

RECORDS: Shares major league single-game record for most strikeouts (nine-inning game)—20 (May 6, 1998). ... Holds N.L. record for most strikeouts in consecutive games—33 (May 6 [20] and 11 [13], 1998).

HONORS: Named N.L. Rookie Pitcher of the Year by The Sporting News (1998). ... Named N.L. Rookie of the Year by Baseball Writers' Association of America (1998).

STATISTICAL NOTES: Led Florida State League with 14 hit batsmen and seven balks in 1996. ... Pitched 2-0 one-hit, complete-game victory against Houston (May 6, 1998). ... Struck out 20 batters in one game (May 6, 1998). ... Struck out 16 batters in one game (August 26, 1998). ... Pitched 1-0 one-hit, complete-game victory against Milwaukee (May 25, 2001). ... Tied for N.L. lead with 16 hit batsmen in 2002.

MISCELLANEOUS: Struck out and had sacrifice hit in two appearances as pinch hitter (2000). ... Appeared in one game as pinch runner (2001).

CAREER HITTING (MLB): 38-for-214 (.178), 17 R, 1 2B, 0 3B, 4 HR, 19 RBI.

Year League	W	L	Pct.	ERA	G	GS	CG	ShO	Sv.-Opp.	IP	H	R	ER	HR	BB-IBB	SO
1995— Gulf Coast Cubs (GCL).....	0	0	...	0.00	1	1	0	0	0-...	3.0	0	0	0	0	1-0	2
— Williamsport (NY-Penn)...	0	0	...	10.38	2	2	0	0	0-...	4.1	5	8	5	0	5-0	5
1996— Daytona (FSL).................	10	2	•.833	2.91	22	22	0	0	0-...	114.1	72	51	37	6	70-0	136
1997— Orlando (Sou.)................	6	7	.462	4.50	19	19	0	0	0-...	94.0	58	49	47	2	79-2	106
— Iowa (A.A.).........................	4	2	.667	4.68	10	10	0	0	0-...	57.2	35	35	30	2	52-0	80
1998— Iowa (PCL)........................	1	0	1.000	0.00	1	1	0	0	0-...	5.0	1	0	0	0	2-0	11
— Chicago (N.L.)...................	13	6	.684	3.40	26	26	1	1	0-0	166.2	117	69	63	14	85-1	233
1999— Chicago (N.L.)...................								Did not play.								
2000— Daytona (FSL).................	2	0	1.000	1.50	2	2	0	0	0-...	12.0	3	2	2	0	5-0	17
— Iowa (PCL)........................	0	0	...	2.57	1	1	0	0	0-...	7.0	4	2	2	1	4-0	7
— Chicago (N.L.)...................	8	7	.533	4.80	23	23	1	0	0-0	137.0	112	77	73	17	87-0	132
2001— Chicago (N.L.)...................	12	6	.667	3.36	28	28	1	1	0-0	174.1	127	70	65	16	92-3	217
2002— Chicago (N.L.)...................	12	11	.522	3.66	33	33	4	1	0-0	213.2	169	92	87	22	97-5	217
Major League totals (4 years).....	45	30	.600	3.75	110	110	7	3	0-0	691.2	525	308	288	69	361-9	799

DIVISION SERIES RECORD

Year League	W	L	Pct.	ERA	G	GS	CG	ShO	Sv.-Opp.	IP	H	R	ER	HR	BB-IBB	SO
1998— Chicago (N.L.)..................	0	1	.000	1.80	1	1	0	0	0-0	5.0	3	1	1	0	4-1	5

WOODARD, STEVE P

PERSONAL: Born May 15, 1975, in Hartselle, Ala. ... 6-4/217. ... Throws right, bats left. ... Full name: Steve Larry Woodard Jr.

HIGH SCHOOL: Hartselle (Ala.).

TRANSACTIONS/CAREER NOTES: Selected by Milwaukee Brewers organization in fifth round of free-agent draft (June 2, 1994). ... On disabled list (August 14-September 11, 1999). ... Traded by Brewers with P Bob Wickman and P Jason Bere to Cleveland Indians for 1B/OF Richie Sexson, P Paul Rigdon, P Kane Davis and a player to be named later (July 28, 2000); Brewers acquired 2B Marcos Scutaro to complete deal (August 30). ... On Cleveland disabled list (April 10-30, 2001); included rehabilitation assignment to Akron (April 30). ... Released by Indians (December 12, 2001). ... Signed by Texas Rangers organization (January 14, 2002). ... Released by Rangers (June 3, 2002). ... Signed by Philadelphia Phillies organization (June 4, 2002). ... Released by Phillies (July 24, 2002). ... Signed by St. Louis Cardinals organization (July 25, 2002). ... Granted free agency (October 15, 2002).

RECORDS: Shares A.L. record for most strikeouts in first major league game—12 (July 28, 1997).

HONORS: Named Texas League Pitcher of the Year (1997).

CAREER HITTING (MLB): 15-for-126 (.119), 6 R, 3 2B, 0 3B, 0 HR, 6 RBI.

Year League	W	L	Pct.	ERA	G	GS	CG	ShO	Sv.-Opp.	IP	H	R	ER	HR	BB-IBB	SO
1994— Arizona Brewers (Ariz.)....	•8	0	*1.000	2.40	15	12	2	0	0-...	82.2	68	29	22	3	13-1	85
1995— Beloit (Midw.)..................	7	4	.636	4.54	21	21	0	0	0-...	115.0	113	68	58	12	31-0	94
1996— Stockton (Calif.)..............	12	9	.571	4.02	28	•28	0	0	0-...	*181.1	201	89	81	14	33-1	142
1997— El Paso (Texas)................	14	3	.824	3.17	19	19	*6	•1	0-...	136.1	136	56	48	8	25-2	97
— Tucson (PCL).....................	1	0	1.000	0.00	1	1	0	0	0-...	7.0	3	0	0	0	1-0	6
— Milwaukee (A.L.)...............	3	3	.500	5.15	7	7	0	0	0-0	36.2	39	25	21	5	6-0	32
1998— Milwaukee (N.L.)...............	10	12	.455	4.18	34	26	0	0	0-0	165.2	170	83	77	19	33-4	135
1999— Milwaukee (N.L.)...............	11	8	.579	4.52	31	29	2	0	0-0	185.0	219	101	93	23	36-7	119
2000— Milwaukee (N.L.)...............	1	7	.125	5.96	27	11	1	0	0-0	93.2	125	70	62	16	33-4	65
— Cleveland (A.L.)■............	3	3	.500	5.67	13	11	0	0	0-0	54.0	57	35	34	10	11-1	35
2001— Cleveland (A.L.)...............	3	3	.500	5.20	29	10	0	0	0-0	97.0	129	60	56	10	17-1	52
— Akron (East.)....................	0	0	...	3.00	1	1	0	0	0-...	3.0	3	1	1	0	1-0	2
— Buffalo (I.L.)....................	4	2	.667	2.39	6	6	1	0	0-...	37.2	36	11	10	2	1-1	32
2002— Texas (A.L.)■..................	0	0	...	6.62	14	0	0	0	0-1	17.2	20	13	13	4	8-1	14
— Scranton/W.B. (I.L.)■......	3	1	.750	2.16	15	1	0	0	5-...	25.0	17	6	6	1	6-1	13
— Memphis (PCL)■.............	2	3	.400	6.30	7	6	1	0	0-...	40.0	53	28	28	7	3-0	42
A.L. totals (4 years).....................	9	9	.500	5.44	63	28	0	0	0-1	205.1	245	133	124	29	42-3	133
N.L. totals (3 years).....................	22	27	.449	4.70	92	66	3	0	0-0	444.1	514	254	232	58	102-15	319
Major League totals (6 years).....	31	36	.463	4.93	155	94	3	0	0-1	649.2	759	387	356	87	144-18	452

WOODWARD, CHRIS SS BLUE JAYS

PERSONAL: Born June 27, 1976, in Covina, Calif. ... 6-0/185. ... Bats right, throws right. ... Full name: Christopher Michael Woodward.

HIGH SCHOOL: Northview (Covina, Calif.).

JUNIOR COLLEGE: Mount San Antonio (Calif.).

TRANSACTIONS/CAREER NOTES: Selected by Toronto Blue Jays organization in 54th round of free-agent draft (June 2, 1994). ... On Syracuse disabled list (May 2-17 and May 21-June 6, 1999). ... On Toronto disabled list (July 1-26, 2001); included rehabilitation assignment to Syracuse (July 20-26). ... On Toronto disabled list (June 21-July 11, 2002); included rehabilitation assignment to Dunedin (July 8-11).

STATISTICAL NOTES: Led Pioneer League shortstops with 106 putouts, 202 assists and 338 total chances in 1995. ... Led South Atlantic League shortstops with 214 putouts in 1996. ... Hit three home runs in one game (August 7, 2002).

2002 GAMES PLAYED BY POSITION (MLB): SS—79; 2B—6; 1B—3; 3B—2; DH—2.

		BATTING														FIELDING	
Year Team (League)	Pos.	G	AB	R	H	2B	3B	HR	RBI	BB	SO	SB-CS	Avg.	OBP	SLG	E	Avg.
1995—Medicine Hat (Pio.)....	SS	•72	241	44	56	8	0	3	21	33	41	9-4	.232	.336	.303	30	.911
1996—Hagerstown (S.Atl.)....	SS	123	424	41	95	24	2	1	48	43	70	11-3	.224	.300	.297	30	.951
1997—Dunedin (FSL)..........	SS	91	314	38	92	13	4	1	38	52	52	4-8	.293	.397	.369	12	.972
1998—Knoxville (Sou.)..........	SS	73	253	36	62	12	0	3	27	26	47	3-5	.245	.319	.328	11	.971
—Syracuse (I.L.)..........	SS	25	85	9	17	6	0	2	6	7	20	1-1	.200	.261	.341	4	.961
1999—Syracuse (I.L.)..........	SS-2B	75	281	46	82	20	3	1	20	38	49	4-1	.292	.378	.395	11	.966
—Toronto (A.L.)............	SS-3B	14	26	1	6	1	0	0	2	2	6	0-0	.231	.276	.269	2	.944
2000—Toronto (A.L.)............	SS-3B-1B-2B	37	104	16	19	7	0	3	14	10	28	1-0	.183	.254	.337	5	.963
—Syracuse (I.L.)...........	2B-3B-SS	37	143	23	46	13	2	5	25	11	30	2-0	.322	.370	.545	2	.988
2001—Toronto (A.L.)............	2-3-S-1-DH	37	63	9	12	3	2	2	5	1	14	0-1	.190	.203	.397	8	.933
—Syracuse (I.L.)...........	3B-SS-1B-2B	51	193	29	59	14	3	11	31	16	40	0-0	.306	.360	.580	9	.950
2002—Toronto (A.L.)............	S-2-1-3-D	90	312	48	86	13	4	13	45	26	72	3-0	.276	.330	.468	15	.964
—Dunedin (FSL)...........	SS	2	6	1	2	0	0	0	0	0	0	0-0	.333	.429	.333	0	1.000
Major League totals (4 years)		178	505	74	123	24	6	18	66	39	120	4-1	.244	.297	.422	30	.958

WOOTEN, SHAWN 1B/C ANGELS

PERSONAL: Born July 24, 1972, in Glendora, Calif. ... 5-10/225. ... Bats right, throws right. ... Full name: William Shawn Wooten.

HIGH SCHOOL: South Hills (Covina, Calif.).

JUNIOR COLLEGE: Mount San Antonio College (Calif.).

TRANSACTIONS/CAREER NOTES: Selected by Detroit Tigers organization in 18th round of free-agent draft (June 3, 1993). ... Released by Tigers (June 19, 1995). ... Signed by Moose Jaw, Prairie League (1995). ... Signed by California Angels organization (February 26, 1997). ... Angels franchise renamed Anaheim Angels for 1997 season. ... On Anaheim disabled list (March 21-July 11, 2002); included rehabilitation assignment to Salt Lake (May 28-June 1) and Rancho Cucamonga (June 28-July 11).

STATISTICAL NOTES: Led South Atlantic League third basemen with .938 fielding percentage in 1994. ... Led Eastern League third basemen with 91 putouts and 356 total chances in 1999.

2002 GAMES PLAYED BY POSITION (MLB): DH—26; 1B—16; C—2; 3B—1.

		BATTING														FIELDING	
Year Team (League)	Pos.	G	AB	R	H	2B	3B	HR	RBI	BB	SO	SB-CS	Avg.	OBP	SLG	E	Avg.
1993—Bristol (Appl.)............	1B-3B-OF	52	177	26	62	12	2	8	39	24	20	1-2	*.350	.432	.576	10	.956
—Fayetteville (S.Atl.).....	1B-3B	5	16	2	4	0	0	1	5	3	3	0-0	.250	.368	.438	0	1.000
1994—Fayetteville (S.Atl.).....	3B-1B	121	439	45	118	25	4	3	61	27	84	1-3	.269	.324	.364	24	†.938
1995—Jacksonville (Sou.).....	3B	20	70	4	9	1	0	2	7	1	17	0-0	.129	.151	.229	5	.921
—Lakeland (FSL)..........	3B	38	135	11	31	10	1	2	11	10	28	0-1	.230	.291	.363	7	.942
—Moose Jaw (PRA)■...		52	201	38	75	12	2	11	55	18	26	3-...	.373	...	.617	...	...
1996—Moose Jaw (PRA)......		77	292	44	89	17	0	12	57	18	46	2-0	.305	.348	.486	...	...
1997—Cedar Rapids (Mid.)■	C-1B	108	353	43	102	23	1	15	75	49	71	0-1	.289	.379	.487	0	1.000
1998—Lake Elsinore (Calif.)..	1B-3B-2B	105	395	56	116	31	0	16	74	38	82	0-2	.294	.357	.494	1	.999
—Midland (Texas)..........	1B	8	28	3	9	4	0	1	6	3	4	0-0	.321	.387	.571	1	.967
1999—Erie (East.)................	3B-C-1B	137	518	70	151	27	1	19	88	50	102	3-1	.292	.360	.458	22	.940
2000—Erie (East.)................	C-3B-1B	51	191	32	56	12	2	9	35	17	30	4-1	.293	.350	.518	9	.970
—Edmonton (PCL)........	C-3B	66	252	43	89	21	3	11	42	18	38	0-0	.353	.401	.591	7	.982
—Anaheim (A.L.)..........	C-1B	7	9	2	5	1	0	0	1	0	0	0-0	.556	.556	.667	0	1.000
2001—Anaheim (A.L.)..........	DH-C-1B-3B	79	221	24	69	8	1	8	32	5	42	2-0	.312	.332	.466	2	.992
2002—Anaheim (A.L.)..........	DH-1B-C-3B	49	113	13	33	8	0	3	19	6	24	2-0	.292	.331	.442	0	1.000
—Salt Lake (PCL)..........	1B-3B-C	10	42	2	11	2	0	0	7	0	11	0-0	.262	.279	.310	1	.976
—Rancho Cuca. (Calif.).	1B	6	18	2	4	3	0	0	3	4	4	0-0	.222	.348	.389	0	1.000
Major League totals (3 years)		135	343	39	107	17	1	11	52	11	66	4-0	.312	.337	.464	2	.994

DIVISION SERIES RECORD

		BATTING														FIELDING	
Year Team (League)	Pos.	G	AB	R	H	2B	3B	HR	RBI	BB	SO	SB-CS	Avg.	OBP	SLG	E	Avg.
2002—Anaheim (A.L.)..........	DH	3	9	4	6	0	0	1	2	0	1	0-0	.667	.667	1.000	0	...

CHAMPIONSHIP SERIES RECORD

		BATTING														FIELDING	
Year Team (League)	Pos.	G	AB	R	H	2B	3B	HR	RBI	BB	SO	SB-CS	Avg.	OBP	SLG	E	Avg.
2002—Anaheim (A.L.)..........	DH	3	8	1	2	0	0	0	1	0	3	0-0	.250	.250	.250	0	...

WORLD SERIES RECORD

NOTES: Member of World Series championship team (2002).

		BATTING														FIELDING	
Year Team (League)	Pos.	G	AB	R	H	2B	3B	HR	RBI	BB	SO	SB-CS	Avg.	OBP	SLG	E	Avg.
2002—Anaheim (A.L.)..........	1B	3	2	0	1	0	0	0	0	0	0	0-0	.500	.500	.500	0	1.000

W

WORRELL, TIM P GIANTS

PERSONAL: Born July 5, 1967, in Pasadena, Calif. ... 6-4/230. ... Throws right, bats right. ... Full name: Timothy Howard Worrell. ... Brother of Todd Worrell, pitcher with St. Louis Cardinals (1985-92) and Los Angeles Dodgers (1993-97).

HIGH SCHOOL: Maranatha (Sierra Madre, Calif.).

COLLEGE: Biola (Calif.).

TRANSACTIONS/CAREER NOTES: Selected by San Diego Padres organization in 20th round of free-agent draft (June 5, 1989). ... On disabled list (April 19, 1994-remainder of season). ... On San Diego disabled list (April 24-September 1, 1995); included rehabilitation assignments to Rancho Cucamonga (May 3-17 and August 1-10) and Las Vegas (May 17-June 1 and August 10-30). ... Traded by Padres with OF Trey Beamon to Detroit Tigers for P Dan Miceli, P Donne Wall and 3B Ryan Balfe (November 19, 1997). ... Traded by Tigers with OF David Roberts to Cleveland Indians for OF Geronimo Berroa (June 24, 1998). ... Traded by Indians to Oakland Athletics for a player to be named later (July 12, 1998); Indians acquired SS Adam Robinson to complete deal (July 27, 1998). ... On Oakland disabled list (July 20-August 8, 1999); included rehabilitation assignment to Modesto (August 5-8). ... Granted free agency (October 29, 1999). ... Signed by Baltimore Orioles organization

(February 4, 2000). ... Released by Orioles (May 1, 2000). ... Signed by Chicago Cubs organization (May 8, 2000). ... Traded by Cubs to San Francisco Giants for 3B Bill Mueller (November 19, 2000). ... On San Francisco disabled list (July 9-26, 2001); included rehabilitation assignment to Arizona League Giants (July 22-26).

STATISTICAL NOTES: Pitched 2-0 no-hit victory for Las Vegas against Phoenix (September 5, 1992).

CAREER HITTING (MLB): 8-for-76 (.105), 6 R, 1 2B, 0 3B, 0 HR, 4 RBI.

Year League	W	L	Pct.	ERA	G	GS	CG	ShO	Sv.-Opp.	IP	H	R	ER	HR	BB-IBB	SO
1990— Charleston, S.C. (S.Atl.) ...	5	8	.385	4.64	20	19	3	0	0-...	110.2	120	65	57	6	28-2	68
1991— Waterloo (Midw.)	8	4	.667	3.34	14	14	3	2	0-...	86.1	70	36	32	5	33-0	83
— High Desert (Calif.)...........	5	2	.714	4.24	11	11	2	0	0-...	63.2	65	32	30	2	33-0	70
1992— Wichita (Texas)	8	6	.571	2.86	19	19	1	1	0-...	125.2	115	46	40	8	32-0	109
— Las Vegas (PCL)	4	2	.667	4.26	10	10	1	1	0-...	63.1	61	32	30	4	19-0	32
1993— Las Vegas (PCL)	5	6	.455	5.48	15	14	2	0	0-...	87.0	102	61	53	13	26-1	89
— San Diego (N.L.)	2	7	.222	4.92	21	16	0	0	0-0	100.2	104	63	55	11	43-5	52
1994— San Diego (N.L.)	0	1	.000	3.68	3	3	0	0	0-0	14.2	9	7	6	0	5-0	14
1995— Rancho Cuca. (Calif.)	0	2	.000	5.16	9	3	0	0	1-...	22.2	25	17	13	2	6-1	17
— Las Vegas (PCL)	0	2	.000	6.00	10	3	0	0	0-...	24.0	27	21	16	1	17-0	18
— San Diego (N.L.)	1	0	1.000	4.72	9	0	0	0	0-0	13.1	16	7	7	2	6-0	13
1996— San Diego (N.L.)	9	7	.563	3.05	50	11	0	0	1-2	121.0	109	45	41	9	39-1	99
1997— San Diego (N.L.)	4	8	.333	5.16	60	10	0	0	3-7	106.1	116	67	61	14	50-2	81
1998— Detroit (A.L.)■..................	2	6	.250	5.98	15	9	0	0	0-1	61.2	66	42	41	11	19-2	47
— Cleveland (A.L.)■............	0	0	...	5.06	3	0	0	0	0-0	5.1	6	3	3	0	2-0	2
— Oakland (A.L.)■..............	0	1	.000	4.00	25	0	0	0	0-2	36.0	34	17	16	5	8-1	33
1999— Oakland (A.L.)	2	2	.500	4.15	53	0	0	0	0-5	69.1	69	38	32	6	34-1	62
— Modesto (Calif.)	0	0	...	0.00	1	1	0	0	0-...	2.0	0	0	0	0	0-0	5
2000— Baltimore (A.L.)■............	2	2	.500	7.36	5	0	0	0	0-0	7.1	12	6	6	3	5-3	5
— Iowa (PCL)■....................	2	0	1.000	5.06	6	0	0	0	0-...	10.2	9	6	6	3	5-1	7
— Chicago (N.L.)..................	3	4	.429	2.47	54	0	0	0	3-6	62.0	60	20	17	7	24-8	52
2001— San Francisco (N.L.)■.....	2	5	.286	3.45	73	0	0	0	0-3	78.1	71	33	30	4	33-4	63
— Arizona Giants (Ariz.)	0	0	...	0.00	1	1	0	0	0-...	3.0	1	0	0	0	1-0	2
2002— San Francisco (N.L.)	8	2	.800	2.25	80	0	0	0	0-1	72.0	55	21	18	3	30-2	55
A.L. totals (3 years)	6	11	.353	4.91	101	9	0	0	0-8	179.2	187	106	98	25	68-7	149
N.L. totals (8 years).....................	29	34	.460	3.72	350	40	0	0	7-19	568.1	540	263	235	50	230-22	429
Major League totals (10 years)...	35	45	.438	4.01	451	49	0	0	7-27	748.0	727	369	333	75	298-29	578

DIVISION SERIES RECORD

Year League	W	L	Pct.	ERA	G	GS	CG	ShO	Sv.-Opp.	IP	H	R	ER	HR	BB-IBB	SO
1996— San Diego (N.L.)	0	0	...	2.45	2	0	0	0	0-1	3.2	4	1	1	0	1-0	2
2002— San Francisco (N.L.)	0	0	...	12.00	3	0	0	0	0-0	3.0	7	6	4	2	2-0	3
Division series totals (2 years)...	0	0	...	6.75	5	0	0	0	0-1	6.2	11	7	5	2	3-0	5

CHAMPIONSHIP SERIES RECORD

Year League	W	L	Pct.	ERA	G	GS	CG	ShO	Sv.-Opp.	IP	H	R	ER	HR	BB-IBB	SO
2002— San Francisco (N.L.)	2	0	1.000	2.08	4	0	0	0	0-0	4.1	2	1	1	1	0-0	3

WORLD SERIES RECORD

Year League	W	L	Pct.	ERA	G	GS	CG	ShO	Sv.-Opp.	IP	H	R	ER	HR	BB-IBB	SO
2002— San Francisco (N.L.)	1	1	.500	3.18	6	0	0	0	0-0	5.2	4	3	2	1	1-0	4

WRIGHT, DAN — P — WHITE SOX

PERSONAL: Born December 14, 1977, in Longview, Texas. ... 6-5/225. ... Throws right, bats right. ... Full name: Jonathan Daniel Wright.

HIGH SCHOOL: Sullivan South (Kingsport, Tenn.).

COLLEGE: Arkansas.

TRANSACTIONS/CAREER NOTES: Selected by Cleveland Indians organization in 19th round of free-agent draft (June 4, 1996); did not sign. ... Selected by Chicago White Sox organization in second round of free-agent draft (June 2, 1999); choice received from Baltimore Orioles as part of compensation for signing of Type A free-agent OF Albert Belle.

CAREER HITTING (MLB): 0-for-4 (.000), 0 R, 0 2B, 0 3B, 0 HR, 0 RBI.

Year League	W	L	Pct.	ERA	G	GS	CG	ShO	Sv.-Opp.	IP	H	R	ER	HR	BB-IBB	SO
1999— Bristol (Appl.)....................	2	0	1.000	1.00	10	0	0	0	1-...	18.0	14	8	2	1	9-1	18
— Burlington (Midw.)	0	0	...	6.00	2	0	0	0	0-...	6.0	5	4	4	1	3-0	3
2000— Winston-Salem (Caro.).....	9	8	.529	3.74	21	21	1	0	0-...	132.1	135	64	55	4	50-0	106
— Birmingham (Sou.)...........	2	4	.333	2.49	7	7	0	0	0-...	43.1	28	15	12	3	24-0	31
2001— Birmingham (Sou.)...........	7	7	.500	2.82	20	20	0	0	0-...	134.0	112	54	42	6	41-0	128
— Chicago (A.L.)	5	3	.625	5.70	13	12	0	0	0-0	66.1	78	45	42	12	39-1	36
2002— Chicago (A.L.)	14	12	.538	5.18	33	33	1	1	0-0	196.1	200	124	113	32	71-1	136
Major League totals (2 years).....	19	15	.559	5.31	46	45	1	1	0-0	262.2	278	169	155	44	110-2	172

WRIGHT, JAMEY — P

PERSONAL: Born December 24, 1974, in Oklahoma City. ... 6-5/234. ... Throws right, bats right. ... Full name: Jamey Alan Wright.

HIGH SCHOOL: Westmoore (Moore, Okla.).

TRANSACTIONS/CAREER NOTES: Selected by Colorado Rockies organization in first round (28th pick overall) of free-agent draft (June 3, 1993). ... On Colorado disabled list (May 15-June 8, 1997); included rehabilitation assignment to Salem (June 1-8). ... Traded by Rockies with C Henry Blanco to Milwaukee Brewers as part of three-way deal in which Rockies received 3B Jeff Cirillo, P Scott Karl and cash from Brewers, Oakland Athletics received P Justin Miller and cash from Rockies and Brewers received P Jimmy Haynes to A's (December 13, 1999). ... On Milwaukee disabled list (March 28-May 23, 2000); included rehabilitation assignments to Huntsville (May 6-13) and Indianapolis (May 14-20). ... On disabled list (May 25-June 10, 2001). ... On Milwaukee disabled list (April 11-May 24, 2002); included rehabilitation assignment to Indianapolis (May 9-20). ... Traded by Brewers with cash to St. Louis Cardinals for OF Chris Morris and a player to be named later (August 29, 2002); Brewers acquired P Mike Matthews to complete deal (September 11, 2002). ... Granted free agency (November 1, 2002).

STATISTICAL NOTES: Led N.L. pitchers with 18 hit batsmen in 2000. ... Tied for N.L. lead with 20 hit batsmen in 2001.

MISCELLANEOUS: Appeared in one game as pinch hitter (2001).

CAREER HITTING (MLB): 43-for-314 (.137), 19 R, 11 2B, 1 3B, 1 HR, 13 RBI.

Year League	W	L	Pct.	ERA	G	GS	CG	ShO	Sv.-Opp.	IP	H	R	ER	HR	BB-IBB	SO
1993—Arizona Rockies (Ariz.).....	1	3	.250	4.00	8	8	0	0	0-...	36.0	35	19	16	1	9-0	26
1994—Asheville (S.Atl.)..............	7	•14	.333	5.97	28	27	2	0	0-...	143.1	*188	107	*95	6	59-1	103
1995—Salem (Caro.)..................	10	8	.556	2.47	26	26	2	1	0-...	•171.0	160	74	47	7	72-3	95
—New Haven (East.).............	0	1	.000	9.00	1	1	0	0	0-...	3.0	6	6	3	0	3-0	0
1996—New Haven (East.)............	5	1	.833	0.81	7	7	1	1	0-...	44.2	27	7	4	0	12-0	54
—Colorado Springs (PCL)...	4	2	.667	2.72	9	9	0	0	0-...	59.2	53	20	18	3	22-0	40
—Colorado (N.L.)................	4	4	.500	4.93	16	15	0	0	0-0	91.1	105	60	50	8	41-1	45
1997—Colorado (N.L.)................	8	12	.400	6.25	26	26	1	0	0-0	149.2	198	113	104	19	71-3	59
—Salem (Caro.)..................	0	1	.000	9.00	1	1	0	0	0-...	1.0	1	1	1	0	1-0	1
—Colorado Springs (PCL)...	1	0	1.000	1.64	2	2	0	0	0-...	11.0	9	3	2	1	5-0	11
1998—Colorado (N.L.)................	9	14	.391	5.67	34	34	1	0	0-0	206.1	235	143	130	24	95-3	86
1999—Colorado (N.L.)................	4	3	.571	4.87	16	16	0	0	0-0	94.1	110	52	51	10	54-3	49
—Colorado Springs (PCL)...	5	7	.417	6.46	17	16	2	0	0-...	100.1	133	87	72	13	38-2	75
2000—Huntsville (Sou.)■..........	2	0	1.000	0.00	2	2	0	0	0-...	12.1	7	0	0	0	5-0	10
—Indianapolis (I.L.)............	0	0	...	1.80	1	1	0	0	0-...	5.0	8	5	1	0	3-0	7
—Milwaukee (N.L.).............	7	9	.438	4.10	26	25	0	0	0-0	164.2	157	81	75	12	88-5	96
2001—Milwaukee (N.L.).............	11	12	.478	4.90	33	33	1	1	0-0	194.2	201	115	106	26	98-10	129
2002—Indianapolis (I.L.)............	1	1	.500	4.11	3	3	0	0	0-...	15.1	16	7	7	3	5-0	13
—Milwaukee (N.L.).............	5	13	.278	5.35	19	19	1	1	0-0	114.1	115	72	68	15	63-8	69
—St. Louis (N.L.)................	2	0	1.000	4.80	4	3	0	0	0-0	15.0	15	8	8	2	12-1	8
Major League totals (7 years).....	50	67	.427	5.17	174	171	4	2	0-0	1030.1	1136	644	592	116	522-34	541

WRIGHT, JARET — P — INDIANS

PERSONAL: Born December 29, 1975, in Anaheim, Calif. ... 6-2/230. ... Throws right, bats right. ... Full name: Jaret Samuel Wright. ... Son of Clyde Wright, pitcher with California Angels (1966-73), Milwaukee Brewers (1974) and Texas Rangers (1975).

HIGH SCHOOL: Katella (Anaheim, Calif.).

TRANSACTIONS/CAREER NOTES: Selected by Cleveland Indians organization in first round (10th pick overall) of free-agent draft (June 2, 1994). ... On disabled list (June 19-September 23, 1996). ... On suspended list (May 10-16, 1999). ... On disabled list (July 19-August 3 and August 9-September 10, 1999); included rehabilitation assignments to Buffalo (September 2) and Akron (September 6). ... On Cleveland disabled list (May 12-27 and June 3, 2000-remainder of season); included rehabilitation assignments to Buffalo (July 29-August 2) and Akron (August 3-10). ... On Cleveland disabled list (March 31-May 19 and September 1, 2001-remainder of season); included rehabilitation assignments to Buffalo (April 30-May 12) and Akron (May 13-19). ... On Buffalo disabled list (July 4-August 9 and August 19-Septmeber 1, 2001) ... On Cleveland disabled list (March 30-July 20, 2002); included rehabilitation assignments to Buffalo (June 17-July 7 and July 11-19).

CAREER HITTING (MLB): 4-for-14 (.286), 2 R, 0 2B, 0 3B, 0 HR, 1 RBI.

Year League	W	L	Pct.	ERA	G	GS	CG	ShO	Sv.-Opp.	IP	H	R	ER	HR	BB-IBB	SO
1994—Burlington (Appl.)............	0	1	.000	5.40	4	4	0	0	0-...	13.1	13	10	8	1	9-0	16
1995—Columbus (S.Atl.)............	5	6	.455	3.00	24	24	0	0	0-...	129.0	93	55	43	9	79-0	113
1996—Kinston (Caro.)................	7	4	.636	2.50	19	19	0	0	0-...	101.0	65	32	28	1	55-0	109
1997—Akron (East.)..................	3	3	.500	3.67	8	8	1	0	0-...	54.0	43	26	22	4	23-2	59
—Buffalo (A.A.)....................	4	1	.800	1.80	7	7	1	1	0-...	45.0	30	16	9	4	19-0	47
—Cleveland (A.L.)................	8	3	.727	4.38	16	16	0	0	0-0	90.1	81	45	44	9	35-0	63
1998—Cleveland (A.L.)................	12	10	.545	4.72	32	32	1	1	0-0	192.2	207	109	101	22	87-4	140
1999—Cleveland (A.L.)................	8	10	.444	6.06	26	26	0	0	0-0	133.2	144	99	90	18	77-1	91
—Buffalo (I.L.)....................	0	0	...	0.00	1	1	0	0	0-...	3.0	0	0	0	0	0-0	4
—Akron (East.)..................	1	0	1.000	0.00	1	1	0	0	0-...	5.0	3	0	0	0	1-0	6
2000—Cleveland (A.L.)................	3	4	.429	4.70	9	9	1	1	0-0	51.2	44	27	27	6	28-0	36
—Buffalo (I.L.)....................	0	0	...	0.00	1	1	0	0	0-...	2.0	0	0	0	0	1-0	1
—Akron (East.)..................	0	0	...	3.38	2	2	0	0	0-...	8.0	4	3	3	0	3-0	5
2001—Buffalo (I.L.)....................	3	1	.750	4.71	7	7	0	0	0-...	28.2	25	18	15	3	13-0	28
—Akron (East.)..................	0	0	...	1.29	1	1	0	0	0-...	7.0	2	1	1	1	0-0	4
—Cleveland (A.L.)................	2	2	.500	6.52	7	7	0	0	0-0	29.0	36	22	21	2	22-0	18
2002—Buffalo (I.L.)....................	5	3	.625	3.88	10	10	1	0	0-...	55.2	57	27	24	5	24-0	43
—Cleveland (A.L.)................	2	3	.400	15.71	8	6	0	0	0-0	18.1	40	34	32	3	19-0	12
Major League totals (6 years).....	35	32	.522	5.50	98	96	2	2	0-0	515.2	552	336	315	60	268-5	360

DIVISION SERIES RECORD

Year League	W	L	Pct.	ERA	G	GS	CG	ShO	Sv.-Opp.	IP	H	R	ER	HR	BB-IBB	SO
1997—Cleveland (A.L.)................	2	0	1.000	3.97	2	2	0	0	0-0	11.1	11	6	5	0	7-1	10
1998—Cleveland (A.L.)................	0	1	.000	12.46	1	1	0	0	0-0	4.1	7	6	6	2	2-0	6
1999—Cleveland (A.L.)................	0	1	.000	22.50	1	0	0	0	0-0	2.0	4	5	5	1	1-0	1
Division series totals (3 years)...	2	2	.500	8.15	4	3	0	0	0-0	17.2	22	17	16	3	10-1	17

CHAMPIONSHIP SERIES RECORD

RECORDS: Shares single-inning record for most home runs allowed—3 (October 12, 1997, third inning).

Year League	W	L	Pct.	ERA	G	GS	CG	ShO	Sv.-Opp.	IP	H	R	ER	HR	BB-IBB	SO
1997—Cleveland (A.L.)................	0	0	...	15.00	1	1	0	0	0-0	3.0	6	5	5	3	2-0	3
1998—Cleveland (A.L.)................	0	1	.000	8.10	2	1	0	0	0-0	6.2	7	6	6	1	8-0	4
Champ. series totals (2 years)....	0	1	.000	10.24	3	2	0	0	0-0	9.2	13	11	11	4	10-0	7

WORLD SERIES RECORD

Year League	W	L	Pct.	ERA	G	GS	CG	ShO	Sv.-Opp.	IP	H	R	ER	HR	BB-IBB	SO
1997—Cleveland (A.L.)................	1	0	1.000	2.92	2	2	0	0	0-0	12.1	7	4	4	2	10-0	12

W

WRIGHT, RON — 1B

PERSONAL: Born January 21, 1976, in Delta, Utah. ... 6-1/230. ... Bats right, throws right. ... Full name: Ronald Wade Wright.

HIGH SCHOOL: Kamiakin (Kennewick, Wash.).

TRANSACTIONS/CAREER NOTES: Selected by Atlanta Braves organization in seventh round of free-agent draft (June 2, 1994). ... Traded by Braves with OF Corey Pointer and a player to be named later to Pittsburgh Pirates for P Denny Neagle (August 28, 1996); Pirates acquired P Jason Schmidt to complete deal (August 30, 1996). ... On Calgary disabled list (July 24-September 2, 1997). ... On Nashville disabled list (April

29-September 8, 1998); included rehabilitation assignment to Gulf Coast Pirates (August 3-6). ... On Altoona disabled list (April 26-May 3 and May 23, 1999-remainder of season). ... Claimed on waivers by Cincinnati Reds (October 14, 1999). ... Granted free agency (October 18, 2000). ... Signed by Tampa Bay Devil Rays organization (November 10, 2000). ... Granted free agency (October 15, 2001). ... Signed by Seattle Mariners organization (December 1, 2001). ... On Tacoma disabled list (July 16-August 1, 2002). ... Granted free agency (October 15, 2002).

STATISTICAL NOTES: Led South Atlantic League first basemen with 99 assists in 1995. ... Led International League first basemen with 980 putouts, 66 assists and 1,054 total chances in 2001.

2002 GAMES PLAYED BY POSITION (MLB): DH—1.

		BATTING														FIELDING	
Year Team (League)	**Pos.**	**G**	**AB**	**R**	**H**	**2B**	**3B**	**HR**	**RBI**	**BB**	**SO**	**SB-CS**	**Avg.**	**OBP**	**SLG**	**E**	**Avg.**
1994— GC Braves (GCL)	1B	45	169	10	29	9	0	1	16	10	21	1-0	.172	.218	.243	6	.986
1995— Macon (S.Atl.)	1B	135	537	93	143	23	1	•32	104	62	118	2-0	.266	.343	.492	18	.984
1996— Durham (Caro.)	1B	66	240	47	66	15	2	20	62	37	71	1-0	.275	.363	.604	7	.987
— Greenville (Sou.)	1B-DH	63	232	39	59	11	1	16	52	38	73	1-0	.254	.360	.517	6	.988
— Carolina (Sou.)■	1B	4	14	1	2	0	0	0	0	2	7	0-1	.143	.250	.143	2	.941
1997— Calgary (PCL)	1B-DH	91	336	50	102	31	0	16	63	24	81	0-2	.304	.348	.539	3	.995
1998— Nashville (PCL)	1B-DH	17	56	6	12	3	0	0	9	9	18	0-0	.214	.328	.268	2	.986
— GC Pirates (GCL)	DH-1B	3	10	4	6	0	0	2	5	2	0	0-0	.600	.615	1.200	0	1.000
1999— Altoona (East.)	DH-1B	24	80	2	17	6	0	0	4	9	27	0-0	.213	.300	.288	1	.991
2000— Chattanooga (Sou.)	1B	79	237	36	63	18	0	12	50	37	70	2-2	.266	.367	.494	6	.989
— Louisville (I.L.)	1B	18	60	10	12	5	0	2	13	8	18	0-0	.200	.294	.383	1	.992
2001— Durham (I.L.)■	1B	121	439	63	115	27	0	20	75	51	103	2-2	.262	.340	.460	8	*.992
2002— Tacoma (PCL)	1B	99	359	52	98	20	1	15	57	39	89	0-1	.273	.351	.460	4	.989
— Seattle (A.L.)	DH	1	3	0	0	0	0	0	0	0	1	0-0	.000	.000	.000	...	...
Major League totals (1 year)		1	3	0	0	0	0	0	0	0	1	0-0	.000	.000	.000	...	...

WUNSCH, KELLY — P — WHITE SOX

PERSONAL: Born July 12, 1972, in Houston. ... 6-5/225. ... Throws left, bats left. ... Full name: Kelly Douglas Wunsch.

HIGH SCHOOL: Bellaire (Texas).

COLLEGE: Texas A&M.

TRANSACTIONS/CAREER NOTES: Selected by Atlanta Braves organization in 54th round of free-agent draft (June 4, 1990); did not sign. ... Selected by Milwaukee Brewers organization in first round (26th pick overall) of free-agent draft (June 3, 1993); pick received as compensation for Toronto Blue Jays signing Type-A free agent Paul Molitor. ... On El Paso disabled list (April 4-May 13, 1996; and April 8-May 7, 1998). ... On Stockton disabled list (June 19-September 10, 1996). ... On Louisville disabled list (July 10-17, 1999). ... Granted free agency (October 15, 1999). ... Signed by Chicago White Sox organization (November 15, 1999). ... On disabled list (June 18, 2001-remainder of season). ... On Chicago disabled list (March 27-May 18, 2002); included rehabilitation assignments to Charlotte (April 4-11 and April 21-May 18).

CAREER HITTING (MLB): 0-for-0 (.000), 0 R, 0 2B, 0 3B, 0 HR, 0 RBI.

Year League	**W**	**L**	**Pct.**	**ERA**	**G**	**GS**	**CG**	**ShO**	**Sv.-Opp.**	**IP**	**H**	**R**	**ER**	**HR**	**BB-IBB**	**SO**
1993— Beloit (Midw.)	1	5	.167	4.83	12	12	0	0	0-...	63.1	58	39	34	5	39-1	61
1994— Beloit (Midw.)	3	10	.231	6.16	17	17	0	0	0-...	83.1	88	69	57	11	47-1	77
— Helena (Pio.)	4	2	.667	5.12	9	9	1	0	0-...	51.0	52	39	29	7	30-0	57
1995— Beloit (Midw.)	4	7	.364	4.20	14	14	3	1	0-...	85.2	90	47	40	7	37-0	66
— Stockton (Calif.)	5	6	.455	5.33	14	13	1	1	0-...	74.1	89	51	44	4	39-0	62
1996—									Did not play.							
1997— Stockton (Calif.)	7	9	.438	3.46	24	22	2	2	0-...	143.0	141	65	55	11	62-0	98
1998— El Paso (Texas)	5	6	.455	5.95	17	17	1	1	0-...	101.1	127	81	67	11	31-0	70
— Louisville (I.L.)	3	1	.750	3.83	9	8	0	0	0-...	51.2	53	23	22	6	15-0	36
1999— Huntsville (Sou.)	4	1	.800	1.95	22	3	0	0	1-...	50.2	40	13	11	1	23-1	35
— Louisville (I.L.)	2	1	.667	4.75	16	2	0	0	0-...	41.2	52	23	22	4	14-0	20
2000— Chicago (A.L.)■	6	3	.667	2.93	*83	0	0	0	1-5	61.1	50	22	20	4	29-1	51
2001— Chicago (A.L.)	2	1	.667	7.66	33	0	0	0	0-2	22.1	21	19	19	4	9-1	16
2002— Charlotte (I.L.)	1	0	1.000	2.25	10	2	0	0	0-...	12.0	13	3	3	0	5-0	9
— Chicago (A.L.)	2	1	.667	3.41	50	0	0	0	0-1	31.2	26	12	12	3	19-1	22
Major League totals (3 years)	10	5	.667	3.98	166	0	0	0	1-8	115.1	97	53	51	11	57-3	89

DIVISION SERIES RECORD

Year League	**W**	**L**	**Pct.**	**ERA**	**G**	**GS**	**CG**	**ShO**	**Sv.-Opp.**	**IP**	**H**	**R**	**ER**	**HR**	**BB-IBB**	**SO**
2000— Chicago (A.L.)	0	1	.000	0.00	3	0	0	0	0-0	.2	2	1	0	0	0-0	0

YAN, ESTEBAN — P — DEVIL RAYS

PERSONAL: Born June 22, 1975, in Campina Del Seibo, Dominican Republic. ... 6-4/255. ... Throws right, bats right. ... Full name: Esteban Luis Yan.

HIGH SCHOOL: Escuela Hicayagua (Dominican Republic).

TRANSACTIONS/CAREER NOTES: Signed as non-drafted free agent by Atlanta Braves organization (November 21, 1990). ... Traded by Braves with OF Roberto Kelly and OF Tony Tarasco to Montreal Expos for OF Marquis Grissom (April 6, 1995). ... Contract sold by Expos to Baltimore Orioles organization (April 6, 1996). ... Selected by Tampa Bay Devil Rays in first round (18th pick overall) of expansion draft (November 18, 1997). ... On Tampa Bay disabled list (June 17-July 15, 1999); included rehabilitation assignment to St. Petersburg (July 10-15). ... On Tampa Bay disabled list (June 22-July 12, 2001); included rehabilitation assignment to Orlando (July 5-12).

STATISTICAL NOTES: Led South Atlantic League with six balks in 1994. ... Hit home run in first major league at-bat (June 4, 2000).

MISCELLANEOUS: Holds Tampa Bay Devil Rays all-time records for most strikeouts (351) and most games pitched (266). ... Shares Tampa Bay Devil Rays all-time record for most wins (26).

CAREER HITTING (MLB): 1-for-1 (1.000), 1 R, 0 2B, 0 3B, 1 HR, 1 RBI.

Year League	**W**	**L**	**Pct.**	**ERA**	**G**	**GS**	**CG**	**ShO**	**Sv.-Opp.**	**IP**	**H**	**R**	**ER**	**HR**	**BB-IBB**	**SO**
1991— San Pedro (DSL)	4	1	.800	3.63	18	11	0	0	0-...	72.0	61	36	29	...	26-...	34
1992— San Pedro (DSL)	12	3	.800	1.32	16	16	7	4	0-...	115.2	85	37	17	1	23-...	86
1993— Danville (Appl.)	4	7	.364	3.03	14	•14	0	0	0-...	71.1	73	46	24	4	24-1	50
1994— Macon (S.Atl.)	11	12	.478	3.27	28	•28	4	•3	0-...	170.2	155	85	62	15	34-1	121
1995— West Palm Beach (FSL)■	6	8	.429	3.07	24	21	1	0	1-...	137.2	139	63	47	3	33-0	89

Year	League	W	L	Pct.	ERA	G	GS	CG	ShO	Sv.-Opp.	IP	H	R	ER	HR	BB-IBB	SO
1996—	Bowie (East.)■	0	2	.000	5.63	9	1	0	0	0-...	16.0	18	12	10	2	8-0	15
—	Baltimore (A.L.)	0	0	...	5.79	4	0	0	0	0-0	9.1	13	7	6	3	3-1	7
—	Rochester (I.L.)	5	4	.556	4.27	22	10	0	0	1-...	71.2	75	37	34	6	18-0	61
1997—	Rochester (I.L.)	11	5	.688	3.10	34	12	0	0	2-...	119.0	107	54	41	13	37-0	131
—	Baltimore (A.L.)	0	1	.000	15.83	3	2	0	0	0-0	9.2	20	18	17	3	7-0	4
1998—	Tampa Bay (A.L.)■	5	4	.556	3.86	64	0	0	0	1-5	88.2	78	41	38	11	41-2	77
1999—	Tampa Bay (A.L.)	3	4	.429	5.90	50	1	0	0	0-3	61.0	77	41	40	8	32-4	46
—	St. Petersburg (FSL)	0	0	...	0.00	2	2	0	0	0-...	4.0	3	1	0	0	1-0	0
2000—	Tampa Bay (A.L.)	7	8	.467	6.21	43	20	0	0	0-2	137.2	158	98	95	26	42-0	111
2001—	Tampa Bay (A.L.)	4	6	.400	3.90	54	0	0	0	22-31	62.1	64	34	27	7	11-1	64
—	Orlando (Sou.)	0	0	...	3.00	2	2	0	0	0-...	3.0	3	1	1	0	0-0	4
2002—	Tampa Bay (A.L.)	7	8	.467	4.30	55	0	0	0	19-27	69.0	70	35	33	10	29-1	53
Major League totals (7 years)		26	31	.456	5.26	273	23	0	0	42-68	437.2	480	274	256	68	165-9	362

YOSHII, MASATO — P — EXPOS

PERSONAL: Born April 20, 1965, in Osaka, Japan. ... 6-2/215. ... Throws right, bats right.

HIGH SCHOOL: Minoshima (Japan).

TRANSACTIONS/CAREER NOTES: Played for Kintetsu Buffaloes of Japan Pacific League (1985-94). ... Played for Yakult Swallows of Japan Central League (1995-97). ... Signed as non-drafted free agent by New York Mets (January 13, 1998). ... Traded by Mets to Colorado Rockies for P Bobby M. Jones and P Lariel Gonzalez (January 14, 2000). ... Released by Rockies (March 28, 2001). ... Signed by Montreal Expos (April 13, 2001).

CAREER HITTING (MLB): 25-for-204 (.123), 10 R, 3 2B, 0 3B, 1 HR, 13 RBI.

Year	League	W	L	Pct.	ERA	G	GS	CG	ShO	Sv.-Opp.	IP	H	R	ER	HR	BB-IBB	SO
1985—	Kintetsu (Jap. Pac.)	0	1	.000	21.00	2	...	...	...	0-...	3.0	...	...	7	...	3-...	1
1986—	Kintetsu (Jap. Pac.)	0	0	...	23.14	2	...	...	...	0-...	2.1	...	...	6	...	2-...	2
1987—	Kintetsu (Jap. Pac.)	2	1	.667	4.75	13	...	...	...	0-...	36.0	...	...	19	...	12-...	23
1988—	Kintetsu (Jap. Pac.)	10	2	.833	2.69	50	...	...	...	24-...	80.1	...	...	24	...	44-...	44
1989—	Kintetsu (Jap. Pac.)	5	5	.500	2.99	47	...	...	...	20-...	84.1	...	...	28	...	37-...	44
1990—	Kintetsu (Jap. Pac.)	8	9	.471	3.39	45	...	...	...	15-...	74.1	...	...	28	...	30-...	55
1991—	Kintetsu (Jap. Pac.)	2	1	.667	3.42	21	...	...	...	2-...	26.1	...	...	10	...	6-...	13
1992—	Kintetsu (Jap. Pac.)	1	0	1.000	2.31	9	...	...	...	0-...	11.2	...	...	3	...	2-...	4
1993—	Kintetsu (Jap. Pac.)	5	5	.500	2.67	22	...	...	...	0-...	104.2	...	...	31	...	25-...	66
1994—	Kintetsu (Jap. Pac.)	7	7	.500	5.47	21	...	...	...	0-...	97.0	...	...	59	...	37-...	42
1995—	Yakult (Jap. Cen.)■	10	7	.588	3.12	25		...	...	0-...	147.1	...	...	51	...	39-...	91
1996—	Yakult (Jap. Cen.)	10	7	.588	3.24	25	9	...	...	0-...	180.1	...	...	65	...	47-...	145
1997—	Yakult (Jap. Cen.)	13	6	.684	2.99	28	26	6	2	0-...	174.1	149	61	58	...	48-...	104
1998—	New York (N.L.)■	6	8	.429	3.93	29	29	1	0	0-0	171.2	166	79	75	22	53-5	117
1999—	New York (N.L.)	12	8	.600	4.40	31	29	1	0	0-0	174.0	168	86	85	25	58-3	105
2000—	Colorado (N.L.)■	6	15	.286	5.86	29	29	0	0	0-0	167.1	201	112	109	32	53-6	88
2001—	Montreal (N.L.)■	4	7	.364	4.78	42	11	0	0	0-0	113.0	127	65	60	18	26-2	63
2002—	Montreal (N.L.)	4	9	.308	4.11	31	20	1	0	0-0	131.1	143	66	60	15	32-2	74
Major League totals (5 years)		32	47	.405	4.62	162	118	3	0	0-0	757.1	805	408	389	112	222-18	447

DIVISION SERIES RECORD

Year	League	W	L	Pct.	ERA	G	GS	CG	ShO	Sv.-Opp.	IP	H	R	ER	HR	BB-IBB	SO
1999—	New York (N.L.)	0	0	...	6.75	1	1	0	0	0-0	5.1	6	4	4	2	0-0	3

CHAMPIONSHIP SERIES RECORD

Year	League	W	L	Pct.	ERA	G	GS	CG	ShO	Sv.-Opp.	IP	H	R	ER	HR	BB-IBB	SO
1999—	New York (N.L.)	0	1	.000	4.70	2	2	0	0	0-0	7.2	9	4	4	0	3-1	4

YOUNG, DMITRI — OF/1B — TIGERS

PERSONAL: Born October 11, 1973, in Vicksburg, Miss. ... 6-2/235. ... Bats both, throws right. ... Full name: Dmitri Dell Young.

HIGH SCHOOL: Rio Mesa (Oxnard, Calif.).

TRANSACTIONS/CAREER NOTES: Selected by St. Louis Cardinals organization in first round (fourth pick overall) of free-agent draft (June 3, 1991). ... On disabled list (June 2-9, 1994). ... On Arkansas suspended list (August 1-11 and August 17-27, 1995). ... On Louisville disabled list (July 14-24, 1996). ... On St. Louis disabled list (May 11-29, 1997); included rehabilitation assignment to Louisville (May 25-29). ... Traded by Cardinals to Cincinnati Reds for P Jeff Brantley (November 10, 1997). ... Selected by Tampa Bay Devil Rays in first round (16th pick overall) of expansion draft (November 18, 1997). ... Traded by Devil Rays to Reds (November 18, 1997), completing deal in which Reds traded OF Mike Kelly to Devil Rays for a player to be named later (November 11, 1997). ... Traded by Reds to Detroit Tigers for OF Juan Encarnacion and P Luis Pineda (December 11, 2001). ... On disabled list (April 23-May 14 and July 6, 2002-remainder of season).

STATISTICAL NOTES: Led Texas League with 14 intentional bases on balls received in 1994. ... Led Texas League first basemen with 15 errors in 1994. ... Tied for American Association lead with eight bases on balls received in 1996. ... Led American Association first basemen with 1,091 putouts, 1,182 total chances and 102 double plays in 1996. ... Had 18-game hitting streak (April 20-May 13, 2000). ... Had 18-game hitting streak (May 17-June 5, 2002). ... Career major league grand slams: 2.

2002 GAMES PLAYED BY POSITION (MLB): DH—35; 1B—15; 3B—1; OF—1.

			BATTING														FIELDING	
Year	Team (League)	Pos.	G	AB	R	H	2B	3B	HR	RBI	BB	SO	SB-CS	Avg.	OBP	SLG	E	Avg.
1991—	Johnson City (Appl.)	3B	37	129	22	33	10	0	2	22	21	28	2-1	.256	.364	.380	5	.932
1992—	Springfield (Midw.)	3B	135	493	74	153	*36	6	14	72	51	94	14-13	.310	.378	.493	42	.879
1993—	St. Petersburg (FSL)	3B-1B	69	270	31	85	13	3	5	43	24	28	3-4	.315	.369	.441	10	.972
—	Arkansas (Texas)	1B-3B	45	166	13	41	11	2	3	21	9	29	4-4	.247	.294	.392	7	.982
1994—	Arkansas (Texas)	OF-1B	125	453	53	123	33	2	8	54	36	60	0-3	.272	.330	.406	†16	.971
1995—	Arkansas (Texas)	OF-DH	97	367	54	107	18	6	10	62	30	46	2-4	.292	.347	.455	9	.931
—	Louisville (A.A.)	OF	2	7	3	2	0	0	0	0	1	1	0-0	.286	.375	.286	1	.750
1996—	Louisville (A.A.)	1B	122	459	*90	153	31	8	15	64	34	67	16-5	*.333	.378	.534	8	.993
—	St. Louis (N.L.)	1B	16	29	3	7	0	0	0	2	4	5	0-1	.241	.353	.241	1	.976

			BATTING														FIELDING	
Year	Team (League)	Pos.	G	AB	R	H	2B	3B	HR	RBI	BB	SO	SB-CS	Avg.	OBP	SLG	E	Avg.
1997—	St. Louis (N.L.)..........	1B-OF-DH	110	333	38	86	14	3	5	34	38	63	6-5	.258	.335	.363	13	.981
—	Louisville (A.A.)..........	OF-1B	24	84	10	23	7	0	4	14	13	15	1-1	.274	.371	.500	1	.985
1998—	Cincinnati (N.L.)■......	OF-1B	144	536	81	166	48	1	14	83	47	94	2-4	.310	.364	.481	12	.976
1999—	Cincinnati (N.L.).........	OF-1B-DH	127	373	63	112	30	2	14	56	30	71	3-1	.300	.352	.504	4	.982
2000—	Cincinnati (N.L.).........	OF-1B-DH	152	548	68	166	37	6	18	88	36	80	0-3	.303	.346	.491	8	.981
2001—	Cincinnati (N.L.).........	OF-1B-3B	142	540	68	163	28	3	21	69	37	77	8-5	.302	.350	.481	16	.967
2002—	Detroit (A.L.)■...........	DH-1B-3B-OF	54	201	25	57	14	0	7	27	12	39	2-0	.284	.329	.458	4	.972
American League totals (1 year)			54	201	25	57	14	0	7	27	12	39	2-0	.284	.329	.458	4	.972
National League totals (6 years)			691	2359	321	700	157	15	72	332	192	390	19-19	.297	.351	.468	54	.977
Major League totals (7 years)			745	2560	346	757	171	15	79	359	204	429	21-19	.296	.349	.467	58	.977

DIVISION SERIES RECORD

			BATTING														FIELDING	
Year	Team (League)	Pos.	G	AB	R	H	2B	3B	HR	RBI	BB	SO	SB-CS	Avg.	OBP	SLG	E	Avg.
1996—	St. Louis (N.L.)..........								Did not play.									

CHAMPIONSHIP SERIES RECORD

			BATTING														FIELDING	
Year	Team (League)	Pos.	G	AB	R	H	2B	3B	HR	RBI	BB	SO	SB-CS	Avg.	OBP	SLG	E	Avg.
1996—	St. Louis (N.L.)..........	PH-1B	4	7	1	2	0	1	0	2	0	2	0-0	.286	.286	.571	0	1.000

YOUNG, ERIC — 2B — BREWERS

PERSONAL: Born May 18, 1967, in New Brunswick, N.J. ... 5-8/180. ... Bats right, throws right. ... Full name: Eric Orlando Young.

HIGH SCHOOL: New Brunswick (N.J.).

COLLEGE: Rutgers.

TRANSACTIONS/CAREER NOTES: Selected by Los Angeles Dodgers organization in 43rd round of free-agent draft (June 5, 1989). ... Selected by Colorado Rockies organization in first round (11th pick overall) of expansion draft (November 17, 1992). ... On Colorado disabled list (March 22-April 22, 1996); included rehabilitation assignments to New Haven (April 5-10), Salem (April 10-13) and Colorado Springs (April 13-22). ... Traded by Rockies to Dodgers for P Pedro Astacio (August 19, 1997). ... On disabled list (July 13-31, 1998). ... On Los Angeles disabled list (July 24-August 13, 1999); included rehabilitation assignment to San Bernardino (August 8-13). ... Traded by Dodgers with P Ismael Valdes to Chicago Cubs for P Terry Adams, P Chad Ricketts and a player to be named later (December 12, 1999); Dodgers acquired P Brian Stephenson to complete deal (December 16, 1999). ... Granted free agency (November 7, 2001). ... Signed by Milwaukee Brewers (January 17, 2002).

RECORDS: Shares modern major league record for most stolen bases in one game—6 (June 30, 1996). ... Shares major league record for most stolen bases in one inning—3 (June 30, 1996, third inning).

HONORS: Named second baseman on The Sporting News N.L. All-Star team (1996). ... Named second baseman on The Sporting News N.L. Silver Slugger team (1996).

STATISTICAL NOTES: Led Florida State League second basemen with 24 errors in 1990. ... Led Texas League in caught stealing with 26 in 1991. ... Led Texas League second basemen with .974 fielding percentage in 1991. ... Tied for N.L. lead in errors by second baseman with 11 in 1995. ... Led N.L. in caught stealing with 19 in 1996 and 22 in 1999. ... Led N.L. second basemen with 109 double plays in 1996 and 111 in 1997.

MISCELLANEOUS: Holds Colorado Rockies all-time record for most stolen bases (180).

2002 GAMES PLAYED BY POSITION (MLB): 2B—123; OF—2; DH—2.

			BATTING														FIELDING	
Year	Team (League)	Pos.	G	AB	R	H	2B	3B	HR	RBI	BB	SO	SB-CS	Avg.	OBP	SLG	E	Avg.
1989—	GC Dodgers (GCL).....	2B	56	197	53	65	11	5	2	22	33	16	*41-10	.330	.432	.467	*15	.939
1990—	Vero Beach (FSL).......	2B-OF	127	460	*101	132	23	7	2	50	69	35	*76-16	.287	.384	.380	†25	.937
1991—	San Antonio (Texas)...	2B-OF	127	461	82	129	17	4	3	35	67	36	*70-26	.280	.373	.354	13	†.974
—	Albuquerque (PCL).....	2B	1	5	0	2	0	0	0	0	0	0	0-0	.400	.400	.400	0	1.000
1992—	Albuquerque (PCL).....	2B	94	350	61	118	16	5	3	49	33	18	28-11	.337	.393	.437	•20	.961
—	Los Angeles (N.L.).....	2B	49	132	9	34	1	0	1	11	8	9	6-1	.258	.300	.288	9	.957
1993—	Colorado (N.L.)■.......	2B-OF	144	490	82	132	16	8	3	42	63	41	42-19	.269	.355	.353	18	.964
1994—	Colorado (N.L.)..........	OF-2B	90	228	37	62	13	1	7	30	38	17	18-7	.272	.378	.430	2	.981
1995—	Colorado (N.L.)..........	2B-OF	120	366	68	116	21	•9	6	36	49	29	35-12	.317	.404	.473	‡11	.974
1996—	New Haven (East.).......	2B	3	15	0	1	0	0	0	0	0	3	0-0	.067	.067	.067	0	1.000
—	Salem (Caro.)............	2B	3	10	2	3	3	0	0	0	3	1	2-0	.300	.462	.600	2	.875
—	Colo. Springs (PCL)...	2B	7	23	4	6	1	1	0	3	5	1	0-0	.261	.393	.391	3	.917
—	Colorado (N.L.)..........	2B	141	568	113	184	23	4	8	74	47	31	*53-19	.324	.393	.421	12	.985
1997—	Colorado (N.L.)..........	2B	118	468	78	132	29	6	6	45	57	37	32-12	.282	.363	.408	15	.978
—	Los Angeles (N.L.)■..	2B	37	154	28	42	4	2	2	16	14	17	13-2	.273	.347	.364	3	.979
1998—	Los Angeles (N.L.).....	2B-DH	117	452	78	129	24	1	8	43	45	32	42-13	.285	.355	.396	13	.976
1999—	Los Angeles (N.L.).....	2B	119	456	73	128	24	2	2	41	63	26	51-22	.281	.371	.355	9	.984
—	San Bern. (Calif.)........	2B	3	12	0	3	0	0	0	0	0	2	0-0	.250	.250	.250	2	.833
2000—	Chicago (N.L.)■.........	2B	153	607	98	180	40	2	6	47	63	39	54-7	.297	.367	.399	15	.979
2001—	Chicago (N.L.)............	2B	149	603	98	168	43	4	6	42	42	45	31-14	.279	.333	.393	12	.981
2002—	Milwaukee (N.L.)■.....	2B-OF-DH	138	496	57	139	29	3	3	28	39	38	31-11	.280	.338	.369	12	.979
Major League totals (11 years)			1375	5020	819	1446	267	42	58	455	528	361	408-139	.288	.362	.393	131	.978

DIVISION SERIES RECORD

			BATTING														FIELDING	
Year	Team (League)	Pos.	G	AB	R	H	2B	3B	HR	RBI	BB	SO	SB-CS	Avg.	OBP	SLG	E	Avg.
1995—	Colorado (N.L.)..........	2B	4	16	3	7	1	0	1	2	2	2	1-0	.438	.500	.688	3	.875

ALL-STAR GAME RECORD

	AB	R	H	2B	3B	HR	RBI	BB	SO	SB-CS	Avg.	OBP	SLG	E	Avg.
All-Star Game totals (1 year)	1	0	0	0	0	0	0	0	0	0-0	.000	.000	.000	0	1.000

Y

YOUNG, KEVIN — 1B — PIRATES

PERSONAL: Born June 16, 1969, in Alpena, Mich. ... 6-3/225. ... Bats right, throws right. ... Full name: Kevin Stacey Young.
HIGH SCHOOL: Washington (Kansas City, Kan.).
JUNIOR COLLEGE: Kansas City Kansas Community College.
COLLEGE: Southern Mississippi.
TRANSACTIONS/CAREER NOTES: Selected by Pittsburgh Pirates organization in seventh round of free-agent draft (June 4, 1990). ... On Pittsburgh disabled list (July 24-August 8, 1995). ... Released by Pirates (March 26, 1996). ... Signed by Kansas City Royals organization (April 1, 1996). ... Released by Royals (December 5, 1996). ... Signed by Pirates (March 31, 1997). ... On suspended list (September 28-30, 2000).
STATISTICAL NOTES: Led New York Pennsylvania League shortstops with 79 putouts in 1990. ... Tied for Southern League lead in errors by third baseman with 26 in 1991. ... Tied for American Association lead in being hit by pitch with 11 in 1992. ... Led American Association third basemen with 300 assists, 32 errors, 436 total chances and 41 double plays in 1992. ... Led N.L. first basemen with .998 fielding percentage in 1993. ... Had 15-game hitting streak (April 23-May 8, 1999). ... Led N.L. first basemen with 1,334 putouts in 1998. ... Led N.L. first basemen with 1,413 putouts and 1,533 total chances in 1999. ... Career major league grand slams: 3.
2002 GAMES PLAYED BY POSITION (MLB): 1B—144.

			BATTING														FIELDING	
Year	Team (League)	Pos.	G	AB	R	H	2B	3B	HR	RBI	BB	SO	SB-CS	Avg.	OBP	SLG	E	Avg.
1990—	Welland (NY-Penn)	SS	72	238	46	58	16	2	5	30	31	36	10-2	.244	.342	.391	26	.883
1991—	Salem (Caro.)	3B	56	201	38	63	12	4	6	28	20	34	3-2	.313	.390	.502	12	.925
—	Carolina (Sou.)	3B-1B	75	263	36	90	19	6	3	33	15	38	9-3	.342	.394	.494	‡28	.907
—	Buffalo (A.A.)	3B-1B	4	9	1	2	1	0	0	2	0	0	1-0	.222	.273	.333	2	.857
1992—	Buffalo (A.A.)	3B-1B	137	490	*91	154	29	6	8	65	67	67	18-12	.314	.406	.447	†32	.932
—	Pittsburgh (N.L.)	3B-1B	10	7	2	4	0	0	0	4	2	0	1-0	.571	.667	.571	1	.800
1993—	Pittsburgh (N.L.)	1B-3B	141	449	38	106	24	3	6	47	36	82	2-2	.236	.300	.343	3	†.998
1994—	Pittsburgh (N.L.)	1B-3B-OF	59	122	15	25	7	2	1	11	8	34	0-2	.205	.258	.320	3	.987
—	Buffalo (A.A.)	3B-1B	60	228	26	63	14	5	5	27	15	45	6-2	.276	.327	.447	4	.982
1995—	Calgary (PCL)	3B-1B-DH	45	163	24	58	23	1	8	34	15	21	6-3	.356	.403	.656	12	.950
—	Pittsburgh (N.L.)	3B-1B	56	181	13	42	9	0	6	22	8	53	1-3	.232	.268	.381	12	.933
1996—	Omaha (A.A.)■	1B-3B-DH	50	186	29	57	11	1	13	46	12	41	3-0	.306	.358	.586	5	.985
—	Kansas City (A.L.)	1B-OF-3B-DH	55	132	20	32	6	0	8	23	11	32	3-3	.242	.301	.470	1	.995
1997—	Pittsburgh (N.L.)■	1B-3B-OF	97	333	59	100	18	3	18	74	16	89	11-2	.300	.332	.535	5	.993
1998—	Pittsburgh (N.L.)	1B	159	592	88	160	40	2	27	108	44	127	15-7	.270	.328	.481	8	.994
1999—	Pittsburgh (N.L.)	1B	156	584	103	174	41	6	26	106	75	124	22-10	.298	.387	.522	*23	.985
2000—	Pittsburgh (N.L.)	1B-DH	132	496	77	128	27	0	20	88	32	96	8-3	.258	.311	.433	*17	.986
2001—	Pittsburgh (N.L.)	1B	142	449	53	104	33	0	14	65	42	119	15-11	.232	.310	.399	7	.994
2002—	Pittsburgh (N.L.)	1B	146	468	60	115	26	1	16	51	50	101	4-6	.246	.322	.408	13	.991
American League totals (1 year)			55	132	20	32	6	0	8	23	11	32	3-3	.242	.301	.470	1	.995
National League totals (10 years)			1098	3681	508	958	225	17	134	576	313	825	79-46	.260	.325	.440	92	.990
Major League totals (11 years)			1153	3813	528	990	231	17	142	599	324	857	82-49	.260	.324	.441	93	.990

YOUNG, MIKE — 2B — RANGERS

PERSONAL: Born October 19, 1976, in Covina, Calif. ... 6-1/190. ... Bats right, throws right. ... Full name: Michael B. Young.
HIGH SCHOOL: Bishop Amat (La Puente, Calif.).
COLLEGE: UC Santa Barbara.
TRANSACTIONS/CAREER NOTES: Selected by Toronto Blue Jays organization in fifth round of free-agent draft (June 3, 1997). ... Traded by Blue Jays with P Darwin Cubillan to Texas Rangers for P Esteban Loaiza (July 19, 2000).
STATISTICAL NOTES: Led South Atlantic League second basemen with .978 fielding percentage in 1998. ... Led A.L. second basemen with 419 assists, 726 total chances and 97 double plays in 2002.
2002 GAMES PLAYED BY POSITION (MLB): 2B—152; SS—11; 3B—4; DH—1.

			BATTING														FIELDING	
Year	Team (League)	Pos.	G	AB	R	H	2B	3B	HR	RBI	BB	SO	SB-CS	Avg.	OBP	SLG	E	Avg.
1997—	St. Catharines (NY-P)	SS-2B	74	276	49	85	18	3	9	48	33	59	9-5	.308	.392	.493	18	.946
1998—	Hagerstown (S.Atl.)	2B-SS-OF	*140	522	86	147	33	5	16	87	55	96	16-8	.282	.354	.456	13	†.977
1999—	Dunedin (FSL)	2B-SS	129	495	86	155	•36	3	5	83	61	78	30-6	.313	.389	.428	22	.961
2000—	Tennessee (Sou.)	2B-SS	91	345	51	95	24	5	6	47	36	72	16-5	.275	.340	.426	16	.965
—	Tulsa (Texas)■	SS	43	188	30	60	13	5	1	32	17	28	9-3	.319	.368	.457	7	.965
—	Texas (A.L.)	2B	2	2	0	0	0	0	0	0	0	1	0-0	.000	.000	.000	0	...
2001—	Oklahoma (PCL)	2B-SS	47	189	28	55	8	0	8	28	20	34	3-3	.291	.358	.460	6	.968
—	Texas (A.L.)	2B	106	386	57	96	18	4	11	49	26	91	3-1	.249	.298	.402	8	.984
2002—	Texas (A.L.)	2-S-3-D	156	573	77	150	26	8	9	62	41	112	6-7	.262	.308	.382	9	.988
Major League totals (3 years)			264	961	134	246	44	12	20	111	67	204	9-8	.256	.303	.389	17	.986

ZAMBRANO, CARLOS — P — CUBS

PERSONAL: Born June 1, 1981, in Carabobo, Venezuela. ... 6-5/250. ... Throws right, bats right. ... Full name: Carlos Alberto Zambrano.
TRANSACTIONS/CAREER NOTES: Signed as non-drafted free agent by Chicago Cubs organization (July 12, 1997). ... On Chicago disabled list (May 10-June 7, 2002); included rehabilitation assignment to Iowa (May 30-June 6). ... On suspended list (August 3-9, 2002).
CAREER HITTING (MLB): 1-for-32 (.031), 0 R, 1 2B, 0 3B, 0 HR, 0 RBI.

Year	League	W	L	Pct.	ERA	G	GS	CG	ShO	Sv.-Opp.	IP	H	R	ER	HR	BB-IBB	SO
1998—	Arizona Cubs (Ariz.)	0	1	.000	3.15	14	2	0	0	1-...	40.0	39	17	14	0	25-3	36
1999—	Lansing (Midw.)	13	7	.650	4.17	27	24	2	1	0-...	153.1	150	87	71	9	62-1	98
2000—	West Tenn (Sou.)	3	1	.750	1.34	9	9	0	0	0-...	60.1	39	14	9	2	21-0	43
—	Iowa (PCL)	2	5	.286	3.97	34	0	0	0	6-...	56.2	54	30	25	3	40-2	46
2001—	Iowa (PCL)	10	5	.667	3.88	26	25	1	0	0-...	150.2	124	73	65	9	68-1	155
—	Chicago (N.L.)	1	2	.333	15.26	6	1	0	0	0-1	7.2	11	13	13	2	8-0	4
2002—	Iowa (PCL)	0	0	...	0.00	3	3	0	0	0-...	9.0	2	0	0	0	6-0	11
—	Chicago (N.L.)	4	8	.333	3.66	32	16	0	0	0-0	108.1	94	53	44	9	63-2	93
Major League totals (2 years)		5	10	.333	4.42	38	17	0	0	0-1	116.0	105	66	57	11	71-2	97

ZAMBRANO, VICTOR P DEVIL RAYS

PERSONAL: Born August 6, 1975, in Los Teques, Venezuela. ... 6-0/203. ... Throws right, bats right. ... Full name: Victor Manuel Zambrano.
HIGH SCHOOL: Manve Maria Billolobo (Los Teques, Venezuela).
TRANSACTIONS/CAREER NOTES: Signed as non-drafted free agent by New York Yankees organization (August 19, 1993). ... Released by Yankees organization (February 7, 1996). ... Signed by Tampa Bay Devil Rays organization (March 14, 1996).
CAREER HITTING (MLB): 0-for-1 (.000), 0 R, 0 2B, 0 3B, 0 HR, 0 RBI.

Year League	W	L	Pct.	ERA	G	GS	CG	ShO	Sv.-Opp.	IP	H	R	ER	HR	BB-IBB	SO
1996— GC Devil Rays (GCL)■	0	0	...	8.10	1	0	0	0	0-...	3.1	4	4	3	0	0-0	6
1997— GC Devil Rays (GCL)	0	0	...	0.00	2	0	0	0	0-...	3.0	1	0	0	0	0-0	2
— Princeton (Appl.)	0	2	.000	1.82	20	0	0	0	0-...	29.2	18	13	6	1	9-1	36
1998— Charleston, S.C. (S.Atl.)	6	4	.600	3.38	48	2	0	0	0-...	77.1	72	32	29	5	20-1	89
1999— St. Petersburg (FSL)	0	2	.000	4.00	7	0	0	0	0-...	9.0	10	6	4	1	5-0	15
— Orlando (Sou.)	7	2	.778	4.59	40	4	0	0	1-...	82.1	92	55	42	5	38-2	81
2000— Durham (I.L.)	0	6	.000	5.03	53	0	0	0	8-...	62.2	72	38	35	9	29-2	55
2001— Durham (I.L.)	1	2	.333	2.08	29	0	0	0	12-...	30.1	26	10	7	2	12-1	29
— Tampa Bay (A.L.)	6	2	.750	3.16	36	0	0	0	2-6	51.1	38	21	18	6	18-0	58
2002— Tampa Bay (A.L.)	8	8	.500	5.53	42	11	0	0	1-3	114.0	120	77	70	15	68-5	73
— Durham (I.L.)	0	1	.000	1.93	10	0	0	0	1-...	14.0	9	4	3	2	4-0	15
Major League totals (2 years)	14	10	.583	4.79	78	11	0	0	3-9	165.1	158	98	88	21	86-5	131

RECORD AS POSITION PLAYER

			BATTING														FIELDING	
Year	Team (League)	Pos.	G	AB	R	H	2B	3B	HR	RBI	BB	SO	SB-CS	Avg.	OBP	SLG	E	Avg.
1994—	GC Yankees (GCL)	SS-2B	50	175	23	63	5	1	0	16	13	43	6-2	.360	.405	.400	21	.911
1995—	GC Yankees (GCL)	2B-SS	27	78	10	16	3	1	0	5	5	15	2-3	.205	.262	.269	4	.959

ZAUN, GREGG C ASTROS

PERSONAL: Born April 14, 1971, in Glendale, Calif. ... 5-10/190. ... Bats both, throws right. ... Full name: Gregory Owen Zaun. ... Nephew of Rick Dempsey, catcher with six major league teams (1969-92).
HIGH SCHOOL: St. Francis (La Canada, Calif.).
TRANSACTIONS/CAREER NOTES: Selected by Baltimore Orioles organization in 17th round of free-agent draft (June 5, 1989). ... On Bowie disabled list (June 17-July 15, 1993). ... Traded by Orioles to Florida Marlins (August 23, 1996), completing deal in which Marlins traded P Terry Mathews to Orioles for a player to be named later (August 21, 1996). ... Traded by Marlins to Texas Rangers for a player to be named later or cash (November 23, 1998); Marlins received cash to complete deal (April 15, 1999). ... Traded by Rangers with OF Juan Gonzalez and P Danny Patterson to Detroit Tigers for P Justin Thompson, P Francisco Cordero, OF Gabe Kapler, C Bill Haselman, 2B Frank Catalanotto and P Alan Webb (November 2, 1999). ... Traded by Tigers to Kansas City Royals for a player to be named later or cash (March 7, 2000). ... On Kansas City disabled list (April 15-May 29, 2000); included rehabilitation assignment to Omaha (May 16-29). ... On Kansas City disabled list (March 31-July 23, 2001); included rehabilitation assignments to Gulf Coast Royals (July 3-12) and Omaha (July 13-23). ... Granted free agency (November 5, 2001). ... Signed by Houston Astros (December 11, 2001).
STATISTICAL NOTES: Led Appalachian League catchers with 460 putouts and 501 total chances in 1990. ... Led Midwest League catchers with 697 putouts and 796 total chances in 1991. ... Led Carolina League catchers with 746 putouts, 91 assists, 18 errors, 855 total chances and 10 double plays in 1992. ... Led International League catchers with 750 putouts, 841 total chances and 11 double plays in 1994. ... Tied for N.L. lead with 12 double plays by catcher in 1998. ... Career major league grand slams: 1.
2002 GAMES PLAYED BY POSITION (MLB): C—44.

			BATTING														FIELDING	
Year	Team (League)	Pos.	G	AB	R	H	2B	3B	HR	RBI	BB	SO	SB-CS	Avg.	OBP	SLG	E	Avg.
1990—	Wausau (Midw.)	C	37	100	3	13	0	1	1	7	7	17	0-0	.130	.194	.180	3	.990
—	Bluefield (Appl.)	C-3B-SS-P	61	184	29	55	5	2	2	21	23	15	5-5	.299	.378	.380	10	.980
1991—	Kane County (Midw.)	C	113	409	67	112	17	5	4	51	50	41	4-4	.274	.353	.369	16	.980
1992—	Frederick (Caro.)	C-2B	108	383	54	96	18	6	6	52	42	45	3-5	.251	.324	.376	†18	.979
1993—	Bowie (East.)	C-DH-2-3-P	79	258	25	79	10	0	3	38	27	26	4-7	.306	.373	.380	10	.979
—	Rochester (I.L.)	C	21	78	10	20	4	2	1	11	6	11	0-0	.256	.302	.397	4	.975
1994—	Rochester (I.L.)	C	123	388	61	92	16	4	7	43	56	72	4-2	.237	.337	.353	9	*.989
1995—	Rochester (I.L.)	C-DH	42	140	26	41	13	1	6	18	14	21	0-3	.293	.367	.529	3	.989
—	Baltimore (A.L.)	C	40	104	18	27	5	0	3	14	16	14	1-1	.260	.358	.394	3	.987
1996—	Baltimore (A.L.)	C	50	108	16	25	8	1	1	13	11	15	0-0	.231	.309	.352	3	.987
—	Rochester (I.L.)	C-DH	14	47	11	15	2	0	0	4	11	6	0-2	.319	.441	.362	2	.965
—	Florida (N.L.)■	C	10	31	4	9	1	0	1	2	3	5	1-0	.290	.353	.419	0	1.000
1997—	Florida (N.L.)	C-1B	58	143	21	43	10	2	2	20	26	18	1-0	.301	.415	.441	8	.978
1998—	Florida (N.L.)	C-2B	106	298	19	56	12	2	5	29	35	52	5-2	.188	.274	.292	8	.986
1999—	Texas (A.L.)■	C-DH	43	93	12	23	2	1	1	12	10	7	1-0	.247	.314	.323	3	.984
2000—	Kansas City (A.L.)■	C-1B-2B	83	234	36	64	11	0	7	33	43	34	7-3	.274	.390	.410	5	.988
—	Omaha (PCL)	C	9	25	7	7	3	0	0	3	4	3	1-1	.280	.379	.400	0	1.000
2001—	GC Royals (GCL)	C	6	18	3	1	0	0	0	1	7	5	0-0	.056	.320	.056	0	1.000
—	Omaha (PCL)	C	11	43	5	12	4	0	1	8	3	3	0-0	.279	.333	.442	1	.985
—	Kansas City (A.L.)	C-DH	39	125	15	40	9	0	6	18	12	16	1-2	.320	.377	.536	5	.975
2002—	Houston (N.L.)■	C	76	185	18	41	7	1	3	24	12	36	1-0	.222	.275	.319	5	.985
American League totals (5 years)			255	664	97	179	35	2	18	90	92	86	10-6	.270	.359	.410	19	.985
National League totals (4 years)			250	657	62	149	30	5	11	75	76	111	8-2	.227	.310	.338	21	.984
Major League totals (8 years)			505	1321	159	328	65	7	29	165	168	197	18-8	.248	.335	.374	40	.985

DIVISION SERIES RECORD

			BATTING														FIELDING	
Year	Team (League)	Pos.	G	AB	R	H	2B	3B	HR	RBI	BB	SO	SB-CS	Avg.	OBP	SLG	E	Avg.
1997—	Florida (N.L.)								Did not play.									

CHAMPIONSHIP SERIES RECORD

			BATTING														FIELDING	
Year	Team (League)	Pos.	G	AB	R	H	2B	3B	HR	RBI	BB	SO	SB-CS	Avg.	OBP	SLG	E	Avg.
1997—	Florida (N.L.)	C	1	0	0	0	0	0	0	0	0	0	0-0	...	...	...	0	1.000

WORLD SERIES RECORD

NOTES: Member of World Series championship team (1997).

			BATTING														FIELDING	
Year	Team (League)	Pos.	G	AB	R	H	2B	3B	HR	RBI	BB	SO	SB-CS	Avg.	OBP	SLG	E	Avg.
1997—	Florida (N.L.)	PH-C-PR	2	2	0	0	0	0	0	0	0	0	0-0	.000	.000	.000	0	1.000

RECORD AS PITCHER

Year	League	W	L	Pct.	ERA	G	GS	CG	ShO	Sv.-Opp.	IP	H	R	ER	HR	BB-IBB	SO
1990—	Bluefield (Appl.)	0	0	...	0.00	1	0	0	0	0-...	1.0	1	0	0	0	1-0	1
1993—	Bowie (East.)	0	0	...	0.00	1	0	0	0	0-...	2.1	1	0	0	0	0-0	0

ZEILE, TODD 3B

PERSONAL: Born September 9, 1965, in Van Nuys, Calif. ... 6-1/200. ... Bats right, throws right. ... Full name: Todd Edward Zeile. ... Husband of Julianne McNamara, Olympic gold-medal gymnast (1984). ... Name pronounced ZEEL.

HIGH SCHOOL: Hart (Newhall, Calif.).

COLLEGE: UCLA.

TRANSACTIONS/CAREER NOTES: Selected by Kansas City Royals organization in 30th round of free-agent draft (June 6, 1983); did not sign. ... Selected by St. Louis Cardinals organization in supplemental round ("sandwich pick" between second and third round 55th pick overall) of free-agent draft (June 2, 1986); pick received as compensation for New York Yankees signing Type C free-agent IF Ivan DeJesus. ... On St. Louis disabled list (April 23-May 9, 1995); included rehabilitation assignment to Louisville (May 6-9). ... Traded by Cardinals with cash to Chicago Cubs for P Mike Morgan, 3B/OF Paul Torres and C Francisco Morales (June 16, 1995). ... Granted free agency (December 21, 1995). ... Signed by Philadelphia Phillies (December 22, 1995). ... Traded by Phillies with OF Pete Incaviglia to Baltimore Orioles for two players to be named later (August 29, 1996); Phillies acquired P Calvin Maduro and P Garrett Stephenson to complete deal (September 4, 1996). ... Granted free agency (October 27, 1996). ... Signed by Los Angeles Dodgers (December 8, 1996). ... Traded by Dodgers with C Mike Piazza to Florida Marlins for OF Gary Sheffield, 3B Bobby Bonilla, C Charles Johnson, OF Jim Eisenreich and P Manuel Barrios (May 15, 1998). ... Traded by Marlins to Texas Rangers for 3B Jose Santo and P Dan DeYoung (July 31, 1998). ... Granted free agency (October 28, 1999). ... Signed by New York Mets (December 11, 1999). ... Traded by Mets to Colorado Rockies as part of three-way deal in which Mets traded P Glendon Rusch to Milwaukee Brewers, Rockies traded 1B/OF Ross Gload and P Craig House to Mets, Brewers traded P Jeff D'Amico, OF Jeromy Burnitz, IF Lou Collier, OF/1B Mark Sweeney and cash to Mets, Mets traded OF Benny Agbayani, IF/OF Lenny Harris and cash to Rockies and Rockies traded OF Alex Ochoa to Brewers (January 21, 2002). ... Granted free agency (October 28, 2002).

RECORDS: Holds N.L. single-season record for fewest putouts by third baseman (150 or more games)—83 (1993). ... Shares modern N.L. single-game record for most errors by first baseman—4 (August 7, 1996).

HONORS: Named Midwest League co-Most Valuable Player (1987).

STATISTICAL NOTES: Led New York-Pennsylvania League with six sacrifice flies in 1986. ... Led New York-Pennsylvania League catchers with 66 assists and tied for league lead with seven double plays in 1986. ... Led Texas League catchers with 687 putouts and 761 total chances in 1988. ... Led American Association catchers with .992 fielding percentage and 17 passed balls in 1989. ... Had 17-game hitting streak (June 21-July 10, 1999). ... Tied for A.L. third baseman lead with 25 errors in 1999. ... Career major league grand slams: 9.

2002 GAMES PLAYED BY POSITION (MLB): 3B—139.

			BATTING														FIELDING	
Year	Team (League)	Pos.	G	AB	R	H	2B	3B	HR	RBI	BB	SO	SB-CS	Avg.	OBP	SLG	E	Avg.
1986—	Erie (NY-Penn)	C	70	248	40	64	14	1	14	*63	37	52	5-1	.258	.352	.492	8	.983
1987—	Springfield (Midw.)	C-3B	130	487	94	142	24	4	25	*106	70	85	1-3	.292	.380	.511	14	.985
1988—	Arkansas (Texas)	C-OF-1B	129	430	95	117	33	2	19	75	83	64	6-5	.272	.388	.491	10	.987
1989—	Louisville (A.A.)	C-3B-1B	118	453	71	131	26	3	19	85	45	78	0-1	.289	.350	.486	6	†.991
—	St. Louis (N.L.)	C	28	82	7	21	3	1	1	8	9	14	0-0	.256	.326	.354	4	.971
1990—	St. Louis (N.L.)	C-3B-1B-OF	144	495	62	121	25	3	15	57	67	77	2-4	.244	.333	.398	15	.980
1991—	St. Louis (N.L.)	3B	155	565	76	158	36	3	11	81	62	94	17-11	.280	.353	.412	*25	.943
1992—	St. Louis (N.L.)	3B	126	439	51	113	18	4	7	48	68	70	7-10	.257	.352	.364	13	.960
—	Louisville (A.A.)	3B	21	74	11	23	4	1	5	13	9	13	0-0	.311	.381	.595	5	.918
1993—	St. Louis (N.L.)	3B	157	571	82	158	36	1	17	103	70	76	5-4	.277	.352	.433	33	.923
1994—	St. Louis (N.L.)	3B	113	415	62	111	25	1	19	75	52	56	1-3	.267	.348	.470	12	.960
1995—	Louisville (A.A.)	1B	2	8	0	1	0	0	0	0	0	2	0-0	.125	.125	.125	1	.923
—	St. Louis (N.L.)	1B	34	127	16	37	6	0	5	22	18	23	1-0	.291	.378	.457	7	.980
—	Chicago (N.L.)■	3B-OF-1B	79	299	34	68	16	0	9	30	16	53	0-0	.227	.271	.371	12	.939
1996—	Philadelphia (N.L.)■	3B-1B	134	500	61	134	24	0	20	80	67	88	1-1	.268	.353	.436	14	.972
—	Baltimore (A.L.)■	3B	29	117	17	28	8	0	5	19	15	16	0-0	.239	.326	.436	3	.964
1997—	Los Angeles (N.L.)■	3B	160	575	89	154	17	0	31	90	85	112	8-7	.268	.365	.459	*26	.931
1998—	Los Angeles (N.L.)	3B-1B	40	158	22	40	6	1	7	27	10	24	1-1	.253	.300	.437	6	.930
—	Florida (N.L.)■	3B	66	234	37	68	12	1	6	39	31	34	2-3	.291	.374	.427	5	.971
—	Texas (A.L.)■	3B	52	180	26	47	14	1	6	28	28	32	1-0	.261	.358	.450	12	.915
1999—	Texas (A.L.)	3B-DH-1B	156	588	80	172	41	1	24	98	56	94	1-2	.293	.354	.488	‡25	.941
2000—	New York (N.L.)■	1B	153	544	67	146	36	3	22	79	74	85	3-4	.268	.356	.467	10	.992
2001—	New York (N.L.)	1B	151	531	66	141	25	1	10	62	73	102	1-0	.266	.359	.373	11	.992
2002—	Colorado (N.L.)■	3B-P	144	506	61	138	23	0	18	87	66	92	1-1	.273	.353	.425	*21	.942
American League totals (3 years)			237	885	123	247	63	2	35	145	99	142	2-2	.279	.351	.473	40	.938
National League totals (13 years)			1684	6041	793	1608	308	19	198	888	768	1000	50-49	.266	.349	.422	214	.970
Major League totals (14 years)			1921	6926	916	1855	371	21	233	1033	867	1142	52-51	.268	.349	.428	254	.967

DIVISION SERIES RECORD

			BATTING														FIELDING	
Year	Team (League)	Pos.	G	AB	R	H	2B	3B	HR	RBI	BB	SO	SB-CS	Avg.	OBP	SLG	E	Avg.
1996—	Baltimore (A.L.)	3B	4	19	2	5	1	0	0	0	2	5	0-0	.263	.333	.316	2	.867
1998—	Texas (A.L.)	3B	3	9	0	3	0	0	0	0	0	2	0-1	.333	.333	.333	0	1.000
1999—	Texas (A.L.)	3B	3	10	0	1	0	0	0	0	2	1	0-0	.100	.250	.100	2	.714
2000—	New York (N.L.)	1B	4	14	0	1	1	0	0	0	4	3	0-0	.071	.278	.143	0	1.000
Division series totals (4 years)			14	52	2	10	2	0	0	0	8	11	0-1	.192	.300	.231	4	.933

CHAMPIONSHIP SERIES RECORD

RECORDS: Shares A.L. single-series record for most home runs—3 (1996).

		BATTING														FIELDING	
Year Team (League)	Pos.	G	AB	R	H	2B	3B	HR	RBI	BB	SO	SB-CS	Avg.	OBP	SLG	E	Avg.
1996— Baltimore (A.L.)	3B	5	22	3	8	0	0	3	5	2	1	0-0	.364	.417	.773	1	.909
2000— New York (N.L.)	1B	5	19	1	7	3	0	1	8	2	4	0-0	.368	.409	.684	0	1.000
Championship series totals (2 years)		10	41	4	15	3	0	4	13	4	5	0-0	.366	.413	.732	1	.980

WORLD SERIES RECORD

		BATTING														FIELDING	
Year Team (League)	Pos.	G	AB	R	H	2B	3B	HR	RBI	BB	SO	SB-CS	Avg.	OBP	SLG	E	Avg.
2000— New York (N.L.)	1B	5	20	1	8	2	0	0	1	1	5	0-0	.400	.429	.500	0	1.000

ZERBE, CHAD — P — GIANTS

PERSONAL: Born April 27, 1972, in Findlay, Ohio. ... 6-0/200. ... Throws left, bats left. ... Full name: William Chad Zerbe.

HIGH SCHOOL: Vivian Gaither (Tampa).

JUNIOR COLLEGE: Hillsborough Community College (Fla.).

TRANSACTIONS/CAREER NOTES: Selected by Los Angeles Dodgers organization in 17th round of free-agent draft (June 3, 1991). ... Released by Dodgers (December 10, 1996). ... Signed by Arizona Diamondbacks organization (January 28, 1997). ... Released by Diamondbacks (May 20, 1997). ... Signed by Sonoma County, Western League (1997). ... Signed by San Francisco Giants organization (November 26, 1997). ... Granted free agency (October 16, 1998). ... Re-signed by Giants organization (March 4, 1999). ... Granted free agency (October 15, 1999). ... Re-signed by Giants organization (October 22, 1999). ... On Shreveport disabled list (May 9-June 7, 2000).

CAREER HITTING (MLB): 3-for-15 (.200), 1 R, 0 2B, 0 3B, 0 HR, 2 RBI.

Year League	W	L	Pct.	ERA	G	GS	CG	ShO	Sv.-Opp.	IP	H	R	ER	HR	BB-IBB	SO
1991— Gulf Coast Dodgers (GCL)	0	2	.000	2.20	16	1	0	0	0-...	32.2	31	19	8	1	15-0	23
1992— Great Falls (Pio.)	8	3	.727	2.14	15	15	1	1	0-...	92.1	75	27	22	2	26-0	70
1993— Bakersfield (Calif.)	0	10	.000	5.91	14	12	1	0	0-...	67.0	83	60	44	2	47-0	41
— Vero Beach (FSL)	1	0	1.000	6.57	10	0	0	0	0-...	12.1	12	10	9	0	13-1	11
1994— Vero Beach (FSL)	5	5	.500	3.39	18	18	1	0	0-...	98.1	88	50	37	6	32-0	68
1995— San Bernardino (Calif.)	11	7	.611	4.57	28	27	1	0	0-...	163.1	168	103	83	15	64-0	94
1996— San Antonio (Texas)	4	6	.400	4.50	17	11	1	0	1-...	86.0	98	52	43	9	37-0	38
1997— High Desert (Calif.)■	1	6	.143	7.43	9	8	0	0	0-...	36.1	61	49	30	7	15-0	26
— Sonoma County (West.)■	4	5	.444	5.40	14	13	2	0	0-...	90.0	117	70	54	7	36-1	52
1998— San Jose (Calif.)■	2	0	1.000	3.35	23	0	0	0	1-...	37.2	37	16	14	3	12-0	28
1999— Bakersfield (Calif.)	7	7	.500	3.64	21	21	0	0	0-...	126.0	124	66	51	4	33-0	81
— Shreveport (Texas)	1	3	.250	1.96	7	6	0	0	0-...	41.1	32	13	9	2	10-0	16
2000— Shreveport (Texas)	2	1	.667	2.33	9	9	0	0	0-...	38.2	37	11	10	1	9-0	34
— Fresno (PCL)	7	3	.700	4.32	17	11	0	0	0-...	81.1	94	46	39	5	17-0	41
— San Francisco (N.L.)	0	0	...	4.50	4	0	0	0	0-0	6.0	6	3	3	1	1-0	5
2001— Fresno (PCL)	3	4	.429	3.55	17	0	0	0	5-...	25.1	28	13	10	2	9-0	17
— San Francisco (N.L.)	3	0	1.000	3.92	27	1	0	0	0-0	39.0	41	21	17	3	10-0	22
2002— Fresno (PCL)	0	0	...	0.00	3	3	0	0	0-...	10.1	8	0	0	0	3-0	5
— San Francisco (N.L.)	2	0	1.000	3.04	50	0	0	0	0-1	56.1	52	22	19	3	21-2	26
Major League totals (3 years)	5	0	1.000	3.46	81	1	0	0	0-1	101.1	99	46	39	7	32-2	53

WORLD SERIES RECORD

Year League	W	L	Pct.	ERA	G	GS	CG	ShO	Sv.-Opp.	IP	H	R	ER	HR	BB-IBB	SO
2002— San Francisco (N.L.)	1	0	1.000	3.00	3	0	0	0	0-0	6.0	6	3	2	0	0-0	0

ZIMMERMAN, JEFF — P — RANGERS

PERSONAL: Born August 9, 1972, in Kelowna, B.C. ... 6-1/200. ... Throws right, bats right. ... Full name: Jeffery Ross Zimmerman.

HIGH SCHOOL: John G. Diefenbaker (Vancouver).

COLLEGE: Texas Christian, then Simon Fraser (B.C.).

TRANSACTIONS/CAREER NOTES: Signed by Winnipeg, Northern League (May 1997). ... Signed as non-drafted free agent by Texas Rangers organization (January 6, 1998). ... On Texas disabled list (March 22, 2002-entire season); included rehabilitation assignments to Charlotte (July 7-12) and Tulsa (July 13-24).

CAREER HITTING (MLB): 0-for-0 (.000), 0 R, 0 2B, 0 3B, 0 HR, 0 RBI.

Year League	W	L	Pct.	ERA	G	GS	CG	ShO	Sv.-Opp.	IP	H	R	ER	HR	BB-IBB	SO
1997— Winnipeg (Nor.)	9	2	.818	2.82	18	16	3	0	0-...	118.0	94	49	37	7	35-0	140
1998— Charlotte (FSL)■	2	1	.667	1.26	10	0	0	0	0-...	14.1	10	2	2	1	1-0	14
— Tulsa (Texas)	3	1	.750	1.29	41	0	0	0	9-...	63.0	38	16	9	5	20-3	67
1999— Oklahoma (PCL)	1	0	1.000	0.00	2	0	0	0	1-...	3.2	0	0	0	0	0-0	2
— Texas (A.L.)	9	3	.750	2.36	65	0	0	0	3-7	87.2	50	24	23	9	23-1	67
2000— Texas (A.L.)	4	5	.444	5.30	65	0	0	0	1-3	69.2	80	45	41	10	34-3	74
2001— Texas (A.L.)	4	4	.500	2.40	66	0	0	0	28-31	71.1	48	19	19	10	16-1	72
2002— Charlotte (FSL)	0	0	...	0.00	2	0	0	0	0-...	2.0	0	0	0	0	1-0	2
— Tulsa (Texas)	0	0	...	0.00	3	0	0	0	0-...	3.0	2	0	0	0	1-0	3
Major League totals (3 years)	17	12	.586	3.27	196	0	0	0	32-41	228.2	178	88	83	29	73-5	213

DIVISION SERIES RECORD

Year League	W	L	Pct.	ERA	G	GS	CG	ShO	Sv.-Opp.	IP	H	R	ER	HR	BB-IBB	SO
1999— Texas (A.L.)	0	0	...	0.00	1	0	0	0	0-0	1.0	1	0	0	0	0-0	1

ALL-STAR GAME RECORD

	W	L	Pct.	ERA	GS	CG	ShO	Sv.-Opp.	IP	H	R	ER	HR	BB-IBB	SO
All-Star Game totals (1 year)	0	0	...	0.00	0	0	0	0-0	1.0	0	0	0	0	2-0	0

ZINTER, ALAN — C — ASTROS

PERSONAL: Born May 19, 1968, in El Paso, Texas. ... 6-2/200. ... Bats both, throws right. ... Full name: Alan Michael Zinter.
HIGH SCHOOL: J.M. Hanks (El Paso, Texas).
COLLEGE: Arizona.
TRANSACTIONS/CAREER NOTES: Selected by San Diego Padres organization in 23rd round of free-agent draft (June 2, 1986); did not sign. ... Selected by New York Mets organization in first round (24th pick overall) of free-agent draft (June 5, 1989). ... Traded by Mets to Detroit Tigers organization for 1B Rico Brogna (March 31, 1994). ... Granted free agency (October 16, 1995). ... Signed by Boston Red Sox organization (December 13, 1995). ... Granted free agency (October 15, 1996). ... Signed by Seattle Mariners organization (December 11, 1996). ... Granted free agency (October 15, 1997). ... Signed by Chicago Cubs organization (December 4, 1997). ... Granted free agency (October 15, 1998). ... Re-signed by Cubs organization (November 13, 1998). ... Contract sold by Cubs to Seibu Lions of Japan Pacific League (April 28, 1999). ... Signed by Cubs organization (November 7, 1999). ... On Iowa disabled list (May 26-June 10, 2000). ... Traded by Cubs to Arizona Diamondbacks for future considerations (August 23, 2000). ... Granted free agency (October 18, 2000). ... Signed by Houston Astros organization (January 8, 2001).
HONORS: Named catcher on The Sporting News college All-America team (1989).
STATISTICAL NOTES: Tied for Eastern League lead with 11 passed balls in 1991. ... Tied for Pacific Coast League lead with 9 intentional bases on balls in 1997.
2002 GAMES PLAYED BY POSITION (MLB): 1B—8; C—1.

		BATTING														FIELDING	
Year Team (League)	Pos.	G	AB	R	H	2B	3B	HR	RBI	BB	SO	SB-CS	Avg.	OBP	SLG	E	Avg.
1989—Pittsfield (NY-Penn)	C	12	41	11	15	2	1	2	12	12	4	0-1	.366	.500	.610	0	1.000
—St. Lucie (FSL)	C-1B-OF	48	159	17	38	10	0	3	32	18	31	0-1	.239	.311	.358	8	.964
1990—St. Lucie (FSL)	C	98	333	63	97	19	6	7	63	54	70	8-1	.291	.386	.447	11	.981
—Jackson (Texas)	C	6	20	2	4	1	0	0	1	3	11	1-0	.200	.304	.250	0	1.000
1991—Williamsport (East.)	C	124	422	44	93	13	6	9	54	59	106	3-3	.220	.319	.344	10	.983
1992—Binghamton (East.)	1B	128	431	63	96	13	5	16	50	70	117	0-0	.223	.337	.387	12	.988
1993—Binghamton (East.)	1B-OF-C-3B	134	432	68	113	24	4	24	87	90	105	1-0	.262	.386	.502	11	.986
1994—Toledo (I.L.)■	1B-DH-OF-C	134	471	66	112	29	5	21	58	69	*185	13-5	.238	.344	.454	8	.989
1995—Toledo (I.L.)	1B-DH-OF-C	101	334	42	74	15	4	13	48	36	102	4-1	.222	.297	.407	5	.991
1996—Pawtucket (I.L.)	1B-DH-C-3B	108	357	78	96	19	5	26	69	58	123	5-1	.269	.373	.569	6	.990
1997—Tacoma (PCL)	1B-DH-3B-C	110	404	69	116	19	4	20	70	64	113	3-1	.287	.388	.502	9	.986
1998—Iowa (PCL)■	1-C-3-D-O	129	419	82	130	23	1	23	81	75	116	3-5	.310	.416	.535	10	.987
1999—Iowa (PCL)	1B-C	14	51	7	13	2	0	3	8	5	13	0-0	.255	.321	.471	0	1.000
—Seibu (Jp. East.)■		18	61	15	19	5	0	5	11	17	17	1-...	.311	...	.639	...	...
—Seibu (Jap. Pac.)	C	61	173	20	35	8	0	8	28	35	59	2-0	.202	...	.387	...	...
2000—Iowa (PCL)	1B-C-OF-3B	90	233	27	53	12	2	14	35	39	78	0-0	.227	.339	.476	7	.981
—Tucson (PCL)■	1B-OF	11	36	9	13	5	1	1	5	8	8	0-0	.361	.477	.639	0	1.000
2001—New Orleans (PCL)■	1B-C-OF	104	332	58	88	16	0	19	65	33	85	1-1	.265	.334	.485	4	.993
2002—New Orleans (PCL)	1B	63	225	30	52	14	0	11	39	22	64	2-0	.231	.298	.440	1	.998
—Houston (N.L.)	1B-C	39	44	5	6	2	0	2	3	0	19	0-0	.136	.136	.318	0	1.000
Major League totals (1 year)		39	44	5	6	2	0	2	3	0	19	0-0	.136	.136	.318	0	1.000

ZITO, BARRY — P — ATHLETICS

PERSONAL: Born May 13, 1978, in Las Vegas, Nev. ... 6-4/215. ... Throws left, bats left. ... Full name: Barry William Zito.
HIGH SCHOOL: University (San Diego).
JUNIOR COLLEGE: Pierce Junior College (Calif.).
COLLEGE: UC Santa Barbara, then Southern California.
TRANSACTIONS/CAREER NOTES: Selected by Texas Rangers organization in third round of free-agent draft (June 2, 1998); did not sign. ... Selected by Oakland Athletics organization in first round (ninth pick overall) of free-agent draft (June 2, 1999).
HONORS: Named A.L. Pitcher of the Year by The Sporting News (2002). ... Named lefthanded pitcher on The Sporting News A.L. All-Star team (2002). ... Named A.L Cy Young Award winner by Baseball Writers' Association of America (2002).
CAREER HITTING (MLB): 0-for-9 (.000), 0 R, 0 2B, 0 3B, 0 HR, 0 RBI.

Year League	W	L	Pct.	ERA	G	GS	CG	ShO	Sv.-Opp.	IP	H	R	ER	HR	BB-IBB	SO
1999—Visalia (Calif.)	3	0	1.000	2.45	8	8	0	0	0-...	40.1	21	13	11	3	22-0	62
—Midland (Texas)	2	1	.667	4.91	4	4	0	0	0-...	22.0	22	15	12	1	11-0	29
—Vancouver (PCL)	1	0	1.000	1.50	1	1	0	0	0-...	6.0	5	1	1	0	2-0	6
2000—Sacramento (PCL)	8	5	.615	3.19	18	18	0	0	0-...	101.2	88	44	36	4	45-0	91
—Oakland (A.L.)	7	4	.636	2.72	14	14	1	1	0-0	92.2	64	30	28	6	45-2	78
2001—Oakland (A.L.)	17	8	.680	3.49	35	•35	3	2	0-0	214.1	184	92	83	18	80-0	205
2002—Oakland (A.L.)	*23	5	.821	2.75	35	*35	1	0	0-0	229.1	182	79	70	24	78-2	182
Major League totals (3 years)	47	17	.734	3.04	84	84	5	3	0-0	536.1	430	201	181	48	203-4	465

DIVISION SERIES RECORD

Year League	W	L	Pct.	ERA	G	GS	CG	ShO	Sv.-Opp.	IP	H	R	ER	HR	BB-IBB	SO
2000—Oakland (A.L.)	1	0	1.000	1.59	1	1	0	0	0-0	5.2	7	1	1	0	2-0	5
2001—Oakland (A.L.)	0	1	.000	1.13	1	1	0	0	0-0	8.0	2	1	1	1	1-0	6
2002—Oakland (A.L.)	1	0	1.000	4.50	1	1	0	0	0-0	6.0	5	3	3	0	4-0	8
Division series totals (3 years)	2	1	.667	2.29	3	3	0	0	0-0	19.2	14	5	5	1	7-0	19

ALL-STAR GAME RECORD

	W	L	Pct.	ERA	GS	CG	ShO	Sv.-Opp.	IP	H	R	ER	HR	BB-IBB	SO
All-Star Game totals (1 year)	0	0	...	0.00	0	0	0	0-0	.1	0	0	0	0	0-0	0

ALOU, FELIPE — GIANTS

PERSONAL: Born May 12, 1935, in Haina, Dominican Republic. ... 6-1/195. ... Batted right, threw right. ... Full name: Felipe Rojas Alou. ... Father of Moises Alou, outfielder, Chicago Cubs; brother of Jesus Alou, major league outfielder with four teams (1965-75 and 1978-79); brother of Matty Alou, major league outfielder with six teams (1960-74); and uncle of Mel Rojas, pitcher with five major league teams (1990-99).

COLLEGE: Santo Domingo (Dominican Republic).

TRANSACTIONS/CAREER NOTES: Signed as free agent by New York Giants organization (November 14, 1955). ... Giants franchise moved from New York to San Francisco (1958). ... Traded by Giants with P Billy Hoeft, C Ed Bailey and a player to be named later to Milwaukee Braves for P Bob Hendley, P Bob Shaw and C Del Crandall (December 3, 1963); Braves acquired IF Ernie Bowman to complete deal (January 8, 1964). ... On disabled list (June 24-July 25, 1964). ... Braves franchise moved from Milwaukee to Atlanta (1966). ... Traded by Braves to Oakland Athletics for P Jim Nash (December 3, 1969). ... Traded by A's to New York Yankees for P Rob Gardner and P Ron Klimkowski (April 9, 1971). ... Contract sold by Yankees to Montreal Expos (September 5, 1973). ... Contract sold by Expos to Milwaukee Brewers (December 7, 1973). ... Released by Brewers (April 29, 1974).

HONORS: Named first baseman on The Sporting News N.L. All-Star team (1966).

STATISTICAL NOTES: Led N.L. with 355 total bases in 1966. ... Career major league grand slams: 2.

				BATTING											FIELDING			
Year	Team (League)	Pos.	G	AB	R	H	2B	3B	HR	RBI	Avg.	BB	SO	SB	PO	A	E	Avg.
1956—	Lake Charles (Evan.)	OF	5	9	1	2	0	0	0	1	.222	...	...	0	6	1	0	1.000
—	Cocoa (FSL)	OF-3B	119	445	111	169	15	6	21	99	*.380	68	40	*48	199	60	23	.918
1957—	Minneapolis (A.A.)	OF	24	57	7	12	2	0	0	3	.211	5	8	1	32	1	1	.971
—	Springfield (East.)	OF-3B	106	359	45	110	14	3	12	71	.306	27	29	18	215	26	9	.964
1958—	Phoenix (PCL)	OF	55	216	61	69	16	2	13	42	.319	17	24	10	150	3	3	.981
—	San Francisco (N.L.)	OF	75	182	21	46	9	2	4	16	.253	19	34	4	126	2	2	.985
1959—	San Francisco (N.L.)	OF	95	247	38	68	13	2	10	33	.275	17	38	5	111	2	3	.974
1960—	San Francisco (N.L.)	OF	106	322	48	85	17	3	8	44	.264	16	42	10	156	5	7	.958
1961—	San Francisco (N.L.)	OF	132	415	59	120	19	0	18	52	.289	26	41	11	196	10	2	.990
1962—	San Francisco (N.L.)	OF	154	561	96	177	30	3	25	98	.316	33	66	10	262	7	8	.971
1963—	San Francisco (N.L.)	OF	157	565	75	159	31	9	20	82	.281	27	87	11	279	9	4	.986
1964—	Milwaukee (N.L.)■	OF-1B	121	415	60	105	26	3	9	51	.253	30	41	5	329	12	5	.986
1965—	Milwaukee (N.L.)	0-1-3-S	143	555	80	165	29	2	23	78	.297	31	63	8	626	43	6	.991
1966—	Atlanta (N.L.)	1-0-3-S	154	*666	*122	*218	32	6	31	74	.327	24	51	5	935	64	13	.987
1967—	Atlanta (N.L.)	1B-OF	140	574	76	157	26	3	15	43	.274	32	50	6	864	34	9	.990
1968—	Atlanta (N.L.)	OF	160	*662	72	•210	37	5	11	57	.317	48	56	12	379	8	8	.980
1969—	Atlanta (N.L.)	OF	123	476	54	134	13	1	5	32	.282	23	23	4	260	4	3	.989
1970—	Oakland (A.L.)■	OF-1B	154	575	70	156	25	3	8	55	.271	32	31	10	290	11	7	.977
1971—	Oakland (A.L.)	OF	2	8	0	2	1	0	0	0	.250	0	1	0	7	0	0	1.000
—	New York (A.L.)■	OF-1B	131	461	52	133	20	6	8	69	.289	32	24	5	506	23	4	.992
1972—	New York (A.L.)	1B-OF	120	324	33	90	18	1	6	37	.278	22	27	1	669	54	7	.990
1973—	New York (A.L.)	1B-OF	93	280	25	66	12	0	4	27	.236	9	25	0	512	31	7	.987
—	Montreal (N.L.)■	OF-1B	19	48	4	10	1	0	1	4	.208	2	4	0	30	3	0	1.000
1974—	Milwaukee (A.L.)■	OF	3	3	0	0	0	0	0	0	.000	0	2	0	0	0	1	.000
American League totals (5 years)			503	1651	180	447	76	10	26	188	.271	95	110	16	1984	119	26	.988
National League totals (13 years)			1579	5688	805	1654	283	39	180	664	.291	328	596	91	4553	203	70	.985
Major league totals (17 years)			2082	7339	985	2101	359	49	206	852	.286	423	706	107	6537	322	96	.986

CHAMPIONSHIP SERIES RECORD

				BATTING											FIELDING			
Year	Team (League)	Pos.	G	AB	R	H	2B	3B	HR	RBI	Avg.	BB	SO	SB	PO	A	E	Avg.
1969—	Atlanta (N.L.)	PH	1	1	0	0	0	0	0	0	.000	0	0	0	...	...	...	...

WORLD SERIES RECORD

				BATTING											FIELDING			
Year	Team (League)	Pos.	G	AB	R	H	2B	3B	HR	RBI	Avg.	BB	SO	SB	PO	A	E	Avg.
1962—	San Francisco (N.L.)	OF	7	26	2	7	1	1	0	1	.269	1	4	0	8	0	1	.889

ALL-STAR GAME RECORD

			BATTING										FIELDING			
Year	League	Pos.	AB	R	H	2B	3B	HR	RBI	Avg.	BB	SO	SB	PO	A	E	Avg.
1962—	National	OF	0	0	0	0	0	0	1	...	0	0	0	0	0	0	...
1966—	National							Did not play.									
1968—	National	OF	0	0	0	0	0	0	0	...	0	0	0	0	0	0	...
All-Star Game totals (2 years)			0	0	0	0	0	0	1	...	0	0	0	0	0	0	...

RECORD AS MANAGER

BACKGROUND: Spring training instructor, Montreal Expos (1976). ... Coach, Expos (1979-80, 1984 and October 8, 1991-May 22, 1992).

HONORS: Named Florida State League Manager of the Year (1990). ... Named N.L. Manager of the Year by The Sporting News (1994). ... Named N.L. Manager of the Year by Baseball Writers' Association of America (1994).

		REGULAR SEASON				POSTSEASON							
						Playoff		Champ. Series		World Series		All-Star Game	
Year	Team (League)	W	L	Pct.	Pos.	W	L	W	L	W	L	W	L
1977—	West Palm Beach (Florida State)	77	55	.583	1st (S)	1	2	—	—	—	—	—	—
1978—	Memphis (Southern)	71	73	.493	2nd (W)	—	—	—	—	—	—	—	—
1981—	Denver (American Association)	76	60	.559	2nd (W)	4	0	—	—	—	—	—	—
1982—	Wichita (American Association)	70	67	.511	2nd (W)	—	—	—	—	—	—	—	—
1983—	Wichita (American Association)	65	71	.478	3rd (W)	—	—	—	—	—	—	—	—
1985—	Indianapolis (American Association)	61	81	.430	4th (E)	—	—	—	—	—	—	—	—
1986—	West Palm Beach (Florida State)	80	55	.593	1st (S)	3	3	—	—	—	—	—	—

MAJOR LEAGUE MANAGERS

Year Team (League)	REGULAR SEASON W	L	Pct.	Pos.	POSTSEASON Playoff W	L	Champ. Series W	L	World Series W	L	All-Star Game W	L
1987—West Palm Beach (Florida State)	75	63	.543	2nd (S)	—	—	—	—	—	—	—	—
1988—West Palm Beach (Florida State)	41	27	.603	2nd (E)	—	—	—	—	—	—	—	—
—(Second half)	30	36	.455	3rd (E)	2	2	—	—	—	—	—	—
1989—West Palm Beach (Florida State)	39	31	.557	T2nd (E)	—	—	—	—	—	—	—	—
—(Second half)	35	33	.515	2nd (E)	—	—	—	—	—	—	—	—
1990—West Palm Beach (Florida State)	49	19	.721	1st (E)	—	—	—	—	—	—	—	—
—(Second half)	43	21	.672	1st (E)	3	3	—	—	—	—	—	—
1991—West Palm Beach (Florida State)	33	31	.516	4th (E)	—	—	—	—	—	—	—	—
—(Second half)	39	28	.582	2nd (E)	6	1	—	—	—	—	—	—
1992—Montreal (N.L.)	70	55	.560	2nd (E)	—	—	—	—	—	—	—	—
1993—Montreal (N.L.)	94	68	.580	2nd (E)	—	—	—	—	—	—	—	—
1994—Montreal (N.L.)	74	40	.649		—	—	—	—	—	—	—	—
1995—Montreal (N.L.)	66	78	.458	5th (E)	—	—	—	—	—	—	1	0
1996—Montreal (N.L.)	88	74	.543	2nd (E)	—	—	—	—	—	—	—	—
1997—Montreal (N.L.)	78	84	.481	4th (E)	—	—	—	—	—	—	—	—
1998—Montreal (N.L.)	65	97	.401	4th (E)	—	—	—	—	—	—	—	—
1999—Montreal (N.L.)	68	94	.420	4th (E)	—	—	—	—	—	—	—	—
2000—Montreal (N.L.)	67	95	.414	4th (E)	—	—	—	—	—	—	—	—
2001—Montreal (N.L.)	21	32	.396		—	—	—	—	—	—	—	—
Major league totals (9 years)	691	717	.491		—	—	—	—	—	—	1	0

NOTES:

1977—Lost to St. Petersburg in semifinals.
1978—Memphis tied one game.
1981—Defeated Omaha in league championship.
1986—Defeated Winter Haven, two games to none, in semifinals; lost to St. Petersburg, three games to one, in league championship.
1988—Defeated Vero Beach, two games to none, in first round; lost to Osceola, two games to none, in semifinals.
1990—Defeated Lakeland, two games to one, in semifinals; lost to Vero Beach, two games to one, in league championship.
1991—Defeated Vero Beach, two games to one, in first round; defeated Lakeland, two games to none, in semifinals; defeated Clearwater, two games to none, in league championship.
1992—Replaced Montreal manager Tom Runnells with club in fourth place and record of 17-20 (May 22).
1994—Montreal was in first place in N.L. East at time of season-ending strike (August 12).
2001—Replaced as Montreal manager by Jeff Torborg, with team in fifth place (May 31).

BAKER, DUSTY

PERSONAL: Born June 15, 1949, in Riverside, Calif. ... 6-2/200. ... Batted right, threw right. ... Full name: Johnnie B. Baker Jr.
HIGH SCHOOL: Del Campo (Fair Oaks, Calif.).
COLLEGE: American River College (Calif.).
TRANSACTIONS/CAREER NOTES: Selected by Atlanta Braves organization in 26th round of free-agent draft (June 6, 1967). ... On West Palm Beach restricted list (April 5-June 13, 1968). ... On Atlanta military list (January 24-April 3, 1969 and June 17-July 3, 1972). ... Traded by Braves with 1B/3B Ed Goodson to Los Angeles Dodgers for OF Jimmy Wynn, 2B Lee Lacy, 1B/OF Tom Paciorek and IF Jerry Royster (November 17, 1975). ... Released on waivers by Dodgers (February 10, 1984); San Francisco Giants claim rejected (February 16, 1984). ... Granted free agency (February 21, 1984). ... Signed by Giants (April 1, 1984). ... On restricted list (April 2-11, 1984). ... Traded by Giants to Oakland Athletics for P Ed Puikunas and C Dan Winters (March 24, 1985). ... Granted free agency (November 10, 1986).
RECORDS: Shares major league records for most plate appearances, most at-bats and most times faced pitcher as batsman in one inning—3 (September 20, 1972, second inning); and most stolen bases in one inning—3 (June 27, 1984, third inning).
HONORS: Named outfielder on The Sporting News N.L. All-Star team (1980). ... Named outfielder on The Sporting News N.L. Silver Slugger team (1980-81). ... Won N.L. Gold Glove as outfielder (1981).
STATISTICAL NOTES: Led N.L. outfielders with 407 total chances in 1973. ... Career major league grand slams: 4.

Year Team (League)	Pos.	G	BATTING AB	R	H	2B	3B	HR	RBI	Avg.	BB	SO	SB	FIELDING PO	A	E	Avg.
1967—Austin (Texas)	OF	9	39	6	9	1	0	0	1	.231	2	7	0	17	0	1	.944
1968—W.Palm Beach (FSL)	OF	6	21	2	4	0	0	0	2	.190	1	4	0	6	2	0	1.000
—Greenwood (W. Car.)	OF	52	199	45	68	11	3	6	39	.342	23	39	6	82	1	3	.965
—Atlanta (N.L.)	OF	6	5	0	2	0	0	0	0	.400	0	1	0	0	0	0	...
1969—Shreveport (Texas)	OF	73	265	40	68	5	1	9	31	.257	36	41	2	135	10	3	.980
—Richmond (Int'l)	OF-3B	25	89	7	22	4	0	0	8	.247	11	22	3	40	9	4	.925
—Atlanta (N.L.)	OF	3	7	0	0	0	0	0	0	.000	0	3	0	2	0	0	1.000
1970—Richmond (I.L.)	OF	118	461	97	150	29	3	11	51	.325	53	45	10	236	10	7	.972
—Atlanta (N.L.)	OF	13	24	3	7	0	0	0	4	.292	2	4	0	11	1	3	.800
1971—Richmond (I.L.)	OF-3B	80	341	62	106	23	2	11	41	.311	25	37	10	136	13	4	.974
—Atlanta (N.L.)	OF	29	62	2	14	2	0	0	4	.226	1	14	0	29	1	0	1.000
1972—Atlanta (N.L.)	OF	127	446	62	143	27	2	17	76	.321	45	68	4	344	8	4	.989
1973—Atlanta (N.L.)	OF	159	604	101	174	29	4	21	99	.288	67	72	24	*390	10	7	.983
1974—Atlanta (N.L.)	OF	149	574	80	147	35	0	20	69	.256	71	87	18	359	10	7	.981
1975—Atlanta (N.L.)	OF	142	494	63	129	18	2	19	72	.261	67	57	12	287	10	3	.990
1976—Los Angeles (N.L.)■	OF	112	384	36	93	13	0	4	39	.242	31	54	2	254	3	1	.996
1977—Los Angeles (N.L.)	OF	153	533	86	155	26	1	30	86	.291	58	89	2	227	8	3	.987
1978—Los Angeles (N.L.)	OF	149	522	62	137	24	1	11	66	.262	47	66	12	250	13	4	.985
1979—Los Angeles (N.L.)	OF	151	554	86	152	29	1	23	88	.274	56	70	11	289	14	3	.990
1980—Los Angeles (N.L.)	OF	153	579	80	170	26	4	29	97	.294	43	66	12	308	5	3	.991
1981—Los Angeles (N.L.)	OF	103	400	48	128	17	3	9	49	.320	29	43	10	181	8	2	.990
1982—Los Angeles (N.L.)	OF	147	570	80	171	19	1	23	88	.300	56	62	17	226	7	6	.975
1983—Los Angeles (N.L.)	OF	149	531	71	138	25	1	15	73	.260	72	59	7	249	4	5	.981
1984—San Fran. (N.L.)■	OF	100	243	31	71	7	2	3	32	.292	40	27	4	112	1	3	.974
1985—Oakland (A.L.)■	1B-OF-DH	111	343	48	92	15	1	14	52	.268	50	47	2	465	29	5	.990
1986—Oakland (A.L.)	OF-DH-1B	83	242	25	58	8	0	4	19	.240	27	37	0	90	4	0	1.000
American League totals (2 years)		194	585	73	150	23	1	18	71	.256	77	84	2	555	33	5	.992
National League totals (17 years)		1845	6532	891	1831	297	22	224	942	.280	685	842	135	3518	103	54	.985
Major league totals (19 years)		2039	7117	964	1981	320	23	242	1013	.278	762	926	137	4073	136	59	.986

DIVISION SERIES RECORD

Year	Team (League)	Pos.	G	AB	R	H	2B	3B	HR	RBI	Avg.	BB	SO	SB	PO	A	E	Avg.
				BATTING											FIELDING			
1981	—Los Angeles (N.L.).....	OF	5	18	2	3	1	0	0	1	.167	2	0	0	12	0	0	1.000

CHAMPIONSHIP SERIES RECORD

RECORDS: Shares single-game record for most grand slams—1 (October 5, 1977). ... Shares single-inning record for most runs batted in—4 (October 5, 1977, fourth inning). ... Shares N.L. single-game record for most hits—4 (October 7, 1978).
NOTES: Named N.L. Championship Series Most Valuable Player (1977).

Year	Team (League)	Pos.	G	AB	R	H	2B	3B	HR	RBI	Avg.	BB	SO	SB	PO	A	E	Avg.
				BATTING											FIELDING			
1977	—Los Angeles (N.L.).....	OF	4	14	4	5	1	0	2	8	.357	2	3	0	3	0	0	1.000
1978	—Los Angeles (N.L.).....	OF	4	15	1	7	2	0	0	1	.467	3	0	0	5	0	0	1.000
1981	—Los Angeles (N.L.).....	OF	5	19	3	6	1	0	0	3	.316	1	0	0	10	0	1	.909
1983	—Los Angeles (N.L.).....	OF	4	14	4	5	1	0	1	1	.357	2	0	0	9	0	0	1.000
Championship series totals (4 years)			17	62	12	23	5	0	3	13	.371	8	3	0	27	0	1	.964

WORLD SERIES RECORD

NOTES: Member of World Series championship team (1981).

Year	Team (League)	Pos.	G	AB	R	H	2B	3B	HR	RBI	Avg.	BB	SO	SB	PO	A	E	Avg.
				BATTING											FIELDING			
1977	—Los Angeles (N.L.).....	OF	6	24	4	7	0	0	1	5	.292	0	2	0	11	0	1	.917
1978	—Los Angeles (N.L.).....	OF	6	21	2	5	0	0	1	1	.238	1	3	0	12	0	0	1.000
1981	—Los Angeles (N.L.).....	OF	6	24	3	4	0	0	0	1	.167	1	6	0	13	0	0	1.000
World Series totals (3 years)			18	69	9	16	0	0	2	7	.232	2	11	0	36	0	1	.973

ALL-STAR GAME RECORD

Year	League	Pos.	AB	R	H	2B	3B	HR	RBI	Avg.	BB	SO	SB	PO	A	E	Avg.
			BATTING											FIELDING			
1981	—National.....................	OF	2	0	1	0	0	0	0	.500	0	0	0	2	0	0	1.000
1982	—National.....................	OF	2	0	0	0	0	0	0	.000	0	0	0	0	0	0	...
All-Star Game totals (2 years)			4	0	1	0	0	0	0	.250	0	0	0	2	0	0	1.000

RECORD AS MANAGER

BACKGROUND: Coach, San Francisco Giants (1988-92). ... Manager, Scottsdale Scorpions, Arizona Fall League (1992, record: 20-22, second place/Northern Division).
HONORS: Named N.L. Manager of the Year by Baseball Writers' Association of America (1993, 1997 and 2000). ... Coach, N.L. All-Star team (1994 and 1997). ... Named N.L. Manager of the Year by THE SPORTING NEWS (1997 and 2000).

Year	Team (League)	W	L	Pct.	Pos.	Playoff W	Playoff L	Champ. Series W	Champ. Series L	World Series W	World Series L	All-Star Game W	All-Star Game L
		REGULAR SEASON				POSTSEASON							
1993	—San Francisco (N.L.)................................	103	59	.636	2nd (W)	—	—	—	—	—	—	—	—
1994	—San Francisco (N.L.)................................	55	60	.478		—	—	—	—	—	—	—	—
1995	—San Francisco (N.L.)................................	67	77	.465	4th (W)	—	—	—	—	—	—	—	—
1996	—San Francisco (N.L.)................................	68	94	.420	4th (W)	—	—	—	—	—	—	—	—
1997	—San Francisco (N.L.)................................	90	72	.556	1st (W)	0	3	—	—	—	—	—	—
1998	—San Francisco (N.L.)................................	89	74	.546	2nd (W)	—	—	—	—	—	—	—	—
1999	—San Francisco (N.L.)................................	86	76	.531	2nd (W)	—	—	—	—	—	—	—	—
2000	— San Francisco (N.L.)................................	97	65	.599	1st (W)	1	3	—	—	—	—	—	—
2001	— San Francisco (N.L.)................................	90	72	.556	2nd (W)	—	—	—	—	—	—	—	—
2002	— San Francisco (N.L.)................................	95	66	.590	2nd (W)	3	2	4	1	3	4	—	—
Major league totals (10 years)	....	840	715	.540		4	8	4	1	3	4	—	—

NOTES:
1994—San Francisco was in second place in N.L. West at time of season-ending strike (August 12).
1997—Lost to Florida in N.L. divisional playoff.
2000—Lost to New York Mets in N.L. divisional playoff.
2001—Defeated Atlanta in N.L. divisional playoff; defeated St. Louis in N.L. Championship Series; lost to Anaheim in World Series.

BOCHY, BRUCE — PADRES

PERSONAL: Born April 16, 1955, in Landes de Boussac, France. ... 6-4/225. ... Batted right, threw right. ... Full name: Bruce Douglas Bochy. ... Brother of Joe Bochy, catcher in Minnesota Twins organization (1969-72). ... Name pronounced BO-chee.
HIGH SCHOOL: Melbourne (Fla.).
JUNIOR COLLEGE: Brevard Community College (Fla.).
COLLEGE: Florida State.
TRANSACTIONS/CAREER NOTES: Selected by Chicago White Sox organization in eighth round of free-agent draft (January 9, 1975); did not sign. ... Selected by Houston Astros organization in secondary phase of free-agent draft (June 4, 1975). ... Traded by Astros to New York Mets for two players to be named later (February 11, 1981); Astros acquired IF Randy Rodgers and C Stan Hough to complete deal (April 3, 1981). ... Released by Mets (January 21, 1983). ... Signed by San Diego Padres organization (February 23, 1983). ... On disabled list (April 13-May 6, 1987). ... Granted free agency (November 9, 1987).
STATISTICAL NOTES: Tied for Florida State League lead with 12 passed balls in 1977.

			BATTING												FIELDING			
Year	Team (League)	Pos.	G	AB	R	H	2B	3B	HR	RBI	Avg.	BB	SO	SB	PO	A	E	Avg.
1975—	Covington (Appal.)	C	37	145	31	49	9	0	4	34	.338	11	18	0	231	36	4	.985
1976—	Columbus (Sou.)	C	69	230	9	53	6	0	0	16	.230	14	30	0	266	45	6	.981
—	Dubuque (Midwest)	C-1B	30	103	9	25	4	0	1	8	.243	12	11	1	165	25	5	.974
1977—	Cocoa (FSL)	C	128	430	40	109	18	2	3	35	.253	35	50	0	*492	67	12	.979
1978—	Columbus (Sou.)	C	79	261	25	70	10	2	7	34	.268	13	30	0	419	49	7	.985
—	Houston (N.L.)	C	54	154	8	41	8	0	3	15	.266	11	35	0	268	35	8	.974
1979—	Houston (N.L.)	C	56	129	11	28	4	0	1	6	.217	13	25	0	198	29	7	.970
1980—	Houston (N.L.)	C-1B	22	22	0	4	1	0	0	0	.182	5	7	0	19	1	0	1.000
1981—	Tidewater (I.L.)■	C	85	269	23	61	11	2	8	38	.227	22	47	0	253	35	3	.990
1982—	Tidewater (I.L.)	C	81	251	32	57	11	0	15	52	.227	19	47	2	427	57	5	.990
—	New York (N.L.)	C-1B	17	49	4	15	4	0	2	8	.306	4	6	0	92	8	4	.962
1983—	Las Vegas (PCL)■	C	42	145	28	44	8	1	11	33	.303	15	25	3	157	21	3	.983
—	San Diego (N.L.)	C	23	42	2	9	1	1	0	3	.214	0	9	0	51	5	0	1.000
1984—	Las Vegas (PCL)	C	34	121	18	32	7	0	7	22	.264	17	13	0	189	17	2	.990
—	San Diego (N.L.)	C	37	92	10	21	5	1	4	15	.228	3	21	0	147	12	2	.988
1985—	San Diego (N.L.)	C	48	112	16	30	2	0	6	13	.268	6	30	0	148	11	2	.988
1986—	San Diego (N.L.)	C	63	127	16	32	9	0	8	22	.252	14	23	1	202	22	2	.991
1987—	San Diego (N.L.)	C	38	75	8	12	3	0	2	11	.160	11	21	0	95	7	4	.962
1988—	Las Vegas (PCL)	C	53	147	17	34	5	0	5	13	.231	17	28	1	207	19	3	.987
Major league totals (9 years)			358	802	75	192	37	2	26	93	.239	67	177	1	1220	130	29	.979

CHAMPIONSHIP SERIES RECORD

			BATTING												FIELDING			
Year	Team (League)	Pos.	G	AB	R	H	2B	3B	HR	RBI	Avg.	BB	SO	SB	PO	A	E	Avg.
1980—	Houston (N.L.)	C	1	1	0	0	0	0	0	0	.000	0	0	0	5	1	0	1.000

WORLD SERIES RECORD

			BATTING												FIELDING			
Year	Team (League)	Pos.	G	AB	R	H	2B	3B	HR	RBI	Avg.	BB	SO	SB	PO	A	E	Avg.
1984—	San Diego (N.L.)	PH	1	1	0	1	0	0	0	0	1.000	0	0	0	...	...	...	...

RECORD AS MANAGER

BACKGROUND: Player/coach, Las Vegas, San Diego Padres organization (1988). ... Coach, Padres (1993-94).

HONORS: Named N.L. Manager of the Year by The Sporting News (1996 and 1998). ... Named N.L. Manager of the Year by Baseball Writers' Association of America (1996).

		REGULAR SEASON				POSTSEASON							
						Playoff		Champ. Series		World Series		All-Star Game	
Year	Team (League)	W	L	Pct.	Pos.	W	L	W	L	W	L	W	L
1989—	Spokane (Northwest)	41	34	.547	1st (N)	2	1	—	—	—	—	—	—
1990—	Riverside (California)	35	36	.493	4th (S)	—	—	—	—	—	—	—	—
—	(Second half)	29	42	.408	5th (S)	—	—	—	—	—	—	—	—
1991—	High Desert (California)	31	37	.456	3rd (S)	—	—	—	—	—	—	—	—
—	(Second half)	42	26	.618	1st (S)	6	2	—	—	—	—	—	—
1992—	Wichita (Texas)	39	29	.574	1st (W)	—	—	—	—	—	—	—	—
—	(Second half)	31	37	.456	4th (W)	6	1	—	—	—	—	—	—
1995—	San Diego (N.L.)	70	74	.486	3rd (W)	—	—	—	—	—	—	—	—
1996—	San Diego (N.L.)	91	71	.562	1st (W)	0	3	—	—	—	—	—	—
1997—	San Diego (N.L.)	76	86	.469	4th (W)	—	—	—	—	—	—	—	—
1998—	San Diego (N.L.)	98	64	.605	1st (W)	3	1	4	2	0	4	—	—
1999—	San Diego (N.L.)	74	88	.457	4th (W)	—	—	—	—	—	—	0	1
2000—	San Diego (N.L.)	76	86	.469	5th (W)	—	—	—	—	—	—	—	—
2001—	San Diego (N.L.)	79	83	.488	4th (W)	—	—	—	—	—	—	—	—
2002—	San Diego (N.L.)	66	96	.407	5th (W)	—	—	—	—	—	—	—	—
Major league totals (8 years)		630	648	.493		3	4	4	2	0	4	0	1

NOTES:

1989—Defeated Southern Oregon in league championship.

1991—Defeated Bakersfield, three games to none, in semifinals; defeated Stockton, three games to two, in league championship.

1992—Defeated El Paso, two games to one, in semifinals; defeated Shreveport, four games to none, in league championship.

1996—Lost to St. Louis in N.L. divisional playoff.

1998—Defeated Houston in N.L. divisional playoff; defeated Atlanta in N.L. Championship Series; lost to New York Yankees in World Series.

BOONE, BOB — REDS

PERSONAL: Born November 19, 1947, in San Diego. ... 6-2/207. ... Batted right, threw right. ... Full name: Robert Raymond Boone. ... Son of Ray Boone, major league infielder with six teams (1948-60); brother of Rodney Boone, minor league catcher/outfielder (1972-75); father of Bret Boone, second baseman, Seattle Mariners; and father of Aaron Boone, third baseman, Cincinnati Reds.

HIGH SCHOOL: Crawford (San Diego).

COLLEGE: Stanford.

TRANSACTIONS/CAREER NOTES: Selected by Philadelphia Phillies organization in 20th round of free-agent draft (June 5, 1969). ... On military list (May 26, 1970-remainder of season). ... On disabled list (April 10-June 4, 1971). ... Contract sold by Phillies to California Angels (December 6, 1981). ... Granted free agency (November 12, 1986). ... Re-signed by Angels (May 1, 1987). ... Granted free agency (October 24, 1988). ... Signed by Kansas City Royals (November 30, 1988). ... On disabled list (May 17-July 20, 1990). ... Granted free agency (November 5, 1990). ... Signed by Oakland Athletics organization (May 31, 1993). ... Released by A's (June 1, 1993).

RECORDS: Holds major league career record for most years by catcher (100 or more games)—15.

HONORS: Named catcher on The Sporting News N.L. All-Star team (1976). ... Won N.L. Gold Glove at catcher (1978-79). ... Won A.L. Gold Glove at catcher (1982 and 1986-1989).

STATISTICAL NOTES: Tied for Carolina League lead in double plays by third baseman with 18 in 1969. ... Led Northwest League catchers with 18 passed balls and 13 double plays in 1972. ... Led N.L. catchers with 924 total chances in 1974. ... Led N.L. catchers with .991 fielding percentage in 1978. ... Led A.L. catchers with 745 total chances in 1982 and 823 in 1989. ... Led A.L. catchers with 12 double plays in 1983, 15 in 1985 and 16 in 1986. ... Career major league grand slams: 2.

Year	Team (League)	Pos.	G	AB	R	H	2B	3B	HR	RBI	Avg.	BB	SO	SB	PO	A	E	Avg.
				BATTING											FIELDING			
1969—	Ral./Dur. (Caro.)	3B	80	300	45	90	13	1	5	46	.300	19	24	0	71	160	20	.920
1970—	Reading (East.)	3B	20	80	12	23	2	0	2	10	.288	7	9	0	28	38	7	.904
1971—	Reading (East.)	3B-C-SS	92	328	41	87	14	3	4	37	.265	28	28	1	206	138	17	.953
1972—	Eugene (N'West)	C	138	513	77	158	32	4	17	67	.308	45	35	2	*699	*77	*24	.970
—	Philadelphia (N.L.)	C	16	51	4	14	1	0	1	4	.275	5	7	1	66	7	5	.936
1973—	Philadelphia (N.L.)	C	145	521	42	136	20	2	10	61	.261	41	36	3	868	*89	10	.990
1974—	Philadelphia (N.L.)	C	146	488	41	118	24	3	3	52	.242	35	29	3	*825	77	*22	.976
1975—	Philadelphia (N.L.)	C-3B	97	289	28	71	14	2	2	20	.246	32	14	1	459	48	5	.990
1976—	Philadelphia (N.L.)	C-1B	121	361	40	98	18	2	4	54	.271	45	44	2	587	39	6	.991
1977—	Philadelphia (N.L.)	C-3B	132	440	55	125	26	4	11	66	.284	42	54	5	654	83	8	.989
1978—	Philadelphia (N.L.)	C-1B-OF	132	435	48	123	18	4	12	62	.283	46	37	2	650	55	8	†.989
1979—	Philadelphia (N.L.)	C-3B	119	398	38	114	21	3	9	58	.286	49	33	1	527	66	8	.987
1980—	Philadelphia (N.L.)	C	141	480	34	110	23	1	9	55	.229	48	41	3	741	88	*18	.979
1981—	Philadelphia (N.L.)	C	76	227	19	48	7	0	4	24	.211	22	16	2	365	32	6	.985
1982—	California (A.L.)■	C	143	472	42	121	17	0	7	58	.256	39	34	0	*650	*87	8	.989
1983—	California (A.L.)	C	142	468	46	120	18	0	9	52	.256	24	42	4	606	*83	*14	.980
1984—	California (A.L.)	C	139	450	33	91	16	1	3	32	.202	25	45	3	660	*71	12	.984
1985—	California (A.L.)	C	150	460	37	114	17	0	5	55	.248	37	35	1	670	71	10	.987
1986—	California (A.L.)	C	144	442	48	98	12	2	7	49	.222	43	30	1	812	*84	11	.988
1987—	Palm Springs (Calif.)	C	3	9	0	1	1	0	0	0	.111	1	0	0	17	4	1	.955
—	California (A.L.)	C-DH	128	389	42	94	18	0	3	33	.242	35	36	0	684	56	*13	.983
1988—	California (A.L.)	C	122	352	38	104	17	0	5	39	.295	29	26	2	506	*66	8	.986
1989—	Kansas City (A.L.)■	C	131	405	33	111	13	2	1	43	.274	49	37	3	*752	64	7	.991
1990—	Kansas City (A.L.)	C	40	117	11	28	3	0	0	9	.239	17	12	1	243	19	4	.985
American League totals (9 years)			1139	3555	330	881	131	5	40	370	.248	298	297	15	5583	601	87	.986
National League totals (10 years)			1125	3690	349	957	172	21	65	456	.259	365	311	23	5742	584	96	.985
Major League totals (19 years)			2264	7245	679	1838	303	26	105	826	.254	663	608	38	11325	1185	183	.986

DIVISION SERIES RECORD

Year	Team (League)	Pos.	G	AB	R	H	2B	3B	HR	RBI	Avg.	BB	SO	SB	PO	A	E	Avg.
				BATTING											FIELDING			
1981—	Philadelphia (N.L.)	C	3	5	0	0	0	0	0	0	.000	0	0	0	10	2	0	1.000

CHAMPIONSHIP SERIES RECORD

Year	Team (League)	Pos.	G	AB	R	H	2B	3B	HR	RBI	Avg.	BB	SO	SB	PO	A	E	Avg.
				BATTING											FIELDING			
1976—	Philadelphia (N.L.)	C	3	7	0	2	0	0	0	1	.286	1	0	0	8	2	0	1.000
1977—	Philadelphia (N.L.)	C	4	10	1	4	0	0	0	0	.400	0	0	0	18	2	0	1.000
1978—	Philadelphia (N.L.)	C	3	11	0	2	0	0	0	0	.182	0	1	0	16	2	1	.947
1980—	Philadelphia (N.L.)	C	5	18	1	4	0	0	0	2	.222	1	2	0	22	3	0	1.000
1982—	California (A.L.)	C	5	16	3	4	0	0	1	4	.250	0	2	0	30	3	0	1.000
1986—	California (A.L.)	C	7	22	4	10	0	0	1	2	.455	1	3	0	33	3	0	1.000
Championship series totals (6 years)			27	84	9	26	0	0	2	9	.310	3	8	0	127	15	1	.993

WORLD SERIES RECORD

NOTES: Member of World Series championship team (1980).

Year	Team (League)	Pos.	G	AB	R	H	2B	3B	HR	RBI	Avg.	BB	SO	SB	PO	A	E	Avg.
				BATTING											FIELDING			
1980—	Philadelphia (N.L.)	C	6	17	3	7	2	0	0	4	.412	4	0	0	49	3	0	1.000

ALL-STAR GAME RECORD

Year	League	Pos.	AB	R	H	2B	3B	HR	RBI	Avg.	BB	SO	SB	PO	A	E	Avg.
			BATTING											FIELDING			
1976—	National	C	2	0	0	0	0	0	0	.000	0	0	0	5	0	0	1.000
1978—	National	C	1	1	1	0	0	0	2	1.000	0	0	0	3	1	0	1.000
1979—	National	C	2	1	1	0	0	0	0	.500	0	0	0	0	0	0	...
1983—	American	C	0	0	0	0	0	0	0	...	0	0	0	1	0	0	1.000
All-Star Game totals (4 years)			5	2	2	0	0	0	2	.400	0	0	0	9	1	0	1.000

RECORD AS MANAGER

BACKGROUND: Coach, Cincinnati Reds (1994). ... Special assistant to general manager, Reds (1998-2000).

		REGULAR SEASON				POSTSEASON							
						Playoff		Champ. Series		World Series		All-Star Game	
Year	Team (League)	W	L	Pct.	Pos.	W	L	W	L	W	L	W	L
1992—	Tacoma (PCL)	26	45	.366	5th (N)	—	—	—	—	—	—	—	—
—	(Second half)	30	42	.417	5th (N)	—	—	—	—	—	—	—	—
1993—	Tacoma (PCL)	32	39	.451	5th (N)	—	—	—	—	—	—	—	—
—	(Second half)	37	35	.514	3rd (N)	—	—	—	—	—	—	—	—
1995—	Kansas City (A.L.)	70	74	.486	2nd (C)	—	—	—	—	—	—	—	—
1996—	Kansas City (A.L.)	75	86	.466	5th (C)	—	—	—	—	—	—	—	—
1997—	Kansas City (A.L.)	36	46	.439	—	—	—	—	—	—	—	—	—
2001—	Cincinnati (N.L.)	66	96	.407	5th (C)	—	—	—	—	—	—	—	—
2002—	Cincinnati (N.L.)	78	84	.481	3rd (C)	—	—	—	—	—	—	—	—
Major League Totals (5 years)		325	386	.457		—	—	—	—	—	—	—	—

NOTES:

1997—Replaced as Kansas City manager by Tony Muser, with club in fourth place (July 9).

BOWA, LARRY — PHILLIES

PERSONAL: Born December 6, 1945, in Sacramento. ... 5-10/155. ... Bats both, throws right. ... Full name: Lawrence Robert Bowa. ... Uncle of Nick Johnson, first baseman, New York Yankees.

HIGH SCHOOL: McClathy (Sacramento).

JUNIOR COLLEGE: Sacramento City College.

TRANSACTIONS/CAREER NOTES: Signed as non-drafted free agent by Philadelphia Phillies organization (October 12, 1965).... On military list (March 7-July 18, 1967).... On disabled list (July 26-September 1, 1973).... On disabled list (May 27-June 23, 1975).... On disabled list (May 25-June 9, 1979).... Traded with 2B Ryne Sandberg to Chicago Cubs for SS Ivan DeJesus (January 27, 1982).... Released by Cubs (August 13, 1985).... Signed by New York Mets (August 20, 1985).... Granted free agency (November 12, 1985).

HONORS: Named shortstop on The Sporting News N.L. All-Star Team (1975 and 1978).... Named shortstop on The Sporting News N.L. All-Star fielding team (1972 and 1978).

STATISTICAL NOTES: Led Eastern League shortstops in double plays with 77 in 1968.... Led Pacific Coast League shortstops with 468 assists and .974 fielding percentage in 1969.... Led N.L. shortstops in total chances with 843 and tied for lead with 97 double plays in 1971.... Led N.L. in sacrifice hits with 18 in 1972.

		BATTING												FIELDING			
Year Team (League)	Pos.	G	AB	R	H	2B	3B	HR	RBI	Avg.	BB	SO	SB	PO	A	E	Avg.
1966—Spartanburg (W. Car.)	SS	97	429	70	134	14	4	2	36	.312	18	44	24	138	284	12	.972
—San Diego (PCL)	SS	5	19	0	6	0	1	0	1	.316	1	3	0	13	20	2	.943
1967—Bakersfield (Calif.)	SS-2B	7	32	4	6	2	0	0	3	.188	1	6	2	15	12	1	.964
—Reading (East.)	SS	22	89	11	25	4	0	0	9	.281	3	17	0	35	79	9	.927
1968—Reading (East.)	SS	133	480	47	116	14	2	3	36	.242	24	27	14	192	•395	24	.961
1969—Eugene (PCL)	SS-2B	135	568	80	163	11	6	1	26	.287	31	56	*48	*215	†469	18	†.974
1970—Philadelphia (N.L.)	SS-2B	145	547	50	137	17	6	0	34	.250	21	48	24	202	418	13	.979
1971—Philadelphia (N.L.)	SS	159	650	74	162	18	5	0	25	.249	36	61	28	272	*560	11	*.987
1972—Philadelphia (N.L.)	SS	152	579	67	145	11	*13	1	31	.250	32	51	17	212	494	9	*.987
1973—Philadelphia (N.L.)	SS	122	446	42	94	11	3	0	23	.211	24	31	10	191	361	12	.979
1974—Philadelphia (N.L.)	SS	162	669	97	184	19	10	1	36	.275	23	52	39	256	462	12	*.984
1975—Philadelphia (N.L.)	SS	136	583	79	178	18	9	2	38	.305	24	32	24	227	403	25	.962
1976—Philadelphia (N.L.)	SS	156	624	71	155	15	9	0	49	.248	32	31	30	180	492	17	.975
1977—Philadelphia (N.L.)	SS	154	624	93	175	19	3	4	41	.280	32	32	32	222	518	13	.983
1978—Philadelphia (N.L.)	SS	156	654	78	192	31	5	3	43	.294	24	40	27	224	502	10	*.986
1979—Philadelphia (N.L.)	SS	147	539	74	130	17	11	0	31	.241	61	32	20	229	448	6	*.991
1980—Philadelphia (N.L.)	SS	147	540	57	144	16	4	2	39	.267	24	28	21	225	449	17	.975
1981—Philadelphia (N.L.)	SS	103	360	34	102	14	3	0	31	.283	26	17	16	117	309	11	.975
1982—Chicago (N.L.)	SS	142	499	50	123	15	7	0	29	.246	39	38	8	210	396	17	.973
1983—Chicago (N.L.)	SS	147	499	73	133	20	5	2	43	.267	35	30	7	230	464	11	*.984
1984—Chicago (N.L.)	SS	133	391	33	87	14	2	0	17	.223	28	24	10	217	378	16	.974
1985—Chicago (N.L.)	SS-2B	72	195	13	48	6	4	0	13	.246	11	20	5	91	197	9	.970
—New York (N.L.)	SS-2B	14	19	2	2	1	0	0	2	.105	2	2	0	9	6	2	.882
Major League totals (16 years)		2247	8418	987	2191	262	99	15	525	.260	474	569	318	3314	6857	211	.980

DIVISION SERIES RECORD

		BATTING												FIELDING			
Year Team (League)	Pos.	G	AB	R	H	2B	3B	HR	RBI	Avg.	BB	SO	SB	PO	A	E	Avg.
1981—Philadelphia (N.L.)	SS	5	17	0	3	1	0	0	1	.176	0	0	0	12	9	1	.955

CHAMPIONSHIP SERIES RECORD

		BATTING												FIELDING			
Year Team (League)	Pos.	G	AB	R	H	2B	3B	HR	RBI	Avg.	BB	SO	SB	PO	A	E	Avg.
1976—Philadelphia (N.L.)	SS	3	8	1	1	1	0	0	1	.125	3	0	0	2	11	0	1.000
1977—Philadelphia (N.L.)	SS	4	17	2	2	0	0	0	1	.118	1	0	0	0	17	0	1.000
1978—Philadelphia (N.L.)	SS	4	18	2	6	0	0	0	0	.333	1	2	0	5	16	0	1.000
1980—Philadelphia (N.L.)	SS	5	19	2	6	0	0	0	0	.316	3	3	1	4	11	1	.938
1984—Chicago (N.L.)	SS	5	15	1	3	1	0	0	1	.200	1	0	0	8	15	0	1.000
Championship series totals (5 years)		21	77	8	18	2	0	0	3	.234	9	5	1	19	70	1	.989

WORLD SERIES RECORD

		BATTING												FIELDING			
Year Team (League)	Pos.	G	AB	R	H	2B	3B	HR	RBI	Avg.	BB	SO	SB	PO	A	E	Avg.
1980—Philadelphia (N.L.)	SS	6	24	3	9	1	0	0	2	.375	0	0	3	5	18	0	1.000

ALL-STAR GAME RECORD

		BATTING											FIELDING			
Year League	Pos.	AB	R	H	2B	3B	HR	RBI	Avg.	BB	SO	SB	PO	A	E	Avg.
1974—National	SS	2	0	0	0	0	0	0	.000	0	0	0	2	0	0	1.000
1975—National	SS	0	1	0	0	0	0	0	...	0	0	0	2	0	0	1.000
1976—National	SS	1	0	0	0	0	0	0	.000	0	0	0	2	1	0	1.000
1978—National	SS	3	1	2	0	0	0	0	.667	0	0	1	2	4	0	1.000
1979—National	SS	2	0	0	0	0	0	0	.000	0	0	0	1	3	0	1.000
All-Star Game totals (5 years)		8	2	2	0	0	0	0	.250	0	0	1	9	8	0	1.000

RECORD AS MANAGER

BACKGROUND: Coach, Phillies (May 11, 1989-96). ... Coach, Anaheim Angels (1997-99). ... Coach, Seattle Mariners (2000).

HONORS: Named N.L. Manager of the Year by The Sporting News (2001). ... Named N.L. Manager of the Year by Baseball Writers' Association of America (2001).

Year	Team (League)	Regular Season W	L	Pct.	Pos.	Playoff W	L	Champ. Series W	L	World Series W	L	All-Star Game W	L
1986—	Las Vegas (PCL)	36	44	.450	3rd (S)	—	—	—	—	—	—	—	—
	—(Second half)	44	28	.611	1st (S)	6	4	—	—	—	—	—	—
1987—	San Diego (N.L.)	65	97	.401	6th (W)	—	—	—	—	—	—	—	—
1988—	San Diego (N.L.)	16	30	.348	—	—	—	—	—	—	—	—	—
2001—	Philadelphia (N.L.)	86	76	.531	2nd (E)	—	—	—	—	—	—	—	—
2002—	Philadelphia (N.L.)	80	81	.497	3rd (E)	—	—	—	—	—	—	—	—
Major League Totals (4 years)		247	284	.465		—	—	—	—	—	—	—	—

NOTES:

1986—Defeated Phoenix, three games to two, in league semifinals; defeated Vancouver, three games to two, to win league championship.

1988—Replaced as Padres manager by Jack McKeon, with club in fifth place (May 28).

BRENLY, BOB — DIAMONDBACKS

PERSONAL: Born February 25, 1954, in Coshocton, Ohio. ... 6-2/205. ... Batted right, threw right. ... Full name: Robert Earl Brenly.

COLLEGE: Ohio University.

TRANSACTIONS/CAREER NOTES: Signed as non-drafted free agent by San Francisco Giants organization (June 21, 1976). ... On disabled list (March 25-May 13, 1982). ... Released by Giants (December 21, 1988). ... Signed by Toronto Blue Jays (January 18, 1989). ... Released by Blue Jays (July 14, 1989). ... Signed by Giants organization (August 2, 1989). ... Granted free agency (November 13, 1989).

STATISTICAL NOTES: Led Midwest League third baseman with 263 assists, 383 total chances and in double plays with 21 in 1977. ... Led California League third baseman in double plays with 30 in 1978. ... Led N.L. catchers in fielding percentage with .995 in 1986. ... Led N.L. catchers in assists with 83 in 1987.

Year	Team (League)	Pos.	G	AB	R	H	2B	3B	HR	RBI	Avg.	BB	SO	SB	PO	A	E	Avg.
			BATTING												FIELDING			
1976—	Great Falls (Pio.)	3B	25	86	16	27	5	1	1	17	.314	12	9	1	10	16	2	.929
	—Fresno (Calif.)	3B	17	60	16	22	3	1	1	9	.367	12	17	1	2	6	1	.889
1977—	Cedar Rapids (Midw.)	3B-OF	136	499	85	135	16	1	22	73	.271	90	108	6	90	†263	‡31	.919
1978—	Fresno (Calif.)	3B	135	489	102	139	34	5	17	89	.284	81	90	12	*118	247	27	.931
1979—	Fresno (Calif.)	3B	56	212	49	65	11	2	9	37	.307	28	31	6	39	133	17	.910
	—Shreveport (Texas)	C-3B-OF-1B	64	193	33	57	8	1	9	30	.295	19	38	0	199	55	7	.973
1980—	Shreveport (Texas)	3B	2	10	2	3	0	0	1	3	.300	0	3	1	1	2	0	1.000
	—Phoenix (PCL)	3B-C-SS-OF	84	287	34	74	9	6	7	45	.258	24	51	2	183	110	20	.936
1981—	Phoenix (PCL)	C-OF-3B	76	257	42	75	11	3	7	41	.292	29	37	2	177	41	9	.960
	—San Francisco (N.L.)	C-3B-OF	19	45	5	15	2	1	1	4	.333	6	4	0	52	6	4	.935
1982—	San Francisco (N.L.)	C-3B	65	180	26	51	4	1	4	15	.283	18	26	6	265	32	12	.961
1983—	San Francisco (N.L.)	C-1B-OF	104	281	36	63	12	2	7	34	.224	37	48	10	465	73	9	.984
1984—	San Francisco (N.L.)	C-1B-OF	145	506	74	147	28	0	20	80	.291	48	52	6	807	76	13	.985
1985—	San Francisco (N.L.)	C-3B-1B	133	440	41	97	16	1	19	56	.220	57	62	1	719	85	17	.979
1986—	San Francisco (N.L.)	C-3B-1B	149	472	60	116	26	0	16	62	.246	74	97	10	688	118	16	†.981
1987—	San Francisco (N.L.)	C-1B-3B	123	375	55	100	19	1	18	51	.267	47	85	10	685	†86	9	.988
1988—	San Francisco (N.L.)	C	73	206	13	39	7	0	5	22	.189	20	40	1	334	27	6	.984
1989—	Toronto (A.L.)■	C-1B	48	88	9	15	3	1	1	6	.170	10	17	0	61	5	1	.985
	—Phoenix (PCL)■	C-3B-1B	27	98	11	25	3	0	2	11	.255	8	12	3	78	16	4	.959
	—San Francisco (N.L.)	C	12	22	2	4	2	0	0	3	.182	1	7	1	31	5	0	1.000
American League totals (1 year)			48	88	9	15	3	1	1	6	.170	10	17	0	61	5	1	.985
National League totals (9 years)			823	2527	312	632	116	6	90	327	.250	308	421	45	4046	508	86	.981
Major League totals (9 years)			871	2615	321	647	119	7	91	333	.247	318	438	45	4107	513	87	.982

CHAMPIONSHIP SERIES RECORD

Year	Team (League)	Pos.	G	AB	R	H	2B	3B	HR	RBI	Avg.	BB	SO	SB	PO	A	E	Avg.
			BATTING												FIELDING			
1987—	San Francisco (N.L.)	C-PH	6	17	3	4	1	0	1	2	.235	3	7	0	28	2	0	1.000

ALL-STAR GAME RECORD

Year	League	Pos.	AB	R	H	2B	3B	HR	RBI	Avg.	BB	SO	SB	PO	A	E	Avg.
			BATTING											FIELDING			
1984—	National	PH	1	0	0	0	0	0	0	.000	0	1	0	...	...	...	...

RECORD AS MANAGER

BACKGROUND: Broadcaster (1990-91). ... Coach, San Francisco Giants (1992-95). ... Broadcaster (1996-2000).

Year	Team (League)	Regular Season W	L	Pct.	Pos.	Playoff W	L	Champ. Series W	L	World Series W	L	All-Star Game W	L
2001—	Arizona (N.L.)	92	70	.568	1st (W)	3	2	4	1	4	3	—	—
2002—	Arizona (N.L.)	98	64	.605	1st (W)	0	3	—	—	—	—	0	0
Major League Totals (2 years)		190	134	.586		3	5	4	1	4	3	0	0

NOTES:

2001—Defeated St. Louis in N.L. divisional playoff; defeated Atlanta in N.L. Championship Series; defeated New York Yankees in World Series.

2002—All-Star Game ended in tie. Lost to St. Louis in N.L. divisional playoff.

COX, BOBBY — BRAVES

PERSONAL: Born May 21, 1941, in Tulsa, Okla. ... 6-0/185. ... Batted right, threw right. ... Full name: Robert Joseph Cox.
HIGH SCHOOL: Selma (Calif.).
JUNIOR COLLEGE: Reedley Junior College (Calif.).
TRANSACTIONS/CAREER NOTES: Signed by Los Angeles Dodgers organization (1959). ... Selected by Chicago Cubs organization from Dodgers organization in Rule 5 minor league draft (November 30, 1964). ... Acquired by Atlanta Braves organization (1966). ... On Austin disabled list (May 8-18 and May 30-June 9, 1966). ... On disabled list (May 1-June 12, 1967). ... Traded by Braves to New York Yankees for C Bob Tillman and P Dale Roberts (December 7, 1967); Roberts later was transferred to Richmond. ... On disabled list (May 28-June 18, 1970). ... Released by Yankees (September 22, 1970). ... Signed by Yankees organization (July 17, 1971). ... Released as player by Fort Lauderdale (August 28, 1971).
STATISTICAL NOTES: Led Alabama-Florida League shortstops with 71 double plays in 1961. ... Led Pacific Coast League third basemen with .954 fielding percentage in 1965.

			BATTING											FIELDING			
Year Team (League)	**Pos.**	**G**	**AB**	**R**	**H**	**2B**	**3B**	**HR**	**RBI**	**Avg.**	**BB**	**SO**	**SB**	**PO**	**A**	**E**	**Avg.**
1960—Reno (California)	2B	125	440	99	112	20	5	13	75	.255	95	129	28	282	*385	*39	.945
1961—Salem (Northwest)	2B	14	44	3	9	2	0	0	2	.205	0	14	0	25	25	2	.962
—Panama City (Al.-Fla.)	2B	92	335	66	102	27	4	17	73	.304	48	72	17	220	247	8	*.983
1962—Salem (Northwest)	3B-2B	*141	514	83	143	26	7	16	82	.278	63	119	7	174	296	28	.944
1963—Albuquerque (Texas)	3B	17	53	5	15	2	0	2	5	.283	3	12	1	8	27	1	.972
—Great Falls (Pio.)	3B	109	407	103	137	*31	4	19	85	.337	73	84	7	82	211	21	*.933
1964—Albuquerque (Texas)	2B	138	523	98	152	29	13	16	91	.291	52	84	8	*322	*415	*28	.963
1965—Salt Lake (PCL)■	3B-2B	136	473	58	125	32	1	12	55	.264	35	96	1	133	337	22	†.955
1966—Tacoma (PCL)	3B-2B	10	34	2	4	1	0	0	4	.118	6	9	0	23	15	0	1.000
—Austin (Texas)■	2B-3B	92	339	35	77	11	1	7	30	.227	25	55	7	140	216	12	.967
1967—Richmond (I.L.)	3B-1B	99	350	52	104	17	4	14	51	.297	34	73	3	84	136	8	.965
1968—New York (A.L.)■	3B	135	437	33	100	15	1	7	41	.229	41	85	3	98	279	17	.957
1969—New York (A.L.)	3B-2B	85	191	17	41	7	1	2	17	.215	34	41	0	50	147	11	.947
1970—Syracuse (I.L.)	3B-SS-2B	90	251	34	55	15	0	9	30	.219	49	40	0	86	163	13	.950
1971—Fort Laud. (FSL)	2B-P	4	9	1	1	0	0	0	0	.111	1	0	0	4	5	0	1.000
Major league totals (2 years)		220	628	50	141	22	2	9	58	.225	75	126	3	148	426	28	.953

RECORD AS PITCHER

Year Team (League)	**W**	**L**	**Pct.**	**ERA**	**G**	**GS**	**CG**	**ShO**	**Sv.**	**IP**	**H**	**R**	**ER**	**BB**	**SO**
1971—Fort Lauderdale (FSL)	0	1	.000	5.40	3	0	0	0	0	10	15	9	6	5	4

RECORD AS MANAGER

BACKGROUND: Minor league instructor, New York Yankees (October 28, 1970-March 24, 1971). ... Player/manager, Fort Lauderdale, Yankees organization (1971). ... Coach, Yankees (1977). ... General manager, Braves (October 1986-1989).
HONORS: Named Major League Manager of the Year by The Sporting News (1985). ... Named A.L. Manager of the Year by Baseball Writers' Association of America (1985). ... Named N.L. Manager of the Year by The Sporting News (1991, 1993, 1999 and 2002). ... Named N.L. Manager of the Year by the Baseball Writers' Association of America (1991).

	REGULAR SEASON				POSTSEASON							
					Playoff		Champ. Series		World Series		All-Star Game	
Year Team (League)	**W**	**L**	**Pct.**	**Pos.**	**W**	**L**	**W**	**L**	**W**	**L**	**W**	**L**
1971—Fort Lauderdale (Florida State)	71	70	.504	4th (E)	—	—	—	—	—	—	—	—
1972—West Haven (East.)	84	56	.600	1st (A)	3	0	—	—	—	—	—	—
1973—Syracuse (International)	76	70	.521	3rd (A)	—	—	—	—	—	—	—	—
1974—Syracuse (International)	74	70	.514	2nd (N)	—	—	—	—	—	—	—	—
1975—Syracuse (International)	72	64	.529	3rd	—	—	—	—	—	—	—	—
1976—Syracuse (International)	82	57	.590	2nd	6	1	—	—	—	—	—	—
1978—Atlanta (N.L.)	69	93	.426	6th (W)	—	—	—	—	—	—	—	—
1979—Atlanta (N.L.)	66	94	.413	6th (W)	—	—	—	—	—	—	—	—
1980—Atlanta (N.L.)	81	80	.503	4th (W)	—	—	—	—	—	—	—	—
1981—Atlanta (N.L.)	25	29	.463	4th (W)	—	—	—	—	—	—	—	—
—(Second half)	25	27	.481	5th (W)	—	—	—	—	—	—	—	—
1982—Toronto (A.L.)	78	84	.481	T6th (E)	—	—	—	—	—	—	—	—
1983—Toronto (A.L.)	89	73	.549	4th (E)	—	—	—	—	—	—	—	—
1984—Toronto (A.L.)	89	73	.549	2nd (E)	—	—	—	—	—	—	—	—
1985—Toronto (A.L.)	99	62	.615	1st (E)	—	—	3	4	—	—	—	—
1990—Atlanta (N.L.)	40	57	.412	6th (W)	—	—	—	—	—	—	—	—
1991—Atlanta (N.L.)	94	68	.580	1st (W)	—	—	4	3	3	4	—	—
1992—Atlanta (N.L.)	98	64	.605	1st (W)	—	—	4	3	2	4	0	1
1993—Atlanta (N.L.)	104	58	.642	1st (W)	—	—	2	4	—	—	0	1
1994—Atlanta (N.L.)	68	46	.596		—	—	—	—	—	—	—	—
1995—Atlanta (N.L.)	90	54	.625	1st (E)	3	1	4	0	4	2	—	—
1996—Atlanta (N.L.)	96	66	.593	1st (E)	3	0	4	3	2	4	1	0
1997—Atlanta (N.L.)	101	61	.623	1st (E)	3	0	2	4	—	—	0	1
1998—Atlanta (N.L.)	106	56	.654	1st (E)	3	0	2	4	—	—	—	—
1999—Atlanta (N.L.)	103	59	.636	1st (E)	3	1	4	2	0	4	—	—
2000—Atlanta (N.L.)	95	67	.586	1st (E)	0	3	—	—	—	—	0	1
2001—Atlanta (N.L.)	88	74	.543	1st (E)	3	0	1	4	—	—	—	—
2002—Atlanta (N.L.)	101	59	.631	1st (E)	2	3	—	—	—	—	—	—
American League totals (4 years)	355	292	.549		—	—	3	4	—	—	—	—
National League totals (17 years)	1450	1112	.566		20	8	27	27	11	18	1	4
Major league totals (21 years)	1805	1404	.562		20	8	30	31	11	18	1	4

NOTES:
1972—Defeated Three Rivers in playoff.
1976—Defeated Memphis, three games to none, in playoffs; defeated Richmond, three games to one, in league championship.
1985—Lost to Kansas City in A.L. Championship Series.
1990—Replaced Atlanta manager Russ Nixon with club in sixth place and record of 25-40 (June 22).
1991—Defeated Pittsburgh in N.L. Championship Series; lost to Minnesota in World Series.
1992—Defeated Pittsburgh in N.L. Championship Series; lost to Toronto in World Series.
1993—Lost to Philadelphia in N.L. Championship Series.
1994—Atlanta was in second place in N.L. East at time of season-ending strike (August 12).
1995—Defeated Colorado in N.L. divisional playoff; defeated Cincinnati in N.L. Championship Series; defeated Cleveland in World Series.
1996—Defeated Los Angeles in N.L. divisional playoff; defeated St. Louis in N.L. Championship Series; lost to New York Yankees in World Series.
1997—Defeated Houston in N.L. divisional playoff; lost to Florida in N.L. Championship Series.
1998—Defeated Chicago Cubs in N.L. divisional playoff; lost to San Diego in N.L. Championship Series.
1999—Defeated Houston in N.L. divisional playoff; defeated New York Mets in N.L. Championship Series; lost to New York Yankees in World Series.
2000—Lost to St. Louis in N.L. divisional playoff.
2001—Defeated Houston in N.L. divisional playoff; lost to Arizona in N.L. Championship Series.
2002—Lost to San Francisco in N.L. divisional playoff.

GARDENHIRE, RON — TWINS

PERSONAL: Born October 24, 1957, in Butzbach, West Germany. ... 6-0/180. ... Bats right, throws right. ... Full name: Ronald Clyde Gardenhire.

HIGH SCHOOL: Okmulgee (Okla.) High School.

JUNIOR COLLEGE: Paris (Texas).

COLLEGE: Texas.

TRANSACTIONS/CAREER NOTES: Selected by New York Mets organization in sixth round of free-agent draft (June 5, 1979). ... On Tidewater disabled list (July 21-31, 1983). ... On disabled list (July 20-August 9 and August 20-September 10, 1984). ... On disabled list (May 2-17, May 25-July 19 and August 16-September 1, 1985); included rehabilitation assignment to Tidewater (June 24-July 13). ... Traded by Mets to Minnesota Twins for P Don Iasparro (November 12, 1986).

			BATTING												FIELDING			
Year	Team (League)	Pos.	G	AB	R	H	2B	3B	HR	RBI	Avg.	BB	SO	SB	PO	A	E	Avg.
1979—	Lynchburg (Caro.)	SS	70	277	36	82	13	3	4	27	.296	21	45	9	120	252	21	.947
1980—	Jackson (Texas)	SS-2B	127	458	58	118	16	6	6	64	.258	45	68	13	168	411	41	.934
1981—	Tidewater (I.L.)	SS-2B-3B	125	414	52	105	17	8	2	40	.254	28	61	28	206	373	33	.946
—	New York (N.L.)	SS-2B-3B	27	48	2	13	1	0	0	3	.271	5	9	2	28	50	2	.975
1982—	New York (N.L.)	SS-2B-3B	141	384	29	92	17	1	3	33	.240	23	55	5	235	399	29	.956
1983—	Tidewater (I.L.)	SS	102	387	63	111	20	6	4	39	.287	34	54	9	202	321	27	.951
—	New York (N.L.)	SS	17	32	1	2	0	0	0	1	.063	1	4	0	13	30	0	1.000
1984—	New York (N.L.)	SS-2B-3B	74	207	20	51	7	1	1	10	.246	9	43	6	98	154	12	.955
1985—	Tidewater (I.L.)	3B-SS-2B	22	71	3	15	2	0	1	10	.211	6	13	0	20	36	5	.918
—	New York (N.L.)	SS-2B-3B	26	39	5	7	2	1	0	2	.179	8	11	0	21	32	4	.930
1986—	Tidewater (I.L.)	2B-SS	96	323	41	89	10	4	4	33	.276	44	48	11	161	288	19	.959
1987—	Portland (PCL)■	1B-3B-2B-SS	117	389	49	106	16	4	6	50	.272	45	70	1	384	126	5	.990
Major League totals (5 years)			285	710	57	165	27	3	4	49	.232	46	122	13	395	665	47	.958

RECORD AS MANAGER

BACKGROUND: Coach, Minnesota Twins (1999-2001).

NOTES: Tied one game (1989, first half).

		REGULAR SEASON				POSTSEASON							
						Playoff		Champ. Series		World Series		All-Star Game	
Year	Team (League)	W	L	Pct.	Pos.	W	L	W	L	W	L	W	L
1988—	Kenosha (Midw.)	41	27	.603	1st (N)	—	—	—	—	—	—	—	—
—	(Second half)	40	32	.556	2nd (N)	3	3	—	—	—	—	—	—
1989—	Orlando (Sou.)	40	31	.563	1st (E)	—	—	—	—	—	—	—	—
—	(Second half)	39	34	.534	4th (E)	1	3	—	—	—	—	—	—
1990—	Orlando (Sou.)	42	30	.583	1st (E)	—	—	—	—	—	—	—	—
—	(Second half)	43	29	.597	2nd (E)	5	4	—	—	—	—	—	—
2002—	Minnesota	94	67	.584	1st (C)	3	2	1	4	—	—	—	—

NOTES:
1988—Defeated Rockford, two games to none, in playoffs; lost to Cedar Rapids, three games to one, in league championship.
1989—Lost to Greenville in playoffs.
1990—Defeated Jacksonville, three games to one, in playoffs; lost to Memphis, three games to two, in league championship.
2002—Defeated Oakland in A.L. divisional playoff; lost to Anaheim in A.L. Championship Series.

HARGROVE, MIKE — ORIOLES

PERSONAL: Born October 26, 1949, in Perryton, Texas. ... 6-0/195. ... Batted left, threw left. ... Full name: Dudley Michael Hargrove.

HIGH SCHOOL: Perryton (Texas).

COLLEGE: Northwestern State, Okla. (degree in physical education and social sciences).

TRANSACTIONS/CAREER NOTES: Selected by Texas Rangers organization in 25th round of free-agent draft (June 6, 1972). ... Traded by Rangers with 3B Kurt Bevacqua and C Bill Fahey to San Diego Padres for OF Oscar Gamble, C Dave Roberts and cash (October 25, 1978). ... Traded by Padres to Cleveland Indians for OF Paul Dade (June 14, 1979). ... Granted free agency (November 12, 1985).

HONORS: Named Western Carolinas League Player of the Year (1973). ... Named A.L. Rookie Player of the Year by THE SPORTING NEWS (1974). ... Named A.L. Rookie of the Year by Baseball Writers' Association of America (1974).

STATISTICAL NOTES: Led New York-Pennsylvania League first basemen with 58 double plays in 1972. ... Led Western Carolinas League with 247 total bases in 1973. ... Led Western Carolinas League first basemen with 118 double plays in 1973. ... Had 23-game hitting streak (April 16-May 15, 1980). ... Led A.L. first basemen with 1,489 total chances in 1980. ... Led A.L. with .432 on-base percentage in 1981. ... Career major league grand slams: 1.

			BATTING											FIELDING			
Year Team (League)	Pos.	G	AB	R	H	2B	3B	HR	RBI	Avg.	BB	SO	SB	PO	A	E	Avg.
1972—Geneva (NY-Penn)	1B	•70	243	38	65	8	0	4	37	.267	52	44	3	*537	•40	10	*.983
1973—Gastonia (W. Car.)	1B	•130	456	88	*160	*35	8	12	82	*.351	68	47	10	*1121	•77	14	*.988
1974—Texas (A.L.)	1B-DH-OF	131	415	57	134	18	6	4	66	.323	49	42	0	638	72	9	.987
1975—Texas (A.L.)	OF-1B-DH	145	519	82	157	22	2	11	62	.303	79	66	4	513	45	13	.977
1976—Texas (A.L.)	1B	151	541	80	155	30	1	7	58	.287	*97	64	2	1222	110	*21	.984
1977—Texas (A.L.)	1B	153	525	98	160	28	4	18	69	.305	103	59	2	1393	100	11	.993
1978—Texas (A.L.)	1B-DH	146	494	63	124	24	1	7	40	.251	*107	47	2	1221	*116	*17	.987
1979—San Diego (N.L.)■	1B	52	125	15	24	5	0	0	8	.192	25	15	0	323	17	5	.986
—Cleveland (A.L.)■	OF-1B-DH	100	338	60	110	21	4	10	56	.325	63	40	2	356	16	2	.995
1980—Cleveland (A.L.)	1B	160	589	86	179	22	2	11	85	.304	111	36	4	*1391	88	10	.993
1981—Cleveland (A.L.)	1B-DH	94	322	43	102	21	0	2	49	.317	60	16	5	766	76	•9	.989
1982—Cleveland (A.L.)	1B-DH	160	591	67	160	26	1	4	65	.271	101	58	2	1293	*123	5	.996
1983—Cleveland (A.L.)	1B-DH	134	469	57	134	21	4	3	57	.286	78	40	0	1098	115	7	.994
1984—Cleveland (A.L.)	1B	133	352	44	94	14	2	2	44	.267	53	38	0	790	83	8	.991
1985—Cleveland (A.L.)	1B-DH-OF	107	284	31	81	14	1	1	27	.285	39	29	1	599	66	6	.991
American League totals (12 years)		1614	5439	768	1590	261	28	80	678	.292	940	535	24	11280	1010	118	.990
National League totals (1 year)		52	125	15	24	5	0	0	8	.192	25	15	0	323	17	5	.986
Major league totals (12 years)		1666	5564	783	1614	266	28	80	686	.290	965	550	24	11603	1027	123	.990

ALL-STAR GAME RECORD

		BATTING										FIELDING			
Year League	Pos.	AB	R	H	2B	3B	HR	RBI	Avg.	BB	SO	SB	PO	A	E	Avg.
1975—American	PH	1	0	0	0	0	0	0	.000	0	0	0	...	...	...	...

RECORD AS MANAGER

BACKGROUND: Minor league coach, Cleveland Indians organization (1986). ... Coach, Indians (1990-July 6, 1991).

HONORS: Named Carolina League Manager of the Year (1987). ... Named Pacific Coast League Manager of the Year (1989). ... Named A.L. Manager of the Year by THE SPORTING NEWS (1995).

	REGULAR SEASON				POSTSEASON							
					Playoff		Champ. Series		World Series		All-Star Game	
Year Team (League)	W	L	Pct.	Pos.	W	L	W	L	W	L	W	L
1987—Kinston (Carolina)	33	37	.471	T3rd (S)	—	—	—	—	—	—	—	—
—(Second half)	42	28	.600	1st (S)	3	3	—	—	—	—	—	—
1988—Williamsport (East.)	66	73	.475	6th	—	—	—	—	—	—	—	—
1989—Colorado Springs (Pacific Coast)	44	26	.629	1st (S)	—	—	—	—	—	—	—	—
—(Second half)	34	38	.472	3rd (S)	2	3	—	—	—	—	—	—
1991—Cleveland (A.L.)	32	53	.376	7th (E)	—	—	—	—	—	—	—	—
1992—Cleveland (A.L.)	76	86	.469	T4th (E)	—	—	—	—	—	—	—	—
1993—Cleveland (A.L.)	76	86	.469	6th (E)	—	—	—	—	—	—	—	—
1994—Cleveland (A.L.)	66	47	.584		—	—	—	—	—	—	—	—
1995—Cleveland (A.L.)	100	44	.694	1st (C)	3	0	4	2	2	4	—	—
1996—Cleveland (A.L.)	99	62	.615	1st (C)	1	3	—	—	—	—	0	1
1997—Cleveland (A.L.)	86	75	.534	1st (C)	3	2	4	2	3	4	—	—
1998—Cleveland (A.L.)	89	73	.549	1st (C)	3	1	2	4	—	—	1	0
1999—Cleveland (A.L.)	97	65	.599	1st (C)	2	3	—	—	—	—	—	—
2000— Baltimore (A.L.)	74	88	.457	4th (E)	—	—	—	—	—	—	—	—
2001— Baltimore (A.L.)	63	98	.391	4th (E)	—	—	—	—	—	—	—	—
2002— Baltimore (A.L.)	67	95	.414	4th (E)	—	—	—	—	—	—	—	—
Major league totals (12 years)	925	872	.515		12	9	10	8	5	8	1	1

NOTES:

1987—Defeated Winston-Salem, two games to none, in playoffs; lost to Salem, three games to one, in league championship.

1989—Lost to Albuquerque in playoffs.

1991—Replaced Cleveland manager John McNamara with club in seventh place and record of 25-52 (July 6).

1994—Cleveland was in second place in A.L. Central at time of season-ending strike (August 12).

1995—Defeated Boston in A.L. divisional playoff; defeated Seattle in A.L. Championship Series; lost to Atlanta in World Series.

1996—Lost to Baltimore in A.L. divisional playoff.

1997—Defeated New York in A.L. divisional playoff; defeated Baltimore in A.L. Championship Series; lost to Florida in World Series.

1998—Defeated Boston in A.L. divisional playoff; lost to New York Yankees in A.L. Championship Series.

1999—Lost to Boston in A.L. divisional playoff.

HOWE, ART — METS

PERSONAL: Born December 15, 1946, in Pittsburgh. ... 6-1/185. ... Batted right, threw right. ... Full name: Arthur Henry Howe Jr.

HIGH SCHOOL: Shaler (Glenshaw, Pa.).

COLLEGE: Wyoming (bachelor of science degree in business administration, 1969).

TRANSACTIONS/CAREER NOTES: Signed as free agent by Pittsburgh Pirates organization (June, 1971). ... On disabled list (August 17-September 2, 1972 and April 13-May 6, 1973). ... Traded by Pirates to Houston Astros (January 6, 1976), completing deal in which Astros traded 2B Tommy Helms to Pirates for a player to be named later (December 12, 1975). ... On disabled list (May 12-June 19, 1982 and March 27, 1983-entire season). ... Granted free agency (November 7, 1983). ... Signed by St. Louis Cardinals (March 21, 1984). ... Released by Cardinals (April 22, 1985).

STATISTICAL NOTES: Tied for Carolina League lead in putouts by third baseman with 95 in 1971. ... Led International League third basemen with 22 errors and 24 double plays in 1972. ... Had 23-game hitting streak (May 1-24, 1981). ... Career major league grand slams: 1.

			BATTING												FIELDING			
Year	Team (League)	Pos.	G	AB	R	H	2B	3B	HR	RBI	Avg.	BB	SO	SB	PO	A	E	Avg.
1971	—Salem (Carolina)	3B-SS	114	382	77	133	27	7	12	79	*.348	82	74	11	‡110	221	21	.940
1972	—Char., W.Va. (I.L.)	3B-2B-SS	109	365	68	99	21	3	14	53	.271	63	69	8	105	248	†24	.936
1973	—Char., W.Va. (I.L.)	3B-2B-SS	119	372	50	85	20	1	8	44	.228	54	70	6	141	229	21	.946
1974	—Char., W.Va. (I.L.)	3B	60	207	26	70	17	4	8	36	.338	31	27	4	35	90	9	.933
	—Pittsburgh (N.L.)	3B-SS	29	74	10	18	4	1	1	5	.243	9	13	0	11	49	4	.938
1975	—Char., W.Va. (I.L.)	3B-2B	11	42	4	15	1	3	0	3	.357	2	4	0	15	23	1	.974
	—Pittsburgh (N.L.)	3B-SS	63	146	13	25	9	0	1	10	.171	15	15	1	19	89	7	.939
1976	—Memphis (I.L.)■	3B-1B	74	259	50	92	21	3	12	59	.355	34	31	1	93	120	14	.938
	—Houston (N.L.)	3B-2B	21	29	0	4	1	0	0	0	.138	6	6	0	17	16	1	.971
1977	—Houston (N.L.)	2B-3B-SS	125	413	44	109	23	7	8	58	.264	41	60	0	213	333	8	.986
1978	—Houston (N.L.)	2B-3B-1B	119	420	46	123	33	3	7	55	.293	34	41	2	240	302	13	.977
1979	—Houston (N.L.)	2B-3B-1B	118	355	32	88	15	2	6	33	.248	36	37	3	188	261	7	.985
1980	—Houston (N.L.)	1-3-2-S	110	321	34	91	12	5	10	46	.283	34	29	1	598	86	10	.986
1981	—Houston (N.L.)	3B-1B	103	361	43	107	22	4	3	36	.296	41	23	1	67	206	9	.968
1982	—Houston (N.L.)	3B-1B	110	365	29	87	15	1	5	38	.238	41	45	2	344	174	7	.987
1983	—								Did not play.									
1984	—St. Louis (N.L.)■	3-1-2-S	89	139	17	30	5	0	2	12	.216	18	18	0	71	80	3	.981
1985	—St. Louis (N.L.)	1B-3B	4	3	0	0	0	0	0	0	.000	0	0	0	5	1	0	1.000
Major league totals (11 years)			891	2626	268	682	139	23	43	293	.260	275	287	10	1773	1597	69	.980

DIVISION SERIES RECORD

			BATTING												FIELDING			
Year	Team (League)	Pos.	G	AB	R	H	2B	3B	HR	RBI	Avg.	BB	SO	SB	PO	A	E	Avg.
1981	—Houston (N.L.)	3B	5	17	1	4	0	0	1	1	.235	2	1	0	6	9	0	1.000

CHAMPIONSHIP SERIES RECORD

			BATTING												FIELDING			
Year	Team (League)	Pos.	G	AB	R	H	2B	3B	HR	RBI	Avg.	BB	SO	SB	PO	A	E	Avg.
1974	—Pittsburgh (N.L.)	PH	1	1	0	0	0	0	0	0	.000	0	0	0	...	...	...	...
1980	—Houston (N.L.)	1B-PH	5	15	0	3	1	1	0	2	.200	2	2	0	29	3	0	1.000
Championship series totals (2 years)			6	16	0	3	1	1	0	2	.188	2	2	0	29	3	0	1.000

RECORD AS MANAGER

BACKGROUND: Coach, Texas Rangers (May 21, 1985-88). ... Scout, Los Angeles Dodgers organization (1994). ... Coach, Colorado Rockies (1995).

		REGULAR SEASON				POSTSEASON							
						Playoff		Champ. Series		World Series		All-Star Game	
Year	Team (League)	W	L	Pct.	Pos.	W	L	W	L	W	L	W	L
1989	—Houston (N.L.)	86	76	.531	3rd (W)	—	—	—	—	—	—	—	—
1990	—Houston (N.L.)	75	87	.463	T4th (W)	—	—	—	—	—	—	—	—
1991	—Houston (N.L.)	65	97	.401	6th (W)	—	—	—	—	—	—	—	—
1992	—Houston (N.L.)	81	81	.500	4th (W)	—	—	—	—	—	—	—	—
1993	—Houston (N.L.)	85	77	.525	3rd (W)	—	—	—	—	—	—	—	—
1996	—Oakland (A.L.)	78	84	.481	3rd (W)	—	—	—	—	—	—	—	—
1997	—Oakland (A.L.)	65	97	.401	4th (W)	—	—	—	—	—	—	—	—
1998	—Oakland (A.L.)	74	88	.457	4th (W)	—	—	—	—	—	—	—	—
1999	—Oakland (A.L.)	87	75	.537	2nd (W)	—	—	—	—	—	—	—	—
2000	—Oakland (A.L.)	91	70	.565	1st (W)	2	3	—	—	—	—	—	—
2001	—Oakland (A.L.)	102	60	.630	2nd (W)	2	3	—	—	—	—	—	—
2002	—Oakland (A.L.)	103	59	.636	1st (W)	2	3	—	—	—	—	—	—
National League totals (5 years)		392	418	.484		—	—	—	—	—	—	—	—
American League totals (7 years)		600	533	.530		6	9	—	—	—	—	—	—
Major league totals (12 years)		992	951	.511		6	9	—	—	—	—	—	—

NOTES:

2000—Lost to New York Yankees in A.L. divisional playoff.

2001—Lost to New York Yankees in A.L. divisional playoff.

2002—Lost to Minnesota in A.L. divisional playoff.

HURDLE, CLINT — ROCKIES

PERSONAL: Born July 30, 1957, in Big Rapids, Mich. ... 6-3/210. ... Batted right, threw right. ... Full name: Clinton Merrick Hurdle.

HIGH SCHOOL: Merritt Island (Fla.).

TRANSACTIONS/CAREER NOTES: Selected by Kansas City Royals organization in first round (ninth pick overall) of free-agent draft (June 4, 1975). ... On disabled list (April 20-May 30 and August 9-September 13, 1981). ... Traded by Royals to Cincinnati Reds for P Scott Brown (December 11, 1981). ... Released by Reds (November 15, 1982). ... Signed by New York Mets organization (April 7, 1983). ... Selected by St. Louis Cardinals (December 10, 1985). ... Granted free agency (November 12, 1986). ... Signed by Mets organization (February 9, 1987).

STATISTICAL NOTES: Tied for Gulf Coast League lead in being hit by pitch with six in 1975. ... Led American Association outfielders with four double plays in 1977. ... Tied for American Association lead in double plays by outfielder with four in 1979. ... Led International League with 12 intentional bases on balls received in 1983.

Year Team (League)	Pos.	G	AB	R	H	2B	3B	HR	RBI	Avg.	BB	SO	SB	PO	A	E	Avg.
		BATTING												FIELDING			
1975—Sarasota Royals (GCL)	OF	49	175	34	48	4	4	1	*31	.274	31	24	1	94	5	2	.980
1976—Waterloo (Midw.)	OF	127	429	89	101	22	5	19	89	.235	18	112	1	179	12	7	.965
1977—Omaha (A.A.)	OF	129	442	85	145	35	3	16	66	.328	96	61	6	198	*17	6	.973
—Kansas City (A.L.)	OF	9	26	5	8	0	0	2	7	.308	2	7	0	17	0	0	1.000
1978—Kansas City (A.L.)	OF-1B-3B	133	417	48	110	25	5	7	56	.264	56	84	1	544	30	12	.980
1979—Omaha (A.A.)	OF	68	220	30	52	13	0	6	29	.236	49	42	2	124	14	4	.972
—Kansas City (A.L.)	OF-3B	59	171	16	41	10	3	3	30	.240	28	24	0	89	2	3	.968
1980—Kansas City (A.L.)	OF	130	395	50	116	31	2	10	60	.294	34	61	0	233	8	10	.960
1981—Kansas City (A.L.)	OF	28	76	12	25	3	1	4	15	.329	13	10	0	59	1	0	1.000
1982—Cincinnati (N.L.)■	OF	19	34	2	7	1	0	0	1	.206	2	6	0	17	2	1	.950
—Indianapolis (A.A.)	OF-1B	88	261	38	64	18	0	12	58	.245	58	63	3	113	7	4	.968
1983—Tidewater (I.L.)■	3B-1B-OF	139	477	82	136	*33	4	22	105	.285	105	109	0	130	149	22	.927
—New York (N.L.)	3B-OF	13	33	3	6	2	0	0	2	.182	2	10	0	1	15	4	.800
1984—Tidewater (I.L.)	1-C-3-O	128	412	60	100	15	1	21	64	.243	79	107	0	1036	60	9	.992
1985—New York (N.L.)	C-OF	43	82	7	16	4	0	3	7	.195	13	20	0	89	7	1	.990
1986—St. Louis (N.L.)■	1-0-C-3	78	154	18	30	5	1	3	15	.195	26	38	0	334	31	3	.992
1987—New York (N.L.)■	1B	3	3	1	1	0	0	0	0	.333	0	1	0	1	0	0	1.000
—Tidewater (I.L.)	1B-OF-C	97	288	38	74	27	0	7	45	.257	47	47	1	275	16	3	.990
American League totals (5 years)		359	1085	131	300	69	11	26	168	.276	133	186	1	942	41	25	.975
National League totals (5 years)		156	306	31	60	12	1	6	25	.196	43	75	0	442	55	9	.982
Major League totals (10 years)		515	1391	162	360	81	12	32	193	.259	176	261	1	1384	96	34	.978

RECORD AS MANAGER

BACKGROUND: Roving hitting instructor, Colorado Rockies (1994-96). ... Hitting coach, Rockies (1997-April 26, 2002).

HONORS: Named Texas League Manager of the Year (1990).

Year Team (League)	W	L	Pct.	Pos.	Playoff W	Playoff L	Champ. Series W	Champ. Series L	World Series W	World Series L	All-Star Game W	All-Star Game L
	REGULAR SEASON				POSTSEASON							
1988—St. Lucie (FSL)	36	34	.514	4th (E)	—	—	—	—	—	—	—	—
—(Second half)	38	31	.551	1st (E)	6	1	—	—	—	—	—	—
1989—St. Lucie (FSL)	42	28	.600	1st (E)	—	—	—	—	—	—	—	—
—(Second half)	37	27	.578	1st (E)	1	2	—	—	—	—	—	—
1990—Jackson (Texas)	35	32	.522	2nd (E)	—	—	—	—	—	—	—	—
—(Second half)	38	30	.559	1st (E)	0	2	—	—	—	—	—	—
1991—Williamsport (Eastern)	60	79	.432	7th	—	—	—	—	—	—	—	—
1992—Tidewater (I.L.)	56	86	.394	4th (W)	—	—	—	—	—	—	—	—
1993—Norfolk (I.L.)	70	71	.496	4th (W)	—	—	—	—	—	—	—	—
2002—Colorado (N.L.)	67	73	.479	4th (W)	—	—	—	—	—	—	—	—

NOTES:

1988—Defeated Lakeland, two games to one, in playoffs; defeated Tampa, two games to none, in playoffs; defeated Osceola, two games to none, to win league championship.

1989—Lost to Port Charlotte in playoffs.

1990—Lost to Shreveport in playoffs.

2002—Replaced Colorado manager Buddy Bell, with club in fifth place and record of 6-16 (April 26).

La RUSSA, TONY — CARDINALS

PERSONAL: Born October 4, 1944, in Tampa. ... 6-0/185. ... Batted right, threw right. ... Full name: Anthony La Russa Jr.

HIGH SCHOOL: Jefferson (Tampa).

COLLEGE: University of Tampa, then South Florida (degree in industrial management), then Florida State (law degree, 1978).

TRANSACTIONS/CAREER NOTES: Signed by Kansas City Athletics organization (June 6, 1962). ... On disabled list (May 9-September 8, 1964; June 3-July 15, 1965; and April 12-May 6 and July 3-September 5, 1967). ... A's franchise moved from Kansas City to Oakland (October 1967). ... Contract sold by A's to Atlanta Braves (August 14, 1971). ... Traded by Braves to Chicago Cubs for P Tom Phoebus (October 20, 1972). ... Contract sold by Cubs to Pittsburgh Pirates organization (March 23, 1974). ... Released by Pirates (April 4, 1975). ... Signed by Chicago White Sox organization (April 7, 1975). ... On disabled list (August 8-18, 1976). ... Contract sold by White Sox to St. Louis Cardinals organization (December 13, 1976). ... Released by Cardinals (September 29, 1977).

STATISTICAL NOTES: Led International League in being hit by pitch with 11 in 1972.

Year Team (League)	Pos.	G	AB	R	H	2B	3B	HR	RBI	Avg.	BB	SO	SB	PO	A	E	Avg.
		BATTING												FIELDING			
1962—Daytona Beach (FSL)	SS	64	225	37	58	7	0	1	32	.258	42	47	11	135	173	38	.890
—Binghamton (East.)	SS-2B	12	43	3	8	0	0	0	4	.186	5	9	2	20	27	8	.855
1963—Kansas City (A.L.)	SS-2B	34	44	4	11	1	1	0	1	.250	7	12	0	29	25	2	.964
1964—Lewiston (N'west)	2B-SS	90	329	50	77	22	1	1	25	.234	53	56	10	188	218	18	.958
1965—Birmingham (Sou.)	2B	75	259	24	50	11	2	1	18	.193	26	37	5	202	161	21	.945
1966—Modesto (California)	2B	81	316	67	92	20	1	7	54	.291	44	37	18	201	212	20	.954
—Mobile (Southern)	2B	51	170	20	50	9	4	4	26	.294	23	24	4	117	133	10	.962
1967—Birmingham (Sou.)	2B	41	139	12	32	6	1	5	22	.230	10	11	3	88	120	5	.977
1968—Oakland (A.L.)	PH	5	3	0	1	0	0	0	0	.333	0	0	0	...	...	...	...
—Vancouver (PCL)	2B	122	455	55	109	16	8	5	29	.240	52	58	4	249	321	14	*.976
1969—Iowa (A.A.)	2B	67	235	37	72	11	1	4	27	.306	42	30	5	177	222	15	.964
—Oakland (A.L.)	PH	8	8	0	0	0	0	0	0	.000	0	1	0	...	...	...	...
1970—Iowa (A.A.)	2B	22	88	13	22	5	0	2	5	.250	9	14	0	52	59	3	.974
—Oakland (A.L.)	2B	52	106	6	21	4	1	0	6	.198	15	19	0	67	89	5	.969

Year Team (League)	Pos.	G	BATTING AB	R	H	2B	3B	HR	RBI	Avg.	BB	SO	SB	FIELDING PO	A	E	Avg.
1971— Iowa (A.A.)	2-3-S-O	28	107	21	31	5	1	2	11	.290	10	11	0	70	85	2	.987
— Oakland (A.L.)	2B-SS-3B	23	8	3	0	0	0	0	0	.000	0	4	0	8	7	2	.882
— Atlanta (N.L.)■	2B	9	7	1	2	0	0	0	0	.286	1	1	0	8	6	1	.933
1972— Richmond (I.L.)	2B	122	389	68	120	13	2	10	42	.308	72	41	0	305	289	20	.967
1973— Wichita (A.A.)■	2B-1B-3B	106	392	82	123	16	0	5	75	.314	60	46	10	423	213	26	.961
— Chicago (N.L.)	PR	1	0	1	0	0	0	0	0	...	0	0	0	...	...	...	...
1974— Char., W.Va. (I.L.)■	2B	139	457	50	119	17	1	8	35	.260	51	50	4	262	*378	17	.974
1975— Denver (A.A.)■	3-O-S-2	118	354	87	99	23	2	7	46	.280	70	46	13	95	91	10	.949
1976— Iowa (A.A.)	3-2-S-1-O-P	107	332	53	86	11	0	4	34	.259	40	43	10	132	160	22	.930
1977— New Orleans (A.A.)■	2B-3B	50	128	17	24	2	2	3	6	.188	20	21	0	66	87	7	.956
American League totals (5 years)		122	169	13	33	5	2	0	7	.195	22	36	0	104	121	9	.962
National League totals (2 years)		10	7	2	2	0	0	0	0	.286	1	1	0	8	6	1	.933
Major league totals (6 years)		132	176	15	35	5	2	0	7	.199	23	37	0	112	127	10	.960

RECORD AS PITCHER

Year Team (League)	W	L	Pct.	ERA	G	GS	CG	ShO	Sv.	IP	H	R	ER	BB	SO
1976— Iowa (A.A.)	0	0	...	3.00	3	0	0	0	0	3	3	1	1	0	0

RECORD AS MANAGER

BACKGROUND: Coach, St. Louis Cardinals organization (June 20-September 29, 1977). ... Coach, Chicago White Sox (July 3, 1978-remainder of season).

RECORDS: Shares major league single-season record for most clubs managed—2 (1986).

HONORS: Named Major League Manager of the Year by The Sporting News (1983). ... Named A.L. Manager of the Year by Baseball Writers' Association of America (1983, 1988 and 1992). ... Named A.L. Manager of the Year by The Sporting News (1988 and 1992). ... Named N.L. Manager of the Year by Baseball Writers' Association of America (2002).

	REGULAR SEASON				POSTSEASON							
					Playoff		Champ. Series		World Series		All-Star Game	
Year Team (League)	W	L	Pct.	Pos.	W	L	W	L	W	L	W	L
1978— Knoxville (Southern)	49	21	.700	1st (W)	—	—	—	—	—	—	—	—
— (Second half)	4	4	.500		—	—	—	—	—	—	—	—
1979— Iowa (American Association)	54	52	.509		—	—	—	—	—	—	—	—
— Chicago (A.L.)	27	27	.500	5th (W)	—	—	—	—	—	—	—	—
1980— Chicago (A.L.)	70	90	.438	5th (W)	—	—	—	—	—	—	—	—
1981— Chicago (A.L.)	31	22	.585	3rd (W)	—	—	—	—	—	—	—	—
— (Second half)	23	30	.434	6th (W)	—	—	—	—	—	—	—	—
1982— Chicago (A.L.)	87	75	.537	3rd (W)	—	—	—	—	—	—	—	—
1983— Chicago (A.L.)	99	63	.611	1st (W)	—	—	1	3	—	—	—	—
1984— Chicago (A.L.)	74	88	.457	T5th (W)	—	—	—	—	—	—	—	—
1985— Chicago (A.L.)	85	77	.525	3rd (W)	—	—	—	—	—	—	—	—
1986— Chicago (A.L.)	26	38	.406		—	—	—	—	—	—	—	—
— Oakland (A.L.)	45	34	.570	T3rd (W)	—	—	—	—	—	—	—	—
1987— Oakland (A.L.)	81	81	.500	3rd (W)	—	—	—	—	—	—	—	—
1988— Oakland (A.L.)	104	58	.642	1st (W)	—	—	4	0	1	4	—	—
1989— Oakland (A.L.)	99	63	.611	1st (W)	—	—	4	1	4	0	1	0
1990— Oakland (A.L.)	103	59	.636	1st (W)	—	—	4	0	0	4	1	0
1991— Oakland (A.L.)	84	78	.519	4th (W)	—	—	—	—	—	—	1	0
1992— Oakland (A.L.)	96	66	.593	1st (W)	—	—	2	4	—	—	—	—
1993— Oakland (A.L.)	68	94	.420	7th (W)	—	—	—	—	—	—	—	—
1994— Oakland (A.L.)	51	63	.447		—	—	—	—	—	—	—	—
1995— Oakland (A.L.)	67	77	.465	4th (W)	—	—	—	—	—	—	—	—
1996— St. Louis (N.L.)	88	74	.543	1st (C)	3	0	3	4	—	—	—	—
1997— St. Louis (N.L.)	73	89	.451	4th (C)	—	—	—	—	—	—	—	—
1998— St. Louis (N.L.)	83	79	.512	3rd (C)	—	—	—	—	—	—	—	—
1999— St. Louis (N.L.)	75	86	.466	4th (C)	—	—	—	—	—	—	—	—
2000— St. Louis (N.L.)	95	67	.586	1st (C)	3	0	1	4	—	—	—	—
2001— St. Louis (N.L.)	93	69	.574	2nd (C)	2	3	—	—	—	—	—	—
2002— St. Louis (N.L.)	97	65	.599	1st (C)	3	0	1	4	—	—	—	—
American League totals (17 years)	1320	1183	.527		—	—	15	8	5	8	3	0
National League totals (7 years)	604	529	.533		11	3	5	12	—	—	—	—
Major League totals (24 years)	1924	1712	.529		11	3	20	20	5	8	3	0

NOTES:

1978—Became Chicago White Sox coach and replaced as Knoxville manager by Joe Jones, with club in third place (July 3).

1979—Replaced as Iowa manager by Joe Sparks, with club in second place (August 3); replaced Chicago manager Don Kessinger with club in fifth place and record of 46-60 (August 3).

1983—Lost to Baltimore in A.L. Championship Series.

1986—Replaced as White Sox manager by interim manager Doug Rader, with club in sixth place (June 20); replaced Oakland manager Jackie Moore (record of 29-44) and interim manager Jeff Newman (record of 2-8) with club in seventh place and record of 31-52 (July 7).

1988—Defeated Boston in A.L. Championship Series; lost to Los Angeles in World Series.

1989—Defeated Toronto in A.L. Championship Series; defeated San Francisco in World Series.

1990—Defeated Boston in A.L. Championship Series; lost to Cincinnati in World Series.

1992—Lost to Toronto in A.L. Championship Series.

1993—On suspended list (October 1-remainder of season).

1994—Oakland was in second place in A.L. West at time of season-ending strike (August 12).

1996—Defeated San Diego in N.L. divisional playoff; lost to Atlanta in N.L. Championship Series.

2000—Defeated Atlanta in N.L. divisional playoff; lost to New York Mets in N.L. Championship Series.

2001—Lost to Arizona in N.L. divisional playoff.

2002—Defeated Arizona in N.L. divisional playoff; lost to San Francisco in N.L. Championship Series.

LITTLE, GRADY — RED SOX

PERSONAL: Born March 3, 1950, in Abilene, Texas. ... 5-11/190. ... Batted right, threw right. ... Full name: William Grady Little. ... Brother of Bryan Little, infielder with Montreal Expos, Chicago White Sox and New York Yankees (1982-86).

HIGH SCHOOL: Garinger (Charlotte, N.C.).

TRANSACTIONS/CAREER NOTES: Selected by Atlanta Braves organization in 12th round of free-agent draft (June 1968).

		BATTING												FIELDING		
Year Team (League)	Pos.	G	AB	R	H	2B	3B	HR	RBI	Avg.	BB	SO	SB	PO	A	E	Avg.
1969—Greenwood (W. Car.)..	C	2	3	0	1	0	0	0	0	.333	0	1	0	9	1	0	1.000
1970—Greenwood (W. Car.)..	C	30	77	8	15	1	0	0	5	.195	25	18	0	169	13	3	.984
1971—Greenwood (W. Car.)..	C	8	11	1	4	2	0	0	1	.364	2	2	0	21	0	0	1.000
—Ft. Lauderdale (FSL)■	C	38	118	8	27	4	1	1	17	.229	18	22	1	240	23	6	.978
1972—West Haven (East.).....	C	34	88	4	17	1	0	0	2	.193	15	18	0	147	11	3	.981
1973—West Haven (East.).....	C	20	42	3	6	0	0	0	1	.143	3	8	0	73	10	1	.988

RECORD AS MANAGER

BACKGROUND: Coach, West Haven, Eastern League (1974). ... Bullpen coach, San Diego Padres (1996). ... Bench coach, Boston Red Sox (1997-99). ... Bench coach, Cleveland Indians (2000-March 11, 2002).

HONORS: Named Carolina League Manager of the Year (1981, 1985 and 1989). ... Named Minor League Manager of the Year by The Sporting News (1992).

MISCELLANEOUS: 8-5 record while filling in for Charlie Manuel (2000 and 2001).

	REGULAR SEASON				POSTSEASON							
					Playoff		Champ. Series		World Series		All-Star Game	
Year Team (League)	W	L	Pct.	Pos.	W	L	W	L	W	L	W	L
1980—Bluefield (Appal.)	29	39	.426	5th	—	—	—	—	—	—	—	—
1981—Hagerstown (Caro.)	37	31	.544	1st (N)	—	—	—	—	—	—	—	—
—(Second half)	33	37	.471	3rd (N)	4	0	—	—	—	—	—	—
1982—Hagerstown (Caro.)	38	29	.567	2nd (N)	—	—	—	—	—	—	—	—
—(Second half)	33	36	.478	3rd (N)	—	—	—	—	—	—	—	—
1983—Charlotte (South.)	33	39	.453	4th (E)	—	—	—	—	—	—	—	—
—(Second half)	36	38	.486	3rd (E)	—	—	—	—	—	—	—	—
1984—Charlotte (South.)	29	43	.403	5th (E)	—	—	—	—	—	—	—	—
—Hagerstown (Caro.)	1	3	.250	—	—	—	—	—	—	—	—	—
1985—Kinston (Caro.)	23	47	.329	4th (S)	—	—	—	—	—	—	—	—
—(Second half)	41	26	.612	1st (S)	0	2	—	—	—	—	—	—
1986—Pulaski (Appal.)	41	25	.621	1st (N)	2	1	—	—	—	—	—	—
1987—Pulaski (Appal.)	39	31	.557	2nd (N)	—	—	—	—	—	—	—	—
1988—Burlington (Midw.)	20	22	.476	—	—	—	—	—	—	—	—	—
—Durham (Caro.)	14	14	.500	2nd (S)	—	—	—	—	—	—	—	—
—(Second half)	38	32	.543	2nd (S)	—	—	—	—	—	—	—	—
1989—Durham (Caro.)	47	23	.671	1st (S)	—	—	—	—	—	—	—	—
—(Second half)	37	31	.544	1st (S)	1	3	—	—	—	—	—	—
1990—Durham (Caro.)	37	33	.529	3rd (S)	—	—	—	—	—	—	—	—
—(Second half)	34	35	.493	4th (S)	—	—	—	—	—	—	—	—
1991—Durham (Caro.)	38	29	.567	3rd (S)	—	—	—	—	—	—	—	—
—(Second half)	41	29	.586	2nd (S)	—	—	—	—	—	—	—	—
1992—Greenville (South.)	49	23	.681	1st (E)	—	—	—	—	—	—	—	—
—(Second half)	51	20	.718	1st (E)	6	2	—	—	—	—	—	—
1993—Richmond (I.L.)	80	62	.563	2nd (W)	1	3	—	—	—	—	—	—
1994—Richmond (I.L.)	80	61	.567	1st (W)	6	1	—	—	—	—	—	—
1995—Richmond (I.L.)	75	66	.532	2nd (W)	2	3	—	—	—	—	—	—
2002—Boston (A.L.)	93	69	.574	2nd (E)	—	—	—	—	—	—	—	—

NOTES:

1981—Defeated Salem, one game to none, in playoffs; defeated Peninsula, three games to none, for League Championship.
1985—Lost to Winston-Salem in playoffs.
1986—Defeated Johson City for League Championship.
1989—Lost to Durham in League Championship.
1992—Defeated Charlotte, three games to none, in playoffs; defeated Chattanooga, three games to two, for League Championship.
1993—Lost to Charlotte in playoffs.
1994—Defeated Charlotte, three games to one, in playoffs; defeated Syracuse, three games to none, for League Championship.
1995—Lost to Norfolk in playoffs.

MACHA, KEN — ATHLETICS

PERSONAL: Born September 29, 1950, in Monroeville, Pa. ... 6-2/220. ... Batted right, threw right. ... Full name: Kenneth Edward Macha.

HIGH SCHOOL: Gateway (Pittsbugh).

COLLEGE: Pittsburgh.

TRANSACTIONS/CAREER NOTES: Selected by Pittsburgh Pirates organization in sixth round of free-agent draft (June 6, 1972). ... Drafted by Montreal Expos (December 4, 1978). ... Contract sold by Expos to Toronto Blue Jays (January 15, 1981). ... Played in Japan (1982-85).

HONORS: Named Eastern League Player of the Year (1974).

STATISTICAL NOTES: Led Eastern League with 32 passed balls in 1973.

Year	Team (League)	Pos.	G	AB	R	H	2B	3B	HR	RBI	Avg.	BB	SO	SB	PO	A	E	Avg.
			BATTING												FIELDING			
1972—	Salem (Caro.)	C-3B	62	197	20	50	7	2	8	33	.254	30	41	2	386	36	13	.970
1973—	Sherbrooke (East.)	C-1-0-3	106	322	40	86	15	0	12	52	.267	42	58	6	551	53	17	.973
1974—	Charl., W.Va. (I.L.)	C-3B	21	65	6	12	3	0	2	10	.185	9	18	1	100	13	4	.966
—	Thetford Mines (East.)	C-3-1-0	117	386	87	133	22	2	21	100	*.345	73	68	22	531	70	6	.990
—	Pittsburgh (N.L.)	C	5	5	1	3	1	0	0	1	.600	0	0	0	1	0	0	1.000
1975—	Charl., W.Va. (I.L.)	1-3-0	138	478	63	128	21	1	14	63	.268	65	76	11	1051	*88	•22	.981
1976—	Charl., W.Va. (I.L.)	3-C-0-1	126	458	68	138	29	1	14	77	.301	55	73	14	232	116	26	.930
1977—	Columbus (I.L.)	0-1-C-3	76	254	51	85	18	2	11	64	.335	41	33	4	187	25	9	.959
—	Pittsburgh (N.L.)	3-1-OF	35	95	2	26	4	0	0	11	.274	6	17	1	72	25	1	.990
1978—	Columbus (I.L.)	3B-OF-C	65	233	34	61	10	1	6	34	.262	36	33	3	62	114	18	.907
—	Pittsburgh (N.L.)	3B	29	52	5	11	1	1	0	5	.212	12	10	2	11	21	1	.970
1979—	Denver (A.A.)■	C-3-0-1	31	102	12	27	1	0	1	10	.265	14	9	5	92	17	8	.932
—	Montreal (N.L.)	3-1-0-C	25	36	8	10	3	1	0	4	.278	2	9	0	24	18	0	1.000
1980—	Montreal (N.L.)	3-1-0-C	49	107	10	31	5	1	1	8	.290	11	17	0	30	43	6	.924
1981—	Toronto (A.L.)	3B-1B-C	37	85	4	17	2	0	0	6	.200	8	15	1	99	36	5	.964
American League totals (1 year)			37	85	4	17	2	0	0	6	.200	8	15	1	99	36	5	.964
National League totals (5 years)			143	295	26	81	14	3	1	29	.275	31	53	3	138	107	8	.968
Major League totals (6 years)			180	380	30	98	16	3	1	35	.258	39	68	4	237	143	13	.967

RECORD AS MANAGER

BACKGROUND: Coach, Montreal Expos (1986). ... Third base coach, Expos (1987-91). ... Bullpen coach/third base coach, California Angels (1992-94). ... Bench coach, Oakland Athletics (1999-2002).

HONORS: Named International League Manager of the Year (1998).

Year	Team (League)	W	L	Pct.	Pos.	Playoff W	Playoff L	Champ. Series W	Champ. Series L	World Series W	World Series L	All-Star Game W	All-Star Game L
		REGULAR SEASON				POSTSEASON							
1995—	Trenton (East.)	73	69	.514	1st (S)	0	3	—	—	—	—	—	—
1996—	Trenton (East.)	86	56	.606	1st (S)	2	3	—	—	—	—	—	—
1997—	Pawtucket (I.L.)	81	60	.574	2nd (E)	1	3	—	—	—	—	—	—
1998—	Pawtucket (I.L.)	77	64	.546	3rd (E)	—	—	—	—	—	—	—	—

NOTES:
1995—Lost to Reading in playoffs.
1996—Lost to Harrisburg in playoffs.
1997—Lost to Rochester in playoffs.

MANUEL, JERRY — WHITE SOX

PERSONAL: Born December 23, 1953, in Hahira, Ga. ... 5-11/180. ... Batted right, threw right.

HIGH SCHOOL: Cordova (Rancho Cordova, Calif.).

TRANSACTIONS/CAREER NOTES: Selected by Detroit Tigers organization in first round (20th pick overall) of free-agent draft (June 6, 1972). ... On disabled list (August 18-September 1, 1978). ... Traded by Tigers to Montreal Expos for C Duffy Dyer (March 14, 1980). ... On disabled list (May 2-July 31, and August 15-September 1, 1981). ... Traded by Expos to San Diego Padres for P Kim Seaman (May 22, 1982). ... Traded by Padres to Expos for a player to be named later (June 8, 1982); Padres acquired P Mike Griffin to complete deal (August 30, 1982). ... Traded by Expos to Chicago Cubs for C Butch Benton (February 4, 1983). ... Granted free agency following 1983 season. ... Signed by Chicago White Sox organization (April 8, 1984). ... Granted free agency following 1985 season. ... Signed by Expos organization for 1986 season. ... On disabled list (June 23-July 17 and July 25-August 4, 1986).

STATISTICAL NOTES: Led Appalachian League shortstops with 303 total chances in 1972. ... Led American Association second basemen with 688 total chances in 1974. ... Led American Association second basemen with 758 total chances and 108 double plays in 1975. ... Led American Association second basemen with 363 assists and 611 total chances in 1979. ... Led American Association shortstops with 612 total chances in 1980.

Year	Team (League)	Pos.	G	AB	R	H	2B	3B	HR	RBI	Avg.	BB	SO	SB	PO	A	E	Avg.
			BATTING												FIELDING			
1972—	Bristol (Appal.)	SS	67	233	31	56	8	8	4	29	.240	19	61	11	*112	*176	15	*.950
1973—	Lakeland (FSL)	SS	117	433	66	109	17	4	2	28	.252	52	98	20	167	349	29	.947
—	Toledo (I.L.)	SS	27	72	8	20	0	0	0	2	.278	3	16	2	44	90	4	.971
1974—	Evansville (A.A.)	2B	127	384	44	81	5	5	1	24	.211	35	74	3	*315	356	17	.975
1975—	Evansville (A.A.)	2B	*137	501	63	115	10	4	4	43	.230	44	101	20	*348	*394	16	.979
—	Detroit (A.L.)	2B	6	18	0	1	0	0	0	0	.056	0	4	0	11	23	2	.944
1976—	Evansville (A.A.)	2B	11	44	6	8	1	0	1	3	.182	2	9	0	25	29	1	.982
—	Detroit (A.L.)	2B-SS	54	43	4	6	1	0	0	2	.140	3	9	1	40	64	8	.929
1977—	Evansville (A.A.)	2B-SS	110	375	52	102	19	7	1	38	.272	45	55	12	198	304	17	.967
1978—	Evansville (A.A.)	2B-SS	114	430	65	113	18	5	7	50	.263	50	83	8	264	321	20	.967
1979—	Evansville (A.A.)	2B-SS	130	460	71	116	26	3	9	75	.252	67	67	8	265	†434	22	.969
1980—	Denver (A.A.)■	SS	128	491	105	136	23	2	3	61	.277	81	62	11	*233	*357	22	.964
—	Montreal (N.L.)	SS	7	6	0	0	0	0	0	0	.000	0	2	0	5	11	1	.941
1981—	Montreal (N.L.)	2B-SS	27	55	10	11	5	0	3	10	.200	6	11	0	37	41	1	.987
1982—	Wichita (A.A.)■	S-3-2-0	71	263	31	67	22	0	3	37	.255	15	34	2	99	152	11	.958
—	San Diego (N.L.)	2B-3B-SS	2	5	0	1	0	1	0	1	.200	1	0	0	1	1	0	1.000
—	Hawaii (PCL)	SS	26	92	8	18	3	1	0	7	.196	11	12	2	41	73	1	.991
1983—	Iowa (A.A.)■	2-0-S-3	85	279	37	74	14	3	3	33	.265	22	46	6	129	143	8	.971
1984—	Denver (A.A.)■	SS-2B-OF	109	335	43	98	14	3	4	40	.293	37	32	7	184	262	18	.961
1985—									Did not play.									
1986—	Indianapolis (A.A.)■	3B-2B	22	41	4	16	2	0	1	9	.390	2	5	0	5	7	1	.923
American League totals (2 years)			60	61	4	7	1	0	0	2	.115	3	13	1	51	87	10	.932
National League totals (3 years)			36	66	10	12	5	1	3	11	.182	7	13	0	43	53	2	.980
Major league totals (5 years)			96	127	14	19	6	1	3	13	.150	10	26	1	94	140	12	.951

DIVISION SERIES RECORD

			BATTING											FIELDING			
Year	Team (League)	Pos.	G	AB	R	H	2B	3B	HR	RBI	Avg.	BB	SO	SB	PO	A	E	Avg.
1981—Montreal (N.L.)		2B	5	14	0	1	0	0	0	0	.071	2	5	0	13	19	3	.914

CHAMPIONSHIP SERIES RECORD

			BATTING											FIELDING			
Year	Team (League)	Pos.	G	AB	R	H	2B	3B	HR	RBI	Avg.	BB	SO	SB	PO	A	E	Avg.
1981—Montreal (N.L.)		PR	1	0	0	0	0	0	0	0	...	0	0	0	...	...	...	...

RECORD AS MANAGER

BACKGROUND: Scout, Chicago White Sox (1985). ... Player/coach, Indianapolis, American Association (1986). ... Roving infield instructor, Montreal Expos organization (1987). ... Minor league field coordinator, Expos (1988-89). ... Coach, Expos (June 3, 1991-1996). ... Coach, Florida Marlins (1997).

HONORS: Named Southern League co-Manager of the Year (1990). ... Named A.L. Manager of the Year by THE SPORTING NEWS (2000). ... Named A.L. Manager of the Year by Baseball Writers' Association of America (2000).

	REGULAR SEASON				POSTSEASON							
					Playoff		Champ. Series		World Series		All-Star Game	
Year Team (League)	W	L	Pct.	Pos.	W	L	W	L	W	L	W	L
1990—Jacksonville (Southern)	38	33	.535	2nd (E)	—	—	—	—	—	—	—	—
—(Second half)	46	27	.630	1st (E)	1	3	—	—	—	—	—	—
1991—Indianapolis (A.A.)	28	22	.560	—	—	—	—	—	—	—	—	—
1998—Chicago (A.L.)	80	82	.494	2nd (C)	—	—	—	—	—	—	—	—
1999—Chicago (A.L.)	75	86	.466	2nd (C)	—	—	—	—	—	—	—	—
2000—Chicago (A.L.)	95	67	.586	1st (C)	0	3	—	—	—	—	—	—
2001—Chicago (A.L.)	83	79	.512	3rd (C)	—	—	—	—	—	—	—	—
2002—Chicago (A.L.)	81	81	.500	2nd (C)	—	—	—	—	—	—	—	—
Major league totals (5 years)	414	395	.512		0	3	—	—	—	—	—	—

NOTES:

1990—Lost to Orlando in playoffs.

1991—Replaced as Indianapolis manager by Pat Kelly (June 2).

2000—Lost to Seattle in A.L. divisional playoff.

McCLENDON, LLOYD — PIRATES

PERSONAL: Born January 11, 1959, in Gary, Ind. ... 6-0/208. ... Batted right, threw right. ... Full name: Lloyd Glenn McClendon.

HIGH SCHOOL: Roosevelt (Gary, Ind.).

COLLEGE: Valparaiso.

TRANSACTIONS/CAREER NOTES: Selected by New York Mets organization in eighth round of free-agent draft (June 3, 1980).... On disabled list (April 4-27, 1982).... Traded by Mets with P Charlie Puleo and OF Jason Felice to Cincinnati Reds for P Tom Seaver (December 16, 1982).... Traded by Reds to Chicago Cubs for OF Rolando Roomes (December 9, 1988).... Traded by Cubs to Pittsburgh Pirates for a player to be named later (September 7, 1990); Cubs acquired P Mike Pomeranz to complete deal (September 28, 1990).... Granted free agency (October 25, 1994).... Signed by Cleveland Indians organization (May 5, 1995).... Granted free agency (October 16, 1995).

STATISTICAL NOTES: Career major league grand slams: 2.

			BATTING											FIELDING			
Year Team (League)	Pos.	G	AB	R	H	2B	3B	HR	RBI	Avg.	BB	SO	SB	PO	A	E	Avg.
1980—Kingsport (Appl.)	C	14	46	7	15	2	0	1	9	.326	5	7	0	19	5	3	.889
—Little Falls (NY-Penn)	C	40	117	25	32	9	1	3	20	.274	32	20	2	203	20	7	.970
1981—Lynchburg (Caro.)	C-3B	103	363	55	91	12	6	7	57	.251	60	68	3	437	74	17	.968
1982—Lynchburg (Caro.)	C-3B	108	384	61	105	25	1	18	78	.273	55	65	4	492	87	15	.975
1983—Waterbury (East.)■	C-3B-1B	123	434	58	114	19	2	15	57	.263	42	64	4	466	99	8	.986
1984—Vermont (East.)	C-1B-3B-OF	60	202	36	56	16	0	7	27	.277	28	28	2	174	24	3	.985
—Wichita (A.A.)	3B-1B-C	48	152	28	45	13	1	6	28	.296	21	33	2	143	45	4	.979
1985—Denver (A.A.)	1B-3B-C-OF	114	379	57	105	18	5	16	79	.277	51	56	4	470	104	17	.971
1986—Denver (A.A.)	1B-OF-C-3B	132	433	75	112	30	1	*24	88	.259	70	75	2	656	45	11	.985
1987—Nashville (A.A.)	1B-C	26	84	11	24	6	0	3	14	.286	17	15	1	72	3	1	.987
—Cincinnati (N.L.)	C-1B-3B-OF	45	72	8	15	5	0	2	13	.208	4	15	1	80	5	2	.977
1988—Cincinnati (N.L.)	C-OF-1B-3B	72	137	9	30	4	0	3	14	.219	15	22	4	197	13	4	.981
—Nashville (A.A.)	OF-C	2	7	0	1	0	0	0	0	.143	1	1	0	12	2	0	1.000
1989—Iowa (A.A.)■	1B-OF-C	34	109	18	35	10	0	4	13	.321	21	19	4	115	6	6	.953
—Chicago (N.L.)	OF-1B-3B-C	92	259	47	74	12	1	12	40	.286	37	31	6	310	18	6	.982
1990—Chicago (N.L.)	OF-1B-C	49	107	5	17	3	0	1	10	.159	14	21	1	120	9	1	.992
—Iowa (A.A.)	1B-3B-OF-C	25	91	14	26	2	0	2	10	.286	8	19	3	125	12	2	.986
—Pittsburgh (N.L.)■	OF	4	3	1	1	0	0	1	2	.333	0	1	0	0	0	0	...
1991—Pittsburgh (N.L.)	OF-1B-C	85	163	24	47	7	0	7	24	.288	18	23	2	163	12	3	.983
1992—Pittsburgh (N.L.)	OF-1B	84	190	26	48	8	1	3	20	.253	28	24	1	136	9	3	.980
1993—Pittsburgh (N.L.)	OF-1B	88	181	21	40	11	1	2	19	.221	23	17	0	98	5	3	.972
1994—Pittsburgh (N.L.)	OF-1B	51	92	9	22	4	0	4	12	.239	4	11	0	46	2	1	.980
1995—Buffalo (A.A.)■	OF-DH-3B	37	108	19	30	6	0	5	19	.278	20	20	0	32	1	2	.943
Major League totals (8 years)		570	1204	150	294	54	3	35	154	.244	143	165	15	1150	73	23	.982

CHAMPIONSHIP SERIES RECORD

RECORDS: Shares records for most hits in one inning—2 (October 13, 1992, second inning); and most singles in one inning—2 (October 13, 1992, second inning).

Year	Team (League)	Pos.	G	AB	R	H	2B	3B	HR	RBI	Avg.	BB	SO	SB	PO	A	E	Avg.
				BATTING											FIELDING			
1989—	Chicago (N.L.)	PH-C-OF	3	3	0	2	0	0	0	0	.667	1	0	0	3	0	0	1.000
1991—	Pittsburgh (N.L.)	PH-1B	3	2	0	0	0	0	0	0	.000	1	0	0	0	0	0	...
1992—	Pittsburgh (N.L.)	OF-PH	5	11	4	8	2	0	1	4	.727	4	1	0	10	0	0	1.000
Championship series totals (3 years)			11	16	4	10	2	0	1	4	.625	6	1	0	13	0	0	1.000

RECORD AS MANAGER

STATISTICAL NOTES: Career major league grand slams: 2.

BACKGROUND: Minor league hitting instructor, Pittsburgh Pirates (1996).... Hitting coach, Pirates (1997-2000).

Year	Team (League)	W	L	Pct.	Pos.	Playoff W	Playoff L	Champ. Series W	Champ. Series L	World Series W	World Series L	All-Star Game W	All-Star Game L
		REGULAR SEASON				POSTSEASON							
2001—	Pittsburgh (N.L.)	62	100	.383	6th (C)	—	—	—	—	—	—	—	—
2002—	Pittsburgh (N.L.)	72	89	.447	4th (C)	—	—	—	—	—	—	—	—
Major league totals (2 years)		134	189	.415		—	—	—	—	—	—	—	—

PENA, TONY — ROYALS

PERSONAL: Born June 4, 1957, in Monte Cristi, Dominican Republic. ... 6-0/190. ... Batted right, threw right. ... Full name: Antonio Francisco Padilla Pena. ... Brother of Ramon Pena, pitcher with Detroit Tigers (1989).

HIGH SCHOOL: Liceo Marti (Monte Cristi, Dominican Republic).

TRANSACTIONS/CAREER NOTES: Signed as non-drafted free agent by Pittsburgh Pirates organization (July 22, 1975). ... Traded by Pirates to St. Louis Cardinals for OF Andy Van Slyke, C Mike LaValliere and P Mike Dunne (April 1, 1987). ... On St. Louis disabled list (April 11-May 22, 1987); included rehabilitation assignment to Louisville (May 19-22). ... Granted free agency (November 13, 1989). ... Signed by Boston Red Sox (November 27, 1989). ... Granted free agency (October 29, 1993). ... Signed by Cleveland Indians organization (February 7, 1994). ... Granted free agency (October 25, 1994). ... Re-signed by Indians organization (December 13, 1994). ... Granted free agency (November 2, 1995). ... Re-signed by Indians (December 6, 1995). ... Granted free agency (November 18, 1996). ... Signed by Chicago White Sox organization (January 10, 1997). ... On Chicago disabled list (June 10-20, 1997). ... Traded by White Sox to Houston Astros for P Julien Tucker (August 15, 1997). ... Granted free agency (October 30, 1997).

HONORS: Named catcher on The Sporting News N.L. All-Star team (1983). ... Won N.L. Gold Glove at catcher (1983-85). ... Won A.L. Gold Glove at catcher (1991).

STATISTICAL NOTES: Led Carolina League catchers with nine double plays and tied for lead with 16 passed balls in 1977. ... Led Eastern League catchers with 14 double plays in 1979. ... Led N.L. catchers with 1,075 total chances in 1983, 999 in 1984 and 1,034 in 1985. ... Led N.L. catchers with 15 double plays in 1984 and 13 in 1989. ... Led N.L. catchers with 100 assists in 1985. ... Led N.L. catchers with 18 errors in 1986. ... Tied for N.L. lead in grounding into double plays with 21 in 1986. ... Led N.L. catchers with .994 fielding percentage in 1988 and .997 in 1989. ... Led A.L. catchers with 864 putouts and 943 total chances in 1990. ... Led A.L. catchers with 929 total chances and 15 double plays in 1991. ... Led A.L. catchers with 12 double plays in 1992. ... Career major league grand slams: 3.

Year	Team (League)	Pos.	G	AB	R	H	2B	3B	HR	RBI	Avg.	BB	SO	SB	PO	A	E	Avg.
				BATTING											FIELDING			
1976—	GC Pirates (GCL)	OF-1B-C-3B	33	110	10	23	2	2	1	11	.209	4	17	5	108	14	4	.968
—	Charl. S.C. (W. Car.)	C	14	49	4	11	2	0	1	8	.224	4	7	0	64	7	2	.973
1977—	Charl. S.C. (W. Car.)	C	29	101	10	24	4	0	3	16	.238	7	21	2	172	19	6	.970
—	Salem (Caro.)	C	84	319	36	88	15	3	7	46	.276	14	60	3	*470	*66	*17	.969
1978—	Shreveport (Texas)	C	104	348	34	80	14	0	8	42	.230	15	96	3	637	54	*25	.965
1979—	Buffalo (East.)	C	134	515	89	161	16	4	34	97	.313	39	83	5	*768	*120	*26	.972
1980—	Portland (PCL)	C	124	452	57	148	24	13	9	77	.327	29	75	5	*639	85	•23	.969
—	Pittsburgh (N.L.)	C	8	21	1	9	1	1	0	1	.429	0	4	0	38	2	2	.952
1981—	Pittsburgh (N.L.)	C	66	210	16	63	9	1	2	17	.300	8	23	1	286	41	5	.985
1982—	Pittsburgh (N.L.)	C	138	497	53	147	28	4	11	63	.296	17	57	2	763	89	16	.982
1983—	Pittsburgh (N.L.)	C	151	542	51	163	22	3	15	70	.301	31	73	6	*976	90	9	.992
1984—	Pittsburgh (N.L.)	C	147	546	77	156	27	2	15	78	.286	36	79	12	*895	*95	9	.991
1985—	Pittsburgh (N.L.)	C-1B	147	546	53	136	27	2	10	59	.249	29	67	12	925	†102	12	.988
1986—	Pittsburgh (N.L.)	C-1B	144	510	56	147	26	2	10	52	.288	53	69	9	824	99	†18	.981
1987—	St. Louis (N.L.)■	C-1B-OF	116	384	40	82	13	4	5	44	.214	36	54	6	624	51	8	.988
—	Louisville (A.A.)	C	2	8	0	3	0	0	0	0	.375	0	2	0	7	1	0	1.000
1988—	St. Louis (N.L.)	C-1B	149	505	55	133	23	1	10	51	.263	33	60	6	796	72	6	†.993
1989—	St. Louis (N.L.)	C-OF	141	424	36	110	17	2	4	37	.259	35	33	5	675	70	2	†.997
1990—	Boston (A.L.)■	C-1B	143	491	62	129	19	1	7	56	.263	43	71	8	†866	74	5	.995
1991—	Boston (A.L.)	C	141	464	45	107	23	2	5	48	.231	37	53	8	*864	60	5	.995
1992—	Boston (A.L.)	C	133	410	39	99	21	1	1	38	.241	24	61	3	*786	57	6	.993
1993—	Boston (A.L.)	C-DH	126	304	20	55	11	0	4	19	.181	25	46	1	698	53	4	.995
1994—	Cleveland (A.L.)■	C	40	112	18	33	8	1	2	10	.295	9	11	0	209	17	1	.996
1995—	Cleveland (A.L.)	C	91	263	25	69	15	0	5	28	.262	14	44	1	508	36	7	.987
1996—	Cleveland (A.L.)	C	67	174	14	34	4	0	1	27	.195	15	25	0	336	27	3	.992
1997—	Chicago (A.L.)■	C-3B	31	67	4	11	1	0	0	8	.164	8	13	0	143	8	0	1.000
—	Houston (N.L.)■	C	9	19	2	4	3	0	0	2	.211	2	3	0	48	6	0	1.000
American League totals (8 years)			772	2285	227	537	102	5	25	234	.235	175	324	21	4410	332	31	.994
National League totals (11 years)			1216	4204	440	1150	196	22	82	474	.274	280	522	59	6850	717	87	.989
Major League totals (18 years)			1988	6489	667	1687	298	27	107	708	.260	455	846	80	11260	1049	118	.991

DIVISION SERIES RECORD

Year	Team (League)	Pos.	G	AB	R	H	2B	3B	HR	RBI	Avg.	BB	SO	SB	PO	A	E	Avg.
				BATTING											FIELDING			
1995—	Cleveland (A.L.)	C	2	2	1	1	0	0	1	1	.500	0	0	0	5	0	0	1.000
1996—	Cleveland (A.L.)	C	1	0	0	0	0	0	0	0	...	0	0	0	1	0	0	1.000
1997—	Houston (N.L.)	C	2	0	0	0	0	0	0	0	...	0	0	0	2	0	0	1.000
Division series totals (3 years)			5	2	1	1	0	0	1	1	.500	0	0	0	8	0	0	1.000

CHAMPIONSHIP SERIES RECORD

Year	Team (League)	Pos.	BATTING G	AB	R	H	2B	3B	HR	RBI	Avg.	BB	SO	SB	FIELDING PO	A	E	Avg.
1987	—St. Louis (N.L.)..........	C	7	21	5	8	0	1	0	0	.381	3	4	1	55	5	0	1.000
1990	—Boston (A.L.).............	C	4	14	0	3	0	0	0	0	.214	0	0	0	22	4	1	.963
1995	—Cleveland (A.L.)..........	C	4	6	1	2	1	0	0	0	.333	1	0	0	15	1	0	1.000
Championship series totals (3 years)			15	41	6	13	1	1	0	0	.317	4	4	1	92	10	1	.990

WORLD SERIES RECORD

Year	Team (League)	Pos.	BATTING G	AB	R	H	2B	3B	HR	RBI	Avg.	BB	SO	SB	FIELDING PO	A	E	Avg.
1987	—St. Louis (N.L.)..........	C-DH	7	22	2	9	1	0	0	4	.409	3	2	1	32	1	1	.971
1995	—Cleveland (A.L.)..........	C	2	6	0	1	0	0	0	0	.167	0	0	0	7	1	0	1.000
World Series totals (2 years)			9	28	2	10	1	0	0	4	.357	3	2	1	39	2	1	.976

ALL-STAR GAME RECORD

Year	League	Pos.	BATTING AB	R	H	2B	3B	HR	RBI	Avg.	BB	SO	SB	FIELDING PO	A	E	Avg.
1982	—National......................	PR-C	1	0	0	0	0	0	0	.000	0	0	1	3	0	0	1.000
1984	—National......................	C	0	0	0	0	0	0	0	...	0	0	0	2	0	0	1.000
1985	—National......................	C	1	0	0	0	0	0	0	.000	0	1	0	4	1	0	1.000
1986	—National......................	PR	0	0	0	0	0	0	0	...	0	0	0	...	...	...	...
1989	—National......................	PH-C	2	0	0	0	0	0	0	.000	0	0	0	2	0	0	1.000
All-Star Game totals (5 years)			4	0	0	0	0	0	0	.000	0	1	1	11	1	0	1.000

RECORD AS MANAGER

BACKGROUND: Bench coach, Houston Astros (2002-May 15, 2002).

Year	Team (League)	REGULAR SEASON W	L	Pct.	Pos.	POSTSEASON Playoff W	Playoff L	Champ. Series W	Champ. Series L	World Series W	World Series L	All-Star Game W	All-Star Game L
1999	—New Orleans (PCL)..................................	55	85	.406	4th (E)	—	—	—	—	—	—	—	—
2000	—New Orleans (PCL)..................................	68	74	.479	3rd (E)	—	—	—	—	—	—	—	—
2001	—New Orleans (PCL)..................................	82	57	.599	1st (E)	3	0	—	—	—	—	—	—
2002	—Kansas City (A.L.)....................................	49	77	.389	4th (C)	—	—	—	—	—	—	—	—

NOTES:

2001—Defeated Iowa in playoffs. Shared League Championship due to stoppage of play in professional baseball.

2002—Replaced Kansas City manager Tony Muser (record of 8-15) and interim manager John Mizerock (record of 5-8) with club in fourth place and record of 18-23 (May 15).

PINIELLA, LOU — DEVIL RAYS

PERSONAL: Born August 28, 1943, in Tampa. ... 6-2/199. ... Batted right, threw right. ... Full name: Louis Victor Piniella. ... Cousin of Dave Magadan, hitting coach, San Diego Padres and third baseman/first baseman with seven major league teams (1986-2001). ... Name pronounced pin-ELL-uh.

HIGH SCHOOL: Jesuit (Tampa).

COLLEGE: Tampa.

TRANSACTIONS/CAREER NOTES: Signed as free agent by Cleveland Indians organization (June 9, 1962). ... Selected by Washington Senators organization from Jacksonville, Indians organization, in Rule 5 major league draft (November 26, 1962). ... On military list (March 9-July 20, 1964). ... Traded by Senators to Baltimore Orioles (August 4, 1964), completing deal in which Orioles traded P Lester (Buster) Narum to Senators for cash and a player to be named later (March 31, 1964). ... On suspended list (June 27-29, 1965). ... Traded by Orioles to Indians for C Camilo Carreon (March 10, 1966). ... On temporarily inactive list (May 19-22, 1967). ... On disabled list (May 22-June 6, 1968). ... On temporarily inactive list (June 6-25, 1968). ... Selected by Seattle Pilots in expansion draft (October 15, 1968). ... Traded by Pilots to Kansas City Royals for OF Steve Whitaker and P John Gelnar (April 1, 1969). ... On military list (August 7-22, 1969). ... On disabled list (May 5-June 8, 1971). ... Traded by Royals with P Ken Wright to New York Yankees for P Lindy McDaniel (December 7, 1973). ... On disabled list (June 17-July 6, 1975; August 23-September 7, 1981; and March 30-April 22, 1983). ... Placed on voluntarily retired list (June 17, 1984).

RECORDS: Shares major league record for most assists by outfielder in one inning—2 (May 27, 1974, third inning).

HONORS: Named A.L. Rookie of the Year by Baseball Writers' Association of America (1969).

STATISTICAL NOTES: Led A.L. in grounding into double plays with 25 in 1972. ... Career major league grand slams: 1.

Year	Team (League)	Pos.	BATTING G	AB	R	H	2B	3B	HR	RBI	Avg.	BB	SO	SB	FIELDING PO	A	E	Avg.
1962	—Selma (Ala.-Fla.).........	OF	70	278	40	75	10	5	8	44	.270	10	57	4	94	6	9	.917
1963	—Peninsula (Caro.)■	OF	143	548	71	170	29	4	16	77	.310	34	70	8	271	*23	8	.974
1964	—Aberdeen (North.)	OF	20	74	8	20	8	3	0	12	.270	6	9	1	37	1	1	.974
	—Baltimore (A.L.)■.......	PH	4	1	0	0	0	0	0	0	.000	0	0	0	...	...	...	...
1965	—Elmira (East.)	OF	126	490	64	122	29	6	11	64	.249	22	57	5	176	5	7	.963
1966	—Portland (PCL)■	OF	133	457	47	132	22	3	7	52	.289	20	52	6	177	11	11	.945
1967	—Portland (PCL)	OF	113	396	46	122	20	1	8	56	.308	23	47	2	199	7	6	.972
1968	—Portland (PCL)	OF	88	331	49	105	15	3	13	62	.317	19	31	0	167	6	7	.961
	—Cleveland (A.L.)..........	OF	6	5	1	0	0	0	0	1	.000	0	0	0	1	0	0	1.000
1969	—Kansas City (A.L.)■ ...	OF	135	493	43	139	21	6	11	68	.282	33	56	2	278	13	7	.977
1970	—Kansas City (A.L.)	OF-1B	144	542	54	163	24	5	11	88	.301	35	42	3	250	6	4	.985
1971	—Kansas City (A.L.)	OF	126	448	43	125	21	5	3	51	.279	21	43	5	201	6	3	.986
1972	—Kansas City (A.L.)	OF	151	574	65	179	*33	4	11	72	.312	34	59	7	275	8	7	.976
1973	—Kansas City (A.L.)	OF-DH	144	513	53	128	28	1	9	69	.250	30	65	5	196	9	3	.986
1974	—New York (A.L.)■.......	OF-DH-1B	140	518	71	158	26	0	9	70	.305	32	58	1	270	16	3	.990
1975	—New York (A.L.)..........	OF-DH	74	199	7	39	4	1	0	22	.196	16	22	0	65	5	1	.986
1976	—New York (A.L.)..........	OF-DH	100	327	36	92	16	6	3	38	.281	18	34	0	199	10	4	.981

Year	Team (League)	Pos.	G	AB	R	H	2B	3B	HR	RBI	Avg.	BB	SO	SB	PO	A	E	Avg.
				BATTING											FIELDING			
1977	— New York (A.L.)	OF-DH-1B	103	339	47	112	19	3	12	45	.330	20	31	2	86	3	2	.978
1978	— New York (A.L.)	OF-DH	130	472	67	148	34	5	6	69	.314	34	36	3	213	4	7	.969
1979	— New York (A.L.)	OF-DH	130	461	49	137	22	2	11	69	.297	17	31	3	204	13	4	.982
1980	— New York (A.L.)	OF-DH	116	321	39	92	18	0	2	27	.287	29	20	0	157	8	5	.971
1981	— New York (A.L.)	OF-DH	60	159	16	44	9	0	5	18	.277	13	9	0	69	2	1	.986
1982	— New York (A.L.)	DH-OF	102	261	33	80	17	1	6	37	.307	18	18	0	68	2	0	1.000
1983	— New York (A.L.)	OF-DH	53	148	19	43	9	1	2	16	.291	11	12	1	67	4	3	.959
1984	— New York (A.L.)	OF-DH	29	86	8	26	4	1	1	6	.302	7	5	0	40	3	0	1.000
Major league totals (18 years)			1747	5867	651	1705	305	41	102	766	.291	368	541	32	2639	112	54	.981

DIVISION SERIES RECORD

Year	Team (League)	Pos.	G	AB	R	H	2B	3B	HR	RBI	Avg.	BB	SO	SB	PO	A	E	Avg.
				BATTING											FIELDING			
1981	— New York (A.L.)	DH-PH	4	10	1	2	1	0	1	3	.200	0	0	0	...	...	...	...

CHAMPIONSHIP SERIES RECORD

Year	Team (League)	Pos.	G	AB	R	H	2B	3B	HR	RBI	Avg.	BB	SO	SB	PO	A	E	Avg.
				BATTING											FIELDING			
1976	— New York (A.L.)	DH-PH	4	11	1	3	1	0	0	0	.273	0	1	0	...	...	...	...
1977	— New York (A.L.)	OF-DH	5	21	1	7	3	0	0	2	.333	0	1	0	9	1	0	1.000
1978	— New York (A.L.)	OF	4	17	2	4	0	0	0	0	.235	0	3	0	13	0	0	1.000
1980	— New York (A.L.)	OF	2	5	1	1	0	0	1	1	.200	2	1	0	5	0	0	1.000
1981	— New York (A.L.)	PH-DH-OF	3	5	2	3	0	0	1	3	.600	0	0	0	0	0	0	...
Championship series totals (5 years)			18	59	7	18	4	0	2	6	.305	2	6	0	27	1	0	1.000

WORLD SERIES RECORD

RECORDS: Shares single-series record for collecting one or more hits in each game (1978).

NOTES: Member of World Series championship team (1977 and 1978).

Year	Team (League)	Pos.	G	AB	R	H	2B	3B	HR	RBI	Avg.	BB	SO	SB	PO	A	E	Avg.
				BATTING											FIELDING			
1976	— New York (A.L.)	DH-OF-PH	4	9	1	3	1	0	0	0	.333	0	0	0	1	0	0	1.000
1977	— New York (A.L.)	OF	6	22	1	6	0	0	0	3	.273	0	3	0	16	1	1	.944
1978	— New York (A.L.)	OF	6	25	3	7	0	0	0	4	.280	0	0	1	14	1	0	1.000
1981	— New York (A.L.)	OF-PH	6	16	2	7	1	0	0	3	.438	0	1	1	7	0	0	1.000
World Series totals (4 years)			22	72	7	23	2	0	0	10	.319	0	4	2	38	2	1	.976

ALL-STAR GAME RECORD

Year	League	Pos.	AB	R	H	2B	3B	HR	RBI	Avg.	BB	SO	SB	PO	A	E	Avg.
			BATTING											FIELDING			
1972	— American	PH	1	0	0	0	0	0	0	.000	0	0	0	...	...	...	...

RECORD AS MANAGER

BACKGROUND: Coach, New York Yankees (June 25, 1984-85). ... Vice-president/general manager, Yankees (beginning of 1988 season-June 22, 1988). ... Special adviser, Yankees (1989).

HONORS: Named A.L. Manager of the Year by Baseball Writers' Association of America (1995 and 2001). ... Named A.L. Manager of the Year by The Sporting News (2001).

Year	Team (League)	W	L	Pct.	Pos.	Playoff W	Playoff L	Champ. Series W	Champ. Series L	World Series W	World Series L	All-Star Game W	All-Star Game L
		REGULAR SEASON				POSTSEASON							
1986	— New York (A.L.)	90	72	.556	2nd (E)	—	—	—	—	—	—	—	—
1987	— New York (A.L.)	89	73	.549	4th (E)	—	—	—	—	—	—	—	—
1988	— New York (A.L.)	45	48	.484	5th (E)	—	—	—	—	—	—	—	—
1990	— Cincinnati (N.L.)	91	71	.562	1st (W)	—	—	4	2	4	0	—	—
1991	— Cincinnati (N.L.)	74	88	.457	5th (W)	—	—	—	—	—	—	0	1
1992	— Cincinnati (N.L.)	90	72	.556	2nd (W)	—	—	—	—	—	—	—	—
1993	— Seattle (A.L.)	82	80	.506	4th (W)	—	—	—	—	—	—	—	—
1994	— Seattle (A.L.)	49	63	.438		—	—	—	—	—	—	—	—
1995	— Seattle (A.L.)	79	66	.545	1st (W)	3	2	2	4	—	—	—	—
1996	— Seattle (A.L.)	85	76	.528	2nd (W)	—	—	—	—	—	—	—	—
1997	— Seattle (A.L.)	90	72	.556	1st (W)	1	3	—	—	—	—	—	—
1998	— Seattle (A.L.)	76	85	.472	3rd (W)	—	—	—	—	—	—	—	—
1999	— Seattle (A.L.)	79	83	.488	3rd (W)	—	—	—	—	—	—	—	—
2000	— Seattle (A.L.)	91	71	.562	2nd (W)	3	0	2	4	—	—	—	—
2001	— Seattle (A.L.)	116	46	.716	1st (W)	3	2	1	4	—	—	—	—
2002	— Seattle (A.L.)	93	69	.574	3rd (W)	—	—	—	—	—	—	—	—
American League totals (13 years)		1064	904	.541		10	7	5	12	—	—	—	—
National League totals (3 years)		255	231	.525		—	—	4	2	4	0	0	1
Major league totals (16 years)		1319	1135	.537		10	7	9	14	4	0	0	1

NOTES:

1988—Replaced New York manager Billy Martin, with club in second place and record of 40-28 (June 23).

1990—Defeated Pittsburgh in N.L. Championship Series; defeated Oakland in World Series.

1994—Seattle was in third place in A.L. West at time of season-ending strike (August 12).

1995—Defeated New York in A.L. divisional playoff; lost to Cleveland in A.L. Championship Series.

1997—Lost to Baltimore in A.L. divisional playoff.

2000—Defeated Chicago White Sox in A.L. divisional playoff; lost to New York Yankees in A.L. Championship Series.

2001—Defeated Cleveland in A.L. divisional playoff; lost to New York Yankees in A.L. Championship Series.

ROBINSON, FRANK — EXPOS

PERSONAL: Born August 31, 1935, in Beaumont, Tex. ... 6-1/194. ... Bats right, throws right.

HIGH SCHOOL: McClymonds (Oakland).

COLLEGE: Xavier.

TRANSACTIONS/CAREER NOTES: Signed by Tulsa, Cincinnati Reds organization (June 19, 1953). ... On temporarily inactive list (April 7-April 18, 1955). ... Traded by Reds to Baltimore Orioles for OF Dick Simpson, P Milt Pappas and P Jack Baldschun (December 9, 1965). ... Traded by Orioles with P Pete Richert to Los Angeles Dodgers for P Doyle Alexander, P Bob O'Brien, C Sergio Robles and 1B/OF Royle Stillman (December 2, 1971). ... Traded by Dodgers with IF Billy Grabarkewitz, IF Bob Valentine, P Bill Singer and P Mike Strahler to California Angels for 3B Ken McMullen and P Andy Messersmith (November 28, 1972). ... Claimed on waivers to Cleveland Indians (September 12, 1974); Indians assigned OF Rusty Torres and C Ken Suarez to Angels to complete deal (December 4, 1974). ... On disabled list (July 4-23, 1975; and April 4-26, 1976). ... Released by Indians (October 5, 1976).

RECORDS: Holds modern major league rookie-season record for most times hit by pitch—20 (1956). ... Shares major league record for most years leading league in intentional bases on balls received—4. ... Shares major league single-game records for most grand slams—2 (June 26, 1970); and fewest putouts by first baseman—0 (July 1, 1971). ... Shares major league record for most runs batted in in two successive innings—8 (June 26, 1970, fifth and sixth innings).

HONORS: Named N.L. Rookie of the Year by The Sporting News (1956). ... Named N.L. Rookie of the Year by Baseball Writers' Association of America (1956). ... Won N.L. Gold Glove as outfielder (1958). ... Named N.L. Player of the Year by The Sporting News (1961). ... Named outfielder on The Sporting News N.L. All-Star team (1961-62). ... Named N.L. Most Valuable Player by Baseball Writers' Association of America (1961). ... Named Major League Player of the Year by The Sporting News (1966). ... Named A.L. Player of the Year by The Sporting News (1966). ... Named outfielder on The Sporting News A.L. All-Star team (1966-67). ... Named A.L. Most Valuable Player by Baseball Writers' Association of America (1966). ... Elected to Hall of Fame (1982).

STATISTICAL NOTES: Led N.L. in being hit by pitch with 20 in 1956, eight in 1960, 11 in 1962, 14 in 1963 and 18 in 1965. ... Hit for the cycle (May 2, 1959). ... Hit three home runs in one game (August 22, 1959). ... Led N.L. first basemen with 111 double plays in 1959. ... Led N.L. with .595 slugging percentage in 1960, .611 in 1961 and .624 in 1962. ... Led N.L. with 23 intentional bases on balls received in 1961, 20 in 1963, 20 in 1964 and tied for lead with 16 in 1962. ... Led N.L. with 10 sacrifice flies in 1961. ... Led A.L. with 367 total bases and .637 slugging percentage in 1966. ... Won A.L. Triple Crown (1966). ... Tied for A.L. lead with seven sacrifice flies in 1966. ... Led A.L. in being hit by pitch with 13 in 1969.

								BATTING							FIELDING		
Year Team (League)	Pos.	G	AB	R	H	2B	3B	HR	RBI	Avg.	BB	SO	SB	PO	A	E	Avg.
1953—Ogden (Pio.)	OF-3B-1B	72	270	70	94	20	6	17	83	.348	53	69	3	105	28	18	.881
1954—Tulsa (Texas)	2B-3B	8	30	4	8	0	0	0	1	.267	...	...	0	17	15	1	.970
—Columbia (S.Atl.)	OF-3B-2B	132	491	*112	165	32	9	25	110	.336	88	65	6	258	63	18	.947
1955—Columbia (S.Atl.)	OF-1B	80	243	50	64	15	7	12	52	.263	41	44	3	203	3	4	.981
1956—Cincinnati (N.L.)	OF	152	572	*122	166	27	6	38	83	.290	64	95	8	323	5	8	.976
1957—Cincinnati (N.L.)	OF-1B	150	611	97	197	29	5	29	75	.322	44	92	10	487	36	6	.989
1958—Cincinnati (N.L.)	OF-3B	148	554	90	149	25	6	31	83	.269	62	80	10	314	24	6	.983
1959—Cincinnati (N.L.)	1B-OF	146	540	106	168	31	4	36	125	.311	69	93	18	1049	78	18	.984
1960—Cincinnati (N.L.)	1B-OF-3B	139	464	86	138	33	6	31	83	.297	82	67	13	775	62	10	.988
1961—Cincinnati (N.L.)	OF-3B	153	545	117	176	32	7	37	124	.323	71	64	22	284	15	3	.990
1962—Cincinnati (N.L.)	OF	162	609	*134	208	*51	2	39	136	.342	76	62	18	315	10	2	.994
1963—Cincinnati (N.L.)	OF-1B	140	482	79	125	19	3	21	91	.259	81	69	26	238	13	4	.984
1964—Cincinnati (N.L.)	OF	156	568	103	174	38	6	29	96	.306	79	67	23	279	7	4	.986
1965—Cincinnati (N.L.)	OF	156	582	109	172	33	5	33	113	.296	70	100	13	282	5	3	.990
1966—Baltimore (A.L.)■	OF-1B	155	576	*122	182	34	2	*49	*122	*.316	87	90	8	282	6	5	.983
1967—Baltimore (A.L.)	OF-1B	129	479	83	149	23	7	30	94	.311	71	84	2	207	8	2	.991
1968—Baltimore (A.L.)	OF-1B	130	421	69	113	27	1	15	52	.268	73	84	11	193	5	7	.966
1969—Baltimore (A.L.)	OF-1B	148	539	111	166	19	5	32	100	.308	88	62	9	367	19	5	.987
1970—Baltimore (A.L.)	OF-1B	132	471	88	144	24	1	25	78	.306	69	70	2	262	11	4	.986
1971—Baltimore (A.L.)	OF-1B	133	455	82	128	16	2	28	99	.281	72	62	3	449	20	11	.977
1972—Los Angeles (N.L.)■	OF	103	342	41	86	6	1	19	59	.251	55	76	2	168	6	6	.967
1973—California (A.L.)■	DH-OF	147	534	85	142	29	0	30	97	.266	82	93	1	38	3	1	.976
1974—California (A.L.)	DH-OF	129	427	75	107	26	2	20	63	.251	75	85	5	0	0	0	...
—Cleveland (A.L.)■	DH-1B	15	50	6	10	1	1	2	5	.200	10	10	0	23	0	1	.958
1975—Cleveland (A.L.)	DH	49	118	19	28	5	0	9	24	.237	29	15	0	...	...	...	...
1976—Cleveland (A.L.)	1B-OF	36	67	5	15	0	0	3	10	.224	11	12	0	11	0	0	1.000
American League totals (10 years)		1203	4137	745	1184	204	21	243	744	.286	667	667	41	1832	72	36	.981
National League totals (11 years)		1605	5869	1084	1759	324	51	343	1068	.300	753	865	163	4514	261	70	.986
Major league totals (21 years)		2808	10006	1829	2943	528	72	586	1812	.294	1420	1532	204	6346	333	106	.984

CHAMPIONSHIP SERIES RECORD

RECORDS: Shares record for most at-bats in one inning—2 (October 3, 1970, fourth inning).

NOTES: Hit home run in first at-bat (October 4, 1969).

								BATTING							FIELDING		
Year Team (League)	Pos.	G	AB	R	H	2B	3B	HR	RBI	Avg.	BB	SO	SB	PO	A	E	Avg.
1969—Baltimore (A.L.)	OF	3	12	1	4	2	0	1	2	.333	3	3	0	2	0	1	.667
1970—Baltimore (A.L.)	OF	3	10	3	2	0	0	1	2	.200	5	2	0	2	0	0	1.000
1971—Baltimore (A.L.)	OF	3	12	2	1	1	0	0	1	.083	1	4	0	7	0	0	1.000
Championship series totals (3 years)		9	34	6	7	3	0	2	5	.206	9	9	0	11	0	1	.917

WORLD SERIES RECORD

RECORDS: Shares career record for most times hit by pitch—3. ... Shares single-game record for most times hit by pitcher—2 (October 8, 1961).

NOTES: Named Most Valuable Player (1966).

								BATTING							FIELDING		
Year Team (League)	Pos.	G	AB	R	H	2B	3B	HR	RBI	Avg.	BB	SO	SB	PO	A	E	Avg.
1961—Cincinnati (N.L.)	OF	5	15	3	3	2	0	1	4	.200	5	3	0	5	0	0	1.000
1966—Baltimore (A.L.)	OF	4	14	4	4	0	1	2	3	.286	2	3	0	6	0	0	1.000
1969—Baltimore (A.L.)	OF	5	16	2	3	0	0	1	1	.188	4	3	0	13	0	0	1.000
1970—Baltimore (A.L.)	OF	5	22	5	6	0	0	2	4	.273	0	5	0	7	0	0	1.000
1971—Baltimore (A.L.)	OF	7	25	5	7	0	0	2	2	.280	1	8	0	12	0	0	1.000
World Series totals (5 years)		26	92	19	23	2	1	8	14	.250	12	22	0	43	0	0	1.000

ALL-STAR GAME RECORD

NOTES: Named Most Valuable Player (1971). ... Member of N.L. All-Star team in 1959 (first game) and 1961 (second game); did not play. ... Named to A.L. team for 1967 game; replaced due to injury.

		BATTING											FIELDING			
Year League	Pos.	AB	R	H	2B	3B	HR	RBI	Avg.	BB	SO	SB	PO	A	E	Avg.
1956—National	OF	2	0	0	0	0	0	0	.000	0	2	0	1	0	0	1.000
1957—National	OF	2	0	0	0	0	0	0	.000	0	0	0	5	0	0	1.000
1959—National	1B	3	1	3	0	0	1	1	1.000	0	0	0	3	0	1	.750
1961—National	OF	1	0	1	0	0	0	0	1.000	0	0	1	2	0	0	1.000
1962—National	OF	3	0	0	0	0	0	0	.000	0	0	0	1	0	0	1.000
1965—National	PH	1	0	0	0	0	0	0	.000	0	1	0	...	...	...	...
1966—American	OF	4	0	0	0	0	0	0	.000	0	1	0	2	0	0	1.000
1967—American		Selected, did not play—injured.														
1969—American	OF	2	0	0	0	0	0	0	.000	0	1	0	0	0	0	...
1970—American	OF	3	0	0	0	0	0	0	.000	0	2	0	1	0	0	1.000
1971—American	OF	2	1	1	0	0	1	2	.500	0	0	0	2	0	0	1.000
1974—American	PH	1	0	0	0	0	0	0	.000	0	0	0	...	...	...	...
All-Star Game totals (11 years)		24	2	5	0	0	2	3	.208	0	7	1	17	0	1	.944

RECORD AS MANAGER

BACKGROUND: Player/manager, Indians (1975). ... Coach, California Angels (July 11, 1997-remainder of season). ... Coach, Baltimore Orioles (1978-May 8, 1978, 1979-80 and 1985-87). ... Coach, Milwaukee Brewers (1984). ... Special assistant to president, Orioles (1988-April 11, 1988).

HONORS: Named A.L. Manager of the Year by The Sporting News (1989).

	REGULAR SEASON				POSTSEASON							
					Playoff		Champ. Series		World Series		All-Star Game	
Year Team (League)	W	L	Pct.	Pos.	W	L	W	L	W	L	W	L
1975—Cleveland (A.L.)	79	80	.497	4th (E)	—	—	—	—	—	—	—	—
1976—Cleveland (A.L.)	81	78	.509	4th (E)	—	—	—	—	—	—	—	—
1977—Cleveland (A.L.)	26	31	.368		—	—	—	—	—	—	—	—
1978—Rochester (I.L.)	56	55	.505	6th	—	—	—	—	—	—	—	—
1981—San Francisco (N.L.)	27	32	.458	5th (W)	—	—	—	—	—	—	—	—
—(Second half)	29	23	.558	3rd (W)	—	—	—	—	—	—	—	—
1982—San Francisco (N.L.)	87	75	.537	3rd (W)	—	—	—	—	—	—	—	—
1983—San Francisco (N.L.)	79	83	.488		—	—	—	—	—	—	—	—
1984—San Francisco (N.L.)	42	64	.396	6th (W)	—	—	—	—	—	—	—	—
1988—Baltimore (A.L.)	54	101	.348	7th (E)	—	—	—	—	—	—	—	—
1989—Baltimore (A.L.)	87	75	.537	2nd (E)	—	—	—	—	—	—	—	—
1990—Baltimore (A.L.)	76	85	.472	5th (E)	—	—	—	—	—	—	—	—
1991—Baltimore (A.L.)	13	24	.481		—	—	—	—	—	—	—	—
2002—Montreal (N.L.)	83	79	.512	2nd (E)	—	—	—	—	—	—	—	—
American League totals (7 years)	416	474	.467		—	—	—	—	—	—	—	—
National League totals (5 years)	347	356	.494		—	—	—	—	—	—	—	—
Major league totals (12 years)	763	830	.479		—	—	—	—	—	—	—	—

NOTES:

1977—Replaced as Cleveland manager by Jeff Torborg, with club in sixth place (June 19).

1978—Replaced interim manager Al Widmer and manager Ken Boyer (May 8).

1984—Replaced as San Francisco manager by Danny Ozark with club in sixth place (August 5).

1988—Replaced Baltimore manager Cal Ripken Sr., with club in seventh place and record of 0-6 (Apil 12).

1991—Replaced as Baltimore manager Johnny Oaks with club in seventh place (May 23).

SCIOSCIA, MIKE — ANGELS

PERSONAL: Born November 27, 1958, in Upper Darby, Pa. ... 6-2/220. ... Batted left, threw right. ... Full name: Michael Lorri Scioscia. ... Name pronounced SO-sha.

HIGH SCHOOL: Springfield (Pa.).

COLLEGE: Penn State.

TRANSACTIONS/CAREER NOTES: Selected by Los Angeles Dodgers organization in first round (19th pick overall) of free-agent draft (June 8, 1976). ... On disabled list (May 19-August 4, 1978; April 10-20, 1980; May 15, 1983-remainder of season; May 6-21, 1984; June 10-July 15, 1986; June 1-16, 1987; and July 5-20, 1991). ... Granted free agency (November 4, 1992). ... Signed by San Diego Padres (February 11, 1993). ... On disabled list (March 29, 1993-entire season). ... Released by Padres (October 15, 1993). ... Signed by Texas Rangers organization (December 14, 1993). ... On voluntary retired list (August 2, 1994).

HONORS: Named catcher on The Sporting News N.L. All-Star team (1990).

STATISTICAL NOTES: Led Midwest League catchers with 20 errors and 12 double plays in 1977. ... Led Pacific Coast League catchers with 791 total chances, 19 double plays and 22 passed balls in 1979. ... Tied for Pacific Coast League lead in being hit by pitch with seven in 1979. ... Led N.L. with 11 passed balls in 1981 and 14 in 1992. ... Led N.L. catchers with 1,016 total chances in 1987, 915 in 1989 and 910 in 1990.

			BATTING											FIELDING			
Year Team (League)	Pos.	G	AB	R	H	2B	3B	HR	RBI	Avg.	BB	SO	SB	PO	A	E	Avg.
1976—Bellingham (N.W.)	C	46	151	25	42	6	0	7	26	.278	36	22	2	202	35	14	.944
1977—Clinton (Midw.)	C-1B	121	364	58	92	20	1	7	44	.253	79	25	9	764	95	†22	.975
1978—San Antonio (Texas)	C	58	204	29	61	16	0	2	34	.299	31	20	3	214	17	4	.983
1979—Albuquerque (PCL)	C	143	461	80	155	34	0	3	68	.336	73	33	5	*690	*86	*15	.981
1980—Albuquerque (PCL)	C	52	160	33	53	11	1	3	33	.331	36	13	3	207	19	5	.978
—Los Angeles (N.L.)	C	54	134	8	34	5	1	1	8	.254	12	9	1	226	26	2	.992

		BATTING												FIELDING			
Year Team (League)	Pos.	G	AB	R	H	2B	3B	HR	RBI	Avg.	BB	SO	SB	PO	A	E	Avg.
1981—Los Angeles (N.L.).....	C	93	290	27	80	10	0	2	29	.276	36	18	0	493	48	7	.987
1982—Los Angeles (N.L.).....	C	129	365	31	80	11	1	5	38	.219	44	31	2	631	57	10	.986
1983—Los Angeles (N.L.).....	C	12	35	3	11	3	0	1	7	.314	5	2	0	55	4	0	1.000
1984—Los Angeles (N.L.).....	C	114	341	29	93	18	0	5	38	.273	52	26	2	701	64	12	.985
1985—Los Angeles (N.L.).....	C	141	429	47	127	26	3	7	53	.296	77	21	3	818	66	•13	.986
1986—Los Angeles (N.L.).....	C	122	374	36	94	18	1	5	26	.251	62	23	3	756	64	15	.982
1987—Los Angeles (N.L.).....	C	142	461	44	122	26	1	6	38	.265	55	23	7	*925	80	11	.989
1988—Los Angeles (N.L.).....	C	130	408	29	105	18	0	3	35	.257	38	31	0	748	63	7	.991
1989—Los Angeles (N.L.).....	C	133	408	40	102	16	0	10	44	.250	52	29	0	*822	*82	11	.988
1990—Los Angeles (N.L.).....	C	135	435	46	115	25	0	12	66	.264	55	31	4	*842	58	10	.989
1991—Los Angeles (N.L.).....	C	119	345	39	91	16	2	8	40	.264	47	32	4	677	51	7	.990
1992—Los Angeles (N.L.).....	C	117	348	19	77	6	3	3	24	.221	32	31	3	641	*74	9	.988
1993—San Diego (N.L.)■.....								Did not play.									
1994—Charlotte (FSL)■........	C	1	2	0	1	0	0	0	0	.500	0	0	0	3	1	0	1.000
Major League totals (13 years)		1441	4373	398	1131	198	12	68	446	.259	567	307	29	8335	737	114	.988

DIVISION SERIES RECORD

		BATTING												FIELDING			
Year Team (League)	Pos.	G	AB	R	H	2B	3B	HR	RBI	Avg.	BB	SO	SB	PO	A	E	Avg.
1981—Los Angeles (N.L.).....	C	4	13	0	2	0	0	0	1	.154	1	2	0	21	3	0	1.000

CHAMPIONSHIP SERIES RECORD

		BATTING												FIELDING			
Year Team (League)	Pos.	G	AB	R	H	2B	3B	HR	RBI	Avg.	BB	SO	SB	PO	A	E	Avg.
1981—Los Angeles (N.L.).....	C	5	15	1	2	0	0	1	1	.133	2	1	0	27	1	0	1.000
1985—Los Angeles (N.L.).....	C	6	16	2	4	0	0	0	1	.250	4	0	0	31	4	1	.972
1988—Los Angeles (N.L.).....	C	7	22	3	8	1	0	1	2	.364	1	2	0	37	4	0	1.000
Championship series totals (3 years)		18	53	6	14	1	0	2	4	.264	7	3	0	95	9	1	.990

WORLD SERIES RECORD

NOTES: Member of World Series championship teams (1981 and 1988).

		BATTING												FIELDING			
Year Team (League)	Pos.	G	AB	R	H	2B	3B	HR	RBI	Avg.	BB	SO	SB	PO	A	E	Avg.
1981—Los Angeles (N.L.).....	C-PH	3	4	1	1	0	0	0	0	.250	1	0	0	7	1	0	1.000
1988—Los Angeles (N.L.).....	C	4	14	0	3	0	0	0	1	.214	0	2	0	28	0	1	.966
World Series totals (2 years)		7	18	1	4	0	0	0	1	.222	1	2	0	35	1	1	.973

ALL-STAR GAME RECORD

		BATTING											FIELDING			
Year League	Pos.	AB	R	H	2B	3B	HR	RBI	Avg.	BB	SO	SB	PO	A	E	Avg.
1989—National......................	C	1	0	0	0	0	0	0	.000	0	0	0	3	0	0	1.000
1990—National......................	C	2	0	0	0	0	0	0	.000	0	1	0	6	0	0	1.000
All-Star Game totals (2 years)		3	0	0	0	0	0	0	.000	0	1	0	9	0	0	1.000

RECORD AS MANAGER

BACKGROUND: Minor league catching coordinator, Dodgers organization (1995-96). ... Bench coach, Dodgers (1997-98). ... Manager, Peoria Javelinas, Dodgers organization (1997).

HONORS: Named A.L. Manager of the Year by THE SPORTING NEWS (2002). ... Named A.L. Manager of the Year by Baseball Writers' Association of America (2002).

	REGULAR SEASON				POSTSEASON							
					Playoff		Champ. Series		World Series		All-Star Game	
Year Team (League)	W	L	Pct.	Pos.	W	L	W	L	W	L	W	L
1999—Albuquerque (PCL)..................................	65	74	.468	3rd (C)	—	—	—	—	—	—	—	—
2000—Anaheim (A.L.)...	82	80	.506	3rd (W)	—	—	—	—	—	—	—	—
2001—Anaheim (A.L.)...	75	87	.463	3rd (W)	—	—	—	—	—	—	—	—
2002—Anaheim (A.L.)...	99	63	.611	2nd (W)	3	1	4	1	4	3	—	—
Major league totals (2 years)............................	256	230	.527		3	1	4	1	4	3	—	—

NOTES:

2002—Defeated New York Yankees in A.L. divisional playoff; defeated Minnesota in A.L. Championship Series; defeated San Francisco in World Series.

SHOWALTER, BUCK RANGERS

PERSONAL: Born May 23, 1956, in DeFuniak Springs, Fla. ... 5-9/195. ... Batted left, threw left. ... Full name: William Nathaniel Showalter III.

JUNIOR COLLEGE: Chipola Junior College (Fla.).

COLLEGE: Mississippi State.

TRANSACTIONS/CAREER NOTES: Selected by New York Yankees organization in fifth round of free-agent draft (June 7, 1977). ... On disabled list (July 1-11 and July 19-August 4, 1981).

STATISTICAL NOTES: Led Southern League first basemen with 1,281 putouts in 1982.

Year	Team (League)	Pos.	G	AB	R	H	2B	3B	HR	RBI	Avg.	BB	SO	SB	PO	A	E	Avg.
				BATTING											FIELDING			
1977—	Fort Lauderdale (FSL)	OF	56	196	32	71	8	1	1	25	.362	36	13	4	96	2	2	.980
1978—	West Haven (East.).....	OF	123	429	52	124	13	2	3	46	.289	55	34	19	192	•15	7	.967
1979—	West Haven (East.).....	1B-OF	129	469	71	131	7	3	6	51	.279	36	30	8	575	52	7	.989
1980—	Nashville (Sou.)..........	OF-1B	142	550	84	*178	19	3	1	82	.324	53	23	6	71	2	1	.986
1981—	Columbus (I.L.)..........	OF	14	37	6	7	1	0	1	3	.189	3	0	0	11	0	1	.917
—	Nashville (Sou.)..........	OF-1B	90	307	46	81	17	6	0	38	.264	46	16	3	201	14	7	.968
1982—	Nashville (Sou.)..........	1B-OF	132	517	66	*152	29	3	3	46	.294	61	42	2	†1282	51	13	.990
1983—	Nashville (Sou.)..........	1B-OF-P	89	297	35	82	13	4	1	37	.276	39	22	1	127	6	2	.985
—	Columbus (I.L.)..........	1B-P	18	63	9	15	3	0	1	8	.238	7	3	1	139	14	1	.994

RECORD AS PITCHER

Year	Team (League)	W	L	Pct.	ERA	G	GS	CG	ShO	Sv.	IP	H	R	ER	BB	SO
1983—	Nashville (Sou.)..................	0	0	...	9.00	1	0	0	0	0	1	2	1	1	0	1
—	Columbus (I.L.)..................	0	0	...	0.00	1	0	0	0	0	2	0	0	0	0	2

RECORD AS MANAGER

BACKGROUND: Minor league coach, New York Yankees organization (1984). ... Coach, Yankees (1990-91). ... Manager/scout, Arizona Diamondbacks (1996-97). ... Broadcaster (2001-02).

HONORS: Named New York-Pennsylvania League Manager of the Year (1985). ... Named Eastern League Manager of the Year (1989). ... Coach, A.L. All-Star team (1992). ... Named A.L. Manager of the Year by The Sporting News (1994). ... Named A.L. Manager of the Year by Baseball Writers' Association of America (1994).

		REGULAR SEASON				POSTSEASON							
						Playoff		Champ. Series		World Series		All-Star Game	
Year	Team (League)	W	L	Pct.	Pos.	W	L	W	L	W	L	W	L
1985—	Oneonta (New York-Pennsylvania)...........	55	23	.705	1st (Y)	3	0	—	—	—	—	—	—
1986—	Oneonta (New York-Pennsylvania)...........	59	18	.766	1st (Y)	0	1	—	—	—	—	—	—
1987—	Fort Lauderdale (Florida State)	85	53	.616	1st (S)	5	1	—	—	—	—	—	—
1988—	Fort Lauderdale (Florida State)	39	29	.574	3rd (E)	—	—	—	—	—	—	—	—
—	(Second half)	30	36	.455	T3rd (E)	—	—	—	—	—	—	—	—
1989—	Albany (East.)	92	48	.657	1st	6	2	—	—	—	—	—	—
1992—	New York (A.L.)	76	86	.469	T4th (E)	—	—	—	—	—	—	—	—
1993—	New York (A.L.)	88	74	.543	2nd (E)	—	—	—	—	—	—	—	—
1994—	New York (A.L.)	70	43	.619		—	—	—	—	—	—	—	—
1995—	New York (A.L.)	79	65	.549	2nd (E)	2	3	—	—	—	—	—	—
1998—	Arizona (N.L.)...	65	97	.401	5th (W)	—	—	—	—	—	—	—	—
1999—	Arizona (N.L.)...	100	62	.617	1st (W)	1	3	—	—	—	—	—	—
2000—	Arizona (N.L.)...	85	77	.525	3rd (W)	—	—	—	—	—	—	—	—
American League totals (4 years)		313	268	.539		2	3	—	—	—	—	—	—
National League totals (3 years)		250	236	.514		1	3	—	—	—	—	—	—
Major league totals (7 years)		563	504	.528		3	6	—	—	—	—	—	—

NOTES:

1985—Defeated Geneva in one-game semifinal playoff; defeated Auburn, two games to none, in league championship.
1986—Lost to Newark in playoffs.
1987—Defeated Lakeland, two games to none, in playoffs; defeated Osceola, three games to one, in league championship.
1989—Defeated Reading, three games to one, in playoffs; defeated Harrisburg, three games to one, in league championship.
1994—New York was in first place in A.L. East at time of season-ending strike (August 12).
1995—Lost to Seattle in A.L. divisional playoff. Named Arizona Diamondbacks manager (November 15).
1999—Lost to New York Mets in N.L. divisional playoff.

TORBORG, JEFF — MARLINS

PERSONAL: Born November 26, 1941, in Westfield, N.J. ... 6-0/195. ... Batted right, threw right. ... Full name: Jeffrey Allen Torborg. ... Father of Doug Torborg, minor league pitcher (1987-88).

HIGH SCHOOL: Westfield (N.J.).

COLLEGE: Rutgers, then Montclair State.

TRANSACTIONS/CAREER NOTES: Signed as non-drafted free agent by Los Angeles Dodgers organization (May 22, 1963). ... Contract sold by Dodgers to California Angels (March 13, 1971). ... On disabled list (June 25-July 27, 1971; May 12-June 13, 1972; and July 13-August 10, 1973). ... Traded by Angels to St. Louis Cardinals for P John Andrews (December 6, 1973). ... Released by Cardinals (March 25, 1974).

Year	Team (League)	Pos.	G	AB	R	H	2B	3B	HR	RBI	Avg.	BB	SO	SB	PO	A	E	Avg.
				BATTING											FIELDING			
1963—	Albuquerque (Texas) ..	C	64	184	19	41	10	3	1	18	.223	15	37	0	349	27	6	.984
1964—	Los Angeles (N.L.).....	C	28	43	4	10	1	1	0	4	.233	3	8	0	80	4	2	.977
1965—	Los Angeles (N.L.).....	C	56	150	8	36	5	1	3	13	.240	10	26	0	300	19	3	.991
1966—	Los Angeles (N.L.).....	C	46	120	4	27	3	0	1	13	.225	10	23	0	269	17	4	.986
1967—	Los Angeles (N.L.).....	C	76	196	11	42	4	1	2	12	.214	13	31	1	413	30	5	.989
1968—	Los Angeles (N.L.).....	C	37	93	2	15	2	0	0	4	.161	6	10	0	206	20	2	.991
1969—	Los Angeles (N.L.).....	C	51	124	7	23	4	0	0	7	.185	9	17	1	251	26	1	.996
1970—	Los Angeles (N.L.).....	C	64	134	11	31	8	0	1	17	.231	14	15	1	275	16	5	.983
1971—	California (A.L.)■........	C	55	123	6	25	5	0	0	5	.203	3	6	0	208	17	3	.987
1972—	California (A.L.)..........	C	59	153	5	32	3	0	0	8	.209	14	21	0	383	28	1	.998
1973—	California (A.L.)..........	C	102	255	20	56	7	0	1	18	.220	21	32	0	611	37	6	.991
American League totals (3 years)			216	531	31	113	15	0	1	31	.213	38	59	0	1202	82	10	.992
National League totals (7 years)			358	860	47	184	27	3	7	70	.214	65	130	3	1794	132	22	.989
Major League totals (10 years)			574	1391	78	297	42	3	8	101	.214	103	189	3	2996	214	32	.990

RECORD AS MANAGER

BACKGROUND: Coach, Cleveland Indians (1975-June 19, 1977). ... Coach, New York Yankees (August 1, 1979-88). ... Broadcaster (1994-2000).

HONORS: Named A.L. Manager of the Year by The Sporting News (1990). ... Named A.L. Manager of the Year by Baseball Writers' Association of America (1990).

	REGULAR SEASON				POSTSEASON							
					Playoff		Champ. Series		World Series		All-Star Game	
Year Team (League)	W	L	Pct.	Pos.	W	L	W	L	W	L	W	L
1977— Cleveland (A.L.)	45	59	.433	5th (E)	—	—	—	—	—	—	—	—
1978— Cleveland (A.L.)	69	90	.434	6th (E)	—	—	—	—	—	—	—	—
1979— Cleveland (A.L.)	43	52	.453		—	—	—	—	—	—	—	—
1989— Chicago (A.L.)	69	92	.429	7th (W)	—	—	—	—	—	—	—	—
1990— Chicago (A.L.)	94	68	.580	2nd (W)	—	—	—	—	—	—	—	—
1991— Chicago (A.L.)	87	75	.537	2nd (W)	—	—	—	—	—	—	—	—
1992— New York (N.L.)	72	90	.444	5th (E)	—	—	—	—	—	—	—	—
1993— New York (N.L.)	13	25	.342		—	—	—	—	—	—	—	—
2001— Montreal (N.L.)	47	62	.431	5th (E)	—	—	—	—	—	—	—	—
2002— Florida (N.L.)	79	83	.488	4th (E)	—	—	—	—	—	—	—	—
American League totals (6 years)	407	436	.483		—	—	—	—	—	—	—	—
National League totals (4 years)	211	260	.448		—	—	—	—	—	—	—	—
Major league totals (10 years)	618	696	.470		—	—	—	—	—	—	—	—

NOTES:
1977—Replaced Cleveland manager Frank Robinson with club in sixth place and record of 26-31 (June 19).
1979—Replaced as Cleveland manager by Dave Garcia with club in sixth place (July 23).
1993—Replaced as New York manager by Dallas Green with club in seventh place (May 19).
2001—Replaced Montreal manager Felipe Alou with club in fifth place and record of 21-32 (May 31).

TORRE, JOE — YANKEES

PERSONAL: Born July 18, 1940, in Brooklyn, N.Y. ... 6-1/210. ... Batted right, threw right. ... Full name: Joseph Paul Torre. ... Brother of Frank Torre, first baseman with Milwaukee Braves (1956-60) and Philadelphia Phillies (1962-63). ... Name pronounced TORE-ee.

HIGH SCHOOL: St. Francis Prep (Brooklyn, N.Y.).

TRANSACTIONS/CAREER NOTES: Signed by Milwaukee Braves organization (August 24, 1959). ... On military list (September 30, 1962-March 26, 1963). ... Braves franchise moved from Milwaukee to Atlanta (1966). ... On disabled list (April 18-May 9, 1968). ... Traded by Braves to St. Louis Cardinals for 1B Orlando Cepeda (March 17, 1969). ... Traded by Cardinals to New York Mets for P Tommy Moore and P Ray Sadecki (October 13, 1974). ... Released as player by Mets (June 17, 1977).

RECORDS: Shares major league single-game record for most times grounded into double play—4 (July 21, 1975).

HONORS: Named catcher on The Sporting News N.L. All-Star team (1964-66). ... Won N.L. Gold Glove at catcher (1965). ... Named Major League Player of the Year by The Sporting News (1971). ... Named N.L. Player of the Year by The Sporting News (1971). ... Named third baseman on The Sporting News N.L. All-Star team (1971). ... Named N.L. Most Valuable Player by Baseball Writers' Association of America (1971).

STATISTICAL NOTES: Led N.L. catchers with .995 fielding percentage in 1964 and .996 in 1968. ... Led N.L. in grounding into double plays with 26 in 1964, 22 in 1965 and 22 in 1967. ... Led N.L. catchers with 12 double plays in 1967. ... Led N.L. with 352 total bases in 1971. ... Hit for the cycle (June 27, 1973). ... Led N.L. first basemen with 102 assists and 144 double plays in 1974. ... Career major league grand slams: 3.

		BATTING												FIELDING			
Year Team (League)	Pos.	G	AB	R	H	2B	3B	HR	RBI	Avg.	BB	SO	SB	PO	A	E	Avg.
1960— Eau Claire (North.)	C	117	369	63	127	23	3	16	74	*.344	70	45	7	636	64	9	.987
— Milwaukee (N.L.)	PH	2	2	0	1	0	0	0	0	.500	0	1	0	...	...	...	...
1961— Louisville (A.A.)	C	27	111	18	38	8	2	3	24	.342	6	9	0	185	14	2	.990
— Milwaukee (N.L.)	C	113	406	40	113	21	4	10	42	.278	28	60	3	494	50	10	.982
1962— Milwaukee (N.L.)	C	80	220	23	62	8	1	5	26	.282	24	24	1	325	39	5	.986
1963— Milwaukee (N.L.)	C-1B-OF	142	501	57	147	19	4	14	71	.293	42	79	1	919	76	6	.994
1964— Milwaukee (N.L.)	C-1B	154	601	87	193	36	5	20	109	.321	36	67	2	1081	94	7	†.994
1965— Milwaukee (N.L.)	C-1B	148	523	68	152	21	1	27	80	.291	61	79	0	1022	73	8	.993
1966— Atlanta (N.L.)	C-1B	148	546	83	172	20	3	36	101	.315	60	61	0	874	87	12	.988
1967— Atlanta (N.L.)	C-1B	135	477	67	132	18	1	20	68	.277	49	75	2	785	81	8	.991
1968— Atlanta (N.L.)	C-1B	115	424	45	115	11	2	10	55	.271	34	72	1	733	48	2	†.997
1969— St. Louis (N.L.)■	1B-C	159	602	72	174	29	6	18	101	.289	66	85	0	1360	91	7	.995
1970— St. Louis (N.L.)	C-3B-1B	•161	624	89	203	27	9	21	100	.325	70	91	2	651	162	13	.984
1971— St. Louis (N.L.)	3B	161	634	97	*230	34	8	24	*137	*.363	63	70	4	*136	271	•21	.951
1972— St. Louis (N.L.)	3B-1B	149	544	71	157	26	6	11	81	.289	54	64	3	336	198	15	.973
1973— St. Louis (N.L.)	1B-3B	141	519	67	149	17	2	13	69	.287	65	78	2	881	128	12	.988
1974— St. Louis (N.L.)	1B-3B	147	529	59	149	28	1	11	70	.282	69	88	1	1173	†121	14	.989
1975— New York (N.L.)■	3B-1B	114	361	33	89	16	3	6	35	.247	35	55	0	172	157	15	.956
1976— New York (N.L.)	1B-3B	114	310	36	95	10	3	5	31	.306	21	35	1	593	52	7	.989
1977— New York (N.L.)	1B-3B	26	51	2	9	3	0	1	9	.176	2	10	0	83	3	1	.989
Major league totals (18 years)		2209	7874	996	2342	344	59	252	1185	.297	779	1094	23	11618	1731	163	.988

ALL-STAR GAME RECORD

		BATTING											FIELDING			
Year League	Pos.	AB	R	H	2B	3B	HR	RBI	Avg.	BB	SO	SB	PO	A	E	Avg.
1963— National							Did not play.									
1964— National	C	2	0	0	0	0	0	0	.000	0	0	0	5	0	0	1.000
1965— National	C	4	1	1	0	0	1	2	.250	0	0	0	5	1	0	1.000
1966— National	C	3	0	0	0	0	0	0	.000	0	1	0	5	0	0	1.000
1967— National	C	2	0	0	0	0	0	0	.000	0	0	0	4	1	0	1.000
1970— National	PH	1	0	0	0	0	0	0	.000	0	0	0	...	...	...	...
1971— National	3B	3	0	0	0	0	0	0	.000	0	1	0	1	0	0	1.000
1972— National	3B	3	0	1	0	0	0	0	.333	0	1	0	1	2	0	1.000
1973— National	1B-3B	3	0	0	0	0	0	0	.000	0	0	0	5	0	0	1.000
All-Star Game totals (8 years)		21	1	2	0	0	1	2	.095	0	3	0	26	4	0	1.000

RECORD AS MANAGER

BACKGROUND: Player/manager, New York Mets (May 31-June 17, 1977).

HONORS: Named Sportsman of the Year by The Sporting News (1996). ... Named co-A.L. Manager of the Year by Baseball Writers' Association of America (1996). ... Named A.L. Manager of the Year by The Sporting News (1998). ... Named A.L. Manager of the Year by Baseball Writers' Association of America (1998).

	REGULAR SEASON				POSTSEASON							
					Playoff		Champ. Series		World Series		All-Star Game	
Year Team (League)	W	L	Pct.	Pos.	W	L	W	L	W	L	W	L
1977— New York (N.L.)	49	68	.419	6th (E)	—	—	—	—	—	—	—	—
1978— New York (N.L.)	66	96	.407	6th (E)	—	—	—	—	—	—	—	—
1979— New York (N.L.)	63	99	.389	6th (E)	—	—	—	—	—	—	—	—
1980— New York (N.L.)	67	95	.414	5th (E)	—	—	—	—	—	—	—	—
1981— New York (N.L.)	17	34	.333	5th (E)	—	—	—	—	—	—	—	—
— (Second half)	24	28	.462	4th (E)	—	—	—	—	—	—	—	—
1982— Atlanta (N.L.)	89	73	.549	1st (W)	—	—	0	3	—	—	—	—
1983— Atlanta (N.L.)	88	74	.543	2nd (W)	—	—	—	—	—	—	—	—
1984— Atlanta (N.L.)	80	82	.494	T2nd (W)	—	—	—	—	—	—	—	—
1990— St. Louis (N.L.)	24	34	.414	6th (E)	—	—	—	—	—	—	—	—
1991— St. Louis (N.L.)	84	78	.519	2nd (E)	—	—	—	—	—	—	—	—
1992— St. Louis (N.L.)	83	79	.512	3rd (E)	—	—	—	—	—	—	—	—
1993— St. Louis (N.L.)	87	75	.537	3rd (E)	—	—	—	—	—	—	—	—
1994— St. Louis (N.L.)	53	61	.465		—	—	—	—	—	—	—	—
1995— St. Louis (N.L.)	20	27	.426	4th (C)	—	—	—	—	—	—	—	—
1996— New York (A.L.)	92	70	.568	1st (E)	3	1	4	1	4	2	—	—
1997— New York (A.L.)	96	66	.593	2nd (E)	2	3	—	—	—	—	1	0
1998— New York (A.L.)	114	48	.704	1st (E)	3	0	4	2	4	0	—	—
1999— New York (A.L.)	98	64	.605	1st (E)	3	0	4	1	4	0	1	0
2000— New York (A.L.)	87	74	.540	1st (E)	3	2	4	2	4	1	1	0
2001— New York (A.L.)	95	65	.594	1st (E)	3	2	4	1	3	4	1	0
2002— New York (A.L.)	103	58	.640	1st (E)	1	3	—	—	—	—	0	0
American League totals (7 years)	685	445	.606		18	11	20	7	19	7	4	0
National League totals (14 years)	894	1003	.471		—	—	0	3	—	—	—	—
Major league totals (21 years)	1579	1448	.522		18	11	20	10	19	7	4	0

NOTES:

1977—Replaced New York manager Joe Frazier with club in sixth place and record of 15-30 (May 31); served as player/manager (May 31-June 18, when released as player).

1982—Lost to St. Louis in N.L. Championship Series.

1990—Replaced St. Louis manager Whitey Herzog (33-47) and interim manager Red Schoendienst (13-11) with club in sixth place and record of 46-58 (August 1).

1994—St. Louis was tied for third place in N.L. Central at time of season-ending strike (August 12).

1995—Replaced as Cardinals manager by interim manager Mike Jorgensen, with club in fourth place (June 16).

1996—Defeated Texas in A.L. divisional playoff; defeated Baltimore in A.L. Championship Series; defeated Atlanta in World Series.

1997—Lost to Cleveland in A.L. divisional playoff.

1998—Defeated Texas in A.L. divisional playoff; defeated Cleveland in A.L. Championship Series; defeated San Diego in World Series.

1999—Defeated Texas in A.L. divisional playoff; defeated Boston in A.L. Championship Series; defeated Atlanta in World Series.

2000—Defeated Oakland in A.L. divisional playoff; defeated Seattle in A.L. Championship Series; defeated New York Mets in World Series.

2001—Defeated Oakland in A.L. divisional playoff; defeated Seattle in A.L. Championship Series; lost to Arizona in World Series.

2002—All-Star Game ended in tie. Lost to Anaheim in A.L. divisional playoff.

TOSCA, CARLOS — BLUE JAYS

PERSONAL: Born September 29, 1953, in Pinar Del Rio, Cuba. ... 5-7/158.

RECORD AS MANAGER

BACKGROUND: Coach, King High School, Tampa, Fla. (1976-77). ... Coach, Oneonta, New York Yankees organization (1978-79). ... Coach, Sarasota, Yankees organization (1986). ... Bench coach, Arizona Diamondbacks (1998-2000). ... Third base coach, Toronto Blue Jays (December 10, 2001-June 3, 2002).

HONORS: Named Gulf Coast League Manager of the Year (1985). ... Named Eastern League Manager of the Year (1996).

	REGULAR SEASON				POSTSEASON							
					Playoff		Champ. Series		World Series		All-Star Game	
Year Team (League)	W	L	Pct.	Pos.	W	L	W	L	W	L	W	L
1980— Gulf Coast Yankees (GCL)	27	35	.435	7th	—	—	—	—	—	—	—	—
1981— Gulf Coast Yankees (GCL)	30	29	.508	7th	—	—	—	—	—	—	—	—
1982— Gulf Coast Yankees (GCL)	42	21	.667	1st	—	—	—	—	—	—	—	—
1983— Greensboro (S. Atl.)	39	33	.542	2nd (N)	—	—	—	—	—	—	—	—
— (Second half)	34	38	.472	3rd (N)	—	—	—	—	—	—	—	—
1984— Greensboro (S. Atl.)	44	28	.611	1st (N)	—	—	—	—	—	—	—	—
— (Second half)	31	41	.431	4th (N)	1	2	—	—	—	—	—	—
1985— Gulf Coast Yankees (GCL)	43	18	.705	1st	—	—	—	—	—	—	—	—
1988— Gulf Coast Royals (GCL)	39	24	.619	1st (N)	0	1	—	—	—	—	—	—
1989— Gulf Coast Royals (GCL)	35	28	.556	3rd (N)	—	—	—	—	—	—	—	—
1990— Gulf Coast Royals (GCL)	25	38	.397	5th (N)	—	—	—	—	—	—	—	—
1991— Baseball City (FSL)	27	39	.409	3rd (C)	—	—	—	—	—	—	—	—
— (Second half)	35	30	.538	2nd (C)	—	—	—	—	—	—	—	—
1992— Gulf Coast Marlins (GCL)	33	27	.550	2nd (C)	—	—	—	—	—	—	—	—
1993— Kane County (Midw.)	39	29	.574	3rd (N)	—	—	—	—	—	—	—	—
— (Second half)	36	33	.522	4th (N)	—	—	—	—	—	—	—	—

Year Team (League)	REGULAR SEASON W	L	Pct.	Pos.	POSTSEASON Playoff W	L	Champ. Series W	L	World Series W	L	All-Star Game W	L
1994—Portland (East.)	60	81	.426	4th (N)	—	—	—	—	—	—	—	—
1995—Portland (East.)	86	56	.606	1st (N)	1	3	—	—	—	—	—	—
1996—Portland (East.)	83	58	.589	1st (N)	4	5	—	—	—	—	—	—
1997—Charlotte (I.L.)	76	65	.539	2nd (N)	1	3	—	—	—	—	—	—
2001—Richmond (I.L.)	68	76	.472	3rd (S)	—	—	—	—	—	—	—	—
2002—Toronto (A.L.)	58	51	.532	3rd (E)	—	—	—	—	—	—	—	—

NOTES:
1984—Lost to Asheville in playoffs.
1985—Championship game rained out.
1988—Lost to Gulf Coast Yankees in championship game.
1995—Lost to New Haven in playoffs.
1996—Defeated Binghamton, three games to two, in playoffs; lost to Harrisburg, three games to one, in league championship.
1997—Lost to Columbus in playoffs.
2002—Replaced Toronto manager Buck Martinez with club in fourth place and record of 20-33 (June 3).

TRACY, JIM — DODGERS

PERSONAL: Born December 31, 1955, in Hamilton, Ohio. ... 6-3/205. ... Batted left, threw right. ... Full name: James Edwin Tracy.
HIGH SCHOOL: Badin (Hamilton, Ohio).
COLLEGE: Marietta College (Ohio).
TRANSACTIONS/CAREER NOTES: Selected by Chicago Cubs organization in fourth round of free-agent draft (January 11, 1977). ... Traded by Cubs to Houston Astros for OF Gary Woods (December 9, 1981).

Year Team (League)	Pos.	G	BATTING AB	R	H	2B	3B	HR	RBI	Avg.	BB	SO	SB	FIELDING PO	A	E	Avg.
1977—Pom. Beach (FSL)	1B-OF	93	261	27	59	13	2	4	34	.226	41	66	1	147	6	4	.975
1978—Pom. Beach (FSL)	1B-OF	78	225	42	55	7	5	6	43	.244	58	34	2	329	27	4	.989
—Midland (Texas)	OF-1B	54	189	34	49	9	2	8	29	.259	20	50	2	174	10	2	.989
1979—Midland (Texas)	1B	86	301	75	107	16	1	15	67	*.355	63	41	7	799	31	6	.993
—Wichita (A.A.)	1B-OF	44	150	26	41	9	1	4	18	.273	21	36	0	364	20	11	.972
1980—Wichita (A.A.)	OF-1B-3B	112	406	66	130	17	6	16	63	.320	67	68	4	428	33	5	.989
—Chicago (N.L.)	OF-1B	42	122	12	31	3	3	3	9	.254	13	37	2	44	0	2	.957
1981—Midland (Texas)	OF-1B	22	73	8	20	3	0	2	7	.274	13	22	0	73	2	0	1.000
—Chicago (N.L.)	OF	45	63	6	15	2	1	0	5	.238	12	14	1	16	0	0	1.000
1982—Tucson (PCL)	OF-1B	133	481	85	153	35	3	12	100	.318	81	83	5	294	14	4	.987
1983—Taiyo (Jap. Cen.)		125	469	61	142	29	2	19	66	.303	32	74	3	...	...	...	...
1984—Taiyo (Jap. Cen.)		3	9	1	2	0	0	1	5	.222	2	1	0	...	...	...	...
—Tucson (PCL)	OF-1B	52	156	22	38	12	3	1	21	.244	31	39	2	67	0	2	.971
Major League totals (2 years)		87	185	18	46	5	4	3	14	.249	25	51	3	60	0	2	.968

RECORD AS MANAGER

BACKGROUND: Minor league field coordinator, Cincinnati Reds (1992). ... Coach, Montreal Expos (1995-98). ... Coach, Los Angeles Dodgers (1999 and 2000).
HONORS: Named Minor League Manager of the Year by THE SPORTING NEWS (1993).

Year Team (League)	REGULAR SEASON W	L	Pct.	Pos.	POSTSEASON Playoff W	L	Champ. Series W	L	World Series W	L	All-Star Game W	L
1987—Peoria (Midw.)	71	69	.507	2nd (S)	—	—	—	—	—	—	—	—
1988—Peoria (Midw.)	29	40	.420	6th (S)	—	—	—	—	—	—	—	—
—(Second half)	41	30	.577	3rd (S)	—	—	—	—	—	—	—	—
1989—Chattanooga (Sou.)	33	38	.465	4th (W)	—	—	—	—	—	—	—	—
—(Second half)	25	43	.368	5th (W)	—	—	—	—	—	—	—	—
1990—Chattanooga (Sou.)	35	36	.493	4th (W)	—	—	—	—	—	—	—	—
—(Second half)	31	42	.425	4th (W)	—	—	—	—	—	—	—	—
1991—Chattanooga (Sou.)	35	32	.522	2nd (W)	—	—	—	—	—	—	—	—
—(Second half)	38	39	.494	3rd (W)	—	—	—	—	—	—	—	—
1993—Harrisburg (East.)	94	44	.681	1st	6	3	—	—	—	—	—	—
1994—Ottawa (I.L.)	70	72	.493	3rd (E)	—	—	—	—	—	—	—	—
2001—Los Angeles (N.L.)	86	76	.531	3rd (W)	—	—	—	—	—	—	—	—
2002—Los Angeles (N.L.)	92	70	.568	3rd (W)	—	—	—	—	—	—	—	—
Major league totals (2 years)	178	146	.549		—	—	—	—	—	—	—	—

NOTES:
1993—Defeated Albany, three games to one, in playoff; defeated Canton-Akron, three games to two, in championship playoff.

TRAMMELL, ALAN — TIGERS

PERSONAL: Born February 21, 1958, in Garden Grove, Calif. ... 6-0/185. ... Batted right, threw right. ... Full name: Alan Stuart Trammell. ... Name pronounced TRAM-ull.
HIGH SCHOOL: Kearney (San Diego).
TRANSACTIONS/CAREER NOTES: Selected by Detroit Tigers organization in second round of free-agent draft (June 8, 1976). ... On disabled list (July 9-31, 1984; June 29-July 17, 1988; June 4-23, 1989; July 18-August 13, 1991; and May 16, 1992-remainder of season). ... Granted free agency (November 6, 1992). ... Re-signed by Tigers (December 2, 1992). ... On disabled list (April 2-17, 1993). ... Granted free agency

(October 28, 1993). ... Re-signed by Tigers (November 3, 1993). ... Granted free agency (October 25, 1994). ... Re-signed by Tigers (April 8, 1995). ... On disabled list (April 21-May 6, 1995). ... Granted free agency (December 21, 1995). ... Re-signed by Tigers (January 24, 1996). ... On disabled list (July 6-July 25 and July 27-September 1, 1996). ... Announced retirement (September 30, 1996).

RECORDS: Shares major league record for most years by shortstop—20 (Detroit, 1977 through 1996, 2,139 games).

HONORS: Named Southern League Most Valuable Player (1977). ... Won A.L. Gold Glove at shortstop (1980-81 and 1983-84). ... Named A.L. Comeback Player of the Year by THE SPORTING NEWS (1983). ... Named shortstop on THE SPORTING NEWS A.L. All-Star team (1987-88 and 1990). ... Named shortstop on THE SPORTING NEWS A.L. Silver Slugger team (1987-88 and 1990).

STATISTICAL NOTES: Led A.L. with 16 sacrifice hits in 1981 and 15 in 1983. ... Had 20-game hitting streak (August 5-22, 1984). ... Had 21-game hitting streak (May 24-June 16, 1987). ... Led A.L. shortstops with 102 double plays in 1990. ... Career major league grand slams: 5.

					BATTING									FIELDING			
Year Team (League)	Pos.	G	AB	R	H	2B	3B	HR	RBI	Avg.	BB	SO	SB	PO	A	E	Avg.
1976—Bristol (Appl.)	SS	41	140	27	38	2	2	0	7	.271	26	20	8	59	131	12	.941
—Montgomery (Sou.)	SS	21	56	4	10	0	0	0	2	.179	7	12	3	40	64	2	.981
1977—Montgomery (Sou.)	SS	134	454	78	132	9	*19	3	50	.291	56	92	4	188	397	27	.956
—Detroit (A.L.)	SS	19	43	6	8	0	0	0	0	.186	4	12	0	15	34	2	.961
1978—Detroit (A.L.)	SS	139	448	49	120	14	6	2	34	.268	45	56	3	239	421	14	.979
1979—Detroit (A.L.)	SS	142	460	68	127	11	4	6	50	.276	43	55	17	245	388	26	.961
1980—Detroit (A.L.)	SS	146	560	107	168	21	5	9	65	.300	69	63	12	225	412	13	.980
1981—Detroit (A.L.)	SS	105	392	52	101	15	3	2	31	.258	49	31	10	181	347	9	.983
1982—Detroit (A.L.)	SS	157	489	66	126	34	3	9	57	.258	52	47	19	259	459	16	.978
1983—Detroit (A.L.)	SS	142	505	83	161	31	2	14	66	.319	57	64	30	236	367	13	.979
1984—Detroit (A.L.)	SS-DH	139	555	85	174	34	5	14	69	.314	60	63	19	180	314	10	.980
1985—Detroit (A.L.)	SS	149	605	79	156	21	7	13	57	.258	50	71	14	225	400	15	.977
1986—Detroit (A.L.)	SS-DH	151	574	107	159	33	7	21	75	.277	59	57	25	238	445	22	.969
1987—Detroit (A.L.)	SS	151	597	109	205	34	3	28	105	.343	60	47	21	222	421	19	.971
1988—Detroit (A.L.)	SS	128	466	73	145	24	1	15	69	.311	46	46	7	195	355	11	.980
1989—Detroit (A.L.)	SS-DH	121	449	54	109	20	3	5	43	.243	45	45	10	188	396	9	.985
1990—Detroit (A.L.)	SS-DH	146	559	71	170	37	1	14	89	.304	68	55	12	232	409	14	.979
1991—Detroit (A.L.)	SS-DH	101	375	57	93	20	0	9	55	.248	37	39	11	131	296	9	.979
1992—Detroit (A.L.)	SS-DH	29	102	11	28	7	1	1	11	.275	15	4	2	46	80	3	.977
1993—Detroit (A.L.)	S-3-O-D	112	401	72	132	25	3	12	60	.329	38	38	12	113	238	9	.975
1994—Detroit (A.L.)	SS-DH	76	292	38	78	17	1	8	28	.267	16	35	3	117	181	10	.968
1995—Detroit (A.L.)	SS-DH	74	223	28	60	12	0	2	23	.269	27	19	3	86	158	5	.980
1996—Detroit (A.L.)	SS-2B-3B-OF	66	193	16	45	2	0	1	16	.233	10	27	6	75	144	6	.973
Major League totals (20 years)		2293	8288	1231	2365	412	55	185	1003	.285	850	874	236	3448	6265	235	.976

CHAMPIONSHIP SERIES RECORD

					BATTING									FIELDING			
Year Team (League)	Pos.	G	AB	R	H	2B	3B	HR	RBI	Avg.	BB	SO	SB	PO	A	E	Avg.
1984—Detroit (A.L.)	SS	3	11	2	4	0	1	1	3	.364	3	1	0	1	8	0	1.000
1987—Detroit (A.L.)	SS	5	20	3	4	1	0	0	2	.200	1	2	0	6	9	1	.938
Championship series totals (2 years)		8	31	5	8	1	1	1	5	.258	4	3	0	7	17	1	.960

WORLD SERIES RECORD

RECORDS: Shares single-game record for batting in all club's runs—4 (October 13, 1984).

NOTES: Named Most Valuable Player (1984). ... Member of World Series championship team (1984).

					BATTING									FIELDING			
Year Team (League)	Pos.	G	AB	R	H	2B	3B	HR	RBI	Avg.	BB	SO	SB	PO	A	E	Avg.
1984—Detroit (A.L.)	SS	5	20	5	9	1	0	2	6	.450	2	2	1	8	9	1	.944

ALL-STAR GAME RECORD

NOTES: Named to A.L. All-Star team for 1984 game; replaced by Alfredo Griffin due to injury. ... Named to A.L. All-Star team for 1988 game; replaced by Cal Ripken Jr. due to injury.

					BATTING								FIELDING			
Year League	Pos.	AB	R	H	2B	3B	HR	RBI	Avg.	BB	SO	SB	PO	A	E	Avg.
1980—American	SS	0	0	0	0	0	0	0	...	0	0	0	0	0	0	...
1984—American							Selected, did not play—injured.									
1985—American	SS	1	0	0	0	0	0	0	.000	0	0	0	0	0	0	...
1987—American	PH	1	0	0	0	0	0	0	.000	0	0	0	...	...	...	...
1988—American							Selected, did not play—injured.									
1990—American	PH	1	0	0	0	0	0	0	.000	0	0	0	...	...	...	...
All-Star Game totals (4 years)		3	0	0	0	0	0	0	.000	0	0	0	0	0	0	...

RECORD AS MANAGER

BACKGROUND: Assistant Director of Baseball Operations, Detroit Tigers (1997-98). ... Hitting coach, Tigers (1999). ... First base coach, San Diego Padres (2000-02).

WEDGE, ERIC — INDIANS

PERSONAL: Born January 27, 1968, in Fort Wayne, Ind. ... 6-3/215. ... Batted right, threw right. ... Full name: Eric Michael Wedge.

HIGH SCHOOL: Northrop (Fort Wayne, Ind.).

COLLEGE: Wichita State.

TRANSACTIONS/CAREER NOTES: Selected by Boston Red Sox organization in third round of free-agent draft (June 5, 1989). ... On Pawtucket disabled list (May 15-22 and May 24-July 10, 1991; and June 3-10 and June 25-July 28, 1992). ... Selected by Colorado Rockies in second round (48th pick overall) of expansion draft (November 17, 1992). ... On Colorado disabled list (March 27-June 17, 1993); included rehabilitation assignments to Central Valley (May 28-June 3) and Colorado Springs (June 3-16). ... On Colorado disabled list (June 17-July 26, 1993). ... Released by Rockies (March 29, 1994). ... Signed by Red Sox organization (May 2, 1994). ... On Pawtucket disabled list (June 21-28, 1994). ... Granted free agency (October 16, 1995). ... Signed by Detroit Tigers organization (1996). ... Granted free agency (October 15, 1996). ... Signed by Philadelphia Phillies organization (1997). ... Granted free agency (October 15, 1997).

STATISTICAL NOTES: Led Eastern League catchers with eight double plays in 1990.

Year	Team (League)	Pos.	G	AB	R	H	2B	3B	HR	RBI	Avg.	BB	SO	SB	PO	A	E	Avg.
			BATTING												FIELDING			
1989—	Elmira (NY-Penn)	C	41	145	20	34	6	2	7	22	.234	15	21	1	283	30	2	.994
—	New Britain (East.)	C	14	40	3	8	2	0	0	2	.200	5	10	0	83	9	0	1.000
1990—	New Britain (East.)	C	103	339	36	77	13	1	5	47	.227	50	54	1	583	62	9	.986
1991—	Pawtucket (I.L.)	C	53	163	24	38	14	1	5	18	.233	25	26	0	282	36	6	.981
—	New Britain (East.)	C	2	8	0	2	0	0	0	2	.250	0	2	0	6	1	0	1.000
—	Winter Haven (FSL)	C	8	21	2	5	0	0	1	1	.238	3	7	1	17	2	0	1.000
—	Boston (A.L.)	PH-DH	1	1	0	1	0	0	0	0	1.000	0	0	0	...	...	...	...
1992—	Pawtucket (I.L.)	C	65	211	28	63	9	0	11	40	.299	32	40	0	209	20	3	.987
—	Boston (A.L.)	DH-C	27	68	11	17	2	0	5	11	.250	13	18	0	19	2	0	1.000
1993—	Cen. Valley (Calif.)■	C	6	23	6	7	0	0	3	11	.304	2	6	0	30	0	0	1.000
—	Colo. Springs (PCL)	C-1B-DH	38	90	17	24	6	0	3	13	.267	16	22	0	134	22	3	.981
—	Colorado (N.L.)	C	9	11	2	2	0	0	0	1	.182	0	4	0	6	1	0	1.000
1994—	Pawtucket (I.L.)■	DH-C-1B	77	255	44	73	14	0	19	59	.286	51	48	0	47	4	1	.981
—	Boston (A.L.)	DH	2	6	0	0	0	0	0	0	.000	1	3	0	...	...	...	...
1995—	Pawtucket (I.L.)	1B-DH-C	108	376	52	88	17	1	20	68	.234	63	96	1	596	46	3	.995
1996—	Toledo (I.L.)	DH-C-1B	96	332	61	78	25	0	15	57	.235	43	81	2	209	15	2	.991
1997—	Scranton/W.B. (I.L.)	C-DH-1B	47	129	25	33	8	1	7	36	.256	22	40	0	137	9	4	.973
American League totals (3 years)			30	75	11	18	2	0	5	11	.240	14	21	0	19	2	0	1.000
National League totals (1 year)			9	11	2	2	0	0	0	1	.182	0	4	0	6	1	0	1.000
Major League totals (4 years)			39	86	13	20	2	0	5	12	.233	14	25	0	25	3	0	1.000

RECORD AS MANAGER

HONORS: Named Carolina League Manager of the Year (1999). ... Named International League Manager of the Year (2001).

		REGULAR SEASON				POSTSEASON							
						Playoff		Champ. Series		World Series		All-Star Game	
Year	Team (League)	W	L	Pct.	Pos.	W	L	W	L	W	L	W	L
1998—	Columbus (SAL)	28	42	.400	4th (S)	—	—	—	—	—	—	—	—
—	(Second half)	31	39	.443	3rd (S)	—	—	—	—	—	—	—	—
1999—	Kinston (Caro.)	37	32	.536	1st (S)	—	—	—	—	—	—	—	—
—	(Second half)	42	26	.618	2nd (S)	1	2	—	—	—	—	—	—
2000—	Akron (East.)	75	68	.524	3rd (S)	—	—	—	—	—	—	—	—
2001—	Buffalo (I.L.)	91	51	.641	1st (N)	2	3	—	—	—	—	—	—
2002—	Buffalo (I.L.)	87	57	.604	2nd (N)	3	3	—	—	—	—	—	—

NOTES:

1999—Lost to Myrtle Beach in playoffs.
2001—Lost to Scranton/Wilkes-Barre in playoffs.
2002—Defeated Scranton/Wilkes-Barre, three games to none, in playoffs; lost to Durham, three games to none, in league championship.

WILLIAMS, JIMY — ASTROS

PERSONAL: Born October 4, 1943, in Santa Maria, Calif. ... 5-11/170. ... Batted right, threw right. ... Full name: James Francis Williams.

COLLEGE: Fresno State College (bachelor of science degree in agribusiness).

TRANSACTIONS/CAREER NOTES: Selected by St. Louis Cardinals organization from Toronto, Boston Red Sox organization (November 29, 1965). ... In military service (July 24, 1966-remainder of season). ... Traded by Cardinals with C Pat Corrales to Cincinnati Reds for C John Edwards (February 8, 1968). ... Selected by Montreal Expos in expansion draft (October 14, 1968). ... On disabled list (May 13-30 and June 24-September 2, 1969). ... On suspended list (June 7-16, 1971). ... Sold to New York Mets organization (June 16, 1971). ... On temporary inactive list (August 12-16, 1971). ... On disabled list (May 15-July 17 and July 29-August 20, 1975).

Year	Team (League)	Pos.	G	AB	R	H	2B	3B	HR	RBI	Avg.	BB	SO	SB	PO	A	E	Avg.
			BATTING												FIELDING			
1965—	Waterloo (Midw.)	SS	115	435	64	125	19	3	2	31	.287	41	74	10	173	*312	26	*.949
1966—	St. Louis (N.L.)	SS-2B	13	11	1	3	0	0	0	1	.273	1	5	0	2	5	0	1.000
1967—	Arkansas (Texas)	SS	28	101	8	21	1	1	0	8	.208	9	14	0	49	80	2	.985
—	Tulsa (PCL)	SS	61	164	18	37	2	0	1	21	.226	18	33	4	87	156	26	.903
—	St. Louis (N.L.)	SS	1	2	0	0	0	0	0	0	.000	0	1	0	6	1	0	1.000
1968—	Indianapolis (PCL)■	SS-2B	120	403	38	91	19	5	2	34	.226	20	59	5	198	323	27	.951
1969—	Vancouver (PCL)■	3B-OF-SS	35	66	7	17	1	1	0	9	.258	4	8	1	17	23	2	.952
1970—	Buff.-Winnipeg (I.L.)	SS-2B-3B	109	361	49	83	15	0	3	18	.230	34	48	5	178	244	30	.934
1971—	Winn.-Tide. (I.L.)■	SS-3B-2B	105	327	40	84	7	4	5	31	.257	38	46	7	120	219	22	.939
1972—									Did not play.									
1973—									Did not play.									
1974—									Did not play.									
1975—	El Paso (Texas)	DH	6	17	3	2	0	0	0	2	.118	2	2	0	...	...	...	...
Major league totals (2 years)			14	13	1	3	0	0	0	1	.231	1	6	0	8	6	0	1.000

RECORD AS MANAGER

BACKGROUND: Coach, Toronto Blue Jays (1980-85). ... Minor league instructor, Atlanta Braves (October 4, 1989-June 25, 1990). ... Coach, Braves (1990-96).

HONORS: Named Pacific Coast League Manager of the Year (1976 and 1979). ... Named A.L. Manager of the Year by THE SPORTING NEWS (1999). ... Named A.L. Manager of the Year by Baseball Writers' Association of America (1999).

		REGULAR SEASON				POSTSEASON							
						Playoff		Champ. Series		World Series		All-Star Game	
Year	Team (League)	W	L	Pct.	Pos.	W	L	W	L	W	L	W	L
1974—	Quad Cities (Midwest)	33	26	.559	1st (S)	—	—	—	—	—	—	—	—
—	(Second half)	32	32	.500	3rd (S)	1	2	—	—	—	—	—	—
1975—	El Paso (Texas)	62	71	.466	3rd (W)	—	—	—	—	—	—	—	—
1976—	Salt Lake City (Pacific Coast)	90	54	.625	1st (E)	2	3	—	—	—	—	—	—
1977—	Salt Lake City (Pacific Coast)	74	65	.532	2nd (E)	—	—	—	—	—	—	—	—
1978—	Springfield (American Association)	70	66	.515	3rd (E)	—	—	—	—	—	—	—	—

Year	Team (League)	W	L	Pct.	Pos.	Playoff W	Playoff L	Champ. Series W	Champ. Series L	World Series W	World Series L	All-Star Game W	All-Star Game L
1979—	Salt Lake City (Pacific Coast)	34	40	.459	4th (S)	—	—	—	—	—	—	—	—
	—(Second half)	46	28	.622	1st (S)	5	0	—	—	—	—	—	—
1986—	Toronto (A.L.)	86	76	.531	4th (E)	—	—	—	—	—	—	—	—
1987—	Toronto (A.L.)	96	66	.593	2nd (E)	—	—	—	—	—	—	—	—
1988—	Toronto (A.L.)	87	75	.537	T3rd (E)	—	—	—	—	—	—	—	—
1989—	Toronto (A.L.)	12	24	.333		—	—	—	—	—	—	—	—
1997—	Boston (A.L.)	78	84	.481	4th (E)	—	—	—	—	—	—	—	—
1998—	Boston (A.L.)	92	70	.568	2nd (E)	1	3	—	—	—	—	—	—
1999—	Boston (A.L.)	94	68	.580	2nd (E)	3	2	1	4	—	—	—	—
2000—	Boston (A.L.)	85	77	.525	2nd (E)	—	—	—	—	—	—	—	—
2001—	Boston (A.L.)	65	53	.551		—	—	—	—	—	—	—	—
2002—	Houston (N.L.)	84	78	.519	2nd (C)	—	—	—	—	—	—	—	—
American League totals (5 years)		695	593	.540		4	5	1	4	—	—	—	—
National League totals (1 year)		84	78	.519		—	—	—	—	—	—	—	—
Major league totals (6 years)		779	671	.537		4	5	1	4				

NOTES:

1974—Lost to Danville in playoffs.
1976—Lost to Hawaii in championship playoff.
1979—Defeated Albuquerque, two games to none, in playoff; defeated Hawaii, three games to none, in championship playoff.
1989—Replaced as Toronto manager by Cito Gaston, with club tied for sixth place (May 15).
1998—Lost to Cleveland in A.L. divisional playoff.
1999—Defeated Cleveland in A.L. divisional playoff; lost to New York Yankees in A.L. Championship Series.
2001—Replaced as manager by Joe Kerrigan with club in second place (August 16).

YOST, NED — BREWERS

PERSONAL: Born August 19, 1954, in Eureka, Calif. ... 6-1/185. ... Batted right, threw right. ... Full name: Edgar Frederick Yost.
JUNIOR COLLEGE: Chabot Junior College.
TRANSACTIONS/CAREER NOTES: Signed as non-drafted free agent by New York Mets organization (June 11, 1974). ... Drafted by Milwaukee Brewers (December 5, 1977). ... On disabled list (July 10-28, 1978). ... On disabled list (July 11-August 15, 1983). ... Traded by Brewers with P Dan Scarpetta to Texas Rangers for C Jim Sundberg (December 8, 1983). ... Released by Rangers (April 1, 1985). ... Signed by Montreal Expos (April 28, 1985). ... Released by Expos (December 19, 1985).

Year	Team (League)	Pos.	G	AB	R	H	2B	3B	HR	RBI	Avg.	BB	SO	SB	PO	A	E	Avg.
			BATTING												FIELDING			
1974—	Batavia (NY-Penn)	C	44	123	14	31	2	2	2	11	.252	13	28	4	199	21	*11	.952
1975—	Wausau (Midw.)	C	79	265	26	51	7	0	6	27	.192	34	69	0	450	42	•19	.963
1976—	Jackson (Texas)	C	83	266	25	53	5	0	3	25	.199	29	56	0	390	42	7	.984
1977—	Jackson (Texas)	C	30	94	7	29	9	0	1	8	.309	10	14	0	145	21	4	.976
	—Tidewater (I.L.)	C	60	165	27	48	8	1	12	31	.291	14	32	0	171	29	3	.985
1978—	Spokane (PCL)	C	89	267	38	70	16	1	7	42	.295	20	45	2	367	49	15	.965
1979—	Vancouver (PCL)	C	130	419	43	110	12	2	3	53	.263	18	75	8	604	64	10	.985
1980—	Vancouver (PCL)	C-1B	80	259	32	80	20	4	2	41	.309	15	40	12	312	34	8	.977
	—Milwaukee (A.L.)	C	15	31	0	5	0	0	0	0	.161	0	6	0	41	5	0	1.000
1981—	Milwaukee (A.L.)	C	18	27	4	6	0	0	3	3	.222	3	6	0	37	6	2	.956
1982—	Milwaukee (A.L.)	C	40	98	13	27	6	3	1	8	.276	7	20	3	121	6	3	.977
1983—	Milwaukee (A.L.)	C	61	196	21	44	5	1	6	28	.224	5	36	1	252	16	8	.971
1984—	Texas (A.L.)■	C	80	242	15	44	4	0	6	25	.182	6	47	1	368	20	2	.995
1985—	Indianapolis (A.A.)■	C-1B	95	267	17	70	15	0	2	24	.262	11	46	1	375	48	12	.972
	—Montreal (N.L.)	C	5	11	1	2	0	0	0	0	.182	0	2	0	24	1	1	.962
1986—	Greenville (Sou.)	C	80	254	35	63	13	0	7	30	.248	19	29	3	502	54	4	*.993
	—Richmond (I.L.)	C	8	17	0	5	0	0	0	0	.294	0	4	0	26	2	0	1.000
1987—	Greenville (Sou.)	C	40	115	6	19	1	0	1	1	.165	8	24	0	197	15	4	.981
	—Richmond (I.L.)	C	9	23	3	7	1	0	1	8	.304	0	6	1	31	4	4	.897
American League totals (5 years)			214	594	53	126	15	4	16	64	.212	21	115	5	819	53	15	.983
National League totals (1 year)			5	11	1	2	0	0	0	0	.182	0	2	0	24	1	1	.962
Major League totals (6 years)			219	605	54	128	15	4	16	64	.212	21	117	5	843	54	16	.982

WORLD SERIES RECORD

Year	Team (League)	Pos.	G	AB	R	H	2B	3B	HR	RBI	Avg.	BB	SO	SB	PO	A	E	Avg.
			BATTING												FIELDING			
1982—	Milwaukee (A.L.)	C	1	0	0	0	0	0	0	0	...	1	0	0	1	0	0	1.000

RECORD AS MANAGER

BACKGROUND: Bullpen coach, Atlanta Braves (1991-98). ... Third base coach, Braves (1999-2002).

Year	Team (League)	W	L	Pct.	Pos.	Playoff W	Playoff L	Champ. Series W	Champ. Series L	World Series W	World Series L	All-Star Game W	All-Star Game L
1988—	Sumter (SAL)	29	40	.420	6th (S)	—	—	—	—	—	—	—	—
	—(Second half)	35	33	.515	4th (S)	—	—	—	—	—	—	—	—
1989—	Sumter (SAL)	30	40	.429	5th (S)	—	—	—	—	—	—	—	—
	—(Second half)	30	41	.423	6th (S)	—	—	—	—	—	—	—	—
1990—	Sumter (SAL)	38	34	.528	4th (S)	—	—	—	—	—	—	—	—
	—(Second half)	35	35	.500	4th (S)	—	—	—	—	—	—	—	—

MANAGERIAL TENDENCIES

OFFENSE

		STOLEN BASES										SACRIFICE BUNTS				HIT & RUN	
				Pitchout	2nd	3rd	Home	Double	Out Percentage				Suc.	Fav.			Suc.
	G	Att.	SB%	Rn Mvg	SB-CS	SB-CS	SB-CS	Steals	0	1	2	Att.	%	Inn.	Sqz.	Att.	%
A.L. Managers																	
Gardenhire, Ron, Min.	161	141	56.0	3	66-50	12-12	1-0	5	14.9	41.8	43.3	49	85.7	3	6	91	24.2
Garner, Phil, Det.	6	4	75.0	0	2-1	1-0	0-0	0	25.0	50.0	25.0	2	100.0	9	0	1	100.0
Hargrove, Mike, Bal.	162	158	69.6	3	93-43	17-3	0-2	1	19.0	30.4	50.6	56	73.2	1	5	90	33.3
Howe, Art, Oak.	162	66	69.7	1	41-18	5-2	0-0	3	18.2	45.5	36.4	29	86.2	5	1	34	29.4
Little, Grady, Bos.	162	108	74.1	2	73-23	7-4	0-1	1	25.0	27.8	47.2	35	74.3	3	1	51	31.4
Manuel, Charlie, Cle.	86	57	50.9	2	27-24	2-3	0-1	0	15.8	33.3	50.9	21	81.0	6	0	32	37.5
Manuel, Jerry, Chi.	162	106	70.8	3	67-27	8-4	0-0	3	26.4	38.7	34.9	76	82.9	1	2	53	32.1
Martinez, Buck, Tor.	53	35	82.9	1	27-5	2-1	0-0	1	20.0	34.3	45.7	13	69.2	4	0	19	10.5
McRae, Hal, T.B.	161	147	69.4	5	93-42	9-2	0-1	2	19.0	27.9	53.1	64	78.1	7	4	76	34.2
Mizerock, John, K.C.	13	13	92.3	1	11-1	1-0	0-0	0	38.5	15.4	46.2	3	100.0	5	0	10	20.0
Muser, Tony, K.C.	23	32	75.0	0	19-7	5-1	0-0	0	28.1	34.4	37.5	11	100.0	7	0	14	50.0
Narron, Jerry, Tex.	162	96	64.6	2	62-30	0-4	0-0	0	20.8	34.4	44.8	59	83.1	8	1	66	30.3
Pena, Tony, K.C.	126	160	65.0	9	89-50	14-6	1-0	4	16.3	36.9	46.9	58	75.9	1	2	92	38.0
Piniella, Lou, Sea.	162	195	70.3	4	116-47	21-9	0-2	10	19.0	41.5	39.5	62	72.6	7	3	73	43.8
Pujols, Luis, Det.	155	105	59.0	3	58-39	4-3	0-1	1	21.9	35.2	42.9	49	69.4	6	1	50	46.0
Scioscia, Mike, Ana.	162	168	69.6	3	102-42	15-8	0-1	4	17.3	35.7	47.0	68	85.3	8	6	128	44.5
Skinner, Joel, Cle.	76	32	71.9	0	22-9	1-0	0-0	0	21.9	37.5	40.6	32	90.6	3	1	13	61.5
Torre, Joe, N.Y.	161	138	72.5	4	82-31	18-7	0-0	2	19.6	37.7	42.8	35	77.1	9	0	60	31.7
Tosca, Carlos, Tor.	109	54	77.8	1	39-7	3-4	0-1	1	22.2	40.7	37.0	15	80.0	4	2	55	43.6
N.L. Managers																	
Baker, Dusty, S.F.	162	95	77.9	4	70-20	4-1	0-0	1	22.1	37.9	40.0	92	82.6	3	0	53	35.8
Baylor, Don, Chi.	83	54	79.6	0	41-10	2-1	0-0	1	24.1	25.9	50.0	63	90.5	3	3	36	38.9
Bell, Buddy, Col.	22	17	64.7	1	10-5	1-1	0-0	0	29.4	23.5	47.1	12	100.0	3	1	10	30.0
Bochy, Bruce, S.D.	162	115	61.7	3	59-40	11-3	1-1	6	16.5	31.3	52.2	63	79.4	3	5	90	40.0
Boone, Bob, Cin.	162	168	69.0	4	100-43	16-5	0-4	2	20.2	32.1	47.6	125	80.0	3	7	68	32.4
Bowa, Larry, Phi.	161	147	70.7	3	91-37	13-6	0-0	4	17.7	36.7	45.6	96	75.0	2	6	55	27.3
Brenly, Bob, Ari.	162	138	66.7	2	85-41	7-1	0-4	2	23.2	31.9	44.9	87	81.6	2	5	58	43.1
Cox, Bobby, Atl.	161	115	66.1	4	70-33	6-4	0-2	1	21.7	29.6	48.7	89	79.8	5	6	61	44.3
Hurdle, Clint, Col.	140	139	66.2	7	82-40	10-5	0-2	3	23.7	29.5	46.8	51	88.2	7	2	94	34.0
Kimm, Bruce, Chi.	78	29	65.5	0	18-8	1-1	0-1	0	13.8	34.5	51.7	41	78.0	2	2	26	34.6
La Russa, Tony, St.L.	162	128	67.2	4	75-29	9-10	2-3	3	30.5	30.5	39.1	108	85.2	3	13	124	43.5
Lachemann, Rene, Chi.	1	1	100.0	0	1-0	0-0	0-0	0	0.0	0.0	100.0	0	...	0	0	0	...
Lopes, Davey, Mil.	15	15	60.0	1	8-6	1-0	0-0	0	13.3	46.7	40.0	9	88.9	3	0	7	28.6
McClendon, Lloyd, Pit.	161	135	63.7	4	71-41	14-8	1-0	8	15.6	40.0	44.4	98	73.5	7	6	104	34.6
Robinson, Frank, Mon.	162	182	64.8	6	102-49	16-14	0-1	2	15.4	36.3	48.4	135	83.7	3	10	100	30.0
Royster, Jerry, Mil.	147	129	65.9	7	77-36	8-7	0-1	2	24.0	35.7	40.3	96	75.0	3	2	59	42.4
Torborg, Jeff, Fla.	162	250	70.8	7	152-62	24-11	1-0	8	22.4	40.4	37.2	82	74.4	5	10	105	39.0
Tracy, Jim, L.A.	162	133	72.2	7	87-32	9-4	0-1	4	22.6	39.8	37.6	84	83.3	2	10	70	34.3
Valentine, Bobby, N.Y.	161	129	67.4	2	78-34	8-5	1-3	1	18.6	37.2	44.2	102	80.4	2	16	92	37.0
Williams, Jimy, Hou.	162	98	72.4	3	63-22	8-3	0-2	2	19.4	31.6	49.0	89	78.7	3	4	60	25.0

DEFENSE

		PITCHOUT			INTENTIONAL BB				DEFENSIVE SUBS				
			Runners		Non-PO		Pct. of	Favorite		Favorite			
	G	Total	Moving	CS%	CS%	IBB	Situations	Score Diff.	Total	Inning	Pos. 1	Pos. 2	Pos. 3
AL Managers													
Gardenhire, Ron, Min	161	14	3	66.7	30.9	19	3.3	-1	41	7	1b-9	rf-9	c-6
Garner, Phil, Det	6	0	0	...	50.0	1	4.0	0	0	0	ph-0	ph-0	ph-0
Hargrove, Mike, Bal	162	41	7	71.4	27.9	28	4.5	-1	19	9	rf-6	cf-5	ss-3
Howe, Art, Oak	162	14	4	75.0	39.1	32	5.4	-1	43	9	lf-17	1b-10	c-8
Little, Grady, Bos	162	51	9	55.6	28.3	24	3.8	0	14	8	2b-7	rf-3	1b-2
Manuel, Charlie, Cle	86	4	0	...	32.4	16	4.7	-2	18	8	rf-10	lf-5	2b-1
Manuel, Jerry, CWS	162	19	6	50.0	26.7	24	4.3	-1	34	8	lf-20	ss-5	cf-5
Martinez, Buck, Tor	53	12	3	33.3	16.7	16	6.3	0	1	9	c-1	ph-0	ph-0
McRae, Hal, TB	161	24	2	0.0	37.1	18	2.6	0	6	9	lf-3	rf-2	3b-1
Mizerock, John, KC	13	0	0	...	60.0	0	0.0	0	1	9	2b-1	ph-0	ph-0
Muser, Tony, KC	23	0	0	...	41.2	2	2.3	-1	2	7	2b-2	ph-0	ph-0
Narron, Jerry, Tex	162	5	0	...	27.5	28	3.8	-2	24	9	cf-10	lf-4	rf-4
Pena, Tony, KC	126	5	1	0.0	23.5	33	6.2	-2	10	8	2b-4	3b-2	rf-2
Piniella, Lou, Sea	162	27	4	75.0	33.0	27	4.9	-1	32	9	lf-17	3b-7	c-3
Pujols, Luis, Det	155	2	1	100.0	29.9	27	3.7	0	11	8	3b-5	lf-3	1b-1

	G	Pitchout Total	Pitchout Runners Moving	Pitchout CS%	Non-PO CS%	Intentional BB IBB	Intentional BB Pct. of Situations	Intentional BB Favorite Score Diff.	Defensive Subs Total	Defensive Subs Favorite Inning	Pos. 1	Pos. 2	Pos. 3
Scioscia, Mike, Ana	162	33	8	75.0	37.2	17	3.1	-1	16	8	cf-5	1b-4	rf-4
Skinner, Joel, Cle	76	0	0	...	31.3	9	2.9	0	10	7	lf-4	cf-3	3b-2
Torre, Joe, NYY	161	19	2	100.0	28.7	33	5.1	0	27	9	rf-8	lf-7	1b-6
Tosca, Carlos, Tor	109	24	5	40.0	35.0	24	5.4	-1	16	9	c-4	cf-4	2b-3
NL Managers													
Baker, Dusty, SF	162	40	5	60.0	28.0	34	6.0	0	16	8	1b-8	cf-4	lf-2
Baylor, Don, ChC	83	15	7	28.6	38.1	26	7.7	-1	14	8	c-4	lf-4	ss-3
Bell, Buddy, Col	22	5	0	...	20.0	6	6.7	-2	2	4	3b-1	lf-1	ph-0
Bochy, Bruce, SD	162	17	0	...	34.5	45	7.2	0	23	9	rf-10	c-3	2b-3
Boone, Bob, Cin	162	24	3	100.0	36.8	50	8.1	-2	11	9	ss-4	lf-3	c-1
Bowa, Larry, Phi	161	16	2	100.0	30.2	40	6.3	-2	16	8	cf-8	1b-4	2b-2
Brenly, Bob, Ari	162	19	1	0.0	36.1	21	3.8	0	22	8	1b-13	cf-4	2b-2
Cox, Bobby, Atl	161	52	8	37.5	36.4	43	7.2	0	15	8	c-5	1b-3	3b-2
Hurdle, Clint, Col	140	13	1	0.0	21.3	32	6.0	-1	23	8	lf-8	3b-4	cf-4
Kimm, Bruce, ChC	78	6	1	100.0	25.7	19	6.1	1	10	8	3b-4	1b-3	c-1
La Russa, Tony, StL	162	13	4	0.0	29.3	29	5.2	-1	15	6	lf-4	cf-4	rf-3
Lachemann, Rene, ChC	1	0	0	...	...	0	0.0	0	0	0	ph-0	ph-0	ph-0
Lopes, Davey, Mil	15	2	0	...	38.5	6	12.8	-1	0	0	ph-0	ph-0	ph-0
McClendon, Lloyd, Pit	161	70	6	50.0	31.1	61	10.1	-1	25	8	3b-12	1b-5	cf-4
Robinson, Frank, Mon	162	25	3	66.7	33.3	61	8.6	-1	29	8	3b-11	1b-6	cf-5
Royster, Jerry, Mil	147	23	0	...	30.3	55	9.5	-2	14	8	lf-4	rf-4	c-3
Torborg, Jeff, Fla	162	23	4	50.0	39.3	33	4.9	0	13	7	rf-4	ss-3	lf-2
Tracy, Jim, LA	162	17	5	40.0	32.3	30	4.6	1	18	9	ss-5	lf-4	2b-3
Valentine, Bobby, NYM	161	43	5	60.0	25.1	40	6.4	-1	14	9	1b-3	ss-3	c-2
Williams, Jimy, Hou	162	50	6	66.7	23.9	53	8.5	-2	23	8	cf-8	lf-5	rf-5

LINEUPS

	G	Starting Lineup: Lineups Used	Starting Lineup: %LHB vs. RHSP	Starting Lineup: %RHB vs. LHSP	Substitutions: #PH	Substitutions: Percent PH Platoon	Substitutions: PH BA	Substitutions: PH HR	Substitutions: #PR	Substitutions: PR SB-CS
AL Managers										
Gardenhire, Ron, Min	161	111	69.3	68.2	121	81.0	.259	3	30	1-1
Garner, Phil, Det	6	3	60.0	77.8	1	100.0	.000	0	1	0-0
Hargrove, Mike, Bal	162	125	36.9	91.7	105	85.7	.167	0	21	2-0
Howe, Art, Oak	162	105	55.6	57.8	126	71.4	.235	5	60	3-0
Little, Grady, Bos	162	120	54.2	76.9	113	84.1	.232	3	41	2-1
Manuel, Charlie, Cle	86	68	55.6	75.8	49	77.6	.179	0	10	0-0
Manuel, Jerry, CWS	162	104	41.4	93.8	77	77.9	.167	2	10	1-0
Martinez, Buck, Tor	53	40	50.3	82.4	27	66.7	.292	2	3	0-0
McRae, Hal, TB	161	126	50.5	66.7	51	54.9	.279	2	13	1-0
Mizerock, John, KC	13	12	42.4	100.0	11	72.7	.000	0	3	1-0
Muser, Tony, KC	23	14	56.8	93.3	20	80.0	.053	0	6	2-0
Narron, Jerry, Tex	162	128	39.7	81.6	131	71.0	.193	0	50	3-1
Pena, Tony, KC	126	102	60.5	82.8	79	86.1	.261	2	23	1-0
Piniella, Lou, Sea	162	128	57.6	80.5	84	89.3	.208	1	99	10-3
Pujols, Luis, Det	155	126	54.5	67.7	46	71.7	.211	0	32	2-2
Scioscia, Mike, Ana	162	101	59.7	74.4	141	76.6	.288	2	46	5-2
Skinner, Joel, Cle	76	64	66.5	75.8	51	80.4	.256	0	19	0-0
Torre, Joe, NYY	161	107	56.9	80.6	80	72.5	.145	1	52	3-2
Tosca, Carlos, Tor	109	91	39.7	82.6	56	58.9	.157	2	20	2-0
NL Managers										
Baker, Dusty, SF	162	118	30.4	77.5	203	72.9	.196	1	29	1-0
Baylor, Don, ChC	83	71	55.2	82.0	111	82.9	.187	1	13	0-0
Bell, Buddy, Col	22	15	47.2	68.5	41	58.5	.189	0	1	0-0
Bochy, Bruce, SD	162	123	57.6	75.5	239	69.0	.190	6	29	3-3
Boone, Bob, Cin	162	130	42.6	69.6	292	62.7	.229	4	35	3-1
Bowa, Larry, Phi	161	109	53.2	73.1	259	75.3	.220	5	15	2-1
Brenly, Bob, Ari	162	141	61.7	62.7	300	79.3	.224	6	28	1-0
Cox, Bobby, Atl	161	105	39.4	96.6	260	71.5	.212	4	30	1-1
Hurdle, Clint, Col	140	100	44.3	71.6	245	64.9	.276	5	19	1-0
Kimm, Bruce, ChC	78	51	51.5	80.2	134	64.9	.252	3	19	0-1
La Russa, Tony, StL	162	116	43.1	70.6	300	58.0	.258	7	22	5-1
Lachemann, Rene, ChC	1	1	66.7	...	1	0.0	.000	0	0	0-0
Lopes, Davey, Mil	15	14	41.4	88.9	28	96.4	.154	0	3	1-1
McClendon, Lloyd, Pit	161	120	33.3	84.1	242	63.2	.199	5	34	1-2
Robinson, Frank, Mon	162	121	46.9	88.6	238	69.7	.197	9	37	3-2
Royster, Jerry, Mil	147	106	39.3	89.7	256	75.4	.268	8	39	2-1
Torborg, Jeff, Fla	162	116	27.8	87.0	253	71.5	.207	1	28	1-2
Tracy, Jim, LA	162	102	42.5	83.5	281	73.7	.280	4	34	1-1
Valentine, Bobby, NYM	161	122	52.7	82.6	309	62.8	.247	6	43	3-5
Williams, Jimy, Hou	162	109	42.9	97.3	250	88.4	.228	3	34	2-1

PITCHING

	STARTERS						RELIEVERS					
	G	Slow Hooks	Quick Hooks	> 120 Pitches	> 140 Pitches	3 Days Rest	Relief App	Mid-Inning Change	Save > 1 IP	1st Batter Platoon Pct	1-Batter App	3 Pit. (<<=2runs)
AL Managers												
Gardenhire, Ron, Min	161	12	27	4	0	2	435	148	1	51.0	16	37
Garner, Phil, Det	6	1	0	2	0	0	15	11	0	60.0	1	1
Hargrove, Mike, Bal	162	8	17	7	0	0	407	170	6	62.7	37	22
Howe, Art, Oak	162	7	12	2	0	0	408	191	8	66.2	46	44
Little, Grady, Bos	162	12	16	2	0	1	338	104	11	59.2	14	30
Manuel, Charlie, Cle	86	4	11	3	0	0	222	92	0	66.2	23	13
Manuel, Jerry, CWS	162	20	20	2	0	0	423	198	10	65.5	43	26
Martinez, Buck, Tor	53	6	7	1	0	0	158	86	4	64.6	16	7
McRae, Hal, TB	161	28	13	10	0	0	306	97	7	57.5	12	12
Mizerock, John, KC	13	1	5	0	0	0	29	3	0	51.7	0	3
Muser, Tony, KC	23	2	3	0	0	0	53	23	2	52.8	4	3
Narron, Jerry, Tex	162	11	25	8	0	1	487	238	5	62.3	49	25
Pena, Tony, KC	126	13	21	7	0	0	339	133	1	59.6	14	13
Piniella, Lou, Sea	162	11	22	8	0	0	343	141	7	61.2	8	29
Pujols, Luis, Det	155	19	10	12	0	0	357	161	8	57.1	29	16
Scioscia, Mike, Ana	162	10	10	5	0	1	400	165	8	67.8	43	33
Skinner, Joel, Cle	76	5	11	1	0	1	199	67	1	62.8	6	6
Torre, Joe, NYY	161	15	15	8	0	2	334	144	13	62.0	24	33
Tosca, Carlos, Tor	109	12	17	1	0	0	303	119	2	62.0	28	23
NL Managers												
Baker, Dusty, SF	162	9	22	19	0	0	418	158	8	66.5	41	37
Baylor, Don, ChC	83	4	9	3	0	0	198	79	5	61.1	15	9
Bell, Buddy, Col	22	2	3	1	0	0	69	24	0	62.3	4	2
Bochy, Bruce, SD	162	14	17	3	0	0	459	208	4	69.3	49	30
Boone, Bob, Cin	162	12	32	3	0	0	462	156	8	65.4	35	29
Bowa, Larry, Phi	161	5	17	8	0	1	450	142	2	63.1	39	27
Brenly, Bob, Ari	162	12	14	14	1	1	422	148	11	67.1	49	28
Cox, Bobby, Atl	161	6	32	5	0	6	469	107	9	53.5	17	54
Hurdle, Clint, Col	140	18	14	3	0	0	437	118	3	57.2	28	23
Kimm, Bruce, ChC	78	7	13	5	0	0	190	48	1	60.5	6	11
La Russa, Tony, StL	162	9	33	5	0	0	472	163	6	63.8	43	46
Lachemann, Rene, ChC	1	0	0	0	0	0	2	2	0	0.0	1	0
Lopes, Davey, Mil	15	1	3	0	0	0	45	17	1	68.9	7	1
McClendon, Lloyd, Pit	161	13	38	0	0	1	459	153	2	67.6	37	40
Robinson, Frank, Mon	162	7	25	9	0	0	437	191	11	61.3	40	28
Royster, Jerry, Mil	147	20	15	6	0	0	401	112	7	56.0	23	21
Torborg, Jeff, Fla	162	15	32	13	0	0	461	125	7	58.6	34	30
Tracy, Jim, LA	162	6	19	3	0	1	423	134	9	61.7	42	37
Valentine, Bobby, NYM	161	13	20	8	0	0	451	139	2	60.8	38	33
Williams, Jimy, Hou	162	4	32	2	0	2	480	164	6	59.8	33	32

2002 Manager Tendencies

One of the things about baseball which appeals to many of us is the game's endless opportunity for analysis. . . and few things are analyzed more than managerial decisions. Major league skippers may not have batting averages and slugging percentages to point to at the end of the season, but when it comes time to judge their performance and production, there's no reason we can't take a look at their statistics.

Which manager posted the best stolen-base success rate?

Which skippers were constantly tinkering with their lineups?

Which managers wore out a path to the pitching mound?

It's questions like these that get our second-guessing juices going, and it's questions like these that inspired the following pages, which look at managerial tendencies in a number of situations. Once again, the skippers are compared based on offense, defense, lineups and pitching use. We don't rank the managers; there is plenty of room for argument on whether certain moves are good or bad. We are simply providing fodder for the discussion.

Offensively, managers have control over bunting, stealing and the timing of hit-and-runs. This section looks at the quantity, timing and success of these moves.

Defensively, this section looks at the success of pitchouts, the frequency of intentional walks, and the pattern of defensive substitutions.

Most managers spend large amounts of their time devising lineups. Here you'll find the number of lineups used, as well as the platoon percentage. The use of pinch-hitters and pinch-runners also is explored.

Finally, how does the manager use pitchers? For starters, this section shows slow and quick hooks, along with the number of times a starter was allowed to throw more than 120 and 140 pitches. For relievers, we look at the number of relief appearances, mid-inning changes and how often a pitcher gets a save going more than one inning (a rare occurrence these days).

For the purposes of this section, it is assumed that a coach filling in for his manager will make his decisions based on what the manager would do in a given situation.

The categories include:

Stolen Base Success Percentage: Stolen bases divided by attempts.

Pitchout Runners Moving: The number of times the opposition is running when a manager calls a pitchout.

Double Steals: The number of double steals attempted in 2002.

Out Percentage: The proportion of stolen bases with that number of outs.

Sacrifice Bunt Attempts: A bunt is considered a sac attempt if no runner is on third, there are no outs, or the pitcher attempts a bunt.

Sacrifice Bunt Success %: A bunt that results in a sacrifice or a hit, divided by the number of attempts.

Favorite Inning: The most common inning in which an event occurred.

Hit-and-Run Success: The hit-and-run results in baserunner advancement with no double play.

Intentional Walk Situation: Runners on base, first base open, and anyone but the pitcher up. The teams must be within two runs of each other, or the tying run must be on base, at bat or on deck.

Defensive Substitutions: Straight defensive substitutions, with the team leading by four runs or less.

Number of Lineups: Based on batting order, 1-8 for National Leaguers, 1-9 for American Leaguers.

Percent LHB vs. RHSP and RHB vs. LHSP: A measure of platooning. A batter is considered to always have the platoon advantage if he is a switch-hitter.

Percent PH platoon: Frequency the manager gets his pinch-hitter the platoon advantage. Switch-hitters always have the advantage.

Score Diff: The most common score differential on which an intentional walk is called for.

Slow and Quick Hooks: A quick hook is the removal of a pitcher who has pitched fewer than six innings and given up three runs or less. A slow hook occurs when a pitcher pitches more than nine innings, or allows seven or more runs, or whose combined innings pitched and runs allowed totals 13 or more.

Mid-Inning Change: The number of times a manager changed pitchers in the middle of an inning.

1-Batter Appearances: The number of times a pitcher was brought in to face only one batter. Called the "Tony La Russa special" because of his penchant for trying to orchestrate specific matchups for specific situations.

3 Pitchers (2 runs or less): The club gives up two runs or less in a game, but uses at least three pitchers.